THE RAILWAY CLEARING HOUSE HANDBOOK OF RAILWAY STATIONS 1904

A Reprint
with an introduction by C.R. Clinker

DAVID & CHARLES REPRINTS

ISBN 0 7153 5120 6
This work was originally published by
The Railway Clearing House in 1904
Reprinted by the present publishers 1970
© 1970 Introduction by C. R. Clinker

Reproduced and Printed in Great Britain by
Redwood Press Limited, Trowbridge & London
for David & Charles (Publishers) Limited
South Devon House Newton Abbot Devon

INTRODUCTION

Prior to 1851 the Railway Clearing House, formed nine years earlier to facilitate inter-company booking and movement of passengers and goods, maintained lists of all stations and distances on lines owned by companies party to the clearing system. These were, of course, for internal use. The public relied for its information upon Bradshaw's *Railway Guide*, maps, local directories and similar sources. Not until the appearance of Mc Corquodale & Co's *Railway & Commercial Gazetteer* first edition in 1868 did the public have a complete list of every railway station, town, village and place in Great Britain.

Meantime, in 1851, Zachary Macaulay, who had entered the service of the Clearing House in 1847, published his *List of all stations on the railways of Great Britain, alphabetically arranged*. A second edition, expanded from 76 to 95 pages and including Irish stations, appeared in 1855. These two books, although like his fine railway maps of the same period published under his own name, were clearly authoritative and at least quasi-official. They were the precursors of a publication which was to continue for a century.

Macaulay died in 1860. Two years later his erstwhile colleagues, Henry Oliver and John Bockett published their *Hand Book of the Stations and Sidings on the Railways in the United Kingdom* as a work of reference for 'Station Masters, Booking and Invoicing Clerks, Shipping Agents and others'. This shewed the location and owning company of each station and siding. Its 29 pages contained about 2,300 entries, plus a four-page appendix dated 1863. The price was 1s 6d paper cover, 2s cloth. Further editions, with appendices of additions and amendments, appeared in 1865 and 1866.

In 1867 a New Edition with over 7,500 entries appeared. In this 'Collieries' were added to the title and tables; the county location also, was shewn for the first time. In 1869 the partners published a 24-page Hand Book of stations provided with cranes; no other information was given.

The seven editions issued between 1872 and 1900 appeared under the names of Henry Oliver and John Airey; Airey had joined the Clearing House staff in 1852 and had already published the first of his invaluable railway maps for which he is better known. The 1872 title now included 'Junctions'. Its 164 pages listed over 10,000 entries with two appendices of 43 pages. The 1876 edition was similar.

The fifth edition, published in 1879, was of considerable wider scope than its predecessors. Not only were there more than 12,500 names, but against each station and public goods depot appeared letters indicating the type of traffic which could be dealt with, viz: G goods, P passengers, F furniture vans, wheeled vehicles, etc, L livestock, T travelling cranes, distinguished from the maximum fixed crane power shewn. The last named was dropped from the remaining editions published under Oliver & Airey's imprint, ie 1883, 1890, 1895 and 1900. The last, and final, edition ran to 412 pages and over 25,000 entries, plus appendices totalling 142 pages. The price was 5s. Both the 1895 and 1900 editions are numbered as the eighth.

Airey's map publishing business was purchased by the Railway Clearing House in 1895. In 1904 the Clearing House produced its first issue of the Hand-Book — the edition here reprinted — on a larger format, 10 x 8 ins, and swollen to 600 pages carrying nearly 35,000 entries. The station accommodation column was augmented by H horse boxes and prize cattle vans, and C carriages by passenger train. The last, of course, referred to gentlemen's private carriages on open trucks.

The next edition, 1912, was re-titled 'Official Hand-Book...'. A large number of private sidings, some apparently omitted from previous issues, were inserted, raising the size by over 100 pages and the entries to 41,500. This issue is of particular interest for its six page list of all the railway companies, joint committees and other bodies whose stations, etc appear in the book. For the first time, nearly all the small number of minor companies not party to the Railway Clearing House are included. Among names now almost forgotten except by railway

historians, will be found the Avonmouth Light, Bideford, Westward Ho! & Appledore, Bishop's Castle, Corris, Dearne Valley, East & West Yorkshire Union, Listowel & Ballybunion, Methley Joint, North Lindsey Light, Princes Dock Joint, Rowrah & Kelton Fell Mineral, Van and Weston, Clevedon & Portishead Light Railways.

Before the following issue of the Hand-Book in 1925, the railway system had been transformed by Grouping under the Railways Act, 1921 and, to a lesser extent, by temporary closure of stations as a wartime economy but which in the event, became permanent in some cases. This issue is, perhaps, of less retrospective value than might be expected. Company names have been changed in accordance with Grouping but the former owning company is not shewn as a section of the new system, eg Glenfield appears as 'LMS' only.

As the book was used mainly by the railway companies — virtually every station was supplied with a copy and supplements — absence of the former owning company in a period of organisational upheaval caused considerable difficulty. On the companies' recommendation the 1929 issue included the new and former names against each entry, eg Glenfield 'LMS(Mid.)' In this issue also, the station accommodation information is elaborated to differentiate between goods depots handling all classes of traffic and those dealing only with minerals or traffic for private sidings; at passenger stations those without parcels facilities are indicated, as are a few goods depots (usually where the passenger station has been closed) which continue to handle parcels. A number of other minor variations from the normal are also shewn.

The 1938 issue has generally been regarded as the peak of the Hand-Books's accuracy and usefulnes Its slightly enlarged pages contained about 45,000 entries. The temporary wartime closures of 1917, eg Brockley Lane, had at last been dropped and, rather belatedly, stations with end-loading docks suitable for motor cars by passenger train had been added, the accommodation letter 'C' being suitably amended.

It was not until 1956 that the next, and most recent, Hand-Book appeared, this time under the imprint of the British Transport Commission (Railway Clearing House); owning company names were replaced by 'Undertaking or Region' and 'Position' by 'Position or Parent Station'. The regional letter is followed supposedly by the pre-1923 owning company of 35 years earlier! – thus, NE(L&Y), Sc(Ne), etc.

However, a number of traps have been laid for the uninitiated and this issue should be used with special care. To conform with railway organisational changes and other domestic circumstances, ownership of some stations has been altered. For example, those between Reading and Ash (also Shalford), originally SE&C appear as LSW, and between Chil-worth & Albury and Reigate as LBSC; the former GN station and depot at Stafford were, by supplementary leaflet, altered to LNW.

Under Nationalisation, a large number of passenger and goods stations, formerly without any distinguishing name, received such names. These appear as separate entries in the 1956 issue and are not always easily related to the 1938 entries. Extensive renamings also, have been carried out, making it difficult to connect the 1938 and 1956 entries; the Leith and Coatbridge-Whifflet areas are particularly affected by this kind of alteration.

Users of the Hand-Book, especially from 1872 onwards, should bear in mind that it was published primarily for railway staff and that the entries, particularly as to names of junctions, conform with RCH usage and *not* with the names of signal boxes controlling such junctions. Thus 'Bristol Junction' between the GW and the Midland companies was, in fact, controlled by South Wales Junction signal box up to 1935 and Bristol East box until 1970.

At the time of writing it is clear that the Hand-Book is being allowed to fade quietly out of existence. The last supplementary leaflet, dated November 1964, was published in March 1965, so the book is now substantially out of date, more particularly as to closure of stations and changes in regional boundaries. Anything like a revival now seems improbable.

1970

C.R. CLINKER

LIST OF
OFFICIAL RAILWAY MAPS AND JUNCTION DIAGRAMS.

Published by THE RAILWAY CLEARING HOUSE,
SEYMOUR STREET, EUSTON SQUARE, LONDON, N.W.

GENERAL MAPS.	SIZE. N. to S.	E. to W.	SCALE.	PRICES. In Sheet. s. d.	FOLDED. 'Pegamoid' Cloth. s. d.	Book-Form s. d.	On Black Roller and Varnished. s. d.	On Spring Roller and Varnished Mahogany Back Board s. d.
	ft. in.	ft. in.		s. d.	s. d.	s. d.	s. d.	s. d.
England and Wales (*Large*)	5 0 ×	4 0	7½ miles to 1 inch	12 6	18 6	20 0	22 6	80 0
do. (*Small*)	3 6 ×	2 6	11 miles to 1 inch	7 0	—	12 0	13 0	60 0
Scotland	3 9 ×	2 6	7½ miles to 1 inch	8 6	13 6	15 0	17 6	65 0
Ireland	3 9 ×	2 6	7½ miles to 1 inch	8 6	13 6	15 0	17 6	65 0

SECTIONAL MAPS.
(*With Distances.*)

NEW SERIES—	SIZE. N. to S.	E. to W.	SCALE.	In Sheet. s. d.	'Pegamoid' Cloth. s. d.	Book-Form s. d.	On Black Roller and Varnished. s. d.	On Spring Roller... s. d.
	ft. in.	ft. in.		s. d.	s. d.	s. d.	s. d.	s. d.
Edinburgh and Glasgow Districts...	2 6 ×	4 0	2 miles to 1 inch	8 6	—	15 0	17 6	75 0
Lancashire and Cheshire Districts	3 9 ×	2 6	2 miles to 1 inch	8 6	—	15 0	17 6	65 0
London and its Environs	3 6 ×	4 3	1 mile to 2 inches	8 6	12 6	15 0	17 6	80 0
Manchester and District	1 3 ×	1 10	1 mile to 1 inch	1 6	—	4 6	5 0	—
Staffordshire and District	2 2 ×	3 6	2 miles to 1 inch	6 0	9 6	11 0	13 6	60 0
Yorkshire District	4 0 ×	3 6	2 miles to 1 inch	11 0	17 6	18 6	22 6	80 0
do. (North Sheet)...	2 0 ×	3 6	2 miles to 1 inch	5 6	9 0	10 6	13 0	60 0
do. (South Sheet)...	2 0 ×	3 6	2 miles to 1 inch	5 6	9 0	10 6	13 0	60 0

SECTIONAL MAPS.
(*With Distances.*)

OLD SERIES—	SIZE. N. to S.	E. to W.	PRICES. In Sheet s. d.	Folded Book-Form. s. d.	On Black Roller and Varnished. s. d.
	ft. in.	ft. in.	s. d.	s. d.	s. d.
Cumberland and Westmorland Districts	1 8 ×	2 2	3 0	6 0	6 6
Durham and Northumberland Districts	2 6 ×	1 10	3 6	7 0	7 6
East of England	2 6 ×	3 6	6 0	12 0	12 6
Gloucestershire and Oxfordshire Districts	1 10 ×	2 6	3 6	7 0	7 6
Scotland (*whole*)	3 8 ×	2 6	6 0	12 0	12 6
South of England	2 6 ×	3 6	6 0	12 0	12 6
South Wales	1 10 ×	3 9	5 6	9 6	10 0
West of England	2 8 ×	3 8	6 0	12 0	12 6

JUNCTION DIAGRAMS.

Railway Junction Diagrams Book (*containing 150 Plates*)....................Price 18s. 6d.

HAND-BOOK OF STATIONS

INCLUDING

JUNCTIONS, SIDINGS, COLLIERIES,

WORKS, &c.,

ON THE

RAILWAYS IN THE UNITED KINGDOM,

SHOWING THE

STATION ACCOMMODATION, CRANE POWER,

COUNTY, COMPANY, AND POSITION.

ALPHABETICALLY ARRANGED.

1904.

Price 8s. 0d.; by Post 8s. 6d.

PUBLISHED BY THE RAILWAY CLEARING HOUSE,
123, SEYMOUR STREET, EUSTON SQUARE,
LONDON, N.W.

Entered at Stationers' Hall.

PRINTED BY McCORQUODALE & Co., LIMITED, LONDON.

NOTES.

CRANE POWER.

The Crane Power shown represents the maximum *fixed* crane power at each Station, but most of the Companies have travelling cranes with a lifting power of five tons and upwards, which can be removed from one Station to another, as circumstances require.

COAL.

Coal traffic can be dealt with at most Goods Stations, and in many instances Coal Sidings are provided adjacent to Passenger Stations.

GAUGES.

The Standard Gauge of the Railways in Great Britain is 4 feet 8½ inches, and in Ireland 5 feet 3 inches. Narrow Gauge Lines, the gauges of which vary, are set out in the List of Railway Companies on pages 4 to 7.

NOTICE:—Every care has been taken to make this work as complete and correct as possible in all respects, but its accuracy is not guaranteed, and neither the Publishers nor the Companies can hold themselves responsible for any liability in cases (if any) of loss arising through the information contained therein being incorrect, nor do the particulars in this Hand-Book affect any arrangements between the Railway Companies in regard to facilities, bookings, rates, routes, etc.

LIST OF RAILWAY COMPANIES,

With abbreviations used in Company Column.

NAME OF COMPANY.	ABBREVIATION.	NAME OF COMPANY.	ABBREVIATION.
Alexandra (Newport and South Wales) Docks and Railway	A. (N. & S. W.) D. & R.	Castlederg and Victoria Bridge, *Light (Gauge 3 feet)*	C. & V. B.
Ashby and Nuneaton Joint	A & N Jt.(L & N W & Mid.)	Cavan and Leitrim, *Light (Gauge 3 feet)*	C. & L.
Axholme Joint (*Light*)	Axholme Jt.(L & Y & N E)	Central London (*Electric*)	C. L.
		Cheadle (North Staffordshire) ...	N.S. (Cheadle)
		Cheshire Lines Committee	C.L.C. (G C, G N, & Mid.)
Ballycastle (*Gauge 3 feet*)	Ballycastle	„ „ „ Southport and Cheshire Lines Extension ...	C.L.C. (S'port. Exten.)
Barry	Barry	City and South London (*Electric*) ...	C. & S.L.
Belfast and County Down	B. & C. D.	Cleator and Workington Junction ...	C. & W. Jn.
Bessbrook and Newry, *Electric (Gauge 3 feet)*	B. & Newry	Clifton Extension Joint... ...	Clif. Ex. Jt.(G. W. & Mid.)
Bideford, Westward Ho! and Appledore	B. W. Ho! & A.	Clogher Valley, *Light (Gauge 3 feet)* ...	Clogher Valley
Birkenhead Joint	B'head Jt. (G W & L N W)	Cockermouth, Keswick, and Penrith...	C. K. & P.
Bishop's Castle	Bishop's Castle	Colne Valley and Halstead	C.V. & H.
Brecon and Merthyr Tydfil Junction...	B. & M.	Cork and Macroom Direct	C. & Macroom
		Cork and Muskerry, *Light (Gauge 3 ft.)*	C. & Muskerry
Brecon & Merthyr, and London & North Western Joint	B. & M. & L. & N. W. Joint	Cork, Bandon, and South Coast ...	C. B. & S.C.
Burry Port and Gwendraeth Valley ...	B. P. & G. V.	Cork, Blackrock, and Passage (*Guage 3 feet*)	C. B. & P.
		Corris (*Gauge 2 feet 3 inches*)	Corris
Caledonian	Cal.	Croydon and Oxted Joint Committee	C. & O. Jt. (L. B. & S. C. and S. E. & C.)
Cambrian	Cam.		
„ Tanat Valley (*Light*)... ...	Cam. (Tanat Valley)		
„ Van	Cam. (Van).	Dearne Valley	Dearne Valley
„ Welshpool and Llanfair, *Light (Gauge 2 feet 6 inches)* ...	Cam. (W. & L.)	Donegal (*Gauge 3 feet*)	Donegal
Carlisle Citadel Station Committee ...	Cit.Sta.Com.(Cal & LNW)	Dornoch, *Light* (Highland)	High. (Dornoch)
Carlisle Dentonholme Station Committee	Dentonholme Sta. Com. (G.&S.W.,Mid.& N.B.)	Dublin, Wicklow, and Wexford ...	D. W. &. W.
		Dumbarton and Balloch Joint... ...	D. & B. Jt. (Cal. & N. B.)
		Dundalk, Newry, and Greenore (London and North Western)... ...	D. N. & G.
Carlisle Goods Traffic Committee ...	Gds. Tfc. Com. (Cal., L. & N W, Mid. & G & SW)	Dundee and Arbroath Joint	D. & A. Jt. (Cal. & N. B.)

LIST OF RAILWAY COMPANIES, with abbreviations used in Company Column—*continued.*

NAME OF COMPANY.	ABBREVIATION.	NAME OF COMPANY.	ABBREVIATION.
East & West Junction and Stratford-upon-Avon, Towcester and Midland Junction	E. & W. Jn.	Great Western and Rhymney Joint ...	G. W. & Rhy. Jt.
East and West Yorkshire Union ...	E. & W. Y. Union.	Gwendraeth Valleys	Gwen. Valleys
East London Joint Committee ...	E. L. Jt. (G. E., L. B. & S. C., Met., M.D., & S. E. & C.)	Halesowen...	Halesowen (G.W. & Mid.)
		Halifax and Ovenden Joint ...	H. & O. Jt (G N & L & Y)
Easton and Church Hope ...	E. & C. H. (G W & L. & S W)	Halifax High Level	H'fax H. L. (G N & L & Y
		Hammersmith and City Joint...	H. & C. Jt (G.W. & Met.)
Festiniog (*Gauge 1 foot 11½ inches*) ...	Festiniog	Highland	High.
Furness	Furness	,, Dornoch (*Light*) ...	High. (Dornoch)
Furness and Midland Joint ...	Fur. & Mid. Jt.	,, Invergarry and Fort Augustus	High (I. & F. A.)
		,, Wick and Lybster (*Light*) ...	High. (W. & L.)
Garstang and Knot End ...	G. & K. E.	Hull, Barnsley, and West Riding Junction Railway and Dock ...	H. & B.
Glasgow and South Western ...	G. & S. W.		
Glasgow and Paisley Joint ...	G & P Jt (Cal & G & S W)	Hundred of Manhood and Selsey (*Light*)	Selsey
Glasgow, Barrhead, and Kilmarnock Joint	G B & K Jt (Cal & G & S W)		
Glasgow District Subway (*Gauge 4 feet*)	Glas. Dist. Sub.	Invergarry and Fort Augustus (High.)	High (I. & F. A.)
Glyn Valley Tramway (*Gauge 2 feet 4½ inches*)	Glyn Valley	Isle of Man (*Gauge 3 feet*)	I. of Man
		Isle of Wight	I. of W.
Great Central	G.C.	Isle of Wight Central	I. of W. Cent.
,, ,, St. Helens Extension ...	G. C. (St. Helens Exten.)		
,, ,, Wigan Junction ...	G. C. (Wigan Jn.)	Jersey Railways Limited (*Gauge 3 feet 6 inches*)	Jersey
Great Eastern	G.E.	Jersey Eastern	Jersey Eastern
Great Northern	G.N.		
Great Northern and City (*Electric*) ...	G.N. & C.	Kent and East Sussex (*Light*)	K. & E. S.
Great Northern and Great Eastern Joint	G.N. & G.E. Jt.	Kilsyth and Bonnybridge Joint ...	K. & B. Jt. (Cal. & N. B.)
Great Northern, and London & North Western Joint	G.N. & L. & N.W. Jt.	Lambourn Valley	L'bourn Valley
		Lancashire and Yorkshire	L. & Y.
Great Northern (Ireland) ...	G.N. (I.)	Lancashire & Yorkshire, and Lancashire Union Joint	L&Y & LU Jt (LY & LNW)
Great North of Scotland ...	G.N. of S.	Lancashire, Derbyshire, and East Coast	L. D. & E. C.
Great Southern and Western ...	G.S. & W.	Lee-on-the-Solent	Lee-on-the-Solent
Great Western	G.W.	Liskeard and Looe	L. & Looe
Great Western and Great Central Joint Committee	G.W. & G.C. Jt.	Listowel and Ballybunion (*Mono Rail*)	L. & B.

LIST OF RAILWAY COMPANIES, with abbreviations used in Company Column—*continued.*

NAME OF COMPANY.	ABBREVIATION.	NAME OF COMPANY.	ABBREVIATION.
Liverpool Overhead (*Electric*)	L'pool. O'head.	Nantybwch and Rhymney Joint ...	N.&R. Jt.(L&NW.& Rhy)
Llanelly and Mynydd Mawr	L. & M. M.	Neath and Brecon	N. & Brecon
London and India Docks	L. & I. Dks.	Norfolk and Suffolk Joint Committee .	N.&S. Jt.(GE&M&GNJt.)
London and North Western	L. & N. W.	Northampton and Banbury Junction...	N. & B. Jn.
„ „ „ Dundalk, Newry, and Greenore	D. N. & G.	North and South Western Junction Joint	N.&S.W.Jn.Jt.(L.&NW, Mid., & N.L.)
London and South Western	L. & S. W.		
London & South Western, and London Brighton & South Coast Joint ...	L. & S W & L B & S C Jt.	North British	N.B.
London, Brighton, and South Coast ...	L. B. & S. C.	North Eastern	N.E.
Londonderry and Lough Swilly (*Gauge 3 feet*)	L. & L. S.	Northern Counties Committee (Midland) ... ... (*The gauge of the Ballymena & Larne, and Ballymena Cushendall & Red Bay Sections, is 3 feet*).	N. C. Com. (Mid.)
London, Tilbury, and Southend ...	L. T. & S.	North London	N.L.
Lynton and Barnstaple (*Gauge 1 foot 11½ inches*)	Lyn. & Barns.	North Staffordshire	N.S.
		„ „ Cheadle ...	N.S. (Cheadle)
		North Union Joint	N.U.Jt.(L.&NW.&L.&Y)
Macclesfield Committee...	Mac. Com. (G. C. & N. S.)	North Wales and Liverpool Joint Committee	N.W. & L. Jt. (G.C. and W. M. & C. Q.)
Manchester and Milford	M. & M.		
Manchester, South Junction, and Altrincham	M. S. J. & A. (GC&LNW)	North Wales Narrow Gauge (*Gauge 1 foot 11½ inches*)	No. Wales N.G.
Manx Northern (*Gauge 3 feet*) ...	Manx Northern		
Marsden (South Shields, Marsden, and Whitburn Colliery)... ...	Marsden		
Maryport and Carlisle	M. & C.	Oldham, Ashton-under-Lyne, and Guide Bridge Junction Joint ...	O. A. & G. B. Jt. (G.C. and L. & N.W.)
Mawddwy	Mawddwy		
Mersey (*Electric*)...	Mersey	Otley and Ilkley Joint	O. & I. Jt. (Mid. & N. E.)
Methley Joint	Meth.Jt.(GN,L&Y&N.E)	Oxford and Aylesbury Tramroad ...	O. & A. Tram.
Metropolitan	Met.		
Metropolitan and Metropolitan District Joint	Met. & Met. Dist. Jt.	Portpatrick and Wigtownshire Joint Committee	P.P.&W.Jt.(Cal.,G&SW, L. & N W., & Mid.)
Metropolitan District	Met. Dist.		
Midland	Mid.	Port Talbot Railway and Docks ...	P. T.
Midland and Great Northern Joint Committee	Mid. & G.N. Jt.	Preston and Longridge Joint ...	P.&L.Jt.(L&NW.& L&Y)
		Preston and Wyre Joint	P.&W.Jt.(L&Y & L&NW)
Midland and South Western Junction	M. & S.W. Jn.	Princes Dock Joint	Princes Dock Joint (Cal. G. & S.W. & N. B.)
Midland Great Western (Ireland) ...	M.G.W.		

LIST OF RAILWAY COMPANIES, with abbreviations used in Company Column—*continued*.

NAME OF COMPANY.	ABBREVIATION.	NAME OF COMPANY.	ABBREVIATION.
Ravenglass and Eskdale (*Gauge 2 feet 9 inches*)	R. & E.	Tanat Valley, *Light* (Cambrian)	Cam. (Tanat Valley)
Rhondda and Swansea Bay	R. & S.B.	Tenbury Joint	Tenbury Jt (G W & LNW)
Rhymney	Rhy.	Timoleague and Courtmacsherry(*Light*)	T. & C.
Rowrah and Kelton Fell Mineral	R. & K. F.	Tottenham and Forest Gate Joint	T.&F.G.Jt.(LT&S&Mid.)
		Tottenham and Hampstead Joint Committee	T. & H. Jt. (G.E. & Mid.)
St. Helens Extension (Great Central)	G. C. (St. Helens Exten.)	Tralee and Dingle, *Light* (*Gauge 3 feet*)	T. & D.
Schull and Skibbereen, *Light* (*Gauge 3 feet*)	S. & S.	Vale of Rheidol, *Light* (*Gauge 2 feet*)	V. of Rheidol
Selsey (Hundred of Manhood and Selsey, *Light*)	Selsey	Vale of Towy Joint	V.of T. Jt.(G W & L.N.W)
Severn and Wye Joint	S. & Wye Jt.(G. W. &Mid.)	Van (Cambrian)	Cam. (Van)
Sheffield and Midland Joint Committee	S. & M. Jt. (G. C. & Mid.)		
Sheppey, *Light* (South Eastern & Chatham)	S. E. & C. (Sheppey)	Waterford and Tramore	W. & T.
Shrewsbury and Hereford Joint	S & H Jt (G W & L N W)	Waterloo and City (*Electric*)	W. & C.
Shrewsbury and Wellington Joint	S & W'tn Jt (GW&LNW)	Welshpool and Llanfair, *Light* (Cambrian) (*Gauge 2 feet 6 inches*)	Cam. (W. & L.)
Shrewsbury and Welshpool Joint	S.&W'plJt.(GW&LNW)	West Clare, *Light* (*Gauge 3 feet*)	West Clare
Sligo, Leitrim, and Northern Counties	S. L. & N. C.	West London Joint	W Lon Jt (G W & L N W)
Somerset and Dorset Joint Committee	S.&D.Jt. (L.&S.W.&Mid)	West London Extension Joint	W.L.E.Jt.(GW,L.&NW, L.&SW,&L.B.&S.C.)
South Eastern and Chatham	S. E. & C.	Weston, Clevedon, and Portishead (*Light*)	W.C. & P.
,, ,,Sheppey(*Light*)	S. E. & C. (Sheppey)	West Riding and Grimsby Joint Committee	W.R.&G.Jt.(G.C.&G.N.)
South Shields, Marsden, and Whitburn Colliery	Marsden	Weymouth and Portland Joint	W.&P.Jt.(G W&L.&SW)
Southport and Cheshire Lines Extension (Cheshire Lines Committee)	C.L.C. (S'port Exten.)	Whitechapel and Bow Joint	W.&B.Jt.(L.T.&S.&MD)
South Wales Mineral	S. Wales Min.	Whitehaven, Cleator, and Egremont Joint	WC&EJt.(Fur.&LNW)
Southwold (*Gauge 3 feet*)	Southwold	Wick and Lybster, *Light* (Highland)	High. (W. & L.)
Swansea and Mumbles	Swan. & Mum.	Wigan Junction (Great Central)	G.C. (Wigan Jn.)
Swinton and Knottingley Joint	S. & K. Jt. (Mid. &.N.E.)	Wirral	Wirral
		Woodside and South Croydon Joint Committee	W. &S.C. Jt.(L.B. & S.C and S.E. & C.)
Taff Bargoed Joint	T.B. Jt. (G.W. & Rhy.)	Wrexham and Minera Joint	W.&M. Jt.(G W&LNW)
Taff Vale	T.V.	Wrexham, Mold, and Connah's Quay	W.M. & C.Q.
Tal-y-llyn (*Gauge 2 feet 3 inches*)	Tal-y-llyn		

HAND-BOOK OF RAILWAY STATIONS, &c.

A

G	P	F	L	H	C	Tons	Cwts	STATIONS, &c.	COUNTY.	COMPANY.	POSITION.
								Abattoir Co.'s Siding	Yorks	Mid.	Bradford.
								Abbey	Warwick	Mid.	See Nuneaton.
								Abbey Dale	Derby	Mid.	See Sheffield, Beauchief and Abbey Dale.
G	P		L	H				Abbeydore	Hereford	G. W.	Pontrilas and Dorstone.
G	P		L	H				Abbeydorney	Kerry	G. S. & W.	Newcastle West and Tralee.
G	P	F	L	H	C			Abbeyfeale	Limerick	G. S. & W.	Newcastle West and Tralee.
								Abbey Foregate	Salop	S & W'tn Jt (GW & LNW)	See Shrewsbury.
G	P		L					Abbey (for West Dereham)	Norfolk	G. E.	Denver Junction and Stoke Ferry.
								Abbeyhill	Edinboro'	N. B.	See Edinboro'.
	P							Abbey Holme Junction	Cumb'land	Cal.—N. B.	Annan and Silloth.
G	P		L	H		1	10	Abbey Junction Station	Cumb'land	N. B. / Cal.	Carlisle and Silloth. / Brayton and Annan.
								Abbey Lane Sidings	Leicester	G. C.	Leicester, Braunstone Gate.
G	P	F	L	H				Abbeyleix	Queens	G. S. & W.	Kilkenny and Maryborough.
								Abbey Mill Siding	Lancs	L. & Y	Burscough Junction.
								Abbey Mill Siding	Lancs	L & Y & LU Jt (LY & LNW)	Same as Birtwistle & Co.'s Siding (Withnell).
								Abbey Mills Lower Junction	Essex	G. E.—L. T. & S.	Same as Bromley Junction.
								Abbey Mills Siding	Essex	L. T. & S.	See London and Thames Haven Petroleum Oil Wharves Co. (London).
								Abbey Mills Upper Junction	Essex	L. T. & S.	Bromley and Plaistow.
								Abbey Siding	Denbigh	L. & N. W.	Llanrwst and Trefriw.
								Abbey Street Mineral Yard	Cheshire	B'head Jt (G W & L N W)	Birkenhead.
G	P		L	H		2	0	Abbey Town	Cumb'land	N. B.	Carlisle and Silloth.
								Reay's Siding	Cumb'land	N. B.	Abbey Town.
G	P							Abbey Wood	Kent	S. E. & C.	Woolwich and Dartford.
								Abbot & Co.'s Wks (Park Wks)	Durham	N. E.	Gateshead.
G	P	F	L	H	C	5	0	Abbotsbury	Dorset	G. W.	Branch from Upwey.
	P*							Abbotsford Ferry	Selkirk	N. B.	Galashiels and Selkirk.
	P							Abbotsham Road	Devon	B. W. Ho! & A.	Bideford and Northam.
								Abbots Wood Junction	Worcester	G. W.—Mid.	Worcester and Ashchurch.
								Abbott & Co.'s Siding	Notts	G. N.	Newark.
G	P		L	H	C			Abbotts Ripton	Hunts	G. N.	Huntingdon and Peterboro'.
								Abden Shipyard	Fife	N. B.	Kinghorn.
								Abell's Siding	Warwick	L. & N. W.	See Hartshill Siding (Nuneaton).
								Abenbury Siding	Denbigh	Cam	See Wrexham.
G	P		L					Aber	Carnarvon	L. & N. W.	Bangor and Rhyl.
								Roberts' & Sons' Siding	Carnarvon	L. & N. W.	Aber and Bangor.
	P							Aberaman	Glamorg'n	T. V.	Aberdare and Mountain Ash.
								Aberaman Branch Junction	Glamorg'n	T. V.	Aberdare.
								Aberaman Colliery	Glamorg'n	G. W.—T. V.	See Powell Duffryn Co. (M'tain Ash).
								Aberaman Gas Works	Glamorg'n	G. W. / T. V.	Mountain Ash. / Aberdare.
G						3	0	Aberangell	Merioneth	Mawddwy	Cemmes Road and Mawddwy.
								Aberavon	Glamorg'n	G. W.	See Port Talbot and Aberavon.
								Aberavon	Glamorg'n	R. & S. B.	See Port Talbot (Aberavon).
	P			H				Aberavon (Sea Side)	Glamorg'n	R. & S. B.	Port Talbot and Briton Ferry.
								Aberavon Junction	Glamorg'n	P. T.—R. & S. B.	Port Talbot Central and Port Talbot (Aberavon).
								Aberavon Tin Plate Co.'s Siding	Glamorg'n	R. & S. B.	Same as Glanwalia Sid. (Pt. Talbot).

EXPLANATION—G *Goods Station.*   P *Passenger and Parcel Station.*   P* *Passenger, but not Parcel or Miscellaneous Traffic.*   F *Furniture Vans, Carriages, Portable Engines, and Machines on Wheels.*   L *Live Stock.*   H *Horse Boxes and Prize Cattle Vans.*   C *Carriages by Passenger Train.*

STATION ACCOMMODATION.						CRANE POWER.		STATIONS, &c.	COUNTY.	COMPANY.	POSITION.
						Tons	Cwts.				
G	P							Aberbaiden Colliery	Glamorg'n	P. T.	Bryndu.
G							}	Aber Bargoed (B. & M.)	Mon	{ B. & M.	Pengam and Rhymney.
G										G. W.	Over B. & M. from Maesycwmmer Jn.
								Lord Tredegar's Siding (B. & M.)	Mon	B. & M.—G. W............	Aber Bargoed and Pengam.
								Aber Bargoed Col. (B. & M.)	Mon	B. & M.—G. W............	Same as Powell Duffryn Co.'s Bargoed New Pits (Pengam).
								Aber Bargoed Junction	Mon	B. & M.	Pengam and Bargoed.
G	P		L	H		0	15	Aberbeeg	Mon	G. W.	Crumlin, Low Level and Ebbw Vale.
								Aberbeeg Colliery (Powells)	Mon	G. W.	Aberbeeg.
								Arral Colliery	Mon	G. W.	Aberbeeg.
								Cwm Colliery	Mon	G. W.	Aberbeeg and Ebbw Vale.
								Graig Fawr Colliery	Mon	G. W.	Aberbeeg and Cwm.
								Llandavel Colliery............	Mon	G. W.	Aberbeeg and Cwm.
								Marine Colliery	Mon	G. W.	Aberbeeg and Cwm.
								Penyfan Colliery..............	Mon	G. W.	Aberbeeg.
G	P		L					Aberbran (N. & B.)	Brecon ...	{ N. & Brecon	Brecon and Devynock.
										Mid.	Over Neath and Brecon Line.
								Aber Branch Junction	Glamorg'n	Rhy.	Caerphilly and Llanbradach.
G	P	F	L	H	C	2	0	Abercairny	Perth	Cal	Crieff and Perth.
G	P					1	10	Abercanaid	Glamorg'n	G. W. & Rhy. Jt.	Merthyr and Quaker's Yard.
								Crawshay Bros.—			
								Castle Pit (GW&Rhy. Jt.)	Glamorg'n	G. W. & Rhy. Jt.—L&NW	Abercanaid and Aberfan.
								Cyfarthfa Works	Glamorg'n	G. W. & Rhy. Jt.	Branch from Cyfarthfa Level Crossing Junction.
								Gethin Pit(G. W. & Rhy. Jt.)	Glamorg'n	G. W. & Rhy. Jt.—L&NW	Abercanaid and Aberfan.
G	P		L			2	0	Abercarn	Mon	G. W.	Newport and Crumlin, Low Level.
								Abercarn (Prince of Wales) Colliery	Mon	G. W.	Abercarn and Cross Keys.
								Abercarn Tin Plate Co.'s Sid	Mon	G. W.	Abercarn.
								Celynen Colliery..............	Mon	G. W.	Abercarn and Newbridge.
	P*							Aberchalder	Inverness	High. (I. & F. A.)	Spean Bridge Jn. & Fort Augustus.
								Aber Colliery	Glamorg'n	G. W.	Ogmore Vale.
								Abercorn	Renfrew..	G. & S. W.	See Paisley.
								Abercorn Basin	Down	B. & C. D.—G. N. (I.)	See Belfast.
								Abercorn Brick Works........	Edinboro'	N. B.	Edinboro', Portobello.
								Abercorn Junction............	Renfrew..	G. & S. W.	Paisley, Abercorn and Cardonald.
								Abercorn Pits	Renfrew..	Cal	Paisley, St. James.
								Abercorris Slate Quarry	Merioneth	Corris	Maespoeth Jn. & Abercwmeiddaw Qy.
G	P							Abercrave (N. & B.)	Brecon ...	{ N. & Brecon	Colbren and Ynisygeinon Junction.
										Mid.	Over Neath and Brecon Line.
								Abercrave Colliery (N. & B.)	Brecon ...	N. & Brecon—Mid.	Abercrave.
								Gwaunclawdd Col. (N. & B.)	Brecon ...	N. & Brecon—Mid.	Abercrave and Ystradgynlais.
								International Abercrave Col (N. & B.)	Brecon ...	N. & Brecon—Mid.	Abercrave.
								International Purification Syndicate (N. & B.)	Brecon ...	N. & Brecon—Mid.	Abercrave.
								Abercwmboi Colliery	Glamorg'n	G.W.—T. V.	See Powell Duffryn Co. (M'tain Ash).
								Abercwmeiddaw Quarry	Merioneth	Corris	Branch from Maespoeth Junction.
G	P	F	L	H	C			Abercynon	Glamorg'n	T. V.	Merthyr and Pontypridd.
								Guest, Keen & Nettlefold's Dowlais Cardiff Colliery..	Glamorg'n	T. V.	Pontypridd and Traveller's Rest.
								Merthyr Local Board Siding	Glamorg'n	T. V.	Stormstown Junction.
								Stormstown Junc. & Siding	Glamorg'n	T. V.	Abercynon and Pontypridd.
								Abercynon, Upper	Glamorg'n	T. V.	Same as Traveller's Rest.
								ABERDARE—			
G	P	F	L	H	C	10	0	(Station)	Glamorg'n	G. W.	Mountain Ash and Hirwain.
G	P	F	L	H	C	10	0	(Station)	Glamorg'n	T. V.	Terminus of Aberdare Branch.
								Aberaman Branch Junction	Glamorg'n	T. V.	Aberaman and Aberdare.
								Aberaman Gas Works	Glamorg'n	T. V.	Over Powell Duffryn Co.'s Line.
								Aberdare Colliery	Glamorg'n	T. V.	Cwmbach Branch.
								Aberdare Gas Works	Glamorg'n	T. V.	Aberdare and Mountain Ash.
								Aberdare Works & Cols.	Glamorg'n	{ G. W.	Aberdare and Mountain Ash.
										T. V.	Aberdare and Aberaman.
								Abernant Colliery	Glamorg'n	T. V.	Cwmbach Branch.
								Bwllfa Dare or Bwllfa No. 1 Colliery	Glamorg'n	T. V.	Near Aberdare.
								Bwllfa Dare or Bwllfa No. 2 Col. (Nantmelyn Col.)	Glamorg'n	T. V.	Near Aberdare.
								Cwmaman Colliery............	Glamorg'n	T. V.	Aberdare and Mountain Ash.
								Cwmbach Colliery	Glamorg'n	T. V.	Cwmbach Branch.
								Cwmbach Siding	Glamorg'n	G. W.	Aberdare.

EXPLANATION—**G** *Goods Station.*   **P** *Passenger and Parcel Station.*   **P*** *Passenger, but not Parcel or Miscellaneous Traffic.*
F *Furniture Vans, Carriages, Portable Engines, and Machines on Wheels.*   **L** *Live Stock.*
H *Horse Boxes and Prize Cattle Vans.*   **C** *Carriages by Passenger Train.*

STATION ACCOMMODATION.						CRANE POWER.		STATIONS, &c.	COUNTY.	COMPANY.	POSITION.
						Tons	Cwts.	ABERDARE—continued.			
.	.	.	.	.	.			Cynon Tin Plate Works (Mill Street Tin Works)	Glamorg'n	T. V.	Near Aberdare.
.	.	.	.	.	.			Gadlys Colliery	Glamorg'n	G. W.	Aberdare and Mountain Ash.
.	.	.	.	.	.			Gadlys Estate Brick Works	Glamorg'n	G. W.	Aberdare and Hirwain.
.	.	.	.	.	.			Gadlys Junction	Glamorg'n	G. W.—T.V.	Hirwain and Aberdare.
.	.	.	.	.	.			Gadlys Tin Works............	Glamorg'n	T. V.	Near Aberdare.
.	.	.	.	.	.			Gadlys Works (Waynes Merthyr Col.)	Glamorg'n	T. V.	Aberdare and Aberaman.
.	.	.	.	.	.			Gloucester Street Siding ...	Glamorg'n	T. V.	Near Aberdare
.	.	.	.	.	.			Hek's Siding.................	Glamorg'n	T. V.	Near Aberdare.
.	.	.	.	.	.			Lletty Shenkin Colliery.....	Glamorg'n	T. V.	Aberaman and Mountain Ash.
.	.	.	.	.	.			Old Duffryn Colliery	Glamorg'n	T. V.	Cwmbach Branch.
								Powell Duffryn Co.—			
.	.	.	.	.	.			Cwmneol Colliery	Glamorg'n	T. V.	Aberdare and Mountain Ash.
.	.	.	.	.	.			Fforchaman Colliery	Glamorg'n	T. V.	Aberdare and Mountain Ash.
.	.	.	.	.	.			Treaman Colliery............	Glamorg'n	T. V.	Mountain Ash and Aberaman.
.	.	.	.	.	.			Tin Plate Works Siding ...	Glamorg'n	{ G. W. / T. V.	Aberdare and Hirwain. / Aberdare.
.	.	.	.	.	.			Tirfounder Level............	Glamorg'n	T. V.	Mountain Ash and Aberaman.
.	.	.	.	.	.			Wadsworth's Siding.........	Glamorg'n	T. V.	Near Aberdare.
.	.	.	.	.	.			Waynes Merthyr Colliery...	Glamorg'n	G. W.	Aberdare and Hirwain.
.	.	.	.	.	.			Werfa Colliery.................	Glamorg'n	T. V.	Cwmbach Branch.
.	.	.	.	.	.			Aberdare Gas Works...........	Glamorg'n	G. W.	Same as Aberaman Gas Works (Mountain Ash).
.	.	.	.	.	.			Aberdare Gas Works...........	Glamorg'n	T. V.	Aberdare.
.	.	.	.	.	.			Aberdare Merthyr Colliery...	Glamorg'n	G. W.	Hirwain.
								ABERDEEN—			
G	.	.	.	.	.	10	0	Albert Quay	Aberdeen	{ Cal. / N. B.	Extension from Guild Street. / Over Cal. from Kinnaber Junction.
.	.	.	.	.	.			Craiginches Siding (Cal.)	Kinc'rdine	Cal.—N. B.	Cove and Aberdeen.
G	.	F	L	.	.	4	0	Deeside.....................	Aberdeen	G. N. of S.	Branch—Ferryhill Jn. & Jt. Station.
.	.	.	.	.	.			Denburn Junction	Aberdeen	Cal.—G. N. of S.	Cove and Dyce.
.	P	.	.	.	.			Don Street	Aberdeen	G. N. of S.	Aberdeen and Dyce.
.	.	.	L	.	.			Ferryhill Cattle Bank (Cal.)	Aberdeen	{ Cal. / N. B.	Cove and Aberdeen. / Over Cal. from Kinnaber Junction.
.	.	.	.	.	.			Ferryhill Junction............	Aberdeen	Cal.—G. N. of S.	Cove and Culter.
.	.	.	.	.	.			Gas Works (Cal.)	Aberdeen	Cal.—N. B.	Extension from Guild Street.
G	.	F	L	.	.	15	0 }	Guild Street (Cal.)............	Aberdeen	{ Cal. / N. B.	Aberdeen. / Over Cal. from Kinnaber Junction.
G	.	F	L	.	.	15	0 }				
G	.	.	.	.	.	15	0	Harbour	Aberdeen	{ Cal. / N. B.	Extension from Guild Street. / Over Cal. from Kinnaber Junction.
.	.	.	.	.	.			Harper's (Ltd.) Tramway...	Kinc'rdine	Cal.—N. B.	Aberdeen.
.	P	.	.	.	.			Holburn Street	Aberdeen	G. N. of S.	Aberdeen and Culter.
.	P	.	.	.	.			Hutcheon Street............	Aberdeen	G. N. of S.	Aberdeen and Dyce.
.	P	.	.	H	C	.	. }	Joint Station (Cal. & G. N. of S.)	Aberdeen	{ Cal. / G. N. of S. / N. B.	Aberdeen. / Ferryhill Junction & Kittybrewster. / Over Cal. from Kinnaber Junction.
.	P	.	.	H	C	.	. }				
.	P	.	.	H	C	.	. }				
G	P	F	L	H	C	5	0	Kittybrewster.................	Aberdeen	G. N. of S.	Aberdeen and Dyce.
.	P	.	.	.	.			Ruthrieston.................	Aberdeen	G. N. of S.	Aberdeen and Culter.
.	P	.	.	.	.			Schoolhill.................	Aberdeen	G. N. of S.	Aberdeen and Dyce.
G	.	.	.	.	.	5	0	Upper Dock....................	Aberdeen	{ Cal. / N. B.	Extension from Guild Street. / Over Cal. from Kinnaber Junction.
G	.	.	.	.	.	75	0	Victoria Dock...................	Aberdeen	{ Cal. / N. B.	Extension from Guild Street. / Over Cal. from Kinnaber Junction.
G	.	F	L	.	.	10	0	Waterloo	Aberdeen	G. N. of S.	Branch from Kittybrewster.
.	P	.	.	.	.			Woodside.....................	Aberdeen	G. N. of S.	Aberdeen and Dyce.
.	.	.	.	.	.			Aberdeen Wharf..............	Northumb	N. E.	Newcastle-on-Tyne.
G	.	.	.	.	.			Aberderfyn..................	Denbigh...	G. W.	Ruabon and Legacy.
.	.	.	.	.	.			Jenkins' and Jones' Siding	Denbigh...	G. W.	Aberderfyn.
.	.	.	.	.	.			Rhos Gas Works	Denbigh...	G. W.	Aberderfyn.
G	P	F	L	H	C	3	0	Aberdour..................	Fife........	N. B.	Inverkeithing and Burntisland.
.	.	.	.	.	.			Lochties Quarry..............	Fife........	N. B.	Aberdour.
.	P	F	L	H	C	.	.	Aberdovey	Merioneth	Cam.	Machynlleth and Barmouth.
G	.	.	L	.	.	3	0	Aberdovey Harbour	Merioneth	Cam.	Branch from Aberdovey.
G	P	.	.	.	.			Aberdylais	Glamorg'n	G. W.	Hirwain and Neath.
.	.	.	.	.	.			Aberdylais Tin Works......	Glamorg'n	G. W.	Aberdylais and Resolven.
G	P	.	.	.	.			Aberedw	Radnor ...	Cam.	Builth Wells and Three Cocks.
G	P	.	.	.	.			Abererch	Carnarvon	Cam.	Afon Wen and Pwllheli.
G	P	.	.	.	.	1	10	Aberfan (for Merthyr Vale)..	Glamorg'n	G. W. & Rhy. Jt.	Merthyr and Quakers Yard.
.	.	.	.	.	.			Derwen Merthyr Colliery...	Glamorg'n	G. W. & Rhy. Jt.	Aberfan and Quakers Yard.
.	.	.	.	.	.			Merthyr Vale Colliery	Glamorg'n	G. W. & Rhy. Jt.	Aberfan and Quakers Yard.

EXPLANATION—G *Goods Station.*   P *Passenger and Parcel Station.*   P* *Passenger, but not Parcel or Miscellaneous Traffic.*
F *Furniture Vans, Carriages, Portable Engines, and Machines on Wheels.*   L *Live Stock.*
H *Horse Boxes and Prize Cattle Vans.*   C *Carriages by Passenger Train.*

STATION ACCOMMODATION.						CRANE POWER.		STATIONS, &c.	COUNTY.	COMPANY.	POSITION.
G	P	F	L	H	C	Tons 5	Cwts 0	Aberfeldy	Perth	High	Branch from Ballinluig.
.	.	.	.	.	.	.	.	Aberfeldy Distillery	Perth	High	Aberfeldy.
G	P	.	.	.	.	.	.	Aberffrwd	Cardigan	V. of Rheidol	Aberystwyth and Devil's Bridge.
G	P	F	L	H	C	3	0	Aberfoyle	Perth	N. B.	Branch from Buchlyvie Junction.
.	.	.	.	.	.	.	.	Aberfoyle Slate Quarries...	Perth	N. B.	Near Aberfoyle.
								ABERGAVENNY—			
G	P	F	L	H	C	5	0	(Station)	Mon	G. W.	Hereford and Pontypool Road.
.	.	.	.	.	.	.	.	Asylum Sid. (L. & N. W.)	Mon	L. & N. W.—G. W.	Abergavenny Jn. Sta. & Brecon Rd.
G	P	F	L	H	C	5	0	Brecon Road	Mon	L. & N. W.	Abergavenny Junc. and Merthyr.
.	.	.	.	.	.	.	.	Gas Works	Mon	L. & N. W.	Brecon Road and Govilon.
.	.	.	.	.	.	.	.	Junction	Mon	G. W.—L. & N. W.	Abergavenny Jn. Sta. & Brecon Rd.
.	P	.	.	.	.	.	.)	Junction Station	Mon	{ G. W.	Hereford and Pontypool Road.
G	P	.	L	H	C					{ L. & N. W.	Brecon Road and Hereford.
.	.	.	.	.	.	.	.	Workhouse Siding	Mon	L. & N. W.	Brecon Road and Govilon.
G	P	F	L	H	C	5	0	Abergele	Denbigh	L. & N. W.	Bangor and Rhyl.
.	.	.	.	.	.	.	.	Abergorchwy or Abergorki Col	Glamorg'n	T. V.	Treorchy.
.	.	.	.	.	.	.	.	Abergrange Saw Mills	Stirling	Cal.	Grangemouth.
G	P	.	L	.	C	.	.	Abergwili	Carmarth'.	L. & N. W.	Carmarthen and Llandilo.
.	.	.	.	.	.	.	.	Abergwili Junction	Carmarth'.	G. W.—L. & N. W.	Carmarthen and Llandilo Bridge.
G	P	.	L	H	.	1	10	Abergwynfi	Glamorg'n	G. W.	Branch from Tondu.
.	.	.	.	.	.	.	.	Avon Colliery	Glamorg'n	G. W.	Abergwynfi.
.	.	.	.	.	.	.	.	Treshenkin Colliery	Glamorg'n	G. W.	Abergwynfi.
G	P	.	.	.	.	.	.	Abergynolwyn	Merioneth	Tal-y-llyn	Terminus.
G	P	F	L	H	C	2	10	Aberlady	Hadding'n	N. B.	Longniddry and Gullane.
.	P	.	.	.	.	.	.	Aberlady Junction	Hadding'n	N. B.	Longniddry and Drem.
G	P	.	.	.	.	.	.	Aberllefenny	Merioneth	Corris	Corris and Ratgoed Quarry.
.	.	.	.	.	.	.	.	Aberllefenny Quarry	Merioneth	Corris	Near Aberllefenny.
G	P	F	L	H	C	4	0	Aberlour	Banff	G. N. of S.	Craigellachie and Boat of Garten.
G	P	.	L	H	C	8	0	Abermule	Montgom	Cam.	Newtown and Welshpool.
.	.	.	.	.	.	.	.	Abermule Junction	Montgom	Cam.	Junction with Kerry Branch.
G	P	.	.	.	.	.	.	Abernant	Glamorg'n	G. W.	Hirwain and Merthyr.
.	.	.	.	.	.	.	.	Blaennant Colliery	Glamorg'n	G. W.	Abernant and Llwydcoed.
.	.	.	.	.	.	.	.	Tunnel Pit	Glamorg'n	G. W.	Abernant and Merthyr.
.	.	.	.	.	.	.	.	Werfa Colliery	Glamorg'n	G. W.	Abernant and Merthyr.
.	.	.	.	.	.	.	.	Abernant Brick Works	Glamorg'n	G. W.	Glyn Neath.
.	.	.	.	.	.	.	.	Abernant Colliery	Glamorg'n	T. V.	Aberdare.
.	.	.	.	.	.	.	.	Abernant Colliery	Mon	L. & N.W.	Same as Bargoed Col. Co's Sid (Argoed)
G	P	F	L	H	C	1	0	Abernethy	Perth	N. B.	Perth and Ladybank.
.	.	.	.	.	.	.	.	Aberpergwm Colliery	Glamorg'n	G. W.	Glyn Neath.
.	.	.	.	.	.	.	.	Aber Rhondda Colliery	Glamorg'n	T. V.	Porth.
G	P	F	L	H	C	1	10	Abersychan and Talywain	Mon	G.W. & L. & N. W. Jt.	Pontypool and Brynmawr.
								Hoskin & Llewellyn—			
.	.	.	.	.	.	.	.	Abersychan Elled Col. GW	Mon	G. W.—L. & N. W.	Abersychan & Talywain.
.	.	.	.	.	.	.	.	Golynos Colliery (G.W.)	Mon	G. W.—L. & N. W.	Abersychan & Talywain.
.	.	.	.	.	.	.	.	Paton's Chemical Wks.(GW)	Mon	G. W.—L. & N. W.	Abersychan & Talywain.
								Varteg Deep Black Vein Co.'s			
.	.	.	.	.	.	.	.	Lower Varteg Col. (GW)	Mon	G. W.—L. & N. W.	Abersychan & Talywain.
.	.	.	.	.	.	.	.	Abersychan & Talywain Junc.	Mon	G. W.—L. & N. W.	Pontypool and Brynmawr.
.	.	.	.	.	.	.	.	Abersychan Elled Colliery	Mon	G. W.	Talywain.
.	.	.	.	.	.	.	.	Abersychan Elled Col. (G.W.)	Mon	G. W.—L. & N. W.	See Hoskin and Llewellyn (Abersychan and Talywain).
G	P	.	L	.	.	2	0	Abersychan, Low Level	Mon	G.W.	Pontypool and Blaenavon.
G	P	F	L	H	C	1	10)	Aberthaw	Glamorg'n	{ Barry	Barry and Bridgend.
G	P	.	L	H	.	.	.)			{ T. V.	Terminus of Bch. from Cowbridge.
.	.	.	.	.	.	.	.	Aberthaw Lime Works	Glamorg'n	T. V.	Aberthaw.
G	P	F	L	.	.	6	0	Abertillery	Mon	G. W.	Aberbeeg and Blaina.
.	.	.	.	.	.	.	.	Arral Griffin Colliery	Mon	G. W.	Abertillery and Aberbeeg.
.	.	.	.	.	.	.	.	Cwmtillery Colliery	Mon	G. W.	Branch from Abertillery.
.	.	.	.	.	.	.	.	Glan Ebbw Tin Plate Wks	Mon	G. W.	Abertillery.
.	.	.	.	.	.	.	.	Gray Colliery	Mon	G. W.	Branch from Abertillery.
.	.	.	.	.	.	.	.	Greenmeadow Colliery	Mon	G. W.	Branch from Abertillery.
.	.	.	.	.	.	.	.	Havodvan Colliery	Mon	G. W.	Abertillery and Aberbeeg.
								Lancaster, Speir & Co.'s			
.	.	.	.	.	.	.	.	Rose Heyworth Col. (GW)	Mon	G. W—L. & N. W.	Abertillery and Blaina.
.	.	.	.	.	.	.	.	Tillery Colliery	Mon	G. W.	Branch from Abertillery.
.	.	.	.	.	.	.	.	Vivian Colliery	Mon	G. W.	Abertillery and Aberbeeg.
.	.	.	.	.	.	.	.	Williams Foundry Siding	Mon	G. W.	Branch from Abertillery.
.	.	.	.	.	.	.	.	Aber Tin Plate Co.'s Sid (Mid)	Glamorg'n	Mid.—G.W.—L. & N. W.	Llansamlet.
G	P	F	L	H	C	1	10	Abertridwr	Glamorg'n	Rhy.	Caerphilly and Senghenith.
.	.	.	.	.	.	.	.	Windsor Colliery	Glamorg'n	Rhy	Abertridwr and Senghenith.
.	.	.	.	.	.	.	.	Abertwsswg Siding (B. & M.)	Mon	B. & M.—G.W.	Rhymney.
.	.	.	.	.	.	.	.	Aber Wagon Co.'s Sid. (Mid.)	Glamorg'n	Mid.—G.W.—L. & N. W.	Six Pit Junction.

EXPLANATION—G *Goods Station.*   P *Passenger and Parcel Station.*   P* *Passenger, but not Parcel or Miscellaneous Traffic.*
F *Furniture Vans, Carriages, Portable Engines, and Machines on Wheels.*   L *Live Stock.*
H *Horse Boxes and Prize Cattle Vans.*   C *Carriages by Passenger Train.*

Station Accommodation						Crane Power		Stations, &c.	County	Company	Position
						Tons	Cwts				
G	P	F	L	H	C	5	0	Aberystwyth	Cardigan..	Cam.	Terminus.
G	P	F	L	H	.	5	0	Aberystwyth	Cardigan..	M. & M.	Terminus.
G	P	F	L	H	C	.	.	Aberystwyth	Cardigan..	V. of Rheidol	Adjoining Cam. & M. & M. Stations.
.	.	.	.	.	.	.	.	Aberystwyth Gas Co.'s Sid.	Cardigan..	Cam.	Aberystwyth and Bow Street.
G	.	.	.	.	.	8	0	Aberystwyth Harbour	Cardigan..	M. & M.	Aberystwyth Sta. & Llanrhystyd Rd.
.	.	.	.	.	.	.	.	Aberystwyth Harbour	Cardigan..	V. of Rheidol	Adjoining M. & M. Station.
.	.	.	.	.	.	.	.	Aberystwyth Junction	Cardigan..	Cam.—M. & M.	Bow Street and Llanrhystyd Road.
G	P	F	L	H	C	8	0	Abingdon	Berks	G. W.	Branch from Radley.
.	.	.	.	.	.	.	.	Abingdon Gas Works	Berks	G. W.	Abingdon.
.	.	.	.	.	.	.	.	Morland's Siding	Berks	G. W.	Abingdon.
.	.	.	.	.	.	.	.	Thomas & Co.'s Siding	Berks	G. W.	Abingdon.
G	P	F	L	H	C	3	0	Abington	Lanark ..	Cal.	Lockerbie and Carstairs.
G	P	F	L	H	C	1	10	Aboyne	Aberdeen	G. N. of S.	Banchory and Ballater.
.	.	.	.	.	.	.	.	Abram	Lancs	G. C. (Wigan Jn.)	See Bickershaw and Abram.
.	.	.	.	.	.	.	.	Abram Coal Co.'s—			
.	.	.	.	.	.	.	.	Abram Colliery, North	Lancs	L. & N. W.	Leigh and Bedford.
.	.	.	.	.	.	.	.	Abram Colliery, South	Lancs	L. & N. W.	Leigh and Bedford.
.	.	.	.	.	.	.	.	Abram Collieries	Lancs	G. C. (Wigan Jn.)	West Leigh and Bedford.
G	P	F	L	H	C	1	5	Aby (for Claythorpe)	Lincoln	G. N.	Boston and Louth.
.	.	.	.	.	.	.	.	Academy Park Flour Mill	Forfar	Cal.	Montrose.
.	.	.	.	.	.	.	.	Academy Park Saw Mill	Forfar	Cal.	Montrose.
G	P	F	L	H	C	8	0	Accrington	Lancs	L. & Y.	Blackburn and Burnley.
.	.	.	.	.	.	.	.	Accrington Corporation Sid.	Lancs	L. & Y.	Accrington.
.	.	.	.	.	.	.	.	Accrington Brick & Tile Co.'s Siding	Lancs	L. & Y.	Huncoat.
.	.	.	.	.	.	.	.	Accrington Gas and Water Board Siding	Lancs	L. & Y.	Great Harwood.
G	P	F	L	H	C	.	.	Achanalt	Ross&Cro'	High.	Dingwall and Kyle of Lochalsh.
.	.	.	.	.	.	.	.	Acharn Siding	Perth	Cal.	See Killin.
G	P	F	L	H	C	1	10	Achill	Mayo	M. G. W.	Bch. from Manulla Junc. Station.
.	.	.	.	.	.	.	.	Achindarroch Depot	Argyll	Cal.	See Duror.
.	P	.	.	.	.	.	.	Ach-na-Cloich	Argyll	Cal.	Callander and Oban.
G	P	F	L	H	C	2	0	Achnasheen	Ross&Cro'	High.	Dingwall and Kyle of Lochalsh.
G	P	F	L	H	C	.	.	Achnashellach	Ross&Cro'	High.	Dingwall and Kyle of Lochalsh.
G	P	.	L	H	.	.	.	Achterneed	Ross&Cro'	High.	Dingwall and Kyle of Lochalsh.
.	.	.	.	.	.	.	.	Ackers, Whitley & Co.'s Bickershaw or Plank Lane Colliery	Lancs	L. & N. W.	Leigh and Bedford.
.	.	.	.	.	.	.	.	Acklam Foundry	Yorks	N. E.	Middlesbro'.
.	.	.	.	.	.	.	.	Acklam Iron Works, Coke Ovens and Wharf	Yorks	N. E.	Middlesbro'.
.	.	.	.	.	.	.	.	Acklam Warrant Store and Wharf	Yorks	N. E.	See Connal's (Middlesbro'.)
G	P	F	L	H	C	1	0	Acklington	Northumb	N. E.	Morpeth and Berwick.
.	.	.	.	.	.	.	.	Amble Junction Siding	Northumb	N. E.	Acklington and Chevington.
.	.	.	.	.	.	.	.	Acklington Colliery	Northumb	N. E.	Amble.
.	.	.	.	.	.	.	.	Ackroyd Bros.' Morley Main Colliery	Yorks	L. & N. W.	Morley.
.	.	.	.	.	.	.	.	Ackton Hall Colliery	Yorks	Mid.	Normanton (for South Traffic). Oakenshaw (for North Traffic).
.	.	.	.	.	.	.	.	Ackton Hall Colliery (L. & Y.)	Yorks	L. & Y.—G.N.—N.E.	Featherstone.
G	P	F	L	H	C	8	0	Ackworth (S. & K. Jt.)	Yorks	S.&K.Jt.(Mid. & N. E.)	Moorthorpe and Pontefract.
.	P	.	.	H	C	.	.	Ackworth (S. & K. Jt.)	Yorks	G. C.	Over S. & K. Jt. from Swinton Junc.
.	P	.	.	H	C	.	.	Ackworth (S. & K. Jt.)	Yorks	G. N.	Over S. & K. Jt. Line.
G	P	F	L	H	C	1	10	Acle	Norfolk	G. E.	Norwich and Yarmouth, Vauxhall.
.	.	.	.	.	.	.	.	Acme Lathe & Products Co.'s Siding	Lancs	Trafford Park Estate	Manchester.
.	.	.	.	.	.	.	.	Acme Manufacturing Co.'s Sid.	Lanark	N. B.	Shettleston.
.	.	.	.	.	.	.	.	Acme Package Co.'s Siding	Lanark	Cal.	Glasgow, South Side.
.	.	.	.	.	.	.	.	Acme Steel Foundry Co.'s Sid.	Lanark	N. B.	Shettleston.
.	.	.	.	.	.	.	.	Acme Wood Flooring Co.'s Siding	Essex	G E—G N—L&NW—Mid	London, Victoria Docks.
.	P	.	.	.	.	.	.	Acocks Green & South Yardley	Worcester	G. W.	Birmingham and Leamington.
.	.	.	.	.	.	.	.	ACREFAIR—			
.	.	.	.	.	.	.	.	Bower's Brick Works Sid.	Denbigh	G. W.	Acrefair.
G	P	F	.	.	.	1	0	High Level	Denbigh	G. W.	Ruabon and Llangollen.
.	.	.	.	.	.	.	.	Hughes & Lancaster's Sid.	Denbigh	G. W.	Rhos and Acrefair, Low Level.
G	.	.	.	.	.	.	.	Low Level	Denbigh	G. W.	Rhos and Trevor Junction.
.	.	.	.	.	.	.	.	Acton	Middlesex	G. W.— N. S. W. Jn.Jt.	See London.
.	.	.	.	.	.	.	.	Acton and Willesden Brick Works	Middlesex	G. W.	London, Acton.
G	P	.	L	H	.	1	10	Acton Bridge	Cheshire..	L. & N. W.	Crewe and Warrington.

EXPLANATION—G *Goods Station.*   P *Passenger and Parcel Station.*   P* *Passenger, but not Parcel or Miscellaneous Traffic.*
F *Furniture Vans, Carriages, Portable Engines, and Machines on Wheels.*   L *Live Stock.*
H *Horse Boxes and Prize Cattle Vans.*   C *Carriages by Passenger Train.*

STATION ACCOMMODATION.						CRANE POWER.		STATIONS, &c.	COUNTY.	COMPANY.	POSITION.
						Tons	Cwts.				
.	.	.	.	.	.	.	.	Acton Bridge—continued.			
								Evans, R., & Co.'s Grange			
.	.	.	.	.	.	.	.	Lane Siding	Cheshire...	L. & N. W.	Acton Bridge and Hartford.
.	.	.	.	.	.	.	.	Moulton's Siding	Cheshire...	L. & N. W.	Acton Bridge and Preston Brook.
.	.	.	.	.	.	.	.	Acton Coal Depot	Middlesex	G. W.—N.&S. W. Jn.Jt.	See London.
.	.	.	.	.	.	.	.	Acton Exchange Sids. (G.W.)	Middlesex	G. W.—N. L.	London, Acton.
.	.	.	.	.	.	.	.	Acton Grange Junction	Cheshire...	B'head Jt.—L. & N. W.	Daresbury and Warrington.
.	.	.	.	.	.	.	.	Acton Grange Junction	Lancs	{ B'head Jt.—Manchester Ship Canal	{ See Manchester Ship Canal Co. (Warrington).
.	.	.	.	.	.	.	.	Acton Green	Middlesex	Met. Dist.	See London, Chiswick Park and Acton Green.
.	.	.	.	.	.	.	.	Acton Junction	Middlesex	L.&S.W.—N.S.W.Jn.Jt.	London, Gunnersbury and Acton.
.	.	.	.	.	.	.	.	Acton, South	Middlesex	N. & S. W. Jn. Jt. (L. & N. W., Mid. & N. L.)	See London, South Acton.
.	.	.	.	.	.	.	.	Acton, South, North Junction	Middlesex	Met. Dist.—N S W Jn.Jt.	See London, South Acton, North Jn.
.	.	.	.	.	.	.	.	Acton Wells Junction	Middlesex	{ G.W.—N.&S.W. Jn. Jt. L. N. W.—N S WJn. Jt. Mid.—N.&S. W. Jn. Jt.	London, Acton and Willesden Junc. London, Willesden Jn. (HL)&Acton. London, Harlesden and Acton.
.	.	.	.	.	.	.	.	Acton, West	Middlesex	Met. Dist.	See Ealing Common & West Acton.
.	.	.	.	.	.	.	.	Adamantine Clinker Wks. Sid.	Lincoln	G. N.	Little Bytham.
.	.	.	.	.	.	.	.	Adamson's, D., Siding (G. C.)	Cheshire...	G. C.—Mid.	Newton (for Hyde).
.	.	.	.	.	.	.	.	Adamson's, J., & Co.'s Siding	Cheshire...	S. & M. Jt. (G. C. & Mid.)	Hyde.
.	.	.	.	.	.	.	.	Adams' Siding (G. & P. Jt.)	Lanark	{ Cal. G. & S. W.	Glasgow, Kinning Park. Glasgow, Eglinton Street.
.	.	.	.	.	.	.	.	Adams, T., & Co.'s Siding	Glo'ster	G. W.—Mid.	Gloucester Docks.
.	.	.	.	.	.	.	.	Adam Street (Rhy.)	Glamorg'n	Rhy.— L. & N. W.	See Cardiff.
G	P	F	L	H	C	.	.	Adare	Limerick.	G. S. & W.	Limerick and Newcastle West.
.	.	.	.	.	.	.	.	Adare Colliery	Glamorg'n	T. V.	Trealaw.
.	P	.	.	.	.	.	.	Adavoyle	Armagh	G. N. (I.)	Dundalk and Goragh Wood.
.	.	.	.	.	.	.	.	Adcock's, J. P. Siding	Leicester..	Mid.	Ashby-de-la-Zouch.
G	P	F	L	H	C	5	0	Adderbury	Oxon	G. W.	Kings Sutton and Chipping Norton.
.	.	.	.	.	.	.	.	Hook Norton Ironstone Sid.	Oxon	G. W.	Adderbury.
G	P	F	L	H	C	.	.	Adderley	Salop	G. W.	Nantwich and Market Drayton.
.	.	.	.	.	.	.	.	Adderley Green	Staffs	N. S.	Branch from Botteslow Junction.
.	.	.	.	.	.	.	.	Adderley Green Colliery	Staffs	N. S.	Adderley Green.
.	.	.	.	.	.	.	.	Chatterley-Whitfield Cols—			
.	.	.	.	.	.	.	.	Mossfield Colliery	Staffs	N. S.	Adderley Green.
.	.	.	.	.	.	.	.	Ubberley Colliery	Staffs	N. S.	Adderley Green.
.	.	.	.	.	.	.	.	Hulme Colliery	Staffs	N. S.	Adderley Green.
.	.	.	.	.	.	.	.	Lawn Colliery	Staffs	N. S.	Adderley Green.
.	.	.	.	.	.	.	.	Mossfield Colliery	Staffs	N. S.	Adderley Green.
.	.	.	.	.	.	.	.	Stirrup & Pye's Siding	Staffs	N. S.	Adderley Green.
.	.	.	.	.	.	.	.	Adderley Park	Warwick.	L. & N. W.	See Birmingham.
								Adderley Park Brick Co.'s			
.	.	.	.	.	.	.	.	Siding (L. & N. W.)	Warwick.	L. & N. W.—Mid.	Birmingham, Adderley Park.
G	P	.	L	.	.	1	10	Addiewell	Edinboro'	{ Cal. N. B.	Holytown and Edinboro'. Branch from Addiewell Junction.
.	.	.	.	.	.	.	.	Addiewell Oil Works	Edinboro'	N. B.	Near Addiewell.
G	.	.	.	.	.	.	.	Cuthill Siding	L'thgow	N. B.	Whitburn and Addiewell.
.	.	.	.	.	.	.	.	Foulshiels Brick Works	L'lithgow	N. B.	Whitburn and Addiewell.
.	.	.	.	.	.	.	.	Foulshiels Colliery	L'lithgow	N. B.	Whitburn and Addiewell.
.	.	.	.	.	.	.	.	Addiewell Junction	L'lithgow	N. B.	Whitburn and Bents.
.	.	.	.	.	.	.	.	Addiewell Pits & Oil Works	Edinboro'	Cal.	West Calder.
G	P	.	L	H	C	1	10	Addingham	Yorks	Mid.	Skipton and Ilkley.
.	.	.	.	.	.	.	.	Addington	N'hamptn	L. & N. W.	See Ringstead and Addington.
.	.	.	.	.	.	.	.	Addiscombe Road	Surrey	S. E. & C.	See Croydon.
								Addison Colliery and Coke			
.	.	.	.	.	.	.	.	Ovens	Durham	N. E.	Blaydon.
.	.	.	.	.	.	.	.	Addison Road (W.L. Jt.)	Middlesex	WLJt—LSW—LB&SC	See London, Kensington.
G	P	F	L	H	C	5	0	Addlestone	Surrey	L. & S.W.	Weybridge and Chertsey.
.	.	.	.	.	.	.	.	Coxes Lock Mill Siding	Surrey	L. & S.W.	Addlestone.
.	.	.	.	.	.	.	.	Addlestone Junction	Surrey	L. & S.W.	Weybridge and Addlestone.
.	.	.	.	.	.	.	.	Adelaide and Windsor	Antrim	G. N. (I.)	See Belfast.
.	.	.	.	.	.	.	.	Adelaide Colliery	Durham	N. E.	Shildon.
.	.	.	.	.	.	.	.	Adelaide Works (C. L. C.)	Cheshire...	C. L. C.—L. & N. W.	See Salt Union, Ltd. (Northwich).
G	P	F	L	H	C	1	15	Adisham (for Wingham)	Kent	S. E. & C.	Canterbury and Dover.
G	P	F	L	H	C	1	10	Adlestrop	Glo'ster	G. W.	Oxford and Evesham.
G	P	.	.	.	.	10	0	Adlington	Cheshire...	L. & N. W.	Macclesfield and Stockport.
G	P	F	L	H	C	5	0	Adlington	Lancs	L. & Y.	Bolton and Chorley.
.	.	.	.	.	.	.	.	Davies & Eckersley's Sid.	Lancs	L. & Y.	Adlington and Blackrod.
								Duxbury Park Colliery			
.	.	.	.	.	.	.	.	(L. & Y. and L. U. Jt.)	Lancs	L. & Y.	Near Adlington.

EXPLANATION—G *Goods Station.*   P *Passenger and Parcel Station.*   P* *Passenger, but not Parcel or Miscellaneous Traffic.*
F *Furniture Vans, Carriages, Portable Engines, and Machines on Wheels.*   L *Live Stock.*
H *Horse Boxes and Prize Cattle Vans.*   C *Carriages by Passenger Train.*

STATION ACCOMMODATION.						CRANE POWER.	STATIONS, &c.	COUNTY.	COMPANY.	POSITION.
						Tons Cwts.	Adlington—*continued.*			
..	..	..	..	..	..		Ellerbeck Colliery Co.'s Ellerbeck Colliery (L. & Y. and L. U. Jt.)..........	Lancs	L. & Y.	Near Adlington.
..	..	..	..	..	..		Grindford Bar Siding	Lancs	L. & Y.	Near Adlington.
..	..	..	..	..	..		Meadow Pit Siding	Lancs	L. & Y.	Adlington.
..	..	..	..	..	..		Wigan Coal and Iron Co.'s Brink's Colliery (L. & Y. and L. U. Jt.)	Lancs	L. & Y.	Near Adlington.
..	..	..	..	..	..		Adlington........................	Lancs	L&Y&LUJt. (LNW&LY)	See White Bear (Adlington).
..	..	..	..	..	..		Adlington Junction	Lancs	L.&Y.—L. & Y. & L.U.Jt.	Chorley and Boar's Head.
..	..	..	..	..	..		Adlington's Flour Mill	Derby	Mid.	Ilkeston Town.
..	..	..	..	..	..		Adlington's Flour Mill	Notts	Mid.	Sutton Junction Station.
..	P	..	..	..	..		Admaston	Salop	S.&W'tn.Jt.(GW&LNW)	Shrewsbury and Wellington.
..	..	..	..	..	..		Admiralty Siding	Dorset	W.&P.Jt.(GW&L&SW)	Portland.
G	P	..	..	..	..		Adolphus Street (G. N.)	Yorks	G. N.—G. C.	See Bradford.
G	P	..	..	..	..		Adoon *(Book to Ballinamore)*..	Leitrim	C. & L.	Mohill and Ballinamore.
..	..	..	..	..	..		Adrain, Chambers & Co.'s Sid.	Derby	Mid.	Killamarsh.
G	P	F	L	H	C		Advie............................	Inverness	G. N. of S.	Craigellachie and Boat of Garten.
..	..	..	..	..	..		Adwalton	Yorks	G. N.	See Drighlington and Adwalton.
..	..	..	..	..	..		Adwick Junction	Yorks	W.R.&G.Jt. (G.C.&G.N.)	Bramwith and Hampole.
..	..	..	..	..	..		Adwick-le-Street	Yorks	W.R.&G.Jt. (G.C.&G.N.)	See Carcroft and Adwick-le-Street.
..	..	..	..	..	..		Adwick Siding (G.C.)	Yorks	G.C.—Mid.	Same as Manvers Main Col. No. 1 Pit.
G	P	..	..	..	..		Afon Wen (Cam.)	Carnarvon	{ Cam. { L. & N. W.	Portmadoc and Pwllheli. Over Cam. from Afon Wen Junc.
..	..	..	..	..	..		Afon Wen Junction	Carnarvon	Cam.—L. & N. W.	Criccieth and Carnarvon.
..	..	..	..	..	..		Afton Pit	Ayr	G. & S.W.	New Cumnock.
..	..	..	..	..	..		Agate & Son's Siding	Sussex	L. B. & S. C.	Horsham.
..	..	..	..	..	..		Agecroft Colliery	Lancs	L. & Y.	Brindle Heath.
..	..	..	..	..	..		Agglament Patent Fuel Co.'s Siding	Glamorg'n	GW—LNW—Mid—RSB	Swansea.
G	P	..	L	H	..	3 0	Aghadowey	Derry	N. C. Com. (Mid.)........	Macfin Junction and Magherafelt.
..	..	..	..	..	..		Agnes Pit......................	Cumb'land	WC&EJt.(Fur&L&NW)	See Cleator Iron Ore Co. (Eskett).
..	..	..	..	..	..		Aigburth	Lancs	{ C L C. (G C, G N & Mid) { L. & N. W.	Same as Mersey Road. See Mossley Hill (for Aigburth).
..	..	..	..	..	..		Aikbank Junction	Cumb'land	M. & C.	Wigton and Leegate.
..	..	..	..	..	..		Aikenhead Colliery	Lanark	Cal.	Glasgow, Cathcart.
..	..	..	..	..	..		Ailsa Shipbuilding Co.'s Sid.	Ayr	G. & S.W.	Troon Harbour.
G	P	..	L	H	..		Ainderby	Yorks	N. E.	Northallerton and Leyburn.
..	..	..	..	..	..		Ainscough Siding	Lancs	L. & Y.	Burscough Junction.
..	..	..	..	..	..		Ainsdale	Lancs	C.L.C. (S'port. Exten.)..	See Seaside (for Ainsdale).
G	P	..	..	..	..	}	Ainsdale (L. & Y.)	Lancs	{ L. & Y. { L. & N. W.	Liverpool and Southport. Over L. & Y. from Bootle Junction.
..	P	..	..	..	..					
..	..	..	..	..	..		Marshall's Siding	Lancs	L. & Y.	Ainsdale.
..	..	..	..	..	..		Mill Siding	Lancs	L. & Y.	Ainsdale.
..	..	..	..	..	..		Ainsworth & Son's Siding	Cumb'land	WC&E Jt. (Fur&L&NW)	Moor Row.
..	..	..	..	..	..		Ainsworth's Margaret Pit	Cumb'land	WC&EJt. (Fur&L&NW)	See Cleator Iron Ore Co. (Eskett).
..	..	..	..	..	..		Ainsworth's Pottery	Durham ...	N. E.	Stockton-on-Tees, North Shore.
							AINTREE—			
G	P	..	L	H	..	5 0	(Station)	Lancs	C.L.C. (G.C., G.N.& Mid.)	Liverpool and Southport.
G	P	..	L	H	..	1 10	(Station)	Lancs	L. & Y.	Liverpool and Ormskirk.
..	..	..	..	..	..		(Station)	Lancs	L. & N. W.	See Liverpool, Walton (for Aintree).
..	P*	..	..	..	..		Cinder Lane	Lancs	L. & Y.	Fazakerley Junction and N. Mersey.
..	..	..	..	..	..		Hartley's Brick Works......	Lancs	C.L.C. (G.C., G.N.& Mid.)	Aintree (C. L. C.).
..	..	..	..	..	..		Junction	Lancs	C. L. C. (S'port. Exten.).	Aintree and Southport.
..	..	..	..	..	..		Junction	Lancs	C. L. C.—L. & Y.	Aintree and Maghull.
..	..	..	..	..	..		Smith's or Hartley's Brick Siding	Lancs	L. & Y.	Aintree (North Mersey Branch).
							AIRDRIE—			
G	P	F	L	H	C	15 0	(Station)	Lanark ...	Cal.	Branch near Whifflet.
..	..	..	..	..	..	25 0	Albert Boiler & Engineering Works	Lanark ...	Cal.	Calder and Airdrie.
..	..	..	..	..	..		Alert Foundry	Lanark ...	N. B.	Branch from Airdrie, South.
..	..	..	..	..	..		Bellsdyke Colliery............	Lanark ...	N. B.	Branch from Airdrie, South.
..	..	..	..	..	..		Branch Junction	Lanark ...	Cal.	Whifflet and Langloan.
..	..	..	..	..	..		Calderbank Colliery	Lanark ...	N. B.	Branch—Rawyards & Brownieside.
..	..	..	..	..	..		Calderbank Steel Works ...	Lanark ...	N. B.	Branch—Rawyards & Brownieside.
..	..	..	..	..	..	10 0	Caledonian Wire Rope Co.'s Siding	Lanark ...	Cal.	Calder and Airdrie.
G	..	..	..	..	..		Carlisle Road Siding	Lanark ...	N. B.	Clarkston & Airdrie, South.
..	..	..	..	..	..		Chapelside Boiler Works ...	Lanark ...	N. B.	Commonhead & Airdrie, North.
..	..	..	..	..	..		Chapelside Foundry	Lanark ...	N. B.	Commonhead and Airdrie, North.

EXPLANATION—G *Goods Station.*   P *Passenger and Parcel Station.*   P* *Passenger, but not Parcel or Miscellaneous Traffic.*
F *Furniture Vans, Carriages, Portable Engines, and Machines on Wheels.*   L *Live Stock.*
H *Horse Boxes and Prize Cattle Vans.*   C *Carriages by Passenger Train.*

STATION ACCOMMODATION.						CRANE POWER.		STATIONS, &c.	COUNTY.	COMPANY.	POSITION.
						Tons	Cwts.				
	P							AIRDRIE—*continued.*			
	P							Commonhead	Lanark ...	N. B.	Coatbridge & Rawyards.
G								Commonhead Siding.........	Lanark ...	N. B.	Commonhead.
								Craigneuk Cols. Nos. 5 & 6	Lanark ...	Cal.	Branch near Airdrie.
								Dalmacoulter Quarry	Lanark ...	N. B.	Branch—Commonhead & Rawyards.
								Gartness Colliery	Lanark ...	Cal.	Branch near Airdrie.
								Gas Works	Lanark ...	N. B.	Commonhead and Airdrie, North.
								Henderson's Siding	Lanark ...	N. B.	Airdrie, South.
								Junction	Lanark ...	Cal.	Calder and Airdrie.
G			L			5	0	North	Lanark ...	N. B.	Branch from Commonhead.
								North Western Bolt, Rivet, and Nut Co.'s Siding ...	Lanark ...	Cal.	Airdrie.
								North West Rivet Works ...	Lanark ...	N. B.	Bellsdyke Branch.
								Paterson & Son's Siding ...	Lanark ...	N. B.	Commonhead and Airdrie, North.
								Roughcraig Colliery	Lanark ...	N. B.	Branch—Commonhead & Rawyards.
								Roughcraig Quarry	Lanark ...	N. B.	Branch—Commonhead & Rawyards.
								Scottish Steel Grit Works	Lanark ...	N. B.	Branch from Airdrie, South.
								Shanks & Son's Wood Yard	Lanark ...	N. B.	Commonhead & Airdrie, North.
								Sharp's Locomotive Works	Lanark ...	N. B.	Airdrie, South
	P			H	C			South........................	Lanark ...	N. B.	Coatbridge, Sunnyside & Bathgate Upper.
G		F	L					South Sidings	Lanark ...	N. B.	Airdrie, South Station.
								Standard Works Siding (Airdrie Iron Co.)	Lanark ...	N. B.	Airdrie, North.
								Steel Foundry................	Lanark ...	N. B.	Branch from Airdrie, South.
								Stevenson & Mackay's Sid.	Lanark ...	N. B.	Commonhead and Airdrie, North.
								Thrushbush Quarry	Lanark ...	N. B.	Branch—Commonhead & Rawyards.
								Victoria Engine Works ...	Lanark ...	N. B.	Branch from Airdrie, South.
								Airdrie Cotton Mills	Lanark ...	N. B.	Rawyards.
								Airdriehill Colliery	Lanark ...	N. B.	Same as Stanrigg Pit, No. 5 Siding (Rawyards).
								Airdriehill Quarry............	Lanark ...	N. B.	Rawyards.
								Airdriehouse Brick Works ...	Lanark ...	N. B.	Coatbridge, Sunnyside.
								Airdrie Iron Co.'s Siding......	Lanark ...	N. B.	Same as Standard Works Siding (Airdrie, North).
								Aird's Siding	Glo'ster ...	G. W.	Bristol, Avonmouth Docks.
								Aird's Siding	Middlesex	G. W.— L. & N. W.	London, Chelsea Basin.
								Aird's Siding	Somerset..	G. W.	Sandford and Banwell.
								Aire & Calder Chemical Wks. (Hunt Bros.)	Yorks	N. E.	Castleford.
								Aire & Calder Glass Bottle Works (E. Breffit & Co.)— Ashton Works	Yorks	N. E.	Castleford.
								Rye Bread Works	Yorks	N. E.	Castleford.
								Airedale Carriage & Wgn. Wks	Yorks	Mid.	Leeds, Kirkstall.
G	P	F	L	H	C	2	0	Airth...........................	Stirling ...	Cal.	Larbert and Alloa.
								Aitken Colliery	Fife.........	N. B.	Kelty.
								Aitkenhead Colliery	Lanark ...	Cal.	Baillieston.
								Aitkenhead's Siding	Lanark ...	Cal.	High Blantyre.
								Aitken's Brewery (N.B.)......	Stirling ...	N. B.—Cal.	Same as Falkirk Brewery (Falkirk, Grahamston).
								Aizlewood's Corn Mills (G.C.)	Yorks	G. C.—G. N.—Mid. ...	Sheffield, Bridgehouses.
								Aizlewood's, J., Siding.........	Yorks	Mid.	Sheffield, Pond Street.
G	P	F	L	H	C	1	0	Akeld	Northumb	N. E.	Alnwick and Coldstream.
								Akeroyd and Son's Siding ...	Yorks	G. N.	Woodkirk.
								Albert Basin	Down	G. N. (I.)	See Newry.
								Albert Boiler & Engineering Works	Lanark ...	Cal.	See Airdrie.
								Albert Dock	Edinboro'	Cal.—N. B.	See Leith.
								Albert Dock (N.E.)	Yorks	N. E.—L. & N. W.	See Hull.
								Albert Dock	Essex	GE—GW—L&NW—Mid	See London, Victoria & Albert Dks.
								Albert Dock (L. & I. D.)	Essex	L. & I. D—G. E.—G N. —GW—L & NW—Mid	See London, Royal Albert Dock.
G						12	0	Albert Edward Dock	Northumb	N. E.	Branch from Percy Main.
								Albert Harbour (G. & S. W.)	Renfrew ...	G. & S. W.—N.B.	See Greenock.
								Albert Hill Bge. & Boiler Wks.	Durham ...	N. E.	Darlington, Hope Town.
								Albert Hill Forge Co.'s Wks.	Durham ...	N. E.	Darlington, Hope Town.
								Albert Hill Foundry	Durham ...	N. E.	Darlington, Hope Town.
								Albert Hill Wagon Works ...	Durham ...	N. E.	See Darlington Wagon & Engineering Co. (Darlington).
								Albert Oil Mills Co.'s Sid (G.E.)	Norfolk ...	G. E.— G. N.— Mid. ...	Lynn Docks.
								Albert Park	Lancs	Mid.	See Withington and Albert Park.

EXPLANATION—G *Goods Station.*   P *Passenger and Parcel Station.*   P* *Passenger, but not Parcel or Miscellaneous Traffic.*
F *Furniture Vans, Carriages, Portable Engines, and Machines on Wheels.*   L *Live Stock.*
H *Horse Boxes and Prize Cattle Vans.*   C *Carriages by Passenger Train.*

STATION ACCOMMODATION.						CRANE POWER.		STATIONS, &c.	COUNTY.	COMPANY.	POSITION.
						Tons	Cwts				
.	.	.	.	.	.	.	.	Albert Quay	Aberdeen	Cal.—N.B.	See Aberdeen, Guild Street.
.	.	.	.	.	.	.	.	Albert Quay	Cork	C.B. & S.C.	See Cork.
.	.	.	.	.	.	.	.	Albert Shaft Works (C. L. C.)	Cheshire	C.L.C.—L. & N. W.	See Salt Union Ltd. (Northwich).
.	.	.	.	.	.	.	.	Albert Street	Cork	C. B. & P.	See Cork.
G	P	.	.	.	.	5	0	Albion	Staffs	L & N. W.	Birmingham and Wolverhampton.
.	.	.	.	.	.	.	.	Lees Siding	Staffs	L & N. W.	Albion and Dudley Port.
.	.	.	.	.	.	.	.	Miles Druce & Co.'s Siding	Staffs	L & N. W.	Albion and Dudley Port.
.	.	.	.	.	.	.	.	Page & Sons' Siding	Staffs	L & N. W.	Albion and Dudley Port.
.	.	.	.	.	.	.	.	Parkes & Co.'s Albion Wks.	Staffs	L & N. W.	Albion and Dudley Port.
.	.	.	.	.	.	.	.	Stone Bros.' Siding	Staffs	L & N. W.	Albion and Dudley Port.
.	.	.	.	.	.	.	.	Stringer Bros.' Siding	Staffs	L & N. W.	Albion and Dudley Port.
.	.	.	.	.	.	.	.	Tupper & Co.'s Britannia Works	Staffs	L & N. W.	Albion and Dudley Port.
.	.	.	.	.	.	.	.	West Bromwich Gas Co.'s Siding	Staffs	L & N. W.	Albion and Oldbury.
.	.	.	.	.	.	.	.	Williams & Co.'s Old Union Pits & Furnaces.	Staffs	L & N. W.	Albion and Oldbury.
.	.	.	.	.	.	.	.	Albion Brick and Tile Works	Northumb	N. E.	Blyth.
.	.	.	.	.	.	.	.	Albion Carriage and Wagon Works Siding	Glo'ster	G. W.	Grange Court.
.	.	.	.	.	.	.	.	Albion Clay Co.'s Sid. (Mid.)	Leicester	Mid.— L. & N. W.	Woodville.
.	.	.	.	.	.	.	.	Albion Colliery	Glamorg'n	T. V.	Cilfynydd.
.	.	.	.	.	.	.	.	Albion Corn Mill	Lancs	L. & N. W.	Same as Hamilton's Sid. (Oldham).
.	.	.	.	.	.	.	.	Albion Dry Dock	Glamorg'n	GW—LNW—Mid—RSB	See Victoria Dry Dks. Co. (Swansea).
.	.	.	.	.	.	.	.	Albion Foundry	Staffs	L. & N. W.	Hednesford.
.	.	.	.	.	.	.	.	Albion Iron Works	Lancs	L. & N. W.	See Monks, Hall & Co. (Wigan).
.	.	.	.	.	.	.	.	Albion Mill Co.'s Siding	Lancs	L. & Y.	Helmshore.
.	.	.	.	.	.	.	.	Albion Saw Mill (G. Clark and Co.)	Durham	N. E.	West Hartlepool.
.	.	.	.	.	.	.	.	Albion Siding	Lancs	L. & N. W.	Same as Atherton Urban District Council Siding (Atherton).
.	.	.	.	.	.	.	.	Albion Siding	Leicester	Mid.	See Wright, W. T., & Co.'s (Sileby).
.	.	.	.	.	.	.	.	Albion Spinning Co.'s Siding	Lancs	L. & Y.	Hollinwood.
.	.	.	.	.	.	.	.	Albion Steel Works Siding	Glamorg'n	G. W.	Briton Ferry.
.	.	.	.	.	.	.	.	Albion Works	Staffs	L. & N. W.	Same as Parkes & Co.'s Sid. (Albion).
.	.	.	.	.	.	.	.	Albright and Wilson's Works Siding	Worcester	G. W.	Oldbury.
G	P	F	L	H	C	5	0	Albrighton	Salop	G. W.	Wellington and Wolverhampton.
.	.	.	.	.	.	.	.	Albury	Surrey	S. E. & C.	See Chilworth and Albury.
G	P	F	L	H	C	1	10	Alcester (Mid)·	Warwick	{ Mid. { G. W.	Evesham and Redditch. Over Mid. from Alcester Junction.
.	.	.	.	.	.	.	.	Alcester Junction	Warwick	G. W.— Mid.	Bearley and Alcester Station.
.	.	.	.	.	.	.	.	Aldam Junction	Yorks	G. C.	Dovecliffe and Wombwell.
.	.	.	.	.	.	.	.	Aldby Limestone Quarry	Cumb'land	W C & E Jt. (Fur & L N W)	See Whitehaven Hematite Iron Co.'s Sidings (Cleator Moor).
G	P	F	.	H	C	1	10	Aldeburgh	Suffolk	G. E.	Branch from Saxmundham.
G	P	.	L	.	.	.	.	Aldeby	Norfolk	G. E.	Beccles and Yarmouth, South Town.
G	P	.	L	.	.	.	.	Alderbury Junction	Wilts	L. & S.W.	Salisbury and Dean.
G	P	F	L	H	C	5	0	Aldergrove	Antrim	G. N. (I.)	Antrim and Lisburn.
G	P	F	L	H	C	2	0	Alderley Edge	Cheshire	L. & N. W.	Crewe and Stockport.
.	.	.	.	.	.	.	.	Aldermaston	Berks	G. W.	Reading and Newbury.
.	.	.	.	.	.	.	.	Aldersey's Siding	Cheshire	L. & N. W.	Same as Jones' Sid. (Tattenhall Rd.).
.	.	.	.	.	.	.	.	Aldersgate Street (Met.)	Middlesex	Met.—G. N.—G. W.—Mid.—S. E. & C.	See London.
								ALDERSHOT—			
.	.	.	.	.	.	.	.	Aldershot Brick Co.'s Sid.	Hants	L. & S.W.	Aldershot.
.	.	.	.	.	.	.	.	Aylwards Siding	Hants	L. & S.W.	Aldershot.
.	.	.	.	.	.	.	.	Gas Co.'s Siding	Surrey	L. & S.W.	Tongham.
.	.	.	.	.	.	.	.	Government Sids. (L & S W)	Hants	L. & S. W.—S. E. & C.	Aldershot.
G	P	F	L	H	C	8	0	Junction	Hants	L. & S.W.—S. E. & C.	Aldershot Town and Ash.
.	P	.	.	.	.	.	.	North Camp	Surrey	S. E. & C.	Guildford and Reading.
.	P	.	.	.	.	.	.	North Camp and Ash Vale	Surrey	L. & S.W.	Woking and Aldershot.
G	P	F	L	H	C	5	0	Town & Camp (L. & S. W.)	Hants	{ L. & S. W. { S. E. & C.	Woking and Farnham. Over L. & S. W. from Aldershot Jn.
.	.	.	.	.	.	.	.	Aldgate (Met.)	Middlesex	Met.— G. W.	See London.
.	.	.	.	.	.	.	.	Aldgate East	Midd'esex	Met. & Met. Dist. Jt.	See London.
.	.	.	.	.	.	.	.	Aldgate East Junction	Middlesex	Met.—Met.&Met.Dist.Jt	London, Bishopsgate and Aldgate East Station.
.	.	.	.	.	.	.	.	Aldgate Junction	Middlesex	Met.—Met.&Met.Dist.Jt.	London, Aldgate and Mark Lane.
.	P	.	.	.	.	.	.	Aldgate. North Curve Junc.	Middlesx	Met.	London, Bishopsgate and Aldgate.
.	.	.	.	.	.	.	.	Aldin Grange	Durham	N. E.	Durham Pass. and Blackhill.
.	.	.	.	.	.	.	.	Aldin Grange Siding	Durham	N. E.	Witton Gilbert.

EXPLANATION—G *Goods Station.* P *Passenger and Parcel Station.* P* *Passenger, but not Parcel or Miscellaneous Traffic.*
F *Furniture Vans, Carriages, Portable Engines, and Machines on Wheels.* L *Live Stock.*
H *Horse Boxes and Prize Cattle Vans.* C *Carriages by Passenger Train.*

STATION ACCOMMODATION.						CRANE POWER.		STATIONS, &c.	COUNTY.	COMPANY.	POSITION.
						Tons	Cwts				
..	..	..	..	..	..	..	..	Aldington Siding	Worcester	G. W.	Evesham.
..	..	..	..	..	..	..	..	Aldin's Siding....................	Surrey ...	L. & S.W.	Richmond.
G	P	F	L	H	C	1	10	Aldridge	Staffs	Mid.	Sutton Coldfield and Walsall.
..	..	..	..	..	..	..	..	Aldridge Col. Co.'s Siding .	Staffs	Mid.	Aldridge and Brownhills.
..	..	..	..	..	..	..	..	Leighswood Colliery	Staffs	Mid.	Near Aldridge.
..	..	..	..	..	..	..	..	Aldridge Cols., Nos. 1 & 2	Staffs	L. & N. W.	Pelsall.
..	..	..	..	..	..	..	..	Aldridge Col. Co.'s Brick Sid.	Staffs	L. & N. W.	Pelsall.
..	..	..	..	..	..	..	..	Aldwarke	Yorks	G. C.	See Parkgate and Aldwarke.
..	..	..	..	..	..	..	..	Aldwarke Main Colliery	Yorks	G. C.—Mid.—G. N.	See Brown, J., & Co.
..	..	..	..	..	..	..	..	Alert Foundry	Lanark ..	N.B.	Airdrie, North.
..	..	..	..	..	..	..	..	Alexander's Bottle Works ...	Durham ..	N. E.	Blaydon.
..	..	..	..	..	..	..	..	Alexander's Siding	Somerset	S.&D.Jt.(L.&S.W.& Mid)	Ashcot.
..	..	..	..	..	..	..	..	Alexandra & Bentinck Docks.	Norfolk ..	GE—G N—Mid—MGNJt	See Lynn Docks.
..	..	..	..	..	..	..	..	Alexandra and Langton Dock.	Lancs	Mid.	See Liverpool.
..	..	..	..	..	..	..	..	Alexandra Colliery...............	Lancs	L. & N. W.	See St. Helens Col. Co. (St. Helens)
..	..	..	..	..	..	..	..	Alexandra Dock	Lancs	L. & Y.	See Liverpool, North Mersey and Alexandra Dock.
..	..	..	..	..	..	..	..	Alexandra Dock	Lancs	L'pool O'head—L & N W.	See Liverpool.
..	..	..	..	..	..	..	..	Alexandra Dock	Yorks	H. & B.—N. E.	See Hull.
..	..	..	..	..	..	..	..	Alexandra Dock Junction ...	Mon	G. W.	See Newport.
..	..	..	..	..	..	..	..	Alexandra Docks (A. D. & R.)	Mon	A.(N.&S.W)D.&R.—G.W	See Newport.
..	..	..	..	..	..	..	..	Alexandra Dk. Timber Depôt.	Lancs	L. & N. W.	See Liverpool.
..	P	..	..	..	..	..	..	Alexandra Palace (G. N.)	Middlesex	{ G. N. .... / N. L. .... }	Branch, Highgate and Finchley. / Over G. N. from Canonbury Junc.
G	P	..	..	..	..	..	..	Alexandra Park	Lancs	G. C.	Manchester, Central & Guide Bge.
..	..	..	..	..	..	..	..	Alexandra Park (G. N.)	Middlesex	G. N.—N. L.—S. E. & C.	See Wood Green (Alexandra Park).
..	..	..	..	..	..	..	..	Alexandra Park (N. B.)	Lanark ...	G. & S. W.—N. B.	See Glasgow.
..	..	..	..	..	..	..	..	Alexandra Park Siding	Middlesex	G. N.	Wood Green.
..	..	..	..	..	..	..	..	Alexandra Pit	Lancs	L. & Y.	See Wigan Coal & Iron Co. (Hindley)
..	..	..	..	..	..	..	..	Alexandra Pit (L. & N.W.)..	Lancs	L.&N.W.—G.C.(Wig. Jn)	See Wigan Coal & Iron Co. (Wigan)
G	P	F	L	H	C	3	0	Alexandria	Dumbartn	D. & B. Jt. (Cal. & N. B.).	Dumbarton & Balloch.
..	..	..	..	..	..	..	..	Alexandria Gas Works......	Dumbartn	D. & B. Jt. (Cal. & N. B.).	Alexandria & Balloch.
..	..	..	..	..	..	..	..	Alexandria Manure Siding.	Dumbartn	D. & B. Jt. (Cal. & N. B.).	Branch from Alexandria.
..	..	..	..	..	..	..	..	Croftengea and Alexandria Works.	Dumbartn	D. & B. Jt. (Cal. & N. B.).	Alexandria and Balloch.
..	..	..	..	..	..	..	..	Dillichip Works	Dumbartn	D. & B. Jt. (Cal. & N. B.).	Branch from Alexandria.
..	..	..	..	..	..	..	..	Ferryfield Print Works ...	Dumbartn	D. & B. Jt. (Cal. & N. B.).	Alexandria and Balloch.
..	..	..	..	..	..	..	..	Lennox Foundry...............	Dumbartn	D. & B. Jt. (Cal. & N. B.).	Alexandria and Balloch.
G	P	F	L	H	C	4	0	Alford	Aberdeen..	G. N. of S.	Branch from Kintore.
G	P	F	L	H	C	5	0	Alford	Lincoln	G. N.	Boston and Louth.
..	..	..	..	..	..	..	..	Alfred Dock Shipping Sheds	Cheshire..	B'head Jt—CLC—NW&L	Birkenhead.
G	P	F	L	H	C	1	10	Alfreton & South Normanton.	Derby ...	Mid.	Clay Cross and Trent.
..	..	..	..	..	..	..	..	Blackwell Col.Co.'s Alfreton Colliery	Derby	Mid.	Branch near Alfreton.
..	..	..	..	..	..	..	..	Alfreton Colliery...................	Derby	Mid.	See Blackwell Col. Co. (Alfreton and South Normanton).
..	..	..	..	..	..	..	..	Alfreton Iron Works............	Derby	Mid.	See Oakes & Co.'s Iron Works (Pye Bridge).
G	P	F	L	H	C	1	10	Algarkirk and Sutterton.......	Lincoln...	G. N.	Spalding and Boston.
..	..	..	..	..	..	..	..	Alice Pit	Cumb'land	C. & W. Jn.	Linefoot.
..	..	..	..	..	..	..	..	Allan Bros. Siding	Northumb	N. E.	Tweedmouth.
..	..	..	..	..	..	..	..	Allan, Cockshut & Co.'s or Wallpaper Manufacturing Co.'s Siding	Middlesex	L. & N. W.	London, Old Ford.
G	P	F	L	H	C	..	..	Allanfearn	Inverness	High.	Inverness and Nairn.
G	P	F	L	H	C	1	10	Allangrange	Ross & Cro'	High.	Muir of Ord and Fortrose.
..	..	..	..	..	..	..	..	Allanrigg Colliery...............	L'lithgow	N. B.	Crofthead.
..	..	..	..	..	..	..	..	Allan's Crwys Siding	Glamorg'n	Rhy	Cardiff.
..	..	..	..	..	..	..	..	Allanshaw Colliery	Lanark ...	{ Cal. / N. B. }	Hamilton, Central. / Hamilton.
..	..	..	..	..	..	..	..	Allanton Colliery	Lanark ...	Cal.	Larkhall.
..	..	..	..	..	..	..	..	Allanton Colliery	Lanark ...	N. B.	Morningside.
..	..	..	..	..	..	..	..	Allanton Fire Clay & Bk. Wks	Lanark ...	Cal.—N. B.	Morningside.
..	..	..	..	..	..	..	..	Allanton Foundry	Lanark ...	Cal.	Morningside.
..	..	..	..	..	..	..	..	Allanwood Paper Mill Siding	Cumb'land	N. E.	Heads Nook.
..	..	..	..	..	..	..	..	Allen & Sons Siding	Suffolk ...	G. E.	Sudbury.
G	P	F	L	H	C	2	0	Allendale	Northumb	N. E.	Branch from Hexham.
..	..	..	..	..	..	..	..	Allen, Edgar, & Co.'s Siding.	Yorks	L. D. & E. C.—Mid.	Sheffield, Tinsley Road.
..	..	..	..	..	..	..	..	Allen, Edgar,&Co.'s Sid.(G.C.)	Yorks	G. C.—Mid.	Tinsley.
..	..	..	..	..	..	..	..	Allensbank Siding	Glamorg'n	T.V.	Cardiff.
..	..	..	..	..	..	..	..	Allen, W. H., Son & Co.'s Siding (Mid.)	Beds.	Mid.—L. & N. W.	Bedford.

EXPLANATION—G *Goods Station.*   P *Passenger and Parcel Station.*   P* *Passenger, but not Parcel or Miscellaneous Traffic.*
F *Furniture Vans, Carriages, Portable Engines, and Machines on Wheels.*   L *Live Stock.*
H *Horse Boxes and Prize Cattle Vans.*   C *Carriages by Passenger Train.*

STATION ACCOMMODATION.						CRANE POWER.		STATIONS, &c.	COUNTY.	COMPANY.	POSITION.
						Tons	Cwts.	Allerdale Coal Co.—			
.	.	.	.	.	.	.	.	Brigham Limestone Siding	Cumb'land	L. & N. W.	Brigham.
.	.	.	.	.	.	.	.	Lowther Pit	Cumb'land	L. & N. W.	Brigham.
.	.	.	.	.	.	.	.	William Pit	Cumb'land	L. & N. W.	Camerton.
.	.	.	.	.	.	.	.	Allerdean Siding	Durham	N. E.	Redheugh.
.	.	.	.	.	.	.	.	Allerford Siding	Somerset	G. W.	Same as Victory Siding (Norton Fitzwarren).
.	P	.	.	.	.	.	.	Aller Siding	Devon	G. W.	Kingskerswell.
G	P	F	L	H	C	5	0	Allerton	Lancs	L. & N. W.	Garston and Liverpool.
.	.	.	.	.	.	.	.	Allerton	Yorks	N. E.	York and Knaresborough.
.	.	.	.	.	.	.	.	Allerton Bywater Colliery	Yorks	N. E.	Ledstone.
.	.	.	.	.	.	.	.	Allerton Haigh Moor Colliery	Yorks	N. E.	Same as Locke & Co.'s Col. (Kippax).
.	.	.	.	.	.	.	.	Allerton Junction	Lancs	C. L. C.—L. & N. W.	Hunt's Cross and Liverpool.
.	.	.	.	.	.	.	.	Allerton Main Colliery	Yorks	N. E.	Same as Bower's Allerton Main Colliery (Kippax).
.	.	.	.	.	.	.	.	Allerton Sidings	Lancs	C.L.C.(G.C,G.N, & Mid.)	See Garston.
.	.	.	.	.	.	.	.	Allhallows Colliery	Cumb'land	M. & C.	Mealsgate.
.	.	.	.	.	.	.	.	Allhusens Works	Durham	N. E.	See United Alkali Co. (Gateshead).
								Alliance Coal & Cannel Co.'s			
.	.	.	.	.	.	.	.	Alliance Colliery	Lancs	G. C. (Wigan Junction)	Wigan.
.	.	.	.	.	.	.	.	Alliance Steel Foundry	Yorks	N. E.	South Bank.
.	.	.	.	.	.	.	.	Alliance Works	Durham	N. E.	See Darlington Wagon & Engineering Co. (Darlington).
.	.	.	.	.	.	.	.	Allington Junction	Lincoln	G. N.	Grantham and Sedgebrook.
.	.	.	.	.	.	.	.	Allington Siding	Kent	S. E. & C.	Maidstone, West.
.	.	.	.	.	.	.	.	Allison & Co.'s Siding	Lanark	N. B.	Shettleston.
								ALLOA—			
G	.	F	L	.	.	3	0	(Station)	Clackman'	Cal.	Branch Terminus.
G	P	F	L	H	C	6	0	(Station, N. B.)	Clackman'	N. B.	Stirling and Dunfermline.
.	P	.	.	H	C	.	.		Clackman'	Cal.	Over N. B. from Longcarse Junc.
.	.	.	.	.	.	.	.	Alloa Brewery (Arrol's)	Clackman'	N. B.	Alloa and Clackmannan Road.
.	.	.	.	.	.	.	.	Alloa Iron Co.'s Siding	Clackman'	Cal.	Alloa.
.	.	.	.	.	.	.	.	Bailey's Pottery	Clackman'	N. B.	Alloa.
.	.	.	.	.	.	.	.	Bass Crest Brewery Siding	Clackman'	Cal.	Alloa.
.	.	.	.	.	.	.	.	British Electric Plant Co.'s Siding	Clackman'	Cal.	Alloa.
.	.	.	.	.	.	.	.			N. B.	Alloa and Longcarse Junction.
G	.	.	.	.	.	20	0	Cousin's Stone Siding	Clackman'	N. B.	Alloa and Tillicoultry.
G	.	.	.	.	.	3	0	Dock	Clackman'	N. B.	Branch from Passenger Station.
.	.	.	.	.	.	.	.	Harbour and Ferry	Clackman'	N. B.	Extension from Goods Station.
.	.	.	.	.	.	.	.	Kelliebank Ship Yard	Clackman'	Cal.	Alloa.
.	.	.	.	.	.	.	.	Longcarse Junction	Clackman'	Cal.—N.B.	Airth and Alloa.
.	.	.	.	.	.	.	.	Paton's Wool Store	Clackman'	N.B.	Alloa and Tillicoultry.
.	.	.	.	.	.	.	.	Richardson's Moss Litter Co.'s Siding	Stirling	Cal.	Airth and Alloa.
G	.	.	.	.	.	.	.	Sauchie Colliery	Clackman'	N.B.	Alloa and Tillicoultry.
G	.	.	.	.	.	.	.	Sauchie General Siding	Clackman'	N. B.	Alloa and Tillicoultry.
G	.	F	L	.	.	2	0	South	Stirling	Cal.	Branch Terminus near Airth.
.	.	.	.	.	.	.	.	Sunnyside Foundry (Melvins)	Clackman'	N. B.	Alloa and Tillicoultry.
.	.	.	.	.	.	.	.	Throsk Siding	Stirling	Cal.	Airth and Alloa.
.	.	.	.	.	.	.	.	West Junction	Clackman'	N. B.	Alloa and Stirling.
.	.	.	.	.	.	.	.	Whinhill Brick Works	Clackman'	N. B.	Alloa and Clackmannan Road.
.	.	.	.	.	.	.	.	Whinhill Colliery	Clackman'	N. B.	Alloa and Clackmannan Road.
.	.	.	.	.	.	.	.	Younger's Ale Siding	Clackman'	N. B.	Alloa.
.	.	.	.	.	.	.	.	Younger's Bottling Stores & Old Malt Barns	Clackman'	Cal.	Alloa.
.	.	.	.	.	.	.	.	Younger's Maltings	Clackman'	N. B.	Alloa.
.	.	.	.	.	.	.	.	Alloa Branch Junction	Stirling	Cal.	Larbert and Bannockburn.
G	.	.	.	.	.	.	.	Alloa Coal Co.'s Siding	Stirling	Cal.	Stirling, Cowpark.
.	.	.	.	.	.	.	.	Allscott Siding	Salop	S.&W' tn Jt (GW&LNW)	Shrewsbury and Wellington.
.	.	.	.	.	.	.	.	Allsopp & Son's Sidings	Staffs	L&NW—Mid—GN—NS.	Burton-on-Trent.
.	.	.	.	.	.	.	.	Allsup & Son's Siding	Lancs	N U Jt(L & NW & L & Y)	Preston, Charles Street.
.	.	.	.	.	.	.	.	Alma Colliery	Derby	Mid.	Hasland.
G	P	F	.	H	C	.	.	Alma Colliery	Durham	N. E.	Pelton.
G	P	.	L	H	C	3	0	Almeley	Hereford	G. W.	Titley and Eardisley.
.	P	.	.	.	.	.	.	Almondbank	Perth	Cal.	Perth and Methven.
G	.	.	.	.	.	.	.	Huntingtower Siding	Perth	Cal.	Perth and Almondbank.
.	P	.	.	.	.	.	.	Ruthven Road	Perth	Cal.	Perth and Almondbank.
G	.	.	.	.	.	.	.	Tibbermuir and Powbridge	Perth	Cal.	Almondbank and Methven.
G	.	.	.	.	.	.	.	Almond Junction Station	Stirling	N. B.	Bowhouse and Bo'ness Junction.
G	.	.	.	.	.	.	.	Blackbraes Siding	Stirling	N. B.	Branch from Almond Junction.
.	.	.	.	.	.	.	.	Canal Siding	Stirling	N. B.	Branch from Almond Junction.

EXPLANATION—G *Goods Station.*   P *Passenger and Parcel Station.*   P* *Passenger, but not Parcel or Miscellaneous Traffic.*
F *Furniture Vans, Carriages, Portable Engines, and Machines on Wheels.*   L *Live Stock.*
H *Horse Boxes and Prize Cattle Vans.*   C *Carriages by Passenger Train.*

STATION ACCOMMODATION.						CRANE POWER.		STATIONS, &c.	COUNTY.	COMPANY.	POSITION.
						Tons	Cwts	Almond Jn. Sta.—*continued.*			
								Craigend Colliery	Stirling ...	N. B.	Branch from Almond Junction.
G	.	.	.	.	.	.	.	Craigend Siding............	Stirling ...	N. B.	Branch from Almond Junction.
.	.	.	.	.	.	.	.	Maddiston Brick Works ...	Stirling ...	N. B.	Branch from Almond Junction.
.	.	.	.	.	.	.	.	Maddiston Quarry........	Stirling ...	N. B.	Branch from Almond Junction.
G	.	.	.	.	.	.	.	Maddiston Siding	Stirling ...	N. B.	Branch from Almond Junction.
.	.	.	.	.	.	.	.	Manuelrigg Colliery	Stirling ...	N. B.	Branch from Almond Junction.
G	.	.	.	.	.	.	.	Parkhall Siding	Stirling ...	N. B.	Branch from Almond Junction.
.	.	.	.	.	.	.	.	Shieldhill Basin	Stirling ...	N. B.	Branch from Almond Junction.
.	.	.	.	.	.	.	.	Shieldhill Colliery	Stirling ...	N. B.	Branch from Almond Junction.
.	.	.	.	.	.	.	.	Shieldhill Exchange Sids.	Stirling ...	N. B.	Branch from Almond Junction.
.	.	.	.	.	.	.	.	Almond's Siding (Belvoir Brick Works)	Notts	G. N.	See Lowfield Sidings (Newark).
.	.	.	.	.	.	.	.	Almond's Standish Brewery	Lancs	L. & N. W.	Wigan.
.	.	.	.	.	.	.	.	Almond Valley Junction......	Perth	Cal.	Perth and Luncarty.
G	P	F	L	H	C	1	0	Alne (*Junc. for Easingwold*)	Yorks	N. E.	York and Thirsk.
G	P	F	L	H	C	1	10	Alness	Ross & Cro'	High.	Dingwall and Invergordon.
G	P	F	L	H	C	5	0	Alnmouth	Northumb	N. E.	Berwick and Morpeth.
.	.	.	.	.	.	.	.	Shortridge Farm Siding ...	Northumb	N. E.	Warkworth and Alnmouth.
G	P	F	L	H	C	4	0	Alnwick	Northumb	N. E.	Alnmouth and Coldstream.
.	.	.	.	.	.	.	.	Alnwick Gas Works	Northumb	N. E.....	Alnwick.
.	.	.	.	.	.	.	.	Alnwick Timber Yard	Northumb	N. E.	Alnwick.
.	.	.	.	.	.	.	.	Broomhill Collieries Coal Depôt.	Northumb	N. E.	Alnwick.
.	.	.	.	.	.	.	.	Radcliffe Coal Co.'s New Coal Depôt	Northumb	N. E.	Alnwick.
.	.	.	.	.	.	.	.	Summit Siding	Northumb	N. E.	Alnwick and Edlingham.
.	.	.	.	.	.	.	.	Alperton	Middlesex	Met. Dist.	See Perivale-Alperton.
.	.	.	.	.	.	.	.	Alpha Engine Works	Lanark	Cal.	Motherwell.
.	.	.	.	.	.	.	.	Alpha Mill Co.'s Siding	Lancs	L. & N. W.	Denton.
.	.	.	.	.	.	.	.	Alphington Road	Devon	G. W.	See Exeter.
.	.	.	.	.	.	.	.	Alps Quarry	Glamorg'n	Barry	Wenvoe.
G	P	F	.	H	C	.	.	Alresford	Essex	G. E.	Colchester and Clacton-on-Sea.
G	P	F	L	H	C	1	10	Alresford	Hants	L. & S.W.	Alton and Winchester.
G	P	.	L	H	C	1	0	Alrewas	Staffs	L. & N. W.	Burton and Lichfield.
G	P	F	L	H	.	5	0	Alsager	Cheshire...	N. S.	Crewe and Harecastle.
.	.	.	.	.	.	.	.	Barker's Siding	Cheshire...	N. S.	Alsager.
.	.	.	.	.	.	.	.	Bibbey's Sand Pits	Cheshire...	N. S.	Lawton Junction.
.	P	.	.	.	.	.	.	Alsager Road	Cheshire...	N. S.	Alsager Junction and Audley.
G	P	.	L	.	.	.	.	Alsop-en-le-dale	Derby	L. & N. W.	Ashbourne and Buxton.
.	.	.	.	.	.	.	.	Hall & Boardman's Siding	Derby	L. & N. W.	Alsop-en-le-dale and Hartington.
G	P	F	L	H	C	3	0	Alston	Cumb'land	N. E.	Branch from Haltwhistle.
.	.	.	.	.	.	.	.	Alston Lime Siding and Depôt	Cumb'land	N. E.	Alston.
.	.	.	.	.	.	.	.	Alston Quarry..................	Cumb'land	N. E.	Alston.
.	.	.	.	.	.	.	.	Alstone Coal Wharf	Glo'ster ...	Mid.	Cheltenham.
.	.	.	.	.	.	.	.	Altami Siding..................	Flint	L. & N. W.	See Parry & Co. (Mold).
G	P	F	L	H	C	5	0	Altcar and Hillhouse	Lancs	C. L. C. (S'port. Exten.)	Aintree and Southport.
G	P	F	L	H	C	5	0		Lancs	L. & Y.	Over C. L. C. from Hillhouse Junc.
G	P*	.	.	H	C	5	0	Altcar Rifle Range (L. & Y.)	Lancs	L. & Y.	Hightown and Formby.
.	P	.	.	.	.	.	.		Lancs	L. & N. W.	Over L. & Y. from Bootle Junction.
.	.	.	.	.	.	.	.	Altham Colliery Co.'s Siding	Lancs	L. & Y.	Great Harwood.
G	P	F	L	H	C	.	.	Althorne	Essex	G. E.	Wickford and Southminster.
.	.	.	.	.	.	.	.	Althorpe	Lincoln	G. C.	Thorne and Barnetby.
G	P	F	L	H	C	10	0	Althorp Park	N'hampt'n	L. & N. W.	Northampton and Rugby.
G	P	F	L	H	C	.	.	Altnabreac	Caithness	High	Helmsdale and Wick.
G	P	.	.	.	.	.	.	Altofts and Whitwood	Yorks	Mid.	Altofts Junction and Methley.
.	.	.	.	.	.	.	.	Briggs' Colliery	Yorks	Mid.	Altofts and Whitwood.
.	.	.	.	.	.	.	.	Altofts Junction	Yorks	Mid.—N. E.	Normanton and Castleford.
G	P	F	L	H	C	5	0	Alton..........................	Hants......	L. & S.W.	Farnham and Winchester.
.	.	.	.	.	.	.	.	Alton Brewery Siding	Hants......	L. & S.W.	Alton.
G	P	.	L	H	.	8	0	Alton	Staffs	N. S.	Leek and Uttoxeter.
.	.	.	.	.	.	.	.	Alton Heights Colliery........	Lanark	Cal.	Lesmahagow.
.	.	.	.	.	.	.	.	Alton Heights Junction	Lanark	Cal.	Lesmahagow and Coalburn.
.	.	.	.	.	.	.	.	Alton Heights Lime Works..	Lanark	Cal.	Lesmahagow.
.	.	.	.	.	.	.	.	Alton Heights Saw Mill	Lanark	Cal.	Lesmahagow.
.	.	.	.	.	.	.	.	Altrincham	Cheshire...	C.L.C.(G.C., G.N. & Mid.)	Same as Hale.
.	.	.	.	.	.	.	.	Altrincham	Cheshire...	L. & N. W.	See Broadheath (Altrincham).
G	P	F	L	H	C	5	0	Altrincham and Bowdon (M. S. J. & A.)	Cheshire...	M S J & A (G C & LNW)	Timperley and Hale.
.	P	.	.	.	.	.	.			C.L.C.(G.C., G.N. & Mid)	Over M. S. J. & A. Line.
.	.	.	.	.	.	.	.	Altrincham, Deansgate Junc.	Cheshire...	C. L. C.—M. S. J. & A...	Baguley and Altrincham.
.	.	.	.	.	.	.	.	Altrincham Junction	Cheshire...	C. L. C.—M. S. J. & A...	Northwich and Altrincham.

EXPLANATION—**G** *Goods Station.*   **P** *Passenger and Parcel Station.*   **P*** *Passenger, but not Parcel or Miscellaneous Traffic.*
F *Furniture Vans, Carriages, Portable Engines, and Machines on Wheels.*   **L** *Live Stock.*
H *Horse Boxes and Prize Cattle Vans.*   **C** *Carriages by Passenger Train.*

G	P	F	L	H	C	Tons	Cwts	STATIONS, &c.	COUNTY.	COMPANY.	POSITION.
.	.	.	.	.	.			Alty's Siding	Lancs	P.&W.Jt. (L&Y&L&NW)	Lytham.
G	P	F	L	H	C	5	0	Alva	Clackman'	N. B.	Branch from Cambus.
.	.	.	.	.	.			Alvanley	Cheshire...	C.L.C. (G.C., G.N.& Mid)	See Helsby and Alvanley.
G	P	.	.	.	.			Alvechurch	Worcester	Mid.	Barnt Green and Redditch.
.	.	.	.	.	.			Alverstoke	Hants	L. & S.W.	See Gosport Road and Alverstoke.
G	P	.	.	.	.			Alverstone	I. of W.	I of W. Cent.	Sandown and Newport.
G	P	.	.	.	.			Alverthorpe	Yorks	G. N.	Wakefield and Ossett.
G	P	F	L	H	C	5	0	Alves	Moray	High	Elgin and Forres.
G	P	F	L	H	C	1	10	Alvescot	Oxon	G. W.	Witney and Fairford.
.	.	.	.	.	.			Alyn Brick, Tile,&Terra Cotta Co.'s Tryddyn Lodge Siding	Flint	L. & N. W.	Coed Talon.
.	.	.	.	.	.			Alyn Steel Tin Plate Works..	Flint	L. & N. W.	Mold.
G	P	F	L	H	C	2	10	Alyth	Perth	Cal.	Branch Terminus near Alyth Junc.
G	.	.	.	.	.			Porterockney Siding	Perth	Cal.	Jordanstone and Alyth.
G	P	F	L	H	C	2	0	Alyth Junction Station	Forfar	Cal.	Coupar Angus and Forfar.
G	.	.	.	.	.			Drumkilbo Siding	Forfar	Cal.	Alyth Junc. and Eassie.
G	P	F	L	H	C	5	0	Ambergate	Derby	Mid.	Derby and Chesterfield.
.	.	.	.	.	.			Buckland Hollow Siding (Duke of Devonshire Sid.)	Derby	Mid.	Ambergate and Butterley.
.	.	.	.	.	.			Bull Bridge Brick Co.'s Sid.	Derby	Mid.	Ambergate and Pye Bridge.
.	.	.	.	.	.			Bull Bridge Canal Wharf..	Derby	Mid.	Near Ambergate.
.	.	.	.	.	.			Bull Bridge Lime Works (Eaton's W. Siding)	Derby	Mid.	Ambergate and Butterley.
.	.	.	.	.	.			Burgon's Mill	Derby	Mid.	Ambergate and Butterley.
.	.	.	.	.	.			Butterley Cl. & Ir. Co.'s Sid.	Derby	Mid.	Ambergate and Wingfield.
.	.	.	.	.	.			Butterley Co.'s Lime Works	Derby	Mid.	Ambergate and Wingfield.
.	.	.	.	.	.			Clay Cross Cl. & Ir. Co.'s Sid.	Derby	Mid.	Ambergate and Wingfield.
.	.	.	.	.	.			Clay Cross Co.'s Lime Works	Derby	Mid.	Ambergate.
.	.	.	.	.	.			Crich Lime Works	Derby	Mid.	Ambergate.
.	.	.	.	.	.			Glossop's Siding	Derby	Mid.	Ambergate.
.	.	.	.	.	.			Johnson & Nephew's Siding	Derby	Mid.	Ambergate and Whatstandwell.
.	.	.	.	.	.			Ambergate Yard	Lincoln	G. N.	Grantham.
G	P	F	L	H	C	1	0	Amberley	Sussex	L. B. & S. C.	Pulborough and Arundel.
.	.	.	.	.	.			Pepper & Son's Siding	Sussex	L. B. & S. C.	Amberley.
.	.	.	.	.	.			Amberswood	Lancs	L. & N. W.	See Hindley and Amberswood.
.	.	.	.	.	.			Amberswood Colliery	Lancs	L. & N. W.	Same as Atherton's (Hindley & A.)
.	.	.	.	.	.			Amberswood East Junction	Lancs	G.C.(Wig.Jn.)—L.&N.W	Bickershaw and Hindley.
.	.	.	.	.	.			Amberswood East Siding	Lancs	L. & N. W.	Same as Crompton and Shawcross Hindley Colliery (Hindley and Amberswood).
.	.	.	.	.	.			Amberswood West Junction	Lancs	G.C.(Wig.Jn.)—L.&N.W	Bickershaw and Brynn.
.	.	.	.	.	.			Amberswood West Siding (G.C., Wigan Junction)	Lancs	G.C.(Wig.Jn.)—L.&N.W	Same as Crompton & Shawcross' Strangeways Hall Colliery.
G	P	F	L	H	C	3	0	Amble	Northumb	N. E.	Branch from Amble Branch Junc.
.	.	.	.	.	.			Acklington Colliery	Northumb	N. E.	Amble.
.	.	.	.	.	.			Radcliffe Newburgh Col.	Northumb	N. E.	Amble.
.	.	.	.	.	.			Amble Branch Junction	Northumb	N. E.	Acklington and Chevington.
.	.	.	.	.	.			Amble Junction Siding	Northumb	N. E.	Acklington. / Chevington.
.	.	.	.	.	.			Amblecote Siding	Staffs	G. W.	See Hall, J., & Co.'s (Stourbridge).
G	P	.	.	.	.		3 0	Ambleside	W'morlnd	Furness / L. & N. W.	Steamer fr. Windermere Lake Side. / Steamer from Bowness.
.	.	.	.	.	.			Amelia Pit	Northumb	N. E.	Same as Shankhouse Col.(Annitsford)
.	.	.	.	.	.			Amen Corner Siding	Berks	L. & S.W.	Bracknell.
.	.	.	.	.	.			American Radiator Co.'s Siding (G.E.)	Essex	GE—GN—L&NW—Mid.	London, Silvertown.
.	.	.	.	.	.			America Wharf	Essex	L. T. & S.	See Anglo-AmericanOilCo(Purfleet).
G	P	F	L	H	C	1 10		Amersham (Met.)	Bucks	Met. / G. C.	Rickmansworth and Aylesbury. / Over Met. Line.
.	P	.	.	H	C		.				
G	P	F	L	H	C	5	0	Amesbury	Wilts	L. & S.W.	Branch from Grateley.
.	.	.	.	.	.			Amiens Street	Dublin	G. N. (I.)	See Dublin.
.	.	.	.	.	.			Amiens Street Junction	Dublin	D. W. & W. (C. of D. Junc.)—G. S. & W.	Dublin.
.	.	.	.	.	.			Amington Colliery	Warwick	L. N. W.—Mid.	Same as Glascote Colliery Co.'s Sid.
G	P	.	L	H	.	3	0	Amisfield	Dumfries	Cal.	Lockerbie and Dumfries.
G	P	F	L	H	C	3	0	Amlwch	Anglesey	L. & N. W.	Branch from Gaerwen.
G	P	.	.	.	.			Ammanford	Carmarth'	G. W.	Pantyffynnon and Garnant.
.	.	.	.	.	.			Ammanford Colliery	Carmarth'	G. W.	Ammanford and Pontamman.
.	.	.	.	.	.			Ammanford Color Works...	Carmarth'	G. W.	Pontamman.
G	.	.	.	.	.			Pontamman	Carmarth'	G. W.	Ammanford and Glanamman.
.	.	.	.	.	.			Pontamman Chemical Wks.	Carmarth'	G. W.	Ammanford and Glanamman.
.	.	.	.	.	.			Amman Iron Co.'s Sid. (Mid.)	Glamorg'n	Mid.—G. W.—L. & N. W.	Brynamman.

EXPLANATION—G *Goods Station.*   P *Passenger and Parcel Station.*   P* *Passenger, but not Parcel or Miscellaneous Traffic.*
F *Furniture Vans, Carriages, Portable Engines, and Machines on Wheels.*   L *Live Stock.*
H *Horse Boxes and Prize Cattle Vans.*   C *Curriages by Passenger Train.*

STATION ACCOMMODATION.						CRANE POWER.		STATIONS, &c.	COUNTY.	COMPANY.	POSITION.
G	P	.	L	H	.	Tons	Cwts	Amotherby	Yorks	N. E.	Malton and Thirsk.
G	P	.	L	H	C	.	.	Ampleforth	Yorks	N. E.	Malton and Thirsk.
								Ampthill	Beds	L. & N. W.	See Millbrook (for Ampthill).
G	P	F	L	H	C	1	10	Ampthill	Beds	Mid.	Bedford and Luton.
G	P	.	L	H		10	0	Ancaster	Lincoln	G. N.	Sleaford and Grantham.
.	.	.	.	.	.	.	.	Anchor Brick Works (Stein's Brick Works)	Stirling	Cal.	Denny, Ingliston.
.	.	.	.	.	.	.	.	Anchor Chemical Works	Lanark	Cal.	Glasgow, Buchanan Street.
.	.	.	.	.	.	.	.	Anchor Fuel Works or Maindy Fuel Works	Glamorg'n	T. V.	Cardiff Docks.
.	.	.	.	.	.	.	.	Anchor Maltings	Herts	G. E.	See Taylor & Sons(Bishops Stortford)
.	.	.	.	.	.	.	.	Anchor Paper Works	Stirling	Cal.	Denny.
.	.	.	.	.	.	.	.	Anchor Siding	Stirling	Cal.	Denny.
.	.	.	.	.	.	.	.	Ancoats	Lancs	Mid.	See Manchester.
.	.	.	.	.	.	.	.	Ancoats Junction	Lancs	L. & Y.— Mid.	Manchester.
.	.	.	.	.	.	.	.	Anderson & Co.'s Foundry	Edinboro'	N. B.	Musselburgh.
.	.	.	.	.	.	.	.	Anderson & Henderson's Saw Mills	Renfrew	Cal.	Glasgow, Kinning Park.
.	.	.	.	.	.	.	.	Anderson & Son's Timber Sid. (N. E.)	Cumb'land	N. E.—L. & N. W.—Mid.	Carlisle.
.	.	.	.	.	.	.	.	Anderson's Siding	Lincoln	G. N. & G. E. Jt	Lea.
.	.	.	.	.	.	.	.	Anderson's Siding	Renfrew	Cal.	Glasgow, West Street.
.	.	.	.	.	.	.	.	Anderson's Siding	Sussex	L. B & S. C.	Slinfold.
.	.	.	.	.	.	.	.	Anderston Brass Foundry (Steven & Struther's) (N.B.)	Lanark	N. B.—Cal.	Glasgow, Stobcross.
.	.	.	.	.	.	.	.	Anderston Cross	Lanark	Cal.	See Glasgow.
.	.	.	.	.	.	.	.	Anderston Foundry	Durham	N. E.	Port Clarence.
								ANDOVER—			
G	P	F	L	H	C	10	0	Junction Sta. (L. & S. W.)	Hants	L. & S. W.	Basingstoke and Salisbury.
										M. & S. W. Jn.	Over L. & S. W. from Red Posts Jn.
.	.	.	.	.	.	.	.	Red Posts Junction	Hants	L. & S.W.—M. & S.W. Jn.	Andover Junc. Sta. and Weyhill.
G	P	F	L	H	C	1	10	Town (L. & S. W.)	Hants	L. & S. W.	Andover Junction and Romsey.
										M. & S. W. Jn.	Over L. & S.W. from Red Posts Jn.
G	P	F	L	H	C	1	10	Andoversford	Glo'ster	G. W.	Bourton-on-Water and Cheltenham.
G	P	F	L	H	C	5	0	Andoversford and Dowdeswell	Glo'ster	M. & S. W. Jn.	Cirencester and Cheltenham.
.	.	.	.	.	.	.	.	Andoversford Junction	Glo'ster	G. W.—M. & S. W. Jn.	Charlton Kings and Cirencester.
.	.	.	.	.	.	.	.	Andrew, J. H., & Co.'s Siding (G. C.)	Yorks	G. C.—G. N.	Sheffield, Bridgehouses.
.	.	.	.	.	.	.	.	Andrews & Baby's Siding	Glamorg'n	GW—LNW—Rhy.—TV	Cardiff.
.	.	.	.	.	.	.	.	Andrews & Co.'s Siding	Down	B. & C. D.	Comber.
.	.	.	.	.	.	.	.	Andrews House Colliery	Durham	N. E.	Redheugh.
.	P	.	.	.	.	.	.	Anerley (L. B. & S. C.)	Kent	L. B. & S. C.	Norwood and Sydenham.
										G. E.	Over L.B. & S. C. from New Cross Jn.
.	.	.	.	.	.	.	.	Angel	Middlesex	C. & S. L.	See London.
G	P	.	.	.	.	3	0	Angel Road	Middlesex	G. E.	Tottenham and Waltham Cross.
.	.	.	.	.	.	.	.	Glover and Mains Siding	Middlesex	G. E.	Angel Road.
.	.	.	.	.	.	.	.	London Fireproof Wall Co.'s Siding	Middlesex	G. E.	Angel Road.
.	.	.	.	.	.	.	.	Martin & Co.'s Siding	Middlesex	G. E.	Angel Road.
.	.	.	.	.	.	.	.	Stacey's Siding	Middlesex	G. E.	Angel Road.
.	.	.	.	.	.	.	.	Tottenham and Edmonton Gas Co.'s Siding	Middlesex	G. E.	Angel Road.
G	.	.	.	.	.	15	0	Angerstein Wharf	Kent	S. E. & C.	Branch—Blackheath & Charlton.
.	.	.	.	.	.	.	.	AngloAmericanOilCo.'sSid.	Kent	S. E. & C.	Angerstein Wharf Branch.
G	P	F	L	H	C	.	.	Angerton	Northumb	N. B.	Reedsmouth and Morpeth.
.	.	.	.	.	.	.	.	Anglesea Colliery	Staffs	L. & N. W.	See Cannock Chase Colliery Co. (Hednesford).
								Anglo-American Oil Co.—			
.	.	.	.	.	.	.	.	America Wharf	Essex	L. T. & S.	Purfleet.
.	.	.	.	.	.	.	.	Caspian Wharf	Essex	L. T. & S.	Purfleet.
.	.	.	.	.	.	.	.	Depôt	Cheshire	Birkenhead Jt.—C.L.C. —N. W. & L.	Birkenhead.
.	.	.	.	.	.	.	.	Depôt	Cornwall	G. W.	Bodmin.
.	.	.	.	.	.	.	.	Depôt	Devon	L. & S. W.	Plymouth, Cattewater Harbour.
.	.	.	.	.	.	.	.	Depôt	Surrey	L. & S. W.	Kingston.
.	.	.	.	.	.	.	.	Siding	Durham	N. E.	Blaydon.
.	.	.	.	.	.	.	.	Siding	Durham	N. E.	Darlington, Hope Town.
.	.	.	.	.	.	.	.	Siding	Durham	N. E.	Sunderland, South Dock.
.	.	.	.	.	.	.	.	Siding	Glo'ster	Clif. Ex. Jt.(G.W. & Mid.)	Bristol, Avonmouth Docks.
.	.	.	.	.	.	.	.	Siding	Kent	S. E. & C.	Angerstein Wharf.
.	.	.	.	.	.	.	.	Siding	Lancs	L. & N. W.	Manchester, London Road.
.	.	.	.	.	.	.	.	Siding	Northumb	N. E.	Blyth.
.	.	.	.	.	.	.	.	Siding	Staffs	L. & N. W.	Wolverhampton.

EXPLANATION—G *Goods Station.*   P *Passenger and Parcel Station.*   P* *Passenger, but not Parcel or Miscellaneous Traffic.*
F *Furniture Vans, Carriages, Portable Engines, and Machines on Wheels.*   L *Live Stock.*
H *Horse Boxes and Prize Cattle Vans.*   C *Carriages by Passenger Train.*

Station Accommodation						Crane Power		STATIONS, &c.	COUNTY.	COMPANY.	POSITION.
						Tons	Cwts.	Anglo-American Oil Co.—*continued.*			
.	.	.	.	.	.	.	.	Siding	Warwick	Mid.	Birmingham.
.	.	.	.	.	.	.	.	Siding	W'morlnd	L. & N. W.	See Kendal Bonded Stores Co (Kendal)
.	.	.	.	.	.	.	.	Siding	Yorks	N. E.	Hull.
.	.	.	.	.	.	.	.	Siding	Yorks	N. E.	York.
.	.	.	.	.	.	.	.	Siding (G. C.)	Lancs	G. C.—Mid.	Manchester, Ardwick.
.	.	.	.	.	.	.	.	Siding (G. E.)	Norfolk	G.E.—G.N.—Mid.	Lynn Docks.
.	.	.	.	.	.	.	.	Siding (N. E.)	Cumb'land	N. E.—L. & N. W.—Mid.	Carlisle.
.	.	.	.	.	.	.	.	Store Siding	Yorks	N. E.	Castleford.
.	.	.	.	.	.	.	.	Store Siding	Yorks	N. E.	Scarborough.
.	.	.	.	.	.	.	.	Anglo - Continental Guano Works (G. E.)	Essex	GE—GN—L&NW—Mid.	London, Silvertown.
.	.	.	.	.	.	.	.	Anglo-Swiss Milk Co.'s Sid.	Bucks	L. & N. W.	Buckingham.
G	P	F	L	H	C	1	10	Angmering	Sussex	L. B. & S. C.	Ford Junction and Worthing.
.	.	.	.	.	.	.	.	Anker Mills	Warwick	L. & N. W.	Same as Fielding & Johnson's Siding (Nuneaton).
.	.	.	.	.	.	.	.	Ankers & Son's Boiler Works	Lancs	L. & N. W.—S. & M. Jt.	Widnes.
.	.	.	.	.	.	.	.	Anlaby Road Junction	Yorks	N. E.	Hessle and Botanic Gardens.
.	P	.	.	.	.	.	.	Annadale (*Book to Drumshambo*)	Leitrim	C. & L.	Ballinamore and Drumshambo.
G	P	F	L	H	C	2	10	Annaghmore	Armagh	G. N. (I.)	Portadown and Dungannon.
G	P	F	L	H	C	5	0	Annan	Dumfries	Cal.	Brayton and Kirtlebridge.
G	P	F	L	H	C	3	0		Dumfries	G. & S. W.	Dumfries and Gretna.
.	.	.	.	.	.	.	.	Cochran & Co.'s Siding	Dumfries	G. & S. W.	Annan and Cummertrees.
.	.	.	.	.	.	.	.	Corsehill Quarry	Dumfries	Cal.	Annan and Kirtlebridge.
.	.	.	.	.	.	.	.	Gulliland Quarry	Dumfries	Cal.	Annan and Kirtlebridge.
.	.	.	.	.	.	.	.	Jackson's Siding	Dumfries	Cal.	Shawhill Junction.
.	.	.	.	.	.	.	.	Newbie Brick Works	Dumfries	G. & S. W.	Annan and Cummertrees.
.	.	.	.	.	.	.	.	Shawhill Siding	Dumfries	Cal.	Bowness and Annan.
.	.	.	.	.	.	.	.			G. & S. W.	Annan Junction.
.	.	.	.	.	.	.	.	Warmanbie Quarry	Dumfries	Cal.	Annan and Kirtlebridge.
.	.	.	.	.	.	.	.	Annandale Pit	Ayr	G. & S. W.	Gatehead.
.	.	.	.	.	.	.	.	Annandale's Mill	Edinboro'	N. B.	Polton.
.	.	.	.	.	.	.	.	Annan Junction	Dumfries	Cal.— G. & S. W.	Bowness and Annan.
.	.	.	.	.	.	.	.	Annanlea Qry (Woodhead Qry)	Dumfries	Cal.	Kirkpatrick.
G	P	F	L	H	C	3	0	Annbank	Ayr	G. & S. W.	Mauchline and Ayr.
.	.	.	.	.	.	.	.	Annbank Brick Works	Ayr	G. & S. W.	Annbank and Drongan.
.	.	.	.	.	.	.	.	Annbank, Nos. 9 and 10 (Muirburn Colliery)	Ayr	G. & S. W.	Annbank and Drongan.
.	.	.	.	.	.	.	.	Auchincruive, Nos. 1 & 2	Ayr	G. & S. W.	Annbank and Monkton.
.	.	.	.	.	.	.	.	Drumley, Nos. 1 and 2	Ayr	G. & S. W.	Annbank.
.	.	.	.	.	.	.	.	Sundrum, Nos. 3 and 4 (Drumdow Colliery)	Ayr	G. & S. W.	Annbank and Drongan.
.	.	.	.	.	.	.	.	Annbank Junction	Ayr	G. & S. W.	Annbank and Auchincruive.
.	.	.	.	.	.	.	.	Annesley	Notts	G. C.	See Hollin Well and Annesley.
.	.	.	.	.	.	.	.	Annesley	Notts	G. N.	Same as Newstead.
G	P	.	L	.	.	.	.	Annesley	Notts	Mid.	Newstead and Kirkby.
.	.	.	.	.	.	.	.	Annesley Colliery	Notts	Mid.	Nottingham and Mansfield Branch.
.	.	.	.	.	.	.	.	Annesley Colliery (G. N.)	Notts	G. N.—G. C.	Newstead.
.	.	.	.	.	.	.	.	Annesley Junction	Notts	G. C.—G. N.	Chesterfield and Hucknall.
.	.	.	.	.	.	.	.	Annesley Jn. with London Ex.	Notts	G. C.	Kirkby and Hucknall Town.
.	.	.	.	.	.	.	.	Annesley Sidings	Notts	G. N.	Newstead.
G	P	F	L	H	C	1	10	Annfield Plain	Durham	N. E.	Washington and Consett.
.	.	.	.	.	.	.	.	Annfield Plain Coal & Lime Depots	Durham	N. E.	Annfield Plain.
.	.	.	.	.	.	.	.	East Castle Col. & Ck. Wks.	Durham	N. E.	Annfield Plain.
.	.	.	.	.	.	.	.	East Pontop Cols. & Ck. Wks.	Durham	N. E.	Annfield Plain.
.	.	.	.	.	.	.	.	Kyo Sand Quarry	Durham	N. E.	Annfield Plain.
.	.	.	.	.	.	.	.	Pontop Col. & Coke Works	Durham	N. E.	Annfield Plain.
.	.	.	.	.	.	.	.	So. Derwent Col. & Ck. Wks.	Durham	N. E.	Annfield Plain.
.	.	.	.	.	.	.	.	So. Derwent Col. Saw Mill.	Durham	N. E.	Annfield Plain.
.	.	.	.	.	.	.	.	So. Derwent Col. (Willie Pit)	Durham	N. E.	Annfield Plain.
.	.	.	.	.	.	.	.	South Moor Col. & Bk. Wks.	Durham	N. E.	Annfield Plain.
.	.	.	.	.	.	.	.	Charlie Pit	Durham	N. E.	Annfield Plain.
.	.	.	.	.	.	.	.	Louisa Pit	Durham	N. E.	Annfield Plain.
.	.	.	.	.	.	.	.	Morrison Pit	Durham	N. E.	Annfield Plain.
.	.	.	.	.	.	.	.	Oxhill Siding	Durham	N. E.	Annfield Plain.
.	.	.	.	.	.	.	.	South Pontop Colliery	Durham	N. E.	Annfield Plain.
.	.	.	.	.	.	.	.	So. Tanfield Col. & Ck. Wks.	Durham	N. E.	Annfield Plain.
.	.	.	.	.	.	.	.	West Shield Row Col. and Coke Works	Durham	N. E.	Annfield Plain.
.	.	.	.	.	.	.	.	West Stanley Colliery	Durham	N. E.	Annfield Plain.
.	.	.	.	.	.	.	.	West Stanley Col. & Ck. Wks.	Durham	N. E.	Annfield Plain.

EXPLANATION—G *Goods Station.*   P *Passenger and Parcel Station.*   P* *Passenger, but not Parcel or Miscellaneous Traffic.*
F *Furniture Vans, Carriages, Portable Engines, and Machines on Wheels.*   L *Live Stock.*
H *Horse Boxes and Prize Cattle Vans.*   C *Carriages by Passenger Train.*

STATION ACCOMMODATION.						CRANE POWER.		STATIONS, &c.	COUNTY.	COMPANY.	POSITION.
						Tons	Cwts.				
.	.	.	.	.	.	1	0	Annick Lodge Siding	Ayr	G. & S.W.	Cunninghamhead.
G	P	.	.	.	.	1	0	Ann tsford	Northumb	N. E.........................	Newcastle and Morpeth.
.	.	.	.	.	.	.	.	Annitsford Village Siding..	Northumb	N. E.	Annitsford.
.	.	.	.	.	.	.	.	Ann Pit...........................	Northumb	N. E.	Annitsford.
.	.	.	.	.	.	.	.	Cramlington Col.&Bk.Wks.	Northumb	N. E.	Annitsford.
.	.	.	.	.	.	.	.	Damdykes Siding	Northumb	N. E.	Annitsford.
.	.	.	.	.	.	.	.	Dudley Colliery	Northumb	N. E.	Annitsford.
.	.	.	.	.	.	.	.	Hartford Col. (Scott Pit) ...	Northumb	N. E.	Annitsford.
.	.	.	.	.	.	.	.	Lamb Pit	Northumb	N. E.	Annitsford.
.	.	.	.	.	.	.	.	ShankhouseCol.(AmeliaPit)	Northumb	N. E.	Annitsford.
.	.	.	.	.	.	.	.	Wrightson Colliery	Northumb	N. E.	Annitsford.
.	.	.	.	.	.	.	.	Ann Pit...........................	Northumb	N. E.	Annitsford.
G	P	F	.	.	.	5	0	Ansdell.............................	Lancs	P.&W.Jt.(L&Y&L&NW)	Blackpool, Central and Lytham.
.	.	.	.	.	.	.	.	Fairhaven Estate Siding ...	Lancs	P.&W.Jt.(L&Y&L&NW)	Ansdell.
.	.	.	.	.	.	.	.	Ans'ey Hall Coal & Iron Co.'s Colliery (Mid.)	Warwick.	Mid.— L. & N. W.	Stockingford.
G	.	F	L	H	C	1	10	Anstruther	Fife	N. B.............................	Leven and St. Andrews.
.	P	.	.	.	.	.	.	Anstruther, New	Fife	N. B.	Leven and St. Andrews.
G	P	F	L	H	C	2	10 }	Antrim	Antrim ...	{ G. N. (I.)	Branch from Knockmore Junction.
G	P	F	L	H	C	2	10 }		Antrim ...	{ N. C. Com. (Mid.)	Belfast and Ballymena.
.	.	.	.	.	.	.	.	Antrim Iron Ore Co.'s Siding	Antrim ...	N. C. Com. (Mid.)	Cargan.
.	.	.	.	.	.	.	.	Antrim Iron Ore Co.'s Siding	Antrim ...	N. C. Com. (Mid.)	Parkmore.
.	.	.	.	.	.	.	.	Antrim Iron Ore Co.'s Siding	Antrim ...	N. C. Com. (Mid.)	Rathkenny.
.	.	.	.	.	.	.	.	Antrim Junction	Antrim ...	G N (I.)—N C Com. (Mid)	Aldergrove and Cookstown.
.	.	.	.	.	.	.	.	Antwerp, Hamburg, & Rotterdam Wharf.................	Northumb	N. E.	Newcastle-on-Tyne.
.	.	.	.	.	.	.	.	Apedale	Staffs	N. S.	Branch—Silverdale and Newcastle.
.	.	.	.	.	.	.	.	Midland Coal Coke & Iron Co.'s Apedale Sidings ...	Staffs	N. S.	Branch—Silverdale and Newcastle.
.	.	.	.	.	.	.	.	Whitebarn Colliery	Staffs	N. S.	Apedale.
.	.	.	.	.	.	.	.	Apethorne Junction	Cheshire.	C. L. C.—S. & M. Jt.	Godley and Woodley.
.	.	.	.	.	.	.	.	Apex Tile and Brick Works	Somerset..	S.&D.Jt.(L.&S.W.&Mid)	Highbridge.
G	P	F	L	H	C	10	0	Apperley Bridge & Rawdon	Yorks	Mid.............................	Leeds and Keighley.
G	P	F	L	H	C	.	.	Appin	Argyll......	Cal	Connel Ferry and Ballachulish.
.	.	.	.	.	.	.	.	Appin Fire Clay Works ...	Fife	N. B.	Townhill Junction Station.
G	P	F	L	H	C	5	0	Appleby	Lincoln ...	G. C.	Thorne and Barnetby.
G	P	F	L	H	C	1	10 }	Appleby	W'morlnd	{ Mid.	Kirkby Stephen and Carlisle.
G	P	F	L	H	C	5	0 }		W'morlnd	{ N. E.	Kirkby Stephen and Penrith.
.	.	.	.	.	.	.	.	Appleby, North Junction ...	W'morlnd	Mid.— N. E.	Carlisle and Kirkby Stephen.
.	.	.	.	.	.	.	.	Appleby & Co.'s Works	Derby	Mid.	Eckington & Renishaw.
.	.	.	.	.	.	.	.	Appleby & Sons' Siding	Lancs	L. & Y.	Blackburn.
.	.	.	.	.	.	.	.	Appleby Iron Co.'s Siding ...	Lincoln ...	G. C.	Frodingham & Scunthorpe.
G	P	F	L	H	C	1	10	Appledore	Kent	S. E. & C.	Hastings and Ashford.
.	.	.	.	.	.	.	.	Applehurst Junction............	Yorks	N. E.—W. R. & G. Jt. ...	Moss and Bramwith.
.	P	.	.	.	.	.	.	App'eton	Lancs	L. & N. W.	St. He'ens and Widnes.
G	P	.	L	.	.	4	0	Appley Bridge	Lancs	L. & Y.	Wigan and Southport.
.	.	.	.	.	.	.	.	Appley Bridge Brick & Tile Co.'s Siding.................	Lancs	L. & Y.	Appley Bridge.
.	.	.	.	.	.	.	.	Corn Mill Siding	Lancs	L. & Y.	Appley Bridge.
.	.	.	.	.	.	.	.	Green Slate Siding	Lancs	L. & Y.	Appley Bridge
.	.	.	.	.	.	.	.	Grove Chemical Co.'s Sid....	Lancs	L. & Y.	Appley Bridge.
.	.	.	.	.	.	.	.	Platt's Siding	Lancs	L. & Y.	Near Appley Bridge.
.	.	.	.	.	.	.	.	West Lancashire Floor Cloth and Linoleum Co.'s Siding	Lancs	L. & Y.	Appley Bridge.
.	.	.	.	.	.	.	.	Arbirlot	Forfar.....	D. & A. Jt. (Cal & N. B.)	See Elliot Junction.
								ARBROATH—			
G	P	F	L	H	C	7	0	(Station)	Forfar.....	Cal.	Dundee and Aberdeen.
G	P	F	L	H	C	7	0	(Station)	Forfar.....	D. & A. Jt. (Cal & N. B.)	Dundee and Aberdeen.
G	.	F	L	.	.	7	0	(Station)	Forfar.....	N.B.	Dundee and Aberdeen.
G	.	.	.	.	.	5	0	Brown & Co.'s Saw Mill....	Forfar.....	D. & A. Jt. (Cal & N. B.)	Arbroath Harbour Branch.
.	.	.	.	.	.	.	.	Corporation Manure Loading Bank	Forfar.....	N.B.	St. Vigean's Junction.
G	.	.	.	.	.	.	.	Harbour (Cal.)	Forfar.....	{ Cal	Arbroath.
									Forfar.....	{ N.B.	Over Cal. from D. & A. Joint Sta.
G	.	.	.	.	.	.	.	Letham Mill Siding........	Forfar.....	Cal.	Colliston and Arbroath.
G	.	.	.	.	.	.	.	St. Vigean's Depôt............	Forfar.....	N. B.	St. Vigean's Junction.
.	.	.	.	.	.	.	.	St. Vigean's Junction	Forfar.....	Cal.—D. & A. Jt.—N. B.	Arbroath and Letham Grange.
G	.	.	.	.	.	15	0	Shanks & Sons' Siding	Forfar.....	D. & A. Jt.—N.B.	St. Vigean's Junction.
G	.	.	.	.	.	.	.	Waulkmill Siding	Forfar.....	Cal.	Colliston and Arbroath.
.	.	.	.	.	.	.	.	Arbuckle Siding................	Lanark ...	N.B.	See Rawyards.
G	P	.	L	H	.	.	.	Ardagh.....	Limerick..	G. S. & W.	Limerick and Newcastle West.

STATION ACCOMMODATION.						CRANE POWER.		STATIONS, &c.	COUNTY.	COMPANY.	POSITION.
						Tons	Cwts.				
G	P	.	.	.	.	.	.	Ardara Road	Donegal	Donegal	Donegal and Killybegs.
.	P*	.	.	.	.	.	.	Arddleen	Montgom	Cam.	Oswestry and Welshpool.
G	P	F	L	H	C	3	0	Ardee	Louth	G. N. (I.)	Branch from Dromin Junction.
.	.	.	.	.	.	.	.	Ardeer Chemical Works	Ayr	Cal.	Stevenston.
.	.	.	.	.	.	.	.	Ardeer Explosives Works	Ayr	Cal.— G. & S.W.	Same as Nobels Explosives Works (Stevenston).
.	.	.	.	.	.	.	.	Ardeer Factory	Ayr	Cal.—G. & S. W.	Stevenston.
.	.	.	.	.	.	.	.	Ardeer Foundry	Ayr	G. & S.W.	Stevenston.
.	.	.	.	.	.	.	.	Ardeer Iron Works	Ayr	Cal.— G. & S.W.	Stevenston.
.	.	.	.	.	.	.	.	Arden Colliery	Lanark	N. B.	Rawyards.
G	P	.	L	H	.	.	.	Ardfert	Kerry	G. S. & W.	Newcastle West and Tralee.
G	P	.	L	H	C	2	10	Ardglass	Down	B. & C. D.	Branch from Downpatrick.
.	.	.	.	.	.	.	.	ArdgowanDistillery(G.&S.W.)	Renfrew	G. & S.W.— N. B.	Greenock, Lynedoch Street.
G	P	F	L	H	C	5	0	Ardingly	Sussex	L. B. & S. C.	Hayward's Heath & Horsted Keynes.
G	P	F	L	H	C	1	0	Ardleigh	Essex	G. E.	Colchester and Ipswich.
G	P	F	L	H	C	1	0	Ardler	Forfar	Cal.	Coupar Angus and Forfar.
.	.	.	.	.	.	.	.	Ardler Junction	Forfar	Cal.	Ardler and Alyth Junction.
G	P	.	L	H	.	1	10	Ardlui (Head of Loch Lomond)	Dumbartn	N. B.	Craigendoran and Crianlarich.
G	P	.	L	.	.	.	.	Ardmore	Derry	N. C. Com. (Mid.)	Limavady and Dungiven.
.	.	.	.	.	.	.	.	Ardoch Quarry	Dumbartn	N. B.	Cardross.
G	P	.	L	H	C	.	.	Ardrahan (G. S. & W.)	Galway	{ G. S. & W.	Athenry and Ennis.
										{ M. G. W.	Over G. S. & W. from Athenry.
								ARDROSSAN—			
G	P	F	L	H	C	4	0	(Station)	Ayr	Cal.	Kilwinning and Ardrossan Harbour.
G	P	F	L	H	C	1	10	(Station)	Ayr	G. & S.W.	Stevenston and Largs.
.	.	.	.	.	.	.	.	Ardrossan Foundry	Ayr	Cal.— G. & S.W.	Ardrossan Harbour.
.	.	.	.	.	.	.	.	Branch Junction	Ayr	G. & S.W.	Kilwinning and Dalry.
.	.	.	.	.	.	.	.	Christie & Co.'s Siding	Ayr	Cal.— G. & S.W.	Ardrossan Harbour.
.	.	.	.	.	.	.	.	Christie's Saw Mill	Ayr	Cal.— G. & S.W.	Ardrossan Harbour.
.	.	.	.	.	.	.	.	Gas Works	Ayr	G. & S.W.	South Beach & West Kilbride.
G	.	F	L	.	.	30	0 }	Harbour	Ayr	{ Cal.	Near Ardrossan.
G	P	.	L	H	C	30	0 }			{ G. & S. W.	Near Ardrossan.
.	.	.	.	.	.	.	.	Junction	Ayr	Cal.— G. & S.W.	Ardrossan, Cal. & G. & S.W. Stas.
G	P	.	L	H	C	.	.	Pier	Ayr	{ Cal.	Ardrossan.
										{ G. & S. W.	Ardrossan.
.	.	.	.	.	.	.	.	Russell & Fullarton's Sid.	Ayr	Cal.— G. & S.W.	Ardrossan Harbour.
.	.	.	.	.	.	.	.	Shipbuilding Co.'s Siding	Ayr	Cal.— G. & S.W.	Ardrossan Harbour.
.	P	.	.	.	.	.	.	South Beach	Ayr	G. & S.W.	Saltcoats and Ardrossan.
.	.	.	.	.	.	.	.	Weighs	Ayr	Cal.	Ardrossan.
.	.	.	.	.	.	.	.	Young's Engine Works	Ayr	Cal.— G. & S.W.	Ardrossan Harbour.
.	.	.	.	.	.	.	.	Ardsheal Quarry	Argyll	Cal.	Kentallen.
.	.	.	.	.	.	.	.	Ardsley	Yorks	G. C.	See Stairfoot (for Ardsley).
G	P	F	L	H	C	10	0 }	Ardsley (G.N.)	Yorks	{ G. N.	Wakefield and Leeds.
.	P	.	.	.	.	.	. }			{ L. & Y.	Over G. N. from Wakefield Junc.
.	.	.	.	.	.	.	.	ArdsleyCol.(Holliday's Col.)	Yorks	G. N.	Ardsley.
.	.	.	.	.	.	.	.	Exchange Sidings	Yorks	G. N.	Ardsley and Lofthouse.
.	.	.	.	.	.	.	.	Yorkshire Iron & Coal Co.'s Ironworks	Yorks	G. N.	Ardsley.
G	P	F	L	H	C	.	.	Ardsollus and Quin (G.S.&W.)	Clare	{ G. S. & W.	Limerick and Ennis.
										{ M. G. W.	Over G. S. & W. from Athenry.
.	.	.	.	.	.	.	.	Ardwick	Lancs	G. C.—L. & N. W.	See Manchester.
.	.	.	.	.	.	.	.	Ardwick Junction	Lancs	G. C.—L. & N. W.	Manchester.
.	.	.	.	.	.	.	.	Ardwick Junction	Lancs	L. & Y.—L. & N. W.	Manchester.
G	P	F	L	H	C	.	.	Arenig	Merioneth	G. W.	Bala and Festiniog.
.	.	.	.	.	.	.	.	Arfon Brick Co.'s Siding	Carnarvon	L. & N. W.	See Seiont Siding (Carnarvon).
G	P	.	.	.	.	.	.	Argoed	Mon	L. & N. W.	Nantybwch and Tredegar Jn. Sta.
.	.	.	.	.	.	.	.	Argoed Coal Co.'s Siding (Cwm Creeich Colliery)	Mon	L. & N. W.	Argoed and Holly Bush.
.	.	.	.	.	.	.	.	Bargoed Colliery Co.'s Sid. (Abernant Colliery)	Mon	L. & N. W.	Bedwellty Pits and Holly Bush.
.	.	.	.	.	.	.	.	Argoed Colliery	Glamorg'n	R. & S. B.	Pontrhydyfen.
.	.	.	.	.	.	.	.	Argyle Street	Glamorg'n	Swan. & Mum.	See Swansea.
G	P	.	L	.	.	.	.	Arigna	Roscom'n	C. & L.	Branch from Ballinamore.
G	P	.	L	.	.	.	. }			{ Cal.	Steamer from Oban.
G	P	.	L	.	.	.	. }	Arisaig	Inverness	{ High.	Steamer from Kyle of Lochalsh.
G	P	F	L	H	C	.	. }			{ N. B.	Fort William and Mallaig.
G	.	.	.	.	.	.	. }				
.	.	.	.	.	.	.	.	Beasdale Siding	Inverness	N. B.	Lochailort and Arisaig.
G	P	F	L	H	C	3	0	Arkholme	Lancs	Fur. & Mid. Jt.	Borwick and Melling.
.	.	.	.	.	.	.	.	Arkleston Junction	Renfrew	G. & P. Jt.—G. & S. W.	Paisley.
G	P	F	L	H	C	3	0	Arklow	Wicklow	D. W. & W.	Wicklow and Wexford.
G	P	.	.	.	.	.	.	Arksey (G. N.)	Yorks	{ G. N.	Doncaster and York.
										{ L. & Y.	Over G. N. from Askern Junction.

EXPLANATION—G *Goods Station.*   P *Passenger and Parcel Station.*   P* *Passenger, but not Parcel or Miscellaneous Traffic.*
F *Furniture Vans, Carriages, Portable Engines, and Machines on Wheels.*   L *Live Stock.*
H *Horse Boxes and Prize Cattle Vans.*   C *Carriages by Passenger Train.*

STATION ACCOMMODATION.						CRANE POWER.		STATIONS. &c.	COUNTY.	COMPANY.	POSITION.
						Tons	Cwts.				
								Arkwright Street	Notts	G. C.	See Nottingham.
G	P	F	L	H	C			Arkwright Town	Derby ...	L. D. & E. C.	Chesterfield and Langwith Junction.
.	.	.	.	.	.	.	.	Bonds Main Colliery	Derby ...	L. D. & E. C.	Branch from Arkwright Town.
.	.	.	.	.	.	.	.	Calow Colliery	Derby ...	L. D. & E. C.	Branch from Arkwright Town.
.	.	.	.	.	.	.	.	Oaks Colliery	Derby ...	L. D. & E. C.	Near Arkwright Town.
G	.	F	L			.	.	Arlecdon (for Rowrah)........	Cumb'land	C. & W. Jn.	Distington and Rowrah Junction.
.	.	.	.	.	.	.	.	Parkside Mining Co.'s Sids.	Cumb'land	C. & W. Jn.................	Arlecdon and Rowrah Junction.
.	.	.	.	.	.	.	.	Rowrah Limestone Siding (Dixon's)	Cumb'land	C. & W. Jn.	Branch—Arlecdon and Rowrah Jn.
.	.	.	.	.	.	.	.	Arledter Size & Chemical Co.'s Siding	Lancs	L. & N. W.—S. & M. Jt.	Widnes.
G	P	F	L	H	C	1	15	Arlesey and Shefford Road	Beds	G. N.	Hitchin and Sandy.
.	.	.	.	.	.	.	.	Gault Brick Co.'s Siding....	Beds	G. N.	Arlesey and Shefford Road.
.	.	.	.	.	.	.	.	London and Arlesey Brick Co.'s Siding	Beds	G. N.	Arlesey and Shefford Road.
.	.	.	.	.	.	.	.	Arlesey Brick Co.'s Siding	Beds	G. N.	Three Counties.
G	P	F	L	H	C	.	.	Arley	Staffs ...	G. W.	Bewdley and Bridgnorth.
G	P	F	L	H	C	.	.	Arley and Fillongley.........	Warwick..	Mid.	Nuneaton and Whitacre.
.	.	.	.	.	.	.	.	Arley Colliery Co.'s Siding	Warwick..	Mid.	Arley and Stockingford.
.	.	.	.	.	.	.	.	Arley Colliery..................	Lancs	L. & N. W.	See Fletcher, Burrows & Co's Gibfield and Arley Colliery (Atherton).
.	.	.	.	.	.	.	.	Arley Pit	Lancs	L. & N. W.	Same as Pearson & Knowles Coal & Ir. Co.'s Crow Orchard Col. (Wigan)
.	.	.	.	.	.	.	.	Arley Pit (L. & N. W.).........	Lancs	L & NW.—G.C (Wig.Jn.)	See Wigan Coal & Iron Co. (Wigan).
G	P	.	L	H		1	10	Armadale	L'lithgow	N. B.	Airdrie South and Bathgate Upper.
.	.	.	.	.	.	.	.	Armadale Brick Works ...	L'lithgow	N. B.	Bch.—Bathgate Upper & Armadale.
.	.	.	.	.	.	.	.	Armadale Collieries	L'lithgow	N. B.	Bch.—Bathgate Upper & Armadale.
.	.	.	.	.	.	.	.	Atlas Brick Works...........	L'lithgow	N. B.	Bch.—Bathgate Upper & Armadale.
.	.	.	.	.	.	.	.	Barbauchlaw Brick Works.	L'lithgow	N. B.	Bch.—Bathgate Upper & Armadale.
.	.	.	.	.	.	.	.	Bathville Brick Works......	L'lithgow	N. B.	Bch.—Bathgate Upper & Armadale.
.	.	.	.	.	.	.	.	Bathville Collieries	L'lithgow	N. B.	Bch.—Bathgate Upper & Armadale.
.	.	.	.	.	.	.	.	Bathville Foundry............	L'lithgow	N. B.	Bch.—Bathgate Upper & Armadale.
.	.	.	.	.	.	.	.	Bathville Steel & Wgn. Wks.	L'lithgow	N. B.	Bch.—Bathgate Upper & Armadale.
.	.	.	.	.	.	.	.	Boghead Brick Works	L'lithgow	N. B.	Bathgate Upper and Armadale.
.	.	.	.	.	.	.	.	Etna Brick Works............	L'lithgow	N. B.	Bch.—Bathgate Upper & Armadale.
.	.	.	.	.	.	.	.	Hartrigg Colliery	L'lithgow	N. B.	Armadale and West Craigs.
.	.	.	.	.	.	.	.	Northrigg Collieries	L'lithgow	N. B.	Bathgate Upper and Armadale.
.	.	.	.	.	.	.	.	Polkemmet Collieries	L'lithgow	N. B.	West Craigs and Armadale.
.	.	.	.	.	.	.	.	Armadale Junction	L'lithgow	N. B.	Bathgate Upper and Armadale.
G	P	.	L			.	.	Armadale (Skye)	Inverness	Cal.	Steamer from Oban.
G	P	.	L			.	.			High.	Steamer from Kyle of Lochalsh.
G	P	.	L			.	.			N. B.	Steamer from Mallaig.
G	P	F	L	H	C	4	10	Armagh	Armagh ...	G. N. (I.)	Clones and Portadown.
G	P	F	L	H	C	1	10	Armathwaite	Cumb'land	Mid.	Appleby and Carlisle.
.	.	.	.	.	.	.	.	Barron Wood Siding	Cumb'land	Mid.	Armathwaite and Lazonby.
G	P	.	.	H	C	1	10	Armitage	Staffs	L. & N. W.	Lichfield and Stafford.
.	.	.	.	.	.	.	.	Elmhurst Siding	Staffs	L. & N. W.	Armitage and Lichfield.
.	.	.	.	.	.	.	.	Armitage Bros. Siding......	Yorks	E. & W. Y. Union ...	See Thorpe Siding (Robin Hood).
.	.	.	.	.	.	.	.	Armitage, G., & Son's Siding	Yorks	E. & W. Y. Union	See Thorpe Siding (Robin Hood).
.	.	.	.	.	.	.	.	Armitage, J., & Son's Siding	Yorks	G. C.	Deepcar (for Stocksbridge).
.	.	.	.	.	.	.	.	Armitage, J., & Son's Siding	Yorks	Mid.	Sheffield, Pond Street.
.	.	.	.	.	.	.	.	Armley and Wortley (G. N.).	Yorks	G. N.—L. & Y.	See Leeds.
.	.	.	.	.	.	.	.	Armley Bridge Siding	Yorks	Mid.—N. E.	Leeds, Wellington Street.
.	.	.	.	.	.	.	.	Armley (for Farnley & Wortley)	Yorks	Mid.	See Leeds.
.	.	.	.	.	.	.	.	Armley Junction	Yorks	Mid.—N. E.	Leeds.
.	.	.	.	.	.	.	.	Armley Road Depôts	Yorks	N. E.	Leeds, Wellington Street.
.	.	.	.	.	.	.	.	Armley Sidings (Mid.)	Yorks	Mid.—N. E.	Leeds, Armley.
.	.	.	.	.	.	.	.	Armour's Warehouse	Cheshire ...	B'headJt—CLC—NW&L	Birkenhead.
G	P	.	L			.	.	Armoy	Antrim	Ballycastle	Ballymoney and Ballycastle.
.	.	.	.	.	.	.	.	Armstrong, Addison & Co.'s Timber Yard	Durham ...	N. E.	Sunderland, Monkwearmouth.
.	.	.	.	.	.	.	.	Armstrong, Whitworth & Co— Battery Siding	Cumb'land	N. B.........................	Silloth.
.	.	.	.	.	.	.	.	Elswick Ordnance & Engineering Wks Blast Furnaces Ship Yard & Wharf (N.E.)	Northumb	N. E.—N. B.	Newcastle-on-Tyne.
.	.	.	.	.	.	.	.	Siding	Northumb	N. E.	Scotswood.
.	.	.	.	.	.	.	.	Siding	Northumb	N. E.	Walker.
.	.	.	.	.	.	.	.	Siding (G. C.)	Lancs	GC—GW—L&NW—Mid	Manchester, Openshaw.
G	P	.	L	H		1	5	Arnage	Aberdeen	G. N. of S.	Dyce and Fraserburgh.
.	.	.	.	.	.	.	.	Arniston Colliery and Brick Works	Edinboro'	N. B.	Gorebridge.

EXPLANATION—G Goods Station.   P Passenger and Parcel Station.   P* Passenger, but not Parcel or Miscellaneous Traffic.
F Furniture Vans, Carriages, Portable Engines, and Machines on Wheels.   L Live Stock.
H Horse Boxes and Prize Cattle Vans.   C Carriages by Passenger Train.

STATION ACCOMMODATION.						CRANE POWER.	STATIONS, &c.	COUNTY.	COMPANY.	POSITION.
						Tons Cwts				
.	.	.	.	.	.	. .	Arnloss Siding	Stirling ...	N. B.	See Slamannan.
.	.	.	.	.	.	. .	Arnold	Notts	G. N.	See Daybrook (for Arnold & Bestwood)
.	.	.	.	.	.	. .	Arnold & Co.'s Siding (G.N.)	Beds	G. N. — L. & N. W.	Luton.
.	.	.	.	.	.	. .	Arnold & Son's Siding (G.N.)	Yorks	G. N.— G. C.— Mid. ...	Same as Belmont Siding (Doncaster).
.	.	.	.	.	.	. .	Arnold, Perrett, & Co.'s Brewery	Glo'ster ...	Mid.	Wickwar.
.	.	.	.	.	.	. .	Arnold's Billington Siding ...	Beds	L. & N. W.	Leighton, Grovebury Crossing.
.	.	.	.	.	.	. .	Arnott's Boiler Works	Lanark ...	Cal.	Same as Coatbridge Boiler Works.
G	P	F	L	H	C	3 0	Arnside...........................	W'morlnd.	Furness......................	Ulverston and Carnforth.
.	.	.	.	.	.	. .	Waterslack Siding.....	Lancs	Furness......................	Arnside and Silverdale.
.	.	.	.	.	.	. .	Arpley	Lancs	L. & N. W.	See Warrington.
.	.	.	.	.	.	. .	Arral Colliery	Mon	G. W.	Aberbeeg.
G	P	F	.	L	H	. .	Arral Griffin Colliery............	Mon	G. W.	Abertillery.
G	P	F	L	H	C	2 0	Arram	Yorks	N. E.	Beverley and Driffield.
G	.	.	L	.	.	. .	Arrochar and Tarbet............	Dumbartn	N. B.	Craigendoran and Ardlui.
.	.	.	.	.	.	. .	Glen Douglas Siding........	Dumbartn	N. B.	Arrochar and Whistlefield.
.	.	.	.	.	.	. .	Arrol's Roof & Bridge Building Works .... }	Lanark ...	{ Cal. .... { N. B.	Glasgow, Buchanan Street. Glasgow, Sighthill.
.	.	.	.	.	.	. .	Arrol's Siding...................	Clackman'	N. B.	Same as Alloa Brewery.
.	.	.	.	.	.	. .	Arrol's (Sir Wm.) New Sid.	Lanark ...	Cal.	Glasgow, London Road.
.	.	.	.	.	.	. .	Arrow Patent Fuel Works ...	Mon	A (N & S W) D & R— G W	Newport, Alexandra Docks.
.	.	.	.	.	.	. .	Arscott Colliery	Salop	S. & W'pl Jt. (GW & LNW)	Same as Smallshaw's Sid. (Hanwood).
G	P	.	L	H	.	1 10	Arthington	Yorks	N. E.	Leeds and Starbeck.
G	P	.	.	.	.	. .	Arthog	Merioneth	Cam.	Barmouth Junction and Dolgelley.
.	.	.	.	.	.	. .	Arthurfield Siding..............	Fife	N. B.	Kingskettle.
.	.	.	.	.	.	. .	Arthur Pit Siding	Fife	N. B.	Whitemyre Junction Station.
.	.	.	.	.	.	. .	Arthur Street	Renfrew ..	Cal.	See Greenock, Regent Street.
G	P	F	L	H	C	5 0	Arundel	Sussex ...	L. B. & S. C.	Pulborough and Ford Junction.
G	P	F	L	H	C	1 0	Arva Road	Cavan ...	M. G. W.	Crossdoney and Killeshandra.
.	.	.	.	.	.	. .	Asby Colliery	Cumb'land	W C & E Jt. (Fur. & L N W)	Lamplugh.
G	P	F	L	H	C	5 0	Ascot and Sunninghill	Berks	L. & S.W.	Staines and Reading.
.	.	.	.	.	.	. .	Ascot Gas Co.'s Siding......	Berks	L. & S.W.	Ascot.
.	.	.	.	.	.	. .	Drake and Mount's Siding	Berks	L. & S.W.	Ascot.
.	.	.	.	.	.	. .	West Sidings	Berks	L. & S.W.	Ascot.
G	P	.	.	.	.	. .	Ascott-under-Wychwood......	Oxon	G. W.	Oxford and Adlestrop.
G	P	.	.	.	.	. .	Asfordby	Leicester..	Mid.	Leicester and Melton.
G	P	F	L	H	C	. .	Ash	Surrey ...	S. E. & C.	Guildford and Reading.
.	.	.	.	.	.	. .	Ashbee & Sons	Glo'ster ...	G. W.—Mid.	Gloucester Docks.
G	P	F	L	H	C	10 0	Ashbourne	Derby	L. & N. W. & N. S. Jt. ...	Buxton and Rocester.
.	.	.	.	.	.	. .	Ashbourne Junction	Derby	L. & N. W.— N. S.	Buxton and Rocester.
.	.	.	.	.	.	. .	Ashburnham Tin Works	Carmarth'.	B. P. & G. V.	Burry Port.
G	P	F	L	H	C	2 0	Ashburton.	Devon ...	G. W.	Branch from Ashburton Junction.
.	.	.	.	.	.	. .	Ashburton Grove	Middlesex	G. N.	See London.
.	.	.	.	.	.	. .	Ashburton Junction	Devon ...	G. W.	Totnes and Newton Abbot.
G	P	F	L	H	C	. .	Ashbury and North Lew......	Devon ...	L. & S.W.	Okehampton and Bude.
.	.	.	.	.	.	. .	Ashburys (for Belle Vue).....	Lancs	G. C.	See Manchester.
.	.	.	.	.	.	. .	Ashburys Junctions	Lancs	G. C.—Mid.—S. & M. Jt.	Manchester.
G	P	F	L	H	C	1 10 }	Ashby-de-la-Zouch (Mid.) ...	Leicester..	{ Mid. .... { L. & N. W.	Leicester and Burton. Over Mid. from Overseal & Moira Jn.
G	P	F	L	H	C	. . }				
.	.	.	.	.	.	. .	Adcock's, J. P., Siding......	Leicester..	Mid.	Melbourne Branch.
.	.	.	.	.	.	. .	Brown & Co.'s Skin Works	Leicester..	Mid.	Ashby-de-la-Zouch.
.	.	.	.	.	.	. .	Burton Brewery Co.'s Sid.	Leicester..	Mid.	Melbourne Branch.
.	.	.	.	.	.	. .	Castle Soap Works (New Hydroleine Co.'s Siding)	Leicester..	Mid.	Melbourne Branch.
.	.	.	.	.	.	. .	Holywell Mill	Leicester..	Mid.	Ashby-de-la-Zouch.
.	.	.	.	.	.	. .	Thornley's Coal Wharf......	Leicester..	Mid.	Melbourne Branch.
.	.	.	.	.	.	. .	Ticknall Tramway Wharf	Leicester..	Mid.	Melbourne Branch.
G	P	F	L	H	C	. .	Ashby Magna	Leicester..	G. C.	Leicester and Lutterworth.
.	.	.	.	.	.	. .	Ashby's Siding	Middlesex	L. & S.W.	Ashford.
G	P	F	L	H	C	1 10	Ashchurch	Glo'ster ...	Mid.	Cheltenham and Defford.
.	.	.	.	.	.	. .	Midland Railway Co.'s Provender Stores	Glo'ster ...	Mid.	Ashchurch.
G	P	.	.	.	.	. .	Ashcot	Somerset..	S. & D. Jt. (L. & S. W. & Mid)	Glastonbury and Highbridge.
.	.	.	.	.	.	. .	Alexander's Siding	Somerset..	S. & D. Jt. (L. & S. W. & Mid)	Ashcot and Shapwick.
.	.	.	.	.	.	. .	Ashdown Forest.................	Sussex ...	L. B. & S. C.	See Forest Row (for Ashdown Forest).
.	.	.	.	.	.	. .	Ashes Quarry	Durham ..	N. E.	Stanhope Kilns.
G	P	.	L	H	.	. .	Ashey	I. of W...	I. of W. Cent.	Ryde and Newport.
.	.	.	.	.	.	. .	Ashfield Siding	Perth	Cal.	See Kinbuck.
							ASHFORD—			
.	.	.	.	.	.	. .	Chart Siding	Kent	S. E. & C.	Pluckley and Ashford, East.
G	P	F	L	H	C	8 0	East	Kent	S. E. & C.	Tonbridge and Folkestone.
.	.	.	.	.	.	. .	Gas Siding	Kent	S. E. & C.	Pluckley and Ashford, East.

EXPLANATION—G *Goods Station.*   P *Passenger and Parcel Station.*   P* *Passenger, but not Parcel or Miscellaneous Traffic.*
F *Furniture Vans, Carriages, Portable Engines, and Machines on Wheels.*   L *Live Stock.*
H *Horse Boxes and Prize Cattle Vans.*   C *Carriages by Passenger Train.*

STATION ACCOMMODATION.						CRANE POWER.		STATIONS, &c.	COUNTY.	COMPANY.	POSITION.
						Tons	Cwts	ASHFORD—continued.			
G	.	F	L	.	.	10	0	Junction	Kent	S. E. & C.	Hothfield and Ashford, East.
G	P	.	.	.	.	5	0	West	Kent	S. E. & C.	Branch—Hothfield & Ashford, East.
								Ashford	Middlesex	L. & S.W.	Twickenham and Staines.
								Ashby's Siding	Middlesex	L. & S.W.	Ashford.
G	P	F	L	H	C	.	.	Ash Green	Surrey	L. & S.W.	Guildford and Farnham.
G	P	.	L	H	C	2	0	Ashington	Northumb	N. E.	Bedlington& Newbiggin-by-the-Sea.
.	.	.	.	.	.	.	.	Ashington Colliery	Northumb	N. E.	Ashington.
.	.	.	.	.	.	.	.	Coneygarth Siding	Northumb	N. E.	Ashington.
.	.	.	.	.	.	.	.	Linton Colliery	Northumb	N. E.	Ashington.
.	.	.	.	.	.	.	.	Potland Siding	Northumb	N. E.	Ashington.
.	.	.	.	.	.	.	.	Woodhorn Colliery	Northumb	N. E.	Ashington.
.	.	.	.	.	.	.	.	Ashington Junction	Northumb	N. E.	Longhirst.
.	.	.	.	.	.	.	.	Ash Junction	Surrey	L. & S.W.—S. E. & C.	Guildford and Aldershot.
G	P	.	L	.	.	5	0	Ashley	Cheshire	C.L.C.(G.C. G.N. & Mid).	Northwich and Altrincham.
G	P	F	L	H	C	.	.	Ashley and Weston	N'hamptn	L. & N. W.	Market Harboro' and Stamford.
	P	.	.	.	.	.	.	Ashley Hill	Glo'ster	G. W.	Bristol and Pilning.
G	P	.	L	H	.	3	0 }	Ashperton (G. W.)	Hereford	{ G. W. / Mid.	Worcester and Hereford. / Over G. W. Line.
G	.	.	L	.	.	3	0 }				
.	.	.	.	.	.	.	.	Ash Road Siding	Kent	S. E. & C.	Sandwich.
G	P	F	L	H	C	.	.	Ashtead	Surrey	L.&S.W. & L.B. & S.C.Jt.	Epsom and Leatherhead.
G	P	.	.	.	.	2	0	Ashton	Devon	G. W.	Heathfield and Exeter.
.	.	.	.	.	.	.	.	Ashton	Lancs	L. & N. W.	See Dukinfield and Ashton.
.	.	.	.	.	.	.	.	Ashton Branch Junction	Lancs	G. C.	See Guide Bridge.
.	.	.	.	.	.	.	.	Ashton Corporation Siding (L. & N.W.)	Lancs	L. & N. W.—O. A. & G.B.	Ashton-under-Lyne, Oldham Road.
G	P	.	.	H	C	5	0	Ashton-in-Makerfield	Lancs	G. C. (St. Helens Exten.)	Lowton St. Mary's and St. Helens.
.	.	.	.	.	.	.	.	Borron & Co.'s Glass Bottle Wks(Newton-le-Willows)	Lancs	G. C. (St. Helens Exten.)	Ashton-in-Makerfield.
.	.	.	.	.	.	.	.	Evans, R., & Co.—			
.	.	.	.	.	.	.	.	Haydock Colliery	Lancs	G. C. (St. Helens Exten.)	Ashton-in-Makerfield.
.	.	.	.	.	.	.	.	Leigh Colliery	Lancs	G. C. (St. Helens Exten.)	Ashton-in-Makerfield.
.	.	.	.	.	.	.	.	New Boston Branch (for Haydock Collieries)	Lancs	G. C. (St. Helens Exten.)	Ashton-in-Makerfield.
.	.	.	.	.	.	.	.	New Boston Colliery	Lancs	G. C. (St. Helens Exten.)	Ashton-in-Makerfield.
.	.	.	.	.	.	.	.	Old Boston Colliery	Lancs	G. C. (St. Helens Exten.)	Ashton-in-Makerfield.
.	.	.	.	.	.	.	.	Pewfall Colliery	Lancs	G. C. (St. Helens Exten.)	Ashton-in-Makerfield.
.	.	.	.	.	.	.	.	Princess Colliery	Lancs	G. C. (St. Helens Exten.)	Ashton-in-Makerfield.
.	.	.	.	.	.	.	.	Queen Colliery	Lancs	G. C. (St. Helens Exten.)	Ashton-in-Makerfield.
.	.	.	.	.	.	.	.	Wood Colliery	Lancs	G. C. (St. Helens Exten.)	Ashton-in-Makerfield.
.	.	.	.	.	.	.	.	Ashton-in-Makerfield	Lancs	L. & N. W.	See Brynn (for Ashton-in-Makerfield)
.	.	.	.	.	.	.	.	Ashton Keynes	Wilts	M. & S. W. Jn.	See Cerney and Ashton Keynes.
.	.	.	.	.	.	.	.	Ashton Moss Col. (L.&N.W.)	Lancs	L. & N. W.—G. C.	Same as New Moss Col. (Guide Bge.)
.	.	.	.	.	.	.	.	Ashton Moss Junction	Lancs	L. & Y.—O. A. & G. B.	Droylsden and Ashton, Oldham Rd.
.	.	.	.	.	.	.	.	Ashton-on-Mersey	Cheshire	M.S.J.&A. (G.C. & LNW)	See Sale and Ashton-on-Mersey.
.	.	.	.	.	.	.	.	Ashton Pit	Lancs	L. & N. W.	See Garswood Cl. & Ir. Co. (Garswood)
.	.	.	.	.	.	.	.	Ashton, R., & Co.'s Bk. Wks.	Flint	W. M. & C. Q.	Buckley.
.	.	.	.	.	.	.	.	Ashton Road Cattle & Mineral Yard	Lancs	Mid.	See Manchester.
.	.	.	.	.	.	.	.	Ashton's Green Colliery	Lancs	L. & N. W.	Same as Bromilow, Foster & Co.'s Siding (St. Helens)
.	.	.	.	.	.	.	.	Ashton's Siding	Lancs	L. & Y.	Oldham, Werneth.
.	.	.	.	.	.	.	.	Ashton's Works (C. L. C.)	Cheshire	C. L. C. — L. & N. W.	See Salt Union Ltd. (Northwich).
G	P	.	.	.	.	.	.	Ashton-under-Hill	Glo'ster	Mid.	Ashchurch and Evesham.
								ASHTON-UNDER-LYNE—			
.	.	.	.	.	.	.	.	Broad Oak Colliery	Lancs	O A & G B (GC & L & N W)	Oldham Road and Park Bridge.
G	P	F	L	H	C	10	0 }	Charlestown (L. & Y.)	Lancs	{ L. & Y. / L. & N. W.	Miles Platting and Stalybridge. / Over L. & Y. Line.
.	P	.	.	H	C	.	. }				
.	.	.	.	.	.	.	.	Corporation Sid.(L.&N.W.)	Lancs	L. & N. W.—O. A. & G.B.	Oldham Road.
.	.	.	.	.	.	.	.	Junction with L. & N. W. Goods Branch	Lancs	L. & N. W.—O. A. & G. B.	Ashton (L&NW) Goods & Guide Bge.
G	.	F	L	H	C	10	0	Oldham Road	Lancs	L. & N. W.	Branch—Guide Bridge and Oldham.
.	P	.	.	.	.	.	.	Oldham Road	Lancs	O A & G B (GC & L & N W)	Guide Bridge and Oldham.
G	P	F	L	H	C	5	0 }	Park Parade (G. C.)	Lancs	{ G. C. / L. & N. W.	Guide Bridge and Stalybridge. / Over G. C. Line.
G	P	F	L	.	.	5	0 }				
.	.	.	.	.	.	.	.	Ridyard's Siding	Lancs	O A & G B (GC & L & N W)	Oldham Road.
.	.	.	.	.	.	.	.	Ashton Vale Colliery	Somerset	G. W.	Clifton Bridge.
.	.	.	.	.	.	.	.	Ashton Works	Yorks	N. E.	See Aire & Calder Glass Bottle Wks. (Castleford).
G	P	F	L	H	C	.	.	Ashurst	Kent	L. B. & S. C.	Oxted and Groombridge.
.	.	.	.	.	.	.	.	Ash Vale	Surrey	L. & S.W.	See Aldershot, North Camp & Ash Vale.
G	P	F	L	H	C	.	.	Ashwater	Devon	L. & S.W.	Okehampton and Launceston.

STATION ACCOMMODATION.						CRANE POWER.		STATIONS, &c.	COUNTY.	COMPANY.	POSITION.
						Tons	Cwts.				
G	P	F	L	H	C	1	10	Ashwell	Cambs	G. N.	Hitchin and Cambridge.
G	P	.	L	H	C	1	10	Ashwell	Rutland	Mid.	Peterboro' and Melton.
								Sheepbridge Co.'s Cottesmore Iron Ore Mines	Rutland	Mid.	Ashwell.
G	P	.	.	.	.			Ashwellthorpe	Norfolk	G. E.	Forncett and Wymondham.
.	.	.	.	.	.			Ashwood Basin(EarlDudley's)	Staffs	G. W.	See Round Oak.
								Ashwood Dale Siding—			
.	.	.	.	.	.			Buxton Lime Firms' Co.	Derby	Mid.	{ Buxton. Miller's Dale.
.	.	.	.	.	.			Buxton New Lime Co.	Derby	Mid.	Buxton.
.	.	.	.	.	.			Ashworth, Kirk & Co.'s Siding	Notts	Mid.	Nottingham.
.	.	.	.	.	.			Ashworth, Kirk & Co.'s Siding	Yorks	H. & B.	Hull, Sculcoates.
.	.	.	.	.	.			Ashworth's (Fernhill) Siding	Lancs	L. & Y.	Bury, High Level.
.	.	.	.	.	.			Ashworth's Siding	Lancs	L. & Y.	Clough Fold.
G	P	F	L	H	C	3	0	Askam	Lancs	Furness	Barrow and Foxfield.
.	.	.	.	.	.			Askam Brick Works	Lancs	Furness	Near Askam Iron Works.
G	.	.	.	.	.			Askam Iron Works	Lancs	Furness	Barrow and Askam.
G	P	.	L	H	.			Askeaton	Limerick	G. S. & W.	Ballingrane and Foynes.
.	.	.	.	.	.			Asken Bridge Junction	Staffs	G. W.	Kingswinford Branch.
G	P	F	L	H	C	5	0 }	Askern (L. & Y.)	Yorks	{ L. & Y. G. N.	Knottingley and Doncaster. Over N. E. and L. & Y. Lines.
.	P	.	.	H	C						
.	.	.	.	.	.			Askern Junction	Yorks	G. N.—L. & Y.	Doncaster and Knottingley.
G	P	.	L	H	C	2	0	Askrigg	Yorks	N. E.	Leyburn and Hawes.
G	P	F	L	H	C			Aslockton	Notts	G. N.	Grantham and Nottingham.
G	P	F	L	H	C	5	0	Aspatria	Cumb'land	M. & C.	Bullgill and Brayton.
.	.	.	.	.	.			Warthole Lime Works	Cumb'land	M. & C.	Aspatria and Bullgill.
.	.	.	.	.	.			Aspden Colliery (Simpson's)	Lancs	L. & Y.	Church and Oswaldtwistle.
.	.	.	.	.	.			Aspden's Siding	Lancs	L. & Y.	Blackburn.
.	.	.	.	.	.			Asphaltic Limestone Concrete Co.'s Siding	Derby	Mid.	Peak Forest.
.	.	.	.	.	.			Aspull	Lancs	L. & Y.	See Dicconson Lane and Aspull.
.	.	.	.	.	.			Assheton-Smith's Port Dinorwic Quay	Carnarvon	L. & N. W.	Port Dinorwic.
								Associated Portland Cement Manufacturers'—			
.	.	.	.	.	.			Siding	Beds	G. N.	Three Counties.
.	.	.	.	.	.			Norton Siding	Herts	G. N.	Baldock.
.	.	.	.	.	.			Hilton, Anderson &Co's Bch.	Essex	L. T. & S.	Grays.
.	.	.	.	.	.			Astbury Siding	Cheshire	N. S.	Mow Cop.
.	.	.	.	.	.			Astell Bros'. Sid. (L. & N.W.)	Beds	L. & N. W.—Mid.	Bedford.
.	P	.	.	.	.			Astley (L. & N. W.)	Lancs	{ L. & N. W. G. W.	Kenyon Junction and Manchester. Over L. & N. W. from Walton Jn.
								Astley & Tyldesley Coal and Salt Co.—			
.	.	.	.	.	.			Jackson's Siding	Lancs	L. & N. W.	Tyldesley.
.	.	.	.	.	.			Siding	Lancs	L. & N. W.	Bolton.
G	.	.	.	.	.	10	0	Astley Bridge	Lancs	L. & Y.	Branch—Bolton and The Oaks.
.	P	.	.	.	.			Aston	Warwick	L. & N. W.	Birmingham and Lichfield.
.	.	.	.	.	.			Aston (Goods)	Warwick	L. & N. W.	See Birmingham.
G	P	.	.	.	.		}	Aston by Stone (N. S.)	Staffs	{ N. S. L. & N. W.	Colwich and Stone. Over N. S. Line.
.	P	.	.	.	.						
.	.	.	.	.	.			Aston Church Road Siding	Warwick	Mid.	Birmingham, Saltley.
.	.	.	.	.	.			Aston Hall Coal and Brick Co.'s Colliery	Flint	L. & N. W.	See Dundas Siding (Queen's Ferry).
.	.	.	.	.	.			Aston Hall Col. & Brick Wks.	Flint	W. M. & C. Q.	Hawarden.
.	.	.	.	.	.			Aston Magna Siding	Worcester	G. W.	Moreton in Marsh.
G	P	F	L	H	C	1	0	Aston Rowant	Oxon	G. W.	Watlington and Chinnor.
.	.	.	.	.	.			Astrop Siding	N'hampton	G. W.	See Hickman's, Sir A., Siding (Kings Sutton).
.	.	.	.	.	.			Astwood Bank	Warwick	Mid.	See Studley and Astwood Bank.
G	P	F	L	H	C	1	10	Aswarby (for Scredington)	Lincoln	G. N.	Bourne and Sleaford.
.	.	.	.	.	.			Burton Brick Sid. (Sleaford & District Brk. & Tile Sid.)	Lincoln	G. N.	Aswarby and Sleaford.
G	P	F	L	H	C			Athboy	Meath	M. G. W.	Branch from Kilmessan.
G	P	.	.	.	.			Athelney	Somerset	G. W.	Durston and Yeovil.
G	P	F	L	H	C	0	15	Athenry (M. G. W.)	Galway	{ M. G. W. G. S. & W.	Galway and Athlone. Over M. G. W. Line.
.	.	.	.	.	.			Athenry Junction	Galway	G. S. & W.—M. G. W.	Tuam and Galway.
G	P	F	L	H	C	5	0	Atherstone	Warwick	L. & N. W.	Lichfield and Nuneaton.
.	.	.	.	.	.			Baddesley Colliery	Warwick	L. & N. W.	Atherstone and Polesworth.
								ATHERTON—			
G	P	.	L	H	.	10	0	(Station)	Lancs	L. & N. W.	Bolton and Kenyon Junction.

EXPLANATION—G *Goods Station.* P *Passenger and Parcel Station.* P* *Passenger, but not Parcel or Miscellaneous Traffic.*
F *Furniture Vans, Carriages, Portable Engines, and Machines on Wheels.* L *Live Stock.*
H *Horse Boxes and Prize Cattle Vans.* C *Carriages by Passenger Train.*

STATION ACCOMMODATION.						CRANE POWER.		STATIONS, &c.	COUNTY.	COMPANY.	POSITION.
						Tons	Cwts.	ATHERTON—continued.			
G	P	.	L	.	.	10	0	(Central)	Lancs	L. & Y.	Pendleton and Hindley.
.	.	.	.	.	.	.	.	Earl of Ellesmere's Wharton Hall Colliery	Lancs	L. & Y.	Near Atherton, Central.
.	.	.	.	.	.	.	.	Fletcher Burrows & Co.—			
.	.	.	.	.	.	.	.	Chanters Colliery	Lancs	L. & N. W.	Howe Bridge and Tyldesley.
.	.	.	.	.	.	.	.	Gibfield & Arley Colliery	Lancs	L. & N. W.	Atherton and West Leigh.
.	.	.	.	.	.	.	.	Lovers' Lane Colliery ...	Lancs	L. & N. W.	Atherton and West Leigh.
.	.	.	.	.	.	.	.	Tyldesley Coal Co.'s Peelwood Colliery	Lancs	L. & Y.	Atherton Central and Walkden.
.	.	.	.	.	.	.	.	Urban District Council (Albion) Siding	Lancs	L. & N. W.	Atherton and Chequerbent.
.	.	.	.	.	.	.	.	Atherton Colliery No. 1	Lancs	L. & N. W.	See Hulton Col. Co. (Chequerbent).
.	.	.	.	.	.	.	.	Atherton Colliery No. 2, Pretoria or New Pit, Chequerbent Bank Siding	Lancs	L. & N. W.	See Hulton Col. Co. (Chequerbent).
.	.	.	.	.	.	.	.	Atherton Siding (L. & N.W.)	Lancs	L. & N. W. — G. W.	See Fletcher, Burrows & Co. (Warrington).
.	.	.	.	.	.	.	.	Atherton's Cruckmeole or Shorthill Colliery	Salop	S.&W'pl Jt.(GW&LNW)	Hanwood.
.	.	.	.	.	.	.	.	Atherton's Siding	Lancs	L. & N. W.	Widnes.
.	.	.	.	.	.	.	.	Atherton's Amberswood Col.	Lancs	L. & N. W.	Hindley and Amberswood.
.	.	.	.	.	.	.	.	Atherton's Siding	Lancs	L. & Y.	Bury, High Level.
G	P	F	L	H	C	5	0	Athlone	W'meath..	G. S. & W.	Branch from Portarlington.
G	P	F	L	H	C	5	0	Athlone	W'meath..	M. G. W.	Galway and Mullingar.
.	.	.	.	.	.	.	.	Athlone Junction	W'meath..	G. S. & W.—M. G. W...	Clara and Roscommon.
G	P	F	L	H	C	1	10	Athy	Kildare ...	G. S. & W.	Bagnalstown and Kildare.
.	.	.	.	.	.	.	.	Atkins' Siding	Surrey ...	S. E. & C.	Whyteleafe.
.	.	.	.	.	.	.	.	Atlantic Patent Fuel Co.'s Sid.	Glamorg'n	GW—LNW—Mid—RSB	Swansea.
.	.	.	.	.	.	.	.	Atlantic Works	Lancs	L. & N. W.	Same as Richards & Co.'s Siding (Broadheath, Altrincham).
.	.	.	.	.	.	.	.	Atlas Blast Furnaces (Mid)..	Yorks	Mid.—G. C.	See Brown, J., & Co. (Sheffield).
.	.	.	.	.	.	.	.	Atlas Brick, Pipe and Tile Co.'s Siding	Staffs	L. & N. W.	Same as Barnett & Beddows' Siding (Pelsall).
.	.	.	.	.	.	.	.	Atlas Brick & Tile Co.'s Siding	Middlesex	Mid.	London, Harlesden.
.	.	.	.	.	.	.	.	Atlas Brick Works	L'lithgow	N. B.	Armadale.
.	.	.	.	.	.	.	.	Atlas Chemical Works	Lancs	L. & N. W —S. & M. Jt..	See United Alkali Co. (Widnes).
.	.	.	.	.	.	.	.	Atlas Engine Works (Sharp, Stewart & Co.) (N. B.)	Lanark ...	N. B.—G. & S. W.	Glasgow, Sighthill.
.	.	.	.	.	.	.	.	Atlas Forge Iron Works	Lancs	L. & N. W.	See Walmsley's (Bolton).
.	.	.	.	.	.	.	.	Atlas Foundry and Brick Machine Works	Yorks	N. E.	Middlesbro'.
.	.	.	.	.	.	.	.	Atlas Machinery Works	Lanark ...	N. B.	Clarkston.
.	.	.	.	.	.	.	.	Atlas Rivet Wks. (McFarlane and Whitfield)................	Durham ...	N. E.	Redheugh.
.	.	.	.	.	.	.	.	Atlas Works	Derby	Mid.	See Fletcher, G. & Co.'s, Masson & Atlas Works (Derby).
G	P	.	.	H	.	.	.	Atlas Works (Mid.)	Yorks	Mid.—G. C.	See Brown, J., & Co. (Sheffield).
G	P	.	L	H	.	.	.	Attadale	Ross & Cro'	High	Strathcarron and Stromeferry.
.	P	.	.	.	.	.	.	Attanagh	Queen's ...	G. S. & W.	Kilkenny and Maryborough.
.	.	.	.	.	.	.	.	Attenboro'	Notts	Mid.	Nottingham and Trent Junction.
.	.	.	.	.	.	.	.	Attenborough & Timms—			
.	.	.	.	.	.	.	.	Siding	N'hamptn	L. & N. W.	Brixworth.
.	.	.	.	.	.	.	.	Siding	N'hamptn	Mid.	Finedon.
.	.	.	.	.	.	.	.	Attenborough's Siding	Lincoln ...	G. N.	Same as Carlton Iron Ore Co.'s Siding (Caythorpe).
.	.	.	.	.	.	.	.	Atterby's Brick Siding........	Durham ...	N. E.	Stockton-on-Tees, South Shore.
.	.	.	.	.	.	.	.	Attercliffe	Yorks	G. C.—L.D. & E.C.—Mid	See Sheffield.
.	.	.	.	.	.	.	.	Attercliffe Junction	Yorks	G. C.	Sheffield.
.	.	.	.	.	.	.	.	Attercliffe Road (Mid.)........	Yorks	Mid.—L. D. & E. C.	See Sheffield.
.	.	.	.	.	.	.	.	Attimore Hall Siding	Herts......	G. N.	Hatfield.
G	P	F	L	H	C	1	0	Attleborough	Norfolk ...	G. E.	Norwich and Thetford.
.	.	.	.	.	.	.	.	Gaymer & Son's Siding......	Norfolk ...	G. E.	Attleborough.
.	.	.	.	.	.	.	.	Long, Mann & Co.'s Siding	Norfolk ...	G. E.	Attleborough.
G	P	F	.	.	.	.	.	Attlebridge	Norfolk ...	Mid. & G. N. Jt.	Norwich, City & Melton Constable.
G	P	.	L	H	.	1	0	Attymon	Galway ...	M. G. W.	Athlone and Athenry.
.	.	.	.	.	.	.	.	Auchencarroch Quarry........	Dumbartn	N. B.	Jamestown.
.	.	.	.	.	.	.	.	Auchencrow Siding	Berwick ...	N. B.	See Reston.
G	P	.	L	H	.	2	0	Auchendinny	Edinboro'	N. B.	Hawthornden Junc. and Penicuik.
.	.	.	.	.	.	.	.	Dalmore Mill Siding	Edinboro'	N. B.	Auchendinny and Rosslyn Castle.
G	P	.	L	H	.	.	.	Auchengray	Lanark ...	Cal.	Carstairs and Edinburgh.

STATION ACCOMMODATION.						CRANE POWER.		STATIONS, &c.	COUNTY.	COMPANY.	POSITION.
						Tons	Cwts.				
.	.	.	.	.	.			Auchengray Colliery............	Lanark ...	N.B.	Longriggend.
.	.	.	.	.	.			Auchenharvie Washer	Ayr	Cal.—G. & S. W.	Stevenston.
.	.	.	.	.	.			Auchenharvie Brick Works.	Ayr	Cal.—G. & S. W.	Stevenston.
.	.	.	.	.	.			Auchenharvie Col. Nos. 1, 4 & 5.	Ayr	Cal.—G. & S. W.	Stevenston.
.	.	.	.	.	.			Auchenharvie Mine	Ayr	Cal.	Stevenston.
G	P	.	L	H	.	1	10	Auchenheath	Lanark ...	Cal.	Larkhall and Lesmahagow.
.	.	.	.	.	.			Auchenheath Quarry No. 1	Lanark ...	Cal.	Auchenheath and Tillietudlem.
.	.	.	.	.	.			Auchenheath Quarry No. 2	Lanark ...	Cal.	Tillietudlem and Auchenheath.
.	.	.	.	.	.			Netherton Lime Works ...	Lanark ...	Cal.	Auchenheath and Lesmahagow.
.	.	.	.	.	.			Auchenlee Quarry & Bk. Wks.	Lanark ...	Cal.	Omoa.
G	P	F	L	H	C	3	0	Auchenmade	Ayr	Cal.	Giffen and Kilwinning.
.	.	.	.	.	.			Auchenmade Qry.&Bk. Wks	Ayr	Cal.	Auchenmade and Lissens.
G	.	.	.	.	.			Lissens	Ayr	Cal.	Giffen and Kilwinning.
.	.	.	.	.	.			Lylestone Quarry & Bk. Wks.	Ayr	Cal.	Lissens and Kilwinning.
.	.	.	.	.	.			Auchenraith Colliery............	Lanark ...	{ Cal. / N.B.	High Blantyre. / Hamilton, Burnbank.
.	.	.	.	.	.			Auchenraith Junction	Lanark ...	Cal.	Hamilton West and High Blantyre.
.	.	.	.	.	.			Auchenreoch Colliery	Stirling ...	N. B.	Gavell.
.	.	.	.	.	.			Auchinbaird Colliery............	Clackman'	N. B.	Sauchie.
G	P	F	L	H	C	3	0	Auchincruive	Ayr	G. & S. W.	Mauchline and Ayr.
.	.	.	.	.	.			Auchincruive Nos. 1 & 2 ...	Ayr	G. & S.W.	Annbank.
G	P	.	L	H	.			Auchindachy	Banff	G. N. of S.	Keith and Craigellachie.
G	P	F	L	H	C	3	0	Auchinleck	Ayr	G. & S.W.	Mauchline and Old Cumnock.
.	.	.	.	.	.			Gilmilnscroft Branch Depôt	Ayr	G. & S.W.	Gilmilnscroft Branch.
.	.	.	.	.	.			Gilmilnscroft, Nos. 1, 2, 3 & 4	Ayr	G. & S.W.	Gilmilnscroft Branch.
.	.	.	.	.	.			Highhouse Pits	Ayr	G. & S.W.	Auchinleck and Mauchline.
.	.	.	.	.	.			Auchinleck Junction	Ayr	G. & S.W.	Auchinleck and Old Cumnock.
.	.	.	.	.	.			Auchlochan Collieries	Lanark ...	Cal.	Coalburn.
.	.	.	.	.	.			Muirburn Siding	Lanark ...	Cal.	Coalburn.
.	.	.	.	.	.			Stocksbriggs	Lanark ...	Cal.	Coalburn.
G	P	F	L	H	C	1	10	Auchmacoy	Aberdeen.	G. N. of S.	Ellon and Boddam.
G	P	.	L	H	C	1	5	Auchmuty Mills	Fife	N. B.	Markinch.
G	P	.	L	H	C	1	5	Auchnagatt	Aberdeen.	G. N. of S.	Dyce and Fraserburgh.
.	.	.	.	.	.			Auchren Lime Works	Lanark ...	Cal.	Lesmahagow.
.	.	.	.	.	.			Auchrie Siding	Forfar ...	Cal.	Rosemill.
G	P	F	L	H	C	1	10	Auchterarder	Perth	Cal.	Stirling and Perth.
G	P	.	L	H	.	2	0	Auchterhouse	Forfar ...	Cal.	Dundee and Newtyle.
G	.	.	.	.	.			Pitnappie Siding	Forfar ...	Cal.	Auchterhouse and Newtyle.
G	P	.	L	H	.	1	5	Auchterless	Aberdeen.	G. N. of S.	Inveramsay and Macduff.
G	P	F	L	H	C	2	0	Auchtermuchty	Fife	N. B.	Kinross Junction and Ladybank.
G	.	.	L	.	.	1	10	Auchtertool	Fife	N. B.	Branch—Kinghorn and Kirkcaldy.
.	.	.	.	.	.			Auckland Pk. Col. & Ck. Ovens	Durham ...	N. E.	Shildon.
.	P	.	.	.	.			Audenshaw	Lancs	L. & N. W.	Denton and Droylsden.
.	.	.	.	.	.			Audenshaw Junction............	Lancs	G. C.—O. A. & G. B......	Same as Guide Bridge West Junc.
G	P	F	L	H	C	1	0	Audlem............................	Cheshire..	G. W.	Nantwich and Market Drayton.
G	P	.	.	.	.	2	0	Audley	Staffs	N. S.	Alsager Junction and Keele.
.	.	.	.	.	.			Audley Colliery	Staffs	N. S.	See Rigby & Co. (Diglake).
G	P	F	L	H	C	1	0	Audley End	Essex	G. E.	Bishops Stortford and Cambridge
.	P	.	.	.	.			Aughacasla.......................	Kerry	T. & D.	Castlegregory Jn. and Castlegregory.
G	P	.	L	.	.	2	0	Augher	Tyrone.....	Clogher Valley	Aughnacloy and Fivemiletown.
G	P	.	L	.	.	2	0	Aughnacloy.......................	Tyrone.....	Clogher Valley	Tynan and Fivemiletown.
G	P	F	L	H	C	3	0	Aughrim	Wicklow..	D. W. & W.	Woodenbridge Junc. and Shillelagh.
.	.	.	.	.	.			Aughton	Lancs	L. & Y.	See Town Green and Aughton.
G	P	F	L	H	C	4	0	Auldbar Road....................	Forfar ...	Cal.	Forfar and Stonehaven.
G	P	F	L	H	C			Auldearn..........................	Nairn	High.	Nairn and Forres.
G	P	F	L	H	C	3	0	Auldgirth..........................	Dumfries..	G. & S. W.	Dumfries and Thornhill.
.	.	.	.	.	.			Dumfries County Council Sid	Dumfries..	G. & S. W.	Auldgirth.
.	.	.	.	.	.			Auldhouseburn Colliery........	Ayr	Cal.	Muirkirk.
.	.	.	.	.	.			Auldhouseburn Sidings.........	Ayr	Cal.	Muirkirk.
.	.	.	.	.	.			Auldton Colliery..................	Lanark ...	Cal.	Dalserf.
G	P	.	L	.	.	}		Aultbea..........................	Ross & Cro'	{ Cal. / High. / N. B.	Steamer from Oban. / Steamer from Kyle of Lochalsh. / Steamer from Mallaig.
G	P	.	L	.	.						
G	P	.	L	.	.						
G	P	F	L	H	C			Aultmore	Banff	High	Keith and Buckie.
G	P	.	L	.	.			Aunascaul........................	Kerry	T. & D.	Castlegregory Junction and Dingle.
.	.	.	.	.	.			Austin Brothers' Siding	Yorks	N. E.	Castleford.
.	.	.	.	.	.			Australia Wharf.................	Essex	L. T. & S.	Same as Purfleet Wharf and Saw Mills Co.'s Siding (Purfleet)
G	P	F	.	H	C			Authorpe	Lincoln ...	G. N.	Boston and Louth.
.	.	.	.	.	.			Aveland's (Lord) Sid. (Mid.)	Rutland ...	Mid.—L. & N. W.	Luffenham.
.	.	.	.	.	.			Aveling & Porter's Siding......	Kent	S. E. &. C.	Strood.
.	.	.	.	.	.			Avenue	Warwick..	L. & N. W.	See Leamington.

STATION ACCOMMODATION.						CRANE POWER.	STATIONS, &c.	COUNTY.	COMPANY.	POSITION.
						Tons Cwts.				
.	.	.	.	.	.	. .	Avenue Colliery	Derby	Mid.	Clay Cross.
.	.	.	.	.	.	. .	Avenuehead Sand Siding	Lanark	N. B.	Bridgend.
.	.	.	.	.	.	. .	Avenue Siding	Northumb	N. E.	Hartley.
.	.	.	.	.	.	. .	Avenue (Malthouse) Siding	Warwick	L. & N. W.	Same as Thomas & Co's (Leamington)
.	.	.	.	.	.	. .	Avery's or Watt & Co.'s Siding	Staffs	L. & N. W.	Soho.
G	P	F	L	H	C	1 10	Aviemore	Inverness	High.	Kingussie and Boat of Garten.
G	P	F	L	H	C	1 10	Avoch	Ross & Cro'	High.	Muir of Ord and Fortrose.
G	P	.	L	H	.	3 0	Avonbridge	Stirling	N. B.	Airdrie, Commonhead and Blackston.
.	.	.	.	.	.	. .	Avoncliffe Siding	Wilts	G. W.	Bradford-on-Avon.
.	.	.	.	.	.	. .	Avon Colliery	Glamorg'n	G. W.	Abergwynfi.
.	.	.	.	.	.	. .	Avondale Tin Plate Works	Mon	G. W.	Upper Pontnewydd.
.	.	.	.	.	.	. .	Avon Foundry	Lanark	Cal.	Stonehouse.
.	.	.	.	.	.	. .	Avonhead Colliery	Lanark	N. B.	Longriggend.
.	.	.	.	.	.	. .	Avon Lodge	Hants	L. & S. W.	Ringwood and Christchurch.
.	.	.	.	.	.	. .	Avon Merthyr Colliery	Glamorg'n	{ P. T.	Cwmavon.
									S. Wales Min.	Briton Ferry and Cymmer.
.	.	.	.	.	.	. .	Avon Mouth Colliery	Glamorg'n	S. Wales Min.	Branch near Cymmer.
.	.	.	.	.	.	. .	Avonmouth Docks	Glo'ster	G. W.— Mid.	See Bristol.
.	.	.	.	.	.	. .	Avonside Engine Works	Glo'ster	Mid.	Bristol, St. Philips.
.	.	.	.	.	.	. .	Avon Street Depôt	Glo'ster	Mid.	See Bristol.
.	.	.	.	.	.	. .	Avon Vale Quarry	Glamorg'n	S. Wales Min.	Avon Vale and Cymmer.
G	P	F	L	.	.	. .	Avonwick	Devon	G. W.	Brent and Kingsbridge.
.	.	.	.	.	.	. .	Awe Crossing	Argyll	Cal.	Taynuilt and Loch Awe.
G	P	.	L	H	.	. .	Awre Junction	Glo'ster	G. W.	Gloucester and Chepstow.
G	P	.	.	.	.	. .	Awsworth	Notts	G. N.	Kimberley and Ilkeston.
.	.	.	.	.	.	. .	Awsworth Iron Works (Bennerley Iron Works)	Notts	G. N.	Awsworth.
							Awsworth Iron Co.—			
.	.	.	.	.	.	. .	Ironstone Siding	Leicester	Mid.	Holwell Wharf.
.	.	.	.	.	.	. .	Siding	Notts	Mid.	Ilkeston.
.	.	.	.	.	.	. .	Awsworth Junction	Notts	G. N.	Kimberley and Awsworth.
G	P	F	L	H	C	3 0	Axbridge	Somerset	G. W.	Yatton and Wells.
G	P	F	L	H	C	5 0	Axminster	Devon	L. & S. W.	Yeovil and Exeter.
G	.	.	.	.	.	. .	Coaxden Siding	Devon	L. & S. W.	Axminster.
.	.	.	.	.	.	. .	Axwell Park Col. (Hannington & Co.)	Durham	N. E.	Swalwell.
G	P	.	L	H	C	1 10	Aycliffe	Durham	N. E.	Darlington and Ferryhill.
.	.	.	.	.	.	. .	Aycliffe Lime Works	Durham	N. E.	Aycliffe.
.	.	.	.	.	.	. .	Chapman's Siding	Durham	N. E.	Aycliffe Lime Works.
.	.	.	.	.	.	. .	Ord & Maddison's Siding	Durham	N. E.	Aycliffe Lime Works.
							AYLESBURY—			
G	P	F	L	H	C	5 0	(Station)	Bucks	L. & N. W.	Branch from Cheddington.
G	P	F	L	H	C	5 0 }	(Station, G. W. & Met. Jt.)	Bucks	{ G. W. & Met. Jt.	Princes Risboro'. & Verney Junction.
.	P	.	.	H	C	. . }			G. C.	Over Met. Line.
.	.	.	.	.	.	. .	Aylesbury Gas Co.'s Siding	Bucks	L. & N. W.	Aylesbury and Marston Gate.
G	.	.	.	.	.	. .	Hartwell Siding	Bucks	Met.	Aylesbury.
.	.	.	.	.	.	. .	Junction	Bucks	G. W.—G. W. & Met. Jt.	Princes Risboro' and Ay'esbury.
.	.	.	.	.	.	. .	North Junction	Bucks	G. W. & Met. Jt.—Met.	Aylesbury and Waddesdon Manor.
.	.	.	.	.	.	. .	South Junction	Bucks	G. W. & Met. Jt.—Met.	Aylesbury and Stoke Mandeville.
.	.	.	.	.	.	. .	Aylesbury Brewery Co.'s Sid.	Bucks	L. & N. W.	Buckingham.
G	P	F	L	H	C	4 0	Aylesford	Kent	S. E. & C.	Maidstone and Strood.
.	.	.	.	.	.	. .	New Hythe Siding	Kent	S. E. & C.	Snodland and Aylesford.
.	.	.	.	.	.	. .	Aylestone Road	Leicester	Mid.	See Leicester.
.	.	.	.	.	.	. .	Aylestone Road Gas Works	Leicester	Mid.	Leicester, East.
G	P	F	L	H	C	1 10	Aylsham	Norfolk	G. E.	Wroxham and County School.
G	P	F	L	H	C	1 0	Aylsham Town	Norfolk	Mid. & G. N. Jt.	Melton Constable & North Walsham Town.
.	.	.	.	.	.	. .	Aylwards Siding	Hants	L. & S. W.	Aldershot.
G	P	.	L	H	.	. .	Aylwardstown	Kilkenny	D. W. & W.	New Ross and Waterford.
G	P	F	L	H	C	2 0	Aynho	N'hampt'n	G. W.	Oxford and Banbury.
G	P	F	L	H	C	. .	Ayot	Herts	G. N.	Hatfield and Luton.
.	.	.	.	.	.	. .	Robinson's Wood Siding	Herts	G. N.	Ayot and Wheathampstead.
							AYR—			
.	P	.	F	.	.	. .	(Station)	Ayr	{ G. & S. W.	Troon and Maybole.
G	.	.	L	H	C	6 0 }		Ayr	G. & S. W.	Branch from Falkland Junction.
.	.	.	.	.	.	. .	Belmont Siding	Ayr	G. & S. W.	Ayr (Passengers) and Dalrymple.
.	.	.	L	.	.	. .	Cattle Market	Ayr	G. & S. W.	Ayr (Passengers) and Dalrymple.
.	.	.	.	.	.	. .	Chemical Co.'s Siding	Ayr	G. & S. W.	Ayr Harbour.
.	.	.	.	.	.	. .	Corporation Siding	Ayr	G. & S. W.	Ayr Harbour.
G	.	.	L	.	.	25 0	Harbour	Ayr	G. & S. W.	Branch from Newton Junction.
.	.	.	.	.	.	. .	Harbour North Junction	Ayr	G. & S. W.	Prestwick and Ayr Harbour.
.	.	.	.	.	.	. .	Harbour South Junction	Ayr	G. & S. W.	Prestwick and Ayr Harbour.

EXPLANATION—G *Goods Station.*   P *Passenger and Parcel Station.*   P* *Passenger, but not Parcel or Miscellaneous Traffic.*
F *Furniture Vans, Carriages, Portable Engines, and Machines on Wheels.*   L *Live Stock.*
H *Horse Boxes and Prize Cattle Vans.*   C *Carriages by Passenger Train.*

STATION ACCOMMODATION.						CRANE POWER.	STATIONS, &c.	COUNTY.	COMPANY.	POSITION.
						Tons Cwts.	AYR—continued.			
							Hawkhill Chemical Works (Walker & Co.'s Siding)..	Ayr	G. & S.W.	Ayr and Auchincruive.
G	P					2 0	Newtonhead Depôt	Ayr	G. & S.W.	Newton Junc. and Blackhouse Junc.
G		F					Newton-on-Ayr	Ayr	G. & S.W.	Ayr (Passengers) and Troon.
						2 0	Townhead Depôt	Ayr	G. & S.W.	Ayr (Passengers) and Dalrymple.
							Wyllie's Chemical Works...	Ayr	G. & S.W.	Falkland Junction.
							Ayresome Iron Wks. & Wharf	Yorks	N. E.	Middlesbro'.
							Ayresome Warrant Store and Wharf	Yorks	N. E.	See Connal's (Middlesbro').
							Ayre's Quay Gas Works ...	Durham ..	N. E.	Pallion.
							Ayre's Siding	Herts	L. & N. W.	See Bushey Lodge Siding (Watford).
							Ayrshire Foundry	Ayr	Cal.—G. & S. W.	Stevenston.
							Ayrton Rolling Mills	Yorks	N. E.	Middlesbro'.
G	P	F	L	H	C	2 0	Aysdalegate Mines	Yorks	N. E.	Slapewath.
G	P	F	L	H	C	5 0	Aysgarth	Yorks	N. E.	Leyburn and Hawes.
							Ayton	Berwick ..	N. B.	Dunbar and Berwick.
							Ayton, Great	Yorks	N. E.	See Great Ayton.
							Ayton Junction	Yorks	N. E.	Nunthorpe and Pinchingthorpe.

B

STATION ACCOMMODATION.						CRANE POWER.	STATIONS, &c.	COUNTY.	COMPANY.	POSITION.
							Babbington Brick Works ...	Notts	Mid.	Nottingham, Basford.
							Babbington Coal Co.—			
							Bulwell Colliery	Notts	Mid.	Nottingham, Bulwell.
							Cinder Hill Colliery	Notts	Mid.	Nottingham, Basford.
							Siding	Derby	Mid.	Tibshelf & Newton.
							Babbington Colliery (G.N.).	Notts	G. N.—G. C.	See Cinder Hill & Babbington Col. (Nottingham).
							Babcock & Wilcox's Siding (G. & S. W.)	Renfrew ...	G. & S.W. — Cal. ...	Same as Porterfield Sid. (Renfrew).
	P						Backhouses Siding............	Yorks	N. E.	Cattal.
							Backworth	Northumb	N. E.	Newcastle and Blyth.
							Backworth Coal Depôt & Sid.	Northumb	N. E.	Newcastle-on-Tyne.
G	P						Backworth Colliery	Northumb	N. E.	Holywell.
G	P		L	H	C	10 0	Bacton	Hereford	G. W.	Pontrilas and Dorstone.
							Bacup	Lancs	L. & Y.	Stacksteads and Britannia.
							Greenwood's Siding	Lancs	L. & Y.	Bacup.
							Holt's Siding	Lancs	L. & Y.	Bacup.
							Baddesley Colliery............	Warwick..	L. & N. W.	Atherstone.
							Baddesley Col. (Baxterley Park Colliery)	Warwick..	Mid.	Kingsbury.
G	P	F	L	H	C	6 0	Badminton	Glo'ster ...	G. W.	Wootton Bassett and Patchway.
G						1 10	Badnall Wharf (for Eccleshall)	Staffs	L. & N. W.	Crewe and Stafford.
							Badsey	Worcester	G. W.	See Littleton and Badsey.
G	P		L	H		2 0	Baggrow	Cumb'land	M. & C.	Aspatria and Mealsgate.
							Baghill (S. & K. Jt.)............	Yorks	S & K Jt.—GC—GN—LY	See Pontefract.
G	P					5 0	Bagillt	Flint	L. & N. W.	Chester and Rhyl.
							Mitchell's Bettisfield Col.	Flint	L. & N. W.	Bagillt and Holywell.
							Baglan Bay Engineering Wks.	Glamorg'n	R. & S. B.	Briton Ferry.
							Baglan Bay Tin Works	Glamorg'n	G. W.	Briton Ferry.
							Bagley & Co.'s Siding	Yorks	L. & Y.	Knottingley.
							Bagnall's Forge&Engine Wks.	Durham ..	N. E.	Hylton.
							Bagnall's Castle Engine Wks.	Staffs	L. & N. W.	Stafford.
G	P	F	L	H	C	1 10	Bagnalstown	Carlow	G. S. & W.	Carlow and Kilkenny.
							Bagnor	Berks	L'bourn Valley	See Stockcross and Bagnor.
							Bagshaw, G. & J., Siding ...	Norfolk ...	G. E.	Haddiscoe.
G	P	F	L	H	C	1 10	Bagshot	Surrey ...	L. & S.W.	Ascot and Farnborough.
							Bagthorpe Junction	Notts	G. C.—G.N.	Nottingham.
G	P	F	L	H	C	5 0	Baguley (C. L. C.)	Cheshire.	C. L. C. (GC,GN,& Mid.) / L. & N. W.	Northenden and Skelton Junction. / Over C. L. C. Line.
G	P	F	L	H	C		Bagworth and Ellistown	Leicester..	Mid.	Leicester and Burton.
							Bagworth Brick Co.'s Sid.	Leicester..	Mid.	Bagworth and Ellistown.
							Bagworth Colliery (Mid.)...	Leicester..	Mid.—L. & N. W.	Bagworth and Ellistown.
							Desford Coal Co.'s Sid. (Mid)	Leicester..	Mid.—L. & N. W.	Bagworth and Desford.
							Ellistown Colliery & Brick Works (Mid.)	Leicester..	Mid.—L. & N. W.	Bagworth and Bardon Hill.
							Ibstock Colliery (Mid.)	Leicester..	Mid.—L. & N. W.	Bagworth and Bardon Hill.
							Nailstone Colliery (Mid.) ...	Leicester..	Mid.—L. & N. W.	Bagworth and Bardon Hill.

EXPLANATION—G *Goods Station.*   P *Passenger and Parcel Station.*   P* *Passenger, but not Parcel or Miscellaneous Traffic.*
F *Furniture Vans, Carriages, Portable Engines, and Machines on Wheels.*   L *Live Stock.*
H *Horse Boxes and Prize Cattle Vans.*   C *Carriages by Passenger Train.*

G	P	F	L	H	C	Tons	Cwts	STATIONS, &c.	COUNTY.	COMPANY.	POSITION.
								Bagworth Brick Co.'s Siding	Leicester	Mid.	Bagworth and Ellistown.
								Bagworth Colliery (Mid.)	Leicester	Mid.—L. & N. W.	Bagworth and Ellistown.
G	P	F	L	H	C	1	10	Baildon	Yorks	Mid.	Shipley and Guiseley.
								Bailey & Clapham's Siding	Yorks	Mid.	Keighley.
								Baileyfield Siding	Edinboro'	N. B.	Edinburgh, Portobello.
G	P	F	L	H	C			Bailey Gate	Dorset	S.&D.Jt.(L.&S.W.&Mid)	Wimborne and Blandford.
								Carter's Siding	Dorset	S.&D.Jt.(L.&S.W.&Mid)	Bailey Gate and Wimborne.
								Bailey's Pottery	Clackman'	N. B.	Alloa.
								Bailey's Siding	Mon	L. & N. W.	Brynmawr.
								Bailey's Siding	Somerset	G. W.	Bristol, Portishead.
								Bailey's Siding	Somerset	G. W.	Frome.
								Bailey, W. H., & Co.'s Siding	Lancs	Trafford Park Estate	Manchester.
	P							Bailiff Bridge	Yorks	L. & Y.	Brighouse and Wyke.
								Bailliesmuir Colliery	Lanark	Cal. / Cal.—N. B.	Newmains. / Morningside.
								Baillie's Quarry	Lanark	N. B.	Forrestfield.
G	P	F	L	H	C	1	10	Baillieston	Lanark	Cal.	Coatbridge and Rutherglen.
								Aitkenhead Colliery	Lanark	Cal.	Branch near Baillieston.
								Braehead Bk & Silicate Wks.	Lanark	Cal.	Branch near Baillieston.
								Braehead Colliery	Lanark	Cal.	Branch near Baillieston.
								Braehead Quarry	Lanark	Cal.	Branch near Baillieston.
								Bredisholm Brick Works	Lanark	Cal.	Branch near Baillieston.
								Bredisholm Chemical Wks.	Lanark	Cal.	Branch near Baillieston.
								Bredisholm Cols. Nos.1,2,3, 4, 5, & 6 (Newland's Col.)	Lanark	Cal.	Branch near Baillieston.
								Bredisholm Quarry	Lanark	Cal.	Branch near Baillieston.
								Calderbank Cols. Nos. 1 & 2	Lanark	Cal.	Mount Vernon & Baillieston.
								Calder Blacking Mill	Lanark	Cal.	Branch near Baillieston.
								Calder Forge	Lanark	Cal.	Branch nr. Baillieston (Drumpeller).
								Cuilhill Basin	Lanark	Cal.	Baillieston and Langloan.
								Drumpark Brick Works	Lanark	Cal.	Baillieston and Langloan.
								Drumpark Colliery	Lanark	Cal.	Baillieston and Langloan.
								Ellismuir Brick Works	Lanark	Cal.	Baillieston and Langloan.
								Ellismuir Cols. Nos. 2 & 3	Lanark	Cal.	Baillieston and Langloan.
								Tennochside Collieries Nos. 1, 2, and 3.	Lanark	Cal.	Branch near Baillieston.
								Tennochside Junction	Lanark	Cal.	Baillieston and Langloan.
								Baillieston	Lanark	N. B.	See Easterhouse (for Baillieston).
								Bain & Co.'s— Collieries	Cumb'land	C. & W. Jn.	High Harrington.
								Ehen Valley Branch Pits Nos. 6 and 11	Cumb'land	WC&E Jt.(Fur.&L&NW)	Gillfoot.
								Harrington Iron Works	Cumb'land	C. & W. Jn. / L. & N. W.	High Harrington. / Harrington.
								Limestone Quarry	Cumb'land	R. & K. F.	Rowrah Junc. and Kelton Fell.
								No. 4 Pit	Cumb'land	WC&E Jt.(Fur.&L&NW)	Parton.
G	P	F	L	H	C	2	0	Bainton	Yorks	N. E.	Market Weighton and Driffield.
								Baird & Co.'s— Kelton Iron Mines	Cumb'land	R. & K. F.	Kelton Fell.
								Knockmurton Iron Mines	Cumb'land	R. & K. F.	Kelton Fell.
								Baird & Stevenson's Siding	Fife	N. B.	Same as Collinswell Siding (Burntisland).
								Baird, H., & Co.'s Siding	Lanark	N. B.	Same as Wordie's Siding (Glasgow).
								Baird's Knockmurton Mines	Cumb'land	WC&EJt(Fur.&L&NW)	Rowrah.
								Baird's Wood Yard (N.B.)	Stirling	N. B.—Cal.	Falkirk, Grahamston.
								Baker & Co.'s Siding	Glamorg'n	G W—LNW—Rhy.—TV	Cardiff.
								Baker, J., & Co.'s Iron Works	Yorks	Mid.	Same as Brinsworth Iron Works (Masbro').
								Baker's Store Yard	Yorks	N. E.	Middlesbro'.
								Baker Street	Renfrew	Cal.	See Greenock.
								Baker Street (Met.)	Middlesex	Met.—G. W.	See London.
G	P	F	L	H	C	5	0	Bakewell	Derby	Mid.	Rowsley and Miller's Dale.
G	P	F	L	H	C	4	0	Bala	Merioneth	G. W.	Bala Junction and Festiniog.
								Balaclava Colliery— Tingley Colliery	Yorks	G. N.	Tingley.
								West Ardsley Colliery	Yorks	G. N.	Tingley.
G	P		L	H		1	10	Balado	Kinross	N. B.	Kinross Junc. & Rumbling Bridge.
								M'Nab's Siding	Kinross	N. B.	Kinross Junction and Balado.
								Balbardie Nos. 1 and 2 Cols.	L'lithgow	N. B.	Bathgate, Lower.
								Balbardie Sand Pit Sidings	L'lithgow	N. B.	Bathgate, Upper.
								Balbirnie Paper Mills	Fife	N. B.	Markinch.
G	P	F	L	H	C			Balbriggan	Dublin	G. N. (I)	Dublin and Drogheda.

EXPLANATION—G *Goods Station.*   P *Passenger and Parcel Station.*   P* *Passenger, but not Parcel or Miscellaneous Traffic.*
F *Furniture Vans, Carriages, Portable Engines, and Machines on Wheels.*   L *Live Stock.*
H *Horse Boxes and Prize Cattle Vans.*   C *Carriages by Passenger Train.*

STATION ACCOMMODATION.						CRANE POWER.	STATIONS, &c.	COUNTY.	COMPANY.	POSITION.
						Tons Cwts.				
.	.	.	.	.	.	. .	Balby Junction	Yorks	G. C.—G.N.	Doncaster.
.	.	.	.	.	.	. .	Balby Siding	Yorks	G. C.	Doncaster.
.	.	.	.	.	.	. .	Balcarres Colliery	Fife	N. B.	Largoward.
.	.	.	.	.	.	. .	Balcarres Str. Manure Depôt (Edinburgh Cleansing Department Siding)	Edinboro'	N. B.	Edinburgh, Morningside Road.
.	.	.	.	.	.	. .	Balcarres Street Works (Mackenzie & Moncur)	Edinboro'	N. B.	Edinburgh, Morningside Road.
G	P	.	.	.	.	5 0	Balcombe	Sussex	L. B. & S. C.	Three Bridges & Haywards Heath.
.	.	.	.	.	.	. .	Baldastard Colliery	Fife	N. B.	Montrave.
G	P	F	L	H	C	3 0	Baldersby	Yorks	N. E.	Thirsk and Melmerby.
G	P	.	L	H	.	. .	Balderton	Cheshire	G. W.	Chester and Wrexham.
G	P	F	L	H	C	1 15	Baldock	Herts	G. N.	Hitchin and Cambridge.
.	.	.	.	.	.	. .	Norton Siding (Associated Portland Cement Manufacturers' Siding)	Herts	G. N.	Baldock and Hitchin.
.	.	.	.	.	.	. .	Page's Malting Siding	Herts	G. N.	Baldock.
G	P	.	L	H	.	2 0	Baldovan	Forfar	Cal.	Dundee and Newtyle.
G	P	.	L	H	.	. .	Baldoyle and Sutton	Dublin	G. N. (I)	Howth Branch.
G	P	.	L	H	C	1 10	Baldragon	Forfar	Cal.	Dundee and Newtyle.
							Baldwin's, Ltd.—			
.	.	.	.	.	.	. .	Elba Colliery	Glamorg'n	G. W.—L. & N. W.	Gowerton.
.	.	.	.	.	.	. .	Elba Steel Works	Glamorg'n	G. W.—L. & N. W.	Gowerton.
.	.	.	.	.	.	. .	Landore Steel Works or Swansea Hematite Iron Works	Glamorg'n	G. W.	Landore.
.	.	.	.	.	.	. .	Landore Steel Works or Swansea Hematite Iron Works (Mid.)	Glamorg'n	Mid.—G.W.—L. & N.W.	Upper Bank.
.	.	.	.	.	.	. .	Lower Mills Works	Mon	G. W.	Pontypool Road.
.	.	.	.	.	.	. .	Panteg Steel and Sheet Works	Mon	G. W.	Panteg.
.	.	.	.	.	.	. .	Phœnix Works	Mon	G. W.	Pontypool Road.
.	.	.	.	.	.	. .	Siding	Glamorg'n	P. T.—R. & S. B.	Cwmavon.
G	P	.	L	.	.	2 0	Balerno	Edinboro'	Cal.	Mid Calder and Currie.
.	.	.	.	.	.	. .	Haggs Siding	Edinboro'	Cal.	Mid Calder and Curriehill.
.	.	.	.	.	.	. .	Kaimes Quarry	Edinboro'	Cal.	Mid Calder and Curriehill.
.	.	.	.	.	.	. .	Ravelrig Quarry	Edinboro'	Cal.	Mid Calder and Balerno.
G	P	F	L	H	C	3 0	Balfron	Stirling	N. B.	Balloch and Stirling.
.	.	.	.	.	.	. .	Drumquhurn Siding	Stirling	N. B.	Balfron and Gartness.
G	P	F	L	H	C	3 0	Balgonie Colliery	Fife	N. B.	Thornton.
.	.	.	.	.	.	. .	Balgowan	Perth	Cal.	Crieff and Perth, North.
.	P	.	.	.	.	. .	Balham (L. B. & S. C.)	Surrey	{ L. B. & S. C. / L. & N. W.	Clapham Junction & Crystal Palace. / Over L.B.& S.C. from Clapham Junc.
G	P	.	L	H	.	2 0	Balhousie Sidings	Perth	Cal.	See Perth.
.	P	.	.	.	.	. .	Balla	Mayo	M. G. W.	Claremorris and Westport.
G	P	F	L	H	C	3 0	Ballabeg	I. of Man	I. of Man	Douglas and Port Erin.
G	P	F	L	H	C	. .	Ballachulish	Argyll	Cal.	Branch from Connel Ferry.
G	P	F	L	H	C	0 10	Ballachulish Ferry	Argyll	Cal.	Connel Ferry and Ballachulish.
.	.	.	.	.	.	. .	Ballaghaderreen	Mayo	M. G. W.	Branch from Kilfree Junction.
G	P	F*	L	.	.	. .	Ballantyne's Mill	Peebles	N. B.	Peebles.
G	P	F	L	H	C	4 0	Ballasalla	I. of Man	I. of Man	Douglas and Port Erin.
.	.	.	.	.	.	. .	Ballater	Aberdeen	G. N. of S.	Branch from Aberdeen.
G	P	.	L	.	.	. .	Ballathie Siding	Perth	Cal.	See Cargill.
.	.	.	.	.	.	. .	Ballaugh	I. of Man	Manx Northern	St. John's and Ramsey.
.	.	.	.	.	.	. .	Balleece Siding	Wicklow	D. W. & W.	Rathdrum.
.	.	.	.	.	.	. .	Ballencrieff Siding	Hadding'n	N. B.	See Drem.
G	P	F	L	H	C	1 10	Ballina	Mayo	M. G. W.	Manulla Junction and Killala.
G	P	.	L	.	.	. .	Ballinamallard	Ferm'nagh	G. N. (I.)	Enniskillen and Omagh.
G	P	.	.	.	.	. .	Ballinamore	Donegal	Donegal	Stranorlar and Glenties.
G	P	.	L	.	.	2 0	Ballinamore	Leitrim	C. & L.	Belturbet and Dromod.
G	P	.	.	.	.	. .	Ballinascarthy Station & Junc.	Cork	C. B. & S. C.—T. & C.	Clonakilty Jn. & Courtmacsherry.
G	P	F	L	H	C	2 0	Ballinasloe	Galway	M. G. W.	Athlone and Athenry.
G	P	F	L	.	.	. .	Ballincollig	Cork	C. & Macroom	Cork and Kilcrea.
G	P	F	L	H	C	3 0	Ballindalloch	Elgin&Mo'	G. N. of S.	Craigellachie and Boat of Garten.
.	P	.	.	.	.	. .	Ballindangan	Cork	G. S. & W.	Mitchelstown and Glanworth.
.	.	.	.	.	.	. .	Ballindarg Siding (Cal.)	Forfar	Cal.—N. B.	See Kirriemuir.
G	P	.	L	.	.	1 0	Ballinderry	Antrim	G. N. (I.)	Antrim and Lisburn.
G	P	.	L	.	.	2 0	Ballindine	Mayo	G. S. & W.	Tuam and Claremorris.
G	P	F	L	H	C	. .	Ballineen and Enniskean	Cork	C. B. & S. C.	Bandon and Dunmanway.
.	P	.	.	.	.	. .	Ballineesteenig	Kerry	T. & D.	Castlegregory Junction and Dingle.
.	G	P	.	.	.	. .	Ballinglen	Wicklow	D. W. & W.	Woodenbridge and Shillelagh.

EXPLANATION—G *Goods Station.*　　P *Passenger and Parcel Station.*　　P* *Passenger, but not Parcel or Miscellaneous Traffic.*
F *Furniture Vans, Carriages, Portable Engines, and Machines on Wheels.*　　F* *Furniture Vans excepted.*　　L *Live Stock.*
H *Horse Boxes and Prize Cattle Vans.*　　C *Carriages by Passenger Train.*

Station Accommodation						Crane Power		Stations, &c.	County.	Company.	Position.
G	P	F	L	H	C	Tons	Cwts.				
G	P	F	L	H	C	.	.	Ballingrane Junction Station	Limerick..	G. S. & W.	Limerick and Newcastle West.
G	P	.	.	.	.	.	.	Ballinhassig....................	Cork	C. B. & S. C.	Cork and Bandon.
G	P	F	L	H	C	1	0	Ballinlough....................	Roscom'n	M. G. W.	Roscommon and Claremorris.
G	P	F	L	H	C	5	0	Ballinluig.....................	Perth ...	High	Dunkeld and Blair Atholl.
.	P	.	.	.	.	.	.	Ballinosare	Kerry ...	T. & D.......................	Castlegregory Junction and Dingle.
G	P	F	L	H	C	2	0	Ballinrobe	Mayo ...	M. G. W.	Branch from Claremorris.
.	P	.	.	.	.	.	.	Ballintogher	Sligo ...	S. L. & N. C.	Manorhamilton and Collooney.
.	P	.	.	.	.	.	.	Balliol Road (Bootle)	Lancs ...	L. & N. W.	See Liverpool, Bootle. (Balliol Rd.).
G	P	F	L	H	C	3	0	Balloch........................	Dumbartn	D. & B. Jt. (Cal. & N.B.)	Dumbarton and Balloch Pier.
G	P	.	.	.	.	5	0	Balloch Pier	Dumbartn	D. & B. Jt. (Cal. & N.B.)	Branch from Dalreoch.
.	.	.	.	.	.	.	.	Ballochmyle Quarry	Ayr	G. & S.W.	Mauchline.
.	.	.	.	.	.	.	.	Ballochnie Siding	Lanark ...	N. B.	See Rawyards.
G	P	F	L	.	.	1	10	Ballybay	Monaghan	G. N. (I.)	Dundalk and Clones.
G	P	.	L	.	.	.	.	Ballybeg	Meath......	G. N. (I.)	Navan and Kells.
G	P	.	L	.	.	.	.	Ballybofey	Donegal ..	Donegal	Stranorlar and Glenties.
G	P	.	.	.	.	.	.	Ballyboley	Antrim ...	N. C. Com. (Mid.)	Ballymena and Larne.
.	.	.	.	.	.	.	.	Ballybrack	Dublin ...	D. W. & W.	See Killiney and Ballybrack.
.	P	.	.	.	.	.	.	Ballybrack	Kerry	G. S. & W.	Killarney and Tralee.
G	P	F	L	H	C	1	10	Ballybrophy	Queen's ..	G. S. & W.	Maryborough and Thurles.
G	P	P	F	L	.	.	.	Ballybunion	Kerry	L. & B.	Terminus.
G	P	F	L	H	C	.	.	Ballycar and Newmarket (G. S. & W.)	Clare	G. S. & W. / M. G. W.	Limerick and Ennis. / Over G. S. & W. from Athenry.
G	P	.	L	H	C	.	.	Ballycarry	Antrim ...	N. C. Com. (Mid.)	Carrickfergus and Larne.
G	P	.	L	H	C	2	0	Ballycastle	Antrim ...	Ballycastle	Terminus.
G	P	F	L	H	C	3	0	Ballyclare	Antrim ...	N. C. Com. (Mid.)	Branch from Ballyclare Junction.
.	.	.	.	.	.	.	.	Paper Mill Siding	Antrim ...	N. C. Com. (Mid.)	Near Ballyclare.
G	P	.	.	H	.	3	0	Ballyclare (Narrow Gauge)...	Antrim ...	N. C. Com. (Mid.)	Ballyboley and Doagh.
G	P	.	L	H	.	2	0	Ballyclare Junction Station...	Antrim ...	N. C. Com. (Mid.)	Antrim and Greenisland.
.	P	.	.	.	.	.	.	Ballycloughan..................	Antrim ...	N. C. Com. (Mid.)	Ballymena and Knockanally.
G	P	.	L	.	.	.	.	Ballyconnell	Cavan	C. & L.	Belturbet and Ballinamore.
G	P	.	L	H	.	.	.	Ballycumber	Kings	G. S. & W.	Portarlington and Athlone.
G	P	.	L	.	.	.	.	Ballydehob	Cork	S. & S.	Schull and Skibbereen.
G	P	.	L	.	.	.	.	Ballyduff	Cork	G. S. & W.	Fermoy and Lismore.
.	P	.	.	.	.	.	.	Ballyduff (Book to Ballinamore)	Leitrim ...	C. & L.	Ballinamore and Drumshambo.
.	P	.	.	.	.	.	.	Ballygarvey....................	Antrim ...	N. C. Com. (Mid.)	Ballymena and Knockanally.
G	P	.	L	.	.	2	0	Ballygawley	Tyrone ...	Clogher Valley	Aughnacloy and Fivemiletown.
G	P	.	L	H	C	2	0	Ballygowan	Down ...	B. & C. D.	Comber and Ballynahinch Junc.
.	.	.	.	.	.	.	.	Dufferin Stone Co.'s Siding	Down ...	B. & C. D.	Ballygowan and Comber.
.	.	.	.	.	.	.	.	Gill's Siding	Down ...	B. & C. D.	Ballygowan and Comber.
.	.	.	.	.	.	.	.	Robb & Co.'s Quarry	Down ...	B. & C. D.	Ballygowan and Comber.
G	P	.	L	H	C	1	0	Ballyglunin...................	Galway ...	G. S. & W.	Athenry and Tuam.
G	P	.	L	.	.	1	0	Ballyhaise Junction Station..	Cavan	G. N. (I.)	Clones and Cavan.
G	P	F	L	H	C	.	.	Ballyhale	Kilkenny..	G. S. & W.	Waterford and Kilkenny.
G	P	F	L	H	C	2	0	Ballyhaunis	Mayo	M. G. W.	Roscommon and Claremorris.
G	P	.	.	.	.	.	.	Ballyheady (Book to Bawnboy Rd.)	Cavan	C. & L.	Ballyconnell and Bawnboy Road.
.	P	.	.	.	.	.	.	Ballyheather	Tyrone ...	Donegal	Londonderry and Strabane.
G	P	F	L	H	C	.	.	Ballyhooly	Cork	G. S. & W.	Mallow and Fermoy.
.	P	.	.	.	.	.	.	Ballykelly	Derry	N. C. Com. (Mid.)	Londonderry and Coleraine.
G	P	.	L	.	.	.	.	Ballyliffin....................	Donegal ..	L. & L. S	Buncrana and Carndonagh.
.	.	.	.	.	.	.	.	Ballymaccarrett Junctions....	Down ...	B. & C. D.—G. N. (I.) ...	Belfast.
G	P	.	L	.	.	.	.	Ballymagan	Donegal ..	L. & L. S..	Buncrana and Carndonagh.
G	P	F	L	H	C	.	.	Ballymagorry	Tyrone ...	Donegal	Londonderry and Strabane.
.	P	.	.	.	.	.	.	Ballymartle	Cork	C. B. & S. C.	Kinsale Junc. Station and Kinsale.
G	P	F	L	H	C	3	0	Ballymena	Antrim ...	N. C. Com. (Mid.)	Antrim and Coleraine.
G	.	.	L	H	.	3	0	Ballymena (Harryville)........	Antrim ...	N. C. Com. (Mid.)	Ballymena and Larne.
G	P	F	L	H	C	2	0	Ballymoe	Galway ...	M. G. W.	Roscommon and Claremorris.
G	P	F	L	H	C	6	0	Ballymoney Station & Junc.	Antrim ...	Ballycastle .... / N. C. Com. (Mid.)	Junction with N. C. Com. (Mid.) / Coleraine and Ballymena.
G	P	F	L	H	C	1	10	Ballymote	Sligo	M. G. W.	Longford and Sligo.
.	P	.	.	.	.	.	.	Ballymurry	Roscom'n	M. G. W.	Athlone and Roscommon.
G	P	.	L	H	C	4	0	Ballynahinch	Down ...	B. & C. D.	Branch from Ballynahinch Junction.
G	P	.	.	.	C	.	.	Ballynahinch Junc. Station..	Down ...	B. & C. D.	Belfast and Downpatrick.
G	P	.	L	.	.	.	.	Ballynahinch	Galway ...	M. G. W.	Galway and Clifden.
G	P	.	.	.	.	.	.	Ballynashee	Antrim ...	N. C. Com. (Mid.)	Larne and Ballymena.
G	P	.	L	H	C	.	.	Ballynoe	Down ...	B. & C. D.	Downpatrick and Ardglass.
G	P	.	L	.	.	.	.	Ballynure	Antrim ...	N. C. Com. (Mid.)	Ballyboley and Doagh.
G	P	F	L	H	.	.	.	Ballyragget	Kilkenny	G. S. & W.	Kilkenny and Maryborough.
G	P	F	L	H	C	2	0	Ballyroney	Down ...	G. N. (I.)	Branch from Banbridge.
G	P	F	L	.	.	2	10	Ballyshannon	Donegal ..	G. N. (I.)	Bundoran Junction and Bundoran.
G	P	F	L	H	C	1	10	Ballysodare (M. G. W.)	Sligo........	M. G. W. .... / G. S. & W. .... / S. L. & N. C.	Longford and Sligo. / Over M. G. W. from Collooney. / Over M. G. W. from Carrignagat Jn.

STATION ACCOMMODATION.						CRANE POWER.		STATIONS, &c.	COUNTY.	COMPANY.	POSITION.
						Tons	Cwts				
G	P	.	L	.	.			Ballyvary	Mayo	M. G. W.	Manulla Junc. Station and Foxford.
G	P	F	L	H	C	1	10	Ballywillan	Longford	M. G. W.	Mullingar and Cavan.
G	P	.	L	.	.			Balmacarra	Ross & Cro'	Cal.	Steamer from Oban.
G	P	.	L	.	.					High.	Steamer from Kyle of Lochalsh.
G	P	.	L	.	.					N. B.	Steamer from Mallaig.
.	G	P	.	.	.			Balmforth's Siding (G. N.)	Beds	G. N.— L. & N. W.	Luton.
.	G	P	.	.	.			Balmoral	Antrim	G. N. (I.)	Belfast and Lisburn.
G	P	.	L	.	.			Balmoral Siding	Renfrew	Cal.	Glasgow, Whiteinch.
								Balmore	Stirling	N. B.	Maryhill and Kilsyth.
								Balmossie	Forfar	Cal.	See Barnhill.
								Balm Road Siding	Yorks	Mid.	Leeds, Hunslet.
								Balmuckety Siding (Cal.)	Forfar	Cal.—N. B.	See Kirriemuir.
								Balmule Siding	Fife	N. B.	See Whitemyre Junction Station.
.	P	.	.	.	.			Balnacoul	Elgin&Mo'	High.	Orbliston and Fochabers Town.
G	P	.	L	H	C			Balne	Yorks	N. E.	Selby and Doncaster.
								Balne Lane Junction	Yorks	G. N.	Wakefield.
								Balornock Junction	Lanark	Cal.	Glasgow.
G	P	F	L	H	C	2	0	Balquhatson Colliery	Stirling	N. B.	Slamannan.
G	P	.	L	.	.	5	0	Balquhidder	Perth	Cal.	Callander and Oban.
								Balshaw Lane and Euxton	Lancs	L. & N. W.	Preston and Wigan.
								Baltic Saw Mill (Harrison & Singleton)	Durham	N. E.	West Hartlepool.
G	P	.	L	H	C			Baltimore	Cork	C. B. & S. C.	Terminus.
G	P	F	L	H	C			Baltinglass	Wicklow	G. S. & W.	Sallins and Tullow.
								Balwill Siding	Stirling	N. B.	See Buchlyvie.
G	P	.	L	H	.	10	0	Bamber Bridge	Lancs	L. & Y.	Preston and Blackburn.
								Dewhirst's Siding	Lancs	L. & Y.	Bamber Bridge.
G	P	F	L	H	C			Bamford	Derby	Mid.	Dore and Chinley.
								Derwent Valley Water Wks.	Derby	Mid.	Near Bamford.
								Bamford & Son's Siding	Staffs	N S.	Uttoxeter.
.	P	.	.	.	.			Bamfurlong	Lancs	L. & N. W.	Warrington and Wigan.
								Bamfurlong Colliery	Lancs	L. & N. W.	See Cross, Tetley & Co. (Wigan).
G	P	F	L	H	C	5	0	Bampton	Devon	G. W.	Morebath Junction and Tiverton.
								Cove Siding	Devon	G. W.	Tiverton and Bampton.
G	P	F	L	H	C	1	10	Bampton	Oxon	G. W.	Witney and Fairford.
G	P	F	L	H	C			Banagher	Kings	G. S. & W.	Branch from Clara.
.	P	.	.	.	.			Banavie	Inverness	N. B.	Fort William and Mallaig.
								Banavie Junction	Inverness	N. B.	Fort William and Banavie.
G	P	.	L	H	.	1	10	Banavie Pier	Inverness	N. B.	Branch from Banavie Junction.
G	P	F	L	H	C	5	0	Banbridge	Down	G. N. (I.)	Scarva and Ballyroney.
								BANBURY—			
G	P	F	L	H	C	10	0	(Station, G. W.)	N'hamptn	G. W.	Oxford and Leamington.
.	P	.	.	H	C	.	.			G. C.	Over G. W. from Banbury Junction.
G	P	F	L	H	C	5	0	(Station, L. & N. W.)	N'hamptn	L. & N. W.	Branch from Verney Junction.
										N. & B. Jn.	Over L. N.W. from Cockley Brake Jn.
								Claridge's Sid. (Gunn's Sid.)	N'hamptn	L. & N. W.	Banbury and Farthinghoe.
								Gas Co.'s Siding	N'hamptn	G. W.	Banbury.
										L. & N. W.	Banbury and Farthinghoe.
								Junction	N'hamptn	G. C.—G. W.	Rugby and Oxford.
								Junction	N'hamptn	G. W.—L. & N. W.	Banbury, G. W. and L. & N. W. Stations.
								Samuelson & Co.'s Siding	N'hamptn	G. W.	Banbury.
G	P	F	L	H	C	7	0	Banbury Street	Warwick	L. & N. W.	See Birmingham.
G	P	F	L	H	C	5	0	Banchory	Kinc'rdine	G. N. of S.	Aberdeen and Aboyne.
								Bandon	Cork	C. B. & S. C.	Cork and Bantry.
								Bandon Hill	Surrey	L. B. & S. C.	See Waddon (for Beddington and Bandon Hill).
G	P	F	L	H	C	2	10	Banff	Banff	G. N. of S.	Branch from Tillynaught.
.	P	.	.	.	.			Banff Bridge	Banff	G. N. of S.	Inveramsay and Macduff.
G	P	F	L	H	C	5	0	Bangor	Carnarvon	L. & N. W.	Holyhead and Rhyl.
								Dixon & Co.'s Siding	Carnarvon	L. & N. W.	Aber and Bangor.
								Lord Penrhyn's—			
								Penlan Mill	Carnarvon	L. & N. W.	Aber and Bangor.
								Port Penrhyn Quay	Carnarvon	L. & N. W.	Aber and Bangor.
G	P	.	L	H	C	2	0	Bangor	Down	B. & C. D.	Branch from Belfast.
G	P	F	L	H	C			Bangor-on-Dee	Flint	Cam.	Wrexham and Ellesmere.
								Bangour Railway Sidings	L'lithgow	N. B.	Uphall.
								Bank	Middlesex	C. L.—C. & S.L.—W. & C.	See London.
								Bank Brick Works	Ayr	G. & S. W.	New Cumnock.
								Bankend Colliery & Lime Wks (Sitehill Colliery)	Lanark	Cal.	Coalburn.
								Bank Farm Siding	Yorks	N. E.	Eston.

EXPLANATION—**G** *Goods Station.* **P** *Passenger and Parcel Station.* **P*** *Passenger, but not Parcel or Miscellaneous Traffic.*
F *Furniture Vans, Carriages, Portable Engines, and Machines on Wheels.* **L** *Live Stock.*
H *Horse Boxes and Prize Cattle Vans.* **C** *Carriages by Passenger Train.*

STATION ACCOMMODATION.						CRANE POWER.		STATIONS, &c.	COUNTY.	COMPANY.	POSITION.
						Tons	Cwts.				
.	.	.	.	.	.	.	.	Bankfield and Canada Dock	Lancs	L. & Y.	See Liverpool.
.	.	.	.	.	.	.	.	Bankfield Mill....................	Yorks	L. & N. W.	Same as Hirst & Son's Siding (Delph).
.	.	.	.	.	.	.	.	Bankfield Siding	Lancs	L. & Y.	Clitheroe.
.	.	.	.	.	.	.	.	Bankfoot Ovens	Durham ...	N. E.	See Pease & Partners (Crook).
.	.	.	.	.	.	.	.	Bank Hall ....?..................	Lancs	L. & Y.	See Liverpool.
.	.	.	.	.	.	.	.	Bank Hall Colliery	Lancs	L. & Y.	Burnley, Bank Top.
.	.	.	.	.	.	.	.	Bankhead........................	Aberdeen	G. N. of S.	Aberdeen and Dyce.
G	P	.	L	H	.	.	.	Bankhead........................	Lanark ...	Cal.	Carstairs and Dolphinton.
.	.	.	.	.	.	.	.	Bankhouse Siding	Lancs	L. & Y.	Shaw and Crompton.
.	.	.	.	.	.	.	.	Bank Junction	Ayr	G. & S.W.	New Cumnock and Old Cumnock.
.	.	.	.	.	.	.	.	Bankmill Siding	Edinboro'	N. B.	Penicuik.
G	P	.	.	H	.	1	0	Banknock	Stirling ...	K. & B. Jt. (Cal. & N. B.)	Kilsyth and Bonnybridge.
.	.	.	.	.	.	.	.	Banknock Colliery............	Stirling ...	K. & B. Jt. (Cal. & N. B.)	Banknock.
.	.	.	.	.	.	.	.	Burnbank Colliery and Fire Clay Works	Stirling ...	K. & B. Jt. (Cal. & N. B.)	Banknock.
.	.	.	.	.	.	.	.	Coneypark Siding	Stirling ...	K. & B. Jt. (Cal. & N. B.)	Banknock and Colzium.
.	.	.	.	.	.	.	.	Bank Nos. 1 and 2..............	Ayr	G. & S.W.	New Cumnock.
.	.	.	.	.	.	.	.	Bank Quay	Lancs	L. & N. W.	See Warrington.
G	P	.	L	H	.	5	0	Banks	Lancs	L. & Y.	Preston and Southport.
.	.	.	.	.	.	.	.	Banks & Co.'s Pottery Works (Mid.)	Derby ...	Mid.—L. & N. W.	Same as Hilltop Pottery Co.'s Siding (Woodville).
.	.	.	.	.	.	.	.	Banks, T., & Co.'s Sidings ...	Lancs	P & L Jt.(L&N W & L & Y)	Longridge. / Preston, Deepdale.
.	.	.	.	.	.	.	.	Bankton Colliery	Hadding'n	N. B.	Prestonpans.
.	.	.	.	.	.	.	.	Bank Top.........................	Durham ...	N. E.	See Darlington.
.	.	.	.	.	.	.	.	Bank Top.........................	Lancs	L. & Y.	See Burnley.
.	.	.	.	.	.	.	.	Bannister and Co.'s—			
.	.	.	.	.	.	.	.	Cressey Street Siding	Lincoln ...	G. C.	Grimsby Town.
.	.	.	.	.	.	.	.	Railway Street Siding	Lincoln ...	G. C.	Grimsby Town.
.	.	.	.	.	.	.	.	Repairing Siding (G.C.) ...	Lincoln ...	G. C.—G. N.	Grimsby Docks.
.	.	.	.	.	.	.	.	Siding	Lincoln ...	G. C.	Cleethorpes.
G	P	F	L	H	C	3	0	Bannockburn	Stirling ...	Cal.	Larbert and Stirling.
.	.	.	.	.	.	.	.	Bannockburn Siding..........	Stirling ...	Cal.	Bannockburn.
.	.	.	.	.	.	.	.	Bannockburn Colliery	Stirling ...	Cal.	Plean Junction.
.	.	.	.	.	.	.	.	Bannockburn Colliery, No. 3	Stirling ...	Cal.	Plean Junction.
G	P	.	L	H	.	.	.	Bansha	Tipperary	G. S. & W.	Clonmel and Tipperary.
G	P	.	.	.	.	5	0	Banstead and Burgh Heath..	Surrey ...	L. B. & S. C.	Sutton and Epsom Downs.
.	.	.	.	.	.	.	.	Banstead Downs	Surrey ...	S. E. & C.	See Chipstead and Banstead Downs.
G	P	F	L	H	C	.	.	Banteer	Cork	G. S. & W.	Mallow and Killarney.
.	.	.	.	.	.	.	.	Bantocks Siding	Staffs	G. W.	Wolverhampton.
.	.	.	.	.	.	.	.	Banton Siding	Stirling ...	K. & B. Jt. (Cal. & N. B.)	See Colzium.
G	P	F	L	H	C	4	0	Bantry	Cork	C. B. & S. C.	Terminus.
.	.	.	.	.	.	.	.	Banwell	Somerset.	G. W.	See Sandford and Banwell.
G	P	F	L	H	C	.	.	Barassie	Ayr	G. & S.W.	Irvine and Troon.
.	.	.	.	.	.	.	.	Railway Works Siding......	Ayr	G. & S.W.	Branch from Barassie Junction.
.	.	.	.	.	.	.	.	Barassie Mid Junction	Ayr	G. & S.W.	Irvine and Troon.
.	.	.	.	.	.	.	.	Barassie North Junction	Ayr	G. & S.W.	Irvine and Troon.
.	.	.	.	.	.	.	.	Barassie South Junction	Ayr	G. & S.W.	Irvine and Troon (Passengers).
.	.	.	.	.	.	.	.	Barbadoes Siding	Perth	N. B.	See Gartmore.
.	.	.	.	.	.	.	.	Barbauchlaw Brick Works ...	L'lithgow	N. B.	Armadale.
G	P	F	L	H	C	.	.	Barbers Bridge	Glo'ster ...	G. W.	Gloucester and Newent.
.	.	.	.	.	.	.	.	Barber, Walker & Co.'s—			
.	.	.	.	.	.	.	.	Brinsley Colliery	Derby	Mid.	Langley Mill and Eastwood.
.	.	.	.	.	.	.	.	High Park Colliery	Derby	Mid.	Langley Mill and Eastwood.
.	.	.	.	.	.	.	.	Moor Green Colliery	Derby	Mid.	Langley Mill and Eastwood.
.	.	.	.	.	.	.	.	Selston Colliery	Derby	Mid.	Langley Mill and Eastwood.
.	.	.	.	.	.	.	.	Siding	Notts	G. N.	Eastwood and Langley Mill.
.	.	.	.	.	.	.	.	Underwood Colliery	Derby	Mid.	Langley Mill and Eastwood.
.	.	.	.	.	.	.	.	Barblues No. 10 Col. (Blair-muckhill Colliery)	Lanark ...	N. B.	Westcraigs.
G	P	F	L	H	C	3	0	Barbon	W'morlnd	L. & N. W.	Ingleton and Low Gill.
.	.	.	.	.	.	.	.	Barclay, Curle & Co.'s Ship-building Yard	Renfrew... / Lanark....	Cal. .... / N. B.	Same as Clydeholm Ship Yard (Glasgow).
.	.	.	.	.	.	.	.	Barclay's Engineering Works	Ayr	G. & S.W.	Kilmarnock.
G	P	F	L	H	C	.	.	Barcombe........................	Sussex ...	L. B. & S. C.	Lewes and Newick.
G	G	P	.	L	.	.	.	Barcombe Mills	Sussex ...	L. B. & S. C.	Lewes and Uckfield.
.	.	.	.	.	.	.	.	Catt & Co.'s Siding	Sussex ...	L. B. & S. C.	Barcombe Mills.
.	.	.	.	.	.	.	.	Wilmshurst's Siding........	Sussex ...	L. B. & S. C.	Barcombe Mills.
G	P	F	L	H	C	.	.	Bardney	Lincoln ...	G. N.	Boston and Lincoln.
.	.	.	.	.	.	.	.	Hall's Brick Siding	Lincoln ...	G. N	Bardney.
G	P	.	.	.	.	.	.	Bardon Hill	Leicester..	Mid.	Leicester and Burton.

G	P	F	L	H	C	Crane Power (Tons Cwts)	STATIONS, &c.	COUNTY.	COMPANY.	POSITION.
							Bardon Hill—*continued.*			
							Cliff Hill Granite Co.'s Sids. (Mid.)	Leicester..	Mid.—L. & N. W.	Bardon Hill.
							Ellis & Everard's Granite Works (Mid.)	Leicester..	Mid.—L. & N. W.	Bardon Hill.
G	P		L	H	C	2 0	Bardon Mill	Northumb	N. E.	Carlisle and Hexham.
							Blackett Colliery	Northumb	N. E.	Haltwhistle and Bardon Mill.
G	P	F	L	H	C	2 0	Bardsey	Yorks	N. E.	Leeds and Wetherby.
							Bardykes Colliery—			
							Hallside Private Siding	Lanark	Cal.	Newton.
							Spittalhill Qry. & Bk. Wks.	Lanark	Cal.	Newton.
G	P						Bare Lane	Lancs	L. & N. W.	Hest Bank and Morecambe.
							Barepot Siding	Cumb'land	L. & N. W.	Same as Derwent Rolling Mills (Workington Bridge).
G	P					1 0	Bargeddie	Lanark	N. B.	Shettleston and Coatbridge.
							Bartonshill Brick Works	Lanark	N. B.	Branch from Bargeddie.
							Drumpellier No. 11 Colliery	Lanark	N. B.	Bargeddie and Blairhill.
							Heatheryknowe Colliery	Lanark	N. B.	Branch from Heatheryknowe Weighs
G							Lochwood Colliery	Lanark	N. B.	Branch from Heatheryknowe Weighs
							Lochwood Siding	Lanark	N. B.	Branch from Heatheryknowe Weighs
							Mainhill Siding	Lanark	N. B.	Branch from Bargeddie.
G	P	F	L	H	C	1 10	Barglachan, Nos. 1 and 2	Ayr	G. & S.W.	Lugar.
	P				H	C	1 10	Bargoed (Rhymney)	Glamorg'n	Rhy.	Pengam and Rhymney.
									B. & M.	Over Rhymney Line.
G		F	L			1 10			L. & N. W.	Over Rhy. from Rhy. Jt. Line Junc.
							Bargoed Colliery Co.'s Siding (Abernant Colliery)	Mon	L. & N. W.	Argoed.
							Bargoed New Pits (Aber Bargoed Colliery) (B. & M.)	Mon	B. & M.—G. W.	See Powell Duffryn Co. (Pengam).
							Bargoed, North Junction	Glamorg'n	Rhy.	Bargoed and Darran.
							Bargoed, South Junction	Glamorg'n	B. & M.—Rhy.	Pengam and Bargoed.
G	P	F	L	H	C		Barham	Kent	S. E. & C.	Canterbury and Shorncliffe.
							Wingmore Siding	Kent	S. E. & C.	Elham and Barham.
							Baring, Brown & Co.'s Siding	Edinboro'	N. B.	Leith, Bonnington.
							Barker & Son's Siding	Herts	G. N.	Hitchin.
							Barker & Son's Welsh Whittle Colliery	Lancs	L. & N. W.	Coppull.
							Barker, J. C., Grain, Cake, and Manure Warehouse	Yorks	N. E.	Driffield.
							Barker's Brick Yard	Yorks	Mid.	Ingleton.
							Barker's Siding	Staffs	N. S.	Alsager.
							Barker's Slag Wks. & Gas Wks.	Durham	N. E.	Ferryhill.
G	P	F	L	H	C		Barkfield Siding	Lancs	L. & Y.	See L. & Y. Railway Co. (Freshfield).
	P						Barking (L. T. & S.)	Essex	L. T. & S.	Plaistow and Grays.
									G. E.	Over L. T. & S. from Forest Gate Jn.
							Barking, East Junction	Essex	L. T. & S.	Barking and Rainham.
							Barking, Tanner St. Junction	Essex	L. T. & S.	Barking and East Ham.
G	P						Barking Side	Essex	G. E.	Woodford and Ilford.
							Barkip Branch Junction	Ayr	G. & S.W.	Beith and Glengarnock.
G	P	F	L	H	C		Barkisland	Yorks	L. & Y.	See Ripponden and Barkisland.
							Barkstone	Lincoln	G. N.	Grantham and Newark.
							Barkus Quarry	Northumb	N. B.	Barrasford.
							Barkworth & Spalding's Sid.	Glo'ster	G. W.— Mid.	Gloucester Docks.
G	P		L	H		1 10	Barlaston (N.S.)	Staffs	N. S.	Stoke and Stone.
	P								L. & N. W.	Over N. S. Line.
							Barlborough Brickyard	Derby	L. D. & E. C.	Clown.
							Barlborough Colliery	Derby	L. D. & E. C.	Clown.
									Mid.	Barrow Hill and Staveley Works.
							Barley Brook Siding	Lancs	L. & Y.	Wigan.
							Barlow Depôt	Durham	N. E.	Same as High Thornley Depôts (Derwenthaugh).
G	P						Barmby	Yorks	H. & B.	Cudworth and Howden.
G	P	F	L	H	C		Barming	Kent	S. E. & C.	Otford Junction and Maidstone.
G	P	F	L	H	C	0 10	Barmouth	Merioneth	Cam.	Aberdovey and Harlech.
G	P						Barmouth Junction Station	Merioneth	Cam.	Barmouth and Towyn.
G	P						Barmston Depôts	Durham	N. E.	Washington.
G	P	F	L	H	C	4 18	Barnack	N'hamptn	G. N.	Stamford and Wansford Junction.
	P*						Ufford Bridge Siding	N'hamptn	G. N.	Stamford and Wansford Junction.
							Barnack	N'hamptn	Mid.	See Uffington and Barnack.
G	P		L	H			Barnagh	Limerick	G. S. & W.	Newcastle West and Tralee.
							Barnard Bros.' Siding	Essex	G. E.	Newport.
G	P	F	L	H	C	10 0	Barnard Castle	Durham	N. E.	Darlington and Kirkby Stephen.

EXPLANATION—G *Goods Station.*   P *Passenger and Parcel Station.*   P* *Passenger, but not Parcel or Miscellaneous Traffic.*
F *Furniture Vans, Carriages, Portable Engines, and Machines on Wheels.*   L *Live Stock.*
H *Horse Boxes and Prize Cattle Vans.*   C *Carriages by Passenger Train.*

Station Accommodation						Crane Power		STATIONS, &c.	COUNTY.	COMPANY.	POSITION.
						Tons	Cwts.				
.	.	.	.	.	.	.	.	Barnard Castle—*continued.*			
.	.	.	.	.	.	.	.	Broomielaw Siding	Durham ...	N. E.	Barnard Castle.
.	.	.	.	.	.	.	.	Dents Gate Siding	Durham ...	N. E.	Barnard Castle.
.	.	.	.	.	.	.	.	Harmire Sid. (Hoggs Sid.)	Durham ...	N. E.	Barnard Castle.
G	P	.	L	H	.	.	.	Barnby Dun	Yorks	G. C.	Doncaster and Thorne.
.	.	.	.	.	.	.	.	Hatfield Lane Siding........	Yorks	G. C.	Barnby Dun.
.	.	.	.	.	.	.	.	Milnthorpe's Malt Kiln ...	Yorks	G. C.	Barnby Dun.
.	.	.	.	.	.	.	.	Barn, Bye and Pear Tree Lane Collieries	Worcester	G. W.	Netherton.
.	.	.	.	.	.	.	.	Barnby Siding.................	Suffolk ...	G. E.	See Carlton Colville.
.	.	.	.	.	.	.	.	Barncluith Colliery	Lanark ...	Cal.	Hamilton, Central.
G	P	F	.	.	.	.	.	Barnehurst	Kent	S. E. & C.	Blackheath and Dartford.
G	P	F	L	H	C	5	0	Barnes	Surrey ...	L. & S.W.	London (Waterloo) and Richmond.
.	.	.	.	.	.	.	.	Barnes Coke Yard (L. & N.W.)	Mon	L. & N. W.—G. W.	Brynmawr.
.	.	.	.	.	.	.	.	Barnes Deep Pit (L. & N. W.)	Mon	L. & N. W.—G. W.	Brynmawr.
.	.	.	.	.	.	.	.	Barnes, F. J., Siding	Dorset......	W.&P.Jt.(G.W.&L&SW)	Portland.
.	.	.	.	.	.	.	.	Barnes, J. G.& W.,Sid.(G.W.)	Mon	G. W.—L. & N. W.	Same as Coalbrookvale West Siding.
.	P	.	.	.	.	.	.	Barnesmore	Donegal ..	Donegal	Stranorlar and Donegal.
.	.	.	.	.	.	.	.	Barnes Siding	Cheshire..	L. & N. W.	Cheadle.
.	.	.	.	.	.	.	.	Barnes' Siding	Yorks	G. N.	Stanningley.
.	.	.	.	.	.	.	.	BARNET—			
.	.	.	.	.	.	.	.	Gas Works	Herts	G. N.	New Barnet and Hadley Wood.
G	P	F	L	H	C	10	0	High (G. N.)	Herts	{ G. N.	Branch from Finsbury Park.
.	P	.	.	.	.	.	.			N.L.	Over G. N. from Canonbury Junc.
G	P	F	L	H	C	10	0	New (G. N.)	Herts	{ G. N.	King's Cross and Hatfield.
.	P	.	.	.	.	.	.			N.L.	Over G. N. from Canonbury Junc.
.	P*	.	.	.	.	.	.			S. E. & C.	Over G. N. from King's Cross Junc.
G	P	F	L	H	C	5	0	Barnetby	Lincoln ...	G. C.	Gainsboro' and Grimsby.
.	.	.	.	.	.	.	.	Birch's Stone Siding	Lincoln ...	G. C.	Barnetby.
.	.	.	.	.	.	.	.	Melton Ross Siding	Lincoln ...	G. C.	Barnetby.
.	.	.	.	.	.	.	.	Truswell Brewery Co.'s Sid.	Lincoln ...	G. C.	Barnetby.
.	.	.	.	.	.	.	.	Barnett & Beddows Atlas Brick, Pipe, and Tile Co.'s Siding	Staffs ...	L. & N. W.	Pelsall.
G	P	F	L	H	C	.	.	Barnham	Suffolk ...	G. E.	Bury and Thetford.
.	.	.	.	.	.	.	.	Grafton, Duke of, Siding ...	Norfolk ...	G. E.	Barnham.
.	.	.	.	.	.	.	.	Trollope & Son's Siding......	Suffolk ...	G. E.	Barnham.
G	P	F	L	H	C	.	.	Barnham Junction Station ...	Sussex ...	L. B. & S. C.	Chichester and Ford Junction.
G	P	F	L	H	C	1	10	Barnhill	Forfar....	Cal.	Dundee and Forfar.
G	.	.	.	.	.	.	.	Balmossie......................	Forfar....	Cal.	Barnhill and Kingennie.
.	.	.	.	.	.	.	.	Barnhill (N. B.)	Lanark ...	N. B.—G. & S. W.	See Glasgow.
.	.	.	.	.	.	.	.	Barnhill Mineral Depôt	Lanark ...	N. B.	Glasgow, Barnhill.
.	.	.	.	.	.	.	.	Barnhill Siding	Perth ...	Cal.	Perth, South.
.	.	.	.	.	.	.	.	Barningham's Siding............	Lancs ...	L. & Y.	Same as Steel Railway Journal Box Co.'s (Pendleton).
G	P	F	L	H	C	5	0	Barnoldswick	Yorks	Mid.	Branch—Earby and Foulridge.
.	.	.	.	.	.	.	.	Barnsbury (N. L.)	Middlesex	N. L.—L. & N. W.	See London, Caledonian Road and Barnsbury.
.	.	.	.	.	.	.	.	BARNSLEY—			
G	.	F	L	.	.	10	0	(Station)	Yorks	G. C.	Bch.—Summer Lane & Court House.
G	P	F	L	H	C	8	0	(Station, L. & Y.)	Yorks	{ L. & Y.	Branch from Horbury Junction.
G	.	F	L	.	.	8	0		Yorks	G. C.	Over L. & Y. Line.
.	.	.	.	.	.	.	.	Barnsley Brewery Siding...	Yorks	G. C.	Oakwell.
.	.	.	.	.	.	.	.	Barnsley Co-operative Sid.	Yorks	G. C.	Summer Lane.
.	.	.	.	.	.	.	.	Barnsley Main Col. Co.'s Sid	Yorks	Mid.	Barnsley and Cudworth.
.	.	.	.	.	.	.	.	Cockram Rd. (Court House) Junction	Yorks	G. C.— Mid.	Court House and Penistone.
.	.	.	.	.	.	.	.	Corporation Siding............	Yorks	G. C.	Barnsley.
.	P	F	L	H	C	.	.	Court House Joint Station	Yorks	{ G. C.	Over Midland Line.
G	P	F	L	H	C	10	0		Yorks	Mid.	Branch from Cudworth.
.	.	.	.	.	.	.	.	Craik's Siding	Yorks	G. C.	Barnsley.
.	.	.	.	.	.	.	.	Darfield West or Quarry Jn.	Yorks	G. C.—Mid.	L. & Y. Station and Cudworth.
.	.	.	.	.	.	.	.	Gas Co.'s Siding	Yorks	G. C.	Barnsley.
.	.	.	.	.	.	.	.	Gullet (Nightsoil) Siding ...	Yorks	G. C.	Barnsley.
.	.	.	.	.	.	.	.	Junction	Yorks	G. C.—L. & Y.	Stairfoot and Darton.
.	.	.	.	.	.	.	.	Mount Osborne West Junc.	Yorks	G. C.—Mid.	Court House and Mexboro'.
.	.	.	.	.	.	.	.	Needham's Siding	Yorks	G. C.	Barnsley.
G	.	.	.	.	.	2	0	Oakwell......................	Yorks	G. C.	Stairfoot and Staincross.
G	.	.	.	.	.	2	0	Old Mill Lane	Yorks	G. C.	Staincross and Barnsley.
.	.	.	.	.	.	.	.	Old Oaks Col. Co.'s Siding...	Yorks	Mid.	Barnsley and Cudworth.
.	.	.	.	.	.	.	.	Pindar Oaks Siding	Yorks	G. C.	Barnsley.
.	.	.	.	.	.	.	.	Pogmoor Siding	Yorks	G. C.	Summer Lane.

EXPLANATION—G *Goods Station.*   P *Passenger and Parcel Station.*   P* *Passenger, but not Parcel or Miscellaneous Traffic.*
F *Furniture Vans, Carriages, Portable Engines, and Machines on Wheels.*   L *Live Stock.*
H *Horse Boxes and Prize Cattle Vans.*   C *Carriages by Passenger Train.*

STATION ACCOMMODATION.						CRANE POWER.	STATIONS, &c.	COUNTY.	COMPANY.	POSITION.
						Tons Cwts.	BARNSLEY—continued.			
.	.	.	.	.	.	. .	Ryland's Glass & Engineering Co.'s Siding	Yorks	Mid.	Barnsley and Cudworth.
G	P	.	.	.	.	5 0	Summer Lane	Yorks	G. C.	Court House and Penistone.
.	.	.	.	.	.	. .	Wilkinson's Malt Kiln Sid.	Yorks	G. C.	Barnsley.
.	.	.	.	.	.	. .	Barnsley Brewery Siding......	Yorks	G. C.	Barnsley, Oakwell.
.	.	.	.	.	.	. .	Barnsley Co-operative Siding	Yorks	G. C.	Barnsley, Summer Lane.
.	.	.	.	.	.	. .	Barnsley Gas Works	Yorks	G. C.	Staincross (for Mapplewell).
.	.	.	.	.	.	. .	Barnsley Junction	Yorks	G. C.	Penistone and Silkstone.
.	.	.	.	.	.	. .	Barnsley Main Colliery........	Yorks	G. C.	Stairfoot (for Ardsley).
.	.	.	.	.	.	. .	Barnsley Main Col. Co.'s Sid.	Yorks	Mid.	Barnsley, Court House.
.	.	.	.	.	.	. .	Barnsmuir Colliery	Stirling ...	N. B.	Slamannan.
							BARNSTAPLE—			
G	P	F	L	H	C	10 0	(Station)	Devon	G. W.	Terminus.
.	.	.	.	.	.	. .	Junction	Devon	G. W.—L. & S. W.	Barnstaple (G. W.) and Barnstaple (L. & S. W.).
G	P	F	L	H	C	10 0}	Junction Sta. (L. & S. W.)	Devon	{ L. & S. W.	Exeter and Bideford.
.	P					}			{ G. W.	Over L. & S. W. from Barnstaple Jn.
G	.	.	.	.	.	. .	Pilton Yard	Devon	L. & B.	Barnstaple.
.	.	.	.	.	.	. .	Rolles Quay Siding	Devon	L. & S.W.	Barnstaple Junction Station.
.	.	.	.	.	.	. .	Shapland and Petters Siding	Devon	L. & S.W.	Barnstaple Junction Station.
.	P	.	.	.	.	. .	Town and Quay	Devon	{ L. & S. W.	Barnstaple Junc. Sta. & Ilfracombe.
									{ L. & B.	Adjoining L. & S. W. Station.
.	.	.	.	.	.	. .	Barnston	Cheshire..	N. W. & L. Jt. (G. C. & W. M. & C. Q.)	See Storeton (for Barnston).
G	P	F	L	H	C	. .	Barnstone....................	Notts	G. N. & L. & N. W. Jt.	Melton Mowbray and Nottingham.
.	.	.	.	.	.	. .	Barnstone Lime Co.'s Sid.	Notts	G. N. & L. & N. W. Jt.	Barnstone and Harby.
							Barnstone Blue Lias Lime Co.'s—			
.	.	.	.	.	.	. .	Hotchley Hill Siding........	Notts	G. C.	East Leake.
.	.	.	.	.	.	. .	Normanton Hill Siding......	Notts	G. C.	East Leake.
G	P	F	L	H	C	. .	Barnt Green..................	Worcester	Mid.	Birmingham and Bromsgrove.
G	P	F	L	H	C	1 10	Barnton (for Cramond Brig)..	Edinboro'	Cal.	Branch near Craigleith.
.	.	.	.	.	.	. .	Barnton Junction	Edinboro'	Cal.	Craigleith and Davidson's Mains.
G	P	.	L	H	.	. .	Barnwell...	N'hamptn.	L. & N. W.	Peterborough and Wellingborough.
.	.	.	.	.	.	. .	Barnwell Junction Station ...	Cambs ...	G. E.	See Cambridge.
.	.	.	.	.	.	. .	Barnwood Junction	Glo'ster ...	G. W.	Gloucester and Cheltenham.
.	.	.	.	.	.	. .	Baron's Lane Siding	Essex	G. E.	See Cold Norton
.	.	.	.	.	.	. .	Baron's Product Co.'s Siding	Glo'ster ...	Mid.	Woodchester.
.	.	.	.	.	.	. .	Baron's Quay Siding (C. L. C.)	Cheshire..	C. L. C.—L. & N. W.	Same as Moore & Brock's Siding (Northwich).
.	.	.	.	.	.	. .	Baron's Quay Works (C. L. C.)	Cheshire...	C. L. C.—L. & N. W. ...	See Salt Union, Ltd. (Northwich).
.	.	.	.	.	.	. .	Barrachnie Siding	Lanark ...	N. B.	Easterhouse.
.	.	.	.	.	.	. .	Barrack Street (G. N., I.) ...	Louth	G. N. (I)—D. N. & G. ...	See Dundalk.
G	P	.	.	.	.	. .	Barras	W'morlnd	N. E.	Barnard Castle & Kirkby Stephen.
							Bowes Gannister and Freestone Co.'s Siding	W'morlnd	N. E.	Barras and Bowes.
.	.	.	.	.	.	. .	Summit Siding	W'morlnd	N. E.	Barras and Bowes.
G	P	.	.	.	.	. .	Barrasford	Northumb	N. B.	Reedsmouth and Hexham.
.	.	.	.	.	.	. .	Barkus Quarry	Northumb	N. B.	Barrasford and Wark.
.	.	.	.	.	.	. .	Gunnerton Quarry	Northumb	N. B.	Barrasford and Wark.
.	.	.	.	.	.	. .	Barraway Siding	Cambs ...	G. E.	See Soham.
.	.	.	.	.	.	. .	Barr Col. and Brick Works...	Ayr	Cal.	Giffen.
.	.	.	.	.	.	. .	Barrett, J., Siding............	Essex	G. E.	Brentwood and Warley.
G	P	F	L	H	C	15 0	Barrhead	Renfrew...	G B & K Jt (Cal & G & S W)	Glasgow and Neilston.
.	P	.	.	.	.	. .	Barrhead, Central	Renfrew...	G. & S.W.	Branch from Paisley Canal Line.
.	.	.	.	.	.	. .	Barrhead North Junction ...	Renfrew...	G.&S.W.—G.B.&K.Jt.	Potterhill and Nitshill.
.	.	.	.	.	.	. .	Barrhead South Junction ...	Renfrew...	G.&S.W.—G.B.&K.Jt...	Barrhead (Central) and Nitshill.
G	P	.	L	H	.	1 10	Barrhill........................	Ayr	G. & S.W.	Girvan and New Luce.
.	.	.	.	.	.	. .	Barrington Colliery & Brick Works	Northumb	N. E.	Bedlington.
.	.	.	.	.	.	. .	Barrington Road Junction ...	Surrey ...	L. B. S. C.—S. E. & C ...	London, Denmark Hill and Brixton.
G	P	.	L	H	.	4 0	Barrmill	Ayr	G B & K Jt (Cal & G & S W)	Lugton and Beith.
.	.	.	.	.	.	. .	Dockra Lime Works	Ayr	G B & K Jt (Cal & G & S W)	Barrmill and Beith.
.	.	.	.	.	.	. .	Dockra Pit	Ayr	G B & K Jt (Cal & G & S W)	Barrmill and Beith.
.	.	.	.	.	.	. .	Barrmill Junction	Ayr	Cal.—G. B. & K. Jt.	Giffen and Lugton.
.	.	.	.	.	.	. .	Barrmill Siding	Ayr	Cal.	See Giffen.
.	.	.	.	.	.	. .	Barron Wood Siding............	Cumb'land	Mid.	Armathwaite.
							BARROW—			
G	.	F	L	.	.	10 0	(Station)	Lancs	Furness......................	Branch—Barrow Central and Roose.
.	.	.	.	.	.	. .	Barrow and Calcutta Jute Co.'s Siding	Lancs	Furness......................	Near Barrow Goods.

EXPLANATION—G *Goods Station.*   P *Passenger and Parcel Station.*   P* *Passenger, but not Parcel or Miscellaneous Traffic.*
F *Furniture Vans, Carriages, Portable Engines, and Machines on Wheels.*   L *Live Stock.*
H *Horse Boxes and Prize Cattle Vans.*   C *Carriages by Passenger Train.*

STATION ACCOMMODATION.						CRANE POWER.		STATIONS, &c.	COUNTY.	COMPANY.	POSITION.
						Tons	Cwts				
								BARROW—*continued.*			
								Barrow Cement and Flag Co.'s Siding	Lancs	Furness	Near Barrow Central.
								British Griffin Chilled Iron and Steel Co.'s Siding	Lancs	Furness	Near Barrow Central.
								Burnip & McDougall's Oil Works	Lancs	Furness	Near Barrow Goods.
								Caird, D. (Exors. of) Siding	Lancs	Furness	Near Barrow Goods.
	P	F		H	C			Central	Lancs	Furness	Main Line
								Clarke & Robinson's Siding	Lancs	Furness	Near Barrow Central.
								Corporation Electric Light Works	Lancs	Furness	Near Barrow Central.
								Corporation Gas Works	Lancs	Furness	Near Barrow Goods.
								Corporation Store Yard	Lancs	Furness	Near Barrow Central.
								Crossfield, F. J., & Co.'s Timber Yard	Lancs	Furness	Barrow Docks.
G						120	0	Dawson's, W. & J., Tim. Yd.	Lancs	Furness	Near Barrow Central.
								Docks	Lancs	Furness	Branch—Barrow Goods and Roose.
								Furness Brk. & Tl. Co.'s Sid.	Lancs	Furness	Near Barrow Central.
								Gradwell, W., & Co.'s Creosote Works	Lancs	Furness	Branch from Barrow Goods.
								Hindpool Saw Mills	Lancs	Furness	Near Barrow Goods.
								Hatton & Co.'s Boiler Works	Lancs	Furness	Branch from Barrow Goods.
								Hawcoat Mineral Siding	Lancs	Furness	Branch near Barrow Central.
								Hindpool Barrow Hematite Steel Co.'s Works	Lancs	Furness	Near Barrow Goods.
								Hunter's, C. W., Siding	Lancs	Furness	Near Barrow Goods.
								Kellner Partington Paper Pulp Co.'s Works	Lancs	Furness	Piel Branch.
								Petroleum Works	Lancs	Furness	Barrow, Ramsden Dock.
G	P	F	L	H	C	25	0	Ramsden Dock	Lancs	Furness	Branch—Barrow Goods and Roose.
								Sandscale Mineral Siding	Lancs	Furness	Branch—Barrow and Askam.
						120	0	Vickers Sons & Maxim's Naval Construction Wks.	Lancs	Furness	Branch near Barrow Goods.
								Waddington & Son's F'dry	Lancs	Furness	Near Barrow Goods.
								Walmsley & Smith's Corn Mill	Lancs	Furness	Near Barrow Goods.
								Wire Works (B. H. S. Co.)	Lancs	Furness	Barrow Goods & Hawcoat Min. Sid.
								Barrow Brick Works (Bryn-cethin Brick Works)	Glamorg'n	G. W.	Tondu.
								Barrow Bros'. Brick Works	Leicester	Mid.	Syston.
								Barrow Colliery	Yorks	{ G. C. Mid.	Worsboro'. Wombwell.
								Barrowden	N'hampton	L. & N. W.	See Wakerley and Barrowden.
								Barrow End Brick Yard	Leicester	Mid.	See Wright, W. T., & Co. (Sileby).
G	P	F	L	H		5	0	Barrow (for Tarvin)	Cheshire	C L C (G C, G N & Mid.)	Northwich and Chester.
	P							Barrow Haven	Lincoln	G. C.	New Holland & Barton-on-Humber.
								Barrow Hill (G. C.)	Derby	G. C.— L. & N. W.	See Staveley Works (for Barrow Hill).
G	P	F	L	H	C	10	0	Barrow Hill & Staveley Works	Derby	Mid.	Chesterfield and Masboro'
								Barlboro' Colliery	Derby	Mid.	Barrow Hill and Creswell.
								Bell House Siding	Derby	Mid.	Barrow Hill and Clown.
								Firth & Co.'s Siding	Derby	Mid.	Whittington.
								Hartington Colliery	Derby	Mid.	Barrow Hill and Bolsover.
								Ireland Colliery	Derby	Mid.	Barrow Hill and Bolsover.
								Markham Colliery	Derby	Mid.	Barrow Hill and Bolsover.
								New Whittington Siding	Derby	Mid.	Barrow Hill and Staveley Works.
								Oxcroft Colliery Co.	Derby	Mid.	Clown Branch.
								Seymour Colliery	Derby	Mid.	Barrow Hill and Bolsover.
								Staveley Coal & Iron Co.— Ireland Coke Works	Derby	Mid.	Barrow Hill and Bolsover.
								Iron Works	Derby	Mid.	Barrow Hill and Staveley Works.
								North Staveley Colliery	Derby	Mid.	Barrow Hill and Killamarsh.
								West Staveley Siding	Derby	Mid.	Whittington and Staveley.
								Barrow Lime Works	Leicester	Mid.	See Ellis, J., & Son's (Mount Sorrel Jn)
								Barrowmouth Cement and Plaster Works (Furness)	Cumb'land	Furness—L. & N. W.	Whitehaven.
G	P	F	L	H	C			Barrow-on-Soar and Quorn	Leicester	Mid.	Loughboro' and Leicester.
								Barrow Road Siding	Leicester	Mid.	See Wright, W. T., & Co. (Sileby)
								Barrows & Sons' Siding	Staffs	L. & N. W.	Tipton.
								Barrow's Siding	Surrey	S. E. & C.	Redhill Junction Station.
								Barr's Court, North & South Junctions	Hereford	G. W.—S. & H. Jt.	Hereford.

EXPLANATION—G *Goods Station.*   P *Passenger and Parcel Station.*   P* *Passenger, but not Parcel or Miscellaneous Traffic.*
F *Furniture Vans, Carriages, Portable Engines, and Machines on Wheels.*   L *Live Stock.*
H *Horse Boxes and Prize Cattle Vans.*   C *Carriages by Passenger Train.*

STATION ACCOMMODATION.						CRANE POWER.	STATIONS, &c.	COUNTY.	COMPANY.	POSITION.
						Tons Cwts.				
G	P	F	L	H	C	1 10	Barry...............	Forfar.....	D. & A. Jt. (Cal. & N. B.)	Dundee and Arbroath.
G	P	.	.	.	.	5 0	Buddon Siding	Forfar.....	D. & A. Jt. (Cal. & N. B.)	Barry and Monifieth.
G	.	.	.	.	.		Military Stores Siding	Forfar.....	D. & A. Jt. (Cal. & N. B.)	Barry.
							BARRY—			
G	P	F	L	H	C	12 0	(Station)	Glamorg'n	Barry...........................	Cadoxton and Llantwit Major.
.	P	.	.	.	.		Dock	Glamorg'n	Barry...........................	Barry and Cadoxton.
.	.	.	.	.	.	50 0	Docks	Glamorg'n	Barry...........................	Barry.
G	P	F	.	H	C	. .	Island	Glamorg'n	Barry...........................	Branch from Barry.
.	P*	.	.	.	.		Junction	Glamorg'n	Barry...........................	Jn. with Vale of Glamorgan Section.
.	.	.	.	.	.		Pier	Glamorg'n	Barry...........................	Extension from Barry Island.
.	.	.	.	.	.		Syndicate Siding	Glamorg'n	Barry...........................	Barry and Barry Dock.
.	.	.	.	.	.		Barry, Ostlere, & Shepherd's Siding	Fife........	N. B.	Kirkcaldy.
.	.	.	.	.	.		Barry Rhondda Colliery	Glamorg'n	Barry...........................	See Pwllgwaun Siding (Pontypridd).
G	P	F	L	H	C	. .	Barskimming Quarry	Ayr	G. & S. W.	Mauchline.
.	.	.	.	.	.		Bartlow............................	Cambs	G. E.	Cambridge and Haverhill.
G	P	F	L	H	C	. .	Barton	Hereford ..	G. W.	See Hereford.
G	.	F	.	.	.		Barton	Lancs	L. & Y.	Hillhouse Junction and Southport.
.	.	.	.	.	.		Marquis Siding	Lancs	L. & Y.	Barton and Hillhouse Junction.
.	.	.	.	.	.		Rydings Siding	Lancs	L. & Y.	Near Barton.
G	.	F	.	.	.		Barton	Yorks	N. E.	Bch.—Darlington and Piercebridge
.	.	.	.	.	.		Barton Engine Shed Sid....	Yorks	N. E.	Barton.
.	.	.	.	.	.		Barton Limestone Co's Stone Crushing Plant Siding ...	Yorks	N. E.	Barton.
.	.	.	.	.	.		Barton Quarry.................	Yorks	N. E.	Barton.
.	.	.	.	.	.		Cleasby Siding	Yorks	N. E.	Barton.
.	.	.	.	.	.		Coniscliffe Siding	Durham ...	N. E.	Barton.
.	.	.	.	.	.		Barton & Brecon Curve Junc.	Hereford ..	G. W.—Mid.	Hereford.
G	P	.	.	.	.		Barton and Broughton	Lancs	L. & N. W.	Lancaster and Preston.
G	P	F	L	H	C	1 10	Barton and Walton (Mid). ...	Staffs	Mid.	Burton and Tamworth.
G	P	F	L	H	C	. .		Staffs	L. & N. W.	Over Midland Line.
.	.	.	.	.	.		Bass & Co.'s Sand Siding...	Staffs	Mid.	Near Wichnor.
G	P	F	L	H	C	. .	Barton Hill	Yorks	N. E.	York and Malton.
.	.	.	.	.	.		Bartonholme Lye	Ayr	Cal.	Kilwinning.
.	.	.	.	.	.		Bartonholm, No. 1............	Ayr	G. & S. W.	Kilwinning.
G	P	.	L	H	.		Barton-le-Street	Yorks	N. E.	Malton and Thirsk.
.	P	.	.	.	.		Barton Moss (L. & N. W.) ...	Lancs	L. & N. W.	Kenyon Junction and Manchester.
.	.	.	.	.	.				G. W.	Over L. & N. W. from Walton Junc.
G	P	F	L	H	C	4 0	Barton-on-Humber	Lincoln ...	G. C.	Branch from New Holland.
.	.	.	.	.	.		Bartonshill Brick Works	Lanark ...	N. B.	Bargeddie.
.	.	.	.	.	.		Barton's Siding	Warwick..	L. & N. W.	See Toy Siding (Birmingham).
.	.	.	.	.	.		Bartram & Sons' Ship Yard...	Durham ...	N. E.	Sunderland, South Dock.
.	.	.	.	.	.		Barugh Quarry	Cumb'land	C. & W. Jn.	High Harrington.
.	.	.	.	.	.		Barwell (L. & N. W.)	Leicester..	L. & N. W.— Mid.	See Elmesthorpe (for Barwell and Earl Shilton).
.	.	.	.	.	.		Barwood Siding	Stirling ...	K. & B. Jt. (Cal. & N. B.)	Kilsyth, New.
G	P	F	L	H	C	3 0	Baschurch	Salop	G. W.	Shrewsbury and Ruabon.
.	.	.	.	.	.		Basford	Notts	Mid.	See Nottingham.
.	.	.	.	.	.		Basford and Bulwell............	Notts	G. N.	See Nottingham.
.	.	.	.	.	.		Basford Chemical Works......	Notts	Mid.	Nottingham, Basford.
.	.	.	.	.	.		Basford East Junction.........	Notts	G. N.	Nottingham.
.	.	.	.	.	.		Basford West Junction.........	Notts	G. C. & G. N. Jt.—G. N.	Nottingham.
.	.	.	.	.	.		Bashall & Co.'s Farington Mill	Lancs	N.U.Jt.(L.N.W.&L.&Y.)	Leyland.
.	.	.	.	.	.		Basic Phosphate Co.'s Works	Durham ...	N. E.	Stillington
.	P	.	.	.	.		Basin	Kerry	T. & D.	Tralee and Castlegregory Junction.
G	P	F	L	H	C	10 0	Basingstoke	Hants	G. W.	Branch from Reading.
.	.	.	.	.	.				L. & S. W.	Woking and Winchester.
.	.	.	.	.	.		Thorneycroft's Steam Carriage & Wagon Co.'s Sid.	Hants	L. & S.W.	Near Basingstoke.
.	.	.	.	.	.		Basingstoke Junction	Hants	G. W.—L. & S. W.	Basingstoke (G. W.) and Basingstoke (L. & S. W.).
.	P	.	.	.	.		Bason Bridge	Somerset..	S .&D.Jt.(L.&S.W.& Mid)	Highbridge and Glastonbury.
							BASSALEG—			
G	P	.	.	.	.		(Station, B. & M.)	Mon	B. & M.	Bassaleg Junction and Machen.
.	P	.	.	.	.			Mon	G.W. (A.(NSW)D.&R.)	Over B. & M. from Bassaleg Junc.
.	P	.	.	.	.		(Station, G. W.)...............	Mon	G. W.	Newport and Crumlin, Low Level.
.	.	.	.	.	.				L. & N. W.	Over G. W. from Nine Mile Point Junction.
.	.	.	.	.	.		Junction	Mon	A (N&SW) D & R—B & M	Alexandra Dock & Bassaleg Station.
.	.	.	.	.	.		Junction	Mon	B. & M.—G. W.	Bassaleg Station and Newport.
.	.	.	.	.	.		Nettlefold's Rogerstone Works	Mon	B. & M.	Bassaleg.

EXPLANATION—G *Goods Station.*　　P *Passenger and Parcel Station.*　　P* *Passenger, but not Parcel or Miscellaneous Traffic.*
F *Furniture Vans, Carriages, Portable Engines, and Machines on Wheels.*　　L *Live Stock.*
H *Horse Boxes and Prize Cattle Vans.*　　C *Carriages by Passenger Train.*

STATION ACCOMMODATION.						CRANE POWER.		STATIONS, &c.	COUNTY.	COMPANY.	POSITION.
						Tons	Cwts				
								Bass & Co.—			
..	..	..	..	..	..			Ale Stores	Durham ...	N. E.	Stockton, South.
..	..	..	..	..	..			Ale Stores	Yorks	N. E.	Middlesbro'.
..	..	..	..	..	..			Breweries (Mid.)	Staffs	Mid.—LNW—G.N—NS.	Burton-on-Trent.
..	..	..	..	..	..			Sand Siding	Staffs	Mid.	Barton and Walton.
..	..	..	..	..	..			Shobnall Maltings (Mid.)	Staffs	Mid.—LNW—G.N—NS.	Burton-on-Trent.
..	..	..	..	..	..			Siding	Essex	G. E.	Woolwich, North.
..	..	..	..	..	..			Siding	Lincoln	G. N.	Sleaford.
..	..	..	..	..	..			Siding (Mid.)	Staffs	Mid.—LNW—G.N—NS.	Burton-on-Trent.
..	..	..	..	..	..			Bass Crest Brewery	Clackman'	Cal.	Alloa.
G	P	F	L	H	C	1	10	Bassenthwaite Lake	Cumb'land	C. K. & P. (L. & N.W. and N. E. Working Cos.)	Keswick and Cockermouth.
..	..	..	..	..	..			Bat and Ball	Kent	S. E. & C.	See Sevenoaks.
..	..	..	..	..	..			Batchelor & Co.'s Artillery Street Siding	Warwick..	Mid.	Birmingham, Lawley Street.
..	..	..	..	..	..			Batchelor & Snowden's Siding	Glamorg'n	T. V.	Ynysybwl.
..	..	..	..	..	..			Bate & Rudd's Siding	Lancs	L. & N. W.	St. Helens.
..	..	..	..	..	..			Bateman, J., Siding	Hunts	G. N. & G. E. Jt.	Somersham.
..	..	..	..	..	..			Bates & Co.'s Siding	Lancs	L. & Y.	Meol's Cop.
..	..	..	..	..	..			Bates & Co.'s Siding	Lancs	L. & N. W.	St. Helens.
..	..	..	..	..	..			Bates Broad Oak Brick, Tile, and Colliery Co.'s Siding	Lancs	L. & N. W.	St. Helens.
..	..	..	..	..	..			Bates Siding	Yorks	G. C.	Hazlehead Bridge.
								BATH—			
G	P	F	L	H	C	5	0	(Station)	Somerset..	G. W.	Bristol and Chippenham.
								(Station, Mid.)	Somerset..	{ Mid.	Branch from Mangotsfield.
G	P	F	L	H	C	10	0			{ S & D Jt (L & S W & Mid)	Over Midland from Bath Junction.
..	..	..	..	..	..			Bath Brewery Co.'s Sid.	Somerset..	Mid.	Weston.
..	..	..	..	..	..			Bath Gas Co.'s Siding	Somerset..	Mid.	Bath and Weston.
..	..	..	..	..	..			Bath Gas Works	Somerset..	Mid.	Bath.
..	..	..	..	..	..			Bath Stone Firms	Somerset..	G. W.	Adjoining Westmoreland Siding.
..	..	..	..	..	..			Bladwell's Stone Siding	Somerset..	Mid.	Bath and Weston.
..	..	..	..	..	..	3	0	Bonded Stores	Somerset..	G. W.	Adjoining Goods Station.
..	..	..	..	..	..			Bonded Stores	Somerset..	Mid.	Bath.
..	..	..	..	..	..			Burgess', T., Siding	Somerset..	Mid.	Bath and Weston.
..	..	..	..	..	..			Marsh, Son & Gibbs' Sid.	Somerset..	Mid.	Bath and Weston.
..	..	..	..	..	..			Stothert and Pitt's Siding	Somerset..	Mid.	Bath and Weston.
..	..	..	..	..	..			Victoria Brick & Tile Co.'s Siding (May's Siding)	Somerset..	S. & D. Jt. (L. & S. W. & Mid)	Bath Junction and Midford.
G	.	F	.	.	.	12	0	Westmoreland Siding	Somerset..	G. W.	Bath.
..	..	..	..	..	..			Windebank, J., & Son's Sid.	Somerset..	Mid.	Bath and Weston.
..	..	..	..	..	..			Junction	Somerset..	Mid.—S. & D. Jt.	Bath Station and Midford.
G	P	.	.	.	.			Bathampton	Somerset..	G. W.	Bath and Chippenham.
..	..	..	..	..	..			Bath & Son's Siding	Glamorg'n	GW—LNW—Mid—RSB	Swansea.
..	..	..	..	..	..			Bath, A., Siding	Middlesex	G. E.	Lower Edmonton.
								BATHGATE—			
..	..	..	..	..	..			Balbardie No. 1 Colliery	L'lithgow	N. B.	Bathgate, Lower and Westfield.
..	..	..	..	..	..			Balbardie No. 2 Colliery	L'lithgow	N. B.	Branch from Bathgate, Lower.
..	..	..	..	..	..			Balbardie Sand Pits	L'lithgow	N. B.	Bathgate, Upper.
..	..	..	..	..	..			Bathgate Chemical Works	L'lithgow	N. B.	Bathgate, Upper and Whitburn.
..	..	..	..	..	..			Bathgate Foundry	L'lithgow	N. B.	Bathgate, Lower & Bathgate, Upper.
..	..	..	..	..	..			Boghead Colliery	L'lithgow	N. B.	Bathgate, Upper and Armadale.
..	..	..	..	..	..			Colinshiel Colliery	L'lithgow	N. B.	Branch—Bathgate, Lower and Westfield.
..	..	..	..	..	..			Couston Siding	L'lithgow	N. B.	Bathgate, Lower and Westfield.
..	..	..	..	..	..			East Junction	L'lithgow	N. B.	Bathgate, Upper & Bathgate, Lower.
..	..	..	..	..	..			Easton Col. (Hopetoun Col.)	L'lithgow	N. B.	Branch—Bathgate, Lower and Westfield.
..	..	..	..	..	..			Gall's Mill Siding	L'lithgow	N. B.	Bathgate, Lower.
..	..	..	..	..	..			Hopetoun Steel Works	L'lithgow	N. B.	Bathgate, Lower.
G	P	.	.	.	.			Lower	L'lithgow	N. B.	Bathgate, Upper and Blackston.
..	..	..	..	..	..			Mosside Collieries	L'lithgow	N. B.	Branch from Bathgate, Upper.
..	..	..	..	..	..			Owen Stone Co.'s Siding	L'lithgow	N. B.	Bathgate, Upper and Livingstone.
..	..	..	..	..	..			Riddochhill Colliery	L'lithgow	N. B.	Branch from Bathgate, Upper.
..	..	..	..	..	..			Seafield Oil Works	L'lithgow	N. B.	Branch—Bathgate, Upper and Livingstone.
G	P	F	L	H	C	5	0	Upper	L'lithgow	N. B.	Ratho and Airdrie.
..	..	..	..	..	..			West Junction	L'lithgow	N. B.	Bathgate, Lower & Bathgate, Upper.
..	..	..	..	..	..			West Lothian Rolling Mills & Shovel Works	L'lithgow	N. B.	Bathgate, Lower & Bathgate, Upper.
..	..	..	..	..	..			Bathgate Junction	Edinboro'	N. B.	Ratho and Broxburn Junction.
..	..	..	..	..	..			Bathgate's Siding	Lancs	L. & N. W.	Garston Docks.

EXPLANATION—G *Goods Station.*   P *Passenger and Parcel Station.*   P* *Passenger, but not Parcel or Miscellaneous Traffic.*
F *Furniture Vans, Carriages, Portable Engines, and Machines on Wheels.*   L *Live Stock.*
H *Horse Boxes and Prize Cattle Vans.*   C *Carriages by Passenger Train.*

STATION ACCOMMODATION.						CRANE POWER.		STATIONS, &c.	COUNTY.	COMPANY.	POSITION.
						Tons	Cwts.				
.	.	.	.	.	.	.	.	Bath Stone Firms	Somerset..	G. W.	Bath.
.	.	.	.	.	.	.	.	Bath Stone Firms	Wilts	G. W.	{ Box. { Chippenham.
.	.	.	.	.	.	.	.	Bathville Brick Works	L'lithgow	N. B.	Armadale.
.	.	.	.	.	.	.	.	Bathville Collieries	L'lithgow	N. B.	Armadale.
.	.	.	.	.	.	.	.	Bathville Foundry	L'lithgow	N. B.	Armadale.
.	.	.	.	.	.	.	.	Bathville Steel & Wgn. Wks.	L'lithgow	N. B.	Armadale.
								BATLEY—			
G	P	F	L	H	C	10	0	(Station)	Yorks	L. & N. W.	Dewsbury and Leeds.
G	P	F	L	H	C	10	0			G. N.	Dewsbury and Dudley Hill.
G	.	F	L	.	.	10	0	(Station, G. N.)	Yorks	G. C.	Over G. N. from Wakefield Junc.
.	P	.	.	.	.					L. & Y.	Over G. N. from Wakefield Junc.
.	.	.	.	.	.	.	.	Howley Park Colliery	Yorks	L. & N. W.	Batley and Morley.
.	.	.	.	.	.	.	.	Junction	Yorks	G. N.—L. & N. W.	Ossett and Dewsbury.
.	.	.	.	.	.	.	.	Soothill Wood Col.(G.N.)	Yorks	G. N.—G. C.	Batley and Woodkirk.
.	P	.	.	.	.	.	.	Upper	Yorks	G. N.	Ossett and Dudley Hill.
.	.	.	.	.	.	.	.	West End Colliery	Yorks	L. & N. W.	Batley and Morley.
.	.	.	.	.	.	.	.	Batley Carr	Yorks	L. & N. W	See Staincliffe and Batley Carr.
G	P	.	L	.	.	10	0			G. N.	Dewsbury and Batley.
.	P	.	.	.	.			Batley Carr (G.N.)	Yorks	L. & Y.	Over G. N. from Wakefield Junc.
.	.	.	.	.	.	.	.	Baton Colliery	Lanark	N. B.	Shotts.
.	.	.	.	.	.	.	.	Batonrigg Colliery	Lanark	N. B.	Shotts.
G	P	.	.	.	.	.	.	Battersby Junction Station	Yorks	N. E.	Ingleby and Kildale.
.	.	.	.	.	.	.	.	Battersby Siding	Yorks	N. E.	Battersby Junction Station.
.	.	.	.	.	.	.	.	Battersea	Surrey	W.L.E.Jt.(GW,L&NW, L.&S.W. & L.B.&S.C.).	See London.
.	.	.	.	.	.	.	.	Battersea Park	Surrey	L. B. & S. C.	See London.
.	.	.	.	.	.	.	.	Battersea Park Rd. (S.E.&C.)	Surrey	S. E. & C.—G. N.— Mid.	See London.
.	.	.	.	.	.	.	.	Battersea Pier Junction	Surrey	S. E. & C.	London, Grosvenor Road and Battersea Park Road.
.	.	.	.	.	.	.	.	Battersea Pier (L.B.& S.C.)	Surrey	L. B. & S. C.—L. & N. W.	Same as London, Grosvenor Road.
.	.	.	.	.	.	.	.	Battersea, Queens Road	Surrey	L. & S.W.	See London, Queen's Road.
.	.	.	.	.	.	.	.	Battersea Wharf (L.B.& S.C.)	Surrey	L B & S C—G N—L & S W — Mid.	See London.
.	P	.	.	.	.	.	.	Batterstown	Meath	M. G. W.	Dublin and Navan.
.	.	.	.	.	.	.	.	Battery Siding	Cumb'land	N. B.	See Armstrong, Whitworth & Co. (Silloth).
G	P	F	L	H	C	4	0	Battle	Sussex	S. E. & C.	Tunbridge Wells and Hastings.
.	.	.	.	.	.	.	.	Crowhurst Park Siding	Sussex	S. E. & C.	Battle and West St. Leonards.
.	.	.	.	.	.	.	.	Mountfield Siding	Sussex	S. E. & C.	Robertsbridge and Battle.
.	.	.	.	.	.	.	.	Sub-Wealden Gypsum Co.'s Siding	Sussex	S. E. & C.	Robertsbridge and Battle.
.	.	.	.	.	.	.	.	Battleblent Siding	Hadding'n	N. B.	See Dunbar.
G	P	F	L	H	C	1	10	Battlesbridge	Essex	G. E.	Wickford and Southminster.
.	.	.	.	.	.	.	.	Batts Foundry	Yorks	N. E.	{ Ruswarp. { Whitby.
G	P	F	L	H	C	5	0	Battyeford and Mirfield	Yorks	L. & N. W.	Cleckheaton and Huddersfield.
.	.	.	.	.	.	.	.	Baty, J., & Son's Siding	Cumb'land	N. E.	Carlisle.
G	P	.	L	.	.	.	.	Bawnboy Road & Templeport	Cavan	C. & L.	Belturbet and Ballinamore.
.	.	.	.	.	.	.	.	Bawsey Siding	Norfolk	Mid. & G. N. Jt.	Grimston Road.
G	P	F	L	H	C	1	0	Bawtry	Yorks	G. N.	Retford and Doncaster.
.	.	.	.	.	.	.	.	Bawtry Road Junction	Yorks	G. C.—N. E.	Same as Thorne Junction.
.	.	.	.	.	.	.	.	Baxendale & Co.'s Siding	Lancs	Trafford Park Estate	Manchester.
.	.	.	.	.	.	.	.	Baxendale & Son's Bee Mills	Lancs	C.L.C. (G.C., G.N. & Mid)	Liverpool, Huskisson.
.	.	.	.	.	.	.	.	Baxendell, R., & Son's Siding	Lancs	Manchester Ship Canal	Manchester.
G	P	.	.	.	.	10	0	Baxenden	Lancs	L. & Y.	Bury and Accrington.
.	.	.	.	.	.	.	.	Baxenden Colliery Siding	Lancs	L. & Y.	Baxenden.
.	.	.	.	.	.	.	.	Lancashire Brick & Terra-Cotta Co.'s Siding	Lancs	L. & Y.	Baxenden.
.	.	.	.	.	.	.	.	Nichol's Chemical Co.'s Sid.	Lancs	L. & Y.	Baxenden.
.	.	.	.	.	.	.	.	Baxterley Park Colliery	Warwick.	Mid.	Same as Baddesley Col. (Kingsbury).
.	.	.	.	.	.	.	.	Baxter's Siding (N. B.)	Lanark	N. B.—Cal.	Glasgow, Great Western Road.
.	.	.	.	.	.	.	.	Baxter Wood Junction	Durham	N. E.	Witton Gilbert and Durham Pass.
.	.	.	.	.	.	.	.	Baxter Works	Lancs	L. & N. W.	See United Alkali Co. (St. Helens).
.	.	.	.	.	.	.	.	Baxton Bank Depôts	Durham	N. E.	Waskerley.
G	P	F	L	H	C	5	0	Bay Horse	Lancs	L. & N. W.	Lancaster and Preston.
.	.	.	.	.	.	.	.	Bayley's Siding	Staffs	L. & N. W.	Wolverhampton.
.	.	.	.	.	.	.	.	Bayliff's Foundry	Cheshire	Birkenhead Jt.—C. L. C.—N. W. & L.	Birkenhead.
.	.	.	.	.	.	.	.	Bayliss, Jones, & Bayliss Sid.	Salop	S&W'pl. Jt.(GW&LNW)	Minsterley.
.	.	.	.	.	.	.	.	Bayliss Siding	Warwick..	Mid.	Lifford.
.	.	.	.	.	.	.	.	Bayly's Siding	Devon	L. & S.W.	Plymouth, Oreston.

EXPLANATION—G *Goods Station.*   P *Passenger and Parcel Station.*   P* *Passenger, but not Parcel or Miscellaneous Traffic.*
F *Furniture Vans, Carriages, Portable Engines, and Machines on Wheels.*   L *Live Stock.*
H *Horse Boxes and Prize Cattle Vans.*   C *Carriages by Passenger Train.*

STATION ACCOMMODATION.						CRANE POWER.		STATIONS, &c.	COUNTY.	COMPANY.	POSITION.
G	P	F	L	H	C	Tons	Cwts.				
G	P	F	L	H	C	1	0	Bayly's Siding and Wharf ...	Devon	G. W.	Plymouth, Sutton Harbour.
.	.	.	.	.	.	.	.	Baynards	Surrey	L. B. & S. C.	Guildford and Horsham.
.	.	.	.	.	.	.	.	Cranleigh Brick & Tile Co.'s Siding (Miles E. A.)	Surrey	L. B. & S. C.	Baynards.
.	.	.	.	.	.	.	.	Bayswater (Queen's Road) ...	Middlesex	Met.	See London.
.	.	.	.	.	.	.	.	Beadle Bros.' Siding	Kent	S. E. & C.	Charlton.
.	.	.	.	.	.	.	.	Beadle Bros.' Siding............	Kent	S. E. & C.	Plumstead.
.	.	.	.	.	.	.	.	Beadles Siding	Kent	S. E. & C.	Erith.
.	.	.	.	.	.	.	.	Beadman, Son & Co.'s Wagon Repairing Works	Yorks	Mid.	Keighley.
G	P	F	L	H	C	5	0	Beag Siding......................	Pembroke	G. W.	See Llanycefn.
.	.	.	.	.	.	.	.	Beal	Northumb	N. E.	Berwick and Belford.
.	.	.	.	.	.	.	.	Beales, H. F., Siding (G. E.)	Cambs	G. E.—L. & N. W.—Mid.	Same as Coldham Brick Co.'s Siding (Cambridge).
.	.	.	.	.	.	.	.	Beale, P., & Co.'s Siding	Cambs	G. E.—G. N.—Mid.	Cambridge.
G	P	F	L	H	C	1	0	Bealings	Suffolk ...	G. E.	Ipswich and Woodbridge.
G	P	F	L	H	C	1	10	Beamish	Durham ...	N. E.	Birtley and Annfield Plain.
.	.	.	.	.	.	.	.	Beamish Air and Mary Col.	Durham ...	N. E.	Beamish.
.	.	.	.	.	.	.	.	Beamish, E., Stanley Col.	Durham ...	N. E.	Beamish.
.	.	.	.	.	.	.	.	Beamish Sawmill and Store House	Durham ...	N. E.	Beamish.
.	.	.	.	.	.	.	.	Chop Hill Colliery	Durham ...	N. E.	Beamish.
.	.	.	.	.	.	.	.	Beard, G. T.	Glo'ster ...	G. W.	Gloucester Docks.
.	.	.	.	.	.	.	.	Beardmore's Ship Yard	Dumbart'n	Cal.	Dalmuir.
G	P	.	L	H	.	1	10	Bearley	Warwick..	G. W.	Stratford-on-Avon and Hatton.
.	.	.	.	.	.	.	.	Bearpark Colliery, Coke, Brick, and Chemical Works........	Durham ...	N. E.	Witton Gilbert.
G	P	.	L	H	.	3	0	Bearsden	Dumbart'n	N. B.	Maryhill and Milngavie.
G	P	F	L	H	C	5	0	Bearsted	Kent	S. E. & C.	Maidstone and Ashford.
.	.	.	.	.	.	.	.	Beart's Sand Pit................	Beds	G. N.	Sandy.
.	P*	.	.	.	.	.	.	Beasdale	Inverness..	N. B.	Fort William and Mallaig.
.	.	.	.	.	.	.	.	Beasdale Siding	Inverness..	N. B.	See Arisaig.
.	.	.	.	.	.	.	.	Beattie's Siding	Edinboro'.	Cal.	Edinburgh, Lothian Road.
G	P	F	L	H	C	4	10	Beattock	Dumfries..	Cal.	Lockerbie and Carstairs.
G	.	.	.	.	.	.	.	Greskine Siding	Dumfries..	Cal.	Beattock and Elvanfoot.
G	.	.	L	.	.	.	.	Summit	Dumfries..	Cal.	Beattock and Elvanfoot.
.	.	.	.	.	.	.	.	Beaty Bros'. Siding	Cumb'land	Mid.	Cumwhinton.
.	.	.	.	.	.	.	.	Beaty's Brick Siding	Cumb'land	Mid.	Cumwhinton.
.	.	.	.	.	.	.	.	Beauchamp Mines	Lincoln ...	G. C.	Frodingham & Scunthorpe.
.	.	.	.	.	.	.	.	Beauchief and Abbey Dale ...	Derby	Mid.	See Sheffield.
G	P	.	L	.	.	1	0	Beaufort	Mon	L. & N. W.	Abergavenny and Merthyr.
.	.	.	.	.	.	.	.	Beaufort Road Boiler Works	Cheshire...	Birkenhead Jt.—C.L.C.—N. W. & L.	See Cammell, Laird, & Co. (Birkenhead).
.	.	.	.	.	.	.	.	Beaufort Tin Plate Co.'s Siding (Mid.)	Glamorg'n	Mid.—G.W.—L. & N. W.	Morriston.
G	P	F	L	H	C	.	.	Beaulieu Road	Hants	L. & S.W.	Southampton and Brockenhurst.
G	P	F	L	H	C	1	10	Beauly	Inverness..	High.	Inverness and Dingwall.
.	.	.	.	.	.	.	.	Beaumaris	Anglesey..	L. & N. W.	By Road from Bangor.
G	P	.	L	.	.	.	.	Beaumont	Jersey	Jersey	St. Helier and St. Aubin.
G	P	.	.	.	.	.	.	Beauparc	Meath......	G. N. (I.)	Drogheda and Navan.
G	P	.	.	.	.	10	0	Bebington and New Ferry ...	Cheshire...	B'head Jt (GW&L&NW)	Birkenhead and Hooton.
G	P	.	.	.	.	.	.	Bebside	Northumb	N. E.	Blyth and Morpeth.
.	.	.	.	.	.	.	.	Bebside Colliery	Northumb	N. E.	Bebside.
G	P	F	L	H	C	6	0	Beccles	Suffolk ...	G. E.	Halesworth and Yarmouth.
.	.	.	.	.	.	.	.	Crisp, J., & Son's Siding ...	Suffolk ...	G. E.	Beccles Station.
.	P	.	.	.	.	.	.	Beckenham Hill.................	Kent	S. E. & C.	Nunhead and Shortlands.
.	.	.	.	.	.	.	.	Beckenham Junction...........	Kent	S. E. & C.	New Beckenham and Beckenham Junction Station.
G	P	F	L	H	C	8	0	Beckenham Junction Station.	Kent	S. E. & C.	Penge and Bromley.
G	P	F	L	H	C	.	.	Beckermet	Cumb'land	W.C.& E Jt.(Fur.&LNW)	Moor Row and Sellafield.
.	.	.	.	.	.	.	.	Beckett & Co.'s Siding.........	Cheshire...	L. & N. W.	See Douglas Siding (Hartford).
G	P	.	L	.	.	.	.	Beckfoot	Cumb'land	R. & E.	Ravenglass and Boot.
G	P	F	L	H	C	1	10	Beckford	Glo'ster ...	Mid.	Ashchurch and Evesham.
G	P	F	L	H	C	1	10	Beckingham.......................	Notts	G. N. & G. E. Jt.	Doncaster and Gainsboro'.
.	.	.	.	.	.	.	.	Beckley	Sussex......	K. & E. S.	See Northiam (for Beckley & Sandh'st)
.	.	.	.	.	.	.	.	Beckton	Essex	G. E.	See London.
.	.	.	.	.	.	.	.	Beckton Junction	Essex	G. E.—L. & I. Dks......	London, Custom House & Gallions.
G	P	.	L	H	C	.	.	Bective	Meath......	M. G. W.	Dublin and Navan.
G	P	F	L	H	C	1	0	Bedale	Yorks	N. E.	Northallerton and Leyburn.
.	.	.	.	.	.	.	.	Beddgelert	Carnarvon	No. Wales N. G.	Same as Snowdon.
.	.	.	.	.	.	.	.	Beddington	Surrey ...	L. B. & S. C.	See Waddon (for Beddington and Bandon Hill).

EXPLANATION—G *Goods Station.*   P *Passenger and Parcel Station.*   P* *Passenger, but not Parcel or Miscellaneous Traffic.*
F *Furniture Vans, Carriages, Portable Engines, and Machines on Wheels.*   L *Live Stock.*
H *Horse Boxes and Prize Cattle Vans.*   C *Carriages by Passenger Train.*

STATION ACCOMMODATION.						CRANE POWER.		STATIONS, &c.	COUNTY.	COMPANY.	POSITION.
						Tons	Cwts				
.	P	.	.	.	.	.	.	Beddington Lane	Surrey ...	L. B. & S. C.	Croydon and Wimbledon.
.	.	.	.	.	.	.	.	Hall & Co.'s Siding	Surrey ...	L. B. & S. C.	Beddington Lane.
.	.	.	.	.	.	.	.	Beddow & Son's Victoria Brick Works	Staffs	L. & N. W. ...	Pelsall.
.	.	.	.	.	.	.	.	Bede Metal Works...............	Durham ...	N. E.	Jarrow.
								BEDFORD—			
G	P	F	L	H	C	10	0	(Station)	Beds	L. & N. W.	Bletchley and Cambridge.
G	P	F	L	H	C	10	0	(Station)	Beds	Mid.	Wellingboro' and Luton.
.	.	.	.	.	.	.	.	Allen, W. H., Son & Co.'s Siding (Mid.)	Beds	Mid.— L. & N. W.	Near Bedford.
.	.	.	.	.	.	.	.	Astell Bros' Sid. (L.&N.W.)	Beds	L. & N. W.—Mid.	Bedford.
.	.	.	.	.	.	.	.	Bedford Gas Co.'s Siding	Beds	Mid.	Near Bedford.
.	.	.	.	.	.	.	.	Church & Son's Sid. (Mid.)	Beds	Mid.—L. & N. W.	Bedford.
.	.	.	.	.	.	.	.	Forder and Son's Brick Works (Elstow Siding)...	Beds	Mid.	Bedford and Ampthill.
.	.	.	.	.	.	.	.	Franklin's Wagon Shed ...	Beds	L. & N. W.	Bedford.
.	.	.	.	.	.	.	.	Grafton & Co.'s Siding	Beds	Mid.	Bedford and Hitchin.
.	.	.	.	.	.	.	.	Hall's Siding	Beds	L. & N. W.	Bedford.
.	.	.	.	.	.	.	.	Hipwell, W., & Sons' Siding (Mid)	Beds	Mid.—L. & N. W.	Bedford.
.	.	.	.	.	.	.	.	Howard's, J. & F., Works	Beds	L. & N. W.—Mid.	Bedford.
.	.	.	.	.	.	.	.	Junction	Beds	L. & N. W.—Mid.	Bedford L. & N. W. & Mid. Stations
.	.	.	.	.	.	.	.	Rogers' Siding (L. & N. W.)	Beds	L. & N. W.—Mid.	Bedford.
.	.	.	.	.	.	.	.	Smith's Timber Co.'s Siding (Mid.)	Beds	Mid.—L. & N. W.	Bedford.
.	.	.	.	.	.	.	.	Wheeldon's Siding............	Beds	L. & N. W.—Mid.	Bedford.
.	.	.	.	.	.	.	.	Bedford............	Lancs	G. C. (Wigan Jn.)	See West Leigh and Bedford.
.	.	.	.	.	.	.	.	Bedford............	Lancs	L. & N. W.	See Leigh and Bedford.
.	.	.	.	.	.	.	.	Bedford Colliery	Lancs	L. & N. W.	Same as Speakman's (Leigh & Bedford).
.	P	.	.	.	.	.	.	Bedford Well Waterworks ...	Sussex ...	L. B. & S. C.	Eastbourne.
.	.	.	.	.	.	.	.	Bedhampton Siding (L B & S C)	Hants ...	L. B. & S. C.—L. & S. W.	Havant.
G	P	.	L	H	.	1	10	Bedlington	Northumb	N. E.	Morpeth and Blyth.
.	.	.	.	.	.	.	.	Barrington Col. & Bk. Wks.	Northumb	N. E.	Bedlington.
.	.	.	.	.	.	.	.	Bedlington Brick Co.'s Sid.	Northumb	N. E.	Bedlington.
.	.	.	.	.	.	.	.	Bedlington Col. " A " Pit...	Northumb	N. E.	Bedlington.
.	.	.	.	.	.	.	.	Bedlington Col.(Doctor Pit)	Northumb	N. E.	Bedlington.
.	.	.	.	.	.	.	.	Furnace Road Siding	Northumb	N. E.	Bedlington.
.	.	.	.	.	.	.	.	West Sleekburn Col. "E" Pit	Northumb	N. E.	Bedlington.
G	P	.	.	.	.	.	.	Bedlinog	Glamorg'n	T. B. Jt. (G. W. & Rhy.)	Llancaiach and Dowlais.
.	.	.	.	.	.	.	.	Ffaldcaiach Sidings	Glamorg'n	T. B. Jt. (G. W. & Rhy.)	Bedlinog and Llancaiach.
.	.	.	.	.	.	.	.	Gilfach Main Quarry.........	Glamorg'n	T. B. Jt. (G. W. & Rhy.)	Bedlinog and Llancaiach.
.	.	.	.	.	.	.	.	Guest, Keen, & Nettlefold— Bedlinog Colliery	Glamorg'n	T. B. Jt. (G. W. & Rhy.)	Branch—Bedlinog & Cwm Bargoed.
.	.	.	.	.	.	.	.	Nantwen Colliery	Glamorg'n	T. B. Jt. (G. W. & Rhy.)	Bedlinog and Llancaiach.
.	.	.	.	.	.	.	.	Bedlinog Colliery	Glamorg'n	T. B. Jt. (G. W. & Rhy.)	See Guest, Keen, & Nettlefold (Bedlinog).
.	P	.	.	.	.	.	.	Bedminster	Somerset..	G. W.	Bristol and Flax Bourton.
.	.	.	.	.	.	.	.	Bedminster, Easton, Kingswood & Parkfield Co.'s Sid.	Glo'ster ...	Mid.	Same as Parkfield Col (Mangotsfield).
G	P	.	L	.	.	.	.	Bedwas	Mon	B. & M.	Pengam and Bassaleg.
.	.	.	.	.	.	.	.	Bryngwyn Colliery	Mon	B. & M.	Bedwas and Maesycwmmer.
.	.	.	.	.	.	.	.	Diamond Llantwit Colliery	Mon	B. & M.	Bedwas and Machen.
.	.	.	.	.	.	.	.	Price & Wills' Siding.........	Mon	B. & M.	Bedwas and Maesycwmmer.
.	P	.	.	.	.	.	.	Bedwellty Pits	Glamorg'n	L. & N. W.	Nantybwch and Tredegar Jn. Sta.
.	.	.	.	.	.	.	.	Bedwellty Pits	Glamorg'n	L. & N. W.	See Tredegar Ir. & Cl.Co. (Tredegar).
G	P	F	L	H	C	1	5	Bedworth	Warwick..	L. & N. W.	Coventry and Nuneaton.
.	.	.	.	.	.	.	.	Bedworth Brick, Tile & Timber Co.'s Sid.(LNW)	Warwick..	L. & N. W.—Mid.	Bedworth and Chilvers Coton.
.	.	.	.	.	.	.	.	Hawkesbury & Bedworth Brick & Tile Co.'s Blockley's Siding (L. & N. W.)	Warwick..	L. & N. W.—Mid.	Bedworth and Chilvers Coton.
.	.	.	.	.	.	.	.	Newdigates Col.(L.&N.W.)	Warwick..	L. & N. W.—Mid.	Bedworth and Hawkesbury Lane.
.	.	.	.	.	.	.	.	Stanley Bros. Charity Col. (L. & N. W.)	Warwick..	L. & N. W.—Mid.	Bedworth and Chilvers Coton.
.	.	.	.	.	.	.	.	Wilson's (Exors. of) Exhall Colliery (L. & N. W.) ...	Warwick..	L. & N. W.—Mid.	Bedworth and Hawkesbury Lane.
G	P	.	L	H	.	3	0	Bedwyn............	Wilts	G. W.	Hungerford and Devizes.
.	.	.	.	.	.	.	.	Beeby's Brick Co.'s Siding ...	Hunts ...	G. N.	Fletton.
.	.	.	.	.	.	.	.	Beech & Son's Pottery	Staffs	N. S.	Longton.
G	P	.	.	.	.	1	10	Beechburn	Durham ...	N. E.	Crook and Wear Valley Junction.
.	.	.	.	.	.	.	.	Beechburn Colliery	Durham ...	N. E.	Crook.

EXPLANATION—G *Goods Station.*   P *Passenger and Parcel Station.*   P* *Passenger, but not Parcel or Miscellaneous Traffic.*
F *Furniture Vans, Carriages, Portable Engines, and Machines on Wheels.*   L *Live Stock.*
H *Horse Boxes and Prize Cattle Vans.*   C *Carriages by Passenger Train.*

STATION ACCOMMODATION.						CRANE POWER.		STATIONS, &c.	COUNTY.	COMPANY.	POSITION.
						Tons	Cwts				
..	..	..	..	..	..	..	..	Beechburn Station Siding ...	Durham ...	N. E.	Crook.
..	..	..	..	..	..	..	..	Beeding Siding	Sussex ...	L. B. & S. C.	Shoreham.
								Bee Hive Works (Jenkins &			
..	..	..	..	..	..	..	..	Co.) (G. C.)	Notts	G. C.—G. N.—Mid.	Retford.
..	..	..	..	..	..	..	..	Beeley, Thos., & Son's Sid.(GC)	Cheshire...	G. C.—Mid.	Newton (for Hyde).
..	..	..	..	..	..	..	..	Beer	Devon ...	L. & S. W.	See Seaton and Beer.
..	..	..	..	..	..	..	..	Beeson's Siding	Beds	L. & N. W.	Blunham.
G	P	F	L	H	C	1	10	Beeston	Notts	Mid.	Derby and Nottingham.
..	..	..	..	..	..	..	..	Beeston Brewery Co.'s Sid.	Notts	Mid.	Near Beeston.
..	..	..	..	..	..	..	..	Beeston Foundry Co.'s Sid.	Notts	Mid.	Near Beeston.
..	..	..	..	..	..	..	..	Clarke's Siding	Notts	Mid.	Beeston.
..	..	..	..	..	..	..	..	Beeston (G. N.)	Yorks	G. N.—L. & Y.	See Leeds.
G	P	F	L	H	C	5	0	Beeston Castle and Tarporley	Cheshire...	L. & N. W.	Chester and Crewe.
..	..	..	..	..	..	..	..	Lord Tollemache's Siding...	Cheshire...	L. & N. W.	Beeston Castle and Tattenhall Road.
..	..	..	..	..	..	..	..	Beeston Colliery	Yorks	Mid.	See Charlesworth, J. & J., Collieries (Woodlesford).
..	..	..	..	..	..	..	..	Beeston Junction	Yorks	G. N.	Leeds.
..	..	..	..	..	..	..	..	Beeston Pit	Yorks	E. & W. Y. Union	Robin Hood.
..	..	..	..	..	..	..	..	Beeston Quarry	Yorks	E. & W. Y. Union	Robin Hood.
..	..	..	..	..	..	..	..	Begg & Co.'s Siding............	Glamorg'n	GW—L&NW—Rhy—TV	Cardiff.
G	P	..	..	..	..	5	0	Beighton (G. C.)	Derby	{ G. C.	Sheffield and Chesterfield.
G	..	..	..	..	..	5	0			{ L. & N. W.	Over G. N. and G. C. Lines.
..	..	..	..	..	..	..	..	Beighton Brick Co.'s Siding	Derby	G. C.	Beighton.
..	..	..	..	..	..	..	..	Holbrook Colliery (G. C.)...	Derby	G. C.—L. & N. W.	Beighton.
..	..	..	..	..	..	..	..	Waddington's Paper Mills	Yorks	G. C.	Beighton.
..	..	..	..	..	..	..	..	Beighton Junctions	Derby	G. C.—Mid.—L.D.& E.C.	Sheffield and Chesterfield.
..	..	..	..	..	..	..	..	Beighton Junc. with Chesterfield Line	Derby	G. C.	Beighton and Killamarsh.
G	P	F	L	H	C	6	0	Beith	Ayr	{ G. & S. W.	Johnstone and Dalry.
G	P	F	L	H	C	4	0		Ayr	{ G B & K Jt(Cal & G&SW)	Branch from Lugton.
..	..	..	..	..	..	..	..	Muir's Siding	Ayr	G. & S. W.	Beith and Glengarnock.
..	..	..	..	..	..	..	..	West of Scotland Furniture Co.'s Siding	Ayr	G B & K Jt(Cal & G & S W)	Beith.
G	P	..	..	..	..	1	15	Bekesbourne	Kent	S. E. & C.	Canterbury and Dover.
G	P	..	L	..	..	2	0	Belcoo	Ferm'nagh	S. L. & N. C.	Enniskillen and Glenfarne.
								BELFAST—			
G	P	F	L	..	..			(Station)	Antrim ...	Mid.	By Steamer from Barrow & Heysham.
G	P	F	L	H	C	10	0	(Station)	Antrim ...	P&WJt.(L&Y & L&NW)	By Steamer from Fleetwood.
G	..	..	..	..	..	30	0	Abercorn Basin	Down	B. & C. D.—G. N. (I.) ...	Over Harbour Commissioners' Line.
..	P	..	..	..	..	..	..	Adelaide and Windsor	Antrim ...	G. N. (I.)	Great Victoria Street and Lisburn.
..	..	..	..	..	..	..	..	Ballymaccarrett Junctions	Down	B. & C. D.—G. N. (I.) ...	Sydenham and Queen's Bridge.
..	..	..	..	..	..	..	..	Central Junction	Antrim ...	G. N. (I.)	Balmoral and Great Victoria Street.
G	..	..	..	..	..	30	0	Clarendon Dock	Antrim ...	G. N. (I.)	Over Harbour Commissioners' Line.
G	..	..	..	..	..	..	..	Donegal Quay	Antrim ...	G. N. (I.)	Over Harbour Commissioners' Line.
..	..	..	..	..	..	..	..	Donegal Quay Junction......	Antrim ...	G. N. (I.)—Harb. Com...	Queen's Bge. and Dufferin Dk. Junc.
G	..	..	..	..	..	..	..	Dufferin Dock	Antrim ...	G. N. (I.)	Over Harbour Commissioners' Line.
..	..	..	..	..	..	..	..	Dufferin Dock Junction......	Antrim ...	G. N. (I)—N. C. Com. (Mid.)—Harb. Com. ...	York Road and Donegal Quay Junc
..	P	..	..	H	C	..	..	Great Victoria Street	Antrim ...	G. N. (I.)	Terminus.
G	P	..	..	..	..	..	..	Greencastle	Antrim ...	N. C. Com. (Mid.)	Belfast and Carrickfergus.
G	..	F	L	..	..	6	0	Grosvenor Street	Antrim ...	G. N. (I.)	Terminus.
G	..	..	L	..	..	..	..	Queen's Bridge	Antrim ...	G. N. (I.)	Central Junc. and Donegal Quay Jn.
G	P	..	L	H	C	4	0	Queen's Quay	Down	B. & C. D.	Terminus.
..	..	..	..	..	..	..	..	Queen's Quay	Down	G. N. (I.)	Over Harbour Commissioners' Line.
G	P	F	L	H	C	5	0	York Road	Antrim ...	N. C. Com. (Mid.)	Terminus.
G	P	F	L	H	C	1	0	Belford	Northumb	N. E.	Morpeth and Berwick.
..	..	..	..	..	..	..	..	Cragmill Siding	Northumb	N. E.	Belford.
..	..	..	..	..	..	..	..	Belford Siding	Yorks	N. E.	Scarborough.
..	P	..	..	..	..	..	..	Belgrave and Birstall	Leicester..	G. C.	Loughboro' and Leicester.
..	..	..	..	..	..	..	..	Belgrave Road..............	Leicester..	G. N.	See Leicester.
								Belhaven Estate Collieries—			
..	..	..	..	..	..	..	..	Meadowhead Colliery......	Lanark ...	Cal.	Shieldmuir.
..	..	..	..	..	..	..	..	Nether Johnstone Collieries	Lanark ...	Cal.	Shieldmuir.
..	..	..	..	..	..	..	..	Over Johnstone Colliery ..	Lanark ...	Cal.	Shieldmuir.
..	..	..	..	..	..	..	..	Over Johnstone Farm Sid..	Lanark ...	Cal.	Shieldmuir.
..	..	..	..	..	..	..	..	Belhaven Works	Lanark ...	Cal.	Wishaw, Central.
..	..	..	..	..	..	..	..	Bellaggio Siding	Sussex ...	L. B. & S. C.	East Grinstead.
..	..	..	..	..	..	..	..	Bellahouston	Lanark ...	G. & S. W.	See Glasgow.
..	..	..	..	..	..	..	..	Bellahouston Junction	Lanark ...	Cal.—G.&S. W.—G&PJt.	Glasgow.
..	..	..	..	..	..	..	..	Bell & Sime's Wood Yard ...	Forfar ...	{ Cal	Dundee, West.
..	..	..	..	..	..	..	..			{ N. B.	Dundee, Tay Bridge.
..	..	..	..	..	..	..	..	Bell & Son's Siding	Edinboro'	N. B.	Leith, Bonnington.

EXPLANATION—G *Goods Station.*   P *Passenger and Parcel Station.*   P* *Passenger, but not Parcel or Miscellaneous Traffic.*
F *Furniture Vans, Carriages, Portable Engines, and Machines on Wheels.*   L *Live Stock.*
H *Horse Boxes and Prize Cattle Vans.*   C *Carriages by Passenger Train.*

STATION ACCOMMODATION.						CRANE POWER.	STATIONS, &c.	COUNTY.	COMPANY.	POSITION.
						Tons Cwts				
G	P	.	L	H	C	3 0	Bellarena	Derry	N. C. Com. (Mid.)	Londonderry and Coleraine.
							Bell Brothers—			
.	.	.	.	.	.	. .	Clarence Iron & Steel Wks.	Durham ...	N. E.	Port Clarence.
.	.	.	.	.	.	. .	Clarence Soda Works ...	Durham ...	N. E.	Port Clarence.
.	.	.	.	.	.	. .	Parson Byers Quarry........	Durham ...	N. E.	Stanhope.
G	P	F	L	H	.	. .	Bell Busk	Yorks	Mid.	Lancaster and Skipton.
G	P	.	L	.	.	2 10	Belleek	Ferm'nagh	G. N. (I.)	Bundoran Junction and Bundoran.
.	.	.	.	.	.	. .	Belle Vue................	Lancs	G. C.	See Manchester, Ashburys (for Belle Vue).
.	.	.	.	.	.	. .	Belle Vue................	Lancs	L. & N. W.	See Manchester, Longsight (for Belle Vue).
G	P	.	.	.	.	. .	Belle Vue................	Lancs	S. & M. Jt. (G. C. & Mid.)	Ashburys and Romiley.
.	.	.	.	.	.	. .	Kendall & Gent's Siding ...	Lancs	S. & M. Jt. (G. C. & Mid.)	Belle Vue.
.	.	.	.	.	.	. .	Belle Vue Brick Co.'s Siding.	Cambs......	L. & N. W.	See Coates & Rutley's (Gamlingay).
.	.	.	.	.	.	. .	Belle Vue Field Siding........	Durham ...	N. E.	West Hartlepool.
.	.	.	.	.	.	. .	Belle Vue Saw Mill	Lanark ...	Cal.	Wishaw.
.	.	.	.	.	.	. .	Belle Vue Siding	Yorks	L. & Y.	Darton.
.	.	.	.	.	.	. .	Bellfield Colliery	Lanark ...	Cal.	Coalburn.
.	.	.	.	.	.	. .	Bellfield Junction	Ayr	G. & S. W.	Riccarton and Kilmarnock.
.	.	.	.	.	.	. .	Bellfield Saw Mill	Renfrew ...	Cal.	Glasgow, Whiteinch.
.	.	.	.	.	.	. .	Bellfield Siding	Edinboro'	N. B.	Same as Boglehole Sid. (Musselburgh)
.	.	.	.	.	.	. .	Bellgrove (N. B.)	Lanark ...	N. B.—G. & S. W.	See Glasgow.
.	.	.	.	.	.	. .	Bellgrove East Junction	Lanark ...	N. B.	Glasgow.
.	.	.	.	.	.	. .	Bell House Siding	Derby	Mid.	Barrow Hill and Staveley Works.
.	P	.	.	.	.	. .	Bellingham	Kent	S. E. & C.	Nunhead and Shortlands.
G	P	F	L	H	C	3 0	Bellingham	No'thumb	N. B.	Riccarton and Reedsmouth.
.	.	.	.	.	.	. .	Bellman Park Siding	Lancs	L. & Y.	Clitheroe.
.	.	.	.	.	.	. .	Bellsdyke Colliery	Lanark ...	N. B.	Airdrie, North.
G	P	F	L	H	C	1 10	Bellshill	Lanark ...	{ Cal.	Holytown and Ruthergl'en.
G	P	F	L	H	C	3 0			{ N. B.	Bothwell and Coatbridge.
.	.	.	.	.	.	. .	Bellshill Colliery	Lanark ...	Cal.	Bellshill and Uddingston.
.	.	.	.	.	.	. .	Bothwell Park Colliery......	Lanark ...	N. B.	Bellshill and Bothwell.
.	.	.	.	.	.	. .	East Parkhead Colliery ...	Lanark ...	N. B.	Branch from Bellshill.
.	.	.	.	.	.	. .	Hamilton Palace Colliery...	Lanark ...	N. B.	Branch—Bellshill and Bothwell.
.	.	.	.	.	.	. .	Milnwood Colliery	Lanark ...	Cal.	Holytown and Bellshill.
.	.	.	.	.	.	. .	Rosehall Cols., Nos. 7, 13 & 21	Lanark ...	N. B.	Branch—Bellshill and Whifflet.
.	.	.	.	.	.	. .	Rosehall South Lye (Gilmour's Manure Siding)...	Lanark ...	N. B.	Branch—Bellshill and Whifflet.
.	.	.	.	.	.	. .	Bell's, H., Siding	Lincoln ...	G. N.	Grantham.
.	.	.	.	.	.	. .	Bellside Brick Works	Lanark ...	Cal	Omoa.
.	.	.	.	.	.	. .	Bellside Colliery	Lanark ...	Cal.	Omoa.
.	.	.	.	.	.	. .	Bellside Quarries	Lanark ...	Cal.	Omoa.
.	.	.	.	.	.	. .	Bellside Saw Mills...........	Lanark ...	Cal.	Omoa.
.	.	.	.	.	.	. .	Bell's Siding	Durham ...	N. E.	Same as Norton Junction Siding (Norton-on-Tees).
G	P	.	.	.	.	. .	Bellurgan................	Louth	D. N. & G.	Dundalk and Greenore.
.	P	.	.	.	.	. .	Belmisthorpe	Rutland ...	G. N.	See Ryhall and Belmisthorpe.
G	P	.	.	.	.	5 0	Belmont	Surrey	L. B. & S. C.	Sutton and Epsom Downs.
G	P	.	L	H	C	. .	Belmont and Cloghan	King's	G. S. & W.	Clara and Banagher.
.	.	.	.	.	.	. .	Belmont Junction	Durham ...	N. E.	Durham.
.	.	.	.	.	.	. .	Belmont Siding	Ayr	G. & S.W.	Ayr.
.	.	.	.	.	.	. .	Belmont Siding (Arnold & Son) (G. N.)................	Yorks	G.N.—G.C.—Mid.	Doncaster.
G	P	F	L	H	C	10 0	Belper	Derby	Mid.	Derby and Chesterfield.
.	.	.	.	.	.	. .	Belper Gas Co.'s Siding ...	Derby	Mid.	Belper.
.	.	.	.	.	.	. .	Belper's (Lord) Siding	Notts	Mid.	Kegworth.
.	P	.	.	.	.	. .	Bel Royal	Jersey......	Jersey	St. Helier and St. Aubin.
G	P	F	L	H	C	1 10	Belses	Roxburgh	N. B.	Galashiels and Hawick.
.	.	.	.	.	.	. .	Greenend Siding............	Roxburgh	N. B.	Be'ses and St. Boswells.
.	.	.	.	.	.	. .	Standhill Siding	Roxburgh	N. B.	Belses and Hassendean.
.	.	.	.	.	.	. .	Belsham & Sons' Siding	Essex	G. E.	Braintree.
.	.	.	.	.	.	. .	Belston Junction	Ayr	G. & S.W.	Drongan and Ochiltree.
.	.	.	.	.	.	. .	Belton	Lincoln ...	G. C.	See Crowle (for Epworth & Belton).
G	P	.	.	.	.	. .	Belton	Suffolk ...	G. E.	Beccles and Yarmouth, South Town.
.	.	.	.	.	.	. .	Beltonford Siding	Hadding'n	N. B.	See Dunbar.
G	P	.	L	.	.	2 0	Belturbet	Cavan ...	{ C. & L.	Near Belturbet Station (G. N., I).
G	P	F	L	H	C				{ G. N. (I.)	Branch from Ballyhaise Junc. Sta.
G	P	F	L	H	C	5 0	Belvedere	Kent	S. E. & C.	Woolwich and Dartford.
.	.	.	.	.	.	. .	Belvelly Siding	Cork	G. S. & W.	Carrigaloe.
.	.	.	.	.	.	. .	Be'voir	Leicester..	G. N. & L. & N. W. Jt. ...	See Redmile (for Belvoir).
.	.	.	.	.	.	. .	Belvoir Brick Works...........	Notts	G. N.	Same as Almond's Siding (Newark, Lowfield Sidings).

EXPLANATION—G *Goods Station.* P *Passenger and Parcel Station.* P* *Passenger, but not Parcel or Miscellaneous Traffic.*
F *Furniture Vans, Carriages, Portable Engines, and Machines on Wheels.* L *Live Stock.*
H *Horse Boxes and Prize Cattle Vans.* C *Carriages by Passenger Train.*

STATION ACCOMMODATION.						CRANE POWER.		STATIONS, &c.	COUNTY.	COMPANY.	POSITION.
						Tons	Cwts				
								Belvoir Plaster Co.'s Siding...	Notts	G. N.	See Lowfield Sidings (Newark).
G	P		L	H		10	0	Bembridge	I. of W	I. of W.	Branch from Brading.
G	P		L	H				Bempton	Yorks	N. E.	Scarborough and Bridlington.
								Benarty Colliery	Fife	N. B.	Kelty.
								Ben Cruachan Quarries	Argyll	Cal.	Loch Awe.
								Bendall's Siding	Glo'ster	Mid.	See Huntingford Mills (Charfield).
G	P	F	L	H	C			Benderloch	Argyll	Cal.	Connel Ferry and Ballachulish.
G	P		L	H				Benfleet	Essex	L. T. & S.	Tilbury and Southend-on-Sea.
								Benfleet Brickfields Siding	Essex	L. T. & S.	Benfleet.
G	P	F						Bengeworth	Worcester	Mid.	Ashchurch and Evesham.
								Benhar Junction	Lanark	Cal.	Shotts and Fauldhouse.
								Benhar Weighs	Lanark	Cal.	Fauldhouse.
G	P	F	L	H	C			Beningbrough	Yorks	N. E.	York and Thirsk.
								Newton Siding	Yorks	N. E.	Beningbrough.
								Bennerley Ironworks	Notts	G. N.	Same as Awsworth Iron Works (Awsworth).
								Bennerley Sidings—			
								Davis, E. P., Siding	Notts	Mid.	Ilkeston.
								Digby Colliery Co.'s Siding	Notts	Mid.	Ilkeston.
								Giltbrook Chemical Works	Notts	Mid.	Ilkeston.
								Nottingham Corporation Chemical Works	Notts	Mid.	Ilkeston.
								Bennett & Son's Siding (G. C.)	Lincoln	G. C.—G. N.	Same as Pyewipe Sid. (Grimsby Dks.)
								Bennett, J. L., & Son's Siding	Norfolk	G. E.	Downham.
								Bennett's (Birch Vale) Siding	Derby	S. & M. Jt. (G. C. & Mid.)	Hayfield.
								Bennett's Brick Siding	Derby	G. N.	Derby.
G	P		L	H				Bennettsbridge	Kilkenny	G. S. & W.	Waterford and Kilkenny.
								Bennett's Iron Foundry	Lancs	L. & N. W.	Manchester, London Road.
								Bennett's Iron Foundry (G.C.)	Lancs	G. C.—Mid.	Manchester, Ardwick.
								Bennett's Saw Mills (G. C.)	Lincoln	G. C.—G. N.	Grimsby.
								Bennett's Siding	Lancs	G. C.	Manchester, Ardwick.
								Ben-Nevis Distillery Siding (Old Distillery)	Inverness	N. B.	Fort William.
								Bennie, D., & Son's Works ...	Lanark	{ Cal. { N. B.	Glasgow, Buchanan Street. Glasgow, Sighthill.
G	P							Ben Rhydding	Yorks	O. & I. Jt. (Mid & N. E.)	Otley and Ilkley.
	P							Bensham	Durham	N. E.	Durham and Newcastle.
								Benskin's Watford Brewery Co.'s Siding	Herts	L. & N. W.	Watford.
								Benstead's Siding	Kent	S. E. & C.	Maidstone, West.
								Bent Colliery	Lanark	Cal.	Hamilton, Central.
G	P	F	L	H	C	5	0	Bentham	Yorks	Mid.	Skipton and Lancaster.
								Low Bentham Timber Sid.	Yorks	Mid.	Bentham.
								Bentinck Colliery	Notts	Mid.	Pinxton.
								Bentinck Colliery (G. C.)	Notts	G. C.—G. N.—L. & N. W.	Kirkby and Pinxton.
								Bentinck Dock	Norfolk	G. E.—G. N.—Mid.—Mid & G. N. Jt.	See Lynn, Alexandra & Bentinck Dks.
G	P	F	L	H	C	5	0	Bentley	Hants	L. & S.W.	Farnham and Winchester.
G	P	F	L	H	C			Bentley	Suffolk	G. E.	Colchester and Ipswich.
								Bentley, J., & Co.'s Siding	Lancs	Manchester Ship Canal	Manchester.
								Bentley's, J., Brick, Tile, and Pottery Siding	Lancs	L. & Y.	Longton Bridge.
								Bentley's Siding	Leicester	Mid.	Leicester, East.
								Bentley's Yorkshire Breweries	Yorks	Mid.	Woodlesford.
G	P					3	0	Benton	Northumb	N. E.	Newcastle and Backworth.
								Holystone Siding	Northumb	N. E.	Benton.
								Benton Quarry	Northumb	N. E.	Forest Hall.
								Bentrigg Colliery	Lanark	Cal.	Netherburn.
								Bent Rigg Lane Siding	Yorks	N. E.	Stainton Dale.
G	P		L	H				Bents	L'lithgow	N. B.	Bathgate, Upper and Morningside.
G	P		L	H				Bentworth and Lasham	Hants	L. & S.W.	Basingstoke and Alton.
								Benwell Colliery	Northumb	N. E.	Elswick.
G								Benwick	Cambs	G. E.	Branch from Whittlesea.
G	P	F	L	H	C	1	10	Beragh	Tyrone	G. N. (I.).	Dungannon and Omagh.
G	P	F	L	H	C	1	10	Bere Alston	Devon	L. & S.W.	Exeter and Plymouth.
G	P	F	L	H	C	1	10	Bere Ferrers	Devon	L. & S.W.	Exeter and Plymouth.
G	P	F	L	H	C	1	10	Berkeley	Glo'ster	S. & Wye Jt. (G. W. & Mid)	Berkeley Road and Sharpness.
G	P	F	L	H	C	1	10	Berkeley Road	Glo'ster	Mid.	Gloucester and Bristol.
								Berkeley Road Junction	Glo'ster	Mid.—S. & Wye Jt.	Gloucester and Sharpness.
	P							Berkeley Road Junction Sta.	Glo'ster	S. & Wye Jt.(G. W.&Mid)	Berkeley Rd. Junction & Sharpness.
								Berk, F. W., & Co.'s District Chemical Co.'s Sid. (G.E.)...	Essex	GE—G N—L N W—Mid	London, Silvertown.
G	P	F	L	H	C	5	0	Berkhamsted	Herts	L. & N. W.	Bletchley and Watford.

EXPLANATION—G *Goods Station.*   P *Passenger and Parcel Station.*   P* *Passenger, but not Parcel or Miscellaneous Traffic.*
F *Furniture Vans, Carriages, Portable Engines, and Machines on Wheels.*   L *Live Stock.*
H *Horse Boxes and Prize Cattle Vans.*   C *Carriages by Passenger Train.*

STATION ACCOMMODATION.						CRANE POWER.		STATIONS, &c.	COUNTY.	COMPANY.	POSITION.
						Tons	Cwts				
G	P							Berkswell	Warwick..	L. & N. W.	Birmingham and Coventry.
								Bermondsey	Surrey	S. E. & C.	See London, Spa Road (Bermondsey).
								Bermondsey, South	Surrey	L. B. & S. C.	See London, South Bermondsey.
								Bernard Road Depôt (G. C.)	Yorks	G. C.—G. N.	See Sheffield, Lumley Street (for Bernard Road Depôt).
								Bernard Road Siding (Central Depôt) (Mid.)	Yorks	Mid.—G. C.	See Sheffield Corporation.
								Bernard's, D., Brewery	Edinboro'	N. B.	Edinburgh, Gorgie.
								Bernard's, T. & J., Siding	Edinboro'	N. B.	Same as Edinburgh Brewery (Edinburgh).
G	P	F	L	H	C			Bernard, T., & Co.'s Siding	Edinboro'	N. B.	Leith, South.
G	P		L	H		5	0	Berrington	Salop	G. W.	Shrewsbury and Buildwas.
								Berrington and Eye	Hereford..	S & H Jt. (G. W. & L N W)	Craven Arms and Hereford.
								Berry & Co.'s Siding (G.C.)	Notts	G. C.—G. N.—Mid.	Worksop.
G	P					5	0	Berry Brow	Yorks	L. & Y.	Huddersfield and Penistone.
								Berryhill Colliery	Lanark	Cal.	Wishaw.
								Berryhill Nos. 2 & 3	Ayr	G. & S. W.	Lugar.
								Berry Hill Sand Co's Sid. (Mid)	Notts	Mid.— G. C.	See Mansfield Sand Co.'s Siding (Mansfield).
								Berry Hill Siding	Staffs	N. S.	Stoke and Bucknall.
								Berry Yard Sugar Refinery (Westburn Sugar Refinery)	Renfrew..	Cal.	Greenock, Upper.
								Bersham Colliery	Denbigh..	G. W.	Wrexham.
								Bertha Pit	Cumb'land	L. & N. W.	See Flimby Colliery Co. (Flimby).
								Berthlwyd Colliery	Glamorg'n	L. & N. W.	Penclawdd.
G	P		L	H		1	10	Bervie	Kinc'rdine	N. B.	Branch from Montrose.
G	P	F	L	H	C			Berwick	Sussex	L. B. & S. C.	Lewes and Polegate.
								Cuckmere Brick Co.'s Siding	Sussex	L. B. & S. C.	Berwick.
G	P	F	L	H	C	5	0	Berwick Station & Junction	Berwick	N. B.—N. E.	Edinburgh and Newcastle.
								Berwig Quarry	Denbigh	G. W.	Minera.
	P							Berwyn	Denbigh	G. W.	Llangollen and Corwen.
G	P		L					Bescar Lane	Lancs	L. & Y.	Wigan and Southport.
	P							Bescot	Staffs	L. & N. W.	Birmingham and Wolverhampton.
G	P										
G	P	F	L	H	C	1	10	Bessbrook	Armagh	{ B. & Newry { G. N. (I.)	Terminus. Goragh Wood and Dundalk.
								Bessemer, H., & Co.'s Wks (Mid)	Yorks	Mid.—G. C.	Sheffield, Wicker.
								Bestwood Coal & Iron Co.'s Sid.	Notts	Mid.	Nottingham, Bulwell.
G	P							Bestwood Colliery Station	Notts	G. N.	Daybrook and Hucknall.
								Bestwood Colliery (G.N.)	Notts	G. N.— G. C.	Bestwood and Bulwell Forest.
								Bestwood Iron Works	Notts	G. N.	Bestwood and Bulwell Forest.
								Bestwood Junction	Notts	G. C. & G. N. Jt.—G. N.	Bulwell Common and Bestwood.
								Bestwood Park	Notts	G. N.	See Daybrook (for Arnold and Bestwood Park).
								Beswick	Lancs	L. & Y.	See Manchester.
G	P	F	L	H	C	8	0	Beswick and Son's Siding	Derby	Mid.	Peak Forest.
								Betchworth	Surrey	S. E. & C.	Red Hill and Dorking.
								Brockham Brick Co.'s Sid.	Surrey	S. E. & C.	Betchworth and Box Hill.
								Dorking Lime Co.'s Siding	Surrey	S. E. & C.	Betchworth.
								Bethell's Siding	N'hamptn	G. C.	Woodford and Hinton.
G	P	F	L	H	C	5	0	Bethesda	Carnarvon	L. & N. W.	Branch from Bangor.
								Bethesda Gas Works	Carnarvon	L. & N. W.	Bethesda.
								Bethnal Green Junc. Station	Middlesex	G. E.	See London.
G	P		L			1	10	Betley Road	Cheshire...	L. & N. W.	Crewe and Stafford.
G	P	F	L	H	C	1	0	Bettisfield	Flint	Cam.	Whitchurch and Ellesmere.
	P							Bettisfield Colliery	Flint	L. & N. W.	Same as Mitchell's Siding (Bagillt).
G	P							Bettws (Llangeinor)	Glamorg'n	P. T.	Maesteg and Pont-y-Rhyll.
								Bettws Garmon	Carnarvon	No. Wales N.G.	Dinas and Snowdon.
								Bettws Llantwit Merthyr Col.	Glamorg'n	P. T.	Lletty Brongu.
								Bettws Llantwit Siding	Glamorg'n	G. W.	Llangeinor.
G	P	F	L	H	C	5	0	Bettws-y-Coed	Carnarvon	L. & N. W.	Blaenau Festiniog and Llandudno Junction Station.
								Beuther's Patent Axle Box and Foundry Co.'s Siding	Warwick..	L. & N. W.	Birmingham, Curzon Street.
								Beuther's Patent Axle Box & Foundry Co.'s Sid. (Mid.)	Warwick..	Mid.—G. W.	Birmingham, Lawley Street.
								Bevan & Son's Chemical Wks. (G. W.)	Carmarth'	G. W.—L. & N. W.	Llanelly.
								Bevan's Castle Chemical Co.'s Siding (G. W.)	Carmarth'	G. W.—L. & N. W.	Llanelly.
								Bevan's Castle Chemical Works	Carmarth'	L. & M. M.	Llanelly.

EXPLANATION—G *Goods Station.*   P *Passenger and Parcel Station.*   P* *Passenger, but not Parcel or Miscellaneous Traffic.*
F *Furniture Vans, Carriages, Portable Engines, and Machines on Wheels.*   L *Live Stock.*
H *Horse Boxes and Prize Cattle Vans.*   C *Carriages by Passenger Train.*

STATION ACCOMMODATION.						CRANE POWER.	STATIONS, &c.	COUNTY.	COMPANY.	POSITION.
G	P	F	L	H	C	Tons 6 Cwts 0	Beverley	Yorks	N. E.	Hull and Driffield.
.	.	.	.	.	.		Glossop and Bulay's Siding	Yorks	N. E.	Beverley.
.	.	.	.	.	.		Stephenson, R., & Son's Sid.	Yorks	N. E.	Beverley.
.	.	.	.	.	.		Thirsk, J., & Sons' Siding ..	Yorks	N. E.	Beverley.
.	.	.	.	.	.		Beverley Road	Yorks	H. & B.	See Hull.
.	.	.	.	.	.		Beverley's (Lord) Siding	Yorks	L. & Y.	Goole.
.	.	.	.	.	.		Beves & Co.'s Siding	Sussex	L. B. & S. C.	Kingston Wharf.
.	.	.	.	.	.		Bevois Park Sidings	Hants	L. & S.W.	See Southampton.
G	P	F	L	H	C	1 10	Bewdley	Worcester	G. W.	Shrewsbury and Hartlebury.
.	.	.	.	.	.		Bewick Main Colliery	Durham	N. E.	Birtley.
.	.	.	.	.	.		Bewsey and Dallam Forge Iron Works	Lancs	C. L. C. (G C, G N, & Mid.)	See Pearson & Knowles Coal & Iron Co. (Warrington).
.	.	.	.	.	.		Bewsey Forge Ir. Wks (LNW)	Lancs	L. & N. W.—G. W.	
G	P	F	L	H	C	5 0	Bexhill	Sussex	L. B. & S. C.	Hastings and Polegate.
.	.	.	.	.	.		Bexhill Electric Light Works Siding	Sussex	L. B. & S. C.	Bexhill.
.	.	.	.	.	.		Bexhill Gas Co.'s Siding	Sussex	L. B. & S. C.	Bexhill and St. Leonard's.
G	P	F	L	H	C	5 0	Bexhill-on-Sea	Sussex	S. E. & C.	Branch from Crowhurst.
G	P	F	L	H	C	.	Bexley	Kent	S. E. & C.	Hither Green and Dartford.
G	P	.	.	.	.		Bexleyheath	Kent	S. E. & C.	Blackheath and Dartford.
.	.	.	.	.	.		Beyer, Peacock and Co.'s Siding (G. C.)	Lancs	G.C.—G.W.—L.&N.W.—Mid.	Manchester, Openshaw.
.	.	.	.	.	.		Bibbey's Sand Pits	Cheshire	N. S.	Alsager.
.	.	.	.	.	.		Bibbington's Lime Works	Derby	L. & N. W.	Dove Holes.
.	.	.	.	.	.		Bibbington's South Works	Derby	Mid.	Peak Forest.
.	.	.	.	.	.		Bibby & Son's Siding	Lancs	L. & N. W.	Liverpool, Waterloo.
.	.	.	.	.	.		Bibby & Son's Siding	Lancs	L. & N. W.—S. & M. Jt.	Widnes.
.	.	.	.	.	.		Bibby, Sons & Co.'s Siding	Lancs	L. & N. W.	Garston Docks.
.	.	.	.	.	.		Bibby, Sons & Co.'s Siding	Lancs	L. & N. W.	St. Helens.
.	.	.	.	.	.		Bibby's Siding	Lancs	S. & M. Jt. (G. C. & Mid.)	Widnes.
G	P	F	L	H	C	5 0	Bicester	Oxon	L. & N. W.	Oxford and Verney Junction Station.
.	P	.	.	.	.		Bickershaw and Abram	Lancs	G. C. (Wigan Jn.)	Lowton St. Mary's and Wigan.
.	.	.	.	.	.		Bickershaw Branch	Lancs	L. & N. W.	Pennington and Platt Bridge.
.	.	.	.	.	.		Bickershaw Branch Junction.	Lancs	G. C. (Wigan Jn.)	West Leigh and Bickershaw.
.	.	.	.	.	.		Bickershaw Collieries	Lancs	G. C. (Wigan Jn.)	West Leigh and Bedford.
.	.	.	.	.	.		Bickershaw Colliery	Lancs	L. & N. W.	Same as Ackers, Whitley & Co.'s Bickershaw or Plank Lane Colliery (Leigh and Bedford).
G	P	.	.	.	.		Bickleigh	Devon	G. W.	Plymouth and Tavistock.
.	.	.	.	.	.		Bickleigh	Devon	G. W.	See Cadeleigh and Bickleigh.
G	P	F	L	H	C	.	Bickley	Kent	S. E. & C.	Bromley and Swanley.
.	.	.	.	.	.		Bicknor Siding	Glo'ster	S. & Wye Jt. (G. W. & Mid)	Lydbrook.
.	.	.	.	.	.		Bicslade Siding	Glo'ster	S. & Wye Jt. (G. W. & Mid)	See Speech House Road.
.	.	.	.	.	.		Biddick Lane Siding	Durham	N. E.	Washington.
G	P	.	.	.	.	1 10	Biddulph	Staffs	N. S.	Ford Green and Congleton.
.	.	.	.	.	.		Heath & Son's Bradley Green Colliery	Staffs	N. S.	Biddulph.
.	.	.	.	.	.		Biddulph Valley Iron Works and Colliery	Staffs	N. S.	See Heath & Sons (Black Bull).
G	P	.	.	.	.		Bideford	Devon	B. W. Ho ! & A.	Adjoining L. & S.W. Station.
G	P	F	L	H	C	10 0			L. & S.W.	Barnstaple and Torrington.
G	P	.	L	.	.		Bidford	Warwick	E. & W. Jn.	Stratford-on-Avon and Broom.
G	.	.	L	.	.	5 0	Bidston	Cheshire	N. W. & L. Jt. (G. C. and W. M. & C. Q.)	Bidston Junction and Upton.
.	.	.	.	.	.				Wirral	Seacombe and West Kirby.
.	P	.	.	.	.		Bidston (Wirral)	Cheshire	G. C.	Over Wirral from Bidston Junction.
.	.	.	.	.	.		Bidston Junction	Cheshire	N. W. & L. Jt.—Wirral	Neston and Birkenhead.
.	P	.	.	.	.		Bieldside	Aberdeen	G. N. of S.	Aberdeen and Banchory.
.	.	.	.	.	.		Bierley Siding	Yorks	G. N.—L. & Y.	Bradford, Low Moor.
G	P	F	L	H	C	4 10	Biggar	Lanark	Cal.	Symington and Peebles.
.	.	.	.	.	.		Causewayend Siding	Lanark	Cal.	Biggar and Coulter.
.	.	.	.	.	.		Biggarford Colliery	Lanark	Cal.	Omoa.
G	P	F	L	H	C	5 0	Biggleswade	Beds	G. N.	Hitchin and Sandy.
.	.	.	.	.	.		Biglis	Glamorg'n	T. V.	Same as Cadoxton.
.	.	.	.	.	.		Biglis Junction	Glamorg'n	Barry—T. V.	Cadoxton and Sully.
.	.	.	.	.	.		Bigrigg	Cumb'land	WC & E Jt. (Fur. & LNW)	See Woodend (for Cleator & Bigrigg).
G	.	.	.	.	.		Bigrigg	Cumb'land	WC & E Jt. (Fur. & LNW)	Bigrigg Mineral Branch.
.	.	.	.	.	.		Bigrigg Mineral Branch	Cumb'land	WC & E Jt. (Fur. & LNW)	Branch near Moor Row.
.	.	.	.	.	.		Bigrigg Pits	Cumb'land	WC & E Jt. (Fur. & LNW)	See Lord Leconfield's (Moor Row).
G	P	.	.	.	.	5 0	Bigsweir	Mon	G. W.	Chepstow and Monmouth.
G	P	.	L	H	.		Bilbster	Caithness	Highland	Georgemas and Wick.
G	P	.	.	.	.		Billacombe	Devon	G. W.	Plymstock and Yealmpton.

EXPLANATION—G Goods Station.   P Passenger and Parcel Station.   P* Passenger, but not Parcel or Miscellaneous Traffic.
F Furniture Vans, Carriages, Portable Engines, and Machines on Wheels.   L Live Stock.
H Horse Boxes and Prize Cattle Vans.   C Carriages by Passenger Train.

STATION ACCOMMODATION.						CRANE POWER.		STATIONS, &c.	COUNTY.	COMPANY.	POSITION.
						Tons	Cwts.				
G	P	F	L	H	C	5	0	Billericay	Essex	G. E.	Shenfield and Southend-on-Sea.
								Billiemain's Siding	Berwick	N. B.	See Reston.
G	P			H				Billing	N'hamptn	L. & N. W.	Northampton and Wellingborough.
								Mead & Sons' Clifford Hill Mills or Little Houghton Crossing	N'hamptn	L. & N. W.	Billing and Northampton.
G	P	F	L	H	C	1	10	Billingboro'	Lincoln	G. N.	Bourne and Sleaford.
								Millthorpe Siding	Lincoln	G. N.	Rippingale and Billingboro.
G	P	F	L	H	C			Billingham Junction Station	Durham	N. E.	Stockton and West Hartlepool.
								Smith's Brick Yard	Durham	N. E.	Billingham Junction Station.
								Billingsgate Fish Market	Yorks	H. & B.—N. E.	Hull.
G	P	F	L	H	C	5	0	Billingshurst	Sussex	L. B. & S. C.	Horsham and Arundel.
								Puttock & Peacock's Siding	Sussex	L. B. & S. C.	Billingshurst.
								Billington Siding	Beds	L. & N. W.	Same as Arnold's (Leighton, Grovebury Crossing).
								Billup's Siding	Hunts	G. N. & G. E. Jt.	See Somersham.
								Billyford Farm Siding	Hadding'n	N. B.	Ormiston.
								Bilson Junction	Glo'ster	G. W.—S. & Wye Joint.	Bullo Pill and Drybrook Road.
G								Bilson Junction Station	Glo'ster	G. W.	Forest of Dean Branch.
								Churchway Colliery	Glo'ster	G. W.	Bilson Jn.—Forest of Dean Branch.
								Crump Meadow Colliery	Glo'ster	G. W.	Bilson Jn.—Forest of Dean Branch.
								Duck Colliery	Glo'ster	G. W.	Bilson Jn.—Forest of Dean Branch.
								East Slade Colliery	Glo'ster	G. W.	Bilson Jn.—Forest of Dean Branch.
								Foxes Bridge Colliery	Glo'ster	G. W.	Bilson Jn.—Forest of Dean Branch.
								Lightmoor Colliery	Glo'ster	G. W.	Bilson Jn.—Forest of Dean Branch.
								New Bowson Colliery	Glo'ster	G. W.	Bilson Jn.—Forest of Dean Branch.
								Trafalgar Siding	Glo'ster	G. W.	Bilson Jn.—Forest of Dean Branch.
								Bilston	Staffs	L. & N. W.	See Ettingshall Road and Bilston.
G	P							Bilston and Deepfields	Staffs	G. W.	Wolverhampton and Dudley.
								Bilston Gas Works	Staffs	G. W.	Bilston & Deepfields and Priestfield.
								Bradley's Capponfield Sid.	Staffs	G. W.	Bilston and Deepfields.
								Hickman's Spring Vale Sid.	Staffs	G. W.	Bilston and Deepfields.
								Staffordshire Steel & Ingot Iron Works Siding	Staffs	G. W.	Bilston and Deepfields.
G	P	F	L	H	C	20	0	Bilston and Ettingshall	Staffs	G. W.	Wolverhampton and Birmingham.
								Bilton Harrogate Gas Works	Yorks	N. E.	Starbeck.
								Bilton Junction	Yorks	N. E.	Harrogate and Ripon.
								Bilton Wharf	Warwick	L. & N. W.—Mid.	See Rugby Portland Cement Co.'s Siding (Rugby).
								Binchester Col. & Coke Ovens	Durham	N. E.	Spennymoor.
								Bindley & Co.'s Brewery (Mid.)	Staffs	Mid.—L&NW—GN—NS	Burton-on-Trent.
G	P	F	L	H	C	1	0	Binegar	Somerset	S. & D. Jt. (L. & S. W. & Mid)	Shepton Mallet and Radstock.
								Read & Son's Siding	Somerset	S. & D. Jt. (L. & S. W. & Mid)	Binegar.
G	P	F	L	H	C	1	10	Bingham	Notts	G. N.	Grantham and Nottingham.
	P							Bingham Road	Notts	G. N. & L. & N. W. Jt.	Melton Mowbray and Nottingham.
								Saxondale Siding	Notts	G. N. & L. & N. W. Jt.	Bingham Road and Saxondale Junc.
G	P	F	L	H	C	10	0	Bingley	Yorks	Mid.	Leeds and Skipton.
								Bingswood Printing Co.'s Sid.	Cheshire	L. & N. W.	Whaley Bridge.
								Binny Quarry	L'lithgow	N. B.	See Young's Oil Co. (Uphall).
G	P	F	L	H	C	2	0	Binton	Warwick	E. & W. Jn.	Stratford-on-Avon and Broom.
								Birchall Siding	Herts	G. N.	Cole Green.
								Birch & Co.'s Brewery	Lancs	L. & N. W.	Rainford Village.
								Birch's Stone Siding	Lincoln	G. C.	Barnetby.
								Birch Coppice Colliery (Morris & Shaw)	Warwick	Mid.	Kingsbury.
								Birchenwood Colliery Co.—Siding	Staffs	N. S.	Harecastle.
								Summit Siding	Staffs	N. S.	Harecastle.
	P*							Birchfield Platform	Elgin&Mo'	G. N. of S.	Craigellachie and Elgin.
								Birchfield Siding	Lancs	L. & Y.	Burscough Junction.
								Birchgrove Colliery Co.'s Siding (Mid.)	Glamorg'n	Mid.—G.W.—L. & N. W.	Glais. Six Pit Junction.
								Birchgrove Steel Co.'s Sid. (Mid.)	Glamorg'n	Mid.—G.W.—L. & N. W.	Glais.
G	P							Birchills	Staffs	L. & N. W.	Rugeley and Walsall.
								Caswell & Bowden's Siding	Staffs	L. & N. W.	Birchills and Bloxwich.
								Griffin, Jones & Co.'s Castle Brick Works	Staffs	L. & N. W.	Birchills and Bloxwich.
								Leamore Brick Co.'s Wilks Siding	Staffs	L. & N. W.	Birchills and Bloxwich.
								Birchills Blast Furnaces	Staffs	L. & N. W.	Same as Russell & Co.'s Siding (Bloxwich).

EXPLANATION—G *Goods Station.*   P *Passenger and Parcel Station.*   P* *Passenger, but not Parcel or Miscellaneous Traffic.*
F *Furniture Vans, Carriages, Portable Engines, and Machines on Wheels.*   L *Live Stock.*
H *Horse Boxes and Prize Cattle Vans.*   C *Carriages by Passenger Train.*

STATION ACCOMMODATION.						CRANE POWER.	STATIONS, &c.	COUNTY.	COMPANY.	POSITION.
						Tons Cwts.				
G	P	F	L	H	C	2 0	Birchington-on-Sea	Kent	S. E. & C.....................	Herne Bay and Margate.
..	..	..	..	..	..		Birch Rock Colliery	Glamorg'n	L. & N. W.	Same as Graigola Merthyr Colliery (Gorseinon).
..	P	..	..	..	..		Birch Vale	Derby.....	S. & M. Jt. (G. C. & Mid.)	New Mills and Hayfield.
..	..	..	..	..	..		Birch Vale Siding	Derby	S. & M. Jt. (G. C. & Mid.)	See Hayfield.
..	..	..	..	..	..		Birchwood New Colliery ...	Derby	Mid.	Pye Bridge.
..	..	..	..	..	..		Birchwood Upper Colliery ...	Notts	Mid.	Pinxton.
..	..	..	..	..	..		Bird & Nicholls' Siding	Staffs	L. & N. W.	Bloxwich.
..	..	..	..	..	..		Bird & Son's Siding	Glamorg'n	GW—LNW—Rhy—TV.	Cardiff.
G	P	..	L	H	..	0 15	Birdbrook	Essex	C. V. & H.	Haverhill and Halstead.
..	P	..	L	H	..		Bird, F. & A., Siding (G. E.)	Norfolk ...	G. E.—G. N.—Mid.	Lynn Harbour.
G	P	..	L	H	..		Birdhill	Tipperary	G. S. & W.	Killaloe and Limerick.
G	P	..	..	H	C		Birdingbury	Warwick..	L. & N. W.	Leamington and Rugby.
..	..	..	..	..	..		Bird-in-Hand Junction	Mon	G. W.—L. & N. W.	Tredegar Junction.
..	..	..	..	..	..		Bird-in-Hand Siding	Mon	G. W.—L. & N. W.	Tredegar Junction.
..	..	..	..	..	..		Birdsfield Brick Works........	Lanark ...	N. B.	Hamilton, Burnbank.
G	P	F	L	H	C	5 0	Birdwell & Hoyland Common	Yorks	G. C.	Sheffield and Barnsley.
..	..	..	..	..	..		Hoyland Brick Works	Yorks	G. C.	Birdwell and Hoyland Common.
..	..	..	..	..	..		Hoyland Silkstone Colliery	Yorks	G. C.	Birdwell and Hoyland Common.
							Newton, Chambers & Co.—			
..	..	..	..	..	..		Rockingham Colliery ..	Yorks	G. C.	Birdwell and Hoyland Common.
..	..	..	..	..	..		Rockingham Gas Works	Yorks	G. C.	Birdwell and Hoyland Common.
..	..	..	..	..	..		Wharncliffe Silkstone Col. .	Yorks	G. C.	Birdwell and Hoyland Common.
							Wharncliffe Silkstone New Coke Works	Yorks	G. C.	Birdwell and Hoyland Common.
..	..	..	..	..	..		Birdwell and Pilley Wharf ...	Yorks	Mid.	See Wombwell.
G	P	..	..	..	..	1 5	Birkdale (L. & Y.)	Lancs	{ L. & Y.	Liverpool and Southport.
..	P	..	..	..	..				L. & N. W.	Over L. & Y. from Bootle Junction.
..	..	..	..	..	..		Lloyd's Siding.................	Lancs	L. & Y.	Near Birkdale.
G	P	..	L	H	C	5 0	Birkdale Palace	Lancs	C. L. C. (S'port Exten.)..	Liverpool and Southport.
							BIRKENHEAD—			
..	..	..	..	..	..		Abbey Street Mineral Yard	Cheshire...	B'head Jt(GW & L & NW)	Terminus—Birkenhead Joint Line.
..	..	..	..	..	..		Alfred Dock Shipping Sheds	Cheshire...	B'head Jt—CLC—NW&L	Over Dock Board Lines.
..	..	..	..	..	..		Anglo-American Oil Co.'s Depôt	Cheshire...	B'head Jt—CLC—NW&L	Over Dock Board Lines.
..	..	..	..	..	..		Armour's Warehouse	Cheshire...	B'head Jt—CLC—NW&L	Over Dock Board Lines.
..	..	..	..	..	..		Bayliff's Foundry	Cheshire...	B'head Jt—CLC—NW&L	Over Dock Board Lines.
..	..	..	..	..	..		Blackpool Street Min. Yard	Cheshire...	B'head Jt(GW & L & NW)	Terminus—Birkenhead Joint Line.
..	..	..	..	..	..		British and Chicago Raw Hide Co.'s Warehouse	Cheshire...	B'head Jt—CLC—NW&L	Over Dock Board Lines.
..	..	..	..	..	..		Buchanan's Flour Mills......	Cheshire...	B'head Jt—CLC—NW&L	Over Dock Board Lines.
							Cammell Laird & Co.—			
							Beaufort Road Boiler Works	Cheshire...	B'head Jt—CLC—NW&L	Over Dock Board Lines.
..	..	..	..	..	..		Gillbrook Yard Boiler Works	Cheshire...	B'head Jt—CLC—NW&L	Over Dock Board Lines.
..	..	..	..	..	..		Monk's Ferry Shipbuilding Yard (B'head Jt.)	Cheshire...	B'head Jt.—C. L. C.	Terminus—Birkenhead Joint Line.
G	..	..	L	..	..	1 10	Canning Street Town	Cheshire...	{ B'head Jt(GW&L&NW)	Terminus—Birkenhead Joint Line.
G	..	..	..	..	..				C. L. C.	Shore Road.
G	..	..	L	..	..				G. W.	Terminus—Birkenhead Joint Line.
G	..	F	..	..	..	3 0	Cathcart Street	Cheshire...	B'head Jt(G W & L & NW)	Terminus—Birkenhead Joint Line.
G	P	..	..	..	..		Central	Cheshire...	Mersey	Green Lane and Hamilton Square.
..	..	..	..	..	..		Chain Testing Works	Cheshire...	B'head Jt—CLC—NW&L	Over Dock Board Lines.
..	..	..	..	..	..		Cheshire Creamery Co.'s Warehouse	Cheshire...	B'head Jt—CLC—NW&L	Over Dock Board Lines.
..	..	..	..	..	..		Coal Tips..................	Cheshire...	B'head Jt—CLC—NW&L	Over Dock Board Lines.
..	..	..	..	..	..		Corporation Gas Works (B'head Jt.)	Cheshire...	B'head Jt.—C. L. C.......	Terminus—Birkenhead Joint Line.
..	..	..	..	..	..		Currie & Rowland's Manure Works	Cheshire...	B'head Jt—CLC—NW&L	Over Dock Board Lines.
G	P	..	L	..	..		Docks	Cheshire...	Wirral	Bidston and Birkenhead Park.
G	..	..	..	..	..		Duke Street.................	Cheshire...	B'head Jt.—C.L.C.	Over Dock Board Lines.
G	..	..	..	..	..	5 0	Duke Street..................	Cheshire...	N. W. & L. Jt. (G.C. and W. M. & C.Q.)	Birkenhead.
G	..	..	..	..	..	5 0	East and West Float.........	Cheshire...	B'head Jt—CLC—NW&L	Over Dock Board Lines.
..	..	..	..	..	..		East and West Float Depôt	Cheshire..	C.L.C. (GC, GN, & Mid.)	Shore Road.
G	..	..	..	..	..		Egerton Dock	Cheshire...	C.L.C.—G. W.—N W & L	Over Dock Board Lines.
G	..	F	L	..	..	20 0	Egerton Dock	Cheshire...	L. & N. W.	Terminus—Birkenhead Joint Line.
..	..	..	..	..	..		English McKenna Process Co.'s Siding	Cheshire...	B'head Jt—CLC—NW&L	Over Dock Board Lines.
..	..	..	..	..	..		Gordon's, A., Warehouse...	Cheshire...	B'head Jt—CLC—NW&L	Over Dock Board Lines.

EXPLANATION—G *Goods Station.*   P *Passenger and Parcel Station.*   P* *Passenger, but not Parcel or Miscellaneous Traffic.*
F *Furniture Vans, Carriages, Portable Engines, and Machines on Wheels.*   L *Live Stock.*
H *Horse Boxes and Prize Cattle Vans.*   C *Carriages by Passenger Train.*

		Station Accommodation.				Crane Power.		Stations, &c.	County.	Company.	Position.
						Tons	Cwts.				
								BIRKENHEAD—*continued.*			
								Grandidge's Timber Depôt	Cheshire...	B'head Jt—CLC—NW&L	Over Dock Board Lines.
								Grange Lane Mineral Yard	Cheshire...	B'head Jt (GW & L & NW)	Terminus—Birkenhead Joint Line.
	P							Green Lane	Cheshire...	Mersey	Central and Rock Ferry.
	P							Hamilton Square	Cheshire...	Mersey	B'head (Central) & L'pool (James St.).
								Hamilton Square Junction	Cheshire...	Mersey	Central & Hamilton Square Station.
								Holt's, A., Warehouses	Cheshire...	B'head Jt—CLC—NW&L	Over Dock Board Lines.
								Jackson Street Mineral Yard	Cheshire...	B'head Jt (GW & L & NW)	Terminus—Birkenhead Joint Line.
								Junction	Cheshire...	B'head Jt.—Dock Board	Near Cathcart Street.
								Junction	Cheshire...	Dock Board—Wirral	Near Docks Station.
								Lewis's Copper Wharf	Cheshire...	B'head Jt—CLC—NW&L	Over Dock Board Lines.
								L'pool Manure Co.'s Works	Cheshire...	B'head Jt—CLC—NW&L	Over Dock Board Lines.
								Liverpool Petroleum Storage Co.'s Warehouse	Cheshire...	B'head Jt—CLC—NW&L	Over Dock Board Lines.
								L'pool Storage Co.'s Depôt	Cheshire...	B'head Jt—CLC—NW&L	Over Dock Board Lines.
								Logan's Copper Wharf	Cheshire...	B'head Jt—CLC—NW&L	Over Dock Board Lines.
								Mersey Tunnel Railway Electrical Power Works	Cheshire..	B'head Jt—CLC—-NW&L	Over Dock Board Lines.
								Monk's Ferry Cl. Co.'s Sid.	Cheshire...	B'head Jt (GW & L & NW)	Terminus—Birkenhead Joint Line.
								Morpeth Branch Dock	Cheshire...	B'head Jt.—N.W. & L.	Over Dock Board Lines.
G		F	L			40	0	Morpeth Dock	Cheshire...	C. L. C. (GC.,GN.& Mid.)	Over Joint Line from Helsby Junc.
G		F	L			12	0	Morpeth Dock	Cheshire...	{ G.W.	Terminus—Birkenhead Joint Line.
G		F	L			40	0	Morpeth Dk.&South Reserve	Cheshire...	{ L. & N. W.	Terminus—Birkenhead Joint Line.
								Mortimer, J. L., & Co.'s Warehouse	Cheshire...	B'head Jt—CLC—NW&L	Over Dock Board Lines.
								National Oil Co.'s Warehouse	Cheshire...	B'head Jt—CLC—NW&L	Over Dock Board Lines.
								Nelson & Son's Warehouse	Cheshire...	B'head Jt—CLC—NW&L	Over Dock Board Lines.
								Northern Guano Co.'s Works	Cheshire..	B'head Jt—CLC—NW&L	Over Dock Board Lines.
G	P							Park Joint Station & Junc.	Cheshire...	{ Mersey	Hamilton Square and Docks, Pass.
	P									{ Wirral	Bidston and Birkenhead.
								Paul Bros.' Flour Mills	Cheshire...	B'head Jt—CLC—NW&L	Over Dock Board Lines.
								Penk's Westons Siding	Cheshire...	B'head Jt(G W & L & NW)	Rock Ferry.
								Powell & Sing's Warehouse	Cheshire...	B'head Jt—CLC—NW&L	Over Dock Board Lines.
G	P					1	10	Rock Ferry (B'head Jt.)	Cheshire...	{ B'head Jt(GW&L&NW)	Birkenhead and Hooton.
	P									{ Mersey	Over B'head Jt. from Rock Ferry Jn.
								Rock Ferry Junction	Cheshire...	B'head Jt.—Mersey	Rock Ferry Station & Birkenhead.
								Rosenthall's, M., Warehouse	Cheshire...	B'head Jt—CLC—NW&L	Over Dock Board Lines.
								Seacombe Grain Warehouses	Cheshire...	B'head Jt—CLC—NW&L	Over Dock Board Lines.
								Shore Road	Cheshire...	B'head Jt(GW&L&NW)	Over Dock Board Lines.
G		F	L			40	0	Shore Road	Cheshire...	C L C (G C, G N & Mid.)	Over Birkenhead Jt. Line from Helsby Junction.
								Taylor's Siding (B'head Jt.)	Cheshire...	B'head Jt.—C. L. C.	Birkenhead.
	P							Town (Grange Road)	Cheshire...	{ B'head Jt.(GW&L N W)	Birkenhead (Woodside) and Hooton.
G						1	0			{ L. & N. W.	Terminus—Birkenhead Joint Line.
								Tunnel Road Mineral Yard	Cheshire...	B'head Jt(G W & L & N W)	Terminus—Birkenhead Joint Line.
								Uveco Cereals Co.'s Siding	Cheshire...	B'head Jt—CLC—NW&L	Over Dock Board Lines.
								Vernon & Son's Flour Mills	Cheshire...	B'head Jt—CLC—NW&L	Over Dock Board Lines.
								Vittoria Wharf Shipping Sheds	Cheshire...	B'head Jt—CLC—NW&L	Over Dock Board Lines.
								Wallasey Dock Shipping Sheds	Cheshire...	B'head Jt—CLC—NW&L	Over Dock Board Lines.
								Wallasey Gas & Water Wks	Cheshire...	B'head Jt—CLC—NW&L	Over Dock Board Lines.
								Wallasey Lairages	Cheshire...	B'head Jt—-CLC—NW&L	Over Dock Board Lines.
								Wilson, J. H., & Co.'s Crane Works	Cheshire...	B'head Jt—CLC—NW&L	Over Dock Board Lines.
	P	F	L	H	C			Woodside	Cheshire...	B'head Jt.(GW & L&NW)	Terminus—Birkenhead Joint Line.
								Woodside Ferry	Cheshire...	B'head Jt.(GW & L&NW)	Ferry from Liverpool.
								Woodside Lairages	Cheshire...	B'head Jt—CLC—NW&L	Over Dock Board Lines.
								Birkenhead Coal Tips	Cheshire...	B'head Jt—CLC—NW&L	Birkenhead.
								Birkenhead Corporation Gas Works (B'head Jt.)	Cheshire...	B'head Jt.—C. L. C.	Birkenhead, Cathcart Street.
G	P	F	L	H	C	10	0	Birkenshaw & Tong	Yorks	G. N.	Morley and Bradford.
								Birkenshaw Brick Wks. (Mid.)	Derby	Mid.—L. & N. W.	Same as Coton Pk. Brk. Co. (Gresley).
								Birkenshaw Col. & Brk. Wks.	Lanark	Cal.	Stonehouse.
								Birkhead Siding	Durham	N. E.	Redheugh.
								Birkrigg Colliery	Lanark	Cal.	Dalserf.
								Birkrigg New Colliery	Lanark	Cal.	Dalserf.
								Birley Collieries (G. C.)	Yorks	G. C.—L. & N. W.	Woodhouse.
								Birkshall Gas Works	Yorks	G. N.	See Bradford Corporation (Bradford)

EXPLANATION—G *Goods Station.*   P *Passenger and Parcel Station.*   P* *Passenger, but not Parcel or Miscellaneous Traffic.*
F *Furniture Vans, Carriages, Portable Engines, and Machines on Wheels.*   L *Live Stock.*
H *Horse Boxes and Prize Cattle Vans.*   C *Carriages by Passenger Train.*

\multicolumn{6}{c}{STATION ACCOMMODATION.}						CRANE POWER.		STATIONS, &c.	COUNTY.	COMPANY.	POSITION.
						Tons	Cwts				
G	P							BIRMINGHAM— Adderley Park	Warwick..	L. & N. W.	Coventry and New Street.
								Adderley Park Brick Co.'s Siding (L. & N. W.)	Warwick..	L. & N. W.—Mid.	Adderley Park.
								Anglo-American Oil Co.'s Siding	Warwick..	Mid.	Lawley Street.
G		F				20	0	Aston (Goods)	Warwick..	L. & N. W.	Windsor Street Wharf Branch.
								Aston Church Road Siding	Warwick..	Mid.	Saltley.
G		F	L			20	0	Banbury Street	Warwick..	L. & N. W.	Branch—Adderley Park and New Street.
								Batchelor & Co.'s Artillery Street Siding	Warwick..	Mid.	Near Lawley Street.
								Beuther's Patent Axle Box and Foundry Co.'s Siding	Warwick..	L. & N. W.	Aston and Stechford.
								Beuther's Patent Axle Box and Foundry Co.'s Siding (Mid.)	Warwick..	Mid.— G. W.	Near Lawley Street.
								Birmingham Oxygen Co.'s Sid ng	Warwick..	Mid.	Near Lawley Street.
								Bonded Warehouse	Warwick..	Mid.	Birmingham, Central.
G	P		L			10	0	Bordesley	Warwick..	G. W.	Snow Hill and Small Heath.
	P							Bordesley Junction	Warwick..	G. W.— Mid.	Small Heath and Saltley.
	P							Brighton Road	Warwick..	L. & N. W.	Camp Hill and Moseley.
								Brotherton & Co.'s Chemical Works	Warwick..	{ L. & N. W. { Mid.	Aston (Pass.) and Vauxhall. Near Lawley Street.
G	P		L			5	0	Camp Hill	Warwick..	Mid.	Saltley and Worcester.
								Carr's Siding	Warwick..	Mid.	Lawley Street.
G		F	L			20	0	Central Stat on	Warwick..	Mid.	Branch from Church Road.
	P							Church Road	Warwick..	Mid.	Five Ways and Selly Oak.
								Compressed Air Co.'s Siding	Warwick..	Mid.	Lawley Street.
								Corporation— Granary	Warwick..	Mid.	Central Station.
								Nechell's Gas Works	Warwick..	L. & N. W.	Aston (Pass.) and Vauxhall.
								Nechell's Gas Wks (Mid.)	Warwick..	Mid.—G. W.	Duddeston Sidings.
								Saltley Gas Department Siding (Mid.)	Warwick..	Mid.—G.W.—L. & N. W.	Lawley Street and Saltley.
								Siding	Warwick..	L. & N. W.	Harborne.
								Windsor Street Gas Works (L. & N. W.)	Warwick..	L. & N. W.—Mid.	Windsor Street Wharf Branch.
G		F	L			20	0	Curzon Street	Warwick..	L. & N. W.	Bch.—Adderley Park and New Str.
								Duddeston Sidings	Warwick..	Mid.	Birmingham.
								Ellis, J., & Son's Siding	Warwick..	Mid.	Camp Hill.
								Evans & Co.'s Siding	Warwick..	L. & N. W.	Windsor Street Wharf Branch.
G		F	L			20	0	Fazeley Street	Warwick..	L. & N. W.	Branch Adderley Pk. and New Str.
	P							Five Ways	Warwick..	Mid.	Church Road and New Street.
								Grand Junction	Warwick..	L. & N. W.— Mid.	New Street and Saltley.
G	P							Hag'ey Road	Warwick..	L. & N. W.	Harborne and Monument Lane.
G	P	F	L	H	C	5	0	Harborne	Warwick..	L. & N. W.	Branch from Monument Lane.
								Harborne	Warwick..	Mid.	See Somerset Road (for Harborne).
								Highgate Coal Wharf	Warwick..	Mid.	Camp Hill and Saltley.
G	P	F	L	H	C	25	0	Hockley	Warwick..	G. W.	Snow Hill and Soho.
G								Hockley Bas'n	Warwick..	G. W.	Near Hockley Station.
								Hockley Bonded Stores	Warwick..	G. W.	Hockley.
	P							Icknie'd Port Road	Warwick..	L. & N. W.	Harborne and Monument Lane.
G		F	L	H		20	0	Lawley Street	Warwick..	Mid.	Branch near Saltley.
								Lewis's, E. C., Siding	Warwick..	G. W.	Small Heath and Sparkbrook.
								Metropolitan Amalgamated Railway Carriage & Wagon Co.— Britannia Works (LNW)	Warwick..	L. & N. W.— Mid.	Adderley Park.
								Siding	Warwick..	L. & N. W.	Aston and Stechford.
								Works (Mid.)	Warwick..	Mid.—G.W.—L. & N. W.	Near Lawley Street.
								Midland Brick Co.'s Britannia Brick Works or Garrison Farm Siding	Warwick..	L. & N. W.	Adderley Park and New Street.
								Midland Railway Carriage & Wgn. Co.'s Wks (Mid.)	Warwick..	Mid.—G.W—.L.& N.W..	Near Lawley Street.
								Mitchell & Butler's Siding	Warwick..	L. & N. W.	Monument Lane and New Street.
								Mitchell's, Wm., Siding	Warwick..	Mid.	Near Lawley Street.
G	P	F				20	0	Monument Lane	Warwick..	L. & N. W.	New Street and Wolverhampton.
	P	F		H	C			New Street (L. & N. W. & Mid. Jt.)	Warwick..	{ L. & N. W. { Mid.	Coventry and Wolverhampton. Over L. & N. W. Line.

EXPLANATION—G *Goods Station.*   P *Passenger and Parcel Station.*   P* *Passenger, but not Parcel or Miscellaneous Traffic.*
F *Furniture Vans, Carriages, Portable Engines, and Machines on Wheels.*   L *Live Stock.*
H *Horse Boxes and Prize Cattle Vans.*   C *Carriages by Passenger Train.*

STATION ACCOMMODATION.						CRANE POWER.	STATIONS, &c.	COUNTY.	COMPANY.	POSITION.
						Tons Cwts.	BIRMINGHAM—continued.			
.	.	.	.	.	.	. .	New Street Junction.........	Warwick..	L. & N. W.— Mid.	New Street Station and Five Ways.
.	.	.	.	.	.	. .	Patent Enamel Co.'s Siding	Warwick..	Mid.	Selly Oak.
.	P	.	.	.	.	. .	Power, F.A., & Son's Siding	Warwick..	Mid.	Near Lawley Street.
G	P	.	.	.	.	. .	Rotton Park Road	Warwick..	L. & N. W.	Harborne and Monument Lane.
							Saltley......................	Warwick..	Mid.	Camp Hill and Whitacre.
							Saltley Carriage & Wagon Works (Mid.)	Warwick..	Mid.—G. W.	Saltley.
.	P	.	.	.	.	. .	Saltley Wharf................	Warwick..	Mid.	Saltley.
G	P	.	.	.	.	8 0	Small Heath & Sparkbrook	Warwick..	G. W.	Birmingham and Acocks Green.
.	P	F	L	H	C	. .	Small Heath Mileage Depôt	Warwick..	G. W.	Near Small Heath and Sparkbrook.
G	.	.	.	.	.	. .	Snow Hill....................	Warwick..	G. W.	Leamington and Wolverhampton.
.	P	.	.	.	.	. .	Soho Pool	Warwick..	L. & N. W.	Branch from Soho Road.
							Somerset Rd. (for Harborne)	Warwick..	Mid.	Church Road and Selly Oak.
							Sutton and Ash's Siding...	Warwick..	L. & N. W.	New Street and Monument Lane.
.	.	.	.	.	.	. .	Toy Siding...................	Warwick..	L. & N. W.	Monument Lane and Winson Green.
.	.	.	.	.	.	. .	Barton's Siding............	Warwick..	L. & N. W.	Toy Siding.
.	.	.	.	.	.	. .	Grice, Grice & Son's Sid.	Warwick..	L. & N. W.	Toy Siding.
.	.	.	.	.	.	. .	Piggott's Siding............	Warwick..	L. & N. W.	Toy Siding.
G	P	.	.	.	.	. .	Vauxhall and Duddeston ...	Warwick..	L. & N. W.	New Street and Lichfield.
							Watson, Todd & Co.'s Siding (L. & N. W.).....	Warwick..	L. & N. W.— Mid........	New Street and Monument Lane.
G	.	.	.	.	.	10 0	Windsor Street Wharf	Warwick..	L. & N. W.	Branch near Aston, Passengers.
.	P	.	.	.	.	. .	Winson Green...............	Warwick..	L. & N. W.	New Street and Wolverhampton.
.	.	.	.	.	.	. .	Wolseley Tool & Motor Car Co.'s Siding	Warwick..	L. & N. W.	Adderley Park.
.	.	.	.	.	.	. .	Wright & Eagle Range Sid.	Warwick..	L. & N. W.	Aston.
.	.	.	.	.	.	. .	Birmingham Carriage and Wagon Co.'s Siding	Cheshire...	B'head Jt. (G W & L N W)	Chester.
.	.	.	.	.	.	. .	Birmingham Carriage and Wagon Works.................	Staffs	G. W.	Handsworth and Smethwick.
							Birmingham Corporation—			
.	.	.	.	.	.	. .	Granary	Warwick..	Mid.	Birmingham, Central Station.
.	.	.	.	.	.	. .	Hollymoor Asylum Branch.	Worcester	Halesowen (G.W.& Mid.)	Rubery.
.	.	.	.	.	.	. .	Nechell's Gas Works	Warwick..	L. & N. W.	Birmingham, Curzon Street.
.	.	.	.	.	.	. .	Nechell's Gas Works (Mid.)	Warwick..	Mid.—G. W.	Birmingham, Lawley Street.
.	.	.	.	.	.	. .	Saltley Gas Department Siding (Mid.)	Warwick..	Mid.—G.W.—L. & N. W.	Birmingham, Saltley.
.	.	.	.	.	.	. .	Siding	Warwick..	L. & N. W.	Birmingham, Harborne.
.	.	.	.	.	.	. .	Water Works	Warwick..	Mid.	Whitacre.
.	.	.	.	.	.	. .	Water Works	Worcester	Halesowen (G. W. & Mid.)	Rubery.
.	.	.	.	.	.	. .	Windsor Street Gas Works } (L. & N. W.) .... }	Warwick..	L. & N. W. – Mid.	Birmingham, Windsor Str. Wharf.
.	.	.	.	.	.	. .	Birmingham Oxygen Co.'s Siding	Warwick..	Mid.	Birmingham, Lawley Street.
.	.	.	.	.	.	. .	Birmingham Tame and Rea Distr ct Drainage Board Sid	Warwick..	Mid.	Water Orton.
							Birmingham Wagon Co.'s Sid. (G. E.)	N'hampt n	G E—G N—L&NW—Mid	Peterboro'.
.	P*	.	.	.	.	. .	Birnie Road	Kinc'rdine	N. B.	Montrose and Bervie.
G	P	F	L	H	C	2 0	Birr	King's.....	G. S. & W.	Branch from Roscrea.
G	P	.	L	H	.	10 0	Birstal	Yorks	L. & N. W.	Branch from Batley.
.	.	.	.	.	.	. .	Kench's Siding	Yorks	L. & N. W.	Birstal and Carlinghow.
.	.	.	.	.	.	. .	Birstal	Yorks	G. N.	See Howden Clough (for Birstal).
.	.	.	.	.	.	. .	Birstal (Upper)	Yorks	L. & N. W.	See Upper Birstal.
.	.	.	.	.	.	. .	Birstall	Leicester..	G. C.	See Be'grave and Birstall.
G	P	F	L	H	C	5 0	Birstwith	Yorks	N. E.	Harrogate and Pateley Bridge.
G	P	F	L	H	C	5 0	Birtley	Durham ...	N. E.	Gateshead and Durham, Pass.
.	.	.	.	.	.	. .	Bewick Main Colliery	Durham ...	N. E.	Birtley.
.	.	.	.	.	.	. .	Birtley Brick & Tile Works	Durham ...	N. E.	Birtley.
.	.	.	.	.	.	. .	Birtley Grange Brick Wks.	Durham ...	N. E.	Birtley.
.	.	.	.	.	.	. .	Birtley Iron Works	Durham ...	N. E.	Birtley.
.	.	.	.	.	.	. .	Birtley Iron Wks. Gas Wks.	Durham ...	N. E.	Birtley.
.	.	.	.	.	.	. .	Black Fell Siding	Durham ...	N. E.	Birtley.
.	.	.	.	.	.	. .	Black House Siding	Durham ...	N. E.	Birtley.
.	.	.	.	.	.	. .	Blue Barns Manure Siding	Durham ...	N. E.	Birtley.
.	.	.	.	.	.	. .	Blythe's Brick Works	Durham ...	N. E.	Birtley.
.	.	.	.	.	.	. .	Durham Turnpike Depôts..	Durham ...	N. E.	Birtley.
.	.	.	.	.	.	. .	Eighton Banks Hauling Engine	Durham ...	N. E.	Birtley.
.	.	.	.	.	.	. .	Ouston Colliery "A" Pit and Gas Works	Durham ...	N. E.	Birtley.

EXPLANATION—G Goods Station.　　P Passenger and Parcel Station.　　P* Passenger, but not Parcel or Miscellaneous Traffic.
F Furniture Vans, Carriages, Portable Engines. and Machines on Wheels.　　L Live Stock.
H Horse Boxes and Prize Cattle Vans.　　C Carriages by Passenger Train.

STATION ACCOMMODATION.						CRANE POWER.		STATIONS, &c.	COUNTY.	COMPANY.	POSITION.
						Tons	Cwts				
								Birtley—*continued.*			
								Ouston Colliery "E" Pit (Birtley Colliery)	Durham ...	N. E.	Birtley.
								Ouston Grain Warehouse and Saw Mill	Durham ...	N. E.	Birtley.
								Ouston Manure Depôt	Durham ...	N. E.	Birtley.
								Ouston Road Coal Siding...	Durham ...	N. E.	Birtley.
								Pelaw Grange Saw Mill ...	Durham ...	N. E.	Birtley.
								Pelaw Grange Sid. & Depôts	Durham ...	N. E.	Birtley.
								Ravensworth Bk. & Tl. Wks.	Durham ...	N. E.	Birtley.
								Urpeth Collieries ("B" and "C" Pits) and Coke Ovens	Durham ...	N. E.	Birtley.
								White Hill Bank Head Sid.	Durham ...	N. E.	Birtley.
								White Hill Manure Depôts	Durham ...	N. E.	Birtley.
								Whitehouse Siding	Durham ...	N. E.	Birtley.
								Birtley Colliery	Durham ...	N. E.	Same as Ouston Col. "E" Pit (Birtley)
								Birtwistle & Co.'s Abbey Mill Siding	Lancs	L&Y&LU Jt (LY & LNW)	Withnell.
								Bishop & Co.'s Siding	Lancs	L. & N. W.	St. Helens.
								Bishop & Son's—			
								Cow Lane Malt Kiln	Notts	G. N. & Mid. Jt.	Newark.
								Spital Maltings	Notts	G. N. & Mid. Jt.	Newark.
G	P	F	L	H	C	10	0	Bishop Auckland	Durham ...	N. E.	Darlington and Crook.
								Cleveland Flour Mills	Durham ...	N. E.	Bishop Auckland.
								Lingford, Gardiner & Co.'s Engine Works.............	Durham ...	N. E.	Bishop Auckland.
								N. E. R. Permanent Way Shops.....................	Durham ...	N. E.	Bishop Auckland.
								N. E. R. Permanent Way Dept. New Shops............	Durham ...	N. E.	Bishop Auckland.
								South Church Siding.........	Durham ...	N. E.	Bishop Auckland.
								Stobart & Co 's Coal Depôt.	Durham ...	N. E.	Bishop Auckland.
								Tenters Street Depôts	Durham ...	N. E.	Bishop Auckland.
								Wilson's Forge & Steel Wks.	Durham ...	N. E.	Bishop Auckland.
								Bishop Auckland and District Gas Co.'s Siding.............	Durham ...	N. E.	Same as Fyland's Bridge Gas Works (West Auckland).
G	P					2	0	Bishopbriggs	Lanark ...	N. B.	Falkirk and Glasgow, Queen Street.
								Crowhill Brick Works	Lanark ...	N. B.	Bishopbriggs and Cowlairs.
								Hunter's Hill Quarry........	Lanark ...	N. B.	Bishopbriggs and Cowlairs.
								Turnbull's Siding	Lanark ...	N. B.	Bishopbriggs and Cowlairs.
								Bishophouse Junction	Yorks	N. E.	Pilmoor.
								Bishopley Cragg Siding	Durham ...	N. E.	Frosterley.
								Bishopley Quarry	Durham ...	N. E.	Frosterley.
								Bishopley Junction Siding ...	Durham ...	N. E.	Frosterley.
								Bishopley Lime Works........	Durham ...	N. E.	Frosterley.
								Bishop Middleham Quarry Sidings	Durham ...	N. E.	{ Ferryhill. { Sedgefield.
G	P	F	L	H	C			Bishopsbourne.................	Kent	S. E. & C.	Canterbury and Shorncliffe.
G	P	F	L	H	C	6	0	Bishop's Castle	Salop	Bishop's Castle	Terminus.
								Bishop's Castle Junction	Salop	Bishop's Castle—S& H Jt.	Same as Stretford Bridge Junc.
								Bishopsgate	Middlesex	G. E.	See London.
								Bishopsgate (Met.).............	Middlesex	Met.—G. W.	See London.
								Bishopsgate Junction	Middlesex	E. L. Jt.—G. E.	London, Shoreditch & Bishopsgate, Pass.
G	P	F	L	H	C	4	0	Bishops Lydeard	Somerset..	G. W.	Taunton and Watchet.
G	P		L			2	0	Bishop's Nympton & Molland	Devon ...	G. W.	Dulverton and South Molton.
								Bishop's Road Sta. & Junc....	Middlesex	G. W.—Met.	See London, Paddington.
								Bishop's Seat Siding............	Durham ...	N. E.	Parkhead.
G	P	F	L	H	C	7	0	Bishops Stortford.............	Herts	G. E.	London and Cambridge.
								Taylor & Son's Sids.—			
								Anchor Maltings............	Herts	G. E.	Bishops Stortford.
								South Mill	Herts	G. E.	Bishops Stortford.
								Bishopstoke..................	Hants	L. & S.W.	See Eastleigh and Bishopstoke.
G	P	F	L					Bishopstone.................	Sussex ...	L. B. & S. C.	Newhaven and Seaford.
G	P	F	L	H	C	5	0	Bishops Waltham	Hants	L. & S.W.	Branch from Botley.
								Edwards' Siding	Hants	L. & S.W.	Bishops Waltham.
G	P	F	L	H	C	2	0	Bishopton.....................	Renfrew...	Cal.	Paisley and Greenock.
								Bishopwearmouth Steam Mills	Durham ...	N. E.	Millfield.
G	P							Bispham.....................	Lancs	P. & W Jt. (L & Y & L&NW)	Blackpool, Talbot Road & Poulton.
								Bispham Hall Coal Co.'s Sid...	Lancs	L. & Y.	Orrell.
								Bitterley Siding	Salop	S & H Jt (G W & L & N W)	Ludlow.

EXPLANATION—**G** *Goods Station.*   P *Passenger and Parcel Station.*   P* *Passenger, but not Parcel or Miscellaneous Traffic.*
F *Furniture Vans, Carriages, Portable Engines, and Machines on Wheels.*   L *Live Stock.*
H *Horse Boxes and Prize Cattle Vans.*   C *Carriages by Passenger Train.*

STATION ACCOMMODATION.						CRANE POWER.	STATIONS, &c.	COUNTY.	COMPANY.	POSITION.
						Tons Cwts.				
G	P	.	.	.	.		Bittern	Hants	L. & S.W.	Southampton and Fareham.
G	P	F	L	H	C	1 10	Bitton	Glo'ster	Mid.	Mangotsfield and Bath.
.	P	.	.	.	.		Blaby	Leicester	L. & N. W.	Leicester and Nuneaton.
G	P	.	.	.	.	1 0	Black Bank	Cambs.	G. E.	Peterboro' and Ely.
.	.	.	.	.	.		Black Banks Chemical Works	Durham	N. E.	Darlington, Bank Top.
.	.	.	.	.	.		Blackbeck Siding	Lancs	Furness (Private)	Same as Dickson's Siding (Haverthwaite).
.	.	.	.	.	.		Black Boy Brick Works	Durham	N. E.	Shildon.
.	.	.	.	.	.		Black Boy Colliery	Durham	N. E.	Shildon.
.	.	.	.	.	.		Blackbraes Siding	Stirling	N. B.	See Almond Junction Station.
.	.	.	.	.	.		Blackbridge Siding	Herts	G. N.	Hatfield.
.	.	.	.	.	.		Blackbrook Branch	Lancs	L. & N. W.	Garswood and St. Helens Junction.
.	.	.	.	.	.		Blackbrook Colliery	Lancs	L. & N. W.	St. Helens.
G	P	.	.	.	.		Black Bull	Staffs	N. S.	Ford Green and Congleton.
							Chell Sidings—			
							Chatterley-Whitfield			
.	.	.	.	.	.		Collieries	Staffs	N. S.	Black Bull.
.	.	.	.	.	.		Tunstall Cl.& Ir.Co.'s Sid	Staffs	N. S.	Black Bull.
							Heath & Sons'—			
							Biddulph Valley Iron			
.	.	.	.	.	.		Works and Colliery	Staffs	N. S.	Black Bull.
.	.	.	.	.	.		Brown Lees Colliery	Staffs	N. S.	Black Bull.
.	.	.	.	.	.		Whitfield's Collieries	Staffs	N. S.	Black Bull.
.	.	.	.	.	.		Black Bull Siding	Yorks	N. E.	{ Marishes Road. Pickering.
							BLACKBURN—			
G	.	F	L	.	.	30 0	(Station)	Lancs	L. & N. W.	Branch—Blackburn (L. & Y.) and Cherry Tree Junction.
G	P	F	L	H	C	10 0			{ L. & Y.	Preston and Accrington.
.	P	F	.	H	C	. .	(Station, L. & Y.)	Lancs	{ L. & N. W.	Over L. & Y. from Cherry Tree Jn.
G	P	F	L	H	C	10 0			{ Mid.	Over L. & Y. Line.
.	.	.	.	.	.		Appleby & Son's Siding	Lancs	L. & Y.	Blackburn.
.	.	.	.	.	.		Aspden's Siding	Lancs	L. & Y.	Daisyfield Siding.
.	.	.	.	.	.		Clifton & Kersley Co.'s Sid.	Lancs	L. & Y.	Daisyfield Siding.
.	.	.	.	.	.		Corporation Sid. (L & Y)	Lancs	L. & Y.—L. & N. W.	Blackburn.
G	.	.	.	.	.	40 0	Daisyfield Siding	Lancs	L. & Y.	Blackburn.
.	.	.	.	.	.		Factory Hill Sid. (L. & Y.)	Lancs	L. & Y.—L. & N. W.	Blackburn.
.	.	.	.	.	.		Greenwood Sid. (L. & Y.)	Lancs	L. & Y.—L. & N. W.	Blackburn.
.	.	.	.	.	.		King's Str. Cl.Sids. (L.& Y.)	Lancs	L. & Y.—L. & N. W.	Blackburn.
							L. & Y. Co.'s Permanent			
.	.	.	.	.	.		Way Stores	Lancs	L. & Y.	Blackburn.
.	.	.	.	.	.		Wigan Cl. & Iron Co.'s Sid.	Lancs	L. & Y.	Blackburn.
.	.	.	.	.	.		Blackburn Foundry	Fife	N. B.	Whitemyre Junction Station.
.	.	.	.	.	.		Blackburn Siding	Stirling	N. B.	Dumgoyne.
.	.	.	.	.	.		Blackburn Valley Junction	Yorks	G. C.—Mid	Sheffield and Barnsley.
.	.	.	.	.	.		Blackbyres Junction	Renfrew	G. & S.W.	Potterhill and Barrhead.
.	.	.	.	.	.		Black Cabin Siding	Durham	N. E.	Waskerley.
.	.	.	.	.	.		Black, C., & Son's Siding	Yorks	Mid.	Sheffield, Queen's Road.
.	.	.	.	.	.		Black Carr Junction	Yorks	G. N.—G. N. & G. E. Jt.	Doncaster.
G	P	.	.	.	.		Black Dog Siding	Wilts	G. W.	Chippenham and Calne.
.	P*	.	.	.	.		Blackdyke	Cumb'land	N. B.	Carlisle and Silloth.
.	.	.	.	.	.		Blacker's Siding	Yorks	Axholme Jt. (L & Y & N E)	{ Eastoft. Reedness Junction.
.	.	.	.	.	.		Blackett Colliery	Northumb	N. E.	{ Bardon Mill. Haltwhistle.
.	.	.	.	.	.		Black Fell Siding	Durham	N. E.	Birtley.
.	.	.	.	.	.		Blackfield Depôts and Siding	Durham	N. E.	Tow Law.
G	P	F	L	H	C	1 10	Blackford	Perth	Cal.	Stirling and Perth.
.	.	.	.	.	.		Blackford Hill	Edinboro'	N. B.	See Edinburgh.
.	.	.	.	.	.		Blackfriars	Surrey	S. E. & C.	See London.
.	.	.	.	.	.		Blackfriars (Met. Dist.)	Middlesex	Met. Dist.—L. & N. W.	See London.
.	.	.	.	.	.		Blackfriars Junction	Surrey	S. E. & C.	London, Ludgate Hill & London Bge.
.	.	.	.	.	.		Blackhall Junction	Lanark	N. B.	Morningside and Crofthead.
.	.	.	.	.	.		Blackhall Weighs	Lanark	N. B.	Croftend and Morningside.
.	.	.	.	.	.		Blackheath	Worcester	G. W.	See Rowley Regis and Blackheath.
G	P	F	L	H	C	10 0	Blackheath	Kent	S. E. & C.	New Cross and Woolwich.
.	P	.	.	.	.		Blackheath Hill	Kent	S. E. & C.	Nunhead and Greenwich.
.	.	.	.	.	.		Blackheath Junction	Kent	S. E. & C.	Blackheath and Charlton.
G	P	F	L	H	C	5 0	Blackhill	Durham	N. E.	Rowley and Newcastle.
.	.	.	.	.	.		Blackhill Coal & Lime Depôt	Durham	N. E.	Blackhill.
.	.	.	.	.	.		Blackhill Drift	Durham	N. E.	Blackhill.
.	.	.	.	.	.		Bradley Coke Ovens	Durham	N. E.	Blackhill

EXPLANATION—G *Goods Station.*   P *Passenger and Parcel Station.*   P* *Passenger, but not Parcel or Miscellaneous Traffic.*
F *Furniture Vans, Carriages, Portable Engines, and Machines on Wheels.*   L *Live Stock.*
H *Horse Boxes and Prize Cattle Vans.*   C *Carriages by Passenger Train.*

STATION ACCOMMODATION.						CRANE POWER.		STATIONS, &c.	COUNTY.	COMPANY.	POSITION.
						Tons	Cwts				
								Blackhill—*continued.*			
..	..	..	..	..	..	..	.	Bradley Coebery Shops ...	Durham ...	N. E.	Blackhill.
..	..	..	..	..	..	..	.	Bunker's Hill Farm Depôt	Durham ...	N. E.	Blackhill.
								Consett Iron & Steel Wks., Furnaces, Mills, Shops and Stores	Durham ...	N. E.	Blackhill.
								Consett Iron Co.'s Granary.	Durham ...	N. E.	Blackhill.
								Consett Iron Wks. High Yd.	Durham ...	N. E.	Blackhill.
								Consett Iron Wks. Jn. Sid. (Consett Iron Works Low Yard)	Durham ...	N. E.	Blackhill.
								Crook Hall Foundry & Coke Ovens	Durham ...	N. E.	Blackhill.
								Crook Hall Slag Mill	Durham ...	N. E.	Blackhill.
								Delves Brick Works & Coke Ovens	Durham ...	N. E.	Blackhill.
								Derwent Colliery	Durham ...	N. E.	Blackhill.
								Hunter Colliery	Durham ...	N. E.	Blackhill.
								Medomsley Colliery	Durham ...	N. E.	Blackhill.
								Medomsley Edge Depôts ...	Durham ...	N. E.	Blackhill.
								Medomsley N. E. Railway Co.'s Depôt	Durham ...	N. E.	B'ackhill.
								Shotley Bridge Siding	Durham ...	N. E.	Blackhill.
								Templetown Coke, Ballast, Washing and Screening Works	Durham ...	N. E.	Blackhill.
..	..	..	..	..	..	..	.	Blackhill Brick Works	Lanark	N. B.	Summerston.
..	..	..	..	..	..	..	.	Blackhill Colliery	Lanark	N. B.	Summerston.
								Blackhill Gas Works	Lanark	Cal.—N. B.—G. & S. W.	Same as Provan Gas Wks. (Glasgow).
								Blackhill Junction	Lanark	Cal.	Glasgow.
								Blackhill Quarry	Kinc'rdine	Cal.	Cove.
								Black Horse Drove Siding ...	Norfolk	G. E.	See Hilgay.
G	.	.	.	.	.	.	}	Black Horse Road	Essex	{ Mid. / T & F G Jt. (LT&S & Mid)	} South Tottenham and Walthamstow.
.	P	.	.	.	.	.	}				
								Pearson & Co.'s Siding	Essex	Mid.	South Tottenham and Black Horse Road.
..	..	..	..	..	..	..	.	Black Horse Siding	Lancs	L. & N. W.	See Wigan Coal & Iron Co. (Wigan).
..	..	..	..	..	..	..	.	Blackhouse Junction	Ayr	G. & S. W.	Ayr and Auchincruive.
..	..	..	..	..	..	..	.	Black House Siding	Durham	N. E.	Birtley.
..	..	..	..	..	..	..	.	Blacklands Junction	Ayr	G. & S. W.	Irvine and Stevenston.
.	P	.	.	.	.	.		Black Lane	Lancs	L. & Y.	Bolton and Bury.
								Tootal, Broadhurst & Lee's Siding	Lancs	L. & Y.	Black Lane.
								Black Lion Crossing	Glamorg'n	T. V.	Same as Merthyr Vale Colliery (Merthyr Vale).
G	P	.	.	.	.	.		Black Mill	Glamorg'n	G. W.	Tondu and Nantymoel.
								Blackmill Siding (N.B.)	Stirling	N. B.—Cal.	Falkirk, Grahamston.
G	P	.	.	.	.	.		Blackmoor	Devon	Lyn. & Barns.	Barnstaple and Lynton.
								Blackmore's Siding	Notts	Mid.	Sutton-in-Ashfield.
.	P	.	.	.	.	.		Black Park Colliery	Denbigh	G. W.	Chirk.
								Blackpill	Glamorg'n	Swan. & Mum.	Mumbles Road and Mumbles.
								BLACKPOOL—			
.	P	.	.	.	.	.		Central	Lancs	P. & W. Jt. (L&Y & L&NW)	Branch from Kirkham.
								Corporation (Abattoir) Sid.	Lancs	P. & W. Jt. (L&Y & L&NW)	Talbot Road.
								Corporation Gas Siding	Lancs	P. & W. Jt. (L&Y & L&NW)	Central.
								Corporation Yard	Lancs	P. & W. Jt. (L&Y & L&NW)	Talbot Road.
G	P	.	.	.	C	3	0	South Shore, Lytham Road	Lancs	P. & W. Jt. (L&Y & L&NW)	Blackpool Central and Kirkham.
.	P	.	.	.	.	.		South Shore, Waterloo Rd.	Lancs	P. & W. Jt. (L&Y & L&NW)	Blackpool Central and Kirkham.
G	.	.	.	.	.	.		Stoney Hill Siding	Lancs	P. & W. Jt. (L&Y & L&NW)	Blackpool Central and Lytham.
G	P	F	L	H	C	10	0	Talbot Road	Lancs	P. & W. Jt. (L&Y & L&NW)	Branch from Poulton.
								Blackpool Street Mineral Yard	Cheshire	B'head Jt. (GW & L&NW)	Birkenhead.
								Black Prince Colliery	Durham	N. E.	Tow Law.
								Blackridge Colliery	Lanark	Cal.	Salisburgh.
.	P	.	.	.	.	.		Blackrock	Cork	C. B. & P.	Cork and Passage.
.	P	.	.	.	.	.		Blackrock	Dublin	D. W. & W.	Kingstown & Dublin, Westland Row.
								Black Rock Junction	Glamorg'n	T. V.	See Ocean Coal Co. (Ynysybwl).
								Black Rock Siding	Derby	L. & N. W.	Same as Drabble & Co.'s Siding (Steeplehouse).
								Black Rock Siding	Lancs	L. & N. W.	Mossley.
								Black Rock Siding	Pembroke	G. W.	Tenby.
G	P	.	L	H	.	10	0	Blackrod	Lancs	L. & Y.	Adlington and Bolton.
G	P	F	L	H	C	.	.	Blacksboat	Elgin & Mo'	G. N. of S.	Craigellachie and Boat of Garten.

EXPLANATION—G *Goods Station.*   P *Passenger and Parcel Station.*   P* *Passenger, but not Parcel or Miscellaneous Traffic.*
F *Furniture Vans, Carriages, Portable Engines, and Machines on Wheels.*   L *Live Stock.*
H *Horse Boxes and Prize Cattle Vans.*   C *Carriages by Passenger Train.*

STATION ACCOMMODATION.						CRANE POWER.		STATIONS, &c.	COUNTY.	COMPANY.	POSITION.
						Tons	Cwts				
								Black's Foundry	Durham	N. E.	Same as North Eastern Foundry (South Shields).
	P							Blackston	Stirling	N. B.	Slamannan and Bo'ness.
								Blackston Colliery	Stirling	N. B.	Blackston and Bowhouse.
								Blackston Weighs	Stirling	N. B.	Near Blackston.
								Blackstone & Co.'s Sid. (G.N.)	Lincoln	G. N.—L. & N.W.—Mid.	Same as Rutland Engineering Works (Stamford).
								Blackstone Brick Works	Renfrew	Cal.	Linwood.
								Blackstone Junction	Renfrew	Cal.	Paisley and Houston.
								Blackstone Mains Siding	Renfrew	Cal.	Linwood.
								Blackstone Sidings	Renfrew	Cal.	Linwood.
								Blacktongue Colliery No. 2	Lanark	N. B.	Rawyards.
								Black Vein Colliery	Mon	G. W.	Nantyglo.
								Black Vein Colliery (Old and New)	Mon	G. W.	Risca.
								Black Vein Colliery	Mon	L. & N. W.	Same as Graham Bros. & Co.'s Sid (Brynmawr).
								Blackwall	Middlesex	G. E.	See London.
								Blackwall Depôt	Middlesex	G. N.	Same as East India Docks Good Depôt and Coal Wharf (London)
G	P	F	L	H	C	4	0	Blackwater	I. of W	I. of W. Cent.	Newport and Sandown.
G	P							Blackwater and Yo.k Town	Hants	S. E. & C.	Guildford and Reading.
	P							Blackweir	Clare	West Clare	Miltown Malbay and Kilkee.
								Blackweir Siding	Glamorg'n	T. V.	Cardiff.
G	P							Blackwell	Derby	Mid.	See Westhouses and Blackwell.
								Blackwell	Worcester	Mid.	Birmingham and Bromsgrove.
								Blackwell Colliery Co.—			
								Alfreton Colliery	Derby	Mid.	Alfreton and South Normanton.
								"A" Winning Colliery	Derby	Mid.	Westhouses and Blackwell.
								"B" Winning Colliery	Derby	Mid.	Westhouses and Blackwell.
								Sutton Colliery	Notts	Mid.	Whiteboro'.
								Blackwell Colliery (G. C.)	Derby	G. C.—G. N.—L. & N. W.	Same as Winning "B" Colliery (Kirkby and Pinxton).
G	P	F	L	H	C	1	0	Blackwood	Lanark	Cal.	Branch Terminus nr. Tillietudlem.
								Blackwood Quarry	Lanark	Cal.	Branch near Blackwood.
								Dunduff Quarry	Lanark	Cal.	Branch near Blackwood.
								Kirkmuirhill Tile Works	Lanark	Cal.	Branch near Blackwood.
								Townhead Siding	Lanark	Cal.	Branch near Blackwood.
G	P		L					Blackwood	Mon	L. & N. W.	Nantybwch and Tredegar Junction, Station.
								Budd & Company's Marsh Siding	Mon	L. & N. W.	Argoed and Blackwood.
								Cwmgelly Siding	Mon	L. & N. W.	Argoed and Blackwood.
								Matthews' Libanus Colliery	Mon	L. & N. W.	Blackwood and Tredegar Junction.
								Rock Colliery	Mon	L. & N. W.	Argoed and Blackwood.
								Budd & Co.	Mon	L. & N. W.	Rock Colliery.
								Pond's	Mon	L. & N. W.	Rock Colliery.
								Treharne's Rock Foundry	Mon	L. & N. W.	Argoed and Blackwood.
G	P		L	H	C	1	10	Blacon	Cheshire	G. C.	Chester & Connah's Quay & Shotton.
								Bladen's Siding	Lanark	Cal.	Glasgow, Tollcross.
								Bladnoch Siding	Wigtown	P.P.&W.Jt.(Cal., G&SW, L. & N. W., & Mid.)	Wigtown and Kirkinner.
								Bladwell's Stone Siding	Somerset	Mid.	Bath.
								BLAENAU FESTINIOG—			
G	P	F	L	H	C	5	0	(Station)	Merioneth	{ G. W.	Branch from Bala Junction Station.
G	P	F	L	H	C					{ L. & N. W.	Branch from Llandudno Junc. Sta.
								Dinas Quarries Extension (Rhiwbryfdir)	Merioneth	Festiniog	Blaenau Festiniog.
								Duffws Quarries Extension	Merioneth	Festiniog	Blaenau Festiniog.
								Exchange Sidings	Merioneth	{ Festiniog—G. W.	Blaenau Festiniog.
										{ Festiniog—L. & N. W.	Blaenau Festiniog.
								Greaves' Siding	Merioneth	L. & N. W.	Blaenau Festiniog & Roman Bridge.
G	P		L		C			Junction Station	Merioneth	Festiniog	Tan-y-Grisiau and Duffws.
								Oakeley's—			
								Coronation Siding	Merioneth	L. & N. W.	Blaenau Festiniog & Roman Bridge.
								New York Siding	Merioneth	L. & N. W.	Blaenau Festiniog & Roman Bridge.
								Town	Merioneth	Festiniog	Same as Duffws.
								BLAENAVON—			
G	P	F	L	H	C	2	0	(Station)	Mon	G. W.	Branch from Pontypool.
G	P	F	L	H	C	1	0	(Station, L. & N. W.)	Mon	{ L. & N. W.	Abersychan and Brynmawr.
	P									{ G. W.	Over L. & N. W. from Abersychan and Talywain Junction.

EXPLANATION—G Goods Station.   P Passenger and Parcel Station.   P* Passenger, but not Parcel or Miscellaneous Traffic.
F Furniture Vans, Carriages, Portable Engines, and Machines on Wheels.   L Live Stock.
H Horse Boxes and Prize Cattle Vans.   C Carriages by Passenger Train.

STATION ACCOMMODATION.						CRANE POWER.	STATIONS, &c.	COUNTY.	COMPANY.	POSITION.
						Tons Cwts.	BLAENAVON—continued.			
.	.	.	.	.	.	. .	Blaenavon Iron Works—			
.	.	.	.	.	.	. .	Furnace (L. & N. W.)...	Mon	L. & N. W.— G. W.	Blaenavon and Waenavon.
.	.	.	.	.	.	. .	Tyre Mill (L. & N. W.)...	Mon	L. & N. W.—G. W.	Blaenavon and Waenavon.
.	.	.	.	.	.	. .	Vipond & Co.'s Varteg Hill Colliery	Mon	L. & N. W.	Blaenavon and Varteg.
.	.	.	.	.	.	. .	Blaenavon Branch	Glamorg'n	P. T.	Bch.—Cwmavon and Tonmawr Jn.
.	.	.	.	.	.	. .	Blaenavon Colliery	Glamorg'n	S. Wales Min.	Branch—Briton Ferry and Cymmer.
.	.	.	.	.	.	. .	Blaenavon Iron & Coal Co.—			
.	.	.	.	.	.	. .	Jaynes Branch	Mon	L. & N. W.	Brynmawr.
.	.	.	.	.	.	. .	Milfraen Hill Colliery ...	Mon	L. & N. W.	Brynmawr.
.	.	.	.	.	.	. .	Blaen-Cae-Gurwen Col. (Mid.)	Glamorg'n	Mid.—G.W.—L.& N.W / Mid.—G.W.—L.& N.W	Brynamman. (For Goods.) / Gurnos. (For Coal.)
.	.	.	.	.	.	. .	Blaen Cae Siding	Carnarvon	L. & N. W.	See Robinson's Slate Qry. (Nantlle).
.	.	.	.	.	.	. .	Blaenclydach	Glamorg'n	T. V.	See Trealaw.
.	.	.	.	.	.	. .	Blaenclydach Colliery	Glamorg'n	T. V.	Trealaw.
.	.	.	.	.	.	. .	Blaenclydach Mileage Siding	Glamorg'n	T. V.	Trealaw.
.	.	.	.	.	.	. .	Blaendare Brick Wks. & Cols.	Glamorg'n	G. W.	Blaendare Junction Station. / Pontypool.
G	.	.	.	.	.	. .	Blaendare Junction Station...	Mon	G. W.	Crumlin, High Level & Pontypool.
.	.	.	.	.	.	. .	Blaendare Brick Works & Collieries	Glamorg'n	G. W.	Branch from Trosnant Junction.
.	.	.	.	.	.	. .	Viaduct Works Siding	Mon	G. W.	Blaendare and Crumlin, High Level.
G	P	F	.	.	.	1 10	Blaengarw	Glamorg'n	G. W.	Branch from Brynmenyn.
.	.	.	.	.	.	. .	International Colliery	Glamorg'n	G. W.	Blaengarw.
.	.	.	.	.	.	. .	Ocean Colliery	Glamorg'n	G. W.	Blaengarw.
.	.	.	.	.	.	. .	Victoria Colliery	Glamorg'n	G. W.	Blaengarw.
.	.	.	.	.	.	. .	Blaengwawr Level Colliery ...	Glamorg'n	G. W.	Dare Junction.
G	P	.	L	H	.	7 0	Blaengwynfi	Glamorg'n	R. & S. B.	Port Talbot and Treherbert.
.	.	.	.	.	.	. .	Corrwg Rhondda Colliery..	Glamorg'n	R. & S. B.	Blaengwynfi.
.	.	.	.	.	.	. .	New Glyncorrwg Colliery...	Glamorg'n	R. & S. B.	Blaengwynfi.
.	.	.	.	.	.	. .	Blaennant Colliery	Glamorg'n	G. W.	Abernant.
G	P	.	L	H	.	7 0	Blaenrhondda	Glamorg'n	R. & S. B.	Port Talbot and Treherbert.
.	.	.	.	.	.	. .	Hendrewen Rhondda Col...	Glamorg'n	R. & S. B.	Blaenrhondda.
.	.	.	.	.	.	. .	Blaenrhondda Branch Junc.	Glamorg'n	T. V.	Near Treherbert.
.	.	.	.	.	.	. .	Blaenrhondda Colliery (North Dunraven Colliery)	Glamorg'n	T. V.	Treherbert.
.	.	.	.	.	.	. .	Blaensychan Colliery	Mon	G. W.	Pontnewynydd.
G	P	F	.	H	C	. .	Blagdon	Somerset..	G. W.	Branch from Congresbury.
.	.	.	.	.	.	. .	Bristol Water Wks. Co.'s Sid.	Somerset	G. W.	Blagdon.
G	P	.	L	H	.	2 0 } / 2 0 }	Blaina (G. W.)	Mon	G. W. / L. & N. W.	Aberbeeg and Nantyglo. / Over G. W. from Nantyglo Junc.
G	.	.	.	.	.	. .	Blaina Iron Wks.&Cols(GW)	Mon	G. W.—L. & N. W.	Blaina.
.	.	.	.	.	.	. .	Blaina Tin Plate Wks.(GW)	Mon	G. W.—L. & N. W.	Blaina.
.	.	.	.	.	.	. .	Lancaster & Co.—			
.	.	.	.	.	.	. .	Cinder Colliery (G. W.)...	Mon	G. W.—L. & N. W.	Blaina.
.	.	.	.	.	.	. .	Henwain Colliery (G.W.)	Mon	G. W.—L. & N. W.	Blaina.
.	.	.	.	.	.	. .	Lower Deep Col. (G.W.)	Mon	G. W.—L. & N. W.	Blaina.
.	.	.	.	.	.	. .	North Griffin Col. (G.W.)	Mon	G. W.—L. & N. W.	Blaina.
.	.	.	.	.	.	. .	South Griffin Col. (G.W.)	Mon	G. W.—L. & N. W.	Blaina.
.	.	.	.	.	.	. .	Pyle & Blaina Wks. (G.W.)	Mon	G. W.—L. & N. W.	Blaina. (For Outwards Traffic.)
.	.	.	.	.	.	. .	Stone's Sun or North Blaina Colliery (G. W.)	Mon	G. W.—L. & N. W.	Blaina. (For Outwards Traffic.)
.	.	.	.	.	.	. .	Blaina Wharf	Mon	A(N.&S. W.)D.&R.—GW	Newport, Alexandra Docks.
.	.	.	.	.	.	. .	Blainscough Colliery Co.—			
.	.	.	.	.	.	. .	Blainscough Colliery	Lancs	L. & N. W.	Coppull.
.	.	.	.	.	.	. .	Darlington Siding	Lancs	L. & N. W.	Coppull.
.	.	.	.	.	.	. .	Blainscough Hall Col. Co's Sid.	Lancs	P.&L. Jt. (L&NW.& L&Y)	Preston, Deepdale
.	.	.	.	.	.	. .	Blainscough Hall Siding	Lancs	P&WJt (L.&Y.& L.&N.W	Same as Rigby & Holmes' Siding (Kirkham).
G	P	F	L	H	C	2 0	Blairadam	Fife	N. B.	Dunfermline and Kinross Junction.
.	.	.	.	.	.	. .	Blairadam Colliery	Fife	N. B.	Kelty.
G	P	F	L	H	C	5 0	Blair Atholl	Perth	High	Dunkeld and Kingussie.
.	.	.	.	.	.	. .	Blair Branch Junction	Ayr	G. & S. W.	Dalry and Montgreenan.
.	.	.	.	.	.	. .	Blairenbathie Colliery	Fife	N. B.	Kelty.
.	.	.	.	.	.	. .	Blairenbathie Siding	Fife	N. B.	Kelty.
.	.	.	.	.	.	. .	Blairfordell Colliery	Fife	N. B.	Kelty.
.	.	.	.	.	.	. .	Blair Foundry	Ayr	G. & S. W.	Hurlford.
G	P	F	L	H	C	4 10	Blairgowrie	Perth	Cal.	Branch Terminus nr. Coupar Angus.
.	P*	.	.	.	.	. .	Rosemount	Perth	Cal.	Coupar Angus and Blairgowrie.
.	.	.	.	.	.	. .	Blairhall Colliery	Fife	N. B.	East Grange.
.	.	.	.	.	.	. .	Blairhill and Gartsherrie	Lanark	N. B.	See Coatbridge.

EXPLANATION—G Goods Station.   P Passenger and Parcel Station.   P* Passenger, but not Parcel or Miscellaneous Traffic.
F Furniture Vans, Carriages, Portable Engines, and Machines on Wheels.   L Live Stock.
H Horse Boxes and Prize Cattle Vans.   C Carriages by Passenger Train.

STATION ACCOMMODATION.						CRANE POWER.		STATIONS, &c.	COUNTY.	COMPANY.	POSITION.
						Tons	Cwts.				
.	.	.	.	.	.	.	.	Blairingone Colliery and Fire Clay Works	Kinross ...	N. B.	Dollar.
.	.	.	.	.	.	.	.	Blairmuckhill Colliery	Lanark	N. B.	Same as Barblues No. 10 Colliery (Westcraigs).
.	.	.	.	.	.	.	.	Blair, Nos. 2 and 9.	Ayr	G. & S. W.	Dalry.
.	.	.	.	.	.	.	.	Blair, No. 4	Ayr	G. & S. W.	Dalry.
.	.	.	.	.	.	.	.	Blair, Nos. 5 and 7	Ayr	G. & S. W.	Dalry.
.	.	.	.	.	.	.	.	Blair's Engineering Works and Depôts	Durham ...	N. E.	Stockton, North Shore.
.	.	.	.	.	.	.	.	Blair's Sheer Legs Siding ...	Durham ...	N. E.	Stockton, North Shore.
G	P	F	.	H	C	.	.	Blakedown	Worcester	G. W.	See Churchill and Blakedown.
G	P†	.	.	.	.	4	0	Blake Hall	Essex	G. E.	Loughton and Ongar.
.	.	.	.	.	.	.	.	Blakeney	Glo'ster ...	G. W.	Branch from Awre Junction.
.	.	.	.	.	.	.	.	Forest of Dean Navigation Colliery	Glo'ster ...	G. W.	Branch from Awre Junction.
G	P	.	L	H	.	.	.	Howbeach Colliery	Glo'ster ...	G. W.	Branch from Awre Junction.
.	.	.	.	.	.	.	.	Blakesley	N'hamptn	E. & W. Ju.	Greens Norton and Byfield.
.	.	.	.	.	.	.	.	Blakesley's New Premier Brk. and Pipe Works	Leicester..	Mid.	Glenfield.
.	.	.	.	.	.	.	.	Blakesley's Coronet Brick Co.'s Siding	Derby	A&N Jt. (L&NW&Mid.)	Measham.
G	P	.	L	H	.	5	0	Blake Street	Warwick..	L. & N. W.	Birmingham and Lichfield.
.	P	.	.	.	.	.	.	Blakey Junction Sidings	Yorks	N. E.	Rosedale, East.
.	.	.	.	.	.	.	.	Blanchardstown	Dublin	M. G. W.	Dublin and Clonsilla.
.	.	.	.	.	.	.	.	Bland & Co.'s Siding	Glamorg'n	GW—L.N.W—Rhy—TV	Cardiff.
G	P	F	L	H	C	10	0	Bland & Co.'s Timber Yard..	Somerset..	S.&D.Jt.(L.&S.W.&Mid)	Highbridge.
.	.	.	.	.	.	.	.	Blandford	Dorset	S.&D.Jt.(L.&S.W.&Mid)	Wimborne and Templecombe.
G	P	F	L	H	C	1	10	Bland's Timber Yard	Glamorg'n	G. W.	Cardiff.
.	.	.	.	.	.	.	.	Blanefield	Stirling ...	N. B.	Lennoxtown and Killearn.
G	P	F	L	H	C	1	10	Blanefield Printing Co.'s Sid.	Stirling ...	N. B.	Branch from Blanefield.
G	P	.	.	.	.	3	0	Blankney and Metheringham	Lincoln	G. N. & G. E. Jt.	Lincoln and Sleaford.
.	.	.	.	.	.	.	.	Blantyre	Lanark ...	Cal.	Hamilton and Newton.
.	.	.	.	.	.	.	.	Blantyre Foundry	Lanark ...	Cal.	Blantyre.
.	.	.	.	.	.	.	.	Blantyre Oil Works (Stonefield Oil Works)	Lanark ...	Cal.	Blantyre.
.	.	.	.	.	.	.	.	Blantyre Saw Mills	Lanark ...	Cal.	Blantyre.
.	.	.	.	.	.	.	.	Bothwell Castle Cols., Nos. 3 & 4	Lanark ...	Cal.	Blantyre and Newton.
.	.	.	.	.	.	.	.	Craighead Colliery	Lanark ...	Cal.	Hamilton (West) and Blantyre.
.	.	.	.	.	.	.	.	Blantyre Branch Junction ...	Lanark ...	N. B.	Bothwell and Burnbank.
.	.	.	.	.	.	.	.	Blantyre Collieries	Lanark ...	Cal.	High Blantyre.
.	.	.	.	.	.	.	.	Blantyre Colliery	Lanark ...	N. B.	Hamilton, Burnbank.
.	.	.	.	.	.	.	.	Blantyre Co-operative Society's Siding	Lanark ...	Cal.	High Blantyre.
.	.	.	.	.	.	.	.	Blantyre Ferme Colliery	Lanark ...	Cal.	Uddingston.
.	.	.	.	.	.	.	.	Blantyre Junction	Lanark ...	Cal.	Hamilton (West) and Blantyre.
G	P	.	.	.	.	.	.	Blarney	Cork	C. & Muskerry	Branch from Coachford Junction.
G	P	.	.	H	.	.	.			G. S. & W.	Cork and Mallow.
G	P	F	L	H	C	5	0	Blaydon (N. E.)	Durham	N. E.	Hexham and Newcastle.
										N. B.	Over N. E. from Hexham.
.	.	.	.	.	.	.	.	Addison Col. & Coke Ovens	Durham ...	N. E.	Blaydon.
.	.	.	.	.	.	.	.	Alexander's Bottle Works..	Durham ...	N. E.	Blaydon.
.	.	.	.	.	.	.	.	Anglo American Oil Co.'s Sid.	Durham ...	N. E.	Blaydon.
.	.	.	.	.	.	.	.	Blaydon Burn Collieries ...	Durham ...	N. E.	Blaydon.
.	.	.	.	.	.	.	.	Blaydon Burn Depôts	Durham ...	N. E.	Blaydon.
.	.	.	.	.	.	.	.	Blaydon Burn High Bk. Wks.	Durham ...	N. E.	Blaydon.
.	.	.	.	.	.	.	.	Blaydon Burn Low Bk. Wks.	Durham ...	N. E.	Blaydon.
.	.	.	.	.	.	.	.	Blaydon Burn Village Depôt	Durham ...	N. E.	Blaydon.
.	.	.	.	.	.	.	.	Blaydon Engine Sheds	Durham ...	N. E.	Blaydon.
.	.	.	.	.	.	.	.	Blaydon Forge Works	Durham ...	N. E.	Blaydon.
.	.	.	.	.	.	.	.	Blaydon Goods Marshalling Sidings	Durham ...	N. E.	Blaydon.
.	.	.	.	.	.	.	.	Blaydon Haugh Coke Ovens	Durham ...	N. E.	Blaydon.
.	.	.	.	.	.	.	.	Blaydon Haugh Rd. Siding	Durham ...	N. E.	Blaydon.
.	.	.	.	.	.	.	.	Blaydon Iron Works	Durham ...	N. E.	Blaydon.
.	.	.	.	.	.	.	.	Blaydon Manure and Alkali Co.'s Works	Durham ...	N. E.	Blaydon.
.	.	.	.	.	.	.	.	Blaydon Mineral Marshalling Sidings	Durham ...	N. E.	Blaydon.
.	.	.	.	.	.	.	.	Blaydon Saw Mills Depôt ...	Durham ...	N. E.	Blaydon.
.	.	.	.	.	.	.	.	Globe Ir. Wks (Douglas Bros.)	Durham ...	N. E.	Blaydon.
.	.	.	.	.	.	.	.	Greenside Colliery	Durham ...	N. E.	Blaydon.

EXPLANATION—G *Goods Station.*   P *Passenger and Parcel Station.*   P* *Passenger, but not Parcel or Miscellaneous Traffic.*

P† *Parcels only.*   F *Furniture Vans, Carriages, Portable Engines, and Machines on Wheels.*   L *Live Stock.*

H *Horse Boxes and Prize Cattle Vans.*   C *Carriages by Passenger Train.*

STATION ACCOMMODATION.						CRANE POWER.	STATIONS, &c.	COUNTY.	COMPANY.	POSITION.
						Tons Cwts.	Blaydon (N. E.)—continued.			
·	·	·	·	·	·	· ·	Harriman's Sanitary Pipe Works	Durham ...	N. E.	Blaydon.
·	·	·	·	·	·	· ·	Hoyles' Lamp Black Works	Durham ...	N. E.	Blaydon.
·	·	·	·	·	·	· ·	Nicholson's Timber Yard...	Durham ...	N. E.	Blaydon.
·	·	·	·	·	·	· ·	Pioneer Foundry (Smith, Patterson & Co.)	Durham ...	N. E.	Blaydon.
·	·	·	·	·	·	· ·	Renshaw's Metal Refinery	Durham ...	N. E.	Blaydon.
·	·	·	·	·	·	· ·	Stargate Col. & Brick Wks.	Durham ...	N. E.	Blaydon.
·	·	·	·	·	·	· ·	Stella Coal Co.'s Emma or Towneley Col. & Depôts..	Durham ...	N. E.	Blaydon.
·	·	·	·	·	·	· ·	Blaydon Main Colliery and Coke Ovens	Durham ...	N. E.	Derwenthaugh.
·	·	·	·	·	·	· ·	Bleachfield Siding (Craig's Cooperage Siding) (N.B.)..	Stirling	N. B.—Cal.	Falkirk, Grahamston.
·	P	·	·	·	·	· ·	Bleadon and Uphill	Somerset..	G. W.	Yatton and Highbridge.
·	P	·	·	·	·	· ·	Bleak Hills Siding	Notts	Mid.	See Duke of Portland's (Mansfield).
G	P	·	·	·	·	· ·	Bleasby	Notts	Mid.	Lincoln and Nottingham.
G	P	·	·	·	·	· ·	Bledlow	Bucks	G. W.	Thame and Princes R.sboro'.
G	P	F	L	H	C	2 0	Blencow	Cumb'land	C. K. & P. (L. & N. W. & N. E. Working Cos.)	Penrith and Keswick.
·	·	·	·	·	·	· ·	Blencowe & Co.'s Brewery	Staffs	L. & N. W.	Cannock.
G	P	F	L	H	C	5 0	Blenheim and Woodstock	Oxon	G. W.	Branch from Kidlington Junction.
·	·	·	·	·	·	· ·	Blenkinsopp's Collieries	Northumb	N. E.	Same as Byron Cols. (Greenhead).
·	P	·	·	·	·	· ·	Blennervil e	Kerry	T. & D.	Tralee and Castlegregory Junction.
G	P	F	L	H	C	· ·	Bletchington	Oxon	G. W.	Oxford and Banbury.
G	P	F	L	H	C	5 0	Bletchley	Bucks	L. & N. W.	Blisworth and Watford.
·	·	·	·	·	·	· ·	Blewitt & Co.'s Quinton Col.	Staffs	L. & N. W.	Wyrley and Church Bridge.
G	P	·	L	·	·	· ·	Blidworth and Rainworth	Notts	Mid.	Mansfield and Southwell.
·	·	·	·	·	·	· ·	Bliss & Son's Siding	Oxon	G. W.	Chipping Norton.
							BLISWORTH—			
G	P	F	L	H	C	5 0	(Station)	N'hampton	L. & N. W.	Bletchley and Rugby.
G	P	·	L	H	·	· ·	(Station, N. & B. Jn.)	N'hampton	{ N. & B. Jn. / E. & W. Jn.	Blisworth Junction. / Over N. & B. Jn. from Greens Norton Junction.
·	·	·	·	·	·	· ·	Gayton Sidings	N'hampton	L. & N. W.	Blisworth and Weedon.
·	·	·	·	·	·	· ·	Brown & Butcher's North ampton Brick and Tile Co.'s Siding	N'hampton	L. & N. W.	Gayton Sidings.
·	·	·	·	·	·	· ·	King's Blisworth and Stowe Brick and Tile Works	N'hampton	L. & N. W.	Gayton Sidings.
·	·	·	·	·	·	· ·	Sparrow's Siding	N'hampton	L. & N. W.	Gayton Sidings.
·	·	·	·	·	·	· ·	Junction	N'hampton	L. & N. W.—N. & B. Jn.	Northampton and Towcester.
·	·	·	·	·	·	· ·	Phipps (Exors.) Siding	N'hampton	L. & N. W.	Blisworth and Northampton.
·	·	·	·	·	·	· ·	Wheldon's Sid. (N & B Jn.)	N'hampton	N. & B. Jn.—L. & N. W.	Blisworth and Towcester.
·	·	·	·	·	·	· ·	Blisworth & Stowe Brick and Tile Works	N'hampton	L. & N. W.	Same as King's Siding (Blisworth, Gayton Sidings).
·	·	·	·	·	·	· ·	Blochairn	Lanark ..	N. B.	See Glasgow.
·	·	·	·	·	·	· ·	Blochairn Iron & Steel Works (Steel Co. of Scotland's Wks)	Lanark ...	Cal.	Glasgow, Buchanan Street.
·	·	·	·	·	·	· ·	Blochairn Iron & Steel Works (Steel Co. of Scotland's Works) (N.B.)	Lanark ...	N. B.—G. & S. W.	Glasgow, Blochairn.
·	·	·	·	·	·	· ·	Blochairn Sand Quarry (N.B.)	Lanark ...	N. B.—G. & S. W.	Glasgow, Blochairn.
·	·	·	·	·	·	· ·	Blochairn Siding	Lanark ...	Cal.	Glasgow, Buchanan Street.
G	P	·	L	H	·	1 10	Blockley	Worcester	G. W.	Oxford and Worcester.
·	·	·	·	·	·	· ·	Blockley's Siding (L.&N. W.)	Warwick..	L. & N. W.—Mid.	Same as Hawkesbury and Bedworth Brick & Tile Co.'s Siding.
·	·	·	·	·	·	· ·	Blockley's Hadley Lodge Sid.	Salop	L. & N. W.	Wombridge.
·	·	·	·	·	·	· ·	Blocksage's, T., Siding	Cheshire..	G. C.	See Victoria Sid. (Newton, for Hyde).
G	P	·	L	·	·	· ·	Blodwell Junction Station	Salop	Cam. (Tanat Valley)	Porthywaen and Llangynog.
·	·	·	·	·	·	· ·	Blodwell Junctions	Salop	Ca.n—Cam(Tanat Valley)	Nantmawr and Llanyblodwell.
·	P	·	·	·	·	· ·	Bloomfield	Down	B. & C. D.	Belfast and Knock.
·	·	·	·	·	·	· ·	Bloomfield	Staffs	G. W.	Same as Princes End.
·	·	·	·	·	·	· ·	Bloomfield Basin	Staffs	L. & N. W.	See Tipton.
·	·	·	·	·	·	· ·	Bloomfield Forge	Lanark ..	Cal.	Shieldmuir.
·	·	·	·	·	·	· ·	Blotoft Siding	Lincoln	G. N. & G. E. Jt.	Helpringham.
·	·	·	·	·	·	· ·	Blowers Green Colliery	Worcester	G. W.	Netherton.
G	P	·	L	H	·	1 5	Blowick	Lancs	L. & Y.	Southport and Burscough Bridge.
·	·	·	·	·	·	· ·	L. & Y. Co.'s Permanent Way Stores	Lancs	L. & Y.	Blowick.

EXPLANATION—G Goods Station.   P Passenger and Parcel Station.   P* Passenger, but not Parcel or Miscellaneous Traffic.
F Furniture Vans, Carriages, Portable Engines, and Machines on Wheels.   L Live Stock.
H Horse Boxes and Prize Cattle Vans.   C Carriages by Passenger Train.

STATION ACCOMMODATION.						CRANE POWER.	STATIONS, &c.	COUNTY.	COMPANY.	POSITION.
						Tons Cwts.	Blowick—*continued.*			
							Southport Gas Works	Lancs	L. & Y.	Blowick.
							Blowith Siding	Yorks	N. E.	Rosedale, East.
							Blows Down Siding	Beds	G. N.	Dunstable.
G	P	F	L	H	C	5 0	Bloxham	Oxon	G. W.	Kings Sutton and Chipping Norton.
							Bloxholme Siding	Lincoln	G. N. & G. E. Jt.	Digby.
G	P	F	L	H	C	12 0	Bloxwich	Staffs	L. & N. W.	Rugeley and Walsall.
							Bird & Nicholls' Siding	Staffs	L. & N. W.	Birchills and Bloxwich.
							Bunch & Son's Staffordshire Iron Works	Staffs	L. & N. W.	Birchills and Bloxwich.
							Delaville Spelter Co.'s Sid.	Staffs	L. & N. W.	Birchills and Bloxwich.
							Essington Farm Col. Co.'s Spring Hill Colliery	Staffs	L. & N. W.	Bloxwich and Wyrley
							Holly Bank (Essington) Col.	Staffs	L. & N. W.	Bloxwich and Wyrley.
							Norton Cannock Colliery	Staffs	L. & N. W.	Bloxwich and Wyrley.
							Norton Cannock Col., No. 2	Staffs	L. & N. W.	Bloxwich and Wyrley.
							Parker & Son's Siding	Staffs	L. & N. W.	Birchills and Bloxwich.
							Russell & Co.'s Birchills Blast Furnaces	Staffs	L. & N. W.	Birchills and Bloxwich.
							Thomas' Brick Works	Staffs	L. & N. W.	Birchills and Bloxwich.
							Thomas' Hatherton Blast Furnaces	Staffs	L. & N. W.	Birchills and Bloxwich.
							Turner's Tramway Siding	Staffs	L. & N. W.	Bloxwich.
							Walsall Glue Co.'s Siding	Staffs	L. & N. W.	Birchills and Bloxwich.
	P						Blucher Pit	Northumb	N. E.	Lemington.
							Blue Anchor	Somerset	G. W.	Watchet and Minehead.
							Blue Barns Manure Siding	Durham	N. E.	Birtley.
							Blue Bell Colliery	Northumb	N. E.	Holywell.
							Blue Bell Co-operative Siding	Northumb	N. E.	Holywell.
G	P		L				Bluestone	Norfolk	Mid. & G. N. Jt.	Melton Constable and North Walsham Town.
							Blundell & Son's Sid. (L&NW)	Lancs	L. & N. W.—G. W.	Warrington, Bank Quay.
G	P					4 0	Blundell, J., & Son's Siding	Lancs	L. & Y.	Liverpool, Marsh Lane & Strand Rd.
	P						Blundellsands and Crosby (L. & Y.)	Lancs	{ L. & Y. { L. & N. W.	Liverpool and Southport. Over L. & Y. from Bootle Junc.
G	P		L	H		1 5	Blundell's Siding	Lancs	L. & Y.	Pemberton.
							Blunham	Beds	L. & N. W.	Bedford and Cambridge.
G	P					5 0	Beeson's Siding	Beds	L. & N. W.	Blunham and Sandy.
G	P	F	L	H	C		Blunsdon	Wilts	M. & S. W. Jn.	Swindon Town and Cirencester.
G	P	F	L	H	C	10 0	Bluntisham	Hunts	G. E.	Ely and St. Ives.
							Blyth	Northumb	N. E.	Branch from Newsham.
							Albion Brick & Tile Works	Northumb	N. E.	Blyth.
							Anglo-American Oil Co.'s Siding	Northumb	N. E.	Blyth.
							Blyth Brick Works (Links Road Siding)	Northumb	N. E.	Blyth.
							Blyth Gas Co.'s Siding	Northumb	N. E.	Blyth.
							Blyth Shipbuilding Co's Sid.	Northumb	N. E.	Blyth.
							Cowpen Colliery & Depôts	Northumb	N. E.	Blyth.
							Cowpen Mill Pit	Northumb	N. E.	Blyth.
							Import Dock Siding	Northumb	N. E.	Blyth.
							Northern Counties Electric Works	Northumb	N. E.	Blyth.
G	P	F	L	H	C	5 0	Blyth Bridge	Staffs	N. S.	Stoke and Uttoxeter.
							Foxfield Colliery	Staffs	N. S.	Blyth Bridge.
G	P						Blythburgh	Suffolk	Southwold	Wenhaston and Walberswick.
							Blythe's Brick Works	Durham	N. E.	Birtley.
							Blythe's Siding	Lancs	L. & Y.	Church and Oswaldtwistle.
G	P	F	L	H	C		Blyton (for Corringham)	Lincoln	G. C.	Gainsboro' and Brigg.
							Jeffery's Malt Kiln	Lincoln	G. C.	Blyton (for Corringham).
							Boam, J., & Co.'s Brick Yard	Lincoln	Mid.	Edmondthorpe and Wymondham.
							Boam's, Joseph, Siding	Norfolk	Mid. & G. N. Jt.	Gayton Road.
							Board of Police Sidings	Lanark	Cal.	Glasgow, Buchanan Street.
							Board's Siding	Somerset	S.&D. Jt. (L.&S.W.&Mid)	Bridgwater.
G	P		L	H		1 10	Board's Siding	Somerset	S.&D. Jt. (L.&S.W.&Mid)	Edington Junction Station.
	P						Boarhills	Fife	N. B.	Anstruther and St. Andrews.
	P						Boar's Head	Lancs	{ L&Y&LUJt(LY&LNW) { L. & N. W.	Boar's Head Junc. and Blackburn. Preston and Wigan.
							Boar's Head Junction	Lancs	L&Y.&L.U.Jt.—L.N.W.	Red Rock and Wigan.
G	P	F	L	H	C	1 10	Boat of Garten Station & Junc.	Inverness	{ G. N. of S. { High.	Branch from Craigellachie. Aviemore and Forres.
							Boazman's, H., Siding	Cumb'land	Mid.	Newbiggin.

EXPLANATION—G *Goods Station.*   P *Passenger and Parcel Station.*   P* *Passenger, but not Parcel or Miscellaneous Traffic.*
F *Furniture Vans, Carriages, Portable Engines, and Machines on Wheels.*   L *Live Stock.*
H *Horse Boxes and Prize Cattle Vans.*   C *Carriages by Passenger Train.*

STATION ACCOMMODATION.						CRANE POWER.		STATIONS, &c.	COUNTY.	COMPANY.	POSITION.
						Tons	Cwts.				
.	.	.	.	.	.			Bobbers Mill Siding (W. Richards & Son's)	Notts	Mid.	Nottingham, Radford.
G	P	F	L	H	C	5	0	Boddam	Aberdeen	G. N. of S.	Branch from Ellon.
G	P	.	L	H		5	0	Bodfari	Flint	L. & N. W.	Denbigh and Mold.
G	P	.	.	.				Bodiam (for Staplecross and Ewhurst)	Sussex	K. & E. S.	Robertsbridge and Tenterden Town.
G	P	F	L	H	C	5	0 }	Bodmin	Cornwall	{ G. W.	Bodmin Road and Wadebridge.
G	P	F	L	H	C	2	0 }			{ L. & S. W.	Branch from Wadebridge.
.	.	.	.	.	.			Anglo-American Oil Co.'s Depôt	Cornwall	G. W.	Bodmin.
G	P	F	L	H	C	8	0	Bodmin Road Sta. and Junc.	Cornwall	G. W.	Plymouth and Truro.
G	P	F	L	H	C	1	10	Bodorgan	Anglesey	L. & N. W.	Bangor and Holyhead.
.	.	.	.	.	.			Boedryngallt Colliery	Glamorg'n	T. V.	See Davis & Son's Ferndale No. 3 Col.
.	.	.	.	.	.			Bog Coal Depôts	Cumb'land	N. E.	Carlisle.
.	.	.	.	.	.			Bog Coke Ovens	Cumb'land	N. E.	{ Brampton Junction. / Lambley.
.	.	.	.	.	.			Bog Colliery	Lanark	Cal.	Larkhall.
.	.	.	.	.	.			Bogend Pit	Ayr	Cal.	Kilwinning.
.	.	.	.	.	.			Bogend Siding	Ayr	Cal.—G. & S. W.	Kilwinning.
.	.	.	.	.	.			Boghead Brick Works	L'lithgow	N. B.	Armadale.
.	.	.	.	.	.			Boghead Colliery	L'lithgow	N. B.	Bathgate, Upper.
.	.	.	.	.	.			Bog Junction	Cumb'land	Car. Goods Tfc. Com.—M. & C.—N. E.	Carlisle.
.	.	.	.	.	.			Boglehole Sid. (Bellfield Sid.)	Edinboro'	N. B.	See Musselburgh.
G	P	F	L	H	C	10	0	Bognor	Sussex	L. B. & S. C.	Branch from Barnham Junction.
.	P	.	.	.	.			Bogside	Ayr	Cal.	Kilwinning and Irvine.
.	.	.	.	.	.			Bogside	Ayr	G. & S. W.	See Irvine.
G	P	.	L	H		1	5	Bogside	Fife	N. B.	Alloa and Dunfermline.
.	.	.	.	.	.			Bogside Colliery	Ayr	Cal.	Kilwinning.
.	.	.	.	.	.			Bogside Pit	Ayr	G. & S. W.	Kilwinning,
.	.	.	.	.	.			Bogside Pit (Craig's)	Ayr	G. & S. W.	Gatehead.
.	.	.	.	.	.			Bogside Sand Lye	Ayr	G. & S. W.	Irvine.
.	.	.	.	.	.			Bog Siding	Cumb'land	N. E.	Carlisle.
.	.	.	.	.	.			Bog Siding	Hadding'n	N. B.	Ormiston.
.	.	.	.	.	.			Bogston	Renfrew	Cal.	See Greenock.
.	.	.	.	.	.			Bogton Quarry	Lanark	Cal.	Thorntonhall.
G	P	F	L	H	C			Boher	Limerick	G. S. & W.	Tipperary and Limerick.
.	.	.	.	.	.			Bolckow, Vaughan & Co.'s Iron Works and Wharf	Yorks	N. E.	Middlesbro'.
.	.	.	.	.	.			Bold	Lancs	L. & N. W.	See Farnworth and Bold.
.	.	.	.	.	.			Bold Colliery	Lancs	L. & N. W.	See Collins Green Col. Co. (Earlestown)
.	.	.	.	.	.			Bold Hall Estate Siding	Lancs	L. & N. W.	See Wigan Cl. & Ir. Co. (St. Helens).
G	.	.	.	.	.			Boldon	Durham	N. E.	Washington and Tyne Dock.
.	.	.	.	.	.			Hedworth Lane Siding	Durham	N. E.	Boldon.
.	.	.	.	.	.			Hylton Lane Depôt & Sid.	Durham	N. E.	Boldon.
.	.	.	.	.	.			Boldon Brick Works	Durham	N. E.	Brockley Whins.
.	.	.	.	.	.			Boldon Colliery	Durham	N. E.	Brockley Whins.
.	.	.	.	.	.			Bold Venture Lime Siding	Lancs	L. & Y.	Chatburn.
.	.	.	.	.	.			Bold Venture Siding	Derby	Mid.	See United Alkali Co. (Peak Forest).
.	.	.	.	.	.			Bollihope Quarry	Durham	N. E.	Frosterley.
G	P	.	.	H	.	5	0	Bollington	Cheshire	Mac. Com.(G. C. & N. S.)	Romiley and Macclesfield.
G	P	F	L	H	C	3	0 }	Bolsover	Derby	{ L. D. & E. C.	Chesterfield and Langwith Junction.
G	P	.	L	.	.	0	10 }			{ Mid.	Staveley Town and Pleasley.
.	.	.	.	.	.			Bolsover Colliery	Derby	L. D. & E. C.	Branch from Bolsover.
.	.	.	.	.	.			Bolsover Col. & Brick Wks.	Derby	Mid.	Doe Lea Branch.
.	.	.	.	.	.			Home Grown Fruit Preserving Co.'s Siding	Derby	L. D. & E. C.	Bolsover.
.	.	.	.	.	.			Markham Col. (L.D.&E.C.)	Derby	L. D. & E. C.—G. E.	Branch from Bolsover.
.	.	.	.	.	.			Bolsover Colliery Co.—Creswell Colliery (Mid.)	Derby	Mid.—G. C.	Elmton and Creswell.
.	.	.	.	.	.			Crown Farm Sidings	Notts	Mid.	Mansfield.
.	.	.	.	.	.			Boltgate Siding	Yorks	Axholme Jt (L & Y & N E)	Luddington.
								BOLTON—			
.	P	F	.	H	C			(Station)	Lancs	L. & N. W.	Branch from Kenyon Junction.
G	P	F	L	H	C	40	0	(Station, L. & Y.)	Lancs	{ L. & Y. / Mid.	Manchester and Preston. / Over L. & Y. Line.
.	.	.	.	.	.			Astley and Tyldesley Coal and Salt Co.'s Siding	Lancs	L. & N. W.	Lever Street Yard.
.	.	.	.	.	.			Bolton Iron & Steel Co.'s Siding	Lancs	L. & N. W.	Bolton.
.	.	.	.	.	.			Bradshaw Gate Siding	Lancs	L. & Y.	Bolton.
G	.	.	.	.	.	1	10	Bridgeman Street	Lancs	L. & N. W.	Branch from Kenyon Junction.

EXPLANATION—G *Goods Station.*   P *Passenger and Parcel Station.*   P* *Passenger, but not Parcel or Miscellaneous Traffic.*
F *Furniture Vans, Carriages, Portable Engines, and Machines on Wheels.*   L *Live Stock.*
H *Horse Boxes and Prize Cattle Vans.*   C *Carriages by Passenger Train.*

STATION ACCOMMODATION.						CRANE POWER.	STATIONS, &c.	COUNTY.	COMPANY.	POSITION.
						Tons Cwts.	BOLTON—continued.			
.	.	.	.	.	.	. .	Bullfield Gas Siding	Lancs	L. & Y.	Bolton.
.	.	.	.	.	.	5 10	Bullfield Manure Siding ...	Lancs	L. & Y.	Bolton.
G	.	.	.	.	.	10 0	Bullfield Siding	Lancs	L. & Y.	Bolton and Lostock Junction.
.	.	.	.	.	.	. .	Burnden Siding	Lancs	L. & Y.	Bolton.
.	.	.	.	.	.	. .	Clive Street Siding	Lancs	L. & Y.	Bolton.
							Corporation—			
.	.	.	.	.	.	. .	Gas Works	Lancs	L. & Y.	Bullfield Siding.
.	.	.	.	.	.	. .	Gas Works	Lancs	L. & Y.	Craddock Lane Siding.
.	.	.	.	.	.	. .	Siding	Lancs	L. & Y.	Bullfield Siding.
.	.	.	.	.	.	. .	Siding	Lancs	L. & Y.	Craddock Lane Siding.
.	.	.	.	.	.	. .	Siding	Lancs	L. & Y.	Lostock Jn. Sta. & Red Moss Jn.
.	.	.	.	.	.	. .	Craddock Lane Gas Siding	Lancs	L. & Y.	Bolton.
G	.	.	.	.	.	10 0	Craddock Lane Manure Sid.	Lancs	L. & Y.	Bolton.
G	.	F	L	.	.	20 0	Craddock Lane Siding	Lancs	L. & Y.	Bolton and The Oaks.
G	.	F	L	.	.	. .	Crook Street	Lancs	L. & N. W.	Branch from Kenyon Junction.
.	.	.	.	.	.	. .	Deansgate.....................	Lancs	L. & N. W.	Branch from Kenyon Junction.
.	.	.	.	.	.	. .	Earl Bradford's Siding	Lancs	L. & Y.	Bolton.
.	.	.	.	.	.	. .	Fletcher, Burrows & Co.'s Siding	Lancs	L. & N. W.	Bolton.
.	.	.	.	.	.	. .	Garswood Hall Colliery Co.'s Siding............	Lancs	L. & Y.	Bolton.
.	.	.	.	.	.	. .	Hulton Colliery Co.'s Siding	Lancs	L. & N. W.	Bolton.
.	.	.	.	.	.	. .	Knowles & Son's Siding.....	Lancs	L. & Y.	Bolton.
.	.	.	.	.	.	. .	L. & Y. Co.'s Permanent Way Stores	Lancs	L. & Y.	Bolton.
.	.	.	.	.	.	. .	L. & Y. Wgn. Dept.'s Sid.	Lancs	L. & Y.	Bolton.
.	.	.	.	.	.	. .	Lecturers Close and Hulme Trust Siding	Lancs	L. & N. W.	Bolton.
.	.	.	.	.	.	. .	Briggs' Coal Yard	Lancs	L. & N. W.	Lecturers Close & Hulme Trust Sid.
.	.	.	.	.	.	. .	Earl of Ellesmere's Cols.	Lancs	L. & N. W.	Lecturers Close & Hulme Trust Sid.
.	.	.	.	.	.	. .	Hick, Hargreaves & Co.'s Soho Iron Works	Lancs	L. & N. W.	Lecturers Close & Hulme Trust Sid.
.	.	.	.	.	.	. .	Ramsden's Siding	Lancs	L. & N. W.	Lecturers Close & Hulme Trust Sid.
.	.	.	.	.	.	. .	Roscoe's Siding	Lancs	L. & N. W.	Lecturers Close & Hulme Trust Sid.
.	.	.	.	.	.	. .	Walmsley's Siding........	Lancs	L. & N. W.	Lecturers Close & Hulme Trust Sid.
G	.	.	.	.	.	10 0	Lever Street Yard............	Lancs	L. & N. W.	Branch from Kenyon Junction.
.	.	.	.	.	.	. .	Locomotive Siding	Lancs	L. & Y.	Bolton.
.	.	.	.	.	.	. .	Magee, Marshall & Co.'s Sid	Lancs	L. & N. W.	Bolton.
G	P	.	.	.	.	. .	Mayor Street Siding........	Lancs	L. & Y.	Bolton.
.	.	.	.	.	.	. .	Rumworth and Daubhill ...	Lancs	L. & N. W.	Bolton and Kenyon Junction.
.	.	.	.	.	.	. .	Wagon Works	Lancs	L. & Y.	Bolton.
.	.	.	.	.	.	. .	Walmsley's Atlas Forge Iron Works	Lancs	L. & N. W.	Bolton.
.	.	.	.	.	.	. .	Wigan Coal & Iron Co.'s Sid.	Lancs	L. & Y. — L. & N. W. ...	Bolton.
G	P	F	L	H	C	1 10	Bolton	Yorks	Mid.	See Wath and Bolton.
							Bolton Abbey	Yorks	Mid.	Skipton and Ilkley.
.	.	.	.	.	.	. .	Duke of Devonshire's Hambleton Siding	Yorks	Mid.	Near Bolton Abbey.
.	.	.	.	.	.	. .	Hambleton Quarries (J. Green & Son)	Yorks	Mid.	Near Bolton Abbey.
G	P	F	L	H	C	1 10	Bolton-le-Sands	Lancs	L. & N. W.	Lancaster and Penrith.
.	P	.	.	H	C	. .	Bolton-upon-Dearne (S&K Jt)	Yorks	S. & K. Jt. (Mid. & N. E.)	Swinton Junction and Moorthorpe.
.	P	.	.	.	.	. .		Yorks	G. C.	Over S. & K. Jt. from Swinton Jn.
G	P	F	L	H	C	. .	Hickleton Main Col. (S&KJt)	Yorks	S. & K. Jt.—G. C.	Near Bolton-upon-Dearne.
.	P	.	.	H	C	. .			N. E.	York and Leeds.
.	P	.	.	.	.	. .	Bolton Percy (N.E.)	Yorks	G. C.	Ov. N E fr. Knottingley Ferry Bge. Jn.
.	P	.	.	.	.	. .			G. N.	Over N. E. and S. & K. Jt. Lines.
.	P	.	.	.	.	. .			Mid.	Ov. NE fr. Knottingley Ferry Bge. Jn.
.	.	.	.	.	.	. .	Bolton's Copper Works.........	Staffs	N. S.	{ Froghall. { Oakamoor.
.	.	.	.	.	.	. .	Bolton Street (Bury)............	Lancs	L. & Y.	Same as Bury, High Level Station.
.	.	.	.	.	.	. .	Bolton, T., & Son's Mersey Copper Works	Lancs	L. & N. W.—S. & M. Jt.	Widnes.
.	.	.	.	.	.	. .	Boltsburn Depôt & Siding ...	Durham ...	N. E.	Parkhead.
.	.	.	.	.	.	. .	Boltslaw Siding	Durham ...	N. E.	Parkhead.
.	.	.	.	.	.	. .	Bomford's Siding	Worcester	G. W.	Fladbury.
G	P	F	L	H	C	3 0	Bonar Bridge	Ross & Cro'	High	Tain and Golspie.
G	P	F	L	H	C	5 0	Boncath	Pembroke	G. W.	Whitland and Cardigan.
.	.	.	.	.	.	. .	Mercantile Co.'s Siding	Pembroke	G. W.	Boncath.
.	.	.	.	.	.	. .	Bond End Branch (Mid.)......	Staffs	Mid—L&NW—G N—N S	Burton-on-Trent.
.	.	.	.	.	.	. .	Bond End Wharf (Mid.)	Staffs	Mid—L&NW—G N—N S	Burton-on-Trent.

EXPLANATION—G *Goods Station.*   P *Passenger and Parcel Station.*   P* *Passenger, but not Parcel or Miscellaneous Traffic.*
F *Furniture Vans, Carriages, Portable Engines, and Machines on Wheels.*   L *Live Stock.*
H *Horse Boxes and Prize Cattle Vans.*   C *Carriages by Passenger Train.*

STATION ACCOMMODATION.						CRANE POWER.		STATIONS, &c.	COUNTY.	COMPANY.	POSITION.
						Tons	Cwts.	Bond's Foundry	Durham	N. E.	Tow Law.
								Bond's Main Colliery	Derby	{ L. D. & E. C.	Arkwright Town.
										{ Mid.	Hasland.
								Bond's Main Colliery (G. C.)	Derby	G. C.—G. N.—L. & N. W.	Grassmoor.
								Bond Street	Middlesex	C. L.	See London.
								Bone Phosphate Chemical Co. —			
								Siding	Flint	L. & N. W.	See Muspratt's Siding (Flint).
								Siding	Lancs	L. & N. W.	Widnes.
								Bo'NESS—			
G	P	F	L	H	C	5	0	(Station)	L'thgow	N. B.	Manuel and Bo'ness Harbour.
								Bo'ness Distillery (Calder's Distillery)	L'thgow	N. B.	Bo'ness and Kinniel.
G						3	0	Bo'ness Harbour and Dock	L'thgow	N. B.	Branch from Manuel.
								Bridgeness Colliery	L'thgow	N. B.	Branch from Bo'ness.
								Bridgeness Pott'ry (McNay's Pottery)	L'thgow	N. B.	Bridgeness Branch.
								Bryson & Co.'s Wood Yard	L'thgow	N. B.	Bo'ness and Kinniel.
								Calder, Dixon & Co.'s Wood Yard	L'thgow	N. B.	Bo'ness and Kinniel.
								Denholm & Co.'s Wood Yd.	L'thgow	N. B.	Bo'ness and Kinniel.
								Dk Foundry (Bo'ness Pott'ry)	L'thgow	N. B.	Bridgeness Branch.
								Donaldson's Wood Yard	L'thgow	N. B.	Bo'ness.
								Forth Bank Foundry	L'thgow	N. B.	Bridgeness Branch.
								Forth Chemical Manure Wks (Oven's Chemical Works)	L'thgow	N. B.	Bo'ness and Kinniel.
								Grange Colliery	L'thgow	N. B.	Bridgeness Branch.
								Grange Foundry	L'thgow	N. B.	Bridgeness Branch.
								High Junction	L'thgow	N. B.	Polmont and Manuel.
G			L					Junction Station	L'thgow	N. B.	Linlithgow and Falkirk.
								Kennedy & Co.'s Wood Yard	L'thgow	N. B.	Bo'ness and Kinniel.
								Kinniel Colliery	L'thgow	N. B.	Bo'ness and Manuel.
								Love and Stewart's—			
								Foundry Wood Yard	L'thgow	N. B.	Bridgeness Branch.
								Grangepans Wood Yard	L'thgow	N. B.	Bridgeness Branch.
								Station Wood Yard	L'thgow	N. B.	Bo'ness.
								Low Junction	L'thgow	N. B.	Bo'ness Junction Station & Bo'ness.
								Northern Trading Co.'s Sid.	L'thgow	N. B.	Bo'ness and Kinniel.
								Smith, Marshall, & Co.'s Wood Yard	L'thgow	N. B.	Bo'ness and Kinniel.
								Snab Siding	L'thgow	N. B.	Bo'ness and Kinniel.
								Thomson & Balfour's Wood Yard	L'thgow	N. B.	Bridgeness Branch.
								Timber Pond Siding	L'thgow	N. B.	Near Bo'ness Siding.
								Tod's Mill Siding	L'thgow	N. B.	Manuel and Kinniel.
								West Lothian Pottery	L'thgow	N. B.	Bridgeness Branch.
								Bo'ness Pottery Siding	L'thgow	N. B.	Same as Dock Foundry (Bo'ness).
								Bonhill Siding (N. B.)	Dumbartn	N. B.—Cal.	See Jamestown.
								Bon Lea Foundry	Yorks	N. E.	Stockton, South.
								Bonnington	Edinboro'	Cal.—N. B.	See Leith.
								Bonnington Bond Siding	Edinboro'	N. B.	Leith, Bonnington.
								Bonnington, East Junction	Edinboro'	N. B.	Edinburgh.
								Bonnington, North Junction	Edinboro'	N. B.	Leith.
								Bonnington, South Junction	Edinboro'	N. B.	Edinburgh.
								BONNYBRIDGE—			
G	P		L	H	C	3	0	(Station)	Stirling	Cal.	Branch near Greenhill.
G	P		L	H		2	0	(Station, E. & G.)	Stirling	N. B.	Falkirk & Lenzie Junction Station.
								Bonnybridge Foundry	Stirling	Cal.	Bonnybridge.
								Smith & Wellstood Siding	Stirling	Cal.	Bonnybridge Foundry.
								Ure's Foundry	Stirling	Cal.	Bonnybridge Foundry.
								Bonnybridge Silica Co.'s Sid. (Griffith's Bk. Works)	Stirling	N. B.	Bonnybridge and Castlecary.
G								Bonnymuir Siding	Stirling	Cal.	Greenhill and Larbert.
								Bonnyrigg Colliery	Stirling	K. & B. Jt. (Cal. & N. B.)	Bonnybridge, Central and Denny-loanhead.
								Bonnyside Brick Works (Dougall's)	Stirling	N. B.	Near Bonnybridge.
								Broomrigg Col. (Denny-loanhead Col.)	Stirling	K. & B. Jt. (Cal. & N. B.)	Bonnybridge, Central and Denny-loanhead.
G	P		L	H		2	0	Central	Stirling	K. & B. Jt. (Cal. & N. B.)	Kilsyth and Bonnywater Junction.
								Milnquarter Brick Works (Stein's Brick Works)	Stirling	N. B.	Bonnybridge and Castlecary.
								Woodlea Siding (Lochview Foundry)	Stirling	N. B.	Bonnybridge.

EXPLANATION—G *Goods Station.*   P *Passenger and Parcel Station.*   P* *Passenger, but not Parcel or Miscellaneous Traffic.*
F *Furniture Vans, Carriages, Portable Engines, and Machines on Wheels.*   L *Live Stock.*
H *Horse Boxes and Prize Cattle Vans.*   C *Carriages by Passenger Train.*

G	P	F	L	H	C	Tons	Cwts	STATIONS, &c.	COUNTY.	COMPANY.	POSITION.
								Bonnymuir Siding	Stirling	Cal.	See Bonnybridge.
G	P	F	L			1	10	Bonnyrigg	Edinboro'	N. B.	Hardengreen and Peebles.
								Hopefield Sid.(Polton No. 1)	Edinboro'	N. B.	Bonnyrigg and Hawthornden.
								Philip's Siding	Edinboro'	N. B.	Bonnyrigg and Hawthornden.
								Polton No. 2 Colliery	Edinboro'	N. B.	Near Bonnyrigg.
								Bonnyrigg Colliery	Stirling	K. & B. Jt. (Cal. & N. B.)	Bonnybridge, Central.
								Bonnyside Bk Wks (Dougall's)	Stirling	N. B.	Bonnybridge (E. & G.)
								Bonnyton Fire Clay Works	Ayr	G. & S.W.	Kilmarnock.
								Bonnyton Pit	Ayr	G. & S.W.	Kilmarnock.
								Bonnywater Junction	Stirling	Cal.—K. & B. Jt.	Larbert and Bonnybridge, Central.
								Bonshaw Brick Works	Dumfries	Cal.	Kirtlebridge.
G	P			H	C			Bontnewydd	Merioneth	G. W.	Bala and Dolgelley.
								Bonville's Court Colliery	Pembroke	G. W.	Saundersfoot.
								Booker's Siding	Berks	G. W.	Steventon.
G	P	F	L	H	C	2	0	Bookham	Surrey	L. & S.W.	Leatherhead and Guildford.
G	P		L			5	0	Boosbeck	Yorks	N. E.	Middlesbro' and Loftus.
								Carr's Tilery & Brick Wks.	Yorks	N. E.	Boosbeck.
								Petch's Siding	Yorks	N. E.	Boosbeck.
								South Skelton Mines	Yorks	N. E.	Boosbeck.
								Stanghow Depôts	Yorks	N. E.	Boosbeck.
								Stanghow Mines	Yorks	N. E.	Boosbeck.
								Wilkinson's Siding	Yorks	N. E.	Boosbeck.
G	P		L					Boot	Cumb'land	R. & E.	Terminus.
	P							Booterstown	Dublin	D. W. & W.	Kingstown & Dublin, Westland Row.
								Bootham Junction	Yorks	N. E.	York and Stamford Bridge.
								Boothorpe Pipe Co.'s Sid. (Mid.)	Leicester	Mid.—L. & N. W.	Woodville.
								Boothstown	Lancs	L. & N.W.	See Ellenbrook (for Boothstown).
G	P	F	L	H	C	5	0	Bootle	Cumb'land	Furness	Millom and Sellafield.
								Bootle (Balliol Road)	Lancs	L. & N.W.	See Liverpool.
								Bootle (L. & Y.)	Lancs	L. & Y.—L. & N. W.	See Liverpool.
								Bootle Junction	Lancs	L. & Y.—L. & N. W.	Liverpool.
								Bopeep Junction	Sussex	L. B. & S. C.—S. E. & C.	St. Leonards.
								Borax Consolidated Works	Flint	W. M. & C. Q.	Same as Wepre Wks. (Connahs Quay).
								Border Counties Chemical Works (Maxwell & Co.'s)	Cumb'land	N. B.	Silloth.
								Border Counties Junction	Northumb	N. E.	Near Hexham.
								Border Siding	Forfar	Cal.	Leysmill.
								Bordesley	Warwick'	G. W.	See Birmingham.
								Bordesley Junction	Warwick	G. W.—Mid.	Birmingham.
								Borestone Siding	Ayr	G. & S.W.	Dalry.
								Boro' Green	Kent	S. E. & C.	See Wrotham and Boro' Green.
								Borough	Surrey	C. & S. L.	See London.
G	P	F	L	H	C	5	0	Boroughbridge	Yorks	N. E.	Pilmoor and Knaresboro'.
								Humberton Siding	Yorks	N. E.	Boroughbridge.
								Roecliffe Siding	Yorks	N. E.	Boroughbridge.
								Borough Foundry	Durham	N. E.	South Shields.
								Borough Market Junction	Surrey	S. E. & C.	London, Cannon Str. & London Bge.
								Borough Road (S. E. & C.)	Surrey	SE&C–GN–L&SW–Mid.	See London.
G	P		L	H				Borris	Carlow	G. S. & W.	Bagnalstown and Palace East.
G	P*							Borrobol	Sutherl'nd	High.	Kinbrace and Kildonan.
								Borron & Co.'s Bottle Works	Lancs	L. & N.W	Earlestown.
								Borron & Co.'s Glass Bottle Wks. (Newton-le-Willows)	Lancs	G. C. (St. Helens Exten.)	Ashton-in-Makerfield.
G	P	F	L	H	C			Borrowash	Derby	Mid.	Derby and Trent.
G	P	F		H	C			Borrows & Sons' Siding	Lancs	L. & N.W.	St. Helens.
G	P	F	L	H	C	3	0	Borth	Cardigan	Cam.	Aberystwyth and Machynlleth.
G	P	F	L	H	C			Borwick	Lancs	Fur. & Mid. Jt.	Carnforth and Arkholme.
								Boscarne Junction	Cornwall	G. W.—L. & S. W.	Bodmin, G.W., & Bodmin, L. & S.W.
G	P		L	H		1	8	Boscombe	Hants	L. & S. W.	See Bournemouth.
G	P							Bosham	Sussex	L. B. & S. C.	Chichester and Havant.
								Bosley	Cheshire	N. S.	Macclesfield and Leek.
								Bostock & Co.'s Siding	Lancs	L. & N.W.	Garston Docks.
G	P	F	L	H	C	5	0	Boston	Lincoln	G. N.	Peterboro' and Grimsby.
								Boston Gas Co.'s Siding	Lincoln	G. N.	Boston.
								Cooper & Son's Siding	Lincoln	G. N.	Boston.
								Sherwin's Brick Siding	Lincoln	G. N.	Boston.
								Simonds & Son's Siding	Lincoln	G. N.	Boston.
G		F				15	0	Boston Dock	Lincoln	G. N.	Branch—Boston and Kirton.
	P							Boston Road (for Brentford and Hanwell)	Middlesex	Met. Dist.	South Ealing and Osterley.
								Boston Spa	Yorks	N. E.	Same as Thorp Arch.

EXPLANATION—G *Goods Station.* P *Passenger and Parcel Station.* P* *Passenger, but not Parcel or Miscellaneous Traffic.*
F *Furniture Vans, Carriages, Portable Engines, and Machines on Wheels.* L *Live Stock.*
H *Horse Boxes and Prize Cattle Vans.* C *Carriages by Passenger Train.*

STATION ACCOMMODATION.						CRANE POWER.		STATIONS, &c.	COUNTY.	COMPANY.	POSITION.
						Tons	Cwts.				
..	..	..	..	..	..			Botanic Gardens.................	Lanark ...	Cal.	See Glasgow.
..	..	..	..	..	..			Botanic Gardens.................	Yorks ...	N. E.	See Hull.
..	..	..	..	..	..			Botanic Gardens Junction ...	Yorks ...	N. E.	Hull.
G	P	F	L	H	C	3	0	Bothwell	Lanark ...	Cal.	Branch near Fallside.
G	P	F	L	H	C	3	0			N. B.	Shettleston and Hamilton.
..	..	..	..	..	..			Bothwell Castle Colliery ...	Lanark ...	N.B.	Bothwell.
..	..	..	..	..	..			Craighead Colliery...........	Lanark ...	N.B.	Bothwell and Burnbank.
..	..	..	..	..	..			Bothwell Castle Cols. Nos. 3 & 4	Lanark ...	Cal.	Blantyre.
..	..	..	..	..	..			Bothwell Junction	Lanark ...	N. B.	Bothwell and Bellshill.
..	..	..	..	..	..			Bothwell Park Brick Works..	Lanark ...	Cal.	Uddingston.
..	..	..	..	..	..			Bothwell Park Colliery.......	Lanark ...	Cal.	Uddingston.
..	..	..	..	..	..			Bothwell Park Colliery.......	Lanark ...	N. B.	Bellshill.
..	..	..	..	..	..			Bothwell Park Quarry	Lanark ...	Cal.	Uddingston.
..	..	..	..	..	..			Bothwell Sidings	Lanark ...	N. B.	Coatbridge, Whifflet.
..	..	..	..	..	..			Bothwell Top Sidings	Lanark ...	N. B.	Coatbridge, Whifflet.
..	..	..	..	..	..			Bothy Siding (N. B.)	Stirling ...	N. B.—Cal.	Falkirk, Grahamston.
G	P	F	L	H	C	2	0	Botley	Hants ...	L. & S.W.	Eastleigh and Fareham.
..	..	..	..	..	..			Knowle Siding	Hants ...	L. & S.W.	Botley.
..	..	..	..	..	..			Botolph Bridge Siding	N'hamptn	G. N.	Peterboro'.
G	P	F	L	H	C	..	..	Bottesford	Leicester..	G. N.	Grantham and Nottingham.
..	..	..	..	..	..			Denton Siding..............	Lincoln ...	G. N.	Branch—Bottesford & Sedgebrook.
..	..	..	..	..	..			Welby's Siding	Lincoln ...	G. N.	Branch—Bottesford & Sedgebrook.
..	..	..	..	..	..			Woolsthorpe Siding	Leicester..	G. N.	Branch—Bottesford & Sedgebrook.
..	..	..	..	..	..			Bottesford, North Junction...	Leicester..	G. N.—G N & L & NWJt	Newark and Melton Mowbray.
..	..	..	..	..	..			Bottesford, South Junction...	Leicester..	G. N.—G N & L & N W Jt	Newark and Melton Mowbray.
..	..	..	..	..	..			Botteslow Junction	Staffs	N. S.	Berry Hill and Bucknall.
G	P	F	L	H	C	..	..	Bottisham and Lode	Cambs......	G. E.	Cambridge and Fordham.
..	..	..	..	..	..			Bottle House Point Ship Yard (Sir Raylton Dixon & Co.)	Yorks	N. E.	Middlesbro'.
..	..	..	..	..	..			Bottom Hall Siding	Yorks	L. & N. W.	Same as Shaw's Siding (Huddersfield).
..	..	..	..	..	..			Bottom's Mill	Lancs	L. & N. W.	Same as Mayall's Siding (Mossley).
..	..	..	..	..	..			Boucher's Siding	Glamorg'n	T. V.	Cadoxton.
G	P	F	L	H	C	4	0	Boughrood	Radnor ...	Cam.	Llanidloes and Three Cocks.
G	P	F	L	H	C	3	0	Boughton	Notts	L. D. & E. C.	Langwith Junction and Tuxford.
..	..	..	..	..	..			Boultham Gate Siding	Lincoln ...	Mid.	Lincoln.
..	..	..	..	..	..			Boultham Junction	Lincoln ...	G. N. & G. E. Jt.	Lincoln.
..	..	..	..	..	..			Boulton, A., & Co...............	Salop	G. W.	Much Wenlock.
..	..	..	..	..	..			Boulton & Co.'s Siding........	Staffs	N. S.	Same as Port Vale Sid. (Longport).
..	..	..	..	..	..			Boundary Road Stone Depôt	Lancs	L. & N. W.	See St. Helens Corporation Sidings (St. Helens).
G	P	F	L	H	C	10	0	Bourne (G. N.)	Lincoln ...	G. N.	Essendine and Sleaford.
										Mid.	Over G. N. from Bourne West Jn.
										Mid. & G. N. Jt...........	Over G. N. from Bourne Junctions.
..	..	..	..	..	..			Bourne Brick & Tile Co.'s Siding (M. & G. N. Jt.)	Lincoln ...	Mid. & G. N. Jt.—G. N.	Bourne.
..	..	..	..	..	..			South Lincolnshire Brk. and Tile Co.'s Keeble's Siding	Lincoln ...	Mid. & G. N. Jt.	Bourne.
..	..	..	..	..	..			Bourne Junctions	Lincoln ...	G. N.—Mid. & G. N. Jt.	Essendine and Spalding.
G	P	F	L	H	C	1	10	Bourne End.......................	Bucks......	G. W.	Maidenhead and High Wycombe.
..	..	..	..	..	..			Thomas & Green's Siding ..	Bucks......	G. W.	Bourne End and Wooburn Green.
								BOURNEMOUTH—			
G	P	..	..	..	..			Boscombe	Hants	L. & S.W.	Christchurch and Bournemouth.
..	..	..	..	..	..			Bourne Valley Sid. (L.S.W.)	Dorset......	L. & S.W.—S. & D. Jt....	Bournemouth, West.
..	P	..	..	..	..			Branksome (L. & S. W.) ...	Dorset......	L. & S.W.	Bournemouth (West) and Poole.
										S & DJt.(L&SW& Mid.)	Over L. & S.W. from Broadstone Jn.
..	..	..	..	..	..			Branksome Junction.........	Dorset......	L. & S.W.	Branksome & Bournemouth, Central.
G	..	..	..	..	..			Branksome Sidings	Hants	L. & S.W.	Bournemouth, West.
G	P	F	L	H	C	10	0	Central	Hants	L. & S.W.	Christchurch & Bournemouth, West.
..	..	..	..	..	..			Gas Works Junction	Hants	L. & S.W.	Bournemouth (Central) & Branksome.
..	..	..	..	..	..			Pottery Siding..................	Dorset......	L. & S.W.	Branksome Junction.
G	P	F	..	H	C	10	0	West (L. & S.W.)............	Hants	L. & S.W.	Bournemouth (Central) and Poole.
										S & DJt.(L & SW& Mid.)	Over L. & S.W. from Broadstone Jn.
..	..	..	..	..	..			West Junction	Hants	L. & S.W.	Bournemouth (West) & Branksome.
..	P	..	..	..	..			Bourne Valley Sid. (L. & S.W.)	Dorset......	L. & S.W.—S. & D. Jt.	Bournemouth, West.
..	P	..	..	..	..			Bournville	Worcester	Mid.	King's Norton and Selly Oak.
..	..	..	..	..	..			Bournville Village Trust Sid.	Worcester	Mid.	Lifford.
G	P	F	L	H	C	1	10	Bourton-on-the-Water	Glo'ster ...	G. W.	Chipping Norton Jn. & Cheltenham.
..	..	..	..	..	..			Bourtreehill Fire Clay Works	Ayr	G. & S.W.	Dreghorn.
..	..	..	..	..	..			Bourtreehill, Nos. 6, 7, and 8 (Capringstone Collieries) ...	Ayr	G. & S.W.	Dreghorn.
..	..	..	..	..	..			Bousteads Grassing	Cumb'land	M. & C.......................	Same as Carlisle Gas Works (Carlisle).

EXPLANATION—G *Goods Station.*   P *Passenger and Parcel Station.*   P* *Passenger, but not Parcel or Miscellaneous Traffic.*
F *Furniture Vans, Carriages, Portable Engines, and Machines on Wheels.*   L *Live Stock.*
H *Horse Boxes and Prize Cattle Vans.*   C *Carriages by Passenger Train.*

STATION ACCOMMODATION.						CRANE POWER.	STATIONS, &c.	COUNTY.	COMPANY.	POSITION.
G	P	F	L	H	C	Tons Cwts. 2 0	Bovey	Devon	G. W.	Heathfield & Moreton Hampstead.
.	.	.	.	.	.	. .	Bovey Granite & Pottery Sids	Devon	G. W.	Heathfield and Bovey.
.	.	.	.	.	.	. .	Bovil Colliery	Mon	B. & M.	Machen.
G	P	F	L	H	C	1 10	Bow	Devon	L. & S.W.	Exeter and Okehampton.
							Bow—			
.	.	.	.	.	.	. .	(Station)	Middlesex	Mid.—N. L.	See London.
.	.	.	.	.	.	. .	Coal Depôt	Middlesex	L. & N. W.	See London.
.	.	.	.	.	.	. .	Junction	Middlesex	G. E.—L. T. & S.	London, Stepney and Bromley.
.	.	.	.	.	.	. .	Junction	Middlesex	G. E.—N. L.	London, Burdett Road and Bow.
.	.	.	.	.	.	. .	Junction	Middlesex	N. L.	London, Bow and South Bromley.
.	.	.	.	.	.	. .	Locomotive Works and Carriage Sidings	Middlesex	N. L.	London, Bow.
.	.	.	.	.	.	. .	Tilbury Branch Junction	Middlesex	N. L.	London, Bow and Old Ford.
.	.	.	.	.	.	. .	Bowbridge Siding	Notts	G. N.	See Cafferata & Co. (Newark).
.	.	.	.	.	.	. .	Bow Common Gas Works	Middlesex	G. E.—N.L.—G.N.—G.W—L. & N. W.	See Gas Light & Coke Co. (London).
.	.	.	.	.	.	. .	Bowdon	Cheshire	C. L. C. (G.C, G.N, & Mid.)	Same as Hale.
.	.	.	.	.	.	. .	Bowdon	Cheshire	M.S.J. & A. (G. C. & Mid.)	See Altrincham and Bowdon.
.	.	.	.	.	.	. .	Bowdon Close Colliery	Durham	N. E.	Willington.
.	.	.	.	.	.	. .	Bowen's Chemical Wks. (G W)	Carmarth'	G. W.— L. & N. W.	Llanelly.
G	P	F	L	H	C	2 0	Bower	Caithness	High	Helmsdale and Wick.
.	.	.	.	.	.	. .	Bower's Brick Work Siding	Denbigh	G. W.	Acrefair, High Level.
.	.	.	.	.	.	. .	Bower's (Tatham) Brick Works	Denbigh	G. W.	Ruabon.
.	.	.	.	.	.	. .	Bower's Col. (Allerton Main Col)	Yorks	N. E.	Kippax.
.	.	.	.	.	.	. .	Bowershall Colliery	Fife	N. B.	Townhill Junction Station.
.	.	.	.	.	.	. .	Bower's Siding	Durham	N. E.	West Hartlepool.
G	P	.	L	H	C	. .	Bowes	Yorks	N. E.	Barnard Castle and Kirkby Stephen.
.	.	.	.	.	.	. .	Summit Siding	W'morlnd	N. E.	Barras and Bowes.
.	.	.	.	.	.	. .	Bowes Bridge Junction	Durham	N. E.	Redheugh.
.	.	.	.	.	.	. .	Bowesfield Junction	Durham	N. E.	Stockton, South.
.	.	.	.	.	.	. .	Bowesfield Metal Yard	Durham	N. E.	Stockton, South.
.	.	.	.	.	.	. .	Bowesfield Steel Works	Durham	N. E.	Stockton, South.
.	.	.	.	.	.	. .	Bowes Gannister & Freestone Co.'s Siding	W'morlnd	N. E.	Barras.
.	.	.	.	.	.	. .	Bowes House Farm Siding	Durham	N. E.	{ Fencehouses. { Penshaw.
.	P	.	.	.	.	.	Bowes Park (G. N.)	Middlesex	{ G. N. { N. L. { S. E. & C.	Wood Green and Enfield. Over G. N. from Canonbury Jn. Over G. N. from King's Cross Jn.
.	P	.	.	.	.	.				
.	P*	.	.	.	.	.				
.	.	.	.	.	.	. .	Bowhill Colliery	Fife	N. B.	Cardenden.
G	P	.	.	.	.	1 10	Bowhouse	Stirling	N. B.	Blackston and Bo'ness.
.	.	.	.	.	.	. .	Bowhouse Saw Mill (Mungall's)	Stirling	N. B.	Bowhouse.
.	.	.	.	.	.	. .	Candie Colliery	Stirling	N. B.	Bowhouse and Blackston.
.	.	.	.	.	.	. .	East Roughrigg Colliery	Stirling	N. B.	Branch—Bowhouse & Causewayend.
.	.	.	.	.	.	. .	Muiravonside Colliery	Stirling	N. B.	Branch—Bowhouse & Causewayend.
.	.	.	.	.	.	. .	Redford Colliery	Stirling	N. B.	Bowhouse and Blackston.
.	.	.	.	.	.	. .	Standburn Siding	Stirling	N. B.	Branch—Bowhouse & Causewayend.
.	.	.	.	.	.	. .	Bowker, A. & J., Sid. (G. E.)	Norfolk	G. E.—G. N.—Mid.	Lynn Harbour.
G	P	.	L	H	.	. .	Bowland	Edinboro'	N. B.	Edinburgh and Galashiels.
G	.	.	.	.	.	. .	Bowshank Siding	Edinboro'	N. B.	Bowland and Stow.
.	.	.	.	.	.	. .	Bowley and Collett's Siding	Glo'ster	Mid.	Gloucester.
							BOWLING—			
G	P	.	L	.	.	5 0	(Station)	Dumbartn	Cal.	Clydebank and Dumbarton.
G	P	F	L	H	C	5 0	(Station)	Dumbartn	N. B.	Kilbowie and Dumbarton.
G	.	.	.	.	.	4 0	Basin	Dumbartn	N. B.	Near Bowling.
G	.	.	.	.	.	. .	Dumbuck Siding (Milton Paper Co.)	Dumbartn	N. B.	Bowling and Dumbarton.
.	.	.	.	.	.	. .	Frisky Wharf	Dumbartn	N. B.	Bowling.
G	.	.	.	.	.	4 0	Harbour	Dumbartn	Cal.	Bowling.
.	.	.	.	.	.	. .	Inner Basin	Dumbartn	Cal.	Bowling.
.	.	.	.	.	.	. .	Little Mill Distillery	Dumbartn	Cal.—N.B.	Near Bowling.
.	.	.	.	.	.	. .	Scott & Co.'s Shipbuilding Yard	Dumbartn	N. B.	Bowling.
.	.	.	.	.	.	. .	Bowling	Yorks	G. N.	See Bradford.
.	.	.	.	.	.	. .	Bowling Iron Works	Yorks	G. N.	Bradford, Bowling.
.	.	.	.	.	.	. .	Bowling Junction	Yorks	G. N.—L. & Y.	Bradford and Low Moor.
.	.	.	.	.	.	. .	Bowling Junction Station	Yorks	L. & Y.	See Bradford.
.	.	.	.	.	.	. .	Bowman & Co.'s Victoria Chemical Works	Lancs	L. & N. W.—S. & M. Jt.	Widnes.
.	.	.	.	.	.	. .	Bowne & Shaw's Limestone Quarry	Derby	Mid.	Wirksworth.

EXPLANATION—G Goods Station.   P Passenger and Parcel Station.   P* Passenger, but not Parcel or Miscellaneous Traffic.
F Furniture Vans, Carriages, Portable Engines, and Machines on Wheels.   L Live Stock.
H Horse Boxes and Prize Cattle Vans.   C Carriages by Passenger Train.

STATION ACCOMMODATION.						CRANE POWER.		STATIONS, &c.	COUNTY.	COMPANY.	POSITION.
						Tons	Cwts.				
G	P	.	L	H	.	3	0	Bowness	Cumb'land	Cal.	Brayton and Annan.
G	P	.	.	.	.			Bowness	W'morlnd	{ Furness	Steamer fr. Windermere, Lake Side.
										{ L. & N. W.	By road from Windermere.
.	.	.	.	.	.			Bow Road.....................	Middlesex	G. E.	See London.
.	.	.	.	.	.			Bow Road Siding............	Middlesex	W. & B. Jt. (L T & S & M D)	See London.
.	.	.	.	.	.			Bowshank Siding	Edinboro'	N. B.	See Bowland.
G	P	.	.	H	C			Bow Street	Cardigan..	Cam.	Aberystwyth and Borth.
.	.	.	.	.	.			Bowyer & Priestley's Siding..	Hunts......	G. N.	Offord and Buckden.
G	P	F	L	H	C	6	0	Box	Wilts	G. W.	Chippenham and Bath.
.	.	.	.	.	.			Bath Stone Firms	Wilts	G. W.	Box and Corsham.
.	.	.	.	.	.			Farleigh Down Siding	Wilts	G. W.	Box and Bathampton.
G	P	.	.	.	.			Boxford......................	Berks	L'bourn Valley	Newbury and Lambourn.
.	P	.	.	.	.			Box Hill	Surrey ...	S. E. & C.	Red Hill and Dorking.
.	P	.	.	.	.			Boxhill and Burford Bridge...	Surrey ...	L. B. & S. C.	Epsom and Dorking.
.	.	.	.	.	.			Boxmoor	Herts	Mid.	Same as Hemel Hempstead.
G	P	F	L	H	C	2	0	Boxmoor & Hemel Hempstead	Herts	L. & N. W.	Bletchley and Watford.
.	.	.	.	.	.			Boxmoor District Gas Co.'s Sid	Herts	Mid.	Hemel Hempsted.
.	.	.	.	.	.			Boxmoor Wharf	Herts	Mid.	Same as Heath Pk. (Hemel Hempst'd)
.	.	.	.	.	.			Boyce & Son's Siding	Norfolk ...	G. E.	Downham.
.	.	.	.	.	.			Boyce's Bridge	Cambs ...	G. E.	See Wisbech Tramway.
.	.	.	.	.	.			Boyd's, J. & T., Siding	Lanark ...	N. B.	Same as Shettleston Iron Works (Shettleston).
.	.	.	.	.	.			Boyd's, W. H., Siding	Lancs	G. C.	Manchester, Openshaw.
G	P	F	L	H	C	3	0	Boyle..........................	Roscom'n	M. G. W.	Longford and Sligo.
.	.	.	.	.	.			Boys & Boden's Siding	Staffs	L. & N. W.	Darlaston.
.	.	.	.	.	.			Boythorpe Lane Wharf	Derby	Mid.	See Chesterfield.
.	.	.	.	.	.			Braby, F., & Co.'s Works ...	Lanark ...	{ Cal.	Glasgow, Buchanan Street.
										{ N. B.	Glasgow, Sighthill.
.	P	.	.	.	.			Braceboro' Spa.	Lincoln ...	G. N.	Bourne and Essendine.
.	.	.	.	.	.			Bracebridge Brick Siding (Lincoln Brick & Tile Co.)	Lincoln ...	G. N.	Waddington.
.	.	.	.	.	.			Bracebridge Gas Works	Lincoln ...	G. N.	Lincoln.
.	.	.	.	.	.			Brackenhill Junction	Ayr.........	G. & S. W.	Mauchline and Auchinleck.
.	.	.	.	.	.			Brackenhills Siding	Ayr.........	Cal.	See Giffen.
.	.	.	.	.	.			Brackenhirst Manure Depôt.	Lanark ...	N. B.	Greengairs.
.	.	.	.	.	.			Brackenhirst Quarry	Lanark ...	N. B.	Greengairs.
G	P	F	L	H	C	5	0	Brackley	N'hamptn	L. & N. W.	Banbury & Verney Junction Station.
.	.	.	.	.	.			Hopcraft and Norris Siding	N'hamptn	L. & N. W.	Brackley and Fulwell.
G	P	F	L	H	C	10	0	Brackley (Central)............	N'hamptn	G. C.	Rugby and Aylesbury.
.	.	.	.	.	.			Brackley Siding or Middle Hulton Colliery	Lancs	L. & N. W.	See Earl of Ellesmere's (Plodder Lane)
G	P	F	L	H	C	5	0	Bracknell	Berks	L. & S.W.	Staines and Reading.
.	.	.	.	.	.			Amen Corner Siding	Berks	L. & S.W.	Bracknell.
.	.	.	.	.	.			Down Mill Siding	Berks	L. & S.W.	Bracknell.
.	.	.	.	.	.			Lawrence's Siding	Berks	L. & S.W.	Bracknell.
G	P	F	L	H	C	.	.	Bradbury	Durham ...	N. E.	Darlington and Ferryhill.
.	P	.	.	.	.			Bradfield	Essex	G. E.	Manningtree and Harwich.
								BRADFORD—			
G	P	F	L	H	C	20	0 }	(Station, Mid.)................	Yorks	{ Mid.	Branch from Shipley Junction.
.	P	.	.	.	.		.			{ N. E.	Over Mid. from Milner Wood Junc.
G	.	F	L	.	.	20	0	Adolphus Street (G. N.) ...	Yorks	{ G. N.	Terminus.
										{ G. C.	Over G. N. from Wakefield Junc.
.	.	.	.	.	.			Bierley Siding................	Yorks	G. N.—L. & Y.	Low Moor.
.	.	.	.	.	.			Bonded Stores................	Yorks	Mid.	Valley Station.
G	.	.	.	.	.			Bowling	Yorks	G. N.	Laister Dyke & Bowling Junction.
.	.	.	.	.	.			Bowling Iron Works	Yorks	G. N.	Bowling.
.	P	.	.	.	.			Bowling Junction Station ...	Yorks	L. & Y.	Bradford and Low Moor.
.	.	.	.	.	.			Bradford Abattoir Co.'s Sid.	Yorks	Mid.	Manningham.
.	.	.	.	.	.			Bradford Co-operative Society's Siding	Yorks	G. N.	Dudley Hill.
G	.	F	L	.	.	25	0	Bridge Street (L. & Y.) ...	Yorks	{ L. & Y.	Exchange Sta. and Bowling Junc.
										{ L. & N. W.	Over L. & Y. Line.
G	.	F	L	.	.	10	0 }	Broomfield (L. & Y.)	Yorks	{ L. & Y.	Bch.—Exchange Sta. & Mill Lane Jn.
G	.	F	L	.	.	3	0 }			{ L. & N. W.	Over L. & Y. Line.
G	.	F	L	H	.	10	0 }	City Road (G. N.)	Yorks	{ G. N.	Branch near Horton Park.
G	.	F	L	.	.	10	0 }			{ G. C.	Over G. N. from Wakefield Junc.
G	P	F	L	H	C	10	0	Clayton	Yorks	G. N.	Bradford and Queensbury.
.	.	.	.	.	.			Cliffs Brick Siding............	Yorks	G. N.	Laister Dyke and Eccleshill.
.	.	.	.	.	.			Corporation Destructor Siding (G. N.)	Yorks	G. N.—G. C.	Adolphus Street and Laister Dyke.
.	.	.	.	.	.			Corporation Siding (Birkshall Gas Works)............	Yorks	G. N.	Laister Dyke and Bowling.

EXPLANATION—G *Goods Station.*   P *Passenger and Parcel Station.*   P* *Passenger, but not Parcel or Miscellaneous Traffic.*
F *Furniture Vans, Carriages, Portable Engines, and Machines on Wheels.*   L *Live Stock.*
H *Horse Boxes and Prize Cattle Vans.*   C *Carriages by Passenger Train.*

Station Accommodation.						Crane Power.		STATIONS, &c.	COUNTY.	COMPANY.	POSITION.
						Tons	Cwts.	BRADFORD—continued.			
								Corporation Slaughter-houses	Yorks	Mid.	Manningham.
G	P	F	L	H	C	10	0	Dudley Hill (G.N.)	Yorks	{ G. N.	Morley and Bradford.
										L. & Y.	Over G. N. Line.
G	P	F	L	H	C	10	0	Eccleshill	Yorks	G. N.	Shipley Branch.
								Ellis Robinson's Siding	Yorks	G. N.	Great Horton.
	P			H	C			Exchange (L. & Y.)	Yorks	{ L. & Y.	Terminus.
										G. N.	Over L. & Y. from Mill Lane Junc.
						5	0	Fagley Siding	Yorks	G. N.	Laister Dyke and Eccleshill.
								Filtration & Sewage Works	Yorks	Mid.	Manningham.
G	P					10	0	Frizinghall	Yorks	Mid.	Bradford and Shipley.
								Gas Works	Yorks	Mid.	Bradford and Manningham.
G	P	F	L	H	C	4	0	Great Horton	Yorks	G. N.	Bradford and Queensbury.
								Hammerton Street Junc.	Yorks	G. N.	Adolphus Street and Laister Dyke.
								Hammerton Str. Sids. (GN)	Yorks	G. N.—G. C.	Adolphus Str. & Hammerton Str. Jn.
								Hodgson's Loom Works	Yorks	Mid.	Near Frizinghall.
								Holden & Son's Sid. (G. N.)	Yorks	G. N.—G. C.	City Road.
	P							Horton Park	Yorks	G. N.	St. Dunstan's and Great Horton.
G	P	F		H	C	10	0	Idle	Yorks	G. N.	Shipley Branch.
G	P	F	L	H	C	10	0	Laister Dyke (G. N.)	Yorks	{ G. N.	Leeds and Bradford.
										L. & Y.	Over G. N. from Bowling Junction.
G		F	L	H	C	10	0	Lister's Sid. (Shetcliffe Mill)	Yorks	G. N.	Dudley Hill and Birkenshaw.
G	P	F	L	H	C	5	0	Low Moor	Yorks	G. N.	Branch near Low Moor Junction.
G	P		L	H				Low Moor (L. & Y.)	Yorks	{ L. & Y.	Halifax and Bradford.
G			L			8	0			G. N.	Over L. & Y. Line.
										L. & N. W.	Over L. & Y. Line.
								Low Moor Colliery	Yorks	L. & Y.	Near Low Moor Station.
								Low Moor Junction	Yorks	G. N.—L. & Y.	Dudley Hill and Low Moor Station.
G	P					5	0	Manchester Road	Yorks	G. N.	Laister Dyke and Great Horton.
	P							Manningham	Yorks	Mid.	Bradford and Shipley.
								Manningham Sidings	Yorks	Mid.	Manningham.
								Mill Lane Junction	Yorks	G. N.—L. & Y.	St. Dunstan's & Exchange Station.
								Newbigging Siding	Yorks	L. & Y.	Low Moor.
								Obank & Son's Siding	Yorks	G. N.	Idle.
								Ripley's Siding (Hall Lane Coal Siding)	Yorks	G. N.	Bowling Sta. and Bowling Junc.
	P							Sharp's Siding	Yorks	L. & Y.	Low Moor (Fork Line).
								St. Dunstan's	Yorks	G. N.	Laister Dyke and Exchange Station.
								St. James' Market Sids.(GN)	Yorks	G. N.—G. C.	Adolphus Street and Laister Dyke.
								Taylor and Parson's Siding	Yorks	G. N.	Great Horton.
	P							Thackley	Yorks	G. N.	Shipley Branch.
								Thornton & Crebbin's Siding (G. N.)	Yorks	G. N.—G. C.	Adolphus Street and Laister Dyke.
G		F				4	0	Trafalgar Street	Yorks	Mid.	Bradford.
								Union Foundry	Yorks	G. N.	Dudley Hill and Laister Dyke.
								Valley	Yorks	Mid.	Bradford, Goods.
G		F	L			3	0	Vicar Lane (L. & Y.)	Yorks	{ L. & Y.	Terminus.
										L. & N. W.	Over L. & Y. Line.
								Vint & Bros.' Siding	Yorks	G. N.	Idle and Eccleshill.
								Bradford Abattoir Co.'s Sid.	Yorks	Mid.	Bradford Station.
								Bradford & Son's Siding	Somerset	{ G. W.	Yeovil, Hendford.
										L. & S. W.	Crewkerne.
								Bradford Bonded Stores	Yorks	Mid.	Bradford Station.
								Bradford Colliery Co.'s Siding	Lancs	L. & Y.	Manchester, Beswick.
								Bradford Co-operative Society's Siding	Yorks	G. N.	Bradford, Dudley Hill.
								Bradford Corporation—			
								Birkshall Gas Works	Yorks	G. N.	Bradford, Laister Dyke.
								Destructor Siding (G.N.)	Yorks	G. N.—G. C.	Bradford, Adolphus Street.
								Slaughter-houses	Yorks	Mid.	Bradford Station.
								Bradford Filtration and Sewage Works	Yorks	Mid.	Bradford Station.
								Bradford Gas Works	Yorks	Mid.	Bradford Station.
G	P	F	L	H	C	6	0	Bradford-on-Avon	Wilts	G. W.	Trowbridge and Bathampton.
								Avoncliffe Siding	Wilts	G. W.	Bradford and Bathampton.
								Bradford Road Gas Works	Lancs	L. & Y.	See Manchester Corporation.
								Bradford South Junction	Wilts	G. W.	Trowbridge and Holt.
								Bradford West Junction	Wilts	G. W.	Trowbridge and Bradford.
G	P	F	L	H	C	10	0	Brading	I. of W.	I. of W.	Ryde and Sandown.
								Bradley (L. & N. W.)	Yorks	L. & N. W.—L. & Y.	See Huddersfield.
								Bradley & Co.'s Siding	Staffs	G. W.	Brettell Lane.

EXPLANATION—G *Goods Station.*   P *Passenger and Parcel Station.*   P* *Passenger, but not Parcel or Miscellaneous Traffic.*
F *Furniture Vans, Carriages, Portable Engines, and Machines on Wheels.*   L *Live Stock.*
H *Horse Boxes and Prize Cattle Vans.*   C *Carriages by Passenger Train.*

STATION ACCOMMODATION.						CRANE POWER.	STATIONS, &c.	COUNTY.	COMPANY.	POSITION.
						Tons Cwts.				
	P						Bradley & Co.'s Works.........	Worcester	G. W.	Stourbridge.
	P						Bradley & Moxley	Staffs	G. W.	Wolverhampton and Birmingham.
							Bradley Bros. Whinstone Sid.	Yorks	N. E.	Kildale.
							Bradley Coke Ovens	Durham ...	N. E.	Blackhill.
							Bradley Coebery Shops	Durham ...	N. E.	Blackhill.
G	P					5 0	Bradley Fold	Lancs	L. & Y.	Bolton and Bury.
							Bradley Fold Siding........	Lancs	L. & Y.	Bradley Fold.
							Darcy Lever Colliery........	Lancs	L. & Y.	Bradley Fold.
							Fletcher's Siding	Lancs	L. & Y.	Bradley Fold.
							Bradley Green Colliery........	Staffs	N. S.	See Heath & Sons (Biddulph).
							Bradley Manufacturing Co.'s Siding	Lancs	L. & N. W.	Wigan.
							Bradley's Capponfield Siding	Staffs	G. W.	Bilston & Deepfields.
							Bradley's Chemical Works ...	Derby	Mid.	See Tyson & Bradley's Chemical Works (Chesterfield).
							Bradley Siding	Salop	G. W.	Much Wenlock.
							Bradley's Siding...................	Notts	G. N.	Newark.
							Bradley's Siding...................	Staffs	L. & N. W.	Darlaston.
							Bradley's Siding...................	Yorks	N. E.	Same as Newton Qry. (Great Ayton).
							Bradley's, T. & A., Iron Works	Notts	Mid.	Newark.
							Bradley Wood Junction	Yorks	L. & Y.—L. & N. W. ...	Brighouse and Huddersfield.
							Bradninch	Devon	G. W.	See Hele and Bradninch.
							Bradshaw Gate Siding	Lancs	L. & Y.	Bolton.
G	P						Bradwell	Bucks	L. & N. W.	Newport Pagnell and Wolverton.
							Bradwell	Derby	Mid.	See Hope (for Castleton & Bradwell).
							Bradwell Hall Bk. & Tile Wks.	Staffs	N. S.	See Hem Heath Sids. (Chesterton).
							Bradwell Sidings (N. S.)	Staffs	N. S.—L. & N. W.	Chatterley.
							Braehead Bk & Silicate Wks.	Lanark ...	Cal.	Baillieston.
							Braehead Brick Works.........	L'lithgow	Cal. / N. B.	Fauldhouse. / Crofthead.
							Braehead Colliery	Lanark ...	Cal.	Baillieston.
							Braehead Colliery	L'lithgow	N. B.	Crofthead.
							Braehead Quarry	Lanark ...	Cal.	Baillieston.
							Braehead Quarry	L'lithgow	Cal. / N. B.	Fauldhouse. / Crofthead.
							Braes Siding	Warwick	L. & N. W.	Same as Rugby Brick and Tile Co.'s Siding (Rugby).
G	P	F	L	H	C		Brafferton	Yorks	N. E.	Boroughbridge and Pilmoor.
							Braichgoch Quarry	Merioneth	Corris	Maespoeth Junction and Abercwmeiddaw Quarry.
							Braich-y-Cymmer Colliery ...	Glamorg'n	G. W.	Pont-y-rhyll.
							Braidenhill Nos. 1 & 2 Collieries	Lanark ...	N. B.	Greengairs.
							Braidhurst Colliery	Lanark ...	Cal.	Motherwell.
G	P		L	H		4 10	Braidwood	Lanark ...	Cal.	Carstairs and Law Junction.
							Braidwood Saw Mills	Lanark ...	Cal.	Braidwood.
							Braidwood Tile Works	Lanark ...	Cal.	Braidwood.
							Braidwood Weighs............	Lanark ...	Cal.	Braidwood.
							Craigenhill Lime Works ...	Lanark ...	Cal.	Cleghorn and Braidwood.
							Lee Brick Works (Fiddlersgill Brick Works)	Lanark ...	Cal.	Cleghorn and Braidwood.
							Meadow Brick Works	Lanark ...	Cal.	Braidwood.
							Nellfield Brick Works	Lanark ...	Cal.	Braidwood.
							Nellfield Saw Mills	Lanark ...	Cal.	Braidwood.
G	P	F	L	H	C	5 0	Braintree	Essex	G. E.	Witham and Bishops Stortford.
							Belsham & Son's Siding ...	Essex	G. E.	Braintree.
							Brown, J., & Son's Siding	Essex	G. E.	Braintree.
							Walford & Co.'s Siding......	Essex	G. E.	Braintree.
G	P	F	L	H	C	1 10	Braithwaite........................	Cumb'land	C. K. & P. (L. & N. W. & N. E. Working Cos.)	Keswick and Cockermouth.
							Braithwaite & Co.'s Siding ...	Glo'ster ...	Mid.	Ryeford.
	P						Bramber	Sussex	L. B. & S. C.	Shoreham and Horsham.
							Brambledown Siding	Kent	S. E. & C. (Sheppey)......	Minster (Sheppey).
G	P					0 15	Bramford	Suffolk	G. E.	Ipswich and Haughley.
							Coe, A., Siding	Suffolk	G. E.	Bramford.
							Fison, J., & Co.'s Siding ...	Suffolk	G. E.	Bramford.
							Packard & Co.'s Siding....	Suffolk	G. E.	Bramford.
	P						Bramhall	Cheshire.	L. & N. W.	Cheadle Hulme and Macclesfield.
							Bramhall Moor Lane............	Cheshire.	Mid.	See Hazel Grove.
G	P		L			2 0	Bramley	Hants	G. W.	Mortimer and Basingstoke.
							Bramley (G. N.)	Yorks	G. N.—L. & Y.	See Leeds.
G	P	F	L	H	C	1 0	Bramley and Wonersh	Surrey	L. B. & S. C.	Guildford and Horsham.
							Street's Siding	Surrey	L. B. & S. C.	Bramley and Wonersh.

EXPLANATION—G *Goods Station.*   P *Passenger and Parcel Station.*   P* *Passenger, but not Parcel or Miscellaneous Traffic.*
F *Furniture Vans, Carriages, Portable Engines, and Machines on Wheels.*   L *Live Stock.*
H *Horse Boxes and Prize Cattle Vans.*   C *Carriages by Passenger Train.*

STATION ACCOMMODATION.						CRANE POWER.		STATIONS, &c.	COUNTY.	COMPANY.	POSITION.
						Tons	Cwts.				
.	P	.	.	.	.	.	.	Brampford Speke	Devon	G. W.	Exeter and Tiverton.
.	P	.	.	.	.	.	.	Brampton........................	N'hamptn*	L. & N. W.	See Pitsford and Brampton.
G	P	.	.	.	.	.	.	Brampton........................	Suffolk ...	G. E.	Ipswich and Beccles.
.	.	.	.	.	.	.	.	Brampton Colliery............	Derby	Mid.	Chesterfield.
G	P	F	L	H	C	2	0	Brampton Junction Station...	Cumb'land	N. E.	Carlisle and Hexham.
.	.	.	.	.	.	.	.	Bog Coke Ovens..............	Cumb'land	N. E.	Brampton Junction and Lambley.
.	.	.	.	.	.	.	.	Brampton Coal Staithes ...	Cumb'land	N. E.	Brampton Junction and Lambley.
.	.	.	.	.	.	.	.	Clesket Siding	Cumb'land	N. E.	Brampton Junction and Lambley.
.	.	.	.	.	.	.	.	Clowsgill Holme Siding ...	Cumb'land	N. E.	Brampton Junction and Lambley.
.	.	.	.	.	.	.	.	Forest Head Lime Quarry..	Cumb'land	N. E.	Brampton Junction and Lambley.
.	.	.	.	.	.	.	.	Halton Lea Gate...............	Cumb'land	N. E.	Brampton Junction and Lambley.
.	.	.	.	.	.	.	.	Kirkhouse Collieries (Naworth Collieries)............	Cumb'land	N. E.	Brampton Junction and Lambley.
.	.	.	.	.	.	.	.	Kirkhouse Dutch Barn Factory and Saw Mills...	Cumb'land	N. E.	Brampton Junction and Lambley.
.	.	.	.	.	.	.	.	Kirkhouse Siding	Cumb'land	N. E.	Brampton Junction and Lambley.
.	.	.	.	.	.	.	.	Midge Holme Coke Ovens..	Cumb'land	N. E.	Brampton Junction and Lambley.
.	.	.	.	.	.	.	.	Midge Holme Sidings	Cumb'land	N. E.	Brampton Junction and Lambley.
.	.	.	.	.	.	.	.	Whitescut Siding	Cumb'land	N. E.	Brampton Junction and Lambley.
.	.	.	.	.	.	.	.	Brampton Siding	Staffs	N. S.	Newcastle.
.	.	.	.	.	.	.	.	Brampton Wharf	Derby	Mid.	See Chesterfield.
G	.	F	L	.	.	.	.	Bramwell & Son's Siding.....	Lancs	L. & N. W.	St. Helens.
.	.	.	.	.	.	.	.	Bramwith........................	Yorks	W R & G Jt. (G C & G N)	Thorne and Wakefield.
G	P	F	L	H	C	.	.	Milnthorpe's Malt Kiln ...	Yorks	W R & G Jt. (G C & G N)	Bramwith and Stainforth Junction.
.	.	.	.	.	.	.	.	Brancepeth	Durham ...	N. E.	Durham and Bishop Auckland.
.	.	.	.	.	.	.	.	Brancepeth Colliery	Durham ...	N. E.	Willington.
.	.	.	.	.	.	.	.	Brancker's Siding (L. & Y.)..	Lancs	L. & Y.—L. & N. W.....	Same as Orrell Colliery (Gathurst).
.	.	.	.	.	.	.	.	Brancliffe Lime Quarry ...	Notts	G. C.	Shireoaks.
.	.	.	.	.	.	.	.	Branders Siding........	Hadding'n	N. B.	Pencaitland.
G	P	F	L	H	C	1	0	Brandon	Suffolk ...	G. E.	Ely and Thetford.
G	P	F	L	H	C	3	0	Brandon and Wolston	Warwick..	L. & N. W.	Coventry and Rugby.
.	.	.	.	.	.	.	.	Brandon Bridge Building Wks.	Lanark ...	Cal.	Motherwell.
G	P	F	L	.	.	2	0	*Brandon Colliery Station......	Durham ...	N. E.	Durham Pass. and Brancepeth.
.	.	.	.	.	.	.	.	Brandon Colliery	Durham ...	N. E.	Brandon Colliery Station.
.	.	.	.	.	.	.	.	Brandon Pipe & Brick Wks.	Durham ...	N. E.	Brandon Colliery Station.
.	.	.	.	.	.	.	.	Broompark Colliery	Durham ...	N. E.	Brandon Colliery Station.
.	.	.	.	.	.	.	.	Browney Colliery	Durham ...	N. E.	Brandon Colliery Station.
.	.	.	.	.	.	.	.	Littleburn Colliery	Durham ...	N. E.	Brandon Colliery Station.
.	.	.	.	.	.	.	.	Brand's Colliery...............	Derby	Mid.	See Butterley Co. (Codnor Park).
.	.	.	.	.	.	.	.	Brand's Siding	Lanark ...	Cal.	Wishaw, Central.
.	.	.	.	.	.	.	.	Brand's Siding	Yorks	N. E.	Malton.
.	.	.	.	.	.	.	.	Brand's Slag Works—			
.	.	.	.	.	.	.	.	Cargo Fleet Iron and Brick Works and Wharf	Yorks	N. E.	South Bank.
.	.	.	.	.	.	.	.	Imperial Iron Works	Yorks .:....	N. E.	South Bank.
.	.	.	.	.	.	.	.	Redcar Iron Works	Yorks	N. E.	Tod Point.
.	.	.	.	.	.	.	.	Brandwood Siding..............	Lancs	L. & Y.	Stacksteads.
.	.	.	.	.	.	.	.	Brandy Bridge Junction	Glamorg'n	G. W. & T. V. Jt.—T.V.	Merthyr.
.	.	.	.	.	.	.	.	Branksome	Dorset.....	L. & S. W.	See Bournemouth, West.
.	.	.	.	.	.	.	.	Branksome Sidings	Hants	L. & S. W.	See Bournemouth, West.
G	P	.	.	.	.	2	0	Bransford Road (G.W.)........	Worcester	G. W.	Worcester and Hereford.
G	.	.	.	.	.	2	0			Mid.	Over G. W. Line.
.	.	.	.	.	.	.	.	Bransgrove's Kenton Lane Siding	Middlesex	L. & N. W.	Harrow & Wealdstone.
.	P	.	.	.	.	.	.	Branston	Staffs	Mid.	Burton and Tamworth.
G	P	F	L	H	C	1	10	Branston & Heighington	Lincoln ...	G. N. & G. E. Jt.	Lincoln and Sleaford.
.	.	.	.	.	.	.	.	Branston's—			
.	.	.	.	.	.	.	.	Maltings (G. N.)............	Notts	G. N—Mid.	Newark.
.	.	.	.	.	.	.	.	Riverside Malt Kilns	Notts	G. N. & Mid. Jt.	Newark.
.	.	.	.	.	.	.	.	Bransty..........................	Cumb'land	Furness—L. & N. W. ...	See Whitehaven.
G	P	.	L	H	.	.	.	Bransty Quarry	Cumb'land	L. & N. W.	Whitehaven.
.	.	.	.	.	.	.	.	Branthwaite	Cumb'land	WC&E Jt.(Fur.&L&NW)	Marron Junction and Moor Row.
.	.	.	.	.	.	.	.	Brasside Brick & Tile Works	Durham ...	N. E.	Leamside.
.	.	.	.	.	.	.	.	Brasside Manure Siding (Whitfield's)	Durham ...	N. E.	Leamside.
G	P	.	.	.	.	.	.	Brasted	Kent	S. E. & C.	Dunton Green and Westerham.
.	P	.	.	.	.	.	.	Bratton	Wilts	G. W.	See Edington and Bratton.
G	P	F	L	H	C	1	10	Bratton Fleming	Devon	Lyn. & Barns..............	Barnstaple and Lynton.
G	P	F	L	H	C	1	10	Braughing	Herts	G. E.	St. Margarets & Buntingford.

* Roundabouts and Show Vans cannot be dealt with at this Station. Live Stock from the South should be invoiced and sent to Brancepeth Station.

EXPLANATION—**G** Goods Station.   **P** Passenger and Parcel Station.   **P*** Passenger, but not Parcel or Miscellaneous Traffic.
F Furniture Vans, Carriages, Portable Engines, and Machines on Wheels.   **L** Live Stock.
H Horse Boxes and Prize Cattle Vans.   **C** Carriages by Passenger Train.

STATION ACCOMMODATION.						CRANE POWER.	STATIONS, &c.	COUNTY.	COMPANY.	POSITION.
						Tons Cwts				
G	P	F	L	H	C	5 0	Braunston	N'hamptn	L. & N. W.	Leamington and Weedon.
G	P	F	L	H	C	. .	Braunston & Willoughby (for Daventry)	Warwick..	G. C.	Rugby and Brackley.
							Braunston Gate	Leicester..	G. C.	See Leicester.
G	P	F	L	H	C	2 0	Braunton	Devon	L. & S. W.	Barnstaple and Ilfracombe.
G	P	F	L	H	C	3 0	Bray	Wicklow..	D. W. & W.	Kingstown and Wicklow.
.	.	.	.	.	.	. .	Bray & Co.'s Siding	Hunts	G. N.	Fletton.
.	P					. .	Braysdown Colliery	Somerset..	S.&D. Jt. (L.&S. W. & Mid)	Radstock.
.	P					. .	Braystones	Cumb'land	Furness	Sellafield and Whitehaven.
G	P	F	L	H	C	3 0	Brayton (M. & C.)	Cumb'land	M. & C.	Aspatria and Leegate.
								Cumb'land	Cal.	Over M. & C. from Brayton Junc.
.	.	.	.	.	.	. .	Domain, No. 3 Pit	Cumb'land	M. & C.	Aspatria and Baggrow.
.	.	.	.	.	.	. .	No. 4 Pit	Cumb'land	M. & C.—Cal.	Brayton Station.
.	.	.	.	.	.	. .	Brayton Junction	Cumb'land	Cal.—M. & C.	Annan and Maryport.
.	.	.	.	.	.	. .	Brayton Siding	Yorks	N. E.	Wistow.
G	P	F	L	H	C	. .	Breadsall	Derby	G. N.	Ilkeston and Derby.
.	.	.	.	.	.	. .	Break's Siding	W'morlnd	L. & N. W.	See Kendal Bonded Stores Siding (Kendal).
.	.	.	.	.	.	. .	Breakwater Junction	Yorks	N. E.	Tod Point and South Bank.
G	P	.	L	H	.	. .	Breamore	Hants	L. & S. W.	Salisbury and Wimborne.
G	P	F	L	H	C	5 0}	Brechin (Cal.)	Forfar	Cal.	Branch near Bridge of Dun.
G	.	F	L	.	.	5 0}			N. B.	Over Cal. from Broomfield Junction.
G	.	.	.	.	.	. .	Kincraig Siding (Cal.)	Forfar	Cal.—N. B.	Bridge of Dun and Brechin.
.	.	.	.	.	.	. .	Breck Road	Lancs	L. & N. W.	See Liverpool.
							BRECON—			
									B. & M.	Branch from Talyllyn.
.	P	F	.	H	C		Free Street (B. & M.)	Brecon	Cam.	Over B. & M. from Talyllyn Junc.
									Mid.	Ov. Cam. & B.& M.fr. Three Cocks Jn.
									N. & Brecon	Over B. & M. from Brecon Junction.
.	.	.	.	.	.	. .	Junction	Brecon	B. & M.—N. & B.	Free Street and Cradoc.
									B. & M.	Branch from Talyllyn.
G	.	F	L	.	.	2 0	Watton (B. & M.)	Brecon	Cam.	Over B. & M. from Talyllyn Junc.
									Mid.	Over Cam. & B. & M. from Three Cocks Junction.
.	.	.	.	.	.	. .	Brecon Boat Siding	Mon	L. & N. W.	Same as Powell's Ellwood Colliery Co.'s Siding (Brynmawr).
.	.	.	.	.	.	. .	Brecon Curve Junctions	Hereford..	G. W.—Mid.—S. & H. Jt.	Hereford.
.	.	.	.	.	.	. .	Brecon Road	Mon	L. & N. W.	See Abergavenny.
G	P	.	L	.	.	1 10	Bredbury	Cheshire..	S. & M. Jt. (G. C. & Mid.)	Ashburys and Romiley.
.	.	.	.	.	.	. .	Bredbury Colliery Co.'s Sid.	Cheshire..	S. & M. Jt. (G. C. & Mid.)	Bredbury.
.	.	.	.	.	.	. .	Lingard Lane Colliery	Cheshire..	S. & M. Jt. (G. C. & Mid.)	Near Bredbury.
.	.	.	.	.	.	. .	Bredbury Junction	Cheshire..	C. L. C.—S. & M. Jt.	Stockport and Romiley.
.	.	.	.	.	.	. .	Brediland Siding	Renfrew..	G. & S. W.	Paisley, Ferguslie.
.	.	.	.	.	.	. .	Bredisholm Branch	Lanark	N. B.	Broomhouse.
.	.	.	.	.	.	. .	Bredisholm Brick Works	Lanark	Cal.	Baillieston.
.	.	.	.	.	.	. .	Bredisholm Chemical Works	Lanark	Cal.	Baillieston.
.	.	.	.	.	.	. .	Bredisholm Collieries, Nos. 1, 2, 3, 4, 5, & 6 (Newlands Col.)	Lanark	Cal.	Baillieston.
.	.	.	.	.	.	. .	Bredisholm Colliery	Lanark	N. B.	Broomhouse.
.	.	.	.	.	.	. .	Bredisholm Quarry	Lanark	Cal.	Baillieston.
									N. B.	Broomhouse.
G	P	.	L	.	.	1 10	Bredon	Worcester	Mid.	Cheltenham and Defford.
.	.	.	.	.	.	. .	Bredon Lime Works	Leicester..	Mid.	Worthington.
.	.	.	.	.	.	. .	Breedon	Leicester..	Mid.	See Tonge and Breedon.
.	.	.	.	.	.	. .	Breffit, E., & Co.'s Sidings	Yorks	N. E.	Same as Aire & Calder Glass Bottle Works (Castleford).
.	P					. .	Breich	Edinboro'	Cal.	Holytown and Edinboro'.
.	.	.	.	.	.	. .	Breich Oil Works	L'lithgow	Cal.	Same as Hermand Oil Works (New) (West Calder).
G	P	F	L	H	C	1 10	Brent	Devon	G. W.	Totnes and Plymouth.
G	P	F	L	H	C	10 0	Brentford	Middlesex	L. & S. W.	Kew Bridge and Hounslow.
.	.	.	.	.	.	. .	Brentford	Middlesex	Met. Dist.	See Boston Road (for Brentford and Hanwell).
.	.	.	.	.	.	. .	Brentford Gas Co.'s Works	Middlesex	G. W.	Southall.
G	P	F	L	.	.	18 0	Brentford Station and Dock..	Middlesex	G. W.	Branch from Southall.
.	.	.	.	.	.	. .	Brent Gas Works	Middlesex	Mid.	London, Cricklewood.
.	.	.	.	.	.	. .	Brent Junction	Devon	G. W.	Totnes and Plymouth.
.	.	.	.	.	.	. .	Brent Junction (Mid.)	Middlesex	Mid.—L. & S. W.	London, Kew Bridge and Hendon.
G	P	.	L	.	.	. .	Brent Knoll	Somerset..	G. W.	Weston-super-Mare & Highbridge.
.	.	.	.	.	.	. .	Brent North Junction	Middlesex	G. C.—Met.	London (Marylebone) and Harrow.
.	.	.	.	.	.	. .	Brent South Junction	Middlesex	G. C.—Met.	London (Marylebone) and Harrow.
G	P	F	L	H	C	. .	Brentor	Devon	L. & S. W.	Okehampton and Tavistock.

EXPLANATION—G *Goods Station.*   P *Passenger and Parcel Station.*   P* *Passenger, but not Parcel or Miscellaneous Traffic.*
F *Furniture Vans, Carriages, Portable Engines, and Machines on Wheels.*   L *Live Stock.*
H *Horse Boxes and Prize Cattle Vans.*   C *Carriages by Passenger Train.*

G	P	F	L	H	C	Tons	Cwts	STATIONS, &c.	COUNTY.	COMPANY.	POSITION.
G	P	F	L	H	C	5	0	Brentwood and Warley	Essex	G. E.	London and Chelmsford.
								Barrett, J., Siding	Essex	G. E.	Brentwood & Warley.
								Brentwood Gas Co.'s Siding	Essex	G. E.	Brentwood & Warley.
								Brown, J., Siding	Essex	G. E.	Brentwood & Warley.
								Daldy & Co.'s Siding	Essex	G. E.	Brentwood & Warley.
								Essex County Council Sid..	Essex	G. E.	Brentwood & Warley.
								Fielder & Co.'s Siding	Essex	G. E.	Brentwood & Warley.
								Girardot & Co.'s Siding	Essex	G. E.	Brentwood & Warley.
								Taylor, Dr., Siding	Essex	G. E.	Brentwood & Warley.
								Brereton Colliery	Staffs	L. & N. W.	Hednesford.
								Bretby Brick & Pipe Co.'s Siding (Mid.)	Derby	Mid.—L. & N. W.	Swadlincote.
								Bretby Colliery Wharf (Newhall Park Colliery) (Mid.)	Derby	Mid.—L. & N. W.	See Earl of Carnarvon's (Swadlincote).
								Bretby New Colliery (Mid.)	Derby	Mid.—L. & N. W.	See Earl of Carnarvon's (Swadlincote)
								Bretherton's Siding	Lancs	L. & N. W.	Rainhill.
G	P		L			5	0	Brettell Lane	Staffs	G. W.	Dudley and Stourbridge.
								Bradley & Co.'s Siding	Staffs	G. W.	Kingswinford Branch.
								Brettell Lane Sand Siding	Staffs	G. W.	Kingswinford Branch.
G						5	0	Bromley Basin	Staffs	G. W.	Kingswinford Branch.
								Corbyns Hall Sidings	Staffs	G. W.	Kingswinford Branch.
								Earl Dudley's Siding	Staffs	G. W.	Kingswinford Branch.
								Glaze & Co.'s Siding	Staffs	G. W.	Kingswinford Branch.
								Hall, J., & Co.'s Siding	Staffs	G. W.	Kingswinford Branch.
								Harris & Pearson's Siding	Staffs	G. W.	Dudley and Stourbridge Junction.
								Harrison's, G. K., Siding	Staffs	G. W.	Dudley and Stourbridge Junction.
								Hindley Fire Brick Co.'s Works	Staffs	G. W.	Kingswinford Branch.
								Kingswinford Branch	Staffs	G. W.	Branch from Kingswinford Junc.
								Kingswinford Junction	Staffs	G. W.	Brettell Lane and Brierley Hill.
								Moor Lane Siding	Staffs	G. W.	Dudley and Stourbridge Junction.
								Roberts & Cooper's Leys Sid.	Staffs	G. W.	Kingswinford Branch.
								Stourbridge Glazed Brick and Fire Clay Co.'s Colliery and Siding	Staffs	G. W.	Kingswinford Branch.
								Walker's, Jno., Siding	Staffs	G. W.	Kingswinford Branch.
								Brewer's Siding (L. & N. W.)	Staffs	L. & N. W.—G. W.—Mid.	Walsall.
								Breydon Junction	Norfolk	G. E.	Yarmouth.
G	P		L	H				Bricket Wood	Herts	L. & N. W.	St. Albans and Watford.
								Taylor's Siding	Herts	L. & N. W.	Bricket Wood and Watford.
								Bricklayers' Arms (S. E. & C.)	Surrey	S. E. & C.—L. & N. W.	See London.
								Bricklayers' Arms Junction	Surrey	L. B. & S. C.—S. E. & C.	London, New Cross and Bricklayers' Arms.
G	P	F	L	H	C	2	0	Brick Pit or Crown Collieries	Glo'ster	S. & Wye Jt. (G. W. & Mid.)	Parkend.
								Bridestowe	Devon	L. & S. W.	Okehampton and Tavistock.
								Machine Drying and Peat Fuel Co.'s Siding	Devon	L. & S. W.	Bridestowe.
G	P	F	L	H	C			Bridge	Kent	S. E. & C.	Canterbury and Shorncliffe.
G	P		L					Bridge End	Derry	L. & L. S.	Londonderry and Buncrana.
G	P							Bridgefoot	Cumb'land	W C & E Jt (Fur. & L & N W)	Marron Junction and Moor Row.
								Bridge House Junction	Durham	N. E.	Durham, Pass. and Croxdale.
								Bridgehouses (G.C.)	Yorks	G. C.—G. N.	See Sheffield.
								Bridgeman Street	Lancs	L. & N. W.	See Bolton.
								Bridge Mill Siding	Ayr	G. & S. W.	Girvan.
								Bridge Mills Siding	Derby	G. C.	Dinting.
G	P	F	L	H	C	10	0	Bridgend (G.W.)	Glamorg'n	{ G. W. / Barry	Cardiff and Neath. / Over G. W. from Bridgend Junc.
								Jenkins' & Sons' Lime and Timber Sidings	Glamorg'n	G. W.	Bridgend.
								McGaul's Siding	Glamorg'n	G. W.	Bridgend.
								Price's, R., Siding	Glamorg'n	G. W.	Bridgend.
								Price's Tan Yard	Glamorg'n	G. W.	Bridgend.
								Sheppard, C., & Son's Sid.	Glamorg'n	G. W.	Bridgend.
								South Wales Portland Cement & Lime Co.'s Sid.	Glamorg'n	G. W.	Bridgend.
G								Bridgend	Lanark	N. B.	Sunnyside and Kirkintilloch Basin.
								Avenuehead Sand Siding	Lanark	N. B.	Bridgend and Gartgill.
								Drumcavil Sand Siding	Lanark	N. B.	Bridgend and Gartgill.
G								Leckethill Siding	Lanark	N. B.	Bridgend and Glenboig.
G								Muckroft Siding	Lanark	N. B.	Bridgend and Garngaber.
								Bridgend Junction	Lanark	N. B.	Bridgend and Waterside Junc.
								Bridgend Junction	Glamorg'n	Barry—G. W.	Southerndown Road and Bridgend.

EXPLANATION—G *Goods Station.*   P *Passenger and Parcel Station.*   P* *Passenger, but not Parcel or Miscellaneous Traffic.*
F *Furniture Vans, Carriages, Portable Engines, and Machines on Wheels.*   L *Live Stock.*
H *Horse Boxes and Prize Cattle Vans.*   C *Carriages by Passenger Train.*

STATION ACCOMMODATION.						CRANE POWER.		STATIONS, &c.	COUNTY.	COMPANY.	POSITION.
						Tons	Cwts				
..	..	..	..	..	..	..	..	Bridgend Junction (for Llynvi and Ogmore Section).........	Glamorg'n	G. W.	Bridgend & Pyle (Main Line).
..	..	..	..	..	..	..	..	Bridgeness Colliery	L'lithgow	N. B.	Bo'ness.
..	..	..	..	..	..	..	..	Bridgeness Pottery (McNay's)	L'lithgow	N. B.	Bo'ness.
G	P	F	L	H	C	3	10	Bridge of Allan	Stirling ...	Cal.	Stirling and Perth.
..	..	..	..	..	..	..	..	Cornton Siding	Stirling ...	Cal.	Stirling and Bridge of Allan.
G	P	F	L	H	C	..	..	Bridge of Dee	Kirkcud...	G. & S.W.	Castle Douglas and Kirkcudbright.
G	P	F	L	H	C	3	0	Bridge of Dun	Forfar ...	Cal.	Forfar and Stonehaven.
G	P	F	L	H	C	1	10	Bridge of Earn	Perth	N. B.	Ladybank and Perth.
..	..	..	..	..	..	..	..	Bridge of Earn Junction	Perth	N. B.	Glenfarg and Perth.
G	P	F	L	H	C	1	10	Bridge of Orchy	Argyll ...	N. B.	Crianlarich and Fort William.
G	P	F	L	H	C	3	0	Bridge of Weir	Renfrew ...	G. & S.W.	Johnstone and Greenock.
..	..	..	..	..	..	..	..	Bridge Road Depôt	Durham ...	N. E.	Stockton, South.
..	..	..	..	..	..	..	..	Bridgerule	Devon......	L. & S.W.	See Whitstone and Bridgerule.
G	P	..	..	..	..	5	0	Bridges	Cornwall ..	G. W.	Newquay and Par.
..	..	..	..	..	..	..	..	Treffrys Siding	Cornwall ..	G. W.	Extension from Bridges.
..	..	..	..	..	..	..	..	Bridgeside Works	Edinboro'	N. B.	Edinburgh, Leith Walk.
..	..	..	..	..	..	..	..	Bridge Street	Armagh ...	D. N. & G.—G. N. (I.)..	See Newry.
..	..	..	..	..	..	..	..	Bridge Street	Lanark ...	Cal.—Glas. Dist. Sub.	See Glasgow.
..	..	..	..	..	..	..	..	Bridge Street	N'hamptn.	L. & N. W.—Mid.—G. N.	See Northampton.
..	..	..	..	..	..	..	..	Bridge Street (L. & Y.)	Yorks	L. & Y.— L. & N. W.	See Bradford.
..	..	..	..	..	..	..	..	Bridge Street Junction	Lanark ,..	Cal.—G. & P. Jt.	Glasgow.
..	..	..	..	..	..	..	..	Bridgeton	Lanark ...	Cal.	See Glasgow.
..	..	..	..	..	..	..	..	Bridgeton Cross...............	Lanark ...	Cal.—N. B.	See Glasgow.
..	..	..	..	..	..	..	..	Bridgeton Cross Junction ...	Lanark ...	Cal.	Glasgow.
..	..	..	..	..	..	..	..	Bridgeton Cross Mineral Depôt	Lanark ...	Cal.	Glasgow, Bridgeton.
..	..	..	..	..	..	..	..	Bridgeton Cross North Junc.	Lanark ...	N. B.	Glasgow.
..	..	..	..	..	..	..	..	Bridgewater Siding	Cheshire...	L. & N. W.	See Manchester Ship Canal Co. (Preston Brook).
..	..	..	..	..	..	..	..	Bridge Yard Siding	Lancs	L. & N. W.	See Widnes Foundry (Widnes).
G	P	F	L	H	C	4	10	Bridgnorth	Salop	G. W.	Shrewsbury and Hartlebury.
								BRIDGWATER—			
G	P	F	L	H	C	8	0	(Station)	Somerset..	G. W.	Highbridge and Taunton.
G	P	F	L	H	C	10	0	(Station)	Somerset..	S.&D.Jt.(L.&S.W.&Mid)	Branch from Edington.
..	..	..	..	..	..	..	..	Board's Siding...............	Somerset..	S.&D.Jt.(L.&S.W.&Mid)	Bridgwater.
G	..	..	..	..	..	1	10	Wharf	Somerset..	S.&D.Jt.(L.&S.W.&Mid)	Branch near Bridgwater.
G	..	..	..	..	..	8	0	Wharf and Docks	Somerset..	G. W.	Branch from Bridgwater.
..	..	..	..	..	..	..	..	Bridgwood's Pottery..........	Staffs	N. S.	Longton.
G	P	F	L	H	C	5	0	Bridlington	Yorks	N. E.	Driffield and Filey.
..	..	..	..	..	..	..	..	Bridlington Gas Co.'s Sid.	Yorks	N. E.	Bridlington.
..	..	..	..	..	..	..	..	Medforth & Hutchinson's Siding	Yorks	N. E.	Bridlington.
								BRIDPORT—			
G	P	F	L	H	C	5	0	(Station)	Dorset.....	G. W.	Maiden Newton and West Bay.
..	P	..	..	..	..	..	..	East Street	Dorset.....	G. W.	Bridport and West Bay.
G	P	..	L	..	..	..	..	West Bay.....................	Dorset.....	G. W.	Branch from Maiden Newton.
G	P	..	L	H	..	6	0	Brierfield	Lancs	L. & Y.	Colne and Burnley.
..	..	..	..	..	..	..	..	Hargreaves' Siding	Lancs	L. & Y.	Brierfield.
..	..	..	..	..	..	..	..	Tunstill's Siding.............	Lancs	L. & Y.	Brierfield.
..	P	..	..	..	..	..	..	Brierley Hill	Staffs	G. W.	Dudley and Stourbridge Junction.
..	..	..	..	..	..	..	..	Brierley Junction	Yorks	Dearne Valley—H. & B.	Grimethorpe and Hemsworth.
..	..	..	..	..	..	..	..	Brierley Siding	Glo'ster ...	S.&WyeJt.(G.W.&Mid.)	Lydbrook, Upper.
..	..	..	..	..	..	..	..	Brierlow Siding	Derby	L. & N. W.	Same as Spencer's (Hindlow).
G	P	F	L	H	C	5	0	Brigg.............................	Lincoln ...	G. C.	Gainsboro' and Barnetby.
..	..	..	..	..	..	..	..	Briggs' Coal Yard	Lancs	L. & N. W.	See Lecturer's Close and Hulme Trust Siding (Bolton).
..	..	..	..	..	..	..	..	Briggs' Colliery	Yorks	Mid.	Altofts & Whitwood.
..	..	..	..	..	..	..	..	Briggs, H., & Sons' Siding ...	Yorks	N. E.	Same as Mexboro' Main Collieries (Castleford).
..	..	..	..	..	..	..	..	Briggs' Siding..................	Derby	L. & N. W.	See Buxton Lime Firms Co. (Hindlow).
G	P	F	L	H	C	3	0	Brigham (L. & N. W.)	Cumb'land	L. & N. W. / M. & C.	Cockermouth and Workington. / Over L. & N. W. from Brigham Jn.
								Allerdale Coal Co.—			
..	..	..	..	..	..	..	..	Brigham Limestone Sid.	Cumb'land	L. & N. W.	Brigham and Broughton Cross.
..	..	..	..	..	..	..	..	Lowther Pit Colliery	Cumb'land	L. & N. W.	Camerton and Marron Junction.
..	..	..	..	..	..	..	..	Brigham Junction	Cumb'land	L. & N. W.—M. & C......	Marron Junction and Cockermouth.
..	..	..	..	..	..	..	..	Brigham Limestone Siding ...	Cumb'land	L. & N. W.	See Allerdale Coal Co. (Brigham).
G	P	F	L	H	C	10	0	Brighouse (L. & Y.)	Yorks	L. & Y. / G. N. / L. & N. W.	Halifax and Huddersfield. / Over L. & Y. from Wakefield Junc. / Over L. & Y. from Bradley Wood Jn.
G	P	F	L	H	C	10	0				
G	..	F	L	..	..	10	0				
..	..	..	..	..	..	..	..	Bright Bros.' Siding	Lancs	L. & Y.	Wardleworth.

EXPLANATION—G Goods Station.   P Passenger and Parcel Station.   P* Passenger, but not Parcel or Miscellaneous Traffic.
F Furniture Vans, Carriages, Portable Engines, and Machines on Wheels.   L Live Stock.
H Horse Boxes and Prize Cattle Vans.   C Carriages by Passenger Train.

STATION ACCOMMODATION.						CRANE POWER.		STATIONS, &c.	COUNTY.	COMPANY.	POSITION.
						Tons	Cwts.				
G	P	F	.	H	C	1	0	Brightlingsea	Essex	G. E.	Branch from Wyvenhoe.
								BRIGHTON—			
G	P	F	L	H	C	12	0	Central	Sussex	L. B. & S. C.	Lewes and Worthing.
G	.	.	.	.	.	5	0	Holland Road	Sussex	L. B. & S. C.	Near Brighton.
								Hollingdean Road Siding (Brighton Corporation)	Sussex	L. B. & S. C.	Brighton and Lewes Road.
G	P	F	L	H	C	10	0	Hove	Sussex	L. B. & S. C.	Brighton and Shoreham.
.	.	.	.	.	.	.	.	Hove Electric Lighting Co.'s Siding	Sussex	L. B. & S. C.	Hove and Brighton.
G	P	.	.	.	.	10	0	Kemp Town	Sussex	L. B. & S. C.	Branch from London Road.
.	P	.	.	.	.			Kemp Town Junction	Sussex	L. B. & S. C.	London Road and Falmer.
.	P	.	.	.	.			Lewes Road	Sussex	L. B. & S. C.	Brighton and Kemp Town.
.	.	.	.	.	.			London Road	Sussex	L. B. & S. C.	Brighton and Falmer.
G	.	.	.	.	.			Montpelier Junction	Sussex	L. B. & S. C.	Brighton (Central) and London Rd.
.	.	.	.	.	.			Top Yard	Sussex	L. B. & S. C.	Brighton.
.	.	.	.	.	.			Brighton Brick & Tile Works and Quarry	Fife	N. B.	Springfield.
.	.	.	.	.	.			Brighton Corporation Siding	Sussex	L. B. & S. C.	Falmer.
.	.	.	.	.	.			Brighton Road	Worcester	Mid.	See Birmingham.
.	.	.	.	.	.			Brightside	Yorks	Mid.	See Sheffield.
.	.	.	.	.	.			Brightside and Carbrook Co-operative Society Sid. (G.C.)	Yorks	G. C.—Mid.	Sheffield, Broughton Lane.
.	.	.	.	.	.			Brightside Junction	Yorks	L. D. & E. C.—Mid.	Tinsley Road and Sheffield.
.	.	.	.	.	.			Brightside Wharf	Yorks	Mid.	See Sheffield.
.	.	.	.	.	.			Brightside Works	Yorks	L.D.&E.C.— Mid. —G.C.	Same as Jessop, W., & Son's Siding (Sheffield).
G	P	F	L	.	.	.	.	Brill	Bucks	O. & A. Tram.	Terminus of Tramroad from Quainton Road.
.	.	.	.	.	.			Brimington (G. C.)	Derby	G. C.— L. & N. W.	See Sheepbridge and Brimington.
G	P	F	L	H	C	8	0	Brimscombe	Glo'ster	G. W.	Gloucester and Swindon.
G	P	.	.	.	.			Brimsdown	Middlesex	G. E.	Tottenham and Waltham Cross.
G	.	.	.	.	.	10	0	Fry Bros.' Siding	Middlesex	G. E.	Brimsdown.
.	.	.	.	.	.			Brindle Heath	Lancs	L. & Y.	Pendleton and Clifton Junction.
.	.	.	.	.	.			Agecroft Colliery	Lancs	L. & Y.	Pendleton and Clifton Junction.
.	.	.	.	.	.			Brindle Heath Race Course	Lancs	L. & Y.	Brindle Heath.
.	.	.	.	.	.			Knowles, A., & Sons Pendleton Colliery	Lancs	L. & Y.	Brindle Heath and Clifton Junction.
.	.	.	.	.	.			Locomotive Sidings	Lancs	L. & Y.	Agecroft and Brindle Heath.
.	.	.	.	.	.			Sun Paper Mill Co.'s Siding	Lancs	L. & Y.	Brindle Heath.
.	P	.	.	H	C			Brinkburn	Northumb	N. B.	Scotsgap and Rothbury.
.	.	.	.	.	.			Brinkburn (Goods) Siding	Northumb	N.B.	See Rothbury.
G	P	F	L	H	C			Brinklow	Warwick	L. & N. W.	Nuneaton and Rugby.
G	P	F	L	H	C	1	10	Brinks Colliery	Lancs	L&Y&LU Jt(LY&LNW)	See Wigan Coal and Iron Co.
								Brinkworth	Wilts	G. W.	Wootton Bassett and Patchway.
G	P	.	L	H	.	4	0	Brinnington Junction	Cheshire	C. L. C.—S. & M. Jt.	Stockport and Reddish.
.	.	.	.	.	.			Brinscall	Lancs	L&Y&LU Jt(LY&LNW)	Heapey and Withnell.
.	.	.	.	.	.			Withnell Mill Sidings	Lancs	L&Y&LUJt(L&Y&LNW)	Brinscall and Withnell.
.	.	.	.	.	.			Leigh's	Lancs	L&Y&LUJt(L&Y&LNW)	Withnell Mill Sidings.
.	.	.	.	.	.			Marriage and Pinnock's	Lancs	L&Y&LUJt(L&Y&LNW)	Withnell Mill Sidings.
.	.	.	.	.	.			Parke's Brick & Fire Clay Co.'s	Lancs	L&Y&LUJt(L&Y&LNW)	Withnell Mill Sidings.
.	.	.	.	.	.			Waring Bros.	Lancs	L&Y&LUJt(L&Y&LNW)	Withnell Mill Sidings.
.	.	.	.	.	.			Wood's Siding	Lancs	L&Y&LUJt(L&Y&LNW)	Brinscall and Heapey.
.	.	.	.	.	.			Brinsley Colliery	Notts	Mid.	See Barber, Walker & Co. (Langley Mill and Eastwood).
.	.	.	.	.	.			Brinsley Colliery (G.N.)	Notts	G.N.— G. C.	Eastwood and Langley Mill.
.	.	.	.	.	.			Brinsley Jn.(Codnor Park Jn.)	Derby	G.N.— Mid.	Eastwood Road and Codnor Park.
.	.	.	.	.	.			Brinsley Sidings	Derby	G.N.	Same as Codnor Park Iron Works.
.	.	.	.	.	.			Brinsworth Iron Works (Baker, J., & Co.)	Yorks	Mid.	Masboro' and Rotherham.
.	.	.	.	.	.			Brisbane's, Thomas, Wood Yard	Stirling	N. B.	Stirling, Cowpark.
G	P	.	L	.	.			Brislington	Somerset	G. W.	Bristol and Radstock.
								BRISTOL—			
.	.	.	.	.	.			Aird's Siding	Glo'ster	G. W.	Avonmouth Docks and Pilning.
.	P	.	.	.	.			Anglo-American Oil Co.'s Siding	Glo'ster	Clif. Ex. Jt. (G. W. & Mid.)	Near Avonmouth Docks.
.	.	.	.	.	.			Avonmouth Docks	Glo'ster	Clif. Ex. Jt.(G. W.& Mid.)	Terminus.
G	.	.	L	.	.	30	0	Avonmouth Docks	Glo'ster	{ G. W. / Mid.	Shirehampton and Pilning. / Terminus.
.	.	.	.	.	.			Avonside Engine Works	Glo'ster	Mid.	Bristol.
G	.	.	.	.	.			Avon Street Depôt	Glo'ster	Mid.	Lower Wharf.

EXPLANATION—G *Goods Station.*   P *Passenger and Parcel Station.*   P* *Passenger, but not Parcel or Miscellaneous Traffic.*
F *Furniture Vans, Carriages, Portable Engines, and Machines on Wheels.*   L *Live Stock.*
H *Horse Boxes and Prize Cattle Vans.*   C *Carriages by Passenger Train.*

STATION ACCOMMODATION.						CRANE POWER.		STATIONS, &c.	COUNTY.	COMPANY.	POSITION.
						Tons	Cwts	BRISTOL—*continued.*			
..	..	..	..	..	..	..	..	Bailey's Siding	Somerset..	G. W.	Portishead.
..	..	..	..	..	..	..	..	Bristol Dock Co.'s Avonmouth Dock Siding	Glo'ster ...	Clif. Ex. Jt. (G. W. & Mid.)	Avonmouth Docks.
..	..	..	..	..	..	..	..	Bristol Wagon and Carriage Wks.Co.'s Sid.(Mid)	Glo'ster ...	Mid.—G.W.	Bristol.
..	..	..	..	..	..	..	..	Cattybrook Brick Co.'s Sid.	Glo'ster ...	G. W.	Bristol.
..	..	..	..	..	..	..	..	Coal Pit Heath Coal Co.'s Siding (Hewitt's Yard)..	Glo'ster ...	Mid.	Bristol.
..	..	..	..	..	..	..	..	Crimea Siding.................	Glo'ster ...	G. W.	Temple Meads.
..	..	..	..	..	..	..	..	East Depôt	Glo'ster ...	G. W.	Temple Meads and St. Ann's Park.
G	P	..	..	..	..	5	0	Fishponds.....................	Glo'ster ...	Mid.	Bristol and Mangotsfield.
..	..	..	..	..	..	..	..	Fishponds Coal Co.'s Siding	Glo'ster ...	Mid.	Near Fishponds Station.
..	..	..	..	..	..	..	..	Great Western Colliery ...	Glo'ster ...	G. W.	Bristol.
G	..	..	..	..	..	35	0	Harbour	Glo'ster ...	G. W.	Branch from Temple Meads.
..	P	F	..	H	C	..	..	Joint Station	Glo'ster ...	{ G. W. .... { Mid.	Bath and Bridgwater. Terminus.
..	..	..	..	..	..	..	..	Junction	Glo'ster ...	G. W.— Mid.	Keynsham & Joint Passenger Sta.
G	..	..	L	..	..	10	0	Kingsland Road...............	Glo'ster ...	G. W.	East Depôt & Joint Passenger Sta.
..	..	..	..	..	..	..	..	Kingswood Colliery(Peckett & Son's Siding)	Glo'ster ...	Mid.	Bristol and Fishponds.
..	..	..	..	..	..	..	..	Malago Vale Colliery	Somerset..	G. W.	Bedminster and Portishead Junc.
..	..	..	..	..	..	..	..	Mardon & Son's Paper Works	Glo'ster ...	Mid.	Bristol.
..	..	..	..	..	..	..	..	Marsh Siding	Somerset..	G. W.	Loop Line.
G	P	F	L	H	C	6	0	Portishead	Somerset..	G. W.	Branch from Bristol.
G	..	..	..	..	..	4	0	Portishead Docks	Somerset..	G. W.	Extension from Portishead Station.
..	..	..	..	..	..	..	..	Portishead Gas Works	Somerset..	G. W.	Portishead.
..	..	..	..	..	..	..	..	Proctor's Siding	Glo'ster ...	G. W.	Redcliffe Wharf.
G	..	F	L	..	..	12	0	Pylle Hill...................	Somerset..	G. W.	Joint Pass. Sta. & Bedminster.
G	..	..	..	..	..	..	..	Redcliffe Wharf	Glo'ster ...	G. W.	Temple Meads and Bristol Station.
..	..	..	..	..	..	..	..	Robinson & Co.'s Siding ...	Glo'ster ...	G. W.	Harbour.
G	P	F	L	H	C	20	0	St. Philips	Glo'ster ...	Mid.	Branch from Lawrence Hill Junc.
G	..	..	..	..	..	6	0	St. Philips Marsh Depôt ...	Glo'ster ...	G. W.	East Depôt and Pylle Hill.
..	..	..	..	..	..	..	..	Sneyd Park Junction	Glo'ster ...	Clif. Ex. Jt.(G.W. & Mid.)	Avonmouth and Clifton Down.
..	..	..	..	..	..	..	..	South Liberty Colliery	Somerset..	G. W.	Portishead Jn. and Flax Bourton.
..	P	..	..	..	..	..	..	Staple Hill	Glo'ster ...	Mid.	Mangotsfield and Fishponds.
..	..	..	..	..	..	..	..	Stapleton Road Gas Wks (Bristol Gas Co.)	Glo'ster ...	{ G. W. .... { Mid.	Bristol and Montpelier. Montpelier and Fishponds.
G	..	F	..	..	..	12	0	Temple Meads...............	Glo'ster ...	G. W.	Bristol Junction and Harbour.
..	..	..	..	..	..	..	..	Westerleigh Sidings	Glo'ster ...	Mid.	Bristol and Yate.
..	..	..	..	..	..	..	..	Western Petroleum Co.'s Siding	Glo'ster ...	Clif. Ex. Jt. (G.W. & Mid.)	Near Avonmouth Docks.
..	..	..	..	..	..	..	..	Bristol Channel Steam Packet Co.'s Pockett's Siding	Glamorg'n	GW—LNW—Mid—RSB	Swansea.
..	..	..	..	..	..	..	..	Bristol Dock Committee's Avonmouth Dock Sidings...	Glo'ster ...	Clif. Ex. Jt.(G.W. & Mid.)	Bristol, Avonmouth Docks.
..	..	..	..	..	..	..	..	Bristol Gas Co.'s Siding	Glos'ter ...	G. W.— Mid	Same as Stapleton Road Gas Works.
..	..	..	..	..	..	..	..	Bristol Steam Navigation Co.	Glos'ter ...	G. W.	Gloucester Docks.
..	..	..	..	..	..	..	..	Bristol Wagon and Carriage Works Co.'s Siding (Mid)..	Glo'ster ...	Mid.—G.W.	Bristol.
..	..	..	..	..	..	..	..	Bristol Wagon Co.'s Siding	Glamorg'n	GW—L&NW—Rhy—TV	Cardiff.
..	..	..	..	..	..	..	..	Bristol Water Works Co.'s Sid.	Somerset..	G. W.	Blagdon.
..	..	..	..	..	..	..	..	Britain Colliery	Derby......	Mid.	See Butterley Co. (Codnor Park).
..	P	..	..	..	..	..	..	Britannia	Lancs	L. & Y.	Bacup and Facit.
..	..	..	..	..	..	..	..	Britannia Stone Siding......	Lancs	L. & Y.	Bacup and Facit.
..	..	..	..	..	..	..	..	Brook's Siding	Lancs	L. & Y.	Britannia.
..	..	..	..	..	..	..	..	Britannia Brick Works.......	Warwick..	L. & N. W.	See Midland Brick Co.(Birmingham).
..	..	..	..	..	..	..	..	Britannia Engineering Works	Ayr	G. & S.W.	Kilmarnock.
..	..	..	..	..	..	..	..	Britannia Foundry, Forge, Nut and Bolt Works.........	Yorks	N. E.	Middlesbro'.
..	..	..	..	..	..	..	..	Britannia Iron & Steel Works and Wharf	Yorks	N. E.	Middlesbro'.
..	..	..	..	..	..	..	..	Britannia Sidings	Lancs	L. & Y.	Ince.
..	..	..	..	..	..	..	..	Britannia Works	Staffs	L. & N. W.	Same as Tupper & Co.'s Sid. (Albion).
..	..	..	..	..	..	..	..	Britannia Works (L. & N. W.)	Warwick..	L. & N. W.—Mid..........	See Metropolitan Amalgamated Railway Carriage and Wagon Co. (Birmingham).
..	..	..	..	..	..	..	..	Britannic Colliery	Glamorg'n	G. W.	Gilfach.
G	P	..	L	..	C	1	10	Brithdir (Rhy)	Glamorg'n	{ Rhy. .... { L. & N. W.	Bargoed and Tirphil. Over Rhy. from Rhymney Joint Line Junction.
G	..	..	L	..	..	1	10				

STATION ACCOMMODATION.	CRANE POWER.	STATIONS, &c.	COUNTY.	COMPANY.	POSITION.
	Tons Cwts.	Brithdir (Rhy.)—continued.			
. . . .	. .	Cefn Brithdir Colliery	Glamorg'n	Rhy.	Brithdir and Bargoed.
		Powell Duffryn Co.—			
. . . .	. .	Coedymoeth Colliery......	Glamorg'n	Rhy.	Brithdir.
. . . .	. .	Elliot Pit	Glamorg'n	Rhy.	Brithdir.
. . . .	. .	White Rose, No. 2 Col.	Glamorg'n	Rhy.	Brithdir.
. . . .	. .	British Alizarine Co.'s Sid. (G. E.)	Essex	GE—GN—L&NW—Mid.	London, Silvertown.
. . . .	. .	British & Chicago Raw Hide Co.'s Warehouse	Cheshire...	B'head Jt—CLC—NW&L	Birkenhead.
. . . .	. .	British Chemical Works	Dumbartn	{ Cal. .... { N. B.	Clydebank. Clydebank, East.
. . . .	. .	British Cyanide Co.	Worcester	G. W.	Oldbury.
. . . .	. .	British Dyewood & Chemical } Co.'s Siding .... }	Lanark ...	N. B.	{ Same as Carntyne Dye Works { (Glasgow).
. . . .	. .	British Electric Car Co.'s Sid.	Lancs	Trafford Park Estate ...	Manchester.
. . . .	. .	British Electric Plant Co.'s Sid	Clackman'	Cal.—N. B.	Alloa.
. . . .	. .	British Gas Light Co. (N. S.)	Staffs	N. S.—L. & N. W.	See Cliff Vale Siding (Etruria).
. . . .	. .	British Gas Light Co.'s Sid....	Yorks	H. & B.	Hull, Sculcoates.
. . . .	. .	British Griffin Chilled Iron and Steel Co.'s Siding	Lancs	Furness........................	Barrow.
. . . .	. .	British Hydraulic Foundry ...	Lanark ...	Cal.—N. B.	Glasgow, Whiteinch.
. . . .	. .	British Insulated and Helsby Cables Co.'s Siding............	Lancs	L. & N. W.	Prescot.
. . . .	. .	British Mannesman Tube Co.'s Siding	Glamorg'n	G. W.	Landore.
. . . .	. .	British Mannesman Tube Co.'s Siding (Mid.)............	Glamorg'n	Mid.—G.W.—L. & N. W.	Upper Bank.
. . . .	. .	British Moss Litter Charcoal and Manure Co.'s Siding ...	Lancs	L. & N. W.	Glazebury.
. . . .	. .	British Museum	Middlesex	C. L.	See London.
. . . .	. .	British Oil and Cake Mills ...	Edinboro'	N. B.	Leith, South.
. . . .	. .	British Plate Works	Lancs	L. & N. W.	See Pilkington Bros. (St. Helens).
. . . .	. .	British Rhondda Colliery	Glamorg'n	G. W.	Glyn Neath.
. . . .	. .	British Thomson-Houston Co.'s Siding	Warwick...	L. & N. W.—Mid.	Rugby.
. . . .	. .	British Tube Works	Lanark ...	{ Cal. .... { N. B.	Langloan. Coatbridge, Whifflet.
. . . .	. .	British Wagon Co.'s Sid. (G.C.)	Yorks	G. C.—G. N.	Rotherham and Masboro'.
. . . .	. .	British Wagon Works (G. C.)	Yorks	G. C.—G. N.	Doncaster.
. . . .	. .	British Westinghouse Co.'s Siding	Renfrew...	Cal............................	Yoker.
. . . .	. .	British Westinghouse Electric & Manufacturing Co.'s Sid.	Lancs	Trafford Park Estate......	Manchester.
		BRITON FERRY—			
G P	3 0	(Station)	Glamorg'n	G. W.	Neath and Bridgend.
G P	7 0	(Station)	Glamorg'n	R. & S. B.	Port Talbot and Neath.
G	2 0	(Station)	Glamorg'n	S. Wales Min.	Terminus.
. . . .	. .	Albion Steel Works	Glamorg'n	G. W.	Briton Ferry.
. . . .	. .	Baglan Bay Engineering Works	Glamorg'n	R. & S. B.	Briton Ferry.
. . . .	. .	Baglan Bay Tin Works...	Glamorg'n	G. W.	Briton Ferry.
. . . .	. .	Briton Ferry Steel Works	Glamorg'n	G. W.	Briton Ferry.
. . . .	. .	Briton Ferry Works	Glamorg'n	G. W.	Briton Ferry.
. . . .	. .	Cambrian Coke Siding	Glamorg'n	G. W.	Briton Ferry.
G	1 10	Dock	Glamorg'n	G. W.	Briton Ferry.
. . . .	. .	Dock Junction.................	Glamorg'n	G. W.—R. & S. B.........	Neath and Port Talbot.
. . . .	. .	Ferry Tin Plate Works (Vernon Siding)	Glamorg'n	R. & S. B.	Briton Ferry.
G	2 0	Glyncorrwg Engineering Works	Glamorg'n	G. W.—S. Wales Min....	Briton Ferry.
. . . .	. .	Gwynne & Co.'s Gwalia Tin Plate Works............	Glamorg'n	G. W.	Briton Ferry.
. . . .	. .	Junction	Glamorg'n	G. W.—S. Wales Min. ...	Briton Ferry Station and Neath Harbour Junction.
. . . .	. .	Junction	Glamorg'n	R. & S. B.—S. Wales Min.	Court Sart and Cymmer.
. . . .	. .	Taylor & Son's Foundry...	Glamorg'n	G. W.	Briton Ferry.
. . . .	. .	Villier's Tin Plate Works...	Glamorg'n	G. W.	Briton Ferry.
. . . .	. .	Warren's Chemical Works...	Glamorg'n	G. W.	Briton Ferry.
. . . .	. .	Wern Tin Plate Co.'s Wks....	Glamorg'n	G. W.	Briton Ferry.
. . . .	. .	Briton Ferry Chemical Works	Glamorg'n	R. & S. B.	Jersey Marine.
. P	. .	Briton Ferry Road..............	Glamorg'n	G. W.	Neath and Swansea.

EXPLANATION—G *Goods Station.*   P *Passenger and Parcel Station.*   P* *Passenger, but not Parcel or Miscellaneous Traffic.*
F *Furniture Vans, Carriages, Portable Engines, and Machines on Wheels.*   L *Live Stock.*
H *Horse Boxes and Prize Cattle Vans.*   C *Carriages by Passenger Train.*

STATION ACCOMMODATION.						CRANE POWER.	STATIONS, &c.	COUNTY.	COMPANY.	POSITION.
						Tons Cwts.	Brittain's or Manystones Qry.	Derby......	L. & N. W.	See Wirksworth Stone & Mineral Co. (Longcliffe).
G	P					2 0	Brixham	Devon......	G. W.	Branch from Churston.
							Brixton (S. E. & C.)	Surrey ...	SE&C—GN—LSW—Mid	See London.
							Brixton Coal Depôt	Surrey ...	Mid.	See London.
							Brixton, East	Surrey ...	L. B. & S. C.	See London, East Brixton.
G	P						Brixton Road	Devon......	G. W.	Plymstock and Yealmpton.
G	P	F	L	H	C	1 10	Brixworth..................	N'hamptn	L. & N. W.	Market Harboro' and Northampton.
							Attenborough & Timms Sid.	N'hamptn	L. & N. W.	Brixworth and Lamport.
							Broadbent & Co.'s Siding......	Leicester..	Mid.	Leicester, West Bridge.
							Broadbent & Co.'s Slag Wool Works	Yorks	N. E.	See Redcar Iron Works (Tod Point).
							Broadbent's Saw Mills, Timber Yards and Depôts	Durham ..	N. E.	Stockton, North Shore.
							Broadbent's Siding	Yorks......	G. C.	Hazlehead Bridge.
							Broadbottom	Cheshire..	G. C.	See Mottram and Broadbottom.
G	P	F	L	H	C	4 0	Broadclyst	Devon......	L. & S. W.	Yeovil and Exeter.
G	P					10 0	Broadfield	Lancs	L. & Y.	Bury and Heywood.
							Broadfoot's Foundry (Inchholm Brass Foundry)........	Renfrew ...	Cal.	Glasgow, Whiteinch.
G	P		L		C	· ·			Cal.	Steamer from Oban.
G	P		L		C	· ·	Broadford..................	Inverness..	High.	Steamer from Kyle of Lochalsh.
G	P		L		C	· ·			N. B.	Steamer from Mallaig.
							Broad Green	Lancs	L. & N. W.	See Liverpool.
							Broad Green Siding	Lancs	L. & N. W.	See Wigan Coal & Iron Co. (Liverpool).
G	P	F	L	H	C	5 0	Broadheath (Altrincham)	Cheshire...	L. & N. W.	Stockport and Warrington.
							Richards & Co.'s Atlantic Works	Lancs	L. & N. W.	Broadheath (Altrincham) and Dunham Massey.
							Broadheath Junction...........	Cheshire...	C. L. C.—L. & N. W. ...	Baguley and Warrington.
							Broadhurst & Son's Sid.(LNW)	Staffs	L. & N. W.—G. W.—Mid.	Walsall.
G	P					5 0	Broadley	Lancs	L. & Y.	Rochdale and Facit.
							Hey's Siding	Lancs	L. & Y.	Broadley.
							Broad Oak Brick, Tile, and Colliery Co.'s Siding	Lancs......	L. & N. W.	Same as Bates' Broad Oak Bk., Tile & Colliery Co.'s Sid. (St. Helens).
							Broad Oak Colliery	Glamorg'n	G. W.	Loughor.
							Broad Oak Colliery	Lancs	O. A. & G. B. Jt. (G. C. and L. & N. W.).........	Ashton, Oldham Road.
							Broad Oaks Siding (Markham & Co.)	Derby......	Mid.	Chesterfield.
							Broadrigg Colliery	Lanark ...	N. B.	Greengairs.
G	P	F	L	H	C	5 0	Broadstairs..................	Kent	S. E. & C.	Margate and Ramsgate.
							Northdown Siding.............	Kent	S. E. & C.	Margate (West) and Broadstairs.
							Broadstone	Dublin ...	M. G. W.	See Dublin.
G	P						Broadstone Junction Station	Dorset......	L. & S.W.—S. & D. Jt.	Poole and Blandford.
							Broad Street	Lancs	L. & Y.	See Pendleton.
							Broad Street	Middlesex	L. & N. W.—N. L.	See London.
							Broadwath Depôts..............	Cumb'land	N. E.	Heads Nook.
							Broadwath Siding	Cumb'land	N. E.	Heads Nook.
							Broadway..................	Middlesex	H. & C. Jt.—Met Dist....	See London, Hammersmith (Broadway).
G	P	F	L	H	C	5 0	Broadwey..................	Dorset......	G. W.	Upwey Junction and Abbotsbury.
							Broadwood Quarry	Durham ...	N. E	Frosterley.
G	P		L				Brock	Lancs	L. & N. W.	Lancaster and Preston.
G	P	F	L	H	C	5 0	Brockenhurst	Hants	L. & S.W.	Southampton and Christchurch.
							Brockenshaw's Dock Siding	Cumb'land	C. & W. Jn.	Workington.
							Brockham Brick Co.'s Siding	Surrey ...	S. E. & C.	Betchworth.
							Brockhampton & Stream Hall Siding	Hereford ..	G. W.	Bromyard.
G	P		L	H		2 10	Brockholes	Yorks	L. & Y.	Huddersfield and Penistone.
							Brockhurst	Hants	L. & S.W.	See Fort Brockhurst.
							Brocklebank Dock	Lancs	L'pool O'head	See Liverpool.
G	P	F	L	H	C		Brocklesby	Lincoln ...	G. C.	Barnetby and Grimsby.
							Brocklesby Junction............	Lincoln ...	G. C.	Brocklesby Station and Ulceby.
	P						Brockley (L. B. & S. C.)	Kent	L. B. & S. C.	New Cross and Forest Hill.
									G. E.	Over L. B. & S. C. from New Cross Jn.
G	P					· ·	Brockley Lane	Kent	G. N.	Over Met. and S. E. & C. Lines.
									S. E. & C.	Nunhead and Greenwich.
							Martin's Siding	Kent	S. E. & C.	Nunhead Jn. Sta. & Brockley Lane.
G	P		L	H		0 15	Brockley Whins..............	Durham ...	N. E.	Newcastle and Sunderland.
							Boldon Brick Works.........	Durham ...	N. E.	Brockley Whins.
							Boldon Colliery	Durham ...	N. E.	Brockley Whins.

STATION ACCOMMODATION.						CRANE POWER.		STATIONS, &c.	COUNTY.	COMPANY.	POSITION.
						Tons	Cwts				
								Brocton................	Staffs......	L. & N. W.	See Milford and Brocton.
G	P	F	L	H	C	5	0	Brodie	Elgin&Mo'	High....................	Nairn and Forres.
								Brodsworth............	Yorks......	H. & B.	See Pickburn and Brodsworth.
	P							Brofiskin Siding (G. W.)	Glamorg'n	G. W.—T. V.	Mwyndy.
	P							Broighter................	Derry	N. C. Com. (Mid.)	Limavady Junction and Limavady.
G	P		L	H		2	0	Bromborough	Cheshire...	B'head Jt. (G W & L N W)	Birkenhead and Hooton.
G	P		L	H		1	10	Bromfield	Cumb'land	Cal.	Brayton and Annan.
G	P	F	L	H	C	5	0	Bromfield..............	Salop	S & H Jt (G W & L N W)	Craven Arms and Hereford.
								Bromfield Hall Siding	Flint	L. & N. W.	Same as Mold Gas and Water Co.'s Siding (Mold).
								Bromford Lane	Worcester	L. & N. W.	See Oldbury and Bromford Lane.
								Bromilow, Foster, & Co.'s Ashtons Green Colliery......	Lancs	L. & N. W.	St. Helens.
								Bromilow Pit	Lancs	L. & N. W.	See Wigan Coal & Iron Co. (Wigan).
								Bromley (L. T. & S.)	Middlesex	L. T. & S.—G. E.—N. L.	See London.
								Bromley Basin	Staffs......	G. W.	See Brettell Lane.
G	P		L	H		10	0	Bromley Cross	Lancs......	L. & Y.	Bolton and Blackburn.
								Bromley Junction	Essex	G. E.—L. T. & S.	London, Canning Town & Bromley.
								Bromley Junction	Middlesex	L. T. & S.—N. L.	London, Bromley and Bow.
G	P	F	L	H	C	10	0	Bromley, North	Kent	S. E. & C.	Branch from Grove Park.
G	P	F	L	H	C	10	0	Bromley, South	Kent	S. E. & C.	Beckenham and Bickley.
								Bromley, South	Middlesex	N. L.	See London, South Bromley.
G	P				C	1	10	Brompton................	Yorks	N. E.	Northallerton and Stockton.
								Brompton (Gloucester Road)	Middlesex	Met—Met Dist—L & N W	See London, Gloucester Road.
								Brompton and Fulham........	Middlesex	L. & N. W.	See London.
								Brompton, West............	Middlesex	Met. Dist.—W. L. E. Jt.	See London, West Brompton.
G	P	F	L	H	C	5	0	Bromsgrove	Worcester	Mid.	Birmingham and Droitwich.
G								Bromshall	Staffs	N. S.	Uttoxeter and Stoke.
								Bromshall Junction	Staffs	G. N.—N. S.	Stafford Common and Uttoxeter.
G	P	F	L	H	C	1	0	Bromyard	Hereford ..	G. W.	Worcester and Leominster.
								Brockhampton and Stream Hall Siding	Hereford ..	G. W.	Bromyard and Suckley.
								Brondesbury	Middlesex	Met.	See London, Kilburn—Brondesbury.
								Brondesbury (L. & N. W.) ...	Middlesex	L. & N. W.—N. L.	See London.
								Brondesbury (Mid.)	Middlesex	Mid.—S. E. & C.	See London, West End and Brondesbury.
G	P		L					Bronwydd Arms............	Carmarth'	G. W.	Carmarthen and Pencader.
								Brook & Co.'s Siding........	Yorks	G. C.	Deepcar (for Stocksbridge).
								Brook & Son's Siding	Yorks	L. & Y.	Lightcliffe.
								Brook Colliery..............	Glamorg'n	G. W.	Same as Gwaun Cae Gurwen Colliery (Garnant).
								Brookdale Works (C. L. C.) ...	Cheshire...	C. L. C.—L. & N. W.......	See Salt Union, Ltd. (Northwich).
								Brooke & Son's Fieldhouse Siding (L. & N. W.)	Yorks	L. & N. W.—L. & Y.......	Huddersfield.
G	P		L					Brookeborough	Ferm'nagh	Clogher Valley	Fivemiletown and Maguiresbridge.
								Brookfield Siding	Derby	G. C.	Dinting.
								Brookhouse Siding..............	Lancs	L. & N. W.	See Widnes Foundry (Widnes).
	P							Brookland	Kent	S. E. & C.	Appledore and Lydd.
G	P					5	0	Brooklands	Cheshire...	M S J & A (GC & L NW)	Manchester and Timperley.
								Brook Lane Exchange Siding	Cheshire...	G. W.—L. & N. W........	Chester.
G	P							Brookmount................	Antrim ...	G. N. (I.)	Antrim and Lisburn.
								Brooks & Pickup's Colliery ...	Lancs	L. & Y.	Townley.
								Brooksbottom Siding............	Lancs	L. & Y.	Summerseat.
G	P	F	L	H	C			Brooksby	Leicester..	Mid.	Leicester and Melton Mowbray.
								Brookside or Bugle Horn Colliery.....................	Lancs	L. & N. W.	See Unsworth & Cowburn's (Wigan).
								Brook's Siding	Hadding'n	N. B.	Ormiston.
								Brook's Siding	Lancs	L. & Y.	Britannia.
G	P	F	L	H	C	1	10	Brookwood	Surrey ...	L. & S.W.	Woking and Farnborough.
								National Rifle Association's Siding (Bisley Camp)......	Surrey ...	L. & S.W.	Private Branch from Brookwood.
								Necropolis Station	Surrey ...	L. & S.W.	Branch to Brookwood Cemetery.
G	P							Broom	Warwick..	E. & W. Jn.	Terminus.
G	P							Broom	Warwick..	Mid.	Alcester and Evesham.
								Broom Junction	Warwick..	E. & W. Jn.— Mid.	Stratford-on-Avon and Wixford.
G	P		L	H		1	10	Broome	Salop	L. & N. W.	Craven Arms & Llandrindod Wells.
								Broomfield (L. & Y.)	Yorks	L. & Y.—L. & N. W. ...	See Bradford.
								Broomfield Colliery (L.&N.W.)	Lancs	L.&N.W.—G.C.(Wig.Jn)	See Wigan Coal & Iron Co. (Wigan).
								Broomfield Junction	Forfar......	Cal.—N.B.	Dubton Junction and Montrose.
								Broomfield Sidings	Forfar......	N.B.	See Montrose.
								Broomfleet Siding	Yorks	N. E.	See Staddlethorpe.
G*								Broomhedge Siding	Antrim ...	G. N. (I.)	Lisburn and Moira.

EXPLANATION—G Goods Station.   G *—Minerals only.   P Passenger and Parcel Station.
P* Passenger, but not Parcel or Miscellaneous Traffic.   F Furniture Vans, Carriages, Portable Engines, and Machines on Wheels.
L Live Stock.   H Horse Boxes and Prize Cattle Vans.   C Carriages by Passenger Train.

G	P	F	L	H	C	Tons	Cwts	STATIONS, &c.	COUNTY.	COMPANY.	POSITION.
G	P	F	L	H	C	.	.	Broomhill	Inverness	High	Boat of Garten and Grantown.
G	P	.	.	.	.	1	10	Broomhill	Northumb	N. E.	Chevington and Amble.
.	.	.	.	.	.			Broomhill Colliery	Northumb	N. E.	Broomhill.
.	.	.	.	.	.			Broomhill Cols. Coal Depôt...	Northumb	N. E.	Alnwick.
.	.	.	.	.	.			Broomhill Siding	Ayr	G. & S. W.	Same as Todhills Siding (Glengarnock and Kilbirnie).
.	.	.	.	.	.			Broomhill Siding	Lancs	P.&L.Jt.(L&NW.&L&Y.)	Same as Tootal Height Quarry Co.'s Siding (Longridge).
.	.	.	.	.	.			Broomhill Sidings	Notts	G.N.	Butlers Hill.
.	.	.	.	.	.			Broomhope Siding	Northumb	N.B.	Reedsmouth.
G	P	.	.	.	.			Broomhouse	Lanark	N.B.	Shettleston and Bothwell.
.	.	.	.	.	.			Bredisholm Branch	Lanark	N.B.	Broomhouse and Maryville.
.	.	.	.	.	.			Bredisholm Colliery	Lanark	N.B.	Branch—Broomhouse & Maryville.
.	.	.	.	.	.			Bredisholm Quarry	Lanark	N.B.	Branch—Broomhouse & Maryville.
.	.	.	.	.	.			Broomhouse Colliery	Lanark	N.B.	Broomhouse and Maryville.
.	.	.	.	.	.			Clydeside Colliery	Lanark	N.B.	Broomhouse and Maryville.
.	.	.	.	.	.			Daldowie Colliery	Lanark	N.B.	Near Broomhouse.
.	P	.	.	.	.			Broomieknowe	Edinboro'	N.B.	Hardengreen and Polton.
.	.	.	.	.	.			Broomielaw Siding	Durham	N. E.	Barnard Castle.
.	.	.	.	.	.			Broomlands, No. 8	Ayr	G. & S. W.	Dreghorn.
G	P	F	L	H	C	1	0	Broomlee (for West Linton)	Peebles	N.B.	Leadburn and Dolphinton.
.	.	.	.	.	.			Leslie's Saw Mill	Peebles	N.B.	Broomlee.
.	.	.	.	.	.			Broomloan Siding	Lanark	G & P Jt (Cal & G & S W)	Glasgow, Govan.
.	.	.	.	.	.			Broompark Colliery	Durham	N. E.	Brandon Colliery Station.
.	.	.	.	.	.			Broomrigg Colliery (Denny-loanhead Colliery Siding)...	Stirling	K.& B. Jt. (Cal. & N. B.)	Bonnybridge, Central.
.	.	.	.	.	.			Broomside Colliery	Lanark	Cal.	Same as Dalzell, Lesmahagow (Motherwell).
.	.	.	.	.	.			Broomside Farm Siding	Lanark	Cal.	Motherwell.
.	.	.	.	.	.			Broomside Junction	Durham	N. E.	Pittington.
.	.	.	.	.	.			Broomside Junction & Siding	Durham	N. E.	Sherburn Colliery Station.
G	P	F	L	H	C	2	0	Brora	Sutherl'nd	High.	Golspie and Helmsdale.
.	.	.	.	.	.			Broseley	Salop	G. W.	See Ironbridge and Broseley.
.	.	.	.	.	.			Brosna Mills Siding	Kings	G. S. & W.	Roscrea and Birr.
								Brotherton & Co.—			
.	.	.	.	.	.			Chemical & Cement Wks.	Yorks	G. N. & L. & Y. Jt.	Wakefield, Kirkgate.
.	.	.	.	.	.			Chemical Works	Warwick	L. & N. W. / Mid.	Birmingham, Curzon Street. / Birmingham, Lawley Street.
.	.	.	.	.	.			Chemical Works	Yorks	Mid.	Leeds, Hunslet.
.	.	.	.	.	.			Chemical Works (Mid.)	Yorks	Mid—†L & Y—L N W— / N. E. / G. N.	Leeds, Hunslet Lane. / (See Appendix to follow).
.	.	.	.	.	.			Siding	Yorks	E. & W. Y. U.	Rothwell.
G	P	.	L	.	.	5	0	Brotton	Yorks	N. E.	Saltburn and Loftus.
.	.	.	.	.	.			Brotton Mines	Yorks	N. E.	Brotton.
.	.	.	.	.	.			Huntcliffe Mines	Yorks	N. E.	Brotton.
.	.	.	.	.	.			Kilton Ironstone Mines	Yorks	N. E.	Brotton.
.	.	.	.	.	.			Kilton Thorpe Depôts	Yorks	N. E.	Brotton.
.	.	.	.	.	.			Lingdale Depôts	Yorks	N. E.	Brotton.
.	.	.	.	.	.			Lingdale Mines	Yorks	N. E.	Brotton.
.	.	.	.	.	.			Lumpsey Depôts	Yorks	N. E.	Brotton.
.	.	.	.	.	.			Lumpsey Mines	Yorks	N. E.	Brotton.
G	P	F	L	H	C	3	0	Brough (N.E.)	Yorks	N. E. / G. C. / L. & N. W.	Hull and Selby. / Over N. E. from Thorne Junction. / Over N. E. from Leeds.
.	P	.	.	H	C	.	.				
.	P	.	.	.	.						
.	.	.	.	.	.			Wiley's Siding	Yorks	N. E.	Brough.
G	P	F	L	H	C	4	0	Broughton	Lancs	Furness.	Foxfield and Coniston.
.	.	.	.	.	.			Broughton	Lancs	L. & N. W.	See Barton and Broughton.
G	P	F	L	H	C	3	0	Broughton	Peebles	Cal.	Symington and Peebles.
G	P	F	L	H	C			Broughton Astley	Leicester	Mid.	Rugby and Leicester.
.	.	.	.	.	.			Broughton Colliery	Denbigh	G. W.	Plas Power.
.	.	.	.	.	.			Broughton Copper Co.'s Ditton Copper Works	Lancs	L. & N. W —S. & M. Jt.	Widnes.
.	P	.	.	.	.			Broughton Cross	Cumb'land	L. & N. W.	Cockermouth and Workington.
G	P	.	L	.	.			Broughton Hall	Flint	L. & N. W.	Chester and Mold.
.	.	.	.	.	.			Ratcliffe's (Exors.) Siding	Flint	L. & N. W.	Broughton Hall and Saltney Wharf
.	.	.	.	.	.			Broughton Lane	Yorks	G. C.	See Sheffield.
.	.	.	.	.	.			Broughton Lane Sid. (G. C.)	Yorks	G. C.— Mid.	See Ward's, T. W. (Sheffield).
.	.	.	.	.	.			Broughton Moor Colliery	Cumb'land	L. & N. W.	Flimby.
.	.	.	.	.	.			Broughton Solway Coke Wks.	Denbigh	G. W.	Plas Power.
G	P	F	L	H	C	3	0	Broughty Ferry	Forfar	D. & A. Jt. (Cal. & N. B.)	Dundee and Arbroath.
.	.	.	.	.	.			Broughty Ferry Junction	Forfar	Cal.—D.&A.Jt.(Cal&NB)	Dundee and Forfar.

EXPLANATION—G *Goods Station.*   P *Passenger and Parcel Station.*   P* *Passenger, but not Parcel or Miscellaneous Traffic.*
F *Furniture Vans, Carriages, Portable Engines, and Machines on Wheels.*   L *Live Stock.*
H *Horse Boxes and Prize Cattle Vans.*   C *Carriages by Passenger Train.*   † *For Local Traffic only.*

STATION ACCOMMODATION.						CRANE POWER.	STATIONS, &c.	COUNTY.	COMPANY.	POSITION.
						Tons Cwts	Brown & Butcher's Northampton Brick & Tile Co.'s Siding	N'hamptn	L. & N. W.	See Gayton Sidings (Blisworth).
							Brown & Co.'s Chemical Works (G. N.)	Lincoln	G. N.—G. C.	Grimsby Town.
							Brown & Co.'s Saw Mill	Forfar	D & A. Jt. (Cal. & N. B.)	See Arbroath.
							Brown & Co.'s Siding	Lancs	L. & Y.	Liverpool, Sandhills.
							Brown & Co.'s Siding	Surrey	L. B. & S. C.	Waddon.
							Brown & Co.'s Skin Works	Leicester	Mid.	Ashby-de-la-Zouch.
							Brown & Glegg's Siding	Edinboro'	Cal.	Edinburgh, Lothian Road.
							Brown & Goodman's Siding	Hunts	{ G. N. & G. E. Jt.	Godmanchester.
									{ Mid.	Huntingdon.
							Brown & Munro's Siding	Lanark	Cal.	Glasgow, Tollcross.
							Brown Bayley's Steel Works (G. C.)	Yorks	G. C.—Mid.	Sheffield, Broughton Lane.
							Brown, Bros., & Co.'s Siding	Edinboro'	N. B.	Edinburgh, Leith Walk.
							Brown, H., & Sons' Siding	Beds	G. N.	Luton.
							Brown, J., & Co.'s Siding	Edinboro'	N. B.	Same as Harpersbrae Sid (Penicuik).
							Brown, J., & Co.—			
			.		.		Aldwarke Main Colliery	Yorks	Mid.	Parkgate and Rawmarsh.
			.		.		Aldwarke Main Col. (G.C.)	Yorks	G. C.—G. N.	Parkgate and Aldwarke.
							Atlas Blast Furnaces (Mid.)	Yorks	Mid.—G. C.	Sheffield, Wicker.
							Atlas Works (Mid.)	Yorks	Mid.—G. C.	Sheffield, Wicker.
							Carr House Colliery	Yorks	Mid.	Masboro' and Rotherham.
							Rotherham Main Colliery	Yorks	Mid.	Masboro' and Rotherham.
							Brown, J., & Son's Siding	Essex	G. E.	Braintree.
							Brown, John, & Co.'s Shipbuilding & Engineering Works	Dumbartn	Cal.—N. B.	{ Same as Clydebank Shipbuilding and Engineering Works.
							Brown, J., Siding	Essex	G. E.	Brentwood and Warley.
							Brown, Lenox & Co.'s Siding	Glamorg'n	A. (N. & S. W.) D. & R.	Same as Newbridge Wks (Glyntaff).
							Brown's Depôt	Yorks	N. E.	South Bank.
							Brown's Foundry	Durham	N. E.	Stockton, North Shore.
							Brown's Gresty Mill	Cheshire	L. & N. W.	Crewe.
							Brown's House Quarry	Durham	N. E.	Frosterley.
							Brown's Saw Mill	Durham	N. E.	Same as Stranton Saw Mill (West Hartlepool).
							Brown's Saw Mills	Fife	N. B.	Buckhaven.
							Brown's, T. & J., Timber Yard	Carmarth'	G. W.—L. & N. W.	Llanelly.
			.				Brown's Timber Yard	Edinboro'	N. B.	Edinburgh, St. Leonard's.
							Brown's, W. & G., Siding (Lodge Lane Mill)	Derby	G. N.	Derby, Friar Gate.
							Brown's, W. H. & P. W., Sid. (G. N.)	Beds	G. N.—L. & N. W.	Luton.
.	P*	.	.	.	.		Browndown	Hants	Lee-on-the Solent	Fort Brockhurst & Lee-on-the-Solent.
.		.	.	.	.		Browney Colliery	Durham	N. E.	Brandon Colliery Station.
							Brownhill Colliery, No. 21	Lanark	Cal.	Omoa.
							BROWNHILLS—			
G	P	F	L	H	C	5 0	(Station)	Staffs	L. & N. W.	Lichfield and Walsall.
G	P	F	L	H	C	. .	(Station)	Staffs	Mid.	Walsall Wood Branch.
G	.	.	.	.	.	. .	Basin	Staffs	L. & N. W.	Lichfield and Walsall.
.	.	.	.	.	.	. .	Cannock & Rugeley Col.	Staffs	Mid.	Walsall Wood Branch.
							Cannock Chase Colliery	Staffs	Mid.	Walsall Wood Branch.
							Conduit Colliery	Staffs	Mid.	Walsall Wood Branch.
.	.	.	.	.	.		Conduit Colliery Co.'s Norton Canes Siding	Staffs	L. & N. W.	Norton Branch.
.	.	.	.	.	.		Coppice Colliery Co.'s Five Ways Colliery	Staffs	L. & N. W.	Norton Branch.
							Harrison's Sidings—			
.	.	.	.	.	.		No. 1, or Old Brownhills Colliery	Staffs	L. & N. W.	Norton Branch.
.	.	.	.	.	.		Wyrley Grove Colliery	Staffs	L. & N. W.	Norton Branch.
							Watling Street Colliery (Owen & Dutson's Sid.)	Staffs	Mid.	Near Brownhills.
							Brownhills Colliery	Staffs	N. S.	See Heath and Son's (Longport).
.	.	.	.	.	.		Brownieside Junction	Lanark	N. B.	Clarkston and Plains.
.	.	.	.	.	.		Brownieside Weighs	Lanark	N. B.	Rawyards and Caldercruix.
.	.	.	.	.	.		Brownieside Colliery	Lanark	N. B.	Brownieside Weighs and Plains.
.	.	.	.	.	.		Craighead Quarry	Lanark	N. B.	Brownieside Junction.
G	.	.	L	.	.	1 10	Plains Siding	Lanark	N. B.	Brownieside Junction & Caldercruix.
.	.	.	.	.	.		Brownlee Colliery	Lanark	Cal.	Law Junction.

EXPLANATION—G *Goods Station.*　　P *Passenger and Parcel Station.*　　P* *Passenger, but not Parcel or Miscellaneous Traffic.*
F *Furniture Vans, Carriages, Portable Engines, and Machines on Wheels.*　　L *Live Stock.*
H *Horse Boxes and Prize Cattle Vans.*　　C *Carriages by Passenger Train.*

						Tons	Cwt.	STATIONS, &c.	COUNTY.	COMPANY.	POSITION.
						.	.	Brown Lees Colliery	Staffs	N. S.	See Heath and Son's (Black Bull).
						.	.	Brownlee's Sleeper Mill	Stirling	Cal.	Grangemouth.
G	P	F	L	H	C	1	0	Brownlie & Co.'s Siding	Ayr	G. & S.W.	Kilmarnock.
						.	.	Broxbourne and Hoddesdon	Herts	G. E.	London and Bishops Stortford.
						.	.	Hoddesdon Gas&Cl.Co.'s Sid	Herts	G. E.	Broxbourne and Hoddesdon.
						.	.	Rochford's Siding	Herts	G. E.	Broxbourne and Cheshunt.
G			L			2	0	Broxburn	L'lithgow	N. B.	See Holygate (for Broxburn).
						.	.	Broxburn Junction Station	L'lithgow	N. B.	Ratho and Linlithgow.
						.	.	Broxburn Oil Works	L'lithgow	N. B.	Branch from Broxburn Junction.
						.	.	Greendyke's Siding	L'lithgow	N. B.	Broxburn Junc. & Broxburn Oil Wks.
						.	.	Niddrie Castle Oil Works (Oakbank Oil Co.)	L'lithgow	N. B.	Broxburn Junc. and Winchburgh.
						.	.	Broxburn Oil Wks. (Holygate Branch)	L'lithgow	N. B.	Holygate.
G	P	F	L	H	C	5	0	Broxton	Cheshire	L. & N. W.	Chester and Whitchurch.
						.	.	Broxtowe Colliery	Notts	{ G. N. / Mid.	Nottingham, Basford and Bulwell. / Nottingham, Basford.
						.	.	Bruce, Alex.,&Co.'s Sid.(G.C.)	Lincoln	G. C.—G. N.	Grimsby Docks.
						.	.	Bruce & Son's Siding	Edinboro'	N. B.	Edinburgh, Leith Walk.
						.	.	Bruce & Son's Siding	Yorks	N. E.	Hull, Stepney.
						.	.	Bruce, Boyd & Co.'s Siding	Edinboro'	N. B.	Leith, South.
						.	.	Brucefield Siding	Fife	N. B.	Forest Mill.
	P					.	.	Bruce Grove	Middlesex	G. E.	Seven Sisters and Enfield Town.
G	P	F	L	H	C	2	0	Brucklay	Aberdeen	G. N. of S.	Dyce and Fraserburgh.
G	P					.	.	Bruckless	Donegal	Donegal	Donegal and Killybegs.
G	P					2	0	Brundall	Norfolk	G. E.	Norwich and Yarmouth, Vauxhall.
						.	.	Brundrit & Co.'s Wright's Sid.	Carnarvon	L. & N. W.	Penmaenmawr.
								Brunner, Mond & Co.—			
						.	.	Alkali Works (C. L. C.)	Cheshire	C. L. C.— L. & N. W.	Northwich.
						.	.	Bleach Works (C. L. C.)	Cheshire	C. L. C.— L. & N. W.	Northwich.
						.	.	Chemical Works	Cheshire	C.L.C.(G.C.,G.N.,&Mid.)	Winnington.
						.	.	Chemical Works (C.L.C.)	Cheshire	C. L. C.— L. & N. W.	Northwich.
						.	.	Newton, Nos. 1 and 2 Sids.	Cheshire	L. & N. W.	Middlewich.
						.	.	Salt Works (C. L. C.)	Cheshire	C. L. C.— L. & N. W.	Northwich.
						.	.	Siding (G. E.)	Essex	GE—GN—L&NW—Mid.	London, Silvertown.
						.	.	Works	Cheshire	N. S.	Ettiley Heath.
						.	.	Brunswick	Lancs	C.L.C.(G.C.,G.N. & Mid.)	See Liverpool.
						.	.	Brunswick Dock	Lancs	L'pool O'head—L.&N.W.	See Liverpool.
						.	.	Brunswick Rock Asphalte Co.'s Siding	Essex	G. E.	London, Stratford.
						.	.	Brunswick South Depôt	Lancs	L. & N. W.	Liverpool.
						.	.	Brunswick Street Brick and Tile Works	Durham	N. E.	Darlington, Bank Top.
						.	.	Brunswick Street Wharf	Cheshire	N. S.	See Congleton.
						.	.	Brunswick Works	Staffs	G. W.	{ See Patent Shaft and Axletree Co. (Wednesbury).
						.	.	Brunswick Works (L. & N.W)	Staffs	L. & N. W.—Mid.	}
						.	.	Bruntcliffe Colliery	Yorks	G. N.	Same as Haigh's Victoria Colliery (Morley).
						.	.	Brunton Farm Siding	Northumb	N. E.	Gosforth.
G	P	F	L	H	C	.	.	Bruree	Limerick	G. S. & W.	Charleville and Limerick.
						.	.	Brush Electrical Engineering Co.'s Siding	Leicester	Mid.	Loughboro'.
						.	.	Brusselton Quarry	Durham	N. E.	Shildon.
						.	.	Brusselton (New Winning) Pit	Durham	N. E.	West Auckland.
G	P	F	L	H	C	3	0	Bruton	Somerset	G. W.	Yeovil and Westbury.
						.	.	Bryan, Donkin & Clench's Sid.	Derby	L. D. & E. C.	Chesterfield.
						.	.	Bryant & May's Siding	Essex	G. E.	London, Devonshire Street.
						.	.	Bryant & Son's Siding	Norfolk	G. E.	Same as Eccles Bge. Sid.(Eccles Rd).
								BRYMBO—			
G	P					.	.	(Station)	Denbigh	W. M. & C. Q.	Brymbo Branch.
G	P					1	0 }	(Station, G. W.)	Denbigh	{ G. W. / L. & N. W.	Wrexham and Coed Poeth. / Over G. W. from Brymbo Junc.
	P					.	. }				
						.	.	Chemical Works Siding	Denbigh	G. W.—W. M. & C. Q.	Brymbo.
						.	.	Colliery	Denbigh	{ G. W. / W. M. & C. Q.	Branch from Brymbo. / Brymbo Branch.
						.	.	Iron and Steel Works	Denbigh	{ G. W. / W. M. & C. Q.	Branch from Brymbo. / Brymbo Branch.
						.	.	Vron Brick Works	Denbigh	G. W.	Brymbo.
						.	.	Vron Colliery	Denbigh	G. W.	Brymbo.
						.	.	Vron Col. & Brick Works	Denbigh	W. M. & C. Q.	Brymbo Branch.
						.	.	Branch Junctions	Denbigh	W. M. & C. Q.	Wrexham and Gwersyllt.
						.	.	Junction	Denbigh	G. W.—W. & M. Jt.	Wrexham and Coed Talon.

EXPLANATION—G Goods Station.   P Passenger and Parcel Station.   P* Passenger, but not Parcel or Miscellaneous Traffic.
F Furniture Vans, Carriages, Portable Engines, and Machines on Wheels.   L Live Stock.
H Horse Boxes and Prize Cattle Vans.   C Carriages by Passenger Train.

G	P	F	L	H	C	Tons	Cwts	STATIONS, &c.	COUNTY.	COMPANY.	POSITION.
								Brymbo Siding	Oxon	G. W.	Hook Norton.
G	P	.	L	.	C	.	.	Bryn	Glamorg'n	P. T.	Port Talbot and Maesteg.
.	.	.	.	.	.	.	.	Bryn Brick Works	Glamorg'n	P. T.	Bryn and Maesteg.
.	.	.	.	.	.	.	.	Bryn Navigation Colliery	Glamorg'n	P. T.	Bryn.
.	.	.	.	.	.	.	.	Dyffryn Rhondda Golden Vein Colliery	Glamorg'n	P. T.	Bryn.
.	.	.	.	.	.	.	.	Varteg Colliery	Glamorg'n	P. T.	Bryn and Maesteg.
								BRYNAMMAN—			
G	P	F	L	H	C	.	.	(Station)	Carmarth'	G. W.	Branch from Pantyffynnon.
G	P	.	.	.	.	.	.	(Station, Mid.)	Carmarth'	{ Mid. / G. W.	Branch from Ynisygeinon Junction. / Over Mid. Line.
.	.	.	.	.	.	.	.	Blaen-cae-Gwrwen Colliery (Mid.)	Glamorg'n	Mid.—G. W.—L. & N. W.	Brynamman and Gwys.
.	.	.	.	.	.	.	.	Cwmteg Colliery Co.'s Siding (Mid.)	Glamorg'n	Mid.—G. W.—L. & N. W.	Near Brynamman.
.	.	.	.	.	.	.	.	Glynbeudy Tin Plate Wks.	Carmarth'	G. W.	Brynamman and Garnant.
.	.	.	.	.	.	.	.	Junction	Carmarth'	G. W.—Mid.	Garnant and Gwys.
.	.	.	.	.	.	.	.	Lange's Anthracite Colliery	Carmarth'	G. W.	Brynamman and Garnant.
.	.	.	.	.	.	.	.	Pantycelyn Colliery (J. J. Thomas & Son) (Mid.)	Glamorg'n	Mid.—G. W.—L. & N. W.	Near Brynamman.
.	.	.	.	.	.	.	.	Bryncethin Brick Works	Glamorg'n	G. W.	Same as Barrow Brk.Wks. (Tondu).
.	.	.	.	.	.	.	.	Bryncethin Junction	Glamorg'n	G. W.	Tondu.
.	.	.	.	.	.	.	.	Bryn Chemical Works (G. W.)	Carmarth'	G. W.—L. & N. W.	Llanelly.
.	.	.	.	.	.	.	.	Bryncoch and Wernddu Col. (Marchowel Colliery) (Mid.)	Glamorg'n	Mid.—G. W.—L. & N. W.	Pontardawe.
.	.	.	.	.	.	.	.	Bryncoch Colliery	Glamorg'n	Rhy	Same as North Wingfield Sid. (Darran)
G	.	.	.	.	.	.	.	Bryndu	Glamorg'n	P. T.	Margam Junction and Cefn Junc.
.	.	.	.	.	.	.	.	Aberbaiden Colliery	Glamorg'n	P. T.	Bryndu and Cefn Junction.
.	.	.	.	.	.	.	.	Bryndu & Port Talbot Col. and Coke Ovens	Glamorg'n	P. T.	Bryndu and Margam Junction.
.	.	.	.	.	.	.	.	Cefn Colliery	Glamorg'n	P. T.	Bryndu and Cefn Junction.
.	.	.	.	.	.	.	.	Margam Moors Sid. (Heolydelaid Siding)	Glamorg'n	P. T.	Bryndu and Margam Junction.
.	.	.	.	.	.	.	.	Tonphillip Colliery	Glamorg'n	P. T.	Bryndu and Cefn Junction.
.	.	.	.	.	.	.	.	Bryndu Colliery Junction	Glamorg'n	G. W.	Tondu and Kenfig Hill.
.	.	.	.	.	.	.	.	Bryn Eglwys Siding	Merioneth	L. & N. W.	Gwyddelwern.
G	P	.	.	.	.	.	.	Brynglas	Merioneth	Tal-y-llyn	Rhydyronen and Dolgoch.
G	P	.	.	.	.	.	.	Bryngwyn	Carnarvon	No. Wales N. G.	Branch from Tryfan Junction.
.	P*	.	.	.	.	.	.	Bryngwyn	Montgom	Cam.	Llanymynech and Llanfyllin.
.	.	.	.	.	.	.	.	Bryngwyn Colliery	Mon	B. & M.	Bedwas.
.	.	.	.	.	.	.	.	Bryngwyn Steel Works	Glamorg'n	G. W.	See Lewis & Son's (Gorseinon).
.	.	.	.	.	.	.	.	Brynhenllysg Colliery Co.'s Colliery (Mid.)	Brecon	{ Mid.—G.W.—L.&N.W. / Mid.—G.W.—L.&N.W.	Gwys. / Gurnos.
G	P	.	L	.	.	.	.	Brynkinalt Colliery	Denbigh	G. W.	Chirk.
.	.	.	.	.	.	.	.	Brynkir	Carnarvon	L. & N. W.	Afon Wen and Carnarvon.
.	.	.	.	.	.	.	.	Brynllynfell Colliery (Mid.)	Glamorg'n	Mid.—G. W.—L. & N. W.	Gurnos.
.	.	.	.	.	.	.	.	Bryn Malley Colliery	Denbigh	G. W.—W. M. & C. Q.	Moss.
								BRYNMAWR—			
G	P	F	L	H	C	1	10	(Station, L. & N. W.)	Brecon	{ L. & N. W. / G. W.	Abergavenny and Merthyr. / Ov. L N W fr. Abersychan & Talywain.
.	P	.	.	H	C						
.	.	.	.	.	.	.	.	Bailey's Siding	Mon	L. & N. W.	Brynmawr and Clydach.
.	.	.	.	.	.	.	.	Barnes Coke Yard (L&NW)	Mon	L. & N. W.—G. W.	Brynmawr and Nantyglo Junction.
.	.	.	.	.	.	.	.	Barnes Deep Pit (L&NW)	Mon	L. & N. W.—G. W.	Brynmawr and Nantyglo Junction.
								Blaenavon Iron & Cl. Co.—			
.	.	.	.	.	.	.	.	Jayne's Branch	Mon	L. & N. W.	Blaenavon and Waenavon.
.	.	.	.	.	.	.	.	Milfraen Hill Colliery	Mon	L. & N. W.	Blaenavon and Waenavon.
.	.	.	.	.	.	.	.	Graham Bros. & Co.'s Black Vein Colliery	Mon	L. & N. W.	Brynmawr and Nantyglo Junction.
.	.	.	.	.	.	.	.	Junction	Mon	L.&N.W.—N.&B.Ir.Co.	Brynmawr and Nantyglo.
.	.	.	.	.	.	.	.	Llyn Colliery (Forge Pit)	Mon	L. & N. W.	Brynmawr and Nantyglo Junction.
.	.	.	.	.	.	.	.	Morgan's Coal Yard (LNW)	Mon	L. & N. W.—G. W.	Brynmawr and Nantyglo Junction.
.	.	.	.	.	.	.	.	Nantyglo Iron Wks. (LNW)	Mon	L. & N. W.—G. W.	Brynmawr and Nantyglo Junction.
.	.	.	.	.	.	.	.	Nantyglo Lion Tin Works	Mon	L. & N. W.	Brynmawr and Nantyglo Junction.
.	.	.	.	.	.	.	.	Powell's Ellwood Col. Co.'s Brecon Boat Siding	Mon	L. & N. W.	Brynmawr and Clydach.
.	.	.	.	.	.	.	.	Stone's Siding	Mon	L. & N. W.	Brynmawr.
.	.	.	.	.	.	.	.	Waen Nantyglo Colliery	Mon	L. & N. W.	Brynmawr and Waenavon.
.	.	.	.	.	.	.	.	Williams' New Clydach Col.	Mon	L. & N. W.	Brynmawr and Waenavon.
.	.	.	.	.	.	.	.	Brynmelyn Quarry	Glamorg'n	G. W.	Garnant.
G	P	.	.	.	.	.	.	Brynmenyn	Glamorg'n	G. W.	Tondu and Black Mill.
.	.	.	.	.	.	.	.	Brynmenyn Colliery	Glamorg'n	G. W.	Brynmenyn.
.	.	.	.	.	.	.	.	Ynisawdre Siding	Glamorg'n	G. W.	Brynmenyn and Tondu.

EXPLANATION—G *Goods Station.*   P *Passenger and Parcel Station.*   P* *Passenger, but not Parcel or Miscellaneous Traffic.*
F *Furniture Vans, Carriages, Portable Engines, and Machines on Wheels.*   L *Live Stock.*
H *Horse Boxes and Prize Cattle Vans.*   C *Carriages by Passenger Train.*

STATION ACCOMMODATION.						CRANE POWER.		STATIONS, &c.	COUNTY.	COMPANY.	POSITION.
						Tons	Cwts.				
..	..	..	..	..	..	..	..	Brynmenyn Junction............	Glamorg'n	G. W.	Brynmenyn and Tondu.
..	P	..	..	..	..	..	..	Brynmill Road....................	Glamorg'n	Swan. & Mum.	Swansea and Mumbles Road.
..	P	..	..	..	..	..	..	Brynn (for Ashton-in-Makerfield)	Lancs	L. & N. W.	St. Helens and Wigan.
..	..	..	..	..	..	..	..	Brynn Hall Colliery............	Lancs	L. & N. W.	Garswood.
..	..	..	..	..	..	..	..	Brynn Tramway.................	Mon	L. & N. W.	Tredegar Junction.
..	..	..	..	..	..	..	..	Brynteg Colliery...............	Glamorg'n	N. & Brecon	Seven Sisters.
..	..	..	..	..	..	..	..	Bryn Tin Works (Mid.)	Glamorg'n	Mid.—G.W.—L. & N. W.	Pontardawe.
G	..	..	..	..	..	..	..	Brynygwynon.....................	Glamorg'n	G. W.	Llantrisant and Pencoed.
..	..	..	..	..	..	..	..	Bryson & Co.'s Siding	Stirling	Cal.	Grangemouth.
..	..	..	..	..	..	..	..	Bryson & Co.'s Wood Yard...	L'lithgow	N. B.	Bo'ness.
G	P	..	L	H	..	..	..	Bubwith	Yorks	N. E.	Selby and Market Weighton.
..	..	..	..	..	..	..	..	Buccleuch Brick & Tile Wks.	Dumfries	G. & S. W.	Sanquhar.
..	..	..	..	..	..	..	..	Buchanan's Flour Mills........	Cheshire	B'head Jt—CLC—NW&L	Birkenhead.
..	..	..	..	..	..	..	..	Buchanan Street.................	Lanark	Cal.—Glas. Dist. Sub.	See Glasgow.
G	P	F	L	H	C	3	0	Buchlyvie	Stirling	N. B.	Balloch and Stirling.
G	..	..	..	..	..	..	..	Balwill Siding.................	Stirling	N. B.	Buchlyvie and Balfron.
G	..	..	..	..	..	..	..	Mye Siding	Stirling	N. B.	Buchlyvie and Port of Monteith.
..	..	..	..	..	..	..	..	Buchlyvie Junction	Stirling	N. B.	Balfron and Port of Monteith.
..	..	..	..	..	..	..	..	Buckden	Hunts	G. N.	See Offord and Buckden.
G	P	..	L	..	..	..	..	Buckden	Hunts	Mid.	Huntingdon and Thrapston.
G	P	..	..	..	..	..	..	Buckenham	Norfolk	G. E.	Norwich and Yarmouth, Vauxhall.
G	P	F	L	H	C	5	0	Buckfastleigh	Devon	G. W.	Totnes and Ashburton.
G	P	F	L	H	C	3	0	Buckhaven	Fife	N. B.	Thornton and Methil.
..	..	..	..	..	..	..	..	Brown's Saw Mill	Fife	N. B.	Bch.—Buckhaven & Wemyss Castle.
..	..	..	..	..	..	..	..	Cameron Junction Siding...	Fife	N. B.	Bch.—Buckhaven & Wemyss Castle.
..	..	..	..	..	..	..	..	Isabella Colliery	Fife	N. B.	Bch.—Buckhaven & Wemyss Castle.
..	..	..	..	..	..	..	..	Muiredge Brick Works.....	Fife	N. B.	Bch.—Buckhaven & Wemyss Castle.
..	..	..	..	..	..	..	..	Muiredge Colliery	Fife	N. B.	Bch.—Buckhaven & Wemyss Castle.
G	..	..	..	..	..	..	..	Muiredge Siding.............	Fife	N. B.	Bch.—Buckhaven & Wemyss Castle.
..	..	..	..	..	..	..	..	Rosie Colliery	Fife	N. B.	Bch.—Buckhaven & Wemyss Castle.
..	..	..	..	..	..	..	..	Buckhill Pit...................	Cumb'land	C. & W. Jn.	Great Broughton.
G	P	..	..	..	..	..	..	Buckhurst Hill	Essex	G. E.	Stratford and Loughton.
G	P	F	L	H	C	4	0	Buckie	Banff	{ G. N. of S.	Portsoy and Elgin.
G	P	F	L	H	C	5	0			{ High	Keith and Portessie.
..	..	..	..	..	..	..	..	Buckingham	Bucks	G. C.	See Finmere (for Buckingham).
G	P	F	L	H	C	10	0	Buckingham	Bucks	L. & N. W.	Banbury and Verney Junc. Station.
..	..	..	..	..	..	..	..	Anglo Swiss Milk Co.'s Sid.	Bucks	L. & N. W.	Buckingham and Fulwell.
..	..	..	..	..	..	..	..	Aylesbury BreweryCo.'sSid.	Bucks	L. & N. W.	Buckingham and Fulwell.
..	..	..	..	..	..	..	..	Condensed Peptonized Milk Co.'s Siding.................	Bucks	L. & N. W.	Buckingham and Fulwell.
..	..	..	..	..	..	..	..	Gough's Siding	Bucks	L. & N. W.	Buckingham and Fulwell.
..	..	..	..	..	..	..	..	Buckingham Junction Sidings	Forfar	N. B.	Dundee, Tay Bridge.
..	..	..	..	..	..	..	..	Buckingham Junction West..	Forfar	Cal.—N. B.	Dundee.
..	..	..	..	..	..	..	..	Buckingham Point Sidings ...	Forfar	N. B.	See Dundee.
..	..	..	..	..	..	..	..	Buckland Hollow Siding	Derby	Mid.	See Duke of Devonshire's(Ambergate)
..	..	..	..	..	..	..	..	Buckland Junction............	Kent	S. E. & C.	Martin Mill and Dover Priory.
..	..	..	..	..	..	..	..	Buckley	Flint	L. & N. W.	See Padeswood and Buckley.
G	..	..	..	..	..	2	0	Buckley	Flint	W. M. & C. Q.	Connah's Quay and Wrexham.
..	..	..	..	..	..	..	..	Ashton, R., & Co.'s Bk. Wks.	Flint	W. M. & C. Q.	Buckley and Connah's Quay.
..	..	..	..	..	..	..	..	Buckley Bk. & Tl. Co.'s Sid.	Flint	W. M. & C. Q.	Buckley and Connah's Quay.
..	..	..	..	..	..	..	..	Buckley Collieries	Flint	W. M. & C. Q.	Buckley and Connah's Quay.
..	..	..	..	..	..	..	..	Castle Fire-Brick Co.'s Sid.	Flint	W. M. & C. Q.	Buckley and Connah's Quay.
..	..	..	..	..	..	..	..	Catherall & Co.'s Brick Sid.	Flint	W. M. & C. Q.	Buckley and Connah's Quay.
..	..	..	..	..	..	..	..	Etna Brick Works............	Flint	W. M. & C. Q.	Buckley and Connah's Quay.
..	..	..	..	..	..	..	..	Ewloe Barn Brick Works...	Flint	W. M. & C. Q.	Buckley and Connah's Quay.
..	..	..	..	..	..	..	..	Globe Brick Works	Flint	W. M. & C. Q.	Buckley and Connah's Quay.
..	..	..	..	..	..	..	..	Hancock & Co.'s Brick Sid.	Flint	W. M. & C. Q.	Buckley.
..	..	..	..	..	..	..	..	Knowle Lane Siding	Flint	W. M. & C. Q.	Branch from Buckley.
..	..	..	..	..	..	..	..	Lane End Colliery	Flint	W. M. & C. Q.	Branch from Buckley.
..	..	..	..	..	..	..	..	Main Colliery Co.'s Siding..	Flint	W. M. & C. Q.	Buckley and Connah's Quay.
..	..	..	..	..	..	..	..	Mount Pleasant Colliery & Brick Works	Flint	W. M. & C. Q.	Buckley and Connah's Quay.
..	..	..	..	..	..	..	..	Northop Hall Siding.........	Flint	W. M. & C. Q.	Buckley and Connah's Quay.
..	..	..	..	..	..	..	..	Old Ewloe Brick Works ...	Flint	W. M. & C. Q.	Buckley and Connah's Quay.
..	..	..	..	..	..	..	..	Parry's Brick Works	Flint	W. M. & C. Q.	Buckley and Connah's Quay.
..	..	..	..	..	..	..	..	Sandycroft Colliery & Brick Works	Flint	W. M. & C. Q.	Buckley and Connah's Quay.
..	..	..	..	..	..	..	..	South Buckley Rock Brick Co.'s Siding	Flint	W. M. & C. Q.	Buckley and Connah's Quay.
..	..	..	..	..	..	..	..	Watkinson&Son'sMountain Colliery......................	Flint	W. M. & C. Q.	Branch from Buckley.

EXPLANATION— G *Goods Station.*   P *Passenger and Parcel Station.*   P* *Passenger, but not Parcel or Miscellaneous Traffic.*
F *Furniture Vans, Carriages, Portable Engines, and Machines on Wheels.*   L *Live Stock.*
H *Horse Boxes and Prize Cattle Vans.*   C *Carriages by Passenger Train.*

STATION ACCOMMODATION.						CRANE POWER.		STATIONS, &c.	COUNTY.	COMPANY.	POSITION.
						Tons	Cwts.				
G	P	F	L	H	C	.	.	Buckley Junction Station (W. M. & C. Q.)	Flint	W. M. & C. Q. .... / G. C.	Hawarden and Wrexham. / Over W. M. C. Q. from Hawarden Bridge Junction.
.	.	.	.	.	.	.	.	Buckley Wells Siding	Lancs	L. & Y.	Bury, High Level.
.	.	.	.	.	.	.	.	Buckminster Sidings............	Lincoln ...	Mid.	See Holwell Iron Co. (South Witham)
G	P	.	.	.	.	1	10	Bucknall and Northwood......	Staffs	N. S.	Stoke and Ford Green.
G	P	F	L	H	C	5	0	Bucknell	Salop	L. & N. W.	Craven Arms & Llandrindod Wells.
G	P	F	L	H	C	3	0	Buckpool	Barff	G. N. of S.	Portsoy and Elgin.
G	P	F	L	H	C	4	0	Bucksburn	Aberdeen..	G. N. of S.	Aberdeen and Dyce.
								Budd & Co.—			
.	.	.	.	.	.	.	.	Marsh Siding	Mon	L. & N. W.	Blackwood.
.	.	.	.	.	.	.	.	Siding	Mon	L. & N. W.	See Rock Colliery (Blackwood).
.	.	.	.	.	.	.	.	Buddon Siding	Forfar......	D. & A. Jt. (Cal. & N. B.)	See Barry.
.	.	.	.	.	.	.	.	Budd's Road Siding (Mid.)...	Glamorg'n	Mid.—G. W.—L. & N. W.	Gurnos.
G	P	F	L	H	C	2	0	Bude	Cornwall ..	L. & S. W.	Branch from Halwill Junction.
.	.	.	.	.	.	.	.	Bude Basin Siding............	Cornwall ..	L. & S. W.	Bude.
G	P	F	L	H	C	2	0	Budleigh Salterton	Devon	L. & S. W.	Branch from Tipton St. John's.
.	.	.	.	.	.	.	.	Buenos Ayres	Kent	S. E. & C.	Same as Birchington-on-Sea.
								BUGLE—			
G	P	.	.	.	.	2	0	(Station)	Cornwall ..	G. W.	Newquay and Par.
.	.	.	.	.	.	1	10	Carbean Siding	Cornwall ..	G. W.	Branch from Goonbarrow Junction.
.	.	.	.	.	.	.	.	Carbis Siding	Cornwall ..	G. W.	Bugle Junction.
.	.	.	.	.	.	.	.	Caudledown Siding	Cornwall ..	G. W.	Goonbarrow Junc. and Carbean Sid.
.	.	.	.	.	.	.	.	Cleaves Siding	Cornwall ..	G. W.	Goonbarrow Junc. and Carbean Sid.
.	.	.	.	.	.	.	.	Gunheath Siding	Cornwall ..	G. W.	Goonbarrow Junc. and Carbean Sid.
.	.	.	.	.	.	.	.	Imperial Goonbarrow Siding	Cornwall ..	G. W.	Goonbarrow Junc. and Carbean Sid.
.	.	.	.	.	.	.	.	Junction	Cornwall ..	G. W.	Newquay and Par.
.	.	.	.	.	.	.	.	Martin's Siding	Cornwall ..	G. W.	Extension from Bugle.
.	.	.	.	.	.	.	.	Old Beam Siding	Cornwall ..	G. W.	Goonbarrow Junc. and Carbean Sid.
.	.	.	.	.	.	.	.	Rosemellyn Siding............	Cornwall ..	G. W.	Bugle Junction and Carbis Siding.
.	.	.	.	.	.	.	.	Rossvear Siding	Cornwall ..	G. W.	Goonbarrow Junction.
.	.	.	.	.	.	.	.	Wheal Anna Siding	Cornwall ..	G. W.	Goonbarrow Junction.
.	.	.	.	.	.	.	.	Wheal Henry Siding.........	Cornwall ..	G. W.	Goonbarrow Junction.
.	.	.	.	.	.	.	.	Wheal Rose Siding	Cornwall ..	G. W.	Extension from Bugle.
.	.	.	.	.	.	.	.	Bugle Horn Colliery	Lancs	L. & N. W.	Same as Unsworth & Cowburn's Brookside Colliery (Wigan).
.	P	.	.	.	.	.	.	Bugsworth	Derby	Mid.	Chapel-en-le-Frith and New Mills.
.	.	.	.	.	.	.	.	Building Material Co.	Lancs	L. & N. W.	See Spekeland Rd. Sids. (Liverpool.)
								Building Material Supply Stores Siding	Salop	L. & N. W.	Shrewsbury.
G	P	F	L	H	C	.	.	Buildwas	Salop	G. W.	Shrewsbury and Hartlebury.
.	.	.	.	.	.	.	.	Griffith's Sand Siding	Salop	G. W.	Buildwas.
G	P	.	L	H	.	2	0	Builth Road......................	Radnor ...	L. & N. W. / Cam.	Llandilo and Llandrindod Wells. / Builth Wells & Newbridge-on-Wye.
G	P	.	.	.	.	.	.				
.	.	.	.	.	.	.	.	Rhoseferig Siding	Brecon ...	L. & N. W.	Builth Road and Cilmery.
.	.	.	.	.	.	.	.	Thomas Siding	Radnor ...	Cam.	Newbridge and Builth Road.
.	.	.	.	.	.	.	.	Builth Road Junction	Radnor ...	Cam.	Builth Road and Newbridge.
.	.	.	.	.	.	.	.	Builth Road Junction	Radnor ...	Cam.—L. & N. W.	Newbridge and Llandrindod Wells.
G	P	F	L	H	C	5	0	Builth Wells	Radnor ...	Cam.	Llanidloes and Three Cocks.
G	P	.	.	.	.	.	.	Bulford.............................	Essex	G. E.	Witham and Braintree.
.	P	.	.	.	.	.	.	Bulkington	Warwick..	L. & N. W.	Nuneaton and Rugby.
.	.	.	.	.	.	.	.	Bull Bridge Brick Co.'s Siding	Derby	Mid.	Ambergate.
.	.	.	.	.	.	.	.	Bull Bridge Canal Wharf......	Derby	Mid.	Ambergate.
.	.	.	.	.	.	.	.	Bull Bridge Lime Works (Eaton's, W.)	Derby	Mid.	Ambergate.
.	P*	.	.	.	.	.	.	Buller's O'Buchan Platform...	Aberdeen..	G. N. of S.	Ellon and Boddam.
.	.	.	.	.	.	.	.	Bullfield Gas Siding	Lancs	L. & Y.	Bolton.
.	.	.	.	.	.	.	.	Bullfield Manure Siding	Lancs	L. & Y.	Bolton.
.	.	.	.	.	.	.	.	Bullfield Siding	Lancs	L. & Y.	See Bolton.
G	P	F	L	H	C	3	0	Bullgill.............................	Cumb'land	M. & C.	Dearham Bridge and Aspatria.
.	.	.	.	.	.	.	.	Warthole Lime Works......	Cumb'land	M. & C.	Bullgill and Aspatria.
.	.	.	.	.	.	.	.	Bullhouse Colliery...............	Yorks	G. C.	Hazlehead Bridge.
G	.	.	.	.	.	.	.	Bullo Pill..........................	Glo'ster ...	G. W.	Newnham and Lydney.
.	.	.	.	.	.	.	.	Bullo Pill Docks..............	Glo'ster ...	G. W.	Branch from Bullo Pill.
.	.	.	.	.	.	.	.	National Trading Co.	Glo'ster ...	G. W.	Bullo Pill.
.	.	.	.	.	.	.	.	Bullough's Siding	Lancs	L. & Y.	See Darwen.
.	.	.	.	.	.	.	.	Bulls Head Siding	Lancs	L. & N. W.	See Evans, R., & Co.'s Coal Yard (Newton-le-Willows).
.	.	.	.	.	.	.	.	Bulls Metal & Melloid Siding	Renfrew...	Cal.	Glasgow, Whiteinch.
.	.	.	.	.	.	.	.	Bulwell..............................	Notts	G. N.	See Nottingham, Basford and Bulwell.
.	.	.	.	.	.	.	.	Bulwell..............................	Notts	Mid.	See Nottingham.

EXPLANATION—G *Goods Station.*   P *Passenger and Parcel Station.*   P* *Passenger, but not Parcel or Miscellaneous Traffic.*
F *Furniture Vans, Carriages, Portable Engines, and Machines on Wheels.*   L *Live Stock.*
H *Horse Boxes and Prize Cattle Vans.*   C *Carriages by Passenger Train.*

STATION ACCOMMODATION.						CRANE POWER.		STATIONS, &c.	COUNTY.	COMPANY.	POSITION.
						Tons	Cwts.				
G	P	.	.	.	.	.	.	Bulwell Common..................	Notts	G. C.	See Nottingham.
.	.	.	.	.	.	.	.	Bulwell Forest	Notts	G. N.	Daybrook and Annesley Junction.
.	.	.	.	.	.	.	.	Rigley's Siding	Notts	G. N.	Bulwell Forest.
.	.	.	.	.	.	.	.	Bulwell Junctions	Notts	G. C.—G. C. & G. N. Jt.	Nottingham.
.	.	.	.	.	.	.	.	Bumsted & Chandler's Siding	Staffs	L. & N. W.	Hednesford.
.	.	.	.	.	.	.	.	Bunch & Son's Staffordshire Iron Works..................	Staffs	L. & N. W.	Bloxwich.
G	P	F	L	H	C	.	.	Bunchrew	Inverness	High	Inverness and Dingwall.
G	P	.	L	.	.	.	.	Buncrana	Donegal ...	L. & L. S.	Londonderry and Carndonagh.
G	P	F	L	.	.	.	.	Bundoran	Donegal ...	G. N. (I.)	Branch from Bundoran Junction Station.
G	P	.	L	.	.	.	.	Bundoran Junction Station...	Tyrone	G. N. (I.)	Enniskillen and Omagh.
.	.	.	.	.	.	.	.	Bundy, W. N., Siding	Cambs ...	G. E.	Whittlesea.
G	P	.	.	.	.	.	.	Bunessan	Argyll ...	Cal.	Steamer from Oban.
G	P	F	L	H	C	1	10	Bungay	Suffolk	G. E.	Beccles and Tivetshall.
.	.	.	.	.	.	.	.	Bunker's Hill Colliery	Staffs	N. S.	See Rigby & Co. (Diglake).
.	.	.	.	.	.	.	.	Bunker's Hill Farm Depôt ...	Durham ..	N. E.	Blackhill.
G	P	F	L	H	C	1	10	Buntingford	Herts	G. E.	Branch from St. Margaret's.
.	.	.	.	.	.	.	.	Sworder, J. & C., Siding ...	Herts	G. E.	Buntingford.
G	.	F	L	.	.	5	0	Burbage	Wilts	G. W.	Savernake and Pewsey.
.	.	.	.	.	.	.	.	Burbage	Wilts	M. & S. W. Jn.	See Grafton and Burbage.
G	P	.	L	H	.	.	.	Burdale	Yorks	N. E.	Malton and Driffield.
.	.	.	.	.	.	.	.	Burdett Road	Middlesex	G. E.	See London.
.	.	.	.	.	.	.	.	Burdin's Siding (L&Y&GNJt)	Yorks	L. & Y. & G. N. Jt.—N. E.	Knottingley.
.	.	.	.	.	.	.	.	Burdon's Coal Depôts.........	Durham ..	N. E.	Castle Eden.
G	P	.	L	H	.	1	10	Bures	Essex	G. E.	Sudbury and Marks Tey.
.	.	.	.	.	.	.	.	Burford Bridge	Surrey	L. B. & S. C.	See Boxhill and Burford Bridge.
.	.	.	.	.	.	.	.	Burgess's, T., Siding	Somerset..	Mid.	Bath.
G	P	F	L	H	C	5	0	Burgess Hill	Sussex	L. B. & S. C.	Brighton and Hayward's Heath.
G	P	.	L	H	.	1	0	Burgh	Cumb'land	N. B.	Carlisle and Silloth.
G	P	F	L	H	C	1	5	Burgh	Lincoln	G. N.	Boston and Louth.
G	P	F	L	H	C	3	0	Burghclere	Hants	G. W.	Newbury and Winchester.
.	.	.	.	.	.	.	.	Forder's Lime Works Siding	Hants	G. W.	Burghclere.
G	P	F	L	H	C	5	0	Burghead	Elgin&Mo'	High	Alves and Hopeman.
.	.	.	.	.	.	.	.	Burgh Heath	Surrey	{ L. B. & S. C.	See Banstead and Burgh Heath.
.	.	.	.	.	.	.	.			{ S. E. & C.	See Kingswood and Burgh Heath.
.	.	.	.	.	.	.	.	Burghlee Siding	Edinboro'	N. B.	Loanhead.
.	.	.	.	.	.	.	.	Burgh Lye	Ayr	G. & S. W.	Irvine.
.	.	.	.	.	.	.	.	Burgh Lye	Renfrew...	Cal.	Paisley, St. James.
.	.	.	.	.	.	.	.	Burgon's Mill	Derby	Mid.	Ambergate.
.	.	.	.	.	.	.	.	Burgoyne's Siding...............	Mon	G. W.	Little Mill Junction.
.	.	.	.	.	.	.	.	Buriton Siding	Hants	L. & S. W.	See Petersfield.
.	.	.	.	.	.	.	.	Burke's Siding	Lincoln	G. N.	Caythorpe.
.	.	.	.	.	.	.	.	Burkitt's, W. & S., Sid. (Mid.)	Notts	Mid.—G. C.	Langwith.
G	P	.	L	.	.	.	.	Burleigh Street	Yorks	H. & B.	See Hull.
G	P	F	L	H	C	1	10	Burlescombe	Devon	G. W.	Wellington and Tiverton Junction.
.	.	.	.	.	.	.	.	Burley	Yorks	O. & I. Jt. (Mid. & N. E.)	Otley and Ilkley.
.	.	.	.	.	.	.	.	Burley Depôts..................	Yorks	N. E.	Leeds and Headingley.
.	.	.	.	.	.	.	.	Burley Junction	Yorks	Mid.—O. & I. Jt.	Menston and Burley Station.
.	.	.	.	.	.	.	.	Burlington Slate Quarries ...	Lancs	Furness	Kirkby.
.	.	.	.	.	.	.	.	Burnage	Lancs	L. & N. W.	See Levenshulme and Burnage.
.	.	.	.	.	.	.	.	Burnard & Algers Wharf.....	Devon	L. & S.W.	Plymouth, Cattewater Harbour.
.	.	.	.	.	.	.	.	Burnbank......................	Lanark ...	N. B.	See Hamilton.
.	.	.	.	.	.	.	.	Burnbank Colliery and Fire-Clay Works	Stirling ...	K. & B. Jt. (Cal. & N.B.)	Banknock.
.	.	.	.	.	.	.	.	Burnbrae Dye Works	Dumbartn	N. B.	Milngavie.
.	.	.	.	.	.	.	.	Burnden Siding	Lancs	L. & Y.	See Bolton.
.	.	.	.	.	.	.	.	Burnell's Siding	Cheshire..	B'head Jt. (G W&L&NW)	Ellesmere Port.
G	P	.	.	.	.	3	0	Burneside......................	W'morlnd	L. & N. W.	Oxenholme and Windermere.
.	.	.	.	.	.	.	.	Croppers' Paper Mills	W'morlnd	L. & N. W.	Burneside.
.	.	.	.	.	.	.	.	Burnet's Siding	Lanark ...	G.&P.Jt.(Cal.&G.&S.W.)	Same as Moorepark Boiler Works (Glasgow).
.	.	.	.	.	.	.	.	Burnett's Wagon Wks. (G.C.)	Yorks	G. C.—G. N.—Mid.	Doncaster.
G	P	.	.	.	.	.	.	Burnfoot	Donegal ...	L. & L. S.	Londonderry and Buncrana.
.	.	.	.	.	.	.	.	Burnfoot Lye	Ayr	G. & S. W.	New Cumnock.
G	P	.	.	.	.	.	.	Burngullow	Cornwall ..	G. W.	Plymouth and Truro.
.	.	.	.	.	.	.	.	Parkyn & Peters' Siding ...	Cornwall ..	G. W.	Burngullow and Drinnick Mill.
.	.	.	.	.	.	.	.	Pochin's Siding	Cornwall ..	G. W.	Burngullow.
.	.	.	.	.	.	.	.	West of England Siding ...	Cornwall ..	G. W.	Burngullow.
.	.	.	.	.	.	.	.	Burngullow Junction	Cornwall ..	G. W.	St. Austell and Grampound Road.
G	P	F	L	H	C	1	10	Burnham	Somerset..	S.&D.Jt.(L.&S. W.&Mid)	Terminus.
.	P	.	.	.	.	.	.	Burnham Beeches	Bucks	G. W.	Slough and Taplow.

EXPLANATION—G *Goods Station.*   P *Passenger and Parcel Station.*   P* *Passenger, but not Parcel or Miscellaneous Traffic.*
F *Furniture Vans, Carriages, Portable Engines, and Machines on Wheels.*   L *Live Stock.*
H *Horse Boxes and Prize Cattle Vans.*   C *Carriages by Passenger Train.*

STATION ACCOMMODATION.					CRANE POWER.	STATIONS, &c.	COUNTY.	COMPANY.	POSITION.
					Tons Cwts.				
G	P	F	L	H C	2 0	Burnham Market	Norfolk ...	G. E.	Heacham and Wells.
						Peterstone Siding	Norfolk ...	G. E.	Wells and Burnham Market.
G	P	F	L	H C	1 10	Burnham-on-Crouch	Essex	G. E.	Wickford and Southminster.
G						Cricksea Ferry Siding	Essex	G. E.	Wickford and Southminster.
						Burnhead Quarry Sidings ...	Lanark ...	N. B.	Rawyards.
	P					Burn Hill	Durham ...	N. E.	Crook and Consett.
						Burnhouse Junction	Durham ...	N. E.	Spennymoor and Byers Green.
						Burnhouse Manure Siding ..	Lanark ...	Cal.	Mossend.
						Burnhouse Siding	Edinboro'	Cal.	Camps.
						Burnhouse Sidings (for Carron Works) (N.B.) ...	Stirling ...	N.B.—Cal.	Falkirk, Grahamston.
						Burnhouse Weighs	Lanark ...	Cal.	Mossend.
						Burnip & MacDougall's Oil Works ...	Lancs	Furness	Barrow.
						BURNLEY—			
						Bank Hall Colliery	Lancs	L. & Y.	Burnley.
G	P	F	L	H C	10 0	Bank Top	Lancs	L. & Y.	Rose Grove and Colne.
	P					Barracks	Lancs	L. & Y.	Rose Grove and Burnley, Bank Top.
						Burnley Barracks Mineral Siding	Lancs	L. & Y.	Burnley Barracks.
						Burnley Corporation Siding	Lancs	L. & Y.	Burnley and Brierfield.
						Duckett, J., & Son	Lancs	L. & Y.	Burnley Barracks Mineral Siding.
						Greenwood & Sons	Lancs	L. & Y.	Burnley Barracks Mineral Siding.
G	P				10 0	Manchester Road	Lancs	L. & Y.	Rose Grove and Townley.
						Burn Moor Collieries ("D." and "Lady Ann" Pits)...	Durham ...	N. E.	{ Fencehouses. { Penshaw.
						Burn Moor or New Lambton Brk., Sanitary & Tl. Wks.	Durham ...	N. E.	{ Fencehouses. { Penshaw.
						Burn Moor or New Lambton Coke Ovens	Durham ...	N. E.	{ Fencehouses. { Penshaw.
						Burn Moor or New Lambton Gas Works	Durham ...	N. E.	{ Fencehouses. { Penshaw.
						Burn Moor Siding	Durham ...	N. E.	{ Fencehouses. { Penshaw.
G	P	F	L	H C	. .	Burnmouth	Berwick ...	N. B.	Dunbar and Berwick.
						Burnmouth Junction	Berwick ...	N. B.	Berwick and Ayton.
						Burn Naze Siding	Lancs	P&W.Jt.(L.&Y.&L&NW)	Same as United Alkali Co.'s Fleetwood Salt Works (Fleetwood.)
						Burnockhill Colliery	Ayr	G. & S.W.	Ochiltree.
						Burnopfield Colliery Coke and Brick Works	Durham ...	N. E.	Redheugh.
						Burn Road Siding	Durham ...	N. E.	West Hartlepool.
						Burns & Co.'s Siding	Cumb'land	N. B.	Carlisle, Canal.
G		F	L		3 0	Burnside	Lanark ...	Cal.	Newton and Cathcart.
						Burns Joinery Wks. & Bk. Yd.	Durham ...	N. E.	West Hartlepool.
						Burns Siding	Fife	N. B.	Inverkeithing.
						Burnt Ash	Kent	S. E. & C.	See Lee for Burnt Ash.
						Burntbroom Colliery	Lanark ...	Cal.	Same as Mount Vernon Colliery (Mount Vernon).
						Burntbroom Sand Pits	Lanark ...	Cal.	Mount Vernon.
G	P		L	H C	1 0	Burnt Fen	Cambs......	G. E.	Ely and Thetford.
G						Burnt House	Cambs......	G. E.	Branch from Whittlesea.
						Burntisland—			
G	P	F	L	H C	6 0	(Station)	Fife	N.B.	Inverkeithing and Kirkcaldy.
						Collinswell Siding (Baird & Stevenson's)	Fife	N. B.	Burntisland and Aberdour.
G						Docks	Fife	N. B.	Burntisland.
						Newbigging Siding (Carron Iron Co.)	Fife	N. B.	Burntisland and Aberdour.
						Pettycur Siding	Fife	N. B.	Burntisland and Kinghorn.
						Pier	Fife	N. B.	Burntisland.
	P					Burnt Mill	Cork	C. & Muskerry	St. Anns and Donoughmore.
G	P			H C	5 0	Burnt Mill	Essex	G. E.	London and Bishops Stortford.
						Burnyeat, Brown & Co.'s Sirhowy Valley Colliery ...	Mon	L. & N. W.	Penllwyn Tramway (Nine Mile Point)
						Burradon Colliery	Northumb	N. E.	Killingworth.
						Burringham	Lincoln ...	G. C.	See Gunness and Burringham.
G	P			H C	. .	Burrington	Somerset	G. W.	Congresbury and Blagdon.
						Burrows & Son's Siding (G.C.)	Yorks	G.C.—Mid.	Sheffield, Broughton Lane.
						Burrows Junction	Glamorg'n	P. T.—R. & S. B	Port Talbot.
						Burrows Lodge	Glamorg'n	G. W.	Same as Wind Street (Swansea).
						Burrows Sidings	Glamorg'n	G. W.—R. & S. B.	Swansea.

EXPLANATION—G Goods Station.   P Passenger and Parcel Station.   P* Passenger, but not Parcel or Miscellaneous Traffic.
F Furniture Vans, Carriages, Portable Engines, and Machines on Wheels.   L Live Stock.
H Horse Boxes and Prize Cattle Vans.   C Carriages by Passenger Train.

STATION ACCOMMODATION.						CRANE POWER.	STATIONS, &c.	COUNTY.	COMPANY.	POSITION.
G	.	.	.	.	.	Tons 3 Cwts. 0	Burry Port	Carmarth'	B. P. & G. V.	Pontyeats and Sandy Junction.
.	.	.	.	.	.		Ashburnham Tin Works ...	Carmarth'	B. P. & G. V.	Burry Port.
.	.	.	.	.	.		Craiglon Colliery	Carmarth'	B. P. & G. V.	Burry Port.
.	.	.	.	.	.		Cwm Capel Colliery	Carmarth'	B. P. & G. V.	Branch—Burry Port and Sandy Jn.
.	.	.	.	.	.		Elliott's Metal Works	Carmarth'	B. P. & G. V.	Burry Port.
.	.	.	.	.	.		Gwscwm Colliery	Carmarth'	B. P. & G. V.	Burry Port and Pontyeats.
.	.	.	.	.	.		New Lodge Siding............	Carmarth'	B. P. & G. V.	Burry Port and Sandy Junction.
.	.	.	.	.	.		Newpool Siding	Carmarth'	B. P. & G. V.	Burry Port and Sandy Junction.
.	.	.	.	.	.		Pembrey White-Lead Wks.	Carmarth'	B. P. & G. V.	Burry Port.
.	.	.	.	.	.		Pwll Siding	Carmarth'	B. P. & G. V.	Burry Port and Sandy-Junction.
.	.	.	.	.	.		Trimsaran Works and Col.	Carmarth'	B. P. & G. V.	Branch from Trimsaran Junction.
.	.	.	.	.	.		Tymawr Siding	Carmarth'	B. P. & G. V.	Burry Port and Pontyeats.
.	.	.	.	.	.		Burry Port	Carmarth'	G. W.	See Pembrey and Burry Port.
.	.	.	.	.	.		Burry Tin Works (G. W.) ...	Carmarth'	G. W.— L & N. W.	See Thomas, R. & Co. (Llanelly).
G	P	.	L	H	.	4 0	Burscough Bridge	Lancs	L. & Y.	Wigan and Southport.
.	.	.	.	.	.		Martland's Siding	Lancs	L. & Y.	Burscough Bridge.
G	P	F	L	H	C	5 0	Burscough Junction Station.	Lancs	L. & Y.	Preston and Ormskirk.
.	.	.	.	.	.		Abbey Mill Siding	Lancs	L. & Y.	Burscough Junction Station.
.	.	.	.	.	.		Ainscough's Siding	Lancs	L. & Y.	Burscough Junction Station.
.	.	.	.	.	.		Birchfield Siding	Lancs	L. & Y.	Burscough Junction Station.
.	.	.	.	.	.		Brick Field Siding............	Lancs	L. & Y.	Burscough Junction Station.
.	.	.	.	.	.		Burscough Abbey Siding ...	Lancs	L. & Y.	Burscough Junction Station.
.	.	.	.	.	.		Ordnance Stores Siding ...	Lancs	L. & Y.	Burscough Junction Station.
.	.	.	.	.	.		Platt's Siding	Lancs	L. & Y.	Burscough Junction Station.
G	P	.	L	.	.		Bursledon........................	Hants	L. & S.W.	Southampton and Fareham.
.	.	.	.	.	.		Hooper and Co.'s Siding ...	Hants	L. & S.W.	Bursledon.
G	P	F	.	H	C	5 0	Burslem	Staffs	N. S.	Hanley and Tunstall (Loop Line).
G	P	F	L	H	C	1 10	Burston	Norfolk ...	G. E.	Ipswich and Norwich.
.	.	.	.	.	.		Burt and Burt's Siding ...	Dorset......	L. & S.W.	Swanage.
.	.	.	.	.	.		Burt, Boulton, & Heywood's—			
.	.	.	.	.	.		Creosote Works	Durham ...	N. E.	West Hartlepool.
.	.	.	.	.	.		Creosoting Works	Lincoln ...	G. C.	Grimsby Docks.
.	.	.	.	.	.		Siding (G. E.)..	Essex	G E—G N—L N W—Mid.	London, Silvertown.
.	.	.	.	.	.		Timber Creosote Yard	Mon	A.(N.&S.W.)D.&R.—G W	Newport, Alexandra Docks.
.	.	.	.	.	.		Burton	Cheshire...	N. W. & L. Jt. (G. C. and W. M. & C. Q.)	See Burton Point (for Burton and Puddington).
G	P	F	L	H	C	3 0	Burton Agnes....................	Yorks	N. E.	Bridlington and Driffield.
.	.	.	.	.	.		Burton, A. J., Siding	Middlesex	G. E.	Bush Hill Park.
G	P	F	L	H	C	2 0	Burton and Holme.............	W'morlnd	L. & N. W.	Lancaster and Penrith.
.	.	.	.	.	.		Shepherd & Son's Holme Mills	W'morlnd	L. & N. W.	Burton & Holme and Milnthorpe.
.	.	.	.	.	.		Burton & Son's Plymouth Whf.	Glamorg'n	G. W.	Cardiff.
.	.	.	.	.	.		Burton Brewery Co.'s Siding	Leicester..	Mid.	Ashby.
.	.	.	.	.	.		Burton Brewery Co.'s Sid (Mid)	Staffs	Mid—L N W—G N—N S	Burton-on-Trent.
.	.	.	.	.	.		Burton Brick Siding (Sleaford & District Brick & Tile Sid.)	Lincoln ...	G. N.	Aswarby.
G	P	.	L	H	.		Burton Constable	Yorks	N. E.	Hull and Hornsea.
.	.	.	.	.	.		Burton Dassett Siding	Warwick..	E. & W. Jn.	Kineton.
.	.	.	.	.	.		Burton Ironstone Co.'s Siding	N'hamptn	Mid.	Cranford.
G	P	.	L	H	.		Burton Joyce	Notts	Mid.	Nottingham and Newark.
.	.	.	.	.	.		Burton Lane Coal Siding......	Yorks	N. E.	York.
.	.	.	.	.	.		Burton Lane Junction	Yorks	N. E.	York, Pass. and Bootham Junction.
.	.	.	.	.	.		Burton Latimer	N'hamptn	Mid.	See Isham & Burton Latimer.
.	.	.	.	.	.		Burton Latimer Gas Co.'s Sid.	N'hamptn	Mid.	Isham & Burton Latimer.
.	.	.	.	.	.		BURTON-ON-TRENT—			
.	.	.	.	.	.		Allsopp & Sons—			
.	.	.	.	.	.		Breweries (Mid.)	Staffs	Mid—L N W—G N—N S	Guild Street, Hay, & Sanders Bchs.
.	.	.	.	.	.		Shobnall Maltings (L. & N. W.)	Staffs	L N W—Mid—G N—N S	Dallow Lane Branch.
.	.	.	.	.	.		Sidings (L. & N.W.)	Staffs	L. & N. W.—G.N.—N.S.	Horninglow Street Branch.
.	.	.	.	.	.		Sidings (Mid.)	Staffs	Mid—L N W—G N—N S	Station Street and Repton.
.	.	.	.	.	.		Bass & Co.'s (Mid.)—			
.	.	.	.	.	.		Breweries	Staffs	Mid—L N W—G N—N S	Bond End, Guild Street, Hay, and Sanders Branches.
.	.	.	.	.	.		Shobnall Maltings........	Staffs	Mid—L N W—G N—N S	Shobnall Branch.
.	.	.	.	.	.		Siding	Staffs	Mid—L N W—G N—N S	Station Street and Repton.
.	.	.	.	.	.		Bindley & Co.'s Brewery (Mid.)	Staffs	Mid—L N W—G N—N S	Bond End Branch.
.	.	.	.	.	.		Bond End Branch (Mid.)..	Staffs	Mid—L N W—G N—N S	Station Street and Branston.
.	.	.	.	.	.		Bond End Wharf (Mid.)...	Staffs	Mid—L N W—G N—N S	Bond End Branch.
.	.	.	.	.	.		Burton Brewery Co.'s Sids. (Mid.)	Staffs	Mid—L N W—G N—N S	Hay and Sanders Branches.

EXPLANATION—G *Goods Station.*   P *Passenger and Parcel Station.*   P* *Passenger, but not Parcel or Miscellaneous Traffic.*
F *Furniture Vans, Carriages, Portable Engines, and Machines on Wheels.*   L *Live Stock.*
H *Horse Boxes and Prize Cattle Vans.*   C *Carriages by Passenger Train.*

STATION ACCOMMODATION.						CRANE POWER.		STATIONS, &c.	COUNTY.	COMPANY.	POSITION.
						Tons	Cwts	BURTON-ON-TRENT—*continued*.			
.	.	.	.	.	.			Burton-on-Trent Screening & Storing Co.'s Sidings (Mid.)	Staffs	Mid—G N—N S	Station Street and Repton.
.	.	.	.	.	.			Burton Pure Ice & Cold Storage Co.'s Sid. (Mid.)	Staffs	Mid—L N W—G N—N S	Horninglow Branch.
.	.	.	.	.	.			Charrington & Co.'s Sidings (Mid.)	Staffs	Mid—L N W—G N—N S	Bond End Branch.
.	.	.	.	.	.			Clay Mills Siding	Staffs	Mid.	Station Street and Repton.
.	.	.	.	.	.			Cooper & Co.'s Crescent Brewery (Mid.)	Staffs	Mid—L N W—G N—N S	Horninglow Branch.
.	.	.	.	.	.			Dallow Lane Bch. (L&NW)	Staffs	L N W—Mid—G N—N S	Stretton Junc. and Shobnall Junc.
.	.	.	.	.	.			Dallow Lane Whf. (LNW)	Staffs	L N W—Mid—G N—N S	Dallow Lane Branch.
.	.	.	.	.	.			Dixie Sidings (L. & N. W.)	Staffs	L. & N. W.—G.N.—N. S.	Wetmoor Junction and Hawkins Lane Junction.
.	.	.	.	.	.			Dixie Sidings (Mid.)	Staffs	Mid.— L. & N. W.—G. N	Station Street and Wetmoor Junc.
.	.	.	.	.	.			Eadie Sidings (Mid.).........	Staffs	Mid—L N W—G N—N S	Bond End Branch.
.	.	.	.	.	.			English Grain Co.'s Siding (Mid.)	Staffs	Mid.—G.N.—N.S...........	Station Street and Repton.
.	.	.	.	.	.			Everard & Co.'s Trent Brewery Sid. (Mid.)	Staffs	Mid—L N W—G N—N S	Bond End Branch.
.	.	.	.	.	.			Evershed's Siding (Mid.)...	Staffs	Mid—L N W—G N—N S	Bond End Branch.
.	.	.	.	.	.			Gas Works (Mid)	Staffs	Mid—L N W—G N—N S	Hay Branch.
.	.	.	.	.	.			General Forage and Grain Drying Co.'s Sid. (Mid.)	Staffs	Mid—L N W—G N—N S	Bond End Branch.
.	.	.	.	.	.			Grout & Co.'s Sid. (L&NW)	Staffs	L N W—Mid—G N—N S	Dallow Lane Branch.
.	.	.	.	.	•			Guild Street Branch (Mid.)	Staffs	Mid—L N W—G N—N S	Station Street and Repton.
.	.	.	.	.	.			Hallam & Son's Siding (L. & N. W.)................	Staffs	L N W—Mid—G N—N S	Dallow Lane Branch.
G	.	F	L	.	.	5	0	Hawkins Lane (G. N.)	Staffs	{ G. N.	Over N. S. from Dove Junction.
										L. & N. W.	Over Mid. & N. S. Lines.
										N. S.	Over G. N. Line.
.	.	.	.	.	.			Hawkins Lane Junctions...	Staffs	L&NW—GN—Mid.—NS	Horninglow Street & Wetmoor Jn.
.	.	.	.	.	.			Hay Branch (Mid.)	Staffs	Mid—L&NW—GN—NS	N. S. Junc. & Wetmoor Junc.
.	.	.	.	.	.			Hay Wharf (Mid.)	Staffs	Mid—L&NW—GN—NS	Hay Branch.
.	.	.	.	.	.			Hodge's, G., Siding (Mid.)	Staffs	Mid.—L&NW—GN—NS	Guild Street Branch.
.	P	.	.	.	.			Horninglow, (N.S.)	Staffs	{ N. S.	Tutbury and Station Street.
										G. N.	Over N. S. from Dove Junction.
.	.	.	.	.	.			Horninglow Branch (Mid.)	Staffs	Mid—L&NW—GN—NS	Branch from N.S. Junction.
G	.	F	L	.	.	5	0	Horninglow Str. (L.&N.W.)	Staffs	{ L. & N. W.	Over Mid. Line.
										N. S.	Over L.N.W.from Hawkins Lane Jn.
										G. N.	Over N. S. from Dove Junction.
.	.	.	.	.	.			Horninglow Wharf (Mid.)...	Staffs	Mid—L&NW—GN—NS	Horninglow Branch.
									Ind Coope & Co.'s (Mid.)—			
.	.	.	.	.	.			Shobnall Maltings	Staffs	Mid.—L. & N. W.—N. S.	Station Street and Branston.
.	.	.	.	.	.			Siding	Staffs	Mid—L&NW—GN—NS	Mosley Street Branch.
.	.	.	.	.	.			Junction	Staffs	Mid.—N. S.	Station Street and Tutbury.
.	.	.	.	.	.			Kind's Siding (L.&N.W.)...	Staffs	L&NW—Mid—GN—NS	Dallow Lane Branch.
.	.	.	.	.	.			Kottingham & Moor Street Wharf (L. & N. W.)	Staffs	L&NW—Mid—GN—NS	Bond End Branch.
.	.	.	.	.	.			Leicester Junctions	Staffs	Mid.	Station Street and Overseal.
.	.	.	.	.	.			Lowe & Son's Sid. (Mid.) ...	Staffs	Mid.—G.N.—N.S...........	Station Street and Repton.
.	.	.	.	.	.			Lowe & Son's Curzon Street Siding (Mid.)	Staffs	Mid—L&NW—GN—NS	Station Street and Repton.
.	.	.	.	.	.			Magee Marshall & Co.'s Brewery (Mid.)	Staffs	Mid.—L&NW—GN—NS	Bond End Branch.
								MarstonThompson&Son's—			
.	.	.	.	.	.			Horninglow Street Maltings (Mid.)	Staffs	Mid.—L. & N. W.—G.N.	Guild Street Branch.
.	.	.	.	.	.			Sidings (Mid.)	Staffs	Mid.—G.N.—N. S.	Station Street and Repton.
.	.	.	.	.	.			Sidings (Mid.)	Staffs	Mid—L&NW—GN—NS	Shobnall Branch.
.	.	.	.	.	.			Meakin's Siding (Mid.)	Staffs	Mid—L&NW—GN—NS	Leicester Junction.
.	.	.	.	.	.			Morton & Co.'s Sid. (Mid.)	Staffs	Mid—L&NW—GN—NS	Station Street and Repton.
.	.	.	.	.	.			Mosley Street Branch (Mid)	Staffs	Mid—L&NW—GN—NS	Station Street and Branston.
.	.	.	.	.	.			New Branch (Mid.)	Staffs	Mid—L&NW—GN—NS	Branch from Bond End Branch.
.	.	.	.	.	.			North Junction	Staffs	G. N.—N.S.	Hawkins Lane and Stretton Junc.
.	.	.	.	.	.			Peach & Co.'s Welcome Siding (Mid.)	Staffs	Mid—L&NW—GN—NS	Bond End Branch.
.	.	.	.	.	.			Perks & Son's Timber Yard Sidings (Mid.)...............	Staffs	Mid—L&NW—GN—NS	Bond End Branch.
.	.	.	.	.	.			Renwick & Hunt's Siding (Mid.)	Staffs	Mid.—L. & N. W.—G. N.	Horninglow Branch.

EXPLANATION—G *Goods Station.*   P *Passenger and Parcel Station.*   P* *Passenger, but not Parcel or Miscellaneous Traffic.*
F *Furniture Vans, Carriages, Portable Engines, and Machines on Wheels.*   L *Live Stock.*
H *Horse Boxes and Prize Cattle Vans.*   C *Carriages by Passenger Train.*

G	P	F	L	H	C	Tons	Cwts	STATIONS, &c.	COUNTY.	COMPANY.	POSITION.
								BURTON-ON-TRENT—*continued*.			
								Riley & Son's Timber Siding (Mid.)	Staffs	Mid—L&NW—GN—NS	Bond End Branch.
								Robinson's Siding (Mid.)	Staffs	Mid—L&NW—GN—NS	Bond End Branch.
								Robinson's Brewery (Mid.)	Staffs	Mid.—L. & N. W.	Bond End Branch.
								Ryknield Engine Co's Siding (Mid.)	Staffs	Mid.—L. & N. W.	Shobnall Branch.
								Salt & Co's Sidings (Mid.)	Staffs	Mid—L&NW—GN—NS	Bond End and Hay Branches.
								Sanders Branch (Mid.)	Staffs	Mid—L&NW—GN—NS	Branch from Hay Branch.
								Shobnall Branch (Mid.)	Staffs	Mid—L&NW—GN—NS	Station Street and Branston.
								Shobnall Junction	Staffs	L. & N. W.—Mid.	Dallow Lane Whf & Bond End Whf.
								Shobnall Wharf (Mid.)	Staffs	Mid—L&NW—GN—NS	Shobnall Branch.
								South Junction	Staffs	G. N.—N. S.	North Junc. & Hawkins Lane Junc.
G	P	F	L	H	C	10	0	Station Street (Mid.)	Staffs	Mid.	Derby and Birmingham.
	P		F		H	C				G. N.	Over N. S. & Mid. Lines.
	P	P	F		H	C				L. & N. W.	Over Mid. Line.
G	P		F	L	H	C	10	0		N. S.	Over Mid. from Burton Junction.
								Staton's Siding (L & N W)	Staffs	L&NW—Mid—GN—NS	Dallow Lane Branch.
								Stretton Junction	Staffs	L. & N. W.—N. S.	Dallow Lane Wharf and Dove Junc.
								Thornewell & Warham's Siding (Mid.)	Staffs	Mid—L&NW—GN—NS	Bond End Branch.
								Trent Cold Storage & Ice Co.'s Siding (Mid.)	Staffs	Mid—L N W—G N—N S	Station Street and Repton.
								Truman, Hanbury & Buxton's Siding (Mid.)	Staffs	Mid—L&NW—GN—NS	Station Street and Repton.
								Walker, P., & Son's Brewery (Mid.)	Staffs	Mid—L&NW—GN—NS	Shobnall Branch.
								Walker's, P. (Trustees of) Siding (Mid.)	Staffs	Mid.—L&NW—GN—NS	Bond End Branch.
								Wetmoor Junction	Staffs	L. & N. W.—Mid.	Horninglow Street and Repton.
								Wetmoor Road	Staffs	G. N.	North Junction and Hawkins Lane.
								Wetmoor Sidings (Mid.)	Staffs	Mid.—G.N.	Station Street and Repton.
								Worthington & Co.'s Siding (Mid.)	Staffs	Mid—L&NW—GN—NS.	Bond End, Hay, and Sanders Bchs.
								Worthington & Co.'s Siding (Mid.)	Staffs	Mid—L. & N. W.	Station Street and Branston.
								Yeoman, Cherry, Curtis & Co.'s Siding (L.&N.W.)	Staffs	L. & N. W.—N. S.	Dallow Lane Branch.
								Burton-on-Trent Screening & Storing Co.'s Sidings (Mid.)	Staffs	Mid.—G N.—N. S.	Burton-on-Trent.
G	P	F	L	H	C			Burton Point (for Burton and Puddington)	Cheshire	N. W. & L. Jt. (G. C. and W. M. & C. Q.)	Connahs Quay and Neston.
G	P		L	H	C	1	10	Burtonport	Donegal	L. & L. S.	Terminus.
G	P	F	L	H	C	5	0	Burton Salmon (N. E.)	Yorks	N. E.	York & Knottingley, Ferrybridge Jn.
	P			H	C					G. C.	Over N.E. from Knottingley, Ferrybridge Junction.
G	P			H	C					G. N.	Over N. E. and S. & K. Jt. Lines.
	P									Mid.	Over N. E. Line.
								Burton Salmon Junction	Yorks	N. E.	York and Knottingley.
								Burton Siding	Lincoln	G. N. & G. E. Jt.	Same as Gate Burton Siding (Lea).
G	P	F	L	H	C			Burwell	Cambs	G. E.	Cambridge and Fordham.
								BURY—			
								Ashworth's (Fernhill) Sid.	Lancs	L. & Y.	Bury.
								Atherton's Siding	Lancs	L. & Y.	Bury.
								Buckley Wells Siding	Lancs	L. & Y.	Bury.
								Bury Saw Mill	Lancs	L. & Y.	Bury.
								Corporation Gas Works	Lancs	L. & Y.	Bury and Black Lane.
								Corporation Siding	Lancs	L. & Y.	Bury.
G	P	F	L	H		10	0	High Level	Lancs	L. & Y.	Clifton Junction and Accrington.
								L.&Y. Co.'s Locomotive Sid.	Lancs	L. & Y.	Bury.
G	P	F	L	H	C	10	0	Low Level	Lancs	L. & Y.	Bolton and Rochdale.
								Paper Co.'s Siding	Lancs	L. & Y.	Bury and Broadfield.
								Peel Mill Co.'s Siding	Lancs	L. & Y.	Near Bury.
								Tottington Junction	Lancs	L. & Y.	Bury and Summerseat.
								BURY ST. EDMUNDS—			
G	P	F	L	H	C	10	0	(Station)	Suffolk	G. E.	Cambridge and Ipswich.
	P							East Gate	Suffolk	G. E.	Sudbury and Bury St. Edmunds.
								Gough, J., & Son's Siding	Suffolk	G. E.	Bury St. Edmunds.
								Hewitt, W.R.,&Co.'s Siding	Suffolk	G. E.	Bury St. Edmunds.
								Ridley & Browne's Siding	Suffolk	G. E.	Bury St. Edmunds.
								Bury Street Junction	Middlesex	G. E.	Lower Edmonton.
								Busbie Colliery Junction	Ayr	G. & S.W.	Crosshouse and Dreghorn.

EXPLANATION—G *Goods Station.*　　P *Passenger and Parcel Station.*　　P* *Passenger, but not Parcel or Miscellaneous Traffic.*
F *Furniture Vans, Carriages, Portable Engines, and Machines on Wheels.*　　L *Live Stock.*
H *Horse Boxes and Prize Cattle Vans.*　　C *Carriages by Passenger Train.*

STATION ACCOMMODATION.						CRANE POWER.	STATIONS, &c.	COUNTY.	COMPANY.	POSITION.
						Tons Cwts.	Busbiehead No. 2	Ayr	G. & S.W.	Crosshouse.
							Busbie Junction	Ayr	G. & S.W.	Kilmarnock and Crosshouse.
G	P		L	H		1 10	Busby	Lanark	Cal.	Pollokshaws and East Kilbride.
							Busby Junction	Renfrew	Cal.—G. B. & K. Jt.	Busby and Pollokshaws.
							Busby Siding	Yorks	N. E.	Sexhow.
G	P			H	C		Bush	Louth	D. N. & G.	Dundalk and Greenore.
G	P						Bushbury	Staffs	L. & N. W.	Stafford and Wolverhampton.
							Bushbury Junction	Staffs	G. W.—L. & N. W.	Bushbury Sta. & Wolverhampton.
G	P					5 0	Bushey	Herts.	L. & N. W.	Willesden and Watford.
							Bushey Colliery Siding	Yorks	G. N.	Gildersome.
							Bushey Lane Junction	Lancs	L. & Y.	Rainford and Skelmersdale.
							Bushey Lodge Sidings	Herts.	L. & N. W.	Watford.
							Ayre's Siding	Herts.	L. & N. W	Bushey Lodge Sidings.
							Tibbles (Vi-Cocoa) Siding	Herts.	L. & N. W.	Bushey Lodge Sidings.
							Bushey Park	Middlesex	L. & S.W.	See Teddington and Bushey Park.
G	P						Bush Hill Park	Middlesex	G. E.	Enfield Town & Lower Edmonton.
							Burton, A. J., Siding	Middlesex	G. E.	Bush Hill Park.
							Drake, G. J., Siding	Middlesex	G. E.	Bush Hill Park.
							Butcher Pit (L. & N. W.)	Lancs	L. N. W.—G.C. (Wig. Jn.)	See Wigan Coal & Iron Co. (Wigan).
							Butcherwood Colliery	Notts	G N—Mid—GC—LD&EC	Same as Stanton Iron Works Co.'s Teversall Colliery (Teversall).
							Bute Docks	Glamorg'n	G. W—L N W—Rhy—TV	See Cardiff.
							Bute Docks Gas Works	Glamorg'n	G. W—L N W—Rhy—TV	Cardiff.
							Bute Engineering and Dry Dock Co.'s Siding	Glamorg'n	G. W—L N W—Rhy—TV	Cardiff.
							Bute East Dock Junction	Glamorg'n	Cardiff—T. V.	Cardiff.
							Bute Estate Siding	Glamorg'n	T. V.	Cardiff.
							Bute Lime Works (G.W.)	Glamorg'n	G. W.—T. V.	Mwyndy.
							Bute Merthyr Colliery	Glamorg'n	T. V.	Treherbert.
							Bute Workshops Siding	Glamorg'n	T. V.	Cardiff.
							Butler & Co.'s Trustees' Sid.	Yorks	G. N.	Stanningley.
	P						Butler's Hill	Notts	G. N.	Daybrook and Hucknall.
							Broomhill Sidings	Notts	G. N.	Butler's Hill.
							Butler's Hill Siding	Notts	G. N.	Hucknall.
							Butler's Siding	Staffs	G. W.	Wolverhampton.
							Butler Street	Lancs	L. & Y.	See Preston.
							Butlin & Co.—			
							Furnaces	N'hamptn	L. & N. W.	Wellingboro'.
							Iron Works	N'hamptn	Mid.	Wellingboro'.
							Wollaston Iron Ore Siding.	N'hamptn	L. & N. W.	Wellingboro'.
							Butt & Son's Siding	Middlesex	{ G. E. { GN—GW—LNW—Mid	London, Millwall Docks. London, Poplar.
							Butterfield & Co.'s Siding	Yorks	Mid.	Keighley.
G						2 0	Butterknowle	Durham	N. E.	Branch from West Auckland.
							Butterknowle Colliery	Durham	N. E.	Butterknowle.
							Cockfield Stone Quarry	Durham	N. E.	Butterknowle.
							Crake Scarr Colliery	Durham	N. E.	Butterknowle.
							Gordon House Colliery	Durham	N. E.	Butterknowle.
							Lands Lane Siding	Durham	N. E.	Butterknowle.
							Millfield Grange Colliery	Durham	N. E.	Butterknowle.
							New Copley Colliery	Durham	N. E.	Butterknowle.
							Storey Lodge Colliery	Durham	N. E.	Butterknowle.
							West Tees Colliery No. 2	Durham	N. E.	Butterknowle.
							Woodland Colliery	Durham	N. E.	Butterknowle.
							Woodland Junction	Durham	N. E.	Butterknowle.
G	P	F	L	H	C		Butterley	Derby	Mid.	Pye Bridge and Ambergate.
							Butterley Co.—			
							Brand's Colliery	Derby	Mid.	Butterley and Pye Bridge.
							Butterley Works	Derby	Mid.	Butterley.
							Hartshay Colliery	Derby	Mid.	Butterley.
							Pentrich Colliery	Derby	Mid.	Butterley and Ambergate.
							Swanwick Colliery	Derby	Mid.	Butterley and Pye Bridge.
							Butterley Co.—			
							Brand's Colliery	Derby	Mid.	{ Butterley. { Codnor Park.
							Brick Yard	Notts	Mid.	Kirkby-in-Ashfield.
							ButterleyCoal & Ir.Co.'sSid.	Derby	Mid.	Ambergate.
							Butterley Works	Derby	Mid.	{ Butterley. { Codnor Park.
							Coal and Iron Works	Derby	Mid.	Codnor Park.
							Dale Quarry	Derby	Mid.	Wirksworth.
							Hartshay Colliery	Derby	Mid.	Butterley.

EXPLANATION—G *Goods Station.*   P *Passenger and Parcel Station.*   P* *Passenger, but not Parcel or Miscellaneous Traffic.*
F *Furniture Vans, Carriages, Portable Engines, and Machines on Wheels.*   L *Live Stock.*
H *Horse Boxes and Prize Cattle Vans.*   C *Carriages by Passenger Train.*

Station Accommodation.						Crane Power.	Stations, &c.	County.	Company.	Position.
						Tons Cwts	Butterley Co.—*continued.*			
.	.	.	.	.	.	. .	Ironstone Siding	Derby	Mid.	Codnor Park.
.	.	.	.	.	.	. .	Langley Collieries	Derby	Mid.	Langley Mill and Eastwood.
.	.	.	.	.	.	. .	Lime Works	Derby	Mid.	Ambergate.
.	.	.	.	.	.	. .	Marehay Colliery	Derby	Mid.	Ripley.
.	.	.	.	.	.	. .	New Colliery (Kirkby Col.)	Notts	Mid.	Kirkby-in-Ashfield.
.	.	.	.	.	.	. .	Plumptre Colliery	Derby	Mid.	Langley Mill and Eastwood.
.	.	.	.	.	.	. .	Roscoe Collieries	Derby	Mid.	Langley Mill and Eastwood.
.	.	.	.	.	.	. .	Sand Siding	Notts	Mid.	Kirkby-in-Ashfield.
.	.	.	.	.	.	. .	Whiteley's Siding	Derby	Mid.	Ripley.
.	.	.	.	.	.	. .	Butterley Works	Derby	Mid.	{ See Butterley Co. (Butterley). { See Butterley Co. (Codnor Park).
.	.	.	.	.	.	. .	Butter's Siding (G.& P. Jt.)	Lanark	{ Cal. { G. & S. W.	Glasgow, Kinning Park. Glasgow, General Terminus.
.	.	.	.	.	.	. .	Buttery Hatch Col. (B. & M.)	Mon	B. & M.—G. W.	Pengam.
G	P	F	L	H	C	. .	Buttevant and Doneraile	Cork	G. S. & W.	Charleville and Mallow.
G	P	.	L	.	.	. .	Buttington	Montgom	{ Cam. { S & W'pl Jt (GW&LNW)	Welshpool and Pool Quay. Shrewsbury and Welshpool.
.	.	.	.	.	.	. .	Buttington Junction	Montgom	Cam.—S. & W'pl Jt.	Welshpool and Shrewsbury.
.	.	.	.	.	.	. .	Butts Junction	Hants	L. & S.W.	Alton and Alresford.
.	.	.	.	.	.	. .	Butts Siding	Worcester	G. W.	See Worcester.
G	P	F	L	H	C	5 0	Buxted	Sussex	L. B. & S. C.	Uckfield and Crowborough.
							BUXTON—			
G	P	F	L	H	C	5 0	(Station)	Derby	Mid.	Branch from Miller's Dale.
G	P	F	L	H	C	10 0	(Station)	Derby	L. & N. W.	Ashbourne and Stockport.
.	.	.	.	.	.	. .	Ashwood Dale Siding	Derby	Mid.	Buxton and Miller's Dale.
.	.	.	.	.	.	. .	Buxton Lime Firms Co.	Derby	Mid.	Ashwood Dale Siding.
.	.	.	.	.	.	. .	Buxton New Lime Co.	Derby	Mid.	Ashwood Dale Siding.
.	.	.	.	.	.	. .	Gas Works	Derby	Mid.	Buxton and Miller's Dale.
.	.	.	.	.	.	. .	Junction	Derby	L. & N. W.—Mid.	Buxton and Miller's Dale.
.	.	.	.	.	.	. .	Buxton Central Works	Derby	Mid.	See Buxton Lime Firms Co. (Miller's Dale).
G	P	F	L	H	C	. .	Buxton Lamas	Norfolk	G. E.	Wroxham and Aylsham.
.	.	.	.	.	.	. .	Buxton Lime Firms Co.—			
.	.	.	.	.	.	. .	Ashwood Dale Siding	Derby	Mid.	{ Buxton. { Miller's Dale.
.	.	.	.	.	.	. .	Briggs' Siding	Derby	L. & N. W.	Hindlow.
.	.	.	.	.	.	. .	Buxton Central Works	Derby	Mid.	Miller's Dale.
.	.	.	.	.	.	. .	Crusher Siding	Derby	L. & N. W.	Hindlow.
.	.	.	.	.	.	. .	East Buxton Siding	Derby	Mid.	Miller's Dale.
.	.	.	.	.	.	. .	Grin Branch	Derby	L. & N. W.	Ladmanlow.
.	.	.	.	.	.	. .	Gritstone Siding	Derby	L. & N. W.	Ladmanlow.
.	.	.	.	.	.	. .	Hoffman's Siding	Derby	L. & N. W.	Hindlow.
.	.	.	.	.	.	. .	Miller's Dale Lime Siding	Derby	Mid.	Miller's Dale.
.	.	.	.	.	.	. .	New South Works	Derby	Mid.	Peak Forest.
.	.	.	.	.	.	. .	Siding	Cheshire	L. & N. W.	Whaley Bridge.
.	.	.	.	.	.	. .	Siding	Cheshire	Mac. Com. (G. C. & N. S.)	Marple, Rose Hill.
.	.	.	.	.	.	. .	Siding	Derby	L. & N. W.	Ladmanlow.
.	.	.	.	.	.	. .	Whaley or Gisbourne Col.	Cheshire	L. & N. W.	Whaley Bridge.
.	.	.	.	.	.	. .	Buxton New Lime Co.'s Sid.	Derby	Mid.	See Ashwood Dale Siding (Buxton)
.	.	.	.	.	.	. .	Bwlch Siding (N. & B.)	Brecon	N. & Brecon—Mid.	Penwyllt.
.	.	.	.	.	.	. .	Bwllfa Dare or Bwllfa No. 1 Colliery	Glamorg'n	{ G. W. { T. V.	Dare Junction Station. Aberdare.
.	.	.	.	.	.	. .	Bwllfa Dare or Bwllfa No. 2 Col. (Nantmelyn Col.)	Glamorg'n	{ G. W. { T. V.	Dare Junction Station. Aberdare.
.	.	.	.	.	.	. .	Byass, R. B., & Co.'s Siding	Glamorg'n	G. W.—P. T.—R. & S. B.	Same as Mansel Sid. (Port Talbot).
.	.	.	.	.	.	. .	Byer Moor Col. Coke Wks & Qry	Durham	N. E.	Redheugh.
G	P	F	L	H	C	1 0	Byer's Green	Durham	N. E.	Bishop Auckland and Spennymoor.
.	.	.	.	.	.	. .	Byer's Green Colliery	Durham	N. E.	Byer's Green.
.	.	.	.	.	.	. .	Byer's Green Old Station and Engine Shed Siding (Todhill's Siding)	Durham	N. E.	Byer's Green.
.	.	.	.	.	.	. .	Byer's Green Ventilating Shaft Siding	Durham	N. E.	Byer's Green.
G	P	.	L	H	.	. .	Byfield	N'hamptn	E. & W. Jn.	Morton Pinkney & Fenny Compton.
G	P	F	L	H	C	. .	Byfleet and Woodham	Surrey	L. & S.W.	Weybridge and Woking.
.	P	.	.	.	.	. .	Byfleet Junction	Surrey	L. & S.W.	Weybridge and Byfleet.
.	P	.	.	.	.	. .	Byker	Northumb	N. E.	Newcastle & Tynemouth (Riverside).
.	P	.	.	.	.	. .	Byker & Heaton Cl. Co.'s Depôt	Northumb	N. E.	Newcastle-on-Tyne.
G	P	.	.	.	.	. }	Bynea (G. W.)	Carmarth'	{ G. W. { L. & N. W.	Llanelly and Pontardulais. Over G. W. from Llandilo Junction
G	.	.	.	.	.	. }	Bynea Brick Works	Carmarth'	G. W.	Branch from Bynea.

STATION ACCOMMODATION.						CRANE POWER.		STATIONS, &c.	COUNTY.	COMPANY.	POSITION.
						Tons	Cwts.				
								Bynea (G. W.)—continued.			
..	..	..	..	..	..			Carnarvon Colliery (G. W.)	Carmarth'	G. W.—L. & N. W.	Branch from Genwen Junction.
..	..	..	..	..	..			Genwen Colliery (G. W.) ...	Carmarth'	G. W.—L. & N. W.	Bynea and Llanelly.
..	..	..	..	..	..			Genwen Junction	Carmarth'	G. W.	Bynea and Llanelly.
..	..	..	..	..	..			Glynea Brick Works	Carmarth'	G. W.	Bynea and Llanelly.
..	..	..	..	..	..			Glynea Colliery (G. W.) ...	Carmarth'	G. W.—L. & N. W.	Bynea and Llanelly.
..	..	..	..	..	..			Pencoed Colliery..............	Carmarth'	G. W.	Bynea and Llanelly.
..	..	..	..	..	..			St. David's Tin Plate Works (G. W.)	Carmarth'	G. W.—L. & N. W.	Branch from Bynea.
..	..	..	..	..	..			Byrehill Junction	Ayr	G. & S. W.	Irvine and Kilwinning.
..	..	..	..	..	..			Byron Brick Co.'s Siding......	Derby	Mid.	Palterton and Sutton.
..	..	..	..	..	..			Byron Cols. (Blenkinsopp's)	Northumb	N. E.	Greenhead.

C

STATION ACCOMMODATION.						CRANE POWER.		STATIONS, &c.	COUNTY.	COMPANY.	POSITION.
..	..	..	..	..	..			Cabra Siding	Dublin	G. S. & W.	See Dublin.
..	..	..	..	..	..			Cadbury Bros.' Siding	Worcester	Mid.	Lifford.
..	..	..	..	..	..			Cadbury's Brick Yard	Worcester	Mid.	Lifford.
..	..	..	..	..	..			Cadder	Lanark ...	N. B.	Lenzie Junction and Cowlairs.
..	..	..	..	..	..			Cadder Siding...............	Lanark ...	N. B.	Lenzie Junction Station.
..	..	..	..	..	..			Cadeby Colliery (G. C.)	Yorks	G. C.—Mid.	Conisborough.
..	..	..	..	..	..			Cadeby Main Colliery	Yorks	H. & B.	Denaby and Conisborough.
G	P	.	L	.	.	5	0	Cadeleigh and Bickleigh ...	Devon	G. W.	Exeter and Tiverton.
..	..	..	..	..	..			Cadge & Colman's Sid. (G. E.)	Hunts	G. E.—L. & N. W.—Mid.	Peterboro'.
.	P	.	.	.	.			Cadger's Loan Quarry	Stirling ...	Cal.	Plean Junction.
.	P	.	.	.	.			Cadishead	Lancs	C.L.C. (G C, G N, & Mid.)	Glazebrook and Partington.
..	..	..	..	..	..			Cadley Hill Colliery (Mid.) ...	Derby	Mid.—L. & N. W.........	See Hall's Collieries (Swadlincote).
								CADOXTON—			
G	.	F	L	H	C	5	0	(Station)	Glamorg'n	T. V.	Cadoxton Pass. and Penarth.
G	P	.	.	.	.	5	0	(Station, Barry)	Glamorg'n	{ Barry / T. V.	Barry and Cogan. / Over Barry from Biglis Junction.
.	P	.	.	.	.						
..	..	..	..	..	..			Boucher's Siding...............	Glamorg'n	T. V.	Cadoxton.
..	..	..	..	..	..			Junction	Glamorg'n	Barry	Cadoxton and Wenvoe.
..	..	..	..	..	..			New Dock Brick Co.'s Sid.	Glamorg'n	T. V.	Cadoxton.
..	..	..	..	..	..			Cadoxton Junction..............	Glamorg'n	G. W.—N. & Brecon......	Neath.
..	..	..	..	..	..			Cadzow Colliery	Lanark ...	Cal.	Hamilton, Central.
..	..	..	..	..	..			Cae Bleyddyn Pits	Flint	L. & N. W.	Same as Coed Talon Colliery Co.'s Siding (Coed Talon).
..	..	..	..	..	..			Caeglas Colliery	Carmarth	L. & M. M.	Cwmblawd.
..	..	..	..	..	..			Cae Harris	Glamorg'n	T. B. Jt. (G. W. & Rhy.)	See Dowlais.
..	..	..	..	..	..			Caello Brick Works	Denbigh ...	G. W.	Coed Poeth.
..	..	..	..	..	..			Caepompren Siding	Carmarth'	B. P. & G. V.	Pontyeats.
G	P	.	.	.	.			Caerau	Glamorg'n	G. W.	Tywith and Cymmer.
..	..	..	..	..	..			Caerau Colliery	Glamorg'n	G. W.	Caerau.
..	..	..	..	..	..			Coegnant Colliery	Glamorg'n	G. W.	Caerau.
..	..	..	..	..	..			Caerbryn Colliery	Carmarth'	G. W.	Pantyffynnon.
.	P	.	.	.	.			Caergwrle Castle (WM & CQ)	Flint	{ W. M. & C. Q. / G. C.	Buckley and Wrexham. / Over W. M. & C. Q. from Hawarden Bridge Junction.
..	..	..	..	..	..			Lassell and Sharman's Brewery Siding	Denbigh ..	W. M. & C. Q.	Hope Village and Cefn-y-bedd.
..	..	..	..	..	..			Caergynydd Colliery	Glamorg'n	L. & N. W................	See Dunvant Quarry (Dunvant).
G	P	.	L	H	.	1	10	Caerleon	Mon	G. W.	Newport and Pontypool Road.
..	..	..	..	..	..			St. Julian's Brick Works...	Mon	G. W.	Caerleon and Newport, High Street.
								CAERPHILLY—			
G	P	F	L	H	C	5	0	(Station, Rhy.)	Glamorg'n	{ Rhy. / G W (A (N & SW) D&R) / B. & M. / L. & N. W.	Cardiff and Ystrad Mynach. / Over B. & M. and Rhy. Lines. / Over Rhy. from Caerphilly Junction. / Over Rhy. from Rhy. Joint Line Jn.
.	P	.	.	H	C						
G	.	F	L	.	.	5	0				
G	.	F	L	H	C	5	0				
..	..	..	..	..	..			Colliery and Brick Works (Wernddu Colliery and Brick Works)	Glamorg'n	Rhy.	Caerphilly and Llanishen.
..	..	..	..	..	..			East Junction..................	Glamorg'n	Rhy.	Caerphilly and Cardiff.
..	..	..	..	..	..			Junction	Glamorg'n	B. & M.—Rhy.	Machen and Caerphilly.
..	..	..	..	..	..			Penrhos Siding (Furnace Blwm Siding)	Glamorg'n	Rhy.	Caerphilly and Taffs Well.
..	..	..	..	..	..			Tunnel North Siding	Glamorg'n	Rhy.	Caerphilly and Llanishen.
..	..	..	..	..	..			West Junction................	Glamorg'n	Rhy.	Caerphilly and Taffs Well.

EXPLANATION—G *Goods Station.* P *Passenger and Parcel Station.* P* *Passenger, but not Parcel or Miscellaneous Traffic.*
F *Furniture Vans, Carriages, Portable Engines, and Machines on Wheels.* L *Live Stock.*
H *Horse Boxes and Prize Cattle Vans.* C *Carriages by Passenger Train.*

STATION ACCOMMODATION.						CRANE POWER.		STATIONS, &c.	COUNTY.	COMPANY.	POSITION.
						Tons	Cwts.				
G	P	.	L	H	.	1	0 }	Caersws Junction Station ...	Montgom	{ Cam.	Newtown and Machynlleth.
G	P	.	L	.	.	.	. }			{ Cam. (Van)	Junction with Cam.
G	P	.	L	H	.	5	0	Caerwys	Flint	L. & N. W.	Denbigh and Mold.
.	.	.	.	.	.	.	.	Denbighshire Portland Cement Co.'s Siding	Flint	L. & N. W.	Caerwys and Nannerch.
.	.	.	.	.	.	.	.	Cafferata and Co.'s Sidings...	Notts	G. N.	Newark.
.	.	.	.	.	.	.	.	Caffin and Co.'s Siding	Sussex	L. B. & S. C.	Three Bridges.
G	P	F	L	H	C	4	0	Cahir	Tipperary	G. S. & W.	Clonmel and Tipperary.
G	P	F	L	H	C	1	0	Cahirciveen	Kerry	G. S. & W.	Farranfore and Valentia Harbour.
.	.	.	.	.	.	.	.	Caia ....:	Denbigh ..	Cam.	See Wrexham.
.	.	.	.	.	.	.	.	Caird & Co.'s Foundry	Renfrew ..	Cal.	Greenock, Regent Street.
.	.	.	.	.	.	.	.	Caird & Co.'s Sid. (G. & S.W.)	Renfrew ..	G. & S.W.—N. B.	Greenock, Albert Harbour.
.	.	.	.	.	.	.	.	Caird, D. (Exors. of) Siding	Lancs	Furness	Barrow.
G	P	.	L	.	.	.	.	Cairnbulg....................	Aberdeen	G. N. of S.	Fraserburgh and St. Combs.
.	.	.	.	.	.	.	.	Cairngryffe Siding	Lanark	Cal.	See Grange Siding (Carstairs).
.	P*	.	.	.	.	.	.	Cairnie Platform...............	Aberdeen	G. N. of S.	Inveramsay and Keith.
.	.	.	.	.	.	.	.	Cairn Street Siding	Glamorg'n	Rhy.	Cardiff.
.	.	.	.	.	.	.	.	Cairn Valley Junction	Dumfries..	G. & S.W.	Dumfries and Holywood.
G	P	.	.	.	.	.	.	Caister-on-Sea................	Norfolk	Mid. & G. N. Jt.	Yarmouth Beach and North Walsham Town.
.	.	.	.	.	.	.	.	Caistor	Lincoln ...	G. C.	See Moortown (for Caistor).
.	.	.	.	.	.	.	.	Cakemoor Brick Works	Worcester	G. W.	Rowley Regis and Blackheath.
G	P	.	L	H	.	.	.	Calbourne and Shalfleet	I. of W...	I. of W. Cent...............	Freshwater and Newport.
.	.	.	.	.	.	.	.	Calcot Mill Siding	Berks ...	G. W.	Theale.
G	P	F	L	H	C	1	5	Calcots.......................	Elgin&Mo'	G. N. of S.	Portsoy and Elgin.
G	P	.	L	H	.	2	0	Caldarvan....................	Dumbartn	N. B.	Balloch and Stirling.
.	.	.	.	.	.	.	.	Gallangad Siding	Dumbartn	N. B.	Caldarvan and Drymen.
G	P	F	L	H	C	4	0	Calder	Lanark	Cal.	Whifflet, High Level and Airdrie.
.	.	.	.	.	.	.	.	Climax Engineering Works	Lanark ...	Cal.	Calder and Airdrie.
.	.	.	.	.	.	.	.	Clydeside Tube Works	Lanark	Cal.	Whifflet, High Level and Calder.
.	.	.	.	.	.	.	.	Imperial Tube Works (Rochsolloch Tube Works)......	Lanark	Cal.	Calder and Airdrie.
.	.	.	.	.	.	.	.	Union Tube Works	Lanark	Cal.	Whifflet, High Level and Calder.
.	.	.	.	.	.	.	.	Victoria Iron & Steel Wks.	Lanark	Cal.	Whifflet, High Level and Calder.
.	.	.	.	.	.	.	.	Calder & Co.'s Timber Yard..	Durham ...	N. E.	Sunderland, South Dock.
G	P	.	.	.	.	3	0	Calderbank	Lanark	Cal.	Whifflet, High Level and Newhouse.
.	.	.	.	.	.	.	.	Calderbank Steel Works	Lanark	Cal.	Calderbank.
.	.	.	.	.	.	.	.	Craigneuk Collieries, Nos. 3, 4, 9, 10, and 11........	Lanark	Cal.	Calderbank.
.	.	.	.	.	.	.	.	Monkland Collieries	Lanark	Cal.	Calderbank.
.	.	.	.	.	.	.	.	Calderbank Cols. Nos. 1 & 2..	Lanark	Cal.	Baillieston.
.	.	.	.	.	.	.	.	Calderbank Colliery	Lanark	N. B.	Airdrie, North.
.	.	.	.	.	.	.	.	Calderbank Steel Works	Lanark	{ Cal.	Calderbank.
.	.	.	.	.	.	.	.			{ N. B.	Airdrie, North.
.	.	.	.	.	.	.	.	Calder Blacking Mill.........	Lanark	Cal.	Baillieston.
.	.	.	.	.	.	.	.	Calder Brick & Fire Clay Wks.	Lanark	Cal.—N. B.	Coatbridge, Whifflet.
.	.	.	.	.	.	.	.	Calder, Chas., & Co.'s Timber Yard }	Yorks	N. E.	{ See Whitehouse Siding and Depôt (South Bank).
.	.	.	.	.	.	.	.	Calder Chemical Works ...	Lanark	Cal.	Coatbridge, Whifflet.
.	.	.	.	.	.	.	.	Calder Collieries	Lanark	Cal.	Coatbridge, Whifflet.
G	P	.	L	H	.	2	10	Caldercruix	Lanark	N. B.	Airdrie, South and Bathgate, Upper.
.	.	.	.	.	.	.	.	Caldercruix New Bch. Sid.	Lanark	N. B.	Near Caldercruix.
.	.	.	.	.	.	.	.	Caldercruix Paper Mills ...	Lanark	N. B.	Caldercruix and Plains.
.	.	.	.	.	.	.	.	Ford Colliery	Lanark	N. B.	Caldercruix and Plains.
.	.	.	.	.	.	.	.	Glengowan Print Works ...	Lanark	N. B.	Branch from Caldercruix.
G	.	.	.	.	.	.	.	Stepends Siding	Lanark	N. B.	Caldercruix and Plains.
.	.	.	.	.	.	.	.	Caldercruix Colliery	Lanark	N. B.	Longriggend.
.	.	.	.	.	.	.	.	Caldercruix Junction	Lanark	N. B.	Caldercruix and Plains.
.	.	.	.	.	.	.	.	Calder Dixon & Co.—			
.	.	.	.	.	.	.	.	Commercial Street Yard ...	Yorks	N. E.	Middlesbro'.
.	.	.	.	.	.	.	.	Creosote Works	Edinboro'	Cal.—N.B.	Granton.
.	.	.	.	.	.	.	.	Timber Siding	Fife	N. B.	Methil.
.	.	.	.	.	.	.	.	West Whf. & Timber Yard	Yorks	N. E.	Middlesbro'.
.	.	.	.	.	.	.	.	Wood Yard	L'lithgow	N. B.	Bo'ness.
.	.	.	.	.	.	.	.	Calder, East	Edinboro'	N. B.	See East Calder.
.	.	.	.	.	.	.	.	Calder Forge	Lanark ...	Cal.	Baillieston.
.	.	.	.	.	.	.	.	Calderhead Foundry	Lanark	Cal.	Shotts.
.	.	.	.	.	.	.	.	Calderhead, Nos. 1 & 3 Cols.	Lanark	N. B.	Shotts.
.	.	.	.	.	.	.	.	Calder Iron Works	Lanark	Cal.—N. B.	Coatbridge, Whifflet.
.	.	.	.	.	.	.	.	Calder's Distillery Siding ...	L'lithgow	N. B.	Same as Bo'ness Distillery Siding.
.	.	.	.	.	.	.	.	Calder Siding	Yorks	Meth.Jt.(GN,L&Y&N.E)	Stanley.
.	.	.	.	.	.	.	.	Caldervale Forge	Lanark ...	N. B.	Clarkston.

EXPLANATION—G *Goods Station.*   P *Passenger and Parcel Station.*   P* *Passenger, but not Parcel or Miscellaneous Traffic.*
F *Furniture Vans, Carriages, Portable Engines, and Machines on Wheels.*   L *Live Stock.*
H *Horse Boxes and Prize Cattle Vans.*   C *Carriages by Passenger Train.*

STATION ACCOMMODATION.						CRANE POWER.	STATIONS, &c.	COUNTY.	COMPANY.	POSITION.
						Tons Cwts.	Caldew Junction	Cumb'land	Cal.—Gds. Tfc. Com. ...	Carlisle.
						.. ..	Caldicot Siding (Severn Tin Plate Works)	Mon	G. W.	Severn Tunnel Junction Station.
						.. ..	Caldon Low	Staffs	N. S.	Froghall.
G	P	F	L	H	.	4 10	Caldwell	Renfrew ...	G B & K Jt (Cal. & G & S W)	Neilston and Stewarton.
.	.	.	.	.	.	.. ..	Caldwell & Almond's Wharf...	Devon	L. & S. W.	Plymouth, Cattewater Harbour.
.	.	.	.	.	.	.. ..	Caldwell's Paper Mills	Fife	N. B.	Inverkeithing.
.	P	.	.	.	.	.. ..	Caledon	Armagh ...	G. N. (I.)	See Tynan and Caledon.
.	P	.	.	.	.	.. ..	Caledon	Tyrone ...	Clogher Valley	Tynan and Aughnacloy.
.	.	.	.	.	.	.. ..	Caledonia & Baltic Saw Mills	Renfrew...	Cal.	Paisley, St. James.
.	.	.	.	.	.	.. ..	Caledonia Engine Works (Craig's Engineering Works)	Renfrew...	Cal.	Paisley, St. James.
.	.	.	.	.	.	.. ..	Caledonia Fire-Clay Works...	Renfrew...	Cal.	Paisley, St. James.
.	.	.	.	.	.	.. ..	Caledonian Bolt & Rivet Wks.	Lanark ...	Cal.	Motherwell.
.	.	.	.	.	.	.. ..	Caledonian Brewery	Edinboro'	Cal.	Edinburgh, Lothian Road.
.	.	.	.	.	.	.. ..	Caledonian Distillery (Haymarket Distillery)	Edinboro'	{ Cal. / N. B.	Edinburgh, Lothian Road. / Edinburgh, Haymarket.
.	.	.	.	.	.	.. ..	Caledonian Forge	Ayr	Cal.	Irvine.
.	.	.	.	.	.	.. ..	Caledonian Iron Works	Lanark ...	Cal.	Glasgow, Bridgeton.
.	.	.	.	.	.	.. ..	Caledonian Pottery (Murray & Co.)	Lanark ...	Cal.	Glasgow, Rutherglen.
.	.	.	.	.	.	.. ..	Caledonian Railway Co.'s Creosoting Works	Stirling ...	Cal.	Greenhill.
.	.	.	.	.	.	.. ..	Electric and Gas Works ...	Edinboro'	Cal.	Edinburgh, Lothian Road.
.	.	.	.	.	.	.. ..	Gas Works	Lanark ...	Cal.	{ Glasgow, Dawsholm. / Glasgow, Kinning Park.
.	.	.	.	.	.	.. ..	Laundry Siding	Edinboro'	Cal.	Edinburgh, Lothian Road.
.	.	.	.	.	.	.. ..	Loco. Works and Stores ...	Lanark ...	Cal.	Glasgow, Buchanan Street.
.	.	.	.	.	.	.. ..	Permanent Way Workshops	Lanark ...	Cal.	Motherwell.
.	.	.	.	.	.	.. ..	Loco. Shops	Lanark ...	Cal.	Motherwell.
.	.	.	.	.	.	.. ..	Caledonian Road	Middlesex	G. N.	See London, Holloway & Cal. Road.
.	.	.	.	.	.	.. ..	Caledonian Road	Middlesex	L. & N. W.	See London.
.	.	.	.	.	.	.. ..	Caledonian Rd. & Barnsbury (N.L.)	Middlesex	N. L.—L. & N. W.	See London.
.	.	.	.	.	.	.. ..	Caledonian Road, Goods ...	Middlesex	G. N.	See London.
.	.	.	.	.	.	.. ..	Caledonian Saw Mills	Lanark ...	Cal.	Lanark.
.	.	.	.	.	.	.. ..	Caledonian Saw Mills (Cal.)...	Stirling ...	Cal.—N. B.	Grangemouth.
.	.	.	.	.	.	.. ..	Caledonian Tube Works	Lanark ...	N. B.	Coatbridge, Sheepford.
.	.	.	.	.	.	.. ..	Caledonian Wire Rope Co's Sid.	Lanark ...	Cal.	See Airdrie.
.	.	.	.	.	.	.. ..	Caledon Shipbuilding Yard...	Forfar......	{ Cal. / N. B.	Dundee, West. / Dundee, Tay Bridge.
.	.	.	.	.	.	.. ..	California Pit	Lancs	L. & Y.	See Wigan Cl. & Ir. Co. (Hindley).
.	.	.	.	.	.	.. ..	California Pit (L. & N. W.)...	Lancs	L & NW—G.C. (Wig. Jn.)	See Wigan Coal & Iron Co. (Wigan).
.	.	.	.	.	.	.. ..	California Siding.................	Berks	S. E. & C.	Wellington College.
.	.	.	.	.	.	.. ..	California Siding.................	Staffs	N. S.	Stoke-on-Trent.
							CALLANDER—			
G	.	F	L	.	.	6 0	(Station)	Perth	Cal.	Dunblane and Oban.
G	.	.	.	.	.	.. ..	Cambusmore Siding	Perth	Cal.	Callander and Doune.
.	P	.	.	H	C	.. ..	Dreadnought	Perth	Cal.	Dunblane and Oban.
.	.	.	.	.	.	.. ..	Callander & Sons' Tannery ...	Edinboro'	N. B.	Leith, Bonnington.
.	.	.	.	.	.	.. ..	Callendar Col. & Brick Works	Stirling ...	N. B.	Falkirk, High.
.	.	.	.	.	.	.. ..	Callendar Iron Foundry (N.B.)	Stirling ...	N. B.—Cal.	Falkirk, Grahamston.
G	P	F	L	H	C	2 0	Calne	Wilts	G. W.	Branch from Chippenham.
.	.	.	.	.	.	.. ..	Calow Colliery	Derby	{ L. D. & E. C. / Mid. / G. C.	Arkwright Town. / Hasland. / Grassmoor.
G	P	.	L	H	.	.. ..	Calthwaite	Cumb'land	L. & N. W.	Carlisle and Penrith.
.	P	F	L	H	C	10 0	Calva Junction	Cumb'land	C. & W. Jn.	Cloffocks Junction and Seaton.
G	P	.	L	.	.	10 0	Calveley	Cheshire...	L. & N. W.	Chester and Crewe.
G	P	F	L	H	C	.. ..	Calverley and Rodley	Yorks	Mid.	Leeds and Shipley.
G	P	F	L	H	C	.. ..	Calvert	Bucks......	G. C.	Brackley and Aylesbury.
G	P	.	.	.	.	.. ..	Itter's Siding	Bucks......	G. C.	Calvert.
.	.	.	.	.	.	.. ..	Cam	Glo'ster ...	Mid.	Coaley Junction and Dursley.
.	.	.	.	.	.	.. ..	Daniel's, T. H. & J., Siding	Glo'ster ...	Mid.	Near Cam.
.	.	.	.	.	.	.. ..	Hunt & Winterbotham's Sid.	Glo'ster ...	Mid.	Near Cam.
G	P	F	L	H	C	5 0	Camberley and York Town (for Sandhurst)	Surrey ...	L. & S. W.	Ascot and Farnborough.
.	.	.	.	.	.	.. ..	Camberwell New Road (S. E. & C.)	Surrey ...	SE&C—GN—LSW—Mid	See London.
.	.	.	.	.	.	.. ..	Cambois Brick Works	Northumb	N. E.	North Blyth.
.	.	.	.	.	.	.. ..	Cambois Colliery.................	Northumb	N. E.	North Blyth.
.	.	.	.	.	.	.. ..	Cambois Co-operative Store ...	Northumb	N. E.	North Blyth.

EXPLANATION—G *Goods Station.*   P *Passenger and Parcel Station.*   P* *Passenger, but not Parcel or Miscellaneous Traffic.*
F *Furniture Vans, Carriages, Portable Engines, and Machines on Wheels.*   L *Live Stock.*
H *Horse Boxes and Prize Cattle Vans.*   C *Carriages by Passenger Train.*

STATION ACCOMMODATION.						CRANE POWER.		STATIONS, &c.	COUNTY.	COMPANY.	POSITION.
						Tons	Cwts.				
								Cambois Shipping Staithes ...	Northumb	N. E.	North Blyth.
G	P	F	L	H	C	4	0	Camborne	Cornwall ..	G. W.	Truro and Penzance.
								Dolcoath Siding	Cornwall ..	G. W.	Camborne and Carn Brea.
								Roskear Goods Bch. & Sids.	Cornwall ..	G. W.	Branch near Camborne.
								Cambrian Asphalte Works ...	Denbigh..	L. & N. W.	Conway.
								Cambrian Coke Siding	Glamorg'n	G. W.	Briton Ferry.
								Cambrian Colliery	Glamorg'n	G. W.	Penygraig.
								Cambrian Foundry	Glamorg'n	G. W.	Llantrisant.
								Cambrian Lubricants Co's Wks	Glamorg'n	GW—LNW—Mid—RSB	Swansea.
								Cambrian Siding	Carnarvon	L. & N. W.	Llanberis.
								Cook & D'dol Slate Qry. Co.	Carnarvon	L. & N. W.	Cambrian Siding.
								Llanberis Slate Quarry Co.	Carnarvon	L. & N. W.	Cambrian Siding.
								Upper Glynrhonwy Qry. Co.	Carnarvon	L. & N. W.	Cambrian Siding.
								Cambrian Siding	Mon	A (N & S W) D & R—G W	Same as Spittle's Foundry (Newport)
								Cambria Road Junction	Surrey	L. B. & S. C.—S. E. & C.	London, Denmark Hill & Loughboro' Junction.
								Cambria Tin Plate Siding ...	Glamorg'n	L. & N. W.	Gorseinon.
								CAMBRIDGE—			
G	.	F	L	.	.	10	0	(Station)	Cambs	G. N.	Branch near Cambridge Pass.
G	.	F	L	.	.	10	0	(Station)	Cambs	L. & N. W.	Branch, Bedford and Cambridge Jn.
G	P	F	L	H	C	10	0	(Station, G. E.)	Cambs	G. E.	Great Chesterford and Ely.
	P			H	C					G. N.	Over G. E. from Shepreth Junction.
	P	F		H	C					L. & N. W.	Over G. E. from Cambridge Junc.
G	P	F	L	H	C	10	0			Mid.	Over G. E. from St. Ives Junction.
G	P	.	.	.	.			Barnwell Junction Station	Cambs	G. E.	Cambridge and Fordham.
								Beale & Co.'s Siding	Cambs	G. N.	Cambridge, Goods.
								Beales, P.,&Co.'s Sid.(G.E.)	Cambs	G. E.—Mid.	Cambridge Station.
								Cambridge Brick Co.'s Siding (G. E.)	Cambs	G. E.—L. & N. W.—Mid.	Cambridge and Barnwell Junction.
								Cambridge Corporation Sid.	Cambs	G. N.	Cambridge, Goods.
								Cambridge Gas Co.'s Siding (G. E.)	Cambs	G. E.—Mid.	Cambridge and Barnwell Junction.
								Coldham Brick Co.'s Siding (Beale's, H. F.,Sid.) (GE)	Cambs	G. E.—L. & N. W.—Mid.	Cambridge and Barnwell Junction.
								Coldham Lane Sid. (G.E.)	Cambs	G. E.—Mid.	Cambridge and Waterbeach.
								Commercial Brewery Co.'s Siding	Cambs	G. E.	Barnwell Junction and Quy.
								Coote & Warren's Sid.(G.E.)	Cambs	G. E.—Mid.	Cambridge and Barnwell Junction.
								Foster Bros.' Siding	Cambs	G. N.	Cambridge, Goods.
								Foster Bros.' Sid. (G. E.)..	Cambs	G. E.—L. & N. W.—Mid.	Cambridge Station.
								Hallack & Bond's Siding...	Cambs	L. & N. W.	Cambridge and Lords Bridge.
								Junction	Cambs	G. E.—L. & N. W.	Cambridge Pass. Sta. and Bedford.
G	.	.	.	.	.	5	0	Mill Road Wharf	Cambs	Mid.	Over G. E. from St. Ives Junction.
								Vinter, J. O., & Son's Siding (G. E.)	Cambs	G. E.—Mid.	Cambridge Station.
								Watts & Son's Sid. (G.E.)	Cambs	G. E.—L. & N. W.—Mid.	Cambridge and Barnwell Junction.
								Cambridge Heath	Middlesex	G. E.	See London.
G	P	.	L	H	.	1	5	Cambus (for Tullibody)	Clackman'	N. B.	Stirling and Alloa.
								Distillery Siding	Clackman'	N. B.	Near Cambus.
								Knox's Brewery	Clackman'	N. B.	Near Cambus.
.	P*							Cambusavie	Sutherl'nd	High. (Dornoch)	The Mound and Dornoch.
								Cambus Junction	Clackman'	N. B.	Cambus and Causewayhead.
G	P	.	L	.	.	3	0	Cambuslang	Lanark	Cal.	Motherwell and Rutherglen.
								Gateside Col. & Brk. Wks.	Lanark	Cal.	Cambuslang and Newton.
								Kirkhill Colliery and Brick Works (Chapel Siding)...	Lanark	Cal.	Cambuslang and Newton.
								Cambusmore Siding	Perth	Cal.	See Callander.
G	P	F	L	H	C	3	0	Cambusnethan	Lanark	Cal.	Wishaw, Central and Newmains.
								Cambusnethan Colliery	Lanark	Cal.	Wishaw, Central.
G	P	.	.	H	C			Cambus O'May	Aberdeen	G. N. of S.	Aboyne and Ballater.
								Cam Cement Co.'s Siding	Cambs	G. N.	Shepreth.
								Camden	Middlesex	L. & N. W.	See London.
								Camden Coal Depôt	Middlesex	L. & N. W.	See London.
								Camden Road (Mid.)	Middlesex	Mid.—S. E. & C.	See London.
								Camden Road, Kentish Town Junction	Middlesex	L. & N. W.—N. L.	London, Willesden Junc. (High Level) and Camden Town.
								Camden Town (N. L.)	Middlesex	N. L.—L. & N. W.	See London.
G	P	F	L	H	C	2	0	Camelford	Cornwall ..	L. & S. W.	Launceston and Wadebridge.
								Camelon	Stirling	Cal.—N. B.	See Falkirk.
								Camelon Branch	Stirling	Cal.—N. B.	Falkirk.
								Camelon Foundry (Camelon Iron Works) (N. B.)	Stirling	N. B.—Cal.	Falkirk, Grahamston.

EXPLANATION—G *Goods Station.*   P *Passenger and Parcel Station.*   P* *Passenger, but not Parcel or Miscellaneous Traffic.*
F *Furniture Vans, Carriages, Portable Engines, and Machines on Wheels.*   L *Live Stock.*
H *Horse Boxes and Prize Cattle Vans.*   C *Carriages by Passenger Train.*

STATION ACCOMMODATION.						CRANE POWER.	STATIONS, &c.	COUNTY.	COMPANY.	POSITION.
						Tons Cwts.	Camelon Iron Works (N. B.)	Stirling ...	N. B.—Cal.	Same as Camelon Foundry (Falkirk)
						. .	Cameron & Co.'s Saw Mill ...	Renfrew ...	Cal.	Greenock, Regent Street.
G	P	F	L	H	C	. .	Cameron Bridge	Fife	N. B.	Thornton and Leven.
						. .	Cameron Bridge Distillery	Fife	N. B.	Cameron Bridge.
						. .	Drumcaldie Distillery	Fife	N. B.	Cameron Bridge.
						. .	Leven Cols., Nos. 1, 2, 3, & 4	Fife	N. B.	Branch—Cameron Bridge & Leven.
						. .	Cameron Colliery	Lanark ...	N. B.	Greengairs.
						. .	Cameron Junction Siding.....	Fife	N. B.	Buckhaven.
G	P	.	L	H		. .	Camerton	Cumb'land	L. & N. W.	Cockermouth and Workington.
						. .	Allerdale Coal Co.'s William Pit	Cumb'land	L. & N. W.	Camerton and Workington Bridge.
						. .	Camerton Colliery & Brick Works Co.'s Siding	Cumb'land	L. & N. W.	Camerton and Marron Junction.
G	P	.				2 0	Camerton	Somerset..	G. W.	Branch from Hallatrow.
						. .	Camerton Collieries	Somerset..	G. W.	Camerton.
						. .	Timsbury Colliery	Somerset..	G. W.	Camerton.
						. .	Camerton Brick Wks. & Col.	Cumb'land	C. & W. Jn.	Seaton.
						. .	Camlachie	Lanark ...	N. B.	See Glasgow.
							Cammell & Co.—			
						. .	Derwent Iron & Steel Wks.	Cumb'land	C. & W. Jn.—L. & N. W.	Workington.
						. .	Frizington Park Mine	Cumb'land	WC&EJt.(Fur.&LNW)	Frizington.
						. .	Kelton Limestone Quarry..	Cumb'land	WC&EJt.(Fur.&LNW)	Rowrah.
						. .	Mowbray Pits	Cumb'land	WC&EJt.(Fur.&LNW)	Frizington.
						. .	Parkhouse Mines	Cumb'land	WC&EJt.(Fur.&LNW)	Moor Row.
						. .	Solway Hematite Iron Wks.	Cumb'land	L. & N. W.—M. & C.......	Maryport.
						. .	Cammell & Co.'s Works	Yorks	G. C.—L. & Y.	Penistone.
							Cammell, C., & Co.—			
						. .	Cyclops Works (Mid.)	Yorks	Mid.—G. C...................	Sheffield, Wicker.
						. .	Grimesthorpe Wks. (Mid.)	Yorks	Mid.—G. C...................	Sheffield, Wicker.
							Cammell, Laird, & Co.—			
						. .	Beaufort Road Boiler Wks.	Cheshire...	B'head Jt—CLC—NW&L	Birkenhead.
						. .	Gillbrook Yard Boiler Wks.	Cheshire...	B'head Jt—CLC—NW&L	Birkenhead.
						. .	Monk's Ferry Shipbuilding Yard (B'head Jt.)	Cheshire...	B'head Jt.—C. L. C.	Birkenhead.
						. .	Siding	Warwick...	L. & N. W.	Foleshill.
G	P	.	L	H	.	. .	Camolin	Wexford...	D. W. & W.	Wicklow and Wexford.
						. .	Campbell & Co.'s Machinery Yard	Yorks	N. E.	{ See Whitehouse Siding and Depôt (South Bank).
						. .	Campbell Road Junction	Middlesex	L. T. & S.—W. & B. Jt..	London, Bromley.
G	P	F	L	H	C	1 10	Camp Colliery..................	Lanark ...	Cal.	Motherwell.
						. .	Campden	Glo'ster ...	G. W.	Oxford and Evesham.
						. .	Campden Gas Works.........	Glo'ster ...	G. W.	Campden.
						. .	Camperdown Dock............	Forfar	{ Cal....................... N. B.	Dundee, West. Dundee, Tay Bridge.
						. .	Camperdown Junction, East..	Forfar	D. & A. Jt.—N. B........	Dundee.
						. .	Camperdown Jute Works......	Forfar	Cal.	Lochee.
						. .	Camperdown Shipbuilding Yard (Gourlay Bros. & Co.)	Forfar	Cal.—N. B.	Dundee.
						. .	Camp Hill	Warwick..	Mid.	See Birmingham.
						. .	Camp Pumping Engine	Lanark ...	Cal.	Motherwell.
G	.	.	L	.		1 10	Camps (for East Calder)	Edinboro'	Cal.	Branch Terminus near Midcalder.
						. .	Burnhouse Siding	Edinboro'	Cal.	Camps.
						. .	Camps Lime Works	Edinboro'	Cal.	Camps.
						. .	Camps Brick Works	Edinboro'	N. B.	East Calder.
G	P	.	L	H		1 10	Campsie Ash	Suffolk ...	G. E.	Same as Wickham Market.
						. .	Campsie Glen	Stirling ...	N. B.	Lennoxtown and Killearn.
						. .	Camps Junctions	Edinboro'	Cal.—N. B.	Midcalder and Uphall.
						. .	Camps Siding	Edinboro'	N. B.	See East Calder.
						. .	Canaan Colliery	Carmarth'	L. & M. M.	Tumble.
						. .	Canada Dock	Lancs	L. & Y.—L'pool O'head— L. & N. W.—Mid.	See Liverpool.
						. .	Canada Dock Timber Depôt..	Lancs	L. & N. W.	See Liverpool.
						. .	Canadian Whf. & Cattle Bank	Forfar	Cal.	Dundee, West.
						. .	Canal	Cumb'land	N. B.	See Carlisle.
						. .	Canal (G. & S. W.).............	Renfrew...	G. & S. W.—N. B.	See Paisley.
G	.	.	.	.		3 0	Canal Basin	Inverness	High.	Branch—Inverness & Clachnaharry.
						. .	Canal Basin....................	Notts	Mid.	Nottingham.
						. .	Canal Junction	Cumb'land	N. B.—N. E.	Carlisle.
						. .	Canal Junction	Renfrew...	G. & S. W.	Elderslie and Ferguslie.
						. .	Canal Junction	Yorks	L&NW—L&NW & NEJt..	Leeds.
						. .	Canal Siding	Lancs	L. & Y.	Wigan.
						. .	Canal Siding	Stirling ...	N. B.	See Almond Junction Station.

EXPLANATION—**G** *Goods Station.*　　**P** *Passenger and Parcel Station.*　　**P*** *Passenger, but not Parcel or Miscellaneous Traffic.*
F *Furniture Vans, Carriages, Portable Engines, and Machines on Wheels.*　　**L** *Live Stock.*
H *Horse Boxes and Prize Cattle Vans.*　　**C** *Carriages by Passenger Train.*

STATION ACCOMMODATION.							CRANE POWER.		STATIONS, &c.	COUNTY.	COMPANY.	POSITION.
							Tons	Cwts.				
									Canal Street Mineral Depôt...	Lanark ...	Cal.	See Glasgow.
									Canal Wharf Siding	Yorks ...	G. C.	Kiveton Park.
									Candermains Siding	Lanark ...	Cal.	Stonehouse.
									CanderriggCols.Nos.1,2,3,4,&5	Lanark ...	Cal.	Stonehouse.
									Candie Colliery	Stirling ...	N. B.	Bowhouse.
									Candy & Co.'s Siding	Devon ...	G. W.	Heathfield.
									Cane Hill	Surrey ...	S. E. & C.	See Coulsdon and Cane Hill.
									Canfield Place Junction	Middlesex	G. C.—Met.	London (Marylebone) and Harrow.
									Canford Siding	Dorset....	L. & S.W.—S. & D. Jt....	Wimborne.
G	P								Canna	Inverness	Cal.	Steamer from Oban.
									Canning Street Town	Cheshire.	B'head Jt.—C.L.C—GW.	See Birkenhead.
									Cannington Shaw & Co.'s Nos. 1 & 2 Works	Lancs	L. & N. W.	St. Helens.
									Canning Town	Essex	G. E.— L. & N. W.	See London.
G	P	F	L	H	C		5	0	Cannock	Staffs	L. & N. W.	Rugeley and Walsall.
									Blencowe & Co.'s Brewery	Staffs	L. & N. W.	Cannock and Hednesford.
									Cannock, Hednesford and District Gas Co.'s Siding	Staffs	L. & N. W.	Cannock and Wyrley.
									Cannock & Leacroft Colliery	Staffs	L. & N. W.	Hednesford.
									Cannock & Rugeley Collieries Nos. 1 & 3	Staffs	L. & N. W.	Hednesford.
									Cannock & Rugeley Colliery .	Staffs	Mid.	Brownhills.
									Cannock & Rugeley Colliery Co.'s Workshop	Staffs	L. & N. W.	Hednesford.
									Cannock Chase Colliery	Staffs	Mid.	Brownhills.
									Cannock Chase Colliery Co.— Anglesea Colliery	Staffs	L. & N. W.	Hednesford.
									Hednesford Colliery	Staffs	L. & N. W.	Hednesford.
									Wharf	Staffs	L. & N. W.	Perry Barr.
									Cannock Old Coppice Colliery	Staffs	L. & N. W.	Same as Hawkins & Sons (Wyrley and Church Bridge).
									Cannock Road Junction	Staffs	G. W.	Wolverhampton.
									Cannock Road Siding	Staffs	G. W.	Wolverhampton.
									Cannon, B., & Co.'s Sid. (Mid)	Lincoln ...	Mid.—G. C.—G. N.	Lincoln.
									Cannon Street..................	Midd'esex	Met.& Met Dist Jt—SE&C	See London.
									Cannon Street..................	Yorks	H. & B.	See Hull.
									Cannon Street, West Junction	Surrey ...	S. E. & C.	London, London Bridge & Waterloo.
									Cannop Stone Works	Glo'ster ...	S.& WyeJt.(G. W. & Mid.)	Same as Thomas & Co.'s Stone Saw Mills (Speech House Road).
G	P		L	H			1	10	Canonbie	Dumfries.	N. B.	Riddings Junc. Station & Langholm.
									Canonbie Colliery	Dumfries.	N. B.	Near Canonbie.
									Canonbury (N. L.).............	Middlesex	N.L.— L. & N. W...........	See London.
									Canonbury Junction	Middlesex	G.N.—N.L.	London, Finsbury Park and Dalston.
									CANTERBURY— Chartham Siding	Kent	S. E. & C.	Selling and Canterbury, East.
G	P	F	L	H	C		7	0	East	Kent	S. E. & C.	Faversham and Dover.
									Howard's Siding	Kent	S. E. & C.	Canterbury, West.
									Junction	Kent	S. E. & C.	Chartham and Canterbury, West.
									Mackeson's Siding	Kent	S. E. & C.	Canterbury, West.
G	P	F	L	H	C				South	Kent	S. E. & C.	Canterbury, West and Shorncliffe.
G	P	F	L	H	C		8	0	West	Kent	S. E. & C.	Ashford and Ramsgate, Town.
									Canterbury Road Junction ...	Surrey ...	S. E. & C.	London, Brixton & Loughboro' Jn.
	P								Cantley	Norfolk ...	G. E.	Norwich & Yarmouth, Vauxhall.
									Canton Sidings	Glamorg'n	G. W.	See Cardiff.
									Canton Siding..................	Glamorg'n	T. V.	See Grangetown.
G	P		L		C				Capecastle	Antrim ...	Ballycastle	Ballymoney and Ballycastle.
									Cape Copper Works	Glamorg'n	R. & S. B.	Jersey Marine.
G	P								Capel	Suffolk ...	G. E.	Hadleigh and Bentley.
									Capel	Surrey ...	L. B. & S. C.	Same as Ockley.
G	P	F	L	H	C				Capel Bangor	Cardigan.	V. of Rhe:dol	Aberystwyth and Devil's Bridge.
									Capeldrae Sid. (Paton's Sid.)	Fife	N. B.	See Kelty.
									Capel Ifan Colliery	Carmarth'.	B. P. & G. V.	Pontyberem.
G	P		L	H					Capenhurst	Cheshire...	B'head Jt.(GW& L & NW)	Chester and Hooton.
									Capewell Horse Nail Co.'s Siding	Middlesex	G. E. / GN—GW—LNW—Mid	London, Millwall Docks. / London, Poplar.
G	P	F	L	H	C				Cappagh	Waterford	G. S. & W.	Dungarvan and Lismore.
G	P	F	L	H	C				Cappoquin	Waterford	G. S. & W.	Dungarvan and Lismore.
									Capringstone Collieries........	Ayr	G. & S.W.	Same as Bourtreehill, Nos. 6, 7 & 8 (Dreghorn.)
									Caprington Junction..........	Ayr	G. & S.W.	Fairlie Branch.
									Caprington, Nos. 40, 41, & 42	Ayr	G. & S.W.	Gatehead.
									Capwell.......................	Cork	C. & Macroom...............	See Cork.

EXPLANATION—G *Goods Station.*   P *Passenger and Parcel Station.*   P* *Passenger, but not Parcel or Miscellaneous Traffic.*
F *Furniture Vans, Carriages, Portable Engines, and Machines on Wheels.*   L *Live Stock.*
H *Horse Boxes and Prize Cattle Vans.*   C *Carriages by Passenger Train.*

STATION ACCOMMODATION.						CRANE POWER.		STATIONS, &c.	COUNTY.	COMPANY.	POSITION.
						Tons	Cwts.				
								Caradog Vale Colliery	Glamorg'n	G. W.	Hendreforgan.
								Caradon Mine	Cornwall	L. & Looe	Moorswater & Cheesewring Quarries.
G	P							Caragh Lake	Kerry	G. S. & W.	Farranfore and Valentia Harbour.
								Carass Siding	L'merick	G. S. & W.	Croom and Patricks Well.
								Carbarns Colliery	Lanark	Cal.	Shieldmuir.
								Carbean Siding	Cornwall	G. W.	See Bugle.
								Carbella Siding	Ayr	G. & S.W.	Lugar.
G	P	F	L	H	C			Carberry	Kildare	M. G. W.	Edenderry Branch.
								Carberry Colliery	Edinboro'	N. B.	Smeaton.
G	P							Carbis Bay	Cornwall	G. W.	St. Ives and St. Erth.
								Carbis Siding	Cornwall	G. W.	Bugle.
								Carbiston Lye	Ayr	G. & S.W.	Hollybush.
								Carbo Syndicate Works (Tudhoe Iron Works	Durham	N. E.	Spennymoor.
								Carbrook Forge (G. C.)	Yorks	G. C.—Mid.	Sheffield, Broughton Lane.
								Carbrook Steel Works	Derby	Mid.	Killamarsh.
G	P	F	L	H	C	10	0	Carcroft and Adwick-le-Street	Yorks	W. R. & G Jt (G C & G N)	Doncaster and Wakefield.
								Carden Colliery	Fife	N. B.	Cardenden.
G	P		L	H		2	0	Cardenden	Fife	N. B.	Thornton and Dunfermline.
								Bowhill Colliery	Fife	N. B.	Cardenden and Lochgelly.
								Carden Colliery	Fife	N. B.	Cardenden and Thornton.
								Clunie Lime Siding	Fife	N. B.	Cardenden and Thornton.
								Denend Colliery	Fife	N. B.	Cardenden and Lochgelly.
								Denend Quarry	Fife	N. B.	Cardenden and Lochgelly.
								Dundonald Colliery	Fife	N. B.	Cardenden and Lochgelly.
								Glencraig Colliery	Fife	N. B.	Cardenden and Lochgelly.
								Minto Colliery	Fife	N. B.	Cardenden and Lochgelly.
								Carden's Siding	Flint	W & MJt(G W & L & N W)	Same as Ffrith Coal and Fire Clay Co.'s (Llanfynydd).
								CARDIFF—			
	P	F	L	H	C			(Station)	Glamorg'n	Rhy.	Adam Street and Caerphilly.
	P			H	C		⎞	(Station, G. W.)	Glamorg'n	G. W.	Newport and Bridgend.
	P						⎠			T. V.	Over G. W. Line.
G		F	L			10	0	Adam Street	Glamorg'n	Rhy.	Cardiff Pass. & Bute Dks. Terminus.
								Allan's Crwys Siding	Glamorg'n	Rhy.	Cardiff.
								Allensbank Siding	Glamorg'n	T. V.	Roath Branch.
								Anchor Fuel Works or Maindy Fuel Works	Glamorg'n	T. V.	Cardiff and Llandaff.
								Andrews & Baby's Siding	Glamorg'n	G W—L N W—Rhy—TV	Over Cardiff Railway.
								Baker & Co.'s Siding	Glamorg'n	G W—L N W—Rhy—TV	Over Cardiff Railway.
								Begg & Co.'s Siding	Glamorg'n	G W—L N W—Rhy—TV	Over Cardiff Railway.
								Bird & Son's Siding	Glamorg'n	G W—L N W—Rhy—TV	Over Cardiff Railway.
								Blackweir Siding	Glamorg'n	T. V.	Cardiff and Llandaff.
								Bland & Co.'s Siding	Glamorg'n	G W—L N W—Rhy—TV	Over Cardiff Railway.
								Blands Timber Yard	Glamorg'n	G. W.	Riverside Branch.
								Bristol Wagon Co.'s Siding	Glamorg'n	G W—L N W— Rhy—TV	Over Cardiff Railway.
								Burton & Son's (Plymouth Wharf)	Glamorg'n	G. W.	Riverside Branch.
G								Bute Docks	Glamorg'n	L. & N. W.	L. & N. W. Goods Branch.
								Bute Docks	Glamorg'n	G. W.—Rhy.—T. V.	Cardiff Docks.
								Bute Docks Gas Works	Glamorg'n	G W—L N W—Rhy—TV	Over Cardiff Railway.
								Bute East Dock Junction	Glamorg'n	Cardiff—T. V.	Bute Dock and Queen Street.
								Bute Engineering & Dry Dock Co.'s Siding	Glamorg'n	G W—L N W—Rhy—TV	Over Cardiff Railway.
								Bute Estate Siding	Glamorg'n	T. V.	Cardiff and Llandaff.
								Bute Workshops Siding	Glamorg'n	T. V.	Cardiff and Llandaff.
								Cairn Street Siding	Glamorg'n	Rhy.	Cardiff.
G		F	L	H	C	12	0	Canton Sidings	Glamorg'n	G. W.	Cardiff and Ely.
								Corporation Electric Lighting Siding	Glamorg'n	G. W.	Canton Sidings.
								Turner's Stone Yard	Glamorg'n	G. W.	Canton Sidings.
								Cardiff & Channel Mills Sid.	Glamorg'n	G W—L N W—Rhy—TV	Over Cardiff Railway.
								Cardiff Grain Co.'s Siding	Glamorg'n	G W—L N W—Rhy—TV	Over Cardiff Railway.
								Cardiff Railway Co.'s Stores	Glamorg'n	G W—L N W—Rhy—TV	Over Cardiff Railway.
								Cathays Coal Yard Siding (Williams')	Glamorg'n	Rhy.	Cardiff.
								Cathays Storage Siding	Glamorg'n	T. V.	Cardiff and Llandaff.
								Cathays Yard	Glamorg'n	T. V.	Cardiff and Llandaff.
								Chemical Co.'s Siding	Glamorg'n	G W—L N W—Rhy—TV	Over Cardiff Railway.
	P*						⎞			G. W.	Cardiff and Riverside Branch.
	P						⎬	Clarence Road (G. W.)	Glamorg'n	Barry	Over T. V. & G. W. from Cogan Jn.
	P						⎠			T. V.	Over G. W. from Penarth Curve Jn.

EXPLANATION—G *Goods Station.*   P *Passenger and Parcel Station.*   P* *Passenger, but not Parcel or Miscellaneous Traffic.*
F *Furniture Vans, Carriages, Portable Engines, and Machines on Wheels.*   L *Live Stock.*
H *Horse Boxes and Prize Cattle Vans.*   C *Carriages by Passenger Train.*

STATION ACCOMMODATION.								CRANE POWER.	STATIONS, &c.	COUNTY.	COMPANY.	POSITION.
								Tons Cwts.	CARDIFF—*continued.*			
.	.	.	.	.	.	.	.		Colliery Supply Co.'s Siding	Glamorg'n	G W—L N W—Rhy—TV	Over Cardiff Railway.
.	.	.	.	.	.	.	.		Cottam & Co.'s Siding	Glamorg'n	G W—L N W—Rhy—TV	Over Cardiff Railway.
.	.	.	.	.	.	.	.		Crockherbtown Junction...	Glamorg'n	Rhy.—T. V.	Adam Street and Llandaff.
.	.	.	.	.	.	.	.		Crown Fuel Works(Maindy)	Glamorg'n	T. V.	Cardiff and Llandaff.
.	.	.	.	.	.	.	.		Crown Fuel Works (Roath Dock)	Glamorg'n	GW—LNW—Rhy—T V	Over Cardiff Railway.
.	.	.	.	.	.	.	.		Crown Preserve Coal Co.'s Fuel Works	Glamorg'n	G W—L N W—Rhy—TV	Over Cardiff Railway.
.	.	.	.	.	.	.	.		Crwys Storage Sidings	Glamorg'n	Rhy.	Cardiff.
.	.	.	.	.	.	.	.		Dampney & Co.'s Siding ...	Glamorg'n	G W—L N W—Rhy—TV	Over Cardiff Railway.
.	.	.	.	.	.	.	.		Dawnay & Co.'s Siding......	Glamorg'n	G W—L N W—Rhy—TV	Over Cardiff Railway.
.	.	.	.	.	.	.	.		Denny, Mott, & Dickson Timber Yard	Glamorg'n	G. W.	Riverside Branch.
G								3 0			G. W.	Branch from Cardiff.
G								3 0 }	Docks	Glamorg'n	Rhy.	Cardiff.
G	P		H					5 0			T. V.	Cardiff.
.	.	.	.	.	.	.	.		Docks Junction	Glamorg'n	G. W.—Rhy.	Cardiff Docks (G. W.) & Adam Str.
.	.	.	.	.	.	.	.		Docks Junction	Glamorg'n	Rhy.—Cardiff	Near Bute Docks Terminus.
.	.	.	.	.	.	.	.		Docks Terminus.............	Glamorg'n	Rhy.	Bute Docks.
.	.	.	.	.	.	.	.		Dowlais Iron & Steel Works (East Moors)	Glamorg'n	G W—L N W—Rhy—TV	Over Cardiff Railway.
.	.	.	.	.	.	.	.		Dumball's Road Coal Siding	Glamorg'n	G. W.	Riverside Branch.
.	.	.	.	.	.	.	.		East Bute Dock	Glamorg'n	G W—L N W—Rhy—TV	Over Cardiff Railway.
.	.	.	.	.	.	.	.		East Junction	Glamorg'n	G. W.—T. V.	Cardiff (G. W.) and Queen Street.
G									Ely Depôt	Glamorg'n	T. V.	Grangetown and Radyr.
.	.	.	.	.	.	.	.		Ely Mileage Siding	Glamorg'n	T. V.	Grangetown and Radyr.
.	.	.	.	.	.	.	.		Fairoak Road Siding (Cemetery Siding)	Glamorg'n	Rhy.	Cardiff.
.	.	.	.	.	.	.	.		Foreign Cattle Lairs	Glamorg'n	G W—L N W—Rhy—TV	Over Cardiff Railway.
.	.	.	.	.	.	.	.		Fownes Forge Co.'s Siding..	Glamorg'n	G W—L N W—Rhy—TV	Over Cardiff Railway.
.	.	.	.	.	.	.	.		Gibbon's Crwys Siding	Glamorg'n	Rhy.	Cardiff.
.	.	.	.	.	.	.	.		Glamorgan Canal Siding ...	Glamorg'n	G. W.	Riverside Branch.
.	.	.	.	.	.	.	.		Glasgow Steamship Co.'s Siding	Glamorg'n	G W—L N W—Rhy—TV	Over Cardiff Railway.
.	.	.	.	.	.	.	.		Gloucester Wagon Co.'s Sid.	Glamorg'n	G W—L N W—Rhy—TV	Over Cardiff Railway.
.	.	.	.	.	.	.	.		Grimes Bros.' Siding........	Glamorg'n	G W—L N W—Rhy—TV	Over Cardiff Railway.
.	.	.	.	.	.	.	.		Guest,Keen & Nettlefold's } Steel Works .... }	Glamorg'n	G. W. / L.& N.W.—Rhy.—T.V.	Newtown and Cardiff Docks. / Over Cardiff Railway.
.	.	.	.	.	.	.	.		Heath Siding (Rhy.)	Glamorg'n	Rhy.—L. & N. W.	Cardiff and Llanishen (*for Down Traffic*).
.	.	.	.	.	.	.	.		Heigham & Co.'s Siding ...	Glamorg'n	G W—L N W—Rhy—TV	Over Cardiff Railway.
.	.	.	.	.	.	.	.		Hill's Dry Dock & Engineering Co.'s Siding............	Glamorg'n	G W—L N W—Rhy—TV	Over Cardiff Railway.
.	.	.	.	.	.	.	.		James' Siding	Glamorg'n	G W—L N W—Rhy—TV	Over Cardiff Railway.
.	.	.	.	.	.	.	.		John Street Siding............	Glamorg'n	T. V.	Cardiff and Cardiff Docks.
.	.	.	.	.	.	.	.		Jones's (F.) Bute Fuel Wks.	Glamorg'n	G W—L N W—Rhy—TV	Over Cardiff Railway.
.	.	.	.	.	.	.	.		Jones's Siding	Glamorg'n	G W—L N W—Rhy—TV	Over Cardiff Railway.
.	.	.	.	.	.	.	.		Junction	Glamorg'n	L. & N. W.—Rhy.	Tyndall Street and Adam Street.
.	.	.	.	.	.	.	.		Junction Dry Dock and Engineering Co.'s Siding	Glamorg'n	G W—L N W—Rhy—TV	Over Cardiff Railway.
.	.	.	.	.	.	.	.		Kestell, J. N., & Co.'s Sid.	Glamorg'n	G W—L N W—Rhy—TV	Over Cardiff Railway.
.	.	.	.	.	.	.	.		Lattey's Siding	Glamorg'n	T. V.	Llandaff and Roath Depôt.
.	.	.	.	.	.	.	.		Leetham & Son's Siding ...	Glamorg'n	G W—L N W—Rhy—TV	Over Cardiff Railway.
.	.	.	.	.	.	.	.		Leon's Crwys Siding	Glamorg'n	Rhy.	Cardiff.
.	.	.	.	.	.	.	.		Moy Road Siding	Glamorg'n	Rhy.	Leon's Crwys Siding.
.	.	.	.	.	.	.	.		Venning's Siding............	Glamorg'n	Rhy.	Leon's Crwys Siding.
.	.	.	.	.	.	.	.		Lincoln Wagon Works......	Glamorg'n	G W—L N W—Rhy—TV	Over Cardiff Railway.
.	.	.	.	.	.	.	.		Lloyd's Testing House	Glamorg'n	G. W.	Riverside Branch.
.	.	.	.	.	.	.	.		L.& N.W.Goods Branch Jn.	Glamorg'n	L. & N. W.—Rhy.	Tyndall Street & Bute Terminus Jn.
.	.	.	.	.	.	.	.		London & South Wales Engineering Co.'s Siding	Glamorg'n	G W—L N W—Rhy—TV	Over Cardiff Railway.
.	.	.	.	.	.	.	.		Maindy Brick Works......	Glamorg'n	T. V.	Cardiff and Llandaff.
.	.	.	.	.	.	.	.		Malting Co.'s Siding.........	Glamorg'n	G W—L N W—Rhy—TV	Over Cardiff Railway.
.	.	.	.	.	.	.	.		Mercantile Pontoon Co.'s Siding	Glamorg'n	G W—L N W—Rhy—TV	Over Cardiff Railway.
.	.	.	.	.	.	.	.		Midland Wagon Co.'s Siding	Glamorg'n	G W—L N W—Rhy—TV	Over Cardiff Railway.
.	.	.	.	.	.	.	.		Mount Stuart Dry Dock & Engineering Co.'s Siding	Glamorg'n	G W—L N W—Rhy—TV	Over Cardiff Railway.
.	.	.	.	.	.	.	.		Newport Road Siding......	Glamorg'n	T. V.	Roath Depôt.
G		F	L	H	C			10 0	Newtown	Glamorg'n	G. W.	Newport and Bridgend.
.	.	.	.	.	.	.	.		Newtown Siding	Glamorg'n	G. W.	Cardiff and Roath.

STATION ACCOMMODATION.						CRANE POWER.	STATIONS, &c.	COUNTY.	COMPANY.	POSITION.
						Tons Cwts.	CARDIFF—continued.			
..	..	..	..	..	..		North Central Wagon Co.'s Siding	Glamorg'n	G W—L N W—Rhy—TV	Over Cardiff Railway.
..	..	..	..	..	..		Penarth Curve, North Jn.	Glamorg'n	G. W.—T. V.	Cardiff (G.W.) and Waterhall Junc.
..	..	..	..	..	..		Penarth Curve, South Jn.	Glamorg'n	G. W.—T. V.	Cardiff and Grangetown.
..	..	..	..	..	..		Pontoon Co.'s Siding.........	Glamorg'n	G W—L N W—Rhy—TV	Over Cardiff Railway.
..	..	..	..	..	..		Poole's Siding	Glamorg'n	G W—L N W—Rhy—TV	Over Cardiff Railway.
G	P	F	L	H	C	5 0	Queen Street	Glamorg'n	T. V.	Cardiff Docks and Llandaff.
..	P	..	..	..	..	⎫			G. W.	Riverside Branch.
..	P	..	..	H	C	⎬	Riverside (G. W.)	Glamorg'n	Barry	Over T.V. & G.W. from Cogan Junc.
..	P	..	..	..	..	⎭			T. V.	Over G. W. from Penarth Curve Jn.
..	P	..	..	..	..		Roath	Glamorg'n	G. W.	Cardiff and Marshfield.
..	..	..	..	..	..		Roath Coal & Mileage Depôt	Glamorg'n	G. W.	Roath and Marshfield.
..	..	..	..	..	..		Roath Depôt	Glamorg'n	T. V.	Roath Branch.
..	..	..	..	..	..		Roath Dock and Basin	Glamorg'n	G W—L N W—Rhy—TV	Over Cardiff Railway.
..	..	..	..	..	..		Roath Dock Storage Sids.	Glamorg'n	T. V.	Roath Branch.
..	..	..	..	..	..		Roath Mileage Siding	Glamorg'n	T. V.	Roath Branch.
..	..	..	..	..	..		Robinson, David, & Co.'s Sid.	Glamorg'n	G W—L N W—Rhy—TV	Over Cardiff Railway.
..	..	..	..	..	..		Rogers & Co.'s Siding	Glamorg'n	G W—L N W—Rhy—TV	Over Cardiff Railway.
..	..	..	..	..	..		Rolling Stock Co.'s Siding	Glamorg'n	G W—L N W—Rhy—TV	Over Cardiff Railway.
G	..	F	..	..	..	5 0	Salisbury Road	Glamorg'n	Rhy.	Cardiff and Llanishen.
..	..	..	..	..	..		Scull & Co.'s Siding.........	Glamorg'n	G W—L N W—Rhy—TV	Over Cardiff Railway.
..	..	..	..	..	..		Shearman & Co.'s Siding...	Glamorg'n	G W—L N W—Rhy—TV	Over Cardiff Railway.
..	..	..	..	..	..		Shields Crwys Cl. Yard Sid.	Glamorg'n	Rhy.	Cardiff.
..	..	..	..	..	..		South Wales Wagon Co.'s Siding	Glamorg'n	G W—L N W—Rhy—TV	Over Cardiff Railway.
..	..	..	..	..	..		Spiller's & Baker's Siding	Glamorg'n	G W—L N W—Rhy—TV	Over Cardiff Railway.
..	..	..	..	..	..		Spiller's Nephews' Biscuit Works	Glamorg'n	T. V.	Roath Branch.
..	..	..	..	..	..		Star Fuel Works	Glamorg'n	T. V.	Cardiff and Llandaff.
..	..	..	..	..	..		Taff Vale Little Dock	Glamorg'n	T. V.	Cardiff Docks.
..	..	..	..	..	..		Taff Vale Railway Co.'s Stores	Glamorg'n	T. V.	Cardiff Docks.
..	..	..	..	..	..		Tharsis Copper Co.'s Siding	Glamorg'n	G W—L N W—Rhy—TV	Over Cardiff Railway.
..	..	..	..	..	..		Thomas' Siding	Glamorg'n	G W—L N W—Rhy—TV	Over Cardiff Railway.
..	..	..	..	..	..		Tydfil Engineering Co.'s Sid.	Glamorg'n	G W—L N W—Rhy—TV	Over Cardiff Railway.
G	..	F	L	..	..	5 0	Tyndall Street................	Glamorg'n	L. & N. W.	Branch from Rhymney Line.
..	..	..	..	..	..		Tyndall Street Junction ...	Glamorg'n	G. W.—Cardiff	Cardiff and Bute Docks.
..	..	..	..	..	..		Tyndall Street Junction ...	Glamorg'n	Rhy.—Cardiff	Cardiff Docks and Adam Street.
..	..	..	..	..	..		Tyneside Engineering Co.'s Siding	Glamorg'n	G W—L N W—Rhy—TV	Over Cardiff Railway.
..	..	..	..	..	..		Watson's Siding..............	Glamorg'n	T. V.	Cardiff Docks and Cardiff.
..	..	..	..	..	..		West Bute Dock............	Glamorg'n	G W—L N W—Rhy—TV	Over Cardiff Railway.
..	..	..	..	..	..		West Canal Wharf	Glamorg'n	G. W.	Riverside Branch.
..	..	..	..	..	..		Western Wagon Co.'s Sid..	Glamorg'n	G W—L N W—Rhy—TV	Over Cardiff Railway.•
..	..	..	..	..	..		West Yard	Glamorg'n	T. V.	Cardiff Docks.
..	..	..	..	..	..		Williams & Son's Siding ...	Glamorg'n	G W—L N W—Rhy—TV	Over Cardiff Railway.
..	..	..	..	..	..		Cardiff Alkali Co.'s Siding ...	Glamorg'n	T. V.	Grangetown.
..	..	..	..	..	..		Cardiff & Channel Mills Sid.	Glamorg'n	G W—L N W—Rhy—TV	Cardiff.
..	..	..	..	..	..		Cardiff and Ogmore Junction	Glamorg'n	G. W.	Blackmill and Ogmore Vale.
..	..	..	..	..	..		Cardiff & South Wales Wagon Co.'s Siding.........	Mon	A. (N & SW) D & R.—GW	Same as Risca Wharf (Newport).
..	..	..	..	..	..		Cardiff Candle Co.'s Works ...	Glamorg'n	T. V.	Grangetown.
..	..	..	..	..	..		Cardiff Colliery	Glamorg'n	T. V.	Same as Guest, Keen & Nettlefold's Dowlais Cardiff Col. (Abercynon).
..	..	..	..	..	..		Cardiff Corporation Electric Lighting Siding	Glamorg'n	G. W.	See Canton Siding (Cardiff).
..	..	..	..	..	..		Cardiff Grain Co.'s Siding...	Glamorg'n	G W—L N W—Rhy—TV	Cardiff.
..	..	..	..	..	..		Cardiff Navigation Colliery ...	Glamorg'n	G. W.	Llantrisant.
..	..	..	..	..	..		Cardiff Railway Co.'s Stores	Glamorg'n	G W—L N W—Rhy—TV	Cardiff.
G	P	F	L	H	C	5 0	Cardigan	Cardigan..	G. W.	Branch from Whitland.
..	..	..	..	..	..		Cardigan Junction	Cardigan..	G. W.	Whitland and Clynderwen.
..	..	..	..	..	..		Cardigan Road	Yorks	N. E.	See Leeds.
G	P	F	L	H	C		Cardington	Beds	Mid.	Hitchin and Bedford.
G	P	..	L	..	..	1 10	Cardonald....................	Renfrew ..	G & P Jt (Cal & G & S W)	Glasgow and Paisley.
..	..	..	..	..	..	60 0	Clyde Engine Works	Renfrew ..	G & P Jt (Cal & G & S W)	Cardonald and Ibrox.
..	..	..	..	..	..		Cockburn's Siding............	Renfrew ..	G & P Jt (Cal & G & S W)	Cardonald and Shields Junction.
..	..	..	..	..	..		Craigton Mineral Siding ...	Renfrew ..	G & P Jt (Cal & G & S W)	Cardonald and Ibrox.
..	..	..	..	..	..		Drumoyne Saw Mills.........	Renfrew ..	G & P Jt (Cal & G & S W)	Cardonald and Ibrox.
..	..	..	..	..	..		Drumoyne Siding (Moore's Works)	Renfrew ..	G & P Jt (Cal & G & S W)	Cardonald and Ibrox.
..	..	..	..	..	..		Flett's Yard...................	Renfrew ..	G & P Jt (Cal & G & S W)	Cardonald and Ibrox.

EXPLANATION—G *Goods Station.*　　　P *Passenger and Parcel Station.*　　　P* *Passenger, but not Parcel or Miscellaneous Traffic.*
F *Furniture Vans, Carriages, Portable Engines, and Machines on Wheels.*　　L *Live Stock.*
H *Horse Boxes and Prize Cattle Vans.*　　C *Carriages by Passenger Train.*

STATION ACCOMMODATION.						CRANE POWER.		STATIONS, &c.	COUNTY.	COMPANY.	POSITION.
						Tons	Cwts.				
								Cardonald—*continued.*			
.	.	.	.	.	.			Grant's Siding (Seafield Engineering Works)	Renfrew ..	G & P Jt (Cal & G & S W)	Cardonald and Paisley.
.	.	.	.	.	.			Hillington Siding	Renfrew ..	G & P Jt (Cal & G & S W)	Cardonald and Shields Junction.
.	.	.	.	.	.			Imperial Siding	Renfrew ..	G & P Jt (Cal & G & S W)	Cardonald and Shields Junction.
.	.	.	.	.	.			Cardonald Junction	Renfrew ..	G & P Jt (Cal & G & S W)	Cardonald and Paisley.
.	.	.	.	.	.			Cardonnel Junction	Glamorg'n	G. W.—R. & S. B.	Briton Ferry Road and Court Sart.
.	.	.	.	.	.			Cardonnel Tin Plate Works ..	Glamorg'n	G. W.	Neath Abbey.
.	.	.	.	.	.			Cardowan Fire Clay Works...	Lanark ...	Cal.	Garnkirk.
.	.	.	.	.	.			Cardowan Manure Siding ...	Lanark ...	Cal.	Steps Road.
G	P	.	L	H	.			Cardrona	Peebles ...	N. B.	Peebles and Galashiels.
G	P	F	L	H	C	3	0	Cardross	Dumbartn	N. B.	Dumbarton and Helensburgh.
.	.	.	.	.	.			Ardoch Quarry	Dumbartn	N. B.	Cardross and Dalreoch.
G	P	F	L	H	C	3	0	Careston	Forfar ...	Cal.	Forfar and Brechin.
G	.	.	L	.	.			Fearn Siding	Forfar......	Cal.	Tannadice and Careston.
.	.	.	.	.	.			Carfin Boiler Works	Lanark ...	Cal.	Newarthill.
.	.	.	.	.	.			Carfin Brick Works	Lanark ...	Cal.	Newarthill.
.	.	.	.	.	.			Carfin Chemical Works........	Lanark ...	Cal.	Newarthill.
.	.	.	.	.	.			Carfin Collieries	Lanark ...	Cal.	Newarthill.
.	.	.	.	.	.			Carfin Collieries, Nos. 6 & 7	Lanark ...	Cal.	Newarthill.
.	.	.	.	.	.			Carfin Colliery, No. 6 Junc.	Lanark ...	Cal.	Holytown and Wishaw, Central.
G	P	.	.	.	.			Cargan	Antrim ...	N. C. Com. (Mid.)......	Ballymena and Parkmore.
.	.	.	.	.	.			Antrim Iron Ore Co.'s Sid.	Antrim ...	N. C. Com. (Mid.)	Cargan.
.	.	.	.	.	.			Crommelin Iron Ore Co's Sid.	Antrim ...	N. C. Com. (Mid.)	Cargan.
G	P	F	L	H	C	3	0	Cargill	Perth ...	Cal.	Perth and Coupar Angus.
G	.	.	.	.	.			Ballathie Siding..............	Perth ...	Cal.	Stanley and Cargill.
.	P	.	.	.	.			Cargo Fleet	Yorks ...	N. E.	Middlesbro' and Saltburn.
.	•	.	.	.	.			Cargo Fleet Iron and Brick Works and Wharf	Yorks ...	N. E.	See Brand's Slag Works (South Bank)
.	.	.	.	.	.			Cargo Fleet Iron Works	Yorks ...	N. E.	Same as Jones & Co.'s Slag Wool Works (South Bank).
.	.	.	.	.	.			Cargo Fleet Salt Wks. & Whf.	Yorks ...	N. E.	South Bank.
.	.	.	.	.	.			Cargo Fleet Timber Yards and Wharves	Yorks ...	N. E.	South Bank.
.	.	.	.	.	.			Cargo Fleet Warrant Stores...	Yorks ...	N. E.	South Bank.
G	P	.	L	H	.			Carham.........	Roxburgh	N. E.	Berwick and Kelso.
.	.	.	.	.	.			Shedlaw Farm Siding	Northumb	N. E.	Carham.
G	P	.	L	H	.			Carisbrooke	I. of W.	I. of W. Cent.	Freshwater and Newport.
G	P	F	L	H	C	5	0	Cark-in-Cartmel	Lancs	Furness.........	Carnforth and Ulverston.
.	.	.	.	.	.			Cartmel	Lancs	Furness.........	Near Cark-in-Cartmel.
.	.	.	.	.	.			Carleton Coal & Brick Siding	Yorks ...	S. & K. Jt. (Mid. & N. E.)	Pontefract.
.	.	.	.	.	.			Carley Lime Works	Durham ...	N. E.	Southwick.
G	P	.	L	H	C			Carlingford	Louth ...	D. N. & G.	Greenore and Newry.
G	P	.	.	.	.			Carlinghow	Yorks ...	L. & N. W	Batley and Birstal.
.	.	.	.	.	.			Carlin How Depôts	Yorks ...	N. E.	Loftus.
.	.	.	.	.	.			Carlin How Engine Shed Sid.	Yorks ...	N. E.	Loftus.
.	.	.	.	.	.			Carlin How Mines	Yorks ...	N. E.	Loftus.
								CARLISLE—			
G	.	F	L	H	.	4	0	(Station)	Cumb'land	Cal.	Carlisle.
G	.	F	L	.	.	5	0	(Station)	Cumb'land	L. & N. W.	Terminus, Lancaster & Carlisle Sect'n.
.	.	.	.	.	.			Anderson & Son's Timber Siding (N. E.)	Cumb'land	N. E.—L. & N. W.—Mid.	London Road Junc. and Canal Junc.
.	.	.	.	.	.			Anglo-American Oil Co.'s Siding (N. E.)	Cumb'land	N. E.—L. & N. W.—Mid.	London Road Junc. and Canal Junc.
.	.	.	.	.	.			Baty, J., & Son's Siding ...	Cumb'land	N. E.	London Road Junc. and Citadel.
.	.	.	.	.	.			Bog Coal Depôts........	Cumb'land	N. E.	London Road Junc. and Canal Junc.
.	.	.	.	.	.			Bog Junction	Cumb'land	Gds. Tfc. Com.—M. & C.	Rome Str. Jn. & M. & C. & N. E. Jn.
.	.	.	.	.	.			Bog Siding	Cumb'land	N. E.	London Road Junc. and Canal Junc.
.	.	.	.	.	.			Burns & Co.'s Siding	Cumb'land	N. B.	Canal.
.	.	.	.	.	.			Caldew Junction..............	Cumb'land	Cal.—Gds. Tfc. Com.	Rockliffe & Dentonholme North Junc.
G	.	F	L	.	.	5	0	Canal	Cumb'land	N. B.	Carlisle, Citadel and Silloth.
.	.	.	.	.	.			Canal Junction	Cumb'land	N. B.—N. E.	Canal Station & London Rd. Station.
.	.	.	.	.	.			Carlisle Co-operative Society's Siding (N. E.)	Cumb'land	N. E.—L. & N. W.—Mid.	London Road Junc. and Canal Junc.
.	.	.	.	.	.			Carr & Co.'s Mill Sid. (N.B.)	Cumb'land	N. B.—L. & N. W.—	Canal.
.	P	F	.	H	C	.	.	Citadel (Cal. & L. & N. W. Jt. Station Committee) ..	Cumb'land	Cal.	Glasgow and Preston.
.	P	F	.	H	C	.	.			L. & N. W.	Terminus, Lancaster & Carlisle Sec.
.	P	F	.	H	C	.	.			G. & S. W.	Over Cal. from Gretna Junction.
.	P	.	.	H	C	.	.			M. & C.	Over Citadel Station Com. Lines.
.	P	.	.	H	C	.	.			Mid.	Over N. E. & Citadel Sta. Com. Lines.
.	P	F	.	H	C	.	.			N. B.	Over Cal. from North Junction.
.	P	F	.	H	C	.	.			N. E.	Over Citadel Station Com. Lines.

EXPLANATION—**G** *Goods Station.*   **P** *Passenger and Parcel Station.*   **P*** *Passenger, but not Parcel or Miscellaneous Traffic.*
F *Furniture Vans, Carriages, Portable Engines, and Machines on Wheels.*   **L** *Live Stock.*
H *Horse Boxes and Prize Cattle Vans.*   **C** *Carriages by Passenger Train.*

STATION ACCOMMODATION.					CRANE POWER.		STATIONS, &c.	COUNTY.	COMPANY.	POSITION.
					Tons	Cwts.	CARLISLE—continued.			
.	.	.	.	.	.	.	Corporation Siding...........	Cumb'land	Gds. Tfc. Com. (Cal., L. & N W, Mid. & G & SW)	Carlisle.
.	.	.	.	.	.	.	Cowan, Sheldon & Co.'s Works (N. E.)...............	Cumb'land	N. E.—L. & N. W.—Mid.	London Road Junction and Citadel.
G	.	F	L H	C	10	0	Creighton's Siding (N. B)....	Cumb'land	N. B.—L. & N. W.	Canal.
.	.		L H	.	.	.	Crown Street	Cumb'land	M. & C.	Branch—South of Citadel Station.
G	.	F	L H	.	10	0	Currock Junction	Cumb'land	M. & C.	Crown Street and Cummersdale.
.	.	.	.	.	.	.	Dalston Road Depôt & Sid.	Cumb'land	N. E.	London Road Junc. and Canal Junc.
.	.	.	.	.	.	.	Dentonholme	Cumb'land	G. & S.W.—Mid.	Branch—Rome Str. Jn. & Caldew Jn.
.	.	.	.	.	.	.	Dentonholme, North and South Junctions	Cumb'land	Dentonholme Sta. Com. —Gds. Tfc. Com....	Rome Street Junc. & Caldew Junc.
.	.	.	.	.	.	.	Deaton Str. Coal Depôts..	Cumb'land	N. E.	London Road Junc. and Canal Junc.
.	.	.	.	.	.	.	Electric Lighting Station	Cumb'land	Gds. Tfc. Com. (Cal., L. & NW, Mid. & G & SW)	Carlisle.
.	.	.	.	.	.	.	Engine Sheds (Currock Jn.)	Cumb'land	G. & S.W.	Over M. & C. from Rome Street Junc.
.	.	.	.	.	.	.	Etterby Sidings	Cumb'land	Cal.	Carlisle and Rockliffe.
.	.	.	.	.	.	.	Forks Junction	Cumb'land	M. & C.	Currock Junc. & Rome Street Junc.
.	.	.	.	.	.	.	Gas Works (Carlisle Goods Traffic Committee)	Cumb'land	Gds. Tfc. Com.—NB—NE	Carlisle.
.	.	.	.	.	.	.	Gas Works (Bousteads Grassing)	Cumb'land	M. & C.	Carlisle.
.	.	.	.	.	.	.	Guaranteed Manure Co.'s Siding (N.B.)	Cumb'land	N. B.—L. & N. W.	Canal.
.	.	.	.	.	.	.	Hewitson, John, Sid. (N E.)	Cumb'land	N. E.—Mid.	London Road Junction and Citadel Station.
.	.	.	.	.	.	.	Junction	Cumb'land	Cal.—Gds. Tfc. Com. ...	Caldew Junc. and Rome Street Junc.
.	.	.	.	.	.	.	Junction	Cumb'land	Gds. Tfc. Com.—L. & N.W.	Rome Street Junction and Penrith.
.	.	.	.	.	.	.	Junction	Cumb'land	M. & C.—N. E.	Dalston and London Road.
.	.	.	.	.	.	.	Junctions	Cumb'land	Cit. Sta. Com.—Cal.—L. & N.W--M.&C.—NE	Near Citadel Station.
G	.	F	L H	.	5	0	London Road	Cumb'land	N. E.	Carlisle, Citadel and Scotby.
.	.	.	.	.	.	.	London Road Coal Depôts	Cumb'land	N. E.	London Road.
.	.	.	.	.	.	.	London Road Junction......	Cumb'land	L. & N. W.—N. E.	Penrith and London Road.
.	.	.	.	.	.	.	Niven's, T., Siding	Cumb'land	N. B.	Canal.
.	.	.	.	.	.	.	N.B. Railway Engine Shed Yard	Cumb'land	N. B.	Carlisle and Harker.
.	.	.	.	.	.	.	North Junction	Cumb'land	Cal.—N. B.	Citadel Station and Harker.
G	.	F	L H	.	5	0	Petterill (Mid.)	Cumb'land	Mid. / G. & S. W.	Terminus. / Over N. E. & Mid. from Rome Street Junction.
.	.	.	.	.	.	.	Petterill Junction	Cumb'land	Mid.—N. E.	Scotby and Citadel Station.
.	.	.	.	.	.	.	Port Carlisle Junction	Cumb'land	Cal.—N. B.	Carlisle (Citadel) and Silloth.
.	.	.	.	.	.	.	Rome Street Junction	Cumb'land	Gds. Tfc. Com.—M.&C— N. E.	Dentonholme South Junction and London Road.
.	.	.	.	.	.	.	South End Co-operative Society's Siding	Cumb'land	Mid.	London Road Junc. and Citadel Sta.
.	.	.	.	.	.	.	Timber Yard (N. B.).........	Cumb'land	N. B.—L. & N. W.	Canal.
.	.	.	.	.	.	.	Willow Holme Junction ...	Cumb'land	Cal.—Gds. Tfc. Com. ...	Port Carlisle Junction and Dentonholme North Junction.
.	.	.	.	.	.	.	Carlisle Brick & Tile Works (Lonsdale Siding)	Cumb'land	Mid.	Cumwhinton.
.	.	.	.	.	.	.	Carlisle Farmers Manure Co.'s Siding	Cumb'land	N. B.	Kirkbride.
.	.	.	.	.	.	.	Carlisle Pier	Dublin ...	D. W. & W.	Branch from Kingstown.
.	.	.	.	.	.	.	Carlisle Road Siding	Lanark ...	Cal.	Lesmahagow.
.	.	.	.	.	.	.	Carlisle Road Siding	Lanark ...	N. B.	See Airdrie.
G	P	F	L H	C	1	0	Carlow	Carlow ...	G. S. & W.	Bagnalstown and Kildare.
G	P	.	L H	.	.	.	Carlton	Durham ...	N. E.	Stockton and Ferryhill.
.	.	.	.	.	.	.	Newfall Chemical Works ...	Durham ...	N. E.	Carlton.
.	.	.	.	.	.	.	Carlton	Notts	G. N.	See Gedling and Carlton.
G	P	F	L H	C	2	0	Carlton	Yorks	H. & B.	Cudworth and Howden.
G	P	.	L H	.	.	.	Carlton and Netherfield	Notts	Mid.	Nottingham and Newark.
.	.	.	.	.	.	.	Carlton Basic Phosphate Co.'s Works	Durham ...	N. E.	Stillington.
G	P	.	L	.	.	.	Carlton Colville	Suffolk ...	G. E.	Lowestoft and Beccles.
.	.	.	.	.	.	.	Barnby Siding..................	Suffolk ...	G. E.	Carlton Colville and Beccles.
.	.	.	.	.	.	.	Carlton Iron Ore Co.'s Siding (Attenborough's)..............	Lincoln ...	G. N.	Caythorpe.
.	.	.	.	.	.	.	Carlton Iron Works	Durham ...	N. E.	Stillington.
.	.	.	.	.	.	.	Carlton Junction..............	Durham ...	N. E.	Carlton.

EXPLANATION—G *Goods Station.*   P *Passenger and Parcel Station.*   P* *Passenger, but not Parcel or Miscellaneous Traffic.*
F *Furniture Vans, Carriages, Portable Engines, and Machines on Wheels.*   L *Live Stock.*
H *Horse Boxes and Prize Cattle Vans.*   C *Carriages by Passenger Train.*

STATION ACCOMMODATION.						CRANE POWER.	STATIONS, &c.	COUNTY.	COMPANY.	POSITION.
						Tons Cwts.	Carlton Main Colliery Co.—			
.	.	.	.	.	.	. .	Carlton Main Colliery	Yorks	H. & B. .... / Mid. / S. & K. Jt. (Mid. & N. E.)	Cudworth, North. / Cudworth. / Moorthorpe.
.	.	.	.	.	.	. .	Frickley Colliery..............	Yorks	S. & K. Jt. (Mid. & N. E.)	Moorthorpe.
.	.	.	.	.	.	. .	Grimethorpe Colliery	Yorks	Dearne Valley .... / G. C. .... / Mid.	Grimethorpe. / Stairfoot. / Cudworth.
.	.	.	.	.	.	. .	Carlton Main New Colliery ...	Yorks	S. & K. Jt. (Mid. & N. E.)	Moorthorpe.
G	P	F	L	H	C	5 0	Carlton-on-Trent..............	Notts	G. N.	Newark and Retford.
G	P	F	L	H	C	4 10	Carluke......................	Lanark ..	Cal.	Carstairs and Law Junction.
.	.	.	.	.	.	. .	Castlehill Colliery	Lanark ..	Cal.	Branch from Castlehill Iron Works Junction.
.	.	.	.	.	.	. .	Castlehill Iron Works Junc.	Lanark ...	Cal.	Carluke and Law Junction.
.	.	.	.	.	.	. .	Gas Works	Lanark ...	Cal.	Carluke and Law Junction.
.	.	.	.	.	.	. .	Hallcraig Brick Works......	Lanark ...	Cal.	Branch near Law Junction.
.	.	.	.	.	.	. .	Hallcraig Tile Works	Lanark ...	Cal.	Branch near Law Junction.
.	.	.	.	.	.	. .	Milton Brick Works	Lanark ...	Cal.	Braidwood and Carluke.
.	.	.	.	.	.	. .	Milton Colliery	Lanark ...	Cal.	Carluke.
.	.	.	.	.	.	. .	Moorfield Siding............	Lanark ...	N. B.	Castlehill Branch.
.	.	.	.	.	.	. .	Raesgill Foundry	Lanark ...	Cal.	Carluke and Law Junction.
.	.	.	.	.	.	. .	Whiteshaw Tile Works......	Lanark ...	Cal.	Branch near Law Junction.
G	.	.	L	.	.	3 0	Carluke (Castlehill)	Lanark ...	N. B.	Branch—Crofthead & Morningside.
.	.	.	.	.	.	. .	Castlehill Colliery	Lanark ...	N. B.	Castlehill Junc. and Castlehill Sta.
.	.	.	.	.	.	. .	Hyndshaw Colliery	Lanark ...	N. B.	Castlehill Junc. and Castlehill Sta.
.	.	.	.	.	.	. .	Carmacoup Colliery	Lanark ...	Cal.	Inches.
							CARMARTHEN—			
G	P	F	L	H	C	2 0	Junction Station..............	Carmarth'	G. W.	Ferryside and Whitland.
.	.	.	.	.	.	. .	Myrtle Hill Junction........	Carmarth'	G. W.	Carmarthen Junc. and Carmarthen.
G	P	F	L	H	C	2 0	Town (G. W.)	Carmarth'	G. W. / L. & N. W.	Carmarthen Junction and Pencader. / Over G. W. from Abergwili Junc.
.	.	.	.	.	.	. .	Carmarthenshire Dock	Carmarth'	L. & M. M.	See Llanelly.
.	.	.	.	.	.	. .	Carmarthen Valley Junction .	Carmarth'	G. W.—L. & N. W.	Ffairfach and Llandilo.
.	.	.	.	.	.	. .	Carmuirs Colliery	Stirling ...	Cal.	Larbert.
.	.	.	.	.	.	. .	Carmuirs Colliery	Stirling ...	N. B.	Falkirk, Grahamston.
.	.	.	.	.	.	. .	Carmuirs East Junction	Stirling ...	Cal.—N. B.	Falkirk.
.	.	.	.	.	.	. .	Carmuirs Iron Foundry (N.B.)	Stirling ...	N. B.—Cal.	Falkirk, Grahamston.
.	.	.	.	.	.	. .	Carmuirs West Junction	Stirling ...	Cal.	Greenhill and Larbert.
G	P	F	L	H	C	2 0	Carmyle	Lanark ...	Cal.	Coatbridge and Rutherglen.
.	.	.	.	.	.	. .	Carmyle Sand Pit	Lanark ...	Cal.	Carmyle Junction and Carmyle.
.	.	.	.	.	.	. .	Foxley Colliery	Lanark ...	Cal.	Carmyle.
.	.	.	.	.	.	. .	Kenmuir Colliery	Lanark ...	Cal.	Mount Vernon and Carmyle.
.	.	.	.	.	.	. .	Kenmuirhill Colliery No. 1	Lanark ...	Cal.	Mount Vernon and Carmyle.
.	.	.	.	.	.	. .	Carmyle Junction	Lanark ...	Cal.	Mount Vernon and Carmyle.
G	P	F	L	H		. .	Carmyllie	Forfar.....	D. & A. Jt. (Cal. & N. B.)	Branch from Elliot Junction.
G	P*					. .	Denhead	Forfar.....	D. & A. Jt. (Cal. & N. B.)	Carmyllie and Elliot Junction.
G						3 0	Quarry Sidings	Forfar.....	D. & A. Jt. (Cal. & N. B.)	End of Carmyllie Branch.
.	P	.	.	.	.	. .	Carnaby	Yorks	N. E.	Bridlington and Driffield.
.	P	.	.	.	.	. .	Carnalea	Down	B. & C. D.	Helen's Bay and Bangor.
G	P	F	L	H	C	5 0	Carnarvon	Carnarvon	L. & N. W.	Afon Wen and Bangor.
.	.	.	.	.	.	. .	Carnarvon Gas Co.'s Siding	Carnarvon	L. & N. W.	Carnarvon and Dinas Junction.
.	.	.	.	.	.	. .	Peblig Siding	Carnarvon	L. & N. W.	Carnarvon and Pont Rug.
.	.	.	.	.	.	. .	Seiont Sidings................	Carnarvon	L. & N. W.	Carnarvon and Pont Rug.
.	.	.	.	.	.	. .	Arfon Brick Co.'s	Carnarvon	L. & N. W.	Seiont Sidings.
.	.	.	.	.	.	. .	Glanmorfa	Carnarvon	L. & N. W.	Seiont Sidings.
.	.	.	.	.	.	. .	Lake & Co.'s	Carnarvon	L. & N. W.	Seiont Sidings.
.	.	.	.	.	.	. .	Carnarvon Colliery (G. W.)...	Carmarth'	G. W. — L. & N. W.	Bynea.
							Carnarvon's, Earl of—			
.	.	.	.	.	.	. .	Bretby Colliery Wharf(Newhall Park Colliery) (Mid.)	Derby	Mid.—L. & N. W.	Swadlincote.
.	.	.	.	.	.	. .	New Bretby Colliery (Mid.)	Derby	Mid.—L. & N. W.	Swadlincote.
G	P	.	.	H		4 0	Carn Brea....................	Cornwall..	G. W.	Redruth and Camborne.
.	.	.	.	.	.	. .	Carn Brea Yard	Cornwall..	G. W.	Carn Brea.
.	.	.	.	.	.	. .	Cook's Kitchen Yard	Cornwall..	G. W.	North Crofty Mineral Branch.
.	.	.	.	.	.	. .	Illogan Highway Siding ...	Cornwall..	G. W.	Carn Brea.
.	.	.	.	.	.	. .	North Crofty Mineral Bch.	Cornwall..	G. W.	Carn Brea.
.	.	.	.	.	.	. .	Tuckingmill Yard	Cornwall..	G. W.	North Crofty Mineral Branch.
.	.	.	.	.	.	. .	Carnbroe Brick Works........	Lanark ...	Cal.	Coatbridge, Whifflet.
.	.	.	.	.	.	. .	Carnbroe Chemical Works ...	Lanark ...	Cal.—N. B.	Coatbridge, Whifflet.
.	.	.	.	.	.	. .	Carnbroe Colliery	Lanark ...	Cal.	Coatbridge, Whifflet.
.	.	.	.	.	.	. .	Carnbroe Iron Works	Lanark ...	Cal.—N. B.	Coatbridge, Whifflet.
.	.	.	.	.	.	. .	Carnbroe Weighs	Lanark ...	N. B.	Whifflet and Bellshill.

EXPLANATION—G *Goods Station.*   P *Passenger and Parcel Station.*   P* *Passenger, but not Parcel or Miscellaneous Traffic.*
F *Furniture Vans, Carriages, Portable Engines, and Machines on Wheels.*   L *Live Stock.*
H *Horse Boxes and Prize Cattle Vans.*   C *Carriages by Passenger Train.*

G	P	F	L	H	C	Tons	Cwts	STATIONS, &c	COUNTY.	COMPANY.	POSITION.
G	P		L					Carndonagh	Donegal	L. & L. S.	Terminus.
								Carne Point Wharves	Cornwall	G. W.	See Fowey.
								CARNFORTH—			
								Carnforth Hematite Iron Works	Lancs	Furness & Mid. Joint...	Near Carnforth Station.
										L. & N. W.	Burton & Holme and Carnforth.
	P			H	C			Joint Passengers	Lancs	Furness	Terminus.
										L. & N. W.	Lancaster and Penrith.
										Mid.	Terminus.
								Junction	Lancs	Fur.—Fur. & Mid. Joint	Silverdale and Borwick.
								Junction	Lancs	Furness— L. & N. W.	Carnforth Station and Lancaster.
G		F	L			10	0	L. & N. W. & Fur. Jt. Goods	Lancs	Furness	Near Passenger Station.
										L. & N. W.	Branch near Passenger Station.
										Furness & Mid. Joint...	Carnforth.
								Watson & Hartley's Siding (Furness & Mid. Joint)	Lancs	Fur. & Mid. Jt.—L.N.W.	Near Carnforth Station.
G	P		L	H		1	0	Carno	Montgom.	Cam.	Newtown and Machynlleth.
								Carnock Colliery	Stirling	Cal.	Plean Junction Station.
G	P	F	L	H	C	3	0	Carnoustie	Forfar	D. & A Jt. (Cal. & N. B.)	Dundee and Arbroath.
G								Panbride Siding	Forfar	D. & A. Jt. (Cal. & N. B.)	Carnoustie and Easthaven.
	P							Carntyne	Lanark	N. B.	Parkhead and Coatbridge.
								Carntyne Dye Works (British Dyewood & Chem. Co.'s Sid.)	Lanark	N. B.	Glasgow, Parkhead.
								Carntyne Foundry and Engineering Works	Lanark	N. B.	Glasgow, Parkhead.
								Carntyne Iron & Steel Works	Lanark	N. B.	Glasgow, Parkhead.
								Carntyne Sidings	Lanark	N. B.	See Glasgow.
G	P		L	H		1	10	Carnwath	Lanark	Cal.	Carstairs and Edinburgh.
								Carolina Port Sidings	Forfar	Cal.	Dundee, West.
										N. B.	Dundee, Tay Bridge.
								Carpella Siding	Cornwall	G. W.	Drinnick Mill.
								Carpenter's Road	Essex	G. E.	See London.
								Carr & Co.'s Mill Siding(N.B.)	Cumb'land	N.B.—L.&N.W.	Carlisle.
								Carr & Co.'s Siding	Cumb'land	N. B.	Silloth.
								Carr & Co.'s Siding (G. C.)	Lincoln	G. C.—G. N.	Grimsby Docks.
G	P	F	L	H	C			Carr Bridge	Inverness	High.	Inverness and Aviemore.
								Carr Bridge Siding	Lancs	L. & N. W.	Same as Lawton's Sid. (Glazebury).
								Carr Close Siding	Notts	Mid.	See Ilkeston Corporation (Ilkeston).
								Carr House Colliery	Yorks	Mid.	See Brown, J. & Co's Sidings (Masboro' & Rotherham).
G	P		L			3	0	Carrichue	Derry	N. C. Com. (Mid.)	Londonderry and Coleraine.
								Carrick & Wardale's Siding	Durham	N. E.	Redheugh.
G	P		L	H	C	2	0	Carrickfergus	Antrim	N. C. Com. (Mid.)	Belfast and Larne.
G	P	F	L			3	0	Carrickmacross	Monaghan	G. N. (I.)	Branch from Inniskeen.
G	P							Carrickmines	Dublin	D. W. & W.	Dublin, Harcourt Street and Bray.
G	P							Carrickmore	Tyrone	G. N. (I.)	Dungannon and Omagh.
G	P	F	L	H	C	1	10	Carrick-on-Shannon	Leitrim	M. G. W.	Longford and Sligo.
G	P	F	L	H	C	4	0	Carrick-on-Suir	Tipperary	G. S. & W.	Clonmel and Waterford.
								Carriers Dock	Lancs	G. W.	Liverpool.
G	P		L	H				Carrigaline	Cork	C. B. & P.	Monkstown and Crosshaven.
G	P							Carrigaloe	Cork	G. S. & W.	Queenstown Junc. and Queenstown.
								Belvelly Siding	Cork	G. S. & W.	Near Carrigaloe.
G	P							Carrigans	Donegal	G. N. (I.)	Strabane and Londonderry.
								Carrignagat Junction	Sligo	M. G. W.—S. L. & N. C.	Sligo and Manorhamilton.
G	P							Carrigrohane	Cork	C. & Muskerry	Cork and Coachford Junction.
G	P		L	H				Carrigtwohill	Cork	G. S. & W.	Cork and Youghal.
								Carrington (G. C.)	Notts	G. C.—G. N.	See Nottingham.
								Carrington, Shaw & Co.'s Sid.	Lancs	L. & Y.	Skelmersdale.
								Carrington Sidings	Lancs	C. L. C. (G.C, G. N. & Mid.)	Partington.
	P							Carr Mill	Lancs	L. & N. W.	St. Helens and Wigan.
G	P		L	H	C			Carrog	Merioneth	G. W.	Llangollen and Corwen.
								Carrog Slate Siding (Corwen Slate Siding)	Merioneth	G. W.	Carrog and Corwen.
								Penarth Quarry Siding	Merioneth	G. W.	Carrog.
	P							Carroll's Cross	Waterford	G. S. & W.	Dungarvan and Waterford.
G	P	F	L	H	C	4	0	Carron	Elgin&Mo'	G. N. of S.	Craigellachie and Boat of Garten.
								Carronbank Iron Works	Stirling	Cal.	Denny.
G	P	F	L	H	C	1	10	Carronbridge	Dumfries	G. & S. W.	Dumfries and Sanquhar.
								Carronhall Cols. Nos. 5 & 6 (N. B.)	Stirling	N. B.—Cal.	Falkirk, Grahamston.
								Carron Iron Co.'s— Jack Trees Siding	Cumb'land	W.C.&E.Jt.(Fur&LNW)	Crossfield.
								Newbigging Siding	Fife	N. B.	Burntisland.

EXPLANATION—G *Goods Station.*   P *Passenger and Parcel Station.*   P* *Passenger, but not Parcel or Miscellaneous Traffic.*
F *Furniture Vans, Carriages, Portable Engines, and Machines on Wheels.*   L *Live Stock.*
H *Horse Boxes and Prize Cattle Vans.*   C *Carriages by Passenger Train.*

STATION ACCOMMODATION.						CRANE POWER.	STATIONS, &c.	COUNTY.	COMPANY.	POSITION.
						Tons Cwt.	Carron Iron Works (N.B.)...	Stirling ...	N. B.— Cal.	Falkirk, Grahamston.
							Carron Iron Wks Bch. Jn.(N B)	Stirling ...	N. B.— Cal.	Falkirk, Grahamston.
							Carron Lye	Lanark ...	N. B.	Rawyards.
							Carronrigg Colliery	Stirling ...	Cal.	Denny.
							Carronshore Siding (N. B.) ...	Stirling ...	N. B.—Cal.	Falkirk, Grahamston.
							Carron Works (N. B.)	Stirling ...	N. B.—Cal.	See Burnhouse Sids (for Carron Wks.)
G	P	.	L				Carrowen	Donegal ...	L. & L. S.	Tooban Junction and Letterkenny.
G	P	.	L	H			Carrowmore	Sligo ...	G. S. & W.	Collooney and Claremorris.
							Carrow Works	Norfolk ...	G. E.	Same as Colman, J. & J., Siding (Norwich).
							Carr's Col. and Brick Yard...	Yorks	N. E.	Lemington.
							Carr's Siding	Warwick..	Mid.	Birmingham, Lawley Street.
							Carr's Tilery & Brick Works	Yorks	N. E.	Boosbeck.
							Carr's, W. H., Siding	Essex	G. E.	Weeley.
							Carr's, W. H., Siding	Suffolk ...	G. E.	Ipswich, Derby Road.
							Carr's, W. H., Siding	Suffolk ...	G. E.	Leiston.
G	P	.					Carsaig	Argyll ...	Cal.	Steamer from Oban.
.	P						Carsbreck	Perth	Cal.	Greenloaning and Blackford.
							Carsehead Brick Works	Ayr.........	G. & S. W.	Dalry.
							Carsehead No. 2..............	Ayr	G. & S. W.	Dalry.
.	P						Carshalton	Surrey ...	L. B. & S. C.	Hackbridge and Sutton.
G	P	F	L	H	C	1 10	Carstairs	Lanark ...	Cal.	Lockerbie and Law Junction.
							Carstairs Sand Pit..... ...	Lanark ...	Cal.	Carstairs and Cleghorn.
							Grange Siding	Lanark ...	Cal.	Thankerton and Carstairs.
							Cairngryffe Siding	Lanark ...	Cal.	Grange Siding.
G							Pettinain Siding	Lanark ...	Cal.	Grange Siding.
							Lampit's Siding	Lanark ...	Cal.	Carstairs and Bankhead.
							Monteith's Siding	Lanark ...	Cal.	Carstairs.
							Carter & Barringer's Siding (Mid.)	Notts	Mid.—G. C.	See Mansfield Sand Co.'s Siding (Mansfield).
							Carter's Brick Works	Durham ...	N. E.	Wingate.
							Carter's Siding	Dorset.....	S. & D. Jt. (L. & S. W & Mid.)	Bailey Gate.
							Carterthorne Colliery	Durham ...	N. E.	Evenwood.
							Cart Harbour	Renfrew ...	G. & S. W.	See Paisley.
							Cart Junction................	Renfrew ...	G. & S. W.	Johnstone and Houston.
							Cartmel	Lancs ...	Furness...	See Cark-in-Cartmel.
							Cartsburn Junction	Renfrew ...	G. & S. W.	Greenock and Upper Port Glasgow.
							Cartsburn Siding (G. & S. W.)	Renfrew ...	G. & S. W.— N. B.	Greenock, Lynedoch Street.
							Cartsdyke	Renfrew ...	Cal.	See Greenock.
							Cartsdyke Saw Mills..........	Renfrew ...	Cal.	Greenock, Regent Street.
							Cartside	Renfrew ...	G. & S. W.	See Johnstone.
							Cartside Junction	Renfrew ...	G. & S. W.	Elderslie and Johnstone, North.
							Cartwright Colliery Co.'s New Hall Field Colliery (Mid.)	Derby	Mid.—L. & N. W.	Swadlincote.
							Carvill Bros.' Siding...........	Down	G. N. (I.)	Newry.
G	P	.	L	.	.	10 0	Carville.....................	Northumb	N. E.	Newcastle and Tynemouth.
							Carville Electric Supply Co.'s Siding...............	Northumb	N. E.	Carville.
							Northumberland Forge Sid.	Northumb	N. E.	Carville.
							Tyne Pontoon Co.'s Siding	Northumb	N. E.	Carville.
							Wallsend & Hebburn Coal Co.'s Siding.................	Northumb	N. E.	Carville.
							Carway Junction	Carmarth'	B. P. & G. V.	Burry Port and Pontyeats.
							Casebourne & Co.'s Siding ...	Durham ...	N. E.	West Hartlepool.
							Casebourne, W. H., & Co.'s Depôts & Creosote Works...	Yorks	N. E.	Castleford.
							Cash & Son's Siding	Notts	Mid.	Mansfield.
G	P	.	L	H	C		Cashelnagore	Donegal ...	L. & L. S.	Letterkenny and Burtonport.
							Caspian Wharf	Essex	L. T. & S.	See Anglo-American Oil Co. (Purfleet).
							Cassell's Gold Extracting Co.'s Siding	Lanark ...	N. B.	Glasgow, Ruchill.
G	P	F	L	H	C	0 10	Cassillis	Ayr.........	G. & S. W.	Ayr and Maybole.
							Castella Siding	Glamorg'n	T. V.	Cross Inn.
							Castlandhill Siding	Fife	N. B.	North Queensferry.
G	P	F	L	H	C	1 5	Castle Ashby and Earls Barton	N'hampt'n	L. & N. W.	Northampton and Wellingboro'.
G	P	F	L	H	C	2 0	Castlebar	Mayo ...	M. G. W.	Claremorris and Westport.
G	P	F	L	H	C		Castlebellingham	Louth	G. N. (I.)	Drogheda and Dundalk.
G	P	F	L			3 0	Castleblaney	Monaghan	G. N. (I.)	Dundalk and Clones.
							Castle Brick Works	Staffs	L. & N. W.	Same as Griffin, Jones & Co.'s Siding (Birchills).
G	P	F	L	H	C		Castle Bromwich	Warwick	Mid.	Birmingham and Whitacre.
G	P						Castle Bytham	Lincoln ...	Mid.	South Witham & Little Bytham Jn.

EXPLANATION—G *Goods Station.*   P *Passenger and Parcel Station.*   P* *Passenger, but not Parcel or Miscellaneous Traffic.*
F *Furniture Vans, Carriages, Portable Engines, and Machines on Wheels.*   L *Live Stock.*
H *Horse Boxes and Prize Cattle Vans.*   C *Carriages by Passenger Train.*

STATION ACCOMMODATION.						CRANE POWER.		STATIONS, &c.	COUNTY.	COMPANY.	POSITION.
						Tons	Cwts.				
								Castle Bytham—*continued.*			
								Rippon & Co.'s Lime & Stone Siding	Lincoln ...	Mid.	Castle Bytham.
G	P		L					Castle Caereinion	Montgom	Cam. (W. & L.)	Welshpool and Llanfair Caereinion.
G	P							Castlecaldwell	Ferm'nagh	G. N. (I.)	Bundoran Junc. and Bundoran.
								Castle Car Works	Salop	L. & N. W.	Same as Milnes & Co.'s Siding (Wombridge).
G	P	F	L	H	C	10	0	Castle Cary	Somerset..	G. W.	Yeovil and Westbury.
G	P	F	L	H	C	1	5	Castlecary	Dumbartn	N. B.	Falkirk and Lenzie Junction.
								Castlecary Fire-Clay Co.'s Siding	Dumbartn	N.B.	Castlecary.
								Glenyards Brick Works ...	Stirling ...	N. B.	Bonnybridge and Castlecary.
G								Greenhill Upper Junc. Sids.	Stirling ...	N. B.	Bonnybridge and Castlecary.
G								Netherwood Siding	Dumbartn	N. B.	Castlecary and Dullatur.
								Castlecary Siding (Stein's Brick Works)	Stirling ...	Cal.	Greenhill.
								Castle Coch Siding	Glamorg'n	Rhy.	Taffs Well.
								Castle (Cille) Colliery	Carmarth'	L. & M. M.	Llanelly.
								Castle (Cille) Colliery (G.W.)	Carmarth'	G. W.—L. & N. W.	Llanelly.
								Castle Colliery Co.'s Sid.(GW)	Carmarth'	G. W.— L. & N. W.	Llanelly.
G	P	F	L	H				Castleconnel	Limerick..	G. S. & W.	Limerick and Killaloe.
G	P		L	H		2	0	Castledawson	Derry	N. C. Com. (Mid.)	Cookstown Junc. and Magherafelt
G	P							Castlederg	Tyrone	C. & V. B.	Branch from Victoria Bridge.
G	P	F	L	H	C	1	10	Castle Donington & Shardlow	Leicester..	Mid.	Trent and Weston-on-Trent.
G	P	F	L	H	C	7	0	Castle Douglas	Kirkcud..	G. & S.W.	Dumfries and Kirkcudbright.
								Castle Douglas Branch Junc.	Dumfries..	G. & S.W.	Dumfries and Lochanhead.
								Castle Douglas Junction	Kirkcud..	G.&S. W.—P. P. & W. Jt.	Castle Douglas and Crossmichael.
G	P		L	H	C	3	0	Castle Eden	Durham ...	N. E.	Ferryhill and Hartlepool.
								Burdon's Coal Depôts	Durham ...	N. E.	Castle Eden.
								Crimdon Siding	Durham ...	N. E.	Castle Eden.
								Nimmo & Son's Brewery	Durham ...	N. E.	Castle Eden.
								Sunderland & South Shields Water Co.'s Pumping Station (Nimmo's Sid.)	Durham ...	N. E.	Castle Eden.
								Wellfield Siding	Durham ...	N. E.	Castle Eden.
								Castle Engine Works	Staffs	L. & N. W.	Same as Bagnall's Sid. (Stafford).
								Castlefield Junction	Lancs	M S J & A (G C & L& NW)	Manchester.
G	P		L	H	C			Castlefinn	Donegal	Donegal	Strabane and Stranorlar.
								Castle Fire Brick Co.'s Siding	Flint	W. M. & C. Q.	Buckley.
								CASTLEFORD—			
	P			H				(Station)	Yorks	L. & Y.	Methley Junction Sta. & Pontefract.
G	P	F	L	H	C	5	0	(Station, N. E.)	Yorks	{ N. E. / G. N.	Burton Salmon and Normanton. / Over N. E. from Methley Junction.
								Aire and Calder Chemical Works (Hunt Bros.)	Yorks	N. E	Castleford, Whitwood Branch.
								Aire and Calder Glass Bottle Wks. (E. Breffit & Co.)— Ashton Works	Yorks	N. E.	Castleford.
								Rye Bread Works	Yorks	N. E.	Castleford, East Branch.
								Anglo-American Oil Co.'s Store	Yorks	N. E.	Castleford.
								Austin Bros.' Siding	Yorks	N. E.	Castleford.
								Casebourne, W. H., & Co.'s Depôts & Creosote Works	Yorks	N. E.	Castleford, Whitwood Branch.
								Castleford & Whitwood Gas Light, and Coke Co.'s Sid.	Yorks	N. E.	Castleford, East Branch.
								Castleford No. 3 Siding	Yorks	N. E.	Castleford.
								Clokie & Co.'s Siding	Yorks	N. E.	Castleford, Whitwood Branch.
G								Cutsyke Siding (L. & Y.)	Yorks	L. & Y.—Mid.	Castleford.
								Fawcett's, T. P., Siding	Yorks	N. E.	Castleford.
								Glasshoughton Col. (L.&Y.)	Yorks	L. & Y.—G N—Mid—N E	Castleford.
								Healdfield Brick Co.'s Sid.	Yorks	N. E.	Castleford.
								Lumb, J.,&Co.'s Glass Bottle Works, Nos. 1, 2, & 3 Sids.	Yorks	N. E.	Castleford.
								Mexbro' Main Collieries (Briggs, H., & Sons)	Yorks	N. E.	Castleford.
								Moss Street Goods Yards & Sidings	Yorks	N. E.	Castleford, Whitwood Branch.
								Pope and Pearson's West Riding Collieries	Yorks	N. E.	Castleford.
								Red Hill Brick Works (Hartley, J., & Co.)	Yorks	N. E.	Castleford.

EXPLANATION—G *Goods Station.*　　P *Passenger and Parcel Station.*　　P* *Passenger, but not Parcel or Miscellaneous Traffic.*
F *Furniture Vans, Carriages, Portable Engines, and Machines on Wheels.*　　L *Live Stock.*
H *Horse Boxes and Prize Cattle Vans.*　　C *Carriages by Passenger Train.*

STATION ACCOMMODATION.						CRANE POWER.		STATIONS, &c.	COUNTY.	COMPANY.	POSITION.
						Tons	Cwts.	CASTLEFORD—continued.			
.	.	.	.	.	.			Ridge Field Brick Co.'s Sid.	Yorks	N. E.	Castleford, Cutsyke Branch.
.	.	.	.	.	.			Victoria Brick Co.'s Siding	Yorks	N. E.	Castleford.
.	.	.	.	.	.			Wheldale Coal Co.'s Siding	Yorks	N. E.	Castleford.
.	.	.	.	.	.			Whitwood Chemical Co.'s Siding	Yorks	N. E.	Castleford.
.	.	.	.	.	.			Whitwood Chemical Co.'s Siding (L. & Y.)	Yorks	L. & Y.—Mid.	Castleford and Methley Junction.
.	.	.	.	.	.			Whitwood Collieries	Yorks	N. E.	Castleford.
.	.	.	.	.	.			Whitwood Col. (L. & Y.)...	Yorks	L. & Y.—G. N.—Mid. ...	Castleford and Methley Junction.
.	.	.	.	.	.			Castle Foregate	Salop	G. W.	See Shrewsbury.
.	.	.	.	.	.			Castle Foregate	Salop	L. & N. W.	See Shrewsbury, New Yard.
G	P	.	L	H	.			Castlegregory	Kerry	T. & D.	Branch from Castlegregory Junc.
G	P	.	L	.	.			Castlegregory Junction	Kerry	T. & D.	Tralee and Dingle.
G	P	.	L	.	.			Castlegrove	Galway ...	G. S. & W.	Tuam and Claremorris.
G	P	F	L	H	C	1	0	Castle Hedingham	Essex	C. V. & H.	Halstead and Haverhill.
.	.	.	.	.	.			Castlehill	Lanark ...	N. B.	See Carluke.
.	.	.	.	.	.			Castlehill Branch Junction ...	Lanark ...	N. B.	Crofthead and Carluke, Castlehill.
.	.	.	.	.	.			Castlehill Colliery	Lanark ...	Cal. N. B.	Carluke. Carluke, Castlehill.
.	.	.	.	.	.			Castlehill Iron Works Junc.	Lanark ...	Cal.	Carluke.
.	.	.	.	.	.			Castlehill Junction.............	Ayr	G. & S. W.	Saltcoats and Ardrossan.
.	.	.	.	.	.			Castlehill Siding (Hopetoun Branch)............................	L'lithgow	N. B.	See Young's Oil Co. (Uphall).
G	P	F	L	H	C	5	0	Castle Howard	Yorks	N. E.	York and Malton.
.	.	.	.	.	.			Castle Howard Sand Co.'s Quarry (Kilner's Siding)	Yorks	N. E.	Castle Howard & Hutton's Ambo.
.	.	.	.	.	.			Crambeck Coal Depôt	Yorks	N. E.	Castle Howard.
.	.	.	.	.	.			Crambeck Siding	Yorks	N. E.	Castle Howard.
.	.	.	.	.	.			Castle Howard Sand Co.'s Quarry (Kilner's Siding)	Yorks	N. E.	Castle Howard. Hutton's Ambo.
G	P	.	L	H	.	1	0	Castleisland......................	Kerry	G. S. & W.	Branch from Gortatlea.
G	P	.	L	H	.			Castle Kennedy	Wigtown..	P.P.&W.Jt.(Cal.G&SW., L. & N. W. & Mid.)......	Stranraer and Glenluce.
G	P	.	L	.	.			Castlemaine......................	Kerry	G. S. & W.	Farranfore & Valentia Harbour.
G	.	.	L	.	.	3	0	Castlemilk	Dumfries..	Cal.	Carlisle and Lockerbie.
.	P	.	.	.	.			Castle Mill	Denbigh...	Glyn Valley	Chirk and Glynceiriog.
.	.	.	.	.	.			Castle Mill Siding	Staffs	G. W.	Dudley.
.	.	.	.	.	.			Castle Pit (G.W. & Rhy. Jt.)	Glamorg'n	GW & Rhy. Jt.—L&NW	See Crawshay Bros'. (Abercanaid).
.	.	.	.	.	.			Castle Pond Sidings	Mon	G. W.	Talywain.
.	.	.	.	.	.			Castle Quarry	Flint	L. & N. W.	Dyserth.
G	P	F	L	H	C	1	10	Castlerea	Roscom'n..	M. G. W.	Roscommon and Claremorris.
G	P	.	L	H	.			Castlerock......................	Derry	N. C. Com. (Mid.)	Londonderry and Coleraine.
.	.	.	.	.	.			Castle Soap Works (New Hydroleine Co.'s Siding) ...	Leicester ..	Mid.	Ashby-de-la-Zouch.
G	P	F	L	H	.	3	0	Castlethorpe	Bucks	L. & N. W.	Bletchley and Blisworth.
.	.	.	.	.	.			Castleton	Derby	Mid.	See Hope (for Castleton & Bradwell).
G	P	.	L	H	C	3	0	Castleton	Lancs	L. & Y.	Manchester and Rochdale.
.	.	.	.	.	.			L. & Y. Co.'s Railway Stores Siding	Lancs	L. & Y.	Castleton.
.	.	.	.	.	.			Magee, Marshall & Co.'s Sid.	Lancs	L. & Y.	Castleton.
.	.	.	.	.	.			Tweedales & Smalley's Sid.	Lancs	L. & Y.	Castleton.
G	P	F	L	H	C	5	0	Castleton......	Yorks	N. E.	Stokesley and Whitby.
.	.	.	.	.	.			Commondale Brick & Pipe Co.'s Siding..............	Yorks	N. E.	Castleton.
.	.	.	.	.	.			Commondale Whinstone Co.'s Siding	Yorks	N. E.	Castleton.
.	.	.	.	.	.			Grayson, Lowood & Co.'s Siding	Yorks	N. E.	Castleton.
.	.	.	.	.	.			Castleton Siding................	Edinboro'	N. B.	Fushiebridge.
.	.	.	.	.	.			Castleton Siding................	Lancs	L. & Y.	Rochdale.
.	.	.	.	.	.			Castleton Stone Siding........	Dorset......	W.&P.Jt.(GW&L.&SW)	See Portland.
G	P	F*	L	.	.			Castletown	I. of Man..	I. of Man	Douglas and Port Erin.
.	.	.	.	.	.			Castletown	Queen's ...	G. S. & W.	See Mountrath and Castletown.
G	P	F	L	H	C			Castletown	W'meath...	M. G. W.	Mullingar and Athlone.
.	.	.	.	.	.			Castletown Brick Works	Durham ...	N. E.	Southwick.
G	P	F	L	H	C			Castletownroche	Cork	G. S. & W.	Mallow and Fermoy.
.	.	.	.	.	.			Castletown Ship Yard	Durham ...	N. E.	Southwick.
.	.	.	.	.	.			Castle Wharf	Durham ...	N. E.	Stockton, South.
.	.	.	.	.	.			Castner, Kellner & Co.'s Sid ..	Cheshire...	L. & N. W.	Runcorn Docks.
G	P	.	.	.	.			Castor (L. & N. W.)	N'hamptn	L. & N. W. .... G. N.	Peterboro' and Wellingboro'. Over L. & N. W. from Longville Jn.
.	P	.	.	.	.						

STATION ACCOMMODATION.						CRANE POWER.	STATIONS, &c.	COUNTY.	COMPANY.	POSITION.
						Tons Cwts.	Caswell & Bowden's Siding...	Staffs	L. & N. W.	Birchills.
G	P	F	L	H	C	. .	Catchpole & Sons' Siding ...	Kent	L. B. & S. C.	London, Deptford Wharf.
G	P	F	L	H	C	4 0	Catcliffe	Yorks	L. D. & E. C.	Killamarsh and Sheffield.
G	P	P	.	L		. .	Caterham	Surrey ...	S. E. & C.	Branch from Purley.
			L			. .	Catfield	Norfolk ...	Mid. & G. N. Jt.	Yarmouth Beach & N. Walsham Tn.
	P					. .	Catford	Kent	S. E. & C.	Nunhead and Shortlands.
G	P					. .	Catford Bridge	Kent	S. E. & C.	Lewisham and Beckenham.
						. .	Cathays Coal Yard Siding (Williams)	Glamorg'n	Rhy.	Cardiff.
						. .	Cathays Storage Siding	Glamorg'n	T. V.	Cardiff.
						. .	Cathays Yard	Glamorg'n	T. V.	Cardiff.
						. .	Cathcart	Renfrew...	Cal.	See Glasgow.
						. .	Cathcart Street	Cheshire...	B'head Jt. (G W & L NW)	See Birkenhead.
						. .	Cathcart Street Depôt	Renfrew...	Cal.	Greenock, Regent Street.
						. .	Cathcart, West Junction	Renfrew...	Cal.	Glasgow.
						. .	Catherall & Co.'s Brick Siding	Flint	W. M. & C. Q.	Buckley.
						. .	Catlings Siding	Middlesex	L. & S. W.	Shepperton.
G	P	.	L	H	.	1 10	Caton	Lancs	Mid.	Settle and Lancaster.
						. .	Claughton Brick Co.'s Sid.	Lancs	Mid.	Near Caton.
						. .	Claughton Manor Siding ...	Lancs	Mid.	Near Caton.
						. .	Lunesdale Siding	Lancs	Mid.	Near Caton.
G	P	F	L	H	C	3 0	Catrine	Ayr	G. & S. W.	Branch from Brackenhill Junction.
G	P	F	L	H	C	1 0	Cattal	Yorks	N. E.	York and Knaresborough.
						. .	Backhouse's Siding	Yorks	N. E.	Cattal.
						. .	Catt & Co.'s Siding	Sussex ...	L. B. & S. C.	Barcombe Mills.
						. .	Catterall	Lancs	L. & N. W.	See Garstang and Catterall.
G	P	F	L	H	C	1 10	Catterick Bridge	Yorks	N. E.	Richmond and Darlington.
						. .	Cattewater Harbour	Devon ...	L. & S. W.	See Plymouth.
						. .	Cattewater Junction	Devon ...	G. W. — L. & S. W.	Plymouth, North Road and Cattewater Harbour.
						. .	Cattle Sales Sid. (L & N. W.)	Warwick	L. & N. W.—Mid.	Same as Dewis's Siding (Coventry).
						. .	Cattybrook Brick Co.'s Siding	Glo'ster ...	{ G. W.	Bristol.
									{ Mid.	Mangotsfield.
						. .	Caucasian Oil Co.'s Siding ...	N'hamptn	Mid.	Peterboro'.
							Caucasian Petroleum Export Co.—			
						. .	Siding	Lancs	Trafford Park Estate......	Manchester.
						. .	Siding	Surrey	L. & S. W.	Wandsworth Town.
						. .	Caudledown Siding	Cornwall ..	G. W.	Bugle.
						. .	Caudwell's Siding	Notts	Mid.	Same as King's Mill Siding.
						. .	Caudwell's, E., Siding	Notts	Mid.	Southwell.
G	P	.	L	H		1 5	Cauldcots	Forfar	N. B.	Arbroath and Montrose.
	P*					. .	Cauldhame Colliery	Ayr	G. & S. W.	Same as Springhill Col. (Dreghorn).
						. .	Causeland	Cornwall ..	L. & Looe.	Moorswater and Looe.
							CAUSEWAYEND—			
G	P					3 0	(Station)	Stirling ...	N. B.	Blackston and Bo'ness.
G						. .	Basin	Stirling ...	N. B.	Near Causewayend.
						. .	Incline Top Siding	Stirling ...	N. B.	Bowhouse and Causewayend.
						. .	Junction	Stirling ...	N. B.	Bowhouse and Almond Junction.
						. .	Linlithgow Foundry	Stirling ...	N. B.	Near Causewayend.
						. .	Causewayend Siding	Lanark ...	Cal.	Biggar.
						. .	Causewayend Siding	Wigtown..	P.P. & W. Jt. (Cal., G & SW, L. & N. W., & Mid.)	Newton Stewart and Wigtown.
G	P	F	L	H	C	3 0	Causewayhead	Clackman'	N. B.	Stirling and Alloa.
G	P	F	L	H	C	3 0 }	Cavan Station and Junction	Cavan	{ G. N. (I.)	Branch from Clones.
G	P	F	L	H	C	1 5 }			{ M. G. W.	Branch from Inny Junction.
G	P	F	L	H	C	. .	Cavendish	Suffolk ...	G. E.	Haverhill and Sudbury.
						. .	Caville Bridge Siding	Yorks	N. E.	Eastrington.
						. .	Cawburn Siding (Constable's Limestone Quarries)	L'lithgow	N.B.	Drumshoreland.
						. .	Cawdor (New) Colliery	Carmarth'	G. W.	Same as Cwmtrupit (Garnant).
						. .	Cawdor (Old) Colliery	Carmarth'	G. W.	Garnant.
						. .	Cawdor Sidings	Derby	Mid.	Matlock Bridge.
						. .	Cawdron Siding	Cornwall ..	G. W.	Launceston.
G	P	.	L	H	C	. .	Cawood	Yorks	N. E.	Branch from Selby.
						. .	South Lane Siding	Yorks	N. E.	Cawood.
G	P	F	L	H	C	. .	Cawston	Norfolk ...	G. E.	Wroxham and County School.
						. .	Cawthorne Basin Siding	Yorks	L. & Y.	Darton.
G	P	F	L	H	C	5 0	Caythorpe	Lincoln ...	G. N.	Grantham and Lincoln.
						. .	Burke's Siding	Lincoln ...	G. N.	Caythorpe and Leadenham.
						. .	Carlton Iron Ore Co.'s Sid. (Attenborough's Siding)	Lincoln ...	G. N.	Caythorpe and Honington.

EXPLANATION—G *Goods Station.*   P *Passenger and Parcel Station.*   P* *Passenger, but not Parcel or Miscellaneous Traffic.*
F *Furniture Vans, Carriages, Portable Engines, and Machines on Wheels.*   L *Live Stock.*
H *Horse Boxes and Prize Cattle Vans.*   C *Carriages by Passenger Train.*

STATION ACCOMMODATION.						CRANE POWER.	STATIONS, &c.	COUNTY.	COMPANY.	POSITION.
						Tons Cwts.	Caythorpe—continued.			
.	.	.	.	.	.	. .	Fulbeck Sidings...............	Lincoln ...	G. N.	Caythorpe and Leadenham.
							Caythorpe Ironstone			
.	.	.	.	.	.	. .	Mines...............	Lincoln ...	G. N.	Fulbeck Sidings.
.	.	.	.	.	.	. .	Yorkshire Iron & Coal Co.	Lincoln ...	G. N.	Fulbeck Sidings.
.	P	.	.	.	.	. .	Cayton	Yorks ...	N. E.	Seamer and Hull.
G	P	F	L	H	.	2 0	Cefn	Brecon ...	B. & M. & L. & N. W. Joint	Abergavenny and Merthyr.
							Crawshay Brothers—			
.	.	.	.	.	.	. .	Cy-farth-fa Works........	Glamorg'n	B. & M. & L. & N. W. Joint	Cefn and Merthyr.
.	.	.	.	.	.	. .	Llwyncelyn Siding	Glamorg'n	B. & M. & L. & N. W. Joint	Cefn and Merthyr.
.	.	.	.	.	.	. .	Vaynor Limestone Quarry	Glamorg'n	B. & M. & L. & N. W. Joint	Cefn and Pontsarn.
.	.	.	.	.	.	. .	Ynysfach Siding............	Glamorg'n	B. & M. & L. & N. W. Joint	Cefn and Merthyr.
G	P	.	.	.	.	. .	Cefn	Denbigh...	G. W.	Ruabon and Chirk.
							Dennis Siding (Cefn Quarry			
.	.	.	.	.	.	. .	Siding)	Denbigh...	G. W.	Cefn.
.	.	.	.	.	.	. .	Cefn Brithdir Colliery	Glamorg'n	Rhy.	Brithdir.
.	.	.	.	.	.	. .	Cefn Colliery	Glamorg'n	P. T.	Bryndu.
.	.	.	.	.	.	. .	Cefn Cribbwr Brick Siding..	Glamorg'n	G. W.	Kenfig Hill.
.	.	.	.	.	.	. .	Cefngyfelach Colliery	Glamorg'n	G. W.	Same as Tirdonkin Col. Co. (Landore)
.	.	.	.	.	.	. .	Cefn Junction	Glamorg'n	G. W.—P. T.	Tondu and Port Talbot.
.	.	.	.	.	.	. .	Cefn Mawr Siding..............	Glamorg'n	G. W.	Resolven.
.	.	.	.	.	.	. .	Cefn Merthyr Siding	Glamorg'n	B. & M. & L. & N. W. Joint	Same as Merthyr T. V. Junction.
.	.	.	.	.	.	. .	Cefn Quarry Siding	Denbigh...	G. W.	Same as Dennis Siding (Cefn).
G	P	F	L	H	C	1 10	Cefn-y-bedd (W. M. & C. Q.)..	Flint	{ W. M. & C. Q.	Wrexham and Buckley.
									G. C.	Over W. M. & C. Q. from Hawarden Bridge Junction.
.	.	.	.	.	.	. .	Llay Hall Col. & Brick Wks.	Flint	W. M. & C. Q.	Caergwrle Castle and Cefn-y-bedd.
.	.	.	.	.	.	. .	Cefn-y-coed Colliery	Flint	L. & N. W.	Coed Talon.
.	.	.	.	.	.	. .	Celbridge	Kildare ...	G. S. & W.	See Hazlehatch and Celbridge.
.	.	.	.	.	.	. .	Celluloid Siding	Glamorg'n	P. T.	Port Talbot (Central).
.	.	.	.	.	.	. .	Celtic Park	Lanark ...	Cal.	See Glasgow, Parkhead (for Celtic Pk.)
.	.	.	.	.	.	. .	Celynen Colliery	Mon	G. W.	Abercarn.
.	.	.	.	.	.	. .	Celyn Wood Colliery	Flint	L. & N. W.	See Phœnix Coal and Cannel Co. (Coed Talon).
.	.	.	.	.	.	. .	Cemetery Hill Siding	Lancs	L. & Y.	Wilpshire.
.	.	.	.	.	.	. .	Cemetery Siding................	Glamorg'n	Rhy.	Same as Fairoak Rd. Sid. (Cardiff).
G	P	F	L	H	C	1 0 }	Cemmes........................	Montgom	Mawddwy	Cemmes Road and Mawddwy.
G							Cemmes Road	Montgom	{ Cam.	Newtown and Machynlleth.
									Mawddwy	Adjoining Cambrian Station.
.	.	.	.	.	.	. .	Central (L. & I. D.)	Essex	L. & I. Dks.—G. E.	See London.
.	.	.	.	.	.	. .	Central Dry Dock	Glamorg'n	GW—LNW—Mid—RSB	Swansea.
							Central Electric Lighting Co.'s			
.	.	.	.	.	.	. .	Siding	Middlesex	G. C.	London, Marylebone.
.	.	.	.	.	.	. .	Central London Railway Sid.	Middlesex	G. W.—L. & N. W.	London, Shepherd's Bush.
.	.	.	.	.	.	. .	Central Treviscoe Siding	Cornwall..	G. W.	Drinnick Mill.
G	.	.	.	.	.	. .	Ceryst	Montgom	Cam. (Van.)	Caersws and Garth.
G	P	F	L	H	C	5 0	Cerney and Ashton Keynes...	Wilts	M. & S. W. Jn.	Swindon Town and Cirencester.
.	.	.	.	.	.	. .	Cessnock	Lanark ...	Glas. Dist. Sub.	See Glasgow.
.	.	.	.	.	.	. .	Cestrian Brick Works	Cheshire...	G. W.	Saltney.
.	.	.	.	.	.	. .	Cethin Pit........................	Glamorg'n	G. W. & Rhy. Jt.	Same as Gethin Pit (Abercanaid).
G	P	.	L	.	.	2 0	Chacewater	Cornwall..	G. W.	Truro and Redruth.
.	.	.	.	.	.	. .	Chaddesden Sidings (Mid.)...	Derby......	Mid.—N. S.	Derby.
G	P	.	.	.	.	. .	Chadwell Heath	Essex	G. E.	Ilford and Romford.
.	.	.	.	.	.	. .	Chadwick's Siding	Lancs	L. & Y.	Liverpool, Great Howard Street.
.	.	.	.	.	.	. .	Chaffer's Siding	Lancs	L. & Y.	Nelson.
.	.	.	.	.	.	. .	Chailey	Sussex ...	L. B. & S. C.	See Newick and Chailey.
							Chain Belt Engineering Co.'s			
.	.	.	.	.	.	. .	Siding	Derby......	L. & N. W.	Derby.
G	P	.	.	.	.	. .	Chalder..........................	Sussex ...	Selsey	Chichester and Selsey.
G	P	.	L	H	.	. . }	Chalfont Road (Met.)	Bucks	{ Met.	Rickmansworth and Aylesbury.
.	P	.	.	H	.	. .			G. C.	Over Met. Line.
.	P	.	.	H	.	. .	Chalfont Road Junction	Bucks	Met.	Chalfont Road and Amersham.
G	P	F	L	H	C	6 0	Chalford	Glo'ster ...	G. W.	Gloucester and Swindon.
.	.	.	.	.	.	. .	Chalk Farm.......................	Middlesex	L. & N. W.—N. L.	See London.
.	.	.	.	.	.	. .	Chalk Farm Junction	Middlesex	L. & N. W.—N. L.	London, Camden.
.	.	.	.	.	.	. .	Chalk Lane Siding..............	Yorks	N. E.	See Hull.
.	.	.	.	.	.	. .	Challoch Junction	Wigtown...	G. & S. W.—P. P. & W.	New Luce and Dunragit.
G	P	F	L	H	C	2 0	Challow..........................	Berks	G. W.	Didcot and Swindon.
.	.	.	.	.	.	. .	Chalmers & Co.'s Siding	Edinboro'	N. B.	Leith, Bonnington.
.	.	.	.	.	.	. .	Chaloner Mines	Yorks	N. E.	Guisboro'.
.	.	.	.	.	.	. .	Chamber Colliery	Lancs	L. & Y.	Same as Incline Sid. (Middleton Jn.)
.	.	.	.	.	.	. .	Chamber's Siding	Kent	S. E. & C.	Faversham.

EXPLANATION—G *Goods Station.*   P *Passenger and Parcel Station.*   P* *Passenger, but not Parcel or Miscellaneous Traffic.*
F *Furniture Vans, Carriages, Portable Engines, and Machines on Wheels.*   L *Live Stock.*
H *Horse Boxes and Prize Cattle Vans.*   C *Carriages by Passenger Train.*

STATION ACCOMMODATION.						CRANE POWER.		STATIONS, &c.	COUNTY.	COMPANY.	POSITION.
						Tons	Cwts.				
.	.	.	.	.	.	.	.	Chamber's Siding	Kent	S. E. & C.	Southfleet.
.	.	.	.	.	.	.	.	Champfleurie Siding (Linlithgow Oil Works Siding) ...	L'lithgow	N. B.	Linlithgow.
.	.	.	.	.	.	.	.	Chance & Hunt's Works	Worcester	G. W.	Oldbury.
.	.	.	.	.	.	.	.	Chance & Hunt's Works (GW)	Staffs	G. W.—L. & N. W.	Wednesbury.
.	.	.	.	.	.	.	.	Chance Bros. & Co.'s Siding	Staffs	L. & N. W.	Spon Lane.
.	.	.	.	.	.	.	.	Chancelot Mill Siding	Edinboro'	Cal.—N. B.	Leith, Bonnington.
.	.	.	.	.	.	.	.	Chancery Lane	Middlesex	C. L.	See London.
G	P	.	L	H	C	.	.	Chandlers Ford	Hants	L. & S.W.	Eastleigh and Romsey.
.:	.	.	.	.	.	.	.	Chandlers Ford Brickfield Siding	Hants	L. & S.W	Chandlers Ford.
.	.	.	.	.	.	.	.	Chanter's Colliery	Lancs	L. & N. W.	See Fletcher, Burrows&Co.(Atherton)
G	P	.	L	.	.	.	.	Chapel	Wexford...	D. W. & W.	Macmine Junction and New Ross.
.	.	.	.	.	.	.	.	Chapel Colliery	Lanark ...	Cal.—N. B.	Morningside.
.	.	.	.	.	.	.	.	Chapel End Sidings (Mid.) ...	Warwick..	Mid.—L. & N. W.	Stockingford.
G	P	F	L	H	C	1	10	Chapel-en-le-Frith	Derby	{ L. & N. W.	Buxton and Stockport.
G	P	F	L	H	C	1	10			{ Mid.	Bakewell and New Mills.
G	P	.	L	H	.	3	0	Chapelhall	Lanark ...	Cal.	Whifflet, High Level & Newhouse.
.	.	.	.	.	.	.	.	Chapelhall Colliery	Lanark ...	Cal.	Calderbank and Chapelhall.
.	.	.	.	.	.	.	.	Lauchope Colliery	Lanark ...	Cal.	Chapelhall and Newhouse.
.	.	.	.	.	.	.	.	Chapel Hill Siding..............	Lancs	P.&L.Jt.(L&NW.&L&Y)	Longridge.
.	.	.	.	.	.	.	.	Kay's................	Lancs	P.&L.Jt.(L&NW.&L&Y)	Chapel Hill Siding.
.	.	.	.	.	.	.	.	Seed & Wallbank's	Lancs	P.&L.Jt.(L&NW.&L&Y)	Chapel Hill Siding.
.	.	.	.	.	.	.	.	Sharple's	Lancs	P.&L.Jt.(L&NW.&L&Y)	Chapel Hill Siding.
.	.	.	.	.	.	.	.	Chapel House Col. (L. & Y.)	Lancs	L. & Y.—L. & N. W. ...	Skelmersdale.
.	.	.	.	.	.	.	.	Chapel New Colliery............	Lanark ...	Cal.	Morningside.
.	.	.	.	.	.	.	.	Chapelside Boiler Works......	Lanark ...	N. B.	Airdrie, North.
.	.	.	.	.	.	.	.	Chapelside Foundry	Lanark ...	N. B.	Airdrie, North.
.	.	.	.	.	.	.	.	Chapel Siding................	Hants	L. & S.W.	Southampton.
.	.	.	.	.	.	.	.	Chapel Siding................	Lanark ...	Cal.	Same as Kirkhill Colliery & Brick Works (Cambuslang).
.	.	.	.	.	.	.	.	Chapel Street	Lancs	L. & Y.	See Southport.
.	.	.	.	.	.	.	.	Chapel Street Mineral Sids...	Renfrew...	Cal.	See Greenock.
G	P	.	.	.	.	.	.	Chapelton	Devon ...	L. & S.W.	Exeter and Barnstaple.
G	P	F	L	H	C	1	10	Chapeltown	Yorks	Mid.	Branch—Brightside and Barnsley.
.	.	.	.	.	.	.	.	Newton, Chambers & Co.— Chapeltown Iron Works.	Yorks	Mid.	Branch from Chapeltown Station.
.	.	.	.	.	.	.	.	Parkgate Oil Works	Yorks	Mid.	Branch from Chapeltown Station.
.	.	.	.	.	.	.	.	Thorncliffe Collieries & Coke Ovens	Yorks	Mid.	Branch from Chapeltown Station.
.	.	.	.	.	.	.	.	Thorncliffe Furnaces	Yorks	Mid.	Branch from Chapeltown Station.
.	.	.	.	.	.	.	.	Thorncliffe Iron Works.....	Yorks	Mid.	Branch from Chapeltown Station.
.	.	.	.	.	.	.	.	Westwood Coke Ovens ...	Yorks	Mid.	Branch from Chapeltown Station.
G	P	F	L	H	C	1	0	Chapeltown & Thorncliffe	Yorks	G. C.	Sheffield and Barnsley.
.	.	.	.	.	.	.	.	Newton, Chambers & Co.— Thorncliffe Colliery	Yorks	G. C.	Chapeltown and Thorncliffe.
.	.	.	.	.	.	.	.	Thorncliffe Siding	Yorks	G. C.	Chapeltown and Thorncliffe.
.	.	.	.	.	.	.	.	Chapeltown Iron Works	Yorks	Mid.	See Newton, Chambers & Co. (Chapeltown).
.	.	.	.	.	.	.	.	Chapman's Public Wharf......	Lancs	S. & M. Jt. (G. C. & Mid.)	Widnes.
.	.	.	.	.	.	.	.	Chapman's Siding	Durham ...	N. E.	See Aycliffe Lime Works.
.	.	.	.	.	.	.	.	Chapman's Siding	Lancs	L. & N. W.	Widnes.
.	.	.	.	.	.	.	.	Chapman's Steam Bakery ...	Lancs	N. E.	Millfield.
.	.	.	.	.	.	.	.	Chapman's Victoria Str. Sid.	Lancs	L. & N. W.—S. & M. Jt.	Widnes.
G	P	F	L	H	C	1	10	Chappel (G. E.)	Essex	{ G. E.	Sudbury and Marks Tey.
.	.	.	.	.	.	.	.			{ C. V. & H.	Over G. E. from Chappel Junction.
.	.	.	.	.	.	.	.	Chappel Junction	Essex	C. V. & H.—G. E.	Colne and Marks Tey.
								CHARD—			
G	P	F	L	H	C	4	0	Joint Station and Junction	Somerset..	{ G. W.	Branch from Taunton.
.	P	.	.	.	.	.	.			{ L. & S. W.................	Branch from Chard Junc. Station.
G	P	F	L	H	C	2	0	Junction Station	Somerset..	L. & S. W.	Yeovil Junction and Exeter.
G	P	F	L	H	C	5	0	Town	Somerset..	L. & S.W.	Branch from Chard Junc. Station.
G	P	F	L	H	C	10	0	Charfield	Glo'ster...	Mid.	Gloucester and Bristol.
.	.	.	.	.	.	.	.	Huntingford Mills	Glo'ster...	Mid.	Berkeley Road and Charfield.
.	.	.	.	.	.	.	.	Bendall's	Glo'ster...	Mid.	Huntingford Mills.
.	.	.	.	.	.	.	.	Kimmin's & Co.	Glo'ster...	Mid.	Huntingford Mills.
G	P	F	L	H	C	5	0	Charing	Kent	S. E. & C.	Maidstone (East) and Ashford.
.	.	.	.	.	.	.	.	Charing Cross	Lanark ...	N. B.	See Glasgow.
.	.	.	.	.	.	.	.	Charing Cross	Middlesex	SE&C—Met Dist—L N W	See London.
.	.	.	.	.	.	.	.	Charing Cross Electrical Supply Association Siding.	Middlesex	G. E.	London, Devonshire Street.
.	.	.	.	.	.	.	.	Charity Colliery (L. & N.W.)	Warwick..	L. & N. W.—Mid.	See Stanley Bros. (Bedworth).

EXPLANATION—G *Goods Station.*   P *Passenger and Parcel Station.*   P* *Passenger, but not Parcel or Miscellaneous Traffic.*
F *Furniture Vans, Carriages, Portable Engines, and Machines on Wheels.*   L *Live Stock.*
H *Horse Boxes and Prize Cattle Vans.*   C *Carriages by Passenger Train.*

STATION ACCOMMODATION.						CRANE POWER.	STATIONS, &c.	COUNTY.	COMPANY.	POSITION.
						Tons Cwts.				
							Charlaw Colliery & Brick Wks.	Durham ...	N. E.	Pelton.
							Charlaw Shield Row Drift ...	Durham ...	N. E.	Pelton.
							Charlaw Shield Row Pit	Durham ...	N. E.	Pelton.
G	P	F	L	H	C	1 10	Charlbury......	Oxon	G. W.	Oxford and Evesham.
							Charles Siding............	Staffs	L. & N. W	Darlaston.
							Charles Street..................	Lancs	L. & N. W.	Same as Manchester, Liverpool Road and Salford.
							Charles Street..................	Lancs	L. & N. W.	See Preston.
							Charles Street Depôts	Yorks	N. E.	Middlesbro'.
G	P	F	L	H	C	1 10	Charlestown...................	Fife	N. B.	Branch from Dunfermline, Lower.
							Charlestown Foundry	Fife	N. B.	Dunfermline (Lower) & Charlestown.
G						5 0	Charlestown Harbour	Fife	N. B.	Charlestown.
							Charlestown Lime Works..	Fife	N. B.	Near Charlestown.
							Charlestown Salt Works ...	Fife	N. B.	Near Charlestown.
G							Merryhill	Fife	N. B.	Dunfermline (Lower) & Charlestown.
							Charlestown Junction	Fife	N. B.	Dunfermline.
G	P	F	L	H	C	3 0	Charlestown...................	Mayo	G. S. & W.	Collooney and Claremorris.
							Charlestown (L. & Y.)	Lancs	L. & Y.— L. & N. W. ...	See Ashton-under-Lyne.
							Charlestown Brk. & Tile Wks.	Yorks	H & O Jt (G N & L & Y)	Halifax, North Bridge.
							Charlesworth's, J. & J.—			
							Beeston Colliery Siding ...	Yorks	Mid.	Woodlesford.
							Collieries	Yorks	Mid.	Rothwell Haigh.
							Kilnhurst Colliery	Yorks	Mid.	Kilnhurst.
							Thrybergh Hall Colliery ...	Yorks	Mid.	Kilnhurst.
							Victoria Colliery............	Yorks	Mid.	Kilnhurst.
G	P	F	L	H	C		Charleville	Cork	G. S. & W.	Mallow and Limerick Junction.
							Charlie Pit	Durham	N. E.	See South Moor Collieries and Brick Works (Annfield Plain).
							Charlotte Street Junction ...	Surrey	S. E. & C.	London, Blackfriars Junction and Borough Road.
	P						Charlton	Kent	S. E. & C.	London Bridge and Woolwich.
							Beadle Bros.' Siding	Kent	S. E. & C.	Charlton.
							Charlton & Wylie's Siding ...	Dumfries..	Cal.	Dumfries.
G	P			H			Charlton Kings (G. W.)	Glo'ster	{ G. W. / M. & S. W. Jn.	Bourton and Cheltenham. Over G. W. from Andoversford Jn.
							Charlton Lias Lime Works ...	Somerset..	S.&D. Jt. (L.&S.W.& Mid)	Shepton Mallet.
							Charlton Pit.................	Lancs	L. & N. W.	See Earl of Ellesmere's (Plodder Lane).
							Charlton Siding	Worcester	G. W.	Fladbury.
							Charlton Works (Mid.).......	Yorks	Mid.—G. C.	Same as Ward's Grimesthorpe Sids.
							Charnwood Granite Co.'s Sid.	Leicester..	L. & N. W.	Shepshed.
							Charrington&Co.'sSids.(Mid.)	Staffs	Mid—L N W—G N—N S	Burton-on-Trent.
G	P					1 10	Chartham...................	Kent	S. E. & C.	Ashford and Canterbury (West).
							Ballast Siding...............	Kent	S. E. & C.	Chilham and Chartham.
							Chartham Siding	Kent	S. E. & C.	Canterbury, East.
G	P		L	H			Chartley & Stowe	Staffs	G. N.	Stafford and Burton.
							Chart Siding	Kent	S. E. & C.	Ashford.
G	P	F	L	H	C		Charwelton	N'hampton	G. C.	Rugby and Brackley.
G	P	F	L	H	C	6 0	Chatburn	Lancs	L. & Y.	Blackburn and Hellifield.
							Bold Venture Lime Siding	Lancs	L. & Y.	Chatburn and Clitheroe.
							CHATHAM—			
	P			H			Central	Kent	S. E. & C.	Branch from Strood.
G						15 0	Dockyard...................	Kent	S. E. & C.	Branch — New Brompton and Rainham.
G	P	F	L	H	C	10 0	Station	Kent	S. E. & C.	Strood and Sittingbourne.
G	P	F	L	H	C	4 0	Chathill	Northumb	N. E.	Morpeth and Berwick.
							Chathill Junction	Northumb	N. E.	Chathill.
							Chatsworth Wagon Works (Hurst, Nelson & Co.'s Sid.)	Derby	Mid.	Sheepbridge and Whittington Moor.
G	P	F	L	H	C	10 0	Chatteris	Cambs	G. N. & G. E. Jt.	St. Ives and March.
G						1 0	Chatteris Dock	Cambs	G. N. & G. E. Jt.	Wimblington and Chatteris.
G	P						Chatterley	Staffs	N. S.	Harecastle and Longport.
							Bradwell Sidings (N. S.)...	Staffs	N. S.—L. & N. W.	Chatterley.
							Chatterley-Whitfield Col. Siding (N.S.)	Staffs	N. S.—L. & N. W.	Chatterley.
							Goldendale Iron Co.—			
							Ravensdale Siding	Staffs	N. S.	Chatterley.
							Yeld Hill Siding	Staffs	N. S.	Chatterley.
							Hardman's Chemical Works	Staffs	N. S.	Chatterley.
							Peake's Brick & Tile Works	Staffs	N. S.	Chatterley.
							Ravensdale Iron Works (Heath & Sons)	Staffs	N. S.	Chatterley.

EXPLANATION—G *Goods Station.*   P *Passenger and Parcel Station.*   P* *Passenger, but not Parcel or Miscellaneous Traffic.*
F *Furniture Vans, Carriages, Portable Engines, and Machines on Wheels.*   L *Live Stock.*
H *Horse Boxes and Prize Cattle Vans.*   C *Carriages by Passenger Train.*

STATION ACCOMMODATION.						CRANE POWER.		STATIONS, &c.	COUNTY.	COMPANY.	POSITION.
						Tons	Cwts.	Chatterley—*continued.*			
.	.	.	.	.	.	.	.	Staffordshire Chemical Co.'s Siding	Staffs	N. S.	Chatterley.
.	.	.	.	.	.	.	.	Timmis' Brick Wks.	Staffs	N. S.	Chatterley.
								Chatterley-Whitfield Cols.—			
.	.	.	.	.	.	.	.	Chell Sidings	Staffs	N. S.	Black Bull.
.	.	.	.	.	.	.	.	Mossfield Colliery	Staffs	N. S.	Adderley Green.
.	.	.	.	.	.	.	.	Siding	Staffs	N. S.	Tunstall.
.	.	.	.	.	.	.	.	Siding (N.S.)	Staffs	N. S.—L. & N. W.	Chatterley.
.	.	.	.	.	.	.	.	Ubberley Colliery	Staffs	N. S.	Adderley Green.
.	.	.	.	.	.	.	.	Chatterton Mine..................	Lincoln ...	G. C.	Frodingham and Scunthorpe.
.	.	.	.	.	.	.	.	Chatterton's Siding.........	Yorks	L. & N. W.	Greenfield.
G	P	F	L	H	C	5	0 }	Cheadle..........................	Cheshire...	C L C (G C, G N, & Mid.)	Stockport and Northenden.
G	P	F	L	H	C	5	0 }		Cheshire...	L. & N. W.	Stockport and Warrington.
.	.	.	.	.	.	.	.	Barnes Siding	Cheshire...	L. & N. W.	Cheadle and Northenden.
.	.	.	.	.	.	.	.	Mosley's Bleach Works ...	Cheshire...	L. & N. W.	Cheadle and Northenden.
G	P	.	.	H	C	.	.	Cheadle..........................	Staffs	N. S. (Cheadle)	Branch from Cresswell.
.	.	.	.	.	.	.	.	Draycott Colliery	Staffs	N. S. (Cheadle)	Cheadle.
G	P	F	L	H	C	10	0	Cheadle Heath	Cheshire...	Mid.	New Mills and Heaton Mersey.
.	.	.	.	.	.	.	.	Stockport Sewage Works...	Cheshire...	Mid.	Cheadle Heath and Heaton Mersey.
G	P	.	L	H	.	.	.	Cheadle Hulme	Cheshire...	L. & N. W.	Crewe and Stockport.
.	.	.	.	.	.	.	.	Lord Vernon's Cl. Wharves	Cheshire...	L. & N. W.	Cheadle Hulme and Bramhall.
.	.	.	.	.	.	.	.	Cheadle Junction	Cheshire...	C. L. C.—Mid.	Cheadle and Cheadle Heath.
G	P	.	.	.	.	.	.	Cheam	Surrey ...	L. B. & S. C.	Epsom and Sutton.
G	P	.	L	H	.	.	.	Checker House	Notts	G. C.	Worksop and Retford.
.	.	.	.	.	.	.	.	Morton Brick Works	Notts	G. C.	Checker House.
								Checkland, Son, & Williams' Donisthorpe Colliery.........	Leicester..	A & N Jt.(L & N W & Mid.)	Donisthorpe.
G	P	F	L	H	C	3	0	Cheddar	Somerset..	G. W.	Yatton and Wells.
G	P	F	L	H	C	.	.	Cheddington	Bucks	L. & N. W.	Bletchley and Watford.
G	P	.	.	H	.	5	0	Cheddleton	Staffs	N. S.	Leek and Uttoxeter.
.	P	.	.	.	.	.	.	Chedworth	Glo'ster ...	M. & S. W. Jn.	Cirencester and Cheltenham.
.	.	.	.	.	.	.	.	Cheesewring Quarries	Cornwall...	L. & Looe.	Terminus.
.	.	.	.	.	.	.	.	Cheetham's Siding............	Lancs	L. & Y.	Middleton Junction Station.
G	P	.	.	.	.	.	.	Chelfham	Devon	Lyn. & Barns.	Barnstaple and Lynton.
G	P	F	L	H	C	0	10	Chelford	Cheshire...	L. & N. W.	Crewe and Stockport.
G	P	.	L	H	.	.	.	Chellaston and Swarkestone..	Derby	Mid.	Derby and Worthington.
								Chell Sidings—			
.	.	.	.	.	.	.	.	Chatterley - Whitfield Collieries....................	Staffs	N. S.	Black Bull.
.	.	.	.	.	.	.	.	Tunstall Coal & Ir.Co.'s Sid.	Staffs	N. S.	Black Bull.
G	P	F	L	H	C	10	0	Chelmsford	Essex	G. E.	London and Colchester.
.	.	.	.	.	.	.	.	Crompton & Co.'s Siding ...	Essex	G. E.	Chelmsford and Ingatestone.
.	.	.	.	.	.	.	.	Gray's, C. H., Siding	Essex	G. E.	Chelmsford.
.	.	.	.	.	.	.	.	Hoffman Manufacturing Co.'s Siding	Essex	G. E.	Chelmsford.
.	.	.	.	.	.	.	.	Marriage, W. H., & Son's Sid	Essex	G. E.	Chelmsford.
.	.	.	.	.	.	.	.	Chelsea and Fulham	Middlesex	W. L. E. Jt.(G W, L & N W, L. & S W, & L. B. & S.C.)	See London.
.	.	.	.	.	.	.	.	Chelsea Basin	Middlesex	G. W.—L. & N.W.........	See London.
G	P	F	L	H	C	.	.	Chelsfield	Kent	S. E. & C.	Chislehurst & Sevenoaks (Tubs Hill).
								CHELTENHAM—			
G	P	F	L	H	C	8	0	(Station)—	Glo'ster ...	G. W.	Branch from Lansdown Junction.
.	.	.	.	.	.	.	.	Alstone Coal Wharf	Glo'ster ...	Mid.	Cheltenham.
.	.	.	.	.	.	.	.	Corporation Siding	Glo'ster ...	G. W.	Cheltenham.
.	.	.	.	.	.	.	.	Gas Works	Glo'ster ...	Mid.	Adjoining High Street Station.
G	P	F	L	.	.	10	0	High Street (Mid.)............	Glo'ster ...	Mid. / M. & S. W. Jn.	Birmingham and Bristol. / Over G. W. and Mid. Lines.
.	P	.	.	H	C	.	.	Lansdown (Mid.)	Glo'ster ...	Mid. / M. & S. W. Jn.	Birmingham and Bristol. / Over G. W. and Mid. Lines.
.	.	.	.	.	.	.	.	Lansdown Junction	Glo'ster ...	G. W.	Cheltenham.
.	.	.	.	.	.	.	.	New Street Coal Yard	Glo'ster ...	G. W.	Cheltenham.
.	.	.	.	.	.	.	.	Shillingford Engineering Wks.(TrustyEngineWks)	Glo'ster ...	Mid.	Near High Street Station.
.	.	.	.	.	.	.	.	Tewkesbury Road Bridge Coal Wharf	Glo'ster ...	Mid.	Cheltenham.
.	.	.	.	.	.	.	.	Webb Bros.' Siding	Glo'ster ...	Mid.	Cheltenham.
.	.	.	.	.	.	.	.	Williams, J., & Co.'s Sid.	Glo'ster ...	Mid.	Cheltenham.
.	.	.	.	.	.	.	.	Chemical Manufacturing Co.'s Siding	Lancs	L. & N. W.—S. & M. Jt.	Widnes.
G	P	F	L	H	C	10	0	Chepstow	Mon	G. W.	Gloucester and Newport.
.	.	.	.	.	.	.	.	Finch's Works and Siding	Mon	G. W.	Chepstow.

EXPLANATION—G *Goods Station.*   P *Passenger and Parcel Station.*   P* *Passenger, but not Parcel or Miscellaneous Traffic.*
F *Furniture Vans, Carriages, Portable Engines, and Machines on Wheels.*   L *Live Stock.*
H *Horse Boxes and Prize Cattle Vans.*   C *Carriages by Passenger Train.*

STATION ACCOMMODATION.						CRANE POWER.		STATIONS, &c.	COUNTY.	COMPANY.	POSITION.
						Tons	Cwts.				
G	P	.	L	H	C	.	.	Chequerbent (for Hulton Park)	Lancs	L. & N. W.	Bolton and Kenyon Junc. Station.
								Hulton Colliery Co.—			
.	.	.	.	.	.	.	.	Atherton Colliery No. 1	Lancs	L. & N. W.	Chequerbent and Rumworth.
.	.	.	.	.	.	.	.	Atherton Colliery No. 2 Pretoria or New Pit Chequerbent Bank Sid	Lancs	L. & N. W.	Atherton and Chequerbent.
.	.	.	.	.	.	.	.	Deep Arley Pit	Lancs	L. & N. W.	Chequerbent and Rumworth.
.	.	.	.	.	.	.	.	Pendlebury Fold Bk. Wks.	Lancs	L. & N. W.	Chequerbent and Rumworth.
.	.	.	.	.	.	.	.	Reserve or Chequerbent Pits	Lancs	L. & N. W.	Chequerbent and Rumworth.
.	.	.	.	.	.	.	.	School Pit	Lancs	L. & N. W.	Chequerbent and Rumworth.
.	.	.	.	.	.	.	.	Workshops	Lancs	L. & N. W.	Chequerbent and Rumworth.
.	.	.	.	.	.	.	.	Chequerbent Bank Siding ...	Lancs	L. & N. W.	See Hulton Colliery Co.'s Atherton Colliery No. 2 (Chequerbent).
.	.	.	.	.	.	.	.	Chequerbent Pits	Lancs	L. & N. W.	See Hulton Col. Co.'s Reserve or Chequerbent Pits (Chequerbent).
G	P	F	L	H	C	2	0	Cheriton Junction	Kent	S. E. & C.	Sandling Junction and Shorncliffe.
.	.	.	.	.	.	.	.	Cherry Burton	Yorks	N. E.	Market Weighton and Beverley.
.	.	.	.	.	.	.	.	Cherryhinton Siding	Cambridge	G. E.	See Fulbourne.
G	P	.	.	.	.	5	0	Cherry Orchard Bk. Co.'s Sid.	Warwick..	L. & N. W.	Kenilworth.
.	P	.	.	.	.			Cherry Tree (L. & Y.)	Lancs	{ L. & Y. .... / L. & N. W.	{ Blackburn and Preston. / Over L. & Y. from Cherry Tree Jn.
.	.	.	.	.	.	.	.	Cherry Tree Junction	Lancs	L.&Y.—L.&Y.& L.U. Jt.	Cherry Tree and Boar's Head.
.	.	.	.	.	.	.	.	Cherry Tree Lane	Yorks	Mid.	See Doncaster.
G	P	F	L	H	C	5	0	Chertsey	Surrey ...	L. & S. W.	Weybridge and Virginia Water.
.	.	.	.	.	.	.	.	Chertsey Gas Co.'s Siding .	Surrey ...	L. & S. W.	Chertsey.
G	P	F	L	H	C	8	0	Chesham	Bucks ...	Met.	Branch from Chalfont Road.
.	.	.	.	.	.	.	.	Cheshire Creamery Co.'s Warehouse	Cheshire...	B'head Jt—CLC—NW&L	Birkenhead.
.	.	.	.	.	.	.	.	Cheshire Siding	Cheshire...	B'head Jt.(GW & L&NW)	Halton.
G	P	F	.	H	C	.	.	Cheshunt	Herts	G. E.	Waltham Cross & Bishops Stortford.
.	.	.	.	.	.	.	.	Cheslyn Hay Colliery	Staffs	L. & N. W.	Same as Hawkins & Son's (Wyrley and Church Bridge).
								CHESTER—			
G	.	F	L	.	.	10	0	(Station)	Cheshire...	G. W.	General Station and Mollington.
G	.	F	L	.	.	10	0	(Station)	Cheshire...	L. & N. W.	Crewe and Rhyl.
.	.	.	.	.	.	.	.	Birmingham Carriage and Wagon Co.'s Siding	Cheshire...	B'head Jt.(G W & L N W)	Chester.
.	.	.	.	.	.	.	.	Brook Lane Exchange Sid.	Cheshire...	G. W.—L. & N. W.	Chester.
.	.	.	.	.	.	.	.	East Junction	Cheshire...	C. L. C.—G. C.	Mickle Trafford and Liverpool Road.
.	P	.	.	H	C	.	.	General	Cheshire...	B'head Jt.(G W & L N W)	Crewe and Rhyl.
.	.	.	.	.	.	.	.	Gloucester Wagon Co.'s Siding	Cheshire...	B'head Jt.(G W & L N W)	Chester and Saltney Wharf.
G	P	.	.	.	.	5	0	Liverpool Road	Cheshire...	G. C.	Northgate and Blacon.
G	P	F	L	H	C	10	0	Northgate	Cheshire...	C.L.C. (G C, G N, & Mid.)	Terminus.
.	.	.	.	.	.	.	.	Percival & Co.'s Siding......	Cheshire...	B'head Jt (G W & L N W)	Chester and Saltney Wharf.
.	.	.	.	.	.	.	.	South Junction	Cheshire...	C. L. C.—G. C.	Northgate and Liverpool Road.
.	.	.	.	.	.	.	.	Walker, Parker & Co.'s Sid.	Cheshire...	B'head Jt (G W & L N W)	Chester and Waverton.
.	.	.	.	.	.	.	.	West Junction	Cheshire...	G. C.	Liverpool Road and Blacon.
.	.	.	.	.	.	.	.	Chester & Co.'s Siding	Renfrew...	G & P Jt (Cal. & G & S W)	Renfrew.
								CHESTERFIELD—			
G	P	F	L	H	C	10	0	(Station)	Derby	L. D. & E. C.	Terminus.
G	P	F	L	H	C	10	0	(Station)	Derby	Mid.	Derby and Sheffield.
G	P	F	L	H	C	10	0	(Station, G. C.)	Derby	{ G. C.	{ Sheffield and Nottingham.
G	.	F	L	.	.	10	0		Derby	{ L. & N. W.	{ Over G. N. and G. C. Lines.
G	.	.	.	.	.	.	.	Boythorpe Lane Wharf...	Derby	Mid.	Brampton Branch.
.	.	.	.	.	.	.	.	Brampton Colliery...........	Derby	Mid.	Brampton Branch.
G	.	.	.	.	.	2	0	Brampton Wharf............	Derby	Mid.	Brampton Branch.
.	.	.	.	.	.	.	.	Broad Oaks Siding (Markham & Co.)	Derby	Mid.	Near Chesterfield.
.	.	.	.	.	.	.	.	Bryan, Donkin & Clench's Siding	Derby	L. D. & E. C.	Chesterfield.
.	.	.	.	.	.	.	.	Chesterfield Brewery	Derby	G. C.	Chesterfield.
.	.	.	.	.	.	.	.	Chesterfield Corporation Siding (Electric Lighting Depôt)	Derby	Mid.	Brampton Branch.
.	.	.	.	.	.	.	.	Chesterfield Gas and Water Board Siding	Derby	Mid.	Brampton Branch.
.	.	.	.	.	.	.	.	Clayton's Tannery............	Derby	Mid.	Near Chesterfield.
.	.	.	.	.	.	.	.	Eastwood's Wagon Works	Derby	Mid.	Near Chesterfield.
.	.	.	.	.	.	.	.	Gibson, Thos., & Co.'s Siding	Derby	Mid.	Near Chesterfield.
.	.	.	.	.	.	.	.	Gothard & Son's Siding...	Derby	Mid.	Brampton Branch.

EXPLANATION—G *Goods Station.*   P *Passenger and Parcel Station.*   P* *Passenger, but not Parcel or Miscellaneous Traffic.*
F *Furniture Vans, Carriages, Portable Engines, and Machines on Wheels.*   L *Live Stock.*
H *Horse Boxes and Prize Cattle Vans.*   C *Carriages by Passenger Train.*

STATION ACCOMMODATION.						CRANE POWER.	STATIONS, &c.	COUNTY.	COMPANY.	POSITION.
						Tons Cwts.	CHESTERFIELD—continued.			
G	.	.	.	.	.	. .	Lordsmill Street Wharf...	Derby	Mid.	Near Chesterfield.
.	.	.	.	.	.	. .	Midland Co.'s Gas Works...	Derby	Mid.	Brampton Branch.
.	.	.	.	.	.	. .	Pearson's, J., London and Oldfield Potteries	Derby	Mid.	Brampton Branch.
.	.	.	.	.	.	. .	Saunder's Brick Works (Storforth Lane Siding)	Derby	Mid.	Near Chesterfield.
.	.	.	.	.	.	. .	Sewage Farm	Derby	G. C.	Chesterfield.
.	.	.	.	.	.	. .	Tadcaster Brewery Co.'s Siding	Derby	G. C.	Chesterfield.
.	.	.	.	.	.	. .	Townrow's, T., Siding	Derby	Mid.	Brampton Branch.
.	.	.	.	.	.	. .	Turner's, J., Siding	Derby	Mid.	Brampton Branch.
.	.	.	.	.	.	. .	Tyson & Bradley's Chemical Works	Derby	Mid.	Brampton Branch.
.	.	.	.	.	.	. .	Universal Weldless Steel Tubes Co.'s Siding	Derby	L. D. & E. C.	Chesterfield.
.	.	.	.	.	.	. .	Walton Colliery Co.'s Siding	Derby	Mid.	Brampton Branch.
G	P	F	L	H	C	5 0	Chester-le-Street	Durham	N. E.	Durham Pass. and Gateshead.
.	.	.	.	.	.	. .	Chester South Moor Colliery	Durham	N. E.	Chester-le-street.
G	P	.	.	.	.	. .	Chester Road	Warwick	L. & N. W.	Birmingham and Lichfield.
G	.	.	.	.	.	5 0	Chesterton	Staffs	N. S.	Branch from Chatterley.
.	.	.	.	.	.	. .	Chesterton Chemical Co.'s Siding	Staffs	N. S.	Chesterton.
.	.	.	.	.	.	. .	Hem Heath Sidings	Staffs	N. S.	Chesterton.
.	.	.	.	.	.	. .	Bradwell Hall Brick and Tile Works	Staffs	N. S.	Hem Heath Sidings.
.	.	.	.	.	.	. .	Hem Heath Mining Co...	Staffs	N. S.	Hem Heath Sidings.
.	.	.	.	.	.	. .	Metallic Tile Co.'s Siding	Staffs	N. S.	Chesterton.
.	.	.	.	.	.	. .	North Staffordshire Brick and Tile Co.'s Siding	Staffs	N. S.	Chesterton.
.	.	.	.	.	.	. .	Parkhouse Colliery	Staffs	N. S.	Chesterton.
.	.	.	.	.	.	. .	Rose Vale Brick & Tl. Wks	Staffs	N. S.	Chesterton.
G	P	.	L	.	.	. .	Chettisham	Cambs	G. E.	Ely and March.
G	P	.	L	H	C	. .	Chevington	Northumb	N. E.	Alnmouth and Morpeth.
.	.	.	.	.	.	. .	Amble Junction Siding	Northumb	N. E.	Acklington and Chevington.
.	.	.	.	.	.	. .	Chicago Raw Hide Co.	Cheshire	B'head Jt.—C. L. C.— N. W. & L.	See British & Chicago Raw Hide Co. (Birkenhead).
G	P	F	L	H	C	5 0	Chichester	Sussex	L. B. & S. C.	Havant and Ford Junction.
G	P	.	.	.	.	. .		Selsey		Terminus.
.	.	.	.	.	.	. .	Hall & Co.'s Siding	Sussex	L. B. & S. C.	Chichester.
.	P	.	.	.	.	. .	Chickenley Heath	Yorks	G. N.	Ossett and Batley.
.	.	.	.	.	.	. .	Chickenley Heath Colliery	Yorks	G. N.	Same as Earlsheaton Colliery (Earlsheaton).
.	.	.	.	.	.	. .	Chiddingfold	Surrey	L. & S. W.	See Witley and Chiddingfold.
.	P	.	.	.	.	. .	Chigwell	Essex	G. E.	Woodford and Ilford.
G	P	F	.	H	C	. .	Chigwell Lane	Essex	G. E.	Loughton and Ongar.
G	P	F	L	H	C	5 0	Chilcompton	Somerset	S. & D. Jt. (L.& S. W. & Mid)	Shepton Mallet and Radstock.
.	.	.	.	.	.	. .	New Rock Colliery	Somerset	S. & D. Jt. (L.& S. W. & Mid)	Chilcompton.
.	.	.	.	.	.	. .	Old Down Siding	Somerset	S. & D. Jt. (L.& S. W. & Mid)	Chilcompton and Binegar.
.	.	.	.	.	.	. .	Child & Sons Siding	Sussex	L. B. & S. C.	Slinfold.
G	P	.	.	.	.	. .	Childwall	Lancs	C. L. C. (GC, GN, & Mid.)	Halewood and West Derby.
G	P	F	L	H	C	4 0	Chilham	Kent	S. E. & C.	Ashford and Canterbury (West).
.	.	.	.	.	.	. .	Chilian Chemical Co's Sid (Mid)	Glamorg'n	Mid.—G. W.—L. & N. W.	Six Pit Junction.
.	.	.	.	.	.	. .	Chillington Co.'s Siding	Staffs	G. W.	Wolverhampton.
G	P	F	L	H	C	. .	Chiltern Green (for Luton Hoo)	Beds	Mid.	St. Albans and Luton.
.	.	.	.	.	.	. .	Chilton Branch Junction	Durham	N. E.	Ferryhill and Sedgefield.
.	.	.	.	.	.	. .	Chilton Buildings Siding	Durham	N. E.	Leasingthorne.
.	.	.	.	.	.	. .	Chilton Colliery	Durham	N. E.	Leasingthorne.
.	.	.	.	.	.	. .	Chilton Lime Works & Quarry	Durham	N. E.	Ferryhill.
.	.	.	.	.	.	. .	Chilton Moor Stores	Durham	N. E.	Fencehouses. Penshaw.
.	P	.	.	.	.	. .	Chilvers Coton	Warwick	L. & N. W.	Coventry and Nuneaton.
G	P	F	L	H	C	5 0	Chilworth and Albury	Surrey	S. E. & C.	Dorking and Guildford.
G	P	F	.	.	.	. .	Chingford	Essex	G. E.	Branch from Clapton.
G	P	F	L	H	C	1 10	Chinley	Derby	Mid.	Bakewell and New Mills.
G	P	F	L	H	C	1 0	Chinnor	Oxon	G. W.	Watlington and Princes Risborough.
G	P	F	L	H	C	7 0	Chippenham	Wilts	G. W.	Swindon and Bath.
.	.	.	.	.	.	. .	Bath Stone Firms	Wilts	G. W.	Chippenham.
.	.	.	.	.	.	. .	Saxby & Farmer	Wilts	G. W.	Chippenham.
.	.	.	.	.	.	. .	Wiltshire Bacon Curing Sid	Wilts	G. W.	Chippenham.
G	P	F	L	H	C	1 10	Chipping Norton	Oxon	G. W.	Chipping Norton Jn & Kings Sutton.
.	.	.	.	.	.	. .	Bliss & Son's Siding	Oxon	G. W.	Chipping Norton.

EXPLANATION—G *Goods Station.* P *Passenger and Parcel Station.* P* *Passenger, but not Parcel or Miscellaneous Traffic.*
F *Furniture Vans, Carriages, Portable Engines, and Machines on Wheels.* L *Live Stock.*
H *Horse Boxes and Prize Cattle Vans.* C *Carriages by Passenger Train.*

STATION ACCOMMODATION.						CRANE POWER.	STATIONS, &c.	COUNTY.	COMPANY.	POSITION.
						Tons Cwts.	*Chipping Norton—continued.*			
..	..	..	..	..	..	.. ..	Chipping Norton Gas Wks.	Oxon	G. W.	Chipping Norton.
..	..	..	..	..	..	.. ..	Sarsden Siding	Oxon	G. W.	Chipping Norton & Chipping Norton Junction.
G	P	F	L	H	C	5 0	Chipping Norton Junc. Sta.	Oxon	G. W.	Oxford and Evesham.
G	P	F	L	H	C	6 0	Chipping Sodbury	Glo'ster ...	G. W.	Wootton Bassett and Patchway.
G	P					.. ..	Chipstead & Banstead Downs	Surrey	S. E. & C.	Purley and Tattenham Corner.
G	P					2 0	Chirk	Denbigh ..	{ Glyn Valley .... { G. W.	Adjoining G. W. Station.
G	P	F	L	H	C	1 10				Gobowen and Ruabon.
..	..	..	..	..	..	.. ..	Black Park Colliery	Denbigh ..	G. W.	Chirk and Llangollen Road.
..	..	..	..	..	..	.. ..	Brynkinalt Colliery	Denbigh ..	G. W.	Chirk and Llangollen Road.
..	..	..	..	..	..	.. ..	Glyn Valley Junction	Denbigh ..	G. W.	Chirk.
..	..	..	..	..	..	.. ..	Chirk Castle Lime Works ...	Denbigh...	G. W.	Llangollen Road.
G	P	F	L	H	C	1 10	Chirnside	Berwick ...	N. B.	Reston and Duns.
..	..	..	..	..	..	.. ..	Chirnside Bridge Paper Mills	Berwick ...	N. B.	Near Chirnside.
..	..	..	..	..	..	.. ..	Chirton	Wilts	G. W.	See Patney and Chirton.
G	P	F	L	H	C	5 0	Chiseldon	Wilts	M. & S. W. Jn.	Swindon Town and Marlboro'.
..	..	..	..	..	..	.. ..	Chisholm & Co.'s Siding	Lanark ...	Cal.	Glasgow, Bridgeton.
G	P.	F	L	H	C	.. ..	Chislehurst	Kent	S. E. & C.	Hither Green and Sevenoaks (Tubs Hill).
..	..	..	..	..	..	.. ..	Chisnall Hall Colliery	Lancs	L. & N. W.	See Pearson & Knowles Coal & Iron Co.'s Coppull Hall Sid. (Coppull).
..	..	..	..	..	..	.. ..	Chiswick	Middlesex	{ N.& S.W. Jn. Jt(L&NW, { Mid., & N. L.)	} See London, Hammersmith and Chiswick.
G	P					.. ..	Chiswick and Grove Park ...	Middlesex	L. & S. W.	Barnes and Kew Bridge.
..	..	..	..	..	..	.. ..	Chiswick Junction..............	Middlesex	L. & S. W.	Kew Bridge and Gunnersbury.
..	..	..	..	..	..	.. ..	Chiswick Park & Acton Green	Middlesex	Met. Dist.	See London.
..	..	..	..	..	..	.. ..	Chloride Electric Syndicate Siding	Lancs	L. & Y.	Clifton Junction.
G	P	F	L	H	C	2 0	Chollerford	Northumb	N. B.	Reedsmouth and Hexham.
G	P	.	L	.	.	3 0	Chollerton	Northumb	N. B.	Reedsmouth and Hexham.
..	..	..	..	..	..	.. ..	Cocklaw Quarry	Northumb	N. B.	Chollerton and Chollerford.
G	P	F	L	H	C	6 0	Cholsey and Moulsford........	Berks	G. W.	Reading and Didcot.
..	..	..	..	..	..	.. ..	Chop Hill Colliery	Durham ...	N. E.	Beamish.
G	P	F	L	.	C	1 10	Choppington	Northumb	N. E.	Morpeth and Blyth.
..	..	..	..	..	..	.. ..	Choppington Colliery	Northumb	N. E.	Choppington.
..	..	..	..	..	..	.. ..	Foggo & Son's Brick Works	Northumb	N. E.	Choppington.
..	..	..	..	..	..	.. ..	Hogarth & Co.'s Brick Wks.	Northumb	N. E.	Choppington.
..	..	..	..	..	..	.. ..	Howard Pit	Northumb	N. E.	Choppington.
..	..	..	..	..	..	.. ..	Netherton Hall Colliery ...	Northumb	N. E.	Choppington.
..	..	..	..	..	..	.. ..	Scott's Brick Works	Northumb	N. E.	Choppington.
..	..	..	..	..	..	.. ..	Simpson's Brick Works ...	Northumb	N. E.	Choppington.
..	..	..	..	..	..	.. ..	Chopwell Col. & Coke Ovens	Durham ...	N. E.	Derwenthaugh.
..	..	..	..	..	..	.. ..	Chopwell Depôt	Durham ...	N. E.	Derwenthaugh.
							CHORLEY—			
G		F	L	.	.	5 0	(Station)	Lancs	L. & N. W.	Branch—Boar's Head & Blackburn.
G	P	F	L	H	C	10 0	(Station, L. & Y.)	Lancs	{ L. & Y.	Bolton and Preston.
.	P	.	.	H	C	.. ..			{ L. & N. W.	Over L. & Y. Line.
..	..	..	..	..	..	.. ..	Chorley Railway Wgn Co.'s Wks(Whittle's Sid)(L&Y)	Lancs	L. & Y.—L. & N. W. ...	Chorley.
..	..	..	..	..	..	.. ..	Junction	Lancs	L.&Y.—L.&Y.& L.U. Jt.	Chorley and Heapey.
..	..	..	..	..	..	.. ..	Ryland's Dacca Twist Co.'s Siding(L.& Y.& L. U. Jt.)	Lancs	L. & Y.	Chorley.
G	P					.. ..	Chorley Wood (Met.)............	Herts	{ Met.	Rickmansworth and Aylesbury.
.	P					.. ..			{ G. C.	Over Met. Line.
G	P	F	.	H	C	5 0	Chorlton-cum-Hardy............	Lancs	C. L. C.(G C, G N,& Mid.)	Manchester and Stockport.
..	..	..	..	..	..	.. ..	Chorlton-cum-Hardy Junction	Lancs	C. L. C.—G. C.—Mid.	Manchester and Stockport.
..	..	..	..	..	..	.. ..	Chowbent West Junction Sid.	Lancs	L. & N. W.	See Wigan Coal & Iron Co. (Leigh and Bedford).
G	P	F	L	H	C	1 10	Christ's Hospital, West Horsham	Sussex ...	L. B. & S. C.	Horsham and Billingshurst.
G	P	F	L	H	C	10 0	Christchurch (for Southbourne-on-Sea)	Hants	L. & S.W.	Brockenhurst and Bournemouth.
..	..	..	..	..	..	.. ..	Christie & Co.'s Siding........	Ayr	Cal.— G. & S.W.	Ardrossan.
..	..	..	..	..	..	.. ..	Christie & Co.'s Siding (G.C.)	Lincoln ...	G. C.—G. N.	Grimsby Docks.
..	..	..	..	..	..	.. ..	Christie's Saw Mill	Ayr	Cal.—G. & S. W.	Ardrossan.
..	..	..	..	..	..	.. ..	Christie's Sleeper Mill Siding (Cal.)	Stirling ...	Cal.—N. B.	Grangemouth.
G	P	F	L	H	C	5 0	Christon Bank................	Northumb	N. E.	Berwick and Morpeth.
..	..	..	..	..	..	.. ..	Falloden Siding & Depôt...	Northumb	N. E.	Christon Bank.
G	P	F	L	H	C	5 0	Christow	Devon......	G. W.	Exeter and Ashton.

EXPLANATION—**G** *Goods Station.*   **P** *Passenger and Parcel Station.*   **P*** *Passenger, but not Parcel or Miscellaneous Traffic.*
F *Furniture Vans, Carriages, Portable Engines, and Machines on Wheels.*   **L** *Live Stock.*
H *Horse Boxes and Prize Cattle Vans.*   **C** *Carriages by Passenger Train.*

Station Accommodation						Crane Power		STATIONS, &c.	COUNTY.	COMPANY.	POSITION.
G	P	F	L	H	C	Tons	Cwts				
G	P	.	.	H	.	3	0	Chudleigh	Devon	G. W.	Newton Abbot and Ashton.
G	P	.	.	.	.	10	0	Church and Oswaldtwistle ...	Lancs	L. & Y.	Blackburn and Accrington.
.	.	.	.	.	.			Aspden Colliery (Simpson's)	Lancs	L. & Y.	Church and Rishton.
.	.	.	.	.	.			Blythe's Siding	Lancs	L. & Y.	Church.
.	.	.	.	.	.			Metcalfe's Siding	Lancs	L. & Y.	Church.
.	.	.	.	.	.			Church & Son's Siding (Mid.)	Beds	Mid.—L. & N. W.	Bedford.
.	.	.	.	.	.			Church Bridge	Staffs	L. & N. W.	See Wyrley and Church Bridge.
G	P	F	.	H	C			Churchbury	Middlesex	G. E.	Edmonton and Cheshunt.
.	.	.	.	.	.			London Brick Co.'s Siding	Middlesex	G. E.	Churchbury.
G	P	.	.	.	.			Church Cross	Cork	S. & S.	Schull and Skibbereen.
.	P	.	.	.	.			Churchdown	Glo'ster	G. W.—Mid.	Cheltenham and Gloucester.
G	P	F	L	H	C			Church End (G. N.)	Middlesex	G. N.—N. L.	See Finchley.
G	P	F	L	H	C					N. E.	York and Leeds.
.	P	.	.	H	C					G. C.	Over N. E. from Ferrybridge Junc.
.	P	.	.	H	C			Church Fenton (N. E.)	Yorks	G. N.	Over N. E. & S. & K. Jt. Lines.
.	P	.	.	.	.					L. & Y.	Over N. E. from Altofts Junction.
.	P	.	.	.	.					Mid.	Over N. E. from Ferrybridge Junc.
.	.	.	.	.	.			Church, G., & Son's Sid. (Mid.)	Beds	Mid.—L. & N. W.	Bedford.
.	.	.	.	.	.			Church Gresley Col. (Mid.)	Derby	Mid.—L. & N. W.	See Moira Colliery Co. (Moira).
G	P	.	L	H	C			Church Hill	Donegal	L. & L. S.	Letterkenny and Burtonport.
G	P	.	.	.	.	1	10	Churchill and Blakedown	Worcester	G. W.	Worcester and Wolverhampton.
.	.	.	.	.	.			Churchill Sidings	Renfrew	Cal.	Greenock, Regent Street.
.	.	.	.	.	.			Church Iron Works	Lancs	G. C. (Wigan Jn.)	Wigan.
.	.	.	.	.	.					L. & N. W.	Same as Ellison's Siding (Wigan).
.	.	.	.	.	.			Church Pit	Northumb	N. E.	Wallsend.
.	.	.	.	.	.			Church Road	Lancs	L. & N. W.	See Garston.
G	P	.	L	.	.			Church Road (B. & M.)	Mon	B. & M.	Newport and Machen.
.	P	.	.	.	.					GW (A.(N&SW)D&R)	Over B. & M. from Bassaleg Junc.
.	.	.	.	.	.			Church Road	Warwick	Mid.	See Birmingham.
.	.	.	.	.	.			Church Road Junctions	Dublin	GN(I)—GS&W—L&NW	See Dublin.
.	.	.	.	.	.			Church Siding	Bucks	O. & A. Tram.	Wotton.
.	.	.	.	.	.			Church Street (G. N.)	Beds	G. N.—L. & N. W.	See Dunstable.
.	.	.	.	.	.			Church Street Jt. Coal Depôt	Yorks	H. & O. Jt. (G. N. & L. & Y.)	See Halifax.
G	P	F	L	H	C	2	10	Church Stretton	Salop	S. & H. Jt (G. W. & L. N. W.)	Craven Arms and Shrewsbury.
.	P	.	.	.	.			Churchtown	Lancs	L. & Y.	Preston and Southport.
.	P	.	.	.	.			Church Village	Glamorg'n	T. V.	Llantrisant and Pontypridd.
.	.	.	.	.	.			Churchway Colliery	Glo'ster	G. W.	Bilson Junction.
G	P	F	.	H	C			Churn	Berks	G. W.	Upton and Compton.
								(Used only when Camp is open.)			
.	.	.	.	.	.			Churn Road Siding	Kent	S. E. & C.	Horsmonden.
G	P	F	L	H	C	2	0	Churston Station & Junction	Devon	G. W.	Kingswear and Torquay.
.	P	.	.	.	.			Churwell	Yorks	L. & N. W.	Dewsbury and Leeds.
.	.	.	.	.	.			Churwell Colliery & Brick Wks.	Yorks	L. & N. W.	Same as Fitton & Robinson's (Morley)
G	P	.	L	H	.			Chwilog (for Nevin)	Carnarvon	L. & N. W.	Afon Wen and Carnarvon.
.	.	.	.	.	.			Cilely Colliery	Glamorg'n	G. W.	Tonyrefail.
G	P	.	.	.	.			Cilfrew	Glamorg'n	N. & Brecon	Neath and Crynant.
.	.	.	.	.	.			Cilfrew Tin Works	Glamorg'n	N. & Brecon	Cilfrew.
.	.	.	.	.	.			Ty-Isaf Quarry	Glamorg'n	N. & Brecon	Cilfrew and Crynant.
G	P	.	L	H	.			Cilfynydd	Glamorg'n	T. V.	Pontypridd and Nelson.
.	.	.	.	.	.			Albion Colliery	Glamorg'n	T. V.	Pontypridd and Abercynon.
.	.	.	.	.	.			Cilgwyn Slate Qry. Co.'s Sid.	Carnarvon	L. & N. W.	Nantlle.
.	.	.	.	.	.			Cille Colliery	Carmarth'	G. W. — L. & M. M. — L. & N. W.	Same as Castle Colliery (Llanelly).
G	P	F	.	.	.			Cilmery	Brecon	L. & N. W.	Llandilo and Llandrindod Wells.
.	.	.	.	.	.			Cil-yr-ychen Lime Works	Carmarth'	G. W.	Llandebie.
.	.	.	.	.	.			Cinder Colliery (G. W.)	Mon	G. W.—L. & N. W.	See Lancaster & Co. (Blaina).
G	P†	F	.	.	.	6	0	Cinderford	Glo'ster	G. W.	Forest of Dean Branch.
G	P	F	L	H	C	6	0			S. & Wye Jt. (G. W. & Mid)	Branch—Bilson Jn. & Drybrook Rd.
.	.	.	.	.	.			Whimsey Mineral Siding	Glo'ster	G. W.	Cinderford.
.	.	.	.	.	.			Cinderford Junction	Glo'ster	G. W.—S. & Wye Jt.	Bilson and Drybrook Road.
.	.	.	.	.	.			Cinder Hill & Babbington Col. (G. N.)	Notts	G. N.—G. C.	Nottingham, Basford and Bulwell,
.	.	.	.	.	.			Cinder Hill Colliery	Notts	Mid.	See Babbington Cl.Co.(Nottingham).
.	.	.	.	.	.			Cinder Lane	Lancs	L. & Y.	See Aintree.
.	.	.	.	.	.			Cinder Lane (Stores) Siding	Lancs	L. & Y.	Fazakerley.
.	.	.	.	.	.			Circle Siding	Lanark	N. B.	Coatbridge, Sheepford.
G	P	F	L	H	C	12	0	Cirencester	Glo'ster	G. W.	Branch from Kemble Junction.
G	P	F	L	H	C	5	0			M. & S. W. Jn.	Swindon Town and Cheltenham.
.	.	.	.	.	.			Citadel (Cal. & L.& N.W. Jt. Sta. Com.)	Cumb'land	Cal.—LNW—G&SW—M&C—Mid—NB—NE	See Carlisle.
.	.	.	.	.	.			City	Middlesex	W. & C.	See London, Mansion House (City).
.	.	.	.	.	.			City of Birmingham Gas Wks.	Staffs	G. W.	Swan Village.

EXPLANATION—**G** *Goods Station.*   **P** *Passenger and Parcel Station.*   **P*** *Passenger, but not Parcel or Miscellaneous Traffic.*

P† *Parcels only.*   **F** *Furniture Vans, Carriages, Portable Engines, and Machines on Wheels.*   **L** *Live Stock.*

H *Horse Boxes and Prize Cattle Vans.*   **C** *Carriages by Passenger Train.*

\	Station Accommodation.						Crane Power.	STATIONS, &c.	COUNTY.	COMPANY.	POSITION.
							Tons Cwts.	City Road	Middlesex	C. & S. L.	See London.
								City Road (G.N.)	Yorks	G. N.—G. C.	See Bradford.
								City Saw Mills Siding	Lanark	N. B.	Glasgow, Port Dundas.
								City Station (Royal Mint St.)	Middlesex	Mid.	See London.
								Clachan Manure Depôt	Lanark	N. B.	Greengairs.
								Clachan Quarry	Lanark	N. B.	Greengairs.
	P							Clachnaharry	Inverness	High	Inverness and Dingwall.
G	P	F	L	H	C			Clackmannan and Kennet	Clackman'	N. B.	Alloa and Kincardine.
								Clackmannan Colliery	Clackman'	N. B.	Clackmannan Road.
G	P		L	H				Clackmannan Road	Clackman'	N. B.	Alloa and Dunfermline.
								Clackmannan Colliery	Clackman'	N. B.	Alloa and Clackmannan Road.
								Tullygarth Colliery	Clackman'	N. B.	Clackmannan Road and Forest Mill.
G	P	F		H	C		1 10	Clacton-on-Sea	Essex	G. E.	Branch from Colchester.
								Martin's, J. W., Siding	Essex	G. E.	Clacton-on-Sea.
G	P		L	H	C			Clady	Donegal	Donegal	Strabane and Stranorlar.
G	P	F	L	H	C		2 0	Clandon	Surrey	L. & S.W.	Surbiton and Guildford.
G								Merrow Siding	Surrey	L. & S.W.	Clandon.
								Clandown Colliery	Somerset	S. & D. Jt. (L. & S. W. & Mid)	Radstock.
G	P	F	L	H	C			Clapham	Yorks	Mid.	Settle and Lancaster.
								Clapham Bros.' Siding	Yorks	Mid.	Keighley.
								Clapham Common	Surrey	C. & S. L.	See London.
								Clapham Junction Station	Surrey	{ L. & S.W.—L.B. & S.C. —W. L. E. Jt. G. N.—S. E. & C.	} See London.
								Clapham Road	Surrey	C. & S. L.	See London.
								Clapham Road (S. E. & C.)	Surrey	S. E. & C.—G. N.—L. & S. W.—Mid.	See London.
								Clapham Road and North Stockwell	Surrey	L. B. & S. C.	See London.
								Clapp's Wharf (Kohla Tile Co.)	Mon	A. (N & S W) D & R—G W	Newport, Alexandra Docks.
								Clapton	Middlesex	G. E.	See London.
G	P	F	L	H	C		1 0	Clara	Kings	{ G. S. & W. M. G. W.	Portarlington and Athlone. Branch from Streamstown Junction.
G	P	F	L	H	C		1 10				
								Clara Junction	Kings	G. S. & W.—M. G. W.	Tullamore and Streamstown.
								Clara Pit (L. & N. W.)	Warwick	L. & N. W.— Mid.	Same as Griff Colliery Co.'s New Colliery (Nuneaton).
								Clara Vale Colliery	Northumb	N. E.	Wylam.
G	P		L				1 10	Clarbeston Road	Pembroke	G. W.	Whitland and New Milford.
								Clarboro' Junction	Notts	G. C.	Retford and Leverton.
	P							Clarboro' Siding	Notts	G. C.	Retford.
G	P	F	L	H	C		1 10	Clar Bridge	Donegal	Donegal	Stranorlar and Donegal.
								Clare	Suffolk	G. E.	Haverhill and Sudbury.
								Clare & Ridgway's Siding	Lancs	L. & N. W.	Sankey Bridges.
G	P		L	H			1 10	Clarecastle (G. S. & W.)	Clare	{ G. S. & W. M. G. W.	Limerick and Ennis. Over G. S. & W. from Athenry.
								Claremont	Surrey	L. & S.W.	See Esher and Claremont.
								CLAREMORRIS—			
G		F	L	H			3 0	(Station)	Mayo	G. S. & W.	Tuam and Collooney.
G	P	F	L	H	C		3 0	(Station M. G. W.)	Mayo	{ M. G. W. G. S. & W.	Roscommon and Westport. Over M. G. W. Line.
G	P		L				3 0				
								Junctions	Mayo	G S. & W.—M. G. W.	Tuam and Castlebar.
								Clarence Depôts	Durham	N. E.	Stockton, North Shore.
								Clarence Dock	Lancs	L'pool O'head	See Liverpool.
								Clarence Iron & Steel Works	Durham	N. E.	See Bell Bros. (Port Clarence).
								Clarence Road (G. W.)	Glamorg'n	G. W.—Barry—T. V.	See Cardiff.
								Clarence Salt Works	Durham	N. E.	See Salt Union Ltd. (Port Clarence).
								Clarence Soda Works	Durham	N. E.	See Bell Bros. (Port Clarence).
								Clarence Street	Mon	G. W.	See Pontypool.
								Clarence Victualling Yard	Hants	L. & S.W.	Gosport.
								Clarence Yard (G. N)	Middlesex	G. N.—N. L.	See London.
								Clarendon Dock	Antrim	G. N. (I.)	See Belfast.
								Claridge's Sid. (Gunn's Sid.)	N'hamptn	L. & N. W.	Banbury.
								Clark & Reas' Siding	Denbigh	G. W.	Wheatsheaf Junction.
								Clark, G., & Co.'s Saw Mill	Durham	N. E.	Same as Albion Saw Mill (West Hartlepool).
								Clark's, R. H., Siding	Suffolk	G. E.	Yarmouth, South Town.
								Clark's Crank & Forging Co.'s Siding (G. N.)	Lincoln	G. N.—G. C.—Mid.	Lincoln.
								Clarke & Robinson's Siding	Lancs	Furness	Barrow.
								Clarke, Chapman & Co.'s Wks	Durham	N. E.	Same as Victoria Wks. (Gateshead).
								Clarke, G., & Son's Siding	Middlesex	{ G. E. GN—GW—LNW—Mid	London, Millwall Docks. London, Poplar.

EXPLANATION—**G** *Goods Station.*   **P** *Passenger and Parcel Station.*   **P*** *Passenger, but not Parcel or Miscellaneous Traffic.*
F *Furniture Vans, Carriages, Portable Engines, and Machines on Wheels.*   **L** *Live Stock.*
H *Horse Boxes and Prize Cattle Vans.*   **C** *Carriages by Passenger Train.*

STATION ACCOMMODATION.						CRANE POWER.		STATIONS, &c.	COUNTY.	COMPANY.	POSITION.
						Tons	Cwts.				
.	.	.	.	.	.			Clarke, Nicholls & Coombs' Sid	Middlesex	G. E.	London, Stratford.
.	.	.	.	.	.			Clarke's Siding	Notts	Mid.	Beeston.
.	.	.	.	.	.			Clarke Street Siding (Handyside & Co.)	Derby	Mid.	Derby.
G	P	.	.	.	.	3	0	Clarkston	Lanark	N. B.	Airdrie South and Caldercruix.
.	.	.	.	.	.			Atlas Machinery Works	Lanark	N. B.	Clarkston.
.	.	.	.	.	.			Caldervale Forge	Lanark	N. B.	Branch from Clarkston.
.	.	.	.	.	.			Gartness Colliery	Lanark	N. B.	Branch from Clarkston.
.	.	.	.	.	.			Gartness Siding	Lanark	N. B.	Branch from Clarkston.
.	.	.	.	.	.			Moffat Paper Mill	Lanark	N. B.	Branch—Clarkston&BrowniesideJn.
.	.	.	.	.	.			Springbank Colliery	Lanark	N. B.	Branch—Clarkston&BrowniesideJn.
.	.	.	.	.	.			Springbank Sidings	Lanark	N B.	Branch—Clarkston&BrowniesideJn.
.	.	.	.	.	.			Springfield Shaft Works	Lanark	N. B.	Branch—Clarkston&BrowniesideJn.
G	P	.	L	H	.	2	0	Clarkston (for Eaglesham)	Renfrew	Cal.	Pollokshaws and Busby.
G	P	.	L	H	.			Clatford (L. & S. W.)	Hants	{ L. & S. W. / M. & S. W. Jn.	Romsey and Andover. / Over L. & S. W. from Andover Junc.
.	.	.	.	.	.			Tasker's Siding	Hants	L. & S.W.	Clatford.
.	.	.	.	.	.			Claughton Brick Co.'s Siding	Yorks	Mid.	Caton.
.	.	.	.	.	.			Claughton Manor Siding	Yorks	Mid.	Caton.
G	P	.	.	.	.			Claverdon	Warwick	G. W.	Stratford-on-Avon and Hatton.
G	P	.	L	.	.			Claxby and Usselby	Lincoln	G. C.	Market Rasen and Barnetby.
.	.	.	.	.	.			Clay & Co.'s Colliery	Derby	Mid.	Same as Morton Colliery (Doe Hill).
.	.	.	.	.	.			Clay & Newman's Sid. (G.W.)	Worcester	G. W.—Mid.	See Salt Union Ltd. (Droitwich).
G	P	.	L	H	.	1	10	Clay Cross	Derby	Mid.	Derby and Chesterfield.
.	.	.	.	.	.			Avenue Colliery	Derby	Mid.	Clay Cross and Chesterfield.
.	.	.	.	.	.			Clay Cross Colliery Co.'s Col. Nos. 1, 2, 3, 4, 7, 9 & 11	Derby	Mid.	Clay Cross.
.	.	.	.	.	.			Clay Cross Co.'s Ironworks	Derby	Mid.	Clay Cross.
.	.	.	.	.	.			Colney Green Siding	Derby	Mid.	Clay Cross and Chesterfield.
.	.	.	.	.	.			Danesmoor (Clay Cross Colliery No. 7)	Derby	Mid.	Clay Cross and Doe Hill.
.	.	.	.	.	.			Knighton's Sidings	Derby	Mid.	Clay Cross.
.	.	.	.	.	.			Clay Cross Cl. & Ir. Co.'s Sid.	Derby	Mid.	Ambergate.
.	.	.	.	.	.			Clay Cross Colliery Co.— Cols. Nos. 1, 2, 3, 4, 7, 9, & 11	Derby	Mid.	Clay Cross.
.	.	.	.	.	.			Collieries Nos. 5 & 6	Derby	Mid.	Doe Hill.
.	.	.	.	.	.			Clay Cross Co.— Iron Works	Derby	Mid.	Clay Cross.
.	.	.	.	.	.			Lime Works	Derby	Mid.	Ambergate.
.	.	.	.	.	.			Claydale Brick Co.'s Siding	Herts	Mid.	Hemel Hempsted.
G	P	F	L	H	C			Claydon	Bucks	L. & N. W.	Oxford and Verney Junc. Station.
G	P	F	L	H	C			Claydon	Suffolk	G. E.	Ipswich and Haughley.
.	.	.	.	.	.			Moy, T., & Co.'s Siding	Suffolk	G. E.	Claydon.
.	.	.	.	.	.			Claye's Siding	Durham	N. E.	Darlington, Bank Top.
.	.	.	.	.	.			Claye's, S. J., Wagon Works	Derby	Mid.	Long Eaton.
G	P	F	L	H	C	2	0	Claygate	Surrey	L. & S.W.	Surbiton and Guildford.
.	.	.	.	.	.			Claygates	Dumfries	N. B.	See Gilnockie (for Claygates).
.	.	.	.	.	.			Clay, J., & Son's Siding	Yorks	L. & Y.	Sowerby Bridge.
.	.	.	.	.	.			Clay Lane Iron Works and Wharf	Yorks	N. E.	South Bank.
.	.	.	.	.	.			Clay Mills	Staffs	N. S.	See Stretton and Clay Mills.
.	.	.	.	.	.			Clay Mills Siding	Staffs	Mid.	Burton-on-Trent.
.	.	.	.	.	.			Clayphon Siding (Mid.)	Glamorg'n	Mid.—G.W.—L. & N.W.	Gurnos.
G	P	F	L	H	C			Claypole	Lincoln	G. N.	Grantham and Newark.
.	.	.	.	.	.			Clay's Siding	Yorks	L. & Y.	Luddendenfoot.
.	.	.	.	.	.			Claythorpe	Lincoln	G. N.	See Aby (for Claythorpe).
.	.	.	.	.	.			Clayton	Yorks	G. N.	See Bradford.
.	.	.	.	.	.			Clayton & Shuttleworth's Siding (G.C.)	Lincoln	G. C.—G. N.—Mid.	Lincoln.
.	.	.	.	.	.			Clayton's Brick Yard (Gwersyllt Brick Works)	Denbigh	G. W.	Moss.
.	.	.	.	.	.			Clayton's Stone Siding	Yorks	G. N.	Cullingworth.
.	.	.	.	.	.			Clayton's Tannery	Derby	Mid.	Chesterfield.
.	.	.	.	.	.			Clayton's Wagon Wks. (G.C.)	Yorks	G. C.—Mid.	Mexbro'.
.	.	.	.	.	.			Clayton & Welsh's Siding	Durham	N. E.	Gateshead.
.	.	.	.	.	.			Clayton Bridge (L. & Y.)	Lancs	L. & Y.—L. & N. W.	See Manchester.
.	.	.	.	.	.			Clayton Junction	Yorks	L. & Y.	Shepley and Denby Dale.
.	.	.	.	.	.			Clayton Tin Plate Works	Glamorg'n	G. W. & L. & N. W. Jt.	Pontardulais.
G	P	F	L	H	C	5	0	Clayton West	Yorks	L. & Y.	Branch—Shepley and Denby Dale.
.	.	.	.	.	.			Park Mill Colliery Siding	Yorks	L. & Y.	Clayton West.
.	.	.	.	.	.			Cleasby Siding	Yorks	N. E.	Barton.
.	.	.	.	.	.			Cleator	Cumb'land	WC&EJt.(Fur.&LNW)	See Woodend (for Cleator & Bigrigg).

EXPLANATION—G *Goods Station.*   P *Passenger and Parcel Station.*   P* *Passenger, but not Parcel or Miscellaneous Traffic.*
F *Furniture Vans, Carriages, Portable Engines, and Machines on Wheels.*   L *Live Stock.*
H *Horse Boxes and Prize Cattle Vans.*   C *Carriages by Passenger Train.*

STATION ACCOMMODATION.						CRANE POWER.	STATIONS, &c.	COUNTY.	COMPANY.	POSITION.
						Tons Cwts	Cleator Iron Ore Co.—			
.	.	.	.	.	.	. .	Agnes Pit...................	Cumb'land	W C & E Jt.(Fur.& LNW)	Eskett.
.	.	.	.	.	.	. .	Ainsworth's Margaret Pit	Cumb'land	W C & E Jt.(Fur.& LNW)	Eskett.
.	.	.	.	.	.	. .	Eskett Pit	Cumb'land	W C & E Jt.(Fur.& LNW)	Eskett.
.	.	.	.	.	.	. .	No. 11 Siding	Cumb'land	W C & E Jt.(Fur.& LNW)	Moor Row.
G	P	F	L	H	C	1 0	Cleator Moor	Cumb'land	C. & W. Jn.	Cleator Moor Jn. & Moresby Parks.
G	P	F	L	H		2 0			WC&EJt.(Fur.&LNW)	Marron Junction and Moor Row.
.	.	.	.	.	.	. .	Dacre's Siding..............	Cumb'land	W C & E Jt.(Fur.& LNW)	Crossfield and Cleator Moor.
.	.	.	.	.	.	. .	Heathcote's Siding	Cumb'land	W C & E Jt.(Fur.& LNW)	Cleator Moor and Frizington.
.	.	.	.	.	.	. .	Urban District Council Gas Works	Cumb'land	W C & E Jt.(Fur.& LNW)	Cleator Moor and Frizington.
							Whitehaven Hematite Iron Co.—			
.	.	.	.	.	.	. .	Aldby Limestone Quarry	Cumb'land	W C & E Jt.(Fur.& LNW)	Cleator Moor and Frizington.
.	.	.	.	.	.	. .	Works	Cumb'land	C. & W. Jn.	Cleator Moor.
.	.	.	.	.	.	. .	Works, North Side........	Cumb'land	W C & E Jt.(Fur.& LNW)	Cleator Moor and Frizington.
.	.	.	.	.	.	. .	Works, South Side........	Cumb'land	W C & E Jt.(Fur.& LNW)	Cleator Moor and Frizington.
.	.	.	.	.	.	. .	Cleator Moor Junction	Cumb'land	C.& W. Jn.—W.C.& E.Jt.	Cleator Moor Station & Moor Row.
.	.	.	.	.	.	. .	Cleaves Siding....................	Cornwall ..	G. W.	Bugle.
							CLECKHEATON—			
G	P	F	L	H		10 0	(Station)	Yorks	L. & N. W.	Huddersfield and Leeds.
G	P	.	L	H		10 0		Yorks	L. & Y.	Bradford and Mirfield.
G	P	.	L	H		10 0	(Station, L. & Y.)...........		G. N.	Over L. & Y. from Wakefield.
G	.	.	L			10 0			L. & N. W.	Over L. & Y. from Heaton Lodge Jn.
.	.	.	.	.	.	. .	Clee Hill	Salop	S.&H.Jt.(G.W.& L.N.W)	Branch from Ludlow.
.	.	.	.	.	.	. .	Clee Hill Dhu Stone Co.'s Sid.	Salop	S.&H.Jt.(G.W.& L.N.W)	Ludlow.
.	.	.	.	.	.	. .	Clee Hill Granite Co.'s Siding	Salop	S.&H.Jt.(G.W.& L.N.W)	Ludlow.
G	P	F	.	H	C	5 0	Cleethorpes	Lincoln ...	G. C.	Branch from Grimsby.
.	.	.	.	.	.	. .	Bannister & Co.'s Siding...	Lincoln ...	G. C.	Cleethorpes.
.	.	.	.	.	.	. .	Cleethorpes Gas Co.'s Sid.	Lincoln ...	G. C.	Cleethorpes.
G	P					. .	Cleeve	Glo'ster ..	Mid.	Cheltenham and Ashchurch.
.	.	.	.	.	.	. .	Clegg Street	Lancs	G. C.—L. & N. W.—O.A. & G. B. Jt.—L. & Y...	See Oldham.
G	P	.	L	H	C	1 10	Cleghorn	Lanark ...	Cal.	Carstairs and Law Junction.
.	.	.	.	.	.	. .	Cleghorn Terra Cotta Works	Lanark ...	Cal.	Cleghorn and Braidwood.
.	.	.	.	.	.	. .	Silvermuir Siding	Lanark ...	Cal.	Cleghorn and Lanark.
.	.	.	.	.	.	. .	Cleghorn & Wilkinson's Siding (C. L. C.)	Cheshire...	C. L. C.—L. & N. W.	Northwich.
G	P	F	L	H	C	4 10	Cleland	Lanark ...	Cal.	Holytown and Morningside.
.	.	.	.	.	.	. .	Cleland Pits, Nos. 40, 43, 44, and 45	Lanark ...	Cal.	Newarthill and Cleland.
.	.	.	.	.	.	. .	Cleland Pottery (Omoa Pottery)	Lanark ...	Cal.	Newarthill and Cleland.
.	.	.	.	.	.	. .	Cleland Townhead (Silverburn Colliery)............	Lanark ...	Cal.	Branch near Cleland.
.	.	.	.	.	.	. .	Spindleside Colliery No. 5	Lanark ...	Cal.	Cleland and Newmains.
.	.	.	.	.	.	. .	Sunnyside Colliery............	Lanark ...	Cal.	Cleland.
.	.	.	.	.	.	. .	Westwood Colliery (Murdestoun Colliery)	Lanark ...	Cal.	Cleland and Newmains.
.	.	.	.	.	.	. .	Cleland Collieries	Lanark ...	Cal.	Newarthill.
G	P	F	L	H	C	. .	Clenchwarton	Norfolk ...	Mid. & G. N. Jt.	South Lynn and Sutton Bridge.
G	P	.	L	H	C	5 0	Cleobury Mortimer	Salop	G. W.	Tenbury and Bewdley.
.	.	.	.	.	.	. .	Clerk & Son's Siding.........	Lanark ...	Cal.	Glasgow, Tollcross.
.	.	.	.	.	.	. .	Clesket Siding	Cumb'land	N. E.	Brampton Junction Station. Lambley.
G	P	F	L	H	C	8 0	Clevedon	Somerset..	G. W.	Branch from Yatton.
G	P					. .			W. C. & P.	Near G. W. Station.
.	.	.	.	.	.	. .	Cleveland Bolt & Nut Co.'s Sid.	Yorks	N. E.	Middlesbro'.
.	.	.	.	.	.	. .	Cleveland Brick Works	Yorks	N. E.	South Bank.
.	.	.	.	.	.	. .	Cleveland Bridge and Engineering Co.'s Siding	Durham ...	N. E.	Darlington, Bank Top.
.	.	.	.	.	.	. .	Cleveland Chemical Works...	Yorks	N. E.	Middlesbro'.
.	.	.	.	.	.	. .	Cleveland Chemical Works (J. Thomas, Jr., & Co.)......	Yorks	N. E.	Middlesbro'.
.	.	.	.	.	.	. .	Cleveland Flour Mills	Durham ...	N. E.	Bishop Auckland.
.	.	.	.	.	.	. .	Cleveland Iron & Steel Works	Yorks	N. E.	South Bank.
.	.	.	.	.	.	. .	Cleveland Port Brick Works.	Yorks	N. E.	Same as Evans & Son's Foundry (South Bank).
.	.	.	.	.	.	. .	Cleveland Road Siding........	Durham ...	N. E.	West Hartlepool.
.	.	.	.	.	.	. .	Cleveland Salt Works	Yorks	N. E.	Middlesbro'.
.	.	.	.	.	.	. .	Cleveland Ship Yard............	Yorks	N. E.	Middlesbro'.
.	.	.	.	.	.	. .	Cleveland Slag & Concrete Wks	Yorks	N. E.	Middlesbro'.

EXPLANATION—G *Goods Station.*   P *Passenger and Parcel Station.*   P* *Passenger, but not Parcel or Miscellaneous Traffic.*
F *Furniture Vans, Carriages, Portable Engines, and Machines on Wheels.*   L *Live Stock.*
H *Horse Boxes and Prize Cattle Vans.*   C *Carriages by Passenger Train.*

STATION ACCOMMODATION.						CRANE POWER.		STATIONS, &c.	COUNTY.	COMPANY.	POSITION.
						Tons	Cwts.				
.	.	.	.	.	.	.	.	Cleveland Steam Flour Mill	Yorks	N. E.	Stockton, South.
.	.	.	.	.	.	.	.	Cleveland Wire Mills	Yorks	N. E.	Middlesbro'.
.	P	.	.	.	.	.	.	Cleveleys	Lancs	P.&W.Jt.(L&Y & L&NW)	Fleetwood and Preston.
G	P	.	L	.	.	.	.	Cliburn	W'morlnd	N. E.	Appleby and Penrith.
.	.	.	.	.	.	.	.	Wetherigg's Pottery Depôts and Brick & Tile Works	W'morlnd	N. E.	Cliburn and Clifton.
G	P	.	L	H	.	.	.	Cliddesden	Hants	L. & S.W.	Basingstoke and Alton.
G	P	F	L	H	C	1	0	Clifden	Galway	M. G. W.	Terminus.
G	P	.	L	H	C	.	.	Cliff Common	Yorks	N. E.	Selby and Market Weighton.
.	.	.	.	.	.	.	.	Malt Kiln Siding	Yorks	N. E.	Cliff Common.
G	P	F	L	H	C	.	.	Cliffe	Kent	S. E. & C.	Gravesend and Port Victoria.
.	.	.	.	.	.	.	.	Cliffe's Siding	Lancs	L. & Y.	Liverpool, Great Howard Street.
.	.	.	.	.	.	.	.	Cliff Hill Granite Co.'s Sidings (Mid.)	Leicester..	Mid.—L. & N. W.	Bardon Hill.
.	.	.	.	.	.	.	.	Cliff House Field Siding	Durham	N. E.	West Hartlepool.
.	.	.	.	.	.	.	.	Cliff House Foundry	Durham	N. E.	West Hartlepool.
.	.	.	.	.	.	.	.	Cliff House Old Pottery	Durham	N. E.	West Hartlepool.
.	.	.	.	.	.	.	.	Cliff House Sid.(Newburn Jn.)	Durham	N. E.	See West Hartlepool.
G	P	.	L	.	.	.	.	Clifford	Hereford	G. W.	Dorstone and Hay.
.	.	.	.	.	.	.	.	Clifford Hill Mills	N'hampton	L. & N. W.	Same as Mead & Son's Sid. (Billing).
.	.	.	.	.	.	.	.	Clifford Siding	Warwick..	E. & W. Jn.	See Stratford-on-Avon.
.	.	.	.	.	.	.	.	Cliff Rigg Quarry	Yorks	N. E.	Great Ayton.
.	.	.	.	.	.	.	.	Cliff's Brick Siding	Yorks	G. N.	Bradford, Laister Dyke.
.	.	.	.	.	.	.	.	Cliff Siding	Warwick.	Mid.	Same as Hathern Station Brick and Terra Cotta Co.'s Sid.(Wilnecote)
.	.	.	.	.	.	.	.	Cliff Vale Siding	Staffs	N. S.	Etruria.
.	.	.	.	.	.	.	.	Cliff Vale Wharf	Staffs	N. S.	Stoke-on-Trent.
G	P	F	L	H	C	5	0	Clifton	W'morlnd	N. E.	Appleby and Penrith.
.	.	.	.	.	.	.	.	Redhills Lime Works	Cumb'land	N. E.	Over L. & N. W. from Clifton Junc.
.	.	.	.	.	.	.	.	Wetheriggs Pottery Depôts and Brick & Tile Works.	W'morlnd	N. E.	Cliburn and Clifton.
G	P	F	L	H	C	.	.	Clifton (N. S.)	Derby	N. S.	Rocester and Ashbourne.
.	P	.	.	.	.	.	.			L. & N. W.	Over N. S. Line.
.	.	.	.	.	.	.	.	Mayfield Siding (Simpson Bros.' Mill)	Derby	N. S.	Clifton.
.	.	.	.	.	.	.	.	Clifton & Kersley Colliery	Lancs	L. & N. W.	Patricroft.
.	.	.	.	.	.	.	.	Clifton & Kersley Colliery Co.'s Siding	Lancs	L. & Y.	Manchester, Miles Platting.
.	.	.	.	.	.	.	.	Clifton & Kersley Co.— Robin Hood Siding	Lancs	L. & Y.	Clifton Junction Station.
.	.	.	.	.	.	.	.	Siding	Lancs	L. & Y.	Blackburn.
.	.	.	.	.	.	.	.	Siding	Lancs	L. & Y.	Halliwell.
.	.	.	.	.	.	.	.	Unity Brook Siding	Lancs	L. & Y.	Dixon Fold.
G	P	F	L	H	C	5	0	Clifton & Lowther	W'morlnd	L. & N. W.	Lancaster and Penrith.
.	.	.	.	.	.	.	.	Lord Lonsdale's Timber Yard (Lowther Siding)	W'morlnd	L. & N. W.	Clifton and Shap.
.	.	.	.	.	.	.	.	Clifton & Lowther Junction	W'morlnd	L. & N. W.—N. E.	Penrith and Clifton.
G	P	F	L	H	C	.	.	Clifton Bridge	Somerset	G. W.	Bristol and Portishead.
.	.	.	.	.	.	.	.	Ashton Vale Colliery	Somerset..	G. W.	Portishead Junc. & Clifton Bridge.
.	.	.	.	.	.	.	.	Giles & Son's Works	Somerset..	G. W.	Portishead Junc. & Clifton Bridge.
.	.	.	.	.	.	.	.	Clifton Chemical Works	Lanark	N. B.	Coatbridge, Sheepford.
.	.	.	.	.	.	.	.	Clifton Colliery	Notts	G. C.—Mid.	Nottingham.
.	.	.	.	.	.	.	.	Clifton Colliery Junction	Notts	G. C.—Clifton Col. Co.	Nottingham.
G	P	F	.	H	C	5	0	Clifton Down	Glo'ster	Clif. Ex. Jt. (G.W. & Mid.)	Montpelier and Avonmouth Docks.
.	.	.	.	.	.	.	.	Clifton Hall Col. (L. & N. W.)	Lancs	L. & N. W.—L. & Y.	Patricroft.
.	.	.	.	.	.	.	.	Cliftonhill Foundry	Lanark	N. B.	Coatbridge, Sheepford.
.	.	.	.	.	.	.	.	Clifton Iron Works	Lanark	N. B.	Coatbridge, Sheepford.
G	P	.	L	H	.	1	10	Clifton Junction Station	Lancs	L. & Y.	Manchester and Bolton.
.	.	.	.	.	.	.	.	Chloride Electric Syndicate Siding	Lancs	L. & Y.	Clifton Junction Station.
.	.	.	.	.	.	.	.	Clifton & Kersley Co's Robin Hood Siding	Lancs	L. & Y.	Clifton Junction Station.
.	.	.	.	.	.	.	.	Pepper Hill Carriage Sid.	Lancs	L. & Y.	Clifton Junction and Dixon Fold.
.	.	.	.	.	.	.	.	Pilkington Tile & Pottery Co.'s Siding	Lancs	L. & Y.	Clifton Junction Station.
.	.	.	.	.	.	.	.	Clifton Maybank	Dorset	G. W.	See Yeovil.
.	.	.	.	.	.	.	.	Clifton Maybank Junction	Dorset	G. W.—L. & S. W.	Yeovil.
G	P	.	L	H	.	.	.	Clifton Mill	Warwick..	L. & N. W.	Market Harboro' and Rugby.
.	.	.	.	.	.	.	.	Clifton (Molyneux) Junction	Lancs	L. & Y.—L. & N. W.	Clifton and Patricroft.
G	P	F	L	H	C	3	0	Clifton-on-Trent	Notts	L. D. & E. C.	Tuxford and Lincoln.
.	P	.	.	.	.	.	.	Clifton Road (Brighouse)	Yorks	L. & Y.	Wyke and Bradley Wood Junction.
.	.	.	.	.	.	.	.	Clifton Siding	Edinboro'	N. B.	See Ratho.

EXPLANATION—G *Goods Station.*   P *Passenger and Parcel Station.*   P* *Passenger, but not Parcel or Miscellaneous Traffic.*
   F *Furniture Vans, Carriages, Portable Engines, and Machines on Wheels.*   L *Live Stock.*
   H *Horse Boxes and Prize Cattle Vans.*   C *Carriages by Passenger Train.*

STATION ACCOMMODATION.						CRANE POWER.	STATIONS, &c.	COUNTY.	COMPANY.	POSITION.
						Tons Cwts.				
.	.	.	.	.	.	. .	Clifton's Siding	Lancs	P. & W. Jt. (L&Y& L&NW)	Lytham.
.	.	.	.	.	.	. .	Climax Engineering Works ..	Lanark ..	Cal.	Calder.
.	.	.	.	.	.	. .	Climpy Colliery	Lanark ..	Cal.	Wilsontown.
.	.	.	.	.	.	. .	Clints Limestone Quarry	Cumb'land	W C& E Jt. (Fur. & LNW)	Same as Lonsdale Hematite Smelting Co.'s Siding (Gillfoot).
.	.	.	.	.	.	. .	Clippens Branch Junction ...	Renfrew..	G. & S.W.	Johnstone and Houston.
.	.	.	.	.	.	. .	Clippens Siding	Renfrew..	G. & S.W.	Johnstone.
.	.	.	.	.	.	. .	Clippens Works	Renfrew..	Cal.	Linwood.
G	P	.	L	H	.	. .	Clipston and Oxenden	N'hamptn	L. & N. W.	Market Harboro' and Northampton.
G	.	F	L	H	C	. .	Clipstone Siding...............	Notts	L. D. & E. C.	Warsop and Edwinstowe.
G	P	F	L	H	C	10 0	Clitheroe (L. & Y.)............	Lancs	{ L. & Y. ...... Mid.	Blackburn and Chatburn. Over L. & Y. line.
.	.	.	.	.	.	. .	Bankfield Siding............	Lancs	L. & Y.	Clitheroe.
.	.	.	.	.	.	. .	Bellman Park Siding	Lancs	L. & Y.	Near Clitheroe.
.	.	.	.	.	.	. .	Foulsyke's Siding	Lancs	L. & Y.	Clitheroe.
.	.	.	.	.	.	. .	Gas Works Siding	Lancs	L. & Y.	Near Clitheroe.
.	.	.	.	.	.	. .	Horrocksford Branch	Lancs	L. & Y.	Clitheroe and Chatburn.
.	.	.	.	.	.	. .	Primrose Siding	Lancs	L. & Y.	Near Clitheroe.
.	.	.	.	.	.	. .	Clive Street Siding	Lancs	L. & N. W.	Bolton.
.	.	.	.	.	.	. .	Cliviger Siding	Lancs	L. & Y.	Holme.
.	P	.	.	.	.	. .	Clock Face	Lancs	L. & N. W.	St. Helens and Widnes.
G	P	.	.	.	.	. .	Clock House.....................	Kent	S. E. & C.	New Beckenham and Elmers End.
G	P	.	L	H	.	1 10	Clocksbriggs	Forfar	Cal.	Forfar and Stonehaven.
.	.	.	.	.	.	. .	Cloddfar Coed Siding	Carnarvon	L. & N. W.	See Robinson's Slate Quarries (Nantlle).
.	.	.	.	.	.	. .	Cloddfar Grai Siding............	Carnarvon	L. & N. W.	Same as Coedmadoc Slate Co.'s Siding (Nantlle).
G	P	F	L	H	C	1 10	Cloghan	Donegal ...	Donegal.	Stranorlar and Glenties.
.	.	.	.	.	.	. .	Cloghan	Kings	G. S. & W.	See Belmont and Cloghan.
G	P	.	L	.	.	. .	Clogher	Tyrone ...	Clogher Valley	Aughnacloy and Fivemiletown.
G	P	.	.	.	.	. .	Cloghroe	Cork	C. & Muskerry	Coachford Junction and Coachford.
.	.	.	.	.	.	. .	Clokie & Co.'s Siding	Yorks	N. E.	Castleford.
G	P	F	L	H	C	. .	Clonakilty	Cork	C. B. & S. C.	Branch from Clonakilty Jn. Station.
.	P	.	.	.	.	. .	Clonakilty Junction Station	Cork	C. B. & S. C.	Bandon and Ballinascarthy.
.	.	.	.	.	.	. .	Clonbeith Junction	Ayr	G. & S.W.	Doura Branch.
.	.	.	.	.	.	. .	Clonbeith Qry. (Eglinton Qry.)	Ayr	G. & S.W.	Kilwinning.
.	P	.	.	.	.	. .	Clondalkin	Dublin ...	G. S. & W.	Dublin and Kildare.
G	P	F	.	H	C	. .	Clondulane	Cork	G. S. & W.	Fermoy and Lismore.
G	P	F	L	H	C	2 10	Clones	Monaghan	G. N. (I.)	Dundalk and Enniskillen.
.	P	.	.	.	.	. .	Clonhugh	W'meath	M. G. W.	Mullingar and Longford.
.	.	.	.	.	.	. .	Clonliffe Mills Siding............	Dublin ...	M. G. W.	Dublin.
.	P	.	L	.	.	. .	Clonmany	Donegal ...	L. & L. S.	Buncrana and Carndonagh.
G	P	F	L	H	C	3 0	Clonmel	Tipperary	G. S. & W.	Waterford and Tipperary.
G	P	.	L	H	.	. .	Clonsilla	Dublin ...	M. G. W.	Dublin and Mullingar.
.	P	.	.	.	.	. .	Clontarf	Dublin ...	G. N. (I.)	Dublin and Malahide.
G	P	F	L	H	C	1 10	Closeburn	Dumfries..	G. & S.W.	Dumfries and Thornhill.
.	.	.	.	.	.	. .	Closeburn Quarry	Dumfries..	G. & S.W.	Closeburn and Thornhill.
.	.	.	.	.	.	. .	Cloud Hill Lime Works	Leicester..	Mid.	Worthington.
.	P	.	.	.	.	. .	Clough Fold	Lancs	L. & Y.	Rawtenstall and Bacup.
.	.	.	.	.	.	. .	Ashworth's Siding............	Lancs	L. & Y.	Clough Fold.
.	.	.	.	.	.	. .	Gas Works	Lancs	L. & Y.	Clough Fold.
.	.	.	.	.	.	. .	Hareholme Siding	Lancs	L. & Y.	Clough Fold.
.	.	.	.	.	.	. .	Union Siding	Lancs	L. & Y.	Rawtenstall and Waterfoot.
G	P	F	L	H	C	. .	Cloughjordan	Tipperary	G. S. & W.	Roscrea and Nenagh.
.	.	.	.	.	.	. .	Clough Mill Siding	Yorks	L. & N. W.	Grotton and Springhead.
.	P	.	.	.	.	. .	Clough Road	Antrim ...	N. C. Com. (Mid.)	Ballymena and Parkmore.
.	.	.	.	.	.	. .	Clough's Siding	Lancs	P & W Jt (L & Y & L & NW)	Lytham.
G	P	.	L	H	C	1 10	Cloughton	Yorks	N. E.	Scarborough and Whitby.
G	P	.	L	H	.	2 10	Clovenfords	Selkirk ...	N. B	Peebles and Galashiels.
							CLOWN OR CLOWNE—			
G	P	.	L	.	C	. .	(Station)	Derby	Mid.	Staveley Town and Elmton.
G	P	F	L	H	C	3 0	(Station, L. D. & E. C.) ...	Derby	{ L. D. & E. C. .... G. E.	Langwith Junction and Sheffield. Over L. D. & E. C. from Lincoln, Pye Wipe Junction (for Coal only).
.	.	.	.	.	.	. .	Barlborough Brickyard......	Derby	L. D. & E. C.	Clown.
.	.	.	.	.	.	. .	Barlborough Colliery........	Derby	L. D. & E. C.	Branch from Clown.
.	.	.	.	.	.	. .	Junction	Derby	L. D. & E. C.— Mid.	Creswell and Clown Station.
.	.	.	.	.	.	. .	Southgate Colliery (Mid.)...	Derby	Mid.—L. D. & E. C.	Near Clown Station.
.	.	.	.	.	.	. .	Clowsgill Holme Siding	Cumb'land	N. E.	{ Brampton Junction Station. Lambley.
.	.	.	.	.	.	. .	Clunas & Co.'s Siding	Edinboro'	N. B.	Edinburgh, Leith Walk.
G	P	.	L	H	.	. .	Clunes	Inverness	High.	Inverness and Dingwall.

EXPLANATION—G Goods Station.   P Passenger and Parcel Station.   P* Passenger, but not Parcel or Miscellaneous Traffic.
F Furniture Vans, Carriages, Portable Engines, and Machines on Wheels.   L Live Stock.
H Horse Boxes and Prize Cattle Vans.   C Carriages by Passenger Train.

STATION ACCOMMODATION.						CRANE POWER.		STATIONS, &c.	COUNTY.	COMPANY.	POSITION.
						Tons	Cwts.				
.	.	.	.	.	.	.	.	Clune Siding	Ayr	G. & S.W.	See Monkton.
.	.	.	.	.	.	.	.	Clunie Lime Siding	Fife	N. B.	Cardenden.
.	.	.	.	.	.	.	.	Clutha Iron Works (G.&P.Jt.)	Lanark	{ Cal.	Glasgow, Kinning Park.
										{ G. & S. W.	Glasgow, General Terminus.
G	P	F	L	H	C	1	10	Clutton	Somerset..	G. W.	Bristol and Radstock.
.	.	.	.	.	.	.	.	Fry's Bottom Colliery	Somerset..	G. W.	Clutton.
.	.	.	.	.	.	.	.	Greyfield Colliery	Somerset..	G. W.	Clutton.
G	P	.	.	.	.	.	.	Clydach	Brecon	L. & N. W.	Abergavenny and Merthyr.
.	.	.	.	.	.	.	.	Clydach Lime Wks(Cuckoos Nest Siding)	Brecon	L. & N. W.	Clydach and Gilwern.
.	.	.	.	.	.	.	.	Gellavellin Siding	Brecon	L. & N. W.	Clydach and Brynmawr.
.	.	.	.	.	.	.	.	Llanelly Lime & Stone Co.'s Siding	Brecon	L. & N. W.	Clydach and Brynmawr.
.	.	.	.	.	.	.	.	Clydach Branch Junction	Glamorg'n	T. V.	Same as Ynysybwl Branch Junc.
.	.	.	.	.	.	.	.	Clydach Court Junction	Glamorg'n	T. V.	Pontypridd and Ynysybwl.
.	.	.	.	.	.	.	.	Clydach Court Loop Junc.	Glamorg'n	T. V.	Ynysybwl and Abercynon.
G	P	.	.	.	.	.	.	Clydach-on-Tawe (Mid.)	Glamorg'n	{ Mid.	Morriston and Glais.
										{ G. W.	Over Midland line.
.	.	.	.	.	.	.	.	Clydach Foundry & Tin Plate Co'sSiding(J.Player & Co.) (Mid.)	Glamorg'n	Mid.—G. W.—L.& N.W.	Clydach-on-Tawe.
								Cory Yeo & Co.— Graigola MerthyrCo'sUpper & Lower Cols. (Mid)	Glamorg'n	Mid.—G. W.—L.& N.W.	Clydach-on-Tawe.
.	.	.	.	.	.	.	.	Hill's Merthyr Col. (Mid)	Glamorg'n	Mid.—G. W.—L.& N.W.	Clydach-on-Tawe.
.	.	.	.	.	.	.	.	Glanyrafan Sidings (Mid.)	Glamorg'n	Mid.—G. W.—L.& N.W.	Clydach-on-Tawe.
.	.	.	.	.	.	.	.	Davies, J., & Co. (Mid.)	Glamorg'n	Mid.—G. W.—L.& N.W.	Glanyrafan Sidings.
.	.	.	.	.	.	.	.	Park Tin Plate Co. (Mid)	Glamorg'n	Mid.—G. W.—L.&N. W.	Glanyrafan Sidings.
.	.	.	.	.	.	.	.	Graig Cwm Colliery (Mid.)	Glamorg'n	Mid.—G. W.—L.& N.W.	Clydach-on-Tawe.
.	.	.	.	.	.	.	.	GraigolaCol (Gueret's)(Mid)	Glamorg'n	Mid.—G. W.—L.& N.W.	Near Clydach-on-Tawe.
.	.	.	.	.	.	.	.	Meadows, Bros. & Co.'s Sid. (Mid.)	Glamorg'n	Mid.—G. W.—L.& N.W.	Clydach-on-Tawe.
.	.	.	.	.	.	.	.	MondNickel Co.'s Sid.(Mid)	Glamorg'n	Mid.— G. W.—L.&N.W.	Near Clydach-on-Tawe.
.	.	.	.	.	.	.	.	Moody Bros.&Co'sCol.(Mid)	Glamorg'n	Mid.—G. W.—L.& N.W.	Near Clydach-on-Tawe.
.	.	.	.	.	.	.	.	West Glamorgan Canister Co.'s Siding (Mid.)	Glamorg'n	Mid.—G. W.—L.& N.W.	Near Clydach-on-Tawe.
.	.	.	.	.	.	.	.	Clydach Vale Colliery	Glamorg'n	G. W.	Penygraig.
.	.	.	.	.	.	.	.	Clydach Vale Colliery (Phillipp's Siding)	Glamorg'n	T. V.	Trealaw.
.	.	.	.	.	.	.	.	Clydach Vale Siding	Glamorg'n	T. V.	Trealaw.
								CLYDEBANK—			
G	P	.	L	.	.	5	0	(Station)	Dumbartn	Cal.	Glasgow (Central, Low Level) and Dumbarton.
.	.	.	.	.	.	.	.	British Chemical Works	Dumbartn	{ Cal.	Clydebank and Kilbowie Road.
										{ N. B.	Clydebank, East.
.	P	.	.	.	.	.	.	Central	Dumbartn	N. B.	Partick and Bowling.
.	.	.	.	.	.	.	.	Clydebank Saw Mill Sid.	Dumbartn	Cal.	Kilbowie Road and Dalmuir.
.	.	.	.	.	.	.	.	Clydebank Shipbuilding and Engineering Wks. (Brown, J., & Co.'s)	Dumbartn	{ Cal.	Clydebank and Kilbowie Road.
										{ N. B.	Near Clydebank, East.
.	.	.	.	.	.	.	.	Dalmuir Bridge and Roofing Works	Dumbartn	Cal.	Clydebank.
G	P	.	L	H	.	.	.	East	Dumbartn	N. B.	Branch—Yoker and Clydebank, Central.
.	.	.	.	.	.	.	.	Clyde Boiler Works	Lanark	Cal.	Motherwell.
.	.	.	.	.	.	.	.	Clydebridge Steel Works	Lanark	Cal.	Glasgow, Rutherglen.
.	.	.	.	.	.	.	.	Clyde Engine Works	Renfrew	G & P. Jt. (Cal. & G & S W)	See Cardonald.
.	.	.	.	.	.	.	.	Clydeholm Ship Yard (Barclay, Curle & Co.)	Renfrew	Cal.	Glasgow, Whiteinch.
.	.	.	.	.	.	.	.		Lanark	N. B.	Glasgow, Whiteinch.
.	.	.	.	.	.	.	.	Clyde Iron Works & Collieries	Lanark	Cal.	Glasgow, Rutherglen.
.	.	.	.	.	.	.	.	Clyde Junction	Lanark	Cal.	Glasgow.
.	.	.	.	.	.	.	.	Clyde Junction	Lanark	G. & S. W.	Glasgow.
.	.	.	.	.	.	.	.	Clyde Lead Works (G.&P.Jt.)	Lanark	{ Cal.	Glasgow, Kinning Park.
										{ G. & S. W.	Glasgow, General Terminus.
.	.	.	.	.	.	.	.	Clyde Nail Works	Lanark	Cal.	Newton.
.	.	.	.	.	.	.	.	Clyde Patent Wire Rope Co.'s Siding	Lanark	Cal.	Glasgow, Bridgeton.
.	.	.	.	.	.	.	.	Clyde Pottery Co.'s Siding (G. & S. W.)	Renfrew	G. & S. W.—N. B.	Port Glasgow, Inchgreen.
.	.	.	.	.	.	.	.	Clydesdale Colliery	Lanark	Cal.	Shieldmuir.
.	.	.	.	.	.	.	.	Clydesdale Distillery	Lanark	Cal.	Same as Wishaw Distillery.
.	.	.	.	.	.	.	.	Clydesdale Dye Works	Lanark	Cal.	Glasgow, Bridgeton.

EXPLANATION—G Goods Station.   P Passenger and Parcel Station.   P* Passenger, but not Parcel or Miscellaneous Traffic.
F Furniture Vans, Carriages, Portable Engines, and Machines on Wheels.   L Live Stock.
H Horse Boxes and Prize Cattle Vans.   C Carriages by Passenger Train.

STATION ACCOMMODATION.						CRANE POWER.	STATIONS, &c.	COUNTY.	COMPANY.	POSITION.
						Tons Cwts.	Clydesdale Iron & Steel Wks.	Lanark ...	Cal.	Mossend.
							Clydesdale Tube Works	Lanark ...	Cal.	Glasgow, Bridgeton.
							Clydesdale Wagon Works ...	Lanark ...	Cal.	Shieldmuir.
							Clydesdale Weighs	Lanark ...	Cal.	Glasgow, South Side.
							Clyde Shipbuilding and Engineering Works	Renfrew ..	Cal.	Port Glasgow.
							Clydeside Colliery	Lanark ...	N. B.	Broomhouse.
							Clydeside Iron Works...... ...	Renfrew...	Cal.	Same as Clyde Structural Iron Wks. (Glasgow).
							Clydeside Tube Works........	Lanark ...	Cal.	Calder.
							Clyde Steel and Engineering Works	Lanark ...	N. B.	Hamilton.
							Clyde Structural Iron Works (Clydeside Iron Works) ...	Renfrew...	Cal.	Glasgow, Whiteinch.
							Clyde Sugar Refinery Store..	Renfrew...	Cal.	Greenock, Upper.
							Clyde Trust Works	Dumbartn	Cal.	Dalmuir.
							Clyde Tube Works	Lanark ...	N. B.	Coatbridge, Sheepford.
							Clyde Valley Electric Works	Lanark ...	Cal.	Motherwell.
							Clyde Valley Electric Works	Renfrew...	Cal.	Yoker.
							Clyde Villa Crane (Cal.)	Lanark ...	Cal.—G. & S. W.	See Glasgow.
G	P	F	L	H	C	1 10	Clynderwen......................	Carmarth'	G. W.	Whitland and New Milford.
G	P	.	L	.	.		Coachford......................	Cork	C. & Muskerry	Terminus.
G	P	.	.	.	.		Coachford Junction Station...	Cork	C. & Muskerry	Cork and Coachford.
G	P	.	.	.	.	1 15	Coalbrookdale..................	Salop	G. W.	Madeley and Buildwas.
							Coalbrookdale Co.'s Siding	Salop	G. W.	Coalbrookdale.
							Coalbrookdale Co.'s Tile Wks.	Salop	G. W.	Lightmoor.
							Coalbrookvale— East Siding (G. W.)	Mon	G. W.—L. & N. W.	Nantyglo.
							West Siding (J. G. & W. Barnes) (G.W.)	Mon	G. W.—L. & N. W.	Nantyglo.
G	P	.	.	.	.	2 0	Coalburn	Lanark ...	Cal.	Lesmahagow and Muirkirk.
							Auchlochan Collieries	Lanark ...	Cal.	Lesmahagow and Coalburn.
							Muirburn Siding	Lanark ...	Cal.	Lesmahagow and Coalburn.
							Stocksbriggs	Lanark ...	Cal.	Lesmahagow and Coalburn.
							Bankend Colliery & Lime Works (Sitehill Colliery)	Lanark ...	Cal.	Coalburn and Muirkirk.
							Bellfield Colliery	Lanark ...	Cal.	Lesmahagow and Coalburn.
							Dalwhannie or Dalquhandy Colliery No. 1............	Lanark ...	Cal.	Coalburn and Muirkirk.
							Dalwhannie or Dalquhandy Colliery No. 2 (Cummerhead Siding)	Lanark ...	Cal.	Coalburn and Muirkirk.
							Galawhistle Pit	Ayr	Cal.	Coalburn and Muirkirk.
							Poneil Colliery and Lime Works	Lanark ...	Cal.	Lesmahagow and Coalburn.
							Spierslack Colliery	Ayr	Cal.	Coalburn and Muirkirk.
							Coales & Son's Siding (Shipley Wharf)	Bucks ...	L. & N. W.	Newport Pagnell.
G	P	.	L	H	.	1 10	Coaley Junction Station	Glo'ster ...	Mid.	Gloucester and Bristol.
							Workman's, J., Mill.........	Glo'ster ...	Mid.	Near Coaley Junc. Station.
							Coal Hills Siding	Derby ...	L. & N. W.	See Hopton Wood Stone Co. (Steeplehouse).
G	P	F	L	H	C	3 0	Coalisland	Tyrone ...	G. N. (I.)	Dungannon and Cookstown.
.	P	.	.	.	.		Coalpit Heath	Glo'ster ...	G. W.	Wootton Bassett and Patchway.
							Coalpit Heath Coal Co.'s Siding (Hewitt's Yard)	Glo'ster ...	Mid.	Bristol, St. Philips.
							Coalpit Heath Colliery.........	Glo'ster ...	Mid.	Mangotsfield.
G	P	F	L	H	C	.	Coalport	Salop	{ G. W. { L. & N. W.	Shrewsbury and Bridgnorth.
G	P	.	L	H	.	.		Salop		Branch from Hadley.
							Coalport China Factory ...	Salop	L. & N. W.	Coalport and Madeley Market.
							Exley & Sons' Siding	Salop	G. W.	Coalport.
							Coal, Salt & Tanning Co.'s Siding (G. C.)	Lincoln	G. C.—G. N.	Grimsby Docks.
							Coal Supply Co.'s Siding......	Lincoln	G. C.	Grimsby Town.
G	P	F	L	H	C	5 0	COALVILLE— (Station)	Leicester..	Mid.	Leicester and Burton.
							Coleorton Colliery (Mid.)...	Leicester..	Mid.—L. & N. W.	Ashby and Swannington.
G	P	F	L	H	C	5 0	East	Leicester..	L. & N. W.	Loughboro' and Nuneaton.
							Ellis & Son's Cake, etc., Stores (Mid.)	Leicester..	Mid.—L. & N. W.	Near Coalville Station.
							Hewes Bros.' Brick Works	Leicester..	Mid.	Near Coalville Station.
							Junction	Leicester..	A. & N. Jt.— Mid.	Coalville and Hugglescote.

EXPLANATION—G Goods Station.   P Passenger and Parcel Station.   P* Passenger, but not Parcel or Miscellaneous Traffic.
F Furniture Vans, Carriages, Portable Engines, and Machines on Wheels.   L Live Stock.
H Horse Boxes and Prize Cattle Vans.   C Carriages by Passenger Train.

STATION ACCOMMODATION.						CRANE POWER.		STATIONS, &c.	COUNTY.	COMPANY.	POSITION.
						Tons	Cwts.	COALVILLE—continued.			
.	.	.	.	.	.	.	.	Midland Brick and Terra Cotta Works (Mid.)......	Leicester..	Mid.—L. & N. W.	Near Coalville Station.
.	.	.	.	.	.	.	.	Snibston Col. (Mid.).........	Leicester..	Mid.—L. & N. W.	Near Coalville Station.
.	.	.	.	.	.	.	.	South Leicestershire Col. & Brk. Co.'s Sid.(A.&N.Jt.)	Leicester..	Mid.	Coalville and Hugglescote.
.	.	.	.	.	.	.	.	Stableford's Bk. W'ks(Mid)	Leicester..	Mid.—L. & N. W.	Near Coalville Station.
.	.	.	.	.	.	.	.	Stableford's Wgn Wks(Mid)	Leicester..	Mid.—L. & N. W.	Near Coalville Station.
.	.	.	.	.	.	.	.	Swannington Pumping Co.'s Siding (Mid.)	Leicester..	Mid.—L. & N. W.	Near Swannington.
.	.	.	.	.	.	.	.	Watter's Flour Mills (Mid.)	Leicester..	Mid.—L. & N. W.	Near Coalville Station.
.	.	.	.	.	.	.	.	Whitwick Colliery............	Leicester..	L. & N. W.	Coalville, East and Whitwick.
.	.	.	.	.	.	.	.	Whitwick Colliery & Brick Works (Mid.)	Leicester..	Mid.—L. & N. W.	Near Coalville Station.
.	.	.	.	.	.	.	.	Wootton Bros.' Foundry	Leicester..	Mid.	Near Coalville Station.
G	P	.	L	H	.	1	0	Coanwood	Northumb	N. E.	Haltwhistle and Alston.
.	.	.	.	.	.	.	.	Coanwood Colliery............	Northumb	N. E.	Coanwood.
.	.	.	.	.	.	.	.	Coanwood Whinstone Qry.	Northumb	N. E.	Coanwood and Lambley.
.	.	.	.	.	.	.	.	Featherstone Colliery	Northumb	N. E.	Coanwood.
.	.	.	.	.	.	.	.	Coatbank Engineering Wks.	Lanark ...	Cal.	Coatbridge, Whifflet.
								COATBRIDGE—			
G	P	F	L	H	C	6	0	(Station)	Lanark ...	Cal.	Motherwell and Buchanan Street.
.	.	.	.	.	.	.	.	Airdriehouse Brick Works	Lanark ...	N. B.	Branch—Sunnyside & Commonhead.
.	P	.	.	.	.	.	.	Blairhill and Gartsherrie...	Lanark ...	N. B.	Shettleston and Coatbridge, Sunnyside.
.	.	.	.	.	.	.	.	Boiler Works (Arnott's) ...	Lanark ...	Cal.	Coatbridge and Langloan.
.	.	.	.	.	.	.	.	Bothwell Sidings	Lanark ...	N. B.	Near Whifflet.
.	.	.	.	.	.	.	.	Bothwell Top Sidings	Lanark ...	N. B.	Near Whifflet.
.	.	.	.	.	.	.	.	British Tube Works	Lanark ...	N. B.	Branch—Sheepford Jn. & Whifflet.
.	.	.	.	.	.	.	.	Calder Brick and Fire- Clay Works..............	Lanark ...	Cal. / N. B.	Whifflet. / Palacecraig Branch.
.	.	.	.	.	.	.	.	Calder Chemical Works...	Lanark ...	Cal.	Whifflet.
.	.	.	.	.	.	.	.	Calder Collieries.............	Lanark ...	Cal.	Whifflet.
.	.	.	.	.	.	.	.	Calder Iron Works	Lanark ...	Cal. / N. B.	Whifflet. / Palacecraig Branch.
.	.	.	.	.	.	.	.	Caledonian Tube Works ...	Lanark ...	N. B.	Branch from Sheepford.
.	.	.	.	.	.	.	.	Carnbroe Brick Works......	Lanark ...	Cal.	Whifflet.
.	.	.	.	.	.	.	.	Carnbroe Chemical Works	Lanark ...	Cal. / N. B.	Whifflet. / Whifflet and Bellshill.
.	.	.	.	.	.	.	.	Carnbroe Colliery	Lanark ...	Cal.	Whifflet.
.	.	.	.	.	.	.	.	Carnbroe Iron Works	Lanark ...	Cal. / N. B.	Whifflet. / Whifflet and Bellshill.
G	P	F	L	.	.	7	0	Central	Lanark ...	N. B.	Blairhill and Whifflet.
G	.	.	.	.	.	.	.	Central Engine Works......	Lanark ...	N. B.	Langloan Branch.
.	.	.	.	.	.	.	.	Circle Siding	Lanark ...	N. B.	Branch from Sheepford.
.	.	.	.	.	.	.	.	Clifton Chemical Works ...	Lanark ...	N. B.	Branch—Sheepford and Coatdyke Goods Depôt.
.	.	.	.	.	.	.	.	Cliftonhill Foundry	Lanark ...	N. B.	Sheepford & Coatdyke Goods Depôt.
.	.	.	.	.	.	.	.	Clifton Iron Works	Lanark ...	N. B.	Branch from Sheepford.
.	.	.	.	.	.	.	.	Clyde Tube Works	Lanark ...	N. B.	Branch—Sheepford and Coatdyke Goods Depôt.
.	.	.	.	.	.	.	.	Coatbank Engineering Works	Lanark ...	Cal.	Whifflet.
.	.	.	.	.	.	.	.	Coatdyke Foundry............	Lanark ...	N. B.	Branch from Sheepford.
G	.	.	.	.	.	3	0	Coatdyke Goods & Mineral Depôt (Sheepford Locks Siding)	Lanark ...	N. B.	Extension from Sheepford.
.	.	.	.	.	.	.	.	Coats' Iron & Steel Works	Lanark ...	N. B.	Sheepford Branch.
.	.	.	.	.	.	.	.	Coats' Tube Works	Lanark ...	N. B.	Sheepford Branch.
.	.	.	.	.	.	.	.	Craig Siding	Lanark ...	N. B.	Whifflet.
.	.	.	.	.	.	.	.	Crown Iron Works............	Lanark ...	N. B.	Sheepford & Coatdyke Goods Depôt.
.	.	.	.	.	.	.	.	Douglas Support Sidings...	Lanark ...	N. B.	Rosehall Branch.
.	.	.	.	.	.	.	.	Drumpellier Colliery	Lanark ...	N. B.	Langloan Branch.
.	.	.	.	.	.	.	.	Drumpellier No. 3 Colliery	Lanark ...	N. B.	Heatheryknowe and Sunnyside.
.	.	.	.	.	.	.	.	Drumpellier Iron and Steel Works	Lanark ...	N. B.	Langloan Branch.
.	.	.	.	.	.	.	.	Dundyvan Basin............	Lanark ...	Cal. / N. B.	Whifflet. / Near Whifflet.
.	.	.	.	.	.	.	.	Dundyvan Foundry	Lanark ...	N. B.	Branch—Sheepford Jn. & Whifflet.
.	.	.	.	.	.	.	.	Dundyvan House - to - House Electric Light Works	Lanark ...	N. B.	Langloan Branch.

EXPLANATION—G Goods Station.   P Passenger and Parcel Station.   P* Passenger, but not Parcel or Miscellaneous Traffic.
F Furniture Vans, Carriages, Portable Engines, and Machines on Wheels.   L Live Stock.
H Horse Boxes and Prize Cattle Vans.   C Carriages by Passenger Train.

STATION ACCOMMODATION.						CRANE POWER.		STATIONS, &c.	COUNTY.	COMPANY.	POSITION.
						Tons	Cwts.	**COATBRIDGE**—continued.			
								Dundyvan Iron Works	Lanark	N. B.	Branch—Sheepford Jn. & Whifflet.
								Dundyvan Rivet Works	Lanark	N. B.	Branch—Sheepford Jn. & Whifflet.
								Dundyvan Wood Yard	Lanark	N. B.	Branch—Sheepford Jn. & Whifflet.
								Eglinton Silica Brick Wks.	Lanark	N. B.	Branch—Sheepford Jn. & Whifflet.
								Faskine Brick Works	Lanark	N. B.	Palacecraig Branch.
								Gartgill	Lanark	N. B.	Sunnyside and Kirkintilloch Basin.
								Gartliston Brick and Fire-Clay Works	Lanark	N. B.	Gartgill and Bridgend.
								Gartsherrie No. 1 Colliery	Lanark	N. B.	Heatheryknowe and Sunnyside.
								Gartsherrie No. 8 Colliery	Lanark	N. B.	Heatheryknowe and Sunnyside.
								Gartsherrie Iron Works	Lanark	N. B.	Sunnyside and Gartgill.
								Gartverrie Fire-Clay Works	Lanark	N. B.	Gartgill and Bridgend.
								Gas Works	Lanark	N. B.	Kipps Branch.
								Gilchrist & Son's Siding	Lanark	Cal.	Coatbridge.
								Glenboig Fire-Clay Works—			
								Old Works	Lanark	N. B.	Gartgill and Bridgend.
								Star Works	Lanark	N. B.	Gartgill and Bridgend.
G								Glenboig General Siding for Garnqueen	Lanark	N. B.	Gartgill and Bridgend.
G								Gunnie Sidings	Lanark	N. B.	Sunnyside and Gartgill.
								Hollandhurst Colliery	Lanark	N. B.	Sunnyside and Gartgill.
								Hudson's Boiler Works	Lanark	N. B.	Sheepford & Coatdyke Goods Depôt
								Imperial Tube Works	Lanark	N. B.	Branch near Coatdyke.
								Iron Works	Lanark	N. B.	Branch—Sheepford Jn. & Whifflet.
								Kipps Byre Colliery	Lanark	N. B.	Branch—Sunnyside & Commonhead.
								Kipps Sidings	Lanark	N. B.	Sunnyside and Commonhead.
								Lanarkshire Chain, Cable, and Anchor Works (Strathearn's Weldless Chain Works)	Lanark	N. B.	Gartgill and Bridgend.
								Langloan Branch	Lanark	N. B.	Branch—Coatbridge (Central) and Whifflet.
								Langloan Iron & Chemical Works	Lanark	N. B.	Terminus—Langloan Branch.
								Leaend Weighs	Lanark	N. B.	Commonhead and Sunnyside.
								Lochrin Iron Works	Lanark	{ Cal. / N. B.	Whifflet. / Near Whifflet.
								Lochrin Ir. Wks. Timber Sid	Lanark	N. B.	Near Whifflet.
								Loudon & Inglis Siding	Lanark	Cal.	Whifflet.
								North British Iron Works (Ellis's)	Lanark	{ Cal. / N. B.	Whifflet. / Sheepford Junction and Sheepford.
								Palacecraig Branch	Lanark	N. B.	Branch from Whifflet.
								Palacecraig Brick Works	Lanark	N. B.	Palacecraig Branch.
								Palacecraig Colliery	Lanark	N. B.	Palacecraig Branch.
								Phœnix Iron Works	Lanark	N. B.	Branch from Sheepford.
								Pottery Siding	Lanark	N. B.	Sheepford.
								Purdie & Son's Siding	Lanark	Cal.	Coatbridge.
								Rochsolloch Brick Works (Coatdyke Brick Works)	Lanark	N. B.	Extension from Sheepford.
								Rochsolloch Iron Works	Lanark	N. B.	Extension from Sheepford.
								Rosehall Brick Works	Lanark	N. B.	Whifflet and Bellshill.
								Rosehall Collieries Nos. 10 and 11	Lanark	N. B.	Whifflet and Bellshill.
								Scotia Iron Works	Lanark	N. B.	Branch from Sheepford.
								Sharp's Siding	Lanark	N. B.	Sunnyside and Coatbridge, Central.
G						3	0	Sheepford	Lanark	N. B.	Branch—Coatbridge (Central) and Whifflet.
								Sheepford Branch Junction	Lanark	N. B.	Coatbridge (Central) and Whifflet.
								Slaughter-house Siding	Lanark	N. B.	Branch—Sheepford Jn. & Whifflet.
G								Southend Sidings	Lanark	N. B.	Sunnyside and Blairhill.
								Souterhouse Brick Works	Lanark	N. B.	Branch—Sheepford Jn. & Whifflet.
								Souterhouse Colliery	Lanark	N. B.	Branch—Sheepford Jn. & Whifflet.
								Speedwell Iron Works	Lanark	N. B.	Whifflet.
								Stobcross Rivet Works	Lanark	N. B.	Sheepford Junction and Whifflet.
								Strachan's Siding	Lanark	Cal.	Whifflet.
								Summerlee Iron Works	Lanark	Cal.	Coatbridge.
								Summerlee Iron Works	Lanark	N. B.	Sunnyside and Blairhill.
								Sunnyside—			
	P	F		H	C			(Station)	Lanark	N. B.	Glasgow (College) & Airdrie, South.
								Engine Works (Lamberton's Siding)	Lanark	N. B.	Sunnyside.

EXPLANATION—G *Goods Station.*   P *Passenger and Parcel Station.*   P* *Passenger, but not Parcel or Miscellaneous Traffic.*
F *Furniture Vans, Carriages, Portable Engines, and Machines on Wheels.*   L *Live Stock.*
H *Horse Boxes and Prize Cattle Vans.*   C *Carriages by Passenger Train.*

STATION ACCOMMODATION.						CRANE POWER.	STATIONS, &c.	COUNTY.	COMPANY.	POSITION.
						Tons	Cwts				

STATION ACCOMMODATION.						CRANE POWER.		STATIONS, &c.	COUNTY.	COMPANY.	POSITION.
						Tons	Cwts	COATBRIDGE—continued.			
								Sunnyside—continued.			
G	.	.	.	.	.	3	0	Goods and Mineral Depôt	Lanark ...	N. B.	Sunnyside, Pass. & Coatbridge Central
.	.	.	.	.	.			Junction	Lanark ...	N. B.	Sunnyside and Gartgill.
.	.	.	.	.	.			Tin-Plate Works	Lanark ...	Cal.—N. B.	Whifflet.
.	.	.	.	.	.			Vulcan Boiler Works	Lanark ...	Cal.	Coatbridge.
.	.	.	.	.	.			Waverley Iron & Steel Wks.	Lanark ...	N. B.	Sunnyside and Commonhead.
								Whifflet—			
G	P	.	.	.	.	1	10	(Station)	Lanark ...	N. B.	Coatbridge (Central) and Bothwell.
.	.	.	.	.	.			Central Junction	Lanark ...	N. B.	Whifflet and Bellshill.
.	.	.	.	.	.			Forge Siding	Lanark ...	N. B.	Near Whifflet.
.	.	.	.	.	.			Foundry (Tennant's Foundry)	Lanark ...	{ Cal. { N. B.	Whifflet. Branch from Whifflet Central Jn.
.	P	.	.	.	.			High Level	Lanark ...	Cal.	Langloan and Airdrie.
G	P	.	.	.	.	3	0	Low Level	Lanark ...	Cal.	Motherwell and Coatbridge.
.	.	.	.	.	.			North Junction	Lanark ...	Cal.—N. B.	Mossend and Coatbridge.
.	.	.	.	.	.			Coatbridge Gas Works	Lanark ...	N. B.	Coatbridge, Sunnyside.
.	.	.	.	.	.			Coatbridge Iron Works	Lanark ...	{ Cal. { N. B.	Langloan.
.	.	.	.	.	.			Coatbridge Tin Plate Works	Lanark ...	Cal.—N. B.	Coatbridge, Whifflet.
.	P	.	.	.	.			Coatdyke	Lanark ...	N. B.	Coatbridge, Whifflet.
.	.	.	.	.	.						Coatbridge, Sunnyside and Airdrie, South.
.	.	.	.	.	.			Coatdyke Brick Works	Lanark ...	N. B.	Same as Rochsolloch Brick Works (Coatbridge).
.	.	.	.	.	.			Coatdyke Foundry	Lanark ...	N. B.	Coatbridge, Sheepford.
.	.	.	.	.	.			Coatdyke Goods and Mineral Depôt (Sheepford Locks Sid)	Lanark ...	N. B.	Coatbridge, Sheepford.
.	.	.	.	.	.			Coates & Rutley's Belle Vue Brick Co.'s Dennis Siding...	Cambs	L. & N. W.	Gamlingay.
.	.	.	.	.	.			Coates Park Colliery	Derby	Mid.	Pye Bridge.
.	.	.	.	.	.			Coatham Iron Works	Yorks	N. E.	Tod Point.
.	.	.	.	.	.			Coatham Lane Depôts	Yorks	N. E.	Redcar.
.	.	.	.	.	.			Coat's Iron and Steel Works	Lanark ...	N. B.	Coatbridge, Sheepford.
.	.	.	.	.	.			Coat's Siding	Renfrew	G. & S. W.	Paisley, Ferguslie.
.	.	.	.	.	.			Coat's Tube Works	Lanark ...	N. B.	Coatbridge, Sheepford.
.	.	.	.	.	.			Coatyburn Siding	Hadding'n	N. B.	See Haddington.
.	.	.	.	.	.			Coaxden Siding	Dorset	L. & S. W.	See Axminster.
G	P	.	.	.	.			Cobbinshaw	Edinboro'	Cal.	Carstairs and Edinburgh.
.	.	.	.	.	.			Cobbinshaw Lime Works...	Edinboro'	Cal.	Auchengray and Cobbinshaw.
.	.	.	.	.	.			Cobbinshaw, South	Edinboro'	Cal.	Branch near Cobbinshaw.
.	.	.	.	.	.			Mungall's Siding	Edinboro'	Cal.	Cobbinshaw.
.	.	.	.	.	.			Tarbrax Oil Works	Lanark ...	Cal.	Branch near Cobbinshaw.
.	.	.	.	.	.			Viewfield Colliery	Lanark ...	Cal.	Branch near Cobbinshaw.
.	.	.	.	.	.			Woolford's Siding	Lanark ...	Cal.	Branch near Cobbinshaw.
G	P	F	L	H	C	2	0	Cobden Mill Siding	Denbigh	G. W.—W. M. & C. Q.	Wrexham.
.	.	.	.	.	.			Cobham and Stoke D'Abernon	Surrey	L. & S. W.	Surbiton and Guildford.
.	P	.	.	.	.			Coborn Road (for Old Ford)..	Middlesex	G. E.	See London.
G	P	.	.	.	.			Cobre Yard	Glamorg'n	R. & S. B.	See Swansea.
.	.	.	.	.	.			Cobridge	Staffs	N. S.	Hanley and Burslem.
.	.	.	.	.	.			Sneyd Col. & Brick Works..	Staffs	N. S.	Cobridge.
.	.	.	.	.	.			Cochran & Co.'s Siding	Dumfries	G. & S. W.	Annan.
.	.	.	.	.	.			Cochrane & Co.'s Sidings	Staffs	G. W.	Round Oak.
.	.	.	.	.	.			Cochrane Bros.' Siding	Selkirk	N. B.	Same as Netherdale Sid. (Galashiels).
.	.	.	.	.	.			Cochrane's, J. & W., Siding..	Selkirk	N. B.	Same as Mid Mill Sid. (Galashiels).
G	P	.	L	H	C	1	10	Cockburnspath	Berwick	N. B.	Dunbar and Berwick.
G	.	.	.	.	.			Pease Siding	Berwick	N. B.	Cockburnspath and Reston.
.	.	.	.	.	.			Cockburn's Siding	Renfrew	G & P Jt (Cal & G & S W)	Cardonald.
								COCKERMOUTH—			
G	.	F	.	.	.	4	0	Station (C. K. & P. and L. & N. W. Jt.)	Cumb'land	{ C.K.&P. & L. & N.W.Jt. { M. & C.	Bch—Cockermouth Pass & Brigham. Over L. & N. W. from Brigham.
.	P	F	L	H	C	.	.	Station (C. K. & P. and L. & N. W. Jt.)	Cumb'land	{ C.K.&P. & L. & N.W.Jt. { M. & C.	Keswick and Workington. Over LNW&CK&P from Brigham.
.	.	.	.	.	.			Junction	Cumb'land	C. K. & P.—L. & N. W..	Keswick and Workington.
G	P	.	.	.	.			Cockett	Glamorg'n	G. W.	Landore and Llanelly.
.	P	.	.	.	.			Cockfield	Durham	N. E.	Barnard Castle & Bishop Auckland.
G	P	F	.	H	C			Cockfield	Suffolk	G. E.	Bury St. Edmunds and Sudbury.
.	.	.	.	.	.			Jennings', F. H., Siding	Suffolk	G. E.	Cockfield.
.	.	.	.	.	.			Cockfield Stone Quarry	Durham	N. E.	Cockfield.
G	P	.	L	H	.			Cocking	Sussex	L. B. & S. C.	Midhurst and Chichester.
.	.	.	.	.	.			Cocklaw Quarry	Northumb	N. B.	Chollerton.
.	.	.	.	.	.			Cockley Brake Junction	N'hampt'n	L. & N. W.—N. & B. Jn.	Banbury and Towcester.
.	.	.	.	.	.			Cockram Road Junction	Yorks	G. C.—Mid.	Barnsley.

EXPLANATION—G *Goods Station.* P *Passenger and Parcel Station.* P* *Passenger, but not Parcel or Miscellaneous Traffic.*
F *Furniture Vans, Carriages, Portable Engines, and Machines on Wheels.* L *Live Stock.*
H *Horse Boxes and Prize Cattle Vans.* C *Carriages by Passenger Train.*

STATION ACCOMMODATION.						CRANE POWER.		STATIONS, &c.	COUNTY.	COMPANY.	POSITION.
						Tons	Cwts				
								Cockshute Sidings (N. S.) ...	Staffs	N. S.—L. & N. W.	Stoke-on-Trent.
G	P	F	L	H	C	1	10	Codford	Wilts	G. W.	Salisbury and Westbury.
								Codnor	Derby	Mid.	See Crosshill and Codnor.
G	P	F	L	H	C	0	15	Codnor Park and Ironville ...	Derby	Mid.	Clay Cross and Trent.
								Butterley Co.—			
								Brand's Colliery	Derby	Mid.	Near Codnor Park Station.
								Britain Colliery	Derby	Mid.	Near Codnor Park Station.
								Butterley Works	Derby	Mid.	Near Codnor Park Station.
								Coal and Iron Works ...	Derby	Mid.	Near Codnor Park Station.
								Gullet Siding	Derby	Mid.	Near Codnor Park Station.
								Ironstone Siding	Derby	Mid.	Near Codnor Park Station.
G	P	F	L	H	C	5	0	Codnor Park (for Ironville and Jacksdale)	Notts	G. N.	Eastwood and Pinxton.
								Codnor Park Collieries (G N)	Derby	G. N.—G. C.	Codnor Park and Eastwood.
								Codnor Park Iron Works (Brinsley Sidings)	Derby	G. N.	Codnor Park and Eastwood.
								Pye Hill Siding	Notts	G. N.	Codnor Park.
								Ridding's Colliery (G. N.)	Notts	G. N.—G. C.	Codnor Park and Pye Hill.
								Codnor Park Junction	Derby	G. N.	Same as Brinsley Junction.
G	P	F	L	H	C	4	0	Codsall	Staffs	G. W.	Wolverhampton and Wellington.
								Coedcae Colliery (Lewis Merthyr Colliery)	Glamorg'n	T. V.	Porth.
								Coedmadoc Slate Co.'s Cloddfar Grai Siding	Carnarvon	L. & N. W.	Nantlle.
	P							Coedpenmaen	Glamorg'n	T. V.	Pontypridd and Nelson.
G	P			H*		4	0	Coed Poeth	Denbigh	G. W.	Wrexham and Minera.
								Caello Brick Works	Denbigh	G. W.	Brymbo and Minera.
								Smelt Sid. (English Electric Carbon Co.'s)	Denbigh	G. W.	Brymbo and Minera.
										L. & N. W.	Branch from Hope.
G	P					5	0 }	Coed Talon (L. & N. W.)	Flint		
	P									G. W.	Over L. & N. W. from Coed Talon Jn.
								Alyn Brick, Tile, & Terra-Cotta Co.'s Tryddyn Lodge Siding	Flint	L. & N. W.	Coed Talon and Llanfynydd.
								Cefn-y-coed Colliery	Flint	L. & N. W.	Coed Talon and Llanfynydd.
								Coed Talon Colliery Co.'s Cae Bleyddyn Pits	Flint	L. & N. W.	Coed Talon and Mold.
								Erith Brick, Tile, & Terra-Cotta Co.'s Siding	Flint	L. & N. W.	Coed Talon and Padeswood.
								Nerquis Old Col. Level Sid.	Flint	L. & N. W.	Coed Talon and Mold.
								Davies'	Flint	L. & N. W.	Nerquis Old Colliery Level Siding.
								Edwards'	Flint	L. & N. W.	Nerquis Old Colliery Level Siding.
								Griffiths'	Flint	L. & N. W.	Nerquis Old Colliery Level Siding.
								Phœnix Coal & Cannel Co.—			
								Celyn Wood Colliery	Flint	L. & N. W.	Coed Talon and Mold.
								New North Leeswood Col.	Flint	L. & N. W.	Coed Talon and Mold.
								South Level Sidings	Flint	L. & N. W.	Coed Talon and Llanfynydd.
								Darbyshire's Siding	Flint	L. & N. W.	South Level Sidings.
								Peter's Siding	Flint	L. & N. W.	South Level Sidings.
								Pontybodkin Coal and Cannel Colliery	Flint	L. & N. W.	South Level Sidings.
								Coed Talon Junction	Flint	L. & N. W.—W. & M. Jt.	Coed Talon and Brymbo.
								Coedybrain Quarry	Glamorg'n	Rhy.	Llanbradach.
								Coedybrain Siding	Denbigh	G. W.	Moss.
								Coedygric Junction	Mon	G. W.	Pontypool.
								Coedymoeth Colliery (B.&M.)	Mon	B. & M.—G. W.	New Tredegar and White Rose.
								Coedymoeth Colliery	Glamorg'n	Rhy.	See Powell Duffryn Co. (Brithdir).
								Coegnant Colliery	Glamorg'n	G. W.	Caerau.
								Coe's, A., Siding	Suffolk	G. E.	Bramford.
G	P							Cogan	Glamorg'n	Barry	Barry and Cogan Junction.
								Cogan Junction	Glamorg'n	Barry—T. V.	Cogan and Grangetown.
								Coghlan Steel & Iron Co.'s Sid.	Derby	Mid.	Leeds, Hunslet Lane.
								Coity Junction	Glamorg'n	Barry—G. W.	Southerndown Road and Tondu.
								Coke Ovens Junction	Suffolk	G. E.—N. & S. Jt.	Lowestoft.
								Colaton Raleigh Siding	Devon	L. & S.W.	East Budleigh.
G	P	F	L	H	C			Colbinstown	Wicklow	G. S. & W.	Sallins and Tullow.
										N. & Brecon	Penwyllt and Neath.
G	P							Colbren Junction Sta. (N.&B.)	Brecon	Mid.	Over Neath and Brecon Line.
G	P	F	L					Colby	I. of Man	I. of Man	Douglas and Port Erin.
								COLCHESTER—			
G	P	F	L	H	C			(Station)	Essex	G. E.	Chelmsford and Ipswich.
								Colchester Brewery Co.'s Sid.	Essex	G. E.	Hythe.

EXPLANATION—G Goods Station.   P Passenger and Parcel Station.   P* Passenger, but not Parcel or Miscellaneous Traffic.
F Furniture Vans, Carriages, Portable Engines, and Machines on Wheels.   L Live Stock.
H Horse Boxes and Prize Cattle Vans.   H* By special arrangement only.   C Carriages by Passenger Train.

STATION ACCOMMODATION.						CRANE POWER.		STATIONS, &c.	COUNTY.	COMPANY.	POSITION.
						Tons	Cwts				
G	P	F	.	.	.	15	0	COLCHESTER—continued. Hythe	Essex	G. E.	Colchester and Wyvenhoe.
.	.	.	.	.	.	.	.	Marriage & Son's Siding....	Essex	G. E.	Hythe.
G	P	F	.	H	C	6	0	Nickoll & Co.'s Siding	Essex	G. E.	Hythe.
.	.	.	.	.	.	.	.	St. Botolphs	Essex	G. E.	Branch—Colchester and Hythe.
.	.	.	.	.	.	.	.	Colchester Brewery Co.'s Sid.	Essex	G. E.	Colchester, Hythe.
G	P	.	L	.	.	1	0	Colchester Brewery Co.'s Sid.	Suffolk	G. E.	Eye.
.	.	.	.	.	.	.	.	Coldham	Cambs	G. E.	Wisbech and March.
.	.	.	.	.	.	.	.	Coldham Brick Co.'s Siding (Beale's, H. F., Sid.) (G.E.)	Cambs	G. E.—L. & N. W.—Mid	Cambridge.
.	.	.	.	.	.	.	.	Coldham Lane Siding (G. E.)	Cambs	G. E.—Mid.	Cambridge.
.	.	.	.	.	.	.	.	Cold Harbour Siding	Devon	G. W.	Tiverton Junction Station.
.	.	.	.	.	.	.	.	Cold Hesleden Siding	Durham	N. E.	Haswell.
.	.	.	.	.	.	.	.	Coldingham	Berwick	N. B.	See Reston (for Coldingham and St. Abbs).
G	P	F	L	H	C	.	.	Cold Norton (for Purleigh and Stow-Maries)	Essex	G. E.	Wickford and Maldon.
G	.	.	L	.	.	.	.	Baron's Lane Siding	Essex	G. E.	Cold Norton and Maldon, West.
G	P	F	L	H	C	1	0	Coldstream	Northumb	N. E.	Berwick and Kelso.
.	.	.	.	.	.	.	.	Learmouth Siding and Depôt	Northumb	N. E.	Coldstream.
G	P	F	L	H	C	1	10	Cole	Somerset	S.&D.Jt.(L.&S.W.& Mid)	Templecombe and Glastonbury.
G	P	.	.	.	.	.	.	Colebrooke	Ferm'nagh	Clogher Valley	Fivemiletown and Maguiresbridge.
G	.	.	.	.	.	2	0	Coleburn's Siding	Elgin&Mo	G. N. of S.	Craigellachie and Elgin.
G	P	F	L	H	C	2	0	Coleford	Glo'ster	{ G. W.	Branch from Monmouth.
G	P	F	L	H	C	1	10			{ S&WyeJt (G.W.& Mid.)	Branch—Coleford Junc. & Milkwall.
.	.	.	.	.	.	.	.	Whitecliffe Lime Works	Glo'ster	G. W.	Coleford and Newland.
.	.	.	.	.	.	.	.	Coleford Branch Junction	Glo'ster	S.&WyeJt.(G.W.& Mid.)	Parkend and Speech House Road.
.	.	.	.	.	.	.	.	Coleford Junction	Glo'ster	G. W.—S. & Wye Jt.	Monmouth and Cinderford.
G	P	.	L	H	C	.	.	Coleford Junction	Devon	L. & S.W.	Yeoford Junction and Bow.
.	.	.	.	.	.	.	.	Cole Green	Herts	G. N.	Hatfield and Hertford.
.	P	.	.	.	.	.	.	Birchall Siding	Herts	G. N.	Cole Green and Hatfield.
.	.	.	.	.	.	.	.	Coleham	Salop	S & H Jt (G W & L & N W)	See Shrewsbury.
.	.	.	.	.	.	.	.	Colehouse Lane	Somerset	W. C. & P.	Weston-super-Mare and Clevedon.
.	.	.	.	.	.	.	.	Coleorton Colliery (Mid.)	Leicester	Mid.—L. & N. W.	Coalville.
G	P	F	L	H	C	2	0	Coleraine Junction Station	Derry	N. C. Com. (Mid.)	Londonderry and Ballymena.
G	P	.	.	.	.	.	.	Coleshill	Warwick	Mid.	Whitacre and Hampton.
.	.	.	.	.	.	.	.	Maxstoke Siding	Warwick	Mid.	Near Coleshill Station.
G	P	.	L	.	.	.	.	Cole's Siding	Derby	G. N.	Derby.
.	.	.	.	.	.	.	.	Colfin	Wigtown	P.P.&W.Jt.(Cal.,G&SW, L. & N. W. & Mid.)	Portpatrick and Stranraer.
G	P	.	.	.	.	.	.	Colinshiel Colliery	L'lithgow	N. B.	Bathgate, Lower.
G	.	.	.	.	.	1	10	Colinton	Edinboro'	Cal.	Currie & Edinburgh.
.	.	.	.	.	.	.	.	Colinton Paper Mill (West Colinton Paper Mill)	Edinboro'	Cal.	Colinton.
G	P	.	.	.	.	.	.	Coll	Argyll	Cal.	Steamer from Oban.
.	.	.	.	.	.	.	.	College	Lanark	G. & S.W.—N. B.	See Glasgow.
.	.	.	.	.	.	.	.	College East Junction	Lanark	G. & S.W.—N. B.	Glasgow, Sydney Street or College East Junction.
G	P	.	.	.	.	0	15	College North Junction	Lanark	N. B.	Glasgow.
.	.	.	.	.	.	.	.	Collessie	Fife	N. B.	Ladybank and Perth.
.	.	.	.	.	.	.	.	Collett & Co.'s Siding	Glo'ster	Mid.	Gloucester.
.	.	.	.	.	.	.	.	Colley's Malt Kiln	Yorks	N. E.	Tadcaster.
.	.	.	.	.	.	.	.	Collier's, W. H., Siding	Essex	G. E.	Marks Tey.
.	.	.	.	.	.	.	.	Colliertree Siding	Lanark	N. B.	Rawyards.
.	P	.	.	.	.	.	.	Colliery Supply Co.'s Siding	Glamorg'n	GW—LNW—Rhy.—TV.	Cardiff.
.	.	.	.	.	.	.	.	Collin	Antrim	N. C. Com. (Mid.)	Ballymena and Larne.
G	P	F	L	H	C	5	0	Collingbourne	Wilts	M. & S. W. Jn.	Savernake and Andover.
G	P	F	L	H	C	.	.	Collingham	Notts	Mid.	Nottingham and Lincoln.
G	P	.	L	H	.	2	0	Collingham Bridge	Yorks	N. E.	Leeds and Wetherby.
.	P	.	.	.	.	.	.	Collins Green	Lancs	L. & N. W.	Kenyon Junc. Station and Liverpool.
.	.	.	.	.	.	.	.	Collins Green Colliery Co.— Bold Colliery	Lancs	L. & N. W.	Earlestown.
.	.	.	.	.	.	.	.	Collins Green Colliery	Lancs	L. & N. W.	Earlestown.
.	.	.	.	.	.	.	.	Collins Green Siding	Lancs	L. & N. W.	See Evans, R., & Co. (Earlestown).
.	.	.	.	.	.	.	.	Collin's, J. W., Siding	Norfolk	G. E.	Downham.
.	.	.	.	.	.	.	.	Collinswell Siding (Baird & Stevenson's)	Fife	N. B.	Burntisland.
G	P	.	L	H	C	1	10	Colliston	Forfar	Cal.	Forfar and Arbroath.
G	P	.	L	H	.	.	.			{ G. S. & W.	Claremorris and Sligo.
G	P	F	L	H	C	1	0	Collooney	Sligo	{ M. G. W.	Longford and Sligo.
G	P	.	L	.	.	.	.			{ S. L. & N. C.	Manorhamilton and Sligo.

EXPLANATION—G Goods Station.　　P Passenger and Parcel Station.　　P* Passenger, but not Parcel or Miscellaneous Traffic.
F Furniture Vans, Carriages, Portable Engines, and Machines on Wheels.　L Live Stock.
H Horse Boxes and Prize Cattle Vans.　　C Carriages by Passenger Train.

STATION ACCOMMODATION.						CRANE POWER.		STATIONS, &c.	COUNTY.	COMPANY.	POSITION.
						Tons	Cwts				
								Collooney Junction	Sligo	{ G. S. & W.—M. G. W... { G. S. & W.—S. L. & N. C.	Charlestown and Ballysodare. Charlestown and Enniskillen.
								Collyshot Collieries	Lanark ...	N. B.	Same as Coltness Col. (Morningside).
								Collyshot Mine	Lanark ...	Cal.	{ Morningside. { Newmains. { Wishaw.
								Colman's, J. & J., Siding (Carrow Works)	Norfolk ...	G. E.	Norwich.
G	P	F	L	H	C	3	0	Colnbrook...........................	Middlesex	G. W.	West Drayton and Staines.
G	P	F	L	H	C	2	0	Colne	Essex	C. V. & H.	Halstead and Chappel.
G	P	F	L	H	C	10	0 }	Colne Station and Junction...	Lancs	{ L. & Y. { Mid.	Branch from Burnley. Branch from Skipton.
G	P	F	L	H	C	10	0 }				
								Colney Green Siding	Derby	Mid.	Clay Cross.
								Colney Hatch	Middlesex	G. N.	See New Southgate and Friern Barnet (for Colney Hatch).
								Colney Hatch Asylum Siding (London County Lunatic Asylum)	Middlesex	G. N.	New Southgate.
								Colney Heath	Herts	G. N.	See Smallford (for Colney Heath).
								Colonial Stove & Iron Wks. (Dobbie, Forbes & Co.)......	Stirling ...	Cal.	Larbert.
								Coltbridge Junction	Edinboro'	Cal.	Edinburgh.
	P*							Coltfield Platform	Elgin&Mo'	High	Alves and Burghead.
								Colthurst, Symons & Co.'s Brick Works	Somerset.	S.&D.Jt. (L.&S.W.&Mid)	Highbridge and Burnham.
G	P	F	L	H	C			Coltishall	Norfolk ...	G. E.	Wroxham and Aylsham.
								Coltman & Son's Siding	Leicester ..	Mid.	Loughborough.
								Coltness Cols. (Collyshot Cols)	Lanark ...	N. B.	Morningside.
								Coltness Iron Works.............	Lanark ...	N. B.	Morningside.
								Coltness Iron Works & Cols..	Lanark ...	Cal.	{ Morningside. { Newmains.
								Colton Coal Depôt	Fife	N. B.	Same as Pittencrieff Colliery Siding.
								Colton Siding	Fife	N. B.	See Whitemyre Junction Station.
								Colville's Iron & Steel Works	Lanark ...	Cal.	Same as Dalzell Iron & Steel Works.
G	P	F	L	H	C	1	10 }	Colwall (G.W.)	Hereford..	{ G. W. { Mid.	Worcester and Hereford. Over G. W. Line.
G		F	L			1	10 }				
G								Colwich............................	Staffs	N. S.	Near Colwich Junction.
G	P	F	L	H	C		. }	Colwich (L. & N. W.)	Staffs	{ L. & N. W. { N. S.	Lichfield and Stafford. Over L. & N. W. from Colwich Jn.
	P	F	L	H	C		. }				
								Colwich Brick & Tile Co.'s Siding	Staffs	L. & N. W.	Colwich and Rugeley, Trent Valley.
								Colwich Junction	Staffs	L. & N. W.—N. S.	Lichfield and Hixon.
								Colwick	Notts	Mid.	See Carlton and Netherfield.
								Colwick (G. N.)	Notts	G. N.—L. & N. W.	See Netherfield and Colwick.
G	P	F	L	H	C	5	0	Colwyn Bay	Denbigh ..	L. & N. W.	Bangor and Rhyl.
	P							Colyford	Devon	L. & S.W.	Seaton Junction and Seaton.
G	P		L			5	0	Colyton	Devon	L. & S.W.	Seaton Junction and Seaton.
G	P		L	H		1	10	Colzium	Stirling ...	K. & B. Jt. (Cal. & N. B.)	Kilsyth and Bonnybridge, Central.
G								Banton Siding..................	Stirling ...	K. & B. Jt. (Cal. & N. B.)	Colzium and Banknock.
G	P		L	H	C	2	10	Comber	Down	B. & C. D.	Belfast and Downpatrick.
								Andrews & Co.'s Siding ...	Down	B. & C. D.	Comber.
								Combe's Siding ...	Oxon	G. W.	Handboro'.
G	P		L	H	C			Combpyne	Devon	L. & S.W.	Axminster and Lyme Regis.
								Commercial BreweryCo.'sSid.	Cambs ...	G. E.	Cambridge, Barnwell Junction Sta.
								Commercial Foundry and Engineering Works	Yorks	N. E.	Middlesbro'.
								Commercial Road	Middlesex	L. T. & S.	See London.
								Commercial Road Junction...	Middlesex	G. E.—L. T. & S.	London, Leman Street & Shadwell.
								Commercial Street Yard	Yorks	N. E.	See Calder, Dixon & Co. (Middlesbro').
								Common Branch Junction ...	Ayr	G. & S.W.	Auchinleck and Lugar.
								Common Branch Junction ...	Glamorg'n	T. V.	Llantrisant.
	P							Commondale	Yorks	N. E.	Near Castleton.
								Commondale Brick & Pipe Co.'s Siding	Yorks	N. E.	Castleton.
								Commondale Whinstone Co.'s Siding	Yorks	N. E.	Castleton.
	P							Commondyke	Ayr	G. & S.W.	Auchinleck and Lugar.
								Commonhead	Lanark ...	N. B.	See Airdrie.
								Commonhead Siding.............	Lanark ...	N. B.	See Airdrie.
								Common Junction	Glamorg'n	G. W.—T. V.	Llantrisant.
								Common Pits, Nos. 5, 6, 7, 10, 11, 12, 14, 15, and 16	Ayr	G. & S.W.	Lugar.

EXPLANATION—G *Goods Station.*   P *Passenger and Parcel Station.*   P* *Passenger, but not Parcel or Miscellaneous Traffic.*
F *Furniture Vans, Carriages, Portable Engines, and Machines on Wheels.*   L *Live Stock.*
H *Horse Boxes and Prize Cattle Vans.*   C *Carriages by Passenger Train.*

STATION ACCOMMODATION.						CRANE POWER.		STATIONS, &c.	COUNTY.	COMPANY.	POSITION.
						Tons	Cwts.				
G	P	F	L	H	C	3	0	Compressed Air Co.'s Siding	Warwick..	Mid.	Birmingham, Lawley Street.
G	P	F	L	H	C	3	0	Compton	Berks	G. W.	Didcot and Newbury.
						.	.	Comrie	Perth	Cal.	Crieff and Balquhidder.
						.	.	Condensed Peptonized Milk Co.'s Siding	Bucks	L. & N. W.	Buckingham.
	P					.	.	Conder Green (Private)	Lancs	L. & N. W.	Glasson Dock and Lancaster.
G	P	F	L	H	C	.	.	Condover	Salop	S.&H.Jt(G.W.&L&NW)	Craven Arms and Shrewsbury.
						.	.	Conduit Colliery	Staffs	Mid.	Brownhills.
						.	.	Conduit Colliery Co.'s Norton Canes Siding	Staffs	L. & N. W.	Brownhills.
						.	.	Coneygarth Siding	Northumb	N. E.	Ashington.
						.	.	Coneygre Siding	Staffs	L. & N. W.	Same as Earl of Dudley's Siding. (Dudley).
						.	.	Coneypark Siding	Stirling	K. & B. Jt. (Cal. & N. B.)	Banknock.
G	P	F	L	H	C	5	0	Congleton (N. S.)	Cheshire.	{ N. S. { L. & N. W.	Macclesfield and Harecastle. Over N. S. Line.
G						.	.	Brunswick Street Wharf	Cheshire.	N. S.	Branch near Congleton.
						.	.	Heath & Son's Wharf	Cheshire.	N. S.	Congleton (Brunswick).
						.	.	Ward's Basin	Cheshire.	N. S.	Congleton (Brunswick).
G	P	.	L	.	.	2	0	Congresbury	Somerset.	G. W.	Yatton and Cheddar.
						.	.	Conisborough	Yorks	H. & B.	See Denaby and Conisborough.
G	P	.	L	H	C	2	0	Conisborough (G. C.)	Yorks	{ G. C. { Mid.	Barnsley and Doncaster. Over G. C. from Swinton Junction.
						.	.	Cadeby Colliery (G. C.)	Yorks	G. C.— Mid.	Conisborough.
						.	.	Kilner's Siding (G. C.)	Yorks	G. C.— Mid.	Conisborough.
						.	.	Coniscliffe Siding	Durham	N. E.	Barton.
	P					.	.	Conishead Priory	Lancs	Furness	Branch from Ulverston.
G	P	F	L	H	C	3	0	Coniston	Lancs	Furness	Branch from Foxfield.
								CONNAH'S QUAY—			
G	P	.				.	.	(Station)	Flint	L. & N. W.	Chester and Rhyl.
G	.	.	.	.	.	12	0	(Station and Dock)	Flint	W. M. & C. Q.	Buckley & Hawarden Bridge Junc.
						.	.	Central Brick Works	Flint	W. M. & C. Q.	Connah's Quay.
						.	.	Darbyshire's Brick Works (Wepre Hall Brick Wks.)	Flint	W. M. & C. Q.	Hawarden & Connah's Quay & Shotton
						.	.	East Junction	Flint	L. & N. W.— W. M.&C.Q.	Rhyl and Connah's Quay.
						.	.	Princes Brick Works	Flint	W. M. & C. Q.	Connah's Quay.
						.	.	Princes Dentith Siding	Flint	L. & N. W.	Connah's Quay and Queen's Ferry.
						.	.	Rowley's Shotton Bk. Wks.	Flint	W. M. & C. Q.	Connah's Quay and Hawarden.
						.	.	Wepre Works (Borax Consolidated Works)	Flint	W. M. & C. Q.	Connah's Quay & Hawarden Bridge.
						.	.	West Junction	Flint	L. & N. W.— W. M.&C.Q.	Rhyl and Connah's Quay.
						.	.	Williams' Brick Works	Flint	W. M. & C. Q.	Connah's Quay.
	P	.	.	.	.	.	.	Connah's Quay and Shotton (W. M. & C. Q.)	Flint	{ W. M. & C. Q. { G. C.	Hawarden Bge. Junc. & Hawarden. Over W. M. & C. Q. from Hawarden Bridge Junction.
								Connal's—			
						.	.	Acklam Warrant Store and Wharf	Yorks	N. E.	Middlesbro'.
						.	.	Ayresome Warrant Store and Wharf	Yorks	N. E.	Middlesbro'.
						.	.	Connal's Pig Iron Store	Renfrew..	Cal.	Glasgow, Kinning Park.
						.	.	Connal's Pig Iron Store (G. & P. Jt.)	Lanark	{ Cal. { G. & S. W.	Glasgow, Kinning Park. Glasgow, General Terminus.
G	P	F	L	H	C	2	0	Connaught Road (L. & I. Dks.)	Essex	L. & I. Dks.— G. E.	See London.
						.	.	Connel Ferry	Argyll	Cal.	Callander and Oban.
						.	.	Connel, North	Argyll	Cal.	See North Connel.
						.	.	Connell & Co.'s Rosin Works	Lancs	L. & N. W.	Widnes.
						.	.	Connell & Co.'s Shipbuilding Yard	Renfrew..	Cal.— N. B.	{ Same as Scotstoun Shipbuilding { Yard (Glasgow).
G	P	F	L	H	C	1	10	Conniberry Junction	Queens	G. S. & W.	Maryborough.
G	P					.	.	Conon	Ross & Cro'	High	Dingwall and Inverness.
G	P		L	H		.	.	Cononley	Yorks	Mid.	Skipton and Keighley.
	P	P				.	.	Consall	Staffs	N. S.	Cheddleton and Froghall.
G	P	F	L	H	C	1	10	Consett	Durham	N. E.	Annfield Plain and Blackhill.
						.	.	Consett Iron & Steel Works, Furnaces, Mills, Shops and Stores	Durham	N. E.	Blackhill.
						.	.	Consett Iron Co.'s Granary	Durham	N. E.	Blackhill.
						.	.	Consett Iron Wks., High Yard	Durham	N. E.	Blackhill.
						.	.	Consett Iron Works Junction Sidings (Low Yard)	Durham	N. E.	Blackhill.
						.	.	Consolidated Engineering Wks	Bucks	G. W.	Slough.

EXPLANATION—G Goods Station.　　P Passenger and Parcel Station.　　P* Passenger, but not Parcel or Miscellaneous Traffic.
F Furniture Vans, Carriages, Portable Engines, and Machines on Wheels.　　L Live Stock.
H Horse Boxes and Prize Cattle Vans.　　C Carriages by Passenger Train.

STATION ACCOMMODATION.						CRANE POWER.	STATIONS, &c.	COUNTY.	COMPANY.	POSITION.
						Tons Cwts.	Consolidated Oil Co.'s—			
..	..	..	..	..	..	.. ..	Nene Siding	N'hamptn	Mid.	Peterborough.
..	..	..	..	..	..	.. ..	Siding	Kent	L. B. & S. C.	London, Deptford Wharf.
..	..	..	..	..	..	.. ..	Siding	W'morlnd	L. & N. W.	See Kendal Bonded Stores Co. (Kendal).
							Consolidated Petroleum Co.'s—			
..	..	..	..	..	..	.. ..	Oil Store	Durham ...	N. E.	Darlington, Hope Town.
..	..	..	..	..	..	.. ..	Siding (G. E.)................	Essex	G. E.—G. N.—G. W.— L. & N. W.—Mid. ...	London, Victoria & Albert Docks.
..	..	..	..	..	..	.. ..	Siding	Yorks	N. E.	Hull.
..	..	..	..	..	..	.. ..	Siding	Yorks	N. E.	York, Foss Islands.
							Consolidated Petroleum Store			
..	..	..	..	..	..	.. ..	Siding	Yorks	N. E.	Scarborough.
G	P	F	L	H	C	10 0	Constable Burton	Yorks	N. E.	Northallerton and Leyburn.
							Constable's Limestone			
..	..	..	..	..	..	.. ..	Quarries	Derby	Mid.	Same as Cawdor Sids.(Matlock Bge.)
G	P	.	L	.	.	5 0	Conway	Carnarvon	L. & N. W.	Bangor and Rhyl.
..	..	..	..	..	..	.. ..	Cambrian Asphalte Works.	Denbigh	L. & N. W.	Branch from Llandudno Junction.
..	..	..	..	..	..	.. ..	Lewis (Executors) Siding	Denbigh...	L. & N. W.	Branch from Llandudno Junction.
							Llandudno Junction Brick			
..	..	..	..	..	..	.. ..	Syndicate Siding	Denbigh...	L. & N. W.	Branch from Llandudno Junction.
G	P						Conway Morfa..................	Carnarvon	L. & N. W.	Bangor and Rhyl.
G						5 0	Conway Quay	Carnarvon	L. & N. W.	Bangor and Rhyl.
G	P	.	L			2 0	Conwil	Carmarth'	G. W.	Carmarthen and Pencader.
							Cook & D'dol Slate Quarry			
..	..	..	..	..	..	.. ..	Co.'s Siding	Carnarvon	L. & N. W.	See Cambrian Siding (Llanberis).
..	..	..	..	..	..	.. ..	Cook & Son's Outer Siding ..	Durham ...	N. E.	Washington.
..	..	..	..	..	..	.. ..	Cook, E., & Co.'s Siding	Middlesex	G. E.	London, Devonshire Street.
..	..	..	..	..	..	.. ..	Cook, F. R., & Co.'s Siding...	Suffolk ...	G. E.	Stowmarket.
..	..	..	..	..	..	.. ..	Cook's Brick Siding	Surrey ...	L. & S. W.	Oxshott.
..	..	..	..	..	..	.. ..	Cook's Kitchen Yard...........	Cornwall..	G. W.	Carn Brea.
							Cooke's Tinsley Iron & Wire			
..	..	..	..	..	..	.. ..	Works	Yorks	L. D. & E. C.—Mid.	Sheffield, Tinsley Road.
							Cooke's Tinsley Iron & Wire			
..	..	..	..	..	..	.. ..	Works (G.C.)	Yorks	G. C.—Mid.	Sheffield, Broughton Lane.
..	..	..	..	..	..	.. ..	Cooke, Verdin & Co.'s Siding	Cheshire...	L. & N. W.	Middlewich.
G	P	.	L	H		.. ..	Cookham	Berks ...	G. W.	Maidenhead and High Wycombe.
G	P	.	L	H	.	1 0	Cooksbridge....................	Sussex	L. B. & S. C.	Lewes and Plumpton.
G	P	F	L	H	C	5 0	Cookstown	Tyrone	N. C. Com. (Mid.)	Branch from Cookstown Junction.
G	P	F	L	H	C	3 0			G. N. (I.)	Branch from Dungannon.
G	P		L	H			Cookstown Junction Station	Antrim	N. C. Com. (Mid.)	Antrim and Ballymena.
..	..	..	..	..	..	.. ..	Cook Street	Lanark ...	G. & S. W.	See Glasgow.
..	..	..	..	..	..	.. ..	Coombe & Co.'s Siding	Essex	G. E.	Leytonstone.
G	P	.	.	.	.	.. ..	Coombe and Malden	Surrey ...	L. & S. W.	Wimbledon and Surbiton.
	P*						Coombe Junction Station......	Cornwall..	L. & Looe	Moorswater and Looe.
.	P	.	.	.	.	.. ..	Coombe Lane	Surrey ...	W. & S. C. Jt.(L. B. & S. C. and S. E. & C.).........	Woodside and Selsdon Road.
							Cooper & Co.'s Crescent			
..	..	..	..	..	..	.. ..	Brewery (Mid.)	Staffs ...	Mid—L&NW—G N—N S	Burton-on-Trent.
..	..	..	..	..	..	.. ..	Cooper & Son's Siding	Lincoln ...	G. N.	Boston.
							Co-operative Wholesale Society's—			
..	..	..	..	..	..	. .	Dunston Flour Mill	Durham ...	N. E.	Redheugh.
							Lard Refinery & Egg Ware-			
..	..	..	..	..	..	.. ..	house	Durham ...	N. E.	West Hartlepool.
..	..	..	..	..	..	.. ..	Siding	Lancs	Manchester Ship Canal...	Manchester.
..	..	..	..	..	..	.. ..	Siding	Lancs	L. & Y.	Crossens.
..	..	..	..	..	..	.. ..	Siding	Lancs	L. & Y.	Liverpool, North Docks.
..	..	..	..	..	..	.. ..	Siding	Lancs	L. & Y.	Middleton Junction.
..	..	..	..	..	..	.. ..	Siding	Lancs	P & L Jt.(L & NW & L & Y)	Longridge.
..	..	..	..	..	..	.. ..	Siding (G. E.)	Essex	GE—GN—L & NW—Mid	London, Silvertown.
..	..	..	..	..	..	.. ..	Soap and Candle Works ...	Lancs	C.L.C.(G.C.,G.N.& Mid.)	Glazebrook.
..	..	..	..	..	..	.. ..	Warehouse	Northumb	N. E.	Newcastle-on-Tyne.
G	P	.	L	H	C	2 10	Cooper Bridge (L. & Y.) ...	Yorks	L. & Y.	Brighouse and Mirfield.
									G. N.	Over L. & Y. from Wakefield.
..	..	..	..	..	..	.. ..	Cooper, H., & Co.'s Works	Yorks	L. D. & E. C.—Mid.	Sheffield, Tinsley Road.
..	..	..	..	..	..	.. ..	Cooper House Siding............	Yorks	L. & Y.	Same as Sowerby Bridge Gas Works (Luddendenfoot).
..	..	..	..	..	..	.. ..	Cooper's Lodge Junction......	Staffs	L & N W—Cannock Chase Co.	Branch from Hednesford.
..	..	..	..	..	..	.. ..	Coote & Sons' Siding...........	Hunts......	G. E.	St. Ives.
..	..	..	..	..	..	.. ..	Coote & Warren's Sidings ...	Cambs......	G. E.—Mid.	Cambridge.

EXPLANATION—G *Goods Station.*   P *Passenger and Parcel Station.*   P* *Passenger, but not Parcel or Miscellaneous Traffic.*
F *Furniture Vans, Carriages, Portable Engines, and Machines on Wheels.*   L *Live Stock.*
H *Horse Boxes and Prize Cattle Vans.*   C *Carriages by Passenger Train.*

STATION ACCOMMODATION.						CRANE POWER.	STATIONS, &c.	COUNTY.	COMPANY.	POSITION.
						Tons Cwts.				
G	P	F	L	.	.	1 10	Cootehill	Cavan	G. N. (I.)	Branch from Shantona Junction.
.	.	.	.	.	.		Copeland Road	Lanark	Glas. Dist. Sub.	See Glasgow.
.	.	.	.	.	.		Copenhagen Junction	Middlesex	G. N.	London, King's Cross and Finsbury Park.
G	P	.	.	H	.		Copgrove	Yorks	N. E.	Knaresboro' and Boroughbridge.
.	P	.	.	.	.		Copley	Yorks	L. & Y.	Halifax and Sowerby Bridge.
.	.	.	.	.	.		Copley Hill	Yorks	L. & N. W.	See Leeds.
G	.	.	.	.	.		Copley Hill Sidings	Yorks	G. N.	Leeds, Holbeck.
G	P	F	L	H	C				N. E.	York and Leeds.
.	P	.	.	H	C				G. C.	Over N. E. from Knottingley Ferry Bridge Junction.
							Copmanthorpe (N. E.)	Yorks		
.	P	.	.	H	C				G. N.	Over N. E. & S. & K. Jt. Lines.
.	P	.	.	.	.				Mid.	Over N. E. Line.
.	.	.	.	.	.		Copperas Bank Forge & Depôts	Durham	N. E.	Pallion.
.	.	.	.	.	.		Copperas Siding	Northumb	N. E.	Lemington.
.	.	.	.	.	.		Copper Mill Junction	Essex	G. E.	London, Lea Bridge.
.	.	.	.	.	.		Copper Miners' Tin Plate Co.'s Siding	Glamorg'n	R. & S. B.	Cwmavon.
.	.	.	.	.	.		Copper Pit Colliery	Glamorg'n	G. W.	Morriston.
.	.	.	.	.	.		Coppice Colliery Co.'s Five Ways Colliery	Staffs	L. & N. W.	Brownhills.
G	P	.	L	H	.	5 0	Copplestone	Devon	L. & S. W.	Exeter and Barnstaple.
G	P	.	L	.	.	5 0	Coppull	Lancs	L. & N. W.	Preston and Wigan.
.	.	.	.	.	.		Barker & Son's Siding (Welch Whittle Colliery)	Lancs	L. & N. W.	Coppull and Balshaw Lane.
							Blainscough Colliery Co.—			
.	.	.	.	.	.		Blainscough Colliery	Lancs	L. & N. W.	Coppull and Standish.
.	.	.	.	.	.		Darlington Siding	Lancs	L. & N. W.	Coppull and Balshaw Lane.
							Pearson & Knowles Cl. & Ir. Co.'s Coppull Hall Sid.	Lancs	L. & N. W.	Coppull and Standish.
.	.	.	.	.	.		Chisnall Hall Colliery	Lancs	L. & N. W.	Coppull Hall Siding.
.	.	.	.	.	.		Hicbibi Brick Works	Lancs	L. & N. W.	Coppull Hall Siding.
.	.	.	.	.	.		Worthington Hall Colliery Co.'s Siding	Lancs	L. & N. W.	Coppull and Standish.
.	.	.	.	.	.		Coppull Hall Siding	Lancs	L. & N. W.	See Pearson & Knowles Coal & Iron Co. (Coppull).
.	.	.	.	.	.	•	Coppy Crooks Colliery Wharf Siding	Durham	N. E.	West Auckland.
.	.	.	.	.	.		Coppy Hall or Stubbers Green Colliery	Staffs	L. & N. W.	Pelsall.
.	.	.	.	.	.		Copy Brick Works	Denbigh	G. W.	Rhos.
.	.	.	.	.	.		Copy Pit Siding	Yorks	L. & Y.	Holme.
G	P	.	.	.	.	1 10	Corbet	Down	G. N. (I)	Banbridge and Ballyroney.
.	P	.	.	.	.		Corbets Lane Junction	Surrey	L. B. & S. C.—S. E. & C.	London, New Cross & London Bge.
G	.	.	.	.	.		Corbiere	Jersey	Jersey	Terminus.
G	P	F	L	H	C	6 0	Corbiere Quarries	Jersey	Jersey	Near Corbiere.
							Corbridge	Northumb	N. E.	Newcastle and Hexham.
.	.	.	.	.	.		Dilston Siding	Northumb	N. E.	Corbridge.
G	P	F	L	H	C	5 0	Corby	Lincoln	G. N.	Peterboro' and Grantham.
.	.	.	.	.	.		Corby	N'hampton	Mid.	See Weldon and Corby.
.	.	.	.	.	.		Corbyns Hall Sidings	Staffs	G. W.	Brettell Lane.
.	.	.	.	.	.		Corby Siding	Cumb'land	N. E.	See Wetheral.
.	.	.	.	.	.		Cordale Siding	Dumbartn	D. & B. Jt. (Cal. & N. B.)	Renton.
.	.	.	.	.	.		Cordes & Co.'s Nail Works	Mon	G. W.	Newport, Dock Street.
.	.	.	.	.	.		Cordner's Landsale Depôts	Durham	N. E.	Sunderland, South Dock.
G	P	F	L	H	C	1 10	Corfe Castle	Dorset	L. & S. W.	Wareham and Swanage.
.	.	.	.	.	.		Eldons Siding	Dorset	L. & S. W.	Corfe Castle.
.	.	.	.	.	.		Furzebrook Siding	Dorset	L. & S. W.	Corfe Castle.
							CORK—			
G	P	F	L	H	C	5 0	Albert Quay	Cork	C. B. & S. C.	Terminus.
G	P	.	L	H	.		Albert Street	Cork	C. B. & P.	Terminus.
G	P	F	L	.	.	3 0	Capwell	Cork	C. & Macroom.	Terminus.
.	.	.	.	.	.		Gouldings Siding	Cork	G. S. & W.	Cork and Blarney.
.	.	.	L	.	.		Kilbarry	Cork	G. S. & W.	Lower Glanmire Road and Blarney.
.	P	F	L	H	C		Lower Glanmire Road	Cork	G. S. & W.	Queenstown and Mallow.
G	.	F	L	H	C	7 0	Penrose Quay	Cork	G. S. & W.	Cork.
.	.	.	.	.	.		Rathpeacon	Cork	G. S. & W.	Cork and Blarney.
G	P	.	L	.	.		Western Road	Cork	C. and Muskerry	Terminus.
.	.	.	.	.	.		Corkerhill Engine Sheds	Lanark	G. & S. W.	Glasgow, Bellahouston.
.	.	.	.	.	.		Corkickle (Furness)	Cumb'land	Furness—L. & N. W.	See Whitehaven.
.	P	.	.	.	.		Cornabrone (Book to Drumshambo)	Leitrim	C. & L.	Ballinamore and Drumshambo.
.	.	.	.	.	.		Cornard's Siding	Suffolk	G. E.	Same as Sudbury, Goods.

EXPLANATION—G Goods Station.   P Passenger and Parcel Station.   P* Passenger, but not Parcel or Miscellaneous Traffic.
F Furniture Vans, Carriages, Portable Engines, and Machines on Wheels.   L Live Stock.
H Horse Boxes and Prize Cattle Vans.   C Carriages by Passenger Train.

Station Accommodation						Crane Power		STATIONS, &c.	COUNTY.	COMPANY.	POSITION.
						Tons	Cwts.				
								Cornbrook	Lancs	C. L. C.—M. S. J. & A.	See Manchester.
								Cornbrook Junction	Lancs	C. L. C.—M. S. J. & A.	Manchester.
								Cornbrook Junction	Lancs	C.L.C.—Man. Ship Canal	Manchester.
								Corncockle Quarry	Dumfries	Cal.	Nethercleugh.
								Cornelly Quarry Siding	Glamorg'n	G. W.	Pyle.
								Corner's Siding	Yorks	Axholme Jt (L & Y & N E)	Reedness Junction.
								Cornforth Lane Siding (Snowdon's)	Durham	N. E.	Coxhoe.
								Corngreave's Siding	Staffs	G. W.	Cradley Heath and Cradley.
G	P		L	H		1	5	Cornhill	Banff	G. N. of S.	Grange and Banff.
	P							Cornholme	Yorks	L. & Y.	Todmorden and Burnley.
								Cornish, D., & Co.'s Siding	Essex	G. E.	Shenfield and Hutton Junc. Station.
								Cornsay Colliery, Coke Ovens, and Brick Works	Durham	N. E.	Waterhouses.
								Cornsilloch Colliery & Brick Works	Lanark	Cal.	Dalserf.
								Cornton Siding	Stirling	Cal.	Bridge of Allan.
								Cornubia Works	Lancs	L. & N. W.—S. & M. Jt.	Same as Dennis & Co. (Widnes).
								Cornwall Junction	Devon	G. W.	Plymouth.
								Cornwall Siding	Carnarvon	L. & N. W.	Same as South Dorothea Slate Co.'s Siding (Nantlle).
G	P							Cornwood	Devon	G. W.	Plymouth and Totnes.
G	P	F	L					Corofin	Clare	West Clare	Ennis and Miltown Malbay.
								Coronation Siding	Durham	N. E.	Wearhead.
								Coronation Siding	Merioneth	L. & N. W.	See Oakeley's (Blaenau Festiniog).
								Coronet Brick Co.'s Siding	Derby	A & N Jt. (L & N W & Mid.)	Same as Blakesley's Sid. (Measham).
G	P		L	H				Corpach	Inverness	N. B.	Fort William and Mallaig.
G	P	F	L	H	C			Corpusty and Saxthorpe	Norfolk	Mid. & G. N. Jt.	Melton Constable & North Walsham Town.
G	P							Corran (Ardgour)	Argyll	Cal.	Steamer from Oban.
								Corringham	Lincoln	G. C.	See Blyton (for Corringham).
								Corringham Light Railway Siding (Kynoch & Co.'s)	Essex	L. T. & S.	Thames Haven.
G	P							Corris	Merioneth	Corris	Machynlleth and Aberllefenny.
	P							Corrour	Inverness	N. B.	Crianlarich and Fort William.
								Corrour Siding	Perth	N. B.	See Rannoch.
								Corrugated Iron Co.—			
								Shrubbery Works	Staffs	G. W.	Wolverhampton.
								Stour Valley Works	Staffs	G. W.	Wolverhampton.
								Corrwg Fechan Colliery	Glamorg'n	S. Wales Min.	Branch near Glyncorrwg.
								Corrwg Rhondda Colliery	Glamorg'n	R. & S. B.	Blaengwynfi.
								Corsebar Junction	Renfrew	G. & S. W.	Paisley, Canal and Potterhill.
								Corsehill, Nos. 10 and 11	Ayr	G. & S. W.	Dreghorn.
								Corsehill Quarry	Dumfries	Cal.	Annan.
								Corsehill Tile Works	Ayr	G. & S. W.	Dreghorn.
G	P					2	0	Corsham	Wilts	G. W.	Chippenham and Bath.
								Yockney & Co.'s Siding	Wilts	G. W.	Corsham.
G	P	F	L	H	C	2	0	Corstorphine	Edinboro'	N. B.	Branch—Haymarket and Saughton.
								Cort and Paul's Iron Works	Leicester	Mid.	Syston.
								Cortis Siding	Sussex	L. B. & S. C.	Worthing.
G	P	F	L	H	C			Corton	Suffolk	N.&S.Jt.(GE&M&GNJt.)	Yarmouth and Lowestoft.
								Corton Wood Colliery	Yorks	G. C. / Mid.	Wath. / Wombwell.
G	P	F	L	H	C	5	0	Corwen (G. W.)	Merioneth	G. W. / L. & N. W.	Llangollen and Bala. / Over G. W. from Corwen Junction.
								Corwen Junction	Merioneth	G. W.— L. & N. W.	Bala and Denbigh.
								Corwen Slate Co.'s Siding	Merioneth	G. W.	Same as Carrog Slate Siding.
								Cory & Son—			
								Coal Stores (G. E.)	Essex	G E—G N—L&NW—Mid	London, Victoria and Albert Docks.
								Siding	Essex	Mid.	London, Victoria Docks.
								Cory, Bros. & Co.—			
								Gelli Colliery	Glamorg'n	T. V.	Ystrad.
								Penrikyber or Penrhiwceiber Colliery	Glamorg'n	T. V.	Penrhiwceiber.
								Pentre Colliery	Glamorg'n	T. V.	Ystrad.
								Tydraw Colliery	Glamorg'n	T. V.	Treherbert.
								Tynybedw Colliery	Glamorg'n	T. V.	Treorchy.
								Cory Briquette Fuel Co.'s Wks	Glamorg'n	G. W.—L. & N. W.— Mid.—R. & S. B.	Swansea.
								Cory Bros.' Resolven Siding	Glamorg'n	G. W.	Resolven.
								Corys' Navigation Col. Co.'s Mountain Colliery	Glamorg'n	L. & N. W.	Gorseinon.

EXPLANATION—G *Goods Station.*   P *Passenger and Parcel Station.*   P* *Passenger, but not Parcel or Miscellaneous Traffic.*
F *Furniture Vans, Carriages, Portable Engines, and Machines on Wheels.*   L *Live Stock.*
H *Horse Boxes and Prize Cattle Vans.*   C *Carriages by Passenger Train.*

STATION ACCOMMODATION.						CRANE POWER.	STATIONS, &c.	COUNTY.	COMPANY.	POSITION.
						Tons Cwts.	Cory, Yeo, & Co.—			
							Graigola MerthyrCol. (Mid.)	Glamorg'n	Mid.—G. W.—L. & N. W.	Clydach-on-Tawe.
G	P		L				Hill's Merthyr Col. (Mid.)..	Glamorg'n	Mid.—G. W.—L. & N. W.	Clydach-on-Tawe.
G	P		L				Coryton	Devon	G. W.	Tavistock and Launceston.
							Coseley	Staffs	L. & N. W.	See Deepfields and Coseley.
G	P	F	L	H	C	5 0	Cosham(L&S W & LB&SCJt.)	Hants	L. & S. W.	Fareham and Portsmouth.
							Cosham Junction	Hants	L. & S W & L B & S C Jt. —L. B. & S. C.	Cosham and Havant.
							Cossall	Notts	Mid.	See Ilkeston Junction and Cossall.
							Cossall Colliery Co.—			
							Siding	Derby	Mid.	Ilkeston.
							Trowell Moor Colliery	Notts	Mid.	Trowell.
							Cossey	Norfolk	Mid. & G. N. Jt.	See Drayton (for Cossey).
G	P	F	L	H	C		Cossington	Somerset	S.&D.Jt.(L.&S.W.&Mid)	Edington Junc. and Bridgwater.
							Cotcastle	Lanark	Cal.	See Stonehouse.
G	P						Cotehill	Cumb'land	Mid.	Appleby and Carlisle.
							Knott Hill Plaster Works	Cumb'land	Mid.	Near Cotehill Station.
							Robinson & Co's Plaster Wks	Cumb'land	Mid.	Near Cotehill Station.
G	P	F	L	H	C		Cotham	Notts	G. N.	Newark and Bottesford North Jn.
G	P		L				Cotherston	Yorks	N. E.	Barnard Castle and Middleton.
							Coton Hill	Salop	G. W.	See Shrewsbury.
							Coton Park Brick Co.'s Sid. (Birkenshaw Brick Works) (Mid.)	Derby	Mid.—L. & N. W.	Gresley.
G	P		L	H			Cottage Siding	Glamorg'n	T. V.	Cross Inn.
							Cottam	Notts	G. C.	Retford and Lincoln.
							Cottam & Co.'s Siding	Glamorg'n	GW—L&NW—Rhy—TV	Cardiff.
							Cottesmore Iron Ore Mines	Rutland	Mid.	Ashwell.
G	P		L	H	C	0 15	Cottingham	Yorks	N. E.	Hull and Beverley.
							Cottingham GasCo.'s Siding	Yorks	N. E.	Cottingham.
							Hull Corporation Water-works	Yorks	N. E.	Cottingham.
							Cottis & Son's Siding	Essex	G. E.	Epping.
							Cotton & Co.'s Victoria Works	Cheshire	L. & N. W.	Holmes Chapel.
G	P	F	L	H	C		Coughton	Warwick	Mid.	Evesham and Redditch.
G	P		L	H			Coulsdon and Cane Hill	Surrey	S. E. & C.	Croydon and Red Hill.
G	P		L	H			Coulter	Lanark	Cal.	Symington and Peebles.
G	P		L				Council Hill Siding	Oxon	G. W.	Hook Norton.
G	P		L			1 0	Coundon	Durham	N. E.	Bishop Auckland and Spennymoor.
							Coundon Depôt	Durham	N. E.	{ Ferryhill. { Leasingthorne.
G	P		L			1 5	Coundon Road	Warwick	L. & N. W.	Coventry and Nuneaton.
G	P						Counter Drain	Lincoln	Mid. & G. N. Jt.	Spalding and Bourne.
G	P		L	H			Countesthorpe	Leicester	Mid.	Rugby and Leicester.
G	P						County School	Norfolk	G. E.	North Elmham and Fakenham.
G	P	F	L	H	C	6 0	Coupar Angus	Perth	Cal.	Perth and Forfar.
							Gentle's Siding	Perth	Cal.	Coupar Angus.
							Panton's Siding	Perth	Cal.	Coupar Angus.
							Wigglesworth Siding	Perth	Cal.	Coupar Angus.
							Court House Joint Station	Yorks	G. C.—Mid.	See Barnsley.
							Court House Junction	Yorks	G. C.—Mid.	Barnsley, Cockram Road.
G	P			H	C		Courtmacsherry	Cork	T. & C.	Terminus.
G	P	F	L	H	C	7 0	Court Sart	Glamorg'n	R. & S. B.	Port Talbot and Swansea.
G						2 0	Glyncorrwg Engineering Works	Glamorg'n	R. & S. B.	Court Sart.
							Court Sart Briton Ferry Junc.	Glamorg'n	R. & S. B.—S. Wales Min.	Court Sart and Cymmer.
							Court Sart Junction	Glamorg'n	G. W.—R. & S. B.	Briton Ferry and Neath.
							Couse and Bailey's Siding	Staffs	G. W.	West Bromwich.
							Cousin's Stone Siding	Clackman'	N. B.	Alloa.
							Cousland Lime Works	Hadding'n	N. B.	Ormiston.
							Coussmaker's Siding	Surrey	L. & S.W.	Wanborough.
							Couston Siding	L'lithgow	N. B.	Bathgate, Lower.
G	P						Cove	Kinc'rdine	Cal.	Stonehaven and Aberdeen.
							Blackhill Quarry	Kinc'rdine	Cal.	Portlethen and Cove.
							Cove Fish, Manure, & Oil Co.'s Siding	Kinc'rdine	Cal.	Portlethen and Cove.
							Cove Quarry	Kinc'rdine	Cal.	Portlethen and Cove.
G	P	F	L	H	C	10 0	Coventry	Warwick	{ L. & N. W. { Mid.	Birmingham and Rugby. Over L. & N. W. from Nuneaton.
G	P†	F	L	H	C	5 0				
							CoventryCorporation Lighting Station	Warwick	Mid.	Coventry.
							Coventry Cotton Mills	Warwick	Mid.	Coventry.

EXPLANATION—G Goods Station.   P Passenger and Parcel Station.   P* Passenger, but not Parcel or Miscellaneous Traffic.
P† Parcels only.   F Furniture Vans, Carriages, Portable Engines, and Machines on Wheels.   L Live Stock.
H Horse Boxes and Prize Cattle Vans.   C Carriages by Passenger Train.

STATION ACCOMMODATION.						CRANE POWER.	STATIONS, &c.	COUNTY.	COMPANY.	POSITION.
						Tons Cwts.	Coventry—*continued.*			
..	..	..	..	..	..	.. ..	Coventry Electric Light Storage Co.	Warwick..	Mid.	Coventry.
..	..	..	..	..	..	.. ..	Dewis Siding (Cattle Sales Siding) (L. & N. W.)	Warwick..	L. & N. W.—Mid.	Coventry and Coundon Road.
..	..	..	..	..	..	.. ..	Seaman & Co.'s Siding	Warwick..	Mid.	Coventry.
..	..	..	..	..	..	.. ..	Webster's Brick Wks. Railway Co.'s Sid.(L.& N.W.)	Warwick..	Mid.	Coventry and Nuneaton.
..	..	..	..	..	..	.. ..	Whitley Coal Wharf	Warwick..	L. & N. W.	Coventry and Brandon.
..	..	..	..	..	..	.. ..	Wyken Colliery	Warwick..	L. & N. W.	Hawkesbury Lane and Longford.
..	..	..	..	..	..	.. ..	CoventryCorporationGasWks.	Warwick..	L. & N. W.	Foleshill.
..	..	..	..	..	..	.. ..	Cove Quarry	Dumfries..	Cal.	Kirkpatrick.
..	..	..	..	..	..	.. ..	Cove Quarry	Kinc'rdine	Cal.	Cove.
..	..	..	..	..	..	.. ..	Cove Siding	Devon	G. W.	Bampton.
..	..	..	..	..	..	.. ..	Cowan & Co.'s Siding	Edinboro'	N. B.	Edinburgh, Leith Walk.
..	..	..	..	..	..	.. ..	Cowan,Sheldon & Co.'s Works (N. E.)	Cumb'land	N. E.—L. & N. W.—Mid.	Carlisle.
G	P	F	L	H	C	1 5	Cowbit	Lincoln ...	G. N. & G. E. Jt.	Spalding and March.
G	P	F	L	H	C	2 10	Cowbridge	Glamorg'n	T. V.	Aberthaw and Llantrisant.
..	..	..	..	..	..	.. ..	Cowbridge and Aberthaw Railway Junction	Glamorg'n	T. V.	Cowbridge and Ystradowen.
..	..	..	..	..	..	.. ..	Cowbridge Road Junction ...	Glamorg'n	Barry.............................	Southerndown Road and Bridgend.
..	..	..	..	..	..	.. ..	Cowcaddens........................	Lanark ...	Glas. Dist. Sub.	See Glasgow.
G	P	F	L	H	C		Cowden..........................	Kent	L. B. & S. C.	Oxted and Groombridge.
							COWDENBEATH—			
..	..	..	..	..	..	.. ..	Cowdenbeath Brick Works	Fife	N. B.	Cowdenbeath (Old) and Lochgelly.
..	..	..	..	..	..	.. ..	Cowdenbeath Colliery	Fife	N. B.	Cowdenbeath (Old) and Lochgelly.
..	..	..	..	..	..	.. ..	Cowdenbeath Gas Works...	Fife	N. B.	Cowdenbeath (Old).
..	..	..	..	..	..	.. ..	Donibristle Colliery	Fife	N. B.	Cowdenbeath (Old) and Crossgates.
..	..	..	..	..	..	.. ..	Foulford Colliery	Fife	N. B.	Cowdenbeath (Old) and Lochgelly.
..	..	..	..	..	..	.. ..	Kirkford Colliery	Fife	N. B.	Cowdenbeath (New) and Crossgates.
..	..	..	..	..	..	.. ..	LumphinnansWestColliery	Fife	N. B.	Cowdenbeath (Old) and Lochgelly.
..	..	..	..	..	..	.. ..	Mossbeath Colliery	Fife	N. B.	Cowdenbeath (New) and Crossgates.
..	P	..	..	..	..	.. ..	New	Fife	N. B.	Dunfermline and Kinross Junction.
..	..	..	..	..	..	.. ..	Newton Colliery...............	Fife	N. B.	Cowdenbeath (Old) and Auchtertool.
G	..	F	L	..	..	3 0	Old................................	Fife	N. B.	Dunfermline and Thornton.
..	..	..	..	..	..	.. ..	Raith Colliery..................	Fife	N. B.	Cowdenbeath (Old) and Crossgates.
..	..	..	..	..	..	.. ..	Cowell, G., Siding............	Durham ...	N. E.	Stockton, South.
G	P	..	L	H	..		Cowes	I. of W.	{ I. of W. Cent.	Terminus.
G	P	F	L	H	C	5 0 }			{ L. & S. W.	Steamer from Southampton.
..	..	..	..	..	..	.. ..	Cowglen Siding	Fife	N. B.	Steelend.
..	..	..	..	..	..	.. ..	Cowie	Stirling ...	Cal.	See Plean (for Cowie).
..	..	..	..	..	..	.. ..	Cowlairs	Lanark ...	N. B.	See Glasgow.
..	..	..	..	..	..	.. ..	Cowlairs Co-operative Society's Siding	Lanark ...	N. B.	Glasgow, Cowlairs.
..	..	..	..	..	..	.. ..	Cowlairs Junctions	Lanark ...	N. B.	Glasgow.
..	..	..	..	..	..	.. ..	Cow Lane Junction	Surrey ...	L. B. & S. C.—S. E. & C.	London, Peckham Rye and Nunhead.
..	..	..	..	..	..	.. ..	Cow Lane Maltings	Notts	G. N. & Mid. Jt.	See Gilstrap Earp & Co.'s (Newark).
..	..	..	..	..	..	.. ..	Cow Lane Malt Kiln..........	Notts	G. N. & Mid. Jt.	See Bishop & Son's (Newark).
..	..	..	..	..	..	.. ..	Cowley Bridge Junction	Devon	G. W.—L. & S. W.	Exeter.
..	..	..	..	..	..	.. ..	Cowpark	Stirling ...	N. B.	See Stirling.
..	..	..	..	..	..	.. ..	Cowpen Bewley Siding........	Durham ...	N. E.	Greatham.
							Cowpen Collieries—			
..	..	..	..	..	..	.. ..	Hannah Col.(NewshamCol.)	Northumb	N. E.	Newsham.
..	..	..	..	..	..	.. ..	Isabella Colliery...............	Northumb	N. E.	Newsham.
..	..	..	..	..	..	.. ..	Cowpen Colliery and Depôts.	Northumb	N. E.	Blyth.
..	..	..	..	..	..	.. ..	Cowpen Mill Pit................	Northumb	N. E.	Blyth.
..	..	..	..	..	..	.. ..	Cowpen Salt Works	Durham ...	N. E.	See United Alkali Co.(PortClarence).
..	..	..	..	..	..	.. ..	Cowper's (Lord) Siding	Herts	G. N.	Hatfield.
G	P	F	L	..	..	3 0	Cowton	Yorks	N. E.	Northallerton and Darlington.
G	P	..	..	..	..	10 0	Coxbench	Derby	Mid.	Little Eaton and Ripley.
..	..	..	..	..	..	.. ..	Slater's Stone Quarry	Derby	Mid.	Near Coxbench Station.
..	..	..	..	..	..	.. ..	Cox Bros'. Flax and JuteWks.	Forfar	Cal.	Lochee.
..	..	..	..	..	..	.. ..	Cox's Lane Siding	Staffs	G. W.	Same as Hingley & Son's Siding (Netherton).
..	..	..	..	..	..	.. ..	Cox's Quarry	Mon	{ G. W.	Cross Keys.
									{ L. & N. W.	Nine Mile Point.
..	..	..	..	..	..	.. ..	Coxes Lock Mill Siding........	Surrey ...	L. & S. W.	Addlestone.
G	P	..	..	..	..	.. ..	Cox Green	Durham ...	N. E.	Sunderland and Penshaw.
G	..	..	..	H	C	1 0	Coxhoe	Durham ...	N. E.	Branch from Ferryhill.
..	..	..	..	..	..	.. ..	Cornforth Lane Siding (Snowdon's)...................	Durham ...	N. E.	Coxhoe.

EXPLANATION—G *Goods Station.*   P *Passenger and Parcel Station.*   P* *Passenger, but not Parcel or Miscellaneous Traffic.*
F *Furniture Vans, Carriages, Portable Engines, and Machines on Wheels.*   L *Live Stock.*
H *Horse Boxes and Prize Cattle Vans.*   C *Carriages by Passenger Train.*

STATION ACCOMMODATION.						CRANE POWER.		STATIONS, &c.	COUNTY.	COMPANY.	POSITION.
						Tons	Cwts.	Coxhoe— *continued.*			
.	.	.	.	.	.	.	.	Coxhoe Gas Works	Durham ...	N. E.	Coxhoe.
.	.	.	.	.	.	.	.	Coxhoe Lime Works and Quarries	Durham ...	N. E.	Coxhoe.
.	.	.	.	.	.	.	.	East Hetton (Kelloe) Col. Clay Mills & Brick Wks.	Durham ...	N. E.	Coxhoe.
.	.	.	.	.	.	.	.	North Eastern Pumping Engine Siding	Durham ...	N. E.	Coxhoe.
.	.	.	.	.	.	.	.	Raisby Hill Basic Works ...	Durham ...	N. E.	Coxhoe.
.	.	.	.	.	.	.	.	Raisby Hill Depôts	Durham ...	N. E.	Coxhoe.
.	.	.	.	.	.	.	.	Raisby Hill High Quarries	Durham ...	N. E.	Coxhoe.
.	.	.	.	.	.	.	.	Raisby Hill Low Quarry ...	Durham ...	N. E.	Coxhoe.
.	.	.	.	.	.	.	.	Coxhoe Branch Junction	Durham ...	N. E.	Ferryhill and Shincliffe.
.	P	.	.	.	.	.	.	Coxhoe Bridge	Durham ...	N. E.	Ferryhill and Hartlepool.
.	.	.	.	.	.	.	.	Coxlodge Colliery Brick Wks. and Depôts	Northumb	N. E.	Gosforth.
.	.	.	.	.	.	.	.	Coxon's Saw Mills	Durham ...	N. E.	West Hartlepool.
G	P	F	L	H	C	1	0	Coxwold	Yorks	N. E.	Malton and Thirsk.
.	.	.	.	.	.	.	.	Coylton Colliery	Ayr	G. & S.W.	Hollybush.
.	.	.	.	.	.	.	.	Craddock Lane Gas Siding ...	Lancs	L. & Y.	Bolton.
.	.	.	.	.	.	.	.	Craddock Lane Manure Sid.	Lancs	L. & Y.	Bolton.
.	.	.	.	.	.	.	.	Craddock Lane Siding	Lancs	L. & Y.	See Bolton.
.	.	.	.	.	.	.	.	Craddock Smith & Co.'s Sid.	Durham ...	N. E.	Stockton, South.
.	.	.	.	.	.	.	.	Cradley	Staffs	G. W.	See Cradley Heath and Cradley.
G	P	.	L	.	.	5	0	Cradley Heath & Cradley.....	Staffs	G. W.	Stourbridge Jn. and Smethwick Jn.
.	.	.	.	.	.	.	.	Corngreaves Siding	Staffs	G. W.	Old Hill and Cradley.
.	.	.	.	.	.	.	.	Cradley Park Siding..........	Worcester	G. W.	Stourbridge Junc. & Cradley Heath.
.	.	.	.	.	.	.	.	Earl Dudley Siding	Staffs	G. W.	Near Cradley Heath.
.	.	.	.	.	.	.	.	Ever's & Son (Homer Hill).	Staffs	G. W.	Cradley Heath and Cradley.
.	.	.	.	.	.	.	.	Griffin, W., Siding	Staffs	G. W.	Near Cradley Heath.
.	.	.	.	.	.	.	.	Harper and Moore's Colliery and Fire Brick Works ...	Worcester	G. W.	Stourbridge Junc. & Cradley Heath.
.	.	.	.	.	.	.	.	Hayes Colliery	Worcester	G. W.	Stourbridge Junc. & Cradley Heath.
.	.	.	.	.	.	.	.	King Bros.' Siding	Worcester	G. W.	Stourbridge Junc. & Cradley Heath.
.	.	.	.	.	.	.	.	King, J., & Co.'s Siding ...	Worcester	G. W.	Stourbridge Junc. & Cradley Heath.
.	.	.	.	.	.	.	.	Mobberley & Perry's Siding	Worcester	G. W.	Stourbridge Junc. & Cradley Heath.
.	.	.	.	.	.	.	.	Netherend Siding	Worcester	G. W.	Lye & Cradley Heath.
.	.	.	.	.	.	.	.	Oldnall Colliery	Worcester	G. W.	Stourbridge Junc. & Cradley Heath.
.	.	.	.	.	.	.	.	Swindell & Collis Siding ...	Staffs	G. W.	Old Hill.
.	.	.	.	.	.	.	.	Witley Coal Co.'s Siding ...	Staffs	G. W.	Cradley Heath and Old Hill.
.	.	.	.	.	.	.	.	Cradley Park Siding...........	Worcester	G. W.	Cradley Heath and Cradley.
G	P	.	.	.	.	.	.	Cradoc (N. & B.).................	Brecon ...	{ N. & Brecon .... Mid.	Brecon and Devynock. Over Neath and Brecon Line.
.	.	.	.	.	.	.	.	Ely Place Siding (N. & B.)	Brecon ...	N. & Brecon—Mid.........	Cradoc and Brecon Junction.
.	P	.	.	.	.	.	.	Mount Street Siding (N&B)	Brecon ...	N. & Brecon—Mid.........	Cradoc and Brecon Junction.
.	P	.	.	.	.	.	.	Craggaknock	Clare	West Clare	Miltown Malbay and Kilkee.
.	.	.	.	.	.	.	.	Craggs and Sons' Wharf ...	Yorks	N. E.	Middlesbro'.
.	.	.	.	.	.	.	.	Craghead Col. & Brick Works	Durham ...	N. E.	Pelton.
.	.	.	.	.	.	.	.	Cragmill Siding	Northumb	N. E.	Belford.
G	P	.	.	.	.	.	.	Craigavad	Down	B. & C. D.	Holywood and Bangor.
.	.	.	.	.	.	.	.	Craigavon Colliery..............	Glamorg'n	P. T.	Port Talbot (Central).
.	.	.	.	.	.	.	.	Craigddu Quarry	Merioneth	G. W.	Tanymanod.
G	P	F	L	H	C	1	5	Craigellachie	Banff	G. N. of S.	Keith and Boat of Garten.
.	.	.	.	.	.	.	.	Craigend Colliery	Stirling ...	N. B.	Almond Junction.
G	P	.	L	H	C	1	10	Craigendoran	Dumbartn	N. B.	Helensburgh and Cardross.
.	P	.	.	.	.	.	.	Craigendoran (West High.)...	Dumbartn	N. B.	Cardross and Helensburgh, Upper.
.	.	.	.	.	.	.	.	Craigendoran Junction	Dumbartn	N. B.	Cardross and Craigendoran.
.	.	.	.	.	.	.	.	Craigend Siding	Stirling ...	N. B.	See Almond Junction.
.	.	.	.	.	.	.	.	Craigenhill Lime Works	Lanark ...	Cal.	Braidwood.
.	.	.	.	.	.	.	.	Craighall Depôt	Lanark ...	N. B.	See Glasgow.
.	.	.	.	.	.	.	.	Craighead Colliery..............	Lanark ...	{ Cal. N. B.	Blantyre. Bothwell.
.	.	.	.	.	.	.	.	Craighead Quarry	Lanark ...	N. B.	Brownieside Weighs.
.	.	.	.	.	.	.	.	Craigiau Quarry (Creigiau Quarry).........................	Glamorg'n	T. V.	Cross Inn.
.	.	.	.	.	.	.	.	Craigielea Chemical Works...	Renfrew...	Cal.	Paisley, St. James.
.	.	.	.	.	.	.	.	Craiginches Siding (Cal.) ...	Kinc'rdine	Cal.—N. B.	Aberdeen, Guild Street.
G	P	.	L	.	.	2	0	Craigleith.........................	Edinboro'	Cal.	Edinburgh and Leith.
.	.	.	.	.	.	.	.	Craigleith Quarry	Edinboro'	Cal.	Craigleith.
.	.	.	.	.	.	.	.	Craiglockhart	Edinboro'	N. B.	See Edinburgh.
.	.	.	.	.	.	٠	.	Craiglon Colliery	Carmarth'	B. P. & G. V.	Burry Port.
.	.	.	.	.	.	.	.	Craigmillar	Edinboro'	N. B.	See Duddingston and Craigmillar.

EXPLANATION—G *Goods Station.*   P *Passenger and Parcel Station.*   P* *Passenger, but not Parcel or Miscellaneous Traffic.*
F *Furniture Vans, Carriages, Portable Engines, and Machines on Wheels.*   L *Live Stock.*
H *Horse Boxes and Prize Cattle Vans.*   C *Carriages by Passenger Train.*

STATION ACCOMMODATION.						CRANE POWER.		STATIONS, &c.	COUNTY.	COMPANY.	POSITION.
						Tons	Cwts				
..	..	..	..	..	..	..	..	Craigmillar Brewery Siding (Murray's Brewery)	Edinboro'	N. B.	Duddingston and Craigmillar.
..	P	..	..	..	..	..	..	Craigmore	Armagh ...	B. & Newry	Bessbrook and Newry.
..	..	..	..	..	..	..	..	Craignethan Siding	Lanark ...	Cal.	Netherburn.
..	..	..	..	..	..	..	..	Craigneuk Collieries Nos. 3, 4, 9, 10, and 11	Lanark ...	Cal.	Calderbank.
..	..	..	..	..	..	..	..	Craigneuk Cols. Nos. 5 & 6 ...	Lanark ...	Cal.	Airdrie.
G	P	..	..	..	..	..	..	Craignure........................	Argyll ...	Cal.	Steamer from Oban.
G	P	F	L	H	C	2	0	Craigo	Forfar	Cal.	Forfar and Stonehaven.
..	..	..	..	..	..	..	..	Craig's Cooperage Sid. (N.B.)	Stirling ...	N. B.—Cal.	Same as Bleachfield Sid. (Falkirk).
..	..	..	..	..	..	..	..	Craig's Engineering Works...	Renfrew...	Cal.	Same as Caledonia Engine Works.
..	..	..	..	..	..	..	..	Craig Siding	Lanark ...	N. B.	Coatbridge, Whifflet.
..	..	..	..	..	..	..	..	Craig's Siding	Lancs	L. & N. W.—S. & M. Jt.	Widnes.
..	..	..	..	..	..	..	..	Craig's Siding	Stirling ...	Cal.	See Stirling.
..	..	..	..	..	..	..	..	Craigton Mineral Sidings ...	Renfrew...	G.&P. Jt. (Cal.&G.&S.W.)	Cardonald.
..	..	..	..	..	..	..	..	Craig-yr-Hesk Qry.(Mackays)	Glamorg'n	T. V.	Pontypridd.
..	..	..	..	..	..	..	..	Craik's Siding..................	Yorks	G. C.	Barnsley.
G	P	F	L	H	C	1	0	Crail	Fife	N. B.	Anstruther and St. Andrews.
..	P	..	..	..	..	..	..	Crakehall	Yorks	N. E.	Northallerton and Leyburn.
..	..	..	..	..	..	..	..	Crake Scarr Colliery	Durham	N. E.	Butterknowle.
..	..	..	..	..	..	..	..	Crambeck Coal Depôt	Yorks	N. E.	Castle Howard.
..	..	..	..	..	..	..	..	Crambeck Siding	Yorks	N. E.	Castle Howard.
G	P	F	L	H	C	1	0	Cramlington	Northumb	N. E.	Newcastle and Morpeth.
..	..	..	..	..	..	..	..	Cramlington (Ann) Colliery and Brick Works	Northumb	N. E.	Annitsford.
..	..	..	..	..	..	..	..	Cramond Brig	Edinboro'	Cal.	See Barnton (for Cramond Brig.)
..	..	..	..	..	..	..	..	Crampton's Siding	Kent	S. E. & C.	Sevenoaks (Bat and Ball).
G	P	F	L	H	C	1	10	Cranbrook	Kent	S. E. & C.	Paddock Wood and Hawkhurst.
..	..	..	..	..	..	..	..	Crane's Brick Works...........	Leicester..	A & N Jt (L & N W & Mid)	Heather and Ibstock.
..	..	..	..	..	..	..	..	Crane's Siding	Staffs	L. & N. W.	Wolverhampton.
..	..	..	..	..	..	..	..	Crane Street	Mon	G. W.	See Pontypool.
..	..	..	..	..	..	..	..	Cranfield Bros.' Siding	Norfolk ...	G. E.	Downham.
G	P	F	..	H	C	..	..	Cranford	N'hamptn	Mid.	Kettering and Thrapston.
..	..	..	..	..	..	..	..	Burton Ironstone Co.'s Sid.	N'hamptn	Mid.	Kettering and Cranford.
..	..	..	..	..	..	..	..	Cranford Ironstone Co.'s Sidings (Cranford, East)	N'hamptn	Mid.	Kettering and Thrapston.
..	..	..	..	..	..	..	..	Kettering Coal & Iron Co.'s Siding (Cranford, West)	N'hamptn	Mid.	Kettering and Cranford.
..	..	..	..	..	..	..	..	Cran, John, & Co.— Shipbuilding Yard............	Edinboro'	Cal.—N. B.	Leith, North.
..	..	..	..	..	..	..	..	Siding	Edinboro'	Cal.—N. B.	Leith, South.
G	P	..	..	..	..	..	..	Crank	Lancs	L. & N. W.	Rainford and St. Helens.
..	..	..	..	..	..	..	..	Crank Hall Siding	Staffs	L. & N. W.	Same as South Staffordshire Waterworks (Wednesbury).
..	..	..	..	..	..	..	..	Crankley Siding	Yorks	N. E.	Easingwold.
G	P	F	L	H	C	5	0	Cranleigh	Surrey.....	L. B. & S. C.	Guildford and Horsham.
..	..	..	..	..	..	..	..	Cranleigh Brick & Tile Co.'s Siding (Miles, E. A.).........	Surrey	L. B. & S. C.	Baynards.
G	P	..	..	..	..	..	..	Cranley Gardens (G. N.)	Middlesex	G. N. .... / N. L.	Highgate and Alexandra Palace. / Over G. N. from Canonbury Junc.
..	P	..	..	..	..	..	..				
G	P	..	L	..	..	..	..	Cranmore	Somerset..	G. W.	Wells and Witham.
..	..	..	..	..	..	..	..	Doulting Siding	Somerset..	G. W.	Cranmore and Shepton Mallet.
..	..	..	..	..	..	..	..	Mendip Granite and Asphalte Co......................	Somerset..	G. W.	Cranmore.
..	..	..	..	..	..	..	..	Cransley (New) Iron and Steel Co.'s Works	N'hamptn	Mid.	Kettering.
..	..	..	..	..	..	..	..	Cranstonhill Engine Works...	Lanark ...	G.&P. Jt.(Cal.&G.&S.W.)	Glasgow, Govan.
G	P	F	L	H	C	..	..	Crathes	Kinc'rdine	G. N. of S.	Aberdeen and Banchory.
..	P	..	..	..	..	..	..	Cratloe (G. S. & W.)	Clare	G. S. & W. .... / M. G. W.	Limerick and Ennis. / Over G. S. & W. from Athenry.
G	P	..	L	H	C	..	..	Craughwell (G. S. & W.)	Galway	G. S. & W. .... / M. G. W.	Athenry and Ennis. / Over G. S. & W. from Athenry.
G	P	F	L	H	C	5	0	Craven Arms and Stokesay (S. & H. Jt.)	Salop	S & H Jt.(G W & L N W) / Bishop's Castle.............	Hereford and Shrewsbury. / Over S. & H. Joint from Stretford
G	P	F	L	..	..	5	0				Bridge Junction.
..	..	..	..	..	..	..	..	Craven Arms Gas Siding ...	Salop	L. & N. W.	Craven Arms and Stokesay.
..	..	..	..	..	..	..	..	Craven Arms & Stokesay Jn.	Salop	L. & N. W.—S. & H. Jt.	Broome and Craven Arms Station.
..	..	..	..	..	..	..	..	Craven Lime Co.— Salt Lake Siding	Yorks......	Mid.	Ribblehead.
..	..	..	..	..	..	..	..	Stainforth Siding	Yorks......	Mid.	Settle.
..	..	..	..	..	..	..	..	Craven Lime Siding	Yorks......	L. & N. W.	Ingleton.
..	..	..	..	..	..	..	..	Craven's Siding	Lancs	L. & N. W.	St. Helens.

EXPLANATION—G *Goods Station.*   P *Passenger and Parcel Station.*   P* *Passenger, but not Parcel or Miscellaneous Traffic.*
F *Furniture Vans, Carriages, Portable Engines, and Machines on Wheels.*   L *Live Stock.*
H *Horse Boxes and Prize Cattle Vans.*   C *Carriages by Passenger Train.*

STATION ACCOMMODATION.						CRANE POWER.		STATIONS, &c.	COUNTY.	COMPANY.	POSITION.
						Tons	Cwts.				
G	P	.	L	H	.	2	0	Craven's Siding	Yorks	G. C.	Sheffield, Darnall (for Handsworth).
.	.	.	.	.	.	.	.	Crawford	Lanark	Cal.	Lockerbie and Carstairs.
.	.	.	.	.	.	.	.	Crawford Pit	Lancs	L. & Y.	See Wigan Coal & Iron Co.(Hindley).
.	.	.	.	.	.	.	.	Crawford Pit (L. & N. W.)	Lancs	L.&N.W—G.C.(Wig.Jn.)	See Wigan Coal & Iron Co. (Wigan).
.	.	.	.	.	.	.	.	Crawford Street Manure Depôt	Lanark	Cal.	Glasgow, West Street.
G	P	F	L	H	C	5	0	Crawley	Sussex	L. B. & S. C.	Horsham and Three Bridges.
.	.	.	.	.	.	.	.	Longley's Siding	Sussex	L. B. & S. C.	Crawley.
.	.	.	.	.	.	.	.	Nightingale's Siding	Sussex	L. B. & S. C.	Crawley.
.	.	.	.	.	.	.	.	Crawley & Co.'s Siding	Cambs	G. E.	Fulbourne.
.	.	.	.	.	.	.	.	Crawley Engine Siding	Durham	N. E.	Stanhope Kilns.
								Crawshay Brothers—			
.	.	.	.	.	.	.	.	Castle Pit (G. W. & Rhy. Jt.)	Glamorg'n	G W & Rhy.Jt.—L & N W	Abercanaid.
.	.	.	.	.	.	.	.	Cy-farth-fa Works	Glamorg'n	B.&M. & L.&N.W. Joint / G. W. & Rhy. Jt. / G. W.—T.V.	Cefn. / Abercanaid. / Merthyr.
.	.	.	.	.	.	.	.	Gethin Pit(G.W.& Rhy. Jt.)	Glamorg'n	G W & Rhy.Jt.—L & N W	Abercanaid.
.	.	.	.	.	.	.	.	Llwyncelyn Siding	Glamorg'n	B.&M.& L. & N. W. Joint	Cefn.
.	.	.	.	.	.	.	.	Vaynor Limestone Quarry	Glamorg'n	B.&M.& L. & N. W. Joint	Cefn.
.	.	.	.	.	.	.	.	Ynysfach Siding	Glamorg'n	B.&M.& L. & N. W. Joint	Cefn.
G	P	.	.	.	.	.	.	Cray (N. & B.)	Brecon	N. & Brecon / Mid.	Devynock and Penwyllt. / Over Neath & Brecon Line.
G	P	.	.	.	.	5	0	Cray Water Works (N.&B.)	Brecon	N. & Brecon—Mid.	Cray and Penwyllt.
.	.	.	.	.	.	.	.	Crayford	Kent	S. E. & C.	Hither Green and Dartford.
.	.	.	.	.	.	.	.	Creek Junction	Kent	S. E. & C.	Barnehurst and Dartford.
.	.	.	.	.	.	.	.	Gravel Pits Co.'s Siding	Kent	S. E. & C.	Bexley and Crayford.
.	.	.	.	.	.	.	.	Land & Brick Co.'s Siding	Kent	S. E. & C.	Bexley and Crayford.
G	P	F	L	H	C	.	.	Creagan	Argyll	Cal.	Connel Ferry and Ballachulish.
.	P	.	.	.	.	.	.	Creagh	Cork	C. B. & S. C.	Skibbereen and Baltimore.
.	P	.	.	.	.	.	.	Creagh (Book to Drumshambo)	Leitrim	C. & L.	Ballinamore and Drumshambo.
G	P	.	.	.	.	.	.	Credenhill	Hereford	Mid.	Hereford and Eardisley.
.	.	.	.	.	.	.	.	Pontithel Chemical Co.'s Works	Hereford	Mid.	Credenhill and Moorhampton.
G	P	F	L	H	C	5	0	Crediton (L. & S. W.)	Devon	L. & S. W. / G. W.	Exeter and Okehampton. / Over L. S. W. from Cowley Bge. Jn.
G	.	F	L	.	.	5	0				
.	.	.	.	.	.	.	.	Creech Junction	Somerset	G. W.	Durston and Taunton.
.	.	.	.	.	.	.	.	Creech Siding	Somerset	G. W.	Same as Sommerville Sid. (Taunton)
G	P	.	L	H	C	1	10	Creeslough	Donegal	L. & L. S.	Letterkenny and Burtonport.
G	P	F	L	H	C	8	0	Creetown	Kirkcud	P.P.&W.Jt.(Cal.,G & SW, L. & N. W., & Mid.)	Newton Stewart & Castle Douglas.
G	P	F	L	H	C	.	.	Creighton's Siding (N. B.)	Cumb'land	N.B.— L. & N. W.	Carlisle.
.	.	.	.	.	.	.	.	Creigiau	Glamorg'n	Barry	Wenvoe and Efail-Isaf.
.	.	.	.	.	.	.	.	Creigiau Quarry	Glamorg'n	T. V.	Same as Craigiau Quarry (Cross Inn)
.	.	.	.	.	.	.	.	Crelake Siding	Devon	G. W.	Tavistock.
.	.	.	.	.	.	.	.	Cremer's Brick & Flint Siding	Kent	S. E. & C.	Newington.
.	.	.	.	.	.	.	.	Cremorne Wharf	Middlesex	G. W.—L. & N. W.	London, Chelsea Basin.
.	.	.	.	.	.	.	.	Crescent Brewery (Mid.)	Staffs	Mid—L N W—G N—N S	Same as Cooper & Co's. (Burton-on-Trent).
.	.	.	.	.	.	.	.	Crescent Cattle Docks	N'hampton	Mid.	Peterboro'.
.	.	.	.	.	.	.	.	Crescent Wharf	N'hampton	Mid.	See Peterboro'.
G	P	F	L	H	C	.	.	Cressage	Salop	G. W.	Shrewsbury and Buildwas.
.	.	.	.	.	.	.	.	Cressey Street Siding	Lincoln	G. C.	See Bannister & Co. (Grimsby).
.	P	.	.	.	.	.	.	Cressington and Grassendale	Lancs	C.L.C.(G.C.,G.N.,&Mid.)	Garston and Liverpool (Central).
G	P	F	L	H	C	5	0	Cresswell	Staffs	N. S.	Stoke and Uttoxeter.
.	.	.	.	.	.	.	.	Cresswell Junction	Staffs	N. S.	Cresswell and Leigh.
.	.	.	.	.	.	.	.	Creswell (Mid.)	Derby	Mid.— G. C.	See Elmton and Creswell.
G	P	.	.	H	.	.	.	Creswell and Welbeck	Derby	L. D. & E. C.	Langwith Junction and Clown.
.	.	.	.	.	.	.	.	Creswell Colliery (Bolsover Colliery Co.) (Mid.)	Derby	Mid.—G. C.	Elmton and Creswell.
.	.	.	.	.	.	.	.	Creswell Col. Jn. (L. D.&E.C.)	Derby	L. D. & E. C. / G. E.	Branch from Creswell & Welbeck. / Over L. D. & E. C. from Lincoln, Pye Wipe Junction (for Coal only).
G	P	.	.	.	.	.	.	Crew	Tyrone	C. & V. B.	Castlederg and Victoria Bridge.
								CREWE—			
G	P	F	L	H	C	10	0	(Station, L. & N. W.)	Cheshire	L. & N. W. / G.W. / N. S.	Stafford and Warrington. / Over L. & N. W. from Nantwich Jn. / Over L. & N. W. from Crewe Junc.
.	.	.	.	.	.	.	.	Brown's Gresty Mill	Cheshire	L. & N. W.	Crewe and Willaston.
.	.	.	.	.	.	.	.	Coal Yard	Cheshire	L. & N. W.	Crewe.
.	.	.	.	.	.	.	.	Exchange Sidings (L&NW)	Cheshire	L. & N. W.—G.W.—N. S.	Crewe.
.	.	.	.	.	.	.	.	Junction	Cheshire	L. & N. W. — N. S.	Crewe and Radway Green.
.	.	.	.	.	.	.	.	Lloyd's Cattle Market Sid.	Cheshire	L. & N. W.	Crewe.

EXPLANATION—**G** Goods Station.   **P** Passenger and Parcel Station.   **P*** Passenger, but not Parcel or Miscellaneous Traffic.
F Furniture Vans, Carriages, Portable Engines, and Machines on Wheels.   **L** Live Stock.
H Horse Boxes and Prize Cattle Vans.   **C** Carriages by Passenger Train.

STATION ACCOMMODATION.						CRANE POWER.	STATIONS, &c.	COUNTY.	COMPANY.	POSITION.
						Tons Cwts.	**CREWE**—continued.			
.	.	.	.	.	.	. .	Lord Crewe's Siding	Cheshire...	L. & N. W.	Crewe.
.	.	.	.	.	.	. .	Sidings	Cheshire...	N. S.	Crewe and Radway Green.
G	.	F	.	.	.	5 0	Wharf	Cheshire...	N. S.	Branch from L. N. W. North of Crewe.
.	.	.	.	.	.	. .	Crewe Junction Sidings	Edinboro'	Cal.	See Granton.
G	P	F	L	H	C	10 0	Crewkerne	Somerset..	L. & S. W.	Yeovil Junction and Exeter.
.	.	.	.	.	.	. .	Bradford & Son's Siding ...	Somerset..	L. & S. W.	Crewkerne.
G	.	.	.	.	.	10 0	Hewish Siding	Somerset..	L. & S. W.	Crewkerne.
.	.	.	.	.	.	. .	Creyke's Crossing	Yorks	N. E.	Goole.
G	P	F	L	H	C	0 10	Crianlarich	Perth	Cal.	Callander and Oban.
G	P	F	L	H	C	1 10		Perth	N. B.	Helensburgh and Fort William.
.	.	.	.	.	.	. .	Crianlarich Junction............	Perth	Cal.—N. B.	Oban and Ardlui.
.	.	.	.	.	.	. .	Cribbw Ballast Sidings	Glamorg'n	G. W.	Tondu.
.	.	.	.	.	.	. .	Cribbw Coke Ovens & Brick Works	Glamorg'n	G. W.	Tondu.
G	P	F	L	H	C	1 0	Criccieth	Carnarvon	Cam.	Harlech and Pwllheli.
G	.	.	.	.	.	4 0	Wern Siding	Carnarvon	Cam.	Portmadoc and Criccieth.
.	.	.	.	.	.	. .	Crich Lime Works	Derby	Mid.	Ambergate.
.	.	.	.	.	.	. .	Crick	N'hamptn	L. & N. W.	See Kilsby and Crick.
G	P	F	L	H	C	5 0	Cricklade	Wilts.......	M. & S. W. Jn.	Swindon Town and Cirencester.
.	.	.	.	.	.	. .	Cricklewood..................	Middlesex	Met.	See London, Willesden Green and Cricklewood.
.	.	.	.	.	.	. .	Cricklewood (Mid.)	Middlesex	Mid.—S. E. & C.	See London.
.	.	.	.	.	.	. .	Cricksea Ferry Siding	Essex	G. E.	See Burnham-on-Crouch.
.	.	.	.	.	.	. .	Cridling Stubbs Siding........	Yorks	L. & Y.	Womersley.
G	P	F	L	H	C	5 0	Crieff	Perth	Cal.	Crieff Junction and Balquhidder.
.	.	.	.	.	.	. .	Strathearn Manure Works	Perth	Cal.	Crieff.
.	.	.	.	.	.	. .	Veitch's Siding	Perth	Cal.	Crieff.
G	P	.	L	H	.	2 0	Crieff Junction Station........	Perth	Cal.	Stirling and Perth.
G	P	.	L	H	.	3 0	Crigglestone	Yorks	L. & Y.	Wakefield and Barnsley.
.	.	.	.	.	.	. .	Crigglestone Coal Co.'s Siding (L. & Y.)...	Yorks	L. & Y.—N. E.	Crigglestone.
.	.	.	.	.	.	. .	Haigh Moor Coal Co.'s Sid.	Yorks	L. & Y.	Crigglestone.
.	.	.	.	.	.	. .	Crimdon Siding	Durham ...	N. E.	Castle Eden.
.	.	.	.	.	.	. .	Crimea Siding..................	Glo'ster ...	G. W.	Bristol, Temple Meads.
.	.	.	.	.	.	. .	Crimea Siding..................	Middlesex	G. W.	London, Paddington.
.	.	.	.	.	.	. .	Crimple Junction	Yorks	N. E.	Pannal and Harrogate.
.	.	.	.	.	.	. .	Crimple Siding	Yorks	N. E.	See Starbeck.
.	.	.	.	.	.	. .	Crimstane Siding	Berwick ...	N. B.	See Duns.
.	.	.	.	.	.	. .	Crindau Gas Works (G.W.)...	Mon	G. W.— L. & N. W.	Newport, Dock Street.
.	.	.	.	.	.	. .	Crindau Glass Works (G.W.)	Mon	G. W.— L. & N. W.	Newport, Dock Street.
.	.	.	.	.	.	. .	Crisp, J., & Son's Siding......	Suffolk ...	G. E.	Beccles.
.	.	.	.	.	.	. .	Crockherbtown Junction	Glamorg'n	Rhy.—T. V.	Cardiff, Adam Street and Llandaff.
G	.	.	.	.	.	. .	Croesnewydd	Denbigh ...	G. W.	Wrexham and Minera.
G	P	.	L	.	.	. .	Croft (L. & N. W.)	Leicester..	L. & N. W.	Leicester and Nuneaton.
G	.	.	L	.	.	. .			Mid.	Over L. & N. W. Line.
.	.	.	.	.	.	. .	Croft Granite Co.'s Siding (L. & N. W.)...	Leicester..	L. & N. W.—Mid.	Croft and Narboro'.
.	.	.	.	.	.	. .	Croft & Son's Railway Quarry	Lancs	P.&L. Jt. (L&NW.&L&Y)	Longridge.
.	.	.	.	.	.	. .	Croft's Quarry Siding	Lancs	P & L Jt(L & NW & L&Y)	Preston, Deepdale.
.	.	.	.	.	.	. .	Croft Depôt	Durham ...	N. E.	Branch from Darlington.
G	.	.	.	.	.	. .	Croftengea & Alexandria Wks.	Dumbartn	D. & B. Jt. (Cal. & N. B.)	Alexandria.
.	.	.	.	.	.	. .	Croftengea Siding (N. B.) ...	Dumbartn	N. B.—Cal.	Jamestown.
G	P	F	L	H	.	1 10	Crofthead......................	L'lithgow	N. B.	Bathgate, Upper and Morningside.
.	.	.	.	.	.	. .	Allanrigg Colliery	L'lithgow	N. B.	Crofthead and Morningside.
.	.	.	.	.	.	. .	Braehead Brick Works......	L'lithgow	N. B.	East Benhar Branch.
.	.	.	.	.	.	. .	Braehead Colliery	L'lithgow	N. B.	East Benhar Branch.
.	.	.	.	.	.	. .	Braehead Quarry	L'lithgow	N. B.	East Benhar Branch.
.	.	.	.	.	.	. .	Crofthead Colliery	L'lithgow	N. B.	Stonehead Branch.
.	.	.	.	.	.	. .	Cultrigg Pits	L'lithgow	N. B.	East Benhar Branch.
.	.	.	.	.	.	. .	East Benhar Branch	L'lithgow	N. B.	Branch from Crofthead.
.	.	.	.	.	.	. .	East Benhar Siding	L'lithgow	N. B.	East Benhar Branch.
.	.	.	.	.	.	. .	Eastfield Brick Works	L'lithgow	N. B.	Stonehead Branch.
.	.	.	.	.	.	. .	Eastfield Quarry	L'lithgow	N. B.	Stonehead Branch.
.	.	.	.	.	.	. .	Falahill Colliery	L'lithgow	N. B.	East Benhar Branch.
.	.	.	.	.	.	. .	Falahill Quarry	L'lithgow	N. B.	East Benhar Branch.
.	.	.	.	.	.	. .	Leavenseat Branch	L'lithgow	N. B.	Branch—Bents and Crofthead.
.	.	.	.	.	.	. .	Leavenseat Lime Works ...	L'lithgow	N. B.	Leavenseat Branch.
.	.	.	.	.	.	. .	Leavenseat Oil Works	L'lithgow	N. B.	Leavenseat Branch.
G	.	.	.	.	.	. .	Longridge Siding	L'lithgow	N. B.	Bents and Crofthead.
.	.	.	.	.	.	. .	Stonehead Branch (Crofthead Branch)	L'lithgow	N. B.	Branch—Bents and Crofthead.

EXPLANATION—G *Goods Station.*   P *Passenger and Parcel Station.*   P* *Passenger, but not Parcel or Miscellaneous Traffic.*
F *Furniture Vans, Carriages, Portable Engines, and Machines on Wheels.*   L *Live Stock.*
H *Horse Boxes and Prize Cattle Vans.*   C *Carriages by Passenger Train.*

STATION ACCOMMODATION.						CRANE POWER.	STATIONS, &c.	COUNTY.	COMPANY.	POSITION.
						Tons Cwts.				
.	P	.	.	.	.	. .	Crofton	Cumb'land	M. & C.	Wigton and Curthwaite.
G	P	.	L	H	.	. .	Crofton	Yorks	L. & Y.	Wakefield and Pontefract.
.	.	.	.	.	.	. .	Crofton	Yorks	W. R. & G. Jt. (G.C.&G.N.)	See Hare Park and Crofton.
.	P	.	.	.	.	. .	Crofton Junction	Yorks	L. & Y.—W. R. & G. Jt.	Wakefield and Hare Park.
.	P	.	.	.	.	. .	Crofton Park (for Ladywell)	Kent	S. E. & C.	Nunhead and Shortlands.
.	.	.	.	.	.	. .	Croft Pit (Furness)	Cumb'land	Furness—L. & N. W.	Whitehaven.
.	P	.	L	H	C	. .	Croft Spa	Durham	N. E.	Northallerton and Darlington.
.	.	.	.	.	.	. .	Croftyguinea Siding	Glamorg'n	T. V.	Same as St. Fagan's Road Siding (Cross Inn).
G	P	.	.	.	.	. .	Crogan	Argyll	Cal.	Steamer from Oban.
G	P	.	L	H	C	. .	Crolly	Donegal	L. & L. S.	Letterkenny and Burtonport.
G	P	F	L	H	C	3 0	Cromdale	Inverness	G. N. of S.	Craigellachie and Boat of Garten.
G	P	F	L	H	C	1 10	Cromer	Norfolk	G. E.	Branch from Norwich.
G	P	F	L	H	C	1 0	Cromer Beach	Norfolk	Mid. & G. N. Jt.	Branch from Melton Constable.
.	.	.	.	.	.	. .	Cromer Gas Co.'s Siding	Norfolk	Mid. & G. N. Jt.	Cromer Beach.
.	.	.	.	.	.	. .	Cromer Urban District Council's Works	Norfolk	Mid. & G. N. Jt.	Cromer Beach.
G	.	.	.	.	.	5 0	Cromford	Derby	{ L. & N. W.	Buxton and High Peak Junction.
.	P	.	.	.	.	}			Mid.	Ambergate and Rowsley.
.	.	.	.	.	.	. .	Cromford Canal Wharf	Derby	Mid.	Near Cromford.
.	.	.	.	.	.	. .	Killer Bros.' Siding	Derby	L. & N. W.	Cromford and Steeplehouse.
.	.	.	.	.	.	. .	Cromford Moor Siding	Derby	L. & N. W.	Same as Killer's Sid. (Steeplehouse).
.	.	.	.	.	.	. .	Crommelin Iron Ore Co.'s Sid.	Antrim	N. C. Com. (Mid.)	Cargan.
.	.	.	.	.	.	. .	Crompton	Lancs	L. & Y.	See Shaw and Crompton.
.	.	.	.	.	.	. .	Crompton & Co.'s Siding	Essex	G. E.	Chelmsford.
.	.	.	.	.	.	. .	Crompton & Co.'s Siding	Lancs	L. & Y.	Croston.
.	.	.	.	.	.	. .	Crompton & Shawcross—			
.	.	.	.	.	.	. .	Fir Tree House Colliery	Lancs	L. & N. W.	Wigan.
.	.	.	.	.	.	. .	Grange Colliery	Lancs	G. C. (Wigan Jn.)	Hindley and Platt Bridge.
.	.	.	.	.	.	. .	Hindley Colliery	Lancs	G. C. (Wigan Jn.)	Hindley and Platt Bridge.
.	.	.	.	.	.	. .	Hindley Colliery (Amberswood East Siding)	Lancs	L. & N. W.	Hindley and Amberswood.
.	.	.	.	.	.	. .	Moss Colliery	Lancs	L. & N. W.	Wigan.
.	.	.	.	.	.	. .	Moss Colliery	Lancs	G. C. (Wigan Jn.)	Hindley and Platt Bridge.
.	.	.	.	.	.	. .	Strangeways Hall Col. or Amberswood West Siding (G. C., Wigan Junction)	Lancs	G C (Wig. Jn.)—L & N W	Hindley and Platt Bridge.
.	.	.	.	.	.	. .	Crompton's Siding	Lancs	L. & Y.	Shaw.
.	.	.	.	.	.	. .	Cromwells Siding	Mon	G. W.	Risca.
.	.	.	.	.	.	. .	Cronbane Siding	Wicklow	D. W. & W.	Ovoca.
G	P	.	L	H	.	1 0	Cronberry	Ayr	G. & S.W.	Lugar and Muirkirk.
.	.	.	.	.	.	. .	Cronberry Junction	Ayr	G. & S.W.	Lugar and Cronberry.
.	.	.	.	.	.	. .	Cronberry No. 1	Ayr	G. & S.W.	Lugar.
.	.	.	.	.	.	. .	Cronberry Tile Works	Ayr	G. & S.W.	Lugar.
G	P	F	L	H	C	5 0	Crone & Taylor's Siding	Lancs	L. & N. W.	St. Helens.
.	.	.	.	.	.	. .	Crook	Durham	N. E.	Bishop Auckland and Tow Law.
.	.	.	.	.	.	. .	Beechburn Colliery	Durham	N. E.	Crook.
.	.	.	.	.	.	. .	Beechburn Station Siding	Durham	N. E.	Crook.
.	.	.	.	.	.	. .	Crook Brk. & Tile Co.'s Sid.	Durham	N. E.	Crook.
.	.	.	.	.	.	. .	East Bitchburn Colliery	Durham	N. E.	Crook.
.	.	.	.	.	.	. .	Eclipse Silica Brick Works	Durham	N. E.	Crook.
.	.	.	.	.	.	. .	Hargill Colliery	Durham	N. E.	Crook.
.	.	.	.	.	.	. .	Low Beechburn Colliery	Durham	N. E.	Crook.
.	.	.	.	.	.	. .	Pease & Partner's—			
.	.	.	.	.	.	. .	Bankfoot Ovens	Durham	N. E.	Crook.
.	.	.	.	.	.	. .	Brick Works	Durham	N. E.	Crook.
.	.	.	.	.	.	. .	General Shops	Durham	N. E.	Crook.
.	.	.	.	.	.	. .	Lucy (Grahamsley) Col.	Durham	N. E.	Crook.
.	.	.	.	.	.	. .	Roddymoor Colliery	Durham	N. E.	Crook.
.	.	.	.	.	.	. .	Stanley Colliery	Durham	N. E.	Crook.
.	.	.	.	.	.	. .	Wagon Shops	Durham	N. E.	Crook.
.	.	.	.	.	.	. .	White Lea Colliery	Durham	N. E.	Crook.
.	.	.	.	.	.	. .	Wooley Colliery	Durham	N. E.	Crook.
.	.	.	.	.	.	. .	Woodifield Colliery	Durham	N. E.	Crook.
.	.	.	.	.	.	. .	Crook Bank Colliery	Durham	N. E.	Redheugh.
.	.	.	.	.	.	. .	Crookgate Siding	Durham	N. E.	Redheugh.
.	.	.	.	.	.	. .	Crook Hall Foundry and Coke Ovens	Durham	N. E.	Blackhill.
.	.	.	.	.	.	. .	Crook Hall Slag Mill	Durham	N. E.	Blackhill.
.	.	.	.	.	.	. .	Crooklands Siding	Lancs	Furness	See Dalton.
G	P	.	L	H	.	1 5	Crook of Devon (for Fossoway)	Kinross	N. B.	Kinross Jn. Sta. & Rumbling Bridge.
.	.	.	.	.	.	. .	Crook Rise Siding	Yorks	Mid.	Rylstone.

EXPLANATION—G *Goods Station.* P *Passenger and Parcel Station.* P* *Passenger, but not Parcel or Miscellaneous Traffic.*
F *Furniture Vans, Carriages, Portable Engines, and Machines on Wheels.* L *Live Stock.*
H *Horse Boxes and Prize Cattle Vans.* C *Carriages by Passenger Train.*

STATION ACCOMMODATION.						CRANE POWER.		STATIONS, &c.	COUNTY.	COMPANY.	POSITION.
						Tons	Cwts.				
								Crook's Sand Siding	Lancs	L. & Y.	Ormskirk.
G	P	F	L	H	C	2	0	Crookston	Renfrew	G. & S.W.	Bellahouston and Paisley, Canal.
G	P	F	L					Crookstown Road	Cork	C. & Macroom	Kilcrea and Macroom.
								Crook Street	Lancs	L. & N.W.	See Bolton.
G	P	F	L	H	C			Croom	Limerick	G. S. & W.	Charleville and Limerick.
								Cropper's Paper Mills	W'morlnd	L. & N.W.	Burneside.
G	P	F	L	H	C	2	0	Cropredy	Oxon	G. W.	Banbury and Leamington.
G	P	F*	L					Crosby	I. of Man	I. of Man	Douglas and Peel.
								Crosby (L. & Y.)	Lancs	L. & Y.—L. & N.W.	See Blundellsands and Crosby.
G	P	F	L	H	C	1	10	Crosby Garrett	W'morlnd	Mid.	Kirkby Stephen and Appleby.
								Griseburne Ballast Siding	W'morlnd	Mid.	Near Crosby Garrett.
								Crosfield & Son's Factory Lane Siding (L. & N. W.)	Lancs	L. & N. W.—G. W.	Warrington (Bank Quay).
								Crosfield & Son's Soap Works	Lancs	L. & N.W.	Warrington (Arpley)
								Cross & Son's Siding	Lanark	Cal.	Glasgow, Port Dundas.
								Cross' Chemical Works	Stirling	Cal.—N. B.	Falkirk, Camelon.
								Cross, Tetley & Co.—			
								Bamfurlong Colliery	Lancs	L. & N.W.	Wigan.
								Mains Colliery	Lancs	L. & N.W.	Wigan.
G	P	F	L	H	C	2	0	Crossdoney	Cavan	M. G. W.	Cavan and Mullingar.
G	P							Crossens	Lancs	L. & Y.	Preston and Southport.
								Co-operative Wholesale Society's Siding	Lancs	L. & Y.	Crossens.
G								Crossfield	Cumb'land	WC & EJt.(Fur.&L&NW)	Marron Junction and Moor Row.
								Carron Iron Co.'s Jack Trees Siding	Cumb'land	WC & EJt.(Fur.&L&NW)	Cleator Moor and Crossfield.
								Crossfield Mines, Nos. 2 & 3 Pits	Cumb'land	WC & EJt.(Fur.&L&NW)	Cleator Moor and Moor Row.
								Lord Leconfield's No. 4 Pit	Cumb'land	WC & EJt.(Fur.&L&NW)	Cleator Moor and Crossfield.
								Stirling's Coal Pit	Cumb'land	WC & EJt.(Fur.&L&NW)	Cleator Moor and Moor Row.
								Stirling's Nos. 4,5,6 & 12 Pits	Cumb'land	WC & EJt.(Fur.&L&NW)	Cleator Moor and Moor Row.
								Crossfield, F.J., & Co.'s Timber Yard	Lancs	Furness	Barrow.
								Crossflat Sidings	Ayr	Cal.	Muirkirk.
G	P		L	H	C	4	0	Crossgar	Down	B. & C. D.	Belfast and Downpatrick.
G	P	F	L	H	C	0	15	Crossgates	Fife	N. B.	Dunfermline and Kinross Junction.
								Fordell Colliery	Fife	N. B.	Crossgates and Cowdenbeath, New.
								Hill of Beath Colliery and Brick Works	Fife	N. B.	Crossgates and Cowdenbeath, New.
								Mossend Foundry	Fife	N. B.	Crossgates and Cowdenbeath, New.
G	P		L					Cross Gates	Yorks	N. E.	Leeds and Selby.
G								Cross Hands	Carmarth'	G. W.	See Pantyffynnon.
G								Cross Hands	Carmarth'	L. & M. M.	Terminus.
								New Cross Hands Colliery	Carmarth'	L. & M. M.	Cross Hands.
G	P		L	H				Crosshaven	Cork	C. B. & P.	Terminus.
								Crosshill	Renfrew	Cal.	See Glasgow.
	P							Crosshill and Codnor	Derby	Mid.	Heanor and Ripley.
								Crosshill Colliery	Fife	N. B.	Kelty.
								Crosshills	Yorks	Mid.	See Kildwick and Crosshills.
								Crosshills Siding	Yorks	N. E.	Wistow.
G	P	F	L	H	C	2	0	Crosshouse	Ayr	G. & S.W.	Kilmarnock and Dalry.
								Busbiehead No. 2	Ayr	G. & S.W.	Crosshouse and Dreghorn.
								Plan Collieries	Ayr	G. & S.W.	Crosshouse and Dreghorn.
								Plan Fire-Clay Works	Ayr	G. & S.W.	Crosshouse and Dreghorn.
								Southhook Colliery	Ayr	G. & S.W.	Crosshouse and Dreghorn.
								Southhook Fire-Clay Works	Ayr	G. & S.W.	Crosshouse and Dreghorn.
								Woodhill No. 8	Ayr	G. & S.W.	Hillhead Branch.
								Crosshouse Junction (Busbie)	Ayr	G. & S.W.	Kilmarnock and Crosshouse.
G	P							Cross Inn	Glamorg'n	T. V.	Pontypridd and Llantrisant.
								Castella Siding	Glamorg'n	T. V.	Treferig Branch.
								Cottage Siding	Glamorg'n	T. V.	Cross Inn and Llantrisant.
								Craigiau or Creigiau Quarry	Glamorg'n	T. V.	Cross Inn and Radyr.
								Gelynog Colliery	Glamorg'n	T. V.	Near Cross Inn.
								Glyn Colliery	Glamorg'n	T. V.	Treferig Branch.
								Pantycorrwg or Pantygored Siding	Glamorg'n	T. V.	Cross Inn and Radyr.
								St. Fagan's Road Siding (Croftyguinea Siding)	Glamorg'n	T. V.	Cross Inn and Radyr.
								South Cambria Colliery	Glamorg'n	T. V.	Cross Inn and Radyr.
								Torycoed Colliery	Glamorg'n	T. V.	Cross Inn and Radyr.
								Treferig Siding	Glamorg'n	T. V.	Treferig Branch.
								Cross Inn No. 1 Railway Junc.	Glamorg'n	T. V.	Cross Inn and Llantwit.

EXPLANATION—G *Goods Station.*   P *Passenger and Parcel Station.*   P* *Passenger, but not Parcel or Miscellaneous Traffic.*
F *Furniture Vans, Carriages, Portable Engines, and Machines on Wheels.*   F* *Furniture Vans excepted.*   L *Live Stock.*
H *Horse Boxes and Prize Cattle Vans.*   C *Carriages by Passenger Train.*

STATION ACCOMMODATION.						CRANE POWER.	STATIONS, &c.	COUNTY.	COMPANY.	POSITION.
						Tons Cwts.				
.	P	.	.	.	.	. .	Cross Keys	Mon	G. W.	Newport and Crumlin, Low Level.
.	.	.	.	.	.	. .	Cox's Quarry	Mon	G. W.	Cross Keys and Abercarn.
.	.	.	.	.	.	. .	Cross Lane (L. & N. W.)	Lancs	L. & N. W.—G.C.—G.W.	See Manchester.
.	.	.	.	.	.	. .	Crosslee	Renfrew	G. & S.W.	See Houston (for Crosslee).
.	.	.	.	.	.	. .	Crossley & Son's Siding	Yorks	H. & O. Jt. (G.N.&L.&Y.)	Halifax, North Bridge.
.	.	.	.	.	.	. .	Crossley's Siding (G. C.)	Lancs	GC—GW—L&NW—Mid	Manchester, Openshaw.
G	P	.	L	H	.	1 0	Crossmichael	Kirkcud	P.P.&W.Jt.(Cal.,G&SW, L. & N. W. & Mid.)	Newton Stewart & Castle Douglas.
G	P	.	.	.	.	3 0	Crossmyloof	Renfrew	G B & K Jt(Cal&G&SW)	Strathbungo and Pollokshaws.
G	P	.	.	.	.	. .	Cross Roads	Antrim	N. C. Com. (Mid.)	Ballymena and Parkmore.
.	.	.	.	.	.	. .	Cross Street Siding	Notts	G. N.	Newark.
							Cross, Tetley & Co.—			
.	.	.	.	.	.	. .	Bamfurlong Colliery	Lancs	L. & N. W.	Wigan.
.	.	.	.	.	.	. .	Mains Colliery	Lancs	L. & N. W.	Wigan.
.	.	.	.	.	.	. .	Crosswell's Brewery Siding	Glamorg'n	G. W.	Ely (for Llandaff).
.	.	.	.	.	.	. .	Crosta's Siding	Notts	Mid.	Nottingham.
G	P	F	L	H	C	5 0	Croston	Lancs	L. & Y.	Preston and Ormskirk.
.	.	.	.	.	.	. .	Crompton & Co.'s Siding	Lancs	L. & Y.	Croston and Rufford.
							Littlewood Brick and Tile			
.	.	.	.	.	.	. .	Co.'s Siding	Lancs	L. & Y.	Near Croston.
.	.	.	.	.	.	. .	Crouch End (G.N.)	Middlesex	G. N.—N. L.	See London.
.	.	.	.	.	.	. .	Crouch Hill	Middlesex	T. & H Jt. (G. E. & Mid.)	See London.
G	P	F	L	H	C	1 10	Crowborough & Jarvis Brook	Sussex	L. B. & S. C.	Buxted and Eridge.
G	P	.	L	.	.	. .	Crowcombe	Somerset	G. W.	Taunton and Watchet.
G	P	.	.	.	.	5 0	Crowden	Derby	G. C.	Guide Bridge and Penistone.
.	.	.	.	.	.	. .	Crowhill Brick Works	Lanark	N. B.	Bishopbriggs.
.	P	.	.	.	.	. .	Crowhurst	Sussex	S. E. & C.	Battle and Hastings.
.	.	.	.	.	.	. .	Crowhurst Junction, East	Surrey	C. & O. Jt.—S. E. & C.	Oxted and Edenbridge.
.	.	.	.	.	.	. .	Crowhurst Junction, North	Surrey	C. & O. Jt.—L. B. & S.C.	East Grinstead and Oxted.
.	.	.	.	.	.	. .	Crowhurst Park Siding	Sussex	S. E. & C.	Battle.
.	.	.	.	.	.	. .	Crowhurst Siding	Surrey	S. E. & C.	Edenbridge.
.	.	.	.	.	.	. .	Crowland	Lincoln	G. N. & G. E. Jt.	See Postland (for Crowland).
G	P	F	L	H	C	. .	Crowle	Lincoln	Axholme Jt.(L.&Y.&N.E)	Branch near Goole.
.	.	.	.	.	.	. .	Spilman's Siding	Yorks	Axholme Jt.(L.&Y.&N.E)	Crowle.
G	P	F	L	H	C	1 10	Crowle (for Epworth&Belton)	Lincoln	G. C.	Thorne and Barnetby.
							Crowle Brick and Tile Co.'s			
.	.	.	.	.	.	. .	Siding	Lincoln	G. C.	Crowle (for Epworth and Belton).
.	.	.	.	.	.	. .	Dymond's Siding	Lincoln	G. C.	Crowle (for Epworth and Belton).
.	.	.	.	.	.	. .	Crowley & Co.'s Siding (G.C.)	Yorks	G. C.— Mid.	Meadow Hall and Wincobank.
.	.	.	.	.	.	. .	Crown Collieries	Glo'ster	S. &Wye Jt.(G.W.& Mid)	Parkend.
.	.	.	.	.	.	. .	Crowndale Stone Co.	Flint	W & M Jt (G W&L&NW)	Llanfynydd.
.	.	.	.	.	.	. .	Crown Farm Sidings	Notts	Mid.	See Bolsover Col. Co. (Mansfield).
.	.	.	.	.	.	. .	Crowhurst Brick Siding	Surrey	L. B. & S. C.	Lingfield.
.	.	.	.	.	.	. .	Crow Nest Junction	Lancs	L. & Y.	Hindley and Daisy Hill.
							Crow Nest or Hewlett Pit			
.	.	.	.	.	.	. .	(L. & Y.)	Lancs	L. & Y.—L. & N. W.	See Wigan Coal & Iron Co. (Hindley)
.	.	.	.	.	.	. .	Crown Fuel Works (Maindy)	Glamorg'n	T. V.	{ Cardiff. Llandaff.
.	.	.	.	.	.	. .	Crown Fuel Wks. (Roath Dk.)	Glamorg'n	G W—LNW—Rhy.—TV	Cardiff.
.	.	.	.	.	.	. .	Crown Glass Works	Lancs	L. & N. W.	See Pilkington Bros. (St. Helens).
.	.	.	.	.	.	. .	Crown Iron Works	Lanark	N. B.	Coatbridge, Sheepford.
							Crown Preserve Coal Co.'s			
.	.	.	.	.	.	. .	Fuel Works	Glamorg'n	G W—LNW—Rhy.—TV	Cardiff.
.	.	.	.	.	.	. .	Crown Street	Lancs	L. & N. W.	See Liverpool.
.	.	.	.	.	.	. .	Crown Street	Cumb'land	M. & C.	See Carlisle.
.	.	.	.	.	.	. .	Crow Orchard Col.or Arley Pit	Lancs	L. & N. W.	See Pearson & Knowles Coal & Iron Co. (Wigan).
G	P	.	.	.	.	. .	Crow Park (for Sutton-on-Trent)	Notts	G. N.	Newark and Retford.
.	.	.	.	.	.	. .	Crow Road	Lanark	Cal.	See Glasgow.
.	.	.	.	.	.	. .	Crows House Brick Works	Durham	N. E.	Thornley Colliery Station.
							Crowther, J. F. & J., Siding			
.	.	.	.	.	.	. .	(L. & Y.)	Yorks	L. & Y.—L. & N. W.	Heckmondwike.
.	.	.	.	.	.	. .	Crowthorne	Berks	S. E. & C.	See Wellington College (for Crowthorne).
.	.	.	.	.	.	. .	Crowthorn Junction	Lancs	L. & N. W.—O. A. & G. B.	Oldham and Stockport.
.	P	.	.	.	.	. .	Croxall	Staffs	Mid.	Tamworth and Burton.
G	P	.	.	.	.	. .	Croxdale	Durham	N. E.	Ferryhill and Durham, Pass.
.	.	.	.	.	.	. .	Croxdale Colliery	Durham	N. E.	Croxdale.
.	.	.	.	.	.	. .	Croxley Green Siding	Herts	L. & N. W.	Same as Dickinson & Co.'s Siding (Watford).
G	P	F	L	H	C	1 5	Croy	Dumbartn	N. B.	Falkirk and Glasgow.

EXPLANATION—G Goods Station.   P Passenger and Parcel Station.   P* Passenger, but not Parcel or Miscellaneous Traffic.
F Furniture Vans, Carriages, Portable Engines, and Machines on Wheels.   L Live Stock.
H Horse Boxes and Prize Cattle Vans.   C Carriages by Passenger Train.

STATION ACCOMMODATION.						CRANE POWER.	STATIONS, &c.	COUNTY.	COMPANY.	POSITION.
						Tons Cwts.	CROYDON—			
	P						Addiscombe Road	Surrey ...	S. E. & C.	Branch from Woodside Junction.
G	P	F	L	H	C	10 0	East	Surrey ...	L. B. & S. C.—S. E. & C.	New Cross and Redhill.
							Gas Co.'s Siding	Surrey ...	L. B. & S. C.	West Croydon & Mitcham Junction.
							Hall & Co.'s Siding	Surrey ...	L. B. & S. C.	Croydon, East.
	P			H	C				L. B. & S. C.	South Croydon and Norwood.
	P						New (L. B. & S. C.)	Surrey ...	G. E.	Over L. B. & S. C. from New Cross Jn.
	P			H	C				L. & N. W.	Over L. B. & S. C. from Clapham Jn.
	P						South	Surrey ...	L. B. & S. C.	Norwood Junction and Stoats Nest.
							South Junction	Surrey ...	C. & O. Jt.—L. B. & S. C.	East Croydon and Sanderstead.
							Waddon Marsh Siding	Surrey ...	L. B. & S. C.	West Croydon.
	P	F		H	C		West	Surrey ...	L. B. & S. C.	Norwood and Sutton.
							Croydon Corporation Siding .	Surrey ...	L. B. & S. C.	Norwood Junction.
							Croydon Gas Co.'s Siding ...	Surrey ...	L. B. & S. C.	Croydon, West.
							Croysdale's Siding	Yorks	L. & Y.	Whitley Bridge.
							Cruckmeole or Shorthill Col.	Salop ...	S & W'pl. Jt(GW & LNW)	Same as Atherton's (Hanwood).
G	P	F	L	H	C	5 0	Cruden Bay..................	Aberdeen	G. N. of S.	Ellon and Boddam.
							Brick Works	Aberdeen	G. N. of S.	Cruden Bay and Boddam.
G	P	F	L	H	C	1 10	Crudgington	Salop ...	G. W.	Wellington and Market Drayton
							Cruick's Fire-Clay Works ...	Fife	N. B	Inverkeithing.
G	P		L			2 0	Crumlin	Antrim ...	G. N. (I.)	Antrim and Lisburn.
	P						Crumlin (High Level)	Mon	G. W.	Pontypool and Tredegar Junction.
G	P		L				Crumlin (Low Level)..........	Mon	G. W.	Newport and Aberbeeg.
							Crumlin Junction	Mon	G. W.	Crumlin, High Level and Blaendare.
							Crump Meadow Colliery	Glo'ster ...	G. W.	Bilson Junction.
							Crump Meadow Sidings	Glo'ster ...	S. & Wye Jt. (GW & Mid)	Drybrook Road.
G	P					5 0	Crumpsall....................	Lancs	L. & Y.	Manchester and Prestwich.
							Crundall's Siding	Kent	S. E. & C.	Queenborough.
G	P	F	L	H	C		Crusheen (G. S. & W.)	Clare	G. S. & W.	Athenry and Ennis.
									M. G. W.	Over G. S. & W. from Athenry.
							Crusher Siding	Derby	L. & N. W.	SeeBuxtonLimeFirmsCo.(Hindlow).
							Crwys Storage Sidings.........	Glamorg'n	Rhy.	Cardiff.
G	P	F	L	H	C		Crymmych Arms	Pembroke	G. W.	Whitland and Cardigan.
G	P		L				Crynant	Glamorg'n	N. & Brecon.	Neath and Colbren.
							Crynant Colliery..............	Glamorg'n	N. & Brecon	Crynant.
							Llwynonn Colliery	Glamorg'n	N. & Brecon	Crynant.
							CRYSTAL PALACE—			
	P			H	C		East	Kent	L. B. & S. C.	Sydenham and Gipsy Hill.
G	P					1 15	High Level and Upper Norwood	Surrey ...	S. E. & C.	Branch from Nunhead Jn. Station.
G	P	F	L	H	C	4 10			L. B. & S. C.	Gipsy Hill and Norwood Junction.
	P			H	C		West (L. B. & S. C.).........	Kent	L. & N. W.	Over L. B. & S. C. from Clapham Jn.
	P*								S. E. & C.	Over L. B. & S. C. from Norwood, Bromley Junction.
							Crystal Palace District Gas Co.'s Siding....................	Kent	S. E. & C.	Lower Sydenham.
G							Crythan Waiting Room	Glamorg'n	S. Wales Min...............	Briton Ferry and Cymmer.
							Cuckmere Brick Co.'s Siding	Sussex ...	L. B. & S. C.	Berwick.
							Cuckoo's Nest Siding	Brecon ...	L. & N. W.	Same as Clydach Lime Works (Clydach).
G	P	F	L	H		5 0	Cuddington	Cheshire.	C.L.C. (G.C., G.N. & Mid.)	Northwich and Chester.
							Cudlip & Son's Paper Mills...	Derby......	Mid.	Little Eaton.
							CUDWORTH—			
G	P	F	L	H	C	5 0	(Station, Mid.)	Yorks	Mid.	Masboro' and Normanton.
	P								H. & B.	Over Mid. from Cudworth, Pass. Jn.
							Carlton Main Colliery	Yorks	H. & B.	Cudworth, North.
							Carlton Main Colliery Co.—			
							Carlton Main Colliery.....	Yorks	Mid.	Cudworth and Royston.
							Grimethorpe Colliery	Yorks	Mid.	Cudworth and Darfield.
							Dobson & Wallis' Siding....	Yorks	Mid.	Cudworth.
							Goods Junction	Yorks	H. & B.—Mid.	Hemsworth and Cudworth Station.
							Grimethorpe Branch	Yorks	Mid.	Cudworth and Darfield.
							Monckton Main Colliery....	Yorks	H. & B.	Cudworth, North.
							Monk Bretton Colliery......	Yorks	H. & B.	Cudworth, North.
							Monk Bretton Col. (Mid.)	Yorks	Mid.—† H. & B.	Cudworth and Barnsley.
							Nall & Co.'s Siding (Mid.)	Yorks	Mid.—† H. & B.	Cudworth and Barnsley.
							New Oaks Colliery	Yorks	H. & B.	Near Stairfoot Junction.
G							North	Yorks	H. & B.	Cudworth, Passengers and Upton.
							Passenger Junction	Yorks	H. & B.—Mid.	Upton and Cudworth Station.
							South Hiendley Colliery (Musgrave Siding)........	Yorks	H. & B.	Cudworth and Hemsworth.
							Storr's Mill	Yorks	Mid.	Cudworth and Darfield.

EXXPLANATION—G *Goods Station.*   P *Passenger and Parcel Station.*   P* *Passenger, but not Parcel or Miscellaneous Traffic.*
F *Furniture Vans, Carriages, Portable Engines, and Machines on Wheels.*   L *Live Stock.*
H *Horse Boxes and Prize Cattle Vans.*   C *Carriages by Passenger Train.*   † *For Local Traffic only.*

STATION ACCOMMODATION.						CRANE POWER.	STATIONS, &c.	COUNTY.	COMPANY.	POSITION.
						Tons Cwts.	CUDWORTH—continued.			
.	.	.	.	.	.	. .	Wharncliffe Woodmoor Colliery .... }	Yorks	{ H. & B.	Cudworth and Hemsworth.
									{ Mid.	Cudworth and Royston.
.	.	.	.	.	.	. .	Yorkshire and Derbyshire Coal & Iron Co.'s Carlton Main Colliery	Yorks	Mid.	Near Barnsley.
.	.	.	.	.	.	. .	Cuilhill Basin	Lanark ...	Cal.	Baillieston.
G	P	F	L	H	C	5 0	Culcheth	Lancs	G. C. (Wigan Jn.)	Glazebrook and Lowton St. Mary's.
G	P	.	.	.	.	. .	Culgaith	Cumb'land	Mid.	Langwathby and New Biggin.
G	P	F	L	H	C	2 0	Culham	Oxon	G. W.	Oxford and Didcot.
G	P	.	L	H	.	2 0	Culkerton..........................	Glo'ster ...	G. W.	Kemble Junction and Tetbury.
G	P	F	L	H	C	1 5	Cullen	Banff	G. N. of S.	Portsoy and Elgin.
G	P	F	L	H	C	. .	Cullercoats	Northumb	N. E.	Newcastle and Shields.
G	P	F	L	H	C	10 0	Cullingworth	Yorks	G. N.	Keighley and Bradford.
.	.	.	.	.	.	. .	Clayton's Stone Siding......	Yorks	G. N.	Cullingworth and Wilsden.
G	P	.	L	H	C	. .	Cullion	Derry	Donegal	Londonderry and Strabane.
G	P	F	L	H	C	. .	Culloden Moor	Inverness..	High.	Inverness and Aviemore.
G	P	F	L	H	C	6 0	Cullompton	Devon	G. W.	Exeter and Taunton.
G	P	.	L	.	.	1 10	Culloville	Monaghan	G. N. (I.)	Dundalk and Clones.
.	P	.	.	.	.	. .	Cullum & Co.'s Siding	Suffolk ...	G. E.	Eye.
G	P	.	L	H	.	2 0	Cullybackey.......................	Antrim ...	N. C. Com. (Mid.)	Coleraine and Ballymena.
.	.	.	.	.	.	. .	Cullyveat Quarry	Dumfries..	Cal.	Locharbriggs.
G	P	.	.	.	.	. .	Culmore	Derry	N. C. Com. (Mid.)	Londonderry and Coleraine.
G	P	.	L	.	.	1 0	Culmstock	Devon	G. W.	Branch from Tiverton Junc. Station.
G	P	.	L	H	.	3 0	Culrain	Ross & Cro'	High.	Bonar Bridge and Golspie.
G	P	.	L	H	.	. .	Culter	Aberdeen	G. N. of S.	Aberdeen and Banchory.
.	P	.	.	.	.	. .	Cultra	Down	B. & C. D.	Holywood and Bangor.
.	.	.	.	.	.	. .	Cultrigg Colliery	L'lithgow	Cal.	Fauldhouse.
.	.	.	.	.	.	. .	Cultrigg Pits	L'lithgow	N. B.	Crofthead.
G	P	.	.	.	.	. .	Cults	Aberdeen	G. N. of S.	Aberdeen and Banchory.
.	.	.	.	.	.	. .	Cults Lime Works	Fife	N. B.	Springfield.
.	.	.	.	.	.	. .	Cults Siding	Fife	N. B.	See Springfield.
.	.	.	.	.	.	. .	Culver Junction	Sussex......	L. B. & S. C.	Lewes and Barcombe.
G	P	F	L	H	C	. .	Culworth	N'hampton	G. C.	Rugby and Brackley.
.	.	.	.	.	.	. .	Culworth Junction...............	N'hampton	G. C.	Woodford and Banbury.
G	P	F	L	H	C	2 0	Cumbernauld	Dumbartn	Cal.	Coatbridge and Larbert.
.	.	.	.	.	.	. .	Cumbernauld Fire Clay Wks	Dumbartn	Cal.	Cumbernauld.
.	.	.	.	.	.	. .	Madgescroft Siding	Lanark ...	Cal.	Glenboig and Cumbernauld.
.	.	.	.	.	.	. .	Maryburgh Siding	Lanark ...	Cal.	Glenboig and Cumbernauld.
.	.	.	.	.	.	. .	Cumberworth	Yorks	L. & Y.	See Denby Dale and Cumberworth.
.	.	.	.	.	.	. .	Cummerhead Siding	Lanark ...	Cal.	Same as Dalwhannie or Dalquhandy Colliery No. 2 (Coalburn).
G	P	F	.	H	C	2 0	Cummersdale	Cumb'land	M. & C.	Dalston and Carlisle.
G	P	F	L	H	C	1 0	Cummertrees	Dumfries..	G. & S. W.	Annan and Dumfries.
.	.	.	.	.	.	. .	Cummertrees Lime Siding	Dumfries..	G. & S. W.	Cummertrees.
.	.	.	.	.	.	. .	Cumming & Co.'s Blacking Works	Derby	Mid.	Sheepbridge.
.	.	.	.	.	.	. .	Cumming & Co.'s Siding	Lanark ...	Cal.	Glasgow, Dawsholm.
.	.	.	.	.	.	. .	Cumming's Blacking Mill (NB)	Stirling ...	N. B.—Cal.	Falkirk, Grahamston.
.	.	.	.	.	.	. .	Cumming's Siding...............	W'morlnd	L. & N. W.	See Kendal Bonded Stores Co. (Kendal).
.	.	.	.	.	.	. .	Cummings, W., & Co.'s Sid.	Derby	Mid.	Sheepbridge.
G	P	F	L	H	C	1 10	Cumnock (A. & C.)...............	Ayr	G. & S. W.	Annbank and Muirkirk.
.	.	.	.	.	.	. .	Glengyron Pit....................	Ayr	G. & S. W.	Cumnock (A. & C.) and Skares.
.	.	.	.	.	.	. .	Cumnock Junction	Ayr	G. & S. W.	Old and New Cumnock.
.	.	.	.	.	.	. .	Cumnock, New	Ayr	G. & S. W.	See New Cumnock.
.	.	.	.	.	.	. .	Cumnock, Old	Ayr	G. & S. W.	See Old Cumnock.
.	.	.	.	.	.	. .	Cumpsty's Siding	W'morlnd	L. & N. W.	See Kendal Bonded Stores Co. (Kendal).
G	P	F	.	.	.	. .	Cumwhinton	Cumb'land	Mid.	Appleby and Carlisle.
.	.	.	.	.	.	. .	Beaty Bros.' Siding	Cumb'land	Mid.	Near Cumwhinton.
.	.	.	.	.	.	. .	Beaty's Brick Siding	Cumb'land	Mid.	Cumwhinton and Cotehill.
.	.	.	.	.	.	. .	Carlisle Brick and Tile Works (Lonsdales Sid.)	Cumb'land	Mid.	Cumwhinton and Cotehill.
.	.	.	.	.	.	. .	Hamilton's T., Brick and Tile Works	Cumb'land	Mid.	Cumwhinton and Cotehill.
.	.	.	.	.	.	. .	Howe & Co.'s Sidings	Cumb'land	Mid.	Cumwhinton and Cotehill.
.	.	.	.	.	.	. .	Cunliffe's Brick Works........	N'hamptn	Mid.	Kettering.
.	.	.	.	.	.	. .	Cunliffe's Siding.................	Surrey ...	L. & S. W.	Worcester Park.
G	P	F	L	H	.	3 0	Cunninghamhead	Ayr	G. & S. W.	Dalry and Kilmarnock.
.	.	.	.	.	.	. .	Annick Lodge Siding	Ayr	G. & S. W.	Cunninghamhead.
.	.	.	.	.	.	. .	Warwickhill Colliery	Ayr	G. & S. W.	Branch from Cunninghamhead.

EXPLANATION—G *Goods Station.*   P *Passenger and Parcel Station.*   P* *Passenger, but not Parcel or Miscellaneous Traffic.*
F *Furniture Vans, Carriages, Portable Engines, and Machines on Wheels.*   L *Live Stock.*
H *Horse Boxes and Prize Cattle Vans.*   C *Carriages by Passenger Train.*

Station Accommodation.						Crane Power.	STATIONS, &c.	COUNTY.	COMPANY.	POSITION.
						Tons Cwts.	Cunningham's, J. & J., Siding	Edinboro'	N. B.	Leith, South.
							Cunningham's Siding	Perth	Cal.	Perth, South.
G	P	F	L	H	C	3 0	Cupar	Fife	N. B.	Ladybank and Dundee, Tay Bridge.
							Newmill Siding	Fife	N. B.	Cupar and Dairsie.
	P						Curling Pond	Perth	Cal.	Greenloaning and Blackford.
							Curragh Siding	Kildare	G. S. & W.	See Kildare.
	P						Curraheen	Kerry	T. & D.	Tralee and Castlegregory Junction.
G	P		L	H		1 10	Currie	Edinboro'	Cal.	Midcalder and Juniper Green.
G							Kinleith Siding	Edinboro'	Cal.	Currie and Juniper Green.
							Currie & Co.'s Siding	Edinboro'	Cal.	Leith, South.
							Currie & Co.'s Siding	Edinboro'	N. B.	Edinburgh, Scotland Street.
							Currie & Co.'s Siding	Lanark	Cal.	Glasgow, General Terminus.
							Currie & Rowland's Manure Works	Cheshire	B'headJt—CLC—NW&L	Birkenhead.
G	P		L	H		4 10	Curriehill	Edinboro'	Cal.	Carstairs and Edinburgh.
							Currieside Colliery (Hawkwoodburn)	Lanark	Cal.	Shotts.
							Currock Junction	Cumb'land	M. & C.	See Carlisle Engine Sheds.
G	P		L	H			Curry	Sligo	G. S. & W.	Collooney and Claremorris.
G	P		L	H		5 0	Curthwaite	Cumb'land	M. & C.	Wigton and Dalston.
							Curwen's Siding	Lancs	P.&L. Jt. (L&NW&L&Y)	Preston, Maudlands.
							Curzon Street	Warwick	L. & N. W.	See Birmingham.
							Curzon Street Siding	Staffs	Mid.—L&NW—GN—NS	See Lowe & Son's Siding (Burton).
							Custom House	Essex	G. E.—L. & I. Dks.	See London.
							Custom House	Lancs	L'pool O'head	See Liverpool.
							Custom House Quay	Edinboro'	Cal.—N. B.	See Leith.
							Custon Hall Chemical Works	Stirling	Cal.	Denny.
							Cuthill Siding	L'lithgow	N. B.	See Addiewell.
							Cuthlie	Forfar	D. & A. Jt. (Cal. & N. B.)	See Elliot Junction.
							Cutler & Son's Siding	Middlesex	{ G. E.	London, Millwall Docks.
									{ GN—GW—LNW—Mid	London, Poplar.
							Cutsyke Junction	Yorks	L. & Y.—N. E.	Pontefract and Castleford.
							Cutsyke Siding (L. & Y.)	Yorks	L. & Y.—Mid.	See Castleford.
G	P	F	L	H	C		Cuxton	Kent	S. E. & C.	Strood and Maidstone.
							Martin, Earle & Co.'s Cement Works	Kent	S. E. & C.	Cuxton and Strood.
							Weeke's Siding	Kent	S. E. & C.	Cuxton and Halling.
G	P						Cwm	Mon	G. W.	Aberbeeg and Ebbw Vale.
G						0 10	Cwmaman	Glamorg'n	G. W.	Branch from Dare Junction.
							Cwmaman Colliery	Glamorg'n	{ G. W.	Dare Junction.
									{ T. V.	Aberdare.
G							Cwmavon	Glamorg'n	{ P. T.	Near Port Talbot.
G	P		L	H		7 0			{ R. & S. B.	Port Talbot and Cymmer.
							Avon Merthyr Colliery	Glamorg'n	P. T.	Blaenavon Branch.
							Baldwin's Siding	Glamorg'n	P. T.—R. & S. B.	Cwmavon.
							Copper Miners Tin Plate Co.'s Siding	Glamorg'n	R. & S. B.	Cwmavon.
							Cwmavon Bk. Wks. Co.'s Sid	Glamorg'n	R. & S. B.	Cwmavon.
							Cwmpelena Colliery	Glamorg'n	P. T.	Whitworth Branch.
							Express Steel Co.'s Siding	Glamorg'n	R. & S. B.	Cwmavon.
							Gwenffrwd Quarry	Glamorg'n	P. T.	Blaenavon.
							Llantwit Merthyr Colliery	Glamorg'n	P. T.	Blaenavon.
							Mercantile Colliery	Glamorg'n	P. T.	Whitworth.
							New Forest Colliery	Glamorg'n	P. T.	Blaenavon.
							Prosser's Quarry (New Forest Quarry)	Glamorg'n	P. T.—S. Wales Min.	Blaenavon Branch.
							Rio Tinto Co.'s Siding	Glamorg'n	P. T.—R. & S. B.	Cwmavon.
							Tonmawr Junction	Glamorg'n	P. T.—S. Wales Min.	Cwmavon and Cymmer.
							Tyn-y-Cwm Quarry	Glamorg'n	P. T.	Blaenavon Branch.
							Whitworth Colliery	Glamorg'n	P. T.	Whitworth Branch.
							Ynysavon Colliery	Glamorg'n	P. T.	Cwmavon and Tonmawr Junction.
							Ynysdavid Sidings	Glamorg'n	P. T.	Cwmavon.
	P						Cwmavon	Mon	G. W.	Pontypool and Blaenavon.
							Vipond & Co's Varteg Hill Col	Mon	G. W.	Pontypool and Blaenavon.
							Cwmbach Branch Junction	Glamorg'n	T. V.	Mountain Ash and Aberaman.
							Cwmbach Colliery	Glamorg'n	T. V.	Aberdare.
							Cwmbach Siding	Glamorg'n	G. W.	Aberdare.
G	P		L	H			Cwm Bargoed	Glamorg'n	T. B. Jt. (G. W. & Rhy.)	Bedlinog and Dowlais.
							Cwm Bargoed Colliery	Glamorg'n	T. B. Jt. (G. W. & Rhy.)	Cwm Bargoed and Dowlais.
							Guest, Keen & Nettlefold— Fochriw or Fforchriw Col.	Glamorg'n	T. B. Jt. (G. W. & Rhy.)	Branch from Cwm Bargoed.
							Tunnel Pit	Glamorg'n	T. B. Jt. (G. W. & Rhy.)	Cwm Bargoed.

EXPLANATION—G *Goods Station.*   P *Passenger and Parcel Station.*   P* *Passenger, but not Parcel or Miscellaneous Traffic.*
F *Furniture Vans, Carriages, Portable Engines, and Machines on Wheels.*   L *Live Stock.*
H *Horse Boxes and Prize Cattle Vans.*   C *Carriages by Passenger Train.*

STATION ACCOMMODATION.						CRANE POWER.		STATIONS, &c.	COUNTY.	COMPANY.	POSITION.
						Tons	Cwts.				
G								Cwmblawd	Carmarth'	L. & M. M.	Llanelly and Cross Hands.
								Caeglas Colliery	Carmarth'	L. & M. M.	Cwmblawd.
G	P					2	0	Cwmbran (G. W.)	Mon	{ G. W.	Newport and Pontypool.
G										L. & N. W.	Over G. W. from Hereford.
								Cwmbran Brick Wks. (GW)	Mon	G. W.— L. & N. W.	Cwmbran.
								Gibbs & Finch's Vitriol Wks. (G.W.)	Mon	G. W.—L. & N. W.	Cwmbran.
								Guest, Keen & Nettlefold's Works & Collieries (GW)	Mon	G. W.—L. & N. W	Cwmbran.
								Henllis Fire Brick Wks (GW)	Mon	G. W.—L. & N. W.	Cwmbran.
								Hill & Co.'s (Oakfields) Wire Works (G. W.)	Mon	G. W.— L. & N. W.	Cwmbran.
								Cwmbran Junction	Mon	G. W.	Upper Pontnewydd and Cwmbran.
								Cwmbwrla Siding	Glamorg'n	G. W.	Landore.
								Cwm Capel Colliery	Carmarth'	B. P. & G. V.	Burry Port.
								Cwm Cerwyn Sid. (East End)	Glamorg'n	P. T.	Maesteg.
								Cwmclydach Colliery	Glamorg'n	T. V.	Trealaw.
								Cwm Colliery	Glamorg'n	G. W. & Rhy. Jt.	Merthyr.
								Cwm Colliery	Mon	G. W.	Aberbeeg.
								Cwm Creeich Colliery	Mon	L. & N. W.	Same as Argoed Cl. Co.'s Sid. (Argoed)
								Cwm Cynon Colliery	Glamorg'n	G. W.—T. V.	See Nixon's (Mountain Ash).
								Cwmfelin Siding	Glamorg'n	G. W.	Landore.
								Cwmffrwd Colliery	Mon	G. W.	Talywain.
								Cwmffrwdoer Colliery	Mon	G. W.	Pontnewynydd.
								Cwmgelly Siding	Mon	L. & N. W.	Blackwood.
								Cwm Glo Colliery	Glamorg'n	G. W. & Rhy. Jt.	Merthyr.
								Cwmgorse Colliery	Glamorg'n	G. W.	Garnant.
								Cwm-Gwinea Colliery	Glamorg'n	P. T.	Port Talbot (Central).
G								Cwmmawr	Carmarth'	B. P. & G. V.	Terminus.
								Cwmneol Colliery	Glamorg'n	G. W.—T. V.	See Powell Duffryn Co.
								Cwmpark Colliery	Glamorg'n	T. V.	See Ocean Coal Co. (Treorchy).
								Cwmpelena Colliery	Glamorg'n	P. T.	Cwmavon.
								Cwmpennar Colliery	Glamorg'n	G. W.	See Powell Duffryn Co (Mountain Ash)
								Cwmphil Siding (Rees Morgan's Siding) (Mid.)	Glamorg'n	Mid.—G. W.—L. & N. W.	Gurnos.
	P							Cwm Prysor	Merioneth	G. W.	Arenig and Trawsfynydd.
								Cwm Siding	Glamorg'n	T. V.	Ynysybwl.
								Cwm Tawe Clay Works (Morgan & Son) (Mid.)	Glamorg'n	Mid.—G. W.—L. & N. W.	Pontardawe.
								Cwmteg Col. Co.'s Sid. (Mid.)	Glamorg'n	Mid.—G. W.—L. & N. W.	Brynamman
								Cwmtillery Colliery	Mon	G. W.	Abertillery.
								Cwmtrupit (New Cawdor) Col.	Carmarth'	G. W.	Garnant.
G	P		L			1	10	Cwm-y-Glo	Carnarvon	L. & N. W.	Carnarvon and Llanberis.
								Cwrt-y-Bettws Colliery	Glamorg'n	G. W.	Neath Abbey.
								Cyanide Co.'s Siding	Fife	N. B.	Same as Kirkland Siding (Leven).
								Cyclops Foundry	Renfrew	Cal.	Glasgow, Whiteinch.
								Cyclops Iron Works	Staffs	L. & N. W.	See Russell & Co.'s (Walsall).
								Cyclops Works (Mid.)	Yorks	Mid.—G. C.	See Cammell, C., & Co. (Sheffield).
								Cyfarthfa Junc. & Iron Works	Glamorg'n	T. V.	Merthyr.
								Cyfarthfa Level Crossing Jn.	Glamorg'n	G. W. & Rhy. Jt.	Merthyr and Abercanaid.
								Cyfarthfa Siding	Glamorg'n	G. W.	Merthyr.
								Cyfarthfa Works	Glamorg'n	{ B. & M. & L. & N. W. Jt.— G. W.—G. W. & Rhy. Jt.—T.V.	See Crawshay Bros.
G	P							Cyfronydd	Montgom	Cam. (W. & L.)	Welshpool & Llanfair Caereinion.
								Cymerau Quarry	Merioneth	Corris	Corris and Ratgoed Quarry.
								CYMMER—			
G	P							(Station)	Glamorg'n	G. W.	Caerau and Abergwynfi.
G	P		L	H		7	0	(Station)	Glamorg'n	R. & S. B.	Port Talbot and Treherbert.
G								(Station)	Glamorg'n	S. Wales Min.	Briton Ferry and Glyncorrwg.
								Duffryn Rhondda Colliery	Glamorg'n	R. & S. B.	Cymmer.
								Glenavon Colliery	Glamorg'n	G. W.	Cymmer.
								Glyncorrwg Gas Works	Glamorg'n	R. & S. B.	Cymmer.
								Glyncymmer Colliery	Glamorg'n	G. W.	Cymmer.
								Junction	Glamorg'n	G. W.—R. & S. B.	Nantyffyllon and Blaengwynfi.
								Junction	Glamorg'n	G. W.—S. Wales Min.	Maesteg and Glyncorrwg.
								Cymmer Colliery or Old Cymmer Colliery	Glamorg'n	T. V.	Porth.
								Cymmer Level or New Cymmer Colliery	Glamorg'n	T. V.	Porth.
								Cymmer Upper Colliery	Glamorg'n	T. V.	Porth.
G	P							Cynghordy	Carmarth'	L. & N. W.	Llandilo and Llandrindod Wells.

EXPLANATION—G *Goods Station.*   P *Passenger and Parcel Station.*   P* *Passenger, but not Parcel or Miscellaneous Traffic.*
F *Furniture Vans, Carriages, Portable Engines, and Machines on Wheels.*   L *Live Stock.*
H *Horse Boxes and Prize Cattle Vans.*   C *Carriages by Passenger Train.*

STATION ACCOMMODATION.						CRANE POWER.		STATIONS, &c.	COUNTY.	COMPANY.	POSITION.
						Tons	Cwts				
G	.	.	.	.	.	.	.	Cynheidre (for Pontyeats)......	Carmarth'	L. & M. M.	Llanelly and Cross Hands.
.	.	.	.	.	.	.	.	Cynllwynddu Colliery	Glamorg'n	T. V.	See Davis & Son's Ferndale No. 8 Colliery (Ferndale).
.	.	.	.	.	.	.	.	Cynon Colliery	Glamorg'n	R. & S. B.	Pontrhydyfen.
.	.	.	.	.	.	.	.	Cynon Tin Plate Works (Mill Street Tin Works)............	Glamorg'n	T. V.	Aberdare.
G	P	F	L	.	.	1	0	Cynwyd..............................	Merioneth	G. W.	Corwen and Bala.

D

.	.	.	.	.	.	.	.	Dacca Twist Co.'s Siding (L. & Y. & L. U. Jt.) ...... }	Lancs	{ L. & Y. .... { L. & N. W.	Same as Ryland's (Chorley). Same as Ryland's (Heapey).
G	P	F	L	H	C	15	0	Dacre...............................	Yorks	N. E.	Harrogate and Pateley Bridge.
.	.	.	.	.	.	.	.	Dacre's Siding	Cumb'land	WC&EJt. (Fur.&LNW)	Cleator Moor.
.	.	.	.	.	.	.	.	Daddry Shields Siding........	Durham ...	N. E.	St. John's Chapel.
G	.	.	.	.	.	.	.	Dafen	Carmarth'	G. W.	Branch from Llanelly.
.	.	.	.	.	.	.	.	Dafen Tin Works	Carmarth'	G. W.	Dafen.
.	.	.	.	.	.	.	.	Gelly Colliery	Carmarth'	G. W.	Dafen.
.	.	.	.	.	.	.	.	Glyncoed Colliery	Carmarth'	G. W.	Dafen.
.	.	.	.	.	.	.	.	St. George's Colliery.......	Carmarth'	G. W.	Dafen.
G	P	F	L	H	C	3	0	Dagenham	Essex	L. T. & S.	Barking and Upminster.
.	.	.	.	.	.	.	.	Dagenham Docks Siding (Williams' & Son's)	Essex	L. T. & S.	Rainham.
G	P	F	L	H	C	.	.	Daggons Road	Dorset.....	L. & S. W.	Salisbury and Wimborne.
.	.	.	.	.	.	.	.	Eustace & Colly's Siding ...	Dorset.....	L. & S. W.	Daggons Road.
.	.	.	.	.	.	.	.	Daglish & Co.'s Siding.......	Lancs	L. & N. W.	St. Helens.
G	P	F	L	H	C	3	0	Dailly	Ayr	G. & S. W.	Maybole and Girvan.
.	.	.	.	.	.	.	.	Dalquharran Brick Works	Ayr	G. & S. W.	Dailly and Kilkerran.
.	.	.	.	.	.	.	.	Dalquharran Colliery	Ayr	G. & S. W.	Dailly and Kilkerran.
.	.	.	.	.	.	.	.	Kilgrammie No. 1	Ayr	G. & S. W.	Dailly.
.	.	.	.	.	.	.	.	Maxwell Pit	Ayr	G. & S. W.	Dailly and Kilkerran.
.	.	.	.	.	.	.	.	Dainton Siding	Devon	G. W.	Totnes.
G	P	.	L	H	.	2	0	Dairsie	Fife.........	N. B.	Cupar and Dundee, Tay Bridge.
.	.	.	.	.	.	.	.	Dairycoates Junction	Yorks	N. E.	Hessle and Hull, Goods.
.	P	.	.	.	.	.	.	Daisy Bank	Staffs	G. W.	Wolverhampton and Dudley.
.	.	.	.	.	.	.	.	Daisy Colliery....................	Lancs	L. & Y.	See Pearson & Knowles Coal & Iron Co. (Ince).
G	P	.	.	.	.	40	0	Daisy Field	Lancs	L. & Y.	Blackburn and Clitheroe.
.	.	.	.	.	.	.	.	Daisy Field Siding	Lancs	L. & Y.	Blackburn.
.	P	.	.	.	.	.	.	Daisy Hill	Lancs	L. & Y.	Pendleton and Hindley.
.	.	.	.	.	.	.	.	Daisy Hill Siding	Durham ...	N. E.	Pelton.
G	P	.	.	H	.	2	0	Dalbeallie........................	Elgin&Mo'	G. N. of S.	Craigellachie and Boat of Garten.
G	.	.	.	.	.	.	.	Tamdhu Siding	Elgin&Mo'	G. N. of S.	Dalbeallie.
G	P	F	L	H	C	7	0	Dalbeattie	Kirkcud...	G. & S. W.	Castle Douglas and Dumfries.
.	.	.	.	.	.	.	.	Fraser & Young's Siding ..	Kirkcud...	G. & S. W.	Dalbeattie.
.	.	.	.	.	.	.	.	Dalchonzie Siding	Perth	Cal.	St. Fillans.
G	P	.	L	H	.	.	.	Dalcross	Inverness	High..........................	Nairn and Inverness.
.	.	.	.	.	.	.	.	Dalderse Depôt	Stirling ...	Cal.—N. B.	See Falkirk, Grahamston.
.	.	.	.	.	.	.	.	Daldowie Colliery	Lanark ...	{ Cal. .... { N. B.	Mount Vernon. Broomhouse.
.	.	.	.	.	.	.	.	Daldy & Co.'s Siding..........	Essex	G. E.	Brentwood and Warley.
.	.	.	.	.	.	.	.	Dale Abbey	Derby	G. N.	See West Hallam (for Dale Abbey).
.	.	.	.	.	.	.	.	Dale Colliery (G. N.).........	Derby	G. N.—G. C.	Ilkeston.
.	.	.	.	.	.	.	.	Dale Colliery	Derby	Mid.	See Stanton Iron Co. (Stanton Gate).
.	.	.	.	.	.	.	.	Dale Quarry	Derby	Mid.	See Butterley Co. (Wirksworth).
G	P	F	L	H	C	.	.	Dalguise	Perth	High..........................	Dunkeld and Pitlochry.
.	P	.	.	.	.	.	.	Dalhousie	Edinboro'	N. B.	Edinburgh and Galashiels.
.	.	.	.	.	.	.	.	Dalhousie Siding	Edinboro'	N. B.	Hawthornden.
G	P	F	L	H	C	3	0	Dalkeith	Edinboro'	N. B.	Branch from Glenesk Junction.
.	.	.	.	.	.	.	.	Glenesk Colliery...............	Edinboro'	N. B.	Millerhill and Eskbank.
.	.	.	.	.	.	.	.	Glenesk Siding	Edinboro'	N. B.	Millerhill and Eskbank.
G	.	.	L	.	.	.	.	Dalkey	Dublin ...	D. W. & W.	Kingstown and Bray.
G	P	.	L	.	.	.	.	Dallam Forge	Lancs	C. L. C. (G C, G N, & Mid.)	See Pearson & Knowles Coal & Iron Co.'s Bewsey & Dallam Forge (Warrington).

EXPLANATION—G *Goods Station.*   P *Passenger and Parcel Station.*   P* *Passenger, but not Parcel or Miscellaneous Traffic.*
F *Furniture Vans, Carriages, Portable Engines, and Machines on Wheels.*   L *Live Stock.*
H *Horse Boxes and Prize Cattle Vans.*   C *Carriages by Passenger Train.*

STATION ACCOMMODATION.						CRANE POWER.	STATIONS, &c.	COUNTY.	COMPANY.	POSITION.
						Tons Cwts.				
..	..	..	..	..	..	..	Dallam Forge Iron Works (L. & N. W.)	Lancs	L. & N. W.—G. W.	{ See Pearson & Knowles Coal & Ir. Co. (Warrington).
..	..	..	..	..	..	..	Dallam Lane Branch (L & N W)	Lancs	L. & N. W.—G. W.	Warrington.
..	..	..	..	..	..	..	Dallasdhu Siding	Elgin&Mo'	High............................	Forres.
..	..	..	..	..	..	..	Dallow Lane Branch (L & N W)	Staffs	L&NW—Mid—G N—N S	Burton-on-Trent.
..	..	..	..	..	..	..	Dallow Lane Wharf (L & N W)	Staffs	L&NW—Mid—G N—N S	Burton-on-Trent.
..	..	..	..	..	..	..	Dalmacoulter Quarry	Lanark	N. B.	Airdrie, North.
G	P	F	L	H	C	1 10	Dalmally	Argyll......	Cal.	Callander and Oban.
..	..	..	..	..	..	..	Dalmarnock	Lanark	Cal.	See Glasgow.
..	..	..	..	..	..	..	Dalmarnock Chemical Works	Lanark	Cal.	Glasgow, Bridgeton.
..	..	..	..	..	..	..	Dalmarnock Gas Works.........	Lanark	Cal.	Glasgow, Bridgeton.
..	..	..	..	..	..	..	Dalmarnock Junction	Lanark	Cal.	Glasgow.
..	..	..	..	..	..	..	Dalmarnock Sewage Works...	Lanark	Cal.	Glasgow, Bridgeton.
G	P	F	L	H	C	3 0	Dalmellington	Ayr	G. & S.W.	Branch from Dalrymple Junction.
..	..	..	..	..	..	..	Dalmellington Iron Works ...	Ayr	G. & S.W.	Waterside.
G	..	..	L	..	..	2 10	Dalmeny	L'lithgow	N. B.	Haymarket and Inverkeithing.
..	..	..	..	..	..	..	Dalmeny Oil Works	L'lithgow	N. B.	Branch from Dalmeny, Goods.
..	..	..	..	..	..	..	Dudgeon's Manure Siding...	L'lithgow	N. B.	Branch from Dalmeny, Goods.
..	P	F	..	H	C	..	Dalmeny (for South Queensferry)	L'lithgow	N. B.	Haymarket and Inverkeithing.
..	..	..	..	..	..	..	Dalmeny, North Junction ...	L'lithgow	N. B.	Dalmeny and Philpstoun.
..	..	..	..	..	..	..	Dalmeny, South Junction......	L'lithgow	N. B.	Dalmeny, Passengers & Turnhouse
..	..	..	..	..	..	..	Dalmonach Branch Junction	Dumbartn	N. B.	Near Jamestown.
..	..	..	..	..	..	..	Dalmonach Works (N. B.) ...	Dumbartn	N. B.—Cal.	Jamestown.
..	..	..	..	..	..	..	Dalmore Mill Siding	Edinboro'	N. B.	Auchendinny.
G	P	F	L	H	C	3 0	Dalmuir	Dumbartn	{ Cal.	Clydebank and Dumbarton.
G	..	F	L	H	C	3 0			{ N. B.	Kilbowie and Bowling.
..	..	..	..	..	..	..	Beardmore's Shipyard	Dumbartn	Cal.	Dalmuir.
..	..	..	..	..	..	..	Clyde Trust Works	Dumbartn	Cal.	Dalmuir and Old Kilpatrick.
..	..	..	..	..	..	..	Dalmuir Iron Wks. (Somervail & Co.'s Siding)	Dumbartn	N. B.	Near Dalmuir.
..	..	..	..	..	..	..	Glasgow Corporation Sewage Works	Dumbartn	Cal.	Dalmuir.
..	..	..	..	..	..	..	Lidgerwood's Siding	Dumbartn	N. B.	Dalmuir and Kilbowie.
..	..	..	..	..	..	..	Dalmuir Bridge and Roofing Works	Dumbartn	Cal.	Clydebank.
..	P	..	..	..	..	..	Dalmuir Junction Station ...	Dumbartn	N. B.	Dalmuir and Kilbowie.
G	P	..	L	H	..	..	Dalnaspidal	Perth	High.	Blair Atholl and Kingussie.
..	..	..	..	..	..	..	Dalquhandy Siding	Lanark	Cal.	Same as Dalwhannie Col. (Coalburn).
..	..	..	..	..	..	..	Dalquharran Brick Works ...	Ayr	G. & S.W.	Dailly.
..	..	..	..	..	..	..	Dalquharran Colliery	Ayr	G. & S.W.	Dailly.
..	..	..	..	..	..	..	Dalquhurn Siding	Dumbartn	D. & B. Jt. (Cal. & N. B.)	Renton.
G	P	F	L	H	C	..	Dalreoch	Dumbartn	D. & B. Jt. (Cal. & N. B.)	Dumbarton and Alexandria.
G	..	..	..	..	..	3 0	Dalreoch Quarry...............	Dumbartn	D. & B. Jt. (Cal. & N. B.)	Dalreoch and Renton.
..	..	..	..	..	..	..	Dalreoch Siding (N. B.) ...	Dumbartn	N. B.—Cal.	Dalreoch and Cardross.
..	..	..	..	..	..	..	Dennystown Forge	Dumbartn	D. & B. Jt. (Cal. & N. B.)	Dalreoch and Renton.
..	..	..	..	..	..	..	Hardie & Gordon's Siding..	Dumbartn	D. & B. Jt. (Cal. & N. B.)	Dalreoch and Renton.
..	..	..	..	..	..	..	Levenbank Foundry	Dumbartn	D. & B. Jt. (Cal. & N. B.)	Dalreoch.
..	..	..	..	..	..	..	Dalreoch Junction	Dumbartn	D. & B. Jt.—N. B.	Dumbarton and Cardross.
G	P	F	L	H	C	3 0	Dalry...............................	Ayr	G. & S.W.	Johnstone and Kilmarnock.
..	..	..	..	..	..	..	Blair, Nos. 2 and 9............	Ayr	G. & S.W.	Blair Branch.
..	..	..	..	..	..	..	Blair, No. 4......................	Ayr	G. & S.W.	Dalry and Dalry Junction.
..	..	..	..	..	..	..	Blair, Nos. 5 and 7	Ayr	G. & S.W.	Dalry.
..	..	..	..	..	..	..	Borestone Siding	Ayr	G. & S.W.	Swinlees Branch.
..	..	..	..	..	..	..	Carsehead Brick Works ...	Ayr	G. & S.W.	Dalry.
..	..	..	..	..	..	..	Carsehead, No. 2	Ayr	G. & S.W.	Dalry.
..	..	..	..	..	..	..	Dalry Junction	Ayr	G. & S.W.	Dalry and Montgreenan.
G	P	..	L	H	C	2 0	Dalrymple	Ayr	G. & S.W.	Ayr and Maybole.
..	..	..	..	..	..	..	Dalrymple Junction	Ayr	G. & S.W.	Ayr and Dalrymple.
G	..	..	L	..	..	..	Dalrymple Junction Station..	Ayr	G. & S.W.	Ayr and Maybole.
..	..	..	..	..	..	..	Dalry Road	Edinboro'	Cal.	See Edinburgh.
..	..	..	..	..	..	..	Dalry Road Stone Sidings ...	Edinboro'	Cal.	Edinburgh, Lothian Road.
..	..	..	..	..	..	..	Dalry West Junction	Edinboro'	Cal.—N. B.	Same as Haymarket West Junction (Edinburgh).
G	P	..	L	H	..	1 10	Dalserf	Lanark ...	Cal.	Larkhall and Lesmahagow.
..	..	..	..	..	..	..	Auldton Colliery	Lanark ...	Cal.	Dalserf and Netherburn.
..	..	..	..	..	..	..	Birkrigg Colliery	Lanark ...	Cal.	Dalserf and Stonehouse.
..	..	..	..	..	..	..	Birkrigg New Colliery	Lanark ...	Cal.	Dalserf and Stonehouse.
..	..	..	..	..	..	..	Cornsilloch Brick Works...	Lanark ...	Cal.	Dalserf and Netherburn.
..	..	..	..	..	..	..	Cornsilloch Colliery	Lanark ...	Cal.	Dalserf and Netherburn.
..	..	..	..	..	..	..	Millburn Chemical Works	Lanark ...	Cal.	Dalserf and Larkhall.
..	..	..	..	..	..	..	Millburn Colliery	Lanark ...	Cal.	Dalserf and Larkhall.

EXPLANATION—G *Goods Station.*   P *Passenger and Parcel Station.*   P* *Passenger, but not Parcel or Miscellaneous Traffic.*
F *Furniture Vans, Carriages, Portable Engines, and Machines on Wheels.*   L *Live Stock.*
H *Horse Boxes and Prize Cattle Vans.*   C *Carriages by Passenger Train.*

STATION ACCOMMODATION.						CRANE POWER.		STATIONS, &c.	COUNTY.	COMPANY.	POSITION.
						Tons	Cwts.				
								Dalserf—*continued.*			
.	.	.	.	.	.	.	.	Over Dalserf Colliery........	Lanark ...	Cal.	Dalserf and Netherburn.
.	.	.	.	.	.	.	.	Shawsburn Colliery	Lanark ...	Cal.	Dalserf and Stonehouse.
.	.	.	.	.	.	.	.	Shaw's Colliery	Lanark ...	Cal.	Dalserf and Stonehouse.
.	.	.	.	.	.	.	.	Shawsrigg Colliery	Lanark ...	Cal.	Dalserf and Stonehouse.
.	.	.	.	.	.	.	.	Shawsrigg Fire Clay and Enamelling Works......	Lanark ...	Cal.	Dalserf and Stonehouse.
G	P	F	L	H	C	5	0	Dalserf (Over) Colliery	Lanark ...	Cal.	Same as Over Dalserf Col. (Dalserf).
G	P	F	L	H	C	5	0	Dalston	Cumb'land	M. & C.	Curthwaite and Carlisle.
.	.	.	.	.	.	.	.	Dalston, East & West Juncs.	Middlesex	N.L.	London, Mildmay Park & Hackney.
.	.	.	.	.	.	.	.	Dalston Junc. Station (N.L.)	Middlesex	N. L.—L. & N. W.	See London.
.	.	.	.	.	.	.	.	Dalston Road Depôt & Siding	Cumb'land	N. E.	Carlisle.
G	P	F	L	H	C	10	0	Dalton	Lancs	Furness	Ulverston and Barrow.
.	.	.	.	.	.	3	0	Crooklands Siding	Lancs	Furness	Dalton and Lindal.
.	.	.	.	.	.	.	.	Millwood Siding..............	Lancs	Furness	Dalton and Furness Abbey.
.	.	.	.	.	.	5	0	Stainton Mineral Siding ...	Lancs	Furness	Branch from Crooklands.
								Dalton Main Collieries—			
.	.	.	.	.	.	.	.	Roundwood Colliery	Yorks	{ G. C.	Parkgate and Aldwarke.
										{ Mid.	Parkgate and Rawmarsh.
.	.	.	.	.	.	.	.	Silverwood Colliery	Yorks	{ G. C.	Parkgate and Aldwarke.
										{ Mid.	Parkgate and Rawmarsh.
.	.	.	.	.	.	.	.	Dalton's Siding	Derby......	G. C.	Dinting.
.	.	.	.	.	.	.	.	Dalwhannie or Dalquhandy Colliery, No. 1	Lanark ...	Cal.	Coalburn.
.	.	.	.	.	.	.	.	Dalwhannie or Dalquhandy Col, No.2 (Cummerhead Sid)	Lanark ...	Cal.	Coalburn.
G	P	F	L	H	C	2	0	Dalwhinnie	Inverness	High.	Blair Atholl and Kingussie.
.	.	.	.	.	.	.	.	Dalzell & Broomside Colliery	Lanark ...	Cal.	Same as Dalzell, Lesmahagow (Motherwell).
.	.	.	.	.	.	.	.	Dalzell Bridge & Roofing Wks.	Lanark ...	Cal.	Motherwell.
.	.	.	.	.	.	.	.	Dalzell Collieries...............	Lanark ...	Cal.	Motherwell.
.	.	.	.	.	.	.	.	Dalzell Engineering Works	Lanark ...	Cal.	Motherwell.
.	.	.	.	.	.	.	.	Dalzell Estate Siding	Lanark ...	Cal.	Motherwell.
.	.	.	.	.	.	.	.	Dalzell Iron and Steel Works (Colville's)	Lanark ...	Cal.	Motherwell.
.	.	.	.	.	.	.	.	Dalzell Junction	Lanark ...	Cal.	Wishaw South and Flemington.
.	.	.	.	.	.	.	.	Dalzell, Lesmahagow (Dalzell and Broomside Colliery) ...	Lanark ...	Cal.	Motherwell.
.	.	.	.	.	.	.	.	Dalzell Saw Mills	Lanark ...	Cal.	Motherwell.
.	.	.	.	.	.	.	.	Dalzell's Moor Row Mines...	Cumb'land	WC& EJt. (Fur. & L N W)	Moor Row.
.	.	.	.	.	.	.	.	Dalzell Washer	Lanark ...	Cal.	Motherwell.
.	.	.	.	.	.	.	.	Dalzell Washer Works	Lanark ...	Cal.	Shieldmuir.
.	.	.	.	.	.	.	.	Damdykes Siding	Northumb	N. E.	Annitsford.
G	P	.	.	.	.	.	.	Damems	Yorks	Mid.	Keighley and Oxenhope.
.	.	.	.	.	.	.	.	Damhead Junction..............	Edinboro'	Cal.—N. B.	Same as Haymarket West Junction (Edinburgh).
.	.	.	.	.	.	.	.	Dam Lane Junction	Lancs	C.L.C. (G C—G N—Mid.)	Glazebrook.
G	P	.	.	L	H	.	.	Dampney & Co.'s Siding......	Glamorg'n	GW—L&NW—Rhy—TV	Cardiff.
G	P	.	.	L	H	.	.	Danby	Yorks	N. E.	Whitby and Castleton.
.	.	.	.	.	.	.	.	Houlsike Siding................	Yorks	N. E.	Danby and Lealholm.
G	P	.	.	L	H	C	.	Danby Wiske	Yorks	N. E.	Northallerton and Darlington.
G	P	.	.	L	H	C	2	0	Dandaleith	Elgin&Mo'	G. N. of S.	Craigellachie and Elgin.
.	.	.	.	.	.	.	.	Danesmoor (Clay Cross Col. No. 7)	Derby......	Mid.	Clay Cross.
.	.	.	.	.	.	.	.	Daniel's, T. H. & J., Siding	Glo'ster ...	Mid.	Cam.
.	.	.	.	.	.	.	.	Dannatt & Good's Lime Wks.	Yorks	H. & B.	Little Weighton.
.	P	.	.	H	.	.	.	Danygraig	Glamorg'n	R. & S. B.	Swansea and Neath.
.	.	.	.	.	.	.	.	Danygraig Brick Siding	Mon	G. W.	Risca.
.	.	.	.	.	.	.	.	Danygraig Junction	Glamorg'n	R. & S. B.—S. H. Trust	Swansea and Danygraig Station.
.	.	.	.	.	.	.	.	Danygraig Siding	Glamorg'n	G. W.—R. & S. B.	Swansea.
.	.	.	.	.	.	.	.	Darbishire's Siding	Carnarvon	L. & N. W.	Penmaenmawr.
.	.	.	.	.	.	.	.	Darbyshire's Brick Works (Wepre Hall Brick Works)	Flint	W. M. & C. Q.	Connah's Quay.
.	.	.	.	.	.	.	.	Darbyshire's Siding	Flint	L. & N. W.	See South Level (Coed Talon).
.	P	.	.	.	.	.	.	Darcy Lever	Lancs	L. & Y.	Bolton and Bury.
.	.	.	.	.	.	.	.	Darcy Lever Colliery............	Lancs	L. & Y.	Bradley Fold.
.	.	.	.	.	.	.	.	D'Arcy Lime Works	Edinboro'	N. B.	Hardengreen.
.	.	.	.	.	.	.	.	D'Arcy Street Depôts	Durham ...	N. E.	Sunderland, South Dock.
G	.	.	.	.	.	.	.	Dare Junction Station	Glamorg'n	G. W.	Dare Branch, near Aberdare.
.	.	.	.	.	.	.	.	Blaengwawr Level Colliery	Glamorg'n	G. W.	Dare Junction and Cwmaman.
.	.	.	.	.	.	.	.	Bwllfa Dare or Bwllfa No. 1 Colliery........................	Glamorg'n	G. W.	Branch from Dare Junction.

STATION ACCOMMODATION.	CRANE POWER.	STATIONS, &c.	COUNTY.	COMPANY.	POSITION.
	Tons Cwts.	Dare Junction Station—*continued.*			
		Bwllfa Dare or Bwllfa No. 2 Col. (Nantmelyn Col.) ...	Glamorg'n	G. W.	Branch from Dare Junction.
		Cwmaman Colliery	Glamorg'n	G. W.	Branch from Dare Junction.
		Fforchneol Siding	Glamorg'n	G. W.	Branch from Dare Junction.
		Fforchwen Colliery	Glamorg'n	G. W.	Branch from Dare Junction.
		Graig Level Colliery	Glamorg'n	G. W.	Branch from Dare Junction.
		Powell Duffryn Co.'s Fforchaman Colliery	Glamorg'n	G. W.	Branch from Dare Junction.
		Dare Pit	Glamorg'n	T. V.	See Ocean Coal Co. (Treorchy).
P		Daresbury	Cheshire	B'head Jt. (G W & L N W)	Helsby and Warrington.
		Dare Valley Junction	Glamorg'n	T. V.	Near Aberdare.
G P F L H C	5 0	Darfield	Yorks	Mid.	Masbro' and Normanton.
		Dearne Valley Colliery	Yorks	Mid.	Near Darfield.
		Houghton Main Colliery	Yorks	Mid.	Near Darfield.
		Seal, Son & Co.'s Siding	Yorks	Mid.	Near Darfield.
		Darfield Main Colliery	Yorks	G. C.	Wombwell.
		Darfield West or Quarry Junc.	Yorks	G. C.—Mid.	Barnsley.
		Dark Hill Siding	Glo'ster	S. & Wye Jt.(G.W.&Mid.)	See Milkwall.
		Dark Lane Brick Works	Salop	G. W.	Hollinswood.
		Dark Lane Siding	Salop	L. & N. W.	Same as Lewis' Siding (Stirchley).
		Darlaston	Staffs	G. W.	See Wednesbury (for Darlaston).
G	3 0	Darlaston	Staffs	L. & N. W.	Birmingham and Wolverhampton.
		Boys & Boden's Siding	Staffs	L. & N. W.	Darlaston and Wednesbury.
		Bradley's Siding	Staffs	L. & N. W.	Darlaston and Wednesbury.
		Charles' Siding	Staffs	L. & N. W.	Darlaston and Wednesbury.
		Darlaston Brick Co.'s Sid.	Staffs	L. & N. W.	Darlaston and Wednesbury.
		Darlaston Steel & Ir. Co's Sid.	Staffs	L. & N. W.	Darlaston and Wednesbury.
		Elwell's Siding	Staffs	L. & N. W.	Bescot & Wood Green.
		Horton & Son's Siding	Staffs	L. & N. W.	Darlaston and Wednesbury.
		Keay's Sidings	Staffs	L. & N. W.	Darlaston and Wednesbury.
		Lloyd's Siding	Staffs	L. & N. W.	Darlaston and Wood Green.
		Mayer & Co.'s Siding	Staffs	L. & N. W.	Darlaston and Wednesbury.
		Richards, C., & Co.'s Siding	Staffs	L. & N. W.	Darlaston and Wednesbury.
		Richards, W. H., & Co.'s Sid.	Staffs	L. & N. W.	Darlaston and Wednesbury.
		South Staffordshire Tramway Co.'s Siding	Staffs	L. & N. W.	Darlaston and Wednesbury.
		Tolley, Son & Bostock's Sid.	Staffs	L. & N. W.	Darlaston and Wednesbury.
		Walsall Corporation Siding	Staffs	L. & N. W.	Bescot and Newton Road.
		West Bromwich Corporation Siding	Staffs	L. & N. W.	Bescot and Newton Road.
		Wilkes & Co.'s Siding	Staffs	L. & N. W.	Darlaston and Wednesbury.
		Wilkes' Siding	Staffs	L. & N. W.	Darlaston and Willenhall.
		Yardley & Co.'s Siding	Staffs	L. & N. W.	Darlaston and Wednesbury.
P		Darlaston and James Bridge	Staffs	L. & N. W.	Birmingham and Wolverhampton.
		Darlaston Branch	Staffs	L. & N. W.	Darlaston and Wednesbury.
G P	5 0	Darley	Yorks	N. E.	Harrogate and Pateley Bridge.
G P F L H	5 0	Darley Dale	Derby	Mid.	Ambergate and Rowsley.
		Darley Dale and District Stone Co.'s Siding	Derby	Mid.	Near Darley Dale Station.
		Stancliffe Estate Co.'s Sid.	Derby	Mid.	Darley Dale and Rowsley.
		DARLINGTON—			
		Albert Hill Bridge and Boiler Works	Durham	N. E.	Hope Town.
		Albert Hill Forge Co.'s Works	Durham	N. E.	Darlington.
		Albert Hill Foundry	Durham	N. E.	Hope Town.
		Anglo-American Oil Co.'s Siding	Durham	N. E.	Hope Town.
G P F L H C	10 0	Bank Top	Durham	N. E.	Northallerton and Ferryhill.
		Bank Top Depôts	Durham	N. E.	Bank Top.
		Black Banks Chemical Wks.	Durham	N. E.	Bank Top.
		Brunswick Street Brick and Tile Works	Durham	N. E.	Darlington.
		Claye's Siding	Durham	N. E.	Bank Top.
		Cleveland Bridge and Engineering Co.'s Siding	Durham	N. E.	Bank Top.
		Consolidated Petroleum Co.'s Oil Store	Durham	N. E.	Hope Town.
		Corporation Siding	Durham	N. E.	Darlington.
		Darlington Railway Plant & Foundry Co.'s Siding	Durham	N. E.	Bank Top.

EXPLANATION—G *Goods Station.*   P *Passenger and Parcel Station.*   P* *Passenger, but not Parcel or Miscellaneous Traffic.*
F *Furniture Vans, Carriages, Portable Engines, and Machines on Wheels.*   L *Live Stock.*
H *Horse Boxes and Prize Cattle Vans.*   C *Carriages by Passenger Train.*

STATION ACCOMMODATION.						CRANE POWER.	STATIONS, &c.	COUNTY.	COMPANY.	POSITION.
						Tons Cwts.	DARLINGTON—*continued.*			
							Darlington Wagon and Engineering Co.—			
.	.	.	.	.	.	. .	Albert Hill Wagon Wks.	Durham	N. E.	Hope Town.
.	.	.	.	.	.	. .	Alliance Works	Durham	N. E.	Darlington.
.	.	.	.	.	.	. .	Electric Works	Durham	N. E.	Darlington.
.	.	.	.	.	.	. .	Gas Works	Durham	N. E.	Hope Town.
.	.	.	.	.	.	. .	Haughton Bridge Wagon Works and Depôts	Durham	N. E.	Darlington.
.	.	.	.	.	.	. .	Haughton Lane Depôts and Siding	Durham	N. E.	Hope Town.
.	.	.	.	.	.	. .	Haughton Road Brk. Wks.	Durham	N. E.	Hope Town.
G	.	F	L	.	.	10 0	Hope Town	Durham	N. E.	Stockton and Barnard Castle.
.	.	.	.	.	.	. .	Johnson & Boyd's Siding..	Durham	N. E.	Bank Top.
.	.	.	.	.	.	. .	Jubb's Coal Yard	Durham	N. E.	Bank Top.
.	.	.	.	.	.	. .	Jubilee Siding	Durham	N. E.	Hope Town.
.	.	.	.	.	.	. .	Nestfield Nut & Bolt Works	Durham	N. E.	Darlington.
							North Eastern Ry. Co.—			
.	.	.	.	.	.	. .	Carriage Repairing Shops	Durham	N. E.	Bank Top.
.	.	.	.	.	.	. .	Loco. Repairing Shops.	Durham	N. E.	Bank Top.
.	.	.	.	.	.	. .	Loco. Works (North Rd.)	Durham	N. E.	Hope Town.
.	.	.	.	.	.	. .	Oil Gas Works	Durham	N. E.	Bank Top.
.	.	.	.	.	.	. .	Permanent Way Stores...	Durham	N. E.	Hope Town.
.	.	.	.	.	.	. .	Wagon Repairing Shops	Durham	N. E.	Bank Top.
.	.	.	.	.	.	. .	Whessoe Lane Shops	Durham	N. E.	Hope Town.
.	.	.	.	.	.	. .	Northgate Depôts	Durham	N. E.	Hope Town.
.	P	.	.	.	.	. .	North Road	Durham	N. E.	Bank Top and Barnard Castle.
.	.	.	.	.	.	. .	Pease & Partner's Granary and Warehouse	Durham	N. E.	Hope Town.
.	.	.	.	.	.	. .	Richardson, W., & Co.'s Siding	Durham	N. E.	Bank Top.
.	.	.	.	.	.	. .	Rise Carr Rolling Mills ...	Durham	N. E.	Hope Town.
.	.	.	.	.	.	. .	Simpson & Co.'s Siding ...	Durham	N. E.	Bank Top.
.	.	.	.	.	.	. .	Skerne Iron Works	Durham	N. E.	Hope Town.
.	.	.	.	.	.	. .	Pease Tubular Syndicate Construction Co.'s Sid.	Durham	N. E.	Skerne Iron Works.
.	.	.	.	.	.	. .	Standard Wire Co.'s Sid.	Durham	N. E.	Skerne Iron Works.
.	.	.	.	.	.	. .	Wake's, J. F., Siding.....	Durham	N. E.	Skerne Iron Works.
.	.	.	.	.	.	. .	Stephenson, R., & Co.'s (Springfield) Loco. Works	Durham	N. E.	Darlington.
.	.	.	.	.	.	. .	Victoria Implement Works	Durham	N. E.	Darlington.
.	.	.	.	.	.	. .	Weardale Steel, Coal, & Coke Co.'s Siding	Durham	N. E.	Bank Top.
.	.	.	.	.	.	. .	Whessoe Brick Works	Durham	N. E.	Hope Town.
.	.	.	.	.	.	. .	Whessoe Foundry	Durham	N. E.	Hope Town.
.	.	.	.	.	.	. .	Darlington Corporation Sid.	Durham	N. E.	Darlington, Bank Top.
.	.	.	.	.	.	. .	Darlington Electric Works ...	Durham	N. E.	Darlington, Bank Top.
.	.	.	.	.	.	. .	Darlington Gas Works	Durham	N. E.	Darlington, Hope Town.
.	.	.	.	.	.	. .	Darlington Railway Plant and Foundry Co.'s Siding	Durham	N. E.	Darlington, Bank Top.
.	.	.	.	.	.	. .	Darlington Siding	Lancs	L. & N. W.	See Blainscough Col. Co. (Coppull).
							Darlington Wagon & Engineering Co.—			
.	.	.	.	.	.	. .	Albert Hill Wagon Works	Durham	N. E.	Darlington, Hope Town.
.	.	.	.	.	.	. .	Alliance Works	Durham	N. E.	Darlington, Hope Town.
.	.	.	.	.	.	. .	Siding	Cumb'land	W C & E Jt.(Fur.& L N W)	Frizington.
.	.	.	.	.	.	. .	Darnall (for Handsworth)	Yorks	G. C.	See Sheffield.
.	.	.	.	.	.	. .	Darnall Junction	Yorks	G. C.	Sheffield.
.	.	.	.	.	.	. .	Darnconner Lye	Ayr	G. & S.W.	Lugar.
.	.	.	.	.	.	. .	Darngavil Collieries	Lanark	N. B.	Rawyards.
.	.	.	.	.	.	. .	Darnick Siding	Roxburgh	N. B.	See Melrose.
.	.	.	.	.	.	. .	Darnley Brick & Lime Works	Renfrew	G B & K Jt(Cal & G & S W)	Nitshill.
G	P	.	L	.	.	2 10	Darran (Rhymney)	Glamorg'n	{ Rhy. / B. & M.	Bargoed and Deri Junction. / Over Rhymney Line.
.	P	.	.	.	.	. .				
.	.	.	.	.	.	. .	Darran Pit (Rhy.)	Glamorg'n	Rhy.—B. & M.	Darran.
.	.	.	.	.	.	. .	Groesfaen Siding	Glamorg'n	Rhy.	Darran and Bargoed.
.	.	.	.	.	.	. .	North Wingfield Siding (Bryncoch Colliery)	Glamorg'n	Rhy.	Darran and Bargoed.
.	.	.	.	.	.	. .	Darran Brick Siding	Mon	G. W.	Risca.
.	.	.	.	.	.	. .	Darranddu Colliery	Glamorg'n	T. V.	Ynysybwl.
.	.	.	.	.	.	. .	Darran Fawr Colliery	Glamorg'n	G. W.	Pontycymmer.
G	P	F	L	H	C	1 10	Darsham	Suffolk	G. E.	Ipswich and Beccles.

EXPLANATION—G *Goods Station.*   P *Passenger and Parcel Station.*   P* *Passenger, but not Parcel or Miscellaneous Traffic.*
F *Furniture Vans, Carriages, Portable Engines, and Machines on Wheels.*   L *Live Stock.*
H *Horse Boxes and Prize Cattle Vans.*   C *Carriages by Passenger Train.*

STATION ACCOMMODATION.						CRANE POWER.		STATIONS, &c.	COUNTY.	COMPANY.	POSITION.
						Tons	Cwts.				
G	P	F	L	H	C	10	0	Dartford	Kent	S. E. & C.	Woolwich and Gravesend.
.	.	.	.	.	.	.	.	Rutter's Siding	Kent	S. E. & C.	Dartford and Slades Green.
.	.	.	.	.	.	.	.	Turner's Siding	Kent	S. E. & C.	Dartford and Slades Green.
.	.	.	.	.	.	.	.	Dartford Junction	Kent	S. E. & C.	Crayford and Dartford.
.	P	.	.	.	.	.	.	Dartmouth	Devon	G. W.	Ferry from Kingswear.
G	P	.	L	H	.	3	0	Darton	Yorks	L. & Y.	Barnsley and Wakefield.
.	.	.	.	.	.	.	.	Belle Vue Siding	Yorks	L. & Y.	Darton.
.	.	.	.	.	.	.	.	Cawthorne Basin Siding	Yorks	L. & Y.	Silkstone Branch.
.	.	.	.	.	.	.	.	Higham Colliery (L. & Y.)	Yorks	L. & Y.—G. C.	Silkstone Branch.
.	.	.	.	.	.	.	.	Mapplewell Siding	Yorks	L. & Y.	Near Darton.
.	.	.	.	.	.	.	.	North Gawber Siding (L&Y)	Yorks	L. & Y.—G. C.—N. E.	Near Darton.
.	.	.	.	.	.	.	.	Silkstone Branch	Yorks	L. & Y.	Darton and Barnsley.
.	.	.	.	.	.	.	.	Stanhope Silkstone Colliery (L. & Y.)	Yorks	L. & Y.—G. C.	Darton.
G	P	F	L	H	C	5	0	Darvel	Ayr	G. & S. W.	Galston Branch Terminus.
G	P	F	L	H	C	10	0	Darwen	Lancs	L. & Y.	Bolton and Blackburn.
.	.	.	.	.	.	5	0	Bullough's Siding	Lancs	L. & Y.	Hoddlesden Branch.
.	.	.	.	.	.	.	.	Darwen Corporation Siding	Lancs	L. & Y.	Darwen.
.	.	.	.	.	.	.	.	Darwen Iron Co.'s Siding	Lancs	L. & Y.	Darwen and Lower Darwen.
G	.	.	.	.	.	5	0	Hoddlesden	Lancs	L. & Y.	Darwen and Lower Darwen.
.	.	.	.	.	.	.	.	Hoddlesden Siding (Place and Son's Siding)	Lancs	L. & Y.	Hoddlesden Branch.
.	.	.	.	.	.	.	.	Whitaker, W., and Co.'s Siding	Lancs	L. & Y.	Darwen and Lower Darwen.
.	.	.	.	.	.	.	.	Wigan Coal & Iron Co.'s Siding	Lancs	L. & Y.	Darwen.
.	.	.	.	.	.	.	.	Darwen and Mostyn Iron Co.'s Siding	Flint	L. & N. W.	Mostyn.
.	.	.	.	.	.	.	.	Darwen Mill Siding	Lancs	L. & Y.	Spring Vale.
G	P	F	L	H	C	.	.	Datchet	Bucks	L. & S. W.	Staines and Windsor.
.	.	.	.	.	.	.	.	Daubhill	Lancs	L. & N. W.	See Bolton, Rumworth & Daubhill.
G	P	F	L	H	C	.	.	Dauntsey	Wilts	G. W.	Swindon and Chippenham.
G	P	.	L	H	.	.	.	Dava	Elgin&Mo'	High.	Forres and Boat of Garten.
.	.	.	.	.	.	.	.	Davenport	Cheshire	L. & N. W.	See Stockport.
.	.	.	.	.	.	.	.	Daventry	N'hamptn	G. C.	See Braunston and Willoughby (for Daventry).
G	P	F	L	H	C	5	0	Daventry	N'hamptn	L. & N. W.	Leamington and Weedon.
.	.	.	.	.	.	.	.	David, D. R., & Co.'s Siding	Glamorg'n	R. & S. B.	Port Talbot (Aberavon).
.	.	.	.	.	.	.	.	Davidson and Co.'s Glass Works	Durham	N. E.	Redheugh.
G	P	F	L	H	C	5	0	Davidson's Mains	Edinboro'	Cal.	Edinburgh and Barnton.
.	.	.	.	.	.	.	.	Davies & Eckersley's Siding	Lancs	L. & Y.	Adlington.
.	.	.	.	.	.	.	.	Davies Dykes Siding	Lanark	N. B.	See Morningside.
.	.	.	.	.	.	.	.	Davies, E., & Son's Ffrwdwyllt Tin Plate Works	Glamorg'n	G. W.—P. T.—R. & S. B.	Port Talbot.
.	.	.	.	.	.	.	.	Davies, J., & Co.'s Sid. (Mid.)	Glamorg'n	Mid.—G. W.—L. & N. W.	See Glanyrafon Siding (Clydach-on-Tawe).
.	.	.	.	.	.	.	.	Davies' Lime Works	Mon	G. W.	Lliswerry.
.	.	.	.	.	.	.	.	Davies' Siding	Flint	L. & N. W.	See Nerquis Old Colliery Level Siding (Coed Talon).
.	.	.	.	.	.	.	.	Davies' Siding	Lancs	L. & N. W.—S. & M. Jt.	Widnes.
.	.	.	.	.	.	.	.	Davies' Siding	Mon	G. W.	Usk.
.	.	.	.	.	.	.	.	Davies' Treborth Siding	Carnarvon	L. & N. W.	Menai Bridge.
G	P	F	L	H	C	1	10	Daviot	Inverness	High.	Inverness and Aviemore.
								Davis & Son's—			
.	.	.	.	.	.	.	.	Ferndale Nos. 1 & 5 Cols.	Glamorg'n	T. V.	Ferndale.
.	.	.	.	.	.	.	.	Ferndale Nos. 2 & 4 Cols. (Ffaldau Colliery)	Glamorg'n	T. V.	Ferndale.
.	.	.	.	.	.	.	.	Ferndale No. 3 Colliery (Boedryngallt Colliery)	Glamorg'n	T. V.	Ferndale. Ystrad.
.	.	.	.	.	.	.	.	Ferndale Nos. 6 & 7 Cols.—Pendyris Colliery	Glamorg'n	T. V.	Ferndale.
.	.	.	.	.	.	.	.	Tylor's Siding	Glamorg'n	T. V.	Ferndale.
.	.	.	.	.	.	.	.	Ferndale No. 8 Colliery (Cynllwynddu Colliery)	Glamorg'n	T. V.	Ferndale.
.	.	.	.	.	.	.	.	Davis' Ironstone Siding	N'hamptn	Mid.	Same as Storefield Ironstone Siding (Glendon and Rushton).
.	.	.	.	.	.	.	.	Davis', E. P., Siding	N'hamptn	Mid.	Gretton.
.	.	.	.	.	.	.	.		Notts	Mid.	See Bennerley Sidings (Ilkeston).
.	.	.	.	.	.	.	.	Davis Gas Stove Co.'s Sid. (N. B.)	Stirling	N. B.—Cal.	Same as Diamond Foundry (Falkirk, Grahamston).
.	.	.	.	.	.	.	.	Davis Mill Siding	Berks	G. W.	Twyford.

EXPLANATION—G *Goods Station.*   P *Passenger and Parcel Station.*   P* *Passenger, but not Parcel or Miscellaneous Traffic.*
F *Furniture Vans, Carriages, Portable Engines, and Machines on Wheels.*   L *Live Stock.*
H *Horse Boxes and Prize Cattle Vans.*   C *Carriages by Passenger Train.*

STATION ACCOMMODATION.	CRANE POWER.	STATIONS, &c.	COUNTY.	COMPANY.	POSITION.
	Tons Cwts.				
. . . . . .	. .	Davison's Wagon Repairing Shops (St. Helens Colliery)	Durham ...	N. E.	West Auckland.
. . . . . .	. .	Davy & Co.'s Siding	Yorks	G. C.	Meadow Hall and Wincobank.
. . . . . .	. .	Dawdon Colliery	Durham ...	N. E.	Seaham.
. . . . . .	. .	Dawley Parva	Salop	G. W.	See Horsehay and Dawley.
G P F L H C	4 10	Dawlish	Devon	G. W.	Exeter and Totnes.
. . . . . .	. .	Dawnay & Co.'s Siding	Glamorg'n	GW—L&NW—Rhy—TV	Cardiff.
. . . . . .	. .	Dawsholm	Lanark ...	Cal.	See Glasgow.
. . . . . .	. .	Dawsholm Castle Siding	Dumbartn	N. B.	Glasgow, Maryhill.
. . . . . .	. .	Dawsholm Chemical Works	Dumbartn	{ Cal. / N. B.	Glasgow, Dawsholm. / Glasgow, Maryhill.
. . . . . .	. .	Dawsholm Gas Works	Dumbartn	N. B.	Glasgow, Maryhill.
. . . . . .	. .	Dawsholm Gas Works (West of Scotland Chemical Wks.)	Dumbartn	Cal.	Glasgow, Dawsholm.
. . . . . .	. .	Dawsholm Locomotive Siding	Lanark ...	Cal.	Glasgow, Dawsholm.
. . . . . .	. .	Dawsholm Paper Mill	Dumbartn	N. B.	Glasgow, Maryhill.
. . . . . .	. .	Dawson's, R. S., Siding	Lancs	Trafford Park Estate	Manchester.
. . . . . .	. .	Dawson's, W. & J., Timber Yd.	Lancs	Furness	Barrow.
G P F L H C	10 0	Daybrook (for Arnold and Bestwood Park)	Notts	G. N.	Netherfield and Kimberley.
. . . . . .	. .	Daybrook Junction	Notts	G. N.	Daybrook and Sherwood.
. . . . . .	. .	Leen Valley Junction	Notts	G. N.	Daybrook and Bulwell Forest.
. . . . . .	. .	Nottingham Corporation Hospital Siding	Notts	G. N.	Daybrook and Leen Valley Junc.
. . . . . .	. .	Nottingham Guardians' Workhouse Siding	Notts	G. N.	Daybrook and Leen Valley Junc.
G P . L . C	.	Dduallt	Merioneth	Festiniog	Tan-y-Bwlch and Tan-y-Grisiau.
. P	.	Deadwater	Northumb	N. B.	Riccarton and Reedsmouth.
. . . . . .	.	Deadwater Siding	Northumb	N. B.	See Kielder.
. . . . . .	.	Deaf Hill Colliery	Durham ...	N. E.	Trimdon.
G P F L H C	8 0	Deal	Kent	S. E. & C.	Minster and Dover.
G P F L H C	5 0	Dean	Wilts	L. & S.W.	Romsey and Salisbury.
. . . . . .	.	Dean & Chapter Colliery	Durham ...	N. E.	Spennymoor.
. . . . . .	.	Dean & Marsh's Siding	Lancs	L. & N. W.—S. & M. Jt.	Widnes.
. . . . . .	.	Dean Lane Coal Depôts	Durham ...	N. E.	South Shields.
G P	6 0	Dean Lane (Newton Heath)	Lancs	L. & Y.	Miles Platting and Oldham.
. . . . . .	.	Dean Quarry Stone Co.'s Sid.	Durham ...	N. E.	South Shields.
. . . . . .	.	Deansgate	Lancs	G. N.	See Manchester.
. . . . . .	.	Deansgate	Lancs	L. & N. W.	See Bolton.
. . . . . .	.	Deansgate	Lancs	M.S.J. & A. (GC&L&NW)	See Manchester, Knott Mill and Deansgate.
. . . . . .	.	Deansgate Junction	Cheshire...	C. L. C.—M. S. J. & A.	Altrincham.
. . . . . .	.	Deansgate Junction	Lancs	C. L. C.—G. N.	Manchester.
. . . . . .	.	Deanside	Renfrew...	G.&P. Jt.(Cal.&G.&S.W.)	See Renfrew.
. . . . . .	.	Dean's Oil Works	L'lithgow	N. B.	Livingston.
. . . . . .	.	Dean Works	Edinboro'	N. B.	Gorebridge.
G P . L H .	1 0	Dearham	Cumb'land	M. & C.	Bullgill and Papcastle.
G P . L H .		Dearham Bridge	Cumb'land	M. & C.	Maryport and Bullgill.
. . . . . .		Dearham Colliery Junction	Cumb'land	M. & C.	Branch from Dearham Bridge.
. . . . . .		Dearne & Dove's Siding	Yorks	G. C.	Worsboro'.
. . . . . .		Dearness Valley Junction	Durham ...	N. E.	Durham (Passengers) and Brandon.
. . . . . .		Dearne Valley Colliery	Yorks	G. C.	Stairfoot (for Ardsley).
. . . . . .		Dearne Valley Colliery	Yorks	Mid.	Darfield.
. . . . . .		Dechmont Colliery	Lanark ...	Cal.	Newton.
. . . . . .		Decoy Exchange Sids. (G.N.)	Yorks	G. N.—G. E.—L. & N. W.	See Doncaster.
. . . . . .		Dee Bank Siding	Flint	L. & N. W.	Flint.
. . . . . .		Howell's	Flint	L. & N. W.	Dee Bank Siding.
. . . . . .		Walker, Parker, & Co.'s	Flint	L. & N. W.	Dee Bank Siding.
. . . . . .		Dee Clwyd Siding	Merioneth	L. & N. W.	Gwyddelwern.
. . . . . .		Deed & Son's Siding	Surrey	L. B. & S. C.	Mitcham Junction.
. P		Deelis	Kerry	T. & D.	Castlegregory Jn. and Castlegregory.
. . . . . .		Dee Oil Co.'s Candle Works	Cheshire...	G. W.	Saltney.
. . . . . .		Dee Oil Co.'s Oil Works	Cheshire...	G. W.	Saltney.
. . . . . .		Dee Oil Co.'s Siding	Cheshire...	L. & N. W.	Saltney Wharf.
. . . . . .		Deep Arley Pit	Lancs	L. & N. W.	See Hulton Col. Co. (Chequerbent).
G P . L . .	5 0	Deepcar (for Stocksbridge)	Yorks	G. C.	Penistone and Sheffield.
. . . . . .	.	Armitage, J., & Son's Sid.	Yorks	G. C.	Stocksbridge Branch.
. . . . . .	.	Brook & Co.'s Siding	Yorks	G. C.	Stocksbridge Branch.
. . . . . .	.	Gregory's Siding	Yorks	G. C.	Stocksbridge Branch.
. . . . . .	.	Langsett's Siding	Yorks	G. C.	Stocksbridge Branch.
. . . . . .	.	Langsett's Siding (Waterworks Branch)	Yorks	G. C.	Stocksbridge Branch.

EXPLANATION—G *Goods Station.*   P *Passenger and Parcel Station.*   P* *Passenger, but not Parcel or Miscellaneous Traffic.*
F *Furniture Vans, Carriages, Portable Engines, and Machines on Wheels.*   L *Live Stock.*
H *Horse Boxes and Prize Cattle Vans.*   C *Carriages by Passenger Train.*

STATION ACCOMMODATION.	CRANE POWER.	STATIONS, &c.	COUNTY.	COMPANY.	POSITION.
	Tons Cwts.	Deepcar (for Stocksbridge)—*continued.*			
. . . .	. .	Lowood's Siding..............	Yorks	G. C.	Stocksbridge Branch.
. . . .	. .	Public Siding	Yorks	G. C.	Stocksbridge Branch.
. . . .	. .	Stocksbridge Co-operative Society's Siding............	Yorks	G. C.	Stocksbridge Branch.
. . . .	. .	Wharncliffe Colliery........	Yorks	G. C.	Stocksbridge Branch.
. . . .	. .	Deepdale	Lancs	P.&L.Jt.(L&NW.&L&Y.)	See Preston.
. . . .	. .	Deepdale Siding................	Lancs	P.&L.Jt.(L&NW.&L&Y.)	See Wigan Coal & Ir. Co. (Preston).
. . . .	. .	Deep Duffryn Colliery	Glamorg'n	G. W.—T. V.	See Nixon's (Mountain Ash).
. . . .	. .	Deepfields	Staffs	G. W.	See Bilston and Deepfields.
G	P	. . . .	20 0	Deepfields and Coseley	Staffs	L. & N. W.	Birmingham and Wolverhampton.
. . . .	. .	Spring Vale Siding	Staffs	L. & N. W.	Deepfields and Ettingshall Road.
. . . .	. .	Hickman's Brick Works	Staffs	L. & N. W.	Spring Vale Siding.
. . . .	. .	Hickman's Iron Works...	Staffs	L. & N. W.	Spring Vale Siding.
. . . .	. .	Meynell & Son's Siding...	Staffs	L. & N. W.	Spring Vale Siding.
. . . .	. .	Whitehouse & Son's Priorfield Furnace	Staffs	L. & N. W.	Deepfields and Tipton.
. . . .	. .	Deep Navigation or Ocean Navigation Colliery (G. W.)	Glamorg'n	G. W.—Rhy.	Treharris.
. . . .	. .	Deeside	Aberdeen	G. N. of S.	See Aberdeen.
. . . .	. .	Dee Side Colliery Co.'s New Flint Colliery	Flint	L. & N. W.	Flint.
G	P	F L H C	1 10	Defford	Worcester	Mid.	Ashchurch & Bromsgrove.
. . . .	. .	Defiance Pit....................	Ayr	G. & S.W.	Hurlford.
G	P	. . . .	5 0	Deganwy	Carnarvon	L. & N. W.	Llandudno and Llandudno Junction Station.
. . . .	. .	Deighton	Yorks	L. & N. W.	See Huddersfield.
G	P	F L H C	2 0	Delabole	Cornwall..	L. & S.W.	Launceston and Wadebridge.
. . . .	. .	Old Delabole Slate Co.'s Sid	Cornwall	L. & S.W.	Delabole.
G	P	F L H	.	5 0	Delamere	Cheshire...	C. L. C.(GC, G N, & Mid.)	Northwich and Chester.
. . . .	. .	Delaney's Siding................	Yorks	Mid.	Gargrave.
. . . .	. .	Delaney's Siding................	Yorks	Mid.	Horton-in-Ribblesdale.
. . . .	. .	Delaval Colliery and Sidings	Northumb	N. E.	Elswick.
. . . .	. .	Delaval Siding..................	Northumb	N. E.	Scotswood.
. . . .	. .	Delaville Spelter Co.'s Siding	Staffs	L. & N. W.	Bloxwich.
. . . .	. .	Delburn Engineering Works	Lanark ...	Cal.	Motherwell.
G	P	F L H C	.	Delgany	Wicklow..	D. W. & W.	See Greystones and Delgany.
G	P	. L	. .	5 0	Delny	Ross & Cro'	High.	Invergordon and Bonar Bridge.
. . . .	. .	Delph	Yorks	L. & N. W.	Branch from Greenfield.
. . . .	. .	Hirst and Son's Bankfield Mill	Yorks	L. & N. W.	Delph Branch.
. . . .	. .	Mallalieu's Siding	Yorks	L. & N. W.	Delph Branch.
. . . .	. .	Delph Branch	Yorks	L. & N. W.	Greenfield and Saddleworth.
. . . .	. .	Delta Rolling Mills	Durham ...	N. E.	Derwenthaugh.
. . . .	. .	Delves Brick Works & Coke Ovens	Durham ...	N. E.	Blackhill.
G	. . . . . .	. .	Denaby and Conisborough ...	Yorks	H. & B.	Branch from Wrangbrook Junction.
. . . .	. .	Cadeby Main Colliery	Yorks	H. & B.	Denaby & Conisborough.
. . . .	. .	Denaby Main Colliery	Yorks	H. & B.	Denaby & Conisborough.
. . . .	. .	Denaby Main Colliery (G.C.)	Yorks	G. C.—Mid.	Mexboro'.
. . . .	. .	Denbeath Colliery	Fife	N. B.	Methil.
G	P	F L H C	10 0	Denbigh	Denbigh...	L. & N. W.	Corwen and Rhyl.
. . . .	. .	Denbigh Gas Co.'s Siding...	Denbigh...	L. & N. W.	Denbigh and Trefnant.
. . . .	. .	Jones's Graig Quarry	Denbigh...	L. & N. W.	Denbigh and Trefnant.
. . . .	. .	Salusbury & Lloyd's Siding	Denbigh...	L. & N. W.	Denbigh and Trefnant.
. . . .	. .	Denbighshire Portland Cement Co.'s Siding........	Flint	L. & N. W.	Caerwys.
. . . .	. .	Denburn Junction	Aberdeen	Cal.—G. N. of S.—N. B.	Aberdeen.
G	P	. . . .	5 0	Denby	Derby	Mid.	Little Eaton and Ripley.
. . . .	. .	Denby Colliery	Derby	Mid.	Near Denby.
. . . .	. .	Denby Iron & Coal Co.'sSid.	Derby	Mid.	Near Denby.
. . . .	. .	Denby Ironworks	Derby	Mid.	Denby.
. . . .	. .	Drury Lowe's Siding.........	Derby	Mid.	Denby.
. . . .	. .	Kilburn Colliery..............	Derby	Mid.	Little Eaton and Ripley.
. . . .	. .	Ryfield Colliery	Derby	Mid.	Denby.
. . . .	. .	Salterwood Colliery	Derby	Mid.	Little Eaton and Ripley.
G	P	. L H	.	5 0	Denby Dale & Cumberworth	Yorks	L. & Y.	Huddersfield and Penistone.
. . . .	. .	Denby Grange Colliery (L&Y)	Yorks	L. & Y.—N. E.	Horbury Junction.
. . . .	. .	Denby Hall Colliery..........	Derby	Mid.	Ripley.
. . . .	. .	Denend Colliery	Fife	N. B.	Cardenden.
. . . .	. .	Denend Quarry	Fife	N. B.	Cardenden.
. . . .	. .	Denhead	Forfar ...	D. & A. Jt. (Cal. & N. B.)	See Carmyllie.

STATION ACCOMMODATION.	CRANE POWER.	STATIONS, &c.	COUNTY.	COMPANY.	POSITION.
	Tons Cwts.	Denholm & Co.'s Wood Yard	L'lithgow	N. B.	Bo'ness.
G P F L H C	10 0	Denholme	Yorks	G. N.	Bradford and Keighley.
. . . . . .	. .	Denmark Hill	Surrey	L. B. & S. C.—S. E. & C.	See London.
. . . . . .	. .	Dennis & Co.'s Cornubia Wks.	Lancs	L. & N. W.—S. & M. Jt.	Widnes.
. . . . . .	. .	Dennis, W. F., & Co.'s Siding	Middlesex	{ G. E.	London, Millwall Docks.
				GN—GW—LNW—Mid	London, Poplar.
. . . . . .	. .	Dennis Siding	Cambs	L. & N. W.	See Coates & Rutley's (Gamlingay).
. . . . . .	. .	Dennis Siding (Cefn Quarry)	Denbigh	G. W.	Cefn.
G P F L H C	3 0	Denny	Stirling	Cal.	Branch near Larbert.
. . . . . .	. .	Anchor Brick Works (Stein's Brick Works)	Stirling	Cal.	Ingliston.
. . . . . .	. .	Anchor Paper Works	Stirling	Cal.	Denny.
. . . . . .	. .	Anchor Siding	Stirling	Cal.	Ingliston.
. . . . . .	. .	Carronbank Iron Works	Stirling	Cal.	Denny.
. . . . . .	. .	Carronrigg Colliery	Stirling	Cal.	Stoneywood.
. . . . . .	. .	Custon Hall Chemical Wks.	Stirling	Cal.	Stoneywood.
. . . . . .	. .	Denny Weighs	Stirling	Cal.	Denny.
. . . . . .	. .	Herbertshire Brick Works	Stirling	Cal.	Stoneywood.
. . . . . .	. .	Herbertshire No. 2	Stirling	Cal.	Stoneywood.
. . . . . .	. .	Herbertshire No. 3	Stirling	Cal.	Denny.
G		Ingliston	Stirling	Cal.	Branch near Denny.
. . . . . .	. .	Ingliston Junction	Stirling	Cal.	Denny.
. . . . . .	. .	Ingliston Mine	Stirling	Cal.	Ingliston.
. . . . . .	. .	Nethermains Siding	Stirling	Cal.	Stoneywood.
. . . . . .	. .	Quarter Colliery	Stirling	Cal.	Ingliston.
G . . L . .	5 0	Stoneywood	Stirling	Cal.	Branch near Denny.
. . . . . .	. .	Vale Paper Works	Stirling	Cal.	Denny.
. . . . . .	. .	Denny & Co.'s Engineering Works	Dumbartn	D. & B. Jt. (Cal. & N. B.)	Dumbarton.
. . . . . .	. .	Denny, Mott & Dickson Timber Yard	Glamorg'n	G. W.	Cardiff.
. . . . . .	. .	Denny, W., & Bros.' Siding	Dumbartn	Cal.—D. & B. Jt.	Same as Leven Ship Yard (Dumbarton).
G P . L H .	1 10	Dennyloanhead	Stirling	K. & B. Jt. (Cal. & N. B.)	Kilsyth and Bonnybridge, Central.
. . . . . .	. .	Dennyloanhead Colliery	Stirling	K. & B. Jt. (Cal. & N. B.)	Same as Broomrigg Colliery (Bonnybridge).
. . . . . .	. .	Dennystown Forge	Dumbartn	D. & B. Jt. (Cal. & N. B.)	Dalreoch.
. . . . . .	. .	Denny West Junction	Stirling	Cal.	Branch near Larbert.
. P	. .	Denstone	Staffs	N. S.	Oakamoor and Uttoxeter.
G P F L H C	5 0	Dent	Yorks	Mid.	Hawes Jn. Sta. and Ribblehead.
. . . . . .	. .	Dentith Siding	Flint	L. & N. W.	Same as Princes Sid. (Connah's Quay)
G P	10 0	Denton	Lancs	L. & N. W.	Stalybridge and Stockport.
. . . . . .	. .	Alpha Mill Co.'s Siding	Lancs	L. & N. W.	Denton and Reddish.
. . . . . .	. .	Denton & Haughton Gas Wks	Lancs	L. & N. W.	Denton and Reddish.
. . . . . .	. .	Denton Colliery	Lancs	L. & N. W.	Denton and Reddish.
. . . . . .	. .	Dentonholme	Cumb'land	G. & S. W.—Mid.	See Carlisle.
. . . . . .	. .	Dentonholme North and South Junctions	Cumb'land	{ Dentonholme Sta. Com. —Goods Traffic. Com.	} Carlisle.
. . . . . .	. .	Denton Siding	Lincoln	G. N.	Bottesford.
. . . . . .	. .	Denton Street Coal Depôts	Cumb'land	N. E.	Carlisle.
. . . . . .	. .	Dent's Gate Siding	Durham	N. E.	Barnard Castle.
. . . . . .	. .	Dent, T. R. (Watson's) Whf.	Yorks	N. E.	Middlesbro'.
G P	. .	Denver	Norfolk	G. E.	Ely and Lynn.
. . . . . .	. .	Depôt Road Boiler Works	Yorks	N. E.	Middlesbro'.
. . . . . .	. .	Deptford	Kent	S. E. & C.	See London.
. . . . . .	. .	Deptford Branch Junction	Durham	N. E.	Pallion.
. . . . . .	. .	Deptford Depôts	Durham	N. E.	Pallion.
. . . . . .	. .	Deptford Rivet Works	Durham	N. E.	Pallion.
. . . . . .	. .	Deptford Road	Surrey	E. L. Jt. (G. E., L. B. & S. C., Met., M. D., & S. E. & C.)	See London.
. . . . . .	. .	Deptford Wharf	Kent	L. B. & S. C.	See London.
		DERBY—			
G . F L . .	10 0	(Station, L. & N. W.)	Derby	{ L. & N. W.	Branch—Burton Pass. (Mid.) and Derby Pass. (Mid.)
				N. S.	Over Mid. and L. & N. W. Lines.
. P F . H C	. .	(Station, Mid.)	Derby	{ Mid.	Burton and Chesterfield.
				L. & N. W.	Over Mid. Line.
				N. S.	Over Mid. from Willington Junc.
. . . . . .	. .	Bennett's Brick Siding	Derby	G. N.	Derby and Mickleover.
. . . . . .	. .	Bonded Stores	Derby	Mid.	Near Nottingham Road.
. . . . . .	. .	Brown's (W. & G.) Siding (Lodge Lane Mill)	Derby	G. N.	Friar Gate.

EXPLANATION—G *Goods Station.*   P *Passenger and Parcel Station.*   P* *Passenger, but not Parcel or Miscellaneous Traffic.*
F *Furniture Vans, Carriages, Portable Engines, and Machines on Wheels.*   L *Live Stock.*
H *Horse Boxes and Prize Cattle Vans.*   C *Carriages by Passenger Train.*

STATION ACCOMMODATION.						CRANE POWER.		STATIONS, &c.	COUNTY.	COMPANY.	POSITION.
						Tons	Cwts.	**DERBY**—continued.			
..	..	..	..	..	..	..	..	Carriage & Wagon Works...	Derby	Mid.	Near Passenger Station.
..	..	..	..	..	..	..	..	Cattle Docks	Derby	Mid.	Passenger Station and Nottingham Road.
..	..	..	..	..	..	..	..	Chaddesden Sids. (Mid.)	Derby	Mid.—N. S...................	Nottingham Road and Spondon.
..	..	..	..	..	..	..	..	Chain Belt Engineering Co.'s Siding...............	Derby	L. & N. W.	Derby Goods Branch.
..	..	..	..	..	..	..	..	Cheese Warehouse and Siding	Derby	Mid.	Near Passenger Station.
..	..	..	..	..	..	..	..	Clarke Street Sid. (Handyside & Co.)	Derby	Mid.	Fox Street and Nottingham Road.
..	..	..	..	..	..	..	..	Cole's Siding	Derby	G. N.	Derby and Mickleover.
..	..	..	..	..	..	..	..	Co-operative Society's Siding and Warehouse	Derby	Mid.	Near St. Mary's (Wood Street).
..	..	..	..	..	..	..	..	Corporation Depôt & Siding	Derby	Mid.	Near Nottingham Road.
..	..	..	..	..	..	..	..	Derby Coal Co.'s Wagon Repairing Siding	Derby	Mid.	Derby.
..	..	..	..	..	..	..	..	Derby Gas Co.'s Siding...	Derby	Mid.	Litchurch and Spondon Curve.
G	..	..	..	..	..	10	0	Duke Street	Derby	G. N.	Branch from Derby, Pass.
..	..	..	..	..	..	..	..	Eastwood, Swingler & Co.'s Iron Works	Derby	Mid.	Near Passenger Station.
..	..	..	..	..	..	..	..	Eaton's, W., Siding	Derby	Mid.	Pear Tree and Normanton.
..	..	..	..	..	..	..	..	Fletcher, G., & Co.'s Masson and Atlas Works ...	Derby	Mid.	Near Passenger Station.
G	P	F	L	H	C	10	0	Friar Gate	Derby	G. N.	Nottingham and Burton.
..	..	..	..	..	..	..	..	Goods Branch Junction ...	Derby	L. & N. W.—Mid.	Derby Station (L. & N. W.), and Burton Pass. (Mid.)
..	..	..	..	..	..	..	..	Handyside & Co's Works...	Derby	{ G. N. .... / Mid.	Duke Street. / Near St. Mary's Station.
..	..	..	..	..	..	..	..	Holme's Siding	Derby	G. N.	Duke Street.
..	..	..	..	..	..	..	..	Jones, A. G., & Co.'s Siding	Derby	G. N.	Derby and Mickleover.
..	..	..	..	..	..	..	..	Kitchen & Co.'s Works....	Derby	Mid.	Near St. Mary's Station.
..	..	..	..	..	..	..	..	Leys Siding (L. & N. W.)...	Derby	L. & N. W.—N. S.	Derby Goods Branch.
..	..	..	..	..	..	..	..	Litchurch Siding (Derby Gas Co.'s).....................	Derby	Mid.	Derby.
G	..	..	..	..	..	4	0	London Road Wharf	Derby	Mid.	Near Passenger Station.
..	P	..	..	..	..	..	..	Nottingham Road	Derby	Mid.	Passenger Station and Duffield.
G	P	..	..	..	..	..	..	Pear Tree and Normanton.	Derby	Mid.	Derby and Burton.
..	..	..	..	..	..	..	..	Pountain, Girardot, & Forman's Siding	Derby	Mid.	Near St. Mary's Station.
..	..	..	..	H	..	..	..	Race Course Horse Dock...	Derby	Mid.	Near St. Mary's Station.
..	..	..	..	..	..	..	..	Race Course Siding	Derby	G. N.	Derby and Breadsall.
..	..	..	..	..	..	..	..	Robinson & Co.'s Siding....	Derby	G. N.	Derby and Mickleover.
..	..	..	..	..	..	..	..	Roe's Timber Co.'s Siding	Derby	Mid.	London Road Wharf.
..	..	..	..	..	..	..	..	Roe's Timber Co.'s New Wks	Derby	Mid.	Nottingham Road.
G	..	F	L	H	..	15	0	St. Mary's	Derby	Mid.	Branch—Pass. Sta. and Duffield.
..	..	..	..	..	..	..	..	Sharon Chemical Works ...	Derby	Mid.	Near St. Mary's Station.
..	..	..	..	..	..	..	..	Stores and Locomotive Department Siding	Derby	Mid.	Near Passenger Station.
..	..	..	..	..	..	..	..	Telegraph and Signal Department Siding	Derby	Mid.	Near Passenger Station.
..	..	..	..	..	..	..	..	West's Siding...............	Derby	G. N.	Derby and Mickleover.
..	..	..	..	..	..	..	..	Wheeldon's Maltings	Derby	Mid.	Near St. Mary's Station.
..	..	..	..	..	..	..	..	Wilkins & Co.'s Siding ...	Derby	G. N.	Derby and Mickleover.
..	..	..	..	..	..	..	..	Derby Bonded Stores	Derby	Mid.	Derby, St. Mary's.
..	..	..	..	..	..	..	..	Derby Carriage & Wagon Works	Derby	Mid.	Derby, St. Mary's.
..	..	..	..	..	..	..	..	Derby Cheese Warehouse and Siding	Derby	Mid.	Derby, St. Mary's.
..	..	..	..	..	..	..	..	Derby Coal Co.'s Wagon Repairing Siding...............	Derby	Mid.	Derby, St. Mary's.
..	..	..	..	..	..	..	..	Derby Corporation Depôt and Siding	Derby	Mid.	Derby, St. Mary's.
..	..	..	..	..	..	..	..	Derby Gas Co.'s Siding....	Derby	Mid.	Derby, St. Mary's.
..	..	..	..	..	..	..	..	Derby Road.....................	Leicester..	L. & N. W.	See Loughboro'.
..	..	..	..	..	..	..	..	Derby Road.....................	Suffolk ...	G. E.	See Ipswich.
..	..	..	..	..	..	..	..	Derby Road Siding	Derby	G. N.	Ilkeston.
								Derby's (Earl of)—			
..	..	..	..	..	..	..	..	Siding	Lancs	L. & Y.	Rainford Junction.
..	..	..	..	..	..	..	..	Siding	Lancs	P & L Jt. (L&NW & L&Y)	Longridge.
..	..	..	..	..	..	..	..	Treals Siding	Lancs	P & W Jt. (L&Y & L&NW)	Kirkham.
..	..	..	..	..	..	..	..	Yard	Lancs	L. & Y.........................	Liverpool, Sandhills.

EXPLANATION—G *Goods Station.*   P *Passenger and Parcel Station.*   P* *Passenger, but not Parcel or Miscellaneous Traffic.*
F *Furniture Vans, Carriages, Portable Engines, and Machines on Wheels.*   L *Live Stock.*
H *Horse Boxes and Prize Cattle Vans.*   C *Carriages by Passenger Train.*

STATION ACCOMMODATION.						CRANE POWER.		STATIONS, &c.	COUNTY.	COMPANY.	POSITION.
						Tons	Cwts.				
..	..	..	..	..	..	..	..	Derbyshire Silica Fire Brick Co.'s Siding	Derby.....	L. & N. W.	Friden.
..	..	..	..	..	..	..	..	Derby Stores and Locomotive Department Siding	Derby.....	Mid.	Derby, St. Mary's.
..	..	..	..	..	..	..	..	Derby Telegraph and Signal Department Siding	Derby.....	Mid.	Derby, St. Mary's.
G	P	F	L	H	C	6	0	Dereen (Book to Mohill)...........	Leitrim ...	C. & L.	Mohill and Dromod.
G	P	F	L	H	C	6	0	Dereham	Norfolk ...	G. E.	Wymondham and Fakenham.
..	..	..	..	..	..	..	..	Fison & Son's Siding........	Norfolk ...	G. E.	Dereham.
..	..	..	..	..	..	..	..	Deri	Glamorg'n	Rhy.............................	Same as Darran.
..	..	..	..	..	..	..	..	Deri Junction	Glamorg'n	B. & M.—Rhy.	Fochriw and Darran.
..	..	..	..	..	..	..	..	Derlwyn Colliery (B. & M.)...	Mon	B. & M.—G. W.	New Tredegar and White Rose.
..	P	..	..	..	..	..	..	Derramore	Armagh ...	B. & Newry.	Bessbrook and Newry.
..	P	..	..	..	..	..	..	Derrymore	Kerry	T. & D.	Tralee and Castlegregory Junction
G	P	..	L	H	..	..	..	Derryork	Derry	N. C. Com. (Mid.)	Limavady and Dungiven.
G	P	..	L	H	..	3	0	Derry Ormond	Cardigan..	M. & M.	Lampeter and Tregaron.
G	P	F	L	H	C	..	..	Dersingham......................	Norfolk ...	G. E.	Lynn and Hunstanton.
G	P	..	L	..	..	1	10	Dervock	Antrim ...	Ballycastle	Ballymoney and Ballycastle.
G	P	..	L	H	..	..	..	Derwen	Denbigh ..	L. & N. W.	Corwen and Denbigh.
..	..	..	..	..	..	..	..	Derwen Merthyr Colliery......	Glamorg'n	G. W. & Rhy. Jt.	Aberfan.
..	..	..	..	..	..	..	..	Derwent Colliery	Durham ...	N. E.	Blackhill.
G	..	..	..	..	..	..	..	Derwenthaugh	Durham ...	N. E.	Gateshead and Blaydon.
..	..	..	..	..	..	..	..	Blaydon Main Colliery and Coke Ovens	Durham ...	N. E.	Derwenthaugh.
..	..	..	..	..	..	..	..	Chopwell Col. & Coke Ovens	Durham ...	N. E.	Derwenthaugh.
..	..	..	..	..	..	..	..	Chopwell Depôt	Durham ...	N. E.	Derwenthaugh.
..	..	..	..	..	..	..	..	Delta Rolling Mills	Durham ...	N. E.	Derwenthaugh.
..	..	..	..	..	..	..	..	Derwenthaugh Coke Ovens and Shipping Staithes ...	Durham ...	N. E.	Derwenthaugh.
..	..	..	..	..	..	..	..	Derwenthaugh Quay Shipping Staithes	Durham ...	N. E.	Derwenthaugh.
..	..	..	..	..	..	..	..	Garesfield (Spen) Colliery, Coke Ovens, Brick Works and Depôts	Durham ...	N. E.	Derwenthaugh.
..	..	..	..	..	..	..	..	Hannington & Co.'s Siding	Durham ...	N. E.	Derwenthaugh.
..	..	..	..	..	..	..	..	Hannington Brick Works...	Durham ...	N. E.	Derwenthaugh.
..	..	..	..	..	..	..	..	High Thornley Depôts (Barlow Depôt)	Durham ...	N. E.	Derwenthaugh.
..	..	..	..	..	..	..	..	Ramsays Fire-Brick Works	Durham ...	N. E.	Derwenthaugh.
..	..	..	..	..	..	..	..	Snowballs Fire-Brick Works	Durham ...	N. E.	Derwenthaugh.
..	..	..	..	..	..	..	..	Swalwell Bridge Depôts ...	Durham ...	N. E.	Derwenthaugh.
..	..	..	..	..	..	..	..	Swalwell Colliery	Durham ...	N. E.	Derwenthaugh.
..	..	..	..	..	..	..	..	Winlaton Mill Rolling Mills	Durham ...	N. E.	Derwenthaugh.
..	..	..	..	..	..	..	..	Derwent Iron & Steel Works	Cumb'land	C. & W. Jn.—L. & N. W.	See Cammell & Co. (Workington).
..	..	..	..	..	..	..	..	Derwent Rolling Mills (Barepot Siding)	Cumb'land	L. & N. W.	Workington Bridge.
..	..	..	..	..	..	..	..	Derwent Valley Water Works	Derby.....	Mid.	Bamford.
G	P	F	..	..	..	..	..	Derwydd Road (G. W.)	Carmarth'	G. W. / L. & N. W.	Pantyffynnon and Llandilo. / Over G. W. Line.
G	P	F	L	H	C	1	10	Desborough and Rothwell ...	N'hamptn	Mid.	Market Harboro' & Wellingboro'.
..	..	..	..	..	..	..	..	Fisher's Ironstone Siding...	N'hamptn	Mid.	Glendon and Desborough.
..	..	..	..	..	..	..	..	Stanton Iron Co.'s Siding...	N'hamptn	Mid.	Glendon and Desborough.
G	P	..	..	..	..	..	..	Desert	Cork	C. B. & S. C.	Bandon and Dunmanway.
G	P	..	L	H	..	3	0	Desertmartin	Derry	N. C. Com. (Mid.)	Magherafelt and Draperstown.
G	P	F	L	H	C	..	..	Desford	Leicester..	Mid.	Leicester and Burton.
..	..	..	..	..	..	..	..	Ellis, J., & Son's Manure Works	Leicester..	Mid.	Desford.
..	..	..	..	..	..	..	..	Merrylees' Siding	Leicester..	Mid.	Near Desford.
..	..	..	..	..	..	..	..	Desford Coal Co.'s Sid. (Mid.)	Leicester..	Mid.—L. & N. W.	Bagworth.
G	P	..	L	H	..	..	..	Dess	Aberdeen..	G. N. of S.	Banchory and Aboyne.
..	..	..	..	..	..	..	..	Deuchar's Brewery...............	Edinboro'	N. B.	Duddingston and Craigmillar.
G	P	F	L	H	C	..	..	Devil's Bridge	Cardigan..	V. of Rheidol	Terminus.
G	P	F	L	H	C	10	0	Devizes	Wilts	G. W.	Woodboro' and Trowbridge.
..	..	..	..	..	..	..	..	Devon Colliery....................	Clackman'	N. B.	Sauchie.
G	P	F	L	H	C	15	0	Devonport	Devon ...	G. W. / L. & S. W.	Plymouth and Saltash. / Tavistock and Plymouth.
G	P	F	L	H	C	10	0				
..	..	..	..	..	..	..	..	H. M. Dockyards, North and South.....................	Devon ...	G. W. / L. & S. W.	See Keyham Junction. / Over G.W. fr. Devonport Junction.
G	..	..	..	..	..	5	0	Stonehouse Pool	Devon ...	L. & S. W.	Branch from Devonport.
..	..	..	..	..	..	..	..	Devonport Junction	Devon.....	G. W.—L. & S. W.	Plymouth, North Rd. & Devonport.
..	..	..	..	..	..	..	..	Devon Quarry....................	Clackman'	N. B.	Sauchie.
G	P	..	L	H	..	..	..	Devon Road......................	Limerick..	G. S. & W.	Newcastle West and Tralee.

STATION ACCOMMODATION.						CRANE POWER.		STATIONS, &c.	COUNTY.	COMPANY.	POSITION.
						Tons	Cwts				
.	.	.	.	.	.	.	.	Devonshaw Siding	Kinross ...	N. B.	Rumbling Bridge.
								Devonshire's (Duke of)—			
.	.	.	.	.	.	.	.	Buckland Hollow Siding ...	Derby	Mid.	Ambergate.
.	.	\.	.	.	.	.	.	Hambleton Siding	Yorks	Mid.	Bolton Abbey.
.	.	.	.	.	.	.	.	Siding	Sussex ...	L. B. & S. C.	Eastbourne.
.	.	.	.	.	.	.	.	Devonshire Street	Middlesex	G. E.	See London.
.	.	.	.	.	.	.	.	Devonside Colliery..............	Clackman'	N. B.	Tillicoultry.
.	.	.	.	.	.	.	.	Devons Road	Middlesex	L. & N. W.	See London.
G	P	F	L	H	C	1	0	Devynock (N. & B.)	Brecon ...	{ N. & Brecon .... / Mid.	Brecon and Penwyllt. / Over Neath and Brecon Line.
.	.	.	.	.	.	.	.	Dewar & Son's Siding	Perth	N. B.	Perth.
.	.	.	.	.	.	.	.	Dewhurst's Siding	Lancs	L. & Y.	Bamber Bridge.
.	.	.	.	.	.	.	.	Dewing & Kersley's Siding ...	Norfolk ...	G. E.	Wells.
								Dewis Siding (Cattle Sales Siding) (L. & N. W.)....	Warwick ...	L. & N. W.—Mid.	Coventry.
								DEWSBURY—			
G	P	F	L	H	C	10	0	(Station)	Yorks	L. & N. W.	Huddersfield and Leeds.
G	P	F	L	H	C	5	0	(Station)	Yorks	L. & Y.	Branch near Thornhill.
G	P	F	L	H	C	8	0 }	(Station, G. N.)	Yorks	{ G. N. .... / G. C.	Ossett and Batley. / Over G. N. from Wakefield Junc.
G	.	F	L	.	.	8	0 }				
.	.	.	.	.	.	.	.	Corporation Gas Siding......	Yorks	L. & Y.	Dewsbury and Wakefield.
.	.	.	.	.	.	.	.	Gas Works (L. & Y.)........	Yorks	L. & Y.—G. N.	Dewsbury and Dewsbury Junction.
.	.	.	.	.	.	.	.	Junction	Yorks	G. N.—L. & Y.	Dewsbury and Thornhill.
.	.	.	.	.	.	.	.	Junction	Yorks	L. & Y.—L. & N. W. ...	Mirfield and Dewsbury.
.	.	.	.	.	.	.	.	Turner's Siding (L. & Y.)...	Yorks	L. & Y.—G. N.	Dewsbury and Thornhill.
.	.	.	.	.	.	.	.	Dewshill Colliery	Lanark ...	Cal.	Salisburgh.
.	.	.	.	.	.	.	.	Dewshill Siding	Lanark ...	Cal.	Salisburgh.
.	.	.	.	.	.	.	.	Dewsnap Siding..............	Cheshire...	G. C.	Guide Bridge.
.	.	.	.	.	.	.	.	Diamond Anthracite Mine Co's Colliery (Mid.)	Brecon ...	Mid.—G. W.—L. & N. W.	Gurnos.
.	.	.	.	.	.	.	.	Diamond Foundry (Davis Gas Stove Co.) (N. B.)	Stirling ...	N. B.—Cal.	Falkirk, Grahamston.
.	.	.	.	.	.	.	.	Diamond Grit Works	Yorks	N. E.	Middlesbro'.
.	.	.	.	.	.	.	.	Diamond Hall Pottery and Depôts	Durham ...	N. E.	Pallion.
.	.	.	.	.	.	.	.	Diamond Llantwit Colliery ...	Mon	B. & M.	Bedwas.
.	P	.	.	.	.	.	.	Dicconson Lane and Aspull...	Lancs	L. & Y.	Hindley and Blackrod.
.	.	.	.	.	.	.	.	Dickens House Drift..........	Durham ...	N. E.	Waterhouses.
.	.	.	.	.	.	.	.	Dickinson & Co.'s Croxley Green Siding	Herts	L. & N. W.	Watford.
.	.	.	.	.	.	.	.	Dickinson & Co.'s Siding......	Yorks	Mid.	Keighley.
.	.	.	.	.	.	.	.	Dick, Kerr & Co.'s English Electric Manufacturing Co.'s Siding..................	Lancs	N.U.Jt.(L.&NW.&L.&Y.)	Preston.
.	.	.	.	.	.	.	.	Dickson's Siding..............	Tyrone ...	G. N. (I.)	Dungannon and Trew.
.	.	.	.	.	.	.	.	Dickson's Siding (Blackbeck Siding) (private)	Lancs	Furness........................	Haverthwaite.
G	P	F	L	H	C	8	0	Didcot	Berks	G. W.	Reading and Oxford.
.	.	.	.	.	.	.	.	Rich's Siding	Berks	G. W.	Didcot and Upton.
G	P	F	.	H	C	1	10	Didsbury	Lancs	Mid.	Manchester and Stockport.
G	P	F	L	H	C	1	10	Digby	Lincoln ...	G. N. & G. E. Jt.	Lincoln and Sleaford.
.	.	.	.	.	.	.	.	Bloxholme Siding	Lincoln ...	G. N. & G. E. Jt.	Digby and Ruskington.
.	.	.	.	.	.	.	.	Digby Colliery (G. N.)	Notts	G. N.—G. C.	Kimberley.
.	.	.	.	.	.	.	.	Digby Colliery Co.'s Siding...	Notts	Mid.	See Bennerley Sidings (Ilkeston).
.	.	.	.	.	.	.	.	Digby Siding (private)	Devon ...	L. & S.W.	Topsham.
G	P	.	L	.	.	5	0	Diggle	Yorks	L. & N. W.	Huddersfield and Stalybridge.
.	.	.	.	.	.	.	.	Hutchinson Hollingworth & Co.'s Siding	Yorks	L. & N. W.	Diggle and Saddleworth.
.	.	.	.	.	.	.	.	Diggles North & South Sidings	Lancs	L. & N. W.	See West Leigh Coal Co's (Wigan).
.	.	.	.	.	.	.	.	Diglake	Staffs	N. S.	Alsager Junction and Keele Junc.
.	.	.	.	.	.	.	.	Diglake Colliery..............	Staffs	N. S.	Diglake.
.	.	.	.	.	.	.	.	Jamage Colliery (Wedgewood's)	Staffs	N. S.	Diglake.
								Rigby & Co.'s—			
.	.	.	.	.	.	.	.	Audley Colliery	Staffs	N. S.	Audley and Jamage Junction.
.	.	.	.	.	.	.	.	Bunkers Hill Colliery ...	Staffs	N. S.	Diglake.
.	.	.	.	.	.	.	.	Digswell Siding	Herts	G. N.	Hatfield.
.	.	.	.	.	.	.	.	Dillichip Works	Dumbart'n	D. & B. Jt. (Cal. & N. B.)	Alexandria.
.	.	.	.	.	.	.	.	Dillwyn & Co.'s Siding (Mid.)	Glamorg'n	Mid.—G. W.—L. & N. W.	Six Pit.
.	.	.	.	.	.	.	.	Dillwyn & Co.'s Spelter Wks. Siding	Glamorg'n	G. W. & Mid. Jt.	Swansea Valley Junction.
.	.	.	.	.	.	.	.	Dilston Siding..................	Northumb	N. E.	Corbridge.

EXPLANATION—G *Goods Station.*   P *Passenger and Parcel Station.*   P* *Passenger, but not Parcel or Miscellaneous Traffic.*
F *Furniture Vans, Carriages, Portable Engines, and Machines on Wheels.*   L *Live Stock.*
H *Horse Boxes and Prize Cattle Vans.*   C *Carriages by Passenger Train.*

STATION ACCOMMODATION.						CRANE POWER.	STATIONS, &c.	COUNTY.	COMPANY.	POSITION.
						Tons Cwts				
G	P	.	.	.	.	. .	Dinas	Carnarvon	{ L. & N.W.	Afon Wen and Carnarvon.
G	P	.	.	.	.	1 10			{ No. Wales N. G.	Adjoining L. & N. W. Station.
							Exchange Sidings	Carnarvon	L.N.W.—No.WalesN.G.	Dinas.
.	P	.	.	.	.	.	Dinas	Glamorg'n	T. V.	Ystrad and Porth.
.	.	.	.	.	.	.	Dinas Colliery	Glamorg'n	T. V.	Porth.
.	.	.	.	.	.	.	Dinas Isha Colliery	Glamorg'n	G. W.	Penygraig.
.	.	.	.	.	.	.	Dinas Main Collieries	Glamorg'n	G. W.	Gilfach.
G	P	.	.	H	.	.	Dinas Powis	Glamorg'n	Barry	Barry and Cogan.
.	.	.	.	.	.	.	Dinas Quarries Extension (Rhiwbryfdir)	Merioneth	Festiniog	Blaenau Festiniog.
.	.	.	.	.	.	.	Dinas Siding	Glamorg'n	G. W.	Glyn Neath.
G	P	.	.	.	.	.	Dingestow	Mon	G. W.	Pontypool Road and Monmouth.
G	P	.	L	H	.	.	Dingle	Kerry	T. & D.	Terminus.
.	.	.	.	.	.	.	Dingle (Park Road)	Lancs	L'pool O'head	See Liverpool.
G	P	F	L	H	C	2 0	Dingwall	Ross & Cro'	High.	Inverness and Invergordon.
G	P	F	L	H†	C†	5 0	Dinmore	Hereford	S & H Jt. (G W & L N W)	Craven Arms and Hereford.
G	P	F	L	H	C	3 0	Dinnet	Aberdeen	G. N. of S.	Aboyne and Ballater.
.	.	.	.	.	.	.	Dinnington Colliery	Northumb	N. E.	Killingworth.
.	P	.	.	.	.	.	Dinsdale	Durham	N. E.	Darlington, Bank Top & Eaglescliffe.
.	.	.	.	.	.	.	Dinsdale Moor Iron Works	Durham	N. E.	Fighting Cocks.
.	.	.	.	.	.	.	Dinsdale Wire & Steel Works	Durham	N. E.	Fighting Cocks.
							DINTING—			
G	.	.	L	H	.	5 0	(Station)	Derby	G. C.	Guide Bridge and Penistone.
.	P	.	.	.	.	.	(Station)	Derby	G. C.	Guide Bridge and Penistone.
.	.	.	.	.	.	.	Bridge Mills Siding	Derby	G. C.	Dinting.
.	.	.	.	.	.	.	Brookfield Siding	Derby	G. C.	Dinting.
.	.	.	.	.	.	.	Dalton's Siding	Derby	G. C.	Dinting.
.	.	.	.	.	.	.	East Junction	Derby	G. C.	Hadfield and Glossop.
.	.	.	.	.	.	.	Lower Barn Siding	Derby	G. C.	Dinting.
.	.	.	.	.	.	.	Mersey Mills Siding	Derby	G. C.	Dinting.
.	.	.	.	.	.	.	Potter's Siding	Derby	G. C.	Dinting.
.	.	.	.	.	.	.	South Junction	Derby	G. C.	Dinting and Glossop.
.	.	.	.	.	.	.	Waterside Mills Siding	Derby	G. C.	Dinting.
.	.	.	.	.	.	.	West Junction	Derby	G. C.	Mottram and Glossop.
G	P	F	L	H	C	5 0	Dinton	Wilts	L. & S.W.	Salisbury and Templecombe.
G	P	.	L	H	.	.	Dinwoodie	Dumfries	Cal.	Lockerbie and Carstairs.
.	.	.	.	.	.	.	Dipton Colliery	Durham	N. E.	Redheugh.
G	P	.	L	H	.	1 10	Dirleton	Hadding'n	N. B.	Drem and North Berwick.
.	.	.	.	.	.	.	Dirrans Saw Mill	Ayr	Cal.—G. & S. W.	Kilwinning.
.	.	.	.	.	.	.	Dirrans Siding	Ayr	G. & S. W.	Kilwinning.
G	P	F	L	H	C	10 0	Disley	Cheshire	L. & N. W.	Buxton and Stockport.
G	P	F	L	H	C	1 10	Diss	Norfolk	G. E.	Ipswich and Norwich.
.	.	.	.	.	.	.	Distillers Co.'s Siding	L'lithgow	N. B.	South Queensferry.
G	P	F	L	H	C	1 0	Distington	Cumb'land	{ C. & W. Jn.	Workington and Moresby Parks.
G	.	F	L	.	.	.			{ WC&EJt(Fur.&L&NW)	Parton and Ullock.
G	.	.	.	.	.	.	Distington Iron Works	Cumb'land	WC&EJt.(Fur.&L&NW)	Parton and Ullock.
.	.	.	.	.	.	.	Distington Junction	Cumb'land	C.&W.Jn.—W. C.& E.Jt.	High Harrington and Ullock.
.	.	.	.	.	.	.	District Chemical Co.'s Siding (G. E.)	Essex	GE—GN—L&NW—Mid.	Same as Berk & Co.'s Sid. (London).
G	P	.	.	.	.	.	Ditchford	N'hamptn	L. & N. W.	Peterboro' and Wellingboro'.
G	P	F	L	H	C	1 10	Ditchingham	Norfolk	G. E.	Tivetshall and Beccles.
.	.	.	.	.	.	.	Ditton	Lancs	C. L. C. (G C,G N, & Mid.)	See Hough Green (for Ditton).
G	P	F	L	H	C	. .	Ditton	Lancs	L. & N. W.	Garston and Warrington.
.	.	.	.	.	.	.	Ditton Brook Iron Works (Bibby & Son's)	Lancs	S. & M. Jt. (G. C. & Mid.)	Widnes.
.	.	.	.	.	.	.	Ditton Brook Siding	Lancs	L. & Y.	Upholland.
.	.	.	.	.	.	.	Ditton Copper Works	Lancs	L. & N. W.—S. & M. Jt.	Same as Broughton Copper Co.'s Siding (Widnes).
.	.	.	.	.	.	.	Ditton Extract Wks.(Maloney & Co.'s)	Lancs	S. & M. Jt. (G. C. & Mid.)	Widnes.
.	.	.	.	.	.	.	Ditton Land Co.'s Waste Tip Siding	Lancs	S. & M. Jt. (G. C. & Mid.)	Widnes.
.	.	.	.	.	.	.	Ditton Oil Mills	Lancs	L. & N. W.—S. & M. Jt.	Widnes.
.	.	.	.	.	.	.	Dixie Sidings (L. & N. W.)	Staffs	L. & N. W.—G.N.—N. S.	Burton-on-Trent.
.	.	.	.	.	.	.	Dixie Sidings (Mid.)	Staffs	Mid.—L. & N. W—G. N.	Burton-on-Trent.
.	.	.	.	.	.	.	Dixon & Co.'s Siding	Carnarvon	L. & N. W.	Bangor.
.	.	.	.	.	.	.	Dixon, Corbett, Newall & Co.'s Rope Works	Durham	N. E.	Redheugh.

H† C† *Only for Traffic to South Stations and from North Stations. Traffic from South Stations and to North Stations should be booked to and despatched from Ford Bridge.*

EXPLANATION—G *Goods Station.*   P *Passenger and Parcel Station.*   P* *Passenger, but not Parcel or Miscellaneous Traffic.*
F *Furniture Vans, Carriages, Portable Engines, and Machines on Wheels.*   L *Live Stock.*
H *Horse Boxes and Prize Cattle Vans.*   C *Carriages by Passenger Train.*

STATION ACCOMMODATION.						CRANE POWER.		STATIONS, &c.	COUNTY.	COMPANY.	POSITION.
						Tons	Cwts.				
.	P	.	.	.	.	.	.	Dixon Fold	Lancs	L. & Y.	Manchester and Bolton.
.	.	.	.	.	.	.	.	Unity Brook Siding (Clifton and Kersley Co.)	Lancs	L. & Y.	Dixon Fold.
.	.	.	.	.	.	.	.	Dixon, J., & Co.'s Siding.....	Northumb	N. E.	Tweedmouth.
.	.	.	.	.	.	.	.	Dixon (Sir Raylton) & Co.'s Ship Yard..................	Yorks	N. E.	Same as Bottle House Point Ship Yard (Middlesbro').
.	.	.	.	.	.	.	.	Dixon's Limestone Siding ...	Cumb'land	C. & W. Jn.	Same as Rowrah Limestone Siding (Arlecdon).
.	.	.	.	.	.	.	.	Dixon's Siding................	Yorks	G. C.	Oughty Bridge.
.	.	.	.	.	.	.	.	Dixon's Sidings	Lanark ...	Cal.	Same as Govan Iron Works and Collieries (Glasgow).
.	.	.	.	.	.	.	.	Dixon's Siding................	Lancs	L. & N. W.	See Spekeland Rd. Sids. (Liverpool).
.	.	.	.	.	.	.	.	Dixon's Wharf................	Worcester	Mid.	Redditch.
G	P	.	L	H	.	2	0	Doagh	Antrim ...	N.C. Com. (Mid.) ...	Antrim and Greenisland.
G	P	F	L	.	.	.	.	Doagh (*Narrow Gauge*)........	Antrim ...	N.C. Com. (Mid.)	Branch from Ballyboley.
.	.	.	.	.	.	.	.	Dobbie, Forbes & Co.'s Siding	Stirling ...	Cal.	Same as Colonial Stove and Iron Works (Larbert).
.	.	.	.	.	.	.	.	Dobbs Brow Junction	Lancs	L. & Y.	Daisy Hill and Crow Nest Junction.
.	.	.	.	.	.	.	.	Dobcross	Yorks	L. & N. W.	See Saddleworth (for Dobcross).
.	.	.	.	.	.	.	.	Dobson & Wallis' Siding	Yorks	Mid.	Cudworth.
.	.	.	.	.	.	.	.	Dobson, Molle & Co.'s Siding	Edinboro'	N. B.	Edinburgh, Leith Walk.
.	.	.	.	.	.	.	.	Dobson's Siding	Glamorg'n	T. V.	Grangetown.
.	.	.	.	.	.	.	.	Dock Foundry Sid. (Bo'ness Pottery)	L'lithgow	N. B.	Bo'ness.
G	P	F	L	H	C	1	10	Docking	Norfolk ...	G. E.	Heacham and Wells.
.	.	.	.	.	.	.	.	Dock Lane Grain Store (Cal.)	Renfrew...	Cal.—G. & S. W.—N. B.	See Springfield Free Warehouses (Glasgow).
.	.	.	.	.	.	.	.	Dockra Lime Works	Ayr	GB&K Jt(Cal & G &SW)	Barrmill.
.	.	.	.	.	.	.	.	Dockra Pit	Ayr	G B&K Jt(Cal & G &SW)	Barrmill.
.	.	.	.	.	.	.	.	Dock Side Timber Yard	Yorks	N. E.	See Whitehouse Siding and Depôt (South Bank).
.	.	.	.	.	.	.	.	Docks Station	Cheshire...	Wirral	See Birkenhead.
.	.	.	.	.	.	.	.	Docks Station (for Ship Canal)	Lancs	C.L.C.—L.&Y.—L. N. W.	See Manchester.
.	.	.	.	.	.	.	.	Dock Street (G.W.)	Mon	G.W.—B. & M.—L.&NW	See Newport.
.	.	.	.	.	.	.	.	Dock Street Coal Sidings.....	Lancs	N.U. Jt.(L.&NW.&L.&Y)	Preston, Charles Street.
.	.	.	.	.	.	.	.	Dock Street Junction	Lancs	L. & N. W.—N. U. Jt. ...	Preston.
.	.	.	.	.	.	.	.	Dock Street Siding	Yorks	N. E.	Middlesbro'.
.	.	.	.	.	.	.	.	Doctor Pit	Northumb	N. E.	Same as Bedlington Col.(Bedlington)
G	P	F	L	H	C	3	0	Doddington and Harby	Notts	L. D. & E. C.	Tuxford and Lincoln.
.	.	.	.	.	.	.	.	Doddington Siding	Lincoln ...	L. D. & E. C.	Doddington and Harby.
.	.	.	.	.	.	.	.	Thorney & Wigsley Siding	Notts	L. D. & E. C.	Doddington and Harby.
.	.	.	.	.	.	.	.	Dodd's Kinnerton Incline Sid.	Flint	L. & N. W.	Hope.
.	.	.	.	.	.	.	.	Dodman, A., & Co.'s Sid. (GE)	Norfolk ...	G. E.—G. N.—Mid.	Lynn Docks.
G	P	.	.	.	.	.	.	Dodworth	Yorks	G. C.	Penistone and Barnsley.
.	.	.	.	.	.	.	.	Old Silkstone & Dodworth Colliery	Yorks	G. C.	Dodworth.
G	P	F	L	H	C	1	10	Doe Hill	Derby......	Mid.	Clay Cross and Codnor Park.
.	.	.	.	.	.	.	.	Clay Cross Colliery Co's Nos. 5 and 6 Collieries	Derby......	Mid.	Trent and Chesterfield.
.	.	.	.	.	.	.	.	Morton Col. (Clay & Co.)...	Derby......	Mid.	Near Doe Hill.
.	.	.	.	.	.	.	.	Pilsley Colliery	Derby......	Mid.	Near Doe Hill.
G	P	.	L	H	.	1	5	Dogdyke	Lincoln ...	G. N.	Boston and Lincoln.
.	.	.	.	.	.	.	.	Dog Lane Siding (G. C.)	Cheshire...	G. C.—G. N.—Mid.	Guide Bridge.
.	.	.	.	.	.	.	.	Dogton Colliery	Fife	N. B.	Same as Thornton Col. (Thornton).
G	P	.	L	H	.	.	.	Dolau	Radnor ...	L. & N. W.	Craven Arms and Llandrindod Wells.
.	.	.	.	.	.	.	.	Dolau Junction	Carmarth'	G. W.	Llanelly.
.	.	.	.	.	.	.	.	Dolau Siding (G.W.)...........	Carmarth'	G. W.—L. & N. W.	Llanelly.
.	.	.	.	.	.	.	.	Dolcoath Siding	Cornwall..	G. W.	Camborne.
G	P	F	L	H	C	.	.	Doldowlod	Radnor ...	Cam.	Llanidloes and Builth Wells.
G	P	F	L	H	C	5	0	Dolgelley (G. W.)	Merioneth	{ G. W.	Bala and Dolgelley Junction.
										Cam.	Over G. W. from Dolgelley Junc.
.	.	.	.	.	.	.	.	Dolgelley Junction..............	Merioneth	Cam.—G. W.	Barmouth Jn. Sta. & Dolgelley Sta.
G	P	.	.	.	.	.	.	Dolgoch.........................	Merioneth	Tal-y-llyn .	Brynglas and Abergynolwyn.
G	P	F	L	H	C	3	0	Dollar	Clackman'	N. B.	Tillicoultry and Kinross Junction.
.	.	.	.	.	.	.	.	Blairingone Colliery and Fire-Clay Works	Kinross ...	N. B.	Dollar and Rumbling Bridge.
.	.	.	.	.	.	.	.	Dollarbeg Siding	Clackman'	N. B.	Dollar and Rumbling Bridge.
.	.	.	.	.	.	.	.	Dollarbeg Siding...............	Clackman'	N. B.	Dollar.
G	P	F	L	H	C	4	10	Dolphinton	Peebles ...	{ Cal.	Branch Terminus near Carstairs.
G	P	F	L	H	C	1	10		Peebles ...	N. B.	Leadburn and Dolphinton Junction.
.	.	.	.	.	.	.	.	Dolphinton Junction	Peebles ...	Cal.—N. B.	Carstairs and Broomlee.
G	P	.	.	.	.	.	.	Dolwen	Montgom	Cam.	Llanidloes and Moat Lane Junction.

EXPLANATION—G *Goods Station.*   P *Passenger and Parcel Station.*   P* *Passenger, but not Parcel or Miscellaneous Traffic.*
F *Furniture Vans, Carriages, Portable Engines, and Machines on Wheels.*   L *Live Stock.*
H *Horse Boxes and Prize Cattle Vans.*   C *Carriages by Passenger Train.*

Station Accommodation						Crane Power		Stations, &c.	County.	Company.	Position.
G	P	F	L	H	C	Tons	Cwts				
G	P	.	L	.	.	1	10	Dolwyddelen	Carnarvon	L. & N. W.	Blaenau Festiniog and Llandudno Junction Station.
.	.	.	.	.	.			Penllyn Siding	Carnarvon	L. & N. W.	Dolwyddelen and Pont-y-pant.
.	P	.	.	.	.			Dol-y-gaer	Brecon	B. & M.	Brecon and Dowlais.
G	P	.	.	.	.			Dolyhir	Radnor	G. W.	Kington and Radnor.
.	.	.	.	.	.			Old Radnor Lime and Stone Works	Radnor	G. W.	Dolyhir.
.	.	.	.	.	.			Radnorshire Coal Co.	Radnor	G. W.	Dolyhir.
G	P	.	.	.	.			Dolywern	Denbigh	Glyn Valley	Chirk and Glynceiriog.
G	P	.	.	.	.			Donabate	Dublin	G.N. (I.)	Dublin and Drogheda.
G	P	.	L	H	C	2	0	Donaghadee	Down	B. & C. D.	Branch from Comber.
G	P	F	L	H	C	4	10	Donaghmore	Tyrone	G. N. (I.)	Dungannon and Omagh.
.	.	.	.	.	.			Donaldson & Son's Saw Mill	Fife	N. B.	Same as Wemyss Saw Mill (Leven)
.	.	.	.	.	.			Donaldson's Wood Yard	Fife	N. B.	Tayport.
.	.	.	.	.	.			Donaldson's Wood Yard	L'lithgow	N. B.	Bo'ness.
G	P	F	L	H	C	1	0	Donamon	Roscom'n	M. G W.	Roscommon and Claremorris.
G	P	.	.	.	.			Don Bridge	Jersey	Jersey	St. Helier and Corbiere.
								DONCASTER—			
G	P	F	L	H	C	7	0			G. N.	Retford and York.
.	P	.	.	H	C					G. C.	Over G. N. Line.
G	P	F	L	H	C	7	0			G. E.	Over G. N. from Black Carr Junc.
G	P	F	L	H	C	7	0	(Station, G. N.)	Yorks	L. & Y.	Over G. N. from Askern Junction.
G	.	F	L	.	.	7	0			L. & N. W.	Over G.N. from Bottesford North Jn.
G	P	F	L	H	C	1	10			Mid.	Over G. C. and G. N. Lines.
G	P	F	L	.	.	7	0			N. E.	Over G. N. from Shaftholme Junc.
G	P	F	L	H	C	7	0			W.R.&G.Jt. (GC&GN)	Over G. N. Line from North Junc.
.	.	.	.	.	.			Balby Junction	Yorks	G. C.—G. N.	Conisboro' and Rossington.
.	.	.	.	.	.			Balby Siding	Yorks	G. C.	Doncaster.
.	.	.	.	.	.			Belmont Siding (G.N.)	Yorks	G. N.—G. C.—Mid.	Doncaster and Rossington.
.	.	.	.	.	.			Arnold & Son (G.N.)	Yorks	G. N.—G. C.—Mid.	Belmont Siding.
.	.	.	.	.	.			Smith's Wire Works(GN)	Yorks	G. N.—G. C.—Mid.	Belmont Siding.
.	.	.	.	.	.			Black Carr Junction	Yorks	G. N—G. N. & G. E. Jt.	Doncaster and Finningley.
.	.	.	.	.	.			British Wagon Works(G.C.)	Yorks	G. C.—G. N.	Doncaster.
.	.	.	.	.	.			Burnett's Wgn. Wks. (G.C.)	Yorks	G. C.—G. N.— Mid.	Doncaster.
G	.	F	L	.	.	1	10	Cherry Tree Lane	Yorks	Mid.	G. N. Station and Conisboro'.
.	.	.	.	.	.			Decoy Exchange Sidings (G. N.)	Yorks	G. N.-G. E.—L.& N.W.	Doncaster Station & Black Carr Junc.
.	.	.	.	.	.			Doncaster Co-operative Society's Coal Depôt	Yorks	Mid.	Doncaster.
.	.	.	.	.	.			Doncaster Co-operative Society's Siding	Yorks	G. C.	Doncaster.
.	.	.	.	.	.			Farmers Co.'s Siding	Yorks	G. C.	Doncaster.
.	.	.	.	.	.			Great Northern Co.'s Loco-motive, Carriage, Wagon and Stores Department Sidings (G. N.)	Yorks	G. N.— G. C.	Doncaster.
.	.	.	.	.	.			Lincoln Wagon & Engine Co.'s Siding (G. C.)	Yorks	G. C.—G. N.—Mid.	Doncaster.
G	.	.	.	.	.	5	0	Marsh Gate	Yorks	G. C.	Thorne and G. N. Station.
.	.	.	.	.	.			Marsh Gate North Junction	Yorks	G. C.—G. N.	Thorne and G. N. Station.
.	.	.	.	.	.			Marsh Gate North Junction	Yorks	G. N.—W. R. & G. Jt.	G. N. Station and Carcroft.
.	.	.	.	.	.			St. James' South Junction	Yorks	G. C.—G. N.	Conisborough and G. N. Station.
.	.	.	.	.	.			South Yorkshire Coal Co.'s Sid. (Ellis', E., Col.)(G.C.)	Yorks	G. C.—Mid.	Near Doncaster Station.
.	.	.	.	.	.			Stevens' Wagon Wks.(G.C.)	Yorks	G. C.—G. N.	Doncaster.
G	P	F	L	H	C	3	0	Donegal	Donegal	Donegal	Stranorlar and Killybegs.
.	.	.	.	.	.			Donegal Quay	Antrim	G. N. (I.)	See Belfast.
G	P	F	L	H	C			Donemana	Tyrone	Donegal	Londonderry and Strabane.
.	.	.	.	.	.			Doneraile	Cork	G. S. & W.	See Buttevant and Doneraile.
.	.	.	.	.	.			Donibristle Colliery	Fife	N. B.	Cowdenbeath, Old.
G	P	F	L	H	C			Donington-on-Bain	Lincoln	G. N.	Louth and Lincoln.
.	.	.	.	.	.			Donington Pipe and Brick Siding (Mid.)	Derby	Mid.—L. & N. W.	Woodville.
G	P	F	L	H	C	1	10	Donington Road	Lincoln	G. N. & G. E. Jt.	Sleaford and Spalding.
.	.	.	.	.	.			Donington Sanitary Pipe and Fire-Brick Co.'s Sid. (Mid.)	Derby	Mid.—L. & N. W.	Moira.
G	P	.	.	.	.			Donisthorpe	Leicester	A&NJt.(L & N W & Mid.)	Shackerstone and Overseal.
.	.	.	.	.	.			Checkland, Son, & Williams' Donisthorpe Colliery	Leicester	A&NJt.(L & N W & Mid.)	Donisthorpe and Overseal.
.	.	.	.	.	.			Donkin & Co.'s Siding	Northumb	N. E.	Walker Gate.
.	.	.	.	.	.			Donnington	Berks	L'bourn Valley	See Speen (for Donnington).
G	P	F	L	H	.	5	0	Donnington	Salop	L. & N. W.	Shrewsbury and Stafford.

EXPLANATION—G *Goods Station.*   P *Passenger and Parcel Station.*   P* *Passenger, but not Parcel or Miscellaneous Traffic.*
F *Furniture Vans, Carriages, Portable Engines, and Machines on Wheels.*   L *Live Stock.*
H *Horse Boxes and Prize Cattle Vans.*   C *Carriages by Passenger Train.*

STATION ACCOMMODATION.						CRANE POWER.	STATIONS, &c.	COUNTY.	COMPANY.	POSITION.
						Tons Cwts.	Donnington—continued.			
							Lilleshall Coal & Iron Co.'s Iron Works and Colliery	Salop	L. & N. W.	Donnington and Trench Crossing.
G	P	.	L	.	.	. .	Walker's Siding...............	Salop	L. & N. W.	Donnington and Trench Crossing.
.	P	.	.	.	.	. .	Donoughmore	Cork	C. & Muskerry	Terminus.
.	.	.	.	.	.	. .	Don's Siding (Cal.)	Forfar	Cal.—N.B.	Forfar.
.	P	.	.	.	.	. .	Don Street	Aberdeen	G. N. of S.	See Aberdeen.
G	P	F	L	.	.	. .	Dooks	Kerry	G. S. & W.	Killorglin and Glenbeigh.
G	P	F	L	.	.	. .	Doonbeg	Clare	West Clare	Miltown Malbay and Kilrush.
.	P	.	.	.	.	. .	Dooniskey	Cork	C. & Macroom	Kilcrea and Macroom.
G	P	F	L	H	C	10 0 }	Dooran Road	Donegal ..	Donegal	Donegal and Killybegs.
G	P	F	L	H	C	10 0 }	Dorchester	Dorset	{ G. W.	Weymouth and Maiden Newton.
								Dorset	{ L. & S. W.	Wareham and Weymouth.
.	.	.	.	.	.	. .	Chalk Siding	Dorset	L. & S. W.	Dorchester.
.	.	.	.	.	.	. .	Edison and De Matto's Sid.	Dorset	L. & S. W.	Dorchester.
.	.	.	.	.	.	. .	Eldridge, Pope, & Co.'s Brewery	Dorset	L. & S. W.	Dorchester.
.	.	.	.	.	.	. .	Hayward's Siding	Dorset	L. & S. W.	Dorchester.
.	P	.	.	.	.	. .	Dorchester Junction	Dorset	G. W.—L. & S. W.	Weymouth and Dorchester.
G	P	F	L	H	C	5 0 }	Dore and Totley...............	Derby	Mid.	Dronfield and Sheffield.
G	P	F	L	H	C	8 0 }	Dorking	Surrey	{ L. B. & S. C.	Holmwood and Leatherhead.
									{ S. E. & C.	Redhill and Guildford.
.	.	.	.	.	.	. .	Dorking Lime Co.'s Siding ...	Surrey	S. E. & C.	Betchworth.
.	P	.	.	.	.	. .	Dormans	Sussex	L. B. & S. C.	East Grinstead and Oxted.
G	P	F	L	H	C	1 10	Dornoch	Sutherl'nd	High. (Dornoch)............	Branch from The Mound.
G	P	F	L	H	C	1 10	Dornock	Dumfries..	G. & S. W.	Annan and Gretna.
.	.	.	.	.	.	. .	Dorothea Pit (Newbottle) ...	Durham ...	N. E.	{ Fencehouses. { Penshaw.
.	.	.	.	.	.	. .	Dorothea Slate Co.'s Pen-y-Bryn Siding...............	Carnarvon	L. & N. W.	Nantlle.
.	.	.	.	.	.	. .	Dorrator Iron Foundry (N.B)	Stirling ...	N. B.—Cal.	Falkirk, Grahamston.
G	P	F	L	H	C	12 0	Dorridge	Warwick..	G. W.	See Knowle and Dorridge.
.	.	.	.	.	.	. .	Dorrington	Salop	S & H Jt (GW & L & NW)	Craven Arms and Shrewsbury.
G	P	F	L	H	C	. .	Dorsley Bank Siding............	Yorks	N. E.	{ Grosmont. { Sleights.
.	.	.	.	.	.	. .	Dorstone	Hereford ..	G. W.	Pontrilas and Hay.
G	P	.	L	.	.	. .	Dosthill Brick Sid. (T. Stone)	Warwick..	Mid.	Wilnecote.
.	.	.	.	.	.	. .	Doublebois	Cornwall...	G. W.	Plymouth and Truro.
.	.	.	.	.	.	. .	Dougall's Brick Works........	Stirling ...	N. B.	Same as Bonnyside Brick Works (Bonnybridge).
.	.	.	.	.	.	. .	Dougall's Brick Works........	L'lithgow..	N. B.	Same as Winchburgh Brick Works.
G	P	F*	L	.	.	10 0	Dougherty's Siding	Yorks	Axholme Jt. (L&Y & NE)	Reedness Junction.
G	P	F	L	H	C	2 0	Douglas...............	I. of Man..	I. of Man	Terminus.
G	.	.	.	.	.	. .	Douglas...............	Lanark	Cal.	Lanark and Muirkirk.
.	.	.	.	.	.	. .	Lintfieldbank	Lanark	Cal.	Lesmahagow and Inches.
.	.	.	.	.	.	. .	Poneil Junction Siding......	Lanark	Cal.	Douglas and Douglas (West).
G	P	.	L	H	.	1 10	Douglas (West)	Lanark	Cal.	Douglas and Muirkirk.
.	.	.	.	.	.	. .	Douglas Bank Col. (L. & Y.)	Lancs	L. & Y.—L. & N. W.	See Rose Bridge and Douglas Bank Colliery Co. (Gathurst).
.	.	.	.	.	.	. .	Douglas Bros.' Siding	Durham ...	N. E.	Same as Globe Iron Wks (Blaydon).
.	.	.	.	.	.	. .	Douglas Colliery...............	Lanark ...	Cal.	Ponfeigh.
.	.	.	.	.	.	. .	Douglas Junctions	Lanark ...	Cal.	Lanark.
.	.	.	.	.	.	. .	Douglas Park Colliery and Quarry	Lanark ...	Cal.	Uddingston.
.	.	.	.	.	.	. .	Douglas Pits Nos. 1, 2, and 3	Renfrew...	Cal.	Paisley, St. James.
.	.	.	.	.	.	. .	Douglas Siding	Cheshire...	L. & N. W.	Hartford.
.	.	.	.	.	.	. .	Beckett & Co.	Cheshire...	L. & N. W.	Douglas Siding.
.	.	.	.	.	.	. .	Evans, R., & Co.	Cheshire...	L. & N. W.	Douglas Siding.
.	.	.	.	.	.	. .	Douglas Support Sidings.....	Lanark ...	N. B.	Coatbridge, Whifflet.
.	.	.	.	.	.	. .	Doulting Siding	Somerset..	G. W.	Cranmore.
.	.	.	.	.	.	. .	Doulton and Co.'s Siding......	Lancs	L. & N. W.	St. Helens.
G	P	F	L	H	C	4 0	Doune	Perth	Cal.	Dunblane and Callander.
G	P	.	.	.	.	. .	Doura Fire-Clay Works	Ayr	G. & S. W.	Kilwinning.
G	P	.	.	.	.	. .	Dousland	Devon	G. W.	Yelverton Junction and Princetown.
.	.	.	.	.	.	. .	Eggworthy Siding............	Devon	G. W.	Dousland and Princetown.
.	P	.	.	.	.	. .	Dovecliffe...............	Yorks	G. C.	Sheffield and Barnsley.
.	.	.	.	.	.	. .	Dovecotland	Perth	Cal.	Same as Perth, North.
G	P	.	L	H	.	. .	Dove Holes	Derby	L. & N. W.	Buxton and Stockport.
.	.	.	.	.	.	. .	Bibbington's Lime Works..	Derby	L. & N. W.	Dove Holes and Buxton.
.	.	.	.	.	.	. .	Dove Holes Brick Co.'s Sid.	Derby	L. & N. W.	Dove Holes and Chapel-en-le-Frith.
.	.	.	.	.	.	. .	Heathcott & Son's Siding ..	Derby	L. & N. W.	Dove Holes and Chapel-en-le-Frith.
.	.	.	.	.	.	. .	Dove Junction	Staffs	G. N.—N. S.	Egginton Junction and Burton.

EXPLANATION—G Goods Station.   P Passenger and Parcel Station.   P* Passenger, but not Parcel or Miscellaneous Traffic.
F Furniture Vans, Carriages, Portable Engines, and Machines on Wheels.   F* Furniture Vans excepted.   L Live Stock.
H Horse Boxes and Prize Cattle Vans.   C Carriages by Passenger Train.

STATION ACCOMMODATION.						CRANE POWER.		STATIONS, &c.	COUNTY.	COMPANY.	POSITION.
						Tons	Cwts				
								DOVER—			
								Contractors' Siding	Kent	S. E. & C.	Dover Town.
	P					4	0	Harbour	Kent	S. E. & C.	Dover Priory and Dover Pier.
								Junction	Kent	S. E. & C.	Dover Harbour and Folkestone.
								Kent Colliery Works.........	Kent	S. E. & C.	Dover Town and Folkestone Jn. Sta.
	P*							Pier	Kent	S. E. & C.	Extension from Dover.
G	P	F	L	H	C	10	0	Priory	Kent	S. E. & C.	Canterbury and Dover Harbour.
G	P	F	L	H	C	10	0	Town	Kent	S. E. & C.	Folkestone and Dover Pier.
								War Office Siding	Kent	S. E. & C.	Dover Priory.
								Dovercourt	Essex	G. E.	See Harwich.
								Dovey Junction	Cardigan..	Cam.	Machynlleth and Aberystwyth.
								Dowdeswell	Glo'ster ..	M. & S. W. Jn.	See Andoversford and Dowdeswell.
								DOWLAIS—			
G	P	F	L			2	5	(Station, B. & M.)	Glamorg'n	B. & M.	Terminus.
G		F	L			2	5		Glamorg'n	L. & N. W.	Over B. & M. from Ivor Junction.
G	P	F	L	H	C	2	10	(Station, Cae Harris).........	Glamorg'n	T. B. Jt. (G. W. & Rhy.)	Terminus.
								Furnace Tops	Glamorg'n	T. B. Jt. (G. W. & Rhy.)	Branch—Dowlais & Cwm Bargoed.
								Guest, Keen & Nettlefold—			
								Iron & Steel Works	Glamorg'n	B. & M.—T. B. Jt.	Dowlais.
								Ivor Siding (B. & M.)...	Glamorg'n	B. & M.—L. & N. W. ...	Dowlais.
								Pantyscallog Siding	Glamorg'n	B. & M.	Pant and Dowlais.
								Penywern Siding	Glamorg'n	L. & N. W.	Dowlais, High Street.
								Tunnel Pit (B. & M.)......	Glamorg'n	B. & M.—L & N. W.	Dowlais.
								Tylerybont Lime Sids....	Glamorg'n	B. & M.	Pant and Dol-y-gaer.
	P		L	H	C			High Street	Glamorg'n	L. & N. W.	Abergavenny and Merthyr.
								Ivor Junction	Glamorg'n	B. & M.—L. & N. W.	Dowlais and Abergavenny.
								Junction	Glamorg'n	T. B. Jt. (G. W. & Rhy.)	Dowlais and Cwm Bargoed.
								Dowlais Cardiff Colliery	Glamorg'n	T. V.	See Guest, Keen & Nettlefold (Abercynon).
								Dowlais Incline	Glamorg'n	G. W.—T. V.	See Guest, Keen & Nettlefold (Merthyr).
								Dowlais Iron & Steel Works (East Moors)	Glamorg'n	GW—LNW—Rhy.—TV	Cardiff.
								Dowlais Junction	Glamorg'n	T. V.	Merthyr.
G	P							Dowlais Top	Glamorg'n	B. & M.	Fochriw and Pant.
								Rhymney Iron Co.'s Limestone Siding	Glamorg'n	B. & M.	Dowlais Top and Fochriw.
								Dowlais Top Junction	Glamorg'n	B. & M.—L. & N. W.	Dowlais Top and Abergavenny.
								Dowlais Works	Glamorg'n	T. V.	See GuestKeen&Nettlefold(Merthyr)
								Dowlow Siding	Derby	L. & N. W.	Hindlow.
G	P	F	L	H	C	1	0	Downham....................	Norfolk ...	G. E.	Ely and Lynn.
								Bennett, J. L., & Son's Sid.	Norfolk ...	G. E.	Downham.
								Boyce & Son's Siding	Norfolk ...	G. E.	Downham.
								Collins, J. W., Siding	Norfolk ...	G. E.	Downham.
								Cranfield Bros.' Siding	Norfolk ...	G. E.	Downham.
								Haylett, B. F., Siding	Norfolk ...	G. E.	Downham.
								Scarnell, Wood & Co.'s Sid.	Norfolk ...	G. E.	Downham.
								Wenn, Mrs. E., Siding......	Norfolk ...	G. E.	Downham.
G	P		L					Downhill	Derry	N. C. Com. (Mid.)	Londonderry and Coleraine.
								Downing & Co.'s Siding	Glo'ster ...	Mid.	Gloucester Docks.
								Downing's, G. & W. E., Sid.	Glo'ster ...	Mid.	Tewkesbury.
								Down Mill Siding	Berks	L. & S.W.	Bracknell.
G	P		L	H	C	5	0	Downpatrick	Down	B. & C. D.	Belfast and Newcastle.
								Downside Siding	Somerset..	S.&D.Jt. (L.&S.W.&Mid)	Binegar and Shepton Mallet.
G	P	F	L	H	C			Downton	Wilts	L. & S.W.	Salisbury and Wimborne.
								Dowrie Siding....................	Forfar	D. & A. Jt. (Cal. & N. B.)	See Elliot Junction Station.
								Dowson's Slate Yard............	Durham ...	N. E.	Millfield.
								Doxey Road....................	Staffs	G. N.	See Stafford Common.
								"D" Pit Brick & Tile Works	Durham ...	N. E.	{ Fencehouses. / Penshaw.
								Drabble & Co.'sBlackRockSid.	Derby	L. & N. W.	Steeplehouse.
								Dragon Junction	Yorks	N. E.	Starbeck and Harrogate.
								Drake & Mount's Siding	Berks	L. & S.W.	Ascot.
								Drake, G. J., Siding............	Middlesex	G. E.	Bush Hill Park.
G	P	F	L	H	C	3	0	Draperstown	Derry	N. C. Com. (Mid.)	Branch from Magherafelt.
								Draughton Crossing Siding...	N'hamptn	L. & N. W.	Lamport.
								Loder's	N'hamptn	L. & N. W.	Draughton Crossing Siding.
								Stanton Iron Works	N'hamptn	L. & N. W.	Draughton Crossing Siding.
G	P	F	L	H	C	2	0	Drax	Yorks	H. & B.	Cudworth and Howden.
G	P	F	L	H	C			Draycott	Derby	Mid.	Derby and Trent.
G	P	F		H	C	5	0	Draycott	Somerset..	G. W.	Wells and Cheddar.
								Draycott Colliery	Staffs	N. S. (Cheadle)	Cheadle.

EXPLANATION—G *Goods Station.*   P *Passenger and Parcel Station.*   P* *Passenger, but not Parcel or Miscellaneous Traffic.*
F *Furniture Vans, Carriages, Portable Engines, and Machines on Wheels.*   L *Live Stock.*
H *Horse Boxes and Prize Cattle Vans.*   C *Carriages by Passenger Train.*

G	P	F	L	H	C	Tons	Cwts	STATIONS, &c.	COUNTY.	COMPANY.	POSITION.
G	P	F	L	H	C			Drayton	Sussex	L. B. & S. C.	Chichester and Barnham Junction.
G	P	F	L	H	C	1	0	Drayton (for Cossey)	Norfolk	Mid. & G. N. Jt.	Norwich (City) & Melton Constable
G								Drayton Crossing	N'hamptn	L. & N. W.	Market Harboro' and Peterboro'.
.	.	.	.	.	.			Drayton Junction	N'hamptn	G N&L & N W Jt—L&NW	Medbourne and Rockingham.
.	.	.	.	.	.			Drayton Park	Middlesex	G. N. & C.	See London.
.	.	.	.	.	.			Dreadnought	Perth	Cal.	See Callander.
G	P	.	L	H	.	3	0	Dreghorn	Ayr	G. & S. W.	Irvine and Crosshouse.
.	.	.	.	.	.			Bourtreehill Fire Clay Wks.	Ayr	G. & S. W.	Dreghorn and Crosshouse.
.	.	.	.	.	.			Bourtreehill, Nos. 6, 7, & 8 (Capringstone Collieries)	Ayr	G. & S. W.	Dreghorn and Crosshouse.
.	.	.	.	.	.			Broomlands, No. 8	Ayr	G. & S. W.	Dreghorn and Crosshouse.
.	.	.	.	.	.			Corsehill, Nos. 10 & 11	Ayr	G. & S. W.	Dreghorn and Irvine.
.	.	.	.	.	.			Corsehill Tile Works	Ayr	G. & S. W.	Dreghorn and Crosshouse.
.	.	.	.	.	.			Greenwood Brick Works	Ayr	G. & S. W.	Dreghorn and Irvine.
.	.	.	.	.	.			Greenwood Collieries	Ayr	G. & S. W.	Dreghorn and Irvine.
.	.	.	.	.	.			Perceton Fire-Clay Works.	Ayr	G. & S. W.	Perceton Branch.
.	.	.	.	.	.			Perceton Pits	Ayr	G. & S. W.	Perceton Branch.
.	.	.	.	.	.			Springhill Colliery (Cauldhame Colliery)	Ayr	G. & S. W.	Dreghorn and Crosshouse.
.	.	.	.	.	.			Warrix Brick Works	Ayr	G. & S. W.	Dreghorn and Irvine.
.	.	.	.	.	.			Warrix Colliery	Ayr	G. & S. W.	Dreghorn and Irvine.
G	P	F	L	H	C	1	5	Drem	Hadding'n	N. B.	Edinburgh and Dunbar.
G	.	.	.	.	.			Ballencrieff Siding	Hadding'n	N. B.	Drem and Longniddry.
.	.	.	.	.	.			Drem Junction	Hadding'n	N. B.	Drem and East Fortune.
.	.	.	.	.	.			Drews Iron Yard	Mon	G. W.	Lliswerry.
G	P	F	L	H	C	5	0	Driffield	Yorks	N. E.	Beverley and Bridlington.
.	.	.	.	.	.			Barker's, J. C., Grain, Cake and Manure Warehouse.	Yorks	N. E.	Driffield.
.	.	.	.	.	.			Driffield Oil Cake Mill and Coal Siding	Yorks	N. E.	Driffield.
.	.	.	.	.	.			Kelleythorpe (Little Driffield) Siding	Yorks	N. E.	Driffield.
G	P	F	L	H	C	3	0	Drigg	Cumb'land	Furness	Ravenglass and Whitehaven.
G	P	.	.	.	.	1	10	Drighlington and Adwalton	Yorks	G. N.	Morley and Bradford.
.	.	.	.	.	.			Howden Clough Colliery	Yorks	G. N.	Howden Clough and Drighlington.
G	P	.	L	H	.			Drimoleague	Cork	C. B. & S. C.	Dunmanway and Skibbereen.
G	.	.	.	.	.	2	0	Drinnick Mill	Cornwall	G. W.	Burngullow and St. Dennis Junc.
.	.	.	.	.	.			Carpella Siding	Cornwall	G. W.	Drinnick Mill and Burngullow Jn.
.	.	.	.	.	.			Central Treviscoe Siding	Cornwall	G. W.	Drinnick Mill and St. Dennis Junc.
.	.	.	.	.	.			Goonvean Siding	Cornwall	G. W.	Drinnick Mill and St. Dennis Junc.
.	.	.	.	.	.			Great Treviscoe Siding	Cornwall	G. W.	Drinnick Mill and St. Dennis Junc.
.	.	.	.	.	.	1	10	High Street Siding	Cornwall	G. W.	Drinnick Mill and Burngullow Junc.
.	.	.	.	.	.			Little Treviscoe Siding	Cornwall	G. W.	Drinnick Mill and St. Dennis Junc.
.	.	.	.	.	.			Luke's New Siding	Cornwall	G. W.	Drinnick Mill and St. Dennis Junc.
.	.	.	.	.	.			Luke's Old Siding	Cornwall	G. W.	Drinnick Mill and St. Dennis Junc.
.	.	.	.	.	.			Parkandillack Siding	Cornwall	G. W.	Drinnick Mill and St. Dennis Junc.
.	.	.	.	.	.			Slip Siding	Cornwall	G. W.	Drinnick Mill and St. Dennis Junc.
.	.	.	.	.	.			Trethosa Siding	Cornwall	G. W.	Drinnick Mill and St. Dennis Junc.
.	.	.	.	.	.			Varcoes Siding	Cornwall	G. W.	Drinnick Mill and St. Dennis Junc.
.	.	.	.	.	.			West of England Clay Co.'s Sidings	Cornwall	G. W.	Drinnick Mill.
.	.	.	.	.	.			Whitegate Siding	Cornwall	G. W.	Drinnick Mill and St. Dennis Junc.
G	P	.	.	.	.			Dripsey	Cork	C. & Muskerry	Coachford Junction and Coachford.
G	P	F	L	H	C	5	0	Drogheda	Louth	G. N. (I.)	Dublin and Dundalk.
G	P	F	L	H	C	5	0	Droitwich (G.W.)	Worcester	{ G.W. / Mid.	Worcester and Wolverhampton. / Over G. W. Line.
.	P	.	.	H	C						
.	.	.	.	.	.			Salt Union, Ltd.— Clay & Newman's Sid (GW)	Worcester	G. W.—Mid.	Droitwich and Stoke Prior.
.	.	.	.	.	.			Works (G.W.)	Worcester	G. W.—Mid.	Droitwich.
G	.	.	L	.	.	1	10	Droitwich Road	Worcester	Mid.	Bromsgrove and Spetchley.
G	P	.	L	.	.			Dromahair	Sligo	S. L. & N. C.	Manorhamilton and Collooney.
.	P	.	.	.	.			Dromin Junction Station	Louth	G. N. (I.)	Drogheda and Dundalk.
.	P	.	.	.	.			Dromkeen	Limerick	G. S. & W.	Limerick and Tipperary.
G	P	.	L	.	.			Dromod	Leitrim	{ C. & L. / M. G. W.	Adjoining Dromod Sta. (M.G.W.) / Longford and Sligo.
G	P	F	L	H	C	5	0				
G	P	.	.	.	.	2	0	Dromore	Down	G. N. (I.)	Belfast and Banbridge.
G	P	F	L	H	C	1	0	Dromore	Kirkcud	P.P.& W. Jt.(Cal., G. & S. W., L. & N. W. & Mid.)	Newton Stewart and Castle Douglas.
G	P	F	L	.	.	1	10	Dromore Road	Tyrone	G. N. (I.)	Enniskillen and Omagh.
G	P	.	L	.	.	1	10	Dronfield	Derby	Mid.	Sheffield and Chesterfield.
.	.	.	.	.	.			Osborne & Co.'s Siding	Derby	Mid.	Near Dronfield Station.
.	.	.	.	.	.			Slag Reduction Co.'s Siding	Derby	Mid.	Dronfield.

EXPLANATION—G Goods Station.   P Passenger and Parcel Station.   P* Passenger, but not Parcel or Miscellaneous Traffic.
F Furniture Vans, Carriages, Portable Engines, and Machines on Wheels.   L Live Stock.
H Horse Boxes and Prize Cattle Vans.   C Carriages by Passenger Train.

STATION ACCOMMODATION.						CRANE POWER.	STATIONS, &c.	COUNTY.	COMPANY.	POSITION.
G	P	F	L	H	C	Tons 1 Cwts. 10	Drongan	Ayr	G. & S.W.	Annbank and Ochiltree.
.	.	.	.	.	.	. .	Drumsmuddin Pit	Ayr	G. & S.W.	Drongan and Ochiltree.
.	.	.	.	.	.	. .	Polquhairn Colliery	Ayr	G. & S.W.	Rankinston and Ochiltree.
.	.	.	.	.	.	. .	Shieldmains Colliery	Ayr	G. & S.W.	Annbank and Drongan.
.	.	.	.	.	.	. .	Trabboch Colliery	Ayr	G. & S.W.	Annbank and Drongan.
G	P	.	L	H	.	1 10	Dronley	Forfar	Cal.	Dundee and Newtyle.
G	.	F	.	.	C	. .	Drope Junction	Glamorg'n	Barry	Cadoxton and Peterston.
G	P	F	L	H	C	5 0	Drope Siding	Glamorg'n	Barry	Drope Junction and Peterston.
G	P	F	L	H	C	5 0	Droxford (for Hambledon)	Hants	L. & S.W.	Alton and Fareham.
G	.	.	.	.	.	6 0	Droylsden	Lancs	G. C.	See Fairfield (for Droylsden).
.	.	.	.	.	.				L. & Y.	Manchester and Ashton.
.	P	.	.	.	.		Droylsden	Lancs	L. & Y. & L.&N.W. Jt.	Near Droylsden Junction.
G	.	.	L	.	.				L. & N. W.	Branch from Denton.
.	.	.	.	.	.	. .	Droylsden Junction	Lancs	L. & Y.— L. & N.W.	Clayton Bridge and Stockport.
G	P	F	L	H	.	. .	Drum	Aberdeen	G. N. of S.	Aberdeen and Banchory.
.	.	.	.	.	.	. .	Drumbathie Brick Works	Lanark	N. B.	Rawyards.
.	.	.	.	.	.	. .	Drumbowie Junction	Lanark	Cal.	Cleland and Newmains.
.	.	.	.	.	.	. .	Drumbowie Siding	Lanark	N. B.	Greengairs.
.	.	.	.	.	.	. .	Drumbowie Weighs	Lanark	Cal.	Omoa.
G	P	.	L	H	.	. .	Drumburgh	Cumb'land	N. B.	Carlisle, Canal and Silloth.
.	.	.	.	.	.	. .	Drumburgh Junction	Cumb'land	N. B.	Burgh and Kirkbride.
.	.	.	.	.	.	. .	Drumcaldie Distillery	Fife	N. B.	Cameron Bridge.
.	.	.	.	.	.	. .	Drumcavil Sand Siding	Lanark	N. B.	Bridgend.
G	P	.	L	.	.	2 0	Drumchapel	Dumbartn	N. B.	Maryhill and Kilbowie.
.	.	.	.	.	.	. .	Drumchapel Brick Works (Gilmour's Brick Works)	Dumbartn	N. B.	Drumchapel and Maryhill.
G	.	.	.	.	.	. .	Garscadden Siding	Dumbartn	N. B.	Drumchapel and Kilbowie.
.	.	.	.	.	.	. .	Drumclair Colliery	Stirling	N. B.	Slamannan.
.	.	.	.	.	.	. .	Drumcondra	Dublin	G. S. & W.	See Dublin.
.	.	.	.	.	.	. .	Drumdow Colliery	Ayr	G. & S.W.	Same as Sundrum Nos. 3 and 4 (Annbank).
G	P	.	L	.	.	. .	Drumfries	Donegal	L. & L. S.	Buncrana and Carndonagh.
.	.	.	.	.	.	. .	Drumgley Siding	Forfar	Cal.	See Glamis.
.	.	.	.	.	.	. .	Drumgrange Pit	Ayr	G. & S.W.	Waterside.
.	.	.	.	.	.	. .	Drumgray Colliery	Lanark	N. B.	Rawyards.
.	P	.	.	.	.	. .	Drumhawnagh	Cavan	M. G. W.	Ballywillan and Cavan.
.	.	.	.	.	.	. .	Drumkilbo Siding	Forfar	Cal.	See Alyth Junction Station.
.	.	.	.	.	.	. .	Drumley Nos. 1 & 2	Ayr	G. & S.W.	Annbank.
G	P	F	L	H	C	1 10	Drumlithie	Kinc'rdine	Cal.	Forfar and Stonehaven.
G	P	F	L	H	C	1 5	Drummuir	Banff	G. N. of S.	Keith and Craigellachie.
.	.	.	.	.	.	. .	Drumoyne Saw Mills	Renfrew	G & P Jt (Cal & G & S W)	Cardonald.
.	.	.	.	.	.	. .	Drumoyne Sid. (Moore's Wks.)	Renfrew	G & P Jt (Cal & G & S W)	Cardonald.
.	.	.	.	.	.	. .	Drumpark Brick Works	Lanark	Cal.	Baillieston.
.	.	.	.	.	.	. .	Drumpark Colliery	Lanark	Cal.	Baillieston.
.	.	.	.	.	.	. .	Drumpellier Colliery No. 4	Lanark	Cal.	Langloan.
.	.	.	.	.	.	. .	Drumpellier Colliery Sidings	Lanark	N. B.	Coatbridge, Sheepford.
.	.	.	.	.	.	. .	Drumpellier Iron & Steel Wks.	Lanark	Cal. / N. B.	Langloan. / Coatbridge, Sheepford.
.	.	.	.	.	.	. .	Drumpellier No. 3 Colliery	Lanark	N. B.	Coatbridge, Sunnyside.
.	.	.	.	.	.	. .	Drumpellier No. 11 Colliery	Lanark	N. B.	Bargeddie.
.	.	.	.	.	.	. .	Drumpellier Railway & Junc.	Lanark	Cal.	Langloan and Baillieston.
.	.	.	.	.	.	. .	Drumquhurn Siding	Stirling	N. B.	Balfron.
G	P	F	L	H	C	. .	Drumree	Meath	M. G. W.	Dublin and Navan.
G	P	.	L	.	.	. .	Drumshambo	Leitrim	C. & L.	Ballinamore and Arigna.
.	.	.	.	.	.	. .	Drumshangie Long Lye	Lanark	N. B.	Same as Drumshangie Sidings (Rawyards).
.	.	.	.	.	.	. .	Drumshangie Sidings (Drumshangie Long Lye)	Lanark	N. B.	See Rawyards.
G	P	.	L	H	.	3 0	Drumshoreland	L'lithgow	N. B.	Ratho and Bathgate, Upper.
.	.	.	.	.	.	. .	Cawburn Siding	L'lithgow	N. B.	Drumshoreland and Uphall.
.	.	.	.	.	.	. .	Drumshoreland Junction	L'lithgow	N. B.	Drumshoreland and Uphall.
.	.	.	.	.	.	. .	Drumsmuddin Pit	Ayr	G. & S.W.	Drongan.
G	P	F	L	H	C	1 5	Drumsna	Leitrim	M. G. W.	Longford and Sligo.
G	P	.	L	H	.	3 0	Drumsurn	Derry	N. C. Com. (Mid.)	Limavady and Dungiven.
.	.	.	.	.	.	. .	Drury Lowe's Siding	Derby	Mid.	Denby.
G	P	.	L	H	.	. .	Drwsynant	Merioneth	G. W.	Bala and Dolgelley.
G	P	.	L	H	.	. .	Drybridge	Ayr	G. & S.W.	Kilmarnock and Troon.
.	.	.	.	.	.	. .	Parkthorn Siding	Ayr	G. & S.W.	Drybridge and Barassie.
.	.	.	.	.	.	. .	Shewalton Moss Siding	Ayr	G. & S.W.	Drybridge and Barassie.
.	P	.	.	.	.	. .	Drybridge	Banff	High.	Keith and Buckie.
G	P	.	.	.	.	. .	Drybrook Road	Glo'ster	S. & Wye Jt. (G. W. & Mid)	Lydbrook Junction and Cinderford.
.	.	.	.	.	.	. .	Crump Meadow Sidings	Glo'ster	S. & Wye Jt. (G. W. & Mid)	Loop Line—Drybrook Rd. & Tufts Jn.

STATION ACCOMMODATION.						CRANE POWER.		STATIONS, &c.	COUNTY.	COMPANY.	POSITION.
						Tons	Cwts	Drybrook Road—*continued.*			
.	.	.	.	.	.	.	.	Foxes Bridge Sidings	Glo'ster ...	S.&Wye Jt. (G. W. & Mid)	Loop Line—Drybrook Rd.&Tufts Jn.
.	.	.	.	.	.	.	.	Lightmoor Siding	Glo'ster ...	S.&Wye Jt. (G. W. & Mid)	Loop Line—Drybrook Rd.&Tufts Jn.
.	.	.	.	.	.	.	.	Trafalgar Siding	Glo'ster ...	S.&Wye Jt. (G. W. & Mid)	Drybrook Road and Serridge Junc.
.	.	.	.	.	.	.	.	Drybrough's Brewery	Edinboro'	N. B.	Duddingston and Craigmillar.
.	.	.	.	.	.	.	.	Dryclough Junction	Yorks	L. & Y.	Halifax and Copley.
.	.	.	.	.	.	.	.	Drym Colliery	Brecon	N. & Brecon	Onllwyn.
G	P	F	L	H	C	3	0	Drymen	Dumbartn	N. B.	Balloch and Stirling.
.	.	.	.	.	.	.	.	Drypool........................	Yorks	{ H. & B.	Same as Hull, Alexandra Dock.
										{ N. E.	See Hull.
G	P*	.	.	.	.	.	.	Drysllwyn	Carmarth'	L. & N. W.	Carmarthen and Llandilo.
.	.	.	.	.	.	.	.	Dubbs Junction	Ayr	G. & S. W.	Kilwinning and Stevenston.
								DUBLIN—			
G	P	F	L	H	C	3	0	Amiens Street....................	Dublin ...	G. N. (I.)	Terminus.
.	P	.	.	.	.	.	.	Amiens Street Junction ...	Dublin ...	D. W. & W.—G. S. & W.	Westland Row and Drumcondra.
.	P	.	.	.	.	.	.	Amiens Street Junction Sta.	Dublin ...	D. W. & W.	Newcomen Bge. Jn.&Westland Row.
.	P	F	L	H	C	0	15	Broadstone	Dublin ...	M. G. W.	Terminus.
.	.	.	L	H	.	.	.	Cabra Siding	Dublin ...	G. S. & W.	Kingsbridge and Glasnevin Junc.
.	.	.	.	.	.	.	.	Church Road Junctions......	Dublin ...	G N(I.)—GS&W—L&N W	Clontarf and North Wall.
.	.	.	.	.	.	.	.	Clonliffe Mills Siding	Dublin ...	M. G. W.	Liffey Jn. Station and North Wall.
.	P	.	.	.	.	.	.	Drumcondra....................	Dublin ...	G. S. & W.	Kingsbridge and North Wall.
.	.	.	.	.	.	.	.	Dublin Warehouse Co.'s Sid.	Dublin ...	G. S. & W.	Branch—Church Road Junction and North Wall.
.	.	.	.	.	.	.	.	East Wall Siding	Dublin ...	G. S. & W.	Near North Wall.
.	.	.	.	.	.	.	.	Fitzsimon's Siding............	Dublin ...	G. S. & W.	Near North Wall.
.	P	.	.	.	.	.	.	Glasnevin	Dublin ...	G. S. & W.	Kingsbridge and North Wall.
.	.	.	.	.	.	.	.	Glasnevin Junction	Dublin ...	G. S. & W.—M. G. W.	Kingsbridge and North Wall.
.	.	.	.	.	.	.	.	Guinness' Siding	Dublin ...	G. S. & W.	Near Kingsbridge.
G	P	F	L	H	C	20	0	Harcourt Street	Dublin ...	D. W. & W.	Terminus.
.	.	.	.	.	.	.	.	Inchicore (Co.'s Stores)......	Dublin ...	G. S. & W.	Dublin.
G	P	F	L	H	C	10	0	Island Bridge Junction......	Dublin ...	G. S. & W.	Kingsbridge and Clondalkin.
.	P	.	.	.	.	.	.	Kingsbridge	Dublin ...	G. S. & W.	Terminus.
.	P	.	.	.	.	.	.	Lansdowne Road	Dublin ...	D. W. & W.	Bray and Westland Row.
.	P	.	L	.	.	.	.	Liffey Junction Station ...	Dublin ...	M. G. W.	Broadstone and Blanchardstown.
.	.	.	.	.	.	.	.	Newcomen Bridge Junction	Dublin ...	D. W. & W.(C. of D. Jn.)—M. G. W.	Westland Row & Liffey Jn. Station.
.	.	.	.	.	.	.	.	North City Mills..............	Dublin ...	M. G. W.	Branch from Liffey Junction.
.	.	.	.	.	.	.	.	North Strand Road Junc....	Dublin ...	G. S. & W.	Drumcondra and North Wall.
								North Wall—			
G	P	F	L	H	C	.	.	Station	Dublin ...	C. L. C.(G C, G N, & Mid.)	By Steamer from Liverpool.
G	P	F	L	H	C	.	.	Station	Dublin ...	G C—G N—L & Y—Mid.	By Steamer from Liverpool.
G	.	F	.	H	C	1	10	Station	Dublin ...	{ G. S. & W.	Terminus.
G	.	F	L	.	C	5	0			{ M. G. W.	Terminus.
G	P	F	L	H	C	.	.	Station	Dublin ...	Mid.	By Steamer from Heysham.
G	P	F	L	H	C	20	0	Station (L. & N. W.)......	Dublin ...	{ L. & N. W.	Extension from Church Road Junc. and by Steamer from Holyhead.
.										{ G. N. (I.)—G. S. & W.	Over L.&N.W. fr. Church Rd. Juncs.
.	.	.	.	.	.	.	.	Sheriff Street	Dublin ...	G. S. & W.	Drumcondra and North Wall.
.	P	.	.	.	.	.	.	Sydney Parade	Dublin ...	D. W. & W.	Westland Row and Bray.
.	P	.	.	.	.	.	.	Tara Street & Georges Quay	Dublin ...	D. W. & W.	Amiens Street and Westland Row.
.	P	.	.	.	.	.	.	Westland Row	Dublin ...	D. W. & W.	Amiens Street and Kingstown.
.	.	.	.	.	.	.	.	West Road Junction.........	Dublin ...	G. S. & W.—M. G. W.	Church Road Jn. & Glasnevin Jn.
.	.	.	.	.	.	.	.	Dublin Bridge..................	Down	G. N. (I.)	See Newry.
.	.	.	.	.	.	.	.	Dub's Locomotive Wks. (Glasgow Locomotive Works) ...	Lanark ...	Cal.	Glasgow, South Side.
G	P	.	L	H	.	3	0	Dubton Junction(for Hillside)	Forfar	Cal.	Forfar and Stonehaven.
.	.	.	.	.	.	.	.	Pugeston Siding..............	Forfar	Cal.	Bridge of Dun and Dubton Junc.
.	.	.	.	.	.	.	.	Ducie Street	Lancs	G. C.	See Manchester.
.	.	.	.	.	.	.	.	Duck Colliery	Glo'ster ...	G. W.	Bilson Junction.
.	.	.	.	.	.	.	.	Duckett, J., & Son's Siding...	Lancs	L. & Y.	See Burnley Barracks Mineral Siding (Burnley).
.	.	.	.	.	.	.	.	Duckmanton	Derby	L. D. & E. C.	Same as Arkwright Town.
.	.	.	.	.	.	.	.	Duckmanton Siding	Derby	G. C.	Staveley Town.
G	P	F	L	H	C	.	.	Dudbridge	Glo'ster ...	Mid.	Stonehouse and Nailsworth.
.	.	.	.	.	.	.	.	Kimmins, Drew & Co.'s Sid.	Glo'ster ...	Mid.	Dudbridge Junc. and Woodchester.
.	.	.	.	.	.	.	.	Rooksmoor Siding (J. Grist & Co.)	Glo'ster ...	Mid.	Dudbridge Junc. and Woodchester.
.	.	.	.	.	.	.	.	Duddeston	Warwick..	L. & N. W.	See Birmingham, Vauxhall and Duddeston.
.	.	.	.	.	.	.	.	Duddeston Sidings	Warwick..	Mid.	Birmingham, Lawley Street.
.	.	.	.	.	.	.	.	Dudding Hill (for Willesden and Neasden)	Middlesex	Mid.	See London.

EXPLANATION—G *Goods Station.*   P *Passenger and Parcel Station.*   P* *Passenger, but not Parcel or Miscellaneous Traffic.*
F *Furniture Vans, Carriages, Portable Engines, and Machines on Wheels.*   L *Live Stock.*
H *Horse Boxes and Prize Cattle Vans.*   C *Carriages by Passenger Train.*

STATION ACCOMMODATION.						CRANE POWER.		STATIONS. &c.	COUNTY.	COMPANY.	POSITION.
						Tons	Cwts				
G	P	.	L	.	.	3	0	Duddingston and Craigmillar	Edinboro'	N. B.	Newington and Portobello.
.	.	.	.	.	.	.	.	Craigmillar Brewery (Murray's Brewery)	Edinboro'	N. B.	Duddingston and Craigmillar.
.	.	.	.	.	.	.	.	Deuchar's Brewery	Edinboro'	N. B.	Duddingston and Craigmillar.
.	.	.	.	.	.	.	.	Drybrough's Brewery	Edinboro'	N. B.	Duddingston and Craigmillar.
.	.	.	.	.	.	.	.	Edinburgh Malting Co's Sid.	Edinboro'	N. B.	Duddingston and Craigmillar.
.	.	.	.	.	.	.	.	Maclachan's Brewery	Edinboro'	N. B.	Duddingston and Craigmillar.
.	.	.	.	.	.	.	.	Paterson's Brewery	Edinboro'	N. B.	Duddingston and Craigmillar.
.	.	.	.	.	.	.	.	Raeburn's Brewery	Edinboro'	N. B.	Duddingston and Craigmillar.
.	.	.	.	.	.	.	.	Somerville's Brewery	Edinboro'	N. B.	Duddingston and Craigmillar.
.	.	.	.	.	.	.	.	Dudgeon's Manure Siding	L'lithgow	N. B.	Dalmeny.
G	P	F	L	H	C	10	0		Worcester	G. W.	Kidderminster & Wolverhampton.
G	P	F	L	H	C	20	0	Dudley	Worcester	L. & N. W.	Dudley Junction and Walsall.
G	.	F	L	H	.	20	0		Worcester	Mid.	Over L. & N. W. from Walsall Jn.
.	.	.	.	.	.	.	.	Castle Mill Siding	Staffs	G. W.	Dudley and Tipton.
.	.	.	.	.	.	.	.	Dudley's, Earl of, Siding (Coneygre Siding)	Staffs	L. & N. W.	Dudley and Dudley Port.
.	.	.	.	.	.	.	.	Palethorpe's Siding	Staffs	L. & N. W.	Dudley and Dudley Port.
.	.	.	.	.	.	.	.	Dudley Colliery	Northumb	N. E.	Annitsford.
.	.	.	.	.	.	.	.	Dudley Hill (G. N.)	Yorks	G. N.—L. & Y.	See Bradford.
.	.	.	.	.	.	.	.	Dudley Junction	Worcester	G. W.—L. & N. W.	Stourbridge and Dudley.
.	P	.	.	.	.	.	.	Dudley Port, High Level	Staffs	L. & N. W.	Birmingham and Wolverhampton.
.	P	.	.	.	.	.	.	Dudley Port, Low Level	Staffs	L. & N. W.	Dudley and Walsall.
.	.	.	.	.	.	.	.	Dudley, South Side	Worcester	G. W.	Netherton.
.	.	.	.	.	.	.	.	Dudley's (Earl of)—			
.	.	.	.	.	.	.	.	Ashwood Basin	Staffs	G. W.	See Round Oak.
.	.	.	.	.	.	.	.	Coneygre Siding	Staffs	L. & N. W.	Dudley.
.	.	.	.	.	.	.	.	Siding	Staffs	G. W.	Brettell Lane.
.	.	.	.	.	.	.	.	Siding	Staffs	G. W.	Cradley Heath and Cradley.
.	.	.	.	.	.	.	.	Dufferin Dock	Antrim	G. N. (I.)	See Belfast.
.	.	.	.	.	.	.	.	Dufferin Stone Co.'s Siding	Down	B. & C. D.	Ballygowan.
G	P	.	.	.	.	5	0	Duffield	Derby	Mid.	Derby and Ambergate.
.	.	.	.	.	.	.	.	Duffryn, Deep Colliery	Glamorg'n	G. W.—T. V.	See Nixon's Deep Duffryn Colliery (Mountain Ash).
.	.	.	.	.	.	.	.	Duffryn, Lower Colliery	Glamorg'n	G. W.—T. V.	Same as Powell Duffryn Co.'s Lower Duffryn Colliery (Mountain Ash).
.	.	.	.	.	.	.	.	Duffryn Main Siding	Glamorg'n	G. W.	Neath Abbey.
.	.	.	.	.	.	.	.	Duffryn Middle Colliery	Glamorg'n	G. W.—Rhy.—T. V.	See Powell Duffryn Co.'s Middle Duffryn Col. (Mountain Ash).
.	.	.	.	.	.	.	.	Duffryn Rhondda Colliery	Glamorg'n	R. & S. B.	Cymmer.
.	.	.	.	.	.	.	.	Duffryn Siding (T. V.)	Glamorg'n	T. V.—G. W.	Same as Plymouth Works (Merthyr).
.	.	.	.	.	.	.	.	Duffryn Siding	Mon	G. W.	Ebbw Vale.
G	P	F	L	H	C	4	0	Dufftown	Banff	G. N. of S.	Keith and Craigellachie.
G	.	.	.	.	.	2	0	Glendullan Siding	Banff	G. N. of S.	Dufftown and Mortlach.
G	.	.	.	.	.	2	0	Mortlach Siding	Banff	G. N. of S.	Branch from Dufftown.
G	.	.	.	.	.	2	0	Parkmore Siding	Banff	G. N. of S.	Dufftown and Mortlach.
G	P	.	L	.	C	2	10	Duffws (Blaenau Festiniog Tn.)	Merioneth	Festiniog	Terminus.
.	.	.	.	.	.	.	.	Duffws Quarries Extension	Merioneth	Festiniog	Blaenau Festiniog.
.	P	.	.	.	.	.	.	Duirinish	Ross & Cro'	High.	Stromeferry and Kyle of Lochalsh.
.	.	.	.	.	.	.	.	Duke of Devonshire's—			
.	.	.	.	.	.	.	.	Buckland Hollow Siding	Derby	Mid.	Ambergate.
.	.	.	.	.	.	.	.	Hambleton Siding	Yorks	Mid.	Bolton Abbey.
.	.	.	.	.	.	.	.	Siding	Sussex	L. B. & S. C.	Eastbourne.
.	.	.	.	.	.	.	.	Duke of Grafton's Siding	Norfolk	G. E.	Barnham.
.	.	.	.	.	.	.	.	Duke of Portland's—			
.	.	.	.	.	.	.	.	Bleak Hills Siding	Notts	Mid.	Mansfield.
.	.	.	.	.	.	.	.	Sidings (Mid.)	Derby	Mid.— G. C.	Whitwell.
.	.	.	.	.	.	.	.	Dukeries Junction Station	Notts	G. N.—L. D. & E. C.	See Tuxford.
.	.	.	.	.	.	.	.	Dukes Dock	Lancs	G. W.	Liverpool.
.	.	.	.	.	.	.	.	Duke's Siding	Yorks	G. C.	Grange Lane.
.	.	.	.	.	.	.	.	Duke Street	Cheshire	B'head Jt.—C. L. C.—N. W. & L. Jt.	See Birkenhead.
.	.	.	.	.	.	.	.	Duke Street	Derby	G. N.	See Derby.
.	.	.	.	.	.	.	.	Duke Street (N. B.)	Lanark	N. B.—G. & S. W.	See Glasgow.
.	.	.	.	.	.	.	.	Duke's Siding (Motherwell Iron & Steel Co.)	Lanark	Cal.	Motherwell.
.	.	.	.	.	.	.	.	Duke's Victoria Wharves	Devon	L. & S.W.	Plymouth, Cattewater Harbour.
.	P	.	.	.	.	.	.		Cheshire	G. C.	Guide Bridge & Ashton, Park Parade.
G	.	.	.	.	.	10	0	Dukinfield	Cheshire	L. & N. W.	Stalybridge and Stockport.
.	P	.	.	.	.	.	.	Dukinfield and Ashton	Cheshire	L. & N. W.	Stalybridge and Stockport.
.	.	.	.	.	.	.	.	Dukinfield Coal and Cannel Co.'s Siding	Cheshire	G. C.	See Victoria Siding (Newton, for Hyde).

EXPLANATION—G *Goods Station.*   P *Passenger and Parcel Station.*   P* *Passenger, but not Parcel or Miscellaneous Traffic.*
F *Furniture Vans, Carriages, Portable Engines, and Machines on Wheels.*   L *Live Stock.*
H *Horse Boxes and Prize Cattle Vans.*   C *Carriages by Passenger Train.*

G	P	F	L	H	C	Tons	Cwts	STATIONS, &c.	COUNTY.	COMPANY.	POSITION.
.	.	.	.	.	.	.	.	Dukinfield Junction	Cheshire	G. C.—L. & N. W.	Ashton, Park Parade & Stockport.
.	P	.	.	.	.	.	.	Dulcot Sidings	Somerset	G. W.	Wells.
.	P	.	.	.	.	.	.	Duleek	Meath	G. N. (I.)	Drogheda and Navan.
G	P	.	L	H	.	2	0	Dullatur	Dumbartn	N. B.	Falkirk and Lenzie.
.	.	.	.	.	.	.	.	Dullatur Quarry	Dumbartn	N. B.	Dullatur and Croy.
.	.	.	.	.	.	.	.	Nethercroy Siding	Dumbartn	N. B.	Dullatur and Croy.
G	P	F	L	H	C	1	10	Dullingham	Cambs	G. E.	Cambridge and Newmarket.
G	P	F	L	H	C	5	0	Dulverton	Devon	G. W.	Wiveliscombe and South Molton.
.	P	.	.	.	.	.	.	Dulwich	Surrey	S. E. & C.	Herne Hill and Beckenham.
.	P	.	.	.	.	.	.	Dulwich, East	Surrey	L. B. & S. C.	See East Dulwich.
.	.	.	.	.	.	.	.	Dulwich, North	Surrey	L. B. & S. C.	See North Dulwich.
.	.	.	.	.	.	.	.	Dumballs Road Coal Siding	Glamorg'n	G. W.	Cardiff.
								DUMBARTON—			
G	.	F	L	.	.	10	0	(Station)	Dumbartn	Cal.	Branch near Dumbarton, East.
G	P	F	L	H	C	10	0	(Station)	Dumbartn	D. & B. Jt. (Cal. & N. B.)	Glasgow and Balloch.
.	.	.	.	.	.	.	.	Denny & Co.'s Engineering Works	Dumbartn	D. & B. Jt. (Cal. & N. B.)	Dumbarton and Dalreoch.
.	.	.	.	.	.	.	.	Dock Shipyard	Dumbartn	D. & B. Jt. (Cal. & N. B.)	Dumbarton Joint Goods.
.	.	.	.	.	.	.	.	Dumbarton Co-operative Society's Bakery Siding	Dumbartn	Cal.	Branch near Dumbarton, East.
.	P	.	.	.	.	.	.	East	Dumbartn	Cal.	Clydebank and Dumbarton.
.	.	.	.	.	.	.	.	Gas Works	Dumbartn	D. & B. Jt. (Cal. & N. B.)	Branch from Dumbarton.
.	.	.	.	.	.	.	.	Junction	Dumbartn	Cal.—D. & B. Jt.—N. B.	Dumbarton and Bowling.
.	.	.	.	.	.	.	.	Leven Shipyard (Denny, W., & Brothers')	Dumbartn	Cal.	Branch near Dumbarton, East.
.	.	.	.	.	.	.	.	Leven Shipyard (Denny, W., & Brothers')	Dumbartn	D. & B. Jt. (Cal. & N. B.)	Branch from Dumbarton.
.	.	.	.	.	.	.	.	Macmillan & Son's Siding	Dumbartn	D. & B. Jt. (Cal. & N. B.)	Branch from Dumbarton.
.	.	.	.	.	.	.	.	Dumbuck Sid (Milton Paper Co)	Dumbartn	N. B.	See Bowling.
								DUMFRIES—			
G	.	F	L	H	.	5	0	(Station)	Dumfries	Cal.	Branch near Lockerbie.
G	P	F	L	H	C	10	0	(Station, G. & S.W.)	Dumfries	G. & S.W.	Annan and Thornhill.
.	P	F	L	H	C	.	.	(Station, G. & S.W.)	Dumfries	Cal.	Over G. & S.W. from Dumfries Jn.
.	.	.	.	.	.	.	.	Bonded Store Siding	Dumfries	Cal.	Dumfries.
.	.	.	.	.	.	.	.	Charlton & Wylie's Siding	Dumfries	Cal.	Dumfries.
.	.	.	.	.	.	.	.	Dumfries Foundry Siding	Dumfries	G. & S.W.	Dumfries.
.	.	.	.	.	.	.	.	Dumfries Gas Works	Dumfries	G. & S.W.	Dumfries.
.	.	.	.	.	.	.	.	Garland & Rodgers' Siding	Dumfries	G. & S.W.	Dumfries.
.	.	.	.	.	.	.	.	Junction	Dumfries	Cal.— G. & S.W.	Locharbriggs & Dumfries (G. & S.W.).
.	.	.	.	.	.	.	.	Dumfries County Council Sid.	Dumfries	G. & S.W.	Auldgirth.
.	P	.	.	.	.	.	.	Dumfries House	Ayr	G. & S.W.	Annbank and Cumnock.
G	P	.	L	H	C	.	.	Dungoyne	Stirling	N. B.	Lennoxtown and Killearn.
.	.	.	.	.	.	.	.	Blackburn Siding	Stirling	N. B.	Dumgoyne and Killearn.
G	P	.	L	H	.	2	10	Dunadry	Antrim	N. C. Com. (Mid.)	Antrim and Greenisland.
.	.	.	.	.	.	.	.	Dunaskin Brick Works	Ayr	G. & S.W.	Waterside.
.	P	.	.	.	.	.	.	Dunaskin Junction	Ayr	G. & S.W.	Waterside and Dalmellington.
.	P	.	.	.	.	.	.	Dunball	Somerset	G. W.	Bridgwater and Highbridge.
.	.	.	.	.	.	.	.	Pottery Siding	Somerset	G. W.	Bridgwater and Highbridge.
G	.	.	.	.	.	.	.	Wharf	Somerset	G. W.	Bridgwater and Highbridge.
G	P	F	L	H	C	3	0	Dunbar (N. B.)	Hadding'n	N. B.	Edinburgh and Berwick.
.	P	.	.	.	.	.	.	Dunbar (N. B.)	Hadding'n	N. E.	Over N. B. from Berwick.
G	.	.	.	.	.	.	.	Battleblent Siding	Hadding'n	N. B.	Dunbar and East Linton.
G	.	.	L	.	.	.	.	Beltonford Siding	Hadding'n	N. B.	Dunbar and East Linton.
G	.	.	.	.	.	.	.	Oxwellmains Limestone Sid.	Hadding'n	N. B.	Dunbar and Innerwick.
.	.	.	.	.	.	.	.	Oxwellmains Siding	Hadding'n	N. B.	Dunbar and Innerwick.
.	.	.	.	.	.	.	.	West Barns Siding	Hadding'n	N. B.	Dunbar and East Linton.
G	P	F	L	H	C	3	0	Dunblane	Perth	Cal.	Stirling and Perth.
.	.	.	.	.	.	.	.	Springbank Mill	Perth	Cal.	Dunblane and Doune.
G	P	F	L	H	C	.	.	Dunboyne	Meath	M. G. W.	Dublin and Navan.
G	P	F	L	H	C	5	0	Dunbridge	Hants	L. & S.W.	Romsey and Salisbury.
.	.	.	.	.	.	.	.	Kimbridge Junction	Hants	L. & S.W.	Romsey and Dunbridge.
.	.	.	.	.	.	.	.	Duncan Colliery	Fife	N. B.	West Wemyss.
.	.	.	.	.	.	.	.	Duncan, J., Siding	Durham	N. E.	Stockton, South.
G	P	F	L	H	C	.	.	Dunchurch	Warwick	L. & N. W.	Leamington and Rugby.
								DUNDALK—			
G	.	.	L	.	.	3	10	Barrack Street (G. N., I.)	Louth	G. N. (I.)	Terminus.
G	.	F	L	.	.	2	10	Barrack Street (G. N., I.)	Louth	D. N. & G.	Over G. N. (I.) from Dundalk, Windmill Road Junction.
.	.	.	.	.	.	.	.	Brewery	Louth	G. N. (I.)	Dundalk.
.	.	.	.	.	.	.	.	Brick Works	Louth	G. N. (I.)	Dundalk.
.	.	.	.	.	.	.	.	Great Northern Brewery	Louth	G. N. (I.)	Dundalk.
G	P	F	L	H	C	3	0	Junction Station (G. N., I.)	Louth	G. N. (I.)	Drogheda and Goragh Wood.
G	P	F	L	H	C	2	0	Junction Station (G. N., I.)	Louth	D. N. & G.	Over G. N. (I.) from Dundalk, Windmill Road Junction.

EXPLANATION—G *Goods Station.*   P *Passenger and Parcel Station.*   P* *Passenger, but not Parcel or Miscellaneous Traffic.*
F *Furniture Vans, Carriages, Portable Engines, and Machines on Wheels.*   L *Live Stock.*
H *Horse Boxes and Prize Cattle Vans.*   C *Carriages by Passenger Train.*

G	P	F	L	H	C	Tons	Cwts	STATIONS, &c.	COUNTY.	COMPANY.	POSITION.
								DUNDALK—*continued.*			
								Lockington's Siding	Louth	D. N. & G.	Quay Street.
								Lunham's Siding	Louth	G. N. (I.)	Dundalk.
	P			H	C			Quay Street	Louth	D. N. & G.	Bellurgan and Dundalk, Windmill Road Junction.
								Windmill Road Junction	Louth	D. N. & G.—G. N. (I.)	Quay Street and Inniskeen.
								Dundas Sidings	Flint	L. & N. W.	Queensferry.
								Aston Hall Coal and Brick Co.'s Colliery	Flint	L. & N. W.	Dundas Sidings.
								Turner's	Flint	L. & N. W.	Dundas Sidings.
								Willans & Robinson's Ferry Works	Flint	L. & N. W.	Dundas Sidings.
								DUNDEE—			
								Bell & Simes' Wood Yard	Forfar	Cal.—N. B.	Dundee Harbour Line.
								Buckingham Junction Sids.	Forfar	N. B.	Esplanade and Tay Bridge.
								Buckingham Junc., West	Forfar	Cal.—N. B.	Magdalen Green and Tay Bridge.
						1	10	Buckingham Point Sidings	Forfar	N. B.	Esplanade and Tay Bridge.
								Caledon Shipbuilding Yard	Forfar	Cal.—N. B.	Dundee Harbour Line.
G						30	0	Camperdown Dock	Forfar	Cal.—N. B.	Dundee Harbour Line.
								Camperdown Junc., East	Forfar	D. & A. Jt.—N. B.	West Ferry and Tay Bridge.
								Camperdown Shipbuilding Yard (Gourlay Bros.&Co.)	Forfar	Cal.—N. B.	Dundee Harbour Line.
								Canadian Wharf and Cattle Bank	Forfar	Cal.	Dundee Harbour Line.
								Carolina Port Sidings	Forfar	Cal.—N. B.	Dundee Harbour Line.
								Cattle Dock Sidings	Forfar	Cal.—N. B.	Dundee Harbour Line.
G						90	0	Dock Connection	Forfar	Cal.	Dundee West & Camperdown Junc.
G						90	0	Dock Connections	Forfar	N. B.	Tay Bridge & Camperdown Jn., East.
								Dundee Ice & Cold Storage Co.'s Siding	Forfar	Cal.—N. B.	Dundee Harbour Line.
								Dundee Weighs	Forfar	Cal.	Dundee West.
G						30	0	Earl Grey Dock	Forfar	Cal.—N. B.	Dundee Harbour Line.
G	P	F	L	H	C	6	0	East	Forfar	D. & A. Jt. (Cal. & N. B.)	Dundee, West and Broughty Ferry.
G						5	0	East End Mineral Depôt	Forfar	D. & A. Jt. (Cal. & N. B.)	Dundee, East.
								Eastern Co-operative Society's Siding	Forfar	Cal.	Fairmuir.
	P							Esplanade	Forfar	N. B.	Tay Bridge and Wormit.
G						2	0	Esplanade Goods & Mineral Depôt	Forfar	N. B.	Tay Bridge and Wormit.
								Esplanade Junc. and Siding	Forfar	Cal.	Magdalen Green & Dundee West.
G		F	L			3	0	Fairmuir	Forfar	Cal.	Branch near Lochee.
								Fish Curing Depôt	Forfar	Cal.—N. B.	Dundee Harbour Line.
								Fleming, A. B., & Co.'s Oil Works	Forfar	Cal.—N. B.	Dundee Harbour Line.
								Fleming and Barry's Wood Yard	Forfar	Cal.—N. B.	Dundee Harbour Line.
G						3	0	Gas Commissioners' Siding	Forfar	D. & A. Jt. (Cal. & N. B.)	Dundee, East.
						90	0	Harbour Connection	Forfar	D. & A. Jt. (Cal. & N. B.)	Dundee, East.
G						5	0	King William Dock	Forfar	Cal.—N. B.	Dundee Harbour Line.
								Lindsay & Low's Siding	Forfar	Cal.—N. B.	Dundee Harbour Line.
	P							Magdalen Green	Forfar	Cal.	Perth and Dundee.
G		F	L			5	0	Maryfield	Forfar	Cal.	Branch near Lochee.
								Ninewells Junction	Forfar	Cal.	Invergowrie and Magdalen Green.
								Panmure Shipbuilding Yard (Dundee Shipbuilders' Co.)	Forfar	Cal.—N. B.	Dundee Harbour Line.
								Seabraes Saw Mills	Forfar	Cal.	Dundee West.
								Seafield Siding	Forfar	Cal.	Dundee West.
G	P	F	L	H	C			Stannergate	Forfar	D. & A. Jt. (Cal. & N. B.)	Dundee East and Broughty Ferry.
G	P	F	L	H	C	20	0	Tay Bridge	Forfar	N. B.	Esplanade and West Ferry.
G						90	0	Victoria Dock	Forfar	Cal.—N. B.	Dundee Harbour Line.
G	P	F	L	H	C	15	0	West	Forfar	Cal.	Perth and Arbroath.
								West End Mineral Depôt	Forfar	Cal.	Dundee West.
								Dundee Floor Cloth and Linoleum Co.'s Siding	Forfar	Cal.	Liff.
								Dundee Ice & Cold Storage Co.'s Siding	Forfar	Cal. / N.B.	Dundee, West. / Dundee, Tay Bridge.
								Dundee Police Commissioners' Siding	Perth	Cal.	Inchcoonans.
								Dundee Shipbuilders Co.'s Siding	Forfar	Cal.—N. B.	Same as Panmure Shipbuilding Yard (Dundee).

G	P	F	L	H	C	Tons	Cwts	STATIONS, &c.	COUNTY.	COMPANY.	POSITION.
								Dundee Street Cattle Siding	Edinboro'	Cal.	Same as Edinboro' Old Cattle Sid.
								Dundee Street Manure Depôt	Edinboro'	Cal.	Edinburgh, Lothian Road.
								Dundee Terrace Stone Siding	Edinboro'	Cal.	Edinburgh, Lothian Road.
G	P							Dundonald	Down	B. & C. D.	Belfast and Comber.
G	P		L	H	C	2	10	Dundonald Colliery	Fife	N. B.	Cardenden.
G	P		L					Dundrum	Down	B. & C. D.	Downpatrick and Newcastle.
G	P	F	L	H	C			Dundrum	Dublin	D. W. & W.	Dublin (Harcourt Street) and Bray.
G	P	F	L	H	C			Dundrum	Tipperary	G. S. & W.	Thurles and Limerick Junction.
								Dunduff Quarry	Lanark	Cal.	Blackwood.
								Dundyvan Basin	Lanark	Cal.—N. B.	Coatbridge, Whifflet.
								Dundyvan Foundry	Lanark	Cal.	Langloan.
										N. B.	Coatbridge, Whifflet.
								Dundyvan House-to-House Electric Light Works	Lanark	N. B.	Coatbridge, Sheepford.
								Dundyvan Iron Works	Lanark	Cal.	Langloan.
										N. B.	Coatbridge, Whifflet.
								Dundyvan Rivet Works	Lanark	N. B.	Coatbridge, Whifflet.
								Dundyvan Silica Brick Works (Eglinton Silica Brk. Wks)	Lanark	Cal.	Langloan.
								Dundyvan Wood Yard	Lanark	N. B.	Coatbridge, Whifflet.
G	P		L	H	C			Dunfanaghy Road	Donegal	L. & L. S.	Letterkenny and Burtonport.
								DUNFERMLINE—			
								Charlestown Junction	Fife	N. B.	Dunfermline (Lower) & Charlestown.
	P			H	C			Lower	Fife	N. B.	Inverkeithing and Cowdenbeath.
								Phœnix Foundry	Fife	N. B.	Dunfermline (Upper) and Whitemyre Junction.
								Touch North Junction	Fife	N. B.	Dunfermline (Upper) and Townhill.
								Touch South Junction	Fife	N. B.	Dunfermline, Upper and Lower.
G	P	F	L	H	C	10	0	Upper	Fife	N. B.	Stirling and Thornton.
								Dunfermline Gas Works	Fife	N. B.	Netherton.
G	P	F	L	H	C	5	0	Dunford Bridge	Yorks	G. C.	Guide Bridge and Penistone.
G	P	F	L	H	C	5	0	Dungannon	Tyrone	G. N. (I.)	Portadown and Omagh.
G	P	F	L	H	C			Dungarvan	Waterford	G. S. & W.	Waterford and Lismore.
G	P							Dungeness	Kent	S. E. & C.	Branch from Appledore.
G	P	F	L	H	C	3	0	Dungiven	Derry	N. C. Com. (Mid.)	Branch from Limavady Junction.
G	P		L					Dungloe Road	Donegal	L. & L. S.	Letterkenny and Burtonport.
G	P	F	L	H	C	1	0	Dunham	Norfolk	G. E.	Lynn and Dereham.
G	P		L	H		3	0	Dunham Hill	Cheshire	B'head Jt. (G W & L N W)	Chester and Helsby.
G	P		L					Dunham Massey	Cheshire	L. & N. W.	Stockport and Warrington.
G								Dunhampstead	Worcester	Mid.	Bromsgrove and Ashchurch.
G	P	F	L	H	C	5	0	Dunkeld	Perth	High.	Perth and Ballinluig.
	P							Dunkettle	Cork	G. S. & W.	Cork and Queenstown Junction.
G	P	F	L	H	C	3	0	Dunkineely	Donegal	Donegal	Donegal and Killybegs.
								Dunkir Cloth Mill (Playne's)	Gloucester	Mid.	Nailsworth.
G	P	F	L	H	C			Dunlavin	Wicklow	G. S. & W.	Sallins and Tullow.
G	P	F	L	H	C	3	0	Dunleer	Louth	G. N. (I.)	Drogheda and Dundalk.
G	P	F	L	H	C	4	0	Dunlop	Ayr	G B & K Jt (Cal & G & S W)	Stewarton and Neilston.
								Dunlop, D. J., & Co.'s Siding	Renfrew	Cal.	Same as Inch Engineering Works (Greenock).
G	P		L	H		3	0	Dunloy	Antrim	N. C. Com. (Mid.)	Ballymena and Coleraine.
G	P	F	L	H	C			Dunmanway	Cork	C. B. & S. C.	Bandon and Bantry.
								Dunmeer Junction	Cornwall	L. & S. W.	Boscarne Junction and Bodmin.
G								Dunmeer Wharf	Cornwall	L. & S. W.	Branch from Wadebridge.
								Dunmore & Son's Biscuit Manufactory	Leicester	Mid.	Wigston.
								Dunmore Junction	Stirling	Cal.	Airth and South Alloa.
								Dunmore Quarry	Stirling	Cal.	Plean Junction Station.
								Dunmore's Siding	N'hampton	L. & N. W.	Higham Ferrers and Irthlingboro'.
G	P	F	L	H	C	1	10	Dunmow	Essex	G. E.	Bishops Stortford and Braintree.
	P							Dunmurry	Antrim	G. N. (I.)	Belfast and Lisburn.
								Dunn & Son's Grain Siding	Roxburgh	N. B.	Same as Kelso Granary.
								Dunn Bros.' Siding	Notts	Mid.	See Trowell Moor Col. (Trowell).
								Dunnerholme Siding	Lancs	Furness	Kirkby.
								Dunnikier Col. (Panny Pit Sid)	Fife	N. B.	Kirkcaldy, Sinclairtown.
								Dunnikier Foundry	Fife	N. B.	Kirkcaldy.
G	P	F	L	H	C	1	10	Dunning	Perth	Cal.	Stirling and Perth.
								Dunn's Manor Siding	Lincoln	G. C.	Keadby.
G	P	F	L	H	C	2	0	Dunphail	Elgin & Mo'	High.	Forres and Boat of Garten.
G	P	F	L	H	C	2	0	Dunragit	Wigtown	P. P. & W. Jt. (Cal., G & S W, L. & N. W. & Mid.)	Stranraer and Glenluce.
								Dunragit Creamery Siding	Wigtown	P. P. & W. Jt. (Cal., G & S W, L. & N. W. & Mid.)	Dunragit and Glenluce.

EXPLANATION—G *Goods Station.*　　P *Passenger and Parcel Station.*　　P* *Passenger, but not Parcel or Miscellaneous Traffic.*
F *Furniture Vans, Carriages, Portable Engines, and Machines on Wheels.*　　L *Live Stock.*
H *Horse Boxes and Prize Cattle Vans.*　　C *Carriages by Passenger Train.*

STATION ACCOMMODATION.						CRANE POWER.		STATIONS, &c	COUNTY.	COMPANY.	POSITION.
						Tons	Cwts.				
.	.	.	.	.	.	.	.	Dunraven, North and South Collieries	Glamorg'n	T. V.	Treherbert.
.	P	F	.	H	C	.	.	Dunrobin (private)	Sutherl'nd	High.	Golspie and Helmsdale.
.	.	.	.	.	.	.	.	Dunrod Siding	Renfrew ..	Cal.	Inverkip.
G	P	F	L	H	C	5	0	Duns	Berwick ..	N. B.	Reston and St. Boswells.
G	.	.	.	.	.	.	.	Crimstane Siding	Berwick ..	N. B.	Duns and Edrom.
.	.	.	.	.	.	.	.	Duns Gas Works	Berwick ..	N. B.	Duns.
G	P	F	L	H	C	2	0	Dunsandle	Galway ...	M. G. W.	Attymon and Loughrea.
.	.	.	.	.	.	.	.	Dunsiston Colliery	Lanark ...	Cal.	Same as Dunsyston Col. (Salisburgh).
G	P	F	L	H	C	.	.	Dunsland Cross	Devon	L. & S.W.	Okehampton and Bude.
								DUNSTABLE—			
G	P	F	L	H	C	5	0	(Station, L. & N. W.)	Beds	L. & N. W	Branch from Leighton.
.	P	.	.	H	C	.	.			G. N.	Over L. & N. W. from Dunstable Jn.
.	.	.	.	.	.	.	.	Blows Downs Siding........	Beds	G. N.	Dunstable and Luton.
G	P	F	L	H	C	5	0	Church Street (G. N.)	Beds	G. N.	Luton and Dunstable Junction.
.	P	.	.	H	C	.	.			L. & N. W.	Over G. N. from Dunstable Junc.
.	.	.	.	.	.	.	.	Dunstable Gas Co.'s Siding	Beds	L. & N. W.	Dunstable and Stanbridgeford.
.	.	.	.	.	.	.	.	Dunstable Lime Co.'s Siding (Rowe's Siding)	Beds	L. & N. W.	Dunstable and Stanbridgeford.
.	.	.	.	.	.	.	.	Junction	Beds	G. N.—L. & N. W.	Luton and Leighton.
G	.	F	L	.	.	.	.	London Road	Beds	G. N.	Branch—Dunstable Junction and Church Street.
.	.	.	.	.	.	.	.	Waterlow & Son's Siding...	Beds	G. N.	Dunstable, London Road.
.	P	.	.	H	.	.	.	Dunstall Park....................	Staffs	G. W.	Wolverhampton and Shrewsbury.
G	P	F	L	H	C	1	10	Dunster............................	Somerset..	G. W.	Watchet and Minehead.
.	.	.	.	.	.	.	.	Dunston	Lincoln ..	G. N. & G. E. Jt.	See Nocton and Dunston.
.	.	.	.	.	.	.	.	Dunston Colliery	Durham ...	N. E.	Redheugh.
.	.	.	.	.	.	.	.	Dunston Engine Works	Durham ...	N. E.	Redheugh.
.	.	.	.	.	.	.	.	Dunston Flour Mill	Durham ...	N. E.	See Co-operative Wholesale Society's (Redheugh).
.	.	.	.	.	.	.	.	Dunston Staiths	Durham ...	N. E.	Redheugh.
G	P	.	L	H	.	.	.	Dunsyre	Lanark ...	Cal.	Carstairs and Dolphinton.
.	.	.	.	.	.	.	.	Dunsyston Colliery	Lanark ...	Cal.	Salisburgh.
.	.	.	.	.	.	.	.	Duntie Siding	Lanark ...	N. B.	See Morningside.
.	.	.	.	.	.	.	.	Duntillan Colliery	Lanark ...	Cal.	Salisburgh.
.	.	.	.	.	.	.	.	Duntillan Farm Siding........	Lanark ...	Cal.	Salisburgh.
G	P	.	.	.	.	.	.	Dunton Green	Kent	S. E. & C.	Chislehurst and Sevenoaks.
.	.	.	.	.	.	.	.	Wreford's Siding	Kent	S. E. & C.	Dunton Green and Sevenoaks, Tubs Hill.
.	.	.	.	.	.	.	.	Dunton Knoll Quarry	Ayr	Cal.	Irvine.
G	P	.	.	.	.	.	.	Dunvant	Glamorg'n	L. & N. W.	Llandilo and Swansea.
.	.	.	.	.	.	.	.	Dunvant (or Penlan) Quarry	Glamorg'n	L. & N. W.	Dunvant and Gowerton.
.	.	.	.	.	.	.	.	Caergynydd Colliery	Glamorg'n	L. & N. W.	Dunvant Quarry.
.	.	.	.	.	.	.	.	Jones & Son's Brick Wks.	Glamorg'n	L. & N. W.	Dunvant Quarry.
.	.	.	.	.	.	.	.	Richards Dunvant Col.	Glamorg'n	L. & N. W.	Dunvant Quarry.
.	.	.	.	.	.	.	.	Holmes & Co.'s Killan Col.	Glamorg'n	L. & N. W.	Dunvant and Gowerton.
.	.	.	.	.	.	.	.	Dunvant Colliery	Glamorg'n	L. & N. W.	Same as Richard's Colliery (Dunvant Quarry).
G	P	.	.	.	.	.	.	Dunvegan...........................	Inverness..	Cal.	Steamer from Oban.
								DURHAM—			
G	.	F	L	H	.	10	0	(Station)	Durham ...	N. E.	Branch from Belmont Junction. Ferryhill and Newcastle.
.	P	.	.	H	C	.	.				
.	.	.	.	.	.	.	.	Belmont Junction	Durham ...	N. E.	Leamside and Sherburn Colliery.
.	.	.	.	.	.	.	.	Durham City & Shincliffe Brick & Tile Co.'s Brick Works	Durham ...	N. E.	Durham Goods Branch.
G	P	F	L	H	C	3	0	Elvet...............................	Durham ...	N. E.	Terminus (via Murton Branch).
.	.	.	.	.	.	.	.	Grange Iron Works	Durham ...	N. E.	Durham Goods Branch.
.	.	.	.	.	.	.	.	Durham Main Colliery	Durham ...	N. E.	Leamside.
.	.	.	.	.	.	..	.	Durham Ox Junction	Lincoln ..	G. C.—G. N.	Lincoln.
.	.	.	.	.	.	.	.	Durham Turnpike Depôts ...	Durham ...	N. E.	Birtley.
.	.	.	.	.	.	.	.	Durham Turnpike Junction...	Durham ...	N. E.	Washington and Pelton.
.	.	.	.	.	.	.	.	Durie Colliery....................	Fife	N. B.	Leven.
.	.	.	.	.	.	.	.	Durie Foundry	Fife	N. B.	Leven.
G	P	F	L	H	C	.	.	Duror	Argyll	Cal.	Connel Ferry and Ballachulish.
G	.	.	.	.	.	.	.	Achindarroch Depôt	Argyll	Cal.	Duror and Appin.
G	P	F	L	H	C	.	.	Durrow and Stradbally	Waterford	G. S. & W.	Dungarvan and Waterford.
G	P	.	.	.	.	.	.	Durrus Road	Cork	C. B. & S. C.	Drimoleague and Bantry.
G	P	F	L	H	C	.	.	Dursley	Glo'ster ...	Mid.	Branch from Coaley Junction.
.	.	.	.	.	.	.	.	Dursley Gas Co.'s Siding...	Glo'ster ...	Mid.	Dursley and Coaley Junction.
.	.	.	.	.	.	.	.	Lister's Siding..................	Glo'ster ...	Mid.	Dursley and Coaley Junction.
G	P	F	L	H	C	.	.	Durston	Somerset..	G. W.	Highbridge and Taunton.

EXPLANATION—G *Goods Station.*   P *Passenger and Parcel Station.*   P* *Passenger, but not Parcel or Miscellaneous Traffic.*
F *Furniture Vans, Carriages, Portable Engines, and Machines on Wheels.*   L *Live Stock.*
H *Horse Boxes and Prize Cattle Vans.*   C *Carriages by Passenger Train.*

STATION ACCOMMODATION.						CRANE POWER.		STATIONS, &c.	COUNTY.	COMPANY.	POSITION.
						Tons	Cwts.				
.	.	.	.	.	.	.	.	Duston Siding...................	N'hamptn	L. & N. W.	Northampton.
.	.	.	.	.	.	.	.	Phipps (Exors.), Hunsbury Hill Iron Works...........	N'hamptn	L. & N. W.	Duston Siding.
.	.	.	.	.	.	.	.	Rice & Co.	N'hamptn	L. & N. W.	Duston Siding.
.	.	.	.	.	.	.	.	Staveley Coal & Iron Co. or Duston Iron Ore Co......	N'hamptn	L. & N. W.	Duston Siding.
.	.	.	.	.	.	.	.	Duxbury Park Colliery (L. & Y. & L. U. Jt.).....	Lancs	{ L. & Y. { L. & N. W.	Adlington. White Bear (Adlington).
.	.	.	.	.	.	.	.	Duxbury's Siding (Yates, Duxbury & Son's)	Lancs	L. & Y.	Heap Bridge.
G	P	.	L	H	.	.	.	Dyce	Aberdeen.	G. N. of S.	Aberdeen and Kintore.
G	G	.	.	.	.	.	.	Dyce Manure Siding........	Aberdeen.	G. N. of S.	Dyce and Kinaldie.
.	.	.	.	.	.	.	.	Dyehouse Siding	Glo'ster ...	Mid.	Woodchester.
.	.	.	.	.	.	.	.	Dyer and Co.'s Saw Mills......	Peebles ...	N. B.	Peebles.
G	P	F	L	H	C	.	.	Dyffryn	Merioneth	Cam.	Harlech and Barmouth.
.	.	.	.	.	.	.	.	Dyffryn Rhondda Golden Vein Colliery	Glamorg'n	P. T.	Bryn.
.	.	.	.	.	.	.	.	Dyffryn Tin Plate Wks. (Mid)	Glamorg'n	Mid.—G.W.—L. & N.W.	Same as Edwards & Co. (Morriston).
.	.	.	.	.	.	.	.	Dyffryn Yard Sidings	Glamorg'n	P. T.	Port Talbot (Central).
.	.	.	.	.	.	.	.	Dykehead Colliery & Quarry	Lanark ...	Cal.	Larkhall.
.	.	.	.	.	.	.	.	Dykes Branch Junction	Ayr	G. & S. W.	Ochiltree and Skares.
.	.	.	.	.	.	.	.	Dyke's Pit	Ayr	G. & S. W.	Skares.
G	P	.	.	.	.	.	.	Dyke, The	Sussex ...	L. B. & S. C.	Branch—Hove and Portslade.
.	.	.	.	.	.	.	.	Dyllas Colliery	Glamorg'n	G. W.	Llwydcoed.
G	P	F	L	H	C	5	0	Dymock	Glo'ster ...	G. W.	Gloucester and Ledbury.
.	.	.	.	.	.	.	.	Dymond's Siding	Lincoln ...	G. C.	Crowle (for Epworth and Belton).
.	.	.	.	.	.	.	.	Dymond's Siding (L. & Y.)...	Yorks	L. & Y.—L. & N. W.	Same as Liversedge Coal Co.'s Sid. (Liversedge).
G	P	.	L	.	.	.	.	Dynevor	Glamorg'n	G. W.	Neath and Landore.
.	.	.	.	.	.	.	.	Dynevor Tin Works	Carmarth'	G. W.	Pantyffynnon.
G	P	F	L	H	C	3	0	Dysart	Fife	N. B.	Kirkcaldy and Thornton.
.	.	.	.	.	.	.	.	Castle Quarry	Flint	L. & N. W.	Dyserth and Meliden.
.	.	.	.	.	.	.	.	Dysart Colliery Siding (Francis Pit Siding)	Fife	N. B.	Dysart and Thornton.
G	.	.	.	.	.	1	10	Dyserth......................	Flint	L. & N. W.	Branch from Prestatyn.
.	.	.	.	.	.	.	.	Roberts' Siding	Flint	L. & N. W.	Dyserth and Meliden.
								E			
.	.	.	.	.	.	.	.	Eadie Sidings (Mid.)...........	Staffs	Mid—L&NW—GN—NS	Burton-on-Trent.
.	.	.	.	.	.	.	.	Eadies' Siding	Lanark ...	Cal.	Glasgow, South Side.
.	.	.	.	.	.	.	.	Eagle Foundry	Ayr	G. & S. W.	Stevenston.
.	.	.	.	.	.	.	.	Eagle Lane Depôt	Essex	G. E.	Same as George Lane Depôt.
.	.	.	.	.	.	.	.	Eaglesbush Colliery	Glamorg'n	G. W.	Neath.
.	.	.	.	.	.	.	.	Eaglescliffe Foundry	Durham ...	N. E.	Stockton, South.
G	P	.	.	.	.	.	.	Eaglescliffe Junction Station	Durham ...	N. E.	Stockton and Darlington.
.	.	.	.	.	.	.	.	Urlay Nook Siding & Depôt	Durham ...	N. E.	Eaglescliffe Junction Station.
.	.	.	.	.	.	.	.	Witham Hall Farm Siding	Durham ...	N. E.	Eaglescliffe Junction Station.
.	.	.	.	.	.	.	.	Witham Hall Quarry	Durham ...	N. E.	Eaglescliffe Junction Station.
.	.	.	.	.	.	.	.	Eaglescliffe Road Brick and Tile Works	Durham ...	N. E.	Stockton, South.
.	.	.	.	.	.	.	.	Eaglesham	Renfrew ...	Cal.	See Clarkston (for Eaglesham).
.	.	.	.	.	.	.	.	Eagle Tin Plate Works	Glamorg'n	G. W.	Neath.
.	P	.	.	.	.	.	.	Ealing (Broadway)...........	Middlesex	{ G. W. { Met. Dist.	London and Slough. Terminus.
.	P	.	.	.	.	.	.	Ealing Common & West Acton	Middlesex	Met. Dist.	Mill Hill Park and Ealing.
.	P	.	.	.	.	.	.	Ealing, North	Middlesex	Met. Dist.	See North Ealing.
.	.	.	.	.	.	.	.	Ealing, South...............	Middlesex	Met. Dist.	See South Ealing.
.	.	.	.	.	.	.	.	Ealing Town Council Siding	Middlesex	G. W.	West Ealing.
.	.	.	.	.	.	.	.	Ealing, West	Middlesex	G. W.	See West Ealing.
.	.	.	.	.	.	.	.	Eamont Bridge Junction......	Cumb'land	L. & N. W.—N. E.	Penrith.
G	P	.	L	.	.	5	0	Earby (Mid.)	Yorks	{ Mid. { L. & Y.	Colne and Skipton. Over Mid. from Colne Junction.
G	P	.	L	.	.	.	.	Eardington	Salop ...	G. W.	Bridgnorth and Hampton Loade.
G	P	F	L	H	C	1	10	Eardisley (Mid.)..............	Hereford ...	{ Mid. { G. W.	Hereford and Hay. Over Mid. from Eardisley Junction.

STATION ACCOMMODATION.						CRANE POWER.		STATIONS, &c.	COUNTY.	COMPANY.	POSITION.
						Tons	Cwts				
								Eardisley Junction	Hereford ..	G. W.—Mid.	Almeley and Eardisley Station.
G	P			H				Earith Bridge	Hunts	G. E.	Ely and St. Ives.
								Earl Bradford's Siding (Great Lever Siding)	Lancs	L. & Y.	Bolton.
								Earl Fitzwilliam's Low Stubbin Colliery	Yorks	G. C.—G. N. .... Mid.	Rotherham and Masboro'. Masboro' and Rotherham.
								Earl Fitzwilliam's Works ...	Yorks	G. C.	Elsecar.
								Earl Grey Dock	Forfar	Cal.—N. B.	See Dundee.
								Earl of Carnarvon's— Bretby Colliery Wharf (Newhall Park Colliery) (Mid.)	Derby	Mid.—L. & N. W.	Swadlincote.
								New Bretby Colliery (Mid.)	Derby	Mid.—L. & N. W.	Swadlincote.
								Earl of Derby's— Siding	Lancs	L. & Y.	Rainford Junction.
								Siding	Lancs	P. & L. Jt. (L & NW. & L & Y)	Longridge.
								Treals Siding	Lancs	P. & W. Jt. (L & Y & L & NW)	Kirkham.
								Yard	Lancs	L. & Y.	Liverpool, Sandhills.
								Earl of Dudley's— Ashwood Basin	Staffs	G. W.	See Round Oak.
								Coneygre Siding	Staffs	L. & N. W.	Dudley.
								Siding	Staffs	G. W.	Brettell Lane.
								Siding	Staffs	G. W.	Cradley Heath & Cradley.
								Earl of Ellesmere's— Brackley Siding, or Middle Hulton Colliery	Lancs	L. & N. W.	Plodder Lane (for Farnworth).
								Charlton Pit	Lancs	L. & N. W.	Plodder Lane (for Farnworth).
								Ellenbrook Colliery	Lancs	L. & N. W.	Tyldesley.
								Ellesmere Colliery	Lancs	L. & Y.	Walkden.
								Linnyshaw Moss Siding ...	Lancs	L. & Y.	Kearsley.
								Liverpool Street Siding ...	Lancs	L. & N. W.	Manchester, Liverpool Rd. & Salford.
								Sanderson Siding	Lancs	L. & N. W.	Tyldesley.
								Siding	Lancs	L. & Y.	Manchester, Miles Platting.
								Siding	Lancs	L. & N. W.	See Lecturers Close & Hulme Trust Siding (Bolton).
								Walkden Colliery	Lancs	L. & N. W.	Tyldesley.
								Wharton Hall Colliery	Lancs	L. & Y.	Atherton, Central.
								Earl Shilton (L. & N. W.)	Leicester ..	L. & N. W.—Mid.	See Elmesthorpe (for Barwell and Earl Shilton).
								Earls Barton	N'hampton	L. & N. W.	See Castle Ashby and Earls Barton.
								Earl's Court (Met. Dist.)	Middlesex	Met. Dist.—GW—L & NW	See London.
								Earl's Court Junction	Middlesex	Met. Dist.—West Lon. Jt.	London, Kensington, Earls Court Station and Addison Road.
								Earles, G. & T., Siding	Yorks	N. E.	Hull, Wilmington.
								Earle's Shipbuilding Co.'s Yd.	Yorks	H. & B. .... N. E.	Hull, Alexandra Dock. Hull, Drypool.
								Earle's Siding	Lincoln ..	G. C.	New Holland.
G	P		L			5	0	Earlestown (L. & N. W.)	Lancs	L. & N.W. .... G. W.	Kenyon Junc. Sta. and Liverpool. Over L. & N. W. from Walton Junc.
	P										
								Borron & Co.'s Bottle Works	Lancs	L. & N. W.	Earlestown.
								Collins Green Colliery Co.— Bold Colliery	Lancs	L. & N. W.	Collins Green and St. Helens Junc.
								Collins Green Colliery ...	Lancs	L. & N. W.	Collins Green and St. Helens Junc.
								Evans, R., & Co.— Collins Green Siding	Lancs	L. & N. W.	Collins Green and St. Helens Junc.
								Haydock Colliery	Lancs	L. & N. W.	Earlestown and Newton-le-Willows.
								Leigh Colliery	Lancs	L. & N. W.	Earlestown.
								New Boston Colliery	Lancs	L. & N. W.	Earlestown.
								Old Boston Colliery	Lancs	L. & N. W.	Earlestown.
								Pewfall Colliery	Lancs	L. & N. W.	Earlestown.
								Princess Colliery	Lancs	L. & N. W.	Earlestown.
								Queen Colliery	Lancs	L. & N. W.	Earlestown.
								Wood Colliery	Lancs	L. & N. W.	Earlestown.
								Fairclough & Son's Siding	Lancs	L. & N. W.	Earlestown.
								Sankey Sugar Co.'s Siding	Lancs	L. & N. W.	Earlestown and Collins Green.
								Slee & Co.'s Foundry	Lancs	L. & N. W.	Earlestown and Warrington.
								Vicars' Iron Works	Lancs	L. & N. W.	Earlestown and Warrington.
								Vulcan Foundry Co.'s Sid.	Lancs	L. & N. W.	Earlestown and Warrington.
								Whitfield's Siding	Lancs	L. & N. W.	Earlestown.
G	P	F	L	H	C			Earley (S. E. & C.)	Berks	S. E. & C. .... L. & S. W.	Wokingham and Reading. Over S. E. & C. from Wokingham Jn.
								Earlsdyke Sidings	Perth	Cal.	See Perth.
	P							Earlsfield and Summers Town	Surrey	L. & S. W.	London and Wimbledon.

STATION ACCOMMODATION.						CRANE POWER.	STATIONS, &c.	COUNTY.	COMPANY.	POSITION.
						Tons Cwts.				
G	P	.	L	H	C	1 10	Earlsheaton	Yorks	G. N.	Dewsbury and Ossett.
.	.	.	.	.	.	. .	Earlsheaton Col. (Chickenley Heath Colliery)	Yorks	G. N.	Earlsheaton and Ossett.
G	P	F	L	H	C	3 0	Earlston	Berwick	N. B.	Duns and St. Boswells.
.	.	.	.	.	.	. .	Fans Loanend Siding	Berwick	N. B.	Earlston and Gordon.
.	.	.	.	.	.	. .	Earl Street Junction	Middlesex	S. E. & C.	London, Ludgate Hill and St. Paul's
.	P	.	.	.	.	. .	Earlswood	Surrey	L. B. & S. C.	Red Hill and Three Bridges.
.	.	.	.	.	.	. .	Earlswood Asylum Siding	Surrey	L. B. & S. C.	Red Hill and Horley.
.	.	.	.	.	.	. .	Earnock Colliery	Lanark	{ Cal. / N. B.	Hamilton, Central. / Hamilton, Burnbank.
.	.	.	.	.	.	. .	Earnock Quarry (Stewartfield Quarry)	Lanark	Cal.	Meikle Earnock.
.	.	.	.	.	.	. .	Earnock Siding	Lanark	Cal.	Meikle Earnock.
.	.	.	.	.	.	. .	Earnshaw's Siding	Lancs	P.&L.Jt.(L&NW&L&Y)	Longridge.
.	.	.	.	.	.	. .	Earsdon Junction	Northumb	N. E.	Holywell and Percy Main.
.	P	.	.	.	.	. .	Earsham	Norfolk	G. E.	Beccles and Tivetshall.
G	P	.	L	H	.	. .	Earswick	Yorks	N. E.	York and Market Weighton.
.	.	.	.	.	.	. .	Easby Siding	Yorks	N. E.	Richmond.
.	.	.	.	.	.	. .	Easington Colliery	Durham	N. E.	Seaham.
G	P	F	L	H	C	. .	Easingwold	Yorks	N. E.	Branch from Alne.
.	.	.	.	.	.	. .	Crankley Siding	Yorks	N. E.	Easingwold.
.	P	F	L	H	C	3 0	Eassie	Forfar	Cal.	Coupar Angus and Forfar.
.	.	.	.	.	.	. .	East and West Float	Cheshire	B'head Jt.–CLC–NW&L	Birkenhead.
.	.	.	.	.	.	. .	East and West Float Depôt..	Cheshire	C.L.C.(G.C.,G.N.,&Mid.)	See Birkenhead.
.	.	.	.	.	.	. .	East Anglian Cement Co.'s Sid. (G. N.)	Cambs	G. N.—G. E.	Shepreth.
G	P	.	L	.	.	2 0	East Anstey	Devon	G. W.	Dulverton and South Molton.
.	.	.	.	.	.	. .	East Ardsley Colliery	Yorks	G. N.	Same as Ardsley Colliery.
.	.	.	.	.	.	. .	East Balquhatson Colliery	Stirling	N. B.	Slamannan.
G	P	.	L	H	.	. .	East Barkwith	Lincoln	G. N.	Lincoln and Louth.
.	.	.	.	.	.	. .	East Benhar Branch	L'lithgow	N. B.	Crofthead.
.	.	.	.	.	.	. .	East Benhar Siding	L'lithgow	N. B.	Crofthead.
.	.	.	.	.	.	. .	East Bitchburn Colliery	Durham	N. E.	Crook.
G	P	.	L	.	.	1 0	East Boldon	Durham	N. E.	Newcastle and Sunderland.
.	.	.	.	.	.	. .	Hodgson's Brick Works	Durham	N. E.	East Boldon.
.	.	.	.	.	.	. .	Leinster's Brick Works	Durham	N. E.	East Boldon.
.	.	.	.	.	.	. .	White Lea Brick Works	Durham	N. E.	East Boldon.
.	.	.	.	.	.	. .	East Boldon Junction	Durham	N. E.	East Boldon and Brockley Whins.
G	P	F	L	H	C	10 0	Eastbourne	Sussex	L. B. & S. C.	Branch from Polegate.
.	·|	.	.	.	.	. .	Bedford Well Waterworks.	Sussex	L. B. & S. C.	Eastbourne.
.	.	.	.	.	.	. .	Duke of Devonshire's Sid.	Sussex	L. B. & S. C.	Eastbourne.
.	.	.	.	.	.	. .	EastbourneCorporationSid.	Sussex	L. B. & S. C.	Eastbourne.
.	·|	.	.	.	.	. .	Eastbourne Gas Works	Sussex	L. B. & S. C.	Eastbourne.
.	.	.	.	.	.	. .	France & Son's Siding	Sussex	L. B. & S. C.	Eastbourne.
.	.	.	.	.	.	. .	Parsons Bros.' Siding	Sussex	L. B. & S. C.	Eastbourne.
.	.	.	.	.	.	. .	East Brixton	Surrey	L. B. & S. C.	See London.
G	P	F	L	H	C	. .	East Budleigh	Devon	L. & S.W.	Tipton St. John's and Budleigh Salterton.
.	·|	.	.	.	.	. .	Colaton Raleigh Siding	Devon	L. & S.W.	East Budleigh
.	P	.	.	.	.	. .	Eastbury	Berks	L'bourn Valley	Newbury and Lambourn.
.	.	.	.	.	.	. .	East Bute Dock	Glamorg'n	GW–LNW–Rhy--TV	Cardiff.
.	.	.	.	.	.	. .	East Buxton Siding	Derby	Mid.	See Buxton Lime Firms Co. (Miller's Dale).
.	.	.	.	.	.	. .	East Calder	Edinboro'	Cal.	See Camps (for East Calder).
G	.	.	L	.	.	1 10	East Calder	Edinboro'	N. B.	Branch from Uphall.
.	.	.	.	.	.	. .	Camps Brick Works	Edinboro'	N. B.	East Calder and Camps Junction.
G	.	.	.	.	.	. .	Camps Siding	Edinboro'	N. B.	East Calder and Camps Junction.
.	.	.	.	.	.	. .	Torrance's Siding	Edinboro'	N. B.	East Calder and Camps Junction.
.	.	.	.	.	.	. .	East Cannock Colliery	Staffs	L. & N. W.	Hednesford.
.	.	.	.	.	.	. .	East Castle Col. & Coke Wks.	Durham	N. E.	Annfield Plain.
.	P*	.	.	.	.	. .	Eastchurch	Kent	S. E. & C. (Sheppey)	Minster (Sheppey) and Leysdown.
.	.	.	.	.	.	. .	Holford Siding	Kent	S. E. & C. (Sheppey)	Eastchurch and Leysdown.
.	.	.	.	.	.	. .	East Coast Salvage Co.'s Warehouse	Edinboro'	Cal.—N. B.	Leith, North.
.	.	.	.	.	.	. .	Eastcroft Gas Works (G. N.)	Notts	G. N.–L. & N. W.	} See Nottingham Corporation (Nottingham).
.	.	.	.	.	.	. .	Eastcroft Sanitary Sid. (Mid.)	Notts	Mid.—L. & N. W.	
.	.	.	.	.	.	. .	East Croydon	Surrey	L. B. & S. C.—S. E. & C.	See Croydon, East.
.	.	.	.	.	.	. .	East Devon Brick Co.'s Sid.	Devon	L. & S.W.	Exmouth.
.	.	.	.	.	.	. .	East Dock	Edinboro'	Cal.	Leith, North.
.	.	.	.	.	.	. .	East Dock	Glamorg'n	G. W.	See Swansea.
.	.	.	.	.	.	. .	East Dock Junction	Glamorg'n	GW—H'bour Trust Lines	Swansea.
.	.	.	.	.	.	. .	East (Prince of Wales) Dock	Glamorg'n	GW–LNW–Mid–RSB	See Swansea.

EXPLANATION—G Goods Station.   P Passenger and Parcel Station.   P* Passenger, but not Parcel or Miscellaneous Traffic.
F Furniture Vans, Carriages, Portable Engines, and Machines on Wheels.   L Live Stock.
H Horse Boxes and Prize Cattle Vans.   C Carriages by Passenger Train.

STATION ACCOMMODATION.						CRANE POWER.	STATIONS, &c.	COUNTY.	COMPANY.	POSITION.
						Tons Cwts.				
G	P	F	L	.	.	. .	East Dulwich	Surrey	L. B. & S. C.	Peckham Rye and Tulse Hill.
							East End Mineral Depôt	Forfar..	D. & A. Jt. (Cal. & N. B.)	See Dundee, East.
G	P	F	L	H	C	3 0	Easterhouse (for Baillieston)	Lanark ..	N. B.	Shettleston and Coatbridge.
.	.	.	.	.	.	. .	Barrachnie Siding	Lanark ..	N. B.	Shettleston and Easterhouse.
.	.	.	.	.	.	. .	North British Nail & Rivet Works	Lanark	N. B.	Easterhouse.
.	.	.	.	.	.	. .	Eastern Co-operative Society's Siding	Forfar....	Cal.	Dundee, Fairmuir.
.	.	.	.	.	.	. .	Eastern Depôt	Glamorg'n	G. W.	Swansea.
.	.	.	.	.	.	. .	Eastern Pit	Glamorg'n	T. V.	See Ocean Coal Co. (Ystrad).
.	.	.	.	.	.	. .	Eastern Saw Mills	Edinboro'	N. B.	Leith.
.	.	.	.	.	.	. .	Easter Road	Edinboro'	N. B.	See Edinburgh.
.	.	.	.	.	.	. .	Easter Road Junction	Edinboro'	N. B.	Edinburgh.
G	P	.	.	.	.	0 10	East Farleigh	Kent	S. E. & C.	Paddock Wood and Maidstone.
.	.	.	.	.	.	. .	East Ferry Road Engineering Works Co.'s Siding...	Middlesex	G. E. / GN—GW—LNW—Mid	London, Millwall Docks. / London, Poplar.
.	.	.	.	.	.	. .	Eastfield Brick Works	L'lithgow	N. B.	Crofthead.
.	.	.	.	.	.	. .	Eastfield Colliery	Lanark ..	N. B.	Longriggend.
.	.	.	.	.	.	. .	Eastfield Quarry	L'lithgow	N. B.	Crofthead.
.	.	.	.	.	.	. .	Eastfield Siding	Edinboro'	N. B.	Glencorse.
G	P	.	L	H	C	5 0	East Finchley (G. N.)	Middlesex	G. N. / N. L.	Finsbury Park and High Barnet. / Over G. N. from Canonbury Junc.
.	P	.	.	.	.					
G	P	F	L	H	C	. .	East Fortune	Hadding'n	N. B.	Edinburgh and Dunbar.
G	P	.	L	H	.	. .	East Garston	Berks	L'bourn Valley	Newbury and Lambourn.
G	P	.	L	H	C	1 10	Eastgate	Durham ..	N. E.	Bishop Auckland and Wearhead.
.	.	.	.	.	.	. .	Greenfoot Quarry	Durham ..	N. E.	Eastgate.
.	.	.	.	.	.	. .	East Gate	Suffolk ..	G. E.	See Bury St. Edmunds.
.	.	.	.	.	.	. .	East Gawber Hall Colliery ...	Yorks	G. C.	Staincross (for Mapplewell).
G	P	F	L	H	C	2 0	East Grange	Fife	N. B.	Alloa and Dunfermline.
.	.	.	.	.	.	. .	Blairhall Colliery	Fife	N. B.	East Grange and Oakley.
.	.	.	.	.	.	. .	East Greenwich	Kent	S. E. & C.	See Maze Hill (for East Greenwich).
							EAST GRINSTEAD—			
.	.	.	.	.	.	. .	Bellaggio Siding	Sussex	L. B. & S. C.	Dormans and East Grinstead.
G	P	F	L	.	.	5 0	High Level	Sussex	L. B. & S. C.	Three Bridges and Tunbridge Wells.
.	.	.	.	.	.	. .	Imberhorne Siding	Sussex	L. B. & S. C.	Grange Road and East Grinstead.
G	P	F	.	H	C	. .	Low Level	Sussex	L. B. & S. C.	Lingfield and Kingscote.
.	.	.	.	.	.	. .	Stenning & Son's Siding....	Sussex	L. B. & S. C.	East Grinstead.
							EAST HAM—			
G	P	.	.	.	.	. .	Station (L. T. & S.)	Essex	L. T. & S. / Mid.	Plaistow and Barking. / Over L. T. & S. from Woodgrange Park Junction.
.	P	.	.	.	.	. .				
.	.	.	.	.	.	. .	Junction	Essex	L. T. & S.	East Ham and Barking.
.	.	.	.	.	.	. .	Loop North Junction.........	Essex	L. T. & S.	East Ham and Woodgrange Park.
.	.	.	.	.	.	. .	Easthaugh, H. J., Siding ...	Suffolk ..	G. E.	Lowestoft (Central).
G	P	F	L	H	.	. .	Easthaven	Forfar....	D. & A. Jt. (Cal. & N. B.)	Dundee and Arbroath.
.	.	.	.	.	.	. .	East Hecla Works..............	Yorks	G. C.—L.D. & E.C.—Mid.	See Hadfield's Steel Foundry Co.
.	.	.	.	.	.	. .	East Hedley Hope Colliery and Coke Ovens	Durham ...	N. E.	Waterhouses.
.	.	.	.	.	.	. .	East Hetton (Kelloe) Colliery Clay Mills and Brick Wks.	Durham ..	N. E.	Coxhoe.
.	.	.	.	.	.	. .	East Holywell Colliery	Northumb	N. E.	Holywell.
G	P	F	L	H	C	. .	East Horndon	Essex	L. T. & S.	Upminster and Pitsea.
.	.	.	.	.	.	. .	East House Depôts	Durham ..	N. E.	Usworth.
.	.	.	.	.	.	. .	East Howle Colliery Coke and Brick Works	Durham ...	N. E.	Ferryhill.
.	.	.	.	.	.	. .	East India Docks (L. & I. D.)	Middlesex	G E—GN—GW—L&NW —Mid.—N L	See London.
.	.	.	.	.	.	. .	East India Docks Goods Depôt and Coal Wharf	Middlesex	G. N.	See London, Poplar.
.	.	.	.	.	.	. .	East India Harbour	Renfrew..	Cal.	See Greenock.
.	.	.	.	.	.	. .	East India Road...............	Middlesex	N. L.	See London, Poplar.
G	P	F	L	H	C	3 0	East Kilbride	Lanark ..	Cal.	Busby and High Blantyre.
G	P	.	L	H	.	1 10	East Langton	Leicester	Mid.	Market Harboro' and Kibworth.
G	P	F	L	H	C	. .	East Leake	Notts	G. C.	Nottingham and Loughboro'.
.	.	.	.	.	.	. .	Barnstone Blue Lias Lime Co.—			
.	.	.	.	.	.	. .	Hotchley Hill Siding......	Notts	G. C.	East Leake.
.	.	.	.	.	.	. .	Normanton Hill Siding...	Notts	G. C.	East Leake.
.	.	.	.	.	.	. .	Paget's Siding	Notts	G. C.	East Leake.
G	P	F	L	H	C	10 0	Eastleigh and Bishopstoke ...	Hants	L. & S.W.	Winchester and Southampton.
.	.	.	.	.	.	. .	Otterbourne Siding	Hants	L. & S.W.	Eastleigh and Bishopstoke.
.	.	.	.	.	.	. .	Wheeler & Co.'s Siding......	Hants	L. & S.W.	Near Eastleigh and Bishopstoke.

EXPLANATION—G *Goods Station.*   P *Passenger and Parcel Station.*   P* *Passenger, but not Parcel or Miscellaneous Traffic.*
F *Furniture Vans, Carriages, Portable Engines, and Machines on Wheels.*   L *Live Stock.*
H *Horse Boxes and Prize Cattle Vans.*   C *Carriages by Passenger Train.*

STATION ACCOMMODATION.						CRANE POWER.	STATIONS, &c.	COUNTY.	COMPANY.	POSITION.
G	P	F	L	H	C	Tons 3 Cwts. 0	East Linton	Hadding'n	N. B.	Edinburgh and Dunbar.
							East London Water Works—			
.	.	.	.	.	.		Siding	Essex	G. E.	London, Lea Bridge.
.	.	.	.	.	.		Siding (Black Horse Road)	Essex	T.&F.G.Jt. (LT&S&Mid.)	London, St. Pancras.
.	.	.	.	.	.		Siding	Middlesex	L. & S.W.	Sunbury.
.	P*	.	.	.	.		East Margate	Kent	S. E. & C.	Margate, W. & Ramsgate Harbour.
.	.	.	.	.	.		East Markham Siding	Notts	G. N.	Tuxford.
.	.	.	.	.	.		East Minster-on-Sea	Kent	S. E. & C. (Sheppey)	Sheerness East & Minster (Sheppey).
.	.	.	.	.	.		East Molesey	Surrey	L. & S.W.	See Hampton Court & East Molesey.
.	.	.	.	.	.		East Moors	Glamorg'n	GW—L N W—Rhy—TV	Same as Dowlais Iron & Steel Works (Cardiff).
G	P	F	L	H	C	. .	East Norton	Leicester	G. N. & L. & N. W. Jt.	Market Harboro' & Melton Mowbray
							East of Fife Central Junction	Fife	N. B.	Cameron Bridge and Kennoway.
G	P	F	L	H	C	. .	Eastoft	Yorks	Axholme Jt (L & Y & N E)	Branch near Goole.
.	.	.	.	.	.		Blacker's Siding	Yorks	Axholme Jt (L & Y & N E)	Eastoft and Reedness Junction.
.	.	.	.	.	.		Whitgift Siding	Yorks	Axholme Jt (L & Y & N E)	Eastoft.
G	P	.	.	.	.	10 0	Easton	Dorset	E. & C. H. (G W & L & S W)	Branch from Portland.
.	.	.	.	.	.		Quarry Tip Siding	Dorset	E. & C. H. (G W & L & S W)	Easton.
.	.	.	.	.	.		Sheepcroft Siding	Dorset	E. & C. H. (G W & L & S W)	Easton.
.	.	.	.	.	.		Webber & Pangbourne's Sid.	Dorset	E.&C.H.(G.W&L.& S.W)	Easton.
.	.	.	.	.	.		Webber & Pangbourne's Sid.	Dorset	E.&C.H.(G.W&L.& S.W)	Off Quarry Tip Siding.
.	.	.	.	.	.		Easton & Anderson's Siding	Kent	S. E. & C.	Erith.
.	.	.	.	.	.		Easton Col. (Hopetoun Col.)	L'lithgow	N. B.	Bathgate, Lower.
G	P	F	L	H	C	. .	Easton Court (for Little Hereford)	Hereford	TenburyJt(GW&L&NW)	Tenbury and Woofferton.
.	P	.	.	.	.		Easton Lodge	Essex	G. E.	Dunmow and Bishops Stortford.
.	.	.	.	.	.		East Parkhead Colliery	Lanark	{ Cal. { N. B.	Uddingston. Bellshill.
.	.	.	.	.	.		East Pilton Siding	Edinboro'	Cal.	Leith.
.	.	.	.	.	.		East Pit Colliery	Lancs	L. & N. W.	See Latham Bros. (Wigan).
.	.	.	.	.	.		East Pontop Col. & Ck. Wks.	Durham	N. E.	Annfield Plain.
.	P	.	.	.	.		East Putney	Surrey	L. & S.W.	Wimbledon and Putney Bridge.
.	.	.	.	.	.		Eastrigg Colliery	L'lithgow	N. B.	Westfield.
G	P	F	L	H	C	. . }	Eastrington	Yorks	{ H. & B. { N. E.	Howden and Hull. Hull and Selby.
G	P	.	L	H	.					
.	.	.	.	.	.		Caville Bridge Siding	Yorks	N. E.	Eastrington.
.	.	.	.	.	.		East Rosedale	Yorks	N. E.	See Rosedale, East.
.	.	.	.	.	.		East Roughrigg Colliery	Stirling	N. B.	Bowhouse.
G	P	F	L	H	C	1 0	East Rudham	Norfolk	Mid. & G. N. Jt.	South Lynn and Melton Constable.
.	.	.	.	.	.		East Ryhope	Durham	N. E.	See Ryhope, East.
.	.	.	.	.	.		East Sheen	Surrey	L. & S.W.	See Mortlake and East Sheen.
.	.	.	.	.	.		East Slade Colliery	Glo'ster	G. W.	Bilson Junction.
.	.	.	.	.	.		East Smithfield	Essex	L. & I. Dks.	See London Docks (East Smithfield).
.	.	.	.	.	.		East Southsea	Hants	L & S W & L B & S C Jt.	See Portsmouth.
.	.	.	.	.	.		East Street	Dorset	G. W.	See Bridport.
.	.	.	.	.	.		East Street Siding	Derby	G. C.	Grassmoor.
.	.	.	.	.	.		East Sussex County Council Asylum Siding	Sussex	L. B. & S. C.	Hellingly.
.	.	.	.	.	.		East Tanfield Colliery, Coke and Brick Works	Durham	N. E.	Redheugh.
.	.	.	.	.	.		East Usk Junction	Mon	G. W.	Newport.
.	.	.	.	.	.		East Usk Wharf (Gt. Western Wharf)	Mon	G. W.	Newport.
G	P	F	L	H	C	. .	East Ville	Lincoln	G. N.	Boston and Louth.
.	.	.	.	.	.		East Wall Siding	Dublin	G. S. & W.	See Dublin.
.	.	.	.	.	.		East Wheal Rose Siding	Cornwall	G. W.	Treamble.
G	P	F	L	H	C	. .	East Winch	Norfolk	G. E.	Lynn and Swaffham.
.	.	.	.	.	.		Eastwood	Derby	Mid.	See Langley Mill and Eastwood.
G	P	.	.	.	.	4 0	Eastwood	Yorks	L. & Y.	Todmorden and Sowerby Bridge.
.	.	.	.	.	.		Eastwood & Co.'s Siding	Essex	L. T. & S.	Shoeburyness.
.	.	.	.	.	.		Eastwood & Co.'s Siding	Middlesex	L. & N. W.	Sudbury and Wembley.
G	P	F	L	H	C	10 0	Eastwood and Langley Mill	Notts	G. N.	Kimberley and Pinxton.
.	.	.	.	.	.		Barber, Walker & Co.'s Sid.	Notts	G. N.	Eastwood and Codnor Park.
.	.	.	.	.	.		Brinsley Colliery (G. N.)	Notts	G. N.—G. C.	Eastwood and Codnor Park.
.	.	.	.	.	.		High Park Colliery (G. N.)	Notts	G. N.—G. C.	Eastwood and Codnor Park.
.	.	.	.	.	.		Langley Mill Colliery (G.N.)	Notts	G. N.—G. C.	Eastwood and Codnor Park.
.	.	.	.	.	.		Moor Green Colliery (G.N.)	Notts	G. N.—G. C.	Eastwood and Codnor Park.
.	.	.	.	.	.		Plumptre Colliery (G. N.)	Notts	G. N.—G. C.	Eastwood and Codnor Park.
.	.	.	.	.	.		Pollington Colliery (G. N.)	Notts	G. N.—G. C.	Eastwood and Codnor Park.
.	.	.	.	.	.		Selston Colliery (G. N.)	Notts	G. N.—G. C.	Eastwood and Codnor Park.
.	.	.	.	.	.		Stoney Lane Siding	Notts	G. N.	Eastwood and Codnor Park.
.	.	.	.	.	.		Underwood Colliery	Notts	G. N.	Eastwood and Codnor Park.

EXPLANATION—G *Goods Station.*   P *Passenger and Parcel Station.*   P* *Passenger, but not Parcel or Miscellaneous Traffic.*
F *Furniture Vans, Carriages, Portable Engines, and Machines on Wheels.*   L *Live Stock.*
H *Horse Boxes and Prize Cattle Vans.*   C *Carriages by Passenger Train.*

STATION ACCOMMODATION.						CRANE POWER.	STATIONS, &c.	COUNTY.	COMPANY.	POSITION.
						Tons Cwts.	Eastwood's Wagon Works ...	Derby	Mid.	Chesterfield.
							Eastwood's Wagon Works ...	Notts	Mid.	Stapleford and Sandiacre.
							Eastwood, Swingler & Co.'s Iron Works	Derby	Mid.	Derby.
							Eatock Pit	Lancs	L. & Y.	See Wigan Coal & Iron Co. (Hindley).
									L. & N. W.	See Wigan Coal & Iron Co.'s Chowbent West Jn. Siding (Wigan).
G	P						Eaton	Salop	Bishop's Castle	Craven Arms and Bishop's Castle.
							Eaton Siding (G. N.)	Leicester	G. N.—Mid.	Waltham-on-the-Wold.
							Eaton's Siding	Derby	Mid.	Derby, Pear Tree and Normanton.
							Eaton's, W., Siding	Derby	Mid.	Same as Bull Bridge Lime Works (Ambergate).
G	P		L	H			Ebberston	Yorks	N. E.	Pickering and Seamer.
							Ebbw Junction	Mon	G. W.	Newport.
G	P	F	L	H	C	1 15	Ebbw Vale	Mon.	G. W.	Branch from Aberbeeg.
G	P	F	L	H	C	1 0			L. & N. W.	Branch from Beaufort.
							Duffryn Siding	Mon	G. W.	Ebbw Vale and Victoria.
							Ebbw Vale Steel, Iron, and Coal Co.—			
							Gantra Siding	Mon	L. & N. W.	Beaufort and Ebbw Vale.
							Siding	Mon	L. & N. W.	Ebbw Vale.
							Works & Ebbw Vale Col.	Mon	G. W.	Ebbw Vale.
							Waen Llwyd Colliery	Mon	G. W.	Ebbw Vale and Cwm.
							Ebbw Vale Steel, Iron, and Coal Co.—			
							Gantra Siding	Mon	L. & N. W.	Ebbw Vale.
							Siding	Mon	L. & N. W.	Ebbw Vale.
							Siding	Mon	L. & N. W.	Sirhowy.
							Siding	Mon	L. & N. W.	Trevil.
							Works and Ebbw Vale Col.	Mon	G. W.	Ebbw Vale.
G	P		L			3 0	Ebchester	Durham	N. E.	Newcastle and Blackhill.
							Hamsterley Colliery	Durham	N. E.	Ebchester.
							Shotley Bridge Siding	Durham	N. E.	Ebchester and Blackhill.
							Westwood Colliery	Durham	N. E.	Ebchester.
	P						Ebdon Lane	Somerset	W. C. & P.	Weston-super-Mare and Clevedon.
							Ebford Siding(Odam's Manure Siding)	Devon	L. & S. W.	Topsham.
G	P	F	L	H	C	4 10	Ecclefechan	Dumfries	Cal.	Carlisle and Lockerbie.
	P						Eccles (L. & N. W.)	Lancs	L. & N. W.	Kenyon Junc. Sta. and Manchester.
									G. W.	Over L. & N. W. from Walton Junc.
							Ecclesall	Derby	Mid.	See Sheffield, Mill Houses & Ecclesall
							Eccles Bridge Siding (Bryant & Son)	Norfolk	G. E.	Eccles Road.
							Eccles Bros.' Siding	Lancs	P.&L.Jt. (L&NW.&L&Y)	Preston, Deepdale.
G	P		L			2 0	Ecclesfield	Yorks	G. C.	Sheffield and Barnsley.
G	P		L			1 10			Mid.	Chapeltown Branch.
							Newton Chambers & Co.'s Smithy Wood Colliery	Yorks	G. C.	Ecclesfield.
									Mid.	Ecclesfield and Chapeltown.
							Eccleshall	Staffs	L. & N. W.	See Badnall Wharf (for Eccleshall).
							Eccleshill	Yorks	G. N.	See Bradford.
G	P	F	L	H	C	1 0	Eccles Road	Norfolk	G. E.	Norwich and Thetford.
							Eccles Bridge Siding (Bryant & Son)	Norfolk	G. E.	Eccles Road and Harling Road.
							Eccleston Branch	Lancs	L. & N. W.	Peasley Cross and St. Helens.
							Eccleston Hall Coal Yard	Lancs	L. & N. W.	St. Helens.
							Eccleston Hall or Gillers Green Colliery	Lancs	L. & N. W.	St. Helens.
	P						Eccleston Park	Lancs	L. & N. W.	Liverpool and St. Helens.
							Eccleston Pottery Siding	Lancs	L. & N. W.	See Pilkington Bros. (St. Helens).
G	P		L	H		1 10	Eckington	Worcester	Mid.	Defford and Cheltenham.
							ECKINGTON & RENISHAW—			
G	P	F	L	H	C	10 0	(Station)	Derby	Mid.	Chesterfield and Masboro'.
G	P	F	L	H	C	10 0	(Station, G. C.)	Derby	G. C.	Sheffield and Chesterfield.
G		F	L			10 0			L. & N. W.	Over G. N. & G. C. Lines.
							Appleby & Co.'s Works	Derby	Mid.	Eckington and Renishaw.
							Eckington Colliery	Derby	Mid.	Beighton and Staveley.
							Hornthorpe Colliery	Derby	Mid.	Eckington and Renishaw.
							Hornthorpe Colliery (G. C.)	Derby	G. C.—L. & N. W.	Eckington and Renishaw.
							Plumbley Colliery	Derby	Mid.	Eckington and Renishaw.
							Renishaw Colliery	Derby	Mid.	Eckington and Renishaw.
							Renishaw Foundry	Derby	G. C.	Eckington and Renishaw.
							Renishaw Iron Works	Derby	G. C.—Mid.	Eckington and Renishaw.

EXPLANATION—G Goods Station.   P Passenger and Parcel Station.   P* Passenger, but not Parcel or Miscellaneous Traffic.
F Furniture Vans, Carriages, Portable Engines, and Machines on Wheels.   L Live Stock.
H Horse Boxes and Prize Cattle Vans.   C Carriages by Passenger Train.

STATION ACCOMMODATION.						CRANE POWER.	STATIONS, &c.	COUNTY.	COMPANY.	POSITION.
						Tons Cwts.	ECKINGTON & RENISHAW—continued.			
.	.	.	.	.	.	. .	Renishaw Park Collieries...	Derby	Mid.	Eckington and Renishaw.
.	.	.	.	.	.	. .	Renishaw Park Collieries (Eckington Colliery) (GC)	Derby	G. C.—L. & N. W.	Eckington and Renishaw.
.	.	.	.	.	.	. .	Wells, J. & G., Siding	Derby	Mid.	Eckington and Renishaw.
.	.	.	.	.	.	. .	Eckington Colliery	Derby	Mid.	Eckington and Renishaw.
.	.	.	.	.	.	. .	Eckington Colliery (G. C.)	Derby	G. C.—L. & N. W.	Same as Renishaw Park Collieries.
.	.	.	.	.	.	. .	Eclipse Silica Brick Works...	Durham	N. E.	Crook.
.	.	.	.	.	.	. .	Eclipse Works	Lanark	Cal.	Glasgow, Buchanan Street.
G	P	F	L	H	C	. .	Edale	Derby	Mid.	Dore and Chinley.
G	P	.	L	H	.	2 0	Edderton	Ross & Cro'	High.	Tain and Bonar Bridge.
G	P	F	L	H	C	2 0	Eddleston	Peebles	N. B.	Hawthornden Junction and Peebles.
.	.	.	.	.	.	. .	Eddlewood Colliery	Lanark	Cal.	Meikle Earnock.
.	.	.	.	.	.	. .	Ede & Son's Siding	Devon	G. W.	Plymouth, Sutton Harbour.
G	P	F	L	H	C	4 0	Edenbridge	Kent	S. E. & C.	Red Hill and Tonbridge.
.	.	.	.	.	.	. .	Crowhurst Siding	Kent	S. E. & C.	Godstone and Edenbridge.
G	P	F	L	H	C	1 10	Edenbridge Town	Kent	L. B. & S. C.	Oxted and Groombridge.
.	.	.	.	.	.	. .	Eden Colliery	Durham	N. E.	Leadgate.
G	P	F	L	H	C	1 10	Edenderry	Kings	M. G. W.	Branch from Nesbitt Junction.
.	.	.	.	.	.	. .	Edenfield	Lancs	L. & Y.	See Ewood Bridge and Edenfield.
.	P	.	.	.	.	. .	Eden Park	Kent	S. E. & C.	Elmer's End and Hayes.
.	.	.	.	.	.	. .	Edenside Brick Works	Fife	N. B.	Guard Bridge.
.	P	.	.	.	.	. .	Edermine Ferry	Wexford	D. W. & W.	Arklow and Wexford.
.	.	.	.	.	.	. .	Edge & Sons' Works	Salop	G. W.	Same as Lawton Sid. (Shifnal).
.	.	.	.	.	.	. .	Edgefield Siding	Edinboro'	N. B.	Loanhead.
.	.	.	.	.	.	. .	Edge Green Colliery	Lancs	G. C.—L. & N. W.	See Evans, R., & Co. (Golborne).
.	.	.	.	.	.	. .	Edge Hill	Lancs	C.L.C. (G. C.,G. N.& Mid.)	See Liverpool, Wavertree and Edge Hill.
.	.	.	.	.	.	. .	Edge Hill	Lancs	L. & N. W.	See Liverpool.
.	.	.	.	.	.	. .	Edge Hill Fruit & Vegetable Depôt	Lancs	L. & N. W.	See Liverpool.
.	.	.	.	.	.	. .	Edge Lane	Lancs	L. & N. W.	See Liverpool.
.	.	.	.	.	.	. .	Edgeley	Cheshire	L. & N. W.	See Stockport.
.	.	.	.	.	.	. .	Edgeley Bleach Works	Cheshire	L. & N. W.	Same as Sykes' Siding (Stockport).
G	P	F	L	H	C	1 0	Edgeworthstown	Longford	M. G. W.	Longford and Mullingar.
G	P	F	L	H	C	5 0	Edgware	Middlesex	G. N.	Branch from Finchley.
.	.	.	.	.	.	. .	Edgware Road (Met.)	Middlesex	Met.—G. W.	See London.
.	.	.	.	.	.	. .	Edgworth	Lancs	L. & Y.	See Turton and Edgworth.
							EDINBURGH—			
.	P	.	.	.	.	. .	Abbeyhill	Edinboro'	N. B.	Waverley and Leith Walk.
.	.	.	.	.	.	. .	Abercorn Brick Works	Edinboro'	N. B.	Branch from Portobello.
.	.	.	.	.	.	. .	Baileyfield Siding	Edinboro'	N. B.	Portobello and South Leith.
.	.	.	.	.	.	. .	Balcarres Street Manure Depôt (Edinburgh Cleansing Department's Siding)	Edinboro'	N. B.	Craiglockhart & Morningside Road
.	.	.	.	.	.	. .	Balcarres Street Works (Mackenzie & Moncur)...	Edinboro'	N. B.	Craiglockhart & Morningside Road.
.	.	.	.	.	.	. .	Beattie's Siding	Edinboro'	Cal.	Murrayfield and Slateford.
.	.	.	.	.	.	. .	Bernards', D., Brewery	Edinboro'	N. B.	Gorgie and Haymarket.
.	P	.	.	.	.	. .	Blackford Hill	Edinboro'	N. B.	Gorgie and Newington.
.	.	.	.	.	.	. .	Bonnington, East Junction	Edinboro'	N. B.	Bonnington and Heriothill.
.	.	.	.	.	.	. .	Bonnington, South Junction	Edinboro'	N. B.	Bonnington and Powderhall.
.	.	.	.	.	.	. .	Bridgeside Works	Edinboro'	N. B.	Macdonald Road Sidings.
.	.	.	.	.	.	. .	Brown & Glegg's Siding	Edinboro'	Cal.	Morrison Street Mineral Depôt.
.	.	.	.	.	.	. .	Brown Bros. & Co.'s Siding	Edinboro'	N. B.	Rosebank Sidings.
.	.	.	.	.	.	. .	Brown's Timber Yard	Edinboro'	N. B.	St. Leonard's.
.	.	.	.	.	.	. .	Bruce & Son's Siding	Edinboro'	N. B.	Near Easter Road.
.	.	.	.	.	.	. .	Caledonian Brewery	Edinboro'	Cal.	Slateford and Murrayfield.
.	.	.	.	.	.	. .	Caledonian Distillery (Haymarket Distillery)	Edinboro'	{Cal. {N. B.	Branch near Murrayfield. Haymarket.
							Caledonian Railway Co.—			
.	.	.	.	.	.	. .	Electric & Gas Works...	Edinboro'	Cal.	Edinburgh.
.	.	.	.	.	.	. .	Laundry Siding	Edinboro'	Cal.	Edinburgh and Slateford.
.	.	.	.	.	.	. .	Clunas & Co.'s Siding	Edinboro'	N. B.	Leith Walk.
.	.	.	.	.	.	. .	Coltbridge Junction	Edinboro'	Cal.	Dalry Road and Murrayfield.
							Corporation—			
.	.	.	.	.	.	. .	Electric Light Siding ...	Edinboro'	Cal.	Edinburgh.
.	.	.	.	.	.	. .	Electric Works	Edinboro'	N. B.	Macdonald Road Sidings.
.	.	.	.	.	.	. .	Manure Sid. (Tynecastle)	Edinboro'	Cal.	Slateford and Murrayfield.
.	.	.	.	.	.	. .	Cowan & Co.'s Siding	Edinboro'	N. B.	Leith Walk.
.	P	.	.	.	.	. .	Craiglockhart	Edinboro'	N. B.	Gorgie and Morningside Road.

EXPLANATION—G *Goods Station.*   P *Passenger and Parcel Station.*   P* *Passenger, but not Parcel or Miscellaneous Traffic.*
F *Furniture Vans, Carriages, Portable Engines, and Machines on Wheels.*   L *Live Stock.*
H *Horse Boxes and Prize Cattle Vans.*   C *Carriages by Passenger Train.*

STATION ACCOMMODATION.						CRANE POWER.		STATIONS, &c.	COUNTY.	COMPANY.	POSITION.
						Tons	Cwts				
								EDINBURGH—continued.			
								Currie & Co.'s Siding.........	Edinboro'	N. B.	Scotland Street.
	P							Dalry Road	Edinboro'	Cal.	Edinburgh and Leith.
								Dalry Road Stone Siding...	Edinboro'	Cal.	Edinburgh and Leith.
								Dobson, Molle & Co.'s Sid.	Edinboro'	N. B.	Easter Road and Leith Walk.
								Dundee Str. Manure Depôt	Edinboro'	Cal.	Merchiston and Edinburgh.
								Dundee Terrace Stone Sid.	Edinboro'	Cal.	Merchiston and Edinburgh.
	P							Easter Road	Edinboro'	N. B.	Waverley and Leith Walk.
								Easter Road Junction	Edinboro'	N. B.	Easter Road and Portobello.
								Edinburgh Brewery (Bernard's, T. & J., Siding)...	Edinboro'	N. B.	Gorgie.
								Forest's Stone Dressing Sid.	Edinboro'	N. B.	Gorgie.
								Fountain Brewery	Edinboro'	Cal.	Merchiston and Edinburgh.
								Gas Works	Edinboro'	N. B.	Waverley and Abbeyhill.
G	.	L				5	0	Gorgie	Edinboro'	{ Cal.	Slateford and Merchiston.
G	P	F L				3	0			{ N. B.	Saughton and Newington.
								Gorgie Junction	Edinboro'	N. B.	Gorgie and Saughton.
								Harrison Park Siding	Edinboro'	Cal.	Edinburgh and Merchiston.
								Haymarket—			
G	P	F L H C				6	0	(Station)	Edinboro'	N. B.	Waverley and Ratho.
								Central Junction	Edinboro'	N. B.	Haymarket and Gorgie.
								Siding	Edinboro'	Cal.	Branch near Murrayfield.
								West Junction	Edinboro'	Cal.—N. B.	Edinburgh and Saughton.
								West Yard Sidings (Roseburn Sidings)............	Edinboro'	N. B.	Haymarket and Saughton.
								Herdman's Siding	Edinboro'	N. B.	Haymarket.
G								Heriothill Depôt	Edinboro'	N. B.	Trinity and Scotland Street.
								Heriothill Saw Mills	Edinboro'	N. B.	Trinity and Scotland Street.
								Hydraulic Siding	Edinboro'	N. B.	Easter Road and Portobello.
								Jeffrey & Co.'s Siding	Edinboro'	Cal.	Slateford and Murrayfield.
G	P	. L				2	0	Joppa	Edinboro'	N. B.	Portobello and Inveresk Junc. Sta.
								Kinnear, Moodie & Co.'s Stone Sidings	Edinboro'	Cal.	Slateford and Murrayfield.
G	P	F L				4	0	Leith Walk (N. B.)	Edinboro'	{ N. B. .... N B, G N, & N E (E. Coast)	} Waverley and Granton.
								Lindsay & Son's Siding.....	Edinboro'	N. B.	Waverley.
								Scarlett's Siding............	Edinboro'	N. B.	Lindsay & Son's Siding.
								Veitch, Moir & Erskines' Siding	Edinboro'	N. B.	Lindsay & Son's Siding.
								Lochend, North Junction	Edinboro'	N. B.	Abbeyhill and Leith, Central.
								Lochend Siding (Younger & Co.) (Moray Park Sid.)	Edinboro'	N. B.	Abbeyhill and Piershill.
								Lochend South Junction ...	Edinboro'	N. B.	Abbeyhill and Piershill.
								Lochend Steel Works	Edinboro'	N. B.	Easter Road and Portobello.
								London Road Foundry (Miller and Co.)	Edinboro'	N. B.	Abbeyhill and Piershill.
								London Road Junction......	Edinboro'	N. B.	Waverley and Abbeyhill.
								Lonies Siding	Edinboro'	Cal.	Edinburgh and Merchiston.
								Lorimer & Clark's Siding	Edinboro'	Cal.	Slateford and Murrayfield.
G	.	F L				10	0	Lothian Road	Edinboro'	Cal.	Terminus.
								McAndrew & Co.'s Stone Siding	Edinboro'	Cal.	Edinburgh and Murrayfield.
								Macdonald Road Sidings...	Edinboro'	N. B.	Leith Walk and Powderhall.
								McEwan's Malt Barns Sid.	Edinboro'	Cal.	Gorgie.
								McEwan's Siding	Edinboro'	Cal.	Merchiston and Edinburgh.
								McKenzie Bros.' Foundry...	Edinboro'	Cal.	Gorgie.
								McLeod's Siding...............	Edinboro'	Cal.	Morrison Street Mineral Depôt.
								Martin's Stone Siding	Edinboro'	Cal.	Slateford and Murrayfield.
								Mather's Foundry	Edinboro'	Cal.	Edinburgh and Murrayfield.
								Meadowbank Siding	Edinboro'	N. B.	Waverley and Portobello.
	P							Merchiston	Edinboro'	Cal.	Carstairs and Edinburgh.
G	P	. L				5	0	Morningside Road	Edinboro'	N. B.	Gorgie and Portobello.
G	.	L				4	10	Morrison Street Depôts.....	Edinboro'	Cal.	Edinburgh.
G	P					3	0	Murrayfield	Edinboro'	Cal.	Edinburgh and Leith.
G	P	F L				3	0	Newington	Edinboro'	N. B.	Morningside Road and Portobello.
								North British Distillery Co.'s Siding...............	Edinboro'	N. B.	Gorgie.
								N. B. Railway—			
								Engineer's Oil Gas Works	Edinboro'	N. B.	Easter Road and Portobello.
								Engineer's Siding	Edinboro'	N. B.	Easter Road and Portobello.
								Telegraph Depôt	Edinboro'	N. B.	Easter Road and Portobello.
								Old Cattle Sid. (Dundee Str.)	Edinboro'	Cal.	Merchiston and Edinburgh.

EXPLANATION—G *Goods Station.*   P *Passenger and Parcel Station.*   P* *Passenger, but not Parcel or Miscellaneous Traffic.*
F *Furniture Vans, Carriages, Portable Engines, and Machines on Wheels.*   L *Live Stock.*
H *Horse Boxes and Prize Cattle Vans.*   C *Carriages by Passenger Train.*

STATION ACCOMMODATION.						CRANE POWER.		STATIONS, &c.	COUNTY.	COMPANY.	POSITION
						Tons	Cwts.	EDINBURGH—continued.			
	P							Palace Brewery	Edinboro'	N. B.	Rose Lane.
	P							Piershill	Edinboro'	N. B.	Abbeyhill and Portobello.
								Piershill Junction	Edinboro'	N. B.	Portobello and Waverley.
G	P		L	H	C	3	0	Portobello	Edinboro'	N. B.	Edinburgh and Prestonpans.
								Portobello East Junction ...	Edinboro'	N. B.	Portobello and Joppa.
								Portobello West Junction...	Edinboro'	N. B.	Piershill and Portobello.
	P							Powderhall	Edinboro'	N. B.	Leith Walk and Bonnington.
	P			H	C			Princes Street..................	Edinboro'	Cal.	Terminus.
								Robertson's Siding............	Edinboro'	Cal.	Merchiston and Edinburgh.
								Rosebank Foundry	Edinboro'	N. B.	Rosebank Sidings.
								Rosebank Sidings............	Edinboro'	N. B.	Leith Walk and Powderhall.
								Roseburn Brewery............	Edinboro'	Cal.	Slateford and Murrayfield.
G						3	0	Rose Lane	Edinboro'	N. B.	Waverley and Portobello.
								Royal Asylum Siding	Edinboro'	N. B.	Morningside Road.
								St. Andrew's Steel Works (Redpath, Brown & Co.'s)	Edinboro'	N. B.	Easter Road and Leith Walk.
G						4	0	St. Leonard's...................	Edinboro'	N. B.	Branch from Duddingston.
								St. Margaret's Gas Works	Edinboro'	N. B.	Rose Lane and Portobello.
								St. Margaret's Locomotive Works	Edinboro'	N. B.	Rose Lane and Portobello.
G						3	0	Scotland Street	Edinboro'	N. B.	Branch—Piershill and Granton.
								"Scotsman" Siding	Edinboro'	N. B.	Waverley.
								Scottish Mushroom Co.'s Siding	Edinboro'	N. B.	Scotland Street.
								Shrubhill Sid. (Edinburgh & District Tramway Co.)	Edinboro'	N. B.	Leith Walk and Powderhall.
								Sloan & Son's Siding.........	Edinboro'	N. B.	Leith Walk.
								Smith & Ritchie's Siding...	Edinboro'	N. B.	Leith Walk.
								South Leith Junction	Edinboro'	N. B.	Portobello and South Leith.
								Steel's Siding	Edinboro'	Cal.	Edinburgh and Murrayfield.
								Stewardson & Co.'s Siding	Edinboro'	N. B.	Leith Walk.
								Stuart's Granolithic Works	Edinboro'	Cal.	Branch near Murrayfield.
								Swan's Live Stock Mart Siding	Edinboro'	N. B.	Haymarket.
								Thorburn & Co.'s Stone Sid.	Edinboro'	Cal.	Edinburgh and Murrayfield.
								Turner & Son's Siding......	Edinboro'	N. B.	Gorgie and Haymarket.
								Tynecastle Siding	Edinboro'	Cal.	Slateford and Murrayfield.
								Usher & Co.'s Distillery.....	Edinboro'	N. B.	St. Leonard's.
								Usher & Son's Brewery......	Edinboro'	N. B.	St. Leonard's.
								Warriston Junction	Edinboro'	N. B.	Trinity and Scotland Street.
								Watherston & Son's Stone Siding	Edinboro'	Cal.	Edinburgh and Murrayfield.
G	P	F	L	H	C	10	0	Waverley (N. B.)	Edinboro'	{ N. B. { N. E.	Portobello and Haymarket. Over N. B. from Berwick.
	P										
								Waverley Oil & Cake Mills	Edinboro'	Cal.	Merchiston and Edinburgh.
								Westbank Brick Works...	Edinboro'	N. B.	Portobello.
								West End Engine Works...	Edinboro'	Cal.	Merchiston and Edinburgh.
								Wood's Bottle Works	Edinboro'	N. B.	Portobello.
								Edinburgh & District Tramway Co.'s Siding	Edinboro'	N. B.	Same as Shrubhill Sid. (Edinburgh).
								Edinburgh and Leith Gas Co.'s Siding	Edinboro'	{ Cal.—N. B. { N. B.	Granton. Leith, South.
								Edinburgh Brewery Siding (Bernards, T. & J.)	Edinboro'	N. B.	Edinburgh, Gorgie.
								Edinburgh Cleansing Department's Siding	Edinboro'	N. B.	{ Same as Balcarres Street Manure { Depôt (Edinburgh).
								Edinburgh Corporation— Electric Light Siding	Edinboro'	Cal.	Edinburgh, Lothian Road.
								Electric Works	Edinboro'	N. B.	Edinburgh, Leith Walk.
								Manure Siding (Tynecastle)	Edinboro'	Cal.	Edinburgh, Lothian Road.
								Edinburgh Dock...............	Edinboro'	Cal.—N. B.	See Leith.
								Edinburgh Foundry	Edinboro'	Cal.	Same as McKenzie Bros.' Foundry.
								Edinburgh Gas Works	Edinboro'	N. B.	Edinburgh, Waverley.
								Edinburgh Malting Co.'s Sid.	Edinboro'	N. W.	Duddingston & Craigmillar.
G	P	F	L	H	C	1	10	Edington & Bratton	Wilts	G. W.	Westbury and Patney.
								Edington Junction	Somerset..	S.&D.Jt.(L.&S.W.&Mid)	Cossington and Edington Junc. Sta.
G	P		L	H				Edington Junction Station ...	Somerset..	S.&D.Jt.(L.&S.W.&Mid)	Glastonbury and Highbridge.
								Board's Siding	Somerset..	S.&D.Jt.(L.&S.W.&Mid)	Edington Junc. Sta. and Cossington.
								Edison & De Mattos' Siding	Dorset......	L. & S.W.	Dorchester.
G	P		L					Edlingham	Northumb	N. E.	Alnwick and Coldstream.
								Summit Siding	Northumb	N. E.	Edlingham and Alnwick.

EXPLANATION—G *Goods Station.*　　P *Passenger and Parcel Station.*　　P* *Passenger, but not Parcel or Miscellaneous Traffic.*
F *Furniture Vans, Carriages, Portable Engines, and Machines on Wheels.*　　L *Live Stock.*
H *Horse Boxes and Prize Cattle Vans.*　　C *Carriages by Passenger Train.*

G	P	F	L	H	C	Tons	Cwts	STATIONS, &c.	COUNTY.	COMPANY.	POSITION.
	P							Edme Siding	Essex	G. E.	Mistley.
G	P	F	L	H	C	1	10	Edmondstown	Mayo	M. G. W.	Kilfree and Ballaghaderreen.
								Edmondthorpe & Wymondham	Lincoln	Mid.	Saxby and Little Bytham Junction.
								Boam, J., & Co.'s Brk. Yard	Lincoln	Mid.	Near Edmondthorpe & Wymondham.
								Edmonsley Col. & Coke Ovens	Durham	N. E.	Pelton.
								Edmonsley Depôts	Durham	N. E.	Pelton.
								Edmonton, Lower	Middlesex	G. E.	See Lower Edmonton.
								Edmonton, Upper	Middlesex	G. E.	See Silver Str. (for Upper Edmonton).
G	P	F	L	H	C	2	10	Edrom	Berwick	N. B.	Reston and Duns.
G	P	F	L	H	C	1	10	Edwalton	Notts	Mid.	Nottingham and Melton Mowbray.
								Smart's Brick Works	Notts	Mid.	Nottingham and Edwalton.
								Edwards & Co.'s Dyffryn Tin Plate Works (Mid.)	Glamorg'n	Mid.—G. W.—L. & N. W.	Morriston.
								Edwards, H., & Son's Siding	Suffolk	G. E.	Woodbridge.
								Edward's Siding	Flint	L. & N. W.	See Nerquis Old Colliery Level Siding (Coed Talon).
								Edward's Siding	Hants	L. & S. W.	Bishops Waltham.
G	P	F	L	H	C	3	0	Edward Street (G. N., I.)	Down	D. N. & G.—G. N. (I.)	See Newry.
	P			H	C			Edwinstowe (L. D. & E. C.)	Notts	L. D. & E. C.	Langwith Junction and Tuxford.
G	P		L	H	C	2	0		Notts	Mid.	Over L. D. & E. C. from Shirebrook Jn.
G	P	F	L	H	C			Edzell	Forfar	Cal.	Branch Terminus near Brechin.
	P							Efail Isaf	Glamorg'n	Barry	Creigiau and Pontypridd.
								Effingham Junction Station	Surrey	L. & S. W.	Surbiton and Guildford.
								Egerton Dock	Cheshire	C.L.C—G. W.—L.& N.W.—N. W. & L.	See Birkenhead.
G	P	F	L	H	C	5	0	Eggesford	Devon	L. & S. W.	Exeter and Barnstaple.
G		P	F	L	H	C			Egginton	Derby	N. S.	Uttoxeter and Willington Junction.
	P	F	L	H	C			Egginton Joint Station	Derby	G. N.	Derby and Burton.
	P	F		H	C				Derby	N. S.	Uttoxeter and Willington Junction.
								Egginton Junction	Derby	G. N.—N. S.	Derby and Burton.
								Eggworthy Siding	Devon	G. W.	Dousland.
G	P	F	L	H	C	5	0	Egham	Surrey	L. & S. W.	Staines and Reading.
								Paices Siding	Surrey	L. & S. W.	Egham.
G	P		L	H				Eglinton	Derry	N. C. Com. (Mid.)	Londonderry and Coleraine.
								Eglinton Ammonia Works	Ayr	Cal.	Kilwinning.
								Eglinton Chemical Co.'s Wks.	Lanark	Cal.	Langloan.
								Eglinton Chemical Works	Ayr	G. & S. W.	Irvine Harbour.
								Eglinton Fire Clay Works (Kenneth's)	Ayr	G. & S. W.	Kilwinning.
								Eglinton Foundry	Renfrew	Cal.—G. & S. W.	Same as Port Eglinton Foundry (Glasgow).
								Eglinton Foundry (Howie's)	Ayr	G. & S. W.	Kilwinning.
								Eglinton Iron Works & Cols.	Ayr	Cal.—G. & S. W.	Kilwinning.
								Eglinton No. 1	Ayr	G. & S. W.	Kilwinning.
								Eglinton Quarry	Ayr	G. & S. W.	Same as Clonbeith Qry. (Kilwinning)
								Eglinton Silica Brick Works	Lanark	Cal.	Same as Dundyvan Silica Brick Works (Langloan).
								Eglinton Silica Brick Works	Lanark	N. B.	Coatbridge, Whifflet.
								Eglinton Street	Lanark	Cal.—G & P Jt.—G & S W	See Glasgow.
G	P	F	L	H	C			Egloskerry	Cornwall	L. & S. W.	Launceston and Wadebridge.
								Eglwysbach	Denbigh	L. & N. W.	See Tal-y-Cafn and Eglwysbach.
G	P	F	L	H	C	3	0	Egremont (Wirral)	Cheshire	Wirral—G. C.	See Seacombe and Egremont.
G	P		L					Egremont	Cumb'land	WC & EJt. (Fur. & LNW)	Moor Row and Sellafield.
								Egton Bridge	Yorks	N. E.	Whitby and Castleton.
								Ehen Valley Branch	Cumb'land	WC & EJt (Fur. & LNW)	Branch from Gillfoot.
								Ehen Valley Branch Pits—Nos. 1, 2, and 3	Cumb'land	WC & EJt (Fur. & LNW)	See Lindow's (Gillfoot).
								Nos. 6 and 11	Cumb'land	WC & EJt (Fur. & LNW)	See Bain & Co. (Gillfoot).
G	P							Eigg	Inverness	Cal.	Steamer from Oban.
								Eighton Banks Hauling Engine	Durham	N. E.	Birtley.
								Eirw Branch Junction	Glamorg'n	T. V.	Porth and Hafod.
								Eirw Gas Works (Porth Gas Works)	Glamorg'n	T. V.	Porth.
								Elan Junction	Radnor	Cam.	Rhayader and Doldowlod.
								Elba Colliery	Glamorg'n	G. W.—L. & N. W.	See Baldwin's, Ltd. (Gowerton).
								Elba Steel Works	Glamorg'n	G. W.—L. & N. W.	See Baldwin's, Ltd. (Gowerton).
								Elbowend Junction	Fife	N. B.	Charlestown and Netherton.
								Elbowend Siding	Fife	N. B.	Netherton.
	P*							Elburton Cross	Devon	G. W.	Plymstock and Yealmpton.
G	P					2	0	Elderslie	Renfrew	G. & S. W.	Paisley and Johnstone.

STATION ACCOMMODATION.						CRANE POWER.		STATIONS, &c.	COUNTY.	COMPANY.	POSITION.
						Tons	Cwts				
.	.	.	.	.	.	.	.	Elderslie Junction	Renfrew	G. & S.W.	Elderslie and Johnstone.
.	.	.	.	.	.	.	.	Elderslie Shipyard & Graving Dock	Renfrew	Cal.	Glasgow, Whiteinch.
.	.	.	.	.	.	.	.	Elders Navigation Oakwood Colliery	Glamorg'n	G. W.	Troedyrhiew Garth.
.	.	.	.	.	.	.	.	Eldon Colliery	Durham	N. E.	Same as South Durham Col. (Shildon).
.	.	.	.	.	.	.	.	Eldon Lane Brick Works	Durham	N. E.	Shildon.
.	.	.	.	.	.	.	.	Eldon's Siding	Dorset	L. & S.W.	Corfe Castle.
.	.	.	.	.	.	.	.	Eldred & Co.'s Lime Siding	Rutland	Mid.	Ketton.
.	.	.	.	.	.	.	.	Eldred's Lime Siding	Lincoln	G. N.	Stamford.
.	.	.	.	.	.	.	.	Eldridge, Pope & Co.'s Brewery	Dorset	L. & S.W.	Dorchester.
.	.	.	.	.	.	.	.	Electrical Copper Co.'s Siding	Lancs	S. & M. Jt. (G. C. & Mid.)	Widnes.
.	.	.	.	.	.	.	.	Electric Construction Corporation Siding	Staffs	L. & N. W.	Wolverhampton.
.	.	.	.	.	.	.	.	Electric Supply Co.'s Siding	Northumb	N. E.	Carville.
.	.	.	.	.	.	.	.	Electro Chemical Co.'s Siding	Lancs	L. & N. W.	St. Helens.
.	.	.	.	.	.	.	.	Electrolytic Alkali Co.'s Sid.	Cheshire	L. & N. W.	Middlewich.
.	.	.	.	.	.	.	.	Electrozone Works	Durham	N. E.	Seaham.
.	.	.	.	.	.	.	.	Elemore Colliery	Durham	N. E.	Hetton.
.	.	.	.	.	.	.	.	Elephant and Castle	Surrey	C. & S. L.—S. E. & C.— G. N.—L. & S. W.—Mid.	See London.
.	.	.	.	.	.	.	.	Elgey's Timber Yard	Durham	N. E.	Seaham.
G	P	F	L	H	C	5	0	Elgin	Elgin&Mo'	G. N. of S.	Craigellachie and Lossiemouth.
G	P	F	L	H	C	5	0	Elgin	Elgin&Mo'	High.	Keith and Forres.
.	.	.	.	.	.	.	.	Elgin Junction	Elgin&Mo'	G. N. of S.—High	Buckie and Forres.
.	.	.	.	.	.	.	.	Elgin and Wellwood Colliery	Fife	N. B.	Townhill Junction Station.
.	.	.	.	.	.	.	.	Elgin Siding	Fife	N. B.	See Whitemyre Junction Station.
G	P	F	L	H	C	.	.	Elham	Kent	S. E. & C.	Canterbury and Shorncliffe.
.	.	.	.	.	.	.	.	Elham Valley Brick Siding	Kent	S. E. & C.	Elham and Barham.
.	.	.	.	.	.	.	.	Ottinge Siding	Kent	S. E. & C.	Lyminge and Elham.
G	P	F	L	H	C	3	0	Elie	Fife	N. B.	Leven and Anstruther.
.	.	.	.	.	.	.	.	Eling	Hants	L. & S.W.	See Totton and Eling.
.	.	.	.	.	.	.	.	Eling Tramway	Hants	L. & S.W.	Totton and Eling.
.	.	.	.	.	.	.	.	Elizabeth Dock	Cumb'land	L. & N. W.—M. & C.	See Maryport.
G	P	F	L	H	C	8	0	Elland (L. & Y.)	Yorks	L. & Y.	Halifax and Brighouse.
G	P	F	L	H	C	8	0	Elland (L. & Y.)	Yorks	G. N.	Over L. & Y. from Wakefield Junc.
G	.	F	L	.	.	8	0	Elland (L. & Y.)	Yorks	L. & N. W.	Over L. & Y. from Bradley Wood Jn.
.	.	.	.	.	.	.	.	Waterhouse's Sid. (L. & Y.)	Yorks	L. & Y.—G. N.	Near Elland.
.	.	.	.	.	.	.	.	Ellangowan Paper Mills	Dumbartn	N. B.	Milngavie.
.	.	.	.	.	.	.	.	Elled Colliery	Mon	G. W.	Pontnewynydd.
.	.	.	.	.	.	.	.	Elled Colliery (G. W.)	Mon	G. W.—L. & N. W.	See Abersychan, Elled Colliery.
.	.	.	.	.	.	.	.	Ellenboro' Colliery	Cumb'land	L. & N. W.—M. & C.	Maryport.
.	P	.	.	.	.	.	.	Ellenbrook (for Boothstown)	Lancs	L. & N. W.	Manchester and Tyldesley.
.	.	.	.	.	.	.	.	Ellenbrook Colliery	Lancs	L. & N. W.	See Earl of Ellesmere's (Tyldesley).
.	.	.	.	.	.	.	.	Ellen Pit	Cumb'land	M. & C.	Bullgill and Aspatria.
.	.	.	.	.	.	.	.	Ellerbeck Colliery Co.—			
.	.	.	.	.	.	.	.	Ellerbeck Colliery (L.&Y. & L. U. Jt.)	Lancs	L. & Y. — L. & N. W.	Adlington. — White Bear (Adlington).
.	.	.	.	.	.	.	.	Rawlinson's Siding (L. & Y. & L. U. Jt.)	Lancs	L. & N. W.	White Bear (Adlington).
G	P	F	L	H	C	2	0	Ellesmere	Salop	Cam.	Whitchurch and Oswestry.
.	.	.	.	.	.	.	.	Ellesmere Colliery	Lancs	L. & Y.	See Earl of Ellesmere's (Walkden).
.	.	.	.	.	.	.	.	Ellesmere Junction	Salop	Cam.	Near Ellesmere Station.
G	P	.	L	H	.	5	0	Ellesmere Port	Cheshire	B'head Jt. (G W & L N W)	Helsby and Hooton.
.	.	.	.	.	.	.	.	Burnell's Siding	Cheshire	B'head Jt. (G W & L N W)	Ellesmere Port and Ince.
.	.	.	.	.	.	.	.	Ship Canal Sidings	Cheshire	B'head Jt. (G W & L N W)	Ellesmere Port.
.	.	.	.	.	.	.	.	Shropshire Union Co.'s Siding connecting with M. S. Canal	Cheshire	B'head Jt. (G W & L N W)	Ellesmere Port.
.	.	.	.	.	.	.	.	Smelting Corporation Stanlow Works	Cheshire	B'head Jt. (G W & L N W)	Ellesmere Port and Ince.
.	.	.	.	.	.	.	.	Ellesmere's, Earl of—			
.	.	.	.	.	.	.	.	Brackley Siding or Middle Hulton Colliery	Lancs	L. & N. W.	Plodder Lane (for Farnworth).
.	.	.	.	.	.	.	.	Charlton Pit	Lancs	L. & N. W.	Plodder Lane (for Farnworth).
.	.	.	.	.	.	.	.	Ellenbrook Colliery	Lancs	L. & N. W.	Tyldesley.
.	.	.	.	.	.	.	.	Ellesmere Colliery	Lancs	L. & Y.	Walkden.
.	.	.	.	.	.	.	.	Linnyshaw Moss Siding	Lancs	L. & Y.	Kearsley.
.	.	.	.	.	.	.	.	Liverpool Street Siding	Lancs	L. & N. W.	Manchester, Liverpool Rd. & Salford
.	.	.	.	.	.	.	.	Sanderson Siding	Lancs	L. & N. W.	Tyldesley.
.	.	.	.	.	.	.	.	Siding	Lancs	L. & Y.	Manchester, Miles Platting.

STATION ACCOMMODATION.						CRANE POWER.	STATIONS, &c.	COUNTY.	COMPANY.	POSITION.
						Tons Cwts.	**Ellesmere's, Earl of**—*continued.*			
.	.	.	.	.	.	. .	Siding	Lancs	L. & N. W.	See Lecturers Close & Hulme Trust Siding (Bolton).
.	.	.	.	.	.	. .	Walkden Colliery	Lancs	L. & N. W.	Tyldesley.
.	.	.	.	.	.	. .	Wharton Hall Colliery	Lancs	L. & Y.	Atherton, Central.
G	P	F	.	.	.	. .	Ellingham	Norfolk	G. E.	Beccles and Tivetshall.
G	P	F	L	H	.	1 10	Elliot Junction Station	Forfar	D. & A. Jt. (Cal. & N. B.)	Dundee and Arbroath.
G	P*	.	.	.	.	. .	Arbirlot	Forfar	D. & A. Jt. (Cal. & N. B.)	Elliot Junction Sta. and Carmyllie.
G	P*	.	L	.	.	. .	Cuthlie	Forfar	D. & A. Jt. (Cal. & N. B.)	Elliot Junction Sta. and Carmyllie.
G	.	.	.	.	.	. .	Dowrie Siding	Forfar	D. & A. Jt. (Cal. & N. B.)	Elliot Junction Sta. and Easthaven.
.	.	.	.	.	.	. .	Elliot Pit	Glamorg'n	Rhy.	See Powell Duffryn Co. (Brithdir).
.	.	.	.	.	.	. .	Elliot Pit (B. & M.)	Mon	B. & M.—G.W.	New Tredegar and White Rose.
.	.	.	.	.	.	. .	Elliotstown	Mon	{ B. & M.	Same as New Tredegar & White Rose.
.	.	.	.	.	.	. .			{ Rhy.	Same as Tir Phil.
.	.	.	.	.	.	. .	Elliott & Son's Timber Yard (Thornhill Quay)	Durham	N. E.	Sunderland, South Dock.
.	.	.	.	.	.	. .	Elliott's Lodge Mill Colliery.	Yorks	L. & N. W.	Fenay Bridge and Lepton.
.	.	.	.	.	.	. .	Elliotts' Metal Works	Carmarth'	B. P. & G. V.	Burry Port.
							Ellis & Everard—			
.	.	.	.	.	.	. .	Granite Works (Mid.)	Leicester	Mid.—L. & N. W.	Bardon Hill.
.	.	.	.	.	.	. .	Siding	Herts	G. N.	Stevenage.
.	.	.	.	.	.	. .	Siding	Leicester	Mid.	Kibworth.
.	.	.	.	.	.	. .	Siding	N'hampt'n	Mid.	Kettering.
.	.	.	.	.	.	. .	Ellis, E., Colliery (G. C.)	Yorks	G. C.—Mid.	Same as South Yorkshire Coal Co. (Doncaster).
							Ellis, J., & Son—			
.	.	.	.	.	.	. .	Barrow Lime Works	Leicester	Mid.	Mountsorrel Junction.
.	.	.	.	.	.	. .	Cake, etc., Stores (Mid.)	Leicester	Mid.—L. & N. W.	Coalville.
.	.	.	.	.	.	. .	Concrete Works	Leicester	Mid.	Mountsorrel Junction.
.	.	.	.	.	.	. .	Kilby Bridge Siding	Leicester	Mid.	Wigston, L. & H.
.	.	.	.	.	.	. .	Manure Works	Leicester	Mid.	Desford.
.	.	.	.	.	.	. .	Siding	Warwick	Mid.	Birmingham, Camp Hill.
.	.	.	.	.	.	. .	Ellismuir Brick Works	Lanark	Cal.	Baillieston.
.	.	.	.	.	.	. .	Ellismuir Collieries, Nos. 2 & 3	Lanark	Cal.	Baillieston.
.	.	.	.	.	.	. .	Ellison & Mitchel's Chemical Works	Yorks	Mid.	Kilnhurst.
.	.	.	.	.	.	. .	Ellison & Mitchel's Siding	Yorks	Mid.	Killamarsh.
.	.	.	.	.	.	. .	Ellison's Church Iron Works	Lancs	G. C.—L. & N. W.	Wigan.
.	.	.	.	.	.	. .	Ellis, Partridge & Co.'s Brick Works (Mid.)	Leicester	Mid.—L. & N. W.	Woodville.
.	.	.	.	.	.	. .	Ellis Robinson's Siding	Yorks	G. N.	Bradford, Great Horton.
.	.	.	.	.	.	. .	Ellis's Siding	Lanark	Cal.—N. B.	Same as North British Iron Works (Coatbridge).
.	.	.	.	.	.	. .	Ellistown	Leicester	Mid.	See Bagworth and Ellistown.
.	.	.	.	.	.	. .	Ellistown Col. & Bk. Wks. (Mid)	Leicester	Mid.—L. & N. W.	Bagworth.
G	P	F	L	H	C	5 0	Ellon	Aberdeen	G. N. of S.	Dyce and Fraserburgh.
.	.	.	.	.	.	. .	Elm Bridge	Cambs	G. E.	See Wisbech Tramway.
G	P	.	.	.	.	. .	Elmers End	Kent	S. E. & C.	New Beckenham & Addiscombe Rd.
.	.	.	.	.	.	. .	Elmers End Junction	Kent	S. E. & C.	Elmers End and Woodside.
G	P	F	L	H	C	1 10	Elmesthorpe (for Barwell & Earl Shilton) (L. & N. W.)	Leicester	{ L. & N. W.	Leicester and Nuneaton.
G	P	F	L	.	.	1 10			{ Mid.	Over L. & N. W. Line.
.	.	.	.	.	.	. .	Enderby & Stoney Stanton Granite Co.'s New Shilton Siding (L. & N. W.)	Leicester	L. & N. W.—Mid.	Elmesthorpe and Croft.
.	.	.	.	.	.	. .	Mountsorrel Granite Co.'s Siding (Stoney Stanton Siding) (L. & N. W.)	Leicester	L. & N. W.—Mid.	Elmesthorpe and Croft.
.	.	.	.	.	.	. .	Elmham	Norfolk	G. E.	See North Elmham.
.	.	.	.	.	.	. .	Elmhurst Siding	Staffs	L. & N. W.	Armitage.
.	.	.	.	.	.	. .	Elms Colliery (Holme House Colliery)	Lancs	L. & N. W.	{ Same as Wigan Cannel Co.'s Siding (Wigan).
.	P	.	.	.	.	. .	Elmstead	Kent	S. E. & C.	Grove Park and Chislehurst.
G	P	F	L	H	C	5 0	Elmswell	Suffolk	G. E.	Bury and Haughley.
G	P	F	L	H	C	1 5	Elmton and Creswell (Mid.)	Derby	{ Mid.	Mansfield and Worksop.
									{ G. C.	Over Mid. from Shireoaks Junctions.
.	.	.	.	.	.	. .	Bolsover Colliery Co.'s Creswell Colliery (Mid.)	Derby	Mid.—G. C.	Elmton and Langwith.
.	.	.	.	.	.	. .	Norwood Siding (Mid.)	Derby	Mid.—G. C.	Elmton and Langwith.
G	P	F	L	H	C	. .	Elrington	Northumb	N. E.	Hexham and Allendale.
.	.	.	.	.	.	. .	Glendue Quarry	Northumb	N. E.	Elrington.
G	P†	.	L	.	.	5 0	Elsecar	Yorks	G. C.	Branch from Elsecar Junction.
.	.	.	.	.	.	. .	Earl Fitzwilliam's Works	Yorks	G. C.	Elsecar.

EXPLANATION—G *Goods Station.*   P *Passenger and Parcel Station.*   P* *Passenger, but not Parcel or Miscellaneous Traffic.*
P† *Parcels and Miscellaneous Traffic only.*   F *Furniture Vans, Carriages, Portable Engines, and Machines on Wheels.*
L *Live Stock.*   H *Horse Boxes and Prize Cattle Vans.*   C *Carriages by Passenger Train.*

STATION ACCOMMODATION.						CRANE POWER.		STATIONS, &c.	COUNTY.	COMPANY.	POSITION.
						Tons	Cwts.				
								Elsecar—continued.			
.	.	.	.	.	.	.	.	Elsecar Gas Co.'s Siding ...	Yorks	G. C.	Elsecar.
.	.	.	.	.	.	.	.	Elsecar High Pit (Plantain or Simon Wood Colliery)	Yorks	G. C.	Elsecar.
.	.	.	.	.	.	.	.	Elsecar Low Pit (Hemingfield Colliery)	Yorks	G. C.	Elsecar.
.	.	.	.	.	.	.	.	Hemingfield Fan Siding ...	Yorks	G. C.	Elsecar.
.	.	.	.	.	.	.	.	Hoyland Silkstone Coke Ovens	Yorks	G. C.	Elsecar.
.	.	.	.	.	.	.	.	Lidgett Colliery	Yorks	G. C.	Elsecar.
.	.	.	.	.	.	.	.	Milton Iron Foundry	Yorks	G. C.	Elsecar.
.	.	.	.	.	.	.	.	Smith's Brick Works (Skiers' Spring Siding)	Yorks	G. C.	Elsecar.
G	P	F	L	H	C	1	10	Elsecar Junction	Yorks	G. C.	Wath and Elsecar.
.	.	.	.	.	.	.	.	Elsecar & Hoyland	Yorks	Mid.	Chapeltown and Barnsley.
.	.	.	.	.	.	.	.	Hoyland Curve Siding	Yorks	Mid.	Near Elsecar & Hoyland.
.	.	.	.	.	.	.	.	Hoyland Silkstone Colliery	Yorks	Mid.	Near Elsecar and Hoyland.
G	P	F	L	H	C	0	15	Elsenham	Essex	G. E.	Cambridge and Bishops Stortford.
G	P	F	L	H	C	.	.	Elsham	Lincoln	G. C.	Thorne and Barnetby.
.	.	.	.	.	.	.	.	Worlaby Siding	Lincoln	G. C.	Elsham.
G	P	.	L	H	.	1	10	Elslack (Mid.)	Yorks	Mid.	Colne and Skipton.
.	P	.	.	.	.					L. & Y.	Over Mid. from Colne Junction.
.	.	.	.	.	.	.	.	Elson Brick Siding	Salop	Cam.	Overton-on-Dee.
G	P	F	L	H	C	.	.	Elsted	Sussex	L. & S.W.	Petersfield and Midhurst.
.	.	.	.	.	.	.	.	Elstob Lane Siding	Durham	N. E.	Stillington.
.	.	.	.	.	.	.	.	Elstow Brick Works	Beds	Mid.	See Forder & Son (Bedford).
G	P	F	L	H	C	1	10	Elstree	Herts	Mid.	St. Albans & Hendon.
.	.	.	.	.	.	.	.	Elstree Brick & Tile Co's Sid	Herts	Mid.	Near Elstree Station.
.	.	.	.	.	.	.	.	Newton's, P., Siding	Herts	Mid.	Elstree.
.	P	.	.	.	.	.	.	Elswick	Northumb	N. E.	Newcastle and Scotswood.
.	.	.	.	.	.	.	.	Benwell Colliery	Northumb	N. E.	Elswick.
.	.	.	.	.	.	.	.	Delaval Colliery & Sidings	Northumb	N. E.	Elswick.
G	.	.	.	.	.	50	0	Elswick Works	Northumb	N. E.	Elswick.
.	.	.	.	.	.	.	.	Elswick Gas Works	Northumb	N. E.	Newcastle-on-Tyne.
.	.	.	.	.	.	.	.	Elswick Ordnance & Engineering Works, Blast Furnaces, Shipyard & Whf. (NE)	Northumb	N. E.—N. B.	Newcastle-on-Tyne.
G	P	.	.	.	.	.	.	Eltham and Mottingham	Kent	S. E. & C.	Hither Green and Dartford.
.	.	.	.	.	.	.	.	Elthorne	Middlesex	G. W.	See Hanwell and Elthorne.
G	P	.	.	.	.	.	.	Elton	Cheshire	B'head.Jt.(GW&L&NW)	See Ince and Elton.
G	P	.	L	.	.	.	.	Elton	N'hamptn	L. & N.W.	Peterboro' and Wellingboro'
.	.	.	.	.	.	.	.	Elton & Orston	Notts	G. N.	Grantham and Nottingham.
.	.	.	.	.	.	.	.	Orston Siding	Notts	G. N.	Elton and Aslockton.
.	.	.	.	.	.	.	.	Elton Head Farm Siding	Lancs	L. & N.W.	Rainhill.
.	.	.	.	.	.	.	.	Eltringham Colliery	Northumb	N. E.	Same as West Mickley Col. (Prudhoe)
G	P	F	L	H	C	1	10	Elvanfoot	Lanark	Cal.	Lockerbie and Carstairs.
.	.	.	.	.	.	.	.	Elvet	Durham	N. E.	See Durham.
.	.	.	.	.	.	.	.	Elwell's Siding	Staffs	L. & N.W.	Darlaston.
.	.	.	.	.	.	.	.	Elworth Works	Cheshire	N. S.	Same as Fodens' (Ettiley Heath).
.	.	.	.	.	.	.	.	Elwy Siding	Flint	L. & N.W.	Same as Williams' (Rhyl).
G	P	F	L	H	C	1	10	Ely	Cambs	G. E.	Cambridge and Lynn.
.	.	.	.	.	.	.	.	Ely Depôt	Glamorg'n	T. V.	See Cardiff.
G	P	.	L	.	.			Ely (for Llandaff) (G.W.)	Glamorg'n	G. W.	Cardiff and St. Fagans.
.	P	.	.	.	.					Barry	Over G.W. from St. Fagans East Jn.
.	.	.	.	.	.	.	.	Crosswell's Brewery Siding	Glamorg'n	G. W.	Ely.
.	.	.	.	.	.	.	.	Owen, T., & Co. (Ely Paper Mills) Siding	Glamorg'n	G. W.	Ely.
.	.	.	.	.	.	.	.	Ely Harbour	Glamorg'n	T. V.	Same as Penarth Harbour.
.	.	.	.	.	.	.	.	Ely Mileage Siding	Glamorg'n	T. V.	Cardiff.
.	.	.	.	.	.	.	.	Ely Paper Mills Siding	Glamorg'n	G. W.—T. V.	Same as Owen, T., & Co.'s Siding.
.	.	.	.	.	.	.	.	Ely Pits Colliery	Glamorg'n	G. W.	Penygraig.
.	.	.	.	.	.	.	.	Ely Place Siding (N. & B.)	Brecon	N. & Brecon—Mid.	Cradoc.
.	.	.	.	.	.	.	.	Ely Tin Plate Works Siding	Glamorg'n	G. W.—T. V.	Llantrisant.
.	P	.	.	.	.	.	.	Emalough	Kerry	T. & D.	Castlegregory Junction and Dingle.
G	P	.	L	H	.	1	15	Embleton	Cumb'land	C. K. & P. (L. & N.W. & N. E. Working Cos.)	Cockermouth and Keswick.
G	P	.	.	.	.	.	.	Embo	Suther'nd	High. (Dornoch)	The Mound and Dornoch.
G	P	.	L	H	.	1	10	Embsay	Yorks	Mid.	Skipton and Ilkley.
.	.	.	.	.	.	.	.	Skipton Rock Co.'s Quarry	Yorks	Mid.	Embsay and Bolton Abbey.
.	.	.	.	.	.	.	.	Emley Moor Siding	Yorks	L. & Y.	Skelmanthorpe.
G	P	.	L	H	.	.	.	Emly	Tipperary	G. S. & W.	Limerick Junction and Charleville.
.	.	.	.	.	.	.	.	Emlyn Colliery	Carmarth'	G. W.	Pantyffynnon.

EXPLANATION—G Goods Station.   P Passenger and Parcel Station.   P* Passenger, but not Parcel or Miscellaneous Traffic.
F Furniture Vans, Carriages, Portable Engines, and Machines on Wheels.   L Live Stock.
H Horse Boxes and Prize Cattle Vans.   C Carriages by Passenger Train.

G	P	F	L	H	C	Tons	Cwts	STATIONS, &c.	COUNTY.	COMPANY.	POSITION.
.	.	.	.	.	.	.	.	EmlynIronWks(PhillipsC.D.)	Glo'ster	G. W.—Mid.	Gloucester.
.	.	.	.	.	.	.	.	Emma or Towneley Colliery and Depôts	Durham	N. E.	Same as Stella Coal Co. (Blaydon).
G	P	.	L	H	.	.	.	Emneth	Norfolk	G. E.	Wisbech and Lynn.
.	.	.	.	.	.	.	.	Empire Brick & Tile Co.'s Sid.	Staffs	L. & N. W.	Pelsall.
.	.	.	.	.	.	.	.	Empire Colliery	Glamorg'n	G. W.	Glyn Neath.
.	.	.	.	.	.	.	.	Empire Indurated Stone Co.'s Siding	Leicester	L. & N. W.— Mid.	Narboro'.
G	P	F	L	H	C	5	0	Emsworth	Hants	L. B. & S. C.	Havant and Chichester.
.	.	.	.	.	.	.	.	Emu Works Siding	Glamorg'n	R. & S. B.	Jersey Marine.
G	P	.	.	.	.	.	.	Emyvale Road	Tyrone	Clogher Valley	Tynan and Aughnacloy.
.	.	.	.	.	.	.	.	Enborne Junction	Berks	G. W.	Newbury and Kintbury.
.	.	.	.	.	.	.	.	Enderby & Stoney Stanton Granite Co.— New Shilton Sid. (L.&N.W.)	Leicester	L. & N. W.—Mid.	Elmesthorpe.
.	.	.	.	.	.	.	.	Siding	Leicester	L&NW—L&NW&MidJt.	Narboro'.
.	.	.	.	.	.	.	.	Enderby Branch	Leicester	L. & N. W. & Mid. Jt.	Croft and Narboro'.
G	P	F	L	H	C	5	0	Endon	Staffs	N. S.	Stoke and Leek.
.	.	.	.	.	.	.	.	Energlyn Sidings	Glamorg'n	Rhy.	Caerphilly and Penyrheol.
G	P	F	L	H	C	1	10	Enfield	Meath	M. G. W.	Dublin and Mullingar.
G	P	F	L	H	C	1	0	Enfield (G. N.)	Middlesex	G. N.	Branch from Wood Green.
.	P	.	.	.	.					N. L.	Over G. N. from Canonbury Junc.
.	P*	.	.	.	.					S. E. & C.	Over G. N. from King's Cross Junc.
.	.	.	.	.	.	.	.	Enfield Gas Co.'s Siding	Middlesex	G. E.	Ponders End.
G	P	.	.	.	.	3	0	Enfield Lock for Enfield Highway	Middlesex	G. E.	Tottenham and Broxbourne.
G	P	F	.	.	.	1	0	Enfield Town	Middlesex	G. E.	Branch from Bethnal Green.
.	.	.	.	.	.	.	.	English Bros.' Siding	Cambs	G. E.	Wisbech.
.	.	.	.	.	.	.	.	English Bros.' Siding (G. E.)	Hunts	G E—G N—L N W—Mid	Peterboro'.
.	.	.	.	.	.	.	.	English Crown Spelter Works	Glamorg'n	R. & S. B.	Swansea.
.	.	.	.	.	.	.	.	English Electric Carbon Co.'s Siding	Denbigh	G. W.	Same as Smelt Siding (Coed Poeth).
.	.	.	.	.	.	.	.	English Electric Manufacturing Co.'s Siding	Lancs	N.U.Jt.(L.&N.W.&L&Y)	Same as Dick, Kerr & Co.'s (Preston).
.	.	.	.	.	.	.	.	English Grain Co.'s Sid. (Mid.)	Staffs	Mid.—G.N.—N.S.	Burton-on-Trent.
.	.	.	.	.	.	.	.	English, J. H., Siding	Suffolk	G. E.	Stowmarket.
.	.	.	.	.	.	.	.	English McKenna Process Co.'s Siding	Cheshire	B'head Jt.—C. L. C.— N. W. & L.	Birkenhead.
.	.	.	.	.	.	.	.			Wirral	Seacombe & Egremont.
G	P	F	L	.	.	2	0	Ennis (G. S. & W.)	Clare	G. S. & W.	Limerick and Athenry.
.	.	.	.	.	.	.	.			M. G. W.	Over G. S. & W. from Athenry.
G	P	.	L	.	.	3	0	Ennis	Clare	West Clare	Adjoining G. S. & W. Station.
G	P	F	L	H	C	3	0	Enniscorthy	Wexford	D. W. & W.	Arklow and Wexford.
G	.	.	.	.	.	.	.	St. John's Siding	Wexford	D. W. & W.	Enniscorthy.
.	.	.	.	.	.	.	.	Enniskean	Cork	C. B. & S. C.	See Ballineen and Enniskean.
G	P	F	L	.	.	1	0	Enniskillen Station & Junction	Ferm'nagh	G. N. (I.)	Clones and Omagh.
G	P	F	L	.	.	3	0			S. L. & N. C.	Junction with G. N. (I.)
G	P	F	L	.	.	.	.	Ennistymon	Clare	West Clare	Ennis and Miltown Malbay.
.	.	.	.	.	.	.	.	Ensor & Co.'s Pipe Works (Mid.)	Derby	Mid.—L. & N. W.	Woodville.
G	P	F	L	H	C	.	.	Enthorpe	Yorks	N. E.	Market Weighton and Driffield.
G	P	.	L	H	.	5	0	Entwistle	Lancs	L. & Y.	Blackburn and Bolton.
.	.	.	.	.	.	.	.	Entwistle Bros.' Siding	Lancs	L. & Y.	Kearsley.
.	.	.	.	.	.	.	.	Entwistle, R., & Co.'s Siding	Lancs	L. & Y.	Spring Vale.
G	P	.	L	H	.	.	.	Enzie	Banff	High.	Keith and Buckie.
G	P	F	L	H	C	1	10	Epping	Essex	G. E.	Loughton and Ongar.
.	.	.	.	.	.	.	.	Cottis & Son's Siding	Essex	G. E.	Epping.
.	.	.	.	.	.	.	.	Epping Gas Co.'s Siding	Essex	G. E.	Epping.
.	.	.	.	.	.	.	.	Eppleton Colliery	Durham	N. E.	Hetton.
G	P	F	L	H	C	5	0	Epsom	Surrey	L. & S. W.	Wimbledon and Leatherhead.
G	P	F	L	H	C	5	0		Surrey	L. B. & S. C.	Sutton and Leatherhead.
.	.	.	.	.	.	.	.	Hall & Co.'s Siding	Surrey	L. B. & S. C.	Epsom.
.	.	.	.	.	.	.	.	Stone & Co.'s Brick Works	Surrey	L. B. & S. C.	Epsom.
G	P	F	L	H	C	.	.	Epsom Downs	Surrey	L. B. & S. C.	Branch from Sutton.
.	.	.	.	.	.	.	.	Gadson's Siding	Surrey	L. B. & S. C.	Epsom Downs.
.	.	.	.	.	.	.	.	Kerr's Siding	Surrey	L. B. & S. C.	Banstead and Epsom Downs.
.	.	.	.	.	.	.	.	Epsom Junction	Surrey	L. & S. W.—L. B. & S. C.	Epsom, L. & S. W. and L. B. & S. C. Station.
.	.	.	.	.	.	.	.	Epworth	Lincoln	G. C.	See Crowle (for Epworth & Belton).
.	.	.	.	.	.	.	.			G. N. & G. E. Jt.	See Haxey and Epworth.
.	.	.	.	.	.	.	.	Era Welsh Slate Co.'s Siding	Merioneth	Corris	Esgairgeiliog.
G	P	.	L	.	.	.	.	Erdington	Warwick	L. & N. W.	Birmingham and Lichfield.

EXPLANATION—G *Goods Station.*   P *Passenger and Parcel Station.*   P* *Passenger, but not Parcel or Miscellaneous Traffic.*
F *Furniture Vans, Carriages, Portable Engines, and Machines on Wheels.*   L *Live Stock.*
H *Horse Boxes and Prize Cattle Vans.*   C *Carriages by Passenger Train.*

STATION ACCOMMODATION.						CRANE POWER.	STATIONS, &c.	COUNTY.	COMPANY.	POSITION.
						Tons Cwts.	Erewash Furnaces...............	Derby	Mid.	Trowell.
							Erewash Valley Brick, Pipe, and Pottery Co.'s Siding ...	Notts	G. N.	Newthorpe.
							Erichsen, Lindhard & Co's Saw Mill and Timber Yard	Durham ...	N. E.	West Hartlepool.
G	P	F	L	H	C	5 0	Eridge	Sussex ...	L. B. & S. C.	Groombridge and Crowborough.
							Erimus Steam Mill	Yorks	N. E.	Middlesbrough.
							ERITH—			
G	P	F	L	H	C	4 0	(Station)	Kent	S. E. & C.	Woolwich and Dartford.
							Beadle's Siding	Kent	S. E. & C.	Erith and Slades Green.
							Easton & Anderson's Sid.	Kent	S. E. & C.	Erith and Slades Green.
							Erith Wharf	Kent	S. E. & C.	Branch—Erith and Slades Green.
							Junction	Kent	S. E. & C.	Barnehurst and Erith.
							North End Siding	Kent	S. E. & C.	Erith and Slades Green.
							White's Brick Siding	Kent	S. E. & C.	Erith and Slades Green.
							Erith Brick, Tile, and Terra Cotta Co.'s Siding	Flint	L. & N. W.	Coed Talon.
G	P	F	L	H	C	3 0	Errol	Perth	Cal.	Perth and Dundee.
G	P	P		L	H		Erwood	Radnor ...	Cam.	Builth Wells and Three Cocks.
G	P	P		L			Eryholme	Yorks	N. E.	Darlington and Northallerton.
							Ness's Siding	Yorks	N. E.	Eryholme.
G	P	F	L	H	C	⎫	Escrick (N. E.)	Yorks	{ N. E.	York and Selby.
	P	P		H	C	⎬			{ G. N.	Over N. E. from Shaftholme Junc.
G	P						Esgairgeiliog	Merioneth	Corris.	Machynlleth and Corris.
							Era Welsh Slate Co.'s Sid.	Merioneth	Corris.	Esgairgeiliog.
							Esh Colliery & Coke Ovens...	Durham ...	N. E.	Waterhouses.
G	P	F	L	H	C		Esher and Claremont	Surrey ...	L. & S. W.	Surbiton and Weybridge.
G	P	P		L	H	C	1 10	Esholt	Yorks	Mid.	Shipley and Guiseley.
	P	P			H	C		Eskbank	Edinboro'	N. B.	Portobello and Hardengreen.
					H	C		Glenesk Siding	Edinboro'	N. B.	Millerhill and Eskbank.
							Eskbank Carpet Works (Stewart Bros.' Siding) ...	Edinboro'	N. B.	Hardengreen.
	P						Eskbridge	Edinboro'	N. B.	Hawthornden and Penicuik.
							Eskbridge Siding	Edinboro'	N. B.	Penicuik.
G	P			L			Eskdale Green	Cumb'land	R. & E.	Ravenglass and Boot.
G							Eskett	Cumb'land	WC.&E.Jt.(Fur.&LNW)	Branch from Eskett Junction.
							Cleator Iron Ore Co.—			
							Agnes Pit....................	Cumb'land	WC.&E.Jt.(Fur.&LNW)	Eskett Branch.
							Ainsworth's Margaret Pit	Cumb'land	WC.&E.Jt.(Fur.&LNW)	Eskett Branch.
							Eskett Pit	Cumb'land	WC.&E.Jt.(Fur.&LNW)	Eskett Branch.
							Eskett Branch	Cumb'land	WC.&E.Jt.(Fur.&LNW)	Frizington and Yeathouse.
							Eskett Junction	Cumb'land	WC.&E.Jt.(Fur.&LNW)	Eskett Station and Frizington.
							Eskett Mining Co.'s Siding...	Cumb'land	WC.&E.Jt.(Fur.&LNW)	See Postlethwaite's (Winder).
							Eskett Pit	Cumb'land	WC.&E.Jt.(Fur.&LNW)	See Cleator Iron Ore Co. (Eskett).
G	P						Eskmeals	Cumb'land	Furness	Millom and Sellafield.
							Vickers, Sons & Maxim's Gun Range Siding........	Cumb'land	Furness	Branch near Eskmeals.
							Eskmill Siding	Edinboro'	N. B.	Penicuik.
							Esk Valley Junction............	Edinboro'	N. B.	Hardengreen and Broomieknowe.
							Esperston Lime Works	Edinboro'	N. B.	Fushiebridge.
							Esplanade	Forfar......	N. B.	See Dundee.
							Espley & Co.'s Saw Mills......	Worcester	Mid.	Evesham.
							Espley's Brick Works	Warwick..	G. W.	Stratford-on-Avon.
G	P	F	L	H	C	1 10	Essendine.	Rutland ...	G. N.	Peterboro' and Grantham.
							Wilsthorpe Siding............	Lincoln ...	G. N.	Essendine and Thurlby.
							Essex County Council Siding	Essex	G. N.	Brentwood and Warley.
	P						Essexford	Monaghan	G. N. (I.)	Inniskeen and Carrickmacross.
							Essex Road	Middlesex	G. N. & C.	See London.
							Essington Colliery	Staffs	L. & N. W.	Same as Holly Bank Col. (Bloxwich).
							Essington Farm Colliery Co.'s Spring Hill Colliery	Staffs	L. & N. W.	Bloxwich.
G	P			L	H		Esslemont	Aberdeen	G. N. of S.	Dyce and Fraserburgh.
G	P			L	H	C		Eston	Yorks	N. E.	Branch from Cargo Fleet Junction.
							Bank Farm Siding............	Yorks	N. E.	Eston.
							Normanby Bk. & Tl. Wks.	Yorks	N. E.	Eston.
							Normanby Depôts	Yorks	N. E.	Eston.
							Ormesby Metallic Brick Co.'s Siding.............	Yorks	N. E.	Eston.
							Eston Grange Farm Siding	Yorks	N. E.	Same as Fisher's Siding (South Bank).
							Eston Mines and Jetty........	Yorks	N. E.	South Bank.
G	P	F	L	H	C	4 0	Etchingham	Sussex ...	S. E. & C.	Tunbridge Wells and Hastings.
G	P						1 10	Etherley	Durham ...	N. E.	Bishop Auckland and Crook.

EXPLANATION—G *Goods Station.*   P *Passenger and Parcel Station.*   P* *Passenger, but not Parcel or Miscellaneous Traffic.*
F *Furniture Vans, Carriages, Portable Engines, and Machines on Wheels.*   L *Live Stock.*
H *Horse Boxes and Prize Cattle Vans.*   C *Carriages by Passenger Train.*

STATION ACCOMMODATION.						CRANE POWER.	STATIONS, &c.	COUNTY.	COMPANY.	POSITION.
						Tons Cwts.	Etherley—*continued*.			
.	.	.	.	.	.	. .	Etherley (George) Colliery and Coke Ovens	Durham ...	N. E.	Etherley.
						. .	Etherley Goods Wharf (New Carterthorne Colliery) ...	Durham ...	N. E.	Etherley.
.	.	.	.	.	.	. .	Jane Colliery	Durham ...	N. E.	Etherley.
.	.	.	.	.	.	. .	Witton Park Depôts	Durham ...	N. E.	Etherley.
.	.	.	.	.	.	. .	Witton Park Iron Works ..	Durham ...	N. E.	Etherley.
.	.	.	.	.	.	. .	Witton Park Slag Works ..	Durham ...	N. E.	Etherley.
.	.	.	.	.	.	. .	Etherley Grange and Wood-house Colliery..............	Durham ...	N. E.	West Auckland.
.	.	.	.	.	.	. .	Etna Brick Works..............	Flint	W. M. & C. Q.	Buckley.
.	.	.	.	.	.	. .	Etna Brick Works	L'lithgow	N. B.	Armadale.
.	.	.	.	.	.	. .	Etna Iron and Steel Works...	Lanark ...	Cal.	Shieldmuir.
.	.	.	.	.	.	. .	Etna Works (Mid.)	Yorks	Mid.—G. C.	Same as Spear & Jackson's (Sheffield)
.	.	.	.	.	.	. .	Eton	Berks	G. W.—L. & S. W.	See Windsor and Eton.
G	P	.	.	.	.	\\	Etruria (N. S.)	Staffs	{ N. S.	Stoke and Harecastle.
G		.	.	.	.	//			{ L. & N. W.	Over N. S. Line.
.	.	.	.	.	.	. .	Cliff Vale Siding	Staffs	N. S.	Etruria.
.	.	.	.	.	.	. .	British Gas Light Co. ...	Staffs	N. S.	Cliff Vale Siding.
.	.	.	.	.	.	. .	North Central Wagon Co.	Staffs	N. S.	Cliff Vale Siding.
.	.	.	.	.	.	. .	Renshaw & Co.	Staffs	N. S.	Cliff Vale Siding.
							Shelton Ir., Steel, & Cl. Co.—			
.	.	.	.	.	.	. .	Granville Siding	Staffs	N. S.	Etruria.
.	.	.	.	.	.	. .	Siding	Staffs	N. S.	Etruria.
.	.	.	.	.	.	. .	Woolliscroft & Sons' Brick and Tile Works	Staffs	N. S.	Etruria.
.	.	.	.	.	.	. .	Etterby Sidings	Cumb'land	Cal.	Carlisle.
G	.	L	.	.	.	7 10	Ettiley Heath (for Sandbach)	Cheshire...	N. S.	Harecastle and Sandbach.
.	.	.	.	.	.	. .	Brunner, Mond & Co.'s Wks.	Cheshire...	N. S.	Ettiley Heath.
.	.	.	.	.	.	. .	Foden's Elworth Works ...	Cheshire...	N. S.	Ettiley Heath.
.	.	.	.	.	.	. .	Hassall Green Siding	Cheshire...	N. S.	Ettiley Heath and Lawton Junction.
.	.	.	.	.	.	. .	Malkin's Bank	Cheshire...	N. S.	Ettiley Heath.
.	.	.	.	.	.	. .	Ettingshall	Staffs	G. W.	See Bilston and Ettingshall.
G	P	.	.	.	.	10 0	Ettingshall Road and Bilston	Staffs	L. & N. W.	Birmingham and Wolverhampton.
G	P	F	L	H	C	. .	Ettington	Warwick...	E. & W. Jn.	Kineton and Stratford-on-Avon.
.	.	.	.	.	.	. .	Ettrick Mill Siding	Selkirk ...	N. B.	Selkirk.
G	P	F	L	H	C	. .	Etwall	Derby	G. N.	Derby and Burton.
.	.	.	.	.	.	. .	Etwall Gas Works............	Derby	G. N.	Etwall and Mickleover.
.	.	.	.	.	.	. .	Eustace and Colly's Sidings	Dorset......	L. & S.W.	Daggons Road.
.	.	.	.	.	.	. .	Euston	Middlesex	L. & N. W.	See London.
G	P	F	L	H	C	5 0	Euxton	Lancs	L. & Y.	Euxton Junction and Chorley.
.	.	.	.	.	.	. .	Euxton	Lancs	L. & N. W.	See Balshaw Lane and Euxton.
.	.	.	.	.	.	. .	Euxton Junction	Lancs	L&Y—L&NW—NU Jt.	Preston and Wigan.
.	.	.	.	.	.	. .	Evans', A. & W., Mill	Leicester..	Mid.	Leicester, West Bridge.
.	.	.	.	.	.	. .	Evans & Co.'s Siding............	Lancs	L. & N. W.	Widnes.
.	.	.	.	.	.	. .	Evans & Co.'s Siding	Warwick..	L. & N. W.	Birmingham, Aston.
.	.	.	.	.	.	. .	Evans & Co.'s Trent Valley Maltings	Staffs	L. & N. W.	Lichfield.
.	.	.	.	.	.	. .	Evans & Son's Foundry (Cleveland Port Brick Works and Siding)	Yorks	N. E.	South Bank.
.	.	.	.	.	.	. .	Evans' Grain Warehouse Siding (G. W.)	Carmarth..	G. W.—L. & N. W.	Llanelly.
							Evans, R., & Co.—			
.	.	.	.	.	.	. .	Bull's Head Siding............	Lancs	L. & N. W.	Newton-le-Willows.
.	.	.	.	.	.	. .	Coal Yard Siding	Lancs	L. & N. W.	St. Helens.
.	.	.	.	.	.	. .	Coal Yard Siding (L & N W)	Lancs	L. & N. W.—G. W.	Warrington, Bank Quay.
.	.	.	.	.	.	. .	Collins Green Siding	Lancs	L. & N. W.	Earlestown.
.	.	.	.	.	.	. .	Douglas Siding	Cheshire...	L. & N. W.	Hartford.
.	.	.	.	.	.	. .	Edge Green Colliery	Lancs	G.C.(St.H.Ex.)—L&NW	Golborne.
.	.	.	.	.	.	. .	Golborne Colliery	Lancs	G.C.(St.H.Ex.)—L&NW	Golborne.
.	.	.	.	.	.	. .	Grange Lane Siding	Cheshire...	L. & N. W.	Acton Bridge.
.	.	.	.	.	.	. .	Havannah Colliery............	Lancs	L. & N. W.	St. Helens.
.	.	.	.	.	.	. .	Haydock Colliery	Lancs	{ G. C. (St. Helens Exten.)	Ashton-in-Makerfield.
									{ L. & N. W.	Earlestown.
.	.	.	.	.	.	. .	Haydock or Old Fold Colliery Siding	Lancs	L. & N. W.	St. Helens.
.	.	.	.	.	.	. .	Leigh Colliery	Lancs	{ G. C. (St. Helens Exten.)	Ashton-in-Makerfield.
									{ L. & N. W.	Earlestown.
.	.	.	.	.	.	. .	New Boston Branch (for Haydock Collieries)	Lancs	G. C. (St. Helens Exten.)	Ashton-in-Makerfield.

EXPLANATION—**G** *Goods Station.*   **P** *Passenger and Parcel Station.*   **P*** *Passenger, but not Parcel or Miscellaneous Traffic.*
F *Furniture Vans, Carriages, Portable Engines, and Machines on Wheels.*   **L** *Live Stock.*
H *Horse Boxes and Prize Cattle Vans.*   **C** *Carriages by Passenger Train.*

STATION ACCOMMODATION.						CRANE POWER.	STATIONS, &c.	COUNTY.	COMPANY.	POSITION.
						Tons Cwts.	Evans, R., & Co.—*continued.*			
.	.	.	.	.	.	. .	New Boston Colliery	Lancs	G. C. (St. Helens Exten.)	Ashton-in-Makerfield.
									L. & N. W.	Earlestown.
.	.	.	.	.	.	. .	Old Boston Colliery	Lancs	G. C. (St. Helens Exten.)	Ashton-in-Makerfield.
									L. & N. W.	Earlestown.
.	.	.	.	.	.	. .	Pewfall Colliery	Lancs	G. C. (St. Helens Exten.)	Ashton-in-Makerfield.
									L. & N. W.	Earlestown.
.	.	.	.	.	.	. .	Princess Colliery...............	Lancs	G. C. (St. Helens Exten.)	Ashton-in-Makerfield.
									L. & N. W.	Earlestown.
.	.	.	.	.	.	. .	Queen Colliery...................	Lancs	G. C. (St. Helens Exten.)	Ashton-in-Makerfield.
									L. & N. W.	Earlestown.
.	.	.	.	.	.	. .	Siding	Flint	L. & N. W.	Rhyl.
.	.	.	.	.	.	. .	Siding	Lancs	L. & N. W.	Rainhill.
.	.	.	.	.	.	. .	Siding	Lancs	L. & N. W.	Garston Docks.
.	.	.	.	.	.	. .	Sidings	Cheshire...	L. & N. W.	Over and Wharton.
.	.	.	.	.	.	. .	Wood Colliery..............	Lancs	G. C. (St. Helens Exten.)	Ashton-in-Makerfield.
									L. & N. W.	Earlestown.
.	.	.	.	.	.	. .	Evedon Siding	Lincoln	G. N. & G. E. Jt.	Ruskington.
.	.	.	.	.	.	. .	Evelyn's Siding	Kent	S. E. & C.	Same as Longfield Sid. (Meopham).
G	P	.	.	.	.	. .	Evenwood	Durham	N. E.	Bishop Auckland & Barnard Castle.
.	.	.	.	.	.	. .	Carterthorne Colliery	Durham	N. E.	Evenwood.
.	.	.	.	.	.	. .	Evenwood Mill..............	Durham	N. E.	Evenwood.
.	.	.	.	.	.	. .	Moor Hill Colliery.............	Durham	N. E.	Evenwood.
.	.	.	.	.	.	. .	Morley Colliery	Durham	N. E.	Evenwood.
.	.	.	.	.	.	. .	Pit Close Colliery	Durham	N. E.	Evenwood.
.	.	.	.	.	.	. .	Randolph Colliery	Durham	N. E.	Evenwood.
.	.	.	.	.	.	. .	West Carterthorne Colliery	Durham	N. E.	Evenwood.
.	.	.	.	.	.	. .	West Tees Colliery	Durham	N. E.	Evenwood.
.	.	.	.	.	.	. .	West Tees No. 1 Colliery...	Durham	N. E.	Evenwood.
.	.	.	.	.	.	. .	Everard & Co.'s Trent Brewery Siding (Mid.)	Staffs	Mid—L&NW—G N—N S	Burton-on-Trent.
.	.	.	.	.	.	. .	Evercreech Junction.............	Somerset..	S.&D. Jt. (L.&S. W. & Mid)	Evercreech Junction Station and Evercreech, New.
G	P	F	L	H	C	10 0	Evercreech Junction Station	Somerset..	S.&D. Jt. (L.&S. W. & Mid)	Templecombe and Glastonbury.
.	.	.	.	.	.	. .	Farrance & Boyton's Bk. Sid.	Somerset..	S.&D. Jt. (L.&S. W. & Mid)	Evercreech Junction.
.	.	.	.	.	.	. .	Somerset Bk. & Tl. Co.'s Sid.	Somerset..	S.&D. Jt. (L.&S. W. & Mid)	Evercreech Junction.
G	P	.	L	H	.	1 10	Evercreech, New	Somerset..	S.&D. Jt. (L.&S. W. & Mid)	Evercreech Jn. Sta. & Shepton Mallet.
G	P	F	L	H	C	5 0	Everingham......................	Yorks	N. E.	Selby and Market Weighton.
.	.	.	.	.	.	. .	Shipton Lane Siding	Yorks	N. E.	Everingham and Market Weighton.
.	.	.	.	.	.	. .	Everitt Allen & Co.'s Siding..	Staffs	L. & N. W.	Soho.
.	.	.	.	.	.	. .	Evers & Sons (Homer Hill) ...	Staffs	G. W.	Cradley Heath and Cradley.
.	.	.	.	.	.	. .	Evershed's Siding (Mid.).....	Staffs	Mid—L & NW—G N—N S	Burton-on-Trent.
G	P	F	L	H	C	1 10	Evershot	Dorset......	G. W.	Yeovil and Weymouth.
G	P	F	L	H	C	5 0	Evesham	Worcester	G. W.	Oxford and Worcester.
G	P	F	L	H	C	5 0		Worcester	Mid.	Ashchurch and Alcester.
.	.	.	.	.	.	. .	Aldington Siding	Worcester	G. W.	Evesham and Littleton.
.	.	.	.	.	.	. .	Espley & Co.'s Saw Mills...	Worcester	Mid.	Near Evesham Station.
.	.	.	.	.	.	. .	Evesham Junction	Worcester	G. W.—Mid.	Evesham G. W. and Mid. Stations.
.	.	.	.	.	.	. .	Eveson's Coal and Coke Yard	Worcester	G. W.	Stourbridge.
.	.	.	.	.	.	. .	Ewell...............................	Kent	S. E. & C.	See Kearsney (for River and Ewell).
G	P	F	L	H	C	5 0	Ewell...............................	Surrey	L. & S.W.	Wimbledon and Leatherhead.
G	P	.	.	.	.	0 15		Surrey	L. B. & S. C.	Sutton and Epsom.
.	.	.	.	.	.	. .	Hall & Davidson's Siding...	Surrey	L. & S.W.	Ewell.
.	.	.	.	.	.	. .	Ewen & Tomlinson's Siding..	Herts	G. N.	Hertford.
.	.	.	.	.	.	. .	Ewenny Siding	Glamorg'n	Barry	Southerndown Road.
G	P	.	L	H	C	. .	Ewesley	Northumb	N. B.	Scotsgap and Rothbury.
.	.	.	.	.	.	. .	Ewhurst	Sussex	K. & E. S.	See Bodiam (for Staplecross and Ewhurst).
.	.	.	.	.	.	. .	Ewloe Barn Brick Works......	Flint	W. M. & C. Q.	Buckley.
G	P	.	.	.	.	5 0	Ewood Bridge and Edenfield	Lancs	L. & Y.	Bacup and Stubbins.
.	.	.	.	.	.	. .	Horncliffe Siding	Lancs	L. & Y.	Near Ewood Bridge.
G	.	.	.	.	.	2 0	Irwell Vale Siding............	Lancs	L. & Y.	Near Ewood Bridge.
.	.	.	.	.	.	. .	Excelsior Iron & Steel Works	Lanark ...	Cal.	Shieldmuir.
.	.	.	.	.	.	. .	Excelsior Stone Co.'s Siding..	N'hampton	Mid	Finedon.
.	.	.	.	.	.	. .	Excelsior Wire Rope Works	Glamorg'n	T. V.	Llandaff.
							EXETER—			
G	.	.	L	.	.	5 0	Alphington Road	Devon	G. W.	Exeter and Heathfield.
G	.	.	.	.	.	. .	Basin...............................	Devon	G. W.	Branch—St. Thomas and Exminster.
.	.	.	.	.	.	. .	Basin Junction	Devon	G. W.	St. Thomas.
.	.	.	.	.	.	. .	Cowley Bridge Junction ...	Devon	G. W.—L. & S. W.	Exeter, St. David's and Crediton.
.	.	.	.	.	.	. .	Junction	Devon	G. W.—L. & S. W.	Exeter, St. David's & Queen Street.
G	P	F	L	H	C	10 0	Queen Street	Devon	L. & S.W.	Yeovil Junction and Crediton.

STATION ACCOMMODATION.						CRANE POWER.		STATIONS, &c.	COUNTY.	COMPANY.	POSITION.
						Tons	Cwts				
								EXETER—*continued.*			
G	P	F	L	H	C	10	0 ⎫	St. David's (G.W.)	Devon	{ G. W.	Bristol and Plymouth.
.	P	.	.	.	.	.	. ⎭			{ L. & S. W.	Over G. W. Line.
.	P	.	.	.	.	.	.	St. Thomas	Devon	G. W.	St. David's and Exminster.
.	.	.	.	.	.	.	.	Exeter Brick & Tile Co.'s Sid.	Devon	L. & S.W.	Topsham.
.	.	.	.	.	.	.	.	Exeter's (Marquis of) Iron-stone Siding	N'hamptn	Mid.	Stamford.
.	.	.	.	.	.	.	.	Exhall	Warwick	L. & N. W.	See Longford and Exhall.
.	.	.	.	.	.	.	.	Exhall Colliery (L. & N. W.)	Warwick	L. & N. W.—Mid.	Same as Wilson's (Exors. of) Siding (Bedworth).
.	.	.	.	.	.	.	.	Exley & Son's Siding	Salop	G. W.	Coalport.
G	P	.	L	.	.	.	.	Exminster	Devon	G. W.	Exeter and Teignmouth.
G	P	F	L	H	C	5	0	Exmouth	Devon	L. & S.W.	Branch from Exeter.
.	.	.	.	.	.	.	.	Dock Line	Devon	L. & S.W.	Exmouth.
.	.	.	.	.	.	.	.	East Devon Brick Co.'s Sid.	Devon	L. & S.W.	Exmouth.
.	.	.	.	.	.	.	.	Exmouth Junction	Devon	L. & S.W.	Exeter and Pinhoe.
.	.	.	.	.	.	.	.	Express Steel Co.'s Siding	Glamorg'n	R. & S. B.	Cwmavon.
G	P	.	.	.	.	.	.	Eyarth	Denbigh	L. & N. W.	Corwen and Denbigh.
G	P	F	L	H	C	1	0	Eye	Suffolk	G. E.	Branch from Mellis.
.	.	.	.	.	.	.	.	Colchester Brewery Co.'s Sid.	Suffolk	G. E.	Eye.
.	.	.	.	.	.	.	.	Cullum & Co.'s Siding	Suffolk	G. E.	Eye.
.	.	.	.	.	.	.	.	Savill & Co.'s Siding	Suffolk	G. E.	Eye.
.	.	.	.	.	.	.	.	Tacon, Sir Thomas, Siding	Suffolk	G. E.	Eye.
.	.	.	.	.	.	.	.	Eye	Hereford	S & H Jt (G W & L N W)	See Berrington and Eye.
G	P	F	L	H	C	1	0	Eye Green	N'hampton	Mid. & G. N. Jt.	Peterboro' and Wisbech.
.	.	.	.	.	.	.	.	Northam Brick Co.'s Sid.	N'hampton	Mid. & G. N. Jt.	Eye Green.
.	.	.	.	.	.	.	.	Star Pressed Brick Co.'s Sid.	N'hampton	Mid. & G. N. Jt.	Eye Green.
G	P	F	L	H	C	.	.	Eyemouth	Berwick	N. B.	Branch from Burnmouth Junction.
G	P	F	L	H	C	1	15	Eynsford	Kent	S. E. & C.	Swanley and Sevenoaks.
G	P	F	L	H	C	1	10	Eynsham	Oxford	G. W.	Yarnton and Witney.
.	.	.	.	.	.	.	.	Eyre & Co.'s Siding (G E)	Norfolk	G. E.—G. N.—Mid.	Lynn Harbour.

F

G	P	.	.	.	.	10	0	Facit	Lancs	L. & Y.	Rochdale and Bacup.
.	.	.	.	.	.	.	.	Heys Siding	Lancs	L. & Y.	Facit.
.	.	.	.	.	.	.	.	Factory Basin	Staffs	G. W.	Tipton.
.	.	.	.	.	.	.	.	Factory Hill Siding (L. & Y.)	Lancs	L. & Y.—L. & N. W.	Blackburn.
.	.	.	.	.	.	.	.	Factory Junction	Surrey	L. B. & S. C.—S. E. & C.	London, Battersea Park and Wandsworth Road.
.	.	.	.	.	.	.	.	Factory Lane Siding	Lancs	L. & N. W.—G. W.	See Crossfield & Sons (Warrington).
.	.	.	.	.	.	.	.	Fagley Siding	Yorks	G. N.	See Bradford.
G	P	.	L	.	.	.	.	Fahan	Donegal	L. & L. S.	Londonderry and Buncrana.
.	P	.	.	.	.	.	.	Failsworth	Lancs	L. & Y.	Dean Lane and Hollinwood.
G	P	.	.	.	.	.	.	Fairbourne	Merioneth	Cam.	Llwyngwril and Barmouth Junc.
.	.	.	.	.	.	.	.	Fairclough & Son's Siding	Lancs	L. & N. W.	Earlestown.
G	P	.	L	H	.	5	0	Fairfield (for Droylsden)	Lancs	G. C.	Manchester and Guide Bridge.
.	.	.	.	.	.	.	.	Fairfield Branch Junction	Ayr	G. & S.W.	Kilmarnock and Gatehead.
.	.	.	.	.	.	.	.	Fairfield Junction	Lancs	G. C.	Fairfield and Guide Bridge.
.	.	.	.	.	.	.	.	Fairfield Shipbuilding Yard and Engineering Works	Lanark	G.&P.Jt.(Cal.&G.&S.W.)	Glasgow, Govan.
.	.	.	.	.	.	.	.	Fairfield Siding	Stirling	N. B.	Kippen.
G	P	F	L	H	C	1	10	Fairford	Glo'ster	G. W.	Branch from Yarnton.
.	.	.	.	.	.	.	.	Fairhaven Estate Co.'s Siding	Lancs	P.&W.Jt.(L&Y&L&NW)	Ansdell.
.	.	.	.	.	.	.	.	Fairhill Colliery	Lanark	Cal.	Hamilton, Central.
.	.	.	.	.	.	.	.	Fairholm Colliery	Lanark	Cal.	Quarter Road.
G	P	F	L	H	C	2	0	Fairlie	Ayr	G. & S.W.	Ardrossan and Largs.
.	.	.	.	.	.	.	.	Fairlie Branch Junction	Ayr	G. & S.W.	Kilmarnock and Gatehead.
.	.	.	.	.	.	.	.	Fairlie No. 3	Ayr	G. & S.W.	Gatehead.
.	P	.	.	.	.	.	.	Fairlie Pier	Ayr	G. & S.W.	Branch from Fairlie Pier Junction.
.	.	.	.	.	.	.	.	Fairlie Pier Junction	Ayr	G. & S.W.	Fairlie and Largs.
.	.	.	.	.	.	.	.	Fairlie's Chemical Works	Stirling	Cal.—N. B.	Falkirk, Camelon.
G	P	F	L	H	C	.	.	Fairlop	Essex	G. E.	Woodford and Ilford.
.	.	.	.	.	.	.	.	Fairmile	Surrey	L. & S.W.	See Oxshott and Fairmile.
.	.	.	.	.	.	.	.	Fairmuir	Forfar	Cal.	See Dundee.
.	.	.	.	.	.	.	.	Fairmuir Junction	Forfar	Cal.	Dundee and Newtyle.

EXPLANATION—G *Goods Station.*   P *Passenger and Parcel Station.*   P* *Passenger, but not Parcel or Miscellaneous Traffic.*
F *Furniture Vans, Carriages, Portable Engines, and Machines on Wheels.*   L *Live Stock.*
H *Horse Boxes and Prize Cattle Vans.*   C *Carriages by Passenger Train.*

STATION ACCOMMODATION.						CRANE POWER.		STATIONS, &c.	COUNTY.	COMPANY.	POSITION.
						Tons	Cwts.				
.	.	.	.	.	.			Fairoak Road Sid. (Cemetery Siding)	Glamorg'n	Rhy.	Cardiff.
G	P	F	L	H	C	1	0	Fairwood Tin Plate Works	Glamorg'n	G. W.—L. & N. W.	See Glasbrook Bros.' (Gowerton).
G	P	F	L	H	C	1	0	Fakenham	Norfolk	G. E.	Dereham and Wells.
								Fakenham Town	Norfolk	Mid. & G. N. Jt.	South Lynn & Melton Constable.
G								Langor Bridge Siding	Norfolk	Mid. & G. N. Jt.	Fakenham Town.
								Falahill	Edinboro'	N. B.	Edinburgh and Galashiels.
.	.	.	.	.	.			Falahill Colliery	L'lithgow	{ Cal.	Fauldhouse.
										{ N. B.	Crofthead.
.	.	.	.	.	.			Falahill Quarry	L'lithgow	N. B.	Crofthead.
G	P	.	L	H	C	1	10	Falcarragh	Donegal	L. & L. S.	Letterkenny and Burtonport.
.	.	.	.	.	.			Falcon Branch	Cumb'land	WC&EJt.(Fur.&L&NW)	Branch off Gillfoot Branch.
.	.	.	.	.	.			Falcon Junction	Surrey	L. B. & S. C.—W. L. E. Jt.	London, Clapham Junction.
.	.	.	.	.	.			Falcon Lane	Surrey	L. & N. W.	See London, Clapham Junction.
.	.	.	.	.	.			Falcon Pit	Cumb'land	WC&EJt.(Fur.&L&NW)	See Wyndham Mining Co. (Gillfoot).
								FALKIRK—			
.	.	.	.	.	.			Baird's Wood Yard (N.B.)	Stirling	N. B.—Cal.	Springfield Branch.
.	.	.	.	.	.			Blackmill Siding (N. B.)	Stirling	N. B.—Cal.	Over Carron Co.'s Line from Burnhouse Siding.
.	.	.	.	.	.			Bleachfield Siding (Craig's Cooperage Sid.) (N. B.)	Stirling	N. B.—Cal.	Branch from Grahamston.
.	.	.	.	.	.			Bothy Siding (N.B.)	Stirling	N. B.—Cal.	Over Carron Co.'s Line from Burnhouse Siding.
.	.	.	.	.	.			Burnhouse Sidings for Carron Works (N. B.)	Stirling	N. B.—Cal.	Grahamston and Larbert Junction.
.	.	.	.	.	.			Callendar Colliery and Brick Works	Stirling	N. B.	Branch from High Falkirk.
.	.	.	.	.	.			Callendar Iron Foundry (N. B.)	Stirling	N. B.—Cal.	Polmont and Larbert Junction.
								Camelon—			
G	.	.	.	.	.	3	0	(Station)	Stirling	Cal.	Branch Terminus near Larbert.
G	.	.	.	.	.	3	0	(Station)	Stirling	N. B.	Branch from Falkirk, High.
.	P	.	.	.	.			(Station)	Stirling	N. B.	Grahamston and Larbert.
.	.	.	.	.	.			Branch	Stirling	{ Cal.	Branch—Greenhill and Larbert.
										{ N. B.	Branch from Falkirk.
.	.	.	.	.	.			Chemical Works	Stirling	{ Cal.	Camelon Branch.
										{ N. B.	Rough Castle Branch and Camelon.
.	.	.	.	.	.			Co-operative Society's Sid	Stirling	N. B.	Camelon Branch.
.	.	.	.	.	.			Foundry (Camelon Iron Works) (N.B.)	Stirling	N. B.—Cal.	Grahamston and Larbert Junction.
.	.	.	.	.	.			Carmuirs Colliery	Stirling	N. B.	Grahamston and Larbert Junction.
.	.	.	.	.	.			Carmuirs East Junction	Stirling	Cal.—N. B.	Greenhill and Grahamston.
.	.	.	.	.	.			Carmuirs Iron Foundry (N. B.)	Stirling	N. B.—Cal.	Grahamston and Larbert Junction.
.	.	.	.	.	.			Carronhall Cols, Nos. 5 & 6 (N. B.)	Stirling	N. B.—Cal.	{ Over Carron Co.'s Line from Burnhouse Siding.
.	.	.	.	.	.			Carron Iron Works (N. B.)	Stirling	N. B.—Cal.	Over Carron Co.'s Line from Burnhouse Siding.
.	.	.	.	.	.			Carron Iron Works Branch Junction (N. B.)	Stirling	N. B.—Cal.	Grahamston.
.	.	.	.	.	.			Carronshore Siding (N.B.)	Stirling	N. B.—Cal.	Over Carron Co.'s Line from Burnhouse Siding.
.	.	.	.	.	.			Cross' Chemical Works	Stirling	{ Cal.	Camelon Branch.
										{ N. B.	Camelon.
.	.	.	.	.	.			Cumming's Blacking Mill (N. B.)	Stirling	N. B.—Cal.	Grahamston and Larbert Junction.
G	.	.	.	.	.	3	0	Dalderse Depôt (N. B.)	Stirling	{ N. B.	Branch from Grahamston.
G	.	.	.	.	.	2	0			{ Cal.	Over N. B. Line.
.	.	.	.	.	.			Diamond Foundry (Davis Gas Stove Co.) (N. B.)	Stirling	N. B.—Cal.	Springfield Branch.
.	.	.	.	.	.			Dorrator Iron Foundry (N. B.)	Stirling	N. B.—Cal.	Grahamston and Larbert Junction.
.	.	.	.	.	.			Fairlie's Chemical Works	Stirling	Cal.—N. B.	Camelon Branch.
.	.	.	.	.	.			Falkirk Brewery (Aitken's Brewery) (N. B.)	Stirling	N. B.—Cal.	Branch from Grahamston.
.	.	.	.	.	.			Falkirk Iron Works (N.B)	Stirling	N. B.—Cal.	Springfield Branch.
.	.	.	.	.	.			Goschen Siding (N.B.)	Stirling	N. B.—Cal.	Over Carron Co.'s Line from Burnhouse Siding.
.	.	.	.	.	.			Gothic Iron Foundry, (R. & A. Main's) (N. B.)	Stirling	N. B.—Cal.	Grahamston and Larbert.
G	P	F	L	H	C	10	0	Grahamston (N. B.)	Stirling	{ N. B.	Polmont and Larbert Junction.
										{ Cal.	Over N. B. from Carmuirs East Jn.

STATION ACCOMMODATION.						CRANE POWER.		STATIONS, &c.	COUNTY.	COMPANY.	POSITION.
						Tons	Cwts.	FALKIRK—*continued.*			
								Grahamston Iron Works (N.B.)	Stirling	N. B.—Cal.	Branch from Grahamston.
								Grangemouth Branch Junc.	Stirling	Cal.—N.B.	Grangemouth and Larbert.
								Grangemouth Iron Co.'s Grange Iron Works (N.B.)	Stirling	N. B.—Cal.	Grahamston and Larbert Junction.
G	P	F	L	H	C	1	5	High Station	Stirling	N. B.	Polmont and Glasgow.
								Hurlet & Campsie Alum Co.'s Siding	Stirling	N. B.	Camelon Branch.
								Kinnaird Siding (N.B.)	Stirling	N. B.—Cal.	Over Carron Co.'s Line from Burnhouse Siding.
								Lime Wharf Chemical Works	Stirling	Cal.	Camelon Branch.
								Lochland Siding (Larbert Junction Sidings) (N.B.)	Stirling	N. B.—Cal.	Grahamston and Larbert Junction.
								Lock No. 16 Siding	Stirling	{ Cal. / N. B.	Camelon Branch. / Camelon.
								New Engineering Wks (NB)	Stirling	N. B.—Cal.	Over Carron Co.'s Line from Burnhouse Siding.
								New Foundry (N.B.)	Stirling	N. B.—Cal.	Over Carron Co.'s Line from Burnhouse Siding.
								North Gate Siding (N.B.)	Stirling	N. B.—Cal.	Over Carron Co.'s Line from Burnhouse Siding.
								Parkhouse Iron Works (NB)	Stirling	N. B.—Cal.	Branch from Grahamston.
								Port Downie Iron Works	Stirling	{ Cal. / N. B.	Camelon Branch. / Camelon.
								Roughlands Siding (N.B.)	Stirling	N. B.—Cal.	Over Carron Co.'s Line from Burnhouse Siding.
								Salton Iron Foundry (N. B.)	Stirling	N. B.—Cal.	Springfield Branch.
								Scottish Central Iron Works (N.B.)	Stirling	N. B.—Cal.	Grahamston and Larbert Junction.
								Sinclair's Cooperage Siding	Stirling	N. B.	Camelon.
								Smith & Lochland's Siding (N.B.)	Stirling	N. B.—Cal.	Larbert Junction Sidings.
G						2	0	Springfield Branch (N.B.)	Stirling	N. B.—Cal.	Branch from Grahamston.
								Springfield Depôt (N. B.)	Stirling	N. B.—Cal.	Springfield Branch.
								Summerford Iron Works	Stirling	N. B.	Camelon.
								Sunnyside Blacking Mills (N.B.)	Stirling	N. B.—Cal.	Grahamston and Larbert Junction.
								Sunnyside Iron Foundry (N. B.)	Stirling	N. B.—Cal.	Grahamston and Larbert Junction.
								Vernon Patent Horse Shoe Co.'s Siding (N.B.)	Stirling	N. B.—Cal.	Grahamston and Larbert Junc.
								Wilkie's Coal Siding	Stirling	N. B.	Camelon.
								William Pit (N.B.)	Stirling	N. B.—Cal.	Over Carron Co.'s Line from Burnhouse Siding.
								Falkirk Brewery (Aitken's Brewery) (N.B.)	Stirling	N. B.— Cal.	Falkirk, Grahamston.
								Falkirk Iron Works (N. B.)	Stirling	N. B.— Cal.	Falkirk, Grahamston.
								Falkland Junction	Ayr	G. & S.W.	Prestwick and Ayr.
G	P		L	H	C	1	10	Falkland Road	Fife	N. B.	Thornton and Ladybank Junction.
								Forthar's Siding	Fife	N. B.	Falkland Road and Kingskettle.
								Lochmuir Shunting Siding	Fife	N. B.	Markinch and Falkland Road.
								Falk's Junction	Cheshire	C. L. C. (GC, GN, & Mid.)	Winsford and Over.
								Fallaw's Quarry	Forfar	Cal.	Rosemill.
	P*							Falloden	Northumb	N. E.	Berwick and Morpeth.
								Falloden Siding and Depôt	Northumb	N. E.	Christon Bank.
G	P	F	L	H	C	5	0	Fallowfield	Lancs	G. C.	Manchester (Central) & Guide Bge.
								Leach & Co.'s Siding	Lancs	G. C.	Fallowfield.
	P							Fallside	Lanark	Cal.	Motherwell and Rutherglen.
								Fallside Quarry & Brick Works	Lanark	Cal.	Uddingston.
G	P	F	L					Falmer	Sussex	L. B. & S. C.	Brighton and Lewes.
								Brighton Corporation Sid.	Sussex	L. B. & S. C.	Falmer.
G	P	F	L	H	C	3	0	Falmouth	Cornwall	G. W.	Branch from Penwithers Junction.
								Falsgrave	Yorks	N. E.	See Scarborough.
G	P	F	L	H	C			Falstone	Northumb	N. B.	Riccarton and Reedsmouth.
G	P	F	L	H	C			Fambridge	Essex	G. E.	Wickford and Southminster.
G	P		L	H	C			Fangfoss	Yorks	N. E.	York and Market Weighton.
								Fans Loanend Siding	Berwick	N. B.	See Earlston.
								Farcet	Hunts	G. N.	See Yaxley and Farcet.
								Farcet Brick Co.'s Siding	Hunts	G. N.	Fletton.
G	P	F	L	H	C	5	0	Fareham	Hants	L. & S.W.	Eastleigh and Portsmouth.
G	P	F	L	H	C	5	0	Faringdon	Berks	G. W.	Branch from Uffington.

EXPLANATION—G *Goods Station.*   P *Passenger and Parcel Station.*   P* *Passenger, but not Parcel or Miscellaneous Traffic.*
F *Furniture Vans, Carriages, Portable Engines, and Machines on Wheels.*   L *Live Stock.*
H *Horse Boxes and Prize Cattle Vans.*   C *Carriages by Passenger Train.*

STATION ACCOMMODATION.						CRANE POWER.		STATIONS, &c.	COUNTY.	COMPANY.	POSITION.
						Tons	Cwts.				
G	.	F	L	.	.	5	0	Faringdon Siding	Hants	L. & S.W.	Alton and Tisted.
G	P	.	.	.	.	.	.	Farington	Lancs	N.U.Jt.(L.&NW.&L.&Y)	Preston and Euxton.
.	.	.	.	.	.	.	.	Farington East Junction	Lancs	L. & Y.—N. U. Jt.	Bamber Bridge and Preston.
.	.	.	.	.	.	.	.	Farington West Junction	Lancs	L. & Y.—N. U. Jt.	Midge Hall and Preston.
.	.	.	.	.	.	.	.	Farington Mill	Lancs	N.U.Jt.(L.&NW.&L.&Y)	Same as Bashall & Co's Sid. (Leyland).
.	.	.	.	.	.	.	.	Farleigh Down Siding	Wilts	G. W.	Box.
.	P*	.	.	.	.	.	.	Farlington Junction	Hants	L. & S.W.—L. B. & S.C.	Havant and Portsmouth.
.	.	.	.	.	.	.	.	Farlington Race Station (L. B. & S. C.)	Hants	{ L. B. & S. C. / L. & S. W.	Havant and Portsmouth. / Over L. B. & S. C. Line.
.	.	.	.	.	.	.	.	Farme Colliery & Brick Works	Lanark	Cal.	Glasgow, Bridgeton.
.	.	.	.	.	.	.	.	Farme Depôt	Lanark	Cal.	Glasgow, Bridgeton.
.	.	.	.	.	.	.	.	Farmer & Co.'s Siding (G. E.)	Essex	GE—GN—L&NW—Mid.	London, Silvertown.
.	.	.	.	.	.	.	.	Farmers Co.'s Siding	Yorks	G. C.	Doncaster.
G	P	F	L	H	C	5	0	Farnborough	Hants	L. & S.W.	Woking and Basingstoke.
G	P	F	L	H	C	5	0	Farnborough (for Frimley)	Hants	S. E. & C.	Guildford and Reading.
.	P	.	.	H	C	.	.	Farnborough Junction	Hants	L. & S.W.	Brookwood and Farnborough.
G	P	.	L	H	.	.	.	Farncombe	Surrey	L. & S.W.	Guildford and Godalming.
G	P	F	L	H	C	5	0	Farnell Road	Forfar	Cal.	Forfar and Stonehaven.
.	.	.	.	.	.	.	.	Farnham	Surrey	L. & S.W.	Aldershot and Alton.
.	.	.	.	.	.	.	.	Wrecclesham Siding	Hants	L. & S.W.	Near Farnham.
G	P	F	L	H	C	5	0	Farnham Junction	Surrey	L. & S.W.	Aldershot and Farnham.
.	.	.	.	.	.	.	.	Farningham Road & Sutton-at-Hone	Kent	S. E. & C.	Swanley and Chatham.
.	.	.	.	.	.	.	.	Farnley	Yorks	Mid.	See Leeds, Armley (for Farnley and Wortley).
.	.	.	.	.	.	.	.	Farnley & Wortley	Yorks	L. & N. W.	See Leeds.
.	.	.	.	.	.	.	.	Farnley Iron Co.—			
.	.	.	.	.	.	.	.	Helm Colliery	Yorks	L. & N. W.	Huddersfield.
.	.	.	.	.	.	.	.	Siding	Yorks	L. & N. W.	Leeds, Farnley and Wortley.
G	P	F	L	H	C	1	10	Farnsfield	Notts	Mid.	Mansfield and Southwell.
.	.	.	.	.	.	.	.	Newark Waterworks Pumping Station	Notts	Mid.	Near Farnsfield.
G	P	F	L	H	C	5	0	Farnworth	Lancs	C L C (G.C, G N, & Mid.)	Warrington (Central) and Garston.
G	P	.	.	H	C	1	0	Farnworth	Lancs	L. & N. W.	See Plodder Lane (for Farnworth).
.	.	.	.	.	.	.	.	Farnworth & Bold	Lancs	L. & N. W.	St. Helens and Widnes.
.	.	.	.	.	.	.	.	Walton & Wood's Farnworth Brick Co.'s Siding	Lancs	L. & N. W.	Farnworth and Clock Face.
.	P	.	.	.	.	.	.	Farnworth and Halshaw Moor	Lancs	L. & Y.	Manchester and Bolton.
.	.	.	.	.	.	.	.	Farnworth Brick Co.'s Siding	Lancs	L. & N. W.	Same as Walton and Woods' Siding (Farnworth & Bold).
G	P	.	L	.	.	.	.	Farranalleen	Tipperary	G. S. & W.	Clonmel and Thurles.
.	.	.	.	.	.	.	.	Farrance and Boyton's Brick Siding	Somerset	S.&D. Jt. (L.&S.W. & Mid)	Evercreech Junction.
G	P	.	L	H	.	.	.	Farranfore	Kerry	G. S. & W.	Killarney and Tralee.
G	P	.	.	.	.	.	.	Farrangalway	Cork	C. B. & S. C.	Kinsale Junction Sta. and Kinsale.
.	.	.	.	.	.	.	.	Farrar's Siding	Notts	G. N. & Mid. Jt.	Newark.
.	.	.	.	.	.	.	.	Farringdon Street (Met.)	Middlesex	Met.—G N.—GW.—Mid.—S. E. & C.	See London.
.	.	.	.	.	.	.	.	Farrington Colliery	Somerset	G. W.	Hallatrow.
G	P	.	.	H	.	.	.	Farthinghoe (L. & N. W.)	N'hamptn	{ L. & N. W. / N. & B. Jn.	Banbury and Verney Junc. Station. / Over L. & N. W. from Cockley Brake Junction.
.	.	.	.	.	.	.	.	Farworth Siding	Yorks	N. E.	{ Levisham. / Pickering.
.	.	.	.	.	.	.	.	Fasey, A., & Son's Siding	Essex	G. E.	Leytonstone.
.	.	.	.	.	.	.	.	Faskine Brick Works	Lanark	N. B.	Coatbridge, Whifflet.
.	.	.	.	.	.	.	.	Fatfield Gears Siding	Durham	N. E.	Washington.
.	.	.	.	.	.	.	.	Fauld Brick Works	Durham	N. E.	South Shields.
.	.	.	.	.	.	.	.	Faulder's Siding	Lancs	C.L.C. (G.C, G.N. & Mid.)	Stockport, Wellington Road.
.	.	.	.	.	.	.	.	Fauldhead Pit	Dumfries	G. & S.W.	Kirkconnel.
G	P	F	L	H	C	1	0	Fauldhouse	L'lithgow	Cal.	Holytown and Edinburgh.
.	.	.	.	.	.	.	.	Benhar Weighs	Lanark	Cal.	Shotts and Fauldhouse.
.	.	.	.	.	.	.	.	Braehead Brick Works	L'lithgow	Cal.	Branch near Fauldhouse.
.	.	.	.	.	.	.	.	Braehead Quarry	L'lithgow	Cal.	Branch near Fauldhouse.
.	.	.	.	.	.	.	.	Cultrigg Colliery	L'lithgow	Cal.	Branch near Fauldhouse.
.	.	.	.	.	.	.	.	Falahill Colliery	L'lithgow	Cal.	Branch near Fauldhouse.
.	.	.	.	.	.	.	.	Handaxwood Pit	L'lithgow	Cal.	Branch near Fauldhouse.
.	.	.	.	.	.	.	.	Leadloch Colliery	L'lithgow	Cal.	Branch near Fauldhouse.
.	.	.	.	.	.	.	.	Leavenseat Qry. & Lime Wks	Edinboro'	Cal.	Fauldhouse and Breich.
.	.	.	.	.	.	.	.	Fauldmoor Siding (Sandysykes Brick & Tile Works)	Cumb'land	N. B.	Lyneside.
G	P	F	L	H	C	7	0	Faversham	Kent	S. E. & C.	Sittingbourne and Canterbury, East.

EXPLANATION— G *Goods Station.*   P *Passenger and Parcel Station.*   P* *Passenger, but not Parcel or Miscellaneous Traffic.*
F *Furniture Vans, Carriages, Portable Engines, and Machines on Wheels.*   L *Live Stock.*
H *Horse Boxes and Prize Cattle Vans.*   C *Carriages by Passenger Train.*

STATION ACCOMMODATION.						CRANE POWER.	STATIONS, &c.	COUNTY.	COMPANY.	POSITION.
						Tons Cwts.	**Faversham**—*continued.*			
							Chamber's Siding	Kent	S. E. & C.	Faversham.
							Graveney Siding..............	Kent	S. E. & C.	Faversham and Whitstable Town.
							Faversham Junction	Kent	S. E. & C.	Faversham and Selling.
							Fawcett's, E. M., Siding	Yorks	N. E.	Selby.
							Fawcett's, T. P., Siding	Yorks	N. E.	Castleford.
G	P						Fawkham (for Hartley and Longfield)................	Kent	S. E. & C.	Farningham Road and Chatham.
							Fawkham Junction	Kent	S. E. & C.	Farningham Road and Fawkham.
G	P		L	H		3 0	Fawley	Hereford..	G. W.	Gloucester and Hereford.
G	P	F	L	H	C	4 10	Fay Gate	Sussex ...	L. B. & S. C.	Horsham and Three Bridges.
							FAZAKERLEY—			
	P						(Station)	Lancs	L. & Y.	Liverpool and Rainford.
							Cinder Lane (Stores) Siding	Lancs	L. & Y.	Fazakerley.
							Junction	Lancs	L. & Y.	Rainford and Liverpool.
							L. & Y. Railway Wagon Department's Siding......	Lancs	L. & Y.	Fazakerley.
							North Junction	Lancs	C. L. C.—Mid.	Liverpool.
							Railway Signal Siding	Lancs	L. & Y.	Near Fazakerley.
							South Junctions	Lancs	C.L.C. (G.C., G.N.& Mid.)	Liverpool.
							Fazeley Street................	Warwick..	L. & N. W.	See Birmingham.
G	P	F	L	H	C	1 10	Fearn................	Ross & Cro'	High.	Invergordon and Tain.
							Fearn Siding	Forfar....	Cal.	See Careston.
G	P	F	L	H	C	3 0	Featherstone	Yorks	L. & Y.	Wakefield and Pontefract.
							Ackton Hall Col. Co.'s Sid. (L. & Y.)	Yorks	L. & Y.—N. E.	Featherstone.
							Featherstone District Council Siding	Yorks	L. & Y.	Featherstone.
							FeatherstoneMainCol(L&Y)	Yorks	L. & Y.—G. N.—N. E.	Featherstone and Sharlston.
							Snydale Colliery (Victoria Colliery) (L. & Y.)	Yorks	L. & Y.—G.N.—N. E.	Featherstone.
							Featherstone Colliery	Northumb	N. E.	Coanwood.
							Featherstone Main Colliery...	Yorks	Mid.	{ Normanton. { Oakenshaw.
							Featherstone Main Col. (L&Y)	Yorks	L. & Y.—G. N.—N. E.	Featherstone.
G	P	F	L		C	2 0	Featherstone Park	Northumb	N. E.	Haltwhistle and Alston.
							Feaver and Luff Cake Mills...	Somerset..	S.&D.Jt.(L.&S.W.&Mid.)	Highbridge.
							Feddlerland Colliery	Lanark ...	N. B.	Rawyards.
							Fedw Colliery................	Mon	B. & M.	Machen.
G							Felinfoel	Carmarth'	L. & M. M.	Llanelly and Cross Hands.
							Quarry Mawr................	Carmarth'	L. & M. M.	Felinfoel.
	P						Felin Hen	Carnarvon	L. & N. W.	Bangor and Bethesda.
							FELIXSTOWE—			
G	P	F		H	C	2 0	Beach	Suffolk ...	G. E.	Branch from Westerfield.
							Dock Junction	Suffolk ...	G E—Felixstowe Dk.&Ry	Felixstowe Dock and Felixstowe.
	P						Pier	Suffolk ...	G. E.	Branch from Westerfield.
G	P	F		H	C	5 0	Town	Suffolk ...	G. E.	Branch from Westerfield.
G	P					3 0	Felling	Durham ...	N. E.	Newcastle and South Shields.
							Felling Colliery and Shipping Staiths................	Durham ...	N. E.	Felling.
							Felling Shore Brick Works	Durham ...	N. E.	Felling.
							Holzapfels Composition Co.'s Siding	Durham ...	N. E.	Felling.
							Tate, Brown & Co.'s Siding (Heworth Quarries)	Durham ...	N. E.	Felling.
G	P		L				Felmingham	Norfolk ...	Mid. & G. N. Jt.	Melton Constable and North Walsham Town.
G	P						Felstead	Essex ...	G. E.	Braintree and Bishops Stortford.
G	P	F	L	H	C	2 0	Feltham	Middlesex	L. & S. W.	Twickenham and Staines.
							Feltham Junction	Middlesex	L. & S. W.	Hounslow and Feltham.
G	P						Fenagh (*Book to Ballinamore*) ..	Leitrim ...	C. & L.	Ballinamore and Mohill.
G	P					1 10	Fenay Bridge and Lepton ...	Yorks	L. & N. W.	Huddersfield and Kirkburton.
							Elliott's Lodge Mill Colliery	Yorks	L. & N. W.	Fenay Bridge and Kirkburton.
							Fence Colliery................	Lanark ...	Cal.	Tillietudlem.
							Fence Colliery................	Yorks	Mid.	Woodhouse Mill.
G	P	F	L	H	C	5 0	Fencehouses	Durham ...	N. E.	Newcastle and Leamside.
							Bowes House Farm Siding	Durham ...	N. E.	Penshaw and Fencehouses.
							Burn Moor Collieries "D" and "Lady Ann" Pits ...	Durham ...	N. E.	Penshaw and Fencehouses.
							Burn Moor or New Lambton Brick, Sanitary, and Tile Works	Durham ...	N. E.	Penshaw and Fencehouses.

EXPLANATION—G *Goods Station.*   P *Passenger and Parcel Station.*   P* *Passenger, but not Parcel or Miscellaneous Traffic.*
F *Furniture Vans, Carriages, Portable Engines, and Machines on Wheels.*   L *Live Stock.*
H *Horse Boxes and Prize Cattle Vans.*   C *Carriages by Passenger Train.*

STATION ACCOMMODATION.						CRANE POWER.	STATIONS, &c.	COUNTY.	COMPANY.	POSITION.
						Tons	Cwts.			
								Fencehouses—*continued.*		
								Burn Moor or New Lambton Coke Ovens	Durham ...	N. E.	Penshaw and Fencehouses.
								Burn Moor or New Lambton Gas Works	Durham ...	N. E.	Penshaw and Fencehouses.
								Burn Moor Siding	Durham ...	N. E.	Penshaw and Fencehouses.
								Chilton Moor Stores	Durham ...	N. E.	Penshaw and Fencehouses.
								Dorothea Pit (Newbottle)...	Durham ...	N. E.	Penshaw and Fencehouses.
								"D" Pit Brick & Tile Works	Durham ...	N. E.	Penshaw and Fencehouses.
								Fencehouses Depôts	Durham ...	N. E.	Penshaw and Fencehouses.
								Herrington Pit	Durham ...	N. E.	Penshaw and Fencehouses.
								Houghton Collieries Old and New Pits	Durham ...	N. E.	Penshaw and Fencehouses.
								Houghton Lime Works ...	Durham ...	N. E.	Penshaw and Fencehouses.
								Houghton Pit	Durham ...	N. E.	Penshaw and Fencehouses.
								Lumley Brick Works	Durham ...	N. E.	Penshaw and Fencehouses.
								Lumley 2nd Pit Depôt	Durham ...	N. E.	Penshaw and Fencehouses.
								Lumley 3rd Pit	Durham ...	N. E.	Penshaw and Fencehouses.
								Lumley 6th Pit Depôt	Durham ...	N. E.	Penshaw and Fencehouses.
								Lumley 6th Pit Gas Works	Durham ...	N. E.	Penshaw and Fencehouses.
								Margaret Pit (Newbottle)	Durham ...	N. E.	Penshaw and Fencehouses.
								Newbottle Manure Siding	Durham ...	N. E.	Penshaw and Fencehouses.
								New Herrington Brick Works	Durham ...	N. E.	Penshaw and Fencehouses.
								New Herrington Colliery...	Durham ...	N. E.	Penshaw and Fencehouses.
								New Lambton Siding	Durham ...	N. E.	Penshaw and Fencehouses.
								New Penshaw Siding	Durham ...	N. E.	Penshaw and Fencehouses.
								Nicholson's Pit Pumping Engine	Durham ...	N. E.	Fencehouses.
								Pea Flat Pumping Engine	Durham ...	N. E.	Penshaw and Fencehouses.
								Philadelphia Locomotive Works	Durham ...	N. E.	Penshaw and Fencehouses.
								Philadelphia Siding	Durham ...	N. E.	Penshaw and Fencehouses.
								Rainton Crossing Siding ...	Durham ...	N. E.	Fencehouses.
								Rainton Junction Gas Wks	Durham ...	N. E.	Fencehouses.
								Sunnyside Siding (Lambton Line)	Durham ...	N. E.	Penshaw and Fencehouses.
								Wapping Siding............	Durham ...	N. E.	Penshaw and Fencehouses.
G	P	F	L	H				Fenchurch Street	Middlesex	G. E.	See London.
G	P							Fencote	Hereford ..	G. W.	Bromyard and Leominster.
G	P					4	0	Feniscowles	Lancs.	{ L.&Y. & L.U.Jt. (L.&Y. & L.&N.W.) .... }	Blackburn and Boar's Head.
G	P		L			1	10	Fenit............	Kerry	G. S. & W.	Branch near Tralee.
								Feniton............	Devon......	L. & S.W.	Same as Sidmouth Junction Station.
G	P		L	H				Fenit Pier	Kerry	G. S. & W.	Branch near Tralee.
G			L	H		5	0	Fenn's Bank	Flint	Cam.	Whitchurch and Ellesmere.
G	P		L	H				Fenny Bentley	Derby	L. & N.W.	Ashbourne and Buxton.
G	P	F	L	H	C			Fenny Compton	Warwick..	{ E. & W. Jn. G. W. }	Fenny Compton Jn. and Kineton. Banbury and Leamington.
G	P	F	L	H	C	1	0	Fenny Compton Junction ...	Warwick..	E. & W. Jn.—G. W.	Stratford-on-Avon and Banbury.
								Fenny Stratford	Bucks......	L. & N.W.	Bedford and Bletchley.
	P							Rowland Bros.' Siding	Bucks......	L. & N.W.	Fenny Stratford & Woburn Sands.
	P							Fenton	Staffs	N. S.	Longton and Stoke.
								Fenton Manor	Staffs	N. S.	Stoke and Bucknall.
G	P	F	L	H	C			Fenton Tileries Co.'s Works	Staffs	N. S.	Stoke-on-Trent.
								Ferbane............	Kings	G. S. & W.	Clara and Banagher.
								Fergushill No. 17	Ayr	G. & S.W.	Kilwinning.
								Fergushill No. 22	Ayr	G. & S.W.	Kilwinning.
								Fergushill Nos. 23 & 28 ...	Ayr	G. & S.W.	Kilwinning.
								Fergushill Nos. 26, 29, & 30 ...	Ayr	G. & S.W.	Kilwinning.
								Ferguslie	Renfrew...	G. & S.W.	See Paisley.
								Ferguslie Fire-Clay Works ...	Renfrew...	G. & S.W.	Paisley, Ferguslie.
								Ferguslie Junction	Renfrew...	G. & S.W.	Ferguslie and Elderslie.
G	P	F	L	H	C	5	0	Ferme Park Sidings	Middlesex	G. N.	London, Finsbury Park.
G	P	F	L		C	5	0	Fermoy	Cork	G. S. & W.	Mallow and Waterford.
G	P	F	L		C	5	0	Ferndale	Glamorg'n	T. V.	Pontypridd and Maerdy.
								Davis & Son—			
								Ferndale, Nos. 1 & 5 Cols.	Glamorg'n	T. V.	Ferndale and Tylorstown.
								Ferndale, Nos. 2 & 4 Collieries (Ffaldau Col.)	Glamorg'n	T. V.	Ferndale and Maerdy.
								Ferndale, No. 3 Colliery (Boedryngallt Colliery)	Glamorg'n	T. V.	Ystrad.

EXPLANATION—G *Goods Station.*   P *Passenger and Parcel Station.*   P* *Passenger, but not Parcel or Miscellaneous Traffic.*
F *Furniture Vans, Carriages, Portable Engines, and Machines on Wheels.*   L *Live Stock.*
H *Horse Boxes and Prize Cattle Vans.*   C *Carriages by Passenger Train.*

STATION ACCOMMODATION.						CRANE POWER.		STATIONS, &c.	COUNTY.	COMPANY.	POSITION.
						Tons	Cwts	Ferndale—continued.			
								Davis & Son—continued.			
								Ferndale, Nos. 6 & 7 Cols.	—		
								Pendyris Colliery	Glamorg'n	T. V.	Ferndale and Tylorstown.
								Tylor's Siding..........	Glamorg'n	T. V.	Ferndale and Tylorstown.
								Ferndale, No. 8 Colliery (Cynllwynddu Colliery)	Glamorg'n	T. V.	Ferndale and Tylorstown.
								Ferndale Gas Works........	Glamorg'n	T. V.	Ferndale and Maerdy.
								Tylorstown Siding...........	Glamorg'n	T. V.	Tylorstown and Ynishir.
								Ferndale Collieries............	Glamorg'n	T. V.	See Davis & Son.
								Fernhill Colliery............	Glamorg'n	T. V.	Treherbert.
G	P		L	H		3	0	Fernhill Heath (G. W.)	Worcester	{ G. W. / Mid.	Worcester and Kidderminster. / Over G. W. from Stoke Prior Junc.
	P			H				Fernhill Siding	Lancs	L. & Y.	Same as Ashworth's Siding (Bury).
	P							Ferniegair	Lanark ...	Cal.	Hamilton and Larkhall.
	P							Ferniegair Colliery..........	Lanark ...	Cal.	Larkhall.
								Ferniegair Siding	Lanark ...	Cal.	See Larkhall.
G	P	F	L	H	C	3	0	Ferns	Wexford	D. W. & W.	Arklow and Wexford.
	P							Ferns Lock	Kildare	M. G. W.	Dublin and Mullingar.
G	P		L	H	C			Ferriby (N. E.)	Yorks	{ N. E. / G. C.	Hull and Selby. / Over N. E. from Thorne Junction.
	P			H	C						
	P							Ferry	Lancs	Furness	Steamer from Windermere, Lake Side.
G	P							Ferry	Norfolk	Mid. & G. N. Jt.	Sutton Bridge and Wisbech.
								Ferrybridge (L & Y & G N Jt.)	Yorks	L & Y & G N Jt.—H&B—NE	See Knottingley (for Ferrybridge).
G	P		L	H		5	0	Ferrybridge, (for Knotting-ley) (S. & K. Jt.)............	Yorks	{ S. & K. Jt. (Mid. & N. E.) / G. C. / G. N.	Burton Salmon and Pontefract. / Over S. & K. Jt. from Swinton Jn. / Over N. E. & S. & K. Jt. Lines.
	P			H							
	P			H							
								Ferrybridge Junction	Yorks	N. E.—S. & K. Jt	Knottingley.
								Ferryfield Print Works........	Dumbart'n	D. & B. Jt. (Cal. & N. B.)	Alexandria.
G	P	F	L	H	C	1	0	Ferryhill	Durham	N. E.	Darlington and Durham.
								Barker's Slag Works and Gas Works	Durham	N. E.	Coxhoe Junction.
								Bishop Middleham Quarry Sidings	Durham	N. E.	Ferryhill and Sedgefield.
								Chilton Lime Wks. & Quarry	Durham	N. E.	Ferryhill.
								Coundon Depôt	Durham	N. E.	Leasingthorne and Ferryhill.
								East Howle Colliery, Coke & Brick Works	Durham	N. E.	Ferryhill.
								Ferryhill Coal Depôt........	Durham	N. E.	Ferryhill.
								Ferryhill Engine Works ...	Durham	N. E.	West Cornforth.
								Ferryhill North Slag Wks..	Durham	N. E.	Ferryhill.
								Ferryhill Sand Quarry (Routledge's)	Durham	N. E.	Ferryhill.
								Ferryhill South Slag Wks..	Durham	N. E.	Ferryhill.
								Mainsforth Lime Works ...	Durham	N. E.	Ferryhill.
								N. E. R. Co.'s New Gas Wks.	Durham	N. E.	Ferryhill.
								Ferryhill Cattle Bank (Cal.)..	Aberdeen.	Cal.—N. B.	See Aberdeen.
								Ferryhill Junction...............	Aberdeen.	Cal.—G. N. of S.	Aberdeen.
G	P	F	L	H	C	1	10	Ferryside	Carmarth'	G. W.	Llanelly and Carmarthen.
G	P							Ferry Siding	Sussex ...	Selsey	Chichester and Selsey.
								Ferry Tin Plate Works (Vernon Siding)	Glamorg'n	R. & S. B.	Briton Ferry.
								Ferry Works	Flint	L. & N. W.	Same as Willans & Robinson's Siding (Queensferry).
G	P	F	L	H	C	1	10	Festiniog	Merioneth	G. W.	Bala and Blaenau Festiniog.
G	P	F	L	H	C	2	0	Fethard	Tipperary	G. S. & W.	Clonmel and Thurles.
								Fettykil Siding	Fife	N. B.	Leslie.
G	P							Ffairfach (G. W.)	Carmarth'	{ G. W. / L. & N. W.	Pantyffynnon and Llandilo. / Over G. W. Line.
								Ffairfach Gas Works........	Carmarth'	G. W.	Pantyffynnon and Llandilo.
								Ffaldau Colliery...............	Glamorg'n	T. V.	See Davis & Son's Ferndale No. 2 and 4 Collieries.
								Ffaldau Nos. 1 & 2 Collieries	Glamorg'n	G. W.	Pontycymmer.
								Ffaldcaiach Sidings	Glamorg'n	T. B. Jt. (G. W. & Rhy.)	Bedlinog.
								Fforchaman Colliery	Glamorg'n	G. W.—T. V.	See Powell Duffryn Co.
								Fforchlas Quarry	Glamorg'n	S. Wales Min.	Briton Ferry and Cymmer.
								Fforchneol Siding...............	Glamorg'n	G. W.	Dare Junction Station.
								Fforchriw Colliery...............	Glamorg'n	T. B. Jt. (G. W. & Rhy.)	Same as Guest, Keen & Nettlefold's Fochriw Colliery (Cwm Bargoed).
								Fforchwen Colliery	Glamorg'n	G. W.	Dare Junction Station.
								Ffors-y-go Colliery...............	Denbigh	G. W.	Moss.

EXPLANATION—G *Goods Station.*   P *Passenger and Parcel Station.*   P* *Passenger, but not Parcel or Miscellaneous Traffic.*
F *Furniture Vans, Carriages, Portable Engines, and Machines on Wheels.*   L *Live Stock.*
H *Horse Boxes and Prize Cattle Vans.*   C *Carriages by Passenger Train.*

STATION ACCOMMODATION.						CRANE POWER.	STATIONS, &c.	COUNTY.	COMPANY.	POSITION.
						Tons Cwts				
	P						Ffosygo Brick Works	Denbigh	W. M. & C. Q.	Moss.
	P						Ffridd Gate	Merioneth	Corris	Machynlleth and Corris.
	P						Ffrith	Flint	W. & M. Jt. (G.W.&LNW)	Brymbo and Llanfynydd.
							Ffrith Coal and Fire-Clay Co.'s Siding (Carden's Siding)	Flint	W.&M.Jt. (G.W.&LNW)	Llanfynydd.
							Ffrith Quarry	Flint	W.&M.Jt. (G.W.&LNW)	Same as Woolliscroft's (Llanfynydd).
							Ffrwd Branch	Denbigh	G. W.	Brymbo and Wrexham.
							Ffrwd Colliery	Denbigh	G. W.—W. M. & C. Q.	Moss.
							Ffrwd Iron Works (Sparrow, J., & Son's)	Denbigh	G. W.—W. M. & C. Q.	Moss.
							Ffrwd Junction	Denbigh	W. M. & C. Q.	Cefn-y-bedd and Gwersyllt.
							Ffrwdwyllt Tin Plate Works	Glamorg'n	G. W.—P. T.—R. & S. B.	Same as Davies, E., & Son's Ffrwd-wyllt Tin Plate Wks. (Port Talbot)
							Fiddle Bridge Siding	Herts	G. N.	Hatfield.
							Fiddlersgill Brick Works	Lanark	Cal.	Same as Lee Brick Wks. (Braidwood).
G	P	F	L	H	C	. .	Fiddown	Kilkenny	G. S. & W.	Clonmel and Waterford.
G	P					5 0	Fidler's Ferry and Penketh	Lancs	L. & N. W.	Garston and Warrington.
							Field & Mackay's Siding	Salop	S & H Jt (G W & L N W)	Same as Titterstone Siding (Ludlow).
							Fielden's Siding	Lancs	L. & Y.	Todmorden.
							Fielden's Withnell Brick & Terra Cotta Co.'s Siding	Lancs	L. U. Jt. (L. Y. & L.N.W.)	Withnell.
							Fielder & Co.'s Siding	Essex	G. E.	Brentwood and Warley.
							Fieldhouse Siding (L. & N.W.)	Yorks	L. & N. W.—L. & Y.	Same as Brooke & Son's Siding (Huddersfield).
							Fielding & Johnson's Anker Mills	Warwick	L. & N. W.	Nuneaton.
							Fielding & Platt's Works	Glo'ster	Mid.	Gloucester Docks.
							Fieldon's Bridge Brick Yard	Durham	N. E.	West Auckland.
							Fieldon's Bridge Junction	Durham	N. E.	West Auckland.
							Fields Sand Siding	Worcester	G. W.	Kidderminster.
							Fields Sidings	Staffs	L. & N. W.	Hednesford.
							Fife Coal Co.—			
							Kelty Weighs Siding	Fife	N. B.	Kelty.
							Mary Pit	Fife	N. B.	Kelty.
							Fife Forge Co.'s Siding	Fife	N. B.	Same as Ingleside Foundry (Kirkcaldy).
G			L			1 0	Fighting Cocks	Durham	N. E.	Darlington and Stockton.
							Dinsdale Moor Iron Works	Durham	N. E.	Fighting Cocks.
							Dinsdale Wire & Steel Wks.	Durham	N. E.	Fighting Cocks.
							Goosepool Siding	Durham	N. E.	Fighting Cocks.
							Graham's Brick Yard	Durham	N. E.	Fighting Cocks.
							Middleton Iron Works	Durham	N. E.	Fighting Cocks.
G	P	F	L	H	C	1 10	Filey	Yorks	N. E.	Scarborough and Bridlington.
G	P	F	L	H	C	2 0	Filleigh	Devon	G. W.	Barnstaple and South Molton.
G	P						Fillongley	Warwick	Mid.	See Arley and Fillongley.
							Filton	Glo'ster	G. W.	Bristol and Pilning.
G	P	F	L	H	C	5 0	Fimber	Yorks	N. E.	See Sledmere and Fimber.
	P						Finchley, Church End (G. N.)	Middlesex	{ G. N. / N. L. }	Finsbury Park and High Barnet. Over G. N. from Canonbury Junc.
							Finchley, East (G. N.)	Middlesex	G. N.—N. L.	See East Finchley.
							Finchley Road	Middlesex	Met.—Mid.—S. E. & C.	See London.
							Finchley Road and Frognal (L. & N. W.)	Middlesex	L. & N. W.—N. L.	See London.
							Finchley Road Junction	Middlesex	Met.—Mid.	London, Finchley Rd. & West End.
							Finch, J.& H., Siding (G.E.)	Norfolk	G. E.—G. N.—Mid.	Lynn Docks.
							Finch's Works and Siding	Mon	G. W.	Chepstow.
							Findlay & Co.'s Sid. (G.&P. Jt.)	Lanark	{ Cal. / G. & S. W. }	Glasgow, Kinning Park. Glasgow, General Terminus.
G	P		L	H		3 0	Findochty	Banff	G. N. of S.	Portsoy and Elgin.
							Findon Hill Depôt	Durham	N. E.	Pelton.
G	P		L			1 10	Finedon	N'hamptn	Mid.	Wellingboro' and Market Harboro'.
							Attenborough&Timm's Sid.	N'hamptn	Mid.	Near Finedon.
							Excelsior Stone Co.'s Siding	N'hamptn	Mid.	Near Finedon.
							Islip Iron Co.'s Siding	N'hamptn	Mid.	Near Finedon.
	P*						Fingask Platform	Aberdeen	G. N. of S.	Inverurie and Oldmeldrum.
G	P						Finghall Lane	Yorks	N. E.	Northallerton and Leyburn.
G	P	F	L	H	C		Finmere (for Buckingham)	Oxon	G. C.	Brackley and Aylesbury.
							Finnieston	Lanark	N. B.	See Glasgow.
							Finnieston Quay	Lanark	Cal.—N. B.	Same as Queen's Dock (Glasgow).
G	P	F	L	H	C	1 0	Finningham	Suffolk	G. E.	Haughley and Norwich.
							Ford's Siding	Suffolk	G. E.	Finningham.
G	P	F	L	H	C	5 0	Finningley	Yorks	G. N. & G. E. Jt.	Doncaster and Gainsboro'.

EXPLANATION—G *Goods Station.*   P *Passenger and Parcel Station.*   P* *Passenger, but not Parcel or Miscellaneous Traffic.*
F *Furniture Vans, Carriages, Portable Engines, and Machines on Wheels.*   L *Live Stock.*
H *Horse Boxes and Prize Cattle Vans.*   C *Carriages by Passenger Train.*

STATION ACCOMMODATION.						CRANE POWER.		STATIONS, &c.	COUNTY.	COMPANY.	POSITION.
						Tons	Cwts				
.	.	.	.	.	.	.	.	Finnockbog Siding	Renfrew	Cal.	Inverkip.
.	.	.	.	.	.	.	.	Finsbury Park	Middlesex	G. N. & C.	See London.
.	.	.	.	.	.	.	.	Finsbury Park (G. N.)	Middlesex	G. N.—N. L.—S. E. & C.	See London.
.	.	.	.	.	.	.	.	Finsbury Park Stoneyard Siding	Middlesex	G. N.	London, Finsbury Park.
G	P	F	L	.	.	2	0	Fintona	Tyrone	G. N. (I.)	Branch from Fintona Junc. Station.
.	P	.	.	.	.	.	.	Fintona Junction Station	Tyrone	G. N. (I.)	Enniskillen and Omagh.
G	P	F	L	H	C	1	10	Fintown	Donegal	Donegal	Stranorlar and Glenties.
.	.	.	.	.	.	.	.	Firbank's or Leighton Sand Co.'s Siding	Beds	L. & N. W.	Leighton (Grovebury Crossing).
G	P	.	L	.	.	.	.	Firmount	Cork	C. & Muskerry	St. Ann's and Donoughmore.
G	P	F	L	H	C	1	5	Firsby	Lincoln	G. N.	Boston and Louth.
.	.	.	.	.	.	.	.	Mill Siding	Lincoln	G. N.	Firsby Station.
.	P	.	.	.	.	.	.	First Tower	Jersey	Jersey	St. Helier and St. Aubyn.
.	.	.	.	.	.	.	.	Firth & Co.'s Siding	Derby	Mid.	Barrow Hill and Staveley Works.
.	.	.	.	.	.	.	.	Firth, T., & Son's Siding (Norfolk & East & West Gun Works) (Mid.)	Yorks	Mid.—G. C.	Sheffield, Wicker.
.	.	.	.	.	.	.	.	Fir Tree House Colliery	Lancs	L. & N. W.	See Crompton and Shawcross Sidings (Wigan).
.	.	.	.	.	.	.	.	Fir Tree House Foundry	Lancs	{ G.C. (Wigan Jn.) / L. & N. W.	Hindley and Platt Bridge. / Same as Wright's Siding (Wigan).
.	.	.	.	.	.	.	.	Fisher & Co.'s Paper Mill	Warwick	Mid.	Kettlebrook.
.	.	.	.	.	.	.	.	Fishergate	Lancs	N U Jt (L & N W & L & Y)	See Preston.
.	.	.	.	.	.	.	.	Fisher, Henderson & Co.'s Tannery	Renfrew	Cal.	Greenock, Regent Street.
.	.	.	.	.	.	.	.	Fisherrow Siding	Edinboro'	N. B.	See Musselburgh.
.	.	.	.	.	.	.	.	Fisher's Ironstone Co.'s Siding	N'hamptn	Mid.	Thrapston.
.	.	.	.	.	.	.	.	Fisher's Ironstone Siding	N'hamptn	Mid.	Desboro' and Rothwell.
.	.	.	.	.	.	.	.	Fisher's Siding	Lancs	L. & N. W.	St. Helens.
.	.	.	.	.	.	.	.	Fisher's Siding (Eston Grange Farm Siding)	Yorks	N. E.	South Bank.
.	.	.	.	.	.	.	.	Fisherton	Wilts	G. W.—L. & S. W.	See Salisbury.
G	P	F	L	H	C	1	10	Fishguard & Goodwick	Pembroke	G. W.	Branch from Clynderwen.
.	.	.	.	.	.	.	.	Fishponds	Glo'ster	Mid.	See Bristol.
.	.	.	.	.	.	.	.	Fishponds Coal Co.'s Siding	Glo'ster	Mid.	Bristol, Fishponds.
G	P	.	.	.	.	.	.	Fiskerton	Notts	Mid.	Nottingham and Newark.
								Fison and Sons—			
.	.	.	.	.	.	.	.	Siding	Norfolk	G. E.	Dereham.
.	.	.	.	.	.	.	.	Siding (G. E.)	Norfolk	G. E.—G. N.—Mid.	Lynn Docks.
.	.	.	.	.	.	.	.	Two Mile Bottom Siding	Norfolk	G. E.	Thetford.
.	.	.	.	.	.	.	.	Fison, J., & Co.'s Siding	Suffolk	G. E.	Bramford.
G	P	F	L	H	C	.	.	Fittleworth	Sussex	L. B. & S. C.	Pulborough and Petworth.
.	.	.	.	.	.	.	.	Fitton & Robinson's Churwell Colliery & Brick Works or Ward's Siding	Yorks	L. & N. W.	Morley.
.	.	.	.	.	.	.	.	Fitzsimon's Siding	Dublin	G. S. & W.	Dublin.
.	.	.	.	.	.	.	.	Fitzwilliam Colliery	Yorks	W. R. & G. Jt. (G. C. & G. N.)	Same as Hemsworth Colliery.
.	.	.	.	.	.	.	.	Fitzwilliam's (Earl) Low Stubbin Colliery	Yorks	{ G. C.—G. N. / Mid.	Rotherham and Masboro'. / Masboro' and Rotherham.
.	.	.	.	.	.	.	.	Fitzwilliam's (Earl) Works	Yorks	G. C.	Elsecar.
.	.	.	.	.	.	.	.	Five Fords Siding	Denbigh	Cam.	Marchwiel.
G	P	.	L	H	C	.	.	Five Mile House	Lincoln	G. N.	Lincoln and Boston.
G	P	.	L	.	.	.	.	Fivemiletown	Tyrone	Clogher Valley	Aughnacloy and Maguiresbridge.
.	.	.	.	.	.	.	.	Five Ways	Warwick	Mid.	See Birmingham.
.	.	.	.	.	.	.	.	Five Ways Colliery	Staffs	L. & N. W.	Same as Coppice Colliery Co.'s Siding (Brownhills).
G	P	.	L	H	.	.	.	Fladbury	Worcester	G. W.	Worcester and Evesham.
.	.	.	.	.	.	.	.	Bomford's Siding	Worcester	G. W.	Fladbury.
.	.	.	.	.	.	.	.	Charlton Siding	Worcester	G. W.	Fladbury and Evesham.
G	P	F	L	H	C	.	.	Flamborough	Yorks	N. E.	Scarborough and Bridlington.
.	.	.	.	.	.	.	.	Flass Junction and Siding	Durham	N. E.	Waterhouses.
.	.	.	.	.	.	.	.	Flavel Range and Imperial Stoves Siding	Warwick	G. W.	Leamington.
G	P	F	.	H	C	3	0	Flax Bourton	Somerset	G. W.	Bristol and Nailsea.
.	.	.	.	.	.	.	.	Flaxley Siding	Yorks	N. E.	Wistow.
G	P	F	L	H	C	5	0	Flaxton	Yorks	N. E.	York and Malton.
G	P	.	.	H	C	.	.	Flecknoe	Warwick	L. & N. W.	Leamington and Weedon.
G	P	F	L	H	C	3	0	Fledborough	Notts	L. D. & E. C.	Tuxford and Lincoln.
G	P	F	L	H	C	.	.	Fleet	Hants	L. & S.W.	Woking and Basingstoke.
G	P	.	L	.	.	.	.	Fleet	Lincoln	Mid. & G. N. Jt.	Sutton Bridge & Spalding.
.	.	.	.	.	.	.	.	Fleet's Colliery	Hadding'n	N. B.	Ormiston.

EXPLANATION—G Goods Station.   P Passenger and Parcel Station.   P* Passenger, but not Parcel or Miscellaneous Traffic.
F Furniture Vans, Carriages, Portable Engines, and Machines on Wheels.   L Live Stock.
H Horse Boxes and Prize Cattle Vans.   C Carriages by Passenger Train.

STATION ACCOMMODATION.						CRANE POWER.	STATIONS, &c.	COUNTY.	COMPANY.	POSITION.
						Tons Cwts.	FLEETWOOD—			
G	P	F	L	H	C	35 0	(Station)	Lancs	P.&W.Jt.(L&Y&L&NW)	Branch from Preston.
							Fleetwood and Blackpool Electric Tramway Co.'s Siding	Lancs	P.&W.Jt.(L&Y&L&NW)	Fleetwood and Cleveleys.
							Fleetwood Electric Lighting Co.'s Siding	Lancs	P.&W.Jt.(L&Y&L&NW)	Fleetwood and Cleveleys.
							Fleetwood Estate Co.'s Sid.	Lancs	P.&W.Jt.(L&Y&L&NW)	Fleetwood and Cleveleys.
							L. & Y. Co.'s Locomotive Siding	Lancs	P.&W.Jt.(L&Y&L&NW)	Fleetwood.
							Riley's Saw Mill..............	Lancs	P.&W.Jt.(L&Y&L&NW)	Fleetwood and Cleveleys.
							United Alkali Co.'s Fleetwood Salt Works or Burn Naze Siding	Lancs	P.&W.Jt.(L&Y&L&NW)	Fleetwood and Cleveleys.
G						25 0	Wyre Dock	Lancs	L. & Y.	Branch—Fleetwood Sta.&Cleveleys.
	P						Wyre Dock	Lancs	P.&W.Jt.(L&Y&L&NW)	Fleetwood and Preston.
							Wyre Dock Junction.........	Lancs	L. & Y.—P. & W. Jt......	Wyre Dock Goods and Preston.
							Fleming, A.B.,&Co.'s OilWks.	Forfar	{ Cal.	Dundee, West.
									N. B.	Dundee, Tay Bridge.
							Fleming & Barry's Wood Yard	Forfar	{ Cal.	Dundee, West.
									N. B.	Dundee, Tay Bridge.
	P						Fleming & Co.'s Works........	Edinboro'	Cal.—N. B.	Granton.
							Flemington	Lanark ...	Cal.	Law Junction and Motherwell.
							Fletcher, Burrows & Co.—			
							Atherton Siding (L.&N.W.)	Lancs	L. & N. W.— G. W.	Warrington, Bank Quay.
							Chanter's Colliery	Lancs	L. & N. W.	Atherton.
							Gibfield and Arley Colliery	Lancs	L. & N. W.	Atherton.
							Lover's Lane Colliery	Lancs	L. & N. W.	Atherton.
							Siding	Lancs	L. & N. W.	Bolton.
							Fletcher, G., & Co.'s Masson and Atlas Works	Derby	Mid.	Derby.
							Fletcher Pit..............	Cumb'land	W C & E Jt.(Fur.& LNW)	Same as Postlethwaite's Moor Row Mining Co.'s Siding (Moor Row.)
							Fletcher, Russell & Co.'s Wilderspool Siding	Lancs	L. & N. W.	Warrington, Arpley.
							Fletcher's Holme Mill Siding (Spring Gardens)	Durham ...	N. E.	West Auckland.
							Fletcher's Siding	Hadding'n	N. B.	Same as Lempock Well Siding (Saltoun).
							Fletcher's Siding	Lancs	L. & Y.	Bradley Fold.
G		F					Fletton	Hunts......	G. N.	Huntingdon and Peterboro'.
							Beeby's Brick Co.'s Siding	Hunts......	G. N.	Fletton and Yaxley.
							Bray & Co.'s Siding	Hunts......	G. N.	Fletton.
							Farcet Brick Co.'s Siding	Hunts......	G. N.	Fletton and Yaxley.
							Fletton Brick Co.'s Siding	Hunts......	G. N.	Fletton.
							Fletton Crown Brick Co.'s Siding	Hunts......	G. N.	Fletton and Yaxley.
							Hicks, Gardener & Co.'s Sid.	Hunts......	G. N.	{ Fletton and Longville Junction. Fletton and Yaxley.
							London Brick Co.'s Sidings	Hunts......	G. N.	Fletton.
							New Peterboro' Brick Co.'s Sidings	Hunts......	G. N.	Fletton and Yaxley.
							Norman Cross Brick Co.'s Siding	Hunts......	G. N.	Fletton and Yaxley.
							Plowman's, T. & M., Siding	Hunts......	G. N.	Fletton and Yaxley.
							Yaxley Brick Co.'s Siding	Hunts......	G. N.	Fletton and Yaxley.
							Fletts Yard..............	Renfrew ...	G & P Jt.(Cal. & G & S W)	Cardonald.
							Fleur-de-Lis Siding (B. & M.)	Mon	B. & M.—G. W.	Pengam.
							Flewitt's Siding	Lancs	L. & N. W.	Widnes.
G	P		L				Flimby	Cumb'land	L. & N. W.	Maryport and Workington.
							Broughton Moor Colliery...	Cumb'land	L. & N. W.	Flimby and Maryport.
							Flimby Colliery Co.—			
							Bertha Pit	Cumb'land	L. & N. W.	Flimby and Maryport.
							Coke Ovens	Cumb'land	L. & N. W.	Flimby and Maryport.
							Robin Hood Pit	Cumb'land	L. & N. W.	Flimby and Maryport.
							Watergate Pit..............	Cumb'land	L. & N. W.	Flimby and Maryport.
							Gillhead Coal, Gannister & Fire Brick Co.'s Siding...	Cumb'land	L. & N. W.	Flimby and Maryport.
							North Western Storing Co.'s Siding	Cumb'land	L. & N. W.	Flimby and Maryport.
							St. Helens Colliery No. 2 and Brick Co.'s Works...	Cumb'land	L. & N. W.	Flimby and Siddick.

EXPLANATION—G *Goods Station.*   P *Passenger and Parcel Station.*   P* *Passenger, but not Parcel or Miscellaneous Traffic.*
F *Furniture Vans, Carriages, Portable Engines, and Machines on Wheels.*   L *Live Stock.*
H *Horse Boxes and Prize Cattle Vans.*   C *Carriages by Passenger Train.*

STATION ACCOMMODATION.						CRANE POWER.	STATIONS, &c.	COUNTY.	COMPANY.	POSITION.
G	P	F	L	H	C	Tons Cwts. 3 10	Flint	Flint	L. & N. W.	Chester and Rhyl.
							Dee Bank Siding	Flint	L. & N. W.	Bagillt and Holywell.
							Howell	Flint	L. & N. W.	Dee Bank Siding.
							Walker, Parker & Co.	Flint	L. & N. W.	Dee Bank Siding.
							Dee Side Colliery Co.'s New Flint Colliery	Flint	L. & N. W.	Flint and Bagillt.
							Muspratt's Siding	Flint	L. & N. W.	Flint and Bagillt.
							Bone Phosphate Chemical Co.	Flint	L. & N. W.	Muspratt's Siding.
							United Alkali Co.	Flint	L. & N. W.	Muspratt's Siding.
							North Wales Paper Mill Co.'s Siding	Flint	L. & N. W.	Flint and Connah's Quay.
							Flintshire Oil Co.'s Siding	Flint	L. & N. W.	Saltney Wharf.
G	P					1 5	Flitwick	Beds	Mid.	Bedford and Luton.
							Franklin's Sand Siding	Beds	Mid.	Near Flitwick Station.
G	P	F	L	H	C	5 0	Flixton	Lancs	C.L.C. (G C, G N, & Mid.)	Warrington & Manchester (Central).
G	P	F	L	H	C	3 0	Float	W'meath	M. G. W.	Mullingar and Cavan.
							Float Junction	Lanark	Cal.	Thankerton and Carstairs.
							Flockton Coal Co.'s Siding	Yorks	L. & Y.	Same as Hartley Bank Col. (Horbury).
							Flockton Points Siding	Yorks	L. & Y.	Horbury Junction.
G	P	F		H	C	1 10	Flordon	Norfolk	G. E.	Norwich and Tivetshall.
							Florence Colliery	Staffs	N. S.	Trentham.
G	P		L				Florencecourt	Ferm'nagh	S. L. & N. C.	Enniskillen and Belcoo.
G	P		L				Floriston	Cumb'land	Cal.	Carlisle and Lockerbie.
							Mossband Siding	Cumb'land	Cal.	Floriston and Gretna.
							Flower & Son's Siding	Warwick	G. W.	Stratford-on-Avon.
G	P						Flushdyke	Yorks	G. N.	Wakefield and Ossett.
							Low Laithes Colliery	Yorks	G. N.	Flushdyke.
							Old Roundwood Colliery	Yorks	G. N.	Flushdyke and Alverthorpe.
G	P	F	L	H	C	1 5	Fochabers	Banff	G. N. of S.	Portsoy and Elgin.
G	P	F	L	H	C	3 0	Fochabers Town	Elgin&Mo'	High.	Branch from Orbliston.
G	P						Fochriw	Glamorg'n	B. & M.	Dowlais Top and Deri Junction.
							Fochriw Sid. & Col. (B.&M.)	Glamorg'n	B. & M.—Rhy.	Dowlais Top and Deri Junction.
							Guest, Keen & Nettlefold's Fochriw Col. (B. & M.)	Glamorg'n	B. & M.—L. & N.W.	Fochriw.
							Pantywaen Junc. & Quarry	Glamorg'n	B. & M.	Fochriw and Dowlais Top.
							Fochriw Colliery (B. & M.)	Glamorg'n	B. & M.—L. & N. W.	See Guest, Keen & Nettlefold (Fochriw).
							Fochriw or Fforchriw Colliery	Glamorg'n	T. B. Jt. (G. W. & Rhy.)	See Guest, Keen & Nettlefold (Cwm Bargoed).
G	P	F	L	H	C		Fockerby	Lincoln	Axholme Jt. (L&Y&NE)	Branch near Goole.
							Pindar's Siding	Lincoln	Axholme Jt. (L&Y&NE)	Fockerby.
							Fodderty Junction	Ross & Cro'	High.	Dingwall and Achterneed.
							Foden's Elworth Works	Cheshire	N. S.	Ettiley Heath.
G	P		L	H	C		Foggathorpe	Yorks	N. E.	Selby and Market Weighton.
							Foggo & Sons' Brick Works	Northumb	N. E.	Choppington.
G	P					1 10	Foleshill	Warwick	L. & N. W.	Coventry and Nuneaton.
							Cammell, Laird & Co.'s Sid.	Warwick	L. & N. W.	Foleshill and Coundon Road.
							Coventry Corporation Gas Works	Warwick	L. & N. W.	Foleshill and Longford.
							Webster's Brick Works Railway Co.'s Siding	Warwick	L. & N. W.	Foleshill and Coundon Road.
							Foley's Siding	Hereford	G. W.	Stoke Edith.
							FOLKESTONE—			
	P						Central	Kent	S. E. & C.	Shorncliffe and Folkestone Jn. Sta.
							FolkestoneCement Co.'s Sid.	Kent	S. E. & C.	Junction Station and Harbour.
G	P	F	L	H	C	8 0	Harbour	Kent	S. E. & C.	Branch from Folkestone Junc. Sta.
G	P	F	L	H	C	4 0	Junction Station	Kent	S. E. & C.	Shorncliffe and Dover Town.
G	P						Fontburn	Northumb	N. B.	Brinkburn and Ewesley.
							Font Siding	Northumb	N. B.	Longwitton.
G						4 0	Forcett	Yorks	N. E.	Branch near Piercebridge.
							Forcett Engine Shed	Yorks	N. E.	Forcett.
							Forcett Park Siding	Yorks	N. E.	Forcett.
							Forcett Quarry	Yorks	N. E.	Forcett.
							Forcett Valley Siding	Yorks	N. E.	Forcett.
							Lowfield Siding	Yorks	N. E.	Forcett.
G	P						Ford	Devon	L. & S.W.	Tavistock and Devonport.
G	P	F	L	H	C	10 0	Ford Bridge	Hereford	S & H Jt (G W & L N W)	Craven Arms and Hereford.
							Ford Colliery	Lanark	N. B.	Caldercruix.
							Fordell Colliery	Fife	N. B.	Crossgates.
G	P		L	H			Forden	Montgom	Cam.	Montgomery and Welshpool.
							Kilkewydd Siding	Montgom	Cam.	Welshpool and Forden.

EXPLANATION—G *Goods Station.*   P *Passenger and Parcel Station.*   P* *Passenger, but not Parcel or Miscellaneous Traffic.*
F *Furniture Vans, Carriages, Portable Engines, and Machines on Wheels.*   L *Live Stock.*
H *Horse-Boxes and Prize Cattle Vans.*   C *Carriages by Passenger Train.*

STATION ACCOMMODATION.						CRANE POWER.	STATIONS, &c.	COUNTY.	COMPANY.	POSITION.
						Tons Cwts.	Forder & Son—			
.	.	.	.	.	.	. .	Elstow Brick Works	Beds	Mid.	Bedford.
.	.	.	.	.	.	. .	Lime and Cement Works...	Beds	Mid.	Harlington.
.	.	.	.	.	.	. .	Sewell Lime Works	Beds	L. & N. W.	Stanbridgeford.
.	.	.	.	.	.	. .	Siding	Beds	L. & N. W.	Millbrook (for Ampthill).
.	.	.	.	.	.	. .	Siding	Warwick.	L. & N. W.	Nuneaton.
.	.	.	.	.	.	. .	Westoning Brick Works...	Beds	Mid.	Harlington.
.	.	.	.	.	.	. .	Forder's Lime Works	Hants ...	G. W.	Burghclere.
G	P	.	.	.	.	10 0	Ford Green and Smallthorne	Staffs ...	N. S.	Bucknall and Black Bull.
.	.	.	.	.	.	. .	Heath & Son's Norton Iron Works	Staffs ...	N. S.	Ford Green.
.	.	.	.	.	.	. .	Taylor & Son's Works	Staffs ...	N. S.	Ford Green.
G	P	F	L	H	C	1 10	Fordham	Cambs.....	G. E.	Ely and Newmarket.
.	.	.	.	.	.	. .	Stevenson & Co.'s Siding ...	Cambs.....	G. E.	Fordham and Burwell.
.	.	.	.	.	.	. .	Fordham's Siding	Herts ...	G. N.	Royston.
G	P	F	L	H	C	5 0	Fordingbridge....................	Hants ...	L. & S. W.	Salisbury and Wimborne.
.	.	.	.	.	.	. .	Ford Junction	Sussex ...	L. B. & S. C.	Arundel and Ford Junc. Station.
G	P	F	L	H	C	. .	Ford Junction Station	Sussex ...	L. B. & S. C.	Angmering and Barnham Junction.
.	.	.	.	.	.	. .	Ford Limestone Qry. & Bk. Wks	Durham ...	N. E.	Hylton.
G	P	F	L	H	C	1 10	Fordoun	Kinc'rdine	Cal.	Forfar and Stonehaven.
.	.	.	.	.	.	. .	Ford Paper Works..............	Durham ...	N. E.	Hylton.
.	.	.	.	.	.	. .	Ford's Colliery	Derby ...	Mid.	Same as Marehay Main Col. (Ripley)
.	.	.	.	.	.	. .	Ford's Siding	Kent	S. E. & C.	Maidstone.
.	.	.	.	.	.	. .	Ford's Siding	Suffolk ...	G. E.	Finningham.
.	.	.	.	.	.	. .	Foregate Street	Worcester	G. W.	See Worcester.
.	.	.	.	.	.	. .	Forest Brick Siding	Sussex ...	S. E. & C.	Frant.
.	.	.	.	.	.	. .	Forester & Co.'s Yard (G. W.)	Carmarth'	G. W.—L. & N. W.	Llanelly.
G	P	F	.	.	.	3 0	Forest Gate	Essex	G. E.	Stratford and Romford.
G	P	.	.	.	.	. .	Forest Gate Junction	Essex	G. E.—L. T. & S.	Stratford and Barking.
G	P	.	.	.	.	. .	Forest Hall	Northumb	N. E.	Newcastle and Morpeth.
.	.	.	.	.	.	. .	Benton Quarry	Northumb	N. E.	Forest Hall.
.	.	.	.	.	.	. .	Forest Head Lime Quarry ...	Cumb'land	N. E.	{ Brampton Junction Station. / Lambley.
G	P	.	.	.	.	10 0 }	Forest Hill (L. B. & S. C.) ...	Kent	{ L. B. & S. C. / G. E. / S. E. & C.	New Cross and Norwood Junction. / Over L. B. & S. C. from New Cross Jn. / Over L.B. & S. C. from Corbet's Lane Junction.
.	P	.	.	.	.	. . }				
.	P*	.	.	.	.	. . }				
.	.	.	.	.	.	. .	Forest Level	Glamorg'n	G. W.—T. V.	Mountain Ash.
G	P	.	L	H	.	1 0	Forest Mill	Clackman'	N. B.	Alloa and Dunfermline.
G	.	.	.	.	.	. .	Brucefield Siding	Fife	N. B.	Forest Mill and Bogside.
.	.	.	.	.	.	. .	Forest of Dean Navigation Col.	Gloucester	G. W.	Blakeney.
.	.	.	.	.	.	. .	Forest of Dean Stone Firms Sid	Gloucester	S. & Wye Jt. (G. W. & Mid.)	Parkend.
.	.	.	.	.	.	. .	Forest Rock Granite Co.'s Sid.	Leicester ..	L. & N. W.	Whitwick.
G	P	F	L	H	C	5 0	Forest Row (for Ashdown Forest)	Sussex ...	L. B. & S. C.	East Grinstead and Tunbridge Wells.
G	P	F	L	H	C	6 0 }	Forfar (Cal.)	Forfar ...	{ Cal. .... / N. B.	Coupar Angus and Stonehaven. / Over Caledonian from Arbroath Jn.
G	.	F	L	.	.	5 0 }				
.	.	.	.	.	.	. .	Don's Siding (Cal.)...........	Forfar ...	Cal.—N. B.	Forfar.
.	.	.	.	.	.	. .	Forfar Gas Works (Cal.) ...	Forfar ...	Cal.—N. B.	Forfar.
.	.	.	.	.	.	. .	Forfar Weighs	Forfar ...	Cal.	Forfar.
G	.	.	.	.	.	. .	Old Station Sidings (Cal.)...	Forfar ...	Cal.—N. B.	Forfar.
.	.	.	.	.	.	. .	Forfar Junction	Forfar ...	Cal.	Forfar and Clocksbriggs.
G	P	F	L	H	C	2 0	Forgandenny	Perth ...	Cal.	Stirling and Perth.
G	.	.	.	.	.	. .	Kirkton Siding	Perth ...	Cal.	Forgandenny and Perth.
G	P	.	.	.	.	. .	Forge Mills	Warwick.	Mid.	Birmingham and Tamworth.
.	.	.	.	.	.	. .	Forge Mills Sidings	Notts ...	Mid.	Nottingham, Bulwell.
.	.	.	.	.	.	. .	Forge Pit..........................	Mon	G. W.—L. & N. W.	Same as Llyn Colliery.
G	P	.	L	H	.	1 0	Forge Valley	Yorks ...	N. E.	Pickering and Scarborough.
.	.	.	.	.	.	. .	Forkneuk Pit	L'lithgow	N. B.	See Young's Oil Co. (Uphall).
.	.	.	.	.	.	. .	Forks Junction	Cumb'land	M. & C.	Carlisle.
G	P	.	L	H	.	3 10 }	Formby (L. & Y.)	Lancs ...	{ L. & Y. .... / L. & N. W.	Liverpool and Southport. / Over L. & Y. from Bootle Junction.
.	P	.	.	H	.	. . }				
.	.	.	.	.	.	. .	Woollard's Siding	Lancs ...	L. & Y.	Formby.
G	P	.	.	.	.	1 0	Forncett	Norfolk	G. E.	Norwich and Tivetshall.
G	P	F	L	H	C	5 0	Forres	Elgin&Mo'	High.	Elgin and Nairn.
.	.	.	.	.	.	. .	Dallasdhu Siding	Elgin&Mo'	High.	Forres and Dunphail.
G	P	.	L	H	.	. .	Forrestfield	Lanark ...	N. B.	Caldercruix and Bathgate, Upper.
.	.	.	.	.	.	. .	Baillie's Quarry	Lanark ...	N. B.	Near Forrestfield.
.	.	.	.	.	.	. .	Forrest's Stone Dressing Sid.	Edinboro'	N. B.	Edinburgh, Gorgie.
.	.	.	.	.	.	. .	Forrestt & Son's Siding	Essex ...	G. E.	Wyvenhoe.
G	P	F	L	H	C	. .	Forsinard	Sutherl'nd	High.	Helmsdale and Wick.
.	.	.	.	.	.	. .	Forster's Siding and Depôt...	Durham ...	N. E.	Pallion.

EXPLANATION—**G** *Goods Station.*   **P** *Passenger and Parcel Station.*   **P*** *Passenger, but not Parcel or Miscellaneous Traffic.*
F *Furniture Vans, Carriages, Portable Engines, and Machines on Wheels.*   **L** *Live Stock.*
H *Horse Boxes and Prize Cattle Vans.*   **C** *Carriages by Passenger Train.*

STATION ACCOMMODATION.						CRANE POWER.	STATIONS, &c.	COUNTY.	COMPANY.	POSITION.
G	P	F	L	H	C	Tons Cwts. . .	Fort Augustus	Inverness	High. (I. & F. A.)	Spean Bridge Junction and Fort Augustus Pier.
G	P	F	L	H	C	. .	Fort Augustus Pier	Inverness	High. (I. & F. A.)	Branch from Spean Bridge Junction.
.	P	.	.	.	.	}	Fort Brockhurst.................	Hants	Lee-on-the-Solent	Adjoining L. & S.W. Station.
.	P	.	.	.	.				L. & S.W.	Fareham and Gosport.
G	P	F	L	H	C	1 10	Forteviot.........................	Perth	Cal.	Stirling and Perth.
G	P	F	L	H	C	1 10	Fort George.....................	Inverness	High.	Branch from Gollanfield.
.	.	.	.	.	.	. .	Forth (N. E.)	Northumb	N. E.—N. B.	See Newcastle.
.	.	.	.	.	.	. .	Forth & Clyde Junction	Dumbartn	D. & B. Jt.—N. B.	Balloch and Jamestown.
.	.	.	.	.	.	. .	Forthar's Siding	Fife	N. B.	Falkland Road.
.	.	.	.	.	.	. .	Forth Bank Foundry	L'lithgow	N. B.	Bo'ness.
.	.	.	.	.	.	. .	Forth Bank Siding	Stirling ...	Cal.	Stirling.
.	.	.	.	.	.	. .	Forth Cattle Docks (N. E.)...	Northumb	N. E.—N. B.	See Newcastle.
.	.	.	.	.	.	. .	Forth Chemical Manure Wks. (Ovens) ...	L'lithgow	N. B.	Bo'ness.
.	.	.	.	.	.	. .	Forth Coal & Lime Depôt ...	Northumb	N. E.	Newcastle-on-Tyne.
.	.	.	.	.	.	. .	Forth Gas Wks. Sid. & Depôt	Northumb	N. E.	Newcastle-on-Tyne.
.	.	.	.	.	.	. .	Forth Goods Junction	Northumb	N. E.	Newcastle-on-Tyne.
.	.	.	.	.	.	. .	Forth HydraulicEngineHouse	Northumb	N. E.	Newcastle-on-Tyne.
.	.	.	.	.	.	. .	Forth N. E. R. Oil Gas Wks.	Northumb	N. E.	Newcastle-on-Tyne.
.	.	.	.	.	.	. .	Forth Provender Warehouse.	Northumb	N. E.	Newcastle-on-Tyne.
.	.	.	.	.	.	. .	Forth Saw Mills (M'Pherson & M'Laren's) (Cal.)	Stirling ...	Cal.—N. B.	Grangemouth.
.	.	.	.	.	.	. .	Forth Side Sidings	Stirling ...	Cal.	Stirling.
.	.	.	.	.	.	. .	Fortisset Colliery	Lanark ...	N. B.	Shotts.
.	.	.	.	.	.	. .	Fortisset Mains Siding	Lanark ...	N. B.	See Shotts.
.	P	.	.	.	.	. .	Fort Matilda	Renfrew ...	Cal.	Greenock and Gourock.
.	.	.	.	.	.	. .	Forton Junction.................	Hants	L. & S.W.	Gosport and Fort Brockhurst.
.	.	.	.	.	.	. .	Fortrigg Colliery	Lanark ...	N. B.	Shotts.
G	P	F	L	H	C	1 10	Fortrose	Ross & Cro'	High	Branch from Muir of Ord.
G	P	F	L	H	C	3 0	Fort William	Inverness	N. B.	Spean Bridge and Mallaig.
.	.	.	.	.	.	. .	Ben Nevis Distillery (Old Distillery)	Inverness	N. B.	Spean Bridge and Fort William.
.	.	.	.	.	.	. .	Glenlochy Distillery	Inverness	N. B.	Mallaig Junction & Fort William.
.	.	.	.	.	.	. .	Nevis Distillery	Inverness	N. B.	Spean Bridge and Fort William.
.	.	.	.	.	.	. .	Torlundy Siding	Inverness	N. B.	Spean Bridge and Fort William.
G	P	F	.	H	C	. .	Forty Hill	Middlesex	G. E.	Edmonton and Cheshunt.
.	P	.	.	.	.	. .	Foryd	Flint	L. & N. W.	Bangor and Rhyl.
G	.	.	.	.	.	5 0	Foryd Pier	Flint	L. & N. W.	Branch from Rhyl.
.	.	.	.	.	.	. .	Jones & Son's Siding	Flint	L. & N. W.	Foryd Pier.
G	P	F	L	H	C	5 0	Foss Cross	Glo'ster ...	M. & S. W. Jn.	Cirencester and Cheltenham.
.	.	.	.	.	.	. .	Fosse Road Wharf...............	Leicester..	Mid.	Leicester, West Bridge.
.	.	.	.	.	.	. .	Foss Islands....................	Yorks	N. E.	See York.
.	.	.	.	.	.	. .	Fossoway.........................	Kinross ...	N. B.	See Crook of Devon (for Fossoway).
.	.	.	.	.	.	. .	Foster & Co.'s Brick Works...	Northumb	N. E.	Holywell.
.	.	.	.	.	.	. .	Foster & Co.'s Siding (Mid.)	Lincoln ...	Mid.—G. C.—G. N.	Lincoln.
.	.	.	.	.	.	. .	Foster Bros.' Mill	Glo'ster ...	G. W.—Mid.	Gloucester Docks.
.	.	.	.	.	.	. .	Foster Bros.' Siding	Cambs.....	G. N.	Cambridge.
.	.	.	.	.	.	. .	Foster Bros.' Siding (G. E.)...	Cambs.....	G. E.—L. & N. W.—Mid.	Cambridge.
.	.	.	.	.	.	. .	Foster, Dent & Co.'s Siding...	Lancs	S. & M. Jt. (G. C. & Mid.)	Widnes.
.	.	.	.	.	.	. .	Foster Siding	Salop	G. W.	Madeley.
.	.	.	.	.	.	. .	Foster, W., & Co.'s Copper Works	Glamorg'n	G.W.—Mid.—L. & N. W.	Same as Pascoe, Grenfell & Son's Copper Works.
.	.	.	.	.	.	. .	Foster, Williams & Co.'s Siding (L. & Y.)	Lancs	L. & Y.—L. & N. W. ...	Same as Moss Pit Sid.(Skelmersdale)
.	P	.	.	.	.	. .	Fota	Cork	G. S. & W.	Queenstown Junc. and Queenstown.
.	.	.	.	.	.	. .	Fotherby & Son's Siding	Leicester..	L. & N. W.	Shepshed.
.	.	.	.	.	.	. .	Fothergill's Upper Llwydcoed Siding	Glamorg'n	G. W.	Same as Upper Llwydcoed Colliery (Llwydcoed).
.	.	.	.	.	.	. .	Foulford Colliery	Fife	N. B.	Cowdenbeath, Old.
.	.	.	.	.	.	. .	Foulford Junction...............	Fife	N. B.	Cowdenbeath (Old) and Lochgelly.
G	P	.	.	.	.	1 10	Foulridge (Mid.)................	Lancs	Mid.	Colne and Skipton.
.	P	.	.	.	.	}			L. & Y.	Over Mid. from Colne Junction.
G	P	F	L	H	C	1 10	Foulsham	Norfolk ...	G. E.	Aylsham and North Elmham.
.	.	.	.	.	.	. .	Foulshiels Brick Works	L'lithgow	Cal.	West Calder.
.	.	.	.	.	.	. .			N. B.	Addiewell.
.	.	.	.	.	.	. .	Foulshiels Colliery......	L'lithgow	Cal.	West Calder.
.	.	.	.	.	.	. .			N.B.	Addiewell.
.	.	.	.	.	.	. .	Foulsykes Siding	Lancs	L. & Y.	Clitheroe.
.	.	.	.	.	.	. .	Fountain Brewery	Edinboro'	Cal.	Edinburgh, Lothian Road.
.	.	.	.	.	.	. .	Fountain Brick Works........	Glamorg'n	G. W.	Tondu.

EXPLANATION—G *Goods Station.*   P *Passenger and Parcel Station.*   P* *Passenger, but not Parcel or Miscellaneous Traffic.*
F *Furniture Vans, Carriages, Portable Engines, and Machines on Wheels.*   L *Live Stock.*
H *Horse Boxes and Prize Cattle Vans.*   C *Carriages by Passenger Train.*

STATION ACCOMMODATION.						CRANE POWER.		STATIONS, &c.	COUNTY.	COMPANY.	POSITION.
						Tons	Cwts.				
G	P	F	L	H	C	1	5	Fountainhall Junction	Edinboro'	N. B.	Fountainhall and Stow.
G	P	.	L	H	.	.	.	Fountainhall Junction Station	Edinboro'	N. B.	Edinburgh and Galashiels.
G	P	F	L	H	C	5	0	Four Ashes	Staffs	L. & N. W.	Stafford and Wolverhampton.
G	P	F	L	H	C	.	.	Four Crosses	Montgom	Cam.	Oswestry and Welshpool.
G	G	.	.	.	.	.	.	Four Oaks	Warwick..	L. & N. W.	Birmingham and Lichfield.
G	P	.	L	H	.	5	0	Four Roads	Carmarth'	Gwen Valleys	Terminus.
.	.	.	.	.	.	.	.	Fourstones	Northumb	N. E.	Carlisle and Hexham.
.	.	.	.	.	.	.	.	Fourstones Colliery	Northumb	N. E.	Fourstones.
.	.	.	.	.	.	.	.	Fourstones Lime Kilns	Northumb	N. E.	Fourstones.
.	.	.	.	.	.	.	.	Prudham Quarry..............	Northumb	N. E.	Fourstones.
.	.	.	.	.	.	.	.	South Tyne Paper Mills ...	Northumb	N. E.	Fourstones.
G	P	.	.	.	H	2	0	Fowey	Cornwall..	G. W.	Branch from Par and Lostwithiel.
.	.	.	.	.	.	2	0	Carne Point Wharves	Cornwall..	G. W.	Fowey and Lostwithiel.
.	.	.	.	.	.	5	0	Fowey Wharves................	Cornwall..	G. W.	Fowey.
.	.	.	.	.	.	.	.	Fowler & Co.'s Siding (Mid.)	Yorks......	Mid.—L.&N.W.—N.E. / G. N.	Leeds, Hunslet Lane. (See Appendix to follow).
G	P	.	L	H	.	.	.	Fowlis	Ross & Cro'	High	Invergordon and Dingwall.
.	.	.	.	.	.	.	.	Fownes Forge & Engineering Co.'s Siding	Durham ...	N. E.	Tyne Dock.
.	.	.	.	.	.	.	.	Fownes Forge Co.'s Siding ...	Glamorg'n	GW—L&NW—Rhy—TV	Cardiff.
G	P	.	L	.	.	.	.	Foxcote Colliery................	Somerset..	G. W.—S. & D. Jt.	Radstock.
.	.	.	.	.	.	.	.	Foxdale	I. of Man.	Manx Northern	Branch from St. John's.
.	.	.	.	.	.	.	.	Foxes Bridge Colliery	Glo'ster ...	G. W.	Bilson Junction.
.	.	.	.	.	.	.	.	Foxes Bridge Siding	Glo'ster ...	S.&Wye Jt. (G.W. & Mid)	Drybrook Road.
.	.	.	.	.	.	.	.	Foxfield Colliery	Staffs	N. S.	Blyth Bridge.
.	P	.	.	H	.	.	.	Foxfield Junction Station ...	Lancs	Furness....................	Barrow and Millom.
G	P	.	L	H	.	2	0	Foxford.............................	Mayo	M. G. W.	Manulla Junction and Killala.
G	P	.	L	H	C	1	10	Foxhall	Donegal ...	L. & L. S.	Letterkenny and Burtonport.
.	.	.	.	.	.	.	.	Foxhole Col. Co.'s Sid. (Mid.)	Glamorg'n	Mid.—G. W.—L. & N. W.	Same as Llanerch Col. (Upper Bank).
G	P	.	L	H	.	.	.	Foxley Colliery	Lanark ...	Cal.	Carmyle.
G	P	.	L	.	.	.	.	Foxrock	Dublin ...	D. W. & W.	Dublin, Harcourt Street and Bray.
G	P	.	.	.	.	1	10	Fox's Bridge	Cork	C. & Muskerry	St. Ann's and Donoughmore.
.	.	.	.	.	.	.	.	Foxton (G. E.)	Cambs......	G. E. / G. N.	Cambridge and Shepreth Junction. Over G. E. from Shepreth Junction.
.	.	.	.	.	.	.	.	Foyle Road	Derry	G. N. (I.)	See Londonderry.
G	P	F	L	.	.	1	5	Foynes	Limerick..	G. S. & W.	Branch from Ballingrane.
.	.	.	.	.	.	.	.	Foynes Pier....................	Limerick..	G. S. & W.	Branch from Ballingrane.
G	P	F	L	H	C	5	0	Framlingham	Suffolk ...	G. E.	Branch from Wickham Market.
.	.	.	.	.	.	.	.	Frampton..........................	Dorset......	G. W.	See Grimstone and Frampton.
.	.	.	.	.	.	.	.	Framwellgate Colliery and Coke Ovens....................	Durham ...	N. E.	Leamside.
.	.	.	.	.	.	.	.	France & Son's Siding	Sussex......	L. B. & S. C.	Eastbourne.
.	.	.	.	.	.	.	.	Francis & Jenkins' Works (G. W.)	Carmarth'	G. W.—L. & N. W.	Llanelly.
.	.	.	.	.	.	.	.	Francis Pit	Fife	N. B.	Same as Dysart Colliery.
.	.	.	.	.	.	.	.	Francis Siding	Cambs......	G. E.	Quy.
.	.	.	.	.	.	.	.	Frankland Brick Works	Durham ...	N. E.	Leamside.
.	.	.	.	.	.	.	.	Frankland Junction	Durham ...	N. E.	Leamside.
.	.	.	.	.	.	.	.	Frankley Sid. (Kellet & Son)	Worcester	Halesowen (G. W. & Mid.)	Rubery.
.	.	.	.	.	.	.	.	Franklin's Sand Siding........	Beds	Mid.	Flitwick.
.	.	.	.	.	.	.	.	Franklin's Wagon Shed	Beds	L. & N. W.	Bedford.
G	P	.	L	H	.	.	.	Frankton	Salop	Cam.	Oswestry and Ellesmere.
G	P	.	.	.	.	.	.	Fransham	Norfolk ...	G. E.	Dereham and Swaffham.
G	P	F	L	H	C	4	0	Frant...............................	Sussex......	S. E. & C.	Tunbridge Wells and Hastings.
.	.	.	.	.	.	.	.	Forest Brick Siding	Sussex......	S. E. & C.	Tunbridge Wells and Frant.
.	.	.	.	.	.	.	.	Fraser and Young's Siding ...	Kirkcud...	G. & S. W.	Dalbeattie.
G	P	F	L	H	C	4	0	Fraserburgh......................	Aberdeen	G. N. of S.	Branch from Maud.
.	.	.	.	.	.	.	.	Fraser Junior's Siding	Fife	N. B.	Kirkcaldy, Sinclairtown.
.	.	.	.	.	.	.	.	Fratton Junction Station.....	Hants	L. & S W & L B & S C Jt.	See Portsmouth.
.	.	.	.	.	.	.	.	Frazer & Son's Siding	Durham ...	N. E.	Hebburn.
.	.	.	.	.	.	.	.	Freakley's Golds Green Sid.	Staffs	L. & N. W.	Great Bridge.
.	.	.	.	.	.	.	.	Free & Co.'s Siding	Suffolk ...	G. E.	Stowmarket.
.	.	.	.	.	.	.	.	Free Rodwell & Co.'s Siding	Essex	G. E.	Mistley.
G	P	.	.	.	.	5	0	Free Street (B. & M.)	Brecon ...	B&M—Cam—Mid—N&B	See Brecon.
G	P	F	L	H	C	1	5	Fremington	Devon	L. & S.W.	Barnstaple and Bideford.
G	P	.	.	.	.	.	.	French Drove & Gedney Hill	Lincoln ...	G. N. & G. E. Jt.	Spalding and March.
G	P	.	.	.	.	.	.	Freshfield (L. & Y.)	Lancs.......	L. & Y. / L. & N. W.	Liverpool and Southport. Over L. & Y. from Bootle Junction.
.	.	.	.	.	.	.	.	Barkfield Sid.(L.&Y.Ry.Co)	Lancs	L. & Y.	Freshfield.
G	P	F	L	H	C	.	.	Freshford.........................	Wilts	G. W.	Trowbridge and Bathampton.
G	P	F	L	H	C	.	.	Freshwater	I. of W. ...	I. of W. Cent.	Terminus.
.	.	.	.	.	.	.	.	Frew's Foundry	Lanark ...	Cal.	Hamilton, Central.

EXPLANATION—G *Goods Station.*   P *Passenger and Parcel Station.*   P* *Passenger, but not Parcel or Miscellaneous Traffic.*
F *Furniture Vans, Carriages, Portable Engines, and Machines on Wheels.*   L *Live Stock.*
H *Horse Boxes and Prize Cattle Vans.*   C *Carriages by Passenger Train.*

STATION ACCOMMODATION.						CRANE POWER.		STATIONS, &c.	COUNTY.	COMPANY.	POSITION.
						Tons	Cwts				
								Freystrop Colliery	Pembroke.	G. W.	Johnston.
								Friar Gate	Derby	G. N.	See Derby.
								Friar's Goose Works	Durham ...	N. E.	See United Alkali Co. (Gateshead).
								Friarton Brick Works	Perth	Cal.	Perth, South.
								Friarton Gas Works and Manure Depôt (Cal.)	Perth	Cal.—N. B.	Perth, South.
								Friarton Goods Yard and Sidings (Cal.)	Perth	Cal.—N. B.	See Perth.
								Friary	Devon	L. & S.W.	See Plymouth.
								Friary Junction	Devon	G. W.—L. & S. W.	Plymouth.
G	P	F	L	H	C	1	10	Frickley (S. & K. Jt.)	Yorks	S. & K. Jt.(Mid. & N. E.) / G. C.	Swinton Junction and Moorthorpe. / Over S. & K. Jt. from Swinton Junc.
.	P	.	.	H	C	.	.				
								Hickleton Main Colliery (S. & K. Jt.)	Yorks	S. & K. Jt.—G.C.	Frickley and Bolton-upon-Dearne.
								Frickley Colliery...............	Yorks	S. & K. Jt. (Mid. & N. E.)	See Carlton Main Colliery Co. (Moorthorpe).
G	.	.	L	.	.	0	15	Friden	Derby	L. & N. W.	Buxton and Cromford.
								Derbyshire Silica Fire Brick Co.'s Siding	Derby	L. & N. W.	Friden and Parsley Hay.
								Friern Barnet	Middlesex	G. N.	See New Southgate and Friern Barnet.
G	P					5	0	Friezland	Yorks	L. & N. W.	Huddersfield and Stalybridge.
								Frimley	Hants	S. E. & C.	See Farnborough (for Frimley).
G	P	F	L	H	C	1	10	Frimley	Surrey	L. & S.W.	Ascot and Farnham.
								Frimley Junction	Surrey	L. & S.W.	Brookwood and Frimley.
G	P							Frinton-on-Sea	Essex	G. E.	Colchester and Walton-on-the-Naze.
G	P	.	L	H		2	0	Friockheim	Forfar	Cal.	Forfar and Arbroath.
								Friockheim Junction............	Forfar	Cal.	Friockheim and Leysmill.
								Frisby	Leicester..	Mid.	Leicester and Melton.
.	P							Frisky Wharf	Dumbartn	N. B.	Bowling.
								Frizinghall	Yorks	Mid.	See Bradford.
G	P	.	L	H	.	3	0	Frizington	Cumb'land	WC&EJt. (Fur. & LNW)	Marron Junction and Moor Row.
								Cammell & Co.'s Sidings—Frizington Park Mine ...	Cumb'land	WC&EJt. (Fur. & LNW)	Frizington and Yeathouse.
								Mowbray Pits	Cumb'land	WC&EJt. (Fur. & LNW)	Mowbray Branch.
								Darlington Wagon & Engineering Co.'s Siding	Cumb'land	WC&EJt. (Fur. & LNW)	Frizington and Cleator Moor.
								Old Parkside Mining Co.'s Sidings	Cumb'land	WC&EJt. (Fur. & LNW)	Frizington.
								Trio Mining Co.'s Pit	Cumb'land	WC&EJt. (Fur. & LNW)	Mowbray Branch.
								Vivian's Boring and Exploration Co.'s Siding ...	Cumb'land	WC&EJt. (Fur.& LNW)	Frizington and Cleator Moor.
G	P	F	L	H	C	1	10	Frocester	Glo'ster ...	Mid.	Gloucester and Bristol.
G	P	F	L	H	C	5	0	Frodingham & Scunthorpe ...	Lincoln ...	G. C.	Thorne and Barnetby.
								Appleby Iron Co.'s Siding..	Linco'n ...	G. C.	Frodingham and Scunthorpe.
								Beauchamp Mines	Lincoln ...	G. C.	Frodingham and Scunthorpe.
								Chatterton Mine...............	Lincoln ...	G. C.	Glebe Branch.
								Frodingham Iron and Steel Co.'s Chemical Works ...	Lincoln ...	G. C.	Frodingham and Scunthorpe.
								Frodingham Iron & Steel Co.'s Siding..................	Lincoln ...	G. C.	Frodingham and Scunthorpe.
								Glebe Mine	Lincoln ...	G. C.	Glebe Branch.
								Gunhouse Wharf	Lincoln ...	G. C.	Branch from Gunhouse Junction.
								Lindsey Iron Works	Lincoln ...	G. C.	Frodingham and Scunthorpe.
								Lord St. Oswald's Mine ...	Lincoln ...	G. C	Glebe Branch.
								Midland Ironstone Co.'s Sid.	Lincoln ...	G. C.	Frodingham and Scunthorpe.
								Normanby Mine...............	Lincoln ...	G. C.	Glebe Branch.
								North Lincolnshire Iron Co.'s Siding	Lincoln ...	G. C.	Frodingham and Scunthorpe.
								Redbourn Hill Works	Lincoln ...	G. C.	Frodingham and Scunthorpe.
								Sheepbridge Mine	Lincoln ...	G. C.	Glebe Branch.
								Sir Berkeley Sheffield's Sid.	Lincoln ...	G. C.	Frodingham and Scunthorpe.
								Trent Iron Works	Lincoln ...	G. C.	Frodingham and Scunthorpe.
								Warren Mines...............	Lincoln ...	G. C.	Glebe Branch.
								Winn's Siding..:............	Lincoln ...	G. C.	Frodingham and Scunthorpe.
G	P	F	L	H	C	3	0	Frodsham	Cheshire..	B'head Jt. (G W & L N W)	Chester and Warrington.
								Frodsham Junction	Cheshire..	B'head Jt.—L. & N. W.	Frodsham and Runcorn.
.	P					5	0	Froghall	Staffs	N. S.	Leek and Uttoxeter.
								Bolton's Copper Works ...	Staffs	N. S.	Froghall.
								Caldon Low...............	Staffs	N. S.	Froghall.
								Frogmore	Herts	L. & N. W.	See Park Street and Frogmore.
								Frognal (L. & N. W.)	Middlesex	L. & N. W.—N. L.	See London, Finchley Rd. & Frognal.

EXPLANATION—G Goods Station. P Passenger and Parcel Station. P* Passenger, but not Parcel or Miscellaneous Traffic.
F Furniture Vans, Carriages, Portable Engines, and Machines on Wheels. L Live Stock.
H Horse Boxes and Prize Cattle Vans. C Carriages by Passenger Train.

STATION ACCOMMODATION.						CRANE POWER.	STATIONS, &c.	COUNTY.	COMPANY.	POSITION.
G	P	F	L	H	C	Tons 7 Cwts. 0	Frome	Somerset..	G. W.	Westbury and Witham.
.	.	.	.	.	.		Bailey's Siding	Somerset..	G. W.	Frome.
.	.	.	.	.	.		Frome Gas Works	Somerset..	G. W.	Frome and Mells Road.
.	.	.	.	.	.		Market House Siding	Somerset..	G. W.	Frome and Mells Road.
.	.	.	.	.	.		Somerset StoneQuarries Sid.	Somerset..	G. W.	Frome and Mells Road.
G	P	F	L	H	C	. .	Fronfraith Siding	Montgom	Cam.	Kerry.
G	P	.	.	.	.	3 0	Frongoch	Merioneth	G. W.	Bala and Festiniog.
G	P	.	.	.	.		Frosterley	Durham ..	N. E.	Stanhope and Bishop Auckland.
.	.	.	.	.	.		Bishopley Cragg Siding	Durham ..	N. E.	Frosterley.
.	.	.	.	.	.		Bishopley Quarry	Durham ..	N. E.	Frosterley.
.	.	.	.	.	.		Bishopley Junction Siding	Durham ..	N. E.	Frosterley.
.	.	.	.	.	.		Bishopley Lime Works	Durham ..	N. E.	Frosterley.
.	.	.	.	.	.		Bollihope Quarry	Durham ..	N. E.	Frosterley.
.	.	.	.	.	.		Broadwood Quarry	Durham ..	N. E.	Frosterley.
.	.	.	.	.	.		Brown's House Quarry	Durham ..	N. E.	Frosterley.
.	.	.	.	.	.		Frosterley Limestone Qry.	Durham ..	N. E.	Frosterley.
.	.	.	.	.	.		Harehope Mining & Quarrying Co.'s Siding	Durham ..	N. E.	Frosterley.
.	.	.	.	.	.		Miln House Quarry	Durham ..	N. E.	Frosterley.
.	.	.	.	.	.		Rogerley Quarry	Durham ..	N. E.	Frosterley.
.	.	.	.	.	.		South Bishopley Quarry	Durham ..	N. E.	Frosterley.
.	.	.	.	.	.		Fry Bros.' Siding	Middlesex	G. E.	Brimsdown.
.	.	.	.	.	.		Fry's Bottom Colliery	Somerset..	G. W.	Clutton.
.	.	.	.	.	.		Fryer's, E., Siding	Somerset..	Mid.	Weston (near Bath).
.	.	.	.	.	.		Fryer's Siding	Glo'ster	S.&Wye Jt. (G.W & Mid)	Milkwall.
G	.	.	L	.	.		Fryston	Yorks	N. E.	Castleford and Burton Salmon.
.	.	.	.	.	.		Fryston Coal Co.'s Siding	Yorks	N. E.	Fryston.
.	.	.	.	.	.		Fulbeck Sidings	Lincoln	G. N.	Caythorpe.
.	.	.	.	.	.		Caythorpe Ironstone Mines	Lincoln	G. N.	Fulbeck Sidings.
.	.	.	.	.	.		Yorkshire Iron & Coal Co.	Lincoln	G. N.	Fulbeck Sidings.
G	P	.	L	.	.	1 10	Fulbourne	Cambs	G. E.	Cambridge and Newmarket.
G	.	.	.	.	.		Cherryhinton Siding	Cambs	G. E.	Cambridge and Fulbourne.
.	.	.	.	.	.		Crawley & Co.'s Siding	Cambs	G. E.	Fulbourne and Cambridge.
.	.	.	.	.	.		Teversham Siding	Cambs	G. E.	Fulbourne and Cambridge.
.	.	.	.	.	.		Fulham	Middlesex	L. & N.W. WL.E.Jt.(GW,L&NW, L.&SW,&L.B.&S.C.)	See London, Brompton & Fulham. See London, Chelsea and Fulham.
.	.	.	.	.	.		Fulham Gas Co.'s Siding	Middlesex	G. W.—L & N. W.	Same as Imperial Gas Light & Coke Co. (London).
.	.	.	.	.	.		Fulham Junction	Middlesex	L. & S.W.—Met. Dist.	London, Putney Bridge.
.	.	.	.	.	.		Fuller, A., Siding	Hunts	G. N. & G. E. Jt.	Warboys.
.	.	.	.	.	.		Fullers Earth Union Siding	Somerset	S & D Jt (L & S W & Mid.)	Wellow.
G	P	F	L	H	C		Fullerton Junction (L & S W)	Hants	L. & S. W. M. & S. W. Jn.	Romsey and Andover. Over L & S.W. from Andover Jn.
.	.	.	.	.	.		Fullwood Junction	Lanark ..	Cal.	Holytown and Mossend.
.	P	.	.	.	.		Fulwell and Hampton Hill	Middlesex	L. & S.W.	Twickenham and Shepperton.
G	P	.	L	H	.		Fulwell and Westbury	Bucks	L. & N. W.	Banbury and Verney Junc. Station.
.	.	.	.	.	.		Fulwell Junction	Middlesex	L. & S.W.	Strawberry Hill and Fulwell.
.	.	.	.	.	.		Fulwell Lime Works	Durham ..	N. E.	Sunderland, Monkwearmouth.
.	.	.	.	.	.		Fulwood Moss Siding	Renfrew..	Cal.	See Houston.
.	.	.	.	.	.		Furnace Blwm Siding	Glamorg'n	Rhy.	Same as Penrhos Siding.
.	.	.	.	.	.		Furnace Road Siding	Northumb	N. E.	Bedlington.
.	.	.	.	.	.		Furner's Siding	Kent	S. E. & C.	Dartford.
.	P	F	.	H	C		Furness Abbey	Lancs	Furness	Ulverston and Barrow.
.	P	.	.	.	.		Furness Brick & Tile Co.'s Sid.	Lancs	Furness	Barrow.
.	.	.	.	.	.		Furness Vale	Cheshire..	L. & N. W.	Buxton and Stockport.
.	.	.	.	.	.		Furness, Withy & Co.'s Ship Yd	Durham ..	N. E.	Hartlepool.
.	.	.	.	.	.		Furniss Siding (G. C.)	Yorks	G. C.—G. N.	Sheffield, Park.
G	P	.	L	H	.		Furzebrook Siding	Dorset	L. & S.W.	Corfe Castle.
.	.	.	.	.	.		Fushiebridge	Edinboro'	N. B.	Edinburgh and Galashiels.
.	.	.	.	.	.		Castleton Siding	Edinboro'	N. B.	Esperton Lime Works Siding.
.	.	.	.	.	.		Esperton Lime Works	Edinboro'	N. B.	Branch from Fushiebridge.
.	.	.	.	.	.		Vogrie Col. & Brick Works	Edinboro'	N. B.	Gorebridge and Fushiebridge.
G	P	.	.	.	.		Futterhills Siding	Glo'ster	S.&Wye Jt.(G.W. & Mid)	See Milkwall.
.	.	.	.	.	.		Fyfin	Tyrone ..	C. & V. B.	Castlederg and Victoria Bridge.
.	.	.	.	.	.		Fylands Bridge Gas Works (Bishop Auckland & District Gas Co.)	Durham ...	N. E.	West Auckland.
.	.	.	.	.	.		Fylands Bridge Loco. Sheds (N. E. R.)	Durham ..	N. E.	West Auckland.
G	P	F	L	H	.		Fyling Hall	Yorks	N. E.	Scarborough and Whitby.
G	P	F	L	H	C	1 5	Fyvie	Aberdeen	G. N. of S.	Inveramsay and Turriff.

EXPLANATION—G *Goods Station.*   P *Passenger and Parcel Station.*   P* *Passenger, but not Parcel or Miscellaneous Traffic.*
F *Furniture Vans, Carriages, Portable Engines, and Machines on Wheels.*   L *Live Stock.*
H *Horse Boxes and Prize Cattle Vans.*   C *Carriages by Passenger Train.*

STATION ACCOMMODATION.					CRANE POWER.	STATIONS, &c.	COUNTY.	COMPANY.	POSITION.
					Tons Cwts.				
								G	
.	.	.	.	.	.	Gadlys Colliery	Glamorg'n	G. W.	Aberdare.
.	.	.	.	.	.	Gadlys Estate Brick Works	Glamorg'n	G. W.	Aberdare.
.	.	.	.	.	.	Gadlys Junction	Glamorg'n	G. W.—T. V.	Aberdare.
.	.	.	.	.	.	Gadlys Tin Works	Glamorg'n	T. V.	Aberdare.
.	.	.	.	.	.	Gadlys Works	Glamorg'n	T. V.	Aberdare.
.	.	.	.	.	.	Gadson's Siding	Surrey	L. B. & S. C.	Epsom Downs.
.	.	.	.	.	.	Gaer Junction	Mon	G. W.	Newport.
G	P	.	L	H	.	Gaerwen	Anglesey	L. & N. W.	Bangor and Holyhead.
G	.	.	L	.	3 0	Gagie	Forfar	Cal.	Dundee and Forfar.
.	.	.	.	.	.	Wellbank Quarry	Forfar	Cal.	Gagie and Monikie.
.	.	.	.	.	.	Gailes	Ayr	G. & S. W.	See Irvine.
.	P	.	.	.	.	Gailey	Staffs	L. & N. W.	Stafford and Wolverhampton.
G	P	.	L	.	5 0	Gainford	Durham	N. E.	Darlington and Barnard Castle.
						GAINSBOROUGH—			
G	P	F	L	H C	20 0	(Station)	Lincoln	{ G. C.	Retford and Barnetby.
G	P	F	L	H C	10 0			G. N. & G. E. Jt.	Lincoln and Doncaster.
.	.	.	.	.	.	Marshall's Siding	Lincoln	G. C.	Gainsborough.
.	.	.	.	.	.	Newsum, Sons & Co.'s Sid.	Lincoln	G. N. & G. E. Jt.	Gainsborough (Trent Wharf Yard).
.	.	.	.	.	.	North Junction	Lincoln	G. C.— G. N. & G. E. Jt.	Gainsborough Sta. and Beckingham.
.	.	.	.	.	.	Pearson Brothers' Siding	Lincoln	G. N. & G. E. Jt.	Gainsborough (Trent Wharf Yard).
.	.	.	.	.	.	South Junction	Lincoln	G. C.— G. N. & G. E. Jt.	Sturton and Gainsborough Station.
.	.	.	.	.	.	Trent Wharf Sidings	Lincoln	G. N. & G. E. Jt.	Gainsborough.
G	P	.	L	.	.			{ Cal.	Steamer from Oban.
G	P	.	L	. C	.	Gairloch	Ross & Cro'	High.	Steamer from Kyle of Lochalsh.
G	P	.	L	.	.			N. B.	Steamer from Mallaig.
G	P	.	L	H C	.	Gairlochy	Inverness	High (I. & F. A.).	Spean Bridge Jn. & Fort Augustus.
G	P	.	L	.	.	Gaisgill	W'morlnd	N. E.	Darlington and Tebay.
.	.	.	.	.	.	Galafoot Gas Works	Selkirk	N. B.	Galashiels.
G	P	F	L	H C	6 0	Galashiels	Selkirk	N. B.	Edinburgh and St. Boswells.
.	.	.	.	.	.	Galafoot Gas Works	Selkirk	N. B.	Galashiels and Lindean.
.	.	.	.	.	.	Mid Mill Siding (J. & W. Cochrane)	Selkirk	N. B.	Galashiels.
.	.	.	.	.	.	Netherdale Sid. (Cochrane Bros.)	Selkirk	N. B.	Galashiels and Lindean.
.	.	.	.	.	.	Paterson's Wood Yard	Selkirk	N. B.	Bowland and Galashiels.
.	.	.	.	.	.	Roberts & Co.'s Mill	Selkirk	N. B.	Galashiels.
.	.	.	.	.	.	Sanderson & Murray's Sid. (Skin Works)	Selkirk	N. B.	Bowland and Galashiels.
.	.	.	.	.	.	Galawhistle Pit	Ayr	Cal.	Coalburn.
.	P	.	.	.	.	Galgate	Lancs	L. & N. W.	Lancaster and Preston.
G	P	.	.	.	.	Gallagh Road	Derry	L. & L. S.	Londonderry and Buncrana.
.	.	.	.	.	.	Gallangad Siding	Dumbartn	N. B.	Caldarvan.
.	.	.	.	.	.	Gallions (L. & I. D.)	Essex	L. & I. Dks.—G. E.	See London.
.	.	.	.	.	.	Galloway's Siding	Lancs	L. & N. W.	Manchester, London Road.
.	.	.	.	.	.	Galloway's Siding (G. C.)	Lancs	G. C.—Mid.	Manchester, Ardwick.
.	.	.	.	.	.	Gallowgate	Lanark	G. & S. W.	See Glasgow.
.	.	.	.	.	.	Gallowgate, Central	Lanark	N. B.	See Glasgow.
.	.	.	.	.	.	Gallowgate, Central Junction	Lanark	G. & S. W.— N. B.	Glasgow.
.	.	.	.	.	.	Gallowhill Sidings	Renfrew	G & P Jt (Cal & G & S W)	Paisley, Greenlaw.
.	.	.	.	.	.	Gallows Close	Yorks	N. E.	Scarborough, Falsgrave.
.	.	.	.	.	.	Gall's Mill	L'lithgow	N. B.	Bathgate, Lower.
.	.	.	.	.	.	Gallsworthy & Son's Sidings (Mid.)	Lincoln	Mid.—G. C.—G. N.	Lincoln.
G	P	F	L	H C	3 0	Galston	Ayr	G. & S. W.	Hurlford and Newmilns.
.	.	.	.	.	.	Galston Colliery	Ayr	G. & S. W.	Near Galston.
.	.	.	.	.	.	Gauchalland, No. 2	Ayr	G. & S. W.	Hurlford and Galston.
.	.	.	.	.	.	Gauchalland, No. 4	Ayr	G. & S. W.	Hurlford and Galston.
.	.	.	.	.	.	Maxwood Colliery	Ayr	G. & S. W.	Galston and Newmilns.
.	.	.	.	.	.	Galston Branch Junction	Ayr	G. & S. W.	Hurlford and Galston.
.	.	.	.	.	.	Galton Junction	Staffs	G. W.—L. & N. W.	Smethwick
.	.	.	.	.	.	Galty-fedw Slate Quarry Co.'s Siding	Carnarvon	L. & N. W.	Nantlle.
G	P	F	L	H C	5 0	Galway	Galway	M. G. W.	Athlone and Clifden.
.	.	.	.	.	.	Gamble's Flour Mill	Notts	Mid.	Nottingham, Bulwell.

EXPLANATION—G Goods Station.   P Passenger and Parcel Station.   P* Passenger, but not Parcel or Miscellaneous Traffic.
F Furniture Vans, Carriages, Portable Engines, and Machines on Wheels.   L Live Stock.
H Horse Boxes and Prize Cattle Vans.   C Carriages by Passenger Train.

G	P	F	L	H	C	Tons	Cwts	STATIONS, &c.	COUNTY	COMPANY	POSITION
G	P	F	L	H	C	1	5	Gamble's Sidings	Lancs	L. & N. W.	St. Helens.
.	.	.	.	.	.			Gamlingay	Cambs	L. & N. W.	Bedford and Cambridge.
								Coates & Rutley's Belle Vue Brick Co.'s Dennis Siding	Cambs	L. & N. W.	Gamlingay and Potton.
.	.	.	.	.	.			Gamston Brick Siding	Notts	G. N.	Retford.
.	.	.	.	.	.			Gane Sand Quarry	Lanark	Cal.	Glenboig.
.	.	.	.	.	.			Gane Siding	Lanark	Cal.	Glenboig.
G	P	.	L	H	.	1	10	Ganton	Yorks	N. E.	Malton and Scarborough.
.	.	.	.	.	.			Gantra Siding	Mon	L. & N. W.	See Ebbw Vale Steel, Iron & Coal Co. (Ebbw Vale).
.	.	.	.	.	.			Gantree Siding	Yorks	N. E.	{ Grosmont. { Sleights.
G	P	F	L	.	.			Gaol Siding (West Siding)	L'lithgow	N. B.	Linlithgow.
G	P	.	.	.	.			Gara Bridge	Devon	G. W.	Branch from Kingsbridge.
.	.	.	.	.	.			Garadice (Book to Ballinamore)	Leitrim	C. & L.	Bawnboy Road and Ballinamore.
.	.	.	.	.	.			Gardden Lodge Junction	Denbigh	G. W.	Ruabon.
.	.	.	.	.	.			Garden Lane Siding	Durham	N. E.	South Shields.
.	.	.	.	.	.			Gardner's Siding	Anglesey	L. & N. W.	Valley.
G	P	F	L	H	C	1	10	Garelochhead	Dumbartn	N. B.	Craigendoran and Ardlui.
.	.	.	.	.	.			Garesfield (Spen) Col., Coke Ovens, Brick Wks. & Depôts	Durham	N. E.	Derwenthaugh.
G	P	F	L	H	C	5	0	Garforth	Yorks	N. E.	Leeds and York.
.	.	.	.	.	.			Garforth Colliery	Yorks	N. E.	Garforth.
.	.	.	.	.	.			Garforth Mill	Yorks	N. E.	Garforth.
.	.	.	.	.	.			Gargieston Siding (Third Part Siding)	Ayr	G. & S.W.	Gatehead.
G	P	.	L	H	.	5	0	Gargrave	Yorks	Mid.	Skipton and Hellifield.
.	.	.	.	.	.			Delaney's Sidings	Yorks	Mid.	Skipton and Gargrave.
G	P	.	L	H	.	3	0	Gargunnock	Stirling	N. B.	Stirling and Balloch.
.	.	.	.	.	.			Garland and Roger's Siding	Dumfries	G. & S.W.	Dumfries.
.	.	.	.	.	.			Garland and Roger's Siding	Edinburgh	N. B.	Leith, South.
G	.	F	L	.	.	1	10	Garliestown	Wigtown	P.P.&W.Jt. (Cal., G&SW, L. & N. W. & Mid.)	Branch from Millisle.
G	P	F	L	H	C	2	0	Garmouth	Elgin&Mo'	G. N. of S.	Portsoy and Elgin.
G	P	.	L	.	.			Garnant	Carmarth'	G. W.	Pantyffynnon and Brynamman.
.	.	.	.	.	.			Brynmelyn Quarry	Glamorg'n	G. W.	Branch from Garnant.
.	.	.	.	.	.			Cawdor (Old) Colliery	Carmarth'	G. W.	Near Glanamman.
.	.	.	.	.	.			Cwmgorse Colliery	Glamorg'n	G. W.	Gwaun Cae Gurwen.
.	.	.	.	.	.			Cwmtrupit (New Cawdor) Colliery	Carmarth'	G. W.	Garnant and Gwaun Cae Gurwen.
.	.	.	.	.	.			Garnant Iron & Tin Plate Works Siding	Carmarth'	G. W.	Garnant and Gwaun Cae Gurwen.
.	.	.	.	.	.			Gellyceidrim Colliery	Carmarth'	G. W.	Garnant and Glanamman.
.	.	.	.	.	.			Glanamman Siding	Carmarth'	G. W.	Glanamman and Ammanford.
G	.	.	.	.	.			Glangarnant Colliery	Carmarth'	G. W.	Garnant and Gwaun Cae Gurwen.
.	.	.	.	.	.			Gors-y-Garnant	Carmarth'	G. W.	Garnant and Gwaun Cae Gurwen.
.	.	.	.	.	.			Gwaun Cae Gurwen Colliery (Brook Colliery)	Glamorg'n	G. W.	Gwaun Cae Gurwen.
.	.	.	.	.	.			Noyadd Colliery	Glamorg'n	G. W.	Garnant and Brynamman.
.	.	.	.	.	.			Raven Colliery	Carmarth'	G. W.	Garnant.
G	P	.	.	.	.			Raven Iron & Tin Plate Wks.	Carmarth'	G. W.	Glanamman.
.	.	.	.	.	.			Garneddwen	Merioneth	Corris	Corris and Aberllefenny.
.	.	.	.	.	.			Garner's Siding	Cheshire	C. L. C. (G.C., G.N. & Mid.)	Winsford and Over.
								GARNGABER—			
G	.	.	.	.	.			High Junction	Dumbartn	N. B.	Garngaber Jn. Sta. & Lenzie Jn. Sta.
.	.	.	.	.	.			Junction Station	Dumbartn	N. B.	Croy and Lenzie Junction Station.
.	.	.	.	.	.			Low Junction	Dumbartn	N. B.	Bridgend and Garngaber Junc. Sta.
G	.	.	.	.	.			Wester Gartshore Colliery	Dumbartn	N. B.	Croy and Garngaber Junction Sta.
G	.	.	.	.	.			Wester Gartshore Farm Sid.	Dumbartn	N. B.	Croy and Garngaber Junction Sta.
.	.	.	.	.	.			Whitelaw's Siding	Dumbartn	N. B.	Croy and Garngaber Junction Sta.
.	.	.	.	.	.			Woodilee Asylum Siding	Dumbartn	N. B.	Croy and Garngaber Junction Sta.
.	.	.	.	.	.			Garngad (N. B.)	Lanark	N. B.—G. & S. W.	See Glasgow.
.	.	.	.	.	.			Garngoch Colliery	Glamorg'n	G. W.—L. & N. W.	See Glasbrook Bros. (Gowerton).
G	P	.	.	.	.	3	0	Garnkirk	Lanark	Cal.	Coatbridge & Glasgow(BuchananStr)
.	.	.	.	.	.			Cardowan Fire-Clay Works	Lanark	Cal.	Garnkirk and Steps Road.
.	.	.	.	.	.			Garnkirk Weighs	Lanark	Cal.	Garnkirk.
.	.	.	.	.	.			Gartloch Distillery (Garnkirk Distillery)	Lanark	Cal.	Garnkirk.
.	.	.	.	.	.			Heathfield Fire-Clay Works	Lanark	Cal.	Gartcosh and Garnkirk.
.	.	.	.	.	.			Saracen Tube Works	Lanark	Cal.	Garnkirk and Steps Road.
.	.	.	.	.	.			Garnkirk Distillery	Lanark	Cal.	Same as Gartloch Distillery (Garnkirk).

EXPLANATION—G *Goods Station.* P *Passenger and Parcel Station.* P* *Passenger, but not Parcel or Miscellaneous Traffic.*
F *Furniture Vans, Carriages, Portable Engines, and Machines on Wheels.* L *Live Stock.*
H *Horse Boxes and Prize Cattle Vans.* C *Carriages by Passenger Train.*

Station Accommodation.						Crane Power.		STATIONS, &c.	COUNTY.	COMPANY.	POSITION.
						Tons	Cwts.				
.	.	.	.	.	.	.	.	Garn Mill Colliery..............	Carmarth'	G. W.	Pantyffynnon.
.	.	.	.	.	.	.	.	Garnqueen	Lanark ...	N. B............................	See Glenboig General Siding (for Garnqueen).
.	.	.	.	.	.	.	.	Garnqueen Brick Works (Hayhill Brick Works)......	Lanark ...	Cal.	Glenboig.
.	.	.	.	.	.	.	.	Garnqueen Junction, North...	Lanark ...	Cal.	Gartsherrie and Glenboig.
.	.	.	.	.	.	.	.	Garnqueen Junction, South...	Lanark ...	Cal.—N. B.	Glenboig & Coatbridge (Sunnyside).
.	.	.	.	.	.	.	.	Garrett & Son's Siding	Suffolk	G. E.	Leiston.
.	.	.	.	.	.	.	.	Garriongill Collieries Nos. 1, 4, and 10 Pits	Lanark ...	Cal.	Wishaw.
.	.	.	.	.	.	.	.	Garriongill Junction	Lanark ...	Cal.	Law Junction and Wishaw (South).
.	.	.	.	.	.	.	.	Garriongill Siding	Lanark ...	N. B.	Morningside.
.	.	.	.	.	.	.	.	Garriongill Weighs	Lanark ...	Cal.	Law Junction Station.
.	.	.	.	.	.	.	.	Garrison Farm Siding	Warwick..	L. & N. W.	See Midland Brick Co. (Birmingham).
.	.	.	.	.	.	.	.	Garrochburn	Ayr.........	G. & S.W.	See Mauchline.
.	.	.	.	.	.	.	.	Garroway's Siding...............	Lanark ...	N. B.	Glasgow, Camlachie.
.	P	.	.	.	.	.	.	Garrynadur	Kerry	T. & D.	Castlegregory Junction and Dingle.
.	.	.	.	.	.	.	.	Garscadden Siding	Dumbartn	N. B.	See Drumchapel.
.	.	.	.	.	.	.	.	Garscube Brick and Cement Siding (N.B.)	Dumbartn	N. B.—Cal.	Glasgow, Maryhill.
.	.	.	.	.	.	.	.	Garscube Brick Works (N.B.)	Lanark ...	N. B.—Cal.	Glasgow, Great Western Road.
.	.	.	.	.	.	.	.	Garscube Siding..................	Dumbartn	N. B.	See Glasgow.
.	.	.	.	.	.	.	.	Garsdale	Yorks......	Mid.	See Hawes Junction and Garsdale.
.	.	.	.	.	.	.	.	Garside's Saw Mills	Derby	G. C.	Glossop.
.	.	.	.	.	.	.	.	Garside's Siding	Beds	L. & N. W.	Leighton, Grovebury Crossing.
G	P	F	L	H	C	2	10	Garstang	Lancs	G. & K. E.	Garstang Junction and Pilling.
G	P	.	L	H	C	.	.	Garstang and Catterall........	Lancs	L. & N. W.	Lancaster and Preston.
.	.	.	.	.	.	.	.	Garstang & Catterall Junction	Lancs	G. & K. E.—L. & N. W.	Garstang and Preston.
								GARSTON—			
G	P	F	L	H	C	5	0	(Station)	Lancs	C.L.C.(G. C,G. N,& Mid.)	Warrington and Liverpool.
G	.	F	L	.	.	.	.	(Station)	Lancs	L. & N. W.	Garston Dock and Warrington.
.	.	.	.	.	.	.	.	Allerton Sidings................	Lancs	C. L. C. (G C, G N, & Mid.)	Branch, Allerton Jn. & Hunt's Cross.
.	.	.	.	.	.	.	.	Bathgate's Siding	Lancs	L. & N. W.	Garston Docks.
.	.	.	.	.	.	.	.	Bibby, Sons & Co.'s Siding	Lancs	L. & N. W.	Garston Docks.
.	.	.	.	.	.	.	.	Bostock & Co.'s Siding ...	Lancs	L. & N. W.	Garston Docks.
.	P	.	.	.	.	.	.	Church Road	Lancs	L. & N. W.	Garston Dock and Warrington.
G	P	F	L	H	C	40	0	Docks...............................	Lancs	L. & N. W.	Branch from Allerton.
.	.	.	.	.	.	.	.	Evans, R., & Co.'s Siding...	Lancs	L. & N. W.	Garston Docks.
.	.	.	.	.	.	.	.	Garston Graving Dock and Shipbuilding Co.'s Siding (Grayson's Siding).........	Lancs	L. & N. W.	Garston Docks.
.	.	.	.	.	.	.	.	Garston Land Co.'s Siding	Lancs	L. & N. W.	Garston Docks.
.	.	.	.	.	.	.	.	Garston Tanning Co.'s Sid.	Lancs	L. & N. W.	Garston Docks.
.	.	.	.	.	.	.	.	Healey's Siding	Lancs	L. & N. W.	Garston Docks.
.	.	.	.	.	.	.	.	Junction	Lancs	C. L. C.—L. & N. W. ...	Liverpool and Warrington.
.	.	.	.	.	.	.	.	King & Son's Siding	Lancs	L. & N. W.	Garston Docks.
.	.	.	.	.	.	.	.	Liverpool United Gas Co.'s Works	Lancs	L. & N. W.	Garston Docks.
.	.	.	.	.	.	.	.	Morton & Co.'s Siding......	Lancs	L. & N. W.	Garston Docks.
.	.	.	.	.	.	.	.	Rawlinson & Son's Siding	Lancs	L. & N. W.	Garston Docks.
.	.	.	.	.	.	.	.	Rio Tinto Ore Co.'s Siding	Lancs	L. & N. W.	Garston Docks.
.	.	.	.	.	.	.	.	Roberts & Co.'s Siding ...	Lancs	L. & N. W.	Garston Docks.
.	.	.	.	.	.	.	.	Rosebridge & Douglas Bank Colliery Co.'s Siding ...	Lancs	L. & N. W.	Garston Docks.
.	.	.	.	.	.	.	.	Smith's Siding	Lancs	L. & N. W.	Garston Docks.
.	.	.	.	.	.	.	.	Turner & Moss' Siding......	Lancs	L. & N. W.	Garston Docks.
.	.	.	.	.	.	.	.	Wigan Coal & Iron Co.'s Sid.	Lancs	L. & N. W.	Garston Docks.
.	.	.	.	.	.	.	.	Wilson Bros.' Bobbin Co.'s Siding	Lancs	L. & N. W.	Garston Docks.
.	.	.	.	.	.	.	.	Wood & Son's Siding	Lancs	L. & N. W.	Garston Docks.
G	P	F	L	H	C	.	.	Garswood	Lancs	L. & N. W.	St. Helens and Wigan.
.	.	.	.	.	.	.	.	Brynn Hall Colliery	Lancs	L. & N. W.	Brynn and Wigan.
.	.	.	.	.	.	.	.	Garswood Coal & Iron Co.— Ashton Pit	Lancs	L. & N. W.	Garswood and Brynn.
.	.	.	.	.	.	.	.	Park Lane Colliery	Lancs	L. & N. W.	Pemberton Branch.
.	.	.	.	.	.	.	.	Garswood Hall Colliery......	Lancs	L. & N. W.	Brynn and Wigan.
.	.	.	.	.	.	.	.	Latham & Worthington's Norley Quarry	Lancs	L. & N. W.	Pemberton Branch.
.	.	.	.	.	.	.	.	May Mill Spinning Co.'s Sid.	Lancs	L. & N. W.	Pemberton Branch.
.	.	.	.	.	.	.	.	Norley Colliery	Lancs	L. & N. W.	Pemberton Branch.
.	.	.	.	.	.	.	.	Higginbottom's	Lancs	L. & N. W.	Norley Colliery.
.	.	.	.	.	.	.	.	Orrell Colliery Co.	Lancs	L. & N. W.	Norley Colliery.

EXPLANATION—G Goods Station.   P Passenger and Parcel Station.   P* Passenger, but not Parcel or Miscellaneous Traffic.
F Furniture Vans, Carriages, Portable Engines, and Machines on Wheels.   L Live Stock.
H Horse Boxes and Prize Cattle Vans.   C Carriages by Passenger Train.

STATION ACCOMMODATION.						CRANE POWER.		STATIONS, &c.	COUNTY.	COMPANY.	POSITION.
						Tons	Cwts.	Garswood—*continued.*			
·	·	·	·	·	·	·	·	Pemberton Colliery Co.'s Pemberton Collieries	Lancs	L. & N. W.	Pemberton Branch.
·	·	·	·	·	·	·	·	Stone's Park Colliery	Lancs	L. & N. W.	Brynn and Garswood.
·	·	·	·	·	·	·	·	Winstanley Colliery	Lancs	L. & N. W.	Pemberton Branch.
·	·	·	·	·	·	·	·	Worsley Mesnes Colliery ...	Lancs	L. & N. W.	Pemberton Branch.
·	·	·	·	·	·	·	·	Worsley Mesnes Iron Wks.	Lancs	L. & N. W.	Pemberton Branch.
·	·	·	·	·	·	·	·	Garswood Coal & Iron Co.— Ashton Pit	Lancs	L. & N. W.	Garswood.
·	·	·	·	·	·	·	·	Long Lane Colliery	Lancs	{ G. C. { L. & N. W.	Golborne. Wigan.
·	·	·	·	·	·	·	·	Park Lane Colliery	Lancs	L. & N. W.	Garswood.
·	·	·	·	·	·	·	·	Garswood Hall Colliery	Lancs	{ G. C. (St. Helens Exten.) { L. & N. W.	Golborne. Garswood.
G	P'	·	·	·	·	3	0	Garswood Hall Colliery Co.'s Siding	Lancs	L. & Y.	Bolton.
·	·	·	·	·	·	·	·	Gartcosh	Lanark ...	Cal.	Coatbridge and Buchanan Street.
·	·	·	·	·	·	·	·	Gartcosh Asylum Siding (Gartcosh New Siding)...	Lanark ...	Cal.	Gartsherrie and Gartcosh.
·	·	·	·	·	·	·	·	Gartcosh Fire Clay and Brick Works	Lanark ...	Cal.	Gartcosh and Garnkirk.
·	·	·	·	·	·	·	·	Gartcosh Iron Works	Lanark ...	Cal.	Gartcosh and Glenboig.
·	·	·	·	·	·	·	·	Gartcosh New Siding	Lanark ...	Cal.	Same as Gartcosh Asylum Siding.
G	P	F	L	H	C	2	0	Gartgill	Lanark ...	N. B.	See Coatbridge.
·	·	·	·	·	·	·	·	Garth	Brecon ...	L. & N. W.	Llandilo and Llandrindod Wells.
G	P	·	·	·	·	·	·	Garth Brick Works	Brecon ...	L. & N. W.	Garth and Llangammarch Wells.
G	·	·	·	·	·	·	·	Garth	Glamorg'n	P. T.	Maesteg and Pont-y-rhyll.
·	·	·	·	·	·	·	·	Garth Colliery	Glamorg'n	P. T.	Garth.
·	·	·	·	·	·	·	·	Garth and Van Road	Montgom	Cam. (Van).	Branch from Cambrian at Caersws.
·	·	·	·	·	·	·	·	Garth Colliery	Glamorg'n	{ G. W. { P. T.	Troedyrhiew Garth. Garth.
·	·	·	·	·	·	·	·	Garth Fire-Clay Works ...	Denbigh ...	G. W.	Trevor.
·	·	·	·	·	·	·	·	Garth Siding	Mon	B. & M.	Rhiwderin.
·	·	·	·	·	·	·	·	Garth Works	Glamorg'n	Rhy.	Taffs Well.
·	·	·	·	·	·	·	·	Gartliston Brick and Fire- Clay Works...............	Lanark ...	{ Cal. { N. B.	Glenboig. Coatbridge, Gartgill.
·	·	·	·	·	·	·	·	Gartloch Distillery (Garnkirk Distillery)	Lanark ...	Cal.	Garnkirk.
G	P	F	L	H	C	1	10	Gartly	Aberdeen	G. N. of S.	Inveramsay and Keith.
G	P	·	L	H	·	3	0	Gartmore	Perth	N. B.	Buchlyvie and Aberfoyle.
G	·	·	·	·	·	·	·	Barbadoes Siding	Perth	N. B.	Buchlyvie and Gartmore.
G	P	·	L	H	·	·	·	Gartness	Stirling ...	N. B.	Balloch and Stirling.
·	·	·	·	·	·	·	·	Gartness Colliery	Lanark ...	{ Cal. { N. B.	Airdrie. Clarkston.
·	·	·	·	·	·	·	·	Gartness Junction	Stirling ...	N. B.	Killearn and Balfron.
·	·	·	·	·	·	·	·	Gartness Sidings	Lanark ...	N. B.	Clarkston.
G	P	·	L	H	·	·	·	Garton	Yorks	N. E.	Malton and Driffield.
G	P	·	·	·	·	·	·	Garton Bros.' Siding	Lancs	L. & N. W.	Newton-le-Willows.
·	·	·	·	·	·	·	·	Gartsherrie	Lanark ...	Cal.	Coatbridge and Buchanan Street.
·	·	·	·	·	·	·	·	Gartsherrie Collieries	Lanark ...	Cal.	Gartsherrie and Gartcosh.
·	·	·	·	·	·	·	·	Gartsherrie Iron Works ...	Lanark ...	Cal.	Coatbridge and Gartsherrie.
·	·	·	·	·	·	·	·	Kilgarth Slag Hill Siding..	Lanark ...	Cal.	Gartsherrie and Gartcosh.
·	·	·	·	·	·	·	·	Lanarkshire Chain Cable & Anchor Works (Strathearn's Weldless Chain Works)	Lanark ...	Cal.	Gartsherrie.
·	·	·	·	·	·	·	·	Gartsherrie	Lanark ...	N. B.	See Blairhill and Gartsherrie.
·	·	·	·	·	·	·	·	Gartsherrie Iron Works ...	Lanark ...	{ Cal. { N. B.	Gartsherrie. Coatbridge, Gartgill.
·	·	·	·	·	·	·	·	Gartsherrie Junction.........	Lanark ...	Cal.—N. B.	Gartcosh and Coatbridge, Sunnyside.
·	·	·	·	·	·	·	·	Gartsherrie No. 1 Colliery ...	Lanark ...	N. B.	Coatbridge, Sunnyside.
·	·	·	·	·	·	·	·	Gartsherrie No. 8 Colliery ...	Lanark ...	N. B.	Coatbridge, Sunnyside.
G	·	·	·	·	·	·	·	Gartshore	Dumbartn	N. B.	Croy and Lenzie Junction Station.
·	·	·	·	·	·	·	·	Gartshore Colliery	Dumbartn	N. B.	Branch from Gartshore.
·	·	·	·	·	·	·	·	Gartshore No. 9 Colliery ...	Dumbartn	N. B.	Gartshore & Lenzie Junction Station.
·	·	·	·	·	·	·	·	Gartside's Brewery (G. C.)	Lancs	G. C.—G. N.—Mid.	Guide Bridge.
·	·	·	·	·	·	·	·	Gartverrie Fire-Clay Works...	Lanark ...	N. B.	Coatbridge, Gartgill.
G	P	·	L	H	C	3	0	Garvagh	Derry	N. C. Com. (Mid.)	Macfin Junction and Magherafelt.
G	P	F	L	H	C	2	0	Garve	Ross & Cro'	High.	Dingwall and Kyle of Lochalsh.
·	·	·	·	·	·	·	·	Garvel Dock	Renfrew ...	Cal.	Same as James Watt Dock (Greenock).
·	·	·	·	·	·	·	·	Garvel Dock (G. & S. W.) ...	Renfrew ...	G. & S. W.—N. B.	Same as James Watt Dock (Port Glasgow).

EXPLANATION—**G** *Goods Station.*   **P** *Passenger and Parcel Station.*   **P*** *Passenger, but not Parcel or Miscellaneous Traffic.*
F *Furniture Vans, Carriages, Portable Engines, and Machines on Wheels.*   **L** *Live Stock.*
H *Horse Boxes and Prize Cattle Vans.*   **C** *Carriages by Passenger Train.*

STATION ACCOMMODATION.						CRANE POWER.		STATIONS, &c.	COUNTY.	COMPANY.	POSITION.
						Tons	Cwts.	Garvel Dock Junction	Renfrew ...	G. & S.W.	Greenock, Lynedoch Street and James Watt Dock.
.	.	.	.	.	.	.	.	Garw Colliery	Glamorg'n	G. W.	Pontyrhyll.
.	.	.	.	.	.	.	.	Gascoigne Wood Junction ...	Yorks	N. E.	South Milford and Hambleton.
.	.	.	.	.	.	.	.	Gas Factory Junction	Middlesex	G. E.—L. T. & S.	Same as Bow Junction (London).
.	.	.	.	.	.	.	.	Gaskell, Deacon & Co.'s Wks.	Lancs	L. & N. W.—S. & M. Jt.	See United Alkali Co. (Widnes).
.	.	.	.	.	.	.	.	Gask Lime Siding	Fife..........	N. B.	Townhill Junction Station.
								Gas Light & Coke Co.—			
.	.	.	.	.	.	.	.	Bow Common Gas Works..	Middlesex	G. E.	London, Bow Road.
.	.	.	.	.	.	.	.	Bow Common Gas Wks(NL)	Middlesex	NL—GN—GW—L&NW	London, Bow.
.	.	.	.	.	.	.	.	Siding	Derby	Mid.	Langley Mill.
.	.	.	.	.	.	.	.	Siding	Surrey ...	L. & S.W.	London, Nine Elms.
.	.	.	.	.	.	.	.	Siding (G. E.)	Essex	GE—GN—L&NW—Mid.	London, Beckton.
.	.	.	.	.	.	.	.	Siding (G. E.)	Essex	GE—GN—L&NW—Mid.	London, Silvertown.
								Gas Residual Products Co.'s			
.	.	.	.	.	.	.	.	Siding	Ayr	G. & S.W.	Irvine Harbour.
.	.	.	.	.	.	.	.	Gas Water Branch Junction	Ayr	G. & S.W.	Cronberry and Muirkirk.
G	P	F	L	H	C	1	10	Gateacre (for Woolton)........	Lancs	C.L.C. (G C, G N, & Mid.)	Halewood and West Derby.
.	.	.	.	.	.	.	.	Gate Burton Siding	Lincoln	G. N. & G. E. Jt.	Lea.
G	P	F	L	H	C	1	10	Gatehead	Ayr	G. & S.W.	Kilmarnock and Troon.
.	.	.	.	.	.	.	.	Annandale Pit.................	Ayr	G. & S.W.	Gatehead.
.	.	.	.	.	.	.	.	Bogside Pit (Craig's)	Ayr	G. & S.W.	Gatehead and Kilmarnock.
.	.	.	.	.	.	.	.	Caprington Nos. 40 and 42	Ayr	G. & S.W.	Fairlie Branch.
.	.	.	.	.	.	.	.	Caprington No. 41	Ayr	G. & S.W.	Fairlie Branch.
.	.	.	.	.	.	.	.	Fairlie No. 3	Ayr	G. & S.W.	Lathmill Siding.
								Gargieston Siding (Third			
.	.	.	.	.	.	.	.	Part Siding)	Ayr	G. & S.W.	Gatehead and Kilmarnock.
.	.	.	.	.	.	.	.	Lathmill Siding	Ayr	G. & S.W.	Gatehead and Drybridge.
.	.	.	.	.	.	.	.	Moorfield Pit	Ayr	G. & S.W.	Gatehead and Kilmarnock.
.	.	.	.	.	.	.	.	Moorfield Tile Works	Ayr	G. & S.W.	Gatehead and Kilmarnock.
.	.	.	.	.	.	.	.	Windyedge Pit	Ayr	G. & S.W.	Gatehead.
.	.	.	.	.	.	.	.	Gatelawbridge Brick Works	Dumfries..	G. & S.W.	Thornhill.
.	.	.	.	.	.	.	.	Gatelawbridge Quarry	Dumfries..	G. & S.W.	Thornhill.
								GATESHEAD—			
G	.	F	L	.	.	10	0	(Station)	Durham ...	N. E.	Newcastle and Felling.
								Abbot & Co.'s Works (Park			
.	.	.	.	.	.	.	.	Works)	Durham ...	N. E.	Gateshead.
.	.	.	.	.	.	.	.	Clayton & Welsh's Siding	Durham ...	N. E.	Gateshead.
.	.	.	.	.	.	.	.	Corporation Depôts	Durham ...	N. E.	Gateshead.
.	P	.	.	.	.	.	.	East	Durham ...	N. E.	Newcastle and Felling.
.	.	.	.	.	.	.	.	Goodall, Bates, & Co.'s Sid.	Durham ...	N. E.	Gateshead.
								North Eastern Railway—			
.	.	.	.	.	.	.	.	Carriage & Wagon Shops	Durham ...	N. E.	Gateshead.
.	.	.	.	.	.	.	.	Locomotive Shops	Durham ...	N. E.	Gateshead.
								Locomotive Stores			
.	.	.	.	.	.	.	.	Department...............	Durham ...	N. E.	Gateshead.
.	.	.	.	.	.	.	.	Permanent Way Shops...	Durham ...	N. E.	Gateshead.
.	.	.	.	.	.	.	.	Permanent Way Stores...	Durham ...	N. E.	Gateshead.
.	.	.	.	.	.	.	.	Oakwellgate Siding	Durham ...	N. E.	Gateshead.
.	.	.	.	.	.	.	.	Park Lane Sidings.........	Durham ...	N. E.	Gateshead.
.	.	.	.	.	.	.	.	Redheugh Colliery...........	Durham ...	N. E.	Gateshead.
								United Alkali Co.'s Wks.—			
.	.	.	.	.	.	.	.	Allhusen's Works	Durham ...	N. E.	Gateshead.
.	.	.	.	.	.	.	.	Friar's Goose Works	Durham ...	N. E.	Gateshead.
								Victoria Works (Clarke,			
.	.	.	.	.	.	.	.	Chapman & Co.)............	Durham ...	N. E.	Gateshead.
.	P	.	.	.	.	.	.	West	Durham ...	N. E.	Newcastle and Low Fell.
.	.	.	.	.	.	.	.	Gateshead Workhouse Siding	Durham ...	N. E.	Redheugh.
G	P	.	L	H	.	1	10	Gateside	Fife..........	N. B.	Kinross Junction and Ladybank.
								Gateside Saw Mill (Shuttle			
.	.	.	.	.	.	.	.	Mill)	Fife..........	N. B.	Gateside and Strathmiglo.
.	.	.	.	.	.	.	.	Gateside Colliery&Brick Wks.	Lanark ...	Cal.	Cambuslang.
.	.	.	.	.	.	.	.	Gateside Pit	Dumfries..	G. & S.W.	Kirkconnel.
.	.	.	.	.	.	.	.	Gate's Siding	Beds........	Mid.	Harlington.
.	.	.	.	.	.	.	.	Gatewen Colliery	Denbigh	G. W.—W. M. & C. Q.	Plas Power.
G	P	.	.	.	.	.	.	Gathurst	Lancs	L. & Y.	Wigan and Southport.
								Orrell Col. (Brancker's Sid.)			
.	.	.	.	.	.	.	.	(L. & Y.)	Lancs	L. & Y.—L. & N. W.	Wigan and Gathurst.
.	.	.	.	.	.	.	.	Pagefield Forge Co.'s Sid...	Lancs	L. & Y.	Gathurst.
.	.	.	.	.	.	.	.	Pagefield Siding	Lancs	L. & Y.	Gathurst and Wigan.
.	.	.	.	.	.	.	.	Walker Bros.	Lancs	L. & Y.	Pagefield Siding.
.	.	.	.	.	.	.	.	Wigan Rolling Mills......	Lancs	L. & Y.	Pagefield Siding.

EXPLANATION—G *Goods Station.*   P *Passenger and Parcel Station.*   P* *Passenger, but not Parcel or Miscellaneous Traffic.*
F *Furniture Vans, Carriages, Portable Engines, and Machines on Wheels.*   L *Live Stock.*
H *Horse Boxes and Prize Cattle Vans.*   C *Carriages by Passenger Train.*

STATION ACCOMMODATION.						CRANE POWER.	STATIONS, &c.	COUNTY.	COMPANY.	POSITION.
						Tons Cwts.	Gathurst—continued.			
							Rosebridge & Douglas Bank Colliery Co.'s Douglas Bank Colliery (L. & Y.)...	Lancs	L. & Y.—L. & N. W. ...	Near Gathurst.
	P*			H			Gatwick (Open on Race Days only)	Surrey ...	L. B. & S. C.	Horley and Three Bridges.
							Gauchalland, Nos. 2 and 4 ...	Ayr	G. & S. W.	{ Galston (for Inwards Traffic). { Hurlford (for Outwards Traffic).
							Gault Brick Co.'s Siding	Beds	G. N.	Arlesey.
G	P						Gaunt & Co.'s Siding............	Yorks	G. N.	Stanningley.
							Gavell	Stirling ...	N. B.	Kirkintilloch and Kilsyth.
							Auchenreoch Colliery	Stirling ...	N. B.	Torrance and Gavell.
							Gavell Colliery	Stirling ...	N. B.	Gavell and Kilsyth.
							Haughrigg Colliery	Stirling ...	N. B.	Gavell.
							Inchterff Sand Siding	Stirling ...	N. B.	Torrance and Gavell.
							Neilston Colliery	Stirling ...	N. B.	Gavell and Kilsyth.
							Netherinch Sand Siding ...	Stirling ...	N. B.	Torrance and Gavell.
							Gay and Wilson's Siding......	Norfolk ..	Mid. & G. N. Jt.	Grimston Road.
							Gaymer, W., & Son's Siding	Norfolk ..	G. E.	Attleboro'.
G	P		L				Gaythorn Gas Works............	Lancs	M S J & A (G C & L & N W)	Manchester, Oxford Road.
							Gayton Road	Norfolk ...	Mid. & G. N. Jt.	South Lynn and Melton Constable.
							Boam, Joseph, Siding	Norfolk ...	Mid. & G. N. Jt.	Gayton Road.
							Gayton Sidings	N'hamptn	L. & N. W.	Blisworth.
							Brown & Butcher's North-ampton Brick and Tile Co.'s Siding	N'hamptn	L. & N. W.	Gayton Sidings.
							King's Blisworth & Stowe Brick & Tile Works	N'hamptn	L. & N. W.	Gayton Sidings.
G	P	F	L	H	C		Sparrow's Siding	N'hamptn	L. & N. W.	Gayton Sidings.
G	P						Geashill...........................	Kings	G. S. & W.	Portarlington and Athlone.
							Geddington	N'hamptn	Mid.	Kettering and Manton.
G	P	F	L	H	C		Gedling	Notts	Mid.	See Carlton and Netherfield.
							Gedling and Carlton	Notts ., ...	G. N.	Netherfield and Kimberley.
							Gedling Colliery	Notts	G. N.	Gedling and Daybrook.
G	P	F	L	H	C		New Digby Colliery	Notts	G. N.	Gedling and Carlton.
							Gedney	Lincoln ..	Mid. & G. N. Jt...........	Sutton Bridge and Spalding.
							Gedney Hill	Lincoln ..	G. N. & G. E. Jt.	See French Drove and Gedney Hill.
							Geldard Junction	Yorks	G. N. & N. E. Jt.—Mid.	Leeds.
G	P	F			C	1 10	Geldard's Foundry.............	Durham ...	N. E.	Spennymoor.
							Geldeston	Norfolk ...	G. E.	Beccles and Tivetshall.
							Gellavellin Siding	Brecon ..	L. & N. W.	Clydach.
							Gelli Colliery	Glamorg'n	T. V.	See Cory Bros. & Co. (Ystrad.)
							Gelli Tarw Junction	Glamorg'n	G. W.	Aberdare and Hirwain.
							Gellyceidrim Colliery	Carmarth'	G. W.	Garnant.
							Gelly Colliery	Carmarth'	G. W.	Dafen.
							Gellydeg Sidings	Mon	G. W.	Pontnewynydd.
							Gellygroes Junction	Mon	G. W.—L. & N. W.	See Tredegar Junc., Sirhowy Junc.
							Gellyhave Colliery	Mon	G. W.	Rhymney Junction Station.
							Gellyonen Col. Co.'s Cols. (Mid.)	Glamorg'n	Mid.—G.W.—L. & N. W.	Pontardawe.
							Gellyrhaidd Junction	Glamorg'n	G. W.	Tonyrefail and Llantrisant.
							Gelynog Colliery................	Glamorg'n	T. V.	Cross Inn.
							General Forage and Grain Drying Co.'s Siding (Mid.)	Staffs	Mid.—L&NW—GN—NS	Burton-on-Trent.
							General Oil Storage Co.'s Sid.	Lancs	Trafford Park Estate......	Manchester.
							General Terminus (Cal.)	Lanark ...	Cal.—G. & S. W.—N. B.	See Glasgow.
							Gentle's Siding	Perth	Cal.	Coupar Angus.
							Genwen Colliery (G. W.) ...	Carmarth'	G. W.—L. & N. W.	Bynea.
							Genwen Junction	Carmarth'	G. W.	Bynea.
							George Colliery	Durham ...	N. E.	Same as Etherley Colliery and Coke Ovens (Etherley).
G	P						George Lane (Woodford)	Essex	G. E.	Stratford and Loughton.
G							George Lane Depôt (Eagle Lane)	Essex	G. E.	George Lane and Snaresbrook.
G	P		L	H		2 0	Georgemas	Caithness..	High.	Helmsdale and Wick.
							George Pit	Glamorg'n	G. W.—T. V.—Rhy.	Same as Powell Duffryn Co.'s Lower Duffryn Col. (Mountain Ash).
							Georges Quay	Dublin ..	D. W. & W.	See Dublin, Tara Street and Georges Quay.
							Georges Road	Lancs	C. L. C. (G C, G N & Mid.)	Same as Wellington Rd. (Stockport).
							Georges Str. Mineral Depôt.	Edinburgh	Cal.	See Leith.
							George Street Siding	Lancs	L. & Y.	See Knowles, A., & Sons (Manchester).
							George Street Wharf (G. C.)	Yorks	G. C.—G. N.	Rotherham and Masboro'.

EXPLANATION—G *Goods Station.* P *Passenger and Parcel Station.* P* *Passenger, but not Parcel or Miscellaneous Traffic.*
F *Furniture Vans, Carriages, Portable Engines, and Machines on Wheels.* L *Live Stock.*
H *Horse Boxes and Prize Cattle Vans.* C *Carriages by Passenger Train.*

STATION ACCOMMODATION.						CRANE POWER.	STATIONS, &c.	COUNTY.	COMPANY.	POSITION.
						Tons Cwts.				
..	P	..	..	..	..		Gerard's Bridge	Lancs	L. & N. W.	Rainford and St. Helens.
..	..	..	..	..	..		Gerard's Bridge Plate Glass Works	Lancs	G. C. (St. Helens Exten.)	See Pilkington Bros. (St. Helens).
..	..	..	..	..	..		Gerard's Bridge Siding........	Lancs	L. & N. W.	See Pilkington Bros. (St. Helens).
..	..	..	..	..	..		Gerard's Bridge Works........	Lancs	L. & N. W.	See United Alkali Co. (St. Helens).
..	..	..	..	..	..		Germiston High and Low Jns.	Lanark ...	Cal.	Glasgow.
..	..	..	..	..	..		Germiston Sand Siding	Lanark ...	Cal.	Glasgow, Buchanan Street.
									N. B.	Glasgow, Sighthill.
..	..	..	..	..	..		Germiston Siding	Lanark ...	Cal.	Glasgow, Buchanan Street.
									N. B.	Glasgow, Sighthill.
..	..	..	..	..	..		Gethin Pit (G.W. & Rhy.Jt.)	Glamorg'n	G W & Rhy. Jt.—L&NW	See Crawshay Bros. (Abercanaid).
..	..	..	..	..	..		Giants Hall Colliery (L&NW)	Lancs	L&N W—G.C. (Wig.Jn.)	See Wigan Coal & Iron Co. (Wigan).
..	..	..	..	..	..		Gibbon's Crwys Siding	Glamorg'n	Rhy.	Cardiff.
..	..	..	..	..	..		Gibbon's Siding	Staffs	L. & N. W.	Wolverhampton.
..	..	..	..	..	..		Gibbs & Canning's Brick & Pipe Works..................	Warwick..	L. & N. W.	Tamworth.
									Mid.	Kettlebrook.
..	..	..	..	..	..		Gibbs & Co.'s Manure and Vitriol Manufactory (G.E.)	Essex	GE—GN—L&NW—Mid.	London, Silvertown.
..	..	..	..	..	..		Gibbs & Finch's Vitriol Wks. (G. W.)...................	Mon	G. W.—L. & N. W.	Cwmbran.
..	..	..	..	..	..		Gibbs Bros.' Cement Works	Leicester..	Mid.	Mountsorrel Junction.
..	..	..	..	..	..		Gibbs Bros.' Siding	Leicester..	L. & N. W.	Shepshed.
..	..	..	..	..	..		Gibbs, Finch & Co.'s Wharf..	Devon	L. & S. W.	Plymouth, Cattewater Harbour.
..	..	..	..	..	..		Gibbshill Siding	Renfrew ...	G. & S. W.	Greenock, Lynedoch Street.
G	P	F	L	H	C	..	Gibbstown	Meath	M. G. W.	Navan and Kingscourt.
..	..	..	..	..	..		Gibfield Colliery	Lancs	L. & N. W.	See Fletcher, Burrows & Co.'s (Atherton).
..	..	..	..	..	..		Gibson & Co.'s Siding	Derby......	Mid.	Chesterfield.
..	..	..	..	..	..		Gibson & Preston's Patent Slab Works (Mid.).........	Warwick..	Mid.—L. & N. W.	Stockingford.
..	..	..	..	..	..		Gibson's Flour Mills	Bucks......	G. W.	Slough.
..	..	..	..	..	..		Gibson's Siding	Lincoln ...	G. N.	Sleaford.
..	..	..	..	..	..		Gidlow Jackson Middle Works	Lancs	L. & N. W.	Wigan.
..	..	..	..	..	..		Gidlow Lane Col. (L & N W)	Lancs	L.&N W—G.C.(Wig.Jn.)	See Wigan Coal & Iron Co. (Wigan).
..	..	..	..	..	..		Gidlow Works..................	Lancs	L. & N. W.	Same as Rylands and Sons' Siding (Wigan).
G	P	..	..	..	..		Giffen.............................	Ayr	Cal.	Barrmill and Ardrossan.
..	..	..	..	..	..		Barr Colliery & Brick Wks	Ayr	Cal.	Barrmill and Giffen.
G	..	..	..	..	..		Barrmill Siding	Ayr	Cal.	Lugton and Giffen.
G	..	..	..	..	..		Brackenhills Siding	Ayr	Cal.	Giffen and Glengarnock.
..	..	..	..	..	..		Giffen Weighs	Ayr	Cal.	Giffen.
G	..	..	L	..	..		Gree Depôt	Ayr	Cal.	Giffen and Lugton.
..	..	..	..	..	..		Muirhouse Siding	Ayr	Cal.	Branch near Brackenhills.
..	..	..	..	..	..		Whitespot New Quarry	Ayr	Cal.	Giffen and Glengarnock.
..	..	..	..	..	..		Whitespot Quarry	Ayr	Cal.	Barkip Branch.
..	..	..	..	..	..		Giffen Junction	Ayr	Cal.	Giffen.
G	P	..	L	H	..	3 0	Giffnock	Renfrew ...	Cal.	Pollokshaws and Busby.
..	..	..	..	..	..		Giffnock Quarries	Renfrew ...	Cal.	Thornliebank and Giffnock.
..	..	..	..	..	..		Washwalls Chemical Works	Renfrew ...	Cal.	Thornliebank and Giffnock.
G	P	..	L	H	..	2 0	Gifford	Hadding'n	N. B.	Branch from Ormiston.
..	..	..	..	..	..		Gigantic Wheel Co.'s Siding (West Kensington)	Middlesex	Mid.	London, St. Pancras.
..	P	..	L	H	C		Giggleswick.....................	Yorks	Mid.	Skipton and Lancaster.
..	..	..	..	..	..		Gilbertfield Brick Works......	Lanark ...	Cal.	Newton.
..	..	..	..	..	..		Gilbertfield Colliery	Lanark ...	Cal.	Newton.
..	..	..	..	..	..		Gilbertson & Co.'s Sid. (Mid.)	Glamorg'n	Mid.—G.W.—L.&N.W.	Pontardawe.
..	..	..	..	..	..		Gilbertson & Page's Siding...	Herts	G. E.	Hertford.
..	..	..	..	..	..		Gilchrist & Son's Siding	Lanark ...	Cal.	Coatbridge.
G	P	F	L	..	..	10 0	Gildersome	Yorks	G. N.	Morley and Dudley Hill.
G	P	F	L	..	..	5 0			L. & N. W.	Cleckheaton and Leeds.
..	..	..	..	..	..		Bushey Colliery Siding.....	Yorks	G. N.	Gildersome and Drighlington.
..	..	..	..	..	..		Hudson's Siding..............	Yorks.......	G. N.	Gildersome.
..	..	..	..	..	..		Giles & Sons' Works	Somerset..	G. W.	Clifton Bridge.
G	P	F	L	H	C	..	Gileston	Glamorg'n	Barry	Barry and Bridgend.
G	P	..	..	..	..		Gilfach	Glamorg'n	G. W.	Branch from Hendreforgan.
..	..	..	..	..	..		Britannic Colliery	Glamorg'n	G. W.	Gilfach Branch.
..	..	..	..	..	..		Dinas Main Collieries	Glamorg'n	G. W.	Gilfach Branch.
..	..	..	..	..	..		Gilfach Goch Colliery	Glamorg'n	G. W.	Gilfach Branch.
..	..	..	..	..	..		Gilfach New Steam Colliery	Glamorg'n	G. W.	Gilfach Branch.
..	..	..	..	..	..		Glamorgan Colliery	Glamorg'n	G. W.	Gilfach Branch.
..	..	..	..	..	..		Gilfach Colliery	Carmarth'	L. & M. M.	Branch from Cross Hands.
G	P	..	..	..	..		Gilfach Colliery	Glamorg'n	Rhy.	Pengam and Bargoed.

EXPLANATION—G *Goods Station.*　P *Passenger and Parcel Station.*　P* *Passenger, but not Parcel or Miscellaneous Traffic.*
F *Furniture Vans, Carriages, Portable Engines, and Machines on Wheels.*　L *Live Stock.*
H *Horse Boxes and Prize Cattle Vans.*　C *Carriages by Passenger Train.*

STATION ACCOMMODATION.	CRANE POWER.	STATIONS, &c.	COUNTY.	COMPANY.	POSITION.
	Tons Cwts				
. . . . . .		Gilfach Colliery (Cartwright's) (B. & M.)	Mon	B. & M.—G. W.	Pengam.
. . . . . .		Gilfach Main Quarry............	Glamorg'n	T. B. Jt. (G. W. & Rhy.)	Bedlinog.
. . . . . .		Gilfach Quarry (B. & M.)......	Mon	B. & M.—G. W.	Pengam.
. . . . . .		Gillbrook Yard Boiler Works	Cheshire...	B'head Jt—CLC—NW&L	See Cammell, Laird & Co. (Birkenhead).
. . . . . .		Giller's Green Colliery	Lancs	L. & N. W.	Same as Eccleston Hall Colliery (St. Helens).
.G.		Gillfoot Branch	Cumb'land	W C & E Jt. (Fur. & LN W)	Branch from Gillfoot.
. . . . . .		Gillfoot Station and Junction	Cumb'land	W C & E Jt. (Fur. & LN W)	Moor Row and Sellafield.
. . . . . .		Bain & Co.'s Ehen Valley Branch Pits Nos. 6 & 11	Cumb'land	W C & E Jt. (Fur. & LN W)	Ehen Valley Branch.
. . . . . .		Lindow's— Ehen Valley Branch Pits Nos. 1, 2, and 3	Cumb'land	W C & E Jt. (Fur. & LN W)	Ehen Valley Branch.
. . . . . .		Rowfoot Pit	Cumb'land	W C & E Jt. (Fur. & LN W)	Ehen Valley Branch.
. . . . . .		Lonsdale Hematite Smelting Co.'s Siding (Clint's Limestone Quarry)	Cumb'land	W C & E Jt. (Fur. & LN W)	Egremont and Woodend.
. . . . . .		Millom & Askam Iron Co.'s Ullbank Branch	Cumb'land	W C & E Jt. (Fur. & LN W)	Beckermet and Egremont.
. . . . . .		Townhead Mining Co.'s Sidings	Cumb'land	W C & E Jt. (Fur. & LN W)	Gillfoot Branch.
. . . . . .		Ullcoats Mining Co.'s Sid.	Cumb'land	W C & E Jt. (Fur. & LN W)	Beckermet and Egremont.
. . . . . .		Wyndham Mining Co.'s— East Siding	Cumb'land	W C & E Jt. (Fur. & LN W)	Gillfoot and Egremont.
. . . . . .		Falcon Pit	Cumb'land	W C & E Jt. (Fur. & LN W)	Gillfoot Branch.
. . . . . .		Nos. 1, 4, and 6 Pits	Cumb'land	W C & E Jt. (Fur. & LN W)	Gillfoot Branch.
. . . . . .		Orgill Pit	Cumb'land	W C & E Jt. (Fur. & LN W)	Gillfoot Branch.
. . . . . .		Gillhead Coal, Gannister, and Fire-Brick Co.'s Siding......	Cumb'land	L. & N. W.	Flimby.
G P F L H C	1 0	Gilling	Yorks	N. E.	Thirsk and Malton.
. . . . . .		Sunbeck Junction	Yorks	N. E.	Pilmoor and Gilling.
G P F L H C	5 0	Gillingham	Dorset.....	L. & S. W.	Salisbury and Templecombe.
. . . . . .		Gillingham Brick & Pottery Co.'s Siding	Dorset......	L. & S. W.	Gillingham.
. . . . . .		Gillingham	Kent	S. E. & C.	See New Brompton and Gillingham.
. . . . . .		Gill's Siding	Down	B. & C. D.	Ballygowan.
G P F L H C	3 0	Gilmerton....................	Edinboro'	N. B.	Millerhill and Roslin.
. . . . . .		Gilmilnscroft Branch Depôt ..	Ayr	G. & S. W.	Auchinleck.
. . . . . .		Gilmilnscroft Branch Junction	Ayr	G. & S. W.	Auchinleck and Lugar.
. . . . . .		Gilmilnscroft Nos. 1, 2, 3, & 4	Ayr	G. & S. W.	Auchinleck.
. . . . . .		Gilmour's Brick Works........	Dumbartn	N. B.	Same as Drumchapel Brick Works (Drumchapel).
. . . . . .		Gilmour's Manure Siding.....	Lanark ...	N. B.	Same as Rosehall South Lye (Bellshill).
. . . . . .		Gilmour Street	Renfrew...	G & P Jt (Cal & G S W)	See Paisley.
G P . . L H		Gilnockie (for Claygates)	Dumfries..	N. B.	Riddings Junction and Langholm.
. . . . . .		Gilpin & Co.'s Siding	Staffs	L. & N. W.	Wyrley and Church Bridge.
G P F L H C	3 0	Gilsland	Northumb	N. E.	Carlisle and Hexham.
. . . . . .		Gilstrap, Earp, & Co.'s— Cow Lane Maltings	Notts	G. N. & Mid. Jt............	Newark.
. . . . . .		Maltings (G. N.).............	Notts	G. N.—Mid.	Newark.
. . . . . .		Massey Sidings	Notts	G. N. & Mid. Jt.	Newark.
. . . . . .		Paston Siding	N'hampton	G. N.	Peterboro'.
. . . . . .		Siding	Lincoln ...	G. C.	Grimsby Town.
. . . . . .		Siding (G. C.)	Notts	G. C.—G. N.—Mid.	Retford.
. . . . . .		Giltbrook Chemical Works ...	Notts	{ Mid. / G. N.	See Bennerley Sidings, (Ilkeston). / See Nottingham Corporation Sidings (Kimberley).
. . . . . .		Gilwen Colliery (Mid.)	Glamorg'n	Mid.—G. W.—L. & N. W.	Gurnos.
. P		Gilwern........................	Brecon ...	L. & N. W.	Abergavenny and Merthyr.
. . . . . .		Gilwern Quarry	Mon	L. & N. W.	Govilon.
. . . . . .		Gilwern Tin Plate Wks. (Mid.)	Glamorg'n	Mid.—G. W.—L. & N. W.	Same as Thomas' Siding (Swansea).
. . . . . .		Gimson & Co.'s Sid. (Mid.) ...	Leicester..	Mid.—L. & N. W.	Leicester, East.
G P	5 0 }	Gipsy Hill (L. B. & S. C.) ...	Surrey ...	{ L. B. & S. C. / L. & N. W. ...:	Streatham Hill and Crystal Palace. / Over L. B. & S. C. from Clapham Junc.
. P					
. . . . . .		Gipsy Inn Siding	Durham ...	N. E.	Leasingthorne.
. . . . . .		Girardot & Co.'s Siding......	Essex	G. E.	Brentwood and Warley.
G.		Girtford Siding	Beds	L. & N. W.	Bedford and Cambridge.
		GIRVAN—			
G P F L H C	3 0	(Station)	Ayr	G. & S. W.	Maybole and Pinwherry.

EXPLANATION—G *Goods Station.*   P *Passenger and Parcel Station.*   P* *Passenger, but not Parcel or Miscellaneous Traffic.*
F *Furniture Vans, Carriages, Portable Engines, and Machines on Wheels.*   L *Live Stock.*
H *Horse Boxes and Prize Cattle Vans.*   C *Carriages by Passenger Train.*

STATION ACCOMMODATION.						CRANE POWER.	STATIONS, &c.	COUNTY.	COMPANY.	POSITION.
						Tons Cwts.	GIRVAN—continued.			
.	.	.	.	.	.	. .	Bridge Mill Siding	Ayr	G. & S.W.	Girvan and Killochan.
.	.	.	.	.	.	. .	Harbour	Ayr	G. & S.W.	Girvan.
.	.	.	.	.	.	. .	Junction	Ayr	G. & S.W.	Girvan and Killochan.
.	.	.	.	.	.	. .	Gisbourne Colliery	Cheshire	L. & N. W.	Same as Buxton Lime Firms Co.'s Whaley Col. (Whaley Bridge).
G	P	F	L	H	C	5 0	Gisburn	Yorks	L. & Y.	Chatburn and Hellifield.
.	.	.	.	.	.	. .	Gittus Siding	Yorks	G. C.	Penistone.
.	.	.	.	.	.	. .	Gladsmuir	Hadding'n	N. B.	See Macmerry (Gladsmuir).
.	.	.	.	.	.	. .	Gladstone Siding	Yorks	N. E.	Pateley Bridge.
G	P	.					Glais (Mid.)	Glamorg'n	Mid. / G. W.	Swansea and Pontardawe. / Over Midland Line.
.	.	.	.	.	.	. .	Birchgrove Colliery Co.'s Siding (Mid.)	Glamorg'n	Mid.—G. W.—L. & N.W.	Glais and Llansamlet.
.	.	.	.	.	.	. .	Birchgrove Steel Co.'s Sid. (Mid.)	Glamorg'n	Mid.—G.W.—L. & N.W.	Glais.
.	.	.	.	.	.	. .	Llwynddu Colliery & Brick Co.'s Siding (Mid.)	Glamorg'n	Mid.—G.W.—L. & N. W.	Glais and Pontardawe.
.	.	.	.	.	.	. .	Sister's Pit (Lewis Graigola Colliery Co.) (Mid.)	Glamorg'n	Mid.—G.W.—L. & N. W.	Glais and Llansamlet.
.	.	.	.	.	.	. .	Yniscedwyn Tin Plate Co.'s Siding (Mid.)	Glamorg'n	Mid.—G. W.—L. & N. W.	Glais.
G	P	.	L	.	C	. .	Glaisdale	Yorks	N. E.	Whitby and Castleton.
.	.	.	.	.	.	. .	Glaisdale Old Iron Works	Yorks	N. E.	Glaisdale.
.	.	.	.	.	.	. .	Glaisdale Whinstone Quarry Co.'s Siding	Yorks	N. E.	Glaisdale.
G	P	F	L	H	C	3 0	Glamis	Forfar	Cal.	Coupar Angus and Forfar.
G	.	.	.	.	.	. .	Drumgley Siding	Forfar	Cal.	Glamis and Forfar.
.	.	.	.	.	.	. .	Glamorgan Canal Siding	Glamorg'n	G. W.	Cardiff.
.	.	.	.	.	.	. .	Glamorgan Colliery	Glamorg'n	T. V.	Same as Llwynypia Col. (Trealaw).
.	.	.	.	.	.	. .	Glamorgan Colliery	Glamorg'n	G. W.	Gilfach.
.	.	.	.	.	.	. .	Glamorganshire Steam Joinery Works and Siding	Glamorg'n	G. W.	Llantrisant.
.	.	.	.	.	.	. .	Glamorgan Works	Glamorg'n	G. W. & L. & N. W. Jt.	Same as Webb, Shakespeare, and Williams' Siding (Pontardulais).
G	P	.	.	.	.	. .	Glanamman	Carmarth'	G. W.	Pantyffynnon and Garnant.
.	.	.	.	.	.	. .	Glanamman Siding	Carmarth'	G. W.	Garnant.
.	.	.	.	.	.	. .	Glanant Colliery	Glamorg'n	G. W.	Tondu.
G	P	.	.	.	.	. .	Glan Conway	Denbigh	L. & N. W.	Blaenau Festiniog & Llandudno Jn Sta.
G	P	.	.	.	.	. .	Glandyfi	Cardigan	Cam.	Machynlleth and Aberystwyth.
.	.	.	.	.	.	. .	Glan Ebbw Tin Plate Works	Mon	G. W.	Abertillery.
.	.	.	.	.	.	. .	Glangarnant Colliery	Carmarth'	G. W.	Garnant.
.	.	.	.	.	.	. .	Glanmore Foundry (G. W.)	Carmarth'	G. W.—L. & N. W.	Llanelly.
.	.	.	.	.	.	. .	Glanmorfa Siding	Carnarvon	L. & N. W.	See Seiont Siding (Carnarvon).
.	.	.	.	.	.	. .	Glanmwrwg Colliery (G. W.)	Carmarth'	G. W.—L. & N. W.	Llangennech.
.	P	.	.	.	.	. .	Glanrafon	Cardigan	V. of Rheidol	Aberystwyth and Devil's Bridge.
.	P	.	.	.	.	. .	Glanrafon Siding	Carnarvon	No. Wales N. G.	Quellyn Lake and Snowdon.
.	P	.	.	.	.	. .	Glanrhyd	Carmarth'	V. of T. Jt. (GW & L.N.W)	Llandilo and Llandovery.
.	.	.	.	.	.	. .	Glanrhyd Tin Plate Co.'s Sid. (Mid.)	Glamorg'n	Mid.—G.W.—L. & N. W.	Pontardawe.
.	.	.	.	.	.	. .	Glantawe Iron and Tin Plate Works (Mid.)	Glamorg'n	Mid.—G.W.—L. & N. W.	Pontardulais.
G	P	.	L	H	.	1 0	Glanton	Northumb	N. E.	Alnwick and Coldstream.
.	.	.	.	.	.	. .	Glanwalia Siding (Aberavon Tin Plate Co.)	Glamorg'n	R. & S. B.	Port Talbot (Aberavon).
G	P	.	L	H	.	. .	Glanworth	Cork	G. S. & W.	Fermoy and Mitchelstown.
.	.	.	.	.	.	. .	Glanyrafan Siding (Mid.)	Glamorg'n	Mid.—G.W.—L. & N. W.	Clydach-on-Tawe.
.	.	.	.	.	.	. .	Davies, J., & Co. (Mid.)	Glamorg'n	Mid.—G.W.—L. & N. W.	Glanyrafan Siding.
.	.	.	.	.	.	. .	Park Tin Plate Co. (Mid.)	Glamorg'n	Mid.—G. W.—L. & N. W.	Glanyrafan Siding.
.	.	.	.	.	.	. .	Glanyrafon Siding	Radnor	Cam.	Pantydwr.
.	P	.	.	.	.	. .	Glapwell	Derby	Mid.	Bolsover and Pleasley.
.	.	.	.	.	.	. .	Glapwell Colliery	Derby	Mid.	Palterton and Sutton.
G	P	.	L	H	.	2 0	Glarryford	Antrim	N. C. Com. (Mid.)	Ballymena and Coleraine.
.	.	.	.	.	.	. .	Glasbrook Brothers—			
.	.	.	.	.	.	. .	Fairwood Tin Plate Works	Glamorg'n	G. W.—L. & N. W.	Gowerton.
.	.	.	.	.	.	. .	Garngoch Colliery	Glamorg'n	G. W.—L. & N. W.	Gowerton.
.	.	.	.	.	.	. .	Gorseinon Colliery	Glamorg'n	L. & N. W.	Gowerton.
.	.	.	.	.	.	. .	Glasbrook, Sons, & Co.'s Timber Yard	Glamorg'n	GW—LNW—Mid.—RSB	Swansea.
G	P	F	L	H	C	5 0	Glasbury-on-Wye	Brecon	Mid.	Hay and Three Cocks.
.	.	.	.	.	.	. .	Glascote Colliery Co.'s Amington Colliery	Warwick	L. & N. W. / Mid.	Tamworth. / Kettlebrook.

EXPLANATION—G Goods Station.   P Passenger and Parcel Station.   P* Passenger, but not Parcel or Miscellaneous Traffic.
F Furniture Vans, Carriages, Portable Engines, and Machines on Wheels.   L Live Stock.
H Horse Boxes and Prize Cattle Vans.   C Carriages by Passenger Train.

STATION ACCOMMODATION.						CRANE POWER.	STATIONS, &c.	COUNTY.	COMPANY.	POSITION.
						Tons Cwts.	**GLASGOW—**			
.	.	.	.	.	.		Acme Package Co.'s Siding	Lanark	Cal.	Rutherglen and Gushetfaulds.
.	P	.	.	.	.		Adams' Siding	Lanark	G & P Jt—(Cal & G & S W)	Eglinton Str. Goods & Pollokshields.
.	.	.	.	.	.		Aikenhead Colliery	Lanark	Cal.	Cathcart and Burnside.
.	P	.	.	.	.		Alexandra Park (N. B.)	Lanark	{ N. B.	Springburn and Bellgrove.
									G. & S. W.	Over N. B. from Sydney Street Jn.
.	.	.	.	.	.		Anchor Chemical Works	Lanark	Cal.	St. Rollox and Robroyston.
.	.	.	.	.	.		Anderson and Henderson's Saw Mills	Renfrew	Cal.	Kinning Park.
.	.	.	.	.	.		Anderson's Siding	Renfrew	Cal.	West Street.
.	.	.	.	.	.		Anderston Brass Foundry (Steven & Struther's)(NB)	Lanark	N. B.—Cal.	Yorkhill and Stobcross Junction.
.	P	.	.	.	.		Anderston Cross	Lanark	Cal.	Central Sta. (Low Level) & Maryhill.
.	.	.	.	.	.		Arrol's Roof and Bridge Building Works	} Lanark..	{ Cal.	St. Rollox.
									N. B.	Germiston Siding.
.	.	.	.	.	.		Arrol's, Sir William, New Siding	Lanark	Cal.	London Road.
.	.	.	.	.	.		Atlas Engine Wks (Sharp, Stewart & Co.) (N.B.)	Lanark	N. B.—G. & S. W.	Springburn and Barnhill.
.	.	.	.	.	.		Balmoral Siding	Renfrew	Cal.	Scotstoun, West and Scotstoun.
.	.	.	.	.	.		Balornock Junction	Lanark	Cal.	Kennyhill and Springburn Park.
G	P	.	.	.	.	1 10	Barnhill (N. B.)	Lanark	{ N. B.	Springburn and Bellgrove.
									G. & S. W.	Over N. B. from Sydney Street Jn.
.	.	.	.	.	.		Barnhill Mineral Depôt	Lanark	N. B.	Near Barnhill.
G	P	.	L	H	.	2 0	Baxter's Siding (N.B.)	Lanark	N. B.—Cal.	Great Western Road.
.	.	.	.	.	.		Bellahouston	Lanark	G. & S.W.	Glasgow and Paisley, Canal.
.	.	.	.	.	.		Bellahouston Junction	Renfrew	Cal.—G & P Jt.—G & S W	Rutherglen and Paisley.
.	.	.	.	.	.		Beltfield Saw Mills	Renfrew	Cal.	Whiteinch and Partick, West.
.	P	.	L	H	.		Bellgrove (N. B.)	Lanark	{ N. B.	Coatbridge and College.
									G. & S. W.	Over N. B. from Sydney Street Jn.
.	.	.	.	.	.		Bellgrove East Junction	Lanark	N. B.	College and Duke Street.
.	.	.	.	.	.		Bennie, D., & Son's Works	Lanark	{ Cal.	St. Rollox.
									N. B.	Germiston Siding.
.	.	.	.	.	.		Blackhill Junction	Lanark	Cal.	Kennyhill and Springburn Park.
G	.	.	.	.	.		Bladen's Siding	Lanark	Cal.	Tollcross and Parkhead.
.	.	.	.	.	.		Blochairn	Lanark	N. B.	Branch from Garngad.
.	.	.	.	.	.		Blochairn Iron and Steel Works (Steel Co. of Scotland's Works)	Lanark	Cal.	Branch near Kennyhill.
.	.	.	.	.	.		Blochairn Iron and Steel Works (Steel Co. of Scotland's Works) (N.B.)	Lanark	N. B.—G. & S. W.	Branch from Garngad.
.	.	.	.	.	.		Blochairn Sand Qry. (N.B.)	Lanark	N. B.—G. & S. W.	Branch from Garngad.
.	.	.	.	.	.		Blochairn Siding	Lanark	Cal.	Buchanan Street.
.	.	.	.	.	.		Board of Police Sidings	Lanark	Cal.	St. Rollox.
.	P	.	.	.	.		Botanic Gardens	Lanark	Cal.	Central Sta. (Low Level) & Maryhill.
.	.	.	.	.	.		Braby, F., & Co.'s Works	Lanark	{ Cal.	St. Rollox.
									N. B.	Germiston Siding.
.	P	.	.	.	.	}	Bridge Street	Lanark	{ Cal.	Eglinton Street and Central Station (High Level).
.	P*	.	.	.	.	}			Glas. Dist. Sub.	St. Enoch and West Street.
.	.	.	.	.	.		Bridge Street Junction	Lanark	Cal.—G. & P. Jt.	Central Sta. & Eglinton Str., Goods.
G	.	F	.	.	.	12 0	Bridgeton	Lanark	Cal.	Rutherglen and St. Rollox.
.	P	.	.	.	.	}	Bridgeton Cross	Lanark	{ Cal.	Rutherglen and Central Station (Low Level).
.	P	.	.	H	C	}			N. B.	Branch from College North Junc.
.	.	.	.	.	.		Bridgeton Cross Junction	Lanark	Cal.	Bridgeton Cross and Glasgow Green.
.	.	.	.	.	.		Bridgeton Cross Mineral Depôt	Lanark	Cal.	Rutherglen & Central Sta. (Low Lev.)
.	.	.	.	.	.		Bridgeton Cross North Jn.	Lanark	N. B.	College and Bridgeton Cross.
.	.	.	.	.	.		British Hydraulic Foundry	} Lanark	{ Cal.	Whiteinch and Scotstoun.
									N. B.	Extension from Whiteinch.
.	.	.	.	.	.		Broadfoot's Foundry (Inchholm Brass Foundry)	Renfrew	Cal.	Whiteinch and Partick, West.
.	.	.	.	.	.		Broomloan Siding	Lanark	G & P Jt (Cal & G & S W)	Govan and Ibrox.
.	.	.	.	.	.		Brown & Munro's Siding	Lanark	Cal.	Tollcross.
G	P	F	L	H	C	25 0}	Buchanan Street	Lanark	{ Cal.	Terminus.
.	P*	.	.	.	.	}			Glas. Dist. Sub.	St. Enoch and Cowcaddens.
.	.	.	.	.	.		Bulls Metal and Melloid Siding	Renfrew	Cal.	Yoker and Scotstoun, West.
.	.	.	.	.	.		Butters Bros.' Siding	Lanark	G & P Jt (Cal & G & S W)	Pollokshields and Ibrox.
.	.	.	.	.	.		Caledonian Iron Works	Lanark	Cal.	Bridgeton.

EXPLANATION—G *Goods Station.*   P *Passenger and Parcel Station.*   P* *Passenger, but not Parcel or Miscellaneous Traffic.*
F *Furniture Vans, Carriages, Portable Engines, and Machines on Wheels.*   L *Live Stock.*
H *Horse Boxes and Prize Cattle Vans.*   C *Carriages by Passenger Train.*

STATION ACCOMMODATION.						CRANE POWER.		STATIONS, &c.	COUNTY.	COMPANY.	POSITION.
						Tons	Cwts.	GLASGOW—*continued.*			
.	.	.	.	.	.	.	.	Caledonian Pottery (Murray & Co.)	Lanark ...	Cal.	Rutherglen.
								Caledonian Railway Co.'s—			
.	.	.	.	.	.	.	.	Gas Works	Lanark ...	Cal.	Dawsholm.
.	.	.	.	.	.	.	.	Gas Works	Lanark ...	Cal.	Bridge Street Junction.
								Locomotive Works and Stores	Lanark	Cal.	St. Rollox.
G	.	F	L	.	.	15	0	Camlachie	Lanark	N. B.	College and Parkhead.
.	.	.	.	.	.	3	0	Canal Street Mineral Depôt	Lanark	Cal.	St. Rollox, West.
								Carntyne Dye Works (British Dyewood and Chemical Co.)	Lanark	N. B.	Parkhead and Carntyne.
								Carntyne Foundry and Engineering Works	Lanark	N. B.	Parkhead and Carntyne.
.	.	.	.	.	.	.	.	Carntyne Iron & Steel Wks.	Lanark	N. B.	Parkhead and Carntyne.
G	.	.	.	.	.	2	0	Carntyne Sidings	Lanark	N. B.	Carntyne.
								Cassell's Gold Extracting Co.'s Siding	Lanark	N. B.	Possilpark and Ruchill.
G	P	.	.	.	.	10	0	Cathcart	Renfrew...	Cal.	Cathcart Circle Railway.
.	.	.	.	.	.	.	.	Cathcart West Junction ...	Renfrew...	Cal.	Cathcart and Muirend.
.	.	.	L	.	.	.	.	Cattle Bank	Lanark	Cal.	St. Rollox.
								Central—			
.	P	F	.	H	C	.	.	High Level (Gordon Str.)	Lanark ...	Cal.	Terminus.
.	P	.	.	.	.	.	.	Low Level	Lanark ...	Cal.	Rutherglen and Maryhill.
								Station Junction	Lanark ...	Cal.	Rutherglen and Central Station (High Level).
.	P*	.	.	.	.	.	.	Cessnock	Lanark ...	Glas. Dist. Sub.	Kinning Park and Copeland Road.
.	P	.	.	.	.	.	.	Charing Cross	Lanark ...	N. B.	College and Partick.
.	.	.	.	.	.	.	.	Chisholm & Co.'s Siding	Lanark ...	Cal.	Bridgeton.
.	.	.	.	.	.	.	.	City Saw Mills	Lanark ...	N. B.	Port Dundas Branch.
.	.	.	.	.	.	.	.	Clerk & Son's Siding	Lanark ...	Cal.	Tollcross and Parkhead.
.	.	.	.	.	.	.	.	Clutha Iron Works	Lanark ...	G & P Jt (Cal & G & S W)	Pollokshields and Ibrox.
.	.	.	.	.	.	.	.	Clyde Bridge Steel Works	Lanark ...	Cal.	Rutherglen and Carmyle.
.	.	.	.	.	.	.	.	Clyde Iron Works & Cols.	Lanark ...	Cal.	Rutherglen and Carmyle.
.	.	.	.	.	.	.	.	Clyde Junction	Lanark ...	Cal.	Rutherglen and Dalmarnock.
.	.	.	.	.	.	.	.	Clyde Junction	Lanark ...	G. & S.W.	St. Enoch and Eglinton Street, Passengers.
.	.	.	.	.	.	.	.	Clyde Lead Works	Renfrew...	G & P Jt (Cal & G & S W)	Pollokshields and Ibrox.
.	.	.	.	.	.	.	.	Clyde Patent Wire Rope Co.'s Siding	Lanark ...	Cal.	Branch near Rutherglen.
.	.	.	.	.	.	.	.	Clyde Structural Iron Works (Clydeside Iron Works)	Renfrew...	Cal.	Scotstoun and Scotstoun, West.
.	.	.	.	.	.	60	0	Clyde Villa Crane (Cal.)	Renfrew...	Cal.—G. & S. W.	General Terminus.
.	.	.	.	.	.	.	.	Clydeholm Ship Yard (Barclay, Curle & Co.)	Renfrew...	Cal.	Whiteinch and Scotstoun.
.	.	.	.	.	.	.	.		Lanark ...	N. B.	Extension from Whiteinch.
.	.	.	.	.	.	.	.	Clydesdale Dye Works	Lanark ...	Cal.	Branch near Rutherglen.
.	.	.	.	.	.	.	.	Clydesdale Tube Works	Lanark ...	Cal.	Branch near Rutherglen.
.	.	.	.	.	.	.	.	Clydesdale Weighs	Lanark ...	Cal.	Rutherglen and Gushetfaulds.
G	.	F	.	.	.	6	0	College	Lanark ...	G. & S. W.	Branch from St. John's Junction.
G	P	F	.	H	C	7	0			N. B.	Bellgrove and Partick.
.	.	.	.	.	.	.	.	College, East Junction	Lanark ...	G. & S. W.—N. B.	Same as Sydney Street Junction.
.	.	.	.	.	.	.	.	College, North Junction ...	Lanark ...	N. B.	College and Bellgrove.
.	.	.	.	.	.	.	.	Connal's Pig Iron Store	Renfrew...	Cal.	Kinning Park.
.	.	.	.	.	.	.	.	Connal's Pig Iron Store	Lanark ...	G & P Jt (Cal & G & S W)	Pollokshields and Ibrox.
G	.	.	.	.	.	2	0	Cook Street	Lanark ...	G. & S.W.	Bridge Street Junc. & Pollokshields.
.	.	.	.	.	.	.	.	Cooperage Siding	Lanark ...	N. B.	Ruchill.
.	P*	.	.	.	.	.	.	Copeland Road	Lanark ...	Glas. Dist. Sub.	Cessnock and Govan Cross.
.	.	.	.	.	.	.	.	Corkerhill Engine Sheds...	Lanark ...	G. & S.W.	Bellahouston and Crookston.
.	P*	.	.	.	.	.	.	Cowcaddens	Lanark ...	Glas. Dist. Sub.	Buchanan Str. and St. George's Cross.
								Cowlairs—			
G	P	.	.	.	.	.	.	(Station)	Lanark ...	N. B.	Lenzie Jn. Sta. & Glasgow, Queen Str.
								Co-operative Society's Siding	Lanark ...	N. B.	Cowlairs.
.	.	.	.	.	.	.	.	East Junction	Lanark ...	N. B.	Bishopbriggs and Possilpark.
.	.	.	.	.	.	.	.	North Junction	Lanark ...	N. B.	Possilpark and Cowlairs.
.	.	.	.	.	.	.	.	West Junction	Lanark ...	N. B.	Cowlairs and Springburn.
G	.	.	.	.	.	10	0	Craighall Depôt	Lanark ...	N. B.	Extension fr. Port Dundas Branch.
.	.	.	.	.	.	.	.	Cranstonhill Engine Works	Lanark ...	G & P Jt (Cal & G & S W)	Govan and Ibrox.
.	.	.	.	.	.	.	.	Crawford Street Manure Depôt	Lanark ...	Cal.	Branch near West Street.

EXPLANATION—G *Goods Station.*   P *Passenger and Parcel Station.*   P* *Passenger, but not Parcel or Miscellaneous Traffic.*
F *Furniture Vans, Carriages, Portable Engines, and Machines on Wheels.*   L *Live Stock.*
H *Horse Boxes and Prize Cattle Vans.*   C *Carriages by Passenger Train.*

STATION ACCOMMODATION.						CRANE POWER.		STATIONS, &c.	COUNTY.	COMPANY.	POSITION.
						Tons	Cwts				
								GLASGOW—continued.			
	P							Cross & Son's Siding	Lanark	Cal.	Port Dundas.
	P							Crosshill	Lanark	Cal.	Cathcart Circle Railway.
								Crow Road	Lanark	Cal.	Maryhill and Partick (West).
								Cumming & Co.'s Siding	Lanark	Cal.	Dawsholm.
								Currie & Co.'s Siding	Lanark	Cal.	General Terminus.
	P							Cyclops Foundry	Renfrew	Cal.	Whiteinch and Scotstoun.
								Dalmarnock	Lanark	Cal.	Rutherglen and Central Station (Low Level).
								Dalmarnock Chemical Wks	Lanark	Cal.	Bridgeton.
								Dalmarnock Gas Works	Lanark	Cal.	Bridgeton.
								Dalmarnock Junction	Lanark	Cal.	Rutherglen and Cambuslang.
								Dalmarnock Sewage Works	Lanark	Cal.	Bridgeton.
G	P							Dawsholm	Lanark	Cal.	Branch near Maryhill.
								Dawsholm Castle Siding	Dumbartn	N. B.	Maryhill and Drumchapel.
								Dawsholm Chemical Works	Dumbartn	{ Cal. / N. B.	Branch near Maryhill. / Maryhill and Great Western Road.
								Dawsholm Gas Works	Dumbartn	N. B.	Maryhill and Great Western Road.
								Dawsholm Gas Wks. (West of Scotland Chemical Works)	Dumbartn	Cal.	Branch near Maryhill.
								Dawsholm Locomotive Sid.	Lanark	Cal.	Branch near Maryhill.
								Dawsholm Paper Mill	Dumbartn	N. B.	Maryhill.
								Dub's Locomotive Works (Glasgow Loco. Works)	Lanark	Cal.	Rutherglen and Gushetfaulds.
	P							Duke Street (N. B.)	Lanark	{ N. B. / G. & S. W.	Alexandra Park and Bellgrove. / Over N. B. from Sydney Street Jn.
								Eadie's Siding	Lanark	Cal.	Gushetfaulds.
	P							Eclipse Works	Lanark	Cal.	St. Rollox.
	P							Eglinton Street	Lanark	{ Cal. / G. & S. W.	Gushetfaulds&Central Sta(HighLev) / St. Enoch and Shields Road.
G		F	L	H		25	0	Eglinton Street	Lanark	G & P Jt (Cal & G & S W)	Bridge Str. Junc. and Pollokshields.
								Elderslie Shipyard and Graving Dock	Renfrew	Cal.	Whiteinch.
								Fairfield Shipbuilding Yard and Engineering Works	Lanark	G & P Jt (Cal & G & S W)	Govan and Ibrox.
								Farme Col. & Brick Works	Lanark	Cal.	Branch near Rutherglen.
								Farme Depôt	Lanark	Cal.	Branch near Rutherglen.
	P							Findlay & Co.'s Siding	Lanark	G & P Jt (Cal & G & S W)	Shields Road and Ibrox.
	P							Finnieston	Lanark	N. B.	College and Partick.
								Gallowgate	Lanark	G. & S. W.	Eglinton Street, Pass. and Sydney Street Junction.
	P							Gallowgate, Central	Lanark	N. B.	College and Bridgeton Cross.
								Gallowgate, Central Junc.	Lanark	G. & S. W.—N. B.	Gallowgate & Gallowgate, Central.
G	P			H		3	0	Garngad (N. B.)	Lanark	{ N. B. / G. & S. W.	Springburn and Bellgrove. / Over N. B. from Sydney Str. Junc.
								Garroway's Siding	Lanark	N. B.	Camlachie.
								Garscube Brick and Cement Siding (N.B.)	Dumbartn	N. B.—Cal.	Maryhill and Drumchapel.
G								Garscube Bk. Wks. (N.B.)	Lanark	N. B.—Cal.	Knightswood Branch.
								Garscube Siding	Dumbartn	N. B.	Maryhill and Dalmuir.
								General Terminus—			
G / G / G						30 / 30 / 8	0 / 0 / 0	(Station, Cal.)	Lanark	{ Cal. / G. & S. W. / N. B.	Terminus on River Clyde. / Over Cal. from Shields Junction. / Over Cal. from Scotland Str. Junc.
G								Quay (Cal.)	Renfrew	{ Cal. / N.B.	General Terminus. / Over Cal. from Scotland Str. Junc.
								Weighs (Cal.)	Lanark	Cal.—N. B.	General Terminus.
								Germiston, High Junction	Lanark	Cal.	Kennyhill and St. Rollox.
								Germiston, Low Junction	Lanark	Cal.	Kennyhill and Buchanan Street.
								Germiston Sand Quarry	Lanark	Cal.	St. Rollox.
								Germiston Sand Siding	Lanark	N. B.	Germiston Siding.
								Germiston Siding	Lanark	N. B.	Branch—Cowlairs Junc. & Sighthill.
G								Germiston Sidings	Lanark	Cal.	St. Rollox.
	P							Glasgow Cross	Lanark	Cal.	Rutherglen & Central Station (Low Level).
								Glasgow District Subway Co.'s Siding	Lanark	G & P Jt (Cal & G & S W)	Bridge Street and Pollokshields.
	P							Glasgow Green	Lanark	Cal.	Rutherglen & Central Station (Low Level).
								Glasgow Portland Cement Siding	Dumbartn	N. B.	Maryhill.

EXPLANATION—G *Goods Station.*   P *Passenger and Parcel Station.*   P* *Passenger, but not Parcel or Miscellaneous Traffic.*
F *Furniture Vans, Carriages, Portable Engines, and Machines on Wheels.*   L *Live Stock.*
H *Horse Boxes and Prize Cattle Vans.*   C *Carriages by Passenger Train.*

STATION ACCOMMODATION.						CRANE POWER.	STATIONS, &c.	COUNTY.	COMPANY.	POSITION.
						Tons Cwts.	GLASGOW—continued.			
.	.	.	.	.	.	. .	Glasgow Postal Telegraph Siding	Lanark ...	Cal.	Kinning Park.
.	.	.	.	.	.	. .	Glasgow Railway Engineering Works	Lanark ...	G & P Jt (Cal & G & S W)	Govan and Ibrox.
.	.	.	.	.	.	. .	Glasgow Telephone Siding	Lanark ...	Cal.	Kinning Park.
.	.	.	.	.	.	. .	Glasgow Tube Works (Marshall's)	Lanark ...	Cal.	Branch near Rutherglen.
.	.	.	.	.	.	. .	Glebe Street Mineral Depôt	Lanark ...	Cal.	St. Rollox.
.	P	.	.	.	.	. .	Gorbals	Lanark ...	G B & K Jt. (Cal. & G & S W)	Gorbals Junction & Strathbungo.
.	.	.	.	.	.	. .	Gorbals Junction	Lanark ...	G. & S.W.—G.B. & K. Jt.	St. Enoch and Strathbungo.
G	P	F	L	H	C	10 0	Govan	Lanark ...	G & P Jt (Cal & G & S W)	Branch from Ibrox.
.	.	.	.	.	.	. .	Govan Brick Works	Lanark ...	Cal.	Rutherglen and Gushetfaulds.
.	.	.	.	.	.	. .	Govan Crane Works	Lanark ...	G & P Jt (Cal & G & S W)	Govan and Ibrox.
.	P*	.	.	.	.	. .	Govan Cross	Lanark ...	Glas. Dist. Sub.	Copeland Road and Merkland Street.
.	.	.	.	.	.	. .	Govan Electrical Works ...	Lanark ...	G & P Jt (Cal & G & S W)	Govan and Ibrox.
.	.	.	.	.	.	. .	Govan Iron Works & Collieries (Dixon's Sidings)	Lanark ...	Cal.	Rutherglen and Gushetfaulds.
.	.	.	.	.	.	. .	Govan Tube Works	Lanark ...	G & P Jt (Cal & G & S W)	Govan and Ibrox.
.	.	.	.	.	.	. .	Great Western Col. (N. B.)	Lanark ...	N. B.—Cal.	Knightswood Branch.
G	P	.	.	.	.	1 10	Great Western Road (N.B.)	Lanark ...	{ N. B.	Partick and Maryhill.
G	.	.	.	.	.	1 10			{ Cal.	Over N.B. from Sighthill Junction.
.	.	.	.	.	.	. .	Great Western Steam Laundry Siding	Lanark ...	N. B.	Jordanhill and Whiteinch.
.	.	.	.	.	.	. .	Greenshield's Siding	Lanark ...	Cal.	Branch near West Street.
.	P	.	.	.	.	. .	Gushetfaulds	Lanark ...	Cal.	Rutherglen & Central (High Level).
.	.	.	.	.	.	. .	Gushetfaulds Junction	Lanark ...	Cal.	Rutherglen & Central Station (High Level).
G	.	.	.	.	.	3 0	Haghill (N. B.)	Lanark ...	{ N. B.	Sighthill and Bellgrove.
									{ G. & S. W.	Over N. B. from Sydney Str. Junc.
.	.	.	.	.	.	. .	Haghill Refuse Wks. (N.B.)	Lanark ...	N. B.—G. & S. W.	Haghill and Parkhead Junction.
.	P*	.	.	.	.	. .	Hillhead	Lanark ...	Glas. Dist. Sub.	Partick Cross and Kelvin Bridge.
.	.	.	.	.	.	. .	Hood & Co.'s Siding	Lanark ...	Cal.	Rutherglen and Gushetfaulds.
.	.	.	.	.	.	. .	Howden & Co.'s Siding	Lanark ...	G & P Jt (Cal & G & SW)	Bridge Street and Pollokshields.
.	.	.	.	.	.	. .	Hunter, Hardin, and Wilson's Siding	Lanark ...	Cal.—N. B.	Germiston Sidings.
.	.	.	.	.	.	. .	Hunter Str. Mineral Depôt	Lanark ...	N. B.	College.
.	.	.	.	.	.	. .	Hutchesontown Saw Mills	Lanark ...	Cal.	Rutherglen and Gushetfaulds.
.	.	.	.	.	.	1 10	Hutchison, Main & Co.'s Siding	Lanark ...	N. B.	Cowlairs.
.	.	.	.	.	.	. .	Hydepark Works (Neilson, Reid, & Co.)	Lanark ...	N. B.	Cowlairs Junction and Sighthill.
G	P	.	.	H	C	2 0	Hyndland	Lanark ...	N. B.	Branch—Partick and Jordanhill.
.	.	.	.	.	.	. .	Ibrox Brick Works	Lanark ...	G & P Jt (Cal & G & S W)	Govan.
.	.	.	.	.	.	. .	Ibrox Flour Mill..............	Renfrew ...	G & P Jt (Cal & G & S W)	Pollokshields and Ibrox.
.	.	.	.	.	.	. .	Inglefield Siding	Lanark ...	Cal.	Gushetfaulds.
.	.	.	.	.	.	. .	James Street Siding	Lanark ...	Cal.	Port Dundas.
.	P	.	.	.	.	. .	Jordanhill	Lanark ...	N. B.	Partick and Clydebank.
.	.	.	.	.	.	. .	Jordanhill Bk. Wks. (N.B.)	Lanark ...	N. B.—Cal.	Knightswood Branch.
.	.	.	.	.	.	. .	Jordanvale Siding	Renfrew ...	Cal.	Whiteinch and Scotstoun.
G	P	F	L	H	C	2 0	Kelvin Bridge	Lanark ...	{ Cal.	Central Sta. (Low Level) & Maryhill.
.	P*	.	.	.	.	. .			{ Glas. Dist. Sub.	Hillhead and St. George's Cross.
.	.	.	.	.	.	. .	Kelvindale Paper Mill	Lanark ...	Cal.	Branch near Maryhill.
G	.	.	.	.	.	. .	Kelvinhaugh Depôt (N.B.)	Lanark ...	N. B.—Cal.	Partick and Stobcross Junction.
.	.	.	.	.	.	. .	Kelvinhaugh Junction	Lanark ...	N. B.	Finnieston and Yorkhill.
.	.	.	.	.	.	. .	Kelvinhaugh Manure Siding (N. B.)...........	Lanark ...	N. B.—Cal.	Partick and Stobcross Junction.
G	P	.	L	H	C	3 0	Kelvinside	Lanark ...	Cal.	Maryhill and Partick, West.
.	.	.	.	.	.	. .	Kelvinside Electric Power Siding	Lanark ...	N. B.	Hyndland.
.	.	.	.	.	.	. .	Kennedy's Siding (N.B.)...	Lanark ...	N. B.—Cal.	Knightswood Branch.
.	.	.	.	.	.	. .	Kennedy's Timber Siding...	Lanark ...	Cal.	Kinning Park.
G	.	.	.	.	.	3 0	Kennyhill	Lanark ...	Cal.	Rutherglen and St. Rollox.
G	.	.	.	.	.	4 0	Kingston Dock (Cal.)........	Lanark ...	Cal.—G. & S. W.—N. B.	General Terminus.
G	.	.	.	.	.	5 0	Kinning Park	Renfrew ...	Cal.	Branch near Pollokshields.
.	P*	.	.	.	.	. .	Kinning Park	Renfrew ...	Glas. Dist. Sub.	Shields Road and Cessnock.
.	.	.	.	.	.	. .	Kinning Park Saw Mills...	Renfrew ...	Cal.	Kinning Park.
G	P	F	L	H	C	2 0	Kirklee	Lanark ...	Cal.	Central Sta. (Low Level) & Maryhill.
.	.	.	.	.	.	. .	Knightswood Branch (N.B.)	Lanark ...	N. B.—Cal.	Branch from Great Western Road.
.	.	.	.	.	.	. .	Knightswood Brick Works (N.B.)	Lanark ...	N. B.—Cal.	Knightswood Branch.
.	.	.	.	.	.	. .	Knightswood, North Junc.	Dumbartn	N. B.	Maryhill and Drumchapel.

EXPLANATION—G *Goods Station.*   P *Passenger and Parcel Station.*   P* *Passenger, but not Parcel or Miscellaneous Traffic.*
F *Furniture Vans, Carriages, Portable Engines, and Machines on Wheels.*   L *Live Stock.*
H *Horse Boxes and Prize Cattle Vans.*   C *Carriages by Passenger Train.*

STATION ACCOMMODATION.						CRANE POWER.		STATIONS, &c.	COUNTY.	COMPANY.	POSITION.
						Tons	Cwts.	GLASGOW—continued.			
								Knightswood Quarry (N.B.)	Lanark	N. B.—Cal.	Knightswood Branch.
								Knightswood, South Junc.	Dumbartn	N. B.	Great Western Road and Maryhill.
								Laidlaw & Sons' Siding	Lanark	Cal.	Buchanan Street.
								Lamb & Crawford's Yard	Lanark	G & P Jt (Cal & G & S W)	Bridge Street and Pollokshields.
								Lambhill Forge	Lanark	Cal.	Branch near Possil.
								Lambhill Foundry	Lanark	Cal.	Branch near Possil.
	P							Langside and Newlands	Renfrew	Cal.	Cathcart Circle Railway.
								Langside Junction	Lanark	Cal.—G. B. & K. Jt.	Gushetfaulds and Strathbungo.
								Laurel Siding (Rodgerson's)	Renfrew	Cal.	Scotstoun, West.
								Linthouse Shipbuilding Yard (Stephen's)	Lanark	G & P Jt (Cal & G & S W)	Govan.
G	P							Lochburn	Lanark	N. B.	Cowlairs and Maryhill.
								Lochburn Iron Works	Lanark	{ Cal. / N. B.	Branch near Possil. / Possilpark and Lochburn.
G						4	0	London Road	Lanark	Cal.	Rutherglen and St. Rollox.
								McEwan & Son's Siding	Renfrew	Cal.	Whiteinch and Scotstoun.
								McGhie's Cement Works	Lanark	Cal.	Branch near Rutherglen.
								Mackie & Co.'s Siding	Lanark	N. B.	Port Dundas Branch.
								Maclehose & Co.'s Sid. (N.B.)	Lanark	N. B.—Cal.	Great Western Road.
								McLellan's Siding	Lanark	Cal.	Kinning Park.
								McMoran's Siding	Lanark	Cal.	Gushetfaulds.
								Main's, A. & J., Siding	Lanark	N. B.	Branch from Possilpark.
								Mallsmire Brick & Fire Clay Works	Lanark	Cal.	Rutherglen and Gushetfaulds.
G	P	F	L	H	C	5	0	Maryhill	Lanark	{ Cal. / N. B.	Central Sta. (Low Level) and Possil. / Cowlairs and Clydebank.
G	P	F	L	H	C	3	0				
								Maryhill, Central Junction	Lanark	N. B.	Maryhill and Great Western Road.
								Maryhill, East Junction	Lanark	N. B.	Maryhill and Lochburn.
								Maryhill Iron Works	Lanark	Cal.	Maryhill and Possil.
G						5	0	Mavisbank Quay (Cal.)	Renfrew	Cal.—G. & S. W.—N. B.	General Terminus.
								Maxwell Junction	Renfrew	Cal.	Gushetfaulds and Ibrox.
G	P		L			3	0	Maxwell Park	Lanark	Cal.	Cathcart Circle Railway.
								Meadowside Ship Yard	Renfrew	Cal.	Partick, West.
	P*							Merkland Street	Lanark	Glas. Dist. Sub.	Govan Cross and Partick Cross.
								Merlin Iron Works	Renfrew	Cal.	Scotstoun and Scotstoun, West.
								Midwharf Siding	Lanark	Cal.	Port Dundas.
								Millcroft Brick Works	Lanark	Cal.	Rutherglen and Gushetfaulds.
								Milngavie Junction	Dumbartn	N. B.	Maryhill and Bearsden.
								Montgomerie & Strachan's Siding	Lanark	Cal.	Polmadie.
								Moorepark Boiler Works (Burnett's)	Lanark	G & P Jt (Cal & G & S W)	Govan and Ibrox.
								Moorepark Siding	Lanark	G & P Jt (Cal & G & S W)	Govan and Ibrox.
								Morrison and Mason's Sid.	Lanark	Cal.	Polmadie.
G	P					3	0	Mount Florida	Renfrew	Cal.	Cathcart Circle Railway.
								Muirhouse Junction	Renfrew	Cal.	Eglinton Street and Pollokshields, West.
								Muirhouse Siding	Renfrew	Cal.	Bridge Street and Strathbungo.
								Muir's Siding	Lanark	G B & K Jt (Cal & G & S W)	Strathbungo Junction.
								National Telephone Siding	Lanark	Cal.	Kinning Park.
						20	0	N. B. Railway Locomotive Works	Lanark	N. B.	Cowlairs.
						3	0	N. B. Railway Stores Department Sidings	Lanark	N. B.	Cowlairs.
								North British Tube Works	Lanark	G & P Jt (Cal & G & S W)	Govan and Ibrox.
								Nursery Brick Works	Lanark	G B & K Jt (Cal & G & S W)	Strathbungo Junction.
G	P	F	L	H	C	5	0	Parkhead	Lanark	N. B.	College and Coatbridge.
	P							Parkhead (for Celtic Park)	Lanark	Cal.	Carmyle and Bridgeton Cross.
								Parkhead Iron & Steel Forge & Rolling Mills	Lanark	{ Cal. / N. B.	Bridgeton and Kennyhill. / Parkhead and Sword Street Depôt.
								Parkhead Junction	Lanark	N. B.	Carntyne and Bellgrove.
								Park Ship Yard (Ritchie, Graham & Milne)	Renfrew	Cal.	Whiteinch and Scotstoun.
								Partick—			
G		F	L			10	0	(Station)	Lanark	Cal.	Maryhill and Partick, West.
G	P	F	L			3	0	(Station)	Lanark	N. B.	Stobcross and Maryhill.
G	P	F	L	H	C	3	0	Central	Lanark	Cal.	Central Sta. (Low Lev.) & Clydebank.
								Electric Light Siding	Lanark	Cal.	Partick, West.
								Junction	Lanark	N. B.	Partick and Hyndland.
								Saw Mills (Robinson, Dunn & Co.'s Wood Yd.)	Lanark	Cal.	Partick, West.

EXPLANATION—G *Goods Station.*   P *Passenger and Parcel Station.*   P* *Passenger, but not Parcel or Miscellaneous Traffic.*
F *Furniture Vans, Carriages, Portable Engines, and Machines on Wheels.*   L *Live Stock.*
H *Horse Boxes and Prize Cattle Vans.*   C *Carriages by Passenger Train.*

STATION ACCOMMODATION.						CRANE POWER.	STATIONS, &c.	COUNTY.	COMPANY.	POSITION.
						Tons Cwts.	GLASGOW—continued.			
							Partick—continued.			
							Ship Yard	Lanark ...	Cal.	Whiteinch.
G	P					3 0	West	Lanark ...	Cal.	Central Sta. (Low Level)&Clydebank
	P*						West, Mineral Depôt ..,	Lanark ...	Cal.	Central Sta. (Low Level)&Clydebank
							Partick Cross	Lanark ...	Glas. Dist. Sub.	Merkland Street and Hillhead.
							Paterson's Siding	Lanark ...	Cal.	St. Rollox, West.
G							Paterson's Siding	Lanark ...	G B & K Jt (Cal & G & S W)	Strathbungo Junction.
							Peacock Siding	Lanark ...	Cal.	St. Rollox, West.
							Phœnix Malting Works.....	Lanark ...	N. B.	Possilpark and Lochburn.
							Phœnix Tube Works (Menzies')	Lanark ...	Cal.	Branch near Rutherglen.
G						3 0	Pinkston Depôt	Lanark ...	N. B.	Port Dundas Branch.
							Pinkston Electric Power Station	Lanark ...	Cal.	St. Rollox, West.
							Pinkston Power Station Sid.	Lanark ...	N. B.	Port Dundas Branch.
							Plantation Foundry	Renfrew...	G & P Jt (Cal & G & S W)	Pollokshields and Ibrox.
G						60 0	Plantation Quay (Cal.)	Lanark ...	Cal.—G. & S. W.—N. B.	General Terminus.
							Pointhouse Shipbuilding Yard (Inglis & Co.'s Shipbuilding Yard)	Lanark ...	Cal.	Partick, Central & Partick, West.
							Pointhouse Shipbuilding Yard (Inglis & Co.'s Shipbuilding Yard) (N. B.) ...	Lanark ...	N. B.—Cal.	Stobcross.
							Pollok Junction	Lanark ...	G. & P. Jt.—G. & S. W.	Ibrox & Eglinton Str. Passengers.
G	P		L			3 0	Pollokshaws, East	Renfrew...	Cal.	Cathcart Circle Railway.
	P						Pollokshields	Lanark ...	G & P Jt (Cal & G & S W)	Eglinton Street Goods & Ibrox.
	P						Pollokshields, East	Lanark ...	Cal.	Cathcart Circle Railway.
							Pollokshields Junction......	Lanark ...	Cal.	Eglinton Street and Queen's Park.
	P						Pollokshields, West	Renfrew...	Cal.	Cathcart Circle Railway.
							Polmadie Brick Works......	Lanark ...	Cal.	Polmadie.
							Polmadie Saw Mills	Lanark ...	Cal.	Polmadie.
							Polmadie Sidings	Lanark ...	Cal.	Rutherglen and Gushetfaulds.
G							Port Dundas	Lanark ...	Cal.	Branch from St. Rollox.
G						3 0		Lanark ...	N. B.	Branch from Cowlairs.
							Port Dundas Distillery......	Lanark ...	N. B.	Port Dundas Branch.
G							Port Eglinton Depôt.........	Renfrew...	G. & S. W.	Eglinton Str. Passengers & Shields.
							Port Eglinton Foundry (Eglinton Foundry) (McLaren's)	Renfrew...	Cal.	Branch near West Street.
									G. & S. W.	Port Eglinton Depôt.
							Port Eglinton Junction ...	Lanark ...	G. & S. W.	Eglinton Str., Passengers & Shields.
G	P		L	H		2 0	Possil......................	Lanark ...	Cal.	Springburn and Maryhill.
							Possil Brick Works	Lanark ...	N. B.	Bishopbriggs and Cowlairs.
							Possil Junction	Lanark ...	Cal.	Springburn Park and Possil.
G	P						Possilpark	Lanark ...	N. B.	Maryhill and Cowlairs.
G						130 0	Princes Dock	Lanark ...	Princes Dock Joint (Cal, G & S W, & N B)	Branch from Ibrox.
G						130 0	Princes Dock (Cal.)	Lanark ...	Cal.—G. & S. W.—N. B.	General Terminus.
							Provan Gas Works (Blackhill Gas Works)	Lanark ...	Cal.	Kennyhill and St. Rollox.
							Provan Gas Works (Blackhill Gas Works) (N. B.)...	Lanark ...	N. B.—G. & S. W.	Barnhill and Garngad.
							Provan Mill Distillery	Lanark ...	Cal.	Kennyhill and St. Rollox.
G							Provan Mill Siding	Lanark ...	Cal.	Robroyston and St. Rollox.
G						130 0	Queen's Dock (Finnieston Quay)	Lanark ...	Cal.—N. B.	Stobcross.
	P						Queen's Park	Renfrew...	Cal.	Cathcart Circle Railway.
							Queen Street—			
G	P			H	C	5 0	High Level (N. B.)	Lanark ...	N. B. / N B, G N, & N E (E. Coast)	Terminus—Edinburgh & Glasgow Line.
	P						Low Level	Lanark ...	N. B.	College and Partick.
							Regent Flour Mills........	Lanark ...	Cal.	Partick, Central.
							Roberts' Siding	Lanark ...	N. B.	Cowlairs.
							Robinson & Hunter's Sid.	Lanark ...	Cal.	West Street.
							Roxburgh Enamelling Wks.	Renfrew...	Cal.	Scotstoun and Scotstoun, West.
G		F	L			6 0	Ruchill...	Lanark ...	N. B.	Branch from Possilpark.
G							Ruchill Hospital Siding....	Lanark ...	Cal.	Branch near Possil.
							Ruchill Manure Siding......	Lanark ...	N. B.	Ruchill.
G	P	F	L	H	C	5 0	Rutherglen	Lanark ...	Cal.	Motherwell and Glasgow, Central.
							Rutherglen Brick Works....	Lanark ...	Cal.	Branch near Rutherglen.
							Rutherglen Weighs	Lanark ...	Cal.	Rutherglen.
G			L			3 0	Rutherglen, West	Lanark ...	Cal.	Rutherglen and Gushetfaulds.

EXPLANATION—G Goods Station.　　P Passenger and Parcel Station.　　P* Passenger, but not Parcel or Miscellaneous Traffic.
F Furniture Vans, Carriages, Portable Engines, and Machines on Wheels.　　L Live Stock.
H Horse Boxes and Prize Cattle Vans.　　C Carriages by Passenger Train.

STATION ACCOMMODATION.						CRANE POWER.	STATIONS, &c.	COUNTY.	COMPANY.	POSITION.
						Tons Cwts.	GLASGOW—continued.			
.	.	.	.	.	.	. .	St. Andrew's Cross Electrical Works	Lanark ...	G B & K Jt (Cal & G & S W)	South Side.
.	P	F	.	H	C	. . }	St. Enoch	Lanark ...	G. & S. W.	Branch from Clyde Junction.
.	P*								Glas. Dist. Sub.	Buchanan Street and Bridge Street.
.	P*						St. George's Cross	Lanark ...	Glas. Dist. Sub.	Kelvin Bridge and Cowcaddens.
							St. John's Junction & Sids.	Lanark ...	G. & S. W.—N. B.	Gallowgate & Sydney Street Junc.
							St. John's Siding	Lanark ...	G. & S. W.	Gallowgate and Sydney Street Junc.
							St. Rollox—			
.	P						(Station)	Lanark ...	Cal.	Coatbridge and Buchanan Street.
.		.	L				Cattle Bank	Lanark ...	Cal.	St. Rollox.
							Chemical Works	Lanark ...	Cal.	St. Rollox.
									N. B.	Port Dundas Branch.
G		.	L			5 0	East	Lanark ...	Cal.	St. Rollox.
.							Manure Depôt	Lanark ...	Cal.	St. Rollox.
							Mineral Depôt	Lanark ...	Cal.	St. Rollox.
							Weighs	Lanark ...	Cal.	St. Rollox.
G		.				5 0	West	Lanark ...	Cal.	St. Rollox.
.							Saltmarket Junction	Lanark ...	G. & S. W.	St. Enoch and Gallowgate.
.							Saracen Foundry	Lanark ...	N. B.	Branch from Possil park.
.							Scotia Bolt & Rivet Works	Lanark ...	Cal.	Branch near Rutherglen.
.							Scotland Street Junction	Lanark ...	Cal.—G. & S. W.	General Term. & Eglinton Str., Pass.
.	P						Scotstoun	Renfrew ...	Cal.	Central Station (Low Level) and Clydebank.
							Scotstoun Flour Mills	Lanark ...	Cal.	Partick, Central.
							Scotstoun Iron Works	Renfrew ...	Cal.	Scotstoun and Scotstoun, West.
							Scotstoun Shipbuilding {	Renfrew ...	Cal.	Scotstoun and Scotstoun, West.
							Yard (Connell & Co.)... {	Lanark ...	N. B.	Extension from Whiteinch.
.	P*						Scotstoun Show Yard	Renfrew ...	N. B.	Jordanhill and Scotstounhill.
G		F	L	H	C	5 0	Scotstoun Show Yard Sid.	Renfrew ...	N. B.	Jordanhill and Whiteinch.
							Scotstoun Steel & Malleable			
							Foundry	Renfrew ...	Cal.	Scotstoun and Scotstoun, West.
G	P	F	L	H	C	3 0	Scotstoun, West	Renfrew ...	Cal.	Central Station (Low Level) and Clydebank.
							Scottish Plaster Works	Lanark ...	Cal.	Branch near Rutherglen.
							Sentinel Siding	Lanark ...	Cal.	Polmadie.
							Shaw's Siding	Lanark ...	Cal.	Maryhill and Possil.
							Shawfield Chemical Works	Lanark ...	Cal.	Rutherglen and Gushetfaulds.
.	P						Shawlands	Renfrew ...	Cal.	Cathcart Circle Railway.
.	P						Shearer's Graving Dock	Renfrew ...	Cal.	Scotstoun, West.
							Shields	Lanark ...	G. & S. W.	Eglinton St., (Pass.) & Bellahouston.
							Shields Junction	Lanark ...	Cal.—G. & P. Jt.	Rutherglen and Paisley.
									G. & P. Jt.—G. & S. W.	Paisley and St. Enoch.
.	P*						Shields Road	Lanark ...	Glas. Dist. Sub.	West Street and Kinning Park.
G	P					. . }	Shields Road (G. & S. W.)	Lanark ...	G. & S. W.	Eglinton Street, Passengers & Ibrox.
G									N. B.	Over G. & S. W. from College East Jn.
G		F	L			15 0	Sighthill (N. B.)	Lanark ...	N. B.	Branch from Cowlairs Junction.
									N B, G N, & N E (E. Coast)	
.							Sighthill, East Junction	Lanark ...	Cal.—N. B.	Buchanan Street & Cowlairs Junc.
.							Sighthill Junction	Lanark ...	N. B.	Springburn and Sighthill.
.							Skaterigg Siding (N.B.)	Dumbartn	N. B.—Cal.	Knightswood Branch.
							Slater Rodger & Co.'s			
							Bonded Store	Lanark ...	Cal.	General Terminus.
G		F	L			15 0	Smellie's Siding	Renfrew ...	Cal.	Partick, West.
G		F	L			10 0	South Side	Lanark ...	Cal.	Branch from Gushetfaulds Junction.
G	P	F				5 0	South Side	Lanark ...	G B & K Jt (Cal & G & S W)	Gorbals and Strathbungo.
							Springburn (N. B.)	Lanark ...	N. B.	Cowlairs Junction and Barnhill.
G		F	L			3 0			G. & S. W.	Over N. B. from Sydney Street Jn.
							Springburn Park	Lanark ...	Cal.	Steps Road and Possil.
							Springfield Free Warehouses (Cal.)	Renfrew ...	Cal.—G. & S. W.—N. B.	General Terminus.
							Dock Lane Grain Store (Cal.)	Renfrew ...	Cal.—G. & S. W.—N. B.	Springfield Free Warehouses.
							McHarg's Store (Cal.)...	Renfrew ...	Cal.—G. & S. W.—N. B.	Springfield Free Warehouses.
G						6 0	Springfield Quay (Cal.)	Lanark ...	Cal.—G. & S. W.—N. B.	General Terminus.
							Star Iron Works	Lanark ...	Cal.	St. Rollox.
							Stewart, D. Y., & Co.'s Sid.	Lanark ...	Cal.	St. Rollox.
G	P	.	L			15 0 }	Stobcross	Lanark ...	Cal.	Central (Low Level) and Maryhill.
G		F	L			15 0 }			N. B.	Branch—Yorkhill and Finnieston.
.							Stobcross Junction	Lanark ...	N. B.	Finnieston and Yorkhill.
.	.	.	.				Stobcross Weighs	Lanark ...	Cal.	Central (Low Level) and Maryhill.
.							Stobhill Hospital Siding	Lanark ...	Cal.	Springburn Park.

EXPLANATION—G Goods Station.   P Passenger and Parcel Station.   P* Passenger, but not Parcel or Miscellaneous Traffic.
F Furniture Vans, Carriages, Portable Engines, and Machines on Wheels.   L Live Stock.
H Horse Boxes and Prize Cattle Vans.   C Carriages by Passenger Train.

STATION ACCOMMODATION.							CRANE POWER.	STATIONS, &c.	COUNTY.	COMPANY.	POSITION.
							Tons Cwts.	GLASGOW—continued.			
								Stockwell Street Junction..	Lanark ...	G. & S.W.	St. Enoch and Gallowgate.
	P							Stonelaw Colliery	Lanark ...	Cal.	Rutherglen.
								Strathbungo	Lanark ...	G B & K Jt (Cal & G & S W)	Gorbals and Pollokshaws.
								Strathbungo Junction	Lanark ...	Cal.—G. B. & K. Jt.	General Terminus and Pollokshaws.
								Strathclyde Junction	Lanark ...	Cal.	Rutherglen and Dalmarnock.
								Strathclyde Siding	Lanark ...	Cal.	Bridgeton.
								Sword Str. Mineral Depôt	Lanark ...	N. B.	Camlachie and Bellgrove.
								Sydney Street or College East Junction..............	Lanark ...	G. & S.W.—N. B.	Gallowgate and Bellgrove.
								Temple Bk. Works (N.B.)	Lanark ...	N. B.—Cal.	Knightswood Branch.
								Temple Gas Works	Lanark ...	Cal.	Dawsholm.
								Temple Gas Works (N.B.)	Lanark ...	N. B.—Cal.	Great Western Road and Maryhill.
								Temple Iron Works (N.B.)	Lanark ...	N. B.—Cal.	Knightswood Branch.
								Temple Saw Mills (Robinson, Dunn & Co.'s Wood Yard) (N.B.)	Lanark ...	N. B.—Cal.	Knightswood Branch.
								Temple Siding (N.B.)......	Lanark ..	N. B.—Cal.	Knightswood Branch.
								Tennants' Siding (United Alkali Co.)	Lanark ...	Cal.	St. Rollox.
								Tharsis Sulphur & Copper Co.'s Siding	Lanark ...	Cal.	St. Rollox.
								Thaw & Campbell's Siding (N. B.)	Lanark ...	N. B.—G. & S. W.	Haghill.
G	P						2 0	Tollcross	Lanark ...	Cal.	Carmyle and Bridgeton Cross.
								Tollcross Estate Siding ..	Lanark ...	Cal.	Tollcross and Parkhead.
								Torry Glen Brick Works...	Lanark ...	Cal.	Rutherglen and Gushetfaulds.
								Trader's Siding	Lanark ...	G & P Jt (Cal & G & S W)	Govan and Ibrox.
								Tradeston Gas Works	Renfrew ...	Cal.	West Street.
								Tradeston Saw Mills.........	Lanark ...	G & P Jt (Cal & G & S W)	Bridge Street and Pollokshields.
								Train's Siding	Lanark ...	Cal.	Bridgeton.
	P							Victoria Park	Renfrew ...	N. B.	Branch from Whiteinch, West Junc.
								Walker's Siding (N.B.)......	Lanark ...	N. B.—Cal.	Great Western Road.
								Watson & Son's Siding.....	Lanark ...	G B & K Jt(Cal & G & S W)	South Side.
G							3 0	West Street......................	Renfrew ...	Cal.	Gushetfaulds & General Terminus.
	P*							West Street......................	Renfrew ...	Glas. Dist. Sub.	Bridge Street and Shields Road.
								West Street Junction	Lanark ...	Cal.	Gushetfaulds and General Terminus.
G	P	F	L	H	C		3 0	Whiteinch— (Station)	Renfrew ...	Cal.	Central Station (Low Level) and Clydebank.
G		F	L				3 0	(Station, for Scotstoun)...	Renfrew ...	N. B.	Bch. from Whiteinch, West Junc.
								East Junction	Lanark ...	N. B.	Partick and Great Western Road.
								Galvanizing Works	Renfrew ...	Cal.	Whiteinch and Partick, West.
								Loop Sidings	Lanark ...	N. B.	Partick and Whiteinch.
								Shipbuilding Yard (Reid & Co.)............	Renfrew ... Lanark ...	Cal. N. B.	Whiteinch and Scotstoun. Extension from Whiteinch.
								West Junction	Lanark ...	N. B.	Jordanhill and Scotstounhill.
								Wordie's Siding (H. Baird & Co.)	Lanark ...	N. B.	Germiston Siding.
								Wylie & Lochhead's Paper Works	Renfrew ...	Cal.	Partick, West.
	P							Yorkhill	Lanark ...	N. B.	Queen Street (Low Level) & Partick.
								Yorkhill Sidings (N.B.) ...	Lanark ...	N. B.—Cal.	Yorkhill and Stobcross Junction.
								Young's Siding (N.B.)	Lanark ...	N. B.—Cal.	Great Western Road.
								Glasgow Cattle Bank	Lanark ...	Cal.	Glasgow, Buchanan Street.
								Glasgow Corporation Sewage Works	Dumbartn	Cal.	Dalmuir.
								Glasgow District Subway Co.'s Siding (G. & P. Jt.)	Lanark ...	Cal. G. & S. W.	Glasgow, Kinning Park. Glasgow, Cook Street.
								Glasgow Iron & Steel Works (Motherwell)	Lanark ...	Cal.	Same as Motherwell Ir. & Steel Wks.
								Glasgow Iron & Steel Works (Wishaw)	Lanark ...	Cal.	Same as Wishaw Iron Works.
								Glasgow Portland Cement Sid	Dumbartn	N. B.	Glasgow, Maryhill.
								Glasgow Postal Telegraph Sid.	Lanark ...	Cal.	Glasgow, Kinning Park.
								Glasgow Powder Magazine ...	Lanark ...	Cal.	Steps Road.
								Glasgow Railway Engineering Works	Lanark ...	G & P Jt.(Cal. & G & S W)	Glasgow, Govan.
								Glasgow Rolling Stock and Plant Works	Lanark ...	Cal.	Motherwell.
								Glasgow Steamship Co.'s Sid.	Glamorg'n	GW—L&NW—Rhy—TV	Cardiff.
								Glasgow Telephone Siding ...	Lanark ...	Cal.	Glasgow, Kinning Park.

EXPLANATION—G *Goods Station.*   P *Passenger and Parcel Station.*   P* *Passenger, but not Parcel or Miscellaneous Traffic.*
F *Furniture Vans, Carriages, Portable Engines, and Machines on Wheels.*   L *Live Stock.*
H *Horse Boxes and Prize Cattle Vans.*   C *Carriages by Passenger Train.*

STATION ACCOMMODATION.						CRANE POWER.	STATIONS, &c.	COUNTY.	COMPANY.	POSITION.
						Tons Cwts.	Glasgow Tube Works (Marshall's)	Lanark	Cal.	Glasgow, Bridgeton.
							Glasnevin	Dublin	G. S. & W.	See Dublin.
							Glasnevin Junction	Dublin	G. S. & W.—M. G. W.	Dublin.
G	P	F	L	H	C	1 5	Glassaugh	Banff	G. N. of S.	Portsoy and Elgin.
G	P		L	H			Glassel	Aberdeen	G. N. of S.	Banchory and Aboyne.
G	P					2 0	Glassford	Lanark	Cal.	Hamilton and Strathaven.
							Glasshoughton Col. (L. & Y.)	Yorks	L & Y—G N—Mid—N E	Castleford.
							Glass Houses Siding	Yorks	N. E.	Pateley Bridge.
G	P		L			2 10	Glasslough	Monaghan	G. N. (I.)	Clones and Armagh.
G	P		L	H	C	3 0	Glasson Dock	Lancs	L. & N. W.	Branch from Lancaster.
G	P		L	H	C		Glasterlaw	Forfar	Cal.	Forfar and Stonehaven.
							Glasterlaw Junction	Forfar	Cal.	Guthrie and Farnell Road.
G	P	F	L	H	C	10 0	Glastonbury & Street	Somerset	S.&D.Jt.(L.&S.W.& Mid)	Templecombe and Highbridge.
							Snow & Co.'s Siding	Somerset	S.&D.Jt.(L.&S.W.& Mid)	Glastonbury.
							Glaze & Co.'s Siding	Staffs	G. W.	Brettell Lane.
							Glazebrook—			
G	P	F	L	H	C	5 0	(Station)	Lancs	C. L. C. (G C, G N,& Mid.)	Warrington and Manchester.
							Co-operative Wholesale Society's Soap & Candle Works	Lancs	C. L. C. (G C, G N,& Mid.)	Irlam (Over Ship Canal Line).
							Dam Lane Junction	Lancs	C. L. C. (G C, G N,& Mid.)	Glazebrook and Warrington.
							East Junction	Lancs	C. L. C. (G C, G N,& Mid.)	Glazebrook Station and Irlam.
							Junction	Lancs	C. L. C.—Ship Canal	Glazebrook Station and Irlam.
							Moss Junction	Lancs	C.L.C.—G.C.(Wigan Jn.)	Warrington and Lowton St. Mary's.
							Risley Siding	Lancs	C. L. C. (G C, G N,& Mid.)	Glazebrook.
							Ainscough Estate, Tenants of	Lancs	C. L. C. (G C, G N,& Mid.)	Risley Siding.
							Marchioness of Headfort, Tenants of	Lancs	C. L. C. (G C, G N,& Mid.)	Risley Siding.
							West Junction	Lancs	C.L.C.—G.C.(Wigan Jn.)	Glazebrook and Lowton St. Mary's.
G	P						Glazebury (L. & N. W.)	Lancs	L. & N. W.	Kenyon Junc. Sta. and Manchester.
	P								G. W.	Over L. & N. W. from Walton Junc.
							British Moss Litter, Charcoal, & Manure Co.'s Sid.	Lancs	L. & N. W.	Astley and Glazebury.
							Griendtsveen Moss Litter Co.'s Siding	Lancs	L. & N. W.	Astley and Glazebury.
							Knowles' Siding	Lancs	L. & N. W.	Astley and Glazebury.
							Lawton's Carr Bridge Sid.	Lancs	L. & N. W.	Glazebury and Kenyon Junc. Sta.
							Gleadell's Malt Kilns	Lincoln	G. C.	Kirton Lindsey.
							Glebe Branch	Lincoln	G. C.	Frodingham and Scunthorpe.
							Glebe Colliery	Staffs	N. S.	Longton.
							Glebe Mine	Lincoln	G. C.	Frodingham and Scunthorpe.
							Glebe Refinery Co.'s Siding (G. & S. W.)	Renfrew	G. & S.W.—N. B.	Greenock, Albert Harbour.
							Glebe Sand Siding	Cumb'land	C. & W. Jn.	High Harrington.
							Glebe Street Mineral Depôt	Lanark	Cal.	Glasgow, St. Rollox.
							Gledholt	Yorks	L. & N. W.	See Huddersfield.
G	P					1 10	Glemsford	Suffolk	G. E.	Haverhill and Sudbury.
	P						Glenageary	Dublin	D. W. & W.	Kingstown and Bray.
							Glenavon Colliery	Glamorg'n	G. W.	Cymmer.
G	P		L			2 0	Glenavy	Antrim	G. N. (I.)	Antrim and Lisburn.
G	P		L	H			Glenbarry	Banff	G. N. of S.	Grange and Banff.
G	P	F	L	H	C		Glenbeigh	Kerry	G. S. & W.	Farranfore and Valentia Harbour.
G	P						Glenboig	Lanark	Cal.	Coatbridge and Larbert.
							Gane Sand Quarry	Lanark	Cal.	Glenboig and Cumbernauld.
							Gane Siding	Lanark	Cal.	Glenboig and Cumbernauld.
							Garnqueen Brick Works (Hayhill Brick Works)	Lanark	Cal.	Glenboig and Gartcosh.
							Gartliston Brick and Fire-Clay Works	Lanark	Cal.	Gartsherrie and Glenboig.
							Glenboig Old Brick Works	Lanark	Cal.	Glenboig.
							Glenboig Star Brick Works	Lanark	Cal.	Glenboig.
							Glenboig Weighs	Lanark	Cal.	Glenboig.
							Greenfoot Sand Quarry	Lanark	Cal.	Glenboig and Cumbernauld.
							Greenfoot Siding	Lanark	Cal.	Glenboig and Cumbernauld.
							Glenboig Fire-Clay Works Siding (Old Works)	Lanark	Cal.	Same as Glenboig Old Brick Works (Glenboig).
									N.B.	Coatbridge, Gartgill.
							Glenboig Fire-Clay Works Siding (Star Works)	Lanark	Cal.	Same as Glenboig Star Brick Works (Glenboig).
									N.-B.	Coatbridge, Gartgill.

EXPLANATION—G *Goods Station.*   P *Passenger and Parcel Station.*   P* *Passenger, but not Parcel or Miscellaneous Traffic.*
F *Furniture Vans, Carriages, Portable Engines, and Machines on Wheels.*   L *Live Stock.*
H *Horse Boxes and Prize Cattle Vans.*   C *Carriages by Passenger Train.*

STATION ACCOMMODATION.						CRANE POWER.	STATIONS, &c.	COUNTY.	COMPANY.	POSITION.
						Tons Cwts.	Glenboig General Siding (for Garnqueen)	Lanark ...	N. B.	See Coatbridge, Gartgill.
							Glenbrook.......................	Cork	C. B. & P.	Cork and Carrigaline.
G	P	.	L	.	.	3 0	Glenbuck	Ayr	Cal.	Douglas and Muirkirk.
							Glenbuck Col. & Lime Wks.	Ayr	Cal.	Inches and Muirkirk.
							Glenbuck Pit	Ayr	G. & S. W.	Muirkirk.
							Glenburnie Siding	Fife	N. B.	See Newburgh.
	P*						Glencarron Platform	Ross & Cro'	High.	Strathcarron and Achnasheen.
G	P	F	L	H	C	3 0	Glencarse	Perth	Cal.	Perth and Dundee.
							Pitfour Brick Works.........	Perth	Cal.	Glencarse.
							Glencleland Colliery	Lanark ...	Cal.	Shieldmuir.
G	P	F	L	H	C	3 0	Glencorse	Edinboro'	N. B.	Branch from Millerhill.
							Eastfield Siding	Edinboro'	N. B.	Extension from Glencorse.
							Mauricewood Siding	Edinboro'	N. B.	Extension from Glencorse.
							Penicuik Gas Works	Edinboro'	N. B.	Extension from Glencorse.
							Glencraig Colliery	Fife	N. B.	Cardenden.
G	P	F	L	H	C		Glendon & Rushton	N'hamptn	Mid.	Market Harboro' and Wellingboro'.
							Glendon Ironstone Siding (Pain's)	N'hamptn	Mid.	Glendon and Rushton.
							Glendon Siding, East	N'hamptn	Mid.	Near Glendon and Rushton.
							Glendon Siding, West	N'hamptn	Mid.	Near Glendon and Rushton.
							Storefield Ironstone Siding (Davis & Co.)	N'hamptn	Mid.	Near Glendon and Rushton.
							Glen Douglas Siding............	Dumbartn	N. B.	See Arrochar and Tarbet.
							Glendue Quarry	Northumb	N. E.	Elrington.
							Glendullan Siding	Banff ...	G. N. of S.	See Dufftown.
G	P	.	L	H	.		Glenealy	Wicklow ..	D. W. & W.	Wicklow and Arklow.
G	P	.	L	.	.				Cal.	Steamer from Oban.
G	P	.	L	.	.		Glenelg	Inverness	High.	Steamer from Kyle of Lochalsh.
G	P	.	L	.	.				N. B.	Steamer from Mallaig.
							Glenesk Colliery	Edinboro'	N. B.	Dalkeith.
							Glenesk Junction	Edinboro'	N. B.	Millerhill and Eskbank.
							Glenesk Siding	Edinboro'	N. B.	See Dalkeith.
							Glenesk Siding	Edinboro'	N. B.	See Eskbank.
G	P	F	L	H	C	1 5	Glenfarg	Fife	N. B.	Kinross Junction and Perth.
G	P	.	L	.	.		Glenfarne	Leitrim ..	S. L. & N. C.	Enniskillen and Manorhamilton.
G	P						Glenfield	Leicester ..	Mid.	Desford and West Bridge.
							Blakesley's New Premier Brick and Pipe Works ...	Leicester ..	Mid.	Glenfield.
							Glenfield Premier Brick & Terra-Cotta Co.'s Siding	Leicester ..	Mid.	Near Glenfield.
							Groby Granite Co.'s Siding	Leicester ..	Mid.	Glenfield and Ratby.
							Patent Victoria Stone Co.'s Siding	Leicester ..	Mid.	Near Glenfield.
							Glenfield Works	Ayr	G. & S. W.	Kilmarnock, Riccarton.
G	P	F	L	H	C		Glenfinnan	Inverness	N. B.	Fort William and Mallaig.
G	P	F	L	H	C	3 0	Glengarnock	Ayr	Cal.	Giffen and Kilbirnie.
							Glengarnock Chemical Wks.	Ayr	Cal.	Glengarnock.
							Glengarnock Iron & Steel Works	Ayr	Cal.	Glengarnock.
G	P	F	L	H	C	3 0	Glengarnock and Kilbirnie ...	Ayr	G. & S. W.	Paisley and Dalry.
							Glengarnock Chemical Wks.	Ayr	G. & S. W	Beith and Glengarnock.
							Glengarnock Iron & Steel Works	Ayr	G. & S. W.	Beith and Glengarnock.
							Todhills Siding (Broomhill Siding)	Ayr	G. & S. W.	Glengarnock and Dalry.
							Whitespot Quarry	Ayr	G. & S. W.	Barkip Branch.
							Glengarnock Chemical Works	Ayr	Cal ... / G. & S. W.	Glengarnock. / Glengarnock and Kilbirnie.
							Glengarnock Ir. & Steel Wks.	Ayr	Cal ... / G. & S. W.	Glengarnock. / Glengarnock and Kilbirnie.
							Glengowan Print Works	Lanark ...	N. B.	Caldercruix.
							Glengyron Pit	Ayr	G. & S. W.	Cumnock (A. & C.).
							Gleniffer Depôt	Renfrew ...	G. & S. W.	See Paisley.
							Glenlochy Crossing	Argyll ...	Cal.	Tyndrum and Dalmally.
							Glenlochy Distillery	Inverness..	N. B.	Fort William.
G	P	F	L	H	C	1 0	Glenluce	Wigtown..	P.P.&W.Jt.(Cal.,G&SW, L. & N. W. & Mid.) ...	Stranraer and Newton Stewart.
							Glenmorangie Siding	Ross & Cro'	High.	Tain.
G	P	.	.	.	.		Glenmore	Donegal ...	Donegal	Stranorlar and Glenties.
	P						Glenmore	Kerry ...	T. & D.	Castlegregory Junc. and Dingle.
							Glenochil	Clackman'	N. B.	See Menstrie and Glenochil.

EXPLANATION—G Goods Station.   P Passenger and Parcel Station.   P* Passenger, but not Parcel or Miscellaneous Traffic.
F Furniture Vans, Carriages, Portable Engines, and Machines on Wheels.   L Live Stock.
H Horse Boxes and Prize Cattle Vans.   C Carriages by Passenger Train.

Station Accommodation						Crane Power		STATIONS, &c.	COUNTY.	COMPANY.	POSITION.
						Tons	Cwts				
.	.	.	.	.	.	.	.	Glenochil Distillery	Clackman'	N. B.	Menstrie and Glenochil.
.	.	.	.	.	.	.	.	Glen Parva	Leicester..	L. & N. W.	See Wigston.
.	.	.	.	.	.	.	.	Glen Ship Yard	Renfrew...	Cal.	Greenock, Regent Street.
.	.	.	.	.	.	.	.	Glentarras Distillery	Dumfries..	N. B.	Langholm.
G	P	F	L	H	C	3	0	Glenties	Donegal ...	Donegal	Branch from Stranorlar.
G	P	.	L	H	.	.	.	Glenwhilly	Wigtown..	G. & S. W.	Barrhill and New Luce.
.	.	.	.	.	.	.	.	Glenyards Brick Works	Stirling ...	N. B.	Castlecary.
.	.	.	.	.	.	.	.	Glespin Colliery	Lanark ...	Cal.	Inches.
.	.	.	.	.	.	.	.	Globe Brick Works	Flint	W. M. & C. Q.	Buckley.
.	.	.	.	.	.	.	.	Globe Chemical Works	Lancs	L. & N. W.—S. & M. Jt.	Widnes.
.	.	.	.	.	.	.	.	Globe Dry Dock	Glamorg'n	GW—LNW—Mid—RSB	See Victoria Dry Docks Co. (Swansea).
.	.	.	.	.	.	.	.	Globe Iron & Steel Works...	Lanark ...	Cal.	Motherwell.
.	.	.	.	.	.	.	.	Globe Iron Works	Lancs	G. C. & L & N W. Jt.	Same as Summer's Sid. (Stalybridge).
.	.	.	.	.	.	.	.	Globe Ir. Wks. (Douglas Bros.')	Durham ...	N. E.	Blaydon.
.	.	.	.	.	.	.	.	Globe Road & Devonshire Str.	Middlesex	G. E.	See London.
.	.	.	.	.	.	.	.	Globe Siding	N'hamptn	Mid.	See Loddington Ir. Ore Co. (Kettering)
.	.	.	.	.	.	.	.	Globe Works	Lancs	G C (St. Helens Exten.)— L. & N. W.	See United Alkali Co. (St. Helens).
.	.	.	.	.	.	.	.	Glodwick Road (L. & N. W.)	Lancs	L. & N. W.—G. C.	See Oldham.
G	P	.	L	H	.	.	.	Glogue	Pembroke	G. W.	Whitland and Cardigan.
.	.	.	.	.	.	.	.	Glogue Slate Quarries Sid.	Pembroke	G. W.	Glogue.
.	.	.	.	.	.	.	.	Glorat Lime Siding	Stirling ...	N. B.	Milton.
G	P	F	L	H	C	5	0	Glossop	Derby ...	G. C.	Branch from Dinting.
.	.	.	.	.	.	.	.	Garsides' Saw Mill	Derby ...	G. C.	Glossop.
.	.	.	.	.	.	.	.	Glossop and Bulay's Siding ..	Yorks	N. E.	Beverley.
.	.	.	.	.	.	.	.	Glossop's Siding	Derby ...	Mid.	Ambergate.
								GLOUCESTER—			
G	P	F	L	H	C	5	0	(Station)	Glo'ster	G. W.	Swindon and Hereford.
G	P	F	L	H	C	10	0	(Station)	Glo'ster	Mid.	Birmingham and Bristol.
.	.	.	.	.	.	.	.	Adams, T., & Co.'s Siding	Glo'ster	G. W.—Mid.	Gloucester Docks.
.	.	.	.	.	.	.	.	Ashbee & Sons	Glo'ster	G. W.—Mid.	Gloucester Docks.
.	.	.	.	.	.	.	.	Barkworth & Spalding's Sid.	Glo'ster	G. W.—Mid..	Gloucester Docks.
.	.	.	.	.	.	.	.	Beard, G. T.	Glo'ster	G. W.	Gloucester Docks.
.	.	.	.	.	.	.	.	Bowley & Collett's Siding...	Glo'ster	Mid.	Gloucester Docks.
.	.	.	.	.	.	.	.	Bristol Steam Navigat'n Co.	Glo'ster	G. W.	Gloucester Docks.
.	.	.	.	.	.	.	.	Collett & Co.'s Siding	Glo'ster	Mid.	Tuffley and Gloucester Docks.
.	.	.	.	.	.	.	.	Corporation Siding	Glo'ster	G. W.	Gloucester Docks.
G	.	.	.	.	.	10	0	Docks	Glo'ster	G. W.	Near Gloucester Station.
G	.	.	.	.	.	.	.		Glo'ster	Mid.	Branch—Gloucester and Haresfield.
G	.	.	.	.	.	.	.	Docks Branch, West	Glo'ster	Mid.	West side of Docks.
.	.	.	.	.	.	.	.	Downing & Co.'s Siding	Glo'ster	Mid.	Gloucester Docks.
.	.	.	.	.	.	.	.	Emlyn Iron Works (Phillips, C. D.)	Glo'ster	G. W.—Mid.	Gloucester.
.	.	.	.	.	.	.	.	Fielding & Platt's Works...	Glo'ster	Mid.	Gloucester Docks.
.	.	.	.	.	.	.	.	Foster Bros.' Mill	Glo'ster	G. W.	Gloucester Docks.
.	.	.	.	.	.	.	.	Gloucester Carriage and Wagon Works	Glo'ster	G. W.—Mid.	Gloucester Docks.
.	.	.	.	.	.	.	.	Gloucester Joinery Co.	Glo'ster	G. W.—Mid.	Gloucester Docks.
.	.	.	.	.	.	.	.	Goodwins' Siding	Glo'ster	Mid.	Gloucester Docks.
.	.	.	.	.	.	.	.	Gopsill, Brown & Co.	Glo'ster	G. W.	Gloucester Docks.
.	.	.	.	.	.	.	.	Griggs & Co.	Glo'ster	G. W.—Mid.	Gloucester Docks.
.	.	.	.	.	.	.	.	Hearn's Siding	Glo'ster	Mid.	Gloucester.
.	.	.	.	.	.	.	.	Hempstead Wharf Gas Co.'s Siding	Glo'ster	Mid.	Gloucester.
G	.	.	.	.	.	.	.	High Orchard Wharf	Glo'ster	Mid.	Gloucester Docks.
G	.	.	.	.	.	10	0	Hudson & Co.	Glo'ster	G. W.—Mid.	Gloucester Docks.
.	.	.	.	.	.	.	.	Llanthony Wharf Yard...	Glo'ster	G. W.	Gloucester Docks.
.	.	.	.	.	.	.	.	Matthews' & Co.'s Yard...	Glo'ster	Mid.	Gloucester Docks.
.	.	.	.	.	.	.	.	New Coal Depôt	Glo'ster	G. W.	Gloucester.
.	.	.	.	.	.	.	.	Nicks & Co.	Glo'ster	G. W.—Mid.	Gloucester Docks.
.	.	.	.	.	.	.	.	Philpott & Co.	Glo'ster	G. W.—Mid.	Gloucester Docks.
.	.	.	.	.	.	.	.	Price, Walker & Co.'s Sid.	Glo'ster	G. W.—Mid.	Gloucester Docks.
.	.	.	.	.	.	.	.	Priday, Metford & Co.	Glo'ster	G. W.—Mid.	Gloucester Docks.
.	.	.	.	.	.	.	.	Reynolds & Co.	Glo'ster	G. W.—Mid.	Gloucester Docks.
.	.	.	.	.	.	.	.	Robinson, T., & Co.	Glo'ster	G. W.—Mid.	Gloucester Docks.
.	.	.	.	.	.	.	.	Romans & Co.'s Siding	Glo'ster	G. W.—Mid.	Gloucester Docks.
.	.	.	.	.	.	.	.	Sessions & Sons' Siding...	Glo'ster	G. W.—Mid.	Gloucester Docks.
.	.	.	.	.	.	.	.	Smith Bros.	Glo'ster	G. W.—Mid.	Gloucester Docks.
.	.	.	.	.	.	.	.	Spillers & Baker's Stores...	Glo'ster	G. W.—Mid.	Gloucester Docks.
.	.	.	.	.	.	.	.	Summers & Scott's Siding	Glo'ster	G. W.—Mid.	Gloucester Docks.
.	.	.	.	.	.	.	.	Tramway Junction	Glo'ster	G. W.—Mid.	Gloucester and Cheltenham.
.	.	.	.	.	.	.	.	Tuffley Docks Branch	Glo'ster	Mid.	Gloucester and Haresfield.

EXPLANATION—G *Goods Station.*   P *Passenger and Parcel Station.*   P* *Passenger, but not Parcel or Miscellaneous Traffic.*
F *Furniture Vans, Carriages, Portable Engines, and Machines on Wheels.*   L *Live Stock.*
H *Horse Boxes and Prize Cattle Vans.*   C *Carriages by Passenger Train.*

STATION ACCOMMODATION.	CRANE POWER.	STATIONS, &c.	COUNTY.	COMPANY.	POSITION.
	Tons Cwts.	**GLOUCESTER**—continued.			
		Tuffley Wharf	Glo'ster	Mid.	Tuffley Junction & Gloucester Dks.
		Turner, Nott & Co.	Glo'ster	G. W.—Mid.	Gloucester Docks.
		Wait, James, & Co.	Glo'ster	G. W.—Mid.	Gloucester Docks.
		Whitfield's Brick Siding	Glo'ster	Mid.	Tuffley Branch.
		Gloucester Carriage & Wgn { Works	Worcester	G. W.	Worcester.
		Gloucester Carriage & Wgn { Works	Glo'ster	G. W.—Mid.	Gloucester Docks.
		Gloucester Joinery Co.	Glo'ster	G. W.—Mid.	Gloucester Docks.
		Gloucester Road	Middlesex	Met—Met.Dist.—L&NW	See London.
		Gloucester Street Siding	Glamorg'n	T. V.	Aberdare.
		Gloucester Wagon Co.—			
		Siding	Cheshire	B'head Jt.(G.W.&L NW)	Chester.
		Siding	Brecon	G. W.	Hirwain.
		Siding	Glamorg'n	GW—LNW—Rhy.—TV	Cardiff.
		Gloucester Wagon Works	Glamorg'n	G. W.	Swansea.
		Gloucester Wharf	Mon	G. W.	Newport, Dock Street.
P		Glounagalt Bridge	Kerry	T. & D.	Castlegregory Junction and Dingle.
		Glover & Mains Siding	Middlesex	G. E.	Angel Road.
		Glover's Flour Mill	Derby	L. D. & E. C.	Killamarsh.
		Glover's Siding	Lancs	L. & N. W.	St. Helens.
		Glover, W. T., & Co.'s Siding	Lancs	Trafford Park Estate	Manchester.
		Glubbs Brick & Tile Co.'s Sid.	Devon	L. & S.W.	Whitstone and Bridgerule.
		Glynbeudy Tin Plate Works	Carmarth'	G. W.	Brynamman.
		Glyn Castle Colliery	Glamorg'n	G. W.	Resolven.
G P	2 0	Glynceiriog	Denbigh	Glyn Valley	Terminus.
		Glyncoed Colliery	Carmarth'	G. W.	Dafen.
		Glyn Colliery	Glamorg'n	T. V.	Cross Inn.
G		Glyncorrwg	Glamorg'n	S. Wales Min.	Cymmer and Glyncorrwg Colliery.
		Glyncorrwg Colliery (S. Wales Min.)	Glamorg'n	S. Wales Min.—G. W.	Terminus.
		Glyncorrwg (New) Colliery	Glamorg'n	R. & S. B.	Blaengwynfi.
		Glyncorrwg Engineering Wks	Glamorg'n	{ G. W.—S. Wales Min. { R. & S. B.	See Briton Ferry. See Court Sart.
		Glyncorrwg Gas Works	Glamorg'n	R. & S. B.	Cymmer.
		Glyncymmer Colliery	Glamorg'n	G. W.	Cymmer.
G P F L H C		Glynde	Sussex	L. B. & S. C.	Polegate and Lewes.
		Newington & Co.'s Siding	Sussex	L. B. & S. C.	Glynde.
		Sussex Portland Cement Co.'s Siding	Sussex	L. B. & S. C.	Glynde.
G P . . H .	1 10	Glyndyfrdwy	Merioneth	G. W.	Llangollen and Corwen.
		Moelferna & Deeside Slate Quarry	Merioneth	G. W.	Glyndyfrdwy.
		Glynea Coal & Brick Works	Carmarth'	G. W.	Bynea.
		Glynea Colliery (G. W.)	Carmarth'	G. W.—L. & N. W.	Bynea.
		Glyne Siding	Sussex	L. B. & S. C.	Same as Hastings and St. Leonards Gas Co.'s Siding (Hastings).
		Glyn Gwyn Colliery	Glamorg'n	T. V.	Penrhiwceiber.
G P		Glynn	Antrim	N. C. Com. (Mid.)	Carrickfergus and Larne.
		Glynnantddu Colliery	Mon	G. W.	Pontnewynydd.
G P . L H		Glyn Neath	Glamorg'n	G. W.	Hirwain and Neath.
		Abernant Brick Works	Glamorg'n	G. W.	Glyn Neath and Hirwain.
		Aberpergwm Colliery	Glamorg'n	G. W.	Glyn Neath.
		British Rhondda Colliery	Glamorg'n	G. W.	Glyn Neath.
		Dinas Siding	Glamorg'n	G. W.	Glyn Neath.
		Empire Colliery	Glamorg'n	G. W.	Glyn Neath.
		Penrhiew Colliery	Glamorg'n	G. W.	Glyn Neath.
		Glyn Pits	Mon	G. W.	Pontypool, Crane Street.
		Glyn-rhonwy Slate Co.'s Sid.	Carnarvon	L. & N. W.	Llanberis.
G	4 0	Glyntaff	Glamorg'n	A. (N. & S. W.) D. & R.	Pontypridd Junc. & Penrhos Junc.
		Groeswen Colliery	Glamorg'n	A. (N. & S. W.) D. & R.	Pontypridd Junc. & Penrhos Junc.
		Newbridge Works (Brown, Lenox & Co.)	Glamorg'n	A. (N. & S. W.) D. & R.	Pontypridd Junc. & Penrhos Junc.
		Pontypridd Gas Works	Glamorg'n	A. (N. & S. W.) D. & R.	Pontypridd Junc. & Penrhos Junc.
		Pontypridd Interchange Sidings	Glamorg'n	A. (N. & S. W.) D. & R.	Pontypridd Junc. & Penrhos Junc.
		Glyn Valley Junction	Denbigh	G. W.	Chirk.
G P . L H		Gnosall	Staffs	L. & N. W.	Shrewsbury and Stafford.
		Goatfoot Colliery	Ayr	G. & S.W.	Hurlford.
G P . L H C	2 0	Goathland	Yorks	N. E.	Whitby and Pickering.
		Goathland Whinstone Sid.	Yorks	N. E.	Goathland.
		Newton Dale Siding	Yorks	N. E.	Levisham and Goathland.
		Raindale Siding	Yorks	N. E.	Levisham and Goathland.

EXPLANATION—G *Goods Station.*   P *Passenger and Parcel Station.*   P* *Passenger, but not Parcel or Miscellaneous Traffic.*
F *Furniture Vans, Carriages, Portable Engines, and Machines on Wheels.*   L *Live Stock.*
H *Horse Boxes and Prize Cattle Vans.*   C *Carriages by Passenger Train.*

STATION ACCOMMODATION.						CRANE POWER.	STATIONS, &c.	COUNTY.	COMPANY.	POSITION.
G	P	F	L	H	C	Tons Cwts 2 0	Gobowen	Salop	G. W.	Shrewsbury and Ruabon.
.	P	.	.	H	C	.	Godalming	Surrey	L. & S. W.	Guildford and Petersfield.
G	.	F	L	.	.	5 0	Godalming	Surrey	L. & S. W.	Branch from Farncombe.
G	.	.	.	.	.	.	Peasmarsh Siding	Surrey	L. & S. W.	Guildford and Godalming.
.	.	.	.	.	.	.	Godalming	Surrey	S. E. & C.	See Shalford (for Godalming).
.	.	.	.	.	.	.	Goddard, Massey & Warner's Siding (Mid.)	Notts	Mid.—L. & N. W.	Nottingham.
.	.	.	.	.	.	.	Godley & Gouldings Sid. (G.C.)	Notts	G. C.—G. N.—Mid.	Worksop.
.	.	.	.	.	.	.	Godley Junction	Cheshire	C. L. C.--G. C.	Woodley and Penistone.
.	P	.	.	.	.	.	Godley Junction Station	Cheshire	C.L.C.(G C, G N, & Mid.) G. C.	Junction with G. C. Guide Bridge and Penistone.
G	P	F	L	H	C	1 0	Godmanchester (G N & G E Jt)	Hunts	G. N. & G. E. Jt.	Huntingdon Junction and St. Ives.
.	P	.	.	H	C	.			Mid.	Over G. N. & G. E. Joint Line.
.	.	.	.	.	.	.	Brown & Goodman's Siding	Hunts	G. N. & G. E. Jt.	Godmanchester.
.	.	.	.	.	.	.	Veasey's, C., Siding	Hunts	G. N. & G. E. Jt.	Godmanchester.
.	P	.	.	.	.	.	Godmanchester	Hunts	Mid.	See Huntingdon (for Godmanchester).
.	.	.	.	.	.	.	Godnow Bridge	Lincoln	G. C.	Thorne and Barnetby.
G	P	F	L	H	C	.	Godshill	I. of W.	I. of W. Cent.	Merstone Junc. & Ventnor (Town).
G	P	F	L	H	C	4 0	Godstone	Surrey	S. E. & C.	Red Hill and Tonbridge.
.	.	.	.	.	.	.	Williams' Brick Siding	Surrey	S. E. & C.	Godstone and Nutfield.
.	P	.	.	.	.	.	Godwin's Siding	Herts	Mid.	Hemel Hempsted.
G	P	.	L	H	.	2 10	Gogar	Edinboro'	N. B.	Haymarket and Ratho.
.	.	.	.	.	.	.	Goitre Siding	Montgom	Cam.	Kerry.
.	P*	.	.	.	.	.	Golant	Cornwall	G. W.	Fowey and Lostwithiel.
G	P	.	L	.	.	5 0	Golborne	Lancs	G. C. (St. Helens Exten.) L. & N. W.	Lowton St. Mary's and St. Helens. Warrington and Wigan.
.	.	.	.	.	.	.	Evans, R., & Co.—			
.	.	.	.	.	.	.	Edge Green Colliery	Lancs	G. C. (St. Helens Exten.) L. & N. W.	Golborne. Bamfurlong and Golborne.
.	.	.	.	.	.	.	Golborne Colliery	Lancs	G. C. (St. Helens Exten.) L. & N. W.	Golborne. Bamfurlong and Golborne.
.	.	.	.	.	.	.	Garswood Coal & Iron Co.'s Long Lane Colliery	Lancs	G. C. (St. Helens Exten.)	Golborne.
.	.	.	.	.	.	.	Garswood Hall Colliery	Lancs	G. C. (St. Helens Exten.)	Golborne.
.	.	.	.	.	.	.	Golborne Mills Co.'s Siding (Parkside Mills)	Lancs	L. & N. W.	Golborne and Lowton.
.	P	.	.	.	.	.	Golborne Colliery	Lancs	GC (St.H.Ex.)—L & N W	See Evans, R., & Co. (Golborne).
.	P	.	.	.	.	.	Golcar	Yorks	L. & N. W.	Huddersfield and Stalybridge.
.	.	.	.	.	.	.	Goldendale Iron Co.—			
.	.	.	.	.	.	.	Ravensdale Siding	Staffs	N. S.	Chatterley.
.	.	.	.	.	.	.	Yeld Hill Siding	Staffs	N. S.	Chatterley.
G	P	F	L	H	C	.	Golden Grove	Carmarth'	L. & N. W.	Carmarthen and Llandilo.
G	P	.	.	.	.	.	Goldenhill	Staffs	N. S.	Tunstall and Kidsgrove.
.	.	.	.	.	.	.	Goldie & Co.'s Siding	Lanark	N. B.	Rawyards.
.	.	.	.	.	.	.	Golding Davis Works	Lancs	L. & N. W—S. & M. Jt.	See United Alkali Co. (Widnes).
.	.	.	.	.	.	.	Golding Davis Waste Tip Sid.	Lancs	S. & M. Jt. (G. C. & Mid.)	Widnes.
.	.	.	.	.	.	.	Goldmire Quarry Siding	Lancs	Furness	Park.
G	P	.	L	H	.	.	Goldsbro'	Yorks	N. E.	York and Knaresborough.
.	.	.	.	.	.	.	Golds Green Siding	Staffs	L. & N. W.	Same as Freakley's Sid. (Gt. Bridge).
.	P	.	.	.	.	.	Gold's Siding	Lanark	Cal.	Law Junction Station.
G	P	.	.	.	.	.	Golfa	Montgom	Cam. (W. & L.)	Welshpool & Llanfair Caereinion.
G	P	.	.	.	.	.	Sylfaen Farm Siding	Montgom	Cam. (W. & L.)	Golfa and Castle Caereinion.
G	P	F	L	H	C	5 0	Gollanfield	Inverness	High.	Nairn and Inverness.
G	P	F	L	H	C	2 0	Golspie	Sutherl'nd	High.	Bonar Bridge and Helmsdale.
.	.	.	.	.	.	.	Golynos Colliery (G. W.)	Mon	G. W. G. W.—L. & N. W.	Talywain. See Hoskin & Llewellyn (Abersychan and Talywain).
G	P	.	L	.	.	5 0	Gomersal	Yorks	L. & N. W.	Cleckheaton and Leeds.
G	P	F	L	H	C	4 0	Gomshall and Shere	Surrey	S. E. & C.	Dorking and Guildford.
.	.	.	.	.	.	.	Goodall, Bates & Co.'s Siding	Durham	N. E.	Gateshead.
.	.	.	.	.	.	.	Goodman's Yard	Middlesex	G. E.	See London.
G	P	.	.	.	.	.	Goodmayes	Essex	G. E.	Stratford and Romford.
.	.	.	.	.	.	.	Goodwick	Pembroke	G. W.	See Fishguard and Goodwick.
.	.	.	.	.	.	.	Goodwin's Siding	Glo'ster	Mid.	Gloucester.
G	P	F	L	H	C	.	Goold's Cross	Tipperary	G. S. & W.	Thurles and Limerick Junction.
.	.	.	.	.	.	.	GOOLE—			
G	P	F	L	H	C	5 0			N. E.	Staddlethorpe and Thorne.
.	P	.	.	H	C	.	(Station, N. E.)	Yorks	G. C.	Over N. E. from Thorne Junction.
.	P	.	.	H	C	.			L. & Y.	Over N. E. from Goole Junction.
.	.	.	.	.	.	.	Creyke's Crossing	Yorks	N. E.	Goole.
G	.	F	L	.	.	50 0	Docks (L. & Y.)	Yorks	L. & Y. N. E.	Terminus. Over L. & Y. from Goole Junction.

EXPLANATION—G Goods Station.   P Passenger and Parcel Station.   P* Passenger, but not Parcel or Miscellaneous Traffic.
F Furniture Vans, Carriages, Portable Engines, and Machines on Wheels.   L Live Stock.
H Horse Boxes and Prize Cattle Vans.   C Carriages by Passenger Train.

STATION ACCOMMODATION.						CRANE POWER.	STATIONS, &c.	COUNTY.	COMPANY.	POSITION.
						Tons Cwts.	GOOLE—continued.			
.	.	.	.	.	.	. .	Junction	Yorks	L. & Y.— N. E.	Rawcliffe and Goole.
.	.	.	.	.	.	. .	Lord Beverley's Siding	Yorks	L. & Y.	Rawcliffe and Goole.
.	.	.	.	.	.	. .	Marshland Junction	Yorks	Axholme Jt.—N. E.	Goole and Reedness.
.	.	.	.	.	.	. .	Milnthorpe's Siding	Yorks	N. E.	Goole.
.	.	.	.	.	.	. .	Newman & Owston's Siding	Yorks	N. E.	Goole and Thorne.
.	.	.	.	.	.	. .	Peat Moss Works	Yorks	N. E.	Creyke's Crossing.
.	.	.	.	.	.	. .	Potter's Grange Junction	Yorks	N. E.	Goole.
.	.	.	.	.	.	. .	Goole Fields Siding	Yorks	Axholme Jt (L & Y & N E)	Reedness Junction.
.	.	.	.	.	.	. .	Goonbarrow Junction	Cornwall	G. W.	Bugle and Bridges.
.	.	.	.	.	.	. .	Goonvean Siding	Cornwall	G. W.	Drinnick Mill.
.	.	.	.	.	.	. .	Goose Hill Junction	Yorks	L. & Y.— Mid.	Normanton.
.	.	.	.	.	.	. .	Goosepool Siding	Durham	N. E.	Fighting Cocks.
G	P	.	.	.	.	5 0	Goostrey	Cheshire	L. & N. W.	Crewe and Stockport.
.	P	.	.	.	.	. .	Gopsill, Brown & Co.	Glo'ster	G. W.	Gloucester Docks.
G	P	.	.	.	.	. .	Goragh Wood	Armagh	G. N. (I.)	Newry and Armagh.
.	.	.	.	.	.	. .	Gorbals	Lanark	G B & K Jt (Cal & G & SW)	See Glasgow.
.	.	.	.	.	.	. .	Gorbals Junction	Lanark	G & S W—G. B. & K. Jt.	Glasgow.
G	P	F	L	H	C	. .	Gordon	Berwick	N. B.	Duns and St. Boswells.
.	.	.	.	.	.	. .	Gordon House Colliery	Durham	N. E.	Butterknowle.
.	.	.	.	.	.	. .	Gordon's, A., Warehouse	Cheshire	B'head Jt—CLC—NW&L	Birkenhead.
.	.	.	.	.	.	. .	Gordon Street	Lanark	Cal.	Same as Glasgow, Central.
G	P	F	L	H	C	1 10	Gorebridge	Edinboro'	N. B.	Edinburgh and Galashiels.
.	.	.	.	.	.	. .	Arniston Col. & Brick Wks.	Edinboro'	N. B.	Hardengreen and Gorebridge.
.	.	.	.	.	.	. .	Dean Works	Edinboro'	N. B.	Hardengreen and Gorebridge.
.	.	.	.	.	.	. .	Gorebridge Gas Works	Edinboro'	N. B.	Gorebridge.
.	.	.	.	.	.	. .	Gored Merthyr Colliery	Glamorg'n	G. W.	Resolven.
G	P	.	L	H	.	. .	Goresbridge	Carlow	G. S. & W.	Bagnalstown and Palace East.
G	P	F	L	H	C	2 0	Gorey	Wexford	D. W. & W.	Arklow and Wicklow.
.	P	.	.	.	.	. .	Gorey Pier	Jersey	Jersey Eastern	Terminus.
.	P	.	.	.	.	. .	Gorey Village	Jersey	Jersey Eastern	St. Helier and Gorey Pier.
.	.	.	.	.	.	. .	Gorgie	Edinboro'	Cal.— N. B.	See Edinburgh.
.	.	.	.	.	.	. .	Gorgie Junction	Edinboro'	N. B.	Edinburgh.
G	P	F	L	H	C	. .	Goring	Sussex	L. B. & S. C.	Worthing and Ford Junction.
G	P	F	L	H	C	6 0	Goring and Streatley	Oxon	G. W.	Reading and Oxford.
G	P	.	.	.	.	. .	Gorleston, North	Suffolk	N. & S. Jt. (GE & M & GN Jt.)	Yarmouth and Lowestoft.
.	.	.	.	.	.	. .	North Gorleston Junction	Suffolk	GE—M & GN Jt—N & S Jt	Yarmouth and Gorleston, North.
G	P	F	L	H	C	5 0	Gorleston-on-Sea	Suffolk	N. & S. Jt. (GE & M & GN Jt.)	Yarmouth and Lowestoft.
G	P	F	L	H	C	. .	Gormanston	Meath	G. N. (I.)	Dublin and Drogheda.
G	P	.	L	H	.	. .	Gorseinon	Glamorg'n	L. & N. W.	Llandilo and Swansea.
.	.	.	.	.	.	. .	Cambria Tin Plate Siding	Glamorg'n	L. & N. W.	Gorseinon and Pontardulais.
.	.	.	.	.	.	. .	Cory's Navigation Colliery Co.'s Mountain Colliery	Glamorg'n	L. & N. W.	Gorseinon and Pontardulais.
.	.	.	.	.	.	. .	Graigola Merthyr Colliery (Birch Rock Colliery)	Glamorg'n	L. & N. W.	Gorseinon and Pontardulais.
.	.	.	.	.	.	. .	Grovesend Steel Works	Glamorg'n	L. & N. W.	Gorseinon and Pontardulais.
.	.	.	.	.	.	. .	Grovesend Tin Plate Works	Glamorg'n	L. & N. W.	Gorseinon and Pontardulais.
.	.	.	.	.	.	. .	Jones' Siding	Glamorg'n	L. & N. W.	Gorseinon and Pontardulais.
.	.	.	.	.	.	. .	Lewis & Sons'— Bryngwyn Steel Works	Glamorg'n	L. & N. W.	Gorseinon and Gowerton.
.	.	.	.	.	.	. .	Tin Plate Works	Glamorg'n	L. & N. W.	Gorseinon and Pontardulais.
.	.	.	.	.	.	. .	Williams & Sons' Grovesend Colliery	Glamorg'n	L. & N. W.	Gorseinon and Pontardulais.
.	.	.	.	.	.	. .	Gorseinon Colliery	Glamorg'n	L. & N. W.	See Glasbrook Bros. (Gowerton).
.	.	.	.	.	.	. .	Gorsgoch Colliery	Carmarth'	L. & M. M.	Llanelly and Gilfach Colliery.
.	.	.	.	.	.	. .	Gors-y-Garnant	Carmarth'	G. W.	See Garnant.
G	P	F	L	H	C	. .	Gort (G. S. & W.)	Galway	{ G. S. & W. / M. G. W.	Ennis and Athenry. / Over G. S. & W. from Athenry.
.	P	.	.	.	.	. .	Gortatlea	Kerry	G. S. & W.	Tralee and Killarney.
.	.	.	.	.	.	. .	Gorton	Lancs	G. C.	See Manchester.
.	.	.	.	.	.	. .	Gorton Junction	Lancs	G. C.	Gorton and Hyde Road.
.	.	.	.	.	.	. .	Gorton Siding	Edinboro'	N. B.	See Hawthornden.
G	P	F	L	H	C	1 10	Gosberton	Lincoln	G. N. & G. E. Jt.	Spalding and Sleaford.
.	.	.	.	.	.	. .	Quadring Siding	Lincoln	G. N. & G. E. Jt.	Donington Road and Gosberton.
.	.	.	.	.	.	. .	Goschen Siding (N. B.)	Stirling	N. B.—Cal.	Falkirk, Grahamston.
.	.	.	.	.	.	. .	Gosforth	Cumb'land	Furness	Seascale.
G	P	.	.	.	.	. .	Gosforth	Northumb	N. E.	Newcastle and Backworth.
.	.	.	.	.	.	. .	Brunton Farm Siding	Northumb	N. E.	Gosforth.
.	.	.	.	.	.	. .	Coxlodge Col. Brick Works and Depôts	Northumb	N. E.	Gosforth.
.	.	.	.	.	.	. .	Gosforth Colliery	Northumb	N. E.	Gosforth.
.	.	.	.	.	.	. .	Hazelrigg Colliery	Northumb	N. E.	Gosforth.

EXPLANATION—G *Goods Station.*   P *Passenger and Parcel Station.*   P* *Passenger, but not Parcel or Miscellaneous Traffic.*
F *Furniture Vans, Carriages, Portable Engines, and Machines on Wheels.*   L *Live Stock.*
H *Horse Boxes and Prize Cattle Vans.*   C *Carriages by Passenger Train.*

STATION ACCOMMODATION.						CRANE POWER.	STATIONS, &c.	COUNTY.	COMPANY.	POSITION.
						Tons Cwts.	Gospel Oak	Middlesex	L & N W—N L—T & H Jt.	See London.
G	P	F	L	H	C	10 0	Gosport...........................	Hants......	L. & S.W.	Branch from Fareham.
							Royal Clarence Victualling Yard	Hants......	L. & S.W.	Extension from Gosport Station.
	P						Gosport Road and Alverstoke	Hants......	L. & S.W.	Fareham and Stokes Bay.
							Gossage and Son's—			
							East Siding	Lancs	L. & N. W.	Widnes.
							West Siding	Lancs	L. & N. W.—S. & M. Jt..	Widnes.
							Gossops Siding	Yorks	Axholme Jt. (L & Y & N E)	Reedness Junction.
							Goss's Siding	Mon	G. W.	Newport.
							Goss's Siding	Mon	A. (N & S W) D & R—G W	Same as Llanarth Wharf (Newport).
G	P		L				Goswick	Northumb	N. E.	Belford and Berwick.
G							Gotham	Notts	G. C.	Nottingham and Loughboro'.
							Paradise Siding	Notts	G. C.	Gotham.
							Sheppard's Siding	Notts	G. C.	Gotham.
							Stocker's Siding	Notts	G. C.	Gotham.
							Gotham Branch Junction ...	Notts	G. C.	Ruddington and Gotham.
							Gothard & Son's Siding ...	Derby......	Mid.	Chesterfield.
							Gothic Iron Foundry (R. & A. Mains) (N. B.)	Stirling ...	N. B.—Cal.	Falkirk, Grahamston.
G	P	F	L	H	C		Gott's Field	Yorks	G. N.	See Leeds.
							Goudhurst	Kent	S. E. & C.	Paddock Wood and Hawkhurst.
							Pattenden Siding	Kent	S. E. & C.	Goudhurst and Cranbrook.
							Gough, J., & Son's Siding	Suffolk ...	G. E.	Bury St. Edmunds.
							Gough's Siding	Bucks	L. & N. W.	Buckingham.
							Gould & Co.'s Siding	Cumb'land	N. B.	Same as Whitem's Sid. (Kirkbride).
							Goulding's Siding	Cork	G. S. & W.	Cork.
							Gould's Siding	N'hamptn	Mid.	Same as Olney Lime Wks. (Olney).
G	P		L	H			Gourdon	Kinc'rdine	N. B.	Montrose and Bervie.
							Gourlay Bros. & Co.'s Ship-building Yard	Forfar	Cal.—N. B.	Same as Camperdown Shipbuilding Yard (Dundee).
G	P	F	L	H	C	5 0	Gourock	Renfrew ...	Cal.	Extension from Greenock.
							Govan	Lanark ...	G & P Jt (Cal & G & S W)	See Glasgow.
							Govan Brick Works	Lanark ...	Cal.	Glasgow, Gushetfaulds.
							Govan Crane Works	Lanark ...	G & P Jt (Cal & G & S W)	Glasgow, Govan.
							Govan Cross	Lanark ..	Glas. Dist. Sub.	See Glasgow.
							Govan Electrical Works	Lanark ..	G & P Jt (Cal & G & S W)	Glasgow, Govan.
							Govan Iron Works & Collieries (Dixon's Sidings) ...	Lanark ..	Cal.	Glasgow, Gushetfaulds.
G	P						Govan Tube Works	Lanark ..	G & P Jt (Cal & G & S W)	Glasgow, Govan.
							Govilon	Mon......	L. & N. W.	Abergavenny and Merthyr.
							Gilwern Quarry	Mon	L. & N. W.	Govilon and Gilwern.
							Govilon Canal Wharf........	Mon	L. & N. W.	Govilon and Abergavenny.
							Gowdall Junction	Yorks	H. & B.	Kirk Smeaton and Carlton.
G	P		L	H	C		Gower Street (Met.)	Middlesex	Met.—G. W.	See London.
G	P		L			}	Gowerton	Glamorg'n	{ G. W.	Landore and Llanelly.
									{ L. & N. W.	Llandilo and Swansea.
							Baldwin's, Ltd.—			
							Elba Colliery	Glamorg'n	G. W.—L. & N. W.	Gowerton.
							Elba Steel Works	Glamorg'n	G. W.—L. & N. W.	Gowerton.
							Glasbrook Bros.—			
							Fairwood Tin Plate Wks.	Glamorg'n	G. W.—L. & N. W.	Gowerton.
							Garngoch Colliery	Glamorg'n	G. W.—L. & N. W.	Gowerton.
							Gorseinon Colliery	Glamorg'n	L. & N. W.	Gowerton and Gorseinon.
							Loughor Colliery.............	Glamorg'n	G. W.	Gowerton and Loughor.
							Marker's Siding	Glamorg'n	L. & N. W.	Gowerton and Penclawdd.
G	P	F	L	H	C		Gowhole Goods Junction	Derby......	Mid.	New Mills and Bugsworth.
G	P		L	H			Gowran	Kilkenny..	G. S. & W.	Bagnalstown and Kilkenny.
G	P						Goxhill	Lincoln ...	G. C.	Barnetby and New Holland.
G	P						Goxhill	Yorks	N. E.	Hull and Hornsea.
							Goyt Mill Co.'s Siding	Derby......	L. & N. W.	Whaley Bridge.
	P*						Grace & Co.'s Paper Mill ...	Durham ...	N. E.	Swalwell.
							Gracehill	Antrim ...	Ballycastle	Ballymoney and Ballycastle.
							Gradwell, W., & Co.—			
							Creosote Works	Lancs	Furness	Barrow.
							Hindpool Saw Mills	Lancs	Furness	Barrow.
G	P	F	L	H	C		Grafham	Hunts......	Mid.	Huntingdon and Thrapston.
G	P	F	L	H	C	5 0	Grafton & Burbage	Wilts	M. & S. W. Jn.	Savernake and Andover.
							Grafton & Co.'s Siding	Beds	Mid.	Bedford.
							Grafton (Duke of) Siding ...	Norfolk ...	G. E.	Barnham.
							Graham & Co.'s Siding........	Lancs	P.&L.Jt. (L & N W. & L & Y)	Preston, Deepdale.
							Graham & Morton's Stores ...	Stirling ...	Cal.	Stirling.

EXPLANATION—G *Goods Station.* P *Passenger and Parcel Station.* P* *Passenger, but not Parcel or Miscellaneous Traffic.*
F *Furniture Vans, Carriages, Portable Engines, and Machines on Wheels.* L *Live Stock.*
H *Horse Boxes and Prize Cattle Vans.* C *Carriages by Passenger Train.*

STATION ACCOMMODATION.						CRANE POWER.	STATIONS, &c.	COUNTY.	COMPANY.	POSITION.
						Tons Cwts.				
.	.	.	.	.	.		Graham Bros. & Co.'s Siding (Black Vein Colliery)	Mon	L. & N. W.	Brynmawr.
.	.	.	.	.	.		Graham Morton & Co.'s Sid.	Yorks	G. N.	Leeds, Hunslet.
.	.	.	.	.	.		Graham's Brick Yard	Durham	N. E.	Fighting Cocks.
.	.	.	.	.	.		Grahamsley Colliery	Durham	N. E.	Same as Pease & Partners' Lucy Colliery (Crook).
.	.	.	.	.	.		Graham's Navigation Colliery	Mon	L. & N. W.	Sirhowy.
.	.	.	.	.	.		Graham's Siding (L. & N. W.)	Staffs	L. & N. W.—G. W.	Wednesbury.
.	.	.	.	.	.		Grahamston (N. B.)	Stirling	N. B.—Cal.	See Falkirk.
.	.	.	.	.	.		Grahamston Iron Wks. (N.B.)	Stirling	N. B.—Cal.	Falkirk, Grahamston.
.	.	.	.	.	.		Graham Street Junction	Edinboro'	N. B.	Bonnington Pass. and Bonnington Goods.
.	.	.	.	.	.		Graig Cwm Colliery (Mid.) ...	Glamorg'n	Mid.—G. W.—L. & N. W.	Clydach-on-Tawe.
.	.	.	.	.	.		Graigddu Brick Works Siding	Mon	G. W.	Pontnewynydd.
.	.	.	.	.	.		Graig Fawr Colliery	Mon	G. W.	Aberbeeg.
.	.	.	.	.	.		Graig Level Colliery	Glamorg'n	G. W.	Dare Junction.
.	.	.	.	.	.		Graigola Col. (Gueret's) (Mid.)	Glamorg'n	Mid.—G. W.—L. & N. W.	Clydach-on-Tawe.
.	.	.	.	.	.		Graigola Merthyr Colliery (Birch Rock Colliery)	Glamorg'n	L. & N. W.	Gorseinon.
.	.	.	.	.	.		Graigola Merthyr Co.'s Upper & Lower Cols. (Mid)	Glamorg'n	Mid.—G. W.—L. & N. W.	{ See Cory, Yeo & Co.'s Collieries (Clydach-on-Tawe).
.	.	.	.	.	.		Graigola Merthyr Co.'s Patent Fuel Works	Glamorg'n	GW—LNW—Mid—RSB	Swansea.
.	.	.	.	.	.		Graig Quarry	Denbigh	L. & N. W.	Same as Jones' Siding (Denbigh).
.	.	.	.	.	.		Graig-yr-Hesk Quarry	Glamorg'n	T. V.	Same as Craig-yr-Hesk Quarry (Pontypridd).
G	P	F	L	H	.	2 0	Grampound Road	Cornwall ..	G. W.	Truro and St. Austell.
G	P	.	.	.	.		Grandborough Road	Bucks	Met.	Aylesbury and Verney Junction.
.	.	.	.	.	.		Grandidge's Timber Depôt ...	Cheshire..	B'head Jt—CLC—NW&L	Birkenhead.
.	.	.	.	.	.		Grand Junction	Warwick..	L. & N. W.—Mid.	Birmingham.
G	P	F	L	H	C	3 0	Grandtully	Perth	High.	Ballinluig and Aberfeldy.
.	.	.	.	.	.		Grane Brick & Stone Co.'s Sid.	Lancs	L. & Y.	Grane Road.
G	.	.	.	.	.	5 0	Grane Road	Lancs	L. & Y.	Haslingden and Helmshore.
.	.	.	.	.	.		Grane Bk. & Stone Co.'s Sid.	Lancs	L. & Y.	Grane Road.
.	.	.	.	.	.		Haslingden Gas Co.'s Sid.	Lancs	L. & Y.	Grane Road.
G	P	.	L	H	.	1 10	Grange	Banff	G. N. of S.	Huntly and Keith.
.	P	.	.	.	.		Grange	Kilkenny..	G. S. & W.	Clonmel and Waterford.
.	.	.	.	.	.		Grange (Low Level)	Glamorg'n	T. V.	See Grangetown.
.	.	.	.	.	.		Grange Brick Works............	Ayr	G. & S.W.	Kilmarnock.
.	.	.	.	.	.		Grange Colliery	Lancs	G. C. (Wigan Jn.)	See Crompton & Shawcross (Hindley and Platt Bridge).
.	.	.	.	.	.		Grange Colliery	L'lithgow	N. B.	Bo'ness.
.	.	.	.	.	.		Grange Colliery	Yorks	G. C.	See Newton Chambers & Co. (Grange Lane).
G	P	.	.	.	.		Grange Con............	Wicklow..	G. S. & W.	Sallins and Tullow.
G	P	F	L	H	C	1 10	Grange Court	Glo'ster ...	G. W.	Gloucester and Hereford.
.	.	.	.	.	.		Albion Carriage & Wagon Works Siding	Glo'ster ...	G. W.	Grange Court.
.	.	.	.	.	.		Grange Foundry............	Ayr	G. & S.W.	Kilmarnock.
.	.	.	.	.	.		Grange Foundry............	L'lithgow	N. B.	Bo'ness.
.	.	.	.	.	.		Grange Gas Works (High and Low Levels)	Glamorg'n	T. V.	Grangetown.
G	P	.	.	.	.		Grange Hill	Essex	G. E.	Woodford and Ilford.
.	.	.	.	.	.		Grange Iron Works	Durham	N. E.	Durham.
.	.	.	.	.	.		Grange Iron Works (N. B. ...	Stirling	N. B.—Cal.	Same as Grangemouth Iron Co. (Falkirk).
G	P	.	.	.	.		Grange Lane	Yorks	G. C.	Sheffield and Barnsley.
.	.	.	.	.	.		Duke's Siding	Yorks	G. C.	Grange Lane.
.	.	.	.	.	.		Grange Lane Colliery	Yorks	G. C.	Grange Lane.
.	.	.	.	.	.		Greasboro' Colliery............	Yorks	G. C.	Grange Lane.
.	.	.	.	.	.		Newton Chambers & Co.— Grange Colliery	Yorks	G. C.	Grange Lane.
.	.	.	.	.	.		Scholes' Colliery	Yorks	G. C	Grange Lane.
.	.	.	.	.	.		Grange Lane Mineral Yard ...	Cheshire...	B'head Jt. (G W & L N W)	Birkenhead.
.	.	.	.	.	.		Grange Lane Siding	Cheshire...	L. & N. W.	See Evans, R., & Co. (Acton Bridge).
G	P	F	L	H	C	5 0	Grangemouth (Cal.)	Stirling ...	{ Cal. { N. B.	Branch near Grahamston. Over Cal. fr. Grangemouth Bch. Jn.
.	.	.	.	.	.		Abergrange Saw Mills	Stirling ...	Cal.	Grangemouth.
.	.	.	.	.	.		Brownlee's Sleeper Mill ...	Stirling ...	Cal.	Grangemouth Harbour.
.	.	.	.	.	.		Bryson & Co.'s Siding	Stirling ...	Cal.	Grangemouth.
.	.	.	.	.	.		Caledonian Saw Mills (Cal.)	Stirling ...	Cal.—N. B.	Grangemouth Harbour.
.	.	.	.	.	.		Christie's Sleeper Mill (Cal.)	Stirling ...	Cal.—N. B.	Grangemouth Harbour.

EXPLANATION—G *Goods Station.*   P *Passenger and Parcel Station.*   P* *Passenger, but not Parcel or Miscellaneous Traffic.*
F *Furniture Vans, Carriages, Portable Engines, and Machines on Wheels.*   L *Live Stock.*
H *Horse Boxes and Prize Cattle Vans.*   C *Carriages by Passenger Train.*

Station Accommodation.	Crane Power.	Stations, &c.	County.	Company.	Position.
	Tons Cwts.	Grangemouth (Cal.)—*continued.*			
		Forth Saw Mills (M'Pherson & M'Laren's) (Cal.).........	Stirling ...	Cal.—N. B.	Grangemouth Harbour.
G	25 0	Grangemouth Harbour (Cal.)	Stirling ...	Cal.—N. B.	Grangemouth.
. . . .		Grangemouth Saw Mill (Muirhead & Son) (Cal.)	Stirling ...	Cal.—N. B.	Grangemouth.
. . . .		Kirkwood & Co.'s Siding...	Stirling ...	Cal.	Grangemouth.
. . . .		Lauriston Iron Works (Thornbridge Sid.) (Cal.)	Stirling ...	Cal.—N. B.	Grahamston and Grangemouth.
. . . .		Scottish Co-operative Wholesale Society's Soap Works (Cal.)	Stirling ...	Cal.—N. B.	Grangemouth.
. . . .		Watt, Torrance & Co.'s Saw Mill (Cal.)	Stirling ...	Cal.—N. B.	Grangemouth.
. . . .		Grangemouth Branch Junc....	Stirling ...	Cal.—N. B.	Falkirk.
. . . .		Grangemouth Iron Co.'s Grange Iron Works (N.B.)	Stirling ...	N. B.—Cal.	Falkirk, Grahamston.
G P F L H C	3 0	Grange-over-Sands............	Lancs	Furness	Carnforth and Ulverston.
. . . .		Meathop Mineral Siding ...	W'morlnd	Furness	Grange-over-Sands and Arnside.
. . . .		Grangepans Wood Yard	L'lithgow	N. B.	See Love & Stewart's (Bo'ness).
. . . .		Grange Quarry	Durham ...	N. E.	Trimdon.
. . . .		Grange Road	Cheshire...	B'head Jt.—L. & N. W.	See Birkenhead Town.
G P F L H C		Grange Road	Sussex ...	L. B. & S. C.	East Grinstead and Three Bridges.
. . . .		Grange Siding....................	Lanark ...	Cal.	Carstairs.
. . . .		Cairngryffe Siding	Lanark ...	Cal.	Carstairs.
. . . .		Pettinain Siding............	Lanark ...	Cal.	Carstairs.
. . . .		Grange Siding....................	Perth	Cal.	Inchture.
. P		Grangetown	Yorks ...	N. E.	Middlesbro' and Redcar.
G P P P . . .		Grangetown (T. V.)	Glamorg'n	T. V. / Barry	Cardiff and Penarth Dock. / Over T. V. from Cogan Junction.
G . F . . C	2 10	Canton Siding	Glamorg'n	T. V.	Grangetown and Radyr.
. . . .		Cardiff Alkali Co.'s Siding	Glamorg'n	T. V.	Grangetown and Canton Siding.
. . . .		Cardiff Candle Co.'s Works	Glamorg'n	T. V.	Grangetown and Penarth Harbour.
. . . .		Dobson's Siding	Glamorg'n	T. V.	Grangetown and Canton Siding.
. . . .		Grange Gas Works (High Level)	Glamorg'n	T. V.	Grangetown and Penarth Harbour.
G		Grange Gas Works (Low Level)	Glamorg'n	T. V.	Grangetown and Penarth Harbour.
. . . .		Grange, Low Level	Glamorg'n	T. V.	Grangetown and Penarth Harbour.
. . . .		Windsor Slipway	Glamorg'n	T. V.	Grangetown and Penarth Harbour.
. . . .		Grangetown Junction	Glamorg'n	T. V.	Grangetown and Penarth Dock.
. . . .		Grange Wharf....................	Staffs ...	N. S.	Branch—Etruria and Longport.
. . . .		Heath & Son's Colliery ...	Staffs ...	N. S.	Grange Wharf.
. . . .		Granite Concrete Co.'s Siding	Lancs	N.U.Jt. (L & N W & L & Y)	Preston.
. . . .		Grant & Co.'s Siding	Staffs ...	Mid.	Burton-on-Trent.
G P F L H C	10 0	Grantham............	Lincoln ...	G. N.	Peterborough and Newark.
. . . .		Ambergate Yard	Lincoln ...	G. N.	Branch near Grantham.
. . . .		Bell's, H., Siding............	Lincoln ...	G. N.	Branch from Ambergate Yard.
. . . .		Grantham Canal Station ...	Lincoln ...	G. N.	Same as Ambergate Yard.
. . . .		Grantham Waterworks (Saltersford Siding)	Lincoln ...	G. N.	Grantham and Great Ponton.
. . . .		Hornsby & Son's Siding ...	Lincoln ...	G. N.	Grantham.
. . . .		Lee & Grinling's Siding ...	Lincoln ...	G. N.	Grantham and Sedgebrook.
. . . .		Wheeldon's Siding	Lincoln ...	G. N.	Grantham and Sedgebrook.
G . . F L . .	5 0	Granton....................	Edinboro'	Cal. / N. B.	Branch near Leith. / Branch from Edinburgh.
G P F L H C	10 0				
. . . .		Calder, Dixon & Co.'s Creosote Works	Edinboro'	Cal. / N. B.	Granton. / West Beach Line.
G		Crewe Junction Sidings ...	Edinboro'	Cal.	Craigleith and Granton.
. . . .		Edinburgh and Leith Gas Corporation Sidings ...	Edinboro'	Cal. / N. B.	Granton. / West Beach Line.
. . . .		Fleming & Co.'s Works......	Edinboro'	Cal. / N. B.	Granton. / West Beach Line.
G	20 0	Granton Gas Works	Edinboro'	Cal.	Granton.
G	10 0	Granton Harbour	Edinboro'	Cal.—N. B.	Extension from Granton.
. . . .		Granton Middle Pier	Edinboro'	Cal.—N. B.	Extension from Granton.
. . . .		Granton Mineral Wharf ...	Edinboro'	Cal.—N. B.	Same as Granton West Pier.
. . . .		Granton Timber Co.'s Sid.	Edinboro'	Cal. / N. B.	Granton. / West Beach Line.
G	20 0	Granton Western Wharf ... Granton West Pier (Mineral Wharf)	Edinboro' Edinboro'	Cal. Cal.—N. B.	Granton. Extension from Granton.

Station Accommodation						Crane Power.		Stations, &c.	County.	Company.	Position.
						Tons	Cwts.	Granton—*continued.*			
..	..	..	..	..	..	..	..	Hawthorn & Co.'s Siding ...	Edinboro'	{ Cal.	Granton.
										N. B.	West Beach Line.
..	..	..	..	..	..	..	..	Mushet & Co.'s Works	Edinboro'	{ Cal.	Granton.
										N. B.	West Beach Line.
..	..	..	..	..	..	..	..	West Beach Line	Edinboro'	Cal.—N. B.	Extension from Granton.
..	..	..	..	..	..	..	..	Granton Junction	Edinboro'	Cal.—N. B.	Granton, Cal. and N. B. Stations.
..	P	..	..	..	..	..	..	Granton Road	Edinboro'	Cal.	Edinburgh and Leith.
G	P	F	L	H	C	1	10	} Grantown .... {	Elgin&Mo'	High.	Forres and Boat of Garten.
G	P	F	L	H	C	1	5		Inverness	G. N. of S.	Craigellachie and Boat of Garten.
								Grantown-on-Spey	Elgin&Mo'	High.	Same as Grantown.
G	P	F	L	H	C	1	5	Grantshouse	Berwick ...	N. B.	Dunbar and Berwick.
..	..	..	..	..	..	..	..	Grant's Siding	Lancs	L. & Y.	Ramsbottom.
..	..	..	..	..	..	..	..	Grant's Siding (Seafield Engineering Works)	Renfrew ...	G & P Jt (Cal & G & S W)	Cardonald.
..	..	..	..	..	..	..	..	Granville Colliery (Mid.)	Derby	Mid.—L. & N. W.	Woodville.
..	..	..	..	..	..	..	..	Granville Siding................	Staffs	N. S.	See Shelton Iron, Steel, & Coal Co. (Etruria).
..	..	..	..	..	..	..	..	Grassendale	Lancs	C. L. C. (G C, G N & Mid)	See Cressington and Grassendale.
..	..	..	..	..	..	..	..	Grassholme Siding............	Yorks	N. E.	Mickleton.
G	P	F	L	H	C	3	0	Grassington and Threshfield	Yorks	Mid.	Branch—Embsay and Skipton.
G	P	..	..	..	..	..	..	} Grassmoor (G. C.) {	Derby	{ G. C.	Chesterfield and Nottingham.
G										L. & N. W.	Over G. N. and G. C. Lines
..	..	..	..	..	..	..	..	Bond's Main Colliery (G.C.)	Derby	G. C.—G. N.—L. & N. W.	Grassmoor.
..	..	..	..	..	..	..	..	Calow Colliery................	Derby	G. C.	Grassmoor.
..	..	..	..	..	..	..	..	East Street Siding............	Derby	G. C.	Grassmoor.
..	..	..	..	..	..	..	..	Grassmoor Collieries (G. C.)	Derby	G. C.—G. N.—L. & N. W.	Grassmoor.
..	..	..	..	..	..	..	..	Grassmoor No. 6 Pit	Derby	G. C.	Grassmoor.
..	..	..	..	..	..	..	..	Grassmoor Collieries (G. C.)..	Derby	G. C.—G. N.—L. & N. W.	Grassmoor.
..	..	..	..	..	..	..	..	Grassmoor Colliery (Mid.)..	Derby	Mid.—L. D. & E. C.	Hasland.
..	..	..	..	..	..	..	..	Grassmoor Junction	Cambs......	G. E.—G. N. & G. E. Jt.	March.
G	P	F	L	H	C	4	0	Grateley	Hants	L. & S.W.	Andover Junction and Salisbury.
..	..	..	..	..	..	..	..	Gravel Lane	Surrey	S. E. & C.	See London.
..	P	..	..	..	..	..	..	Gravelly Hill	Warwick..	L. & N. W.	Birmingham and Lichfield.
..	..	..	..	..	..	..	..	Graveney Siding	Kent	S. E. & C.	Faversham.
								GRAVESEND—			
G	P	F	L	H	C	10	0	Central	Kent	S. E. & C.	Dartford and Strood.
						2	15	Pier	Kent	S. E. & C.	Branch from Farningham Road.
..	P	..	..	..	..	..	..	Town Pier	Kent	L. T. & S.	Ferry from Tilbury.
..	..	..	..	..	..	..	..	Uralite Co.'s Siding	Kent	S. E. & C.	Gravesend Central and Cliffe.
G	P	F	L	H	C	..	..	West	Kent	L. T. & S.	Ferry from Tilbury.
G	P	F	L	H	C	10	0	West Street	Kent	S. E. & C.	Branch from Farningham Road.
..	..	..	..	..	..	..	..	Gray, C. H., Siding	Essex	G. E.	{ Chelmsford. Witham.
..	..	..	..	..	..	..	..	Gray Colliery	Mon	G. W.	Abertillery.
G	P	..	L	H	..	..	..	Grayrigg	W'morlnd	L. & N. W.	Lancaster and Penrith.
								Gray's—			
..	..	..	..	..	..	..	..	Central Ship Yard............	Durham ...	N. E.	West Hartlepool.
..	..	..	..	..	..	..	..	Graving Dock	Durham ...	N. E.	West Hartlepool.
..	..	..	..	..	..	..	..	Old Ship Yard................	Durham ...	N. E.	West Hartlepool.
..	..	..	..	..	..	..	..	Gray's Brickyard	Northumb	N. E.	Newcastle-on-Tyne.
..	..	..	..	..	..	..	..	Gray's Grain Store............	Stirling ...	Cal.	Stirling.
G	P	F	L	H	C	3	0	Grays	Essex	L. T. & S.	Barking and Tilbury.
								Associated Portland Cement Manufacturers' Siding (Hilton, Anderson & Co.'s Branch)	Essex	L. T. & S.	Grays.
..	..	..	..	..	..	..	..	Gray's Chalk Quarries	Essex	L. T. & S.	Grays.
..	..	..	..	..	..	..	..	Seabrooke's Siding	Essex	L. T. & S.	Grays.
..	..	..	..	..	..	..	..	Wall's Siding	Essex	L. T. & S.	Grays.
..	..	..	..	..	..	..	..	West Thurrock Siding......	Essex	L. T. & S.	Grays and Purfleet.
..	..	..	..	..	..	..	..	Wouldham Cement Co.'s Sid	Essex	L. T. & S.	Grays.
..	..	..	..	..	..	..	..	Grayson, Lowood & Co.'s Sid.	Yorks	N. E.	Castleton.
..	..	..	..	..	..	..	..	Grayson's Siding	Lancs	L. & N. W.	Same as Garston Graving Dock and Shipbuilding Co.'s Siding (Garston Docks).
..	..	..	..	..	..	..	..	Grazebrooks Siding	Worcester	G. W.	Netherton.
..	..	..	..	..	..	..	..	Greasbro' Colliery..............	Yorks	{ G. C.	Grange Lane.
										Mid.	Masbro' and Rotherham.
..	..	..	..	..	..	..	..	Greasley	Notts	G. N.	See Newthorpe, Greasley, and Shipley Gate.
G	P	..	..	H	..	..	..	Great Alne	Warwick..	G. W.	Alcester and Bearley.

EXPLANATION—G *Goods Station.*   P *Passenger and Parcel Station.*   P* *Passenger, but not Parcel or Miscellaneous Traffic.*
F *Furniture Vans, Carriages, Portable Engines, and Machines on Wheels.*   L *Live Stock.*
H *Horse Boxes and Prize Cattle Vans.*   C *Carriages by Passenger Train.*

STATION ACCOMMODATION.						CRANE POWER.	STATIONS, &c.	COUNTY.	COMPANY.	POSITION.
						Tons Cwts.				
G	P	F	L	H	C	5 0	Great Ayton	Yorks	N. E.	Middlesbro' and Battersby.
.	.	.	.	.	.	. .	Cliff Rigg Quarry	Yorks	N. E.	Great Ayton.
.	.	.	.	.	.	. .	Gribdale Quarry...............	Yorks	N. E.	Great Ayton.
.	.	.	.	.	.	. .	Newton Qry.(Bradley'sSid.)	Yorks	N. E.	Great Ayton.
G	P	.	L	H	.	. .	Great Barr	Staffs	L. & N. W.	Birmingham and Wolverhampton.
.	.	.	.	.	.	. .	Hamstead Colliery	Staffs	L. & N. W.	Great Barr and Newton Road.
G	P	F	L	H	C	. .	Great Bentley	Essex	G. E.	Colchester and Clacton-on-Sea.
.	.	.	.	.	.	. .	Simmon's Siding	Essex	G. E.	Great Bentley.
.	.	.	.	.	.	. .	Great Bowdon Sidings	Leicester ..	Mid.	Market Harboro'.
							GREAT BRIDGE—			
G	P	.	L	.	.	10 0	(Station)	Staffs	G. W.	Dudley and Swan Village.
G	P	F	L	H	C	15 0 ⎫	(Station, L. & N. W.)	Staffs	⎰ L. & N. W.	Dudley and Walsall.
G	.	F	L	H	.	15 0 ⎭			⎱ Mid.	Over L. & N. W. from Walsall Junc.
.	.	.	.	.	.	. .	Freakley's Golds Green Sid.	Staffs	L. & N. W.	Great Bridge and Wednesbury.
.	.	.	.	.	.	. .	Horsley Iron Co.'s Siding (L. & N. W.)	Staffs	L. & N. W.—Mid.	Great Bridge and Dudley Port.
.	.	.	.	.	.	. .	Junction	Staffs	G. W.—L. & N. W.	Great Bridge and Dudley.
.	.	.	.	.	.	. .	Stonehewer & Co.'s Siding (L. & N. W.)	Staffs	L. & N. W.—Mid.	Great Bridge and Dudley Port.
G	P	.	L	H	.	. .	Great Bridgeford	Staffs	L. & N. W.	Crewe and Stafford.
G	P	F	L	H	.	. .	Great Broughton	Cumb'land	C. & W. Jn.	Workington and Linefoot Junction.
.	.	.	.	.	.	. .	Buckhill Pit..................	Cumb'land	C. & W. Jn.	Great Broughton and Seaton.
.	.	.	.	.	.	. .	Great Central Co.'s Limestone Siding	Derby	Mid.	Peak Forest.
.	.	.	.	.	.	. .	Great Central Co-operative Engineering & Ship Repairing Co.'s Siding (G. C.)......	Lincoln ...	G. C.—G. N.	Grimsby.
							Great Central Railway Co.—			
.	.	.	.	.	.	. .	Bonded Stores..................	Yorks	G. C.	Sheffield, Bridgehouses.
.	.	.	.	.	.	. .	Engineer's Siding	Yorks	G. C.	Sheffield, Park.
.	.	.	.	.	.	. .	Loco., Carriage, & Wagon Department & General Stores Siding (G.C.)......	Lancs	G C—GW—LN W—Mid.	Manchester, Openshaw.
.	.	.	.	.	.	. .	Locomotive Stores	Yorks	G. C.	Sheffield, Bridgehouses.
.	.	.	.	.	.	. .	Oil Gas Works	Yorks	G. C.	Sheffield, Park.
G	P	F	L	.	.	1 10	Great Chesterford	Essex	G. E.	Cambridge and Bishops Stortford.
.	.	.	.	.	.	. .	Littlebury Siding	Essex	G. E.	Great Chesterford and Audley End.
G	P	.	L	H	.	. .	Great Coates	Lincoln ...	G. C.	Barnetby and Grimsby.
.	.	.	.	.	.	. .	Great Cornards Siding	Suffolk ...	G. E.	Sudbury.
G	P	F	L	H	C	. .	Great Dalby..................	Leicester ..	G. N. & L. & N. W. Jt.	Market Harboro' & Melton Mowbray.
.	.	.	.	.	.	. .	Greatfields Siding	Sussex ...	L. B. & S. C.	Polegate.
G	P	.	.	.	.	. .	Great Glen	Leicester ..	Mid.	Leicester and Market Harboro'.
.	.	.	.	.	.	. .	Great Grimsby	Lincoln ...	G. C.—G. N.	See Grimsby.
G	P	.	L	H	.	. .	Greatham	Durham ...	N. E.	Stockton and West Hartlepool.
.	.	.	.	.	.	. .	Cowpen Bewlay Siding......	Durham ...	N. E.	Greatham.
.	.	.	.	.	.	. .	Greatham Salt & Brine Wks.	Durham ...	N. E.	Greatham.
G	P	.	L	H	.	8 0	Great Harwood	Lancs	L. & Y.	Loop—Blackburn and Burnley.
.	.	.	.	.	.	. .	Accrington Gas and Water Board Siding	Lancs	L. & Y.	Great Harwood.
.	.	.	.	.	.	. .	Altham Col. Co.'s Siding...	Lancs	L. & Y.	Great Harwood.
.	.	.	.	.	.	. .	Martholme Colliery	Lancs	L. & Y.	Great Harwood.
.	P	.	.	.	.	. .	Great Haywood (N. S.)	Staffs	⎰ N. S.	Colwich and Hixon.
									⎱ L. & N. W.	Over N. S. Line.
.	.	.	.	.	.	. .	Great Horton	Yorks	G. N.	See Bradford.
.	.	.	.	.	.	. .	Great Howard Street	Lancs	L. & Y.	See Liverpool.
.	.	.	.	.	.	. .	Great Lever Siding	Lancs	L. & Y.	Same as Earl Bradford's Sid.(Bolton).
.	P	.	.	.	.	. .	Great Linford	Bucks	L. & N. W.	Newport Pagnell and Wolverton.
.	.	.	.	.	.	. .	Great Longstone...............	Derby	Mid.	Same as Longstone.
G	P	F	L	H	C	1 10 ⎫	Great Malvern (G. W.)......	Worcester	G. W.—Mid.	See Malvern, Great.
.	P	.	.	H	C	. . ⎭	Great Missenden (Met.)	Bucks	⎰ Met.	Rickmansworth and Aylesbury.
									⎱ G. C.	Over Metropolitan Line.
.	.	.	.	.	.	. .	Great Mountain Colliery ...	Carmarth	L. & M. M.	Tumble.
.	.	.	.	.	.	. .	Great Northern Brewery ...	Louth	G. N. (I.)	Dundalk.
.	.	.	.	.	.	. .	Great Northern Co.'s Loco., Carriage, Wagon & Stores Departments Sids. (G. N.).	Yorks	G. N.—G. C.	Doncaster.
G	P	.	L	H	C	. .	Great Ormesby	Norfolk ...	Mid. & G. N. Jt...........	North Walsham Town & Yarmouth Beach.
G	P	F	L	H	C	5 0	Great Ponton	Lincoln ...	G. N.	Peterboro' and Grantham.
.	.	.	.	.	.	. .	Great Rocks Lime Works ...	Derby	Mid.	Peak Forest.
G	P	.	L	H	.	. .	Great Shefford	Berks	L'bourn Valley	Newbury and Lambourn.
G	P	.	.	H	C	. .	Great Somerford...............	Wilts	G. W.	Dauntsey and Malmesbury.

EXPLANATION—G *Goods Station.*   P *Passenger and Parcel Station.*   P* *Passenger, but not Parcel or Miscellaneous Traffic.*
F *Furniture Vans, Carriages, Portable Engines, and Machines on Wheels.*   L *Live Stock.*
H *Horse Boxes and Prize Cattle Vans.*   C *Carriages by Passenger Train.*

STATION ACCOMMODATION.	CRANE POWER.	STATIONS, &c.	COUNTY.	COMPANY.	POSITION.
	Tons Cwts	Great Treviscoe Siding	Cornwall ..	G. W.	Drinnick Mill.
		Great Victoria Street	Antrim ...	G. N. (I.)	See Belfast.
		Great Western Carriage Wks.	Wilts	G. W.	Swindon.
		Great Western Colliery	Glos'ter	G. W.	Bristol.
		Great Western Colliery	Glamorg'n	T. V.	Same as Gyfeillon Colliery (Hafod).
		Great Western Colliery (N.B.)	Lanark ...	N. B.—Cal.	Glasgow, Great Western Road.
		Great Western Docks	Devon	G. W.	Plymouth.
		Great Western Loco. Works..	Glo'ster	G. W.	Swindon.
		Great Western Nail Works Sid.	Salop	G. W.	Oakengates.
		Great Western Road (N.B.)..	Lanark	N. B.—Cal.	See Glasgow.
		Great Western Road Siding..	Lanark ...	Cal.	See Glasgow.
		Great Western Siding	Glo'ster	S. & Wye Jt.(G. W. & Mid.)	Speech House Road.
		Great Western Steam Laundry Siding	Lanark	N. B.	Glasgow, Whiteinch.
		Great Western Wharf	Mon	G. W.	Same as East Usk Wharf (Newport).
		Great Wyrley Colliery	Staffs	L. & N. W.	Wyrley and Church Bridge.
		Greaves, Bull & Lakin—			
		Siding	Warwick..	L. & N. W.	Southam and Long Itchington.
		Works	Warwick..	G. W.	Southam Road and Harbury.
		Works	Warwick..	G. W.	Wilmcote.
		Greave's Siding	Merioneth	L. & N. W.	Blaenau Festiniog.
		Gree Depôt	Ayrshire...	Cal.	See Giffen.
		Greenall, Whitley & Co.'s Wilderspool Brewery	Lancs	L. & N. W.	Warrington, Arpley.
		Green & Co.'s Pottery Works (Mid.)	Derby	Mid.—L. & N. W.	Woodville.
		Green, J., & Sons' Siding	Yorks	Mid.	Same as Hambleton Quarries (Bolton Abbey).
		Green's, H., Siding	Lancs	L. & N. W.	Manchester, London Road.
		Green's, H., Siding (G. C.)..	Lancs	G.C.—Mid.	Manchester, Ardwick.
		Green's, R. & H., Siding	Middlesex	Mid.	London, Poplar.
G P		Green's Siding	Hereford ..	G. W.	Westbrook and Clifford.
		Green's Siding	Lancs	L. & N. W.	Tyldesley.
		Ramsden's Shakerley Col.	Lancs	L. & N. W.	Green's Siding.
		Tyldesley Coal Co.'s Tyldesley Colliery	Lancs	L. & N. W.	Green's Siding.
		Green's Siding	Yorks	G. N.—L. & Y.	Wakefield, Kirkgate.
		Green's Siding	Yorks	Mid.	Rylstone.
		Green's Wharf (Mid.)	Warwick..	Mid.—L. & N. W.	Stockingford.
		Green Ayre	Lancs	Mid.	See Lancaster.
		Greenbank (C. L. C.)	Cheshire.	C. L. C.—L. & N. W.	See Hartford and Greenbank.
		Greenbank	Lancs	L. & N. W.	See Preston.
		Greenbank Works	Lancs	L. & N. W.	See United Alkali Co. (St. Helens).
		Greencastle	Antrim	N. C. Com. (Mid.)	See Belfast.
		Greencastle	Down	{ D. N. & G.	By Steamer from Greenore.
G P . L				{ L. & N. W.	By Steamer from Holyhead via Greenore.
		Greendykes Siding	L'lithgow	N. B.	Broxburn Junction.
		Greenend Siding	Roxburgh	N. B.	Belses.
		Greener's Glass Works	Durham ..	N. E.	Millfield.
G P	5 - 0	Greenfield	Yorks	L. & N. W.	Huddersfield and Stalybridge.
		Chatterton's Siding	Yorks	L. & N. W.	Delph Branch.
		Whitehead's Royal George Siding	Yorks	L. & N. W.	Greenfield and Mossley.
		Greenfield Colliery	Lanark	Cal.	Hamilton, Central.
		Greenfield Colliery, No. 7	Lanark	N. B.	Shettleston.
		Greenfield Foundry	Lanark	N. B.	Hamilton, Burnbank.
		Greenfield's Siding	Salop	G. W.	Shrewsbury.
		Greenfoot Quarry	Durham	N. E.	Eastgate.
		Greenfoot Sand Quarry	Lanark	Cal.	Glenboig.
		Greenfoot Siding	Lanark	Cal.	See Glenboig.
		Greenford Green	Middlesex	Met. Dist.	See Sudbury Hill (for Greenford Green).
G	3 0	Greengairs	Lanark	N. B.	North Monkland Railway—Coatbridge and Slamannan.
		Brackenhirst Manure Depôt	Lanark	N. B.	Coatbridge and Greengairs.
		Brackenhirst Quarry	Lanark	N. B.	Coatbridge and Greengairs.
		Braidenhill No. 1 Colliery	Lanark	N. B.	Coatbridge and Greengairs.
		Braidenhill No. 2 Colliery	Lanark	N. B.	Coatbridge and Greengairs.
		Broadrigg Colliery	Lanark	N. B.	Greengairs and Slamannan.
		Cameron Colliery	Lanark	N. B.	Coatbridge and Greengairs.
		Clachan Manure Depôt	Lanark	N. B.	Coatbridge and Greengairs.

EXPLANATION—G Goods Station.   P Passenger and Parcel Station.   P* Passenger, but not Parcel or Miscellaneous Traffic.
F Furniture Vans, Carriages, Portable Engines, and Machines on Wheels.   L Live Stock.
H Horse Boxes and Prize Cattle Vans.   C Carriages by Passenger Train.

Station Accommodation						Crane Power		Stations, &c.	County	Company	Position
						Tons	Cwts	Greengairs—*continued.*			
								Clachan Quarry	Lanark	N. B.	Coatbridge and Greengairs.
								Drumbowie Siding	Lanark	N. B.	Coatbridge and Greengairs.
								Kipps Brick Works	Lanark	N. B.	Coatbridge and Greengairs.
								Kipps Quarry	Lanark	N. B.	Coatbridge and Greengairs.
								Kirkstyle Quarry	Lanark	N. B.	Coatbridge and Greengairs.
								Langdales Junction	Lanark	N. B.	Greengairs and Slamannan.
								Meikle Drumgray Colliery	Lanark	N. B.	Coatbridge and Greengairs.
								North Glentore Colliery	Lanark	N. B.	Greengairs and Slamannan.
						3	0	Rigghead Siding	Lanark	N. B.	Greengairs and Slamannan.
								Ryden Mains Quarry	Lanark	N. B.	Greengairs and Slamannan.
								Ryden Quarry	Lanark	N. B.	Coatbridge and Greengairs.
								Shyflat Manure Siding	Lanark	N. B.	Coatbridge and Greengairs.
								Sun Tube Works	Lanark	N. B.	Coatbridge and Greengairs.
								Greengate Brick & Tile Co.'s Siding	Lancs	L. & N. W.	St. Helens.
								Greenhaff & Co.'s Siding	Leicester	Mid.	Same as Launt Pottery Works (Worthington).
G	P	F	L	H	C	5	0	Greenhall Brick Works	Lanark	Cal.	High Blantyre.
								Greenhead	Northumb	N. E.	Carlisle and Hexham.
								Byron Cols. (Blenkinsopp's)	Northumb	N. E.	Greenhead.
G	P		L	H				Greenhill	Stirling	Cal.	Coatbridge and Larbert.
								Caledonian Railway Co.'s Creosoting Works	Stirling	Cal.	Greenhill.
								Castlecary Siding (Stein's Brick Works)	Stirling	Cal.	Greenhill and Cumbernauld.
								Greenhill Brick Works	Lanark	Cal.	Omoa.
								Greenhill Collieries (Windyedge Colliery No. 4)	Lanark	Cal.	Omoa.
								Greenhill, Lower Junction	Stirling	Cal.	Greenhill and Larbert.
								Greenhill Quarry	Lanark	Cal.	Omoa.
								Greenhill, Upper Junction	Stirling	Cal.—N. B.	Lower Greenhill and Castlecary.
G								Greenhill, Upper Junc. Sids.	Stirling	N. B.	See Castlecary.
	P							Greenhill, Upper Siding	Stirling	Cal.	Branch from Greenhill.
								Greenhithe	Kent	S. E. & C.	Dartford and Gravesend Central.
								Greenhough's Siding	Lancs	L. & N. W.—S. & M. Jt.	Widnes.
G	P		L	H				Greening & Sons' Siding	Lancs	L. & N. W.	Warrington, Bank Quay.
								Greenisland	Antrim	N. C. Com. (Mid.)	Belfast and Carrickfergus.
								Greenland Colliery	Mon	G. W.	Pontnewynydd.
								Greenland Creosote Works and Saw Mill	Durham	N. E.	West Hartlepool.
								Greenland Depôts	Yorks	N. E.	Redcar.
								Greenland Sleeper Saw Mill	Durham	N. E.	See Lauder, R., & Co. (West Hartlepool).
								Green Lane	Cheshire	Mersey	See Birkenhead.
								Green Lane Manure Siding	Yorks	N. E.	Marske.
								Green Lane Mill Sid. (Mallinson, Barraclough & Co.)	Yorks	Mid.	Yeadon.
								Green Lanes	Middlesex	T. & H. Jt. (G. E. & Mid.)	See London, Harringay Park, Green Lanes.
G	P		L	H		2	0	Green Lanes Junction	Middlesex	G W—H&C Jt (G W & Met)	Royal Oak and Westbourne Park.
G								Greenlaw	Berwick	N. B.	Duns and St. Boswells.
								Greenside Quarry	Berwick	N. B.	Greenlaw.
								Lintmill Siding	Berwick	N. B.	Greenlaw and Marchmont.
G	P	F	L	H	C	2	10	Greenlaw	Renfrew	G & P Jt (Cal & G & S W)	See Paisley.
								Greenloaning	Perth	Cal.	Stirling and Perth.
G	P							Greenmeadow Colliery	Mon	G. W.	Abertillery.
								Greenmount	Lancs	L. & Y.	Bury and Holcombe Brook.
								GREENOCK—			
G		F	L			25	0	Albert Harbour (G. & S.W.)	Renfrew	{ G. & S. W.	Branch near Princes Pier.
										N. B.	Over G. & S.W. fr. College, East Jn.
						3	0	Ardgowan Distillery (G. & S. W.)	Renfrew	G. & S.W. — N. B.	Lynedoch Street.
								Arthur Street Siding	Renfrew	Cal.	Cartsdyke and Greenock, Central.
G			L					Baker Street	Renfrew	Cal.	Cartsdyke and Greenock, Central.
								Berry Yard Sugar Refinery (Westburn Sugar Refinery)	Renfrew	Cal.	Upper Greenock.
G	P					12	0	Bogston	Renfrew	Cal.	Port Glasgow & Greenock, Central.
								Caird & Co.'s Foundry	Renfrew	Cal.	Greenock, Arthur Street.
								Caird & Co.'s Sid. (G.&S.W.)	Renfrew	G. & S.W. — N. B.	Albert Harbour.
								Cameron & Co.'s Saw Mill	Renfrew	Cal.	Greenock (James Watt Dock).

EXPLANATION—G *Goods Station.*   P *Passenger and Parcel Station.*   P* *Passenger, but not Parcel or Miscellaneous Traffic.*
F *Furniture Vans, Carriages, Portable Engines, and Machines on Wheels.*   L *Live Stock.*
H *Horse Boxes and Prize Cattle Vans.*   C *Carriages by Passenger Train.*

G	P	F	L	H	C	Tons	Cwts	STATIONS, &c.	COUNTY.	COMPANY.	POSITION.
								GREENOCK—*continued.*			
								Cartsburn Sid. (G. & S. W.)	Renfrew	G. & S W.— N. B.	Lynedoch Street.
	P							Cartsdyke	Renfrew	Cal.	Port Glasgow & Greenock, Central.
								Cartsdyke Saw Mills	Renfrew	Cal.	Cartsdyke and Greenock, Central.
								Cathcart Street Depôt	Renfrew	Cal.	Greenock, Central.
	P			H	C	4	10	Central	Renfrew	Cal.	Port Glasgow and Gourock.
								Chapel Street Mineral Sid.	Renfrew	Cal.	Greenock, Central.
								Churchill Siding	Renfrew	Cal.	Bogston and Cartsdyke.
								Clyde Sugar Refinery Store	Renfrew	Cal.	Upper Greenock.
G								Custom House Quay	Renfrew	Cal.	Greenock, Regent Street.
G								East India Harbour	Renfrew	Cal.	Greenock.
								Fisher, Henderson & Co.'s Tannery	Renfrew	Cal.	Bogston and Cartsdyke.
								Foundry	Renfrew	Cal.	Greenock, Regent Street.
								Gibbshill Siding	Renfrew	G. & S. W.	Lynedoch Str. & Upper Port Glasgow
								Glebe Refinery Co.'s Siding (G. & S. W.)	Renfrew	G. & S. W.— N. B.	Albert Harbour.
								Glen Ship Yard	Renfrew	Cal.	Port Glasgow and Bogston.
								Greenock Felt Work Co.'s Siding	Renfrew	Cal.	Regent Street.
								Greenock Saccharine Co.'s Sid. (Brewers' Sugar Co.)	Renfrew	Cal.	Upper Greenock.
								Harbour Branch Junction	Renfrew	G. & S. W.	Princes Pier and Lynedoch Street.
								Inch Engineering and Ship-building Wks. (Dunlop & Co.)	Renfrew	Cal.	Bogston.
								James Watt Dock (Garvel Dock)	Renfrew	Cal.	Branch near Bogston.
								John Street Depôt	Renfrew	Cal.	Cartsdyke and Greenock, Central.
								Kincaid's Siding	Renfrew	Cal.	Greenock, Regent Street.
								Kingston Yard	Renfrew	Cal.	Bogston.
								Ladyburn Saw Mills	Renfrew	Cal.	Greenock (James Watt Dock).
G						1	10	Ladyburn Sidings	Renfrew	Cal.	Bogston and Cartsdyke.
G	P	F				4	0	Lynedoch Street (G & S W)	Renfrew	G. & S. W.	Princes Pier and Kilmalcolm.
G		F				4	0			N. B.	Over G. & S. W. fr. College, East Jn.
								Murdieston Siding (Paper Mill Branch)	Renfrew	Cal.	Upper Greenock.
								Newark Sail Cloth Co.'s Siding	Renfrew	Cal.	Port Glasgow and Bogston.
								Orchard Sugar Refinery Co.'s Store	Renfrew	Cal.	Greenock, Victoria Harbour.
								Overton Paper Mill	Renfrew	Cal.	Upper Greenock.
								Poynter's Sid. (G. & S. W.)	Renfrew	G. & S. W.— N. B.	Lynedoch Street.
	P			H	C			Princes Pier (G. & S. W.)	Renfrew	G. & S. W.	Greenock Branch, Terminus.
	P									N. B.	Steamer from Craigendoran.
G		F	L			25	0	Regent Street	Renfrew	Cal.	Cartsdyke and Greenock, Central.
								Regent Str. Mineral Depôt	Renfrew	Cal.	Greenock, Central.
								Scott & Co.'s Siding— East Yard	Renfrew	Cal.	Cartsdyke and Greenock, Central.
								Foundry and Engineering Works	Renfrew	Cal.	Cartsdyke and Greenock, Central.
								Mid Yard	Renfrew	Cal.	Port Glasgow and Wemyss Bay.
G	P	F	L	H	C	5	0	Upper Greenock	Renfrew	Cal.	Branch near Cartsdyke.
						100	0	Victoria Harbour	Renfrew	Cal.	
								Walker & Co.'s Sugar Refinery	Renfrew	Cal.	Greenock, West.
	P							West	Renfrew	Cal.	Greenock and Gourock.
								West Harbour	Renfrew	Cal.	Branch from Victoria Harbour.
G						3	0	West Mineral Depôt	Renfrew	Cal.	Greenock and Gourock.
								Greenock Felt Work Co.'s Sid.	Renfrew	Cal.	Greenock, Regent Street.
								Greenock Foundry	Renfrew	Cal.	Greenock, Regent Street.
								Greenock Gas Wks. (G & S W)	Renfrew	G. & S. W.— N. B.	Port Glasgow, Inchgreen.
								Greenock, James Watt Dock (G. & S. W.)	Renfrew	G. & S. W.— N. B.	See Port Glasgow, Inchgreen.
								Greenock Saccharine Co.'s Sid (Brewers' Sugar Co.)	Renfrew	Cal.	Greenock, Regent Street.
								Greenock West Mineral Depôt	Renfrew	Cal.	Greenock.
G	P	F	L	H	C	3	0	Greenodd	Lancs	Furness	Ulverston and Lake Side.
G	P	F	L	H	C	10	0	Greenore (D. N. & G.)	Louth	D. N. & G.	Terminus.
										L. & N. W.	By Steamer from Holyhead.
G	P		L	H		3	0	Green Road	Cumb'land	Furness	Foxfield and Millom.
								Underhill Mineral Siding	Cumb'land	Furness	Foxfield and Millom.

STATION ACCOMMODATION.						CRANE POWER.	STATIONS, &c.	COUNTY.	COMPANY.	POSITION.
						Tons Cwts.				
							Greenshields' Siding	Lanark	Cal.	Glasgow, West Street.
							Greenside (G. N.)	Yorks	G. N.—L. & Y.	See Pudsey.
							Greenside Brick Works	Lanark	Cal.	Omoa.
							Greenside Colliery	Durham	N. E.	Blaydon.
							Greenside Colliery	Lanark	Cal.	Omoa.
							Greenside Quarry	Berwick	N. B.	Greenlaw.
							Green Slate Siding	Lancs	L. & Y.	Appley Bridge.
	P						Green's Norton Junction	N'hamptn	E. & W. Jn.—N. & B. Jn.	Blakesley and Towcester.
							Greenwich	Kent	S. E. & C.	London Bridge and Woolwich.
							Greenwich, Maze Hill	Kent	S. E. & C.	See Maze Hill (for East Greenwich).
	P						Greenwich, North	Middlesex	G. E.	See London, North Greenwich.
							Greenwich Park	Kent	S. E. & C.	Branch from Nunhead.
							Greenwood & Batley's Siding (G. N.)	Yorks	G.N.—G.C.—Mid.—N.E.	See Leeds.
							Greenwood & Sons' Siding	Lancs	L. & Y.	See Duckett, J., & Son, Burnley Barracks Mineral Sid. (Burnley).
							Greenwood Brick Works	Ayr	G. & S. W.	Dreghorn.
							Greenwood Collieries	Ayr	G. & S. W.	Dreghorn.
							Greenwood, G. L., & Co.'s Sid.	Yorks	Mid.	Keighley.
							Greenwood's Sarn Terra Cotta Brick and Tile Works	Salop	S & W'pl.Jt.(G W&LNW)	Westbury.
							Greenwood's Corn Mill	Lancs	L. & Y.	Town Green.
							Greenwood Siding (L. & Y.)	Lancs	L. & Y.—L. & N. W.	Blackburn.
							Greenwood's Siding	Lancs	L. & Y.	Bacup.
G	P		L	H		10 0	Greetland (L. & Y.)	Yorks	{ L. & Y.	Halifax and Brighouse.
G	P		L	H		10 0			G. N.	Over L. & Y. from Wakefield Junc.
G			L			5 0			L. & N. W.	Over L. & Y. from Bradley Wood Jn.
							Greetwell Junction	Lincoln	G. N.—G.N. & G. E. Jt.	Lincoln.
							Gregor Bros.' Siding	Glamorg'n	GW—LNW—Mid—RSB	Swansea.
							Gregory & Son's Siding	Derby	Mid.	Sheffield, Mill Houses and Ecclesall.
							Gregory, J., & Son's Siding	Derby	Mid.	Sheffield, Heeley.
							Gregory, Riddish, & Co.'s Sid	Durham	N. E.	Leadgate.
							Gregory's Siding	Yorks	G. C.	Deepcar (for Stocksbridge).
	P						Gregson Lane Siding	Lancs	L. & Y.	Hoghton.
							Gresford	Denbigh	G. W.	Chester and Wrexham.
							Gresford Mill Siding	Denbigh	G. W.	See Rossett.
							Greskine Siding	Dumfries	Cal.	See Beattock.
G	P	F	L	H	C		Gresley (Mid.)	Derby	{ Mid.	Burton and Ashby-de-la-Zouch.
									L. & N. W.	Over Mid. Line.
							Coton Park Brick Co.'s Birkenshaw Brk. Wks. (Mid.)	Derby	Mid.—L. & N. W.	Near Gresley.
							Gresley Brewery Co.'s Sid. (Thompson & Son) (Mid.)	Derby	Mid.—L. & N. W.	Near Gresley.
							Mansfield's, H.R., Sid.(Mid)	Derby	Mid.—L. & N. W.	Near Gresley.
							Netherseal Colliery (Mid.)	Leicester	Mid.—L. & N. W.	Near Gresley.
							Netherseal Wharf (Mid.)	Derby	Mid.—L. & N. W.	Near Gresley.
							Gresty Mill	Cheshire	L. & N. W.	Same as Brown's Siding (Crewe).
G	P	F	L	H	C	2 0	Gretna	Cumb'land	{ Cal	Carlisle and Lockerbie.
G	P		L	H					N. B.	Branch from Longtown Junction.
G			L				Quintinshill	Dumfries	Cal.	Gretna and Kirkpatrick.
G	P	F	L	H	C	1 10	Gretna Green	Dumfries	{ G. & S. W.	Carlisle and Annan.
	P								N. B.	Over G. & S. W. from Gretna Junc.
							Gretna Junction	Cumb'land	Cal.—N. B.	Longtown and Gretna.
							Gretna Junction	Dumfries	Cal.—G. & S. W.	Gretna Green and Gretna.
G	P		L	H			Gretton	N'hamptn	Mid.	Kettering and Manton.
							Davis, E. P., Siding	N'hamptn	Mid.	Near Gretton.
	P						Greve d'Azette	Jersey	Jersey Eastern	St. Helier and Gorey.
							Greyfield Colliery	Somerset	G. W.	Clutton.
							Greyrigg Colliery	Lanark	N. B.	Rawyards.
G	P		L	H			Greystones and Delgany	Wicklow	D. W. & W.	Bray and Wicklow.
							Gribdale Quarry	Yorks	N. E.	Great Ayton.
							Grice, Grice & Sons' Siding	Warwick	L. & N. W.	See Toy Siding (Birmingham).
							Griendtsveen Moss Litter Co.'s Siding	Lancs	L. & N. W.	Glazebury.
							Griff Branch (L. & N. W.)	Warwick	L. & N. W.—Mid.	Bedworth and Chilvers Coton.
							Griff Brick Yard (L. & N. W)	Warwick	L. & N. W.—Mid.	See Haunchwood Brick and Tile Co. (Nuneaton).
							Griff Colliery Co.—			
							Griff New Colliery or Clara Pit (L. & N. W.)	Warwick	L. & N. W.—Mid.	Nuneaton.
							Griff Old Col. (L. & N. W.)	Warwick	L. & N. W.—Mid.	Nuneaton.
							Griff Granite Co.'s Sid.(LNW)	Warwick	L. & N. W.—Mid.	Nuneaton.

EXPLANATION—G *Goods Station.*   P *Passenger and Parcel Station.*   P* *Passenger, but not Parcel or Miscellaneous Traffic.*
F *Furniture Vans, Carriages, Portable Engines, and Machines on Wheels.*   L *Live Stock.*
H *Horse Boxes and Prize Cattle Vans.*   C *Carriages by Passenger Train.*

STATION ACCOMMODATION.						CRANE POWER.	STATIONS, &c.	COUNTY.	COMPANY.	POSITION.
						Tons Cwts.	Griffin, Jones & Co.'s Castle Brick Works	Staffs	L. & N. W.	Birchills.
						·	Griffin's Siding	Warwick..	L. & N. W.	Napton and Stockton.
						·	Griffin, W., Siding	Staffs	G. W.	Cradley Heath and Cradley.
						·	Griffiths' Brick Works	Yorks	N. E.	Middlesbro'.
						·	Griffiths' Brick Works	Stirling ...	N. B.	Same as Bonnybridge Silica Co.'s Siding.
G	P	·	·	·	·	·	Griffiths' Crossing	Carnarvon	L. & N. W.	Bangor and Carnarvon.
						·	Parkia Brick Co.'s Siding (Lord Penrhyn's)	Carnarvon	L. & N. W.	Griffiths Crossing and Carnarvon.
						·	Griffiths' Sand Siding	Salop	G. W.	Buildwas.
						·	Griffiths' Siding	Flint	L. & N. W.	See Nerquis Old Colliery Level Siding (Coed Talon).
							Griffithstown (G. W.)	Mon	G. W.—L. & N.W.	See Panteg and Griffithstown.
						·	Griffiths, W., & Co.'s Siding (G. E.)	Essex	G E—GN—L&NW—Mid	London, Silvertown.
						·	Griggs & Co.	Glo'ster ...	G. W.—Mid.	Gloucester Docks.
						·	Griggs, J., & Co.'s Siding ...	Lancs	Trafford Park Estate...	Manchester.
						·	Grimes Bros.' Siding	Glamorg'n	GW—LNW—Rhy—TV	Cardiff.
						·	Grimesthorpe Gas Wks (Mid)	Yorks	Mid.—G. C.	See United Gas Light Co. (Sheffield).
						·	Grimesthorpe Junction........	Yorks	Mid.	See Sheffield.
						·	Grimesthorpe Sidings (Mid.)	Yorks	Mid.—G. C.	See Ward's, T. W., Sidings (Sheffield).
						·	Grimesthorpe Works (Mid.)..	Yorks	Mid.—G. C.	See Cammell, C., & Co. (Sheffield.)
G		·	·	·	·	·	Grimethorpe	Yorks	Dearne Valley..............	Brierley Junction and Houghton.
						·	Carlton Main Colliery Co.'s Grimethorpe Colliery......	Yorks	Dearne Valley..............	Grimethorpe and Houghton.
						·	Grimethorpe Branch	Yorks	Mid.	Cudworth.
						·	Grimethorpe Colliery............	Yorks	Dearne Val.—G.C.—Mid.	See Carlton Main Colliery Co.
G	P	F	L	H	C	·	Grimoldby	Lincoln ...	G. N.	Louth and Mablethorpe.
G	P	·	·	·	·	·	Grimsargh	Lancs	P & L Jt(L & N W & L& Y)	Longridge and Preston.
						·	Whittingham Asylum Sid.	Lancs	P & L Jt(L& N W & L& Y)	Grimsargh and Longridge.
							GRIMSBY—			
G	·	F	L	·	·	10 0	(Station)	Lincoln ...	G. N.	Near North Junction.
						·	Bannister and Co.'s— Cressey Street Siding ...	Lincoln ...	G. C.	Grimsby Town.
						·	Railway Street Siding ...	Lincoln ...	G. C.	Grimsby Town.
						·	Repairing Siding (G. C.)	Lincoln ...	G. C.—G. N.	Grimsby Docks.
						·	Bennett's Saw Mills (G. C.)	Lincoln ...	G. C.—G. N.	Grimsby Docks.
						·	Brown & Co.'s Chemical Works (G. N.)................	Lincoln ...	G. N.—G. C.	Grimsby Station.
						·	Bruce, Alex., & Co.'s Siding (G. C.)	Lincoln ...	G. C.—G. N.	Grimsby Docks.
						·	Burt, Boulton & Heywood's Creosoting Works	Lincoln ...	G. C.	Grimsby Docks.
						·	Carr & Co.'s Siding (G. C.)	Lincoln ...	G. C.—G. N.	Grimsby Docks.
						·	Christie & Co.'s Sid. (G. C.)	Lincoln ...	G. C.—G. N.	Grimsby Docks.
	P	·	·	·	·	·	Docks	Lincoln ...	G. C.	Town, Passengers and Cleethorpes.
G	·	F	L	H	C	70 0	Docks Royal (G. C.)	Lincoln ...	{ G. C. / G. N.	Bch.—Dks., Passengers & New Clee. / Over G. C. from Grimsby Junction.
G	·	F	L	·	·	70 0	Gas Works (G. N.)	Lincoln ...	G. N.—G. C.	Grimsby and Waltham.
						·	Gilstrap, Earp & Co.'s Siding	Lincoln ...	G. C.	Grimsby Town.
							Great Central Co-operative Engineering and Ship-Repairing Co.'s Siding (G. C.).............	Lincoln ...	G. C.—G. N.	Grimsby Docks.
							Grimsby Coal, Salt, and Tanning Co.'s Siding (G. C.)	Lincoln ...	G. C.—G. N.	Grimsby Docks.
							Grimsby Coal Supply Co.'s Siding	Lincoln ...	G. C.	Grimsby Town.
							Grimsby Co-operative Society's Siding	Lincoln ...	G. C.	Grimsby Town.
							Grimsby Corporation Electric Light Works...	Lincoln ...	G. N.	Grimsby and Waltham.
						·	Grimsby Corporation Nightsoil Siding (G. C.)	Lincoln ...	G. C.—G. N.	Grimsby Docks.
						·	Grimsby Fish Manure and Oil Co.'s Biscuit Factory (G. C.)................	Lincoln ...	G. C.—G. N.	Grimsby Docks.

EXPLANATION—G *Goods Station.*   P *Passenger and Parcel Station.*   P* *Passenger, but not Parcel or Miscellaneous Traffic.*
F *Furniture Vans, Carriages, Portable Engines, and Machines on Wheels.*   L *Live Stock.*
H *Horse Boxes and Prize Cattle Vans.*   C *Carriages by Passenger Train.*

STATION ACCOMMODATION.						CRANE POWER.	STATIONS, &c.	COUNTY.	COMPANY.	POSITION.
						Tons Cwts.	GRIMSBY—continued.			
.	.	.	.	.	.	. .	Grimsby Ice Co.'s Siding (G. C.)	Lincoln ...	G. C.—G. N.	Grimsby Docks.
.	.	.	.	.	.	. .	Holles Street Siding	Lincoln ...	G. C.	Grimsby Town.
.	.	.	.	.	.	. .	Humber Street Sid. (G. C.)	Lincoln ...	G. C.—G. N.	Grimsby Docks.
.	P	.	.	.	.	. .	Knott & Barker's Saw Mills	Lincoln ...	G. C.	Grimsby Docks.
.	.	.	.	.	.	. .	New Clee	Lincoln ...	G. C.	Town, Passengers and Cleethorpes.
.	.	.	.	.	.	. .	Norfolk & Sons' Siding	Lincoln ...	G. C.	Grimsby Town.
.	.	.	.	.	.	. .	North Junction	Lincoln ...	G. C.—G. N.	Docks, Passengers and Louth.
.	.	.	.	.	.	. .	Old Gas House Siding	Lincoln ...	G. C.	Grimsby Town.
.	.	.	.	.	.	. .	Orby Bradley's Siding	Lincoln ...	G. C.	Grimsby Town.
.	.	.	.	.	.	. .	Pyewipe Manure Works (G. C.)	Lincoln ...	G. C.—G. N.	Grimsby Docks.
.	.	.	.	.	.	. .	Schofield, Hagerup & Doughty's Shipbuilding Works (G. C.)	Lincoln ...	G. C.—G. N.	Grimsby Docks.
.	.	.	.	.	.	. .	Shepherd, A., & Co.'s Saw Mills	Lincoln ...	G. C.	Grimsby Docks.
.	.	.	.	.	.	. .	Soames & Sons' Siding	Lincoln ...	G. C.	Grimsby Town.
.	P	.	.	H	C	. .	South Junction	Lincoln ...	G. C.—G. N.	Town, Passengers and Louth.
G	.	F	L	H	C	7 10	Town (G. C.)	Lincoln ...	{ G. C.	Barnetby and Docks, Passengers.
.	P	F	L	H	C				G. C.	Town, Pass. and Docks, Passengers.
									G. N.	Over G. C. from South Junction.
.	.	.	.	.	.	. .	Worms, Josse & Co.'s— Repairing Siding (G. C.)	Lincoln ...	G. C.—G. N.	Grimsby Town.
.	.	.	.	.	.	. .	Siding (G. C.)	Lincoln ...	G. C.—G. N.	Grimsby Town.
.	.	.	.	.	.	. .	Grimsby Coal, Salt, and Tanning Co.'s Siding (G. C.) ...	Lincoln ...	G. C.—G. N.	Grimsby Docks.
.	.	.	.	.	.	. .	Grimsby Cl. Supply Co.'s Sid.	Lincoln ...	G. C.	Grimsby Town.
.	.	.	.	.	.	. .	Grimsby Co-operative Society's Siding	Lincoln ...	G. C.	Grimsby Town.
.	.	.	.	.	.	. .	Grimsby Corporation Electric Light Works	Lincoln ...	G. N.	Grimsby Town.
.	.	.	.	.	.	. .	Grimsby Corporation Night-soil Siding (G. C.)	Lincoln ...	G. C.—G. N.	Grimsby Docks.
.	.	.	.	.	.	. .	Grimsby Fish Manure and Oil Co.'s Biscuit Factory (G. C.)	Lincoln ...	G. C.—G. N.	Grimsby Docks.
.	.	.	.	.	.	. .	Grimsby Gas Works (G. N.)	Lincoln ...	G. N.—G. C.	Grimsby Town.
.	.	.	.	.	.	. .	Grimsby Ice Co.'s Sid. (G C)	Lincoln ...	G. C.—G. N.	Grimsby Docks.
G	P	F	L	H	C	1 10	Grimston	Leicester..	Mid.	Nottingham and Melton Mowbray.
G	P	.	.	.	.	. .	Grimstone and Frampton	Dorset ...	G. W.	Yeovil and Weymouth.
G	P	.	L	H	.	. .	Grimston Road	Norfolk ...	Mid. & G. N. Jt.	South Lynn and Melton Constable.
.	.	.	.	.	.	. .	Bawsey Siding	Norfolk ...	Mid. & G. N. Jt.	Grimston Road and Gayton Road.
.	.	.	.	°	.	. .	Gay & Wilson's Siding	Norfolk ...	Mid. & G. N. Jt.	Bawsey Siding.
.	.	.	.	.	.	. .	Grin Branch	Derby ...	L. & N. W.	See Buxton Lime Firms Co. (Ladmanlow).
G	P	.	L	.	.	4 0	Grindford Bar Siding	Lancs ...	L. & Y.	Adlington.
G	P	.	L	H	.	. .	Grindleford	Derby ...	Mid.	Dore and Chinley.
G	P	.	.	.	.	. .	Grindley	Staffs ...	G. N.	Stafford and Burton.
.	.	.	.	.	.	. .	Grinkle	Yorks ...	N. E.	Whitby and Loftus.
.	.	.	.	.	.	. .	Grinsdale Bridge Siding	Cumb'land	N. B.	Kirkandrews.
.	.	.	.	.	.	. .	Grinstead, East	Sussex ...	L. B. & S. C.	See East Grinstead.
.	.	.	.	.	.	. .	Grinstead, West	Sussex ...	L. B. & S. C.	See West Grinstead.
.	.	.	.	.	.	. .	Gripper & Wightman's Siding	Herts ...	G. N.	Hertford.
G	P	.	.	.	.	. .	Griseburne Ballast Siding ...	W'morlnd	Mid.	Crosby Garrett.
.	.	.	.	.	.	. .	Gristhorpe	Yorks ...	N. E.	Scarborough and Filey.
.	.	.	.	.	.	. .	Grist's, J., Siding	Glo'ster ...	Mid.	Same as Rooksmoor Siding (Dudbridge).
.	.	.	.	.	.	. .	Gritstone Siding	Derby ...	L. & N. W.	See Buxton Lime Firms Co. (Ladmanlow).
.	.	.	.	.	.	. .	Groby Granite Co.'s Siding...	Leicester..	Mid.	Glenfield.
.	.	.	.	.	.	. .	Groesfaen Siding	Glamorg'n	Rhy.	Darran.
G	P	.	L	.	.	. .	Groeslon	Carnarvon	L. & N. W.	Afon Wen and Carnarvon.
.	.	.	.	.	.	. .	Jones' & Ingham's Tudor Siding	Carnarvon	L. & N. W.	Groeslon and Penygroes.
G	.	.	.	.	.	. .	Groeswen Colliery	Glamorg'n	A. (N. & S. W.) D. & R.	Glyntaff.
.	.	.	.	.	.	. .	Grogley Junction and Siding	Cornwall..	L. & S.W.	Branch from Wadebridge.
.	.	.	.	.	.	. .	Gronant Siding	Flint ...	L. & N. W.	Prestatyn.
.	.	.	.	.	.	. .	Groom's Siding (G.W.)	Hereford..	G. W.—L. & N. W.—Mid.	Hereford.
.	.	.	.	.	.	. .	Groom, Sons & Co.'s Siding...	Salop ...	S & W'tn Jt(GW&L&NW)	Wellington.

Station Accommodation.						Crane Power.		Stations, &c.	County.	Company.	Position.
						Tons	Cwts				
G	P	F	L	H	C	5	0	Groombridge	Sussex	L. B. & S. C.	East Grinstead & Tunbridge Wells.
G	P							Groomsport Road	Down	B. & C. D.	Comber and Donaghadee.
G	P	F	L	H	C	5	0	Grosmont	Yorks	N. E.	Whitby and Pickering.
.	.	.	.	.	.			Dorsley Bank Siding	Yorks	N. E.	Sleights and Grosmont.
.	.	.	.	.	.			Gantree Siding	Yorks	N. E.	Sleights and Grosmont.
.	.	.	.	.	.			Newbiggin Siding	Yorks	N. E.	Sleights and Grosmont.
.	.	.	.	.	.			Woodlands Sid. (Harrison's)	Yorks	N. E.	Sleights and Grosmont.
.	.	.	.	.	.			Grosvenor Road	Middlesex	L. B. & S.C.—S. E. & C.—GN—GW—LNW—Mid	See London.
.	.	.	.	.	.			Grosvenor Street	Antrim	G. N. (I.)	See Belfast.
G	P	.	.	.	.	1	10	Grotton and Springhead	Yorks	L. & N. W.	Greenfield and Oldham.
.	.	.	.	.	.			Clough Mill Siding	Yorks	L. & N. W.	Grotton and Lees.
.	.	.	.	.	.			Livingstone Spinning Co.'s Siding	Yorks	L. & N. W.	Grotton and Lees.
.	.	.	.	.	.			Springhead Spinning Co.'s Siding	Yorks	L. & N. W.	Grotton and Lees.
.	.	.	.	.	.			Grout & Co.'s Sid.(L. & N.W.)	Staffs	L&NW—Mid—GN—NS	Burton-on-Trent.
.	P	.	.	.	.			Grouville	Jersey	Jersey Eastern	St. Helier and Gorey.
.	.	.	.	.	.			Grovebury Crossing	Beds	L. & N. W.	See Leighton.
.	.	.	.	.	.			Grove Chemical Co.'s Siding	Lancs	L. & Y.	Appley Bridge.
G	P	.	L	H	C			Grove Ferry	Kent	S. E. & C.	Canterbury West & Ramsgate Town.
G	P	.	.	H	.			Grove Park	Kent	S. E. & C.	Hither Green and Chislehurst.
.	.	.	.	.	.			Grove Park Junction	Kent	S. E. & C.	Grove Park and Chislehurst.
.	.	.	.	.	.			Grove Park	Middlesex	L. & S.W.	See Chiswick and Grove Park.
.	.	.	.	.	.			Grove Rake Mines	Durham	N. E.	Parkhead.
.	.	.	.	.	.			Grove Road	Middlesex	L. & S.W.	See London, Hammersmith.
.	.	.	.	.	.			Grovesend Colliery	Glamorg'n	L. & N. W.	Same as Williams & Son's Siding (Gorseinon).
.	.	.	.	.	.			Grovesend Steel Works	Glamorg'n	L. & N. W.	Gorseinon.
.	.	.	.	.	.			Grovesend Tin Plate Works	Glamorg'n	L. & N. W.	Gorseinon.
.	.	.	.	.	.			Grove Siding	Kent	S. E. & C.	Minster (Sheppey) and Eastchurch.
.	.	.	.	.	.			Guaranteed Manure Co.'s Siding (N. B.)	Cumb'land	N. B.—L. & N. W.	Carlisle.
G	P	.	L	H	C	2	0	Guard Bridge	Fife	N. B.	St. Andrews and Leuchars Junction.
.	.	.	.	.	.			Edenside Brick Works	Fife	N. B.	St. Andrews and Guard Bridge.
.	.	.	.	.	.			Seggie Siding	Fife	N. B.	Guard Bridge and Leuchars Junc.
G	P	.	L	H	.	1	10	Guay	Perth	High.	Dunkeld and Blair Atholl.
.	.	.	.	.	.			Gueret's, L., Colliery (Mid.)	Glamorg'n	Mid.—G. W.—L. & N.W.	Same as Graigola Colliery (Clydach-on-Tawe).
G	P	.	L	H	C	2	0	Guernsey	Guernsey	{ G. W.	Steamer from Weymouth.
G	P	.	.	.	.	4	0			{ L. & S. W.	Steamer from Southampton.
.	.	.	.	.	.			Guest & Dewsbury's South Wales Potteries (G. W.)	Carmarth'	G. W.—L. & N. W.	Llanelly.
								Guest, Keen & Nettlefold—			
.	.	.	.	.	.			Bedlinog Colliery	Glamorg'n	T. B. Jt. (G. W. & Rhy.)	Bedlinog.
.	.	.	.	.	.			Dowlais Cardiff Colliery	Glamorg'n	T.V.	Abercynon.
.	.	.	.	.	.			Dowlais Incline	Glamorg'n	G. W.—T.V.	Merthyr.
.	.	.	.	.	.			Dowlais Iron & Steel Works	Glamorg'n	{ B. & M.—T. B. Jt.	Dowlais.
.	.	.	.	.	.					{ T. V.	Merthyr.
.	.	.	.	.	.			Dowlais Works	Glamorg'n	T.V.	Merthyr.
.	.	.	.	.	.			Fochriw Colliery (B. & M.)	Glamorg'n	B. & M.—L. & N. W.	Fochriw.
.	.	.	.	.	.			Fochriw or Fforchriw Col.	Glamorg'n	T. B. Jt. (G. W. & Rhy.)	Cwm Bargoed.
.	.	.	.	.	.			Ivor Siding (B. & M.)	Glamorg'n	B. & M.—L. & N. W.	Dowlais.
.	.	.	.	.	.			London Works	Staffs	L. & N. W.	Soho.
.	.	.	.	.	.			Nantwen Colliery	Glamorg'n	T. B. Jt. (G. W. & Rhy.)	Bedlinog.
.	.	.	.	.	.			Pantyscallog Siding	Glamorg'n	B. & M.	Dowlais.
.	.	.	.	.	.			Penywern Siding	Glamorg'n	L. & N. W.	Dowlais.
.	.	.	.	.	.			Steel Works	Glamorg'n	G W—LN W—Rhy—TV	Cardiff.
.	.	.	.	.	.			Tunnel Pit	Glamorg'n	T. B. Jt. (G. W. & Rhy.)	Cwm Bargoed.
.	.	.	.	.	.			Tunnel Pit (B. & M.)	Glamorg'n	B. & M.—L. & N. W.	Dowlais.
.	.	.	.	.	.			Tylerybont Lime Sidings	Glamorg'n	B. & M.	Dowlais.
.	.	.	.	.	.			Works & Collieries (G.W.)	Mon	G. W.—L. & N. W.	Cwmbran.
.	.	.	.	.	.			Works and Sidings	Mon	G. W.	Rogerstone.
.	.	.	.	.	.			Guestling Siding	Sussex	S. E. & C.	Ore.
G	P	.	L	H	C	.	.	Guestwick	Norfolk	Mid. & G. N. Jt.	Melton Constable & Norwich (City).
								GUIDE BRIDGE—			
G	.	.	L	.	.	10	0	(Station)	Lancs	L. & N. W.	Branch—Stalybridge & Stockport.
G	P	.	L	H	.	10	0			{ G. C.	Manchester and Penistone.
G	P	.	L	H	.	10	0	(Station, G. C.)	Lancs	{ G. N.	Over G. C. Line.
	P	.	.	H	.					{ L. & N. W.	Over G. C. Line.
G	.	.	L	.	.	10	0			{ Mid.	Over G. C. Line.
.	.	.	.	.	.			Ashton Branch Junction	Lancs	G. C.	Guide Bridge Station & Dukinfield.

EXPLANATION—G *Goods Station.*   P *Passenger and Parcel Station.*   P* *Passenger, but not Parcel or Miscellaneous Traffic.*
F *Furniture Vans, Carriages, Portable Engines, and Machines on Wheels.*   L *Live Stock.*
H *Horse Boxes and Prize Cattle Vans.*   C *Carriages by Passenger Train.*

STATION ACCOMMODATION.						CRANE POWER.		STATIONS, &c.	COUNTY.	COMPANY.	POSITION.
						Tons	Cwts.	GUIDE BRIDGE—continued.			
								Dewsnap Siding	Cheshire...	G. C.	Guide Bridge.
								Dog Lane Siding (G. C.)	Cheshire...	G. C.—G. N.—Mid.	Guide Bridge.
								East Junction	Lancs	G. C.—O. A. & G. B.	Guide Bridge & Ashton, Oldham Rd.
								Gartside's Brewery (G. C.)	Lancs	G. C.—G. N.—Mid	Guide Bridge.
								Guide Bridge Spinning Co.'s Sid. (O. A. & G. B.)	Lancs	O. A. & G. B.—G. N.	Guide Bridge.
	P							Guide Bridge Wagon Wks.	Cheshire	G. C.	Guide Bridge.
								Hooley Hill	Lancs	L. & N. W.	Stalybridge and Stockport.
								Junction	Lancs	G. C.—L. & N. W.	Ashton, Park Parade & Stockport.
								New Moss Colliery Co.'s Ashton Moss Col. (L&NW)	Lancs	L. & N. W.—G. C.	Ashton, Oldham Road and Denton.
								Planet Foundry Co.'s Sid. (L. & N. W.)	Lancs	L. & N. W.—G. C.	Denton and Hooley Hill.
								Princes Dock (G. C.)	Lancs	G. C.—G. N.	Guide Bridge.
								West Junction (Audenshaw Junction)	Lancs	G. C.—O. A. & G. B.	Fairfield and Ashton, Oldham Rd.
								GUILDFORD—			
G	P	F	L	H	C	10	0	(Station, L. & S. W.)	Surrey	L. & S. W.	Woking and Godalming.
										L. B. & S. C.	Over L. & S. W. from Peasmarsh Jn.
										S. E. & C.	Over L. & S. W. from Shalford Junc.
	P							Junction	Surrey	S. E. & C.	Guildford.
								London Road	Surrey	L. & S.W.	Guildford and Surbiton.
								Guild Street (Cal.)	Aberdeen	Cal.—N. B.	See Aberdeen.
								Guild Street Branch (Mid.)	Staffs	Mid.—L&NW—GN—NS	Burton-on-Trent.
								Guinness' Siding	Dublin	G. S. & W.	Dublin.
G	P	F	L	H	C	6	0	Guisboro'	Yorks	N. E.	Branch from Middlesbro'.
								Chaloner Mines	Yorks	N. E.	Guisboro'.
								Hutton Gate Depôt & Sid.	Yorks	N. E.	Guisboro'.
G	P	F	L	H	C	10	0	Guiseley	Yorks	Mid.	Shipley and Menston.
								Ings Mill Co.'s Siding	Yorks	Mid.	Near Guiseley.
								Moon, A., & Son's Siding	Yorks	Mid.	Near Guiseley.
								Taylor, Jas., Siding	Yorks	Mid.	Guiseley.
G	P	F	L	H	C	2	0	Gullane	Hadding'n	N. B.	Branch from Aberlady Junction.
								Gullet (Nightsoil) Siding	Yorks	G. C.	Barnsley.
								Gullet Siding	Derby	Mid.	See Butterley Co. (Codnor Park).
								Gulliland Quarry	Dumfries..	Cal.	Annan.
								Gulston's Siding	Carmarth'	G. W.	Pantyffynnon.
								Gunheath Siding	Cornwall ..	G. W.	Bugle.
								Gunhouse Junction	Lincoln ...	G. C.	Frodingham and Gunness.
								Gunhouse Wharf	Lincoln ...	G. C.	Frodingham & Scunthorpe.
	P							Gunnersbury (L. & S. W.)	Middlesex	L. & S. W.	Addison Road and Richmond.
										G. W.—Met.	Over L. & S. W. from Hammersmith Junction.
										N & S W Jn Jt.(L & NW, Mid., & N L)	Over L. & S. W. from Acton Junc.
								Gunnerton Quarry	Northumb	N. B.	Barrasford.
								Gunnerton Siding	Northumb	N. B.	See Wark.
G	P	F	L	H	C			Gunness and Burringham	Lincoln	G. C.	Thorne and Barnetby.
								Gunnie Sidings	Lanark ...	N. B.	See Coatbridge, Sunnyside.
								Gunn's Siding	N'hamptn	L. & N. W.	Same as Claridge's Siding (Banbury).
G	P	F	L	H	C			Gunton	Norfolk ...	G. E.	North Walsham and Cromer.
G								Gunville Siding	I. of W. ...	I. of W. Cent.	Yarmouth and Newport.
G								Gurnos (Mid.)	Glamorg'n	Mid.	Ystalyfera and Gwys.
										G. W.	Over Midland Line.
								Blaen-Cae-Gurwen Colliery (Mid.)	Glamorg'n	Mid.—G. W.—L. & N. W.	Gurnos and Brynamman.
								Brynhenllysk Colliery Co.'s Colliery (Mid.)	Brecon ...	Mid.—G. W.—L. & N. W.	Gurnos and Gwys.
								Brynllynfell Colliery (Mid.)	Glamorg'n	Mid.—G. W.—L. & N. W.	Gurnos.
								Budd's Road Siding (Mid.)	Glamorg'n	Mid.—G. W.—L. & N. W.	Gurnos and Ystalyfera.
								Clayphon Siding (Mid.)	Glamorg'n	Mid.—G. W.—L. & N. W.	Yniscedwyn Branch.
								Cwmphil Siding (Rees Morgan's Siding) (Mid.)	Glamorg'n	Mid.—G. W.—L. & N. W.	Gurnos and Gwys.
								Diamond Anthracite Mine Co.'s Colliery (Mid.)	Brecon ...	Mid.—G. W.—L. & N. W.	Yniscedwyn Branch.
								Gilwen Colliery (Mid.)	Glamorg'n	Mid.—G. W.—L. & N. W.	Gurnos and Gwys.
								Gurnos Anthracite Col. (Mid)	Glamorg'n	Mid.—G. W.—L. & N. W.	Yniscedwyn Branch.
								Gurnos Brick Co.'s Sid. (Mid)	Glamorg'n	Mid.—G. W.—L. & N. W.	Gurnos and Gwys.
								Gurnos Foundry (Mid.)	Glamorg'n	Mid.—G. W.—L. & N. W.	Gurnos.
								Gurnos Tin Plate Co.'s Siding (Mid.)	Glamorg'n	Mid.—G. W.—L. & N. W.	Gurnos and Gwys.

EXPLANATION—G *Goods Station.*   P *Passenger and Parcel Station.*   P* *Passenger, but not Parcel or Miscellaneous Traffic.*
F *Furniture Vans, Carriages, Portable Engines, and Machines on Wheels.*   L *Live Stock.*
H *Horse Boxes and Prize Cattle Vans.*   C *Carriages by Passenger Train.*

STATION ACCOMMODATION.						CRANE POWER.		STATIONS, &c.	COUNTY.	COMPANY.	POSITION.
						Tons	Cwts	Gurnos (Mid.)—continued.			
.	.	.	.	.	.			Gwaun-Cae-Gurwen Colliery (Mid.)	Glamorg'n	Mid.—G. W.—L. & N. W.	Gurnos and Brynamman.
.	.	.	.	.	.			Hendreforgan Col. (Mid.)	Glamorg'n	Mid.—G. W.—L. & N. W.	Gurnos and Gwys.
.	.	.	.	.	.			Henllys Vale Colliery (Mid.)	Glamorg'n	Mid.—G. W.—L. & N. W.	Gurnos and Gwys.
.	.	.	.	.	.			Pantmawr Col. Sid. (Mid.)	Glamorg'n	Mid.—G. W.—L. & N. W.	Gurnos.
.	.	.	.	.	.			Penygorof Siding (Mid.)	Glamorg'n	Mid.—G. W.—L. & N. W.	Yniscedwyn Branch.
.	.	.	.	.	.			Phœnix Tin Plate Co.'s Siding (Mid.)	Glamorg'n	Mid.—G. W.—L. & N. W.	Gurnos and Gwys.
.	.	.	.	.	.			Pwllbach Colliery (Mid.)	Glamorg'n	Mid.—G. W.—L. & N. W.	Gurnos and Ystalyfera.
.	.	.	.	.	.			Pwllbach Siding (Mid.)	Glamorg'n	Mid.—G. W.—L. & N. W.	Gurnos.
.	.	.	.	.	.			South Wales Anthracite Colliery Co.'s Yniscedwyn Colliery (Mid.)	Glamorg'n	Mid.—G. W.—L. & N. W.	Yniscedwyn Branch.
.	.	.	.	.	.			Tirbach Colliery and Brick Works (Mid.)	Glamorg'n	Mid.—G. W.—L. & N. W.	Gurnos and Ystalyfera.
.	.	.	.	.	.			Twrch Brk. Co.'s Sid. (Mid.)	Glamorg'n	Mid.—G. W.—L. & N. W.	Gurnos and Gwys.
.	.	.	.	.	.			Yniscedwyn Tin Plate Co.'s Siding (Mid)	Glamorg'n	Mid.—G. W.—L. & N. W.	Yniscedwyn Branch.
.	.	.	.	.	.			Ystradowen Colliery (Mid.)	Glamorg'n	Mid.—G. W.—L. & N. W.	Gurnos and Gwys.
G	P	.	.	.	.			Gurteen	Cork	C. & Muskerry	Coachford Junction and Coachford.
.	.	.	.	.	.			Gushetfaulds	Lanark	Cal.	See Glasgow.
.	.	.	.	.	.			Gushetfaulds Junction	Lanark	Cal.	Glasgow.
G	P	F	L	H	C			Guthrie	Forfar	Cal.	Forfar and Stonehaven.
.	.	.	.	.	.			Guthrie Junction	Forfar	Cal.	Guthrie and Glasterlaw.
G	P	.	L	.	.	0	12	Guyhirne	Cambs.	G. N. & G. E. Jt.	Spalding and March.
G	.	.	L	.	.	1	5	Twenty Foot River Siding	Cambs.	G. N. & G. E. Jt.	March and Guyhirne.
.	.	.	.	.	.			Gwaelodywaen Colliery(B&M)	Mon	B. & M.—G.W.	Pengam.
.	.	.	.	.	.			Gwalia Tin Plate Works	Glamorg'n	G. W.	Same as Gwynne & Co.'s Tin Plate Works (Briton Ferry).
G	.	.	.	.	.			Gwaun Cae Gurwen	Glamorg'n	G. W.	Branch from Garnant.
.	.	.	.	.	.			Gwaun Cae Gurwen Colliery (Brook Colliery)	Glamorg'n	G. W.	Garnant.
.	.	.	.	.	.			Gwaun-Cae-Gurwen Col.(Mid)	Glamorg'n	Mid.—G.W.—L. & N. W.	Gurnos.
.	.	.	.	.	.			Gwaunclawdd Colliery (N&B)	Brecon	N. & Brecon—Mid.	Abercrave.
.	.	.	.	.	.			Gwaun-y-bara Siding	Glamorg'n	B. & M.	Machen.
G	P	.	L	H	C			Gweedore	Donegal	L. & L. S.	Letterkenny and Burtonport.
.	.	.	.	.	.			Gwenallt Colliery	Mon	G. W.	Pontnewynydd.
.	.	.	.	.	.			Gwenffrwd Quarry	Glamorg'n	P. T. / S. Wales Min.	Cwmavon. / Briton Ferry and Cymmer.
.	.	.	.	.	.			Gwernllwyn Colliery	Glamorg'n	P. T.	Lletty Brongu.
.	.	.	.	.	.			Gwernydd Colliery (G. W.)	Carmarth'	G. W.—L. & N. W.	Llangennech.
G	P	.	.	.	.			Gwersyllt and Wheatsheaf (W. M. & C. Q.)	Denbigh	W. M. & C. Q. / G. C.	Buckley and Wrexham. / Over W. M. & C. Q. from Hawarden Bridge Junction.
	P										
.	.	.	.	.	.			Gwersyllt Brick Works	Denbigh	W. M. & C. Q.	Gwersyllt and Wrexham.
.	.	.	.	.	.			Gwersyllt Colliery	Denbigh	W. M. & C. Q.	Gwersyllt and Cefn-y-bedd.
.	.	.	.	.	.			Gwersyllt Brick Works	Denbigh	G. W. / W. M. & C. Q.	Same as Clayton's Brick Yard (Moss). / Gwersyllt and Wheatsheaf.
.	.	.	.	.	.			Gwersyllt Colliery	Denbigh	G. W. / W. M. & C. Q.	Moss. / Gwersyllt and Wheatsheaf.
G	P	.	L	H	.			Gwinear Road	Cornwall	G. W.	Camborne and Penzance.
.	.	.	.	.	.			Gwrhay Colliery	Mon	G. W.	Tredegar Junction.
.	.	.	.	.	.			Gwscwm Colliery	Carmarth'	B. P. & G. V.	Burry Port.
G	P	.	L	H	.			Gwyddelwern	Merioneth	L. & N. W.	Corwen and Denbigh.
.	.	.	.	.	.			Bryn Eglwys Siding	Merioneth	L. & N. W.	Gwyddelwern and Corwen.
.	.	.	.	.	.			Dee Clwyd Siding	Merioneth	L. & N. W.	Gwyddelwern and Derwen.
.	.	.	.	.	.			Gwynne & Co.'s Gwalia Tin Plate Works	Glamorg'n	G. W.	Briton Ferry.
.	.	.	.	.	.			Gwyn's Drift Colliery (Mid.)	Glamorg'n	Mid.—G. W.—L. & N. W.	See South Wales Primrose Coal Co. (Pontardawe).
G	P	.	.	.	.			Gwys (Mid.)	Brecon	Mid. / G. W.	Brynamman and Ystalyfera. / Over Midland Line.
.	.	.	.	.	.			Brynhenllysk Colliery Co.'s Colliery (Mid.)	Brecon	Mid.—G. W.—L. & N. W.	Near Gwys.
.	.	.	.	.	.			Hendreforgan Col. (Mid.)	Glamorg'n	Mid.—G. W.—L. & N. W.	Gwys and Gurnos.
.	.	.	.	.	.			Henllys Vale Col. (Mid.)	Glamorg'n	Mid.—G. W.—L. & N. W.	Near Gwys.
.	.	.	.	.	.			Gyfeillon Colliery (Great Western Colliery)	Glamorg'n	T. V.	Hafod.

EXPLANATION—G *Goods Station.*   P *Passenger and Parcel Station.*   P* *Passenger, but not Parcel or Miscellaneous Traffic.*
F *Furniture Vans, Carriages, Portable Engines, and Machines on Wheels.*   L *Live Stock.*
H *Horse Boxes and Prize Cattle Vans.*   C *Carriages by Passenger Train.*

STATION ACCOMMODATION.						CRANE POWER.	STATIONS, &c.	COUNTY.	COMPANY.	POSITION.
						Tons Cwts.	**H**			
G	P	F	L	H	C	5 0	Habergham Siding	Lancs	L. & Y.	Rose Grove.
							Habrough	Lincoln	G. C.	Barnetby and Grimsby.
							Immingham Siding	Lincoln	G. C.	Habrough.
							Habrough Junction	Lincoln	G. C.	Habrough and Ulceby.
G	P	F	L	H	C		Hackbridge	Surrey	L. B. & S. C.	Sutton and Mitcham Junction.
							Hackney	Middlesex	N. L.	See London.
							Hackney Coal Depôt	Middlesex	L. & N. W.	See London.
							Hackney Downs	Middlesex	G. E.	See London.
							Hackney Wick	Middlesex	G. N.	See London.
							Hackney Wick Junction	Middlesex	G. E.—N. L.	London, Victoria Park or Hackney Wick Junction.
G	P	F	L	H	C		Haconby Siding	Lincoln	G. N.	Morton Road.
							Haddenham	Cambs	G. E.	Ely and St. Ives.
							Jewson's, F., Siding	Cambs	G. E.	Sutton and Haddenham.
							Porter's, J., Siding	Cambs	G. E.	Haddenham.
G	P	F	L	H	C	3 0	Haddington	Hadding'n	N. B.	Branch from Longniddry.
G							Coatyburn Siding	Hadding'n	N. B.	Longniddry and Haddington.
G							Laverocklaw Siding	Hadding'n	N. B.	Longniddry and Haddington.
G	P	F	L	H	C		Haddiscoe	Norfolk	G. E.	Norwich and Lowestoft.
							Bagshaw's, G. & J., Siding	Norfolk	G. E.	Haddiscoe.
G	P		L	H		5 0	Hadfield (for Hollingworth)	Derby	G. C.	Guide Bridge and Penistone.
							Hadfield Mills (Rhodes Sid.)	Derby	G. C.	Hadfield (for Hollingworth).
							Hadfield's Steel Foundry Co.—			
							East Hecla Works	Yorks	L. D. & E. C.—Mid.	Sheffield, Tinsley Road.
							East Hecla Works (G. C.)	Yorks	G. C.—Mid.	Tinsley.
							Tinsley Works	Yorks	L. D. & E. C.—Mid.	Sheffield, Tinsley Road.
							Tinsley Works (G. C.)	Yorks	G. C.—Mid.	Tinsley.
G	P			H			Hadham	Herts	G. E.	St. Margaret's and Buntingford.
G	P	F	L	H	C	5 0	Hadleigh	Suffolk	G. E.	Branch from Bentley.
	P						Wilson, T. W. (Exors, of) Sid.	Suffolk	G. E.	Hadleigh.
							Hadley	Salop	L. & N. W.	Shrewsbury and Stafford.
G	P						Hadley Lodge Siding	Salop	L. & N. W.	Same as Blockley's Sid. (Wombridge).
	P					}	Hadley Wood (G. N.)	Middlesex	{ G. N. / N. L.	New Barnet and Hatfield. / Over G. N. from Canonbury Junc.
G	P						Hadlow Road	Cheshire	B'head Jt. (G W & L N W)	Hooton and West Kirby.
G	P		L	H	C		Hadnall	Salop	L. & N. W.	Shrewsbury and Whitchurch.
							Hadnock Siding	Hereford	G. W.	Symond's Yat.
G	P						Hafod	Denbigh	G. W.	See Johnstown and Hafod.
	P					}	Hafod (T.V.)	Glamorg'n	{ T. V. / Barry	Pontypridd and Porth. / Over T. V. from Hafod Junction.
							Coke Ovens Sidings	Glamorg'n	T. V.	Pontypridd and Hafod.
							Gyfeillon Colliery (Great Western Colliery)	Glamorg'n	T. V.	Pontypridd and Hafod.
							Hafod Colliery	Glamorg'n	T. V.	Hafod and Porth.
							Tymawr Colliery	Glamorg'n	T. V.	Pontypridd and Hafod.
							Hafod Junction	Glamorg'n	Barry—T.V.	Pontypridd and Hafod.
							Hafod Junction	Glamorg'n	G. W.	Swansea.
							Hafod Rhondda Colliery	Glamorg'n	Barry	Hafod Junction.
							Hafod Siding	Glamorg'n	G. W.	See Vivian & Sons (Swansea).
							Hafod-y-bwch Colliery	Denbigh	G. W.	Johnstown and Hafod.
							Haggerston (N.L.)	Middlesex	N. L.—L. & N. W.	See London.
							Haggie's, D. H. G., Rope Wks.	Durham	N. E.	Sunderland, Monkwearmouth.
							Hagg Lane Siding	Yorks	N. E.	See Milford Junction Station.
							Haggs Siding	Edinboro'	Cal.	Balerno.
							Haghill (N. B.)	Lanark	N. B.—G. & S. W.	See Glasgow.
							Haghill Refuse Works (N. B.)	Lanark	N. B.—G. & S. W.	Glasgow, Haghill.
G	P			H	C		Hagley	Worcester	G. W.	Dudley and Kidderminster.
G	P	F	L	H	C	3 0	Hagley Road	Warwick	L. & N. W.	See Birmingham.
							Haigh	Yorks	L. & Y.	Horbury Junction and Barnsley.
							Haigh Colliery (L. & Y.)	Yorks	L. & Y.—N. E.	Haigh.
							Woolley Colliery (L. & Y.)	Yorks	L. & Y.—G. C.—N. E.	Near Haigh.
							Haigh Brewery	Lancs	L. & N. W.	Same as Sumner & Co's Sid. (Wigan).
							Haigh Foundry	Lancs	L. & N. W.	Same as Petford's Siding (Wigan).
							Haigh Junction	Lancs	L & Y & L U Jt.—L. & N. W.	Red Rock.
							Haigh Moor Coal Co.'s Siding	Yorks	L. & Y.	Crigglestone.

EXPLANATION—G *Goods Station.*   P *Passenger and Parcel Station.*   P* *Passenger, but not Parcel or Miscellaneous Traffic.*
F *Furniture Vans, Carriages, Portable Engines, and Machines on Wheels.*   L *Live Stock.*
H *Horse Boxes and Prize Cattle Vans.*   C *Carriages by Passenger Train.*

\multicolumn{6}{c}{STATION ACCOMMODATION.}	CRANE POWER.	STATIONS, &c.	COUNTY.	COMPANY.	POSITION.
						Tons Cwts.	Haigh Moor Colliery Co.'s Sid.	Yorks	E. & W. Y. Union	Same as Newmarket Haigh Moor Colliery Co.'s Sid. (Robin Hood).
							Haigh Saw Mills (L. & N. W.)	Lancs	L & N W– G C (Wig. Jn.)	See Wigan Coal & Iron Co. (Wigan).
							Haigh's Victoria Colliery (Bruntcliffe Colliery)	Yorks	G. N.	Morley.
							Hailes Quarry	Edinboro'	Cal.	Slateford.
							Hailey Brickfields Siding	Herts	G. E.	St. Margarets.
G	P	F	L	H	C	5 0	Hailsham	Sussex	L. B. & S. C.	Polegate and Hellingly.
G	P		L				Hainault	Essex	G. E.	Woodford and Ilford.
							Hainton	Lincoln	G. N.	Same as South Willingham.
G	P					2 0	Hairmyres	Lanark	Cal.	Busby and East Kilbride.
							Hairmyres Limestone Qry.	Lanark	Cal.	Hairmyres.
G	P		L			0 18	Halbeath	Fife	N. B.	Dunfermline & Cowdenbeath, New
G	P					5 0	Hale	Cheshire	C.L.C. (G C, G N, & Mid.)	Altrincham and Northwich.
							Hale	Lancs	L. & N. W.	See Halebank (for Hale).
	P						Halebank (for Hale)	Lancs	L. & N. W.	Garston and Warrington.
							Hale End	Essex	G. E.	See Higham Park and Hale End.
G	P	F	L	H	C	6 0	Halesowen (G. W.)	Worcester	{ G. W. / Mid.	Branch from Old Hill. / Branch from Northfield.
G						12 0	Halesowen Basin	Worcester	G. W.	Branch from Halesowen.
							Somer's Siding	Worcester	G. W.	Halesowen Basin Branch.
							Halesowen Junction	Worcester	G. W.—Halesowen	Old Hill and Northfield.
							Hales Siding (L. & N. W.)	Staffs	L. & N. W.— G.W.— Mid.	Walsall.
G	P	F	L	H	C	1 0	Halesworth	Suffolk	{ G. E. / Southwold	Ipswich and Beccles. / Terminus (Darsham and Brampton).
	P						Halewood	Lancs	C.L.C.(G C, G N, & Mid.)	Warrington and Garston.
	P						Haley's Foundry	Yorks	G. N.	Bramley.
							HALIFAX—			
G	P	F	L	H	C	10 0	(Station) (L. & Y.)	Yorks	{ L. & Y. / G. N. / L. & N. W.	Huddersfield and Bradford. / Over L. & Y. from Bowling Junc. / Over L. & Y. from Bradley Wood Jn.
	P	F	L	H	C					
G		F	L			10 0				
							Charlestown Brick & Tile Siding	Yorks	H & O Jt (G N & L & Y)	North Bridge.
							Church Street Coal Depôt	Yorks	H & O Jt (G N & L & Y)	North Bridge and Shaw Syke.
							Corporation Brick and Gas Works	Yorks	H & O Jt (G N & L & Y)	North Bridge.
							Crossley & Son's Siding	Yorks	H & O Jt (G N & L & Y)	North Bridge and Ovenden.
G	P	F	L	H	C	10 0	Holmfield	Yorks	H & O Jt (G N & L & Y)	Bradford and Halifax.
							Holmfield Junction	Yorks	G N—H & O Jt (G N&L&Y)	Queensbury and Ovenden.
							Holmfield Junction	Yorks	H'fax H. L.—H. & O. Jt.	Holmfield and Pellon.
							Junction	Yorks	H. & O. Jt.—L. & Y.	North Bridge and Shaw Syke.
G	P	F	L			10 0	North Bridge	Yorks	H & O Jt (G N & L & Y)	Holmfield and Shaw Syke.
	P						Ovenden	Yorks	H & O Jt (G N & L & Y)	Holmfield and North Bridge.
G	P	F	L	H	C	10 0	Pellon	Yorks	H'fax H. L. (G N & L & Y)	Branch near Holmfield.
G	P						St. Paul's	Yorks	H'fax H. L. (G N & L & Y)	Branch near Holmfield.
G			F	L	H	10 0	South Parade	Yorks	{ G. N. / L. & Y.	Branch near Shaw Syke. / Branch near Shaw Syke.
G			F	L		8 0				
							Webster & Son's Siding	Yorks	H'fax H. L. (G N & L & Y)	Wheatley.
G						2 0	Wheatley	Yorks	H'fax H. L. (G N & L & Y)	Holmfield and Pellon.
							Halifax Corporation Brick and Gas Works	Yorks	H. & O. Jt. (G. N. & L. & Y.)	Halifax, North Bridge.
							Halifax Siding	Suffolk	G. E.	Ipswich.
G	P	F	L	H	C	3 0	Halkirk	Caithness	High.	Helmsdale and Wick.
							Halkyn Lime Co.—			
							Halkyn Siding	Flint	L. & N. W.	Rhydymwyn.
							Hendre Siding	Flint	L. & N. W.	Rhydymwyn.
							Hall & Boardman's—			
							Brick Yard (Mid.)	Derby	Mid.—L. & N. W.	Swadlincote.
							Pipe Works (Mid.)	Derby	Mid.—L. & N. W.	Swadlincote.
							Siding	Derby	L. & N. W.	Alsop-en-le-dale.
							Hall & Co.'s—			
							Siding	Surrey	L. B. & S. C.	Beddington Lane.
							Siding	Sussex	L. B. & S. C.	Chichester.
							Siding	Surrey	L. B. & S. C.	East Croydon.
							Siding	Surrey	L. B. & S. C.	Epsom.
							Siding	Surrey	L. B. & S. C.	Mitcham.
							Siding	Surrey	L. B. & S. C.	Redhill.
							Siding	Surrey	L. B. & S. C.	Stoats Nest.
							Hall & Davidson's Siding	Surrey	L. & S.W.	Ewell.
							Hall & Pickles' Siding	Lancs	Manchester Ship Canal	Manchester.
							Hall & Shaw's Works	Lancs	L. & N. W.—S. & M. Jt.	See United Alkali Co. (Widnes).
							Hall & Stell's Siding	Yorks	Mid.	Keighley.

EXPLANATION—G Goods Station.   P Passenger and Parcel Station.   Pᵃ Passenger, but not Parcel or Miscellaneous Traffic.
F Furniture Vans, Carriages, Portable Engines, and Machines on Wheels.   L Live Stock.
H Horse Boxes and Prize Cattle Vans.   C Carriages by Passenger Train.

STATION ACCOMMODATION.						CRANE POWER.		STATIONS, &c.	COUNTY.	COMPANY.	POSITION.
						Tons	Cwts.				
.	.	.	.	.	.	.	.	Hall, J., & Co.—			
.	.	.	.	.	.	.	.	Amblecote Siding	Staffs	G. W.	Stourbridge.
.	.	.	.	.	.	.	.	Siding	Staffs	G. W.	Brettell Lane.
.	.	.	.	.	.	.	.	Hall's Brick Siding	Lincoln	G. N.	Bardney.
.	.	.	.	.	.	.	.	Hall's Collieries (Mid.)—			
.	.	.	.	.	.	.	.	Cadley Hill Colliery (Mid.)	Derby	Mid.—L. & N. W.	Swadlincote.
.	.	.	.	.	.	.	.	Swadlincote Old Col.(Mid.)	Derby	Mid.—L. & N. W.	Swadlincote.
.	.	.	.	.	.	.	.	Hall's Colliery	Derby	Mid.	New Mills.
.	.	.	.	.	.	.	.	Hall's Malt Kilns	Yorks	G. C.	Kiveton Park.
.	.	.	.	.	.	.	.	Halls' Siding	Beds	L. & N. W.	Bedford.
.	.	.	.	.	.	.	.	Hall's Siding	Lancs	L. & N. W.	Oldham, Glodwick Road.
.	.	.	.	.	.	.	.	Hall's Tramroad Junction	Mon	G. W.	Cross Keys and Risca.
.	.	.	.	.	.	.	.	Hallack & Bonds' Siding	Cambs	L. & N. W.	Cambridge.
.	.	.	.	.	.	.	.	Hallam & Son's Sid.(L&N.W.)	Staffs	L&NW—Mid.—GN—NS	Burton-on-Trent.
.	.	.	.	.	.	.	.	Hallamfield Siding	Derby	G. N.	Ilkeston.
.	.	.	.	.	.	.	.	Hallam Fields Siding	Derby	Mid.	See Stanton Iron Co. (Stanton Gate).
G	P	F	L	H	C	.	.	Hallaton	Leicester	G. N. & L. & N. W. Jt.	Melton Mowbray & Market Harboro'.
G	P	F	L	H	C	3	0	Hallatrow	Somerset	G. W.	Clutton and Welton.
.	.	.	.	.	.	.	.	Farrington Colliery	Somerset	G. W.	Hallatrow.
.	.	.	.	.	.	.	.	Hard Stone Firms Siding	Somerset	G. W.	Hallatrow.
.	.	.	.	.	.	.	.	Old Mills Colliery	Somerset	G. W.	Hallatrow.
.	.	.	.	.	.	.	.	Hall Carr Siding	Lancs	L. & Y.	Rawtenstall.
.	.	.	.	.	.	.	.	Hallcraig Brick Works	Lanark	Cal.	Carluke.
.	.	.	.	.	.	.	.	Hallcraig Junction	Lanark	Cal.	Carluke and Law Junction.
.	.	.	.	.	.	.	.	Hallcraig Tile Works	Lanark	Cal.	Carluke.
.	.	.	.	.	.	.	.	Hall End Colliery	Warwick	Mid.	Same as Birch Coppice Colliery (Kingsbury).
.	.	.	.	.	.	.	.	Hall Green Sand and Gravel Siding	Cumb'land	C. & W. Jn.	High Harrington.
G	P	F	L	H	C	.	.	Halling	Kent	S. E. & C.	Strood and Maidstone, West.
.	.	.	.	.	.	.	.	Hilton, Anderson & Co.'s Siding	Kent	S. E. & C.	Halling.
G	P	.	L	H	.	.	.	Hallington	Lincoln	G. N.	Louth and Lincoln.
G	.	.	.	.	.	10	0	Halliwell	Lancs	L. & Y.	Branch—Bolton and The Oaks.
.	.	.	.	.	.	.	.	Clifton & Kearsley Co.'s Sid.	Lancs	L. & Y.	Halliwell.
.	.	.	.	.	.	.	.	L. & Y. Railway Stores Sid.	Lancs	L. & Y.	Halliwell.
.	.	.	.	.	.	.	.	Hall Lane Coal Siding	Yorks	G. N.	Same as Ripley's Siding (Bradford).
.	P	.	.	.	.	.	.	Hall Road (L. & Y.)	Lancs	{ L. & Y. / L. & N. W.	Liverpool and Southport. / Over L. & Y. from Bootle Junction.
.	.	.	.	.	.	.	.	Hall Royd Siding	Yorks	G. C.	Silkstone.
.	.	.	.	.	.	.	.	Hallside Colliery (Hallside East Farm Siding)	Lanark	Cal.	Newton.
.	.	.	.	.	.	.	.	Hallside East Farm Siding	Lanark	Cal.	Same as Hallside Colliery (Newton).
.	.	.	.	.	.	.	.	Hallside Private Siding	Lanark	Cal.	See Bardykes Colliery (Newton).
.	.	.	.	.	.	.	.	Hallside Steel Works	Lanark	Cal.	Same as Newton Steel Works (Newton).
.	.	.	.	.	.	.	.	Hallyard's Siding	Edinboro'	N. B.	Ratho.
G	P	.	.	.	.	.	.	Halmerend	Staffs	N. S.	Alsager Junc. and Keele Junc.
G	P	F	.	.	.	.	.	Halsall	Lancs	L. & Y.	Barton and Southport.
.	.	.	.	.	.	.	.	Halshaw Moor	Lancs	L. & Y.	See Farnworth and Halshaw Moor.
G	P	F	L	H	C	2	0	Halstead	Essex	C. V. & H.	Chappel and Haverhill.
G	P	F	L	H	C	5	0	Halton	Cheshire	B'head Jt. (G W & L N W)	Helsby and Warrington.
.	.	.	.	.	.	.	.	Cheshire Siding	Cheshire	B'head Jt. (G W & L N W)	Frodsham and Halton.
.	.	.	.	.	.	.	.	Speakman's Sutton Dock	Cheshire	B'head Jt. (G W & L N W)	Frodsham and Halton.
G	P	.	.	.	.	1	10	Halton	Lancs	Mid.	Lancaster and Skipton.
.	.	.	.	.	.	.	.	Halton & Co.'s Sid. (L & N W)	Lancs	L. & N. W.—G. W.	Warrington, Bank Quay.
G	P	.	L	.	.	1	5	Halton Holgate	Lincoln	G. N.	Firsby and Spilsby.
.	.	.	.	.	.	.	.	Halton Lea Gate	Cumb'land	N. E.	Brampton Junction and Lambley.
G	P	F	L	H	C	3	0	Haltwhistle	Northumb	N. E.	Carlisle and Hexham.
.	.	.	.	.	.	.	.	Blackett Colliery	Northumb	N. E.	Haltwhistle and Bardon Mill.
.	.	.	.	.	.	.	.	South Tyne Col. & Bk. Wks.	Northumb	N. E.	Haltwhistle.
G	P	F	L	H	C	.	.	Halwill Junction Station	Devon	L. & S.W.	Okehampton and Bude.
.	.	.	.	.	.	.	.	Hambledon	Hants	L. & S.W.	See Droxford (for Hambledon).
G	P	.	L	H	.	1	10	Hambleton	Yorks	N. E.	Selby and Milford Junction.
.	.	.	.	.	.	.	.	Hambleton Quarries (J. Green & Son's)	Yorks	Mid.	Bolton Abbey.
.	.	.	.	.	.	.	.	Hambleton Siding	Yorks	Mid.	See Duke of Devonshire's (Bolton Abbey).
.	.	.	.	.	.	.	.	Hamburg, Antwerp, & Rotterdam Wharf	Northumb	N. E.	Newcastle-on-Tyne.
.	.	.	.	.	.	.	.	Ham Hill & Doulting Stone Co.'s Siding	Somerset	G. W.	Yeovil, Hendford.

EXPLANATION—G Goods Station.   P Passenger and Parcel Station.   P* Passenger, but not Parcel or Miscellaneous Traffic.
F Furniture Vans, Carriages, Portable Engines, and Machines on Wheels.   L Live Stock.
H Horse Boxes and Prize Cattle Vans.   C Carriages by Passenger Train.

Station Accommodation.						Crane Power.		Stations, &c.	County.	Company.	Position.
						Tons	Cwts.	HAMILTON—			
G	P	F	L	H	C	3	0	(Station)	Lanark	N. B.	Branch from Shettleston.
								Allanshaw Colliery	Lanark	Cal. / N. B.	Hamilton, Central & Hamilton West. Peacock Cross Station.
								Auchenraith Colliery	Lanark	N. B.	Branch—Bothwell and Burnbank.
								Barncluith Colliery	Lanark	Cal.	Hamilton, Central and Ferniegair.
								Bent Colliery	Lanark	Cal.	Branch near Hamilton, West.
								Birdsfield Brick Works	Lanark	N. B.	Branch—Bothwell and Burnbank.
								Blantyre Colliery	Lanark	N. B.	Branch—Bothwell and Burnbank.
G	P		L			1	10	Burnbank	Lanark	N. B.	Bothwell and Hamilton.
								Cadzow Colliery	Lanark	Cal.	Branch near Hamilton, West.
G	P	F	L	H	C	3	0	Central	Lanark	Cal.	Larkhall and Newton.
								Clyde Steel & Engineering Works	Lanark	N. B.	Peacock Cross and Hamilton.
								Corporation Refuse Siding	Lanark	Cal.	Hamilton, West and Blantyre.
								Earnock Colliery	Lanark	Cal. / N.B.	Hamilton, West and Blantyre. Burnbank and Peacock Cross.
								Fairhill Colliery	Lanark	Cal.	Branch near Hamilton, West.
								Frew's Foundry	Lanark	Cal.	Hamilton, West.
								Greenfield Colliery	Lanark	Cal.	Hamilton, West and Blantyre.
								Greenfield Foundry	Lanark	N. B.	Branch—Bothwell and Burnbank.
								Hamilton Colliery	Lanark	Cal.	Hamilton, West.
	P							Peacock Cross	Lanark	N. B.	Bothwell and Hamilton.
								Silverton Colliery	Lanark	Cal.	Hamilton, Central and Ferniegair.
								Wellhall Colliery	Lanark	N. B.	Burnbank and Peacock Cross.
G	P					4	10	West	Lanark	Cal.	Hamilton, Central and Newton.
								Whistleberry Colliery	Lanark	Cal.	Hamilton, West and Blantyre.
								Whitehill Colliery	Lanark	Cal.	Hamilton, West and Blantyre.
								Hamilton Corporation Refuse Siding	Lanark	Cal.	Hamilton.
								Hamilton Corporation Refuse Siding	Lanark	Cal.	Larkhall.
								Hamilton Junction	Lanark	Cal.	Newton.
								Hamilton Palace Colliery	Lanark	Cal. / N. B.	Uddingston. Bellshill.
G	P		L	H				Hamilton's Bawn	Armagh	G. N. (I.)	Goragh Wood and Armagh.
								Hamilton's Brick & Tile Wks.	Cumb'land	Mid.	Cumwhinton.
								Hamilton's Siding	Lancs	L. & Y.	Oldham, Mumps.
								Hamilton's Albion Corn Mill	Lancs	L. & N. W.	Oldham, Glodwick Road.
								Hamilton Square	Cheshire	Mersey	See Birkenhead.
	P							Ham Lane	Somerset	W. C. & P.	Weston-super-Mare and Clevedon.
								Hamlett's Siding	Cheshire	C. L. C. (G C, G N, & Mid.)	Winsford and Over.
								Hammersmith (Broadway)	Middlesex	H. & C. Jt.—Met. Dist.	See London.
								Hammersmith and Chiswick	Middlesex	N.&S.W.Jn.Jt.(L.&NW, Mid., & N. L.)	See London.
								Hammersmith Branch Junc.	Middlesex	N.&S.W.Jn.Jt.(L.&NW, Mid., & N. L.)	London, Acton and South Acton.
								Hammersmith (Grove Road) (L. & S. W.)	Middlesex	L. & S.W.—G. W.—Met	See London.
								Hammersmith Junction	Middlesex	H. & C. Jt.—L. & S. W.	London, Shepherd's Bush&GroveRd.
G	P							Hammerton	Yorks	N. E.	York and Knaresboro'.
								Hammerton Street Junction	Yorks	G. N.	Bradford.
								Hammerton Str. Sids. (G. N.)	Yorks	G. N.—G. C.	Bradford, Adolphus Street.
G	P							Hammerwich	Staffs	L. & N. W.	Lichfield and Walsall.
G	P	F		H	C			Hampden Pk.(for Willingdon)	Sussex	L. B. & S. C.	Polegate and Eastbourne.
G	P							Hampole	Yorks	W.R.&G.Jt.(G.C.&G.N.)	Doncaster and Wakefield.
								Hampole Siding	Yorks	H. & B.	Pickburn & Brodsworth.
								Hampstead's(Borough of)Sid.	Middlesex	L. & N. W.	London, Finchley Road and Frognal.
								Hampstead Heath (L. & N.W.)	Middlesex	L. & N. W.—N. L.	See London.
G	P	F	L	H	C	3	0	Hampstead Norris	Berks	G. W.	Didcot and Newbury.
	P							Hampstead Road Junction	Middlesex	L. & N. W—N. L.	London, Camden.
G	P	F	L	H	C	10	0	Hampsthwaite	Yorks	N. E.	Harrogate and Pateley Bridge.
								Hampton	Middlesex	L. & S.W.	Twickenham and Shepperton.
								Hampton Water Works	Middlesex	L. & S.W.	Hampton.
G	P	F	L	H	C	5	0	Hampton	Warwick	L. & N. W. / Mid.	Birmingham and Coventry. Whitacre and Hampton Junction.
G	P	F	L	H	C						
								Packington's Siding	Warwick	Mid.	Hampton and Coleshill.
								Hampton Junction	Warwick	L. & N. W.—Mid.	Coventry and Whitacre.
G	P	F	L	H	C	5	0	HamptonCourt&East Molesey	Surrey	L. & S.W.	Branch from Hampton Court Junc.
								Hampton Court Gas Co.'s Sid.	Middlesex	L. & S.W.	Teddington.
								Hampton Court Junction	Surrey	L. & S.W.	Surbiton and Esher.
								Hampton Hill	Middlesex	L. & S.W.	See Fulwell and Hampton Hill.

EXPLANATION—G *Goods Station.*   P *Passenger and Parcel Station.*   P* *Passenger, but not Parcel or Miscellaneous Traffic.*
F *Furniture Vans, Carriages, Portable Engines, and Machines on Wheels.*   L *Live Stock.*
H *Horse Boxes and Prize Cattle Vans.*   C *Carriages by Passenger Train.*

STATION ACCOMMODATION.						CRANE POWER.		STATIONS, &c.	COUNTY.	COMPANY.	POSITION.
						Tons	Cwts.				
G	P	.	.	.	.	.	.	Hampton Loade	Salop	G. W.	Hartlebury and Bridgnorth.
.	.	.	.	.	.	.	.	Hampton-on-Sea	Kent	S. E. & C.	See Herne Bay and Hampton-on-Sea.
.	P	.	.	.	.	.	.	Hampton Wick	Middlesex	L. & S.W.	Kingston and Teddington.
.	.	.	.	.	.	.	.	Hamstead Colliery	Staffs	L. & N. W.	Great Barr.
.	.	.	.	.	.	.	.	Hamsteel's Colliery, Coke Ovens and Brick Works	Durham	N. E.	Waterhouses.
.	.	.	.	.	.	.	.	Hamsterley Colliery	Durham	N. E.	Ebchester.
G	P	.	L	H	C	.	.	Ham Street and Orlestone	Kent	S. E. & C.	Hastings and Ashford.
.	.	.	.	.	.	.	.	Ruckinge Siding	Kent	S. E. & C.	Ham Street and Ashford.
.	.	.	.	.	.	.	.	Ham Street Bank Siding	Kent	S. E. & C.	Ham Street and Ashford.
.	.	.	.	.	.	.	.	Hamwood Siding	Somerset	S.&D.Jt.(L.&S.W.& Mid)	Binegar and Shepton Mallet.
G.	.	F	L	H	.	5	0	Hamworthy	Dorset	L. & S.W.	Branch from Hamworthy Junction.
G	.	.	.	.	.	10	0	Hamworthy Wharf	Dorset	L. & S.W.	Hamworthy.
.	.	.	.	.	.	.	.	Sydenham & Co.'s Siding	Dorset	L. & S.W.	Hamworthy.
G	P	F	L	H	C	.	.	Hamworthy Junction Station	Dorset	L. & S.W.	Wimborne and Wareham.
.	.	.	.	.	.	.	.	Kinson Pottery Co.'s Siding	Dorset	L. & S.W.	Hamworthy Junction Station.
.	.	.	.	.	.	.	.	Lytchett Brick Works	Dorset	L. & S.W.	Hamworthy Junction Station.
.	.	.	.	.	.	.	.	Hancock & Co.'s Brick Siding	Flint	W. M. & C. Q.	Buckley.
.	.	.	.	.	.	.	.	Handaxwood Pit	L'lithgow	Cal.	Fauldhouse.
G	P	F	L	H	C	1	10	Handborough	Oxon	G. W.	Oxford and Evesham.
.	.	.	.	.	.	.	.	Combe's Siding	Oxon	G. W.	Handborough and Charlbury.
G	P	.	.	.	.	5	0	Handforth	Cheshire	L. & N. W.	Crewe and Stockport.
.	.	.	.	.	.	.	.	Handley & Co.'s Siding	Lancs	L. & N. W.	Widnes.
.	.	.	.	.	.	.	.	Handon Hold Colliery	Durham	N. E.	Pelton.
.	.	.	.	.	.	.	.	Handsworth	Yorks	G. C.	See Sheffield, Darnall (for Handsworth).
G	P	.	L	H	.	10	0	Handsworth and Smethwick	Staffs	G. W.	Birmingham and Wednesbury.
.	.	.	.	.	.	.	.	Birmingham Carriage and Wagon Works	Staffs	G. W.	Handsworth and Smethwick Junc.
.	.	.	.	.	.	.	.	Sandwell Park Colliery	Staffs	G. W.	Handsworth and West Bromwich.
.	P	.	.	.	.	.	.	Handsworth Wood	Staffs	L. & N. W.	Perry Barr and Soho Road.
.	.	.	.	.	.	.	.	Handyside & Co.'s Siding	Derby	Mid.	Same as Clarke Street Sid. (Derby).
.	.	.	.	.	.	.	.	Handyside & Co.'s Works	Derby	G. N.—Mid.	Derby.
.	.	.	.	.	.	.	.	Hanger Lane Junction	Middlesex	Met. Dist.	Ealing Common and North Ealing.
G	P	F	L	H	C	10	0	Hanley	Staffs	N. S.	Etruria and Burslem.
G	.	.	.	.	.	.	.	York Street Wharf	Staffs	N. S.	Hanley.
.	.	.	.	.	.	.	.	Hanley Borough Colliery	Staffs	N. S.	Bucknall.
.	.	.	.	.	.	.	.	Hannah Col. (Newsham Col.)	Northumb	N. E.	See Cowpen Collieries (Newsham).
G	P	.	.	.	.	.	.	Hannington	Wilts	G. W.	Swindon and Highworth.
.	.	.	.	.	.	.	.	Hannington & Co.'s Colliery	Durham	N. E.	Same as Axwell Park Colliery (Swalwell).
.	.	.	.	.	.	.	.	Hannington & Co.'s Siding	Durham	N. E.	Derwenthaugh.
.	.	.	.	.	.	.	.	Hannington Brick Works	Durham	N. E.	Derwenthaugh.
.	.	.	.	.	.	.	.	Hanson's Brewery	Notts	Mid.	Kimberley.
.	.	.	.	.	.	.	.	Hanwell	Middlesex	Met. Dist.	See Boston Road (for Brentford and Hanwell).
.	P	.	.	.	.	.	.	Hanwell and Elthorne	Middlesex	G. W.	London (Paddington) and Slough.
G	P	F	L	H	C	1	10	Hanwood	Salop	S&W'pl.Jt. (GW&LNW)	Shrewsbury and Welshpool.
.	.	.	.	.	.	.	.	Atherton's Cruckmeole or Shorthill Colliery	Salop	S&W'pl.Jt. (GW&LNW)	Hanwood and Plealey Road.
.	.	.	.	.	.	.	.	Smallshaw's Arscott Col.	Salop	S&W'pl.Jt. (GW&LNW)	Hanwood and Yockleton.
G	P	.	L	.	.	5	0	Hapton	Lancs	L. & Y.	Accrington and Burnley.
.	.	.	.	.	.	.	.	Riley's Siding	Lancs	L. & Y.	Hapton.
.	.	.	.	.	.	.	.	Harborne	Warwick	{ L. & N. W.	See Birmingham.
.	.	.	.	.	.	.	.			{ Mid.	See Birmingham, Somerset Road (for Harborne).
.	.	.	.	.	.	.	.	Harboro' Siding	Derby	L. & N. W.	Same as Swann, Ratcliffe & Co.'s Siding (Longcliffe).
G	P	.	L	H	.	4	10	Harburn	Edinboro'	Cal.	Carstairs and Edinburgh.
.	.	.	.	.	.	.	.	Harburn Lime Works	Edinboro'	Cal.	Cobbinshaw and Harburn.
.	.	.	.	.	.	.	.	Harbury	Warwick	G. W.	See Southam Road and Harbury.
.	.	.	.	.	.	.	.	Harby	Notts	L. D. & E. C.	See Doddington and Harby.
G	P	F	L	H	C	5	0	Harby and Stathern	Leicester	G. N. & L. & N. W. Jt.	Melton Mowbray and Nottingham
.	.	.	.	.	.	.	.	Stathern Ironstone Siding	Leicester	G. N. & L. & N. W. Jt.	Harby and Long Clawson.
.	.	.	.	.	.	.	.	Harcourt Street	Dublin	D. W. & W.	See Dublin.
G	.	.	.	.	.	1	10	Hardengreen	Edinboro'	N. B.	Edinburgh and Galashiels.
.	.	.	.	.	.	.	.	D'Arcy Lime Works	Edinboro'	N. B.	Newbattle Branch.
.	.	.	.	.	.	.	.	Eskbank Carpet Works (Stewart Bros.)	Edinboro'	N. B.	Hardengreen.
.	.	.	.	.	.	.	.	Kippielaw Siding	Edinboro'	N. B.	Newbattle Branch.
.	.	.	.	.	.	.	.	Lady Victoria Pit	Edinboro'	N. B.	Newbattle Branch.
.	.	.	.	.	.	.	.	Lingerwood Nos. 1 & 2 Sids.	Edinboro'	N. B.	Newbattle Branch.

EXPLANATION—G *Goods Station.*　　P *Passenger and Parcel Station.*　　P* *Passenger, but not Parcel or Miscellaneous Traffic.*
F *Furniture Vans, Carriages, Portable Engines, and Machines on Wheels.*　　L *Live Stock.*
H *Horse Boxes and Prize Cattle Vans.*　　C *Carriages by Passenger Train.*

STATION ACCOMMODATION.						CRANE POWER.	STATIONS. &c.	COUNTY.	COMPANY.	POSITION.
						Tons Cwt	**Hardengreen—**continued.			
.	.	.	.	.	.	. .	Newbattle Branch	Edinboro'	N. B.	Bch.—Hardengreen & Gorebridge.
.	.	.	.	.	.	. .	Newbattle Brick Works	Edinboro'	N. B.	Newbattle Branch.
.	.	.	.	.	.	. .	Newbattle Colliery	Edinboro'	N. B.	Newbattle Branch.
.	.	.	.	.	.	. .	Shaw's Depôt	Edinboro'	N. B.	Newbattle Branch.
.	.	.	.	.	.	. .	Hardengreen Junction	Edinboro'	N. B.	Eskbank and Dalhousie.
.	.	.	.	.	.	. .	Hardham Brick Siding	Sussex	L. B. & S. C.	Pulborough.
.	.	.	.	.	.	. .	Hardham Junction	Sussex	L. B. & S. C.	Pulborough and Amberley.
.	.	.	.	.	.	. .	Hardie & Gordon's Siding	Dumbartn	D. & B. Jt. (Cal. & N. B.)	Dalreoch.
G	P	F	L	H	C	1 0	Hardingham	Norfolk	G. E.	Wymondham and Dereham.
.	.	.	.	.	.	. .	Hardingstone Junction	N'hamptn	L. & N. W.— Mid.	Northampton.
.	.	.	.	.	.	. .	Hardman's Chemical Works	Staffs	N. S.	{ Chatterley. / { Milton.
.	.	.	.	.	.	. .	Hardshaw Brook Works, East and West	Lancs	L. & N. W.	See United Alkali Co. (St. Helens).
.	.	.	.	.	.	. .	Hard Stone Firms Siding	Somerset	G. W.	Hallatrow.
.	.	.	.	.	.	. .	Hardwick	Derby	Mid.	See Rowthorn and Hardwick.
.	.	.	.	.	.	. .	Hardwick Collieries	Derby	Mid.	Hasland.
.	.	.	.	.	.	. .	Hardwick Colliery (G. C.)	Derby	G. C.—G. N.—L. & N. W.	Heath.
.	.	.	.	.	.	. .	Hardwicke Quarry (Tytherington Stone Co.)	Glo'ster	Mid.	Tytherington.
G	.	.	L	.	.	. .	Hardwick Road Siding	Norfolk	Mid. & G. N. Jt.	South Lynn and Melton Constable.
.	.	.	.	.	.	. .	Hardy's Brewery	Notts	Mid.	Kimberley.
.	.	.	.	.	.	. .	Hardy's Siding	Derby	Mid.	Langley Mill.
G	P	F	L	H	C	5 0 }	Harecastle(forKidsgrove)(NS)	Staffs	{ N. S.	Longport and Congleton.
G	.	F	L	.	.	5 0 }			{ L. & N. W.	Over N. S. Line.
.	.	.	.	.	.	. .	Birchenwood Colliery Co.— Siding	Staffs	N. S.	Harecastle.
.	.	.	.	.	.	. .	Summit Siding	Staffs	N. S.	Harecastle Junction & Goldenhill.
.	.	.	.	.	.	. .	Trubshaw Sidings	Staffs	N. S.	Harecastle.
.	.	.	.	.	.	. .	Pooley & Son's Works	Staffs	N. S.	Trubshaw Siding.
.	.	.	.	.	.	. .	Settle's, J., Siding	Staffs	N. S.	Trubshaw Siding.
.	.	.	.	.	.	. .	Hareholme Siding	Lancs	L. & Y.	Clough Fold.
.	.	.	.	.	.	. .	Harehope Mining & Quarrying Co.'s Siding	Durham	N. E.	Frosterley.
.	.	.	.	.	.	. .	Harelaw Lime Siding	Hadding'n	N. B.	Longniddry.
G	P	.	L	H	.	. .	Hare Park and Crofton	Yorks	W. R.&G.Jt.(G.C.&G.N.)	Doncaster and Wakefield.
.	.	.	.	.	.	. .	Sharlston West Colliery	Yorks	W. R.&G.Jt.(G.C.&G.N.)	Hare Park and Crofton.
.	.	.	.	.	.	. .	Hare Park Junction	Yorks	W. R.&G.Jt.(G.C.&G.N.)	Hare Park and Wakefield.
.	P	.	.	.	.	. .	Haresfield	Glo'ster	Mid.	Gloucester and Stonehouse.
.	.	.	.	.	.	. .	Hareshaw Colliery	Lanark	Cal.	Salisburgh.
.	.	.	.	.	.	. .	Hareshaw Silica Brick Works	Lanark	Cal.	Salisburgh.
.	.	.	.	.	.	. .	Hargill Colliery	Durham	N. E.	Crook.
.	.	.	.	.	.	. .	Hargreaves' Colliery	Lancs	L. & Y.	Near Baxenden.
.	.	.	.	.	.	. .	Hargreaves, G., & Co.'s Siding (Whinney Hill Plastic Brick Co.'s Siding)	Lancs	L. & Y.	Huncoat.
.	.	.	.	.	.	. .	Hargreaves' Siding	Lancs	L. & Y.	Brierfield.
.	.	.	.	.	.	. .	Hargreaves' Siding	Lancs	L. & Y.	Waterfoot (for Newchurch).
G	P	.	L	H	.	. .	Harker	Cumb'land	N. B.	Hawick and Carlisle.
G	.	.	.	.	.	. .	Kingmoor Siding	Cumb'land	N. B.	Harker and Carlisle.
.	.	.	.	.	.	. .	Harkess, W., & Son's Ship Yard	Yorks	N. E.	Middlesbro'.
G	P	.	L	H	.	. .	Harlech	Merioneth	Cam.	Pwllheli and Barmouth.
.	.	.	.	.	.	. .	Harlesden	Middlesex	L. & N. W.	Same as London, Willesden Junc.
.	.	.	.	.	.	. .	Harlesden (for West Willesden and Stonebridge Park)	Middlesex	Mid.	See London.
G	P	F	L	H	C	8 0	Harleston	Norfolk	G. E.	Beccles and Tivetshall.
G	P	F	L	H	C	1 0	Harling Road	Norfolk	G. E.	Norwich and Thetford.
G	P	F	L	H	C	1 10	Harlington	Beds	Mid.	Bedford and Luton.
.	.	.	.	.	.	. .	Forder & Son— Lime and Cement Works	Beds	Mid.	Harlington and Leagrave.
.	.	.	.	.	.	. .	Westoning Brick Works	Beds	Mid.	Harlington and Flitwick.
.	.	.	.	.	.	. .	Gate's Siding	Beds	Mid.	Near Harlington.
.	.	.	.	.	.	. .	Harlington	Middlesex	G. W.	See Hayes and Harlington.
G	P	F	L	H	C	1 0	Harlow	Essex	G. E.	Broxbourne and Bishops Stortford.
.	.	.	.	.	.	. .	Harlow & Sawbridgeworth Gas Light & Coke Co.'s Siding	Essex	G. E.	Harlow.
.	.	.	.	.	.	. .	Harmire Siding (Hogg's Sid.)	Durham	N. E.	Barnard Castle.
G	P	F	L	H	C	1 0	Harmston	Lincoln	G. N.	Lincoln and Grantham.
G	P	.	.	.	.	. .	Harold Wood	Essex	G. E.	Chelmsford and Stratford.
.	.	.	.	.	.	. .	King & Son's Siding	Essex	G. E.	Harold Wood.

EXPLANATION—G *Goods Station.*   P *Passenger and Parcel Station.*   P* *Passenger, but not Parcel or Miscellaneous Traffic.*
F *Furniture Vans, Carriages, Portable Engines, and Machines on Wheels.*   L *Live Stock.*
H *Horse Boxes and Prize Cattle Vans.*   C *Carriages by Passenger Train.*

Station Accommodation						Crane Power		Stations, &c.	County	Company	Position
G	P	F	L	H	C	Tons	Cwts				
G	P	F	L	H	C	1	0	Harpenden	Herts	G. N.	Hatfield and Luton.
G	P	F	L	H	C					Mid.	Bedford and St. Albans.
.	.	.	.	.	.	.	.	Harper & Moore's Colliery and Fire Brick Works	Worcester	G. W.	Cradley Heath and Cradley.
G	P	.	.	.	.	.	.	Harperley	Durham	N. E.	Bishop Auckland and Wolsingham.
.	.	.	.	.	.	.	.	MacNiel's Siding	Durham	N. E.	Harperley.
.	.	.	.	.	.	.	.	Harperley Depôts	Durham	N. E.	Witton-le-Wear.
.	.	.	.	.	.	.	.	Harpersbrae Siding (Brown, J., & Co.)	Edinboro'	N. B.	Penicuik.
.	.	.	.	.	.	.	.	Harper's (Ltd.) Tramway	Kinc'rdine	Cal.—N. B.	Aberdeen, Guild Street.
G	.	.	.	.	.	.	.	Harpur Hill	Derby	L. & N. W.	Hindlow and Ladmanlow.
.	.	.	.	.	.	.	.	Harraton Colliery & Depôt	Durham	N. E.	Washington.
.	.	.	.	.	.	.	.	Harraton Hall Depôt	Durham	N. E.	Washington.
G	P	F	L	H	C	5	0	Harrietsham	Kent	S. E. & C.	Maidstone (East) and Ashford.
.	.	.	.	.	.	.	.	Harriman's Sanitary Pipe Works	Durham	N. E.	Blaydon.
.	.	.	.	.	.	.	.	Harringay (G. N.)	Middlesex	G. N.—N. L.—S. E. & C.	See London.
.	.	.	.	.	.	.	.	Harringay Park (Green Lanes)	Middlesex	Mid.—T. & H. Jt.	See London.
G	P	.	L	H	.	2	0	Harrington	Cumb'land	L. & N. W.	Whitehaven and Workington.
.	.	.	.	.	.	.	.	Bain & Co.'s Harrington Iron Works	Cumb'land	L. & N. W.	Harrington and Parton.
.	.	.	.	.	.	.	.	Harrington Gas Works	Cumb'land	L. & N. W.	Harrington.
.	.	.	.	.	.	.	.	Little's Wagon Repairing Works	Cumb'land	L. & N. W.	Harrington.
.	.	.	.	.	.	.	.	Harrington Harbour	Cumb'land	C. & W. Jn.	Branch from Harrington Junction.
.	.	.	.	.	.	.	.	Harrington Iron Works	Cumb'land	C. & W. Jn.	See Bain & Co.'s Sidings (High Harrington).
.	.	.	.	.	.	.	.			L. & N. W.	Same as Bain & Co.'s (Harrington).
.	.	.	.	.	.	.	.	Harrington Junction	Cumb'land	C. & W. Jn.	Workington and Distington.
G	P	F	L	H	C	1	5	Harringworth	N'hampton	Mid.	Kettering and Manton.
.	.	.	.	.	.	.	.	Harris & Pearson's Siding	Staffs	G. W.	Brettell Lane.
.	.	.	.	.	.	.	.	Harris' Deepwater Wharf	Yorks	N. E.	South Bank.
.	.	.	.	.	.	.	.	Harris' Siding	Beds	L. & N. W.	Leighton, Grovebury Crossing.
.	.	.	.	.	.	.	.	Harrison, Ainslie & Co.'s Siding	Lancs	Furness	Haverthwaite.
.	.	.	.	.	.	.	.	Harrison & Camm's Works	Yorks	Mid.	Same as Holmes' Wagon Works (Masboro' & Rotherham).
.	.	.	.	.	.	.	.	Harrison & Singleton's Siding	Durham	N. E.	Same as Baltic Saw Mill (West Hartlepool).
.	.	.	.	.	.	.	.	Harrison, Blair & Co.'s Chemical Works	Lancs	L. & Y.	Kearsley.
.	.	.	.	.	.	.	.	Harrison's, J. & C., Siding	Glamorg'n	GW—LNW—Mid—RSB	Swansea.
.	.	.	.	.	.	.	.	Harrison, J., & Son's Siding	Yorks	N. E.	See Packet Wharf Slate Yard (Middlesbro').
.	.	.	.	.	.	.	.	Harrison's—			
.	.	.	.	.	.	.	.	No. 1 or Old Brownhills Col.	Staffs	L. & N. W.	Brownhills.
.	.	.	.	.	.	.	.	Wyrley Grove Colliery	Staffs	L. & N. W.	Brownhills.
.	.	.	.	.	.	.	.	Harrison's, G. K., Siding	Staffs	G. W.	Brettell Lane.
.	.	.	.	.	.	.	.	Harrison's, G. K., Siding	Worcester	G. W.	Lye.
.	.	.	.	.	.	.	.	Harrison's Siding	Yorks	N. E.	Same as Woodland's Siding.
.	.	.	.	.	.	.	.	Harrison Park Siding	Edinboro'	Cal.	Edinburgh, Lothian Road.
G	P	F	L	H	C	10	0	Harristown	Kildare	G. S. & W.	Sallins and Tullow.
G	P	.	.	H	C					N. E.	Leeds and Ripon.
.	P	.	.	H	C			Harrogate (N. E.)	Yorks	G. N.	Over L. & Y. and N. E. Lines.
.	P	.	.	H	C					L. & Y.	Over N. E. from Leeds.
.	P	.	.	.	.					Mid.	Over N. E. from Leeds.
.	.	.	.	.	.	.	.	Crimple Junction	Yorks	N. E.	Harrogate and Pannal.
.	.	.	.	.	.	.	.	Dragon Junction	Yorks	N. E.	Harrogate and Starbeck.
.	.	.	.	.	.	.	.	Harrop Benson's Foundry	Glamorg'n	G. W. & L. & N. W. Jt.	Pontardulais.
G	P	F	L	H	C	5	0	Harrow and Wealdstone	Middlesex	L. & N. W.	Watford and London (Willesden Jn).
.	.	.	.	.	.	.	.	Bransgrove's Kenton Lane Siding	Middlesex	L. & N. W.	Harrow and Stanmore.
.	.	.	.	.	.	.	.	Ingall, Parsons, Clive & Co.'s Siding	Middlesex	L. & N. W.	Harrow and Stanmore.
.	.	.	.	.	.	.	.	Harrowby's Siding	Staffs	N. S.	Sandon.
.	.	.	.	.	.	.	.	Harrow Lane Junction	Middlesex	G. E.—N. L.	Same as Millwall Docks Junction (London).
G	P	F	L	H	C	1	10	Harrow-on-the-Hill (Met.)	Middlesex	Met.	Baker Street and Rickmansworth.
.	P	.	.	H	C					G. C.	Over Met. Line.
.	.	.	.	.	.	.	.	Harrow, South	Middlesex	Met. Dist.	See South Harrow.
.	.	.	.	.	.	.	.	Harrow, South Junction	Middlesex	Met.	Harrow-on-the-Hill and Canfield Place Junction.

EXPLANATION—G *Goods Station.*   P *Passenger and Parcel Station.*   P* *Passenger, but not Parcel or Miscellaneous Traffic.*
F *Furniture Vans, Carriages, Portable Engines, and Machines on Wheels.*   L *Live Stock.*
H *Horse Boxes and Prize Cattle Vans.*   C *Carriages by Passenger Train.*

STATION ACCOMMODATION.						CRANE POWER.	STATIONS, &c.	COUNTY.	COMPANY.	POSITION.
						Tons Cwts.				
G	P	F	L	H	C	. . }	Harryville	Antrim	N. C. Com. (Mid.)	See Ballymena (Harryville).
G	P	.	.	H	C	. . }	Harston (G. E.)	Cambs	{ G. E.	Cambridge and Shepreth Junction.
									{ G. N.	Over G. E. from Shepreth Junction.
.	P	.	.	.	.		Hart	Durham	N. E.	Hartlepool and Castle Eden.
.	P	.	.	.	.		Hartburn Junction	Durham	N. E.	Stockton, N. E. Pass & S. & D. Pass.
G	P	F	L	H	C	5 0	Hartfield	Sussex	L. B. & S. C.	East Grinstead & Tunbridge Wells.
G	P	F	L	H	C	0 15	Hartford	Cheshire	L. & N. W.	Crewe and Warrington.
.	.	.	.	.	.		Douglas Siding	Cheshire	L. & N. W.	Hartford and Acton Bridge.
.	.	.	.	.	.		Beckett & Co.	Cheshire	L. & N. W.	Douglas Siding.
.	.	.	.	.	.		Evans, R., & Co.	Cheshire	L. & N. W.	Douglas Siding.
.	.	.	.	.	.		Hartford	Lancs	L. & Y.	See Oldham.
G	P	.	L	H	.	5 0 }	Hartford & Greenbank (C LC)	Cheshire	{ C. L. C. (G C, G N, & Mid.)	Northwich and Chester.
G	P	.	.	.	.	5 0 }			{ L. & N. W.	Over C. L. C. Line.
.	.	.	.	.	.		Hartford Colliery (Scott Pit)	Northumb	N. E.	Annitsford.
.	.	.	.	.	.		Hartford Junction	Cheshire	C. L. C.—L. & N. W.	Northwich and Warrington.
.	.	.	.	.	.		Harthill	Lanark	N. B.	See West Craigs (for Harthill).
.	.	.	.	.	.		Harthill Dewar Siding	Lanark	N. B.	West Craigs.
.	.	.	.	.	.		Harthill Siding	Lanark	N. B.	See West Craigs.
.	.	.	.	.	.		Harting	Sussex	L. & S.W.	See Rogate and Harting.
G	P	F	L	H	C	5 0	Hartington	Derby	L. & N. W.	Ashbourne and Buxton.
.	.	.	.	.	.		Hartington Colliery (G. C.)	Derby	G. C.—G.N.—L. & N. W.	Staveley Town.
.	.	.	.	.	.		Hartington Colliery	Derby	Mid.	Barrow Hill and Staveley Works.
.	.	.	.	.	.		Hart, J. B., Siding	Suffolk	G. E.	Woodbridge.
G	P	F	L	H	C	1 10	Hartlebury	Worcester	G. W.	Worcester and Kidderminster.
G	P	F	L	H	C	5 0	Hartlepool	Durham	N. E.	Castle Eden and West Hartlepool.
.	.	.	.	.	.		Corporation Destructor Works	Durham	N. E.	Hartlepool.
.	.	.	.	.	.		Fish Quay	Durham	N. E.	Hartlepool.
.	.	.	.	.	.		Furness, Withy & Co.'s Ship Yard	Durham	N. E.	Hartlepool.
.	.	.	.	.	.		Hartlepool Coal Depôts	Durham	N. E.	Hartlepool.
.	.	.	.	.	.		Hartlepool Ropery Co.'s Rope Works	Durham	N. E.	Hartlepool.
.	.	.	.	.	.		Jobson, R., & Co's Repairing Works	Durham	N. E.	Hartlepool.
.	.	.	.	.	.		Millbank Foundry	Durham	N. E.	Hartlepool.
.	.	.	.	.	.		Richardson, Westgarth & Co.'s Engine Works	Durham	N. E.	Hartlepool.
.	.	.	.	.	.		Trechmann's Cement Wks.	Durham	N. E.	Hartlepool.
.	.	.	.	.	.		Trinity Junction	Durham	N. E.	Hartlepool.
.	.	.	.	.	.		Tweddle, A., & Co.'s Coal Dust Mill	Durham	N. E.	Hartlepool.
.	.	.	.	.	.	3 0	Victoria Dock Sidings	Durham	N. E.	Hartlepool.
.	.	.	.	.	.		Hartlepools Cement Works	Durham	N. E.	See Longhill Sids. (West Hartlepool).
.	.	.	.	.	.		Hartlepools Concrete Works	Durham	N. E.	See Longhill Sids. (West Hartlepool).
.	.	.	.	.	.		Hartlepools Pulp & Paper Co.'s Works	Durham	N. E.	West Hartlepool.
.	.	.	.	.	.		Hartlepool, West	Durham	N. E.	See West Hartlepool.
.	.	.	.	.	.		Hartley	Kent	S. E. & C.	See Fawkham (for Hartley and Longfield).
G	P	.	.	.	.		Hartley	Northumb	N. E.	Backworth and Blyth.
.	.	.	.	.	.		Avenue Siding	Northumb	N. E.	Hartley.
.	.	.	.	.	.		Hartley & Co.'s Siding	Yorks	N. E.	Same as Red Hill Brick Works (Castleford).
.	.	.	.	.	.		Hartley Bank Colliery (Flockton Coal Co.)	Yorks	L. & Y.	Horbury & Ossett.
.	.	.	.	.	.		Hartley Row	Hants	L. & S.W.	See Winchfield (for Hartley Row).
.	.	.	.	.	.		Hartley's Brick Siding	Lancs	L. & Y.	See Smith's or Hartley's Brick Siding (Aintree).
.	.	.	.	.	.		Hartley's Brick Works	Lancs	C. L. C. (G C, G N, & Mid.)	Aintree.
.	.	.	.	.	.		Hartley's Preserve Works	Lancs	C. L. C. (G C, G N, & Mid.)	Liverpool, Walton-on-the-Hill.
.	.	.	.	.	.		Hartley's Siding	Lancs	L. & Y.	Liverpool, Preston Road.
.	.	.	.	.	.		Harton Colliery	Durham	N. E.	South Shields.
G	P	.	L	H	C		Harton Road	Salop	G. W.	Much Wenlock and Craven Arms.
.	.	.	.	.	.		Hartrigg Colliery	Lanark	Cal.	Hartwood.
.	.	.	.	.	.		Hartrigg Colliery	L'lithgow	N. B.	Armadale.
.	.	.	.	.	.		Hartshay Colliery	Derby	Mid.	Butterley.
.	P	.	.	.	.		Hartshill and Woodside	Worcester	G. W.	Dudley and Stourbridge Junction.
.	.	.	.	.	.		Hartshill Brick & Tile Co.'s Works	Staffs	N. S.	Newcastle-under-Lyme.
.	.	.	.	.	.		Hartshill Granite and Brick Works (Mid.)	Warwick	Mid.—L. & N. W.	Same as Jee's (Stockingford).

EXPLANATION—G *Goods Station.*   P *Passenger and Parcel Station.*   P* *Passenger, but not Parcel or Miscellaneous Traffic.*
F *Furniture Vans, Carriages, Portable Engines, and Machines on Wheels.*   L *Live Stock.*
H *Horse Boxes and Prize Cattle Vans.*   C *Carriages by Passenger Train.*

STATION ACCOMMODATION.						CRANE POWER.	STATIONS, &c.	COUNTY.	COMPANY.	POSITION.
						Tons Cwts.				
.	.	.	.	.	.	.	Hartshill Siding..............	Staffs	N. S.	Newcastle-under-Lyme.
.	.	.	.	.	.	.	Hartshill Siding..............	Warwick...	L. & N. W.	Nuneaton.
.	.	.	.	.	.	.	Abell's	Warwick...	L. & N. W.	Hartshill Siding.
.	.	.	.	.	.	.	Jee's	Warwick...	L. & N. W.	Hartshill Siding.
.	.	.	.	.	.	.	Hartside Siding ..•.......	Edinboro'	N. B.	See Oxton.
.	.	.	.	.	.	.	Hartwell Siding..............	Bucks	Met.	See Aylesbury.
G	P	F	L	H	C	2 0	Hartwood.....................	Lanark ...	Cal.	Holytown and Edinburgh.
.	.	.	.	.	.	.	Hartrigg Colliery...	Lanark ...	Cal.	Hartwood.
.	.	.	.	.	.	.	Hartwood Asylum Siding...	Lanark ...	Cal.	Hartwood.
.	.	.	.	.	.	.	Ladylands Colliery...........	Lanark ...	Cal.	Hartwood and Shotts.
.	.	.	.	.	.	.	Hartwoodhill Colliery	Lanark ...	N. B.	Shotts.
.	.	.	.	.	.	.	Hartwoodhill Junction........	Lanark ...	N. B.	West Craigs and Shotts.
.	.	.	.	.	.	.	Hartwoodhill Siding..........	Lanark ...	N. B.	Shotts.
.	.	.	.	.	.	.	Harty Road Siding	Kent	S. E. & C. (Sheppey)......	Leysdown.
.	.	.	.	.	.	.	Harum Siding.................	Yorks	N. E.	Helmsley.
.	.	.	.	.	.	.	Harvest Lane Coal Depôt...	Yorks	G. C.	Sheffield, Park.
.	.	.	.	.	.	.	Harvey's Distillery	Renfrew...	Cal.—N. B.	Same as Yoker Distillery (Yoker).
.	.	.	.	.	.	.	Harvey's Siding..............	Lancs	L. & Y.	Liverpool, Preston Road.
G	P	.	.	.	.	.	Harvington	Worcester	Mid.	Evesham and Alcester.
							HARWICH—			
G	P	F	L	H	C	10 0	(Station)	Essex	G. E.	Branch from Manningtree.
G	P	.	.	.	.	.	Dovercourt	Essex	G. E.	Manningtree and Harwich.
G	P	F	L	H	C	30 0	Parkeston Quay	Essex	G. E.	Manningtree and Harwich.
G	P	.	L	.	.	.	Haselour	Staffs	Mid.	Tamworth and Burton.
G	.	.	.	.	.	.	Hasland	Derby	Mid.	Clay Cross and Chesterfield.
.	.	.	.	.	.	.	Alma Colliery.............	Derby	Mid.	Grassmoor Branch.
.	.	.	.	.	.	.	Bonds Main Colliery........	Derby	Mid.	Bonds Main Branch.
.	.	.	.	.	.	.	Calow Colliery.............	Derby	Mid.	Branch from Grassmoor Colliery.
.	.	.	.	.	.	.	Grassmoor Colliery (Mid.)	Derby	Mid.—L. D. & E. C.	Grassmoor Branch.
.	.	.	.	.	.	.	Hardwick Collieries	Derby	Mid.	Grassmoor Branch.
.	.	.	.	.	.	.	Ling's Colliery.............	Derby	Mid.	Grassmoor Branch.
.	.	.	.	.	.	.	Ling's Row Siding...........	Derby	Mid.	Grassmoor Branch.
.	.	.	.	.	.	.	Ling's Siding Wharf........	Derby	Mid.	Extension from Alma Colliery.
.	.	.	.	.	.	.	Williamthorpe Colliery ...	Derby	Mid.	Grassmoor Branch.
G	P	F	L	H	C	5 0	Haslemere	Surrey ...	L. & S.W.	Guildford and Petersfield.
G	P	.	L	H	.	7 0	Haslingden	Lancs	L. & Y.	Bury and Accrington.
.	.	.	.	.	.	.	Haslingden Gas Co.'s Siding	Lancs	L. & Y.	Grane Road.
.	.	.	.	.	.	.	Hassall Green Siding	Staffs	N. S.	Ettiley Heath.
G	P	F	L	H	C	3 0	Hassendean	Roxburgh	N. B.	Galashiels and Hawick.
.	.	.	.	.	.	.	Hassockrig Colliery	Lanark ...	N. B.	Shotts.
G	P	F	L	H	C	1 10	Hassocks	Sussex.:..	L. B. & S. C.	Brighton and Hayward's Heath.
.	.	.	.	.	.	.	Hudson's Siding............	Sussex.....	L. B. & S. C.	Hassocks.
G	P	F	L	H	C	5 0	Hassop	Derby	Mid.	Rowsley and Miller's Dale.
.	.	.	.	.	.	.	Monsal Dale Siding	Derby	Mid.	Hassop.
G	P	F	L	H	C	8 0	Hastings (S. E. & C.)	Sussex ...	{ S. E. & C.	Branch from Tonbridge.
									{ L. B. & S. C.	Over S. E. & C. from Bopeep Junc.
.	.	.	.	.	.	.	Hastings & St. Leonards Gas Co.'s Sid. (Glyne Sid.)	Sussex.....	L. B. & S. C.	Bexhill and St. Leonards.
G	P	F	L	H	C	2 0	Haswell	Durham ...	N. E.	Hartlepool and Sunderland.
.	.	.	.	.	.	.	Cold Hesleden Siding	Durham ...	N. E.	Haswell.
.	.	.	.	.	.	.	Horden Collieries	Durham ...	N. E.	Haswell.
.	.	.	.	.	.	.	Murton Colliery	Durham ...	N. E.	Haswell.
.	.	.	.	.	.	.	Shotton Brick Works and Manure Siding	Durham ...	N. E.	Haswell.
.	.	.	.	.	.	.	Shotton Col. & Brick Wks.	Durham ...	N. E.	Haswell.
.	.	.	.	.	.	.	South Hetton Colliery	Durham ...	N. E.	Haswell.
.	.	.	.	.	.	.	Tuthil Lime Stone Quarries	Durham ...	N. E.	Haswell.
G	P	F	L	.	C	2 0	Hatch	Somerset..	G. W.	Taunton and Chard.
.	.	.	.	.	.	.	Hatcham	Surrey ...	L. B. & S. C.	See London, Old Kent Road and Hatcham.
G	P	F	L	H	C	5 0	Hatch End	Middlesex	L. & N. W.	See Pinner and Hatch End.
.	.	.	.	.	.	.	Hatfield	Herts	G. N.	King's Cross and Hitchin.
.	.	.	.	.	.	.	Attimore Hall Siding	Herts	G. N.	Hatfield and Cole Green.
.	.	.	.	.	.	.	Blackbridge Siding	Herts	G. N.	Ayot and Wheathampstead.
.	.	.	.	.	.	.	Digswell Siding	Herts	G. N.	Hatfield and Cole Green.
.	.	.	.	.	.	.	Fiddle Bridge Siding	Herts	G. N.	Hatfield and Smallford.
.	.	.	.	.	.	.	Horn's Siding...............	Herts	G. N.	Hatfield and Ayot.
.	.	.	.	.	.	.	Lord Cowper's Siding	Herts	G. N.	Hatfield and Cole Green.
.	.	.	.	.	.	.	Lord Salisbury's Siding ...	Herts	G. N.	Hatfield and Cole Green.
.	.	.	.	.	.	.	Marshmoor Siding	Herts	G. N.	Hatfield and Potter's Bar.
.	.	.	.	.	.	.	Mount Pleasant Siding......	Herts	G. N.	Hatfield and Cole Green.
.	.	.	.	.	.	.	Peart's Siding................	Herts	G. N.	Hatfield and Cole Green.

EXPLANATION—G *Goods Station.*   P *Passenger and Parcel Station.*   P* *Passenger, but not Parcel or Miscellaneous Traffic.*
F *Furniture Vans, Carriages, Portable Engines, and Machines on Wheels.*   L *Live Stock.*
H *Horse Boxes and Prize Cattle Vans.*   C *Carriages by Passenger Train.*

STATION ACCOMMODATION.						CRANE POWER.	STATIONS, &c.	COUNTY.	COMPANY.	POSITION.
						Tons Cwts.	Hatfield—*continued.*			
.	.	.	.	.	.	. .	Smart's Brickfield Siding	Herts	G. N.	Hatfield and Cole Green.
.	.	.	.	.	.	. .	Smart's Twentieth Mile Siding	Herts	G. N.	Hatfield and Cole Green.
.	.	.	.	.	.	. .	Hatfield	Yorks	G. C.	See Stainforth and Hatfield.
.	.	.	.	.	.	. .	Hatfield Lane Siding	Yorks	G. C.	Barnby Dun.
G	P	.	L	H	.	. .	Hatfield Peverel	Essex	G. E.	Chelmsford and Witham.
G	P	.	L	H	.	. .	Hathern	Notts	Mid.	Trent and Loughboro'.
.	.	.	.	.	.	. .	Hathern Station Brick and Terra Cotta Co.'s Siding	Notts	Mid.	Near Hathern.
.	.	.	.	.	.	. .	Hathern Station Brick and Terra Cotta Co.—Cliff Siding	Warwick	Mid.	Wilnecote.
.	.	.	.	.	.	. .	Siding	Notts	Mid.	Hathern.
G	P	F	L	H	C	10 0	Hathersage	Derby	Mid.	Dore and Chinley.
.	.	.	.	.	.	. .	Hatherton Blast Furnaces	Staffs	L. & N. W.	Same as Thomas' Siding (Bloxwich).
.	.	.	.	.	.	. .	Hatherton Siding (L & N W)	Staffs	L. & N. W.—G. W.—Mid	Walsall.
.	.	.	.	.	.	. .	Stokes & Co.	Staffs	L. & N. W.—G. W.—Mid	Hatherton Siding.
.	.	.	.	.	.	. .	Walsall Hardware Co.	Staffs	L. & N. W.—G. W.	Hatherton Siding.
.	.	.	.	.	.	. .	Hattersley Bros.' Stove Grate Works (G.C.)	Yorks	G. C.—Mid.	Mexboro'.
G	P	.	L	H	.	1 10	Hatton	Aberdeen	G. N. of S.	Ellon and Boddam.
.	.	.	.	.	.	. .	Hatton & Co.'s Boiler Works	Lancs	Furness	Barrow.
G	P	F	L	H	C	. .	Hatton Junction Station	Warwick	G. W.	Birmingham and Leamington.
.	.	.	.	.	.	. .	Hatton's Wood Brick Co.'s Sid	Lancs	Trafford Park Estate	Manchester.
.	.	.	.	.	.	. .	Haugh Colliery	Stirling	K. & B. Jt.—N. B.	Kilsyth.
.	.	.	.	.	.	. .	Haugh Col. and Coking Ovens	Stirling	K. & B. Jt.—N. B.	Kilsyth.
.	.	.	.	.	.	. .	Haughhead Junction	Lanark	Cal.	Hamilton, Central and Ferniegair.
.	.	.	.	.	.	. .	Haughhead Colliery	Lanark	Cal.	Newton.
G	P	F	.	H	C	1 0	Haughley	Suffolk	G. E.	Ipswich and Bury St. Edmunds.
.	.	.	.	.	.	. .	Haughrigg Colliery	Stirling	K. & B. Jt. (Cal. & N.B.) N. B.	Kilsyth. Gavell.
G	P	.	.	.	.	. .	Haughton	Staffs	L. & N. W.	Shrewsbury and Stafford.
.	.	.	.	.	.	. .	Haughton Bridge Wagon Works and Depôts	Durham	N. E.	Darlington, Bank Top.
.	.	.	.	.	.	. .	Haughton Lane Depôts & Sid.	Durham	N. E.	Darlington, Bank Top.
.	.	.	.	.	.	. .	Haughton Road Brick Wks.	Durham	N. E.	Darlington, Bank Top.
.	.	.	.	.	.	. .	Haunchwood Brk. & Tl. Co.—Griff Brk. Yard (L.& N.W.)	Warwick	L. & N. W.—Mid.	Nuneaton.
.	.	.	.	.	.	. .	Heath End Brick & Tile Works (L. & N. W.)	Warwick	L. & N. W.—Mid.	Nuneaton.
.	.	.	.	.	.	. .	Nowell's Siding (Mid.)	Warwick	Mid.—L. & N. W.	Stockingford.
.	.	.	.	.	.	. .	Haunchwood (or Nowell) Brick & Col. Co.'s Siding (Hickman's, Sir A.) (Mid.)	Warwick	Mid.—L. & N. W.	Stockingford.
.	.	.	.	.	.	. .	Havannah Colliery	Lancs	L. & N. W.	See Evans, R., & Co. (St. Helens)
G	P	F	L	H	C	5 0	Havant (L. B. & S. C.)	Hants	L. B. & S. C. L. & S. W.	Portsmouth and Chichester. Over L. B. & S. C. Line.
.	.	.	.	.	.	. .	Bedhampton Sid. (L B & SC)	Hants	L. B. & S. C.—L. & S. W.	Havant and Portsmouth.
.	.	.	.	.	.	. .	Havant Junction	Hants	L. & S.W.—L. B. & S. C.	Havant and Rowland's Castle.
G	P	.	L	.	.	. .	Havenhouse	Lincoln	G. N.	Wainfleet and Skegness.
G	P	.	L	.	.	. .	Haven Street	I. of Wight	I. of W. Cent.	Ryde and Newport.
G	P	F	L	H	C	10 0	Haverfordwest	Pembroke	G. W.	Whitland and New Milford.
G	P	F	L	.	.	0 15	Haverhill	Suffolk	C. V. & H. G. E.	Terminus. Sudbury and Cambridge.
G	P	F	L	H	C	1 10				
.	.	.	.	.	.	. .	Withersfield Siding	Suffolk	G. E.	Haverhill and Bartlow.
.	.	.	.	.	.	. .	Haverhill Junction	Suffolk	C. V. & H.—G. E.	Birdbrook and Haverhill.
.	.	.	.	.	.	. .	Haverstock Hill (Mid.)	Middlesex	Mid.—S. E. & C.	See London.
G	P	F	L	H	C	3 0	Haverthwaite	Lancs	Furness	Ulverston and Lake Side.
.	.	.	.	.	.	. .	Dickson's Sid. (Blackbeck Siding) (*private*)	Lancs	Furness	Haverthwaite and Greenodd.
.	.	.	.	.	.	. .	Harrison, Ainslie & Co.'s Siding	Lancs	Furness	Branch near Haverthwaite.
G	P	.	.	.	.	1 0	Haverton Hill	Durham	N. E.	Billingham and Port Clarence.
.	.	.	.	.	.	. .	Hemingway's Girder Wks.	Durham	N. E.	Haverton Hill.
.	.	.	.	.	.	. .	N. E. R. Loco. Sheds	Durham	N. E.	Haverton Hill.
.	.	.	.	.	.	. .	South Durham Salt Works (Salt Union Ltd.)	Durham	N. E.	Haverton Hill.
.	.	.	.	.	.	. .	Tees Salt Works	Durham	N. E.	Haverton Hill.
.	.	.	.	.	.	. .	Tennant's Salt Works	Durham	N. E.	Haverton Hill.
.	.	.	.	.	.	. .	Watson's Brick Works	Durham	N. E.	Haverton Hill.
.	.	.	.	.	.	. .	Havodvan Colliery	Mon	G. W.	Abertillery.

EXPLANATION—G *Goods Station.*   P *Passenger and Parcel Station.*   P* *Passenger, but not Parcel or Miscellaneous Traffic.*
F *Furniture Vans, Carriages, Portable Engines, and Machines on Wheels.*   L *Live Stock.*
H *Horse Boxes and Prize Cattle Vans.*   C *Carriages by Passenger Train.*

STATION ACCOMMODATION.						CRANE POWER.		STATIONS, &c.	COUNTY.	COMPANY.	POSITION.
G	P	F	L	H	C	Tons	Cwts.	Hawarden (W. M. & C. Q.)	Flint	{ W. M. & C. Q.	Buckley & Hawarden Bridge Junc.
.	P	.	.	H	C	.	.			{ G. C.	Over W. M. & C. Q. from Hawarden Bridge Junction.
.	.	.	.	.	.	.	.	Aston Hall Col. & Brk. Wks.	Flint	W. M. & C. Q.	Connah's Quay and Hawarden.
.	.	.	.	.	.	.	.	Hawarden Bridge East Junc.	Flint	G. C.—N. W. & L. Jt. ...	Chester and Neston.
.	.	.	.	.	.	.	.	Hawarden Bridge Junction..	Flint	G. C.—W. M. & C. Q. ...	Chester and Hawarden.
.	.	.	.	.	.	.	.	Hawarden Bridge North Jn.	Flint	{ N. W. & L. Jt. (G. C. & W. M. & C. Q.) }	Connah's Quay & Shotton and Burton Point.
.	.	.	.	.	.	.	.	Hawarden Bridge West Junc.	Flint	G. C.—N. W. & L. Jt. ..	Connah's Quay & Shotton & Neston.
.	.	.	.	.	.	.	.	Hawarden Bridge Siding......	Flint	G. C.	Same as Summer's Sid. (Saughall).
.	.	.	.	.	.	.	.	Hawarden Bridge (Public) Siding	Flint	G. C.	Saughall.
.	.	.	.	.	.	.	.	Hawcoat Mineral Siding	Lancs	Furness	Barrow.
G	P	.	L	H	C	.	.	Hawes Junction & Garsdale..	Yorks	Mid.	Settle and Appleby.
G	P	F	L	H	C	5	0	Hawes Station & Junction ...	Yorks	{ Mid.	Branch from Hawes Junc. Station.
										{ N. E.	Branch from Northallerton.
G	P	F	L	H	C	5	0	Hawick........................	Roxburgh	N. B.	Galashiels and Carlisle.
.	.	.	.	.	.	.	.	Mansfield Gas Works	Roxburgh	N. B.	Hawick.
.	.	.	.	.	.	.	.	Mansfield Siding	Roxburgh	N. B.	Hawick.
.	.	.	.	.	.	.	.	Hawkesbury and Bedworth Brick & Tile Co.'s Blockley's Siding (L. & N. W.)...	Warwick	L. & N. W.—Mid.	Bedworth.
G	P	.	.	.	.	.	.	Hawkesbury Lane	Warwick	L. & N. W.	Coventry and Nuneaton.
.	.	.	.	.	.	.	.	Hawke's (Lord) Siding........	Yorks	L. & Y.	Womersley.
.	.	.	.	.	.	.	.	Hawke's Siding	Warwick	L. & N. W.	Kenilworth.
.	.	.	.	.	.	.	.	Hawkhead	Renfrew	G. & S. W.	See Paisley.
.	.	.	.	.	.	.	.	Hawkhill Chemical Works (Walker & Co.)	Ayr	G. & S. W.	Ayr.
.	.	.	.	.	.	.	.	Hawkhill Junction	Ayr	G. & S. W.	Ayr, Passengers and Prestwick.
.	.	.	.	.	.	.	.	Hawkhill Siding	Fife	N. B.	Kincardine.
G	P	F	L	H	C	1	10	Hawkhurst	Kent	S. E. & C.	Branch from Paddock Wood.
.	.	.	.	.	.	.	.	Hawkins & Son's Cannock Old Coppice or Cheslyn Hay Colliery	Staffs	L. & N. W.	Wyrley and Church Bridge.
.	.	.	.	.	.	.	.	Hawkins Lane (G. N.)	Staffs	G. N.—L. & N. W.—N. S.	See Burton-on-Trent.
.	.	.	.	.	.	.	.	Hawkins Lane Junctions......	Staffs	L&NW—G N—Mid—N S	Burton-on-Trent.
.	.	.	.	.	.	.	.	Hawkshead Siding	Middlesex	G. N.	Potter's Bar.
.	.	.	.	.	.	.	.	Hawkshead Street Junction..	Lancs	L. & Y.	Southport.
.	.	.	.	.	.	.	.	Hawksworth Quarry	Yorks	N. E.	Horsforth.
.	.	.	.	.	.	.	.	Hawkwoodburn	Lanark	Cal.	Same as Currieside Colliery (Shotts).
.	.	.	.	.	.	.	.	Hawn's Hendon Depôts	Durham	N. E.	Sunderland, South Docks.
G	P	.	.	.	.	10	0	Haworth	Yorks	Mid.	Keighley and Oxenhope.
G	P	.	L	H	.	.	.	Hawsker	Yorks	N. E.	Scarborough and Whitby.
.	.	.	.	.	.	.	.	Hawthorn & Co.'s Siding......	Edinboro'	Cal.—N. B.	Granton.
G	P	.	L	H	.	2	0	Hawthornden & Rosewell ...	Edinboro'	N. B.	Hardengreen and Peebles.
.	.	.	.	.	.	.	.	Dalhousie Siding	Edinboro'	N. B.	Bonnyrigg and Hawthornden.
G	.	.	.	.	.	.	.	Gorton Siding	Edinboro'	N. B.	Hawthornden and Rosslyn Castle.
.	.	.	.	.	.	.	.	Whitehill Colliery, Fire-Clay & Brick Works	Edinboro'	N. B.	Hawthornden and Rosslynlee.
.	.	.	.	.	.	.	.	Hawthornden Junction	Edinboro'	N. B.	Bonnyrigg and Rosslynlee.
.	.	.	.	.	.	.	.	Hawthorn, Leslie & Co.'s Sid.	Northumb	N. E.	{ Newcastle-on-Tyne. { St. Peter's.
G	P	.	L	H	.	.	.	Haxby	Yorks	N. E.	York and Malton.
G	P	F	L	H	C	5	0	Haxey & Epworth	Lincoln	G. N. & G. E. Jt.	Doncaster and Gainsboro'.
G	P	F	L	H	C	1	10	Hay (Mid.)	Hereford	{ Mid.	Hereford and Three Cocks.
										{ G. W.	Over Mid. from Hay Junction.
.	.	.	.	.	.	.	.	Williams, R., & Son's Timber Siding	Hereford	G. W.—Mid.	Near Hay.
.	.	.	.	.	.	.	.	Hay Junction	Hereford	G. W.—Mid.	Dorstone and Hay.
.	.	.	.	.	.	.	.	Hay Branch (Mid.)	Staffs	Mid—L&NW—GN—NS	Burton-on-Trent.
G	.	.	.	.	.	.	.	Haybridge	Salop	L. & N. W.	Shrewsbury and Stafford.
.	.	.	.	.	.	.	.	Haybridge Iron Co.'s Siding	Salop	L. & N. W.	Hadley and Wellington.
.	.	.	.	.	.	.	.	Haybridge Iron Co.— Old Park Siding.............	Salop	{ G. W. .... { L. & N. W.	Hollinswood. Stirchley.
.	.	.	.	.	.	.	.	Siding	Salop	{ G. W. .... { L. & N. W.	Wellington. Haybridge.
.	P	.	.	.	.	.	.	Hayburn Wyke	Yorks	N. E.	Scarborough and Whitby.
G	P	.	.	.	.	.	.	Haydock	Lancs	G. C. (St. Helens Exten.)	Lowton St. Mary's and St. Helens.
.	.	.	.	.	.	.	.	Haydock Colliery	Lancs	{ G. C.(St. Helens Exten.)	See Evans, R., & Co. (Ashton-in-Makerfield).
.	.	.	.	.	.	.	.			{ L. & N. W.	See Evans, R., & Co. (Earlestown).

EXPLANATION—G *Goods Station.*   P *Passenger and Parcel Station.*   P* *Passenger, but not Parcel or Miscellaneous Traffic.*
F *Furniture Vans, Carriages, Portable Engines, and Machines on Wheels.*   L *Live Stock.*
H *Horse Boxes and Prize Cattle Vans.*   C *Carriages by Passenger Train.*

STATION ACCOMMODATION.						CRANE POWER.	STATIONS, &c.	COUNTY.	COMPANY.	POSITION.
						Tons Cwts.	Haydock or Old Fold Col. Sid.	Lancs	L. & N. W.	See Evans, R., & Co. (St. Helens).
	P			H			Haydock Park Race Course Station (For Race traffic only)	Lancs	G. C. (St. Helens Exten.)	Lowton St. Mary's and St. Helens.
G	P	F	L	H	C	5 0	Haydon Bridge	Northumb	N. E.	Carlisle and Hexham.
							Whinstone Quarry Siding	Northumb	N. E.	Haydon Bridge.
							Haydon Square	Middlesex	L. & N. W.	See London.
G	P						Haydon's Road	Surrey	L. & S W & L B & S C Jt.	Wimbledon and Tooting.
							Neal's Siding	Surrey	L. & S W & L B & S C Jt.	Wimbledon and Tooting.
G	P	F	L	H	C	7 0	Hayes	Kent	S. E. & C.	Branch from Elmer's End.
G	P					6 0	Hayes and Harlington	Middlesex	G. W.	London (Paddington) and Slough.
							Hayes Colliery	Worcester	G. W.	Cradley Heath and Cradley.
							Hayes Victoria Cotton Mills	Lancs	L. & N. W.	Leigh and Bedford.
G	P	F	L	H	C	5 0	Hayfield	Derby	S. & M. Jt. (G. C. & Mid.)	Branch from New Mills.
							Bennett's Siding	Derby	S. & M. Jt. (G. C. & Mid.)	Birch Vale.
G							Birch Vale Siding	Derby	S. & M. Jt. (G. C. & Mid.)	Hayfield.
							Hayfield Printing Co.—			
							High Level Siding	Derby	S. & M. Jt. (G. C. & Mid.)	Hayfield.
							Low Level Siding	Derby	S. & M. Jt. (G. C. & Mid.)	Hayfield.
							Slack's Crossing Siding	Derby	S. & M. Jt. (G. C. & Mid.)	Hayfield.
							Hayhill Brick Works	Lanark	Cal.	Same as Garnqueen Brick Works (Glenboig).
							Hayhole Lead Works	Northumb	N. E.	Northumberland Dock.
							Hayhurst & Marsden's Siding	Lancs	P.&L.Jt.(L&NW.&L&Y)	Longridge.
G	P		L	H		15 0	Hayle	Cornwall	G. W.	Truro and Penzance.
							Hayle Wharves	Cornwall	G. W.	Hayle.
							Haylett, B. F., Siding	Norfolk	G. E.	Downham.
G	P	F	L	H	C	1 10	Hayling Island	Hants	L. B. & S. C.	Branch from Havant.
							Hayling Oyster Co.'s Sid.	Hants	L. B. & S. C.	Havant and Hayling Island.
							Hayling, North	Hants	L. B. & S. C.	See North Hayling.
							Haymarket	Edinboro'	N. B.	See Edinburgh.
							Haymarket Central Junction	Edinboro'	N. B.	Edinburgh.
							Haymarket Distillery	Edinboro'	Cal.—N. B.	Same as Caledonian Distillery (Edinburgh).
							Haymarket Siding	Edinboro'	Cal.	Edinburgh, Lothian Road.
							Haymarket West Junction	Edinboro'	Cal.—N. B.	Edinburgh.
							Haymarket West Yard Sidings (Roseburn Sidings)	Edinboro'	N. B.	Edinburgh, Haymarket.
							Hay, Merricks & Co.'s Gunpowder Works	Edinboro'	N. B.	Rosslyn Castle.
							Hayston Sand Siding	Stirling	N. B.	Torrance.
G	P	F	L	H	C	4 10	Haywards Heath	Sussex	L. B. & S. C.	Brighton and Three Bridges.
							Jenner & Higg's Siding	Sussex	L. B. & S. C.	Haywards Heath.
							Hayward's Siding	Dorset	L. & S.W.	Dorchester.
							Hayward, Tyler & Howard's Sidings (G. N.)	Beds	G. N.—L. & N. W.	Luton.
							Hay Wharf (Mid.)	Staffs	Mid—L&NW—GN—NS	Burton-on-Trent.
G	P						Haywood	Lanark	Cal.	Branch near Auchengray.
							Haywood & Co.'s Pipe Works (Mid.)	Leicester	Mid.—L. & N. W.	Moira.
							Hazard Colliery	Durham	N. E.	Hetton.
G	P	F	L	H	C	5 0	Hazel Grove	Cheshire	L. & N. W.	Buxton and Stockport.
							Stockport Guardians' Woodmoor Siding	Cheshire	L. & N. W.	Stockport (Davenport) and Hazel Grove.
	P						Hazel Grove	Cheshire	Mid.	New Mills and Heaton Mersey.
G						5 0	Bramhall Moor Lane	Cheshire	Mid.	New Mills and Heaton Mersey.
							Hazelrigg Colliery	Northumb	N. E.	Gosforth.
G	P						Hazelwell	Worcester	Mid.	King's Heath and Lifford.
G	P	F	L	H	C		Hazelwood	Derby	Mid.	Duffield and Wirksworth.
G	P	F	L	H	C		Hazlehatch and Celbridge	Kildare	G. S. & W.	Dublin and Kildare.
G	P					5 0	Hazlehead Bridge	Yorks	G. C.	Guide Bridge and Penistone.
							Bates' Siding	Yorks	G. C.	Hazlehead Bridge.
							Broadbent's Siding	Yorks	G. C.	Hazlehead Bridge.
							Bullhouse Colliery	Yorks	G. C.	Hazlehead Bridge.
							Hepworth Colliery	Yorks	G. C.	Hazlehead Bridge.
							Hepworth Iron Co.'s Siding	Yorks	G. C.	Hazlehead Bridge.
							Tinker's Siding	Yorks	G. C.	Hazlehead Bridge.
G	P	F	L	H	C		Heacham	Norfolk	G. E.	Lynn and Hunstanton.
							Lewis, A., Siding	Norfolk	G. E.	Heacham.
G	P	F	L	H	C	4 0	Headcorn	Kent	S. E. & C.	Tonbridge and Ashford.
							Headfield Junction	Yorks	G. N.— L. & Y.	Same as Dewsbury Junction.
G	P		L				Headford Junction Station	Kerry	G. S. & W.	Mallow and Killarney.
G	P		L	H		10 0	Headingley	Yorks	N. E.	Leeds and Harrogate.

EXPLANATION—G Goods Station.   P Passenger and Parcel Station.   P* Passenger, but not Parcel or Miscellaneous Traffic.
F Furniture Vans, Carriages, Portable Engines, and Machines on Wheels.   L Live Stock.
H Horse Boxes and Prize Cattle Vans.   C Carriages by Passenger Train.

STATION ACCOMMODATION.						CRANE POWER.	STATIONS, &c.	COUNTY.	COMPANY.	POSITION.
						Tons Cwts.				
G	P	.	.	.	.	. .	Heads Nook....................	Cumb'land	N. E.	Carlisle and Brampton.
.	.	.	.	.	.	. .	Allanwood Paper Mill Sid.	Cumb'land	N. E.	Heads Nook.
.	.	.	.	.	.	. .	Broadwath Depôts............	Cumb'land	N. E.	Heads Nook.
.	.	.	.	.	.	. .	Broadwath Siding	Cumb'land	N. E.	Heads Nook.
.	P	.	.	.	.	. .	Headwood	Antrim	N. C. Com. (Mid.)	Ballymena and Larne.
.	.	.	.	.	.	. .	Healdfield Brick Co.'s Siding	Yorks	N. E.	Castleford.
G	P	.	.	.	.	10 0	Healey	Lancs	L. & Y.	See Shawclough and Healey.
.	.	.	.	.	.	. .	Healey House	Yorks	L. & Y.	Lockwood and Meltham.
.	.	.	.	.	.	. .	Healey Mills Siding	Yorks	L. & Y.	See Horbury & Ossett.
.	.	.	.	.	.	. .	Healey's Siding	Lancs	L. & N. W.	Garston Docks.
.	.	.	.	.	.	. .	Healey's Siding	Leicester..	Mid.	Kirby Muxloe.
G	P	.	L	H	.	. .	Healing	Lincoln ...	G. C.	Barnetby and Grimsby.
.	.	.	.	.	.	. .	Healing & Son's Siding.....	Glo'ster ..	Mid.	Tewkesbury.
G	P	.	.	.	.	. .	Healy's Bridge	Cork	C. & Muskerry	Cork and Coachford Junction.
G	P	F	L	H	C	10 0 ⎫	Heanor	Derby	{ G. N.	Branch—Ilkeston & West Hallam.
G	P	.	.	.	.	5 0 ⎬			{ Mid.	Langley Mill and Ripley.
G	.	.	.	.	.	1 5	Heanor Junction	Derby	Mid.	Shipley Gate and Langley Mill.
.	.	.	.	.	.	. .	Heap Bridge	Lancs	L. & Y.	Branch—Bury and Broadfield.
.	.	.	.	.	.	. .	Duxbury's Siding (Yates, Duxbury & Son's Siding)	Lancs	L. & Y.	Heap Bridge.
.	.	.	.	.	.	. .	Wrigley's Siding	Lancs	L. & Y.	Heap Bridge.
G	P	.	.	.	.	4 0	Heapey	Lancs	L&Y&LUJt(LY&LNW)	Boar's Head and Blackburn.
.	.	.	.	.	.	. .	Ryland's Dacca Twist Co.'s Siding (L. & Y. & L.U. Jt.)	Lancs	L. & N. W.	Heapey and Chorley.
G	P	F	L	H	C	1 10 ⎫	Hearn's Siding	Glo'ster ...	Mid.	Gloucester.
G	.	F	L	.	.	1 10 ⎬	Heath (G. C.)	Derby	{ G. C.	Chesterfield and Nottingham.
									{ L. & N. W.	Over G. N. and G. C. Lines.
.	.	.	.	.	.	. .	Hardwick Colliery (G.C.)...	Derby	G. C.—G. N.—L. & N.W.	Heath.
.	.	.	.	.	.	. .	Heath Junction	Derby	G. C.	Grassmoor and Heath.
							Heath & Son's—			
.	.	.	.	.	.	. .	Biddulph Valley Iron Works and Colliery............	Staffs	N. S.	Black Bull.
.	.	.	.	.	.	. .	Bradley Green Colliery.....	Staffs	N. S.	Biddulph.
.	.	.	.	.	.	. .	Brownhills Colliery	Staffs	N. S.	Longport.
.	.	.	.	.	.	. .	Brown Lees Colliery	Staffs	N. S.	Black Bull.
.	.	.	.	.	.	. .	Colliery	Staffs	N. S.	Grange Wharf.
.	.	.	.	.	.	. .	Norton Iron Works	Staffs	N. S.	Ford Green.
.	.	.	.	.	.	. .	Ravensdale Iron Works ...	Staffs	N. S.	Chatterley.
.	.	.	.	.	.	. .	Wharf	Cheshire...	N. S.	Congleton (Brunswick).
.	.	.	.	.	.	. .	Heathcote's Siding	Cumb'land	WC&EJt.(Fur.&LNW)	Cleator Moor.
.	.	.	.	.	.	. .	Heathcott & Son's Siding ...	Derby	L. & N. W.	Dove Holes.
.	.	.	.	.	.	. .	Heath End Brick & Tile Works (L. & N. W.) ⎱	Warwick..	L. & N. W.—Mid.	{ See Haunchwood Brick and Tile Co. (Nuneaton).
.	.	.	.	.	.	. .	Heath End Colliery	Leicester..	Mid.	Worthington.
G	P	F	L	H	C	1 10	Heather and Ibstock.........	Leicester..	A & N Jt.(L&NW & Mid.)	Shackerstone and Hugglescote Jn.
.	.	.	.	.	.	. .	Crane's Brick Works........	Leicester..	A & N Jt.(L&NW & Mid.)	Heather and Shackerstone.
.	.	.	.	.	.	. .	Heather Brick & Tile Co.'s Siding	Leicester..	A & N Jt.(L&NW & Mid.)	Heather and Hugglescote.
.	.	.	.	.	.	. .	National Brick Co.'s Siding	Leicester..	A & N Jt.(L&NW & Mid.)	Heather and Shackerstone.
.	.	.	.	.	.	. .	Wain's Brick Works	Leicester..	A & N Jt.(L&NW & Mid.)	Heather and Shackerstone.
.	.	.	.	.	.	. .	Heatherbell Colliery	Lanark ...	Cal.	Salisburgh.
.	.	.	.	.	.	. .	Heathery Colliery	Lanark ...	Cal.	Shieldmuir.
.	.	.	.	.	.	. .	Heatheryknowe Colliery	Lanark ...	N. B.	Bargeddie.
.	.	.	.	.	.	. .	Heatheryknowe Weighs	Lanark ...	N. B.	Shettleston and Coatbridge.
							HEATHFIELD—			
G	P	.	L	.	.	3 0	(Station)	Devon	G. W.	Newton Abbot and Moreton Hampstead.
.	.	.	.	.	.	. .	Candy & Co.'s Siding	Devon	G. W.	Heathfield.
.	.	.	.	.	.	. .	Junction	Devon	G. W.	Newton Abbot and Moreton Hampstead.
G	P	F	L	H	C	7 0	Heathfield	Sussex ...	L. B. & S. C.	Rotherfield and Polegate.
.	.	.	.	.	.	. .	Strickland's Siding	Sussex ...	L. B. & S. C.	Heathfield.
.	.	.	.	.	.	. .	Heathfield Fire-Clay Works	Lanark ...	Cal. '	Garnkirk.
.	.	.	.	.	.	. .	Heath Junction	Glamorg'n	Rhy.—Cardiff	Cardiff and Llanishen.
.	.	.	.	.	.	. .	Heath Park, for Boxmoor (Boxmoor Wharf)	Herts	Mid.	See Hemel Hempsted.
.	.	.	.	.	.	. .	Heath Siding (Rhy.)............	Glamorg'n	Rhy.—L. & N. W.	{ Cardiff (for down traffic). Llanishen (for up traffic).
.	P	.	.	.	.	. .	Heath Town	Staffs	Mid.	Wolverhampton and Walsall.
.	.	.	.	.	.	. .	Heath Town Junction	Staffs	L. & N. W.—Mid.	Walsall and Wolverhampton.
G	P	F	L	H	C	1 0	Heatley and Warburton	Cheshire...	L. & N. W.	Stockport and Warrington.
.	.	.	.	.	.	. .	Heaton	Northumb	N. E.	See Newcastle-on-Tyne.

EXPLANATION—G *Goods Station.*　　P *Passenger and Parcel Station.*　　P* *Passenger, but not Parcel or Miscellaneous Traffic.*
F *Furniture Vans, Carriages, Portable Engines, and Machines on Wheels.*　　L *Live Stock.*
H *Horse Boxes and Prize Cattle Vans*　　C *Carriages by Passenger Train.*

STATION ACCOMMODATION.						CRANE POWER.		STATIONS, &c.	COUNTY.	COMPANY.	POSITION.
						Tons	Cwts.				
.	.	.	.	.	.	.	.	Heaton & Byker Coal Co.'s Depôt	Northumb	N. E.	Same as Byker & Heaton Coal Co.'s Depôt (Newcastle-on-Tyne).
.	P	.	.	.	.	.	.	Heaton Chapel	Lancs	L. & N. W.	Manchester and Stockport.
.	.	.	.	.	.	.	.	Heaton Junction	Northumb	N. E.	Newcastle and Morpeth.
.	.	.	.	.	.	.	.	Heaton Junction Manure Loading Wharf	Northumb	N. E.	Newcastle-on-Tyne.
.	.	.	.	.	.	.	.	Heaton Jn. Metal Refinery	Northumb	N. E.	Newcastle-on-Tyne.
.	.	.	.	.	.	.	.	Heaton Jn. or Walker Gate Carriage & Wagon Shops	Northumb	N. E.	Walker Gate.
.	.	.	.	.	.	.	.	Heaton Junction Public Sid.	Northumb	N. E.	Newcastle-on-Tyne.
.	.	.	.	.	.	.	.	Heaton Lodge Junction	Yorks	L. & Y.—L. & N. W.	Mirfield and Huddersfield.
.	P	.	.	.	.	.	.	Heaton Mersey	Lancs	Mid.	Manchester and Stockport.
.	.	.	.	.	.	.	.	Heaton Mersey, East Junc.	Lancs	C. L. C.—Mid.	Stockport & Heaton Mersey Station.
G	.	.	.	.	.	.	.	Heaton Mersey Wharf	Lancs	Mid.	Heaton Mersey.
.	.	.	.	.	.	.	.	Heaton Norris	Lancs	{ C.L.C.(G C, G N, & Mid.) L. & N. W.	Same as Wellington Rd. (Stockport). See Stockport.
.	P	.	.	.	.	.	.	Heaton Park	Lancs	L. & Y.	Manchester and Prestwich.
G	P	F	L	.	.	5	0	Hebburn	Durham	N. E.	Pelaw and South Shields.
.	.	.	.	.	.	.	.	Frazer & Son's Siding	Durham	N. E.	Hebburn.
.	.	.	.	.	.	.	.	Reyrolle & Co.'s Siding	Durham	N. E.	Hebburn.
.	.	.	.	.	.	.	.	Rope & Sail Co.'s Siding	Durham	N. E.	Hebburn.
.	.	.	.	.	.	.	.	Sproat, Marley & Co.'s Sid.	Durham	N. E.	Hebburn.
.	.	.	.	.	.	.	.	Tharsis Sulphur & Copper Co.'s Siding	Durham	N. E.	Hebburn.
.	.	.	.	.	.	.	.	United Alkali Co.'s Siding	Durham	N. E.	Hebburn.
.	.	.	.	.	.	.	.	Hebburn Collieries	Durham	N. E.	Jarrow.
G	P	F	L	H	C	10	0	Hebden Bridge	Yorks	L. & Y.	Sowerby Bridge and Todmorden.
.	.	.	.	.	.	.	.	Hebden Bge. Gas Co.'s Sid.	Yorks	L. & Y.	Hebden Bridge.
G	P	.	L	H	C	.	.	Heck	Yorks	N. E.	Selby and Doncaster.
G	P	F	L	H	C	1	10	Heckington	Lincoln	G. N.	Boston and Sleaford.
								HECKMONDWIKE—			
G	P	F	L	H	C	5	0	(Station)	Yorks	L. & N. W.	Cleckheaton and Huddersfield.
G	P	F	L	H	C	10	0			{ L. & Y.	Bradford and Mirfield.
G	P	F	L	H	C	10	0	(Station, L. & Y.)	Yorks	G. N.	Over L. & Y. from Wakefield.
G	.	F	L	.	.	9	0			L. & N. W.	Over L.&Y. from Heaton Lodge Jn.
.	.	.	.	.	.	.	.	Crowther, J. F. & J., Siding (L. & Y.)	Yorks	L. & Y.—L. & N. W.	Heckmondwike and Mirfield.
.	.	.	.	.	.	.	.	Park Farm Siding (L. & Y.)	Yorks	L. & Y.—L. & N. W.	Heckmondwike and Mirfield.
.	.	.	.	.	.	.	.	SpringwellBreweryCo.'sSid	Yorks	L. & Y.	Near Heckmondwike.
.	P	.	.	.	.	.	.	Heddon-on-the-Wall	Northumb	N. E.	Hexham and Newcastle.
.	.	.	.	.	.	.	.	Heddon Bank Farm Siding	Northumb	N. E.	Heddon-on-the-Wall.
.	.	.	.	.	.	.	.	Heddon Col. & Fire Brk. Sid	Northumb	N. E.	Heddon-on-the-Wall.
.	.	.	.	.	.	.	.	Jackson's (Sir John) Siding	Northumb	N. E.	Heddon-on-the-Wall.
G	P	.	L	H	C	1	0	Hedgeley	Northumb	N. E.	Alnwick and Coldstream.
.	.	.	.	.	.	.	.	Hedley Hill Col. & Coke Ovens	Durham	N. E.	Waterhouses.
.	.	.	.	.	.	.	.	Hedley Hope Colliery	Durham	N. E.	Tow Law.
G	P	F	L	H	C	1	10	Hednesford	Staffs	L. & N. W	Rugeley and Walsall.
.	.	.	.	.	.	.	.	Albion Foundry	Staffs	L. & N. W.	Hednesford and Rugeley Town.
.	.	.	.	.	.	.	.	Brereton Colliery	Staffs	L. & N. W.	Hednesford and Rugeley Town.
.	.	.	.	.	.	.	.	Bumsted & Chandler's Sid.	Staffs	L. & N. W.	Branch from Hednesford.
.	.	.	.	.	.	.	.	Cannock and Leacroft Col.	Staffs	L. & N. W.	Norton Branch.
.	.	.	.	.	.	.	.	Cannock & RugeleyColliery Co.'s Workshop Siding	Staffs	L. & N. W.	Branch from Hednesford.
.	.	.	.	.	.	.	.	Cannock and Rugeley Collieries, Nos. 1 and 3	Staffs	L. & N. W.	Branch from Hednesford.
								Cannock Chase Col. Co.—			
.	.	.	.	.	.	.	.	Anglesea Colliery	Staffs	L. & N. W.	Brownhills and Hammerwich.
.	.	.	.	.	.	.	.	Hednesford Colliery	Staffs	L. & N. W.	Branch from Hednesford.
.	.	.	.	.	.	.	.	East Cannock Colliery	Staffs	L. & N. W.	Hednesford and Cannock.
								Fields—			
.	.	.	.	.	.	.	.	Littleworth Brick Wks.	Staffs	L. & N. W.	Branch from Hednesford.
.	.	.	.	.	.	.	.	Siding	Staffs	L. & N. W.	Hednesford and Rugeley Town.
.	.	.	.	.	.	.	.	Midland Carriage & Wagon Co.'s Siding	Staffs	L. & N. W.	Hednesford and Rugeley Town.
.	.	.	.	.	.	.	.	Rugeley Gas Co.'s Siding	Staffs	L. & N. W.	Hednesford and Rugeley Town.
.	.	.	.	.	.	.	.	South Staffordshire Fire Brick Co.'s Siding	Staffs	L. & N. W.	Branch from Hednesford.
.	.	.	.	.	.	.	.	West Cannock Colliery	Staffs	L. & N. W.	Hednesford and Cannock.
.	.	.	.	.	.	.	.	Hednesford Colliery	Staffs	L. & N. W.	See Cannock Chase Colliery Co. (Hednesford).
G	P	.	L	H	C	3	0	Hedon	Yorks	N. E.	Hull and Withernsea.
.	.	.	.	.	.	.	.	Hedworth Barium Co.'s Sid.	Durham	N. E.	Tyne Dock.

EXPLANATION—G Goods Station.   P Passenger and Parcel Station.   P* Passenger, but not Parcel or Miscellaneous Traffic.
F Furniture Vans, Carriages, Portable Engines, and Machines on Wheels.   L Live Stock.
H Horse Boxes and Prize Cattle Vans.   C Carriages by Passenger Train.

STATION ACCOMMODATION.						CRANE POWER.	STATIONS, &c.	COUNTY.	COMPANY.	POSITION.
						Tons Cwts				
.	.	.	.	.	.	. .	Hedworth Lane Siding	Durham	N. E.	Boldon.
.	.	.	.	.	.	. .	Heeley	Yorks	Mid.	See Sheffield.
.	.	.	.	.	.	. .	Heenan and Froude (G.W.)	Worcester	G. W.—Mid.	Worcester.
.	.	.	.	.	.	. .	Hefford's Siding	Leicester	G. N.	Leicester, Belgrave Road.
.	.	.	.	.	.	. .	Heigham & Co.'s Siding	Glamorg'n	GW—LNW—Rhy—TV	Cardiff.
G	P	.	.	.	.	2 0	Heighington	Durham	N. E.	Darlington and Bishop Auckland.
						. .	Whiley Hill Siding	Durham	N. E.	Heighington.
.	.	.	.	.	.	. .	Heighington	Lincoln	G. N. & G. E. Jt.	See Branston and Heighington.
.	.	.	.	.	.	. .	Heights Quarry	Durham	N. E.	Parkhead.
.	.	.	.	.	.	. .	Heiton Siding	Roxburgh	N. B.	See Roxburgh.
.	.	.	.	.	.	. .	Hek's Siding	Glamorg'n	T. V.	Aberdare.
G	P	.	L	.	.	4 0	Hele and Bradninch	Devon	G. W.	Exeter and Taunton.
G	P	.	.	.	C	. .	Helen's Bay	Down	B. & C. D.	Holywood and Bangor.
G	P	F	L	H	C	5 0	Helensburgh	Dumbartn	N. B.	Branch from Craigendoran Junction.
G	P	F	L	H	C	1 10	Helensburgh, Upper	Dumbartn	N. B.	Craigendoran and Ardlui.
G						. .	Helland Siding	Cornwall	L. & S.W.	Branch from Wadebridge.
G	P	F	L			. .	Hellesdon	Norfolk	Mid. & G. N. Jt.	Norwich, City & Melton Constable.
G	P	F	L	H		}	Hellifield (Mid.)	Yorks	{ Mid.	Skipton and Settle.
G	P	.	L	H		}		Yorks	{ L. & Y.	Over Midland Line.
.	.	.	.	.	.	. .	Hellifield Junction	Yorks	L. & Y.—Mid.	Clitheroe and Settle.
G	P	.	.	.	.	5 0	Hellingly	Sussex	L. B. & S. C.	Rotherfield and Polegate.
.	.	.	.	.	.	. .	East Sussex County Council Asylum Siding	Sussex	L. B. & S. C.	Hellingly.
.	.	.	.	.	.	. .	Hellpout Mill Siding	Leicester	A & N Jt. (L & N W & Mid.)	Shackerstone.
.	.	.	.	.	.	. .	Hellwith Bridge Siding	Yorks	Mid.	Horton-in-Ribblesdale.
.	.	.	.	.	.	. .	Helm Colliery	Yorks	L. & N. W.	See Farnley Iron Co. (Huddersfield).
G	P	F	L	H	C	. . }	Helmdon	N'hamptn	{ G. C.	Rugby and Brackley.
G	P	F	L	H	C	2 10 }			{ N. & B. Jn.	Towcester and Banbury.
G	P	F	L	H	C	1 0	Helmsdale	Sutherl'nd	High.	Golspie and Wick.
G	P	.	L	H		10 0	Helmshore	Lancs	L. & Y.	Bury and Accrington.
.	.	.	.	.	.	. .	Albion Mill Co.'s Siding	Lancs	L. & Y.	Helmshore.
.	.	.	.	.	.	. .	Porritt, J., & Son's Siding	Lancs	L. & Y.	Helmshore.
G	P	F	L	H	C	1 10	Helmsley	Yorks	N. E.	Gilling and Kirby Moorside.
.	.	.	.	.	.	. .	Harum Siding	Yorks	N. E.	Helmsley.
G	P	F	L	H	C	1 10	Helpringham	Lincoln	G. N. & G. E. Jt.	Spalding and Sleaford.
.	.	.	.	.	.	. .	Blotoft Siding	Lincoln	G. N. & G. E. Jt.	Donington Road and Helpringham.
G	P	F	L	H	C	1 10	Helpston	N'hamptn	Mid.	Peterboro' and Stamford.
.	.	.	.	.	.	. .	Towgood & Son's Paper Mills	N'hamptn	Mid.	Near Helpston.
G	P	.	L	H		10 0	Helsby	Cheshire	B'head Jt. (GW & LNW)	Chester and Warrington.
.	.	.	.	.	.	. .	Runcorn and Helsby Red Sandstone Co.'s Siding	Cheshire	B'head Jt. (GW & LNW)	Helsby.
.	.	.	.	.	.	. .	Helsby Junction	Cheshire	B'head Jt.—C. L. C.	Hooton and Helsby.
G	.	.	L	.	.	5 0	Helsby and Alvanley	Cheshire	C. L. C. (G C, G N, & Mid.)	Mouldsworth and Helsby Junction.
.	.	.	.	.	.	. .	Runcorn and Helsby Stone Co.'s Siding	Cheshire	C. L. C. (G C, G N, & Mid.)	Helsby.
.	.	.	.	.	.	. .	Telegraph Manufacturing Co.'s Siding	Cheshire	C. L. C. (G C, G N, & Mid.)	Helsby.
G	P	F	L	H	C	4 0	Helston	Cornwall	G. W.	Branch from Gwinear Road.
.	.	.	.	.	.	. .	Hemel Hempstead	Herts	L. & N. W.	See Boxmoor and Hemel Hempstead.
G	P	F	L	H	C	1 10	Hemel Hempsted	Herts	Mid.	Branch from Harpenden.
.	.	.	.	.	.	. .	Boxmoor District Gas Co.'s Siding	Herts	Mid.	Near Hemel Hempsted.
.	.	.	.	.	.	. .	Claydale Brick Co.'s Siding	Herts	Mid.	Near Hemel Hempsted.
.	.	.	.	.	.	. .	Godwin's Siding	Herts	Mid.	Near Hemel Hempsted.
G						. .	Heath Park for Boxmoor (Boxmoor Wharf)	Herts	Mid.	Near Hemel Hempsted.
.	.	.	.	.	.	. .	Hem Heath Sidings	Staffs	N. S.	Chesterton.
.	.	.	.	.	.	. .	Bradwell Hall Brick and Tile Works	Staffs	N. S.	Hem Heath Sidings.
.	.	.	.	.	.	. .	Hem Heath Mining Co.	Staffs	N. S.	Hem Heath Sidings.
G	P	.	L	H		. .	Hemingbrough	Yorks	N. E.	Hull and Selby.
.	.	.	.	.	.	. .	Smith & Co.'s Malt Kiln	Yorks	N. E.	Hemingbrough.
.	.	.	.	.	.	. .	Hemingfield Colliery	Yorks	G. C.	Same as Elsecar Low Pit.
.	.	.	.	.	.	. .	Hemingfield Fan Siding	Yorks	G. C.	Elsecar.
.	.	.	.	.	.	. .	Hemingway's Girder Works	Durham	N. E.	Haverton Hill.
.	.	.	.	.	.	. .	Hempstead Wharf Gas Co.'s Siding	Glo'ster	Mid.	Gloucester.
G	P	.	L	.	.	. .	Hemsby	Norfolk	Mid. & G. N. Jt.	North Walsham Town and Yarmouth Beach.
G	P	F	L	H	C	10 0	Hemsworth	Yorks	W. R. & G. Jt. (G.C. & G.N.)	Doncaster and Wakefield.
.	.	.	.	.	.	. .	Hemsworth Colliery (Fitzwilliam Colliery)	Yorks	W. R. & G. Jt. (G.C. & G.N.)	Hemsworth and Nostell.

EXPLANATION—G *Goods Station.*　　P *Passenger and Parcel Station.*　　P* *Passenger, but not Parcel or Miscellaneous Traffic.*
F *Furniture Vans, Carriages, Portable Engines, and Machines on Wheels.*　　L *Live Stock.*
H *Horse Boxes and Prize Cattle Vans.*　　C *Carriages by Passenger Train.*

STATION ACCOMMODATION.						CRANE POWER.		STATIONS, &c.	COUNTY.	COMPANY.	POSITION.
						Tons	Cwts.				
G	P	F	.	H	C	.	.	Hemsworth and South Kirkby	Yorks	H. & B.	Cudworth and Howden.
								Hemsworth Junction	Yorks	H. & B.—W. R. & G. Jt.	Upton and Hemsworth.
G	P	.	L	.	.	1	0	Hemyock	Devon	G. W.	Branch from Tiverton Jn. Station.
.	.	.	.	.	.	.	.	Whitehall Siding	Devon	G. W.	Hemyock.
.	.	.	.	.	.	.	.	Henderson's Chemical Works	Ayr	G. & S.W.	Irvine Harbour.
.	.	.	.	.	.	.	.	Henderson's Siding	Lanark	N. B.	Airdrie, North.
.	.	.	.	.	.	.	.	Hendford	Somerset	G. W.	See Yeovil.
G	P	F	L	H	C	1	10	Hendon (Mid.)	Middlesex	{ Mid.	London and St. Alban's.
.	P*									S. E. & C.	Over Met. and Midland Lines.
.	.	.	.	.	.	.	.	Hendon Dock	Durham	N. E.	See River Wear Commissioners (Sunderland).
.	.	.	.	.	.	.	.	Hendon Gas Works (Sunderland Gas Co.)	Durham	N. E.	Sunderland, South Dock.
.	.	.	.	.	.	.	.	Hendon Paper Works	Durham	N. E.	Sunderland, South Dock.
G	P	.	.	.	.	.	.	Hendreforgan	Glamorg'n	G. W.	Llantrisant and Gilfach.
.	.	.	.	.	.	.	.	Caradog Vale Colliery	Glamorg'n	G. W.	Hendreforgan and Black Mill.
.	.	.	.	.	.	.	.	Hendreforgan Col. (Mid.)	Glamorg'n	Mid.—G. W.—L. & N. W.	{ Gurnos. Gwys.
.	.	.	.	.	.	.	.	Hendre Siding	Flint	L. & N. W.	See Halkyn Lime Co.(Rhydymwyn).
.	.	.	.	.	.	.	.	Hendrewen Colliery	Glamorg'n	G. W.	South Rhondda.
.	.	.	.	.	.	.	.	Hendrewen Rhondda Colliery	Glamorg'n	R. & S. B.	Blaenrhondda.
.	.	.	.	.	.	.	.	Hendry's Siding	Ayr	G. & S.W.	Kilwinning.
G	.	.	.	.	.	.	.	Hendy Siding (G. W.)	Carmarth'	{ G. W.	Pontardulais and Llangennech.
										L. & N. W.	Over G. W. from Llandilo Junction.
.	.	.	.	.	.	.	.	Hendy Tin Plate Wks. (GW)	Carmarth'	G. W.—L. & N. W.	Hendy Siding.
.	.	.	.	.	.	.	.	Talyclyn Colliery and Brick Works (G. W.)	Carmarth'	G. W.—L. & N. W.	Hendy Siding.
.	.	.	.	.	.	.	.	Hendy Tin Plate Wks.(G.W.)	Carmarth'	G. W.—L. & N. W.	Hendy Siding.
G	P	F	L	H	C	1	10	Henfield	Sussex	L. B. & S. C.	Partridge Green and Steyning.
.	.	.	.	.	.	.	.	Hengoed	Glamorg'n	G. W.	Same as Rhymney Junction Station.
.	.	.	.	.	.	.	.	Hengoed Junction	Glamorg'n	G. W.—Rhy.	Llancaiach and Pengam.
G	P	.	.	.	.	.	.	Hengoed Junc. Station (Rhy.)	Glamorg'n	{ Rhy.	Ystrad Mynach and Pengam.
G	.	.	.	.	.	.	.			L. & N. W.	Over Rhy. fr. Rhymney Jt. Line Jn.
.	.	.	.	.	.	.	.	North Hengoed Colliery	Glamorg'n	Rhy.	Hengoed and Pengam.
G	P	.	.	.	.	.	.	Heniarth Gate	Montgom	Cam. (W. & L.)	Welshpool and Llanfair Caereinion.
.	.	.	.	.	.	.	.	Henley & Co.'s Old Wks.(G E)	Essex	GE—GN—L&NW—Mid.	London, Silvertown.
G	P	F	L	H	C	5	0	Henley-in-Arden	Warwick	G. W.	Branch from Rowington Junction.
G	P	F	L	H	C	10	0	Henley-on-Thames	Oxon	G. W.	Branch from Twyford.
.	.	.	.	.	.	.	.	Henley, W. T., Telegraph Works Co.'s Siding (G. E.)	Essex	GE—GN—L&NW—Mid.	Woolwich, North.
G	P	.	L	H	.	6	0	Henllan	Carmarth'	G. W.	Llandyssil and Newcastle Emlyn.
.	.	.	.	.	.	.	.	Henllis Fire-Brick Wks.(GW)	Mon	G. W.—L. & N. W.	Cwmbran.
.	.	.	.	.	.	.	.	Henllys Vale Colliery (Mid.)	Glamorg'n	Mid.—G. W.—L. & N. W.	{ Gurnos. Gwys.
G	P	.	.	.	.	.	.	Henlow	Beds	Mid.	Hitchin and Bedford.
.	.	.	.	.	.	.	.	Plowman & Son's Siding	Beds	Mid.	Henlow and Shefford.
G	P	.	L	H	.	.	.	Hensall (L. & Y.)	Yorks	{ L. & Y.	Goole and Knottingley.
.	P	.	.	.	.	.	.			H. & B.	Over L. & Y. from Hensall Junc.
.	.	.	.	.	.	.	.	Hensall Junction	Yorks	H. & B.—L. & Y.	Carlton and Knottingley.
G	P	F	L	H	C	1	0	Henstridge	Somerset	S.& D.Jt.(L.&S.W.&Mid)	Blandford and Templecombe.
.	.	.	.	.	.	.	.	Henwain Colliery (G.W.)	Mon	G. W.—L. & N. W.	See Lancaster & Co. (Blaina).
.	.	.	.	.	.	.	.	Henwick (G. W.)	Worcester	G. W.—Mid.	See Worcester.
.	.	.	.	.	.	.	.	Henwick Hall Siding	Yorks	N. E.	{ Selby. Temple Hirst.
.	.	.	.	.	.	.	.	Heol-lladron Junction	Brecon	B. & M.	Near Brecon.
.	.	.	.	.	.	.	.	Heolydelaid Siding	Glamorg'n	P. T.	Same as Margam Moors Sid(Bryndu).
G	P*	.	.	.	.	.	.	Hepscott	Northumb	N. E.	Morpeth and Blyth.
.	.	.	.	.	.	.	.	Hepscott Isabella Colliery	Northumb	N. E.	Hepscott.
.	.	.	.	.	.	.	.	Hepworth Colliery	Yorks	G. C.	Hazlehead Bridge.
.	.	.	.	.	.	.	.	Hepworth Iron Co.'s Siding	Yorks	G. C.	Hazlehead Bridge.
.	.	.	.	.	.	.	.	Herbert's Brick Works	Leicester	Mid.	Syston.
.	.	.	.	.	.	.	.	Herbertshire Brick Works	Stirling	Cal.	Denny.
.	.	.	.	.	.	.	.	Herbertshire Pits Nos. 2 & 3	Stirling	Cal.	Denny.
.	.	.	.	.	.	.	.	Herbert's Siding	Mon	G. W.	Newport, High Street.
.	.	.	.	.	.	.	.	Herbert Street	Staffs	G. W.	See Wolverhampton.
.	.	.	.	.	.	.	.	Herculaneum Dock	Lancs	L'pool O'head	See Liverpool.
.	.	.	.	.	.	.	.	Herculaneum Dock Coal Cranes & Tips (M.D & H.B.)	Lancs	C. L. C. (G C, G N, & Mid.)	Liverpool, Brunswick.
.	.	.	.	.	.	.	.	Herdman's Siding	Edinboro'	N. B.	Edinburgh, Haymarket.
.	.	.	.	.	.	.	.	Herdshill Colliery	Lanark	{ Cal.	{ Morningside. Newmains.
										N. B.	Morningside.

EXPLANATION—G *Goods Station.*   P *Passenger and Parcel Station.*   P* *Passenger, but not Parcel or Miscellaneous Traffic.*
F *Furniture Vans, Carriages, Portable Engines, and Machines on Wheels.*   L *Live Stock.*
H *Horse Boxes and Prize Cattle Vans.*   C *Carriages by Passenger Train.*

STATION ACCOMMODATION.						CRANE POWER.		STATIONS, &c.	COUNTY.	COMPANY.	POSITION.
G	P	F	L	H	C	Tons	Cwts				
								HEREFORD—			
G	P	F	L	H	C	10	0	(Station, S. & H. Joint) ...	Hereford ..	S & H Jt (GW & L N W)	Abergavenny and Craven Arms.
.	P	.	.	H	C	.	.			Mid.	Over S. & H. Jt. Lines.
.	.	.	.	.	.	.	.	Barr's Court Junc., North	Hereford ..	G. W.—S. & H. Jt.	Barton and Craven Arms.
.	.	.	.	.	.	.	.	Barr's Court Junc., South	Hereford..	G. W.—S. & H. Jt.	Rotherwas Junc. & Hereford Sta.
G	.	.	L	.	.	.	.	Barton	Hereford ..	G. W.	Barr's Court North Jn. & Red Hill Jn.
.	.	.	.	.	.	.	.	Brecon Curve Junction......	Hereford..	G. W.—Mid.	Hereford Station and Moorfields.
.	.	.	.	.	.	.	.	Brecon Curve Junction......	Hereford..	G. W.—S. & H. Jt.	Barton and Hereford Station.
.	.	.	.	.	.	.	.	Corporation Siding (G. W.)	Hereford..	G. W.—L. & N. W.	Hereford Station.
.	.	.	.	.	.	.	.	Gas Works (G. W.)	Hereford..	G. W.—L. & N. W.—Mid.	Barton.
.	.	.	.	.	.	.	.	Groom's Siding (G. W.) ...	Hereford..	G. W.—L. & N. W.—Mid.	Barton.
G	.	F	L	.	.	5	0	Moorfields	Hereford ..	Mid.	Over G. W. and S. & H. Jt. Lines.
.	.	.	.	.	.	.	.	Moorfields Exchange Sidings (Mid.)	Hereford..	Mid.—G. W.—L. & N. W.	Over G. W. and Mid. from Brecon Curve Junction.
.	.	.	.	.	.	.	.	Red Hill Junction	Hereford..	G. W.—L. & N. W.	Tram Inn and Hereford Station.
.	.	.	.	.	.	.	.	Rotherwas Junction	Hereford..	G. W.—L. & N. W.	Holme Lacy and Hereford Station.
.	.	.	.	.	.	.	.	Shelwick Junction............	Hereford..	G. W.—S. & H. Jt.	Withington and Hereford Station.
.	.	.	.	.	.	.	.	Show Yard Siding (G. W.)	Hereford..	G. W.—L. & N. W.	Hereford.
.	.	.	.	.	.	.	.	Stone Siding (G. W.)	Hereford..	G. W.—L. & N. W.	Hereford.
.	.	.	.	.	.	.	.	Wagon Works (G. W.)......	Hereford..	G. W.—L. & N. W.	Hereford.
.	.	.	.	.	.	.	.	Watkins Bros.' Siding	Hereford..	G. W.	Hereford.
G	P	F	L	H	C	.	.	Heriot	Edinboro'	N. B.	Edinburgh and Galashiels.
.	.	.	.	.	.	.	.	Heriothill Depôt	Edinboro'	N. B.	See Edinburgh.
.	.	.	.	.	.	.	.	Heriothill Saw Mills..........	Edinboro'	N. B.	Edinburgh, Scotland Street.
.	.	.	.	.	.	.	.	Hermand Brick Works........	Edinboro'	Cal.	West Calder.
.	.	.	.	.	.	.	.	Hermand Oil Works (New) (Breich Oil Works)	L'lithgow	Cal..............................	West Calder.
G	P	.	L	H	.	1	10	Hermitage	Berks	G. W.	Didcot and Newbury.
G	P	F	L	H	C	7	0	Herne Bay & Hampton-on-Sea	Kent	S. E. & C....................	Faversham and Margate.
								HERNE HILL—			
G	P	.	.	.	.	.	.	(Station, S. E. & C.)	Surrey ...	S. E. & C.	Brixton and Penge.
.	P	.	.	.	.	.	.			L. & S. W.	Over L. B. & S. C. and S. E. & C. from Streatham Junction.
.	.	.	.	.	.	.	.	North Junction	Surrey ...	S. E. & C.	Brixton and Herne Hill.
.	.	.	.	.	.	.	.	Poplar Walk Siding	Surrey ...	S. E. & C.	Herne Hill.
.	.	.	.	.	.	.	.	Sorting Sidings	Surrey ...	S. E. & C.	Herne Hill and Loughboro' Junc.
.	.	.	.	.	.	.	.	South Junction	Surrey ...	S. E. & C.	Herne Hill and Dulwich.
G	P	.	L	H	.	.	.	Herriard	Hants ...	L. & S.W.	Basingstoke and Alton.
.	.	.	.	.	.	.	.	Herringfleet Junction Station	Suffolk ...	G. E.	Beccles and Yarmouth, South Town.
.	.	.	.	.	.	.	.	Herrington Pit	Durham ...	N. E.	Fencehouses. Penshaw.
.	.	.	.	.	.	.	.	Hersham	Surrey ...	L. & S.W	See Walton and Hersham.
G	P	F	L	H	C	4	10	Hertford	Herts	G. E.	Branch from Broxbourne.
G	P	F	L	H	C	5	0			G. N.	Branch from Hatfield.
.	.	.	.	.	.	.	.	Ewen & Tomlinson's Siding	Herts	G. N.	Hertford.
.	.	.	.	.	.	.	.	Gilbertson & Page Siding	Herts	G. E.	Hertford.
.	.	.	.	.	.	.	.	Gripper & Wightman's Sid.	Herts	G. N.	Hertford Station and Junction.
.	.	.	.	.	.	.	.	King's Meads Siding	Herts	G. N.	Hertford Station and Junction.
.	.	.	.	.	.	.	.	McMullen & Son's Siding	Herts	G. N.	Hertford.
.	.	.	.	.	.	.	.	Manser & Co.'s Siding	Herts	G. N.	Hertford Station and Junction.
G	P	.	.	.	.	.	.	Hertford Junction...............	Herts	G. E.—G. N.	Ware and Hertford G. N.
.	.	.	.	.	.	.	.	Hertingfordbury	Herts	G. N.	Hatfield and Hertford.
.	.	.	.	.	.	.	.	Hertingfordbury Gravel Sid.	Herts	G. N.	Hertingfordbury.
.	.	.	.	.	.	.	.	Page & Welch's Siding	Herts	G. N.	Hertingfordbury and Hertford.
.	.	.	.	.	.	.	.	Webb & Co.'s Siding........	Herts	G. N.	Hertingfordbury and Hertford.
G	P	.	L	H	C	.	.	Hesketh Bank	Lancs	L. & Y.	Preston and Southport.
.	.	.	.	.	.	.	.	Tarleton Branch...............	Lancs	L. & Y.	Branch from Hesketh Bank.
G	P	.	L	H	.	.	.	Hesketh Park	Lancs	L. & Y.	Preston and Southport.
G	P	.	L	H	.	.	.	Hesleden	Durham ...	N. E.	Castle Eden and Hartlepool.
.	.	.	.	.	.	.	.	Hesleden Bank Siding	Durham ...	N. E.	Hesleden.
G	P	F	L	H	C	.	.	Heslerton	Yorks	N. E.	Malton and Scarborough.
.	P	.	.	.	.	.	.	Hessay	Yorks	N. E.	York and Knaresborough.
G	P	F	L	H	C	5	0	Hessle (N. E.)......................	Yorks	N. E.	Hull and Selby.
.	P	.	.	H	C	.	.			G. C.	Over N. E. from Thorne Junction.
G	P	.	.	H	.	.	.	Hest Bank	Lancs	L. & N. W.	Lancaster and Penrith.
.	P	.	.	.	.	.	.	Heston-Hounslow	Middlesex	Met. Dist.	Osterley and Hounslow Barracks.
G	P	F	L	H	C	10	0	Heswall..............................	Cheshire..	B'head Jt.(GW & LNW)	Hooton and West Kirby.
G	P	.	L	H	.	5	0	Heswall Hills	Cheshire..	N. W. & L. Jt. (G. C. and W. M. & C. Q.)	Neston and Birkenhead.
G	P	.	L	.	.	.	.	Hethersett	Norfolk ..	G. E.	Norwich and Wymondham.
G	P	.	L	.	.	3	0	Hetton	Durham ...	N. E.	Murton Junction & Durham, Elvet.
.	.	.	.	.	.	.	.	Elemore Colliery...............	Durham ...	N. E.	Hetton.

EXPLANATION—G *Goods Station.*　　P *Passenger and Parcel Station.*　　P* *Passenger, but not Parcel or Miscellaneous Traffic.*
F *Furniture Vans, Carriages, Portable Engines, and Machines on Wheels.*　　L *Live Stock.*
H *Horse Boxes and Prize Cattle Vans.*　　C *Carriages by Passenger Train.*

STATION ACCOMMODATION.						CRANE POWER.	STATIONS, &c.	COUNTY.	COMPANY.	POSITION.
						Tons Cwts.	Hetton—*continued.*			
.	.	.	.	.	.	. .	Eppleton Colliery	Durham ...	N. E.	Hetton.
.	.	.	.	.	.	. .	Hazard Colliery	Durham ...	N. E.	Hetton.
.	.	.	.	.	.	. .	Hetton Colliery	Durham ...	N. E.	Hetton.
.	.	.	.	.	.	. .	North Hetton Colliery	Durham ...	N. E.	Hetton.
G	P	F	L	H	C	. .	Hever	Kent	L. B. & S. C.	Oxted and Groombridge.
.	P	.	.	.	.	. .	Heversham	W'morlnd	Furness.........................	Arnside and Hincaster Junction.
.	.	.	.	.	.	. .	Hewes Bros.' Brick Works ...	Leicester..	Mid.	Coalville.
.	.	.	.	.	.	. .	Hewish Siding	Somerset..	L. & S.W.	See Crewkerne.
.	.	.	.	.	.	. .	Hewitson's, John, Sid. (N.E.)	Cumb'land	N. E.—Mid.	Carlisle.
.	.	.	.	.	.	. .	Hewitt & Renshaw's Siding...	Cheshire..	C. L. C.—L. & N. W.	Northwich.
.	.	.	.	.	.	. .	Hewitt's Yard....................	Glo'ster ...	Mid.	Same as Coal Pit Heath Coal Co.'s Siding (Bristol).
.	.	.	.	.	.	. .	Hewitt, W. R., & Co.'s Sid.	Suffolk ...	G. E.	{ Bury St. Edmunds. { Stowmarket.
.	.	.	.	.	.	. .	Hewlett Pit (L. & Y.)	Lancs	L. & Y.—L. & N. W.	Same as Wigan Coal and Iron Co.'s Crow Nest Siding.
.	.	.	.	.	.	. .	Heworth Colliery	Durham ...	N. E.	Pelaw Junction Station.
.	.	.	.	.	.	. .	Heworth Quarries	Durham ...	N. E.	Same as Tate, Brown & Co.'s Siding (Felling).
G	P	F	L	H	C	5 0	Hexham (N. E.)	Northumb	{ N. E. .... { N. B.	Reedsmouth and Newcastle. Over N. E. from Hexham Junction.
.	.	.	.	.	.	. .	Hexham Junction	Northumb	N. B.—N. E.	Wall and Hexham.
.	.	.	.	.	.	. .	Hexthorpe Junction	Yorks	G. C.	Conisboro' and Doncaster.
.	.	.	.	.	.	. .	Heyes' Siding	Lancs	L. & N. W.	Widnes.
G	P	F	L	H	C	3 0	Heyford	Oxon	G. W.	Oxford and Banbury.
.	.	.	.	.	.	. .	Heysham Harbour Contractors Siding	Lancs	Mid.	Morecambe.
.	.	.	.	.	.	. .	Heys Siding	Lancs	L. & Y.	Broadley.
.	.	.	.	.	.	. .	Heys Siding	Lancs	L. & Y.	Facit.
G	P	F	L	H	C	1 10	Heytesbury	Wilts	G. W.	Salisbury and Warminster.
G	P	F	L	H	C	10 0	Heywood	Lancs	L. & Y.	Bury and Rochdale.
.	.	.	.	.	.	. .	L. & Y. Rly. Wagon Co.'s Siding	Lancs	L. & Y.	Heywood.
.	.	.	.	.	.	. .	Hibaldstow	Lincoln ...	G. C.	See Scawby and Hibaldstow.
.	.	.	.	.	.	. .	Hibel Road	Cheshire..	L. & N. W. & N. S. Jt. ...	See Macclesfield.
.	.	.	.	.	.	. .	Hicbibi Brick Works	Lancs	L. & N. W.	See Pearson & Knowles Coal & Iron Co.'s Coppull Hall Sid. (Coppull).
.	.	.	.	.	.	. .	Hick, Hargreaves & Co.'s Soho Iron Works	Lancs	L. & N. W.	{ See Lecturer's Close and Hulme { Trust Siding (Bolton).
G	P	F	L	.	.	. .	Hickleton and Thurnscoe ...	Yorks	H. & B.	Wrangbrook Junction and Wath.
.	.	.	.	.	.	. .	Hickleton Main Colliery ...	Yorks	H. & B.	Hickleton and Wath.
.	.	.	.	.	.	. .	Hickleton Main Colliery (S. & K. Jt.)	Yorks	S. & K. Jt.—G. C.	{ Bolton-on-Dearne. { Frickley.
							Hickman's—			
.	.	.	.	.	.	. .	Brick Works	Staffs	L. & N. W.	See Spring Vale Siding (Deepfields and Coseley).
.	.	.	.	.	.	. .	Iron Works	Staffs	L. & N. W.	See Spring Vale Siding (Deepfields and Coseley).
.	.	.	.	.	.	. .	Siding	Staffs	G. W.	See Spring Vale Siding (Bilston and Deepfields).
.	.	.	.	.	.	. .	Hickman's, H. T., Siding ...	Worcester	G. W.	Lye.
.	.	.	.	.	.	. .	Hickman's Timber Depôt......	Staffs	G. W.	Wolverhampton.
							Hickman's, Sir A.—			
.	.	.	.	.	.	. .	Astrop Siding.................	N'hampt'n	G. W.	Kings Sutton.
.	.	.	.	.	.	. .	Haunchwood (or Nowell) Brick & Colliery Co.'s Siding (Mid.)	Warwick..	Mid.—L. & N. W.	Stockingford.
.	.	.	.	.	.	. .	Tunnel Pit (Mid.)	Warwick..	Mid.—L. & N. W.	Stockingford.
.	.	.	.	.	.	. .	Hicks & Co.'s Siding	Essex	G. E.	Stansted.
.	.	.	.	.	.	. .	Hicks, Gardener & Co.'s Sid.	Hunts......	G. N.	Fletton.
.	.	.	.	.	.	. .	Hickson's Works	Cheshire...	C. L. C. (G.C., G.N. & Mid.)	{ See Salt Union Ltd. (Winnington). { See Salt Union Ltd. (Winsford and Over).
							Higginbottom's—			
.	.	.	.	.	.	. .	Norley Colliery	Lancs	L. & N. W.	Garswood.
.	.	.	.	.	.	. .	Prescot Colliery or Lancaster's Siding.................	Lancs	L. & N. W.	Huyton Quarry.
.	.	.	.	.	.	. .	Whiston Colliery	Lancs	L. & N. W.	Huyton Quarry.
.	.	.	.	.	.	. .	Higginshaw Gas Siding ...	Lancs	L. & Y.	Oldham, Mumps.
G	P	F	L	H	C	1 10	Higham	Kent	S. E. & C.	Gravesend and Strood.
.	.	.	.	.	.	. .	Ballast Pit Siding	Kent	S. E. & C.	Higham.

EXPLANATION—G *Goods Station.*   P *Passenger and Parcel Station.*   P* *Passenger, but not Parcel or Miscellaneous Traffic.*
F *Furniture Vans, Carriages, Portable Engines, and Machines on Wheels.*   L *Live Stock.*
H *Horse Boxes and Prize Cattle Vans.*   C *Carriages by Passenger Train.*

STATION ACCOMMODATION.						CRANE POWER.	STATIONS, &c.	COUNTY.	COMPANY.	POSITION.
						Tons Cwts.				
G	P	F	.	H	C	1 10	Higham	Suffolk ...	G. E.	Newmarket & Bury St. Edmunds.
G	P	F	L	H	C	1 15	Higham Colliery (L. & Y.) ...	Yorks	L. & Y.—G. C.	Darton.
							Higham Ferrers & Irthling-boro'	N'hampton	L. & N. W.	Peterboro' and Wellingboro'.
.	.	.	.	.	.		Dunmore's Siding	N'hampton	L. & N. W.	Ditchford and Higham Ferrers.
.	.	.	.	.	.		Irthlingboro' Brick & Tile Co.'s Siding	N'hampton	L. & N. W.	Higham Ferrers and Ditchford.
.	.	.	.	.	.		Irthlingboro' Iron Ore Co.'s Siding	N'hampton	L. & N. W.	Higham Ferrers and Ditchford.
.	.	.	.	.	.		Metropolitan Brick & Tile Co.'s Siding	N'hampton	L. & N. W.	Higham Ferrers and Ditchford.
G	P	F	L	H	C	1 10	Higham Ferrers (for Irthling-boro')	N'hampton	Mid.	Branch from Wellingboro'.
.	P						Higham-on-the-Hill	Leicester..	A & N Jt. (L & N W & Mid.)	Nuneaton and Shackerstone.
G	P						Highams Park & Hale End ...	Essex	G. E.	Wood Street and Chingford.
.	.	.	.	.	.		High Barmston Depôt	Durham ..	N. E.	Washington.
.	P	.	L	H	.		High Barnet (G. N.)	Herts	G. N.—N. L.	See Barnet, High.
G	P	.	L	H	.		High Blaithwaite	Cumb'land	M. & C.	Aikbank Junction and Mealsgate.
G	P	.	L	H	.	2 0	High Blantyre	Lanark ...	Cal.	Hamilton and Strathaven.
.	.	.	.	.	.		Aitkenhead Siding	Lanark ...	Cal.	High Blantyre.
.	.	.	.	.	.		Auchenraith Colliery	Lanark ...	Cal.	Blantyre and High Blantyre.
.	.	.	.	.	.		Blantyre Collieries	Lanark ...	Cal.	Near High Blantyre.
.	.	.	.	.	.		Blantyre Co-operative Society's Siding	Lanark ...	Cal.	Blantyre and High Blantyre.
.	.	.	.	.	.		Greenhall Brick Works	Lanark ...	Cal.	High Blantyre.
.	.	.	.	.	.		Sydes Siding	Lanark ...	Cal.	High Blantyre.
.	.	.	.	.	.		Udston Colliery	Lanark ...	Cal.	High Blantyre & Meikle Earnock.
							HIGHBRIDGE—			
G	P	F	L	H	C	4 0	(Station)	Somerset..	G. W.	Bristol and Bridgwater.
G	P	F	L	H	C	1 10	(Station)	Somerset..	S. & D. Jt. (L. & S W & Mid)	Glastonbury and Burnham.
.	.	.	.	.	.		Apex Tile & Brick Works	Somerset..	S.&D.Jt.(L.&S.W.& Mid.)	Highbridge and Burnham.
.	.	.	.	.	.		Bland & Co.'s Timber Yard	Somerset..	S.&D.Jt.(L.&S.W.& Mid.)	Highbridge Wharf.
.	.	.	.	.	.		Feaver & Luff Cake Mills...	Somerset..	S.&D.Jt.(L.&S.W.& Mid.)	Highbridge Wharf.
.	.	.	.	.	.		Gas Works	Somerset..	G. W.	Highbridge.
.	.	.	.	.	.		Junction	Somerset..	G. W.—S. & D. Jt.	Highbridge and Burnham.
.	.	.	.	.	.		Norris Siding	Somerset..	S.&D.Jt.(L.&S.W.& Mid.)	Highbridge Wharf.
.	.	.	.	.	.		Pitts, A. G., Brick Works	Somerset..	S.&D.Jt.(L.&S.W.& Mid.)	Highbridge Wharf.
G	.	.	L	.	.	10 0	Wharf	Somerset..	S.&D.Jt.(L.&S.W.& Mid.)	Branch—Burnham and Highbridge.
.	.	.	.	.	.		High Brooms Siding	Kent	S. E. & C.	Southborough.
.	.	.	.	.	.		Highbury & Islington (N. L.)	Middlesex	N. L.—L. & N. W.	See London.
.	.	.	.	.	.		Highbury Coal Depôt	Middlesex	L. & N. W.	See London.
.	.	.	.	.	.		Highbury Vale	Middlesex	G. N.	See London.
.	.	.	.	.	.		High Carr Siding	Staffs	N. S.	Talk-o'-th'-Hill.
G	P	F	L	H	C	3 0	Highclere	Hants	G. W.	Newbury and Winchester.
G	P	F	L	.	.		Higher Buxton	Derby	L. & N. W.	Ashbourne and Stockport.
.	.	.	.	.	.		High Falkirk	Stirling ...	N. B.	See Falkirk.
G	P	.	L	H	C		High Field	Yorks	N. E.	Selby and Market Weighton.
.	.	.	.	.	.		Highfield Siding	Durham ..	N. E.	Same as Victoria Garesfield Colliery Coke and Brick Works (Rowlands Gill).
.	.	.	.	.	.		Highfield Siding	Lancs	L. & N. W.	See Scowcroft & Co. (Plodder Lane).
.	.	.	.	.	.		Highgate (G. N.)	Middlesex	G. N.—N. L.	See London.
.	.	.	.	.	.		Highgate Coal Wharf	Warwick..	Mid.	Birmingham, Camp Hill.
.	.	.	.	.	.		Highgate Road Coal Depôt ...	Middlesex	Mid.	See London.
.	.	.	.	.	.		Highgate Road (for Parliament Hill)	Middlesex	Mid.—T. & H. Jt.	See London.
.	.	.	.	.	.		Highgate Road Junction	Middlesex	Mid.—T. & H. Jt.	London, Kentish Town and Highgate Road.
G	P	.	L	H	.		High Harrington	Cumb'land	C. & W. Jn.	Workington and Distington.
.	.	.	.	.	.		Bain & Co.— Collieries	Cumb'land	C. & W. Jn.	Branch from High Harrington.
.	.	.	.	.	.		Harrington Iron Works	Cumb'land	C. & W. Jn.	Branch from High Harrington.
.	.	.	.	.	.		Barugh Quarry	Cumb'land	C. & W. Jn.	High Harrington and Distington.
.	.	.	.	.	.		Glebe Sand Siding	Cumb'land	C. & W. Jn.	Branch from High Harrington.
.	.	.	.	.	.		Hall Green Sand & Gravel Siding	Cumb'land	C. & W. Jn.	High Harrington and Distington.
.	.	.	.	.	.		High Hazels Colliery (G. C.)	Yorks	G. C.—L. & N. W.	Sheffield, Darnall (for Handsworth).
.	.	.	.	.	.		Highhouse Pits	Ayr	G. & S.W.	Auchinleck.
G	P	F	L	H	C	2 0	Highlandman	Perth	Cal.	Crieff Junction and Crieff.
.	.	.	.	.	.		High Lane	Cheshire...	L. & N. W.	See Middlewood (for High Lane).
.	P	.	.	.	.		High Lane	Cheshire...	Mac. Com. (G. C. & N. S.)	Romiley and Macclesfield.
.	.	.	.	.	.		Contractor's Siding	Cheshire...	Mac. Com. (G. C. & N. S.)	High Lane.

EXPLANATION—G *Goods Station.*   P *Passenger and Parcel Station.*   P* *Passenger, but not Parcel or Miscellaneous Traffic.*
F *Furniture Vans, Carriages, Portable Engines, and Machines on Wheels.*   L *Live Stock.*
H *Horse Boxes and Prize Cattle Vans.*   C *Carriages by Passenger Train.*

G	P	F	L	H	C	Tons	Cwts	STATIONS, &c.	COUNTY.	COMPANY.	POSITION.
								Highlea Siding (Polwarth's)	Hadding'n	N. B.	Humbie.
G	P		L	H				Highley	Salop	G. W.	Hartlebury and Bridgnorth.
								Highley Mining Co.'s Sid.	Salop	G. W.	Highley.
								Kinlett Siding	Salop	G. W.	Highley and Arley.
								High Meadow Siding	Hereford	G. W.	Same as Slaughter Sid. (Symonds Yat).
								High Orchard Wharf	Glo'ster	Mid.	See Gloucester.
								High Park Colliery	Derby	Mid.	See Barber, Walker & Co. (Langley Mill and Eastwood).
								High Park Colliery (G. N.)	Notts	G. N.—G. C.	Eastwood and Langley Mill.
								High Peak Junction	Derby	L. & N. W.—Mid.	Buxton and Ambergate.
								High Peak Silica Co.'s Siding	Derby	L. & N. W.	See Wragg & Son's Siding (Parsley Hay).
								High Quarry	Yorks	N. E.	Lartington.
	P							High Shields	Durham	N. E.	Newcastle and South Shields.
								High Shields Depôt	Durham	N. E.	South Shields.
								High Stoop Siding and Depôt	Durham	N. E.	Tow Law.
								High Street (Kensington)	Middlesex	Met.—Met. Dist.—Mid.	See London.
								High Street Siding	Cornwall	G. W.	See Drinnick Mill.
								High Thornley Depôts (Barlow Depôt)	Durham	N. E.	Derwenthaugh.
G	P			H				Hightown (L. & Y.)	Lancs	L. & Y.	Liverpool and Southport.
	P			H						L. & N. W.	Over L. & Y. from Bootle Junction.
								Sniggery Siding	Lancs	L. & Y.	Near Hightown.
G	P	F	L	H	C	2	0	Highworth	Wilts	G. W.	Branch from Swindon.
								Highworth Junction	Wilts	G. W.	Swindon and Shrivenham.
G	P	F	L	H	C	10	0	High Wycombe	Bucks	G. W. & G. C. Jt.	Aylesbury and Maidenhead.
								High Wycombe Junction	Bucks	G. W. & G. C. Jt.—G. W.	High Wycombe and Loudwater.
								Hilda Colliery & Fuel Works	Durham	N. E.	South Shields.
								Hilda Depôts	Durham	N. E.	South Shields.
								Hilda Shipping Staithes	Durham	N. E.	South Shields.
G	P							Hildenborough	Kent	S. E. & C.	Sevenoaks and Tonbridge.
								Weald Siding	Kent	S. E. & C.	Hildenborough and Sevenoaks, Tubs Hill.
G						4	10	Hilden Siding	Antrim	G. N. (I.)	Belfast and Lisburn.
								Hildyard's Siding	Yorks	N. E.	Ottringham.
G	P		L	H		1	0	Hilgay	Norfolk	G. E.	Ely and Lynn.
G								Black Horse Drove	Norfolk	G. E.	Hilgay Fen and Littleport.
								Hillam Gates Siding (Yorkshire Plaster Co.)	Yorks	N. E.	Milford Junction Station.
								Hill & Co.'s (Oakfield's) Wire Works (G. W.)	Monmouth	G. W.—L. & N. W.	Cwmbran.
								Hill & Co.'s Storing Ground	Yorks	N. E.	Middlesbro'.
								Hill & Smith's Siding	Staffs	G. W.	Round Oak.
								Hill, Evans & Co.'s Sid. (G.W.)	Worcester	G. W.—Mid.	Worcester.
								Hill, J., & Son's Siding	Yorks	Mid.	Keighley.
								Hill's Dry Dock & Engineering Co.'s Siding	Glamorg'n	G W—L N W—Rhy—TV	Cardiff.
								Hill's Merthyr Colliery (Mid.)	Glamorg'n	Mid.—G. W.—L. & N. W.	See Cory, Yeo, & Co.'s Collieries (Clydach-on-Tawe).
								Hill's Plymouth Col. (T. V.)	Glamorg'n	T. V.—G. W.	Same as Plymouth Works and Collieries (Merthyr).
								Hill's Plymouth Siding	Glamorg'n	G. W.	Merthyr.
								Hill Colliery	Lanark	Cal.	Same as South Linrigg Colliery. (Netherburn).
G	P							Hill End	Herts	G. N.	Hatfield and St. Albans.
								Owen & Co.'s Siding	Herts	G. N.	Hill End.
								Hill Farm Siding	Renfrew	Cal.	Inverkip.
G	P		L			1	10	Hillfoot	Dumbartn	N. B.	Bearsden and Milngavie.
								Hillhead	Lanark	Glas. Dist. Sub.	See Glasgow.
								Hillhead Collieries	Ayr	G. & S. W.	Kilmarnock.
								Hillhead Colliery	Lanark	N. B.	Longriggend.
								Hillhead Fire-Clay Works	Ayr	G. & S. W.	Kilmarnock.
								Hill Head Manure Siding	Northumb	N. E.	Killingworth.
								Hillhouse	Lancs	C. L. C. (S'port Exten.)	See Altcar and Hillhouse.
								Hillhouse	Yorks	L. & Y. and L. & N. W. Jt.	See Huddersfield.
								Hillhouse Junction	Lancs	C. L. C.—L. & Y.	Altcar and Barton.
								Hillhouserigg Colliery	Lanark	N. B.	Shotts.
G	P	F	L	H	C			Hillington (for Sandringham)	Norfolk	Mid. & G. N. Jt.	South Lynn and Melton Constable.
								Hillington Siding	Renfrew	G & P Jt (Cal & G & S W)	Cardonald.
								Hillman's Siding	Sussex	L. B. & S. C.	{ Partridge Green. / West Grinstead.

EXPLANATION—G *Goods Station.*   P *Passenger and Parcel Station.*   P* *Passenger, but not Parcel or Miscellaneous Traffic.*
F *Furniture Vans, Carriages, Portable Engines, and Machines on Wheels.*   L *Live Stock.*
H *Horse Boxes and Prize Cattle Vans.*   C *Carriages by Passenger Train.*

_	_	_	_	_	_	Tons	Cwts	STATIONS, &c.	COUNTY.	COMPANY.	POSITION.
.	.	.	.	.	.			Hill of Beath Colliery and Brick Works	Fife	N. B.	Crossgates.
G	P	.	L	H	C	.	.	Hill of Down	Meath	M. G. W.	Dublin and Mullingar.
.	.	.	.	.	.			Hill of Drumgray Colliery	Lanark	N. B.	Rawyards.
G	P	F	L	H	C	2	0	Hillsborough	Down	G. N. (I.)	Belfast and Banbridge.
.	.	.	.	.	.			Hillside	Forfar	Cal.	See Dubton Junction.
G	P	.	L	H	.	2	0	Hillside	Forfar	N. B.	Montrose and Laurencekirk.
.	.	.	.	.	.			Kinnaber Junction Sidings	Forfar	N. B.	Hillside and Craigo.
.	.	.	.	.	.			Hilltop Pottery Co.'s Siding (Banks & Co.) (Mid.)	Derby	Mid.—L. & N. W.	Woodville.
.	.	.	.	.	.			Hillwood Quarry	Edinboro'	N. B.	Ratho.
.	.	.	.	.	.			Hilsea Junction	Hants	L. & S W & L B & S C Jt.—L. B. & S. C.	See Portcreek or Hilsea Junction.
.	.	.	.	.	.			Hilton, Anderson & Co.'s Bch.	Essex	L. T. & S.	Same as Associated Portland Cement Manufacturers' Siding (Grays).
.	P	.	.	.	.			Hilton, Anderson & Co.'s Sid.	Kent	S. E. & C.	Halling.
.	.	.	.	.	.			Hilton House	Lancs	L. & Y.	Hindley and Blackrod.
.	.	.	.	.	.			Scot Lane Siding (L. & Y.)	Lancs	L. & Y.—L. & N. W.	Hilton House.
.	.	.	.	.	.			Hilton Junction	Perth	Cal.—N. B.	Perth and Bridge of Earn.
G	.	.	L	.	.			Hincaster Junction	W'morlnd	Furness—L. & N. W.	Arnside and Penrith.
.	.	.	.	.	.			Hincaster Siding	W'morlnd	L. & N. W.	Lancaster and Penrith.
.	.	.	.	.	.			Hinchcliffe Lime Siding	Yorks	W. R. & G. Jt. (G.C.&G.N.)	South Elmsall.
G	P	F	L	H	C	1	10	Hinckley (L. & N. W.)	Leicester	{ L. & N. W. { Mid.	Leicester and Nuneaton. Over L. & N. W. Line.
.	.	.	.	.	.			Hincksman's Cotton Mill	Lancs	L. & N. W.	Preston, Charles Street.
G	P	.	L	H	C	2	0	Hinderwell	Yorks	N. E.	Whitby and Middlesbro'.
G	P	F	L	H	C	5	0	Hindley	Lancs	L. & Y.	Wigan and Bolton.
.	.	.	.	.	.			Wigan Coal & Iron Co.—			
.	.	.	.	.	.			Alexandra Pit	Lancs	L. & Y.	Near Hindley.
.	.	.	.	.	.			California Pit	Lancs	L. & Y.	Near Hindley.
.	.	.	.	.	.			Crawford Pit	Lancs	L. & Y.	Near Hindley.
.	.	.	.	.	.			Crow Nest or Hewlett Pit (L. & Y.)	Lancs	L. & Y.—L. & N. W.	Near Hindley.
.	.	.	.	.	.			Eatock Pit	Lancs	L. & Y.	Hindley and Daisy Hill.
.	.	.	.	.	.			Hindley Pit	Lancs	L. & Y.	Hindley.
.	.	.	.	.	.			Iron and Steel Works	Lancs	L. & Y.	Near Hindley.
.	.	.	.	.	.			Kirkless Hall Coal and Iron Sidings	Lancs	L. & Y.	Near Hindley.
.	.	.	.	.	.			Ladies' Lane Col. (L. & Y.)	Lancs	L. & Y.—L. & N. W.	Hindley.
.	.	.	.	.	.			Meadow Pit	Lancs	L. & Y.	Hindley.
.	.	.	.	.	.			Washpit Siding	Lancs	L. & Y.	Hindley.
.	.	.	.	.	.			Woodshaw Pit	Lancs	L. & Y.	Hindley.
G	.	.	L	.	.	5	0	Hindley and Amberswood	Lancs	L. & N. W.	Preston and Tyldesley.
.	.	.	.	.	.			Atherton's Amberswood Colliery	Lancs	L. & N. W.	Hindley & Amberswood & Brynn.
.	.	.	.	.	.			Crompton & Shawcross Hindley Colliery (Amberswood East Siding)	Lancs	L. & N. W.	{ Hindley and Amberswood and Brynn.
.	.	.	.	.	.			Hindley Brick & Tile Co.'s Siding	Lancs	L. & N. W.	{ Hindley and Amberswood and Brynn.
G	P	.	.	.	.	10	0	Hindley and Platt Bridge	Lancs	G. C. (Wigan Jn.)	Lowton St. Mary's and Wigan.
.	.	.	.	.	.			Crompton & Shawcross—			
.	.	.	.	.	.			Grange Colliery	Lancs	G. C. (Wigan Jn.)	Hindley and Platt Bridge.
.	.	.	.	.	.			Hindley Colliery	Lancs	G. C. (Wigan Jn.)	Hindley and Platt Bridge.
.	.	.	.	.	.			Moss Colliery	Lancs	G. C. (Wigan Jn.)	Hindley and Platt Bridge.
.	.	.	.	.	.			Strangeways Hall Col. or Amberswood West Sid. (G. C., Wigan Jn.)	Lancs	G C (Wig. Jn.)—L & N W	Hindley and Platt Bridge.
.	.	.	.	.	.			Fir Tree House Foundry	Lancs	G. C. (Wigan Jn.)	Hindley and Platt Bridge.
.	.	.	.	.	.			Hindley Field Colliery	Lancs	G. C. (Wigan Jn.)	Hindley and Platt Bridge.
.	.	.	.	.	.			Moss Hall Colliery	Lancs	G. C. (Wigan Jn.)	Hindley and Platt Bridge.
.	.	.	.	.	.			Scowcroft & Co.'s Hindley Green Colliery	Lancs	G. C. (Wigan Jn.)	Hindley and Platt Bridge.
.	.	.	.	.	.			Victoria Colliery Co.'s Victoria Colliery	Lancs	G. C. (Wigan Jn.)	Hindley and Platt Bridge.
.	.	.	.	.	.			Wigan Junction Collieries and Brick Works	Lancs	G. C. (Wigan Jn.)	Hindley and Platt Bridge.
.	.	.	.	.	.			Hindley Brick & Tile Co.'s Sid.	Lancs	L. & N. W.	Hindley and Amberswood.
.	.	.	.	.	.			Hindley Colliery	Lancs	G. C. (Wigan Jn.)	See Crompton and Shawcross (Hindley and Platt Bridge).
.	.	.	.	.	.			Hindley Colliery	Lancs	L. & N. W.	See Pearson & Knowles Coal & Iron Co. (Wigan).

EXPLANATION—G *Goods Station.*   P *Passenger and Parcel Station.*   P* *Passenger, but not Parcel or Miscellaneous Traffic.*
F *Furniture Vans, Carriages, Portable Engines, and Machines on Wheels.*   L *Live Stock.*
H *Horse Boxes and Prize Cattle Vans.*   C *Carriages by Passenger Train.*

Station Accommodation.						Crane Power.	STATIONS, &c.	COUNTY.	COMPANY.	POSITION.
						Tons Cwts	Hindley Colliery (Ambers-wood East Siding)	Lancs	L. & N. W.	See Crompton and Shawcross (Hindley and Ambersswood).
							Hindley Field Colliery	Lancs	G. C. (Wigan Jn.)	Hindley and Platt Bridge.
									L. & N. W.	Wigan.
	P						Hindley Fire Brick Co.'s Wks.	Staffs	G. W.	Brettell Lane.
	P						Hindley Green	Lancs	L. & N. W.	Tyldesley and Wigan.
							Hindley Green Colliery	Lancs	G C (Wig. Jn.)—L & N W	See Scowcroft & Co.
							Hindley Junction	Lancs	L. & Y.—L. & N. W.	Hindley and Standish.
G	P		L	H		1 10	Hindlow	Derby	L. & N. W.	Ashbourne and Buxton.
							Buxton Lime Firms Co.—			
							Briggs' Siding	Derby	L. & N. W.	Hindlow and Hurdlow.
							Crusher Siding	Derby	L. & N. W.	Harpur Hill and Ladmanlow.
							Hoffman's Siding	Derby	L. & N. W.	Branch from Harpur Hill.
							Dowlow Siding	Derby	L. & N. W.	Hindlow and Hurdlow.
							Spencer's Brierlow Siding	Derby	L. & N. W.	Hindlow and Hurdlow.
G	P						Hindolvestone	Norfolk	Mid. & G. N. Jt.	Melton Constable & Norwich (City).
							Hindpool Barrow Hematite Steel Co.'s Works	Lancs	Furness	Barrow.
							Hindpool Saw Mills	Lancs	Furness	See Gradwell, W., & Co. (Barrow).
							Hindsward Colliery	Ayr	G. & S.W.	Skares.
							Hingley & Son's Siding (Cox's Lane Siding)	Staffs	G. W.	Netherton.
							Hinks Hay Siding	Salop	G. W.—L. & N. W.	See Stirchley Iron Co.
G	P		L				Hinton	N'hamptn	G. C.	See Woodford and Hinton.
G	P	F	L	H	C		Hinton	Worcester	Mid.	Ashchurch and Evesham.
G	P						Hinton Admiral	Hants	L. & S.W.	Brockenhurst and Christchurch.
G	P					5 0	Hipperholme (L. & Y.)	Yorks	L. & Y.	Halifax and Bradford.
									G. N.	Over L. & Y. from Bowling Junction.
							Stone Siding	Yorks	L. & Y.	Halifax and Bradford.
							Hipwell, W., & Son's Sid. (Mid)	Beds	Mid.—L. & N. W.	Bedford.
							Hirst & Son's Bankfield Mill	Yorks	L. & N. W.	Delph.
							Hirstrigg Colliery	Lanark	Cal.	Salisburgh.
G	P	F	L	H	C	1 0	Hirwain	Brecon	G. W.	Aberdare and Neath.
							Aberdare Merthyr Colliery	Glamorg'n	G. W.	Hirwain and Glyn Neath.
							Gloucester Wagon Co.	Brecon	G. W.	Hirwain and Glyn Neath.
							Penderyn Tramway	Brecon	G. W.	Hirwain.
							Pond Siding	Glamorg'n	G. W.	Hirwain and Glyn Neath.
							Tower (Duffryn Aberdare) Colliery	Glamorg'n	G. W.	Hirwain and Glyn Neath.
G	P		L	H		1 0	Histon	Cambs	G. E.	St. Ives and Cambridge.
	P			H					Mid.	Over G. N. & G.E. Jt. and G.E. Lines.
							HITCHIN—			
G		F	L			1 10	(Station)	Herts	Mid.	Branch from Bedford.
G	P	F	L	H	C	10 0	(Station, G. N.)	Herts	G. N.	King's Cross and Huntingdon.
	P			H	C				Mid.	Over G. N. from Hitchin Junction.
							Barker & Son's Siding	Herts	G. N.	Hitchin.
							Gas Works	Herts	G. N.	Hitchin.
							Junction	Herts	G. N.—Mid.	Hatfield and Bedford.
							Ransom's Lime Siding	Herts	G. N.	Hitchin and Three Counties.
	P						Hither Green	Kent	S. E. & C.	St. John's and Grove Park.
							Hither Green Exchange Sidings (S. E. & C.)	Kent	S. E. & C.	Hither Green and Grove Park.
									G. E.	Over S. E. & C. from New Cross Jn.
							Hither Green Junction	Kent	S. E. & C.	St. John's and Hither Green.
	P						Hixon (N. S.)	Staffs	N. S.	Colwich and Weston.
									L. & N. W.	Over N. S. Line.
							Hobb's Point Pier Siding	Pembroke	G. W.	See Pembroke Dock.
							Hockham	Norfolk	G. E.	See Wretham and Hockham.
G	P	F	L	H	C		Hockley	Essex	G. E.	Wickford and Southend-on-Sea.
							Hockley	Warwick	G. W.	See Birmingham.
							Hockley Basin	Warwick	G. W.	See Birmingham.
							Hockley Bonded Stores	Warwick	G. W.	Birmingham, Hockley.
							Hockley Hall and Whateley Colliery Co.	Warwick	Mid.	Same as Kingsbury Col. (Kingsbury).
							Hockley Hall Col. & Bk. Wks.	Warwick	Mid.	Wilnecote.
							Hodbarrow Mineral Siding	Cumb'land	Furness	Millom Iron Works.
							Hoddesdon	Herts	G. E.	See Broxbourne and Hoddesdon
							Hoddesdon Gas & Cl. Co.'s Sid.	Herts	G. E.	Broxbourne.
							Hoddlesden	Lancs	L. & Y.	See Darwen.
							Hoddlesden Junction	Lancs	L. & Y.	Darwen and Lower Darwen.
							Hoddlesden Sid. (Place & Son's)	Lancs	L. & Y.	Darwen.
							Hodge's, G., Siding (Mid.)	Staffs	Mid—L & N W—G N—N S	Burton-on-Trent.
							Hodgson's Brick Works	Durham	N. E.	East Boldon.

STATION ACCOMMODATION.						CRANE POWER.	STATIONS, &c.	COUNTY.	COMPANY.	POSITION.
						Tons Cwts.	Hodgson's Loom Works	Yorks	Mid.	Bradford (Frizinghall).
							Hodkin & Jones' Siding	Yorks	Mid.	Sheffield, Queen's Road.
G	P	F	L	H	C	4 0	Hodnet	Salop	G. W.	Wellington and Market Drayton.
							Hodroyd Colliery	Yorks	{ G. C.	Notton and Royston.
									{ Mid.	Royston and Notton.
G	P	F				6 0	Hoe Street (Walthamstow)	Essex	G. E.	Hackney Downs and Chingford.
							Walthamstow Urban District Council Siding	Essex	G. E.	Hoe Street.
							Hoffman Manufacturing Co.'s Siding	Essex	G. E.	Chelmsford.
							Hoffman's Siding	Derby	L. & N. W.	See Buxton Lime Firms Co. (Hindlow).
							Hogarth & Co.'s Brick Works	Northumb	N. E.	Choppington.
							Hogg's Siding	Durham	N. E.	Same as Harmire Sid (Barnard Castle)
G	P		L	H	C	5 0	Hoghton	Lancs	L. & Y.	Preston and Blackburn.
							Gregson Lane Siding	Lancs	L. & Y.	Near Hoghton.
							Hoghton Tower Siding	Lancs	L. & Y.	Near Hoghton.
							Hogswell Siding	Essex	G. E.	See Woodham Ferris.
G	P	F	L	H	C	2 0	Hoist Sidings	Yorks	G. N. & L. & Y. Jt.	Wakefield, Kirkgate.
							Holbeach	Lincoln	Mid. & G. N. Jt.	Sutton Bridge and Spalding.
							Holbeck	Yorks	G. N.—Mid.—GC—L&Y	See Leeds.
							Holbeck Junction	Yorks	G.N.—G.N. & L. & Y. Jt.	Leeds.
							Holbeck Junction	Yorks	G. N. & N. E. Jt.—Mid.	Leeds.
							Holbeck Junction Station	Yorks	N. E.	See Leeds.
							Holborn Viaduct	Middlesex	S. E. & C.	See London.
							Holbrook Colliery	Derby	Mid.	Killamarsh.
							Holbrook Colliery (G. C.)	Derby	G. C.—L. & N. W.	Beighton.
							Holburn Street	Aberdeen	G. N. of S.	See Aberdeen.
G	P					10 0	Holcombe Brook	Lancs	L. & Y.	Branch from Bury.
							Holden & Son's Siding (G.N.)	Yorks	G. N.—G. C.	Bradford, City Road.
							Hole & Co.—			
							Siding (Mid.)	Notts	{ Mid.	Newark.
									{ G. N.	(See Appendix to follow).
							Spital Maltings	Notts	G. N. & Mid. Jt.	Newark.
							Holehouse Junction	Ayr	G. & S. W.	Hollybush and Patna.
							Holes Bay Junction	Dorset	L. & S. W.	See Poole (for Longfleet).
							Holford Siding	Kent	S. E. & C. (Sheppey)	Eastchurch.
							Holgate Dock	Yorks	N. E.	York.
G	P		L		C		Holkham	Norfolk	G. E.	Heacham and Wells.
	P						Holland Arms	Anglesey	L. & N. W.	Amlwch and Gaerwen.
							Hollandhurst Colliery	Lanark	N. B.	Coatbridge, Sunnyside.
							Holland Moss Siding	Lancs	L. & Y.	Rainford Junction.
							Holland Park	Middlesex	C. L.	See London.
							Holland Road	Sussex	L. B. & S. C.	See Brighton.
							Holles Street Siding	Lincoln	G. C.	Grimsby Town.
							Holliday's Colliery	Yorks	G. N.	Same as Ardsley Colliery.
G	P	F	L	H	C	2 0	Hollingbourne	Kent	S. E. & C.	Maidstone and Ashford.
							Hollingdean Road Siding	Sussex	L. B. & S. C.	Brighton.
							Hollingworth	Derby	G. C.	See Hadfield (for Hollingworth).
G						10 0	Hollins	Lancs	L. & Y.	Darwen and Lower Darwen.
							Hollins & Co.'s Sidings (Mid)	Notts	Mid.—G. C.	Same as Pleasley Vale Sidings (Mansfield Woodhouse).
G							Hollinswood	Salop	G. W.	Shifnal and Oakengates.
							Dark Lane Brick Works	Salop	G. W.	Hollinswood and Oakengates.
							Haybridge Iron Co.'s Old Park Siding	Salop	G. W.	Hollinswood.
							Johnston's Ballast Siding	Salop	G. W.	Over Old Park Branch.
							Johnston's Ballast Siding	Salop	G. W.	Hollinswood.
							Lewis's, W., Works	Salop	G. W.	Hollinswood.
							Lilleshall Coal & Iron Co.—			
							Ironworks & Colliery	Salop	G. W.	Hollinswood,
							Priors Lee Siding	Salop	G. W.	Hollinswood.
							Snedshill Works	Salop	G. W.	Hollinswood.
							Midland Iron Works (C. & W. Walker)	Salop	G. W.	Over Private Line from Hollinswood.
							Randlay Brick Works	Salop	G. W.	Over Old Park Branch.
							Stirchley Iron Co.—			
							Hinks Hay Siding	Salop	G. W.	Over Old Park Branch.
							Old Park Siding	Salop	G. W.	Over Old Park Branch.
							Wrekin Chemical Wks. Sid.	Salop	G. W.	Over Old Park Branch.
							Hollinswood Siding	Salop	L. & N. W.	See Lilleshall Coal and Iron Co. (Oakengates).
	P*						Hollin Well and Annesley	Notts	G. C.	Chesterfield and Nottingham.

STATION ACCOMMODATION.						CRANE POWER.		STATIONS, &c.	COUNTY.	COMPANY.	POSITION.
						Tons	Cwts.				
G	P	.	L	H	.	10	0	Hollinwood	Lancs	L. & Y.	Miles Platting and Oldham.
.	.	.	.	.	.	.	.	Albion Spinning Co.'s Sid.	Lancs	L. & Y.	Hollinwood.
.	.	.	.	.	.	.	.	Holloway and Caledonian Road (G. N.)	Middlesex	G. N.—S. E. & C.	See London.
.	.	.	.	.	.	.	.	Holloway Bros.' Siding........	Derby	Mid.	Ilkeston Town.
.	.	.	.	.	.	.	.	Holloway, Cattle	Middlesex	G. N.	See London.
.	.	.	.	.	.	.	.	Holloway's Siding	Staffs	G. W.	Wolverhampton.
.	.	.	.	.	.	.	.	Holly Bank (Essington) Col.	Staffs	L. & N. W.	Bloxwich.
G	P	F	L	H	C	2	0	Hollybush	Ayr	G. & S.W.	Ayr and Dalmellington.
.	.	.	.	.	.	.	.	Carbiston Lye	Ayr	G. & S.W.	Potterston Junction.
.	.	.	.	.	.	.	.	Coylton Colliery.............	Ayr	G. & S.W.	Potterston Junction.
.	.	.	.	.	.	.	.	Percleuan Lye	Ayr	G. & S.W.	Potterston Junction.
.	.	.	.	.	.	.	.	Potterston Lyes	Ayr	G. & S.W.	Potterston Junction.
.	P	.	.	.	.	.	.	Holly Bush	Mon	L. & N. W.	Nantybwch and Tredegar Junc. Sta.
.	.	.	.	.	.	.	.	Tredegar Iron & Coal Co.'s Pochin Pits	Mon	L. & N. W.	Holly Bush and Bedwellty Pits.
.	.	.	.	.	.	.	.	Williams' (Executors of) Holly Bush Colliery	Mon	L. & N. W.	Holly Bush and Bedwellty Pits.
.	.	.	.	.	.	.	.	Holly Bush Colliery	Mon	L. & N. W.	Same as Williams' (Exors. of) Siding (Holly Bush).
G	P	.	.	.	.	.	.	Hollyhill	Cork	S. & S.	Schull and Skibbereen.
.	.	.	.	.	.	.	.	Hollym Gate Siding	Yorks	N. E.	Withernsea.
.	.	.	.	.	.	.	.	Hollymoor Asylum Siding ...	Worcester	Halesowen (G. W. & Mid.).	See Birmingham Corporation (Rubery).
G	P	F	L	H	C	.	.	Hollymount	Mayo	M. G. W.	Claremorris and Ballinrobe.
.	.	.	.	.	.	.	.	Holman, Mitchell & Co.'s Sid.	Lancs	L. & N. W.	St. Helens.
.	.	.	.	.	.	.	.	Holmbank Siding	Edinboro'	N. B.	Rosslynlee.
G	P	F	L	H	C	1	0	Holme	Hunts	G. N.	Huntingdon and Peterboro'.
.	P	.	.	.	.	.	.	Holme	Lancs	L. & Y.	Burnley and Todmorden.
.	.	.	.	.	.	.	.	Cliviger Siding	Lancs	L. & Y.	Near Holme.
.	.	.	.	.	.	.	.	Copy Pit Siding	Lancs	L. & Y.	Near Holme.
.	.	.	.	.	.	.	.	Holme	W'morl'nd	L. & N. W.	See Burton and Holme.
G	P	F	L	H	C	.	.	Holme	Yorks	N. E.	Selby and Market Weighton.
G	P	F	L	H	C	1	0	Holme Hale.............	Norfolk ...	G. E.	Thetford and Swaffham.
.	.	.	.	.	.	.	.	Holme House Colliery	Lancs	L. & N. W.	Same as Wigan Cannel Co.'s Elms Colliery (Wigan).
G	P	F	L	H	C	.	.	Holme Lacy.............	Hereford ..	G. W.	Gloucester and Hereford.
.	.	.	.	.	.	.	.	Holme Mills.............	W'morl'nd	L. & N. W.	Same as Shepherd & Son's Siding (Burton and Holme).
.	P	.	.	.	.	.	.	Holmes	Yorks	Mid.	Sheffield and Rotherham.
.	.	.	.	.	.	.	.	Holmes & Co.'s Killan Col.	Glamorg'n	L. & N. W.	Dunvant.
.	.	.	.	.	.	.	.	Holmes Blast Furnaces (Parkgate Iron & Steel Co.)	Yorks	Mid.	Masboro' and Rotherham.
.	.	.	.	.	.	.	.	Holmes Blast Siding (G. C.)..	Yorks	G. C.—G. N.	Rotherham and Masboro'.
G	P	F	L	H	C	5	0	Holmes Chapel	Cheshire..	L. & N. W.	Crewe and Stockport.
.	.	.	.	.	.	.	.	Cotton & Co.'s Victoria Works	Cheshire..	L. & N. W.	Holmes Chapel and Goostrey.
.	.	.	.	.	.	.	.	Holmes Junction	Yorks	G. C.	Holmes Blast Sid. and Rotherham.
.	.	.	.	.	.	.	.	Holmes No. 4	Ayr	G. & S.W.	Hurlford.
.	.	.	.	.	.	.	.	Holmes Oil Works.............	L'lithgow	N. B.	Uphall.
.	.	.	.	.	.	.	.	Holmes Pottery Works(Shaw, G., & Son)	Yorks	Mid.	Masboro' and Rotherham.
.	.	.	.	.	.	.	.	Holmes Siding.............	Derby	G. N.	Derby.
.	.	.	.	.	.	.	.	Holmes Siding (G. C.)	Notts	G. C.—G. N.—Mid.	Retford.
.	.	.	.	.	.	.	.	Holmes Station Siding	Yorks	Mid.	Masboro' and Rotherham.
.	.	.	.	.	.	.	.	Holmes Steel Wks. (P. Stubs)	Yorks	Mid.	Masboro' and Rotherham.
.	.	.	.	.	.	.	.	Holmes Wagon Works (Harrison & Camm)	Yorks	Mid.	Masboro' and Rotherham.
.	.	.	.	.	.	.	.	Holmethorpe Siding	Surrey ...	S. E. & C.	Red Hill.
.	.	.	.	.	.	.	.	Holmfield.............	Yorks	H & O Jt (G N & L & Y)	See Halifax.
.	.	.	.	.	.	.	.	Holmfield Junction	Yorks	G. N.—H. & O. Jt.	Halifax.
.	.	.	.	.	.	.	.	Holmfield Junction	Yorks	H'fax H. L.—H. & O. Jt.	Halifax.
G	P	.	L	H	.	10	0	Holmfirth	Yorks	L. & Y.	Branch from Huddersfield.
.	.	.	.	.	.	.	.	Holm Junction	Ayr	G. & S.W.	Saltcoats and Ardrossan.
.	.	.	.	.	.	.	.	Holmside Colliery	Durham ...	N. E.	Pelton.
G	P	F	L	H	C	4	0	Holmsley	Hants	L. & S.W.	Brockenhurst and Wimborne.
.	.	.	.	.	.	.	.	Holmstone Camp Siding	Kent	S. E. & C.	Lydd.
G	P	F	L	H	C	5	0	Holmwood	Surrey ...	L. B. & S. C.	Dorking and Horsham.
G	P	F	L	H	C	2	0	Holsworthy	Devon ...	L. & S.W.	Okehampton and Bude.
G	P	F	L	H	C	.	.	Holt	Norfolk ...	Mid. & G. N. Jt.	Melton Constable and Cromer.
.	.	.	.	.	.	.	.	Kelling Heath Siding	Norfolk ...	Mid. & G. N. Jt.	Holt.
.	.	.	.	.	.	.	.	Norfolk County Council Sid.	Norfolk ...	Mid. & G. N. Jt.	Holt.

STATION ACCOMMODATION.						CRANE POWER.	STATIONS, &c.	COUNTY.	COMPANY.	POSITION.
						Tons Cwts.				
G	P	.	.	.	.	1　0	Holt	Wilts	G. W.	Melksham and Trowbridge.
G	P	.	.	.	.	. .	Holtby	Yorks	N. E.	York and Market Weighton.
G	P	.	L	H	.	. .	Holton	Lincoln	G. C.	Market Rasen and Barnetby.
G	P	.	L	H	.	. .	Holton-le-Clay	Lincoln	G. N.	Louth and Grimsby.
.	.	.	.	.	.	. .	Holt's, A., Warehouses	Cheshire	B'head Jt—CLC—NW&L.	Birkenhead.
.	.	.	.	.	.	. .	Holt's Siding	Lancs	L. & Y.	Bacup.
.	.	.	.	.	.	. .	Holt Town Sidings & Works	Lancs	L. & Y.	See Manchester Corporation.
.	.	.	.	.	.	. .	Holwell Co.'s Siding (G. N.)	Leicester	G. N.—Mid.	Waltham-on-the-Wold.
							Holwell Iron Co.—			
.	.	.	.	.	.	. .	Buckminster Siding	Lincoln	Mid.	South Witham.
							Potter Hill, Kettleby Mines			
.	.	.	.	.	.	. .	Iron Ore Siding	Leicester	Mid.	Holwell Junction Station.
G	.	.	.	.	.	. .	Sidings	Leicester	Mid.	Holwell Junction Station.
.	.	.	.	.	.	. .	Holwell Junction Station	Leicester	Mid.	Grimston and Melton Mowbray.
							Holwell Iron Co.—			
							Potter Hill, Kettleby			
.	.	.	.	.	.	. .	Mines Iron Ore Siding	Leicester	Mid.	Holwell Branch.
.	.	.	.	.	.	. .	Sidings	Leicester	Mid.	Holwell Junction Station.
.	.	.	.	.	.	. .	Lion Brick & Tile Co.'s Sid.	Leicester	Mid.	Holwell Branch.
							Stanton Iron Co.'s Iron Ore			
G	.	.	.	.	.	. .	Siding	Leicester	Mid.	Holwell Branch.
.	.	.	.	.	.	. .	Holwell Wharf	Leicester	Mid.	Holwell Branch.
							Awsworth Iron Co.'s Iron-			
G	.	.	.	.	.	. .	stone Siding	Leicester	Mid.	Holwell Branch.
.	.	.	.	.	.	3　0	Holygate (for Broxburn)	L'lithgow	N. B.	Branch from Drumshoreland.
							Broxburn Oil Works (Holy-			
.	.	.	.	.	.	. .	gate Branch)	L'lithgow	N. B.	Extension from Holygate.
G	P	F	L	H	C	80　0	Holyhead	Anglesey	L. & N. W.	Terminus—Chester and Holyhead Section.
							Holyhead & North Wales Gas			
.	.	.	.	.	.	. .	and Water Corporation Sid.	Carnarvon	L. & N. W.	Nantlle.
.	.	.	.	.	.	. .	Holystone Siding	Northumb	N. E.	Benton.
							Holytown Collieries and Brick			
.	P	.	.	H	C	. .	Works	Lanark	Cal.	Newarthill.
G	P	F	L	H	C	5　0	Holytown Junction Station	Lanark	Cal.	Bellshill and Wishaw, Central.
G	.	.	L	.	.	1　0	Holywell	Flint	L. & N. W.	Chester and Rhyl.
.	.	.	.	.	.	. .	Holywell	Northumb	N. E.	Percy Main and Seghill.
.	.	.	.	.	.	. .	Backworth Colliery	Northumb	N. E.	Holywell.
.	.	.	.	.	.	. .	Blue Bell Colliery	Northumb	N. E.	Holywell.
.	.	.	.	.	.	. .	Blue Bell Co-operative Sid.	Northumb	N. E.	Holywell.
.	.	.	.	.	.	. .	Earsdon Junction	Northumb	N. E.	Holywell and Percy Main.
.	.	.	.	.	.	. .	East Holywell Colliery	Northumb	N. E.	Holywell.
.	.	.	.	.	.	. .	Foster & Co.'s Brick Works	Northumb	N. E.	Holywell.
.	.	.	.	.	.	. .	Prospect Hill Siding	Northumb	N. E.	Holywell.
.	.	.	.	.	.	. .	Holywell Green	Yorks	L. & Y.	See Stainland and Holywell Green.
.	.	.	.	.	.	. .	Holywell Mill	Leicester	Mid.	Ashby-de-la-Zouch.
G	P	.	L	H	C	. .	Holywood	Down	B. & C. D.	Belfast and Bangor.
G	P	F	L	H	C	3　0	Holywood	Dumfries	G. & S. W.	Dumfries and Thornhill.
.	.	.	.	.	.	. .	Portrack Siding	Dumfries	G. & S. W.	Holywood and Auldgirth.
.	.	.	.	.	.	. .	Holzapfel's Composition Sid.	Durham	N. E.	Felling.
.	.	.	.	.	.	. .	Home Farm Colliery	Lanark	Cal.	Larkhall.
.	.	.	.	.	.	. .	Homer Hill Siding	Staffs	G. W.	Same as Evers & Sons (Cradley Heath and Cradley).
G	P	F	L	H	C	1　10	Homersfield	Norfolk	G. E.	Beccles and Tivetshall.
.	.	.	.	.	.	. .	Homerton	Middlesex	N. L.	See London.
G	P	F	L	H	C	1　10	Honeybourne	Glo'ster	G. W.	Worcester and Moreton-in-Marsh.
G	P	.	L	H	.	. .	Honing (for Worstead)	Norfolk	Mid. & G. N. Jt.	North Walsham Town & Yarmouth Beach.
G	P	F	L	H	C	. .	Honington	Lincoln	G. N.	Grantham and Lincoln.
.	.	.	.	.	.	. .	Stanton Iron Wks.Co.'s Sid.	Lincoln	G. N.	Honington and Barkstone.
G	P	F	L	H	C	5　0	Honiton	Devon	L. & S.W.	Yeovil Junction and Exeter.
G	P	.	L	H	.	5　0	Honley	Yorks	L. & Y.	Huddersfield and Penistone.
G	P	.	.	.	.	. .	Honor Oak	Surrey	S. E. & C.	Nunhead and Crystal Palace.
.	P	.	.	.	.	. .	Honor Oak Park (L. B. & S. C.)	Kent	{ L. B. & S. C.	New Cross and Forest Hill.
									{ G. E.	Over L. B. & S. C. from New Cross Junction.
G	P	F	L	H	C	5　0	Hood & Co.'s Siding	Lanark	Cal.	Glasgow, Gushetfaulds.
.	.	.	.	.	.	. .	Hook	Hants	L. & S.W.	Woking and Basingstoke.
.	.	.	.	.	.	. .	Hook Brick & Tile Co.'s Sid.	Hants	L. & S.W.	Hook.
G	P	F	L	H	C	5　0	Hook Norton	Oxon	G. W.	Kings Sutton and Chipping Norton.
.	.	.	.	.	.	. .	Brymbo Siding	Oxon	G. W.	Hook Norton and Bloxham.
.	.	.	.	.	.	. .	Council Hill Siding	Oxon	G. W.	Hook Norton and Bloxham.

EXPLANATION—G *Goods Station.*　　P *Passenger and Parcel Station.*　　P* *Passenger, but not Parcel or Miscellaneous Traffic.*
F *Furniture Vans, Carriages, Portable Engines, and Machines on Wheels.*　　L *Live Stock.*
H *Horse Boxes and Prize Cattle Vans.*　　C *Carriages by Passenger Train.*

STATION ACCOMMODATION.	CRANE POWER.	STATIONS, &c.	COUNTY.	COMPANY.	POSITION.
	Tons Cwts.	Hook Norton—*continued.*			
. . . . . .	. .	Hook Norton Ironstone Co.'s Siding	Oxon	G. W.	Hook Norton.
. . . . . .	. .	South Hill Siding	Oxon	G. W.	Hook Norton and Chipping Norton.
. . . . . .	. .	Hook Norton Ironstone Siding	Oxon	G. W.	{ Adderbury. { Hook Norton.
G P		Hoole	Lancs	L. & Y.	Preston and Southport.
. . . . . .		Hooley Hill	Lancs	L. & N. W.	See Guide Bridge.
. . . . . .		Hooper & Co.'s Siding	Hants	L. & S. W.	Bursledon.
. . . . . .		Hooper & Son's Siding	Glo'ster	Mid.	Stonehouse.
. . . . . .		Hooper's Telegraph & India Rubber Works	Middlesex	{ G. E. { GN—GW—LNW—Mid	London, Millwall Docks. London, Poplar.
G P F L H C	2 10	Hooton	Cheshire	B'head Jt. (G W & L N W)	Birkenhead and Chester.
. . . . . .		West Cheshire Water Co.'s Siding	Cheshire	B'head Jt. (G W & L N W)	Hooton.
. . . . . .	.	Hopcraft & Norris' Siding	N'hampton	L. & N. W.	Brackley.
		HOPE—			
G P	1 0	(Station)	Flint	L. & N. W.	Chester and Mold.
. . . . . .		(Station, W. M. & C. Q.)	Flint	W. M. & C. Q.—G. C.	See Penyfford (for Hope).
. . . . . .		Dodd's Kinnerton Incline Siding	Flint	L. & N. W.	Hope and Kinnerton.
. P		Exchange Station	Flint	L. & N. W.	Chester and Mold.
. P		Exchange Station (W. M. & C. Q.)	Flint	{ W. M. & C. Q. { G. C.	Buckley and Wrexham. Over W. M. & C. Q. from Hawarden Bridge Junction.
. . . . . .		Junction	Flint	L. & N. W.—W. M. & C. Q.	Mold and Wrexham.
G P . L H .	1 0	Village (W. M. & C. Q.)	Flint	{ W. M. & C. Q. { G. C.	Connahs Quay and Wrexham. Over W. M. & C. Q. from Hawarden Bridge Junction.
G P F L H C	2 0	Hope (for Castleton & Bradwell)	Derby	Mid.	Dore and Chinley.
. . . . . .		Hope Cottage Siding	Northumb	N. E.	Killingworth.
. . . . . .		Hopefield Siding (Polton No. 1 Siding)	Edinboro'	N. B.	Bonnyrigg.
G P F L H C	5 0	Hopeman	Elgin&Mo'	High.	Branch from Alves.
. . . . . .		Hope Street	Lancs	L. & Y.	See Manchester.
. . . . . .		Hopetoun Branch	L'lithgow	N. B.	Uphall.
. . . . . .		Hopetoun Colliery	L'lithgow	N. B.	Same as Easton Colliery (Bathgate, Lower).
. . . . . .		Hopetoun Mines	L'lithgow	N. B.	See Young's Oil Co. (Uphall).
. . . . . .		Hopetoun Oil Works (Niddry Oil Works)	L'lithgow	N. B.	See Young's Oil Co. (Uphall).
. . . . . .		Hopetoun Quarry	L'lithgow	N. B.	Winchburgh.
. . . . . .		Hopetoun Steel Works	L'lithgow	N. B.	Bathgate, Lower.
. . . . . .		Hope Town	Durham	N. E.	See Darlington.
G P		Hopton	Suffolk	N.&S.Jt.(GE&M&GNJt.)	Yarmouth and Lowestoft.
G P F L H C	5 0	Hopton Heath	Salop	L. & N. W.	Craven Arms & Llandrindod Wells.
. . . . . .		Hopton Quarry	Derby	L. & N. W.	See Hopton Wood Stone Co. (Steeple-house).
. . . . . .		Hopton Bone Works	Derby	L. & N. W.	Same as Taylor's Sid. (Longcliffe).
		Hopton Wood Stone Co.—			
. . . . . .		Coal Hills Siding	Derby	L. & N. W.	Steeplehouse.
. . . . . .		Hopton Quarry	Derby	L. & N. W.	Steeplehouse.
. . . . . .		Middle Peak Siding	Derby	L. & N. W.	Steeplehouse.
. . . . . .		Horbling	Lincoln	G. N.	Same as Billingboro'.
G P . L H .	7 0	Horbury & Ossett (L. & Y.)	Yorks	{ L. & Y. { G. N.	Wakefield and Mirfield. Over L. & Y. from Wakefield.
. . . . . .		Hartley Bank Colliery (Flockton Coal Co.'s Sid)	Yorks	L. & Y.	Near Horbury and Ossett.
G	5 0	Healey Mills Siding	Yorks	L. & Y.	Horbury and Ossett.
. . . . . .		Horbury Gas Co.'s Siding	Yorks	L. & Y.	Near Horbury and Ossett.
. . . . . .		Horbury Wagon Co.'s Sid.	Yorks	L. & Y.	Horbury and Ossett.
. . . . . .		Yorkshire Railway Wagon Co.'s Siding	Yorks	L. & Y.	Horbury and Ossett.
. P		Horbury Junc. Sta. (L. & Y.)	Yorks	{ L. & Y. { G. N.	Wakefield and Mirfield. Over L. & Y. from Wakefield.
. . . . . .		Denby Grange Col. (L.& Y.)	Yorks	L. & Y.—N. E.	Horbury Junction & Crigglestone.
. . . . . .		Flockton Points Siding	Yorks	L. & Y.	Horbury Junction Station.
. . . . . .		Horbury Junction Iron Co.'s Siding (Co-operative Society's Siding)	Yorks	L. & Y.	Horbury Junction Station.
. . . . . .		Marsden & Son's Siding	Yorks	L. & Y.	Horbury Junction Station.
. . . . . .		Roberts' Siding	Yorks	L. & Y.	Near Horbury Junction Station.

EXPLANATION—G *Goods Station.*   P *Passenger and Parcel Station.*   P* *Passenger, but not Parcel or Miscellaneous Traffic.*
F *Furniture Vans, Carriages, Portable Engines, and Machines on Wheels.*   L *Live Stock.*
H *Horse Boxes and Prize Cattle Vans.*   C *Carriages by Passenger Train.*

STATION ACCOMMODATION.						CRANE POWER.		STATIONS, &c.	COUNTY.	COMPANY.	POSITION.
						Tons	Cwts.				
G	P							Horden Collieries	Durham ...	N. E.	Haswell.
G								Horderley	Salop	Bishop's Castle	Craven Arms and Bishop's Castle.
G								Horeb	Carmarth'	L. & M. M.	Llanelly and Cross Hands.
								Sylen Mountain Colliery ...	Carmarth'	L. & M. M.	Horeb.
G	P	F	L	H	C	4	10	Horeham Road	Sussex	L. B. & S. C.	See Waldron and Horeham Road.
								Horley	Surrey	L. B. & S. C.	Three Bridges and Red Hill.
								Horley Gas Co.'s Siding ...	Surrey	L. B. & S. C.	Horley.
G	P	F	L	H	C	1	10	Hornby..........................	Lancs	Mid.	Lancaster and Skipton.
G	P	F	L	H	C	5	0	Horncastle	Lincoln	G. N.	Branch—Boston and Lincoln.
								Roberts & Son's Siding ...	Lincoln	G. N.	Horncastle.
								Threlfall's Siding	Lincoln	G. N.	Horncastle.
G	P	F	L	H	C	3	0	Hornchurch....................	Essex	L. T. & S.	Barking and Upminster.
								Horncliffe Siding	Lancs	L. & Y.	Ewood Bridge.
								Horner, R., Siding	Essex	G. E.	Southminster.
								Horninglow (N. S.)	Staffs	N. S.—G. N.	See Burton-on-Trent.
								Horninglow Branch (Mid.)	Staffs	Mid—L & NW—GN—NS	Burton-on-Trent.
								Horninglow Street (L & N W)	Staffs	L. & N. W.—G. N.—N S	See Burton-on-Trent.
								Horninglow Street Maltings (Mid.)	Staffs	Mid.—L. & N. W.—G. N.	See Marston, Thompson & Son (Burton-on-Trent).
								Horninglow Wharf (Mid.) ...	Staffs	Mid—L & NW—GN—NS	Burton-on-Trent.
	P	F		H	C			Hornsby & Son's Siding	Lincoln	G. N.	Grantham.
G	P		L			2	0	Hornsea	Yorks	N. E.	Branch from Wilmington.
								Hornsea Bridge	Yorks	N. E.	Hull and Hornsea.
								Hornsea Brick Co.'s Siding	Yorks	N. E.	Hornsea Bridge.
								Hornsea Gas Co.'s Siding...	Yorks	N. E.	Hornsea Bridge.
G	P	F	L			10	0	Hornsey (G. N.)................	Middlesex	G. N. .... / N. L. .... / S. E. & C.	King's Cross and New Barnet. / Over G. N. from Canonbury Junc. / Over Met. and G. N. Lines.
	P										
	P*										
								Hornsey Gas Works	Middlesex	G. N.	Hornsey.
								Hornsey Road................	Middlesex	T. & H. Jt. (G. E. & Mid.)	See London.
								Horn's Siding	Herts	G. N.	Hatfield.
								Hornthorpe Colliery	Derby	Mid.	Eckington and Renishaw.
G	P		L	H		4	10	Hornthorpe Colliery (G. C.)...	Derby	G. C.—L. & N. W........	Eckington and Renishaw.
G	P		L	H				Horrabridge.....................	Devon	G. W.	Plymouth and Tavistock.
								Horringford	I. of Wight	I. of W. Cent.	Sandown and Newport.
G	P		L					Horrocksford Branch	Lancs	L. & Y.	Clitheroe.
G	P	F	L	H	C			Horse and Jockey	Tipperary	G. S. & W.	Clonmel and Thurles.
								Horsebridge (L. & S. W.).....	Hants	L. & S. W. .... / M. & S. W. Jn.	Romsey and Andover. / Over L. & S. W. from Andover Jn.
G	P		L			1	10	Horsehay and Dawley	Salop	G. W.	Wellington and Coalbrookdale.
								Horsehay Co.'s Siding	Salop	G. W.	Horsehay.
G	P		L	H		1	10	Horseleap......................	W'meath..	M. G. W.	Streamstown Junction and Clara.
								Horsemoor Siding	Cambs	G. E.	March.
								Horsenden	Middlesex	Met. Dist.	See Sudbury Town (for Horsenden).
								Horsforth	Yorks	Mid.	See Leeds, Newlay and Horsforth.
G	P	F	L	H	C	10	0	Horsforth	Yorks	N. E.	Leeds and Harrogate.
								Hawksworth Quarry	Yorks	N. E.	Horsforth.
								Mosley Siding	Yorks	N. E.	Horsforth.
								Woodside Siding	Yorks	N. E.	Horsforth.
G	P	F	L	H	C	10	0	Horsham	Sussex	L. B. & S. C.	Three Bridges and Pulborough.
								Agate & Son's Siding	Sussex	L. B. & S. C.	Horsham.
								Nightingale's Siding	Sussex	L. B. & S. C.	Horsham.
								Horsley Ir. Co.'s Sid. (L&NW)	Staffs	L. & N. W.—Mid.	Great Bridge.
G	P	F	L	H	C	2	0	Horsley, Ripley and Ockham	Surrey	L. & S.W.	Surbiton and Guildford.
G	P	F	L	H	C			Horsmonden	Kent	S. E. & C.	Paddock Wood and Hawkhurst.
								Churn Road Siding	Kent	S. E. & C.	Horsmonden and Paddock Wood.
G	P	F		H	C			Horsted Keynes	Sussex	L. B. & S. C.	West Hoathly and Sheffield Park.
G	P	F	L	H	C			Horton & Son's Siding	Staffs	L. & N. W.	Darlaston.
G	P	F	L	H	C			Horton-in-Ribblesdale	Yorks	Mid.	Settle and Hawes Junction.
								Delaney's Siding	Yorks	Mid.	Near Horton.
								Hellwith Bridge Siding ...	Yorks	Mid.	Near Horton.
								Horton Lime Works	Yorks	Mid.	Near Horton.
								Ribblesdale Lime and Flag Co.'s Siding	Yorks	Mid.	Horton and Settle.
								Horton Park	Yorks	G. N.	See Bradford.
G	P		L	H		7	0	Horwich	Lancs	L. & Y.	Branch from Blackrod.
								L. & Y. Co.'s Carriage Sid.	Lancs	L. & Y.	Horwich.
								L. & Y. Co.'s Locomotive Siding	Lancs	L. & Y.	Horwich.
								Locomotive Works Junc....	Lancs	L. & Y.	Horwich Branch.
								Mason & Son's Siding	Lancs	L. & Y.	Horwich.
								Mason's, W. E., Siding....	Lancs	L. & Y.	Horwich.

EXPLANATION—G *Goods Station.*   P *Passenger and Parcel Station.*   P* *Passenger, but not Parcel or Miscellaneous Traffic.*
F *Furniture Vans, Carriages, Portable Engines, and Machines on Wheels.*   L *Live Stock.*
H *Horse Boxes and Prize Cattle Vans.*   C *Carriages by Passenger Train.*

STATION ACCOMMODATION						CRANE POWER		STATIONS, &c.	COUNTY.	COMPANY.	POSITION.
						Tons	Cwts				
G	P	.	L	.	.	.	.	Hoscar	Lancs	L. & Y.	Parbold and Burscough Bridge.
.	.	.	.	.	.	.	.	Hose	Leicester	G. N. & L. & N. W. Jt.	See Long Clawson and Hose.
								Hoskin & Llewellyn—			
.	.	.	.	.	.	.	.	Abersychan Elled Colliery (G.W.)	Mon	G. W.—L. & N. W.	Abersychan and Talywain.
.	.	.	.	.	.	.	.	Golynos Colliery (G.W.)	Mon	G. W.—L. & N. W.	Abersychan and Talywain.
.	.	.	.	.	.	.	.	Hotchley Hill Siding	Notts	G. C.	See Barnstone Blue Lias Lime Co.'s Siding (East Leake).
G	P	F	L	H	C	5	0	Hothfield	Kent	S. E. & C.	Maidstone and Ashford.
.	P	.	.	.	.	.	.	Hotwells	Glo'ster	Clif. Ex. Jt. (G.W. & Mid.)	Branch from Sea Mills.
G	P	.	L	H	C	1	0	Hougham	Lincoln	G. N.	Grantham and Newark.
G	P	F	L	H	C	5	0	Hough Green (for Ditton)	Lancs	C. L. C. (G C, G N, & Mid.)	Warrington and Garston.
.	.	.	.	.	.	.	.	Hough Green Junction	Lancs	C. L. C.—S. & M. Jt.	Hough Green and Widnes.
.	.	.	.	.	.	.	.	Houghton	Leicester	G. N.	See Ingersby (for Houghton).
G	.	.	.	.	.	.	.	Houghton	Yorks	Dearne Valley	Branch from Brierley Junction.
.	.	.	.	.	.	.	.	Houghton Main Colliery	Yorks	Dearne Valley	Near Houghton.
.	.	.	.	.	.	.	.	Houghton Cols. Old & New Pits	Durham	N. E.	{ Fencehouses. / Penshaw.
.	.	.	.	.	.	.	.	Houghton Lime Works	Durham	N. E.	{ Fencehouses. / Penshaw.
.	.	.	.	.	.	.	.	Houghton Main Colliery	Yorks	{ G. C. / Mid.	Stairfoot (for Ardsley). / Darfield.
.	.	.	.	.	.	.	.	Houghton Pit	Durham	N. E.	{ Fencehouses. / Penshaw.
.	.	.	.	.	.	.	.	Houghton's Siding	Lancs	L. & N. W.	Sankey Bridges.
.	.	.	.	.	.	.	.	Houlder Bros.' Depôt	Mon	A (N & S W) D & R—G W	Newport, Alexandra Docks.
.	.	.	.	.	.	.	.	Houldsworth Pit	Ayr	G. & S. W.	Waterside.
.	.	.	.	.	.	.	.	Houlsike Siding	Yorks	N. E.	{ Danby. / Lealholm.
.	.	.	.	.	.	.	.	Hounslow	Middlesex	Met. Dist.	See Heston-Hounslow.
G	P	F	L	H	C	5	0	Hounslow and Whitton	Middlesex	L. & S. W.	Kew Bridge and Feltham.
.	P	.	.	.	.	.	.	Hounslow Barracks	Middlesex	Met. Dist.	Terminus—Bch. fr. Mill Hill Park.
.	P	.	.	.	.	.	.	Hounslow Town	Middlesex	Met. Dist.	Terminus—Bch. fr. Mill Hill Park.
G	P	.	L	H	.	2	0	Houston	Renfrew	Cal.	Houston and Bishopton.
.	.	.	.	.	.	.	.	Fulwood Moss Siding	Renfrew	Cal.	Houston and Bishopton.
.	.	.	.	.	.	.	.	South Barr Siding	Renfrew	Cal.	Paisley and Greenock.
G	P	F	L	H	C	2	0	Houston (Crosslee)	Renfrew	G. & S. W.	Paisley and Greenock.
.	.	.	.	.	.	.	.	Hove	Sussex	L. B. & S. C.	See Brighton.
.	.	.	.	.	.	.	.	Hove Electric Lighting Co.'s Siding	Sussex	L. B. & S. C.	Brighton.
G	P	F	L	H	C	0	15	Hovingham Spa	Yorks	N. E.	Malton and Thirsk.
.	.	.	.	.	.	.	.	Howard & Kyte's Siding	Glamorg'n	T. V.	Llandaff.
.	.	.	.	.	.	.	.	Howard Conduit Co.'s Siding	Lancs	Trafford Park Estate	Manchester.
.	.	.	.	.	.	.	.	Howard Pit	Northumb	N. E.	Choppington.
.	.	.	.	.	.	.	.	Howards & Son's Siding	Essex	G. E.	London, Devonshire Street.
.	.	.	.	.	.	.	.	Howard's, J. & F., Works	Beds	L. & N. W.—Mid.	Bedford.
.	.	.	.	.	.	.	.	Howard's Siding	Kent	S. E. & C.	Canterbury, West.
.	.	.	.	.	.	.	.	Howbeach Colliery	Glo'ster	G. W.	Blakeney.
G	P	F	L	H	C	2	0	Howden	Yorks	H. & B.	Cudworth and Hull.
G	P	F	L	H	C	6	0	Howden (N. E.)	Yorks	{ N. E. / L. & N. W.	Hull and Selby. / Over N. E. from Leeds.
.	P	.	.	.	.	.	.	Thorpe Hall Siding	Yorks	N. E.	Howden.
.	.	.	.	.	.	.	.	Howden & Co.'s Sid. (G & P Jt)	Lanark	{ Cal. / G. & S. W.	Glasgow, Kinning Park. / Glasgow, Cook Street.
.	P	.	.	.	.	.	.	Howden Clough (for Birstal)	Yorks	G. N.	Batley and Dudley Hill.
.	.	.	.	.	.	.	.	Howden Clough Colliery	Yorks	G. N.	Drighlington and Adwalton.
.	.	.	.	.	.	.	.	Howden Colliery	Hadding'n	N. B.	Ormiston.
.	.	.	.	.	.	.	.	Howden Col. & Brick Works	Durham	N. E.	Witton-le-Wear.
.	.	.	.	.	.	.	.	Howdon Dock	Northumb	N. E.	Same as Northumberland Dock.
G	P	.	L	H	.	.	.	Howdon-on-Tyne	Northumb	N. E.	Newcastle and Tynemouth.
.	.	.	.	.	.	.	.	Howe & Co.'s Siding	Cumb'land	Mid.	Cumwhinton.
.	P	.	.	.	.	.	.	Howe Bridge	Lancs	L. & N. W.	Tyldesley and Wigan.
.	.	.	.	.	.	.	.	Howell & Co.'s Iron Wks. (G.C.)	Yorks	G. C.—Mid.	Same as Sheffield Tube Wks. (Tinsley)
.	.	.	.	.	.	.	.	Howell & Son's Timber Yard (G. W.)	Carmarth'	G. W.—L. & N. W.	Llanelly.
.	.	.	.	.	.	.	.	Howell, Coath & Co.'s Lime Works	Carmarth'	G. W.	Porthcawl.
.	.	.	.	.	.	.	.	Howell, J. C., & Co.'s Electric Works (G. W.)	Carmarth'	G. W.—L. & N. W.	Llanelly.
.	.	.	.	.	.	.	.	Howell's Siding	Flint	L. & N. W.	See Dee Bank Siding (Flint).
.	.	.	.	.	.	.	.	Howford Tile Works	Northumb	N. B.	Wall.
.	.	.	.	.	.	.	.	Howick	Lancs	L. & Y.	See Hutton and Howick.

EXPLANATION—G *Goods Station.*   P *Passenger and Parcel Station.*   P* *Passenger, but not Parcel or Miscellaneous Traffic.*
F *Furniture Vans, Carriages, Portable Engines, and Machines on Wheels.*   L *Live Stock.*
H *Horse Boxes and Prize Cattle Vans.*   C *Carriages by Passenger Train.*

STATION ACCOMMODATION.						CRANE POWER.		STATIONS, &c.	COUNTY.	COMPANY.	POSITION.
						Tons	Cwts				
								Howie & Co.'s Siding	Ayr	G. & S.W.	Same as Eglinton Foundry (Kilwinning).
								Howlett, T. S., Siding	Norfolk	G. E.	Watton.
								Howley Park & Great Finsdale Quarry	Yorks	G. N.	Woodkirk.
								Howley Park Colliery	Yorks	L. & N. W.	Batley.
								Howley Park Co-operative Society's Siding	Yorks	G. N.	Woodkirk.
								Howls or Tibbington's Siding	Staffs	L. & N. W.	Wednesbury.
G	P		L	H		3	0	How Mill	Cumb'land	N. E.	Carlisle and Hexham.
								Howmuir Colliery	Lanark	Cal.	Omoa.
G	P		L	H				Howsham	Lincoln	G. C.	Market Rasen and Barnetby.
G	P			H				Howth	Dublin	G. N. (I.)	Branch from Howth Junction.
	P			H				Howth Junction Station	Dublin	G. N. (I.)	Dublin and Malahide.
G	P					3	0	Howwood	Renfrew	G. & S.W.	Johnstone and Dalry.
	P			H				Hoy	Caithness	High.	Georgemas and Thurso.
G	P					5	0	Hoylake	Cheshire	Wirral	Bidston and West Kirby.
								Hoylake and West Kirby Gas and Water Co.'s Siding	Cheshire	Wirral	Hoylake.
								Hoylake & West Kirby Urban District Council Electricity Works Siding	Cheshire	Wirral	Hoylake.
								Hoyland	Yorks	G. C. Mid.	Same as Birdwell & Hoyland Common. See Elsecar and Hoyland.
								Hoyland Brick Works	Yorks	G. C.	Birdwell and Hoyland Common.
								Hoyland Common	Yorks	G. C. Mid.	See Birdwell & Hoyland Common. See Wentworth & Hoyland Common.
								Hoyland Curve Siding	Yorks	Mid.	Elsecar and Hoyland.
								Hoyland, E. & J., Siding	Yorks	G. C.	See Wombwell Pottery Siding (Wombwell).
								Hoyland Nether	Yorks	G. C.	Same as Birdwell & Hoyland Common.
								Hoyland Silkstone Coke Ovens	Yorks	G. C.	Elsecar.
								Hoyland Silkstone Colliery	Yorks	G. C. Mid.	Birdwell and Hoyland Common. Elsecar and Hoyland.
								Hoyles Lamp-Black Works	Durham	N. E.	Blaydon.
G	P		L	H				Hubbert's Bridge	Lincoln	G. N.	Boston and Sleaford.
G	P	F	L	H	C	1	10	Hucknall	Notts	G. N. Mid.	Daybrook and Annesley Junction. Nottingham and Mansfield.
G	P		L			1	15				
								Butler's Hill Siding	Notts	G. N.	Hucknall.
								Hucknall Colliery, No. 1	Notts	G. N. Mid.	Bestwood and Butler's Hill. Near Hucknall.
								Hucknall Colliery, No. 2	Notts	G. N. Mid.	Butler's Hill and Hucknall. Near Hucknall.
								Hucknall Huthwaite	Derby	Mid.	See Whiteborough (for Hucknall Huthwaite).
								Hucknall Huthwaite Local Board Siding	Derby	Mid.	Westhouses and Blackwell.
								Hucknall New Colliery	Derby	Mid.	See New Hucknall Colliery (Westhouses and Blackwell).
G	P	F		H	C			Hucknall Town	Notts	G. C.	Chesterfield and Nottingham.
								Hucknall Colliery	Notts	G. C.	Hucknall Town.
								HUDDERSFIELD—			
G	P	F	L	H	C	10	0	(Station, L&Y & LNW Jt.)	Yorks	L. & Y. & L. & N. W. Jt. G. C.	Dewsbury and Stalybridge. Over L. & Y. from Penistone Junc.
	P							Bradley (L. & N. W.)	Yorks	L. & N. W. L. & Y.	Huddersfield Station and Dewsbury. Over L. & N. W. from Bradley Wood Junction.
								Brooke & Son's Fieldhouse Siding (L. & N. W.)	Yorks	L. & N. W.—L. & Y.	Hillhouse and Bradley.
G	P							Deighton	Yorks	L. & N. W.	Huddersfield Station & Kirkburton.
								Farnley Ir. Co.'s Helm Col.	Yorks	L. & N. W.	Bradley and Mirfield.
G						2	10	Gledholt	Yorks	L. & N. W.	Huddersfield Station & Stalybridge.
G		F	L			10	0	Hillhouse	Yorks	L. & Y. & L. & N. W. Jt.	Huddersfield Station & Dewsbury.
G	P	F	L	H	C	1	5	Kirkheaton	Yorks	L. & N. W.	Huddersfield Station & Kirkburton.
G	P		L	H		5	0	Longwood and Milnsbridge	Yorks	L. & N. W.	Huddersfield Station & Stalybridge.
								Shaw & Shaw's Scarwood Siding	Yorks	L. & N. W.	Longwood and Golcar.
								Shaw's Bottom Hall Siding	Yorks	L. & N. W.	Longwood and Golcar.
								Springwood Junction	Yorks	L & Y—L & Y & L & N W Jt.—L. & N W	Huddersfield Station & Stalybridge.
								Huddersfield Corporation Sid.	Lancs	L. & N. W.	Micklehurst.
								Huddersfield Corporation Sid.	Yorks	L. & N. W.	Marsden.

EXPLANATION—G Goods Station.   P Passenger and Parcel Station.   P* Passenger, but not Parcel or Miscellaneous Traffic.
F Furniture Vans, Carriages, Portable Engines, and Machines on Wheels.   L Live Stock.
H Horse Boxes and Prize Cattle Vans.   C Carriages by Passenger Train.

STATION ACCOMMODATION.						CRANE POWER.		STATIONS, &c.	COUNTY.	COMPANY.	POSITION.
						Tons	Cwts				
.	.	.	.	.	.	.	.	Huddleston Siding	Yorks	N. E.	Micklefield.
.	.	.	.	.	.	.	.	Hudson & Co.	Glo'ster ..	G. W.—Mid.	Gloucester Docks.
.	.	.	.	.	.	.	.	Hudson Dock	Durham ..	N. E.	See River Wear Commissioners (Sunderland).
.	.	.	.	.	.	.	.	Hudson's Boiler Works........	Lanark ..	N. B.	Coatbridge, Sheepford.
.	.	.	.	.	.	.	.	Hudson's Siding................	Surrey ...	L. B. & S. C.	London, New Cross.
.	.	.	.	.	.	.	.	Hudson's Siding................	Sussex ...	L. B. & S. C.	Hassocks.
.	.	.	.	.	.	.	.	Hudson's Siding................	Yorks	G. N.	Gildersome.
.	.	.	.	.	.	.	.	Hudswell, Clarke & Co.'s Siding (Mid.)	Yorks	Mid.—N.E. / G. N.	Leeds, Hunslet Lane. See Appendix to follow).
.	.	.	.	.	.	.	.	Hues' Siding	Lancs	L. & N. W.	Widnes.
G	P	F	L	H	C	1	5	Hugglescote	Leicester..	A & N Jt. (L & N W & Mid.)	Shackerstone and Hugglescote Jn.
.	.	.	.	.	.	.	.	South Leicestershire Colliery and Brick Co.'s Siding ...	Leicester..	A & N Jt. (L & N W & Mid)	Hugglescote and Coalville, East.
.	.	.	.	.	.	.	.	Hugglescote Junction	Leicester..	A. & N. Jt.—L. & N. W.	Shackerstone and Loughboro'.
.	.	.	.	.	.	.	.	Hughes & Co.'s Siding	N'hamptn	L. & N. W.	See Weston Wharf (Northampton).
.	.	.	.	.	.	.	.	Hughes & Lancaster's Siding	Denbigh ..	G. W.	Acrefair, Low Level.
.	.	.	.	.	.	.	.	Hughes' Timber Yard (G. W.)	Carmarth'	G. W.—L. & N. W.	Llanelly.
.	.	.	.	.	.	.	.	Hugo Colliery....................	Fife	N. B.	West Wemyss.
.	.	.	.	.	.	.	.	Huish Colliery	Somerset..	G. W.	Radstock.
								HULL—			
G	.	.	.	.	.	80	0	Albert Dock (N. E.)	Yorks	N. E. / L. & N. W.	Hull, Goods. Over N. E. from Leeds.
G	P	F	L	.	.	100	0	Alexandra Dock	Yorks	H. & B. .... N. E.	Terminus. Drypool.
G	.	.	.	.	.	20	0				
.	.	.	.	.	.	.	.	Anglo-American Oil Co.'s Siding	Yorks	N. E.	Hull, Goods.
.	.	.	.	.	.	.	.	Ashworth, Kirk & Co.'s Sid.	Yorks	H. & B.	Sculcoates.
.	P	.	.	.	.	.	.	Beverley Road	Yorks	H. & B.	Willerby and Cannon Street. Near Neptune Street.
.	.	.	.	.	.	.	.	Billingsgate Fish Market...	Yorks	H. & B. / N. E.	Hull, Goods. Hull and Withernsea.
.	P	.	.	.	.	.	.	Botanic Gardens	Yorks	N. E.	Hull.
.	.	.	.	.	.	.	.	Botanic Gardens Junction	Yorks	N. E.	Hull.
.	.	.	.	.	.	.	.	British Gas Light Co.'s Sids	Yorks	H. & B.	Sculcoates.
.	.	.	.	.	.	.	.	Bruce, J., & Son's Siding...	Yorks	N. E.	Stepney.
G	.	.	.	.	.	.	.	Burleigh Street	Yorks	H. & B.	Branch near Alexandra Dock.
G	P	F	.	H	C	4	0	Cannon Street................	Yorks	H. & B.	Terminus.
G	.	F	.	.	.	3	0	Chalk Lane Siding............	Yorks	N. E.	Hull.
.	.	.	.	.	.	.	.	Co-operative Wholesale Society's Siding	Yorks	N. E.	Hull.
.	P	.	L	H	C	.	.	Corporation Pier	Yorks	G. C.	Ferry from New Holland.
.	.	.	.	.	.	.	.	Corporation Water Works	Yorks	H. & B.	Neptune Street and Willerby.
G	.	F	.	.	.	8	0	Creek..............................	Yorks	G. C.	Ferry from New Holland.
.	.	.	.	.	.	.	.	Drypool	Yorks	H. & B.	Same as Alexandra Dock.
G	.	.	.	.	.	20	0	Drypool	Yorks	N. E.	Branch from Southcoates.
.	.	.	.	.	.	.	.	Earle's, G. & T., Siding ...	Yorks	N. E.	Wilmington.
.	.	.	.	.	.	.	.	Earle's Shipbuilding Co.'s Yard	Yorks	H. & B. / N. E.	Alexandra Dock. Drypool.
.	.	.	.	.	.	.	.	Hull Coal Supply Association Siding........	Yorks	N. E.	Southcoates.
G	.	.	.	.	.	25	0	Humber Dock (N.E.)........	Yorks	N. E. / L. & N. W.	Hull, Goods. Over N. E. from Leeds.
G	.	F	.	.	.	25	0	Kingston Street................	Yorks	G. C.	Over N. E. from Thorne Junction.
.	.	.	.	.	.	.	.	Kingston Street (N. E.) ...	Yorks	N. E.—L & Y—L & N W.	See Railway Str. and Kingston Str.
G	.	F	L	H	C	20	0	Neptune Street	Yorks	H. & B.	Branch from Springbank Junction.
.	P	.	L	H	C	.	.	Paragon Street (N. E.)......	Yorks	N. E.	Terminus.
.	P	.	.	H	C	.	.			G. C.	Over N. E. from Thorne Junction.
.	P	.	.	H	C	.	.			L. & Y.	Over N. E. from Goole.
.	P	.	.	H	C	.	.			L. & N. W.	Over N. E. from Leeds.
G	.	.	.	.	.	8	0	Prince's Dock (N.E.).........	Yorks	N. E. / L. & N. W.	Hull, Goods. Over N. E. from Leeds.
G	.	.	.	.	.	3	0	Queen's Dock (N. E.)	Yorks	N. E. / L. & N. W.	Hull, Goods. Over N. E. from Leeds.
G	.	.	.	.	.	25	0	Railway Dock (N. E.).......	Yorks	N. E. / L. & N. W.	Hull, Goods. Over N. E. from Leeds.
G	.	F	L	H	.	15	0	Railway Street and Kingston Street (N. E.)	Yorks	N. E. / L. & Y.—L. & N. W.	Branch from Dairycoates Junction. Over N. E. Line.
G	.	F	L	.	.	15	0				
G	.	.	.	.	.	25	0	St. Andrew's Dock (N. E.)	Yorks	N. E. / L. & N. W.	Hull, Goods. Over N. E. from Leeds.
G	.	F	L	.	.	10	0	Sculcoates......................	Yorks	H. & B / N. E.	Branch, Willerby & Alexandra Dock. Hull and Withernsea.
G	.	.	.	.	.	10	0				
G	P	.	.	.	.	5	0	Southcoates	Yorks	N. E.	Hull and Withernsea.

EXPLANATION—G *Goods Station.*   P *Passenger and Parcel Station.*   P* *Passenger, but not Parcel or Miscellaneous Traffic.*
F *Furniture Vans, Carriages, Portable Engines, and Machines on Wheels.*   L *Live Stock.*
H *Horse Boxes and Prize Cattle Vans.*   C *Carriages by Passenger Train.*

STATION ACCOMMODATION.						CRANE POWER.	STATIONS, &c.	COUNTY.	COMPANY.	POSITION.
						Tons Cwts.	HULL—continued.			
							Springbank Junction	Yorks	H. & B.	Willerby and Neptune Street.
							Springhead Loco. Siding	Yorks	H. & B.	Willerby and Springbank Junction.
G	P					2 10	Stepney	Yorks	N. E.	Hull and Withernsea.
							Sutton Southcoates and Drypool Gas Co.'s Sid.	Yorks	N. E.	Wilmington.
G						45 0	Victoria Dock	Yorks	N. E.	Drypool.
G						25 0	William Wright Dk. (N.E.)	Yorks	{ N. E. { L. & N. W.	Hull, Goods. Over N. E. from Leeds.
G	P		L			5 0	Wilmington	Yorks	N. E.	Hull and Hornsea.
							Hull & Liverpool Red Oxide Co.'s Siding	Lancs	L. & N. W.	St. Helens.
G	P	F	L	H	C	1 10	Hullavington	Wilts	G. W.	Wootton Bassett and Patchway.
							Hull Coal Supply Association Siding	Yorks	N. E.	Hull, Southcoates.
							Hull Corporation Water Wks.	Yorks	{ H. & B. { N.E.	Hull, Neptune Street. Cottingham.
							Hull Steam Shipping Co.'s Wharf	Northumb	N. E.	Newcastle-on-Tyne.
							Hulme Advertising Match Co.'s Siding	Lancs	C. L. C. (G C, G N, & Mid.)	Irlam.
							Hulme Colliery	Staffs	N. S.	Adderley Green.
							Hulme's Siding	Lancs	L. & N. W.	Widnes.
							Hulme Trust Siding	Lancs	L. & N. W.	See Lecturers Close or Hulme Trust Siding (Bolton).
							Hulton Colliery Co.—			
							Atherton Colliery No. 1	Lancs	L. & N. W.	Chequerbent.
							Atherton Colliery No. 2 Pretoria or New Pit Chequerbent Bank Siding	Lancs	L. & N. W.	Chequerbent.
							Coal Wharf	Lancs	L. & N. W.	Liverpool, Edge Hill.
							Deep Arley Pit	Lancs	L. & N. W.	Chequerbent.
							Pendlebury Fold Bk. Wks.	Lancs	L. & N. W.	Chequerbent.
							Reserve or Chequerbent Pits	Lancs	L. & N. W.	Chequerbent.
							School Pit	Lancs	L. & N. W.	Chequerbent.
							Siding	Lancs	L. & N. W.	Bolton.
							Workshops	Lancs	L. & N. W.	Chequerbent.
							Hulton Park	Lancs	L. & N. W.	See Chequerbent (for Hulton Park).
							Humber Dock (N. E.)	Yorks	N. E.—L. & N. W.	See Hull.
							Humberstone	Leicester	G. N.	See Leicester.
							Humberstone Road	Leicester	L. & N. W.—Mid.	See Leicester.
							Humber Street Siding (G. C.)	Lincoln	G. C.—G. N.	Grimsby Docks.
							Humberton Siding	Yorks	N. E.	Boroughbridge.
G	P		L	H			Humbie	Hadding'n	N. B.	Ormiston and Gifford.
							Highlea Siding (Polwarths)	Hadding'n	N. B.	Saltoun and Humbie.
G	P						Hummerbeck Colliery Wharf	Durham	N. E.	West Auckland.
							Huncoat	Lancs	L. & Y.	Accrington and Burnley.
							Accrington Brick and Tile Co.'s Siding	Lancs	L. & Y.	Huncoat.
							Hargreaves, G., & Co.'s Siding (Whinney Hill Plastic Brick Co.'s Siding)	Lancs	L. & Y.	Huncoat.
							Huncoat Bk. & Terra Cotta Co.'s Siding	Lancs	L. & Y.	Huncoat.
G	P						Hundred End	Lancs	L. & Y.	Preston and Southport.
G	P	F	L	H	C	8 0	Hungerford	Berks	G. W.	Newbury and Devizes.
G	P	F	L	H	C	1 0	Hunmanby	Yorks	N. E.	Scarboro' and Bridlington.
							Parker's Siding	Yorks	N. E.	Hunmanby.
G	P						Whitaker & Son's Siding	Yorks	N. E.	Hunmanby.
							Hunnington	Worcester	Halesowen (G. W. & Mid.)	Halesowen and Northfield.
							Hunsbury Hill Iron Works	N'hampton	L. & N. W.	See Phipps (Exors.) (Northampton).
							Hunslet	Yorks	G.N.—Mid.—N. E.—E.& W. Y.U.—L. & Y.	See Leeds.
							Hunslet and Stourton Sidings	Yorks	Mid.	Leeds, Hunslet Lane.
							Hunslet Engine Co.'s Siding (Mid.)	Yorks	{ Mid.—N. E. { G. N.	Leeds, Hunslet Lane. (See Appendix to follow).
							Hunslet Exchange Sidings	Yorks	G. N.— N. E.	See Leeds.
							Hunslet Lane	Yorks	Mid.	See Leeds.
G	P	F	L	H	C	1 0	Hunstanton	Norfolk	G. E.	Branch from Lynn.
G	P						Hunston	Sussex	Selsey	Chichester and Selsey.
							Hunt & Hunt's or Morris & Griffin's Siding (L. & N.W.)	Staffs	L. & N. W.—G. W.	Wolverhampton.

STATION ACCOMMODATION.						CRANE POWER.		STATIONS, &c.	COUNTY.	COMPANY.	POSITION.
						Tons	Cwts.				
.	.	.	.	.	.			Hunt & Winterbotham's Sid.	Glo'ster ...	Mid.	Cam.
.	.	.	.	.	.			Hunt Bros.' Siding	Yorks	N. E.	Same as Aire and Calder Chemical Works (Castleford).
.	.	.	.	.	.			Huntcliffe Mines	Yorks	N. E.	Brotton.
.	.	.	.	.	.			Hunter & Co.'s Siding	Northumb	N. E.	Walker.
.	.	.	.	.	.			Hunter Colliery	Durham ...	N. E.	Blackhill.
.	.	.	.	.	.			Hunter, Hardin & Wilson's } Siding	Lanark ...	{ Cal.	{ Glasgow, Buchanan Street.
										N. B.	Glasgow, Sighthill.
.	.	.	.	.	.			Hunter's, C. W., Siding	Lancs	Furness	Barrow.
.	.	.	.	.	.			Hunter's Hill Quarry	Lanark	N. B.	Bishopbriggs.
.	.	.	.	.	.			Hunter's Repairing Shop and Siding	Warwick..	G. W.	Leamington.
.	.	.	.	.	.			Hunter's Wagon Works	Warwick..	L. & N. W.—Mid.	Rugby.
.	.	.	.	.	.			Hunter Street Mineral Depôt	Lanark	N. B.	Glasgow, College.
.	.	.	.	.	.			Hunthill Junction	Lanark	Cal.	Blantyre and East Kilbride.
								HUNTINGDON—			
G	P	F	L	H	C	10	0	(Station)	Hunts	G. N.	Hitchin and Peterboro'.
	P							(Station)	Hunts	G. N. & G. E. Jt.	G. N. Station and Godmanchester.
G	P	F	L	H	C	1	0	(Station)	Hunts	Mid.	Branch from Kettering.
.	.	.	.	.	.			Brown & Goodman's Siding	Hunts	Mid.	Huntingdon.
.	.	.	.	.	.			Junction	Hunts	G. N.—G. N. & G. E. Jt.	Offord and Godmanchester.
.	.	.	.	.	.			Junction	Hunts	G. N. & G. E. Jt.—Mid.	Godmanchester and Buckden.
.	.	.	.	.	.			Veasey's, Chas., Siding	Hunts	Mid.	Huntingdon.
.	.	.	.	.	.			Huntingford Mills	Glo'ster	Mid.	Charfield.
.	.	.	.	.	.			Bendall & Co.	Glo'ster	Mid.	Huntingford Mills.
.	.	.	.	.	.			Kimmins & Co.	Glo'ster	Mid.	Huntingford Mills.
.	.	.	.	.	.			Huntingtower Siding	Perth	Cal.	See Almondbank.
.	.	.	.	.	.			Huntley & Palmer's Siding...	Berks	G. W.—L & SW—S E & C	Reading.
G	P	F	L	H	C	4	0	Huntly	Aberdeen	G. N. of S.	Inveramsay and Keith.
.	.	.	.	.	.			Hunton's Brick Works (Old and New)	Durham	N. E.	Stockton, North Shore.
.	.	.	.	.	.			Hunt's Cross	Lancs	C. L. C. (G C, G N, & Mid.)	Garston and Warrington.
	P							Hunwick	Durham	N. E.	Durham and Bishop Auckland.
G	P							Hunwick Colliery	Durham	N. E.	Hunwick.
.	.	.	.	.	.			Hunwick Tilery & Bk. Wks.	Durham	N. E.	Hunwick.
.	.	.	.	.	.			Newfield Colliery Coke and Brick Works	Durham	N. E.	Hunwick.
.	.	.	.	.	.			Newton Cap Colliery Coke and Brick Works	Durham	N. E.	Hunwick.
.	.	.	.	.	.			Rough Lea Colliery Coke, Brick, and Pipe Works...	Durham	N. E.	Hunwick.
.	.	.	.	.	.			West Hunwick Colliery and Brick Works	Durham	N. E.	Hunwick.
G	P	.	L	H	C			Hurdlow	Derby	L. & N. W.	Ashbourne and Buxton.
.	.	.	.	.	.			Hurlet & Campsie Alum Wks.	Stirling	N. B.	Lennoxtown.
.	.	.	.	.	.			Hurlet & Campsie Alum Co.'s Siding	Stirling	N. B.	Falkirk, Camelon.
G	P	F	L			3	0	Hurlford	Ayr	G. & S.W.	Kilmarnock and Mauchline.
.	.	.	.	.	.			Blair Foundry	Ayr	G. & S.W.	Hurlford.
.	.	.	.	.	.			Defiance Pit	Ayr	G. & S.W.	Mayfield Branch.
.	.	.	.	.	.			Gauchalland, No. 2	Ayr	G. & S.W.	Hurlford and Galston.
.	.	.	.	.	.			Gauchalland, No. 4	Ayr	G. & S.W.	Hurlford and Galston.
.	.	.	.	.	.			Goatfoot Colliery	Ayr	G. & S.W.	Hurlford and Galston.
.	.	.	.	.	.			Holmes, No. 4.	Ayr	G. & S.W.	Mayfield Branch.
.	.	.	.	.	.			Hurlford Fire-Clay Works	Ayr	G. & S.W.	Hurlford and Galston.
.	.	.	.	.	.			Hurlford Mineral Sidings..	Ayr	G. & S.W.	Mayfield Branch.
.	.	.	.	.	.			Loudoun, No. 1	Ayr	G. & S.W.	Mayfield Branch.
.	.	.	.	.	.			Mayfield Saw Mill	Ayr	G. & S.W.	Hurlford Junction.
.	.	.	.	.	.			Moss Siding	Ayr	G. & S.W.	Hurlford.
.	.	.	.	.	.			Portland Iron Works	Ayr	G. & S.W.	Hurlford.
.	.	.	.	.	.			Portland No. 4 & Bk. Wks.	Ayr	G. & S.W.	Kilmarnock and Hurlford.
.	.	.	.	.	.			Portland, Nos. 5 and 8	Ayr	G. & S.W.	Hurlford and Galston.
.	.	.	.	.	.			Portland, Nos. 6 and 7	Ayr	G. & S.W.	Riccarton and Galston.
.	.	.	.	.	.			Skerrington, Nos. 19 and 20	Ayr	G. & S.W.	Mayfield Branch.
.	.	.	.	.	.			Hurlingham	Middlesex	Met. Dist.	See London, Putney Bridge and Hurlingham.
G	G	P	F	L	H	C		Hurn	Hants	L. & S.W.	Ringwood and Christchurch.
G	G	P	F	L	H	C	5	0	Hurstbourne	Hants	L. & S.W.	Basingstoke and Andover Junction.
.	.	.	.	.	.			Hurstbourne Junction	Hants	L. & S.W.	Hurstbourne and Andover Junc.
.	.	.	.	.	.			Hurst Green Junction	Surrey	C. & O. Jt.—L. B. & S. C.	Oxted and Edenbridge Town.
.	.	.	.	.	.			Hurst, Nelson & Co.'s } Wagon Works	Derby	Mid.	{ Same as Chatsworth Wagon Works (Sheepbridge).

EXPLANATION—G *Goods Station.*   P *Passenger and Parcel Station.*   P* *Passenger, but not Parcel or Miscellaneous Traffic.*
F *Furniture Vans, Carriages, Portable Engines, and Machines on Wheels.*   L *Live Stock.*
H *Horse Boxes and Prize Cattle Vans.*   C *Carriages by Passenger Train.*

STATION ACCOMMODATION.						CRANE POWER.		STATIONS, &c.	COUNTY.	COMPANY.	POSITION.
						Tons	Cwts.				
G	P		L	H				Hurst's, W., Siding (L. & Y.)	Yorks	L.&Y.—G.N.—L.&N.W.	Mirfield.
								Hurworth Burn	Durham	N. E.	Stockton and Sunderland.
								Huskisson	Lancs	C. L. C. (G C, G N, & Mid.)	See Liverpool.
								Huskisson Dock	Lancs	L'pool O'head	See Liverpool.
G	P							Huskisson Junction	Lancs	C. L. C.—Dock Line	Liverpool.
								Husthwaite Gate	Yorks	N. E.	Thirsk and Malton.
								Hutcheon Street	Aberdeen	G. N. of S.	See Aberdeen.
								Hutchesontown Saw Mills	Lanark	Cal.	Glasgow, South Side.
								Hutchinson, Hollingworth & Co.'s Siding	Yorks	L. & N. W.	Diggle.
								Hutchinson's Estate Siding	Lancs	S. & M. Jt. (G. C. & Mid.)	Widnes.
								Hutchinson's Siding	Derby	Mid.	Sutton Junction Station.
								Hutchinson's Trustees West Bank Siding	Lancs	L. & N. W.—S. & M. Jt.	Widnes.
								Hutchinson's Works	Lancs	L. & N. W.	See United Alkali Co. (Widnes).
								Hutchison & Co.'s Flour Mills	Fife	N. B.	Kirkcaldy.
								Hutchison & Co.'s Maltings	Fife	N. B.	Kirkcaldy.
								Hutchison, Main & Co.'s Sid.	Lanark	N. B.	See Glasgow, Cowlairs.
	P							Hutton	Essex	G. E.	See Shenfield & Hutton Junc. Sta.
G	P		L	H		0	15	Hutton and Howick	Lancs	L. & Y.	Preston and Longton Bridge.
	P							Hutton Cranswick	Yorks	N. E.	Hull and Driffield.
								Hutton Gate	Yorks	N. E.	Middlesbro' and Guisbro'.
								Hutton Gate Depôt and Sid.	Yorks	N. E.	Guisbro'.
G	P		L	H	C			Huttonrigg Colliery	Lanark	Cal.	Mossend.
								Huttons Ambo	Yorks	N. E.	York and Malton.
								Castle Howard Sand Co.'s Quarry (Kilner's Siding)	Yorks	N. E.	Huttons Ambo and Castle Howard.
G	P	F	L	H	C	5	0	Huyton	Lancs	L. & N. W.	Kenyon Junction Sta. and Liverpool.
G	P							Huyton and Roby Gas Works	Lancs	L. & N. W.	Huyton Quarry.
								Huyton Quarry	Lancs	L. & N. W.	Kenyon Junction Sta. and Liverpool.
								Electric Lamp Works	Lancs	L. & N. W.	Willis Branch.
								Higginbottom's— Prescot Colliery or Lancaster's Siding	Lancs	L. & N. W.	Huyton Quarry and Rainhill.
								Whiston Colliery	Lancs	L. & N. W.	Huyton Quarry and Huyton.
								Huyton & Roby Gas Works	Lancs	L. & N. W.	Huyton Quarry and Huyton.
								Scraton's Pottery	Lancs	L. & N. W.	Willis Branch.
								Shaw's Huyton Quarry Iron Works	Lancs	L. & N. W.	Willis Branch.
								Tushingham Bros.' Bk. Wks.	Lancs	L. & N. W.	Willis Branch.
								Willis Branch	Lancs	L. & N. W.	Huyton Quarry and Huyton.
								Huyton Quarry Iron Works	Lancs	L. & N. W.	Same as Shaw's (Huyton Quarry).
								Hyde	Cheshire	G. C.	See Newton (for Hyde).
G	P	F				20	0	Hyde	Cheshire	S. & M. Jt. (G. C. & Mid.)	Guide Bridge and Marple.
								Adamson, J., & Co.'s Siding	Cheshire	S. & M. Jt. (G. C. & Mid.)	Hyde.
								Tinker, Shenton & Co.'s Sid.	Cheshire	S. & M. Jt. (G. C. & Mid)	Hyde.
								Hyde Junction	Cheshire	G. C.—S. & Mid. Jt.	Guide Bridge and Hyde.
	P							Hyde Junction Station	Cheshire	S. & M. Jt. (G. C. & Mid.)	Guide Bridge and Hyde.
								Hyde Mill Siding	Beds	G. N.	Luton Hoo.
								Hydepark Works (Neilson, Reid & Co.'s Siding)	Lanark	N. B.	Glasgow, Sighthill.
G	P					5	0	Hyde Road	Lancs	G. C.	Manchester (Central) & Guide Bridge.
								Legh Brick Co.'s Siding	Lancs	G. C.	Hyde Road.
								Parkfield Brick Kiln	Lancs	G. C.	Hyde Road.
								Rowland & Co.'s Siding	Lancs	G. C.	Hyde Road.
								Hyde Road Coal Depôt	Lancs	L. & N. W.	Manchester, Longsight.
								Hyde Road Junction	Lancs	G. C.	Hyde Road and Gorton.
								Hydraulic Stone & Cement Co.'s Siding	Lancs	L. & N. W.—S. & M. Jt.	Widnes.
G	P							Hykeham	Lincoln	Mid.	Lincoln and Newark.
								Hykeham Foundry Co.'s Sid.	Lincoln	Mid.	Hykeham.
G	P		L	H	C	3	0	Hylton	Durham	N. E.	Sunderland and Penshaw.
								Bagnall's Forge & Engine Works	Durham	N. E.	Hylton.
								Ford Limestone Quarry and Brick Works	Durham	N. E.	Hylton.
								Ford Paper Works	Durham	N. E.	Hylton.
								Offerton Depôt & Siding	Durham	N. E.	Hylton and Penshaw.
								Reay & Usher's Forge	Durham	N. E.	Hylton.
								Hylton Colliery	Durham	N. E.	Southwick.
								Hylton Lane Depôt & Siding	Durham	N. E.	Boldon.
								Hyndland	Lanark	N. B.	See Glasgow.

EXPLANATION—G *Goods Station.*   P *Passenger and Parcel Station.*   P* *Passenger, but not Parcel or Miscellaneous Traffic.*
F *Furniture Vans, Carriages, Portable Engines, and Machines on Wheels.*   L *Live Stock.*
H *Horse Boxes and Prize Cattle Vans.*   C *Carriages by Passenger Train.*

G	P	F	L	H	C	Tons	Cwts	STATIONS, &c.	COUNTY.	COMPANY.	POSITION.
								Hyndshaw Colliery	Lanark	N. B.	Carluke, Castlehill.
								Hythe	Essex	G. E.	See Colchester.
G	P	F	L	H	C			Hythe	Kent	S. E. & C.	Sandling and Sandgate.

I

G	P	F	L	H	C	Tons	Cwts	STATIONS, &c.	COUNTY.	COMPANY.	POSITION.
	P							Ibrox	Lanark	G & P Jt (Cal & G & S W)	Cardonald and Shields Road.
								Ibrox Brick Works	Lanark	G & P Jt (Cal & G & S W)	Glasgow, Govan.
								Ibrox Flour Mills (G. & P. Jt.)	Lanark	Cal. / G. & S. W.	Glasgow, Kinning Park. / Glasgow, Eglinton Street.
								Ibrox Junction	Lanark	G & P Jt (Cal & G & S W)	Pollokshields and Cardonald.
								Ibstock	Leicester	A & N Jt. (L & N W & Mid.)	See Heather and Ibstock.
								Ibstock Colliery (Mid.)	Leicester	Mid.—L. & N. W.	Bagworth.
								Ickles Dock	Yorks	Mid.	See Masboro' and Rotherham.
								Ickles Siding (Steel, Peech, & Tozer's) (G.C.)	Yorks	G. C.—G. N.	Rotherham and Masboro'.
								Icknield Port Road	Warwick	L. & N. W.	See Birmingham.
G	P	F						Ide	Devon	G. W.	Exeter and Heathfield.
								Idle	Yorks	G. N.	See Bradford.
G	P	F	L	H	C			Idridgehay	Derby	Mid.	Duffield and Wirksworth.
G	P	F	L	H	C	1	0	Ilderton	Northumb	N. E.	Alnwick and Coldstream.
								Ilex Siding	Lancs	L. & Y.	Rawtenstall.
G	P	F	L			2	0	Ilford	Essex	G. E.	Stratford and Romford.
								Page, R., Siding	Essex	G. E.	Ilford.
G	P	F	L	H	C	10	0	Ilfracombe	Devon	L. & S.W.	Branch from Barnstaple.
G	P	F	L	H	C	10	0	Ilkeston	Derby	G. N.	Derby and Nottingham.
								Dale Colliery (G. N.)	Derby	G. N.	Stanton Branch.
								Derby Road	Derby	G. N.	Ilkeston and Stanton Branch.
								Hallamfields Siding	Derby	G. N.	Part of Stanton Iron Works Sidings.
								Ilkeston Colliery (G. N.)	Derby	G. N.—G. C.	Stanton Branch.
								Manners Colliery (G. N.)	Derby	G. N.—G. C.	Ilkeston and Marlpool.
								Nutbrook Colliery	Derby	G. N.	Ilkeston and Marlpool.
								Shipley Colliery	Derby	G. N.	Ilkeston and Marlpool.
								Stanton Iron Co.'s Works	Derby	G. N.	Branch—Ilkeston & West Hallam.
								Ilkeston Colliery	Derby	Mid.	Stanton Gate.
	P		L					Ilkeston Junction and Cossall	Notts	Mid.	Shipley Gate and Stanton Gate.
G	P	F	L	H	C	5	0	Ilkeston Town	Derby	Mid.	Branch from Ilkeston Jn. & Cossall.
								Adlington's Flour Mill	Notts	Mid.	Near Ilkeston Town.
								Awsworth Iron Co.'s Siding	Notts	Mid.	Bennerley Junction and Kimberley.
								Bennerley Sidings—			
								Davis, E. P., Siding	Notts	Mid.	Near Ilkeston Town.
								Digby Colliery Co.'s Sid.	Notts	Mid.	Bennerley Junction and Kimberley.
								Giltbrook Chemical Wks.	Notts	Mid.	Bennerley Junction and Kimberley.
								Nottingham Corporation Chemical Works	Notts	Mid.	Branch from Bennerley Junction.
								Cossall Colliery Co.'s Siding	Notts	Mid.	Near Ilkeston Junction and Cossall.
								Holloway Bros.' Siding	Derby	Mid.	Ilkeston.
								Ilkeston Corporation—			
								Carr Close Siding	Notts	Mid.	Adjoining Ilkeston Town.
								Gas Siding	Notts	Mid.	Adjoining Ilkeston Town.
G	P	F	L	H	C	5	0	Ilkley	Yorks	O. & I. Jt. (Mid. & N. E.)	Burley and Addingham.
								Walker, F., Siding	Yorks	O. & I. Jt. (Mid. & N. E.)	Ilkley.
								Ilkley Junction	Yorks	Mid.—O. & I. Jt.	Addingham and Ben Rhydding.
								Illingworth, Ingham & Co.'s Siding	Lancs	Trafford Park Estate	Manchester.
								Illogan Highway Siding	Cornwall	G. W.	Carn Brea.
								Ilmington	Warwick	G. W.	See Longdon Road.
								Ilminster	Somerset	G. W.	Taunton and Chard.
G	P	F	L	H	C	12	0	Ilott Canal Wharf	Leicester	Mid.	Swannington and Ashby.
								Imberhorne Siding	Sussex	L. B. & S. C.	East Grinstead.
								Immingham Siding	Lincoln	G. C.	Habrough.
								Imperial Boiler Works	Durham	N. E.	Stockton, South.
								Imperial Cold Stores Siding	Middlesex	G. E.	London, Seven Sisters.
								Imperial Depôts	Yorks	N. E.	South Bank.
								Imperial Dock	Edinboro'	Cal.—N. B.	See Leith.
								Imperial Gas Light and Coke Co.'s Siding	Middlesex	G. W.—L. & N. W.	London, Chelsea and Fulham.

EXPLANATION—G *Goods Station.* P *Passenger and Parcel Station.* P* *Passenger, but not Parcel or Miscellaneous Traffic*
F *Furniture Vans, Carriages, Portable Engines, and Machines on Wheels.* L *Live Stock.*
H *Horse Boxes and Prize Cattle Vans.* C *Carriages by Passenger Train.*

STATION ACCOMMODATION.						CRANE POWER.		STATIONS, &c.	COUNTY.	COMPANY.	POSITION.
						Tons	Cwts.	Imperial Goonbarrow Siding	Cornwall ..	G. W.	Bugle.
								Imperial Iron Works............	Yorks	N. E.	See Brand's Slag Wks.(South Bank).
								Imperial Siding	Renfrew ...	G & P Jt (Cal & G & S W)	Cardonald.
								Imperial Steel Works	Yorks	G. C.	Tinsley.
								Imperial Tube Works	Lanark ...	N. B.	Coatbridge, Sheepford.
								Imperial Tube Works (Rochsolloch Tube Works).........	Lanark ...	Cal.	Calder.
	P							Ince	Lancs	L. & Y.	Wigan and Bolton.
								Britannia Sidings	Lancs	L. & Y.	Ince.
								Ince Forge Siding	Lancs	L. & Y.	Ince.
								Moss Hall Colliery............	Lancs	L. & Y.	Ince.
								Pearson & Knowles Coal & Iron Co.—			
								Daisy Colliery	Lancs	L. & Y.	Westwood Siding.
								Moss Hall Siding	Lancs	L. & Y.	Westwood Siding.
								Moss Side Iron Works ...	Lancs	L. & Y.	Westwood Siding.
								Westwood Siding	Lancs	L. & Y.	Near Ince.
G	P			H				Ince and Elton	Cheshire...	B'head Jt. (G W & L N W)	Helsby and Hooton.
								Ince Forge Co.'s Siding	Lancs	L. & N. W.	Same as Melling Bros.' Sid.(Wigan).
								Ince Hall Coal Co.'s Siding	Lancs	L. & N. W.	Preston, Charles Street.
								Ince Iron Works...............	Lancs	L. & N. W.	Wigan.
								Ince Moss Colliery	Lancs	L. & N. W.	See Pearson & Knowles Coal and Iron Co. (Wigan).
								Ince Wagon and Iron Works	Lancs	G. C. (Wigan Jn.)	Wigan.
								Ince Wagon Works	Lancs	L. & N. W.	Wigan.
G	P		L	H				Inch	Wexford ..	D. W. & W.	Arklow and Wexford.
G	P	F	L	H	C	2	0	Inchbare	Forfar......	Cal.	Brechin and Edzell.
								Inchbelly Sand Siding	Stirling ...	N. B.	Kirkintilloch.
G			L			2	0	Inchcoonans	Perth	Cal.	Perth and Dundee.
								Dundee Police Commissioners' Siding	Perth	Cal.	Inchcoonans.
								Inchcoonans Brick Works	Perth	Cal.	Inchcoonans.
								Inch Engineering & Shipbuilding Works (Dunlop & Co.)	Renfrew ...	Cal.	Greenock, Regent Street.
G	P		L	H		1	10	Inches	Lanark ...	Cal.	Douglas and Muirkirk.
								Carmacoup Colliery	Lanark ...	Cal.	Inches.
								Glespin Colliery	Lanark ...	Cal.	Douglas, West and Inches.
								Inchgreen (G. & S. W.)	Renfrew ...	G. & S.W. — N. B.	See Port Glasgow.
								Inchgreen Junction	Renfrew ...	G. & S.W.	Inchgreen and James Watt Dock.
								Inchholm Brass Foundry......	Renfrew ...	Cal.	Same as Broadfoot's Foundry (Glasgow).
								Inchicore (Co.'s Stores)........	Dublin ...	G. S. & W.	Dublin.
G	P		L					Inch Road	Donegal ...	L. & L. S.	Londonderry and Buncrana.
								Inchterff Sand Siding	Stirling ...	N. B.	Gavell.
G	P	F	L	H	C	2	0	Inchture	Perth	Cal.	Perth and Dundee.
								Grange Siding	Perth	Cal.	Inchture and Errol.
								Kinnaird Siding	Perth	Cal.	Branch near Inchture.
								Incline Siding (Chamber Col.)	Lancs	L. & Y.	Middleton Junction Station.
								Incline Top Siding	Stirling ...	N. B.	Causewayend.
								Ind, Coope & Co.—			
								Shobnall Maltings (Mid.)...	Staffs	Mid.—L. & N. W.—N. S.	Burton-on-Trent.
								Siding	Essex	G. E.	London, Stratford.
								Siding	Essex	G. E.	Romford.
								Siding (Mid.)	Staffs	Mid.—L&NW—GN—NS	Burton-on-Trent.
								Indestructible Rolled Steel Axle Box Works	Lanark ...	Cal.	Wishaw.
								India Rubber, Gutta Percha, and Telegraph Co.'s Siding (G. E.)	Essex	GE—GN—L&NW—Mid.	London, Silvertown.
								Ingall, Parsons, Clive & Co.'s Siding	Middlesex	L. & N. W.	Harrow and Wealdstone.
G	P	F	L	H	C	1	10	Ingatestone	Essex	G. E.	Brentwood and Chelmsford.
G	P	F	L	H	C			Ingersby (for Houghton)	Leicester..	G. N.	Leicester Branch.
								Ingestre (N. S.)	Staffs	N. S.—L. & N. W.	See Weston and Ingestre.
G	P	F	L	H	C			Ingestre (for Weston)	Staffs	G. N.	Stafford and Burton.
								Weston Salt Works	Staffs	G. N.	Ingestre.
G	P	F		H	C			Ingham	Suffolk ...	G. E.	Bury St. Edmunds and Thetford.
								Seven Hills Siding............	Suffolk ...	G. E.	Ingham and Barnham.
								Ingham's Fire Brick Co.'s Brick and Pipe Works (Ravenslodge Siding)	Yorks	L. & N. W.	Ravensthorpe and Thornhill.
								Ingham's Siding	Yorks	L. & Y.	Thornhill.

EXPLANATION—G *Goods Station.*   P *Passenger and Parcel Station.*   P* *Passenger, but not Parcel or Miscellaneous Traffic.*
F *Furniture Vans, Carriages, Portable Engines, and Machines on Wheels.*   L *Live Stock.*
H *Horse Boxes and Prize Cattle Vans.*   C *Carriages by Passenger Train.*

G	P	F	L	H	C	Crane Power (Tons Cwts)	STATIONS, &c.	COUNTY.	COMPANY.	POSITION.
G	P	F	L	H			Ingilbys Siding	Yorks	N. E.	Pateley Bridge.
	P						Ingleby	Yorks	N. E.	Battersby Junction and Yarm.
							Ingle, E., & Son's Siding	Yorks	L. & Y.	Womersley.
							Inglefield Siding	Lanark	Cal.	Glasgow, South Side.
							Ingleside Foundry (Fife Forge Co.)	Fife	N. B.	Kirkcaldy, Sinclairtown.
							INGLETON—			
G	P	F	L	H	C	1 10	(Station)	Yorks	L. & N. W.	Branch from Low Gill.
G	P	F	L	H	C	2 0	(Station, Mid.)	Yorks	Mid.	Branch from Clapham.
G	P	F	L				(Station, Mid.)	Yorks	L. & N. W.	Over Mid. from Ingleton Junction.
							Barker's Brick Yard	Yorks	Mid.	Clapham and Ingleton.
							Craven Lime Siding	Yorks	L. & N. W.	Ingleton.
							Scott's Siding	Yorks	Mid.	Near Ingleton.
							Junction	Yorks	L. & N. W.—Mid.	Low Gill and Hellifield.
							Inglis & Co.'s Shipbuilding Yard	Lanark	Cal.—N. B.	Same as Pointhouse Shipbuilding Yard (Glasgow).
							Inglis Siding	Edinboro'	N. B.	Leith, Bonnington.
							Ingliston	Stirling	Cal.	See Denny.
							Ingliston Branch Junction	Edinboro'	N. B.	Ratho and Kirkliston.
							Ingliston Junction	Stirling	Cal.	Denny.
							Ingliston Mine	Stirling	Cal.	Denny.
							Ingliston Pit	Edinboro'	N. B.	Ratho.
G	P	F	L	H	C	5 0	Ingrow	Yorks	G. N.	Keighley and Bradford.
G	P					5 0	Ingrow	Yorks	Mid.	Keighley and Oxenhope.
							Ing's Mill Co.'s Siding	Yorks	Mid.	Guiseley.
							Ing's Road Junction	Yorks	G. N.—L. & Y.	Wakefield.
							Inholmes Park Siding	Sussex	L. B. & S. C.	Wivelsfield.
							Inkerman Brick Works	Renfrew	Cal.	Paisley, St. James.
G	P	F	L	H	C	4 0	Innerleithen	Peebles	N. B.	Peebles and Galashiels.
							Waverley Mills	Peebles	N. B.	Innerleithen.
							Innerleven Salt Works	Fife	N. B.	Methil.
G	P		L	H		2 0	Innerpeffray	Perth	Cal.	Crieff and Perth.
G	P	F	L	H	C		Innerwick	Hadding'n	N. B.	Dunbar and Berwick.
							Innes' Siding	Surrey	L. B. & S. C.	Morden.
							Innishannon	Cork	C. B. & S. C.	See Upton and Innishannon.
G	P		L			1 10	Inniskeen	Monaghan	G. N. (I.)	Dundalk and Clones.
	P						Inns Coal and Grain Siding	Herts	G. N.	Stevenage.
							Inny Junction Station	W'meath	M. G. W.	Multyfarnham & Edgeworthstown.
G	P	F	L	H	C	1 5	Insch	Aberdeen	G. N. of S.	Inveramsay and Keith.
G	P						Instow	Devon	L. & S. W	Barnstaple and Bideford.
							Intake Siding	Derby	L. & N. W.	Same as Shaw Bros.' Siding (Steeplehouse).
							International Abercrave Colliery (N. & B.)	Brecon	N. & Brecon—Mid.	Abercrave.
							International Colliery	Glamorg'n	G. W.	Blaengarw.
							International Purification Syndicate (N. & B.)	Brecon	N. & Brecon—Mid.	Abercrave.
							Intractable Ore Co.'s Siding	Lancs	S. & M. Jt. (G. C. & Mid.)	Widnes.
G	P	F	L	H	C		Inver	Donegal	Donegal	Donegal and Killybegs.
G	P		L	H			Inveramsay	Aberdeen	G. N. of S.	Inverurie and Keith.
G	P	F	L	H	C	2 0	Inveresk	Edinboro'	N. B.	Edinburgh and Dunbar.
							Wallyford Colliery	Edinboro'	N. B.	Inveresk and Prestonpans.
							Inveresk Paper Mills	Edinboro'	N. B.	Musselburgh.
G	P	F	L	H	C		Invergarry	Inverness	High (I. & F. A.)	Spean Bge. Junc. & Fort Augustus.
G	P	F	L	H	C	1 10	Invergordon	Ross & Cro'	High.	Dingwall and Tain.
G							Harbour Branch	Ross & Cro'	High.	Invergordon.
							Invergordon Bone Meal Sid.	Ross & Cro'	High.	Invergordon.
G	P		L	H		3 0	Invergowrie	Perth	Cal.	Perth and Dundee.
							Kingoodie Siding	Perth	Cal.	Longforgan and Invergowrie.
							Mylnefield Quarry	Perth	Cal.	Longforgan and Invergowrie.
G	P		L				Inverie	Inverness	Cal.	Steamer from Oban.
G	P		L				Inverie	Inverness	High.	Steamer from Kyle of Lochalsh.
G	P		L				Inverie	Inverness	N. B.	Steamer from Mallaig.
G	P		L	H		3 0	Inverkeilor	Forfar	N. B	Arbroath and Montrose.
G	P	F	L	H	C	3 0	Inverkeithing	Fife	N. B.	Dalmeny and Dunfermline.
							Burns' Siding	Fife	N. B.	Inverkeithing and North Queensferry, Goods.
							Caldwell's Paper Mills	Fife	N. B.	Inverkeithing and North Queensferry, Goods.
							Cruick's Fire-Clay Works	Fife	N. B.	Inverkeithing and North Queensferry, Goods.
							Inverkeithing Harbour	Fife	N. B.	Branch from Inverkeithing.

EXPLANATION—G *Goods Station.*   P *Passenger and Parcel Station.*   P* *Passenger, but not Parcel or Miscellaneous Traffic.*
F *Furniture Vans, Carriages, Portable Engines, and Machines on Wheels.*   L *Live Stock.*
H *Horse Boxes and Prize Cattle Vans.*   C *Carriages by Passenger Train.*

STATION ACCOMMODATION.						CRANE POWER.		STATIONS, &c.	COUNTY.	COMPANY.	POSITION.
						Tons	Cwts.	Inverkeithing—continued.			
								Inverkeithing Harbour Branch Sidings	Fife	N. B.	Branch from Inverkeithing.
								Inverkeithing Shipbuilding Yard	Fife	N. B.	Branch from Inverkeithing.
								Inverkeithing, Central Junc.	Fife	N. B.	Inverkeithing and Aberdour.
								Inverkeithing, East Junction	Fife	N. B.	Dunfermline and Aberdour.
								Inverkeithing, North Junc.	Fife	N. B.	Dunfermline and Inverkeithing.
								Inverkeithing, South Junc.	Fife	N. B.	North Queensferry and Inverkeithing.
G	P	F	L	H	C	1	0	Inverkip	Renfrew	Cal.	Port Glasgow and Wemyss Bay.
								Dunrod Siding	Renfrew	Cal.	Ravenscraig and Inverkip.
								Finnochbog Siding	Renfrew	Cal.	Inverkip and Wemyss Bay.
								Hill Farm Siding	Renfrew	Cal.	Ravenscraig and Inverkip.
G	P	F	L	H	C	5	0	Inverness	Inverness	High.	Nairn and Dingwall.
G								Harbour Branch	Inverness	High.	Inverness.
G	P	F	L	H	C			Invershin	Sutherl'nd	High.	Bonar Bridge and Golspie.
								Invertiel Junction	Fife	N. B.	Kinghorn and Kirkcaldy.
								Invertiel Siding	Fife	N. B.	Kirkcaldy.
G	P		L	H				Inverugie	Aberdeen	G. N. of S.	Maud and Peterhead.
G	P	F	L	H	C	4	0	Inverurie	Aberdeen	G. N. of S.	Aberdeen and Inveramsay.
G								Port Elphinstone	Aberdeen	G. N. of S.	Kintore and Inverurie.
G	P							Iona	Argyll	Cal.	Steamer from Oban.
								IPSWICH—			
G	P	F	L	H	C	10	0	(Station)	Suffolk	G. E.	Colchester and Haughley.
								Carr, W. H., Siding	Suffolk	G. E.	Derby Road.
G	P	F		H	C			Derby Road	Suffolk	G. E.	Ipswich and Felixstowe.
								Halifax Siding	Suffolk	G. E.	Ipswich and Bentley.
								Palfreman, Foster & Co.'s Siding	Suffolk	G. E.	Derby Road.
								Rosher's Brick & Tile Co.'s Siding	Suffolk	G. E.	Westerfield.
G	P							Westerfield	Suffolk	G. E.	Ipswich and Woodbridge.
G	P	F	L	H	C	1	10	Irchester	N'hamptn	Mid.	Bedford and Wellingboro'.
								Stanton Iron Co.'s Siding	N'hamptn	Mid.	Irchester Junction.
								Ireland & Knight's Mancetter Quarries (Mid.)	Warwick	Mid.—L. & N. W.	Stockingford.
								Ireland Coke Works	Derby	Mid.	See Staveley Coal & Iron Co. (Barrow Hill).
								Ireland Colliery	Derby	Mid.	Barrow Hill and Staveley Works.
								Ireland Colliery (G.C.)	Derby	G. C.—G. N.—L. & N. W.	Staveley Town.
								Irelands Siding	Lancs	L. & N. W.	Widnes.
G	P	F	L	H	C	5	0	Irlam	Lancs	C. L. C. (G C, G N, & Mid.)	Warrington and Manchester.
								Hulme Advertising Match Co.'s Siding	Lancs	C. L. C. (GC, GN, & Mid.)	Irlam.
								Royle's Siding	Lancs	C. L. C. (GC, GN, & Mid.)	Irlam.
	P							Irlams-o'-th'-Height	Lancs	L. & Y.	Pendleton and Pendlebury.
G	P							Iron Acton	Glo'ster	Mid.	Yate and Thornbury.
G	P	F	L	H	C	1	10	Ironbridge and Broseley	Salop	G. W.	Shrewsbury and Bridgnorth.
								Jackfield Siding	Salop	G. W.	Ironbridge and Coalport.
								Maw's Siding	Salop	G. W.	Ironbridge and Coalport.
								Ironville	Notts	G. N.	See Codnor Park (for Ironville and Jacksdale).
										Mid.	See Codnor Park and Ironville.
								Irthlingboro'	N'hamptn	L. & N. W.	See Higham Ferrers and Irthlingboro'.
										Mid.	See Higham Ferrers (for Irthlingboro').
								Irthlingboro' Brick and Tile Co.'s Siding	N'hamptn	L. & N. W.	Higham Ferrers and Irthlingboro'.
								Irthlingboro' Iron Ore Co.'s Siding	N'hamptn	L. & N. W.	Higham Ferrers and Irthlingboro'.
G	P		L					Irton Road	Cumb'land	R. & E.	Ravenglass and Boot.
								Irton Siding	Yorks	N. E.	Seamer.
								IRVINE—			
G	P	F	L	H	C	4	0	(Station)	Ayr	Cal.	Branch Terminus, near Kilwinning.
G	P	F	L	H	C	10	0	(Station)	Ayr	G. & S. W.	Dalry and Ayr.
	P*							Bogside	Ayr	G. & S. W.	Irvine and Kilwinning.
								Bogside Sand Lye	Ayr	G. & S. W.	Irvine and Kilwinning.
								Burgh Lye	Ayr	G. & S. W.	Irvine and Kilwinning.
								Caledonian Forge	Ayr	Cal.	Irvine.
								Dunton Knoll Quarry	Ayr	Cal.	Irvine.

EXPLANATION—G *Goods Station.*   P *Passenger and Parcel Station.*   P* *Passenger, but not Parcel or Miscellaneous Traffic.*
F *Furniture Vans, Carriages, Portable Engines, and Machines on Wheels.*   L *Live Stock.*
H *Horse Boxes and Prize Cattle Vans.*   C *Carriages by Passenger Train.*

STATION ACCOMMODATION.						CRANE POWER.	STATIONS, &c.	COUNTY.	COMPANY.	POSITION.
						Tons Cwts.	IRVINE—continued.			
							Eglinton Chemical Works	Ayr	G. & S.W.	Irvine Harbour.
							Forge Co.'s Siding	Ayr	G. & S.W.	Irvine Harbour Branch.
	P*						Gailes	Ayr	G. & S.W.	Irvine and Barassie.
							Gas Residual Products Co.'s Siding	Ayr	G. & S.W.	Irvine Harbour.
G						25 0	Harbour	Ayr	G. & S.W.	Branch from Irvine.
							Harbour Junction	Ayr	G. & S.W.	Irvine.
							Henderson's Chemical Wks.	Ayr	G. & S.W.	Irvine Harbour.
							Junction	Ayr	G. & S.W.	Irvine and Barassie.
							Metallic Oxide Co.'s Siding	Ayr	G. & S.W.	Irvine Harbour.
							Stewart's Foundry	Ayr	G. & S.W.	Irvine Harbour
							United Alkali Co.'s Works	Ayr	G. & S.W.	Irvine Harbour.
							Walker's Siding	Ayr	G. & S.W.	Irvine Harbour.
						3 0	Workshops Siding	Ayr	G. & S.W.	Irvine.
							Irvine's Shipbuilding and Dry Dock Co.'s Harbour Ship Yard	Durham	N. E.	West Hartlepool.
G	P	F	L				Irvinestown	Ferm'nagh	G. N. (I.)	Bundoran Junction and Bundoran.
							Irwell Vale Siding	Lancs	L. & Y.	See Ewood Bridge.
							Isaac's Siding	Cornwall	G. W.	Liskeard.
							Isabella Colliery	Fife	N. B.	Buckhaven.
							Isabella Colliery	Northumb	N. E.	See Cowpen Collieries (Newsham).
							Isca Engineering Works	Mon	G. W.	Newport, Dock Street.
G	P	F	L				Isfield	Sussex	L. B. & S. C.	Lewes and Uckfield.
G	P					1 10	Isham and Burton Latimer	N'hamptn	Mid.	Wellingboro' and Kettering.
							Burton Latimer Gas Co.'s Siding	N'hamptn	Mid.	Isham and Burton Latimer.
							Isham Ironstone Co.'s Sid.	N'hamptn	Mid.	Isham and Burton Latimer.
							Lloyd & Co.'s Siding	N'hamptn	Mid.	Isham and Burton Latimer.
							Wallis', T. & J., Mill	N'hamptn	Mid.	Isham and Burton Latimer.
							Island Bridge Junction	Dublin	G. S. & W.	Dublin.
G	P	F	L	H	C		Isleham	Cambs	G. E.	Fordham and Mildenhall.
							Isle of Thanet Tram Co.'s Sid.	Kent	S. E. & C.	Same as Northdown Siding (Broadstairs).
G	P		L				Isleornsay	Inverness	Cal. — / High. / N. B.	Steamer from Oban. / Steamer from Kyle of Lochalsh. / Steamer from Mallaig.
	P						Isleworth and Spring Grove	Middlesex	L. & S.W.	Kew Bridge and Hounslow.
							Islington (N. L.)	Middlesex	N. L.—L. & N. W.	See London, Highbury & Islington.
							Islington Electric Light Wks.	Middlesex	G. N.	London, Finsbury Park.
G	P	F	L	H	C		Islip	Oxford	L. & N. W.	Oxford & Verney Junction Station.
							Islip Iron Co.'s Sidings	N'hamptn	L. & N. W. / Mid. / Mid.	Thrapston. / Finedon. / Twywell.
							Islwyn Colliery	Mon	G. W.	Tredegar Junction.
G	P	F	L	H	C		Itchen Abbas	Hants	L. & S.W.	Winchester and Farnham.
							Itter, A. W., Siding	Cambs	G. E.	Whittlesea.
							Itter's Siding	Bucks	G. C.	Calvert.
							Ivens Siding	N'hamptn	L. & N. W.	Welton.
							Ivor Junction	Glamorg'n	B. & M.—L. & N. W.	Dowlais.
							Ivor Siding (B. & M.)	Glamorg'n	B. & M.—L. & N. W.	See Guest, Keen & Nettlefold (Dowlais).
G	P		L	H	C	2 0	Ivybridge	Devon	G. W.	Plymouth and Totnes.

𝕁

							Jackfield Siding	Salop	G. W.	Ironbridge and Broseley.
							Jacksdale	Notts	G. N.	See Codnor Park (for Ironville and Jacksdale).
							Jackson & Co.'s Oil & Grease Works	Glamorg'n	GW—LNW—Mid—RSB	Swansea.
							Jackson & Son's Siding	Lancs	P.&L.Jt.(L&NW.& L&Y)	Preston, Deepdale.
							Jackson Bros.' Siding	Yorks	L. & Y. & G. N. Jt.	Knottingley.
							Jackson Dock	Durham	N. E.	See West Hartlepool.
							Jackson's, J. & W., Timber Yard (Fur.)	Cumb'land	Furness—L. & N. W.	Whitehaven, Preston Street.

EXPLANATION—G Goods Station.   P Passenger and Parcel Station.   P* Passenger, but not Parcel or Miscellaneous Traffic.
F Furniture Vans, Carriages, Portable Engines, and Machines on Wheels.   L Live Stock.
H Horse Boxes and Prize Cattle Vans.   C Carriages by Passenger Train.

STATION ACCOMMODATION.						CRANE POWER.		STATIONS, &c.	COUNTY.	COMPANY.	POSITION.
						Tons	Cwts.				
.	.	.	.	.	.	.	.	Jackson's Siding..............	Cumb'land	L. & N. W.	Workington.
.	.	.	.	.	.	.	.	Jackson's Siding..............	Dumfries..	Cal.	Annan.
.	.	.	.	.	.	.	.	Jackson's Siding..............	Lancs	L. & N. W.	See Astley and Tyldesley Coal and Salt Co. (Tyldesley).
.	.	.	.	.	.	.	.	Jackson's Siding..............	Yorks	N. E.	Thirsk.
.	.	.	.	.	.	.	.	Jackson's (Sir John), Siding	Northumb	N. E.	Heddon-on-the-Wall.
.	.	.	.	.	.	.	.	Jackson Street Mineral Yard	Cheshire...	B'head Jt. (G W & L N W)	Birkenhead.
.	.	.	.	.	.	.	.	Jackson, T., Saw Mill	Durham ...	N. E.	Sunderland, South Dock.
.	.	.	.	.	.	.	.	Jack Trees Siding	Cumb'land	W C & E Jt.(Fur.& L N W)	See Carron Iron Co. (Crossfield).
.	.	.	.	.	.	.	.	Jamage Col. (Wedgewood's)..	Staffs	N. S.	Diglake.
.	.	.	.	.	.	.	.	Jamage Junction	Staffs	N. S.	Alsager Junction and Keele Junc.
.	.	.	.	.	.	.	.	James Bridge	Staffs	L. & N. W.	See Darlaston and James Bridge.
.	.	.	.	.	.	.	.	James' Morfa Brk. Wks. (G W)	Carmarth'	G. W.—L. & N. W. ...	Llanelly.
.	.	.	.	.	.	.	.	James' Siding	Glamorg'n	G W—L N W—Rhy—T V	Cardiff.
.	.	.	.	.	.	.	.	James Street	Lancs	G. W.—L'pool O'head— Mersey	See Liverpool.
G	P	.	.	.	.	.	.	James Street Siding	Lanark ...	Cal.	Glasgow, Port Dundas.
G							}	Jamestown (N. B.)............	Dumbartn	{ N. B.	Balloch and Stirling.
G							}			{ Cal.	Over N. B. from Forth & Clyde Jn.
.	.	.	.	.	.	.	.	Auchencarroch Quarry......	Dumbartn	N. B.	Jamestown and Caldarvan.
G	.	.	.	.	.	.	.	Bonhill Siding (N. B.)	Dumbartn	N. B.—Cal.	Branch from Jamestown.
.	.	.	.	.	.	.	.	Croftengea Siding (N. B.)....	Dumbartn	N. B.—Cal.	Balloch and Jamestown.
.	.	.	.	.	.	.	.	Dalmonach Works (N. B.)..	Dumbartn	N. B.—Cal.	Branch from Jamestown.
.	.	.	.	.	.	.	.	Levenbank DyeWks.(N.B.)	Dumbartn	N. B.—Cal.	Balloch and Jamestown.
.	.	.	.	.	.	.	.	Milton Works (N. B.)	Dumbartn	N. B.—Cal.	Dalmonach Branch.
.	.	.	.	.	.	.	.	James Watt Dk. (Garvel Dk.)	Renfrew ...	Cal.	Greenock, Regent Street.
.	.	.	.	.	.	.	.	James Watt Dock (Garvel Dock) (G. & S. W.)	Renfrew ...	G. & S. W.—N. B.	Port Glasgow, Inchgreen.
.	.	.	.	.	.	.	.	Jane Colliery	Durham ...	N. E.	Etherley.
.	.	.	.	.	.	.	.	Jardine Hall Siding	Dumfries..	Cal.	Nethercleugh.
.	.	.	.	.	.	.	.	Jardine's Siding	Lanark ...	Cal.	Newton.
G	P	F	L	H	C	5	0	Jarrow	Durham ...	N. E.	Gateshead and South Shields.
.	.	.	.	.	.	.	.	Bede Metal Works...........	Durham ...	N. E.	Jarrow.
.	.	.	.	.	.	.	.	Hebburn Collieries	Durham ...	N. E.	Jarrow and Hebburn.
.	.	.	.	.	.	.	.	Jarrow Manure Depôts......	Durham ...	N. E.	Jarrow.
.	.	.	.	.	.	.	.	Jarrow Shipping Staithes..	Durham ...	N. E.	Jarrow.
.	.	.	.	.	.	.	.	Jarrow Slag Works	Durham ...	N. E. •	Jarrow.
.	.	.	.	.	.	.	.	Monkton Depôts	Durham ...	N. E.	Jarrow.
.	.	.	.	.	.	.	.	Palmer's Iron Works and Ship Yard	Durham ...	N. E.	Jarrow.
.	.	.	.	.	.	.	.	Pontop and Jarrow Junc.	Durham ...	N. E.	Jarrow.
.	.	.	.	.	.	.	.	Springwell Colliery	Durham ...	N. E.	Jarrow.
.	.	.	.	.	.	.	.	Springwell Quarry	Durham ...	N. E.	Jarrow.
.	.	.	.	.	.	.	.	Wardley Colliery	Durham ...	N. E.	Jarrow.
.	.	.	.	.	.	.	.	Western Road Depôts	Durham ...	N. E.	Jarrow.
.	.	.	.	.	.	.	.	Jarvis Brook	Sussex ...	L. B. & S. C.	See Crowborough and Jarvis Brook.
.	.	.	.	.	.	.	.	Jarvis', D., Siding	Glamorg'n	G W—L N W—Mid—R S B	Swansea.
.	.	.	.	.	.	.	.	Jaynes Branch	Mon	L. & N. W.	See Blaenavon Iron and Coal Co. (Brynmawr).
G	P	F	L	H	C	3	0	Jedburgh	Roxburgh	N. B.	Branch from Roxburgh.
G	P	.	L	H				Jedfoot	Roxburgh	N. B.	Roxburgh and Jedburgh.
.	.	.	.	.	.	.	.	Jee's	Warwick..	L. & N. W.	See Hartshill Siding (Nuneaton).
.	.	.	.	.	.	.	.	Jee's Hartshill Granite & Brick Works (Mid.)..............	Warwick..	Mid.—L. & N. W.	Stockingford.
.	.	.	.	.	.	.	.	Jefferies Siding	Glo'ster ...	G. W.	Stonehouse.
.	.	.	.	.	.	.	.	Jeffery's Malt Kiln	Lincoln ...	G. C.	Blyton (for Corringham).
.	.	.	.	.	.	.	.	Jeffrey & Co.'s Siding	Edinboro'	Cal.	Edinburgh, Lothian Road.
.	.	.	.	.	.	.	.	Jeffries' Siding	Derby	Mid.	Whatstandwell.
.	.	.	.	.	.	.	.	Jellieston Colliery	Ayr	G. & S. W.	Waterside.
.	.	.	.	.	.	.	.	Jenkins & Co.'s Siding (G. C.)	Notts	G. C.—G. N.—Mid.	Same as Bee Hive Works (Retford).
.	.	.	.	.	.	.	.	Jenkins & Jones' Siding ...	Denbigh...	G. W.	Aberderfyn.
.	.	.	.	.	.	.	.	Jenkins & Sons' Lime & Timber Siding	Glamorg'n	G. W.	Bridgend.
.	.	.	.	.	.	.	.	Jenner & Higg's Siding ...	Sussex ...	L. B. & S. C.	Haywards Heath.
.	.	.	.	.	.	.	.	Jennings, F. H., Siding	Suffolk ...	G. E.	Cockfield.
.	.	.	.	.	.	.	.	Jennison's Siding	Lancs	L. & N. W.	Manchester, Longsight.
.	.	.	.	.	.	.	.	Jenny Gray Pit	Fife.........	N. B.	See Lochgelly Collieries, No. 12 Siding (Lochgelly).
.	.	.	.	.	.	.	.	Jenny Lind Brick Works......	Lanark ...	Cal.	Newarthill.
G	P	.	L	H	C	2	0 }	Jepson's Siding	Lincoln ...	G. N.	Spalding.
G	P	.	L	H	C	5	0 }	Jersey	Jersey......	{ G. W.	Steamer from Weymouth.
G	P	.	.	.	.	.	.			{ L. & S. W.	Steamer from Southampton.

EXPLANATION—G Goods Station.   P Passenger and Parcel Station.   P* Passenger, but not Parcel or Miscellaneous Traffic.

F Furniture Vans, Carriages, Portable Engines, and Machines on Wheels.   L Live Stock.

H Horse Boxes and Prize Cattle Vans.   C Carriages by Passenger Train.

STATION ACCOMMODATION.						CRANE POWER.		STATIONS, &c.	COUNTY.	COMPANY.	POSITION.
						Tons	Cwts.				
G	P	.	L	H	.	7	0	Jersey Marine..................	Glamorg'n	R. & S. B.	Port Talbot and Swansea.
.	.	.	.	.	.			Briton Ferry Chemical Wks.	Glamorg'n	R. & S. B.	Jersey Marine.
.	.	.	.	.	.			Cape Copper Works	Glamorg'n	R. & S. B.	Jersey Marine.
.	.	.	.	.	.			Emu Works.....................	Glamorg'n	R. & S. B.	Jersey Marine.
.	.	.	.	.	.			Main Colliery...................	Glamorg'n	R. & S. B.	Jersey Marine.
.	.	.	.	.	.			Neath River Bridge Siding	Glamorg'n	R. & S. B.	Jersey Marine.
.	.	.	.	.	.			Red Jacket Quarry	Glamorg'n	R. & S. B.	Jersey Marine.
.	.	.	.	.	.			Jersey Siding	Glamorg'n	GW—LNW—Mid—RSB.	Swansea.
G	P	F	L	H	C			Jervaulx	Yorks	N. E.	Northallerton and Leyburn.
.	.	.	.	.	.			Jerviston Junction	Lanark ...	Cal.	Motherwell and Mossend.
.	.	.	.	.	.			Jerviston Quarry	Lanark ...	Cal.	Mossend.
.	P	.	.	.	.			Jesmond	Northumb	N. E.	Newcastle and Gosforth.
.	.	.	.	.	.			Jesse Ellis & Co.'s Siding ...	Kent	S. E. & C.	Maidstone.
.	.	.	.	.	.			Jessop, W., & Son—			
.	.	.	.	.	.			Brightside Works	Yorks	L. D. & E. C.—Mid.	Sheffield, Tinsley Road.
.	.	.	.	.	.			Brightside Works (Mid.) ...	Yorks	Mid.—G.C.—L. D. & E.C.	Sheffield, Wicker.
.	.	.	.	.	.			Jewson & Son's Siding	Suffolk ...	G. E.	Yarmouth, South Town.
.	.	.	.	.	.			Jewson's, F., Siding	Cambs......	G. E.	Haddenham.
.	.	.	.	.	.			Joan Croft Junction	Yorks	N. E.	Shaftholme Junction and Moss.
.	.	.	.	.	.			Jobern's Brick Works	Staffs	Mid.	Walsall Wood.
.	.	.	.	.	.			Jobling's Cask Yard	Durham ...	N. E.	Millfield.
.	.	.	.	.	.			Jobson, R., & Co.'s Repairing Works	Durham ...	N. E.	Hartlepool.
G	P	F	L	H	C	.	.	John o' Gaunt	Leicester..	G. N. & L. & N. W. Jt....	Market Harboro' & Melton Mowbray.
.	.	.	.	.	.			John Pit (L. & N. W.)	Lancs	L.&N.W.—G.C.(Wig.Jn.)	See Wigan Coal & Iron Co. (Wigan).
.	.	.	.	.	.			John's, D. W., Siding	Glamorg'n	GW—LNW—Mid—RSB	Swansea.
G	P	.	L	H	.	0	15	Johnshaven	Kinc'rdine	N. B.	Montrose and Bervie.
.	.	.	.	.	.			Johnson & Boyd's Siding...	Durham ...	N. E.	Darlington, Bank Top.
.	.	.	.	.	.			Johnson & Nephew's Siding...	Derby	Mid.	Ambergate.
.	.	.	.	.	.			Johnson Bros.' Sid.(L.&N.W.)	Staffs	L. & N.W.—G. W.—Mid.	Walsall.
.	.	.	.	.	.			Johnson's Siding................	Lancs	L. & Y.	Manchester, Beswick.
G	P	F	L	H	C	1	10	Johnston	Pembroke	G. W.	Whitland and New Milford.
.	.	.	.	.	.			Freystrop Colliery	Pembroke	G. W.	Johnston.
.	.	.	.	.	.			JOHNSTONE—			
G	P	F	L	H	C	30	0	(Station)	Renfrew ...	G. & S.W.	Paisley and Dalry.
G	.	.	L	.	.	2	0	Cartside	Renfrew ...	G. & S.W.	Branch from Cart Junction.
.	.	.	.	.	.			Clippens Siding	Renfrew ...	G. & S.W.	Johnstone and Houston.
.	.	.	.	.	.			Gas Works Siding	Renfrew ...	G. & S.W.	Cartside.
.	.	.	.	.	.			Lang & Son's Siding	Renfrew ...	G. & S.W.	Johnstone and Cart Junction.
.	.	.	.	.	.			Junction	Renfrew ...	G. & S.W.	Elderslie and Johnstone.
G	P	.	.	.	.	2	0	North	Renfrew ...	G. & S.W.	Branch from Cart Junction.
.	.	.	.	.	.			Shanks & Co.'s Siding	Renfrew ...	G. & S.W.	Johnstone and Cart Junction.
.	.	.	.	.	.			Johnstone's Sidings	Limerick	G. S. & W.	Rathkeale.
.	.	.	.	.	.			Johnston's Ballast Siding ...	Salop	G. W.	Hollinswood.
G	P	.	.	.	.			Johnstown and Hafod	Denbigh ...	G. W.	Ruabon and Wrexham.
.	.	.	.	.	.			Hafod-y-bwch Colliery	Denbigh ...	G. W.	Johnstown and Hafod.
.	.	.	.	.	.			Ruabon Cl. & Ck. Co.'s Sid.	Denbigh ...	G. W.	Johnstown and Hafod.
.	.	.	.	.	.			Ruabon Coal Co.'s Brick Works Siding	Denbigh ...	G. W.	Johnstown and Hafod.
.	.	.	.	.	.			John Street Depôt	Renfrew ...	Cal.	Greenock, Regent Street.
.	.	.	.	.	.			John Street Siding	Glamorg'n	T. V.	Cardiff Docks.
.	.	.	.	.	.			Jones, A. G., & Co.'s Siding...	Derby	G. N.	Derby.
.	.	.	.	.	.			Jones & Campbell's Siding ...	Stirling ...	Cal.	Same as Torwood Foundry (Larbert).
.	.	.	.	.	.			Jones & Co.'s Slag Wool Wks. (Cargo Fleet Iron Works)..	Yorks	N. E.	South Bank.
.	.	.	.	.	.			Jones & Ingham's Tudor Sid.	Carnarvon	L. & N. W.	Groeslon.
.	.	.	.	.	.			Jones & Son's Brick Works...	Glamorg'n	L. & N. W.	See Dunvant Quarry (Dunvant).
.	.	.	.	.	.			Jones & Son's Siding............	Carnarvon	L. & N. W.	Pontrhythallt.
.	.	.	.	.	.			Jones & Son's Siding............	Flint	L. & N. W.	Foryd Pier.
.	.	.	.	.	.			Jones & Son's Siding............	Flint	L. & N. W.	Rhyl.
.	.	.	.	.	.			Jones & Son's Rhydwen Sid.	Flint	L. & N. W.	Rhyl.
.	.	.	.	.	.			Jones & Son's Shropshire Maltings (L. & N. W.)	Salop	L. & N. W.—G.W.	Shrewsbury.
.	.	.	.	.	.			Jones, B., Daniel & Co.'s Lime Works	Glamorg'n	G. W.	Stormy.
.	.	.	.	.	.			Jones, M., Bros.' Siding	Glamorg'n	GW—LNW—Mid—RSB	Swansea.
G	.	.	.	.	.			Jones Drove	Cambs......	G. E.	Branch near Whittlesea.
.	.	.	.	.	.			Jones's Aldersey's Siding......	Cheshire...	L. & N. W.	Tattenhall Road.
.	.	.	.	.	.			Jones's (F.) Bute Fuel Works	Glamorg'n	GW—LNW—Rhy.—TV	Cardiff.
.	.	.	.	.	.			Jones's Graig Quarry	Denbigh...	L. & N. W.	Denbigh.
.	.	.	.	.	.			Jones's Longcliffe Quarry......	Derby	L. & N. W.	Longcliffe.
.	.	.	.	.	.			Jones's Siding (Mid.)............	Derby	Mid.—L. & N. W.	Woodville.

EXPLANATION—G *Goods Station.*   P *Passenger and Parcel Station.*   P* *Passenger, but not Parcel or Miscellaneous Traffic.*
F *Furniture Vans, Carriages, Portable Engines, and Machines on Wheels.*   L *Live Stock*
H *Horse Boxes and Prize Cattle Vans.*   C *Carriages by Passenger Train.*

STATION ACCOMMODATION.						CRANE POWER.		STATIONS, &c.	COUNTY.	COMPANY.	POSITION.
						Tons	Cwts.				
.	.	.	.	.	.	.	.	Jones's Siding	Glamorg'n	GW—LNW—Rhy.—TV	Cardiff.
.	.	.	.	.	.	.	.	Jones's Siding	Glamorg'n	L. & N. W.	Gorseinon.
.	.	.	.	.	.	.	.	Joppa	Edinboro'	N. B.	See Edinburgh.
.	.	.	.	.	.	.	.	Jordan Col. (Meadow Hall)	Yorks	G. C.	Meadow Hall and Wincobank.
.	.	.	.	.	.	.	.	Jordan's Foundry (Pillgwenlly Foundry)	Mon	A (N & S W) D & R—G W	Newport, Alexandra Docks.
.	.	.	.	.	.	.	.	Jordanhill	Lanark	N. B.	See Glasgow.
.	.	.	.	.	.	.	.	Jordanhill Brick Works (NB)	Lanark	N. B.—Cal.	Glasgow, Great Western Road.
G	P	.	L	H	.	1	10	Jordanstone	Perth	Cal.	Alyth Junction and Alyth.
.	P	.	.	.	.	.	.	Jordanstown	Antrim	N. C. Com. (Mid.)	Belfast and Carrickfergus.
.	.	.	.	.	.	.	.	Jordan Vale Siding	Renfrew	Cal.	Glasgow, Whiteinch.
.	.	.	.	.	.	.	.	Jubb's Coal Yard	Durham	N. E.	Darlington, Bank Top.
.	.	.	.	.	.	.	.	Jubilee Siding	Durham	N. E.	Darlington, Bank Top.
.	.	.	.	.	.	.	.	Jubilee Siding	Durham	N. E.	West Hartlepool.
.	.	.	.	.	.	.	.	Jubilee Siding	Lancs	L. & Y.	Shaw and Crompton.
.	.	.	.	.	.	.	.	Judkin's Stone Siding	Warwick	A & N Jt. (L & N W & Mid.)	Nuneaton.
.	.	.	.	.	.	.	.	Junction Bridge Mineral Depôt	Edinboro'	N. B.	See Leith, North.
.	.	.	.	.	.	.	.	Junction Dry Dock & Engineering Co.'s Siding	Glamorg'n	GW—LNW—Rhy.—TV	Cardiff.
.	.	.	.	.	.	.	.	Junction Mills	Edinboro'	N. B.	Leith, North.
.	.	.	.	.	.	.	.	Junction Road	Edinboro'	N. B.	See Leith.
.	.	.	.	.	.	.	.	Junction Road	Middlesex	T. & H. Jt. (G. E. & Mid.)	See London.
.	P	.	.	.	.	.	.	Junction Road	Sussex	K. & E. S.	Robertsbridge and Bodiam.
.	.	.	.	.	.	.	.	Junction Road Junction	Middlesex	Mid.—T. & H. Jt.	London, Haverstock Hill & Junction Road.
G	P	.	.	.	.	1	10	Juniper Green	Edinboro'	Cal.	Currie and Edinburgh.
G	P	F	L	H	C	2	0	Justinhaugh	Forfar	Cal.	Forfar and Brechin.

K

STATION ACCOMMODATION.						CRANE POWER.		STATIONS, &c.	COUNTY.	COMPANY.	POSITION.
.	.	.	.	.	.	.	.	Kaimes Colliery	Ayr	G. & S. W.	Muirkirk.
.	.	.	.	.	.	.	.	Kaimes Quarry	Edinboro'	Cal.	Balerno.
G	P	F	L	H	C	.	.	Kanturk	Cork	G. S. & W.	Banteer and Newmarket.
G	P	F	L	H	C	.	.	Katesbridge	Down	G. N. (I.)	Banbridge and Ballyroney.
.	.	.	.	.	.	.	.	Kates Mill	Edinboro'	Cal.	See Slateford.
.	.	.	.	.	.	.	.	Kaye & Co.'s Siding	Warwick	L. & N. W.	Southam and Long Itchington.
.	.	.	.	.	.	.	.	Kay Park Junction	Ayr	G. & S. W.	Hurlford and Kilmarnock.
.	.	.	.	.	.	.	.	Kayser, Ellison & Co.'s Siding (Mid.)	Yorks	Mid.—G.C.	Sheffield, Wicker.
.	.	.	.	.	.	.	.	Kay's Siding	Lancs	P & L Jt. (L & N W & L & Y)	See Chapel Hill Siding (Longridge).
G	.	.	L	H	.	.	.	Keadby	Lincoln	G. C.	Thorne and Barnetby.
.	.	.	.	.	.	.	.	Dunn's Manor Siding	Lincoln	G. C.	Keadby.
.	.	.	.	.	.	.	.	Keadby Junction	Lincoln	G. C.	Crowle and Keadby.
.	P	.	.	.	.	.	.	Kearsley	Lancs	L. & Y.	Manchester and Bolton.
.	.	.	.	.	.	.	.	Earl of Ellesmere's Linnyshaw Moss Siding	Lancs	L. & Y.	Kearsley Branch.
.	.	.	.	.	.	.	.	Entwistle Bros.' Siding	Lancs	L. & Y.	Kearsley.
.	.	.	.	.	.	.	.	Harrison, Blair & Co.'s Chemical Works	Lancs	L. & Y.	Kearsley Branch.
.	.	.	.	.	.	.	.	Stoneclough Col. Co.'s Sid.	Lancs	L. & Y.	Kearsley.
G	P	.	.	.	.	.	.	Kearsley Junction	Lancs	L. & Y.	Kearsley and Dixon Fold.
.	.	.	.	.	.	1	15	Kearsney (for River & Ewell)	Kent	S. E. & C.	Canterbury and Dover.
.	.	.	.	.	.	.	.	Kearsney Junction	Kent	S. E. & C.	Kearsney and Dover Priory.
.	.	.	.	.	.	.	.	Kearsney Loop Junction	Kent	S. E. & C.	Kearsney and Martin Mill.
.	.	.	.	.	.	.	.	Keay's Sidings	Staffs	L. & N. W.	Darlaston.
.	.	.	.	.	.	.	.	Keebles Siding	Lincoln	Mid. & G. N. Jt	Same as South Lincolnshire Brick and Tile Co.'s Siding (Bourne).
G	P	.	L	H	.	.	.	Keele (N.S.)	Staffs	{ N.S. / G.W.	Silverdale and Market Drayton. / Over N. S. Line.
.	.	.	.	.	.	.	.	Keele Park	Staffs	N. S.	Near Keele.
G	P	F	L	H	C	1	0	Kegworth	Notts	Mid.	Derby and Loughborough.
.	.	.	.	.	.	.	.	Lord Belper's Siding	Notts	Mid.	Kegworth and Trent.
								KEIGHLEY—			
G	.	F	L	.	.	10	0	(Station, G.N.)	Yorks	{ G.N. / G.C.	Branch—Ingrow & Keighley Junc. / Over G. N. from Wakefield Junction.
G	P	F	L	H	C	15	0	(Station, Mid.)	Yorks	{ Mid. / G.N.	Leeds and Skipton. / Over Mid. from Keighley Junction.

STATION ACCOMMODATION.							CRANE POWER.		STATIONS, &c.	COUNTY.	COMPANY.	POSITION.
							Tons	Cwts.	KEIGHLEY—continued.			
									Bailey & Clapham's Siding	Yorks	Mid.	Keighley.
									Beadman, Sons & Co.'s Wagon Repairing Works	Yorks	Mid.	Keighley.
									Butterfield & Co.'s Siding	Yorks	Mid.	Keighley.
									Clapham Bros.' Siding	Yorks	Mid.	Keighley.
									Corporation Gas Works	Yorks	Mid.	Keighley.
									Dickinson & Co.'s Siding	Yorks	Mid.	Keighley.
									Greenwood, G. L., & Co.'s Siding	Yorks	Mid.	Keighley.
									Hall & Stell's Siding	Yorks	Mid.	Keighley.
									Hill, J., & Son's Siding	Yorks	Mid.	Keighley.
									Junction	Yorks	G. N.—Mid.	Ingrow and Keighley (Mid.)
									Lund, S., & Son's Siding	Yorks	Mid.	Keighley.
									Mitchell, T., & Son's Siding	Yorks	Mid.	Keighley.
									Rustless Iron Co.'s Siding	Yorks	Mid.	Keighley.
									Senior's, C., Siding	Yorks	Mid.	Keighley.
									Smith, P., & Son— Lawkholme Works	Yorks	Mid.	Keighley.
									Midland Works	Yorks	Mid.	Keighley.
									Whalley, G., & Co.'s Siding	Yorks	Mid.	Keighley.
									Keiller & Son's Siding (G. E.)	Essex	GE—GN—LNW—Mid.	London, Silvertown.
G	P	F	L	H	C		5	0	Keith Station and Junction	Banff	{ High. { G. N. of S.	Junction with G. N. of S. Grange and Dufftown.
G	P	P	F	L	H	C	2	0				
	P								Keith Town	Banff	G. N. of S.	Keith and Craigellachie.
									Kellett & Son's Siding	Worcester	Halesowen (G. W. & Mid.)	Same as Frankley Sidings (Rubery)
									Kelleythorpe Siding (Little Driffield Siding)	Yorks	N. E.	Driffield.
									Kelliebank Ship Yard	Clackman'	Cal.	Alloa.
									Kelling Heath Siding	Norfolk	Mid. & G. N. Jt.	Holt.
									Kellner Partington Paper Pulp Co.'s Works	Lancs	Furness	Barrow.
									Kelloe Colliery	Durham	N. E.	Same as East Hetton Col. (Coxhoe).
G	P		L	H					Kells	Antrim	N. C. Com. (Mid.)	Ballymena and Larne.
G	P								Kells	Kerry	G. S. & W.	Farranfore and Valentia Harbour.
G	P	F	L	H	C		3	0	Kells	Meath	G. N. (I.)	Navan and Oldcastle.
G	P		L				3	0	Kellswater	Antrim	N. C. Com. (Mid.)	Antrim and Ballymena.
									Kelly's Siding	Sussex	S. E. & C.	Rye Harbour.
G	P	F	L	H	C				Kelmarsh	N'hamptn	L. & N. W.	Market Harboro' and Northampton.
									Kelsey Hill Ballast Pit	Yorks	N. E.	Rye Hill.
									Kelsey Hill Gravel Siding	Yorks	N. E.	Keyingham.
G	P	F	L	H	C		4	0	Kelso (N. B.)	Roxburgh	{ N. B. { N. E.	Branch from St. Boswells. Over N. B. from Sprouston Junc.
									Kelso Granary (Dunn & Son's Grain Siding)	Roxburgh	N. B.	Kelso.
									Kelso Junction	Roxburgh	N. B.	St. Boswells and Maxton.
	P								Kelston	Somerset	Mid.	Mangotsfield and Bath.
									Kelton Fell	Cumb'land	R. & K. F.	Terminus.
									Baird & Co.— Kelton Iron Mines	Cumb'land	R. & K. F.	Rowrah Junction and Kelton Fell.
									Knockmurton Iron Mines	Cumb'land	R. & K. F.	Kelton Fell.
									Kelton Iron Mines	Cumb'land	R. & K. F.	See Baird & Co. (Kelton Fell).
									Kelton Limestone Quarry	Cumb'land	WC&EJt. (Fur.&LNW)	See Cammell & Co. (Rowrah).
G	P	F	L	H	C		3	0	Kelty	Fife	N. B.	Dunfermline and Kinross Junction.
									Aitken Colliery	Fife	N. B.	Near Kelty.
									Benarty Colliery	Fife	N. B.	Blairadam and Kelty.
									Blairadam Colliery	Fife	N. B.	Branch from Kelty.
									Blairenbathie Colliery	Fife	N. B.	Branch from Kelty.
									Blairenbathie Siding	Fife	N. B.	Terminus—Blairadam Branch.
									Blairfordell Colliery	Fife	N. B.	Near Kelty.
G									Capeldrae Sid. (Paton's Sid.)	Fife	N. B.	Branch from Kelty.
									Crosshill Colliery	Fife	N. B.	Branch from Kelty.
									Fife Coal Co.— Kelty Weighs Siding	Fife	N. B.	Blairadam Branch.
									Mary Pit	Fife	N. B.	Lochore Branch.
									Kelty Brick Works	Fife	N. B.	Branch from Kelty.
									Kelty Colliery	Fife	N. B.	Branch from Kelty.
									Kingseat Colliery	Fife	N. B.	Kelty and Whitemyre Junction.
									Kinnaird Colliery, No. 1	Kinross	N. B.	Kelty and Blairadam.
									Lassodie Colliery	Fife	N. B.	Kelty and Whitemyre Junction.
									Lassodie Mill Colliery	Fife	N. B.	Kelty and Whitemyre Junction.
									Lindsay Colliery	Fife	N. B.	Kelty and Whitemyre Junction.

EXPLANATION—G *Goods Station.*   P *Passenger and Parcel Station.*   P* *Passenger, but not Parcel or Miscellaneous Traffic.*
F *Furniture Vans, Carriages, Portable Engines, and Machines on Wheels.*   L *Live Stock.*
H *Horse Boxes and Prize Cattle Vans.*   C *Carriages by Passenger Train.*

STATION ACCOMMODATION.						CRANE POWER.		STATIONS, &c.	COUNTY.	COMPANY.	POSITION.
						Tons	Cwts.	**Kelty**—*continued.*			
.	.	.	.	.	.	.	.	Lochore Colliery	Fife	N. B.	Branch from Kelty.
								Lumphinnans Colliery, No.			
.	.	.	.	.	.	.	.	11 Siding	Fife	N. B.	Branch—Lochgelly and Kelty.
.	.	.	.	.	.	.	.	Westfield Siding	Fife	N. B.	Branch from Kelty.
.	.	.	.	.	.	.	.	Kelty Junction	Fife	N. B.	Cowdenbeath (New) and Kelty.
.	.	.	.	.	.	.	.	Kelty Weighs Siding	Fife	N. B.	See Fife Coal Co. (Kelty).
G	P	F	L	H	C	1	10	Kelvedon	Essex	G. E.	Chelmsford and Colchester.
.	.	.	.	.	.	.	.	Kelvin Bridge	Lanark	Cal.—Glas. Dist. Sub.	See Glasgow.
.	.	.	.	.	.	.	.	Kelvindale Paper Mill	Lanark	Cal.	Glasgow, Dawsholm.
.	.	.	.	.	.	.	.	Kelvinhaugh Depôt (N.B.)	Lanark	N. B.—Cal.	See Glasgow.
.	.	.	.	.	.	.	.	Kelvinhaugh Junction	Lanark	N. B.	Glasgow.
.	.	.	.	.	.	.	.	Kelvinhaugh Manure Sid(NB)	Lanark	N. B.—Cal.	Glasgow, Stobcross.
.	.	.	.	.	.	.	.	Kelvinside	Lanark	Cal.	See Glasgow.
.	.	.	.	.	.	.	.	Kelvinside Electric Power Sid	Lanark	N. B.	Glasgow, Hyndland.
.	.	.	.	.	.	.	.	Kelvin Valley East Junction	Stirling	N. B.	Kirkintilloch and Gavell.
.	.	.	.	.	.	.	.	Kelvin Valley East Jn. Sids.	Stirling	N. B.	Kirkintilloch.
.	.	.	.	.	.	.	.	Kelvin Valley West Junction	Stirling	N. B.	Kirkintilloch and Gavell.
.	.	.	.	.	.	.	.	Kemberton Colliery	Salop	G. W.	Madeley.
.	P	F	.	H	C	.	.	Kemble Junction	Wilts	G. W.	Gloucester and Swindon.
G	P	F	L	H	.	1	5	Kemnay	Aberdeen	G. N. of S.	Kintore and Alford.
.	.	.	.	.	.	.	.	Kempson & Co.'s Works	Derby	Mid.	Pye Bridge.
.	.	.	.	.	.	.	.	Kempton Park Race Station	Middlesex	L. & S.W.	Sunbury.
.	.	.	.	.	.	.	.	Kemp Town	Sussex	L. B. & S. C.	See Brighton.
G	P	.	L	.	.	.	.	Kemsing	Kent	S. E. & C.	Otford and Maidstone.
.	.	.	.	.	.	.	.	Kench's Siding	Yorks	L. & N. W.	Birstal.
G	P	F	L	H	C	10	0	Kendal (L. & N. W.)	W'morlnd	{ L. & N. W.	Oxenholme and Windermere.
.	P	.	.	.	.	.	.			Furness	Over L. & N. W. from Hincaster Jn.
.	.	.	.	.	.	.	.	Kendal Bonded Stores Co.	W'morlnd	L. & N. W.	Kendal and Burneside.
.	.	.	.	.	.	.	.	Anglo-American Oil Co.'s			
.	.	.	.	.	.	.	.	Siding	W'morlnd	L. & N. W.	Kendal Bonded Stores Co.
.	.	.	.	.	.	.	.	Break's Siding	W'morlnd	L. & N. W.	Kendal Bonded Stores Co.
.	.	.	.	.	.	.	.	Consolidated Oil Co.'s Sid	W'morlnd	L. & N. W.	Kendal Bonded Stores Co.
.	.	.	.	.	.	.	.	Cumming's Siding	W'morlnd	L. & N. W.	Kendal Bonded Stores Co.
.	.	.	.	.	.	.	.	Cumpsty's Siding	W'morlnd	L. & N. W.	Kendal Bonded Stores Co.
.	.	.	.	.	.	.	.	Kendal Co-operative			
.	.	.	.	.	.	.	.	Society's Coal Wharf	W'morlnd	L. & N. W.	Kendal Bonded Stores Co.
.	.	.	.	.	.	.	.	Manchester Corporation			
.	.	.	.	.	.	.	.	Siding	W'morlnd	L. & N. W.	Kendal Bonded Stores Co.
.	.	.	.	.	.	.	.	Pattinson's Siding	W'morlnd	L. & N. W.	Kendal Bonded Stores Co.
.	.	.	.	.	.	.	.	Pennington's Siding	W'morlnd	L. & N. W.	Kendal Bonded Stores Co.
.	.	.	.	.	.	.	.	Thompson's (Marcelus)			
.	.	.	.	.	.	.	.	Siding	W'morlnd	L. & N. W.	Kendal Bonded Stores Co.
.	.	.	.	.	.	.	.	Thompson's (Miles) Sid.	W'morlnd	L. & N. W.	Kendal Bonded Stores Co.
.	.	.	.	.	.	.	.	Westmorland Woollen			
.	.	.	.	.	.	.	.	Co.'s Siding	W'morlnd	L. & N. W.	Kendal Bonded Stores Co.
.	.	.	.	.	.	.	.	Whitwell, Hargreaves &			
.	.	.	.	.	.	.	.	Co.'s Siding	W'morlnd.	L. & N. W.	Kendal Bonded Stores Co.
.	.	.	.	.	.	.	.	Whitwell, Hargreaves &			
.	.	.	.	.	.	.	.	Co.'s Siding	W'morlnd	L. & N. W.	Kendal and Burneside.
.	.	.	.	.	.	.	.	Whitwell, Mark & Co.'s			
.	.	.	.	.	.	.	.	Siding	W'morlnd	L. & N. W.	Kendal and Burneside.
.	.	.	.	.	.	.	.	Kendal Co-operative	W'morlnd	L. & N. W.	{ See Kendal Bonded Stores Co.
.	.	.	.	.	.	.	.	Society's Coal Wharf			(Kendal).
.	.	.	.	.	.	.	.	Kendall & Gent's Siding	Lancs	S. & M. Jt. (G. C. & Mid.)	Belle Vue.
.	.	.	.	.	.	.	.	Kendall's Siding	Lancs	L. & N. W.	Manchester, London Road.
.	.	.	.	.	.	.	.	Kendall's Siding (G. C.)	Lancs	G. C.—Mid.	Manchester, Ardwick.
G	P	.	.	.	.	.	.	Kenfig Hill	Glamorg'n	G. W.	Tondu and Porthcawl.
.	.	.	.	.	.	.	.	Cefn Cribbw Brick Siding	Glamorg'n	G. W.	Tondu and Kenfig Hill.
G	P	F	L	H	C	5	0	Kenilworth	Warwick	L. & N. W.	Coventry and Leamington.
.	.	.	.	.	.	.	.	Cherry Orchard Brick Co.'s			
.	.	.	.	.	.	.	.	Siding	Warwick	L. & N. W.	Kenilworth and Coventry.
.	.	.	.	.	.	.	.	Hawke's Siding	Warwick	L. & N. W.	Kenilworth and Coventry.
.	.	.	.	.	.	.	.	Kenilworth Gas Co.'s Siding	Warwick	L. & N. W.	Kenilworth and Tile Hill.
.	.	.	.	.	.	.	.	Lockhart's Siding	Warwick	L. & N. W.	Kenilworth and Coventry.
.	.	.	.	.	.	.	.	Streets Siding	Warwick	L. & N. W.	Kenilworth and Tile Hill.
G	P	.	.	.	.	.	.	Kenley	Surrey	S. E. & C	Purley and Caterham.
G	P	F	L	H	C	.	.	Kenmare	Kerry	G. S. & W.	Branch from Headford Junction.
.	.	.	.	.	.	.	.	Kenmuir Colliery	Lanark	Cal.	Carmyle.
.	.	.	.	.	.	.	.	Kenmuirhill Colliery No. 1	Lanark	Cal.	Carmyle.
.	.	.	.	.	.	.	.	Kenmuirhill Colliery No. 2	Lanark	Cal.	Mount Vernon.
.	.	.	.	.	.	.	.	Kennedy & Co.'s Wood Yard	L'lithgow	N. B.	Bo'ness.

EXPLANATION—G *Goods Station.*   P *Passenger and Parcel Station.*   P* *Passenger, but not Parcel or Miscellaneous Traffic.*
F *Furniture Vans, Carriages, Portable Engines, and Machines on Wheels.*   L *Live Stock.*
H *Horse Boxes and Prize Cattle Vans.*   C *Carriages by Passenger Train.*

STATION ACCOMMODATION.						CRANE POWER.	STATIONS, &c.	COUNTY.	COMPANY.	POSITION.
						Tons Cwts.				
..	..	..	..	..	..	.. ..	Kennedy's Siding	Lanark ...	Cal.	Meikle Earnock.
..	..	..	..	..	..	.. ..	Kennedy's Siding (N.B.)......	Lanark ...	N. B.—Cal.	Glasgow, Great Western Road.
..	..	..	..	..	..	.. ..	Kennedy's Timber Siding ...	Lanark ...	Cal.	Glasgow, Kinning Park.
..	..	..	..	..	..	.. ..	Kennet	Clackman'	N. B.	See Clackmannan and Kennet.
G	P	F	L	H	C	2 0	Kennethmont	Aberdeen .	G. N. of S.	Inveramsay and Keith.
..	..	..	..	..	..	.. ..	Kenneth's Fire-Clay Works...	Ayr	G. & S. W.	Same as Eglinton Fire Clay Works (Kilwinning).
G	P	F	L	H	C	1 10	Kennett	Cambs......	G. E.	Newmarket and Bury.
..	..	..	..	..	..	.. ..	Kennington	Middlesex	C. & S. L.	See London.
..	..	..	..	..	..	.. ..	Kennington Junction	Berks	G. W.	Littlemore and Oxford.
G	P	..	..	..	..	.. ..	Kennishead	Renfrew ...	GB&KJt.(Cal&G&SW)	Neilston and Pollokshaws.
G	..	F	L	..	..	.. ..	Kennoway	Fife	N. B.	Cameron Bridge and Montrave.
..	..	..	..	..	..	.. ..	Kennyhill	Lanark ...	Cal.	See Glasgow.
..	..	..	..	..	..	.. ..	Kensal Green Gas Works ..	Middlesex	G. W.	London, Paddington.
..	..	..	..	..	..	.. ..	Kensal Rise (L. & N. W.) ...	Middlesex	L. & N. W.—N. L.	See London.
..	..	..	..	..	..	.. ..	Kensington	Middlesex	GW—LNW—WLon Jt— L & S W—L B & S C..	See London.
..	..	..	..	..	..	.. ..	Kensington and Notting Hill Electric Lighting Co.'s Sid.	Middlesex	G. W.—L. & N. W.	London, Shepherd's Bush.
..	..	..	..	..	..	.. ..	Kensington (Earls Court) Jn.	Middlesex	Met. Dist.—W. Lon. Jt.	London, Earls Court & Addison Rd.
..	..	..	..	..	..	.. ..	Kensington (High Street) ...	Middlesex	Met.—Met. Dist.—Mid...	See London.
..	..	..	..	..	..	.. ..	Kensington (High Street) Jn.	Middlesex	Met.—Met. Dist.	Brompton (Gloucester Road) and Kensington (High Street).
..	..	..	..	..	..	.. ..	Kensington (High Street) Jn.	Middlesex	Met. Dist.—Mid.	Kensington (High Street) and Earls Court.
..	..	..	..	..	..	.. ..	Kensington Junction	Middlesex	L. & S.W.—W. Lon. Jt.	London, Hammersmith and Kensington (Addison Road).
..	..	..	..	..	..	.. ..	Kensington Vestry Siding ...	Middlesex	G. W.—L. & N. W.	London, Shepherd's Bush.
G	P	F	L	H	C	3 0	Kentallen........................	Argyll ...	Cal.	Connel Ferry and Ballachulish.
..	..	..	..	..	..	.. ..	Ardsheal Quarry...............	Argyll ...	Cal.	Kentallen and Ballachulish.
..	..	..	..	..	..	.. ..	Kent Colliery Works	Kent	S. E. & C.	Dover Town.
..	P	..	..	..	..	.. ..	Kent House (Beckenham) ...	Kent	S. E. & C.	Penge and Beckenham.
..	..	..	..	..	..	.. ..	Kentish Town (L. & N. W.)..	Middlesex	L. & N. W.—N. L..........	See London.
..	..	..	..	..	..	.. ..	Kentish Town (Mid.)	Middlesex	Mid.—G. E.—S. E. & C.	See London.
..	..	..	..	..	..	.. ..	Kentish Town Junction	Middlesex	L. & N. W.—N. L.	Same as London, Camden Road Jn.
..	..	..	..	..	..	.. ..	Kenton Lane Siding	Middlesex	L. & N. W.	Same as Bransgrove's Sid. (Harrow and Wealdstone).
..	P	..	..	H	C	.. ..	Kent's Bank	Lancs	Furness.........................	Grange and Ulverston.
..	..	..	..	..	..	.. ..	Kenworthy's Siding	Yorks	L. & Y.	Lockwood.
G	P	F	L	H	C	2 10 }	Kenyon Jn. Station (L&NW)	Lancs	{ L. & N. W.	Liverpool and Manchester.
..	P	..	..	H	C	.. .. }			{ G. W.	Over L. & N. W. from Walton Junc.
..	..	..	..	..	..	.. ..	Kepplehill Colliery	Lanark ...	N. B.	Shotts.
G	P	..	L	H	..	5 0	Kerne Bridge	Hereford ..	G. W.	Ross and Monmouth.
..	..	..	..	..	..	.. ..	Kerr, Stuart & Co.'s Foundry	Staffs	N. S.	Stoke-on-Trent.
..	..	..	..	..	..	.. ..	Kerr's Siding	Surrey ...	L. B. & S. C.	Epsom Downs.
G	P	F	L	H	C	5 0	Kerry	Montgom	Cam.	Branch from Abermule.
..	..	..	..	..	..	.. ..	Fronfraith Siding	Montgom	Cam.	Abermule and Kerry.
..	..	..	..	..	..	.. ..	Goitre Siding	Montgom	Cam.	Abermule and Kerry.
..	..	..	..	..	..	.. ..	Middle Mill Siding	Montgom	Cam.	Abermule and Kerry.
..	..	..	..	..	..	.. ..	Kerse Mill Siding	Stirling ...	Cal.	Stirling.
G	P	..	L	H	..	.. ..	Kershope Foot	Cumb'land	N. B.	Hawick and Carlisle.
G	P	..	L	..	..	.. ..	Kesh	Ferm'nagh	G. N. (I.)	Bundoran Junction and Bundoran.
..	..	..	..	..	..	.. ..	Kestell, J. N., & Co.'s Siding	Glamorg'n	G W—L N W—Rhy—TV	Cardiff.
..	..	..	..	..	..	.. ..	Kesteven Siding	Lincoln ...	G. N. & G. E. Jt.	Saxilby.
G	P	F	L	H	C	4 0	Keswick	Cumb'land	C. K. & P. (L&NW&NE Working Cos.)	Penrith and Cockermouth.
..	P	..	..	..	..	.. ..	Ketley	Salop	G. W.	Wellington and Lightmoor.
..	..	..	..	..	..	.. ..	Ketley Junction	Salop	G. W.	Wellington and Oakengates.
G	P	F	L	H	C	10 0	Kettering	N'hampt n	Mid.	Market Harboro' and Wellingboro'.
..	..	..	..	..	..	.. ..	Cunliffe's Brick Works......	N'hampt n	Mid.	Near Kettering.
..	..	..	..	..	..	.. ..	Ellis & Everard's Siding ...	N'hampt n	Mid.	Kettering.
..	..	..	..	..	..	.. ..	Kettering Iron & Coal Co.'s Siding	N'hampt n	Mid.	Near Kettering.
..	..	..	..	..	..	.. ..	Loddington Iron Ore Co.— Globe Siding	N'hampt n	Mid.	Terminus—Loddington Branch.
..	..	..	..	..	..	.. ..	Loddington Siding	N'hampt n	Mid.	Terminus—Loddington Branch.
..	..	..	..	..	..	.. ..	New Cransley Iron & Steel Co.'s Works......	N'hampt n	Mid.	Loddington Branch.
..	..	..	..	..	..	.. ..	Kettering Iron&CoalCo.'s Sid.	N'hampt n	Mid.	{ Cranford. { Kettering.
G	..	..	..	..	..	.. ..	Kettlebrook	Warwick..	Mid.	Tamworth and Whitacre.
..	..	..	..	..	..	.. ..	Fisher & Co.'s Paper Mill..	Warwick..	Mid.	Tamworth and Wilnecote.

EXPLANATION—G Goods Station.   P Passenger and Parcel Station.   P* Passenger, but not Parcel or Miscellaneous Traffic.
F Furniture Vans, Carriages, Portable Engines, and Machines on Wheels.   L Live Stock.
H Horse Boxes and Prize Cattle Vans.   C Carriages by Passenger Train.

STATION ACCOMMODATION.						CRANE POWER.		STATIONS, &c.	COUNTY.	COMPANY.	POSITION.
						Tons	Cwts				
·	·	·	·	·	·	·	·	Kettlebrook—continued.			
·	·	·	·	·	·	·	·	Gibbs & Canning's Brick and Pipe Works	Warwick..	Mid.	Kettlebrook.
·	·	·	·	·	·	·	·	Glascote Colliery Co.'s Amington Colliery	Warwick..	Mid.	Near Kettlebrook.
·	·	·	·	·	·	·	·	Thompson & Southwick's Foundry	Warwick..	Mid.	Kettlebrook.
·	·	·	·	·	·	·	·	Kettleby Mines Iron Ore Sid.	Leicester..	Mid.	Same as Potter Hill, Kettleby Mines Iron Ore Siding.
G	P	·	L	H	·	·	·	Kettleness	Yorks	N. E.	Whitby and Middlesbro'.
G	P	F	L	H	C	10	0	Ketton (Mid.)	Rutland	Mid. / L. & N. W.	Stamford and Oakham.
·	P	·	·	H	C	·	·				Over Mid. from Luffenham Junc.
·	·	·	·	·	·	·	·	Eldred & Co.'s Lime Siding	Rutland	Mid.	Near Ketton.
·	·	·	·	·	·	·	·	Thorpe's, W. B., Siding	Rutland	Mid.	Near Ketton.
G	·	F	L	H	C	5	0	Kevock Mill	Edinboro'	N. B.	Polton.
G	·	·	·	·	·	·	·	Kew Bridge	Middlesex	N&S.W.Jn.Jt.(L&NW, Mid., & N. L.)	Acton and Old Kew Junction.
G	P	·	L	·	·	·	·	Kew Bridge (L. & S. W.)	Middlesex	L. & S. W. / N&S WJn.Jt.(L&NW, Mid., & N. L.)	Hammersmith and Brentford.
·	P	·	·	·	·	·	·				Over L. & S. W. from Kew East Jn.
G	P	F	L	·	·	·	·	Kew, East Junction	Middlesex	L.&S.W—N&S.WJn.Jt.	London, Kew Bridge and Acton.
·	·	·	·	·	·	·	·	Kew Gardens	Lancs	L. & Y.	Southport and Barton.
·	P	·	·	·	·	·	·	Kew Gardens (L. & S. W.)	Surrey	L. & S. W. / G. W.—Met. / N.&S.WJn.Jt.(L&NW, Mid., & N. L.)	Addison Road and Richmond. / Over L&SW.from Hammersmith Jn. / Over L. & S. W. from Acton Junc.
·	·	·	·	·	·	·	·	Kew New Junction	Middlesex	L. & S.W.	See London, New Kew Junction.
·	·	·	·	·	·	·	·	Kew Old Junction	Middlesex	L.&S.W—N&S.WJn.Jt.	See London, Old Kew Junction.
G	P	·	L	H	C	1	10	Keyham	Devon	G. W.	Devonport and Saltash.
·	·	·	·	·	·	·	·	Keyham Junction (for H.M. Dockyards)	Devon	G. W.	Devonport and Saltash.
G	P	·	L	H	·	·	·	Keyingham	Yorks	N. E.	Hull and Withernsea.
·	·	·	·	·	·	·	·	Kelsey Hill Gravel Siding	Yorks	N. E.	Keyingham.
·	·	·	·	·	·	·	·	Keymer Brick & Tile Co.'s Sid.	Sussex	L. B. & S. C.	Wivelsfield.
·	·	·	·	·	·	·	·	Keymer Junction	Sussex	L. B. & S. C.	Burgess Hill and Wivelsfield.
G	P	·	L	H*	·	·	·	Keynsham	Somerset.	G. W.	Bath and Bristol.
·	·	·	·	·	·	·	·	Kibblesworth Colliery	Durham	N. E.	Redheugh.
G	P	F	L	H	C	1	10	Kibworth	Leicester..	Mid.	Leicester and Market Harboro'.
·	P	·	·	·	·	·	·	Ellis & Everard's Siding	Leicester..	Mid.	Kibworth.
G	P	F	L	H	C	5	0	Kidbrooke	Kent	S. E. & C.	Blackheath and Dartford.
G	P	F	L	H	C	2	0	Kidderminster	Worcester	G. W.	Worcester and Dudley.
·	·	·	·	·	·	·	·	Fields Sand Siding	Worcester	G. W.	Kidderminster.
G	P	F	L	H	C	·	·	Kidlington	Oxon	G. W.	Banbury and Oxford.
·	·	·	·	·	·	·	·	Kidlington Junction	Oxon	G. W.	Banbury and Oxford.
·	P	·	·	·	·	·	·	Kidnall's Colliery	Glo'ster	S. & Wye Jt (G W & Mid)	Same as Norchard Col. (Whitecroft).
·	·	·	·	·	·	·	·	Kidsgrove	Staffs	N. S.	Mow Cop and Goldenhill.
·	·	·	·	·	·	·	·	Kidsgrove Goods (N. S.)	Staffs	N. S.—L. & N. W.	See Harecastle (for Kidsgrove).
G	P	F	L	H	C	1	10	Kidwelly	Carmarth'	G. W.	Llanelly and Carmarthen Junction.
·	·	·	·	·	·	·	·	Stephens & Co.'s Siding	Carmarth'	G. W.	Kidwelly.
·	·	·	·	·	·	·	·	Kidwelly Junction	Carmarth'	B. P. & G. V.	Burry Port and Pontyeats.
·	·	·	·	·	·	·	·	Kidwelly Junction	Carmarth'	G. W.—G. V.	Kidwelly and Mynydd-y-Garreg.
G	P	F	L	H	C	·	·	Kidwelly Quay	Carmarth'	B. P. & G. V.	Terminus.
G	·	·	·	·	·	·	·	Kielder	Northumb	N. B.	Riccarton and Reedsmouth.
·	·	·	·	·	·	·	·	Deadwater Siding	Northumb	N. B.	Riccarton and Kielder.
·	P	·	·	·	·	·	·	Thorlieshope Lime Works	Roxburgh	N. B.	Saughtree and Deadwater.
·	·	·	·	·	·	·	·	Kilbagie	Clackman'	N. B.	Alloa and Kincardine.
·	·	·	·	·	·	·	·	Kilbagie Paper Mill	Clackman'	N. B.	Branch from Kilbagie.
G	P	F	L	H	C	3	0	Kilbarry	Cork	G. S. & W.	See Cork.
G	P	·	L	·	·	·	·	Kilbirnie	Ayr	Cal.	Terminus of Branch from Giffen.
·	·	·	·	·	·	·	·	Knox's Siding	Ayr	Cal.	Kilbirnie.
G	P	·	L	·	·	3	0	Kilbirnie	Ayr	G. & S.W.	See Glengarnock and Kilbirnie.
·	·	·	·	·	·	·	·	Kilbowie	Dumbartn	N. B.	Maryhill and Dumbarton.
·	·	·	·	·	·	·	·	Kilbowie Iron Works	Dumbartn	N. B.	Near Kilbowie.
·	P	·	·	·	·	·	·	Singer Manufact'ng Co.'sSid	Dumbartn	N. B.	Near Kilbowie.
·	·	·	·	·	·	·	·	Kilbowie Road	Dumbartn	Cal.	Glasgow, Central, and Dumbarton.
·	P	·	·	·	·	·	·	Kilbride, East	Lanark	Cal.	See East Kilbride.
·	·	·	·	·	·	·	·	Kilburn	Derby	Mid.	Little Eaton and Ripley.
·	·	·	·	·	·	·	·	Kilburn & Maida Vale(LNW)	Middlesex	L. & N. W.—N. L.	See London.
·	·	·	·	·	·	·	·	Kilburn—Brondesbury	Middlesex	Met.	See London.
·	·	·	·	·	·	·	·	Kilburn Colliery	Derby	Mid.	Denby.
G	P	·	·	·	·	·	·	Kilby Bridge Siding	Leicester..	Mid.	See Ellis, J., & Son (Wigston).
·	·	·	·	·	·	·	·	Kilchoan	Argyll	Cal.	Steamer from Oban.

EXPLANATION—G *Goods Station.*   P *Passenger and Parcel Station.*   P* *Passenger, but not Parcel or Miscellaneous Traffic.*
F *Furniture Vans, Carriages, Portable Engines, and Machines on Wheels.*   L *Live Stock.*
H *Horse Boxes and Prize Cattle Vans.*   H* *By special arrangement only.*   C *Carriages by Passenger Train.*

STATION ACCOMMODATION.						CRANE POWER.		STATIONS, &c.	COUNTY.	COMPANY.	POSITION.
						Tons	Cwts				
G	P		L	H	C	1	10	Kilcock	Kildare	M. G. W.	Dublin and Mullingar.
G	P							Kilcoe	Cork	S. & S.	Schull and Skibbereen.
G	P	F	L	H	C	1	10	Kilconquhar	Fife	N. B.	Leven and Anstruther.
G	P		L	H				Kilcool	Wicklow	D. W. & W.	Bray and Wicklow.
G	P	F	L			2	0	Kilcrea	Cork	C. & Macroom	Cork and Macroom.
G	P	F	L	H	C	6	0	Kildale	Yorks	N. E.	Battersby and Grosmont.
								Bradley Bros.' Whinstone Siding	Yorks	N. E.	Kildale.
G	P	F	L	H	C			Kildare	Kildare	G. S. & W.	Dublin and Portarlington.
	P	F		H	C			Curragh Siding	Kildare	G. S. & W.	Kildare and Newbridge.
G	P	F	L	H	C	3	0	Kildary	Ross & Cro'	High.	Invergordon and Tain.
G	P	F	L	H	C			Kildonan	Sutherl'nd	High.	Helmsdale and Wick.
G	P	F	L	H	C	5	0	Kildwick and Crosshills	Yorks	Mid.	Shipley and Skipton.
								Kildwick Parish Gas Co.'s Siding	Yorks	Mid.	Near Kildwick.
	P							Kilfenora	Kerry	G. S. & W.	Tralee and Fenit.
	P							Kilfree Junction Station	Sligo	M. G. W.	Longford and Sligo.
								Kilgarth Slag Hill Siding	Lanark	Cal.	Gartsherrie.
G	P		L	H				Kilgarvan	Kerry	G. S. & W.	Headford Junction and Kenmare.
G	P		L	H		5	0	Kilgerran	Pembroke	G. W.	Crymmych Arms and Cardigan.
G	P		L	H				Kilgetty	Pembroke	G. W.	Whitland and Tenby.
								Kilgrammie, No. 1	Ayr	G. & S. W.	Dailly.
								Kilham Siding	Northumb	N. E.	Mindrum.
G	P		L					Kilkee	Clare	West Clare	Terminus.
G	P	F	L	H	C	10	0	Kilkenny	Kilkenny	G. S. & W.	Maryborough and Waterford.
G	P	F	L	H	C	3	0	Kilkerran	Ayr	G. & S. W.	Maybole and Girvan.
								Kilkewydd Siding	Montgom	Cam.	Forden.
G	P		L	H		1	0	Killagan	Antrim	N. C. Com. (Mid.)	Ballymena and Coleraine.
G	P	F	L	H	C	2	0	Killala	Mayo	M. G. W.	Branch from Manulla Junc. Station.
G	P	F	L	H	C	1	0	Killaloe	Tipperary	G. S. & W.	Branch from Birdhill.
								KILLAMARSH—			
	P							(Station)	Derby	L. D. & E. C.	Clowne and Sheffield.
G	P		L			1	0	(Station)	Derby	Mid.	Eckington and Treeton.
G	P	F	L	H	C	10	0	(Station, G. C.)	Derby	G. C.	Sheffield and Chesterfield.
G		F	L			10	0		Derby	L. & N. W.	Over G. N. and G. C. Lines.
								Adrain, Chambers & Co.'s Siding	Derby	Mid.	Killamarsh.
								Carbrook Steel Works	Derby	Mid.	Killamarsh.
								Ellison & Mitchel's Siding	Derby	Mid.	Killamarsh and Eckington.
								Glover's Flour Mill	Derby	L. D. & E. C.	Killamarsh.
								Holbrook Colliery	Derby	Mid.	Killamarsh and Eckington.
								Junction	Derby	G. C.	Kiveton Park and Killamarsh.
								Killamarsh Brick and Tile Co.'s Siding	Derby	L. D. & E. C.	Killamarsh.
								Kiveton Park Colliery	Yorks	Mid.	Branch from Killamarsh.
								Sheepbridge Coal and Iron Co.'s Norwood Colliery	Derby	Mid.	Norwood Branch.
								Staveley Coal & Iron Co.'s North Staveley Colliery	Yorks	Mid.	North Staveley Branch.
								West Kiveton Colliery	Derby	Mid.	Branch from Killamarsh.
								Killan Colliery	Glamorg'n	L. & N. W.	Same as Holmes & Co.'s Siding (Dunvant).
G	P	F	L	H	C	5	0	Killarney	Kerry	G. S. & W.	Mallow and Tralee.
G	P		L	H				Killay	Glamorg'n	L. & N. W.	Llandilo and Swansea.
								Richards' Rhydydefed Col.	Glamorg'n	L. & N. W.	Killay and Mumbles Road.
G	P	F	L					Killeagh	Cork	G. S. & W.	Cork and Youghal.
G	P	F	L	H	C	3	0	Killearn	Stirling	N. B.	Lennoxtown and Buchlyvie.
								Killer Bros.' Siding	Derby	L. & N. W.	Cromford.
								Killer's Cromford Moor Sid.	Derby	L. & N. W.	Steeplehouse.
G	P	F	L	H	C	1	10	Killeshandra	Cavan	M. G. W.	Branch from Crossdoney.
G	P	F	L	H	C			Killiecrankie	Perth	High.	Dunkeld and Blair Atholl.
G	P	F	L	H	C	2	0	Killin	Perth	Cal.	Killin Junc. Station and Loch Tay.
								Acharn Siding	Perth	Cal.	Killin and Killin Junction Station.
G								Killin Junction Station	Perth	Cal.	Callander and Oban.
	P							Killiney and Ballybrack	Dublin	D. W. & W.	Kingstown and Bray.
G	P	F	L	H	C	3	0	Killingworth	Northumb	N. E.	Newcastle and Morpeth.
								Burradon Colliery	Northumb	N. E.	Killingworth.
								Dinnington Colliery	Northumb	N. E.	Killingworth.
								Hill Head Manure Siding	Northumb	N. E.	Killingworth.
								Hope Cottage Siding	Northumb	N. E.	Killingworth.
								Killingworth Colliery	Northumb	N. E.	Killingworth.
								Killingworth Saw Mill	Northumb	N. E.	Killingworth.

EXPLANATION—G *Goods Station.*   P *Passenger and Parcel Station.*   P* *Passenger, but not Parcel or Miscellaneous Traffic.*
F *Furniture Vans, Carriages, Portable Engines, and Machines on Wheels.*   L *Live Stock.*
H *Horse Boxes and Prize Cattle Vans.*   C *Carriages by Passenger Train.*

						Tons	Cwts	STATIONS, &c.	COUNTY.	COMPANY.	POSITION.
								Killingworth—*continued.*			
.	.	.	.	.	.	.	.	Scorer's Manure Siding ...	Northumb	N. E.	Killingworth.
.	.	.	.	.	.	.	.	Seaton Burn Colliery	Northumb	N. E.	Killingworth.
G	P	F	L	H	C	3	0	Killochan	Ayr	G. & S.W.	Maybole and Girvan.
.	P	.	.	.	.	.	.	Killonan Junction Station ...	Limerick ..	G. S. & W.	Killaloe and Limerick.
G	P	F	L	H	C	.	.	Killorglin	Kerry	G. S. & W.	Farranfore and Valentia Harbour.
G	P	F	L	H	C	.	.	Killough	Down	B. & C. D.	Downpatrick and Ardglass.
G	P	F	L	.	.	1	10	Killucan	W'meath ..	M. G. W.	Dublin and Mullingar.
G	P	F	L	.	.	.	.	Killumney	Cork	C. & Macroom	Cork and Kilcrea.
G	P	.	L	H	C	.	.	Killurin	Wexford	D. W. & W.	Arklow and Wexford.
G	P	F	L	H	C	3	0	Killybegs	Donegal ..	Donegal	Branch from Stranorlar.
G	P	F	L	H	C	.	.	Killygordon	Donegal ..	Donegal	Strabane and Stranorlar.
G	P	F	L	H	C	.	.	Killylea	Armagh ..	G. N. (I.)	Armagh and Monaghan.
.	P	.	.	.	.	.	.	Killymard	Donegal ..	Donegal	Donegal and Killybegs.
G	P	F	L	H	C	.	.	Killyran (*Book to Bawnboy Road*)	Cavan	C. & L.	Bawnboy Road and Ballinamore.
G	P	.	L	H	.	.	.	Killywhan	Kirkcud ..	G. & S.W.	Dumfries and Castle Douglas.
G	P	.	L	H	C	1	10	Kilmacow	Kilkenny	G. S. & W.	Kilkenny and Waterford.
G	P	F	L	H	C	.	.	Kilmacrenan	Donegal ..	L. & L. S.	Letterkenny and Burtonport.
G	P	F	L	H	.	.	.	Kilmacthomas	Waterford	G. S. & W.	Dungarvan and Waterford.
G	P	F	L	H	C	3	0	Kilmainham Wood	Meath	M. G. W.	Navan and Kingscourt.
G	P	F	L	H	C	.	.	Kilmalcolm	Renfrew ..	G. & S.W.	Paisley and Greenock.
G	P	F	L	H	C	.	.	Kilmallock	Limerick ..	G. S. & W.	Limerick Junction and Charleville.
G	.	F	L	.	.	20	0	KILMARNOCK— (Station)	Ayr	G B & K Jt(Cal & G & SW)	Branch—Kilmaurs & Kilmarnock Jn.
G	P	F	L	H	C	20	0 }	(Station, G. & S.W.)	Ayr	{ G. & S. W.	Dalry and Mauchline.
.	P	.	.	H	C		}			{ G B & K Jt(Cal & G&SW)	Over G. & S. W. from Kilmarnock Jn.
.	.	.	.	.	.	.	.	Barclay's Engineering Wks.	Ayr	G. & S.W.	Kilmarnock.
.	.	.	.	.	.	.	.	Bonnyton Fire-Clay Works	Ayr	G. & S.W.	Kilmarnock and Crosshouse.
.	.	.	.	.	.	.	.	Bonnyton Pit	Ayr	G. & S.W.	Kilmarnock and Crosshouse.
.	.	.	.	.	.	.	.	Britannia Engineering Wks.	Ayr	G. & S.W.	Kilmarnock.
.	.	.	.	.	.	.	.	Brownlie & Co.'s Saw Mills	Ayr	G. & S.W.	Kilmarnock.
.	.	.	.	.	.	.	.	Gas Works	Ayr	G. & S.W.	Kilmarnock.
.	.	.	.	.	.	.	.	Glenfield Works	Ayr	G. & S.W.	Loop Line—Kilmarnock & Gatehead.
.	.	.	.	.	.	.	.	Grange Brick Works	Ayr	G. & S.W.	Kilmarnock and Gatehead.
.	.	.	.	.	.	.	.	Grange Foundry	Ayr	G. & S.W.	Kilmarnock and Gatehead.
.	.	.	.	.	.	.	.	Hillhead Collieries	Ayr	G. & S.W.	Kilmarnock and Crosshouse.
.	.	.	.	.	.	.	.	Hillhead Fire-Clay Works	Ayr	G. & S.W.	Kilmarnock and Crosshouse.
.	.	.	.	.	.	.	.	Junction	Ayr	G. & S.W.	Kilmarnock and Gatehead.
.	.	.	.	.	.	.	.	Junction	Ayr	G. & S.W.—G. B. & K. Jt.	Kilmarnock and Kilmaurs.
.	.	.	.	.	.	.	.	Locomotive Works	Ayr	G. & S.W.	Kilmarnock.
.	.	.	.	.	.	.	.	Paton's Siding	Ayr	G. & S.W.	Kilmarnock.
.	.	.	.	.	.	.	.	Portland Forge Siding	Ayr	G. & S.W.	Kilmarnock.
G	.	F	.	.	.	3	0	Riccarton	Ayr	G. & S.W.	Loop Line—Kilmarnock & Gatehead.
G	.	.	.	.	.	3	0	St. Marnock's Depôt	Ayr	G. & S.W.	Kilmarnock.
G	P	F	L	H	C	2	0	Kilmaurs	Ayr	G B & K Jt(Cal & G & SW)	Kilmarnock and Stewarton.
G	P	.	.	.	.	.	.	Kilmeadan	Waterford	G. S. & W.	Dungarvan and Waterford.
.	.	.	.	.	.	.	.	Kilmersdon Colliery	Somerset..	G. W.	Radstock.
G	P	F	L	H	C	.	.	Kilmessan	Meath	M. G. W.	Dublin and Navan.
G	P	.	L	H	.	.	.	Kilmorna	Kerry	G. S. & W.	Newcastle West and Tralee.
G	P	.	.	.	.	.	.	Kilmurry	Cork	C. & Muskerry.	Coachford Junction and Coachford.
G	P	.	.	.	.	.	.	Kilmurry	Clare	West Clare	Miltown Malbay and Kilkee.
.	.	.	.	.	.	.	.	Kilner & Son's Glass Bottle Works	Yorks	G. N. & L. & Y. Jt.	Wakefield, Kirkgate.
.	.	.	.	.	.	.	.	Kilner's Siding	Yorks	L. & Y.	Thornhill.
.	.	.	.	.	.	.	.	Kilner's Siding	Yorks	N. E.	Same as Castle Howard Sand Co.'s Quarry (Castle Howard).
G	P	F	L	H	C	5	0 }	Kilner's Siding (G. C.)	Yorks	G. C.—Mid.	Conisborough.
G	P	F	L	.	.	4	0 }	Kilnhurst	Yorks	{ G. C. { Mid.	Rotherham and Doncaster. Swinton and Masborough.
.	.	.	.	.	.	.	.	Charlesworth, J. & J., Sids.— Kilnhurst Colliery	Yorks	Mid.	Near Kilnhurst.
.	.	.	.	.	.	.	.	Thrybergh Hall Colliery	Yorks	Mid.	Near Kilnhurst.
.	.	.	.	.	.	.	.	Victoria Colliery	Yorks	Mid.	Near Kilnhurst.
.	.	.	.	.	.	.	.	Ellison & Mitchel's Chemi- cal Works	Yorks	Mid.	Near Kilnhurst.
.	.	.	.	.	.	.	.	Kilnhurst Colliery	Yorks	G. C.	Kilnhurst.
.	.	.	.	.	.	.	.	Sheffield Corporation Sid.	Yorks	G. C.	Kilnhurst.
.	.	.	.	.	.	.	.	Thrybergh Colliery	Yorks	G. C.	Kilnhurst.
.	.	.	.	.	.	.	.	Kilnhurst Colliery	Yorks	{ G. C. { Mid.	Kilnhurst. See Charlesworth's, J. & J. (Kiln- hurst).
.	.	.	.	.	.	.	.	Kilnknowe Junction	Selkirk ...	N. B.	Clovenfords and Galashiels.

EXPLANATION—G *Goods Station.* P *Passenger and Parcel Station.* P* *Passenger, but not Parcel or Miscellaneous Traffic.*
F *Furniture Vans, Carriages, Portable Engines, and Machines on Wheels.* L *Live Stock.*
H *Horse Boxes and Prize Cattle Vans.* C *Carriages by Passenger Train.*

STATION ACCOMMODATION.						CRANE POWER.	STATIONS, &c.	COUNTY.	COMPANY.	POSITION.
						Tons Cwts.				
G			L				Kilnwick Gate	Yorks	N. E.	Beverley and Driffield.
G	P					1 10	Kilpatrick	Dumbartn	N. B.	Dalmuir and Bowling.
							Kilpatrick, Old	Dumbartn	Cal.	See Old Kilpatrick.
							Kilpunt Siding	L'lithgow	N. B.	Ratho.
G	P		L	H		3 0	Kilrea	Derry	N. C. Com. (Mid.)	Macfin Junction and Magherafelt.
G	P		L				Kilroot	Antrim ...	N. C. Com. (Mid.)	Carrickfergus and Whitehead.
G	P	F	L				Kilrush	Clare	West Clare	Branch from Moyasta Junction.
G	P	F	L	H	C	10 0	Kilsby and Crick	N'hamptn	L. & N. W.	Northampton and Rugby.
G	P		L	H			Kilsheelan	Tipperary	G. S. & W.	Clonmel and Waterford.
							KILSYTH—			
G	P*	F	L	H	C	1 10	(Station, N. B.)	Stirling ...	{ N. B. .... ; K. & B. Jt. (Cal. & N.B.)	Branch from Kilsyth Junction. ; Over N. B. from Kilsyth Junction.
							Barwood Siding	Stirling ...	K. & B. Jt. (Cal. & N. B.)	Kilsyth, New and Colzium.
							Gas Works	Stirling ...	K. & B. Jt.—N. B.	Near Kilsyth.
							Haugh Colliery	Stirling ...	K. & B. Jt.—N. B.	Near Kilsyth.
							Haugh Colliery and Coking Ovens	Stirling ...	K. & B. Jt.—N. B.	Near Kilsyth.
							Haughrigg Colliery	Stirling ...	K. & B. Jt. (Cal. & N. B.)	Kilsyth.
							Junction	Stirling ...	K. & B. Jt.—N. B.	Kilsyth, New and Gavell.
	P						New Station	Stirling ...	K. & B. Jt. (Cal. & N. B.)	Gavell and Colzium.
							Young's Coal Depôt	Stirling ...	K. & B. Jt. (Cal. & N. B.)	Kilsyth, New.
G	P	F	L	H	C	3 0	Kiltimagh	Mayo......	G. S. & W.	Collooney and Claremorris.
							Kilton Ironstone Mines	Yorks	N. E.	Brotton.
							Kilton Thorpe Depôts	Yorks	N. E.	Brotton.
	P						Kiltoom	Roscom'n	M. G. W.	Athlone and Claremorris.
G	P						Kiltubrid (Book to Drumshambo)	Leitrim ...	C. & L.	Ballinamore and Drumshambo.
G							Kilvert, N., & Sons' Siding	Lancs	Trafford Park Estate.....	Manchester.
G							Kilwaughter Siding	Antrim ...	N. C. Com. (Mid.)	Larne and Ballyboley.
G	P	F	L	H	C	4 0 }	Kilwinning	Ayr	{ Cal. ; G. & S. W.	Giffen and Ardrossan. ; Dalry and Irvine.
G	P	F	L	H	C	6 0 }				
							Bartonholme Lye	Ayr	Cal.	Kilwinning and Irvine.
							Bartonholm, No. 1	Ayr	G. & S.W.	Eglinton Iron Works.
							Bogend Pit	Ayr	Cal.	Kilwinning.
							Bogend Siding	Ayr	G. & S.W.	Doura Branch.
							Bogside Colliery...............	Ayr	Cal.	Kilwinning and Irvine.
							Bogside Pit	Ayr	G. & S.W.	Eglinton Iron Works.
							Clonbeith Quarry (Eglinton Quarry).........................	Ayr	G. & S.W.	Doura Branch.
							Dirran's Saw Mill	Ayr	{ Cal. ; G. & S. W.	Kilwinning and Irvine. ; Doura Branch.
							Dirran's Siding	Ayr	G. & S.W.	Doura Branch.
							Doura Fire-Clay Works ...	Ayr	G. & S.W.	Doura Branch.
							Eglinton Ammonia Wks.	Ayr	Cal.	Kilwinning and Irvine.
							Eglinton Fire-Clay Works (Kenneth's)	Ayr	G. & S.W.	Doura Branch.
							Eglinton Foundry(Howie's)	Ayr	G. & S.W.	Kilwinning.
							Eglinton Iron Works	Ayr	{ Cal. ; G. & S. W.	Kilwinning and Irvine. ; Doura Branch.
							Eglinton Ir. Wks. & Cols.	Ayr	Cal.—G. & S. W.	Kilwinning and Irvine.
							Eglinton, No. 1	Ayr	G. & S.W.	Eglinton Iron Works.
							Fergushill, No. 17	Ayr	G. & S.W.	Doura Branch.
							Fergushill, No. 22	Ayr	G. & S.W.	Doura Branch.
							Fergushill, Nos. 23 & 28 ...	Ayr	G. & S.W.	Doura Branch.
							Fergushill, Nos. 26, 29, & 30	Ayr	G. & S.W.	Kilwinning.
							Hendry's Siding...............	Ayr	{ Cal. ; G. & S. W.	Kilwinning and Irvine. ; Eglinton Iron Works.
							Ladyha' Pit	Ayr	G. & S.W.	Kilwinning and Irvine.
							Longford Chemical Works (Scottish Acid & Alkali Co.'s Works)	Ayr	{ Cal. ; G. & S. W.	Branch—Byrehill Jn. & Dubbs Jn.
							Misk Pit	Ayr	{ Cal. ; G. & S. W.	Kilwinning and Irvine. ; Eglinton Iron Works.
							Morgan's Siding...............	Ayr	Cal.	Kilwinning.
							Redburn Pits	Ayr	{ Cal. ; G. & S. W.	Kilwinning and Irvine. ; Eglinton Iron Works.
G	P						Kimberley	Norfolk ...	G. E.	Wymondham and Dereham.
G	P	F	L	H	C	10 0 }	Kimberley	Notts	{ G. N. ; Mid.	Nottingham and Ilkeston. ; Ilkeston Junction and Watnall.
G	P	F	L	H	C	1 10 }				
							Digby Colliery (G. N.)......	Notts	G. N.—G. C.	Kimberley and Newthorpe.
							Giltbrook Chemical Works (Nottingham Corporation Siding)	Notts	G. N.	Kimberley and Newthorpe.

STATION ACCOMMODATION.						CRANE POWER.	STATIONS, &c.	COUNTY.	COMPANY.	POSITION.
						Tons Cwts.	Kimberley—*continued.*			
.	.	.	.	.	.	. .	Hanson's Brewery............	Notts	Mid.	Near Kimberley.
.	.	.	.	.	.	. .	Hardy's Brewery............	Notts	Mid.	Near Kimberley.
.	.	.	.	.	.	. .	Lodge Colliery Siding	Notts	G. N.	Kimberley and Newthorpe.
.	.	.	.	.	.	. .	Watnall Colliery (G. N.) ...	Notts	G. N.—G. C.	Basford and Kimberley.
.	.	.	.	.	.	. .	Kimberley Colliery	Notts	Mid.	Nottingham, Basford.
G	P	F	L	H	C	1 10	Kimblesworth Colliery........	Durham ...	N. E.	Plawsworth.
							Kimbolton	Beds	Mid.	Huntingdon and Thrapston.
.	.	.	.	.	.	. .	Kimbridge Junction	Hants	L. & S.W.	Dunbridge.
.	.	.	.	.	.	. .	Kimmins & Co.'s Siding	Glo'ster ...	Mid.	See Huntingford Mills (Charfield).
.	.	.	.	.	.	. .	Kimmins, Drew & Co.'s Sid..	Glo'ster ...	Mid.	Dudbridge.
G	P	.	L	H	.	2 0	Kinaldie	Aberdeen ...	G. N. of S.	Aberdeen and Kintore.
G	P	F	L	H	C	. .	Kinbrace	Sutherl'nd	High.	Helmsdale and Wick.
G	P	.	L	H	.	3 0	Kinbuck	Perth	Cal.	Stirling and Perth.
G	.	.	.	.	.	3 0	Ashfield Siding	Perth	Cal.	Dunblane and Kinbuck.
.	.	.	.	.	.	. .	Kinbuck Sand Pit	Perth	Cal.	Kinbuck.
.	.	.	.	.	.	. .	Kincaid Print Works	Stirling ...	N. B.	Milton.
.	.	.	.	.	.	. .	Kincaid's Siding	Renfrew ...	Cal.	Greenock, Regent Street.
G	P	.	L	H	.	1 10	Kincardine	Fife	N. B.	Branch from Kincardine Bch. Junc.
.	.	.	.	.	.	. .	Hawkhill Siding	Fife	N. B.	Kilbagie and Kincardine.
.	.	.	.	.	.	. .	Kincardine Branch Junction	Clackman'	N. B.	Alloa and Clackmannan.
G	P	F	L	H	C	2 0	Kincraig	Inverness	High.	Kingussie and Boat of Garten.
.	.	.	.	.	.	. .	Kincraig Siding (Cal.)	Forfar	Cal.—N. B.	See Brechin.
.	.	.	.	.	.	. .	Kinds Siding (L. & N. W.)..	Staffs	L&NW—Mid—GN—NS	Burton-on-Trent.
G	P	F	L	H	C	2 0	Kineton	Warwick ...	E. & W. Jn.	Fenny Compton and Stratford-on-Avon.
G	P	.	L	H	.	2 0	Burton Dassett Siding	Warwick ...	E. & W. Jn.	Kineton and Fenny Compton.
.	.	.	.	.	.	. .	Kinfauns	Perth	Cal.	Perth and Dundee.
.	.	.	.	.	.	. .	King & Son's Siding	Essex	G. E.	Harold Wood.
.	.	.	.	.	.	. .	King & Son's Siding	Lancs	L. & N. W.	Garston Docks.
G	P	.	L	H	.	. .	King Bros.' Siding	Worcester	G. W.	Cradley Heath and Cradley.
G	P	F	L	H	C	1 10	King-Edward	Aberdeen	G. N. of S.	Inveramsay and Macduff.
G	P	F	L	H	C	0 15	Kingennie	Forfar	Cal.	Dundee and Forfar.
.	.	.	.	.	.	. .	Kingennie Manure Siding ..	Forfar	Cal.	Kingennie.
G	P	F	L	H	C	. .	Kinghorn	Fife	N. B.	Burntisland and Kirkcaldy.
.	.	.	.	.	.	. .	Abden Ship Yard	Fife	N. B.	Near Kinghorn.
.	.	.	.	.	.	. .	Kingmoor Sidings...........	Cumb'land	N. B.	Harker.
.	.	.	.	.	.	. .	Kingoodie Siding	Perth	Cal.	Invergowrie.
G	P	F	L	H	C	1 0	Kingsbarns	Fife	N. B.	Anstruther and St. Andrews.
G	P	F	L	H	C	6 0	Kingsbridge	Devon	G. W.	Branch from Brent Junction.
G	P	.	.	.	.	. .	Kingsbridge	Dublin ...	G. S. & W.	See Dublin.
.	.	.	.	.	.	. .	Kingsbury	Warwick..	Mid.	Birmingham and Tamworth.
.	.	.	.	.	.	. .	Baddesley (Baxterley Park) Colliery	Warwick..	Mid.	Kingsbury Branch.
.	.	.	.	.	.	. .	Birch Coppice Colliery (Morris & Shaw's)	Warwick..	Mid.	Kingsbury Branch.
.	.	.	.	.	.	. .	Kingsbury Col. (Hockley Hall & Whateley Col. Co.)	Warwick..	Mid.	Kingsbury and Wilnecote.
.	.	.	.	.	.	. .	New Kingsbury Collieries	Warwick..	Mid.	Kingsbury.
G	P	F	L	H	C	10 0	Kingsbury-Neasden	Middlesex	Met.	See London.
.	P	.	.	H	C	. .	Kingscliffe (L. & N. W.) ...	N'hamptn	{ L. & N. W. .... \\ { G. N.	Market Harboro' and Peterboro'. \\ Over L. & N. W. from Longville Jn.
G	P	F	L	H	C	10 0	Kingscote	Sussex ...	L. B. & S. C.	East Grinstead and West Hoathly.
G	P	F	L	H	C	5 0	Kingscourt	Cavan	M. G. W.	Branch from Navan.
.	.	.	.	.	.	. .	King's Cross	Middlesex	G. N.—Met.—Mid.—G W —S. E. & C.	See London.
.	.	.	.	.	.	. .	King's Cross Junction	Middlesex	Met.—Mid.	London, King's Cross & Kentish Town
.	.	.	.	.	.	. .	King's Cross Junctions........	Middlesex	G. N.—Met.	London, King's Cross, York Road and King's Cross (Met.)
.	.	.	.	.	.	. .	King's Dyke Sidings............	Cambs ...	G. E.	Whittlesea.
.	.	.	.	.	.	. .	Kingseat Colliery	Fife	N. B.	Kelty.
G	P	.	.	.	.	. .	King's Heath	Worcester	Mid.	Camp Hill and Lifford.
.	P	.	.	.	.	. .	Kingshouse	Perth	Cal.	Callander and Oban.
.	.	.	.	.	.	. .	King's House Engine Works and Foundry...........	Durham ...	N. E.	Pallion.
.	.	.	.	.	.	. .	King's House Landsale Depôt	Durham ...	N. E.	Pallion.
.	.	.	.	.	.	. .	King's Inch	Renfrew ...	G.&P.Jt.(Cal.&G.&S.W.)	See Renfrew.
.	.	.	.	.	.	. .	Kings, J., & Co.'s Siding......	Worcester	G. W.	Cradley Heath and Cradley.
G	P	.	.	.	.	. .	Kingskerswell	Devon	G. W.	Newton Abbot and Torre.
.	.	.	.	.	.	. .	Aller Siding	Devon	G. W.	Newton Abbot and Torre.
G	P	.	.	.	.	0 15	Kingskettle	Fife	N. B.	Thornton and Ladybank.
.	.	.	.	.	.	. .	Arthurfield Siding............	Fife	N. B.	Near Kingskettle.

EXPLANATION—**G** *Goods Station.*   **P** *Passenger and Parcel Station.*   **P*** *Passenger, but not Parcel or Miscellaneous Traffic.*
F *Furniture Vans, Carriages, Portable Engines, and Machines on Wheels.*   **L** *Live Stock.*
H *Horse Boxes and Prize Cattle Vans.*   **C** *Carriages by Passenger Train.*

STATION ACCOMMODATION.						CRANE POWER.		STATIONS, &c.	COUNTY.	COMPANY.	POSITION.
						Tons	Cwts.				
G	P	.	.	.	.			Kingsknowe	Edinboro'	Cal.	Edinburgh and Midcalder.
								Kingsknowe Stone Depôt ...	Edinboro'	Cal.	Slateford.
G	P	F	L	H	C	1	10	Kingsland	Hereford ..	G. W.	Leominster and Kington.
								Kingsland	Middlesex	L. & N. W.	See London.
.	.	.	.	.	.			Kingsland Road	Glo'ster ...	G. W.	See Bristol.
G	P	.	.	.	.	3	0	King's Langley	Herts	L. & N. W.	Bletchley and Watford.
.	.	.	.	.	.			King's Lynn (G. E.)	Norfolk ...	G. E.—M'd. & G. N. Jt..	See Lynn.
.	.	.	.	.	.			King's Meads Siding	Herts	G. N.	Hertford.
.	.	.	.	.	.			King's Mill Siding	Denbigh..	Cam.	See Wrexham.
.	.	.	.	.	.			King's Mill Sid. (Caudwell's)	Notts	Mid.	{ Mansfield. { Sutton-in-Ashfield.
G	P	.	L	H	.			Kingsmuir	Forfar	Cal.	Dundee and Forfar.
G	P	.	L	H	C	1	10	King's Norton	Worcester	Mid.	Birmingham and Bromsgrove.
.	.	.	.	.	.			King's Norton Metal Co.'s Sid	Worcester	Mid.	Lifford.
.	.	.	.	.	.			King's Blisworth & Stowe Brick and Tile Works	N'hamptn	L. & N. W.	See Gayton Sidings (Blisworth).
.	.	.	.	.	.			King's Street Coal Sids. (L&Y)	Lancs	L. & Y.—L. & N. W.	Blackburn.
G	P	.	.	H	.			King's Sutton	N'hamptn	G. W.	Banbury and Oxford.
.	.	.	.	.	.			Astrop Sid.(Sir A. Hickman)	N'hamptn	G. W.	King's Sutton.
G	P	F	L	H	C	5	0	Kingston	Surrey	L. & S. W.	Wimbledon and Twickenham.
.	.	.	.	.	.			Anglo-American Oil Co.'s Depôt	Surrey	L. & S. W.	Kingston.
.	.	.	.	.	.			Kingston Gas Co.'s Siding	Surrey ...	L. & S. W.	Kingston.
.	.	.	.	.	.			Kingston Dock (Cal.)	Lanark ...	Cal.—G. & S. W.—N. B.	See Glasgow.
.	.	.	.	.	.			Kingston Hill	Surrey ...	L. & S. W.	See Norbiton and Kingston Hill.
.	P	.	.	.	.			Kingston Road	Somerset..	W. C. & P.	Weston-super-Mare and Clevedon.
.	.	.	.	.	.			Kingston Street	Yorks	G. C.	See Hull.
.	.	.	.	.	.			Kingston Street (N. E.)	Yorks	N. E.—L. & Y.—L. & N. W.	See Hull.
G	.	.	.	.	.	6	0	Kingston Wharf	Sussex	L. B. & S. C.	Brighton and Worthing.
.	.	.	.	.	.			Beves & Co.'s Siding	Sussex	L. B. & S. C.	Kingston Wharf.
.	.	.	.	.	.			Kingston Yard	Renfrew..	Cal.	Greenock, Bogston.
G	P	.	.	.	.			Kingstown	Dublin	D. W. & W.	Dublin, Westland Row and Bray.
.	P	.	.	.	.			Kingstown Pier	Dublin	L. & N. W.	Steamer from Holyhead.
.	.	.	.	.	.			King Street Depôt	Renfrew..	G. & S. W.	See Paisley.
.	.	.	.	.	.			King Street Junction	Armagh	G. N. (I.)	Newry.
G	P	F	L	H	C	2	0	Kingswear	Devon	G. W.	Branch from Newton Abbot.
.	.	.	.	.	.	3	0	Kingswear Wharves	Devon	G. W.	Kingswear.
.	.	.	.	.	.			Kingswinford Branch	Staffs	G. W.	Brettell Lane.
.	.	.	.	.	.			Kingswinford Junction	Staffs	G. W.	Brettell Lane.
G	P	.	.	.	.			Kingswood and Burgh Heath	Surrey	S. E. & C.	Purley and Tattenham Corner.
.	.	.	.	.	.			Kingswood Col.(Peckett&Son)	Glo'ster	Mid.	Bristol, Fishponds.
G	P	.	.	.	.			Kingthorpe	Lincoln	G. N.	Lincoln and Louth.
G	P	F	L	H	C	1	10	Kington	Hereford..	G. W.	Leominster and New Radnor.
G	P	F	L	H	C	3	0	Kingussie	Inverness..	High.	Blair Atholl and Boat of Garten.
G	.	.	.	.	.	5	0	King William	Lancs	L. & Y.	Bromley Cross and Turton.
.	.	.	.	.	.			King William Dock	Forfar	Cal.—N. B.	See Dundee.
.	.	.	.	.	.			Kinleith Siding	Edinboro'	Cal.	See Currie.
.	.	.	.	.	.			Kinlett Siding	Salop	G. W.	Highley.
G	P	F	L	H	C	2	0	Kinloss	Elgin&Mo'	High.	Forres and Elgin.
.	.	.	.	.	.			Kinnaber Junction	Forfar	Cal.—N. B.	Stonehaven and Montrose.
.	.	.	.	.	.			Kinnaber Junction Sidings..	Forfar	N. B.	Hillside.
.	.	.	.	.	.			Kinnaird Colliery, No. 1	Kinross ...	N. B.	Kelty.
.	.	.	.	.	.			Kinnaird Siding	Perth	Cal.	Inchture.
.	.	.	.	.	.			Kinnaird Siding (N. B.)	Stirling ...	N. B.—Cal.	Falkirk, Grahamston.
.	.	.	.	.	.			Kinnear, Moodie & Co.'s Stone Sidings	Edinboro'	Cal.	Edinburgh, Lothian Road.
G	P	.	L	H	.			Kinnersley	Hereford ..	Mid.	Hereford and Hay.
G	P	.	L	.	.			Kinnerton	Flint	L. & N. W.	Chester and Rhyl.
.	.	.	.	.	.			Kinnerton Incline Siding....	Flint	L. & N. W.	Same as Dodd's Siding (Hope).
.	P	.	.	.	.			Kinniel	L'lithgow	N. B.	Causewayend and Bo'ness.
.	.	.	.	.	.			Kinniel Colliery	L'lithgow	N. B.	Bo'ness.
.	.	.	.	.	.			Kinniel Weighs	L'lithgow	N. B.	Causewayend and Bo'ness.
.	.	.	.	.	.			Kinning Park	Renfrew..	Cal.—Glas. Dist. Sub.	See Glasgow.
.	.	.	.	.	.			Kinning Park Saw Mill	Renfrew..	Cal.	Glasgow, Kinning Park.
.	.	.	.	.	.			Kinross Junction	Kinross	N. B.	Milnathort and Balado.
.	P	.	L	H	C			Kinross Junction Station	Kinross	N. B.	Loch Leven and Milnathort.
G	P	F	L	H	C	4	0	Kinsale	Cork	C. B. & S. C.	Branch from Kinsale Junc. Station.
G	P	.	.	.	.			Kinsale Junction Station	Cork	C. B. & S. C.	Ballinhassig and Upton.
.	P	.	.	.	.			Kinson Pottery Co.'s Siding..	Dorset	L. & S.W.	Hamworthy Junction.
G	P	F	L	H	C	1	0	Kintbury	Berks	G. W.	Newbury and Hungerford.
G	P	F	L	H	C	3	0	Kintore	Aberdeen	G. N. of S.	Aberdeen and Inveramsay.
.	.	.	.	.	.			Ratchill Siding	Aberdeen	G. N. of S.	Kintore and Kenmay.

EXPLANATION—G *Goods Station.*   P *Passenger and Parcel Station.*   P* *Passenger, but not Parcel or Miscellaneous Traffic.*
F *Furniture Vans, Carriages, Portable Engines, and Machines on Wheels.*   L *Live Stock.*
H *Horse Boxes and Prize Cattle Vans.*   C *Carriages by Passenger Train.*

STATION ACCOMMODATION.						CRANE POWER.		STATIONS, &c.	COUNTY.	COMPANY.	POSITION.
						Tons	Cwts.				
G	P	F	L	H	C	2	0	Kipling Cotes	Yorks	N. E.	Market Weighton and Beverley.
G	P	F	L	H	C	2	0	Kippax	Yorks	N. E.	Leeds and Castleford.
.	.	.	.	.	.	.	.	Bower's Colliery (Allerton Main Colliery)	Yorks	N. E.	Kippax.
.	.	.	.	.	.	.	.	Locke & Co.'s Col. (Allerton Haigh Moor Colliery)	Yorks	N. E.	Kippax.
.	.	.	.	.	.	.	.	Medhurst Coal & Sand Sid.	Yorks	N. E.	Kippax.
G	P	.	L	H	C	3	0	Kippen	Stirling	N. B.	Stirling and Balloch.
.	.	.	.	.	.	.	.	Fairfield Siding	Stirling	N. B.	Kippen and Port of Monteith.
.	.	.	.	.	.	.	.	Kippielaw Siding	Edinboro'	N. B.	Hardengreen.
.	.	.	.	.	.	.	.	Kipps Brick Works	Lanark	N. B.	Greengairs.
.	.	.	.	.	.	.	.	Kipps Byre Colliery	Lanark	N. B.	Coatbridge, Sunnyside.
.	.	.	.	.	.	.	.	Kipps Junction	Lanark	N. B.	Coatbridge, Sunnyside & Greengairs.
.	.	.	.	.	.	.	.	Kipps Quarry	Lanark	N. B.	Greengairs.
.	.	.	.	.	.	.	.	Kipps Sidings	Lanark	N. B.	Coatbridge, Sunnyside.
.	.	.	.	.	.	.	.	Kip Siding	Durham	N. E.	Washington.
G	P	F	.	H	C	.	.	Kirby Cross	Essex	G. E.	Colchester and Walton-on-the-Naze.
G	P	F	L	H	C	3	0	Kirbymoorside	Yorks	N. E.	Helmsley and Pickering.
G	P	.	.	.	.	.	.	Kirby Muxloe	Leicester	Mid.	Leicester and Burton.
.	.	.	.	.	.	.	.	Healey's Siding	Leicester	Mid.	Kirby Muxloe.
G	P	.	.	.	.	.	.	Kirby Park	Cheshire	B'head Jt. (GW&L.N.W.)	Hooton and West Kirby.
.	P	.	.	.	.	.	.	Kirkandrews	Cumb'land	N. B.	Carlisle and Silloth.
.	.	.	.	.	.	.	.	Grinsdale Bridge Siding	Cumb'land	N. B.	Carlisle and Kirkandrews.
G	P	.	L	H	.	1	10	Kirkbank	Roxburgh	N. B.	Roxburgh and Jedburgh.
G	P	.	L	H	.	.	.	Kirkbride	Cumb'land	N. B.	Carlisle and Silloth.
.	.	.	.	.	.	.	.	Carlisle Farmers Manure Co.'s Siding	Cumb'land	N. B.	Drumburgh and Kirkbride.
.	.	.	.	.	.	.	.	Whitem's Sid.(Gould & Co.)	Cumb'land	N. B.	Drumburgh and Kirkbride.
.	.	.	.	.	.	.	.	Kirkbride Junction	Cumb'land	Cal.—N.B.	Silloth and Abbey Junction.
.	.	.	.	.	.	.	.	Kirk Bros.' & Co.— Marsh Sidings	Cumb'land	L. & N. W.	Workington.
.	.	.	.	.	.	.	.	New Yard Iron Works	Cumb'land	L. & N. W.	Workington.
G	P	.	L	H	.	1	10	Kirkbuddo	Forfar	Cal.	Dundee and Forfar.
G	P	F	L	H	C	1	5	Kirkburton	Yorks	L. & N. W.	Branch from Huddersfield.
.	.	.	.	.	.	.	.	Linfit Lane Coal Co.'s Sid.	Yorks	L. & N. W.	Kirkburton and Fenay Bridge.
G	P	.	L	H	.	1	0	Kirkby	Lancs	Furness	Barrow and Foxfield.
.	.	.	.	.	.	.	.	Burlington Slate Quarries	Lancs	Furness	Near Kirkby Station.
.	.	.	.	.	.	.	.	Dunnerholme Siding	Lancs	Furness	Kirkby and Askam.
G	P	.	L	H	.	5	0	Kirkby	Lancs	L. & Y.	Liverpool and Wigan.
.	.	.	.	.	.	.	.	Simonswood Siding	Lancs	L. & Y.	Rainford Junction and Kirkby.
G	P	F	L	H	C	1	10	Kirkby and Pinxton (G. C.)	Notts	G. C.	Chesterfield and Nottingham.
G	.	F	L	.	.	1	10			L. & N. W.	Over G. N. and G. C. Lines.
.	.	.	.	.	.	.	.	Bentinck Colliery (G. C.)	Notts	G. C.—G.N.—L. & N. W.	Kirkby and Pinxton.
.	.	.	.	.	.	.	.	Kirkby and Pinxton Local Board Siding	Notts	G. C.	Kirkby and Pinxton.
.	.	.	.	.	.	.	.	Langton Colliery (G. C.)	Notts	G. C.—G.N.—L. & N. W.	Kirkby and Pinxton.
.	.	.	.	.	.	.	.	New Hucknall Col. (G. C.)	Derby	G. C.—G.N.—L. & N. W.	Kirkby and Pinxton.
.	.	.	.	.	.	.	.	Pinxton Colliery (G.C.)	Derby	G. C.—L. & N. W.	Kirkby and Pinxton.
.	.	.	.	.	.	.	.	South Normanton Col.(G.C.)	Derby	G. C.—G.N.—L. & N. W.	Kirkby and Pinxton.
.	.	.	.	.	.	.	.	Winning B. Colliery (Blackwell Colliery) (G. C.)	Derby	G. C.—G.N.—L. & N. W.	Kirkby and Pinxton.
.	.	.	.	.	.	.	.	Kirkby Colliery	Notts	Mid.	Same as Butterley Co.'s New Colliery (Kirkby-in-Ashfield).
.	.	.	.	.	.	.	.	Kirkby Col.(Summit Pit)(GN)	Notts	G. N.—G.C.—L.D.&E.C.	Sutton-in-Ashfield.
G	P	.	.	.	.	.	.	Kirkby-in-Ashfield	Notts	Mid.	Nottingham and Mansfield.
.	.	.	.	.	.	.	.	Butterley Co.'s— Brickyard	Notts	Mid.	Kirkby Junction.
.	.	.	.	.	.	.	.	New Col. (Kirkby Col.)	Notts	Mid.	Kirkby and Sutton.
.	.	.	.	.	.	.	.	Sand Siding	Notts	Mid.	Kirkby and Sutton.
G	P	F	L	H	C	5	0	Kirkby Lonsdale	Lancs	L. & N. W.	Ingleton and Low Gill.
.	.	.	.	.	.	.	.	Kirkby, North Junction	Notts	G. C.—G. N.	Kirkby and Sutton-in-Ashfield.
.	.	.	.	.	.	.	.	Kirkby Siding	Notts	G. N.	See Sutton-in-Ashfield.
.	.	.	.	.	.	.	.	Kirkby, South Junction	Notts	G. C.—G. N.	Hucknall Town and Sutton-in-Ashfield.
G	P	F	L	H	C	5	0	Kirkby Stephen	W'morlnd.	N. E.	Barnard Castle and Tebay.
G	P	F	L	H	C	1	10	Kirkby Stephen and Ravenstonedale	W'morlnd.	Mid.	Settle and Appleby.
G	P	F	L	H	C	3	0	Kirkby Thore	W'morlnd	N. E.	Appleby and Penrith.
G	P	F	L	H	C	6	0	KIRKCALDY— (Station)	Fife	N. B.	Burntisland and Thornton.
.	.	.	.	.	.	.	.	Barry, Ostlere, and Shepherd's Siding	Fife	N. B.	Kirkcaldy.

EXPLANATION—G *Goods Station.*   P *Passenger and Parcel Station.*   P* *Passenger, but not Parcel or Miscellaneous Traffic.*
F *Furniture Vans, Carriages, Portable Engines, and Machines on Wheels.*   L *Live Stock.*
H *Horse Boxes and Prize Cattle Vans.*   C *Carriages by Passenger Train.*

STATION ACCOMMODATION.						CRANE POWER.		STATIONS, &c.	COUNTY.	COMPANY.	POSITION.
						Tons	Cwts.	**KIRKCALDY**—continued.			
								Dunnikier Col. (Panny Pit)	Fife	N. B.	Branch from Sinclairtown.
								Dunnikier Foundry	Fife	N. B.	Kirkcaldy and Sinclairtown.
								Fraser Junctions Siding	Fife	N. B.	Sinclairtown.
G						18	0	Harbour	Fife	N. B.	Bch. fr. Kirkcaldy Harbour Bch. Jn.
								Harbour Branch Junction	Fife	N. B.	Kirkcaldy and Sinclairtown.
G								Harbour Sidings	Fife	N. B.	Bch. fr. Kirkcaldy Harbour Bch. Jn.
								Hutchison & Co.—			
								Flour Mills	Fife	N. B.	Bch. fr. Kirkcaldy Harbour Bch. Jn.
								Maltings	Fife	N. B.	Bch. fr. Kirkcaldy Harbour Bch. Jn.
								Ingleside Foundry (Fife Forge Co.)	Fife	N. B.	Dunnikier Colliery.
								Invertiel Siding	Fife	N. B.	Kinghorn and Kirkcaldy.
G	P	F	L	H	C	5	0	Sinclairtown	Fife	N. B.	Kirkcaldy and Thornton.
								Victoria Maltings	Fife	N. B.	Kirkcaldy Harbour Branch.
								Victoria Siding	Fife	N. B.	Kirkcaldy Harbour Branch.
								Whitebank Sid. (M'Intosh & Co.'s Cabinet Works)	Fife	N. B.	Top of Kirkcaldy Harbour Branch.
G	P	F	L	H	C	1	10	Kirkconnel	Dumfries	G. & S.W.	New Cumnock and Thornhill.
								Fauldhead Pit	Dumfries	G. & S.W.	Kirkconnel.
								Gateside Pit	Dumfries	G. & S.W.	Kirkconnel and Sanquhar.
G	P	F	L	H	C	1	0	Kirkcowan	Wigtown	P.P.&W.Jt.(Cal.,G&SW, L. & N. W., & Mid.)	Stranraer and Newton Stewart.
G	P	F	L	H	C	5	0	Kirkcudbright	Kirkcud	G. & S.W.	Branch from Castle Douglas.
								Kirkcudbright Branch Junc.	Kirkcud	G. & S.W.	Castle Douglas.
								Kirkdale	Lancs	L. & Y.	See Liverpool.
								Kirk Ella	Yorks	H. & B.	See Willerby and Kirk Ella.
								Kirk Ella Lime Works	Yorks	H. & B.	Willerby and Kirk Ella.
								Kirkford Colliery	Fife	N. B.	Cowdenbeath, Old.
								Kirkgate (G. N. & L. & Y. Jt)	Yorks	GN & L & Y Jt—L & NW	See Wakefield.
G	P	F	L	H	C			Kirkgunzeon	Kirkcud	G. & S.W.	Dumfries and Dalbeattie.
G	P	F	L	H	C	5	0	Kirkham	Lancs	P&W Jt(L&Y&L&NW)	Fleetwood and Preston.
								Derby's (Earl of), Treals Sid.	Lancs	P&W Jt(L&Y & L&NW)	Kirkham and Salwick.
								Moss', T., Siding	Lancs	P&W Jt(L&Y & L&NW)	Kirkham and Singleton.
								Porritt & Son's Siding	Lancs	P&W Jt(L&Y&L&NW)	Kirkham and Wrea Green.
								Richards, Boulder & Co.'s Wesham Mill	Lancs	P&W Jt(L&Y&L&NW)	Kirkham and Singleton.
								Rigby & Holmes' Blainscough Hall Siding	Lancs	P&W Jt (L&Y&L&NW)	Kirkham and Wrea Green.
G	P	F	L	H	C	5	0	Kirkham Abbey	Yorks	N. E.	York and Malton.
								Kirkheaton	Yorks	L. & N. W.	See Huddersfield.
G		F	L			3	0	Kirkhill	Lanark	Cal.	Newton and Cathcart.
								Kirkhill Colliery and Brick Works (Chapel Siding)	Lanark	Cal.	Cambuslang.
								Kirkhouse Branch Junction	Northumb	N. E.	Lambley.
								Kirkhouse Collieries (Naworth Collieries)	Cumb'land	N. E.	Brampton Junction Station.
								Kirkhouse Dutch Barn Factory and Saw Mills	Cumb'land	N. E.	{ Brampton Junction Station. { Lambley.
								Kirkhouse Siding	Cumb'land	N. E.	{ Brampton Junction Station. { Lambley.
G	P		L	H				Kirkinner	Wigtown	P.P.&W.Jt.(Cal.,G&SW, L. & N. W., & Mid.)	Newton Stewart and Whithorn.
G	P	F	L	H		3	0	Kirkintilloch	Dumbartn	N. B.	Lenzie Junction and Lennoxtown.
								Inchbelly Sand Siding	Stirling	N. B.	Kirkintilloch and Gavell.
								Kelvin Valley East Jn. Sids.	Stirling	N. B.	Kirkintilloch and Gavell.
								Kirkintilloch Gas Works	Dumbartn	N. B.	Kirkintilloch.
								Lion Foundry	Dumbartn	N. B.	Kirkintilloch.
								Meiklehill Colliery	Dumbartn	N. B.	Branch from Kirkintilloch.
								Meiklehill Siding	Dumbartn	N. B.	Meiklehill Colliery Branch.
								Middlemuir Junc. Siding	Dumbartn	N. B.	Lenzie Junction and Kirkintilloch.
								Old Foundry (M'Neill's Slag Wool Siding)	Dumbartn	N. B.	Kirkintilloch.
								Woodilee Colliery	Dumbartn	N. B.	Lenzie Junction and Kirkintilloch.
G						3	0	Kirkintilloch Basin	Dumbartn	N. B.	Terminus—Coatbridge and Kirkintilloch Line.
								Basin Foundry	Dumbartn	N. B.	Kirkintilloch Basin.
								Basin Saw Mills	Dumbartn	N. B.	Kirkintilloch Basin.
								Jetty Sid. (Shipment Sid.)	Dumbartn	N. B.	Kirkintilloch Basin.
								Nickel Co.'s Siding	Dumbartn	N. B.	Kirkintilloch Basin.
								South Bank Iron Works	Dumbartn	N. B.	Kirkintilloch Basin.
								Kirk, Knight & Co.'s Siding	Lincoln	G. N.	Sleaford.

EXPLANATION—G *Goods Station.*   P *Passenger and Parcel Station.*   P* *Passenger, but not Parcel or Miscellaneous Traffic.*
F *Furniture Vans, Carriages, Portable Engines, and Machines on Wheels.*   L *Live Stock.*
H *Horse Boxes and Prize Cattle Vans.*   C *Carriages by Passenger Train.*

STATION ACCOMMODATION.						CRANE POWER.		STATIONS, &c.	COUNTY.	COMPANY.	POSITION.
						Tons	Cwts				
.	.	.	.	.	.	.	.	Kirkland Siding..............	Cumb'land	R. & K. F.	Rowrah Junction and Kelton Fell.
.	.	.	.	.	.	.	.	Kirkland Sid(CyanideCo'sSid)	Fife	N. B.	Leven.
.	.	.	.	.	.	.	.	Kirklee	Lanark	Cal.	See Glasgow.
.	.	.	.	.	.	.	.	Kirkless Hall Coal & Iron Sids.	Lancs	L. & Y.	See Wigan Coal & Ir. Co. (Hindley).
.	.	.	.	.	.	.	.	Kirkless Hall Col. (L.&N.W.)	Lancs	L.&N.W.–G.C.(Wig.Jn.)	See Wigan Coal & Iron Co. (Wigan).
.	.	.	.	.	.	.	.	Kirkless Hall Iron & Steel Works (L. & N. W.)	Lancs	L.&N.W.–G.C.(Wig.Jn.)	See Wigan Coal & Iron Co. (Wigan).
.	.	.	.	.	.	.	.	Kirkless Hall Ir. & Steel Wks. Round House Sid. (L&NW)	Lancs	L.&N.W.–G.C.(Wig.Jn.)	See Wigan Coal & Iron Co. (Wigan).
.	.	.	.	.	.	.	.	Kirkless Hall Ore Mine and Slag Siding	Lancs	L. & N. W.	See Wigan Coal & Iron Co. (Wigan).
.	.	.	.	.	.	.	.	Kirkless Stores (L.&N.W.)...	Lancs	L.&N.W.–G.C.(Wig.Jn.)	See Wigan Coal & Iron Co. (Wigan).
G	P	.	L	H	.	.	.	Kirklington	Notts	Mid.	Mansfield and Southwell.
G	P	.	L	H	.	3	0	Kirkliston	L'lithgow	N. B.	Ratho and Dalmeny, Goods.
G	.	.	.	.	.	.	.	Distillery Siding............	L'lithgow	N. B.	Branch from Kirkliston.
.	.	.	.	.	.	.	.	Kirkliston Distillery Works	L'lithgow	N. B.	Extension of Distillery Siding.
G	P	.	L	.	.	.	.	Kirk Michael	I. of Man..	Manx Northern	St. Johns and Ramsey.
.	.	.	.	.	.	.	.	Kirkmuirhill Tile Works.....	Lanark ...	Cal.	Blackwood.
G	P	.	L	.	.	.	.	Kirknewton	Northumb	N. E.	Coldstream and Alnwick.
.	.	.	.	.	.	.	.	Kirkoswald	Cumb'land	Mid.	See Lazonby and Kirkoswald.
G	P	.	L	H	.	4	0	Kirkpatrick	Dumfries..	Cal.	Carlisle and Lockerbie.
.	.	.	.	.	.	.	.	Annanlea Quarry (Wood-head Quarry)	Dumfries..	Cal.	Kirkpatrick and Kirtlebridge.
.	.	.	.	.	.	.	.	Cove Quarry	Dumfries..	Cal.	Kirkpatrick and Kirtlebridge.
.	.	.	.	.	.	.	.	Kirkpatrick Bros.' Siding ...	Lancs	Trafford Park Estate......	Manchester.
G	P	F	L	H	C	.	.	Kirk Smeaton	Yorks	H. & B.	Cudworth and Howden.
.	.	.	.	.	.	.	.	Kirkstall	Yorks	Mid.	See Leeds.
.	.	.	.	.	.	.	.	Kirkstall Forge	Yorks	Mid.	See Leeds.
.	.	.	.	.	.	.	.	Kirkstall Forge Co.'s Siding	Yorks	Mid.	Leeds, Kirkstall Forge.
G	P	.	L	H	C	1	5	Kirkstead	Lincoln ...	G. N.	Boston and Lincoln.
.	.	.	.	.	.	.	.	Kirkstyle Quarry	Lanark ...	N. B.	Greengairs.
.	.	.	.	.	.	.	.	Kirkton Siding	Perth	Cal.	See Forgandenny.
.	.	.	.	.	.	.	.	Kirkwood & Co.'s Siding	Stirling ...	Cal.	Grangemouth.
.	.	.	.	.	.	.	.	Kirkwood Collieries(K.C.Co.)	Lanark ...	Cal.	Langloan.
.	.	.	.	.	.	.	.	Kirkwood Collieries (S.I.Co.)	Lanark ...	Cal.	Langloan.
.	.	.	.	.	.	.	.	Kirkwood's Siding..............	Renfrew ...	GB&KJt(Cal&G&SW)	Same as Darnley Brick and Lime Works (Nitshill).
G	P	F	L	H	C	3	0)	Kirriemuir (Cal.)	Forfar......	{ Cal.	Terminus—Branch near Forfar.
G	.	F	L	.	.	3	0)			{ N. B.	Over Caledonian from Arbroath Jn.
G	.	.	.	.	.	.	.	Ballindarg Siding (Cal.) ...	Forfar......	Cal.—N. B.	Branch near Forfar.
G	.	.	.	.	.	.	.	Balmuckety Siding (Cal.)..	Forfar......	Cal.—N. B.	Branch near Forfar.
G	.	.	.	.	.	.	.	Kirriemuir Jn. & Sid. (Cal.)	Forfar......	Cal.—N. B.	Glamis and Forfar.
G	P	F	L	H	C	4	10	Kirtlebridge	Dumfries..	Cal.	Carlisle and Lockerbie.
.	.	.	.	.	.	.	.	Bonshaw Brick Works	Dumfries..	Cal.	Kirtlebridge and Annan.
G	P	.	L	H	C	.	.	Kirton	Lincoln ...	G. N.	Spalding and Boston.
G	P	F	L	H	C	5	0	Kirton Lindsey	Lincoln ...	G. C.	Gainsboro' and Brigg.
.	.	.	.	.	.	.	.	Gleadell's Malt Kilns	Lincoln ...	G. C.	Kirton Lindsey.
.	.	.	.	.	.	.	.	Kirton Tunnel Lime Works	Lincoln ...	G. C.	Kirton Lindsey.
.	.	.	.	.	.	.	.	Kirton Tunnel Lime Works..	Lincoln ...	G. C.	Kirton Lindsey.
.	.	.	.	.	.	.	.	Kitchen & Co.'s Works......	Derby	Mid.	Derby.
.	.	.	.	.	.	.	.	Kitson & Co.'s Siding (Mid.)	Yorks	{ Mid.—L.&N.W.—N.E.	Leeds, Hunslet Lane.
.	.	.	.	.	.	.	.			{ G. N.	(See Appendix to follow).
.	.	.	.	.	.	.	.	Kittybrewster..............	Aberdeen..	G. N. of S.	See Aberdeen.
G	P	.	L	H	.	10	0	Kiveton Park	Yorks	G. C.	Sheffield and Worksop.
.	.	.	.	.	.	.	.	Canal Wharf	Yorks	G. C.	Kiveton Park.
.	.	.	.	.	.	.	.	Colliery	Yorks	G. C.	Kiveton Park.
.	.	.	.	.	.	.	.	Hall's Malt Kilns	Yorks	G. C.	Kiveton Park.
.	.	.	.	.	.	.	.	Lockwood Blagden Lime Co.'s Siding	Yorks	G. C.	Kiveton Park.
.	.	.	.	.	.	.	.	Noble's Lime Siding	Yorks	G. C.	Kiveton Park.
.	.	.	.	.	.	.	.	Rural District Siding	Yorks	G. C.	Kiveton Park.
.	.	.	.	.	.	.	.	Turner & Son's Lime Siding	Yorks	G. C.	Kiveton Park.
.	.	.	.	.	.	.	.	Kiveton Park Colliery	Yorks	Mid.	Killamarsh.
.	.	.	.	.	.	.	.	Knapton	Norfolk ...	N.&S.Jt.(GE&M&GNJt.)	See Paston and Knapton.
G	P	F	L	H	C	.	.	Knapton	Yorks	N. E.	Malton and Scarborough.
G	P	F	L	H	C	15	0	Knaresboro'	Yorks	N. E.	Starbeck and York.
G	P	F	L	H	C	.	.	Knebworth	Herts	G. N.	Hatfield and Hitchin.
.	.	.	.	.	.	.	.	Rowe's Lime Siding	Herts	G. N.	Knebworth and Stevenage.
.	.	.	.	.	.	.	.	Wallace & Inns Siding......	Herts	G. N.	Welwyn and Knebworth.
.	.	.	.	.	.	.	.	Woolmer Green Siding......	Herts	G. N.	Knebworth and Welwyn.
.	.	.	.	.	.	.	.	Kneeshaw, Lupton & Co.'s Llysfaen Siding	Carnarvon	L. & N. W.	Llysfaen.

EXPLANATION—G *Goods Station.*   P *Passenger and Parcel Station.*   P* *Passenger, but not Parcel or Miscellaneous Traffic.*
F *Furniture Vans, Carriages, Portable Engines, and Machines on Wheels.*   L *Live Stock.*
H *Horse Boxes and Prize Cattle Vans.*   C *Carriages by Passenger Train.*

STATION ACCOMMODATION.						CRANE POWER.		STATIONS, &c.	COUNTY.	COMPANY.	POSITION.
						Tons	Cwts				
								Knight, J., & Son's Sid. (GE)	Essex	G E—G N—L NW—Mid.	London, Silvertown.
G	P	F	L	H	C	5	0	Knighton	Radnor	L. & N. W.	Craven Arms & Llandrindod Wells.
								Knighton Jn. Brk. Wks. (Mid.)	Leicester	Mid.—L. & N. W.	See Leicester Brick Co.
								Knighton's Siding	Derby	Mid.	Clay Cross.
								Knight's Grange Works	Cheshire	C. L. C. (G C, G N, & Mid.)	See Salt Union, Ltd. (Winsford and Over).
								Knight's, W., Siding	Glo'ster	Mid.	Ryeford.
G								Knight's Hill	Surrey	L. & N. W.	Over L. B. & S. C. from Clapham Jn.
								Knightsridge Siding	L'lithgow	N. B.	See Livingston.
								Knightswood Branch (N.B.)	Lanark	N. B.—Cal.	Glasgow, Great Western Road.
								Knightswood Brk. Wks. (N B)	Lanark	N. B.—Cal.	Glasgow, Great Western Road.
								Knightswood, North Junc.	Lanark	N. B.	Glasgow.
								Knightswood Quarry (N. B.)	Lanark	N. B.—Cal.	Glasgow, Great Western Road.
								Knightswood, South Junction	Lanark	N. B.	Glasgow.
G	P	F						Knightwick	Worcester	G. W.	Worcester and Bromyard.
G	P		L	H				Knitsley	Durham	N. E.	Blackhill and Durham.
G	P		L	H		1	10	Knock	Banff	G. N. of S.	Grange and Banff.
	P							Knock	Down	B. & C. D.	Belfast and Comber.
								Knockahaw	Queens	G. S. & W.	See Lisduff (Knockahaw).
G	P							Knockanally	Antrim	N. C. Com. (Mid.)	Ballymena and Parkmore.
								Mountcashel Iron Ore Co.'s Siding	Antrim	N. C. Com. (Mid.)	Knockanally.
	P							Knockane	Cork	C. & Muskerry	St. Anne's and Donoughmore.
G	P	F	L	H	C	5	0	Knockcroghery	Roscom'n	M. G. W.	Athlone and Roscommon.
G	P	F	L	H	C	5	0	Knockholt	Kent	S. E. & C.	Chislehurst and Sevenoaks.
G	P	F	L	H	C			Knocklong	Limerick	G. S. & W.	Limerick Jn. and Charleville.
G	P		L			3	0	Knockloughrim	Derry	N. C. Com. (Mid.)	Macfin Junction and Magherafelt.
								Knockmore Junction	Antrim	G. N. (I.)	Lisburn and Maze.
								Knockmurton Iron Mines	Cumb'land	R. & K. F.	See Baird & Co. (Kelton Fell).
								Knockterra Pit	Ayr	G. & S. W.	Skares.
								Knoll Drift Pit	Yorks	Mid.	Wombwell.
								Knott and Barker's Saw Mills	Lincoln	G. C.	Grimsby Docks.
								Knott Hill Plaster Works	Cumb'land	Mid.	Cotehill.
								KNOTTINGLEY—			
G	P	F	L	H	C	5	0	(Station, for Ferrybridge) (L. & Y. & G. N. Jt.)	Yorks	L. & Y. & G. N. Jt.	Doncaster and Pontefract.
	P									H. & B.	Over L. & Y. from Hensall Junc.
G	P	F	L			5	0			N. E.	Over L. & Y. from Knottingley Jn.
								Bagley & Co.'s Siding	Yorks	L. & Y.	Knottingley Depôt.
								Burdin's Sid. (L&Y&GNJt.)	Yorks	L. & Y. & G. N. Jt.—N. E.	Knottingley.
								Creosoting Sidings	Yorks	L. & Y.	Knottingley Depôt.
G						1	10	Depôt	Yorks	L. & Y.	Knottingley and Whitley Bridge.
								Ferrybridge Junction	Yorks	N. E.—S. & K. Jt.	Burton Salmon and Pontefract.
								Jackson Bros.' Siding	Yorks	L. & Y. & G. N. Jt.	Knottingley.
								Junction	Yorks	L. & Y.—N. E.	Knottingley and Burton Salmon.
								Knottingley (S. & K. Jt.)	Yorks	S. & K. Jt—G. C.	See Ferrybridge (for Knottingley).
								Knott Mill and Deansgate	Lancs	M S J & A (G C & L N W)	See Manchester.
								Knotty Ash and Stanley	Cheshire	C.L.C. (G.C., G.N.&Mid.)	See Liverpool.
G	P		L	H		5	0	Knowesgate	Northumb	N. B.	Reedsmouth and Morpeth.
G	P	F	L	H	C	6	0	Knowle and Dorridge	Warwick	G. W.	Birmingham and Leamington.
								Knowle Lane Siding	Flint	W. M. & C. Q.	Buckley.
								Knowle Siding	Hants	L. & S. W.	Botley.
								Knowles, A., & Son's—			
								George Street Siding	Lancs	L. & Y.	Manchester, Salford.
								Pendleton Colliery	Lancs	L. & Y.	Brindle Heath.
								Siding	Lancs	L. & Y.	Manchester, Miles Platting.
								Knowles & Co.'s Brick and Sanitary Pipe Works (Mid.)	Derby	Mid.—L. & N. W.	Woodville.
								Knowles & Son's Siding	Lancs	L. & Y.	Bolton.
								Knowles, S., & Co.'s Siding	Lancs	L. & Y.	Tottington.
								Knowles Siding	Lancs	L. & N. W.	Manchester, Longsight.
								Knowles Siding	Lancs	L. & N. W.	Glazebury.
								Knownoble Colliery	Lanark	Cal.	Shieldmuir.
								Knownoblehill Colliery	Lanark	Cal.	Omoa.
								Knox's Brewery	Clackman'	N. B.	Cambus.
								Knox's Siding	Ayr	Cal.	Kilbirnie.
	P							Knuckbue	Cork	C. B. & S. C.	Dunmanway and Skibbereen.
G	P							Knucklas	Radnor	L. & N. W.	Craven Arms & Llandrindod Wells.
								Radnor Co.'s Wharf	Radnor	L. & N. W.	Knucklas and Knighton.
G	P	F	L	H	C	5	0	Knutsford (C. L. C.)	Cheshire	C.L.C.(G.C,G.N.&Mid.)	Northwich and Manchester.
	P			H	C					L. & N. W.	Over C. L. C. from Northwich Jn.
								Shaw Heath Siding	Cheshire	C.L.C. (G.C., G.N.& Mid.)	Knutsford.
								Knutton Ir. & Steel Co.'s Sid.	Staffs	N. S.	Pool Dam.

EXPLANATION—G *Goods Station.*   P *Passenger and Parcel Station.*   P* *Passenger, but not Parcel or Miscellaneous Traffic.*
F *Furniture Vans, Carriages, Portable Engines, and Machines on Wheels.*   L *Live Stock.*
H *Horse Boxes and Prize Cattle Vans.*   C *Carriages by Passenger Train.*

STATION ACCOMMODATION.						CRANE POWER.	STATIONS, &c.	COUNTY.	COMPANY.	POSITION.
						Tons Cwts.	Knutton Manor Mining Co.'s			
.	.	.	.	.	.	. .	Siding	Staffs	N. S.	Silverdale.
.	.	.	.	.	.	. .	Kohla Tile Co.'s Wharf	Mon	A (N & S W) D & R—G W	Same as Clapp's Wharf (Newport).
							Kottingham and Moor Street			
.	.	.	.	.	.	. .	Wharf (L. & N. W.)	Staffs	L N W—Mid.—G N—N S	Burton-on-Trent.
.	.	.	.	.	.	. .	Kurtz's Siding	Lancs	L. & Y.	Seaforth and Litherland.
.	.	.	.	.	.	. .	Kurtz Waste Bank Siding ...	Lancs	L. & N. W.	See United Alkali Co. (St. Helens).
.	.	.	.	.	.	. .	Kurtz Works	Lancs	L. & N. W.	See United Alkali Co. (St. Helens).
G	P	.	L	.	.	.	Kyleakin	Inverness	Cal.	Steamer from Oban.
G	P	.	L	L	.	C			High.	Steamer from Kyle of Lochalsh.
G	P	.	L	L	.				N. B.	Steamer from Mallaig.
G	P	F	L	H	C	5 0	Kyle of Lochalsh..........	Ross & Cro'	High.	Branch from Dingwall.
.	.	.	.	.	.	. .	Kynoch & Co.'s Siding	Essex	L. T. & S.	Same as Corringham Light Railway Siding (Thames Haven).
.	.	.	.	.	.	. .	Kynoch's Siding..............	Staffs	L. & N. W.	Witton.
.	.	.	.	.	.	. .	Kyo Sand Quarry	Durham ...	N. E.	Annfield Plain.

L

.	.	.	.	.	.	. .	Lackenby Iron Works	Yorks	N. E.	South Bank.
.	.	.	.	.	.	. .	Lacon & Co.'s Siding (G. E.)	Norfolk ...	G. E.—M. & G. N. Jt.	Yarmouth, Vauxhall.
.	.	.	.	.	.	. .	Ladbroke Grove	Middlesex	H. & C. Jt. (G. W. & Met.)	See London, Notting Hill and Ladbroke Grove.
G	.	.	.	.	.	2 0	Ladies' Lane Colliery (L.&Y.)	Lancs	L. & Y.—L. & N. W.	See Wigan Coal & Iron Co. (Hindley).
.	.	.	.	.	.	. .	Ladmanlow	Derby	L. & N. W.	Branch from Hindlow.
							Buxton Lime Firms Co.—			
.	.	.	.	.	.	. .	Grin Branch	Derby	L. & N. W.	Ladmanlow and Harpur Hill.
.	.	.	.	.	.	. .	Gritstone Siding............	Derby	L. & N. W.	Ladmanlow.
.	.	.	.	.	.	. .	Siding	Derby	L. & N. W.	Ladmanlow and Harpur Hill.
.	.	.	.	.	.	. .	Lady Ann Pit	Durham ...	N. E.	See Burn Moor Collieries (Fencehouses and Penshaw).
G	P	F	L	H	C	3 0	Ladybank..................	Fife	N. B.	Thornton and Perth.
.	.	.	.	.	.	. .	Ladybank Saw Mill	Fife	N. B.	Ladybank and Collessie.
.	.	.	.	.	.	. .	Malt Barns Siding........	Fife	N. B.	Ladybank and Auchtermuchty.
.	.	.	.	.	.	. .	Smith's Saw Mill	Fife	N. B.	Ladybank and Auchtermuchty.
.	.	.	.	.	.	. .	Ladybank Junction	Fife	N. B.	Kingskettle and Collessie.
.	.	.	.	.	.	. .	Ladyburn Saw Mills	Renfrew ...	Cal.	Greenock, Regent Street.
.	.	.	.	.	.	. .	Ladyburn Sidings	Renfrew ...	Cal.	See Greenock.
							Lady Durham or Sherburn			
.	.	.	.	.	.	. .	Colliery and Coke Ovens ...	Durham ...	N. E.	Sherburn Colliery Station.
.	.	.	.	.	.	. .	Ladyha' Pit ....,	Ayr	Cal.—G. & S. W.	Kilwinning.
.	.	.	.	.	.	. .	Ladyland's Colliery	Lanark ...	Cal.	Hartwood.
.	.	.	.	.	.	. .	Ladylands Siding	Stirling ...	N. B.	See Port of Monteith.
.	.	.	.	.	.	. .	Lady Lilian Colliery	Fife........	N. B.	West Wemyss.
.	.	.	.	.	.	. .	Lady Margaret Colliery	Glamorg'n	T. V.	Treherbert.
G	P	.	L	H	.	2 0	Lady Neave Siding	Essex	G. E.	Romford.
.	.	.	.	.	.	. .	Ladysbridge	Banff	G. N. of S.	Grange and Banff.
.	P	.	.	.	.	. .	Lady Victoria Pit	Edinboro'	N. B.	Hardengreen.
.	.	.	.	.	.	. .	Ladywell	Kent	S. E. & C.	Lewisham and Beckenham.
G	P	.	L	H	.	1 10	Lady Windsor Colliery........	Glamorg'n	T. V.	See Ocean Coal Co. (Ynysybwl).
.	.	.	.	.	.	. .	Laffan's Bridge	Tipperary	G. S. & W.	Clonmel and Thurles.
.	P	.	.	.	.	. .	Lager Brewery Co.'s Siding..	Denbigh ...	G. W.	Wrexham.
G	P	F	L	.	.	. .	La Haule	Jersey......	Jersey	St. Helier and St. Aubin.
.	.	.	.	.	.	. .	Lahinch	Clare	West Clare	Ennis and Miltown Malbay.
.	.	.	.	.	.	. .	Laidlaw & Son's Siding	Lanark ...	Cal.	Glasgow, Buchanan Street.
G	P	F	L	H	C	3 0	Laindon	Essex	L. T. & S.	Upminster and Pitsea.
.	.	.	.	.	.	. .	Laira	Devon ...	G. W.	Plymouth.
.	.	.	.	.	.	. .	Laira Junction (G. W.)......	Devon ...	G. W.—L. & S. W.	Plymouth.
G	P	F	L	H	C	1 10	Lairg	Sutherl'nd	High.	Bonar Bridge and Golspie.
.	.	.	.	.	.	. .	Laister Dyke (G. N.)........	Yorks	G. N.—L. & Y.	See Bradford.
.	.	.	.	.	.	. .	Lake & Co.'s Siding	Carnarvon	L. & N. W.	See Seiont Siding (Carnarvon).

G	P	F	L	H	C	Tons	Cwts	STATIONS, &c.	COUNTY.	COMPANY.	POSITION.
G	P	.	L	H	.	1	0	Lakenheath	Suffolk	G. E.	Ely and Thetford.
								Lake Side (Windermere)	Lancs	Furness	See Windermere, Lake Side.
G	P	.	L	H	.			Lamancha	Peebles	N. B.	Leadburn and Dolphinton.
								Lamb & Crawford's Yard (G. & P. Jt.)	Lanark	Cal.	Glasgow, Kinning Park.
										G. & S. W.	Glasgow, Eglinton Street.
								Lamb & Moore's Siding	Lancs	L. & Y.	Same as Newtown and Meadows Siding (Wigan).
								Lamb, R., Siding	Durham	N. E.	Stockton, South.
	P	.						Lambeg	Antrim	G. N. (I.)	Belfast and Lisburn.
								Lamberton's Siding	Lanark	N. B.	Same as Sunnyside Engine Works (Coatbridge).
								Lamberts Wharfage Co.'s Yard	Glamorg'n	GW—LNW—Mid—RSB	Swansea.
								Lambhill Forge	Lanark	Cal.	Glasgow, Possil.
								Lambhill Foundry	Lanark	Cal.	Glasgow, Possil.
G	P	.	L	H	.			Lambley	Northumb	N. E.	Haltwhistle and Alston.
								Bog Coke Ovens	Cumb'land	N. E.	Brampton Junction and Lambley.
								Clesket Siding	Cumb'land	N. E.	Brampton Junction and Lambley.
								Clowsgill Holme Siding	Cumb'land	N. E.	Brampton Junction and Lambley.
								Coanwood Whinstone Qry.	Northumb	N. E.	Coanwood and Lambley.
								Forest Head Lime Quarry	Cumb'land	N. E.	Brampton Junction and Lambley.
								Halton Lea Gate	Cumb'land	N. E.	Brampton Junction and Lambley.
								Kirkhouse Branch Junction	Northumb	N. E.	Lambley.
								Kirkhouse Dutch Barn Factory and Saw Mills	Cumb'land	N. E.	Brampton Junction and Lambley.
								Kirkhouse Siding	Cumb'land	N. E.	Brampton Junction and Lambley.
								Midge Holme Coke Ovens	Cumb'land	N. E.	Brampton Junction and Lambley.
								Midge Holme Sidings	Cumb'land	N. E.	Brampton Junction and Lambley.
								Whitescut Siding	Cumb'land	N. E.	Brampton Junction and Lambley.
G	P	F	L	H	C	1	10	Lambourn	Berks	L'bourn Valley	Terminus.
								Lamb Pit	Northumb	N. E.	Annitsford.
								Lambton Drops Saw Mills and Timber Yards	Durham	N. E.	Pallion.
								Lambton (Lord) or Littletown Colliery Store & Coal Sids.	Durham	N. E.	Sherburn Colliery Station.
								Lambton Shipping Drops	Durham	N. E.	Pallion.
G	P	.						Lamesley	Durham	N. E.	Gateshead and Durham, Pass.
G	P	F	L	H	C	2	10	Lamington	Lanark	Cal.	Lockerbie and Carstairs.
	P	.						La Moye	Jersey	Jersey	St. Helier and Corbiere.
G	P	F	L	H	.	1	10	Lampeter	Cardigan	M. & M.	Pencader and Tregaron.
G	P	.	L	H	.			Lamphey	Pembroke	G. W.	Tenby and Pembroke Dock.
								Lampit's Siding	Lanark	Cal.	Carstairs.
G	P	.	L	H	.			Lamplugh	Cumb'land	WC&EJt.(Fur.&L&NW)	Marron Junction and Moor Row.
								Asby Colliery	Cumb'land	WC&EJt.(Fur.&L NW)	Lamplugh and Rowrah.
G	P	F	L	H	C	1	10	Lamport	N'hamptn	L. & N. W.	Market Harboro' and Northampton.
								Draughton Crossing Siding	N'hamptn	L. & N. W.	Lamport and Kelmarsh.
								Loder's	N'hamptn	L. & N. W.	Draughton Crossing Siding.
								Stanton Iron Co.	N'hamptn	L. & N. W.	Draughton Crossing Siding.
G	P	F	L	H	C	4	10	Lanark	Lanark	Cal.	Terminus near Carstairs.
								Caledonian Saw Mills	Lanark	Cal.	Lanark.
								Douglas Junctions	Lanark	Cal.	Lanark.
								Lanark Oil Works (North British Oil & Candle Wks)	Lanark	Cal.	Cleghorn and Lanark.
								Lanark Saw Mills	Lanark	Cal.	Lanark.
								Todd's Saw Mill	Lanark	Cal.	Lanark.
								Lanarkshire Chain, Cable, and Anchor Works Sid. (Strathearn's Weldless Chain Works)	Lanark	Cal.	Gartsherrie.
										N. B.	Coatbridge, Gartgill.
								Lanarkshire Steel Works	Lanark	Cal.	Motherwell.
								Lancashire & Yorkshire Railway Co.'s—			
								Barkfield Siding	Lancs	L. & Y.	Freshfield.
								Carriage Siding	Lancs	L. & Y.	Horwich.
								Carriage Works	Lancs	L. & Y.	Newton Heath.
								Locomotive Siding	Lancs	L. & Y.	Bury, High Level.
								Locomotive Siding	Lancs	L. & Y.	Horwich.
								Locomotive Siding	Lancs	L. & Y.	Lostock Hall.
								Locomotive Siding	Lancs	L. & Y.	Lower Darwen.
								Locomotive Siding	Yorks	L. & Y.	Mirfield.
								Locomotive Siding	Lancs	L. & Y.	Newton Heath.
								Locomotive Siding	Lancs	P.&W.Jt.(L&Y&L&NW)	Fleetwood.
								Permanent Way Stores	Lancs	L. & Y.	Blackburn.

EXPLANATION—G *Goods Station.*   P *Passenger and Parcel Station.*   P* *Passenger, but not Parcel or Miscellaneous Traffic.*
F *Furniture Vans, Carriages, Portable Engines, and Machines on Wheels.*   L *Live Stock.*
H *Horse Boxes and Prize Cattle Vans.*   C *Carriages by Passenger Train.*

STATION ACCOMMODATION.						CRANE POWER.		STATIONS, &c.	COUNTY.	COMPANY.	POSITION.
						Tons	Cwts.	**Lancashire & Yorkshire Railway Co.'s**—*continued.*			
.	.	.	.	.	.	.	.	Permanent Way Stores ...	Lancs	L. & Y.	Blowick.
.	.	.	.	.	.	.	.	Permanent Way Stores ...	Lancs	L. & Y.	Bolton.
.	.	.	.	.	.	.	.	Permanent Way Stores ...	Lancs	L. & Y.	Ormskirk.
.	.	.	.	.	.	.	.	Permanent Way Stores ...	Lancs	L. & Y.	Wigan.
.	.	.	.	.	.	.	.	Stores	Lancs	L. & Y.	Halliwell.
.	.	.	.	.	.	.	.	Stores Siding	Lancs	L. & Y.	Heywood and Castleton.
.	.	.	.	.	.	.	.	Wagon Co.'s Siding	Lancs	L. & Y.	Manchester, Miles Platting.
.	.	.	.	.	.	.	.	Wagon Department Siding	Lancs	L. & Y.	Heywood.
.	.	.	.	.	.	.	.	Wagon Department Siding	Lancs	L. & Y.	Bolton.
.	.	.	.	.	.	.	.	Wagon Department Siding	Lancs	L. & Y.	Fazakerley.
.	.	.	.	.	.	.	.	Westhead Siding	Lancs	L. & Y.	Lostock Hall.
.	.	.	.	.	.	.	.	Lancashire Asylums Board Winwick Hall Siding	Lancs	L. & N. W.	Skelmersdale.
.	.	.	.	.	.	.	.	Lancashire Brick and Terra Cotta Co.'s Siding	Lancs	L. & Y.	Warrington, Bank Quay.
.	.	.	.	.	.	.	.	Lancashire Dynamo & Motor Co.'s Siding..................	Lancs	Trafford Park Estate.....	Baxenden.
.	.	.	.	.	.	.	.	Lancashire Metal Works	Lancs	L. & N. W.—S. & M. Jt.	Manchester.
								LANCASTER—			See United Alkali Co. (Widnes).
G	P	F	L	H	C	5	0 }	Castle (L. & N. W.)	Lancs	{ L. & N. W. .... / Mid.	Penrith and Preston. / Over L. & N. W. from Lancaster Jn.
.	P	.	.	H	C		. }				
.	.	.	.	.	.	.	.	Corporation Siding	Lancs	Mid.	Lancaster and Halton.
G	P	F	L	H	C	5	0	Gas Works (L. & N. W.) ...	Lancs	L. & N. W.—Mid.	Lancaster Quay.
.	.	.	.	.	.	.	.	Green Ayre	Lancs	Mid.	Halton and Morecambe.
.	.	.	.	.	.	.	.	Junction	Lancs	L. & N. W.—Mid.	Lancaster, Castle Sta. & Green Ayre.
.	.	.	.	.	.	.	.	Metropolitan Amalgamated Railway Carriage and Wagon Co.'s Sid. (Mid.)	Lancs	Mid.—L. & N. W.	Near Lancaster.
G	.	.	.	.	.	3	0	Quay (L. & N. W.)	Lancs	{ L. & N. W. .... / Mid.	Lancaster and Glasson Dock. / Over L. & N. W. from Lancaster Jn.
.	.	.	.	.	.	.	.	Thoms' Siding	Lancs	L. & N. W.	Lancaster and Galgate.
.	.	.	.	.	.	.	.	Williamson's Siding	Lancs	L. & N. W.	Lancaster Quay.
								Lancaster & Co.—			
.	.	.	.	.	.	.	.	Cinder Colliery (G.W.)......	Mon	G. W.—L. & N. W.	Blaina.
.	.	.	.	.	.	.	.	Henwain Colliery (G.W.)...	Mon	G. W.—L. & N. W.	Blaina.
.	.	.	.	.	.	.	.	Lower Deep Colliery (G.W.)	Mon	G. W.—L. & N. W.	Blaina.
.	.	.	.	.	.	.	.	North Griffin Colliery (GW)	Mon	G. W.—L. & N. W.	Blaina.
.	.	.	.	.	.	.	.	South Griffin Colliery (GW)	Mon	G. W.—L. & N. W.	Blaina.
.	.	.	.	.	.	.	.	Lancaster, Speir & Co.'s Rose Heyworth Colliery (G. W.)	Mon	G. W.—L. & N. W.	Abertillery.
.	.	.	.	.	.	.	.	Lancaster's Siding...............	Lancs	L. & N. W.	Same as Higginbottom's Prescot Colliery (Huyton Quarry).
G	P	F	L	H	C	5	0	Lancaster Gate	Middlesex	C. L.	See London.
.	.	.	.	.	.	.	.	Lanchester	Durham ...	N. E.	Durham and Blackhill.
.	.	.	.	.	.	.	.	Lanchester Colliery	Durham ...	N. E.	Lanchester.
.	.	.	.	.	.	.	.	Lanchester Saw Mill.........	Durham ...	N. E.	Lanchester.
.	.	.	.	.	.	.	.	Malton Colliery	Durham ...	N. E.	Lanchester.
G	P	F	L	H	C	.	.	Lancing	Sussex ...	L. B. & S. C.	Brighton and Worthing.
								LANDORE—			
.	.	.	.	.	.	.	.	Baldwin's, Ltd., Landore Steel Works, or Swansea Hematite Iron Works......	Glamorg'n	G. W.	Landore and Llansamlet.
.	.	.	.	.	.	.	.	British Mannesman Tube Co.'s Siding	Glamorg'n	G. W.	Landore and Llansamlet.
.	.	.	.	.	.	.	.	Cwmbwrla Siding	Glamorg'n	G. W.	Landore and Cockett.
.	.	.	.	.	.	.	.	Cwmfelin Siding...............	Glamorg'n	G. W.	Landore and Cockett.
G	P	.	.	.	.	12	0	High Level	Glamorg'n	G. W.	Neath and Llanelly.
.	P	.	.	.	.	.	.	Low Level	Glamorg'n	G. W.	Morriston Branch.
.	.	.	.	.	.	.	.	Millbrook Engineering Co.'s Siding	Glamorg'n	G. W.	Landore, High Level.
.	.	.	.	.	.	.	.	Pascoe, Grenfell, & Son's, or Foster, W., & Co.'s Morfa Copper Works.............	Glamorg'n	G. W.	Landore, Low Level.
.	.	.	.	.	.	.	.	Tirdonkin Colliery Co.'s Cefngyfelach Colliery ...	Glamorg'n	G. W.	Landore and Cockett.
.	.	.	.	.	.	.	.	Vivian & Son's Alkali Works	Glamorg'n	G. W.	Landore, Low Level.
.	.	.	.	.	.	.	.	Vivian's Colliery...............	Glamorg'n	G. W.	Landore, High Level.
.	.	.	.	.	.	.	.	Landore Steel Works.........	Glamorg'n	G. W.	See Baldwin's Ltd. (Landore).
.	.	.	.	.	.	.	.	Landore Steel Works (Mid.)	Glamorg'n	Mid.—G. W.—L. & N. W.	See Baldwin's, Ltd. (Upper Bank).

EXPLANATION—G *Goods Station.*　　P *Passenger and Parcel Station.*　　P* *Passenger, but not Parcel or Miscellaneous Traffic.*
F *Furniture Vans, Carriages, Portable Engines, and Machines on Wheels.*　　L *Live Stock.*
H *Horse Boxes and Prize Cattle Vans.*　　C *Carriages by Passenger Train.*

STATION ACCOMMODATION						CRANE POWER		STATIONS, &c.	COUNTY.	COMPANY.	POSITION.
						Tons	Cwts				
.	.	.	.	.	.			Landowner's Branch	Lancs	S. & M. Jt. (G. C. & Mid.)	Widnes.
.	.	.	.	.	.			Lands Lane Siding	Durham	N. E.	Butterknowle.
.	.	.	.	.	.			Lane End Colliery	Flint	W. M. & C. Q.	Buckley.
.	.	.	.	.	.			Lane End Works	Staffs	N. S.	Longton.
.	.	.	.	.	.			Lanemark Brick Works	Ayr	G. & S. W.	New Cumnock.
.	.	.	.	.	.			Lanemark Collieries	Ayr	G. & S. W.	New Cumnock.
.	.	.	.	.	.			Lane's Siding	Glo'ster	Mid.	Ryeford.
.	.	.	.	.	.			Lane, W. & J., Siding	Cambs	G. E.	Newmarket.
.	.	.	.	.	.			Lang & Son's Siding	Renfrew	G. & S. W.	Johnstone, Cartside.
.	.	.	.	.	.			Lange's Anthracite Colliery	Carmarth'	G. W.	Brynamman.
.	.	.	.	.	.			Lang's Siding	Salop	S.&H. Jt.(G.W.&L.N.W.)	Ludlow.
G	P	.	L	H	.	2	0	Langbank	Renfrew	Cal.	Paisley and Port Glasgow.
.	.	.	.	.	.			Langbyres Junction	Lanark	Cal.	Omoa and Newhouse.
.	.	.	.	.	.			Langdale & Co.'s Siding	Perth	Cal.	Perth, South.
.	.	.	.	.	.			Langdale Manure Co.'s Siding	Northumb	N. E.	St. Peters.
.	.	.	.	.	.			Langdales Junction Siding	Lanark	N. B.	Greengairs.
G	.	.	.	.	.			Langford	Beds	G. N.	Hitchin and Sandy.
.	P*	.	.	.	.			Langford	Essex	G. E.	Witham and Maldon.
G	P	F	.	H	C			Langford	Somerset	G. W.	Congresbury and Blagdon.
G	P	.	.	H	C	2	0	Langho	Lancs	L. & Y.	Blackburn and Clitheroe.
G	P	F	L	H	C	4	0	Langholm	Dumfries	N. B.	Branch from Riddings Junction.
.	.	.	.	.	.			Glentarras Distillery	Dumfries	N. B.	Gilnockie and Langholm.
G	P	.	.	.	.	1	10	Langley	Bucks	G. W.	London, Paddington and Slough.
G	P	.	L	H	.	3	0	Langley	Northumb	N. E.	Hexham and Allendale.
.	.	.	.	.	.			Langley Bridge Canal Lock	Derby	Mid.	Langley Mill and Eastwood.
.	.	.	.	.	.			Langley Collieries	Derby	Mid.	See Butterley Co. (Langley Mill and Eastwood).
G	P	.	.	.	.	1	10	Langley Green & Rood End	Worcester	G. W.	Stourbridge Jn. and Smethwick Jn.
.	.	.	.	.	.			Langley Mill	Notts	G. N.	See Eastwood and Langley Mill.
G	P	F	L	H	C	1	10	Langley Mill and Eastwood	Derby	Mid.	Clay Cross and Trent.
								Barber, Walker & Co.—			
.	.	.	.	.	.			Brinsley Colliery	Derby	Mid.	Langley Mill.
.	.	.	.	.	.			High Park Colliery	Derby	Mid.	Langley Mill.
.	.	.	.	.	.			Moor Green Colliery	Derby	Mid.	Langley Mill.
.	.	.	.	.	.			Selston Colliery	Derby	Mid.	Langley Mill.
.	.	.	.	.	.			Underwood Colliery	Derby	Mid.	Langley Mill.
								Butterley Co.—			
.	.	.	.	.	.			Langley Collieries	Derby	Mid.	Heanor Junction.
.	.	.	.	.	.			Plumptre Colliery	Notts	Mid.	Langley Mill.
.	.	.	.	.	.			Roscoe Collieries	Derby	Mid.	Heanor Junction.
.	.	.	.	.	.			Gas Light & Coke Co.'s Sid.	Derby	Mid.	Langley Mill.
.	.	.	.	.	.			Hardy's Siding	Derby	Mid.	Beggarlee Junction.
.	.	.	.	.	.			High Park Colliery	Derby	Mid.	Langley Mill.
.	.	.	.	.	.			Langley Bridge Canal Lock	Derby	Mid.	Langley Mill.
.	.	.	.	.	.			Langley Mill Brick Co.'s Sid	Derby	Mid.	Beggarlee Junction.
.	.	.	.	.	.			Langley Mill Co-operative Society's Siding	Derby	Mid.	Langley Mill.
.	.	.	.	.	.			Langley Mill Gas Co.'s Sid.	Derby	Mid.	Langley Mill.
.	.	.	.	.	.			New Langley Colliery	Derby	Mid.	Langley Mill.
.	.	.	.	.	.			Oakes & Co.'s Pollington Colliery	Derby	Mid.	Langley Mill and Codnor Park.
.	.	.	.	.	.			Pickersgill & Frost's Siding	Derby	Mid.	Beggarlee Junction.
.	.	.	.	.	.			Smith's Flour Mill	Derby	Mid.	Langley Mill.
.	.	.	.	.	.			Stoneyford Colliery	Derby	Mid.	Langley Mill and Codnor Park.
.	.	.	.	.	.			Turner's, G. R., Wagon Wks.	Derby	Mid.	Langley Mill and Shipley Gate.
.	.	.	.	.	.			Langley Mill Brick Co.'s Sid.	Derby	Mid.	Langley Mill.
.	.	.	.	.	.			Langley Mill Colliery (G. N.)	Notts	G. N.—G. C.	Eastwood and Langley Mill.
.	.	.	.	.	.			Langley Mill Co-operative Society's Siding	Derby	Mid.	Langley Mill.
.	.	.	.	.	.			Langley Mill Gas Co.'s Siding	Derby	Mid.	Langley Mill.
.	.	.	.	.	.			Langley Park Col. & Coke Wks.	Durham	N. E.	Witton Gilbert.
.	.	.	.	.	.			Langley Siding	Herts	G. N.	Stevenage.
G	P	.	L	.	.	1	10	Langloan	Lanark	Cal.	Coatbridge and Rutherglen.
.	.	.	.	.	.			British Tube Works	Lanark	Cal.	Coatbridge and Langloan.
.	.	.	.	.	.			Coatbridge Iron Works	Lanark	Cal.	Coatbridge and Langloan.
.	.	.	.	.	.			Drumpellier Colliery, No. 4	Lanark	Cal.	Langloan and Baillieston.
.	.	.	.	.	.			Drumpellier Ir. & Steel Wks.	Lanark	Cal.	Langloan and Baillieston.
.	.	.	.	.	.			Dundyvan Foundry	Lanark	Cal.	Whifflet and Langloan.
.	.	.	.	.	.			Dundyvan Iron Works	Lanark	Cal.	Coatbridge and Langloan.
.	.	.	.	.	.			Dundyvan Silica Brk. Wks. (Eglinton Silica Bk. Wks.)	Lanark	Cal.	Coatbridge and Langloan.
.	.	.	.	.	.			Eglinton Chemical Co's Wks.	Lanark	Cal.	Coatbridge and Langloan.

EXPLANATION—G *Goods Station.*   P *Passenger and Parcel Station.*   P* *Passenger, but not Parcel or Miscellaneous Traffic.*
F *Furniture Vans, Carriages, Portable Engines, and Machines on Wheels.*   L *Live Stock.*
H *Horse Boxes and Prize Cattle Vans.*   C *Carriages by Passenger Train.*

STATION ACCOMMODATION.						CRANE POWER.	STATIONS, &c.	COUNTY.	COMPANY.	POSITION.
						Tons Cwts.	Langloan—continued.			
.	.	.	.	.	.	. .	Kirkwood Cols. (K. C. Co.)	Lanark ...	Cal.	Langloan and Baillieston.
.	.	.	.	.	.	. .	Kirkwood Collieries (Summerlee Iron Co.)	Lanark ...	Cal.	Langloan and Baillieston.
.	.	.	.	.	.	. .	Langloan Iron & Chemical Works	Lanark ...	Cal.	Langloan and Baillieston.
.	.	.	.	.	.	. .	Langloan Weighs	Lanark ...	Cal.	Langloan.
.	.	.	.	.	.	. .	Victoria Tube Works	Lanark ...	Cal.	Langloan and Baillieston.
.	.	.	.	.	.	. .	Woodside Iron & Steel Wks.	Lanark ...	Cal.	Langloan and Baillieston.
.	.	.	.	.	.	. .	Langloan Branch	Lanark ...	N. B.	Coatbridge, Sheepford.
.	.	.	.	.	.	. .	Langloan Iron & Chemical Works	Lanark ...	{ Cal. { N. B.	Langloan. Coatbridge, Sheepford.
.	.	.	.	.	.	. .	Langloan Junction..............	Lanark ...	N. B.	Coatbridge, Central and Whifflet.
G	P	F	L H C			8 0	Langor Bridge Siding	Norfolk ...	Mid. & G. N. Jt.	Fakenham Town.
G	P	.	L H			. .	Langport	Somerset..	G. W.	Durston and Yeovil.
.	.	.	.	.	.	. .	Langrick	Lincoln ...	G. N.	Boston and Lincoln.
.	.	.	.	.	.	. .	Langsett's Siding	Yorks	G. C.	Deepcar (for Stocksbridge).
.	.	.	.	.	.	. .	Langsett's Siding (Waterworks Branch)	Yorks	G. C.	Deepcar (for Stocksbridge).
.	.	.	.	.	.	. .	Langside and Newlands	Renfrew...	Cal.	See Glasgow.
.	.	.	.	.	.	. .	Langside Junction.............	Lanark ...	Cal.—G. B. & K. Jt......	Glasgow.
.	P	.	.	.	.	. .	Langston	Hants	L. B. & S. C.	Havant and Hayling.
.	.	.	.	.	.	. .	Langton Colliery	Derby	Mid.	Pinxton.
.	.	.	.	.	.	. .	Langton Colliery (G. C.)	Notts	G. C.—G. N.—L. & N.W.	Kirkby and Pinxton.
.	.	.	.	.	.	. .	Langton Dock	Lancs	{ L'pool O'head .... { Mid.	See Liverpool. See Alexandra and Langton Dock (Liverpool).
G	P	F	L H C			5 0	Laugtree Pit (L. & N. W.) ...	Lancs	L & N W—G C (Wig. Jn.)	See Wigan Coal & Iron Co. (Wigan)
G	P	F	L H C			1 10	Langwathby	Cumb'land	Mid.	Appleby and Carlisle.
							Langwith (Mid.)	Derby	{ Mid. { G. C.	Mansfield and Worksop. Over Mid. from Shireoaks Junctions.
.	.	.	.	.	.	. .	Burkitt's, W. & S., Siding (Mid.)	Derby	Mid.—G. C.	Langwith.
.	.	.	.	.	.	. .	Langwith Colliery (Mid.)...	Derby	Mid.—G. C.	Langwith and Elmton.
.	.	.	.	.	.	. .	Sheepbridge Coal and Iron Co.'s Langwith Col.(Mid.)	Derby	Mid.—G. C.	Langwith.
.	.	.	.	.	.	. .	Langwith Colliery (Mid.)......	Derby	Mid.—G. C.	See Sheepbridge Coal & Iron Co. (Langwith).
.	.	.	.	.	.	. .	Langwith Col. (L. D. & E. C.)	Derby	L. D. & E. C.—G. E.	Langwith Junction Station.
.	.	.	.	.	.	. .	Langwith Junction..............	Derby	G. N.—L. D. & E. C.	Sutton-in-Ashfield and Langwith Junction Station.
G	P	F	L H C			3 0	Langwith Junction Station...	Derby	L. D. & E. C.	Chesterfield and Tuxford.
.	.	.	.	.	.	. .	Langwith Col. (L.D. & E.C.)	Derby	L. D. & E. C.—G. E.	Branch from Langwith Junction.
G	P	F	L H C			. .	Langworth	Lincoln ...	G. C.	Lincoln and Market Rasen.
.	.	.	.	.	.	. .	Lanridge Cols.(Linridge Cols.)	Lanark ...	Cal.	Omoa.
.	.	.	.	.	.	. .	Lanridge Junction..............	Lanark ...	Cal.	Omoa and Newhouse.
.	.	.	.	.	.	. .	Lansdown	Glo'ster ...	Mid.	See Cheltenham.
.	.	.	.	.	.	. .	Lansdowne Road	Dublin ...	D. W. & W.	See Dublin.
.	.	.	.	.	.	. .	Lansdown Junction	Glo'ster ...	G. W.	Cheltenham.
G	P	F	L H C			. .	Lapford	Devon	L. & S.W.	Exeter and Barnstaple.
G	P	.	L H			. .	Lapworth	Warwick..	G. W.	Birmingham and Leamington.
G	P	F	L H C			4 10	Larbert	Stirling ...	Cal.	Coatbridge and Stirling.
.	.	.	.	.	.	. .	Carmuirs Colliery	Stirling ...	Cal.	Larbert and Grahamston.
.	.	.	.	.	.	. .	Colonial Stove & Iron Works (Dobbie, Forbes & Co.) ...	Stirling ...	Cal.	Larbert and Grahamston.
.	.	.	.	.	.	. .	Larbert Saw Mill	Stirling ...	Cal.	Larbert.
.	.	.	.	.	.	. .	Larbert Weighs	Stirling ...	Cal.	Larbert.
.	.	.	.	.	.	. .	Stenhousemuir Quarry and Brick Works	Stirling ...	Cal.	Larbert and Bannockburn.
.	.	.	L	.	.	. .	Stenhousemuir Siding (Muirhall Siding)	Stirling ...	Cal.	Larbert and Bannockburn.
.	.	.	.	.	.	. .	Torwood Foundry (Jones & Campbell's)	Stirling ...	Cal.	Larbert.
.	.	.	.	.	.	. .	Larbert Junction	Stirling ...	Cal.—N. B.	Larbert and Grahamston.
.	.	.	.	.	.	. .	Larbert Junction Sids. (N. B.)	Stirling ...	N. B.—Cal.	Same as Lochland Siding (Falkirk).
G	P	F	L H C			1 0	Largo	Fife	N. B.	Leven and Anstruther.
G	.	F	L	.	.	2 0	Largoward	Fife	N. B.	Cameron Bridge and Lochty.
.	.	.	.	.	.	. .	Balcarres Colliery	Fife	N. B.	Largoward and Lochty.
G	P	F	L H C			2 0	Largs	Ayr	G. & S.W.	Branch from Ardrossan.
G	P	F	L H C			4 10	Larkhall	Lanark ...	Cal.	Hamilton and Lesmahagow.
.	.	.	.	.	.	. .	Allanton Colliery	Lanark ...	Cal.	Ferniegair and Larkhall.
.	.	.	.	.	.	. .	Bog Colliery	Lanark ...	Cal.	Ferniegair and Larkhall.

EXPLANATION—G *Goods Station.*　　P *Passenger and Parcel Station.*　　P* *Passenger, but not Parcel or Miscellaneous Traffic.*
F *Furniture Vans, Carriages, Portable Engines, and Machines on Wheels.*　　L *Live Stock.*
H *Horse Boxes and Prize Cattle Vans.*　　C *Carriages by Passenger Train.*

STATION ACCOMMODATION.						CRANE POWER.	STATIONS, &c.	COUNTY.	COMPANY.	POSITION.
						Tons Cwts.	Larkhall—continued.			
							Dykehead Colliery & Quarry	Lanark	Cal.	Ferniegair and Larkhall.
							Ferniegair Colliery	Lanark	Cal.	Motherwell and Ferniegair.
G							Ferniegair Siding	Lanark	Cal.	Motherwell and Ferniegair.
							Hamilton Corporation Refuse Siding	Lanark	Cal.	Motherwell and Ferniegair.
							Home Farm Colliery	Lanark	Cal.	Ferniegair and Larkhall.
							Merryton Col. & Brick Wks.	Lanark	Cal.	Ferniegair and Larkhall.
							Merryton Farm Siding	Lanark	Cal.	Ferniegair and Larkhall.
							Ross Collieries	Lanark	Cal.	Motherwell and Ferniegair.
							Ross Weighs	Lanark	Cal.	Ross Junction.
							Skellyton Colliery	Lanark	Cal.	Ferniegair and Larkhall.
G	P	F	L	H	C	3 0	Larne	Antrim	N. C. Com. (Mid.)	Carrickfergus and Larne Harbour.
G	P		L	H		3 0	Larne (Narrow Gauge)	Antrim	N. C. Com. (Mid.)	Ballyboley and Larne Harbour.
G	P	F	L	H	C	1 0	Larne Harbour	Antrim	N. C. Com. (Mid.)	Terminus (from Belfast).
G	P		L	H			Larne Hbr. (Narrow Gauge)	Antrim	N. C. Com. (Mid.)	Terminus (from Ballymena).
	P						La Rocque	Jersey	Jersey Eastern	St. Helier and Gorey.
G	P	F	L			1 10	Lartington	Yorks	N. E.	Barnard Castle and Kirkby Stephen.
							High Quarry	Yorks	N. E.	Lartington.
							Lartington Quarry Co.'s Freestone Quarry	Yorks	N. E.	Lartington.
							Lasham	Hants	L. & S.W.	See Bentworth and Lasham.
							Lassell & Sharman's Brewery	Denbigh	W. M. & C. Q.	Caergwrle Castle.
							Lassodie Colliery	Fife	N. B.	Kelty.
							Lassodie Mill Colliery	Fife	N. B.	Kelty.
G	P					1 10	Lasswade	Edinboro'	N. B.	Hardengreen and Polton.
							Latchford	Lancs	L. & N. W.	See Warrington.
							Latchford Junction	Lancs	L. & N. W.—Manchester Ship Canal	See Man. Ship Canal Co., Warringt'n.
							Latchmere Junctions	Surrey	W.L.E.Jt.(GW,L&NW, L.&SW,& L.B.&S.C.)	London, Battersea & Clapham Jn.
							Lathalmond Siding	Fife	N. B.	See Townhill Junction Station.
							Latham & Worthington's Norley Quarry	Lancs	L. & N. W.	Garswood.
							Latham Brothers—			
							East Pit Colliery	Lancs	L. & N. W.	Wigan.
							Rose Bridge Colliery	Lancs	L. & N. W.	Wigan.
							Lathbury's Sidings (Mid.)	Staffs	Mid—L&NW—G N—N S	Burton-on-Trent.
							Lathmill Siding	Ayr	G. & S.W.	Gatehead.
							Latimer Road	Middlesex	H. & C. Jt. (G.W. & Met.)	See London.
							Lattey's Siding	Glamorg'n	T. V.	Cardiff.
							Lauchope Colliery	Lanark	Cal.	Chapelhall.
G	P		L	H			Lauder	Berwick	N. B.	Branch from Fountainhall.
							Lauder, R., & Co.—			
							Greenland Sleeper Saw Mill	Durham	N. E.	West Hartlepool.
							Newburn Saw Mills	Durham	N. E.	West Hartlepool.
G	P	F	L	H	C	10 0	Launceston	Cornwall	G. W.	Branch from Tavistock Junction.
G	P	F	L	H	C	2 0		Cornwall	L. & S. W.	Okehampton and Wadebridge.
							Cawdron Siding	Cornwall	G. W.	Lifton and Launceston.
							Trood & Co.'s Siding	Cornwall	L. & S.W.	Launceston.
G	P						Launton	Oxon	L. & N. W.	Oxford and Verney Junction Sta.
							Laurel Siding (Rodgerson's)	Renfrew	Cal.	Glasgow, Whiteinch.
G	P	F	L	H	C	3 0	Laurencekirk	Kinc'rdine	Cal.	Forfar and Stonehaven.
G	P		L	H		2 10	Laurencetown	Down	G. N. (I.)	Scarva and Banbridge.
							Laurieston Iron Works (Thornbridge Siding) (Cal.)	Stirling	Cal.—N. B.	Grangemouth.
G	P		L	H		1 10	Lauriston	Kinc'rdine	N. B.	Montrose and Bervie.
G	P	F	L	H	C		Lavant	Sussex	L. B. & S. C.	Midhurst and Chichester.
							Lavender Hill Junction	Surrey	L. & S.W.—S. E. & C.	London, Clapham Junction.
							Lavender's Siding (L.&N.W.)	Staffs	L. & N. W.—Mid.	Walsall.
G	P	F	L	H	C	1 2	Lavenham	Suffolk	G. E.	Sudbury and Bury St. Edmunds.
G	P						Lavernock	Glamorg'n	T. V.	Penarth and Cadoxton.
							Laverocklaw Siding	Hadding'n	N. B.	See Haddington.
G	P	F	L	H	C	1 10	Lavington	Wilts	G. W.	Westbury and Patney.
							Lavington & Co.'s Siding	Kent	S. E. & C.	Maidstone.
G	P						Lawderdale (Book to Ballinamore)	Leitrim	C. & L.	Ballinamore and Mohill.
G	P	F	L	H	C	1 10	Law Junction Station	Lanark	Cal.	Carstairs and Motherwell.
							Brownlee Colliery	Lanark	Cal.	Branch near Law Junction.
							Garriongill Weighs	Lanark	Cal.	Law Junction and Wishaw, South.
							Gold's Siding	Lanark	Cal.	Carluke and Law Junction.
							Law Collieries, Nos. 3 and 4	Lanark	Cal.	Branch near Law Junction.
							Law Colliery, No. 2	Lanark	Cal.	Carluke and Law Junction.

EXPLANATION—G Goods Station.   P Passenger and Parcel Station.   P* Passenger, but not Parcel or Miscellaneous Traffic.
F Furniture Vans, Carriages, Portable Engines, and Machines on Wheels.   L Live Stock.
H Horse Boxes and Prize Cattle Vans.   C Carriages by Passenger Train.

STATION ACCOMMODATION.						CRANE POWER.		STATIONS, &c.	COUNTY.	COMPANY.	POSITION.
						Tons	Cwts	Law Junction Station—*continued.*			
								Law Junction Weighs	Lanark	Cal.	Carluke and Law Junction.
								Shawfield Colliery	Lanark	Cal.	Branch near Law Junction.
								Lawkholme Works	Yorks	Mid.	See Smith, P., & Son's (Keighley).
	P							Lawley Bank	Salop	G. W.	Wellington and Lightmoor.
								Lawley Street	Warwick	Mid.	See Birmingham.
								Lawn Colliery	Staffs	N. S.	Adderley Green.
								Lawnwood Siding	Lincoln	G. N.	Same as Adamantine Clinker Works (Little Bytham).
G	P	F				12	0	Lawrence & Co.'s Siding	Notts	G. N.	Netherfield and Colwick.
								Lawrence Hill	Glo'ster	G. W.	Bristol and Stapleton Road.
								Lawrence's Siding	Berks	L. & S.W.	Bracknell.
								Lawson Co.'s Yard	Cumb'land	C. & W. Jn.	Workington.
	P							Law's Siding	Lancs	L. & Y.	Shawforth.
								Lawton	Cheshire	N. S.	Harecastle and Wheelock.
								Lawton Junction	Cheshire	N. S.	Crewe and Harecastle.
								Lawton Siding (Edge & Son's Works)	Salop	G. W.	Shifnal.
								Lawton's Carr Bridge Siding	Lancs	L. & N. W.	Glazebury.
								Laycock's, W. S., Siding	Derby	Mid.	Sheffield, Mill Houses and Ecclesall.
								Laygate Lane Siding	Durham	N. E.	South Shields.
								Laygate Lime & Coal Depôts	Durham	N. E.	South Shields.
								Laygate Manure Wharf	Durham	N. E.	South Shields.
G	P							Laytown	Meath	G. N. (I.)	Dublin and Drogheda.
								Lazenby Depôts	Yorks	N. E.	South Bank.
G	P	F	L	H	C	5	0	Lazonby & Kirkoswald	Cumb'land	Mid.	Appleby and Carlisle.
								Long Meg Siding	Cumb'land	Mid.	Lazonby and Little Salkeld.
G	P		L	H				Lea	Lincoln	G. N. & G. E. Jt.	Lincoln and Gainsboro'.
								Anderson's Siding	Lincoln	G. N. & G. E. Jt.	Lea and Gainsboro'.
								Gate Burton Siding	Lincoln	G. N. & G. E. Jt.	Lea and Stow Park.
								Lea & Limehouse Cut Coal Tip (N. L.)	Middlesex	N L—GN—G W—L N W	See London.
								Lea Bridge	Essex	G. E.	See London.
								Lea Bridge District Gas Co.'s Siding	Essex	G. E.	London, Lea Bridge.
G	P	F	L	H	C	1	10	Leach & Co.'s Siding	Lancs	G. C.	Fallowfield.
								Leadburn	Edinboro'	N. B.	Hawthornden and Peebles.
								Leadburn Junction	Edinboro'	N. B.	Leadburn and Eddleston.
G	P	F	L	H	C	6	0	Lead Co.'s Saw Mill	Yorks	N. E.	Middleton-in-Teesdale.
G	P							Leadenham	Lincoln	G. N.	Grantham and Lincoln.
								Leadgate	Durham	N. E.	Consett and Annfield Plain.
								Eden Colliery	Durham	N. E.	Leadgate.
								Gregory, Riddish & Co.'s Siding	Durham	N. E.	Leadgate.
								South Medomsley Colliery, Coke & Brick Works	Durham	N. E.	Leadgate.
G	P					3	0	Leadhills	Lanark	Cal.	Elvanfoot and Wanlockhead.
								Leadloch Colliery	L'lithgow	Cal.	Fauldhouse.
								Leaend Weighs	Lanark	N. B.	Coatbridge.
G	P		L	H		1	10	Leagrave	Beds	Mid.	Bedford and Luton.
G	P					1	10	Lea Green	Lancs	L. & N. W.	Kenyon Junc. Station & Liverpool.
G	P		L	H				Leake	Lincoln	G. N.	Boston and Louth.
G	P		L	H		1	0	Lealholm	Yorks	N. E.	Whitby and Castleton.
								Houlsike Siding	Yorks	N. E.	Lealholm and Danby.
								LEAMINGTON—			
G	P	F	L	H	C	10	0	(Station)	Warwick	G. W.	Birmingham and Banbury.
G	P	F	L	H	C			Avenue	Warwick	L. & N. W.	Birmingham and Weedon.
								Coal Yard	Warwick	L. & N. W.	Leamington (Avenue) and Warwick (Milverton).
								Flavel Range and Imperial Stoves Siding	Warwick	G. W.	Leamington.
								Gas Works	Warwick	G. W.	Leamington.
								Hunter's Repairing Shop and Siding	Warwick	G. W.	Leamington.
								Junction	Warwick	G. W.—L. & N. W.	Leamington and Coventry.
								Milverton	Warwick	L. & N. W.	Same as Warwick (Milverton).
								Smith & Son's Siding	Warwick	L. & N. W.	Kenilworth & Warwick (Milverton).
								Thomas & Co.'s Avenue or Malthouse Siding	Warwick	L. & N. W.	Leamington (Avenue) and Marton.
								Leamore Brick Co.'s Wilk's Siding	Staffs	L. & N. W.	Birchills.
G	P	F	L	H	C	2	0	Leamside	Durham	N. E.	Durham and Sunderland.

EXPLANATION—G *Goods Station.*   P *Passenger and Parcel Station.*   P* *Passenger, but not Parcel or Miscellaneous Traffic.*
F *Furniture Vans, Carriages, Portable Engines, and Machines on Wheels.*   L *Live Stock.*
H *Horse Boxes and Prize Cattle Vans.*   C *Carriages by Passenger Train.*

STATION ACCOMMODATION.	CRANE POWER.	STATIONS, &c.	COUNTY.	COMPANY.	POSITION.
	Tons Cwts.	Leamside—*continued.*			
		Brasside Brick & Tile Wks.	Durham ...	N. E.	Leamside.
		Brasside Manure Siding (Whitfield's)	Durham ...	N. E.	Leamside.
		Durham Main Colliery	Durham ...	N. E.	Leamside.
		Framwellgate Colliery and Coke Ovens	Durham ...	N. E.	Leamside.
		Frankland Brick Works	Durham ...	N. E.	Leamside.
		Frankland Junction	Durham ...	N. E.	Leamside.
		Learmouth Siding & Depôt	Northumb	N. E.	Coldstream.
P		Lea Road	Lancs ...	P.&W.Jt.(L.&Y&L&NW)	Kirkham and Preston.
G		Leasingthorne	Durham ...	N. E.	Chilton Branch.
		Chilton Buildings Siding	Durham ...	N. E.	Leasingthorne.
		Chilton Colliery	Durham ...	N. E.	Leasingthorne.
		Coundon Depôt	Durham ...	N. E.	Leasingthorne and Ferryhill.
		Gipsy Inn Siding	Durham ...	N. E.	Leasingthorne.
		Leasingthorne Colliery Coke and Brick Works	Durham ...	N. E.	Leasingthorne.
		Windlestone Lane Depôts..	Durham ...	N. E.	Leasingthorne.
P		Leasowe	Cheshire..	Wirral	Bidston and West Kirby.
G P F L H C	5 0	Leatherhead	Surrey	{ L. & S. W.	Epsom and Guildford.
				{ L. B. & S. C.	Epsom and Dorking.
		Leatherhead Junction	Surrey	L. & S. W.—L. B. & S. C.	Leatherhead, L. & S. W. & L. B. & S. C. Stations.
		Leat Mill Siding	Devon	G. W.	Lifton.
P		Leaton	Salop	G. W.	Shrewsbury and Ruabon.
		Leavenseat Branch	L'lithgow	N. B.	Crofthead.
		Leavenseat Lime Works	L'lithgow	{ Cal.	Fauldhouse.
				{ N. B.	Crofthead.
		Leavenseat Oil Works	L'lithgow	N. B.	Crofthead.
		Leavenseat Quarry	L'lithgow	Cal.	Fauldhouse.
		Lebus, H., Siding	Middlesex	G. E.	London, Tottenham.
G P F L H C	1 10	Lechlade	Glo'ster ...	G. W.	Witney and Fairford.
		Leckethill Siding	Lanark ...	N. B.	See Bridgend.
G P F L H C	6 0	Leckhampton (G. W.)	Glo'ster ...	{ G. W.	Bourton-on-the-Water & Cheltenham
				{ M. & S. W. Jn.	Over G. W. from Andoversford Jn.
		Leconfields (Lord)—			
		Bigrigg Pits	Cumb'land	W C & E Jt. (Fur.&LNW)	Moor Row.
		Coal Depôt	Cumb'land	W C & E Jt. (Fur.&LNW)	Moor Row.
		No. 4 Pit	Cumb'land	W C & E Jt. (Fur.&LNW)	Crossfield.
		Lecturers Close and Hulme Trust Siding	Lancs	L. & N. W.	Bolton.
		Bridgewater Collieries	Lancs	L. & N. W.	Lecturers Close & Hulme Trust Sid.
		Brigg's Coal Yard	Lancs	L. & N. W.	Lecturers Close & Hulme Trust Sid.
		Hick, Hargreaves & Co.'s Soho Iron Works	Lancs	L. & N. W.	Lecturers Close & Hulme Trust Sid.
		Ramsden's Siding	Lancs	L. & N. W.	Lecturers Close & Hulme Trust Sid.
		Roscoe's Siding	Lancs	L. & N. W.	Lecturers Close & Hulme Trust Sid.
		Walmsley's Siding	Lancs	L. & N. W.	Lecturers Close & Hulme Trust Sid.
G P F L H C	4 0	Ledbury	Hereford	G. W.	Worcester and Hereford.
G P . L H .	3 0	Ledsham	Cheshire..	B'head Jt. (G W & L N W)	Hooton and West Kirby.
G P F L H C	2 0	Ledstone	Yorks	N. E.	Castleford and Garforth.
		Allerton Bywater Colliery..	Yorks	N. E.	Ledstone.
		Lee	Devon	L. & S.W.	See Mortehoe and Lee.
G P	10 0	Lee (for Burnt Ash)	Kent	S. E. & C.	Hither Green and Dartford.
		Lee and Grinling's Siding	Lincoln	G. N.	Grantham.
G P . L		Leebotwood	Salop	S & H Jt. (G W & L N W)	Craven Arms and Shrewsbury.
		Lee Brick Works (Fiddlersgill Brick Works)	Lanark ...	Cal.	Braidwood.
		Leech, Neal & Co.'s Siding	Derby	Mid.	Spondon.
		LEEDS—			
		Airedale Carriage & Wagon Works	Yorks	Mid.	Near Kirkstall.
G P	10 0	Armley (for Farnley and Wortley)	Yorks	Mid.	Holbeck and Kirkstall.
				{ G. N.	Leeds and Bradford.
G P	10 0	Armley and Wortley (G. N.)	Yorks	{ L. & Y.	Over G. N. from Bowling Junction.
		Armley Bridge Siding	Yorks	Mid.—N. E.	Holbeck and Headingley.
		Armley Junction	Yorks	Mid.—N. E.	Kirkstall and Headingley.
		Armley Road Depôts	Yorks	N. E.	Holbeck and Headingley.
		Armley Sidings (Mid.)	Yorks	Mid.—N. E.	Armley.
		Balm Road Siding	Yorks	Mid.	Hunslet.

EXPLANATION—G *Goods Station.*   P *Passenger and Parcel Station.*   P* *Passenger, but not Parcel or Miscellaneous Traffic.*
F *Furniture Vans, Carriages, Portable Engines, and Machines on Wheels.*   L *Live Stock.*
H *Horse Boxes and Prize Cattle Vans.*   C *Carriages by Passenger Train.*

STATION ACCOMMODATION.						CRANE POWER.	STATIONS, &c.	COUNTY.	COMPANY.	POSITION.
						Tons Cwts.	LEEDS—*continued.*			
G	P	.	L	.	.	5 0	Beeston (G. N.)	Yorks	G. N.	Leeds and Wakefield.
									L. & Y.	Over G. N. from Wakefield.
.	.	.	.	.	.	.	Beeston Junction	Yorks	G. N.	Ardsley and Hunslet.
.	.	.	.	.	.	.	Bonded Warehouse	Yorks	Mid.	Hunslet Lane.
G	P	F	L	H	C	10 0	Bramley (G. N.)	Yorks	G. N.	Leeds and Bradford.
									L. & Y.	Over G. N. from Bowling Junction.
							Brotherton & Co.—			
.	.	.	.	.	.	.	Chemical Works............	Yorks	Mid.	Hunslet.
.	.	.	.	.	.	.	Chemical Works (Mid.)...	Yorks	Mid-† L&Y–L N W–N E	Hunslet Lane.
									G.N.	(*See Appendix to follow*).
.	.	.	.	.	.	.	Canal Junction	Yorks	L&NW—L&NW& N E Jt.	Farnley and New Station.
G	.	.	.	.	.	5 0	Cardigan Road	Yorks	N. E.	Leeds and Harrogate.
.	P	F	L	H	C	1 0	Central	Yorks	G. N., L.& Y., L. & N. W. & N. E. Jt.	Terminus.
.	P	.	.	H	C	.		Yorks	G. C.	Over G. N. from Wakefield.
.	.	.	.	.	.	.	Coghlan Steel & Ir.Co.'s Sid.	Yorks	Mid.	Hunslet.
G	.	.	L	.	.	.	Copley Hill	Yorks	L. & N. W.	Dewsbury and Central Station.
.	.	.	.	.	.	.	Copley Hill Sidings	Yorks	G. N.	Holbeck and Beeston.
G	P	.	.	.	.	1 10	Farnley and Wortley......	Yorks	L. & N. W.	Dewsbury and Central Station.
.	.	.	.	.	.	.	Farnley Iron Co.'s Siding...	Yorks	L. & N. W.	Branch from Farnley and Wortley.
.	.	.	.	.	.	.	Fowler & Co.'s Sid. (Mid.)	Yorks	Mid.—L.& N.W.—N.E.	Hunslet Lane.
									G. N.	(*See Appendix to follow*).
.	.	.	.	.	.	.	Geldard Junction	Yorks	G. N. & N. E. Jt.—Mid.	Three Signal Bridge Junction and New Wortley Junction.
G	.	F	L	H	C	10 0	Gotts Field	Yorks	G. N.	Leeds.
.	.	.	.	.	.	.	Graham, Morton & Co.'s Sid.	Yorks	G. N.	Hunslet.
G	.	.	.	.	.	.	Greenwood and Batley's Siding (G. N.)............	Yorks	G. N.—G. C.—Mid.-N.E.	Wellington Street & Geldard Junc.
.	P	.	.	.	.	.	Holbeck	Yorks	Mid.	Whitehall Junction and Armley.
.	P	.	.	.	.	.	Holbeck (G. N.)	Yorks	G. N.	Wortley Junc. and Central Station.
									G. C.—L. & Y.	Over G. N. Line.
.	.	.	.	.	.	.	Holbeck Junction	Yorks	G. N.—G. N.& L. & Y. Jt.	Holbeck Sta. & Three Signal Bge. Jn.
.	.	.	.	.	.	.	Holbeck Junction	Yorks	G. N. & N. E. Jt.—Mid.	Geldard Junc. and Whitehall Junc.
.	P	.	.	.	.	.	Holbeck Junction Station..	Yorks	N. E.	New Station and Headingley.
.	.	.	.	.	.	.	Hudswell, Clarke & Co.'s Siding (Mid.)	Yorks	Mid.—N.E.	Hunslet Lane.
									G. N.	(*See Appendix to follow*).
G	.	F	L	H	C	40 0	Hunslet	Yorks	G. N.	Branch from Beeston Junction.
G	.	.	.	.	.	5 0	Hunslet	Yorks	Mid.	Hunslet, Pass. and Rothwell Haigh.
.	P	.	.	.	.	.	Hunslet (Mid.)	Yorks	Mid.	Holbeck and Methley.
									E. & W. Y. U.—L. & Y.	Over Midland Line.
G	.	F	L	.	.	40 0	Hunslet	Yorks	N. E.	Branch—Marsh Lane & Cross Gates.
.	.	.	.	.	.	.	Hunslet & Stourton Sidings	Yorks	Mid.	Hunslet, Passengers and Rothwell Haigh.
.	.	.	.	.	.	.	Hunslet Engine Co.'s Siding (Mid.)................	Yorks	Mid.—N. E.	Hunslet Lane.
									G. N.	(*See Appendix to follow*).
.	.	.	.	.	.	.	Hunslet Exchange Sidings	Yorks	G. N.—N. E.	Beeston and Marsh Lane.
G	.	F	L	H	C	30 0	Hunslet Lane	Yorks	Mid.	Branch—Hunslet and Whitehall Jn.
.	.	.	.	.	.	.	Junction	Yorks	L&Y&L&NWJt—L&NW	Dewsbury and Whitehall Road.
.	.	.	.	.	.	.	Junction	Yorks	L & N W & N E Jt—Mid.	New Station and Armley.
.	.	.	.	.	.	.	Junction	Yorks	L & N W & N E Jt—N E	New Station and Marsh Lane.
G	P	F	L	H	C	10 0	Kirkstall	Yorks	Mid.	Leeds & Shipley.
G	P	.	.	.	.	.	Kirkstall Forge	Yorks	Mid.	Leeds & Shipley.
.	.	.	.	.	.	.	Kirkstall Forge Co.'s Sid...	Yorks	Mid.	Near Kirkstall Forge.
.	.	.	.	.	.	.	Kitson & Co.'s Sid. (Mid.)	Yorks	Mid.—L.& N. W.—N.E.	Hunslet Lane.
									G. N.	(*See Appendix to follow*).
.	.	.	.	.	.	.	Leeds Bonded Stores........	Yorks	L. & Y.	Wellington Street.
.	.	.	.	.	.	.	Leeds Copper Works	Yorks	Mid.	Hunslet Lane.
.	.	.	L	.	.	.	Leeds Corporation Cattle Market (L. & N. W.)...	Yorks	L. & N. W.—Mid.—N. E.	Dewsbury and Central Station.
							Leeds Corporation GasWks.—			
.	.	.	.	.	.	.	Meadow Lane Sid. (Mid)	Yorks	Mid.—N. E.	Hunslet Lane.
									G. N.	(*See Appendix to follow*).
.	.	.	.	.	.	.	New Wortley Sid. (Mid.)	Yorks	Mid.—N. E.	New Wortley.
									G. N.	(*See Appendix to follow*).
.	.	.	.	.	.	.	Leeds Forge Co.'s Works	Yorks	Mid.	Armley.
.	.	.	.	.	.	.	Leeds Phosphate Co.'s Siding (Mid.)	Yorks	Mid.—L.& N.W.—N.E.	Hunslet.
									G. N.	(*See Appendix to follow*).
.	.	.	.	.	.	.	Leeds Steel Works (W. Scott, Ltd.) (Mid.)......	Yorks	Mid-† L & Y–LNW-NE	Hunslet.
									G. N.	(*See Appendix to follow*).
.	.	.	.	.	.	.	Lowmoor Ironworks Co.'s New Park Pit..............	Yorks	G. N.	Beeston Junction and Hunslet.

EXPLANATION—G *Goods Station.*   P *Passenger and Parcel Station.*   P* *Passenger, but not Parcel or Miscellaneous Traffic.*
F *Furniture Vans, Carriages, Portable Engines, and Machines on Wheels.*   L *Live Stock.*
H *Horse Boxes and Prize Cattle Vans.*   C *Carriages by Passenger Train.*   † *For Local Traffic only.*

G	P	F	L	H	C	Tons	Cwts	STATIONS, &c.	COUNTY.	COMPANY.	POSITION.
								LEEDS—*continued.*			
								Manning, Wardle & Co.'s Siding (Mid.)	Yorks	{ Mid.—L.&N.W.—N.E. / G.N. }	Hunslet Lane. / (*See Appendix to follow*).
G	P	F	L			10	0	Marsh Lane (N.E.)	Yorks	{ N.E. / L.&N.W. }	New Station and Cross Gates. / Over N.E. from Leeds.
	P										
								Middleton Colliery (Mid.)	Yorks	{ Mid.—N.E. / G.N. }	Hunslet. / (*See Appendix to follow*).
								Middleton Estate and Colliery Co.'s Siding	Yorks	G.N.	Beeston.
								Midland Engine Works (J. & H. McLaren)(Mid)	Yorks	{ Mid.—N.E. / G.N. }	Hunslet Lane. / (*See Appendix to follow*).
								Monk Bridge Iron Works (G.N. & N.E. Jt.)	Yorks	{ G.N. & N.E. Jt.—G.C. / —L. & N.W. }	Branch near Geldard Junction.
								Monk Bridge Ir. Wks. (Mid)	Yorks	{ Mid.—L.&N.W.—N.E. / G.N. }	Holbeck. / (*See Appendix to follow*).
G	P					1	10	Neville Hill Sidings	Yorks	N.E.	Marsh Lane.
	P	F		H	C			Newlay and Horsforth	Yorks	Mid.	Leeds and Shipley.
								New Station	Yorks	L.&N.W. & N.E. Jt.	Dewsbury and Marsh Lane.
								New Wortley Junction	Yorks	G.N. & N.E. Jt.—Mid.	Geldard Junction and Armley.
								Nicholson, J., & Son's Chemical Works (Mid.)	Yorks	{ Mid.—†L.&Y.—L N W—NE / G.N. }	Hunslet. / (*See Appendix to follow*).
								Osmondthorpe Colliery	Yorks	N.E.	Marsh Lane.
								Pepper Road Siding	Yorks	Mid.	Hunslet.
								Pitt & Co.'s Sidings	Yorks	Mid.	Newlay and Horsforth.
								Thackeray's Sidings	Yorks	Mid.	Newlay and Kirkstall.
								Three Signal Bridge Junc.	Yorks	GN—L&Y—L&NW—NE	Central and Dewsbury.
								Tunstall & Co.'s Chem. Wks.	Yorks	Mid.	Newlay and Kirkstall.
								Waterloo Main Colliery	Yorks	{ G.N. / N.E. }	Hunslet. / Marsh Lane and Cross Gates.
	P			H	C			Wellington (Mid.)	Yorks	{ Mid. / E. & W.Y.U.—L.& Y. }	Branch—Hunslet and Holbeck. / Over Midland Line.
G		F	L	H	C	10	0	Wellington Bridge (G.N.)	Yorks	{ G.N. / G.C. }	Leeds. / Over G.N. from Wakefield.
G		F	L			10	0				
								Wellington Street—			
G		F	L			10	0	(Station)	Yorks	L.&Y. & L.&N.W. Jt.	Branch from Three Signal Bge. Jn.
G		F	L			15	0	(Station)	Yorks	N.E.	Branch from Geldard Junction.
G		F	L	H	C	25	0	(Station, G.N.)	Yorks	{ G.N. / G.C. }	Branch from Geldard Junction. / Over G.N. from Wakefield.
G		F	L			25	0				
								Whitehall Junction	Yorks	L.&N.W.—Mid.	Dewsbury and Wellington, Pass.
G		F				20	0	Whitehall Road	Yorks	L.&Y. & L.&N.W. Jt.	Branch from Copley Hill.
								Whittaker Bros. & Co.'s Dye Works	Yorks	Mid.	Newlay and Calverley.
								Wortley Junctions	Yorks	G.N.	Beeston and Armley.
								Leeds and Wakefield Brewery Co.'s Siding	Yorks	N.E.	Sherburn-in-Elmet.
								Leeds Bonded Stores	Yorks	L.&Y.	Leeds, Wellington Street.
								Leeds Copper Works	Yorks	E.&W.Y.U.	Rothwell.
								Leeds Copper Works	Yorks	Mid.	Leeds, Hunslet Lane.
								Leeds Corporation Cattle Market (L.&N.W.)	Yorks	L.&N.W.—Mid.—N.E.	Leeds, Wellington Street.
								Leeds Corporation Gas Wks.—			
								Meadow Lane Siding (Mid.)	Yorks	{ Mid.—N.E. / G.N. }	Leeds, Hunslet Lane. / (*See Appendix to follow*).
								New Wortley Siding (Mid.)	Yorks	{ Mid.—N.E. / G.N. }	Leeds, Hunslet Lane. / (*See Appendix to follow*).
								Leeds Fire-Clay Co.'s Siding	Lancs	L.&Y.	Liverpool, Great Howard Street.
								Leeds Forge Co.'s Works	Yorks	Mid.	Leeds, Armley.
								Leeds Phosphate Co.'s Siding (Mid.)	Yorks	{ Mid.—L.&N.W.—N.E. / G.N. }	Leeds, Hunslet. / (*See Appendix to follow*).
								Leeds Road Sid. (Thorpe Rd.)	Yorks	N.E.	Wistow.
								Leeds Steel Works (W. Scott, Ltd.) (Mid.)	Yorks	{ Mid.—†L.&Y.—L N W—NE / G.N. }	Leeds, Hunslet. / (*See Appendix to follow*).
G	P		L	H		3	0	Leegate	Cumb'land	M. & C.	Brayton and Wigton.
G	P	F	L	H	C	5	0	Leek	Staffs	N.S.	Bosley and Froghall.
								Leekbrook Siding	Staffs	N.S.	Leek and Cheddleton.
								Leekbrook Siding	Staffs	N.S.	Leek.
G	P	F	L	H	C	0	15	Leeming Bar	Yorks	N.E.	Northallerton and Bedale.
								Vale of Mowbray Brewery (Plews & Son's)	Yorks	N.E.	Leeming Bar.
	P							Leemount	Cork	C. & Muskerry	Cork and Coachford Junction.
								Leen Valley Junction	Notts	G.N.	Daybrook and Bulwell Forest.
G	P							Lee-on-the-Solent	Hants	Lee-on-the-Solent	Terminus.

EXPLANATION—G *Goods Station.*   P *Passenger and Parcel Station.*   P* *Passenger, but not Parcel or Miscellaneous Traffic.*
F *Furniture Vans, Carriages, Portable Engines, and Machines on Wheels.*   L *Live Stock.*
H *Horse Boxes and Prize Cattle Vans.*   C *Carriages by Passenger Train.*   † *For Local Traffic only.*

STATION ACCOMMODATION.						CRANE POWER.		STATIONS, &c.	COUNTY.	COMPANY.	POSITION.
G	P	F	L	H	C	Tons 10	Cwts 0	Lees	Lancs	L. & N. W.	Greenfield and Oldham.
.	.	.	.	.	.	.	.	Sett Siding	Lancs	L. & N. W.	Lees and Oldham (Glodwick Road).
.	.	.	.	.	.	.	.	Lees, J. B. & S., Timber Depôt	Staffs	G. W.	Swan Village.
.	.	.	.	.	.	.	.	Lee's Siding	Kent	S. E. & C.	Snodland.
.	.	.	.	.	.	.	.	Lees Siding	Lancs	O. A. & G. B. Jt. (G. C. and L. & N. W.)	Park Bridge.
.	.	.	.	.	.	.	.	Lee's Siding	Staffs	L. & N. W.	Albion.
.	.	.	.	.	.	.	.	Leetham & Son's Siding	Glamorg'n	GW—L&NW—Rhy—TV	Cardiff.
G	.	.	.	H	.	.	.	Leetham & Son's Siding	Yorks	N. E.	York.
G	P	.	.	.	.	.	.	Legacy	Denbigh	G. W.	Wrexham and Rhos.
.	.	.	.	.	.	.	.	Legbourne Road	Lincoln	G. N.	Boston and Louth.
.	P	.	.	.	.	.	.	Legh Brick Co.'s Siding	Lancs	G. C.	Hyde Road.
.	.	.	.	.	.	.	.	Le Hocq	Jersey	Jersey Eastern	St. Helier and Gorey.
								LEICESTER—			
.	.	.	.	.	.	.	.	Abbey Lane Sidings	Leicester	G. C.	Leicester.
.	.	.	.	.	.	.	.	Aylestone Road Gas Works	Leicester	Mid.	Leicester.
.	.	.	.	.	.	.	.	Aylestone Rd. Goods Depôt	Leicester	Mid.	Leicester.
G	P	F	L	H	C	10	0	Belgrave Road	Leicester	G. N.	Branch — Melton Mowbray and Market Harboro'.
.	.	.	.	.	.	.	.	Bentley's Siding	Leicester	Mid.	Aylestone Road.
G	.	F	L	H	.	25	0	Bonded Stores	Leicester	L. & N. W.—Mid.	Leicester.
.	.	.	.	.	.	.	.	Braunstone Gate	Leicester	G. C.	Loughborough and Lutterworth.
.	.	.	.	.	.	.	.	Broadbent & Co.'s Siding	Leicester	Mid.	Near West Bridge.
.	.	.	L	.	.	.	.	Cattle Docks (Mid.)	Leicester	{ Mid. L. & N. W.	Knighton Junction. Over Mid. from Wigston Junction.
.	P	.	.	.	.	.	.	Central	Leicester	G. C.	Loughborough and Lutterworth.
G	P	F	L	H	C	20	0	East Station (Queen Street)	Leicester	Mid.	Loughborough & Market Harboro'.
.	.	.	.	.	.	.	.	Evans', A. & W., Mill	Leicester	Mid.	Near West Bridge.
.	.	.	.	.	.	.	.	Fosse Road Wharf	Leicester	Mid.	Near West Bridge.
.	.	.	.	.	.	.	.	Gimson & Co.'s Sid. (Mid.)	Leicester	Mid.—L. & N. W.	Leicester.
G	P	F	L	H	C	10	0	Hefford's Siding	Leicester	G. N.	Leicester and Humberstone.
G	.	.	F	L	.	10	0	Humberstone	Leicester	G. N.	Leicester and Thurnby.
G	P	.	L	.	.	5	0	Humberstone Road	Leicester	{ L. & N. W. Mid.	Branch—North of Mid. Station. Leicester and Syston.
.	.	.	.	.	.	.	.	Leicester Brk. Co.'s Knighton Junction Wks. (Mid.)	Leicester	Mid.—L. & N. W.	Leicester and Wigston.
.	.	.	.	.	.	.	.	Leicester Co-operative Society's Corn Mill (Mid.)	Leicester	Mid.—L. & N. W.	Leicester and Humberstone Road.
								Leicester Corporation—			
.	.	.	.	.	.	.	.	Gas Siding	Leicester	Mid.	Kirby Muxloe and Knighton Junc.
.	.	.	.	.	.	.	.	Siding (Mid.)	Leicester	Mid.—L. & N. W.	Near Cattle Docks.
.	.	.	.	.	.	.	.	L. & N. W. Goods Bch. Jn.	Leicester	L. & N. W.—Mid	Humberstone Road and Syston.
.	P	.	.	H	C	.	.	London Road (Mid.)	Leicester	{ Mid. L. & N. W.	Market Harboro' and Derby. Over Mid. from Wigston Junction.
.	.	.	.	.	.	20	0	Narborough and Enderby Granite Co.'s Siding (L. & N. W. & Mid. Jt.)	Leicester	Mid.	Enderby Branch.
.	.	.	.	.	.	.	.	Nedham Street Wharf	Leicester	Mid.	Leicester and Humberstone Road.
.	.	.	.	.	.	.	.	Norman and Underwood's Siding (Mid.)	Leicester	Mid.—L. & N. W.	Leicester and Knighton Junction.
.	.	.	.	.	.	.	.	Pingle Coal Wharf	Leicester	Mid.	Near West Bridge.
.	.	.	.	.	.	.	.	Richards & Son's Iron Wks.	Leicester	G. N.	Leicester and Humberstone.
.	.	.	.	.	.	.	.	Richards, W., & Son's Iron Works (Mid.)	Leicester	Mid.—L. & N. W.	Humberstone Road and Syston.
.	.	.	.	.	.	.	.	Smith's Timber Co.'s Siding (Mid.)	Leicester	Mid.—L. & N. W.	Passenger Station and Cattle Dock.
.	.	.	.	.	.	.	.	Soar Lane Coal Wharf	Leicester	Mid.	Near West Bridge.
.	.	.	.	.	.	.	.	Taylor & Hubbard's Sid (Mid)	Leicester	Mid.—L. & N. W.	Leicester Goods & Humberstone Rd.
.	.	.	.	.	.	.	.	Watney, Combe, & Co.'s Siding (Mid.)	Leicester	Mid.—L. & N. W.	Leicester.
G	P	.	.	.	.	10	0	West Bridge	Leicester	Mid.	Branch from Desford.
.	.	.	.	.	.	.	.	West Bridge Wharf	Leicester	Mid.	Near West Bridge.
.	.	.	.	.	.	.	.	Leicester Brick Co.'s Knighton Jn. Wks. (Mid.)	Leicester	{ Mid.—L. & N. W. Mid	Leicester, East Sta. (Queen Street). Wigston.
.	.	.	.	.	.	.	.	Leicester Co-operative Society's Corn Mill (Mid.)	Leicester	Mid.—L. & N. W.	Leicester, East Station (Queen Str.)
								Leicester Corporation—			
.	.	.	.	.	.	.	.	Gas Siding	Leicester	Mid.	Leicester, East Station (Queen Str.)
.	.	.	.	.	.	.	.	Siding (Mid.)	Leicester	Mid.—L. & N. W.	Leicester, East Station (Queen Str.)
.	.	.	.	.	.	.	.	Leicester Junctions	Staffs	Mid.	Burton-on-Trent.
.	.	.	.	.	.	.	.	Leicestershire Dairy Co.'s Sid.	Leicester	Mid.	Wigston (South).
G	P	.	L	H	.	.	.	Leigh	Essex	L. T. & S.	Tilbury and Southend-on-Sea.

EXPLANATION—G *Goods Station.*　　P *Passenger and Parcel Station.*　　P* *Passenger, but not Parcel or Miscellaneous Traffic.*
F *Furniture Vans, Carriages, Portable Engines, and Machines on Wheels.*　　L *Live Stock.*
H *Horse Boxes and Prize Cattle Vans.*　　C *Carriages by Passenger Train.*

STATION ACCOMMODATION.						CRANE POWER.		STATIONS, &c.	COUNTY.	COMPANY.	POSITION.
						Tons	Cwts.	Leigh	Lancs	G. C. (Wigan Jn.)	See West Leigh and Bedford.
G	P	F	L	H	C	5	0	Leigh	Staffs	N. S.	Stoke and Uttoxeter.
								Leigham Junction	Surrey	L. B. & S. C.	Tulse Hill and Streatham.
G	P	F	L	H	C	10	0	Leigh and Bedford	Lancs	L. & N. W.	Kenyon Junction Sta. & Tyldesley.
								Abram Coal Co.—			
								Abram Colliery, North	Lancs	L. & N. W.	Pennington and Platt Bridge.
								Abram Colliery, South	Lancs	L. & N. W.	Pennington and Platt Bridge.
								Ackers, Whitley & Co.'s Bickershaw or Plank Lane Colliery	Lancs	L. & N. W.	Pennington and Platt Bridge.
								Hayes' Victoria Cotton Mills	Lancs	L. & N. W.	Atherton and West Leigh.
								Speakman's Bedford Col.	Lancs	L. & N. W.	Leigh and Tyldesley.
								Wigan Coal & Iron Co.— Chowbent West Junction Siding	Lancs	L. & N. W.	Howe Bridge and Hindley Green.
								Eatock Pit	Lancs	L. & N. W.	Chowbent West Junction Siding.
								Priestner Pit	Lancs	L. & N. W.	Chowbent West Junction Siding.
								Sovereign Pit	Lancs	L. & N. W.	Chowbent West Junction Siding.
								Leigh Colliery	Lancs	G. C. (St. Helens Exten.)	See Evans, R., & Co. (Ashton-in-Makerfield).
										L. & N. W.	See Evans, R., & Co. (Earlestown).
G	P	F	L					Leigh Court	Worcester	G. W.	Worcester and Bromyard.
								Leigh's Siding	Lancs	L&Y&LU Jt (LY & LNW)	See Withnell Mill Siding (Brinscall).
								Leighs Wood Branch	Staffs	L. & N. W.	Branch from Pelsall.
								Leighswood Colliery	Staffs	Mid.	Aldridge.
G	P	F	L	H	C	5	0	Leighton	Bucks	L. & N. W.	Bletchley and Watford.
								Arnold's Billington Siding	Beds	L. & N. W.	Grovebury Crossing & Stanbridgeford
								Firbank's or Leighton Sand Co.'s Siding	Beds	L. & N. W.	Grovebury Crossing & Stanbridgeford
								Garside's Siding	Beds	L. & N. W.	Grovebury Crossing and Leighton
G								Grovebury Crossing	Beds	L. & N. W.	Dunstable and Leighton.
								Harris Siding	Beds	L. & N. W.	Grovebury Crossing & Stanbridgeford
								Leighton Gas Works	Beds	L. & N. W.	Grovebury Crossing & Stanbridgeford
								Leighton Gas Works	Beds	L. & N. W.	Leighton, Grovebury Crossing.
								Leighton Sand Co.'s Siding	Beds	L. & N. W.	Same as Firbank's (Leighton.)
								Leinster's Brick Works	Durham	N. E.	East Boldon.
G	P	F	L	H	C	15	0	Leiston	Suffolk	G. E.	Saxmundham and Aldeburgh.
								Carr, W. H., Siding	Suffolk	G. E.	Leiston.
								Garrett & Son's Siding	Suffolk	G. E.	Leiston.
G			L					Sizewell Siding	Suffolk	G. E.	Leiston and Aldeburgh.
								LEITH—			
G						65	0	Albert Dock	Edinboro'	Cal.	South Leith.
G						65	0		Edinboro'	N. B.	South Leith.
								Baring, Brown & Co.'s Sid.	Edinboro'	N. B.	Branch from Bonnington, Goods.
								Bell & Son's Siding	Edinboro'	N. B.	Branch from Bonnington, Goods.
								Bernard, T., & Co.'s Siding	Edinboro'	N. B.	Seafield Siding.
G								Bonnington	Edinboro'	Cal.	South Leith Branch.
G	P					4	0		Edinboro'	N. B.	Leith Walk and North Leith.
								Bonnington Bond Siding	Edinboro'	N. B.	Branch from Bonnington, Goods.
								Bonnington, North Junc.	Edinboro'	N. B.	Trinity and Bonnington.
								British Oil & Cake Mills	Edinboro'	N. B.	Seafield Siding.
								Bruce, Boyd & Co.'s Siding	Edinboro'	N. B.	Edinburgh & Leith Gas Co.'s Siding.
								Callander & Son's Tannery	Edinboro'	N. B.	Branch from Bonnington, Goods.
	P	F	L	H	C			Central	Edinboro'	N. B.	Branch—Abbeyhill and Piershill.
								Chalmers & Co.'s Siding	Edinboro'	N. B.	Branch from Bonnington Goods.
								Chancelot Mill Siding	Edinboro'	Cal	Bonnington and North Leith.
									Edinboro'	N. B	Branch—Bonnington and Trinity.
								Cran, John, & Co.— Shipbuilding Yard	Edinboro'	Cal.—N. B.	Victoria Dock, North Leith.
								Siding	Edinboro'	Cal.—N. B.	Tower Street Siding.
								Cunningham's, J. & J., Sid.	Edinboro'	N. B.	Seafield Siding.
								Currie & Co.'s Siding	Edinboro'	Cal.	Albert Dock.
G						4	0	Custom House Quay	Edinboro'	Cal.	North Leith.
G						4	0		Edinboro'	N. B.	North Leith.
								East Coast Salvage Co.'s Warehouse	Edinboro'	Cal.—N. B.	Victoria Dock, North Leith.
								East Dock	Edinboro'	Cal.	North Leith.
								Eastern Saw Mills	Edinboro'	N. B.	Leith, Central and Piershill.
								East Pilton Siding	Edinboro'	Cal.	Leith.
								Edinburgh & Leith Gas Co.'s Siding	Edinboro'	N. B.	South Leith.

EXPLANATION—G *Goods Station.*   P *Passenger and Parcel Station.*   P* *Passenger, but not Parcel or Miscellaneous Traffic.*
F *Furniture Vans, Carriages, Portable Engines, and Machines on Wheels.*   L *Live Stock.*
H *Horse Boxes and Prize Cattle Vans.*   C *Carriages by Passenger Train.*

STATION ACCOMMODATION.						CRANE POWER.		STATIONS, &c.	COUNTY.	COMPANY.	POSITION.
						Tons	Cwts.	LEITH—*continued.*			
G						10	0 }	Edinburgh Dock	Edinboro'	{ Cal.	South Leith.
G						10	0 }			N. B.	South Leith.
								Garland & Rogers' Siding	Edinboro'	N. B.	South Leith.
						2	0	George Str. Mineral Depôt	Edinboro'	Cal.	North Leith.
								Graham Street Junction	Edinboro'	N. B.	Bonnington, Passengers and Bonnington, Goods.
G							}	Imperial Dock	Edinboro'	{ Cal.	South Leith.
G							}			N. B.	South Leith.
G								Inglis' Siding	Edinboro'	N. B.	Branch from Bonnington, Goods.
								Junction Bridge Mineral Depôt	Edinboro'	N. B.	Bonnington and North Leith.
								Junction Mills Siding	Edinboro'	N. B.	Bonnington and North Leith.
	P							Junction Road	Edinboro'	N. B.	Bonnington and North Leith.
								Leith Chemical Co.'s Siding	Edinboro'	N. B.	South Leith.
								Leith General Warehouse Co.'s Siding	Edinboro'	N. B.	Seafield Siding.
G	P	F	L	H	C	20	0	Leith Walk	Edinboro'	Cal.	South Leith Branch.
						3	0	Lexmount Siding	Edinboro'	Cal.	Newhaven.
								Lochend Road Sidings	Edinboro'	Cal.	South Leith Branch.
								Lothian Coal Co.'s Depôt (Marquis of Lothian's Depôt)	Edinboro'	N. B.	South Leith.
								Menzies & Co.'s Shipbuilding Yard	Edinboro'	Cal.—N.B.	Victoria Dock, North Leith.
								Morton & Co.'s Shipbuilding Yard	Edinboro'	Cal.—N.B.	Victoria Dock, North Leith.
								Newhaven Sidings	Edinboro'	Cal.	North Leith.
								North British Grain Storage and Transit Co.'s Siding	Edinboro'	N. B.	South Leith.
								North British Ice and Cold Storage Co.'s Siding	Edinboro'	Cal.—N. B.	Tower Street Siding.
G	P	F	L	H	C	20	0 }	North Leith	Edinboro'	{ Cal.	Terminus.
G	P	F	L	H	C	3	0 }			N. B.	Branch from Leith Walk.
G						4	0 }	Old Dock	Edinboro'	{ Cal.	North Leith.
G						4	0 }			N. B.	North Leith.
								Oliver's Mineral Siding	Edinboro'	Cal.	Newhaven.
								Ovens & Son's Siding	Edinboro'	Cal.—N. B.	Tower Street Siding.
								Patmore & Co.— New Grain Elevator Warehouse	Edinboro'	Cal.	South Leith.
								Siding	Edinboro'	N. B.	Branch from Bonnington, Goods.
								Peebles, Bruce & Co.'s Sid.	Edinboro'	Cal.	Granton Road and Craigleith.
	P							Pilrig	Edinboro'	Cal.	South Leith Branch.
G						5	0 }	Queen's Dock	Edinboro'	{ Cal.	North Leith.
G						5	0 }			N. B.	North Leith.
								Ramage & Ferguson's Shipbuilding Yard	Edinboro'	Cal.—N. B.	Victoria Dock, North Leith.
								Restalrig Road Sidings	Edinboro'	Cal.	South Leith Branch.
								Seafield Siding	Edinboro'	Cal.—N. B.	Off South Leith Yard.
								Shaw's Siding	Edinboro'	N. B.	Branch from Bonnington, Goods.
								Sinclair's Siding	Edinboro'	N. B.	Branch from Bonnington, Goods.
G		F	L	H		20	0 }	South Leith	Edinboro'	{ Cal.	Terminus.
G	P	F	L			15	0 }			N. B.	Branch from Portobello.
								Stenhouse's Siding	Edinboro'	Cal.—N. B.	Old Dock, North Leith.
								Stewart & Co.'s Siding	Edinboro'	N. B.	Branch from Bonnington, Goods.
								Stocker's Siding	Edinboro'	Cal.—N. B.	Old Dock, North Leith.
								Tower Street Siding	Edinboro'	Cal.—N. B.	Off South Leith Yard.
G	P					2	10	Trinity and Newhaven	Edinboro'	N. B.	Leith Walk and Granton.
								Upper Mineral Siding	Edinboro'	Cal.	Newhaven.
G						10	0 }	Victoria Dock	Edinboro'	{ Cal.	Old Dock, North Leith.
G						10	0 }			N. B.	Old Dock, North Leith.
G							}	Victoria Dock Jetty	Edinboro'	{ Cal.	Old Dock, North Leith.
G							}			N. B.	Old Dock, North Leith.
								Victoria Dock Wharf	Edinboro'	Cal.	Harbour, North Leith.
								West Pier Siding	Edinboro'	Cal.	Harbour, North Leith.
								Younger & Co.'s Siding	Edinboro'	Cal.	South Leith Branch.
								Leith and Newcastle Steam Shipping Co.'s Wharf	Northumb	N. E.	Newcastle-on-Tyne.
								Leith Hill	Surrey	L. B. & S. C.	Same as Holmwood.
								Leith Walk	Edinboro'	Cal.	See Leith.

EXPLANATION—G *Goods Station.*　　P *Passenger and Parcel Station.*　　P* *Passenger, but not Parcel or Miscellaneous Traffic.*
F *Furniture Vans, Carriages, Portable Engines, and Machines on Wheels.*　　L *Live Stock.*
H *Horse Boxes and Prize Cattle Vans.*　　C *Carriages by Passenger Train.*

STATION ACCOMMODATION.	CRANE POWER.	STATIONS, &c.	COUNTY.	COMPANY.	POSITION.
	Tons Cwts.				
. . . . . .	. .	Leith Walk (N. B.)	Edinboro'	{ N. B. { NB, G N, N E (E.Coast)	} See Edinburgh.
G P	. .	Leixlip	Kildare ...	M. G. W.	Dublin and Mullingar.
G P . . . H .	. .	Lelant	Cornwall ..	G. W.	St. Ives and St. Erth.
. . . . . .	. .	Leman Street	Middlesex	G. E.	See London.
G P	1 5	Lemington	Northumb	N. E.	Newcastle and Hexham.
. . . . . .	. .	Blucher Pit	Northumb	N. E.	Lemington.
. . . . . .	. .	Carr's Colliery & Brick Yard	Northumb	N. E.	Lemington.
. . . . . .	. .	Copperas Siding	Northumb	N. E.	Lemington.
. . . . . .	. .	Montague Colliery	Northumb	N. E.	Lemington.
. . . . . .	. .	North Walbottle Colliery...	Northumb	N. E.	Lemington.
. . . . . .	. .	Lemington Point Siding	Northumb	N. E.	Newburn.
. . . . . .	. .	Lempock Well Sid.(Fletcher's)	Hadding'n	N. B.	Saltoun.
G P	. .	Lenaderg	Down ...	G. N. (I.)	Laurencetown and Banbridge.
G P F L H C	5 0	Lenham	Kent	S. E. & C.	Maidstone and Ashford.
. . . . . .	. .	Lennox Foundry..............	Dumbartn	D. & B. Jt. (Cal. & N. B.)	Alexandria.
. . . . . .	. .	Lennox Mill..................	Stirling ...	N. B.	Lennoxtown.
. . . . . .	. .	Lennoxtown—			
. . P . . .	. .	(Station) (Blane Valley) ...	Stirling ...	N. B.	Kirkintilloch and Killearn.
G . . F L H C	2 10	(Station) (Campsie Branch)	Stirling ...	N. B.	Milton and Lennoxtown (B. V.).
. . . . . .	. .	Hurlet & Campsie Alum Works	Stirling ...	N. B.	Milton and Lennoxtown.
. . . . . .	. .	Lennox Mill..................	Stirling ...	N. B.	Extension from Lennoxtown.
. . . . . .	. .	Underwood Chemical Works	Stirling ...	N. B.	Milton and Lennoxtown.
. . . . . .	. .	Lenton	Notts	Mid.	See Nottingham.
G P F L H C	. .	Lentran	Inverness	High.	Inverness and Dingwall.
G P F L H C	. .	Lenwade	Norfolk ...	Mid. & G. N. Jt.	Melton Constable & Norwich (City).
. . . . . .	. .	Lenzie Junction	Dumbartn	N. B.	Bishopbriggs and Croy.
G P . . . L H	3 0	Lenzie Junction Station	Lanark ...	N. B.	Falkirk and Glasgow.
. . . . . .	. .	Cadder Siding	Lanark ...	N. B.	Lenzie Junction & Bishopbriggs.
. . . . . .	. .	Leoch Quarry	Forfar	Cal.	Rosemill.
. . . . . .	. .	Leominster—			
G P F L H C	7 10	(Station)	Hereford ..	S & H Jt (G W & L N W)	Craven Arms and Hereford.
. . . . . .	. .	Bromyard Line Junction...	Hereford ..	G. W.—S. & H. Jt.	Steens Bridge and Craven Arms.
. . . . . .	. .	Kington Line Junction......	Hereford ..	G. W.—S. & H. Jt.	Kingsland and Hereford.
. . . . . .	. .	Leon's Crwys Siding	Glamorg'n	Rhy.	Cardiff.
. . . . . .	. .	Moy Road Siding	Glamorg'n	Rhy.	Leon's Crwys Siding.
. . . . . .	. .	Venning's Siding	Glamorg'n	Rhy.	Leon's Crwys Siding.
. . . . . .	. .	Lepton	Yorks	L. & N. W.	See Fenay Bridge and Lepton.
. . . . . .	. .	Lescher, J. F., Siding	Middlesex	G. E.	London, Spitalfields.
G P F L H C	3 0	Leslie	Fife	N. B.	Branch from Markinch.
. . . . . .	. .	Fettykil Siding	Fife	N. B.	Near Leslie.
. . . . . .	. .	Leslie's Saw Mill	Peebles ...	N. B.	Broomlee.
G P . . . L H	3 0	Lesmahagow	Lanark ...	Cal.	Larkhall and Coalburn.
. . . . . .	. .	Alton Heights Colliery......	Lanark ...	Cal.	Lesmahagow and Coalburn.
. . . . . .	. .	Alton Heights Lime Works	Lanark ...	Cal.	Lesmahagow and Coalburn.
. . . . . .	. .	Alton Heights Saw Mill ...	Lanark ...	Cal.	Lesmahagow and Coalburn.
. . . . . .	. .	Auchren Lime Works	Lanark ...	Cal.	Lesmahagow and Coalburn.
. . . . . .	. .	Carlisle Road Siding........	Lanark ...	Cal.	Lesmahagow and Coalburn.
. . . . . .	. .	Lesmahagow Junction	Lanark ...	Cal.	Motherwell and Fallside.
. . . . . .	. .	Lesmahagow Junction Weighs	Lanark ...	Cal.	Motherwell.
. . P . . .	. .	Les Marais	Jersey	Jersey Eastern	St. Helier and Gorey.
. . . . . .	. .	Lester's Minera LimeCo.'sSid.	Denbigh ...	G. W.	Minera.
G P F L H C	0 15	Letham Grange	Forfar	N. B.	Arbroath Junction and Montrose.
. . . . . .	. .	Letham Mill Siding	Forfar	Cal.	See Arbroath.
G P . . . L H	. .	Lethenty	Aberdeen	G. N. of S.	Inverurie and Old Meldrum.
G P . . . L .	. .	Letterkenny	Donegal ...	L. & L. S.	Londonderry and Burtonport.
G P F L H C	1 10	Letterston	Pembroke	G. W.	Clynderwen and Fishguard.
. . P . . .	. .	Leuchars Junction..............	Fife	N. B.	Dairsie and Leuchars, Old.
G P* . . . L H	. .	Leuchars Junction Station ...	Fife	N. B.	Ladybank and Dundee.
G P* . . . L H	. .	Leuchars, Old	Fife	N. B.	Ladybank and Tayport.
G P F L H C	5 0	Leven...........................	Fife	N. B.	Cameron Bridge and Anstruther.
. . . . . .	. .	Creosote Works	Fife	N. B.	Branch from Leven.
. . . . . .	. .	Durie Colliery	Fife	N. B.	Leven and Largo.
. . . . . .	. .	Durie Foundry	Fife	N. B.	Branch from Leven.
. . . . . .	. .	Kirkland Siding (Cyanide Co.'s Siding)	Fife	N. B.	Branch—Cameron Bridge & Leven.
. . . . . .	. .	Leven Harbour and Docks	Fife	N. B.	Branch from Leven.
. . . . . .	. .	Silverburn Siding	Fife	N. B.	Leven and Largo.
. . . . . .	. .	Wemyss Saw Mill (Donald-son & Son's)..............	Fife	N. B.	Branch from Leven.
. . . . . .	. .	Wilkie & Gibb's Brick Wks.	Fife	N. B.	Leven and Largo.

EXPLANATION—G *Goods Station.*   P *Passenger and Parcel Station.*   P* *Passenger, but not Parcel or Miscellaneous Traffic.*
F *Furniture Vans, Carriages, Portable Engines, and Machines on Wheels.*   L *Live Stock.*
H *Horse Boxes and Prize Cattle Vans.*   C *Carriages by Passenger Train.*

STATION ACCOMMODATION.						CRANE POWER.	STATIONS, &c.	COUNTY.	COMPANY.	POSITION.
						Tons Cwts.				
..	..	..	..	..	..	.. ..	Levenbank Dye Works (N.B.)	Dumbartn	N. B.—Cal.	Jamestown.
..	..	..	..	..	..	.. ..	Levenbank Foundry	Dumbartn	D. & B. Jt. (Cal. & N. B.)	Dalreoch.
..	..	..	..	..	..	.. ..	Leven Cols. Nos. 1, 2, 3, & 4.	Fife	N. B.	Cameron Bridge.
..	..	..	..	..	..	.. ..	Leven Ship Yard (Denny, W, & Bros.' Siding)	Dumbartn	Cal.—D. & B. Jt.	Dumbarton.
G	P	.	L	H	.	5 0	Levenshulme	Lancs	G. C.	Manchester, Central and Guide Bge.
G	P	.	.	.	C	.. ..	Levenshulme and Burnage	Lancs	L. & N. W.	Manchester and Stockport.
..	..	..	..	..	..	.. ..	Lever Bros.' Port Sunlight Sid.	Cheshire	B'head Jt.(G W & L N W)	Spital.
G	P	.	L	H	C	.. ..	Lever Street Yard	Lancs	L. & N. W.	See Bolton.
G	P	.	L	.	.	.. ..	Leverton	Notts	G. C.	Retford and Lincoln.
..	..	..	..	..	..	.. ..	Levisham	Yorks	N. E.	Whitby and Malton.
..	..	..	..	..	..	.. ..	Farworth Siding	Yorks	N. E.	Levisham and Pickering.
..	..	..	..	..	..	.. ..	Newton Dale Siding	Yorks	N. E.	Levisham and Goathland.
..	..	..	..	..	..	.. ..	Raindale Siding	Yorks	N. E.	Levisham and Goathland.
G	P	F	L	H	C	5 0	Lewden Colliery	Yorks	G. C.	Worsboro'.
..	..	..	..	..	..	.. ..	Lewes	Sussex	L. B. & S. C.	Brighton and Polegate.
..	..	..	..	..	..	.. ..	Southerham Siding	Sussex	L. B. & S. C.	Lewes.
..	..	..	..	..	..	.. ..	Strickland's Siding	Sussex	L. B. & S. C.	Lewes.
..	..	..	..	..	..	.. ..	Lewes Road	Sussex	L. B. & S. C.	See Brighton.
..	..	..	..	..	..	.. ..	Lewis & David's Siding	Glamorg'n	R. & S. B.	Port Talbot (Aberavon).
							Lewis & Son's—			
..	..	..	..	..	..	.. ..	Bryngwyn Steel Works	Glamorg'n	L. & N. W.	Gorseinon.
..	..	..	..	..	..	.. ..	Tin Plate Works	Glamorg'n	L. & N. W.	Gorseinon.
..	..	..	..	..	..	.. ..	Lewis, A., Siding	Norfolk	G. E.	Heacham.
..	..	..	..	..	..	.. ..	Lewis' Chemical Wks. (Mid.)	Glamorg'n	Mid.—G. W.—L. & N.W.	Pontardawe.
..	..	..	..	..	..	.. ..	Lewis' Copper Wharf	Cheshire	B'head Jt—CLC—NW&L	Birkenhead.
..	..	..	..	..	..	.. ..	Lewis' Dark Lane Siding	Salop	L. & N. W.	Stirchley.
..	..	..	..	..	..	.. ..	Lewis, E. C., Siding	Warwick	G. W.	Birmingham, Small Heath.
..	..	..	..	..	..	.. ..	Lewis' (Executors) Siding	Denbigh	L. & N. W.	Conway.
..	..	..	..	..	..	.. ..	Lewis Graigola Colliery Co.'s Siding (Mid.)	Glamorg'n	{ Mid.—G. W.—L. & N.W { Mid.—G. W.—L. & N.W	Same as Sister's Pit (Six Pit Junc). Same as Sister's Pit (Glais).
..	..	..	..	..	..	.. ..	Lewis Merthyr Colliery	Glamorg'n	T. V.	Same as Coedcae Colliery (Porth).
..	..	..	..	..	..	.. ..	Lewis' Waste Tip Siding	Lancs	S. & M. Jt. (G. C. & Mid.)	Widnes.
G	P	.	.	.	.	1 5	Lewisham Junction	Kent	S. E. & C.	St. John's and Lewisham Junc. Sta.
.	P	.	.	.	.	.. ..	Lewisham Junction Station	Kent	S. E. & C.	New Cross and Blackheath.
..	..	..	..	..	..	.. ..	Lewisham Road	Kent	S. E. & C.	Nunhead and Greenwich.
G	P	F	L	H	C	5 0	Lexmount Siding	Edinboro'	Cal.	See Leith.
G	P	.	.	.	.	.. ..	Leyburn	Yorks	N. E.	Northallerton and Hawes.
..	..	..	..	..	..	.. ..	Leycett	Staffs	N. S.	Alsager Junc. and Keele Junc.
..	..	..	..	..	..	.. ..	Madeley Coal & Iron Co.'s Leycett Colliery	Staffs	N. S.	Leycett.
..	..	..	..	..	..	.. ..	Leycett Colliery	Staffs	{ L. & N. W. { N. S.	See Madeley Cl. & Ir. Co. (Madeley). See Madeley Cl. & Ir. Co. (Leycett).
G	P	F	L	H	C	10 0	Leyland	Lancs	N.U.Jt.(L&NW.&L.&Y.)	Preston and Euxton.
..	..	..	..	..	..	.. ..	Bashall & Co.'s Farington Mill	Lancs	N.U.Jt. (L.&NW.&L&Y)	Leyland and Farington.
G	P	F	L	H	C	.. ..	Leyny	Sligo	G. S. & W.	Collooney and Claremorris.
.	P*	.	.	.	.	.. ..	Leysdown	Kent	S. E. & C. (Sheppey)	Extension from Queenborough.
..	..	..	..	..	..	.. ..	Harty Road Siding	Kent	S. E. & C. (Sheppey)	Eastchurch and Leysdown.
G	P	.	L	H	.	1 10	Leysmill	Forfar	Cal.	Forfar and Arbroath.
..	..	..	..	..	..	.. ..	Border Siding	Forfar	Cal.	Friockheim and Leysmill.
..	..	..	..	..	..	.. ..	Leysmill Quarry	Forfar	Cal.	Friockheim and Leysmill.
..	..	..	..	..	..	.. ..	Leys Siding	Staffs	G. W.	Same as Roberts & Cooper's (Brettell Lane).
G	P	.	.	.	.	.. ..	Leys Siding (L. & N. W.)	Derby	L. & N. W.—N. S.	Derby.
G	.	.	.	.	.	.. ..	Leyton	Essex	G. E.	Stratford and Loughton.
.	P	.	.	.	.	.}	Leyton	Essex	{ Mid. { T.&F.G.Jt(LT&S&Mid)	} South Tottenham and Leytonstone.
G	P	.	.	.	.	.}				
.	.	.	.	.	.	.. ..	Leytonstone	Essex	G. E.	Stratford and Loughton.
..	..	..	..	..	..	.. ..	Coombe & Co.'s Siding	Essex	G. E.	Leytonstone.
..	..	..	..	..	..	.. ..	Fasey, A., & Son's Siding	Essex	G. E.	Leytonstone.
G	.	.	.	.	.	.}	Leytonstone	Essex	{ Mid. { T.&F.G.Jt(LT&S&Mid)	} Leyton and East Ham.
.	P	.	.	.	.	.}				
.	P	.	.	.	.	.. ..	Lezayre	I. of Man.	Manx Northern	St. John's and Ramsey.
G	P	F	L	H	C	1 10	Lhanbryde	Elgin&Mo'	High.	Elgin and Keith.
..	..	..	..	..	..	.. ..	Libanus Colliery	Mon	L. & N. W.	Same as Matthews Sid.(Blackwood).
							LICHFIELD—			
G	P	F	L	H	C	10 0	City	Staffs	L. & N. W.	Lichfield, T. V. (H. L.) and Walsall.
..	..	..	..	..	..	.. ..	Evans & Co.'s Trent Valley Maltings	Staffs	L. & N. W.	Alrewas and Armitage.
..	..	..	..	..	..	.. ..	Lichfield Brewery Co.'s Siding	Staffs	L. & N. W.	City and Alrewas.

EXPLANATION—G *Goods Station.*   P *Passenger and Parcel Station.*   P* *Passenger, but not Parcel or Miscellaneous Traffic.*
F *Furniture Vans, Carriages, Portable Engines, and Machines on Wheels.*   L *Live Stock.*
H *Horse Boxes and Prize Cattle Vans.*   C *Carriages by Passenger Train.*

STATION ACCOMMODATION.						CRANE POWER.	STATIONS, &c.	COUNTY.	COMPANY.	POSITION.
						Tons Cwts.	LICHFIELD—continued.			
							Richardson's Siding	Staffs	L. & N. W.	City and Trent Valley Stations.
							South Staffordshire Water-works	Staffs	L. & N. W.	City and Hammerwich.
.	P	.	.	.	.		Trent Valley, High Level...	Staffs	L. & N. W.	Burton and Walsall.
.	P	.	L	.	.		Trent Valley, Low Level...	Staffs	L. & N. W.	Nuneaton and Stafford.
							Lidgerwood's Siding...........	Dumbartn	N. B.	Dalmuir.
							Lidgett Colliery	Yorks	G. C.	Elsecar.
							Lidgett's Colliery	Yorks	Mid.	Wentworth and Hoyland Common.
.	P						Lidlington	Beds	L. & N. W.	Bedford and Bletchley.
G	P	.	L	H	.	3 0	Liff	Forfar ...	Cal.	Dundee and Lochee.
							Dundee Floorcloth & Lino-leum Co.'s Siding	Forfar ...	Cal.	Liff.
							Liffey Junction Station........	Dublin ...	M. G. W.	See Dublin.
G	P					1 10	Lifford	Worcester	Mid.	King's Norton and King's Heath.
							Bayliss' Siding	Worcester	Mid.	Near Lifford.
							Bournville Village Trust Sid	Worcester	Mid.	Lifford.
							Cadbury Bros.' Siding	Worcester	Mid.	Selly Oak and King's Norton.
							Cadbury's Brick Yard	Worcester	Mid.	Lifford.
							King's Norton Metal Co.'s Siding	Worcester	Mid.	Near Lifford.
G	P	F	L	H	C	1 10	Lifton	Devon ...	G. W.	Tavistock and Launceston.
							Leat Mill Siding	Devon ...	G. W.	Lifton and Launceston.
							Lifton Quarry Siding	Devon ...	G. W.	Lifton and Launceston.
G	P	.	L	H	C	10 0	Lightcliffe (L. & Y.)	Yorks	{ L. & Y. / G. N.	Halifax and Bradford. / Over L. & Y. from Bowling Junc.
							Brook & Sons' Siding	Yorks	L. & Y.	Lightcliffe.
G							Lightmoor	Salop	G. W.	Shifnal and Coalbrookdale.
							Coalbrookdale Co.'s Tile Works	Salop	G. W.	Lightmoor.
							Lightmoor Colliery	Glo'ster ...	G. W.	Bilson Junction.
							Lightmoor Siding	Glo'ster ...	S.&WyeJt.(G.W.& Mid.)	Drybrook Road.
							Lightshaw Colliery	Ayr	G. & S.W.	Muirkirk.
.	P						Lilbourne	Warwick...	L. & N. W.	Market Harboro' and Rugby.
							Lilleshall Coal and Iron Co.—			
							Hollinswood Siding	Salop	L. & N. W.	Oakengates.
							Ironworks and Colliery......	Salop	{ G. W. / L. & N. W.	Hollinswood. / Donnington.
							Priors Lee Siding	Salop	{ G. W. / L. & N. W.	Hollinswood. / Oakengates.
							Siding (G. N.)..................	Staffs	{ G. N. / L. & N. W.	Stafford Common. / Stafford.
							Snedshill Siding...............	Salop	L. & N. W.	Oakengates.
							Snedshill Works	Salop	G. W.	Hollinswood.
							Lilleshall Co.'s Siding	Salop	G. W.	Presthope.
							Lillie Bridge Sidings...........	Middlesex	W.L.E.Jt.(GW,L&NW, L.&S.W.,&L.B.&S.C.)	London, Kensington.
							Lilliehill Brick & Tile Works	Fife	N. B.	Townhill Junction Station.
							Lilliehill Junction	Fife	N. B.	Whitemyre Junc. Sta. and Steelend.
.	P						Lilliput Road	Glamorg'n	Swan. & Mum.	Mumbles and Mumbles Road.
							Lilyburn Print Works.........	Stirling ...	N. B.	Milton.
							Lily Drift Col. & Coke Ovens	Durham ...	N. E.	Rowland's Gill.
G	P	.	L	H	C	3 0	Limavady	Derry	N. C. Com. (Mid.)	Limavady Junction and Dungiven.
G	P	.	L	.	.		Limavady Junction	Derry	N. C. Com. (Mid.)	Londonderry and Coleraine.
							Limefield Junction..............	Edinboro'	Cal.	West Calder and Newpark.
							Limefield Weighs	Edinboro'	Cal.	West Calder.
							Limehouse	Middlesex	G. E.	See London.
							Limehouse Cut Coal Tip (N.L.)	Middlesex	N L—G N—G W—L N W	See Lea & Limehouse Cut Coal Tip.
G	P	F	L	H	C	20 0	Limerick (G. S. & W.).........	Limerick..	{ G. S. & W. / M. G. W.	Ennis and Tipperary. / Over G. S. & W. from Athenry.
G	P	F	L	H	C	. .	Limerick Junction Station ...	Tipperary	G. S. & W.	Clonmel and Limerick.
							Limerigg Collieries	Stirling ...	N. B.	Slamannan.
							Limerigg Junction...............	Stirling ...	N. B.	Longriggend and Slamannan.
G						1 10	Lime Road	Stirling ...	N. B.	Falkirk and Bonnybridge.
						3 0	Lime Wharf Chemical Wks.	Stirling ...	N. B.	Branch—Lime Road & Bonnybridge.
							Rough Castle Brick Works	Stirling ...	N. B.	Lime Road and Bonnybridge.
						1 10	Rough Castle Oil Works ...	Stirling ...	N. B.	Branch—Lime Road & Bonnybridge.
							Lime Street......................	Lancs	L. & N. W.	See Liverpool.
							Lime Wharf Chemical Works	Stirling ...	{ Cal. / N. B.	Falkirk, Camelon. / See Lime Road.
							Limeylands Colliery	Hadding'n	N. B.	Ormiston.
G	P	.	.	H	.	1 10	Limpley Stoke	Wilts	G. W.	Bathampton and Bradford.

EXPLANATION—G *Goods Station.*   P *Passenger and Parcel Station.*   P² *Passenger, but not Parcel or Miscellaneous Traffic.*
F *Furniture Vans, Carriages, Portable Engines, and Machines on Wheels.*   L *Live Stock.*
H *Horse Boxes and Prize Cattle Vans.*   C *Carriages by Passenger Train.*

Station Accommodation.						Crane Power.		STATIONS, &c.	COUNTY.	COMPANY.	POSITION.
						Tons	Cwts.	Linacre Works	Lancs	Mid.	See Liverpool United Gas Co. (Liverpool).
G	P	F	L	H	C	.	.	Linby	Notts	{ G. N. / Mid.	Daybrook and Annesley Junction. / Nottingham and Mansfield.
								Linby Colliery	Notts	Mid.	Linby and Hucknall.
								Linby Colliery (G. N.)	Notts	G. N.—G. C.	Hucknall and Linby.
								LINCOLN—			
G		F				10	0	(Station)	Lincoln	G. C.	Market Rasen and Lincoln (Mid.)
G	P	F	L	H	C	10	0	(Station, G. N.)	Lincoln	{ G. N. / G. C. / G. E. / L. D. & E. C.	Boston and Doncaster. / Over G. N. Line. / Over G. N. Line. / Over G. N. from Pyewipe Junction.
G	P	F	L	H	C	10	0 }	(Station, Mid.)	Lincoln	{ Mid. / G. C.	Hykeham & Lincoln Junction. / Over Mid. from Lincoln Junction.
	P		L	H	C	.	. }				
								Boultham Gate Siding	Lincoln	Mid.	Near Lincoln.
								Boultham Junction	Lincoln	G. N. & G. E. Jt.	Pyewipe Junc. & Greetwell Junc.
								Bracebridge Gas Works	Lincoln	G. N.	Lincoln and Waddington.
								Cannon, B., & Co.'s Siding (Mid.)	Lincoln	Mid.—G. C.—G. N.	Lincoln.
								Clark's Crank & Forging Co.'s Siding (G. N.)	Lincoln	G. N.—G. C.—Mid.	Lincoln.
								Clayton & Shuttleworth's Siding (G. C.)	Lincoln	G. C.—G. N.—Mid.	Lincoln.
								Durham Ox Junction	Lincoln	G. C.—G. N.	Market Rasen and Lincoln (G. N.)
								Foster & Co.'s Siding (Mid.)	Lincoln	Mid.—G. C.—G. N.	Lincoln.
								Gallsworthy & Son's Siding (Mid.)	Lincoln	Mid.—G. C.—G. N.	Lincoln.
								Greetwell Junction	Lincoln	G. N.—G. N. & G. E. Jt.	Washingboro' and Sincil Junction.
								Junction	Lincoln	G. C.—Mid.	Market Rasen and Lincoln (Mid.)
								Lincoln Leather Co.'s Siding (Mid.)	Lincoln	Mid.—G. N.	Lincoln.
								Lincoln Sewage Farm (GN)	Lincoln	G. N.—G. C.	Lincoln and Washingboro'.
								Lincoln Tannery Co.'s Siding (Mid.)	Lincoln	Mid.—G. N.	Lincoln.
								Lincoln Wgn. Co.'s Sid.(GN)	Lincoln	G. N.—G. C.—Mid.	Lincoln.
								Monk's Abbey Siding (G C)	Lincoln	G. C.—Mid.	Lincoln.
								Newsum, Sons & Co.'s Siding (G. C.)	Lincoln	G. C.—G. N.—Mid.	Lincoln.
								Pelham Street Junction	Lincoln	G. N.	Lincoln and Waddington.
								Poppleton's Siding (Mid.)	Lincoln	Mid.—G. C.—G. N.	Lincoln.
								Pyewipe Junction	Lincoln	{ G.N.—G. N. & G. E. Jt. / GN & GE Jt.—LD & EC	Lincoln Station and Saxilby. / Lincoln Station and Tuxford.
								Robey & Co.'s Siding (G.N.)	Lincoln	G. N.—G. C.—Mid.	Lincoln.
								Ruston, Proctor & Co.— Iron Works (G. C.)	Lincoln	G. C.—G. N.—Mid.	Lincoln.
								New Boiler and Wood Works (Mid.)	Lincoln	Mid.—G. C.—G. N.	Lincoln.
								Sincil Bank Junction	Lincoln	G. N.—G. N. & G. E. Jt.	Lincoln Station and Branston.
								Stone's Place Siding (G.N.& G. E. Jt.)	Lincoln	G. N. & G. E. Jt.—G. C.	Pyewipe Junc. & Greetwell Junc.
								Warriner's Siding	Lincoln	G. C.	Lincoln.
								West Holmes Junction	Lincoln	G. N.—G. N. & G. E. Jt.	Lincoln Station & Boultham Junc.
								Lincoln Brick & Tile Co.'s Sid.	Lincoln	G. N.	Same as Bracebridge Brick Siding (Waddington).
								Lincoln Brick Co.'s Siding	Lincoln	G. N.	Waddington.
								Lincoln Leather Co.'s Sid.(Mid)	Lincoln	Mid.—G. N.	Lincoln.
								Lincoln Tannery Co.'s Sid (Mid)	Lincoln	Mid.—G. N.	Lincoln.
								Lincoln Wagon & Engine Co.'s Siding (G. C.)	Yorks	G. C.—G. N.—Mid.	Doncaster.
								Lincoln Wagon Co.'s Sid.(GN)	Lincoln	G. N.—G. C.—Mid.	Lincoln.
								Lincoln Wagon Works	Glamorg'n	GW—L&NW—Rhy—TV	Cardiff.
G	P		L	H				Lindal	Lancs	Furness	Ulverston and Dalton.
								Lindal Ore Depôt Mineral Sid.(Ulverston Ore Depôt)	Lancs	Furness	Lindal.
G	P		L	H				Lindean	Selkirk	N. B.	Galashiels and Selkirk.
								Lindley's Stone Siding (Mid.)	Notts	Mid.—G. C.	Mansfield.
								Lindows— Ehen Valley Branch Pits Nos. 1, 2, and 3	Cumb'land	WC & E Jt.(Fur. & L N W)	Gillfoot.
								Rowfoot Pit	Cumb'land	WC & E Jt.(Fur. & L N W)	Gillfoot.
								Sir John Pit	Cumb'land	WC & E Jt.(Fur. & L N W)	Moor Row.
								Sykehouse Mines	Cumb'land	WC & E Jt.(Fur. & L N W)	Moor Row.

EXPLANATION—G *Goods Station.* P *Passenger and Parcel Station.* P *Passenger, but not Parcel or Miscellaneous Traffic.*
F *Furniture Vans, Carriages, Portable Engines, and Machines on Wheels.* L *Live Stock.*
H *Horse Boxes and Prize Cattle Vans.* C *Carriages by Passenger Train.*

STATION ACCOMMODATION.						CRANE POWER.	STATIONS, &c.	COUNTY.	COMPANY.	POSITION.
						Tons Cwts				
..	..	..	..	..	..	..	Lindsay & Low's Siding	Forfar....	{ Cal.	Dundee, West.
									N. B.	Dundee, Tay Bridge.
..	..	..	..	..	..	..	Lindsay & Son's Siding	Edinboro'	N. B.	Edinburgh, Waverley.
..	..	..	..	..	..	..	Scarlett's Siding	Edinboro'	N. B.	Lindsay & Son's Siding.
							Veitch, Moir, & Erskine's Siding	Edinboro'	N. B.	Lindsay & Son's Siding.
..	..	..	..	..	..	..	Lindsay Colliery	Fife	N. B.	Kelty.
..	..	..	..	..	..	..	Lindsay Pit (L. & N. W.)	Lancs	LNW—GC (Wig.Jn) L Y	See Wigan Coal & Iron Co. (Wigan).
..	..	..	..	..	..	..	Lindsey Iron Works	Lincoln ...	G. C.	Frodingham and Scunthorpe.
G	..	..	..	..	..	..	Linefoot	Cumb'land	C. & W. Jn.	Linefoot Junction.
..	..	..	..	..	..	..	Alice Pit	Cumb'land	C. & W. Jn.	Linefoot Junction.
..	..	..	..	..	..	..	Linefoot Junction	Cumb'land	C. & W. Jn.—M. & C. ...	Great Broughton and Dearham.
..	..	..	..	..	..	..	Linfit Lane Coal Co.'s Siding	Yorks	L. & N. W.	Kirkburton.
..	..	..	..	..	..	..	Lingard Lane Colliery	Cheshire...	S. & M. Jt. (G. C. & Mid.)	Bredbury.
..	..	..	..	..	..	..	Ling Colliery	Derby	Mid.	Hasland.
..	..	..	..	..	..	..	Lingdale Depôts	Yorks	N. E.	Brotton.
..	..	..	..	..	..	..	Lingdale Mines	Yorks	N. E.	Brotton.
..	..	..	..	..	..	..	Lingerwood Nos. 1 & 2 Siding	Edinboro'	N. B.	Hardengreen.
G	P	F	L	H	C	..	Lingfield	Surrey ...	L. B. & S. C.	East Grinstead and Oxted.
..	..	..	..	..	..	..	Crowhurst Brick Siding ...	Surrey ...	L. B. & S. C.	Lingfield.
..	..	..	..	..	..	..	London and Brighton Brick Co.'s Siding..................	Surrey......	L. B. & S. C.	Lingfield.
..	..	..	..	..	..	..	Lingford, Gardiner & Co.'s Engine Works	Durham ...	N. E.	Bishop Auckland.
..	..	..	..	..	..	..	Ling's Row Siding............	Derby	Mid.	Hasland.
..	..	..	..	..	..	..	Ling's Siding Wharf...........	Derby	Mid.	Hasland.
G	P	F	L	H	C	..	Lingwood	Norfolk ...	G. E.	Yarmouth and Norwich.
G	P	F	..	H	C	..	Link's Road Siding	Northumb	N. E.	Same as Blyth Brick Works (Blyth).
G	P	F	L	H	C	..	Linley	Salop	G. W.	Shrewsbury and Bridgnorth.
G	P	F	L	H	C	2 10	Linlithgow	L'lithgow	N. B.	Edinburgh and Falkirk.
..	..	..	..	..	..	..	Champfleurie Siding (Linlithgow Oil Works)	L'lithgow	N. B.	Branch from Linlithgow Station.
..	..	..	..	..	..	..	Gaol Siding (West Siding)	L'lithgow	N. B.	Linlithgow and Manuel.
..	..	..	..	..	..	..	Linlithgow Foundry	Stirling ...	N. B.	Causewayend.
..	..	..	..	..	..	..	Linlithgow Oil Works	L'lithgow	N. B.	Same as Champfleurie Siding (Linlithgow).
..	..	..	..	..	..	..	Linnyshaw Moss Siding	Lancs	L. & Y.	See Earl of Ellesmere's (Kearsley).
..	..	..	..	..	..	..	Linridge Collieries..............	Lanark ...	Cal.	Same as Lanridge Collieries (Omoa).
..	..	..	..	..	..	..	Linrigg Colliery................	Lanark ...	Cal.	Newhouse.
..	..	..	..	..	..	..	Lintfieldbank Siding...........	Lanark ...	Cal.	See Douglas.
..	..	..	..	..	..	..	Linthorpe Depôts	Yorks	N. E.	Middlesbro'.
..	..	..	..	..	..	..	Linthorpe Iron Works	Yorks	N. E.	Middlesbro'.
..	..	..	..	..	..	..	Linthorpe Wharf	Yorks	N. E.	Middlesbro'.
..	..	..	..	..	..	..	Linthouse Shipbuilding Yard (Stephen's)	Lanark ...	G & P Jt (Cal & G & S W)	Glasgow, Govan.
G	..	..	..	..	..	1 5	Linthwaite	Yorks	L. & N. W	Huddersfield and Stalybridge.
..	..	..	..	..	..	..	Lintmill Siding	Berwick ...	N. B.	See Greenlaw.
G	P	F	L	H	C	1 0	Linton	Cambs......	G. E.	Cambridge and Haverhill.
..	..	..	..	..	..	..	Linton Colliery	Northumb	N. E.	Ashington.
..	..	..	..	..	..	..	Lintz Colliery	Durham ...	N. E.	Lintz Green.
G	P	..	..	..	..	..	Lintz Green	Durham ...	N. E.	Newcastle and Blackhill.
..	..	..	..	..	..	..	Lintz Colliery	Durham ...	N. E.	Lintz Green.
..	..	..	..	..	..	..	South Garesfield Colliery...	Durham ...	N. E.	Lintz Green.
G	..	..	L	..	..	4 0	Linwood	Renfrew ...	{ Cal.	Branch near Houston.
G	..	..	L	..	..	6 0		Renfrew ...	G. & S. W.	Linwood Branch.
..	..	..	..	..	..	..	Blackstone Brick Works ...	Renfrew ...	Cal.	Branch near Houston.
..	..	..	..	..	..	..	Blackstone Mains Siding ...	Renfrew ...	Cal.	Branch near Houston.
..	..	..	..	..	..	..	Blackstone Sidings	Renfrew ...	Cal.	Linwood.
..	..	..	..	..	..	..	Clippens Works	Renfrew ...	Cal.	Branch near Houston.
..	..	..	..	..	..	..	Linwood Brick Works	Renfrew ...	Cal.—G. & S. W.	Linwood.
..	..	..	..	..	..	..	Middleton Farm Siding ...	Renfrew ...	Cal.	Branch near Houston.
..	..	..	..	..	..	..	Linwood Branch Junction ...	Renfrew ...	G. & S.W.	Elderslie and Houston.
..	..	..	..	..	..	..	Lion Brick & Tile Co.'s Siding	Leicester..	Mid.	Holwell Junction.
..	..	..	..	..	..	..	Lion Foundry	Dumbartn	N. B.	Kirkintilloch.
..	..	..	..	..	..	..	Lion Tin Plate Works	Mon	G. W.	Nantyglo.
..	..	..	..	..	..	..	Lion Tin Works	Mon	L. & N. W.	Same as Nantyglo Lion Tin Works (Brynmawr).
G	P	F	L	H	C	5 0	Liphook	Hants	L. & S.W.	Guildford and Petersfield.
..	..	..	..	..	..	..	Lipson Junction................	Devon	G. W.	Plymouth.
G	P	F	L	..	..	2 0	Lisbellaw	Ferm'nagh	G. N. (I.)	Clones and Enniskillen.
G	P	F	L	H	C	4 10	Lisburn	Antrim ...	G. N. (I.)	Belfast and Portadown.

EXPLANATION—G *Goods Station.*   P *Passenger and Parcel Station.*   P* *Passenger, but not Parcel or Miscellaneous Traffic.*
F *Furniture Vans, Carriages, Portable Engines, and Machines on Wheels.*   L *Live Stock.*
H *Horse Boxes and Prize Cattle Vans.*   C *Carriages by Passenger Train.*

G	P	F	L	H	C	Tons	Cwts	STATIONS, &c.	COUNTY.	COMPANY.	POSITION.
G*	P					5	0	Liscard and Poulton (Wirral)	Cheshire...	{ Wirral	Bidston and Seacombe.
	P									G. C.	Over Wirral from Bidston Junction.
	P							Wallasey Gas & Water Wks.	Cheshire...	Wirral	Liscard and Poulton.
G	P							Liscooley	Donegal	Donegal	Strabane and Stranorlar.
G	P		L					Lisduff (Knockahaw)	Queens	G. S. & W.	Maryborough and Thurles.
								Lisduff Siding	Queens	G. S. & W.	Maryborough and Thurles.
G	P							Liselton	Kerry	L. & B.	Listowel and Ballybunion.
G	P	F	L	H	C	10	0	Liskeard	Cornwall..	{ G. W.	Plymouth and Bodmin Road.
G	P									L. & Looe	Adjoining G. W. Station.
								Isaac's Siding	Cornwall	G. W.	Liskeard.
								Liskeard Junction	Cornwall	G. W.—L. & Looe	Liskeard and Looe.
G	P	F	L	H	C	1	10	Lismore	Argyll	Cal.	Steamer from Oban.
G	P		L	H				Lismore	Waterford	G. S. & W.	Fermoy and Dungarvan.
	P							Lisnagry	Limerick..	G. S. & W.	Limerick and Killaloe.
G	P	F	L			1	10	Lisnalinchy	Antrim	N. C. Com. (Mid.)	Ballyclare Junction and Ballyclare.
G	P							Lisnaskea	Ferm'nagh	G. N. (I.)	Clones and Enniskillen.
G	P	F	L	H	C	5	0	Lispole	Kerry	T. & D.	Castlegregory Junction and Dingle.
								Liss	Hants	L. & S.W.	Guildford and Petersfield.
								Lissens	Ayr	Cal.	See Auchenmade.
								Lister's Siding	Glo'ster	Mid.	Dursley.
								Lister's Siding	Yorks	L. & N. W.	See Morley Corporation (Morley).
								Lister's Siding (Shetcliffe Mill)	Yorks	G. N.	Bradford, Dudley Hill.
G	P	F	L	H	C	1	10	Listowel	Kerry	{ G. S. & W.	Newcastle West and Tralee.
G	P	F	L							L. & B.	Adjoining G. S. & W. Station.
G	P	F	L	H	C	3	0	Litchfield	Hants	G. W.	Newbury and Winchester.
								Litchurch Sid. (Derby Gas Co.)	Derby	Mid.	Derby.
								Litherland	Lancs	L. & Y.	See Seaforth and Litherland.
G	P	F	L	H	C	10	0	Littleborough	Lancs	L. & Y.	Rochdale and Todmorden.
								Littleburn Colliery	Durham	N. E.	Brandon Colliery Station.
								Littlebury Siding	Essex	G. E.	Great Chesterford.
G	P	F	L	H	C	5	0	Little Bytham	Lincoln	G. N.	Peterboro' and Grantham.
								Adamantine Clinker Works (Lawnwood Siding)	Lincoln	G. N.	Little Bytham and Corby.
								Little Bytham Junction	Lincoln	Mid.—Mid. & G. N. Jt.	Saxby and Bourne.
								Little Dock	Glamorg'n	T. V.	Same as Taff Vale Little Dock (Cardiff Docks).
								Little Driffield Siding	Yorks	N. E.	Same as Kellythorpe Sid. (Driffield).
G	P					5	0	Little Eaton	Derby	Mid.	Ripley Branch.
								Cudlip & Son's Paper Mills	Derby	Mid.	Near Little Eaton.
								Peckwash Mill (Tempest & Son's Siding)	Derby	Mid.	Derby and Duffield.
G	P	F	L	H	C	2	0	Littleham	Devon	L. & S.W.	Exmouth and Budleigh Salterton.
G	P	F	L	H	C	7	0	Littlehampton	Sussex	L. B. & S. C.	Branch—Arundel and Ford.
								Little Hereford	Hereford...	Tenbury Jt (G W & L N W)	See Easton Court (for Little Hereford).
								Little Houghton Crossing	N'hampton	L. & N. W.	Same as Mead & Son's Clifford Hill Mills (Billing).
	P							Little Hulton	Lancs	L. & N. W.	Bolton and Manchester.
								Little Hulton Mineral	Lancs	L. & N. W.	Branch—Bolton and Manchester.
								Little Ilford Sidings	Essex	L. T. & S.	East Ham and Barking.
	P							Little Island	Cork	G. S. & W.	Cork and Queenstown Junction.
	P							Little Kimble	Bucks	G. W.	Princes Risboro and Aylesbury.
G	P		L			1	0	Little Mill	Northumb	N. E.	Alnmouth and Berwick.
								Little Mill Lime Kilns	Northumb	N. E.	Little Mill.
								Little Mill Whinstone Qry.	Northumb	N. E.	Little Mill.
								Little Mill Distillery	Dumbartn	Cal.—N. B.	Bowling.
G	P							Little Mill Junction Station	Mon	G. W.	Pontypool Road and Usk.
								Burgoyne's Siding	Mon	G. W.	Little Mill Junction Station.
G	P			H		2	0	Littlemore	Oxon	G. W.	Oxford and Thame.
								Oxford County Asylum Sid.	Oxon	G. W.	Littlemore.
								Little Mountain Colliery	Carmarth..	L. & M. M.	Tumble.
G	P	F	L	H	C	1	0	Littleport	Cambs	G. E.	Ely and Downham.
G	P							Little Salkeld	Cumb'land	Mid.	Appleby and Carlisle.
G	P	F	L	H	C	6	0	Little Somerford	Wilts	G. W.	Wootton Bassett and Patchway.
G	P		L					Little Steeping	Lincoln	G. N.	Boston and Louth.
								Littlestone-on-Sea	Kent	S. E. & C.	See New Romney and Littlestone-on-Sea.
G	P							Little Sutton	Cheshire	B'head Jt. (G W & L N W)	Helsby and Hooton.
								Littles Wagon Repairing Wks.	Cumb'land	L. & N. W.	Harrington.
								Littlethorpe Brick & Tile Co.'s Siding	Yorks	N. E.	Strensall.
								Littlethorpe Siding	Yorks	N. E.	Ripon.

EXPLANATION—G *Goods Station.*   G* *Coal and Minerals only.*   P *Passenger and Parcel Station.*
P* *Passenger, but not Parcel or Miscellaneous Traffic.*   F *Furniture Vans, Carriages, Portable Engines, and Machines on Wheels.*
L *Live Stock.*   H *Horse Boxes and Prize Cattle Vans.*   C *Carriages by Passenger Train.*

Station Accommodation.	Crane Power. (Tons Cwts)	STATIONS, &c.	COUNTY.	COMPANY.	POSITION.
G P	2 0	Littleton & Badsey	Worcester	G. W.	Evesham and Honeybourne.
		Littleton Colliery	Staffs	L. & N. W.	Penkridge.
		Littletown Colliery	Durham	N. E.	Sherburn Colliery Station.
		Little Treviscoe Siding	Cornwall	G. W.	Drinnick Mill.
G P F L H C	2 0	Little Weighton	Yorks	H. & B.	Howden and Hull.
		Dannatt & Good's Lime Wks	Yorks	H. & B.	Little Weighton.
		Littlewood Brick & Tile Co.'s Siding	Lancs	L. & Y.	Croston.
G P . L H .	1 10	Littleworth	Lincoln	G. N.	Peterboro' and Spalding.
		Littleworth Brick Works	Staffs	L. & N. W.	See Field's (Hednesford).
		Littleworth Tramway Junc.	Staffs	L. & N. W.	Norton Branch.
		LIVERPOOL—			
G . F L H C	20 0	Alexandra & Langton Dock	Lancs	Mid.	Bootle Branch.
		Alexandra Dock	Lancs	L. & Y.	See North Mersey & Alexandra Dk.
. P		Alexandra Dock	Lancs	L'pool O'head	Liverpool.
G P F . H C	20 0	Alexandra Dock	Lancs	L. & N. W.	Branch from Spellow.
G	7 0	Alexandra Dk. Timber Depot	Lancs	L. & N. W.	Branch from Bootle.
G	10 0	Bankfield and Canada Dock	Lancs	L. & Y.	Branch near Bootle.
. P		Bank Hall	Lancs	L. & Y.	North Docks and Marsh Lane.
		Baxendale & Son's Bee Mills	Lancs	C. L. C. (G C, G N, & Mid.)	Branch near Huskisson.
		Bibby & Son's Siding	Lancs	L. & N. W.	Waterloo.
		Blundell, J., & Son's Siding	Lancs	L. & Y.	Marsh Lane and Strand Road.
. P		Bootle (L. & Y.)	Lancs	{ L. & Y. / L. & N. W. }	Bank Hall and Strand Road. / Over L. & Y. from Bootle Junction.
. P		Bootle (Balliol Road)	Lancs	L. & N. W.	Alexandra Dock and Spellow.
		Bootle Junction	Lancs	L. & Y.—L. & N. W.	Bootle and Spellow.
G P	2 10	Breck Road	Lancs	L. & N. W.	Canada Dock and Edge Hill.
G P		Broad Green	Lancs	L. & N. W.	Kenyon Junction Sta. and Lime Str.
. P		Brocklebank Dock	Lancs	L'pool O'head	Liverpool.
		Brown & Co.'s Siding	Lancs	L. & Y.	Sandhills.
G . F L H .	40 0	Brunswick	Lancs	C. L. C. (G C, G N, & Mid.)	Liverpool and Garston.
. P	5 0	Brunswick Dock	Lancs	{ C. L. C. (G C, G N, & Mid.) / L'pool O'head / L. & N. W. }	Brunswick. / Liverpool. / Over Dock Lines from Park Lane.
G	7 0	Brunswick, South Depôt	Lancs	L. & N. W.	Over Dock Lines from Park Lane.
		Canada Dock	Lancs	L. & Y.	See Bankfield and Canada Dock.
G P F L H C	20 0	Canada Dock	Lancs	{ L'pool O'head / L. & N. W. }	Liverpool. / Branch from Edge Hill.
		Canada Dock	Lancs	Mid.	See Sandon and Canada Dock.
G	10 0	Canada Dock Timber Depot	Lancs	L. & N. W.	Branch from Edge Hill.
G . F	10 0	Carriers Dock	Lancs	G. W.	Liverpool.
. P F . H C	1 10	Central	Lancs	C. L. C. (G C, G N, & Mid.)	Terminus.
. P		Central (Low Level)	Lancs	Mersey	Terminus.
		Chadwick's Siding	Lancs	L. & Y.	Great Howard Street.
. P		Clarence Dock	Lancs	L'pool O'head	Liverpool.
		Cliffe's Siding	Lancs	L. & Y.	Great Howard Street.
		Co-operative Wholesale Society's Siding	Lancs	L. & Y.	North Docks.
G		Crown Street	Lancs	L. & N. W.	Branch from Edge Hill.
. P		Custom House	Lancs	L'pool O'head	Liverpool.
. P		Dingle (Park Road)	Lancs	L'pool O'head	Liverpool.
G . F	10 0	Dukes Dock	Lancs	G. W.	Liverpool.
		Edge Hill	Lancs	C. L. C. (G C, G N, & Mid.)	See Wavertree and Edge Hill.
G . F	10 0	Edge Hill	Lancs	L. & N. W.	{ Branch near Edge Hill, Passengers. / Kenyon Junction Sta. & Lime Str. }
. P					
G	3 0	Edge Hill Fruit & Vegetable Depôt	Lancs	L. & N. W.	Branch near Edge Hill, Passengers.
		Edge Lane	Lancs	L. & N. W.	Canada Dock and Edge Hill.
. P		Exchange and Tithebarn Street (L. & Y.)	Lancs	{ L. & Y. / Mid. }	Terminus. / Over L. & Y. from Hellifield Junc.
		Fazakerley, North Junction	Lancs	C. L. C.—Mid.	West Derby and Alexandra Docks.
		Fazakerley, South Junctions	Lancs	C. L. C. (G C, G N, & Mid.)	West Derby & Walton-on-the-Hill.
G	10 0	Great Howard Street	Lancs	L. & Y.	Sandhills and Exchange.
		Hartley's Preserve Works	Lancs	C. L. C. (G C, G N, & Mid.)	Walton-on-the-Hill.
		Hartley's Siding	Lancs	L. & Y.	Kirkdale and Fazakerley.
		Harvey's Siding	Lancs	L. & Y.	Preston Road.
. P		Herculaneum Dock	Lancs	L'pool O'head	Liverpool.
		Herculaneum Dock Coal Cranes and Tips (M. D. and H. B.)	Lancs	C. L. C. (G C, G N, & Mid.)	Brunswick.
		High Level, Coal	Lancs	L. & Y.	Liverpool.
		Hulton Col. Co.'s Cl. Wharf	Lancs	L. & N. W.	Broad Green and Roby.

EXPLANATION—G *Goods Station.*   P *Passenger and Parcel Station.*   P* *Passenger, but not Parcel or Miscellaneous Traffic.*
F *Furniture Vans, Carriages, Portable Engines, and Machines on Wheels.*   L *Live Stock.*
H *Horse Boxes and Prize Cattle Vans.*   C *Carriages by Passenger Train.*

STATION ACCOMMODATION.						CRANE POWER.	STATIONS, &c.	COUNTY.	COMPANY.	POSITION.
						Tons Cwts.	LIVERPOOL—continued.			
G	.	F	L	H	.	36 0	Huskisson....................	Lancs	C. L. C. (G C, G N, & Mid.)	Terminus of North Extension.
.	P	.	.	.	.	. .	Huskisson Dock	Lancs	L'pool O'head	Liverpool.
G	.	.	.	.	.	1 0	Huskisson Junction	Lancs	C. L. C.—Dock Line	Huskisson Station & Sandon Dock.
.	P	.	.	.	.	. .	James Street	Lancs	G. W.	Liverpool.
.	P	.	.	.	.	. .			Mersey	Liverpool, Central & Hamilton Square.
.	P	.	.	.	.	. .			L'pool O'head	Liverpool.
G	P	F	L	H	C	5 0	Kirkdale	Lancs	L. & Y.	Sandhills and Walton Junction.
.	P	.	.	.	.	. .	Knotty Ash and Stanley ...	Lancs	C. L. C. (G C, G N, & Mid.)	Hunts Cross and West Derby.
.	P	.	.	.	.	. .	Landing Stage	Lancs	B'head Jt. (G W & L N W)	Ferry from Birkenhead.
.	P	.	.	.	.	. .	Landing Stage	Lancs	Wirral	Ferry from Seacombe & Egremont.
.	P	.	.	.	.	. .	Langton Dock................	Lancs	L'pool O'head	Liverpool.
.	.	.	.	.	.	. .	Leeds Fire-Clay Co.'s Siding	Lancs	L. & Y.	Great Howard Street.
.	P	F	.	H	C	1 10	Lime Street	Lancs	L. & N. W.	Terminus, Liverpool & Manchester Section.
.	.	.	.	.	.	. .	Liverpool Corporation Electric Power Station.........	Lancs	L. & N. W.	Stanley and Tue Brook.
.	.	.	.	.	.	. .	Liverpool Corporation Manure Siding	Lancs	L. & Y.	Sandhills.
.	.	.	.	.	.	. .	Liverpool Grain Storage & Transit Co.'s Sidings	Lancs	L. & Y.	North Mersey and Alexandra Dock.
.	.	.	.	.	.	. .			L. & N. W.	Alexandra Dock.
.	.	.	.	.	.	. .			Mid.	Adjoining Alexandra & Langton Dk.
.	.	.	.	.	.	. .	Liverpool United Gas Co.— Linacre Works	Lancs	Mid.	Walton and Alexandra & Langton Dk.
.	.	.	.	.	.	. .	Wavertree Gas Works...	Lancs	L. & N. W.	Broad Green and Edge Hill.
.	.	.	.	.	.	. .	Lord Derby's Yard	Lancs	L. & Y.	Sandhills.
.	.	.	.	.	.	. .	Lord's Siding	Lancs	Mid.	Walton and Alexandra & Langton Dock.
G	.	F	.	.	.	5 0	Love Lane	Lancs	L. & Y.	Same as Great Howard Street.
G	.	.	.	.	.	5 0	Manchester Dock	Lancs	G. W.	Liverpool.
G	P	.	L	H	C	1 10			L. & N. W.	Ferry from Birkenhead.
.	P	.	.	.	.	. .	Marsh Lane and Strand Road (L. & Y.)............	Lancs	L. & Y.	Bootle and Seaforth.
.	.	.	.	.	.	. .			L. & N. W.	Over L. & Y. from Bootle Junction.
.	P	.	.	.	.	. .	Musker's Siding	Lancs	L. & N. W.	Breck Road and Tue Brook.
G	.	F	L	H	.	20 0	Nelson Dock	Lancs	L'pool O'head	Liverpool.
G	.	F	.	.	.	10 0	North Docks	Lancs	L. & Y.	Branch near Sandhills.
.	.	.	.	.	.	. .	North Mersey & Alexandra Dock	Lancs	L. & Y.	Branch near Seaforth.
.	.	.	.	.	.	. .	North Shore Mill Co.'s Sid.	Lancs	C. L. C. (G C, G N, & Mid.)	Branch near Huskisson.
G	.	.	.	.	.	10 0	Oil Co.'s Siding	Lancs	L. & Y.	Sandhills.
.	.	.	.	.	.	. .	Park Lane	Lancs	L. & N. W.	Branch from Edge Hill.
.	P	.	.	.	.	. .	Park Road	Lancs	L'pool O'head	See Dingle, Park Road.
G	P	.	L	H	.	2 10	Pierhead	Lancs	L'pool O'head	Liverpool.
.	P	.	.	.	.	. .	Preston Road	Lancs	L. & Y.	Kirkdale and Fazakerley.
.	.	.	.	.	.	. .	Princes Dock	Lancs	L'pool O'head	Liverpool.
G	.	.	.	.	.	5 0	Rainford Coal Co.'s Siding	Lancs	L. & Y.	Sandhills.
.	.	.	.	.	.	. .	Rathbone Road	Lancs	L. & N. W.	Branch from Edge Hill.
.	P	.	.	.	.	. .	Redfern Street Siding	Lancs	L. & Y.	Sandhills and Bank Hall.
.	P	.	.	.	.	. .	Riverside	Lancs	L. & N. W.	Branch from Edge Hill.
.	P	.	.	.	.	. .	St. James	Lancs	C. L. C. (G C, G N, & Mid.)	Liverpool and Garston.
G	P	.	.	.	.	10 0	St. Michaels	Lancs	C. L. C. (G C, G N, & Mid.)	Liverpool and Garston.
G	P	F	.	.	.	20 0	Sandhills	Lancs	L. & Y.	Kirkdale and Great Howard Street.
.	P	.	.	.	.	. .	Sandon and Canada Dock	Lancs	Mid.	Branch from Huskisson.
.	P	.	.	.	.	. .	Seaforth Sands	Lancs	L'pool O'head	Liverpool.
.	.	.	.	.	.	. .	Sefton Park..................	Lancs	L. & N. W.	Garston and Edge Hill.
G	.	.	.	.	.	10 0	Silcock, R., & Son's Siding	Lancs	L. & Y.	Great Howard Street.
G	.	.	.	.	.	. .	South Docks	Lancs	L. & Y.	Over Dock Line from North Mersey.
.	.	.	.	.	.	. .	Spekeland Road Sidings ...	Lancs	L. & N. W.	Branch from Edge Hill.
.	.	.	.	.	.	. .	Building Material Co. ...	Lancs	L. & N. W.	Spekeland Road Sidings.
.	.	.	.	.	.	. .	Dixon's	Lancs	L. & N. W.	Spekeland Road Sidings.
.	P	.	.	.	.	. .	Spellow........................	Lancs	L. & N. W.	Canada Dock and Edge Hill.
G	P	.	L	H	.	3 0	Stanley	Lancs	C. L. C. (G C, G N, & Mid.)	See Knotty Ash and Stanley.
G	.	.	.	.	.	1 10	Stanley	Lancs	L. & N. W.	Canada Dock and Edge Hill.
.	.	.	.	.	.	. .	Stanley Dock	Lancs	G. W.	Liverpool.
.	.	.	.	.	.	. .	Stanley Land and Brick Co.'s Siding	Lancs	L. & N. W.	Edge Lane and Stanley.
.	P	.	.	.	.	. .	Stubb's Flag Yard...........	Lancs	L. & N. W.	Crown Street.
G	P	.	.	.	.	2 0	Toxteth Dock	Lancs	L'pool O'head	Liverpool.
G	P	.	.	.	.	1 5	Tue Brook	Lancs	L. & N. W.	Canada Dock and Edge Hill.
.	P	.	.	.	.	. .	Walton (for Aintree)........	Lancs	L. & N. W.	Canada Dock and Edge Hill.
G	P	.	.	.	.	7 0	Walton Junction Station...	Lancs	L. & Y.	Kirkdale and Aintree.
.	P	.	.	.	.	. .	Walton-on-the-Hill	Lancs	C. L. C. (G C, G N, & Mid.)	Huskisson and West Derby.

EXPLANATION— G *Goods Station.*   P *Passenger and Parcel Station.*   P* *Passenger, but not Parcel or Miscellaneous Traffic.*
F *Furniture Vans, Carriages, Portable Engines, and Machines on Wheels.*   L *Live Stock.*
H *Horse Boxes and Prize Cattle Vans.*   C *Carriages by Passenger Train.*

G	P	F	L	H	C	Tons	Cwts	STATIONS, &c.	COUNTY.	COMPANY.	POSITION.
								LIVERPOOL—continued.			
								Wapping	Lancs	L. & N. W.	Same as Park Lane.
G		F				10	0	Wapping & Salthouse Dock	Lancs	L. & Y.	Over Dock Line from North Mersey.
	P							Wapping Dock	Lancs	L'pool O'head	Liverpool.
G			L			25	0	Waterloo	Lancs	L. & N. W.	Branch from Edge Hill.
	P							Wavertree	Lancs	L. & N. W.	Garston and Edge Hill.
G		F	L	H		10	0	Wavertree and Edge Hill	Lancs	C. L. C. (G C, G N, & Mid.)	Branch—Wavertree and Edge Hill.
G	P					5	0	West Derby	Lancs	C. L. C. (G C, G N, & Mid.)	Hunts Cross and Aintree.
								White Moss Coal Co.'s Sid.	Lancs	L. & Y.	Kirkdale.
								Wigan Coal & Iron Co.'s Broad Green Siding	Lancs	L. & N. W.	Broad Green and Roby.
								Liverpool and St. Helens Brick Works	Lancs	L. & N. W.	St. Helens.
								Liverpool Corporation—			
								Electric Power Station	Lancs	L. & N. W.	Liverpool, Edge Hill.
								Manure Siding	Lancs	L. & Y.	Liverpool, Sandhills.
								Liverpool Grain Storage & Transit Co.'s Sidings	Lancs	L. & Y.	Liverpool, North Mersey and Alexandra Dock.
										L. & N. W.	Liverpool, Alexandra Dock.
										Mid.	Liverpool, Alexandra & Langton Dk.
								Liverpool Manure Co.'s Wks.	Cheshire	B'head Jt—CLC—NW&L	Birkenhead.
								Liverpool Petroleum Storage Co.'s Warehouse	Cheshire	B'head Jt—CLC—NW&L	Birkenhead.
								Liverpool Road	Cheshire	G. C.	See Chester.
								Liverpool Road and Salford (L. & N. W.)	Lancs	L. & N.W.—G. C.—G.W.	See Manchester.
								Liverpool Road and Salford Junction	Lancs	L. & N. W.—M. S. J. & A.	Manchester.
								Liverpool Silver and Copper Co.'s Siding	Lancs	L. & N. W.—S. & M. Jt.	Widnes.
								Liverpool Storage Co.'s Depôt	Cheshire	B'head Jt—CLC—NW&L	Birkenhead.
								Liverpool Street	Lancs	L. & Y.	See Manchester.
								Liverpool Street	Middlesex	G. E.	See London.
								Liverpool Street Junction	Middlesex	G. E.—Met.	London, Liverpool Street and Moorgate Street.
								Liverpool Street Siding	Lancs	L. & N. W.	See Earl of Ellesmere's (Manchester)
								Liverpool United Gas Co.—			
								Linacre Works	Lancs	Mid.	Liverpool, Alexandra & Langton Dk.
								Wavertree Gas Works	Lancs	L. & N. W.	Liverpool, Edge Hill.
								Works	Lancs	L. & N. W.	Garston Docks.
								Liverpool Warehousing Co.'s Siding (G. B. Taylor)	Lancs	Trafford Park Estate	Manchester.
								Liverpool Wharf	Mon	G. W	Newport, Dock Street.
								LIVERSEDGE—			
G	P		L			5	0	(Station)	Yorks	L. & N. W.	Cleckheaton and Huddersfield.
G	P			H		3	10	(Station, L. & Y.)	Yorks	L. & Y.	Bradford and Mirfield.
G	P			H		3	10		Yorks	G. N.	Over L. & Y. from Wakefield Jn.
G						3	10		Yorks	L. & N. W.	Over L. & Y. from Heaton Lodge Jn.
								Liversedge Coal Co.'s Dymond's Siding (L. & Y.)	Yorks	L.&Y.—G. N.—L.&N.W.	Heckmondwike and Liversedge.
								Stanley Colliery (L. & Y.)	Yorks	L.&Y.—G. N.—L.&N.W.	Liversedge and Cleckheaton.
								Liversedge & Son's Siding	Yorks	N. E.	Selby.
								Liverton Mines	Yorks	N. E.	Loftus.
								Liver Works, Nos. 1 & 2 Sids.	Lancs	L. & N. W.—S. & M. Jt.	See United Alkali Co. (Widnes).
G	P		L	H		3	0	Livingston	L'lithgow	N. B.	Ratho and Bathgate, Upper.
								Dean's Oil Works	L'lithgow	N. B.	Livingston and Bathgate, Upper.
G								Knightsridge Siding	L'lithgow	N. B.	Uphall and Livingston.
								Livingstone Spinning Co.'s Siding	Yorks	L. & N. W.	Grotton and Springhead.
G	P		L	H				Lixnaw	Kerry	G. S. & W.	Newcastle West and Tralee.
G	P		L	H				Llanarthney	Carmarth'	L. & N. W.	Carmarthen and Llandilo.
								Llanarth Wharf (Goss's Sid.)	Mon	A (N & SW) D & R—G W	Newport, Alexandra Docks.
G	P	F	L	H	C			Llanbadarn	Cardigan	V. of Rheidol	Aberystwyth and Devil's Bridge.
G	P	F	L	H	C			Llanbedr & Pensarn	Merioneth	Cam.	Harlech and Barmouth.
G	P	F	L	H	C	1	10	Llanberis	Carnarvon	L. & N. W.	Branch from Carnarvon.
								Cambrian Sidings	Carnarvon	L. & N. W.	Llanberis and Cwm-y-glc.
								Cook & D'dol Slate Qry. Co.	Carnarvon	L. & N. W.	Cambrian Sidings.
								Llanberis Slate Qry. Co.	Carnarvon	L. & N. W.	Cambrian Sidings.
								Upper Glyn-rhonwy Quarry Co.	Carnarvon	L. & N. W.	Cambrian Sidings.
								Glyn-rhonwy Slate Co.'s Siding	Carnarvon	L. & N. W.	Llanberis and Cwm-y-glo.

EXPLANATION—G *Goods Station.*   P *Passenger and Parcel Station.*   P* *Passenger, but not Parcel or Miscellaneous Traffic.*
F *Furniture Vans, Carriages, Portable Engines, and Machines on Wheels.*   L *Live Stock.*
H *Horse Boxes and Prize Cattle Vans.*   C *Carriages by Passenger Train.*

STATION ACCOMMODATION.						CRANE POWER.		STATIONS, &c.	COUNTY.	COMPANY.	POSITION.
						Tons	Cwts				
G	P	.	L	.	.	.	.	Llanberis Slate Qry. Co.'s Sid.	Carnarvon	L. & N. W.	See Cambrian Sidings (Llanberis).
G	P	F	L	H	C	1	10	Llanbister Road	Radnor ...	L. & N. W.	Craven Arms & Llandrindod Wells.
G	.	F	L	.	.	1	10	Llanbradach (Rhy.)	Glamorg'n	{ Rhy. { L. & N. W.	Caerphilly and Ystrad Mynach. Over Rhy. from Rhymney Joint Line Junction.
.	.	.	.	.	.	.	.	Coedybrain Quarry	Glamorg'n	Rhy.	Llanbradach.
.	.	.	.	.	.	.	.	Llanbradach Colliery	Glamorg'n	Rhy.	Llanbradach.
.	.	.	.	.	.	.	.	Pwllypant Quarry (Rhy.)..	Glamorg'n	Rhy.—L. & N. W.	Llanbradach and Caerphilly.
.	.	.	.	.	.	.	.	Trehir Quarry...............	Glamorg'n	Rhy.	Llanbradach.
G	P	.	L	H	.	1	0	Llanbrynmair	Montgom..	Cam.	Newtown and Machynlleth.
.	.	.	.	.	.	.	.	Llancaiach	Glamorg'n	T. V.	Same as Nelson.
G	P	.	L	.	.	.	.	Llancaiach (G. W.)	Glamorg'n	{ G. W. { Rhy.	Quaker's Yard and Rhymney June. Over G. W. from Penallta Junction.
.	P	.	.	.	.	.	.	Llancaiach Colliery (G. W.)	Glamorg'n	G. W.—Rhy.—T. V.	Penallta Junction and Llancaiach.
.	.	.	.	.	.	.	.	Llancaiach Branch Junction	Glamorg'n	T. V.	Same as Stormstown Junction.
.	.	.	.	.	.	.	.	Llancaiach Junction	Glamorg'n	G. W.—T. B. Jt.	Llancaiach and Dowlais.
.	.	.	.	.	.	.	.	Llancaiach Junction	Glamorg'n	G. W.—T. V.	Treharris and Nelson.
G	P	.	L	.	.	3	0	Llandaff (G. W.)	Glamorg'n	G. W.—Barry..............	See Ely (for Llandaff).
.	.	.	.	.	.	.	.	Llandaff (for Whitchurch) ...	Glamorg'n	T. V.	Cardiff and Pontypridd.
.	.	.	.	.	.	.	.	Crown Fuel Wks. (Maindy)	Glamorg'n	T. V.	Llandaff and Cardiff.
.	.	.	.	.	.	.	.	Excelsior Wire Rope Works	Glamorg'n	T. V.	Llandaff and Cardiff.
.	.	.	.	.	.	.	.	Howard & Kyte's Siding ...	Glamorg'n	T. V.	Cardiff and Llandaff.
.	.	.	.	.	.	.	.	Wauntreoda Works	Glamorg'n	T. V.	Cardiff and Llandaff.
.	.	.	.	.	.	.	.	Llandavel Colliery...............	Mon	G. W.	Aberbeeg.
.	.	.	.	.	.	.	.	Llanddu Quarry.................	Montgom	Cam.	Llanymynech.
G	P	.	L	.	.	.	.	Llandebie (G. W.)	Carmarth'	{ G. W. { L. & N. W.	Pantyffynnon and Llandilo. Over G. W. Line.
.	.	.	.	.	.	.	.	Cil-yr-ychen Lime Works...	Carmarth'	G. W.	End of Limestone Branch.
.	.	.	.	.	.	.	.	Limestone Branch	Carmarth'	G. W.	Llandebie and Derwydd Road.
.	.	.	.	.	.	.	.	Penson & Southern's Siding (G. W.)................	Carmarth'	G. W.—L. & N. W.	Llandebie.
.	.	.	.	.	.	.	.	Pistil Lime Works	Carmarth'	G. W.	Branch from Limestone Branch.
G	P	.	.	.	.	.	.	Llandebie Lime Works Siding	Carmarth'	G. W.	Pantyffynon.
G	P	F	L	H	C	8	0	Llandenny	Mon	G. W.	Usk and Monmouth.
.	.	.	.	.	.	.	.	Llanderfel.....................	Merioneth	G. W.	Corwen and Dolgelley.
								LLANDILO—			
G	P	F	L	H	C	4	10	(Station, G. W.)	Carmarth'	{ G. W. { L. & N. W.	Pantyffynnon and Llandovery. ‖ Over G. W. Line.
.	.	.	.	.	.	.	.	Junction	Carmarth'	G. W.—L. & N. W.	Llandilo and Carmarthen.
.	.	.	.	.	.	.	.	Junction	Carmarth'	G. W.—V. of T. Jt.	Llandilo and Llandovery.
.	.	.	.	.	.	.	.	Thomas Bros.' Timber Yard (G. W.)	Glamorg'n	G. W.—L. & N. W.	Llandilo.
G	P	F	L	H	C	1	10	Llandilo Bridge	Carmarth'	L. & N. W.	Carmarthen and Llandilo.
.	.	.	.	.	.	.	.	Llandilo Junction Siding......	Carmarth'	G. W.	Llanelly.
G	P	.	.	.	.	.	.	Llandinam	Montgom	Cam.	Moat Lane and Llanidloes.
.	.	.	.	.	.	.	.	Llandough Brick Works	Glamorg'n	T. V.	Penarth Dock.
.	.	.	.	.	.	.	.	Llandough Coal Yard (Price's)	Glamorg'n	T. V.	Penarth Dock.
.	.	.	.	.	.	.	.	Llandough Lime Works (Thomas & Son)	Glamorg'n	T. V.	Penarth Dock.
.	.	.	.	.	.	.	.	Llandough Storage Sidings...	Glamorg'n	T. V.	Penarth Dock.
G	P	F	L	H	C	3	0	Llandovery.......................	Carmarth'	V. of T. Jt.(GW&L&NW)	Llandilo and Llandovery Junction.
G	P	F	L	H	C	8	0	Llandovery Junction............	Carmarth'	L. & N. W.—V. of T. Jt.	Llandrindod Wells & Llandovery.
G	P	F	L	H	C	1	10	Llandrillo.....................	Merioneth	G. W.	Corwen and Dolgelley.
G	P	F	L	H	C	5	0	Llandrindod Wells..............	Radnor ...	L. & N. W.	Craven Arms and Llandilo.
.	.	.	.	.	.	.	.	Llandudno	Carnarvon	L. & N. W.	Branch from Llandudno Junc. Sta.
.	.	.	.	.	.	.	.	Llandudno Gas Co.'s Siding	Carnarvon	L. & N. W.	Llandudno and Deganwy.
.	.	.	.	.	.	.	.	Llandudno Junction Brick Syndicate Siding	Denbigh...	L. & N. W.	Conway.
G	P	F	L	H	C	.	.	Llandudno Junction Station..	Carnarvon	L. & N. W.	Bangor and Rhyl.
.	P	.	.	.	.	.	.	Llandulas.....................	Denbigh...	L. & N. W.	Bangor and Rhyl.
G	P	F	L	H	C	1	10	Llandyssil.....................	Carmarth'	G. W.	Pencader and Newcastle Emlyn.
								LLANELLY—			
G	P	F	L	H	C	10	0	(Station, .G. W.)...............	Carmarth'	{ G. W. { L. & N. W.	Landore and Carmarthen. Over G. W. from Llandilo Junction.
G	.	F	L	.	.	10	0				
.	.	.	.	.	.	.	.	Bevan & Son's Chemical Works (G. W.)	Carmarth'	G. W.—L. & N. W.	Branch from Llanelly.
.	.	.	.	.	.	.	.	Bevan's Castle Chemical Co.'s Siding (G. W.)	Carmarth'	G. W.—L. & N. W.	Llanelly Dock.
.	.	.	.	.	.	.	.	Bevan's Castle Chemical Works	Carmarth'	L. & M. M.	Llanelly.
.	.	.	.	.	.	.	.	Bowen's Chemical Works (G. W.)........................	Carmarth'	G. W.—L. & N. W.	Branch from Llanelly.

EXPLANATION—G *Goods Station.*　　P *Passenger and Parcel Station.*　　P* *Passenger, but not Parcel or Miscellaneous Traffic.*
F *Furniture Vans, Carriages, Portable Engines, and Machines on Wheels.*　　L *Live Stock.*
H *Horse Boxes and Prize Cattle Vans.*　　C *Carriages by Passenger Train.*

STATION ACCOMMODATION.						CRANE POWER.		STATIONS, &c.	COUNTY.	COMPANY.	POSITION.
						Tons	Cwts	**LLANELLY**—*continued.*			
								Brown's, T. & J., Timber Yard	Carmarth'	G. W.—L. & N. W.	On Neville, Druce & Co.'s Line.
								Bryn Chemical Works (GW)	Carmarth'	G. W.—L. & N. W.	Llanelly.
G						15	0	Carmarthenshire Dock	Carmarth'	L. & M. M.	Llanelly.
								Castle (Cille) Colliery	Carmarth'	L. & M. M.	Llanelly.
								Castle (Cille) Colliery (G. W.)	Carmarth'	G. W.—L. & N. W.	Old Castle Siding.
								Castle Col. Co.'s Sid. (G. W.)	Carmarth'	G. W.—L. & N. W.	Llanelly.
G						5	0	Docks (G. W.)	Carmarth'	{ G. W. / L. & N. W.	Branch from Llanelly. / Over G. W. from Llandilo Junction.
								Dolau Junction	Carmarth'	G. W.	Branch from Llanelly.
								Dolau Siding (G. W.)	Carmarth'	G. W.—L. & N. W.	Branch from Llanelly.
								Evan's Grain Warehouse Siding (G. W.)	Carmarth'	G. W.—L. & N. W.	Llanelly.
								Forester & Co.'s Yard (G. W.)	Carmarth'	G. W.—L. & N. W.	Branch from Llanelly.
								Francis & Jenkins' Works (G. W.)	Carmarth'	G. W.—L. & N. W.	On Neville, Druce & Co.'s Line.
								Glanmore Foundry (G. W.)	Carmarth'	G. W.—L. & N. W.	Llanelly.
								Guest & Dewsbury's South Wales Potteries (G. W.)	Carmarth'	G. W.—L. & N. W.	Llanelly.
								Howell & Son's Timber Yard (G. W.)	Carmarth'	G. W.—L. & N. W.	Branch from Llanelly.
								Howell, J. C., & Co.'s Electric Works (G. W.)	Carmarth'	G. W.—L. & N. W.	Branch from Llanelly.
								Hughes' Timber Yard (G. W.)	Carmarth'	G. W.—L. & N. W.	Llanelly.
								James' Morfa Brick Works (G. W.)	Carmarth'	G. W.—L. & N. W.	Llanelly Dock.
								Junction	Carmarth'	G. W.—Hbr. Comm.	Llanelly and Pembrey.
								Junction	Carmarth'	G. W.—L. & M. M.	Llanelly and Cross Hands.
								Llandilo Junction Siding	Carmarth'	G. W.	Llanelly and Loughor.
								Llanelly Galvanizing Co.'s Works (G. W.)	Carmarth'	G. W.—L. & N. W.	Branch from Llanelly.
								Llanelly Gas Works (G.W.)	Carmarth'	G. W.—L. & N. W.	On Neville, Druce & Co.'s Line.
								Llanelly Steel Co.'s Works	Carmarth'	L. & M. M.	Llanelly.
								Llanelly Steel Co.'s Works (G. W.)	Carmarth'	G. W.—L. & N. W.	Old Castle Siding.
								Machynis Brick Works (G. W.)	Carmarth'	G. W.—L. & N. W.	Branch from Llanelly.
								Neville, Druce & Co.'s Copper Works (G. W.)	Carmarth'	G. W.—L. & N. W.	Llanelly.
								Neville, R., & Co.'s Sid. (GW)	Carmarth'	G. W.—L. & N. W.	On Neville, Druce & Co.'s Line.
								Neville's Copper Works Dock (G. W.)	Carmarth'	G. W.—L. & N. W.	Llanelly Dock.
								North Dock	Carmarth'	G. W.	Llanelly and Pembrey.
G						5	0	North Dock	Carmarth'	L. & M. M.	Over Harbour Commissioners' Line.
								Old Castle Tin Plate Works	Carmarth'	L. & M. M.	Llanelly.
								Old Castle Tin Plate Works (G. W.)	Carmarth'	G. W.—L. & N. W.	Llanelly and Pembrey.
								Old Lodge Tin Plate Works (G. W.)	Carmarth'	G. W.—L. & N. W.	On Neville, Druce & Co.'s Line.
								Samuel Bros.' Shipbuilding Yard	Carmarth'	G. W.	Llanelly.
								Thomas & Clements' Foundry (G. W.)	Carmarth'	G. W.—L. & N. W.	Branch from Llanelly.
								Thomas & Evans & John Dyer	Carmarth'	G. W.	Llanelly.
								Thomas, R., & Co.— Burry Tin Works (G.W.)	Carmarth'	G. W.—L. & N. W.	Branch from Llanelly.
								South Wales Tin Plate Works (G.W.)	Carmarth'	G. W.—L. & N. W.	Llanelly Dock.
								Tregoning & Son's Morfa Tin Plate Works (G. W.)	Carmarth'	G. W.—L. & N. W.	Llanelly Dock.
G						2	0	Victoria Road	Carmarth'	L. & M. M.	Llanelly.
								Waddell, Son & Co.'s Siding (G.W.)	Carmarth'	G. W.—L. & N. W.	On Neville, Druce & Co.'s Line.
								Welsh Tin Plate Stamping Co. (G. W.)	Carmarth'	G. W.—L. & N. W.	On Neville, Druce & Co.'s Line.
								Western Tin Plate Co. (G. W.)	Carmarth'	G. W.—L. & N. W.	Llanelly.

EXPLANATION—G *Goods Station.*   P *Passenger and Parcel Station.*   P* *Passenger, but not Parcel or Miscellaneous Traffic.*
F *Furniture Vans, Carriages, Portable Engines, and Machines on Wheels.*   L *Live Stock.*
H *Horse Boxes and Prize Cattle Vans.*   C *Carriages by Passenger Train.*

G	P	F	L	H	C	Tons	Cwts	Stations, &c.	County.	Company.	Position.
								LLANELLY—continued.			
								Williams & Davies' Timber Yard (G.W.)	Carmarth'	G.W.—L.&N.W.	Llanelly.
								Llanelly Lime Stone Co.'s Sid.	Brecon	L.&N.W.	Clydach.
								Llanerch Colliery (G.W.)	Mon	G.W.—L.&N.W.	Same as Partridge, Jones & Co. (Pontnewynydd).
								Llanerch Colliery (Foxhole Colliery Co.) (Mid.)	Glamorg'n	Mid.—G.W.—L.&N.W.	Upper Bank.
G	P	F	L	H	C	1	0	Llanerch-y-medd	Anglesey	L.&N.W.	Amlwch and Gaerwen.
G	P	F	L	H	C	1	10	Llanfair	Anglesey	L.&N.W.	Bangor and Holyhead.
G	P		L			2	10	Llanfair Caereinion	Montgom	Cam. (W.&L.)	Terminus.
G	P	F	L	H	C	1	0	Llanfairfechan	Carnarvon	L.&N.W.	Bangor and Rhyl.
G	P		L	H				Llanfalteg	Carmarth'	G.W.	Whitland and Cardigan.
G	P		L	H				Llanfechain	Montgom	Cam.	Llanymynech and Llanfyllin.
G	P		L	H				Llanfihangel	Cardigan	Cam.	Borth and Aberystwyth.
G	P	F	L	H	C	5	0	Llanfyllin	Montgom	Cam.	Branch from Llanymynech.
G	P					5	0	Llanfynydd	Flint	W.&M. Jt.(GW&L&NW)	Brymbo and Coed Talon.
								Crowndale Stone Co.	Flint	W.&M. Jt.(GW&L&NW)	Llanfynydd and Ffrith.
								Ffrith Coal and Fire-Clay Co.'s Carden's Siding	Flint	W.&M. Jt.(GW&L&NW)	Ffrith and Brymbo.
								Woolliscroft's Ffrith Quarry or Trimley Hall Siding	Flint	W.&M. Jt.(GW&L&NW)	Llanfynydd and Ffrith.
G	P		L	H				Llanfyrnach	Pembroke	G.W.	Whitland and Cardigan.
G	P		L	H		5	0	Llangadock	Carmarth'	V. of T. Jt. (GW&LNW)	Llandilo and Llandovery.
G	P		L					Llangammarch Wells	Brecon	L.&N.W.	Llandilo and Llandrindod Wells.
G	P		L					Llangedwyn	Denbigh	Cam. (Tanat Valley)	Porthywaen and Llangynog.
G	P	F	L	H	C	1	10	Llangefni	Anglesey	L.&N.W.	Amlwch and Gaerwen.
G	P							Llangeinor	Glamorg'n	G.W.	Brynmenyn and Pontycymmer.
								Bettws Llantwit Siding	Glamorg'n	G.W.	Llangeinor.
G	P							Llangeinor	Glamorg'n	P.T.	See Bettws (Llangeinor).
G						3	0	Llangennech (G.W.)	Carmarth'	G.W. / L.&N.W.	Pontardulais and Llanelly. / Over G.W. from Llandilo Junction.
								Glanmwrwg Colliery (G.W.)	Carmarth'	G.W.—L.&N.W.	Llangennech and Bynea.
								Gwernydd Colliery (G.W.)	Carmarth'	G.W.—L.&N.W.	Llangennech and Bynea.
								Llangennech Timber Yard	Carmarth'	G.W.	Llangennech and Bynea.
								Llangennech Tin Works (G.W.)	Carmarth'	G.W.—L.&N.W.	Llangennech and Bynea.
								Morlais Colliery (G.W.)	Carmarth'	G.W.—L.&N.W.	Llangennech and Pontardulais.
								Morlais Tin Works (G.W.)	Carmarth'	G.W.—L.&N.W.	Llangennech and Bynea.
								Mwrwg Vale Colliery (G.W.)	Carmarth'	G.W.—L.&N.W.	Llangennech and Bynea.
								Plasissa Colliery (G.W.)	Carmarth'	G.W.—L.&N.W.	Llangennech and Bynea.
								Tyisha Saw Mills	Carmarth'	G.W.	Llangennech and Bynea.
G	P		L	H				Llanglydwen	Carmarth'	G.W.	Whitland and Cardigan.
G	P	F	L	H	C	3	0	Llangollen	Denbigh	G.W.	Ruabon and Corwen.
								Pentrefelin Siding	Denbigh	G.W.	Llangollen and Glyndyfrdwy.
G						3	0	Llangollen Road	Denbigh	G.W.	Chirk and Ruabon.
								Chirk Castle Lime Works	Denbigh	G.W.	Ruabon and Llangollen Road.
								Penybont Brick Works	Denbigh	G.W.	Ruabon and Llangollen Road.
G	P							Llangonoyd	Glamorg'n	G.W.	Tondu and Maesteg.
								Llynvi Valley Colliery	Glamorg'n	G.W.	Llangonoyd.
G	P							Llangunllo	Radnor	L.&N.W.	Craven Arms & Llandrindod Wells.
G	P		L	H	C			Llangwyllog	Anglesey	L.&N.W.	Amlwch and Gaerwen.
G	P			H				Llangybi	Carnarvon	L.&N.W.	Afon Wen and Carnarvon.
G	P	F	L					Llangybi	Cardigan	M.&M.	Lampeter and Tregaron.
G	P							Llangynog	Montgom	Cam. (Tanat Valley)	Terminus.
G	P					1	0	Llanharan	Glamorg'n	G.W.	Llantrisant and Bridgend.
								Meiros Colliery	Glamorg'n	G.W.	Llanharan.
G	P							Llanharan Junction	Glamorg'n	G.W.	Llantrisant and Pencoed.
								Llanharry	Glamorg'n	T.V.	Llantrisant and Cowbridge.
	P							Llanharry Lime Works	Glamorg'n	T.V.	Llanharry.
								Llanhilleth	Mon	G.W.	Aberbeeg and Crumlin, Low Level.
								Llanhilleth Colliery (Partridge Jones)	Mon	G.W.	Llanhilleth and Aberbeeg.
								Monk's Quarry Siding	Mon	G.W.	Llanhilleth and Blaendare.
								Llanhilleth Junction	Mon	G.W.	Aberbeeg and Llanhilleth.
G	P	F	L	H	C	4	0	Llanidloes	Montgom	Cam.	Moat Lane and Rhayader.
G	P		L	H				Llanilar	Cardigan	M.&M.	Tregaron and Aberystwyth.
G	P	F	L	H	C			Llanishen (Rhymney)	Glamorg'n	Rhy. / L.&N.W.	Cardiff and Caerphilly. / Over Rhy. from Rhymney Joint Line Junction.
								Heath Siding (Rhy.)	Glamorg'n	Rhy.—L.&N.W.	Cardiff & Llanishen (for up traffic).
G	P							Llanmorlais	Glamorg'n	L.&N.W.	Branch from Gowerton.

EXPLANATION—G Goods Station.   P Passenger and Parcel Station.   P* Passenger, but not Parcel or Miscellaneous Traffic.
F Furniture Vans, Carriages, Portable Engines, and Machines on Wheels.   L Live Stock.
H Horse Boxes and Prize Cattle Vans.   C Carriages by Passenger Train.

STATION ACCOMMODATION.						CRANE POWER.		STATIONS, &c.	COUNTY.	COMPANY.	POSITION.
						Tons	Cwts.				
.	.	.	.	.	.	.	.	Llannerch Siding	Denbigh	L. & N. W.	St. Asaph.
G	P	.	L	.	.	.	.	Llanpumpsaint	Carmarth'	G. W.	Carmarthen and Pencader.
G	P	.	.	.	.	.	.	Llanrhaiadr	Denbigh	L. & N. W.	Corwen and Denbigh.
G	P	.	L	.	.	.	.	Llanrhaiadr Mochnant	Denbigh	Cam. (Tanat Valley)	Porthywaen and Llangynog.
G	P	.	L	H	.	.	.	Llanrhystyd Road	Cardigan	M. & M.	Tregaron and Aberystwyth.
G	P	F	L	H	C	10	0	Llanrwst and Trefriw	Carnarvon	L. & N. W.	Blaenau Festiniog and Llandudno Junction Station.
.	.	.	.	.	.	.	.	Abbey Siding	Denbigh	L. & N. W.	Llanrwst and Tal-y-Cafn.
.	.	.	.	.	.	.	.	Tanlan Siding	Denbigh	L. & N. W.	Llanrwst and Tal-y-Cafn.
G	P	F	L	H	C	1	0	Llansaintffraid	Montgom	Cam.	Llanymynech and Llanfyllin.
								LLANSAMLET—			
G	P	.	.	.	.	.	.	(Station)	Glamorg'n	G. W.	Neath and Landore.
G	.	.	.	.	.	5	0	(Station, Mid.)	Glamorg'n	{ Mid. / G. W.	Swansea and Glais. / Over Midland Line.
.	.	.	.	.	.	.	.	Aber Tin Plate Co's Sid (Mid)	Glamorg'n	Mid.—G. W.—L. & N. W.	Llansamlet and Six Pit.
.	.	.	.	.	.	.	.	Tawe Engineering Co.'s Siding (Mid.)	Glamorg'n	Mid.—G. W.—L. & N. W.	Llansamlet and Glais.
.	.	.	.	.	.	.	.	Velinfran Col. (Richards, J. J., & Co.'s Brick Works) (Mid.)	Glamorg'n	Mid.—G. W.—L. & N. W.	Llansamlet and Glais.
G	P	.	L	.	.	.	.	Llansilin Road	Montgom	Cam. (Tanat Valley)	Porthywaen and Llangynog.
G	P	.	.	H	.	.	.	Llantarnam	Mon	G. W.	Newport and Pontypool Road.
.	.	.	.	.	.	.	.	Star Brick & Tile Works	Mon	G. W.	Llantarnam and Cwmbran.
.	.	.	.	.	.	.	.	Llantarnam Junction	Mon	G. W.	Llantarnam and Pontnewydd.
.	.	.	.	.	.	.	.	Llanthony Wharf Yard	Glo'ster	G. W.	See Gloucester.
								LLANTRISANT—			
G	P	F	L	H	C	6	0	(Station)	Glamorg'n	G. W.	Cardiff and Bridgend.
G	P	F	L	H	C	.	.	(Station)	Glamorg'n	T. V.	Pontypridd and Cowbridge.
.	.	.	.	.	.	.	.	Branch Junction	Glamorg'n	T. V.	Taffs Well and Treforest.
.	.	.	.	.	.	.	.	Cambrian Foundry	Glamorg'n	G. W.	Llantrisant.
.	.	.	.	.	.	.	.	Cardiff Navigation Colliery	Glamorg'n	G. W.	Llantrisant.
.	.	.	.	.	.	.	.	Common Branch Junction	Glamorg'n	T. V.	Llantwit and Cross Inn.
.	.	.	.	.	.	.	.	Common Junction	Glamorg'n	G. W.—T. V.	Tonyrefail and Cross Inn.
.	.	.	.	.	.	.	.	Ely Tin Plate Works Siding	Glamorg'n	{ G. W. / T. V.	Llantrisant. / Llantrisant and Llanharry.
.	.	.	.	.	.	.	.	Glamorganshire Steam Joinery Works & Siding	Glamorg'n	G. W.	Llantrisant.
.	.	.	.	.	.	.	.	Maesaraul Junction	Glamorg'n	G. W.—T. V.	Llantrisant and Cross Inn.
.	.	.	.	.	.	.	.	Noel Bros.' Brick and Pipe Works and Siding	Glamorg'n	G. W.	Llantrisant.
.	.	.	.	.	.	.	.	No. 1 Railway Junction	Glamorg'n	T. V.	Cross Inn and Llantwit.
G	P	.	.	.	.	.	.	Llantwit	Glamorg'n	T. V.	Pontypridd and Llantrisant.
.	.	.	.	.	.	.	.	Llest Llantwit Colliery	Glamorg'n	T. V.	Llantwit and Cross Inn.
.	.	.	.	.	.	.	.	Wallsend Siding	Glamorg'n	T. V.	Llantwit and Cross Inn.
G	P	F	L	H	C	1	10	Llantwit Major	Glamorg'n	Barry	Barry and Bridgend.
.	.	.	.	.	.	.	.	Llantwit Merthyr Colliery	Glamorg'n	P. T.	Cwmavon.
G	P	F	L	H	C	.	.	Llanuwchllyn	Merioneth	G. W.	Bala and Dolgelley.
G	P	.	.	.	.	.	.	Llanvihangel (G. W.)	Mon	{ G. W. / L. & N. W.	Hereford and Abergavenny. / Over G. W. from Hereford.
G	P	.	L	.	.	1	10	Llanwern	Mon	G. W.	Magor and Newport.
G	P	.	L	.	.	.	.	Llanwnda	Carnarvon	L. & N. W.	Afon Wen and Carnarvon.
.	.	.	.	.	.	.	.	Williams & Son's Siding	Carnarvon	L. & N. W.	Llanwnda and Groeslon.
.	.	.	.	.	.	.	.	Llanwonno Colliery	Glamorg'n	T. V.	Ynysybwl.
G	P	.	L	H	.	1	10	Llanwrda	Carmarth'	V. of T. Jt. (GW & L.N.W)	Llandilo and Llandovery.
G	P	F	L	H	C	2	0	Llanwrtyd Wells	Brecon	L. & N. W.	Llandilo and Llandrindod Wells.
G	P	.	L	.	.	.	.	Llanyblodwell	Salop	Cam. (Tanat Valley)	Porthywaen and Llangynog.
G	P	F	L	H	.	3	0	Llanybyther	Carmarth'	M. & M.	Pencader and Lampeter.
G	P	.	.	.	.	.	.	Llanycefn	Pembroke	G. W.	Clynderwen and Fishguard.
G	.	.	.	.	.	.	.	Beag Siding	Pembroke	G. W.	Clynderwen and Llanycefn.
G	P	F	L	H	C	5	0	Llanymynech	Salop	Cam.	Oswestry and Welshpool.
.	.	.	.	.	.	.	.	Llanddu Quarry	Montgom	Cam.	Llanymynech.
.	.	.	.	.	.	.	.	Rock Siding	Salop	Cam.	Llanymynech and Llanyblodwell.
.	.	.	.	.	.	.	.	Llanymynech Junction	Salop	Cam.	Junction with Llanfyllin Branch.
.	.	.	.	.	.	.	.	Llay Hall Col. & Brick Works	Flint	W. M. & C. Q.	Cefn-y-Bedd.
.	.	.	.	.	.	.	.	Llest Llantwit Colliery	Glamorg'n	T. V.	Llantwit.
G	P	.	.	.	.	.	.	Lletty Brongu	Glamorg'n	P. T.	Maesteg and Pont-y-rhyll.
.	.	.	.	.	.	.	.	Bettws Llantwit Merthyr Colliery	Glamorg'n	P. T.	Lletty Brongu.
.	.	.	.	.	.	.	.	Gwernllwyn Colliery	Glamorg'n	P. T.	Lletty Brongu and Bettws (Llangeinor).
.	.	.	.	.	.	.	.	Letty Brongu Colliery	Glamorg'n	P. T.	Lletty Brongu & Bettws (Llangeinor).
.	.	.	.	.	.	.	.	Moel-gilau Colliery	Glamorg'n	P. T.	Lletty Brongu & Bettws (Llangeinor).

EXPLANATION—G *Goods Station.*　　P *Passenger and Parcel Station.*　　P* *Passenger, but not Parcel or Miscellaneous Traffic.*
F *Furniture Vans, Carriages, Portable Engines, and Machines on Wheels.*　　L *Live Stock.*
H *Horse Boxes and Prize Cattle Vans.*　　C *Carriages by Passenger Train.*

Station Accommodation						Crane Power		STATIONS, &c.	COUNTY.	COMPANY.	POSITION.
						Tons	Cwts.				
								Lletty Shenkin Colliery	Glamorg'n	T. V.	Aberdare.
								Llewellyn & Cubitt's Siding	Glamorg'n	T. V.	Same as Rhondda Engine Works (Ystrad).
								Lliswerry	Mon	G. W.	Llanwern and Newport.
								Davies' Lime Works	Mon	G. W.	Lliswerry.
								Drews' Iron Yard	Mon	G. W.	Lliswerry.
	P							Llong	Flint	L. & N. W.	Chester and Mold.
								Llong Colliery	Flint	L. & N. W.	See Parry & Co. (Padeswood).
								Lloyd & Co.'s Siding	N'hamptn	Mid.	Isham and Burton Latimer.
								Lloyd's—			
								Monway Works	Staffs	G. W.	See Patent Shaft and Axletree Co. (Wednesbury).
								Monway Works (L & N W)	Staffs	L. & N. W.—Mid.	See Patent Shaft and Axletree Co. (Wednesbury).
								Old Park Works	Staffs	G. W.	See Patent Shaft and Axletree Co. (Wednesbury).
								Old Park Works (L & N W)	Staffs	L. & N. W.—Mid.	See Patent Shaft and Axletree Co. (Wednesbury).
								Lloyd's Cattle Market Siding	Cheshire	L. & N. W.	Crewe.
								Lloyd's Siding	Lancs	L. & Y.	Birkdale.
								Lloyd's Siding	Staffs	L. & N. W.	Darlaston.
								Lloyd's Testing House {	Glamorg'n	G. W.	Cardiff.
									Staffs	G. W.	Tipton.
								Lloyd's Testing House Works	Cheshire	G. W.	Saltney.
								Lloyd's Test Works	Durham	N. E.	Sunderland, South Dock
G	P							Llwydarth Tin Works Siding	Glamorg'n	G. W.	Troedyrhiew Garth.
								Llwydcoed	Glamorg'n	G. W.	Hirwain and Merthyr.
								Dyllas Colliery	Glamorg'n	G. W.	Llwydcoed and Abernant.
								Upper Llwydcoed Colliery (Fothergill's)	Glamorg'n	G. W.	Llwydcoed and Abernant.
								Llwyncelyn Siding	Glamorg'n	B. & M. & L. & N. W. Joint	See Crawshay Bros. (Cefn).
G	P							Llwynddu Colliery & Brick Co.'s Siding (Mid.)	Glamorg'n	Mid.—G. W.—L. & N. W.	Glais.
								Llwyngwern	Merioneth	Corris	Machynlleth and Corris.
G	P		L	H				Llwyngwern Slate Quarry	Merioneth	Corris	Llwyngwern.
								Llwyngwril	Merioneth	Cam.	Towyn and Barmouth.
	P							Llwynonn Colliery	Glamorg'n	N. & Brecon	Crynant.
								Llwynypia and Tonypandy	Glamorg'n	T. V.	Porth and Treherbert.
								Llwynypia Colliery (Glamorgan Colliery)	Glamorg'n	T. V.	Trealaw.
								Llwynypia Mileage Siding	Glamorg'n	T. V.	See Trealaw.
G	P		L	H				Llwynenion Brick Works (Powell, J., & Co.)	Denbigh	G. W.	Rhos.
								Llynclys	Salop	Cam.	Oswestry and Welshpool.
								Llynclys Junction	Salop	Cam.	Junction with Porthywaen Branch.
								Llyn Colliery (Forge Pit)	Mon	{ G. W. / L. & N. W.	Nantyglo. / Brynmawr.
								Llynvi Gas Co.'s Siding	Glamorg'n	G. W.	See North's (Maesteg).
G	P							Llynvi Valley Colliery	Glamorg'n	G. W.	Llangonoyd.
								Llysfaen	Carnarvon	L. & N. W.	Bangor and Rhyl.
								Kneeshaw, Lupton & Co.'s Llysfaen Siding	Carnarvon	L. & N. W.	Llysfaen and Llandulas.
								Raynes & Co.'s—			
								Penmaenrhos Siding	Carnarvon	L. & N. W.	Llysfaen and Old Colwyn.
								Penybryn Siding	Carnarvon	L. & N. W.	Llysfaen and Old Colwyn.
G	P	F	L	H	C	3	0	Loanend Colliery	Lanark	Cal.	Newton.
								Loanhead	Edinboro'	N. B.	Millerhill and Roslin.
								Burghlee Siding	Edinboro'	N. B.	Loanhead and Roslin.
								Edgefield Siding	Edinboro'	N. B.	Loanhead and Gilmerton.
								Ramsay Pit	Edinboro'	N. B.	Loanhead.
								Standard Siding	Edinboro'	N. B.	Loanhead and Gilmerton.
								Straiton Siding	Edinboro'	N. B.	Loanhead and Gilmerton.
								Loanrigg Colliery and Brick Works	Lanark	N. B.	Rawyards.
								Loanstone Siding	Edinboro'	N. B.	Pomathorn.
								Lobley Hill Siding and Depôt	Durham	N. E.	Redheugh.
G	P	F	L	H	C			Lobnitz & Co.'s Sid. (G & S W)	Renfrew	G. & S. W.—Cal.	Renfrew.
G	P							Lochailort	Inverness	N. B.	Fort William and Mallaig.
G	P	F	L	H	C			Lochaline	Argyll	Cal.	Steamer from Oban.
G	P							Lochanhead	Dumfries	G. & S. W.	Dumfries and Dalbeattie.
G	P		L	H		3	0	Locharbriggs	Dumfries	Cal.	Lockerbie and Dumfries.
								Cullyveat Quarry	Dumfries	Cal.	Locharbriggs and Amisfield.
								Locharbriggs Quarry	Dumfries	Cal.	Locharbriggs.
G	P	F	L	H	C	2	0	Loch Awe	Argyll	Cal.	Callander and Oban.
								Ben Cruachan Quarries	Argyll	Cal.	Dalmally and Loch Awe.
								Loch Awe Weighs	Argyll	Cal.	Callander and Oban.

EXPLANATION—G *Goods Station.*   P *Passenger and Parcel Station.*   P* *Passenger, but not Parcel or Miscellaneous Traffic.*
F *Furniture Vans, Carriages, Portable Engines, and Machines on Wheels.*   L *Live Stock.*
H *Horse Boxes and Prize Cattle Vans.*   C *Carriages by Passenger Train.*

STATION ACCOMMODATION.						CRANE POWER.		STATIONS, &c.	COUNTY.	COMPANY.	POSITION.
						Tons	Cwts.				
G	P	.	.	.	.	.	.	Lochbuie	Argyll	Cal.	Steamer from Oban.
.	.	.	.	.	.	.	.	Lochburn	Lanark	N. B.	See Glasgow.
.	.	.	.	.	.	.	.	Lochburn Iron Works	Lanark	{ Cal.	Glasgow, Possil.
										{ N. B.	Glasgow, Lochburn.
G	P	.	L	H	.	4	0	Lochee	Forfar	Cal.	Dundee and Newtyle.
.	.	.	.	.	.	.	.	Camperdown Jute Works	Forfar	Cal.	Lochee.
.	.	.	.	.	.	.	.	Cox Bros.' Flax & Jute Wks.	Forfar	Cal.	Lochee.
G	P	.	.	.	.	2	0	Lochee, West	Forfar	Cal.	Dundee and Lochee.
.	.	.	.	.	.	.	.	Lochee Saw Mill Co.'s Sid.	Forfar	Cal.	Lochee, West.
.	.	.	.	.	.	.	.	Lochend Collieries	Lanark	N. B.	Longriggend.
.	.	.	.	.	.	.	.	Lochend North & South Jns.	Edinboro'	N. B.	Edinburgh.
.	.	.	.	.	.	.	.	Lochend Road Sidings	Edinboro'	Cal.	Leith, South.
.	.	.	.	.	.	.	.	Lochend Siding	Fife	N. B.	See Steelend.
.	.	.	.	.	.	.	.	Lochend Steel Works	Edinboro'	N. B.	Edinburgh, Leith Walk.
.	.	.	.	.	.	.	.	Lochend (Younger & Co.) Siding (Moray Park Siding)	Edinboro'	N. B.	Edinburgh, Rose Lane.
G	P	.	L	H	.	1	10	Lochgelly	Fife	N. B.	Dunfermline and Thornton.
.	.	.	.	.	.	.	.	Lochgelly Brick Works	Fife	N. B.	Cardenden and Lochgelly.
.	.	.	.	.	.	.	.	Lochgelly Cols. No. 12 Sid.	Fife	N. B.	Cardenden and Lochgelly.
.	.	.	.	.	.	.	.	Jenny Gray Pit	Fife	N. B.	Branch off Lochgelly Cols. No. 12 Sid.
.	.	.	.	.	.	.	.	Milgund Pit	Fife	N. B.	Branch off Lochgelly Cols. No. 12 Sid.
.	.	.	.	.	.	.	.	Nelly Pit	Fife	N. B.	Branch off Lochgelly Cols. No. 12 Sid.
.	.	.	.	.	.	.	.	Mary Pit Colliery	Fife	N. B.	Cowdenbeath and Lochgelly.
.	.	.	.	.	.	.	.	Lochgreen Junction	Ayr	G. & S. W.	Troon and Monkton.
.	.	.	.	.	.	.	.	Lochhead Brick & Fire-Clay Works	Fife	N. B.	Whitemyre Junction Station.
.	.	.	.	.	.	.	.	Lochhead Siding	Fife	N. B.	See Whitemyre Junction Station.
G	P	.	.	.	.	.	.	Loch Hourn	Inverness	{ Cal. High. N. B.	Steamer from Oban. Steamer from Kyle of Lochalsh. Steamer from Mallaig.
G	P	.	.	.	.	.	.	Lochielside	Inverness	N. B.	Fort William and Mallaig.
G	P	.	L	.	.	.	.	Lochinver	Sutherl'nd	{ Cal. High. N. B.	Steamer from Oban. Steamer from Kyle of Lochalsh. Steamer from Mallaig.
G	P	.	L	.	C						
G	P	.	L	.	.						
.	.	.	.	.	.	.	.	Lochland Siding (Larbert Junction Sidings) (N. B.)	Stirling	N. B.—Cal.	Falkirk, Grahamston.
G	P	F	L	H	C	1	15	Loch Leven	Fife	N. B.	Dunfermline and Kinross Junction.
G	P	F	L	H	C	.	.	Lochluichart	Ross & Cro'	High.	Dingwall and Kyle of Lochalsh.
G	P	F	L	H	C	3	0	Lochmaben	Dumfries	Cal.	Lockerbie and Dumfries.
G	P	.	L	.	.			Lochmaddy	Inverness	{ Cal. High. N. B.	Steamer from Oban. Steamer from Kyle of Lochalsh. Steamer from Mallaig.
G	P	.	L	.	C						
G	P	.	L	.	.						
G	.	.	.	.	.	2	0	Lochmill	L'lithgow	N. B.	Linlithgow and Falkirk.
.	.	.	.	.	.	.	.	Lochmuir Shunting Siding	Fife	N. B.	Falkland Road.
.	.	.	.	.	.	.	.	Lochore Colliery	Fife	N. B.	Kelty.
G	P	.	.	.	.	.	.	Loch Pooltiel	Inverness	Cal.	Steamer from Oban.
.	.	.	.	.	.	.	.	Lochrin Iron Works	Lanark	Cal.—N. B.	Coatbridge, Whifflet.
.	.	.	.	.	.	.	.	Lochrin Iron Wks. Timber Sid.	Lanark	N. B.	Coatbridge, Whifflet.
.	.	.	.	.	.	.	.	Lochside Colliery	Fife	N. B.	Townhill Junction Station.
.	.	.	.	.	.	.	.	Lochside Fire-Clay Works	Fife	N. B.	Townhill Junction Station.
.	P*	.	.	.	.	.	.	Lochskerrow	Kirkcud	P.P.&W.Jt.(Cal., G&SW, L. & N. W., & Mid.)	Newton Stewart & Castle Douglas.
G	P	.	L	H	.	1	10	Loch Tay	Perth	Cal.	Branch Terminus near Killin Junc.
.	.	.	.	.	.	.	.	Lochtie's Quarry	Fife	N. B.	Aberdour.
G	.	.	.	.	.	.	.	Loch Torridon	Ross & Cro'	N. B.	Steamer from Mallaig.
G	.	.	F	L	.	2	0	Lochty	Fife	N. B.	Branch from Cameron Bridge.
.	.	.	.	.	.	.	.	Lochty Maltings	Fife	N. B.	Thornton.
.	.	.	.	.	.	.	.	Lochview Foundry	Stirling	N. B.	Same as Woodlea Siding (Bonnybridge, E. & G.).
G	P	F	L	H	C	3	0	Lochwinnoch	Renfrew	G. & S. W.	Paisley and Dalry.
.	.	.	.	.	.	.	.	Lochwood Colliery	Lanark	N. B.	Bargeddie.
.	.	.	.	.	.	.	.	Lochwood Siding	Lanark	N. B.	See Bargeddie.
.	.	.	.	.	.	.	.	Locke & Co.'s Colliery (Allerton Haigh Moor Colliery)	Yorks	N. E.	Kippax.
.	.	.	.	.	.	.	.	Locke & Co.'s Siding	Yorks	L. & Y.—Mid.	Same as St. John's Col. (Normanton).
G	P	F	L	H	C	4	10	Lockerbie	Dumfries	Cal.	Carlisle and Carstairs.
.	.	.	.	.	.	.	.	Milne & McDonald's Siding	Dumfries	Cal.	Lockerbie.
.	.	.	.	.	.	.	.	Lockhart's Siding	Warwick	L. & N. W.	Kenilworth.
G	P	F	L	H	C	.	.	Lockington	Yorks	N. E.	Hull and Driffield.
.	.	.	.	.	.	.	.	Lockington's Siding	Louth	D. N. & G.	Dundalk, Quay Street.
.	.	.	.	.	.	.	.	Lock No. 16 Siding	Stirling	Cal.—N. B.	Falkirk, Camelon.
.	.	.	.	.	.	.	.	Lockoford Siding	Derby	G. C.	Sheepbridge and Brimington.

EXPLANATION—G *Goods Station.*   P *Passenger and Parcel Station.*   P* *Passenger, but not Parcel or Miscellaneous Traffic.*
F *Furniture Vans, Carriages, Portable Engines, and Machines on Wheels.*   L *Live Stock.*
H *Horse Boxes and Prize Cattle Vans.*   C *Carriages by Passenger Train.*

STATION ACCOMMODATION.						CRANE POWER.	STATIONS, &c.	COUNTY.	COMPANY.	POSITION.
						Tons Cwts.	Locksbrook Wharf Timber Co.'s Siding	Somerset..	Mid.	Weston.
G	P	.	L	.	.	5 0	Lockwood	Yorks	L. & Y.	Huddersfield and Penistone.
.	.	.	.	.	.	. .	Kenworthy's Siding	Yorks	L. & Y.	Lockwood.
.	.	.	.	.	.	. .	Springwood Siding	Yorks	L. & Y.	Near Lockwood.
.	.	.	.	.	.	. .	Whiteley & Son's Siding	Yorks	L. & Y.	Lockwood.
.	.	.	.	.	.	. .	Lockwood & Co.'s Lime Wks.	Yorks	G. C.	Warmsworth.
.	.	.	.	.	.	. .	Lockwood Blagden Lime Co.'s Siding	Yorks	G. C.	Kiveton Park.
							Loddington Iron Ore Co.—			
.	.	.	.	.	.	. .	Globe Siding	N'hamptn	Mid.	Kettering.
.	.	.	.	.	.	. .	Loddington Siding	N'hamptn	Mid.	Kettering.
.	.	.	.	.	.	. .	Loddington Siding	N'hamptn	Mid.	See Loddington Iron Ore Co. (Kettering).
G	P	F	L	.	.	6 0	Loddiswell	Devon	G. W.	Brent and Kingsbridge.
.	.	.	.	.	.	. .	Lode	Cambs	G. E.	See Bottisham and Lode.
.	.	.	.	.	.	. .	Loder's Siding	N'hamptn	L. & N. W.	See Draughton Crossing Siding (Lamport).
.	.	.	.	.	.	. .	Loders & Nucoline Siding (GE)	Essex	GE—GN—L&NW—Mid.	London, Silvertown.
.	.	.	.	.	.	. .	Lodge & Flesher's Siding	Yorks	G. N.	Wilsden.
.	.	.	.	.	.	. .	Lodge Colliery Siding	Notts	G. N.	Kimberley.
G	P	F	L	H	C	3 0	Lodge Hill	Somerset..	G. W.	Wells and Cheddar.
.	.	.	.	.	.	. .	Lodge Holes Colliery	Staffs	L. & N. W.	Wednesbury.
.	.	.	.	.	.	. .	Lodge Lane Mill	Derby	G. N.	Same as Brown's, W.& G. Sid.(Derby)
.	.	.	.	.	.	. .	Lodge Mill Colliery	Yorks	L. & N. W.	Same as Elliott's Siding (Fenay Bridge and Lepton).
.	.	.	.	.	.	. .	Lodge's Siding	Yorks	Mid.	Same as Ryhill Colliery (Royston and Notton).
							LOFTHOUSE—			
.	P*	.	.	.	.	. .	(Station)	Yorks	Meth. Jt. (GN,L&Y & N E)	Near Lofthouse South Junction.
G	P	.	L	.	.	5 0	(Station, G. N.)	Yorks	{ G. N.	Wakefield and Leeds.
									{ L. & Y.	Over G. N. from Wakefield.
.	.	.	.	.	.	. .	Alum Works	Yorks	Meth.Jt.(GN,L&Y & N E)	Lofthouse North Junc. and Stanley.
.	.	.	.	.	.	. .	Colliery	Yorks	{ E. & W. Y. Union	Lofthouse.
									{ G. N.	Lofthouse and Ardsley.
.	.	.	.	.	.	. .	Junction	Yorks	E. & W. Y. Union—G.N.	Robin Hood and Lofthouse.
.	.	.	.	.	.	. .	North Junction	Yorks	G. N.—Meth. Jt.	Ardsley and Stanley.
.	.	.	.	.	.	. .	South Junction	Yorks	G. N.—Meth. Jt.	Wakefield and Stanley.
G	P	F	L	H	C	5 0	Lofthouse Colliery Co.'s Sid.	Yorks	Mid.	Rothwell Haigh.
.	.	.	.	.	.	. .	Loftus	Yorks	N. E.	Saltburn and Whitby.
.	.	.	.	.	.	. .	Carlin How Depôts	Yorks	N. E.	Loftus.
.	.	.	.	.	.	. .	Carlin How Engine Shed	Yorks	N. E.	Loftus.
.	.	.	.	.	.	. .	Carlin How Mines	Yorks	N. E.	Loftus.
.	.	.	.	.	.	. .	Liverton Mines	Yorks	N. E.	Loftus.
.	.	.	.	.	.	. .	Loftus Depôts	Yorks	N. E.	Loftus.
.	.	.	.	.	.	. .	Loftus Mines	Yorks	N. E.	Loftus.
.	.	.	.	.	.	. .	North Loftus Mines	Yorks	N. E.	Loftus.
.	.	.	.	.	.	. .	Skinningrove Depôts	Yorks	N. E.	Loftus.
.	.	.	.	.	.	. .	Skinningrove Iron Works	Yorks	N. E.	Loftus.
.	.	.	.	.	.	. .	Logan Junction	Ayr	G. & S. W.	Cumnock (A. & C.) and Cronberry.
.	.	.	.	.	.	. .	Loganlea Cols., Nos. 1, 2, 3, & 4	Edinboro'	Cal.	West Calder.
.	.	.	.	.	.	. .	Logan's Copper Wharf	Cheshire	B'head Jt–CLC–NW & L	Birkenhead.
G	P	.	L	H	.	. .	Logierieve	Aberdeen	G. N. of S.	Dyce and Fraserburgh.
G	P	.	.	H	.	. .	Login	Carmarth'	G. W.	Whitland and Cardigan.
G	P	.	L	.	.	. .	Lombardstown	Cork	G. S. & W.	Mallow and Killarney.
G	P	.	L	H	..	. .	Londesboro'	Yorks	N. E.	York and Market Weighton.
							LONDON—			
.	.	.	.	.	.	. .	Acme Wood Flooring Co.'s Siding	Essex	GE—GN—L&NW—Mid	Victoria Docks.
G	P	F	L	.	.	6 0 }	Acton	Middlesex	{ G. W.	Paddington and Ealing.
G	P	.	.	.	.	. . }			{ N.& S.W.Jn.Jt.(L N W, Mid., & N. L.)	Willesden and Kew Bridge.
.	.	.	.	.	.	. .	Acton & Willesden Brick Works	Middlesex	G. W.	Acton and West London Junction.
.	.	.	.	.	.	. .	Acton Coal Depôt	Middlesex	{ G. W.	Paddington and Ealing.
									{ N&SW.Jn.Jt.(L.&NW, Mid., & N. L.)	Acton and Hammersmith.
.	.	.	.	.	.	. .	Acton Exchange Sid. (GW)	Middlesex	G. W.—N. L.	Acton.
.	.	.	.	.	.	. .	Acton Green	Middlesex	Met. Dist.	See Chiswick Park and Acton Green.
.	.	.	.	.	.	. .	Acton Junction	Middlesex	L. S.—N.& S. W. Jn. Jt.	Gunnersbury and Acton.
.	.	.	.	.	.	. .	Acton Wells Junction	Middlesex	G. W.—N.& S. W. Jn. Jt.	Acton and Willesden Junction.
.	.	.	.	.	.	. .	Acton Wells Junction	Middlesex	L& NW—N.&S.W.Jn.Jt.	Willesden Jn. (High Level) & Acton.

EXPLANATION—G *Goods Station.*   P *Passenger and Parcel Station.*   P* *Passenger, but not Parcel or Miscellaneous Traffic.*
F *Furniture Vans, Carriages, Portable Engines, and Machines on Wheels.*   L *Live Stock.*
H *Horse Boxes and Prize Cattle Vans.*   C *Carriages by Passenger Train.*

Station Accommodation						Crane Power		Stations, &c.	County.	Company.	Position.
						Tons	Cwts				
								LONDON—*continued.*			
								Acton Wells Junction	Middlesex	Mid.—N. & S. W. Jn. Jt.	Harlesden and Acton.
								Addison Road (W. Lon. Jt.)	Middlesex	W. Lon. Jt.—L. & S.W.—L. B. & S. C.	See Kensington.
								Addison Road Junction ...	Middlesex	W. Lon. Jt.—W. L. E. Jt.	Addison Road and Clapham Junc.
								Aird's Siding	Middlesex	G. W.—L. & N. W.	Chelsea Basin.
	P							Aldersgate Street (Met.) ...	Middlesex	Met.	Farringdon Str. and Moorgate Str.
	P*									G. N.—Mid.	Over Met. from Kings Cross Junc.
	P*									G. W.	Over Met. from Bishop's Road.
	P*									S. E. & C.	Over Met. from Snow Hill Junction.
	P							Aldgate (Met.)...............	Middlesex	Met.	Bishopsgate and Mark Lane.
										G. W.	Over Met. from Bishop's Road.
	P							Aldgate East...............	Middlesex	Met. & Met. Dist. Jt.	Mark Lane and St. Marys (Whitechapel).
								Aldgate East Junction ...	Middlesex	Met—Met.& Met. Dist..Jt.	Bishopsgate and Aldgate East Sta.
								Aldgate Junction	Middlesex	Met—Met.& Met. Dist. Jt.	Aldgate and Mark Lane.
								Aldgate, North Curve Junc.	Middlesex	Met.	Bishopsgate and Aldgate.
								Allan Cockshut & Co.'s or Wallpaper Manufacturing Co.'s Siding	Middlesex	L. & N. W.	Old Ford.
								American Radiator Co.'s Siding (G.E.)	Essex	GE—GN—L & NW—Mid.	Silvertown.
	P							Angel	Middlesex	C. & S. L.	Terminus.
								Anglo-Continental Guano Works (G.E.)	Essex	GE—GN—L & NW—Mid.	Silvertown Tram.
G								Ashburton Grove	Middlesex	G. N.	Finsbury Park and Holloway.
								Atlas Brk. & Tile Co.'s Sid.	Middlesex	Mid.	Acton Canal Wharf.
	P							Baker Street (Met.)	Middlesex	Met.	Edgware Road and Portland Road.
	P*									G. W.	Over Met. from Bishop's Road.
	P							Baker Street, East...........	Middlesex	Met.	Portland Rd. & St. John's Wood Rd.
								Baker Street Junction	Middlesex	Met.	Baker Street and Portland Road.
	P*							Bank	Middlesex	C. L.	Terminus.
	P									C. & S. L.	Angel and London Bridge.
								Bank	Middlesex	W. & C.	Same as Mansion House.
								Barnsbury (N. L.)	Middlesex	N. L.—L. & N. W.	See Caledonian Road and Barnsbury.
								Barrington Road Junction	Surrey	L. B. & S. C.—S. E. & C.	Denmark Hill and Brixton.
								Battersea	Surrey	L. & S.W.	See Queen's Road, Battersea.
	P							Battersea	Surrey	W L E Jt. (GW, L & N W, L & S W, & L B & S C)	Clapham Junction and Kensington.
	P							Battersea Park	Surrey	L. B. & S. C.	Victoria and Clapham Junction.
	P							Battersea Park Road (S E&C)	Surrey	S. E. & C.	Victoria and Wandsworth Road.
										G. N.—Mid.	Over Met. and S. E & C. Lines.
								Battersea Pier (L.B.& S.C.)	Surrey	L. B. & S. C.—L. & N. W.	Same as Grosvenor Road.
								Battersea Pier Junction	Surrey	S. E. & C.	Grosvenor Rd. & Battersea Park Rd.
G		F	L			10	0	Battersea Wharf (L B & S C)	Surrey	L. B. & S. C.	Bch.—Wandsworth Rd. & Victoria.
G										G. W.—Mid.	Over Met., S E & C, & L B & S C Lines.
G										L. & S. W.	Over LB&SC from Longhedge Junc.
	P							Bayswater (Queen's Road)	Middlesex	Met.	Praed Street and Notting Hill Gate.
G	P							Beckton	Essex	G. E.	Branch from Custom House.
								Beckton Junction	Essex	G.E.—L. & I. Dks.	Custom House and Gallions.
								Berk, F. W., & Co.'s District Chemical Co.'s Sid. (G.E.)	Essex	GE—GN—L & NW—Mid.	Silvertown.
G	P							Bethnal Green Junc. Sta.	Middlesex	G. E.	Liverpool Street and Stratford.
G		F				5	0	Bishopsgate	Middlesex	G. E.	Terminus. / Liverpool Street & Bethnal Green.
	P							Bishopsgate (Met.)............	Middlesex	Met.	Moorgate Street and Aldgate.
	P*									G. W.	Over Met. from Bishop's Road.
								Bishopsgate Junction	Middlesex	E. L. Jt.—G. E.	Shoreditch and Liverpool Street.
								Bishop's Road Sta. & Junc.	Middlesex	G. W.—Met.	See Paddington.
G		F	L	H		5	0	Blackfriars	Surrey	S. E. & C.	Ludgate Hill and Elephant & Castle.
	P							Blackfriars (Met. Dist.) ...	Middlesex	Met. Dist.	Temple and Mansion House.
										L. & N. W.	Over Met. Dist. from Kensington, Earls Court Junction.
								Blackfriars Junction........	Surrey	S. E. & C.	Ludgate Hill and London Bridge.
	P							Blackwall	Middlesex	G. E.	Branch from Stepney.
								Blackwall (Poplar)...........	Middlesex	G. E.	Branch near Canning Town.
G						1	10	Blackwall Depôt..............	Middlesex	G. N.	Same as East India Docks Goods Depôt and Coal Wharf.
	P*							Bond Street................	Middlesex	C. L.	Marble Arch and Bank.
	P							Borough	Surrey	C. & S. L.	London Bridge & Clapham Common.
								Borough Market Junction	Surrey	S. E. & C.	Waterloo Junction Station and London Bridge.

EXPLANATION—G *Goods Station.*   P *Passenger and Parcel Station.*   P* *Passenger, but not Parcel or Miscellaneous Traffic.*
F *Furniture Vans, Carriages, Portable Engines, and Machines on Wheels.*   L *Live Stock.*
H *Horse Boxes and Prize Cattle Vans.*   C *Carriages by Passenger Train.*

STATION ACCOMMODATION.						CRANE POWER.	STATIONS, &c.	COUNTY.	COMPANY.	POSITION.
						Tons Cwts.	LONDON—continued.			
.	P	.	.	.	.	. .	Borough Road (S. E. & C.)	Surrey ..	{ S. E. & C.	Ludgate Hill and Elephant & Castle.
									G. N.—Mid.	Over Met. and S. E. & C. Lines.
									L. & S. W.	Over L. B. & S. C. & S. E. & C. Lines.
							Bow—			
G	.	F	L	.	.	20 0	(Station)	Middlesex	Mid.	Over G. E. from Tottenham Junc.
.	P	.	.	.	.	. .	(Station)	Middlesex	N. L.	Dalston and Poplar.
.	.	.	.	.	:	. .	Coal Depôt	Middlesex	L. & N. W.	Over N. L. from Camden Junction.
.	.	.	.	.	.	. .	Junction	Middlesex	G. E.—L. T. & S.	Stepney and Bromley.
.	.	.	.	.	.	. .	Junction	Middlesex	G. E.—N. L.	Burdett Road and Bow.
.	.	.	.	.	.	. .	Junction	Middlesex	N. L.	Bow and South Bromley.
.	.	.	.	.	.	. .	Locomotive Works and Carriage Sidings	Middlesex	N. L.	Bow and Poplar.
.	.	.	.	.	.	. .	Tilbury Branch Junction	Middlesex	N. L.	Old Ford and Bow.
G	P	.	.	.	.	5 0 }	Bow Road.......................	Middlesex	{ G. E.	Stepney and Stratford.
.	P	.	.	.	.				W.&B.Jt.(LT&S&MD)	Mile End and Campbell Road Junc.
.	.	.	.	.	.	. .	Brent Gas Works	Middlesex	Mid.	Near Brent Junction.
.	.	.	.	.	.	. .	Brent Junction (Mid.)	Middlesex	Mid.—L. & S. W.	Kew Bridge and Hendon.
.	.	.	.	.	.	. .	Brent Junction, North	Middlesex	G. C.—Met.	Marylebone & Harrow-on-the-Hill.
.	.	.	.	.	.	. .	Brent Junction, South	Middlesex	G. C.—Met.	Marylebone & Harrow-on-the-Hill.
G	.	F	L	H	.	8 0	Bricklayers' Arms(S.E.&C.)	Surrey ...	{ S. E. & C.	Branch—London Bge. & New Cross.
									L. & N. W.	Over S. E. & C. from Longhedge Jn.
.	.	.	.	.	.	. .	Bricklayers' Arms Junction	Surrey ...	L. B. & S. C.—S. E. & C.	New Cross and Bricklayers' Arms.
.	.	.	.	.	.	. .	British Alizarine Co.'s Sid. (G. E.)	Essex	GE—GN—L & NW—Mid.	Silvertown Tram.
.	P*	.	.	.	.	. .	British Museum	Middlesex	C. L.	Marble Arch and Bank.
.	P	.	.	.	.	. .	Brixton (S. E. & C.)	Surrey ...	{ S. E. & C.	Victoria and Herne Hill.
									G. N.—Mid.	Over Met. and S. E. & C. Lines.
									L. & S. W.	Over S. E. & C. from Longhedge Jn.
.	.	.	.	.	.	. .	Brixton Coal Depôt	Surrey	Mid.	Over Met. & S. E. & C. Lines.
.	.	.	.	.	.	. .	Brixton, East	Surrey	L. B. & S. C.	See East Brixton.
.	.	.	.	.	.	. .	Brixton Junction	Surrey	S. E. & C.	Clapham Road and Brixton.
G	.	F	.	.	.	10 0	Broad Street	Middlesex	L. & N. W.	Over N. L. from Camden Junction.
.	P	.	.	.	.	. .	Broad Street (N. L.).........	Middlesex	{ N. L.	City Terminus.
									L. & N. W.	Over N. L. from Camden Junction.
.	.	.	.	.	.	. .	Broadway.......................	Middlesex	H. & C. Jt.—Met. Dist...	See Hammersmith (Broadway).
G	P	F	L	.	.	. . }			{ L. T. & S.	Plaistow and Commercial Road.
.	P	.	.	.	.		Bromley (L. T. & S.)........	Middlesex	G. E.	Over L. T. & S. Line.
.	P	.	.	.	.				N. L.	Over L. T. & S. from Bromley Junc.
.	.	.	.	.	.	. .	Bromley, Campbell Road Junction	Middlesex	L. T. & S.—W. & B. Jt.	Bromley and Bow Road.
.	.	.	.	.	.	. .	Bromley Junction	Essex	G. E.—L. T. & S.	Canning Town and Bromley.
.	.	.	.	.	.	. .	Bromley Junction	Middlesex	L. T. & S.—N. L.	Bromley and Bow.
.	.	.	.	.	.	. .	Bromley, South	Middlesex	N. L.	See South Bromley.
G	.	F	.	.	.	10 0	Brompton and Fulham......	Middlesex	L. & N. W.	Clapham Junction and Kensington.
.	.	.	.	.	.	. .	Brompton (GloucesterRoad)	Middlesex	Met.—Met. Dist.—LNW	See Gloucester Road.
.	.	.	.	.	.	. .	Brompton, West	Middlesex	Met. Dist.—W. L. E. Jt.	See West Brompton.
.	.	.	.	.	.	. .	Brondesbury	Middlesex	Met.	See Kilburn—Brondesbury.
.	P	.	.	.	.	. .	Brondesbury (L. & N. W.)	Middlesex	{ L. & N. W.	Kentish Town and Willesden Junc.
									N. L.	Over L&NW from Kentish Town Jn.
.	.	.	.	.	.	. .	Brondesbury (Mid.)	Middlesex	Mid.—S. E. & C.	See West End and Brondesbury.
.	.	.	.	.	.	. .	Brunner, Mond & Co.'s Sid. (G. E.)	Essex	GE—GN—L & NW—Mid.	Silvertown Tram.
.	.	.	.	.	.	. .	Brunswick Rock Asphalte Co.'s Siding...................	Essex	G. E.	Stratford.
.	.	.	.	.	.	. .	Bryant & May's Siding......	Essex	G. E.	Devonshire Street.
.	P	.	.	.	.	. .	Burdett Road	Middlesex	G. E.	Stepney and Stratford.
.	.	.	.	.	.	. .	Burt, Boulton, and Heywood's Siding (G.E.)......	Essex	GE—GN—L & NW—Mid.	Silvertown Tram.
.	.	.	.	.	.	. .	Butt & Son's Siding	Middlesex	GE-GN-GW-LNW-Mid	Millwall Docks.
G	.	.	.	.	.	6 0	Caledonian Road	Middlesex	G. N.	Branch from Copenhagen Junction.
.	.	.	.	.	.	. .	CaledonianRd.(Pass.)(G.N)	Middlesex	G. N.—S. E. & C.	See Holloway and Caledonian Road.
.	P	.	.	.	.	. .	Caledonian Road and Barnsbury (N. L.)......	Middlesex	{ N. L.	Dalston and Camden Town.
									L. & N. W.	Over N. L. from Camden Junction.
.	.	.	.	.	.	. .	Caledonian Rd. Coal Depôt	Middlesex	L. & N. W.	Over N. L. from Camden Junction.
G	P	.	.	.	.	. . }	Camberwell New Road (S. E. & C.)...............	Surrey ...	{ S. E. & C.	Loughboro' Junction Station and Elephant and Castle.
.	P	.	.	.	.				G. N.—Mid.	Over Met. and S. E. & C. Lines.
.	P	.	.	.	.				L. & S. W.	Over L. B. & S. C. & S. E. & C. Lines.
.	.	.	.	.	.	. .	Cambria Road Junction ...	Surrey ...	L. B. & S. C.—S. E. & C...	Denmark Hill & Loughboro' Jn. Sta.
.	P	.	.	.	.	. .	Cambridge Heath	Middlesex	G. E.	Bethnal Green and Hackney Downs.
G	.	F	.	.	.	20 0	Camden	Middlesex	L. & N. W.	Euston and Willesden Junction.

EXPLANATION—G *Goods Station.*   P *Passenger and Parcel Station.*   P* *Passenger, but not Parcel or Miscellaneous Traffic.*
F *Furniture Vans, Carriages, Portable Engines, and Machines on Wheels.*   L *Live Stock.*
H *Horse Boxes and Prize Cattle Vans.*   C *Carriages by Passenger Train.*

Station Accommodation.						Crane Power.		Stations, &c.	County.	Company.	Position.
						Tons	Cwts.	LONDON—*continued.*			
								Camden Coal Depôt	Middlesex	L. & N. W.	Camden.
	P							Chalk Farm	Middlesex	L. & N. W.	Euston and Willesden Junction.
								Chalk Farm Junction	Middlesex	L. & N. W.—N. L.	Willesden Junc. (Low Level) and Camden Town.
								Hampstead Road Junc.	Middlesex	L. & N. W.—N. L.	Willesden Junction (Low Level) and Camden Town.
	P							Camden Road (Mid.)	Middlesex	Mid.	St. Pancras and Kentish Town.
	P*									S. E. & C.	Over Met. and Mid. Lines.
								Camden Road, Kentish Town Junction	Middlesex	L. & N. W.—N. L.	Willesden Junction (High Level) and Camden Town.
	P							Camden Town (N. L.)	Middlesex	N. L.	Dalston and Chalk Farm.
										L. & N. W.	Over N. L. from Camden Junction.
								Campbell Road Junction	Middlesex	L. T. & S.—W. & B. Jt.	Bromley.
								Canfield Place Junction	Middlesex	G. C.—Met.	Marylebone and Harrow-on-the-Hill.
G						20	0	Canning Town	Essex	G. F.	Stratford and North Woolwich.
G	P					5	0			L. & N. W.	Over N. L. & G. E. from Camden Jn.
	P							Cannon Street	Middlesex	Met. & Met. Dist. Jt.	Mansion House and Monument.
	P									S. E. & C.	City Terminus.
								Cannon Street, West Junc.	Surrey	S. E. & C.	Waterloo Jn. Sta. & London Bridge.
	P							Canonbury (N. L.)	Middlesex	N. L.	Dalston and Camden Town.
										L. & N. W.	Over N. L. from Camden Junction.
								Canonbury Junction	Middlesex	G. N.—N. L.	Finsbury Park and Dalston.
								Canterbury Road Junction	Surrey	S. E. & C.	Brixton & Loughboro' Junc. Station.
								Capewell Horse Nail Co.'s Siding	Middlesex	GE—GN—GW—LNW—Mid	Millwall Docks.
G						3	0	Carpenter's Road	Essex	G. E.	Stratford and Victoria Park Junc.
								Catchpole & Sons' Siding	Surrey	L. B. & S. C.	Deptford Wharf.
	P							Central (L. & I. D.)	Essex	L. & I. Dks.	Custom House and Gallions.
										G. E.	Over L. & I. Docks Line.
								Central Electric Lighting Co.'s Siding	Middlesex	G. C.	Marylebone.
								Central London Railway Siding	Middlesex	G. W.—L. & N. W.	Shepherd's Bush.
								Chalk Farm	Middlesex	L. & N. W.	See Camden.
	P							Chalk Farm	Middlesex	N. L.	Camden Town and Willesden Junc.
								Chalk Farm Junction	Middlesex	L. & N. W.—N. L.	Camden.
	P*							Chancery Lane	Middlesex	C. L.	Marble Arch and Bank.
	P	F		H	C			Charing Cross	Middlesex	S. E. & C.	West End Terminus.
	P							Charing Cross (Met. Dist.)	Middlesex	Met. Dist.	Westminster and Temple.
										L. & N. W.	Over Met. Dist. from Kensington, Earls Court Junction.
								Charing Cross Electrical Supply Association Sid.	Middlesex	G. E.	Devonshire Street.
								Charlotte Street Junction	Surrey	S. E. & C.	Ludgate Hill and Borough Road.
	P							Chelsea and Fulham	Middlesex	W. L. E. Jt. (GW, L. & NW, L. & S. W., & L. B. & S. C.)	Clapham Junction and Kensington.
G						10	0	Chelsea Basin	Middlesex	G. W.—L. & N. W.	Branch from Chelsea and Fulham.
								Chiswick	Middlesex	N. & S. W. Jn. Jt. (L. & NW, Mid., & N. L.)	See Hammersmith and Chiswick.
	P							Chiswick Park and Acton Green	Middlesex	Met. Dist.	Turnham Green and Mill Hill Park.
								City	Middlesex	W. & C.	See Mansion House (City).
	P							City Road	Middlesex	C. & S. L.	Angel and London Bridge.
G						1	15	City Sta. (Royal Mint Str.)	Middlesex	Mid.	Over G. E. from Tottenham Junc.
	P							Clapham Common	Surrey	C. & S. L.	Terminus.
								Clapham Junction—			
	P							(Station)	Surrey	L. B. & S. C.	Victoria and Crystal Palace.
	P							(Station)	Surrey	W. L. E. Jt. (GW, L. & NW, L. & S. W., & L. B. & S. C.)	Terminus.
	P							(Station, L. & S. W.)	Surrey	L. & S. W.	Waterloo and Wimbledon.
	P									G. N.	Over Met., S. E. & C. & L. & S. W. Lines.
	P*									S. E. & C.	Over L. & S. W. fr. Lavender Hill Jn.
								Falcon Junction	Surrey	L. B. & S. C.—W. L. E. Jt.	Croydon and Kensington.
G		F	L			5	0	Falcon Lane	Surrey	L. & N. W.	Branch from Clapham Junction.
								Lavender Hill Junction	Surrey	L. & S. W.—S. E. & C.	Clapham Jn. Sta. & Longhedge Jn.
								Ludgate Junction	Surrey	L. & S. W.—W. L. E. Jt.	Kensington and Clapham Junction.
								West London Junction	Surrey	L. & S. W.—W. L. E. Jt.	Waterloo and Kensington.
	P							Clapham Road	Surrey	C. & S. L.	London Bge. & Clapham Common.
G	P							Clapham Road (S. E. & C.)	Surrey	S. E. & C.	Victoria and Brixton.
	P									G. N.—Mid.	Over Met. and S. E. & C. Lines.
	P									L. & S. W.	Over S. E. & C. from Longhedge Jn.

EXPLANATION—G *Goods Station.*   P *Passenger and Parcel Station.*   P* *Passenger, but not Parcel or Miscellaneous Traffic.*
F *Furniture Vans, Carriages, Portable Engines, and Machines on Wheels.*   L *Live Stock.*
H *Horse Boxes and Prize Cattle Vans.*   C *Carriages by Passenger Train.*

STATION ACCOMMODATION.						CRANE POWER.		STATIONS, &c.	COUNTY.	COMPANY.	POSITION.
						Tons	Cwts				
	P							LONDON—*continued.* Clapham Road and North Stockwell	Surrey	L. B. & S. C.	Wandsworth Road & Peckham Rye.
G	P					3	0	Clapton	Middlesex	G. E.	Hackney Downs and Tottenham.
G								Clarence Yard (G.N.)	Middlesex	{ G. N. / N. L.	Finsbury Park and Holloway. / Over G. N. from Canonbury Junc.
								Clarke, Nicholls & Coombs Siding	Middlesex	G. E.	Stratford.
	P							Clarke, G., & Son's Siding	Middlesex	GE—GN—GW—LNW—Mid	Millwall Docks.
	P							Coborn Road (for Old Ford)	Middlesex	G. E.	Stratford and Liverpool Street.
G		F	L			24	0	Commercial Road	Middlesex	L. T. & S.	Branch from Commercial Road Junc.
								Commercial Road Junction	Middlesex	G. E.—L. T. & S.	Leman Street and Shadwell.
	P							Connaught Road (L. & I. D.)	Essex	{ L. & I. Dks. / G. E.	Custom House and Gallions. / Over L. & I. Docks Line.
								Consolidated Oil Co.'s Sid.	Kent	L. B. & S. C.	Deptford Wharf.
								Consolidated Petroleum Co.'s Siding (G. E.)	Essex	{ G.E.—G.N.—G.W.— / L. & N. W.—Mid.	Victoria Docks.
								Cook, E., & Co.'s Siding	Middlesex	G. E.	Devonshire Street.
								Co-operative Wholesale Society's Siding (G.E.)	Essex	GE—GN—L & NW-Mid.	Silvertown.
								Copenhagen Junction	Middlesex	G. N.	King's Cross and Finsbury Park.
								Copper Mill Junction	Essex	G. E.	Lea Bridge.
								Corbet's Lane Junction	Surrey	L. B. & S. C.—S. E. & C.	New Cross and London Bridge.
								Cory & Son— Coal Stores (G.E.)	Essex	GE—GN—L&NW—Mid	Victoria Docks.
								Siding	Essex	Mid.	Victoria and Albert Docks.
								Cow Lane Junction	Surrey	L. B. & S. C.—S. E. & C.	Peckham Rye and Nunhead.
								Cremorne Wharf	Middlesex	G. W.—L. & N.W.	Chelsea Basin.
								Cricklewood	Middlesex	Met.	See Willesden Green & Cricklewood.
G	P							Cricklewood (Mid.)	Middlesex	{ Mid. / S. E. & C.	Hendon and London (St. Pancras). / Over Met. and Mid. Lines.
	P*										
								Crimea Siding	Middlesex	G. W.	Near Paddington.
	P							Crouch End (G. N.)	Middlesex	{ G. N. / N. L.	Finsbury Park and Finchley. / Over G. N. from Canonbury Junc.
	P							Crouch Hill	Middlesex	T. & H. Jt. (G. E. & Mid.)	Highgate Road & South Tottenham.
	P							Custom House	Essex	{ G. E. / L. & I. Dks.	Stratford and North Woolwich. / Branch from Custom House (G. E).
								Cutler, S., & Son's Siding	Middlesex	GE—GN—GW—LNW—Mid	Millwall Docks.
								Dalston, East Junction	Middlesex	N. L.	Dalston and Mildmay Park.
	P							Dalston Junc. Sta. (N. L.)	Middlesex	{ N. L. / L. & N. W.	Broad Street and Camden Town. / Over N. L. from Camden Junction.
								Dalston, West Junction	Middlesex	N. L.	Dalston and Hackney.
	P							Denmark Hill	Surrey	{ L. B. & S. C. / S. E. & C.	Peckham Rye and Wandsworth Rd. / Brixton and Peckham Rye.
	P										
								Dennis, W. F., & Co.'s Sid.	Middlesex	GE—GN—GW—LNW—Mid	Millwall Docks.
	P							Deptford	Kent	S. E. & C.	London Bridge and Greenwich.
	P							Deptford Road	Surrey	E.L.Jt.(G.E.,L.B.&S.C., Met.,M.D.,&S.E.&C.)	Whitechapel and New Cross.
G						30	0	Deptford Wharf	Kent	L. B. & S. C.	Branch from New Cross.
								Devonshire Street (Pass)	Middlesex	G. E.	See Globe Rd. and Devonshire Str.
G		F				35	0	Devonshire Street	Middlesex	G. E.	Bishopsgate and Stratford.
G								Devons Road	Middlesex	L. & N. W.	Over N. L. from Camden Junction.
								Docks (East Smithfield)	Middlesex	L. & I. Dks.	Branch from Leman Street (G. E).
	P*							Drayton Park	Middlesex	G. N. & C.	Finsbury Park and Moorgate.
G								Dudding Hill (for Willesden and Neasden)	Middlesex	Mid.	Brent Junc. and Acton Wells Junc.
	P							Earls Court (Met. Dist.)	Middlesex	{ Met. Dist. / G. W.—L. & N. W.	Gloucester Road & West Brompton. / Over Met. Dist. from Earls Court Jn.
								Earls Court Junction	Middlesex	Met. Dist.—W. Lon. Jt.	Earls Court and Addison Road.
	P							East Brixton	Surrey	L. B. & S. C.	Peckham Rye and Wandsworth Rd.
								East Ferry Road Engineering Works Co.'s Siding	Middlesex	GE—GN—GW—LNW—Mid	Millwall Docks.
G						60	0	East India Docks (L. & I.D.)	Middlesex	{ G.E. / G.N.—G.W.—L.&N.W / Mid.—N. L.	Branch from Poplar. / Over N. L. and G.E. Lines. / Over G. E. Line.
G								East India Docks, Goods Depôt and Coal Wharf	Middlesex	G. N.	Over N. L. and G. E. Line.
								East India Road	Middlesex	N. L.	See Poplar.
								East London Water Works	Essex	{ G. E. / T & F.G.Jt(LT&S& Mid)	Stratford and Lea Bridge. / South Tottenham & Blackhorse Rd.
	P							Edgware Road (Met.)	Middlesex	{ Met. / G. W.	Praed Street and Baker Street. / Over Met. from Bishop's Road.
	P*										

EXPLANATION—G *Goods Station.*   P *Passenger and Parcel Station.*   P* *Passenger, but not Parcel or Miscellaneous Traffic.*
F *Furniture Vans, Carriages, Portable Engines, and Machines on Wheels.*   L *Live Stock.*
H *Horse Boxes and Prize Cattle Vans.*   C *Carriages by Passenger Train.*

STATION ACCOMMODATION.						CRANE POWER.		STATIONS, &c.	COUNTY.	COMPANY.	POSITION.
						Tons	Cwts.	LONDON—continued.			
..	P	..	..	..	..	..	..	Elephant and Castle	Surrey ...	C. & S. L.	London Bridge & Clapham Common.
..	P	..	..	..	..	..	..	Elephant & Castle(S.E.&C.)	Surrey ...	S. E. & C.	Ludgate Hill & Loughboro Jn. Sta.
										G. N.—Mid.	Over Met. and S. E. & C. Lines.
										L. & S. W.	Over L. B. & S. C. & S. E. & C. Lines.
..	P*	..	..	..	..	..	..	Essex Road	Middlesex	G. N. & C.	Finsbury Park and Moorgate.
..	P	F	..	H	C	1	0	Euston	Middlesex	L. & N. W.	Terminus.
..	..	..	..	..	..	..	..	Factory Junction	Surrey	L. B. & S. C.—S. E. & C.	Battersea Pk. & Wandsworth Road.
..	..	..	..	..	..	..	..	Falcon Junction...............	Surrey	L. B. & S. C.—W.L.E. Jt.	Croydon and Kensington.
..	..	..	..	..	..	..	..	Falcon Lane......................	Surrey	L. & N. W.	See Clapham Junction.
G	..	F	..	..	..	3	0	Farmer & Co.'s Sid. (G.E.)	Essex	GE—GN—L & NW—Mid.	Silvertown Tram.
..	P	..	..	..	..	..	..	Farringdon Street	Middlesex	G. N.	Branch from Met. Station.
..	P	..	..	..	..	..	..	Farringdon Street (Met.)...	Middlesex	Met.	King's Cross and Aldersgate Street.
..	P*	..	..	..	..	..	..			G. N.—Mid.	Over Met. from King's Cross Junc.
..	P*	..	..	..	..	..	..			G. W.	Over Met. from Bishop's Road.
..	P*	..	..	..	..	..	..			S. E. & C.	Over Met. from West Street Junc.
..	P	..	..	..	..	..	..	Fenchurch Street	Middlesex	G. E.	Terminus.
..	P	..	..	..	..	..	..	Ferme Park Sidings	Middlesex	G. N.	Finsbury Park and Hornsey.
G	P	F	L	H	C	..	..	Finchley Road	Middlesex	Met.	Baker Street & Harrow-on-the-Hill.
G	P	..	..	..	..	..	..	Finchley Road (Mid.)	Middlesex	Mid.	St. Pancras and Hendon.
..	P*	..	..	..	..	..	..			S. E. & C.	Over Mid. from King's Cross Junc.
G	P	..	..	..	..	..	..	Finchley Road & Frognal (L. & N. W.)	Middlesex	L. & N. W.	Kentish Town and Willesden Junc.
..	P	..	..	..	..	..	..			N. L.	Over L. & N. W. from Kentish Town Junction.
..	P*	..	..	..	..	..	..	Finchley Road Junction ...	Middlesex	Met.—Mid.	Finchley Road and West End.
G	P	..	..	..	..	10	0	Finsbury Park	Middlesex	G. N. & C.	Adjoining G. N. Station.
..	P	..	..	..	..	..	..	Finsbury Park (G. N.)	Middlesex	G. N.	King's Cross and Barnet.
..	P	..	..	..	..	..	..			N. L.	Over G. N. from Canonbury Junc.
..	P*	..	..	..	..	..	..			S. E. & C.	Over Met. and G. N. Lines.
..	..	..	..	..	..	..	..	Finsbury Park Stoneyard Siding	Middlesex	G. N.	Finsbury Park.
..	..	..	..	..	..	..	..	Frognal (L. & N. W.)	Middlesex	L. & N. W.—N. L.	See Finchley Road and Frognal.
..	..	..	..	..	..	..	..	Fulham............................	Middlesex	L. & N. W.	See Brompton and Fulham.
..	..	..	..	..	..	..	..	Fulham............................	Middlesex	W. L. E. Jt. (G. W., L. & N. W., L. & S.W. and L. B. & S. C.) ...	See Chelsea and Fulham.
..	P	..	..	..	..	..	..	Gallions (L. & I. Dks.)	Essex	L. & I. Dks.	Terminus.
..	..	..	..	..	..	..	..			G. E.	Over L. & I. Docks Line.
..	..	..	..	..	..	..	..	Gas Light and Coke Co.— Bow Common Gas Works	Middlesex	G. E.	Bow Road.
G	..	..	..	..	..	..	..	Bow Common Gas Works (N. L.)	Middlesex	NL—GN—GW—L&NW	Bow and Stepney.
..	..	..	..	..	..	..	..	Siding	Surrey	L. & S.W.	Nine Elms.
..	..	..	..	..	..	..	..	Siding (G. E.)	Essex	GE—GN—L & NW—Mid	Beckton.
..	..	..	..	..	..	..	..	Siding (G.E.)	Essex	GE—GN—L & NW—Mid	Silvertown.
..	..	..	..	..	..	..	..	Gibbs & Co.'s Manure and Vitriol Manufactory (GE)	Essex	GE—GN—L & NW—Mid	Silvertown Tram.
..	..	..	..	..	..	..	..	Gigantic Wheel Co.'s Siding	Middlesex	Mid.	West Kensington.
..	P	..	..	..	..	..	..	Globe Rd. & Devonshire Str.	Middlesex	G. E.	Liverpool Street and Stratford.
..	P	..	..	..	..	..	..	Gloucester Road..............	Middlesex	Met.	High Street and South Kensington.
..	P	..	..	..	..	..	..	Gloucester Road (Met. Dist.)	Middlesex	Met. Dist.	South Kensington and High Street.
										L. & N. W.	Over M. D. from Earl's Court Junc.
G	..	..	..	..	..	2	0	Goodman's Yard..............	Middlesex	G. E.	Minories.
..	P	..	..	..	..	..	..	Gospel Oak	Middlesex	T. & H. Jt. (G. E. & Mid.)	Branch from Highgate Road Junc.
G	P	..	..	..	..	..	..	Gospel Oak (L. & N. W.)...	Middlesex	L. & N. W.	Kentish Town and Willesden Junc.
..	P	..	..	..	..	..	..			N. L.	Over L. & N. W. fr. Kentish Town Jn.
..	P	..	..	..	..	..	..	Gower Street (Met.)	Middlesex	Met.	King's Cross and Baker Street.
..	P*	..	..	..	..	..	..			G. W.	Over Met. from Bishop's Road.
G	..	..	..	..	..	..	..	Gravel Lane....................	Surrey ...	S. E. & C.	Branch—Ludgate Hill and London Bridge.
..	..	..	..	..	..	..	..	Green Lanes....................	Middlesex	T. & H. Jt. (G. E. & Mid.)	See Harringay Park, Green Lanes.
..	..	..	..	..	..	..	..	Green Lanes Junction	Middlesex	G. W.—H. & C. Jt.	Royal Oak and Westbourne Park.
..	..	..	..	..	..	..	..	Green's, R. & H., Siding..	Middlesex	Mid.	Poplar Docks.
..	..	..	..	..	..	..	..	Griffiths, W., & Co's Sid.(GE)	Essex	GE—GN—L & NW—Mid	Silvertown.
..	P	..	..	..	..	..	..	Grosvenor Rd. (L. B. & S.C.)	Middlesex	L. B. & S. C.	Victoria and Battersea Park Road.
										L. & N. W.	Over L. B. & S. C. fr. Longhedge Jn.
..	P	..	..	..	..	..	..	Grosvenor Road (S. E. & C.)	Middlesex	S. E. & C.	Victoria and Wandsworth Road.
										G. N.—Mid.	Over Met. and S. E. & C. Lines.
										G. W.	Over S.E. & C. from Longhedge Jn.
..	P	..	..	..	..	..	..	Grove Road (L. & S. W.)...	Middlesex	L.&S.W.—G.W.—Met...	See Hammersmith (Grove Road).
..	P	..	..	..	..	..	..	Hackney	Middlesex	N. L.	Dalston and Bow.
..	..	..	..	..	..	..	..	Hackney Coal Depôt.........	Middlesex	L. & N. W.	Over N. L. from Camden Junction.

EXPLANATION—G *Goods Station.*　　P *Passenger and Parcel Station.*　　P* *Passenger, but not Parcel or Miscellaneous Traffic.*
F *Furniture Vans, Carriages, Portable Engines, and Machines on Wheels.*　　L *Live Stock.*
H *Horse Boxes and Prize Cattle Vans.*　　C *Carriages by Passenger Train.*

\begin{tabular}{c} STATION \\ ACCOMMODATION. \end{tabular}						\begin{tabular}{c} CRANE \\ POWER. \end{tabular}		STATIONS, &c.	COUNTY.	COMPANY.	POSITION.
						Tons	Cwts				
								LONDON—*continued.*			
G	P					5	0	Hackney Downs	Middlesex	G. E.	Over N.L. from Victoria Park Jn. Seven Sisters and Bethnal Green.
G						4	0	Hackney Wick	Middlesex	G. N.	Bch. from N.L. nr. Victoria Park Jn.
								Hackney Wick (or Victoria Park) Junction	Middlesex	G. E.—N. L.	Stratford and Hackney.
	P							Haggerston (N. L.)	Middlesex	{ N. L. / L. & N. W.	Broad Street and Dalston. Over N. L. from Camden Junction.
G*	P P P							Hammersmith (Broadway)	Middlesex	{ H. & C.Jt.(G.W. & Met.) / Met. Dist.	Branch from Latimer Road. West Kensington & Studland Rd.Jn.
	P							Hammersmith (Grove Rd.) (L. & S.W.)	Middlesex	{ L. & S. W. / G. W.—Met.	Kensington and Richmond. Over L. & S.W. fr. Hammersmith Jn.
G	P					5	0	Hammersmith & Chiswick	Middlesex	N.&S.W.Jn.Jt.(L.&NW, Mid., & N. L.	Branch from Acton.
								Hammersmith Branch Jn.	Middlesex	N.&S.W.Jn.Jt.(L.&NW, Mid., & N. L.)	Acton and South Acton.
								Hammersmith Junction	Middlesex	H. & C. Jt.—L. & S. W.	Shepherd's Bush and Hammersmith (Grove Road).
G	P P							Hampstead Heath (L&NW)	Middlesex	{ L. & N. W. / N. L.	Kentish Town and Willesden Junc. Over L & N W fr. Kentish Town Jn.
								Hampstead Road Junction.	Middlesex	L. & N. W.—N. L.	Willesden Jn. (Low Level) & Camden Town.
G		F			C	5	0	Hampstead's (Borough of) Siding	Middlesex	L. & N. W.	Finchley Road and West End Lane. Harlesden (for West Willesden & Stonebridge Park)
								Harlesden (for West Willesden & Stonebridge Park)	Middlesex	Mid.	Dudding Hill and Acton Wells.
G	P P P*							Harringay (G. N.)	Middlesex	{ G. N. / N. L. / S. E. & C.	Finsbury Park and Hornsey. Over G. N. from Canonbury Junc. Over Metropolitan and G. N. Lines.
G	P							Harringay Pk., Green Lanes	Middlesex	{ Mid. / T & H Jt. (G E &Mid.)	South Tottenham and Highgate Rd.
								Harrow Lane Junction	Middlesex	G. E.—N. L.	Same as Millwall Docks Junction.
	P P*							Hatcham	Surrey	L. B. & S. C.	See Old Kent Road and Hatcham.
G								Haverstock Hill (Mid.)	Middlesex	{ Mid. / S. E. & C.	St. Pancras and Hendon. Over Metropolitan and Mid. Lines.
G						5	0	Haydon Square	Middlesex	L. & N. W.	Over N. L. & G. E. from Camden Jn.
	P							Henley & Co.'s Old Wks (GE)	Essex	GE—GN—L & NW—Mid.	Silvertown.
G								Highbury and Islington (N. L.)	Middlesex	{ N. L. / L. & N. W.	Dalston Junction and Camden Town. Over N. L. from Camden Junction.
G								Highbury Coal Depôt	Middlesex	L. & N. W.	Over N. L. from Camden Junction.
G	P							Highbury Vale	Middlesex	G. N.	Finsbury Park and Holloway.
G	P P P							Highgate (G. N.)	Middlesex	{ G. N. / N. L.	Finsbury Park and Finchley. Over G. N. from Canonbury Junc.
	P P							Highgate Road (for Parliament Hill)	Middlesex	{ Mid. / T. & H. Jt. (G.E. & Mid.)	Kentish Town and Upper Holloway. Kentish Town and Upper Holloway.
								Highgate Road Coal Depôt	Middlesex	Mid.	Highgate Road Station.
G	P P							Highgate Road Junction	Middlesex	Mid.—T. & H. Jt.	Kentish Town & Highgate Road Sta.
								High Street (Kensington)	Middlesex	{ Met / Met. Dist. / Mid	Notting Hill Gate & Gloucester Rd. Terminus. Over L. & S. W. & Met. Dist. Lines.
								High Street (Kensington) Junction	Middlesex	Met.—Met. Dist.	Gloucester Road and High Street.
								High Street (Kensington) Junction	Middlesex	Met. Dist.—Mid.	High Street and Earls Court.
								His Majesty's Naval Depôt Stores	Middlesex	GE—GN—GW—LNW—Mid	West India Docks.
	P							Holborn Viaduct	Middlesex	S. E. & C.	City Terminus.
	P*							Holland Park	Middlesex	C. L.	Shepherd's Bush and Marble Arch.
	P P*							Holloway and Caledonian Road (G. N.)	Middlesex	{ G. N. / S. E. & C.	King's Cross and Finsbury Park. Over Met. and G. N. Lines.
			L					Holloway, Cattle	Middlesex	G. N.	King's Cross and Holloway.
	P							Homerton	Middlesex	N. L.	Dalston and Bow.
								Hooper's Telegraph & India Rubber Works	Middlesex	GE—GN—GW—LNW—Mid	Millwall Docks.
	P							Hornsey Road	Middlesex	T. & H. Jt. (G. E. & Mid.)	Highgate Road & South Tottenham.
								Howards & Son's Siding	Essex	G. E.	Devonshire Street.
								Hudson's Siding	Surrey	L. B. & S. C.	New Cross.
								Hurlingham	Middlesex	Met. Dist	See Putney Bridge and Hurlingham.
								Imperial Cold Stores Siding	Middlesex	G. E.	Seven Sisters.
								Imperial Gas Light and Coke Co.'s Siding	Middlesex	G. W.—L. & N. W.	Chelsea and Fulham.
								Ind Coope & Co.'s Siding	Essex	G. E.	Stratford.

EXPLANATION—G *Goods Station.* G* *Mineral Class Traffic only.* P *Passenger and Parcel Station.*
P* *Passenger, but not Parcel or Miscellaneous Traffic.* F *Furniture Vans, Carriages, Portable Engines, and Machines on Wheels.*
L *Live Stock.* H *Horse Boxes and Prize Cattle Vans.* C *Carriages by Passenger Train.*

STATION ACCOMMODATION.						CRANE POWER.		STATIONS, &c.	COUNTY.	COMPANY.	POSITION.
						Tons	Cwts				
								LONDON—*continued.*			
								India-Rubber, Gutta-Percha & Telegraph Co.'s Siding (G.E.)	Essex	GE—GN—L & NW—Mid.	Silvertown.
								Islington (N. L.)	Middlesex	N. L.—L. & N. W.	See Highbury and Islington.
								Islington Electric Light Works	Middlesex	G. N.	Near Holloway.
	P							Junction Road	Middlesex	T. & H. Jt. (G. E. & Mid.)	Highgate Road & Upper Holloway.
								Junction Road Junction	Middlesex	Mid.—T. & H. Jt.	Haverstock Hill and Junction Road.
	P							Keiller & Son's Sid. (G.E.)	Essex	GE—GN—L & NW—Mid.	Silvertown.
	P							Kennington	Surrey	C. & S. L.	London Bridge & Clapham Common.
								Kensal Green Gas Works	Middlesex	G. W.	Westbourne Park & West London Jn.
	P							Kensal Rise (L. & N. W.)	Middlesex	L. & N. W. / N. L.	Kentish Town and Willesden Junc. / Over L. & N. W. fr. Kentish Town Jn.
								Kensington—			
	P	F		H	C			Addison Rd. (W.Lon. Jt.)	Middlesex	W Lon Jt (G W & L NW) / L. & S. W. / L. B. & S. C.	Uxbridge Road & Earls Court Junc. / Over West London Joint Line. / Over West London Joint Line.
	P			H	C						
	P										
								Addison Road Junction	Middlesex	W. Lon. Jt.—W.L. E. Jt.	Addison Road and Clapham Junc.
								Earls Court Junction	Middlesex	Met. Dist.—W. Lon. Jt.	Earls Court and Addison Road.
								High Street	Middlesex	Met.—Met. Dist.—Mid.	See High Street (Kensington).
								High Street Junction	Middlesex	Met.—Met. Dist.	Gloucester Road and High Street.
								High Street Junction	Middlesex	Met. Dist.—Mid.	High Street and Earls Court.
								Junction	Middlesex	L. & S.W.—W. Lon. Jt.	Hammersmith and Addison Road.
								Lillie Bridge Sidings	Middlesex	W.L.E.Jt.(GW, L&NW, L.&SW, & L.B.&S.C.)	Clapham Junction and Kensington. Branch—Addison Road & Lillie Bge.
G						5	0	Warwick Road	Middlesex	G. W. / L. & N. W.	Clapham Junction and Kensington.
G											
								West	Middlesex	Met. Dist.—Mid.	See West Kensington.
								Kensington & Notting Hill Electric Lighting Co.'s Sid	Middlesex	G. W.—L. & N. W	Shepherd's Bush.
								Kensington Vestry Siding	Middlesex	G. W.—L. & N. W	Shepherd's Bush.
	P							Kentish Town (L. & N. W.)	Middlesex	L. & N. W. / N. L.	Kentish Town Jn. & Willesden Jn. / Over L. & N. W. fr. Kentish Town Jn.
G	P		L					Kentish Town (Mid.)	Middlesex	Mid. / G. E. / S. E. & C.	St. Pancras and Hendon. / Over Mid. from Highgate Road Jn. / Over Met. and Mid. Lines.
	P*										
								Kentish Town Junction	Middlesex	L. & N. W.—N. L.	Same as Camden Road Junction.
G		F	L	H	C	5	0	Kew Bridge	Middlesex	N.&S.W. Jn.Jt.(L.&NW, Mid., & N. L.)	Acton and Old Kew Junction.
								Kew East Junction	Middlesex	L. & S.W.—N&SW Jn Jt	Kew Bridge and Acton.
G	P					5	0	Kilburn and Maida Vale (L. & N. W.)	Middlesex	L. & N. W. / N. L.	Euston and Willesden Junction. / Over L. & N. W. from Chalk Farm Jn.
	P							Kilburn—Brondesbury	Middlesex	Met.	Baker Street & Harrow-on-the-Hill.
G	P	F	L	H	C			Kingsbury—Neasden	Middlesex	Met.	Baker Street & Harrow-on-the-Hill.
G		F	L	H	C	10	0	King's Cross	Middlesex	G. N.	Branch from Copenhagen Junc. / Terminus.
	P	F	L	H	C	0	10				
	P							King's Cross (Met.)	Middlesex	Met. / G. N.—Mid. / G. W. / S. E. & C.	Gower Street and Farringdon Street. / Over Met. from King's Cross Junc. / Over Met. from Bishop's Road. / Over Met. from West Street Junc.
	P*										
	P*										
	P*										
	P*							King's Cross (Suburban) (G. N.)	Middlesex	G. N. / S. E. & C.	King's Cross (Met.) and Holloway. / Over Met. and G. N. Lines.
	P										
	P							King's Cross (York Rd) (GN)	Middlesex	G. N. / S. E. & C.	King's Cross. / Over Met. and G. N. Lines.
	P*										
								King's Cross Junction	Middlesex	Met.—Mid.	King's Cross and Kentish Town.
								King's Cross Junctions	Middlesex	G. N.—Met.	King's Cross (York Road) and King's Cross (Met.)
G		F				5	0	Kingsland	Middlesex	L. & N. W.	Over N. L. from Camden Junction.
								Knight, J., & Son's Sid.(GE)	Essex	GE—GN—L & NW—Mid.	Silvertown Tram.
								Ladbroke Grove	Middlesex	H. & C. Jt. (G. W. & Met.)	See Notting Hill & Ladbroke Grove.
	P*							Lancaster Gate	Middlesex	C. L.	Shepherd's Bush and Marble Arch.
								Latchmere Junctions	Surrey	W.L.E.Jt.(GW, L&NW, L.&SW, & L.B.&S.C.)	Battersea & Clapham Junc. Station.
	P*							Latimer Road	Middlesex	H. & C. Jt. (G. W. & Met.)	Notting Hill and Shepherd's Bush.
								Latimer Road Junction	Middlesex	H. & C. Jt (G. W. & Met.)	Latimer Road and Uxbridge Road.
								Lavender Hill Junction	Surrey	L. & S.W.—S. E. & C.	Clapham Jn. Sta. & Longhedge Jn.
								Lea and Limehouse Cut Coal Tip (N. L.)	Middlesex	N. L. / G.N.—G.W.—L.&N.W	Bow and Poplar. / Over N. L. Line.
								Lea Bridge—			
G	P							(Station)	Essex	G. E.	Stratford and Tottenham.
								Copper Mill Junction	Essex	G. E.	Lea Bridge and Tottenham.

EXPLANATION—G *Goods Station.*   P *Passenger and Parcel Station.*   P* *Passenger, but not Parcel or Miscellaneous Traffic.*
F *Furniture Vans, Carriages, Portable Engines, and Machines on Wheels.*   L *Live Stock.*
H *Horse Boxes and Prize Cattle Vans.*   C *Carriages by Passenger Train.*

STATION ACCOMMODATION.					CRANE POWER.		STATIONS, &c.	COUNTY.	COMPANY.	POSITION.
					Tons	Cwts.	LONDON—continued.			
.	.	.	.	.	.	.	Lea Bridge District Gas Co.'s Siding	Essex	G. E.	Lea Bridge.
.	P	.	.	.	.	.	Lebus, H., Siding	Middlesex	G. E.	Tottenham.
.	.	.	.	.	.	.	Leman Street	Middlesex	G. E.	Fenchurch Street and Stepney.
.	.	.	.	.	.	.	Lescher, J. F., Siding	Middlesex	G. E.	Spitalfields, Goods.
.	.	.	.	.	.	.	Lillie Bridge Sidings	Middlesex	W. L. E. Jt. (GW, L& NW, L.&S. W.&L. B.&S. C.)	Kensington.
.	P	.	.	.	.	.	Limehouse	Middlesex	G. E.	Stepney and Blackwall, Pass.
.	P	.	.	H	C	.	Liverpool Street	Middlesex	G. E.	City Terminus.
.	.	.	.	.	.	.	Liverpool Street Junction	Middlesex	G. E.—Met.	Liverpool Str. Sta. & Moorgate Str.
.	.	.	.	.	.	.	Loders & Nucoline Sid.(GE)	Essex	GE—GN—L & NW—Mid.	Silvertown.
.	.	.	.	.	.	.	London and India Docks Co.'s Siding	Essex	L. & I. Dks.—G. E.—Mid.	Near Swing Bridge, Victoria Docks, South Side.
.	.	.	.	.	.	.	London & Thames Haven Petroleum Oil Wharves Co.'s Abbey Mills Siding	Essex	L. T. & S.	Bromley.
.	P	.	.	.	.	.	London Bridge	Surrey	C. & S. L.	Angel and Clapham Common.
.	P	F	.	H	C	.	London Bridge	Surrey	L. B. & S. C.	Terminus.
.	P	.	.	.	.	.			S. E. & C.	Charing Cross and New Cross.
.	.	.	.	.	.	.	London County Council's Siding (G. E.)	Essex	GE—GN—L&NW—Mid.	Beckton.
.	P	.	.	.	.	.	London Fields	Middlesex	G. E.	Bethnal Green & Hackney Downs.
.	.	.	.	.	.	.	London Keg and Drum Co.'s Siding	Middlesex	GE-GN-GW-LNW-Mid	Millwall Docks.
.	P	.	.	.	.	.	London Necropolis Co.	Surrey	L. & S.W.	Private Station—Waterloo.
.	.	.	.	.	.	.	London Pressed Hinge Co.'s Siding	Middlesex	GE-GN-GW-LNW-Mid	Millwall Docks.
.	.	.	.	.	.	.	Longhedge Junctions	Surrey	LBSC—SE&C—WLE Jt.	Victoria and Kensington.
.	P	.	.	.	.	.	Longhedge Works	Surrey	S. E. & C.	Branch from Stewarts Lane Junc.
.	.	.	.	.	.	.	Loudoun Road (for Swiss Cottage) (L. & N. W.)	Middlesex	L. & N. W.	Euston and Willesden Junction.
.	.	.	.	.	.	.			N. L.	Over L. & N.W. from Chalk Farm Jn.
.	.	.	.	.	.	.	Loughboro' Junction	Surrey	S. E. & C.	Camberwell New Road and Loughboro' Junction Station.
.	P	.	.	.	.	.	Loughboro' Jn. Sta.(SE & C)	Surrey	S. E. & C.	Elephant & Castle and Herne Hill.
.	.	.	.	.	.	.			G. N.—Mid.	Over Met. & S. E. & C. Lines.
.	.	.	.	.	.	.			L. & S. W.	Over L. B. & S. C. & S. E. & C. Lines.
.	.	.	.	.	.	.	Lovibond & Son's Brewery Siding	Middlesex	Mid.	West Kensington.
.	P	.	.	.	.	.	Ludgate Hill (S. E. & C.)	Middlesex	S. E. & C.	Holborn Viaduct & Elephant & Castle
.	.	.	.	.	.	.			G. N.—Mid.	Over Met. & S. E. & C. Lines.
.	.	.	.	.	.	.			L. & S. W.	Over L. B. & S. C. & S. E. & C. Lines.
.	.	.	.	.	.	.	Ludgate Junction	Surrey	L. & S.W.—W. L. E. Jt.	Kensington and Clapham Junction.
.	.	.	.	.	.	.	Lyle & Son's Siding (G.E.)	Essex	GE—GN—L & NW—Mid.	Silvertown Tram.
.	.	.	.	.	.	.	McAndrew, R., & Co.'s Sid.	Middlesex	GE-GN-GW-LNW-Mid	Millwall Docks.
.	.	.	.	.	.	.	McDougall & Co.'s Siding	Middlesex	GE-GN-GW-LNW-Mid	Millwall Docks.
.	.	.	.	.	.	.	McDougall Bros.' Siding	Middlesex	GE-GN-GW-LNW-Mid	Millwall Docks.
.	.	.	.	.	.	.	McVitie & Price's Siding	Middlesex	L. & N. W.	Willesden Junction and Sudbury.
.	.	.	.	.	.	.	Madge's Siding	Surrey	S. E. & C.	Camberwell New Road.
.	.	.	.	.	.	.	Maida Vale (L. & N. W.)	Middlesex	L. & N. W.—N. L.	See Kilburn and Maida Vale.
G	.	F	L	.	10	0	Maiden Lane	Middlesex	L. & N. W.	Over N. L. from Camden Junction.
.	P	.	.	.	.	.	Maiden Lane (N. L.)	Middlesex	N. L.	Dalston and Camden Town.
.	.	.	.	.	.	.			L. & N. W.	Over N. L. from Camden Junction.
.	P	.	.	.	.	.	Manor Way (L. & I. Dks.)	Essex	L. & I. Dks.	Custom House and Gallions.
.	.	.	.	.	.	.			G. E.	Over L. & I. Docks Line.
.	P*	.	.	.	.	.	Mansion House (City)	Middlesex	W. & C.	Terminus.
.	P	.	.	.	.	.	Mansion House (Met. Dist.)	Middlesex	Met. Dist.	Blackfriars and Cannon Street.
.	.	.	.	.	.	.			L. & N. W.	Over Met. Dist. from Kensington, Earls Court Junction.
.	.	.	.	.	.	.	Mansion House Junction	Middlesex	Met. Dist.—Met. & Met. Dist. Jt.	Mansion House and Cannon Street.
.	P*	.	.	.	.	.	Marble Arch	Middlesex	C. L.	Shepherd's Bush and Bank.
.	P	.	.	.	.	.	Mark Lane	Middlesex	Met. & Met. Dist. Jt.	Monument and Aldgate.
.	P	.	.	.	.	.	Marlborough Road	Middlesex	Met.	Baker Street & Harrow-on-the-Hill.
G	P	F	.	H	C	25	0	Marylebone	Middlesex	G. C.	Terminus.
.	.	.	.	.	.	.	Metropolitan Borough of Stepney Siding	Middlesex	G. E.	Devonshire Street.
.	.	.	.	.	.	.	Metropolitan Electric Supply Co.'s Siding	Middlesex	L. & N. W.	Willesden Junction and Sudbury.
.	.	.	.	.	.	.	Metropolitan Junction	Surrey	S. E. & C.	Waterloo Jn. Sta. and London Bge.
.	P	.	.	.	.	.	Mildmay Park (N. L.)	Middlesex	N. L.	Dalston and Camden Town.
.	.	.	.	.	.	.			L. & N. W.	Over N. L. from Camden Junction.

EXPLANATION—G *Goods Station.*   P *Passenger and Parcel Station.*   P* *Passenger, but not Parcel or Miscellaneous Traffic.*
F *Furniture Vans, Carriages, Portable Engines, and Machines on Wheels.*   L *Live Stock.*
H *Horse Boxes and Prize Cattle Vans.*   C *Carriages by Passenger Train.*

STATION ACCOMMODATION.						CRANE POWER.		STATIONS, &c.	COUNTY.	COMPANY.	POSITION.
						Tons	Cwts.	LONDON—continued.			
								Mileage Yard	Middlesex	G. W.	See Paddington.
	P							Mile End	Middlesex	W.&B.Jt.(L.T.&S.&M D)	Stepney Green and Bow Road.
								Millington & Sons' Siding	Middlesex	G. E.	Tottenham.
								Millwall Docks—			
G	P					1	10	Dock Station	Middlesex	G. E.	Millwall Junc. & North Greenwich.
G	P							Junction Station	Middlesex	G. E.	Stepney and Blackwall.
								Junction (Harrow Lane)	Middlesex	G. E.—N. L.	Millwall Dks. Junc. Sta. and Poplar.
										{ G.E.—N. L.	Over Dock Lines.
G						60	0	Millwall Docks	Middlesex	{ G.N.—G.W.—L.&N.W	Over N.L., and Dock Lines.
										{ Mid.	Over G.E., and Dock Lines.
								Minories Junction	Middlesex	Met. & Met. Dist. Jt. ...	Aldgate and Mark Lane.
G								Mitre Bridge	Middlesex	L. & N. W.	Kensington and Willesden Junction.
	P							Monument	Middlesex	Met. & Met. Dist. Jt. ...	Cannon Street and Mark Lane.
								Moore, Nettlefold & Co.'s Siding (G.E.)	Essex	GE—GN—L & NW—Mid.	Silvertown.
	P							Moorgate Street.............	Middlesex	C. & S. L.................	Angel and London Bridge.
	P*							Moorgate Street.............	Middlesex	G. N. & C.	Terminus.
	P									{ Met.	Aldersgate Street and Bishopsgate.
	P							Moorgate Street (Met.)......	Middlesex	{ G. N.—Mid.	Over Met. from King's Cross Junc.
	P									{ G. W.	Over Met. from Bishop's Road.
	P*									{ S. E. & C.	Over Met. from Snow Hill Junction.
	P*							N. A.O. Food Co.'s Siding	Middlesex	GE—GN—GW—LNW—Mid	Millwall Docks.
								Neasden	Middlesex	Met.	See Kingsbury, Neasden.
								Neasden	Middlesex	Mid.	See Dudding Hill (for Willesden and Neasden).
								Neasden Junction	Middlesex	G. C.—Mid.	Harrow and Acton Wells Junction.
								Neasden Jn. & Sids. (G. C.)	Middlesex	G. C.—L. & S. W.........	Neasden Junction and Harrow.
								New Cross—			
	P									{ L. B. & S. C.	London Bridge and Croydon.
	P									{ G. E.	Over LB&SC from East London Jn.
	P							(Station, L. B. & S. C.)..	Surrey ...	{ Met. Dist.	Over LB&SC from New Cross Junc.
	P*									{ S. E. & C.	Over LB&SC from Corbets Lane Jn.
										{ S. E. & C.	London Bridge and St. John's.
	P							(Station, S. E. & C.)	Kent	{ Met.	Over SE&C from East London Junc.
G								Depôt	Surrey ...	G. E.	Over E. L. Jt.and L. B. & S. C. Lines.
								Junction	Kent	E. L. Jt.—S. E. & C. ...	Deptford Road and New Cross.
								Junction	Surrey ...	E. L. Jt.—L. B. & S.C....	Deptford Road and New Cross.
								Newington Vestry Siding...	Surrey ...	S. E. & C.	Walworth Road.
								New Kew Junction	Middlesex	L. & S.W.	Kew Bridge and Gunnersbury.
								New River Co.'s Water-works Siding	Middlesex	Mid.	Dudding Hill and Brent.
G		F	L			20	0	Nine Elms	Surrey ...	L. & S.W..............	London Goods Terminus.
								Nine Elms Gas Co.'s Siding	Surrey ...	L. & S. W.	Nine Elms.
								Nine Elms Stone Masonry Works	Surrey ...	L. & S. W.	Nine Elms.
	P							North Greenwich	Middlesex	G. E.	Branch from Millwall Junction.
								North Kent Junction	Kent	S. E. & C.	Spa Road and Deptford.
								North Pole Junction	Middlesex	G W—L&N W—W L Jt.	Same as West London, North Pole Jn.
								North Stockwell.............	Surrey ...	L. B. & S. C.	See Clapham Rd. & North Stockwell.
	P							Notting Hill and Ladbroke Grove	Middlesex	H. & C. Jt. (G. W. & Met.)	Westbourne Park and Latimer Road.
	P*							Notting Hill Gate	Middlesex	C. L.	Shepherd's Bush and Marble Arch.
	P							Notting Hill Gate	Middlesex	Met.	Bayswater (Queen's Road) and Kensington, High Street.
								Odam's Manure & Chemical Co.'s Siding (G.E.)	Essex	GE—GN—L & NW—Mid.	Silvertown Tram.
								Old Ford	Middlesex	G. E.	See Coborn Road (for Old Ford).
G						20	0	Old Ford	Middlesex	{ L. & N. W.	Over N. L. from Camden Junction.
	P									{ N. L.	Dalston and Bow.
	P							Old Kent Road & Hatcham	Surrey ...	L. B. & S. C.	London Bridge and Peckham Rye.
								Old Kent Road Junction...	Surrey ...	E. L. Jt.—L. B. & S. C.	Deptford Road and Old Kent Road.
								Old Kew Junction............	Middlesex	L&SW.—N&SW Jn. Jt.	Brentford and Acton.
								Old Oak Common West Jn.	Middlesex	G. W.	Westbourne Park and Acton.
								Old Oak Exchange Sidings (N. & S. W. Jn. Jt.)	Middlesex	L & NW—L&SW—N L	Willesden Junction and Acton.
								Old Oak Junction	Middlesex	L&NW—N&SW.Jn.Jt.	Willesden Junction and Acton.
	P							Old Street	Middlesex	C. & S. L.	Angel and London Bridge.
	P*							Old Street	Middlesex	G. N. & C.	Finsbury Park and Moorgate.
	P							Oliver, W., & Son's Siding	Middlesex	GE—GN—GW—LNW—Mid	Millwall Docks.
	P							Oval	Surrey ...	C. & S. L.	London Bridge & Clapham Common.
	P*							Oxford Circus	Middlesex	C. L.	Marble Arch and Bank.

EXPLANATION—G Goods Station.   P Passenger and Parcel Station.   P* Passenger, but not Parcel or Miscellaneous Traffic.
F Furniture Vans, Carriages, Portable Engines, and Machines on Wheels.   L Live Stock.
H Horse Boxes and Prize Cattle Vans.   C Carriages by Passenger Train.

Station Accommodation.						Crane Power.		Stations, &c.	County.	Company.	Position.
						Tons	Cwts	LONDON—*continued.*			
								Paddington—			
G	P	F	L	H	C	12	0	(Station)	Middlesex	G. W.	Terminus.
.	P	.	.	.	.			Bishop's Road Station and Junction	Middlesex	G. W.—Met.	Westbourne Park & Edgware Road.
G	.	.	.	.	.	20	0	Mileage Yard	Middlesex	G. W.	Branch near Westbourne Park.
.	P	.	.	.	.			Praed Street	Middlesex	Met.	Edgware Road and Bayswater (Queen's Road).
								Parliament Hill	Middlesex	Mid.—T. & H. Jt.	See Highgate Road (for Parliament Hill).
.	P	.	.	.	.			Parsons Green..............	Middlesex	Met. Dist................	Walham Green and Putney Bridge.
.	.	.	.	.	.			Patent Indurated Stone Co.'s Siding	Middlesex	GE–GN–GW–LNW–Mid	Millwall Docks.
.	.	.	.	.	.			Patent Victoria Stone Co.'s Siding	Essex	G. E.	Stratford Market.
.	P	.	.	.	.		}	Peckham Rye	Surrey ...	{ L. B. & S. C.	London Bridge & Wandsworth Rd.
.	P	.	.	.	.				Surrey ...	{ S. E. & C.	Brixton and Nunhead.
.	.	.	.	.	.			Peckham Rye Coal Depôt...	Surrey	L. & N. W. & Mid. Jt. ...	Over L. B. & S. C. from Clapham Jn.
								Poplar—			
.	P	.	.	.	.			(Goods)	Middlesex	G. E.	See Blackwall (Poplar).
G	.	F	L	H	.	30	0	(Passengers)	Middlesex	G. E.	Stepney and Blackwall.
G	G	.	F	.	.	30	0	(Dock)	Middlesex	G. N.	Over N. L. from Canonbury Junc.
G	G	.	F	L	.	30	0	(Dock)	Middlesex	L. & N. W.	Over N. L. from Camden Junction.
G	G	.	F	L	.	30	0	(Dock)	Middlesex	N. L.	Terminus.
G	G	.	F	L	.	5	0	(Dock and Station)	Middlesex	G. W.	Over N. L. from Acton Wells Junc.
G	.	.	.	.	.			(Station and Dock)........	Middlesex	Mid.	Branch from G. E. at Poplar.
.	.	.	.	.	.			East India Docks	Middlesex	GE—GN—GW—L & NW —Mid.—N L	See East India Docks.
.	.	.	.	.	.			East India Docks Goods Depôt & Coal Wharf...	Middlesex	G. N.	See East India Docks.
.	P	.	.	H	C			East India Road............	Middlesex	N. L.	Bow and Poplar Dock.
.	.	.	.	.	.			Junction with Dock Co.'s Lines	Middlesex	N. L.	Poplar and Millwall Dock.
.	.	.	.	.	.			Millwall Docks	Middlesex	GE—GN—GW—L & NW —Mid.—N L	See Millwall Docks.
.	.	.	.	.	.			South West India Docks	Middlesex	GE—GN—GW—L & NW —Mid.—N L	See South West India Docks.
.	.	.	.	.	.			West India Docks	Middlesex	GE—GN—GW—L & NW —Mid.—N L	See West India Docks.
.	P	.	.	.	.		}	Portland Road (Met.)	Middlesex	{ Met.	Baker Street and Gower Street.
.	P*	.	.	.	.					{ G. W.	Over Met. from Bishop's Road.
.	P*	.	.	.	.			Portobello Junc. & Sids.	Middlesex	G. W.	Near Westbourne Park.
.	.	.	.	.	.			Post Office	Middlesex	C. L.	Marble Arch and Bank.
.	.	.	.	.	.			Pouparts Junction	Surrey ...	L. B. & S. C.	Clapham Junc. & Longhedge Junc.
.	.	.	.	.	.			Praed Street	Middlesex	Met.	See Paddington.
.	.	.	.	.	.			Praed Street Junction	Middlesex	Met.	Edgware Rd. and Praed Street Sta.
.	.	.	.	.	.			Prior, J., Siding.............	Middlesex	G. E.	Blackwall.
.	.	.	.	.	.			Putney Bridge & Fulham Junction	Middlesex	L. & S.W.—Met. Dist. ...	East Putney and Putney Bridge.
.	P	.	.	.	.			Putney Bridge & Hurlingham	Middlesex	Met. Dist................	Parsons Green and East Putney.
G	P	.	.	.	.	5	0 }	Queen'sPk (WestKilburn) }	Middlesex	{ L. & N. W.	Euston and Willesden Junction.
.	P	.	.	.	.			(L. & N. W.) }	Middlesex	{ N. L.	Over L&N W from Chalk Farm. Jn.
.	P*	.	.	.	.			Queen's Road	Middlesex	C. L.	Shepherd's Bush and Marble Arch.
.	P	.	.	.	.			Queen's Road (Battersea)...	Surrey ...	L. & S.W.	Waterloo and Clapham Junction.
.	.	.	.	.	.			Queen's Road (Bayswater)	Middlesex	Met.	See Bayswater (Queen's Road).
.	P	.	.	.	.			Queen's Road (Peckham)...	Surrey ...	L. B. & S. C.	London Bridge and Peckham Rye.
.	.	.	.	.	.			Rait & Gardiner's Siding ...	Middlesex	GE–GN–GW–LNW–Mid	Millwall Docks.
.	P	.	.	.	.			Ravenscourt Park (L&S.W)	Middlesex	{ L. & S. W. { G. W.—Met { Met. Dist.	Hammersmith and Richmond. Over L&S W from Hammersmith Jn. Over L. & S. W. Line.
.	P	.	.	.	.			Rectory Road	Middlesex	G. E.	Hackney Downs and Seven Sisters.
G	.	.	.	.	.	25	0	Regent's Canal Wharf	Middlesex	G. C.	Marylebone.
.	P	.	.	.	.			Rotherhithe	Surrey ...	E.L.Jt. (G.E.,L.B.&S.C., Met., M. D., & S. E. C.)	Whitechapel and New Cross.
.	.	.	.	.	.			Rowbotham's Siding........	Middlesex	G. W.	Acton and West London Junction.
G	.	F	L	.	.	50	0	Royal Albert Dk. (L.& I. D.)	Essex	{ L. & I. Dks. { GE–GN–GW–LNW–Mid	Branch from Beckton Junction. Over L. & I. Dks. Goods Lines.
G	.	.	.	.	.	5	0	Royal Albert Dk. Coal Hoist	Essex	GE–GN–GW–LNW–Mid	Victoria and Albert Docks.
.	.	.	.	.	.			Royal Mint Street............	Middlesex	G. N.	Bch. from G. E. near Fenchurch Str.
.	.	.	.	.	.			Royal Mint Street............	Middlesex	Mid.	See City Station.
.	P*	.	.	.	.			Royal Oak	Middlesex	G. W.	Bishop's Road and Westbourne Park.

EXPLANATION—**G** *Goods Station.*   **P** *Passenger and Parcel Station.*   **P*** *Passenger, but not Parcel or Miscellaneous Traffic.*
F *Furniture Vans, Carriages, Portable Engines, and Machines on Wheels.*   **L** *Live Stock.*
H *Horse Boxes and Prize Cattle Vans.*   **C** *Carriages by Passenger Train.*

Station Accommodation	Crane Power (Tons Cwts)	Stations, &c.	County	Company	Position
		LONDON—continued.			
G . F L . .	50 0	RoyalVictoriaDk.(L.&I.D.)	Essex	{ L. & I. Dks. .... / GE-GN-GW-LNW-Mid	Beckton Junction and Albert Dock. / Over L. & I. Dks. Goods Lines.
. P		St. Ann's Road	Middlesex	T. & H. Jt. (G. E. & Mid.)	South Tottenham & Highgate Road.
. . . . . .		St. George's, East	Middlesex	G. E.	See Shadwell & St. Georges, East.
. P		St. James' Park (Met. Dist.)	Middlesex	{ Met. Dist. .... / L. & N. W.	Victoria and Westminster. / Over Met. Dist. from Kensington, Earls Court Junction.
. P		St. John's Wood Road	Middlesex	Met.	Baker Street & Harrow-on-the-Hill.
. P		St. Mary's (Whitechapel)...	Middlesex	Met. & Met. Dist. Jt......	Aldgate East and Whitechapel.
. . . . . .		St. Mary's Junction	Middlesex	Met. Dist.—Met. & Met. Dist. Jt.	Whitechapel and St. Mary's.
		St. Pancras—			
G . F . . .	20 0	(Station)	Middlesex	Mid.	Branch from St. Paul's Road Junc.
. P F . H C	. . }	(Station, Mid.)	Middlesex	{ Mid. .... / G. E.	Terminus. / Over Mid. from Highgate Road Jn.
. P . . H C					
. . . . . .		Junction	Middlesex	G. N.—N. L.	Holloway and Camden Town.
. . . . . .		Junction	Middlesex	Mid.—N. L.	St. Pancras Goods & Camden Town.
. P		St. Paul's	Middlesex	S. E. & C.	Loop—LudgateHill & BoroughRoad.
. P		St. Paul's Road Junction...	Middlesex	Mid.	Camden Road and St. Pancras.
. P		St. Quintin Park & Wormwood Scrubbs	Middlesex	L. & N. W.	Kensington and Willesden Junc.
. . . . . .		Saxby & Farmer's Siding...	Middlesex	L. & N. W.	Kilburn and Queen's Park (West Kilburn).
. P		Seven Sisters	Middlesex	G. E.	Hackney Downs and Enfield Town.
. P		Shadwell	Middlesex	E.L.Jt.(G.E.,L.B.&S.C., Met., M.D., & S.E. &c.)	Whitechapel and New Cross.
. P		Shadwell&St.George's,East	Middlesex	G. E.	Fenchurch Street and Stepney.
. P*		Shakespeare Coal Wharf...	Surrey	S. E. & C.	Clapham Road.
				C. L.	Terminus.
G . F . . .	5 0 }	Shepherd's Bush	Middlesex	{ G. W. / H. & C. Jt. (G. W. & Met.) / L. & N. W. / L. & S. W.	West London Junc. & Uxbridge Rd. / Latimer Road and Hammersmith. / Kensington and Willesden Junc. / Kensington and Hammersmith.
. P					
G . P . . .					
. P					
. . . . . .		Shepherd's Bush (Pass.) ...	Middlesex	W.Lon.Jt.(GW & LNW)	See Uxbridge Road (for Shepherd's Bush).
. P		Shoreditch	Middlesex	E.L.Jt.(G.E.,L.B.&S.C., Met. M.D., & S.E. &c.)	Whitechapel and Bishopsgate Junc.
G		Shoreditch	Middlesex	L. & N. W.	Over N. L. from Camden Junction.
. P		Shoreditch (N. L.)............	Middlesex	{ N. L. / L. & N. W.	Broad Street and Dalston. / Over N. L. from Camden Junction.
G P	1 10	Silvertown	Essex	G. E.	Stratford and North Woolwich.
. . . . . .		Silvertown Oil Storage Co.'s Siding (G.E.)	Essex	G. E.—L. & N. W.—Mid.	Silvertown Tram.
. P		Sloane Square (Met. Dist.)	Middlesex	{ Met. Dist. .... / L. & N. W.	South Kensington and Victoria. / Over Met. Dist. from Kensington, Earls Court Junction.
G	5 0	Smithfield	Middlesex	G. W.	Over Met. from Bishop's Road.
. P		Snow Hill (S. E. & C.)	Middlesex	{ S. E. & C. / G. N.—Mid.	Ludgate Hill and West Street Jn. / Over Met. and S. E. & C. Lines.
. . . . . .		Snow Hill Junction	Middlesex	Met.—S. E. & C.	Aldersgate Street and Snow Hill Sta.
. . . . . .		Snow Hill Sidings	Middlesex	L. & S.W.	Snow Hill Station & Farringdon Str.
G	5 0	Somers Town	Middlesex	Mid.	Terminus (Near St. Pancras).
. . . . . .		Somers Town Coal Depôt...	Middlesex	Mid.	Near St. Pancras.
. P		South Acton	Middlesex	N.&S.W.Jn.Jt.(L.&NW, Mid., & N. L.)	Acton and Kew Bridge.
. . . . . .		South Acton, North Junc.	Middlesex	Met Dist—N & SW.Jn.Jt.	Mill Hill Park and Acton.
. P		South Bermondsey	Surrey	L. B. & S. C.	London Bridge and Peckham Rye.
. P		South Bromley	Middlesex	N. L.	Bow and Poplar.
. P		South Docks (Millwall)......	Middlesex	G. E.	Millwall Jn. Sta. & North Greenwich.
. P		South Kensington	Middlesex	Met.	Brompton (Gloucester Road) and Sloane Square.
. P		South Kensington (Met. Dist.)	Middlesex	{ Met. Dist. .... / L. & N. W.	Brompton (Gloucester Road) and Sloane Square. / Over Met. Dist. from Kensington, Earl's Court Junction.
. . . . . .		South Kensington Junction	Middlesex	Met.—Met. Dist.	South Kensington & Sloane Square.
G	. . }	South Tottenham & Stamford Hill	Middlesex	{ Mid. / T & H Jt (G E & Mid.) }	Highgate Road and Tottenham.
. P					
. . . . . .		South Tottenham Junction	Middlesex	G. E.—T. & H. Jt.	Seven Sisters and South Tottenham Station.
. . . . . .		South Tottenham Junction	Middlesex	T. & F. G. Jt.—T. & H. Jt.	Blackhorse Rd. & South Tottenham.

EXPLANATION—G *Goods Station.*   P *Passenger and Parcel Station.*   P* *Passenger, but not Parcel or Miscellaneous Traffic.*
F *Furniture Vans, Carriages, Portable Engines, and Machines on Wheels.*   L *Live Stock.*
H *Horse Boxes and Prize Cattle Vans.*   C *Carriages by Passenger Train.*

HAND-BOOK OF RAILWAY STATIONS, &c   LON—LON   341

G	P	F	L	H	C	Tons	Cwts	STATIONS, &c.	COUNTY.	COMPANY.	POSITION.
								LONDON—*continued.*			
	P							Southwark Park	Surrey	S. E. & C.	London Bridge and Greenwich.
G						60	0	South West India Docks (L. & I. D.)	Middlesex	G.E. G N—G W—L & N W Mid. N. L.	Millwall Dks. Jn. Sta. & Millwall Dks. Over N. L. & Dock Lines. Over G. E. & Dock Lines. Over Dock Lines.
	P							Spa Road (Bermondsey)	Surrey	S. E. & C.	London Bridge and Greenwich.
								Spencer, Chapman and Messel's Chemical Manure Works (G.E.)	Essex	GE—GN—L & NW–Mid.	Silvertown Tram.
								Spitalfields—			
G						4	10	(Station)	Middlesex	G. E.	Bishopsgate and Stratford.
								Coal	Middlesex	G. E.	Branch from Spitalfields, Goods.
								Hoist	Middlesex	G. E.	Spitalfields Coal Branch.
								Hoist Junction	Middlesex	E. L. Jt.—G. E.	Whitechapel and Spitalfields Hoist.
G								Spring Place Sidings	Middlesex	Mid.	Kentish Town.
	P							Stamford Hill	Middlesex	G. E.	Hackney Downs and Seven Sisters.
								Stamford Hill	Middlesex	Mid.—T. & H. Jt.	See So. Tottenham & Stamford Hill.
	P							Stephens, Smith & Co.'s Sid.	Middlesex	GE–GN–GW–LNW-Mid	South West India Docks.
	P							Stepney	Middlesex	G. E.	Fenchurch Street and Stratford.
	P							Stepney Green	Middlesex	W.&B.Jt.(L T. & S. & MD)	Whitechapel and Mile End.
G			L			10	0	Stewart's Lane (S. E. & C.)	Surrey	S. E. & C. G. W.–L. & N. W.–Mid.	Branch from Stewart's Lane Junc. Over S. E. & C. Line.
	P							Stewart's Lane Junction	Surrey	L. B. & S. C.—S. E. & C.	Grosvenor Rd. & Wandsworth Rd.
								Stockwell	Surrey	C. & S. L.	London Bridge & Clapham Common.
								Stockwell, North	Surrey	L. B. & S. C.	See Clapham and North Stockwell.
G	P							Stoke Newington	Middlesex	G. E.	Hackney Downs and Seven Sisters.
								Stonebridge Park	Middlesex	Mid.	See Harlesden (for West Willesden and Stonebridge Park).
								Stoney Street Junction	Surrey	S. E. & C.	Waterloo Junc. Sta. & Cannon Str.
								Stratford—			
G	P	F	L	H	C	10	0	Central	Essex	G. E.	Liverpool Street and Romford.
	P							Low Level	Essex	G. E.	Victoria Park & Stratford Market.
								Stratford Exchange Sidings (G. E.)	Essex	G. E.—N. L.	Stratford.
G	P							Stratford Market	Essex	G. E.	Stratford and North Woolwich.
	P							Stroud Green (G. N.)	Middlesex	G. N. N. L.	Finsbury Park and Highgate. Over G. N. from Canonbury Junc.
								Stuart's Granolithic Stone Co.'s Siding	Middlesex	GE–GN–GW–LNW-Mid	Millwall Docks.
								Studland Road Junction	Middlesex	L. & S.W.—Met. Dist.	Ravenscourt Park & Hammersmith.
								Subway Junction	Middlesex	G. W.	Paddington and Westbourne Park.
								Surrey Canal Junction	Surrey	S. E. & C.	London Bridge and New Cross.
G								Surrey Commercial Docks	Surrey	L. B. & S. C.	Deptford Wharf Branch.
	P							Swiss Cottage	Middlesex	Met.	Baker Street & Harrow-on-the-Hill.
								Swiss Cottage (L. & N. W.)	Middlesex	L. & N. W.—N. L.	See Loudoun Rd. (for Swiss Cottage).
								Tate, H., & Son's Sid. (G.E.)	Essex	GE–GN–L & N W-Mid.	Silvertown.
	P							Temple (Met. Dist.)	Middlesex	Met. Dist. L. & N. W.	Blackfriars and Charing Cross. Over Met. Dist. from Kensington, Earl's Court Junction.
								Temple Mills Sidings (G.E.)	Middlesex	G. E. L.&N.W.—Mid.—N.L.	Stratford and Lea Bridge. Over G. E. Line.
G								Thames Iron Works, Shipbuilding & Engineering Co.'s Siding (G. E.)	Essex	GE–GN–L & NW-Mid	Canning Town.
								Thames Wharf	Essex	Mid.	Victoria Docks.
						10	0	Thames Wharf, Coal	Essex	G. E.	Bch.—Canning Town & Victoria Dks.
								Thames Wharf Junction	Essex	G. E.—Mid.	Canning Town and Victoria Docks.
	P							Tidal Basin	Essex	G. E.	Stratford and North Woolwich.
G	P	F	L	H	C	1	0	Tottenham	Middlesex	G. E.	Stratford and Broxbourne.
								Tottenham, North Junc.	Middlesex	G. E.—T. & H. Jt.	Tottenham and Crouch Hill.
								Tottenham, West Junc.	Middlesex	G. E.—T. & H. Jt.	Lea Bridge and Crouch Hill.
	P*							Tottenham Court Road	Middlesex	C. L.	Marble Arch and Bank.
G		F	L			5	0	Tufnell Park	Middlesex	G. E.	Branch from Tufnell Park Junction.
								Tufnell Park Junction	Middlesex	G. E.—T. & H. Jt.	Junction Road and Upper Holloway.
								Turnham Green Junction	Middlesex	L. & S.W.—Met. Dist.	Turnham Green and Chiswick Park.
G		F			C			United Alkali Co.'s Sid. (GE)	Essex	GE–GN–L & NW-Mid.	Silvertown Tram.
	P							Upper Holloway	Middlesex	Mid. T. & H. Jt. (G. E. & Mid.)	Highgate Rd. & South Tottenham.
	P							Uxbridge Road (for Shepherd's Bush)	Middlesex	W Lon Jt (G W & L N W)	Kensington and West London North Pole Junction.
								Uxbridge Road Junction	Middlesex	H. & C. Jt.—W. Lon. Jt.	Latimer Road and Kensington.

EXPLANATION—G *Goods Station.*   P *Passenger and Parcel Station.*   P* *Passenger, but not Parcel or Miscellaneous Traffic.*
F *Furniture Vans, Carriages, Portable Engines, and Machines on Wheels.*   L *Live Stock.*
H *Horse Boxes and Prize Cattle Vans.*   C *Carriages by Passenger Train.*

G	P	F	L	H	C	Tons	Cwts	STATIONS, &c.	COUNTY.	COMPANY.	POSITION.
								LONDON—*continued.*			
	P							Vallance Road Junction ...	Middlesex	Met. Dist.—W. & B. Jt.	St. Marys and Stepney Green.
	P							Vauxhall	Surrey ...	L. & S.W.	Waterloo and Clapham Junction.
	P	F		H	C		}	Victoria (L. B. & S. C.) ...	Middlesex	L. B. & S. C.	West End Terminus.
	P									L. & N. W.	Over LB&SC from Longhedge Junc.
	P							Victoria (Met. Dist.)	Middlesex	Met. Dist.	Sloane Square and St. James' Park.
										L. & N. W.	Over Met. Dist. from Kensington, Earls Court Junction.
	P	F		H	C			Victoria (S. E. & C.)	Middlesex	S. E. & C.	West End Terminus.
										G. N.—Mid.	Over Met. and S. E. & C. Lines.
										G. W.	Over S E & C from Longhedge Junc.
								Victoria & Albert Docks—			
G		F				12	0	Victoria and Albert	Essex	G. W.	Over N. L., G.E., and L.&I.D. Lines.
G						15	0	Victoria & Albert Docks	Essex	Mid.	Over G. E. from Tottenham Junc.
G								Victoria & Albert Docks (G. E.)	Essex	G. E.	Stratford and North Woolwich.
										G. W.	Over N. L. and G. E. Lines.
										L. & N. W.	Over N.L. and G.E. from Camden Jn.
G						2	0	Victoria Dock	Essex	G. N.	Branch from L.&I.D.&G.E. Stations.
								Victoria Docks Junction...	Essex	G. E.—Mid.	Bch.—Canning Tn. & Custom House.
	P							Victoria Park	Middlesex	G. E.	Branch from Stratford.
	P									N. L.	Dalston and Bow.
								Victoria Park or Hackney Wick Junction	Middlesex	G. E.—N. L.	Stratford and Hackney.
	P							Walham Green	Middlesex	Met. Dist.	West Brompton & Parsons Green.
								Walthamstow Urban District Council Siding	Essex	G. E.	Lea Bridge.
	P							Walworth Road (S. E.& C.)	Surrey ...	S. E. & C.	Elephant & Castle and Loughboro' Junction Station.
										G. N.—Mid.	Over Met. and S. E. & C. Lines.
										L. & S. W.	Over L. B. & S. C. and S.E.&C. Lines.
								Walworth Road Coal Depôt	Surrey	Mid.	Over Met. and S. E. & C. Lines.
	P							Wandsworth Road............	Surrey	L. B. & S. C.	Victoria and Peckham Rye.
G		F				8	0	Wandsworth Road	Surrey	Mid.	Over Met. and S. E. & C. Lines.
								Wandsworth Rd. (S.E.&C.)	Surrey	S. E. & C.	Victoria and Brixton.
	P									G. N.—Mid.	Over Met. and S. E. & C. Lines.
										L. & S. W.	Over S. E. & C. from Longhedge Jn.
	P							Wapping	Middlesex	E. L. Jt.(G.E., L.B.&S.C., Met., M. D.,&S. E.&C.)	Whitechapel and New Cross.
								Warwick Road	Middlesex	G. W.—L. & N. W.	See Kensington.
	P			H	C		}	Waterloo	Surrey	L. & S. W.	Terminus.
	P*									W. & C.	Adjoining L. & S. W. Station.
	P							Waterloo Junction	Surrey	L. & S.W.—S. E. & C. ...	Waterloo L.S.W. & Waterloo Jn. Sta.
	P							Waterloo Junction Station	Surrey	S. E. & C.	Charing Cross and London Bridge.
								Wellington Sidings	Middlesex	G. N.	Highgate and East Finchley.
	P*						}	Westbourne Park	Middlesex	G. W.	Paddington and Ealing.
	P*									H. & C. Jt.(G. W.&Met.)	Royal Oak and Notting Hill.
	P						}	West Brompton	Middlesex	Met. Dist.	Earls Court and Walham Green.
	P									W.L.E.Jt(GW,L&NW, L. & S.W, L. B.&S.C.)	Clapham Junction and Kensington.
G	P	F	L		C		}	West End and Brondesbury (Mid.)	Middlesex	Mid.	St. Pancras and Hendon.
	P*									S. E. & C.	Over Mid. from King's Cross Junc.
	P							West End Lane (L.&N.W.)	Middlesex	L. & N. W.	Kentish Town and Willesden Junc.
										N. L.	Over L.&N.W. fr. Kentish Town Jn.
								Western Electric Co.'s Siding (G.E.)	Essex	G E—G N—L N W—Mid	Silvertown.
	P							West Hampstead	Middlesex	Met., ...	Baker Street & Harrow-on-the-Hill.
								West Ham Gas Co.'s Siding	Essex	G. E.	Stratford Market.
G						3	0	West Ham, South	Essex	G. E.	Custom House and Beckton.
								West India Coal Sidings ...	Middlesex	Mid.	West India Docks.
	P							West India Docks	Middlesex	G. E.	Stepney and Blackwall.
G	P	F	L			40	0	West India Docks	Middlesex	L. & I. Dks.	Millwall.
G						60	0	West India Docks (L.&I.D.)	Middlesex	G. E.	Millwall Junc. and Millwall Docks.
										G. N.—G.W.—L. N. W.	Over N. L. and Docks Lines.
										Mid.	Over G. E. and Docks Lines.
										N. L.	Over Docks Lines.
G	P	F		H	C	5	0 }	West Kensington	Middlesex	Met. Dist.	Hammersmith and Earls Court.
										Mid.	Over L. & S. W. & Met. Dist. Lines.
								West Kensington Junction	Middlesex	Met. Dist.—Mid.	Hammersmith & West Kensington.
								West Kilburn (L. & N. W.)	Middlesex	L. & N. W.—N. L.	See Queen's Park (West Kilburn).
								West London Junction ...	Middlesex	G. W.	Westbourne Park and Acton.
								West London Junction......	Surrey ...	L. & S.W.—W. L. E. Jt.	Waterloo and Kensington.
								West London, North Pole Jn.	Middlesex	G.W.—L.N.W.—W L Jt.	Willesden Junc. and Kensington.

EXPLANATION—**G** *Goods Station.*   **P** *Passenger and Parcel Station.*   **P*** *Passenger, but not Parcel or Miscellaneous Traffic.*
F *Furniture Vans, Carriages, Portable Engines, and Machines on Wheels.*   **L** *Live Stock.*
H *Horse Boxes and Prize Cattle Vans.*   **C** *Carriages by Passenger Train.*

STATION ACCOMMODATION.						CRANE POWER.		STATIONS, &c.	COUNTY.	COMPANY.	POSITION.
						Tons	Cwts.	LONDON—continued.			
.	P	.	.	.	.	.	.	Westminster (Met. Dist.)	Middlesex	{ Met. Dist.	St. James' Park and Charing Cross.
										L. & N. W.	Over Met. Dist. from Kensington, Earls Court Junction.
.	.	.	.	.	.	.	.	West Street Junction	Middlesex	Met.—S. E. & C.	Farringdon Street and Snow Hill.
.	.	.	.	.	.	.	.	West Willesden	Middlesex	Mid.	See Harlesden (for West Willesden and Stonebridge Park).
.	P	.	.	.	.	.	.	Whitechapel	Middlesex	E. L. Jt. (G. E., L. B. & S.C., Met., M. D. & S. E. & C.)	Shoreditch and New Cross.
.	P	.	.	.	.	.	.	Whitechapel	Middlesex	W. & B. Jt. (L. T. & S. & MD)	St. Mary's and Stepney Green.
.	.	.	.	.	.	.	.	Whitechapel Junction	Middlesex	E. . L. Jt.—Met. & Met. Dist. Jt.	Shadwell & St. Mary's (Whitechapel).
.	.	.	.	.	.	.	.	Whitechapel, Vallance Road Junction	Middlesex	Met. Dist.—W. & B. Jt.	St. Mary's and Stepney Green.
G	.	.	.	.	.	2	10	Whitecross Street	Middlesex	Mid.	Branch from Metropolitan near Aldersgate Street.
.	.	.	.	.	.	.	.	Willesden......................	Middlesex	Mid.	See Dudding Hill (for Willesden and Neasden).
.	.	.	.	.	.	.	.	Willesden & Acton Bk. Wks.	Middlesex	G. W.	Same as Acton & Willesden Bk. Wks.
.	.	.	.	.	.	.	.	Willesden Electric Light Works Siding	Middlesex	Mid.	Harlesden and Dudding Hill.
G	P	F	L	H	C	4	0	Willesden Green and Cricklewood	Middlesex	Met.	Baker Street & Harrow-on-the-Hill.
.	.	.	.	.	.	.	.	Willesden Junction— Exchange Sids. (L & N W)	Middlesex	L. & N. W.—L. & S. W.	Willesden Junction.
.	P	.	.	.	.	.	.	High Level (L. & N. W.)	Middlesex	{ L. & N. W.	Kensington and Kentish Town.
										G. W.	Over N. & S. W. Jn. Jt. & L. & N. W. from Acton Wells Junction.
										N. L.	Over L.&N.W. from Kentish Town Junction.
G	P	F	L	H	C	10	0 }	Junction	Middlesex	L & N W—N & S W Jn. Jt.	Euston and Acton.
.	P	.	.	.	.			Low Level (L. & N. W.)	Middlesex	{ L. & N. W.	Euston and Watford.
G	.	F	L	.	.	12	0			N. L.	Over L.&N.W. from Chalk Farm Jn.
.	.	.	.	.	.	.	.	Willow Walk	Surrey	L. B. & S. C.	Bricklayers' Arms.
.	.	.	.	.	.	.	.	Willow Walk Junction....	Surrey	L. B. & S. C.—S. E. & C.	Willow Walk and Deptford.
.	.	.	.	.	.	.	.	Wormwood Scrubbs	Middlesex	L. & N. W.	See St. Quintin Park and Wormwood Scrubbs.
G	.	.	.	.	.	5	0	Worship Street	Middlesex	L. & N. W.	Adjoining Broad Street.
.	.	.	.	.	.	.	.	Yarrow & Co.'s Siding......	Middlesex	GE—GN—GW—LNW—Mid	Millwall Docks.
.	.	.	.	.	.	.	.	York Road (G. N.)............	Middlesex	G. N.—S. E. & C.	See King's Cross.
.	.	.	.	.	.	.	.	Young & Marten's Siding	Essex	G. E.	Stratford.
.	.	.	.	.	.	.	.	London and Arlesey Brick Co.'s Siding....................	Beds	G. N.	Arlesey.
.	.	.	.	.	.	.	.	London and Brighton Brick Co.'s Siding	Surrey	L. B. & S. C.	Lingfield.
.	.	.	.	.	.	.	.	London and India Docks Co.'s Siding	Essex	L. & I. Dks.—G. E.	London, Blackwall.
.	.	.	.	.	.	.	.	London and Manchester Plate Glass Co.'s Siding	Lancs	L. & N. W.	St. Helens.
.	.	.	.	.	.	.	.	London and Oldfield Potteries (Pearson's, J., Siding)	Derby......	Mid.	Chesterfield.
.	.	.	.	.	.	.	.	London and South Wales Engineering Co.'s Siding...	Glamorg'n	G W—L N W—Rhy—T V	Cardiff.
.	.	.	.	.	.	.	.	London and Thames Haven Petroleum Oil Wharves Co.— Abbey Mills Siding	Essex	L. T. & S.	London, Bromley.
.	.	.	.	.	.	.	.	Siding	Essex	L. T. & S......................	Thames Haven.
.	.	.	.	.	.	.	.	London Brick Co.— Siding	Beds	L. & N. W.	Millbrook (for Ampthill).
.	.	.	.	.	.	.	.	Siding	Middlesex	G. E.	Churchbury.
.	.	.	.	.	.	.	.	Sidings	Hunts	G. N.	Fletton.
.	.	.	.	.	.	.	.	London Bridge	Surrey ...	C & SL—LB & SC—SE & C	See London.
.	.	.	.	.	.	.	.	London County Council's Siding (G. E.) .... }	Middlesex	{ G.E.—G.N.—L. & N.W. —Mid. .... }	London, Beckton.
.	.	.	.	.	.	.	.	London County Lunatic Asylum Siding .... }	Middlesex	G. N.	Same as Colney Hatch Asylum Siding (New Southgate).
								LONDONDERRY—			
G	P	F	L	H	C	5	0	(Station)	Derry	Donegal	Terminus.
G	P	F	L	.	.	.	.	(Station)	Derry	Mid.	By Steamer from Heysham.
G	P	F	L	H	C	50	0	(Station)	Derry	P.&W.Jt. (L&Y & L&NW)	Steamer from Fleetwood.
G	.	.	.	.	.	.	.	City	Derry	Donegal	Over Bridge and Harbour Commissioners' Tram Lines.

EXPLANATION—G *Goods Station.*   P *Passenger and Parcel Station.*   P* *Passenger, but not Parcel or Miscellaneous Traffic.*
F *Furniture Vans, Carriages, Portable Engines, and Machines on Wheels.*   L *Live Stock.*
H *Horse Boxes and Prize Cattle Vans.*   C *Carriages by Passenger Train.*

STATION ACCOMMODATION.						CRANE POWER.	STATIONS, &c.	COUNTY.	COMPANY.	POSITION.
						Tons Cwts.	LONDONDERRY—continued.			
G	P	F	L	.	.	3 0	Foyle Road	Derry	G. N. (I.)	Terminus.
G	.	.	.	.	.	1 10			N. C. Com. (Mid.).	Over Bridge and Harbour Commissioners' Tram Lines.
G	P	.	L	.	.	2 0	Graving Dock	Derry	L. & L. S.	Terminus.
G	P	F	L	H	C	3 0	Water Side	Derry	N. C. Com. (Mid.)	Terminus.
.	.	.	.	.	.	. .	Londonderry Brick Siding	Durham	N. E.	Ryhope, East.
.	.	.	.	.	.	. .	Londonderry Granary	Durham	N. E.	Seaham.
.	.	.	.	.	.	. .	Londonderry Limestone Quarry	Durham	N. E.	Seaham.
.	.	.	.	.	.	. .	Londonderry Lime Works	Durham	N. E.	Seaham.
.	.	.	.	.	.	. .	Londonderry Stores	Durham	N. E.	Seaham.
.	.	.	.	.	.	. .	Londonderry Wagon Shops	Durham	N. E.	Seaham.
.	.	.	.	.	.	. .	London Fields	Middlesex	G. E.	See London.
.	.	.	.	.	.	. .	London Fireproof Wall Co.'s Siding	Middlesex	G. E.	Angel Road.
.	.	.	.	.	.	. .	London Keg and Drum Co.'s Siding	Middlesex	G. E.	London, Millwall Docks.
									GN–GW–L & NW–Mid.	London, Poplar.
.	.	.	.	.	.	. .	London Necropolis Co.'s Sta.	Surrey	L. & S.W.	See London.
.	.	.	.	.	.	. .	London Pressed Hinge Co.'s Siding	Middlesex	G. E.	London, Millwall Docks.
									GN–GW–L & NW–Mid.	London, Poplar.
.	.	.	.	.	.	. .	London Road	Beds	G. N.	See Dunstable.
.	.	.	.	.	.	. .	London Road	Cumb'land	N. E.	See Carlisle.
.	.	.	.	.	.	. .	London Road	Lanark	Cal.	See Glasgow.
.	.	.	.	.	.	. .	London Road	Lancs	G. C.—L. & N. W.— M. S. J. & A.	See Manchester.
.	.	.	.	.	.	. .	London Road	Notts	G. N.	See Nottingham.
.	.	.	.	.	.	. .	London Road	Surrey	L. & S.W.	See Guildford.
.	.	.	.	.	.	. .	London Road	Sussex	L. B. & S. C.	See Brighton.
.	.	.	.	.	.	. .	London Road (Mid.)	Leicester	Mid.—L. & N. W.	See Leicester.
.	.	.	.	.	.	. .	London Road Coal Depôts	Cumb'land	N. E.	Carlisle.
.	.	.	.	.	.	. .	London Road Foundry (Miller & Co.'s Siding)	Edinboro'	N. B.	Edinburgh, Rose Lane.
.	.	.	.	.	.	. .	London Road Junction	Cumb'land	L. & N. W.—N. E.	Carlisle.
.	.	.	.	.	.	. .	London Road Junction	Edinboro'	N. B.	Edinburgh.
.	.	.	.	.	.	. .	London Road Junction	Lancs	G. C.—L. & N. W.	Manchester.
.	.	.	.	.	.	. .	London Road Junction	Lancs	L. & N. W.—M. S. J. & A.	Manchester.
.	.	.	.	.	.	. .	London Road Wharf	Derby	Mid.	See Derby.
.	.	.	.	.	.	. .	London Wharf	Northumb.	N. E.	Newcastle-on-Tyne.
.	.	.	.	.	.	. .	London Works	Staffs	L. & N. W.	See Guest, Keen & Nettlefold (Soho).
.	.	.	.	.	.	. .	Longacres Mines	Yorks	N. E.	North Skelton.
.	.	.	.	.	.	. .	Longbottom's Wagon Repairing Siding (G.C.)	Yorks	G. C.—G. N.	Sheffield, Bridgehouses.
G	P	F	L	H	C	10 0	Long Buckby	N'hampton	L. & N. W.	Northampton and Rugby.
.	.	.	.	.	.	. .	Longcarse Junction	Clackman'	Cal.—N. B.	Alloa.
G	P	F	L	H	C	. .	Long Clawson & Hose	Leicester	G. N. & L. & N. W. Jt.	Melton Mowbray and Nottingham.
G	.	.	.	.	.	0 15	Longcliffe	Derby	L. & N. W.	Buxton and Cromford.
.	.	.	.	.	.	. .	Jones's Longcliffe Quarry	Derby	L. & N. W.	Longcliffe and Steeplehouse.
.	.	.	.	.	.	. .	Minninglow Siding	Derby	L. & N. W.	Longcliffe and Friden.
.	.	.	.	.	.	. .	Shaw & Lovegrove's Longcliffe Limestone Co.'s Sid.	Derby	L. & N. W.	Longcliffe and Friden.
.	.	.	.	.	.	. .	Swann, Ratcliffe & Co.'s Harboro' Siding	Derby	L. & N. W.	Longcliffe and Steeplehouse.
.	.	.	.	.	.	. .	Taylor's Hopton Bone Wks.	Derby	L. & N. W.	Longcliffe and Steeplehouse.
.	.	.	.	.	.	. .	Wirksworth Stone & Mineral Co.'s Brittains or Manystones Quarry	Derby	L. & N. W.	Longcliffe and Steeplehouse.
G	P	.	.	H	.	. .	Longdon Road (for Ilmington)	Worcester	G. W.	Moreton-in-Marsh and Shipston-on-Stour.
G	P	.	.	.	.	. .	Longdown	Devon	G. W.	Exeter and Heathfield.
G	P	.	L	.	.	5 0	Long Eaton	Derby	Mid.	Trent and Stapleford.
.	.	.	.	.	.	. .	Claye's, S. J., Wagon Works	Derby	Mid.	Near Long Eaton.
.	.	.	.	.	.	. .	Long Eaton Gas Works	Derby	Mid.	Near Long Eaton.
.	.	.	.	.	.	. .	Toton Sidings	Derby	Mid.	Near Long Eaton.
.	.	.	.	.	.	. .	Trent Girder Yard (Engineer's Siding)	Derby	Mid.	Trent and Attenboro'.
.	.	.	.	.	.	. .	Long Eaton Junction	Derby	Mid.	Trent and Attenboro'.
.	.	.	.	.	.	. .	Longfield	Kent	S. E. & C.	See Fawkham (for Hartley and Longfield).
.	.	.	.	.	.	. .	Longfield Sid. (Evelyn's Sids.)	Kent	S. E. & C.	Meopham.
.	.	.	.	.	.	. .	Longfleet	Dorset	L. & S.W.	See Poole (for Longfleet).
G	P	F	L	H	C	1 0	Longford	Longford	M. G. W.	Mullingar and Sligo.

EXPLANATION—G *Goods Station.*   P *Passenger and Parcel Station.*   P* *Passenger, but not Parcel or Miscellaneous Traffic.*
F *Furniture Vans, Carriages, Portable Engines, and Machines on Wheels.*   L *Live Stock.*
H *Horse Boxes and Prize Cattle Vans.*   C *Carriages by Passenger Train.*

STATION ACCOMMODATION.						CRANE POWER.		STATIONS, &c.	COUNTY.	COMPANY.	POSITION.
						Tons	Cwts.				
.	P	.	.	.	.	.	.	Longford and Exhall............	Warwick..	L. & N. W.	Coventry and Nuneaton.
.	.	.	.	.	.	.	.	Longford Chemical Works (Scottish Acid & Alkali Co.)	Ayr	Cal.—G. & S. W.	Kilwinning.
.	.	.	.	.	.	.	.	Longford Gas Works (L&NW)	Lancs	L. & N. W.—G. W.	Warrington, Bank Quay.
.	.	.	.	.	.	.	.	Longford Wire Co.'s Siding (L. & N. W.)	Lancs	L. & N. W.—G. W.	Warrington, Bank Quay.
G	P	.	L	H	.	1	10	Longforgan	Perth	Cal.	Perth and Dundee.
G	P	.	L	H	.	5	0	Longhaven	Aberdeen	G. N. of S.	Ellon and Boddam.
.	.	.	.	.	.	.	.	Longhedge Junctions	Surrey ...	L. B. & S. C.—S. E. & C.— W. L. E. Jt.	London, Victoria and Kensington.
.	.	.	.	.	.	.	.	Longhedge Works	Surrey ...	S. E. & C.	See London.
.	.	.	.	.	.	.	.	Longhill Foundry	Durham ..	N. E.	West Hartlepool.
.	.	.	.	.	.	.	.	Longhill Sidings.................	Durham ..	N. E.	West Hartlepool.
G	P	F	L	H	C	1	0	Longhirst	Northumb	N. E.	Berwick and Morpeth.
.	.	.	.	.	.	.	.	Ashington Junction	Northumb	N. E.	Longhirst.
.	.	.	.	.	.	.	.	Longhirst Hall Colliery ...	Northumb	N. E.	Longhirst.
.	.	.	.	.	.	.	.	Longholme Siding	Lancs	L. & Y.	Rawtenstall.
G	P	.	.	.	.	5	0	Longhope..........................	Glo'ster ...	G. W.	Gloucester and Hereford.
G	P	F	L	H	C	1	10	Longhoughton	Northumb	N. E.	Berwick and Morpeth.
.	.	.	.	.	.	.	.	Long Itchington	Warwick..	L. & N. W.	See Southam and Long Itchington.
.	.	.	.	.	.	.	.	Long Lane Colliery	Lancs	G C (St. H. Ex.)—L & N W	See Garswood Coal & Iron Co.
.	.	.	.	.	.	.	.	Longley's Siding	Sussex ...	L. B. & S. C.	Crawley.
.	.	.	.	.	.	.	.	Long, Mann & Co.'s Siding..	Norfolk ...	G. E.	Attleboro'.
G	P	.	L	H	.	.	.	Long Marston	Glo'ster ...	G. W.	Stratford-on-Avon & Honeybourne.
G	P	F	L	H	C	1	10	Long Marton	W'morlnd	Mid.	Appleby and Carlisle.
.	.	.	.	.	.	.	.	Long Meg Siding	Cumb'land	Mid.	Lazonby and Kirkoswald.
G	P	F	L	H	C	1	10	Long Melford	Suffolk ...	G. E.	Sudbury and Bury.
G	P	F	L	H	.	2	0	Longmorn.........................	Elgin&Mo'	G. N. of S.	Craigellachie and Elgin.
G	P	.	L	H	C	.	.	Longniddry	Hadding'n	N. B.	Edinburgh and Dunbar.
.	.	.	.	.	.	.	.	Harelaw Lime Siding	Hadding'n	N. B.	Longniddry Station.
.	.	.	.	.	.	.	.	Longniddry West Siding...	Hadding'n	N. B.	Prestonpans and Longniddry.
.	.	.	.	.	.	.	.	Longniddry Junction	Hadding'n	N. B.	Prestonpans and Drem.
G	P	F	L	H	C	.	.	Longparish	Hants	L. & S. W.	Hurstbourne and Fullerton.
.	P	.	.	.	.	.	.	Longpavement	Clare	G. S. & W.	Limerick and Ennis.
G	P	F	L	H	C	10	0 }	Longport (N. S.)	Staffs	{ N. S.	Stoke and Harecastle.
G	.	F	L	.	.	10	0 }			{ L. & N. W.	Over N. S. Line.
.	.	.	.	.	.	.	.	Brownhill's Colliery (Heath & Son's)	Staffs	N. S.	Longport.
.	.	.	.	.	.	.	.	PortVale Sid.(Boulton&Co.)	Staffs	N. S.	Longport.
G	P	F	L	H	C	.	.	Long Preston	Yorks	Mid.	Skipton and Settle.
G	P	.	L	H	.	5	0	Longridge	Lancs	P.&L. Jt. (L&NW.&L&Y)	Branch from Preston.
.	.	.	.	.	.	.	.	Banks & Co.'s Siding	Lancs	P.&L. Jt. (L&NW.&L&Y)	Longridge.
.	.	.	.	.	.	.	.	Chapel Hill Sidings	Lancs	P.&L. Jt. (L&NW.&L&Y)	Longridge and Grimsargh.
.	.	.	.	.	.	.	.	Kay's	Lancs	P.&L. Jt. (L&NW.&L&Y)	Chapel Hill Sidings.
.	.	.	.	.	.	.	.	Seed & Wallbank's	Lancs	P.&L. Jt. (L&NW.&L&Y)	Chapel Hill Sidings.
.	.	.	.	.	.	.	.	Sharple's	Lancs	P.&L. Jt. (L&NW.&L&Y)	Chapel Hill Sidings.
.	.	.	.	.	.	.	.	Co-operative Wholesale Society's Siding	Lancs	P.&L. Jt. (L&NW.&L&Y)	Longridge.
.	.	.	.	.	.	.	.	Croft & Son's Railway Qry.	Lancs	P.&L. Jt. (L&NW.&L&Y)	Longridge.
.	.	.	.	.	.	.	.	Earl of Derby's Siding	Lancs	P.&L. Jt. (L&NW.&L&Y)	Longridge.
.	.	.	.	.	.	.	.	Earnshaw's Siding............	Lancs	P.&L. Jt. (L&NW.&L&Y)	Longridge.
.	.	.	.	.	.	.	.	Hayhurst & Marsden's Sid.	Lancs	P.&L. Jt. (L&NW.&L&Y)	Longridge.
.	.	.	.	.	.	.	.	Longridge Coal Co.'s Siding	Lancs	P.&L. Jt. (L&NW.&L&Y)	Longridge.
.	.	.	.	.	.	.	.	Smith's Victoria Mill	Lancs	P.&L. Jt. (L&NW.&L&Y)	Longridge.
.	.	.	.	.	.	.	.	Tootal Height Quarry Co.'s Broomhill Siding	Lancs	P.&L. Jt. (L&NW.&L&Y)	Longridge.
.	.	.	.	.	.	.	.	Whittle, G., & Co.'s Stonebridge Mill	Lancs	P.&L. Jt. (L&NW.&L&Y)	Longridge and Grimsargh.
.	.	.	.	.	.	.	.	Wigan Coal & Iron Co.'s Sid.	Lancs	P.&L. Jt. (L&NW.&L&Y)	Longridge.
.	.	.	.	.	.	.	.	Wilkinson's Stone Quarry..	Lancs	P.&L. Jt. (L&NW.&L&Y)	Longridge.
.	.	.	.	.	.	.	.	Longridge Siding	L'lithgow	N. B.	See Crofthead.
.	.	.	.	.	.	.	.	Longrigg Coal Crushers' Sid.	Lanark ..	N. B.	Longriggend.
.	.	.	.	.	.	.	.	Longrigg Coke Ovens	Lanark ..	N. B.	Longriggend.
.	.	.	.	.	.	.	.	Longrigg Collieries	Lanark ..	N. B.	Longriggend.
.	.	.	.	.	.	.	.	Longrigg Dross Washers' Sid.	Lanark ..	N. B.	Longriggend.
G	P	.	.	.	.	1	10	Longriggend	Lanark ..	N. B.	Airdrie, Commonhead & Slamannan.
.	.	.	.	.	.	.	.	Auchengray Colliery.........	Lanark ..	N. B.	Longriggend and Slamannan.
.	.	.	.	.	.	.	.	Avonhead Colliery	Lanark ..	N. B.	Longriggend and Whiterigg.
.	.	.	.	.	.	.	.	Caldercruix Colliery	Lanark ..	N. B.	Branch from Longriggend.
.	.	.	.	.	.	.	.	Eastfield Colliery	Lanark ..	N. B.	Branch from Longriggend.
.	.	.	.	.	.	.	.	Hillhead Colliery	Lanark ..	N. B.	Longriggend and Slamannan.
.	.	.	.	.	.	.	.	Lochend Collieries	Lanark ..	N. B.	Branch—Longriggend &Slamannan.

EXPLANATION—G *Goods Station.*　　P *Passenger and Parcel Station.*　　P* *Passenger, but not Parcel or Miscellaneous Traffic.*
F *Furniture Vans, Carriages, Portable Engines, and Machines on Wheels.*　　L *Live Stock.*
H *Horse Boxes and Prize Cattle Vans.*　　C *Carriages by Passenger Train.*

STATION ACCOMMODATION.						CRANE POWER.	STATIONS, &c.	COUNTY.	COMPANY.	POSITION.
						Tons Cwts.	Longriggend—*continued.*			
..	..	..	..	..	..	..	Longrigg Coal Crushers' Sid.	Lanark ...	N. B.	Longriggend and Slamannan.
..	..	..	..	..	..	..	Longrigg Coke Ovens	Lanark ...	N. B.	Longriggend and Slamannan.
..	..	..	..	..	..	..	Longrigg Collieries	Lanark ...	N. B.	Longriggend and Slamannan.
..	..	..	..	..	..	..	Longrigg Dross Washers' Siding	Lanark ...	N. B.	Longriggend and Slamannan.
..	..	..	..	..	..	..	Longriggend Collieries......	Lanark ...	N. B.	Branch from Longriggend.
..	..	..	..	..	..	?	Longrigg Sidings	Lanark ...	N. B.	Longriggend and Slamannan.
..	..	..	..	..	..	..	Meadowfield Siding	Lanark ...	N. B.	Longriggend and Slamannan.
G	..	..	..	..	..	..	Mosslye Siding	Lanark ...	N. B.	Whiterigg and Longriggend.
..	..	..	..	..	..	..	Nimmo & Co.'s Briquette or Patent Fuel Works ...	Lanark ...	N. B.	Branch—Whiterigg & Longriggend.
..	..	..	..	..	..	..	Roughrigg Collieries.........	Lanark ...	N. B.	Longriggend and Slamannan.
..	..	..	..	..	..	..	Longrigg Sidings	Lanark ...	N. B.	Longriggend.
G	P	..	L	H	C	1 5	Longside	Aberdeen	G. N. of S.	Maud and Peterhead.
..	..	..	..	..	..	..	Longsight (for Belle Vue) ...	Lancs ...	L. & N. W.	See Manchester.
G	P	F	L	H	C	1 0	Long Stanton	Cambs...	{ G.E.	St. Ives and Cambridge.
..	P	..	..	H	C	..			{ Mid.	Over G. N. & G. E. Joint and G. E. Lines.
..	P	..	..	..	..	..	Longstone	Derby....	Mid.	Buxton and Rowsley.
G	..	..	..	..	..	..	Longstow	Hunts.....	Mid.	Kimbolton and Grafham.
..	..	..	..	..	..	..	Lord Ancaster's Brick Yard	Rutland...	Mid.	Luffenham and Ketton.
G	P	F	L	H	C	2 0	Long Sutton	Lincoln ...	Mid. & G. N. Jt.	Sutton Bridge and Spalding.
G	P	F	L	..	..	10 0	Longton (N. S.)	Staffs ...	N. S.	Stoke and Uttoxeter.
..	..	..	..	..	..	..	Beech & Son's Pottery ...	Staffs ...	N. S.	Longton.
..	..	..	..	..	..	..	Bridgwood's Pottery........	Staffs ...	N. S.	Longton.
..	..	..	..	..	..	..	Glebe Colliery............	Staffs ...	N. S.	Longton.
..	..	..	..	..	..	..	Lane End Works	Staffs ...	N. S.	Longton.
..	..	..	..	..	..	..	Longton Gas Works	Staffs ...	N. S.	Longton.
..	..	..	..	..	..	..	Longton Hall Colliery	Staffs ...	N. S.	Longton.
..	..	..	..	..	..	..	Longton Mills Co.'s Siding	Staffs ...	N. S.	Longton.
..	..	..	..	..	..	..	Meir Hay Colliery (Park Hall Colliery Co.)	Staffs ...	N. S.	Longton.
..	..	..	..	..	..	..	Millfield Sidings	Staffs ...	N. S.	Longton and Blyth Bridge.
..	..	..	..	..	..	..	Oldfield Colliery............	Staffs ...	N. S.	Longton.
..	..	..	..	..	..	..	Sutherland Wharf.........	Staffs ...	N. S.	Longton.
G	P	F	L	H	C	1 0	Longton Bridge	Lancs ...	L. & Y.	Preston and Southport.
..	..	..	..	..	..	..	Bentley's, J., Brick, Tile, and Pottery Siding	Lancs	L. & Y.	Longton Bridge.
G	P	F	L	H	C	5 0	Longtown.................	Cumb'land	N. B.	Hawick and Carlisle.
..	..	..	..	..	..	..	Longtown Junction	Cumb'land	N. B.	Scotch Dyke and Lyneside.
G	P	..	L	H	C	..	Longville	Salop...	G. W.	Much Wenlock and Craven Arms.
..	..	..	..	..	..	..	Longville Junction	N'hamptn	G. N.—L. & N. W.	Peterboro' and Market Harboro'.
G	P	F	L	H	C	..	Longwitton	Northumb	N. B.	Scotsgap and Rothbury.
..	..	..	..	..	..	..	Font Siding	Northumb	N. B.	Ewesley and Brinkburn.
..	..	..	..	..	..	..	Longwood and Milnsbridge...	Yorks ...	L. & N. W.	See Huddersfield.
..	..	..	..	..	..	..	Lonie's Siding............	Edinboro'	Cal.	Edinburgh, Lothian Road.
G	P	F	L	H	C	1 5	Lonmay	Aberdeen.	G. N of S.	Dyce and Fraserburgh.
..	..	..	..	..	..	..	Lonsdale Dock	Cumb'land	C. & W. Jn.—L. & N. W.	See Workington.
..	..	..	..	..	..	..	Lonsdale Hematite Smelting Co.'s Siding	Cumb'land	L. & N. W.	Whitehaven, Preston Street.
..	..	..	..	..	..	..	Lonsdale Hematite Smelting Co.'s (Clint's Limestone Quarry) Siding	Cumb'land	W C & E Jt. (Fur & L N W)	Gillfoot.
..	..	..	..	..	..	..	Lonsdale Mining Co.'s Winder Pits	Cumb'land	W C & E Jt. (Fur & L N W)	Winder.
..	..	..	..	..	..	..	Lonsdale's Siding	Cumb'land	Mid.	Same as Carlisle Brick and Tile Works (Cumwhinton).
..	..	..	..	..	..	..	Lonsdale's (Lord) Timber Yard (Lowther Siding) ...	W'morlnd	L. & N. W.	Clifton and Lowther.
G	P	..	..	..	..	..	Loo Bridge	Kerry ...	G. S. & W.	Headford Junction and Kenmare.
G	P	F	L	H	C	2 0	Looe	Cornwall..	L. & Looe.	Terminus.
..	..	..	..	..	..	..	Lord Aveland's Siding (Mid.)	Rutland...	Mid.—L. & N. W.	Luffenham.
..	..	..	..	..	..	..	Lord Belper's Siding.........	Notts ...	Mid.	Kegworth.
..	..	..	..	..	..	..	Lord Beverley's Siding........	Yorks ...	L. & Y.	Goole.
..	..	..	..	..	..	..	Lord Cowper's Siding	Herts ...	G. N.	Hatfield.
..	..	..	..	..	..	..	Lord Crewe's Siding	Cheshire	L. & N. W.	Crewe.
..	..	..	..	..	..	..	Lord Derby's— Siding	Lancs ...	L. & Y.	Rainford Junction.
..	..	..	..	..	..	..	Siding	Lancs ...	P.&L.Jt.(L&NW.&L&Y)	Longridge.
..	..	..	..	..	..	..	Treal's Siding..............	Lancs ...	P.&W.Jt.(L&Y&L&NW)	Kirkham.
..	..	..	..	..	..	..	Yard	Lancs ...	L. & Y.	Liverpool, Sandhills.

EXPLANATION—**G** *Goods Station.*   **P** *Passenger and Parcel Station.*   **P*** *Passenger, but not Parcel or Miscellaneous Traffic.*

F *Furniture Vans, Carriages, Portable Engines, and Machines on Wheels.*   **L** *Live Stock.*

H *Horse Boxes and Prize Cattle Vans.*   **C** *Carriages by Passenger Train.*

STATION ACCOMMODATION.						CRANE POWER.		STATIONS, &c.	COUNTY.	COMPANY.	POSITION.
						Tons	Cwts				
.	.	.	.	.	.	.	.	Lord Hawke's Siding	Yorks	L. & Y.	Womersley.
.	.	.	.	.	.	.	.	Lord Lambton or Littletown Colliery Store & Coal Sids.	Durham ...	N. E.	Sherburn Colliery Station.
.	.	.	.	.	.	.	.	Lord Leconfield's—			
.	.	.	.	.	.	.	.	Bigrigg Pits	Cumb'land	WC&EJt.(Fur.&LNW)	Moor Row.
.	.	.	.	.	.	.	.	Coal Depôt	Cumb'land	WC&EJt.(Fur.&LNW)	Moor Row.
.	.	.	.	.	.	.	.	No. 4 Pit	Cumb'land	WC&EJt.(Fur.&LNW)	Crossfield.
.	.	.	.	.	.	.	.	Lord Lonsdale's Timber Yard (Lowther Siding)	W'morlnd	L. & N. W.	Clifton and Lowther.
.	.	.	.	.	.	.	.	Lord Penrhyn's—			
.	.	.	.	.	.	.	.	Parkia Brick Co.'s Siding	Carnarvon	L. & N. W.	Griffith's Crossing.
.	.	.	.	.	.	.	.	Penlan Mill	Carnarvon	L. & N. W.	Bangor.
.	.	.	.	.	.	.	.	Port Penrhyn Quay	Carnarvon	L. & N. W.	Bangor.
.	.	.	.	.	.	.	.	Lord St. Oswald's Mine	Lincoln ...	G. C.	Frodingham and Scunthorpe.
.	.	.	.	.	.	.	.	Lord Salisbury's Siding	Herts	G. N.	Hatfield.
.	.	.	.	.	.	.	.	Lord Tollemache's Siding ...	Cheshire...	L. & N. W.	Beeston Castle and Tarporley.
.	.	.	.	.	.	.	.	Lord Tredegar's—			
.	.	.	.	.	.	.	.	Siding (B. & M.)	Mon	B. & M.—G. W.	Aber Bargoed.
.	.	.	.	.	.	.	.	Siding	Mon	L. & N. W.	Ynysddu.
.	.	.	.	.	.	.	.	Lord Vernon's—			
.	.	.	.	.	.	.	.	Coal Wharves	Cheshire...	L. & N. W.	Cheadle Hulme.
.	.	.	.	.	.	.	.	Coal Wharves	Cheshire...	L. & N. W.	Stockport, Edgeley.
.	.	.	.	.	.	.	.	Coal Wharves	Cheshire...	L. & N. W.	Macclesfield.
.	.	.	.	.	.	.	.	Poynton & Worth Colliery	Cheshire...	L. & N. W.—Mac. Com.	Poynton.
G	P	.	L	.	.	1	5	Lord Wantage's Siding	Berks	G. W.	Wantage Road.
.	.	.	.	.	.	.	.	Lord's Bridge	Cambs ...	L. & N. W.	Bedford and Cambridge.
.	.	.	.	.	.	.	.	Lord's Mill Street Wharf.....	Derby	Mid.	See Chesterfield.
.	.	.	.	.	.	.	.	Lord's Siding	Lancs	L. & N. W.	Manchester, Weaste.
.	.	.	.	.	.	.	.	Lord's Siding	Lancs	Mid.	Liverpool, Alexandra & Langton Dk.
.	P	.	.	.	.	.	.	Lordship Lane (Forest Hill)	Surrey ...	S. E. & C.	Nunhead and Crystal Palace.
.	.	.	.	.	.	.	.	Lord Street	Lancs	C. L. C. (S'port Exten.)..	See Southport.
.	.	.	.	.	.	.	.	Lorimer & Clark's Siding.....	Edinboro'	Cal.	Edinburgh, Lothian Road.
G	P	F	L	H	C	4	0	Loseby	Leicester..	G. N.	Leicester Branch.
G	P	F	L	H	C	4	0	Lossiemouth	Elgin&Mo'	G. N. of S.	Branch from Elgin.
G	P	.	L	H	.	5	0	Lostock Gralam	Cheshire...	C. L. C. (GC, G N, & Mid.)	Northwich and Knutsford.
G	P	.	L	H	.	5	0	Lostock Hall	Lancs	L. & Y.	Preston and Ormskirk.
.	.	.	.	.	.	.	.	L. & Y. Railway Locomotive Siding	Lancs	L. & Y.	Lostock Hall.
.	.	.	.	.	.	.	.	L. & Y. Railway Wagon Departments Siding	Lancs	L. & Y.	Lostock Hall.
G	P	.	L	H	.	3	0	Lostock Junction Station ...	Lancs	L. & Y.	Bolton and Chorley.
G	P	F	L	H	C	2	0	Lostwithiel	Cornwall	G. W.	Bodmin Road and Par.
.	.	.	.	.	.	.	.	Lostwithiel Junction...........	Cornwall	G. W.	Bodmin Road and Par.
G	P	F	L	H	C	.	.	Loth	Sutherl'nd	High.	Helmsdale and Bonar Bridge.
.	.	.	.	.	.	.	.	Lothian Coal Co.'s Depôt (Marquis of Lothian's Depôt) ...	Edinboro'	N. B.	Leith, South.
.	.	.	.	.	.	.	.	Lothian Road	Edinboro'	Cal.	See Edinburgh.
.	.	.	.	.	.	.	.	Loudon & Inglis Siding	Lanark ...	Cal.	Coatbridge, Whifflet.
.	.	.	.	.	.	.	.	Loudoun No. 1	Ayr	G. & S. W.	Hurlford.
.	.	.	.	.	.	.	.	Loudoun No. 3	Ayr	G. & S. W.	Newmilns.
.	.	.	.	.	.	.	.	Loudoun Road (for Swiss Cottage) (L. & N. W.)	Middlesex	L. & N. W.—N. L.	See London.
G	P	.	.	H	.	1	0	Loudwater	Bucks	G. W.	High Wycombe and Maidenhead.
G	P	F	L	H	C	10	0	Loughboro'— (Station)	Leicester..	Mid.	Leicester and Trent.
.	.	.	.	.	.	.	.	Brush Electrical Engineering Co.'s Siding	Leicester..	Mid.	Near Loughboro'.
G	P	F	L	H	C	10	0	Central	Leicester..	G. C.	Nottingham and Leicester.
.	.	.	.	.	.	.	.	Coltman & Son's Siding ...	Leicester..	Mid.	Near Loughboro'.
G	P	F	L	H	C	5	0	Derby Road	Leicester..	L. & N. W.	Branch from Shackerstone.
.	.	.	.	.	.	.	.	Messenger's Siding	Leicester..	L. & N. W.	Loughboro' and Shepshed.
.	.	.	.	.	.	.	.	Moss & Son's Siding	Leicester..	G. C.	Loughboro'.
.	.	.	.	.	.	.	.	Tucker's Brick & Tile Siding	Leicester..	G. C.	Loughboro'.
.	.	.	.	.	.	.	.	Loughboro' Junction	Surrey ...	S. E. & C.	London, Brixton and Camberwell.
.	.	.	.	.	.	.	.	Loughboro' Jn. Sta. (S.E.&C.)	Surrey ...	SE&C—GN—LSW—Mid	See London.
.	P	.	L	.	.	.	.	Loughboro' Water Works ...	Leicester..	L. & N. W.	Shepshed.
G	P	.	L	H	.	.	.	Lough Eske	Donegal ...	Donegal	Stranorlar and Donegal.
G	P	.	L	H	C	.	.	Loughgilly	Armagh ...	G. N. (I.)	Goragh Wood and Armagh.
G	P	.	L	.	.	.	.	Lough Meala	Donegal ...	L. & L. S.	Letterkenny and Burtonport.
.	.	.	.	.	.	.	.	Loughor	Carmarth'	G. W.	Landore and Llanelly.
.	.	.	.	.	.	.	.	Broad Oak Colliery	Carmarth'	G. W.	Loughor.
.	.	.	.	.	.	.	.	Loughor Colliery	Carmarth'	G. W.	Gowerton.

EXPLANATION—G *Goods Station.*   P *Passenger and Parcel Station.*   P* *Passenger, but not Parcel or Miscellaneous Traffic.*
F *Furniture Vans, Carriages, Portable Engines, and Machines on Wheels.*   L *Live Stock.*
H *Horse Boxes and Prize Cattle Vans.*   C *Carriages by Passenger Train.*

STATION ACCOMMODATION.						CRANE POWER.		STATIONS, &c.	COUNTY.	COMPANY.	POSITION.
						Tons	Cwts				
								Loughrea	Galway ...	G. S. & W.	Same as Craughwell.
G	P	F	L	H	C	3	0	Loughrea	Galway ..	M. G. W.	Branch from Attymon.
G	P	F	.	H	C	1	10	Loughton	Essex ...	G. E.	Stratford and Ongar.
G	.	.	.	H	C			Loughton Siding	Bucks ...	L. & N. W.	Bletchley and Blisworth.
.	.	.	.	.	.			Louisa Pit	Durham ...	N. E.	See South Moor Collieries (Annfield Plain).
.	.	.	.	.	.			Lount Fire-Brick & Sanitary Pipe Co.'s Siding	Derby	Mid.	Worthington.
.	.	.	.	.	.			Lount Pottery Works (Greenhaff & Co.)	Leicester ..	Mid.	Worthington.
G	P	F	L	H	C	10	0	Louth	Lincoln ...	G. N.	Boston and Grimsby.
								Love and Stewart's—			
.	.	.	.	.	.			Foundry Wood Yard	L'lithgow	N. B.	Bo'ness.
.	.	.	.	.	.			Grangepans Wood Yard ...	L'lithgow	N. B.	Bo'ness.
.	.	.	.	.	.			Station Wood Yard	L'lithgow	N. B.	Bo'ness.
.	.	.	.	.	.			Love Lane	Lancs ...	L. & Y.	Same as Gt. Howard Str. (Liverpool).
.	.	.	.	.	.			Lovering & Co.'s Prideaux Wood Siding	Cornwall ..	G. W.	St. Blazey.
.	.	.	.	.	.			Lovers' Lane Colliery	Lancs ...	L. & N. W.	See Fletcher, Burrows & Co. (Atherton).
.	.	.	.	.	.			Love's Brick Yard............	Beds	G. N.	Sandy.
.	.	.	.	.	.			Love's Siding	Beds	L. & N. W.	Sandy.
.	.	.	.	.	•			Lovibond & Son's Brewery Siding (West Kensington)	Middlesex	Mid.	London, St. Pancras.
.	.	.	.	.	.			Low & Duff's Siding	Forfar ...	D. & A. Jt. (Cal. & N. B.)	See Monifieth.
.	.	.	.	.	.			Low Barmston Depôt	Durham ...	N. E.	Washington.
.	.	.	.	.	.			Low Beechburn Colliery	Durham ...	N. E.	Crook.
.	.	.	.	.	.			Low Bentham Timber Siding	Yorks ...	Mid.	Bentham.
.	.	.	.	.	.			Lowca Iron Works............	Cumb'land	L. & N. W.	Parton.
G	P	F	L	H	C	.	.	Lowdham	Notts	Mid.	Nottingham and Newark.
								Lowe & Son's—			
.	.	.	.	.	.			Curzon Street Siding (Mid.)	Staffs	Mid.—L&NW—GN—NS	Burton-on-Trent.
.	.	.	.	.	.			Siding (Mid.)	Staffs	Mid.—G. N.—N. S.	Burton-on-Trent.
.	.	.	.	.	.			Lower Barn Siding	Derby	G. C.	Dinting.
.	.	.	.	.	.			Lower Bathgate	L'lithgow	N. B.	See Bathgate, Lower.
G	P	.	.	.	.	5	0	Lower Darwen	Lancs	L. & Y.	Blackburn and Bolton.
.	.	.	.	.	.			L. & Y. Co.'s Locomotive Siding	Lancs	L. & Y.	Lower Darwen.
.	.	.	.	.	.			Lower Deep Colliery (G. W.)	Mon	G. W.—L. & N. W.	See Lancaster & Co. (Blaina).
.	.	.	.	.	.			Lower Duffryn Col. (George Pit)	Glamorg'n	G. W.—T. V.—Rhy.	See Powell Duffryn Co. (M'tain Ash).
								LOWER EDMONTON—			
.	.	.	.	.	.			Bath, A., Siding..............	Middlesex	G. E.	Lower Edmonton and Churchbury.
.	.	.	.	.	.			Bury Street Junction	Middlesex	G. E.	Lower Edmonton & Bush Hill Park.
.	.	.	.	.	.			High Level	Middlesex	G. E.	Seven Sisters and Enfield Town.
.	P	.	.	.	.			Low Level	Middlesex	G. E.	Enfield Town and Tottenham.
G	P	.	.	.	.			Plowman, T. & M., Siding...	Middlesex	G. E.	Lower Edmonton and Churchbury.
.	.	.	.	.	.			Smyth & Co.'s Siding	Middlesex	G. E.	Lower Edmonton and Churchbury.
.	.	.	.	.	.			Lower Farm Siding	Glamorg'n	L. & N. W.	See Tredegar Iron and Coal Co. (Tredegar).
.	.	.	.	.	.			Lower Glanmire Road	Cork	G. S. & W.	See Cork.
.	.	.	.	.	.			Lower Greenhill Junction......	Stirling ...	Cal.	Greenhill.
.	P	.	.	.	.			Lower Ince	Lancs	G. C. (Wigan Jn.)	Lowton St. Mary's and Wigan.
.	.	.	.	.	.			Lower Ince Stone Quarry and Brick Yard	Lancs	G. C. (Wigan Jn.)	Wigan.
.	.	.	.	.	.			Lower Lydbrook Tin Plate Works	Glo'ster ...	S.&Wye Jt.(G.W.& Mid.)	Lydbrook.
.	.	.	.	.	.			Lower Merton Junction	Surrey ...	L.B.&S.C.—L.B.& S.C.& L. & S. W. Jt.	Merton Abbey and Wimbledon.
.	.	.	.	.	.			Lower Mills Works	Mon	G. W.	See Baldwin's, Ltd. (Pontypool).
.	P	.	.	.	.			Lower Penarth	Glamorg'n	T. V.	Penarth and Cadoxton.
G	P	.	.	.	.			Lower Sydenham	Kent	S. E. & C.	Lewisham and New Beckenham.
.	.	.	.	.	.			Crystal Palace District Gas Co.'s Siding	Kent	S. E. & C.	Lower Sydenham & Catford Bridge.
.	.	.	.	.	.			Lower Varteg Colliery (G. W.)	Mon	{ G. W.	Talywain.
										{ G. W.—L. & N. W.	Same as Varteg Deep Black Vein Co. (Abersychan & Talywain).
.	.	.	.	.	.			Lower Wellwood Siding	Ayr	G. & S. W.	Muirkirk.
								LOWESTOFT—			
G	P	F	L	H	C	1	10	Central (G.E.)................	Suffolk ...	{ G. E.	Terminus.
										{ M. & G. N. Jt.	Over G. E. from Coke Ovens Jn.
.	.	.	.	.	.			Coke Ovens Junction.........	Suffolk ...	G. E.—N. & S. Jt.	Lowestoft, Central & Lowestoft, North
.	.	.	.	.	.			Easthaugh, H. J., Siding...	Suffolk ...	G. E.	Lowestoft, South Side.

EXPLANATION—G *Goods Station.*   P *Passenger and Parcel Station.*   P* *Passenger, but not Parcel or Miscellaneous Traffic.*
F *Furniture Vans, Carriages, Portable Engines, and Machines on Wheels.*   L *Live Stock.*
H *Horse Boxes and Prize Cattle Vans.*   C *Carriages by Passenger Train.*

STATION ACCOMMODATION.						CRANE POWER.	STATIONS, &c.	COUNTY.	COMPANY.	POSITION.
						Tons Cwts.	LOWESTOFT—continued.			
G	P	F	L	H	C		North	Suffolk ...	N.&S. Jt.(GE&M&GNJt.)	Yarmouth and Lowestoft.
G	.	.	.	.	.	7 0	South Side	Suffolk ...	G. E.	Lowestoft and Carlton Colville.
.	.	.	.	.	.		Loweth, T. A., Bone Works...	Notts	Mid.	Nottingham, Bulwell.
G	P	.	.	.	.		Low Fell	Durham ...	N. E.	Gateshead and Durham, Passengers.
.	.	.	.	.	.		Lowfield Siding	Yorks	N. E.	Forcett.
.	.	.	.	.	.		Lowfield Sidings..........	Notts	G. N.	Newark.
.	.	.	.	.	.		Belvoir Plaster Co........	Notts	G. N.	Lowfield Sidings.
.	.	.	.	.	.		Simpson & Co.............	Notts	G. N.	Lowfield Sidings.
G	P	.	.	.	.		Low Gill	W'morlnd	L. & N. W.	Lancaster and Penrith.
.	.	.	.	.	.		Low Laithes Colliery......	Yorks	G. N.	Flushdyke.
.	.	.	.	.	.		Low Leyton	Essex	G. E.	Same as Leyton.
.	.	.	.	.	.		Lowmill Siding	Edinboro'	N. B.	Penicuik.
.	.	.	.	.	.		Low Moor	Yorks	G. N.—L. & Y.—L. & N. W.	See Bradford.
.	.	.	.	.	.		Low Moor Colliery	Yorks	L. & Y.	Bradford, Low Moor.
.	.	.	.	.	.		Low Moor Ironworks Co.'s New Park Pit	Yorks	G. N.	Leeds, Beeston.
.	.	.	.	.	.		Low Moor Junction	Yorks	G. N.—L. & Y.	Bradford.
.	.	.	.	.	.		Lowood's Siding..........	Yorks	G. C.	Deepcar (for Stocksbridge).
.	.	.	.	.	.		Lowood's Wharncliffe Brick Works (Wharncliffe Gannister Brick Works) ...	Yorks	N. E.	Middlesbro'.
G	P	.	L	H	.	2 0	Low Row	Cumb'land	N. E.	Carlisle and Hexham.
G	P	.	L	H	.		Low Street	Essex	L. T. & S.	Tilbury and Southend-on-Sea.
.	.	.	.	.	.		Low Stubbin Colliery	Yorks	G. C.—Mid.—G. N.	Same as Earl Fitzwilliam's Siding.
.	.	.	.	.	.		Lowther	W'morlnd	L. & N. W.—N. E.	See Clifton and Lowther.
.	.	.	.	.	.		Lowther Iron Works........	Cumb'land	C. & W. Jn.	Workington.
.	.	.	.	.	.		Lowther Pit...............	Cumb'land	L. & N. W.	See Allerdale Coal Co. (Brigham).
.	.	.	.	.	.		Lowther Siding	W'morlnd	L. & N. W.	Same as Lord Lonsdale's Timber Yard (Clifton and Lowther).
G	P	F	L	H	C		Lowthorpe	Yorks	N. E.	Bridlington and Driffield.
.	P	.	.	.	.		Lowton	Lancs	L. & N. W.	Golborne and Kenyon Junction Sta.
G	P	.	.	.	.	5 0	Lowton St. Mary's..........	Lancs	G. C. (Wigan Jn.)	Glazebrook and Wigan.
.	.	.	.	.	.		Lowton St. Mary's Junction	Lancs	G. C. (Wigan Jn.)—G. C. (St. Helens Exten.) ...	Lowton St. Mary's and Golborne.
.	.	.	.	.	.		Low Town (G. N.)	Yorks	G. N.—L. & Y.	See Pudsey.
.	P	.	.	.	.		Low Wood	W'morlnd	Furness	Steamer fr. Windermere, Lake Side.
G	P	F	L	H	C		Lubenham	Leicester ..	L. & N. W.	Market Harboro' and Rugby.
G	P	.	L	H	.	. }	Lucan	Dublin ...	{ G. S. & W.	Dublin and Kildare.
.	P	.	.	.	.				{ M. G. W.	Dublin and Mullingar.
.	.	.	.	.	.		Lucas Bros.' Fire-Brick Works	Durham ...	N. E.	Redheugh.
G	P	F	L	H	C	0 15	Lucker	Northumb	N. E.	Berwick and Morpeth.
.	.	.	.	.	.		Lucks Explosives Co.'s Siding	Suffolk ...	G. E.	Stowmarket.
.	.	.	.	.	.		Lucy Colliery (Grahamsley Colliery)	Durham ...	N. E.	See Pease & Partners (Crook).
G	P	.	L	H	.		Ludboro'	Lincoln ...	G. N.	Louth and Grimsby.
G	P	.	L	H	.	5 0	Luddendenfoot	Yorks	L. & Y.	Sowerby Bridge and Todmorden.
.	.	.	.	.	.		Clay's Siding	Yorks	L. & Y.	Luddendenfoot.
.	.	.	.	.	.		Sowerby Bridge Gas Works (Whitworth's) (Cooper House Siding)	Yorks	L. & Y.	Near Luddendenfoot.
G	P	F	L	H	C		Luddington	Yorks	Axholme Jt. (L&Y&NE)	Branch near Goole.
.	.	.	.	.	.		Boltgate Siding	Yorks	Axholme Jt. (L&Y&NE)	Luddington.
.	.	.	.	.	.		Ludgate Hill (S. E. & C.) ...	Middlesex	SE&C—GN—LSW—Mid	See London.
.	.	.	.	.	.		Ludgate Junction	Surrey ...	L. & S.W.—W. L. E. Jt.	London, Clapham Junction.
G	P	F	L	H	C	5 0	Ludgershall	Wilts	M. & S. W. Jn.	Savernake and Andover.
G	P	F	L	H	C	5 0	Ludlow	Salop	S & H Jt. (G W & L N W)	Craven Arms and Hereford.
.	.	.	.	.	.		Bitterley Siding	Salop	S & H Jt. (G W & L N W)	Ludlow and Clee Hill.
.	.	.	.	.	.		Clee Hill Dhu Stone Co.'s Siding	Salop	S & H Jt. (G W & L N W)	Ludlow and Clee Hill.
.	.	.	.	.	.		Clee Hill Granite Co.'s Sid.	Salop	S & H Jt. (G W & L N W)	Ludlow and Clee Hill.
.	.	.	.	.	.		Lang's Siding	Salop	S & H Jt. (G W & L N W)	Ludlow and Clee Hill.
.	.	.	.	.	.		Middleton Siding	Salop	S & H Jt. (G W & L N W)	Ludlow and Clee Hill.
.	.	.	.	.	.		Titterstone Siding (Field & Mackay's)	Salop	S & H Jt. (G W & L N W)	Ludlow and Clee Hill.
.	.	.	.	.	.		Ludlow's Colliery	Somerset..	G. W.—S. & D. Jt.	Radstock.
.	.	.	.	.	.		Ludworth Colliery	Durham ...	N. E.	Thornley Colliery Station.
G	P	F	L	H	C	1 10 }	Luffenham (Mid.)	Rutland ...	{ Mid.	Stamford and Oakham.
G	P	F	L	H	C	. }			{ L. & N. W.	Over Mid. from Luffenham Junc.
.	.	.	.	.	.		Aveland's (Lord) Sid. (Mid.)	Rutland ...	Mid.—L. & N. W.	Luffenham.
.	.	.	.	.	.		Molesworth & Springthorpe's Siding	Rutland ...	Mid.	Adjoining Luffenham Station.

EXPLANATION—G *Goods Station.*   P *Passenger and Parcel Station.*   P* *Passenger, but not Parcel or Miscellaneous Traffic.*
F *Furniture Vans, Carriages, Portable Engines, and Machines on Wheels.*   L *Live Stock.*
H *Horse Boxes and Prize Cattle Vans.*   C *Carriages by Passenger Train.*

STATION ACCOMMODATION.						CRANE POWER.	STATIONS, &c.	COUNTY.	COMPANY.	POSITION.
						Tons Cwts.	Luffenham Junction	Rutland ...	L. & N. W.—Mid.	Market Harboro' and Stamford.
.	P	.	.	.	.	. .	Lugar	Ayr	G. & S. W.	Auchinleck and Muirkirk.
.	.	.	.	.	.	. .	Barglachan Nos. 1 and 2 ...	Ayr	G. & S. W.	Lugar Iron Works.
.	.	.	.	.	.	. .	Berryhill No. 2	Ayr	G. & S. W.	Lugar Iron Works.
.	.	.	.	.	.	. .	Carbella Siding	Ayr	G. & S. W.	Cronberry and Muirkirk.
.	.	.	.	.	.	. .	Common Pits Nos. 5, 6, 7, 10, 11, 12, 14, 15, and 16	Ayr	G. & S. W.	Lugar Iron Works.
.	.	.	.	.	.	. .	Cronberry No. 1	Ayr	G. & S. W.	Lugar and Cronberry.
.	.	.	.	.	.	. .	Cronberry Tile Works	Ayr	G. & S. W.	Lugar and Cronberry.
.	.	.	.	.	.	. .	Darnconner Lye	Ayr	G. & S. W.	Lugar Iron Works.
.	.	.	.	.	.	. .	Lugar Brick Works	Ayr	G. & S. W.	Lugar Iron Works.
.	.	.	.	.	.	. .	Lugar Iron Works............	Ayr	G. & S. W.	Branch from Lugar.
.	.	.	.	.	.	. .	Stonebrigg's Siding	Ayr	G. & S. W.	Cronberry and Muirkirk.
.	.	.	.	.	.	. .	Lugsdale Siding	Lancs	L. & N. W.	{ See Widnes. { See United Alkali Co.'s Widnes Alkali Works (Widnes).
G	P	F	L	H	C	3 0	Lugton	Ayr	{ Cal. { G B & K Jt (Cal & G & SW)	Giffen and Clarkston. Barrhead and Stewarton.
G	P	F	L	H	C	1 10				
.	.	.	.	.	.	. .	LugtonBk. Wks. (Reid&Co.)	Ayr	G B & K Jt (Cal & G & S W)	Lugton.
.	.	.	.	.	.	. .	Lugton Junction	Ayr	Cal.—G. B. & K. Jt.......	Uplawmoor and Lugton.
G	P	F	L	H	C	. .	Luib	Perth ...	Cal.	Callander and Oban.
.	.	.	.	.	.	. .	Luke's Old and New Sidings	Cornwall ..	G. W.	Drinnick Mill.
.	.	.	.	.	.	. .	Lumb, J., & Co.'s Glass Bottle Works, Nos. 1, 2, & 3 Sids.	Yorks	N. E.	Castleford.
.	.	.	.	.	.	. .	Lumby Dock	Yorks	N. E.	Milford Junction Station.
.	.	.	.	.	.	. .	Lumley Brick Works	Durham ...	N. E.	{ Fencehouses. { Penshaw.
.	.	.	.	.	.	. .	Lumley Second Pit Depôt ...	Durham ...	N. E.	{ Fencehouses. { Penshaw.
.	.	.	.	.	.	. .	Lumley Sixth Pit Gas Works	Durham ...	N. E.	{ Fencehouses. { Penshaw.
.	.	.	.	.	.	. .	Lumley Sixth Pit Depôt	Durham ...	N. E.	{ Fencehouses. { Penshaw.
.	.	.	.	.	.	. .	Lumley Steel Co.'s Siding ...	Durham ...	N. E.	West Hartlepool.
.	.	.	.	.	.	. .	Lumley Street (for Bernard Road Depôt) (G.C.)	Yorks	G. C. — G. N.	Sheffield, Park.
.	.	.	.	.	.	. .	Lumley Third Pit	Durham ...	N. E.	{ Fencehouses. { Penshaw.
G	P	F	L	H	C	5 0	Lumphanan	Aberdeen	G. N. of S.	Banchory and Aboyne.
.	.	.	.	.	.	. .	Lumphinnans, Central Junc.	Fife........	N. B.	Lochgelly and Cowdenbeath, Old.
.	.	.	.	.	.	. .	Lumphinnans Colliery No. 11	Fife........	N. B.	Kelty.
.	.	.	.	.	.	. .	Lumphinnans, East Junction	Fife........	N. B.	Lochgelly and Cowdenbeath, Old.
.	.	.	.	.	.	. .	Lumphinnans, North Junction	Fife........	N. B.	Kelty and Cowdenbeath, Old.
.	.	.	.	.	.	. .	Lumphinnans, West Colliery	Fife........	N. B.	Cowdenbeath, Old.
.	.	.	.	.	.	. .	Lumpsey Depôts	Yorks	N. E.	Brotton.
.	.	.	.	.	.	. .	Lumpsey Mines	Yorks	N. E.	Brotton.
G	P	F	L	H	C	. .	Lunan Bay	Forfar	N. B.	Arbroath and Montrose.
G	P	.	L	H	.	3 0	Luncarty	Perth	Cal.	Perth and Coupar Angus.
G	P	.	L	H	.	1 10	Lundin Links	Fife........	N. B.	Leven and Anstruther.
.	.	.	.	.	.	. .	Lund, S., & Son's Siding......	Yorks	Mid.	Keighley.
.	.	.	.	.	.	. .	Lund's (C.) Wharf............	Northumb	N. E.	Newcastle-on-Tyne.
.	.	.	.	.	.	. .	Lunedale Whinstone Co.'s Sid.	Durham ...	N. E.	Middleton-in-Teesdale.
.	.	.	.	.	.	. .	Lunesdale Siding	Lancs	Mid.	Caton.
.	.	.	.	.	.	. .	Lunham's Siding	Louth	G. N. (I.)	Dundalk.
G	P	F	L	.	.	2 10	Lurgan	Armagh	G. N. (I.)	Belfast and Portadown.
.	.	.	.	.	.	. .	Lusk	Dublin	G. N. (I.)	See Rush and Lusk.
G	P	.	.	.	.	. .	Lustleigh	Devon	G. W.	Bovey and Moreton Hampstead.
							Luton—			
G	P	F	L	H	C	5 0	(Station)	Beds	Mid.	Bedford and St. Albans.
G	P	F	L	H	C	5 0	(Station, G. N.)	Beds	{ G. N. { L. & N. W.	Hatfield and Dunstable. Over G. N. from Dunstable Junction.
.	.	.	.	.	.	. .	Arnold & Co.'s Siding(G.N.)	Beds	G. N.—L. & N. W.	Luton.
.	.	.	.	.	.	. .	Balmforth's Siding (G. N.)	Beds	G. N.—L. & N. W.	Luton and Luton Hoo.
.	.	.	.	.	.	. .	Brown, H., & Son's Siding	Beds	G. N.	Luton and Dunstable.
.	.	.	.	.	.	. .	Brown's, W. H. & P. W., Siding (G. N.)...........	Beds	G. N.—L. & N. W.	Luton and Dunstable.
.	.	.	.	.	.	. .	Hayward, Tyler & Howard's Sidings (G. N.)	Beds	G. N.—L. & N. W.	Luton and Luton Hoo.
.	.	.	.	.	.	. .	Luton Gas Co.'s Sid. (G.N.)	Beds	G. N.—L. & N. W.	Luton.
.	.	.	.	.	.	. .	West Hydraulic Engineering Co.'s Siding.........	Beds	Mid.	Luton.
.	.	.	.	.	.	. .	William's Siding (G. N.)...	Beds	G. N.—L. & N. W.	Luton.

EXPLANATION—G *Goods Station.*   P *Passenger and Parcel Station.*   P* *Passenger, but not Parcel or Miscellaneous Traffic.*
F *Furniture Vans, Carriages, Portable Engines, and Machines on Wheels.*   L *Live Stock.*
H *Horse Boxes and Prize Cattle Vans.*   C *Carriages by Passenger Train.*

STATION ACCOMMODATION.						CRANE POWER.		STATIONS, &c.	COUNTY.	COMPANY.	POSITION.
						Tons	Cwts.				
G	P	F	L	Ḧ	C	.	.	Luton Hoo	Beds	Mid.	See Chiltern Green (for Luton Hoo).
						.	.	Luton Hoo (for New Mill End)	Beds	G. N.	Hatfield and Luton.
G	P	F	L	H	C	.	.	Hyde Mill Siding	Beds	G. N.	Luton Hoo and Harpenden.
						.	.	Lutterworth	Leicester	G. C.	Leicester and Rugby.
								Lutterworth	Leicester	{ L. & N. W.	See Welford and Lutterworth.
										Mid.	See Ullesthorpe and Lutterworth.
G	P	F	L	H	C	1	10	Lybster	Caithness	High. (W. & L.)	Branch from Wick.
								LYDBROOK—			
						.	.	Bicknor Siding	Glo'ster	S. & Wye Jt. (G. W. & Mid.)	Lydbrook Junc. & Lydbrook, Upper.
						.	.	Brierley Siding	Glo'ster	S. & Wye Jt. (G. W. & Mid)	Lydbrook, Upper & Serridge Junc.
G	P	.	L	H	.			Junction	Glo'ster	G. W.—S. & Wye Jt.	Symonds Yat and Lydbrook, Upper.
.	P	.	.	H	.		}	Junction Station (G. W.)	Glo'ster	{ G. W.	Kerne Bridge and Monmouth.
										S. & Wye Jt.(G. W. & Mid)	Lydbrook Jn. and Lydbrook, Upper.
.	.	.	.	.	.	.	.	Lydbrook Tin Works	Glo'ster	S. & Wye Jt. (G. W. & Mid)	Lydbrook, Upper & Lydbrook, Upper.
.	.	.	.	.	.	.	.	Mierystock Siding	Glo'ster	S. & Wye Jt. (G. W. & Mid)	Lydbrook, Upper & Lydbrook Junc.
.	.	.	.	.	.	.	.	Speculation Sid. (Wye Col.)	Glo'ster	S. & Wye Jt. (G. W. & Mid)	Lydbrook, Upper & Serridge Junc.
G	P	.	.	.	.	1	10	Upper	Glo'ster	S. & Wye Jt. (G. W. & Mid)	Lydbrook, Upper.
.	.	.	.	.	.	.	.	Waterloo Siding (Thomas & Co.)	Glo'ster	S. & Wye Jt. (G. W. & Mid)	Lydbrook Junc. and Drybrook Road.
G	P	F	L	H	C	.	.	Lydd	Kent	S. E. & C.	Appledore and Dungeness.
G	P	F	L	H	C	.	.	Holmstone Camp Siding	Kent	S. E. & C.	Lydd.
G	P	F	L	H	C	2	0 }	Lydford Station & Junction	Devon	{ G. W.	Plymouth and Launceston.
G	P	F	L	H	C					L. & S. W.	Exeter and Plymouth.
G	P	F	L	.	.	6	0	Lydham Heath	Salop	Bishop's Castle	Craven Arms and Bishop's Castle.
G	P	F	L	H	C	5	0	Lydiate	Lancs	C. L. C. (S'port Exten.)	Aintree and Southport (Lord Street).
								LYDNEY—			
G	P	F	L	H	C	7	0	(Station)	Glo'ster	G. W.	Gloucester and Chepstow.
.	P	.	.	.	.	.	.	Junction	Glo'ster	G. W.—S. & Wye Jt.	Lydney and Sharpness.
.	.	.	.	.	.	.	.	Junction Station	Glo'ster	S. & Wye Jt. (G. W. & Mid)	Lydney Town and Severn Bridge.
.	.	.	.	.	.	.	.	Lower Dock and Basin	Glo'ster	S. & Wye Jt. (G. W. & Mid)	Branch near Lydney Junction.
.	.	.	.	.	.	.	.	Lydney Colour Works	Glo'ster	S. & Wye Jt. (G. W. & Mid)	Lydney Junction and Lydney Town.
.	.	.	.	.	.	.	.	Lydney Tin Works (Thomas & Co.)	Glo'ster	S. & Wye Jt. (G. W. & Mid)	Lydney Junction and Lydney Town.
G	.	.	.	.	.	1	10	Town	Glo'ster	S. & Wye Jt. (G. W. & Mid)	Lydney Junction and Whitecroft.
G	P	.	.	H	.	8	0	Upper Dock and Basin	Glo'ster	S. & Wye Jt. (G. W. & Mid)	Branch near Lydney Junction.
G	P	F	L	H	C	5	0	Lye	Worcester	G. W.	Stourbridge and Cradley.
.	.	.	.	.	.	.	.	Harrison, G. K., Siding	Worcester	G. W.	Stourbridge and Cradley.
.	.	.	.	.	.	.	.	Hickman, H. T., Siding	Worcester	G. W.	Stourbridge and Cradley.
.	.	.	.	.	.	.	.	Rhodes, T., & Son Siding	Worcester	G. W.	Stourbridge and Cradley.
.	.	.	.	.	.	.	.	Timmis & Co.'s Siding	Worcester	G. W.	Stourbridge and Cradley.
.	.	.	.	.	.	.	.	Lyle & Son's Siding (G. E.)	Essex	GE—GN—L&NW—Mid.	London, Silvertown.
G	P	F	L	H	C	.	.	Lylestone Quarry & Brk. Wks.	Ayr	Cal.	Auchenmade.
G	P	F	L	H	C	.	.	Lyme Regis	Dorset	L. & S. W.	Branch from Axminster.
.	.	.	.	.	.	.	.	Lyminge	Kent	S. E. & C.	Canterbury and Shorncliffe.
								Lymington—			
.	P	.	.	.	.	0	15	Junction	Hants	L. & S. W.	Brockenhurst and Lymington.
G	P	F	L	H	C	5	0	Pier	Hants	L. & S. W.	Extension from Lymington Town.
G	P	.	L	H	.	1	5	Town	Hants	L. & S. W.	Brockenhurst and Lymington Pier.
G	P	F	L	H	C	.	.	Lymm	Cheshire	L. & N. W.	Stockport and Warrington.
G	P	F	L	H	C	.	.	Lympstone	Devon	L. & S. W.	Exeter and Exmouth.
G	P	F	L	H	C	1	10	Lyndhurst Road	Hants	L. & S. W.	Southampton and Brockenhurst.
.	.	.	.	.	.	.	.	Lyne	Peebles	Cal.	Symington and Peebles.
G	P	.	L	H	.	.	.	Lynedoch Street (G. & S. W.)	Renfrew	G. & S. W.—N. B.	See Greenock.
.	.	.	.	.	.	.	.	Lyneside	Cumb'land	N. B.	Hawick and Carlisle.
.	.	.	.	.	.	.	.	Fauldmoor Siding (Sandysykes Brick & Tile Works)	Cumb'land	N. B.	Longtown and Lyneside.
								LYNN—			
G	P	F	L	H	C	1	0	(Station, G. E.)	Norfolk	{ G. E.	Ely and Hunstanton.
										GN—Mid—Mid&GNJt.	Over G. E. from Lynn Junction.
.	.	.	.	.	.	.	.	Albert Oil Mills Co.'s Siding (G. E.)	Norfolk	G. E.	Lynn Docks.
.	.	.	.	.	.	.	.	Anglo-American Oil Co.'s Siding (G. E.)	Norfolk	G. E.—G. N.—Mid.	Lynn Docks.
.	.	.	.	.	.	.	.	Bird, F. & A., Siding (G.E.)	Norfolk	G. E.—G. N.—Mid.	Lynn Harbour.
.	.	.	.	.	.	.	.	Bowker, A. & J., Sid. (G.E.)	Norfolk	G. E.—G. N.—Mid.	Lynn Harbour.
G	.	F	.	.	.	15	0	Docks (Alexandra & Bentinck), (King's Lynn Dock Co.)	Norfolk	{ G. E.	Branch near Goods Station.
										GN—Mid—Mid&GNJt.	Over G. E. from Lynn Junction.
.	.	.	.	.	.	.	.	Dodman, A., & Co.'s Siding (G. E.)	Norfolk	G. E.—G. N.—Mid.	Lynn Docks Branch.
.	.	.	.	⁼	.	.	.	Eyre & Co.'s Siding (G.E.)	Norfolk	G. E.—G. N.—Mid.	Lynn Harbour.
.	.	.	.	.	.	.	.	Finch's, J. & H., Siding (GE)	Norfolk	G. E.—G. N.—Mid.	Lynn Docks.

EXPLANATION—G *Goods Station.*   P *Passenger and Parcel Station.*   P* *Passenger, but not Parcel or Miscellaneous Traffic.*
F *Furniture Vans, Carriages, Portable Engines, and Machines on Wheels.*   L *Live Stock.*
H *Horse Boxes and Prize Cattle Vans.*   C *Carriages by Passenger Train.*

STATION ACCOMMODATION.						CRANE POWER.		STATIONS, &c.	COUNTY.	COMPANY.	POSITION.
						Tons	Cwts	**LYNN**—*continued.*			
.	.	.	.	.	.			Fison & Son's Siding (G.E.)	Norfolk ...	G. E.—G. N.—Mid.	Lynn Docks Branch.
G	.	.	.	.	.			Harbour (G. E.)	Norfolk ...	{ G. E. .... / GN—Mid-- Mid&GNJt.	Branch near Lynn Station. / Over G. E. from Lynn Junction.
.	.	.	.	.	.			Junction	Norfolk ...	G. E.—Mid. & G. N. Jt.	Lynn and South Lynn.
.	.	.	.	.	.			Lynn Co-operative Society's Coal Siding (G. E.)	Norfolk ...	G. E.—G. N.—Mid.	Lynn Docks Branch.
.	.	.	.	.	.			Lynn Corporation— Ashyard Siding (G.E.)...	Norfolk ...	G. E.—G. N.—Mid.	Lynn Harbour.
.	.	.	.	.	.			Electric Light Wks. (GE)	Norfolk ...	G. E.—G. N.—Mid.	Lynn Docks Branch.
.	.	.	.	.	C			Pattrick & Thompson's Siding (G. E.)	Norfolk ...	G. E.—G. N.—Mid.	Lynn Docks.
.	.	.	.	.	.			Savage Bros.' Siding (G.E.)	Norfolk ...	G. E.—G. N.—Mid.	Lynn Docks.
.	.	.	.	.	.			Springall's, R. F., Sid. (GE)	Norfolk ...	G. E.—G. N.—Mid.	Lynn Harbour.
.	.	.	.	.	.			Vynne & Everett's Sid. (GE)	Norfolk ...	G. E.—G. N.—Mid.	Lynn Harbour.
.	.	.	.	.	.			West Norfolk Farmers' Manure and Chemical Co.'s Siding (G. E.)	Norfolk ...	G. E.—G. N.—Mid.	Lynn Harbour.
.	.	.	.	.	.			Lynn Co-operative Society's Coal Siding (G. E.)	Norfolk ...	G. E.—G. N.—Mid.	Lynn Docks.
.	.	.	.	.	.			Lynn Corporation— Ashyard Siding (G. E.)...	Norfolk ...	G. E.—G. N.—Mid.	Lynn Harbour.
.	.	.	.	.	.			Electric Light Works (G.E.)	Norfolk ...	G. E.—G. N.—Mid.	Lynn Docks.
.	.	.	.	.	.			Lynn, South	Norfolk ...	Mid. & G. N. Jt.	See South Lynn.
G	P	.	.	.	.			Lynton	Devon ...	Lyn. & Barns	Terminus.
G	P	.	.	.	.			Lyons Hall	Hereford ..	G. W.	Titley and Eardisley.
.	.	.	.	.	.			Lyon's Siding	Lancs	L. & N. W.	St. Helens.
.	.	.	.	.	.			Lysaght & Co.'s Siding.........	Staffs	Mid.	Same as Osier Bed Iron Co.'s Siding (Wolverhampton).
.	.	.	.	.	.			Lysaght's Orb Iron Wks. Sid.	Mon	G. W.	Newport, High Street.
.	.	.	.	.	.			Lytchett Brick Works	Dorset...	L. & S.W.	Hamworthy Junction.
G	P	F	L	H	C	5	0	Lytham	Lancs	P.&W.Jt.(L&Y&L&NW)	Blackpool (Central) and Kirkham.
.	.	.	.	.	.			Alty's Siding	Lancs	P.&W.Jt.(L&Y&L&NW)	Lytham.
.	.	.	.	.	.			Clifton's Siding	Lancs	P.&W.Jt.(L&Y&L&NW)	Lytham.
.	.	.	.	.	.			Clough's Siding	Lancs	P.&W.Jt.(L&Y&L&NW)	Lytham.
.	.	.	.	.	.			Mogridge's Siding	Lancs	P.&W.Jt.(L&Y&L&NW)	Wrea Green.
.	.	.	.	.	.			Lytham Old Branch	Lancs	P. & W.Jt.(L&Y&L&NW)	See Blackpool, South Shore.
.	.	.	.	.	.			Lytham Road	Lancs	P. & W.Jt.(L&Y&L&NW)	See Blackpool, South Shore.

M

STATION ACCOMMODATION.						CRANE POWER.		STATIONS, &c.	COUNTY.	COMPANY.	POSITION.
G	P	.	L	H	C	1	5	Maam Cross......................	Galway ...	M. G. W.	Galway and Clifden.
G	P	F	L	H	C			Mablethorpe	Lincoln ...	G. N.	Louth and Sutton-on-Sea.
.	.	.	.	.	.			McAndrew, R., & Co.'s Siding	Middlesex	{ G. E. / GN—GW—LNW—Mid	London, Millwall Docks. / London, Poplar.
.	.	.	.	.	.			McAndrew & Co.'s Stone Sid.	Edinboro'	Cal.	Edinburgh, Lothian Road.
G	P	.	L	H	.	2	10	Macbiehill	Peebles ...	N. B.	Leadburn and Dolphinton.
.	.	.	.	.	.			McBride's Siding	Renfrew ...	Cal.	Port Glasgow.
.	.	.	.	.	.			McCash & Son's Siding	Perth	Cal.	Perth, North.
								MACCLESFIELD—			
G	.	F	L	H	C	8	0	(Station)	Cheshire...	Mac. Com. (G. C. & N.S.)	Branch—Bollington & Central Sta.
.	P	.	.	H	C	.	. }	Central	Cheshire...	{ Mac. Com. (G.C. & N.S.) / N. S.	Bollington and Congleton. / Hibel Road and North Rode.
.	P	F	L	H	C	.	. }				
.	.	.	.	.	.			Gas Works	Cheshire...	N. S.	Macclesfield.
G	.	F	L	.	.	10	0	Hibel Road	Cheshire...	L. & N. W. & N. S. Jt.	Branch near Hibel Road, Passenger.
.	P	F	.	H	C			Hibel Road (L. & N. W.).....	Cheshire...	{ L. & N. W. .... / N. S.	Branch from Cheadle Hulme. / Over L. & N. W. from Junction.
.	.	.	.	.	.			Hibel Road Junction.........	Cheshire...	L. & N. W.—N. S.........	Cheadle Hulme and Congleton.
.	.	.	.	.	.			Junction	Cheshire...	Mac. Com.—N. S.	Macclesfield, Central.
.	.	.	.	.	.			Lord Vernon's Coal Wharves	Cheshire...	L. & N. W.	Macclesfield and Prestbury.
.	.	.	.	.	.			Macdonald Road Siding	Edinboro'	N. B.	Edinburgh, Leith Walk.
.	.	.	.	.	.			McDougall & Co.'s Siding......	Middlesex	{ G. E. / GN—GW—LNW—Mid	London, Millwall Docks. / London, Poplar.
.	.	.	.	.	.			McDougall Bros.' Siding......	Middlesex	{ G. E. / GN—GW—LNW—Mid	London, Millwall Docks. / London, Poplar.

EXPLANATION—G *Goods Station.*   P *Passenger and Parcel Station.*   P* *Passenger, but not Parcel or Miscellaneous Traffic.*
F *Furniture Vans, Carriages, Portable Engines, and Machines on Wheels.*   L *Live Stock.*
H *Horse Boxes and Prize Cattle Vans.*   C *Carriages by Passenger Train.*

G	P	F	L	H	C	Tons	Cwts	STATIONS, &c.	COUNTY.	COMPANY.	POSITION.
G	P	F	L	H	C	1	5	Macduff	Banff	G. N. of S.	Branch from Inveramsay.
.	.	.	.	.	.			McEwan & Son's Siding	Renfrew	Cal.	Glasgow, Whiteinch.
.	.	.	.	.	.			McEwan's Malt Barns Siding	Edinboro'	Cal.	Edinburgh, Lothian Road.
.	.	.	.	.	.			McEwan's Malt Barns Siding	Stirling	N. B.	Stirling, Cowpark.
.	.	.	.	.	.			McEwan's Siding	Edinboro'	Cal.	Edinburgh, Lothian Road.
.	.	.	.	.	.			McFarlane & Whitfield's Sid.	Durham	N. E.	Same as Atlas Rivet Works (Redheugh).
G	P	.	.	H	.			Macfin Junction Station	Derry	N. C. Com. (Mid.)	Coleraine and Ballymena.
.	.	.	.	.	.			McGaul's Siding	Glamorg'n	G. W.	Bridgend.
.	.	.	.	.	.			McGhie's Cement Works	Lanark	Cal.	Glasgow, Bridgeton.
.	.	.	.	.	.			McHarg's Store (Cal.)	Renfrew	Cal.—G. & S. W—N. B.	See Springfield Free Warehouses (Glasgow).
G	P	.	.	.	.			Machen (B. & M.)	Mon	{ B. & M. — { G. W. (A (N&SW) D&R)	Bassaleg and Bedwas. — Over B. & M. from Bassaleg Junc.
	P										
.	.	.	.	.	.			Bovil Colliery	Mon	B. & M.	Church Road and Machen.
.	.	.	.	.	.			Fedw Colliery	Mon	B. & M.	Church Road and Machen.
.	.	.	.	.	.			Gwaun-y-bara Siding	Glamorg'n	B. & M.	Machen and Caerphilly.
.	.	.	.	.	.			Machen Foundry	Mon	B. & M.	Church Road and Machen.
.	.	.	.	.	.			Machen Lime Kilns	Mon	B. & M.	Church Road and Machen.
.	.	.	.	.	.			Machen Tin Works (Machen Forge)	Mon	B. & M.	Branch near Machen.
.	.	.	.	.	.			Pentwyn Siding	Glamorg'n	B. & M.	Caerphilly and Machen.
.	.	.	.	.	.			Rhos Llantwit Colliery	Glamorg'n	B. & M.	Machen and Caerphilly.
.	.	.	.	.	.			Rock Veins Colliery	Glamorg'n	B. & M.	Machen and Caerphilly.
.	.	.	.	.	.			Rudry Brick Works	Glamorg'n	B. & M.	Machen and Caerphilly.
.	.	.	.	.	.			Vedw Colliery	Mon	B. & M.	Machen and Church Road.
.	.	.	.	.	.			Waterloo Tin Plate Works	Glamorg'n	B. & M.	Caerphilly Branch.
.	.	.	.	.	.			Machen Junction	Mon	B. & M.	Machen and Caerphilly.
.	.	.	.	.	.			Machine Drying & Peat Fuel Co.'s Siding	Devon	L. & S.W.	Bridestowe.
.	.	.	.	.	.			Machynis Brick Wks. (G.W.)	Carmarth'	G. W.—L. & N. W.	Llanelly.
G	P	F	L	H	C	5	0	Machynlleth	Montgom	{ Cam. — { Corris	Moat Lane and Aberystwyth. — Adjoining Cambrian Station.
G	P										
.	.	.	.	.	.			M'Intosh & Co.'s Cabinet Wks.	Fife	N. B.	Same as Whitebank Sid. (Kirkcaldy).
.	.	.	.	.	.			MacKay's Quarry	Glamorg'n	T. V.	Same as Craig-yr-Hesk Quarry (Pontypridd).
.	.	.	.	.	.			McKechnie & Co.'s Siding	Lancs	L. & N. W.	Widnes.
.	.	.	.	.	.			McKechnie Works	Lancs	L. & N. W.	See United Alkali Co. (St. Helens).
.	.	.	.	.	.			McKenna Process Co.'s Siding	Cheshire	{ B'head Jt.—C. L. C.— { N. W. & L.—Wirral	{ Same as English McKenna Process { Co.'s Siding.
.	.	.	.	.	.			McKenzie & Hollands' Siding (Vulcan Works) (G. W.)	Worcester	G. W.—Mid.	Worcester.
.	.	.	.	.	.			Mackenzie & Moncur's Siding	Edinboro'	N. B.	Same as Balcarres Street Works (Edinburgh).
.	.	.	.	.	.			McKenzie Bros.' Foundry	Edinboro'	Cal.	Edinburgh, Lothian Road.
.	.	.	.	.	.			Mackenzie, Donald & Son's Siding	Essex	G. E.	Thorpe-le-Soken.
.	.	.	.	.	.			MacKeson's Siding	Kent	S. E. & C.	Canterbury, West.
.	.	.	.	.	.			Mackie & Co.'s Siding	Lanark	N. B.	Glasgow, Port Dundas.
.	.	.	.	.	.			Maclachlan's Brewery	Edinboro'	N. B.	Duddingston and Craigmillar.
.	.	.	.	.	.			McLaren & Co.'s Foundry	Renfrew	Cal.—G. & S. W.	Same as Port Eglinton F'dry (Glasgow)
.	.	.	.	.	.			McLaren, J. & H., Works (Mid.)	Yorks	{ Mid.—N. E.— { G. N.	Same as Midland Engine Wks. (Leeds) — (See Appendix to follow).
.	.	.	.	.	.			McLaren's Cols., Nos. 1 & 2 (B. & M.)	Mon	B. & M.—G. W.	Rhymney.
.	.	.	.	.	.			Maclehose & Co.'s Sid. (N.B.)	Lanark	N. B.—Cal.	Glasgow, Great Western Road.
.	.	.	.	.	.			McLellan's Siding	Lanark	Cal.	Glasgow, Kinning Park.
.	.	.	.	.	.			McLeod's Siding	Edinboro'	Cal.	Edinburgh, Lothian Road.
G	P	.	L	H	.	1	10	Macmerry (Gladsmuir)	Hadding'n	N. B.	Branch from Smeaton Junction.
.	.	.	.	.	.			Penston Colliery	Hadding'n	N. B.	Macmerry and Winton.
.	.	.	.	.	.			Macmillan & Son's Siding	Dumbartn	D. & B. Jt. (Cal. & N. B.)	Dumbarton.
G	P	.	.	.	.			Macmine Junction Station	Wexford	D. W. & W.	Wicklow and Wexford.
.	.	.	.	.	.			McMoran's Siding	Lanark	Cal.	Glasgow, South Side.
.	.	.	.	.	.			McMullen & Son's Siding	Herts	G. N.	Hertford.
.	.	.	.	.	.			M'Nab's Siding	Kinross	N. B.	Balado.
.	.	.	.	.	.			M'Nay's Pottery	L'lithgow	N. B.	Same as Bridgeness Pottery (Bo'ness).
.	.	.	.	.	.			MacNeill's Slag Wool Siding	Dumbartn	N. B.	Same as Old Foundry Siding (Kirkintilloch).
.	.	.	.	.	.			MacNiel's Siding	Durham	N. E.	Harperley.
.	.	.	.	.	.			McOnie's Siding	Renfrew	G. & S.W.	Port Glasgow, Inchgreen.
.	.	.	.	.	.			M'Pherson & M'Laren's Saw Mill (Cal.)	Stirling	Cal.—N. B.	{ Same as Forth Saw Mills (Grange-{ mouth).

EXPLANATION—G *Goods Station.*   P *Passenger and Parcel Station.*   P* *Passenger, but not Parcel or Miscellaneous Traffic.*
F *Furniture Vans, Carriages, Portable Engines, and Machines on Wheels.*   L *Live Stock.*
H *Horse Boxes and Prize Cattle Vans.*   C *Carriages by Passenger Train.*

STATION ACCOMMODATION.						CRANE POWER.		STATIONS, &c.	COUNTY.	COMPANY.	POSITION.
						Tons	Cwts.				
G	P	F	L	.	.	.	.	Macroom	Cork	C. & Macroom	Terminus.
.	.	.	.	.	.	.	.	McVitie & Price's Siding	Middlesex	L. & N. W.	London, Willesden Junction.
G	P	F	L	H	C	1	10	Madderty	Perth	Cal.	Crieff and Perth.
.	.	.	.	.	.	.	.	Maddiston Brick Works	Stirling	N. B.	Almond Junction Station.
.	.	.	.	.	.	.	.	Maddiston Quarry	Stirling	N. B.	Almond Junction Station.
.	.	.	.	.	.	.	.	Maddiston Siding	Stirling	N. B.	See Almond Junction Station.
.	.	.	.	.	.	.	.	Maddocks & Co.'s Works	Salop	G. W.	Oakengates.
G	P	.	L	.	.	2	0	Madeley	Salop	G. W.	Shifnal and Coalbrookdale.
.	.	.	.	.	.	.	.	Foster Siding	Salop	G. W.	Madeley.
.	.	.	.	.	.	.	.	Kemberton Colliery	Salop	G. W.	Shifnal and Madeley.
.	.	.	.	.	.	.	.	Madeley Court Iron Works	Salop	G. W.	Madeley.
.	.	.	.	.	.	.	.	Madeley Wood Co.'s Tile Works	Salop	G. W.	Near Madeley.
G	P	F	L	H	C	1	10	Madeley	Staffs	L. & N. W.	Crewe and Stafford.
.	.	.	.	.	.	.	.	Madeley Coal and Iron Co.'s Leycett Colliery	Staffs	L. & N. W.	Madeley and Whitmore.
.	.	.	.	.	.	.	.	Madeley Heath Tile Co.'s Siding	Staffs	L. & N. W.	Madeley and Whitmore.
.	.	.	.	.	.	.	.	Ridge Hill Brick and Tile Co.'s Siding	Staffs	L. & N. W.	Madeley and Whitmore.
.	.	.	.	.	.	.	.	Madeley Coal and Iron Co.'s } Leycett Colliery	Staffs	{ L. & N. W / N. S.	Madeley. / Leycett.
.	.	.	.	.	.	.	.	Madeley Court Iron Works	Salop	G. W.	Madeley.
.	.	.	.	.	.	.	.	Madeley Junction	Salop	G. W.	Shifnal and Oakengates.
G	P	F	L	H	C	1	5	Madeley Market	Salop	L. & N. W.	Coalport and Hadley.
.	.	.	.	.	.	.	.	Madeley Wood Co.'s Siding	Salop	L. & N. W.	Madeley Market and Coalport.
.	P	.	.	.	.	.	.	Madeley Road	Staffs	N. S.	Stoke and Market Drayton.
.	.	.	.	.	.	.	.	Madeley Wood Co.— Siding	Salop	L. & N. W.	Madeley Market.
.	.	.	.	.	.	.	.	Tile Works	Salop	G. W.	Madeley.
.	.	.	.	.	.	.	.	Madgescroft Siding	Lanark	Cal.	Cumbernauld.
.	.	.	.	.	.	.	.	Madge's Siding	Surrey	S. E. & C.	London, Camberwell New Road.
.	P	.	.	.	.	.	.	Madore	Cork	C. B. & S. C.	Dunmanway and Skibbereen.
G	P	.	L	.	.	.	.	Maenclochog	Pembroke	G. W.	Clynderwen and Fishguard.
G	P	.	L	H	C	.	.	Maentwrog Road	Merioneth	G. W.	Bala and Festiniog.
G	P	F	L	.	.	.	.	Maerdy	Glamorg'n	T. V.	Branch from Porth.
.	.	.	.	.	.	.	.	Maerdy or Mardy Colliery	Glamorg'n	T. V.	Near Maerdy.
.	.	.	.	.	.	.	.	Maesaraul Junction	Glamorg'n	G. W.—T. V.	Llantrisant.
.	.	.	.	.	.	.	.	Maesaraul Siding	Glamorg'n	G. W.	Mwyndy.
.	.	.	.	.	.	.	.	Maesglas Junction	Mon	A. (N&SW.) D&R—G W	Newport.
.	.	.	.	.	.	.	.	Maespoeth Junction	Merioneth	Corris	Machynlleth and Corris.
G	P	F	L	H	C	1	10 }	Maesteg	Glamorg'n	{ G. W. / P. T.	Tondu and Nantyffyllon. / Port Talbot and Pont-y-rhyll.
G	P	.	L	.	C	.	. }				
.	.	.	.	.	.	.	.	Cwm Cerwyn Sid. (East End)	Glamorg'n	P. T.	Maesteg and Bryn.
.	.	.	.	.	.	.	.	Maesteg Gas Works	Glamorg'n	G. W.	Maesteg and Troedyrhiew Garth.
.	.	.	.	.	.	.	.	Norths— Colliery	Glamorg'n	{ G. W. / P. T.	Maesteg. / Maesteg and Garth.
.	.	.	.	.	.	.	.	Llynvi Gas Co.'s Siding	Glamorg'n	G. W.	Maesteg and Nantyffyllon.
.	.	.	.	.	.	.	.	Nantyffyllon Colliery	Glamorg'n	G. W.	Maesteg and Nantyffyllon.
.	.	.	.	.	.	.	.	Tygwynbach Colliery	Glamorg'n	G. W.—P. T.	Maesteg.
G	P	.	L	H	.	.	.	Maes-y-Crugiau	Carmarth	M. & M.	Pencader and Lampeter.
G	P	.	L	.	.	.	.	Maesycwmmer	Mon	B. & M.	Newport and Pengam.
.	.	.	.	.	.	.	.	Viaduct Colliery	Mon	B. & M.	Maesycwmmer.
.	.	.	.	.	.	.	.	Maesycwmmer Chemical Wks.	Mon	G. W.	Rhymney Junction.
.	.	.	.	.	.	.	.	Maesycwmmer Junction	Mon	B. & M.—G. W.	Pengam and Crumlin, High Level.
.	.	.	.	.	.	.	.	Maesymarchog Colliery	Glamorg'n	N. & Brecon	Onllwyn.
.	.	.	.	.	.	.	.	Magdalen Green	Forfar	Cal.	See Dundee.
G	P	.	L	H	C	.	.	Magdalen Road	Norfolk	G. E.	Ely and Lynn.
.	.	.	.	.	.	.	.	Read & Wildbur Siding	Norfolk	G. E.	Magdalen Road.
G	.	.	L	.	.	.	.	St. Germain's Siding	Norfolk	G. E.	Lynn Junction and Magdalen Road.
G	.	.	.	.	.	.	.	Wiggenhall Siding	Norfolk	G. E.	Magdalen Road and Middle Drove.
.	.	.	.	.	.	.	.	Magee, Marshall & Co.'s Brewery (Mid.)	Staffs	Mid.—L&NW—GN—NS	Burton-on-Trent.
.	.	.	.	.	.	.	.	Magee, Marshall & Co.'s Sid.	Lancs	{ L. & Y. / L. & N. W.	Castleton. / Bolton.
G	P	.	.	.	.	.	.	Mageney	Kildare	G. S. & W.	Bagnalstown and Kildare.
G	P	.	L	H	.	3	0	Maghera	Derry	N. C. Com. (Mid.)	Macfin Junction and Magherafelt.
G	P	F	L	H	.	2	10	Magherafelt	Derry	N. C. Com. (Mid.)	Cookstown Junction and Cookstown.
G	P	.	.	H	.	.	.	Magheramorne	Antrim	N. C. Com. (Mid.)	Carrickfergus and Larne.
.	.	.	.	.	.	.	.	Maghull	Lancs	C. L. C. (S'port Exten.).	See Sefton and Maghull.
G	P	.	L	H	.	1	10	Maghull	Lancs	L. & Y.	Liverpool and Ormskirk.

EXPLANATION—G *Goods Station.*   P *Passenger and Parcel Station.*   P* *Passenger, but not Parcel or Miscellaneous Traffic.*
F *Furniture Vans, Carriages, Portable Engines, and Machines on Wheels.*   L *Live Stock.*
H *Horse Boxes and Prize Cattle Vans.*   C *Carriages by Passenger Train.*

STATION ACCOMMODATION.						CRANE POWER.		STATIONS, &c.	COUNTY.	COMPANY.	POSITION.
G	P	.	L	.	.	Tons	Cwts.	Magilligan	Derry	N. C. Com. (Mid.)	Londonderry and Coleraine.
.	.	.	.	.	.	.	.	Magnesium Metal Co.'s Sid.	Lancs	L. & N. W.	Patricroft.
G	P	.	.	.	.	4	0	Magor	Mon	G. W.	Chepstow and Newport.
G	P	.	L	.	.	.	.	Maguiresbridge	Ferm'nagh	{ Clogher Valley	Adjoining G. N. (I.) Station.
G	P	.	L	.	.	.	.			G. N. (I.)	Clones and Enniskillen.
G	P	F	L	H	C	6	0	Maida Vale (L. & N. W.)	Middlesex	L. & N. W.—N. L.	See London, Kilburn & Maida Vale.
.	.	.	.	.	.	.	.	Maidenhead	Berks	G. W.	Twyford and Slough.
.	.	.	.	.	.	.	.	Waltham Siding	Berks	G. W.	Twyford and Maidenhead.
.	.	.	.	.	.	.	.	Maiden Lane	Middlesex	L. & N. W.—N. L.	See London.
G	P	F	L	H	C	1	10	Maiden Newton	Dorset	G. W.	Evershot and Dorchester.
								MAIDSTONE—			
.	.	.	.	.	.	.	.	Allington Siding	Kent	S. E. & C.	Aylesford and Maidstone Barracks.
.	P	.	.	.	.	.	.	Barracks	Kent	S. E. & C.	Strood and Maidstone West.
.	.	.	.	.	.	.	.	Benstead's Siding	Kent	S. E. & C.	Aylesford and Maidstone Barracks.
.	.	.	.	.	.	.	.	Coal Depôt	Kent	Mid.	Over Met. & S. E. & C. Lines.
G	P	F	L	H	C	10	0	East	Kent	S. E. & C.	Otford and Ashford.
.	.	.	.	.	.	.	.	Ford's Siding	Kent	S. E. & C.	Maidstone Barracks and Maidstone West.
.	.	.	.	.	.	.	.	Jesse Ellis & Co.'s Siding	Kent	S. E. & C.	Maidstone Barracks and Maidstone West.
.	.	.	.	.	.	.	.	Lavington & Co.'s Siding	Kent	S. E. & C.	Maidstone Barracks and Maidstone West.
.	.	.	.	.	.	.	.	Pine & Son's Siding	Kent	S. E. & C.	Maidstone Barracks and Maidstone West.
.	.	.	.	.	.	.	.	Ragstone Siding	Kent	S. E. & C.	Aylesford and Maidstone Barracks.
G	P	F	L	H	C	15	0	Tovil Siding	Kent	S. E. & C.	Maidstone and Tovil.
.	.	.	.	.	.	.	.	West	Kent	S. E. & C.	Strood and Paddock Wood.
.	.	.	.	.	.	.	.	West & Wright's Siding	Kent	S. E. & C.	Maidstone Barracks and Maidstone West.
.	.	.	.	.	.	.	.	Main Colliery	Glamorg'n	{ G. W.	Neath Abbey.
.	.	.	.	.	.	.	.			{ R. & S. B.	Jersey Marine.
.	.	.	.	.	.	.	.	Main Colliery Co.'s Siding	Flint	W. M. & C. Q.	Buckley.
.	.	.	.	.	.	.	.	Maindee, East & West Juncs.	Mon	G. W.	Newport and Llanwern.
.	.	.	.	.	.	.	.	Maindy Brick Works	Glamorg'n	T. V.	Cardiff.
.	.	.	.	.	.	.	.	Maindy Colliery	Glamorg'n	T. V.	See Ocean Coal Co. (Ystrad).
.	.	.	.	.	.	.	.	Maindy Fuel Works	Glamorg'n	T. V.	Same as Anchor Fuel Works (Cardiff Docks).
.	.	.	.	.	.	.	.	Mainhill Siding	Lanark	N. B.	Bargeddie.
.	.	.	.	.	.	.	.	Main's, A. & J., Siding	Lanark	N. B.	Glasgow, Possilpark.
.	.	.	.	.	.	.	.	Main's Colliery	Lancs	L. & N. W.	See Cross, Tetley & Co. (Wigan).
.	.	.	.	.	.	.	.	Mainsforth Lime Works	Durham	N. E.	Ferryhill.
.	.	.	.	.	.	.	.	Main's, R. & A., Siding (N. B.)	Stirling	N. B.—Cal.	Same as Gothic Ir. Foundry (Falkirk).
.	.	.	.	.	.	.	.	Mainwaring's Siding	Salop	S & H Jt. (G W & L N W)	Woofferton.
.	.	.	.	.	.	.	.	Maitland, W. F., Siding	Essex	G. E.	Stansted.
.	.	.	.	.	.	.	.	Makin & Bancroft's Treacle Stores	Cheshire	C. L. C. (GC, GN, & Mid.)	Birkenhead, Shore Road.
G	P	F	L	H	C	.	.	Malago Vale Colliery	Somerset	G. W.	Bristol, Portishead.
.	.	.	.	.	.	.	.	Malahide	Dublin	G. N. (I.)	Dublin and Drogheda.
G	P	F	L	H	C	1	10	Malden	Surrey	L. & S.W.	See Coombe & Malden.
G	P	F	L	.	.	1	10	Maldon, East	Essex	G. E.	Terminus.
.	P	.	.	.	.	.	.	Maldon, West	Essex	G. E.	Wickford and Maldon, East.
.	.	.	.	.	.	.	.	Maling & Son's Ford Pottery	Northumb	N. E.	St. Peters.
.	.	.	.	.	.	.	.	Malins Lee	Salop	L. & N. W.	Coalport and Hadley.
G	P	F	L	H	C	5	0	Maliphant Siding	Glamorg'n	G. W.	Swansea.
.	.	.	.	.	.	.	.	Malkins Bank	Cheshire	N. S.	Ettiley Heath.
G	.	.	.	.	.	5	0	Mallaig	Inverness	N. B.	Extension from Fort William.
.	.	.	.	.	.	.	.	Mallaig Pier	Inverness	N. B.	Mallaig.
.	.	.	.	.	.	.	.	Mallaig Junction	Inverness	N. B.	Fort William and Banavie.
G	P	F	L	H	C	1	10	Mallalieu's Siding	Yorks	L. & N. W.	Delph.
G	P	F	L	H	C	1	10	Mallaranny	Mayo	M. G. W.	Westport and Achill.
.	.	.	.	.	.	.	.	Malling	Kent	S. E. & C.	Otford and Maidstone, East.
.	.	.	.	.	.	.	.	Mallinson, Barraclough & Co.'s Siding	Yorks	Mid.	{ Same as Green Lane Mill Siding (Yeadon).
G	P	F	L	H	C	.	.	Mallow	Cork	G. S. & W.	Charleville and Cork.
.	.	.	.	.	.	.	.	Webb's Siding	Cork	G. S. & W.	Mallow.
.	.	.	.	.	.	.	.	Mallsmire Brick and Fire-Clay Works	Lanark	Cal.	Glasgow, South Side.
G	P	F	L	H	C	1	10	Mallwyd	Merioneth	Mawddwy	Cemmes Road and Mawddwy.
.	.	.	.	.	.	.	.	Malmesbury	Wilts	G. W.	Terminus—Branch from Dauntsey.
.	.	.	.	.	.	.	.	Maloney & Co.'s Siding	Lancs	{ L. & N. W.	Widnes.
.	.	.	.	.	.	.	.			{ S. & M. Jt. (G. C. & Mid.)	Same as Ditton Extract Works (Widnes).

EXPLANATION—G *Goods Station.*   P *Passenger and Parcel Station.*   P* *Passenger, but not Parcel or Miscellaneous Traffic.*
F *Furniture Vans, Carriages, Portable Engines, and Machines on Wheels.*   L *Live Stock.*
H *Horse Boxes and Prize Cattle Vans.*   C *Carriages by Passenger Train.*

STATION ACCOMMODATION.						CRANE POWER.		STATIONS, &c.	COUNTY.	COMPANY.	POSITION.
						Tons	Cwts				
G	P	F	L	H	C	10	0	Malpas	Cheshire...	L. & N. W.	Chester and Whitchurch.
.	.	.	.	.	.	.	.	Malt Barns Siding	Fife	N. B.	Ladybank.
.	.	.	.	.	.	.	.	Malthouse Siding	Warwick..	L. & N. W.	Same as Thomas & Co.'s (Leamington)
G	P	F	L	H	C	10	0	Malton	Yorks	N. E.	York and Scarborough.
.	.	.	.	.	.	.	.	Brand's Siding	Yorks	N. E.	Malton.
.	.	.	.	.	.	.	.	Malton Biscuit Mill	Yorks	N. E.	Malton.
.	.	.	.	.	.	.	.	Malton Manure Co.'s Sid.	Yorks	N. E.	Malton.
.	.	.	.	.	.	.	.	Oldfield's Siding	Yorks	N. E.	Malton.
.	.	.	.	.	.	.	.	Pye Pits	Yorks	N. E.	Malton.
.	.	.	.	.	.	.	.	Malton Colliery	Durham ..	N. E.	Lanchester.
								MALVERN—			
.	P	.	.	H	C	.	.	Great (G. W.)	Worcester	{ G. W. .... / Mid.	Worcester and Hereford. / Over G. W. Line.
.	.	.	.	.	.	.	.	Junction	Worcester	G. W.—Mid.	Malvern Wells and Great Malvern.
G	P	F	L	H	C	10	0}	Link (G. W.)	Worcester	{ G. W.	Worcester and Hereford.
.	P	.	.	H	C	.	.}			Mid.	Over G. W. Line.
.	.	.	.	.	.	.	.	Link Gas Works (G.W.) ...	Worcester	G. W.—Mid.	Malvern Link.
G.	.	.	.	.	.	.	.	Sidings	Worcester	Mid.	Tewkesbury and Malvern Junction.
G	P	.	.	.	.	3	0}	Wells	Worcester	{ G. W.	Worcester and Hereford.
G	P	F	L	H	C	5	0}			Mid.	Tewkesbury and Malvern Junction.
.	.	.	.	.	.	.	.	Mancetter Quarries (Mid.) ...	Warwick..	Mid.—L. & N. W.	Same as Ireland & Knight's (Stockingford).
								MANCHESTER—			
.	.	.	.	.	.	.	.	Acme Lathe & Products Co.'s Siding.................	Lancs	Trafford Park Estate......	Trafford Park, Manchester.
G	.	F	.	.	.	20	0	Ancoats	Lancs	Mid.	Branch—Ashburys and Ancoats Jn.
.	.	.	.	.	.	.	.	Ancoats Junction	Lancs	L. & Y.—Mid.	Beswick and Ashburys Junction.
								Anglo-American Oil Co.—			
.	.	.	.	.	.	.	.	Siding	Lancs	L. & N. W.	Ardwick.
.	.	.	.	.	.	.	.	Siding (G. C.)	Lancs	G. C.—Mid.	Ardwick.
G	P	F	L	.	.	25	0}	Ardwick	Lancs	{ G. C.	London Road and Guide Bridge.
G	.	.	.	.	.	20	0}			{ L. & N. W.	London Road and Stockport.
.	.	.	.	.	.	.	.	Ardwick Junction...........	Lancs	G. C.—L. & N. W.........	Guide Bridge and London Road.
.	.	.	.	.	.	.	.	Ardwick Junction...........	Lancs	L. & Y.—L. & N. W. ...	Miles Platting and London Road.
								Armstrong, Whitworth & Co.'s Siding (G.C.)	Lancs	GC—GW—L&NW—Mid	Openshaw.
.	P	.	.	.	.	.	.	Ashburys (for Belle Vue) ...	Lancs	G. C.	London Road and Guide Bridge.
.	.	.	.	.	.	.	.	Ashburys Junction	Lancs	G. C.—Mid.	Ashburys Station and Ancoats.
.	.	.	.	.	.	.	.	Ashburys Junction	Lancs	G. C.—S. & M. Jt.........	London Road and Belle Vue.
G.	.	.	L	.	.	20	0	Ashton Road Cattle and Mineral Yard	Lancs	Mid.	Ancoats Goods Branch.
.	.	.	.	.	.	.	.	Bailey, W. H., & Co.'s Sid.	Lancs	Trafford Park Estate......	Trafford Park, Manchester.
.	.	.	.	.	.	.	.	Baxendale & Co.'s Siding...	Lancs	Trafford Park Estate......	Trafford Park, Manchester.
.	.	.	.	.	.	.	.	Baxendell, R., & Son's Sid.	Lancs	Manchester Ship Canal..	Manchester Docks.
.	.	.	.	.	.	.	.	Bennett's Iron Foundry ...	Lancs	L. & N. W.	Ardwick.
.	.	.	.	.	.	.	.	Bennett's Iron Foundry (GC)	Lancs	G. C.—Mid.	Ardwick.
.	.	.	.	.	.	.	.	Bennett's Siding.............	Lancs	G. C.	Ardwick.
.	.	.	.	.	.	.	.	Bentley, J., & Co.'s Siding	Lancs	Manchester Ship Canal..	Manchester Docks.
G.	.	.	L	.	.	10	0	Beswick	Lancs	L. & Y.	Branch—Ardwick Junction and Miles Platting.
.	.	.	.	.	.	.	.	Beyer, Peacock & Co.'s Siding (G.C.)...................	Lancs	GC—GW—L&NW—Mid	Openshaw.
.	.	.	.	.	.	.	.	Bonded Stores	Lancs	Mid.	Ancoats.
.	.	.	.	.	.	.	.	Boyd's, W. H., Siding	Lancs	G. C.	Openshaw.
.	.	.	.	.	.	.	.	Bradford Col. Co.'s Siding	Lancs	L. & Y.	Beswick.
.	.	.	.	.	.	.	.	British Electric Car Co.'s Siding	Lancs	Trafford Park Estate......	Trafford Park, Manchester.
.	.	.	.	.	.	.	.	British Westinghouse Electric and Manufacturing Co.'s Siding.................	Lancs	Trafford Park Estate......	Trafford Park, Manchester.
.	.	.	.	.	.	.	.	Castlefield Junction	Lancs	MSJ&A (GC&L&NW)	Knott Mill and Liverpool Road Jn.
.	.	.	.	.	.	.	.	Caucasian Petroleum Export Co.'s Siding	Lancs	Trafford Park Estate......	Trafford Park, Manchester.
G	P	F	.	H	C	22	0	Central	Lancs	C.L.C. (G.C., G.N. & Mid.)	Terminus.
G	P	.	.	.	.	2	0}	Clayton Bridge (L. & Y.)...	Lancs	{ L. & Y.	Manchester and Ashton.
.	P	.	.	.	.	.	.}			{ L. & N. W.	Over L. & Y. Line.
.	.	.	.	.	.	.	.	Clifton and Kearsley Colliery Co.'s Siding	Lancs	L. & Y.	Miles Platting.
.	.	.	.	.	.	.	.	Co-operative Wholesale Society's Siding.............	Lancs	Manchester Ship Canal...	Manchester Docks.
G	.	.	.	.	.	.	.	Cornbrook	Lancs	C.L.C. (G.C., G.N. & Mid.)	Manchester, Central and Urmston.
.	.	.	.	.	.	.	.	Cornbrook Junction	Lancs	C. L. C.—M. S. J. & A. ..	Urmston and London Road.

EXPLANATION—G *Goods Station.*   P *Passenger and Parcel Station.*   P* *Passenger, but not Parcel or Miscellaneous Traffic.*
F *Furniture Vans, Carriages, Portable Engines, and Machines on Wheels.*   L *Live Stock.*
H *Horse Boxes and Prize Cattle Vans.*   C *Carriages by Passenger Train.*

G	P	F	L	H	C	Tons	Cwts	STATIONS, &c.	COUNTY	COMPANY	POSITION
								MANCHESTER—continued.			
G								Cornbrook Junction	Lancs	C.L.C.—Man. Ship Canal	Manchester Docks.
G	P	F	L	H	C			Cornbrook Siding	Lancs	MSJ&A (GC&L&NW)	Knott Mill and Old Trafford.
			L					Cross Lane (L. & N.W.)	Lancs	L. & N. W.	Kenyon Junc. Sta. & Liverpool Rd.
	P		L	L						G. C.	Over L. & N.W. & M.S.J. & A. Lines.
										G. W.	Over L. & N. W. from Walton Junc.
								Crossley's Siding (G.C.)	Lancs	GC—GW—L&NW—Mid	Openshaw.
								Dawson's, R. S., Siding	Lancs	Trafford Park Estate	Trafford Park, Manchester.
G		F				25	0	Deansgate	Lancs	G. N.	Branch near Cornbrook.
								Deansgate, G. N. Goods Branch Junction	Lancs	C. L. C.—G. N.	Cornbrook Junction and Deansgate.
G		F				30	0	Docks	Lancs	Manchester Ship Canal	Manchester Docks.
	P*			H	C			Docks Station	Lancs	L. & Y.	Branch from Windsor Bridge Junc.
G		F				3	0	Ducie Street	Lancs	G. C.	Terminus.
								Earl of Ellesmere— Liverpool Street Siding	Lancs	L. & N. W.	Cross Lane and Ordsall Lane.
								Siding	Lancs	L. & Y.	Miles Platting and Philips Park Sid.
	P	F		H	C			Exchange (L. & N. W.)	Lancs	L. & N. W.	Branch from Ordsall Lane.
										G. W.	Over L. & N. W. from Walton Junc.
								Galloway's Siding	Lancs	L. & N. W.	Ardwick.
								Galloway's Siding (G.C.)	Lancs	G. C.—Mid.	Ardwick.
								Gaythorn Gas Works	Lancs	MSJ&A (GC&L&NW)	Oxford Road and Knott Mill.
								General Oil Storage Co.'s Siding	Lancs	Trafford Park Estate	Trafford Park, Manchester.
								Glover, W. T., & Co.'s Sid.	Lancs	Trafford Park Estate	Trafford Park, Manchester.
	P							Gorton	Lancs	G. C.	London Road and Guide Bridge.
								Great Central Locomotive Carriage & Wagon Department and General Stores Siding (G.C.)	Lancs	GC—GW—L&NW—Mid	Openshaw.
								Green's, H., Siding	Lancs	L. & N. W.	Ardwick.
								Green's, H., Siding (G. C.)	Lancs	G. C.—Mid.	Ardwick.
								Griggs, J., & Co.'s Siding	Lancs	Trafford Park Estate	Trafford Park, Manchester.
								Hall & Pickles' Siding	Lancs	Manchester Ship Canal	Manchester Docks.
								Hattons Wood Brick Co.'s Siding	Lancs	Trafford Park Estate	Trafford Park, Manchester.
G						10	0	Hope Street	Lancs	L. & Y.	Victoria and Windsor Bridge.
								Howard Conduit Co.'s Sid.	Lancs	Trafford Park Estate	Trafford Park, Manchester.
								Hyde Road Coal Depôt	Lancs	L. & N. W.	London Road and Stockport.
								Illingworth, Ingham & Co.'s Siding	Lancs	Trafford Park Estate	Trafford Park, Manchester.
								Jennison's Siding	Lancs	L. & N. W.	Longsight.
								Johnson's Siding	Lancs	L. & Y.	Beswick.
								Kendall's Siding	Lancs	L. & N. W.	Ardwick.
								Kendall's Siding (G.C.)	Lancs	G. C.—Mid.	Ardwick.
								Kilvert, N., & Sons' Siding	Lancs	Trafford Park Estate	Trafford Park, Manchester.
								Kirkpatrick Bros.' Siding	Lancs	Trafford Park Estate	Trafford Park, Manchester.
	P							Knott Mill and Deansgate	Lancs	MSJ&A (GC&L&NW)	London Road and Timperley.
								Knowles, A., & Son's— George Street Siding	Lancs	L. & Y.	Salford.
								Siding	Lancs	L. & Y.	Miles Platting and Philips Park Sid.
								Knowles Siding	Lancs	L. & N. W.	Longsight.
								Lancashire & Yorkshire Railway Co.'s Stores Sid.	Lancs	L. & Y.	Miles Platting.
								Lancashire Dynamo & Motor Co.'s Siding	Lancs	Trafford Park Estate	Trafford Park, Manchester.
G		F	L			20	0	Liverpool Road & Salford (L. & N. W.)	Lancs	L. & N. W.	Terminus, Liverpool and Manchester Section.
G		F	L			20	0			G. C.	Over L. & N.W. & M.S.J. & A. Lines.
										G. W.	Over L. & N. W. from Walton Junc.
								Liverpool Rd. & Salford Jn.	Lancs	L. & N. W.—M. S. J. & A.	Kenyon Junc. Sta. & London Road.
								Liverpool Street	Lancs	L. & Y.	Manchester.
	P							Liverpool Warehousing Co.'s Sid. (G. B. Taylor)	Lancs	Trafford Park Estate	Trafford Park, Manchester.
G	P	F	L	H	C	20	0	London Road	Lancs	MSJ&A (GC&L&NW)	Terminus.
	P			H	C			London Road (L. & N. W.)	Lancs	L. & N. W.	Terminus, Crewe & Manchester Sec.
	P			H	C					G. C.	Over L. & N. W. from Ardwick Jn.
	P			H	C					N. S.	Over L. & N. W. from Macclesfield.
								London Road Junction	Lancs	G. C.—L. & N. W.	Ducie Street and Stockport.
								London Road Junction	Lancs	L. & N. W.—M. S. J. & A.	Stockport and Oxford Road.
G	P	F	L	H	C	5	0	Longsight (for Belle Vue)	Lancs	L. & N. W.	London Road and Stockport.
								Lord's Siding	Lancs	L. & N. W.	Weaste Junction Branch.

EXPLANATION—G Goods Station. P Passenger and Parcel Station. P* Passenger, but not Parcel or Miscellaneous Traffic.
F Furniture Vans, Carriages, Portable Engines, and Machines on Wheels. L Live Stock.
H Horse Boxes and Prize Cattle Vans. C Carriages by Passenger Train.

STATION ACCOMMODATION.						CRANE POWER.		STATIONS, &c.	COUNTY.	COMPANY.	POSITION.
						Tons	Cwts.	MANCHESTER—continued.			
								Manchester Corporation—			
.	.	.	.	.	.	.	.	Bradford Road Gas Wks.	Lancs	L. & Y.	Miles Platting and Ancoats Junc.
								Cleansing Department			
.	.	.	.	.	.	.	.	Siding	Lancs	G. C.	Ardwick.
.	.	.	.	.	.	.	.	Holt Town Sids. & Wks.	Lancs	L. & Y.	Beswick.
.	.	.	.	.	.	.	.	Rochdale Road Gas Wks.	Lancs	L. & Y.	Oldham Road.
.	.	.	.	.	.	.	.	Siding	Lancs	L. & N. W.	Philips Park and Clayton Bridge.
.	.	.	.	.	.	.	.	Stuart Street Siding......	Lancs	L. & Y.	Ardwick.
.	.	.	.	.	.	.	.	Tramway Department Sid	Lancs	L. & N. W.	Ardwick.
								Tramway Department			
.	.	.	.	.	.	.	.	Siding (G. C.).............	Lancs	G. C.—Mid.	Ardwick.
.	.	.	.	.	.	.	.	Manchester Patent Fuel Wks	Lancs	Trafford Park Estate......	Trafford Park, Manchester.
.	.	.	.	.	.	.	.	Mather & Platt's Siding...	Lancs	L. & Y.	Miles Platting and Park.
								Metropolitan Amalgamated			
								Railway Carriage & Wa-			
.	.	.	.	.	.	.	.	gon Co.'s Siding (G. C.)	Lancs	GC—GW—L&NW—Mid.	Openshaw.
G	P	.	.	.	.	.	.	Miles Platting (L. & Y.) ...	Lancs	L. & Y. / L. & N. W.	Victoria and Newton Heath. / Over L. & Y. Line.
.	.	.	.	.	.	.	.	Morrell, Mills & Co.'s Sid.	Lancs	Manchester Ship Canal...	Manchester Docks.
.	.	.	.	.	.	.	.	New Barns Junction	Lancs	L. & Y.—Man. Ship Canal	Manchester Docks.
.	.	.	.	.	.	.	.	Newsum, Sons, & Co.'s Sid.	Lancs	Trafford Park Estate......	Trafford Park, Manchester.
.	.	.	.	.	.	.	.	Nuttall, E., & Co.'s Siding	Lancs	Trafford Park Estate......	Trafford Park, Manchester.
G	.	.	.	.	.	10	0	Oldfield Road (L. & N. W.)	Lancs	L. & N. W. .... / G. W.	Kenyon Junc. Sta. & Liverpool Road. / Over L. & N. W. from Walton Junc.
G	.	F	.	.	.	20	0	Oldham Road	Lancs	L. & Y.	Branch from Miles Platting.
G	.	.	.	.	.	10	0	Openshaw......................	Lancs	G. C.	London Road and Guide Bridge.
G	.	.	.	.	.	.	.	Ordsall Lane	Lancs	L. & Y.	Salford.
G	P	F	L	.	.	.	.	Ordsall Lane (for Salford) (L. & N. W.)	Lancs	L. & N. W. .... / G. W.	Kenyon Junc. Sta & Liverpool Road. / Over L. & N. W. from Walton Junc.
G*	P	.	.	.	.	.	.	Oxford Road	Lancs	M S J & A (GC&L&NW)	Timperley and London Road.
.	P	.	.	.	.	.	.	Park (L. & Y.)	Lancs	L. & Y. / L. & N. W.	Miles Platting and Ashton. / Over L. & Y. Line.
.	.	.	.	.	.	.	.	Philips Park Sids. (L. & Y.)	Lancs	L. & Y.—G. C.—L. & N. W. —Mid.	Ardwick Junc. and Miles Platting.
.	.	.	.	.	.	.	.	Pure Oil Co.'s Siding........	Lancs	Trafford Park Estate......	Trafford Park, Manchester.
.	.	.	.	.	.	.	.	Redpath, Brown & Co.'s Sid.	Lancs	Trafford Park Estate......	Trafford Park, Manchester.
.	.	.	.	.	.	.	.	Royce's Siding..................	Lancs	Trafford Park Estate......	Trafford Park, Manchester.
.	.	.	.	.	.	.	.	Russell's, T. E., Siding......	Lancs	Trafford Park Estate......	Trafford Park, Manchester.
G	.	F	L	.	.	25	0	Salford	Lancs	L. & Y.	Victoria and Windsor Bridge.
.	P	.	.	.	.	.	.	Salford (New Bailey Street)	Lancs	L. & Y.	Victoria and Windsor Bridge.
								Salford Corporation Sewage			
.	.	.	.	.	.	.	.	Works	Lancs	L. & N. W.	Weaste Junction Branch.
.	.	.	.	.	.	.	.	Salford Gas Works............	Lancs	L. & Y.	Salford (Liverpool Street).
								Salford Gas Works (Regent's			
.	.	.	.	.	.	.	.	Road)	Lancs	L. & N. W.	Cross Lane and Ordsall Lane.
.	.	.	.	.	.	.	.	Sandars & Co.'s Siding	Lancs	Trafford Park Estate......	Trafford Park, Manchester.
.	P	.	.	.	.	.	.	Seedley (L. & N. W.)	Lancs	L. & N. W. .... / G. W.	Kenyon Junc. Sta. & Liverpool Road. / Over L. & N. W. from Walton Junc.
.	.	.	.	.	.	.	.	Ship Canal Railway	Lancs	C. L. C. .... / L. & Y. .... / L. & N. W.	Cornbrook. / New Barns. / Weaste.
G	.	.	.	.	.	.	.	Ship Canal Station............	Lancs	L. & Y.	Branch from Salford, Windsor Bge.
.	.	.	.	.	.	.	.	Skipwith & Jones' Siding...	Lancs	Trafford Park Estate......	Trafford Park, Manchester.
.	.	.	.	.	.	.	.	Southern, J. W., & Son's Sid.	Lancs	Trafford Park Estate......	Trafford Park, Manchester.
.	.	.	.	.	.	.	.	Swain's Siding..................	Lancs	L. & Y.	Miles Platting.
								Tatton & Fitzgerald's Sid-			
.	.	.	.	.	.	.	.	ing (G. C.)	Lancs	G. C.—L. & N. W.	Ardwick.
.	.	.	.	.	.	.	.	Tetlow & Son's Siding (G.C.)	Lancs	G. C.—L. & N. W.—Mid.	Ardwick.
.	P	.	.	.	.	.	.	Trafford Park..................	Lancs	C. L. C. (GC, GN, & Mid.)	Central Station and Urmston.
.	.	.	.	.	.	.	.	Trafford Park (L. & Y.).....	Lancs	Trafford Park Estate......	Trafford Park, Manchester.
								Trafford Park Enamelling			
.	.	.	.	.	.	.	.	Co.'s Siding	Lancs	Trafford Park Estate......	Trafford Park, Manchester.
.	.	.	.	.	.	.	.	Trafford Park Estate.........	Lancs	Manchester Ship Canal...	Trafford Park, Manchester.
								Trafford Park Estates Wks.			
.	.	.	.	.	.	.	.	Department Siding	Lancs	Trafford Park Estate......	Trafford Park, Manchester.
.	.	.	.	.	.	.	.	Trafford Park Junction......	Lancs	Manchester Ship Canal —Trafford Pk. Estate	Manchester Docks and Trafford Park, Manchester.
								Trafford Park Steel Works			
.	.	.	.	.	.	.	.	Co.'s Siding	Lancs	Manchester Ship Canal...	Manchester Docks.
								Trafford Power & Light			
.	.	.	.	.	.	.	.	Supply Siding..............	Lancs	Trafford Park Estate......	Trafford Park, Manchester.

EXPLANATION—G Goods Station.   G* Traffic for Gaythorn Gas Works only.   P Passenger and Parcel Station.
P* Passenger, but not Parcel or Miscellaneous Traffic.   F Furniture Vans, Carriages, Portable Engines, and Machines on Wheels.
L Live Stock.   H Horse Boxes and Prize Cattle Vans.   C Carriages by Passenger Train.

STATION ACCOMMODATION.						CRANE POWER.	STATIONS, &c.	COUNTY.	COMPANY.	POSITION.
						Tons Cwts.	MANCHESTER—continued.			
.	P	F	.	H	C	. .	Victoria (L. & Y.)	Lancs	L. & Y.	Salford and Miles Platting.
									L. & N. W.	Over L. & Y. Line.
									Mid.	Over L. & Y. Line.
.	.	.	.	.	.	. .	Victoria Junction	Lancs	L. & Y.—L. & N. W......	Miles Platting and Exchange.
.	.	.	.	.	.	. .	Warburton's Siding	Lancs	L. & Y.	Miles Platting.
G	P					}	Weaste (L. & N. W.)........	Lancs	L. & N. W.	Kenyon Junc. Sta. & Liverpool Road.
	P								G. W.	Over L. & N. W. from Walton Jn.
.	.	.	.	.	.	. .	Weaste Junction	Lancs	L&NW—Man. Ship Canal	Manchester Docks.
.	.	.	.	.	.	. .	Wigan Coal & Iron Co.'s Ordsall Lane Siding	Lancs	L. & N. W.	Liverpool Road and Ordsall Lane.
.	.	.	L	.	.	. .	Windsor Bridge (L. & Y.)..	Lancs	L. & Y.	Victoria and Pendleton.
									Mid.	Over L. & Y. Line.
							Manchester Corporation—			
.	.	.	.	.	.	. .	Bradford Road Gas Works	Lancs	L. & Y.	Manchester, Oldham Road.
.	.	.	.	.	.	. .	Cleansing Dept. Siding.....	Lancs	G. C.	Manchester, Ardwick.
.	.	.	.	.	.	. .	Holt Town Sidings & Works	Lancs	L. & Y.	Manchester, Beswick.
.	.	.	.	.	.	. .	Rochdale Road Gas Works	Lancs	L. & Y.	Manchester, Oldham Road.
.	.	.	.	.	.	. .	Siding	W'morlnd	L. & N. W.	See Kendal Bonded Stores Co. (K'dal)
.	.	.	.	.	.	. .	Stuart Street Siding	Lancs	L. & Y.	Manchester, Oldham Road.
.	.	.	.	.	.	. .	Tramway Dept. Siding.....	Lancs	L. & N. W.	Manchester, London Road.
.	.	.	.	.	.	. .	Tramway Dept. Sid. (G. C.)	Lancs	G. C.—Mid.	Manchester, Ardwick.
.	.	.	.	.	.	. .	Manchester Dock	Lancs	G. W.—L. & N. W.	See Liverpool.
.	.	.	.	.	.	. .	Manchester Patent Fuel Wks.	Lancs	Trafford Park Estate......	Manchester.
.	.	.	.	.	.	. .	Manchester Road	Lancs	L. & Y.	See Burnley.
.	.	.	.	.	.	. .	Manchester Road	Yorks	G. N.	See Bradford.
							Manchester Ship Canal Co.—			
.	.	.	.	.	.	. .	Acton Grange Junction ...	Lancs	B'head Jt.—Manchester Ship Canal	Warrington, Bank Quay.
.	.	.	.	.	.	. .	Bridgewater Siding	Cheshire...	L. & N. W.	Preston Brook.
.	.	.	.	.	.	. .	Latchford Junction	Lancs	L&NW—Man. Ship Canal	Warrington, Latchford.
.	.	.	.	.	.	. .	Runcorn Docks Siding	Cheshire...	L. & N. W.	Runcorn Docks.
G	P	F	L	H	C	1 0	Mandle's Siding..............	Cumb'land	M. & C.	Maryport.
G	P	F	L	H	C		Manea	Cambs	G. E.	Ely and March.
G	P	F	L	H			Mangotsfield	Glo'ster ...	Mid.	Gloucester and Bristol.
.	.	.	.	.	.	. .	Cattybrook Brick Co.'s Sid.	Glo'ster ...	Mid.	Near Mangotsfield.
.	.	.	.	.	.	. .	Coalpit Heath Colliery	Glo'ster ...	Mid.	Near Mangotsfield.
G	.	.	.	.	.	. .	Parkfield Col., North and South Pits (Bedminster, Easton, Kingswood and Parkfield Co.)	Glo'ster ...	Mid.	Near Mangotsfield.
.	.	.	.	.	.	. .	Manley	Cheshire...	C. L. C. (G C, G N, & Mid.)	Helsby and Mouldsworth.
.	.	.	.	.	.	. .	Manley Quarry	Cheshire...	C. L. C. (G C, G N, & Mid.)	Branch near Manley.
.	.	.	.	.	.	. .	Manmoel Colliery	Mon	G. W.	Tredegar Junction.
.	.	.	.	.	.	. .	Manner's Colliery	Derby	Mid.	Stanton Gate.
.	.	.	.	.	.	. .	Manner's Colliery (G. N.)......	Derby	G. N.—G. C.	Ilkeston.
.	.	.	.	.	.	. .	Mannieshall Quarry	Lanark	Cal.	Omoa.
.	.	.	.	.	.	. .	Mannieshall Siding	Lanark	Cal.	See Omoa.
.	.	.	.	.	.	. .	Manningham	Yorks	Mid.	See Bradford.
.	.	.	.	.	.	. .	Manningham Sidings...........	Yorks	Mid.	Bradford.
G	P	F	L	H	C	1 10	Manningtree	Essex	G. E.	Colchester and Ipswich.
.	.	.	.	.	.	. .	Manning, Wardle & Co.'s Siding (Mid.)	Yorks	Mid.—L. & N. W.—N. E.	Leeds, Hunslet Lane.
									G. N.	(See Appendix to follow).
G	P	.	L	H	.		Manod	Merioneth	G. W.	Festiniog and Blaenau Festiniog.
G	P	.	L	H			Manorbier......................	Pembroke	G. W.	Tenby and Pembroke Dock.
G	P	.	L	.	.		Manor Cunningham	Donegal ...	L. & L. S.	Tooban Junction and Letterkenny.
G	P	.	L	.	.	1 10	Manorhamilton	Leitrim ...	S. L. & N. C.	Enniskillen and Collooney.
.	.	.	.	.	.	. .	Manor House Siding...........	Yorks	N. E.	Otterington. / Thirsk.
G	P	.	.	.	.		Manor Park	Essex	G. E.	Stratford and Romford.
.	.	.	.	.	.	. .	Manors	Northumb	N. E.	See Newcastle-on-Tyne.
.	.	.	.	.	.	. .	Manors Coal Depôt	Northumb	N. E.	Newcastle-on-Tyne.
.	.	.	.	.	.	. .	Manor Way (L. & I. Dks.)	Essex	L. & I. Dks.—G. E.	See London.
.	.	.	.	.	.	. .	Mansel Sid. (Byass, R. B., & Co)	Glamorg'n	G. W.—P. T.—R. & S. B.	Port Talbot.
.	.	.	.	.	.	. .	Manser & Co.'s Siding	Herts	G. N.	Hertford.
G	P	F	L	H	C	10 0	Mansfield (Mid.)	Notts	Mid.	Nottingham and Shireoaks Junc.
									G. C.	Over Mid. from Shireoaks Junctions.
.	.	.	.	.	.	. .	Bolsover Col. Co.'s Crown Farm Sidings	Notts	Mid.	Near Mansfield.
.	.	.	.	.	.	. .	Cash & Son's Siding	Notts	Mid.	Near Mansfield.
.	.	.	.	.	.	. .	Duke of Portland's Bleak Hills Siding..................	Notts	Mid.	Near Mansfield.

EXPLANATION—G *Goods Station.*   P *Passenger and Parcel Station.*   P* *Passenger, but not Parcel or Miscellaneous Traffic.*
F *Furniture Vans, Carriages, Portable Engines, and Machines on Wheels.*   L *Live Stock.*
H *Horse Boxes and Prize Cattle Vans.*   C *Carriages by Passenger Train.*

STATION ACCOMMODATION.						CRANE POWER.	STATIONS, &c.	COUNTY.	COMPANY.	POSITION.
						Tons Cwts.	Mansfield (Mid.)—continued.			
.	.	.	.	.	.	. .	Kings Mill Sid. (Caudwell's)	Notts	Mid.	Near Mansfield.
.	.	.	.	.	.	. .	Lindley's, R., Stone Siding (Mid.)	Notts	Mid.—G. C.	Near Mansfield.
.	.	.	.	.	.	. .	Mansfield Brick & Stone Co.'s Siding.................	Notts	Mid.	Near Mansfield.
							Mansfield Sand Co.'s Siding (Mid.)—			
.	.	.	.	.	.	. .	Berry Hill Sand Co.'s......	Notts	Mid.—G. C.	Near Mansfield.
.	.	.	.	.	.	. .	Carter & Barringer's......	Notts	Mid.—G. C.	Near Mansfield.
.	.	.	.	.	.	. .	Pye's Timber Yard (Mid.)	Notts	Mid.—G. C.	Near Mansfield.
.	.	.	.	.	.	. .	Sanderson & Robinson's Siding	Notts	Mid.	Near Mansfield.
.	.	.	.	.	.	. .	Mansfield Bros.' Tile Works (Mid.)	Derby......	Mid.—L. & N. W.	Woodville.
.	.	.	.	.	.	. .	Mansfield Gas Works	Roxburgh	N. B.	Hawick.
.	.	.	.	.	.	. .	Mansfield Siding................	Roxburgh	N. B.	Hawick.
.	.	.	.	.	.	. .	Mansfield's, H. R., Sids.(Mid.)	Derby	Mid.—L. & N. W.	{ Gresley. { Woodville.
.	.	.	.	.	.	. .	Mansfield's Sanitary Siding (Mid.)	Derby......	Mid.—L. & N. W.	Woodville.
.	.	.	.	.	.	. .	Mansfield's Siding...............	Leicester..	L. & N. W.	Whitwick.
G	P	F	L	H	C	1 10	Mansfield Woodhouse (Mid.)	Notts	{ Mid. { G. C.	Mansfield and Shirebrook. Over Mid. from Shireoaks Junctions.
.	.	.	.	.	.	. .	Pleasley Vale Sidings(Wm. Hollins & Co.) (Mid.) ...	Notts	Mid.—G. C.	Mansfield Woodhouse and Pleasley.
.	.	.	.	.	.	. .	Sherwood Colliery Co.'s Siding (Mid.)	Notts	Mid.—G. C.	Near Mansfield Woodhouse.
.	.	.	.	.	.	. .	Sill's, W., Lime Works ...	Notts	Mid.	Pleasley Junction.
.	.	.	.	.	.	. .	Mansion House (City)	Middlesex	W. & C.	See London.
.	.	.	.	.	.	. .	Mansion House (Met. Dist.)	Middlesex	Met. Dist.—L. & N. W.	See London.
.	.	.	.	.	.	. .	Mansion House Junction......	Middlesex	Met. Dist—Met. & Met. Dist. Joint	London, Mansion House & Cannon Str.
G	P	F	L	H	C	1 10	Manton (for Uppingham)......	Rutland ...	Mid.	Stamford and Oakham.
.	.	.	.	.	.	. .	Manton Sidings	Notts	Mid.	See Wigan Coal and Iron Co. (Worksop).
.	.	.	.	.	.	. .	Manton Wood Colliery (G. C.)	Notts	G. C.—G. N.	Worksop.
.	P	.	.	.	.	. .	Manuel (E. & G.)	Stirling ...	N. B.	Linlithgow and Falkirk.
.	P	.	.	.	.	. .	Manuel (Monkland Railway)	Stirling ...	N. B.	Avonbridge and Bo'ness.
.	.	.	.	.	.	. .	Manuelrigg Colliery	Stirling ...	N. B.	Almond Junction Station.
.	P	.	.	.	.	. .	Manulla Junction Station ...	Mayo	M. G. W.	Claremorris and Westport.
.	.	.	.	.	.	. .	Manvers Main Colliery	Yorks	H. & B.	Wath.
.	.	.	.	.	.	. .	Manvers Main Colliery (New)	Yorks	G. C.	Mexboro'.
.	.	.	.	.	.	. .	Manvers Main Col., No. 1 Pit (Adwick Siding) (G. C.) ...	Yorks	G. C.—Mid.	Mexboro'.
.	.	.	.	.	.	. .	Manvers Main Col., No. 2 Pit	Yorks	Mid.	Swinton.
.	.	.	.	.	.	. .	Manvers Main Colliery (Old)	Yorks	G. C.	Mexboro'.
.	.	.	.	.	.	. .	Manvers New Colliery	Yorks	Mid.	Swinton.
.	.	.	.	.	.	. .	Manvers Old Colliery	Yorks	Mid.	Swinton.
.	.	.	.	.	.	. .	Manystones Quarry	Derby......	L. & N. W.	Same as Wirksworth Stone and Mineral Co.'s Brittain's Quarry (Longcliffe).
							Mapperley Colliery Co.—			
.	.	.	.	.	.	. .	Siding	Derby	Mid.	Stanton Gate.
.	.	.	.	.	.	. .	Stanley Colliery (G. N.) ...	Derby......	G. N.—G. C.	West Hallam.
.	.	.	.	.	.	. .	Mapplewell	Yorks	G. C.	See Staincross (for Mapplewell).
.	.	.	.	.	.	. .	Mapplewell Siding	Yorks	L. & Y.	Darton.
G	P	.	L	H		2 0	Marazion	Cornwall..	G. W.	Camborne and Penzance.
.	.	.	.	.	.	. .	Marble Arch	Middlesex	C. L.	See London.
							MARCH—			
G	P	F	L	H	C	1 10	(Station, G. E.)	Cambs ...	{ G. E. { G. N.	Peterboro' and Ely. Over G. E. Line.
.	.	.	.	.	.	. .	Grassmoor Junction	Cambs ...	G. E.—G. N. & G. E. Jt.	Whitemoor and Twenty Foot River Siding.
.	.	.	.	.	.	. .	Horsemoor Siding	Cambs ...	G. E.	March.
.	.	.	.	.	.	. .	Junction	Cambs ...	G. E.—G. N. & G. E. Jt.	March Station and Wimblington.
G	.	.	.	.	.	2 10 }	Whitemoor (G. E.)............	Cambs ...	{ G. E. { G. N.	Spalding and Ely. Over G. E. from March Junction.
G	.	.	.	.	.	. .	Marchington	Staffs	N. S.	Uttoxeter and Tutbury.
G	P	.	.	H		. .	Marchmont	Berwick ...	N. B.	Duns and St. Boswells.
G	P	.	L	H	C	. .	Marchowel Colliery (Mid.) ...	Glamorg'n	Mid.—G. W.—L. & N. W.	Same as Bryncoch and Wernddu Colliery (Pontardawe).

EXPLANATION—G *Goods Station.* P *Passenger and Parcel Station.* P* *Passenger, but not Parcel or Miscellaneous Traffic.*
F *Furniture Vans, Carriages, Portable Engines, and Machines on Wheels.* L *Live Stock.*
H *Horse Boxes and Prize Cattle Vans.* C *Carriages by Passenger Train.*

G	P	F	L	H	C	Tons	Cwts	STATIONS, &c.	COUNTY.	COMPANY.	POSITION.
.	.	.	.	.	.	.	.	Marchwiel	Denbigh	Cam.	Wrexham and Ellesmere.
G	P	F	L	H	C	4	0	Five Fords Siding	Denbigh	Cam.	Marchwiel and Bangor-on-Dee.
G	P	.	L	H	.	.	.	Marden	Kent	S. E. & C.	Tonbridge and Ashford.
.	.	.	.	.	.	.	.	Mardocks	Herts	G. E.	St. Margaret's and Buntingford.
.	.	.	.	.	.	.	.	Mardon & Son's Paper Works	Glo'ster	Mid.	Bristol, St. Philips.
.	.	.	.	.	.	.	.	Mardy Colliery	Glamorg'n	T. V.	Same as Maerdy Colliery (Maerdy).
.	.	.	.	.	.	.	.	Mardy Junction	Glamorg'n	G. W.—G. W. & T. V. Jt.	Merthyr.
.	.	.	.	.	.	.	.	Marefield, North Junction	Leicester	G. N.—G. N. & L. N. W. Jt.	Loseby and Melton Mowbray.
.	.	.	.	.	.	.	.	Marefield, South Junction	Leicester	G. N.—G. N. & L. N. W. Jt.	Loseby and Market Harboro'.
.	.	.	.	.	.	.	.	Marehay Colliery	Derby	Mid.	See Butterley Co. (Ripley).
G	P	.	.	.	.	.	.	Marehay Main Col. (Ford's)	Derby	Mid.	Ripley.
.	.	.	.	.	.	.	.	Marfleet	Yorks	N. E.	Hull and Withernsea.
.	.	.	.	.	.	.	.	Margam Colliery	Glamorg'n	G. W.	Port Talbot and Aberavon.
.	.	.	.	.	.	.	.	Margam Copper Works	Glamorg'n	G. W.	Port Talbot and Aberavon.
.	.	.	.	.	.	.	.	Margam Forge	Glamorg'n	P. T.	Port Talbot.
.	.	.	.	.	.	.	.	Margam Junction	Glamorg'n	G. W.—P. T.	Pyle and Port Talbot.
.	.	.	.	.	.	.	.	Margam Moors Siding (Heolydelaid Siding)	Glamorg'n	P. T.	Bryndu.
.	.	.	.	.	.	.	.	Margam Sand Siding	Glamorg'n	G. W.	Port Talbot and Aberavon.
.	.	.	.	.	.	.	.	Margam Siding	Glamorg'n	R. & S. B.	See Vivian & Sons' (Port Talbot).
.	.	.	.	.	.	.	.	Margaret Pit (Newbottle)	Durham	N. E.	{ Fencehouses. { Penshaw.
.	.	.	.	.	.	.	.	MARGATE—			
.	.	.	.	.	.	.	.	East	Kent	S. E. & C.	See East Margate.
.	P	.	.	.	.	.	.	Marshall & Co.'s Siding	Kent	S. E. & C.	Margate, West.
G	P	F	L	H	C	10	0	Sands	Kent	S. E. & C.	Branch from Ramsgate.
G	P	F	L	H	C	10	0	West	Kent	S. E. & C.	Herne Bay and Ramsgate.
.	.	.	.	.	.	.	.	Marine Colliery	Mon	G. W.	Aberbeeg.
.	P	.	.	.	.	.	.	Marino	Down	B. & C. D.	Holywood and Bangor.
G	P	.	L	H	.	.	.	Marishes Road	Yorks	N. E.	Malton and Pickering.
.	.	.	.	.	.	.	.	Black Bull Siding	Yorks	N. E.	Marishes Road and Pickering.
.	.	.	.	.	.	.	.	Maritime Colliery	Glamorg'n	T. V.	Pontypridd.
.	.	.	.	.	.	.	.	Mark Cross	Sussex	L. B. & S. C.	See Rotherfield and Mark Cross.
.	.	.	.	.	.	.	.	Marker's Siding	Glamorg'n	L. & N. W.	Gowerton.
G	P	F	L	H	C	1	10	Market Bosworth	Leicester	A&N Jt.(L.&N.W.&Mid.)	Nuneaton and Shackerstone.
.	.	.	.	.	.	.	.	Market Branch	Wilts	L. & S.W.	Salisbury.
G	P	F	L	H	C	5	0	Market Drayton (G. W.)	Salop	{ G. W. { N. S.	Wellington and Nantwich. Over G. W. from Market Drayton Jn.
.	.	.	.	.	.	.	.	Market Drayton Junction	Salop	G. W.—N. S.	Market Drayton Station & Pipe Gate.
.	.	.	.	.	.	.	.	MARKET HARBORO'—			
G	P	F	L	H	C	5	0	(Station)	Leicester	Mid.	East Langton and Desboro'.
G	P	F	L	H	C	5	0 }	(Station, L. & N. W.)	Leicester	{ L. & N. W. { G. N.	Rugby and Stamford. Over L. & N. W. from Welham Junc.
G	.	.	.	.	.	.	}				
.	.	.	.	.	.	.	.	Great Bowdon Sidings	Leicester	Mid.	Market Harboro'.
G	P	F	L	.	.	.	.	Junction	Leicester	L. & N. W.—Mid.	Market Harboro' and Wigston.
.	.	.	.	.	.	.	.	Market Hill	Armagh	G. N. (I.)	Goragh Wood and Armagh.
.	.	.	.	.	.	.	.	Market House Siding	Somerset	G. W.	Frome.
G	P	F	L	H	C	5	0	Market Rasen	Lincoln	G. C.	Lincoln and Barnetby.
G	P	F	L	H	C	5	0	Market Weighton	Yorks	N. E.	York and Beverley.
.	.	.	.	.	.	.	.	Shipton Lane Siding	Yorks	N. E.	Market Weighton and Everingham.
.	.	.	.	.	.	.	.	Markham & Co.'s Siding	Derby	Mid.	Same as Broad Oaks Siding (Chesterfield).
.	.	.	.	.	.	.	.	Markham Cols. Nos. 1 & 2 (GC)	Derby	G.C.—G. N.—L. & N. W.	Staveley Town.
.	.	.	.	.	.	.	.	Markham Colliery	Derby	Mid.	Barrow Hill and Staveley Works.
.	.	.	.	.	.	.	.	Markham Col. (L. D. & E. C.)	Derby	L. D. & E. C.—G. E.	Bolsover.
G	P	F	L	H	C	2	0	Markinch	Fife	N. B.	Thornton and Ladybank.
.	.	.	.	.	.	.	.	Auchmuty Mills	Fife	N. B.	Branch—Markinch and Leslie.
.	.	.	.	.	.	.	.	Balbirnie Paper Mills	Fife	N. B.	Branch—Markinch and Leslie.
.	.	.	.	.	.	.	.	Rothes Siding	Fife	N. B.	Branch—Markinch and Leslie.
.	.	.	.	.	.	.	.	Rothesfield Siding	Fife	N. B.	Branch—Markinch and Leslie.
.	.	.	.	.	.	.	.	Markinch Junction	Fife	N. B.	Markinch and Leslie.
.	.	.	.	.	.	.	.	Mark Lane	Middlesex	Met. & Met. Dist. Jt.	See London.
G	P	F	L	H	C	1	0	Marks Tey	Essex	G. E.	Colchester and Chelmsford.
.	.	.	.	.	.	.	.	Collier, W. H., Siding	Essex	G. E.	Marks Tey.
G	P	F	L	H	C	1	10	Marlboro'	Wilts	{ G. W. { M. & S. W. Jn.	Branch from Savernake. Swindon Town and Savernake.
G	P	F	L	H	C	1	10 }				
.	P	.	.	.	.	.	.	Marlborough Road	Middlesex	Met.	See London.
G	P	.	.	.	.	.	.	Marlesford	Suffolk	G. E.	Wickham Market & Framlingham.
.	.	.	.	.	.	.	.	Marley Hill Colliery Coke and Brick Works	Durham	N. E.	Redheugh.
.	.	.	.	.	.	.	.	Marley Hill Depôt	Durham	N. E.	Redheugh.
.	.	.	.	.	.	.	.	Marling's, Sir Wm., Siding	Glo'ster	Mid.	Ryeford.

EXPLANATION—G *Goods Station.* P *Passenger and Parcel Station.* P* *Passenger, but not Parcel or Miscellaneous Traffic.*
F *Furniture Vans, Carriages, Portable Engines, and Machines on Wheels.* L *Live Stock.*
H *Horse Boxes and Prize Cattle Vans.* C *Carriages by Passenger Train.*

STATION ACCOMMODATION.							CRANE POWER.	STATIONS, &c.	COUNTY.	COMPANY.	POSITION.
							Tons Cwts.				
G	P	F	L	H	H	C	2 0	Marlow	Bucks	G. W.	Branch from Bourne End.
.	P	.	.	.	H	C	. .	Marlpool (for Shipley Hall)	Derby	G. N.	Branch—Ilkeston and West Hallam.
G	P	.	L	.	.	.	1 10	Marple	Cheshire	S. & M. Jt. (G. C. & Mid.)	Romiley and New Mills.
G	P	.	.	.	.	.	. .	Marple (Rose Hill)	Cheshire	Mac. Com. (G. C. & N. S.)	Romiley and Macclesfield.
.	.	.	.	.	.	.	. .	Buxton Lime Firms Co.'s Siding	Cheshire	Mac. Com. (G. C. & N. S.)	Rose Hill.
.	.	.	.	.	.	.	. .	Tymm's Siding	Cheshire	Mac. Com. (G. C. & N. S.)	Rose Hill.
.	.	.	.	.	.	.	. .	Marple Junction	Cheshire	Mac. Com.—S. & M. Jt.	Romiley and Rose Hill.
.	.	.	.	.	.	.	. .	Marquis of Exeter's Ironstone Siding	N'hamptn	Mid.	Stamford.
.	.	.	.	.	.	.	. .	Marquis of Lothian's Depôt	Edinboro'	N. B.	Same as Lothian Coal Co.'s Depôt (Leith).
.	.	.	.	.	.	.	. .	Marquis's Siding	Lancs	L. & Y.	Barton.
.	.	.	.	.	.	.	. .	Marriage & Pinnock's Siding	Lancs	L Y & LU Jt. (LY & LNW)	See Withnell Mill Sidings (Brinscall).
.	.	.	.	.	.	.	. .	Marriage & Son's Siding	Essex	G. E.	Colchester, Hythe.
.	.	.	.	.	.	.	. .	Marriage, W. H., & Son's Sid.	Essex	G. E.	Chelmsford.
.	.	.	.	.	.	.	. .	Marron Junction	Cumb'land	L. & N. W.—W. C. & E. Jt.	Bridgefoot and Workington.
.	P	.	.	.	.	.	. .	Marsden	Durham	Marsden	Terminus.
G	P	.	.	.	.	.	10 0	Marsden	Yorks	L. & N. W.	Huddersfield and Stalybridge.
.	.	.	.	.	.	.	. .	Huddersfield Corporation Siding	Yorks	L. & N. W.	Marsden and Diggle.
.	.	.	.	.	.	.	. .	Marsden & Son's Siding	Yorks	L. & Y.	Horbury Junction Station.
.	.	.	.	.	.	.	. .	Marsden Limestone Quarry and Lime Works	Durham	N. E.	South Shields.
.	.	.	.	.	.	.	. .	Marsden Manure Siding	Durham	N. E.	South Shields.
.	.	.	.	.	.	.	. .	Marsden Paper Mills	Durham	N. E.	South Shields.
.	.	.	.	.	.	.	. .	Marshall & Co.'s Siding	Kent	S. E. & C.	Margate, West.
.	.	.	.	.	.	.	. .	Marshall & Son's Siding	Lancs	L. & N. W.	St. Helens.
.	.	.	.	.	.	.	. .	Marshall Green Colliery and Brick Works	Durham	N. E.	Witton-le-Wear.
.	.	.	.	.	.	.	. .	Marshall Green Saw Mill	Durham	N. E.	Witton-le-Wear.
.	.	.	.	.	.	.	. .	Marshall's Siding	Lanark	Cal.	Same as Motherwell Boiler Works.
.	.	.	.	.	.	.	. .	Marshall's Siding	Lancs	L. & Y.	Ainsdale.
.	.	.	.	.	.	.	. .	Marshall's Siding	Lincoln	G. C.	Gainsboro'.
.	.	.	.	.	.	.	. .	Marshall's Siding	Warwick	L. & N. W.	Same as Tamworth Colliery Co.'s Siding (Tamworth).
.	.	.	.	.	.	.	. .	Marshall's Tube Works	Lanark	Cal.	Same as Glasgow Tube Works (Glasgow).
.	.	.	.	.	.	.	. .	Marshall's Wagon Works	Notts	Mid.	Nottingham, Lenton.
.	.	.	.	.	.	.	. .	Marsh & Co.'s Brick Works	Durham	N. E.	Washington.
G	P	F	L	H	.	C	2 0	Marsh Brook	Salop	S & H Jt (G W & L N W)	Craven Arms and Shrewsbury.
.	.	.	.	.	.	.	. .	Marsh Farm Junction	Salop	G. W.—S. & H. Jt.	Buildwas and Craven Arms.
G	P	.	L	H	.	.	. .	Marshfield	Mon	G. W.	Newport and Cardiff.
.	.	.	.	.	.	.	. .	Marsh Gate	Yorks	G. C.	See Doncaster.
.	.	.	.	.	.	.	. .	Marsh Gate, North Junctions	Yorks	G.C.—G.N.—W R & G Jt.	Doncaster.
G	P	.	L	H	.	.	. .	Marsh Gibbon & Poundon	Bucks	L. & N. W.	Oxford and Verney Junction Station.
.	.	.	.	.	.	.	. .	Marsh House Coal and Lime Works (L. & N. W.)	Lancs	L & NW—G. C. (Wig. Jn.)	See Wigan Coal & Iron Co. (Wigan).
.	.	.	.	.	.	.	. .	Marshland Junction	Yorks	Axholme Jt.—N. E.	Goole.
.	.	.	.	.	.	.	. .	Marsh Lane and Strand Road (L. & Y.)	Lancs	L. & Y.—L. & N. W.	See Liverpool, Marsh Lane and Strand Road.
.	.	.	.	.	.	.	. .	Marsh Lane (N. E.)	Yorks	N. E.—L. & N. W.	See Leeds.
G	P	.	.	.	.	.	. .	Marsh Mills	Devon	G. W.	Plymouth and Tavistock.
.	.	.	.	.	.	.	. .	Milling Co.'s Works	Devon	G. W.	Marsh Mills.
.	.	.	.	.	.	.	. .	Marshmoor Siding	Herts	G. N.	Hatfield.
.	.	.	.	.	.	.	. .	Marsh Siding	Somerset	G. W.	Bristol, Temple Meads.
.	.	.	.	.	.	.	. .	Marsh Siding	Mon	G. W.	Same as Budd & Co.'s (Blackwood).
.	.	.	.	.	.	.	. .	Marsh Sidings	Cumb'land	L. & N. W.	See Kirk, Bros. & Co. (Workington).
.	.	.	.	.	.	.	. .	Marsh, Son & Gibb's Siding	Somerset	Mid.	Bath.
.	.	.	.	.	.	.	. .	Marsh Wire Works	Yorks	N. E.	Middlesbro'.
G	P	F	L	H	.	C	1 0	Marske	Yorks	N. E.	Redcar and Saltburn.
.	.	.	.	.	.	.	. .	Green Lane Manure Siding	Yorks	N. E.	Marske.
.	.	.	.	.	.	.	. .	Toft's Siding	Yorks	N. E.	Marske.
.	.	.	.	.	.	.	. .	Upleatham Mines	Yorks	N. E.	Marske.
.	.	.	.	.	.	.	. .	Marson Street Goods Depôt (L. & N. W.)	Lancs	L. & N. W.—G. W.	See Warrington.
.	.	.	.	.	.	.	. .	Marston, Thompson & Son's Sidings (Mid.)	Staffs	Mid.—L&NW—GN—NS	Burton-on-Trent.
G	P	.	L	H	.	.	. .	Marston Gate	Herts	L. & N. W.	Aylesbury and Cheddington.
G	P	.	L	H	.	.	. .	Marston Green	Warwick	L. & N. W.	Birmingham and Coventry.
.	.	.	.	.	.	.	. .	Marston Hall Works (C.L.C.)	Cheshire	C. L. C.—L. & N. W.	See Salt Union, Ltd. (Northwich).
.	.	.	.	.	.	.	. .	Marston Junction	Derby	N. S.	Tutbury and Burton.

EXPLANATION—G Goods Station. P Passenger and Parcel Station. P* Passenger, but not Parcel or Miscellaneous Traffic.
F Furniture Vans, Carriages, Portable Engines, and Machines on Wheels. L Live Stock.
H Horse Boxes and Prize Cattle Vans. C Carriages by Passenger Train.

STATION ACCOMMODATION.						CRANE POWER.		STATIONS, &c.	COUNTY.	COMPANY.	POSITION.
						Tons	Cwts.				
G	P	.	L	H	.	1	10	Marston Lane Siding	Hereford ..	G. W.	See Pembridge.
G	P	.	L	H	.	.	.	Marston Magna	Somerset..	G. W.	Sparkford and Yeovil.
G	P	.	L	H	.	.	.	Marston Moor	Yorks	N. E.	York and Knaresboro'.
.	.	.	.	.	.	.	.	Wilstrop Siding	Yorks	N. E.	Marston Moor.
.	.	.	.	.	.	.	.	Marston Old Works (C. L. C.)	Cheshire...	C. L. C.—L. & N. W.	See Salt Union, Ltd. (Northwich).
.	.	.	.	.	.	.	.	Marston Siding (C. L. C.).....	Cheshire...	C. L. C.—L. & N. W.	See Thompson's (Northwich).
.	.	.	.	.	.	.	.	Marston Works (C. L. C.)......	Cheshire...	C. L. C.—L. & N. W.	See Salt Union, Ltd. (Northwich).
G	P	F	L	H	C	.	.	Martham (for Rollesby)	Norfolk ...	Mid. & G. N. Jt.	North Walsham Town & Yarmouth Beach.
.	.	.	.	.	.	.	.	Martholme Colliery	Lancs	L. & Y.	Great Harwood.
.	.	.	.	.	.	.	.	Martin & Co.'s Siding	Middlesex	G. E.	Angel Road.
.	.	.	.	.	.	.	.	Martin & Maymon's Siding...	Lancs	P.&L.Jt.(L&NW.&L&Y	Preston, Deepdale.
.	.	.	.	.	.	.	.	Martin Bros.'—			
.	.	.	.	.	.	.	.	Quay	Devon	L. & S.W.	Plymouth, Cattewater Harbour.
.	.	.	.	.	.	.	.	Siding	Devon	G. W.	Plymouth.
.	.	.	.	.	.	.	.	Martin Earle & Co.'s Cement Works	Kent	S. E. & C.	Cuxton.
.	.	.	.	.	.	.	.	Martin, J. W., Siding	Essex	G. E.	Clacton-on-Sea.
.	.	.	.	.	.	.	.	Martin's Siding	Kent	S. E. & C.	Brockley Lane.
.	.	.	.	.	.	.	.	Martin's Siding	N'hamptn	L. & N. W.	Northampton, Castle.
.	.	.	.	.	.	.	.	Martin's Sidings.................	Cornwall ..	G. W.	Bugle.
.	.	.	.	.	.	.	.	Martin's Stone Siding	Edinboro'	Cal.	Edinburgh, Lothian Road.
G	P	F	L	H	C	10	0	Martin Mill	Kent	S. E. & C.	Dover and Deal.
.	.	.	.	.	.	.	.	Martland's Siding	Lancs	L. & Y.	Burscough Bridge.
G	P	F	L	H	C	10	0	Martock	Somerset..	G. W.	Durston and Yeovil.
.	.	.	.	.	.	.	.	Marton	Lincoln ...	G. N. & G. E. Jt.	See Stow Park (for Marton).
G	P	F	L	H	C	.	.	Marton	Warwick...	L. & N. W.	Leamington and Rugby.
.	.	.	.	.	.	.	.	Marton Lane Siding & Depôts	Yorks	N. E.	Nunthorpe.
G	P	F	L	H	C	1	0	Maryborough	Queens ...	G. S. & W.	Kildare and Thurles.
.	.	.	.	.	.	.	.	Maryburgh Siding................	Lanark ...	Cal.	Cumbernauld.
.	.	.	.	.	.	.	.	Maryfield	Forfar	Cal.	See Dundee.
.	.	.	.	.	.	.	.	Maryhill	Lanark ...	Cal.—N. B.	See Glasgow.
.	.	.	.	.	.	.	.	Maryhill, Central Junction...	Lanark ...	N. B.	Glasgow.
.	.	.	.	.	.	.	.	Maryhill, East Junction	Lanark ...	N. B.	Glasgow.
.	.	.	.	.	.	.	.	Maryhill Iron Works...........	Lanark ...	Cal.	Glasgow, Maryhill.
G	P	F	L	H	C	1	10	Marykirk	Kinc'rdine	Cal.	Forfar and Stonehaven.
.	P	.	.	.	.	.	.	Maryland Point	Essex	G. E.	Stratford and Romford.
.	.	.	.	.	.	.	.	Marylebone	Middlesex	G. C.	See London.
.	.	.	.	.	.	.	.	Mary Pit	Fife.........	N. B.	See Fife Coal Co. (Kelty).
.	.	.	.	.	.	.	.	Mary Pit Colliery	Fife.........	N. B.	Lochgelly.
G	P	F	L	H	C	5	0	Maryport (M. & C.)	Cumb'land	M. & C. / L. & N. W.	Maryport Junction and Bullgill. / Over M. & C. from Maryport Junc.
.	.	.	.	.	.	.	.	Cammell & Co.'s Solway Hematite Iron Works	Cumb'land	L. & N. W. / M. & C.	Maryport and Flimby. / Maryport.
G	.	.	.	.	.	.	.	Elizabeth Dock	Cumb'land	L. & N. W.	Maryport.
.	.	.	.	.	.	.	.	Elizabeth Dock	Cumb'land	M. & C.	Branch—Maryport Junc. and Sta.
.	.	.	.	.	.	.	.	Ellenboro' Colliery...........	Cumb'land	L. & N. W. / M. & C.	Maryport and Flimby. / Maryport.
.	.	.	.	.	.	.	.	Mandle's Siding	Cumb'land	M. & C.	Maryport.
G	.	.	.	.	.	.	.	Ritson & Co.'s Timber Yard	Cumb'land	M. & C.	Maryport.
.	.	.	.	.	.	.	.	Senhouse Dock	Cumb'land	L. & N. W.—M. & C.	Maryport.
.	.	.	.	.	.	.	.	Walker's Shipbuilding Yard	Cumb'land	M. & C.	Maryport.
.	.	.	.	.	.	.	.	Wharton's Phœnix Foundry	Cumb'land	M. & C.	Maryport.
G	P	.	.	.	.	.	.	Maryport Junction	Cumb'land	L. & N. W.—M. & C.	Workington and Maryport.
.	P	.	.	.	.	.	.	Mary Tavy	Devon......	G. W.	Tavistock and Lydford.
.	.	.	.	.	.	.	.	Maryville	Lanark ...	N. B.	Shettleston Junction and Bothwell.
.	.	.	.	.	.	.	.	Masboro'	Yorks	G. C.	See Rotherham and Masboro'.
G	P	F	L	H	C	10	0	Masboro' and Rotherham......	Yorks	Mid.	Sheffield and Swinton.
.	.	.	.	.	.	.	.	Brinsworth Iron Works (Baker, J., & Co.)	Yorks	Mid.	Masboro'.
.	.	.	.	.	.	.	.	Brown, J., & Co.—			
.	.	.	.	.	.	.	.	Carr House Colliery	Yorks	Mid.	Masboro'.
.	.	.	.	.	.	.	.	Rotherham Main Colliery	Yorks	Mid.	Masboro'.
.	.	.	.	.	.	.	.	Earl Fitzwilliam's Low Stubbin Colliery	Yorks	Mid.	Masboro'.
.	.	.	.	.	.	.	.	Greasboro' Colliery	Yorks	Mid.	Masboro'.
.	.	.	.	.	.	.	.	Holmes Blast Furnaces (Parkgate Ir. & Steel Co.)	Yorks	Mid.	Masboro'.
.	.	.	.	.	.	.	.	Holmes Pottery Works (Shaw, G., & Son)	Yorks	Mid.	Masboro'.
.	.	.	.	.	.	.	.	Holmes Station Siding	Yorks	Mid.	Holmes.
.	.	.	.	.	.	.	.	Holmes Steel Wks.(P.Stubs)	Yorks	Mid.	Masboro'.

EXPLANATION—G Goods Station.   P Passenger and Parcel Station.   P* Passenger, but not Parcel or Miscellaneous Traffic.
F Furniture Vans, Carriages, Portable Engines, and Machines on Wheels.   L Live Stock.
H Horse Boxes and Prize Cattle Vans.   C Carriages by Passenger Train.

STATION ACCOMMODATION.						CRANE POWER.		STATIONS, &c.	COUNTY.	COMPANY.	POSITION.
						Tons	Cwts.	Masboro' and Rotherham—*continued.*			
..	..	..	..	..	..			Holmes Wagon Works (Harrison & Camm)	Yorks	Mid.	Masboro'.
G	..	..	..	..	..	4	0	Ickles Dock	Yorks	Mid.	Masboro'.
..	..	..	..	..	..			Midland Iron Co.'s Siding	Yorks	Mid.	Masboro'.
..	..	..	..	..	..			North Central Wagon Co.'s Siding	Yorks	Mid.	Masboro'.
..	..	..	..	..	..			Owen & Dyson's Works ...	Yorks	Mid.	Masboro'.
..	..	..	..	..	..			Parkgate Chemical Works	Yorks	Mid.	Masboro'.
..	..	..	..	..	..			Parkgate Steel Works (W. Oxley & Co.)	Yorks	Mid.	Masboro'.
..	..	..	..	..	..			Phœnix Steel Works (Steel, Peech & Tozer)	Yorks	Mid.	Masboro'.
..	..	..	..	..	..			Slag Reduction Co.'s Siding	Yorks	Mid.	Masboro'.
..	..	..	..	..	..			South Yorks Hoop Iron Works (Wilcock & Jones)	Yorks	Mid.	Masboro'.
G	P	..	L	..	..			Masbury	Somerset..	S.&D. Jt.(L.&S. W.& Mid)	Shepton Mallet and Radstock.
..	..	..	..	..	..			Mascall, J. & R., Siding	Yorks	N. E.	See Packet Wharf Slate Yard (Middlesbro').
G	P	F	L	H	C	2	0	Masham	Yorks	N. E.	Branch from Melmerby.
..	..	..	..	..	..			Mason & Son's Siding	Lancs	L. & Y.	Horwich.
..	..	..	..	..	..			Mason, Cash & Co.'s Sid.(Mid.)	Derby	Mid.—L. & N. W.	Woodville.
..	..	..	..	..	..			Mason's, W. E., Siding	Lancs	L. & Y.	Horwich.
..	..	..	..	..	..			Massey's Siding	Derby	A & N Jt.(L & N W & Mid.)	Measham.
..	..	..	..	..	..			Massey Siding	Notts	G. N. & Mid. Jt.	See Gilstrap, Earp & Co. (Newark).
G	P	F	L	H	C			Massingham	Norfolk ...	Mid. & G. N. Jt.	South Lynn and Melton Constable.
..	..	..	..	..	..			Wilson's Stone Siding	Norfolk ...	Mid. & G. N. Jt.	Massingham.
..	..	..	..	..	..			Masson Works	Derby	Mid.	Same as Fletcher, G., & Co.'s Works (Derby).
..	..	..	..	..	..			Mather & Platt's Siding	Lancs	L. & Y.	Manchester, Oldham Road.
..	..	..	..	..	..			Mather's Foundry	Edinboro'	Cal.	Edinburgh, Lothian Road.
..	..	..	..	..	..			Mathew's Mill Siding	Merioneth	Corris	Corris and Aberllefenny.
..	..	..	..	..	..			Mathias' Siding	Glamorg'n	T. V.	Nelson.
..	..	..	..	..	..			Mathieson's Works	Lancs	L. & N. W.—S. & M. Jt.	See United Alkali Co. (Widnes).
G	P	F	L	H	C			Matlock Bath	Derby	Mid.	Ambergate and Miller's Dale.
..	..	..	..	..	..			Shaw Bros.' Siding	Derby	Mid.	Near Matlock Bath.
G	P	F	L	H	C	15	0	Matlock Bridge	Derby	Mid.	Ambergate and Miller's Dale.
..	..	..	..	..	..			Cawdor Siding (Constable's Limestone Quarries)	Derby	Mid.	Near Matlock Bridge.
..	..	..	..	..	..			Matlock Bridge Limestone Co.'s Siding	Derby	Mid.	Matlock Bridge and Darley Dale.
..	..	..	..	..	..			Shaw's Limestone Siding...	Derby	Mid.	Near Matlock Bridge.
..	..	..	..	..	..			Matthews & Co.'s Yard	Glo'ster ...	Mid.	Gloucester.
..	..	..	..	..	..			Matthews Libanus Colliery	Mon	L. & N. W.	Blackwood.
G	P	F	L	H	C	5	0	Mauchline	Ayr	G. & S.W.	Kilmarnock and Auchinleck.
..	..	..	..	..	..			Ballochmyle Quarry	Ayr	G. & S.W.	Mauchline.
..	..	..	..	..	..			Barskimming Quarry	Ayr	G. & S.W.	Mauchline.
G	..	..	L	..	..			Garrochburn	Ayr	G. & S.W.	Mauchline and Hurlford.
..	..	..	..	..	..			Mauchline Junction	Ayr	G. & S.W.	Mauchline and Auchinleck.
G	P	F	L	H	C	1	5	Maud	Aberdeen	G. N. of S.	Aberdeen and Fraserburgh.
..	..	..	..	..	..			Maudlands	Lancs	P. & W. Jt. (L. & Y. & L. & N. W.)..............	See Preston.
..	..	..	..	..	..			Maudlands Junction	Lancs	L. & N. W.—P. & L. Jt.	Preston.
..	..	..	..	..	..			Maudlands Junction	Lancs	L. & N. W.—P. & W. Jt.	Preston.
..	..	..	..	..	..			Mauds Bridge Siding	Yorks	G. C.	Thorne.
..	..	..	..	..	..			Mauricewood Siding	Edinboro'	N. B.	Glencorse.
..	..	..	..	..	..			Mavisbank Quay (Cal.)	Renfrew...	Cal.—G. & S. W.—N. B.	See Glasgow.
..	..	..	..	..	..			Maw & Co.'s Siding	Salop	G. W.	Ironbridge and Broseley.
G	P	..	L	H	..	3	0	Mawcarse	Kinross ...	N. B.	Kinross Junction and Ladybank.
..	..	..	..	..	..			Reid's Saw Mill	Kinross ...	N. B.	Mawcarse.
..	..	..	..	..	..			Mawcarse Junction	Kinross ...	N. B.	Milnathort and Glenfarg.
G	..	..	L	..	..			Mawddwy	Merioneth	Mawddwy	Terminus.
..	..	..	..	..	..			Mawson, Clark & Co.'s Siding	Durham ...	N. E.	Redheugh.
..	..	..	..	..	..			Mawson, Clark & Co.'s Siding	Northumb	N. E.	Newcastle-on-Tyne.
..	..	..	..	..	..			Maxstoke Siding	Warwick..	Mid.	Coleshill.
G	P	..	L	H	..	3	0	Maxton	Roxburgh	N. B.	Galashiels and Kelso.
..	..	..	..	..	..			Maxwell & Co.'s Chemical Wks.	Cumb'land	N. B.	Same as Border Counties' Chemical Works (Silloth).
..	..	..	..	..	..			Maxwell Junction	Renfrew...	Cal.	Glasgow.
..	..	..	..	..	..			Maxwell Park	Lanark ...	Cal.	See Glasgow.
..	..	..	..	..	..			Maxwell Pit.....................	Ayr	G. & S.W.	Dailly.
..	..	..	..	..	..			Maxwell Street Depôts.........	Durham ...	N. E.	South Shields.

EXPLANATION—G *Goods Station.*   P *Passenger and Parcel Station.*   P* *Passenger, but not Parcel or Miscellaneous Traffic.*
F *Furniture Vans, Carriages, Portable Engines, and Machines on Wheels.*   L *Live Stock.*
H *Horse Boxes and Prize Cattle Vans.*   C *Carriages by Passenger Train.*

STATION ACCOMMODATION.						CRANE POWER.	STATIONS, &c.	COUNTY.	COMPANY.	POSITION.
G	P	F	L	H	C	7 0	Maxwelltown	Kirkcud	G. & S.W.	Dumfries and Dalbeattie.
							Maxwood Colliery	Ayr	G. & S.W.	Galston.
G	P	F	L	H	C	3 0	Mayall's Bottom's Mill	Lancs	L. & N. W.	Mossley.
							Maybole	Ayr	G. & S.W.	Ayr and Girvan.
G	P	F	L	H	C	1 10	Mayer & Co.'s Siding	Staffs	L. & N. W.	Darlaston.
							Mayfield	Sussex	L. B. & S. C.	Rotherfield and Heathfield.
							Mayfield Branch Junction	Ayr	G. & S.W.	Hurlford and Galston.
							Mayfield Saw Mill	Ayr	G. & S.W.	Hurlford.
							Mayfield Siding (Simpson Bros.' Mill)	Derby	N. S.	Clifton.
							May Hill	Mon	G. W.	See Monmouth.
							May Mill Spinning Co.'s Sid.	Lancs	L. & N. W.	Garswood.
G	P	.	L	H	C	.	Maynooth	Kildare	M. G. W.	Dublin and Mullingar.
							Mayor Street Siding	Lancs	L. & Y.	Bolton.
							Maypole Cols. & Brick Works	Lancs	G. C. (Wigan Jn.)	West Leigh and Bedford.
							May's Siding	Kent	S. E. & C.	Swanley.
							May's Siding	Somerset	S.&D.Jt.(L.&L.S.W.& Mid.)	Same as Victoria Brick & Tile Co.'s Siding (Bath).
.	P						Maytown	Armagh	B. & Newry	Bessbrook and Newry.
.	P						Maze	Antrim	G. N. (I.)	Belfast and Portadown.
.	P						Maze Hill (for East Greenwich)	Kent	S. E. & C.	Greenwich and Woolwich.
							Mead & Sons' Clifford Hill Mills or Little Houghton Crossing	N'hamptn	L. & N. W.	Billing.
							Meadowbank Siding	Edinboro'	N. B.	Edinburgh, Rose Lane.
							Meadow Bank Works	Cheshire	C. L. C. (G C, G N, & Mid.)	See Salt Union Ltd. (Winsford and Over).
							Meadow Brick Works	Lanark	Cal.	Braidwood.
							Meadow Colliery	Hadd'gton	N. B.	See Ormiston Coal Co.'s Meadow Colliery (Ormiston).
							Meadowfield Siding	Lanark	N. B.	Longriggend.
							Meadow Hall	Yorks	Mid.	See Sheffield, Wincobank and Meadow Hall.
G	P						Meadow Hall and Wincobank	Yorks	G. C.	Sheffield and Barnsley.
							Crowley & Co.'s Siding (GC)	Yorks	G. C.—Mid.	Meadow Hall and Wincobank.
							Davy & Co.'s Siding	Yorks	G. C.	Meadow Hall and Wincobank.
							Gas Siding	Yorks	G. C.	Meadow Hall and Wincobank.
							Jordan Col. (Meadow Hall)	Yorks	G. C.	Meadow Hall and Wincobank.
							Yorkshire Engine Co.'s Siding (G. C.)	Yorks	G. C.—Mid.	Meadow Hall and Wincobank.
							Meadowhead Colliery	Lanark	Cal.	See Belhaven Estate Collieries (Shieldmuir).
							Meadow Lane Siding (Mid.)	Yorks	{ Mid.—N.E. / G. N.	See Leeds Corporation Gas Works (Leeds). (See Appendix to follow).
							Meadow Pit	Lancs	L. & Y.	See Wigan Coal & Iron Co. (Hindley).
							Meadow Pit	Lancs	L. & Y.	Adlington.
							Meadow Pit (L.& N.W.)	Lancs	L & N W—G C (Wig. Jn.)	See Wigan Coal & Iron Co. (Wigan).
							Meadows, Bros. & Co.'s Siding (Mid.)	Glamorg'n	Mid.—G.W.—L. & N. W.	Clydach-on-Tawe.
							Meadowside Ship Yard	Renfrew	Cal.	Glasgow, Partick, Central.
							Meadows' Siding	Cheshire	L. & N. W.	Stockport, Davenport.
							Meadows' Siding	Lancs	L. & N. W.	Stockport, Edgeley.
							Meadow Works	Cheshire	C. L. C. (G C, G N, & Mid.)	See Salt Union Ltd. (Winsford & Over).
							Mead's Siding	Herts	L. & N. W.	Tring.
							Meakin's Siding (Mid.)	Staffs	Mid.—L&NW—GN—NS	Burton-on-Trent.
G	P	F	L	H	C	5 0	Mealsgate	Cumb'land	M. & C.	High Blaithwaite and Baggrow.
							Allhallows Colliery	Cumb'land	M. & C.	Mealsgate and Baggrow.
G	P	F	L	H	C	1 10	Measham	Leicester	A & N Jt. (L & N W & Mid.)	Overseal and Shackerstone.
							Blakesley's Coronet Brick Co.'s Siding	Derby	A & N Jt.(L & N W & Mid.)	Measham and Snarestone.
							Massey's Siding	Leicester	A & N Jt.(L & N W & Mid.)	Measham and Donisthorpe.
							Measham Colliery	Leicester	A & N Jt.(L & N W & Mid.)	Measham and Snarestone.
							Measham Terra Cotta Co.'s Siding	Leicester	A & N Jt.(L & N W & Mid.)	Measham and Snarestone.
							Red Bank Brick Co.'s Sid.	Leicester	A & N Jt.(L & N W & Mid.)	Measham and Snarestone.
G	P	F	L	H	C	.	Meathop Mineral Siding	W'morlnd	Furness	Grange-over-Sands.
							Medbourne	Leicester	G. N. & L. & N. W. Jt.	Melton Mowbray and Drayton Jn.
							Medd's Egg Packing and Pickling Works	Durham	N. E.	West Hartlepool.
G	P	.	L	H	.	.	Medforth & Hutchinson's Sid.	Yorks	N. E.	Bridlington.
							Medge Hall	Yorks	G. C.	Thorne and Barnetby.
							Moss Litter Co.'s Siding	Yorks	G. C.	Medge Hall.

EXPLANATION—G *Goods Station.*   P *Passenger and Parcel Station.*   P* *Passenger, but not Parcel or Miscellaneous Traffic.*
F *Furniture Vans, Carriages, Portable Engines, and Machines on Wheels.*   L *Live Stock.*
H *Horse Boxes and Prize Cattle Vans.*   C *Carriages by Passenger Train.*

STATION ACCOMMODATION.						CRANE POWER.		STATIONS, &c.	COUNTY.	COMPANY.	POSITION.
						Tons	Cwts				
.	.	.	.	.	.			Medhurst Coal and Sand Sid.	Yorks	N. E.	Kippax.
G	.	.	.	.	.			Medina Wharf	I. of W.	I. of W. Cent.	Branch—Mill Hill and Newport.
.	.	.	.	.	.			Medomsley Colliery	Durham	N. E.	Blackhill.
.	.	.	.	.	.			Medomsley Edge Depôts	Durham	N. E.	Blackhill.
.	.	.	.	.	.			Medomsley N. E. Railway Co.'s Depôt	Durham	N. E.	Blackhill.
G	P	F	L	H	C	3	0	Medstead	Hants	L. & S.W.	Alton and Winchester.
.	P	.	.	.	.			Meen Glas	Donegal	Donegal	Stranorlar and Donegal.
.	.	.	.	.	.			Meeting Slack Depôt	Durham	N. E.	Waskerley.
.	.	.	.	.	.			Megget & Son's Siding	Notts	Mid.	Sutton-in-Ashfield.
G	P	.	L	H	.	2	0	Meigle	Perth	Cal.	Alyth Junction and Alyth.
.	.	.	.	.	.			Meikle Drumgray Colliery (Dykehead Branch)	Lanark	N. B.	Rawyards.
.	.	.	.	.	.			Meikle Drumgray Colliery (North Monkland Railway)	Lanark	N. B.	Greengairs.
G	P	.	L	.	.	2	0	Meikle Earnock	Lanark	Cal.	Hamilton and Strathaven.
.	.	.	.	.	.			Earnock Quarry (Stewart-field Quarry)	Lanark	Cal.	High Blantyre and Meikle Earnock.
.	.	.	.	.	.			Earnock Siding	Lanark	Cal.	High Blantyre and Meikle Earnock.
.	.	.	.	.	.			Eddlewood Colliery	Lanark	Cal.	Meikle Earnock and Quarter Road.
.	.	.	.	.	.			Kennedy's Siding	Lanark	Cal.	Meikle Earnock.
.	.	.	.	.	.			Neilsland Colliery	Lanark	Cal.	Meikle Earnock and Quarter Road.
.	.	.	.	.	.			Townhill Siding	Lanark	Cal.	High Blantyre and Meikle Earnock.
.	.	.	.	.	.			Wellbrae Quarry & Siding	Lanark	Cal.	High Blantyre and Meikle Earnock.
.	.	.	.	.	.			Meiklehill Colliery	Dumbartn	N. B.	Kirkintilloch.
.	.	.	.	.	.			Meiklehill Siding	Dumbartn	N. B.	Kirkintilloch.
.	.	.	.	.	.			Meikleriggs Junction	Renfrew	G. & S.W.	Paisley, Ferguslie and Potterhill.
.	P	.	.	.	.			Meir	Staffs	N. S.	Blyth Bridge and Normacot.
.	.	.	.	.	.			Meir Hay Colliery	Staffs	N. S.	See Park Hall Colliery Co. (Longton).
.	.	.	.	.	.			Meiros Colliery	Glamorg'n	G. W.	Llanharan.
G	.	.	.	.	.			Melangoose Mill	Cornwall	G. W.	Branch from St. Dennis Junction.
.	.	.	.	.	.			Meledor Siding	Cornwall	G. W.	Extension from Melangoose Mill.
.	.	.	.	.	.			Pochins Siding	Cornwall	G. W.	St. Dennis Junc. and Drinnick Mill.
.	.	.	.	.	.	1	10	Retew Sidings	Cornwall	G. W.	St. Dennis Junc. & Melangoose Mill.
.	.	.	.	.	.			Trerice Siding	Cornwall	G. W.	St. Dennis Junc. & Melangoose Mill.
.	.	.	.	.	.			Virginia Siding	Cornwall	G. W.	Extension from Melangoose Mill.
.	.	.	.	.	.			Melbourn	Cambs	G. N.	See Meldreth and Melbourn.
G	P	F	L	H	C	1	10	Melbourne	Derby	Mid.	Derby and Worthington.
.	.	.	.	.	.			Melbourne Junction	Derby	Mid.	Derby and Willington.
G	P	F	L	H	C	.	.	Meldon	Northumb	N. B.	Reedsmouth and Morpeth.
.	.	.	.	.	.			Meldon Junction	Devon	L. & S.W.	Okehampton and Bridestowe.
G	P	F	L	H	C	1	10	Meldreth and Melbourn	Cambs	G. N.	Hitchin and Cambridge.
.	.	.	.	.	.			Meldreth Portland Cement & Brick Co.'s Siding	Cambs	G. N.	Meldreth and Melbourn.
.	.	.	.	.	.			Meledor Siding	Cornwall	G. W.	Melangoose Mill.
.	.	.	.	.	.			Melford	Suffolk	G. E.	Same as Long Melford.
G	.	.	.	.	.	1	10	Meliden	Flint	L. & N.W.	Dyserth and Prestatyn.
.	.	.	.	.	.			Roberts' Siding	Flint	L. & N.W.	Meliden and Dyserth.
.	.	.	.	.	.			Melincourt Siding	Glamorg'n	G. W.	Resolven.
.	.	.	.	.	.			Melincrythan Chemical Co.— Acid Siding	Glamorg'n	R. & S. B	Neath.
.	.	.	.	.	.			Siding	Glamorg'n	G. W.	Neath.
.	.	.	.	.	.			Melingriffith Works	Glamorg'n	T. V.	Same as Pentyrch Siding (Taff's Well).
G	P	F	L	H	C	3	0	Melksham	Wilts	G. W.	Chippenham and Holt.
.	.	.	.	.	.			Spencer & Co.'s Siding	Wilts	G. W.	Melksham.
.	.	.	.	.	.			Mellanby, Thos., Siding	Yorks	N. E.	Stockton, South.
G	P	F	L	H	C	1	10	Melling	Lancs	C. & W. Jt. (Fur. & Mid.)	Wennington and Arkholme.
.	.	.	.	.	.			Melling Bros.' Ince Forge Co.'s Siding	Lancs	L. & N.W.	Wigan.
.	.	.	.	.	.			Melling's Siding	Lancs	L. & N.W.	St Helens.
G	P	F	L	H	C	1	0	Mellis	Suffolk	G. E.	Haughley and Norwich.
G	P	.	L	.	.	1	10	Mells Road	Somerset	G. W.	Frome and Radstock.
.	.	.	.	.	.			Newbury Colliery	Somerset	G. W.	Mells Road.
G	P	F	L	H	C	5	0	Melmerby	Yorks	N. E.	Ripon and Northallerton.
G	P	F	L	H	C	1	10	Melrose	Roxburgh	N. B.	Galashiels and St. Boswells.
G	.	.	.	.	.			Darnick Siding	Roxburgh	N. B.	Galashiels and Melrose.
G	P	F	L	H	C	10	0	Meltham	Yorks	L. & Y.	Branch from Huddersfield.
G	P	F	L	H	C	1	10	Melton	Suffolk	G. E.	Ipswich and Wickham Market.
G	P	F	L	H	C	1	0	Melton Constable	Norfolk	Mid. & G. N. Jt.	Fakenham Town and Norwich City.
G	P	F	L	H	C	5	0	Melton Mowbray	Leicester	G. N. & L. & N. W. Jt.	Market Harboro' and Nottingham.
G	P	F	L	H	C	5	0			Mid.	Nottingham and Oakham.

STATION ACCOMMODATION.						CRANE POWER.	STATIONS, &c.	COUNTY.	COMPANY.	POSITION.
						Tons Cwts.				
.	.	.	.	.	.	. .	Melton Ross Siding	Lincoln ...	G. C.	Barnetby.
.	.	.	.	.	.	. .	Melvin's Siding	Clackman'	N. B.	Same as Sunnyside Foundry (Alloa).
.	.	.	.	.	.	. .	Melyn Tin Works	Glamorg'n	G. W.	Neath.
G	P	.	L	.	.	2 10	Menai Bridge	Carnarvon	L. & N. W.	Bangor and Holyhead.
.	.	.	.	.	.	. .	Davies' Treborth Siding ...	Carnarvon	L. & N. W.	Port Dinorwic and Treborth.
							Mendip Granite and Asphalte			
G	P	F	L	.	.	. .	Co.	Somerset..	G. W.	Cranmore.
.	.	.	.	.	.	. .	Menheniot	Cornwall ..	G. W.	Plymouth and Liskeard.
G	P	F	L	H	C	1 10	Mennock Siding..................	Dumfries..	G. & S. W.	See Sanquhar.
.	.	.	.	.	.	. .	Menston	Yorks	Mid.	Guiseley and Otley.
							West Riding County			
.	.	.	.	.	.	. .	Asylum Siding	Yorks	Mid.	Menston.
G	P	.	L	H	.	2 10	Menstrie and Glenochil	Clackman'	N. B.	Cambus and Alva.
G	P	.	.	.	.	. .	Glenochil Distillery	Clackman'	N. B.	Menstrie and Glenochil Station.
.	.	.	.	.	.	. .	Menthorpe Gate...............	Yorks	N. E.	Selby and Market Weighton.
							Menzies & Co.'s Shipbuilding			
.	.	.	.	.	.	. .	Yard	Edinboro'	Cal.—N. B.	Leith, North.
.	.	.	.	.	.	. .	Menzies' Tube Works	Lanark ...	Cal.	Same as Phœnix Tube Works (Glasgow).
G	P	.	.	.	.	. .	Meols	Cheshire...	Wirral	Bidston and West Kirby.
G	P	F	L	H	C	5 0	Meols Cop	Lancs	L. & Y.	Southport and Barton.
.	.	.	.	.	.	. .	Bates & Co.'s Siding........	Lancs	L. & Y.	Meols Cop.
.	.	.	.	.	.	. .	Meols Cop Corporation Sid.	Lancs	L. & Y.	Meols Cop.
.	.	.	.	.	.	. .	Southport Gas Works	Lancs	L. & Y.	Meols Cop.
G	P	F	L	H	C	1 15	Meopham	Kent ...	S. E. & C.	Swanley and Chatham.
.	.	.	.	.	.	. .	Longfield Siding	Kent ...	S. E. & C.	Fawkham and Meopham.
.	.	.	.	.	.	. .	Newington Vestry Siding	Kent ...	S. E. & C.	Meopham.
.	.	.	.	.	.	. .	Mercantile Colliery	Glamorg'n	P. T.	Cwmavon.
.	.	.	.	.	.	. .	Mercantile Co.'s Siding	Pembroke	G. W.	Boncath.
.	.	.	.	.	.	. .	Mercantile Pontoon Co.'s Sid.	Glamorg'n	GW—LNW—Rhy.—TV	Cardiff.
.	.	.	.	.	.	. .	Merchant's Quay	Cumb'land	L. & N. W.	See Workington.
.	.	.	.	.	.	. .	Merchiston	Edinboro'	Cal.	See Edinburgh.
.	.	.	.	.	.	. .	Merkland Street...............	Lanark ...	Glas. Dist. Sub.	See Glasgow.
.	.	.	.	.	.	. .	Merlin Iron Works	Renfrew..	Cal.	Glasgow, Whiteinch.
.	.	.	.	.	.	. .	Merrington Lane Foundry ...	Durham ...	N. E.	Spennymoor.
.	.	.	.	.	.	. .	Merrington Lane Siding	Durham ...	N. E.	Spennymoor.
.	.	.	.	.	.	. .	Merrow Siding	Surrey ...	L. & S. W.	See Clandon.
.	.	.	.	.	.	. .	Merrybent Junction	Durham ...	N. E.	Near Darlington.
.	.	.	.	.	.	. .	Merryhill Siding..............	Fife........	N. B.	See Charlestown.
.	.	.	.	.	.	. .	Merrylee's Siding	Leicester..	Mid.	Desford.
.	.	.	.	.	.	. .	Merryton Col. & Brick Works	Lanark ...	Cal.	Larkhall.
.	.	.	.	.	.	. .	Merryton Farm Siding........	Lanark ...	Cal.	Larkhall.
							Mersey & Calder Extract Co.'s			
.	.	.	.	.	.	. .	Siding	Lancs	L. & N. W.—S. & M. Jt.	Widnes.
.	.	.	.	.	.	. .	Mersey Chemical Works	Lancs	S. & M. Jt. (G. C. & Mid.)	See Pilkington's Mersey Chemical Wks., United Alkali Co. (Widnes)
.	.	.	.	.	.	. .	Mersey Copper Works	Lancs	L. & N. W.—S. & M. Jt.	Same as Bolton, T., & Son's Siding (Widnes).
.	.	.	.	.	.	. .	Mersey Manure Works.........	Lancs	S. & M. Jt. (G. C. & Mid.)	See Pilkington's Mersey Manure Wks., United Alkali Co. (Widnes)
.	.	.	.	.	.	. .	Mersey Mills Siding	Derby....	G. C.	Dinting.
.	P	.	.	.	.	. .	Mersey Road	Lancs	C. L. C. (G C, G N, & Mid.)	Garston and Liverpool.
							Mersey Tunnel Railway			
.	.	.	.	.	.	. .	Electrical Power Works ...	Cheshire...	B'head Jt—CLC—NW&L	Birkenhead.
.	.	.	.	.	.	. .	Mersey White Lead Co.'s Sid.	Lancs	L. & N. W.	Sankey Bridges.
G	P	F	L	H	C	4 0	Merstham	Surrey ...	S. E. & C.	Croydon and Red Hill.
.	.	.	.	.	.	. .	Merstham Lime Siding........	Surrey ...	S. E. & C.	Coulsdon and Merstham.
.	.	.	.	.	.	. .	Peters' Lime Siding	Surrey ...	S. E. & C.	Coulsdon and Merstham.
G	P	.	L	H	.	. .	Merstone Junction Station ...	I. of W.	I. of W. Cent.	Newport and Sandown.
							MERTHYR—			
G	.	F	L	.	.	10 0	(Station)	Glamorg'n	T. V.	Terminus.†
G	P	F	L	H	C	10 0	(Station, G. W.)	Glamorg'n	G. W.	Terminus.
									B. & M.	Over G. W. from Rhydycar Junction.
									L. & N. W.	Over G. W. from Rhydycar Junction.
									Rhy.	Over G. W. from Merthyr Joint Line Junction.
.	P	.	.	.	.	. .	(Station, G. W.)	Glamorg'n	T. V.	Over G. W. from Brandy Bridge Jn.
.	.	.	.	.	.	. .	Brandy Bridge Junction ...	Glamorg'n	G. W. & T. V. Jt.—T. V.	Merthyr and Troedyrhiew.
.	.	.	.	.	.	. .	Crawshay Bros.' Cyfarthfa Works	Glamorg'n	G. W.	Merthyr and Abernant.
									T. V.	Merthyr.
.	.	.	.	.	.	. .	Cwm Colliery	Glamorg'n	G. W. & Rhy. Jt.	Near Merthyr.
.	.	.	.	.	.	. .	Cwm Glo Colliery	Glamorg'n	G. W. & Rhy. Jt.	Near Merthyr.

EXPLANATION—G *Goods Station.*   P *Passenger and Parcel Station.*   P* *Passenger, but not Parcel or Miscellaneous Traffic.*
F *Furniture Vans, Carriages, Portable Engines, and Machines on Wheels.*   L *Live Stock.*
H *Horse Boxes and Prize Cattle Vans.*   C *Carriages by Passenger Train.*

STATION ACCOMMODATION.						CRANE POWER.		STATIONS, &c.	COUNTY.	COMPANY.	POSITION.
						Tons	Cwts	**MERTHYR**—*continued.*			
..	..	..	..	..	..		..	Cyfarthfa Crossing Junc....	Glamorg'n	G. W. & Rhy. Jt.	Merthyr and Abercanaid.
..	..	..	..	..	..		..	Cyfarthfa Junction & Iron Works	Glamorg'n	T. V.	Merthyr and Pentrebach.
..	..	..	..	..	..		..	Cyfarthfa Siding	Glamorg'n	G. W.	Merthyr and Abernant.
..	..	..	..	..	..		..	Dowlais Junction	Glamorg'n	T. V.	Merthyr and Pentrebach.
								Guest, Keen & Nettlefold—			
..	..	..	..	..	..		..	Dowlais Incline	Glamorg'n	G. W.—T. V.	Merthyr.
..	..	..	..	..	..		..	Dowlais Iron & Steel Wrks	Glamorg'n	T. V.	Merthyr and Pentrebach.
..	..	..	..	..	..		..	Dowlais Works	Glamorg'n	T. V.	Merthyr.
..	..	..	..	..	..		..	Hill's Plymouth Siding......	Glamorg'n	G. W.	Merthyr.
..	..	..	..	..	..		..	Junction	Glamorg'n	B&M&L&NW Jt.—T V	Cefn and Troedyrhiew.
..	..	..	..	..	..		..	Junction	Glamorg'n	G. W.—G. W. & Rhy. Jt.	Merthyr and Abercanaid.
..	..	..	..	..	..		..	Mardy Junction	Glamorg'n	G. W.—G. W. & T. V. Jt.	Merthyr and Troedyrhiew.
..	..	..	..	..	..		..	Merthyr Gas Works	Glamorg'n	T. V.	Near Merthyr.
..	..	..	..	..	..		..	Plymouth Works & Cols. (Duffryn Siding) (T. V.)	Glamorg'n	T. V.—G. W.	Troedyrhiew and Pentrebach.
..	..	..	..	..	..		..	Rhydycar Junction	Glamorg'n	B&M&L&NW Jt—G W	Cefn and Merthyr (G. W.).
..	..	..	..	..	..		..	Ynysfach Junction	Glamorg'n	B&M&L&NW Jt.—T V	Cefn and Troedyrhiew.
..	..	..	..	..	..		..	Merthyr Llantwit Colliery ..	Glamorg'n	S. Wales Min..............	Briton Ferry and Cymmer.
..	..	..	..	..	..		..	Merthyr Local Board Siding	Glamorg'n	T. V.	Abercynon.
..	..	..	..	..	..		..	Merthyr Vale	Glamorg'n	G. W. & Rhy. Jt.	See Aberfan (for Merthyr Vale).
G	P	..	..	..	..		..	Merthyr Vale	Glamorg'n	T. V.	Merthyr and Pontypridd.
..	..	..	..	..	..		..	Merthyr Vale Colliery (Black Lion Crossing)...............	Glamorg'n	T. V.	Merthyr Vale and Quaker's Yard.
..	..	..	..	..	..		..	Merthyr Vale Colliery	Glamorg'n	{ G. W. & Rhy. Jt. ...... / T. V.	Aberfan. / Merthyr Vale.
G	P	F	L	H	C		..	Merton Abbey..................	Surrey	L. & S.W. & L. B. & S.C. Jt.	Wimbledon and Tooting.
..	..	..	..	..	..		..	Read & Co.'s Siding	Surrey	L. & S.W. & L.B. & S.C. Jt.	Merton Abbey.
..	P	..	..	..	..		..	Merton Park	Surrey	{ L. B. & S. C. / L.&S.W.&L.B.&S.C.Jt.	Wimbledon and Mitcham. / Wimbledon and Merton Abbey.
..	..	..	..	..	..		..	Messenger's Siding	Leicester	L. & N. W.	Loughboro'.
..	..	..	..	..	..		..	Mesty Croft Sidings	Staffs	L. & N. W.	See Wednesbury.
..	..	..	..	..	..		..	Metallic Oxide Co.'s Siding...	Ayr	G. & S.W.	Irvine Harbour.
..	..	..	..	..	..		..	Metallic Tile Co.'s Siding ...	Staffs	N. S.	Chesterton.
..	..	..	..	..	..		..	Metcalfe's Siding	Lancs	L. & Y.	Church and Oswaldtwistle.
..	..	..	..	..	..		..	Metheringham	Lincoln	G. N. & G. E. Jt.	See Blankney and Metheringham.
G	P	..	L	H	..	1	10	Methil	Fife	N. B.	Branch from Thornton.
..	..	..	..	..	..		..	Calder, Dixon & Co.'s Timber Siding	Fife	N. B.	Branch from Methil.
..	..	..	..	..	..		..	Denbeath Colliery	Fife	N. B.	Branch from Methil.
..	..	..	..	..	..		..	Innerleven Salt Works......	Fife	N. B.	Branch from Methil.
G	..	..	..	..	..	25	0	Methil Dock..................	Fife	N. B.	Extension from Methil.
..	..	..	..	..	..		..	Wemyss Brick Works	Fife	N. B.	Branch from Methil.
								METHLEY—			
G	P	F	L	H	C		..	(Station)	Yorks	Meth. Jt. (GN, L&Y&NE)	Methley, L. & Y. Jn. & Stanley.
G	P	..	..	..	..		..	(Station Mid.)	Yorks	{ Mid. / L. & Y.	Leeds and Normanton. / Over Mid. from Methley Junction.
..	P	..	..	..	..		}				
..	..	..	..	..	..		..	Junction	Yorks	L. & Y.—Meth. Jt.	Methley, L.&Y.&Joint Line Stations.
..	..	..	..	..	..		..	Junction	Yorks	L. & Y.—Mid.	Methley, L. & Y. & Mid. Stations.
..	..	..	..	..	..		..	Junction	Yorks	Meth. Jt.—N. E.	Methley, Joint Line Sta. & Castleford.
..	..	..	..	..	..		..	Junction	Yorks	Mid.—N. E.	Methley, Mid. Station & Castleford.
G	P	..	L	H	..		..	Junction Station	Yorks	L. & Y.	Castleford and Methley, Mid. Junc.
..	..	..	..	..	..		..	Savile Colliery................	Yorks	Mid.	Near Methley.
G	P	F	L	H	C	3	0	Methven	Perth	Cal.	Branch Terminus near Perth.
G	..	..	..	..	..		..	Tippermallo Siding	Perth	Cal.	Methven Junction.
..	..	..	..	..	..		..	Methven Junction	Perth	Cal.	Perth and Crieff.
								Metropolitan Amalgamated Railway Carriage and Wagon Co.—			
..	..	..	..	..	..		..	Britannia Works (L.&N.W.)	Warwick	L. & N. W.—Mid.	Birmingham, Curzon Street.
..	..	..	..	..	..		..	Siding	Staffs	L. & N. W.	Spon Lane.
..	..	..	..	..	..		..	Siding	Warwick	L. & N. W.	Birmingham, Curzon Street.
..	..	..	..	..	..		..	Siding (G. C.)	Lancs	GC—GW—L&NW—Mid	Manchester, Openshaw.
..	..	..	..	..	..		..	Siding (Mid.)	Lancs	Mid.—L. & N. W.	Lancaster.
..	..	..	..	..	..		..	Works (Mid.)	Warwick	Mid.—G.W.—L. & N. W.	Birmingham, Lawley Street.
..	..	..	..	..	..		..	Metropolitan Borough of Stepney Siding	Middlesex	G. E.	London, Devonshire Street.
..	..	..	..	..	..		..	Metropolitan Brick & Tile Co.'s Siding	N'hamptn	L. & N. W.	Higham Ferrers and Irthlingboro'.
..	..	..	..	..	..		..	Metropolitan Electric Supply Co.'s Siding....................	Middlesex	L. & N. W.	London, Willesden Junction.

EXPLANATION—G *Goods Station.*   P *Passenger and Parcel Station.*   P* *Passenger, but not Parcel or Miscellaneous Traffic.*
F *Furniture Vans, Carriages, Portable Engines, and Machines on Wheels.*   L *Live Stock.*
H *Horse Boxes and Prize Cattle Vans.*   C *Carriages by Passenger Train.*

STATION ACCOMMODATION.						CRANE POWER.		STATIONS, &c.	COUNTY.	COMPANY.	POSITION.
						Tons	Cwts				
.	.	.	.	.	.	.	.	Metropolitan Junction	Surrey ...	S. E. & C.	London, Waterloo Junction Station and London Bridge.
.	.	.	.	.	.	.	.	Metropolitan Wagon Co.'s Siding (G. E.)..................	Hunts......	G E—G N—L N W—Mid.	Peterboro'.
G	P	F	L	H	C	10	0	Mexboro' (G.C.)	Yorks	{G.C. .... Mid.	Rotherham and Doncaster. Over G.C. from Swinton Junction.
.	.	.	.	.	.	.	.	Clayton's Wagon Wks. (GC)	Yorks	G. C.—Mid.	Mexboro'.
.	.	.	.	.	.	.	.	Denaby Main Colliery (GC)	Yorks	G. C.—Mid.	Mexboro'.
.	.	.	.	.	.	.	.	East Junction	Yorks	G. C.	Mexboro' and Swinton.
.	.	.	.	.	.	.	.	Hattersley Bros.' Stove Grate Works (G. C.)	Yorks	G. C.—Mid.	Mexboro'.
.	.	.	.	.	.	.	.	Manvers Main Col. (New)	Yorks	G. C.	Mexboro'.
.	.	.	.	.	.	.	.	Manvers Main Col. No. 1 Pit (Adwick Siding) (GC)	Yorks	G. C.—Mid.	Mexboro'.
.	.	.	.	.	.	.	.	Manvers Main Col. (Old)	Yorks	G. C.	Mexboro'.
.	.	.	.	.	.	.	.	South Junction	Yorks	G. C.	Wath and Swinton.
.	.	.	.	.	.	.	.	South Yorkshire Bottle Co.'s Siding	Yorks	G. C.	Mexboro'.
.	.	.	.	.	.	.	.	Verity's Wagon Works (GC)	Yorks	G. C.—Mid.	Mexboro'.
.	.	.	.	.	.	.	.	West Junction................	Yorks	G. C.	Wath and Swinton.
.	.	.	.	.	.	.	.	Mexboro' Main Collieries (Briggs, H., & Sons)	Yorks	N. E.	Castleford.
.	.	.	.	.	.	.	.	Meynell & Son's Siding........	Staffs	L. & N. W.	See Spring Vale Siding (Deepfields and Coseley).
.	.	.	.	.	.	.	.	Mica Boiler Covering Co.'s Sid	Lancs	L. & N. W.—S. & M. Jt.	Widnes.
.	.	.	.	.	.	.	.	Michael Colliery	Fife	N. B.	Wemyss Castle.
G	P	F	L	H	C	4	0	Micheldever	Hants	L. & S.W.	Basingstoke and Winchester.
G	P	F	L	H	C	0	10	Micklefield	Yorks	N. E.	Leeds and Selby.
.	.	.	.	.	.	.	.	Huddleston Siding	Yorks	N. E.	Micklefield.
.	.	.	.	.	.	.	.	Micklefield Lime Co.'s Sid.	Yorks	N. E.	Micklefield.
.	.	.	.	.	.	.	.	Newthorpe Siding	Yorks	N. E.	Micklefield.
.	.	.	.	.	.	.	.	Peckfield Colliery	Yorks	N. E.	Micklefield.
G	P	.	.	.	.	10	0	Micklehurst	Cheshire...	L. & N. W.	Huddersfield and Stalybridge.
.	.	.	.	.	.	.	.	Huddersfield Corporation Siding	Lancs	L. & N. W.	Micklehurst and Friezland.
G	P	F	L	H	C	.	.	Mickleover (for Radbourne)..	Derby	G. N.	Derby and Burton.
.	.	.	.	.	.	.	.	Micklethwaite's, R. K., Brick-yard	Yorks	G. C.	Stairfoot (for Ardsley).
.	.	.	.	.	.	.	.	Micklethwaite's, R. K., Stone Siding	Yorks	G. C.	Stairfoot (for Ardsley).
G	P	.	.	.	.	1	0	Mickleton....................	Yorks	N. E.	Barnard Castle and Middleton.
.	.	.	.	.	.	.	.	Grassholme Siding............	Yorks	N. E.	Mickleton.
.	.	.	.	.	.	.	.	Mickleton Quarry	Yorks	N. E.	Mickleton.
G	P	.	L	.	.	5	0	Mickle Trafford	Cheshire...	{ B'head Jt. (GW&LNW) C.L.C. (GC, GN, & Mid)	Chester and Helsby. Mouldsworth and Chester.
.	P*	.	.	.	.	.	.	Mickley	Northumb	N. E.	Newcastle and Carlisle.
.	.	.	.	.	.	.	.	Mickley Colliery................	Northumb	N. E.	{ Prudhoe. Stocksfield.
G	P	F	L	H	C	2	0	Midcalder.....................	Edinboro'	Cal.	Carstairs and Edinburgh.
.	.	.	.	.	.	.	.	Midcalder Junction Siding	Edinboro'	Cal.	Newpark and Midcalder.
.	.	.	.	.	.	.	.	Selm's Siding	Edinboro'	Cal.	Newpark and Midcalder.
.	.	.	.	.	.	.	.	Midcalder Junction	Edinboro'	Cal.	Newpark and Midcalder.
G	P	F	L	H	C	.	.	Mid Clyth	Caithness	High. (W. & L.)..........	Wick and Lybster.
.	.	.	.	.	.	.	.	Middle Bank Copper Works (Mid.)	Glamorg'n	Mid.—G.W.—L. & N.W.	Upper Bank.
G	P	.	.	.	.	.	.	Middle Drove	Norfolk ...	G. E.	Wisbech and Lynn.
.	.	.	.	.	.	.	.	Middle Duffryn Colliery	Glamorg'n	T. V.	Mountain Ash.
.	.	.	.	.	.	.	.	Middle Duffryn Jn. Sids.(GW)	Glamorg'n	G. W.—Rhy.	Mountain Ash.
.	.	.	.	.	.	.	.	Middleford Junction............	Lancs	L. & Y.	Hutton and Whitehouse Junction.
.	.	.	.	.	.	.	.	Middle Hulton Colliery	Lancs	L. & N. W.	Same as Bridgewater Collieries Brackley Siding (Plodder Lane).
.	.	.	.	.	.	.	.	Middlehurst's Siding	Lancs	L. & N. W.	St. Helens.
.	.	.	.	.	.	.	.	Middle Mill Siding	Montgom	Cam.	Kerry.
.	.	.	.	.	.	.	.	Middlemuir Junction	Dumbartn	N. B.	Lenzie and Kirkintilloch.
.	.	.	.	.	.	.	.	Middlemuir Junction Siding	Dumbartn	N. B.	Kirkintilloch.
.	.	.	.	.	.	.	.	Middle Peak Siding	Derby	L. & N. W.	See Hopton Wood Stone Co. (Steeplehouse).
.	.	.	.	.	.	.	.	Middle Pit Colliery	Somerset...	S. & D. Jt. (L.&S.W. & Mid)	Radstock.
G	P	F	L	H	C	10	0	Middlesbrough	Yorks	N. E.	Stockton and Redcar.
.	.	.	.	.	.	.	.	Acklam Foundry	Yorks	N. E.	Middlesbro'.
.	.	.	.	.	.	.	.	Acklam Iron Works, Coke Ovens and Wharf	Yorks	N. E.	Middlesbro'.

STATION ACCOMMODATION.						CRANE POWER.	STATIONS, &c.	COUNTY.	COMPANY.	POSITION.
						Tons Cwts.	Middlesbrough—*continued.*			
..	..	..	..	..	..		Atlas Foundry and Brick Machine Works	Yorks	N. E.	Middlesbro'.
..		..	..	..	..		Ayresome Iron Works and Wharf	Yorks	N. E.	Middlesbro'.
..		..	..	..	..		Ayrton Rolling Mills........	Yorks	N. E.	Middlesbro'.
..		..	..	..	..		Baker's Store Yard	Yorks	N. E.	Middlesbro'.
..		..	..	..	..		Bass & Co.'s Ale Stores......	Yorks	N. E.	Middlesbro'.
..		..	..	..	..		Bolckow, Vaughan & Co.'s Iron Works and Wharf...	Yorks	N. E.	Middlesbro' Dock.
					..		Bottle House Point Shipyard (Dixon, Sir Raylton, & Co.)	Yorks	N. E.	Middlesbro' Dock.
					..		Britannia Foundry, Forge, Nut and Bolt Works......	Yorks	N. E.	Middlesbro'.
					..		Britannia Iron and Steel Works and Wharf.........	Yorks	N. E.	Middlesbro'.
							Calder, Dixon & Co.'s—			
..		..	..	..	..		Commercial Street Yard	Yorks	N. E.	Middlesbro'.
..		..	..	..	..		West Whf. & Timber Yard	Yorks	N. E.	Middlesbro'.
..		..	..	..	..		Charles Street Depôts	Yorks	N. E.	Middlesbro'.
					..		Chemical Works (North Eastern Steel Works) ...	Yorks	N. E.	Middlesbro'.
..		..	..	..	..		Cleveland Bolt & Nut Co.'s Siding	Yorks	N. E.	Middlesbro'.
..		..	..	..	..		Cleveland Chemical Works	Yorks	N. E.	Middlesbro'.
..		..	..	..	..		Cleveland Chemical Works (J. Thomas, Jnr., & Co.)	Yorks	N. E.	Middlesbro' Dock.
..		..	..	..	..		Cleveland Salt Works	Yorks	N. E.	Middlesbro' Dock.
..		..	..	..	..		Cleveland Ship Yard.........	Yorks	N. E.	Middlesbro'.
..		..	..	..	..		Cleveland Slag & Concrete Works	Yorks	N. E.	Middlesbro'.
..		..	..	..	..		Cleveland Wire Mills	Yorks	N. E.	Middlesbro'.
..		..	..	..	..̤		Commercial Foundry and Engineering Works	Yorks	N. E.	Middlesbro'.
							Connal's—			
..		..	..	..	..		Acklam Warrant Store and Wharf	Yorks	N. E.	Middlesbro'.
							Ayresome Warrant Store and Wharf ....̤..	Yorks	N. E.	Middlesbro'.
..		..	..	..	..		Craggs & Sons' Wharf	Yorks	N. E.	Middlesbro'.
..		..	..	..	..		Dent, T. R. (Watson's) Whf.	Yorks	N. E.	Middlesbro'.
..		..	..	..	..		Depôt Road Boiler Works	Yorks	N. E.	Middlesbro'.
..		..	..	..	..		Diamond Grit Works.........	Yorks	N. E.	Middlesbro'.
..		..	..	..	..		Dock Street Siding	Yorks	N. E.	Middlesbro' Dock.
..		..	..	..	..		Erimus Steam Mill	Yorks	N. E.	Middlesbro'.
..		..	..	..	..̤		Griffiths' Brick Works	Yorks	N. E.	Middlesbro'.
..		..	..	..	..		Harkess, W., & Son's Ship Yard	Yorks	N. E.	Middlesbro' Dock.
..		..	..	..	..		Hill & Co.'s Storing Ground	Yorks	N. E.	Middlesbro'.
..		..	..	..	..		Linthorpe Depôts	Yorks	N. E.	Middlesbro'.
..		..	..	..	..		Linthorpe Ir. Wks. & Whf.	Yorks	N. E.	Middlesbro'.
..		..	..	..	..		Lowood's Wharncliffe Brick Works (Wharncliffe Gannister Brick Works)	Yorks	N. E.	Middlesbro'.
..		..	..	..	..		Marsh Wire Works	Yorks	N. E.	Middlesbro'.
..		..	..	..	..		Middlesbro' Ballast Line ...	Yorks	N. E.	Middlesbro'.
..		..	..	..	..		Middlesbro' Boiler Works..	Yorks	N. E.	Middlesbro'.
..		..	..	..	..		Middlesbro' Coal Depôt ...	Yorks	N. E.	Middlesbro'.
							Middlesbro' Corporation—			
..		..	..	..	..		Asylum Siding	Yorks	N. E.	Middlesbro'.
..		..	..	..	..		Wharf and Store Yard ...	Yorks	N. E.	Middlesbro'.
..		..	..	..	..	30 0	Middlesbro' Dock	Yorks	N. E.	Middlesbro'.
..		..	..	..	..		Middlesbro' Dock Electric Power Station	Yorks	N. E.	Middlesbro'.
..		..	..	..	..		Middlesbro' Engine Sheds	Yorks :...	N. E.	Middlesbro'.
..		..	..	..	..		Middlesbro' Galvanizing Works	Yorks	N. E.	Middlesbro'.
..		..	..	..	..		Middlesbro' Gas Works ...	Yorks	N. E.	Middlesbro'.
..		..	..	..	..		Middlesbro' Manure Sheds	Yorks	N. E.	Middlesbro'.
..		..	..	..	..		Middlesbro' Owners Timber Yard	Yorks	N. E.	Middlesbro' Dock.

EXPLANATION—G *Goods Station.*   P *Passenger and Parcel Station.*   P* *Passenger, but not Parcel or Miscellaneous Traffic.*
F *Furniture Vans, Carriages, Portable Engines, and Machines on Wheels.*   L *Live Stock.*
H *Horse Boxes and Prize Cattle Vans.*   C *Carriages by Passenger Train.*

STATION ACCOMMODATION.						CRANE POWER.		STATIONS, &c.	COUNTY.	COMPANY.	POSITION.
						Tons	Cwts	Middlesbrough—*continued.*			
·	·	·	·	·	·	·	·	Middlesbro' Salt Brine Pumping Works............	Yorks	N. E.	Middlesbro'.
·	·	·	·	·	·	·	·	Mildred's Depôts	Yorks	N. E.	Middlesbro'.
·	·	·	·	·	·	·	·	Newport Engine Sheds......	Yorks	N. E.	Middlesbro'.
·	·	·	·	·	·	·	·	Newport Ironworks Coke Ovens and Wharf	Yorks	N. E.	Middlesbro'.
·	·	·	·	·	·	·	·	Newport Rolling Mills	Yorks	N. E.	Middlesbro'.
·	·	·	·	·	·	·	·	Newport Wire Works	Yorks	N. E.	Middlesbro'.
·	·	·	·	·	·	·	·	North Eastern Dock Yard..	Yorks	N. E.	Middlesbro'.
·	·	·	·	·	·	·	·	North Eastern Steel and Basic Slag Works	Yorks	N. E.	Middlesbro'.
·	·	·	·	·	·	·	·	North Ormesby Road Depôts	Yorks	N. E.	Middlesbro'.
·	·	·	·	·	·	·	·	North Street Depôts	Yorks	N. E.	Middlesbro'.
·	·	·	·	·	·	·	·	North Street Engineering and Boiler Works	Yorks	N. E.	Middlesbro'.
·	·	·	·	·	·	·	·	North Street Engine Works and Scrap Yard	Yorks	N. E.	Middlesbro'.
·	·	·	·	·	·	·	·	North Street Siding	Yorks	N. E.	Middlesbro'.
·	·	·	·	·	·	·	·	Old Town Depôts	Yorks	N. E.	Middlesbro'.
·	·	·	·	·	·	·	·	Packet Wharf	Yorks	N. E.	Middlesbro'.
·	·	·	·	·	·	·	·	Packet Wharf Slate Yard...	Yorks	N. E.	Middlesbro'.
·	·	·	·	·	·	·	·	J. Harrison & Son	Yorks	N. E.	Packet Wharf Slate Yard.
·	·	·	·	·	·	·	·	J. & R. Mascall	Yorks	N. E.	Packet Wharf Slate Yard.
·	·	·	·	·	·	·	·	Patent Lubricating Bag Wks (Tees Oil & Grease Works)	Yorks	N. E.	Middlesbro'.
·	·	·	·	·	·	·	·	Pennyman's Siding	Yorks	N. E.	Middlesbro'.
·	·	·	·	·	·	·	·	Smiles Cement Works	Yorks	N. E.	Middlesbro'.
·	·	·	·	·	·	·	·	Steel Strip & Hoop Works	Yorks	N. E.	Middlesbro'.
·	·	·	·	·	·	·	·	Taylor, Sanderson & Co.'s Brick Works	Yorks	N. E.	Middlesbro'.
·	·	·	·	·	·	·	·	Tees Dock Yard and Wharf	Yorks	N. E.	Middlesbro'.
·	·	·	·	·	·	·	·	Tees Saw Mills & Timber Yd.	Yorks	N. E.	Middlesbro'.
·	·	·	·	·	·	·	·	Thomas & Co.'s Iron Yard..	Yorks	N. E.	Middlesbro'.
·	·	·	·	·	·	·	·	Toll Bar Depôt	Yorks	N. E.	Middlesbro'.
·	·	·	·	·	·	·	·	Toll Bar Siding	Yorks	N. E.	Middlesbro'.
·	·	·	·	·	·	·	·	Vulcan Boiler Works......	Yorks	N. E.	Middlesbro'.
·	·	·	·	·	·	·	·	Vulcan Street Siding	Yorks	N. E.	Middlesbro'.
·	·	·	·	·	·	·	·	Wellington Cast Steel Foundry	Yorks	N. E.	Middlesbro'.
·	·	·	·	·	·	·	·	West Bridge Depôt	Yorks	N. E.	Middlesbro'.
·	·	·	·	·	·	·	·	Westgarth's Engine Works and Wharf	Yorks	N. E.	Middlesbro'.
·	·	·	·	·	·	·	·	West Marsh Iron and Steel Works	Yorks	N. E.	Middlesbro'.
·	·	·	·	·	·	·	·	West Marsh Wharf	Yorks	N. E.	Middlesbro'.
·	·	·	·	·	·	·	·	Yorkshire Tube Works......	Yorks	N. E.	Middlesbro'.
G	P	F	L	H	C	5	0	Middleton	Lancs	L. & Y.	Branch from Middleton Junc. Sta.
·	·	·	·	·	·	·	·	Middleton & Tonge Spinning Co.'s Siding...............	Lancs	L. & Y.	Middleton.
G	P	F	·	H	C	·	·	Middleton	Norfolk ...	G. E.	Lynn and Swaffham.
G	P	·	L	H	·	·	·	Middleton	Northumb	N. B.	Reedsmouth and Morpeth.
G	P	F	L	·	·	·	·	Middleton	W'morlnd	L. & N. W.	Ingleton and Low Gill.
·	·	·	·	·	·	·	·	Middleton Branch Junction	Durham ...	N. E.	Barnard Castle and Lartington.
·	·	·	·	·	·	·	·	Middleton Colliery (Mid.) ...	Yorks	{ Mid.—N.E. { G. N.	{ Leeds, Hunslet Lane. { (See *Appendix to follow*).
·	·	·	·	·	·	·	·	Middleton Estate and Colliery Co.'s Siding...............	Yorks	G. N.	Leeds, Beeston.
·	·	·	·	·	·	·	·	Middleton Farm Siding	Renfrew ...	Cal.	Linwood.
G	P	F	L	H	C	5	0	Middleton-in-Teesdale	Yorks	N. E.	Branch near Barnard Castle.
·	·	·	·	·	·	·	·	Co-operative Society's Depôts	Yorks	N. E.	Middleton-in-Teesdale.
·	·	·	·	·	·	·	·	Lead Co.'s Saw Mill	Yorks	N. E.	Middleton-in-Teesdale.
·	·	·	·	·	·	·	·	Lunedale Whinstone Co.'s Siding	Yorks	N. E.	Middleton-in-Teesdale.
·	·	·	·	·	·	·	·	Ord & Maddison's Quarry...	Yorks	N. E.	Middleton-in-Teesdale.
·	·	·	·	·	·	·	·	Park End Quarries	Yorks	N. E.	Middleton-in-Teesdale.
·	·	·	·	·	·	·	·	Middleton Iron Works	Durham ...	N. E.	Fighting Cocks.
G	P	·	L	·	·	2	0	Middleton Junction Station...	Lancs	L. & Y.	Manchester and Castleton.
·	·	·	·	·	·	·	·	Cheetham's Siding	Lancs	L. & Y.	Middleton Junction.
·	·	·	·	·	·	·	·	Co-operative Wholesale Society's Siding	Lancs	L. & Y.	Middleton Junction and Castleton.

EXPLANATION—G *Goods Station.*   P *Passenger and Parcel Station.*   P* *Passenger, but not Parcel or Miscellaneous Traffic.*
F *Furniture Vans, Carriages, Portable Engines, and Machines on Wheels.*   L *Live Stock.*
H *Horse Boxes and Prize Cattle Vans.*   C *Carriages by Passenger Train.*

STATION ACCOMMODATION.						CRANE POWER.		STATIONS, &c.	COUNTY.	COMPANY.	POSITION.
						Tons	Cwts				
								Middleton Junction Station—*continued.*			
								Incline Sid. (Chamber Col.)	Lancs	L. & Y.	Middleton Junction and Werneth.
G	P	F	L	H	C	5	0	Middleton-on-the-Wolds	Yorks	N. E.	Market Weighton and Driffield.
								Middleton Quay Sheers	Durham	N. E.	See Tidal Basin (West Hartlepool).
								Middleton's Bone Mill Siding (G. C.)	Notts	G. C.—G. N.—Mid.	Worksop.
								Middleton Siding	Derby	L. & N. W.	Same as Spencer & Co.'s Siding (Steeplehouse).
								Middleton Siding	Salop	S & H Jt. (GW & L & NW)	Ludlow.
G	P							Middletown	Montgom	S&W'pl. Jt(GW & L&NW)	Shrewsbury and Welshpool.
								Middletown Siding	Edinboro'	N. B.	See Oxton.
G	P	F	L	H	C	1	0	Middlewich	Cheshire	L. & N. W.	Northwich and Sandbach.
								Brunner, Mond & Co.'s Newton Nos. 1 & 2 Sids.	Cheshire	L. & N. W.	Middlewich and Sandbach.
								Cooke, Verdin & Co.'s Sid.	Cheshire	L. & N. W.	Middlewich and Sandbach.
								Electrolytic Alkali Co.'s Sid.	Cheshire	L. & N. W.	Middlewich and Sandbach.
								Murgatroyd Salt Co.'s Sid.	Cheshire	L. & N. W.	Middlewich and Sandbach.
								Seddon's Siding	Cheshire	L. & N. W.	Middlewich and Sandbach.
	P							Middlewood	Cheshire	Mac. Com. (G. C. & N. S.)	Romiley and Macclesfield.
	P							Middlewood (for High Lane)	Cheshire	L. & N. W.	Buxton and Stockport.
								Middlewood Junction	Cheshire	L. & N. W. & N. S. Jt.— Mac. Com.	Buxton and Poynton.
										L. & N. W.—L. & N. W. & N. S. Jt.	Buxton and Poynton.
								Middle Works	Lancs	L. & N. W.	Same as Gidlow Jackson Sid. (Wigan).
								Middridge Colliery	Durham	N. E.	Shildon.
G	P					5	0	Midford	Somerset	S. & D. Jt. (L. & S. W. & Mid)	Radstock and Bath.
G	P		L			1	5	Midge Hall	Lancs	L. & Y.	Preston and Ormskirk.
								Midge Holme Coke Ovens	Cumb'land	N. E.	Brampton Junction. Lambley.
								Midge Holme Sidings	Cumb'land	N. E.	Brampton Junction. Lambley.
G	P	F		H	C	2	0	Midgham	Berks	G. W.	Reading and Newbury.
G	P	F	L	H	C	10	0	Midhurst	Sussex	L. & S. W.	Branch from Petersfield.
G	P	F	L	H	C	10	0		Sussex	L. B. & S. C.	Selham and Cocking.
								Midhurst Junction	Sussex	L. & S. W.—L. B. & S. C.	Midhurst, L. & S. W. & L. B. & S. C. Sta.
								Midland Brick & Terra Cotta Works	Leicester	Mid.	Coalville.
								Midland Brick Co.— Britannia Brick Works or Garrison Farm Siding	Warwick	L. & N. W.	Birmingham, Curzon Street.
								Siding	N'hampt	Mid.	Wellingboro'.
								Midland Carriage and Wagon Co.'s— Siding	Staffs	L. & N. W.	Hednesford.
								Siding (G. W.)	Salop	G. W.—L. & N. W.	Shrewsbury.
								Midland Coal, Coke, & Ir. Co.— Apedale Sidings	Staffs	N. S.	Apedale.
								Podmore Hall Colliery	Staffs	N. S.	Podmore.
								Midland Colliery	Yorks	Mid.	Woodlesford.
								Midland Co.'s Gas Works	Derby	Mid.	Chesterfield.
								Midland Engine Works (J. & H. McLaren) (Mid.)	Yorks	Mid.—N. E.	Leeds, Hunslet Lane.
										G. N.	(See Appendix to follow).
								Midland Iron Co.'s Siding	Yorks	Mid.	Masboro' and Rotherham.
								Midland Ironstone Co.'s Sid.	Lincoln	G. C.	Frodingham and Scunthorpe.
								Midland Iron Works (C. & W. Walker)	Salop	G. W.	Hollinswood.
								Midland Pottery Co.'s Siding	Lancs	L. & N. W.	St. Helens.
								Midland Railway Carriage & Wagon Co.— Sidings	Derby	Mid.	Stapleford and Sandiacre.
								Works	Cheshire	G. W.	Saltney.
								Works (Mid.)	Warwick	Mid.—G. W.—L. & N. W.	Birmingham, Lawley Street.
								Midland Railway Co.— Bonded Stores Siding	Yorks	Mid.	Sheffield, Wicker.
								Oil Gas Works	Yorks	Mid.	Sheffield, Queen's Road.
								Provender Stores	Glo'ster	Mid.	Ashchurch.
								Provender Stores	Rutland	Mid.	Oakham.
								Midland Road	Worcester	Mid.	See Worcester.
								Midland Spelter Co.'s Siding	Staffs	L. & N. W.	Pelsall.
								Midland Tin Plate Wks. (Mid.)	Glamorg'n	Mid.—G. W.—L. & N. W.	Same as Morriston Tin Plate Co.
								Midland Wagon Co.'s Siding	Glamorg'n	GW—L&NW—Rhy—TV	Cardiff.

EXPLANATION—G *Goods Station.*   P *Passenger and Parcel Station.*   P* *Passenger, but not Parcel or Miscellaneous Traffic.*
F *Furniture Vans, Carriages, Portable Engines, and Machines on Wheels.*   L *Live Stock.*
H *Horse Boxes and Prize Cattle Vans.*   C *Carriages by Passenger Train.*

STATION ACCOMMODATION.						CRANE POWER.		STATIONS, &c	COUNTY.	COMPANY.	POSITION.
						Tons	Cwts.	Midland Wagon Co.'s Siding (G. E.)	Hunts......	GE—GN—L&NW—Mid.	Peterboro'.
G	P	F	L	H	C	.	.	Midleton	Cork	G. S. & W.	Cork and Youghal.
.	.	.	.	.	.	.	.	Mid Mill Siding (J. & W. Cochrane)	Selkirk ...	N. B.	Galashiels.
G	P	.	L	.	.	1	5	Midsomer-Norton & Welton..	Somerset..	G. W.	Bristol and Radstock.
G	P	F	L	H	C	1	10			S & D Jt. (L & SW & Mid)	Shepton Mallet and Radstock.
.	.	.	.	.	.	.	.	Farrington Colliery	Somerset..	G. W.	Hallatrow and Welton.
.	.	.	.	.	.	.	.	Norton Hill Colliery	Somerset..	S. & D. Jt. (L.& S. W. & Mid)	Midsomer-Norton.
.	.	.	.	.	.	.	.	Mid Wharf Siding	Lanark ...	Cal.	Glasgow, Port Dundas.
.	.	.	.	.	.	.	.	Midwood & Son's Siding	Lancs	S. & M. Jt. (G. C. & Mid.)	Widnes.
.	.	.	.	.	.	.	.	Mierystock Siding..............	Glo'ster ...	S. & Wye Jt.(G.W. & Mid)	Lydbrook, Upper.
G	P	F	L	H	C	2	0	Milborne Port	Somerset..	L. & S.W.	Templecombe and Yeovil Junction.
.	.	.	.	.	.	.	.	Milburn's Siding	Cumb'land	L. & N. W.	Workington.
G	P	.	L	H	.	.	.	Milcote (for Weston-on-Avon and Welford-on-Avon)	Warwick..	G. W.	Stratford-on-Avon & Honeybourne.
G	P	F	L	H	C	1	10	Mildenhall	Suffolk ...	G. E.	Branch from Fordham.
.	.	.	.	.	.	.	.	Mildmay Park (N. L.)	Middlesex	N. L.—L. & N. W.	See London.
.	.	.	.	.	.	.	.	Mildred's Depôts	Yorks......	N. E.	Middlesbro'.
.	.	.	.	.	.	.	.	Mileage Yard	Middlesex	G. W.	See London, Paddington.
.	.	.	.	.	.	.	.	Mile End	Middlesex	W. & B. Jt(L.T. & S. & M.D)	See London.
.	.	.	.	.	.	.	.	Miles, E. A., Siding	Surrey ...	L. B. & S. C.	Same as Cranleigh Brick and Tile Co.'s Siding (Baynards).
.	.	.	.	.	.	.	.	Miles, Druce & Co.—			
.	.	.	.	.	.	.	.	Iron Depôt	Staffs ...	G. W.	Withymoor Basin.
.	.	.	.	.	.	.	.	Siding	Staffs ...	L. & N. W.	Albion.
.	.	.	.	.	.	.	.	Miles Platting (L. & Y.)	Lancs	L. & Y.—L. & N. W.	See Manchester.
G	P	.	L	.	.	.	.	Milford	Carlow ...	G. S. & W.	Bagnalstown and Kildare.
G	P	F	L	H	C	.	.	Milford	Surrey ...	L. & S.W.	Godalming and Petersfield.
.	.	.	.	.	.	.	.	Milford	Wilts	L. & S.W.	See Salisbury.
G	P	.	L	.	.	.	.	Milford and Brocton...........	Staffs ...	L. & N. W.	Lichfield and Stafford.
G	P	F	L	H	C	.	.			N. E.	York and Normanton.
.	P	.	.	H	C	.	.			G. C.	Over N. E. from Knottingley, Ferry Bridge Junction.
G	P	.	.	H	C	.	.	Milford Junc. Station (N. E.)	Yorks......	G. N.	Over N. E. & S. & K. Jt. Lines.
.	P	.	.	H	C	.	.			L. & Y.	Over N. E. Line.
.	P	.	.	H	C	.	.			Mid.	Over N. E. Line.
G	.	.	.	.	.	.	.	Hagg Lane Siding	Yorks......	N. E.	Milford Junction.
.	.	.	.	.	.	.	.	Hillam Gates Siding (Yorkshire Plaster Co.)	Yorks......	N. E.	Milford Junction.
.	.	.	.	.	.	.	.	Lumby Dock	Yorks......	N. E.	Milford Junction.
.	.	.	.	.	.	.	.	Smith's, J., Brewery Co.'s Siding	Yorks......	N. E.	Milford Junction.
.	.	.	.	.	.	.	.	Milford-on-Sea	Hants ...	L. & S.W.	See Milton (for Milford-on-Sea).
.	.	.	.	.	.	.	.	Milford, South	Yorks......	N. E.	See South Milford.
.	.	.	.	.	.	.	.	Milfraen Hill Colliery	Mon	L. & N. W.	See Blaenavon Iron and Coal Co. (Brynmawr).
.	.	.	.	.	.	.	.	Milgund Pit.......................	Fife	N. B.	See Lochgelly Collieries, No. 12 Siding (Lochgelly).
G	P	.	.	.	.	.	.	Milkwall	Glo'ster ...	S. & Wye Jt. (G.W. & Mid.)	Coleford and Parkend.
.	.	.	.	.	.	8	0	Dark Hill Siding	Glo'ster ...	S. & Wye Jt. (G.W. & Mid.)	Coleford Branch.
.	.	.	.	.	.	.	.	Fryer's Siding..................	Glo'ster ...	S. & Wye Jt. (G.W. & Mid.)	Milkwall.
.	.	.	.	.	.	8	0	Futterhill's Siding............	Glo'ster ...	S. & Wye Jt. (G.W. & Mid.)	Coleford Branch.
.	.	.	.	.	.	.	.	Point Quarry Sidings	Glo'ster ...	S. & Wye Jt. (G.W. & Mid.)	Coleford Branch.
.	.	.	.	.	.	.	.	Sling Branch	Glo'ster ...	S. & Wye Jt. (G.W. & Mid.)	Branch from Milkwall.
.	.	.	.	.	.	.	.	Turner's Stone Saw Mills...	Glo'ster ...	S. & Wye Jt. (G.W. & Mid.)	Milkwall.
.	.	.	.	.	.	.	.	Millbank Foundry	Yorks......	N. E.	Hartlepool.
.	.	.	.	.	.	.	.	Millbay	Devon ...	G. W.	See Plymouth.
.	.	.	.	.	.	.	.	Millbrook	Cheshire..	L. & N. W.	See Staley and Millbrook.
G	P	.	.	.	.	.	.	Millbrook	Jersey ...	Jersey	St. Helier and St. Aubin.
.	.	.	.	.	.	.	.	Millbrook (L. & S. W.)........	Hants ...	L. & S.W.—M. & S.W. Jn.	See Southampton.
G	P	F	L	H	C	.	.	Millbrook (for Ampthill)	Beds	L. & N. W.	Bedford and Bletchley.
.	.	.	.	.	.	.	.	Forder & Son's Siding	Beds	L. & N. W.	Millbrook and Bedford.
.	.	.	.	.	.	.	.	London Brick Co.'s Siding	Beds	L. & N. W.	Millbrook and Bedford.
.	.	.	.	.	.	.	.	Molesworth & Co.'s Wootton Pillinge Brick Co.'s Sid.	Beds	L. & N. W.	Millbrook and Bedford.
.	.	.	.	.	.	.	.	Millbrook Engineering Co.'s Siding	Glamorg'n	G. W.	Landore.
.	.	.	.	.	.	.	.	Millburn Chemical Works ...	Lanark ...	Cal.	Dalserf.
.	.	.	.	.	.	.	.	Millburn Colliery	Lanark ...	Cal.	Dalserf.
.	.	.	.	.	.	.	.	Millburn Junction	Inverness..	High.	Inverness and Allanfearn.
.	.	.	.	.	.	.	.	Millburn Siding	Dumbartn	D. & B. Jt. (Cal. & N. B.)	Renton.

EXPLANATION—G *Goods Station.*   P *Passenger and Parcel Station.*   P* *Passenger, but not Parcel or Miscellaneous Traffic.*
F *Furniture Vans, Carriages, Portable Engines, and Machines on Wheels.*   L *Live Stock.*
H *Horse Boxes and Prize Cattle Vans.*   C *Carriages by Passenger Train.*

STATION ACCOMMODATION.						CRANE POWER.		STATIONS, &c.	COUNTY.	COMPANY.	POSITION.
						Tons	Cwts.				
.	.	.	.	.	.			Millcroft Brick Works	Lanark	Cal.	Glasgow, South Side.
.	.	.	.	.	.			Miller & Co.'s Siding	Edinboro'	N. B.	Same as London Road Foundry (Edinburgh).
G	P	.	L	H	C	1	5	Millerhill	Edinboro'	N. B.	Portobello and Hardengreen.
.	.	.	.	.	.			Millerhill Junction	Edinboro'	N. B.	Millerhill and Eskbank.
.	.	.	.	.	.			Miller's Brass Foundry	Durham	N. E.	South Shields.
G	P	F	L	H	C	2	0	Miller's Dale	Derby	Mid.	New Mills and Rowsley.
.	.	.	.	.	.			Buxton Central Lime Co.'s Siding	Derby	Mid.	Near Miller's Dale.
								Buxton Lime Firms Co.—			
.	.	.	.	.	.			Ashwood Dale Siding	Derby	Mid.	Miller's Dale and Buxton.
.	.	.	.	.	.			Buxton Central Works	Derby	Mid.	Miller's Dale and Peak Forest.
.	.	.	.	.	.			East Buxton Siding	Derby	Mid.	Near Miller's Dale.
.	.	.	.	.	.			Miller's Dale Lime Sids.	Derby	Mid.	Near Miller's Dale.
.	.	.	.	.	.			Peak Forest Stone Siding	Derby	Mid.	Peak Forest Junction.
.	.	.	.	.	.			Topley Pike Stone Quarry (Newton, Chambers & Co.)	Derby	Mid.	Near Miller's Dale.
.	.	.	.	.	.			Miller's Dale Lime Siding	Derby	Mid.	See Buxton Lime Firms Co. (Miller's Dale).
G	P	.	L	.	.	5	0	Millfield	Durham	N. E.	Sunderland and Pallion.
.	.	.	.	.	.			Bishopwearmouth Steam Mills	Durham	N. E.	Millfield.
.	.	.	.	.	.			Chapman's Steam Bakery	Durham	N. E.	Millfield.
.	.	.	.	.	.			Dowson's Slate Yard	Durham	N. E.	Millfield.
.	.	.	.	.	.			Greener's Glass Works	Durham	N. E.	Millfield.
.	.	.	.	.	.			Jobling's Cask Yard	Durham	N. E.	Millfield.
.	.	.	.	.	.			Millfield Landsale	Durham	N. E.	Millfield.
.	.	.	.	.	.			West End Landsale Depôts	Durham	N. E.	Millfield.
.	.	.	.	.	.			Millfield Depôts	Durham	N. E.	Stockton, North Shore.
.	.	.	.	.	.			Millfield Grange Colliery	Durham	N. E.	Butterknowle.
.	.	.	.	.	.			Millfield Junction	Staffs	N. S.	Longton and Blyth Bridge.
.	.	.	.	.	.			Millfield Sidings	Staffs	N. S.	Longton.
G	P	.	.	.	.			Mill Hill	I. of W.	I. of W. Cent.	Newport and Cowes.
G	P							Mill Hill	Middlesex	G. N.	Finchley and Edgware.
G	P	F	L	H	C	1	10	Mill Hill	Middlesex	Mid.	London and St. Albans.
.	.	.	.	.	.			Mill Hill Gas Works	Middlesex	G. N.	Mill Hill.
.	.	.	.	.	.			War Office Barracks Siding	Middlesex	G. N.	Mill Hill.
G	P	.	.	.	.	8	0	Mill Hill (L. & Y.)	Lancs	L. & Y.	Blackburn and Cherry Tree.
.	P									L. & N. W.	Over L. & Y. from Cherry Tree Jn.
.	P	.	.	.	.			Mill Hill Park	Middlesex	Met. Dist.	Chiswick Park & Ealing Common.
.	.	.	.	.	.			Mill Houses & Ecclesall	Derby	Mid.	See Sheffield.
G	P	F	L	H	C	3	0	Milliken Park	Renfrew	G. & S. W.	Paisley and Dalry.
.	.	.	.	.	.			Milling Co.'s Works	Devon	G. W.	Marsh Mills.
.	.	.	.	.	.			Millington & Son's Siding	Middlesex	G. E.	London, Tottenham.
.	.	.	.	.	.			Millington's Siding	Salop	L. & N. W.	Oakengates.
.	.	.	.	.	.			Millington's Works	Salop	G. W.	Oakengates.
G	P	.	L	H	.			Millisle	Wigtown.	P.P.&W.Jt.(Cal., G&SW, L. & N. W., & Mid.)	Newton Stewart and Whithorn.
.	.	.	.	.	.			Mill Lands Brick & Tile Wks.	Glamorg'n	G. W.	Neath.
.	.	.	.	.	.			Mill Lane Junction	Yorks	G. N.—L. & Y.	Bradford.
.	.	.	.	.	.			Mill Lane Mining Co.'s Siding	Lancs	L. & N. W.	Rainford Village.
.	.	.	.	.	.			Mill Lane Siding	Lancs	L. & N. W.	See Pilkington's (Rainford Village).
G	P	F	L	H	C	5	0	Millom	Cumb'land	Furness	Foxfield and Drigg.
.	.	.	.	.	.			Millom & Askam Iron Co.'s Ullbank Branch	Cumb'land	WC&EJt(Fur & L & NW)	Gillfoot.
G	.	.	.	.	.			Millom Iron Works	Cumb'land	Furness	Branch from Millom.
.	.	.	.	.	.			Hodbarrow Mineral Siding	Cumb'land	Furness	Near Millom Iron Works.
.	.	.	.	.	.			Mill Road Wharf	Cambs	Mid.	See Cambridge.
.	.	.	.	.	.			Mills & Son's Siding	Northumb	N. E.	Newcastle-on-Tyne.
G	.	.	.	.	.			Mill Street	Glamorg'n	G. W.	Hirwain and Dare Junction.
.	.	.	.	.	.			Mill Street	Staffs	L. & N. W.	See Wolverhampton.
.	.	.	.	.	.			Mill Street Mileage & Coal Sidings (G. W.)	Mon	G. W.—L. & N. W.	See Newport.
.	.	.	.	.	.			Mill Street Tin Works	Glamorg'n	T. V.	Same as Cynon Tin Plate Works (Aberdare).
G	P	F	L	H	C	.	.	Millstreet	Cork	G. S. & W.	Mallow and Killarney.
.	.	.	.	.	.			Millthorpe Siding	Lincoln	G. N.	Billingboro'.
G	P	.	.	H	.			Milltimber	Aberdeen	G. N. of S.	Aberdeen and Banchory.
.	P	.	.	.	.			Milltown	Dublin	D. W. & W.	Dublin, Harcourt Street and Bray.
G	P	.	L	.	.	1	0	Milltown	Galway	G. S. & W.	Tuam and Claremorris.
.	P	.	.	.	.			Milltown	Kerry	G. S. & W.	Farranfore and Valentia Harbour.
.	P	.	.	.	.			Millvale	Armagh	B. & Newry	Bessbrook and Newry.

EXPLANATION—G *Goods Station.*   P *Passenger and Parcel Station.*   P* *Passenger, but not Parcel or Miscellaneous Traffic.*
F *Furniture Vans, Carriages, Portable Engines, and Machines on Wheels.*   L *Live Stock.*
H *Horse Boxes and Prize Cattle Vans.*   C *Carriages by Passenger Train.*

Station Accommodation.						Crane Power.		Stations, &c.	County.	Company.	Position.
						Tons	Cwts				
.	.	.	.	.	.	.	.	Millwall Docks	Middlesex	{ G. E.—G. N.—G. W.— L.&N. W—Mid.—N.L. }	} See London.
.	.	.	.	.	.	.	.	Millwall Docks Junction (Harrow Lane)	Middlesex	G. E.—N. L.	{ London, Millwall Docks Junction Station and Poplar.
G	P	F	L	H	C	1	5	Millwood Siding	Lancs	Furness.	Dalton.
.	.	.	.	.	.	.	.	Milnathort	Kinross	N. B.	Kinross Junction and Ladybank.
.	.	.	.	.	.	.	.	Milnathort Spinning Co.'s Siding	Kinross	N. B.	Milnathort.
.	.	.	.	.	.	.	.	Milne & McDonald's Siding	Dumfries	Cal.	Lockerbie.
.	.	.	.	.	.	.	.	Milner Royd Junction	Yorks	L. & Y.	Sowerby Bridge and Copley.
.	.	.	.	.	.	.	.	Milnes & Co.'s Castle Car Works	Salop	L. & N. W.	Wombridge.
G	P	F	L	H	C	3	0	Milne's Siding	Forfar	Cal.	Montrose.
.	.	.	.	.	.	.	.	Milngavie	Dumbartn	N. B.	Branch from Milngavie Junction.
.	.	.	.	.	.	.	.	Burnbrae Dye Works	Dumbartn	N. B.	Bearsden and Milngavie.
.	.	.	.	.	.	.	.	Ellangowan Paper Mills	Dumbartn	N. B.	Milngavie.
.	.	.	.	.	.	.	.	Milngavie Junction	Dumbartn	N. B.	Glasgow.
.	.	.	.	.	.	.	.	Miln House Quarry	Durham	N. E.	Frosterley.
.	.	.	.	.	.	.	.	Milnquarter Brick Works (Stein's)	Stirling	N. B.	Bonnybridge (E. & G.).
G	P	.	L	.	.	5	0	Milnrow	Lancs	L. & Y.	Oldham and Rochdale.
.	.	.	.	.	.	.	.	Milnsbridge	Yorks	L. & N. W.	See Huddersfield, Longwood and Milnsbridge.
G	P	F	L	H	C	3	0	Milnthorpe	W'morlnd	L. & N. W.	Lancaster and Penrith.
.	.	.	.	.	.	.	.	Sedgwick's Siding	W'morlnd	L. & N. W	Milnthorpe and Oxenholme.
.	.	.	.	.	.	.	.	Wakefield & Co.'s Siding	W'morlnd	L. & N. W.	Milnthorpe.
.	.	.	.	.	.	.	.	Milnthorpe's Malt Kiln	Yorks	{ G. C. { W. R.& G Jt (G.C.&G.N.)	Barnby Dun. Bramwith.
.	.	.	.	.	.	.	.	Milnthorpe's Siding	Yorks	N. E.	Goole.
.	.	.	.	.	.	.	.	Milnwood Colliery	Lanark	Cal.	Bellshill.
.	.	.	.	.	.	.	.	Milnwood Iron & Steel Works	Lanark	Cal.	Mossend.
.	.	.	.	.	.	.	.	Milnwood Junction	Lanark	Cal.	Motherwell and Mossend.
.	.	.	.	.	.	.	.	Milton	Hants	L. & S.W.	See New Milton (for Milford-on-Sea).
G	P	.	.	.	.	.	.	Milton	Kent	S. E. & C.	See Sittingbourne and Milton.
.	.	.	.	.	.	.	.	Milton	Staffs	N. S.	Stoke and Leek.
G	P	.	L	.	.	2	0	Hardman's Chemical Wks.	Staffs	N. S.	Milton.
.	.	.	.	.	.	.	.	Milton	Stirling	N. B.	Kirkintilloch and Lennoxtown.
.	.	.	.	.	.	.	.	Glorat Lime Siding	Stirling	N. B.	Milton and Lennoxtown.
.	.	.	.	.	.	.	.	Kincaid Print Works	Stirling	N. B.	Kirkintilloch and Milton.
.	.	.	.	.	.	.	.	Lilyburn Print Works	Stirling	N. B.	Milton and Lennoxtown.
.	.	.	.	.	.	.	.	Milton Brick Works	Lanark	Cal.	Carluke.
.	.	.	.	.	.	.	.	Milton Collieries	Lanark	Cal.	Motherwell.
.	.	.	.	.	.	.	.	Milton Colliery	Lanark	Cal.	Carluke.
.	.	.	.	.	.	.	.	Milton Forge and Engineering Works	Durham	N. E.	West Hartlepool.
.	.	.	.	.	.	.	.	Milton Hall Brick Co.'s Sid.	Essex	G. E.	Southend-on-Sea.
.	.	.	.	.	.	.	.	Milton Iron Foundry	Yorks	G. C.	Elsecar.
.	.	.	.	.	.	.	.	Milton Junction	Lanark	Cal.	Steps Road and St. Rollox.
.	.	.	.	.	.	.	.	Milton Junction	Staffs	N. S.	Bucknall and Ford Green.
.	.	.	.	.	.	.	.	Milton of Campsie	Stirling	N. B.	Same as Milton.
.	P	.	.	.	.	.	.	Milton Paper Co.'s Siding	Dumbartn	N. B.	Same as Dumbuck Sid. (Bowling).
.	.	.	.	.	.	.	.	Milton Road	Somerset	W. C. & P.	Weston-super-Mare and Clevedon.
.	.	.	.	.	.	.	.	Milton Saw Mills (Willson's)	Durham	N. E.	West Hartlepool.
.	.	.	.	.	.	.	.	Milton Siding	Forfar	D. & A. Jt. (Cal. & N. B.)	See Monifieth.
G	P	F	L	.	.	.	.	Milton Works (N. B.)	Dumbartn	N. B.—Cal.	Jamestown.
G	P	.	L	.	.	1	10	Miltown Malbay	Clare	West Clare	Ennis and Kilkee.
G	P	F	L	.	.	.	.	Milverton	Somerset	G. W.	Taunton and Wiveliscombe.
.	.	.	.	.	.	.	.	Milverton	Warwick	L. & N. W.	See Warwick.
G	P	F	L	H	.	2	0	Mindrum	Northumb	N. E.	Coldstream and Alnwick.
G	.	.	.	.	.	3	0	Kilham Siding	Northumb	N. E.	Mindrum.
G	P	F	L	H	C	.	.	Minehead	Somerset	G. W.	Branch from Norton-Fitzwarren.
G	.	.	.	.	.	.	.	Minera	Denbigh	G. W.	Branch from Wrexham.
.	.	.	.	.	.	.	.	Berwig Quarry	Denbigh	G. W.	Coed Poeth and Minera.
.	.	.	.	.	.	.	.	Lester's Minera Lime Co.	Denbigh	G. W.	End of Minera Branch.
.	.	.	.	.	.	.	.	United Minera Mining Co.	Denbigh	G. W.	End of Minera Branch.
.	.	.	.	.	.	.	.	Vicarage Siding	Denbigh	G. W.	Coed Poeth and Minera.
G	P	F	L	H	C	1	10	Minety	Wilts	G. W.	Swindon and Gloucester.
G	P	.	.	.	.	.	.	Minffordd	Merioneth	{ Cam. { Festiniog	Harlech and Portmadoc. Portmadoc and Penrhyn.
G	P	.	L	.	C	5	0				
.	.	.	.	.	.	.	.	Minffordd Exchange Sidings	Merioneth	Cam.—Festiniog	Minffordd.
G	.	.	.	.	.	.	.	Minkie Road	Carmarth'	Gwen. Valleys	Kidwelly Jn. and Mynydd-y-Garreg.
.	.	.	.	.	.	.	.	Minninglow Siding	Derby	L. & N. W.	Longcliffe.

Explanation—G Goods Station.　　P Passenger and Parcel Station.　　P* Passenger, but not Parcel or Miscellaneous Traffic.
F Furniture Vans, Carriages, Portable Engines, and Machines on Wheels.　　L Live Stock.
H Horse Boxes and Prize Cattle Vans.　　C Carriages by Passenger Train.

Station Accommodation						Crane Power		Stations, &c.	County.	Company.	Position.
						Tons	Cwts				
						.	.	Minories Junction	Middlesex	Met. & Met. Dist. Jt. ...	London, Aldgate and Mark Lane.
	P					.	.	Minshull Vernon	Cheshire	L. & N. W.	Crewe and Warrington.
	P*					.	.	Minster (Sheppey)	Kent	S. E. & C. (Sheppey)	Sheerness and Eastchurch.
						.	.	Brambledown Siding	Kent	S. E. & C. (Sheppey)	Minster (Sheppey) and Eastchurch.
G	P	F	L	H	C	.	.	Minster (Thanet)	Kent	S. E. & C.	Canterbury and Ramsgate.
						.	.	Minster, East	Kent	S. E. & C. (Sheppey)	See East Minster-on-Sea.
G	P	F	L	H	C	5	0	Minsterley	Salop	S. &W'pl Jt (GW&LNW)	Branch from Hanwood.
						.	.	Bayliss, Jones & Bayliss' Sid	Salop	S. &W'pl Jt (GW&LNW)	Minsterley and Pontesbury.
G	P	F	L	H	C	1	5	Mintlaw	Aberdeen	G. N. of S.	Maud and Peterhead.
						.	.	Minto Colliery	Fife	N. B.	Cardenden.
						.	.	Mint Street	Middlesex	G. N.	See London, Royal Mint Street.
						.	.	Mirehouse Junction	Cumb'land	Furness—W. C. & E. Jt.	Whitehaven.
						.	.	Mirfield	Yorks	L. & N. W.	See Battyeford and Mirfield.
						.	.			{ L. & Y.	Brighouse and Thornhill.
G	P	F	L	H	C	5	0	Mirfield (L. & Y.)	Yorks	{ G. N.—L. & N. W.	Over L. & Y. Line.
						.	.	Hurst's, W., Siding (L&Y)	Yorks	L.&Y.—G.N.--L.&N.W.	Mirfield and Cleckheaton.
						.	.	L. & Y. Co.'s Locomotive Sid	Yorks	L. & Y.	Mirfield.
						.	.	Sutcliffe's Malt Kiln (L&Y)	Yorks	L. & Y.—G N—L & N W	Mirfield and Cooper Bridge.
						.	.	Mirfield Coal Co.—			
						.	.	Siding	Yorks	L. & N. W.	Ravensthorpe and Thornhill.
						.	.	Siding (L. & Y.)	Yorks	L. & Y.—L. & N. W.	Northorpe.
						.	.	Miskin Colliery	Glamorg'n	T. V.	Mountain Ash.
						.	.	Miskin's Siding	Kent	S. E. & C.	Sharnal Street.
						.	.	Misk Pit	Ayr	Cal.—G. & S. W.	Kilwinning.
G		F	L			5	0	Mislingford	Hants	L. & S. W.	Droxford and Wickham.
G	P	F	L	H	C	5	0	Misterton	Notts	G. N. & G. E. Jt.	Doncaster and Gainsboro'.
						.	.	Misterton Gas Works	Notts	G. N. & G. E. Jt.	Misterton.
						.	.	Newell & Co.'s Siding	Notts	G. N. & G. E. Jt.	Misterton and Walkeringham.
G						10	0	Stockwith Siding	Notts	G. N. & G. E. Jt.	Bch.—Misterton & Walkeringham.
G	P	F		H	C	1	10	Mistley	Essex	G. E.	Manningtree and Harwich.
						.	.	Edme Siding	Essex	G. E.	Mistley.
						.	.	Free, Rodwell & Co.'s Sid.	Essex	G. E.	Mistley.
						.	.	Tendring Hundred Water Works	Essex	G. E.	Mistley.
G	P					5	0	Mitcham	Surrey	L. B. & S. C.	Wimbledon and West Croydon.
						.	.	Hall & Co.'s Siding	Surrey	L. B. & S. C.	Mitcham.
	P					.	.	Mitcham Junction Station ...	Surrey	L. B. & S. C.	Wimbledon and Croydon.
						.	.	Deed & Son's Siding	Surrey	L. B. & S. C.	Mitcham Junction.
G	P		L			1	10	Mitcheldean Road	Hereford	G. W.	Gloucester and Hereford.
						.	.	Mitchell and Butler's Siding	Warwick	L. & N. W.	Birmingham, Monument Lane.
						.	.	Mitchell Main Colliery	Yorks	G. C.	Wombwell.
						.	.	Mitchell, T., & Son's Siding..	Yorks	Mid.	Keighley.
						.	.	Mitchell's Bettisfield Colliery	Flint	L. & N. W.	Bagillt.
						.	.	Mitchell's, W., Siding	Warwick	Mid.	Birmingham, Lawley Street.
G	P	F	L	H	C	.	.	Mitchelstown	Cork	G. S. & W.	Branch from Fermoy.
						.	.	Mitre Bridge	Middlesex	L. & N. W.	See London.
G	P	F	L	H	C	1	10	Moate	W'meath	M. G. W.	Mullingar and Athlone.
	P					.	.	Moat Lane Junction Station	Montgom	Cam.	Newtown and Machynlleth.
						.	.	Moat Quarry	Cumb'land	N. B.	Riddings Junction Station.
G	P		L	H		5	0	Mobberley	Cheshire	C. L. C. (GC, GN, & Mid.)	Altrincham and Northwich.
						.	.	Mobberley & Perry's Siding	Worcester	G. W.	Cradley Heath and Cradley.
	P					.	.	Mochdre and Pabo	Carnarvon	L. & N. W.	Bangor and Rhyl.
						.	.	Moderator Sidings	Mon	G. W.	Newport, Dock Street.
						.	.	Moelferna & Deeside Slate Qry	Merioneth	G. W.	Glyndyfrdwy.
						.	.	Moel-gilau Colliery	Glamorg'n	P. T.	Lletty Brongu.
G	P	F	L	H	C	5	0	Moffat	Dumfries	Cal.	Branch near Beattock.
						.	.	Moffat Paper Mills Siding ...	Lanark	N. B.	Clarkston.
G	P		L	H		.	.	Mogeely	Cork	G. S. & W.	Cork and Youghal.
	P					.	.	Mogridge's Siding	Lancs	P.&W.Jt.(L&Y&L&NW)	Lytham.
G	P		L			.	.	Mohill	Leitrim	C. & L.	Ballinamore and Dromod.
G	P		L			2	10	Moira	Antrim	G. N. (I.)	Belfast and Portadown.
G	P					.	.	Moira	Leicester	A & N Jt.(L & N W & Mid.)	See Overseal and Moira.
G	P					1	10	Moira (Mid.)	Leicester	{ Mid.	Burton and Ashby.
G	P									{ L. & N. W.	Over Mid. from Overseal & Moira Jn.
						.	.	Donington Sanitary Pipe & Fire Brick Co.'s Sid. (Mid)	Leicester	Mid.—L. & N. W.	Near Moira.
						.	.	Haywood & Co.'s Pipe Works (Mid.)	Leicester	Mid.—L. & N. W.	Near Moira.
						.	.	Moira Colliery Co.—			
						.	.	Church Gresley Col. (Mid.)	Derby	Mid.—L. & N. W.	Near Moira.
						.	.	Rawdon Colliery (Mid.)	Leicester	Mid.—L. & N. W.	Near Moira.
						.	.	Reservoir Colliery (Mid.)	Leicester	Mid.—L. & N. W.	Near Moira.

STATION ACCOMMODATION.						CRANE POWER.	STATIONS, &c.	COUNTY.	COMPANY.	POSITION.
						Tons Cwts	Moira (Mid.)—continued.			
.	.	.	.	.	.	. .	Robinson & Dowler's Wadland's Canal Wharf (Mid.)	Derby	Mid.—L. & N. W.........	Near Moira.
.	.	.	.	.	.	. .	Sutton & Co.'s Siding (Mid.)	Leicester..	Mid.—L. & N. W.........	Near Moira.
.	.	.	.	.	.	. .	Tugby & Co.'s Pipe Works (Mid.)	Leicester..	Mid.—L. & N. W.........	Near Moira.
G	P	.	L	.	.	10 0	Molahiffe	Kerry	G. S. & W.	Farranfore and Valentia Harbour.
G	P	F	L	H	C	10 0	Mold	Flint	L. & N. W.	Chester and Denbigh
.	.	.	.	.	.	. .	Alyn Steel Tin Plate Works	Flint	L. & N. W.	Mold and Rhydymwyn.
.	.	.	.	.	.	. .	Mold Gas & Water Co.'s Bromfield Hall Siding ...	Flint	L. & N. W.	Mold and Llong.
.	.	.	.	.	.	. .	Parry & Co.'s Altami or Mold Argoed Siding	Flint	L. & N. W.	Mold and Llong.
.	.	.	.	.	.	. .	Mold Argoed Siding	Flint	L. & N. W.	Same as Parry & Co.'s Altami Siding (Mold).
G	.	.	.	.	.	. .	Mold Jn. (near Saltney Whf.)	Flint	L. & N. W.	Chester and Rhyl.
.	.	.	.	.	.	. .	Mold Junc. (Saltney Ferry)..	Flint	L. & N. W.	See Saltney Ferry (Mold Junction).
.	.	.	.	.	.	. .	Molesworth & Co.'s Wootton Pillinge Brick Co.'s Siding	Beds	L. & N. W.	Millbrook (for Ampthill).
.	.	.	.	.	.	. .	Molesworth & Springthorpe's Siding	Rutland ...	Mid.	Luffenham.
.	.	.	.	.	.	. .	Molland	Devon	G. W.	See Bishops Nympton & Molland.
.	.	.	.	.	.	. .	Moller's Timber Yard	Durham ...	N. E.	Sunderland, South Dock.
G	P	.	.	.	.	. .	Mollington	Cheshire...	B'head Jt. (GW&L&NW)	Chester and Hooton.
G	P	.	.	.	.	5 0	Molyneux Brow	Lancs	L. & Y.	Clifton Jn. Station & Ringley Road.
.	.	.	.	.	.	. .	Molyneux Junction	Lancs	L. & Y.—L. & N. W. ...	See Clifton (Molyneux) Junction.
.	.	.	.	.	.	. .	Monachdy or Monachty Col.	Glamorg'n	T. V.	Same as Mynachdy Col. (Ynysybwl).
G	P	F	L	H	C	4 10	Monaghan	Monaghan	G. N. (I.)	Clones and Armagh.
G	P	.	L	.	.	. .	Monaghan Road	Monaghan	G. N. (I.)	Dundalk and Clones.
G	P	F	L	H	C	. .	Monasterevan	Kildare ...	G. S. & W.	Kildare and Portarlington.
.	.	.	.	.	.	. .	Monckton Main Colliery	Yorks	{ G. C. ... H. & B. ... Mid.	Notton and Royston. / Cudworth, North. / Royston and Notton.
.	.	.	.	.	.	. .	Monckton's Siding...............	N'hamptn	L. & N. W.	Wakerley and Barrowden.
.	P	.	.	.	.	. .	Mond Nickel Co.'s Sid. (Mid.)	Glamorg'n	Mid.—G. W.—L. & N. W.	Clydach-on-Tawe.
.	P	.	.	.	.	. .	Moneycarrie	Derry	N. C. Com. (Mid.)	Garvagh and Aghadowey.
G	P	.	L	H	.	2 0	Moneymore	Derry	N. C. Com. (Mid.)	Cookstown Junction & Cookstown.
G	P	F	L	H	.	2 0	Monifieth	Forfar	D. & A. Jt. (Cal. & N. B.)	Dundee and Arbroath.
G	.	.	.	.	.	. .	Low & Duff's Siding	Forfar	D. & A. Jt. (Cal. & N. B.)	Monifieth.
G	.	.	.	.	.	. .	Milton Siding	Forfar	D. & A. Jt. (Cal. & N. B.)	Monifieth and Broughty Ferry.
G	P	.	L	H	.	2 0	Monikie	Forfar	Cal.	Dundee and Forfar.
.	.	.	.	.	.	. .	Monk & Newells..................	Denbigh...	G. W.	Ruabon.
.	P	.	.	.	.	. .	Monk Bretton.....................	Yorks	Mid.	Cudworth and Barnsley.
.	.	.	.	.	.	. .	Monk Bretton Colliery	Yorks	H. & B.	Cudworth, North.
.	.	.	.	.	.	. .	Monk Bretton Colliery (Mid.)	Yorks	Mid—† H. B.	Cudworth.
.	.	.	.	.	.	. .	Monk Bretton Junction	Yorks	H. & B.—Mid.	Cudworth & Monk Bretton Station.
.	.	.	.	.	.	. .	Monk Bridge Iron Works (G. N. & N. E. Jt.)	Yorks	{ G. N. & N.E. Jt.—G. C. —L. & N. W.	} Leeds, Wellington Street.
.	.	.	.	.	.	. .	Monk Bridge Iron Wks.(Mid.)	Yorks	{ Mid.—L.&N.W.—N.E. G. N.	Leeds, Hunslet Lane. / (See Appendix to follow).
.	.	.	.	.	.	. .	Monkhill	Yorks	L. & Y.	See Pontefract.
.	.	.	.	.	.	. .	Monkland Collieries	Lanark ...	Cal.	Calderbank.
.	.	.	.	.	.	. .	Monkredding Quarry	Ayr	G. & S.W.	Same as Redstone Quarry (Montgreenan).
.	.	.	.	.	.	. .	Monk's Abbey Siding (G.C.)	Lincoln ...	G. C.— Mid.	Lincoln.
G	P	.	.	.	.	1 10	Monkseaton.......................	Northumb	N. E.	Tynemouth and Morpeth.
.	.	.	.	.	.	. .	Red House Siding	Northumb	N. E.	Monkseaton.
.	.	.	.	.	.	. .	Monk's Ferry Coal Co.'s Sid.	Cheshire...	B'head Jt. (G W & L N W)	Birkenhead, Cathcart Street.
.	.	.	.	.	.	. .	Monk's Ferry Shipbuilding Yard (Birkenhead Jt.)	Cheshire...	B'head Jt.—C.L.C.	See Cammell, Laird & Co. (B'head).
.	.	.	.	.	.	. .	Monks, Hall & Co.— Albion Iron Works	Lancs	L. & N. W.	Wigan.
.	.	.	.	.	.	. .	Siding	Lancs	L. & N. W.	Warrington, Arpley.
.	.	.	.	.	.	. .	Monk's Quarry Siding	Mon	G. W.	Llanhilleth.
G	P	.	.	.	.	. .	Monkstown	Cork	C. B. & P.	Cork and Carrigaline.
G	P	F	L	H	C	2 0	Monkton	Ayr	G. & S.W.	Troon and Ayr.
G	.	.	.	.	.	. .	Clune Siding	Ayr	G. & S.W.	Monkton and Annbank.
.	.	.	.	.	.	. .	Monkton Sand Lye	Ayr	G. & S.W.	Monkton and Troon.
.	.	.	.	.	.	. .	Monkton Depôts.................	Durham ...	N. E.	Jarrow.
.	.	.	.	.	.	. .	Monktonhall Junction	Edinboro'	N. B.	New Hailes and Smeaton.
.	.	.	.	.	.	. .	Monkton Junction...............	Ayr	G. & S.W.	Monkton and Prestwick.
.	.	.	.	.	.	. .	Monkwearmouth	Durham ...	N. E.	See Sunderland.

EXPLANATION—G *Goods Station.*   P *Passenger and Parcel Station.*   P* *Passenger, but not Parcel or Miscellaneous Traffic.*
F *Furniture Vans, Carriages, Portable Engines, and Machines on Wheels.*   L *Live Stock.*
H *Horse Boxes and Prize Cattle Vans.*   C *Carriages by Passenger Train.*   † *For local traffic only.*

STATION ACCOMMODATION.						CRANE POWER.		STATIONS, &c.	COUNTY.	COMPANY.	POSITION.
						Tons	Cwts.				
.	.	.	.	.	.	.	.	Monkwearmouth Fire-Brick Works	Durham ...	N. E.	Sunderland, Monkwearmouth.
.	.	.	.	.	.	.	.	Monkwearmouth Junction ...	Durham ...	N. E.	Monkwearmouth and East Boldon.
.	.	.	.	.	.	.	.	Monmore Green	Staffs	L. & N. W.	See Wolverhampton.
								MONMOUTH—			
.	P	.	.	.	.	.	.	Gas Works	Mon	G. W.	Monmouth and Symonds Yat.
.	P	.	.	.	.	.	.	May Hill	Mon	G. W.	Troy and Ross.
.	.	.	.	.	.	.	.	Saw Mills Siding	Mon	G. W.	Monmouth and Symonds Yat.
G	P	F	L	H	C	10	0	Troy	Mon	G. W.	Pontypool Road and Ross.
.	.	.	.	.	.	.	.	Monmouthshire Steel & Tin Plate Co.'s Siding	Mon	G. W.	Same as Pontymister Steel Works (Risca).
.	P	.	.	.	.	.	.	Monsal Dale	Derby......	Mid.	Millers Dale and Rowsley.
.	.	.	.	.	.	.	.	Monsal Dale Siding	Derby......	Mid.	Hassop.
G	P	.	L	.	.	10	0	Montacute	Somerset...	G. W.	Martock and Yeovil.
.	.	.	.	.	.	.	.	Montague Colliery	Northumb	N. E.	Lemington.
.	.	.	.	.	.	.	.	Montague Smith & Co.'s Sid.	Norfolk ...	Mid. & G. N. Jt.	Yarmouth Beach.
.	.	.	.	.	.	.	.	Monteith's Siding	Lanark ...	Cal.	Carstairs.
.	.	.	.	.	.	.	.	Montgomerie & Strachan's Sid	Lanark ...	Cal.	Glasgow, South Side.
G	P	F	L	H	C	8	0	Montgomery	Montgom	Cam.	Welshpool and Newtown.
G	P	F	L	H	C	2	0	Montgreenan	Ayr	G. & S. W.	Dalry and Kilmarnock.
.	.	.	.	.	.	.	.	Redstone Quarry (Monk-redding Quarry)	Ayr	G. & S. W.	Montgreenan and Dalry.
.	P	.	.	.	.	.	.	Monton Green	Lancs	L. & N. W.	Manchester and Tyldesley.
G	P	F	.	H	C	.	.	Montpelier	Glo'ster ...	Clif. Ex. Jt. (G. W. & Mid.)	Bristol and Clifton Down.
.	.	.	.	.	.	.	.	Montpelier Junction	Sussex ...	L. B. & S. C.	Brighton.
G	.	F	L	.	.	2	0	Montrave	Fife	N. B.	Cameron Bridge and Lochty.
.	.	.	.	.	.	.	.	Baldastard Colliery	Fife......	N. B.	Montrave and Largoward.
G	P	F	L	H	C	5	0	Montrose	Forfar	Cal.	Branch Terminus near Dubton Jn.
G	P	F	L	H	C	10	0	Montrose	Forfar	N. B.	Arbroath and Bervie.
.	.	.	.	.	.	.	.	Academy Park Flour Mill..	Forfar	Cal.	Montrose.
.	.	.	.	.	.	.	.	Academy Park Saw Mill ...	Forfar	Cal.	Montrose.
G	.	.	.	.	.	.	.	Broomfield Siding	Forfar	N. B.	Montrose and North Water Bridge.
.	.	.	.	.	.	.	.	Milne's Siding	Forfar	Cal.	Montrose.
.	.	.	.	.	.	.	.	Montrose Gas Co.'s Siding	Forfar	N. B.	Montrose.
G	.	.	.	.	.	.	.	Montrose Harbour Branch Sidings	Forfar	N. B.	Montrose Station and Harbour.
.	.	.	.	.	.	.	.	Muir, Son & Patton's Lime Siding	Forfar	Cal.	Montrose Harbour.
.	.	.	.	.	.	.	.	Victoria Saw Mills	Forfar	Cal.	Montrose.
.	.	.	.	.	.	.	.	Whiteman's Coal Siding ...	Forfar	Cal.	Montrose.
G	.	.	.	.	.	.	.	Montrose Harbour	Forfar	Cal. / N. B.	Montrose. / Branch from Montrose.
.	.	.	.	.	.	.	.	Monument	Middlesex	Met. & Met. Dist. Jt. ...	See London.
.	.	.	.	.	.	.	.	Monument Lane	Warwick..	L. & N. W.	See Birmingham.
.	.	.	.	.	.	.	.	Monway Works	Staffs	G. W.	See Patent Shaft and Axletree Co.'s Lloyd's Works (Wednesbury).
.	.	.	.	.	.	.	.	Monway Works (L. & N. W.)	Staffs	L. & N. W.—Mid.	
G	P	F	L	H	C	1	5	Monymusk	Aberdeen	G. N. of S.	Kintore and Alford.
.	.	.	.	.	.	.	.	Moody Bros. & Co.'s Colliery (Mid.)	Glamorg'n	Mid.—G. W.—L. & N. W.	Clydach-on-Tawe.
.	.	.	.	.	.	.	.	Moon, A., & Son's Siding	Yorks	Mid.	Guiseley.
.	P	.	.	.	.	.	.	Moore	Cheshire...	L. & N. W.	Crewe and Warrington.
.	.	.	.	.	.	.	.	Moore & Brock's Baron's Quay Siding (C. L. C.)	Cheshire...	C. L. C.—L. & N. W.	Northwich.
.	.	.	.	.	.	.	.	Moore, Nettlefold & Co.'s Siding (G. E.)	Essex	GE—GN—L&NW—Mid.	London, Silvertown.
.	.	.	.	.	.	.	.	Moore's Glass Works	Durham ...	N. E.	South Shields.
.	.	.	.	.	.	.	.	Moore's Siding	Glamorg'n	T. V.	Penarth Dock.
.	.	.	.	.	.	.	.	Moore's Works	Renfrew ...	G & P Jt. (Cal & G & S W)	Same as Drumoyne Sidings (Cardonald).
.	.	.	.	.	.	.	.	Moor End Siding	Yorks	N. E.	Thorne.
.	.	.	.	.	.	.	.	Moorepark Boiler Works (Burnett's)	Lanark ...	G & P Jt. (Cal & G & S W)	Glasgow, Govan.
.	.	.	.	.	.	.	.	Moorepark Junction	Lanark ...	G & P Jt. (Cal & G & S W)	Ibrox and Govan.
.	.	.	.	.	.	.	.	Moorepark Siding	Lanark ...	G & P Jt. (Cal & G & S W)	Glasgow, Govan.
.	.	.	.	.	.	.	.	Moorfield Pit	Ayr	G. & S. W.	Gatehead.
.	.	.	.	.	.	.	.	Moorfield Siding	Lanark ...	N. B.	Carluke, Castlehill.
.	.	.	.	.	.	.	.	Moorfield Tile Works	Ayr	G. & S. W.	Gatehead.
G	P	.	L	.	.	.	.	Moorfields	Antrim ...	N. C. Com. (Mid.)	Ballymena and Larne.
.	.	.	.	.	.	.	.	Moorfields	Hereford...	Mid.	See Hereford.
.	.	.	.	.	.	.	.	Moorfields Exchange Sidings (Mid.)	Hereford..	Mid.—G. W.—L. & N. W.	Hereford.
.	.	.	.	.	.	.	.	Moorgate Street	Middlesex	C. & S. L.	See London.

EXPLANATION—G Goods Station.   P Passenger and Parcel Station.   P* Passenger, but not Parcel or Miscellaneous Traffic.
F Furniture Vans, Carriages, Portable Engines, and Machines on Wheels.   L Live Stock.
H Horse Boxes and Prize Cattle Vans.   C Carriages by Passenger Train.

G	P	F	L	H	C	Tons	Cwts	STATIONS, &c.	COUNTY.	COMPANY.	POSITION.
								Moorgate Street	Middlesex	G. N. & C.	See London.
								Moorgate Street (Met.)	Middlesex	Met.—G. N.—G. W.—Mid.—S. E. & C.	See London.
								Moor Green Colliery	Derby	Mid.	See Barber, Walker & Co. (Langley Mill and Eastwood).
								Moor Green Colliery (G. N.)	Notts	G. N.—G. C.	Eastwood and Langley Mill.
G	P	F	L	H	C	5	0	Moorhampton	Hereford	Mid.	Hereford and Hay.
								Moor Hill Colliery	Durham	N. E.	Evenwood.
G	P	F	L					Moorhouse and South Elmsall	Yorks	H. & B.	Wrangbrook Junction and Wath.
								Moor Lane Depôt	Lancs	S. & M. Jt. (G. C. & Mid.)	See Widnes Corporation.
								Moor Lane Junction	Lancs	S. & M. Jt. (G. C. & Mid.)	Widnes.
								Moor Lane Siding	Staffs	G. W.	Brettell Lane.
								Moor Pit, No. 5 (L. & N. W.)	Lancs	L & N W—G C (Wig. Jn.)	See Wigan Coal & Iron Co. (Wigan).
G	P		L	H		3	0	Moor Row	Cumb'land	WC&EJt.(Fur.&LNW)	Frizington and Whitehaven.
								Ainsworth & Son's Siding	Cumb'land	WC&EJt.(Fur.&LNW)	Moor Row and Woodend.
								Cammell & Co.'s Parkhouse Mines	Cumb'land	WC&EJt.(Fur.&LNW)	Pallaflat Branch.
								Cleator Iron Ore Co.'s No. 11 Siding	Cumb'land	WC&EJt.(Fur.&LNW)	Moor Row and Woodend.
								Dalzell's Moor Row Mines	Cumb'land	WC&EJt.(Fur.&LNW)	Moor Row and Whitehaven.
								Lindow's— Sir John Pit	Cumb'land	WC&EJt.(Fur.&LNW)	Bigrigg Branch.
								Sykehouse Mines	Cumb'land	WC&EJt.(Fur.&LNW)	Pallaflat Branch.
								Lord Leconfield's— Bigrigg Pits	Cumb'land	WC&EJt.(Fur.&LNW)	Bigrigg Branch.
								Coal Depôt	Cumb'land	WC&EJt.(Fur.&LNW)	Bigrigg Branch.
								Moss Bay Steel & Ir.Co's Pits	Cumb'land	WC&EJt.(Fur.&LNW)	Bigrigg Branch.
								Pallaflat Co.'s No. 2 Siding	Cumb'land	WC&EJt.(Fur.&LNW)	Pallaflat Branch.
								Postlethwaite's— Moor Row Mining Co.'s Fletcher Pit	Cumb'land	WC&EJt.(Fur.&LNW)	Bigrigg Branch.
								No. 6 Moor Row or Royalty Pit	Cumb'land	WC&EJt.(Fur.&LNW)	Bigrigg Branch.
								Stirling's No. 10 Pit	Cumb'land	WC&EJt.(Fur.&LNW)	Moor Row and Woodend.
								Moor Row Mines	Cumb'land	WC&EJt.(Fur.&LNW)	Same as Dalzell's (Moor Row).
								Moor Row Mining Co.'s Fletcher Pit	Cumb'land	WC&EJt.(Fur.&LNW)	See Postlethwaite's (Moor Row).
								Moor Row or Royalty Pit (No. 6)	Cumb'land	WC&EJt.(Fur.&LNW)	See Postlethwaite's (Moor Row).
								Moors, East	Glamorg'n	T. V.	See East Moors (Cardiff Docks).
G	P		L			5	0	Moorside and Wardley	Lancs	L. & Y.	Pendleton and Hindley.
								Moor Steel and Iron Works	Durham	N. E.	Stockton, North Shore.
								Moor Street Whf. (L.&N.W.)	Staffs	L&NW—Mid—GN—N S	See Kottingham and Moor Street Wharf (Burton-on-Trent).
G						2	0	Moorswater	Cornwall	L. & Looe	Looe and Cheesewring Quarries.
G	P	F	L	H	C	2	0	Moorthorpe & South Kirkby	Yorks	S. & K. Jt. (Mid.&N.E.)	Swinton Junction and Pontefract.
	P			H	C			(S. & K. Jt.)		G. C.	Over S. & K. Jt. from Swinton Jn.
								Carlton Main Colliery Co.— Carlton Main Colliery	Yorks	S. & K. Jt. (Mid. & N. E.)	Near Moorthorpe and South Kirkby.
								Frickley Colliery	Yorks	S. & K. Jt. (Mid. & N. E.)	Near Moorthorpe and South Kirkby.
								South Kirkby Colliery	Yorks	S. & K. Jt. (Mid. & N. E.)	Near Moorthorpe and South Kirkby.
G	P	F	L	H	C	5	0	Moortown (for Caistor)	Lincoln	G. C.	Market Rasen and Barnetby.
G	P		L	H				Morar	Inverness	N. B.	Fort William and Banavie.
								Moray Park Siding	Edinboro'	N. B.	Same as Lochend Sid. (Edinburgh).
G	P	F	L	H	C	5	0	Morchard Road	Devon	L. & S. W.	Exeter and Barnstaple Junction.
G	P	F	L	H				Morcott	Rutland	L. & N. W.	Market Harboro' and Stamford.
	P							Morden	Surrey	L. B. & S. C.	Wimbledon and Croydon.
								Innes Siding	Surrey	L. B. & S. C.	Morden.
								Mordey, Carney & Co.'s Ship Repairing Yard	Mon	A (N & S W) D & R—G W	Newport, Alexandra Docks.
G	P		L			2	0	Morebath	Devon	G. W.	Wiveliscombe and Dulverton.
								Morebath Junction	Devon	G. W	Morebath and Dulverton.
								MORECAMBE—			
G	P	F	L	H	C	5	0	(Station)	Lancs	L. & N. W.	Branch from Lancaster.
G	P	F	L	H	C	5	0	(Station)	Lancs	Mid.	Branch from Wennington Junction.
								Gas Works Siding	Lancs	Mid.	Morecambe and Lancaster.
G	P	F	L	H	C	10	0	Harbour (Mid.)	Lancs	Mid.	Extension from Morecambe.
G			L			10	0			L. & N. W.	Over Mid. from Morecambe Junc.
								Heysham Harbour Contractors' Siding	Lancs	Mid.	Near Morecambe.
								Junction	Lancs	L. & N. W.—Mid.	Lancaster and Morecambe.
								Sewage Works	Lancs	Mid.	Morecambe Harbour.

EXPLANATION—G *Goods Station.*   P *Passenger and Parcel Station.*   P* *Passenger, but not Parcel or Miscellaneous Traffic.*
F *Furniture Vans, Carriages, Portable Engines, and Machines on Wheels.*   L *Live Stock.*
H *Horse Boxes and Prize Cattle Vans.*   C *Carriages by Passenger Train.*

STATION ACCOMMODATION.						CRANE POWER.		STATIONS, &c.	COUNTY.	COMPANY.	POSITION.
						Tons	Cwts.	Moresby Coal Co.—			
..	..	..	..	..	..	..	..	Oatlands Pit	Cumb'land	C. & W. Jn.	Oatlands.
..	..	..	..	..	..	..	..	Walk Mill Pit.................	Cumb'land	C. & W. Jn.	Moresby Parks.
..	..	..	..	..	..	..	..	Moresby Junction	Cumb'land	C. & W. Jn.	Moresby Parks and Cleator Moor.
G	P	.	L	H	.	..	..	Moresby Parks	Cumb'land	C. & W. Jn.	Distington and Cleator Moor.
								Moresby Coal Co.'s Walk			
..	..	..	..	..	..	..	..	Mill Pit.....................	Cumb'land	C. & W. Jn.	Moresby Junction.
G	P	.	.	.	.	5	0	Moreton	Cheshire...	Wirral	Bidston and West Kirby.
								Moreton Brick & Tile Co.'s			
..	..	..	..	..	..	..	..	Siding	Cheshire...	Wirral	Moreton.
G	P	F	L	H	C	..	..	Moreton	Dorset.....	L. & S.W.	Wimborne and Dorchester.
..	..	..	..	..	..	..	..	Moreton Brick Yard	Dorset.....	L. & S.W.	Moreton.
..	..	..	..	..	..	..	..	Moreton Sand Pit	Dorset.....	L. & S.W.	Moreton.
G	P	F	L	H	C	4	0	Moreton-Hampstead	Devon	G. W.	Branch from Newton Abbot.
G	P	F	L	H	C	5	0	Moreton-in-Marsh	Glo'ster ...	G. W.	Oxford and Evesham.
..	..	..	..	..	..	..	..	Aston Magna Siding.........	Worcester	G. W.	Moreton-in-Marsh.
G	P	.	.	.	.	1	0	Moreton-on-Lugg	Hereford ..	S & H Jt (G W & L N W)	Craven Arms and Hereford.
..	..	..	..	..	..	..	..	Morfa Brick Works (G. W.)	Carmarth'	G. W.—L. & N. W.	Same as James' (Llanelly Docks).
..	..	..	..	..	..	..	..	Morfa Colliery....................	Glamorg'n	G. W.—P. T.	Port Talbot.
..	..	..	..	..	..	..	..	Morfa Copper Works...........	Glamorg'n	G. W.	Same as Pascoe, Grenfell & Sons, or Foster, Williams & Co. (Landore).
..	..	..	..	..	..	..	..	Morfa Copper Works (Vivian's Loop Siding)	Glamorg'n	P. T.	Port Talbot (Central).
..	..	..	..	..	..	..	..	Morfa Junction	Carmarth'	G. W.	Llanelly.
..	..	..	..	..	..	..	..	Morfa Siding	Glamorg'n	R. & S. B.	See Vivian & Son's (Port Talbot).
..	..	..	..	..	..	..	..	Morfa Tin Plate Wks. (G. W.)	Carmarth'	G. W.—L. & N. W.	Same as Tregonning & Son's Tin Works (Llanelly Docks).
..	..	..	..	..	..	..	..	Morgan & Son's Siding (Mid.)	Glamorg'n	Mid.—G.W.—L. & N. W.	Same as Cwm Tawe Clay Works (Pontardawe).
..	..	..	..	..	..	..	..	Morgan's Coal Yard (L.N.W.)	Mon	L. & N. W.—G. W.	Brynmawr.
..	..	..	..	..	..	..	..	Morgan's Siding.................	Ayr	G. & S.W.	Kilwinning.
..	..	..	..	..	..	..	..	Morlais Col. & Tin Wks. (G.W.)	Carmarth'	G. W.—L. & N. W.	Llangennech.
..	..	..	..	..	..	..	..	Morlais Junction	Glamorg'n	B. & M.—B. & M. & L. & N. W. Jt.—L. & N. W.	Pontsarn and Abergavenny.
..	..	..	..	..	..	..	..	Morland's Siding	Berks	G. W.	Abingdon.
G	P	.	.	.	.	10	0	Morley	Yorks	{ G. N.	Ardsley and Dudley Hill.
G	P	.	L	H	.	10	0		Yorks	{ L. & N. W.	Dewsbury and Leeds.
..	..	..	..	..	..	..	..	Ackroyd Bros.' Morley Main Colliery	Yorks	L. & N. W.	Morley and Churwell.
..	..	..	..	..	..	..	..	Fitton and Robinson's Churwell Colliery and Brick Works or Ward's Siding	Yorks	L. & N. W.	Churwell and Farnley.
..	..	..	..	..	..	..	..	Haigh's Victoria Colliery (Bruntcliffe Colliery)......	Yorks	G. N.	Morley and Gildersome.
								Morley Corporation—			
..	..	..	..	..	..	..	..	Gas Co.'s Siding	Yorks	L. & N. W.	Morley and Churwell.
..	..	..	..	..	..	..	..	Lister's Siding	Yorks	L. & N. W.	Morley and Churwell.
..	..	..	..	..	..	..	..	Pawson Bros.' Quarry	Yorks	G. N.	Morley.
..	..	..	..	..	..	..	..	Morley & Co.'s Siding	Cheshire...	L. & N. W.	Stockport.
..	..	..	..	..	..	..	..	Morley Colliery	Durham ..	N. E.	Evenwood.
..	..	..	..	..	..	..	..	Morley Main Colliery	Yorks	L. & N. W.	Same as Ackroyd Bros. (Morley).
G	P	.	L	.	.	..	..	Morley's Bridge	Kerry	G. S. & W.	Headford Junction and Kenmare.
G	P	.	L	H	.	..	..	Mormond	Aberdeen	G. N. of S.	Aberdeen and Fraserburgh.
								MORNINGSIDE—			
G	P	.	L	H	.	1	10	(Station)	Lanark ...	Cal.	Branch Terminus, Newmains.
G	P	.	L	H	.	1	10	(Station)	Lanark ...	N. B.	Branch from Bathgate, Upper.
..	..	..	..	..	..	..	..	Allanton Colliery	Lanark ...	N. B.	Branch—Morningside & Crofthead.
..	..	..	..	..	..	..	..	Allanton Fire-Clay and Brick Works	Lanark ...	Cal.—N. B.	Morningside.
..	..	..	..	..	..	..	..	Allanton Foundry	Lanark ...	Cal.	Morningside.
..	..	..	..	..	..	..	..	Bailliesmuir Colliery.........	Lanark ...	{ Cal.	Morningside.
										{ N. B.	Branch from Morningside.
..	..	..	..	..	..	..	..	Chapel Colliery	Lanark ...	{ Cal.	Morningside.
										{ N. B.	Castlehill Junction and Station.
..	..	..	..	..	..	..	..	Chapel New Colliery.........	Lanark ...	Cal.	Morningside.
..	..	..	..	..	..	..	..	Collyshot Mine	Lanark ...	Cal.	Morningside.
..	..	..	..	..	..	..	..	Coltness Collieries (Collyshot Collieries)................	Lanark ...	N. B.	Branch near Morningside.
..	..	..	..	..	..	..	..	Coltness Iron Works........	Lanark ...	N. B.	Branch near Morningside.
..	..	..	..	..	..	..	..	Coltness Iron Works & Cols.	Lanark ...	Cal.	{ Morningside and Newmains. { Morningside and Stirling Road.
G	.	.	.	.	.	..	..	Davies' Dykes Siding	Lanark ...	N. B.	Morningside and Crofthead.

EXPLANATION—G *Goods Station.*   P *Passenger and Parcel Station.*   P* *Passenger, but not Parcel or Miscellaneous Traffic.*
F *Furniture Vans, Carriages, Portable Engines, and Machines on Wheels.*   L *Live Stock.*
H *Horse Boxes and Prize Cattle Vans.*   C *Carriages by Passenger Train.*

STATION ACCOMMODATION.						CRANE POWER.		STATIONS, &c.	COUNTY.	COMPANY.	POSITION.
						Tons	Cwts.	MORNINGSIDE—continued.			
G	.	.	.	.	.	.	.	Duntie Siding	Lanark ...	N. B.	Morningside and Crofthead.
.	.	.	.	.	.	.	.	Garriongill Siding	Lanark ...	N. B.	Coltness Branch.
.	.	.	.	.	.	.	.	Herdshill Colliery	Lanark ...	{ Cal.	Stirling Road.
										N. B.	Branch near Morningside.
.	.	.	.	.	.	.	.	Junction	Lanark ...	Cal.—N. B.	Morningside (Cal.) and Crofthead.
.	.	.	.	.	.	.	.	Morningside Brick Works...	Lanark ...	{ Cal.	Morningside.
										N. B.	Coltness Branch.
.	.	.	.	.	.	.	.	Morningside Collieries	Lanark ...	Cal.	Morningside.
.	.	.	.	.	.	.	.	Morningside Col. No. 10...	Lanark ...	N. B.	Near Morningside.
.	.	.	.	.	.	.	.	Morningside Foundry	Lanark ...	Cal.	Morningside.
G	.	.	.	.	.	3	0	Stirling Road	Lanark ...	Cal.	Morningside and Wishaw (South).
.	.	.	.	.	.	.	.	Stonecraig No. 1 Pit	Lanark ...	Cal.	Morningside.
.	.	.	.	.	.	.	.	Watstonfoot Colliery........	Lanark ...	N. B.	Morningside and Crofthead.
.	.	.	.	.	.	.	.	Morningside Road	Edinboro'	N. B.	See Edinburgh.
G	P	F	L	H	C	10	0	Morpeth (N. E.)..............	Northumb	{ N. E.	Newcastle and Alnwick.
										N. B.	Over N. E. from Morpeth Junction.
.	.	.	.	.	.	.	.	Junction	Northumb	N. B.—N. E.	Meldon and Morpeth.
.	.	.	.	.	.	.	.	Sidings	Northumb	N. E.	Morpeth.
.	.	.	.	.	.	.	.	Morpeth Branch Dock	Cheshire...	B'headJt—CLC—NW&L	Birkenhead.
.	.	.	.	.	.	.	.	Morpeth Dock	Cheshire...	B'headJt—CLC—NW&L	See Birkenhead.
.	.	.	.	.	.	.	.	Morpeth Dock&South Reserve	Cheshire...	G. W.—L. & N. W.	See Birkenhead.
.	.	.	.	.	.	.	.	Morrell, Mills & Co.'s Siding...	Lancs	Manchester Ship Canal...	Manchester.
.	.	.	.	.	.	.	.	Morris & Griffin's Chemical Works	Mon	G. W.	Newport, High Street.
.	.	.	.	.	.	.	.	Morris & Griffin's Glue Works	Mon	G. W.	Newport, High Street.
.	.	.	.	.	.	.	.	Morris & Griffin's Sid.(L&NW)	Staffs	L. & N. W.—G. W.	Same as Hunt & Hunt's Siding (Wolverhampton).
.	.	.	.	.	.	.	.	Morris & Shaw's Colliery......	Warwick..	Mid.	Same as Birch Coppice Colliery (Kingsbury).
.	.	.	.	.	.	.	.	Morrison & Mason's Siding...	Lanark ...	Cal.	Glasgow, South Side.
.	.	.	.	.	.	.	.	Morrison Pit	Durham ...	N. E.	See South Moor Collieries (Annfield Plain).
.	.	.	.	.	.	.	.	Morrison's Haven Siding......	Hadding'n	N. B.	Prestonpans.
.	.	.	.	.	.	.	.	Morrison's Siding	Northumb	N. E.	St. Peter's.
.	.	.	.	.	.	.	.	Morrison Street Cattle Depôt	Edinboro'	Cal.	Edinburgh, Lothian Road.|
.	.	.	.	.	.	.	.	Morrison Street Mineral Depôt	Edinboro'	Cal.	See Edinburgh.
								MORRISTON—			
G	P	.	.	H	.	5	0	(Station)	Glamorg'n	G. W.	Branch from Hafod Junction.
G	P	.	.	.	.	.	.	(Station, Mid.)	Glamorg'n	{ Mid.	Upper Bank and Glais.
										G. W.	Over Mid. Line.
.	.	.	.	.	.	.	.	Beaufort Tin Plate Co.'s Siding (Mid.)	Glamorg'n	Mid.—G. W.—L. & N. W.	Morriston and Upper Bank.
.	.	.	.	.	.	.	.	Copper Pit Colliery	Glamorg'n	G. W.	Morriston and Plas Marl.
.	.	.	.	.	.	.	.	Edwards & Co.'s Dyffryn Tin Plate Works (Mid.)	Glamorg'n	Mid.—G. W.—L. & N. W.	Morriston.
.	.	.	.	.	.	.	.	Morriston Tin Plate Co.'s Midland Tin Plate Works (Mid.)	Glamorg'n	Mid.—G. W.—L. & N. W.	Morriston.
.	.	.	.	.	.	.	.	Pentrefelin Sidings	Glamorg'n	G. W.	Morriston.
.	.	.	.	.	.	.	.	Pentreporth Chemical Wks.	Glamorg'n	G. W.	Morriston.
.	.	.	.	.	.	.	.	Upper Forest & Worcester Steel & Tin Plate Works (Mid.)	Glamorg'n	Mid.—G. W.—L. & N. W.	Morriston.
.	.	.	.	.	.	.	.	Vivian & Son's Spelter Wks.	Glamorg'n	G. W.	Morriston and Plas Marl.
.	.	.	.	.	.	.	.	Williams', Chas., Sid. (Mid)	Glamorg'n	Mid.—G. W.—L. & N. W.	Morriston.
G	P	F	L	H	C	.	.	Morse's, E. & G., Siding	Suffolk ...	G. E.	Oulton Broad.
G	P	F	L	H	C	3	0	Mortehoe and Lee	Devon......	L. & S. W.	Barnstaple and Ilfracombe.
.	.	.	.	.	.	.	.	Mortimer	Berks	G. W.	Reading and Basingstoke.
.	.	.	.	.	.	.	.	Mortimer, J. L., & Co.'s Warehouse	Cheshire...	B'headJt—CLC—NW&L	Birkenhead.
.	P	.	.	.	.	.	.	Mortlach Siding................	Banff	G. N. of S.	See Dufftown.
.	.	.	.	.	.	.	.	Mortlake and East Sheen ...	Surrey ...	L. & S.W.	Clapham Junction and Richmond.
.	.	.	.	.	.	.	.	Mort Liddell Works	Lancs	L. & N. W.—S. & M. Jt.	See United Alkali Co. (Widnes).
.	.	.	.	.	.	.	.	Morton & Co.'s Shipbuilding Yard	Edinboro'	Cal.—N. B.	Leith, North.
.	.	.	.	.	.	.	.	Morton & Co.'s Siding	Lancs	L. & N. W.	Garston Docks.
.	.	.	.	.	.	.	.	Morton & Co.'s Siding (Mid.)	Staffs	Mid.—LNW—GN—NS	Burton-on-Trent.
.	.	.	.	.	.	.	.	Morton Brick Works	Notts	G. C.	Checker House.
.	.	.	.	.	.	.	.	Morton Carr's Siding	Yorks	N. E.	Nunthorpe.
.	.	.	.	.	.	.	.	Morton Colliery (Clay & Co.)	Derby......	Mid.	Doe Hill.

EXPLANATION—G Goods Station.   P Passenger and Parcel Station.   P* Passenger, but not Parcel or Miscellaneous Traffic.
F Furniture Vans, Carriages, Portable Engines, and Machines on Wheels.   L Live Stock.
H Horse Boxes and Prize Cattle Vans.   C Carriages by Passenger Train.

STATION ACCOMMODATION.						CRANE POWER.		STATIONS, &c.	COUNTY.	COMPANY.	POSITION.
						Tons	Cwts.	Morton Grange Siding	Yorks	N. E.	Nunthorpe.
G	P	F	L	H	C	.	.	Morton-Pinkney..................	N'hamptn	E. & W. Jn................	Greens-Norton Junction and Fenny Compton.
G	P	F	L	H	C	1	10	Morton Road	Lincoln ...	G. N.	Bourne and Sleaford.
								Haconby Siding	Lincoln ...	G. N.	Morton Road and Rippingale.
								Morton Siding	Fife	N. B.	Tayport.
								Morton's Siding	Fife	N. B.	Whitemyre Junction Station.
								Morton's Siding	Yorks	G. N.	Thornton.
.	P							Moseley..........................	Worcester	Mid.	Birmingham and King's Heath.
								Moseley Green..................	Glo'ster ...	S. & Wye Jt.(G.W. & Mid.)	Lydney and Drybrook Road.
G	P	F	L	H	C	10	0	Moses Gate	Lancs	L. & Y.	Manchester and Bolton.
								Mosley's Bleach Works........	Cheshire...	L. & N. W.	Cheadle.
								Mosley Siding	Yorks	N. E.	Horsforth.
								Mosley Street Branch (Mid.)	Staffs	Mid.—L N W—G N—N S	Burton-on-Trent.
G						.	}	Moss	Denbigh...	{ G. W.	Wrexham and Ffrwd.
										{ W. M. & C. Q.	Ffrwd Branch.
								Bryn Malley Colliery	Denbigh...	G. W.—W. M. & C. Q....	Ffrwd Branch.
								Clayton's Brick Yard (Gwersyllt Brick Works)	Denbigh...	G. W.	Moss and Wheatsheaf Junction.
								Coedybrain Siding...........	Denbigh...	G. W.	Ffrwd Branch.
								Ffors-y-go Colliery...........	Denbigh...	G. W.	Ffrwd Branch.
								Ffosygo Brick Works	Denbigh...	W. M. & C. Q.	Ffrwd Branch.
								Ffrwd Colliery	Denbigh...	G. W.—W. M. & C. Q....	Ffrwd Branch.
								Ffrwd Iron Works (Sparrow, J., & Son's)........	Denbigh...	{ G. W.	Branch from Moss.
										{ W. M. & C. Q.	Ffrwd Branch.
								Gwersyllt Colliery...........	Denbigh...	G. W.	Branch near Wheatsheaf Junction.
								Westminster Colliery	Denbigh...	{ G. W.	Moss.
										{ W. M. & C. Q.	Ffrwd Branch.
								Windy Hill Siding	Denbigh...	W. M. & C. Q.	Ffrwd Branch.
G	P	.	L	H		.	.	Moss (N. E.)	Yorks	{ N. E.	Selby and Doncaster.
										{ G. N.	Over N. E. from Shaftholme Junc.
								Moss & Gambles' Siding	Yorks	G. C.	Wadsley Bridge.
.	P							Moss and Pentre	Denbigh...	W. M. & C. Q.	Brymbo and Wrexham.
								Moss & Sons' Siding	Leicester..	G. C.	Loughboro'.
								Mossband Colliery	Lanark ...	Cal.	Omoa.
								Mossband Siding	Cumb'land	Cal.	Floriston.
G	P	.	.	H		.	.	Moss Bank	Lancs	L. & N. W.	Rainford and St. Helens.
								Moss Bay Cart Siding	Cumb'land	C. & W. Jn.	Workington.
								Moss Bay Hematite Iron and Steel Co.'s Siding	Cumb'land	L. & N. W.	Workington.
								Moss Bay Iron Works	Cumb'land	C. & W. Jn.	Workington.
								Moss Bay Steel & Iron Co.'s Pits	Cumb'land	WC&E Jt.(Fur.& L&NW)	Moor Row.
								Mossbeath Colliery	Fife	N. B.	Cowdenbeath, Old.
								Mossblown Junction	Ayr	G. & S.W.	Annbank and Auchincruive.
G	P	.	.			5	0	Mossbridge	Lancs	C. L. C. (S'port Exten.)..	Aintree and Southport (Lord Street).
								Moss Colliery	Lancs	G C (Wigan Jn.)—L&NW	See Crompton and Shawcross.
								Moss Colliery	Lancs	L. & N. W.	See Pearson & Knowles Coal and Iron Co. (Wigan).
G	P	F	L	H	C	3	0	Mossend	Lanark ...	Cal.	Motherwell and Coatbridge.
								Burnhouse Manure Siding	Lanark ...	Cal.	Mossend and Whifflet.
								Burnhouse Weighs	Lanark ...	Cal.	Mossend and Whifflet.
								Clydesdale Ir. & Steel Wks.	Lanark ...	Cal.	Mossend and Motherwell.
								Huttonrigg Colliery	Lanark ...	Cal.	Mossend.
								Jerviston Quarry	Lanark ...	Cal.	Mossend and Motherwell.
								Milnwood Iron & Steel Wks.	Lanark ...	Cal.	Mossend and Motherwell.
								Mossend Iron & Steel Wks.	Lanark ...	Cal.	Mossend.
								Riccardjohnstone Siding ...	Lanark ...	Cal.	Jerviston Junc. and Dalzell Junc.
								South Junction	Lanark ...	Cal.	Motherwell and Mossend.
								Thankerton Collieries	Lanark ...	Cal.	Branch near Mossend.
								Woodhall Colliery	Lanark ...	Cal.	Branch near Mossend.
								Woodhall Mine	Lanark ...	Cal.	Branch near Mossend.
								Mossend Foundry	Fife	N. B.	Crossgates.
								Mossfield Colliery	Staffs	N. S.	Adderley Green.
								Mossfield Colliery	Staffs	N. S.	See Chatterley-Whitfield Collieries (Adderley Green).
								Mossfield Colliery (L. & Y.)..	Lancs	L. & Y.—L. & N. W.	Skelmersdale.
								Moss Hall Colliery	Lancs	G. C. (Wigan Jn.)	Hindley and Platt Bridge.
								Moss Hall Colliery.............	Lancs	L. & Y.	Ince.
								Moss Hall Colliery, South ...	Lancs	L. & N. W.	Wigan.
								Moss Hall Siding	Lancs	L. & Y.	See Pearson & Knowles Coal and Iron Co. (Ince).
								Mosside Collieries	L'lithgow	N. B.	Bathgate, Upper.

STATION ACCOMMODATION.						CRANE POWER.		STATIONS, &c.	COUNTY.	COMPANY.	POSITION.
						Tons	Cwts.				
.	.	.	.	.	.	.	.	Moss Junction	Lancs	C L C—G.C. (Wigan Jn.)	Glazebrook.
.	.	.	.	.	.	.	.	Moss Lane Junction	Lancs	L. & Y.........................	Midge Hall and Lostock Hall.
.	P	.	.	.	.	.	.	Mossley............................	Antrim ...	N. C. Com. (Mid.)	Ballyclare Junc. and Greenisland.
G	P	.	L	H	C	5	0	Mossley..............................	Lancs	L. & N. W.	Huddersfield and Stalybridge.
.	.	.	.	.	.	.	.	Black Rock Siding	Lancs	L. & N. W.	Mossley and Stalybridge.
.	.	.	.	.	.	.	.	Mayall's Bottom's Mill.....	Lancs	L. & N. W.	Mossley and Greenfield.
.	.	.	.	.	.	.	.	Scout Siding	Lancs	L. & N. W.	Mossley and Stalybridge.
G	P	F	L	H	C	.	.	Mossley Hill (for Aigburth)...	Lancs	L. & N. W.	Garston and Liverpool.
.	.	.	.	.	.	.	.	Mosslye Siding	Lanark ...	N. B.	See Longriggend.
.	.	.	.	.	.	.	.	Moss Pit Siding (Foster Williams & Co.) (L. & Y.)	Lancs	L. & Y.—L. & N. W.......	Skelmersdale.
G	P	.	.	.	.	.	.	Moss Side..........................	Lancs	P & W Jt(L&Y & L & NW)	Lytham and Preston.
.	.	.	.	.	.	.	.	Moss Side Iron Works	Lancs	{ L. & Y.	See Pearson & Knowles Coal and Iron Co. (Ince).
.	.	.	.	.	.	.	.			{ L. & N. W.	See Pearson & Knowles Coal and Iron Co. (Wigan).
.	.	.	.	.	.	.	.	Moss Side Siding	Lancs	L. & Y.	Skelmersdale.
.	.	.	.	.	.	.	.	Moss Siding......................	Ayr	G. & S.W.	Hurlford.
.	.	.	.	.	.	.	.	Moss Siding.....................	Staffs	L. & N. W.	Same as Orton & Co.'s Sid. (Stafford).
.	.	.	.	.	.	.	.	Moss Street Goods Yards and Sidings	Yorks	N. E.	Castleford.
G	P	.	L	H	.	2	0	Mosstowie	Elgin&Mo'	High.	Elgin and Alves.
.	.	.	.	.	.	.	.	Newton Siding	Elgin&Mo'	High.	Mosstowie and Alves.
.	P	.	.	.	.	.	.	Moss, T., Siding................	Lancs	P&WJt(L&Y & L & NW)	Kirkham.
.	P	.	.	.	.	.	.	Moston	Lancs	L. & Y.	Middleton Junc. & Newton Heath.
.	.	.	.	.	.	.	.	Moston Col.(Platt Bros. & Co's)	Lancs	L. & Y.	Newton Heath.
G	P	.	L	H	C	5	0	Mostyn	Flint	L. & N. W.	Chester and Rhyl.
.	.	.	.	.	.	.	.	Darwen & Mostyn Iron Co.'s Siding	Flint	L. & N. W.	Mostyn and Prestatyn.
G	P	.	L	H	C	5	0	Motherwell	Lanark ...	Cal.	Law Junction and Glasgow.
.	.	.	.	.	.	.	.	Alpha Engine Works	Lanark ...	Cal.	Motherwell.
.	.	.	.	.	.	.	.	Braidhurst Colliery	Lanark ...	Cal.	Motherwell and Mossend.
.	.	.	.	.	.	.	.	Brandon Bridge Building Works	Lanark ...	Cal.	Motherwell.
.	.	.	.	.	.	.	.	Broomside Farm Siding ...	Lanark ...	Cal.	Motherwell and Ferniegair.
.	.	.	.	.	.	.	.	Caledonian Bolt and Rivet Works	Lanark ...	Cal.	Motherwell and Flemington.
.	.	.	.	.	.	.	.	Caledonian Railway Co.'s Permanent Way Workshops	Lanark ...	Cal.	Motherwell.
.	.	.	.	.	.	.	.	Caledonian Railway Locomotive Shops	Lanark ...	Cal.	Motherwell and Mossend.
.	.	.	.	.	.	.	.	Camp Colliery................	Lanark ...	Cal.	Motherwell and Ferniegair.
.	.	.	.	.	.	.	.	Camp Pumping Engine ...	Lanark ...	Cal.	Motherwell and Ferniegair.
.	.	.	.	.	.	.	.	Clyde Boiler Works	Lanark ...	Cal.	Motherwell.
.	.	.	.	.	.	.	.	Clyde Valley Electric Wks.	Lanark ...	Cal.	Motherwell.
.	.	.	.	.	.	.	.	Dalzell Bge. & Roofing Wks.	Lanark ...	Cal.	Motherwell.
.	.	.	.	.	.	.	.	Dalzell Collieries.............	Lanark ...	Cal.	Motherwell and Ferniegair.
.	.	.	.	.	.	.	.	Dalzell Engineering Works	Lanark ...	Cal.	Motherwell.
.	.	.	.	.	.	.	.	Dalzell Estate Siding.........	Lanark ...	Cal.	Motherwell.
.	.	.	.	.	.	.	.	Dalzell Iron & Steel Works (Colville's)	Lanark ...	Cal.	Motherwell.
.	.	.	.	.	.	.	.	Dalzell Lesmahagow (Dalzell & Broomside Colliery)	Lanark ...	Cal.	Motherwell and Ferniegair.
.	.	.	.	.	.	.	.	Dalzell Saw Mills	Lanark ...	Cal.	Motherwell.
.	.	.	.	.	.	.	.	Dalzell Washer	Lanark ...	Cal.	Motherwell.
.	.	.	.	.	.	.	.	Delburn Engineering Wks.	Lanark ...	Cal.	Motherwell and Flemington.
.	.	.	.	.	.	.	.	Duke's Siding (Motherwell Iron & Steel Co.)	Lanark ...	Cal.	Motherwell.
.	.	.	.	.	.	.	.	Glasgow Rolling Stock and Plant Works	Lanark ...	Cal.	Motherwell and Flemington.
.	.	.	.	.	.	.	.	Globe Iron & Steel Works...	Lanark ...	Cal.	Motherwell and Mossend.
.	.	.	.	.	.	.	.	Lanarkshire Steel Works...	Lanark ...	Cal.	Motherwell and Shieldmuir.
.	.	.	.	.	.	.	.	Lesmahagow Junc. Weighs	Lanark ...	Cal.	Motherwell.
.	.	.	.	.	.	.	.	Milton Collieries	Lanark ...	Cal.	Motherwell and Mossend.
.	.	.	.	.	.	.	.	Motherwell Boiler Works (Marshall's)	Lanark ...	Cal.	Jerviston Junc. and Dalzell Junc.
.	.	.	.	.	.	.	.	Motherwell Bridge Building Co.'s Works	Lanark ...	Cal.	Motherwell and Fallside.
.	.	.	.	.	.	.	.	Motherwell Collieries	Lanark ...	Cal.	Motherwell and Fallside.
.	.	.	.	.	.	.	.	Motherwell Crane & Engine Works	Lanark ...	Cal.	Motherwell.

EXPLANATION—G *Goods Station.*   P *Passenger and Parcel Station.*   P* *Passenger, but not Parcel or Miscellaneous Traffic.*
F *Furniture Vans, Carriages, Portable Engines, and Machines on Wheels.*   L *Live Stock.*
H *Horse Boxes and Prize Cattle Vans.*   C *Carriages by Passenger Train.*

STATION ACCOMMODATION.						CRANE POWER.		STATIONS, &c.	COUNTY.	COMPANY.	POSITION.
						Tons	Cwts.	Motherwell—continued.			
.	.	.	.	.	.	.	.	Motherwell Forge Siding...	Lanark ...	Cal.	Motherwell.
.	.	.	.	.	.	.	.	Motherwell Iron & Steel Works (Glasgow Iron and Steel Works, Motherwell)	Lanark ...	Cal.	Motherwell and Mossend.
.	.	.	.	.	.	.	.	Motherwell Quarry	Lanark ...	Cal.	Motherwell and Flemington.
.	.	.	.	.	.	.	.	Motherwell Signal Shops...	Lanark ...	Cal.	Motherwell.
.	.	.	.	.	.	.	.	North Motherwell Collieries	Lanark ...	Cal.	Motherwell and Fallside.
.	.	.	.	.	.	.	.	Parkhead Colliery	Lanark ...	Cal.	Motherwell and Flemington.
.	.	.	.	.	.	.	.	Parkneuk Bridge Building Works	Lanark ...	Cal.	Motherwell and Mossend.
.	.	.	.	.	.	.	.	Pott, Cassells & Williamson's Works...............	Lanark ...	Cal.	Motherwell and Fallside.
.	.	.	.	.	.	.	.	Watson's Pits, Nos. 1,2,3,&4	Lanark ...	Cal.	Motherwell and Fallside.
.	.	.	.	.	.	.	.	Watsonville Colliery	Lanark ...	Cal.	Motherwell and Ferniegair.
.	.	.	.	.	.	.	.	Windmillhill Sidings.........	Lanark ...	Cal.	Motherwell and Flemington.
.	.	.	.	.	.	.	.	Motherwell Iron & Steel Co.'s Siding	Lanark ...	Cal.	Same as Duke's Siding (Motherwell).
.	.	.	.	.	.	.	.	Motherwell Wagon & Rolling Stock Works	Lanark ...	Cal.	Shieldmuir.
.	.	.	.	.	.	.	.	Mottingham...............	Kent	S. E. & C.	See Eltham and Mottingham.
G	P	F	L	H	C	.	.	Mottisfont (L. & S. W.)........	Hants	L. & S. W. / M. & S. W. Jn............	Romsey and Andover. / Over L. & S.W. from Andover Jn.
.	.	.	.	.	.	.	.	Wither's Siding	Hants	L. & S. W.	Near Mottisfont.
G	P	F	L	H	C	5	0	Mottram & Broadbottom......	Cheshire...	G. C.	Guide Bridge and Penistone.
G	P	F	L	H	.	5	0	Mouldsworth	Cheshire...	C.L.C. (G C, G N, & Mid.)	Northwich and Chester.
.	.	.	.	.	.	.	.	Moulsford..................	Berks	G. W.	See Cholsey and Moulsford.
G	P	F	L	H	C	1	5	Moulton	Lincoln ...	Mid. & G. N. Jt............	Sutton Bridge and Spalding.
G	P	.	.	.	.	.	.	Moulton	Yorks	N. E.	Darlington and Richmond.
.	.	.	.	.	.	.	.	Scorton Brick Works	Yorks	N. E.	Moulton and Scorton.
.	.	.	.	.	.	.	.	Moulton's Siding	Cheshire...	L. & N. W.	Acton Bridge.
G	P	F	L	H	C	1	10	Mound, The...............	Sutherl'nd	High.	Bonar Bridge and Golspie.
.	.	.	.	.	.	.	.	Mound (The) Junction	Sutherl'nd	High.—High. (Dornoch)	Rogart and Skelbo.
G	P	F	L	H	C	1	10	Mountain Ash	Glamorg'n	G. W. / T. V.	Quaker's Yard and Aberdare. / Aberdare and Pontypridd.
G	P	F	L	H	C	2	0				
.	.	.	.	.	.	.	.	Aberaman or Aberdare Gas Works	Glamorg'n	G. W.	Over Powell Duffryn Line.
.	.	.	.	.	.	.	.	Forest Level	Glamorg'n	G. W. / T. V.	Mountain Ash and Quaker's Yard. / Pontycynon Junction.
.	.	.	.	.	.	.	.	Middle Duffryn Colliery ...	Glamorg'n	T. V.	Mountain Ash and Aberaman.
.	.	.	.	.	.	.	.	Middle Duffryn Junction Sidings (G. W.)	Glamorg'n	G. W.—Rhy.	Mountain Ash and Aberdare.
.	.	.	.	.	.	.	.	Miskin Colliery	Glamorg'n	T. V.	Mountain Ash.
								Nixon's—			
.	.	.	.	.	.	.	.	Cwm Cynon Colliery......	Glamorg'n	G. W. / T. V.	Mountain Ash and Penrhiwceiber. / Abercynon and Penrhiwceiber.
.	.	.	.	.	.	.	.	Deep Duffryn Colliery ...	Glamorg'n	G. W. / T. V.	Mountain Ash and Penrhiwceiber. / Mountain Ash and Aberaman.
.	.	.	.	.	.	.	.	Navigation Col. (G. W.)	Glamorg'n	G. W.—Rhy.	Mountain Ash and Penrhiwceiber.
.	.	.	.	.	.	.	.	Navigation Colliery	Glamorg'n	T. V.	Mountain Ash and Penrhiwceiber.
.	.	.	.	.	.	.	.	Navigation Sidings	Glamorg'n	T. V.	Mountain Ash and Penrhiwceiber.
								Powell Duffryn Co.—			
.	.	.	.	.	.	.	.	Aberaman Colliery	Glamorg'n	G. W. / T. V.	Mountain Ash and Aberdare. / Aberaman Branch.
.	.	.	.	.	.	.	.	Abercwmboi Colliery ...	Glamorg'n	G. W. / T. V.	Mountain Ash and Aberdare. / Mountain Ash and Aberaman.
.	.	.	.	.	.	.	.	Cwmneol Colliery	Glamorg'n	G. W.	Mountain Ash and Aberdare.
.	.	.	.	.	.	.	.	Cwmpennar Colliery	Glamorg'n	G. W.	Mountain Ash and Aberdare.
.	.	.	.	.	.	.	.	Fforchaman Colliery	Glamorg'n	G. W.—T. V.	Mountain Ash and Aberdare.
.	.	.	.	.	.	.	.	Lower Duffryn Colliery (George Pit) (G.W.) ...	Glamorg'n	G. W.—Rhy.	Mountain Ash and Aberdare.
.	.	.	.	.	.	.	.	Lower Duffryn Colliery (George Pit)	Glamorg'n	T. V.	Mountain Ash and Aberaman.
.	.	.	.	.	.	.	.	Treaman Colliery	Glamorg'n	G. W.—T. V.	Mountain Ash and Aberdare.
.	.	.	.	.	.	.	.	Mountain Ash Junction	Glamorg'n	G. W.—T. V.	Mountain Ash and Aberdare.
.	.	.	.	.	.	.	.	Mountain Ash Gas Works ...	Glamorg'n	T. V.	Same as Penrhiwceiber Gas Works (Penrhiwceiber).
.	.	.	.	.	.	.	.	Mountain Colliery	Flint	W. M. & C. Q ...	Same as Watkinson & Son's Colliery (Buckley).
.	.	.	.	.	.	.	.	Mountain Colliery	Glamorg'n	L. & N. W.	See Cory's Navigation Colliery Co.'s Mountain Colliery (Gorseinon).
.	P	.	.	.	.	.	.	Mountain Stage	Kerry	G. S. & W.	Farranfore and Valentia Harbour.

EXPLANATION—G Goods Station.   P Passenger and Parcel Station.   P* Passenger, but not Parcel or Miscellaneous Traffic.
F Furniture Vans, Carriages, Portable Engines, and Machines on Wheels.   L Live Stock.
H Horse Boxes and Prize Cattle Vans.   C Carriages by Passenger Train.

STATION ACCOMMODATION.						CRANE POWER.	STATIONS, &c.	COUNTY.	COMPANY.	POSITION.
						Tons Cwts.	Mountcashel Iron Ore Co.'s			
							Siding	Antrim ...	N. C. Com. (Mid.)	Knockanally.
G	P	F	L			3 0	Mountcharles	Donegal ...	Donegal	Donegal and Killybegs.
							Mountcow Siding	Lanark ...	Cal.	Salisburgh.
							Mountfield Siding	Sussex	S. E. & C.	Battle.
							Mount Florida	Renfrew ..	Cal.	See Glasgow.
G	P	F	L	H			Mount Gould Junction	Devon ...	G. W.	Plymouth.
G	P		L	H		1 5	Mountmellick	Queens	G. S. & W.	Branch from Maryborough.
							Mount Melville	Fife	N. B.	Anstruther and St. Andrews.
							Mountnessing Siding	Essex	G. E.	See Shenfield and Hutton.
							Mount Osborne West Junc.	Yorks ...	G. C.—Mid.	Barnsley.
							Mount Pleasant	Louth ...	G. N. (I.)	Dundalk and Goragh Wood.
							Mount Pleasant Colliery and			
							Brick Works	Flint	W. M. & C. Q.	Buckley.
G	P	F	L	H	C		Mount Pleasant Siding	Herts ...	G. N.	Hatfield.
							Mountrath and Castletown	Queens	G. S. & W.	Maryborough and Thurles.
							Mount St. Mary	Derby ...	L. D. & E. C.	See Spink Hill (for Mount St. Mary).
							Mount Sorrel	Leicester ..	G. C.	See Swithland Siding (for Mount Sorrel).
							Mount Sorrel Granite Co.—			
							Branch and Siding	Leicester ..	Mid.	Mount Sorrel Junction Station.
							Stoney Stanton Siding			
							(L. & N. W.)	Leicester ..	L. & N. W.—Mid.	Elmesthorpe.
G							Mount Sorrel Junc. Station	Leicester ..	Mid.	Sileby and Barrow-on-Soar.
							Ellis, J., & Son—			
							Barrow Lime Works	Leicester ..	Mid.	Near Mount Sorrel Junc. Station.
							Concrete Works	Leicester ..	Mid.	Near Mount Sorrel Junc. Station.
							Gibbs Bros.' Cement Works	Leicester ..	Mid.	Near Mount Sorrel Junc. Station.
							Mount Sorrel Granite Co.'s			
							Branch and Siding	Leicester ..	Mid.	Near Mount Sorrel Junc. Station.
							Mount Street Siding (N. & B.)	Brecon	N. & Brecon—Mid.	Cradoc.
							Mount Stuart Dry Dock and			
							Engineering Co.'s Siding...	Glamorg'n	GW—L&NW—Rhy—TV	Cardiff.
G	P	,					Mount Vernon	Lanark ...	{ Cal.	Coatbridge and Rutherglen.
									{ N. B.	Shettleston and Bothwell.
							Burntbroom Sand Pits	Lanark ...	Cal.	Mount Vernon.
							Daldowie Colliery	Lanark ...	Cal.	Mount Vernon and Baillieston.
							Kenmuirhill Colliery No. 2	Lanark ...	Cal.	Mount Vernon and Carmyle.
							Mount Vernon Collieries	Lanark ...	N. B.	Branch—Mount Vernon and Broomhouse.
							Mount Vernon Colliery			
							(Burntbroom Colliery) ...	Lanark ...	Cal.	Mount Vernon and Baillieston.
							Mount Vernon Sand Siding	Lanark ...	N. B.	Mount Vernon and Shettleston.
							Mount Vernon Iron & Steel			
							Works	Lanark ...	N. B.	Shettleston.
	P						Mourne Abbey	Cork	G. S. & W.	Mallow and Cork.
							Mowbray Branch	Cumb'land	W.C.&E.Jt.(Fur.&LNW)	Eskett and Frizington.
G	P						Mowbray Pits	Cumb'land	W.C.&E.Jt.(Fur.&LNW)	See Cammell & Co. (Frizington).
							Mow Cop	Cheshire..	N. S.	Harecastle and Congleton.
							Astbury Siding	Cheshire..	N. S.	Mow Cop.
G	P	F	L	H	C	1 10	Moxley	Staffs ...	G. W.	See Bradley and Moxley.
							Moy	Inverness	High.	Inverness and Aviemore.
G	P						Moy	Tyrone ...	G. N. (I.)	See Trew and Moy.
G	P	F	L	H	C		Moyasta Junction Station	Clare	West Clare	Miltown Malbay and Kilkee.
							Moycullen	Galway ...	M. G. W.	Galway and Clifden.
							Moy Road Siding	Glamorg'n	Rhy.	See Leon's Crwys Siding (Cardiff).
							Moy, T., & Co.'s Siding (G.E.)	Hunts	G E—G N—L&NW—Mid	Peterboro'.
							Moy, T., & Co., Siding	Suffolk	G. E.	Claydon.
	P						Moyvalley	Kildare ...	M. G. W.	Dublin and Mullingar.
G	P		L	H		1 10	Muchalls	Kinc'rdine	Cal.	Stonehaven and Aberdeen.
G	P	F	L	H	C	1 10	Much Wenlock	Salop	G. W.	Buildwas and Craven Arms.
							Boulton, A., & Co.	Salop	G. W.	Buildwas and Much Wenlock.
							Bradley Siding	Salop	G. W.	Buildwas and Much Wenlock.
							South Wales and Cannock			
							Chase Coal Co.'s Siding	Salop	G. W.	Buildwas and Much Wenlock.
G							Muckamore	Antrim ...	N. C. Com. (Mid.)	Dunadry and Antrim.
							Muckcroft Siding	Lanark ...	N. B.	See Bridgend.
							Muiravonside Colliery	Stirling ...	N. B.	Bowhouse.
							Muirbeath Colliery	Fife	N. B.	Townhill Junction Station.
							Muirburn Colliery	Ayr	G. & S.W.	Same as Annbank, Nos. 9 & 10 (Annbank).
							Muirburn Siding	Lanark ...	Cal.	See Auchlochan Colliery (Coalburn).

EXPLANATION—G Goods Station.   P Passenger and Parcel Station.   P* Passenger, but not Parcel or Miscellaneous Traffic.
F Furniture Vans, Carriages, Portable Engines, and Machines on Wheels.   L Live Stock.
H Horse Boxes and Prize Cattle Vans.   C Carriages by Passenger Train.

Station Accommodation	Crane Power	Stations, &c.	County	Company	Position
	Tons Cwts	Muircockhall Colliery	Fife	N. B.	Townhill Junction Station.
		Muiredge Brick Works	Fife	N. B.	Buckhaven.
		Muiredge Colliery	Fife	N. B.	Buckhaven.
		Muiredge Siding	Fife	N. B.	See Buckhaven.
G P F L H C	3 0	Muirend	Renfrew	Cal.	Whitecraigs and Cathcart.
		Muirhall Siding	Stirling	Cal.	Same as Stenhousemuir Siding (Larbert).
		Muirhead & Son's Saw Mill (Cal.)	Stirling	Cal.—N. B.	Same as Grangemouth Saw Mill.
		Muirhouse Boiler Works (Shieldmuir Boiler Works)	Lanark	Cal.	Shieldmuir.
		Muirhouse Collieries	Lanark	Cal.	Shieldmuir.
		Muirhouse Engine Works	Lanark	Cal.	Shieldmuir.
		Muirhouse Junction	Renfrew	Cal.	Glasgow.
		Muirhouse Siding	Ayr	Cal.	Giffen.
		Muirhouse Siding	Renfrew	Cal.	Glasgow, South Side.
G P F L H C	3 0	Muirkirk (G. & S. W.)	Ayr	{ G. & S. W. / Cal.	Branch from Auchinleck. / Over G. & S. W. from Muirkirk Jn.
		Auldhouseburn Colliery	Ayr	Cal.	Muirkirk and Glenbuck.
		Auldhouseburn Sidings	Ayr	Cal.	Muirkirk and Glenbuck.
		Crossflat Sidings	Ayr	Cal.	Muirkirk and Glenbuck.
		Glenbuck Pit	Ayr	G. & S. W.	Muirkirk Iron Works.
		Kaimes Colliery	Ayr	G. & S. W.	Muirkirk and Cronberry.
		Lightshaw Colliery	Ayr	G. & S. W.	Muirkirk Iron Works.
		Lower Wellwood Siding	Ayr	G. & S. W.	Muirkirk and Cronberry.
		Muirkirk Iron Works	Ayr	Cal.—G. & S. W.	Muirkirk.
		Upper Wellwood No. 1	Ayr	G. & S. W.	Muirkirk and Auchinleck.
		Muirkirk Junction	Ayr	Cal.—G. & S. W.	Douglas and Muirkirk.
		Muir, Son, & Patton's Lime Siding	Forfar	Cal.	Montrose.
		Muir's Siding	Ayr	G. & S. W.	Beith.
		Muir's Siding	Lanark	G B & K Jt (Cal & G & S W)	Glasgow, Strathbungo.
G P F L H C	5 0	Muir of Ord	Inverness	High.	Inverness and Dingwall.
G P F L H C	1 0	Mulben	Elgin & Mo'	High.	Keith and Elgin.
		Tauchers Siding	Elgin & Mo'	High.	Mulben and Keith.
G P	2 0	Mullafernaghan	Down	G. N. (I.)	Belfast and Banbridge.
P		Mullaghglass	Armagh	B. & Newry	Bessbrook and Newry.
G P . L H		Mullinavat	Kilkenny	G. S. & W.	Waterford and Kilkenny.
G P F L H C	1 10	Mullingar	W'meath	M. G. W.	Dublin and Athlone.
		Mullstane Craig Quarry	Renfrew	G. & S. W.	Paisley, Potterhill.
G P F L H C	1 10	Multyfarnham	W'meath	M. G. W.	Mullingar and Longford.
G P		Mumbles	Glamorg'n	Swan. & Mum.	Terminus.
G P . L / P	}	Mumbles Road	Glamorg'n	{ L. & N. W. / Swan. & Mum.	Llandilo and Swansea. / Swansea and Mumbles.
		Mumbles Road Junction	Glamorg'n	L.&N. W.—Swan.&Mum.	Swansea and Mumbles.
G P F L H C	1 10	Mumby Road	Lincoln	G. N.	Willoughby and Sutton-on-Sea.
		Mumps (L. & Y.)	Lancs	L. & Y.—L. & N. W.	See Oldham.
G P . L		Muncaster	Cumb'land	R. & E.	Ravenglass and Boot.
G P F L H C		Mundesley-on-Sea	Norfolk	N.&S. Jt. (GE&M&GNJt.)	Branch from North Walsham.
		Mundy's Colliery	Derby	Mid.	Same as Shipley Col. (Stanton Gate).
		Mungall's Saw Mill	Stirling	N. B.	Same as Bowhouse Saw Mill.
		Mungall's Siding	Edinboro'	Cal.	Cobbinshaw.
G P F L H C	2 10	Munlochy	Ross & Cro'	High.	Muir of Ord and Fortrose.
		Muntz Metal Co.'s Siding	Staffs	L. & N. W.	Soho.
		Murdestoun Colliery	Lanark	Cal.	Same as Westwood Col. (Cleland).
		Murdieston Siding (Paper Mill Branch)	Renfrew	Cal.	Greenock, Upper.
		Murgatroyd Salt Co.'s Siding	Cheshire	L. & N. W.	Middlewich.
		Murray & Co.'s Pottery	Lanark	Cal.	Same as Caledonian Pottery (Glasgow).
		Murrayfield	Edinboro'	Cal.	See Edinburgh.
		Murray's Brewery	Edinboro'	N. B.	Same as Craigmillar Brewery (Duddingston and Craigmillar).
		Murrayshall Lime Works	Stirling	N. B.	Stirling, Shore Road.
G P F L H C / G P . L H	5 0 }	Murrow	Cambs	{ G. N. & G. E. Jt. / Mid. & G. N. Jt.	Spalding and March. / Peterboro' and Wisbech.
G P F L H C	3 0	Murthly	Perth	High.	Perth and Dunkeld.
		Murthly Asylum Siding	Perth	High.	Murthly.
G P F L H		Murtle	Aberdeen	G. N. of S.	Aberdeen and Banchory.
		Murton Colliery	Durham	N. E.	Haswell.
G P F L H C	1 0	Murton Junction Station	Durham	N. E.	Sunderland and Durham (Elvet).
P		Musgrave	W'morlnd	N. E.	Kirkby Stephen and Appleby.

EXPLANATION—G *Goods Station.*   P *Passenger and Parcel Station.*   P* *Passenger, but not Parcel or Miscellaneous Traffic.*
F *Furniture Vans, Carriages, Portable Engines, and Machines on Wheels.*   L *Live Stock.*
H *Horse Boxes and Prize Cattle Vans.*   C *Carriages by Passenger Train.*

G	P	F	L	H	C	Tons	Cwts	STATIONS, &c.	COUNTY.	COMPANY.	POSITION.
								Musgrave & Son's Siding	Lancs	L. & Y.	Westhoughton.
								Musgrave Siding	Yorks	H. & B.	Same as South Hiendley Colliery (Cudworth).
								Mushet & Co.'s Works	Edinboro'	Cal.--N. B.	Granton.
								Musker's Siding	Lancs	L. & N. W.	Liverpool, Edge Hill.
								Muskham Siding	Notts	G. N.	Newark.
								Muspratt's Siding	Flint	L. & N. W.	Flint.
								Bone Phosphate Chemical Co.	Flint	L. & N. W.	Muspratt's Siding.
								United Alkali Co.	Flint	L. & N. W.	Muspratt's Siding.
								Muspratt's Works	Lancs	L. & N. W.—S. & M. Jt.	See United Alkali Co. (Widnes).
G	P	F	L	H	C	2	0	Musselburgh	Edinboro'	N. B.	Branch from New Hailes.
G								Anderson & Co.'s Foundry	Edinboro'	N. B.	Fisherrow Siding.
								Boglehole Siding (Bellfield Siding)	Edinboro'	N. B.	Musselburgh and New Hailes.
G								Fisherrow Siding	Edinboro'	N. B.	Musselburgh and New Hailes.
								Inveresk Paper Mills	Edinboro'	N. B.	Musselburgh.
								Olive Bank Siding	Edinboro'	N. B.	Fisherrow Siding.
								Stuart's Net Works	Edinboro'	N. B.	Musselburgh.
								West Bush Mills	Edinboro'	N. B.	Fisherrow Siding.
G	P							Muswell Hill (G. N.)	Middlesex	{ G. N. / N L.	Highgate and Alexandra Palace. / Over G. N. from Canonbury Junc.
G	P		L	H	C	2	0	Muthill (G. W.)	Perth	Cal.	Crieff Junction Station and Crieff.
								Mutley (G. W.)	Devon	G. W.—L. & S. W.	See Plymouth.
								Mwrwg Vale Colliery (G. W.)	Carmarth'	G. W.—L. & N. W.	Llangennech.
								Mwyndy	Glamorg'n	G. W.	Branch from Llantrisant.
								Brofiskin Siding (G.W.)	Glamorg'n	G. W.—T. V.	Mwyndy Branch.
								Bute Lime Works (G.W.)	Glamorg'n	G. W.—T. V.	Mwyndy Branch.
								Maesaraul Siding	Glamorg'n	G. W.	Mwyndy Branch.
								Mwyndy Lime Works Siding (G. W.)	Glamorg'n	G. W.—T. V.	Mwyndy Branch.
								Mwyndy Siding (Oxide and Iron Ore Co.) (G. W.)	Glamorg'n	G. W.—T. V.	Mwyndy Branch.
								Scull's Siding (G. W.)	Glamorg'n	G. W.—T. V.	Mwyndy Branch.
								Mye Siding	Stirling	N. B.	See Buchlyvie.
								Myle's Siding	Hadding'n	N. B.	Prestonpans.
								Mylnefield Quarry	Perth	Cal.	Invergowrie.
								Mynachdy Colliery	Glamorg'n	T. V.	Ynysybwl.
G								Mynydd-y-Garreg	Carmarth'	Gwen. Valleys	Kidwelly Junction and Four Roads.
								Myre Siding	L'lithgow	N. B.	See Winchburgh.
								Myrtle Hill Junction	Carmarth'	G. W.	Carmarthen.
G	P					5	0	Mytholmroyd	Yorks	L. & Y.	Todmorden and Sowerby Bridge.

N

G	P	F	L	H	C	Tons	Cwts	STATIONS, &c.	COUNTY.	COMPANY.	POSITION.
G	P	F	L	H	C			Naas	Kildare	G. S. & W.	Sallins and Tullow.
G	P	F	L	H	C			Naburn (N. E.)	Yorks	{ N. E. / G. N.	York and Selby. / Over N. E. from Shaftholme Junc.
								Nadin, J.N., & Co.'s Sid. (Mid.)	Derby	Mid.—L. & N. W.	Same as Stanton Col. (Swadlincote).
G	P		L	H	C	2	0	Nafferton	Yorks	N. E.	Bridlington and Driffield.
								Nornabell's Siding	Yorks	N. E.	Nafferton.
G	P							Nailsea	Somerset	G. W.	Bristol and Yatton.
								Nailstone Colliery (Mid.)	Leicester	Mid.—L. & N. W.	Bagworth.
G	P	F	L	H	C	1	10	Nailsworth	Glo'ster	Mid.	Branch from Stonehouse.
								Dunkirk Cloth Mill (Playne's)	Glo'ster	Mid.	Nailsworth Branch.
G	P	F	L	H	C	3	0	Nairn	Nairn	High.	Forres and Inverness.
								Nall & Co.'s Siding	Yorks	G. C.—L. & Y.	Penistone.
								Nall & Co.'s Siding (Mid.)	Yorks	Mid.—† H. & B.	Cudworth.
G	P		L	H				Nancegollan	Cornwall	G. W.	Gwinear Road and Helston.
G	P	F	L	H	C	5	0	Nannerch	Flint	L. & N. W.	Denbigh and Mold.
G								Nanstallon Wharf	Cornwall	L. & S.W.	Branch from Wadebridge.
G	P		L	H	C			Nantclwyd	Denbigh	L. & N. W.	Corwen and Denbigh.
G	P	F						Nantgaredig	Carmarth'	L. & N. W.	Carmarthen and Llandilo.
								Nantgwyn Colliery	Glamorg'n	G. W.	Same as Naval (Nantgwyn) Colliery (Penygraig).

EXPLANATION—G *Goods Station.*   P *Passenger and Parcel Station.*   P* *Passenger, but not Parcel or Miscellaneous Traffic.*
F *Furniture Vans, Carriages, Portable Engines, and Machines on Wheels.*   L *Live Stock.*
H *Horse Boxes and Prize Cattle Vans.*   C *Carriages by Passenger Train.*   † *For Local Traffic only.*

STATION ACCOMMODATION.						CRANE POWER.	STATIONS, &c.	COUNTY.	COMPANY.	POSITION.
						Tons Cwts				
G	P	.	.	.	.	5 0	Nantlle	Carnarvon	L. & N. W.	Branch from Penygroes.
.	.	.	.	.	.		Cilgwyn Slate Qry. Co.'s Sid.	Carnarvon	L. & N. W.	Nantlle Tram.
.	.	.	.	.	.		Coedmadoc Slate Co.'s Cloddfar Grai Siding	Carnarvon	L. & N. W.	Nantlle Tram.
.	.	.	.	.	.		Dorothea Slate Co.'s Pen-y-Bryn Siding	Carnarvon	L. & N. W.	Nantlle Tram.
.	.	.	.	.	.		Galty-fedw Slate Quarry Co.'s Siding.................	Carnarvon	L. & N. W.	Nantlle Tram.
.	.	.	.	.	.		Holyhead & North Wales Gas & Water Corporation Sid.	Carnarvon	L. & N. W.	Nantlle and Penygroes.
.	.	.	.	.	.		New Vronhenlog Slate Co.'s Siding	Carnarvon	L. & N. W.	Nantlle and Penygroes.
.	.	.	.	.	.		Penyrorsedd Slate Quarries	Carnarvon	L. & N. W.	Nantlle Tram.
							Robinson's Slate Quarries—			
.	.	.	.	.	.		Blaen Cae Siding	Carnarvon	L. & N. W.	Nantlle Tram.
.	.	.	.	.	.		Cloddfar Coed Siding......	Carnarvon	L. & N. W.	Nantlle Tram.
.	.	.	.	.	.		Talysarn Siding	Carnarvon	L. & N. W.	Nantlle Tram.
.	.	.	.	.	.		South Dorothea Slate Co.'s Cornwall Siding	Carnarvon	L. & N. W.	Nantlle Tram.
.	.	.	.	.	.		Tanrallt Siding	Carnarvon	L. & N. W.	Nantlle and Penygroes.
.	.	.	.	.	.		Nantlle Tram.....................	Carnarvon	L. & N. W.	Branch from Penygroes.
G	.	.	.	.	.		Nantmawr	Salop	Cam.	Branch from Llanymynech.
.	.	.	.	.	.		Nantmawr Junction	Montgom	Cam.	Llanymynech and Llanyblodwell.
.	.	.	.	.	.		Nantmelyn Colliery	Glamorg'n	G. W.—T. V.	Same as Bwllfa Dare or Bwllfa No. 2. Colliery.
.	.	.	.	.	.		Nantwen Colliery	Glamorg'n	T. B. Jt. (G. W. & Rhy.)	See Guest, Keen, & Nettlefold (Bedlinog).
G	P	F	L	H	C	5 0	Nantwich (L. & N. W.)	Cheshire ...	{ L. & N. W. .... / G. W.	Crewe and Whitchurch. / Over L. & N. W. from Nantwich Jn.
.	.	.	.	.	.		Nantwich Junction	Cheshire...	G. W.—L. & N. W.	Audlem and Crewe.
G	P	.	L	H	C		Nantybwch	Brecon ...	L. & N. W.	Abergavenny and Merthyr.
.	.	.	.	.	.		Nantybwch Junction............	Brecon ...	L. & N. W.—N. & R. Jt.	Nantybwch and Rhymney.
.	.	.	.	.	.		Nantycafn Colliery...............	Glamorg'n	N. & Brecon	Seven Sisters.
G	P	.	.	H	.		Nantyderry (G. W.)	Mon	{ G. W. .... / L. & N. W.	Pontypool Road and Abergavenny. / Over G. W. from Hereford.
G	P	.	.	.	.	6 0	Nantyffyllon	Glamorg'n	G. W.	Maesteg and Abergwynfi.
G	.	.	.	.	.		Nantyffyllon Colliery	Glamorg'n	G. W.	See North's (Maesteg).
G	P	F	L	H	C	2 0	Nantyglo (G. W.)	Mon	{ G. W. .... / L. & N. W.	Blaina and Brynmawr. / Over G. W. from Nantyglo Junction.
G	.	.	.	.	.	2 0	Black Vein Colliery	Mon	G. W.	Branch from Nantyglo.
							Coalbrookvale—			
.	.	.	.	.	.		East Siding (G. W.)	Mon	G. W.—L. & N. W.	Nantyglo and Blaina.
.	.	.	.	.	.		West Siding (J. G. & W. Barnes) (G. W.)	Mon	G. W.—L. & N. W.	Nantyglo and Blaina.
.	.	.	.	.	.		Lion Tin Plate Works	Mon	G. W.	Branch from Nantyglo.
.	.	.	.	.	.		Llyn Colliery (Forge Pit)...	Mon	G. W.	Branch from Nantyglo.
.	.	.	.	.	.		Pyle & Blaina Works (GW)	Mon	G. W.—L. & N. W.	Nantyglo (for Inwards Traffic).
.	.	.	.	.	.		Stone's Sun or North Blaina Colliery (G. W.)	Mon	G. W.—L. & N. W.	Nantyglo (for Inwards Traffic).
.	.	.	.	.	.		Nantyglo Junction	Mon	G. W.—L. & N. W.	Blaina and Abergavenny.
.	.	.	.	.	.		Nantyglo Iron Works (LNW)	Mon	L. & N. W.—G. W.	Brynmawr.
.	.	.	.	.	.		Nantyglo Lion Tin Works ...	Mon	{ G. W. .... / L. & N. W.	Nantyglo. / Brynmawr.
G	P	.	L	.	.	2 0	Nantymoel	Glamorg'n	G. W.	Branch from Black Mill.
.	.	.	.	.	.		Ocean Colliery..................	Glamorg'n	G. W.	Nantymoel.
G	P	F	L	H	C		Nantyronen	Cardigan..	V. of Rheidol	Aberystwyth and Devil's Bridge.
.	.	.	.	.	.		Nantywrach Siding	Carmarth'	G. W.	Pantyffynnon.
.	.	.	.	.	.		N. A. O. Food Co.'s Siding...	Middlesex	{ G. E. .... / GN—GW—LNW—Mid	London, Millwall Docks. / London, Poplar.
.	.	.	.	.	.		Napier & Miller's Shipbuilding Yard	Renfrew...	Cal.—N. B.	Same as Yoker Shipbuilding Yard.
.	.	.	.	.	.		Napsbury Siding	Herts	Mid.	St. Albans.
G	P	.	L	H	.		Napton and Stockton	Warwick..	L. & N. W.	Leamington and Weedon.
.	.	.	.	.	.		Griffin's Siding	Warwick..	L. & N. W.	Napton and Southam.
.	.	.	.	.	.		Nelson's Siding	Warwick..	L. & N. W.	Napton and Southam.
G	P	F	L	H	C	2 0	Narberth	Pembroke	G. W.	Whitland and Tenby.
G	P	F	L	H	C	1 0	Narborough	Norfolk ...	G. E.	Lynn and Swaffham.
.	.	.	.	.	.		Vynne & Everett's Siding...	Norfolk ...	G. E.	Narborough.
G	P	F	L	H	C	1 10	Narborough (L. & N. W.) ...	Leicester..	{ L. & N. W. .... / Mid.	Leicester and Nuneaton. / Over L. & N. W. Line.
G	.	F	L	.	.	1 10				
.	.	.	.	.	.		Empire Indurated Stone Co.'s Siding	Leicester..	L. & N. W.	Narborough.

EXPLANATION—G *Goods Station.*   P *Passenger and Parcel Station.*   P* *Passenger, but not Parcel or Miscellaneous Traffic.*
F *Furniture Vans, Carriages, Portable Engines, and Machines on Wheels.*   L *Live Stock.*
H *Horse Boxes and Prize Cattle Vans.*   C *Carriages by Passenger Train.*

STATION ACCOMMODATION.							CRANE POWER.		STATIONS, &c.	COUNTY.	COMPANY.	POSITION.
							Tons	Cwts				
									Narborough (L. & N. W.)—continued.			
									Enderby & Stoney Stanton Granite Co.'s—			
.	.	.	.	.	.	.	.	.	Narboro' Quarry............	Leicester..	L. & N. W.	Narborough and Elmesthorpe.
.	.	.	.	.	.	.	.	.	Siding	Leicester..	L. & N. W. & Mid. Jt....	Enderby Branch.
									Narborough and Enderby Granite Co.'s Siding (L. & N. W. & Mid. Jt.)...	Leicester..	{ L. & N. W. .... { Mid.	Narborough. Leicester.
.	P	.	.	.	.	.	.	.	Narrow Water	Down	G. N. (I.)	Newry and Warrenpoint.
.	.	.	.	.	.	.	.	.	Nash & Co.'s Siding	Herts	G. N.	Royston.
.	.	.	.	.	.	.	.	.	Nash's Brick Works Siding..	Bucks......	G. W.	Slough.
G	P	F	L	H	C	.	5	0	Nasmyth, Wilson & Co.'s Sid.	Lancs	L. & N. W.	Patricroft.
.	P	.	.	H	C	.			Nassington (L. & N. W.)......	N'hamptn	{ L. & N. W. .... { G. N.	Market Harboro' and Peterboro'. Over L. & N. W. from Longville Jn.
G	P	.	L	H	.	.	.	.	Nateby	Lancs	G. & K. E.	Garstang and Pilling.
.	.	.	.	.	.	.	.	.	National Brick Co.'s Siding...	Leicester..	A & N Jt. (L & N W & Mid.)	Heather and Ibstock.
.	.	.	.	.	.	.	.	.	National Colliery	Glamorg'n	T. V.	Wattstown.
.	.	.	.	.	.	.	.	.	National Oil Co.'s Warehouse	Cheshire...	B'head Jt—CLC—NW&L	Birkenhead.
.	.	.	.	.	.	.	.	.	National Rifle Association's Siding (Bisley Camp)	Surrey ...	L. & S. W.	Brookwood.
.	.	.	.	.	.	.	.	.	National Telephone Co.'s Sid.	Leicester..	A & N Jt. (L & N W & Mid.)	Nuneaton.
.	.	.	.	.	.	.	.	.	National Telephone Siding ...	Lanark ...	Cal.	Glasgow, Kinning Park.
.	.	.	.	.	.	.	.	.	National Trading Co.	Glo'ster ...	G. W.	Bullo Pill.
.	.	.	.	.	.	.	.	.	Nattrass, F., & Son's Siding..	Durham ...	N. E.	Stockton, South.
.	.	.	.	.	.	.	.	.	Naval Colliery.................	Glamorg'n	T. V.	Same as Pandy Pit (Trealaw).
.	.	.	.	.	.	.	.	.	Naval Ely Colliery............	Glamorg'n	G. W.	Penygraig.
.	.	.	.	.	.	.	.	.	Naval (Nantgwyn) Colliery...	Glamorg'n	G. W.	Penygraig.
G	P	F	L	H	C	.	5	0	Navan	Meath ...	{ G. N. (I.) .... { M. G. W.	Drogheda and Kells. Kilmessan and Kingscourt.
G	P	F	L	H	C	.	4	18	Navan Junction	Meath......	G. N. (I.)—M. G. W. ...	Ballybeg and Kilmessan.
G	P	F	L	H	C	.	.	.	Navenby	Lincoln ...	G. N.	Lincoln and Grantham.
.	.	.	.	.	.	.	.	.	Navigation Colliery	Glamorg'n	G. W.	See North's (Tondu).
.	.	.	.	.	.	.	.	.	Navigation Colliery	Glamorg'n	G. W.—T. V.—Rhy......	See Nixon's (Mountain Ash).
.	P	.	.	.	.	.	.	.	Navigation Sidings	Glamorg'n	T. V.	See Nixon's (Mountain Ash).
.	.	.	.	.	.	.	.	.	Naworth	Cumb'land	N. E.	Carlisle and Hexham.
.	.	.	.	.	.	.	.	.	Naworth Collieries............	Cumb'land	N. E.	Same as Kirkhouse Collieries (Brampton Junction Station).
G	P	F	L	H	C	.			Nawton.......................	Yorks	N. E.	Helmsley and Kirby Moorside.
.	.	.	.	.	.	.	.	.	Neal's Siding	Surrey ...	L. & S. W. & L. B. & S. C. Jt.	Haydon's Road.
.	.	.	.	.	.	.	.	.	Neasden	Middlesex	{ Met. .... { Mid.	See London, Kingsbury-Neasden. See London, Dudding Hill (for Willesden and Neasden).
.	.	.	.	.	.	.	.	.	Neasden Junction	Middlesex	G. C.—Mid..................	London, Harrow & Acton Wells Jn.
.	.	.	.	.	.	.	.	.	Neasden Junc. & Sids. (G.C.)	Middlesex	G. C.—L. & S. W.	London, Neasden Junc., & Harrow.
									NEATH—			
G	P	F	L	H	C	.	10	0	(Station)	Glamorg'n	G. W.	Landore and Port Talbot.
G	.	.	L	.	.	.	1	0	(Station)	Glamorg'n	N. & Brecon	Cadoxton Junction and Crynant.
G	P	F	L	H	C	.	7	0	(Station)	Glamorg'n	R. & S. B.	Branch from Court Sart.
.	.	.	.	.	.	.	.	.	Cadoxton Junction............	Glamorg'n	G. W.—N. & Brecon......	Neath (Low Level) and Crynant.
.	.	.	.	.	.	.	.	.	Eaglesbush Colliery	Glamorg'n	G. W.	Neath and Briton Ferry.
.	.	.	.	.	.	.	.	.	Eagle Tin Plate Works...	Glamorg'n	G. W.	Neath and Briton Ferry.
.	.	.	.	.	.	.	.	.	Junction	Glamorg'n	G. W.	Neath (Low Level) and Aberdylais.
.	P	F	.	.	.	.	.	.	Low Level (G. W.)	Glamorg'n	{ G. W. .... { N. & Brecon	Neath Abbey and Neath Junction. Over G. W. from Cadoxton Junc.
									Melincrythan Chemical Co.—			
.	.	.	.	.	.	.	.	.	Acid Siding.................	Glamorg'n	R. & S. B.	Neath.
.	.	.	.	.	.	.	.	.	Siding	Glamorg'n	G. W.	Neath and Briton Ferry.
.	.	.	.	.	.	.	.	.	Melyn Tin Works	Glamorg'n	G. W.	Neath and Briton Ferry.
.	.	.	.	.	.	.	.	.	Mill Lands Brk. & Tile Wks.	Glamorg'n	G. W.	Neath.
.	.	.	.	.	.	.	.	.	Neath Corporation Gas Works................	Glamorg'n	G. W.	Neath.
.	.	.	.	.	.	.	.	.	Neath Steel Sheet and Galvanizing Co.............	Glamorg'n	G. W.	Neath and Briton Ferry.
.	.	.	.	.	.	.	.	.	Oliver, Thomas & Co.'s Wks.	Glamorg'n	G. W.	Neath.
.	.	.	.	.	.	.	.	.	Vale of Neath Brewery...	Glamorg'n	N. & Brecon	Neath.
G	P	.	.	.	.	.	.	.	Neath Abbey	Glamorg'n	G. W.	Neath and Swansea.
.	.	.	.	.	.	.	.	.	Cardonnel Tin Plate Works	Glamorg'n	G. W.	Neath Abbey & Briton Ferry Road.
.	.	.	.	.	.	.	.	.	Cwrt-y-bettws Colliery	Glamorg'n	G. W.	Swansea and Neath Abbey.
.	.	.	.	.	.	.	.	.	Duffryn Main Siding.........	Glamorg'n	G. W.	Neath Abbey and Neath (Low Level).
.	.	.	.	.	.	.	.	.	Main Colliery	Glamorg'n	G. W.	Neath Abbey.
.	.	.	.	.	.	.	.	.	Neath Harbour Junction	Glamorg'n	R. & S. B.—S. Wales Min.	Neath and Cymmer.
.	.	.	.	.	.	.	.	.	Neath River Bridge Siding ...	Glamorg'n	R. & S. B.	Jersey Marine.

EXPLANATION—G *Goods Station.*   P *Passenger and Parcel Station.*   P* *Passenger, but not Parcel or Miscellaneous Traffic.*
F *Furniture Vans, Carriages, Portable Engines, and Machines on Wheels.*   L *Live Stock.*
H *Horse Boxes and Prize Cattle Vans.*   C *Carriages by Passenger Train.*

STATION ACCOMMODATION.						CRANE POWER.	STATIONS, &c.	COUNTY.	COMPANY.	POSITION.
						Tons Cwts				
.	.	.	.	.	.	. .	Neave (Lady) Siding............	Essex	G. E.	Romford.
.	.	.	.	.	.	. .	Nechell's Gas Works............	Warwick..	L. & N. W.—Mid.—G. W.	See Birmingham Corporation.
.	.	.	.	.	.	. .	Necropolis Station..............	Surrey	L. & S.W.	See Brookwood.
.	.	.	.	.	.	. .	Nedham Street Wharf	Leicester..	Mid.	See Leicester, East.
G	P	F	L	H	C	1 10	Needham......................	Suffolk	G. E.	Ipswich and Haughley.
.	.	.	.	.	.	. .	Needham's Siding	Yorks	G. C.	Barnsley.
.	.	.	.	.	.	. .	Needingworth Junction	Hunts......	G. E.—G. N. & G. E. Jt.	St. Ives.
G	P	F	L	H	C	5 0	Neen Sollars	Salop	G. W.	Tenbury and Bewdley.
.	.	.	.	.	.	. .	Neepsend	Yorks	G. C.	See Sheffield.
.	.	.	.	.	.	. .	Neepsend Gas Works (G. C.)	Yorks	G. C.—G. N.—Mid.	See United Gas Light Co. (Sheffield).
.	.	.	.	.	.	. .	Neepsend Works (G. C.)	Yorks	G.C.—G. N.—L. & N. W.	Same as Sheffield Brick Co.'s Siding (Sheffield).
.	P	.	.	.	.	. .	Neill's Hill	Down	B. & C. D.	Belfast and Knock.
.	.	.	.	.	.	. .	Neill's Hill Siding	Down	B. & C. D.	Belfast and Knock.
.	.	.	.	.	.	. .	Neilsen, Andersen & Co.'s Wharf	Northumb	N. E.	Newcastle-on-Tyne.
.	.	.	.	.	.	. .	Neilsland Colliery	Lanark ...	Cal.	Meikle Earnock.
.	.	.	.	.	.	. .	Neilson, Reid & Co.'s Siding	Lanark ...	N. B.	Same as Hydepark Works (Glasgow).
.	.	.	.	.	.	. .	Neilson's Iron Ore Siding......	N'hamptn	Mid.	Wellingboro'.
G	P	F	L	H	C	3 0	Neilston	Renfrew...	Cal.	Giffen and Clarkston.
G	P	F	L	H	C	4 0	Neilston	Renfrew...	G B & K Jt(Cal & G&SW)	Barrhead and Stewarton.
G	.	.	L	.	.	. .	Netherton Depôt	Renfrew...	Cal.	Neilston and Patterton.
.	.	.	.	.	.	. .	Neilston Colliery	Stirling ...	N. B.	Gavell.
.	.	.	.	.	.	. .	Nellfield Brick Works	Lanark ...	Cal.	Braidwood.
.	.	.	.	.	.	. .	Nellfield Saw Mills	Lanark ...	Cal.	Braidwood.
.	.	.	.	.	.	. .	Nelly Pit	Fife.........	N. B.	See Lochgelly Collieries, No. 12 Siding (Lochgelly).
G	P	F	L	H	C	10 0	Nelson	Lancs	L. & Y.	Colne and Burnley.
.	.	.	.	.	.	. .	Chaffer's Siding	Lancs	L. & Y.	Nelson.
.	.	.	.	.	.	. .	Nelson New Depôt	Lancs	L. & Y.	Nelson.
G	P	.	.	H	.	. .	Nelson	Glamorg'n	T. V.	Pontypridd and Llancaiach Junc.
.	.	.	.	.	.	. .	Mathias' Siding	Glamorg'n	T. V.	Nelson.
.	.	.	.	.	.	. .	Whitehall Quarry	Glamorg'n	T.V.	Nelson.
.	.	.	.	.	.	. .	Nelson & Son's Warehouse ..	Cheshire..	B'head Jt—CLC—NW&L	Birkenhead.
.	.	.	.	.	.	. .	Nelson Dock	Lancs	L'pool O'head	See Liverpool.
.	.	.	.	.	.	. .	Nelson's Siding	Warwick..	L. & N. W.	Napton and Stockton.
G	P	F	L	H	C	2 0	Nenagh	Tipperary	G. S. & W.	Roscrea and Birdhill.
.	.	.	.	.	.	. .	Nene Siding	N'hamptn	Mid.	Same as Consolidated Oil Co.'s Siding (Peterboro').
.	.	.	.	.	.	. .	Nene Sulphate Works	N'hamptn	Mid.	Northampton, Bridge Street.
.	.	.	.	.	.	. .	Neptune Siding	Northumb	N. E.	Same as Wigham, Richardson & Co.'s Siding (Walker).
.	.	.	.	.	.	. .	Neptune Street	Yorks	H. & B.	See Hull.
.	.	.	.	.	.	. .	Nerquis Old Colliery Level Siding......................	Flint	L. & N. W.	Coed Talon.
.	.	.	.	.	.	. .	Davies'	Flint	L. & N. W.	Nerquis Old Colliery Level Siding.
.	.	.	.	.	.	. .	Edwards'	Flint	L. & N. W.	Nerquis Old Colliery Level Siding.
.	.	.	.	.	.	. .	Griffiths'	Flint	L. & N. W.	Nerquis Old Colliery Level Siding.
.	.	.	.	.	.	. .	Nesbitt Junction	Meath.....	M. G. W.	Enfield and Moyvalley.
.	.	.	.	.	.	. .	Ness's Siding	Yorks	N. E.	Eryholme.
.	.	.	.	.	.	. .	Nestfield Nut & Bolt Works..	Durham ...	N. E.	Darlington, Bank Top.
G	P	.	L	.	.	10 0	Neston	Cheshire...	B'head Jt. (G W & L N W)	Hooton and West Kirby.
G	P	F	L	H	C	3 0	Neston and Parkgate	Cheshire...	N.W. & L. Jt. (G. C. and W. M. & C. Q.)	Connah's Quay & Shotton and Birkenhead.
G	P	.	.	.	.	1 10	Netherburn	Lanark ...	Cal.	Larkhall and Lesmahagow.
.	.	.	.	.	.	. .	Bentrigg Colliery	Lanark ...	Cal.	Netherburn and Tillietudlem.
.	.	.	.	.	.	. .	Craignethan Siding	Lanark ...	Cal.	Netherburn and Tillietudlem.
.	.	.	.	.	.	. .	Netherburn Siding	Lanark ...	Cal.	Netherburn.
.	.	.	.	.	.	. .	South Longrigg Colliery (Hill Colliery)................	Lanark ...	Cal.	Dalserf and Netherburn.
.	.	.	.	.	.	. .	Woodside Collieries	Lanark ...	Cal.	Dalserf and Netherburn.
G	P	.	L	H	.	4 10	Nethercleugh	Dumfries..	Cal.	Lockerbie and Carstairs.
.	.	.	.	.	.	. .	Corncockle Quarry	Dumfries..	Cal.	Nethercleugh.
.	.	.	.	.	.	. .	Jardine Hall Siding	Dumfries..	Cal.	Nethercleugh.
.	.	.	.	.	.	. .	Nethercroy Siding............	Dumbartn	N. B.	Dullatur.
.	.	.	.	.	.	. .	Netherdale Siding (Cochrane Bros.)	Selkirk ...	N. B.	Galashiels.
.	.	.	.	.	.	. .	Netherend Siding	Worcester	G. W.	Cradley Heath and Cradley.
.	.	.	.	.	.	. .	Netherfield	Notts	Mid.	See Carlton and Netherfield.
G	P	.	.	.	.	. .	Netherfield & Colwick (G. N.)	Notts	G. N.	Gedling and Nottingham.
									L. & N. W.	Over G. N. from Saxondale Junc.

EXPLANATION—G Goods Station.   P Passenger and Parcel Station.   P* Passenger, but not Parcel or Miscellaneous Traffic.
F Furniture Vans, Carriages, Portable Engines, and Machines on Wheels.   L Live Stock.
H Horse Boxes and Prize Cattle Vans.   C Carriages by Passenger Train.

STATION ACCOMMODATION.						CRANE POWER.		STATIONS, &c.	COUNTY.	COMPANY.	POSITION.
						Tons	Cwts				
.	.	..	.		.	.	.	Netherfield & Colwick (G. N.) —continued.			
.	.	.	.	.	.	.	.	Lawrence & Co.'s Siding ...	Notts	G. N.	Netherfield & Colwick and Nottingham.
.	.	.	.	.	.	.	.	Netherfield Siding............	Notts	G. N.	Netherfield & Colwick and Gedling.
.	.	.	.	.	.	.	.	Nottingham Corporation Sewage Siding	Notts	G. N.	Rectory Junction and Gedling.
.	.	.	.	.	.	.	.	Netherfield & Colwick North Junction	Notts	G. N.	Radcliffe-on-Trent and Gedling.
.	.	.	.	.	.	.	.	Netherfield & Colwick, Rectory Junction	Notts	G. N.	Radcliffe-on-Trent and Gedling.
.	.	.	.	.	.	.	.	Netherfield & Colwick West Junction	Notts	G. N.	Radcliffe-on-Trent and Nottingham.
.	.	.	.	.	.	.	.	Netherinch Sand Siding	Stirling	N. B.	Gavell.
.	.	.	.	.	.	.	.	Netherjohnstone Collieries ...	Lanark ...	Cal.	See Belhaven Estate Collieries (Shieldmuir).
.	.	.	.	.	.	.	.	Netherjohnstone Washer......	Lanark ...	Cal.	Shieldmuir.
.	.	.	.	.	.	.	.	Nethermains Siding	Stirling ...	Cal.	Denny.
.	.	.	.	.	.	.	.	Netherseal Colliery (Mid.) ...	Leicester..	Mid.—L. & N. W.	Gresley.
.	.	.	.	.	.	.	.	Netherseal Wharf (Mid.)......	Derby	Mid.—L. & N. W.	Gresley.
G	.	.	.	.	.	0	15	Netherton	Fife	N. B.	Branch—Dunfermline, Lower and Charlestown.
.	.	.	.	.	.	.	.	Dunfermline Gas Works ...	Fife	N. B.	Dunfermline, Lower & Elbowend Jn.
G	P	.	.	.	.	6	0	Elbowend Siding	Fife	N. B.	Charlestown and Netherton.
.	.	.	.	.	.	.	.	Netherton	Worcester	G. W.	Dudley and Stourbridge Junction.
.	.	.	.	.	.	.	.	Barn, Bye and Pear Tree Lane Collieries	Worcester	G. W.	Netherton and Hartshill.
.	.	.	.	.	.	.	.	Blowers Green Colliery......	Worcester	G. W.	Dudley and Stourbridge Junction.
.	.	.	.	.	.	.	.	Dudley South Side............	Worcester	G. W.	Dudley and Stourbridge Junction.
.	.	.	.	.	.	.	.	Grazebrook Siding............	Worcester	G. W.	Dudley and Stourbridge Junction.
.	.	.	.	.	.	.	.	Hingley & Son's (Cox's Lane Siding)	Worcester	G. W.	Old Hill and Windmill End.
.	.	.	.	.	.	.	.	Stourbridge Glazed Brick & Fire-Clay Co.'s Col. & Sid.	Worcester	G. W.	Dudley and Stourbridge Junction.
G	P	F	L	H	C	10	0	Netherton	Yorks	L. & Y.	Lockwood and Meltham.
.	.	.	.	.	.	.	.	Netherton Depôt	Renfrew...	Cal.	See Neilston.
.	.	.	.	.	.	.	.	Netherton Hall Colliery	Northumb	N. E.	Choppington.
.	.	.	.	.	.	.	.	Netherton Lime Works	Lanark ...	Cal.	Auchenheath.
G	P	.	L	H	.	.	.	Nethertown	Cumb'land	Furness	Ravenglass and Whitehaven.
.	.	.	.	.	.	.	.	Netherwood Siding	Dumbartn	N. B.	See Castlecary.
G	P	F	L	H	C	.	.	Nethy Bridge	Inverness	G. N. of S.	Craigellachie and Boat of Garten.
G	P	F	L	H	C	5	0	Netley	Hants	L. & S.W.	Fareham and Southampton.
.	.	.	.	.	.	.	.	Nettlefold's Branch Junction	Mon	G. W.	Newport, High Str. and Llanwern.
.	.	.	.	.	.	.	.	Nettlefold's Rogerstone Wks.	Mon	B. & M.	Bassaleg.
.	.	.	.	.	.	.	.	Nettlefold's Works Sidings...	Mon	G. W.	See Guest, Keen & Nettlefold (Rogerstone).
.	.	.	.	.	.	.	.	Neville, Druce & Co.'s Copper Works (G. W.)	Carmarth'	G. W.—L. & N. W.	Llanelly.
.	.	.	.	.	.	.	.	Neville Hill Sidings	Yorks	N. E.	Leeds, Marsh Lane.
.	.	.	.	.	.	.	.	Neville, R., & Co.'s Sid.(GW)	Carmarth'	G. W.—L. & N. W.	Llanelly.
.	.	.	.	.	.	.	.	Neville's Copper Works Dock (G. W.)	Carmarth'	G. W.—L. & N. W.	Llanelly.
.	.	.	.	.	.	.	.	Neville's (Skelbrook) Siding..	Yorks	H. & B.	Pickburn and Brodsworth.
.	.	.	.	.	.	.	.	Neville's Siding (L. & N. W.)	Staffs	L. & N. W.—G. W.—Mid.	Walsall.
.	.	.	.	.	.	.	.	Nevin	Carnarvon	L. & N. W	See Chwilog (for Nevin).
.	.	.	.	.	.	.	.	Nevis Distillery	Inverness	N. B.	Fort William.
.	.	.	.	.	.	.	.	Newall's Wire Rope Works...	Durham ...	N. E.	Washington.
								NEWARK—			
G	P	F	L	H	C	10	0	(Station)	Notts	Mid.	Nottingham and Lincoln.
G	P	F	L	H	C	10	0	(Station, G. N.)	Notts	{ G. N.	Grantham and Retford.
G	.	F	L	.	.	10	0		Notts	{ L. & N. W.	Over G. N. from Bottesford North Jn.
.	.	.	.	.	.	.	.	Abbott & Co.'s Siding......	Notts	G. N.	Newark.
								Bishop & Son—			
.	.	.	.	.	.	.	.	Cow Lane Malt Kiln	Notts	G. N. & Mid. Jt.	Joint Curve.
.	.	.	.	.	.	.	.	Spital Maltings	Notts	G. N. & Mid. Jt.	Joint Curve.
.	.	.	.	.	.	.	.	Bradley's, T. W., Iron Wks.	Notts	G. N.—Mid.	Joint Curve.
								Branston's—			
.	.	.	.	.	.	.	.	Maltings (G. N.)............	Notts	G. N.—Mid.	Newark.
.	.	.	.	.	.	.	.	Riverside Malt Kiln	Notts	G. N. & Mid. Jt.	Joint Curve.
								Cafferata & Co.—			
.	.	.	.	.	.	.	.	Bowbridge Siding........	Notts	G. N.	Newark and Cotham.
.	.	.	.	.	.	.	.	Siding	Notts	G. N.	Newark.
.	.	.	.	.	.	.	.	Cross Street Siding	Notts	G. N.	Newark and Cotham.

EXPLANATION—G *Goods Station.*　　P *Passenger and Parcel Station.*　　P* *Passenger, but not Parcel or Miscellaneous Traffic.*
F *Furniture Vans, Carriages, Portable Engines, and Machines on Wheels.*　　L *Live Stock.*
H *Horse Boxes and Prize Cattle Vans.*　　C *Carriages by Passenger Train.*

STATION ACCOMMODATION.						CRANE POWER.	STATIONS, &c.	COUNTY.	COMPANY.	POSITION.
						Tons Cwts	NEWARK—continued.			
.	.	.	.	.	.	. .	Farrar's Siding	Notts	G. N. & Mid. Jt.	Joint Curve.
							Gilstrap, Earp & Co.—			
.	.	.	.	.	.	. .	Cow Lane Maltings......	Notts	G. N. & Mid. Jt.	Joint Curve.
.	.	.	.	.	.	. .	Maltings (G. N.)............	Notts	G. N.—Mid.	Newark.
.	.	.	.	.	.	. .	Massey Sidings	Notts	G. N. & Mid. Jt.	Joint Curve.
							Hole & Co.—			
.	.	.	.	.	.	. .	Siding (Mid.)	Notts	{ Mid. .... { G.N.	Newark. (See Appendix to follow).
.	.	.	.	.	.	. .	Spital Maltings	Notts	G. N. & Mid. Jt.	Joint Curve.
.	.	.	.	.	.	. .	Junction	Notts	G. N.—Mid.	Newark (G.N.) and Newark (Mid.)
.	.	.	.	.	.	. .	Lowfield Sidings.............	Notts	G. N.	Newark and Cotham.
.	.	.	.	.	.	. .	Almond Siding (Belvoir Brick Works).......	Notts	G. N.	Lowfield Sidings.
.	.	.	.	.	.	. .	Belvoir Plaster Co.'s Sid.	Notts	G. N.	Lowfield Sidings.
.	.	.	.	.	.	. .	Simpson & Co.'s Siding...	Notts	G. N.	Lowfield Sidings.
G	.	.	.	.	.	. .	Muskham Siding	Notts	G. N.	Newark and Carlton.
.	.	.	.	.	.	. .	Nicholson & Son's Sid.(Mid).	Notts	{ Mid. .... { G.N.	Newark. (See Appendix to follow).
.	.	.	.	.	.	. .	Parnham & Son's Water Mill (Mid.)	Notts	{ Mid. { G. N.	Nottingham and Newark. (See Appendix to follow).
.	.	.	.	.	.	. .	Quibell Bros.' Siding (G.N.)	Notts	G. N.—Mid.	Newark.
.	.	.	.	.	.	. .	Ransome & Co.'s Siding...	Notts	G. N.	Newark.
.	.	.	.	.	.	. .	Warwick & Richardson's Sid	Notts	G. N. & Mid. Jt.	Joint Curve.
.	.	.	.	.	.	. .	Wheatcroft's Siding.......	Notts	Mid.	Newark.
.	.	.	.	.	.	. .	Newark Sailcloth Co.'s Siding	Renfrew ...	Cal.	Greenock, Regent Street.
.	.	.	.	.	.	. .	Newark Water Works Pumping Station	Notts	Mid.	Farnsfield.
G	.	.	L	.	.	2 0	Newarthill	Lanark ...	Cal.	Holytown and Edinburgh.
.	.	.	.	.	.	. .	Carfin Boiler Works	Lanark ...	Cal.	Holytown and Wishaw, Central.
.	.	.	.	.	.	. .	Carfin Brick Works	Lanark ...	Cal.	Holytown and Wishaw, Central.
.	.	.	.	.	.	. .	Carfin Chemical Works.....	Lanark ...	Cal.	Holytown and Wishaw, Central.
.	.	.	.	.	.	. .	Carfin Collieries	Lanark ...	Cal.	Holytown and Wishaw, Central.
.	.	.	.	.	.	. .	Carfin Collieries, Nos. 6 & 7	Lanark ...	Cal.	Holytown and Wishaw, Central.
.	.	.	.	.	.	. .	Cleland Collieries	Lanark ...	Cal.	Newarthill and Cleland.
.	.	.	.	.	.	. .	Holytown Cols. & Bk. Wks.	Lanark ...	Cal.	Holytown.
.	.	.	.	.	.	. .	Jenny Lind Brick Works...	Lanark ...	Cal.	Holytown and Wishaw, Central.
.	.	.	.	.	.	. .	Nimmo & Co.'s Siding	Lanark ...	Cal.	Holytown.
.	.	.	.	.	.	. .	New Bailey Street.............	Lancs	L. & Y.	See Manchester, Salford.
.	.	.	.	.	.	. .	New Barnet (G. N.)	Herts	G. N.—N. L.—S. E. & C.	See Barnet, New.
.	.	.	.	.	.	. .	New Barns Junction............	Lancs	L. & Y.—Ship Canal......	Manchester, Salford.
.	.	.	.	.	.	. .	New Basford (G. C.)	Notts	G. C.—G. N.	See Nottingham.
.	.	.	.	.	.	. .	Newbattle Branch	Edinboro'	N. B.	Hardengreen.
.	.	.	.	.	.	. .	Newbattle Brick Works	Edinboro'	N. B.	Hardengreen.
.	.	.	.	.	.	. .	Newbattle Colliery	Edinboro'	N. B.	Hardengreen.
.	P	.	.	.	.	. .	New Beckenham	Kent	S. E. & C.	Catford Bridge and Beckenham Jn.
.	.	.	.	.	.	. .	Newbegin Colliery	Yorks	G. C.	See Newton Chambers & Co. (Westw'd)
.	.	.	.	.	.	. .	Newbie Brick Works............	Dumfries.	G. & S.W.	Annan.
G	P	F	L	H	C	. .	New Biggin.	W'morlnd	Mid.	Appleby and Carlisle.
.	.	.	.	.	.	. .	Boazman's, H., Siding	W'morlnd	Mid.	Near New Biggin.
G	P	F	L	H	C	1 0	Newbiggin-by-the-Sea	Northumb	N. E.	Branch from Bedlington.
.	.	.	.	.	.	. .	Woodhorn Siding	Northumb	N. E.	Newbiggin-by-the-Sea.
.	.	.	.	.	.	. .	Newbiggin Siding..............	Yorks	N. E.	{ Grosmont. { Sleights.
G	P	.	L	H	.	. .	Newbigging	Lanark ...	Cal.	Carstairs and Dolphinton.
G	.	.	.	.	.	. .	Todholes Siding	Lanark ...	Cal.	Newbigging and Dunsyre.
.	.	.	.	.	.	. .	Newbigging Siding	Fife.........	N. B.	See Carron Iron Co. (Burntisland).
.	.	.	.	.	.	. .	Newbigging Siding	Yorks	L. & Y.	Bradford, Low Moor.
.	.	.	.	.	.	. .	New Birchwood Colliery	Derby	Mid.	See Seeley's (Pye Bridge).
G	P	F	L	.	.	1 10	Newbliss	Monaghan	G. N. (I.)	Dundalk and Clones.
.	.	.	.	.	.	. .	Newbold's Siding	Warwick.	Mid.	See Rugby Portland Cement Co. (Rugby).
.	.	.	.	.	.	. .	New Boston Branch (for Haydock Collieries)	Lancs	G. C. (St. Helens Exten.)	{ See Evans, R., & Co. (Ashton-in-Makerfield).
.	.	.	.	.	.	. .	New Boston Colliery............	Lancs	{ G. C. (St. Helens Exten.) { L. & N. W.	See Evans, R., & Co. (Ashton-in-Makerfield). See Evans, R., & Co. (Earlestown).
.	.	.	.	.	.	. .	Newbottle Manure Siding ...	Durham ...	N. E.	{ Fencehouses. { Penshaw.
.	.	.	.	.	.	. .	New Bowson Colliery	Glo'ster ...	G. W.	Bilson Junction.
.	.	.	.	.	.	. .	New Brancepeth Colliery Coke Ovens & Brick Works	Durham ...	N. E.	Waterhouses.

EXPLANATION—G Goods Station.   P Passenger and Parcel Station.   P* Passenger, but not Parcel or Miscellaneous Traffic.
F Furniture Vans, Carriages, Portable Engines, and Machines on Wheels.   L Live Stock.
H Horse Boxes and Prize Cattle Vans.   C Carriages by Passenger Train.

STATION ACCOMMODATION.						CRANE POWER.	STATIONS, &c.	COUNTY.	COMPANY.	POSITION.
						Tons Cwts.				
..	..	..	..	..	..	..	New Bretby Colliery (Mid.)	Derby......	Mid.—L. & N. W.	See Earl of Carnarvon's (Swadlincote).
G	P	F	L	H	C	2 0	Newbridge	Kildare ...	G. S. & W.	Dublin and Kildare.
G	P	.	L				Newbridge	Mon	G. W.	Newport and Aberbeeg.
G	P	F	L	H	C	0 15	New Bridge Lime Works ...	Yorks......	N. E.	Pickering.
..	..	..	..	..	..	..	Newbridge-on-Wye	Radnor ...	Cam.	Llanidloes and Builth Wells.
..	..	..	..	..	..	..	Watts' Siding..............	Brecon ...	Cam.	Doldowlod and Newbridge.
..	..	..	..	..	..	..	Newbridge Rhondda Brewery Co.'s Siding	Glamorg'n	T. V.	Pontypridd.
..	..	..	..	..	..	..	New Bridge Street	Northumb	N. E.	See Newcastle-on-Tyne.
..	..	..	..	..	..	..	New Bridge Street Coal Sidings and Depôt..........	Northumb	N. E.	Newcastle-on-Tyne.
..	..	..	..	..	..	..	Newbridge Works (Brown, Lenox & Co.)	Glamorg'n	A. (N. & S. W.) D. & R.	Glyntaff.
G	P					5 0	New Brighton	Cheshire..	Wirral	Terminus.
G	P	F	L	H	C	5 0	New Brompton & Gillingham	Kent	S. E. & C.	Chatham and Sittingbourne.
..	..	..	..	..	..	..	New Broughton Colliery	Denbigh...	G. W.—W. M. & C. Q...	Plas Power.
G	P						New Buildings	Derry	Donegal	Londonderry and Strabane.
G	P	F	L	H	C	2 0	Newburgh	Fife.........	N. B.	Perth and Ladybank.
G	.	.	.	.	.	..	Glenburnie Siding	Fife.........	N. B.	Collessie and Newburgh.
..	..	..	..	..	..	..	Newburgh	Lancs......	L. & Y.	See Parbold (for Newburgh).
G	P					3 0	Newburn	Northumb	N. E.	North Wylam and Lemington.
..	..	..	..	..	..	..	Lemington Point Siding ...	Northumb	N. E.	Newburn.
..	..	..	..	..	..	..	Newburn Hill Sand and Gravel Siding	Northumb	N. E.	Newburn.
..	..	..	..	..	..	..	Newburn Rolling Mills (Spencer's)	Northumb	N. E.	Newburn.
..	..	..	..	..	..	..	Newburn Steel Works (Spencer's)	Northumb	N. E.	Newburn.
..	..	..	..	..	..	..	Newburn Water Works ...	Northumb	N. E.	Newburn.
..	..	..	..	..	..	..	Throckley Colliery & Brick Works	Northumb	N. E.	Newburn.
..	..	..	..	..	..	..	Walbottle Colliery & Brick Works	Northumb	N. E.	Newburn.
..	..	..	..	..	..	..	Newburn Junction	Durham ...	N. E.	Same as Cliff House Siding (West Hartlepool).
..	..	..	..	..	..	..	Newburn Saw Mill	Durham ...	N. E.	See Lauder, R., & Co. (West Hartlepool).
G	P	F	L	H	C	7 0 }	Newbury (G. W.)	Berks	{ G. W. .... L'bourn Valley..........	Reading and Hungerford. Over G. W. from Newbury Junc.
.	P	.	.	.	.	.				
..	..	..	..	..	..	..	Newbury Gas Works	Berks	G. W.	Newbury.
..	..	..	..	..	..	..	Plenty & Sons' Siding.....	Berks	G. W.	Newbury.
..	..	..	..	..	..	..	Skinner's Siding..............	Berks	G. W.	Newbury.
..	..	..	..	..	..	..	Newbury Junction	Berks	G. W.—L'bourn Valley..	Newbury and Lambourn.
..	..	..	..	..	..	..	Newbury Colliery	Somerset..	G. W.	Mells Road.
G	P						Newbury Park	Essex	G. E.	Woodford and Ilford.
G	P	.	L	H			Newby Wiske..............	Yorks......	N. E.	Northallerton and Ripon.
..	..	..	..	..	..	..	New Carterthorne Colliery ...	Durham ...	N. E.	Same as Etherley Goods Wharf (Etherley).
G	P	.	L	H	C	4 0	New Carway Colliery........	Carmarth'	B. P. & G. V.	Pontyeats.
G	P	.	L	H			Newcastle..............	Down	B. & C. D.	Branch from Downpatrick.
..	..	..	..	..	..	..	Newcastle..............	Wicklow..	D. W. & W.	Bray and Wicklow.
..	..	..	..	..	..	..	Newcastle and Gateshead Water Co.'s Siding	Northumb	N. B.	Woodburn.
..	..	..	..	..	..	..	Newcastle Colliery..............	Notts	{ G. N. .... Mid.	Nottingham, Basford and Bulwell. Nottingham, Basford.
G	P	F	L	H	C	6 0	Newcastle Emlyn	Carmarth'	G. W.	Branch from Carmarthen Junction.
..	..	..	..	..	..	..	Newcastle Gas Works	Staffs	N. S.	Pool Dam.
							NEWCASTLE-ON-TYNE—			
..	..	..	..	..	..	..	Aberdeen Wharf..............	Northumb	N. E.	Quayside Branch.
..	..	..	..	..	..	..	Antwerp, Hamburg and Rotterdam Wharf	Northumb	N. E.	Quayside Branch.
..	..	..	..	..	..	..	Backworth Coal Depôt and Siding	Northumb	N. E.	Trafalgar.
..	..	..	..	..	..	..	Byker & Heaton Coal Co.'s Depot	Northumb	N. E.	Newcastle-on-Tyne.
.	P	.	.	H	C	..	Central (N. E.)	Northumb	{ N. E. .... N. B.	Darlington and Berwick. Over N. E. from Hexham Junction.
..	..	..	..	..	..	..	Co-operative Wholesale Society's Warehouse.....	Northumb	N. E.	Quayside Branch.
..	..	..	..	..	..	..	Corporation Depôt..........	Northumb	N. E.	Newcastle-on-Tyne.
..	..	..	..	..	..	..	Elswick Gas Works	Northumb	N. E.	Forth.

EXPLANATION—G *Goods Station.* P *Passenger and Parcel Station.* P* *Passenger, but not Parcel or Miscellaneous Traffic.*
F *Furniture Vans, Carriages, Portable Engines, and Machines on Wheels.* L *Live Stock.*
H *Horse Boxes and Prize Cattle Vans.* C *Carriages by Passenger Train.*

STATION ACCOMMODATION.						CRANE POWER.		STATIONS, &c.	COUNTY.	COMPANY.	POSITION.
						Tons	Cwts	NEWCASTLE-ON-TYNE—*continued.*			
..	..	..	..	..	..	..	..	Elswick Ordnance and Engineering Works, Blast Furnaces, Ship Yard and Wharf (Armstrong, Whitworth & Co.) (N. E.).....	Northumb	N. E.—N. B.	Forth.
G	.	F	L	..	..	20	0	Forth (N. E.)	Northumb	{ N. E.	Branch—Central Sta. & Scotswood.
										N. B.	Over N. E. from Hexham Junction.
..	..	.	L	..	..	..	..	Forth Cattle Dock (N. E.)	Northumb	N. E.—N. B.	Central Sta. and Forth Goods Junc.
..	..	..	..	..	..	..	..	Forth Coal & Lime Depôt...	Northumb	N. E.	Newcastle-on-Tyne.
..	..	..	..	..	..	..	..	Forth Gas Works & Depôt	Northumb	N. E.	Newcastle-on-Tyne.
..	..	..	..	..	..	..	..	Forth Goods Junction	Northumb	N. E.	Scotswood and Central Station.
..	..	..	..	..	..	..	..	Forth Hydraulic Engine House	Northumb	N. E.	Central Sta. and Forth Goods Junc.
..	..	..	..	..	..	..	..	Forth N.E.R. Oil Gas Wks.	Northumb	N. E.	Central Sta. and Forth Goods Junc.
..	..	..	..	..	..	..	..	Forth Provender Warehouse	Northumb	N. E.	Central Sta. and Forth Goods Junc.
..	..	..	..	..	..	..	..	Grain Warehouse	Northumb	N. E.	Quayside Branch.
..	..	..	..	..	..	..	..	Granary	Northumb	N. E.	Same as Trafalgar.
..	..	..	..	..	..	..	..	Gray's Brickyard	Northumb	N. E.	Trafalgar.
..	..	..	..	..	..	..	..	Hawthorne, Leslie & Co.'s Siding	Northumb	N. E.	Forth.
.	P	..	..	..	..	..	..	Heaton	Northumb	N. E.	Newcastle and Tynemouth.
..	..	..	..	..	..	..	..	Heaton Junction	Northumb	N. E.	Newcastle-on-Tyne and Morpeth.
..	..	..	..	..	..	..	..	Heaton Junction Manure Loading Wharf	Northumb	N. E.	Trafalgar.
..	..	..	..	..	..	..	..	Heaton Jn. Metal Refinery	Northumb	N. E.	Trafalgar.
..	..	..	..	..	..	..	..	Heaton Jn. Public Siding	Northumb	N. E.	Trafalgar.
..	..	..	..	..	..	..	..	High Level Bridge	Northumb	N. E.	Central Station and Gateshead.
..	..	..	..	..	..	..	..	Hull Steam Shipping Co.'s Wharf	Northumb	N. E.	Quayside Branch.
..	..	..	..	..	..	..	..	Leith and Newcastle Steam Shipping Co.'s Wharf...	Northumb	N. E.	Quayside Branch.
..	..	..	..	..	..	..	..	London Wharf	Northumb	N. E.	Quayside Branch.
..	..	..	..	..	..	..	..	Lund's (C.) Wharf	Northumb	N. E.	Quayside Branch.
.	P	..	..	..	..	..	..	Manors	Northumb	N. E.	Central Station and Heaton.
..	..	..	..	..	..	..	..	Manor's Coal Depôt	Northumb	N. E.	Central Station.
..	..	..	..	..	..	..	..	Mawson, Clark & Co.'s Sid.	Northumb	N. E.	Newcastle-on-Tyne.
..	..	..	..	..	..	..	..	Mills & Sons' Siding	Northumb	N. E.	Newcastle-on-Tyne.
..	..	..	..	..	..	..	..	Neilsen, Andersen & Co.'s Wharf	Northumb	N. E.	Quayside Branch.
.	P	..	..	..	..	..	..	New Bridge Street	Northumb	N. E.	Terminus of Backworth Line.
..	..	..	..	..	..	..	..	New Bridge Street Coal Sidings and Depôt........	Northumb	N. E.	Newcastle-on-Tyne.
..	..	..	..	..	..	..	..	Newcastle Corporation Electricity Generators Siding	Northumb	N. E.	Trafalgar.
..	..	..	..	..	..	..	..	Newcastle Grain and General Warehousing Co.'s Siding	Northumb	N. E.	Newcastle-on-Tyne Quay.
..	..	..	..	..	..	..	..	Parson's Siding	Northumb	N. E.	Trafalgar.
..	..	..	..	..	..	..	..	Pyman, Bell & Co.'s Wharf	Northumb	N. E.	Quayside Branch.
G	..	..	..	..	..	2	10	Quay	Northumb	N. E.	Branch near Manors.
..	..	..	..	..	..	80	0	Quayside Branch	Northumb	N. E.	Branch near Manors.
..	..	..	..	..	..	..	..	Red Barns Manure Wharf	Northumb	N. E.	Trafalgar.
..	..	..	..	..	..	..	..	South Benwell Colliery...	Northumb	N. E.	Forth and Scotswood.
..	..	..	..	..	..	..	..	Stephenson, R., & Co.'s Sid.	Northumb	N. E.	Forth.
G	.	F	..	..	..	20	0	Trafalgar	Northumb	N. E.	Branch near Manors.
G	P	F	L	H	C	2	0	Newcastleton	Roxburgh	N. B.	Hawick and Carlisle.
G	P	F	L	H	C	10	0 }	Newcastle-under-Lyme (N.S.)	Staffs	{ N. S.	Stoke and Market Drayton.
G										G. W.	Over N. S. Line.
..	..	..	..	..	..	..	..	Brampton Siding	Staffs	N. S.	Newcastle.
..	..	..	..	..	..	..	..	Hartshill Brick and Tile Co.'s Works	Staffs	N. S.	Stoke and Newcastle.
..	..	..	..	..	..	..	..	Hartshill Siding...............	Staffs	N. S.	Stoke and Newcastle.
G	P	F	L	H	C	1	5	Newcastle West	Limerick ..	G. S. & W.	Limerick and Tralee.
G	P	.	..	..	..	..	..	Newchurch	I. of W. ..	I. of W. Cent.	Newport and Sandown.
..	..	..	..	..	..	..	..	Newchurch	Lancs	L. & Y.	See Waterfoot (for Newchurch).
..	..	..	..	..	..	..	..	New Clee	Lincoln ..	G. C.	See Grimsby.
..	..	..	..	..	..	..	..	New Clydach Colliery	Mon	L. & N. W.	See Williams' Sidings (Brynmawr).
..	..	..	..	..	..	..	..	Newcomen Bridge Junction...	Dublin ...	D. W. & W. (C. of D. Jn.) —M. G. W.	Dublin.
..	..	..	..	..	..	..	..	New Copley Colliery	Durham ..	N. E.	Butterknowle.
G	P	..	..	..	..	..	..	Newcourt	Cork	S. & S.	Schull and Skibbereen.

EXPLANATION—G *Goods Station.*   P *Passenger and Parcel Station.*   P* *Passenger, but not Parcel or Miscellaneous Traffic.*
F *Furniture Vans, Carriages, Portable Engines, and Machines on Wheels.*   L *Live Stock.*
H *Horse Boxes and Prize Cattle Vans.*   C *Carriages by Passenger Train.*

STATION ACCOMMODATION.						CRANE POWER.		STATIONS, &c.	COUNTY.	COMPANY.	POSITION.
						Tons	Cwts.				
..	..	..	..	..	..	..	..	New Cransley Ir.&Stl.Co's Wks	N'hamptn	Mid.	Kettering.
..	..	..	..	..	..	..	..	New Cross Hands Colliery ...	Carmarth'	L. & M. M.	Cross Hands.
..	..	..	..	..	..	..	..	New Cross (L. B. & S. C.)......	Surrey	L. B. & S. C.—G. E.—Met. Dist.—S. E. & C.	See London.
..	..	..	..	..	..	..	..	New Cross (S. E. & C.)..........	Kent	S. E. & C.—Met.	See London.
..	..	..	..	..	..	..	..	New Cross Depôt	Surrey	G. E.	See London.
..	..	..	..	..	..	..	..	New Cross Junction	Kent	E. L. Jt.—S. E. & C.	Deptford Road and New Cross.
..	..	..	..	..	..	..	..	New Cross Junction	Surrey	E. L. Jt.—L. B. & S. C.	Deptford Road and New Cross.
..	..	..	..	..	..	..	..	New Croydon	Surrey	L. B. & S. C.	See Croydon, New.
G	P	F	L	H	C	2	0	New Cumnock......................	Ayr	G. & S.W.	Old Cumnock and Thornhill.
..	..	..	..	..	..	..	..	Afton Pit	Ayr	G. & S.W.	Bank Junction.
..	..	..	..	..	..	..	..	Bank Brick Works...........	Ayr	G. & S.W.	Branch from Bank Junction.
..	..	..	..	..	..	..	..	Bank, Nos. 1 and 2	Ayr	G. & S.W.	Branch from Bank Junction.
..	..	..	..	..	..	..	..	Burnfoot Lye	Ayr	G. & S.W.	Bank Junction.
..	..	..	..	..	..	..	..	Lanemark Brick Works ...	Ayr	G. & S.W.	Bank Junction.
..	..	..	..	..	..	..	..	Lanemark Collieries	Ayr	G. & S.W.	Bank Junction.
..	..	..	..	..	..	..	..	Pathhead Colliery	Ayr	G. & S.W.	New Cumnock and Old Cumnock.
..	..	..	..	..	..	..	..	Polquhap Siding.............	Ayr	G. & S.W.	New Cumnock and Old Cumnock.
..	..	..	..	..	..	..	..	Riggfoot Pit	Ayr	G. & S.W.	Bank Junction.
..	..	..	..	..	..	..	..	New Cut and Harbour Road	Glamorg'n	GW—LNW—Mid—RSB	Swansea.
..	..	..	..	..	..	..	..	New Cymmer Colliery	Glamorg'n	T. V.	See Cymmer Level or New Cymmer Colliery (Porth).
..	..	..	..	..	..	..	..	Newdigates Col. (L. & N. W.)	Warwick..	L. & N. W.—Mid.	Bedworth.
..	..	..	..	..	..	..	..	New Digby Colliery	Notts	G. N.	Gedling and Carlton.
..	..	..	..	..	..	..	..	New Dock Brick Co.'s Siding	Glamorg'n	T. V.	Cadoxton.
G	P	F	L	H	C	..	..	Newell & Co.'s Siding	Notts	G. N. & G. E. Jt.	Misterton.
..	..	..	..	..	..	..	..	New Eltham & Pope Street...	Kent	S. E. & C.	Hither Green and Dartford.
G	P	F	L	H	C	5	0	New England Siding	N'hamptn	G. N.	Peterboro'.
..	..	..	..	..	..	..	..	Newent	Glo'ster	G. W.	Gloucester and Ledbury.
..	..	..	..	..	..	..	..	New Expanded Metal Co. (Stranton Works)	Durham	N. E.	West Hartlepool.
..	..	..	..	..	..	..	..	New Explosives Co.'s Siding	Suffolk	G. E.	Stowmarket.
..	..	..	..	..	..	..	..	Newfall Chemical Works......	Durham	N. E.	Carlton.
..	..	..	..	..	..	..	..	New Fancy Colliery	Glo'ster	S.&Wye Jt.(G.W.& Mid.)	Parkend.
..	..	..	..	..	..	..	..	New Ferry	Cheshire...	B'head Jt.(G W & L N W)	See Bebington and New Ferry.
G	..	..	..	..	..	..	..	Newfield Colliery, Coke, and Brick Works	Durham	N. E.	Hunwick.
..	..	..	..	..	..	..	..	Newfields	Staffs	N. S.	Branch—Tunstall and Goldenhill.
..	..	..	..	..	..	..	..	New Fletton Brick Co.'s Sid.	Bucks	L. & N. W.	Woburn Sands.
..	..	..	..	..	..	..	..	New Flint Colliery...............	Flint	L. & N. W.	Same as Dee Side Col. Co.'s (Flint).
..	..	..	..	..	..	..	..	New Forest Colliery	Glamorg'n	P. T. / S. Wales Min.	Cwmavon. Briton Ferry and Cymmer.
..	..	..	..	..	..	..	..	New Forest Quarry	Glamorg'n	P. T.—S. Wales Min.	Same as Prosser's Quarry (Cwmavon).
G	P	F	L	H	C	1	0	New Galloway......................	Kirkcud...	P.P.&W.Jt.(Cal.,G &SW, L. & N. W., & Mid.)..	Newton Stewart & Castle Douglas.
..	..	..	..	..	..	..	..	New Glyncorrwg Colliery......	Glamorg'n	R. & S. B.	Blaengwynfi.
..	P	..	..	..	..	..	..	New Hailes	Edinboro'	N. B.	Portobello and Inveresk.
..	..	..	..	..	..	..	..	New Hailes Junction............	Edinboro'	N. B.	Joppa and Inveresk.
..	..	..	..	..	..	..	..	New Hall Field Colliery (Mid.)	Derby	Mid.—L. & N. W.	Same as Cartwright Colliery Co.'s Siding (Swadlincote).
..	..	..	..	..	..	..	..	New Hall Hey Siding	Lancs	L. & Y.	Rawtenstall.
..	..	..	..	..	..	..	..	Newhall Park Colliery (Mid.)	Derby	Mid.—L. & N. W.	Same as Earl of Carnarvon's Bretby Colliery Wharf (Swadlincote).
G	P	..	..	..	..	..	..	Newham	Cornwall..	G. W.	See Truro.
..	P	..	..	..	..	..	..	Newham	Northumb	N. E.	Berwick and Morpeth.
..	..	..	..	..	..	..	..	Newhaven	Edinboro'	Cal.	Edinburgh and Leith.
..	..	..	..	..	..	..	..	Newhaven	Edinboro'	N. B.	See Trinity and Newhaven.
								NEWHAVEN—			
G	P	F	L	H	C	25	0	Harbour	Sussex	L. B. & S. C.	Newhaven Town and Bishopstone.
..	..	..	..	..	..	..	..	Sussex Portland Cement Co.'s Siding.................	Sussex	L. B. & S. C.	Lewes and Newhaven.
G	P	..	L	..	..	6	0	Town	Sussex	L. B. & S. C.	Lewes and Seaford.
..	..	..	..	..	..	..	..	Wharf	Sussex	L. B. & S. C.	Same as Newhaven Harbour.
..	..	..	..	..	..	..	..	Newhaven Sidings..............	Edinboro'	Cal.	Leith, North.
..	..	..	..	..	..	..	..	New Herrington Colliery and Brick Works	Durham	N. E.	Fencehouses. Penshaw.
G	P	..	..	..	..	10	0	New Hey	Lancs	L. & Y.	Oldham and Rochdale.
G	P	F	L	H	C	12	0	New Holland	Lincoln	G. C.	Branch from Brocklesby.
..	..	..	..	..	..	..	..	Earle's Siding.................	Lincoln	G. C.	New Holland.
..	..	..	..	..	..	..	..	Senior's Siding...............	Lincoln	G. C.	New Holland.
..	P	..	..	..	..	..	..	New Holland Pier	Lincoln	G. C.	Branch from Brocklesby.
G	P	F	L	H	C	1	10	Newhouse...........................	Lanark	Cal.	Chapelhall and Omoa.

STATION ACCOMMODATION.						CRANE POWER.	STATIONS, &c.	COUNTY.	COMPANY.	POSITION.
						Tons Cwts.	Newhouse—*continued.*			
.	.	.	.	.	.	.	Linrigg Colliery	Lanark ...	Cal.	Omoa and Newhouse.
.	.	.	.	.	.	.	Newhouse Colliery............	Lanark ...	Cal.	Newhouse.
.	.	.	.	.	.	.	Newhouse Junction	Lanark ...	Cal.	Omoa and Newhouse.
.	.	.	.	.	.	.	New Hucknall Colliery (G.C.)	Derby	G. C.—G. N.—L. & N. W.	Kirkby and Pinxton.
.	.	.	.	.	.	.	New Hucknall Colliery.......	Derby	Mid.	Westhouses and Blackwell.
.	.	.	.	.	.	.	New Hydroleine Co.'s Siding	Leicester..	Mid.	Same as Castle Soap Works (Ashby).
.	.	.	.	.	.	.	New Hythe Siding	Kent	S. E. & C.	Aylesford.
G	P	F	L	H	C	.	Newick and Chailey	Sussex ...	L. B. & S. C.	Sheffield Park and Barcombe.
.	.	.	.	.	.	.	Newington	Edinboro'	N. B.	See Edinburgh.
G	P	.	L	.	.	.	Newington	Kent	S. E. & C.	Chatham and Sittingbourne.
.	.	.	.	.	.	.	Cremer's Brick & Flint Sid.	Kent	S. E. & C.	Rainham and Newington.
.	.	.	.	.	.	.	Newington & Co.'s Siding ...	Sussex ...	L. B. & S. C.	Glynde.
.	.	.	.	.	.	.	Newington Vestry Siding ...	Kent	S. E. & C.	Meopham.
.	.	.	.	.	.	.	Newington Vestry Siding ...	Surrey ...	S. E. & C.	London, Walworth Road.
.	.	.	.	.	.	.	New Kew Junction	Middlesex	L. & S.W.	London, Kew Bridge & Gunnersbury.
.	.	.	.	.	.	.	New Kilsyth	Stirling ...	K. & B. Jt. (Cal. & N. B.)	See Kilsyth, New.
.	.	.	.	.	.	.	New Kingsbury Collieries ...	Warwick..	Mid.	Kingsbury.
.	.	.	.	.	.	.	New Lambton Siding	Durham ...	N. E.	{ Fencehouses. / Penshaw.
G	P	.	.	.	.	1 10	Newland	Glo'ster ...	G. W.	Monmouth and Coleford.
.	.	.	.	.	.	.	Newlands Colliery	Lanark ...	Cal.	Same as Bredisholm Collieries No. 1, etc. (Baillieston).
.	.	.	.	.	.	.	Newlandside Quarry	Durham ...	N. E.	Stanhope.
G	P	.	L	H	.	.	New Lane	Lancs	L. & Y.	Wigan and Southport.
.	.	.	.	.	.	.	New Langley Colliery	Derby	Mid.	Langley Mill.
.	.	.	.	.	.	.	Newlay & Horsforth	Yorks	Mid.	See Leeds.
.	.	.	.	.	.	.	Newliston Branch Junction...	L'lithgow	N. B.	Ratho and Drumshoreland.
.	.	.	.	.	.	.	Newliston Mine Siding........	L'lithgow	N. B.	Ratho.
.	.	.	.	.	.	.	New Lodge Siding..............	Carmarth'	B. P. & G. V.	Burry Port.
G	P	.	L	H	.	1 10	New Luce	Wigtown..	G. & S. W.	Girvan and Stranraer.
G	P	F	L	H	.	1 5	Newmachar	Aberdeen	G. N. of S.	Aberdeen and Fraserburgh.
G	P	.	L	H	C	1 10	Newmains	Lanark ...	Cal.	Holytown and Morningside.
.	.	.	.	.	.	.	Bailliesmuir Colliery........	Lanark ...	Cal.	Newmains.
.	.	.	.	.	.	.	Collyshot Mine	Lanark ...	Cal.	Newmains.
.	.	.	.	.	.	.	Coltness Iron Works and } Collieries .... }	Lanark ...	Cal.	{ Newmains and Morningside. / Stirling Road and Morningside.
.	.	.	.	.	.	.	Herdshill Colliery	Lanark ...	Cal.	Newmains.
.	.	.	.	.	.	.	Stonecraig No. 1 Pit........	Lanark ...	Cal.	Newmains.
.	.	.	.	.	.	.	New Malden	Surrey.....	L. & S.W.	Same as Coombe and Malden.
.	.	.	.	.	.	.	Newman & Owston's Siding..	Yorks	N. E.	{ Goole. / Thorne.
G	P	F	L	H	C	1 0	Newmarket	Cambs....	G. E.	Cambridge and Bury St. Edmunds.
.	.	.	.	.	.	.	Lane, W. & J., Siding	Cambs....	G. E.	Newmarket.
.	.	.	.	.	.	.	Newmarket (G. S. & W.)......	Clare	G. S. & W.—M. G. W.	See Ballycar and Newmarket.
G	P	F	L	H	C	.	Newmarket	Cork	G. S. & W.	Branch from Banteer.
.	.	.	.	.	.	.	Newmarket Colliery	Yorks	Meth.Jt.(GN,L &Y& NE)	Stanley.
.	.	.	.	.	.	.	Newmarket Haigh Moor & } Spencer Collieries .... }	Yorks	{ E. & W. Y. Union ...... / Mid.	{ Robin Hood. / Rothwell Haigh.
.	.	.	.	.	.	.	Newmarket Silkstone Colliery	Yorks	{ E. & W. Y. Union ...... / Mid.	{ Robin Hood. / Rothwell Haigh.
G	P	F	L	H	C	9 0	New Milford	Pembroke	G. W.	Milford Haven.
G	P	.	L	.	.	.	Newmill	Kinc'rdine	Cal.	Forfar and Stonehaven.
.	.	.	.	.	.	.	New Mill End	Beds	G. N.	See Luton Hoo (for New Mill End).
G	P	F	L	H	C	10 0 }			{ L. & N. W.	Buxton and Stockport.
G	.	.	L	.	.	5 0 }	New Mills	Derby	{ Mid.	Chapel-en-le-Frith and Marple.
.	P	.	.	.	.	. }			{ S. & M. Jt. (G. C. & Mid.)	Marple and Hayfield.
.	.	.	.	.	.	.	Hall's Colliery.................	Derby	Mid.	Gowhole Goods Junction.
.	.	.	.	.	.	.	New Mills Junction	Derby	Mid.—S. & M. Jt.	Marple and Chapel-en-le-Frith.
.	P*	.	.	.	.	.	Newmills	Donegal	L. & L. S.	Letterkenny and Burtonport.
.	.	.	.	.	.	.	Newmill Siding	Fife	N. B.	Cupar.
G	P	F	L	H	C	6 0	Newmilns	Ayr	G. & S.W.	Hurlford and Darvel.
.	.	.	.	.	.	.	Loudoun No. 3	Ayr	G. & S.W.	Newmilns.
G	P	F	L	H	C	.	New Milton (for Milford-on-Sea)	Hants	L. & S.W.	Brockenhurst and Christchurch.
.	.	.	.	.	.	.	New Monckton Colliery	Yorks	Mid.	Royston and Notton.
.	.	.	.	.	.	.	New Moss Colliery Co.'s Ashton Moss Col.(L.& N.W.)	Lancs	L. & N. W.—G. C.	Guide Bridge.
G	P	F	L	H	C	1 10	Newnham	Glo'ster ...	G. W.	Gloucester and Chepstow.
G	P	F	L	H	C	5 0	Newnham Bridge	Worcester	G. W.	Tenbury and Bewdley.
.	.	.	.	.	.	.	New North Leeswood Colliery	Flint	L. & N. W.	See Phœnix Coal & Cannel Co. (Coed Talon).

EXPLANATION—G *Goods Station.*   P *Passenger and Parcel Station.*   P* *Passenger, but not Parcel or Miscellaneous Traffic.*
F *Furniture Vans, Carriages, Portable Engines, and Machines on Wheels.*   L *Live Stock.*
H *Horse Boxes and Prize Cattle Vans.*   C *Carriages by Passenger Train.*

STATION ACCOMMODATION.						CRANE POWER.		STATIONS, &c.	COUNTY.	COMPANY.	POSITION.
						Tons	Cwts.				
.	.	.	.	.	.	.	.	New Oaks Colliery..............	Yorks	{ G. C.	Stairfoot (for Ardsley).
										{ H. & B.	Cudworth, North.
G	P	.	L	H	.	1	10	New Oaks Junction	Yorks	G. C.	Stairfoot and Dovecliffe.
.	.	.	.	.	.	.	.	Newpark	Edinboro'	Cal.	Holytown and Edinburgh.
.	.	.	.	.	.	.	.	Westfield Limestone Pit ...	Edinboro'	Cal.	Newpark.
.	.	.	.	.	.	.	.	New Penshaw Siding	Durham ...	N. E.	{ Fencehouses.
											{ Penshaw.
.	.	.	.	.	.	.	.	New Peterboro' Brick Co.'s Sid. (Peterboro' Brick Co.)	Hunts	G. N.	Fletton.
.	.	.	.	.	.	.	.	New Plas Colliery (B. & M.)...	Mon	B. & M.—G. W.	Pengam.
.	.	.	.	.	.	.	.	New Poole Junction Station..	Dorset......	S.&D.Jt. (L.&S.W.&Mid)	See Broadstone and New Poole.
G	P	.	.	.	.	1	10	Newpool Siding	Carmarth'	B. P. & G. V.	Burry Port.
G	P	F	L	H	C	.	.	Newport	Essex	G. E.	Cambridge and Bishops Stortford.
								Barnard Bros.' Siding	Essex	G. E.	Newport.
G	.	F	L	H	C	8	0	Newport	I. of W.	{ I. of W. Cent.	Cowes and Ryde.
G	P	F	L	H	C	1	0	Newport	Mayo	{ L. & S. W...................	Steamer from Southampton.
										M. G. W.	Westport and Achill.
G	.	.	.	.	.	.	.	NEWPORT—			
								Alexandra Dock Junction (for Alexandra Dock only)	Mon	G. W.	Newport and Marshfield.
G	.	F	.	.	.	40	0	Alexandra Docks (A.D.&R.)	Mon	{ A. (N. & S. W.) D. & R.	Newport.
										{ G. W.	Over A. (N. & S. W.) D. & R.
.	.	.	.	.	.	.	.	Arrow Patent Fuel Works	Mon	A (N & S W) D & R—G W	Alexandra Dock.
.	.	.	.	.	.	.	.	Blaina Wharf..................	Mon	A (N & S W) D & R—G W	Old Dock.
.	.	.	.	.	.	.	.	Burt Boulton & Heywood's Timber Creosote Yard...	Mon	A (N & S W) D & R—G W	Alexandra Dock.
.	.	.	.	.	.	.	.	Clapp's Whf.(KohlaTileCo)	Mon	A (N & S W) D & R—G W	Old Dock.
.	.	.	.	.	.	.	.	Cordes & Co.'s Nail Works	Mon	G. W.	Dock Street and Cwmbran.
.	.	.	.	.	.	.	.	Crindau Gas Works (G.W.)	Mon	G. W.—L. & N. W.	Dock Street and Cwmbran.
.	.	.	.	.	.	.	.	Crindau Glass Wks. (G.W.)	Mon	G. W.—L. & N. W.	Dock Street and Cwmbran.
G	.	F	L	.	.	10	0	Dock Street (G. W.)	Mon	{ G. W.	Cwmbran and Waterloo Junction.
										{ B. & M.	Over G. W. from Bassaleg Junction.
										{ L. & N. W.	Over G. W. from Hereford.
.	.	.	.	.	.	.	.	East Usk Junction............	Mon	G. W.	High Street and Llanwern.
.	.	.	.	.	.	.	.	East Usk Wharf (Great Western Wharf)............	Mon	G. W.	On Nettlefold's Branch.
.	.	.	.	.	.	.	.	Ebbw Junction	Mon	G. W.	Newport and Marshfield.
.	.	.	.	.	.	.	.	Gaer Junction...............	Mon	G. W.	High Street and Bassaleg.
.	.	.	.	.	.	.	.	Gas Works	Mon	G. W.	Dock Street and Cwmbran.
.	.	.	.	.	.	.	.	Gloucester Wharf	Mon	G. W.	Dock Street and Cwmbran.
.	.	.	.	.	.	.	.	Goss' Siding..................	Mon	G. W.	Branch near Dock Street.
G	P	F	L	H	C	5	0	Herbert's Siding..............	Mon	G. W.	High Street and Caerleon.
	P	.	.	H	C	.	.	High Street (G. W.)	Mon	{ G. W.	Gloucester and Cardiff.
	P	.	.	H	C	.	.			{ B. & M.	Over G. W. from Bassaleg Junction.
										{ L. & N. W.	Over G. W. from Nine Mile Point Jn.
.	.	.	.	.	.	.	.	Houlder Bros.' Depôt	Mon	A (N & S W) D & R—G W	Alexandra Dock.
.	.	.	.	.	.	.	.	Isca Engineering Works...	Mon	G. W.	Branch from Dock Street.
.	.	.	.	.	.	.	.	Jordan's Foundry (Pillgwenlly Foundry).........	Mon	A (N & S W) D & R—G W	Old Dock.
.	.	.	.	.	.	.	.	Junction	Mon	A.(N&SW.)D.&R.—GW.	Alexandra Docks and High Street.
.	.	.	.	.	.	.	.	Liverpool Wharf..............	Mon	G. W.	Dock Street and Mill Street.
.	.	.	.	.	.	.	.	Llanarth Wharf(Goss'sSid.)	Mon	A (N & S W) D & R—G W	Old Dock.
.	.	.	.	.	.	.	.	Lysaght's Orb Iron Works	Mon	G. W.	Branch from East Usk Junction.
.	.	.	.	.	.	.	.	Maesglas Junction............	Mon	A.(N&SW.)D.&R.—GW.	Alexandra Docks and Bassaleg.
.	.	.	.	.	.	.	.	Maindee, East & West Jns.	Mon	G. W.	High Street and Llanwern.
G	.	.	.	.	.	10	0	Mill Street Mileage& Coal Sidings (G.W.)	Mon	{ G. W.	Dock Street and Cwmbran.
										{ L. & N. W.	Over G. W. from Hereford.
.	.	.	.	.	.	.	.	Moderator Sidings............	Mon	G. W.	Dock Street and Mill Street.
.	.	.	.	.	.	.	.	Mordey, Carney & Co.'s Ship Repairing Yard...	Mon	A (N & S W) D & R—G W	Alexandra Dock.
.	.	.	.	.	.	.	.	Morris & Griffin's Chemical Works	Mon	G. W.	Nettlefold's Branch.
.	.	.	.	.	.	.	.	Morris & Griffin's Glue Wks	Mon	G. W.	Nettlefold's Branch.
.	.	.	.	.	.	.	.	Nicholas & Co.'s Timber Yard	Mon	A (N & S W) D & R—G W	Alexandra Dock.
.	.	.	.	.	.	.	.	North Central Wagon Co.'s Rhymney Wharf	Mon	A (N & S W) D & R—G W	Old Dock.
.	.	.	.	.	.	.	.	Old Dock......................	Mon	A (N & S W) D & R—G W	Alexandra Dock & Dock Street.
.	.	.	.	.	.	.	.	Old Dock Junction	Mon	G. W.	Near Dock Street.
.	.	.	.	.	.	.	.	Park Junction..................	Mon	G. W.	Newport and Bassaleg.
.	.	.	.	.	.	.	.	Penner Wharf (Phillips & Son's Malt House).........	Mon	A (N & S W) D & R—G W	Old Dock.

EXPLANATION—G *Goods Station.*   P *Passenger and Parcel Station.*   P* *Passenger, but not Parcel or Miscellaneous Traffic.*
F *Furniture Vans, Carriages, Portable Engines, and Machines on Wheels.*   L *Live Stock.*
H *Horse Boxes and Prize Cattle Vans.*   C *Carriages by Passenger Train.*

STATION ACCOMMODATION.						CRANE POWER.		STATIONS, &c.	COUNTY.	COMPANY.	POSITION.
						Tons	Cwts.	NEWPORT—continued.			
								Risca Wharf (Cardiff & South Wales Wagon Co.)	Mon	A (N & S W) D & R—G W	Old Dock.
								River Coal Shipping Jetties	Mon	A (N & S W) D & R—G W	Alexandra Dock.
								Russell's Wharf..............	Mon	A (N & S W) D & R—G W	Old Dock.
								Scott, G., & Co.'s Siding ...	Mon	A (N & S W) D & R—G W	Alexandra Dock.
								Spittle's (Cambrian) F'dry.	Mon	A (N & S W) D & R—G W	Old Dock.
								Tredegar Wharf Co.'s Bch.	Mon	G. W.	Branch near Dock Street.
								Usk Side Engineering & Rivet Works	Mon	G. W.	Branch near Dock Street.
								Waterloo Junction...........	Mon	G. W.	Alexandra Dock Junc. & Dock Str.
G	P	F	L	H	C	5	0	Newport	Salop	L. & N. W.	Shrewsbury and Stafford.
G	P							Newport	Yorks	H. & B.	Howden and Hull.
	P							Newport	Yorks	N. E.	Stockton and Middlesbro'.
G	P	F	L	H	C	2	0	Newport (East)	Fife........	N. B.	Dundee and Tayport.
								Newport Gas Works	Fife........	N. B.	Newport (East) and Tayport.
	P							Newport (West)	Fife........	N. B.	Dundee and Tayport.
								Newport Engine Sheds........	Yorks	N. E.	Middlesbro'.
								Newport Iron Works Coke Ovens & Wharf	Yorks	N. E.	Middlesbro'.
G	P	F	L	H	C	5	0	Newport Pagnell	Bucks	L. & N. W.	Branch from Wolverton.
								Coales & Son's Shipley Wharf	Bucks	L. & N. W.	Newport Pagnell and Great Linford.
								Price's Siding	Bucks	L. & N. W.	Newport Pagnell.
								Newport Road Siding	Glamorg'n	T. V.	Cardiff.
								Newport Rolling Mills........	Yorks	N. E.	Middlesbro'.
								Newport Wire Works	Yorks	N. E.	Middlesbro'.
G	P	F	L	H	C	5	0	Newquay	Cornwall..	G. W.	Branch from Par.
G								Newquay Harbour...........	Cornwall..	G. W.	Extension from Newquay.
								Pollard's Siding	Cornwall..	G. W.	Extension from Newquay.
								Quintrell Downs Siding ...	Cornwall..	G. W.	Newquay and St. Columb Road.
								Trevemper Siding	Cornwall..	G. W.	Tolcarn Junc. and Shepherd's Siding
G	P		L	H		3	0	New Quay Road..............	Carmarth'	M. & M.	Pencader and Lampeter.
G	P	F	L	H	C			New Radnor	Radnor	G. W.	Branch from Titley.
								New River Waterworks	Middlesex	L. & S. W.	Sunbury.
								New Rock Colliery..............	Somerset..	S. & D. Jt. (L. & S. W. & Mid)	Chilcompton.
G	P	F	L	H	C			New Romney and Littlestone-on-Sea	Kent	S. E. & C.	Branch—Lydd and Dungeness.
G	P	F	L	H	C			New Ross....................	Kilkenny..	D. W. & W.	Branch from Macmine Junction.
G	P							Newry	Down	B. & Newry	Adjoining G. N. (I.) Station.
								NEWRY—			
G						2	0	Albert Basin	Down	G. N. (I.)	Branch from King Street Junction.
G			L					Bridge Street	Armagh ..	D. N. & G.	Bridge Street Junction & Greenore.
								Bridge Street Junction......	Armagh ..	D. N. & G.—G. N. (I.)..	Edward Street and Greenore.
								Carvill Bros.' Siding	Down	G. N. (I.)	Edward Street and Dublin Bridge.
	P							Dublin Bridge..............	Down	G. N. (I.)	Goragh Wood and Warrenpoint.
G	P	F	L	H	C	5	0	Edward Street (G. N., I.)....	Down	{ G. N. (I.) / D. N. & G....	Goragh Wood and Warrenpoint. / Over G. N. (I.) from Bridge Str. Jn.
								King Street Junction	Down	G. N. (I.)	Edward Street and Dublin Bridge.
	P							Newseat	Aberdeen	G. N. of S.	Maud and Peterhead.
G	P		L			1	10	Newsham.....................	Northumb	N. E.	Newcastle and Blyth.
								Cowpen Collieries—			
								"Hannah" Colliery (Newsham Colliery)............	Northumb	N. E.	Newsham.
								"Isabella" Colliery	Northumb	N. E.	Newsham.
								Newsham Siding	Durham ..	N. E.	Winston.
								New Sharlston Col. (L. & Y.)	Yorks	L. & Y.—G. N.—N. E.	Sharlston.
								New Sharlston Collieries	Yorks	Mid.	Oakenshaw.
								New Shilton Sid. (L. & N. W.)	Leicester..	L. & N. W. — Mid.	See Enderby & Stoney Stanton Granite Co. (Elmesthorpe).
G	P	F	L	H	C	3	0	Newsholme	Yorks	L. & Y.	Chatburn and Hellifield.
								Newson Garrett & Son's Siding	Suffolk ...	G. E.	Snape.
G	P	F	L	H	C	5	0	New Southgate and Friern Barnet (for Colney Hatch) (G. N.)	Middlesex	{ G. N. / N. L. / S. E. & C.	King's Cross and New Barnet. / Over G. N. from Canonbury Junc. / Over G. N. from King's Cross Junc.
	P										
	P*										
								Colney Hatch Asylum Siding (London County Lunatic Asylum Siding)	Middlesex	G. N.	New Southgate.
								Gas Works Siding	Middlesex	G. N.	New Southgate.
								New South Works..............	Derby	Mid.	See Buxton Lime Firms Co. (Peak Forest).
								New Sovereign Colliery	Yorks	G. C.	Worsboro'.

EXPLANATION—G *Goods Station.*   P *Passenger and Parcel Station.*   P* *Passenger, but not Parcel or Miscellaneous Traffic.*
F *Furniture Vans, Carriages, Portable Engines, and Machines on Wheels.*   L *Live Stock.*
H *Horse Boxes and Prize Cattle Vans.*   C *Carriages by Passenger Train.*

STATION ACCOMMODATION.						CRANE POWER.		STATIONS, &c.	COUNTY.	COMPANY.	POSITION.
G	P	F	L	H	C	Tons	Cwts.				
G	P	F	L	H	C	.	.	Newstead	Notts	{ G. N. .... Mid.	Annesley Junction and Daybrook. Linby and Kirkby-in-Ashfield.
.	.	.	.	.	.	.	.	Annesley Colliery (G. N.)	Notts	G. N.—G. C.	Branch from Annesley Junction.
.	.	.	.	.	.	.	.	Annesley Sidings	Notts	G. N.	Annesley and Newstead.
.	.	.	.	.	.	.	.	Newstead Colliery (G. N.)	Notts	G. N.—G. C.	Newstead and Linby.
.	.	.	.	.	.	.	.	Newstead Colliery Sidings	Notts	Mid.	Near Newstead.
.	.	.	.	.	.	.	.	New Street (L&NW & Mid. Jt.)	Warwick..	L. & N. W.—Mid.	See Birmingham.
.	.	.	.	.	.	.	.	New Street Coal Yard	Glos'ter ...	G. W.	Cheltenham
.	.	.	.	.	.	.	.	New Street Junction	Warwick...	L. & N. W.—Mid.	Birmingham.
.	.	.	.	.	.	.	.	Newsum, Sons & Co.— Siding	Lincoln ...	G. N. & G. E. Jt.	Gainsboro'.
.	.	.	.	.	.	.	.	Siding	Lancs	Trafford Park Estate......	Manchester.
.	.	.	.	.	.	.	.	Siding (G. C.).................	Lincoln ...	G. C.—G. N.—Mid.	Lincoln.
G	P	F	L	H	C	.	.	Newthorpe, Greasley & Shipley Gate	Notts	G. N.	Kimberley and Pinxton.
.	.	.	.	.	.	.	.	Erewash Valley Brick, Pipe, and Pottery Co.'s Siding	Notts	G. N.	Newthorpe, Greasley & Shipley Gate.
.	.	.	.	.	.	.	.	Newthorpe Siding	Yorks	N. E.	Micklefield.
G	P	.	L	H	.	3	0	Newton	Derby	Mid.	See Tibshelf and Newton.
G	P	.	L	H	.	3	0	Newton	Lanark ...	Cal.	Motherwell and Rutherglen.
.	.	.	.	.	.	.	.	Bardykes Colliery— Hallside Private Siding..	Lanark ...	Cal.	Blantyre and Newton.
.	.	.	.	.	.	.	.	Spittalhill Quarry and Brick Works	Lanark ...	Cal.	Blantyre and Newton.
.	.	.	.	.	.	.	.	Clyde Nail Works	Lanark ...	Cal.	Newton.
.	.	.	.	.	.	.	.	Dechmont Colliery..........	Lanark ...	Cal.	Branch near Newton.
.	.	.	.	.	.	.	.	Gilbertfield Brick Works...	Lanark ...	Cal.	Branch near Newton.
.	.	.	.	.	.	.	.	Gilbertfield Colliery	Lanark ...	Cal.	Branch near Newton.
.	.	.	.	.	.	.	.	Hallside Colliery (Hallside East Farm Siding)........	Lanark ...	Cal.	Blantyre and Newton.
.	.	.	.	.	.	.	.	Haughhead Colliery	Lanark ...	Cal.	Uddingston and Newton.
.	.	.	.	.	.	.	.	Jardine's Siding............	Lanark ...	Cal.	Branch near Newton.
.	.	.	.	.	.	.	.	Loanend Colliery	Lanark ...	Cal.	Branch near Newton.
.	.	.	.	.	.	.	.	Newton Colliery No. 1	Lanark ...	Cal.	Uddingston and Newton.
.	.	.	.	.	.	.	.	Newton Colliery No. 2 (Newton Farm Siding)...	Lanark ...	Cal.	Uddingston and Newton.
.	.	.	.	.	.	.	.	Newton Steel Works (Hallside Steel Works)	Lanark ...	Cal.	Newton.
.	.	.	.	.	.	.	.	Steel Co. of Scotland's Wks.	Lanark ...	Cal.	Newton.
.	.	.	.	.	.	.	.	Westburn Colliery	Lanark ...	Cal.	Newton and Cambuslang.
G	P	F	L	H	C	25	0	Newton (for Hyde).............	Cheshire..	G. C.	Guide Bridge and Penistone.
.	.	.	.	.	.	.	.	Adamson's, D., Siding (G.C.)	Cheshire..	G. C.—Mid.	Newton (for Hyde).
.	.	.	.	.	.	.	.	Beeley, Thomas, & Sons' Siding (G. C.)	Cheshire...	G. C.—Mid.	Newton (for Hyde).
.	.	.	.	.	.	.	.	Newton Moor Spinning Co.'s Siding	Cheshire...	G. C.	Newton (for Hyde).
.	.	.	.	.	.	.	.	Victoria Siding	Cheshire...	G. C.	Newton (for Hyde).
.	.	.	.	.	.	.	.	Blocksage's	Cheshire...	G. C.	Victoria Siding.
.	.	.	.	.	.	.	.	Dukinfield Coal & Cannel Co.	Cheshire...	G. C.	Victoria Siding.
G	P	F	L	H	C	8	0	Newton Abbot	Devon	G. W.	Teignmouth and Totnes.
.	.	.	.	.	.	.	.	Stoneycombe Sidings	Devon	G. W.	Newton Abbot and Totnes.
.	.	.	.	.	.	.	.	Teignbridge Siding	Devon	G. W.	Newton Abbot and Teigngrace.
.	.	.	.	.	.	.	.	Newton Abbot Junction	Devon	G. W.	Teignmouth and Totnes.
.	.	.	.	.	.	.	.	Newton Ballast Hill Siding...	Fife	N. B.	St. Fort.
.	.	.	.	.	.	.	.	Newton Cap Colliery Coke & Brick Works	Durham ...	N. E.	Hunwick.
.	.	.	.	.	.	.	.	Newton Chambers & Co.— Chapeltown Iron Works	Yorks	Mid.	Chapeltown.
.	.	.	.	.	.	.	.	Grange Colliery	Yorks	G. C.	Grange Lane.
.	.	.	.	.	.	.	.	Newbegin Colliery..........	Yorks	G. C.	Westwood.
.	.	.	.	.	.	.	.	Parkgate Oil Works	Yorks	Mid.	Chapeltown.
.	.	.	.	.	.	.	.	Rockingham Colliery	Yorks	G. C.	Birdwell and Hoyland Common.
.	.	.	.	.	.	.	.	Rockingham Gas Works ...	Yorks	G. C.	Birdwell and Hoyland Common.
.	.	.	.	.	.	.	.	Smithy Wood Colliery ...	Yorks	G. C.—Mid.	Ecclesfield.
.	.	.	.	.	.	.	.	Tankersley Colliery	Yorks	G. C.	Westwood.
.	.	.	.	.	.	.	.	Thorncliffe Cols.& Ck.Ovens	Yorks	Mid.	Chapeltown.
.	.	.	.	.	.	.	.	Thorncliffe Colliery	Yorks	G. C.	Chapeltown and Thorncliffe.
.	.	.	.	.	.	.	.	Thorncliffe Furnaces..........	Yorks	Mid.	Chapeltown.
.	.	.	.	.	.	.	.	Thorncliffe Iron Works ...	Yorks	Mid.	Chapeltown.
.	.	.	.	.	.	.	.	Thorncliffe Siding	Yorks	G. C.	Chapeltown and Thorncliffe.
.	.	.	.	.	.	.	.	Topley Pike Stone Quarry	Yorks	Mid.	Miller's Dale.

EXPLANATION—G *Goods Station.*   P *Passenger and Parcel Station.*   P* *Passenger, but not Parcel or Miscellaneous Traffic.*
F *Furniture Vans, Carriages, Portable Engines, and Machines on Wheels.*   L *Live Stock,*
H *Horse Boxes and Prize Cattle Vans.*   C *Carriages by Passenger Train.*

STATION ACCOMMODATION.						CRANE POWER.	STATIONS, &c.	COUNTY.	COMPANY.	POSITION.
						Tons Cwts.	Newton Chambers & Co.—*continued.*			
·	·	·	·	·	·	·	Westwood Coke Ovens......	Yorks......	{ G. C.	Westwood.
									{ Mid.	Chapeltown.
·	·	·	·	·	·	·	Newton Colliery.................	Fife........	N. B.	Cowdenbeath, Old.
·	·	·	·	·	·	·	Newton Dale Siding	Yorks......	N. E.	{ Goathland.
										{ Levisham.
·	·	·	·	·	·	·	Newton Farm Siding	Lanark ...	Cal.	Same as Newton Col. No. 2. (Newton).
·	·	·	·	·	·	·	Newtonhead Depôt	Ayr........	G. & S.W.	See Ayr.
·	P	·	·	·	·	·	Newton Heath	Lancs	L. & Y.	Manchester and Rochdale.
·	·	·	·	·	·	·	L. & Y. Railway Carriage Works	Lancs	L. & Y.	Newton Heath.
·	·	·	·	·	·	·	L. & Y. Railway Locomotive Siding	Lancs	L. & Y.	Newton Heath.
·	·	·	·	·	·	·	Moston Colliery Siding (Platt Bros. & Co.)........	Lancs	L. & Y.	Middleton Junc. & Newton Heath.
·	·	·	·	·	·	·	Newton Heath (Dean Lane)	Lancs	L. & Y.	See Dean Lane (Newton Heath).
G	P	·	L	H	·	·	Newtonhill	Kinc'rdine	Cal.	Stonehaven and Aberdeen.
·	·	·	·	·	·	·	Newton Junction	Ayr........	G. & S.W.	Ayr (Pass.) and Prestwick.
·	·	·	·	·	·	·	Newton Junction	Lanark ...	Cal.	Same as Hamilton Junction.
G	P	·	L	H	·	1 10	Newton Kyme	Yorks......	N. E.	Harrogate and Church Fenton.
G	P	F	L	H	C	5 0 }	Newton-le-Willows (L & N W)	Lancs	{ L. & N.W.	Kenyon Junction Sta. & Liverpool.
·	P	·	·	H	C	}			{ G. W.	Over L. & N. W. from Walton Junc.
·	·	·	·	·	·	·	Evans, R., & Co.'s Bull's Head Siding	Lancs	L. & N. W.	Golborne and Lowton.
·	·	·	·	·	·	·	Garton Bros.' Siding........	Lancs	L. & N. W.	Newton-le-Willows & Kenyon Junction Station.
·	·	·	·	·	·	·	Stone's (Executors) Siding	Lancs	L. & N. W.	Newton-le-Willows & Kenyon Junction Station.
·	·	·	·	·	·	·	Newton Moor Spinning Co.'s Siding	Cheshire...	G. C.	Newton (for Hyde).
G	P	F	L	H	C	5 0	Newtonmore	Inverness	High.	Blair Atholl and Kingussie.
·	·	·	·	·	·	·	Newton, Nos. 1 & 2 Sidings	Cheshire...	L. & N. W.	See Brunner Mond & Co. (Middlewich).
·	·	·	·	·	·	·	Newton-on-Ayr	Ayr........	G. & S.W.	See Ayr.
G	P	·	·	·	·	·	Newton Poppleford	Devon......	L. & S.W.	Tipton St. John's and Budleigh Salterton.
·	·	·	·	·	·	·	Newton Qry. (Bradley's Sid.)	Yorks	N. E.	Great Ayton.
·	P	·	·	·	·	·	Newton Road	Staffs	L. & N W	Birmingham and Wolverhampton.
·	·	·	·	·	·	·	Newton's Brickyard	Derby......	L. D. & E. C.	Spink Hill.
·	·	·	·	·	·	·	Newton Siding	Elgin&Mo'	High.	Mosstowie.
·	·	·	·	·	·	·	Newton Siding	Fife........	N. B.	See St. Fort.
·	·	·	·	·	·	·	Newton Siding	Yorks......	N. E.	Beningbrough.
·	·	·	·	·	·	·	Newton's, P., Siding...........	Herts	Mid.	Elstree.
G	P	F	L	H	C	5 0	Newton Stewart................	Wigtown...	P.P.&W.Jt.(Cal.,G&SW, L. & N. W., & Mid.)...	Stranraer and Castle Douglas.
G	P	·	·	·	·	·	Newton Tony	Wilts	L. & S.W.	Branch from Grateley.
·	·	·	·	·	·	·	Newtown	Glamorg'n	G. W.	See Cardiff.
G	P	F	L	H	C	8 0	Newtown	Montgom.	Cam.	Moat Lane and Welshpool.
G	·	·	·	·	·	·	Brick Yard Siding...........	Montgom.	Cam.	Newtown and Moat Lane.
·	·	·	·	·	·	·	Newtown & Meadows Siding (Lamb & Moore's Siding)...	Lancs	L. & Y.	Wigan.
G	P	·	L	H	C	4 0	Newtownards	Down	B. & C. D.	Comber and Donaghadee.
·	·	·	·	·	·	·	Scrabo Stone Siding	Down	B. & C. D.	Newtownards and Comber.
G	P	·	L	·	·	·	Newtownbutler	Ferm'nagh	G. N. (I.)	Clones and Enniskillen.
G	P	·	L	·	·	·	Newtown Cunningham........	Donegal ...	L. & L. S.	Tooban Junction and Letterkenny.
G	P	·	L	H	·	·	Newtownforbes	Longford...	M. G. W.	Longford and Sligo.
·	·	·	·	·	·	·	Newtown Siding	Glamorg'n	G. W.	Cardiff.
G	P	F	L	·	·	1 10	Newtown Stewart	Tyrone ...	G. N. (I.)	Omagh and Strabane.
·	·	·	·	·	·	·	New Tredegar (Rhy.)	Glamorg'n	Rhy.—L. & N. W.........	See Tir Phil (for New Tredegar).
G	P	·	·	·	·	2 0 }	New Tredegar and White Rose (B. & M.) }	Mon	{ B. & M.	Pengam and Rhymney.
G	·	·	·	·	·	2 0 }			{ G. W.	Over B.&M. from Maesycwmmer Jn.
·	·	·	·	·	·	·	Coedymoeth Col. (B. & M.)	Mon	B. & M.—G.W.	Near New Tredegar & White Rose.
·	·	·	·	·	·	·	Derlwyn Colliery (B. & M.)	Mon	B. & M.—G.W.	Near New Tredegar & White Rose.
·	·	·	·	·	·	·	Elliot Pit (B. & M.)	Mon	B. & M.—G.W.	New Tredegar and Pengam.
·	·	·	·	·	·	·	New Tredegar Col. (B&M)	Mon	B. & M.—G.W.	Rhymney and New Tredegar.
·	·	·	·	·	·	·	New Tredegar Steam Coal Pit or Level (B. & M.)...	Mon	B. & M.—G.W.	Rhymney and New Tredegar.
·	·	·	·	·	·	·	White Rose Col. (B. & M.)	Mon	B. & M.—G.W.	Near New Tredegar & White Rose.
·	·	·	·	·	·	·	New Tredegar Branch Junc.	Glamorg'n	Rhy.	Tir Phil and Pontlottyn.
·	·	·	·	·	·	·	New Tredegar Colliery (Rhy.)	Glamorg'n	Rhy.— L. & N. W.........	See Powell Duffryn Co. (Tir Phil).
G	P	·	L	·	·	3 0	Newtyle	Forfar	Cal.	Dundee and Alyth Junction.
·	·	·	·	·	·	·	Newtyle Chemical Works..	Forfar ...	Cal.	Newtyle.
·	·	·	·	·	·	·	New Vronhenlog Slate Co.'s Sid	Carnarvon	L. & N. W.	Nantlle.

EXPLANATION—**G** *Goods Station.* **P** *Passenger and Parcel Station.* **P*** *Passenger, but not Parcel or Miscellaneous Traffic.*
F *Furniture Vans, Carriages, Portable Engines, and Machines on Wheels.* **L** *Live Stock.*
H *Horse Boxes and Prize Cattle Vans.* **C** *Carriages by Passenger Train.*

STATION ACCOMMODATION.						CRANE POWER.	STATIONS, &c.	COUNTY.	COMPANY.	POSITION.
						Tons Cwts.				
.	.	.	.	.	.	. .	New Wandsworth	Surrey ...	L. B. & S. C.	See Wandsworth, New.
.	.	.	.	.	.	. .	New Whittington Siding ...	Derby	Mid.	Barrow Hill and Staveley Works.
.	.	.	.	.	.	. .	New Wortley Junction.........	Yorks	G. N. & N. E. Jt.—Mid.	Leeds.
.	.	.	.	.	.	. .	New Wortley Siding (Mid.)...	Yorks	{ Mid.—N.E.	See Leeds Corporation Gas Works.
									{ G. N.	(See Appendix to follow).
.	.	.	.	.	.	. .	New Yard Iron Works.........	Cumb'land	L. & N. W.	See Kirk Bros.' & Co. (Workington).
.	.	.	.	.	.	. .	New York Siding	Merioneth	L. & N. W.	See Oakeley's (Blaenau Festiniog).
.	.	.	.	.	.	. .	New York Siding (G. C.)......	Yorks	G. C.—G. N.	Rotherham and Masbro'.
.	.	.	.	.	.	. .	New Zealand Colliery	Yorks	Mid.	Normanton.
.	.	.	.	.	.	. .	Nicholas & Co.'s Timber Yard	Mon	A(N.&S.W.)D.&R.—GW	Newport, Alexandra Docks.
.	.	.	.	.	.	. .	Nichol's Chemical Co.'s Siding	Lancs	L. & Y.	Baxenden.
.	.	.	.	.	.	. .	Nichol's Lime Siding............	Surrey	C. & O. Jt. (L. B. & S. C. and S. E. & C.)	Upper Warlingham.
.	.	.	.	.	.	. .	Nicholson & Son's Sid. (Mid.)	Notts	{ Mid.	Newark.
									{ G. N.	(See Appendix to follow).
.	.	.	.	.	.	. .	Nicholson, J., & Son's Chemical Works (Mid.) }	Yorks	{ Mid.—† L&Y–LN W–NE	Leeds, Hunslet Lane.
									{ G. N.	(See Appendix to follow).
.	.	.	.	.	.	. .	Nicholson's Pit Pumping Engine	Durham ...	N. E.	Fencehouses.
.	.	.	.	.	.	. .	Nicholson's Timber Yard	Durham ...	N. E.	Blaydon.
.	.	.	.	.	.	. .	Nickel Co.'s Siding............	Dumbart'n	N. B.	Kirkintilloch Basin.
.	.	.	.	.	.	. .	Nickoll & Co.'s Siding	Essex	G. E.	Colchester, Hythe.
.	.	.	.	.	.	. .	Nicks & Co........................	Glo'ster ...	G. W.—Mid.	Gloucester Docks.
G	P	F	L	H	C	5 0	Nidd Bridge	Yorks	N. E.	Leeds and Ripon.
G	.	.	.	.	.	. .	Niddrie	Edinboro'	N. B.	Duddingston and Millerhill.
.	.	.	.	.	.	. .	Niddrie Colliery	Edinboro'	N. B.	Duddingston and Niddrie.
.	.	.	.	.	.	. .	Niddrie Sanitary Fire-Clay Works	Edinboro'	N. B.	Duddingston and Niddrie.
.	.	.	.	.	.	. .	Niddrie, East Junction........	Edinboro'	N. B.	Portobello and Inveresk.
.	.	.	.	.	.	. .	Niddrie, North Junction......	Edinboro'	N. B.	Duddingston and Portobello.
.	.	.	.	.	.	. .	Niddrie, South Junction	Edinboro'	N. B.	Portobello and Millerhill.
.	.	.	.	.	.	. .	Niddrie, West Junction	Edinboro'	N. B.	Duddingston and Inveresk.
.	.	.	.	.	.	. .	Niddry Castle Oil Works (Oakbank Oil Co.)	L'lithgow	N. B.	Broxburn Junction Station.
.	.	.	.	.	.	. .	Niddry Oil Works	L'lithgow	N. B.	Same as Young's Oil Co.'s Hopetoun Oil Works (Uphall).
G	P	F	L	H	C	. .	Nigg	Ross & Cro'	High.	Invergordon and Bonar Bridge.
.	.	.	.	.	.	. .	Nightingale's Sidings	Sussex	L. B. & S. C.	{ Crawley. / Horsham.
.	.	.	.	.	.	. .	Nimmo's Siding	Durham ...	N. E.	Same as Sunderland & South Shields Water Co.'s Pumping Station (Castle Eden).
.	.	.	.	.	.	. .	Nimmo & Co.'s Briquette or Patent Fuel Works	Lanark ...	N. B.	Longriggend.
.	.	.	.	.	.	. .	Nimmo & Co.'s Siding	Lanark ...	Cal.	Newarthill.
.	.	.	.	.	.	. .	Nimmo & Son's Brewery	Durham ...	N. E.	Castle Eden.
.	.	.	.	.	.	. .	Nine Elms	Surrey	L. & S.W.	See London.
.	.	.	.	.	.	. .	Nine Elms Gas Co.'s Siding ..	Surrey	L. & S.W.	London, Nine Elms.
.	.	.	.	.	.	. .	Nine Elms Stone Masonry Wks	Surrey	L. & S.W.	London, Nine Elms.
G	P	.	.	.	.	. .	Nine Mile Point	Mon	L. & N. W.	Branch from Nantybwch.
.	.	.	.	.	.	. .	Cox's Quarry	Mon	L. & N. W.	Nine Mile Point and Ynysddu.
.	.	.	.	.	.	. .	Penllwyn Tramway	Mon	L. & N. W.	Nine Mile Point and Ynysddu.
.	.	.	.	.	.	. .	Burnyeat, Brown & Co.'s Sirhowy Valley Col.	Mon	L. & N. W.	Penllwyn Tramway.
.	.	.	.	.	.	. .	Southwood Jones&Co'sSid	Mon	L. & N. W.	Penllwyn Tramway.
.	.	.	.	.	.	. .	Nine Mile Point Junction ...	Mon	G. W.—L. & N. W.	Risca and Tredegar Junc. Station.
G	P	.	L	H	.	. .	Ninewells Junction	Forfar ...	Cal.	Dundee.
G	P	.	L	H	.	. .	Ningwood.........................	I. of W. ...	I. of W. Cent...............	Newport and Freshwater.
G	P	F	L	H	C	4 0	Nisbet	Roxburgh	N. B.	Roxburgh and Jedburgh.
.	.	.	.	.	.	. .	Nitshill	Renfrew...	G B & K Jt. (Cal & G & S W)	Pollokshaws and Barrhead.
.	.	.	.	.	.	. .	Darnley Brick & Lime Wks.	Renfrew...	G B & K Jt. (Cal & G & SW)	Nitshill.
.	.	.	.	.	.	. .	Perry & Hope's Siding	Renfrew...	G B & K Jt. (Cal & G & SW)	Nitshill.
.	.	.	.	.	.	. .	Victoria Pits	Renfrew...	G B & K Jt. (Cal & G & SW)	Branch from Nitshill.
.	.	.	.	.	.	. .	Niven's, T., Siding	Cumb'land	N. B.	Carlisle, Canal.
							Nixon's—			
.	.	.	.	.	.	. .	Cwm Cynon Colliery	Glamorg'n	G. W.—T. V.	Mountain Ash.
.	.	.	.	.	.	. .	Deep Duffryn Colliery	Glamorg'n	G. W.—T. V.	Mountain Ash.
.	.	.	.	.	.	. .	Navigation Colliery	Glamorg'n	G. W.—Rhy.—T. V.	Mountain Ash.
.	.	.	.	.	.	. .	Navigation Sidings	Glamorg'n	T. V.	Mountain Ash.
G	P	F	L	H	C	2 0	Nobber	Meath......	M. G. W.	Navan and Kingscourt.
.	.	.	.	.	.	. .	Nobel's Explosives Works	Stirling ...	N. B.	Redding.
.	.	.	.	.	.	. .	Nobel's Explosives Works (Ardeer Explosives Works)	Ayr	Cal.—G. & S. W.	Stevenston.

EXPLANATION—G Goods Station.   P Passenger and Parcel Station.   P* Passenger, but not Parcel or Miscellaneous Traffic.
F Furniture Vans, Carriages, Portable Engines, and Machines on Wheels.   L Live Stock.
H Horse Boxes and Prize Cattle Vans.   C Carriages by Passenger Train.

STATION ACCOMMODATION.						CRANE POWER.	STATIONS, &c.	COUNTY.	COMPANY.	POSITION.
						Tons Cwts.	Noble's Lime Siding	Yorks	G. C.	Kiveton Park.
G	P	F	L	H	C	1 10	Nocton and Dunston............	Lincoln ...	G. N. & G. E. Jt.	Lincoln and Sleaford.
							Noel Bros.' Brick and Pipe Works and Siding	Glamorg'n	G. W.	Llantrisant.
G	P	.	.	.	.		Noel Park and Wood Green ..	Middlesex	G. E.	Seven Sisters and Palace Gates (Wood Green).
G	P	.	.	.	.		Norbiton and Kingston Hill..	Surrey	L. & S. W.	Wimbledon and Kingston.
G	P	F	L	H	C	8 ,0)	Norbury (N. S.)	Derby	{ N. S.	Rocester and Ashbourne.
.	P	.	.	.	.	}			{ L. & N. W.	Over N. S. Line.
.	P	.	.	.	.		Norbury	Surrey	L. B. & S. C.	Streatham Common and Thornton Heath.
							Norchard or Kidnall's Colliery	Glo'ster ...	S. & Wye Jt. (G. W. & Mid.)	Whitecroft.
.	.	.	.	.	.		Norfolk and East and West Gun Works (Mid.)............	Yorks	Mid.—G. C.	Same as Firth, T. & Sons (Sheffield).
.	.	.	.	.	.		Norfolk & Son's Siding.........	Lincoln ...	G. C.	Grimsby.
.	.	.	.	.	.		Norfolk County Council Sid.	Norfolk ...	Mid. & G. N. Jt.	Holt.
G	P	F	L	H	C	0 15	Norham...........................	Northumb	N. E.	Berwick and Kelso.
.	.	.	.	.	.		Norley Colliery	Lancs	L. & N. W.	See Higginbottom's & Orrell Colliery Co. (Garswood).
.	.	.	.	.	.		Norley Quarry.....................	Lancs	L. & N. W.	Same as Latham & Worthington's Siding (Garswood).
.	P	.	.	.	.		Normacot	Staffs	N. S.	Blyth Bridge and Longton.
.	.	.	.	.	.		Norman & Underwood's Siding (Mid.)	Leicester..	Mid.—L. & N. W.	Leicester, East.
.	.	.	.	.	.		Normanby Brick & Tile Wks.	Yorks	N. E.	Eston.
.	.	.	.	.	.		Normanby Depôts	Yorks	N. E.	Eston.
.	.	.	.	.	.		Normanby Gas Works	Yorks	N. E.	Same as South Bank and Normanby Gas Works (South Bank).
.	.	.	.	.	.		Normanby Iron Wks. & Whf.	Yorks	N. E.	South Bank.
.	.	.	.	.	.		Normanby Mine..................	Lincoln ...	G. C.	Frodingham and Scunthorpe.
.	.	.	.	.	.		Norman Cross Brick Co.'s Sid.	Hunts	G. N.	Fletton.
.	.	.	.	.	.		Norman's Siding..................	Lancs	L. & N. W.—S. & M. Jt.	Widnes.
.	.	.	.	.	.		Normanton	Derby	Mid.	See Derby, Pear Tree & Normanton
.	.	.	.	.	.				{ Mid.	Leeds and Cudworth.
G	P	F	L	H	C	15 0	Normanton (Mid.)	Yorks	{ L. & Y.	Over Mid. from Goose Hill Junction.
									{ N. E.	Over Mid. from Altofts Junction.
.	.	.	.	.	.		Ackton Hall Colliery (for South Traffic)	Yorks	Mid.	Snydale Branch.
.	.	.	.	.	.		Featherstone Main Colliery	Yorks	Mid.	Featherstone Branch.
.	.	.	.	.	.		New Zealand Colliery	Yorks	Mid.	Normanton.
.	.	.	.	.	.		Pope & Pearson's Colliery...	Yorks	Mid.	Near Normanton.
.	.	.	.	.	.		St. John's Colliery (Locke & Co.) (L. & Y.)	Yorks	L. & Y.—N. E.	Goose Hill Junction and Wakefield.
.	.	.	.	.	.		St. John's Colliery Sidings (Locke & Co.)	Yorks	Mid.	Near Normanton.
.	.	.	.	.	.		Sharlston Colliery	Yorks	Mid.	Snydale Branch.
.	.	.	.	.	.		Snydale Branch Sidings ...	Yorks	Mid.	Normanton.
.	.	.	.	.	.		West Riding Colliery	Yorks	Mid.	Near Altofts.
.	.	.	.	.	.		Normanton, Goose Hill Junc.	Yorks	L. & Y.—Mid.	Wakefield and Normanton.
.	.	.	.	.	.		Normanton Hill Siding........	Notts	G. C.	See Barnston Blue Lias Lime Co.'s Siding (East Leake).
.	.	.	.	.	.		Nornabell's Siding..............	Yorks	N. E.	Nafferton.
.	.	.	.	.	.		Norris Siding	Somerset..	S. & D. Jt. (L. & S. W. & Mid)	Highbridge.
.	.	.	.	.	.		North Airdrie	Lanark ...	N. B.	See Airdrie, North.
.	P	.	L	H	C		Northallerton	Yorks	N. E.	Darlington and Thirsk.
G	P	F	L	H	.	5 0	Northallerton Low Station ...	Yorks	N. E.	Leeds and Stockton (Adjoins Main Line Station).
.	.	.	.	.	.		Northam	Hants	L. & S. W.	See Southampton.
.	P	.	.	.	.		Northam	Devon	B. W. Ho ! & A.	Terminus.
.	.	.	.	.	.		Northam Brick Co.'s Siding..	N'hampton	Mid. & G. N. Jt.	Eye Green.
.	.	.	.	.	.		Northam Sidings	Hants	L. & S. W.	See Southampton.
							NORTHAMPTON—			
.	P	.	.	H	C		(Station)	N'hampton	Mid.	Branch from Bedford.
							Bonded Warehouse	N'hampton	Mid.	Northampton.
G	P	F	L	H	C	10 0)	Bridge Street (L. & N. W.)	N'hampton	{ L. & N. W.	Blisworth and Wellingboro'.
G	.	.	.	.	.	}			{ G. N.	Over L. & N. W. from Welham Jn.
G	.	F	L	.	.	5 0	Bridge Street	N'hampton	Mid.	Branch near Pass. Station.
G	P	F	.	H	C	10 0)	Castle (L. & N. W.)	N'hampton	{ L. & N. W.	Market Harboro' and Roade.
G	.	.	.	.	.	}			{ G. N.	Over L. & N. W. from Welham Jn.
.	.	.	.	.	.		Duston Siding..................	N'hampton	L. & N. W.	Northampton and Blisworth.
.	.	.	.	.	.		Phipps (Exors.) Hunsbury Hill Iron Works.........	N'hampton	L. & N. W.	Duston Siding.

STATION ACCOMMODATION.						CRANE POWER.	STATIONS, &c.	COUNTY.	COMPANY.	POSITION.
						Tons Cwts.	NORTHAMPTON—continued.			
							Duston Siding—continued.			
.	.	.	.	.	.	. .	Rice & Co.	N'hamptn	L. & N. W.	Duston Siding.
							Staveley Coal & Iron Co.			
.	.	.	.	.	.	. .	or Duston Iron Ore Co.	N'hamptn	L. & N. W.	Duston Siding.
.	.	.	.	.	.	. .	Hardingstone Junction	N'hamptn	L. & N. W.—Mid.	Wellingboro' and Northampton.
.	.	.	.	.	.	. .	Martin's Siding	N'hamptn	L. & N. W.	Northampton.
.	.	.	.	.	.	. .	Nene Sulphate Works	N'hamptn	Mid.	Near Northampton.
.	.	.	.	.	.	. .	Phipps (Exors) Wagon Wks.	N'hamptn	L. & N. W.	Northampton and Blisworth.
.	.	.	.	.	.	. .	Smith's Timber Co.'s Siding	N'hamptn	Mid.	Near Northampton.
.	.	.	.	.	.	. .	Weston Wharf	N'hamptn	L. & N. W.	Bridge Street and Castle Stations.
.	.	.	.	.	.	. .	Hughes & Co.'s Siding	N'hamptn	L. & N. W.	Weston Wharf.
							Northampton Brewery			
.	.	.	.	.	.	. .	Co.'s Siding	N'hamptn	L. & N. W.	Weston Wharf.
							Northampton Gas Co.'s			
.	.	.	.	.	.	. .	Siding	N'hamptn	L. & N. W.	Weston Wharf.
							Northampton Brewery Co.'s			
.	.	.	.	.	.	. .	Siding	N'hamptn	L. & N. W.	See Weston Wharf (Northampton).
							Northampton Brick & Tile }			{ Same as Brown & Butcher's (Blis-
.	.	.	.	.	.	. .	Co.'s Siding }	N'hamptn	L. & N. W.	worth, Gayton Sidings).
.	.	.	.	.	.	. .	Northampton Gas Co.'s Siding	N'hamptn	L. & N. W.	See Weston Wharf (Northampton).
							North Auchinlee Quarry and			
G	P	F	L	H	C	3 0	Brick Works	Lanark	Cal.	Omoa.
G	P	F	L	H	C	3 0	North Berwick	Hadding'n	N. B.	Branch from Drem.
.	.	.	.	.	.	. .	Gas Works	Hadding'n	N. B.	North Berwick and Dirleton.
							North Biddick Brick & Tile			
.	.	.	.	.	.	. .	Co.'s Siding	Durham	N. E.	Washington.
.	.	.	.	.	.	. .	North Biddick Colliery	Durham	N. E.	Washington.
							North Bitchburn Colliery			
							Coke Ovens, and Brick and			
.	.	.	.	.	.	. .	Pipe Works	Durham	N. E.	Witton-le-Wear.
G	.	.	.	.	.	. .	North Blaina Colliery (G.W.)	Mon	G. W.—L. & N. W.	See Stone's Sun or North Blaina Col.
.	.	.	.	.	.	. .	North Blyth	Northumb	N. E.	Branch, Bedlington & North Seaton.
.	.	.	.	.	.	. .	Cambois Brick Works	Northumb	N. E.	North Blyth.
.	.	.	.	.	.	. .	Cambois Colliery	Northumb	N. E.	North Blyth.
.	.	.	.	.	.	. .	Cambois Co-operative Store	Northumb	N. E.	North Blyth.
.	.	.	.	.	.	. .	Cambois Shipping Staithes	Northumb	N. E.	North Blyth.
.	.	.	.	.	.	. .	North Bridge	Yorks	H & O Jt (G N & L & Y)	See Halifax.
							North British Distillery Co.'s			
.	.	.	.	.	.	. .	Siding	Edinboro'	N. B.	Edinburgh, Gorgie.
							North British Grain Storage			
.	.	.	.	.	.	. .	and Transit Co.'s Siding	Edinboro'	N. B.	Leith, South.
							North British Ice & Cold			
.	.	.	.	.	.	. .	Storage Co.'s Siding	Edinboro'	Cal.—N. B.	Leith, South.
							North British Iron Works }		{ Cal.	Coatbridge, Whifflet.
.	.	.	.	.	.	. .	(Ellis's) }	Lanark	{ N. B.	Coatbridge, Sheepford.
							North British Nail & Rivet			
.	.	.	.	.	.	. .	Works	Lanark	N. B.	Easterhouse.
							North British Oil & Candle			
.	.	.	.	.	.	. .	Works	Lanark	Cal.	Same as Lanark Oil Wks. (Lanark).
							North British Railway Co.—			
.	.	.	.	.	.	. .	Engineer's Oil Gas Works	Edinboro'	N. B.	Edinburgh, Leith Walk.
.	.	.	.	.	.	. .	Engineer's Siding	Edinboro'	N. B.	Edinburgh, Leith Walk.
.	.	.	.	.	.	. .	Engineer's Siding	Lanark	N. B.	Shettleston.
.	.	.	.	.	.	. .	Engine Shed Yard	Cumb'land	N. B.	Carlisle, Canal.
.	.	.	.	.	.	. .	Locomotive Works Sidings	Lanark	N. B.	See Glasgow.
.	.	.	.	.	.	. .	Stores Department Sidings	Lanark	N. B.	See Glasgow.
.	.	.	.	.	.	. .	Telegraph Depôt	Edinboro'	N. B.	Edinburgh, Leith Walk.
.	.	.	.	.	.	. .	North British Tube Works	Lanark	G & P Jt (Cal & G & S W)	Glasgow, Govan.
G	P	F	L	H	C	. .	North Camp & Ash Vale	Surrey	L. & S.W.	See Aldershot.
G	P	F	L	H	C	. .	North Cave	Yorks	H. & B.	Howden and Hull.
							North Central Wagon Co.—			
.	.	.	.	.	.	. .	Rhymney Wharf	Mon	A. (N.&S.W.)D & R—GW	Newport, Alexandra Docks.
.	.	.	.	.	.	. .	Siding	Glamorg'n	G. W.	Swansea.
.	.	.	.	.	.	. .	Siding	Glamorg'n	G W—L N W—Rhy—TV	Cardiff.
.	.	.	.	.	.	. .	Siding	Yorks	Mid.	Masboro' and Rotherham.
.	.	.	.	.	.	. .	Siding (N.S.)	Staffs	N. S.—L. & N. W.	See Cliff Vale Siding (Etruria).
.	.	.	.	.	.	. .	North City Mills	Dublin	M. G. W.	Dublin.
							North Close Colliery (Spenny-			
.	.	.	.	.	.	. .	moor Cattle Dock)	Durham	N. E.	Spennymoor.
.	P	.	.	.	.	. .	North Connel	Argyll	Cal.	Connel Ferry and Ballachulish.
.	.	.	.	.	.	. .	North Cooks Kitchen Yard	Cornwall	G. W.	Carn Brea.

EXPLANATION—G Goods Station.   P Passenger and Parcel Station.   P* Passenger, but not Parcel or Miscellaneous Traffic.
F Furniture Vans, Carriages, Portable Engines, and Machines on Wheels.   L Live Stock.
H Horse Boxes and Prize Cattle Vans.   C Carriages by Passenger Train.

STATION ACCOMMODATION.						CRANE POWER.	STATIONS, &c.	COUNTY.	COMPANY.	POSITION.
						Tons Cwts.				
.	.	.	.	.	.	. .	North Crofty Mineral Branch	Cornwall ..	G. W.	Carn Brea.
.	.	.	.	.	.	. .	North Dean (L. & Y.)	Yorks	L.&Y.—G.N.—L.&N.W.	Same as Greetland.
.	.	.	.	.	.	. .	Northdown Siding (Isle of Thanet Tram Co.'s Siding)	Kent	S. E. & C.	Broadstairs.
G	P	.	L	H	.	. .	North Drove	Lincoln ...	Mid.& G. N. Jt.	Spalding and Bourne.
.	P	.	.	.	.	. .	North Dulwich	Surrey ...	L. B. & S. C.	Peckham Rye and Tulse Hill.
.	P	.	.	.	.	. .	North Dunraven Colliery......	Glamorg'n	T. V.	Same as Blaenrhondda Colliery (Treherbert).
.	P	.	.	.	.	. .	North Ealing (for Hanger Hill)	Middlesex	Met. Dist.	Ealing Common & Park Royal.
.	.	.	.	.	.	. .	North Eastern Brick and Tile Works	Yorks	N. E.	South Bank.
.	.	.	.	.	.	. .	North Eastern Dock Yard ...	Yorks	N. E.	Middlesbro'.
.	.	.	.	.	.	. .	North Eastern Foundry (Black's)	Durham ...	N. E.	South Shields.
							North Eastern Marine Engineering Co.—			
.	.	.	.	.	.	. .	Northumberland Engine Works	Northumb	N. E.	Willington Quay.
.	.	.	.	.	.	. .	Siding	Durham ...	N. E.	Sunderland, South Dock.
.	.	.	.	.	.	. .	North Eastern Pumping Engine Siding	Durham ...	N. E.	Coxhoe.
							North Eastern Railway Co.—			
.	.	.	.	.	.	. .	Carriage and Wagon Works	Durham ...	N. E.	Gateshead.
.	.	.	.	.	.	. .	Carriage Repairing Shops...	Durham ...	N. E.	Darlington, Bank Top.
.	.	.	.	.	.	. .	Dock Engineer's Works ...	Durham ...	N. E.	West Hartlepool.
.	.	.	.	.	.	. .	Gas Works	Durham ...	N. E.	Shildon.
.	.	.	.	.	.	. .	Greenland Creosote Works and Saw Mill	Durham ...	N. E.	West Hartlepool.
.	.	.	.	.	.	. .	Hydraulic Engine Works...	Durham ...	N. E.	West Hartlepool.
.	.	.	.	.	.	. .	Locomotive Department (Greensfield)	Durham ...	N. E.	Gateshead.
.	.	.	.	.	.	. .	Locomotive Repairing Shops	Durham ...	N. E.	Darlington, Bank Top.
.	.	.	.	.	.	. .	Locomotive Shed	Durham ...	N. E.	Haverton Hill.
.	.	.	.	.	.	. .	Locomotive Stores Department	Durham ...	N. E.	Gateshead.
.	.	.	.	.	.	. .	Locomotive Works (North Road)	Durham ...	N. E.	Darlington, Hope Town.
.	.	.	.	.	.	. .	New Gas Works	Durham ...	N. E.	Ferryhill.
.	.	.	.	.	.	. .	Oil Gas Works...............	Durham ...	N. E.	Darlington, Bank Top.
.	.	.	.	.	.	. .	Oil Gas Works (Forth)	Northumb	N. E.	Newcastle-on-Tyne.
.	.	.	.	.	.	. .	Permanent Way Department New Shops............	Durham ...	N. E.	Bishop Auckland.
.	.	.	.	.	.	. .	Permanent Way Shops	Durham ...	N. E.	Bishop Auckland.
.	.	.	.	.	.	. .	Permanent Way Shops	Durham ...	N. E.	Gateshead.
.	.	.	.	.	.	. .	Permanent Way Stores ...	Durham ...	N. E.	Darlington, Hope Town.
.	.	.	.	.	.	. .	Stores Department	Durham ...	N. E.	Gateshead.
.	.	.	.	.	.	. .	Wagon Repairing Shops ...	Durham ...	N. E.	Darlington, Bank Top.
.	.	.	.	.	.	. .	Wagon Repairing Shops ...	Durham ...	N. E.	West Hartlepool.
.	.	.	.	.	.	. .	Wagon Shops	Durham ...	N. E.	Seaham.
.	.	.	.	.	.	. .	Wagon Works...............	Durham ...	N. E.	Shildon.
.	.	.	.	.	.	. .	Whessoe Lane Shops.........	Durham ...	N. E.	Darlington, Hope Town.
.	.	.	.	.	.	. .	North Eastern Steel and Basic Slag Works	Yorks	N. E.	Middlesbro'.
G	P	F	L	H	C	1 0	North Elmham	Norfolk ...	G. E.	Dereham and Wells.
.	.	.	.	.	.	. .	North Elmsall................	Yorks	H. & B.	See Upton and North Elmsall.
G	P	F	L	H	C	5 0	Northenden (C. L. C.)	Cheshire...	{ C.L.C.(G.C.,G.N.&Mid) { L. & N. W.	Stockport and Altrincham. Over C. L. C. Line.
.	.	.	.	.	.	. .	Northenden Junction	Cheshire...	C. L. C.—L. & N. W. ...	Northenden and Stockport.
.	.	.	.	.	.	. .	North End Siding	Kent	S. E & C.	Erith.
.	.	.	.	.	.	. .	Northern Brick and Terra Cotta Co.'s Siding	Lancs	L. & Y.	Summerseat.
.	.	.	.	.	.	. .	Northern Counties Electric Works	Northumb	N. E.	Blyth.
.	.	.	.	.	.	. .	Northern Counties Electricity Supply Co.'s Works	Durham ..	N. E.	Spennymoor.
.	.	.	.	.	.	. .	Northern Guano Co.'s Works	Cheshire...	B'head Jt—CLC—N W & L	Birkenhead.
.	.	.	.	.	.	. .	Northern Quarries Lime } Works .... }	Lancs ...... W'morlnd.	Furness. Furness.	Silverdale. Sandside.
.	.	.	.	.	.	. .	Northern Trading Co.'s Siding	L'lithgow.	N. B.	Bo'ness.
.	.	.	.	.	.	. .	Northern Wood Haskinizing Co.'s Siding	Northumb	N. E.	Walker.
.	.	.	.	.	.	. .	Northey's Siding	Devon	G. W.	Plymouth, Sutton Harbour.

EXPLANATION—G *Goods Station.*   P *Passenger and Parcel Station.*   P* *Passenger, but not Parcel or Miscellaneous Traffic.*
F *Furniture Vans, Carriages, Portable Engines, and Machines on Wheels.*   L *Live Stock.*
H *Horse Boxes and Prize Cattle Vans.*   C *Carriages by Passenger Train.*

G	P	F	L	H	C	Tons	Cwts	STATIONS, &c.	COUNTY.	COMPANY.	POSITION.
G	P	.	L	H	.	.	.	Northfield	Worcester	Mid.	Birmingham and Bromsgrove.
.	.	.	.	.	.	.	.	Northfield Colliery	Hadding'n	N. B.	Prestonpans.
.	.	.	.	.	.	.	.	Northfield Siding (G. C.)	Yorks	G. C.—G. N.	Rotherham and Masboro'.
.	.	.	.	.	.	.	.	North Finchley (G.N.)	Middlesex	G. N.—N.L.	See Woodside Pk. (for North Finchley)
G	P	F	L	H	C	5	0	Northfleet	Kent	S. E. & C.	Dartford and Gravesend (Central).
.	.	.	.	.	.	.	.	Northfleet Ballast Co.'s Sid.	Kent	S. E. & C.	Northfleet.
.	.	.	.	.	.	.	.	Swanscombe Siding	Kent	S. E. & C.	Northfleet and Greenhithe.
.	.	.	.	.	.	.	.	Northgate	Cheshire	C.L.C. (G C, GN, & Mid.)	See Chester.
.	.	.	.	.	.	.	.	North Gate Depôts	Durham	N. E.	Darlington, Bank Top
.	.	.	.	.	.	.	.	North Gate Siding (N.B.)	Stirling	N. B.—Cal.	Falkirk, Grahamston.
.	.	.	.	.	.	.	.	North Gawber Siding (L.&Y.)	Yorks	L. & Y.—G. C.—N.E.	Darton.
.	.	.	.	.	.	.	.	North Glentore Colliery	Lanark	N. B.	Greengairs.
.	.	.	.	.	.	.	.	North Gorleston Junction	Suffolk	G.E.—M. & G. N. Jt.— N. & S. Jt.	Gorleston, North.
.	.	.	.	.	.	.	.	North Greenwich	Middlesex	G. E.	See London.
.	.	.	.	.	.	.	.	North Griffin Colliery (G. W.)	Mon	G. W.—L. & N. W.	See Lancaster & Co. (Blaina).
G	P	F	L	H	C	.	.	North Grimston	Yorks	N. E.	Malton and Driffield.
.	.	.	.	.	.	.	.	North Grimston Lime Wks.	Yorks	N. E.	North Grimston.
.	P	.	.	.	.	.	.	North Hayling	Hants	L. B. & S. C.	Havant and Hayling Island.
.	.	.	.	.	.	.	.	North Hendre Lead Mining Co.'s Siding	Flint	L. & N. W.	Rhydymwyn.
.	.	.	.	.	.	.	.	North Hengoed Colliery	Glamorg'n	Rhy.	Hengoed.
.	.	.	.	.	.	.	.	North Hetton Colliery	Durham	N. E.	Hetton.
.	.	.	.	.	.	.	.	North Hylton Lane Depôt	Durham	N. E.	Southwick.
G	P	F	L	H	C	.	.	Northiam (for Beckley and Sandhurst)	Sussex	K. & E. S.	Robertsbridge & Tenterden Town.
.	.	.	.	.	.	.	.	North Johnstone	Renfrew	G. & S.W.	See Johnstone, North.
G	P	.	L	H	.	.	.	North Kelsey	Lincoln	G. C.	Market Rasen and Barnetby.
.	.	.	.	.	.	.	.	North Kent Junction	Kent	S. E. & C.	London, Spa Road and Deptford.
.	.	.	.	.	.	.	.	North Leith	Edinboro'	Cal.—N.B.	See Leith.
.	.	.	.	.	.	.	.	North Lew	Cornwall	L. & S.W.	See Ashbury and North Lew.
.	.	.	.	.	.	.	.	North Lincolnshire Iron Co.'s Siding	Lincoln	G. C.	Frodingham and Scunthorpe.
.	.	.	.	.	.	.	.	North Linrigg Junction	Lanark	Cal.	Omoa and Salisburgh.
.	.	.	.	.	.	.	.	North Loftus Mines	Yorks	N. E.	Loftus.
.	P	.	.	.	.	.	.	North Lonsdale Crossing	Lancs	Furness	Ulverston and Priory.
.	.	.	.	.	.	.	.	North Lonsdale Iron Works	Lancs	Furness	Ulverston.
.	.	.	.	.	.	.	.	North Mersey and Alexandra Dock	Lancs	L. & Y.	See Liverpool.
.	.	.	.	.	.	.	.	North Monkland Junction	Lanark	N. B.	Greengairs and Slamannan.
.	.	.	.	.	.	.	.	North Moss Lane Siding	Lancs	C. L. C. (S'port Exten.)	Woodvale.
.	.	.	.	.	.	.	.	North Motherwell Collieries	Lanark	Cal.	Motherwell.
.	.	.	.	.	.	.	.	North Ockendon Siding	Essex	L. T. & S.	Ockendon.
.	.	.	.	.	.	.	.	Northolt	Middlesex	Met. Dist.	See South Harrow (for Roxeth and Northolt).
.	.	.	.	.	.	.	.	Northop Hall Siding	Flint	W. M. & C. Q.	Buckley.
.	.	.	.	.	.	.	.	North Ormesby Road Depôts	Yorks	N. E.	Middlesbro'.
.	.	.	.	.	.	.	.	North Ormesby Timber Yard	Yorks	N. E.	See Whitehouse Siding and Depôt (South Bank).
G	P	.	L	H	C	.	.	Northorpe	Lincoln	G. C.	Gainsboro' and Brigg.
.	P	.	.	.	.	.	.	Northorpe	Yorks	L. & Y.	Mirfield and Heckmondwike.
.	.	.	.	.	.	.	.	Mirfield Coal Co.'s Sid(L&Y)	Yorks	L. & Y.—L. & N. W.	Northorpe.
G	P	.	L	.	.	5	0	Northorpe	Yorks	L. & N. W.	Cleckheaton and Huddersfield.
.	.	.	.	.	.	.	.	North Pole Junction	Middlesex	G.W.—L.&N.W.—WLJt	Same as London, West London North Pole Junction.
G	.	.	.	.	.	3	0	North Quay Wharves	Devon	G. W.—L. & S. W.	Plymouth, Sutton Harbour.
.	P	.	.	.	.	.	.	North Queensferry	Fife	N. B. / N. B.	Branch from Inverkeithing. / Dalmeny and Inverkeithing.
.	.	.	.	.	.	.	.	Castlandhill Siding	Fife	N. B.	North Queensferry Goods Branch.
.	.	.	.	.	.	.	.	North Riding Maltings	Yorks	N. E.	Stockton, South.
.	.	.	.	.	.	.	.	Northrigg Collieries	L'lithgow	N. B.	Armadale.
.	.	.	.	.	.	.	.	North Road	Devon	G. W. & L. & S. W. Jt.	See Plymouth.
.	.	.	.	.	.	.	.	North Road	Durham	N. E.	See Darlington.
G	P	.	.	H	.	.	.	North Rode	Cheshire	N. S.	Macclesfield and Congleton.
								North's—			
.	.	.	.	.	.	.	.	Colliery	Glamorg'n	G. W.—P. T.	Maesteg.
.	.	.	.	.	.	.	.	Llynvi Gas Co.'s Siding	Glamorg'n	G. W.	Maesteg.
.	.	.	.	.	.	.	.	Nantyffyllon Colliery	Glamorg'n	G. W.	Maesteg.
.	.	.	.	.	.	.	.	Navigation Colliery	Glamorg'n	G. W.	Tondu.
.	.	.	.	.	.	.	.	Parkslip Colliery	Glamorg'n	G. W.	Tondu.
.	.	.	.	.	.	.	.	Works and Coke Ovens	Glamorg'n	G. W.	Tondu.
.	.	.	.	.	.	.	.	Wyndham Pits	Glamorg'n	G. W.	Ogmore Vale.

EXPLANATION—G *Goods Station.*   P *Passenger and Parcel Station.*   P* *Passenger, but not Parcel or Miscellaneous Traffic.*
F *Furniture Vans, Carriages, Portable Engines, and Machines on Wheels.*   L *Live Stock.*
H *Horse Boxes and Prize Cattle Vans.*   C *Carriages by Passenger Train.*

STATION ACCOMMODATION.						CRANE POWER.	STATIONS, &c.	COUNTY.	COMPANY.	POSITION.
						Tons Cwts.				
G	P		L				North Seaton	Northumb	N. E.	Bedlington and Newbiggin.
							North Seaton Colliery	Northumb	N. E.	North Seaton.
						4 0	North Seaton Quarry	Northumb	N. E.	North Seaton.
G	P	F	L	H	C	10 0	North Shields	Northumb	N. E.	Newcastle and Tynemouth.
							Preston Colliery	Northumb	N. E.	North Shields.
							Tynemouth Gas Co.'s Sid.	Northumb	N. E.	North Shields.
							North Shields and Tyne-mouth Coal Co.'s Siding	Northumb	N. E.	{ See Tynemouth Road Coal Depôt (Tynemouth).
							North Shore	Durham ...	N. E.	See Stockton.
							North Shore Flour Mill	Durham ...	N. E.	Stockton, North Shore.
							North Shore Junction	Durham ...	N. E.	Stockton, North Shore.
							North Shore Mill Co.'s Siding	Lancs	C.L.C. (G C, G N, & Mid.)	Liverpool, Huskisson.
G	P					1 10	North Skelton	Yorks	N. E.	Saltburn and Loftus.
							Longacres Mines	Yorks	N. E.	North Skelton.
							North Skelton Mines	Yorks	N. E.	North Skelton.
							North Staffordshire Brick and Tile Co.'s Siding	Staffs	N. S.	Chesterton.
							N. S. Railway Co.'s Stores Department Siding	Staffs	N. S.	Stoke-on-Trent.
							North Staveley Colliery (G.C.)	Yorks	G. C.—L. & N. W.	Woodhouse.
							North Staveley Colliery ...	Yorks	Mid.	See Staveley Coal & Iron Co.
							North Staveley Junction	Yorks	G. C.—Mid.	Kiveton Park and Killamarsh.
							North Stockwell	Surrey ...	L. B. & S. C.	See London, Clapham Road and North Stockwell.
							North Strand Road Junction	Dublin ...	G. S. & W.	Dublin.
							North Street Depôts	Yorks	N. E.	Middlesbro'.
							North Street Engineering and Boiler Works	Yorks	N. E.	Middlesbro'.
							North Street Engine Works and Scrap Yard	Yorks	N. E.	Middlesbro'.
							North Street Siding	Yorks	N. E.	Middlesbro'.
G	P						North Sunderland	Northumb	N. E.	Branch from Chathill.
G	P	F	L	H	C	10 0	North Tawton	Devon ...	L. & S. W.	Exeter and Okehampton.
G	P		L	H	C		North Thoresby	Lincoln ...	G. N.	Louth and Grimsby.
							North Tucking Mill Yard ...	Cornwall...	G. W.	Carn Brea and Camborne.
							Northumberland & Durham Coal Co.'s Siding	Northumb	N. E.	{ See Tynemouth Road Coal Depôt (Tynemouth).
G						3 0	Northumberland Dock	Northumb	N. E.	Branch near Percy Main.
							Hayhole Lead Works	Northumb	N. E.	Northumberland Dock.
							Seaton Delaval Colliery Staithes	Northumb	N. E.	Northumberland Dock.
							White Hill Point	Northumb	N. E.	Northumberland Dock.
							Northumberland Engine Wks.	Northumb	N. E.	Same as North Eastern Marine Engineering Co. (Willington Quay).
							Northumberland Forge.........	Northumb	N. E.	Carville.
							North Walbottle Colliery......	Northumb	N. E.	Lemington.
							North Wales Narrow Gauge Exchange Sidings	Carnarvon	L. & N. W.	Dinas.
							North Wales Paper Mill Co.'s Siding	Flint	L. & N. W.	Flint.
							North Wall	Dublin ...	G. N. (I.)—G. S. & W.—L. & N. W.—M. G. W.	See Dublin.
	P						North Walsall	Staffs	Mid.	Wolverhampton & Sutton Coldfield.
G	P	F	L	H	C	1 0	North Walsham	Norfolk ...	G. E.	Norwich and Cromer.
							North Walsham Junction ...	Norfolk ...	{ G.E.—Mid.&G.N. Jt.—N. & S. Jt.	{ North Walsham Station and Mundesley-on-Sea.
G	P	F	L	H	C	1 0	North Walsham Town	Norfolk ...	Mid. & G. N. Jt.	Melton Constable & Yarmouth Beach.
	P*						North Water Bridge............	Kinc'rdine	N. B.	Montrose and Bervie.
G	P	F		H	C		North Weald	Essex	G. E.	Loughton and Ongar.
							North Western Bolt, Rivet, and Nut Co.'s Siding.........	Lanark ...	Cal.	Airdrie.
							North Western Hematite Iron and Steel Works...............	Cumb'land	C. & W. Jn.	Workington.
							North Western Storage Co.'s Siding	Cumb'land	C. & W. Jn.	Workington.
							North Western Storing Co.'s Siding	Cumb'land	L. & N. W.	Flimby.
							North West Rivet Works	Lanark ...	N. B.	Airdrie, North.
							North Wexford	Wexford...	G. S. & W.	See Wexford, North.
G	P	F	L	H	C	5 0	Northwich (C. L. C.)............	Cheshire...	{ C.L.C.(G C, G N, & Mid.) L. & N. W.	Knutsford and Chester. Over C. L. C. from Hartford Junc.

EXPLANATION—G Goods Station.   P Passenger and Parcel Station.   P* Passenger, but not Parcel or Miscellaneous Traffic.
F Furniture Vans, Carriages, Portable Engines, and Machines on Wheels.   L Live Stock.
H Horse Boxes and Prize Cattle Vans.   C Carriages by Passenger Train.

STATION ACCOMMODATION.						CRANE POWER.		STATIONS, &c.	COUNTY.	COMPANY.	POSITION.
						Tons	Cwts.	**Northwich (C. L. C.)**—*continued.*			
								Brunner, Mond & Co.—			
·	·	·	·	·	·	·	·	Alkali Works (C. L. C.)...	Cheshire...	C. L. C.—L. & N. W. ...	Northwich.
·	·	·	·	·	·	·	·	Bleach Works (C. L. C.)	Cheshire...	C. L. C.—L. & N. W. ...	Northwich.
·	·	·	·	·	·	·	·	Chemical Works (C.L.C.)	Cheshire...	C. L. C.—L. & N. W. ...	Northwich.
·	·	·	·	·	·	·	·	Salt Works (C. L. C.) ...	Cheshire...	C. L. C.—L. & N. W. ...	Northwich.
·	·	·	·	·	·	·	·	Cleghorn & Wilkinson's Siding (C. L. C.)............	Cheshire...	C. L. C.—L. & N. W. ...	Northwich.
··	·	·	·	·	·	·	·	Hewitt & Renshaw's Siding (C. L. C.)............	Cheshire...	C. L. C.—L. & N. W. ...	Northwich.
·	·	·	·	·	·	·	·	Moore & Brock's Baron's Quay Siding (C. L. C.)...	Cheshire...	C. L. C.—L. & N. W. ...	Northwich.
·	·	·	·	·	·	·	·	Novelty Iron Works (C L C)	Cheshire...	C. L. C.—L. & N. W. ...	Northwich.
								Salt Union, Limited—			
·	·	·	·	·	·	·	·	Adelaide Works (C.L.C.)	Cheshire...	C. L. C.—L. & N. W. ...	Northwich Salt Branch.
·	·	·	·	·	·	·	·	Albert ShaftWorks (CLC)	Cheshire...	C. L. C.—L. & N. W. ...	Northwich Salt Branch.
·	·	·	·	·	·	·	·	Ashton's Works (C.L.C.)	Cheshire...	C. L. C.—L. & N. W. ...	Northwich Salt Branch.
·	·	·	·	·	·	·	·	Baron's Quay Wks.(CLC)	Cheshire...	C. L. C.—L. & N. W. ...	Northwich Salt Branch.
·	·	·	·	·	·	·	·	Brookdale Works (C L C)	Cheshire...	C. L. C.—L. & N. W. ...	Northwich Salt Branch.
·	·	·	·	·	·	·	·	Marston Hall Wks. (CLC)	Cheshire...	C. L. C.—L. & N. W. ...	Northwich Salt Branch.
·	·	·	·	·	·	·	·	Marston OldWorks (CLC)	Cheshire...	C. L. C.—L. & N. W. ...	Northwich Salt Branch.
·	·	·	·	·	·	·	·	Marston Works (C.L.C.)	Cheshire...	C. L. C.—L. & N. W. ...	Northwich Salt Branch.
·	·	·	·	·	·	·	·	Rayner's Works (C. L. C.)	Cheshire...	C. L. C.—L. & N. W. ...	Northwich Salt Branch!
·	·	·	·	·	·	·	·	Victoria Works (C. L. C.)	Cheshire...	C. L. C.—L. & N. W. ...	Northwich Salt Branch.
·	·	·	·	·	·	·	·	Wincham Works (C.L.C.)	Cheshire...	C. L. C.—L. & N. W. ...	Northwich Salt Branch.
·	·	·	·	·	·	·	·	Witton Hall Works (CLC)	Cheshire...	C. L. C.—L. & N. W. ...	Northwich Salt Branch.
·	·	·	·	·	·	·	·	Witton Works (C. L. C.)	Cheshire...	C. L. C.—L. & N. W. ...	Northwich Salt Branch.
								Thompson's—			
·	·	·	·	·	·	·	·	Brick Works or Warrington Road Sid. (C.L.C.)	Cheshire...	C. L. C.—L. & N. W. ...	Northwich.
·	·	·	·	·	·	·	·	Marston Siding (C. L. C.)	Cheshire...	C. L. C.—L. & N. W. ...	Northwich.
·	·	·	·	·	·	·	·	White & Co.'s Iron Works (C. L. C.)	Cheshire...	C. L. C.—L. & N. W. ...	Northwich.
G	·	·	·	·	·	·	·	Northwich Junction	Cheshire...	C. L. C.—L. & N. W. ...	Northwich Station and Sandbach.
G	·	·	·	·	·	·	·	Northwich Salt Branch Junction (C. L. C.)	Cheshire...	C.L.C.(G C, G N, & Mid.) / L. & N. W.	Northwich and Lostock Gralam. / Over C. L. C. from Hartford Junc.
·	·	·	·	·	·	·	·	North Wingfield Siding (Bryncoch Colliery)	Glamorg'n	Rhy.	Darran.
G	P	F	L	H	C	1	10	Northwood	Staffs	N. S.	See Bucknall and Northwood.
·	P	·	·	H	C	·	·	Northwood (Met.)	Middlesex	Met. .... / G. C.	Harrow-on-the-Hill and Rickmansworth. / Over Met. Line.
G	P	·	·	·	·	·	·	North Woolwich	Essex	G. E.	See Woolwich, North.
G	P	·	·	·	·	·	·	North Wootton	Norfolk ...	G. E.	Lynn and Hunstanton.
G	P	·	·	H	·	3	0	North Wylam	Northumb	N. E.	Loop—Scotswood and Wylam.
·	P	·	·	·	·	·	·	North Yorkshire Depôts	Yorks	N. E.	Stockton, South.
G	P	·	L	H	·	·	·	Norton	Cheshire...	B'head Jt. (G W & L N W)	Helsby and Warrington.
·	P	·	·	H	·	·	·	Norton (L. & Y.)	Yorks	L. & Y. / G. N.	Knottingley and Doncaster. / Over L. & Y. Line.
·	·	·	·	·	·	·	·	Norton Branch	Staffs	L. & N. W.	Branch from Pelsall.
								NORTON BRIDGE--			
·	P	·	L	H	C	·	·	(Station, L. & N. W.)	Staffs	L. & N. W. .... / N. S.	Crewe and Stafford. / Over L & N W from Norton Bridge Jn.
G	·	F	L	·	·	5	0	(Station, N. S.)	Staffs	N. S. .... / L. & N. W.	Stone and Norton Bridge Junction. / Over N. S. from Norton Bridge Jn.
·	·	·	·	·	·	·	·	Junction	Staffs	L. & N. W.—N. S.	Stafford and Stone.
·	·	·	·	·	·	·	·	Norton Canes Siding	Staffs	L. & N. W.	Same as Conduit Colliery Co.'s Siding (Brownhills).
·	·	·	·	·	·	·	·	Norton Cannock Collieries ...	Staffs	L. & N. W.	Bloxwich.
G	P	·	·	·	·	1	10	Norton, East	Leicester..	G. N. & L. & N. W. Jt...	See East Norton.
·	·	·	·	·	·	·	·	Norton-Fitzwarren	Somerset..	G. W.	Taunton and Wellington.
·	·	·	·	·	·	·	·	Victory Sid. (Allerford Sid.)	Somerset..	G. W.	Norton-Fitzwarren.
G	P	·	L	H	C	·	·	Norton Hill Colliery	Somerset..	S.&D.Jt. (L.&S.W.&Mid)	Midsomer-Norton.
G	·	·	·	·	·	·	·	Norton-in-Hales (N. S.).........	Salop	N.S. / G. W.	Stoke and Market Drayton. / Over N. S. Line.
·	·	·	·	·	·	·	·	Norton Iron Works	Staffs	N. S.	See Heath & Sons (Ford Green).
G	P	·	·	·	·	·	·	Norton Junction Station	Worcester	G. W.	Worcester and Evesham.
G	P	·	·	·	·	·	·	Norton Mains Siding	Edinboro'	N. B.	Ratho.
·	·	·	·	·	·	·	·	Norton-on-Tees	Durham ...	N. E.	Stockton and Billingham.
·	·	·	·	·	·	·	·	Norton Jn. Sid. (Bell's Sid.)	Durham ...	N. E.	Norton-on-Tees.
·	·	·	·	·	·	·	·	Norton Quarry Siding	Edinboro'	N. B.	Ratho.
G	P	·	·	·	·	·	·	Norton Road	Glamorg'n	Swan. & Mum.	Mumbles Road and Mumbles.

EXPLANATION—G *Goods Station.*   P *Passenger and Parcel Station.*   P* *Passenger, but not Parcel or Miscellaneous Traffic.*
F *Furniture Vans. Carriages, Portable Engines, and Machines on Wheels.*   L *Live Stock.*
H *Horse Boxes and Prize Cattle Vans.*   C *Carriages by Passenger Train.*

STATION ACCOMMODATION.						CRANE POWER.		STATIONS, &c.	COUNTY.	COMPANY.	POSITION.
						Tons	Cwts				
.	.	.	.	.	.	.	.	Norton Siding	Herts	G. N.	See Associated Portland Cement Manufacturers' Sid. (Baldock).
								NORWICH—			
G	P	F	L	H	C	10	0	City	Norfolk	Mid. & G. N. Jt.	Terminus.
.	.	.	.	.	.	.	.	Colman, J. & J., Siding (Carrow Works)	Norfolk	G. E.	Trowse.
.	.	.	.	.	.	.	.	Corporation New Mills Sid.	Norfolk	Mid. & G. N. Jt.	Norwich.
G	P	F	.	H	C	8	0	Thorpe	Norfolk	G. E.	Terminus.
G	P	F	L	H	C	1	0	Trowse	Norfolk	G. E.	Wymondham and Norwich, Thorpe.
G	P	F	.	H	C	5	0	Victoria	Norfolk	G. E.	Terminus.
								NORWOOD—			
.	.	.	.	.	.	.	.	Croydon Corporation Sid.	Surrey	L. B. & S. C.	Norwood Junction Station.
.	.	.	.	.	.	.	.	Crystal Palace Line Junc.	Surrey	L. B. & S. C.—S. E. & C.	Crystal Palace & Beckenham Junc.
G	P	F	.	.	.	5	0			L. B. & S. C.	Croydon and Forest Hill.
.	P	.	.	.	.	.	.	Junction Station (LB & SC)	Surrey	G. E.	Over L. B. & S. C. from New Cross Jn.
.	P	.	.	.	.	.	.			L. & N. W.	Over L. B. & S. C. from Clapham Jn.
.	P*	.	.	.	.	.	.			S. E. & C.	Over L. B. & S. C. Line.
.	.	.	.	.	.	.	.	Smith & Son's Siding	Surrey	L. B. & S. C.	Norwood Junction Station.
.	.	.	.	.	.	.	.	Spur Line Junction	Surrey	L. B. & S. C.—S. E. & C.	Norwood Junc. & Beckenham Junc.
.	.	.	.	.	.	.	.	West	Surrey	L. B. & S. C.	See West Norwood.
.	.	.	.	.	.	.	.	Norwood Colliery	Derby	Mid.	See Sheepbridge Coal and Iron Co. (Killamarsh).
.	.	.	.	.	.	.	.	Norwood Colliery	Durham	N. E.	Redheugh.
.	.	.	.	.	.	.	.	Norwood Green	Yorks	L. & Y.	See Wyke and Norwood Green.
.	.	.	.	.	.	.	.	Norwood Siding (Mid.)	Derby	Mid.—G. C.	Elmton and Creswell.
G	P	.	L	H	C	10	0	Nostell	Yorks	W.R.&G.Jt.(G.C.& G.N.)	Doncaster and Wakefield.
.	.	.	.	.	.	.	.	Nostell Colliery	Yorks	W.R.&G.Jt.(G.C.& G.N.)	Nostell Sta. & Nostell South Junc.
.	.	.	.	.	.	.	.	Nostell, North Junction	Yorks	G. C.—W. R. & G. Jt.	Ryhill and Hare Park.
.	.	.	.	.	.	.	.	Nostell, South Junction	Yorks	G. C.—W. R. & G. Jt.	Ryhill and Nostell.
G	P	F	L	H	C	8	0	Notgrove	Glo'ster	G. W.	Bourton-on-the-Water and Cheltenham.
								NOTTINGHAM—			
G	.	F	L	.	.	25	0	(Station)	Notts	G. C.	Arkwright Street and Ruddington.
G	.	F	L	.	.	10	0	(Station)	Notts	L. & N. W.	Branch from G. N. Line.
G	P	F	L	H	C	20	0	(Station)	Notts	Mid.	Derby and Lincoln.
.	P	.	.	.	.	.	.	Arkwright Street	Notts	G. C.	Victoria and Loughboro'.
.	.	.	.	.	.	.	.	Ashworth, Kirk & Co.'s Sid	Notts	Mid.	Eastcroft.
.	.	.	.	.	.	.	.	Babbington Brick Works	Notts	Mid.	Near Basford.
.	.	.	.	.	.	.	.	Babbington Coal Co.'s Bulwell Colliery	Notts	Mid.	Bulwell.
.	.	.	.	.	.	.	.	Bagthorpe Junction	Notts	G. C.—G. N.	Nottingham and Derby.
G	P	F	L	.	.	10	0	Basford	Notts	Mid.	Nottingham and Mansfield.
G	P	F	L	H	C	10	0	Basford and Bulwell	Notts	G. N.	Nottingham and Ilkeston.
.	.	.	.	.	.	.	.	Basford Chemical Works	Notts	Mid.	Near Basford.
.	.	.	.	.	.	.	.	Basford, East Junction	Notts	G. N.	Basford and Daybrook.
.	.	.	.	.	.	.	.	Basford, West Junction	Notts	G. C. & G. N. Jt.—G. N.	Bulwell Common and Basford.
.	.	.	.	.	.	.	.	Bestwood Cl. & Ir. Co.'s Sid.	Notts	Mid.	Bulwell and Hucknall.
.	.	.	.	.	.	.	.	Bobber's Mill Siding (W. Richards & Son)	Notts	Mid.	Radford and Basford.
.	.	.	.	.	.	.	.	Broxtowe Colliery	Notts	G. N.	Basford and Kimberley.
G	P	F	L	H	C	5	0	Bulwell	Notts	Mid.	Nottingham and Mansfield.
G	P	.	.	.	.	.	.	Bulwell Common	Notts	G. C.	Victoria and Hucknall Town.
.	.	.	.	.	.	.	.	Bulwell, North Junction	Notts	G. C.—G. C. & G. N. Jt.	Bulwell Common and Bestwood.
.	.	.	.	.	.	.	.	Bulwell, South Junction	Notts	G. C.—G. C. & G. N. Jt.	Bulwell Common and Basford.
.	.	.	.	.	.	.	.	Canal Basin	Notts	Mid.	Nottingham.
.	.	.	.	.	.	.	.	Canal Wharf	Notts	G. N.	Nottingham.
.	P	.	.	.	.	.	.	Carrington (G. C.)	Notts	G. C.	Victoria and Bulwell Common.
.	.	.	.	.	.	.	.			G. N.	Over G. C. from Bagthorpe Junc.
.	.	.	.	.	.	.	.	Cinder Hill & Babbington Colliery (G.N.)	Notts	G. N.—G. C.	Basford and Kimberley.
.	.	.	.	.	.	.	.	Cinder Hill Colliery (Babbington Coal Co.'s Siding)	Notts	Mid.	Near Basford.
.	.	.	.	.	.	.	.	Clifton Colliery	Notts	G. C.—Mid.	Near Nottingham.
.	.	.	.	.	.	.	.	Clifton Colliery Junction	Notts	G. C.—Col. Co.	Bch. from Nottingham (G.C.) Goods.
.	.	.	.	.	.	.	.			Mid.—Col. Co.	Near Nottingham.
.	.	.	.	.	.	.	.	Corporation Sidings— Cattle Market (Mid.)	Notts	Mid.—G.N.—L. & N. W.	Nottingham and Edwalton.
.	.	.	.	.	.	.	.	Eastcroft Gas Wks. (GN)	Notts	G. N.—L. & N. W.	Nottingham.
.	.	.	.	.	.	.	.	Eastcroft Sanitary Siding (Mid.)	Notts	Mid.—L. & N. W.	Nottingham and Melton Junction.
.	.	.	.	.	.	.	.	Gas Works	Notts	Mid.	Radford and Lenton. Near Basford.
.	.	.	.	.	.	.	.	Health Dept. Siding	Notts	Mid.	Near Basford.

STATION ACCOMMODATION.						CRANE POWER.	STATIONS, &c.	COUNTY.	COMPANY.	POSITION.
						Tons Cwts.	NOTTINGHAM—continued.			
							Corporation Sidings—continued.			
							Sanitary and Works and			
.	.	.	.	.	.	. .	Ways Siding	Notts	Mid.	Radford.
.	.	.	.	.	.	. .	Siding	Notts	Mid.	Bulwell.
.	.	.	.	.	.	. .	Crosta's Siding	Notts	Mid.	Nottingham.
.	.	.	.	.	.	. .	Forge Mill Sidings	Notts	Mid.	Bulwell and Hucknall.
.	.	.	.	.	.	. .	Gamble's Flour Mill	Notts	Mid.	Bulwell.
							Goddard, Massey & Warner's Siding (Mid.)	Notts	Mid.—L. & N. W.	Near Nottingham.
.	.	.	.	.	.	. .	Junction	Notts	G. N.—L. & N. W.	Netherfield and L. & N. W. Station.
.	.	.	.	.	.	. .	Junction	Notts	G. N.—Mid.	Nottingham, G. N. & Mid. Stations.
.	.	.	.	.	.	. .	Kimberley Colliery	Notts	Mid.	Near Basford.
G	P	.	.	.	.	5 0	Lenton	Notts	Mid.	Nottingham and Hucknall.
							London Road—			
.	P	.	.	.	.	. .	(High Level)	Notts	G. N.	Weekday Cross Junction and Netherfield & Colwick.
G	P	F	L	H	C	10 0 }	(Low Level, G. N.)	Notts	{ G. N.	Terminus.
.	P	.	.	H	C	. . }			L. & N. W.	Over G. N. from Saxondale Junc.
.	.	.	.	.	.	. .	Loweth, T. A., Bone Works	Notts	Mid.	Bulwell and Hucknall.
.	.	.	.	.	.	. .	Marshall's Wagon Works	Notts	Mid.	Lenton.
G	P	.	.	.	.	. . }	New Basford (G. C.)	Notts	{ G. C.	Victoria and Bulwell Common.
.	P	.	.	.	.	. . }			G. C.	Over G. C. from Bagthorpe Junc.
.	.	.	.	.	.	. .	Newcastle Colliery	Notts	G. N.	Basford and Kimberley.
							Nottingham Builders' Brick Co.'s Siding	Notts	G. N.	Thorneywood and Nottingham.
.	.	.	.	.	.	. .	Nottingham Patent Brick Co.'s Siding	Notts	G. N.	Daybrook and Sherwood.
.	.	.	.	.	.	. .	Nottingham Patent Brick Co.'s Siding	Notts	G. N.	Thorneywood and Daybrook.
.	P*	.	L	H	.	. .	Nottingham Race Course	Notts	G. N.	Nottingham & Netherfield & Colwick.
G	P	.	L	.	.	12 0	Radford	Notts	Mid.	Nottingham and Mansfield.
.	.	.	.	.	.	. .	Radford Colliery (Wollaton Colliery Co.)	Notts	Mid.	Radford.
.	.	.	.	.	.	. .	Railway & General Engineering Co.'s Sid. (Mid.)	Notts	Mid.—L. & N. W.	Nottingham and Carlton.
G	P	F	L	H	C	. .	St. Ann's Well	Notts	G. N.	Nottingham and Daybrook.
.	.	.	.	.	.	. .	Sankey & Son's Siding	Notts	Mid.	Bulwell.
G	P	F	L	H	C	. .	Sherwood	Notts	G. N.	Nottingham and Daybrook.
G	P	F	L	H	C	. .	Thorneywood	Notts	G. N.	Nottingham and Daybrook.
.	P	.	.	H	C	. .	Trent Lane Junctions	Notts	G. N.	Nottingham & Netherfield & Colwick.
.	.	.	.	.	.	. .	Victoria	Notts	G. C. & G. N. Jt.	Carrington & Weekday Cross Junc.
.	.	.	.	.	.	. .	Wade & Co.'s Siding (Whitemoor)	Notts	Mid.	Radford.
.	.	.	.	.	.	. .	Walker's, J. & T., Bone Wks	Notts	Mid.	Bulwell and Hucknall.
.	.	.	.	.	.	. .	Weekday Cross Junction	Notts	G. C.—G. N.	Victoria and London Road.
.	.	.	.	.	.	. .	Wollaton Colliery	Notts	Mid.	Radford and Trowell.
.	.	.	.	.	.	. .	Wollaton Colliery, No. 2	Notts	Mid.	Radford and Basford.
.	.	.	.	.	.	. .	Nottingham Builders' Brick Co.'s Siding	Notts	G. N.	Nottingham, Thorneywood.
.	.	.	.	.	.	. .	Nottingham Canal Basin	Notts	Mid.	Nottingham.
.	.	.	.	.	.	. .	Nottingham Canal Wharf	Notts	G. N.	Nottingham, London Road.
							Nottingham Corporation—			
.	.	.	.	.	.	. .	Cattle Market (Mid.)	Notts	Mid.—G. N.—L. & N. W.	Nottingham Station.
.	.	.	.	.	.	. .	Chemical Works	Notts	Mid.	See Bennerley Sidings (Ilkeston).
.	.	.	.	.	.	. .	Eastcroft Gas Wks. (G.N.)	Notts	G. N.—L. & N. W.	Nottingham, London Road.
.	.	.	.	.	.	. .	Eastcroft Sanitary Sid(Mid)	Notts	Mid.—L. & N. W.	Nottingham Station.
.	.	.	.	.	.	. .	Gas Works	Notts	Mid.	{ Nottingham, Basford. / Nottingham, Radford.
.	.	.	.	.	.	. .	Giltbrook Chemical Works	Notts	G. N.	Kimberley.
.	.	.	.	.	.	. .	Health Department Siding	Notts	Mid.	Nottingham, Basford.
.	.	.	.	.	.	. .	Hospital Siding	Notts	G. N.	Daybrook.
.	.	.	.	.	.	. .	Sanitary & Wks. & Ways Sid.	Notts	Mid.	Nottingham, Radford.
.	.	.	.	.	.	. .	Sewage Siding	Notts	G. N.	Netherfield and Colwick.
.	.	.	.	.	.	. .	Siding	Notts	Mid.	Nottingham, Bulwell.
.	.	.	.	.	.	. .	Nottingham Guardians' Workhouse Siding	Notts	G. N.	Daybrook.
.	.	.	.	.	.	. .	Nottingham Patent Brick Co.'s Siding	Notts	G. N.	{ Nottingham, Sherwood. / Nottingham, Thorneywood.
.	.	.	.	.	.	. .	Nottingham Road	Derby	Mid.	See Derby.
.	.	.	.	.	.	. .	Notting Hill & Ladbroke Grove	Middlesex	H. & C. Jt. (G.W.& Met.)	See London.
.	.	.	.	.	.	. .	Notting Hill Gate	Middlesex	C. L.—Met.	See London.

EXPLANATION—G Goods Station.   P Passenger and Parcel Station.   P* Passenger, but not Parcel or Miscellaneous Traffic.
F Furniture Vans, Carriages, Portable Engines, and Machines on Wheels.   L Live Stock.
H Horse Boxes and Prize Cattle Vans.   C Carriages by Passenger Train.

STATION ACCOMMODATION.						CRANE POWER.	STATIONS, &c.	COUNTY.	COMPANY.	POSITION.
						Tons Cwts.	Notton	Yorks	Mid.	See Royston and Notton.
G	P					2 0	Notton & Royston	Yorks	G. C.	Barnsley and Wakefield.
							Hodroyd Colliery	Yorks	G. C.	Notton and Royston.
							Monckton Main Colliery ...	Yorks	G. C.	Notton and Royston.
							Ryhill Main Colliery	Yorks	G. C.	Notton and Royston.
							Notton & Royston Junction..	Yorks	G. C.	Notton and Ryhill.
G	P	F	L	H	C	5 0	Novar	Ross & Cro'	High.	Dingwall and Invergordon.
							Novelty Iron Works (C.L.C.)	Cheshire...	C. L. C.—L. & N. W.	Northwich.
							Nowell Colliery (Mid.)	Warwick..	Mid.—L. & N. W.	Same as Sir A. Hickman's Haunchwood Brick & Col. Co.'s Siding.
							Nowell's Siding (Mid.)	Warwick..	Mid.—L. & N. W.	See Haunchwood Brick and Tile Co. (Stockingford).
							Noyadd Colliery	Glamorg'n	G. W.	Garnant.
G	P	.	L	H	C	. .	Nunburnholme	Yorks	N. E.	York and Market Weighton.
							NUNEATON—			
G	P	F	L	H	C	10 0	(Station)	Warwick..	L. & N. W.	Lichfield and Rugby.
G	P	F	L	H	C	5 0	Abbey	Warwick..	Mid.	Leicester and Whitacre.
							Fielding & Johnson's Anker Mills	Warwick..	L. & N. W.	Nuneaton and Chilvers Coton.
							Forder & Son's Siding	Warwick..	L. & N. W.	Nuneaton and Bulkington.
							Griff Colliery Co.—			
							Griff New Colliery or Clara Pit (L. & N. W.)	Warwick..	L. & N. W.—Mid.	Griff Branch.
							Griff Old Col. (L.&N.W.)	Warwick..	L. & N. W.—Mid.	Griff Branch.
							Griff Granite Co.'s Siding (L. & N. W.)	Warwick..	L. & N. W.—Mid.	Griff Branch.
							Hartshill Siding..............	Warwick..	L. & N. W.	Nuneaton and Atherstone.
							Abell's	Warwick..	L. & N. W.	Hartshill Siding.
							Jee's	Warwick..	L. & N. W.	Hartshill Siding.
							Haunchwood Brick & Tile Co.—			
							Griff Bk. Yard (L.&N.W.)	Warwick..	L. & N. W.—Mid.	Griff Branch.
							Heath End Brick & Tile Works (L.&N.W.)	Warwick..	L. & N. W.—Mid.	Griff Branch.
							Joint Line Junction	Warwick..	A. & N. Jt.—Mid.........	Shackerstone and Abbey.
							Judkins' Stone Siding	Warwick..	A&NJt. (L & N W & Mid.)	Nuneaton and Higham-on-the-Hill.
							National Telephone Co.'s Siding	Warwick..	A&NJt. (L & N W & Mid.)	Nuneaton and Higham-on-the-Hill.
							Nuneaton Local Board Sewage Works	Warwick..	L. & N. W.	Nuneaton and Atherstone.
							South Leicester Line Junc.	Warwick..	L. & N. W.—Mid.	Leicester and Abbey
							Stanley Bros.' Brick & Pipe Works (L. & N. W.)	Warwick..	L. & N. W.—Mid.	Griff Branch.
							Swinnerton's Siding	Warwick..	L. & N. W.	Nuneaton.
							Trent Valley Joint Line Jn.	Warwick..	A. & N. Jt.—L. & N. W.	Nuneaton and Shackerstone.
							Trent Valley Junction	Warwick..	L. & N. W.—Mid.	Nuneaton Station and Abbey.
							Nuneaton New Colliery (Mid.)	Warwick..	Mid.—L. & N. W.	See Stanley Bros. (Stockingford).
							Nunhead Junctions	Surrey ...	S. E. & C.	Nunhead Jn. Sta. & Brockley Lane.
G	P						Nunhead Junction Station ...	Surrey ...	S. E. & C.	Peckham Rye and Greenwich Park.
							Nunnery	Yorks	L. & N. W.	See Sheffield.
							Nunnery Colliery	Yorks	L. & N. W.	Sheffield, Nunnery.
							Nunnery Colliery Co.—			
							Nunnery Colliery	Yorks	G. C.	Sheffield, Park.
							Nunnery Colliery	Yorks	L. & N. W.	Sheffield, Nunnery
							Nunnery Colliery	Yorks	Mid.	Sheffield, Wicker.
							Soaphouse Siding (G. C.)...	Yorks	G. C.—G. N.	Sheffield, Park.
G	P	.	L	H	C	. .	Nunnington	Yorks	N. E.	Gilling and Helmsley.
G	P	F	L	H	C	2 0	Nunthorpe	Yorks	N. E.	Middlesbro' and Guisboro'.
							Marton Lane Sid. & Depôts	Yorks	N. E.	Nunthorpe.
							Morton Carr's Siding	Yorks	N. E.	Nunthorpe.
							Morton Grange Siding	Yorks	N. E.	Nunthorpe.
							Nursery Brick Works	Lanark ...	G.B.&K.Jt.(Cal.&G.S W)	Glasgow, Strathbungo.
G	P	F	L	H	C		Nursling (L.&S.W.)	Hants ...	L. & S. W.	Romsey and Redbridge.
									M. & S. W. Jn.	Over L. & S. W. from Andover Jn.
							Nutbrook Colliery	Derby	G. N.	Ilkeston.
G	P						Nutfield	Surrey ...	S. E. & C.	Red Hill and Tonbridge.
							Nuttall & Co.'s Siding	Lancs	L. & N. W.	St. Helens.
							Nuttall, E., & Co.'s Siding ...	Lancs	Trafford Park Estate......	Manchester.

Station Accommodation.						Crane Power.	STATIONS, &c.	COUNTY.	COMPANY.	POSITION.
						Tons Cwts.				
							O			
G	P	F	L	H	C	5 0	Oakamoor....................	Staffs	N. S.	Uttoxeter and Leek.
							Bolton's Copper Works ...	Staffs	N. S.	Oakamoor.
G	.	.	.	.	.	. .	Oakbank	Edinboro'	Cal.	Holytown and Edinburgh.
						. .	Oakbank Oil Works	Edinboro'	Cal.	Newpark and Midcalder.
						. .	Redcraig Siding.............	Edinboro'	Cal.	Newpark and Midcalder.
						. .	Oakbank Oil Co.'s Siding.....	L'lithgow	N. B.	Same as Niddrie Castle Oil Works (Broxburn Junction Station).
						. .	Oak Brick Works Siding......	Mon	G. W.	Pontnewynydd.
							Oakeley's—			
						. .	Coronation Siding	Merioneth	L. & N. W.	Blaenau Festiniog.
						. .	New York Siding	Merioneth	L. & N. W.	Blaenau Festiniog.
G	P	F	L	H	C	5 0	Oakengates	Salop	G. W.	Wellington and Shifnal.
G	P	F	L	H	C	5 0			L. & N. W.	Coalport and Hadley.
						. .	Great Western Nail Works	Salop	G. W.	Oakengates.
							Lilleshall Coal & Iron Co.—			
						. .	Hollinswood Siding	Salop	L. & N. W.	Oakengates and Malins Lee.
						. .	Priors Lee Siding	Salop	L. & N. W.	Oakengates and Malins Lee.
						. .	Snedshill Siding............	Salop	L. & N. W.	Oakengates and Malins Lee.
						. .	Maddocks & Co.'s Works ...	Salop	G. W.	Oakengates.
						. .	Millington's Siding	Salop	L. & N. W.	Oakengates and Priors Lee.
						. .	Millington Works	Salop	G. W.	Oakengates.
G	.	.	L	.	.	3 0	Oakenshaw.....................	Yorks	Mid.	Oakenshaw Junc. and Normanton.
						. .	Ackton Hall Colliery (for South Traffic)	Yorks	Mid.	Featherstone Branch.
						. .	Featherstone Main Colliery	Yorks	Mid.	Featherstone Branch.
						. .	New Sharlston Collieries ...	Yorks	Mid.	Featherstone Branch.
						. .	Sharlston Colliery	Yorks	Mid.	Snydale Branch.
						. .	Snydale Branch Sidings ...	Yorks	Mid.	Oakenshaw and Normanton.
						. .	Oakenshaw Junction............	Yorks	L. & Y.—Mid.	Wakefield and Masboro'.
						. .	Oakenshaw Junction............	Yorks	Mid.—W. R. & G. Jt. ...	Barnsley and Wakefield.
						. .	Oakerthorpe Colliery	Derby	Mid.	Wingfield.
							Oakes & Co.—			
						. .	Alfreton Iron Works........	Derby	Mid.	Pye Bridge.
						. .	Collieries	Derby	Mid.	Pye Bridge.
						. .	Pollington Colliery	Derby	Mid.	Langley Mill & Eastwood.
						. .	Riddings Brick Yard	Derby	Mid.	Pye Bridge.
						. .	Riddings Sanitary Pipe Works	Derby	Mid.	Pye Bridge.
						. .	Riddings Siding	Derby	Mid.	Pye Bridge.
						. .	Oakfields Wire Works (G. W.)	Mon	G. W.—L. & N. W.	Same as Hill & Co.'s Wire Works (Cwmbran).
G	P	F	L	H	C	. .	Oakham	Rutland ...	Mid.	Peterboro' and Melton Mowbray.
						. .	Midland Provender Stores	Rutland ...	Mid.	Oakham.
G	P	.	L	H	.	1 0	Oakington (G. E.)	Cambs ...	G. E.	St. Ives and Cambridge.
.	P	.	.	H	.				Mid.	Over G. N. & G. E. Jt. & G.E. Lines.
G	P	.	.	.	.		Oakleigh Park (G. N.)	Herts ...	G. N.	New Southgate and New Barnet.
.	P	.	.	.	.				N. L.	Over G. N. from Canonbury Junc.
.	P*	.	.	.	.				S. E. & C.	Over G. N. from King's Cross Junc.
G	P	.	L	H	.	1 10	Oakle Street	Glo'ster ...	G. W.	Gloucester and Hereford.
G	P	.	L	H	.	1 10	Oakley	Beds	Mid.	Bedford and Wellingboro'.
G	P	.	L	H	.	1 5	Oakley	Fife	N. B.	Alloa and Dunfermline.
						. .	Oakley Colliery	Fife	N. B.	Branch from Oakley.
						. .	Young's Saw Mill	Fife	N. B.	Oakley.
G	P	F	L	H	C	. .	Oakley	Hants	L. & S.W.	Basingstoke and Andover.
						. .	Oaks, The	Lancs	L. & Y.	See The Oaks.
						. .	Oaks Colliery	Derby	L. D. & E. C.	Arkwright Town.
						. .	Oak Tanning Co.'s Siding (L. & N. W.)	Staffs	L. & N. W.—G.W.—Mid.	Walsall.
						. .	Oak Tree Siding...............	Staffs	N. S.	Talk-o'-th'-Hill.
						. .	Oakwell	Yorks	G. C.	See Barnsley.
						. .	Oakwell Colliery	Derby	G. N.	Same as Ilkeston Colliery (Ilkeston).
						. .	Oakwellgate Siding	Durham ...	N. E.	Gateshead.
						. .	Oakwell Junction	Yorks	G. C.	Stairfoot and Staincross.
						. .	Oakwood Colliery	Glamorg'n	G. W.	Same as Elder's Navigation (Troedyrhiew Garth).

EXPLANATION—G *Goods Station.*　　P *Passenger and Parcel Station.*　　P* *Passenger, but not Parcel or Miscellaneous Traffic.*
F *Furniture Vans, Carriages, Portable Engines, and Machines on Wheels.*　　L *Live Stock.*
H *Horse Boxes and Prize Cattle Vans.*　　C *Carriages by Passenger Train.*

STATION ACCOMMODATION.						CRANE POWER.		STATIONS, &c.	COUNTY.	COMPANY.	POSITION.
						Tons	Cwts.				
G	P	.	L	.	.	5	0	Oakwood Junction...............	Glamorg'n	P. T.	Port Talbot and Cwmavon.
.	.	.	.	.	.			Oakworth......................	Yorks	Mid.	Keighley and Oxenhope.
.	.	.	.	.	.			Oates Siding (G. C.)	Notts	G. C.—G. N.—Mid.	Worksop.
G	P	.	L	H	C	.	.	Oatlands	Cumb'land	C. & W. Jn.	Distington and Rowrah Junction.
								Moresby Coal Co.'s Oat-			
.	.	.	.	.	.			lands Pit	Cumb'land	C. & W. Jn.	Oatlands.
.	.	.	.	.	.			Oatlands Pit	Cumb'land	C. & W. Jn.	See Moresby Coal Co. (Oatlands).
G	P	F	L	H	C	4	10	Oban	Argyll......	Cal.	Terminus.
.	.	.	.	.	.			Oban Electric Works	Argyll......	Cal.	Oban.
.	.	.	.	.	.	5	0	Oban Pier......................	Argyll......	Cal.	Oban.
.	.	.	.	.	.			Obank & Son's Siding	Yorks	G. N.	Bradford, Idle.
G	P	F	L	H	C	.	.	Occumster	Caithness..	High. (W. & L.)	Wick and Lybster.
								Ocean Coal Co.—			
.	.	.	.	.	.			Black Rock Junction	Glamorg'n	T. V.	Ynysybwl.
.	.	.	.	.	.			Cwmpark (Park) Colliery...	Glamorg'n	T. V.	Treorchy.
.	.	.	.	.	.			Dare Pit	Glamorg'n	T. V.	Treorchy.
.	.	.	.	.	.			Eastern Pit	Glamorg'n	T. V.	Ystrad.
.	.	.	.	.	.			Lady Windsor Colliery......	Glamorg'n	T. V.	Ynysybwl.
.	.	.	.	.	.			Maindy Colliery	Glamorg'n	T. V.	Ystrad.
.	.	.	.	.	.			Ocean Colliery	Glamorg'n	G. W.	Nantymoel.
.	.	.	.	.	.			Ocean Colliery	Glamorg'n	G. W.	Blaengarw.
.	.	.	.	.	.			Ocean Dry Dock Co.'s Siding	Glamorg'n	G. W. — L. & N. W. — Mid.—R. & S. B. ...	Swansea.
.	.	.	.	.	.			Ocean Navigation Col. (G.W.)	Glamorg'n	G. W.—Rhy.	Same as Deep Navigation Colliery (Treharris).
G	P	.	L	H	.	1	0	Ochiltree	Ayr	G. & S.W.	Annbank and Cumnock (A. & C.).
.	.	.	.	.	.			Burnockhill Colliery	Ayr	G. & S.W.	Ochiltree and Drongan.
G	P	F	L	H	C	.	.	Ockendon	Essex	L. T. & S.	Upminster and Grays.
.	P	.	.	.	.			North Ockendon Siding ...	Essex	L. T. & S.	Ockendon and Upminster.
.	P	.	.	.	.			Ocker Hill	Staffs	L. & N. W.	Tipton and Wednesbury.
.	.	.	.	.	.			Ockham	Surrey	L. & S.W.	See Horsley, Ripley and Ockham.
G	P	F	L	H	C	5	0	Ockley	Surrey	L. B. & S. C.	Dorking and Horsham.
								Odam's Manure & Chemical			
.	.	.	.	.	.			Co.'s Siding (G. E.)	Essex	GE—GN—L&NW—Mid.	London, Silvertown.
.	.	.	.	.	.			Odam's Manure Siding	Devon	L. & S.W.	Same as Ebford Siding (Topsham).
.	.	.	.	.	.			Offerton Siding & Depôt	Durham ...	N. E.	{ Hylton. { Penshaw.
G	P	F	L	H	C	.	.	Offord & Buckden	Hunts	G. N.	Sandy and Huntingdon.
.	.	.	.	.	.			Bowyer & Priestley's Siding	Hunts	G. N.	Offord and Buckden.
G	P	F	L	H	C	5	0	Ogbourne	Wilts	M. & S. W. Jn.	Swindon Town and Marlboro'.
G	P	F	.	H	C	2	0	Ogmore Vale	Glamorg'n	G. W.	Black Mill and Nantymoel.
.	.	.	.	.	.			Aber Colliery	Glamorg'n	G. W.	Ogmore Vale.
.	.	.	.	.	.			Tynewydd Col. & Coke Ovens	Glamorg'n	G. W.	Ogmore Vale and Nantymoel.
.	.	.	.	.	.			Wyndham Pits (North's)...	Glamorg'n	G. W.	Ogmore Vale and Nantymoel.
G	P	F	L	H	C	5	0	Okehampton	Devon	L. & S.W.	Exeter and Plymouth.
.	.	.	.	.	.			Old Beam Siding	Cornwall ..	G. W.	Bugle.
.	.	.	.	.	.			Old Bescot	Staffs	L. & N. W.	See Wood Green (Old Bescot).
.	.	.	.	.	.			Old Boston Colliery	Lancs	{ G. C.(St. Helens Exten.) { L. & N. W.	See Evans, R., & Co. (Ashton-in-Makerfield). See Evans, R., & Co. (Earlestown).
.	.	.	.	.	.			Old Brownhills Colliery	Staffs	L. & N. W.	Same as Harrison's No. 1. Colliery (Brownhills).
G	P	F	L	.	.	30	0	Oldbury	Worcester	G. W.	Branch—Stourbridge Junction and Smethwick Junction.
.	.	.	.	.	.			Albright & Wilson's Works } Siding }	Worcester	G. W.	{ Branch—Stourbridge Junction { and Smethwick Junction.
.	.	.	.	.	.			British Cyanide Co.	Worcester	G. W.	Branch—Stourbridge Junction and Smethwick Junction.
.	.	.	.	.	.			Chance & Hunt's Works ...	Worcester	G. W.	Branch—Stourbridge Junction and Smethwick Junction.
.	.	.	.	.	.			Oldbury Alkali Works	Worcester	G. W.	Branch—Stourbridge Junction and Smethwick Junction.
.	.	.	.	.	.			Oldbury Basin	Worcester	G. W.	Oldbury.
G	P	F	L	H	.	5	0	Oldbury and Bromford Lane	Worcester	L. & N. W.	Birmingham and Wolverhampton.
G	P	F	L	H	C	3	0	Oldcastle	Meath......	G. N. (I.)	Branch from Drogheda.
.	.	.	.	.	.			Old Castle Tin Plate Works	Carnarth'	GW—L&M M—L & NW	Llanelly.
G	P	.	.	.	.			Old Colwyn	Denbigh ...	L. & N. W.	Bangor and Rhyl.
G	P	F	L	H	C	2	0	Old Cumnock	Ayr	G. & S.W.	Mauchline and Sanquhar.
.	.	.	.	.	.			Old Cymmer Colliery	Glamorg'n	T. V.	See Cymmer Colliery or Old Cymmer Colliery (Porth).
G	P	F	L	H	C	1	10	Old Dalby.......................	Leicester..	Mid.	Nottingham and Melton Mowbray.
.	.	.	.	.	.			Stanton Iron Co.'s Works...	Leicester..	Mid.	Old Dalby and Grimston.

EXPLANATION—G *Goods Station.*   P *Passenger and Parcel Station.*   P* *Passenger, but not Parcel or Miscellaneous Traffic.*
F *Furniture Vans, Carriages, Portable Engines, and Machines on Wheels.*   L *Live Stock.*
H *Horse Boxes and Prize Cattle Vans.*   C *Carriages by Passenger Train.*

STATION ACCOMMODATION.						CRANE POWER.	STATIONS, &c.	COUNTY.	COMPANY.	POSITION.
						Tons Cwts.	Old Delabole Slate Co.'s Sid.	Cornwall ..	L. & S.W.	Delabole.
	P						Old Down Siding	Somerset..	S.&D.Jt.(L.&S.W.&Mid)	Chilcompton.
G	.	F	L	.	.	10 0	Old Duffryn Colliery	Glamorg'n	T. V.	Aberdare.
G	.	F	L	.	.	10 0	Old Ewloe Brick Works	Flint	W. M. & C. Q.	Buckley.
	P	.	.	H	C		Oldfield Colliery	Staffs	N. S.	Longton.
							Oldfield Road (L. & N. W.)..	Lancs	L. & N. W.—G. W.	See Manchester.
	P	.	.	H	C		Oldfield's Siding...............	Yorks	N. E.	Malton.
							Old Fold Siding	Lancs	L. & N. W.	Same as Evans, R., & Co.'s Haydock Colliery (St. Helens).
							Old Ford	Middlesex {	G. E.	SeeLondon,CobornRd.(forOld Ford).
									L. & N. W.—N. L.	See London.
							OLDHAM—			
							Ashton's Siding	Lancs	L. & Y.	Werneth.
G	.	F	L	.	.	10 0 }	Central	Lancs	L. & Y.	Werneth and Mumps.
	P						Clegg Street	Lancs ...... {	G. C.	Over O. A. & G. B. Line.
		.	.	H	C				L. & N. W.	Over O. A. & G. B. Line.
	P	.	.	H	C		Clegg Street (O. A. & G. B.)	Lancs ...... {	O. A. & G. B. Jt. (G. C. and L.& N. W.)	Glodwick Road and Guide Bridge.
									L. & Y.	Over O. A. & G. B. Line.
G	P	F	L	H	C	10 0 }	Corn Mill Siding	Lancs	L. & Y.	Mumps.
	P	.	.	H	C		Corporation Gas Siding ...	Lancs	L. & Y.	Mumps.
							Glodwick Road (L. & N. W.)	Lancs ...... {	L. & N. W.	Oldham Junction and Greenfield.
									G. C.	Over L. & N. W. from Oldham Junc.
							Hall's Siding	Lancs	L. & N. W.	Glodwick Road.
							Hamilton's Albion Corn Mill	Lancs	L. & N. W.	Glodwick Road.
G						5 0	Hamilton's Siding	Lancs	L. & Y.	Mumps.
							Hartford	Lancs	L. & Y.	Mumps and Royton Junction.
							Higginshaw Gas Siding....	Lancs	L. & Y.	Royton Branch.
							Junction	Lancs	L. & Y.—O. A. & G. B. Jt.	Mumps and Clegg Street.
G	P	F	L	H	C	10 0 }	Junction	Lancs	L.N.W.—O. A. & G. B. Jt.	Glodwick Road and Clegg Street.
	P	.	.	H	C		Mumps (L. & Y.)	Lancs ...... {	L. & Y.	Rochdale and Middleton Junc. Loop.
									L. & N. W.	Over L. & Y. from Oldham Junction.
							Platt's Siding	Lancs	L. & Y.	Werneth.
							Rhodes Bank Siding	Lancs	L. & Y.	Near Mumps.
G	P					10 0	Tay Spinning Co.'s Siding...	Lancs	L. & Y.	Near Royton Junction.
							Werneth	Lancs	L. & Y.	Middleton Junc. & Central Station.
							Wormald's Siding	Lancs	L. & Y.	Mumps.
							Oldham Road	Lancs	L. & Y.	See Manchester.
							Oldham Road	Lancs	L.&N.W.—O.A.&G.B.Jt	See Ashton-under-Lyne.
	P						Oldham Road Potato Market	Lancs	L. & Y.	Same as Oldham Road (Manchester).
							Old Hill	Staffs	G. W.	Branch—Stourbridge Junction and Smethwick Junction.
							Old Kent Road and Hatcham	Surrey	L. B. & S. C.	See London.
							Old Kent Road Junction	Surrey	E. L. Jt.—L. B. & S. C.	London, Deptford Road and Old Kent Road.
G	P	F	L	H	C	2 0	Old Kew Junction	Middlesex	L&SW—N.&S.W.Jn.Jt.	London, Brentford and Acton.
							Old Kilpatrick	Dumbartn	Cal.	Clydebank and Dumbarton.
							Old Lodge Tin Plate Works (G. W.)	Carmarth'	G. W.— L. & N. W.	Llanelly.
G	P	F	L	H	C	1 5	Oldmeldrum	Aberdeen	G. N. of S.	Branch from Inverurie.
G	P	F	L	H	C	1 10	Old Milford	Pembroke	G. W.	Branch from Johnston.
							Old Milford Gas Works......	Pembroke	G. W.	Old Milford.
							Old Milford Junction	Pembroke	G. W.—Milford Dk. Co.	Old Milford.
							Old Milford Junction	Pembroke	G. W.—Milford Haven & Estate Co.	Old Milford.
							Old Mill Lane	Yorks	G. C.	See Barnsley.
							Old Mills Colliery	Somerset..	G. W.	Hallatrow.
							Oldnall Colliery	Worcester	G. W.	Cradley Heath and Cradley.
G	P	F	L	H	C	1 5	Old North Road	Cambs ...	L. & N. W.	Bedford and Cambridge.
							Old Oak Common West Junc.	Middlesex	G. W.	London, Westbourne Park & Acton.
							Old Oak Exchange Sidings (N.& S.W. Jn. Jt.)	Middlesex.	L&NW—L&SW—NL	London,Willesden Junc. and Acton.
							Old Oak Junction	Middlesex	L&NW—N.&S.W.Jn.Jt.	London, Willesden Junc. and Acton.
							Old Oaks Colliery	Yorks	Mid.	Barnsley.
							Old Oaks Junction.............	Yorks	G. C.	Barnsley and Staincross.
							Old Parkside Mining Co.'s Siding	Cumb'land	WC& EJt.(Fur.& LNW)	Frizington.
							Old Park Siding	Salop ...... {	G. W.	Hollinswood.
									L. & N. W.	Stirchley.
							Haybridge Iron Co.	Salop	G. W.—L. & N. W.	Old Park Siding.
							Stirchley Iron Co.	Salop ...... {	G. W.	Hollinswood.
									L. & N. W.	Old Park Siding.

EXPLANATION—G Goods Station.   P Passenger and Parcel Station.   P* Passenger, but not Parcel or Miscellaneous Traffic.
F Furniture Vans, Carriages, Portable Engines, and Machines on Wheels.   L Live Stock.
H Horse Boxes and Prize Cattle Vans.   C Carriages by Passenger Train.

STATION ACCOMMODATION.						CRANE POWER.	STATIONS, &c.	COUNTY.	COMPANY.	POSITION.
						Tons Cwts.	Old Park Works	Staffs	G. W.	See Patent Shaft and Axletree Co., Lloyd's Works (Wednesbury).
							Old Park Works (L. & N. W.)	Staffs	L. & N. W.—Mid.	
							Old Plas Colliery (B. & M.)	Mon	B. & M.—G. W.	Pengam.
							Old Radnor Lime and Stone Works	Radnor	G. W.	Dolyhir.
							Old Roundwood Colliery	Yorks	G. N.	Flushdyke.
							Old Side Siding	Lancs	L. & N. W.	See Widnes Foundry (Widnes).
							Old Silkstone and Dodworth Colliery	Yorks	G. C.	Dodworth.
							Old Street	Middlesex	C. & S. L.—G. N. & C.	See London.
	P*						Oldtown	Donegal	L. & L. S.	Letterkenny and Burtonport.
G	P	F	L	H	C		Old Trafford	Lancs	M S J&A(G C & L & N W)	Timperley and London Road.
							Old Trafford Junction	Lancs	C. L. C.—M. S. J. & A.	Manchester, Central and Timperley.
							Old Union Pits and Furnaces	Staffs	L. & N. W.	Same as Williams&Co.'s Sid. (Albion).
							Old Warehouse Siding	Glamorg'n	T. V.	Ynysybwl.
							Old Welton Colliery	Somerset	G. W.	Radstock.
G							Old Woods Wharf	Salop	G. W.	Leaton and Baschurch.
							Olive Bank Siding	Edinboro'	N. B.	Musselburgh.
							Olive Grove Depôt	Yorks	Mid.	See Sheffield Corporation (Sheffield).
							Oliver Bros.' Brewery	Suffolk	G. E.	Sudbury.
							Oliver's Mineral Siding	Edinboro'	Cal.	Leith, North.
							Oliver, Thos., & Co.'s Works	Glamorg'n	G. W.	Neath.
							Oliver, W., & Son's Siding	Middlesex	G. E. / GN—GW—LNW—Mid	London, Millwall Docks. / London, Poplar.
G	P	F	L	H	C	3 0	Ollerton	Notts	L. D. & E. C.	Langwith Junction and Tuxford.
G	P	F	L	H	C	1 0	Olney (Mid.)	Bucks	Mid. / E. & W. Jn.	Bedford and Northampton. / Over Midland from Ravenstone Wood Junction.
G		F	L							
							Olney Lime Works (Gould's Siding)	Bucks	Mid.	Olney and Turvey.
							Olton	Warwick	G. W.	Birmingham and Leamington.
G	P	F	L	H	C	1 10	Omagh	Tyrone	G. N. (I.)	Londonderry and Enniskillen.
G	G	F	L	H		1 10	Omagh Market	Tyrone	G. N. (I.)	Branch near Omagh.
G	P						Omeath	Louth	D. N. & G.	Greenore and Newry.
G	P						Omoa	Lanark	Cal.	Holytown and Edinburgh.
							Auchenlee Qry. & Bk. Wks.	Lanark	Cal.	Omoa.
							Bellside Brick Works	Lanark	Cal.	Omoa and Hartwood.
							Bellside Colliery	Lanark	Cal.	Omoa and Hartwood.
							Bellside Quarries&Bk.Wks.	Lanark	Cal.	Omoa and Hartwood.
							Bellside Saw Mills	Lanark	Cal.	Omoa.
							Biggarford Colliery	Lanark	Cal.	Omoa and Newhouse.
							Brownhill Colliery, No. 21	Lanark	Cal.	Omoa and Newhouse.
							Drumbowie Weighs	Lanark	Cal.	Omoa.
							Greenhill Brick Works	Lanark	Cal.	Omoa and Salisburgh.
							Greenhill Cols. (Windyedge Colliery, No. 4)	Lanark	Cal.	Omoa and Salisburgh.
							Greenhill Quarry	Lanark	Cal.	Omoa and Salisburgh.
							Greenside Brick Works	Lanark	Cal.	Branch near Newhouse.
							Greenside Colliery	Lanark	Cal.	Branch near Newhouse.
							Howmuir Colliery	Lanark	Cal.	Near Mannieshall Siding.
							Knownoblehill Colliery	Lanark	Cal.	Newarthill and Omoa.
							Lanridge Collieries (Linridge Collieries)	Lanark	Cal.	Omoa and Newhouse.
							Mannieshall Quarry	Lanark	Cal.	Omoa and Salisburgh.
G							Mannieshall Siding	Lanark	Cal.	Omoa and Salisburgh.
							Mossband Colliery	Lanark	Cal.	Branch near Mannieshall.
							North Auchinlee Quarry & Brick Works	Lanark	Cal.	Omoa and Salisburgh.
							Omoa Boiler Works	Lanark	Cal.	Omoa.
							Omoa Foundry	Lanark	Cal.	Omoa.
							Omoa Iron Works	Lanark	Cal.	Newarthill and Omoa.
							Omoa Poorhouse Siding	Lanark	Cal.	Omoa.
							Smellie's Saw Mill	Lanark	Cal.	Omoa.
							Tillanburn Siding	Lanark	Cal.	Branch near Mannieshall.
							Omoa Pottery	Lanark	Cal.	Same as Cleland Pottery (Cleland).
G	P	F	L	H	C	1 10	Ongar	Essex	G. E.	Branch from Stratford.
G	P		L	H		2 10	Onibury	Salop	S & H Jt (G W & L N W)	Craven Arms and Hereford.
G	P						Onich	Inverness	Cal.	Steamer from Oban.
G	P		L				Onllwyn	Brecon	N. & Brecon	Neath and Colbren.
							Drym Colliery	Brecon	N. & Brecon	Onllwyn.
							Maesymarchog Colliery	Glamorg'n	N. & Brecon	Branch from Onllwyn.
							Onllwyn Colliery	Glamorg'n	N. & Brecon	Onllwyn.

EXPLANATION—G *Goods Station.* P *Passenger and Parcel Station.* P* *Passenger, but not Parcel or Miscellaneous Traffic.* F *Furniture Vans, Carriages, Portable Engines, and Machines on Wheels.* L *Live Stock.* H *Horse Boxes and Prize Cattle Vans.* C *Carriages by Passenger Train.*

Station Accommodation	Crane Power (Tons Cwts)	Stations, &c.	County	Company	Position
G P . L . .	. .	Oola	Limerick	G. S. & W.	Limerick and Tipperary.
		Openshaw	Lancs	G. C.	See Manchester.
G P F L H C	5 0	Oranmore	Galway	M. G. W.	Athenry and Galway.
		Orbiston Colliery	Lanark	Cal.	Uddingston.
G P F L H C	1 0	Orbliston	Elgin&Mo'	High.	Keith and Elgin.
		Orby Bradley's Siding	Lincoln	G. C.	Grimsby Town.
		Orchard Sugar Refining Co.'s Store	Renfrew	Cal.	Greenock, Regent Street.
		Ord & Maddison's Quarry	Yorks	N. E.	Middleton-in-Teesdale.
		Ord & Maddison's Siding	Durham	N. E.	See Aycliffe Lime Works (Aycliffe).
. P*		Orden's Platform	Banff	G. N. of S.	Banff and Tillynaught.
		Ordnance Crossing Siding	Essex	L. T. & S.	Same as Purfleet Siding (Purfleet).
		Ordsall Lane	Lancs	L. & Y.	See Manchester.
		Ordsall Lane (for Salford) (L. & N. W.)	Lancs	L. & N. W.—G. W.	See Manchester.
		Ordsall Lane Siding	Lancs	L. & N. W.	See Wigan Coal and Iron Co. (Manchester).
		Ordsall Siding (G. C.)	Notts	G. C.—G. N.	Retford.
		Ordsall Siding	Notts	Mid.	Retford.
G P . L . .		Ore	Sussex	S. E. & C.	Hastings and Rye.
		Guestling Siding	Sussex	S. E. & C.	Ore and Winchelsea.
		Oreston	Devon	L. & S.W.	See Plymouth.
		Orgill Pit	Cumb'land	WC&EJt(Fur&L&NW)	See Wyndham Mining Co. (Gillfoot).
		Orgreave's Colliery (G. C.)	Yorks	G. C.—L. & N. W.	Woodhouse.
		Orgreave's Colliery (Mid.)	Yorks	Mid.—L. D. & E. C.	Woodhouse Mill.
		Orlestone	Kent	S. E. & C.	See Ham Street and Orlestone.
		Orme and Muntz Siding	Cheshire	L. & N. W.	Runcorn Docks.
G P	1 0	Ormesby	Yorks	N. E.	Middlesbro' and Guisboro'.
		Ormesby Foundry	Yorks	N. E.	South Bank.
		Ormesby Iron Works & Whf.	Yorks	N. E.	South Bank.
		Ormesby Metallic Brick Co.'s Siding	Yorks	N. E.	Eston.
G P F L H C	2 0	Ormiston	Hadding'n	N. B.	Smeaton and Macmerry.
		Billyford Farm Siding	Hadding'n	N. B.	Ormiston and Smeaton.
		Bog Siding	Hadding'n	N. B.	Ormiston and Smeaton.
		Brook's Siding	Hadding'n	N. B.	Ormiston and Smeaton.
		Cousland Lime Works	Hadding'n	N. B.	Ormiston and Smeaton.
		Fleet's Colliery	Hadding'n	N. B.	Ormiston and Smeaton.
		Howden Colliery	Hadding'n	N. B.	Ormiston and Smeaton.
		Limeylands Colliery	Hadding'n	N. B.	Ormiston and Smeaton.
		Ormiston Coal Co.'s Meadow Colliery	Hadding'n	N. B.	Ormiston and Pencaitland.
		Ormiston Station Colliery	Hadding'n	N. B.	Ormiston.
		Oxenford Colliery	Hadding'n	N. B.	Ormiston and Smeaton.
		Walker's Lye	Hadding'n	N. B.	Ormiston and Smeaton.
		Ormiston Junction	Hadding'n	N. B.	Ormiston and Gifford.
		Ormrod's, A., Siding	Lancs	L. & Y.	Orrell.
G P		Ormside	W'morlnd	Mid.	Kirkby Stephen and Appleby.
G P F L H C	5 0	Ormskirk	Lancs	L. & Y.	Liverpool and Preston.
		Crook's Sand Siding	Lancs	L. & Y.	Ormskirk and Town Green.
		L. & Y. Railway Locomotive Siding	Lancs	L. & Y.	Ormskirk.
		L. & Y. Railway Permanent Way Stores	Lancs	L. & Y.	Ormskirk.
G P F L H C		Orpington	Kent	S. E. & C.	Hither Green and Sevenoaks (Tubs Hill).
G P . L H C	3 0	Orrell	Lancs	L. & Y.	Liverpool and Wigan.
		Bispham Hall Cl. Co.'s Sid.	Lancs	L. & Y.	Orrell.
		Ormrod's, A., Siding	Lancs	L. & Y.	Orrell.
		Orrell Colliery (Brancker's Siding) (L. & Y.)	Lancs	L. & Y.—L. & N. W.	Gathurst.
		Orrell Colliery Co.'s Norley Colliery	Lancs	L. & Y.	Garswocd.
		Orr's Zinc White Siding	Lancs	L. & N. W.	Widnes.
		Orston	Notts	G. N.	See Elton and Orston.
		Orston Siding	Notts	G. N.	Elton and Orston.
G P F L H C		Orton	Elgin&Mo'	High.	Keith and Elgin.
		Orton & Co.'s Moss Siding	Staffs	L. & N. W.	Stafford.
G P F L H C		Orwell	Suffolk	G. E.	Westerfield and Felixstowe.
		Osborne & Co.'s Siding	Yorks	Mid.	Dronfield.
		Osgodby Siding	Yorks	N. E.	{ Riccall / Selby.

EXPLANATION—G Goods Station.   P Passenger and Parcel Station.   P* Passenger, but not Parcel or Miscellaneous Traffic.
F Furniture Vans, Carriages, Portable Engines, and Machines on Wheels.   L Live Stock.
H Horse Boxes and Prize Cattle Vans.   C Carriages by Passenger Train.

STATION ACCOMMODATION.						CRANE POWER.		STATIONS, &c.	COUNTY.	COMPANY.	POSITION.
						Tons	Cwts.				
.	.	.	.	.	.	.	.	Osier Bed Iron Co.'s Siding (Lysaght & Co.)	Staffs	Mid.	Wolverhampton.
.	.	.	.	.	.	.	.	Osmondthorpe Colliery	Yorks	N. E.	Leeds, Marsh Lane.
G	P	F	L	H	C	2	0	Ossett	Yorks	G. N.	Wakefield and Batley.
.	.	.	.	.	.	.	.	Pildacre Colliery	Yorks	G. N.	Ossett and Chickenley Heath.
.	.	.	.	.	.	.	.	Shaw Cross Colliery	Yorks	G. N.	Chickenley Heath and Batley.
.	.	.	.	.	.	.	.	Ossett (L. & Y.)	Yorks	L. & Y.—G. N.	See Horbury and Ossett.
.	P	.	.	.	.	.	.	Osterley and Spring Grove	Middlesex	Met. Dist.	Boston Road and Hounslow.
.	.	.	.	.	.	.	.	Oswaldtwistle	Lancs	L. & Y.	See Church and Oswaldtwistle.
G	P	F	L	H	C	8	0	Oswestry	Salop	Cam.	Whitchurch and Welshpool.
G	P	F	L	H	C	5	0		Salop	G. W.	Branch from Gobowen.
.	.	.	.	.	.	.	.	Thomas' Siding	Salop	Cam.	Oswestry.
.	.	.	.	.	.	.	.	Oswestry Junction	Salop	Cam.—G. W.	Oswestry Station and Gobowen.
G	P	F	.	.	.	1	10	Otford Junction Station	Kent	S. E. & C.	Swanley and Sevenoaks.
.	.	.	.	.	.	.	.	Otford Lime Works	Kent	S. E. & C.	Otford Junction Station.
.	.	.	.	.	.	.	.	Otford, East Junction	Kent	S. E. & C.	Otford Junction Station & Kemsing.
.	.	.	.	.	.	.	.	Otford, North Junction	Kent	S. E. & C.	Otford Junction Sta. & Sevenoaks (Bat & Ball).
.	.	.	.	.	.	.	.	Otford, South Junction	Kent	S. E. & C.	Otford Junction Sta. & Sevenoaks (Bat & Ball).
G	P	F	L	H	C	10	0	Otley	Yorks	O. & I. Jt. (Mid. & N. E.)	Arthington and Ilkley.
.	.	.	.	.	.	.	.	Otley Junction	Yorks	N. E.—O. & I. Jt.	Poole and Otley Station.
.	.	.	.	.	.	.	.	Otterbourne Siding	Hants	L. & S.W.	Eastleigh.
G	P	F	L	H	C	2	0	Otterham	Cornwall	L. & S.W.	Launceston and Wadebridge.
G	P	.	.	.	.	.	.	Otterington	Yorks	N. E.	Thirsk and Northallerton.
.	.	.	.	.	.	.	.	Manor House Siding	Yorks	N. E.	Otterington and Thirsk.
.	P	.	.	.	.	.	.	Otterspool	Lancs	C. L. C. (G C, G N, & Mid.)	Liverpool and Garston.
G	P	F	L	H	C	2	0	Ottery St. Mary	Devon	L. & S.W.	Sidmouth Junction and Sidmouth.
.	.	.	.	.	.	.	.	Ottinge Siding	Kent	S. E. & C.	Elham.
.	.	.	.	.	.	.	.	Ottô Monsted's Works	Middlesex	G. W.	Southall.
G	P	.	L	H	C	.	.	Ottringham	Yorks	N. E.	Hull and Withernsea.
.	.	.	.	.	.	.	.	Hildyard's Siding	Yorks	N. E.	Ottringham.
G	P	F	L	H	C	1	0	Oughterard	Galway	M. G. W.	Galway and Clifden.
G	P	.	.	.	.	5	0	Oughty Bridge	Yorks	G. C.	Penistone and Sheffield.
.	.	.	.	.	.	.	.	Dixon's Siding	Yorks	G. C.	Oughty Bridge.
.	.	.	.	.	.	.	.	Oughty Bridge Timber Sid.	Yorks	G. C.	Oughty Bridge.
.	.	.	.	.	.	.	.	Silica Co.'s Low Yard	Yorks	G. C.	Oughty Bridge.
.	.	.	.	.	.	.	.	Silica Co.'s Top Yard	Yorks	G. C.	Oughty Bridge.
.	.	.	.	.	.	.	.	Wardlow's Siding	Yorks	G. C.	Oughty Bridge.
G	P	.	L	.	.	1	0	Oulton Broad	Suffolk	G. E.	Norwich and Lowestoft.
.	.	.	.	.	.	.	.	Morse, E. & G., Siding	Suffolk	G. E.	Oulton Broad.
G	P	F	L	H	C	5	0	Oundle	N'hampton	L. & N. W.	Peterboro' and Wellingboro'.
.	.	.	.	.	.	.	.	Ouston Colliery "A" Pit and Gas Works	Durham	N. E.	Birtley.
.	.	.	.	.	.	.	.	Ouston Colliery "E" Pit (Birtley Colliery)	Durham	N. E.	Birtley.
.	.	.	.	.	.	.	.	Ouston Grain Warehouse and Saw Mill	Durham	N. E.	Birtley.
.	.	.	.	.	.	.	.	Ouston Junction	Durham	N. E.	Birtley and Chester-le-Street.
.	.	.	.	.	.	.	.	Ouston Manure Depôt	Durham	N. E.	Birtley.
.	.	.	.	.	.	.	.	Ouston Road Coal Siding	Durham	N. E.	Birtley.
.	.	.	.	.	.	.	.	Outram & Co.'s Pottery Works (Mid.)	Derby	Mid.—L. & N. W.	Woodville.
.	.	.	.	.	.	.	.	Outwell Basin	Cambs	G. E.	See Wisbech Tramway.
.	.	.	.	.	.	.	.	Outwell Village	Cambs	G. E.	See Wisbech Tramway.
.	.	.	.	.	.	.	.	Outwood Siding	Lancs	L. & Y.	Ringley Road.
.	.	.	.	.	.	.	.	Ouzlewell Green Siding	Yorks	E. & W. Y. Union	Robin Hood.
.	.	.	.	.	.	.	.	Oval	Surrey	C. & S. L.	See London.
.	.	.	.	.	.	.	.	Ovenden	Yorks	H & O Jt (G N & L & Y)	See Halifax.
.	.	.	.	.	.	.	.	Ovens & Sons' Siding	Edinboro'	Cal.—N. B.	Leith, South.
.	.	.	.	.	.	.	.	Oven's Chemical Works	L'lithgow	N. B.	Same as Forth Chemical Manure Works (Bo'ness).
.	.	.	.	.	.	.	.	Over	Cheshire	C.L.C. (G C, G N, & Mid.)	See Winsford and Over.
G	P	F	L	H	C	1	10	Over and Wharton	Cheshire	L. & N. W.	Branch—Crewe and Warrington.
.	.	.	.	.	.	.	.	Evans, R., & Co.— Siding	Cheshire	L. & N. W.	Hartford and Winsford.
.	.	.	.	.	.	.	.	Siding	Cheshire	L. & N. W.	Over and Wharton Branch.
.	.	.	.	.	.	.	.	Salt Union, Ltd.— Sidings	Cheshire	L. & N. W.	Hartford and Winsford.
.	.	.	.	.	.	.	.	Sidings	Cheshire	L. & N. W.	Over and Wharton Branch.
.	.	.	.	.	.	.	.	Over and Wharton Branch	Cheshire	L. & N. W.	Hartford and Winsford.
.	.	.	.	.	.	.	.	Over Dalserf Colliery	Lanark	Cal.	Dalserf.

EXPLANATION—G *Goods Station.*   P *Passenger and Parcel Station.*   P* *Passenger, but not Parcel or Miscellaneous Traffic.*
F *Furniture Vans, Carriages, Portable Engines, and Machines on Wheels.*   L *Live Stock.*
H *Horse Boxes and Prize Cattle Vans.*   C *Carriages by Passenger Train.*

Station Accommodation.						Crane Power.		STATIONS, &c.	COUNTY.	COMPANY.	POSITION.
						Tons	Cwts.				
								Over Johnstone Colliery	Lanark	Cal.	} See Belhaven Estate Collieries (Shieldmuir).
								Over Johnstone Farm Siding	Lanark	Cal.	
								Over Junction and Sidings	Glo'ster	G. W.	Gloucester and Grange Court.
G		F	L			1	10	Overseal & Moira	Leicester	A & N Jt. (L & N W & Mid.)	Nuneaton and Overseal & Moira Jn.
								Overseal & Moira, East Junc.	Leicester	A. & N. Jt.—Mid.	Shackerstone and Moira.
G	P	F	L	H	C			Overseal & Moira, West Junc.	Leicester	A. & N. Jt.—Mid.	Shackerstone and Gresley.
G	P	F		H	C			Overton	Hants	L. & S.W.	Basingstoke and Andover.
	P				C		}	Overton (L. & N. W.)	Hunts	{ L. & N. W.	Market Harboro' and Peterboro'.
	P				C					{ G. N.	
G	P	F	L	H	C	4	0	Overton-on-Dee	Flint	Cam.	Over L. & N. W. from Longville Jn.
								Elson Brick Siding	Salop	Cam.	Wrexham and Ellesmere.
								Overton Paper Mill	Renfrew	Cal.	Overton-on-Dee and Ellesmere.
								Overtown Forge	Lanark	Cal.	Greenock, Upper.
								Overtown Siding	Lanark	Cal.	Wishaw.
	P							Overtown, Waterloo	Lanark	Cal.	Wishaw.
								Overwood Quarry	Lanark	Cal.	Law Junction and Holytown.
								Over Works Siding	Cheshire	C.L.C. (G C, G N, & Mid.)	Stonehouse.
G	P	F	L	H	C	3	0	Ovoca	Wicklow	D. W. & W.	See Salt Union Ltd. (Winsford and Over).
								Cronebane Siding	Wicklow	D. W. & W.	Wicklow and Arklow.
								Owen & Co.'s Siding	Herts	G. N.	Ovoca.
								Owen & Dutson's Siding	Staffs	Mid.	Hill End.
								Owen & Dyson's Works	Yorks	Mid.	Same as Watling Street Colliery (Brownhills).
								Owen's Siding	Herts	Mid.	Masboro' and Rotherham.
								Owen Stone Co.—			Redbourn.
								Siding	L'lithgow	N. B.	Bathgate, Upper.
								Siding	Surrey	L. & S.W.	Worplesdon.
								Owen, T., & Co.'s Ely Paper Mills	Glamorg'n	{ G. W.	Ely (for Llandaff).
										{ T. V.	Penarth Dock.
								Oxbridge Foundry	Durham	N. E.	Stockton, North Shore.
								Oxcroft Colliery Co.	Derby	Mid.	Barrow Hill and Staveley Works.
								Oxendon	N'hamptn	L. & N. W.	See Clipston and Oxendon.
								Oxenford Colliery	Hadding'n	N. B.	Ormiston.
G	P	F	L	H	C	5	0	Oxenholme	W'morlnd	L. & N. W.	Lancaster and Penrith.
G	P		L	H		10	0	Oxenhope	Yorks	Mid.	Branch from Keighley.
G	G	F	L	H	C	10	0 }	Oxford	Oxon	{ G. W.	Didcot and Banbury.
G	G	F	L	H	C	10	0 }			{ L. & N. W.	Branch from Bletchley.
						3	0	Oxford Gas Works	Oxon	G. W.	Oxford.
								Wolvercot Siding	Oxon	G. W.	Oxford and Yarnton.
								Oxford Junction	Oxon	G. W.—L. & N. W.	Oxford and Yarnton.
								Oxford Circus	Middlesex	C. L.	See London.
								Oxford County Asylum Siding	Oxon	G. W.	Littlemore.
								Oxford Road	Lancs	MSJ&A(GC&L&NW)	See Manchester.
								Oxheys	Lancs	L. & N. W.	See Preston.
								Oxhill Siding	Durham	N. E.	See South Moor Collieries (Annfield Plain).
								Oxide & Iron Ore Co.'s Siding (G. W.)	Glamorg'n	G. W.—T. V.	Same as Mwyndy Siding.
								Oxley & Co.'s Siding	Yorks	Mid.	Same as Parkgate Steel Works (Masboro').
								Oxley, Wm., & Co.'s Sid. (G.C)	Yorks	G. C.—G. N.	Rotherham and Masboro'.
G	P	F	L	H	C	2	0	Oxley Sidings	Staffs	G. W.	Wolverhampton.
								Oxshott & Fairmile	Surrey	L. & S.W.	Surbiton and Guildford.
								Cook's Brick Siding	Surrey	L. & S.W.	Oxshott.
G	P	F	L	H	C			Oxspring Siding	Yorks	G. C.	Penistone.
								Oxted	Surrey	C. & O. Jt. (L. B. & S. C. and S. E. & C.)	Croydon and Edenbridge.
								Oxted Greystone Lime Co.'s Siding	Surrey	{ C. & O. Jt. (L. B. & S. C. and S. E. & C.)	Oxted and Woldingham.
G	P		L	H				Oxton	Berwick	N. B.	Fountainhall and Lauder.
G								Hartside Siding	Edinboro'	N. B.	Fountainhall and Oxton.
G								Middletown Siding	Edinboro'	N. B.	Fountainhall and Oxton.
								Oxwellmains Limestone Sid.	Hadding'n	N. B.	Dunbar.
								Oxwellmains Siding	Hadding'n	N. B.	See Dunbar.
G	P	F	L	H	C	1	5	Oyne	Aberdeen	G. N. of S.	Inveramsay and Keith.
	P							Oystermouth	Glamorg'n	Swan. & Mum.	Mumbles Road and Mumbles.

EXPLANATION—G *Goods Station.*   P *Passenger and Parcel Station.*   P* *Passenger, but not Parcel or Miscellaneous Traffic.*
F *Furniture Vans, Carriages, Portable Engines, and Machines on Wheels.*   L *Live Stock.*
H *Horse Boxes and Prize Cattle Vans.*   C *Carriages by Passenger Train.*

STATION ACCOMMODATION.						CRANE POWER.		STATIONS, &c.	COUNTY.	COMPANY.	POSITION.
						Tons	Cwts				
								P			
·	·	·	·	·	·	·	·	Pabo	Carnarvon	L. & N. W.	See Mochdre and Pabo.
·	·	·	·	·	·	·	·	Pacific Patent Fuel Co.'s Sid.	Glamorg'n	GW—LNW—Mid—RSB	Swansea.
·	·	·	·	·	·	·	·	Packard & Co.'s Siding	Suffolk	G. E.	Bramford.
·	·	·	·	·	·	·	·	Packet Wharf	Yorks	N. E.	Middlesbro'.
·	·	·	·	·	·	·	·	Packet Wharf Slate Yard	Yorks	N. E.	Middlesbro'.
·	·	·	·	·	·	·	·	J. Harrison & Son	Yorks	N. E.	Packet Wharf Slate Yard.
·	·	·	·	·	·	·	·	J. & R. Mascall	Yorks	N. E.	Packet Wharf Slate Yard.
·	·	·	·	·	·	·	·	Packington's Siding	Warwick	Mid.	Hampton.
G	P	·	L	H	·	·	·	Padbury	Bucks	L. & N. W.	Banbury and Verney Junction Sta.
·	·	·	·	·	·	·	·	Paddington	Middlesex	G. W.	See London.
·	·	·	·	·	·	·	·	Paddington, Bishop's Road	Middlesex	G. W.—Met.	See London.
·	·	·	·	·	·	·	·	Paddington, Praed Street	Middlesex	Met.	See London.
G	P	F	L	H	C	4	0	Paddock Wood	Kent	S. E. & C.	Tonbridge and Ashford.
·	·	·	·	·	·	·	·	Paddock Wood Junction	Kent	S. E. & C.	Paddock Wood and Marden.
G	P	·	L	H	·	1	10	Padeswood and Buckley	Flint	L. & N. W.	Chester and Mold.
·	·	·	·	·	·	·	·	Parry & Co.'s Llong Colliery	Flint	L. & N. W.	Padeswood and Llong.
·	·	·	·	·	·	·	·	Ratcliffe's (Executors) Sids.	Flint	L. & N. W.	{ Padeswood and Coed Talon. Padeswood and Hope.
G	P	F	L	H	C	5	0	Padgate	Lancs	C. L. C. (G C, G N, & Mid.)	Warrington and Glazebrook.
G	P	F	L	H	C	10	0	Padiham	Lancs	L. & Y.	Loop—Blackburn and Burnley.
G	P	F	L	H	C	2	0	Padstow	Cornwall	L. & S.W.	Extension from Wadebridge.
·	·	·	·	·	·	·	·	Page & Son's Siding	Staffs	L. & N. W.	Albion.
·	·	·	·	·	·	·	·	Page & Taylor's Siding	Lancs	P. & L. Jt. (L & NW. & L&Y)	Preston, Deepdale.
·	·	·	·	·	·	·	·	Page's Malting Siding	Herts	G. N.	Baldock.
·	·	·	·	·	·	·	·	Page, R., Siding	Essex	G. E.	Ilford.
·	·	·	·	·	·	·	·	Page Bank Colliery Coke Ovens & Brick Works	Durham	N. E.	{ Same as South Brancepeth Col. Ck. Ovens & Bk. Wks. (Spennymoor).
·	·	·	·	·	·	·	·	Pagefield Forge Co.'s Siding	Lancs	L. & Y.	{ Gathurst. Wigan.
·	·	·	·	·	·	·	·	Pagefield Siding	Lancs	L. & Y.	{ Gathurst. Wigan.
·	·	·	·	·	·	·	·	Walker Bros.	Lancs	L. & Y.	Pagefield Siding.
·	·	·	·	·	·	·	·	Wigan Rolling Mills	Lancs	L. & Y.	Pagefield Siding.
·	·	·	·	·	·	·	·	Paget's Siding	Notts	G. C.	East Leake.
·	·	·	·	·	·	·	·	Paices Siding	Surrey	L. & S.W.	Egham.
G	P	F	L	H	C	2	0	Paignton	Devon	G. W.	Torquay and Churston.
·	·	·	·	·	·	·	·	Pain's Ironstone Siding	N'hamptn	Mid.	Weldon and Corby.
·	·	·	·	·	·	·	·	Pain's Siding	N'hamptn	Mid.	Same as Glendon Ironstone Siding.
								PAISLEY—			
G	P	·	·	·	·	·	·	Abercorn	Renfrew	G. & S.W.	Glasgow and Renfrew.
·	·	·	·	·	·	·	·	Abercorn Pits	Renfrew	Cal.	St. James and Houston.
·	·	·	·	·	·	·	·	Arkleston Junction	Renfrew	G. & P. Jt.—G. & S. W.	Cardonald and Paisley, Abercorn.
·	·	·	·	·	·	·	·	Brediland Siding	Renfrew	G. & S.W.	Ferguslie and Elderslie.
·	·	·	·	·	·	·	·	Burgh Lye	Renfrew	Cal.	St. James.
·	·	·	·	·	·	·	·	Caledonia & Baltic SawMills	Renfrew	Cal.	St. James.
·	·	·	·	·	·	·	·	Caledonia Fire-Clay Works	Renfrew	Cal.	Burgh Lye.
G	P	F	L	H	C	6	0	Canal (G. & S. W.)	Renfrew	{ G. & S. W. N. B.	{ Glasgow (Bellahouston) & Johnstone. Over G. & S. W. from College Junc.
G	·	F	L	·	·	6	0				
G	·	·	·	·	·	25	0	Cart Harbour	Renfrew	G. & S.W.	Branch—Abercorn and Renfrew.
·	·	·	·	·	·	·	·	Coat's Siding	Renfrew	G. & S.W.	Ferguslie.
·	·	·	·	·	·	·	·	Craigielea Chemical Works	Renfrew	Cal.	Burgh Lye.
·	·	·	·	·	·	·	·	Craig's Engineering Works (Caledonia Engine Wks.)	Renfrew	Cal.	Burgh Lye.
·	·	·	·	·	·	·	·	Douglas Pits, Nos. 1, 2, & 3	Renfrew	Cal.	St. James and Houston.
G	·	·	·	·	·	3	0	Ferguslie	Renfrew	G. & S.W.	Paisley (Canal) and Johnstone.
·	·	·	·	·	·	·	·	Ferguslie Fire-Clay Works	Renfrew	G. & S.W.	Ferguslie and Elderslie.
·	·	·	·	·	·	·	·	Gallowhill Sidings	Renfrew	G & P Jt (Cal & G & S W)	Gilmour Street and Cardonald.
·	·	·	·	·	·	·	·	Gas Works	Renfrew	G. & S.W.	Gilmour Street and Johnstone.
·	P	·	·	H	C	·	·	Gilmour Street Station & Jn.	Renfrew	Cal.—G & P Jt.—G & S W.	Glasgow and Johnstone.
G	·	·	·	·	·	2	0	Gleniffer Depôt	Renfrew	G. & S.W.	Extension from Potterhill.
G	·	F	L	H	·	15	0	Greenlaw	Renfrew	G & P Jt (Cal & G & S W)	Glasgow and Johnstone.
G	P	·	·	·	·	2	0	Hawkhead	Renfrew	G. & S.W.	Glasgow (Bellahouston) and Paisley, Canal.
·	·	·	·	·	·	·	·	Inkerman Brick Works	Renfrew	Cal.	St. James and Houston.
G	·	·	·	·	·	·	·	King Street Depôt	Renfrew	G. & S.W.	Gilmour Street and Johnstone.

STATION ACCOMMODATION.						CRANE POWER.		STATIONS, &c.	COUNTY.	COMPANY.	POSITION.
						Tons	Cwts.	PAISLEY—*continued.*			
G						2	0	Mullstane Craig Quarry.....	Renfrew...	G. & S.W.	Potterhill and Gleniffer Depôt.
G	P					3	0	Potterhill	Renfrew...	G. & S.W.	Branch—Paisley (Canal) & Ferguslie.
G						2	0	St. James...................	Renfrew...	Cal.	Paisley and Houston.
G								Saucel	Renfrew...	G. & S.W	Glasgow (Bellahouston) and Paisley, Canal.
G								Saucel Distillery.............	Renfrew...	G. & S.W.	Paisley, Saucel.
G						2	0	Stoneybrae	Renfrew...	G. & S.W.	Gilmour Street and Johnstone.
								Underwood Mineral Depôt	Renfrew...	Cal.	Paisley and St. James.
								Walkinshaw Pits	Renfrew...	Cal.	St. James and Houston.
								Walkinshaw Siding	Renfrew...	Cal.	St. James and Houston.
								Wallneuk Junction	Renfrew...	G. & P. Jt.—G. & S. W.	Gilmour Street and Abercorn.
	P							West	Renfrew...	G. & S.W.	Paisley (Canal) and Johnstone.
								Paisley Gas Works............	Renfrew...	G. & S.W.	Paisley, Stoneybrae.
								Palace Brewery	Edinboro'	N. B.	Edinburgh, Rose Lane.
								Palacecraig Branch.........	Lanark ...	N. B.	Coatbridge, Whifflet.
								Palacecraig Brick Works.....	Lanark ...	N. B.	Coatbridge, Whifflet.
								Palacecraig Colliery	Lanark ...	N. B.	Coatbridge, Whifflet.
G	P		L					Palace East Junction	Wexford...	D. W. & W.	Macmine Junction and New Ross.
G	P	F		H†	C†			Palace Gates (Wood Green)..	Middlesex	G. E.	Branch from Seven Sisters.
								Palethorpe's Siding	Staffs	L. & N. W.	Dudley.
								Palfreman, Foster & Co.'s Sid.	Suffolk ...	G. E.	Ipswich, Derby Road.
								Pallaflat Branch............	Cumb'land	WC&EJt.(Fur.&LNW)	Branch off Bigrigg Branch.
								Pallaflat Co.'s No. 2 Siding...	Cumb'land	WC&EJt.(Fur.&LNW)	Moor Row.
G	P	F	L	H	C	1	10	Pallas	Limerick ..	G. S. & W.	Limerick and Tipperary.
G	P	F	L	H	C	3	0	Pallion	Durham ...	N. E.	Sunderland and Penshaw.
								Ayre's Quay Gas Works ...	Durham ...	N. E.	Pallion.
								Copperas Bank Forge and Depôts	Durham ...	N. E.	Pallion.
								Deptford Branch Junction	Durham ...	N. E.	Pallion.
								Deptford Depôts............	Durham ...	N. E.	Pallion.
								Diamond Hall Pottery and Depôts	Durham ...	N. E.	Pallion.
								Forster's Siding and Depôt	Durham ...	N. E.	Pallion.
								Kings House Engine Works and Foundry	Durham ...	N. E.	Pallion.
								Kings House Landsale Depôt	Durham ...	N. E.	Pallion.
								Lambton Drops Saw Mills and Timber Yard	Durham ...	N. E.	Pallion.
								Lampton Shipping Drops...	Durham ...	N. E.	Pallion.
								Pallion Brass Foundry, Engine Wks. & Ship Yard	Durham ...	N. E.	Pallion.
								Pallion Forge (Ray's)	Durham ...	N. E.	Pallion.
								Pallion Foundry............	Durham ...	N. E.	Pallion.
								Sunderland Forge and Engineering Co.'s Siding	Durham ...	N. E.	Pallion.
G	P		L	H				Palmer, Hall & Co.'s Works..	Durham ...	N. E.	Redheugh.
	P		L	H				Palmer's Green & Southgate (G. N.)	Middlesex	G. N.	Wood Green and Enfield.
	P									N. L.	Over G. N. from Canonbury Junc.
	P*									S. E. & C.	Over G. N. from King's Cross Junc.
								Palmer's Ir. Wks. & Ship Yard	Durham ...	N. E.	Jarrow.
								Palmerston Siding (for Pinxton Collieries)	Notts	G. N.	Pinxton Wharf.
G	P		L	H				Palnure	Kirkcud...	PP&WJt.(Cal., G & SW, L. & N. W., & Mid.)	Newton Stewart & Castle Douglas.
G	P	F	L	H	C			Palterton and Sutton	Derby	Mid.	Pleasley and Staveley Town.
								Byron Brick Co.'s Siding...	Derby	Mid.	Near Palterton and Sutton.
								Glapwell Colliery	Derby	Mid.	Doe Lea Branch.
G	P	F	L	H	C			Pampisford	Cambs ...	G. E.	Cambridge and Haverhill.
								Pamplin's Siding	Hants ...	L. & S.W.	Totton and Eling.
								Panbride Siding	Forfar ...	D. & A. Jt. (Cal. & N. B.)	See Carnoustie.
G	P		L	H		5	0	Pandy (G. W.)	Mon	G. W.	Hereford and Abergavenny.
G						5	0			L. & N. W.	Over G. W. from Hereford.
								Pandy Pit (Naval Colliery) ...	Glamorg'n	T. V.	Trealaw.
G	P	F	L	H	C	1	10	Pangbourne	Berks ...	G. W.	Reading and Oxford.
G								Panmure	Forfar	D. & A. Jt. (Cal. & N. B.)	Dundee and Arbroath.
G						1	10	Smieton & Son's Siding ...	Forfar	D. & A. Jt. (Cal. & N. B.)	Panmure.
G						3	0	Taymouth Siding	Forfar	D. & A. Jt. (Cal. & N. B.)	Panmure and Barry.
G								Tennant & Co.'s Siding	Forfar	D. & A. Jt. (Cal. & N. B.)	Panmure and Barry.
								Panmure Shipbuilding Yard (Dundee Shipbuilders Co.	Forfar	Cal.	Dundee, West.
										N.B.	Dundee, Tay Bridge.

EXPLANATION—G *Goods Station.* P *Passenger and Parcel Station.* P* *Passenger, but not Parcel or Miscellaneous Traffic.*
F *Furniture Vans, Carriages, Portable Engines, and Machines on Wheels.* L *Live Stock.*
H *Horse Boxes and Prize Cattle Vans.* H† C† *By special arrangement only.* C *Carriages by Passenger Train.*

STATION ACCOMMODATION.					CRANE POWER.	STATIONS, &c.	COUNTY.	COMPANY.	POSITION.
					Tons Cwts.				
G	P	.	L H	.	5 0	Pannal	Yorks	N. E.	Leeds and Harrogate.
.	.	.	. .	.	.	Crimple Junction	Yorks	N. E.	Pannal and Harrogate.
.	.	.	. .	.	.	Panny Pit	Fife	N. B.	Same as Dunnikier Col. (Kirkcaldy).
.	P	.	. .	.	.	Pant	Glamorg'n	B. & M.	Dowlais Top and Pontsticill.
G	P	.	. .	.	.	Pant	Salop	Cam.	Oswestry and Welshpool.
.	.	.	. .	.	.	Pant Brick Works	Denbigh	G. W.	See Ruabon Coal & Coke Co. (Rhos).
.	.	.	. .	.	.	Pant Junction	Glamorg'n	B. & M.	Dowlais Top and Pontsticill.
G	P	.	L H C	.	2 0	Panteg & Griffithstown(G.W.)	Mon	G. W.	Pontypool, Crane Str. & Cwmbran.
G	.	.	. .	.	2 0			L. & N. W.	Over G. W. from Hereford.
.	.	.	. .	.	.	Baldwin's, Limited, Panteg Steel and Sheet Works...	Mon	G. W.	Panteg & Griffithstown.
G	P	.	. .	.	.	Pant-glas	Carnarvon	L. & N. W.	Afon Wen and Carnarvon.
.	.	.	. .	.	.	Pantmawr Colliery Sid. (Mid.)	Glamorg'n	Mid.—G. W.—L. & N.W.	Gurnos.
.	.	.	. .	.	.	Panton's Siding	Perth	Cal.	Coupar Angus.
.	.	.	. .	.	.	Pantycelyn Colliery (Thomas, J. J., & Son) (Mid.)	Glamorg'n	Mid.—G.W.—L. & N.W.	Brynamman.
.	.	.	. .	.	.	Pantycorrwg Siding (Panty-gored Siding)	Glamorg'n	T. V.	Cross Inn.
G	P	.	. .	.	.	Pantydwr	Radnor	Cam.	Llanidloes and Builth Wells.
.	.	.	. .	.	.	Glanyrafon Siding	Radnor	Cam.	Pantydwr and Tylwch.
G	P	.	L .	.	.	Pantyffynnon (G. W.)	Carmarth'	G. W.	Pontardulais and Llanelly.
.	.	.	. .	.	.			L. & N. W.	Over G. W. Line.
.	.	.	. .	.	.	Caerbryn Colliery	Carmarth'	G. W.	Tirydail and Cross Hands.
G	.	.	. .	.	.	Cross Hands	Carmarth'	G. W.	Branch from Tirydail.
.	.	.	. .	.	.	Dynevor Tin Works	Carmarth'	G. W.	Pantyffynnon.
.	.	.	. .	.	.	Emlyn Colliery	Carmarth'	G. W.	Cross Hands.
.	.	.	. .	.	.	Garn Mill Colliery	Carmarth'	G. W.	Pantyffynnon.
.	.	.	. .	.	.	Gulston's Siding	Carmarth'	G. W.	Tirydail and Cross Hands.
.	.	.	. .	.	.	Llandebie Lime Works Sid.	Carmarth'	G. W.	Tirydail and Cross Hands.
.	.	.	. .	.	.	Nantywrach Siding	Carmarth'	G. W.	Park Siding.
.	.	.	. .	.	.	Pantyffynnon Colliery	Carmarth'	G. W.	Pantyffynnon and Tirydail.
.	.	.	. .	.	.	Park & Blaina Colliery	Carmarth'	G. W.	Pantyffynnon and Tirydail.
.	.	.	. .	.	.	Pontyclerc Brick Works	Carmarth'	G. W.	Pantyffynnon and Tirydail.
.	.	.	. .	.	.	Pontyclerc Colliery	Carmarth'	G. W.	Pantyffynnon and Tirydail.
.	.	.	. .	.	.	Rhos Colliery	Carmarth'	G. W.	Same as Pantycorrwg Sid. (Cross Inn)
.	.	.	. .	.	.	Pantygored Siding	Glamorg'n	T. V.	See Guest, Keen & Nettlefold
.	.	.	. .	.	.	Pantyscallog Siding	Glamorg'n	B. & M.	(Dowlais).
.	.	.	. .	.	.	Pantywaen Junction & Quarry	Glamorg'n	B. & M.	Fochriew.
G	P	.	L H	.	.	Papcastle	Cumb'land	M. & C.	Dearham and Brigham.
.	.	.	. .	.	.	Papcastle Limestone Quarry (M. & C.)	Cumb'land	M. & C.—L. & N. W.	Papcastle.
G	P	F	L H C	.	4 0	Par	Cornwall	G. W.	St. Austell and Lostwithiel.
.	.	.	. .	.	.	Par Dock	Cornwall	G. W.	St. Blazey.
.	.	.	. .	.	.	Par Harbour	Cornwall	G. W.	St. Austell and Par.
.	.	.	. .	.	.	Par Junction	Cornwall	G. W.	St. Austell and Lostwithiel.
.	.	.	. .	.	.	Paradise Siding	Notts	G. C.	Gotham.
.	.	.	. .	.	.	Paragon Street (N. E.)	Yorks	N E—G C—L & Y—LNW	See Hull.
G	P	F	L .	.	4 0	Parbold (for Newburgh)	Lancs	L. & Y.	Wigan and Southport.
.	.	.	. .	.	.	Parbold Quarry	Lancs	L. & Y.	Near Parbold (for Newburgh).
.	.	.	. .	.	.	Pardovan General Siding	L'lithgow	N. B.	See Philpstoun.
.	.	.	. .	.	.	Pardovan Quarry	L'lithgow	N. B.	Philpstoun.
G	P	.	. .	.	.	Parham	Suffolk	G. E.	Wickham Market and Framlingham.
G	P	F	L H C	.	.	Park	Aberdeen	G. N. of S.	Aberdeen and Banchory.
G	.	.	L .	.	.	Park	Lancs	Furness	Barrow and Askam.
.	.	.	. .	.	.	Goldmire Quarry Siding	Lancs	Furness	Dalton and Askam.
.	.	.	. .	.	.	Roanhead Mines (Private)	Lancs	Furness	Barrow and Askam.
.	P	.	. .	.	.	Park	Middlesex	G. E.	Tottenham and Broxbourne.
.	.	.	. .	.	.	Park (G. C.)	Yorks	G. C.—G. N.	See Sheffield.
.	.	.	. .	.	.	Park (L. & Y.)	Lancs	L. & Y.—L. & N. W.	See Manchester.
.	.	.	. .	.	.	Park & Blaina Colliery	Carmarth'	G. W.	Pantyffynnon.
.	.	.	. .	.	.	Parkandillack Siding	Cornwall	G. W.	Drinnick Mill.
G	P	.	. .	.	.	Park Bridge	Lancs	O. A. & G. B. Jt. (G. C. and L. & N. W.)	Ashton, Oldham Road and Oldham.
.	.	.	. .	.	?	Lees Siding	Lancs	O. A. & G. B. Jt. (G. C. and L. & N. W.)	Park Bridge.
.	.	.	. .	.	.	Parkburn Siding	Durham	N. E.	Parkhead.
.	.	.	. .	.	.	Parkbury Siding	Herts	Mid.	Radlett.
.	.	.	. .	.	.	Park Colliery	Glamorg'n	T. V.	Same as Ocean Coal Co.'s Cwmpark Colliery (Treorchy).
.	.	.	. .	.	.	Park Colliery	Lancs	L. & Y.	Skelmersdale.
.	.	.	. .	.	.	Park Colliery	Lancs	L. & N. W.	Same as Stone's Siding (Garswood).

EXPLANATION—G *Goods Station.*   P *Passenger and Parcel Station.*   P* *Passenger, but not Parcel or Miscellaneous Traffic.*
F *Furniture Vans, Carriages, Portable Engines, and Machines on Wheels.*   L *Live Stock.*
H *Horse Boxes and Prize Cattle Vans.*   C *Carriages by Passenger Train.*

STATION ACCOMMODATION.						CRANE POWER.	STATIONS, &c.	COUNTY.	COMPANY.	POSITION.
						Tons Cwts.				
G	P		L				Park Drain	Notts	G. N. & G. E. Jt.	Gainsborough and Doncaster.
G	P	F	L	H	C	6 0	Parkend	Glo'ster	S. & Wye Jt.(G.W. & Mid)	Lydney and Lydbrook.
							Brick Pit or Crown Collieries	Glo'ster	S. & Wye Jt.(G.W. & Mid)	Parkend.
							Forest of Dean Stone Firms Siding	Glo'ster	S. & Wye Jt.(G.W. & Mid)	Parkend Royal Branch.
							New Fancy Colliery	Glo'ster	S. & Wye Jt.(G.W. & Mid)	Drybrook Road and Tufts Junction.
							Parkend Royal Colliery	Glo'ster	S. & Wye Jt.(G.W. & Mid)	Bch.—Parkend & Speech House Rd.
							Payne's Siding	Glo'ster	S. & Wye Jt.(G.W. & Mid)	Parkend and Speech House Road.
							Park End Quarries	Yorks	N. E.	Middleton-in-Teesdale.
							Parker & Son's Siding	Staffs	L. & N. W.	Bloxwich.
							Parker's Siding	Yorks	N. E.	Hunmanby.
							Parkes & Co.'s Albion Works	Staffs	L. & N. W.	Albion.
							Parke's Brick & Fire-Clay Co.'s Siding	Lancs	L.&Y.& L.U. Jt. (L.& Y. and L. & N. W.)	See Withnell Mill Sidings (Brinscall).
							Parkeston Quay	Essex	G. E.	See Harwich.
							Park Farm Siding (L. & Y.)	Yorks	L. & Y. — L. & N. W.	Heckmondwike.
							Parkfield Brick Kiln	Lancs	G. C.	Hyde Road.
							Parkfield Colliery North and South Pits (Bedminster, Easton, Kingswood, and Parkfield Co.)	Glo'ster	Mid.	Mangotsfield.
							Parkfield Works	Durham	N. E.	Stockton, South.
G	P		L	H			Parkgate	Cheshire	B'head Jt.(G W & L N W)	Hooton and West Kirby.
							Wirral Colliery	Cheshire	B'head Jt.(G W & L N W)	Parkgate and Neston.
							Parkgate	Cheshire	N. W. & L. Jt. (G. C. and W. M. & C. Q.)	See Neston and Parkgate.
	P	F	L	H	C		Parkgate and Aldwarke	Yorks	G. C.	Rotherham and Doncaster.
							Brown, J., & Co.'s Aldwarke Main Colliery (G.C.)	Yorks	G. C.—G. N.	Parkgate and Aldwarke.
							Dalton Main Collieries—			
							Roundwood Colliery	Yorks	G. C.	Parkgate and Aldwarke.
							Silverwood Colliery	Yorks	G. C.	Parkgate and Aldwarke.
G	P		L			5 0	Parkgate and Rawmarsh	Yorks	Mid.	Masboro' and Swinton.
							Brown, J., & Co.'s Aldwarke Main Colliery	Yorks	Mid.	Near Parkgate and Rawmarsh.
							Dalton Main Collieries—			
							Roundwood Colliery	Yorks	Mid.	Near Parkgate and Rawmarsh.
							Silverwood Colliery	Yorks	Mid.	Near Parkgate and Rawmarsh.
							Parkgate Chemical Works	Yorks	G. C.—G. N. Mid.	Rotherham and Masboro'. Masboro' and Rotherham.
							Parkgate Iron & Steel Co.—			
							Siding (G. C.)	Yorks	G. C.—G. N.	Rotherham and Masboro'.
							Siding	Yorks	Mid.	Same as Holmes Blast Furnaces (Masboro').
							Parkgate Oil Works	Yorks	Mid.	See Newton, Chambers & Co. (Chapeltown).
							Parkgate Steel Works (W. Oxley & Co.)	Yorks	Mid.	Masboro' and Rotherham.
							Park Gutter Siding	Glo'ster	S. & Wye Jt.(G.W. & Mid)	See Princess Royal Sidings (Whitecroft).
							Park Hall Colliery	Derby	L. D. & E. C.	Spink Hill.
							Park Hall Colliery Co—			
							Meir Hay Colliery	Staffs	N. S.	Longton.
							Weston Coyney Colliery	Staffs	N. S.	Weston Coyney.
							Parkhall Siding	Stirling	N. B.	See Almond Junction Station.
G							Parkhead	Durham	N. E.	Branch from Waskerley.
							Bishop's Seat Siding	Durham	N. E.	Parkhead.
							Boltsburn Depôt & Siding	Durham	N. E.	Parkhead and Waskerley.
							Boltslaw Siding	Durham	N. E.	Parkhead.
							Grove Rake Mines	Durham	N. E.	Parkhead.
							Heights Quarry	Durham	N. E.	Parkhead.
							Parkburn Siding	Durham	N. E.	Parkhead.
							Parkhead Quarry	Durham	N. E.	Parkhead.
							Rispey Mines	Durham	N. E.	Parkhead.
							Rookhope Mill	Durham	N. E.	Parkhead.
							Scutterhill Depôt & Siding	Durham	N. E.	Parkhead and Waskerley.
							Smailes Burn Mine	Durham	N. E.	Parkhead.
							West Slit Siding	Durham	N. E.	Parkhead.
							Wolf Cleugh Siding	Durham	N. E.	Parkhead.
							Parkhead	Lanark	N. B.	See Glasgow.
							Parkhead (for Celtic Park)	Lanark	Cal.	See Glasgow.
							Parkhead Colliery	Lanark	Cal.	Motherwell.

EXPLANATION—G Goods Station.   P Passenger and Parcel Station.   P* Passenger, but not Parcel or Miscellaneous Traffic.
F Furniture Vans, Carriages, Portable Engines, and Machines on Wheels.   L Live Stock.
H Horse Boxes and Prize Cattle Vans.   C Carriages by Passenger Train.

STATION ACCOMMODATION.					CRANE POWER.		STATIONS, &c.	COUNTY.	COMPANY.	POSITION.
					Tons	Cwts.				
..	..	..	..	..			Parkhead Iron & Steel Forge & Rolling Mills	Lanark ...	{ Cal.	Glasgow, Bridgeton.
									{ N. B.	Glasgow, Parkhead.
..	..	..	..	..			Parkhead Junction	Lanark ...	N. B.	Glasgow.
G	P	..	L	H	1	5	Parkhill	Aberdeen	G. N. of S.	Dyce and Fraserburgh.
..	..	..	..	..			Park Hill Colliery (L. & Y.)	Yorks	L. & Y.—N. E.	Wakefield.
..	..	..	..	..			Parkhouse Colliery..............	Staffs	N. S.	Chesterton.
..	..	..	..	..			Parkhouse Iron Works (N.B.)	Stirling ...	N. B.—Cal.	Falkirk, Grahamston.
..	..	..	..	..			Parkhouse Junction	Ayr	G. & S. W.	Ardrossan and West Kilbride.
..	..	..	..	..			Parkhouse Mines	Cumb'land	WC&EJt.(Fur.&LNW)	See Cammell & Co. (Moor Row).
..	..	..	..	..			Parkia Brick Co.'s Siding ...	Carnarvon	L. & N. W.	See Lord Penrhyn's (Griffith's Crossing).
..	..	..	..	..			Park Iron Ore & Coal Co.'s Sid	Glo'ster ...	S. & Wye Jt. (G. W. & Mid)	Whitecroft.
..	..	..	..	..			Park Joint Station & Junction	Cheshire...	Mersey—Wirral	See Birkenhead.
..	..	..	..	..			Park Junction	Mon	G. W.	Newport.
..	..	..	..	..			Park Lane	Lancs	L. & N. W.	See Liverpool.
..	..	..	..	..			Park Lane Colliery	Lancs	L. & N. W.	See Garswood Coal and Iron Co. (Garswood).
..	..	..	..	..			Park Lane Lime Works	Yorks	N. E.	Pickering.
..	..	..	..	..			Park Lane Sidings..............	Durham ...	N. E.	Gateshead.
..	..	..	..	..			Park Mill Colliery	Yorks	L. & Y.	Clayton West.
G	P	..	..	..			Parkmore........................	Antrim ...	N. C. Com. (Mid.)	Ballymena and Retreat.
..	..	..	..	..			Antrim Iron Ore Works ...	Antrim ...	N. C. Com. (Mid.)........	Near Parkmore.
..	..	..	..	..			Parkmore Siding	Banff	G. N. of S.	See Dufftown.
..	..	..	..	..			Parkneuk Bridge Building Works	Lanark ...	Cal.	Motherwell.
..	..	..	..	..			Park Parade (G. C.)	Lancs	G. C.—L. & N. W.	See Ashton-under-Lyne.
..	..	..	..	..			Park Pit	Yorks	N. E.	Same as Skelton Park Pit Depôt and Siding (Slapewath).
..	..	..	..	..			Park Road	Lancs	L'pool O'head	See Liverpool, Dingle (Park Road).
G	..	F	L	..	1	10	Park Royal	Middlesex	G. W.	Westbourne Park and Greenford.
..	..	..	..	..			Royal Agricultural Show Yard Siding	Middlesex	G. W.	Park Royal.
..	P	..	..	..			Park Royal & Twyford Abbey	Middlesex	Met. Dist..................	North Ealing & Perivale-Alperton.
..	..	..	..	..			Parks Bridge Junction.........	Kent	S. E. & C.	St. John's and Hither Green.
..	..	..	..	..			Park Ship Yard (Ritchie, Graham & Milne)	Renfrew ...	Cal.	Glasgow, Whiteinch.
..	..	..	..	..			Parkside Mills	Lancs	L. & N. W.	Same as Golborne Mills Co.'s Siding (Golborne).
..	..	..	..	..			Parkside Mining Co.'s Sidings	Cumb'land	C. & W. Jn.	Arlecdon (for Rowrah).
..	..	..	..	..			Parkslip Colliery	Glamorg'n	G. W.	See Norths' (Tondu).
G	P	..	..	..	1	0	Parkstone (L. & S. W.)........	Dorset......	{ L. & S. W.	Bournemouth and Poole.
									{ S & DJt.(L.& SW&Mid.)	Over L. & S. W. from Broadstone Jn.
..	..	..	..	..			Wragg & Son's South Western Pottery............	Dorset......	L. & S.W.	Parkstone.
G	P	..	..	H			Park Street and Frogmore ...	Herts	L. & N. W.	St. Albans and Watford.
..	..	..	..	..			Park Street Sid. (Silvester's)	Herts	Mid.	St. Albans.
..	..	..	..	..			Parkthorn Siding	Ayr	G. & S.W.	Drybridge.
..	..	..	..	..			Park Tinplate Co.'s Works (Mid.)	Glamorg'n	Mid.—G. W.—L. & N. W.	{ See Glanyrafon Siding (Clydach-on-Tawe).
..	..	..	..	..			Park Works	Durham ...	N. E.	Same as Abbot & Co.'s Works (Gateshead).
..	..	..	..	..			Parkyn & Peter's Siding	Cornwall	G. W.	Burngullow.
..	..	..	..	..			Parliament Hill	Middlesex	Mid.—T. & H. Jt.	See London, Highgate Road (for Parliament Hill).
..	..	..	..	..			Parnham & Son's Water Mill (Mid.)	Notts	{ Mid.	Newark.
									{ G. N.	(See Appendix to follow).
..	..	..	..	..			Parry & Co.— Altami or Mold Argoed Sid.	Flint	L. & N. W.	Mold.
..	..	..	..	..			Llong Colliery.................	Flint	L. & N. W.	Padeswood & Buckley.
..	..	..	..	..			Parry's Brick Works...........	Flint	W. M. & C. Q.	Buckley.
..	..	..	..	..			Parry's Coal Yard	Lancs	L. & N. W.	Thelwall.
G	P	..	L	..	5	0	Parsley Hay......................	Derby	L. & N. W.	Ashbourne and Buxton.
..	..	..	..	..			Wragg & Son's High Peak Silica Co.'s Siding	Derby	L. & N. W.	Parsley Hay and Hartington.
..	..	..	..	..			Parson Byers Quarry...........	Durham ...	N. E.	See Bell Bros. (Stanhope).
..	..	..	..	..			Parsons Green....................	Middlesex	Met. Dist.	See London.
..	..	..	..	..			Parson's Siding	Northumb	N. E.	Newcastle-on-Tyne.
..	..	..	..	..			Parsons Bros.' Siding	Sussex ...	L. B. & S. C.	Eastbourne.
..	..	..	..	..			Partick	Lanark ...	Cal.—N. B.	See Glasgow.
..	..	..	..	..			Partick, Central.................	Lanark ...	Cal.	See Glasgow.
..	..	..	..	..			Partick Cross	Lanark ...	Glas. Dist. Sub.	See Glasgow.
..	..	..	..	..			Partick Electric Light Siding	Lanark ...	Cal.	Glasgow, Whiteinch.

EXPLANATION—G *Goods Station.*   P *Passenger and Parcel Station.*   P* *Passenger, but not Parcel or Miscellaneous Traffic.*
F *Furniture Vans, Carriages, Portable Engines, and Machines on Wheels.*   L *Live Stock.*
H *Horse Boxes and Prize Cattle Vans.*   C *Carriages by Passenger Train.*

STATION ACCOMMODATION.						CRANE POWER.		STATIONS, &c.	COUNTY.	COMPANY.	POSITION.
						Tons	Cwts.				
.	.	.	.	.	.	.	.	Partick Saw Mills	Lanark ...	Cal.	See Robinson, Dunn & Co.'s Wood Yard (Glasgow).
.	.	.	.	.	.	.	.	Partick Ship Yard..............	Lanark ...	Cal.	Glasgow, Whiteinch.
.	.	.	.	.	.	.	.	Partick, West.................	Lanark ...	Cal.	See Glasgow.
.	.	.	.	.	.	.	.	Partick, West, Mineral Depôt	Lanark ...	Cal.	See Glasgow.
G	P	F	L	H	C	5	0	Partington	Lancs	C. L. C. (G C, G N, & Mid.)	Warrington and Stockport.
.	.	.	.	.	.	.	.	Carrington Sidings...........	Lancs	C. L. C. (G C, G N, & Mid.)	Partington.
.	.	.	.	.	.	.	.	Partington Junction	Lancs	C. L. C.—Ship Canal ...	Partington.
G	P	.	L	H	.	3	0	Parton	Cumb'land	L. & N. W.	Whitehaven and Workington.
.	.	.	.	.	.	.	.	Bain & Co.'s No. 4 Pit	Cumb'land	W C & E Jt. (Fur. & L N W)	Parton and Distington.
.	.	.	.	.	.	.	.	Lowca Iron Works............	Cumb'land	L. & N. W.	Parton and Harrington.
.	.	.	.	.	.	.	.	Parton Junction	Cumb'land	L. & N. W.—W.C.& E. Jt.	Distington and Whitehaven.
G	P	.	L	H	.	.	.	Parton	Kirkcud...	P.P.& W.Jt.(Cal., G&SW, L. & N. W., & Mid.)...	Newton Stewart and Castle Douglas.
G	P	F	L	H	C	1	0	Partridge Green.................	Sussex ...	L. B. & S. C.	West Grinstead and Henfield.
.	.	.	.	.	.	.	.	Hillman's Siding	Sussex ...	L. B. & S. C.	Partridge Green.
.	.	.	.	.	.	.	.	Partridge, Jones & Co.'s Llanerch Colliery (G.W.)...	Monmouth	G. W.—L. & N. W.	Pontnewynydd.
.	.	.	.	.	.	.	.	Pascoe, Grenfell & Son's or Foster, W., & Co.'s—			
.	.	.	.	.	.	.	.	Copper Works (Mid.)	Glamorg'n	Mid.—G. W.—L. & N. W.	Upper Bank.
G	P	.	.	.	.	.	.	Morfa Copper Works.........	Glamorg'n	G. W.	Landore.
G	P	.	L	.	.	.	.	Passage....................	Cork	C. B. & P.	Cork and Carrigaline.
.	.	.	.	.	.	.	.	Paston & Knapton	Norfolk ...	N.&S.Jt.(GE&M&GNJt.)	North Walsham and Mundesley-on-Sea.
.	.	.	.	.	.	.	.	Paston Siding.....................	N'hamptn	G. N.	See Gilstrap, Earp & Co. (Peterboro').
G	P	F	L	H	C	1	10	Patchway and Stoke Gifford	Glo'ster ...	G. W.	Bristol and Pilning.
.	.	.	.	.	.	.	.	Pearson & Son...................	Glo'ster ...	G. W.	Patchway and Stoke Gifford.
G	P	F	L	H	C	10	0	Pateley Bridge	Yorks	N. E.	Branch from Harrogate.
.	.	.	.	.	.	.	.	Gladstone Siding	Yorks	N. E.	Pateley Bridge.
.	.	.	.	.	.	.	.	Glass Houses Siding	Yorks	N. E.	Pateley Bridge.
.	.	.	.	.	.	.	.	Ingilby's Siding	Yorks	N. E.	Pateley Bridge.
.	.	.	.	.	.	.	.	Scotgate Ash Stone Co.'s Siding	Yorks	N. E.	Pateley Bridge.
.	.	.	.	.	.	.	.	Patent Axle Box Co.'s Works (Mid.)	Staffs	Mid.—G. W.	Wednesfield.
.	.	.	.	.	.	.	.	Patent Enamel Co.'s Siding..	Worcester	Mid.	{ Birmingham. { Selly Oak.
.	.	.	.	.	.	.	.	Patent Indurated Stone Co.'s Siding.................	Middlesex	{ G. E. { GN—GW—LNW—Mid	London, Millwall Docks. London, Poplar.
.	.	.	.	.	.	.	.	Patent Lubricating Bag Works (Tees Oil and Grease Works)	Yorks	N. E.	Middlesbro'.
.	.	.	.	.	.	.	.	Patent Shaft & Axletree Co.—			
.	.	.	.	.	.	.	.	Brunswick Works...........	Staffs	G. W.	Wednesbury (for Darlaston).
.	.	.	.	.	.	.	.	Brunswick Works (L&NW)	Staffs	L. & N. W.—Mid.	Wednesbury.
.	.	.	.	.	.	.	.	Lloyd's—			
.	.	.	.	.	.	.	.	Monway Works	Staffs	G. W.	Wednesbury (for Darlaston).
.	.	.	.	.	.	.	.	Monway Works (L&NW)	Staffs	L. & N. W.—Mid.	Wednesbury.
.	.	.	.	.	.	.	.	Old Park Works.........	Staffs	G. W.	Wednesbury (for Darlaston).
.	.	.	.	.	.	.	.	Old Park Works (L&NW)	Staffs	L. & N. W.—Mid.	Wednesbury.
.	.	.	.	.	.	.	.	Patent Victoria Stone Co.—			
.	.	.	.	.	.	.	.	Siding	Essex	G. E.	London, Stratford Market.
.	.	.	.	.	.	.	.	Siding	Leicester	Mid.	Glenfield.
.	.	.	.	.	.	.	.	Paterson & Sons' Siding	Lanark ...	N. B.	Airdrie, North.
.	.	.	.	.	.	.	.	Paterson's Brewery	Edinboro'	N. B.	Duddingston and Craigmillar.
.	.	.	.	.	.	.	.	Paterson's Siding	Lanark ...	Cal.	Glasgow, Buchanan Street.
.	.	.	.	.	.	.	.	Paterson's Siding	Lanark ...	G B & K Jt (Cal & G & SW)	Glasgow, Strathbungo.
.	.	.	.	.	.	.	.	Paterson's Wood Yard........	Selkirk ...	N. B.	Galashiels.
.	.	.	.	.	.	.	.	Pather	Lanark ...	Cal.	Wishaw.
.	.	.	.	.	.	.	.	Pather Iron & Steel Works ...	Lanark ...	Cal.	Wishaw.
.	.	.	.	.	.	.	.	Pathhead Colliery	Ayr	G. & S.W.	New Cumnock.
.	.	.	.	.	.	.	.	Patmore & Co.—			
.	.	.	.	.	.	.	.	New Grain Elevator Warehouse........................	Edinboro'	Cal.	Leith, South.
.	.	.	.	.	.	.	.	Siding	Edinboro'	N. B.	Leith, Bonnington.
G	P	.	L	H	C	1	10	Patna	Ayr	G. & S.W.	Ayr and Dalmellington.
.	P	.	.	.	.	.	.	Patney & Chirton	Wilts	G. W.	Devizes and Hungerford.
.	.	.	.	.	.	.	.	Paton's Chemical Wks. (G.W.)	Mon	G. W.— L. & N. W.	Abersychan and Talywain.
.	.	.	.	.	.	.	.	Paton's Siding	Ayr	G. & S.W.	Kilmarnock.
.	.	.	.	.	.	.	.	Paton's Siding	Fife	N. B.	Same as Capeldrae Siding (Kelty).
.	.	.	.	.	.	.	.	Paton's Siding	Mon	G. W.	Pontypool Road.

EXPLANATION—G *Goods Station.*   P *Passenger and Parcel Station.*   P* *Passenger, but not Parcel or Miscellaneous Traffic.*
F *Furniture Vans, Carriages, Portable Engines, and Machines on Wheels.*   L *Live Stock.*
H *Horse Boxes and Prize Cattle Vans.*   C *Carriages by Passenger Train.*

STATION ACCOMMODATION.						CRANE POWER.		STATIONS, &c.	COUNTY.	COMPANY.	POSITION.
						Tons	Cwts.				
								Paton's Wool Store	Clackman'	N. B.	Alloa.
G	P	.	L	H	C	.	.	Patrick's Well....................	Limerick..	G. S. & W.	Limerick and Newcastle West.
G	P	F	L	H	C	5	0	Patricroft (L. & N. W.)	Lancs.......	L. & N. W.	Kenyon Junc. Sta. & Manchester.
	P	.	.	H	C					G. W.	Over L. & N. W. from Walton Junc.
G	.	F	L	H	.	5	0			L. & Y.	Over L. & N. W. from Clifton (Molyneux) Junction.
.	.	..	.	.	.	.	.	Clifton & Kersley Colliery (L. & N. W.)..................	Lancs	L. & N. W.— L. & Y.	Patricroft & Clifton (Molyneux) Jn.
.	.	.	.	.	.	.	.	Clifton Hall Colliery (North) (L. & N. W.)	Lancs	L. & N. W.— L. & Y.	Patricroft & Clifton (Molyneux) Jn.
.	.	.	.	.	.	.	.	Clifton Hall Colliery (South) (L. & N. W.)	Lancs	L. & N. W.— L. & Y.	Patricroft & Clifton (Molyneux) Jn.
.	.	.	.	.	.	.	.	Magnesium Metal Co.'s Sid.	Lancs	L. & N. W.	Patricroft and Eccles.
.	.	.	.	.	.	.	.	Nasmyth, Wilson & Co.'s Siding	Lancs	L. & N. W.	Patricroft and Eccles.
.	.	.	.	.	.	.	.	Pilkington Tile & Pottery Co.'s Siding	Lancs	L. & N. W.	Patricroft & Clifton (Molyneux) Jn.
.	.	.	.	.	.	.	.	Turner's Siding	Lancs	L. & N. W.	Eccles and Monton Green.
.	.	.	.	.	.	.	.	Wigan Coal & Iron Co.'s Sid.	Lancs	L. & N. W.	Eccles and Monton Green.
G	P	.	L	.	.	.	.	Patrington	Yorks	N. E.	Hull and Withernsea.
.	.	.	.	.	.	.	.	Winestead Siding	Yorks	N. E.	Patrington and Ottringham.
.	.	.	.	.	.	.	.	Pattenden Siding	Kent	S. E. & C.	Goudhurst.
G	P	F	L	H	C	3	0	Patterton	Renfrew..	Cal.	Giffen and Clarkston.
.	.	.	.	.	.	.	.	Pattinson & Son's Corn Mill (Furness)	Cumb'land	Furness—L. & N. W. ...	Whitehaven, Preston Street.
.	.	.	.	.	.	.	.	Pattinson's Siding	W'morlnd	L. & N. W.	See Kendal Bonded Stores Co. (Kendal).
.	.	.	.	.	.	.	.	Pattison, Thos., Sidings	Durham ...	N. E.	Stockton, South.
.	.	.	.	.	.	.	.	Pattrick & Thompsons' Siding (G. E.)	Norfolk ...	G. E.—G. N.—Mid.	Lynn Docks.
.	.	.	.	.	.	.	.	Paul Bros.' Flour Mills	Cheshire ..	B'headJt—CLC—NW&L	Birkenhead.
.	.	.	.	.	.	.	.	Paul, R. & W., Siding	Suffolk ...	G. E.	Stowmarket.
.	.	.	.	.	.	.	.	Paull's Siding	Carnarvon	L. & N. W.	Penygroes.
.	.	.	.	.	.	.	.	Pawson Bros.' Quarries........	Yorks	E. & W. Y. Union	Robin Hood.
.	.	.	.	.	.	.	.			G. N.	Morley.
.	.	.	.	.	.	.	.			G. N.	Woodkirk.
.	.	.	.	.	.	.	.	Paye & Welch's Siding........	Herts	G. N.	Hertingfordbury.
.	.	.	.	.	.	.	.	Payne's Siding	Glo'ster ...	S. & Wye Jt. (G. W. & Mid)	Parkend.
.	.	.	.	.	.	.	.	Peach & Co.'s Welcome Siding (Mid.)................	Staffs	Mid—L&NW—GN—NS	Burton-on-Trent.
.	.	.	.	.	.	.	.	Peacock & Barlow's Siding (L. & N. W.)	Lancs	L. & N. W.— G. W.	Warrington, Bank Quay.
.	.	.	.	.	.	.	.	Peacock Cross	Lanark ...	N. B.	See Hamilton.
.	.	.	.	.	.	.	.	Peacock Siding	Lanark ...	Cal.	See Glasgow.
.	.	.	.	.	.	.	.	Peacock's Siding	Durham ...	N. E.	Redheugh.
.	.	.	.	.	.	.	.	Pea Flat Pumping Engine ...	Durham ...	N. E.	Fencehouses. Penshaw.
.	.	.	.	.	.	.	.	Peakdale Siding..................	Derby	Mid.	Peak Forest.
G	P	.	L	.	.	.	.	Peake	Cork	C. & Muskerry	Coachford Junction and Coachford.
.	.	.	.	.	.	.	.	Peake's Brick & Tile Works	Staffs	N. S.	Chatterley.
G	P	.	.	.	.	1	0	Peak Forest.....................	Derby	Mid.	New Mills and Rowsley.
.	.	.	.	.	.	.	.	Asphaltic Limestone Concrete Co.'s Siding	Derby	Mid.	Near Peak Forest.
.	.	.	.	.	.	.	.	Beswick & Son's Siding ...	Derby	Mid.	Peak Forest.
.	.	.	.	.	.	.	.	Bibbington's South Works	Derby	Mid.	Near Peak Forest.
.	.	.	.	.	.	.	.	Buxton Lime Firms Co.'s New South Works.........	Derby	Mid.	Peak Forest.
.	.	.	.	.	.	.	.	Great Central Co.'s Limestone Siding	Derby	Mid.	Peak Forest.
.	.	.	.	.	.	.	.	Great Rocks Lime Works..	Derby	Mid.	Near Peak Forest.
.	.	.	.	.	.	.	.	Peakdale Siding..............	Derby	Mid.	Near Peak Forest.
.	.	.	.	.	.	.	.	Smalldale Siding	Derby	Mid.	Near Peak Forest.
.	.	.	.	.	.	.	.	Southdale Siding	Derby	Mid.	Near Peak Forest.
.	.	.	.	.	.	.	.	Taylor's, S., Siding	Derby	Mid.	Near Peak Forest.
.	.	.	.	.	.	.	.	United Alkali Co.'s Bold Venture Siding	Derby	Mid.	Near Peak Forest.
.	.	.	.	.	.	.	.	Peak Forest Stone Siding ...	Derby	Mid.	Miller's Dale.
G	P	F	L	H	C	1	5	Peakirk..........................	N'hamptn	G. N.	Peterboro' and Spalding.
.	.	.	.	.	.	.	.	Stapleton's Siding	N'hamptn	G. N.	Peakirk.
.	.	.	.	.	.	.	.	Pearson & Co.'s Pottery Sid.	Derby	Mid.	Same as Whittington Moor Potteries (Sheepbridge).
.	.	.	.	.	.	.	.	Pearson & Co.'s Siding........	Essex	T.&F.G.Jt.(LT&S&Mid.)	Black Horse Road.

STATION ACCOMMODATION.						CRANE POWER.		STATIONS, &c.	COUNTY.	COMPANY.	POSITION.
						Tons	Cwts.	Pearson & Knowles Coal & Iron Co.—			
·	·	·	·	·	·		·	Bewsey & Dallam Forge Iron Works	Lancs	C. L. C. (G C, G N, & Mid.)	Warrington, Central.
·	·	·	·	·	·		·	Bewsey Forge Iron Works (L. & N. W.)	Lancs	L. & N. W.— G. W.	Warrington, Bank Quay.
·	·	·	·	·	·		·	Coal Yard (L. & N. W.)	Lancs	L. & N. W.— G. W.	Warrington, Bank Quay.
·	·	·	·	·	·		·	Coppull Hall Siding	Lancs	L. & N. W.	Coppull.
·	·	·	·	·	·		·	Chisnall Hall Colliery	Lancs	L. & N. W.	Coppull Hall Siding.
·	·	·	·	·	·		·	Hicbibi Brick Works	Lancs	L. & N. W.	Coppull Hall Siding.
·	·	·	·	·	·		·	Crow Orchard Col. or Arley Pit	Lancs	L. & N. W.	Wigan.
·	·	·	·	·	·		·	Daisy Colliery	Lancs	L. & Y.	Ince.
·	·	·	·	·	·		·	Dallam Forge Iron Works (L. & N. W.)	Lancs	L. & N. W.— G. W.	Warrington, Bank Quay.
·	·	·	·	·	·		·	Hindley Colliery	Lancs	L. & N. W.	Wigan.
·	·	·	·	·	·		·	Ince Moss Colliery	Lancs	L. & N. W.	Wigan.
·	·	·	·	·	·		·	Moss Hall Siding	Lancs	L. & Y.	Ince.
·	·	·	·	·	·		·	Moss Colliery	Lancs	L. & N. W.	Wigan.
·	·	·	·	·	·		·	Moss Side Iron Works	Lancs	{ L. & Y. / L. & N. W.	Ince. / Wigan.
·	·	·	·	·	·		·	Pumping Siding	Lancs	L. & N. W.	Warrington, Bank Quay.
·	·	·	·	·	·		·	Siding	Lancs	L. & Y.	Southport.
·	·	·	·	·	·		·	Spring Colliery	Lancs	L. & N. W.	Wigan.
·	·	·	·	·	·		·	Westwood Siding	Lancs	L. & Y.	Wigan.
·	·	·	·	·	·		·	Works	Lancs	G. W.	Ince.
·	·	·	·	·	·		·	Pearson & Son	Glo'ster	G. W.	Warrington.
·	·	·	·	·	·		·	Pearson & Son's Siding	Durham	N. E.	Patchway and Stoke Gifford.
·	·	·	·	·	·		·	Pearson & Son's Siding	Glo'ster	Mid.	Seaham.
·	·	·	·	·	·		·	Pearson Bros.' Siding	Lincoln	G. N. & G. E. Jt.	Yate.
·	·	·	·	·	·		·	Pearson's, J., Siding	Derby	Mid.	Gainsboro'.
·	·	·	·	·	·		·				Same as London & Oldfield Potteries (Chesterfield)
·	·	·	·	·	·		·	Pearson's, J. H., Siding	Staffs	G. W.	Withymoor Basin.
·	·	·	·	·	·		·	Pearson's Saw Mill & Timber Yard	Durham	N. E.	West Hartlepool.
·	·	·	·	·	·		·	Pear Tree and Normanton	Derby	Mid.	See Derby.
·	·	·	·	·	·		·	Peart's Siding	Herts	G. N.	Hatfield.
								Pease & Partners'—			
·	·	·	·	·	·		·	Bankfoot Ovens	Durham	N. E.	Crook.
·	·	·	·	·	·		·	Brick Works	Durham	N. E.	Crook.
·	·	·	·	·	·		·	General Shops	Durham	N. E.	Crook.
·	·	·	·	·	·		·	Granary and Warehouse	Durham	N. E.	Darlington, Bank Top.
·	·	·	·	·	·		·	Lucy (Grahamsley) Colliery	Durham	N. E.	Crook.
·	·	·	·	·	·		·	Roddymoor Colliery	Durham	N. E.	Crook.
·	·	·	·	·	·		·	St. Helens Colliery	Durham	N. E.	West Auckland.
·	·	·	·	·	·		·	Stanley Colliery	Durham	N. E.	Crook.
·	·	·	·	·	·		·	Wagon Shops	Durham	N. E.	Crook.
·	·	·	·	·	·		·	White Lea Colliery	Durham	N. E.	Crook.
·	·	·	·	·	·		·	Wooley Colliery	Durham	N. E.	Crook.
·	·	·	·	·	·		·	Pease Siding	Berwick	N. B.	See Cockburnspath.
·	·	·	·	·	·		·	Pease Tubular Syndicate Construction Co.'s Siding	Durham	N. E.	See Skerne Iron Works (Darlington).
·	P	·	·	·	·		·	Peasley Cross	Lancs	L. & N. W.	St. Helens and Widnes.
·	·	·	·	·	·		·	Peasley Cross & Sherdley Col.	Lancs	L. & N. W.	Same as White Cross Colliery Co.'s Siding (St. Helens).
·	·	·	·	·	·		·	Peasmarsh Junction	Surrey	L. & S. W.— L. B. & S. C.	Guildford and Bramley.
·	·	·	·	·	·		·	Peasmarsh Siding	Surrey	L. & S. W.	See Godalming.
·	·	·	·	·	·		·	Peat Fuel Co.'s Siding	Devon	L. & S. W.	Same as Machine Drying and Peat Fuel Co.'s Siding (Bridestowe).
·	·	·	·	·	·		·	Peblig Siding	Carnarvon	L. & N. W.	Carnarvon.
·	·	·	·	·	·		·	Peckett & Son's Siding	Glo'ster	Mid.	Same as Kingswood Colliery (Bristol)
·	·	·	·	·	·		·	Peckfield Colliery	Yorks	N. E.	Micklefield.
·	·	·	·	·	·		·	Peckham	Surrey	L. B. & S. C.	See London, Queens Road (Peckham).
·	·	·	·	·	·		·	Peckham Rye	Surrey	L. B. & S. C.— S. E. & C.	See London.
·	·	·	·	·	·		·	Peckham Rye Coal Depôt	Surrey	L. & N. W. & Mid. Jt.	See London.
·	P*	·	·	·	·		·	Peckwash Mill Siding (Tempest & Sons)	Derby	Mid.	Little Eaton.
G	P	F	L	H	C	6	0	Pedair Ffordd	Montgom	Cam. (Tanat Valley)	Porthywaen and Llangynog.
G	P	F	L	H	C	2	10	Peebles	Peebles	{ Cal. / N. B.	Terminus of Bch. from Symington. / Leadburn and Galashiels.
·	·	·	·	·	·		·	Ballantyne's Mill	Peebles	N. B.	Peebles.
·	·	·	·	·	·		·	Dyer & Co.'s Saw Mills	Peebles	N. B.	Peebles.
·	·	·	·	·	·		·	Peebles Gas Works	Peebles	N. B.	Peebles

EXPLANATION—G Goods Station.   P Passenger and Parcel Station.   P* Passenger, but not Parcel or Miscellaneous Traffic.
F Furniture Vans, Carriages, Portable Engines, and Machines on Wheels.   L Live Stock.
H Horse Boxes and Prize Cattle Vans.   C Carriages by Passenger Train.

STATION ACCOMMODATION.							CRANE POWER.	STATIONS, &c.	COUNTY.	COMPANY.	POSITION.
							Tons Cwts.	Peebles—continued.			
G	.	.	.	.	.	.	. .	Peebles Old Station Sidings	Peebles ...	N. B.	Peebles.
.	.	.	.	.	.	.	. .	Peebles Junction	Peebles ...	Cal.—N.B.	Peebles (Cal.) and Peebles (N. B.).
.	.	.	.	.	.	.	. .	Peebles, Bruce & Co.'s Siding	Edinboro'	Cal.	Leith, North.
.	.	.	.	.	.	.	. .	Peed's Siding	Cambs. ...	G. E.	Whittlesea.
G	P	F*	L	.	.	.	2 0	Peel	I. of Man..	I. of Man	Terminus.
.	.	.	.	.	.	.	. .	Peel Colliery	Staffs	Mid.	Wilnecote.
.	.	.	.	.	.	.	. .	Peel Hall Colliery	Lancs	L. & N. W.	See Roscoe's (Plodder Lane).
.	.	.	.	.	.	.	. .	Peel Hall Siding	Lancs	L. & Y.	Walkden.
.	.	.	.	.	.	.	. .	Peel Mill Co.'s Siding	Lancs	L. & Y.	Bury, High Level.
G	P	.	L	.	.	.	. .	Peel Road	I. of Man..	Manx Northern	St. John's and Ramsey.
.	.	.	.	.	.	.	. .	Peel's Yard	Glamorg'n	G. W.—L. & N. W.—Mid. —R. & S. B.	Swansea.
.	.	.	.	.	.	.	. .	Peelwood Colliery	Lancs	L. & Y.	See Tyldesley Coal Co. (Atherton).
G	P	.	.	.	.	.	. .	Pegswood	Northumb	N. E.	Morpeth and Berwick.
.	.	.	.	.	.	.	. .	Pegswood Colliery & Siding	Northumb	N. E.	Pegswood.
.	.	.	.	.	.	.	. .	Pegwell Bay	Kent	S. E. & C.	See St. Lawrence (for Pegwell Bay).
.	.	.	.	.	.	.	. .	Pelaw Grange Saw Mill	Durham ...	N. E.	Birtley.
.	.	.	.	.	.	.	. .	Pelaw Grange Siding & Depôts	Durham ...	N. E.	Birtley.
G	P	.	.	.	.	.	3 0	Pelaw Junction Station	Durham ...	N. E.	Newcastle and Washington.
.	.	.	.	.	.	.	. .	Heworth Colliery	Durham ...	N. E.	Pelaw Junction Station.
.	.	.	.	.	.	.	. .	Springwell Brick Works	Durham ...	N. E.	Pelaw Junction Station.
.	.	.	.	.	.	.	. .	Standard Brick Co.'s Siding	Durham ...	N. E.	Pelaw Junction Station.
.	.	.	.	.	.	.	. .	Pelham Street Junction	Lincoln ...	G. N.	Lincoln.
.	.	.	.	.	.	.	. .	Pellon	Yorks	H'fax H. L. (G N & L & Y)	See Halifax.
G	P	.	.	.	.	.	1 10	Pelsall	Staffs	L. & N. W.	Lichfield and Walsall.
.	.	.	.	.	.	.	. .	Aldridge Cols., Nos. 1 and 2	Staffs	L. & N. W.	Leighs Wood Branch.
.	.	.	.	.	.	.	. .	Aldridge Col. Co.'s Bk. Sid.	Staffs	L. & N. W.	Leighs Wood Branch.
.	.	.	.	.	.	.	. .	Barnett & Beddows' Atlas Bk., Pipe & Tl. Co.'s Sid.	Staffs	L. & N. W.	Leighs Wood Branch.
.	.	.	.	.	.	.	. .	Beddow & Son's Victoria Brick Works	Staffs	L. & N. W.	Leighs Wood Branch.
.	.	.	.	.	.	.	. .	Coppy Hall or Stubbers Green Colliery	Staffs	L. & N. W.	Leighs Wood Branch.
.	.	.	.	.	.	.	. .	Empire Bk. & Tile Co.'s Sid.	Staffs	L. & N. W.	Leighs Wood Branch.
.	.	.	.	.	.	.	. .	Midland Spelter Co.'s Sid.	Staffs	L. & N. W.	Pelsall and Brownhills.
.	.	.	.	.	.	.	. .	Walsall Wood Colliery Co.— Ryders Hayes or Pelsall Colliery	Staffs	L. & N. W.	Pelsall and Brownhills.
.	.	.	.	.	.	.	. .	Walsall Wood Colliery	Staffs	L. & N. W.	Pelsall and Brownhills.
.	.	.	.	.	.	.	. .	Wilkes Siding	Staffs	L. & N. W.	Pelsall and Brownhills.
.	.	.	.	.	.	.	. .	Pelsall Colliery	Staffs	L. & N. W.	Same as Walsall Wood Col. Co.'s Ryders Hayes Colliery (Pelsall).
G	P	.	.	.	.	.	1 10	Pelton	Durham ...	N. E.	Birtley and Annfield Plain.
.	.	.	.	.	.	.	. .	Alma Colliery	Durham ...	N. E.	Pelton.
.	.	.	.	.	.	.	. .	Charlaw Col. & Brick Wks.	Durham ...	N. E.	Pelton.
.	.	.	.	.	.	.	. .	Charlaw Shield Row Drift..	Durham ...	N. E.	Pelton.
.	.	.	.	.	.	.	. .	Charlaw Shield Row Pit ...	Durham ...	N. E.	Pelton.
.	.	.	.	.	.	.	. .	Craghead Col. & Brick Wks.	Durham ...	N. E.	Pelton.
.	.	.	.	.	.	.	. .	Daisy Hill Siding	Durham ...	N. E.	Pelton.
.	.	.	.	.	.	.	. .	Edmondsley Colliery & Coke Ovens	Durham ...	N. E.	Pelton.
.	.	.	.	.	.	.	. .	Edmondsley Depôts	Durham ...	N. E.	Pelton.
.	.	.	.	.	.	.	. .	Findon Hill Depôts	Durham ...	N. E.	Pelton.
.	.	.	.	.	.	.	. .	Handon Hold Colliery	Durham ...	N. E.	Pelton.
.	.	.	.	.	.	.	. .	Holmside Colliery	Durham ...	N. E.	Pelton.
.	.	.	.	.	.	.	. .	Pelton Colliery	Durham ...	N. E.	Pelton.
.	.	.	.	.	.	.	. .	Pelton New Winning Col.	Durham ...	N. E.	Pelton.
.	.	.	.	.	.	.	. .	Sacriston Colliery	Durham ...	N. E.	Pelton.
.	.	.	.	.	.	.	. .	South Pelaw Colliery	Durham ...	N. E.	Pelton.
.	.	.	.	.	.	.	. .	South Pelaw Junction	Durham ...	N. E.	Pelton.
.	.	.	.	.	.	.	. .	Stella Gill Junction	Durham ...	N. E.	Pelton.
.	.	.	.	.	.	.	. .	Twizell Colliery	Durham ...	N. E.	Pelton.
.	.	.	.	.	.	.	. .	Waldridge Colliery	Durham ...	N. E.	Pelton.
.	.	.	.	.	.	.	. .	West Pelton Alma Colliery	Durham ...	N. E.	Pelton.
.	.	.	.	.	.	.	. .	West Pelton Brick Works..	Durham ...	N. E.	Pelton.
G	P	.	L	H	.	.	5 0	Pemberton	Lancs	L. & Y.	Wigan and Rainford.
.	.	.	.	.	.	.	. .	Blundell's Siding	Lancs	L. & Y.	Near Pemberton.
.	.	.	.	.	.	.	. .	Winstanley Siding	Lancs	L. & Y.	Near Pemberton.
.	.	.	.	.	.	.	. .	Pemberton Branch	Lancs	L. & N. W.	Brynn and Wigan.
.	.	.	.	.	.	.	. .	Pemberton Colliery Co.'s Pemberton Collieries	Lancs	L. & N. W.	Garswood.

EXPLANATION—G *Goods Station.*   P *Passenger and Parcel Station.*   P* *Passenger, but not Parcel or Miscellaneous Traffic.*
F *Furniture Vans, Carriages, Portable Engines, and Machines on Wheels.*   F* *Furniture Vans excepted.*   L *Live Stock.*
H *Horse Boxes and Prize Cattle Vans.*   C *Carriages by Passenger Train.*

G	P	F	L	H	C	Tons	Cwts	STATIONS, &c.	COUNTY.	COMPANY.	POSITION.
.	P	.	.	.	.			Pemberton Junction	Lancs	L. & Y.—L. & N. W.	Pemberton and St. Helens.
G	P	F	L	H	C	1	10	Pembrey and Burry Port	Carmarth'	G. W.	Llanelly and Carmarthen.
.	.	.	.	.	.			Pembrey Junction	Carmarth'	B. P. & G. V.—G. W.	Pembrey and Pontyeats.
.	.	.	.	.	.			Pembrey White Lead Works	Carmarth'	B. P. & G. V.	Burry Port.
G	P	F	L	H	C	6	0	Pembridge	Hereford	G. W.	Leominster and Kington.
G	.	.	.	.	.			Marston Lane Siding	Hereford	G. W.	Pembridge and Titley.
G	P	F	L	H	C	3	0	Pembroke	Pembroke	G. W.	Tenby and Pembroke Dock.
G	P	F	L	H	C	6	0	Pembroke Dock	Pembroke	G. W.	Branch from Whitland.
G	.	F	.	.	.	20	0	Dock Yard Branch	Pembroke	G. W.	Extension from Pembroke Dock Sta.
G	.	F	.	.	.	5	0	Hobb's Point Pier	Pembroke	G. W.	Extension from Pembroke Dock Sta.
.	.	.	.	.	.			Penallta Junction	Glamorg'n	G. W.—Rhy.	Llancaiach and Ystrad Mynach.
.	.	.	.	.	.			Penallta Siding	Glamorg'n	Rhy.	Ystrad Mynach.
G	P	.	.	H	.			Penally	Pembroke	G. W.	Tenby and Pembroke Dock.
								PENARTH—			
.	.	.	.	.	.			Cement Works (Portland Cement Co.'s Siding)	Glamorg'n	T. V.	Lower Penarth and Lavernock.
G	P	.	.	.	.			Dock and Harbour	Glamorg'n	T. V.	Cardiff and Penarth.
.	.	.	.	.	.			Llandough Brick Works	Glamorg'n	T. V.	Penarth Dock and Grangetown.
.	.	.	.	.	.			Llandough Coal Yard (Price's)	Glamorg'n	T. V.	Penarth Dock and Grangetown.
.	.	.	.	.	.			Llandough Lime Works (Thomas & Son)	Glamorg'n	T. V.	Penarth Dock and Grangetown.
.	.	.	.	.	.			Llandough Storage Sidings	Glamorg'n	T. V.	Penarth Dock and Grangetown.
.	P	.	.	.	.			Lower	Glamorg'n	T. V.	Penarth and Cadoxton.
.	.	.	.	.	.			Moore's Siding	Glamorg'n	T. V.	Radyr and Grangetown.
.	.	.	.	.	.			Owen, T., & Co. (Ely Paper Mills) Siding	Glamorg'n	T. V.	Radyr and Grangetown.
.	.	.	.	.	.			Penarth Shipbuilding Co.'s Siding	Glamorg'n	T. V.	Penarth Dock.
.	.	.	.	.	.			Slipway, Penarth Dock	Glamorg'n	T. V.	Penarth Dock.
.	.	.	.	.	.			South Wales Portland Cement Co.'s Siding	Glamorg'n	T. V.	Lower Penarth and Lavernock.
G	P	F	L	H	C	3	0	Town	Glamorg'n	T. V.	Penarth Dock and Cadoxton.
.	.	.	.	.	.			Victoria Wharves	Glamorg'n	T. V.	Penarth Harbour.
.	.	.	.	.	.			Williams' Lime Siding	Glamorg'n	T. V.	Penarth Dock.
.	.	.	.	.	.			Windsor Slipway	Glamorg'n	T. V.	Penarth Harbour and Grangetown.
.	.	.	.	.	.			Penarth Branch Junc. (T.V.)	Glamorg'n	{ T. V. / Rhy. }	Radyr and Llandaff. / Over T. V. from Taffs Well Junc.
.	.	.	.	.	.			Penarth Curve North and South Junctions	Glamorg'n	G. W.—T. V.	Cardiff.
.	.	.	.	.	.			Penarth Dock, Low Level	Glamorg'n	T. V.	Penarth Dock.
.	.	.	.	.	.			Penarth Quarry Siding	Merioneth	G. W.	Carrog.
G	P	F	L	H	C	1	10	Pencader (G. W.)	Carmarth'	{ G. W. / M. & M. }	Carmarthen and Llandyssil. / Over G. W. from Pencader Junction.
G	P	F	L	H	.	1	10				
.	.	.	.	.	.			Pencader Junction	Carmarth'	G. W.—M. & M.	Pencader and Lampeter.
G	P	.	L	H	.			Pencaitland	Hadding'n	N. B.	Ormiston and Gifford.
.	.	.	.	.	.			Brander's Siding	Hadding'n	N. B.	Pencaitland and Ormiston.
G	P	.	.	.	.			Penclawdd	Glamorg'n	L. & N. W	Gowerton and Llanmorlais.
.	.	.	.	.	.			Berthlwyd Colliery	Glamorg'n	L. & N. W.	Penclawdd and Gowerton.
.	.	.	.	.	.			Penlan Colliery	Glamorg'n	L. & N. W.	Penclawdd and Llanmorlais.
G	P	.	L	.	.			Pencoed	Glamorg'n	G. W.	Llantrisant and Bridgend.
.	.	.	.	.	.			Pencoed Brick Works	Glamorg'n	G. W.	Pencoed.
.	.	.	.	.	.			Pencoed Colliery	Glamorg'n	G. W.	Bynea.
.	.	.	.	.	.			Penderyn Tramway	Brecon	G. W.	Hirwain.
.	P	.	.	.	.			Pendlebury	Lancs	L. & Y.	Salford and Swinton.
.	.	.	.	.	.			Pendlebury & Co.'s Sid. (L N W)	Lancs	L. & N. W.—G. W.	Warrington, Bank Quay.
.	.	.	.	.	.			Pendlebury Fold Brick Wks.	Lancs	L. & N. W.	See Hulton Col. Co. (Chequerbent).
.	P	.	.	.	.			Pendleton	Lancs	L. & Y.	Manchester and Bolton.
.	.	.	.	.	.			Steel Railway Journal Box Co.'s Sid. (Barningham's)	Lancs	L. & Y.	Pendleton.
.	P	.	.	.	.			Pendleton, Broad Street	Lancs	L. & Y.	Salford and Swinton.
.	.	.	.	.	.			Pendleton Colliery	Lancs	L. & Y.	See Knowles, A., & Son's (Brindle Heath).
.	.	.	.	.	.			Pendre	Merioneth	Tal-y-llyn	Same as Towyn.
.	.	.	.	.	.			Pendyris Colliery	Glamorg'n	T. V.	See Davis & Son's Ferndale Nos. 6 and 7 Collieries (Ferndale).
								PENGAM—			
G	P	.	.	.	.	1	0	(Station, B. & M.)	Mon	{ B. & M. / G. W. }	Maesycwmmer and Bargoed. / Over B. & M. from Maesycwmmer Jn.
G	.	.	.	.	.	1	0				
G	P	.	.	.	.			(Station, Rhy.)	Glamorg'n	{ Rhy. / L. & N. W. }	Hengoed and Bargoed. / Over Rhy. from Rhy. Joint Line Jn.
G	.	.	.	.	.						
.	.	.	.	.	.			Buttery Hatch Col. (B. & M.)	Mon	B. & M.—G. W.	Maesycwmmer and Pengam.

EXPLANATION—G *Goods Station.*   P. *Passenger and Parcel Station.*   P* *Passenger, but not Parcel or Miscellaneous Traffic.*
F *Furniture Vans, Carriages, Portable Engines, and Machines on Wheels.*   L *Live Stock.*
H *Horse Boxes and Prize Cattle Vans.*   C *Carriages by Passenger Train.*

STATION ACCOMMODATION.						CRANE POWER.		STATIONS, &c.	COUNTY.	COMPANY.	POSITION.
						Tons	Cwts				
								PENGAM—continued.			
..	..	..	..	..	..	..	..	Fleur-de-Lis Siding (B. & M.)	Mon	B. & M.—G. W.	Pengam and Maesycwmmer.
..	..	..	..	..	..	..	..	Gilfach Colliery (Cart-wright's) (B. & M.)	Mon	B. & M.—G. W.	Pengam and Bargoed.
..	..	..	..	..	..	..	..	Gilfach Quarry (B. & M.)...	Mon	B. & M.—G. W.	Pengam and Bargoed.
..	..	..	..	..	..	..	..	Gwaelodywaen Col.(B.&M.)	Mon	B. & M.—G. W.	New Tredegar and Pengam.
..	..	..	..	..	..	..	..	New Plas Colliery (B. & M.)	Mon	B. & M.—G. W.	Maesycwmmer and Pengam.
..	..	..	..	..	..	..	..	Old Plas Colliery (B. & M.)	Mon	B. & M.—G. W.	Maesycwmmer and Pengam.
..	..	..	..	..	..	..	..	Powell Duffryn Co.'s Bargoed New Pits (Aber Bargoed Col.) (B. & M.)	Mon	B. & M.—G. W.	Aber Bargoed and Pengam.
..	..	..	..	..	..	..	..	Rock Coal Siding (B. & M.)	Mon	B. & M.—G. W.	Pengam and Maesycwmmer.
..	..	..	..	..	..	..	..	Spelter Siding (B. & M.) ...	Mon	B. & M.—G. W.	Maesycwmmer and Pengam.
..	..	..	..	..	..	..	..	Wainborfa Colliery (B.&M.)	Mon	B. & M.—G. W.	Pengam.
G	P	F	..	..	..	1	10	Penge	Kent	S. E. & C.	Herne Hill and Beckenham.
G	P	F	..	..	..	5	0	Penge (L. B. & S. C.)	Kent	L. B. & S. C.	Forest Hill and Norwood Junction.
..	P	..	..	..	..	..	..			G. E.	Over L. B. & S. C. from New Cross Jn.
..	..	..	..	..	..	..	..	Penge Junction	Kent	S. E. & C.	Kent House and Beckenham.
G	P	F	L	H	C	3	0	Penicuik	Edinboro'	N. B.	Branch from Hawthornden Junction.
..	..	..	..	..	..	..	..	Bankmill Siding...............	Edinboro'	N. B.	Penicuik.
..	..	..	..	..	..	..	..	Eskbridge Siding	Edinboro'	N. B.	Auchendinny and Penicuik.
..	..	..	..	..	..	..	..	Eskmill Siding	Edinboro'	N. B.	Auchendinny and Penicuik.
..	..	..	..	..	..	..	..	Harpersbrae Siding(Brown, J., & Co.)	Edinboro'	N. B.	Auchendinny and Penicuik.
..	..	..	..	..	..	..	..	Lowmill Siding	Edinboro'	N. B.	Auchendinny and Penicuik.
..	..	..	..	..	..	..	..	Valleyfield Siding	Edinboro'	N. B.	Penicuik.
..	..	..	..	..	..	..	..	Penicuik Gas Works	Edinboro'	N. B.	Glencorse.
								PENISTONE—			
..	P	..	..	H	C	..	..	(Station)	Yorks	G. C.	Sheffield and Guide Bridge.
										L. & Y.	Huddersfield and Sheffield.
G	..	F	L	H	C	5	0	(Station, G. C.)	Yorks	G. C.	Passenger Station and Guide Bridge.
										L. & Y.	Over G. C. from Penistone Junction.
..	P	..	..	H	C	..	..	(Station, G. C.)	Yorks	G. N.	Over G. C. from Retford Junction.
..	..	..	..	..	..	..	..	Cammell & Co.'s Works ...	Yorks	G. C.—L. & Y.	Penistone.
..	..	..	..	..	..	..	..	Gittus Siding	Yorks	G. C.	Penistone.
..	..	..	..	..	..	..	..	Nall & Co.'s Siding	Yorks	G. C.—L. & Y.	Penistone.
..	..	..	..	..	..	..	..	Oxspring Siding.............	Yorks	G. C.	Penistone.
..	..	..	..	..	..	..	..	Penistone Junction	Yorks	G. C.—L. & Y.	Sheffield and Denby Dale.
..	..	..	..	..	..	..	..	Penketh	Lancs	L. & N. W.	See Fidler's Ferry and Penketh.
G	P	F	L	H	C	1	10	Penkridge	Staffs	L. & N. W.	Stafford and Wolverhampton.
..	..	..	..	..	..	..	..	Littleton Colliery	Staffs	L. & N. W.	Penkridge and Gailey.
..	..	..	..	..	..	..	..	Penk's Westons Siding........	Cheshire...	B'head Jt. (G W & L N W)	Birkenhead, Rock Ferry.
..	..	..	..	..	..	..	..	Penlan Colliery	Glamorg'n	L. & N. W.	Penclawdd.
..	..	..	..	..	..	..	..	Penlan Mill	Carnarvon	L. & N. W.	See Lord Penrhyn's (Bangor).
..	..	..	..	..	..	..	..	Penlan Quarry	Glamorg'n	L. & N. W.	Same as Dunvant Quarry (Dunvant).
..	..	..	..	..	..	..	..	Penllwyn Tramway	Mon	L. & N. W.	Nine Mile Point.
..	..	..	..	..	..	..	..	Burnyeat, Brown & Co.'s Sirhowy Valley Colliery	Mon	L. & N. W.	Penllwyn Tramway.
..	..	..	..	..	..	..	..	Southwood, Jones & Co.'s Siding	Mon	L. & N. W.	Penllwyn Tramway.
..	..	..	..	..	..	..	..	Penllwyn Tramway Junction	Mon	G. W.	Nine Mile Point.
..	..	..	..	..	..	..	..	Penllyn Siding	Carnarvon	L. & N. W.	Dolwyddelen.
G	P	F	..	H	C	1	5	Penmaenmawr	Carnarvon	L. & N. W.	Bangor and Rhyl.
..	..	..	..	..	..	..	..	Brundrit & Co's Wrights Sid	Carnarvon	L. & N. W.	Penmaenmawr and Llanfairfechan.
..	..	..	..	..	..	..	..	Darbishire's Siding	Carnarvon	L. & N. W.	Penmaenmawr and Conway.
G	P	F	L	H	C	..	..	Penmaenpool	Merioneth	Cam.	Barmouth Junction and Dolgelley.
..	..	..	..	..	..	..	..	Penmaenrhos Siding	Carnarvon	L. & N. W.	See Raynes & Co. (Llysfaen).
..	..	..	..	..	..	..	..	Pen Mill	Somerset..	G. W.	See Yeovil.
..	..	..	..	..	..	..	..	Pennard	Somerset..	S.&D.Jt.(L.&S.W.& Mid)	See West Pennard.
..	..	..	..	..	..	..	..	Penner Junction...............	Mon	G. W.	Tredegar Junction Station.
..	..	..	..	..	..	..	..	Penner Wharf (Phillips & Son's Malt House)	Mon	A (N & S W) D & R—G W	Newport, Alexandra Docks.
..	..	..	..	..	..	..	..	Penn Farm Siding	Oxon	G. W.	Thame.
..	P	..	..	..	..	..	..	Pennington	Lancs	L. & N. W.	Bolton & Kenyon Junction Station.
..	..	..	..	..	..	..	..	Pennington's Siding	W'morl'nd	L. & N. W.	See Kendal Bonded Stores Co. (Kendal).
G	P	F	L	H	C	1	10	Penns	Warwick..	Mid.	Castle Bromwich & Sutton Coldfield.
..	..	..	..	..	..	..	..	Pennyman's Siding	Yorks	N. E.	Middlesbro'.
..	..	..	..	..	..	..	..	Pennyvennie Nos. 1 & 2	Ayr	G. & S.W.	Waterside.
G	P	..	L	H	..	5	0	Penpergwm (G. W.)	Mon	G. W.	Pontypool Road and Abergavenny.
G	..	..	..	..	..	5	0			L. & N. W.	Over G. W. from Hereford.
..	..	..	..	..	..	..	..	Penpontpren Siding	Montgom	Cam.	Tylwch.

EXPLANATION—G *Goods Station.*   P *Passenger and Parcel Station.*   P* *Passenger, but not Parcel or Miscellaneous Traffic.*
F *Furniture Vans, Carriages, Portable Engines, and Machines on Wheels.*   L *Live Stock.*
H *Horse Boxes and Prize Cattle Vans.*   C *Carriages by Passenger Train.*

STATION ACCOMMODATION.						CRANE POWER.		STATIONS, &c.	COUNTY.	COMPANY.	POSITION.
						Tons	Cwts				
	P							Penrhiew Colliery	Glamorg'n	G. W.	Glyn Neath.
G	P						}	Penrhiwceiber	Glamorg'n	{ G. W.	Quaker's Yard and Mountain Ash.
										(T. V.	Mountain Ash and Pontypridd.
								Cory Bros. & Co.'s Penrikyber or Penrhiwceiber Colliery	Glamorg'n	T. V.	Penrhiwceiber and Abercynon.
								Cwmcynon Colliery	Glamorg'n	T. V.	Penrhiwceiber and Abercynon.
								Glyn Gwyn Colliery	Glamorg'n	T. V.	Penrhiwceiber and Abercynon.
								Penrhiwceiber Gas Works (Mountain Ash Gas Wks.)	Glamorg'n	T. V.	Penrhiwceiber and Mountain Ash.
								Pontcynon Junction	Glamorg'n	T. V.	Penrhiwceiber and Abercynon.
								Ynisboeth Qry. (Richards')	Glamorg'n	T. V.	Penrhiwceiber and Abercynon.
								Penrhiwceiber Colliery	Glamorg'n	T. V.	Same as Cory Bros.' & Co.'s Penrikyber Colliery (Penrhiwceiber).
								Penrhiw Colliery	Glamorg'n	T. V.	Pontypridd.
								Penrhiw Colliery	Mon	G. W.	Tredegar Junction Station.
								Penrhos Brick Wks Sid (N & B)	Brecon	N. & Brecon—Mid	Ystradgynlais.
								Penrhos, North Junction	Glamorg'n	A.(N & SW)D.&R.—Rhy.	Pontypridd and Caerphilly.
								Penrhos Siding (Furnace Blwm Siding)	Glamorg'n	Rhy.	Caerphilly.
								Penrhos, South Junction	Glamorg'n	Barry—Rhy.	St. Fagans and Llanbradach.
G	P		L		C	2	10	Penrhyn	Merioneth	Festiniog	Minffordd and Tan-y-bwlch.
G	P	F	L	H	C	3	0	Penrhyndeudraeth	Merioneth	Cam.	Harlech and Pwllheli.
								Penrhyn's, Lord—			
								Parkia Brick Co.'s Siding	Carnarvon	L. & N. W.	Griffiths Crossing.
								Penlan Mill	Carnarvon	L. & N. W.	Bangor.
								Port Penrhyn Quay	Carnarvon	L. & N. W.	Bangor.
								Penrikyber or Penrhiwceiber Colliery	Glamorg'n	T. V.	See Cory Bros. & Co. (Penrhiwceiber).
								PENRITH—			
G	P	F	L	H	C	5	0	(Station for Ullswater Lake) (L. & N. W.)	Cumb'land	{ L. & N. W.	Carlisle and Lancaster.
										C. K. & P.	Over L. & N. W. from Penrith Junc.
										N. E.	Over L. & N. W. from Clifton Junc.
								Eamont Bridge Junction	Cumb'land	L. & N. W.—N. E.	Penrith and Clifton.
								Junction	Cumb'land	C. K. & P.—L. & N. W.	Blencow and Penrith.
								Redhills Junction	Cumb'land	C. K. & P.—N. E.	Blencow and Clifton.
								Penrose Quay	Cork	G. S. & W.	See Cork.
G	P	F	L	H	C	1	10	Penruddock	Cumb'land	C. K. & P. (L. & N. W. & N. E. Working Cos.)	Penrith and Keswick.
G	P	F	L	H	C	2	0	Penryn	Cornwall	G. W.	Truro and Falmouth.
								Pensarn	Merioneth	Cam.	See Llanbedr and Pensarn.
G	P	F	L	H	C	1	5	Pensford	Somerset	G. W.	Bristol and Clutton.
G	P		L	H	C	2	0	Penshaw	Durham	N. E.	Washington and Leamside.
								Bowes House Farm Siding	Durham	N. E.	Penshaw and Fencehouses.
								Burn Moor Collieries ("D" and Lady Ann Pits)	Durham	N. E.	Penshaw and Fencehouses.
								Burn Moor or New Lambton Bk., Sanitary & Tile Wks.	Durham	N. E.	Penshaw and Fencehouses.
								Burn Moor or New Lambton Coke Ovens	Durham	N. E.	Penshaw and Fencehouses.
								Burn Moor or New Lambton Gas Works	Durham	N. E.	Penshaw and Fencehouses.
								Burn Moor Siding	Durham	N. E.	Penshaw and Fencehouses.
								Chilton Moor Stores	Durham	N. E.	Penshaw and Fencehouses.
								Dorothea Pit (Newbottle)	Durham	N. E.	Penshaw and Fencehouses.
								"D" Pit Brick & Tile Wks.	Durham	N. E.	Penshaw and Fencehouses.
								Fencehouses Depôts	Durham	N. E.	Penshaw and Fencehouses.
								Herrington Pit	Durham	N. E.	Penshaw and Fencehouses.
								Houghton Collieries (Old and New Pits)	Durham	N. E.	Penshaw and Fencehouses.
								Houghton Lime Works	Durham	N. E.	Penshaw and Fencehouses.
								Houghton Pit	Durham	N. E.	Penshaw and Fencehouses.
								Lumley Brick Works	Durham	N. E.	Penshaw and Fencehouses.
								Lumley 2nd Pit Depôt	Durham	N. E.	Penshaw and Fencehouses.
								Lumley 3rd Pit	Durham	N. E.	Penshaw and Fencehouses.
								Lumley 6th Pit Depôt	Durham	N. E.	Penshaw and Fencehouses.
								Lumley 6th Pit Gas Works	Durham	N. E.	Penshaw and Fencehouses.
								Margaret Pit (Newbottle)	Durham	N. E.	Penshaw and Fencehouses.
								Newbottle Manure Siding	Durham	N. E.	Penshaw and Fencehouses.
								New Herrington Brk. Wks.	Durham	N. E.	Penshaw and Fencehouses.
								New Herrington Colliery	Durham	N. E.	Penshaw and Fencehouses.
								New Lambton Siding	Durham	N. E.	Penshaw and Fencehouses.
								New Penshaw Siding	Durham	N. E.	Penshaw and Fencehouses.

EXPLANATION—G *Goods Station.* P *Passenger and Parcel Station.* P* *Passenger, but not Parcel or Miscellaneous Traffic.* F *Furniture Vans, Carriages, Portable Engines, and Machines on Wheels.* L *Live Stock.* H *Horse Boxes and Prize Cattle Vans.* C *Carriages by Passenger Train.*

STATION ACCOMMODATION.						CRANE POWER.		STATIONS, &c.	COUNTY.	COMPANY.	POSITION.
						Tons	Cwts	Penshaw—continued.			
								Offerton Siding and Depôt	Durham	N. E.	Penshaw and Hylton.
								Pea Flat Pumping Engine	Durham	N. E.	Penshaw and Fencehouses.
								Penshaw Brk. & Quarry Sid.	Durham	N. E.	Penshaw.
								Penshaw Foundry Co.'s Sid.	Durham	N. E.	Penshaw.
								Philadelphia Locomotive Works	Durham	N. E.	Penshaw and Fencehouses.
								Philadelphia Siding	Durham	N. E.	Penshaw and Fencehouses.
								Sunnyside Siding (Lambton Line)	Durham	N. E.	Penshaw and Fencehouses.
								Tadcaster Tower Brewery Co.'s Siding	Durham	N. E.	Penshaw.
								Wapping Siding	Durham	N. E.	Penshaw and Fencehouses.
								Whitefield Pit	Durham	N. E.	Penshaw.
								Penshaw Junction	Durham	N. E.	Penshaw and Washington.
G	P	F	L	H	C	4	0	Penshurst	Kent	S. E. & C.	Red Hill and Tonbridge.
								Penson & Southern's Sid. (GW)	Carmarth'	G. W.—L. & N. W.	Llandebie.
								Penston Colliery	Hadding'n	N. B.	Macmerry.
G	P		L	H		2	0	Penton	Cumb'land	N. B.	Hawick and Carlisle.
								Pentre	Glamorg'n	T. V.	Same as Ystrad.
								Pentre Colliery	Glamorg'n	T. V.	See Cory Bros. & Co. (Ystrad).
	P							Pentrebach	Glamorg'n	T. V.	Merthyr and Pontypridd.
G	P		L					Pentrefelin	Denbigh	Cam. (Tanat Valley)	Porthywaen and Llangynog.
								Pentrefelin Colliery	Glamorg'n	G. W.	Morriston.
								Pentrefelin Siding	Denbigh	G. W.	Llangollen.
								Pentreporth Chemical Works	Glamorg'n	G. W.	Morriston.
								Pentrich Colliery	Derby	Mid.	Butterley.
								Pentwyn Colliery	Mon	G. W.	Talywain.
								Pentwyn Junction	Mon	G. W.	Pontypool and Abersychan.
								Pentwyn Siding	Glamorg'n	B. & M.	Machen.
								Pentyrch Siding (Melingriffith Works)	Glamorg'n	T. V.	Taffs Well.
								Penwithers Junction	Cornwall	G. W.	Truro and Chacewater.
								Penwortham Junction	Lancs	L. & Y.	Howick and Whitehouse Junction.
G	P							Penwyllt (N. & B.)	Brecon	N. & Brecon / Mid.	Devynock and Colbren. / Over Neath and Brecon Line.
								Bwlch Siding (N. & B.)	Brecon	N. & Brecon—Mid.	Penwyllt and Devynock.
								Penwyllt Dinas Silica Brick Co.'s Siding (N. & B.)	Brecon	N. & Brecon—Mid.	Penwyllt.
								Penwyllt Lime & Limestone Co.'s Siding (N. & B.)	Brecon	N. & Brecon—Mid.	Penwyllt.
G	P	F	L	H	C	5	0	Penybont	Radnor	L. & N. W.	Craven Arms and Llandrindod Wells.
								Penybont Brick Works	Denbigh	G. W.	Llangollen Road.
G	P		L					Penybontfawr	Montgom	Cam. (Tanat Valley)	Porthywaen and Llangynog.
								Pen-y-Bryn Siding	Carnarvon	L. & N. W.	Same as Dorothea Slate Co.'s Siding (Nantlle).
								Penybryn Siding	Carnarvon	L. & N. W.	See Raynes & Co. (Llysfaen).
								Penyfan Colliery	Mon	G. W.	Aberbeeg.
G	P		L	H		1	0	Penyffordd (for Hope) (W. M. & C. Q.)	Flint	W. M. & C. Q. / G. C.	Connah's Quay and Wrexham. / Over W. M. & C. Q. from Hawarden
	P			H							Bridge Junction.
								Penygorof Siding (Mid.)	Glamorg'n	Mid.—G. W.—L. & N. W.	Gurnos.
G	P	F	L	H	C	2	0	Penygraig	Glamorg'n	G. W.	Branch from Llantrisant.
								Cambrian Colliery	Glamorg'n	G. W.	Penygraig.
								Clydach Vale Colliery	Glamorg'n	G. W.	Near Penygraig.
								Dinas Isha Colliery	Glamorg'n	G. W.	Penygraig and Tonyrefail.
								Ely Pits Colliery	Glamorg'n	G. W.	Penygraig.
								Naval Ely Colliery	Glamorg'n	G. W.	Penygraig and Tonyrefail.
								Naval (Nantgwyn) Colliery	Glamorg'n	G. W.	Near Penygraig.
								Penygraig Colliery	Glamorg'n	G. W.	Penygraig and Tonyrefail.
								Watkin & Philip's Timber Yard	Glamorg'n	G. W.	Penygraig and Tonyrefail.
G	P		L	H		5	0	Penygroes	Carnarvon	L. & N. W.	Afon Wen and Carnarvon.
								Paull's Siding	Carnarvon	L. & N. W.	Penygroes and Nantlle.
G	P	F	L*					Penyrheol	Glamorg'n	Rhy.	Caerphilly and Senghenith.
								Price & Wills' Siding	Glamorg'n	Rhy.	Penyrheol.
								Penyrorsedd Slate Quarries	Carnarvon	L. & N. W.	Nantlle.
								Penywern Siding	Glamorg'n	L. & N. W.	See Guest, Keen & Nettlefold (Dowlais)
G	P	F	L	H	C	3	0	Penzance	Cornwall	G. W.	Terminus.
							5	0	Ponsandane Siding	Cornwall	G. W.	Penzance.
G	P		L	H	C	1	0	Peplow	Salop	G. W.	Wellington and Market Drayton.
								Pepper & Son's Siding	Sussex	L. B. & S. C.	Amberley.

EXPLANATION—G *Goods Station.*   P *Passenger and Parcel Station.*   P* *Passenger, but not Parcel or Miscellaneous* **Traffic.**
F *Furniture Vans, Carriages, Portable Engines, and Machines on Wheels.*   L *Live Stock.*
L* *In full truck loads only.*   H *Horse Boxes and Prize Cattle Vans.*   C *Carriages by Passenger Train.*

Station Accommodation.						Crane Power.		STATIONS, &c.	COUNTY.	COMPANY.	POSITION.
						Tons	Cwts				
.	.	.	.	.	.	.	.	Pepper Hill Carriage Siding..	Lancs	L. & Y.	Clifton Junction.
.	.	.	.	.	.	.	.	Pepper Road Siding	Yorks	Mid.	Leeds, Hunslet.
.	.	.	.	.	.	.	.	Pepper's Lime Quarry	Yorks	N. E.	Wormald Green.
.	.	.	.	.	.	.	.	Perceton Branch Junction ...	Ayr	G. & S.W.	Dreghorn and Crosshouse.
.	.	.	.	.	.	.	.	Perceton Fire-Clay Works ...	Ayr	G. & S.W.	Dreghorn.
.	.	.	.	.	.	.	.	Perceton Pits	Ayr	G. & S.W.	Dreghorn.
.	.	.	.	.	.	.	.	Percival & Co.'s Siding........	Cheshire ..	B'headJt. (G W & L N W)	Chester.
.	.	.	.	.	.	.	.	Percival Lane Siding	Cheshire..	L. & N. W.	Same as Wilson's Siding (Runcorn Docks).
G	P	.	L	.	.	2	0	Percleuan Lye...................	Ayr	G. & S.W.	Hollybush.
.	.	.	.	.	.	.	.	Percy Main	Northumb	N. E.	Newcastle and Tynemouth.
.	P	.	.	.	.	.	.	Earsdon Junction	Northumb	N. E.	Percy Main and Holywell.
.	.	.	.	.	.	.	.	Perivale-Alperton	Middlesex	Met. Dist.	Park Royal and Sudbury Town.
.	.	.	.	.	.	.	.	Perks & Son's Timber Yard Sidings (Mid.).	Staffs	Mid—L N W—G N—N S	Burton-on-Trent.
G	P	F	L	H	C	6	0	Perranporth......................	Cornwall...	G. W.	Newquay and Truro.
G	P	F	L	H	C	2	0	Perranwell	Cornwall...	G. W.	Truro and Falmouth.
.	.	.	.	.	.	.	.	Perry & Hope's Siding	Renfrew ...	G B & K Jt. (Cal & G&SW)	Nitshill.
G	P	.	.	.	.	.	.	Perry Barr	Staffs	L. & N. W.	Birmingham and Wolverhampton.
.	.	.	.	.	.	.	.	Cannock Chase CollieryCo.'s Wharf	Staffs	L. & N. W.	Perry Barr and Great Barr.
.	.	.	.	.	.	.	.	Perseverance Boiler Works...	Durham ...	N. E.	Stockton, North Shore.
G	P	F	L	H	C	5	0	Pershore	Worcester	G. W.	Worcester and Evesham.
.	P	.	.	.	.	.	.	Persley	Aberdeen	G. N. of S.	Aberdeen and Dyce.
								PERTH—			
G	.	F	L	.	.	5	0	(Station)	Perth	N. B.	Branch from South of General Sta.
G	.	.	.	.	.	.	.	Balhousie Sidings	Perth	Cal.	Perth, North.
.	.	.	.	.	.	.	.	Barnhill Siding	Perth	Cal.	Perth and Kinfauns.
.	.	.	.	.	.	.	.	Cunningham's Siding	Perth	Cal.	Perth Harbour.
G	.	.	.	.	.	.	.	Dewar & Son's Siding	Perth	N. B.	Perth.
.	.	.	.	.	.	.	.	Earlsdyke Sidings	Perth	Cal.	Perth, North.
G	.	.	.	.	.	.	.	Friarton Brick Works	Perth	Cal.	Perth Harbour.
G	.	.	.	.	.	.	.	Friarton Gas Works and Manure Depôt (Cal.)	Perth	Cal.—N. B.	Perth Harbour.
.	.	.	.	.	.	.	.	Friarton Goods Yard and Sidings (Cal.)	Perth	Cal.—N. B.	Forgandenny and Perth.
.	P	.	.	H	C	.	.	General	Perth	{ Cal. .... / High .... / N. B.	Stirling and Coupar Angus. / Over Cal. from Stanley Junction. / Over Cal. from Hilton Junction.
G	.	.	.	.	.	.	.	Harbour (Cal.)	Perth	Cal.—N. B.	Branch—Forgandenny and Perth.
.	.	.	.	.	.	.	.	Langdale & Co.'s Siding...	Perth	Cal.	Perth Harbour.
G	.	F	L	.	.	6	0 }	McCash & Son's Siding......	Perth	Cal.	Perth, North.
G	.	F	L	.	.	.	.	North (Dovecotland), (Cal.)	Perth	{ Cal. .... / High	General Station and Luncarty. / Over Cal. from Stanley Junction.
G	P	F	L	.	.	5	0	Perth City Electric Siding	Perth	Cal.	Perth Harbour.
.	.	.	.	.	.	.	.	Princes Street....................	Perth	Cal.	Perth and Dundee.
G	.	.	L	.	.	1	10	Sinclair's Saw Mills	Perth	Cal.	Perth, North.
.	.	.	.	.	.	.	.	South	Perth	Cal.	Forgandenny & Perth General Sta.
.	.	.	.	.	.	.	.	Tay Salmon Fishery Syndicate Siding	Perth	Cal.	Perth.
.	.	.	.	.	.	.	.	Tulloch Siding	Perth	Cal.	Perth and Almondbank.
.	.	.	.	.	.	.	.	Petch's Siding	Yorks	N. E.	Boosbeck.
								PETERBOROUGH—			
G	P	F	L	H	C	10	0 }	(Station, G. E.)	Hunts ...	{ G. E. .... / G. N. .... / L. & N. W. .... / Mid.—Mid. & G. N. Jt.	Branch from March. / Over G.E. from Peterboro' Junction. / Over G.E. from Peterboro' Junction. / Over G.E. Line.
.	P	.	.	H	C	10	0				
G	P	F	L	H	C	10	0				
G	P	F	L	H	C	10	0				
.	P	.	.	H	C	.	.	(Station, G. N.)	N'hampt'n	{ G. N. .... / Mid. .... / Mid. & G. N. Jt.	Huntingdon and Grantham. / Over G. N. Line. / Over G.N. from Peterboro' Junction.
G	P	F	L	H	C	10	0 }				
.	.	.	.	.	.	.	.	Botolph Bridge Siding......	N'hampt'n	G. N.	Peterboro' and Longville Junction.
.	.	.	.	.	.	.	.	Cadge & Colman's Sid. (GE)	Hunts......	G. E.—L. & N. W.—Mid.	Peterboro'.
.	.	.	.	.	.	.	.	Caucasian Oil Co.'s Siding	N'hampt'n	Mid.	Crescent Wharf.
.	.	.	.	.	.	.	.	Consolidated Oil Co.'s Siding (Nene Siding)	N'hampt'n	Mid.	Crescent Wharf.
G	.	.	L	H	.	.	.	Crescent Cattle Docks	N'hampt'n	Mid.	Peterboro' and Walton.
.	.	.	.	.	.	.	.	Crescent Wharf	N'hampt'n	Mid.	Peterboro' and Walton.
.	.	.	.	.	.	.	.	English Bros.' Sid. (G.E.)..	Hunts......	GE—GN—L& NW—Mid	Peterboro'.
.	.	.	.	.	.	.	.	Gilstrap, Earp & Co.'s Paston Siding..............	N'hampt'n	G. N.	Peterboro' and Werrington Junction.
.	.	.	.	.	.	.	.	Junction	N'hampt'n	G. E.—G. N.	Taken as between Peterboro', G. E. and G. N. Stations.

EXPLANATION—G *Goods Station.*   P *Passenger and Parcel Station.*   P* *Passenger, but not Parcel or Miscellaneous Traffic.*
F *Furniture Vans, Carriages, Portable Engines, and Machines on Wheels.*   L *Live Stock.*
H *Horse Boxes and Prize Cattle Vans.*   C *Carriages by Passenger Train.*

STATION ACCOMMODATION.						CRANE POWER.		STATIONS, &c.	COUNTY.	COMPANY.	POSITION.
						Tons	Cwts	PETERBOROUGH—*continued.*			
..	..	..	..	..	..	..	..	Junction	Hunts ...	G. E.—L. & N. W.—Mid.	Taken as at G. E. Station.
..	..	..	..	..	..	..	..	Junction	N'hamptn	G. N.—L. & N. W.	Taken as near G. N. Station (South of).
..	..	..	..	..	..	..	..	Junction	N'hamptn	G. N.—Mid.	Taken as at G. N. Station.
..	..	..	..	..	..	..	..	Junction	N'hamptn	G. N.—Mid. & G. N. Jt.	Peterboro' G. N. Station and Eye Green.
..	..	..	..	..	..	..	..	Junction	N'hamptn	L. & N. W.—Mid.	Taken as near G. E. Station (West of).
..	..	..	..	..	..	..	..	Junction	N'hamptn	Mid.—Mid. & G. N. Jt...	Crescent Wharf and Eye Green.
..	..	..	..	..	..	..	..	Metropolitan Wagon Co.'s Siding (G. E.)...............	Hunts ...	GE—GN—L & NW—Mid	Peterboro'.
..	..	..	..	..	..	..	..	Midland Wagon Co.'s Siding (G. E.)	Hunts ...	GE—GN—L & NW—Mid	Peterboro'.
..	..	..	..	..	..	..	..	Moy, T., & Co.'s Sid. (G.E.)	Hunts ...	GE—GN—L & NW—Mid	Peterboro'.
..	..	..	..	..	..	..	..	New England Siding	N'hamptn	G. N.	Peterboro' & Werrington Junction.
..	..	..	..	..	..	..	..	Phipps & Co.'s Sid (Mid.)...	N'hamptn	Mid.—L. & N. W.	Crescent Wharf.
..	..	..	..	..	..	..	..	Rickett, Cockerell & Co.'s Siding (G. E.)	Hunts ...	GE—L & NW—Mid.	Peterboro'.
..	..	..	..	..	..	..	..	Thompson, S., & Son's Siding (Mid.).....................	N'hamptn	Mid.—L. & N. W.	Crescent Wharf.
G	..	..	..	..	..	5	0	Woodstone Wharf	N'hamptn	L. & N. W.	Peterboro' and Wellingboro'.
..	..	..	..	..	..	..	..	Peterboro' Brick Co.'s Siding	Hunts ...	G. N.	See New Peterboro' Brick Co.'s Sid. (Fletton).
..	..	..	..	..	..	..	..	Peterboro' Corporation Water Works	N'hamptn	G. N.	Tallington.
G	P	F	..	H	C	5	0	Peterchurch	Hereford ..	G. W.	Pontrilas and Dorstone.
G	P	F	L	H	C	5	0	Peterhead	Aberdeen	G. N. of S.	Branch from Maud.
G	P	F	L	H	C	5	0	Petersfield	Hants	L. & S.W.	Guildford and Portsmouth.
G	..	..	..	..	..	..	..	Buriton Siding	Hants	L. & S.W.	Petersfield.
..	..	..	..	..	..	..	..	Peters' Lime Siding	Surrey ...	S. E. & C.	Merstham.
..	..	..	..	..	..	..	..	Peters' Siding	Flint	L. & N. W.	See South Level (Coed Talon).
G	P	..	L	H	..	..	..	Peterston	Glamorg'n	G. W.	Cardiff and Llantrisant.
..	..	..	..	..	..	..	..	Peterston, East & West Juncs.	Glamorg'n	Barry—G. W.	Wenvoe and Peterston.
..	..	..	..	..	..	..	..	Peterstone Siding	Norfolk ...	G. E.	Burnham Market.
..	..	..	..	..	..	..	..	Petford's Haigh Foundry......	Lancs	L. & N. W.	Wigan.
..	..	..	..	..	..	..	..	Pethick's Yard and Quay......	Devon	L. & S.W.	Plymouth, Cattewater Harbour.
..	..	..	..	..	..	..	..	Petolite Fuel Co.'s Siding ...	Glamorg'n	GW—LNW—Mid—RSB	Swansea.
..	..	..	..	..	..	..	..	Petterill (Mid.)	Cumb'land	Mid.—G. & S. W.	See Carlisle.
..	..	..	..	..	..	..	..	Petterill Junction	Cumb'land	Mid.—N. E.	Carlisle.
G	P	F	L	..	..	..	..	Pettigo	Donegal ...	G. N. (I.)	Bundoran Junc. and Bundoran.
..	..	..	..	..	..	..	..	Pettinain Siding...............	Lanark ...	Cal.	See Grange Siding (Carstairs).
..	..	..	..	..	..	..	..	Pettycur Siding	Fife.........	N. B.	Burntisland.
G	P	F	L	H	C	5	0	Petworth	Sussex ...	L. B. & S. C.	Pulborough and Midhurst.
G	P	F	L	H	C	..	..	Pevensey and Westham	Sussex ...	L. B. & S. C.	Polegate and Hastings.
..	..	..	..	..	..	..	..	Pewfall Colliery	Lancs	G. C. (St. Helens Exten.)	See Evans, R., & Co. (Ashton-in-Makerfield).
..	..	..	..	..	..	..	..			L. & N. W.	See Evans, R., & Co. (Earlestown).
G	P	F	L	H	C	1	10	Pewsey	Wilts	G. W.	Hungerford and Devizes.
..	..	..	..	..	..	..	..	Philadelphia Loco. Works ...	Durham ...	N. E.	{ Fencehouses. / Penshaw.
..	..	..	..	..	..	..	..	Philadelphia Siding	Durham ...	N. E.	{ Fencehouses. / Penshaw.
..	..	..	..	..	..	..	..	Philips Park Sids. (L. & Y.)	Lancs	L&Y—GC—LNW—Mid.	See Manchester.
..	..	..	..	..	..	..	..	Philip's Siding	Edinboro'	N. B.	Bonnyrigg.
..	..	..	..	..	..	..	..	Phillipps' Siding...............	Glamorg'n	T. V.	Same as Clydach Vale Colliery (Trealaw).
..	..	..	..	..	..	..	..	Phillips & Son's Malt House	Mon.........	A (N & S W) D & R—G W	Same as Penner Wharf (Newport).
..	..	..	..	..	..	..	..	Phillips & Williams' Siding...	Mon.........	L. & N. W.	Sirhowy.
..	..	..	..	..	..	..	..	Phillips', C. D., Works........	Glo'ster ...	G. W.—Mid.	Same as Emlyn Ir. Wks. (Gloucester).
..	..	..	..	..	..	..	..	Phillips' Siding	Herts	G. N.	Royston.
G	P	..	..	H	..	..	..	Philorth	Aberdeen	G. N. of S.	Dyce and Fraserburgh.
..	..	..	..	..	..	..	..	Philpott & Co.	Glo'ster ...	G. W.—Mid.	Gloucester Docks.
G	P	..	L	H	..	1	10	Philpstoun	L'lithgow	N. B.	Ratho and Linlithgow.
G	..	..	..	..	..	..	..	Pardovan General Siding...	L'lithgow	N. B.	Philpstoun and Linlithgow.
..	..	..	..	..	..	..	..	Pardovan Quarry	L'lithgow	N. B.	Philpstoun and Linlithgow.
..	..	..	..	..	..	..	..	Philpstoun Oil Works (Ross & Co.)	L'lithgow	N. B.	Philpstoun.
..	..	..	..	..	..	..	..	Phipps & Co.'s Siding (Mid.)	N'hamptn	Mid.—L. & N. W.	Peterboro.'
..	..	..	..	..	..	..	..	Phipps (Exors)— Hunsbury Hill Iron Works	N'hamptn	L. & N. W.	See Duston Siding (Northampton).
..	..	..	..	..	..	..	..	Siding	N'hamptn	L. & N. W.	Blisworth.
..	..	..	..	..	..	..	..	Wagon Works	N'hamptn	L. & N. W.	Northampton, Bridge Street.
..	..	..	..	..	..	..	..	Phœnix Bottle Works	Durham ..	N. E.	Sunderland, South Dock.

EXPLANATION—G *Goods Station.*   P *Passenger and Parcel Station.*   P* *Passenger, but not Parcel or Miscellaneous Traffic.*
F *Furniture Vans, Carriages, Portable Engines, and Machines on Wheels.*   L *Live Stock.*
H *Horse Boxes and Prize Cattle Vans.*   C *Carriages by Passenger Train.*

STATION ACCOMMODATION.						CRANE POWER.		STATIONS, &c.	COUNTY.	COMPANY.	POSITION.
						Tons	Cwts.				
								Phœnix Coal & Cannel Co.—			
·	·	·	·	·	·	·	·	Celyn Wood Colliery......	Flint	L. & N. W.	Coed Talon.
·	·	·	·	·	·	·	·	New North Leeswood Col.	Flint	L. & N. W.	Coed Talon.
·	·	·	·	·	·	·	·	Phœnix Dry Dock............	Glamorg'n	GW—LNW—Mid—RSB	Swansea.
·	·	·	·	·	·	·	·	Phœnix Engineering Works	Durham ...	N. E.	Stockton, North Shore.
·	·	·	·	·	·	·	·	Phœnix Foundry	Cumb'land	M. & C.	Same as Wharton's Phœnix Foundry (Maryport).
·	·	·	·	·	·	·	·	Phœnix Foundry	Fife	N. B.	Dunfermline, Upper.
·	·	·	·	·	·	·	·	Phœnix Iron Works	Lanark ...	N. B.	Coatbridge, Sheepford.
·	·	·	·	·	·	·	·	Phœnix Malting Works	Lanark ...	N. B.	Glasgow, Lochburn.
·	·	·	·	·	·	·	·	Phœnix Steel Works (Steel, Peech & Tozer)	Yorks	Mid.	Masbro' and Rotherham.
·	·	·	·	·	·	·	·	Phœnix Tin Plate Co.'s Siding (Mid.)	Glamorg'n	Mid.—G. W.—L. & N. W.	Gurnos.
·	·	·	·	·	·	·	·	Phœnix Tube Wks. (Menzies')	Lanark ...	Cal.	Glasgow, Bridgeton.
G	·	·	·	·	·	·	·	Phœnix Works	Mon	G. W.	See Baldwin's, Ltd., (Pontypool).
·	·	·	·	·	·	·	·	Pickburn & Brodsworth...	Yorks	H. & B.	Wrangbrook Junction and Denaby.
·	·	·	·	·	·	·	·	Hampole Siding	Yorks	H. & B.	Wrangbrook Junction and Pickburn.
G	P	F	L	H	C	5	0	Neville's (Shelbrook) Siding	Yorks	H. & B.	Wrangbrook Junction and Pickburn.
·	·	·	·	·	·	·	·	Pickering............	Yorks	N. E.	Malton and Whitby.
·	·	·	·	·	·	·	·	Black Bull Siding	Yorks	N. E.	Pickering and Marishes Road.
·	·	·	·	·	·	·	·	Farworth Siding............	Yorks	N. E.	Levisham and Pickering.
·	·	·	·	·	·	·	·	New Bridge Lime Works...	Yorks	N. E.	Pickering.
·	·	·	·	·	·	·	·	Park Lane Lime Works ...	Yorks	N. E.	Pickering.
·	·	·	·	·	·	·	·	Pickering Lime Works......	Yorks	N. E.	Pickering.
·	·	·	·	·	·	·	·	Pickering & Co.'s Siding	Fife	N. B.	Same as Thornton Wagon Works (Thornton).
·	·	·	·	·	·	·	·	Pickering & Co.'s Wagon Wks.	Lanark ...	Cal.	Same as Wishaw Wagon Works (Wishaw).
·	·	·	·	·	·	·	·	Pickering & Co.'s Wagon Works	Lanark ...	N. B.	Rawyards.
·	·	·	·	·	·	·	·	Pickering's Siding............	Durham ...	N. E.	West Hartlepool.
·	·	·	·	·	·	·	·	Pickersgill & Frost's Siding	Derby	Mid.	Langley Mill and Eastwood.
G	P	F	L	H	C	1	10	Pickhill Siding	Yorks	N. E.	Sinderby.
·	·	·	·	·	·	·	·	Picton	Yorks	N. E.	Northallerton and Stockton.
G	P	·	·	·	·	·	·	Pidcock & Co.'s Siding (G.C.)	Notts	G. C.—G. N.—Mid.	Retford.
·	·	·	·	·	·	·	·	Piddington	N'hamptn	Mid.	Bedford and Northampton.
G	P	·	L	·	·	·	·	Pidley-cum-Fenton Siding ...	Hunts	G. N. & G. E. Jt.	See Warboys.
G	P	F	L	H	C	5	0	Piel	Lancs	Furness	Branch from Barrow.
·	·	·	·	·	·	·	·	Piercebridge	Durham ...	N. E.	Darlington and Barnard Castle.
·	·	·	·	·	·	·	·	Pier Engine Works	Durham ...	N. E.	Sunderland, South Dock.
·	·	·	·	·	·	·	·	Pierhead	Lancs	L'pool O'head	See Liverpool.
·	·	·	·	·	·	·	·	Piershill	Edinboro'	N. B.	See Edinburgh.
·	·	·	·	·	·	·	·	Piershill Junction	Edinboro'	N. B.	Edinburgh.
·	·	·	·	·	·	·	·	Piggott's Siding	Warwick.	L. & N. W.	See Toy Siding (Birmingham).
·	·	·	·	·	·	·	·	Pildacre Colliery	Yorks	G. N.	Ossett.
								Pilkington Bros.—			
·	·	·	·	·	·	·	·	British Plate Works	Lancs	L. & N. W.	St. Helens.
·	·	·	·	·	·	·	·	Crown Glass Works	Lancs	L. & N. W.	St. Helens.
·	·	·	·	·	·	·	·	Eccleston Pottery Siding...	Lancs	L. & N. W.	St. Helens.
·	·	·	·	·	·	·	·	Gerard's Bridge Plate Glass Works	Lancs	G. C.—(Wigan Junction)	St. Helens.
·	·	·	·	·	·	·	·	Gerard's Bridge Siding ...	Lancs	L. & N. W.	St. Helens.
								Pilkington's—			
·	·	·	·	·	·	·	·	Mill Lane Siding	Lancs	L. & N. W.	Rainford Village.
·	·	·	·	·	·	·	·	Sand Siding	Lancs	L. & N. W.	Rainford Village.
·	·	·	·	·	·	·	·	Yard	Lancs	L. & N. W.	Rainford Village.
·	·	·	·	·	·	·	·	Pilkington's Siding	Lancs	L. & Y.	Town Green.
·	·	·	·	·	·	·	·	Pilkington's Works	Lancs	L. & N. W.—S. & M. Jt.	See United Alkali Co. (Widnes).
·	·	·	·	·	·	·	·	Pilkington Tile and Pottery Co.'s Siding..................	Lancs	{ L. & Y. { L. & N. W.	Clifton Junction. Patricroft.
G	P	·	·	·	·	1	10	Pill	Somerset...	G. W.	Bristol and Portishead.
·	·	·	·	·	·	·	·	Pillgwenlly Foundry............	Mon........	A (N & SW) D. & R.—GW	Same as Jordan's Foundry (Newport).
G	P	F	L	H	C	0	10	Pilling	Lancs	G. & K. E.	Terminus.
G	P	·	·	·	·	·	·	Pilmoor............	Yorks	N. E.	York and Thirsk.
·	·	·	·	·	·	·	·	Bishophouse Junction	Yorks	N. E.	Pilmoor.
·	·	·	·	·	·	·	·	Sessay Wood Junction	Yorks	N. E.	Pilmoor.
·	·	·	·	·	·	·	·	Sessay Wood Siding........	Yorks	N. E.	Pilmoor.
·	·	·	·	·	·	·	·	Sunbeck Junction	Yorks	N. E.	Pilmoor and Gilling.
G	P	F	L	H	C	1	10	Pilning	Glo'ster ...	G. W.	Bristol and Severn Tunnel Junction.
·	·	·	·	·	·	·	·	Pilning Junction	Glo'ster ...	G. W.	Bristol and Severn Tunnel Junction.
·	·	·	·	·	·	·.	·	Pilrig	Edinboro'	Cal.	See Leith.

EXPLANATION—G *Goods Station.*   P *Passenger and Parcel Station.*   P* *Passenger, but not Parcel or Miscellaneous Traffic.*
F *Furniture Vans, Carriages, Portable Engines, and Machines on Wheels.*   L *Live Stock.*
H *Horse Boxes and Prize Cattle Vans.*   C *Carriages by Passenger Train.*

STATION ACCOMMODATION.						CRANE POWER.		STATIONS, &c.	COUNTY.	COMPANY.	POSITION.
						Tons	Cwts.				
G	P	.	.	.	.	.	.	Pilsley	Derby....	G. C.	Chesterfield and Nottingham.
.	.	.	.	.	.	.	.	Pilsley Colliery (G. C.)	Derby....	G. C.—G. N.—L. & N.W.	Pilsley.
.	.	.	.	.	.	.	.	Pilsley Colliery	Derby....	Mid.	Doe Hill.
.	.	.	.	.	.	.	.	Pilsley Colliery (G. C.).........	Derby....	G. C.—G. N.—L. & N.W.	Pilsley.
.	.	.	.	.	.	.	.	Pilsley Junction	Derby....	G. C.	Pilsley and Tibshelf Town.
.	.	.	.	.	.	.	.	Pilton Yard......................	Devon	Lyn. & Barns...........	See Barnstaple.
G	P	F	L	H	C	1	10	Pinchbeck	Lincoln ..	G. N. & G. E. Jt.	Spalding and Sleaford.
G	P	.	.	.	.	.	.	Pinchingthorpe	Yorks	N. E.	Middlesbro' and Guisboro'.
.	.	.	.	.	.	.	.	Powder Magazine	Yorks	N. E.	Pinchingthorpe.
.	.	.	.	.	.	.	.	Pindar Oaks Siding	Yorks	G. C.	Barnsley.
.	.	.	.	.	.	.	.	Pindars Siding	Lincoln ..	Axholme Jt (L & Y & N E)	Fockerby.
.	.	.	.	.	.	.	.	Pine & Son's Siding	Kent	S. E. & C.	Maidstone, West.
.	.	.	.	.	.	.	.	Pinfold Siding	Warwick..	L. & N. W.	Rugby.
.	.	.	.	.	.	.	.	Pingle Coal Wharf..........	Leicester..	Mid.	Leicester, West Bridge.
G	P	.	.	.	.	.	.	Pinhoe	Devon	L. & S.W.	Yeovil Junction and Exeter.
.	.	.	.	.	.	.	.	Poltimore Siding (Sander's Brick Works)............	Devon	L. & S.W.	Pinhoe.
.	P	.	.	.	.	.	.	Pinkhill	Edinboro'	N. B.	Haymarket and Corstorphine.
.	.	.	.	.	.	.	.	Pinkston Depôt	Lanark ..	N. B.	See Glasgow, Port Dundas.
.	.	.	.	.	.	.	.	Pinkston Electric Power Sta.	Lanark ..	Cal.	Glasgow, Buchanan Street.
.	.	.	.	.	.	.	.	Pinkston Power Station Sid.	Lanark ..	N. B.	Glasgow, Port Dundas.
G	P	.	L	H	.	1	10	Pinmore	Ayr	G. & S.W.	Girvan and Barrhill.
G	P	F	L	H	C	1	10	Pinner (Met.)	Middlesex	{ Met.	Harrow-on-the-Hill and Rickmansworth.
.	P	.	.	H	C	.	.			{ G. C.	Over Met. Line.
G	P	.	.	.	.	.	.	Pinner and Hatch End........	Middlesex	L. & N. W.	Watford and Willesden.
.	.	.	.	.	.	.	.	Pinnox Junction..............	Staffs	N. S.	Tunstall.
G	P	F	L	H	C	1	10	Pinwherry	Ayr	G. & S.W.	Girvan and Barrhill.
G	P	.	.	.	.	.	.	Pinxton and Selston	Notts	Mid.	Mansfield and Codnor Park.
.	.	.	.	.	.	.	.	Bentinck Colliery	Notts	Mid.	Near Pinxton.
.	.	.	.	.	.	.	.	Birchwood Upper Colliery..	Notts	Mid.	Near Pinxton.
.	.	.	.	.	.	.	.	Langton Colliery	Notts	Mid.	Near Pinxton.
.	.	.	.	.	.	.	.	Pinxton Colliery..........	Notts	Mid.	Near Pinxton.
.	.	.	.	.	.	.	.	Portland Collieries	Notts	Mid.	Near Pinxton.
.	.	.	.	.	.	.	.	Sleights Colliery	Notts	Mid.	Mansfield and Codnor Park.
.	.	.	.	.	.	.	.	Pinxton (G. C.)	Notts	G. C.—L. & N. W........	See Kirkby and Pinxton.
.	.	.	.	.	.	.	.	Pinxton Collieries	Derby	G. N.	Pinxton Wharf.
.	.	.	.	.	.	.	.	Pinxton Colliery (G. C.)	Derby	G. C.—L. & N. W........	Kirkby and Pinxton.
G	P	F	L	H	C	.	.	Pinxton Wharf	Notts	G. N.	Branch from Kimberley.
.	.	.	.	.	.	.	.	Palmerston Siding (for Pinxton Collieries).........	Notts	G. N.	Codnor Park and Pinxton.
.	.	.	.	.	.	.	.	Pinxton Collieries	Derby	G. N.	Pinxton and Pye Hill.
.	.	.	.	.	.	.	.	Pioneer Foundry (Smith, Patterson & Co.)	Durham ..	N. E.	Blaydon.
G	P	F	L	H	C	5	0	Pipe Gate (N. S.)	Salop	{ N. S.	Stoke and Market Drayton.
G	.	.	.	.	.	.	.			{ G. W.	Over N. S. Line.
G	.	.	.	.	.	.	.	Pirbright Junction	Surrey	L. & S.W.	Brookwood and Farnborough.
G	.	.	L	.	.	.	.	Pirton Sidings	Worcester	Mid.	Wadborough and Defford.
.	.	.	.	.	.	.	.	Pistil Lime Works..............	Carmarth'	G. W.	Llandebie.
G	P	F	L	H	C	1	5	Pitcaple	Aberdeen	G. N. of S.	Inveramsay and Keith.
.	.	.	.	.	.	.	.	Pit Close Colliery	Durham ..	N. E.	Evenwood.
.	P	.	.	.	.	.	.	Pitfodels	Aberdeen	G. N. of S.	Aberdeen and Culter.
.	.	.	.	.	.	.	.	Pitfour Brick Works	Perth	Cal.	Glencarse.
G	P	F	L	H	C	5	0	Pitlochry	Perth	High.	Dunkeld and Blair Atholl.
G	P	.	L	H	.	1	10	Pitlurg	Aberdeen	G. N. of S.	Ellon and Boddam.
.	.	.	.	.	.	.	.	Pitnappie Siding	Forfar	Cal.	See Auchterhouse.
G	P	F	L	H	C	.	.	Pitsea	Essex	L. T. & S.	Tilbury and Southend-on-Sea.
.	.	.	.	.	.	.	.	Pitsea Junction	Essex	L. T. & S.	Benfleet and Stanford.
G	P	F	L	H	C	.	.	Pitsford and Brampton	N'hamptn	L. & N. W.	Market Harboro' and Northampton.
.	.	.	.	.	.	.	.	Pitt & Co.'s Siding	Yorks	Mid.	Leeds, Newlay and Horsforth.
.	.	.	.	.	.	.	.	Pittencrieff Colliery (Colton Coal Depôt)............	Fife	N. B.	Whitemyre Junction Station.
G	P	F	L	H	C	1	10	Pittenweem	Fife	N. B.	Leven and Anstruther.
G	P	.	L	.	.	.	.	Pittington	Durham ..	N. E.	Durham (Elvet) and Sunderland.
.	.	.	.	.	.	.	.	Broomside Junction	Durham ..	N. E.	Pittington.
.	.	.	.	.	.	.	.	Pitts, A. G., Brick Works ...	Somerset..	S.&D.Jt.(L.&S.W.& Mid)	Highbridge.
.	P	.	.	.	.	.	.	Pitts Hill	Staffs	N. S.	Goldenhill and Tunstall.
.	.	.	.	.	.	.	.	Place & Son's Siding........	Lancs	L. & Y.	Same as Hoddlesden Sid. (Darwen).
.	.	.	.	.	.	.	.	Plasycoed Colliery	Mon	G. W.	Pontnewynydd.
G	P	.	L	H	.	.	.	Plaidy	Aberdeen	G. N. of S.	Inveramsay and Macduff.
.	P	.	.	H	.	.	.	Plains	Lanark ..	N. B.	Airdrie, South and Caldercruix.
.	.	.	.	.	.	.	.	Plains Siding	Lanark ..	N. B.	Brownieside Weighs.

EXPLANATION—G Goods Station.   P Passenger and Parcel Station.   P* Passenger, but not Parcel or Miscellaneous Traffic.
F Furniture Vans, Carriages, Portable Engines, and Machines on Wheels.   L Live Stock.
H Horse Boxes and Prize Cattle Vans.   C Carriages by Passenger Train.

G	P	F	L	H	C	Tons	Cwts	STATIONS, &c.	COUNTY.	COMPANY.	POSITION.
.	P	.	.	.	.	.	.	Plaistow (L. T. & S.)	Essex	{ L. T. & S. / N. L.	Commercial Road and Barking. / Over L. T. & S. from Bromley Junc.
.	.	.	.	.	.	.	.	Plan Collieries	Ayr	G. & S. W.	Crosshouse.
.	.	.	.	.	.	.	.	Planet Foundry Co.'s Siding (L. & N. W.)	Lancs	L. & N. W.—G. C.	Guide Bridge.
.	P	.	.	.	.	.	.	Plan Fire-Clay Works	Ayr	G. & S. W.	Crosshouse.
.	.	.	.	.	.	.	.	Plank Lane	Lancs	L. & N. W.	Pennington and Platt Bridge.
.	.	.	.	.	.	.	.	Plank Lane Colliery	Lancs	L. & N. W.	Same as Ackers, Whitley & Co.'s Bickershaw Col. (Leigh & Bedford).
.	.	.	.	.	.	.	.	Plank Lane Junction	Lancs	G. C. (Wigan Jn.)—L N W	West Leigh and Kenyon Jn. Station.
.	.	.	.	.	.	.	.	Plantain or Simon Wood Col.	Yorks	G. C.	Same as Elsecar High Pit (Elsecar).
.	.	.	.	.	.	.	.	Plantation Foundry (G & P Jt.)	Lanark	{ Cal. / G. & S. W.	Glasgow, Kinning Park. / Glasgow, General Terminus.
.	.	.	.	.	.	.	.	Plantation Quay (Cal.)	Lanark	Cal.—G. & S. W.—N. B.	See Glasgow.
G	P	.	.	.	.	.	.	Plasbach Colliery	Carmarth'	B. P. & G. V.	Pontyeats.
.	.	.	.	.	.	.	.	Plashetts	Northumb	N. B.	Riccarton and Reedsmouth.
.	.	.	.	.	.	.	.	Plashetts Colliery	Northumb	N. B.	Plashetts.
.	.	.	.	.	.	.	.	Plasissa Colliery (G. W.)	Carmarth'	G. W.—L. & N. W.	Llangennech.
.	.	.	.	.	.	.	.	Plasmadoc Junction	Denbigh	G. W.	Ruabon.
.	P	.	.	.	.	.	.	Plasmadoc Sidings	Denbigh	G. W.	Ruabon.
G	P	.	.	.	.	.	.	Plas Marl	Glamorg'n	G. W.	Swansea and Morriston.
G	P	.	.	.	.	.	.	Plas Power	Denbigh	{ G. W. / W. M. & C. Q.	Wrexham and Brymbo. / Brymbo and Wrexham.
.	.	.	.	.	.	.	.	Broughton Colliery	Denbigh	G. W.	Plas Power and Brymbo.
.	.	.	.	.	.	.	.	Broughton Solway Coke Works	Denbigh	G. W.	Plas Power and Brymbo.
.	.	.	.	.	.	.	.	Gatewen Colliery	Denbigh	{ G. W. / W. M. & C. Q.	Moss Valley Junction and Moss. / Brymbo Branch.
.	.	.	.	.	.	.	.	New Broughton Colliery	Denbigh	{ G. W. / W. M. & C. Q.	Wrexham and Plas Power. / Brymbo Branch.
.	.	.	.	.	.	.	.	Plas Power Colliery	Denbigh	{ G. W. / W. M. & C. Q.	Plas Power and Brymbo. / Brymbo Branch.
.	.	.	.	.	.	.	.	Plas Power Junction	Denbigh	G. W.—W. M. & C. Q.	Brymbo and Wrexham.
.	.	.	.	.	.	.	.	Plas-yn-wern	Denbigh	G. W.	Rhos.
.	P	.	.	.	.	.	.	Platt Bridge	Lancs	G. C. (Wigan Jn.)	See Hindley and Platt Bridge.
.	.	.	.	.	.	.	.	Platt Bridge	Lancs	L. & N. W.	Tyldesley and Wigan.
.	.	.	.	.	.	.	.	Platt Bros. & Co.'s Siding	Lancs	L. & Y.	Same as Moston Colliery (Newton Heath).
.	.	.	.	.	.	.	.	Platt Bros. & Co.'s Siding	Lancs	L. & Y.	Shaw and New Hey.
.	.	.	.	.	.	.	.	Platt's Siding	Lancs	L. & Y.	Appley Bridge.
.	.	.	.	.	.	.	.	Platt's Siding	Lancs	L. & Y.	Burscough Junction Station.
G	P	.	.	.	.	1	0	Platt's Siding	Lancs	L. & Y.	Oldham, Werneth.
.	.	.	.	.	.	.	.	Plawsworth	Durham	N. E.	Newcastle and Durham.
.	.	.	.	.	.	.	.	Kimblesworth Colliery	Durham	N. E.	Plawsworth.
.	.	.	.	.	.	.	.	Player & Co.'s Foundry (Mid.)	Glamorg'n	Mid.—G. W.—L. & N. W.	Same as Clydach Foundry Tin Plate Co.'s Siding (Clydach-on-Tawe).
.	.	.	.	.	.	.	.	Playne's Cloth Mill	Glo'ster	Mid.	Same as Dunkirk Cloth Mill (Nailsworth).
G	P	.	.	.	.	.	.	Plealey Road	Salop	S. & W'pl Jt. (GW & LNW)	Hanwood and Minsterley.
.	P	.	.	.	.	.	.	Plean (for Cowie)	Stirling	Cal.	Larbert and Bannockburn.
G	.	.	L	.	.	1	10	Plean Junction Station	Stirling	Cal.	Larbert and Bannockburn.
.	.	.	.	.	.	.	.	Bannockburn Colliery	Stirling	Cal.	Plean Junction.
.	.	.	.	.	.	.	.	Bannockburn Colliery No. 3	Stirling	Cal.	Plean Junction.
.	.	.	.	.	.	.	.	Cadgers Loan Quarry	Stirling	Cal.	Branch at Plean Junction.
.	.	.	.	.	.	.	.	Carnock Colliery	Stirling	Cal.	Branch at Plean Junction.
.	.	.	.	.	.	.	.	Dunmore Quarry	Stirling	Cal.	Plean Junction.
.	.	.	.	.	.	.	.	Plean Colliery No. 4	Stirling	Cal.	Plean Junction.
.	.	.	.	.	.	.	.	Plean East Pit & Coke Ovens	Stirling	Cal.	Branch at Plean Junction.
.	.	.	.	.	.	.	.	Plean East Siding	Stirling	Cal.	Branch at Plean Junction.
.	.	.	.	.	.	.	.	Plean Junction Weighs	Stirling	Cal.	Plean Junction.
.	.	.	.	.	.	.	.	Plean Quarry	Stirling	Cal.	Branch at Plean Junction.
.	P	.	.	.	.	.	.	Polmaise Quarry	Stirling	Cal.	Plean Junction.
G	P	F	L	H	C	.	.	Pleasington	Lancs	L. & Y.	Preston and Blackburn.
G	P	.	.	.	.	.	.	Pleasley	Derby	{ G. N. / Mid.	Sutton-in-Ashfield and Shirebrook. / Glapwell and Mansfield.
.	.	.	.	.	.	.	.	Pleasley Colliery	Derby	Mid.	Pleasley and Teversall.
.	.	.	.	.	.	.	.	Pleasley Colliery (G. N.)	Derby	G. N.—G. C.	Pleasley and Skegby.
.	.	.	.	.	.	.	.	Pleasley Vale Sidings (W. Hollins & Co.) (Mid.)	Notts	Mid.—G. C.	Mansfield Woodhouse.
.	P	.	.	.	.	.	.	Pleck	Staffs	L. & N. W.	Walsall and Wolverhampton.
.	.	.	.	.	.	.	.	Pienty & Son's Siding	Berks	G. W.	Newbury.
G	P	F	L	H	C	.	.	Plessey	Northumb	N. E.	Newcastle and Morpeth.

EXPLANATION—G *Goods Station.*   P *Passenger and Parcel Station.*   P* *Passenger, but not Parcel or Miscellaneous Traffic.*
F *Furniture Vans, Carriages, Portable Engines, and Machines on Wheels.*   L *Live Stock.*
H *Horse Boxes and Prize Cattle Vans.*   C *Carriages by Passenger Train.*

STATION ACCOMMODATION.						CRANE POWER.	STATIONS, &c.	COUNTY.	COMPANY.	POSITION.
						Tons Cwts.	Plews & Son's Brewery.........	Yorks	N. E.	Same as Vale of Mowbray Brewery (Leeming Bar).
G	P	F	L	H	C	1 10	Plockton	Ross & Cro'	High.	Dingwall and Kyle of Lochalsh.
G	P	.	.	.	.	5 0	Plodder Lane (for Farnworth)	Lancs	L. & N. W.	Bolton and Manchester.
							Earl of Ellesmere's—			
.	.	.	.	.	.	. .	Brackley Siding or Middle Hulton Colliery	Lancs	L. & N. W.	Plodder Lane and Little Hulton.
.	.	.	.	.	.	. .	Charlton Pit	Lancs	L. & N. W	Plodder Lane and Little Hulton.
.	.	.	.	.	.	. .	Roscoe's Peel Hall Colliery.	Lancs	L. & N. W.	Plodder Lane and Little Hulton.
.	.	.	.	.	.	. .	Scowcroft & Co.'s Highfield Siding	Lancs	L. & N. W.	Plodder Lane and Little Hulton.
G	P	F	L	.	.	6 0	Plowden	Salop	Bishop's Castle	Craven Arms and Bishop's Castle.
.	.	.	.	.	.	. .	Plowman & Son's Siding	Beds	Mid.	Henlow.
.	.	.	.	.	.	. .	Plowman, E., Siding	Essex	G. E.	Rayleigh.
.	.	.	.	.	.	. .	Plowman's, T. & M., Siding...	Hunts......	G. N.	Fletton.
.	.	.	.	.	.	. .	Plowman's, T. & M., Siding...	Middlesex	G. E.	Lower Edmonton.
G	P	.	L	.	.	. .	Pluck	Donegal ...	L. & L. S.	Tooban Junc. and Letterkenny.
G	P	F	L	H	C	5 0	Pluckley	Kent	S. E. & C.	Tonbridge and Ashford.
.	.	.	.	.	.	. .	Pluckley Brick Siding	Kent	S. E. & C.	Pluckley.
G	P	.	L	.	.	5 0	Plumbley	Cheshire ...	C. L. C. (G C, G N, & Mid.)	Northwich and Knutsford.
.	.	.	.	.	.	. .	Plumbley Colliery	Derby	Mid.	Eckington and Renishaw.
G	P	.	L	H	.	5 0	Plumpton.........................	Cumb'land	L. & N. W.	Carlisle and Penrith.
G	P	F	L	H	C	. .	Plumpton..........................	Sussex ...	L. B. & S. C.	Hayward's Heath and Lewes.
.	.	.	.	.	.	. .	Plumpton Siding	Lancs	Furness.....................	Ulverston.
.	.	.	.	.	.	. .	Plumptre Colliery	Derby	Mid.	See Butterley Co. (Langley Mill and Eastwood).
.	.	.	.	.	.	. .	Plumptre Colliery (G.N.)	Notts	G. N.—G. C.	Eastwood and Langley Mill.
.	P	.	.	.	.	. .	Plumstead	Kent	S. E. & C.	Woolwich and Dartford.
.	.	.	.	.	.	. .	Beadle Bros.' Siding	Kent	S. E. & C.	Plumstead.
.	.	.	.	.	.	. .	Woolwich Arsenal Siding..	Kent	S. E. & C.	Plumstead.
G	P	F	L	H	C	1 10	Plumtree	Notts	Mid.	Nottingham and Melton Mowbray.
							PLYMOUTH—			
.	.	.	.	.	.	. .	Anglo-American Oil Co.'s Depôt	Devon	L. & S.W.	Cattewater Harbour Branch.
.	.	.	.	.	.	. .	Bayly's Siding	Devon	G. W.	Sutton Harbour.
.	.	.	.	.	.	. .	Bayly's Siding..................	Devon	L. & S.W.	Oreston and Turnchapel Branch.
.	.	.	.	.	.	. .	Bayly's Wharf	Devon	G. W.	Sutton Harbour.
.	.	.	.	.	.	. .	Burnard & Alger's Wharf...	Devon	L. & S.W.	Cattewater Harbour Branch.
.	.	.	.	.	.	. .	Caldwell & Almond's Wharf	Devon	L. & S.W.	Cattewater Harbour Branch.
G	.	.	.	.	.	. .	Cattewater Harbour	Devon	L. & S.W.	Branch from Cattewater Junction.
.	.	.	.	.	.	. .	Cattewater Junction.........	Devon	G. W.—L. & S. W.	North Road and Plymstock.
.	.	.	.	.	.	. .	Corporation Electric Works	Devon	L. & S.W.	Cattewater Harbour Branch.
.	.	.	.	.	.	. .	Corporation Lime Works...	Devon	L. & S.W.	Cattewater Harbour Branch.
.	.	.	.	.	.	. .	Duke's Victoria Wharves...	Devon	L. & S.W.	Cattewater Harbour Branch.
.	.	.	.	.	.	. .	Ede & Son's Siding	Devon	G. W.	Sutton Harbour.
G	P	F	L	H	C	10 0	Friary	Devon	L. & S.W.	Terminus.
.	.	.	.	.	.	. .	Friary Junction	Devon	G. W.—L. & S. W.	Marsh Mills and Friary.
.	.	.	.	.	.	. .	Gibbs, Finch & Co.'s Wharf	Devon	L. & S.W.	Cattewater Harbour Branch.
G	.	.	.	.	.	12 0	Great Western Docks	Devon	G. W.	Extension from Millbay.
.	.	.	.	.	.	. .	H. M. Admiralty Wharf ...	Devon	L. & S.W.	Turnchapel.
.	.	.	.	.	.	. .	Laira	Devon	G. W.	Friary Junction and Marsh Mills.
.	.	.	.	.	.	. .	Laira Junction (G. W.)......	Devon	G. W.—L. & S. W.	Mutley and Marsh Mills.
.	.	.	.	.	.	. .	Lipson Junction...............	Devon	L. & S.W.	North Road and Sutton Harbour.
.	.	.	.	.	.	. .	Martin Bros.' Quay	Devon	L. & S.W.	Cattewater Harbour Branch.
.	.	.	.	.	.	. .	Martin Bros.' Siding.........	Devon	G. W.	Laira.
G	P	F	L	H	C	10 0	Millbay Station and Docks	Devon	G. W.	Terminus.
.	.	.	.	.	.	. .	Mount Gould Junction......	Devon	G. W.	Lipson Junction and Friary Junc.
.	P	.	.	.	.	. .	Mutley (G. W.)	Devon	{ G. W. ...... { L. & S. W.	North Road and Plympton. Over G. W. from Devonport Junc.
.	.	.	.	.	.	. .	Northey's Siding	Devon	G. W.	Sutton Harbour and Laira Junction.
.	.	.	.	.	.	. .	North Quay Wharves	Devon	{ G. W. ...... { L. & S. W.	Extension from Sutton Harbour. Branch from Friary.
.	P	.	.	H	C	. .	North Road.....................	Devon	G. W. & L. & S.W. Jt. ...	Mutley and Devonport.
G	P	.	.	.	.	. .	Oreston...........................	Devon	L. & S.W.	Friary and Turnchapel.
.	.	.	.	.	.	. .	Pethick's Yard and Quay...	Devon	L. & S.W.	Cattewater Harbour Branch.
G	P	F	L	.	.	. .	Plymstock (L. & S. W.)......	Devon	{ L. & S. W. ...... { G. W.	Friary and Turnchapel. North Road and Billacombe.
.	.	.	.	.	.	. .	Plymstock Junction	Devon	G. W.—L. & S. W.	Billacombe and Plymstock.
.	.	.	.	.	.	. .	South Junction	Devon	G. W.	Plymouth and Devonport.
.	.	.	.	.	.	. .	Sparrow & Co.'s Lime Kilns	Devon	L. & S.W.	Cattewater Harbour Branch.
G	.	.	.	.	.	2 0	Sutton Harbour	Devon	G. W.	Branch from Laira Junction.
G	.	.	.	.	.	10 0	Sutton Harbour	Devon	L. & S.W.	Branch from Friary.

EXPLANATION—G *Goods Station.*   P *Passenger and Parcel Station.*   P* *Passenger, out not Parcel or Miscellaneous Traffic.*
F *Furniture Vans, Carriages, Portable Engines, and Machines on Wheels.*   L *Live Stock.*
H *Horse Boxes and Prize Cattle Vans.*   C *Carriages by Passenger Train.*

STATION ACCOMMODATION.						CRANE POWER.		STATIONS, &c.	COUNTY.	COMPANY.	POSITION.
						Tons	Cwts.	PLYMOUTH—continued.			
G	P	.	.	.	.	.	.	Turnchapel	Devon	L. & S.W.	Branch from Friary.
.	.	.	.	.	.	.	.	West Junction	Devon	G. W.	Devonport Junction and North Rd.
.	.	.	.	.	.	.	.	Plymouth Corporation Electric Works	Devon	L. & S.W.	Plymouth, Cattewater Harbour.
.	.	.	.	.	.	.	.	Plymouth Corporation Lime Works	Devon	L. & S.W.	Plymouth, Cattewater Harbour.
.	.	.	.	.	.	.	.	Plymouth Siding	Glamorg'n	G. W.	Same as Hill's (Merthyr).
.	.	.	.	.	.	.	.	Plymouth Wharf	Glamorg'n	G. W.	Same as Burton & Son's (Cardiff.)
.	.	.	.	.	.	.	.	Plymouth Works and Collieries (Duffryn Siding) (T. V.) ...	Glamorg'n	T. V.—G. W.	Merthyr.
G	P	.	L	.	.	.	.	Plympton	Devon	G. W.	Plymouth and Totnes.
.	.	.	.	.	.	.	.	Plymstock (L. & S. W.) ...	Devon	L. & S.W.—G. W.	See Plymouth.
.	.	.	.	.	.	.	.	Plymstock Junction	Devon	G. W.—L. & S. W.	Plymouth.
.	.	.	.	.	.	.	.	Pochin & Co.'s Chemical Works (L. & N. W.)	Lancs	L. & N. W.—G. W.	Warrington, Bank Quay.
.	.	.	.	.	.	.	.	Pochin Pits	Mon	L. & N. W.	See Tredegar Iron & Coal Co. (Holly Bush).
.	.	.	.	.	.	.	.	Pochin's Siding	Cornwall ..	G. W.	{ Burngullow. { Melangoose Mill.
.	.	.	.	.	.	.	.	Pocket Nook Branch	Lancs	L. & N. W.	Carr Mill and Peasley Cross.
.	.	.	.	.	.	.	.	Pocket Nook Works	Lancs	G. C. (St. Helens Exten.)	See Union Plate Glass Co. (St. Helens.)
.	.	.	.	.	.	.	.	Pockett's Siding.................	Glamorg'n	GW—LNW—Mid—RSB	Same as Bristol Channel Steam Packet Co.'s Siding (Swansea).
G	P	F	L	H	C	5	0	Pocklington......................	Yorks	N. E.	York and Market Weighton.
.	.	.	.	.	.	.	.	Pocklington Flour Mill (Thirsk, J., & Son) ...	Yorks	N. E.	Pocklington.
.	.	.	.	.	.	.	.	Pocklington Gas Works ...	Yorks	N. E.	Pocklington.
.	.	.	.	.	.	.	.	Podmore	Staffs	N. S.	Halmerend and Leycett.
.	.	.	.	.	.	.	.	Midland Coal, Coke & Iron Co.'s Podmore Hall Col.	Staffs	N. S.	Podmore.
.	.	.	.	.	.	.	.	Podmore Hall Colliery	Staffs	N. S.	See Midland Coal, Coke & Iron Co. (Podmore).
.	.	.	.	.	.	.	.	Pogmoor Siding	Yorks	G. C.	Barnsley, Summer Lane.
.	.	.	.	.	.	.	.	Pointhouse Shipbuilding Yard (Inglis & Co.'s Shipbuilding Yard)................	Lanark ..	Cal.	Glasgow, Partick, Central.
.	.	.	.	.	.	.	.	Pointhouse Shipbuilding Yard (Inglis & Co.'s Shipbuilding Yard) (N.B.) ...	Lanark ..	N. B.—Cal.	Glasgow, Stobcross.
.	P	.	.	.	.	.	.	Point Pleasant	Northumb	N. E.	Loop—Newcastle and Percy Main.
.	.	.	.	.	.	.	.	Point Pleasant Junction	Surrey	L. & S.W.	Wandsworth and Putney.
.	.	.	.	.	.	.	.	Point Quarry Sidings	Glo'ster ...	S. & Wye Jt.(G. W. & Mid.)	Milkwall.
G	P	F	L	H	C	.	.	Pokesdown	Hants	L. & S.W.	Christchurch and Bournemouth.
.	P	.	.	.	.	.	.	Polegate	Sussex	L. B. & S. C.	Bexhill and Lewes.
.	.	.	.	.	.	.	.	Greatfield Siding	Sussex	L. B. & S. C.	Polegate and Hailsham.
G	P	F	L	H	C	.	.	Polesworth	Warwick..	L. & N. W.	Lichfield and Nuneaton.
.	.	.	.	.	.	.	.	Pooley Hall Colliery	Warwick..	L. & N. W.	Polesworth and Tamworth.
.	.	.	.	.	.	.	.	Polkemmet Collieries	L'lithgow	N. B.	Armadale.
.	.	.	.	.	.	.	.	Polkemmet Junction............	L'lithgow	N. B.	Bathgate, Upper and Whitburn.
.	.	.	.	.	.	.	.	Polkemmet Weighs	L'lithgow	N. B.	Bathgate, Upper and Armadale.
.	.	.	.	.	.	.	.	Pollard's Siding	Cornwall ..	G. W.	Newquay.
.	.	.	.	.	.	.	.	Pollington Colliery..............	Derby ...	Mid.	See Oakes & Co. (Langley Mill and Eastwood).
.	.	.	.	.	.	.	.	Pollington Colliery (G. N.) ...	Notts	G. N.—G. C.	Eastwood and Langley Mill.
.	.	.	.	.	.	.	.	Pollitt, S., & Co.'s Paper Wks.	Lancs	Furness	Ulverston.
.	.	.	.	.	.	.	.	Pollok Junction	Lanark ...	G. & P. Jt.—G. & S. W.	Glasgow, Ibrox & Eglinton Street.
G	P	F	L	H	C	4	0	Pollokshaws	Renfrew ...	G B & K Jt (Cal & G & S W)	Glasgow, South Side & Kennishead.
.	.	.	.	.	.	.	.	Pollokshaws Weighs	Renfrew ...	G B & K Jt (Cal & G & S W)	Pollokshaws.
.	.	.	.	.	.	.	.	Pollokshaws, East	Renfrew ...	Cal.	See Glasgow.
.	.	.	.	.	.	.	.	Pollokshields	Lanark ...	Cal.—G. & P. Jt.	See Glasgow.
.	.	.	.	.	.	.	.	Pollokshields, East..............	Lanark ...	Cal.	See Glasgow.
.	.	.	.	.	.	.	.	Pollokshields Junction	Lanark ...	Cal.	See Glasgow.
.	.	.	.	.	.	.	.	Pollokshields, West	Renfrew ...	Cal.	Glasgow.
.	.	.	.	.	.	.	.	Polmadie Brick Works........	Lanark ...	Cal.	See Glasgow.
.	.	.	.	.	.	.	.	Polmadie Saw Mills	Lanark ...	Cal.	Glasgow, South Side.
.	.	.	.	.	.	.	.	Polmadie Sidings	Lanark ...	Cal.	Glasgow, South Side.
.	.	.	.	.	.	.	.	Polmaise Colliery	Stirling ...	Cal.	Glasgow, South Side.
.	.	.	.	.	.	.	.	Polmaise Quarry..................	Stirling ...	Cal.	Stirling.
G	P	F	L	H	C	3	0	Polmont	Stirling ...	N. B.	Plean Junction Station.
.	.	.	.	.	.	.	.	Polmont Junction	Stirling ...	N. B.	Linlithgow and Falkirk.
											Polmont and Falkirk.

EXPLANATION—G *Goods Station.*   P *Passenger and Parcel Station.*   P* *Passenger, but not Parcel or Miscellaneous Traffic.*
F *Furniture Vans, Carriages, Portable Engines, and Machines on Wheels.*   L *Live Stock.*
H *Horse Boxes and Prize Cattle Vans.*   C *Carriages by Passenger Train.*

STATION ACCOMMODATION.						CRANE POWER.		STATIONS, &c.	COUNTY.	COMPANY.	POSITION.
						Tons	Cwts				
								Polquhairn Colliery	Ayr	G. & S.W.	Drongan.
								Polquhap Siding	Ayr	G. & S.W.	New Cumnock.
G	P							Polsham	Somerset	S.&D.Jt.(L.&S.W.& Mid)	Wells and Glastonbury.
								Poltimore Siding (Sander's Brick Works)	Devon	L. & S.W.	Pinhoe.
G	P		L	H		4	0	Polton	Edinboro'	N. B.	Branch from Hardengreen.
								Annandale's Mill	Edinboro'	N. B.	Lasswade and Polton.
								Kevock Mill	Edinboro'	N. B.	Lasswade and Polton.
								Springfield Mill	Edinboro'	N. B.	Polton.
								Polton No. 1 Siding	Edinboro'	N. B.	Same as Hopefield Sid. (Bonnyrigg).
								Polton No. 2 Colliery	Edinboro'	N. B.	Bonnyrigg.
								Polwarth's Siding	Hadding'n	N. B.	Same as Highlea Siding (Humbie).
G	P	F	L	H	C	2	0	Pomathorn	Edinboro'	N. B.	Hawthornden and Peebles.
								Loanstone Siding	Edinboro'	N. B.	Rosslynlee and Pomathorn.
G	P		L			1	10	Pomeroy	Tyrone	G. N. (I.)	Dungannon and Omagh.
G	P	F		H	C	2	0	Ponders End	Middlesex	G. E.	Tottenham and Waltham Cross.
								Enfield Gas Co.'s Siding	Middlesex	G. E.	Ponders End.
								Pond's Siding	Mon	L. & N. W.	See Rock Colliery (Blackwood).
								Pond's Wentlooge Colliery	Mon	L. & N. W.	Ynysddu.
								Pond Street (Mid.)	Yorks	Mid.—L. D. & E. C.	See Sheffield.
								Poneil Col. and Lime Works	Lanark	Cal.	Coalburn.
								Poneil Junction Siding	Lanark	Cal.	Douglas.
G	P		L	H		1	10	Ponfeigh	Lanark	Cal.	Lanark and Douglas.
								Douglas Colliery	Lanark	Cal.	Ponfeigh.
								Riggside Colliery	Lanark	Cal.	Ponfeigh and Douglas.
								Ponsandane Siding	Cornwall	G. W.	Penzance.
	P							Pontac	Jersey	Jersey Eastern	St. Helier and Gorey.
								Pontamman	Carmarth'	G. W.	See Ammanford.
								Pontamman Chemical Works	Carmarth'	G. W.	Ammanford.
G	P					3	0	Pontardawe (Mid.)	Glamorg'n	{ Mid. / G. W.	Glais and Ystalyfera. / Over Midland Line.
								Bryncoch & Wernddu Col. (Marchowel Col.) (Mid.)	Glamorg'n	Mid.—G. W.—L. & N. W.	Pontardawe.
								Bryn Tin Works (Mid.)	Glamorg'n	Mid.—G. W.—L. & N. W.	Pontardawe.
								Cwm Tawe Clay Works (Morgan & Son) (Mid.)	Glamorg'n	Mid.—G. W.—L. & N. W.	Pontardawe and Ystalyfera.
								Gellyonen Colliery Co.'s Collieries (Mid.)	Glamorg'n	Mid.—G. W.—L. & N. W.	Pontardawe.
								Gilbertson & Co.'s Sid. (Mid.)	Glamorg'n	Mid.—G. W.—L. & N. W.	Pontardawe.
								Glanrhyd Tin Plate Co.'s Siding (Mid.)	Glamorg'n	Mid.—G. W.—L. & N. W.	Pontardawe.
								Glantawe Iron & Tin Plate Works (Mid.)	Glamorg'n	Mid.—G. W.—L. & N. W.	Pontardawe.
								Lewis' Pontardawe Chemical Works (Mid.)	Glamorg'n	Mid.—G. W.—L. & N. W.	Pontardawe.
								So. Wales Primrose Coal Co.—Gwyn's Drift Col. (Mid.)	Glamorg'n	Mid.—G. W.—L. & N. W.	Pontardawe.
								Waen-y-Coed Sids. (Mid.)	Glamorg'n	Mid.—G. W.—L. & N. W.	Pontardawe.
								Ynismedwy Tin Plate Works (Mid.)	Glamorg'n	Mid.—G. W.—L. & N. W.	Pontardawe and Ystalyfera.
G	P		L	H	C			Pontardulais	Glamorg'n	G. W. & L. & N. W. Jt...	Llandilo and Swansea.
								Clayton Tin Plate Works	Glamorg'n	G. W. & L. & N. W. Jt...	Pontardulais.
								Harrop Benson's Foundry	Glamorg'n	G. W. & L. & N. W. Jt...	Glamorgan Tin Works.
								Teilo Tin Plate Co.'s Siding	Glamorg'n	G. W. & L. & N. W. Jt...	Pontardulais.
								Webb, Shakespeare & Williams' Glamorgan Tin Works	Glamorg'n	G. W. & L. & N. W. Jt...	Pontardulais.
								Pontardulais Junction	Glamorg'n	G. W.—L. & N. W.	Pantyffynnon and Swansea.
								Pontcynon Junction	Glamorg'n	T. V.	Penrhiwceiber.
G	P		L	H				Pontdolgoch	Montgom	Cam.	Newtown and Machynlleth.
								PONTEFRACT—			
G	P	F	L	H	C	5	0	Baghill (S. & K. Jt.)	Yorks	{ S. & K. Jt. (Mid. & N. E.)	Sheffield and York.
	P			H	C					G. C.	Over S. & K. Jt. from Swinton Junc.
	P			H	C					G. N.	Over N. E. & S. & K. Jt. Lines.
G										L. & Y.	Over S. & K. Jt. fr. Pontefract Junc.
								Carleton Coal & Brick Siding	Yorks	S. & K. Jt. (Mid. & N. E.)	Near Pontefract.
								Junction	Yorks	L. & Y.—S. & K. Jt.	Pontefract L. & Y. & S. & K. Jt. Stas.
G	P	F	L	H	C	3	0	Monkhill	Yorks	L. & Y.	Wakefield and Knottingley.
								Prince of Wales Col. (L. & Y.)	Yorks	L & Y—G N—Mid.—N E	Pontefract.
G	P	F	L	H	C	5	0	Pontesbury	Salop	S.&W'pl Jt.(GW& LNW)	Hanwood and Minsterley.
								Snailbeach District Railway Co.'s Exchange Siding	Salop	S.&W'pl Jt.(GW& LNW)	Pontesbury and Minsterley.

EXPLANATION—G *Goods Station.*   P *Passenger and Parcel Station.*   P* *Passenger, but not Parcel or Miscellaneous Traffic.*
F *Furniture Vans, Carriages, Portable Engines, and Machines on Wheels.*   L *Live Stock.*
H *Horse Boxes and Prize Cattle Vans.*   C *Carriages by Passenger Train.*

Station Accommodation						Crane Power		Stations, &c.	County.	Company.	Position.
						Tons	Cwts				
G	P							Pont Fadog	Denbigh	Glyn Valley	Chirk and Glynceiriog.
G	P*							Pontfaen	Denbigh	Glyn Valley	Chirk and Glynceiriog.
G	P							Ponthenry Colliery	Carmarth'	B. P. & G. V.	Pontyeats.
								Ponthir	Mon	G. W.	Caerleon and Llantarnam.
								Ponthir Tin Works Siding	Mon	G. W.	Ponthir.
								Pontithel Chemical Co.'s Siding (Cam.)	Brecon	Cam.—Mid.	Three Cocks.
G	P		L	H				Pontithel Chemical Works	Hereford	Mid.	Credenhill.
G	P	F	L*	H	C	1	10	Pont Llanio	Cardigan	M. & M.	Lampeter and Tregaron.
G		F				1	10	Pontlottyn (Rhy.)	Glamorg'n	Rhy.	Bargoed and Rhymney.
										L. & N. W.	Over Rhy. from Rhymney Joint Line Junction.
	P							Rhymney Merthyr Colliery	Glamorg'n	Rhy.	Pontlottyn.
	P							Pont Marquet	Jersey	Jersey	St. Helier and St. Aubin.
G	P							Pontnewydd	Mon	G. W.	Pontypool Road and Caerleon.
								Pontrhydyrun Tin Works Siding	Mon	G. W.	Pontnewydd and Pontypool Road.
G	P							Pontnewynydd	Mon	G. W.	Pontypool and Blaenavon.
								Blaensychan Colliery	Mon	G. W.	Branch from Pontnewynydd.
								Cwmffrwdoer Colliery	Mon	G. W.	Branch from Pontnewynydd.
								Elled Colliery	Mon	G. W.	Branch from Pontnewynydd.
								Gellydeg Sidings	Mon	G. W.	Branch from Pontnewynydd.
								Glynnantddu Colliery	Mon	G. W.	Branch from Pontnewynydd.
								Graigddu Brick Works Sid.	Mon	G. W.	Branch from Pontnewynydd.
								Greenland Colliery	Mon	G. W.	Branch from Pontnewynydd.
								Gwenallt Colliery	Mon	G. W.	Branch from Pontnewynydd.
								Oak Brick Works Siding	Mon	G. W.	Branch from Pontnewynydd.
								Partridge, Jones & Co.'s Llanerch Colliery (G.W.)	Mon	G. W.—L. & N. W.	Branch from Pontnewynydd.
								Plasycoed Colliery	Mon	G. W.	Branch from Pontnewynydd.
								Pontnewynydd Sheet and Galvanising Co.	Mon	G. W.	Branch from Pontnewynydd.
								Pontypool Tinplate Works	Mon	G. W.	Branch from Pontnewynydd.
								Tirpentwys Colliery	Mon	G. W.	Branch from Pontnewynydd.
								Tygwyn Llantwit Colliery	Mon	G. W.	Branch from Pontnewynydd.
								Pontoon Co.'s Siding	Glamorg'n	GW—LNW—Rhy—TV	Cardiff.
								Pontop and Jarrow Junction	Durham	N. E.	Jarrow.
								Pontop Colliery & Coke Works	Durham	N. E.	Annfield Plain.
G	P		L	H				Pontrhydyfen	Glamorg'n	R. & S. B.	Port Talbot and Cymmer.
								Argoed Colliery Siding	Glamorg'n	R. & S. B.	Pontrhydyfen.
								Cynon Colliery Siding	Glamorg'n	R. & S. B.	Pontrhydyfen.
	P							Pontrhydyrun	Mon	G. W.	Newport and Pontypool.
								Pontrhydyrun Tin Works Sid.	Mon	G. W.	Pontnewydd.
G	P		L			5	0	Pontrhythallt	Carnarvon	L. & N. W.	Carnarvon and Llanberis.
								Jones & Son's Siding	Carnarvon	L. & N. W.	Pontrhythallt and Pont Rug.
G	P	F	L	H	C	5	0	Pontrilas (G. W.)	Hereford	G. W.	Hereford and Abergavenny.
G						5	0			L. & N. W.	Over G. W. from Hereford.
								Pontrilas Chemical Works Siding	Hereford	G. W.	Pontrilas.
								Pontrilas Junction	Hereford	G. W.	Junction with Golden Valley Branch.
	P							Pont Rug	Carnarvon	L. & N. W.	Carnarvon and Llanberis.
	P							Pontsarn (for Vaynor)	Glamorg'n	B. & M. & L. & N. W. Joint	Merthyr and Morlais Junction.
								Pont Shon Norton Junction	Glamorg'n	T. V.	Pontypridd and Abercynon.
								Pontsmill Siding	Cornwall	G. W.	St. Blazey.
	P							Pontsticill	Glamorg'n	B. & M.	Dolygaer and Dowlais.
G								Pontyberem	Carmarth'	B. P. & G. V.	Pontyeats and Cwmmawr.
								Capel Ifan Colliery	Carmarth'	B. P. & G. V.	Pontyberem and Pontyeats.
								Pontyberem Colliery	Carmarth'	B. P. & G. V.	Pontyberem and Cwmmawr.
								Pontyberem	Carmarth'	L. & M. M.	Same as Cwmblawd.
								Pontybodkin Coal & Cannel Colliery	Flint	L. & N. W.	See South Level Sids. (Coed Talon).
								Pontyclerc Brick Works	Carmarth'	G. W.	Pantyffynnon.
								Pontyclerc Colliery	Carmarth'	G. W.	Pantyffynnon.
G	P		L			1	10	Pontycymmer (G. W.)	Glamorg'n	G. W.	Branch from Brynmenyn.
	P									P. T.	Over G. W. from Pont-y-rhyll Junc.
								Darran Fawr Col.	Glamorg'n	G. W.	Pontycymmer and Blaengarw.
								Ffaldau Nos. 1 & 2 Collieries	Glamorg'n	G. W.	Pontycymmer and Blaengarw.
								Pwllcarn Colliery	Glamorg'n	G. W.	Near Blaengarw.
								Victoria Colliery	Glamorg'n	G. W.	Pontycymmer and Blaengarw.
G								Pontyeats	Carmarth'	B. P. & G. V.	Burry Port and Pontyberem.
								Caepomprem Siding	Carmarth'	B. P. & G. V.	Pontyeats and Pontyberem.
								New Carway Colliery	Carmarth'	B. P. & G. V.	Branch from Carway Junction.

EXPLANATION—G *Goods Station.*   P *Passenger and Parcel Station.*   P* *Passenger, but not Parcel or Miscellaneous Traffic.*
F *Furniture Vans, Carriages, Portable Engines, and Machines on Wheels.*   L *Live Stock.*
L* *In full truck loads only.*   H *Horse Boxes and Prize Cattle Vans.*   C *Carriages by Passenger Train.*

STATION ACCOMMODATION.						CRANE POWER.		STATIONS, &c.	COUNTY.	COMPANY.	POSITION.
						Tons	Cwts.	Pontyeats—*continued.*			
..	..	..	..	..	..	..	..	Plasbach Colliery	Carmarth'	B. P. & G. V.	Pontyeats and Burry Port.
..	..	..	..	..	..	..	..	Ponthenry Colliery............	Carmarth'	B. P. & G. V.	Pontyeats and Pontyberem.
..	..	..	..	..	..	..	..	Pontyeats	Carmarth'	L. & M. M.	See Cynheidre (for Pontyeats).
..	..	..	..	..	..	..	..	Pontygwaith Siding	Glamorg'n	T. V.	Wattstown.
								Pontymister Steel Works (Monmouthshire Steel & Tin Plate Co.)	Mon	G. W.	Risca.
G	P	..	..	..	..	..	..	Pontypant	Carnarvon	L. & N. W.	Blaenau Festiniog and Llandudno Junction Station.
								PONTYPOOL— Baldwin's, Ltd.—			
..	..	..	..	..	..	..	..	Lower Mills Works	Mon	G. W.	Pontypool Road and Clarence Street.
..	..	..	..	..	..	..	..	Phœnix Works	Mon	G. W.	Pontypool Road and Clarence Street.
..	..	..	..	..	..	..	..	Blaendare Brick Works and Collieries	Mon	G. W.	Branch from Trosnant Junction.
G	P	..	..	..	..	1	10	Clarence Street	Mon	G. W.	Pontypool Road and Crumlin, High Level.
..	..	..	..	..	..	..	..	Coedygric Junction	Mon	G. W.	Pontypool Road and Panteg.
G	P	F	L	H	C	1	10	Crane Street	Mon	G. W.	Newport and Blaenavon.
..	..	..	..	..	..	..	..	Glyn Pits	Mon	G. W.	Branch from Trosnant Junction.
..	..	..	..	..	..	..	..	Paton's Siding.................	Mon	G. W.	Pontypool Road.
G	P	F	L	H	C	10	0	Road (G. W.)	Mon	G. W.	Newport and Abergavenny.
G	..	..	..	..	..	10	0			L. & N. W.	Over G. W. from Hereford.
..	..	..	..	..	..	..	..	Pontypool Tin Plate Works..	Mon	G. W.	Pontnewynydd.
								PONTYPRIDD—			
	P	..	..	..	..	..	..	(Station)	Glamorg'n	Barry	Efail-Isaf and Hafod Junction.
G	P	F	L	H	C	2	10	(Station, T. V.)	Glamorg'n	T. V.	Merthyr and Cardiff.
..	P	..	..	H	C	..	..			G W (A (N & S W) D & R)	Over B. & M., Rhy., & T. V. Lines.
..	..	..	..	..	..	..	..	Craig-yr-Hesk Quarry (Mackay's)	Glamorg'n	T. V.	Pontypridd and Abercynon.
..	..	..	..	..	..	..	..	Maritime Colliery	Glamorg'n	T. V.	Pontypridd and Hafod.
..	..	..	..	..	..	..	..	Newbridge Rhondda Brewery Co.'s Siding.....	Glamorg'n	T. V.	Pontypridd.
..	..	..	..	..	..	..	..	Penrhiw Colliery	Glamorg'n	T. V.	Pontypridd and Hafod.
..	..	..	..	..	..	..	..	Pontypridd Gas Works	Glamorg'n	A. (N. & S. W.) D. & R.	Glyntaff.
..	..	..	..	..	..	..	..	Pontypridd Interchange Sid.	Glamorg'n	A. (N. & S. W.) D. & R.	Glyntaff.
..	..	..	..	..	..	..	..	Pontypridd Junction............	Glamorg'n	A.(N&SW)D.&R.—T.V.	Glyntaff and Pontypridd.
..	..	..	..	..	..	..	..	Pontypridd North Curve Jn.	Glamorg'n	T. V.	Pontypridd and Abercynon.
G	P	..	..	..	..	..	..	Pontyrhyll (G. W.)..............	Glamorg'n	G. W.	Brynmenyn and Pontycymmer.
..	P	..	..	..	..	..	..			P. T.	Over G. W. from Pontyrhyll Junc.
..	..	..	..	..	..	..	..	Braich-y-Cymmer Colliery	Glamorg'n	G. W.	Pontyrhyll and Pontycymmer.
..	..	..	..	..	..	..	..	Garw Colliery	Glamorg'n	G. W.	Pontyrhyll and Pontycymmer.
..	..	..	..	..	..	..	..	West Rhondda Colliery......	Glamorg'n	G. W.	Pontyrhyll.
..	..	..	..	..	..	..	..	Pontyrhyll Junction	Glamorg'n	G. W.—P. T.	Pontyrhyll and Garth.
G	P	F	L	H	C	10	0	Pool	Yorks	N. E.	Harrogate and Ilkley.
G	..	..	..	..	..	..	..	Pool Dam	Staffs	N. S.	Branch—Newcastle and Silverdale.
..	..	..	..	..	..	..	..	Knutton Iron & Steel Co.'s Siding	Staffs	N. S.	Pool Dam.
..	..	..	..	..	..	..	..	Newcastle Gas Works	Staffs	N. S.	Pool Dam.
..	..	..	..	..	..	..	..	Silvester & Co.'s Foundry..	Staffs	N. S.	Pool Dam.
G	P	F	L	H	C	5	0	Poole (for Longfleet) (L & SW)	Dorset......	L. & S. W.	Bournemouth and Wimborne.
										S & DJt (L&SW & Mid)	Over L. & S. W. from Broadstone Jn.
..	..	..	..	..	..	..	..	Holes Bay Junction	Dorset......	L. & S.W.	Poole and Hamworthy Junction.
G	..	..	..	..	..	..	..	Poole Quay	Dorset......	L. & S.W.	Poole.
..	..	..	..	..	..	..	..	Poole Siding	Somerset..	G. W.	Wellington.
..	..	..	..	..	..	..	..	Poole's Siding....................	Cheshire..	L. & N. W.	Wrenbury.
..	..	..	..	..	..	..	..	Poole's Siding....................	Glamorg'n	G W—LN W—Rhy—T V	Cardiff.
G	P	..	L	..	..	..	..	Poolewe...........................	Ross & Cro'	Cal.	Steamer from Oban.
G	P	..	L	..	..	..	..			High.	Steamer from Kyle of Lochalsh.
G	P	..	..	..	..	..	..			N. B.	Steamer from Mallaig.
..	..	..	..	..	..	..	..	Pooley & Son's Works	Staffs	N. S.	See Trubshaw's Siding (Harecastle).
..	..	..	..	..	..	..	..	Pooley Hall Colliery	Warwick..	L. & N. W.	Polesworth.
G	P	..	L	H	..	..	..	Pool Quay	Montgom	Cam.	Oswestry and Welshpool.
..	..	..	..	..	..	..	..	Pope & Pearson's Collieries...	Yorks	N. E.	Castleford.
..	..	..	..	..	..	..	..	Pope & Pearson's Colliery ...	Yorks	Mid.	Normanton.
..	..	..	..	..	..	..	..	Pope's Siding	Surrey ...	S. E. & C......................	Red Hill.
..	..	..	..	..	..	..	..	Pope Street	Kent	S. E. & C......................	See New Eltham and Pope Street.
..	..	..	..	..	..	..	..	Poplar	Middlesex	G E—G W—Mid.—N L	See London.
..	..	..	..	..	..	..	..	Poplar Dock	Middlesex	GN—GW—L&NW—Mid —N. L.	See London.
..	..	..	..	..	..	..	..	Poplar Walk Siding	Surrey ...	S. E. & C......................	Herne Hill.

EXPLANATION—G *Goods Station.*   P *Passenger and Parcel Station.*   P* *Passenger, but not Parcel or Miscellaneous Traffic.*
F *Furniture Vans, Carriages, Portable Engines, and Machines on Wheels.*   F* *Furniture Vans excepted.*   L *Live Stock.*
H *Horse Boxes and Prize Cattle Vans.*   C *Carriages by Passenger Train.*

\multicolumn{6}{c}{STATION ACCOMMODATION.}						CRANE POWER.	STATIONS, &c.	COUNTY.	COMPANY.	POSITION.
G	P	.	L	H	.	. .	Poppleton	Yorks	N. E.	York and Knaresborough.
.	.	.	.	.	.	. .	Poppleton's Siding (Mid)	Lincoln	Mid.—G. C.—G. N.	Lincoln.
							Porritt & Son's—			
.	.	.	.	.	.	. .	Siding	Lancs	L. & Y.	Helmshore.
.	P	.	.	.	.	. .	Siding	Lancs	P.&W.Jt.(L&Y&L&NW)	Kirkham.
.	P	.	.	.	.	. .	Port	Donegal	Donegal	Donegal and Killybegs.
G	P	F	L	H	C	4 10	Portadown	Armagh	G. N. (I.)	Belfast and Armagh.
G	P	F	L	H	C	. .	Portarlington	Queens	G. S. & W.	Kildare and Maryborough.
G	P	F	L	H	C	. .	Portbury	Somerset	G. W.	Bristol and Portishead.
G	P	.	L	.	.	. .	Port Carlisle	Cumb'land	N. B.	Branch from Drumburgh.
.	.	.	.	.	.	. .	Port Carlisle Junction	Cumb'land	Cal.—N. B.	Carlisle.
.	P	.	.	.	.	. .	Portchester	Hants	L. & S.W.	Fareham and Portsmouth.
G	P	.	L	.	.	1 10	Port Clarence	Durham	N. E.	Branch near Billingham.
.	.	.	.	.	.	. .	Anderston Foundry	Durham	N. E.	Port Clarence.
							Bell Bros.'—			
.	.	.	.	.	.	. .	Clarence Iron&SteelWks.	Durham	N. E.	Port Clarence.
.	.	.	.	.	.	. .	Clarence Soda Works	Durham	N. E.	Port Clarence.
							Clarence Salt Works (Salt			
.	.	.	.	.	.	. .	Union, Ltd.)	Durham	N. E.	Port Clarence.
							Cowpen Salt Works			
.	.	.	.	.	.	. .	(United Alkali Co.)	Durham	N. E.	Port Clarence.
.	.	.	.	.	.	. .	Portcreek or Hilsea Junction	Hants	L.& S.W. & L.B.& S.C.Jt.—L. B. & S. C.	Portsmouth and Havant.
G	P	F	L	H	C	1 0	Port Dinorwic	Carnarvon	L. & N. W.	Bangor and Carnarvon.
							Assheton-Smith's Port Dinorwic Quay	Carnarvon	L. & N. W.	Port Dinorwic and Treborth.
.	.	.	.	.	.	. .	Port Dinorwic Quay	Carnarvon	L. & N. W.	Same as Assheton-Smith's (Port Dinorwic).
.	.	.	.	.	.	. .	Port Downie Iron Works	Stirling	Cal.—N. B.	Falkirk, Camelon.
.	.	.	.	.	.	. .	Port Dundas	Lanark	Cal.—N. B.	See Glasgow.
.	.	.	.	.	.	. .	Port Dundas Distillery	Lanark	N. B.	Glasgow, Port Dundas.
.	.	.	.	.	.	. .	Port Edgar Siding	L'lithgow	N. B.	South Queensferry.
.	.	.	.	.	.	. .	Port Eglinton Depôt	Renfrew	G. & S.W.	See Glasgow.
							Port Eglinton Foundry (Eglinton Foundry, McLaren's)	Renfrew	{ Cal. { G. & S. W.	Glasgow, South Side. / Glasgow, Cook Street.
.	.	.	.	.	.	. .	Port Eglinton Junction	Lanark	G. & S.W.	Glasgow.
.	.	.	.	.	.	. .	Port Elphinstone	Aberdeen	G. N. of S.	See Inverurie.
.	.	.	.	.	.	. .	Porterfield	Renfrew	G.&P.Jt.(Cal.&G.&S.W.)	See Renfrew.
							Porterfield Siding (Babcock & Wilcox's) (G. & S. W.)	Renfrew	G. & S.W.—Cal.	Renfrew.
G	P	F*	L	.	.	. .	Port Erin	I. of Man	I. of Man	Terminus.
.	.	.	.	.	.	. .	Porter, J., Siding	Cambs	G. E.	Haddenham.
.	.	.	.	.	.	. .	Porterockney Siding	Perth	Cal.	See Alyth.
G	P	.	L	.	.	5 0	Portesham	Dorset	G. W.	Upwey and Abbotsbury.
G	P	.	L	H	C	1 5}	Portessie	Banff	{ G. N. of S. { High.	Portsoy and Elgin. / Buckie and Portessie Junction.
G	P	F	L	H	C	1 5}				
.	.	.	.	.	.	. .	Portessie Junction	Banff	G. N. of S.—High	Findochty and Buckie.
							PORT GLASGOW—			
G	P	.	L	.	.	15 0	(Station)	Renfrew	Cal.	Paisley and Greenock.
.	.	.	.	.	.	. .	Clyde Pottery Co.'s Siding (G. & S. W.)	Renfrew	G. & S.W.—N. B.	Inchgreen.
.	.	.	.	.	.	. .	Clyde Shipbuilding and Engineering Works	Renfrew	Cal.	Port Glasgow.
.	.	.	.	.	.	. .	Greenock Gas Works (G. & S. W.)	Renfrew	G. & S.W.—N. B.	Inchgreen.
G	.	F	L	.	.	4 0	Harbour	Renfrew	Cal.	Port Glasgow.
G	.	.	.	.	.	6 0}	Inchgreen (G. & S. W.)	Renfrew	{ G. & S. W. { N. B.	Garvel Dock Branch. / Over G.& S.W. from College East Jn.
G	.	.	.	.	.	6 0}				
.	.	.	.	.	.	25 0	James Watt Dock (Garvel Dock) (G. & S. W.)	Renfrew	{ G. & S. W. { N. B.	Branch from Cartsburn Junction. / Over G.& S.W. from College East Jn.
.	.	.	.	.	.	. .	McBride's Siding	Renfrew	Cal.	Port Glasgow and Greenock.
G	.	.	L	.	.	. .	McOnie's Siding	Renfrew	G. & S.W.	Inchgreen and James Watt Dock.
G	P	F	L	H	C	1 5	Upper	Renfrew	G. & S.W.	Greenock and Kilmalcolm.
G	P	F	L	H	C	2 0}	Portgordon	Banff	G. N. of S.	Portsoy and Elgin.
.	P	.	.	.	.		Porth (T. V.)	Glamorg'n	{ T. V. { Barry	Pontypridd and Treherbert. / Over T. V. from Hafod Junction.
.	.	.	.	.	.	. .	Aber Rhondda Colliery	Glamorg'n	T. V.	Porth and Ynishir.
							Coedcae Colliery (Lewis			
.	.	.	.	.	.	. .	Merthyr Colliery)	Glamorg'n	T. V.	Porth and Hafod.
							Cymmer Colliery or Old			
.	.	.	.	.	.	. .	Cymmer Colliery	Glamorg'n	T. V.	Porth and Hafod.

EXPLANATION—G *Goods Station.*　　P *Passenger and Parcel Station.*　　P* *Passenger, but not Parcel or Miscellaneous Traffic.*
F *Furniture Vans, Carriages, Portable Engines, and Machines on Wheels.*　　L *Live Stock.*
H *Horse Boxes and Prize Cattle Vans.*　　C *Carriages by Passenger Train.*

STATION ACCOMMODATION.						CRANE POWER.		STATIONS, &c.	COUNTY.	COMPANY.	POSITION.
						Tons	Cwts.	**Porth (T. V.)**—*continued.*			
								Cymmer Level or New Cymmer Colliery	Glamorg'n	T. V.	Porth and Hafod.
								Cymmer Upper Colliery	Glamorg'n	T. V.	Porth and Hafod.
								Dinas Colliery	Glamorg'n	T. V.	Dinas and Llwynypia.
								Eirw Gas Works (Porth Gas Works)	Glamorg'n	T. V.	Porth and Hafod.
								Tynewydd Colliery (Troedyrhiew Colliery)	Glamorg'n	T. V.	Porth and Dinas.
								Porth Gas Works	Glamorg'n	T. V.	Same as Eirw Gas Works (Porth).
G	P		L					Porthall	Donegal	G. N. (I.)	Strabane and Londonderry.
G	P		L	H	C	1	10	Porthcawl	Glamorg'n	G. W.	Branch from Pyle.
								Howell, Coath & Co.'s Lime Works	Glamorg'n	G. W.	Porthcawl.
	P*							Porthywaen	Salop	Cam. (Tanat Valley)	Oswestry and Llangynog.
								Porthywaen Junction	Salop	Cam—Cam (Tanat Valley)	Oswestry and Porthywaen.
G								Porthywaen Quarries	Salop	Cam.	Branch from Llynclys.
G	P	F	L	H	C	2	0	Port Isaac Road	Cornwall	L. & S.W.	Launceston and Wadebridge.
								Portishead	Somerset	G. W.	See Bristol.
								Portishead Docks	Somerset	G. W.	See Bristol.
								Portishead Gas Works	Somerset	G. W.	Bristol, Portishead.
G	P		L	H		2	0	Portknockie	Banff	G. N. of S.	Portsoy and Elgin.
G	P	F	L	H	C	10	0	Portland	Dorset	W. & P. Jt. (GW & L & SW)	Terminus.
								Admiralty Siding	Dorset	W. & P. Jt. (GW & L & SW)	Portland.
						10	0	Barnes, F. J., Siding	Dorset	W. & P. Jt. (GW & L & SW)	Portland
								Castleton Stone Siding	Dorset	W. & P. Jt. (GW & L & SW)	Portland.
								Whitehead & Co.'s Siding	Dorset	W. & P. Jt. (GW & L & SW)	Portland.
								Portland Cement Co.'s Siding	Glamorg'n	T. V.	Same as Cement Works (Penarth Town).
								Portland Collieries	Notts	Mid.	Pinxton.
								Portland Forge Siding	Ayr	G. & S.W.	Kilmarnock.
								Portland Iron Works	Ayr	G. & S.W.	Hurlford.
								Portland No. 4 and Brick Wks.	Ayr	G. & S.W.	Hurlford.
								Portland Nos. 5 and 8	Ayr	G. & S.W.	Hurlford.
								Portland Nos. 6 and 7	Ayr	G. & S.W.	Hurlford.
								Portland Road (Met.)	Middlesex	Met.—G. W.	See London.
								Portland's, Duke of—			
								Bleak Hills Siding	Notts	Mid.	Mansfield.
								Sidings (Mid.)	Derby	Mid.—G. C.	Whitwell.
								Portland Works (G. C.)	Notts	G. C.—G. N.—Mid.	Worksop.
G	P		L	H				Portlethen	Kinc'rdine	Cal.	Stonehaven and Aberdeen.
G	P	F	L	H	C	5	0	Portmadoc	Carnarvon	Cam.	Harlech and Pwllheli.
G	P		L		C	2	10	Portmadoc	Carnarvon	Festiniog	Terminus.
								Dock Extension	Carnarvon	Festiniog	Portmadoc.
								Syenite Quarry	Carnarvon	Cam.	Minffordd and Portmadoc.
	P							Portmarnock	Dublin	G. N. (I.)	Dublin and Drogheda.
								Portobello	Edinboro'	N. B.	See Edinburgh.
								Portobello Depôts	Durham	N. E.	Sunderland, Monkwearmouth.
								Portobello East & West Jns.	Edinboro'	N. B.	Edinburgh.
								Portobello Grease Works	Durham	N. E.	Sunderland, Monkwearmouth.
								Portobello Junction and Sids.	Middlesex	G. W.	London, Paddington.
								Portobello Saw Mills	Durham	N. E.	Sunderland, Monkwearmouth.
G	P		L	H		3	0	Port of Monteith	Stirling	N. B.	Stirling and Balloch.
G								Ladyland's Siding	Stirling	N. B.	Port of Monteith and Kippen.
G	P	F	L	H	C			Porton	Wilts	L. & S.W.	Andover Junction and Salisbury.
G	P	F	L	H	C	1	0	Portpatrick	Wigtown.	P.P. & W. Jt. (Cal., G&SW, L. & N. W. & Mid)	Terminus.
								Port Penrhyn Quay	Carnarvon	L. & N. W.	See Lord Penrhyn's (Bangor).
								Portrack Lane Siding	Durham	N. E.	Stockton, North Shore.
								Portrack Siding	Dumfries.	G. & S.W.	Holywood.
G								Portreath	Cornwall	G. W.	Branch from Carn Brea.
G	P		L					Portree	Inverness.	Cal.	Steamer from Oban.
G	P		L		C			Portree	Inverness.	High.	Steamer from Kyle of Lochalsh.
G	P		L					Portree	Inverness.	N. B.	Steamer from Mallaig.
G	P	F	L	H	C	2	0	Portrush	Antrim	N. C. Com. (Mid.)	Branch from Coleraine.
G	P	F*	L					Port St. Mary	I. of Man.	I. of Man	Douglas and Port Erin.
								Portsea Island Gas Co.'s Sid.	Hants	L. & S.W. & L.B. & S.C. Jt.	Portsmouth.
G	P		L	H				Portskewet	Mon	G. W.	Chepstow and Newport.
G	P		L	H		5	0	Portslade	Sussex	L. B. & S. C.	Brighton and Shoreham.
								PORTSMOUTH—			
	P							East Southsea	Hants	L. & S W & L B & S C Jt.	Branch from Fratton Junc. Station.
G	P	F	L			6	0	Fratton Junction Station	Hants	L. & S W & L B & S C Jt.	Havant and Portsmouth Town.

EXPLANATION—G *Goods Station.*   P *Passenger and Parcel Station.*   P* *Passenger, but not Parcel or Miscellaneous Traffic.*
F *Furniture Vans, Carriages, Portable Engines, and Machines on Wheels.*   F* *Furniture Vans excepted.*   L *Live Stock.*
H *Horse Boxes and Prize Cattle Vans.*   C *Carriages by Passenger Train.*

STATION ACCOMMODATION.						CRANE POWER.	STATIONS, &c.	COUNTY.	COMPANY.	POSITION.
						Tons Cwts.	PORTSMOUTH—*continued.*			
..	P	..	..	..	..	.. ..	Harbour	Hants	L. & S W & L B & S C Jt.	Terminus.
..	..	..	..	..	..	.. ..	H.M. Dockyard Siding	Hants	L. & S W & L B & S C Jt.	Portsmouth.
..	..	..	..	..	..	.. ..	H.M. Gunwharf Siding	Hants	L. & S W & L B & S C Jt.	Portsmouth.
G	P	F	L	H	C	10 0	Portsea Island Gas Co.'s Sid.	Hants	L. & S W & L B & S C Jt.	Fratton and Portcreek Junction.
G	P	..	L	H	..	5 0	Town	Hants	L. & S W & L B & S C Jt.	Havant and Portsmouth Harbour.
..	..	..	L	H	..	.. ..	Portsmouth	Lancs	L. & Y.	Burnley and Todmorden.
G	P	..	L	..	..	5 0	Stubley Siding	Lancs	L. & Y.	Near Portsmouth.
..	P	..	L	L	..	.. ..	Portsmouth Arms	Devon	L. & S.W.	Yeoford Junction and Barnstaple.
G	P	F	L	L	C	4 0	Port Soderick	I. of Man..	I. of Man	Douglas and Port Erin.
G	P	..	L	..	..	.. ..	Portsoy	Banff	G. N. of S.	Tillynaught and Elgin.
..	..	..	..	..	..	.. ..	Portstewart	Derry	N. C. Com. (Mid.)	Coleraine and Portrush.
..	..	..	..	..	..	.. ..	Port Sunlight Siding	Cheshire..	B'head Jt. (G W & L N W)	See Lever Bros. (Spital).
..	..	..	..	..	..	.. ..	PORT TALBOT—			
..	..	..	..	..	..	.. ..	Burrows Junction	Glamorg'n	P. T.—R. & S. B.	North Bank and Port Talbot (Aberavon).
G	P	..	L	..	C	.. ..	Celluloid Siding	Glamorg'n	P. T.	Port Talbot and Bryn.
..	..	..	..	..	..	.. ..	Central	Glamorg'n	P. T.	Terminus.
..	..	..	..	..	..	.. ..	Craigavon Colliery	Glamorg'n	P. T.	Port Talbot and Cwmavon.
..	..	..	..	..	..	.. ..	Cwmgwinea Colliery	Glamorg'n	P. T.	Port Talbot and Bryn.
..	..	..	..	..	..	.. ..	David, D. R., & Co.'s Siding	Glamorg'n	R. & S. B.	Over Dock Line.
..	..	..	..	..	..	.. ..	Davies, E., & Son's Ffrwdwyllt Tin Plate Works...	Glamorg'n	G. W.—P. T.—R. & S. B.	Port Talbot.
G	..	..	..	..	..	7 0	Dock	Glamorg'n	R. & S. B.	Branch from Port Talbot.
..	..	..	..	..	..	.. ..	Dyffryn Yard Sidings	Glamorg'n	P. T.	Port Talbot and Bryn.
..	..	..	..	..	..	.. ..	Glanwalia Siding (Aberavon Tin Plate Co.)	Glamorg'n	R. & S. B.	Port Talbot.
..	..	..	..	..	..	.. ..	Graving Dock Siding	Glamorg'n	R. & S. B.	Port Talbot Dock.
..	..	..	..	..	..	.. ..	Iron and Steel Works	Glamorg'n	G. W.—P. T.—R. & S. B.	Port Talbot.
..	..	..	..	..	..	.. ..	Junction	Glamorg'n	G. W.—P. T.	Margam and Port Talbot (North Bank, Goods).
..	..	..	..	..	..	.. ..	Junction	Glamorg'n	G. W.—R & S. B.	Port Talbot G. W. & R. & S. B. Stas.
..	..	..	..	..	..	.. ..	Lewis & David's Siding ...	Glamorg'n	R. & S. B.	Port Talbot.
..	..	..	..	..	..	.. ..	Mansel Siding (Byass, R. B., & Co.)	Glamorg'n	G. W.—P. T.—R. & S. B.	Port Talbot.
..	..	..	..	..	..	.. ..	Margam Colliery	Glamorg'n	G. W.	Margam Junction.
..	..	..	..	..	..	.. ..	Margam Copper Works...	Glamorg'n	G. W.	Port Talbot.
..	..	..	..	..	..	.. ..	Margam Forge	Glamorg'n	P. T.	Oakwood Junction.
..	..	..	..	..	..	.. ..	Margam Sand Siding......	Glamorg'n	G. W.	Port Talbot.
..	..	..	..	..	..	.. ..	Morfa Colliery	Glamorg'n	G. W.—P. T.	Margam Junction.
G	..	..	..	..	..	.. ..	Morfa Copper Works (Vivian's Loop Siding)...	Glamorg'n	P. T.	Margam Junction.
..	..	..	..	..	..	.. ..	North Bank..............	Glamorg'n	P. T.	Branch from Burrows Junction.
G	P	F	L	H	C	7 0	Old Dock Junction	Glamorg'n	G. W.—P. T.	Same as Port Talbot Junction.
G	P	..	..	..	..	7 0 }	Port Talbot (Aberavon) (R. & S. B.) }	Glamorg'n	{ R. & S. B. P. T.	Cymmer and Swansea. Over R. & S. B. Line.
G	P	F	L	H	C	7 0	Port Talbot and Aberavon	Glamorg'n	G. W.	Bridgend and Neath.
..	..	..	..	..	..	.. ..	Taibach Tin Plate Works	Glamorg'n	P. T.	Port Talbot (Central).
..	..	..	..	..	..	.. ..	Talbot Wharf Junction ...	Glamorg'n	P. T.—R. & S. B.	Port Talbot Dock.
..	..	..	..	..	..	.. ..	Tyn-y-ffram Siding	Glamorg'n	P. T.	Port Talbot and Bryn.
..	..	..	..	..	..	.. ..	Vivian & Son's—			
..	..	..	..	..	..	.. ..	Margam Siding	Glamorg'n	R. & S. B.	Over Dock Line.
..	..	..	..	..	..	.. ..	Morfa Siding	Glamorg'n	R. & S. B.	Over Dock Line.
..	..	..	..	..	..	.. ..	Sand Siding	Glamorg'n	R. & S. B.	Port Talbot.
..	..	..	..	..	..	.. ..	Wharf	Glamorg'n	P. T.	Branch from Burrows Junction.
..	P	..	..	..	..	0 15	Port Vale Sid. (Boulton & Co.)	Staffs	N. S.	Longport.
..	..	..	..	..	..	.. ..	Port Victoria	Kent	S. E. & C.	Branch—Gravesend and Higham.
..	..	..	..	..	..	.. ..	Port Victoria Branch Junc.	Kent	S. E. & C.	Gravesend and Higham.
..	..	..	..	..	..	.. ..	Portwood	Lancs	C. L. C. (G C, GN, & Mid.)	See Stockport.
..	..	..	..	..	..	.. ..	Possil	Lanark ..	Cal.	See Glasgow.
..	..	..	..	..	..	.. ..	Possil Brick Works	Lanark ..	N. B.	Glasgow, Cowlairs.
..	..	..	..	..	..	.. ..	Possil Junction	Lanark ..	Cal.	Glasgow.
..	..	..	..	..	..	.. ..	Possilpark	Lanark ..	N. B.	See Glasgow.
G	P	F	L	H	C	4 10	Postland (for Crowland)	Lincoln ..	G. N. & G. E. Jt.	March and Spalding.
..	..	..	..	..	..	.. ..	Postlethwaite's—			
..	..	..	..	..	..	.. ..	Eskett Mining Co.'s Siding	Cumb'land	W C & E Jt.(Fur.& L N W)	Winder.
..	..	..	..	..	..	.. ..	Moor Row Mining Co.'s Fletcher Pit............	Cumb'land	W C & E Jt.(Fur.& L N W)	Moor Row.
..	..	..	..	..	..	.. ..	No. 6 Moor Row or Royalty Pit	Cumb'land	W C & E Jt.(Fur.& L N W)	Moor Row.
..	..	..	..	..	..	.. ..	Post Office	Middlesex	C. L.	See London.
..	..	..	..	..	..	.. ..	Potland Siding	Northumb	N. E.	Ashington.

EXPLANATION—G *Goods Station.*   P *Passenger and Parcel Station.*   P* *Passenger, but not Parcel or Miscellaneous Traffic.*
F *Furniture Vans, Carriages, Portable Engines, and Machines on Wheels.*   L *Live Stock.*
H *Horse Boxes and Prize Cattle Vans.*   C *Carriages by Passenger Train.*

STATION ACCOMMODATION.						CRANE POWER.	STATIONS, &c.	COUNTY.	COMPANY.	POSITION.
						Tons Cwts.	Pott, Cassells, & Williamson's Works	Lanark ...	Cal.	Motherwell.
G	P	F	L	H	C	1 10	Potter Hanworth	Lincoln ...	G. N. & G. E. Jt.	Lincoln and Sleaford.
G	P	.	L	H	.	. .	Potter Heigham	Norfolk ...	Mid. & G. N. Jt.	North Walsham Town & Yarmouth Beach.
.	.	.	.	.	.	. .	Potterhill	Renfrew...	G. & S.W.	See Paisley.
.	.	.	.	.	.	. .	Potterhill Junction	Renfrew...	G. & S.W.	Potterhill and Elderslie.
.	.	.	.	.	.	. .	Potter Hill Kettleby Mines } Iron Ore Siding .... }	Leicester...	Mid.	{ See Holwell Iron Co. (Holwell { Junction Station).
G	P	F	L	H	C	5 0 }	Potter's Bar (G. N.)	Middlesex	{ G. N. { N. L.	New Barnet and Hatfield. Over G. N. from Canonbury Junc.
.	P	.	.	.	.	}				
.	.	.	.	.	.	. .	Hawkshead Siding............	Middlesex	G. N.	Potter's Bar and Hatfield.
.	.	.	.	.	.	. .	Potter's Grange Junction......	Yorks......	N. E.	Goole.
.	.	.	.	.	.	. .	Potter's Siding	Derby......	G. C.	Dinting.
.	.	.	.	.	.	. .	Potterston Junction	Ayr	G. & S.W.	Ayr and Hollybush.
.	.	.	.	.	.	. .	Potterston Lyes	Ayr	G. & S.W.	Hollybush.
G	P	.	L	H	C	5 0	Potto	Yorks......	N. E.	Stockton and Stokesley.
G	P	F	L	H	C	1 5	Potton	Beds	L. & N. W.	Bedford and Cambridge.
.	.	.	.	.	.	. .	Poulton (Wirral)	Cheshire...	Wirral—G. C.	See Liscard and Poulton.
G	P	F	L	H	C	5 0	Poulton	Lancs	P. & W. Jt. (L&Y&L&NW)	Fleetwood and Preston.
.	.	.	.	.	.	. .	Poulton Gas Works	Lancs	P. & W. Jt. (L&Y&L&NW)	Poulton and Singleton.
.	.	.	.	.	.	. .	Seed and Parr's Siding.....	Lancs	P. & W. Jt. (L&Y&L&NW)	Poulton and Cleveleys.
.	.	.	.	.	.	. .	Pounder's Boat-building Yard and Saw Mill	Durham ...	N. E.	West Hartlepool.
.	.	.	.	.	.	. .	Poundon	Bucks	L. & N. W.	See Marsh Gibbon and Poundon.
.	.	.	.	.	.	. .	Pountain, Girardot and Forman's Siding	Derby	Mid.	Derby.
.	.	.	.	.	.	. .	Pouparts Junction	Surrey ...	L. B. & S. C.	London, Battersea Park and Clapham Junction.
.	.	.	.	.	.	. .	Powbridge	Perth	Cal.	See Tibbermuir and Powbridge.
.	.	.	.	.	.	. .	Powderhall	Edinboro'	N. B.	See Edinburgh.
.	.	.	.	.	.	. .	Powell & Sing's Warehouse...	Cheshire...	B'head Jt—CLC—NW&L	Birkenhead.
							Powell Duffryn Co.—			
.	.	.	.	.	.	. .	Aberaman Colliery.........	Glamorg'n	G. W.—T. V.	Mountain Ash.
.	.	.	.	.	.	. .	Abercwmboi Colliery.........	Glamorg'n	G. W.—T. V.	Mountain Ash.
.	.	.	.	.	.	. .	Bargoed New Pits (Aber Bargoed Colliery) (B & M)	Mon	B. & M.—G. W............	Pengam.
.	.	.	.	.	.	. .	Coedymoeth Colliery.........	Glamorg'n	Rhy.	Brithdir.
.	.	.	.	.	.	. .	Cwmneol Colliery	Glamorg'n	{ G. W. { T. V.	Mountain Ash. Aberdare.
.	.	.	.	.	.	. .	Cwmpennar Colliery	Glamorg'n	G. W.	Mountain Ash.
.	.	.	.	.	.	. .	Elliot Pit	Glamorg'n	Rhy.	Brithdir.
.	.	.	.	.	.	. .	Fforchaman Colliery	Glamorg'n	{ G. W. { G. W.—T. V. { T. V.	Dare Junction. Mountain Ash. Aberdare.
.	.	.	.	.	.	. .	Lower Duffryn Colliery (George Pit).................	Glamorg'n	T. V.	Mountain Ash.
.	.	.	.	.	.	. .	Lower Duffryn Colliery (George Pit) (G. W.)......	Glamorg'n	G. W.—Rhy.	Mountain Ash.
.	.	.	.	.	.	. .	New Tredegar Col. (Rhy)..	Glamorg'n	Rhy.—L. & N. W.	Tir Phil.
.	.	.	.	.	.	. .	Treaman Colliery	Glamorg'n	{ G. W.—T. V. { T. V.	Mountain Ash. Aberdare.
.	.	.	.	.	.	. .	White Rose No. 2 Colliery	Glamorg'n	Rhy.	Brithdir.
.	.	.	.	.	.	. .	Powell, J., & Co.................	Denbigh...	G. W.	Same as Llwynenion Brick Works (Rhos).
.	.	.	.	.	.	. .	Powell's Colliery..............	Mon	G. W.	Same as Aberbeeg Col. (Aberbeeg).
.	.	.	.	.	.	. .	Powell's Ellwood Colliery Co.'s Brecon Boat Siding	Mon	L. & N. W.	Brynmawr.
.	.	.	.	.	.	. .	Power, F. A., & Son's Siding	Warwick...	Mid.	Birmingham, Lawley Street.
G	P	.	L	.	.		Powerstock	Dorset......	G. W.	Bridport and Maiden Newton.
.	.	.	.	.	.	. .	Poynters Siding (G. & S. W.)	Renfrew...	G. & S.W.—N. B.	Greenock, Lynedoch Street.
G	P	F	L	H	C	1 0 }	Poynton	Cheshire...	{ L. & N. W. { Mac. Com. (G.C. & N. S.)	Macclesfield and Stockport. Romiley and Macclesfield.
G	P	.	.	.	.	}				
.	.	.	.	.	.	. .	Lord Vernon's Poynton } and Worth Colliery ... }	Cheshire...	{ L. & N. W. { Mac. Com. (G.C. & N. S.)	Poynton and Bramhall. Poynton.
.	.	.	.	.	.	. .	Poynton and Worth Colliery	Cheshire...	L. & N. W.—Mac. Com.	See Lord Vernon's (Poynton).
G	P	F	L	H	C	. .	Poyntzpass	Armagh ...	G. N. (I.)	Newry and Portadown.
.	.	.	.	.	.	. .	Praed Street	Middlesex	Met.	See London, Paddington.
.	.	.	.	.	.	. .	Praed Street Junction	Middlesex	Met.	London, Edgware Road and Praed Street Station.
.	.	.	.	.	.	. .	Pratt, E. R. M., Siding	Norfolk ...	G. E.	Ryston.
.	.	.	.	.	.	. .	Pratt's Depôt	Durham ...	N. E.	Southwick.

EXPLANATION—G *Goods Station.*   P *Passenger and Parcel Station.*   P* *Passenger, but not Parcel or Miscellaneous Traffic.*
F *Furniture Vans, Carriages, Portable Engines, and Machines on Wheels.*   L *Live Stock.*
H *Horse Boxes and Prize Cattle Vans.*   C *Carriages by Passenger Train.*

G	P	F	L	H	C	Tons	Cwts	STATIONS, &c.	COUNTY.	COMPANY.	POSITION.
								Pratt's Siding	Herts	L. & N. W.	Watford.
								Pratt's Siding	Staffs	N. S.	Stoke-on-Trent.
G	P		L	H				Praze	Cornwall	G. W.	Gwinear Road and Helston.
G	P		L	H	C	1	10	Prees	Salop	L. & N. W.	Shrewsbury and Whitchurch.
G	P							Preesgweene	Salop	G. W.	Chirk and Gobowen.
								Premier Gas Engineering Co.'s Siding	Notts	Mid.	Stapleford and Sandiacre.
								Prentice Bros.' Siding	Suffolk	G. E.	Stowmarket.
								Prentice, T. P., & Co.'s Siding	Suffolk	G. E.	Stowmarket.
G	P	F	L	H	C	5	0	Prescot	Lancs	L. & N. W.	Liverpool and St. Helens.
								British Insulated & Helsby Cables Co.'s Siding	Lancs	L. & N. W.	Prescot and Eccleston Park.
								Prescot Colliery or Lancaster's Siding	Lancs	L. & N. W.	See Higginbottom's (Huyton Qry.).
G	P	F	L	H	C	1	10	Prestatyn	Flint	L. & N. W.	Chester and Rhyl.
								Gronant Siding	Flint	L. & N. W.	Prestatyn and Rhyl.
G	P			H	C	5	0	Prestbury	Cheshire	L. & N. W.	Macclesfield and Stockport.
G	P	F	L	H	C	1	8	Presteign	Radnor	G. W.	Branch—Leominster and Kington.
G	P	F	L	H	C			Presthope	Salop	G. W.	Craven Arms and Much Wenlock.
								Lilleshall Co.'s Siding	Salop	G. W.	Presthope and Longville.
								Westwood Siding	Salop	G. W.	Much Wenlock and Presthope.
								PRESTON—			
								Allsup & Son's Siding	Lancs	N.U.Jt.(L.&NW.&L.&Y)	Ribble Branch.
								Banks, T., & Co.'s Siding	Lancs	P.&L.Jt.(L&NW.&L.&Y)	Deepdale and Ribbleton.
								Blainscough Hall Colliery Co.'s Siding	Lancs	P.&L.Jt.(L&NW.&L.&Y)	Deepdale and Ribbleton.
G	P	F	L			25	0	Butler Street	Lancs	L. & Y.	Near Joint Passenger Station.
G		F				20	0	Charles Street	Lancs	L. & N. W.	Branch near Fishergate.
								Corporation Str. Coal Yard	Lancs	N.U.Jt.(L&NW.&L.&Y)	Fishergate and Lancaster.
								Croft's Quarry Siding	Lancs	P.&L.Jt.(L&NW&L&Y)	Deepdale.
								Curwen's Siding	Lancs	P.&L.Jt.(L&NW&L&Y)	Maudlands.
G	P					5	0	Deepdale	Lancs	P.&L.Jt.(L&NW&L&Y)	Fishergate & Longridge.
						25	0	Dick, Kerr & Co.'s English Electric Manufacturing Co.'s Siding	Lancs	N.U.Jt.(L.&NW.&L.&Y)	Ribble Branch.
								Docks	Lancs	N.U.Jt.(L.&NW.&L.&Y)	Branch near Fishergate.
								Dock Street Coal Sidings	Lancs	N.U.Jt.(L.&NW.&L.&Y)	Preston.
								Dock Street Junction	Lancs	L. & N. W.—N. U. Jt.	Lancaster and Fishergate.
								Eccles Bros.' Siding	Lancs	P.&L.Jt.(L&NW.&L.&Y)	Deepdale and Ribbleton.
								Electric Railway & Tramway Carriage Works	Lancs	N.U.Jt.(L.&NW.&L.&Y)	Ribble Branch.
	P	F		H	C			Fishergate	Lancs	N.U.Jt.(L.&NW.&L.&Y)	Lancaster and Wigan.
								Fishergate Junction	Lancs	L. & Y.—N. U. Jt.	Blackburn & Dock Street Junction.
								Graham & Co.'s Siding	Lancs	P.&L.Jt.(L&NW.&L.&Y)	Deepdale and Ribbleton.
								Granite Concrete Co.'s Sid.	Lancs	N.U.Jt.(L.&NW.&L.&Y)	Ribble Branch.
G								Greenbank	Lancs	L. & N. W.	Lancaster & Fishergate.
								Hincksman's Cotton Mill	Lancs	L. & N. W.	Fishergate and Oxheys.
								Ince Hall Coal Co.'s Siding	Lancs	L. & N. W.	Fishergate and Oxheys.
								Jackson & Son's Siding	Lancs	P.&L.Jt.(L&NW.&L.&Y)	Deepdale and Ribbleton.
								Martin & Maymon's Siding	Lancs	P.&L.Jt.(L&NW.&L.&Y)	Deepdale and Ribbleton.
G		F	L			5	0	Maudlands	Lancs	P.&W.Jt.(L&Y&L&NW)	Over P. & L. Joint from Junction near Dock Street.
								Maudlands Junction	Lancs	{ L. & N.W.—P. & L. Jt. / L. & N.W.—P. & W. Jt.	Fishergate and Longridge. / Fishergate Joint Pass. and Lea Road.
G	P		L	H				Oxheys	Lancs	L. & N. W.	Lancaster & Fishergate.
								Page & Taylor's Siding	Lancs	P.&L.Jt.(L&NW.&L.&Y)	Deepdale and Ribbleton.
								Preston Industrial Co-operative Society's Siding	Lancs	P.&L.Jt.(L&NW.&L.&Y)	Deepdale and Ribbleton.
								Railway Key Co.'s Siding	Lancs	P.&L.Jt.(L&NW.&L.&Y)	Deepdale and Ribbleton.
								Ribble Branch	Lancs	N.U.Jt.(L.&NW.&L.&Y)	Branch near Fishergate.
								Smith & Son's Siding	Lancs	P.&L.Jt.(L&NW.&L.&Y)	Deepdale and Ribbleton.
								Turner's Siding	Lancs	L. & N. W.	Preston.
								Ward's, T. W., Siding	Lancs	N.U.Jt.(L.&NW.&L.&Y)	Ribble Branch.
								Waring & Co.'s Siding	Lancs	P.&L.Jt.(L&NW.&L.&Y)	Deepdale and Ribbleton.
								Whitehouse Junc., North	Lancs	L. & Y.	Fishergate and Blackburn.
								Whitehouse Junc., South	Lancs	L. & Y.	Fishergate and Blackburn.
								Whitehouse Junction, West	Lancs	L. & Y.	Fishergate and Longton Bridge.
								Wigan Coal & Iron Co.'s Siding	Lancs	P.&L.Jt.(L&NW.&L.&Y)	Deepdale and Ribbleton.
G	P		L			1	10	Preston Brook	Cheshire	L. & N. W.	Crewe and Warrington.
								Manchester Ship Canal Co.'s Bridgewater Siding	Cheshire	L. & N. W.	Preston Brook and Acton Bridge.

EXPLANATION—G *Goods Station.*   P *Passenger and Parcel Station.*   P* *Passenger, but not Parcel or Miscellaneous Traffic.*
F *Furniture Vans, Carriages, Portable Engines, and Machines on Wheels.*   L *Live Stock.*
H *Horse Boxes and Prize Cattle Vans.*   C *Carriages by Passenger Train.*

STATION ACCOMMODATION.						CRANE POWER.		STATIONS, &c.	COUNTY.	COMPANY.	POSITION.
						Tons	Cwts.				
..	..	..	..	..	..	..	..	Preston Colliery	Northumb	N. E.	North Shields.
..	..	..	..	..	..	..	..	Prestongrange Colliery.........	Hadding'n	N. B.	Prestonpans.
..	..	..	..	..	..	..	..	Preston Industrial Co-operative Society's Siding	Lancs	P.&L.Jt.(L&NW.&L&Y.)	Preston, Deepdale.
..	P	..	..	..	..	..	..	Preston Junction Station......	Lancs	L. & Y.	Preston and Bamber Bridge.
G	P	F	L	H	C	2	0	Prestonpans.................	Hadding'n	N. B.	Edinburgh and Dunbar.
..	..	..	..	..	..	..	..	Bankton Colliery	Hadding'n	N. B.	Tranent Branch.
..	..	..	..	..	..	..	..	Morrison's Haven Siding ...	Hadding'n	N. B.	Prestonpans and Inveresk.
..	..	..	..	..	..	..	..	Myle's Siding	Hadding'n	N. B.	Tranent Branch.
..	..	..	..	..	..	..	..	Northfield Colliery..........	Hadding'n	N. B.	Prestonpans.
..	..	..	..	..	..	..	..	Prestongrange Colliery......	Hadding'n	N. B.	Prestonpans and Inveresk.
G	..	..	..	..	..	1	10	Tranent	Hadding'n	N. B.	Branch from Prestonpans.
..	..	..	..	..	..	..	..	Tranent Collieries	Hadding'n	N. B.	Branch from Prestonpans.
..	..	..	..	..	..	..	..	Prestonpans Junction	Hadding'n	N. B.	Prestonpans and Longniddry.
..	P	..	..	..	..	..	..	Preston Park	Sussex	L. B. & S. C.	Brighton and Hassocks.
..	..	..	..	..	..	..	..	Preston Road	Lancs	L. & Y.	See Liverpool.
..	..	..	..	..	..	..	..	Preston's Siding (G. C.)	Notts	G. C.—G. N.—Mid.	Worksop.
..	..	..	..	..	..	..	..	Preston Street (Fur.)	Cumb'land	Furness—L. & N. W.	See Whitehaven.
G	P	..	..	..	..	10	0	Prestwich	Lancs	L. & Y.	Manchester and Radcliffe.
G	P	F	L	H	C	3	0	Prestwick.................	Ayr	G. & S.W.	Troon and Ayr.
..	..	..	..	..	..	..	..	Pretoria or New Pit (Chequerbent Bank Siding)	Lancs. ...	L. & N. W.	Same as Hulton Colliery Co.'s Atherton Col. No. 2 (Chequerbent).
..	..	..	..	..	..	..	..	Price & Wills' Siding	Glamorg'n	Rhy.	Penyrheol.
..	..	..	..	..	..	..	..	Price & Wills' Siding	Mon	B. & M.	Bedwas.
..	..	..	..	..	..	..	..	Price's Coal Siding	Glamorg'n	T. V.	Same as Llandough Coal Yard (Penarth Dock).
..	..	..	..	..	..	..	..	Price's, R., Siding...........	Glamorg'n	G. W.	Bridgend.
..	..	..	..	..	..	..	..	Price's Siding	Bucks	L. & N. W.	Newport Pagnell.
..	..	..	..	..	..	..	..	Price's Tan Yard	Glamorg'n	G. W.	Bridgend.
..	..	..	..	..	..	..	..	Price, Walker & Co.'s Siding	Glo'ster ...	G. W.—Mid.	Gloucester Docks.
..	..	..	..	..	..	..	..	Priday, Metford & Co.	Glo'ster ...	G. W.—Mid.	Gloucester Docks.
..	..	..	..	..	..	..	..	Prideaux Wood Siding	Cornwall	G. W.	Same as Lovering & Co. (St. Blazey).
..	P	..	..	..	..	..	..	Priestfield.................	Staffs	G. W.	Birmingham and Wolverhampton.
..	..	..	..	..	..	..	..	Priestner Pit	Lancs	L. & N. W.	See Wigan Coal & Iron Co.'s Chowbent West Junc. Siding (Leigh and Bedford).
..	..	..	..	..	..	..	..	Priestner's Siding	Cheshire...	L. & N. W.	Wilmslow.
..	..	..	..	..	..	..	..	Primrose Coal Co. (Mid.)	Glamorg'n	Mid.—G. W.—L & N W	Same as South Wales Primrose Coal Co. (Pontardawe).
..	..	..	..	..	..	..	..	Primrose Colliery (Mid.)	Glamorg'n	Mid.—G. W.—L & N W	Same as South Wales Primrose Colliery (Ystalyfera).
..	..	..	..	..	..	..	..	Primrose Main Colliery......	Yorks	G. C.	Staincross (for Mapplewell).
..	..	..	..	..	..	..	..	Primrose Siding	Lancs	L. & Y.	Clitheroe.
..	..	..	..	..	..	..	..	Prince of Wales Colliery	Mon	G. W.	Same as Abercarn Col. (Abercarn).
..	..	..	..	..	..	..	..	Prince of Wales Col. (L. & Y.)	Yorks	L. & Y.—G. N.—Mid.—N. E.	Pontefract.
..	..	..	..	..	..	..	..	Prince of Wales Dock	Glamorg'n	G.W.—L.&N.W.—Mid.—R. & S. B.	See East or Prince of Wales Dock (Swansea).
..	..	..	..	..	..	..	..	Princes Brick Works...........	Flint	W. M. & C. Q.	Connah's Quay.
..	..	..	..	..	..	..	..	Princes Dentith Siding	Flint	L. & N. W.	Connah's Quay.
..	..	..	..	..	..	..	..	Princes Dock	Lanark	Princes Dock Joint (Cal., G. & S. W. & N. B.)......	See Glasgow.
..	..	..	..	..	..	..	..	Princes Dock (Cal.)	Lanark	Cal.—G. & S. W.—N. B.	See Glasgow.
..	..	..	..	..	..	..	..	Princes Dock	Lancs	L'pool O'head	See Liverpool.
..	..	..	..	..	..	..	..	Princes Dock (N. E.)	Yorks	N. E.—L. & N. W.	See Hull.
..	..	..	..	..	..	..	..	Princes Dock (G. C.)	Lancs	G. C.—G. N.	Guide Bridge.
..	..	..	..	..	..	..	..	Princes End.................	Staffs	G. W.—L. & N. W.	See Tipton.
..	..	..	..	..	..	..	..	Princes Pier	Renfrew ...	G. & S.W.—N. B.	See Greenock.
G	P	F	L	H	C	3	0	Princes Risboro'	Bucks	G. W. & G. C. Jt.	Aylesbury and Maidenhead.
..	..	..	..	..	..	..	..	Princes Risboro' Junction ...	Bucks	G.W.—G. W. & G. C. Jt.	Princes Risboro' and Aylesbury.
..	..	..	..	..	..	..	..	Princess Colliery	Lancs	G. C. (St. Helens Exten.)	See Evans, R., & Co. (Ashton-in-Makerfield).
..	..	..	..	..	..	..	..			L. & N. W.	See Evans, R., & Co. (Earlestown).
..	..	..	..	..	..	..	..	Princess Royal Sidings— Flour Mill	Glo'ster	S.&Wye Jt.(G.W.&Mid.)	Whitecroft.
..	..	..	..	..	..	..	..	Park Gutter Siding	Glo'ster	S.&Wye Jt.(G.W.&Mid.)	Whitecroft.
..	..	..	..	..	..	..	..	Princes Street...............	Edinboro'	Cal.	See Edinburgh.
..	..	..	..	..	..	..	..	Princes Street...............	Perth	Cal.	See Perth.
G	P	F	L	H	C	2	0	Princetown	Devon	G. W.	Branch from Yelverton Junction.
..	..	..	..	..	..	..	..	Royal Oak Siding	Devon	G. W.	Dousland and Princetown.
..	..	..	..	..	..	..	..	Swell Tor Siding	Devon	G. W.	Dousland and Princetown.
..	..	..	..	..	..	..	..	Priorfield Furnace............	Staffs	L. & N. W.	Same as Whitehouse & Son's Siding (Deepfields).

EXPLANATION—G *Goods Station.*   P *Passenger and Parcel Station.*   P* *Passenger, but not Parcel or Miscellaneous Traffic.*
F *Furniture Vans, Carriages, Portable Engines, and Machines on Wheels.*   L *Live Stock.*
H *Horse Boxes and Prize Cattle Vans.*   C *Carriages by Passenger Train.*

STATION ACCOMMODATION.						CRANE POWER.		STATIONS, &c.	COUNTY.	COMPANY.	POSITION.
						Tons	Cwts.				
.	.	.	.	.	.			Prior, J., Siding................	Middlesex	G. E.	London, Blackwall.
.	.	.	.	.	.			Priors Lee Siding	Salop	G. W.—L. & N. W.	See Lilleshall Coal & Iron Co.
.	.	.	.	.	.			Priory	Lancs	Furness	See Conishead Priory.
.	.	.	.	.	.			Priory Junction	Lancs	G. C.	Ashburys and Gorton.
.	.	.	.	.	.			Priory Siding	Lincoln ...	G. N.	Stamford.
.	.	.	.	.	.			Pritchard's Chemical Works	Glamorg'n	G. W.	Swansea.
G	P	F	L	H	C			Prittlewell	Essex	G. E.	Wickford and Southend-on-Sea.
.	P*	.	.	.	.			Privett	Hants	{ Lee-on-the-Solent	Fort Brockhurst and Lee-on-the-Solent.
G	P	F	L	H	C	5	0			{ L. & S. W..................	Alton and Fareham.
.	.	.	.	.	.			Proctor & Ryland's Siding ...	Cheshire...	{ G. W.	Saltney.
										{ L. & N. W.	Saltney Wharf.
.	.	.	.	.	.			Proctor's Siding	Glo'ster ...	G. W.	Bristol, Redcliffe Wharf.
.	.	.	.	.	.			Prospect Hill Siding	Northumb	N. E.	Holywell.
.	.	.	.	.	.			Prospect Pit (L. & N. W.)....	Lancs	L.& N.W.–G.C.(Wig.Jn.)	See Wigan Coal & Iron Co. (Wigan).
.	.	.	.	.	.			Prosser's Quarry (New Forest Quarry)..................	Glamorg'n	P. T.—S. Wales Min. ...	Cwmavon.
.	.	.	.	.	.			Provan Gas Works (Blackhill Gas Works)	Lanark ...	Cal.	Glasgow, Buchanan Street.
.	.	.	.	.	.			Provan Gas Works (Blackhill Gas Works)(N. B.)...........	Lanark ...	N. B.—G. & S. W.	Glasgow, Blochairn.
.	.	.	.	.	.			Provan Mill Distillery	Lanark ...	Cal.	Glasgow, Buchanan Street.
.	.	.	.	.	.			Provan Mill Siding	Lanark ...	Cal.	See Glasgow.
.	.	.	.	.	.			Prudham Quarry	Northumb	N. E.	Fourstones.
G	P	.	L	H	.	3	0	Prudhoe (N. E.)	Northumb	{ N. E.	Newcastle and Hexham.
										{ N. B.	Over N. E. from Hexham Junction.
.	.	.	.	.	.			Mickley Colliery.............	Northumb	N. E.	Prudhoe and Stocksfield.
.	.	.	.	.	.			Prudhoe Colliery	Northumb	N. E.	Prudhoe.
.	.	.	.	.	.			West Mickley Colliery (Eltringham Colliery) ...	Northumb	N. E.	Prudhoe.
.	.	.	.	.	.			West Wylam Colliery	Northumb	N. E.	Prudhoe and Wylam.
.	.	.	.	.	.			West Wylam Junction	Northumb	N. E.	Prudhoe and Wylam.
.	.	.	.	.	.			Puddington	Cheshire...	{ N. W. & L. Jt.(G.C.and W. M. & C. Q.)	{ See Burton Point (for Burton and Puddington.
G	P	F	L	H	C	10	0	Pudsey, Greenside (G. N.) ...	Yorks	{ G. N.	Branch—Bramley and Stanningley.
.	P									{ L. & Y.	Over G. N. Line.
.	.	.	.	.	.			Vicker's Quarry	Yorks	G. N.	Pudsey Greenside and Dudley Hill.
G	P	.	L	.	.	10	0	Pudsey, Low Town (G. N.)	Yorks	{ G. N.	Branch—Bramley and Stanningley.
.	P									{ L. & Y.	Over G. N. Line.
.	.	.	.	.	.			Pugeston Siding.................	Forfar ...	Cal.	Dubton Junction.
G	P	F	L	H	C	10	0	Pulborough	Sussex ...	L. B. & S. C.	Horsham and Arundel.
.	.	.	.	.	.			Hardham Brick Siding ...	Sussex ...	L. B. & S. C.	Pulborough and Fittleworth.
.	.	.	.	.	.			Puleston Mill	Denbigh ...	G. W.	Wrexham.
.	.	.	.	.	.			Pulford's Siding	Cheshire...	G. W.	Rossett.
G	P	.	L	H	C	.	.	Pulham Market	Norfolk ...	G. E.	Tivetshall and Beccles.
G	P							Pulham St. Mary	Norfolk ...	G. E.	Tivetshall and Beccles.
.	.	.	.	.	.			Pumpherston Farm Siding ...	L'lithgow	N. B.	Same as Pumpherston No. 4 Mine (Uphall).
.	.	.	.	.	.			Pumpherston No. 2 Mine......	L'lithgow	N. B.	Uphall.
.	.	.	.	.	.			Pumpherston No. 4 Mine (Pumpherston Farm Sid.)	L'lithgow	N. B.	Uphall.
.	.	.	.	.	.			Pumpherston No. 5 Mine ...	L'lithgow	N. B.	Uphall.
.	.	.	.	.	.			Pumpherston Oil Works	L'lithgow	N. B.	Uphall.
G	P							Puncheston	Pembroke	G. W.	Clynderwen and Fishguard.
.	.	.	.	.	.			Purdie & Son's Siding	Lanark ...	Cal.	Coatbridge.
.	.	.	.	.	.			Pure Oil Co.'s Siding	Lancs	Trafford Park Estate.....	Manchester.
G	P	F	.	H	.			Purfleet	Essex	L. T. & S.	Barking and Tilbury.
.	.	.	.	.	.			Anglo-American Oil Co.— America Wharf	Essex	L. T. & S.	Purfleet.
.	.	.	.	.	.			Caspian Wharf	Essex	L. T. & S.	Purfleet.
.	.	.	.	.	.			Purfleet Siding (Ordnance Crossing Siding)	Essex	L. T. & S.	Purfleet.
.	.	.	.	.	.			Purfleet Wharf & Saw Mills Co.'s Sid.(Australia Whf.)	Essex	L. T. & S.	Purfleet.
.	.	.	.	.	.			Thames Paper Works	Essex	L. T. & S.	Purfleet.
.	.	.	.	.	.			Purleigh	Essex	G. E.	See Cold Norton (for Purleigh and Stow Maries).
G	P	F	L	H	C	8	0	Purley Junction	Surrey ...	S. E. & C.	Purley and Kenley.
G	P	F	L	H	C	.	.	Purley Junction Station	Surrey ...	{ L. B. & S. C.	Croydon and Red Hill.
	P									{ S. E. & C.	Croydon and Red Hill.
G	P	F	L	H	C	.	.	Purley Oaks......................	Surrey ...	L. B. & S. C.	South Croydon and Purley.
G	P	F	L	H	C	.	.	Purton	Wilts	G. W.	Swindon and Gloucester.

EXPLANATION—G *Goods Station.*   P *Passenger and Parcel Station.*   P* *Passenger, but not Parcel or Miscellaneous Traffic.*
F *Furniture Vans, Carriages, Portable Engines, and Machines on Wheels.*   L *Live Stock.*
H *Horse Boxes and Prize Cattle Vans.*   C *Carriages by Passenger Train.*

STATION ACCOMMODATION.						CRANE POWER.	STATIONS, &c.	COUNTY.	COMPANY.	POSITION.
						Tons Cwts.				
..	P	..	..	..	..	.. ..	Putney	Surrey ...	L. & S.W.	Clapham Junction and Richmond.
..	..	..	..	..	..	.. ..	Putney Bridge & Fulham Jn.	Middlesex	L. & S.W.—Met. Dist. ...	East Putney and Putney Bridge.
..	..	..	..	..	..	.. ..	Putney Bridge & Hurlingham	Middlesex	Met. Dist.	See London.
..	..	..	..	..	..	.. ..	Putney East	Surrey ...	L. & S.W.	See East Putney.
G	P	..	L	..	..	1 10	Puxton	Somerset..	G. W.	Bristol and Highbridge.
..	..	..	..	..	..	.. ..	Pwllbach Colliery (Mid.)	Glamorg'n	Mid.—G.W.—L. & N.W.	Gurnos.
..	..	..	..	..	..	.. ..	Pwllbach Siding (Mid.)	Glamorg'n	Mid.—G.W.—L. & N.W.	Gurnos.
..	..	..	..	..	..	.. ..	Pwllcarn Colliery	Glamorg'n	G. W.	Pontycymmer.
..	..	..	..	..	..	.. ..	Pwllglas	Montgom	Cam. (Van).	Same as Treveglwys.
..	..	..	..	..	..	.. ..	Pwllgwaun Siding	Glamorg'n	Barry	Pontypridd.
..	..	..	..	..	..	.. ..	Barry Rhondda Col. Siding	Glamorg'n	Barry	Pwllgwaun Siding.
..	..	..	..	..	..	.. ..	Victoria Brick Works Sid.	Glamorg'n	Barry	Pwllgwaun Siding.
G	P	F	L	H	C	3 0	Pwllheli	Carnarvon	Cam.	Terminus of Coast Section.
..	..	..	..	..	..	.. ..	Pwll Siding	Carmarth'	B. P. & G. V.	Burry Port.
..	..	..	..	..	..	.. ..	Pwllypant Quarry (Rhy.) ...	Glamorg'n	Rhy.—L. & N. W.	Llanbradach.
..	..	..	..	..	..	.. ..	Pwllyrhebog Branch Junction	Glamorg'n	T. V.	Trealaw and Llwynypia.
G	P	..	L	H	..	5 0	Pye Bridge	Notts	Mid.	Clay Cross and Codnor Park.
..	..	..	..	..	..	.. ..	Coates Park Colliery	Derby	Mid.	Near Pye Bridge.
..	..	..	..	..	..	.. ..	Kempson & Co.'s Works ...	Derby	Mid.	Near Pye Bridge.
							Oakes & Co.'s—			
..	..	..	..	..	..	.. ..	Alfreton Iron Works......	Derby	Mid.	Near Pye Bridge.
..	..	..	..	..	..	.. ..	Collieries	Derby	Mid.	Near Pye Bridge.
..	..	..	..	..	..	.. ..	Riddings Brick Yard ...	Derby	Mid.	Near Pye Bridge.
							Riddings Sanitary Pipe			
..	..	..	..	..	..	.. ..	Works	Derby	Mid.	Near Pye Bridge.
..	..	..	..	..	..	.. ..	Riddings Siding	Derby	Mid.	Near Pye Bridge.
..	..	..	..	..	..	.. ..	Pye Bridge Chemical Wks.	Derby	Mid.	Codnor Park and Clay Cross.
..	..	..	..	..	..	.. ..	Riddings Colliery	Derby	Mid.	Pye Bridge.
..	..	..	..	..	..	.. ..	Seeley's New Birchwood Col.	Derby	Mid.	Near Pye Bridge.
..	P	..	..	H	C	.. ..	Pye Hill	Notts	G. N.	Eastwood and Pinxton.
..	..	..	..	..	..	.. ..	Pye Hill Siding	Notts	G. N.	Codnor Park.
..	..	..	..	..	..	.. ..	Pye Pits	Yorks	N. E.	Malton.
..	..	..	..	..	..	.. ..	Pye's Timber Yard (Mid.) ...	Notts	Mid.—G. C.	Mansfield.
..	..	..	..	..	..	.. ..	Pyewipe Junction	Lincoln ...	G. N.—G. N. & G. E. Jt.	Lincoln.
..	..	..	..	..	..	.. ..	Pyewipe Junction	Lincoln ...	G N & G E Jt—L D & E C	Lincoln.
..	..	..	..	..	..	.. ..	Pyewipe Manure Wks. (G.C.)	Lincoln ...	G. C.—G. N.	Grimsby Docks.
G	P	..	L	H	..	1 10⎫	Pyle	Glamorg'n	{ G. W.	Bridgend and Neath.
..	P	..	..	..	..	⎬			{ G. W.	Tondu and Porthcawl.
..	..	..	..	..	..	.. ..	Cornelly Quarry Siding ...	Glamorg'n	G. W.	Pyle.
..	..	..	..	..	..	.. ..	Pyle Sand Siding	Glamorg'n	G. W.	Pyle.
..	..	..	..	..	..	.. ..	Pyle and Blaina Works (GW)	Mon.	{ G. W.—L. & N. W......	Blaina (for Outwards Traffic).
..	..	..	..	..	..	.. ..			{ G. W.—L. & N. W......	Nantyglo (for Inwards Traffic).
..	..	..	..	..	..	.. ..	Pyle Junction	Glamorg'n	G. W.	Bridgend and Pyle.
..	..	..	..	..	..	.. ..	Pyle Junction	Glamorg'n	G. W.—P. T.	Pyle and Bryndu.
G	P	..	L	H	..	1 10	Pylle	Somerset..	S.&D.Jt.(L.&S.W.& Mid)	Evercreech Jn. Sta. & Glastonbury.
..	..	..	..	..	..	.. ..	Pylle Lime Works	Somerset..	S.&D.Jt.(L.&S.W.& Mid)	Pylle and West Pennard.
..	..	..	..	..	..	.. ..	Pylle Hill	Somerset..	G. W.	See Bristol.
..	..	..	..	..	..	.. ..	Pyman, Bell & Co.'s Wharf...	Northumb	N. E.	Newcastle-on-Tyne.
							Pyman's Saw Mill and Timber			
..	..	..	..	..	..	.. ..	Yard	Durham ...	N. E.	West Hartlepool.
..	..	..	..	..	..	.. ..	Pym's Sand Siding	Beds	G. N.—L. & N. W........	Sandy.
..	..	..	..	..	..	.. ..	Pym's Sand Siding	Surrey ...	S. E. & C.	Red Hill.

Q

G	P	..	..	..	..	.. ..	Quadring Siding..................	Lincoln ...	G. N. & G. E. Jt.	Gosberton.
G	P	..	L	H	..	.. ..	Quainton Road	Bucks......	O. & A. Tram	Aylesbury and Brill.
G	P	..	..	H	..	⎫	Quainton Road (Met.)	Bucks......	{ Met.	Aylesbury and Verney Junction.
..	P	..	..	..	..	⎬			{ G. C.	Over Met. Line.
..	..	..	..	..	..	.. ..	Quainton Road Junction	Bucks......	G. C.—Met	Rugby and Quainton Road.
..	..	..	..	..	..	.. ..	Quainton Road Junction	Bucks......	Met.—O. & A. Tram......	Aylesbury and Brill.
G	..	..	..	..	..	.. ..	Quakers Drove....................	Cambs.....	G. E.	Branch near Whittlesea.
							Quaker's Yard—			
..	P	..	..	..	..	.. ..	High Level (G.W.)............	Glamorg'n	{ G. W.	Llancaiach and Mountain Ash.
..	..	..	..	..	..	.. ..			{ Rhy.	Over G. W. from Penallta Junc.

EXPLANATION—G *Goods Station.*   P *Passenger and Parcel Station.*   P* *Passenger, but not Parcel or Miscellaneous Traffic.*
F *Furniture Vans, Carriages, Portable Engines, and Machines on Wheels.*   L *Live Stock.*
H *Horse Boxes and Prize Cattle Vans.*   C *Carriages by Passenger Train.*

STATION ACCOMMODATION.						CRANE POWER.	STATIONS, &c.	COUNTY.	COMPANY.	POSITION.
						Tons Cwts.	Quaker's Yard—*continued.*			
.	.	.	.	.	.	. .	Junction	Glamorg'n	G. W.—G. W. & Rhy Jt.	Quaker's Yard Station and Aberfan.
.	.	.	.	.	.	. .	Junction	Glamorg'n	G. W.—T. V.	Llancaiach and Merthyr.
.	P	.	.	.	.	.⎫	Low Level	Glamorg'n	{ G. W.	Llancaiach.
.	P	.	.	.	.	.⎭			{ T. V.	Pontypridd and Merthyr.
.	.	.	.	.	.	. .	Low Level Junction	Glamorg'n	G. W.	Treharris and Low Level Station.
.	.	.	.	.	.	. .	Quarry Junction	Yorks	G. C.—Mid	Same as Darfield West Jn.(Barnsley).
.	.	.	.	.	.	. .	Quarry Mawr	Carmarth'	L. & M. M.	Felinfoel.
.	.	.	.	.	.	. .	Quarter Colliery	Stirling ...	Cal.	Denny, Ingliston.
G	P	.	.	.	.	3 0	Quarter Road...'	Lanark ...	Cal.	Hamilton and Strathaven.
.	.	.	.	.	.	. .	Fairholm Colliery	Lanark ...	Cal.	Meikle Earnock and Quarter Road.
.	.	.	.	.	.	. .	Quarter Collieries	Lanark ...	Cal.	Meikle Earnock and Quarter Road.
.	.	.	.	.	.	. .	Quarter Iron Works Junc.	Lanark ...	Cal.	Meikle Earnock and Quarter Road.
.	.	.	.	.	.	. .	Quarter Junction Siding	Lanark ...	Cal.	Meikle Earnock and Quarter Road.
.	.	.	.	.	.	. .	Quayside Branch	Northumb	N. E.	See Newcastle-on-Tyne.
.	.	.	.	.	.	. .	Quay Street....................	Louth	D. N. & G.	See Dundalk.
G	P	F	L	H	C	1 15	Queenborough.................	Kent	S. E. & C.	Sittingbourne and Sheerness.
.	.	.	.	.	.	. .	Crundall's Siding	Kent	S. E. & C.	Queenborough and Sheerness Dock-yard.
.	.	.	.	.	.	. .	Queenborough Cement Co.'s Siding	Kent	S. E. & C.	Queenborough.
.	.	.	.	.	.	. .	Queenborough Junction	Kent	SE& C—SE&C (Sheppey)	Queenborough and Sheerness Dock-yard.
G	P*	.	.	.	.	3 0	Queenborough Pier	Kent	S. E. & C.	Branch—Queenborough and Sheer-ness Dockyard.
.	.	.	.	.	.	. .	Queen Colliery	Lancs	{ G. C. (St. Helens Exten.)	See Evans, R., & Co. (Ashton-in-Makerfield).
									{ L. & N. W.	See Evans, R., & Co. (Earlestown).
G	P	.	L	.	.	. .	Queen's Bridge	Antrim ...	G. N. (I.)	See Belfast.
.	.	.	.	.	.	. .	Queensbury	Yorks	G. N.	Bradford and Halifax.
.	.	.	.	.	.	. .	Queen's Dock	Edinboro'	Cal.—N. B.	See Leith.
.	.	.	.	.	.	. .	Queen's Dock (N. E.)	Yorks	N. E.—L. & N. W.	See Hull.
.	.	.	.	.	.	. .	Queen's Dock (Finnieston Quay)...........................	Lanark ...	Cal.—N. B.	See Glasgow.
G	P	.	L	H	.	5 0	Queensferry.....................	Flint	L. & N. W.	Chester and Rhyl.
.	.	.	.	.	.	. .	Dundas Sidings	Flint	L. & N. W.	Queensferry and Sandycroft.
.	.	.	.	.	.	. .	Aston Hall Coal & Brick Co.'s Colliery	Flint	L. & N. W.	Dundas Sidings.
.	.	.	.	.	.	. .	Turner's	Flint	L. & N. W.	Dundas Sidings.
.	.	.	.	.	.	. .	Willans & Robinson's Ferry Works	Flint	L. & N. W.	Dundas Sidings.
.	.	.	.	.	.	. .	Queensferry Junction	Edinboro'	N. B.	Gogar and Ratho.
.	.	.	.	.	.	. .	Queensferry, North	Fife	N. B.	See North Queensferry.
.	.	.	.	.	.	. .	Queensferry, South (Goods)...	L'lithgow	N. B.	See South Queensferry.
.	.	.	.	.	.	. .	Queensferry, South (Pass.) ..	L'lithgow	N. B.	See Dalmeny (for South Queensferry)
.	.	.	.	.	.	. .	Queen's Park	Renfrew...	Cal.	See Glasgow.
.	.	.	.	.	.	. .	Queen's Park (West Kilburn) (L. & N. W.)	Middlesex	L. & N. W.—N. L.	See London.
.	.	.	.	.	.	. .	Queen's Quay	Down	B. & C. D.—G. N. (I.) ...	See Belfast.
.	.	.	.	.	.	. .	Queen's Road	Essex	Mid.—T. & F. G. Jt.	See Walthamstow.
.	.	.	.	.	.	. .	Queen's Road	Middlesex	C. L.	See London.
.	.	.	.	.	.	. .	Queen's Road	Yorks	Mid.	See Sheffield.
.	.	.	.	.	.	. .	Queen's Road (Battersea) ..	Surrey ...	L. & S.W.	See London.
.	.	.	.	.	.	. .	Queen's Road (Bayswater) ..	Middlesex	Met.	See London, Bayswater (Queen's Rd.)
.	.	.	.	.	.	. .	Queen's Road (Peckham)......	Surrey ...	L. B. & S. C.	See London.
G	P	F	L	H	C	5 0	Queenstown	Cork	G. S. & W.	Terminus.
G	P	.	.	.	.	. .	Queenstown Junction Station	Cork	G. S. & W.	Cork and Midleton.
.	.	.	.	.	.	. .	Queen Street	Devon ...	L. & S.W.	See Exeter.
.	.	.	.	.	.	. .	Queen Street	Glamorg'n	T. V.	See Cardiff.
.	.	.	.	.	.	. .	Queen Street	Leicester..	Mid.	Same as Leicester, East Station.
.	.	.	.	.	.	. .	Queen Str. (High Level) (NB)	Lanark ...	{ N. B.	} See Glasgow.
									{ N B,G N, N E (E. Coast)	
.	.	.	.	.	.	. .	Queen Street (Low Level) ...	Lanark ...	N. B.	See Glasgow.
G	P	.	.	.	.	. .	Quellyn Lake	Carnarvon	No. Wales N. G.	Dinas and Snowdon.
.	.	.	.	.	.	. .	Quibell Bros.' Siding (G.N.)...	Notts	G. N.—Mid...................	Newark.
G	P	.	.	.	.	. .	Quilty	Clare	West Clare	Miltown Malbay and Kilkee.
.	.	.	.	.	.	. .	Quin (G. S. & W.)	Clare	G. S. & W.—M. G. W....	See Ardsollus and Quin.
.	.	.	.	.	.	. .	Quintinshill	Dumfries..	Cal.	See Gretna.
.	.	.	.	.	.	. .	Quinton Colliery................	Staffs	L. & N. W.	Same as Blewitt & Co. (Wyrley and Church Bridge).
.	.	.	.	.	.	. .	Quintrell Downs Siding	Cornwall ..	G. W.	Newquay.
.	.	.	.	.	.	. .	Quirk, Barton & Burn's Siding	Lancs	L. & N. W.	St. Helens.

EXPLANATION—G *Goods Station.*   P *Passenger and Parcel Station.*   P* *Passenger, but not Parcel or Miscellaneous Traffic.*
F *Furniture Vans, Carriages, Portable Engines, and Machines on Wheels.*   L *Live Stock.*
H *Horse Boxes and Prize Cattle Vans.*   C *Carriages by Passenger Train.*

G	P	F	L	H	C	Tons	Cwts	STATIONS, &c.	COUNTY.	COMPANY.	POSITION.
G	P	.	L	.	.	.	.	Quorn	Leicester	Mid.	See Barrow-on-Soar and Quorn.
G	P	.	L	.	.	.	.	Quorn & Woodhouse	Leicester	G. C.	Loughboro' and Leicester.
G	P	F	.	.	.	.	.	Quy	Cambs	G. E.	Cambridge and Fordham.
								Francis Siding	Cambs	G. E.	Quy.

R

G	P	F	L	H	C	Tons	Cwts	STATIONS, &c.	COUNTY.	COMPANY.	POSITION.
G	P	.	L	.	.	.	.	Raasay	Inverness	Cal.	Steamer from Oban.
G	P	.	L	.	.	.	.			High.	Steamer from Kyle of Lochalsh.
G	P	.	L	.	.	.	.			N. B.	Steamer from Mallaig.
G	P	F	L	H	C	3	0	Racks	Dumfries	G. & S. W.	Dumfries and Annan.
.	.	.	.	.	.	.	.	Radbourne	Derby	G. N.	See Mickleover (for Radbourne).
.	P	.	.	.	.	.	.	Radcliffe	Lancs	L. & Y.	Whitefield and Bradley Fold.
G	P	F	L	H	C	10	0	Radcliffe Bridge	Lancs	L. & Y.	Salford and Bury.
.	.	.	.	.	.	.	.	Radcliffe Coal Co.'s New Coal Depôt	Northumb	N. E.	Alnwick.
.	.	.	.	.	.	.	.	Radcliffe Newburgh Colliery	Northumb	N. E.	Amble.
G	P	F	L	H	C	.	.	Radcliffe-on-Trent (G. N.)	Notts	G. N.	Grantham and Nottingham.
.	P	F	.	H	C	.	.			L. & N. W.	Over G. N. from Saxondale Junc.
.	.	.	.	.	.	.	.	Radford	Notts	Mid.	See Nottingham.
G	P	F	L	H	C	2	10	Radlett	Herts	Mid.	St. Albans and London.
								Parkbury Siding	Herts	Mid.	Near Radlett.
G	P	.	L	.	.	.	.	Radley	Berks	G. W.	Didcot and Oxford.
.	.	.	.	.	.	.	.	Radnor Co.'s Wharf	Radnor	L. & N. W.	Knucklas.
.	.	.	.	.	.	.	.	Radnorshire Coal Co.	Radnor	G. W.	Dolyhir.
G	P	F	L	H	C	6	0	Radstock	Somerset	G. W.	Frome and Bristol.
G	P	F	L	H	C	5	0		Somerset	S. & D. Jt. (L&SW&Mid.)	Shepton Mallet and Bath.
								Braysdown Colliery	Somerset	S. & D. Jt. (L. & S. W. & Mid)	Radstock and Wellow.
								Clandown Colliery	Somerset	S. & D. Jt. (L. & S. W. & Mid)	Radstock.
								Foxcote Colliery	Somerset	G. W.—S. & D. Jt.	Radstock.
								Huish Colliery	Somerset	G. W.	Radstock.
								Kilmersdon Colliery	Somerset	G. W.	Radstock.
								Ludlow's Colliery	Somerset	G. W.—S. & D. Jt.	Radstock.
								Middle Pit Colliery	Somerset	S. & D. Jt. (L. & S. W. & Mid)	Radstock.
								Old Welton Colliery	Somerset	G. W.	Radstock.
								Radstock Coal Co.'s Siding	Somerset	G. W.	Radstock.
								Tyning's Colliery	Somerset	G. W.—S. & D. Jt.	Radstock.
								Wheeler & Gregory's Wagon Works	Somerset	G. W.—S. & D. Jt.	Radstock.
								Writhlington Colliery	Somerset	G. W.—S. & D. Jt.	Radstock.
G	P	.	.	.	.	.	.	Radway Green	Cheshire	N. S.	Crewe and Harecastle.
G	P	.	.	.	.	.	.	Radyr	Glamorg'n	T. V.	Cardiff and Pontypridd.
								Radyr Quarry	Glamorg'n	T. V.	Radyr and Grangetown.
								Radyr Stores (Taff Vale Railway Co.'s)	Glamorg'n	T. V.	Radyr.
								Waterhall Siding	Glamorg'n	T. V.	Radyr and Cross Inn.
.	.	.	.	.	.	.	.	Raebog Siding	Lanark	N. B.	Rawyards.
.	.	.	.	.	.	.	.	Raeburn's Brewery	Edinboro'	N. B.	Duddingston and Craigmillar.
.	.	.	.	.	.	.	.	Raesgill Foundry	Lanark	Cal.	Carluke.
.	P	.	.	.	.	.	.	Raffeen	Cork	C. B. & P.	Cork and Carrigaline.
G	P	.	L	H	.	4	10	Raglan	Mon	G. W.	Usk and Monmouth.
.	.	.	.	.	.	.	.	Raglan Colliery	Glamorg'n	G. W.	South Rhondda.
.	.	.	.	.	.	.	.	Ragstone Siding	Kent	S. E. & C.	Maidstone, West.
.	P	.	.	.	.	.	.	Raheny	Dublin	G. N. (I.)	Dublin and Malahide.
.	.	.	.	.	.	.	.	Railway & General Engineering Co.'s Siding (Mid.)	Notts	Mid.—L. & N. W.	Nottingham.
.	.	.	.	.	.	.	.	Railway Key Co.'s Siding	Lancs	P. & L. Jt. (L & NW. & L & Y)	Preston, Deepdale.
.	.	.	.	.	.	.	.	Railway Street & Kingston Street (N. E.)	Yorks	N. E.—L. & Y—L. & N. W.	See Hull.
.	.	.	.	.	.	.	.	Railway Street Siding	Lincoln	G. C.	See Bannister & Co.'s Sidings (Grimsby Town).
.	.	.	.	.	.	.	.	Raimes & Co.'s Siding	Durham	N. E.	Stockton, South.
.	.	.	.	.	.	.	.	Rainbow Hill Junction	Worcester	G. W.	Worcester.
.	.	.	.	.	.	.	.	Raindale Siding	Yorks	N. E.	Goathland / Levisham.
.	.	.	.	.	.	.	.	Rainford Coal Co.'s Siding	Lancs	L. & Y.	Liverpool, Sandhills.

EXPLANATION—G *Goods Station.*   P *Passenger and Parcel Station.*   P* *Passenger, but not Parcel or Miscellaneous Traffic.*
F *Furniture Vans, Carriages, Portable Engines, and Machines on Wheels.*   L *Live Stock.*
H *Horse Boxes and Prize Cattle Vans.*   C *Carriages by Passenger Train.*

STATION ACCOMMODATION.						CRANE POWER.		STATIONS, &c.	COUNTY.	COMPANY.	POSITION.
						Tons	Cwts.				
G	P		L	H		3	0	Rainford Junction..............	Lancs	L. & Y.—L. & N. W. ...	Wigan and St. Helens.
	P			H				Rainford Junction Station ...	Lancs	{ L. & Y.	Liverpool and Wigan.
										{ L. & N. W.	Branch from St. Helens.
								Holland Moss Colliery	Lancs	L. & Y.	Near Rainford Junction.
								Lord Derby's Siding	Lancs	L. & Y.	Near Rainford Junction.
G	P		L			1	10	Rainford Coal Siding	Lancs	L. & Y.	Rainford and Kirkby.
								Rainford Village..............	Lancs	L. & N. W.	Rainford Junction and St. Helens.
								Birch & Co.'s Brewery	Lancs	L. & N. W.	Rainford Village & Rainford Jn. Sta.
								Mill Lane Mining Co.'s Sid.	Lancs	L. & N. W.	Crank and Rookery.
								Pilkington's—			
								Mill Lane Siding	Lancs	L. & N. W.	Crank and Rookery.
								Sand Siding	Lancs	L. & N. W.	Crank and Rookery.
G	P	F	L	H	C	1	0	Yard	Lancs	L. & N. W.	Rainford Village & Rainford Jn. Sta.
								Rainham	Essex	L. T. & S.	Barking and Tilbury.
								Dagenham Docks Siding (Williams & Son)........	Essex	L. T. & S.	Rainham.
G	P	F	L	H	C	1	15	Wennington Siding	Essex	L. T. & S.	Rainham.
G	P		L	H		5	0	Rainham	Kent	S. E. & C.	Chatham and Sittingbourne.
								Rainhill	Lancs	L. & N. W.	Kenyon Junction Sta. and Liverpool.
								Bretherton's Siding	Lancs	L. & N. W.	Rainhill.
								Elton Head Farm	Lancs	L. & N. W.	Rainhill and Lea Green.
								Evans, R., & Co.'s Siding	Lancs	L. & N. W.	Rainhill.
								Rainhill Gas & Water Co.'s Siding	Lancs	L. & N. W.	Rainhill and Lea Green.
								Sutton Heath & Lea Green Colliery Co.—			
								East Colliery	Lancs	L. & N. W.	Rainhill and Lea Green.
								Roughdale Works	Lancs	L. & N. W.	Rainhill and Lea Green.
								West Colliery	Lancs	L. & N. W.	Rainhill and Lea Green.
								Rainton Crossing Siding ...	Durham ...	N. E.	Fencehouses.
								Rainton Junction Gas Works	Durham ...	N. E.	Fencehouses.
								Rainworth	Notts	Mid.	See Blidworth and Rainworth.
								Raisby Hill Basic Works.....	Durham ...	N. E.	Coxhoe.
								Raisby Hill Depôts	Durham ...	N. E.	Coxhoe.
								Raisby Hill High Quarries ...	Durham ...	N. E.	Coxhoe.
								Raisby Hill Low Quarry	Durham ...	N. E.	Coxhoe.
								Rait & Gardiner's Siding	Middlesex	{ G. E.	London, Millwall Docks.
										{ GN—GW—LNW—Mid	London, Poplar.
								Raith Colliery Sidings	Fife	N. B.	Cowdenbeath, Old.
								Ramage & Ferguson's Ship-building Yard.............	Edinboro'	Cal.—N. B.	Leith, North.
								Ramford Brick & Tile Co.'s Tickle's Siding	Lancs	L. & N. W.	St. Helens.
	P							Rampside	Lancs	Furness	Barrow and Piel.
								Ramsay Pit	Edinboro'	N. B.	Loanhead.
								Ramsay's Fire-Brick Works	Durham ...	N. E.	Derwenthaugh.
G	P		L	H	C	8	0	Ramsbottom	Lancs	L. & Y.	Bury and Accrington.
								Grant's Siding............	Lancs	L. & Y.	Ramsbottom.
								Ramsbottom Paper Mill ...	Lancs	L. & Y.	Near Ramsbottom.
								Ramsbottom Gas Co.'s Siding	Lancs	L. & Y.	Stubbins.
								Ramsden Bellhouse Siding ...	Essex	G. E.	See Wickford Junction.
								Ramsden Dock	Lancs	Furness	See Barrow.
								Ramsden's—			
								Shakerley Colliery	Lancs	L. & N. W.	See Green's Siding (Tyldesley).
								Siding	Lancs	L. & N. W.	See Lecturers' Close and Hulme Trust Siding (Bolton).
G	P	F	L	H	C	5	0	Ramsey	Hunts......	G. N.	Branch—Huntingdon & Peterboro'.
G	P	F	L	H	C	2	0	Ramsey (High Street)	Hunts......	G. N. & G. E. Jt.	Branch from Somersham.
G	P		L					Ramsey	I. of Man.	Manx Northern	Terminus.
								Ramsgate—			
G	P	F	L	H	C	10	0	Harbour	Kent	S. E. & C.	Branch from Faversham.
G	P	F	L	H	C	8	0	Town	Kent	S. E. & C.	Canterbury (West) & Margate Sands.
G	P		L	H		3	0	Randalstown	Antrim ...	N. C. Com. (Mid.)	Cookstown Junction & Magherafelt.
								Randlay Brick Works	Salop	G. W.	Hollinswood.
								Randley Bk. & Tile Co.'s Sid.	Salop	L. & N. W.	Stirchley.
								Randolph Colliery	Durham ...	N. E.	Evenwood.
								Randolph Colliery	Fife	N. B.	Thornton.
	P							Ranelagh and Rathmines......	Dublin ...	D. W. & W.	Dublin, Harcourt Street and Bray.
G	P		L	H		2	0	Rankinston	Ayr	G. & S.W.	Hollybush and Ochiltree.
								Rankinston Brick Works...	Ayr	G. & S.W.	Rankinston Junction.
								Rankinston Collieries	Ayr	G. & S.W.	Rankinston Junction.
								Rankinston Junction.........	Ayr	G. & S.W.	Rankinston and Ochiltree.

EXPLANATION—G Goods Station.   P Passenger and Parcel Station.   P* Passenger, but not Parcel or Miscellaneous Traffic.
F Furniture Vans, Carriages, Portable Engines, and Machines on Wheels.   L Live Stock.
H Horse Boxes and Prize Cattle Vans.   C Carriages by Passenger Train.

G	P	F	L	H	C	Crane Power (Tons Cwts)	Stations, &c.	County	Company	Position
G	P	F	L	H	C	1 10	Rannoch	Perth	N. B.	Crianlarich and Fort William.
							Corrour Siding	Perth	N. B.	Rannoch and Tulloch.
G	P	F	L	H	C	1 0	Ranskill	Notts	G. N.	Retford and Doncaster.
							Ransome & Co.'s Siding	Notts	G. N.	Newark.
							Ransom's Lime Siding	Herts	G. N.	Hitchin.
							Ransom, W. G., Siding	Suffolk	G. E.	Stowmarket.
	P						Rashenny	Donegal	L. & L. S.	Buncrana and Carndonagh.
G	P		L	H			Raskelf	Yorks	N. E.	York and Thirsk.
G	P						Ratby	Leicester	Mid.	Desford and Leicester, West Bridge.
							Ratchill Siding	Aberdeen	G. N. of S.	Kintore.
							Ratcliffe's (Exors.) Siding	Flint	L. & N. W.	Broughton Hall.
							Ratcliffe's (Exors.) Sidings	Flint	L. & N. W.	Padeswood and Buckley.
							Ratgoed Quarry	Merioneth	Corris.	Terminus.
							Rathbone Road	Lancs	L. & N. W.	See Liverpool.
G	P	F	L	H	C		Rathdrum	Wicklow	D. W. & W.	Wicklow and Arklow.
							Balleece Siding	Wicklow	D. W. & W.	Rathdrum.
G	P						Rathduff	Cork	G. S. & W.	Mallow and Cork.
G	P		L	H		1 5	Rathen	Aberdeen	G. N. of S.	Dyce and Fraserburgh.
	P						Rathgarogue	Wexford	D. W. & W.	Macmine Junction and New Ross.
G	P	F	L	H	C	1 5	Rathkeale	Limerick	G. S. & W.	Newcastle West and Limerick.
							Johnstone's Siding	Limerick	G. S. & W.	Rathkeale and Ardagh.
	P						Rathkenny	Antrim	N. C. Com. (Mid.)	Ballymena and Parkmore.
							Antrim Iron Ore Co.	Antrim	N. C. Com. (Mid.)	Rathkenny.
							Rathmines	Dublin	D. W. & W.	See Ranelagh and Rathmines.
G	P		L	H			Rathmore	Cork	G. S. & W.	Mallow and Killarney.
G	P						Rathnew	Wicklow	D. W. & W.	Wicklow and Arklow.
							Rathnew Brick Works	Wicklow	D. W. & W.	Rathnew.
G	P	F	L	H	C	1 5	Ratho	Edinboro'	N. B.	Edinburgh and Linlithgow.
G							Clifton Siding	Edinboro'	N. B.	Ratho and Drumshoreland.
							Hallyards Siding	Edinboro'	N. B.	Ingliston Pit Branch.
							Hillwood Quarry	Edinboro'	N. B.	Ratho and Broxburn Junction.
							Ingliston Pit Siding	Edinboro'	N. B.	Branch—Ratho and Kirkliston.
							Kilpunt Siding	L'lithgow	N. B.	Newliston Mine Branch.
							Newliston Mine	L'lithgow	N. B.	Branch—Ratho and Drumshoreland.
							Norton Mains Siding	Edinboro'	N. B.	Gogar and Ratho.
							Norton Quarry	Edinboro'	N. B.	Ratho.
							Rathowen	Longford	M. G. W.	See Street and Rathowen.
							Rathpeacon	Cork	G. S. & W.	See Cork.
G	P	F	L	H	C	1 10	Rathven	Banff	High.	Keith and Buckie.
G	P	F	L	H	C		Rathvilly	Carlow	G. S. & W.	Sallins and Tullow.
							Rattery Siding	Devon	G. W.	Totnes and Brent.
G	P		L	H			Rauceby	Lincoln	G. N.	Sleaford and Grantham.
							Rauceby Sand Pit Siding	Lincoln	G. N.	Rauceby.
G	P	F	L	H	C	1 10	Raunds	N'hampton	Mid.	Huntingdon and Thrapston.
							Ravelrig Junction	Edinboro'	Cal.	Midcalder and Curriehill.
							Ravelrig Quarry	Edinboro'	Cal.	Balerno.
							Raven Colliery	Glamorg'n	G. W.	Garnant.
G	P	F	L	H	C	3 10	Ravenglass	Cumb'land	{ Furness / R. & E.	Millom and Sellafield. / Adjoining Furness Station.
G	P		L				Ravenhead Branch	Lancs	L. & N. W.	Peasley Cross and St. Helens.
							Ravenhead Colliery	Lancs	L. & N. W.	See St. Helens Col. Co. (St. Helens).
							Ravenhead Sanitary Pipe and Brick Co.'s Siding	Lancs	L. & N. W.	St. Helens.
							Raven Iron & Tin Plate Wks.	Carmarth'	G. W.	Garnant.
G	P						Ravensbourne	Kent	S. E. & C.	Nunhead and Shortlands.
G	P						Ravenscar	Yorks	N. E.	Scarboro' and Whitby.
							Whitaker's Brick Yard	Yorks	N. E.	Ravenscar.
							Ravenscourt Park (L. & S. W.)	Middlesex	L. & S. W.—G. W.—Met.—Met. Dist.	See London.
G	P						Ravenscraig	Renfrew	Cal.	Greenock, Upper and Wemyss Bay.
							Ravenscraig Sand Quarry	Lanark	Cal.	Shieldmuir.
							Ravensdale Iron Works	Staffs	N. S.	See Heath & Sons (Chatterley).
							Ravensdale Siding	Staffs	N. S.	See Goldendale Iron Co. (Chatterley).
							Ravenslodge Siding	Yorks	L. & N. W.	Same as Ingham's Fire Brick Co.'s Brick & Pipe Works.
							Raven Square	Montgom	Cam. (W. & L.)	See Welshpool.
G	P	F	L	H	C	7 0	Ravensthorpe (L. & Y.)	Yorks	{ L. & Y. / G. N.	Thornhill and Heckmondwike. / Over L. & Y. from Wakefield.
G	P	F	L	H	C	10 0	Ravensthorpe and Thornhill	Yorks	L. & N. W.	Dewsbury and Huddersfield.
							Ingham's Fire Brick Co.'s Brick & Pipe Works (Ravenslodge Siding)	Yorks	L. & N. W.	Ravensthorpe and Dewsbury.

EXPLANATION—G *Goods Station.*   P *Passenger and Parcel Station.*   Pᵖ *Passenger, but not Parcel or Miscellaneous Traffic.*
F *Furniture Vans, Carriages, Portable Engines, and Machines on Wheels.*   L *Live Stock.*
H *Horse Boxes and Prize Cattle Vans.*   C *Carriages by Passenger Train.*

STATION ACCOMMODATION.						CRANE POWER.	STATIONS, &c.	COUNTY.	COMPANY.	POSITION.
						Tons Cwts.	Ravensthorpe and Thornhill—*continued.*			
..	..	..	..	..	..		Mirfield Coal Co.'s Siding	Yorks	L. & N. W.	Ravensthorpe and Dewsbury.
..	..	..	..	..	..		Ravenstonedale	W'morlnd	Mid.	See Kirkby Stephen & Ravenstonedale.
G	P	.	L	H	.	1 10	Ravenstonedale	W'morlnd	N. E.	Tebay and Kirkby Stephen.
..	..	..	..	..	..		Ravenstone Wood Junction..	N'hamptn	E. & W. Jn.—Mid.	Salcey Forest and Olney.
..	..	..	..	..	..		Ravenswood Junction	Roxburgh	N. B.	St. Boswells and Earlston.
..	..	..	..	..	..		Ravensworth Brk. & Tl.Wks.	Durham ...	N. E.	Birtley.
..	..	..	..	..	..		Ravensworth Colliery	Durham ...	N. E.	Redheugh.
G	P	F	L	H	C	5 0	Rawcliffe	Yorks	L. & Y.	Goole and Knottingley.
..	..	..	..	..	..		Rawdon	Yorks	Mid.	See Apperley Bridge and Rawdon.
..	..	..	..	..	..		Rawdon Colliery (Mid.)	Leicester..	Mid.—L. & N. W.	See Moira Colliery Co. (Moira).
..	..	..	..	..	..		Rawlinson & Son's Siding ...	Lancs	L. & N. W.	Garston Docks.
..	..	..	..	..	..		Rawlinson's Siding	Lancs	L&Y&LUJt(LY&LNW)	See Ellerbeck Col. Co. (White Bear, Adlington).
..	..	..	..	..	..		Rawmarsh	Yorks	Mid.	See Parkgate and Rawmarsh.
G	P	F	L	H	C	10 0	Rawtenstall	Lancs	L. & Y.	Stubbins and Bacup.
..	..	..	..	..	..		Hall Carr Siding.............	Lancs	L. & Y.	Rawtenstall.
..	..	..	..	..	..		Ilex Siding	Lancs	L. & Y.	Near Rawtenstall.
..	..	..	..	..	..		Longholme Siding	Lancs	L. & Y.	Near Rawtenstall.
..	..	..	..	..	..		New Hall Hey Siding	Lancs	L. & Y.	Near Rawtenstall.
..	..	..	..	..	..		Townsend Fold Siding	Lancs	L. & Y.	Near Rawtenstall.
..	..	..	..	..	..		Union Mill Siding	Lancs	L. & Y.	Rawtenstall.
G	P	.	L	.	.	3 0	Rawyards	Lanark ...	N. B.	Airdrie, Commonhead & Slamannan.
..	..	..	..	..	..		Airdrie Cotton Mills	Lanark ...	N. B.	Rawyards.
..	..	..	..	..	..		Airdriehill Quarry	Lanark ...	N. B.	Rawyards and Whiterigg.
G	..	..	..	..	..		Arbuckle Siding	Lanark ...	N. B.	Whiterigg and Longriggend.
..	..	..	..	..	..		Arden Colliery	Lanark ...	N. B.	Whiterigg and Longriggend.
G	..	..	..	..	..		Ballochnie Siding	Lanark ...	N. B.	Branch—Rawyards and Whiterigg.
..	..	..	..	..	..		Blacktongue Colliery, No. 2	Lanark ...	N. B.	Branch—Rawyards and Whiterigg.
..	..	..	..	..	..		Burnhead Quarry Sidings..	Lanark ...	N. B.	Rawyards and Plains.
..	..	..	..	..	..		Carron Lye	Lanark ...	N. B.	Branch—Rawyards and Whiterigg.
..	..	..	..	..	..		Colliertree Siding	Lanark ...	N. B.	Rawyards and Brownieside.
..	..	..	..	..	..		Darngavil Collieries	Lanark ...	N. B.	Branch—Rawyards and Whiterigg.
..	..	..	..	..	..		Drumbathie Brick Works..	Lanark ...	N. B.	Branch—Rawyards & Brownieside.
..	..	..	..	..	..		Drumgray Colliery	Lanark ...	N. B.	Branch—Rawyards and Whiterigg.
G	..	..	..	..	..		Drumshangie Sidings (Drumshangie Long Lye)	Lanark ...	N. B.	Branch—Rawyards and Whiterigg.
..	..	..	..	..	..		Feddlerland Colliery	Lanark ...	N. B.	Branch—Rawyards and Whiterigg.
..	..	..	..	..	..		Goldie & Co.'s Siding	Lanark ...	N. B.	Rawyards.
..	..	..	..	..	..		Greyrigg Colliery	Lanark ...	N. B.	Branch—Rawyards and Whiterigg.
..	..	..	..	..	..		Hill of Drumgray Colliery..	Lanark ...	N. B.	Branch—Rawyards and Whiterigg.
..	..	..	..	..	..		Loanrigg Col. & Brick Wks.	Lanark ...	N. B.	Rawyards and Whiterigg.
..	..	..	..	..	..		Meikle Drumgray Colliery	Lanark ...	N. B.	Branch—Rawyards and Whiterigg.
..	..	..	..	..	..		Pickering&Co.'sWgn.Wks.	Lanark ...	N. B.	Rawyards.
..	..	..	..	..	..		Raebog Siding	Lanark ...	N. B.	Branch—Rawyards and Whiterigg.
..	..	..	..	..	..		Rawyards Brick Works ...	Lanark ...	N. B.	Rawyards and Whiterigg.
..	..	..	..	..	..		Stanrigg Brick Works	Lanark ...	N. B.	Branch from Whiterigg.
..	..	..	..	..	..		Stanrigg Colliery	Lanark ...	N. B.	Branch—Rawyards and Whiterigg.
..	..	..	..	..	..		Stanrigg Oil Works	Lanark ...	N. B.	Rawyards and Whiterigg.
..	..	..	..	..	..		Stanrigg Pit No. 5 (Airdriehill Colliery).................	Lanark ...	N. B.	Rawyards and Whiterigg.
..	..	..	..	..	..		Taylor's Sid.(Watt Str.Sid.)	Lanark ...	N. B.	Rawyards.
..	..	..	..	..	..		Upperton Siding	Lanark ...	N. B.	Branch—Rawyards and Whiterigg.
..	..	..	..	..	..		West Glentore Colliery......	Lanark ...	N. B.	Branch—Rawyards and Whiterigg.
..	..	..	..	..	..		Whiterigg Brick Works ...	Lanark ...	N. B.	Branch—Rawyards and Whiterigg.
..	..	..	..	..	..		Whiterigg Park Colliery ...	Lanark ...	N. B.	Branch—Rawyards and Whiterigg.
..	..	..	..	..	..		Rawyards Junction	Lanark ...	N. B.	Commonhead and Whiterigg.
..	..	..	..	..	..		Raybould's Works..............	Cumb'land	L. & N. W.	Workington.
G	P	.	.	.	.		Raydon Wood	Suffolk ...	G. E.	Bentley and Hadleigh.
G	P	F	L	H	C	1 10	Rayleigh	Essex	G. E.	Wickford and Southend-on-Sea.
..	..	..	..	..	..		Plowman, E., Siding	Essex	G. E.	Rayleigh and Hockley.
G	P	F	L	H	C		Rayne	Essex	G. E.	Braintree and Dunmow.
..	..	..	..	..	..		Rayner's Works (C.L.C.)	Cheshire..	C. L. C.—L. & N. W......	See Salt Union Ltd. (Northwich).
..	..	..	..	..	..		Raynes & Co.—			
..	..	..	..	..	..		Penmaenrhos Siding	Carnarvon	L. & N. W.	Llysfaen.
..	..	..	..	..	..		Penybryn Siding	Carnarvon	L. & N. W.	Llysfaen.
..	P	.	.	.	.		Raynes Park	Surrey ...	L. & S. W.	Wimbledon and Surbiton.
G	P	.	.	.	.		Raynham Park	Norfolk ...	Mid. & G. N. Jt.	South Lynn and Melton Constable.
..	..	..	..	..	..		Read & Co.'s Siding	Surrey......	L.&S.W.&L.B.&S.C. Jt.	Merton Abbey.
..	..	..	..	..	..		Read & Sons' Siding	Somerset	S.&D.Jt.(L & SW & Mid.)	Binegar.
..	..	..	..	..	..		Read & Wildbur Siding	Norfolk ...	G. E.	Magdalen Road.

EXPLANATION—G *Goods Station.*　　P *Passenger and Parcel Station.*　　P* *Passenger, but not Parcel or Miscellaneous Traffic.*
F *Furniture Vans, Carriages, Portable Engines, and Machines on Wheels.*　　L *Live Stock.*
H *Horse Boxes and Prize Cattle Vans.*　　C *Carriages by Passenger Train.*

STATION ACCOMMODATION.						CRANE POWER.	STATIONS, &c.	COUNTY.	COMPANY.	POSITION.
						Tons Cwts.	Read, T. M., Siding	Norfolk ...	G. E.	Tivetshall.
							READING—			
G	P	F	L	H	C	10 0	(Station)	Berks	G. W.	Maidenhead and Didcot.
G	P	F	L	H	C	15 0	(Station, S. E. & C.)	Berks	{ S. E. & C.	Extension from Guildford.
									{ L. & S. W.	Over S. E. & C. from Wokingham Jn.
							Gas Works	Berks	G W—L & S W—S E & C	Reading.
							Huntley & Palmer's Siding	Berks	G W—L & S W—S E & C	Reading.
							Junction	Berks	G. W.—L. & S. W.	Reading Sta. and Wokingham Jn.
	P						Junction	Berks	L. & S. W.—S. E. & C. ...	Earley and Reading.
	P						Rearsby	Leicester..	Mid.	Syston and Melton Mowbray.
							Reay & Usher's Forge	Durham ..	N. E.	Hylton.
							Reay's Siding	Cumb'land	N. B.	Abbey Town.
G	P	F	L	H	C	1 0	Recess	Galway ...	M. G. W.	Galway and Clifden.
	P						Recess Hotel Platform	Galway ...	M. G. W.	Galway and Clifden.
							Rectory Junction	Notts	G. N.	Netherfield and Colwick.
							Rectory Road	Middlesex	G. E.	See London.
							Red Bank Brick Co.'s Siding	Derby	A & N Jt. (L & N W & Mid.)	Measham.
							Red Barns Manure Wharf ...	Northumb	N. E.	Newcastle-on-Tyne.
G	P					1 0	Redbourn	Herts	Mid.	Harpenden and Hemel Hempsted.
							Owen's Siding	Herts	Mid.	Redbourn and Hemel Hempsted.
							Redbourn Hill Works	Lincoln ...	G. C.	Frodingham and Scunthorpe.
G	P	F	L	H	C	10 0	Redbridge (L. & S. W.)	Hants	{ L. & S. W.	Southampton and Brockenhurst.
									{ M. & S. W. Jn.	Over L. & S. W. from Andover Jn.
							Redbridge Wharf	Hants	L. & S.W.	Redbridge.
							Schultze Gunpowder Co.'s Siding	Hants	L. & S.W.	Redbridge.
G	P					5 0	Redbrook	Mon	G. W.	Monmouth and Chepstow.
							Redburn Pits	Ayr	Cal.—G. & S. W.	Kilwinning.
G	P	F	L	H	C	5 0	Redcar	Yorks	N. E.	Middlesbro' and Saltburn.
							Coatham Lane Depôts	Yorks	N. E.	Redcar.
							Greenland Depôt	Yorks	N. E.	Redcar.
							Warrenby Depôt & Siding	Yorks	N. E.	Redcar.
							Redcar Iron Works—			
							Brand's Slag Works	Yorks	N. E.	Tod Point.
							Broadbent & Co.'s Slag Wool Works	Yorks	N. E.	Tod Point.
G	P	F	L	H	C	2 0	Redcastle	Ross & Cro'	High.	Muir of Ord and Fortrose.
							Redcliffe Wharf	Glo'ster ...	G. W.	See Bristol.
							Redcraig Siding	Edinboro'	Cal.	Oakbank.
G						1 10	Redding	Stirling ...	N. B.	Polmont and Falkirk.
							Nobel's Explosives Works..	Stirling ...	N. B.	Redding.
							Redding Collieries	Stirling ...	N. B.	Branch from Redding.
							Reddish	Lancs	L. & N. W.—S. & M. Jt...	See Stockport.
							Reddish Junction	Cheshire..	S. & M. Jt. (G. C. & Mid.)	Reddish and Bredbury.
G	P	F	L	H	C	1 10	Redditch	Worcester	Mid.	Barnt Green and Evesham.
							Dixon's Wharf	Worcester	Mid.	Near Redditch.
							Redditch Town and District Gas Co.'s Siding	Worcester	Mid.	Near Redditch.
							Redfern Street Siding	Lancs	L. & Y.	Liverpool, Sandhills.
							Redford Colliery	Stirling ...	N. B.	Bowhouse.
							Redford Siding	Fife	N. B.	Thornton.
G						5 0	Redheugh	Durham ...	N. E.	Gateshead and Blaydon.
							Allerdean Siding	Durham ...	N. E.	Redheugh.
							Andrews House Colliery ...	Durham ...	N. E.	Tanfield Branch.
							Atlas Rivet Works (McFarlane & Whitfield's Siding)	Durham ...	N. E.	Redheugh.
							Birkhead Siding	Durham ...	N. E.	Tanfield Branch.
							Bowes Bridge Junction ...	Durham ...	N. E.	Tanfield Branch.
							Burnopfield Colliery, Coke and Brick Works	Durham ...	N. E.	Tanfield Branch.
							Byer Moor Colliery, Coke Works and Quarry	Durham ...	N. E.	Tanfield Branch.
							Carrick & Wardale's Siding	Durham ...	N. E.	Redheugh.
							Co-operative Wholesale Society's Dunston Flour Mill	Durham ...	N. E.	Redheugh.
							Crook Bank Colliery	Durham ...	N. E.	Tanfield Branch.
							Crookgate Siding	Durham ...	N. E.	Tanfield Branch.
							Davidson & Co.'s Glass Wks.	Durham ...	N. E.	Redheugh.
							Dipton Colliery	Durham ...	N. E.	Tanfield Branch.
							Dixon, Corbett, Newall & Co.'s Rope Works	Durham ...	N. E.	Redheugh.

EXPLANATION—G *Goods Station.*   P *Passenger and Parcel Station.*   P* *Passenger, but not Parcel or Miscellaneous Traffic.*
F *Furniture Vans, Carriages, Portable Engines, and Machines on Wheels.*   L *Live Stock.*
H *Horse Boxes and Prize Cattle Vans.*   C *Carriages by Passenger Train.*

STATION ACCOMMODATION.						CRANE POWER.		STATIONS, &c.	COUNTY.	COMPANY.	POSITION.
						Tons	Cwts.	Redheugh—*continued.*			
..	..	..	..	..	..			Dunston Colliery	Durham ..	N. E.	Redheugh.
..	..	..	..	..	..			Dunston Engine Works ...	Durham ..	N. E.	Redheugh.
..	..	..	..	..	..			Dunston Staithes	Durham ..	N. E.	Redheugh.
..	..	..	..	..	..			East Tanfield Colliery, Coke and Brick Works	Durham ..	N. E.	Tanfield Branch.
..	..	..	..	..	..			Gateshead Workhouse Sid.	Durham ..	N. E.	Redheugh.
..	..	..	..	..	..			Kibblesworth Colliery	Durham ..	N. E.	Tanfield Branch.
..	..	..	..	..	..			Lobley Hill Siding & Depôt	Durham ..	N. E.	Tanfield Branch.
..	..	..	..	..	..			Lucas Bros.' Fire-Brick Wks.	Durham ..	N. E.	Redheugh.
..	..	..	..	..	..			Marley Hill Colliery, Coke and Brick Works	Durham ..	N. E.	Tanfield Branch.
..	..	..	..	..	..			Marley Hill Depôt	Durham ..	N. E.	Tanfield Branch.
..	..	..	..	..	..			Mawson, Clark & Co.'s Sid.	Durham ..	N. E.	Redheugh.
..	..	..	..	..	..			Norwood Colliery	Durham ..	N. E.	Tanfield Branch.
..	..	..	..	..	..			Palmer, Hall & Co.'s Works	Durham ..	N. E.	Redheugh.
..	..	..	..	..	..			Peacock's Siding	Durham ..	N. E.	Tanfield Branch.
..	..	..	..	..	..			Ravensworth Colliery	Durham ..	N. E.	Tanfield Branch.
..	..	..	..	..	..			Redheugh Brick Works ...	Durham ..	N. E.	Redheugh.
..	..	..	..	..	..			Redheugh Gas Works	Durham ..	N. E.	Redheugh.
..	..	..	..	..	..			Redheugh Sheet Iron Co.'s Siding	Durham ..	N. E.	Redheugh.
G	..	..	..	..	..	5	0	Redheugh Tile Shed Depôt	Durham ..	N. E.	Redheugh.
..	..	..	..	..	..			Redheugh Wharf Co.	Durham ..	N. E.	Redheugh.
..	..	..	..	..	..			Sunniside Depôt	Durham ..	N. E.	Tanfield Branch.
..	..	..	..	..	..			Tanfield Branch Junction..	Durham ..	N. E.	Tanfield Branch.
..	..	..	..	..	..			Tanfield Lane Manure Depôts and Siding	Durham ..	N. E.	Tanfield Branch.
..	..	..	..	..	..			Tanfield Lea Colliery and Coke Ovens	Durham ..	N. E.	Tanfield Branch.
..	..	..	..	..	..			Tanfield Moor Colliery	Durham ..	N. E.	Tanfield Branch.
..	..	..	..	..	..			Teams Siding	Durham ..	N. E.	Redheugh.
..	..	..	..	..	..			Thubron's Timber Yard and Creosote Works	Durham ..	N. E.	Redheugh.
..	..	..	..	..	..			Tyne Bolt and Rivet Works	Durham ..	N. E.	Redheugh.
..	..	..	..	..	..			White-le-head Siding	Durham ..	N. E.	Tanfield Branch.
..	..	..	..	..	..			Redheugh Colliery	Durham ..	N. E.	Gateshead.
								RED HILL—			
G	..	F	L	..	..	6	0	(Station)	Surrey	L. B. & S. C.	Red Hill Junction and Earlswood.
G	..	F	L	..	..	8	0	(Station)	Surrey	S. E. & C.	Red Hill Junction and Tonbridge.
..	P	..	..	H	C	..	..	(Station and Junction)	Surrey	{ L. B. & S. C.	Croydon and Three Bridges.
										{ S. E. & C.	Croydon and Tonbridge.
..	..	..	..	..	..			Barrow's Siding	Surrey	S. E. & C.	Red Hill and Reigate.
..	..	..	..	..	..			Hall & Co.'s Siding	Surrey	L. B. & S. C.	Red Hill.
..	..	..	..	..	..			Holmethorpe Siding	Surrey	S. E. & C.	Red Hill and Merstham.
..	..	..	..	..	..			Pope's Siding	Surrey	S. E. & C.	Red Hill and Merstham.
..	..	..	..	..	..			Pym's Siding	Surrey	S. E. & C.	Red Hill and Reigate.
..	..	..	..	..	..			Redhill Gas Co.'s Siding ...	Surrey	L. B. & S. C.	Red Hill.
..	..	..	..	..	..			Silver Sand Siding	Surrey	S. E. & C.	Red Hill and Reigate.
..	..	..	..	..	..			Stenning & Son's Siding ...	Surrey	L. B. & S. C.	Red Hill.
..	..	..	..	..	..			Thornton's Siding	Surrey	S. E. & C.	Red Hill and Merstham.
..	..	..	..	..	..			Trower's Siding	Surrey	S. E. & C.	Red Hill and Merstham.
..	..	..	..	..	..			Red Hill Brick Works (Hartley, J., & Co.)	Yorks	N. E.	Castleford.
..	..	..	..	..	..			Red Hill Junction	Hereford..	G. W.—L. & N. W.	Hereford.
..	P	..	..	..	..			Redhills	Cavan	G. N. (I.)	Clones and Cavan.
..	..	..	..	..	..			Redhills Junction	Cumb'land	C. K. & P.—N. E.	Penrith.
..	..	..	..	..	..			Redhills Lime Works	Cumb'land	N. E.	Clifton.
..	..	..	..	..	..			Red House Siding	Montgom	Cam. (Van).	Caersws and Ceryst.
..	..	..	..	..	..			Red House Siding	Northumb	N. E.	Monkseaton.
..	P	..	..	..	..			Red Jacket Quarry	Glamorg'n	R. & S. B.	Jersey Marine.
G	P	F	L	H	C	..	..	Redland	Glo'ster	Clif. Ex. Jt. (G.W. & Mid.)	Clifton Down and Montpelier.
G	P	F	L	H	C	1	0	Redmile (for Belvoir)	Leicester	G. N. & L. & N. W. Jt.	Bottesford Junc. & Melton Mowbray.
G	P	F	L	H†	C†	3	10	Redmire	Yorks	N. E.	Leyburn and Hawes.
G	P	F	L	H	C	..	..	Rednal	Salop	G. W.	Shrewsbury and Chirk.
..	..	..	..	..	..			Redpath, Brown & Co.'s Sid.	Edinboro'	N. B.	Same as St. Andrew's Steel Works (Edinburgh).
..	..	..	..	..	..			Redpath, Brown & Co.'s Sid.	Lancs	Trafford Park Estate	Manchester.
..	..	..	..	..	..			Red Posts Junction	Hants	L. & S.W.—M. & S.W. Jn.	Andover.
G	P	..	L	..	..	5	0	Red Rock	Lancs	L&Y & LU Jt (LNW&LY)	Blackburn and Boar's Head.
..	..	..	..	..	..			Red Rock (Haigh Junction)...	Lancs	L&Y & LU Jt.—L. & N. W.	Boar's Head and Red Rock.
G	P	F	L	H	C	5	0	Redruth	Cornwall	G. W.	Truro and Penzance.

EXPLANATION—G *Goods Station.*   P *Passenger and Parcel Station.*   P* *Passenger, but not Parcel or Miscellaneous Traffic.*
F *Furniture Vans, Carriages, Portable Engines, and Machines on Wheels.*   L *Live Stock.*
H *Horse Boxes and Prize Cattle Vans.*   H† C† *By special arrangement only.*   C *Carriages by Passenger Train.*

STATION ACCOMMODATION.						CRANE POWER.		STATIONS, &c.	COUNTY.	COMPANY.	POSITION.
						Tons	Cwts				
								Redruth—*continued.*			
G						4	10	Redruth Old Goods Yard...	Cornwall ..	G. W.	Redruth.
								Tresavean Branch & Siding	Cornwall ..	G. W.	Redruth and Carnbrea.
								Redshaw, Chas., Siding	Leicester..	Mid	Wigston, South.
								Redstone Quarry (Monkredding Quarry)	Ayr	G. & S. W.	Montgreenan.
								Red Street	Staffs	N. S.	Talk-o'-th'-Hill Branch.
G	P		L	H	C			Redham	Norfolk ...	G. E.	Norwich and Yarmouth.
G	P		L	H				Reedness Junction Station ..	Yorks	Axholme Jt (L&Y&NE)	Branch near Goole.
								Blacker's Siding..............	Yorks	Axholme Jt (L&Y&NE)	Reedness Junction and Eastoft.
								Corners Siding	Yorks	Axholme Jt (L&Y&NE)	Reedness Junction.
								Dougherty's Siding	Yorks	Axholme Jt(L&Y&NE)	Reedness Junction.
								Goole Fields Siding	Yorks	Axholme Jt (L&Y&NE)	Reedness Junction.
								Gossop's Siding	Yorks	Axholme Jt (L&Y&NE)	Reedness Junction.
								Moss Litter Siding	Yorks	Axholme Jt (L&Y&NE)	Reedness Junction.
								Peat Works	Yorks	Axholme Jt (L&Y&NE)	Reedness Junction.
								Smith's Siding	Yorks	Axholme Jt (L&Y&NE)	Riccarton and Morpeth.
G	P		L	H				Reedsmouth	Northumb	N. B.	Reedsmouth and Woodburn.
								Broomhope Siding	Northumb	N. B.	Bellingham and Wark.
								Reedsmouth Junction	Northumb	N. B.	Lincoln and Market Rasen.
G	P		L	H				Reepham	Lincoln ...	G. C.	County School and Aylsham.
G	P	F	L	H	C	1	10	Reepham	Norfolk ...	G. E.	See Whitwell and Reepham.
								Reepham	Norfolk ...	Mid. & G. N. Jt.	Same as Cwmphil Siding (Gurnos).
								Rees Morgan Siding (Mid.)..	Glamorg'n	Mid.—G.W.—L. & N.W.	Glasgow, Partick, Central.
								Regent Flour Mills	Lanark ...	Cal.	London, Marylebone.
								Regent's Canal Wharf	Middlesex	G. C.	Same as Salford Gas Works (Manchester).
								Regent's Road Gas Works ...	Lancs	L. & N. W.	
								Regent Street....................	Renfrew ...	Cal.	See Greenock.
								Regent Street Mineral Depôt	Renfrew ...	Cal.	Greenock, Regent Street.
								Reid & Co.'s Brick Works ...	Ayr	G B & K Jt (Cal & G & SW)	Same as Lugton Brick Works (Lugton).
								Reid & Co.'s Shipbuilding Yard	Renfrew ...	Cal.	Same as Whiteinch Shipbuilding Yard (Glasgow).
									Lanark ...	N. B.	
								Reid's Saw Mill	Kinross ...	N. B.	Mawcarse.
G	P	F	L	H	C	8	0	Reigate	Surrey ...	S. E. & C.	Red Hill and Guildford.
								Relly Mill Junction	Durham ...	N. E.	Durham, Passengers and Croxdale.
								RENFREW—			
								Chester & Co.'s Siding	Renfrew ...	G.&P.Jt.(Cal.&G.&S.W.)	Kings Inch and Porterfield.
G	P	F	L	H	C	3	0	Deanside	Renfrew...	G.&P.Jt.(Cal.&G.&S.W.)	Kings Inch and Cardonald.
G	P	F	L	H	C	3	0	Fulbar Street (G. & S. W.)	Renfrew	G. & S. W.	Branch from Paisley.
G	.	F	L	H	C	3	0			Cal.	Over G. & S. W. from Arkleston Jn.
								Harbour (G. & S. W.)	Renfrew ...	G. & S.W.—Cal.	Renfrew.
G	P	F	L	H	C	3	0	Kings Inch	Renfrew ...	G.&P.Jt.(Cal.&G.&S.W.)	Cardonald and Porterfield.
								Lobnitz & Co.'s Sid.(G&SW)	Renfrew ...	G. & S.W.—Cal.	Renfrew.
G	P	F	L	H	C	3	0	Porterfield	Renfrew ...	G.&P.Jt.(Cal.&G.&S.W.)	Terminus of Branch from Cardonald.
								Porterfield Siding (Babcock & Wilcox's) (G. & S. W.)	Renfrew ...	G. & S.W.—Cal.	Renfrew and Paisley, Abercorn.
								Simons & Co.'s Sid. (G&SW)	Renfrew ...	G. & S.W.—Cal.	Renfrew.
	P							South	Renfrew ...	G. & S.W.	Renfrew and Paisley.
G	P					15	0	Wharf (G. & S. W.)	Renfrew ...	G. & S. W.	Branch from Paisley.
G	.					15	0			Cal.	Renfrew.
								Renishaw	Derby	G. C.—L. & N. W.—Mid.	See Eckington and Renishaw.
								Renishaw Colliery	Derby	Mid.	Eckington and Renishaw.
								Renishaw Foundry.............	Derby	G. C.	Eckington and Renishaw.
								Renishaw Iron Works	Derby	G. C.—Mid.	Eckington and Renishaw.
								Renishaw Park Collieries......	Derby	Mid.	Eckington and Renishaw.
								Renishaw Park Collieries (Eckington Col.) (G. C.)...	Derby	G. C.—L. & N. W.	Eckington and Renishaw.
								Renshaw & Co.'s Siding......	Staffs	N. S.	See Cliff Vale Siding (Etruria).
								Renshaw's Metal Refinery ...	Durham ...	N. E.	Blaydon.
G	P		L	H		3	0	Renton	Dumbartn	D. & B. Jt. (Cal. & N. B.)	Dumbarton and Balloch.
								Cordale Siding	Dumbartn	D. & B. Jt. (Cal. & N. B.)	Dalreoch and Renton.
								Dalquhurn Siding	Dumbartn	D. & B. Jt. (Cal. & N. B.)	Dalreoch and Renton.
								Millburn Siding	Dumbartn	D. & B. Jt. (Cal. & N. B.)	Renton and Alexandria.
								Renton, B. M., & Co.'s Midland Works (Mid.)	Yorks	Mid.—G. C.	Sheffield, Wicker.
								Renwick & Hunt's Sid. (Mid.)	Staffs	Mid.—L. & N.W.—G. N.	Burton-on-Trent.
G	P		L	H				Repton and Willington (Mid.)	Derby	Mid.	Derby and Burton.
	P			H						L. & N. W	Over Mid. from Wichnor Junction.
								Reserve or Chequerbent Pits	Lancs	L. & N. W.	See Hulton Col. Co. (Chequerbent).
								Reservoir Colliery (Mid.)......	Leicester..	Mid.—L. & N. W.	See Moira Colliery Co. (Moira).

EXPLANATION—G *Goods Station.*   P *Passenger and Parcel Station.*   P* *Passenger, but not Parcel or Miscellaneous Traffic.*
F *Furniture Vans, Carriages, Portable Engines, and Machines on Wheels.*   L *Live Stock.*
H *Horse Boxes and Prize Cattle Vans.*   C *Carriages by Passenger Train.*

STATION ACCOMMODATION.						CRANE POWER.	STATIONS, &c.	COUNTY.	COMPANY.	POSITION.
G	P	.	L	.	.	Tons Cwts.	Resolven	Glamorg'n	G. W.	Hirwain and Neath.
.	.	.	.	.	.		Cefn Mawr Siding	Glamorg'n	G. W.	Resolven and Aberdylais.
.	.	.	.	.	.		Cory Bros.' Resolven Siding	Glamorg'n	G. W.	Resolven.
.	.	.	.	.	.		Glyn Castle Colliery	Glamorg'n	G. W.	Resolven.
.	.	.	.	.	.		Gored Merthyr Colliery ...	Glamorg'n	G. W.	Resolven.
.	.	.	.	.	.		Melincourt Siding	Glamorg'n	G. W.	Resolven and Aberdylais.
.	.	.	.	.	.		Rheola Colliery	Glamorg'n	G. W.	Resolven.
G	P	F	L	H	C	1 10	Restalrig Road Sidings	Edinboro'	Cal.	Leith, South.
G	P	F	L	H	C		Reston (for Coldingham and St. Abbs)	Berwick	N. B.	Dunbar and Berwick.
G	.	.	.	.	.		Auchencrow Siding	Berwick	N. B.	Reston and Chirnside.
G	.	.	.	.	.		Billiemains Sidings	Berwick	N. B.	Reston and Chirnside.
.	.	.	.	.	.		Reston Junction	Berwick	N. B.	Ayton and Grantshouse.
.	.	.	.	.	.		Retailers' Siding	Glamorg'n	T. V.	Same as Incline Top Sid. (Trealaw).
.	.	.	.	.	.		Retew Sidings	Cornwall	G. W.	Melangoose Mill.
							RETFORD—			
G	.	F	L	.	.	5 0	(Station, G. C.)	Notts	{ G. C.	Gainsboro' and Worksop.
									Mid.	Over G. C. from Shireoaks Junction.
G	P	F	L	H	C	10 0			{ G. N.	Newark and Doncaster.
.	P	.	F	H	C				G. C.	Over G. N. Line.
G	.	F	L	.	C	10 0	(Station, G. N.)	Notts	L. & N. W.	Over G. N. fr. Bottesford North Jr.
.	P	.	.	H	C	. .			{ Mid.	Over G. C. from Shireoaks Junction.
.	.	.	.	.	.		Bee Hive Works (Jenkins & Co.) (G.C.)	Notts	G. C.—G. N.—Mid.	Retford.
.	.	.	.	.	.		Clarboro' Siding	Notts	G. C.	Retford.
.	.	.	.	.	.		Gamston Brick Siding	Notts	G. N.	Retford and Tuxford.
.	.	.	.	.	.		Gilstrap, Earp & Co.'s Siding (G. C.)	Notts	G. C.—G. N.—Mid.	Retford.
.	.	.	.	.	.		Holmes Siding (G. C.)	Notts	G. C.—G. N.—Mid.	Retford.
.	.	.	.	.	.		North Junction	Notts	G. C.—G. N.	Worksop and G. N. Station.
.	.	.	.	.	.		Ordsall Siding (G. C.)	Notts	G. C.—G. N.—Mid.	Retford.
.	.	.	.	.	.		Pidcock & Co.'s Sid. (G.C.)	Notts	G. C.—G. N.—Mid.	Retford.
.	.	.	.	.	.		Rushey Siding (G. C.)	Notts	G. C.—G. N.—Mid.	Retford.
.	.	.	.	.	.		South Junction	Notts	G. C.—G. N.	Gainsboro' and G. N. Station.
.	.	.	.	.	.		Welham Siding	Notts	G. C.	Retford.
.	.	.	.	.	.		Worksop and Retford Brewery Co.'s Siding (G. C.)..	Notts	G. C.—Mid.	Retford.
G	.	.	.	.	.		Retreat	Antrim	N. C. Com. (Mid.)	Branch from Ballymena.
.	.	.	.	.	.		Reynolds & Co.	Glo'ster	G. W.—Mid.	Gloucester Docks.
.	.	.	.	.	.		Reyrolle & Co.'s Siding........	Durham	N. E.	Hebburn.
G	P	F	L	H	C	4 0	Rhayader	Radnor	Cam.	Llanidloes and Builth Wells.
.	P	.	.	.	.		Rhee Valley Cement Co.'s Sid	Cambs	G. N.	Shepreth.
.	P	.	.	.	.		Rheidol Falls	Cardigan	V. of Rheidol	Aberystwyth and Devil's Bridge.
.	.	.	.	.	.		Rheola Colliery	Glamorg'n	G. W.	Resolven.
G	P	.	L	H	.	5 0	Rhewl	Denbigh	L. & N. W.	Corwen and Denbigh.
.	.	.	.	.	.		Rhiwbryfdir.....................	Merioneth	Festiniog	Same as Dinas Quarries Extension (Blaenau Festiniog).
G	P	.	.	.	.	}	Rhiwderin (B. & M.)............	Mon.	{ B. & M.	Newport and Machen.
.	P	.	.	.	.				GW (A (N & SW) D & R)	Over B. & M. from Bassaleg Junc.
.	P	.	.	.	.		Garth Siding	Mon	B. & M.	Bassaleg and Rhiwderin.
.	.	.	.	.	.		Rhiwfron	Cardigan	V. of Rheidol	Aberystwyth and Devil's Bridge.
.	.	.	.	.	.		Rhodes Bank Siding	Lancs	L. & Y.	Oldham (Mumps).
.	.	.	.	.	.		Rhodes Siding..................	Derby	G. C.	Same as Hadfield Mills Sid. (Hadfield).
.	.	.	.	.	.		Rhodes, T., & Son's Siding ...	Worcester	G. W.	Lye.
.	.	.	.	.	.		Rhondda Branch Junction ...	Glamorg'n	T. V.	Pontypridd and Hafod.
.	.	.	.	.	.		Rhondda Cutting Junction ...	Glamorg'n	T. V.	Pontypridd and Hafod.
.	.	.	.	.	.		Rhondda Engine Works (Llewellyn & Cubitt's)	Glamorg'n	T. V.	Ystrad.
.	.	.	.	.	.		Rhondda Fach Branch Junc.	Glamorg'n	T. V.	Porth and Hafod.
.	.	.	.	.	.		Rhondda Merthyr Colliery ...	Glamorg'n	T. V.	Treherbert.
G	P	F	L	H	C		Rhoose	Glamorg'n	Barry	Barry and Bridgend.
.	.	.	.	.	.		Rhoose Lime Works	Glamorg'n	Barry	Rhoose.
G	P	.	.	H	.	1 0	Rhos	Denbigh	G. W.	Wrexham and Acrefair (Low Level).
.	.	.	.	.	.		Copy Brick Works	Denbigh	G. W.	Rhos.
.	.	.	.	.	.		Llwynenion Brick Works (Powell, J., & Co.)	Denbigh	G. W.	Rhos and Wrexham.
.	.	.	.	.	.		Plas-yn-wern	Denbigh	G. W.	Rhos and Acrefair (Low Level).
.	.	.	.	.	.		Ruabon Coal & Coke Co.'s Pant Brick Works	Denbigh	G. W.	Rhos and Acrefair (Low Level).
.	.	.	.	.	.		Wrexham Water Co.'s Wks.	Denbigh	G. W.	Rhos.
G	.	.	.	.	.		Wynn Hall Siding............	Denbigh	G. W.	Rhos and Acrefair (Low Level).
.	.	.	.	.	.		Rhos Colliery	Carmarth'	G. W.	Pantyffynnon.

EXPLANATION—G *Goods Station.*　　P *Passenger and Parcel Station.*　　P* *Passenger, but not Parcel or Miscellaneous Traffic:*
F *Furniture Vans, Carriages, Portable Engines, and Machines on Wheels.*　　L *Live Stock.*
H *Horse Boxes and Prize Cattle Vans.*　　C *Carriages by Passenger Train.*

STATION ACCOMMODATION.						CRANE POWER.	STATIONS, &c.	COUNTY.	COMPANY.	POSITION.
						Tons Cwts.	Rhos Gas Works................	Denbigh...	G. W.	Aberderfyn.
							Rhosddu	Denbigh...	W. M. & C. Q.	See Wrexham.
							Rhosferig Siding	Brecon ...	L. & N. W.	Builth Road.
G	P	F	L	H	C	1 10	Rhosgoch	Anglesey..	L. & N. W.	Amlwch and Gaerwen.
G	P						Rhos Llantwit Colliery	Glamorg'n	B. & M.	Machen.
G	P						Rhostryfan	Carnarvon	No. Wales N. G.	Tryfan Junction and Bryngwyn.
G	P						Rhostyllen	Denbigh...	G. W.	Wrexham and Rhos.
G	P	F	L	H	C	5 0	Rhuddlan	Flint	L. & N. W.	Denbigh and Rhyl.
G	P						Rhydmeredydd	Salop ...	Cam.	Llanymynech and Blodwell.
G	P		L	H			Rhydowen	Carmarth'	G. W.	Whitland and Cardigan.
							Rhydwen Siding	Flint	L. & N. W.	Same as Jones & Son's Sid. (Rhyl).
							Rhydycar Junction	Glamorg'n	B&M&L&NW Jt.—GW	Merthyr.
							Rhydy-defed Colliery	Glamorg'n	L. & N. W.	Same as Richards' Siding (Killay).
G	P		L	H		5 0	Rhydymwyn	Flint	L. & N. W.	Denbigh and Mold.
							Halkyn Lime Co.—			
							Halkyn Siding	Flint	L. & N. W.	Rhydymwyn and Nannerch.
							Hendre Siding	Flint	L. & N. W.	Rhydymwyn and Nannerch.
							North Hendre Lead Mining Co.'s Siding	Flint	L. & N. W.	Rhydymwyn and Nannerch.
							Ruby Brick & Tile Co.'s Sid.	Flint	L. & N. W.	Rhydymwyn and Nannerch.
G	P						Rhydyronen	Merioneth	Tal-y-llyn.	Towyn and Brynglas.
G	P	F	L	H	C	5 0	Rhyl	Flint	L. & N. W.	Bangor and Chester.
							Evans, R., & Co.'s Siding ...	Flint	L. & N. W.	Rhyl and Prestatyn.
							Jones & Son's Rhydwen Sid.	Flint	L. & N. W.	Rhyl and Prestatyn.
							Jones & Son's Siding.........	Flint	L. & N. W.	Rhyl and Foryd.
							Roberts' Siding	Flint	L. & N. W.	Rhyl and Prestatyn.
							Williams' Elwy S ding	Flint	L. & N. W.	Rhyl and Prestatyn.
							RHYMNEY—			
G	P					2 0 }	(Station, B. & M.)	Mon	{ B. & M.	Branch from Aber Bargoed.
G						2 0 }			{ G. W.	Over B. & M. from Maesycwmmer Junction.
G	P	F	L	H	C	5 0	(Station, Rhy.)	Glamorg'n	{ Rhy.	Nantybwch and Cardiff.
									{ L. & N. W.	Over Rhymney from Rhymney Joint Line Junction.
							Abertwsswg Siding(B.&M.)	Mon	B. & M.—G. W.	Near Rhymney.
							Junction	Glamorg'n	N. & R. Jt.—Rhy.	Rhymney Bridge and Rhymney.
							McLaren's Col. No. 1 (B&M)	Mon	B. & M.—G. W.	Rhymney and New Tredegar.
							McLaren's Col. No. 2 (B&M)	Mon	B. & M.—G. W.	Near Rhymney.
							Rhymney Iron Co.'s Works (B. & M.)	Mon	B. & M.—G. W.	Near Rhymney.
							Rhymney Iron Co.'s Works	Mon	Rhy.—L. & N. W.	Near Rhymney.
G	P					}	Rhymney Bridge	Brecon	{ L. & N. W.	Abergavenny and Merthyr.
	P								{ N&R Jt.(L&NW&Rhy.)	Nantybwch and Rhymney Junction.
							Taylor's Siding	Brecon	L. & N. W.	Rhymney Bridge.
							Rhymney Bridge Junction ...	Brecon	L. & N. W.—N. & R. Jt.	Merthyr and Nantybwch Junction.
							Rhymney Iron Co.'s Limestone Sidings	Glamorg'n	B. & M.	Dowlais Top.
G	P						Rhymney Junction Station...	Glamorg'n	G. W.	Tredegar Junction & Llancaiach.
							Gellyhave Colliery	Mon	G. W.	Branch from Maesycwmmer Junc.
							Maesycwmmer Chemical Works	Mon	G. W.	Rhymney Junc. & Tredegar Junc.
							Trelyn Colliery	Mon	G. W.	Branch from Maesycwmmer Junc.
							Rhymney Merthyr Colliery...	Glamorg'n	Rhy.	Pontlottyn.
							Rhymney Wharf	Mon.	A (N&S W) D & R—G W	{ See North Central Wagon Co. (Newport).
							Ribble Branch	Lancs	N.U.Jt.(L.&NW.&L.&Y)	Preston.
G	P	F	L	H	C		Ribblehead	Yorks	Mid.	Settle and Appleby.
							Craven Lime Co.'s Salt Lake Siding	Yorks	Mid.	Ribblehead.
							Ribblesdale Lime & Flag Co.'s Siding	Yorks	Mid.	Horton-in-Ribblesdale.
	P						Ribbleton	Lancs	P. & L. Jt.(L&NW.&L&Y)	Longridge and Preston.
							Ribchester	Lancs	L. & Y.	See Wilpshire (for Ribchester).
G	P	F	L	H	C	1 0 }	Riccall (N.E.)	Yorks	{ N. E.	York and Selby.
	P			H	C				{ G. N.	Over N. E. from Shaftholme Junc.
							Osgodby Siding	Yorks	N. E.	Riccall and Selby.
							Riccardjohnstone Siding ...	Lanark ..	Cal.	Mossend.
							Riccarton	Ayr	G. & S. W.	See Kilmarnock.
G	F		L				Riccarton	Roxburgh	N. B.	Hawick and Carlisle.
G							Saughtree Siding	Roxburgh	N. B.	Riccarton and Keilder.
G							Whitrope Siding	Roxburgh	N. B.	Shankend and Riccarton.
							Riccarton Junction	Roxburgh	N. B.	Shankend and Newcastleton.

EXPLANATION—G Goods Station.   P Passenger and Parcel Station.   P* Passenger, but not Parcel or Miscellaneous Traffic.
F Furniture Vans, Carriages, Portable Engines, and Machines on Wheels.   L Live Stock.
H Horse Boxes and Prize Cattle Vans.   C Carriages by Passenger Train.

STATION ACCOMMODATION.						CRANE POWER.		STATIONS, &c.	COUNTY.	COMPANY.	POSITION.
						Tons	Cwts.				
·	·	·	·	·	·	·	·	Rice & Co.'s Siding	N'hamptn	L. & N. W.	See Duston Siding (Northampton).
·	·	·	·	·	·	·	·	Richards & Beick's Siding ...	Glo'ster ...	Mid.	Ryeford.
·	·	·	·	·	·	·	·	Richards & Co.'s Atlantic Works	Lancs	L. & N. W.	Broadheath, Altrincham.
·	·	·	·	·	·	·	·	Richards & Son's Iron Works	Leicester..	G. N.	Leicester, Belgrave Road.
·	·	·	·	·	·	·	·	Richards & Son's Siding	Notts	Mid.	Same as Bobber's Mill Siding (Nottingham).
·	·	·	·	·	·	·	·	Richards, Boulder & Co.'s Wesham Mill	Lancs	P.&W.Jt. (L&Y&L&NW)	Kirkham.
·	·	·	·	·	·	·	·	Richards, C., & Co.'s Siding	Staffs	L. & N. W.	Darlaston.
·	·	·	·	·	·	·	·	Richards Dunvant Colliery...	Glamorg'n	L. & N. W.	See Dunvant Quarry (Dunvant).
·	·	·	·	·	·	·	·	Richards, J.J.,&Co.'s Brick Works (Mid.)	Glamorg'n	Mid.—G. W.—L.&N.W.	Same as Velin-fran Colliery (Llansamlet and Six Pit Junction).
·	·	·	·	·	·	·	·	Richards' Quarry	Glamorg'n	T. V.	Same as Ynisboeth Quarry (Penrhiwceiber).
·	·	·	·	·	·	·	·	Richard's Rhydydefed Colliery	Glamcrg'n	L. & N. W.	Killay.
·	·	·	·	·	·	·	·	Richards, W., & Son's Iron Works (Mid.)	Leicester..	Mid.—L. & N. W.........	Leicester, East.
·	·	·	·	·	·	·	·	Richards, W. H., & Co.'s Sid.	Staffs	L. & N. W.	Darlaston.
·	·	·	·	·	·	·	·	Richardson's Coal Sidings (L. & N. W.)	Lancs	L. & N. W. / L. & N. W.—G. W.	Warrington, Arpley. / Warrington, Bank Quay.
·	·	·	·	·	·	·	·	Richardson's Moss Litter Co.'s Siding	Stirling ...	Cal.	Alloa.
·	·	·	·	·	·	·	·	Richardson's Siding	Staffs	L. & N. W.	Lichfield.
·	·	·	·	·	·	·	·	Richardson, W., & Co.'s Sid.	Durham ...	N. E.	Darlington, Bank Top.
·	·	·	·	·	·	·	·	Richardson, Westgarth & Co.'s Engine Works.................	Durham ...	N. E.	Hartlepool.
G	P	·	L	·	·	2	10	Richboro' Siding	Kent	S. E. & C.	Sandwich.
G	P	F	L	H	C	5	0	Rich-hill	Armagh ...	G. N. (I.)	Portadown and Armagh.
·	P	·	·	·	·	·	·	Richmond (L. & S. W.)	Surrey	L. & S. W. / G. W.—Met.* / Met. Dist. / N.&S.W.Jn.Jt(L&NW Mid., & N. L.)	Clapham Junction and Twickenham. / Over L&SW from Hammersmith Jn. / Over L&SW from Studland Rd. Jn. / Over L. & S. W. from Acton June.
·	P*	·	·	·	·						
·	P	F	·	·	·						
·	·	·	·	·	·	·	·	Aldin's Siding................	Surrey	L. & S. W.	Richmond.
·	·	·	·	·	·	·	·	Richmond Corporation Sid.	Surrey	L. & S. W.	Richmond.
·	·	·	·	·	·	·	·	Richmond Gas Co.'s Siding	Surrey	L. & S. W.	Richmond.
G	P	F	L	H	C	3	0	Richmond	Yorks	N. E.	Terminus of Darlington & Richmond Branch.
·	·	·	·	·	·	·	·	Easby Siding	Yorks	N. E.	Richmond.
·	·	·	·	·	·	·	·	Richmond & Co.'s Sid.(LNW)	Lancs	L. & N. W.—G. W.	Warrington, Bank Quay.
·	·	·	·	·	·	·	·	Richmond Iron & Steel Wks.	Durham ...	N. E.	Stockton, South.
·	·	·	·	·	·	·	·	Rich's Siding	Berks	G. W.	Didcot.
·	·	·	·	·	·	·	·	Rickett, Cockerell & Co.'s Siding (G. E.)................	Hunts	G E—L & N W—Mid	Peterboro'.
G	P	F	L	H	C	1	10	Rickmansworth	Herts	L. & N. W.	Branch from Watford Junc. Station.
G	P	F	L	H	C	1	10	Rickmansworth (Met.)........	Herts	Met. / G. C.	Harrow-on-the-Hill and Aylesbury. / Over Met. Line.
·	P	·	·	H	C	-	-				
·	·	·	·	·	·	·	·	Riddings Brick Yard	Derby	Mid.	See Oakes & Co. (Pye Bridge).
·	·	·	·	·	·	·	·	Riddings Colliery	Derby	Mid.	Pye Bridge.
·	·	·	·	·	·	·	·	Riddings Colliery (G. N.)......	Notts	G. N.—G.C.	Codnor Park (for Ironville and Jacksdale).
G	P	·	L	H	·	·	·	Riddings Junction.............	Cumb'land	N. B.	Scotch Dyke and Penton.
·	·	·	·	·	·	·	·	Riddings Junction Station ...	Cumb'land	N. B.	Hawick and Carlisle.
·	·	·	·	·	·	·	·	Moat Quarry	Cumb'land	N. B.	Riddings Junction and Scotch Dyke.
·	·	·	·	·	·	·	·	Riddings Sanitary Pipe Wks.	Derby	Mid.	See Oakes & Co. (Pye Bridge).
·	·	·	·	·	·	·	·	Riddings Siding	Derby	Mid.	See Oakes & Co. (Pye Bridge).
·	·	·	·	·	·	·	·	Riddochhill Colliery	L'lithgow	N. B.	Bathgate, Upper.
·	·	·	·	·	·	·	·	Ridge Field Brick Co.'s Siding	Yorks	N. E.	Castleford.
·	·	·	·	·	·	·	·	Ridge Hill Brick & Tile Co.'s Siding	Staffs	L. & N. W.	Madeley.
G	P	F	L	H	C	·	·	Ridgmont.....................	Beds	L. & N. W.	Bedford and Bletchley.
G	P	F	L	H	C	3	0	Riding Mill	Northumb	N. E.	Newcastle and Hexham.
·	·	·	·	·	·	·	·	Ridley & Browne's Siding ...	Suffolk ...	G. E.	Bury St. Edmunds.
·	·	·	·	·	·	·	·	Ridley & Co.'s Steel Works	Durham ...	N. E.	Swalwell.
·	·	·	·	·	·	·	·	Ridley & Son's Yard..........	Yorks	N. E.	See Whitehouse Siding and Depôt (South Bank).
·	·	·	·	·	·	·	·	Ridyard's Siding	Lancs	O. A. & G. B. Jt. (G. C. and L. & N. W.)	Ashton, Oldham Road.
·	·	·	·	·	·	·	·	Rigby & Co.—			
·	·	·	·	·	'	·	·	Audley Colliery	Staffs	N. S.	Diglake.
·	·	·	·	·	·	·	·	Bunkers Hill Colliery	Staffs	N. S.	Diglake.

EXPLANATION—G Goods Station.　　P Passenger and Parcel Station.　　P* Passenger, but not Parcel or Miscellaneous Traffic.
F Furniture Vans, Carriages, Portable Engines, and Machines on Wheels.　　L Live Stock.
H Horse Boxes and Prize Cattle Vans.　　C Carriages by Passenger Train.

STATION ACCOMMODATION.						CRANE POWER.	STATIONS, &c.	COUNTY.	COMPANY.	POSITION.
						Tons Cwts.	Rigby & Holmes' Blainscough Hall Siding	Lancs	P.&W.Jt.(L&Y&L&NW)	Kirkham.
G	P	F	L	H	C		Rigg	Dumfries	G. & S.W.	Gretna and Dornock.
							Riggfoot Pit	Ayr	G. & S.W.	New Cumnock.
							Rigghead Siding	Lanark	N. B.	See Greengairs.
							Riggside Colliery	Lanark	Cal.	Ponfeigh.
							Rigley's Siding	Notts	G. N.	Bulwell Forest.
							Riley & Son's Timber Sid. (Mid)	Staffs	Mid—L&NW—GN—NS	Burton-on-Trent.
							Riley's Saw Mill	Lancs	P.&W.Jt.(L&Y&L&NW)	Fleetwood.
							Riley's Siding	Lancs	L. & Y.	Hapton.
G	P	F	L	H	C		Rillington	Yorks	N. E.	Malton and Scarboro'.
G	P	F	L	H	C		Rimington	Yorks	L. & Y.	Chatburn and Hellifield.
							Rimmon Colliery	Lanark	Cal.	Shotts.
	P						Ringley Road	Lancs	L. & Y.	Salford and Bury.
							Outwood Siding	Lancs	L. & Y.	Ringley Road.
G	P						Ringstead and Addington	N'hamptn	L. & N. W.	Peterboro' and Wellingboro'.
G	P	F	L	H	C	5 0	Ringwood	Hants	L. & S.W.	Brockenhurst and Wimborne.
							Uddens Siding	Hants	L. & S.W.	Ringwood and Wimborne.
							Rio Tinto Co.'s Siding	Glamorg'n	P. T.—R. & S. B.	Cwmavon.
							Rio Tinto Ore Co.'s Siding	Lancs	L. & N. W.	Garston Docks.
G	P	F	L	H	C	1 10	Ripley	Derby	Mid.	Branch from Little Eaton Junction.
							Butterley Co.—			
							Marehay Colliery	Derby	Mid.	Branch near Ripley.
							Whiteley's Siding	Derby	Mid.	Branch near Ripley.
							Donley Hall Colliery	Derby	Mid.	Branch near Ripley.
							Marehay Main Col. (Ford's)	Derby	Mid.	Branch near Ripley.
							Ripley Colliery	Derby	Mid.	Branch near Ripley.
							Wainsgrove Colliery	Derby	Mid.	Branch near Ripley.
							Ripley	Surrey	L. & S.W.	See Horsley, Ripley and Ockham.
							Ripley's Siding (Hall Lane Coal Siding)	Yorks	G. N.	Bradford, Bowling.
							Ripley Valley	Yorks	N. E.	Harrogate and Pateley Bridge.
G	P					5 0	Ripon (N. E.)	Yorks	{ N. E.	Harrogate and Thirsk.
G	P	F	L	H	C	5 0 }			{ G. N.	Over L. & Y. and N. E. Lines.
	P			H	C					Ripon.
							Littlethorpe Siding	Yorks	N. E.	
G	P	F	L	H		1 10	Rippingale	Lincoln	G. N.	Bourne and Sleaford.
G	P						Ripple	Worcester	Mid.	Tewkesbury and Malvern.
							Rippon & Co.'s Lime & Stone Siding	Lincoln	Mid.	Castle Bytham.
G	P		L	H		10 0	Ripponden and Barkisland	Yorks	L. & Y.	Sowerby Bridge and Rishworth.
G	P		L			2 0 }	Risca (G. W.)	Mon	{ G. W.	Newport and Crumlin, Low Level.
	P								{ L. & N. W.	Over G. W. fr. Nine Mile Point Jn.
							Black Vein Col. (Old & New)	Mon	G. W.	Risca and Nine Mile Point.
							Brick Works Siding	Mon	G. W.	Risca and Nine Mile Point.
							Cromwell's Siding	Mon	G. W.	Risca and Cross Keys.
							Danygraig Brick Siding	Mon	G. W.	Risca and Nine Mile Point Junction.
							Darran Brick Siding	Mon	G. W.	Risca and Cross Keys.
							Hall's Tramroad Junction	Mon	G. W.	Risca and Cross Keys.
							Lime Kiln Siding	Mon	G. W.	Risca and Cross Keys.
							Pontymister Steel Works (Monmouthshire Steel & Tinplate Co.)	Mon	G. W.	Risca and Rogerstone.
							White, H., & Co.'s Foundry Siding	Mon	G. W.	Risca and Rogerstone.
							Risca Wharf (Cardiff & South Wales Wagon Co.)	Mon	A (N & S W) D & R—G W	Newport, Alexandra Docks.
							Rise Carr Rolling Mills	Durham	N. E.	Darlington, Hope Town.
G	P		L	H		6 0	Rishton	Lancs	L. & Y.	Blackburn and Accrington.
G	P					3 10	Rishworth	Yorks	L. & Y.	Branch from Sowerby Bridge.
							Rishworth, Ingleby & Lofthouse's Mill	Yorks	N. E.	Tadcaster.
							Risley Siding	Lancs	C. L. C. (G C, G N, & Mid.)	Glazebrook.
							Ainscough Estate, Tenants of	Lancs	C. L. C. (G C, G N, & Mid.)	Risley Siding.
							Marchioness of Headfort, Tenants of	Lancs	C. L. C. (G C, G N, & Mid.)	Risley Siding.
							Rispey Mines	Durham	N. E.	Parkhead.
							Ritchie, Graham, & Milne's Ship Yard	Renfrew	Cal.	Same as Park Ship Yard (Glasgow).
							Ritchie's Siding	Fife	N. B.	Same as Tayport Spinning Co.'s Sid.
							Ritson & Co.'s Timber Yard	Cumb'land	M. & C.	Maryport.
							River	Kent	S. E. & C.	See Kearsney (for River and Ewell).

STATION ACCOMMODATION.						CRANE POWER.		STATIONS, &c.	COUNTY.	COMPANY.	POSITION.
						Tons	Cwts.				
.	.	.	.	.	.	.	.	River Don Works (Mid.)	Yorks	Mid.—G. C.—L. D. & E. C.	See Vickers, Sons & Maxim's (Sheffield).
.	.	.	.	.	.	.	.	Riverside	Lancs	L. & N. W.	See Liverpool.
.	.	.	.	.	.	.	.	Riverside (G. W.)	Glamorg'n	G. W.—Barry—T. V. ...	See Cardiff.
.	.	.	.	.	.	.	.	Riverside Malt Kiln	Notts	G. N. & Mid. Jt.	See Branston's Sidings (Newark).
.	.	.	.	.	.	.	.	River Wear Commissioners' Siding (Hudson & Hendon Docks)	Durham ...	N. E.	Sunderland, South Dock.
G	P	F	L	H	C	.	.	Roade	N'hamptn	L. & N. W.	Bletchley and Blisworth.
.	.	.	.	.	.	.	.	Roade Limestone Co.'s Works	N'hamptn	L. & N. W.	Roade and Castlethorpe.
.	.	.	.	.	.	.	.	Roade Junction	N'hamptn	E. & W. Jn—L. & N. W.	Towcester and Blisworth.
.	.	.	.	.	.	.	.	Roanhead Mines (Private) ...	Lancs	Furness	Park.
.	.	.	.	.	.	.	.	Roath	Glamorg'n	G. W.	See Cardiff.
.	.	.	.	.	.	.	.	Roath Branch Junction	Glamorg'n	T. V.	Cardiff and Llandaff.
.	.	.	.	.	.	.	.	Roath Coal and Mileage Depôt	Glamorg'n	G. W.	Cardiff.
.	.	.	.	.	.	.	.	Roath Depôt	Glamorg'n	T. V.	Cardiff.
.	.	.	.	.	.	.	.	Roath Dock and Basin	Glamorg'n	G W—LNW—Rhy—TV	Cardiff.
.	.	.	.	.	.	.	.	Roath Dock Storage Sidings	Glamorg'n	T. V.	Cardiff Docks.
.	.	.	.	.	.	.	.	Roath Mileage Siding	Glamorg'n	T. V.	Cardiff.
.	.	.	.	.	.	.	.	Robb & Co.'s Quarry	Down	B. & C. D.	Ballygowan.
.	.	.	.	.	.	.	.	Roberts & Co.'s Mill	Selkirk ...	N. B.	Galashiels.
.	.	.	.	.	.	.	.	Roberts & Co.'s Siding	Lancs	L. & N. W.	Garston Docks.
.	.	.	.	.	.	.	.	Roberts & Co.'s Siding	Staffs	L. & N. W.	Tipton.
.	.	.	.	.	.	.	.	Roberts & Cooper's (Leys) Sid.	Staffs	G. W.	Brettell Lane.
.	.	.	.	.	.	.	.	Roberts & Son's Siding	Carnarvon	L. & N. W.	Aber.
.	.	.	.	.	.	.	.	Roberts & Son's Siding	Lincoln	G. N.	Horncastle.
.	.	.	.	.	.	.	.	Roberts Bros.' Siding	Lancs	S. & M. Jt. (G. C. & Mid.)	Widnes.
.	.	.	.	.	.	.	.	Roberts, R. K., Siding	Lancs	L. & Y.	Tottington.
.	.	.	.	.	.	.	.	Roberts' Siding	Flint	L. & N. W.	Dyserth.
.	.	.	.	.	.	.	.	Roberts' Siding	Flint	L. & N. W.	Meliden.
.	.	.	.	.	.	.	.	Roberts' Siding	Flint	L. & N. W.	Rhyl.
.	.	.	.	.	.	.	.	Roberts' Siding	Lanark	N. B.	Glasgow, Cowlairs.
.	.	.	.	.	.	.	.	Roberts' Siding	Yorks	L. & Y.	Horbury Junction Station.
.	.	.	.	.	.	.	.	Roberts' Siding	Yorks	L. & Y.	Womersley.
G	P	F	L	H	C	4	0	Robertsbridge (S. E. & C.) ...	Sussex ...	{ S. E. & C.	Tunbridge Wells and Hastings.
G	P	.	.	.	.					{ K. & E. S.	Over S. E. & C. fr. Robertsbridge Jn.
.	.	.	.	.	.	.	.	Smith's Siding	Sussex ...	S. E. & C.	Robertsbridge and Battle.
G	.	.	.	.	.	.	.	Robertsbridge Junction	Sussex ...	K. & E. S.—S. E. & C.	Bodiam and Robertsbridge Station.
.	.	.	.	.	.	.	.	Robertsbridge Mill Siding ...	Sussex ...	K. & E. S.	Robertsbridge Junction & Bodiam.
.	.	.	.	.	.	.	.	Robertson's Siding	Edinboro'	Cal.	Edinburgh, Lothian Road.
G	P	.	.	.	.	5	0	Robey & Co.'s Siding (G.N.).	Lincoln	G. N.—G. C.—Mid.	Lincoln.
.	.	.	.	.	.	.	.	Robin Hood	Yorks	E. & W. Y. Union	Lofthouse Junction and Rothwell.
.	.	.	.	.	.	.	.	Beeston Pit	Yorks	E. & W. Y. Union	Robin Hood.
.	.	.	.	.	.	.	.	Beeston Quarry	Yorks	E. & W. Y. Union	Robin Hood.
.	.	.	.	.	.	.	.	Newmarket Haigh Moor and Spencer Collieries ...	Yorks	E. & W. Y. Union	Robin Hood.
.	.	.	.	.	.	.	.	Newmarket Silkstone Col.	Yorks	E. & W. Y. Union	Robin Hood.
.	.	.	.	.	.	.	.	Ouzlewell Green Siding...	Yorks	E. & W. Y. Union	Robin Hood.
.	.	.	.	.	.	.	.	Pawson Bros.' Thorpe Quarry	Yorks	E. & W. Y. Union	Robin Hood.
.	.	.	.	.	.	.	.	Simon Carves Co.'s Siding	Yorks	E. & W. Y. Union	Robin Hood.
.	.	.	.	.	.	.	.	Thorpe Siding	Yorks	E. & W. Y. Union	Robin Hood.
.	.	.	.	.	.	.	.	Armitage Bros.' Siding...	Yorks	E. & W. Y. Union	Thorpe Siding.
.	.	.	.	.	.	.	.	Armitage, G., & Sons' Sid.	Yorks	E. & W. Y. Union	Thorpe Siding.
.	.	.	.	.	.	.	.	Whitaker & Son's Siding...	Yorks	E. & W. Y. Union	Robin Hood.
.	.	.	.	.	.	.	.	Robin Hood Colliery	Yorks	Mid.	Rothwell Haigh.
.	.	.	.	.	.	.	.	Robin Hood Pit	Cumb'land	L. & N. W.	See Flimby Colliery Co. (Flimby).
G	P	F	L	H	C	1	10	Robin Hood's Bay	Yorks	N. E.	Scarboro' and Whitby.
.	.	.	.	.	.	.	.	Robin Hood Siding	Lancs	L. & Y.	See Clifton & Kersley Co. (Clifton Jn).
.	.	.	.	.	.	.	.	Robinson & Co.'s Plaster Wks.	Cumb'land	Mid.	Cotehill.
.	.	.	.	.	.	.	.	Robinson & Co.'s Siding	Derby ...	G. N.	Derby.
.	.	.	.	.	.	.	.	Robinson & Co.'s Siding	Glo'ster ...	G. W.	Bristol Harbour.
.	.	.	.	.	.	.	.	Robinson & Co.'s Siding	Lancs	L. & Y.	Rochdale.
.	.	.	.	.	.	.	.	Robinson & Co.'s Timber Yard	Yorks	N. E.	See Whitehouse Siding and Depôt (South Bank).
.	.	.	.	.	.	.	.	Robinson & Dowler's Wadlands Canal Wharf (Mid.).	Leicester..	Mid.—L. & N. W.	Moira.
.	.	.	.	.	.	.	.	Robinson & Hunter's Siding	Lanark ...	Cal.	Glasgow, South Side.
.	.	.	.	.	.	.	.	Robinson Bros.' Siding	Derby ...	Mid.	Spondon.
.	.	.	.	.	.	.	.	Robinson, Cook & Co.'s Siding	Lancs	L. & N. W.	St. Helens.
.	.	.	.	.	.	.	.	Robinson, David, & Co.'s Sid.	Glamorg'n	GW—LNW—Rhy—T V	Cardiff.

EXPLANATION—G Goods Station.   P Passenger and Parcel Station.   P* Passenger, but not Parcel or Miscellaneous Traffic.
F Furniture Vans, Carriages, Portable Engines, and Machines on Wheels.   L Live Stock.
H Horse Boxes and Prize Cattle Vans.   C Carriages by Passenger Train.

STATION ACCOMMODATION.						CRANE POWER.	STATIONS, &c.	COUNTY.	COMPANY.	POSITION.
						Tons Cwts.	Robinson, Dunn & Co.'s Wood Yards—			
.	.	.	.	.	.	. .	Partick Saw Mills	Lanark ...	Cal.	Glasgow, Whiteinch.
.	.	.	.	.	.	. .	Temple Saw Mills (N. B.)	Lanark ...	N. B.—Cal.	Glasgow, Great Western Road.
							Robinson, Son & Co.'s Siding			
.	.	.	.	.	.	. .	(L. & N. W.)	Lancs	L. & N. W.—G. W.	Warrington, Bank Quay.
							Robinson, Sons & Co.'s Egg			
.	.	.	.	.	.	. .	Packing & Pickling Works	Durham ...	N. E.	West Hartlepool.
.	.	.	.	.	.	. .	Robinson's Brewery (Mid.)	Staffs	Mid.—L&NW—GN—NS	Burton-on-Trent.
.	.	.	.	.	.	. .	Robinson's Siding	Lincoln ...	G. N.	Spilsby.
.	.	.	.	.	.	. .	Robinson's Siding (Mid.)	Derby	Mid.—L. & N. W.	Woodville.
.	.	.	.	.	.	. .	Robinson's Siding (Mid.)	Staffs	Mid.—L&NW—GN—NS	Burton-on-Trent.
							Robinson's Slate Quarries—			
.	.	.	.	.	.	. .	Blaen Cae Siding	Carnarvon	L. & N. W.	Nantlle.
.	.	.	.	.	.	. .	Cloddfar Coed Siding......	Carnarvon	L. & N. W.	Nantlle.
.	.	.	.	.	.	. .	Talysarn Siding............	Carnarvon	L. & N. W.	Nantlle.
.	.	.	.	.	.	. .	Robinson's Wood Siding	Herts	G. N.	Ayot.
.	.	.	.	.	.	. .	Robinson, T., & Co.	Glo'ster ...	G. W.—Mid.	Gloucester Docks.
G	P	.	.	.	.	2 0	Robroyston	Lanark ...	Cal.	Coatbridge & Glasgow, Buchanan Str.
.	.	.	.	.	.	. .	Robroyston Brick Works...	Lanark ...	Cal.	Steps Road and Robroyston.
.	.	.	.	.	.	. .	Robroyston Quarry	Lanark ...	Cal.	Steps Road and Robroyston.
.	.	.	.	.	.	. .	Robroyston Siding............	Lanark ...	Cal.	Steps Road and Robroyston.
.	.	.	.	.	.	. .	Robroyston Junction, West...	Lanark ...	Cal.	Robroyston and St. Rollox.
.	.	.	.	.	.	. .	Robson's, W. & C., Timber Yard	Durham ...	N. E.	Sunderland, South Dock.
.	P	.	.	.	.	. .	Roby	Lancs	L. & N. W.	Kenyon Junc. Sta. and Liverpool.
G	P	F	L	H	C	10 0	Rocester (N.S.)	Staffs	{ N. S. / L. & N. W.	{ Uttoxeter and Leek. / Over N.S. Line.
G	P	F	L	H	C	10 0	Rochdale	Lancs	L. & Y.	Manchester and Todmorden.
.	.	.	.	.	.	. .	Castleton Siding	Lancs	L. & Y.	Rochdale and Castleton.
.	.	.	.	.	.	. .	Robinson & Co.'s Siding...	Lancs	L. & Y.	Rochdale.
.	.	.	.	.	.	. .	Rochdale Road Gas Works	Lancs	L. & Y.	See Manchester Corporation.
G	P	.	L	.	.	. .	Roche	Cornwall	G. W.	Par and Newquay.
.	P	.	.	.	.	. .	Rochester	Kent	S. E. & C.	Strood and Chatham (Central).
.	P	.	.	.	.	. .	Rochester (Main Line).........	Kent	S. E. & C.	Rochester Bridge (Strood) and Chatham (Main Line).
.	P	.	.	.	.	. .	Rochester Bridge (Strood)...	Kent	S. E. & C.	Sole Street & Chatham (Main Line).
G	P	.	.	.	.	. .	Rochestown	Cork	C. B. & P.	Cork and Passage.
G	P	F	L	H	C	1 10	Rochford	Essex	G. E.	Wickford and Southend-on-Sea.
.	.	.	.	.	.	. .	Rochford, E., Siding	Essex	G. E.	Stansted.
.	.	.	.	.	.	. .	Rochford's Siding	Herts	G. E.	Broxbourne.
							Rochsolloch Brick Works			
.	.	.	.	.	.	. .	(Coatdyke Brick Works)...	Lanark ...	N. B.	Coatbridge, Sheepford.
.	.	.	.	.	.	. .	Rochsolloch Iron Works......	Lanark ...	N. B.	Coatbridge, Sheepford.
.	.	.	.	.	.	. .	Rochsolloch Tube Works ...	Lanark ...	Cal.	Same as Imperial Tube Works (Calder).
G	P	.	L	H	.	. .	Rockcliffe........................	Cumb'land	Cal.	Carlisle and Lockerbie.
.	.	.	.	.	.	. .	Rock Coal Siding (B. & M.)	Mon	B. & M.—G. W.	Pengam.
.	.	.	.	.	.	. .	Rock Colliery	Mon	L. & N. W.	Blackwood.
.	.	.	.	.	.	. .	Budd & Co.	Mon	L. & N. W.	Rock Colliery.
.	.	.	.	.	.	. .	Pond's	Mon	L. & N. W.	Rock Colliery.
G	P	.	L	.	.	. .	Rockcorry	Monaghan	G. N. (I.)	Ballybay and Cootehill.
.	.	.	.	.	.	. .	Rock Ferry (B'head Joint)....	Cheshire...	B'head Jt.—Mersey	See Birkenhead.
.	.	.	.	.	.	. .	Rock Ferry Junction	Cheshire...	B'head Jt.—Mersey	Birkenhead.
.	.	.	.	.	.	. .	Rock Foundry	Mon	L. & N. W.	Same as Treharne's (Blackwood).
G	P	F	L	H	C	5 0	Rockingham (L. & N. W.)......	Leicester..	{ L. & N. W. / G. N.	Market Harboro' and Stamford.
.	P	.	.	H	C					Over L. & N. W. from Longville Jn.
.	.	.	.	.	.	. .	Rockingham Colliery	Yorks	Mid.	Wombwell.
.	.	.	.	.	.	. .	Rockingham Colliery ...... }	Yorks	G. C.	{ See Newton, Chambers & Co. (Bird- / well and Hoyland Common).
.	.	.	.	.	.	. .	Rockingham Gas Works ... }			
.	.	.	.	.	.	. .	Rock Siding	Salop	Cam.	Llanymynech.
.	.	.	.	.	.	. .	Rock Veins Colliery	Glamorg'n	B. & M.	Machen.
.	.	.	.	.	.	. .	Rodbourne Siding	Wilts	G. W.	Swindon.
.	.	.	.	.	.	. .	Roddymoor Colliery	Durham ...	N. E.	See Pease & Partners (Crook).
.	.	.	.	.	.	. .	Rodgerson's Siding	Renfrew ...	Cal.	Same as Laurel Siding (Glasgow).
.	.	.	.	.	.	. .	Rodley	Yorks	Mid.	See Calverley & Rodley.
.	.	.	.	.	.	. .	Rodwell	Dorset.....	W & P. Jt. (GW&L&SW)	See Weymouth.
.	.	.	.	.	.	. .	Roecliffe Siding	Yorks	N. E.	Boroughbridge.
.	.	.	.	.	.	. .	Roe Lane Junction	Lancs	L. & Y.	Southport.
.	.	.	.	.	.	. .	Roe's Timber Co.'s New Works	Derby	Mid.	Derby.
.	.	.	.	.	.	. .	Roe's Timber Co.'s Siding ...	Derby	Mid.	Derby.
G	P	F	L	H	C	1 10	Rogart	Sutherl'nd	High.	Bonar Bridge and Golspie.
G	P	F	L	H	C	. .	Rogate and Harting	Sussex ...	L. & S. W.	Petersfield and Midhurst.

STATION ACCOMMODATION.						CRANE POWER.	STATIONS, &c.	COUNTY.	COMPANY.	POSITION.
						Tons Cwts.				
							Roger & Co.'s Siding	Durham	N. E.	Stockton, South.
							Rogers & Co.'s Siding	Glamorg'n	GW—LNW—Rhy—T V	Cardiff.
							Roger's Siding (L. & N. W.)	Beds	L. & N. W.—Mid.	Bedford.
							Rogerley Quarry	Durham	N. E.	Frosterley.
G	P						Rogerstone	Mon	G. W.	Newport and Risca.
							Guest, Keen, & Nettlefold's Works & Sidings	Mon	G. W.	Rogerstone.
							Rogerstone Works	Mon	B. & M.	Same as Nettlefold's Rogerstone Works (Bassaleg).
							Roker Park	Durham	N. E.	Sunderland, Monkwearmouth.
	P						Rollesby	Norfolk	Mid. & G. N. Jt.	See Martham (for Rollesby).
	P			H			Rolles Quay	Devon	L. & S. W.	Barnstaple Junction Station.
G	P		L	H	C		Rolleston	Notts	Mid.	Nottingham and Newark.
	P						Rolleston-on-Dove (N. S.)	Staffs	N. S.	Burton, Horninglow and Tutbury.
	P								G. N.	Over N. S. from Dove Junction.
	P								L. & N. W.	Over N. S. Line.
							Rolling Stock Co.'s Siding	Glamorg'n	GW—LNW—Rhy—T V	Cardiff.
G	P	F	L	H	C		Rollison & Slater's Siding	Salop	L. & N. W.	Wombridge.
G	P		L				Rolvenden	Kent	K. & E. S.	Robertsbridge & Tenterden Town.
G	P						Romaldkirk	Yorks	N. E.	Barnard Castle and Middleton.
							Roman Bridge	Carnarvon	L. & N. W.	Blaenau Festiniog and Llandudno Junction Station.
							Roman Camp Branch Siding	L'lithgow	N. B.	Uphall.
							Romans & Co.'s Siding	Glo'ster	G. W.—Mid.	Gloucester Docks.
G	P	F	L	H	C	1 0	Rome Street Junction	Cumb'land	Gds. TfcCom—M&C—N E	Carlisle.
G	P	F	L	H	C		Romford	Essex	G. E.	London and Chelmsford.
									L. T. & S.	Branch from Upminster.
							Ind Coope & Co.'s Siding	Essex	G. E.	Romford.
							Neave, Lady, Siding	Essex	G. E.	Romford and Harold Wood.
							Romford Gas & Coke Co's Sid	Essex	G. E.	Romford.
G	P					2 0	Romford Junction	Essex	G. E.—L. T. & S.	Romford and Upminster.
							Romiley	Cheshire	S. & M. Jt. (G. C. & Mid.)	Hyde and Marple.
G	P	F	L	H	C	5 0	Romiley Junction	Cheshire	S. & M. Jt. (G. C. & Mid.)	Bredbury and Romiley.
							Romsey (L. & S. W.)	Hants	L. & S. W.	Eastleigh and Salisbury.
									M. & S. W. Jn.	Over L. & S.W. from Andover Junc.
	P						Rood End	Worcester	G. W.	See Langley Green and Rood End.
G						1 0	Rookery	Lancs	L. & N. W.	Rainford Junc. Sta. and St. Helens.
							Rookery Bridge	Cheshire	L. & N. W.	Crewe and Stockport.
							Vicker's Siding	Cheshire	L. & N. W.	Rookery Bridge and Sandbach.
							Rookhope Mill	Durham	N. E.	Parkhead.
	P			H			Rooksmoor Sid. (J. Grist & Co.)	Glo'ster	Mid.	Dudbridge.
							Roose	Lancs	Furness	Furness Abbey and Barrow.
G	P	F	L	H	C		Ropkins & Co.'s Mill Siding	Cambs	G. E.	Wisbech.
							Ropley	Hants	L. & S. W.	Alton and Winchester.
							Ropner's Shipyard	Durham	N. E.	Stockton, North Shore.
							Roscoe Collieries	Derby	Mid.	See Butterley Co. (Langley Mill and Eastwood).
							Roscoe's— Peel Hall Colliery	Lancs	L. & N. W.	Plodder Lane.
							Siding	Lancs	L. & N. W.	See Lecturers Close and Hulme Trust Siding (Bolton).
G	P	F	L	H	C	2 0	Roscommon	Roscom'n	M. G. W.	Athlone and Claremorris.
G	P	F	L	H	C	2 0	Roscrea	Tipperary	G. S. & W.	Ballybrophy and Birr.
							Rosebank Collieries	Fife	N. B.	Whitemyre Junction Station.
							Rosebank Foundry	Edinboro'	N. B.	Edinburgh, Leith Walk.
							Rosebank Quarry	Fife	N. B.	Whitemyre Junction Station.
							Rosebank Sidings	Edinboro'	N. B.	Edinburgh, Leith Walk.
							Rose Bridge & Douglas Bank Colliery Co.— Douglas Bank Col. (L. & Y.)	Lancs	L. & Y.—L. & N. W.	Gathurst.
							Siding	Lancs	L. & N. W.	Garston Docks.
							Rose Bridge Colliery	Lancs	L. & N. W.	See Latham Bros. (Wigan).
							Roseburn Brewery	Edinboro'	Cal.	Edinburgh, Lothian Road.
							Roseburn Sidings	Edinboro'	N. B.	Same as Haymarket West Yard Sidings (Edinburgh).
G	P					2 0	Rosebush	Pembroke	G. W.	Clynderwen and Fishguard.
G							Rosedale, East	Yorks	N. E.	Branch from Battersby Junc. Sta.
							Blakey Junction Sidings	Yorks	N. E.	Rosedale, East.
							Blowith Siding	Yorks	N. E.	Rosedale, East.
							Rosedale, East Depôts	Yorks	N. E.	Rosedale, East.
							Rosedale, East Mines	Yorks	N. E.	Rosedale, East.
							Rosedale, West Depôts	Yorks	N. E.	Rosedale, East.

EXPLANATION—G *Goods Station.*   P *Passenger and Parcel Station.*   P* *Passenger, but not Parcel or Miscellaneous Traffic.*
F *Furniture Vans, Carriages, Portable Engines, and Machines on Wheels.*   L *Live Stock.*
H *Horse Boxes and Prize Cattle Vans.*   C *Carriages by Passenger Train.*

STATION ACCOMMODATION.						CRANE POWER.		STATIONS, &c.	COUNTY.	COMPANY.	POSITION.
						Tons	Cwts.	Rosedale, East—*continued.*			Rosedale, East.
								Sheriffs Pit	Yorks	N. E.	Branch from Battersby Junc. Sta.
G								Rosedale, West	Yorks	N. E.	Rosedale, East.
G	P	F	L	H	C	10	0	Rose Grove	Lancs	L. & Y.	Burnley and Hapton.
								Habergham Siding...........	Lancs	L. & Y.	Rose Grove.
								Rosehall Brick Works	Lanark ...	N. B.	Coatbridge, Whifflet.
								Rosehall Cols., Nos. 10 & 11..	Lanark ...	N. B.	Coatbridge, Whifflet.
								Rosehall Cols., Nos. 7, 13, & 21	Lanark ...	N. B.	Bellshill.
								Rosehall South Lye (Gilmour's Manure Siding)	Lanark ...	N. B.	Bellshill.
								Rose Heyworth Col. (G. W.)	Mon	G. W.—L. & N. W.	Same as Lancaster, Speir & Co.
								Rose Hill	Cheshire..	Mac. Com. (G. C. & N. S.)	See Marple (Rose Hill).
								Rose Lane	Edinboro'.	N. B.	See Edinburgh.
								Rosemary Hill Colliery.......	Staffs	N. S.	Silverdale.
								Rosemellyn Siding...........	Cornwall ..	G. W.	Bugle.
G			L					Rosemill	Forfar	Cal.	Dundee and Newtyle.
								Auchrie Siding	Forfar	Cal.	Baldragon and Rosemill.
								Fallows Quarry	Forfar	Cal.	Rosemill and Dronley.
								Leoch Quarry	Forfar	Cal.	Baldragon and Dronley.
								Rosemill Manure Works ...	Forfar	Cal.	Baldragon and Rosemill.
								Rosemill Quarry...........	Forfar	Cal.	Baldragon and Rosemill.
								Rosemill Weighs............	Forfar	Cal.	Rosemill.
								Rosemount	Perth	Cal.	See Blairgowrie.
								Rosenthall's, M., Warehouse	Cheshire..	B'head Jt—CLC—NW&L	Birkenhead.
								Rose Pit	Yorks	E. & W. Y. Union........	Rothwell.
								Rose Vale Brick & Tile Works	Staffs	N. S.	Chesterton.
								Rosewell	Edinboro' .	N. B.	See Hawthornden and Rosewell.
								Rosharry (*Book to Mohill*).....	Leitrim ...	C. & L.	Ballinamore and Mohill.
	P							Rosher's Brk. & Tile Co.'s Sid.	Suffolk ...	G. E.	Ipswich, Westerfield.
	P							Rosherville	Kent	S. E. & C.	Southfleet & Gravesend. (West Str.)
								Rosie Colliery	Fife	N. B.	Buckhaven.
								Roskear Goods Branch & Sids.	Cornwall ..	G. W.	Camborne.
G	P	F	L	H	C	3	0	Roslin	Edinboro' .	N. B.	Branch from Millerhill.
								Roslin Colliery	Edinboro' .	N. B.	Roslin and Glencorse.
	P							Ross	Galway	M. G. W.	Galway and Clifden.
G	P	F	L	H	C	10	0	Ross	Hereford ..	G. W.	Gloucester and Hereford.
								Ross & Co.'s Siding	L'lithgow	N. B.	Same as Philpstoun Oil Works (Philpstoun).
								Ross Collieries...............	Lanark ...	Cal.	Larkhall.
G	P	F	L	H	C	1	10	Rossett	Denbigh ..	G. W.	Wrexham and Chester.
G								Gresford Mill Siding........	Denbigh ..	G. W.	Rossett and Wrexham.
								Pulford Siding	Denbigh ..	G. W.	Rossett and Wrexham.
G	P	F	L	H	C			Rossington	Yorks	G. N.	Retford and Doncaster.
								Ross Junction...............	Lanark ...	Cal.	Motherwell and Ferniegair.
G	P							Rosslare	Wexford...	G. S. & W.	Wexford and Rosslare Harbour.
G	P			H				Harbour	Wexford...	G. S. & W.	Branch from Wexford.
								Pier	Wexford...	G. S. & W.	Branch from Wexford.
G	P		L	H		2	0	Rosslyn Castle	Edinboro' .	N. B.	Hawthornden Junc. and Penicuik.
								Hay, Merricks & Co.'s Gunpowder Works	Edinboro' .	N. B.	Rosslyn Castle.
	P								Edinboro' .	N. B.	Hardengreen and Peebles.
G	P		L	H				Rosslynlee	Edinboro' .	N. B.	Rosslynlee and Pomathorn.
								Holmbank Siding	Limerick ..	G. S. & W.	Charleville and Limerick.
	P							Rosstemple	Cornwall ..	G. W.	Bugle.
								Rossvear Siding.............	Lanark ...	Cal.	Larkhall.
								Ross Weighs	Northumb .	N. B.	Branch from Scotsgap.
G	P	F	L	H	C	4	0	Rothbury....................	Northumb .	N. B.	Longwitton and Rothbury.
G		L						Brinkburn (Goods) Siding	Sussex ...	L. B. & S. C.	Eridge and Mayfield.
G	P	F	L	H	C	1	10	Rotherfield and Mark Cross	Yorks	Mid.	See Masbro' and Rotherham.
G	P	F	L	H	C			Rotherham	Yorks	Mid.	Branch near Masbro'.
G	P	F	L	H	C			Rotherham (Westgate)........	Yorks	G. C.	Sheffield and Doncaster.
G	P	F	L	H	C	10	0	Rotherham and Masbro' (G. C.)	Yorks	G. C. / G. N.	Over G. C. Line.
G		F	L			10	0		Yorks	G. C.—G. N.	Rotherham and Masbro'.
								British Wgn. Co.'s Sid. (GC)	Yorks	G. C.—G. N.	Rotherham and Masbro'.
								Earl Fitzwilliam's Low Stubbin Col. (G. C.)	Yorks	G. C.—G. N.	Rotherham and Masbro'.
								George Street Wharf (G C)	Yorks	G. C.—G. N.	Rotherham and Masbro'.
								Holmes Blast Siding (G C)	Yorks	G. C.—G. N.	Rotherham and Masbro'.
								Ickles Siding (Steel, Peech & Tozer's) (G.C.)............	Yorks	G. C.—G. N.	Rotherham and Masbro'.
								New York Siding (G.C.) ...	Yorks	G. C.—G. N.	Rotherham and Masbro'.
								Northfield Siding (G. C.)..	Yorks	G. C.—G. N.	Rotherham and Masbro'.
								Oxley, Wm., & Co.'s Sid. (GC)	Yorks	G. C.—G. N.	Rotherham and Masbro'.

EXPLANATION—G *Goods Station.*   P *Passenger and Parcel Station.*   P* *Passenger, but not Parcel or Miscellaneous Traffic.*
F *Furniture Vans, Carriages, Portable Engines, and Machines on Wheels.*   L *Live Stock.*
H *Horse Boxes and Prize Cattle Vans.*   C *Carriages by Passenger Train.*

STATION ACCOMMODATION.						CRANE POWER.	STATIONS, &c.	COUNTY.	COMPANY.	POSITION.
						Tons Cwts.	Rotherham and Masboro' (GC)—*continued*.			
.	.	.	.	.	.	. .	Parkgate Chemical Works (G. C.)	Yorks	G. C.—G. N.	Rotherham and Masboro'.
.	.	.	.	.	.	. .	Parkgate Iron and Steel Co.'s Siding (G. C.)	Yorks	G. C.—G. N.	Rotherham and Masboro'.
.	.	.	.	.	.	. .	Rotherham Forge and Rolling Mills (G. C.).........	Yorks	G. C.—G. N.	Rotherham and Masboro'.
.	.	.	.	.	.	. .	Rotherham Main Col. (G C)	Yorks	G. C.—G. N.	Rotherham and Masboro'.
.	.	.	.	.	.	. .	Shaw's Siding (G. C.)	Yorks	G. C.—G. N.	Rotherham and Masboro'.
.	.	.	.	.	.	. .	Slag Reduction Co.'s Siding (G. C.)	Yorks	G. C.—G. N.	Rotherham and Masboro'.
.	.	.	.	.	.	. .	Yates, Haywood & Co.'s Siding (G. C.).............	Yorks	G. C.—G. N.	Rotherham and Masboro'.
.	.	.	.	.	.	. .	Rotherham Forge & Rolling Mills (G. C.)	Yorks	G. C.—G. N.	Rotherham and Masboro'.
.	.	.	.	.	.	. .	Rotherham Main Colliery ...	Yorks	Mid.	See Brown, J., & Co., (Masboro' and Rotherham).
.	P	.	.	.	.	. .	Rotherham Main Col. (G. C.)	Yorks	G. C.—G. N.	Rotherham and Masboro'.
.	.	.	.	.	.	. .	Rotherham Road	Yorks	G. C.	Rotherham and Doncaster.
.	.	.	.	.	.	. .	Rotherhithe.....................	Surrey ...	E. L. Jt. (G. E., L. B. & S. C., Met., M. D. & S. E. & C.)	See London.
.	.	.	.	.	.	. .	Rother Vale Collieries	Yorks	Mid.	Woodhouse Mill.
.	.	.	.	.	.	. .	Rotherwas Junction	Hereford ..	G. W.—L. & N. W.	Hereford.
.	.	.	.	.	.	. .	Rotherwood Iron and Steel Co.'s Siding...............	Yorks	Mid.	Woodhouse Mill.
G	P	F	L	H	C	5 0	Rothes	Elgin & Mo'	G. N. of S.	Craigellachie and Elgin.
.	.	.	.	.	.	. .	Rothesfield Siding	Fife	N. B.	Markinch.
.	.	.	.	.	.	. .	Rothes Siding	Fife	N. B.	Markinch.
G	P	.	L	H	C	1 5	Rothiemay	Aberdeen	G. N. of S.	Inveramsay and Keith.
G	P	.	L	H	C	1 5	Rothie Norman	Aberdeen	G. N. of S.	Inveramsay and Macduff.
G	P	.	.	.	.	. .	Rothley	Leicester ..	G. C.	Loughboro' and Leicester.
G	P	.	.	.	.	1 10	Rothwell	N'hampt'n	Mid.	See Desboro' and Rothwell.
.	.	.	.	.	.	. .	Rothwell	Yorks	E. & W. Y. Union......	Lofthouse Junction & Woodlesford.
.	.	.	.	.	.	. .	Brotherton & Co.'s Siding	Yorks	E. & W. Y. Union	Rothwell.
.	.	.	.	.	.	. .	Leeds Copper Works........	Yorks	E. & W. Y. Union	Rothwell.
.	.	.	.	.	.	. .	Lofthouse Colliery............	Yorks	E. & W. Y. Union	Lofthouse.
.	.	.	.	.	.	. .	Rose Pit	Yorks	E. & W. Y. Union	Rothwell.
.	.	.	.	.	.	. .	Rothwell Colliery	Yorks	Mid.	See Charlesworth's, J. & J., Collieries (Rothwell Haigh).
G	.	.	.	.	.	. .	Rothwell Haigh	Yorks	Mid.	Leeds and Woodlesford.
.	.	.	.	.	.	. .	Charlesworth's, J. & J., Collieries—			
.	.	.	.	.	.	. .	Newmarket Silkstone Colliery.................	Yorks	Mid.	Near Rothwell Haigh.
.	.	.	.	.	.	. .	Robin Hood Colliery......	Yorks	Mid.	Near Rothwell Haigh.
.	.	.	.	.	.	. .	Rothwell Colliery	Yorks	Mid.	Near Rothwell Haigh.
.	.	.	.	.	.	. .	Lofthouse Col. Co.'s Siding	Yorks	Mid.	Near Rothwell Haigh.
.	.	.	.	.	.	. .	Newmarket Haigh Moor and Spencer Collieries ...	Yorks	Mid.	Near Rothwell Haigh.
.	.	.	.	.	.	. .	Rothwell Haigh Junction ...	Yorks	E. & W. Y. Union—Mid.	Rothwell and Leeds.
.	.	.	.	.	.	. .	Rotterdam, Antwerp and Hamburg Wharf	Northumb	N. E.	Newcastle-on-Tyne.
.	.	.	.	.	.	. .	Rotton Park Road...............	Warwick..	L. & N. W.	See Birmingham.
.	.	.	.	.	.	. .	Roudham Junction Station...	Norfolk ...	G. E.	Thetford and Wymondham.
.	.	.	.	.	.	. .	Rough Castle Branch Junc.	Stirling ...	N. B.	Lime Road and Bonnybridge.
.	.	.	.	.	.	. .	Rough Castle Brick Works...	Stirling ...	N. B.	Lime Road.
.	.	.	.	.	.	. .	Rough Castle Oil Works ...	Stirling ...	N. B.	See Lime Road.
.	.	.	.	.	.	. .	Roughcraig Colliery	Lanark ...	N. B.	Airdrie, North.
.	.	.	.	.	.	. .	Roughcraig Quarry	Lanark ...	N. B.	Airdrie, North.
.	.	.	.	.	.	. .	Roughdale Works	Lancs	L. & N. W.	See Sutton Heath & Lea Green Colliery Co. (Rainhill).
.	.	.	.	.	.	. .	Roughlands Siding (N.B.) ...	Stirling ...	N. B.—Cal.	Falkirk, Grahamston.
.	.	.	.	.	.	. .	Rough Lea Colliery, Coke, Brick & Pipe Works	Durham ...	N. E.	Hunwick.
.	.	.	.	.	.	. .	Roughrigg Collieries	Lanark ...	N. B.	Longriggend.
.	.	.	.	.	.	. .	Round House Branch	Lancs	L. & N. W.	Wigan.
.	.	.	.	.	.	. .	Round House Siding (L&NW)	Lancs	L. & N. W.—G. C.	Same as Wigan Coal & Iron Co.'s Kirkless Hall Iron & Steel Works (Wigan).
G	P	.	.	.	.	. .	Round Oak	Staffs	G. W.	Dudley and Stourbridge Junction.
G	.	.	.	.	.	. .	Ashwood Basin (Earl Dudley's)	Staffs	G. W.	Round Oak.

EXPLANATION—G *Goods Station.* P *Passenger and Parcel Station.* P* *Passenger, but not Parcel or Miscellaneous Traffic.*
F *Furniture Vans, Carriages, Portable Engines, and Machines on Wheels.* L *Live Stock.*
H *Horse Boxes and Prize Cattle Vans.* C *Carriages by Passenger Train.*

STATION ACCOMMODATION.						CRANE POWER.		STATIONS, &c.	COUNTY.	COMPANY.	POSITION.
						Tons	Cwts.				
								Round Oak—*continued.*			
.	.	.	.	.	.			Cochrane & Co.'s Sidings	Staffs	G. W.	Round Oak and Woodside.
.	.	.	.	.	.			Hill & Smith's Siding	Staffs	G. W.	Dudley and Stourbridge Junction.
.	.	.	.	.	.					G. C.	See Dalton Main Collieries (Parkgate and Aldwarke).
.	.	.	.	.	.			Roundwood Colliery	Yorks	Mid.	See Dalton Main Collieries (Parkgate and Rawmarsh).
.	.	.	.	.	.			Roundwood Colliery	Yorks	G. N.	See Old Roundwood Colliery (Flushdyke).
.	.	.	.	.	.			Routledge's Sand Siding	Durham	N. E.	Same as Ferryhill Sand Quarry (Ferryhill).
G	P	F	L	H	C	1	10	Row	Dumbartn	N. B.	Craigendoran and Ardlui.
.	.	.	.	.	.			Rowbotham's Siding	Middlesex	G. W.	London, Acton.
G	P	.	L	H	.			Rowden Mill	Hereford	G. W.	Bromyard and Leominster.
.	.	.	.	.	.			Rowe's Lime Siding	Herts	G. N.	Knebworth.
.	.	.	.	.	.			Rowe's Siding	Beds	L. & N. W.	Same as Dunstable Lime Co.'s Siding (Dunstable).
G	P	F	L	H	C	.	.	Rowfant	Sussex	L. B. & S. C.	Three Bridges and East Grinstead.
.	.	.	.	.	.			Rowfant Brick Siding	Sussex	L. B. & S. C.	Rowfant.
.	.	.	.	.	.			Rowfoot Pit	Cumb'land	WC&EJt. (Fur.&LNW)	See Lindow's (Gillfoot).
.	.	.	.	.	.			Rowington Junction	Warwick	G. W.	Hatton and Lapworth.
.	.	.	.	.	.			Rowland & Co.'s Siding	Lancs	G. C.	Hyde Road.
.	.	.	.	.	.			Rowland Bros.' Siding	Bucks	L. & N. W.	Fenny Stratford.
G	P	F	L	H	C	5	0	Rowland's Castle	Hants	L. & S. W.	Petersfield and Portsmouth.
.	.	.	.	.	.			Rowlands Castle Brick & Tile Co.'s Siding	Hants	L. & S. W.	Rowlands Castle.
G	P	F	L	H	C	3	0	Rowland's Gill	Durham	N. E.	Scotswood and Blackhill.
.	.	.	.	.	.			Lily Drift Colliery & Coke Ovens	Durham	N. E.	Rowland's Gill.
.	.	.	.	.	.			Victoria Garesfield Colliery, Coke and Brick Works (Highfield Siding)	Durham	N. E.	Rowland's Gill.
.	.	.	.	.	.			Rowland's Siding	Lincoln	G. N. & G. E. Jt.	Lincoln and Saxilby.
G	P	.	L	.	.	1	10	Rowley	Durham	N. E.	Blackhill and Tow Law.
.	.	.	.	.	.			Whitehall Sidings	Durham	N. E	Rowley.
G	P	.	.	.	.	4	10	Rowley Regis & Blackheath	Worcester	G. W.	Langley Green and Old Hill.
.	.	.	.	.	.			Cakemoor Brick Works	Worcester	G. W.	Rowley Regis.
.	.	.	.	.	.			Rowley's Shotton Brick Wks.	Flint	W. M. & C. Q.	Connah's Quay.
.	.	.	.	.	.			Rowntree's Siding	Yorks	N. E.	York.
.	.	.	.	.	.			Rowrah	Cumb'land	C. & W. Jn.	See Arlecdon (for Rowrah).
G	P	.	L	H	.	3	0	Rowrah	Cumb'land	WC&EJt. (Fur.&LNW)	Marron Junction and Moor Row.
.	.	.	.	.	.			Baird's Knockmurton Mines	Cumb'land	WC&EJt. (Fur.&LNW)	Rowrah.
.	.	.	.	.	.			Cammell & Co.'s Kelton Limestone Quarry	Cumb'land	WC&EJt. (Fur.&LNW)	Rowrah and Lamplugh.
.	.	.	.	.	.			Rowrah Limestone Quarries	Cumb'land	WC&EJt. (Fur.&LNW)	Rowrah and Lamplugh.
.	.	.	.	.	.			Wyndham Mining Co.'s Pits	Cumb'land	WC&EJt. (Fur.&LNW)	Rowrah.
.	.	.	.	.	.			Rowrah Junction	Cumb'land	C. & W. Jn.—R. & K. F.	Distington and Kelton Fell.
.	.	.	.	.	.			Rowrah Junction	Cumb'land	R. & K. F.—W. C. & E. Jt.	Kelton Fell and Moor Row.
.	.	.	.	.	.			Rowrah Limestone Siding (Dixon's Siding)	Cumb'land	C. & W. Jn.	Arlecdon (for Rowrah).
G	P	F	L	H	C	10	0	Rowsley	Derby	Mid.	Ambergate and Miller's Dale.
G	P	.	L	H	.			Rowthorn & Hardwick	Derby	Mid.	Pleasley and Staveley Town.
G	P	.	L	H	.			Roxburgh	Roxburgh	N. B.	St. Boswells and Kelso.
G	.	.	L	.	.	1	10	Heiton Siding	Roxburgh	N. B.	Roxburgh and Kelso.
.	.	.	.	.	.			Roxburgh Junction	Roxburgh	N. B.	Rutherford and Kelso.
.	.	.	.	.	.			Roxburgh Enamelling Works	Renfrew	Cal.	Glasgow, Whiteinch.
.	.	.	.	.	.			Roxeth	Middlesex	Met. Dist.	See South Harrow (for Roxeth and Northolt).
.	.	.	.	.	.			Royal Agricultural Show Yard Siding	Middlesex	G. W.	Park Royal.
.	.	.	.	.	.			Royal Albert Dk. (L.&I.Dks.)	Essex	L. & I. Dks.—G. E.—G. N. G. W.—L&NW—Mid.	See London.
.	.	.	.	.	.			Royal Albert Dock Coal Hoist	Essex	G. E.—G. N.—G. W.— L. & N. W.—Mid.	London, Victoria & Albert Docks.
.	.	.	.	.	.			Royal Asylum Siding	Edinboro'	N. B.	Edinburgh, Morningside Road.
.	.	.	.	.	.			Royal Clarence Victualling Yard	Hants	L. & S. W.	Gosport.
.	.	.	.	.	.			Royal Engineers' Siding	Essex	L. T. & S.	Shoeburyness.
.	.	.	.	.	.			Royal George Siding	Yorks	L. & N. W.	Same as Whitehead's Sid(Greenfield).
.	.	.	.	.	.			Royal Mint Street	Middlesex	G. N. / Mid.	See London. / See London, City Station.
.	.	.	.	.	.			Royal Oak	Middlesex	G. W.	See London.

EXPLANATION—G *Goods Station.*   P *Passenger and Parcel Station.*   P* *Passenger, but not Parcel or Miscellaneous Traffic.*
F *Furniture Vans, Carriages, Portable Engines, and Machines on Wheels.*   L *Live Stock.*
H *Horse Boxes and Prize Cattle Vans.*   C *Carriages by Passenger Train.*

STATION ACCOMMODATION.						CRANE POWER.	STATIONS, &c.	COUNTY.	COMPANY.	POSITION.
						Tons Cwts.	Royal Oak Siding	Devon	G. W.	Princetown.
G	P	F	L	H	C	. .	Royal Pier	Hants	L. & S.W.	See Southampton.
.	.	.	.	.	.	. .	Royal Show Ground	Middlesex	L. & N. W.	Branch from Willesden Junc. Sta.
.	.	.	.	.	.	. .	RoyalVictoriaDk.(L.&I.Dks.)	Essex	L. & I. Dks.—G.E.—G.N. G. W.—L&NW—Mid.	See London.
G	P	F	L	H	C	1 10	Roy Bridge	Inverness	N. B.	Crianlarich and Fort William.
.	.	.	.	.	.	. .	Royce's Siding	Lancs	Trafford Park Estate......	Manchester.
G	P	.	.	.	.	. .	Roydmoor Sidings..............	Yorks	S. & K. Jt. (Mid. & N. E.)	Pontefract and Moorthorpe.
.	.	.	.	.	.	. .	Roydon	Essex	G. E.	Broxbourne and Bishops Stortford.
G	P	F	L	H	C	5 0	Royle's Siding	Lancs	C.L.C.(G.C.,G.N. & Mid.)	Irlam.
.	.	.	.	.	.	. .	Royston	Herts	G. N.	Hitchin and Cambridge.
.	.	.	.	.	.	. .	Farmer's Manure Co.'s Sid.	Herts	G. N.	Royston.
.	.	.	.	.	.	. .	Fordham's Siding	Herts	G. N.	Royston.
.	.	.	.	.	.	. .	Nash & Co.'s Siding	Herts	G. N.	Royston.
.	.	.	.	.	.	. .	Phillip's Siding	Herts	G. N.	Royston.
.	.	.	.	.	.	. .	Smith, T. H., & Son's Siding	Herts	G. N.	Royston.
.	.	.	.	.	.	. .	Wilkerson & Son's Siding..	Herts	G. N.	Royston.
.	.	.	.	.	.	. .	Royston	Yorks	G. C.	See Notton and Royston.
G	P	F	L	H	C	1 10	Royston and Notton	Yorks	Mid.	Masboro' and Normanton.
.	.	.	.	.	.	. .	Hodroyd Colliery	Yorks	Mid.	Near Royston and Notton.
.	.	.	.	.	.	. .	Monckton Main Colliery ...	Yorks	Mid.	Cudworth and Oakenshaw.
.	.	.	.	.	.	. .	New Monckton Colliery ...	Yorks	Mid.	Royston and Notton.
.	.	.	.	.	.	. .	Ryhill Col. (Lodge's Siding)	Yorks	Mid.	Near Royston and Notton.
.	.	.	.	.	.	. .	Royston Cement Co.'s Siding	Cambs	G. N.	Shepreth.
G	P	.	L	H	.	5 0	Royton	Lancs	L. & Y.	Branch from Royton Junc. Station.
.	.	.	.	.	.	. .	Woodstock Spinning Co.'s Siding	Lancs	L. & Y.	Royton.
G	P	F	L	H	C	5 0	Royton Junction Station	Lancs	L. & Y.	Oldham and Rochdale.
.	.	.	.	.	.	. .	Ruabon	Denbigh ..	G. W.	Chirk and Wrexham.
.	.	.	.	.	.	. .	Bowers (Tatham) Brk. Wks.	Denbigh..	G. W.	Ruabon and Johnstown & Hafod.
.	.	.	.	.	.	. .	Gardden Lodge Junction ...	Denbigh..	G. W.	Ruabon and Johnstown & Hafod.
.	.	.	.	.	.	. .	Monk & Newell's Works ...	Denbigh..	G. W.	Gardden Lodge Branch.
.	.	.	.	.	.	. .	Plasmadoc Junction	Denbigh..	G. W.	Ruabon and Cefn.
.	.	.	.	.	.	. .	Plasmadoc Sidings	Denbigh..	G. W.	Ruabon (South Yard).
.	.	.	.	.	.	. .	Ruabon Brick and Terra Cotta Co.'s Sidings	Denbigh..	G. W.	Gardden Lodge Branch.
.	.	.	.	.	.	. .	Vauxhall Colliery	Denbigh..	G. W.	Ruabon and Johnstown & Hafod.
.	.	.	.	.	.	. .	Wynnstay Colliery	Denbigh..	G. W.	Ruabon.
.	.	.	.	.	.	. .	Ruabon Coal and Coke Co.— Pant Brick Works	Denbigh..	G. W.	Rhos.
.	.	.	.	.	.	. .	Siding	Denbigh..	G. W.	Johnstown & Hafod.
.	.	.	.	.	.	. .	RuabonCoalCo.'sBrickWorks	Denbigh..	G. W.	Johnstown & Hafod.
G	P	.	.	.	.	. .	Rubery	Worcester	Halesowen (G. W. & Mid.)	Halesowen and Northfield.
.	.	.	.	.	.	. .	Birmingham Corporation— Hollymoor Asylum Bch.	Worcester	Halesowen (G. W. & Mid.)	Near Rubery.
.	.	.	.	.	.	. .	Water Works	Worcester	Halesowen (G. W. & Mid.)	Near Rubery.
.	.	.	.	.	.	. .	Frankley Sidings (Kellet & Son)	Worcester	Halesowen (G. W. & Mid.)	Rubery and Halesowen.
.	.	.	.	.	.	. .	Ruby Brick & Tile Co.'s Siding	Flint	L. & N. W.	Rhydymwyn.
.	.	.	.	.	.	. .	Ruchill	Lanark ..	N. B.	See Glasgow.
.	.	.	.	.	.	. .	Ruchill Hospital Siding	Lanark ..	Cal.	See Glasgow.
.	.	.	.	.	.	. .	Ruchill Manure Siding........	Lanark ..	N. B.	Glasgow, Ruchill.
.	.	.	.	.	.	. .	Ruckinge Siding	Kent	S. E. & C.	Ham Street.
.	.	.	.	.	.	. .	Ruckley Sand Siding	Salop	G. W.	Shifnal.
G	P	F	L	H	C	. .	Ruddington	Notts	G. C.	Nottingham and Loughboro'.
.	.	.	.	.	.	. .	Wilford Brick Co.'s Siding	Notts	G. C.	Ruddington.
G	P	F	L	H	C	. .	Rudgwick	Sussex ..	L. B. & S. C.	Guildford and Horsham.
.	P	.	.	.	.	. .	Rudry Brick Works	Glamorg'n	B. & M.	Machen.
G	P	.	.	.	.	5 0	Rudyard	Staffs	N. S.	Macclesfield and Leek.
G	P	F	L	H	C	5 0	Rufford	Lancs	L. & Y.	Preston and Ormskirk.
.	.	.	.	.	.	. .	Rufford & Co.'s Works	Worcester	G. W.	Stourbridge.
							RUGBY—			
G	P	F	L	H	C	10 0	(Station)	Warwick..	{ L. & N. W. { Mid.	Blisworth and Nuneaton. Branch from Leicester.
.	.	.	.	.	.	. .	British Thomson-Houston Co.'s Siding	Warwick..	L. & N. W.—Mid.	Rugby.
G	P	F	L	H	C	10 0	Central	Warwick..	G. C.	Lutterworth and Brackley.
.	.	.	.	.	.	. .	Hunter's Wagon Works ...	Warwick..	L. & N. W.—Mid.	Rugby.
.	.	.	.	.	.	. .	Junction	Warwick..	L. & N. W.—Mid.	Blisworth and Wigston.
.	.	.	.	.	.	. .	Pinfold Siding..................	Warwick..	L. & N. W.	Rugby and Dunchurch.
.	.	.	.	.	.	. .	Rugby Brick and Tile Co.'s Braes Siding	Warwick..	L. & N. W.	Rugby and Dunchurch.

EXPLANATION—G *Goods Station.*   P *Passenger and Parcel Station.*   P* *Passenger, but not Parcel or Miscellaneous Traffic.*
F *Furniture Vans, Carriages, Portable Engines, and Machines on Wheels.*   L *Live Stock.*
H *Horse Boxes and Prize Cattle Vans.*   C *Carriages by Passenger Train.*

STATION ACCOMMODATION.						CRANE POWER.		STATIONS, &c.	COUNTY.	COMPANY.	POSITION.
						Tons	Cwts.	RUGBY—continued.			
.	.	.	.	.	.	.	.	Rugby Gas Co.'s Siding ...	Warwick..	{ L. & N. W.	Rugby and Brinklow.
										{ Mid.	Rugby.
								Rugby Portland Cement Co.—			
.	.	.	.	.	.	.	.	Bilton Wharf	Warwick..	{ L. & N. W.	Rugby and Dunchurch.
										{ Mid.	Rugby.
						.	.	Newbold's Siding	Warwick..	Mid.	Near Rugby Wharf.
G	.	.	.	.	.	.	.	Rugby Wharf	Warwick..	Mid.	Branch—Rugby and Ullesthorpe.
G	.	.	.	.	.	.	.	Willans & Robinson's Sid.	Warwick..	L. & N. W.	Rugby and Dunchurch.
G	P	F	L	H	C	5	0	Rugeley (Trent Valley)	Staffs	L. & N. W.	Lichfield and Stafford.
						.	.	Rugeley Gas Co.'s Siding......	Staffs	L. & N. W.	Hednesford.
G	P	.	.	.	.	.	.	Rugeley Town	Staffs	L. & N. W.	Rugeley (T. V.) and Walsall.
	P	.	.	.	.	.	.	Rum	Inverness..	Cal.	Steamer from Oban.
G	P	F	L	H	C	3	0	Rumbling Bridge	Kinross ..	N. B.	Tillicoultry and Kinross Junction.
						.	.	Devonshaw Siding	Kinross ..	N. B.	Rumbling Bridge and Dollar.
						.	.	Rumworth and Daubhill	Lancs	L. & N. W.	See Bolton.
G	P	F	L	H	C	5	0	Runcorn	Cheshire...	L. & N. W.	Crewe and Liverpool.
						.	.	Castner, Kellner & Co.'s Sid.	Cheshire...	L. & N. W.	Runcorn Docks.
G	.	.	.	.	.	.	.	Docks	Cheshire...	L. & N. W.	Branch from Runcorn.
								Manchester Ship Canal Co.'s Runcorn Docks Siding ...	Cheshire...	L. & N. W.	Runcorn Docks.
						.	.	Orme & Muntz Siding	Cheshire...	L. & N. W.	Runcorn Docks.
								Runcorn and Helsby Red Sandstone Co.'s Siding...	Cheshire...	L. & N. W.	Runcorn Docks.
						.	.	Salt Union, Limited, Siding	Cheshire...	L. & N. W.	Runcorn Docks.
						.	.	Walker's Siding	Cheshire...	L. & N. W.	Runcorn Docks.
						.	.	Wilson's Percival Lane Sid.	Cheshire...	L. & N. W.	Runcorn Docks.
								Runcorn and Helsby Red } Sandstone Co.'s Siding... }	Cheshire...	{ B'head Jt. (GW & LN W)	Helsby.
										{ L. & N. W.	Runcorn Docks.
								Runcorn and Helsby Stone Co.'s Siding...............	Cheshire...	C. L. C. (G C, G N, & Mid.)	Helsby and Alvanley.
								Runcorn and Widnes Co-operative Society's Siding	Lancs	L. & N. W.	Widnes Dock.
								Runcorn Docks Siding	Cheshire...	L. & N. W	See Manchester Ship Canal Co. (Runcorn).
	P*	.	.	.	.	.	.	Runemede Range	Middlesex	G. W.	Colnbrook and Staines.
	P	.	.	.	.	.	.	Rushall	Staffs	L. & N. W.	Lichfield and Walsall.
G	P	F	L	H	C	.	.	Rush and Lusk	Dublin ...	G. N. (I.)	Dublin and Drogheda.
G	P	.	.	.	.	.	.	Rushbrooke	Cork	G. S. & W.	Queenstown Junc. and Queenstown.
G	P	F	L	H	C	.	.	Rushbury	Salop	G. W.	Much Wenlock and Craven Arms.
G	P	F	L	H	C	5	0	Rushden	N'hamptn	Mid.	Wellingboro' and Higham Ferrers.
						.	.	Rushden Brick & Tile Co.'s Siding	N'hamptn	Mid.	Rushden and Wellingboro'.
						.	.	Rushden District Gas Co.'s Siding	N'hamptn	Mid.	Rushden and Higham Ferrers.
G	P	F	L	H	C	5	0	Rushey Platt	Wilts	M. & S. W. Jn. ...	Swindon Town and Cricklade.
						.	.	Rushey Platt Junction	Wilts	G. W.—M. & S. W. Jn...	Same as Swindon Junction.
						.	.	Rushey Siding (G. C.)	Notts	G. C.—G. N.—Mid. ...	Retford.
						.	.	Rushton	N'hamptn	Mid.	See Glendon and Rushton.
G	P	F	L	H	C	.	.	Rushton	Staffs	N. S.	Macclesfield and Leek.
G	P	F	L	H	C	10	0	Ruskington	Lincoln	G. N. & G. E. Jt.	Sleaford and Lincoln.
						.	.	Evedon Siding..................	Lincoln	G. N. & G. E. Jt.	Ruskington and Sleaford.
G	P†	.	.	.	.	.	.	Ruspidge	Glo'ster	G. W.	Bullo Pill and Bilson Junction.
						.	.	Shakemantle Siding	Glo'ster	G. W.	Forest of Dean Branch.
						.	.	Soudley Siding	Glo'ster	G. W.	Forest of Dean Branch.
								Russell & Co.—			
						.	.	Birchills Blast Furnaces ...	Staffs	L. & N. W.	Bloxwich.
						.	.	Cyclops Iron Works	Staffs	L. & N. W.	Walsall.
						.	.	Russell & Fullarton's Siding	Ayr	Cal.—G. & S. W.	Ardrossan.
						.	.	Russell's Siding	Staffs	L. & N. W.	Wednesbury.
						.	.	Russell's, T. E., Siding	Lancs	Trafford Park Estate......	Manchester.
						.	.	Russell's Wharf	Mon	A (N & S W) D & R—G W	Newport, Alexandra Docks.
						.	.	Rustless Iron Co.'s Siding ...	Yorks	Mid.	Keighley.
								Ruston, Proctor & Co.—			
						.	.	Iron Works (G. C.)	Lincoln	G. C.—G. N.—Mid.	Lincoln.
						.	.	New Boiler & Wood Works (Mid.)..................	Lincoln	Mid.—G. C.—G. N.	Lincoln.
						.	.	Ruswarp	Yorks	N. E.	Whitby and Pickering.
G	P	F	L	.	.	.	.	Ruswarp	Yorks	N. E.	Ruswarp and Whitby.
						.	.	Batt's Foundry	Yorks	N. E.	Ruswarp.
						.	.	Sneaton Siding	Yorks	N. E.	Ruswarp.
						.	.	Whitby Gas Works	Yorks	N. E.	Ruswarp and Whitby.

EXPLANATION—G *Goods Station.*   P *Passenger and Parcel Station.*   P* *Passenger, but not Parcel or Miscellaneous Traffic.*
P† *Parcels only.*   F *Furniture Vans, Carriages, Portable Engines, and Machines on Wheels.*   L *Live Stock.*
H *Horse Boxes and Prize Cattle Vans.*   C *Carriages by Passenger Train.*

STATION ACCOMMODATION.						CRANE POWER.	STATIONS, &c.	COUNTY.	COMPANY.	POSITION.
						Tons Cwt.				
G	P	.	L	H	.		Rutherford	Roxburgh	N. B.	St. Boswells and Kelso.
.	.	.	.	.	.		Rutherglen	Lanark ..	Cal.	See Glasgow.
.	.	.	.	.	.		Rutherglen Brick Works......	Lanark ..	Cal.	Glasgow, Bridgeton.
.	.	.	.	.	.		Rutherglen Weighs	Lanark ..	Cal.	Glasgow, Rutherglen.
G	.	.	.	.	.		Rutherglen, West	Lanark ..	Cal.	See Glasgow.
G	P	F	L	H	C	5 0	Ruthern Bridge Wharf	Cornwall	L. & S.W.	Branch from Grogley Junction.
.	.	.	.	.	.		Ruthin	Denbigh..	L. & N. W.	Corwen and Denbigh.
.	.	.	.	.	.		Ruthin Lime Siding	Denbigh..	L. & N. W.	Ruthin and Rhewl.
.	.	.	.	.	.		Ruthrieston	Aberdeen	G. N. of S.	See Aberdeen.
.	.	.	.	.	.		Ruthven Road	Perth ..	Cal.	See Almondbank.
G	P	F	L	H	C	1 10	Ruthwell	Dumfries..	G. & S.W.	Annan and Dumfries.
.	.	.	.	.	.		Rutland Engineering Works (Blackstone & Co.) (G. N.)	Lincoln	G. N.—L. & N. W.—Mid.	Stamford.
.	.	.	.	.	.		Rutland Street	Glamorg'n	Swan. & Mum.	See Swansea.
.	.	.	.	.	.		Rutter's Siding	Kent ..	S. E. & C.	Dartford.
G	P	F	L	H	C	1 0	Ryburgh	Norfolk ..	G. E.	Dereham and Fakenham.
.	.	.	.	.	.		Smith, F. & G., Siding......	Norfolk ..	G. E.	Ryburgh.
							RYDE—			
G	P	.	.	.	.	5 0	Esplanade(LSW&LBSCJt)	I. of W	{L&SW.&LB.&S.C.Jt. / I. of W. / I. of W. Cent.	Ryde Pier Head & St. John's Road. / Over R.P.&R. from St. John's Road. / Over I. of W. and Ryde Pier & Rly.
.	P	.	.	.	.	2 10	Pier Head(LSW&LBSCJt)	I. of W ...	{L.&S.W.&L.B.&S.C.Jt. / I. of W. / I. of W. Cent.	Steamer from Portsmouth and Stokes Bay. / Over R.P.&R. from St. John's Road. / Over I. of W. and Ryde Pier & Rly.
G	P	F	L	H	C	10 0	St. John's Road (I. of W.)	I. of W	{I. of W. / I. of W. Cent.	Ryde Pier Head and Brading. / Over I. of W. from Smallbrook Jn.
.	.	.	.	.	.		St. John's Road Junction...	I. of W	I. of W.—L. & S. W. & L. B. & S. C. Jt.	Brading and Ryde Pier Head.
.	.	.	.	.	.		Ryden Mains Quarry	Lanark	N. B.	Greengairs.
.	.	.	.	.	.		Ryden Quarry	Lanark	N. B.	Greengairs.
.	.	.	.	.	.		Ryders Hayes or Pelsall Col.	Staffs	L. & N. W.	See Walsall Wood Colliery Co. (Pelsall).
.	.	.	.	.	.		Rydings Siding	Lancs	L. & Y.	Barton.
G	P	F	L	H	C	4 0	Rye	Sussex	S. E. & C.	Hastings and Ashford.
.	.	.	.	.	.		Harbour	Sussex	S. E. & C.	Branch—Winchelsea & Rye.
.	.	.	.	.	.		Kelly's Siding	Sussex	S. E. & C.	Rye Harbour Branch.
.	.	.	.	.	.		Rye Chemical Co.'s Siding	Sussex	S. E. & C.	Rye Harbour Branch.
.	.	.	.	.	.		Rye Bread Works	Yorks	N. E.	See Aire & Calder Glass Bottle Works (Castleford).
.	.	.	.	.	.		Ryecroft Junction	Staffs	L. & N. W.—Mid.	Walsall.
.	.	.	.	.	.		Ryefield Colliery	Derby	Mid.	Denby.
G	P	F	.	H	C	1 10	Ryeford	Glo'ster	Mid.	Stonehouse and Nailsworth.
.	.	.	.	.	.		Braithwaite & Co.'s Siding	Glo'ster ..	Mid.	Ryeford.
.	.	.	.	.	.		Knight's, W., Siding	Glo'ster ..	Mid.	Ryeford.
.	.	.	.	.	.		Lane's Siding	Glo'ster ..	Mid.	Ryeford and Dudbridge.
.	.	.	.	.	.		Richards & Beick's Siding	Glo'ster ..	Mid.	Ryeford.
.	.	.	.	.	.		Sir Wm. Marling's Siding..	Glo'ster ..	Mid.	Near Ryeford.
.	.	.	.	.	.		Webb & Spring's Mills......	Glo'ster ..	Mid.	Near Ryeford.
G	P	.	L	.	.		Rye Hill	Yorks	N. E.	Hull and Withernsea.
.	.	.	.	.	.		Kelsey Hill Ballast Pit......	Yorks	N. E.	Rye Hill.
G	P	.	.	.	.		Rye House	Herts	G. E.	Hertford and Broxbourne.
G	P	.	.	.	.		Ryhall & Belmisthorpe........	Rutland ..	G. N.	Stamford and Essendine.
G	P	.	.	.	.	5 0	Ryhill	Yorks	G. C.	Barnsley and Wakefield.
.	.	.	.	.	.		Ryhill Colliery (Lodge's Sid.)	Yorks	Mid.	Royston and Notton.
.	.	.	.	.	.		Ryhill Main Colliery	Yorks	G. C.	Notton and Royston.
G	P	.	L	H	C	1 10	Ryhope	Durham	N. E.	Murton and Sunderland, South Side.
.	.	.	.	.	.		Ryhope Col. & Brick Works	Durham	N. E.	Ryhope.
.	.	.	.	.	.		Silksworth Colliery & Depôt	Durham	N. E.	Ryhope.
.	P*	.	.	.	.		Ryhope, East	Durham	N. E.	Sunderland and Seaham.
.	.	.	.	.	.		Londonderry Brick Siding	Durham	N. E.	Ryhope, East.
.	.	.	.	.	.		Ryhope Grange Junction...	Durham	N. E.	Sunderland and Ryhope.
.	.	.	.	.	.		Ryknield Engine Co.'s Siding (Mid.)	Staffs	Mid. —L&NW—GN—NS	Burton-on-Trent.
.	.	.	.	.	.		Rylands & Son's Gidlow Wks.	Lancs	L. & N. W.	Wigan.
.	.	.	.	.	.		Ryland's Dacca Twist Co.'s Siding (L.&Y.&L.U.Jt.)	Lancs	{L. & Y. / L. & N. W.	Chorley. / Heapey.
.	.	.	.	.	.		Ryland's Glass and Engineering Co.'s Siding ...	Yorks	{G. C. / Mid.	Stairfoot (for Ardsley). / Barnsley.
G	P	F	L	H	C	.	Rylstone	Yorks	Mid.	Skipton and Grassington.
.	.	.	.	.	.		Crook Rise Siding	Yorks	Mid.	Rylstone and Skipton.
.	.	.	.	.	.		Green's Siding	Yorks	Mid.	Embsay Junction and Rylstone.

EXPLANATION—G *Goods Station.*   P *Passenger and Parcel Station.*   P* *Passenger, but not Parcel or Miscellaneous Traffic.*
F *Furniture Vans, Carriages, Portable Engines, and Machines on Wheels.*   L *Live Stock.*
H *Horse Boxes and Prize Cattle Vans.*   C *Carriages by Passenger Train.*

STATION ACCOMMODATION.						CRANE POWER.	STATIONS, &c.	COUNTY.	COMPANY.	POSITION.
						Tons Cwts.	**Rylstone**—continued.			
							Swinden Lime Works (Spencer's)	Yorks	Mid.	Rylstone and Grassington.
G	P	.	L	.	.	. .	Ryston	Norfolk	G. E.	Denver and Stoke Ferry.
.	.	.	.	.	.	. .	Pratt, E. R. M., Siding	Norfolk	G. E.	Ryston.
.	P	.	.	.	.	. .	Ryton	Durham	N. E.	Newcastle and Hexham.

S

STATION ACCOMMODATION.						CRANE POWER.	STATIONS, &c.	COUNTY.	COMPANY.	POSITION.
.	.	.	.	.	.	. .	Sacriston Colliery	Durham	N. E.	Pelton.
.	.	.	.	.	.	. .	Sadd, J., & Son's Siding	Essex	G. E.	Southend-on-Sea.
G	P	.	L	H	.	1 10	Saddleworth (for Dobcross)	Yorks	L. & N. W.	Huddersfield and Stalybridge.
G	P	F	L	H	C	1 10	Saffron Walden	Essex	G. E.	Audley End and Bartlow.
.	.	.	.	.	.	. .	St. Abbs	Berwick	N. B.	See Reston (for St. Abbs).
G	P	F	L	H	C	6 0	St. Agnes	Cornwall	G. W.	Newquay and Truro.
							St. Albans—			
G	P	F	L	H	C	5 0	(Station)	Herts	G. N.	Branch from Hatfield.
G	P	F	L	H	C	10 0	(Station)	Herts	Mid.	Bedford and London.
G	P	F	L	H	C	10 0	(Station, L. & N. W.)	Herts	{ L. & N. W.	Branch from Watford Junc. Station.
.	P	.	.	H	C				{ G. N.	Over L. & N. W. from St. Albans Jn.
							Junction	Herts	G. N.—L. & N. W.	St. Albans (G. N.) and Watford.
.	.	.	.	.	.	. .	Napsbury Siding	Herts	Mid.	St. Albans and Radlett.
.	.	.	.	.	.	. .	Park Street Sid. (Silvester's)	Herts	Mid.	St. Albans and Radlett.
.	.	.	.	.	.	. .	St. Albans Gas Co.'s Siding	Herts	L. & N. W.	St. Albans and Park Street.
.	.	.	.	.	.	. .	Salvation Army Siding	Herts	G. N.	St. Albans and Hill End.
.	.	.	.	.	.	. .	Sanders' Siding	Herts	G. N.	St. Albans and Hill End.
.	.	.	.	.	.	. .	Sandridge Siding	Herts	Mid.	St. Albans and Harpenden.
.	.	.	.	.	.	. .	Walls' Siding	Herts	Mid.	St. Albans.
G	P	F	L	H	C	3 0	St. Andrews	Fife	N. B.	Anstruther and Leuchars.
							St. Andrew's Cross Electrical Works	Lanark	G B & K Jt (Cal & G & S W)	Glasgow, South Side (G. B. & K.)
.	.	.	.	.	.	. .	St. Andrew's Dock (N. E.)	Yorks	N. E.—L. & N. W.	See Hull.
							St. Andrew's Steel Works (Redpath, Brown & Co.)	Edinboro'	N. B.	Edinburgh, Leith Walk.
G	P	F	L	H	C	5 0	St. Annes-on-the-Sea	Lancs	P. & W. Jt. (L & Y & L & N W)	Blackpool (Central) and Lytham.
.	P	.	.	.	.	. .	St. Annes Park	Somerset	G. W.	Bristol and Keynsham.
G	P	.	L	.	.	. .	St. Ann's	Cork	C. & Muskerry	Coachford Junc. and Blarney.
.	.	.	.	.	.	. .	St. Ann's Road	Middlesex	T. & H. Jt. (G. E. & Mid.)	See London.
.	.	.	.	.	.	. .	St. Ann's Well	Notts	G. N.	See Nottingham.
G	P	.	.	.	.	. .	St. Anthony's	Northumb	N. E.	Loop—Newcastle and Percy Main.
G	P	F	L	H	C	5 0	St. Asaph	Flint	L. & N. W	Denbigh and Rhyl.
							Llannerch Siding	Denbigh	L. & N. W.	St. Asaph and Trefnant.
G	P	.	L	H	.	. .	St. Athan Road	Glamorg'n	T. V.	Cowbridge and Aberthaw.
G	P	.	.	.	.	. .	St. Aubin	Jersey	Jersey	St. Helier and Corbiere.
G	P	F	L	H	C	2 0	St. Austell	Cornwall	G. W.	Burngullow and Par.
							Trenance Siding	Cornwall	G. W.	St. Austell and Burngullow.
G	P	F	L	H	C	7 0	St. Bees	Cumb'land	Furness	Sellafield and Whitehaven.
G	P	.	.	.	.	2 0	St. Blazey	Cornwall	G. W.	Fowey and Newquay.
.	.	.	.	.	.	. .	Par Dock	Cornwall	G. W.	St. Blazey and Fowey.
.	.	.	.	.	.	. .	Pontsmill Siding	Cornwall	G. W.	St. Blazey and Bridges.
.	.	.	.	.	.	. .	Lovering & Co.'s Prideaux Wood Siding	Cornwall	G. W.	St. Blazey and Bridges.
.	.	.	.	.	.	. .	St. Blazey Junction	Cornwall	G. W.	Fowey and Newquay.
G	P	F	L	H	C	3 0	St. Boswells	Roxburgh	N. B.	Galashiels and Hawick.
.	.	.	.	.	.	. .	St. Botolphs	Essex	G. E.	See Colchester.
G	P	F	L	H	C	1 10	St. Budeaux (for Saltash)	Devon	L. & S. W.	Tavistock and Devonport.
G	P	F	L	H	C	5 0	St. Clears	Carmarth'	G. W.	Carmarthen Junc. and Whitland.
G	P	P	L	L	.	5 0	St. Columb Road	Cornwall	G. W.	Newquay and Par.
G	P	.	L	L	.	. .	St. Combs	Aberdeen	G. N. of S.	Branch from Fraserburgh.
G	P	.	L	H	.	. .	St. Cyres (L. & S. W.)	Devon	{ L. & S. W.	Exeter and Crediton.
									{ G. W.	Over L. & S. W. from Exeter.
G	P	.	L	H	.	0 15	St. Cyrus	Kinc'rdine	N. B.	Montrose and Bervie.
.	.	.	.	.	.	. .	St. David's (G. W.)	Devon	G. W.—L. & S. W.	See Exeter.
.	.	.	.	.	.	. .	St. David's Tin Plate Works (G. W.)	Carmarth'	G. W.—L. & N. W.	Bynea.
.	.	.	.	.	.	. .	St. Dennis Junction	Cornwall	G. W.	St. Columb Road and Victoria.

STATION ACCOMMODATION.						CRANE POWER.		STATIONS, &c.	COUNTY.	COMPANY.	POSITION.
G	P			H	C	Tons	Cwts	St. Deny's	Hants	L. & S.W.	See Southampton.
G							}	St. Devereux (G. W.)	Hereford	G. W.	Hereford and Abergavenny.
										L. & N. W.	Over G. W. from Hereford.
								St. Dunstans	Yorks	G. N.	See Bradford.
								St. Edmunds	Suffolk	G. E.	See Bury St. Edmunds.
								St. Enoch	Lanark	G & SW—Glas. Dist. Sub.	See Glasgow.
G	P	F	L	H	C			St. Erth	Cornwall	G. W.	Camborne and Penzance.
								ST. FAGANS—			
G								East & West Junctions	Glamorg'n	Barry—G. W.	Creigiau and St. Fagans.
G	P		L	H			}	Station	Glamorg'n	Barry	Cardiff and Creigiau.
	P						}	Station (G. W.)	Glamorg'n	G. W.	Cardiff and Bridgend.
										Barry	Over G. W. from St. Fagans, East Junction.
								St. Fagan's Road Siding (Croftyguinea Siding)	Glamorg'n	T. V.	Cross Inn.
G	P		L	H	C	2	0	Saintfield	Down	B. & C. D.	Comber and Ballynahinch.
G	P	F	L	H	C	3	0	St. Fillans	Perth	Cal.	Crieff and Lochearnhead.
								Dalchonzie Siding	Perth	Cal.	Comrie and St. Fillans.
G	P	F	L	H	C	1	10	St. Fort	Fife	N. B.	Leuchars Junction Sta. & Dundee.
								Newton Ballast Hill Siding	Fife	N. B.	St. Fort and Wormit.
G								Newton Siding	Fife	N. B.	St. Fort and Wormit.
	P							St. Gabriel's	Glamorg'n	Swan. & Mum.	Swansea and Mumbles Road.
								St. George's Colliery	Carmarth'	G. W.	Dafen.
								St. George's Cross	Lanark	Glas. Dist. Sub.	See Glasgow.
								St. George's, East	Middlesex	G. E.	See London, Shadwell and St. George's, East.
								St. Germain's	I. of Man	Manx Northern	St. John's and Ramsey.
								St. Germain's Siding	Norfolk	G. E.	See Magdalen Road.
G	P	F	L	H	C	2	0	St. German's	Cornwall	G. W.	Plymouth and Liskeard.
G	P							St. Harmons	Radnor	Cam.	Rhayader and Pantydwr.
G	P	F	L	H	C	10	0	St. Helens	I. of W.	I. of W.	Brading and Bembridge.
G		F	L	H	C	10	0	St. Helens Quay	I. of W.	I. of W.	Branch from St. Helens.
								ST. HELENS—			
G	P	F	L	H	C	10	0	(Station)	Lancs	G. C. (St. Helens Exten.)	Extension from Lowton St. Mary's.
G	P	F	L	H	C	20	0	(Station)	Lancs	L. & N. W.	Liverpool and Wigan.
								Bate & Rudd's Siding	Lancs	L. & N. W.	Ravenhead Branch.
								Bates & Co.'s Siding	Lancs	L. & N. W.	St. Helens.
								Bates' Broad Oak Brick, Tile, & Col. Co.'s Siding	Lancs	L. & N. W.	Blackbrook Branch.
								Bibby, Sons & Co.'s Siding	Lancs	L. & N. W.	Ravenhead Branch.
								Bishop & Co.'s Siding	Lancs	L. & N. W.	Pocket Nook Branch.
								Blackbrook Col. Co.'s Siding	Lancs	L. & N. W.	Blackbrook Branch.
								Borrows & Son's Siding	Lancs	L. & N. W.	St. Helens Junction.
								Bramwell & Son's Siding	Lancs	L. & N. W.	Blackbrook Branch.
								Bromilow, Foster & Co.'s Ashton's Green Colliery	Lancs	L. & N. W.	Blackbrook Branch.
								Cannington, Shaw & Co.'s Works, Nos. 1 and 2	Lancs	L. & N. W.	Ravenhead Branch.
	P			H	C			Central	Lancs	G. C. (St. Helens Exten.)	Extension from Lowton St. Mary's.
								Craven's Siding	Lancs	L. & N. W.	Eccleston Branch.
								Crone & Taylor's Siding	Lancs	L. & N. W.	Sutton Oak Branch.
								Daglish & Co.'s Siding	Lancs	L. & N. W.	St. Helens.
								Doulton & Co.'s Siding	Lancs	L. & N. W.	Eccleston Branch.
								Eccleston Coal Yard	Lancs	L. & N. W.	Eccleston Branch.
								Eccleston Hall or Gillers Green Colliery	Lancs	L. & N. W.	Eccleston Branch.
								Electro Chemical Co.'s Sid.	Lancs	L. & N. W.	Blackbrook Branch.
								Evans, R., & Co.—			
								Coal Yard	Lancs	L. & N. W.	St. Helens Junction.
								Havannah Colliery	Lancs	L. & N. W.	Blackbrook Branch.
								Haydock or Old Fold Colliery Siding	Lancs	L. & N. W.	Blackbrook Branch.
								Fisher's Siding	Lancs	L. & N. W.	St. Helens Junction and Lea Green.
								Gamble's Siding	Lancs	L. & N. W.	Gerard's Bridge and Moss Bank.
								Gamble's Siding	Lancs	L. & N. W.	Carr Mill and Garswood.
								Glover's Siding	Lancs	L. & N. W.	Ravenhead Branch.
								Greengate Brick & Tile Co.'s Siding	Lancs	L. & N. W.	Ravenhead Branch.
								Holman, Mitchell & Co.'s Siding	Lancs	L. & N. W.	St. Helens.
								Hull and Liverpool Red Oxide Co.'s Siding	Lancs	L. & N. W.	Ravenhead Branch.

EXPLANATION—G *Goods Station.* P *Passenger and Parcel Station.* P* *Passenger, but not Parcel or Miscellaneous Traffic.*
F *Furniture Vans, Carriages, Portable Engines, and Machines on Wheels.* L *Live Stock.*
H *Horse Boxes and Prize Cattle Vans.* C *Carriages by Passenger Train.*

STATION ACCOMMODATION.						CRANE POWER.	STATIONS, &c.	COUNTY.	COMPANY.	POSITION.
						Tons Cwts.	ST. HELENS—continued.			
•	•	•	•	•	•		Liverpool and St. Helens Brick Works	Lancs	L. & N. W.	Ravenhead Branch.
•	•	•	•	•	•		London and Manchester Plate Glass Co.'s Siding	Lancs	L. & N. W.	Sutton Oak.
•	•	•	•	•	•		Lyon's Siding	Lancs	L. & N. W.	Eccleston Branch.
•	•	•	•	•	•		Marshall & Son's Siding.....	Lancs	L. & N. W.	Pocket Nook Branch.
•	•	•	•	•	•		Melling's Siding..............	Lancs	L. & N. W.	St. Helens.
•	•	•	•	•	•		Middlehurst's Siding........	Lancs	L. & N. W.	Peasley Cross and Sutton Oak.
•	•	•	•	•	•		Midland Pottery Co.'s Siding	Lancs	L. & N. W.	Ravenhead Branch.
•	•	•	•	•	•		Nuttall & Co.'s Siding	Lancs	L. & N. W.	Ravenhead Branch.
							Pilkington Bros.—			
•	•	•	•	•	•		British Plate Works	Lancs	L. & N. W.	Ravenhead Branch.
•	•	•	•	•	•		Crown Glass Works	Lancs	L. & N. W.	Ravenhead Branch.
•	•	•	•	•	•		Eccleston Pottery Siding	Lancs	L. & N. W	Eccleston Branch.
•	•	•	•	•	•		Gerard's Bridge Plate Glass Works	Lancs	G. C. (St. Helens Exten.)	St. Helens.
•	•	•	•	•	•		Gerard's Bridge Siding...	Lancs.	L. & N. W.	Gerard's Bridge.
•	•	•	•	•	•		Quirk, Barton & Burns' Siding	Lancs	L. & N. W.	St. Helens and Peasley Cross.
•	•	•	•	•	•		Ramford Brick & Tile Co.'s Tickle's Siding	Lancs	L. & N. W.	Blackbrook Branch.
•	•	•	•	•	•		Ravenhead Sanitary Pipe and Brick Co.'s Siding...	Lancs	L. & N. W.	Ravenhead Branch.
•	•	•	•	•	•		Robinson, Cook and Co.'s Siding	Lancs	L. & N. W.	Pocket Nook Branch.
							St. Helens Colliery Co.—			
•	•	•	•	•	•		Alexandra Colliery	Lancs	L. & N. W.	Ravenhead Branch.
•	•	•	•	•	•		Ravenhead Colliery	Lancs	L. & N. W.	Ravenhead Branch.
•	•	•	•	•	•		St. Helens Colliery	Lancs	L. & N. W.	Ravenhead Branch.
•	•	•	•	•	•		St. Helens Co-operative Society's Siding	Lancs	L. & N. W.	Eccleston Branch.
•	•	•	•	•	•		St. Helens Copper Co.'s Siding	Lancs	L. & N. W.	Ravenhead Branch.
							St. Helens Corporation—			
•	•	•	•	•	•		Boundary Road Stone Depôt	Lancs	L. & N. W.	Eccleston Branch.
•	•	•	•	•	•		Electric Works	Lancs	L. & N. W.	Eccleston Branch.
•	•	•	•	•	•		Gas Works	Lancs	L. & N. W.	Pocket Nook Branch.
•	•	•	•	•	•		Gas Works	Lancs	L. & N. W.	St. Helens.
•	•	•	•	•	•		Manure Works	Lancs	L. & N. W.	Blackbrook Branch.
•	•	•	•	•	•		Salisbury Street Depôt...	Lancs	L. & N. W.	St. Helens.
•	•	•	•	•	•		St. Helens Smelting Co.'s Siding	Lancs	L. & N. W.	Pocket Nook Branch.
•	•	•	•	•	•		Sutton Metal Co.'s Siding	Lancs	L. & N. W.	St. Helens.
•	•	•	•	•	•		Todd Bros.' Siding	Lancs	L. & N. W.	Peasley Cross and St. Helens.
							Union Plate Glass Co.—			
•	•	•	•	•	•		Pocket Nook Works	Lancs	G. C. (St. Helens Exten.)	St. Helens.
•	•	•	•	•	•		Siding	Lancs	L. & N. W.	Pocket Nook Branch.
							United Alkali Co.—			
•	•	•	•	•	•		Baxter Works...............	Lancs	L. & N. W.	Blackbrook Branch.
•	•	•	•	•	•		Central Stores...............	Lancs	L. & N. W.	Pocket Nook Branch.
•	•	•	•	•	•		Gerard's Bridge Works...	Lancs	L. & N. W.	St. Helens.
•	•	•	•	•	•		Globe Works	Lancs.	{ G.C. (St. Helens Exten.) / L. & N. W. .... }	St. Helens. / Pocket Nook Branch.
•	•	•	•	•	•		Greenbank Works	Lancs	L. & N. W.	Eccleston Branch.
•	•	•	•	•	•		Hardshaw Brook Works (East and West)........	Lancs	L. & N. W.	Pocket Nook Branch.
•	•	•	•	•	•		Kurtz Waste Bank Siding	Lancs	L. & N. W.	Pocket Nook Branch.
•	•	•	•	•	•		Kurtz Works	Lancs	L. & N. W.	Peasley Cross and St. Helens.
•	•	•	•	•	•		McKechnie Works.........	Lancs	L. & N. W.	Ravenhead Branch.
•	•	•	•	•	•		Sutton Lodge Works......	Lancs	L. & N. W.	Ravenhead Branch.
•	•	•	•	•	•		Varley & Co.'s Waterloo Foundry	Lancs........	{ G.C. (St. Helens Exten.) / L. & N. W. .... }	St. Helens. / Pocket Nook Branch.
•	•	•	•	•	•		Webb's Coal Yard	Lancs	L. & N. W.	Pocket Nook Branch.
•	•	•	•	•	•		White Cross Colliery Co.'s Peasley Cross & Sherdley Colliery	Lancs	L. & N. W.	Ravenhead Branch.
•	•	•	•	•	•		Wigan Coal & Iron Co.'s Bold Hall Estate Siding	Lancs	L. & N. W.	Clock Face and Farnworth.
•	•	•	•	•	•		Wood & Co.'s Siding........	Lancs	L. & N. W.	Ravenhead Branch.

EXPLANATION—G *Goods Station.*   P *Passenger and Parcel Station.*   P* *Passenger, but not Parcel or Miscellaneous Traffic.*
F *Furniture Vans, Carriages, Portable Engines, and Machines on Wheels.*   L *Live Stock.*
H *Horse Boxes and Prize Cattle Vans.*   C *Carriages by Passenger Train.*

STATION ACCOMMODATION.						CRANE POWER.	STATIONS, &c.	COUNTY.	COMPANY.	POSITION.
						Tons Cwts.	St. Helens Colliery	Durham	N. E.	See Pease & Partners (West Auckland).
							St. Helens Colliery	Lancs	L. & N. W.	See St. Helens Col. Co. (St. Helens).
							St. Helens Col. Co.'s Ck. Oven	Cumb'land	L. & N. W.	Workington.
							St. Helens Colliery No. 2 and Brick Co.'s Works	Cumb'land	L. & N. W.	Flimby.
							St. Helens Colliery No. 3 William Pit (C. & W. Junc.)	Cumb'land	C. & W. Jn.—L. & N. W.	Workington.
G	P	.	L	H	.	5 0	St. Helens Junction Station	Lancs	L. & N. W.	Kenyon Junc. Station & Liverpool.
G	P	P	.			}	St. Helens Road	Glamorg'n	Swan. & Mum	See Swansea.
							St. Helier	Jersey	{ Jersey / Jersey Eastern	Terminus. / Terminus.
G	P	F	L	H	C	2 0	St. Hilda Colliery Junction	Durham	N. E.	Tyne Dock and South Shields.
							St. Ives	Cornwall	G. W.	Branch from St. Erth.
							St. Ives—			
G	P	F	L	H	C	1 0	(Station, G. E.)	Hunts	{ G. E. / G. N. / Mid.	Cambridge and Huntingdon. / Over G. E. from St. Ives Junction. / Over G.N. & G.E. Jt. & G.E. Lines.
G		.	L	.	.	}				
.	P	.	.	H	C					
							Coote & Son's Siding	Hunts	G. E.	St. Ives.
							Junction	Hunts	G. E.—G. N. & G. E. Jt.	Swavesey and Godmanchester.
							Needingworth Junction	Hunts	G. E.—G. N. & G. E. Jt.	St. Ives and Somersham.
							St. James'	Lancs	C.L.C. (G C, G N, & Mid.)	See Liverpool.
							St. James'	Renfrew	Cal.	See Paisley.
G	P	.	L	H	.	1 10	St. James Deeping	Lincoln	G. N.	Peterboro and Spalding.
							St. James' Market Sids. (G.N.)	Yorks	G. N.	Bradford, Adolphus St.
							St. James' Park (Met. Dist.)	Middlesex	Met. Dist.—L. & N. W.	See London.
							St. James' South Junction	Yorks	G. C.—G. N.	Doncaster.
.	P						St. James Str. (Walthamstow)	Essex	G. E.	Hackney Downs and Chingford.
							St. John's	Devon	L. & S.W.	See Tipton St. John's.
G	P	F*	L				St. John's	I. of Man	I. of Man	Douglas and Peel.
.	P						St. John's	Kent	S. E. & C.	New Cross and Chislehurst.
G	P	.	L	H	C	1 10	St. John's Chapel	Durham	N. E.	Stanhope and Wearhead.
							Daddry Shields Siding	Durham	N. E.	St. John's Chapel.
							St. John's Colliery (G. C.)	Derby	G. C.—G. N.—L. & N. W.	Staveley Town.
							St. John's Colliery (Locke & Co.)	Yorks	L. & Y.—Mid.—N. E.	Normanton.
							St. John's Junction	I. of Man	I. of Man—Manx Northern	Douglas and Ramsey.
							St. John's Junction	Lanark	G. & S.W.	Glasgow.
							St. John's Road (I. of W.)	I. of W.	I. of W.—I. of W. Cent.	See Ryde.
							St. John's Siding	Wexford	D. W. & W.	See Enniscorthy.
							St. John's Sidings	Lanark	G. & S.W.	Glasgow, College.
G	P	.	L				St. John's Station and Junc.	I. of Man	Manx Northern	Ramsey and Foxdale.
G	P	.	L				St. Johnston	Donegal	G. N. (I.)	Strabane and Londonderry.
							St. John's Wood Road	Middlesex	Met.	See London.
							St. Julian's Brick Works	Mon	G. W.	Caerleon.
G	P	F	L	H	C	2 0	St. Kew Highway	Cornwall	L. & S.W.	Launceston and Wadebridge.
	P*						St. Keyne	Cornwall	L. & Looe.	Moorswater and Looe.
G	P	.	L	H	.		St. Lawrence	I. of W.	I. of W. Cent.	Merstone Junc. and Ventnor Town.
.	P						St. Lawrence (for Pegwell Bay)	Kent	S. E. & C.	Minster (Thanet) & Ramsgate Town.
							St. Leonards	Edinboro'	N. B.	See Edinburgh.
							St. Leonards—			
							Bopeep Junction	Sussex	L. B. & S. C.—S. E. & C.	West Marina and Warrior Square.
.	P						Warrior Square (S. E. & C.)	Sussex	{ S. E. & C. / L. B. & S. C.	Battle and Hastings. / Over S. E. & C. from Bopeep Junc.
G	P	F	L	H	C	10 0	West Marina	Sussex	L. B. & S. C.	Bexhill and Hastings.
							St. Leonards, West	Sussex	S. E. & C.	See West St. Leonards.
.	P						St. Luke's	Jersey	Jersey Eastern	St. Helier and Gorey.
							St. Luke's	Lancs	L. & Y.	See Southport.
G	P	F	.	H	C	6 0	St. Margaret's	Herts	G. E.	Hertford and Broxbourne.
							Hailey Brickfield Siding	Herts	G. E.	St. Margarets and Rye House.
.	P						St. Margaret's	Middlesex	L. & S.W.	Richmond and Twickenham.
							St. Margaret's Gas Works	Edinboro'	N. B.	Edinburgh, Rose Lane.
							St. Margaret's Junction	Sussex	L. B. & S. C.	East Grinstead and Dormans.
							St. Margaret's Locomotive Works	Edinboro'	N. B.	Edinburgh, Rose Lane.
G	P	.	L	H	C		St. Marnock's Depôt	Ayr	G. & S.W.	See Kilmarnock.
G	P	F	L	H	C	1 15	St. Mary Church Road	Glamorg'n	T. V.	Cowbridge and Aberthaw.
							St. Mary Cray	Kent	S. E. & C.	Bromley, South & Swanley Jn. Sta.
							St. Mary's	Derby	Mid.	See Derby.
G	P	F	L	H	C		St. Mary's	Hunts	G. N.	Branch—Huntingdon & Peterboro'.
							St. Mary's (Whitechapel)	Middlesex	Met. & Met. Dist. Jt.	See London.
							St. Mary's Junction	Middlesex	Met. Dist.—Met. & Met. Dist. Jt.	London, Whitechapel & St. Marys.

STATION ACCOMMODATION.						CRANE POWER.	STATIONS, &c.	COUNTY.	COMPANY.	POSITION.
						Tons Cwts.	St. Mary's Mill	Selkirk	N. B.	Selkirk.
							St. Michael's	Lancs	C.L.C. (G C, G N, & Mid.)	See Liverpool.
G	P	F	L	H	C	2 0	St. Monans	Fife	N. B.	Leven and Anstruther.
G	P	F	L	H	C	5 0	St. Neots	Hunts	G. N.	Sandy and Huntingdon.
G	P	F	L	H	C	. .	St. Olave's	Suffolk ...	G. E.	Beccles & Yarmouth, South Town.
						. .	St. Oswald's (Lord) Mine......	Lincoln ...	G. C.	Frodingham and Scunthorpe.
							St. Pancras (Mid.)	Middlesex	Mid.—G. E.	See London.
							St. Pancras Junction............	Middlesex	G. N.—N. L.	London, Holloway & Camden Town.
							St. Pancras Junction............	Middlesex	Mid.—N. L.	London, St. Pancras Goods and Camden Town.
							St. Paul's	Middlesex	S. E. & C.	See London.
							St. Paul's	Yorks	H'fax H. L. (G N & L & Y)	See Halifax.
							St. Paul's Road Junction......	Middlesex	Mid.	London, Camden Rd. & St. Pancras.
G	P	.	L	H	.	5 0	St. Peter's	Northumb	N. E.	Loop—Newcastle and Percy Main.
						. .	Hawthorn, Leslie & Co.'s Sid.	Northumb	N. E.	St. Peters.
						. .	Langdale Manure Co.'s Sid.	Northumb	N. E.	St. Peters.
						. .	Maling & Son's Ford Pottery	Northumb	N. E.	St. Peters.
						. .	Morrison's Siding	Northumb	N. E.	St. Peters.
						. .	St. Peter's Oil Gas Works...	Northumb	N. E.	St. Peters.
						. .	Scott's Quarry..................	Northumb	N. E.	St. Peters.
						. .	St. Philip's	Glo'ster ...	Mid.	See Bristol.
						. .	St. Philip's Marsh Depôt	Glo'ster ...	G. W.	See Bristol.
							St. Quintin Park and Wormwood Scrubbs	Middlesex	L. & N. W.	See London.
						. .	St. Rollox........................	Lanark ...	Cal.	See Glasgow.
						. .	St. Rollox Cattle Bank	Lanark ...	Cal.	See Glasgow.
						. .	St. Rollox Chemical Works...	Lanark ...	{ Cal. / N. B.	Glasgow, Buchanan Street. / Glasgow, Port Dundas.
						. .	St. Rollox, East	Lanark ...	Cal.	See Glasgow.
						. .	St. Rollox Manure Depôt......	Lanark ...	Cal.	Glasgow, Buchanan Street.
						. .	St. Rollox Mineral Depôt......	Lanark ...	Cal.	Glasgow, Buchanan Street.
						. .	St. Rollox Weighs	Lanark ...	Cal.	Glasgow, Buchanan Street.
						. .	St. Rollox, West	Lanark ...	Cal.	See Glasgow.
						. .	St. Thomas	Devon	G. W.	See Exeter.
						. .	St. Thomas	Glamorg'n	Mid.	See Swansea.
						. .	St. Vigean's Depôt............	Forfar......	N. B.	See Arbroath.
						. .	St. Vigean's Junction	Forfar......	Cal.—D. & A. Jt.—N. B.	Arbroath.
G	.	.	L	.	.	. .	Salcey Forest	Northamp	E. & W. Jn.	Towcester & Ravenstone Wood Jn.
G	P	F	L	H	C	5 0	Sale and Ashton-on-Mersey...	Cheshire...	M.S.J.&A. (GC& L&NW)	Manchester and Timperley.
G	.	.	.	.	.	. .	Salehurst Siding	Sussex	K. & E. S.	Robertsbridge and Bodiam.
G	P	.	.	.	.	. .	Salen (Loch Sunart)	Argyll......	Cal.	Steamer from Oban.
G	P	.	.	.	.	. .	Salen (Mull)	Argyll......	Cal.	Steamer from Oban.
						. .	Salford	Lancs	L. & Y.	See Manchester.
						. .	Salford (L. & N. W.)............	Lancs	L. & N. W.—G. W.	See Manchester, Liverpool Road and Salford.
						. .	Salford (L. & N. W.)............	Lancs	L. & N. W.—G. W.........	See Manchester, Ordsall Lane (for Salford).
						. .	Salford Corporation Sewage Works	Lancs	L. & N. W.	Manchester, Weaste.
						. .	Salford Gas Works	Lancs	L. & Y.	Manchester, Salford.
						. .	Salford Gas Works (Regent's Road)	Lancs	L. & N. W.	Manchester, Liverpool Road.
						. .	Salford Junction..................	Lancs	L. & N. W.—M. S. J. & A.	See Manchester, Liverpool Road and Salford Junction.
G	P	F	L	H	.	1 10	Salford Priors	Warwick ..	Mid.	Evesham and Alcester.
G	P	.	L	.	.	. .	Salhouse	Norfolk ...	G. E.	Norwich and Cromer.
						. .	Saline Valley Colliery	Fife	N. B.	Same as Sunnybraes Col. (Steelend).
G	.	.	.	.	.	1 10	Salisburgh	Lanark ...	Cal.	Branch from Omoa.
						. .	Blackridge Colliery	Lanark ...	Cal.	Extension from Salisburgh.
						. .	Dewshill Colliery	Lanark ...	Cal.	Extension from Salisburgh.
						. .	Dewshill Siding	Lanark ...	Cal.	Extension from Salisburgh.
						. .	Dunsyston Colliery	Lanark ...	Cal.	Extension from Salisburgh.
						. .	Duntillan Colliery	Lanark ...	Cal.	Extension from Salisburgh.
						. .	Duntillan Farm Siding ...	Lanark ...	Cal.	Extension from Salisburgh.
						. .	Hareshaw Colliery............	Lanark ...	Cal.	Omoa and Salisburgh.
						. .	Hareshaw Silica Brick Wks.	Lanark ...	Cal.	Omoa and Salisburgh.
						. .	Heatherbell Colliery	Lanark ...	Cal.	Omoa and Salisburgh.
						. .	Hirstrigg Colliery	Lanark ...	Cal.	Extension from Salisburgh.
						. .	Mountcow Siding	Lanark ...	Cal.	Extension from Salisburgh.
							SALISBURY—			
G	P	F	L	H	C	12 0 }	Fisherton........................	Wilts	{ G. W. / L. & S. W.	Branch from Westbury. / Andover Junction & Templecombe.
G	P	.	.	H	C	. . }				

EXPLANATION—G Goods Station.   P Passenger and Parcel Station.   P* Passenger, but not Parcel or Miscellaneous Traffic.
F Furniture Vans, Carriages, Portable Engines, and Machines on Wheels.   L Live Stock.
H Horse Boxes and Prize Cattle Vans.   C Carriages by Passenger Train.

STATION ACCOMMODATION.						CRANE POWER.	STATIONS, &c.	COUNTY.	COMPANY.	POSITION.
						Tons Cwts.	SALISBURY—*continued.*			
							Market Branch (L. & S. W.)	Wilts	L. & S.W. — G. W.	Near Fisherton Station.
G	.	F	L	H	.	10 0	Milford	Wilts	L. & S.W.	Terminus.
.	.	.	.	.	.		Milford Junction	Wilts	L. & S.W.	Salisbury and Dean.
.	.	.	.	.	.		Tunnel Junction	Wilts	L. & S.W.	Salisbury and Porton.
.	.	.	.	.	.		Salisbury Road	Glamorg'n	Rhy.	See Cardiff.
.	.	.	.	.	.		Salisbury's (Lord) Siding	Herts	G. N.	Hatfield.
.	.	.	.	.	.		Salisbury Street Depôt	Lancs	L. & N. W.	See St. Helens Corporation (St. Helens).
G	P	F	L	H	C	.	Sallins	Kildare	G. S. & W.	Dublin and Kildare.
G	P	.	L	.	.	.	Sallybrook	Donegal	L. & L. S.	Tooban Junction and Letterkenny.
.	P	.	.	.	.	·	Salt & Co.'s Sidings (Mid.)	Staffs	Mid—L & NW—GN—NS	Burton-on-Trent.
.	P	.	.	.	.		Salt and Sandon	Staffs	G. N.	Stafford and Burton.
							Salt, Sir Titus, Sons & Co.'s Mills	Yorks	Mid.	Shipley.
G	P	.	.	.	.		Saltaire	Yorks	Mid.	Leeds and Skipton.
G	P	F	L	H	C	2 0	Saltash	Cornwall	G. W.	Plymouth and Liskeard.
.	.	.	.	.	.		Saltash	Cornwall	L. & S.W.	See St. Budeaux (for Saltash).
G	P	F	L	H	C	5 0	Saltburn	Yorks	N. E.	Branch—Marske and Brotton.
.	.	.	.	.	.		Saltburn Junction	Yorks	N. E.	Saltburn and Marske.
G	P	F	L	H	C	3 0 }	Saltcoats	Ayr	{ Cal.	} Kilwinning and Ardrossan.
G	P	F	L	H	C	3 0 }			G. & S. W.	
.	.	.	.	.	.		Saltersford Siding	Lincoln	G. N.	Same as Grantham Waterworks (Grantham).
.	.	.	.	.	.		Salters Gate Sid. & Stone Whf.	Durham	N. E.	Waskerley.
.	.	.	.	.	.		Salterwood Colliery	Derby	Mid.	Denby.
G	P	F	L	H	C	.	Saltfleetby	Lincoln	G. N.	Louth and Mablethorpe.
.	P	P	.	.	.		Saltford	Somerset	G. W.	Bristol and Bath.
.	P	.	.	.	.		Salthill	Dublin	D. W. & W.	Kingstown & Dublin, Westland Row.
.	.	.	.	.	.		Salthouse Dock	Lancs	L. & Y.	See Liverpool, Wapping & Salthouse Dock.
.	.	.	.	.	.		Salt Lake Siding	Yorks	Mid.	See Craven Lime Co. (Ribblehead).
.	.	.	.	.	.		Saltley	Warwick	Mid.	See Birmingham.
.	.	.	.	.	.		Saltley Carriage & Wagon Works (Mid.)	Warwick	Mid.—G.W.	Birmingham, Saltley.
.	.	.	.	.	.		Saltley Gas Department Siding (Mid.)	Warwick	Mid.—G. W.—L. & N.W.	See Birmingham Corporation.
.	.	.	.	.	.		Saltley Wharf	Warwick	Mid.	Birmingham, Saltley.
.	.	.	.	.	.		Saltmarket Junction	Lanark	G. & S.W.	Glasgow.
G	P	F	L	H	C	1 0 }	Saltmarshe (N. E.)	Yorks	{ N. E.	Staddlethorpe and Goole.
.	P	.	.	H	C	. . }			G. C.	Over N. E. from Thorne Junction.
G	G	.	L	.	.		Skelton Bridge Siding	Yorks	N. E.	Saltmarshe.
G	G	P	.	.	.	10 0	Saltney	Cheshire	G. W.	Chester and Wrexham.
.	.	.	.	.	.		Cestrian Brick Works	Cheshire	G. W.	Saltney.
.	.	.	.	.	.		Dee Oil Co.'s Candle Works	Cheshire	G. W.	Saltney.
.	.	.	.	.	.		Dee Oil Co.'s Oil Works	Cheshire	G. W.	Saltney.
.	.	.	.	.	.		Junction	Cheshire	G. W.—L. & N. W.	Chester and Flint.
.	.	.	.	.	.		Lloyd's Testing Works	Cheshire	G. W.	Saltney.
.	.	.	.	.	.		Midland Railway Carriage and Wagon Co.'s Works	Cheshire	G. W.	Saltney.
.	.	.	.	.	.		Proctor & Ryland's Siding	Cheshire	G. W.	Saltney.
.	.	.	.	.	.		Riverside Wharf	Cheshire	G. W.	Saltney.
.	.	.	.	.	.		Ten Coal Exchange Co.'s Brick Works	Cheshire	G. W.	Saltney.
.	.	.	.	.	.		Webb & Son's Siding	Cheshire	G. W.	Saltney.
.	.	.	.	.	.		Wood & Son's Chain and Anchor Works	Cheshire	G. W.	Saltney.
.	P	.	.	.	.		Saltney Ferry (Mold Junction)	Flint	L. & N. W.	Chester and Mold.
G	.	.	.	.	.		Saltney Wharf	Cheshire	L. & N. W.	Chester and Rhyl.
.	.	.	.	.	.		Dee Oil Co.'s Siding	Cheshire	L. & N. W.	Saltney Wharf and Chester.
.	.	.	.	.	.		Flintshire Oil Co.'s Siding	Flint	L. & N. W.	Saltney Wharf and Chester.
.	.	.	.	.	.		Proctor & Ryland's Siding	Cheshire	L. & N. W.	Saltney Wharf and Chester.
.	.	.	.	.	.		Webb & Son's Siding	Cheshire	L. & N. W.	Saltney Wharf and Chester.
.	.	.	.	.	.		Salton Iron Foundry (N. B.)	Stirling	N. B.—Cal.	Falkirk, Grahamston.
G	P	.	L	H	.	1 0	Saltoun	Hadding'n	N. B.	Ormiston and Gifford.
.	.	.	.	.	.		Lempock Well Siding (Fletcher's)	Hadding'n	N. B.	Saltoun and Pencaitland.
							Salt Union, Limited—			
.	.	.	.	.	.		Adelaide Works (C. L. C.)	Cheshire	C. L. C.— L. & N. W.	Northwich.
.	.	.	.	.	.		Albert Shaft Wks. (C.L.C.)	Cheshire	C. L. C.— L. & N. W.	Northwich.
.	.	.	.	.	.		Ashton's Works (C. L. C.)	Cheshire	C. L. C.— L. & N. W.	Northwich.
.	.	.	.	.	.		Baron's Quay Wks. (C.L.C.)	Cheshire	C. L. C.—L. & N. W.	Northwich.

EXPLANATION—**G** *Goods Station.*   **P** *Passenger and Parcel Station.*   **P*** *Passenger, but not Parcel or Miscellaneous Traffic.*
F *Furniture Vans, Carriages, Portable Engines, and Machines on Wheels.*   **L** *Live Stock.*
H *Horse Boxes and Prize Cattle Vans.*   **C** *Carriages by Passenger Train.*

						Tons	Cwts	STATIONS, &c.	COUNTY.	COMPANY.	POSITION.
								Salt Union, Limited—continued.			
								Brookdale Works (C. L. C.)	Cheshire...	C. L. C.—L. & N. W. ...	Northwich.
								Clarence Salt Works.........	Durham ...	N. E.	Port Clarence.
								Clay & Newman's Sid.(GW)	Worcester	G. W.—Mid.	Droitwich.
								Hickson's Works	Cheshire...	C.L.C. (G C, G N, & Mid.)	Winsford and Over.
								Hickson's Works	Cheshire...	C.L.C. (G C, G N, & Mid.)	Winnington.
								Knight's Grange Works ...	Cheshire...	C.L.C. (G C, G N, & Mid.)	Winsford and Over.
								Marston Hall Wks. (C.L.C.)	Cheshire...	C. L. C.—L. & N. W. ...	Northwich.
								Marston Old Wks. (C.L.C.)	Cheshire...	C. L. C.—L. & N. W. ...	Northwich.
								Marston Works (C. L. C.)...	Cheshire...	C. L. C.—L. & N. W. ...	Northwich.
								Meadow Bank Works	Cheshire...	C.L.C. (G C, G N, & Mid.)	Winsford and Over.
								Meadow Works	Cheshire...	C.L.C. (G C, G N, & Mid.)	Winsford and Over.
								Over Works	Cheshire...	C.L.C. (G C, G N, & Mid.)	Winsford and Over.
								Rayner's Works(C.L.C.) ...	Cheshire...	C.L.C.—L. & N.W.	Northwich.
								Siding	Cheshire...	L. & N. W.	Runcorn Docks.
								Sidings	Cheshire...	L. & N. W.	Over and Wharton.
								Soap Works	Cheshire...	C.L.C. (G C, G N, & Mid.)	Winsford and Over.
								South Durham Salt Works	Durham ...	N. E.	Haverton Hill.
								Stoke Prior Works...........	Worcester	G. W.—Mid.	Stoke Works.
								Victoria Works (C. L. C.)...	Cheshire...	C. L. C.—L. & N. W. ...	Northwich.
								Warboise Works..............	Cheshire...	C.L.C. (G C, G N, & Mid.)	Winnington.
								Willow Bank Works.........	Cheshire...	C.L.C. (G C, G N, & Mid.)	Winsford and Over.
								Wincham Works (C. L. C.)	Cheshire...	C. L. C.—L. & N. W. ...	Northwich.
								Witton Hall Works (C L C)	Cheshire...	C.L.C.—L. & N. W. ...	Northwich.
								Witton Works (C. L. C.)...	Cheshire...	C. L. C.—L. & N. W. ...	Northwich.
								Works	Cheshire...	N. S.	Ettiley Heath.
								Works (G. W.)	Worcester	G. W.—Mid.	Droitwich.
								Salusbury & Lloyd's Siding...	Denbigh...	L. & N. W.	Denbigh.
								Salvation Army Siding	Herts	G. N.	St. Albans.
G	P	.	L	.	.	.	.	Salwick.........................	Lancs ...	P.&W.Jt. (L&Y&L&NW)	Fleetwood and Preston.
	P							Samarès	Jersey ...	Jersey Eastern	St. Helier and Gorey.
G	P	F	L	H	C	2	0	Sampford Courtenay	Devon ...	L. & S.W.	Exeter and Okehampton.
								Sampford Siding	Devon ...	G. W.	Tiverton Junction Station.
								Samuel Bros.' Shipbuilding Yard	Carmarth'	G. W.	Llanelly.
								Samuelson & Co.'s Siding ...	N'hamptn	G. W.	Banbury.
G	P	F	L	H	C	5	0	Sandal	Yorks ...	W.R.& G.Jt.(G.C.&G.N.)	Doncaster and Wakefield.
.	P	.	.	H	C			Sandal and Walton	Yorks ...	Mid.	Normanton and Masboro'.
								Sandars & Co.'s Siding	Lancs ...	Trafford Park Estate ...	Manchester.
								SANDBACH—			
G	P	F	L	H	C	5	0	(Station)	Cheshire...	L. & N. W.	Crewe and Stockport.
								(Goods)	Cheshire...	N. S.	See Ettiley Heath (for Sandbach).
								(Pass)	Cheshire...	N. S.	See Wheelock and Sandbach.
								Junction	Cheshire...	L. & N. W.—N. S.	Northwich and Ettiley Heath.
								Sander's Branch (Mid.)........	Staffs	Mid.—L&NW—GN—NS	Burton-on-Trent.
								Sander's Brick Works	Devon	L. & S.W.	Same as Poltimore Siding (Pinhoe).
								Sander's Siding	Herts	G. N.	St. Albans.
								Sanderson & Murray's Siding	Selkirk ...	N. B.	Galashiels.
								Sanderson & Robinson's Sid.	Notts	Mid.	Mansfield.
								Sanderson Bros. & Newbould's Siding	Yorks ...	L. D. & E. C.—Mid.	Sheffield, Attercliffe.
.	.	.	.	.	.			Sanderson, H., Siding	Durham ...	N. E.	Stockton, South.
								Sanderson Siding	Lancs ...	L. & N. W.	See Earl of Ellesmere's (Tyldesley).
G	P	F	L					Sanderstead	Surrey ...	C. & O. Jt. (L. B. & S. C. and S. E. & C.)	Croydon and Oxted.
G	.P	F	L	H	C	2	0	Sandford and Banwell	Somerset...	G. W.	Yatton and Cheddar.
.	.	.	.	.	.			Aird's Siding	Somerset..	G. W.	Sandford and Banwell.
								Sandford Pottery Siding	Dorset ...	L. & S.W.	Wareham.
G	P	F	L	H	C			Sandgate	Kent	S. E. & C.	Branch from Sandling Junc. Station.
								Sandhills	Lancs ...	L. & Y.	See Liverpool.
G	P	F	L	H	C			Sandholme	Yorks ...	H. & B.	Howden and Hull.
								Sandholme Brick Works ...	Yorks ...	H. & B.	Sandholme.
								Sandhurst.......................	Berks ...	L. & S.W.	See Camberley & York Town (for Sandhurst).
								Sandhurst	Kent	K. & E. S.	See Northiam (for Beckley and Sandhurst).
								Sandiacre......................	Notts	Mid.	See Stapleford and Sandiacre.
G	P	.	L	H	.	1	10	Sandilands	Lanark ...	Cal.	Lanark and Douglas.
								Sandilands Weighs	Lanark ...	Cal.	Sandilands.
G	P	F	L	H	C	.		Sandling Junction Station ...	Kent	S. E. & C.	Ashford and Folkestone.
								Sandling Park Junction	Kent	S. E. & C.	Westenhanger & Sandling Jn. Sta.
								Sandon	Staffs	G. N.	See Salt and Sandon.

EXPLANATION—G Goods Station.   P Passenger and Parcel Station.   P* Passenger, but not Parcel or Miscellaneous Traffic.
F Furniture Vans, Carriages, Portable Engines, and Machines on Wheels.   L Live Stock.
H Horse Boxes and Prize Cattle Vans.   C Carriages by Passenger Train.

STATION ACCOMMODATION.						CRANE POWER.	STATIONS, &c.	COUNTY.	COMPANY.	POSITION.
G	P P	F	L	H	C	. .	Sandon (N. S.)	Staffs	N. S.	Colwich and Stone.
									L. & N. W	Over N. S. Line.
.	.	.	.	.	.	. .	Harrowby's Siding............	Staffs	N. S.	Sandon.
.	.	.	.	.	.	. .	Sandon and Canada Dock......	Lancs	Mid.	See Liverpool.
G	P	F	L	H	C	10 0	Sandown Station & Junction	I. of W. ...	I. of W.	Ryde and Ventnor.
									I. of W. Cent.	Branch from Merstone Jn. Station.
.	P*	.	.	.	.	. .	Sandplace	Cornwall ...	L. & Looe...............	Moorswater and Looe.
.	.	.	.	.	.	. .	Sandridge Siding	Herts	Mid.	St. Albans and Harpenden.
.	.	.	.	.	.	. .	Sandringham	Norfolk ...	Mid. & G. N. Jt...........	See Hillington (for Sandringham).
.	.	.	.	.	.	. .	Sandscale Mineral Siding......	Lancs	Furness	Barrow.
G	P	.	.	.	.	2 0	Sandsend	Yorks	N. E.	Whitby and Saltburn.
G	P	F	L	H	C	5 0	Sandside	W'morlnd	Furness	Arnside and Hincaster Junction.
.	.	.	.	.	.	. .	Northern Quarries Lime Works	W'morlnd	Furness	Near Sandside.
.	.	.	.	.	.	. .	Sandwell Park Colliery........	Staffs	G. W.	Handsworth and Smethwick.
G	P	F	L	H	C	4 0	Sandwich	Kent	S. E. & C.	Minster (Thanet) and Deal.
.	.	.	.	.	.	. .	Ash Road Siding	Kent	S. E. & C.	Minster (Thanet) and Sandwich.
.	.	.	.	.	.	. .	Richboro' Siding............	Kent	S. E. & C.	Sandwich and Minster (Thanet).
.	.	.	.	.	.	. .	Sandwith Stone Quarries (Fur)	Cumb'land	Furness—L. & N. W. ...	Whitehaven, Preston Street.
G	P	F	L	H	C	1 10	Sandy	Beds	G. N.	Hitchin and Huntingdon.
G	P	F	L	H	C	1 5			L. & N. W.	Bedford and Cambridge.
.	.	.	.	.	.	. .	Beart's Sand Pit..............	Beds	G. N.	Sandy.
.	.	.	.	.	.	. .	Love's Brick Yard	Beds	G. N.	Sandy.
.	.	.	.	.	.	. .	Love's Siding	Beds	L. & N. W.	Sandy and Blunham.
.	.	.	.	.	.	. .	Pym's Sand Siding	Beds	G. N.—L. & N. W.	Sandy.
.	.	.	.	.	.	. .	Sandy Junction	Beds	G. N.—L. & N. W.	Sandy (G. N.) Station and Bedford.
.	.	.	.	.	.	. .	Sandy Junction	Carmarth'	B. P. & G. V.—L. & M. M.	Burry Port and Llanelly.
.	P	.	.	.	.	. .	Sandycove	Dublin ...	D. W. & W.	Kingstown and Bray.
G	P	.	.	H	.	. .	Sandycroft	Flint	L. & N. W.	Chester and Rhyl.
.	.	.	.	.	.	. .	Sandycroft Foundry.........	Flint	L. & N. W.	Sandycroft.
.	.	.	.	.	.	. .	Sandycroft Col. & Brick Wks.	Flint	W. M. & C. Q.	Buckley.
.	.	.	.	.	.	. .	Sandysykes Brick & Tile Wks.	Cumb'land	N. B.	Same as Fauldmoor Sid. (Lyneside).
G	P	F	L	H	C	5 0	Sankey	Lancs	C. L. C. (G C, G N, & Mid.)	Warrington and Garston.
.	.	.	.	.	.	. .	Sankey & Son's Siding........	Notts	Mid.	Nottingham, Bulwell.
G	P	.	.	.	.	. .	Sankey Bridges	Lancs	L. & N. W.	Liverpool and Warrington.
.	.	.	.	.	.	. .	Clare & Ridgway's Siding	Lancs	L. & N. W.	Sankey Bridges and Fidler's Ferry.
.	.	.	.	.	.	. .	Houghton's Siding............	Lancs	L. & N. W.	Sankey Bridges and Fidler's Ferry.
.	.	.	.	.	.	. .	Mersey White Lead Co.'s Siding	Lancs	L. & N. W	Sankey Bridges and Fidler's Ferry.
.	.	.	.	.	.	. .	Sankey Sugar Co.'s Siding ...	Lancs	L. & N. W.	Earlestown.
G	P	F	L	H	C	2 0	Sanquhar	Dumfries..	G. & S.W.	Old Cumnock and Thornhill.
.	.	.	.	.	.	. .	Buccleuch Brick & Tl. Wks.	Dumfries..	G. & S.W.	Sanquhar.
G	.	F	.	.	.	. .	Mennock Siding	Dumfries..	G. & S.W.	Sanquhar and Carronbridge.
.	.	.	.	.	.	. .	Sanquhar Brick & Tl. Wks.	Dumfries..	G. & S.W.	Sanquhar.
G	P	.	L	.	.	. .	Santon	I. of Man	I. of Man	Douglas and Port Erin.
.	.	.	.	.	.	. .	Saracen Foundry	Lanark ...	N. B.	Glasgow, Possilpark.
.	.	.	.	.	.	. .	Saracen Tube Works	Lanark ...	Cal.	Garnkirk.
G	P	.	.	.	.	. .	Sarnau	Carmarth'	G. W.	Carmarthen and Whitland.
.	.	.	.	.	.	. .	Sarn Terra Cotta Brick and Tile Works	Salop	S. & W'pl. Jt. (GW & LNW)	Same as Greenwood's Brick Works (Westbury).
.	.	.	.	.	.	. .	Sarsden Siding	Oxon	G. W.	Chipping Norton.
.	.	.	.	.	.	. .	Satinite Co.'s Siding...........	Lancs	L. & N. W.—S. & M. Jt.	Widnes.
.	.	.	.	.	.	. .	Saucel	Renfrew ..	G. & S.W.	See Paisley.
.	.	.	.	.	.	. .	Saucel Distillery..............	Renfrew ..	G. & S.W.	Paisley, Saucel.
G	P	.	.	.	.	. .	Sauchie.......................	Clackman'	N. B.	Alloa and Tillicoultry.
.	.	.	.	.	.	. .	Auchinbaird Colliery........	Clackman'	N. B.	Sauchie and Tillicoultry.
.	.	.	.	.	.	. .	Devon Colliery	Clackman'	N. B.	Sauchie and Tillicoultry.
.	.	.	.	.	.	. .	Devon Quarry Siding	Clackman'	N. B.	Sauchie and Tillicoultry.
.	.	.	.	.	.	. .	Sauchie Colliery	Clackman'	N. B.	Alloa.
.	.	.	.	.	.	. .	Sauchie General Siding	Clackman'	N. B.	See Alloa.
G	P	F	L	H	C	5 0	Saughall	Flint	G. C.	Chester and Connah's Quay.
.	.	.	.	.	.	. .	Hawarden Bridge (Public) Siding	Flint	G. C.	Near Saughall.
.	.	.	.	.	.	. .	Summer's Hawarden Bridge Siding............	Flint	G. C.	Near Saughall.
.	.	.	.	.	.	. .	Welsh Road Siding	Flint	G. C.	Saughall.
G	P	F	L	H	C	2 10	Saughton	Edinboro'	N. B.	Edinburgh and Ratho.
.	.	.	.	.	.	. .	Saughton Junction	Edinboro'	N. B.	Haymarket and Turnhouse.
.	P	.	.	.	.	. .	Saughtree.....................	Roxburgh	N. B.	Riccarton and Reedsmouth.
.	.	.	.	.	.	. .	Saughtree Siding	Roxburgh	N. B.	See Riccarton.
.	.	.	.	.	.	. .	Saunder's Brick Works (Storforth Lane Siding)	Derby......	Mid.	Chesterfield.

EXPLANATION—G *Goods Station.*   P *Passenger and Parcel Station.*   P* *Passenger, but not Parcel or Miscellaneous Traffic.*
F *Furniture Vans, Carriages, Portable Engines, and Machines on Wheels.*   L *Live Stock.*
H *Horse Boxes and Prize Cattle Vans.*   C *Carriages by Passenger Train.*

STATION ACCOMMODATION.					CRANE POWER.		STATIONS, &c.	COUNTY.	COMPANY.	POSITION.
					Tons	Cwts				
G	P	F	L	H	.	. .	Saundersfoot	Pembroke	G. W.	Whitland and Tenby.
					.	. .	Bonville's Court Colliery ...	Pembroke	G. W. & G. C. Jt.	Saundersfoot and Tenby.
G	P	F	L	H	C	. .	Saunderton	Bucks	G. W. & G. C. Jt.	Princes Risboro' & High Wycombe.
					.	. .	Savage Bros.' Siding (G. E.)	Norfolk	G. E.—G. N.—Mid.	See Lynn.
G	P	F	L	H	C	. . }	Savernake	Wilts	{ G. W.	Hungerford and Devizes.
G	P	F	L	H	C	. . }			{ M. & S. W. Jn.	Marlboro' and Grafton.
					.	. .	Savernake, Wolfhall Junction	Wilts	G. W.—M. & S. W. Jn....	Savernake Station and Grafton.
					.	. .	Savile Colliery..............	Yorks	Mid.	Methley.
					.	. .	Savill & Co.'s Siding	Suffolk	G. E.	Eye.
G	P	F	L	H	C	1 0	Sawbridgeworth	Essex	G. E.	Broxbourne and Bishops Stortford.
					.	. .	Taylor, H. A. & D., Siding	Essex	G. E.	Sawbridgeworth.
G	P	F	L	H	C	1 0	Sawdon..............	Yorks	N. E.	Pickering and Scarboro'.
G	P				.	. .	Sawley	Derby	Mid.	Derby and Trent.
	P				.	. .	Sawley Junction Station	Derby	Mid.	Sawley and Trent.
					.	. .	Sawston Siding	Cambs.....	G. E.	See Whittlesford.
G	P	F	L	H	C	1 10	Saxby	Leicester..	Mid.	Stamford and Melton Mowbray.
					.	. .	Saxby & Farmer's Siding	Middlesex	L. & N. W.	London, Kilburn and Maida Vale.
					.	. .	Saxby & Farmer's Siding.....	Wilts	G. W.	Chippenham.
G	P	F	L	H	C	1 10	Saxham..............	Suffolk	G. E.	Bury and Newmarket.
G	P	F	L	H	C	1 10 }	Saxilby (G. N. & G. E. Jt.)...	Lincoln ...	{ G. N. & G. E. Jt.	Lincoln and Gainsborough.
	P			H	C	. . }			{ G. C.	Over G. N. & G. E. Jt. from Sykes Jn.
					.	. .	Kesteven Siding..............	Lincoln	G. N. & G. E. Jt.	Saxilby and Lincoln.
G	P	F	L	H	C	1 10	Saxmundham	Suffolk	G. E.	Ipswich and Beccles.
					.	. .	Saxon Brick Co.'s Siding......	Cambs.....	G. E.	Whittlesea.
					.	. .	Saxondale Junction	Notts	G. N.—G. N.&L.&N.W.Jt.	Nottingham and Melton Mowbray.
					.	. .	Saxondale Siding	Notts	G. N. & L. & N. W. Jt....	Bingham Road.
					.	. .	Saxthorpe	Norfolk ...	Mid. & G. N. Jt.	See Corpusty and Saxthorpe.
					.	. .	Sayers & Co.'s Foundry	Northumb	N. E.	Walker.
G					.	. .	Scafell	Montgom	Cam.	Newtown and Llanidloes.
G	P	F	L	H	C	1 10	Scalby	Yorks	N. E.	Scarborough and Whitby.
G	P	F	L	H	C	. .	Scalford	Leicester..	G. N. & L. & N. W. Jt....	Melton Mowbray and Nottingham.
					.	. .	Scalford Junction	Leicester..	G.N.—G.N.&L.&N.WJt.	Waltham-on-the-Wold and Melton Mowbray.
							SCARBOROUGH—			
	P			H	C	. .	(Station)	Yorks	N. E.	Hull and Whitby.
					.	. .	Anglo American Oil Store...	Yorks	N. E.	Scarboro'.
					.	. .	Belford Siding	Yorks	N. E.	Scarboro'.
					.	. .	Consolidated Petroleum Store..............	Yorks	N. E.	Scarboro'.
G	.	F	L	.	.	5 0	Falsgrave (Gallows Close)...	Yorks	N. E.	Scarboro' and Seamer.
					.	. .	Scarboro' Gas Co.'s Siding	Yorks	N. E.	Scarboro'.
					.	. .	Scarborough Junction	Yorks	N. E.	Seamer and Scalby.
G	P	F	L	H	C	. .	Scarcliffe	Derby	L. D. & E. C.	Chesterfield and Langwith Junction.
					.	. .	Scarlett's Siding	Edinboro'	N. B.	See Lindsay & Son's (Edinburgh).
					.	. .	Scarnell, Wood & Co.'s Siding	Norfolk ...	G. E.	Downham.
G	P	F	L	H	C	. .	Scarva	Down	G. N. (I.)	Goragh Wood and Portadown.
					.	. .	Scarwood Siding	Yorks	L. & N. W.	Same as Shaw & Shaw's Siding (Huddersfield).
G	P	F	L	H	C	5 0	Scawby & Hibaldstow	Lincoln ...	G. C.	Gainsboro' and Brigg.
					.	. .	Schofield, Hagerup & Doughty's Shipbuilding Works (G.C.)	Lincoln ...	G. C.—G. N.	Grimsby Docks.
G	P	.	L		.	. .	Scholes	Yorks	N. E.	Leeds and Wetherby.
					.	. .	Scholes Colliery	Yorks	G. C.	Grange Lane.
					.	. .	Schoolhill..............	Aberdeen	G. N. of S.	See Aberdeen.
					.	. .	School Pit	Lancs	L. & N. W.	See Hulton Colliery Co. (Chequerbent).
G	P	.	L		.	. .	Schull	Cork	S. & S.	Terminus.
	P				.	. .	Schultze Gunpowder Co.'s Sid.	Hants. ...	L. & S.W.	Redbridge.
G	P	F	L	H	C	1 10	Scopwick and Timberland ...	Lincoln ...	G. N. & G. E. Jt.	Lincoln and Sleaford.
					.	. .	Scorer's Manure Siding	Northumb	N. E.	Killingworth.
G	P	.			.	. .	Scorrier	Cornwall ..	G. W.	Truro and Redruth.
					.	4 0	Wheal Busy Siding	Cornwall ..	G. W.	Scorrier.
	P				.	. .	Scorton	Lancs	L. & N. W.	Lancaster and Preston.
G	P	.	L	H	C	. .	Scorton	Yorks	N. E.	Richmond and Eryholme.
					.	. .	Scorton Brick Works	Yorks	N. E.	Moulton.
G	P	.	L	.	.	1 5 }	Scotby..............	Cumb'land	{ Mid.	Appleby and Carlisle.
G	P	F	L	H	C	2 0 }			{ N. E.	Carlisle and Hexham.
G	P	.	L	H		. .	Scotch Dyke	Cumb'land	N. B.	Hawick and Carlisle.
					.	. .	Scotgate Ash Stone Co.'s Sid.	Yorks	N. E.	Pateley Bridge.
					.	. .	Scotia Bolt and Rivet Works	Lanark ...	Cal.	Glasgow, Bridgeton.
					.	. .	Scotia Iron Works..............	Lanark ...	N. B.	Coatbridge, Sheepford.

EXPLANATION—G *Goods Station.*   P *Passenger and Parcel Station.*   P* *Passenger, but not Parcel or Miscellaneous Traffic.*
F *Furniture Vans, Carriages, Portable Engines, and Machines on Wheels.*   L *Live Stock.*
H *Horse Boxes and Prize Cattle Vans.*   C *Carriages by Passenger Train.*

STATION ACCOMMODATION.						CRANE POWER.	STATIONS, &c.	COUNTY.	COMPANY.	POSITION.
						Tons Cwts.				
.	.	.	.	.	.	. .	Scotland Street	Edinboro'	N. B.	See Edinburgh.
.	.	.	.	.	.	. .	Scotland Street Junction......	Lanark ...	Cal.—G. & S. W.	Glasgow.
.	.	.	.	.	.	. .	Scot Lane Siding (L. & Y.)...	Lancs	L. & Y.—L. & N. W. ...	Hilton House.
G	P	F	L	H	C	. .	Scotscalder	Caithness..	High.	Helmsdale and Wick.
G	P	F	L	H	C	2 0	Scotsgap	Northumb	N. B.	Reedsmouth and Morpeth.
.	.	.	.	.	.	. .	Scotsgap Junction	Northumb	N. B.	Scotsgap and Longwitton.
.	.	.	.	.	.	. .	" Scotsman " Siding	Edinboro'	N. B.	Edinburgh, Waverley.
.	.	.	.	.	.	. .	Scotstoun	Renfrew ...	{ Cal. { N. B.	See Glasgow. See Glasgow, Whiteinch (for Scotstoun).
G	P	.	.	.	.	1 10	Scotstoun Flour Mills	Lanark ...	Cal.	Glasgow, Partick, Central.
.	.	.	.	.	.	. .	Scotstounhill	Renfrew ..	N. B.	Partick and Clydebank.
.	.	.	.	.	.	. .	Scotstoun Iron Works	Renfrew ..	Cal.	Glasgow, Whiteinch.
.	.	.	.	.	.	. .	Scotstoun Shipbuilding Yard (Connell & Co.)	Renfrew ..	Cal.—N. B.	Glasgow, Whiteinch.
.	.	.	.	.	.	. .	Scotstoun Show Yard	Renfrew ..	N. B.	See Glasgow.
.	.	.	.	.	.	. .	Scotstoun Steel and Malleable Foundry	Renfrew ..	Cal.	Glasgow, Whiteinch.
G	P	.	L	H	C	3 0 }	Scotstoun, West	Renfrew ..	Cal.	See Glasgow.
	P						Scotswood (N. E.)	Northumb	{ N. E. { N. B.	Newcastle and Hexham. Over N. E. from Border Jn., Hexham.
.	.	.	.	.	.	. .	Armstrong, Whitworth & Co.'s Siding	Northumb	N. E.	Scotswood.
.	.	.	.	.	.	. .	Delaval Siding	Northumb	N. E.	Scotswood.
.	.	.	.	.	.	. .	South Benwell Colliery ...	Northumb	N. E.	Scotswood.
.	.	.	.	.	.	. .	Scotswood Bridge	Northumb	N. E.	Scotswood and Blaydon.
.	.	.	.	.	.	. .	Scotswood Junction	Northumb	N. E.	Scotswood and Newcastle.
.	.	.	.	.	.	. .	Scott & Co.'s Shipbuilding Yard	Dumbartn	N. B.	Bowling.
.	.	.	.	.	.	. .	Scott & Co.'s Sidings	Renfrew ..	Cal.	Greenock, Regent Street.
.	.	.	.	.	.	. .	Scott & Middleton's Siding...	Durham ...	N. E.	Seaham.
.	.	.	.	.	.	. .	Scott & Smith's Siding	Wilts	G. W.	Warminster.
.	.	.	.	.	.	. .	Scott, G., & Co.'s Siding ...	Mon	A (N & SW) D & R—G W	Newport, Alexandra Docks.
.	.	.	.	.	.	. .	Scott, W., Ltd.— Siding	Yorks	Mid.	Woodlesford.
.	.	.	.	.	.	. .	Works (Mid.)	Yorks	{ Mid.—†L&Y-L&NW-NE { G.N.	Same as Leeds Steel Works (Leeds). (See Appendix to follow).
.	.	.	.	.	.	. .	Scott's Brick Works............	Northumb	N. E.	Choppington.
.	.	.	.	.	.	. .	Scott's Depôt	Durham ...	N. E.	Southwick.
.	.	.	.	.	.	. .	Scott's Quarry	Northumb	N. E.	St. Peters.
.	.	.	.	.	.	. .	Scott's Siding	Lancs	L. & N. W.	Stockport, Reddish.
.	.	.	.	.	.	. .	Scott's Siding	Yorks	Mid.	Ingleton.
.	.	.	.	.	.	. .	Scottish Acid & Alkali Co.'s Works	Ayr	Cal.—G. & S. W.	{ Same as Longford Chemical Works { (Kilwinning).
.	.	.	.	.	.	. .	Scottish Central Ir. Wks.(NB)	Stirling ...	N. B.—Cal.	Falkirk, Grahamston.
.	.	.	.	.	.	. .	Scottish Co-op. Wholesale Society's Soap Works (Cal.)	Stirling ...	Cal.—N. B.	Grangemouth.
.	.	.	.	.	.	. .	Scottish Mushroom Co.'s Sid.	Edinboro'	N. B.	Edinburgh, Scotland Street.
.	.	.	.	.	.	. .	Scottish Plaster Works	Lanark ...	Cal.	Glasgow, Bridgeton.
.	.	.	.	.	.	. .	Scottish Steel Grit Works ...	Lanark ...	N. B.	Airdrie, North.
.	.	.	.	.	.	. .	Scott Pit	Northumb	N. E.	Same as Hartford Col. (Annitsford).
.	.	.	.	.	.	. .	Scout Siding	Lancs	L. & N. W.	Mossley.
.	.	.	.	.	.	. .	Scowcroft & Co.— Highfield Siding............	Lancs	L. & N. W.	Plodder Lane.
.	.	.	.	.	.	. .	Hindley Green Colliery ...	Lancs	{ G. C. (Wigan Jn.) ...... { L. & N. W.	Hindley and Platt Bridge. Wigan.
.	.	.	.	.	.	. .	Scrabo Stone Siding	Down	B. & C. D.	Newtownards.
.	.	.	.	.	.	. .	Scraptoft	Leicester..	G. N.	See Thurnby and Scraptoft.
.	.	.	.	.	.	. .	Scraton's Pottery	Lancs	L. & N. W.	Huyton Quarry.
.	.	.	.	.	.	. .	Scredington	Lincoln ...	G. N.	See Aswarby (for Scredington).
G	P	.	L	H	C	. .	Scremerston......................	Northumb	N. E.	Berwick and Belford.
.	.	.	.	.	.	. .	Scremerston Colliery........	Northumb	N. E.	Tweedmouth and Scremerston.
.	.	.	.	.	.	. .	Scremerston Lime Works	Northumb	N. E.	Scremerston.
.	P	.	.	.	.	. .	Scrooby...........................	Notts	G. N.	Retford and Doncaster.
.	.	.	.	.	.	. .	Scropton Siding	Derby	N. S.	Tutbury.
G	P	.	L	H	.	. .	Scruton	Yorks	N. E.	Northallerton and Leyburn.
.	.	.	.	.	.	. .	Sculcoates	Yorks	H. & B.—N. E.	See Hull.
.	.	.	.	.	.	. .	Scull & Co.'s Siding	Glamorg'n	GW—LNW—Rhy.—TV	Cardiff.
.	.	.	.	.	.	. .	Scull's Siding (G.W.)	Glamorg'n	G. W.—T. V.	Mwyndy.
.	.	.	.	.	.	. .	Scunthorpe	Lincoln ...	G. C.	See Frodingham and Scunthorpe.
.	.	.	.	.	.	. .	Scutterhill Depôt & Siding ...	Durham ...	N. E.	Parkhead.
.	.	.	.	.	.	. .	Seabraes Saw Mills	Forfar	Cal.	Dundee.

EXPLANATION—G Goods Station.   P Passenger and Parcel Station.   P* Passenger, but not Parcel or Miscellaneous Traffic.
F Furniture Vans, Carriages, Portable Engines, and Machines on Wheels.   L Live Stock.
H Horse Boxes and Prize Cattle Vans.   C Carriages by Passenger Train.   † For Local Traffic only.

G	P	F	L	H	C	Crane Power (Tons Cwts)	STATIONS, &c.	COUNTY.	COMPANY.	POSITION.
.	.	.	.	.	.		Seabrooke's Siding	Essex	L. T. & S.	Grays.
G	P	F	L	H	C	5 0	Seacombe & Egremont (Wirral)	Cheshire	{ Wirral	Terminus.
.	P	.	.	H	C				{ G. C.	Over Wirral from Bidston Junction.
.	.	.	.	.	.		English McKenna Process Co.'s Siding	Cheshire	Wirral	Seacombe and Egremont.
.	.	.	.	.	.		Seacombe Pressed Brick & Tile Works	Cheshire	Wirral	Seacombe.
.	.	.	.	.	.		Wallasey Urban District Council Gas Works	Cheshire	Wirral	Seacombe and Egremont.
.	.	.	.	.	.		Seacombe Grain Warehouses	Cheshire	B'head Jt—CLC—NW&L	Birkenhead.
G	P	.	L	H	.		Seacroft	Lincoln	G. N.	Wainfleet and Skegness.
.	.	.	.	.	.		Seafield Engineering Works	Renfrew	G & P Jt (Cal & G & S W)	Same as Grant's Siding (Cardonald).
.	.	.	.	.	.		Seafield Oil Works	L'lithgow	N. B.	Bathgate, Upper.
.	.	.	.	.	.		Seafield Siding	Edinboro'	Cal.—N. B.	Leith, South.
.	.	.	.	.	.		Seafield Siding	Forfar	Cal.	Dundee.
G	P	F	L	H	C	1 10	Seaford	Sussex	L. B. & S. C.	Branch from Lewes.
G	P	F	L	H	C	5 0	Seaforth & Litherland (L.&Y.)	Lancs	{ L. & Y.	Liverpool and Southport.
.	P	.	.	.	.				{ L. & N. W.	Over L. & Y. from Bootle Junction.
.	.	.	.	.	.		Kurtz's Siding	Lancs	L. & Y.	Seaforth and Litherland.
.	.	.	.	.	.		Seaforth Sands	Lancs	L'pool O'head	See Liverpool.
G	P	F	L	H	C	2 0	Seaham	Durham	N. E.	Branch from Sunderland.
.	.	.	.	.	.		Dawdon Colliery	Durham	N. E.	Seaham.
.	.	.	.	.	.		Easington Colliery	Durham	N. E.	Seaham.
.	.	.	.	.	.		Electrozone Works	Durham	N. E.	Seaham.
.	.	.	.	.	.		Elgey's Timber Yard	Durham	N. E.	Seaham.
.	.	.	.	.	.		Londonderry Granary	Durham	N. E.	Seaham.
.	.	.	.	.	.		Londonderry Limestone Quarry	Durham	N. E.	Seaham.
.	.	.	.	.	.		Londonderry Lime Works	Durham	N. E.	Seaham.
.	.	.	.	.	.		Londonderry Stores	Durham	N. E.	Seaham.
.	.	.	.	.	.		Londonderry Wagon Shops	Durham	N. E.	Seaham.
.	.	.	.	.	.		N. E. R. Wagon Shops	Durham	N. E.	Seaham.
.	.	.	.	.	.		Pearson & Son's Siding	Durham	N. E.	Seaham.
.	.	.	.	.	.		Scott & Middleton's Siding	Durham	N. E.	Seaham.
.	.	.	.	.	.		Seaham Collieries	Durham	N. E.	Seaham.
.	.	.	.	.	.		Seaham Colliery Brick Wks.	Durham	N. E.	Seaham.
.	.	.	.	.	.		Seaham Colliery Manure Sid.	Durham	N. E.	Seaham.
.	.	.	.	.	.		Seaham Col. Station Depôt	Durham	N. E.	Seaham.
.	.	.	.	.	.		Seaham Colliery Wagon Shops and Works	Durham	N. E.	Seaham.
.	.	.	.	.	.		Seaham Colliery Workman's Coal Siding and Depôt	Durham	N. E.	Seaham.
.	.	.	.	.	.		Seaham Foundry	Durham	N. E.	Seaham.
.	.	.	.	.	.		Seaham Gas Works	Durham	N. E.	Seaham.
.	.	.	.	.	.		Seaham Hall Siding	Durham	N. E.	Seaham.
.	.	.	.	.	.		Seaham Hbr. Blast Furnace	Durham	N. E.	Seaham.
.	.	.	.	.	.		Seaham Hbr. Bottle Works	Durham	N. E.	Seaham.
.	.	.	.	.	.		Seaham Harbour Depôts	Durham	N. E.	Seaham.
.	.	.	.	.	.		Seaham Harbour Dock Sids.	Durham	N. E.	Seaham.
.	.	.	.	.	.		Seaham Harbour Siding	Durham	N. E.	Seaham.
.	.	.	.	.	.		Seaham Hbr. Timber Yard	Durham	N. E.	Seaham.
.	.	.	.	.	.		Seaham Stores and Granary	Durham	N. E.	Seaham.
.	.	.	.	.	.		South Hetton Junction (Swine Lodge)	Durham	N. E.	Seaham.
.	.	.	.	.	.		South Shields & Sunderland Water Co.'s Pumping Engine	Durham	N. E.	Seaham.
.	P	.	.	.	.		Seaham Colliery Station	Durham	N. E.	Sunderland and Seaham.
.	P	.	.	.	.		Seaham Hall (private)	Durham	N. E.	Branch from Sunderland.
G	P	F	L	H	C	2 0	Seahouses	Northumb	N. E.	Branch from Chathill.
.	.	.	.	.	.		Seal, Son & Co.'s Siding	Yorks	Mid.	Darfield.
.	.	.	.	.	.		Seaman & Co.'s Timber and Joinery Works	Warwick	Mid.	Coventry.
G	P	F	L	H	C	1 10	Seamer	Yorks	N. E.	Malton and Scarboro'.
.	.	.	.	.	.		Irton Siding	Yorks	N. E.	Seamer.
.	P	.	.	.	.		Sea Mills	Glo'ster	Clif. Ex. Jt. (G. W. & Mid)	Clifton Down and Shirehampton.
.	.	.	.	.	.		Seamless Steel Boat Co.'s Sid.	Yorks	G. N.—L. & Y.	Wakefield, Kirkgate.
.	P	.	.	.	.		Seapoint	Dublin	D. W. & W.	Kingstown & Dublin, Westland Row.
G	P	F	L	H	C	3 0	Seascale	Cumb'land	Furness	Ravenglass and Whitehaven.
.	.	.	.	.	.		Gosforth	Cumb'land	Furness	Near Seascale.
.	.	.	.	.	.		Sea Side	Glamorg'n	R. & S. B.	See Aberavon (Sea Side).
.	P	.	.	.	.		Seaside (for Ainsdale)	Lancs	C. L. C. (S'port Exten.)	Aintree and Southport.

EXPLANATION—G *Goods Station.*   P *Passenger and Parcel Station.*   P* *Passenger, but not Parcel or Miscellaneous Traffic.*
F *Furniture Vans, Carriages, Portable Engines, and Machines on Wheels.*   L *Live Stock.*
H *Horse Boxes and Prize Cattle Vans.*   C *Carriages by Passenger Train.*

G	P	F	L	H	C	Tons	Cwts	STATIONS, &c.	COUNTY.	COMPANY.	POSITION.
G	P	.	L	.	.			Seaton	Cumb'land	C. & W. Jn.	Workington and Great Broughton.
								Camerton Brick Works & Colliery	Cumb'land	C. & W. Jn.	Seaton and Great Broughton.
G	P	.	.	.	.			Seaton (D. & S.)	Durham	N. E.	Sunderland and Durham (Elvet).
.	.	.	.	.	.			Seaton Bank Head Depôt	Durham	N. E.	Seaton.
G	P	F	L	H	C			Seaton (L. & N. W.)	Rutland	L. & N. W.	Market Harboro' and Peterboro'.
.	P	.	.	H	C					G. N.	Over L. & N. W. from Longville Jn.
G	P	F	L	H	C	10	0	Seaton and Beer	Devon	L. & S. W.	Branch from Seaton Junction.
.	.	.	.	.	.			Seaton Burn Colliery	Northumb	N. E.	Killingworth.
G	P	F	L	H	C			Seaton Carew	Durham	N. E.	West Hartlepool and Stockton.
.	.	.	.	.	.			Seaton Carew Iron Co.'s Blast Furnaces	Durham	N. E.	West Hartlepool.
.	.	.	.	.	.			Seaton Carew Iron Works & Coke Ovens	Durham	N. E.	West Hartlepool.
G	P	.	L	H	.	1	0	Seaton Delaval	Northumb	N. E.	Blyth and Backworth.
.	.	.	.	.	.			Seaton Delaval Collieries	Northumb	N. E.	Seaton Delaval.
.	.	.	.	.	.			Seaton Delaval Col. Staithes	Northumb	N. E.	Northumberland Dock.
G	P	F	L	H	C	5	0	Seaton Junction Station	Devon	L. & S. W.	Axminster and Honiton.
.	.	.	.	.	.			Seaton, North	Northumb	N. E.	See North Seaton.
G	P	F	L	H	C	5	0	Sedbergh	Yorks	L. & N. W.	Ingleton and Low Gill.
G	P	.	L	H	.			Seddon's Siding	Cheshire	L. & N. W.	Middlewich.
G	P	.	L	H	.	1	10	Sedgebrook	Lincoln	G. N.	Grantham and Nottingham.
.	.	.	.	.	.			Sedgefield	Durham	N. E.	Ferryhill and Stockton.
.	.	.	.	.	.			Bishop Middleham Quarry Sidings	Durham	N. E.	Sedgefield and Ferryhill.
.	.	.	.	.	.			Sedgefield Saw Mill	Durham	N. E.	Sedgefield.
.	.	.	.	.	.			Sedgefield Weigh	Durham	N. E.	Sedgefield.
G	P	.	L	.	.			Sedgeford	Norfolk	G. E.	Heacham and Wells.
.	.	.	.	.	.			Sedgwick's Siding	W'morlnd	L. & N. W.	Milnthorpe.
.	.	.	.	.	.			Seed & Parr's Siding	Lancs	P.&W. Jt. (L&Y & L& NW)	Poulton.
.	.	.	.	.	.			Seed & Wallbank's Siding	Lancs	P.& L. Jt. (L&NW. & L&Y)	See Chapel Hill Siding (Longridge).
.	.	.	.	.	.			Seedley (L. & N.W.)	Lancs	L. & N. W.—G. W.	See Manchester.
								Seeley's Collieries—			
.	.	.	.	.	.			New Birchwood Colliery	Derby	Mid.	Pye Bridge.
.	.	.	.	.	.			Tibshelf Colliery (Nos. 1 & 2, and 3 & 4 Pits)	Derby	Mid.	Tibshelf and Newton.
G	P							Seend	Wilts	G. W.	Devizes and Trowbridge.
G	P	F	L	H	C	5	0	Sefton & Maghull	Lancs	C. L. C. (S'port Exten.)	Aintree and Southport.
.	.	.	.	.	.			Sefton Park	Lancs	L. & N. W.	See Liverpool.
.	.	.	.	.	.			Seggie Siding	Fife	N. B.	Guard Bridge.
G	P							Seghill	Northumb	N. E.	Backworth and Blyth.
.	.	.	.	.	.			Seghill Colliery	Northumb	N. E.	Seghill.
.	.	.	.	.	.			Seiont Siding	Carnarvon	L. & N. W.	Carnarvon.
.	.	.	.	.	.			Arfon Brick Co.	Carnarvon	L. & N. W.	Seiont Siding.
.	.	.	.	.	.			Glanmorfa Siding	Carnarvon	L. & N. W.	Seiont Siding.
.	.	.	.	.	.			Lake & Co.	Carnarvon	L. & N. W.	Seiont Siding.
.	.	.	.	.	.			Selborne	Hants	L. & S. W.	See Tisted (for Selborne).
G	P	F	L	H	C	10	0	Selby (N. E.)	Yorks	N. E.	York and Doncaster.
.	P									G. E.	Over N. E. from Doncaster.
G	P	.	.	H	C					G. N	Over N. E. from Shaftholme Junc.
.	P	.	.	H	C					L. & N. W.	Over N. E. from Leeds.
.	.	.	.	.	.			East Junction	Yorks	N. E.	Selby Station and Cliffe Common.
.	.	.	.	.	.			Fawcett's, E. M., Siding	Yorks	N. E.	Selby.
.	.	.	.	.	.			Government Magazine Sid.	Yorks	N. E.	Selby.
.	.	.	.	.	.			Henwick Hall Siding	Yorks	N. E.	Selby and Temple Hirst.
.	.	.	.	.	.			Liversedge, W., & Son's Sid.	Yorks	N. E.	Selby.
.	.	.	.	.	.			Osgodby Siding	Yorks	N. E.	Selby and Riccall.
.	.	.	.	.	.			Selby Gas Works	Yorks	N. E.	Selby.
.	.	.	.	.	.			Selby Common Siding	Yorks	N. E.	Same as Sherburn Rd. Sid. (Wistow).
G	P	.	L	H	.			Selham	Sussex	L. B. & S. C.	Petworth and Midhurst.
.	P	.	.	.	.			Selhurst	Surrey	L. B. & S. C.	Croydon and Balham.
G	P	F	L	H	C	5	0	Selkirk	Selkirk	N. B.	Branch from Galashiels.
.	.	.	.	.	.			Ettrick Mill	Selkirk	N. B.	Selkirk.
.	.	.	.	.	.			St. Mary's Mill	Selkirk	N. B.	Selkirk.
.	.	.	.	.	.			Yarrow Mill	Selkirk	N. B.	Selkirk.
.	.	.	.	.	.			Selkirk Junction	Selkirk	N. B.	Galashiels and Melrose.
G	P	F	L	H	C	3	0	Sellafield Station and Junc.	Cumb'land	Furness / W. C. & E. Jt.	Ravenglass and St. Bees. / Branch from Moor Row.
G	P	F	L	H	C	1	10	Selling	Kent	S. E. & C.	Faversham and Canterbury, East.
G	P	.	.	.	.	1	10	Selly Oak	Worcester	Mid.	King's Norton and Five Ways.
.	.	.	.	.	.			Patent Enamel Co.'s Siding	Worcester	Mid.	Near Selly Oak.
.	.	.	.	.	.			Selm's Siding	Edinboro'	Cal.	Midcalder.

EXPLANATION—**G** *Goods Station.*   **P** *Passenger and Parcel Station.*   **P*** *Passenger, but not Parcel or Miscellaneous Traffic.*
F *Furniture Vans, Carriages, Portable Engines, and Machines on Wheels.*   **L** *Live Stock.*
H *Horse Boxes and Prize Cattle Vans.*   **C** *Carriages by Passenger Train.*

STATION ACCOMMODATION.						CRANE POWER.	STATIONS. &c.	COUNTY.	COMPANY.	POSITION.
						Tons Cwts.				
G	P	F	L	.	.	10 0	Selsdon Road	Surrey	C. & O. Jt. (L. B. & S. C. and S. E. & C.)	South Croydon and Sanderstead.
									W. & S. C. Jt. (L. B. & S. C. and S. E. & C.)	Coombe Lane and Sanderstead.
							Selsdon Road Junction	Surrey	C. & O. Jt.—W. & S. C. Jt.	Sanderstead and Coombe Lane.
.	P*	.	.	.	.		†Selsey Beach	Sussex	Selsey	Terminus.
G	P	.	.	.	.		Selsey Town	Sussex	Selsey	Chichester and Selsey Beach.
							Selston	Notts	Mid.	See Pinxton and Selston.
							Selston Colliery	Derby	Mid.	See Barber, Walker & Co. (Langley Mill and Eastwood).
							Selston Colliery (G. N.)	Notts	G. N.—G. C.	Eastwood and Langley Mill.
G	P	F	L	H	C	5 0	Semley (for Shaftesbury)	Wilts	L. & S.W.	Salisbury and Templecombe.
G	P	F	L	H	C	1 10	Senghenith	Glamorg'n	Rhy.	Aber Valley Branch.
							Universal Colliery	Glamorg'n	Rhy.	Senghenith.
							Senghenydd	Glamorg'n	Rhy.	Same as Senghenith.
							Senhouse Dock	Cumb'land	L. & N. W.—M. & C.	See Maryport.
							Senior's, C., Siding	Yorks	Mid.	Keighley.
							Senior's Siding	Lincoln	G. C.	New Holland.
							Senior's Siding	Yorks	L. & Y.	Shepley and Shelley.
							Sentinel Siding	Lanark	Cal.	Glasgow, South Side.
							Serridge Junction	Glo'ster	S. & Wye Jt. (G. W. & Mid.)	Drybrook Road & Speech House Rd.
G	P	F	L	H	C	.	Sessay	Yorks	N. E.	York and Thirsk.
							Sessay Wood Jn. and Siding	Yorks	N. E.	Pilmoor.
							Sessions & Son's Siding	Glo'ster	G. W.—Mid.	Gloucester Docks.
G	P	F	L	H	C	5 0	Settle	Yorks	Mid.	Hellifield and Appleby.
							Craven Lime Co's Stainforth Siding	Yorks	Mid.	Near Settle.
							Settle's, J., Siding	Staffs	N. S.	See Trubshaw Sidings (Harecastle).
G	P	.	.	.	.		Settrington	Yorks	N. E.	Malton and Driffield.
							Settrington Lime Works	Yorks	N. E.	Settrington.
							Sett Siding	Lancs	L. & N. W.	Lees.
							Seven Hills Siding	Suffolk	G. E.	Ingham.
.	P	.	.	.	.		Seven Kings	Essex	G. E.	Stratford and Romford.
							SEVENOAKS—			
G	P	F	L	H*	.	1 15	Bat and Ball	Kent	S. E. & C.	Swanley Junction Station and Sevenoaks, Tubs Hill.
							Crampton's Siding	Kent	S. E. & C.	Otford Jn. & Sevenoaks, Bat & Ball.
							Gas Co.'s Siding	Kent	S. E. & C.	Sevenoaks, Bat & Ball.
							Junction	Kent	S. E. & C.	Bat & Ball and Tubs Hill.
G	P	F	L	H	C	4 0	Tubs Hill	Kent	S. E. & C.	Chislehurst and Tonbridge.
G	P	.	.	.	.		Seven Sisters	Glamorg'n	N. & Brecon	Neath and Colbren.
							Brynteg Colliery	Glamorg'n	N. & Brecon	Seven Sisters and Crynant.
							Nantycafn Colliery	Glamorg'n	N. & Brecon	Seven Sisters and Crynant.
							Seven Sisters Colliery	Glamorg'n	N. & Brecon	Seven Sisters.
							Seven Sisters	Middlesex	G. E.	See London.
							Seven Stars	Montgom	Cam. (W. & L.)	See Welshpool.
G	P	F	L	H	C	.	Severn Bridge	Glo'ster	S. & Wye Jt. (G. W. & Mid.)	Lydney and Sharpness.
							Severn Tin Plate Works	Mon	G. W.	Same as Caldicot Siding (Severn Tunnel Junction Station).
G	P	F	L	H	C	6 0	Severn Tunnel Junc. Station	Mon	G. W.	Chepstow and Newport.
							Caldicot Siding (Severn Tin Plate Works)	Mon	G. W.	Severn Tunnel Jn. and Portskewet.
							Sudbrook Brick Works	Mon	G. W.	Severn Tunnel Jn. and Portskewet.
							Walker's Siding (Sudbrook Branch)	Mon	G. W.	Severn Tunnel Jn. and Portskewet.
							Severn Valley Junction	Salop	G. W.—S. & H. Jt.	Shrewsbury.
							Severus Junction	Yorks	N. E.	York, North Junc. and Poppleton.
							Sewell Lime Works	Beds	L. & N. W.	See Forder & Son's (Stanbridgeford).
G	P	.	L	H	C	2 0	Sexhow	Yorks	N. E.	Picton and Stokesley.
							Busby Siding	Yorks	N. E.	Sexhow.
							Seymour Colliery	Derby	Mid.	Barrow Hill and Staveley Works.
G	P	F	L	H	C	.	Shackerstone	Leicester	A & N Jt. (L & N W & Mid.)	Nuneaton & Hugglescote Junction.
							Hellpout Mill	Leicester	A & N Jt. (L & N W & Mid.)	Shackerstone and Heather.
							Shacklegate Junction	Middlesex	L. & S.W.	Teddington and Strawberry Hill.
							Shadwell	Middlesex	E. L. Jt. (G. E., L. B. & S. C., Met., M. D., & S. E. & C.)	See London.
							Shadwell & St. George's, East	Middlesex	G. E.	See London.
							Shaftesbury	Wilts	L. & S.W.	See Semley (for Shaftesbury).
							Shaftholme Junction	Yorks	G. N.—N. E.	Doncaster and Moss.
							Shakemantle Siding	Glo'ster	G. W.	Ruspidge.
							Shakerley Colliery	Lancs	L. & N. W.	Same as Ramsden's Green's Siding (Tyldesley).

EXPLANATION—G *Goods Station.*   P *Passenger and Parcel Station.*   P* *Passenger, but not Parcel or Miscellaneous Traffic.*
F *Furniture Vans, Carriages, Portable Engines, and Machines on Wheels.*   L *Live Stock.*   H *Horse Boxes and Prize Cattle Vans.*
H* *Prize Cattle Vans only.*   C *Carriages by Passenger Train.*   † *Open in Summer months only.*

STATION ACCOMMODATION.						CRANE POWER.		STATIONS, &c.	COUNTY.	COMPANY.	POSITION.
						Tons	Cwts.	Shakespeare Coal Wharf	Surrey	S. E. & C.	London, Clapham Road.
G	P	F	L	H	C	5	0	Shalfleet	I. of W.	I. of W. Cent.	See Calbourne and Shalfleet.
								Shalford (for Godalming)......	Surrey	S. E. & C.	Dorking and Guildford.
								Shalford Junction	Surrey	L. & S.W.—S. E. & C. ...	Guildford and Shalford.
G	P	F	L	H	C	1	10	Shallcross	Cheshire...	L. & N. W.	See Whaley Bridge.
G	P		L	H				Shandon	Dumbartn	N. B.	Craigendoran and Ardlui.
								Shankend	Roxburgh	N. B.	Hawick and Carlisle.
G	P		L	H				Shankhouse Col. (Amelia Pit)	Northumb	N. E.	Annitsford.
G	P	F	L	H	C	10	0	Shankill	Dublin	D. W. & W.	Dublin (Harcourt Street) and Bray.
								Shanklin	I. of W.	I. of W.	Sandown and Ventnor.
								Shanks, A., & Son's Siding ...	Forfar......	Cal.—D. & A. Jt.—N. B.	See Arbroath.
								Shanks & Co.'s Siding	Renfrew ...	G. & S.W.	Johnstone, Cartside.
								Shanks & Son's Wood Yard ...	Lanark ...	N. B.	Airdrie, North.
G	P	F	L	H	C	5	0	Shantona Junction.............	Monaghan	G. N. (I.)	Dundalk and Clones.
								Shap	W'morlnd	L. & N. W.	Lancaster and Penrith.
								Shap Granite & Patent Concrete Co.'s Summit Sid.	W'morlnd	L. & N. W.	Shap and Tebay.
G	P		L	H				Shapland & Petter's Siding...	Devon ...	L. & S.W.	Barnstaple Junction Station.
								Shapwick	Somerset...	S.&D.Jt.(L.&S.W.&Mid)	Glastonbury and Highbridge.
	P							Shardlow	Leicester...	Mid.	See Castle Donington and Shardlow.
								Sharlston	Yorks	L. & Y.	Wakefield and Pontefract.
								New Sharlston Col. (L & Y)	Yorks	L. & Y.—G. N.—N. E. ...	Sharlston.
								Sharlston Colliery	Yorks	Mid.	{ Normanton. { Oakenshaw.
								Sharlston Siding...............	Yorks	L. & Y.	Wakefield and Pontefract.
								Sharlston, West Colliery	Yorks	W.R.&G.Jt.(G.C.&G.N.)	Hare Park and Crofton.
G	P	F	L	H	C			Sharnal Street	Kent	S. E. & C.	Gravesend (Central) & Port Victoria.
								Miskin's Siding	Kent	S. E. & C.	Sharnal Street and Port Victoria.
								Stoke Siding	Kent	S. E. & C.	Sharnal Street and Port Victoria.
								Wybourne Siding	Kent	S. E. & C.	Cliffe and Sharnal Street.
G	P	F	L	H	C			Sharnbrook	Beds	Mid.	Bedford and Wellingboro'.
								Sharon Chemical Works	Derby	Mid.	Derby, St. Marys.
G	P	F	L	H	C			Sharples Siding	Lancs	P.&L.Jt.(L&NW.&L&Y)	See Chapel Hill Siding (Longridge).
								Sharpness Docks	Glo'ster ...	S.&Wye Jt.(G.W. & Mid)	Severn Bridge and Berkeley.
								Sharp's Locomotive Works...	Lanark ...	N. B.	Airdrie, North.
								Sharp's Siding	Lanark ...	N. B.	Coatbridge, Sunnyside.
								Sharp's Siding	Yorks	L. & Y.	Bradford, Low Moor.
								Sharp, Stewart & Co.'s Siding (N. B.)	Lanark ...	N. B.—G. & S. W.	{ Same as Atlas Engine Works { (Glasgow).
G	P					5	0	Shaw and Crompton	Lancs	L. & Y.	Oldham and Rochdale.
								Bankhouse Siding	Lancs	L. & Y.	Shaw.
								Crompton's Siding.........	Lancs	L. & Y.	Shaw.
								Jubilee Siding	Lancs	L. & Y.	Shaw.
								Shaw & Lovegrove's Longcliffe Limestone Co.'s Siding......	Derby	L. & N. W.	Longcliffe.
								Shaw & Shaw's Scarwood Siding	Yorks	L. & N. W.	{ Huddersfield, Longwood and Milnsbridge.
								Shaw & Son's Siding............	Yorks	L. & Y	Stainland and Holywell Green.
								Shaw Bros.' Siding	Derby	Mid.	Matlock Bath.
								Shaw Bros.' Intake Siding ...	Derby	L. & N. W.	Steeplehouse.
								Shaw, G.,& Son's Pottery Wks.	Yorks	Mid.	Same as Holmes Pottery Works (Masboro').
								Shaw's Bottom Hall Siding...	Yorks	L. & N. W.	Huddersfield, Longwood and Milnsbridge.
								Shaw's Colliery	Lanark ...	Cal.	Dalserf.
								Shaw's Depôt	Edinboro'	N. B.	Hardengreen.
								Shaw's Huyton Quarry Iron Works	Lancs	L. & N. W.	Huyton Quarry.
								Shaw's Limestone Siding......	Derby	Mid.	Matlock Bridge.
								Shaw's Siding..................	Edinboro'	N. B.	Leith, Bonnington.
								Shaw's Siding	Lanark ...	Cal.	Glasgow, Maryhill.
								Shaw's Siding (G. C.)	Yorks	G. C.—G. N.	Rotherham and Masboro'.
G	P					5	0	Shaw's Sidings	Somerset...	Mid.	Weston (near Bath).
								Shawclough & Healey	Lancs	L. & Y.	Rochdale and Facit.
								Shaw Cross Colliery	Yorks	G. N.	Ossett.
								Shawfield Chemical Works ...	Lanark ...	Cal.	Glasgow, South Side.
								Shawfield Colliery	Lanark ...	Cal.	Law Junction Station.
G	P					1	10	Shawford & Twyford	Hants	L. & S.W.	Winchester and Southampton.
								Shawford Junction	Hants	L. & S.W.	Shawford and Eastleigh.
G	P							Shawforth	Lancs	L. & Y.	Bacup and Facit.
								Law's Siding	Lancs	L. & Y.	Shawforth.
								Shaw Heath Siding	Cheshire...	C. L. C. (G C, G N, & Mid.)	Knutsford.

EXPLANATION—G *Goods Station.*   P *Passenger and Parcel Station.*   P* *Passenger, but not Parcel or Miscellaneous Traffic.*
F *Furniture Vans, Carriages, Portable Engines, and Machines on Wheels.*   L *Live Stock.*
H *Horse Boxes and Prize Cattle Vans.*   C *Carriages by Passenger Train.*

STATION ACCOMMODATION.						CRANE POWER.		STATIONS, &c.	COUNTY.	COMPANY.	POSITION.
						Tons	Cwts.				
.	.	.	.	.	.	.	.	Shawhill Junction	Dumfries..	Cal.—G. & S. W.	Same as Annan Junction.
.	.	.	.	.	.	.	.	Shawhill Siding	Dumfries..	Cal.—G. & S. W.	Annan.
.	.	.	.	.	.	.	.	Shawlands	Renfrew...	Cal.	See Glasgow.
.	.	.	.	.	.	.	.	Shawsburn Colliery	Lanark ...	Cal.	Dalserf.
.	.	.	.	.	.	.	.	Shawsrigg Colliery............	Lanark ...	Cal.	Dalserf.
.	.	.	.	.	.	.	.	Shawsrigg Fire-Clay and Enamelling Works	Lanark ...	Cal.	Dalserf.
.	.	.	.	.	.	.	.	Shaw Syke (L. & Y.)	Yorks	L.&Y.—G. N.—L.&N.W.	Same as Halifax Station.
.	.	.	.	.	.	.	.	Shearer's Graving Dock	Renfrew...	Cal.	Glasgow, Whiteinch.
.	.	.	.	.	.	.	.	Shearman & Co.'s Siding	Glamorg'n	GW—LNW—Rhy.—TV	Cardiff.
.	.	.	.	.	.	.	.	Shedlaw Farm Siding	Northumb	N. E.	Carham.
.	.	.	.	.	.	.	.	Sheen	Surrey ...	L. & S.W.	See Mortlake and East Sheen.
G	P	F	L	H	C	10	0	Sheepbridge & Brimington (G. C.)	Derby......	G. C.	Sheffield and Chesterfield.
G	.	F	L	.	.	10	0			L. & N. W.	Over G. N. & G. C. Lines from Saxondale Junction.
.	.	.	.	.	.	.	.	Lockoford Siding	Derby......	G. C.	Sheepbridge and Brimington.
.	.	.	.	.	.	.	.	Sheepbridge Siding	Derby......	G. C.	Sheepbridge and Brimington.
G	P	.	L	H	.	1	10	Sheepbridge and Whittington Moor	Derby......	Mid.	Chesterfield and Sheffield.
.	.	.	.	.	.	.	.	Chatsworth Wagon Works (Hurst, Nelson & Co.) ...	Derby......	Mid.	Dunston and Barlow Branch.
.	.	.	.	.	.	.	.	Sheepbridge Coal and Iron Co.'s Cinder Breaker Sid.	Derby......	Mid.	Dunston and Barlow Branch.
.	.	.	.	.	.	.	.	Sheepbridge Co.'s New Pipe Works	Derby......	Mid.	Sheepbridge Branch.
.	.	.	.	.	.	.	.	Sheepbridge Gas Co.'s Wks.	Derby......	Mid.	Sheepbridge Branch.
.	.	.	.	.	.	.	.	Whittington Blacking Mill (Cummings, W., & Co.)..	Derby......	Mid.	Dunston and Barlow Branch.
.	.	.	.	.	.	.	.	Whittington Moor Potteries (Pearson & Co.)	Derby......	Mid.	Dunston and Barlow Branch.
G	.	.	.	.	.	.	.	Whittington Road Public Wharf	Derby......	Mid.	Sheepbridge.
.	.	.	.	.	.	.	.	Sheepbridge Coal & Iron Co.— Cinder Breaker Siding	Derby......	Mid.	Sheepbridge and Whittington Moor.
.	.	.	.	.	.	.	.	Langwith Colliery (Mid.)...	Derby......	Mid.—G. C.	Langwith.
.	.	.	.	.	.	.	.	Norwood Colliery	Derby......	Mid.	Killamarsh.
.	.	.	.	.	.	.	.	Sheepbridge Ir. Ore Co.'s Sid.	Rutland ...	Mid.	Ashwell.
.	.	.	.	.	.	.	.	Sheepbridge Mine	Lincoln ...	G. C.	Frodingham and Scunthorpe.
.	.	.	.	.	.	.	.	Sheepbridge Siding	Derby......	G. C.	Sheepbridge and Brimington.
.	.	.	.	.	.	.	.	Sheepcroft Siding	Dorset ...	E.&C.H.(GW.&L&SW.)	Easton.
.	.	.	.	.	.	.	.	Sheepford	Lanark ...	N. B.	See Coatbridge.
.	.	.	.	.	.	.	.	Sheepford Branch Junction...	Lanark ...	N. B.	Coatbridge, Central and Whifflet.
.	.	.	.	.	.	.	.	Sheepford Locks Siding	Lanark ...	N. B.	Same as Contdyke Goods and Mineral Depôt (Coatbridge).
G	P	F	L	H	C	15	0	Sheerness Dockyard	Kent	S. E. & C.	Branch from Sittingbourne.
.	P*	.	.	.	.	.	.	Sheerness, East	Kent	S. E. & C. (Sheppey)......	Queenborough & Minster (Sheppey).
.	P	.	.	.	.	.	.	Sheerness-on-Sea	Kent	S. E. & C.	Branch from Sheerness Dockyard.
								SHEFFIELD—			
.	.	.	.	.	.	.	.	Aizlewood's Corn Mills (GC)	Yorks	G. C.—G. N.—Mid.	Bridgehouses.
.	.	.	.	.	.	.	.	Allen, Edgar, & Co.'s Siding	Yorks	L. D. & E. C.—Mid.	Tinsley Road.
.	.	.	.	.	.	.	.	Andrew, J. H., & Co.'s Siding (G. C.)	Yorks	G. C.—G. N.	Bridgehouses.
.	P	.	.	.	.	.	.	Attercliffe......................	Yorks	G. C.	Victoria and Rotherham.
										L. D. & E. C.	Goods Terminus.
G	.	F	L	.	.	35	0	Attercliffe	Yorks	Mid.	Branch from Grimesthorpe Junction.
.	.	.	.	.	.	.	.	Attercliffe Junction	Yorks	G. C.	Attercliffe and Darnall.
										Mid.	Pond Str. and Grimesthorpe Junc.
.	P	.	.	.	.	.	.	Attercliffe Road (Mid.)......	Yorks	L. D. & E. C.	Over Mid. from Brightside Junction.
G	P	F	L	H	C	.	.	Beauchief & Abbey Dale ...	Derby......	Mid.	Sheffield and Chesterfield.
.	.	.	.	.	.	.	.	Bessemer, H., & Co.'s Works (Mid.)	Yorks	Mid.—G. C.	Wicker.
.	.	.	.	.	.	.	.	Black, C., & Son's Siding	Yorks	Mid.	Queen's Road.
G	.	F	L	H	C	40	0	Bridgehouses (G. C.)........	Yorks	G. C.	Neepsend and Victoria. Over G. C. Line.
										G. N.	
.	P	.	.	.	.	.	.	Brightside	Yorks	Mid.	Sheffield and Masboro'.
.	.	.	.	.	.	.	.	Brightside and Carbrook Co-operative Sid. (G.C.)	Yorks	G. C.—Mid.	Broughton Lane.
.	.	.	.	.	.	.	.	Brightside Junction	Yorks	L. D. & E. C.—Mid.	Tinsley Road and Attercliffe Road.
G	.	.	.	.	.	5	0	Brightside Wharf	Yorks	Mid.	Wicker and Brightside.
G	P	.	L	.	.	10	0	Broughton Lane..............	Yorks	G. C.	Victoria and Rotherham.
.	.	.	.	.	.	.	.	Brown Bayley's Steel Works (G. C.)	Yorks	G. C.—Mid.	Broughton Lane.

EXPLANATION—G *Goods Station.*   P *Passenger and Parcel Station.*   P* *Passenger, but not Parcel or Miscellaneous Traffic.*
F *Furniture Vans, Carriages, Portable Engines, and Machines on Wheels.*   L *Live Stock.*
H *Horse Boxes and Prize Cattle Vans.*   C *Carriages by Passenger Train.*

Station Accommodation.						Crane Power.		Stations, &c.	County.	Company.	Position.
						Tons	Cwts	SHEFFIELD—continued.			
								Brown, J., & Co.—			
								Atlas Blast Furnaces (Mid.)	Yorks	Mid.—G. C.	Wicker.
								Atlas Works (Mid.)	Yorks	Mid.—G. C.	Wicker.
								Burrows & Son's Sid. (G.C.)	Yorks	G. C.—Mid.	Broughton Lane.
								Cammell, C., & Co.—			
								Cyclops Works (Mid.)	Yorks	Mid.—G. C.	Wicker.
								Grimesthorpe Wks. (Mid)	Yorks	Mid.—G. C.	Wicker.
								Carbrook Forge (G. C.)	Yorks	G. C.—Mid.	Broughton Lane.
G	P†	F	L			10	0	City	Yorks	L. & N. W.	Branch from G. C. Line.
								Cooke's Tinsley Iron and Wire Works (G. C.)	Yorks	G. C.—Mid.	Broughton Lane.
								Cooke's Tinsley Iron & Wire Works	Yorks	L. D. & E. C.—Mid.	Tinsley Road.
								Cooper, H., & Co.'s Works	Yorks	L. D. & E. C.—Mid.	Tinsley Road.
								Corporation Sidings—			
								Bernard Road Siding (Central Depôt) (Mid.)	Yorks	Mid.—G. C.	Pond Street and Attercliffe Road.
								Electric Power Siding	Yorks	G. C.	Bridgehouses.
								Olive Grove Depôt	Yorks	Mid.	Queen's Road.
								Sewage Works	Yorks	Mid.	Wicker.
								Woodside Lane Depôt (G. C.)	Yorks	G. C.—G. N.	Bridgehouses.
G	P					10	0	Craven's Siding	Yorks	G. C.	Darnall (for Handsworth).
								Darnall (for Handsworth)	Yorks	G. C.	Victoria and Woodhouse.
								Darnall Junction	Yorks	G. C.	Attercliffe and Darnall.
								Firth, T., & Son's Siding (Norfolk and East & West Gun Works) (Mid.)	Yorks	Mid.—G. C.	Wicker.
								Furniss' Siding (G. C.)	Yorks	G. C.—G. N.	Park.
								G. C. Railway—			
								Bonded Stores	Yorks	G. C.	Bridgehouses.
								Engineers' Siding	Yorks	G. C.	Park.
								Loco. Stores	Yorks	G. C.	Bridgehouses.
								Oil Gas Works	Yorks	G. C.	Park.
								Gregory & Son's Siding	Yorks	Mid.	Mill Houses and Ecclesall.
								Gregory, J., & Son's Siding	Yorks	Mid.	Near Heeley.
								Grimesthorpe Junction	Yorks	Mid.	Attercliffe Road and Brightside.
								Hadfield's Steel Foundry Co.—			
								East Hecla Works	Yorks	L. D. & E. C.—Mid.	Tinsley Road.
								Tinsley Works	Yorks	L. D. & E. C.—Mid.	Tinsley Road.
G	P	F		H	C	5	0	Harvest Lane Coal Depôt	Yorks	G. C.	Park.
								Heeley	Yorks	Mid.	Sheffield and Chesterfield.
								High Hazels Colliery (G.C.)	Yorks	G. C.—L. & N. W.	Darnall (for Handsworth).
								Hodkin & Jones' Siding	Yorks	Mid.	Queen's Road.
								Jessop, W., & Son's—			
								Brightside Works	Yorks	L. D. & E. C.—Mid.	Tinsley Road.
								Brightside Works (Mid.)	Yorks	Mid.—G.C.—L. D. & E.C.	Wicker.
								Junction with L. & N. W. Goods Branch	Yorks	G. C.—L. & N. W.	Darnall and City.
								Kayser, Ellison & Co.'s Siding (Mid.)	Yorks	Mid.—G. C.	Wicker.
								Laycock's, W. S., Siding	Yorks	Mid.	Mill Houses and Ecclesall.
								Longbottom's Wagon Repairing Siding (G.C.)	Yorks	G. C.—G. N.	Bridgehouses.
								Lumley Street (for Bernard Road Depôt) (G. C.)	Yorks	G. C.—G. N.	Park.
								Midland Railway Bonded Stores Siding	Yorks	Mid.	Wicker.
								Midland Railway Oil Gas Works	Yorks	Mid.	Queen's Road.
G	P					1	10	Mill Houses and Ecclesall	Yorks	Mid.	Sheffield and Chesterfield.
G	P							Neepsend	Yorks	G. C.	Victoria and Wadsley Bridge.
G		F	L	H	C	40	0	Nunnery	Yorks	L. & N. W.	Branch from G. C. Line.
								Nunnery Colliery Co.—			
								Nunnery Colliery	Yorks	G. C.	Park.
								Nunnery Colliery	Yorks	L. & N. W.	Nunnery Branch.
								Nunnery Colliery	Yorks	Mid.	Pond Street and Attercliffe Road.
								Soaphouse Siding (G. C.)	Yorks	G. C.—G. N.	Park.
G								Park (G. C.)	Yorks	{ G. C.	Victoria and Darnall.
										{ G. N.	Over G. C. Line.

STATION ACCOMMODATION.						CRANE POWER.		STATIONS, &c.	COUNTY.	COMPANY.	POSITION.
						Tons	Cwts.	SHEFFIELD—continued.			
G	P	.	L	H	C	5	0	Pond Street (Mid.)	Yorks	Mid.	Chesterfield and Masboro'.
	P	.	.	H	C	.	.			L. D. & E. C.	Over Mid. from Brightside Junction.
G	.	F	L	.	.	5	0	Queen's Road	Yorks	Mid.	Pond Street and Heeley.
.	.	.	.	.	.	.	.	Renton, B. M., & Co.'s Works (Mid.)...............	Yorks	Mid.—G. C.	Wicker.
.	.	.	.	.	.	.	.	Sanderson Bros.' & Newbould's Siding............	Yorks	L. D. & E. C.—Mid.	Attercliffe.
.	.	.	.	.	.	.	.	Sheffield Brick Co.'s Neepsend Works (G. C.)........	Yorks	G. C.—G. N.—L. & N. W.	Bridgehouses.
.	.	.	.	.	.	.	.	Sheffield United Gas Light Co.— Grimesthorpe Gas Works (Mid.)	Yorks	Mid.—G. C.	Wicker.
.	.	.	.	.	.	.	.	Neepsend Gas Wks. (GC)	Yorks	G. C.—G. N.—Mid.	Bridgehouses.
.	.	.	.	.	.	.	.	Smith's, S., Flour Mill (Mid)	Yorks	Mid.—G. C.	Wicker.
.	.	.	.	.	.	.	.	Spear & Jackson's Etna Works (Mid.)	Yorks	Mid.—G. C.	Wicker.
.	.	.	.	.	.	.	.	Tinsley Colliery	Yorks	G. C.	Broughton Lane.
.	.	.	.	.	.	.	.	Tinsley Park Colliery	Yorks	L. D. & E. C.—Mid.	Tinsley Road.
G	P	F	L	H	C	10	0	Tinsley Road	Yorks	L. D. & E. C.	Clown and Sheffield.
G	.	F	L	.	.	10	0			Mid.	Treeton and Sheffield.
.	.	.	.	.	.	.	.	Tunnel Junction	Yorks	G. C.—Mid.	Neepsend and Brightside.
G	.	.	.	.	.	.	.	Upwell Street Wharf	Yorks	Mid.	Wicker and Brightside.
.	.	.	.	.	.	.	.	Vickers, Sons & Maxim's Siding (Mid.)	Yorks	Mid.—G. C.—L. D. &E. C.	Pond Street and Brightside.
.	P	.	.	H	C	.	.			G. C.	Neepsend and Darnall.
.	P	.	.	H	C	.	.	Victoria (G. C.)	Yorks	G. N.	Over G. C. Line.
.	P	.	.	H	C	.	.			L. & Y.	Over G. C. from Penistone Junction.
.	.	.	.	.	.	.	.	Ward's, T. W.— Broughton Lane Sid.(GC)	Yorks	G. C.—Mid.	Broughton Lane.
.	.	.	.	.	.	.	.	Grimesthorpe Sids. (Mid.)	Yorks	Mid.—G. C.	Wicker.
G	.	F	L	.	.	35	0	Wicker	Yorks	Mid.	Tunnel Junc. & Grimesthorpe Junc.
.	.	.	.	.	.	.	.	Wigfull & Son's Corn Mill (G. C.)	Yorks	G. C.—G. N.—Mid.	Bridgehouses.
G	P	.	.	.	.	.	.	Wincobank & Meadow Hall	Yorks	Mid.	Sheffield and Masboro'.
.	.	.	.	.	.	.	.	Woodburn Junction	Yorks	G. C.	Victoria and Attercliffe.
.	.	.	.	.	.	.	.	Woodhouse & Rixson's Sid.	Yorks	L. D. & E. C.—Mid.	Attercliffe.
.	.	.	.	.	.	.	.	Sheffield Brick Co.'s Neepsend Works (G. C.)	Yorks	G. C.—G. N.—L. & N. W.	Sheffield, Bridgehouses.
.	.	.	.	.	.	.	.	Sheffield Corporation— Bernard Road Siding (Central Depôt) (Mid.)	Yorks	Mid.—G. C.	Sheffield, Wicker.
.	.	.	.	.	.	.	.	Electric Power Siding......	Yorks	G. C.	Sheffield, Bridgehouses.
.	.	.	.	.	.	.	.	Olive Grove Depôt......	Yorks	Mid.	Sheffield, Queen's Road.
.	.	.	.	.	.	.	.	Sewage Works	Yorks	G. C.	Tinsley.
.	.	.	.	.	.	.	.			Mid.	Sheffield, Wicker.
.	.	.	.	.	.	.	.	Siding	Yorks	G. C.	Kilnhurst.
.	.	.	.	.	.	.	.	Woodside Lane Depôt(G.C.)	Yorks	G. C.—G. N.	Sheffield, Bridgehouses.
G	P	F	L	H	C	5	0	Sheffield Park............	Sussex	L. B. & S. C.	Horsted Keynes and Newick.
.	.	.	.	.	.	.	.	Sheffield's Siding	Sussex	L. B. & S. C.	Sheffield Park.
.	.	.	.	.	.	.	.	Turner & Sons' Siding	Sussex	L. B. & S. C.	Sheffield Park.
.	.	.	.	.	.	.	.	Sheffield's Brick Works	Cumb'land	M. & C.	Wigton.
.	.	.	.	.	.	.	.	Sheffield's (Sir Berkeley) Sid.	Lincoln	G. C.	Frodingham & Scunthorpe.
.	.	.	.	.	.	.	.	Sheffield Tube Works (Howell & Co.'s Iron Works) (G.C.)	Yorks	G. C.—Mid.	Tinsley.
.	.	.	.	.	.	.	.	Sheffield United Gas Light Co.— Grimesthorpe Gas Works (Mid.)	Yorks	Mid.—G. C.	Sheffield, Wicker.
.	.	.	.	.	.	.	.	Neepsend Gas Works (G.C.)	Yorks	G. C.—G. N.—Mid.	Sheffield, Bridgehouses.
G	P	F	L	H	C	1	10	Shefford	Beds	Mid.	Hitchin and Bedford.
.	.	.	.	.	.	.	.	Shefford Road	Beds	G. N.	See Arlesey and Shefford Road.
G	P	.	L	H	.	1	0	Shelford	Cambs	G. E.	Cambridge and Bishops Stortford.
.	.	.	.	.	.	.	.	Shelley	Yorks	L. & Y.	See Shepley and Shelley.
.	.	.	.	.	.	.	.	Shelton Iron, Steel & Coal Co.— Granville Siding............	Staffs	N. S.	Etruria.
.	.	.	.	.	.	.	.	Siding	Staffs	N. S.	Etruria.
.	.	.	.	.	.	.	.	Shelwick Junction............	Hereford ..	G. W.—S. & H. Jt.	Hereford.
G	P	.	L	H	.	2	0	Shenfield & Hutton Junc. Sta.	Essex	G. E.	Brentwood and Chelmsford.
.	.	.	.	.	.	.	.	Cornish, D., & Co.'s Siding	Essex	G. E.	Shenfield and Hutton Junc. Station
G	.	.	.	.	.	.	.	Mountnessing Siding........	Essex	G. E.	Shenfield and Wickford.
G	P	F	L	H	C	5	0	Shenstone..................	Staffs	L. & N. W.	Birmingham and Lichfield.

EXPLANATION—G *Goods Station.*   P *Passenger and Parcel Station.*   P* *Passenger, but not Parcel or Miscellaneous Traffic.*
F *Furniture Vans, Carriages, Portable Engines, and Machines on Wheels.*   L *Live Stock.*
H *Horse Boxes and Prize Cattle Vans.*   C *Carriages by Passenger Train.*

STATION ACCOMMODATION.						CRANE POWER.	STATIONS, &c.	COUNTY.	COMPANY.	POSITION.
G	P	F	L	H	C	Tons Cwts.				
.	.	.	.	.	.	.	Shenton	Leicester ..	A & N Jt. (L & N W & Mid.)	Nuneaton and Shackerstone.
.	.	.	.	.	.	.	Shepherd, A., & Co.'s Saw Mills	Lincoln ...	G. C.	Grimsby Docks.
.	.	.	.	.	.	.	Shepherd & Blackburn's Sid.	Yorks	L. & Y.	Sowerby Bridge.
.	.	.	.	.	.	.	Shepherd & Son's Holme Mills	W'morlnd	L. & N. W.	Burton and Holme.
.	.	.	.	.	.	.	Shepherd's Bush.................	Middlesex	C. L.—G.W.—H. & C. Jt. —L.&N.W.—L.&S.W.	See London.
.	.	.	.	.	.	.	Shepherd's Bush.................	Middlesex	W Lon Jt (G W & L N W)	See London, Uxbridge Road (for Shepherd's Bush).
G	P	F	L	H	C	1 10	Shepherd's Well...............	Kent	S. E. & C.	Canterbury East and Dover Priory.
G	P	.	.	.	.	10 0	Shepley and Shelley	Yorks	L. & Y.	Huddersfield and Penistone.
.	.	.	.	.	.	.	Senior's Siding	Yorks	L. & Y.	Near Shepley and Shelley.
.	.	.	.	.	.	.	Sheppard, C., & Son's Siding	Glamorg'n	G. W.	Bridgend.
.	.	.	.	.	.	.	Sheppard's Siding	Notts ...	G. C.	Gotham.
G	P	F	L	H	C	.	Shepperton	Middlesex	L. & S. W.	Branch from Twickenham.
.	.	.	.	.	.	.	Catling's Siding...............	Middlesex	L. & S. W.	Shepperton.
G	P	F	L	H	C	1 10	Shepreth	Cambs	G. N.	Hitchin and Cambridge.
.	.	.	.	.	.	.	Cam Cement Co.'s Siding...	Cambs	G. N.	Shepreth and Meldreth.
.	.	.	.	.	.	.	East Anglian Cement Co.'s Siding (G. N.)	Cambs	G. N.—G. E.	Shepreth.
.	.	.	.	.	.	.	Rhee Valley Cement Co.'s Siding	Cambs	G. N.	Shepreth.
.	.	.	.	.	.	.	Royston Cement Co.'s Sid.	Cambs	G. N.	Shepreth.
.	.	.	.	.	.	.	Shepreth Junction..............	Cambs	G. E.—G. N.	Hitchin and Cambridge.
G	P	F	L	H	C	5 0	Shepshed	Leicester ..	L. & N. W.	Loughboro' and Nuneaton.
.	.	.	.	.	.	.	Charnwood Granite Co.'sSid	Leicester ..	L. & N. W.	Shepshed and Loughboro'.
.	.	.	.	.	.	.	Fotherby & Son's Siding ...	Leicester ..	L. & N. W.	Shepshed and Whitwick.
.	.	.	.	.	.	.	Gibbs Bros.' Siding	Leicester ..	L. & N. W.	Shepshed and Loughboro'.
.	.	.	.	.	.	.	Loughboro' Waterworks ...	Leicester ..	L. & N. W.	Shepshed and Whitwick.
G	P	F	L	H	C	8 0 }	Shepton Mallet	Somerset ..	{ G. W.	Witham and Wells.
G	P	F	L	H	C	5 0 }			S. & D. Jt. (L & SW & Mid)	Evercreech and Radstock.
.	.	.	.	.	.	.	Charlton Lias Lime Works	Somerset ..	S.&D. Jt. (L.&S.W & Mid)	Shepton Mallet.
G	P	F	L	H	C	5 0	Sherborne........................	Dorset	L. & S. W.	Templecombe and Yeovil Junction.
G	.	.	.	.	.	.	Sherborne Coal, Timber, Corn, & Coke Co.'s Siding	Dorset......	L. & S. W.	Sherborne.
.	.	.	.	.	.	.	Sherborne Gas Co.'s Siding	Dorset......	L. & S. W.	Sherborne.
G	P	.	L	H	C	2 0	Sherburn Colliery Station ...	Durham ...	N. E.	Ferryhill and Leamside.
.	.	.	.	.	.	.	Broomside Junc. & Siding	Durham ...	N. E.	Sherburn Colliery Station.
.	.	.	.	.	.	.	Lady Durham or Sherburn Colliery and Coke Ovens	Durham ...	N. E.	Sherburn Colliery Station.
.	.	.	.	.	.	.	Littletown Colliery	Durham ...	N. E.	Sherburn Colliery Station.
.	.	.	.	.	.	.	Lord Lambton or Little-town Colliery Store and Coal Sidings	Durham ...	N. E.	Sherburn Colliery Station.
.	.	.	.	.	.	.	Sherburn Colliery	Durham ...	N. E.	Sherburn Colliery Station.
.	.	.	.	.	.	.	Sherburn Colliery Jn. Sid.	Durham ...	N. E.	Sherburn Colliery Station.
.	.	.	.	.	.	.	Sherburn Hill Colliery	Durham ...	N. E.	Sherburn Colliery Station.
.	.	.	.	.	.	.	Sherburn House Colliery ...	Durham ...	N. E.	Sherburn Colliery Station.
G	P	.	.	.	.	.	Sherburn House...............	Durham ...	N. E.	Murton and Durham (Elvet).
.	.	.	.	.	.	.	Sherburn House Brick Wks	Durham ...	N. E.	Sherburn House.
.	.	.	.	.	.	.	Shincliffe Brick Works......	Durham ...	N. E.	Sherburn House.
G	P	.	L	H	.	5 0 }	Sherburn-in-Elmet (N. E.) ...	Yorks	{ N. E.	York and Milford Junction.
.	P	.	.	H	.	}			{ G. N.	Over N. E. and S. & K. Jt. Lines.
.	P	.	.	.	.	}			{ Mid.	Over N. E. Line.
.	.	.	.	.	.	.	Leeds & Wakefield Brewery Co.'s Siding..................	Yorks	N. E.	Sherburn-in-Elmet.
.	.	.	.	.	.	.	Sherburn Road Siding (Selby Common Siding)	Yorks	N. E.	Wistow.
.	.	.	.	.	.	.	Shere	Surrey ...	S. E. & C.	See Gomshall and Shere.
.	.	.	.	.	.	.	Sheriffs Pit	Yorks	N. E.	Rosedale (East).
.	.	.	.	.	.	.	Sheriff Street	Dublin ...	G. S. & W.	See Dublin.
G	P	F	L	H	C	.	Sheringham	Norfolk ..	Mid. & G. N. Jt.	Melton Constable & Cromer Beach.
.	.	.	.	.	.	.	Sherwin's Brick Siding	Lincoln ...	G. N.	Boston.
.	.	.	.	.	.	.	Sherwood	Notts ...	G. N.	See Nottingham.
.	.	.	.	.	.	.	Sherwood Col. Co.'s Sid. (Mid)	Notts	Mid.—G. C.	Mansfield Woodhouse.
.	.	.	.	.	.	.	Shetcliffe Mill Siding	Yorks	G. N.	Same as Lister's Siding (Bradford).
G	P	F	L	H	C	3 0	Shettleston	Lanark ...	N. B.	Glasgow, College and Coatbridge.
.	.	.	.	.	.	.	Acme Manufacturing Co.'s Siding	Lanark ...	N. B.	Carntyne and Shettleston.
.	.	.	.	.	.	.	Acme Steel Foundry Co.'s Siding	Lanark ...	N. B.	Shettleston and Mount Vernon.
.	.	.	.	.	.	.	Allison & Co.'s Siding	Lanark ...	N. B.	Branch from Shettleston.
.	.	.	.	.	.	.	Greenfield Colliery No. 7...	Lanark ...	N. B.	Carntyne and Shettleston.

EXPLANATION—G *Goods Station.*   P *Passenger and Parcel Station.*   P* *Passenger, but not Parcel or Miscellaneous Traffic.*
F *Furniture Vans, Carriages, Portable Engines, and Machines on Wheels.*   L *Live Stock.*
H *Horse Boxes and Prize Cattle Vans.*   C *Carriages by Passenger Train.*

STATION ACCOMMODATION.						CRANE POWER.		STATIONS, &c.	COUNTY.	COMPANY.	POSITION.
						Tons	Cwts.	Shettleston—*continued.*			
.	.	.	.	.	.	.	.	Mount Vernon Iron & Steel Works	Lanark	N. B.	Branch from Shettleston Junction.
.	.	.	.	.	.	.	.	N.B. Railway Engineer's Sid	Lanark	N. B.	Shettleston.
.	.	.	.	.	.	.	.	Shettleston Iron Works (J. & T. Boyd's)	Lanark	N. B.	Carntyne and Shettleston.
.	.	.	.	.	.	.	.	Shettleston Oil & Chemical Works	Lanark	N. B.	Branch from Shettleston Junction.
.	.	.	.	.	.	.	.	Shettleston Junction	Lanark	N. B.	Shettleston and Easterhouse.
.	.	.	.	.	.	.	.	Shettleston Weighs	Lanark	N. B.	Shettleston and Mount Vernon.
.	.	.	.	.	.	.	.	Shewalton Moss Siding	Ayr	G. & S.W.	Drybridge.
G	P	.	L	H	.	.	.	Shide	I. of W.	I. of W. Cent.	Newport and Sandown.
G	P	.	L	.	.	.	.	Shieldaig	Ross & Cro'	High.	Steamer from Kyle of Lochalsh.
.	P	.	.	.	.	.	.	Shieldaig (Loch Torridon)	Ross & Cro'	N. B.	Steamer from Mallaig.
G	.	.	.	.	.	3	0	Shieldhall	Renfrew	G & P Jt (Cal & G & S W)	Branch from Cardonald Junction.
.	.	.	.	.	.	.	.	Shieldhall Timber Bank	Renfrew	G & P Jt (Cal & G & S W)	Shieldhall.
.	.	.	.	.	.	.	.	Shieldhall Wharf	Renfrew	G & P Jt (Cal & G & S W)	Shieldhall.
G	P	F	L	H	C	3	0	Shieldhill	Dumfries	Cal.	Lockerbie and Dumfries.
.	.	.	.	.	.	.	.	Shieldhill Basin Siding	Lanark	N. B.	Almond Junction Station.
.	.	.	.	.	.	.	.	Shieldhill Colliery	Lanark	N. B.	Almond Junction Station.
.	.	.	.	.	.	.	.	Shieldhill Exchange Sidings	Lanark	N. B.	Almond Junction Station.
.	.	.	.	.	.	.	.	Shieldmains Colliery	Ayr	G. & S.W.	Drongan.
G	.	.	.	.	.	.	.	Shieldmuir	Lanark	Cal.	Law Junction and Motherwell.
								Belhaven Estate Collieries—			
.	.	.	.	.	.	.	.	Meadowhead Colliery	Lanark	Cal.	Shieldmuir.
.	.	.	.	.	.	.	.	Netherjohnstone Cols.	Lanark	Cal.	Shieldmuir.
.	.	.	.	.	.	.	.	Netherjohnstone Washer	Lanark	Cal.	Shieldmuir.
.	.	.	.	.	.	.	.	Over Johnstone Colliery	Lanark	Cal.	Shieldmuir.
.	.	.	.	.	.	.	.	Over Johnstone Farm Sid.	Lanark	Cal.	Shieldmuir.
.	.	.	.	.	.	.	.	Bloomfield Forge	Lanark	Cal.	Shieldmuir.
.	.	.	.	.	.	.	.	Carbarns Colliery	Lanark	Cal.	Shieldmuir.
.	.	.	.	.	.	.	.	Clydesdale Colliery	Lanark	Cal.	Shieldmuir.
.	.	.	.	.	.	.	.	Clydesdale Wagon Works	Lanark	Cal.	Shieldmuir.
.	.	.	.	.	.	.	.	Dalzell Washer Works	Lanark	Cal.	Shieldmuir.
.	.	.	.	.	.	.	.	Etna Iron and Steel Works	Lanark	Cal.	Shieldmuir.
.	.	.	.	.	.	.	.	Excelsior Iron & Steel Wks.	Lanark	Cal.	Shieldmuir.
.	.	.	.	.	.	.	.	Glencleland Colliery	Lanark	Cal.	Shieldmuir.
.	.	.	.	.	.	.	.	Heathery Colliery	Lanark	Cal.	Shieldmuir.
.	.	.	.	.	.	.	.	Knownoble Colliery	Lanark	Cal.	Shieldmuir.
.	.	.	.	.	.	.	.	Motherwell Wagon and Rolling Stock Works	Lanark	Cal.	Shieldmuir.
.	.	.	.	.	.	.	.	Muirhouse Boiler Works (Shieldmuir Boiler Wks.)	Lanark	Cal.	Shieldmuir.
.	.	.	.	.	.	.	.	Muirhouse Collieries	Lanark	Cal.	Shieldmuir.
.	.	.	.	.	.	.	.	Muirhouse Engine Works	Lanark	Cal.	Shieldmuir.
.	.	.	.	.	.	.	.	Ravenscraig Sand Quarry	Lanark	Cal.	Shieldmuir.
.	.	.	.	.	.	.	.	Shieldmuir Colliery No. 1	Lanark	Cal.	Shieldmuir.
.	.	.	.	.	.	.	.	Shieldmuir Colliery No. 6 (Wood's Siding)	Lanark	Cal.	Shieldmuir.
.	.	.	.	.	.	.	.	Shieldmuir Weighs	Lanark	Cal.	Wishaw South and Flemington.
.	.	.	.	.	.	.	.	Shields Colliery	Lanark	Cal.	Shieldmuir.
.	.	.	.	.	.	.	.	Stirling's Boiler Works	Lanark	Cal.	Shieldmuir and Flemington.
.	.	.	.	.	.	.	.	Whitegates Siding	Lanark	Cal.	Shieldmuir.
.	.	.	.	.	.	.	.	Shieldmuir Boiler Works	Lanark	Cal.	Same as Muirhouse Boiler Works (Shieldmuir).
G	P	.	L	H	.	1	10	Shield Row	Durham	N. E.	Birtley and Annfield Plain.
.	.	.	.	.	.	.	.	Stanley Siding	Durham	N. E.	Shield Row.
.	.	.	.	.	.	.	.	Shields	Lanark	G. & S.W.	See Glasgow.
.	.	.	.	.	.	.	.	Shields Colliery	Lanark	Cal.	Shieldmuir.
.	.	.	.	.	.	.	.	Shields Crwys Coal Yard	Glamorg'n	Rhy.	Cardiff.
.	.	.	.	.	.	.	.	Shields Junction	Lanark	Cal.—G. & P. Jt.	Glasgow.
.	.	.	.	.	.	.	.	Shields Junction	Lanark	G. & S.W.—G. & P. Jt.	Glasgow.
.	.	.	.	.	.	.	.	Shield's Lime Works	Leicester	Mid.	Worthington.
.	.	.	.	.	.	.	.	Shields, North	Northumb	N. E.	See North Shields.
.	.	.	.	.	.	.	.	Shields Road	Lanark	G. & S. W.—Glas. Dist. Sub.—N. B.	See Glasgow.
.	.	.	.	.	.	.	.	Shields, South	Durham	Marsden—N. E.	See South Shields.
G	P	F	L	H	C	1	0	Shifnal	Salop	G. W.	Oakengates and Wolverhampton.
.	.	.	.	.	.	.	.	Lawton Siding (Edge & Son's Works)	Salop	G. W.	Shifnal and Albrighton.
.	.	.	.	.	.	.	.	Ruckley Sand Siding	Salop	G. W.	Shifnal and Albrighton.
.	.	.	.	.	.	.	.	Upton Siding	Salop	G. W.	Shifnal and Albrighton.

EXPLANATION—G *Goods Station.*   P *Passenger and Parcel Station.*   P* *Passenger, but not Parcel or Miscellaneous Traffic.*
F *Furniture Vans, Carriages, Portable Engines, and Machines on Wheels.*   L *Live Stock.*
H *Horse Boxes and Prize Cattle Vans.*   C *Carriages by Passenger Train.*

STATION ACCOMMODATION.						CRANE POWER.		STATIONS, &c.	COUNTY.	COMPANY.	POSITION.
						Tons	Cwts.				
G	P	F	L	.	.	5	0	Shildon	Durham	N. E.	Darlington and Bishop Auckland.
.	.	.	.	.	.	.	.	Adelaide Colliery	Durham	N. E.	Shildon.
.	.	.	.	.	.	.	.	Auckland Park Colliery and Coke Ovens	Durham	N. E.	Shildon.
.	.	.	.	.	.	.	.	Black Boy Brick Works	Durham	N. E.	Shildon.
.	.	.	.	.	.	.	.	Black Boy Colliery	Durham	N. E.	Shildon.
.	.	.	.	.	.	.	.	Brusselton Quarry	Durham	N. E.	Shildon.
.	.	.	.	.	.	.	.	Eldon Lane Brick Works	Durham	N. E.	Shildon.
.	.	.	.	.	.	.	.	Middridge Colliery	Durham	N. E.	Shildon.
.	.	.	.	.	.	.	.	Shildon Colliery	Durham	N. E.	Shildon.
.	.	.	.	.	.	.	.	Shildon Lodge Colliery	Durham	N. E.	Shildon.
.	.	.	.	.	.	.	.	Shildon N. E. R. Gas Works	Durham	N. E.	Shildon.
.	.	.	.	.	.	.	.	Shildon N. E. R. Wgn. Wks.	Durham	N. E.	Shildon.
.	.	.	.	.	.	.	.	South Durham and Eldon Collieries, Coke Ovens, and Brick Works	Durham	N. E.	Shildon.
.	.	.	.	.	.	.	.	West Durham Wallsend Col.	Durham	N. E.	Shildon.
.	.	.	.	.	.	.	.	Shildon Tunnel Junction	Durham	N. E.	Shildon and Bishop Auckland.
G	P	F	L	H	C	.	.	Shillelagh	Wicklow	D. W. & W.	Branch from Woodenbridge Junc.
.	.	.	.	.	.	.	.	Shillingford Engineering Co.'s (Trusty Engine Works)	Glo'ster	Mid.	Cheltenham.
G	P	F	L	H	C	5	0	Shillingstone	Dorset	S.&D.Jt.(L.&S.W.& Mid)	Templecombe and Wimborne.
G	P	.	L	H	.	.	.	Shilton	Warwick	L. & N. W.	Nuneaton and Rugby.
G	P	.	L	H	.	.	.	Shincliffe	Durham	N. E.	Ferryhill and Leamside.
.	.	.	.	.	.	.	.	Shincliffe Saw Mill	Durham	N. E.	Shincliffe.
.	.	.	.	.	.	.	.	Whitwell Colliery	Durham	N. E.	Shincliffe.
.	.	.	.	.	.	.	.	Shincliffe Brick Works	Durham	N. E.	Sherburn House.
G	P	.	.	.	.	1	10	Shiplake	Oxon	G. W.	Twyford and Henley-on-Thames.
G	P	F	L	H	C	10	0	Shipley	Yorks	Mid.	Leeds and Keighley.
.	.	.	.	.	.	.	.	Salt, Sir Titus, Sons & Co.'s Mills	Yorks	Mid.	Shipley and Saltaire.
.	.	.	.	.	.	.	.	Shipley Stone Siding	Yorks	Mid.	Shipley.
G	P	F	L	H	C	10	0	Shipley & Windhill	Yorks	G. N.	Branch from Laister Dyke.
.	.	.	.	.	.	.	.	Shipley Quarry Siding	Yorks	G. N.	Shipley.
.	.	.	.	.	.	.	.	Shipley Colliery (G. N.)	Derby	G. N.—G. C.	Ilkeston.
.	.	.	.	.	.	.	.	Shipley Colliery (Mundy's)	Derby	Mid.	Stanton Gate.
G	P	.	.	.	.	.	.	Shipley Gate	Derby	Mid.	Clay Cross and Trent.
.	.	.	.	.	.	.	.	Shipley Gate	Notts	G. N.	See Newthorpe, Greasley & Shipley Gate.
.	.	.	.	.	.	.	.	Shipley Hall	Derby	G. N.	See Marlpool (for Shipley Hall).
.	.	.	.	.	.	.	.	Shipley Junction	Yorks	G. N.—Mid.	Laister Dyke and Shipley (Mid.)
.	.	.	.	.	.	.	.	Shipley Wharf	Bucks	L. & N. W.	Same as Coales & Son's Siding (Newport Pagnell).
G	P	.	L	H	.	2	0	Shipston-on-Stour	Worcester	G. W.	Branch from Moreton-in-Marsh.
G	P	F	L	H	C	8	0	Shipton	Oxon	G. W.	Oxford and Moreton-in-Marsh.
.	.	.	.	.	.	.	.	Shipton Lane Siding	Yorks	N. E.	{ Everingham. { Market Weighton.
G	P	F	L	H	C	.	.	Shirdley Hill	Lancs	L. & Y.	Barton and Southport.
								SHIREBROOK—			
G	P	F	L	H	C	.	.	(Station)	Derby	G. N.	Sutton-in-Ashfield & Langwith Jn.
G	P	F	L	H	C	1	10	(Station, Mid.)	Derby	{ Mid. { G. C.	Mansfield and Shireoaks. Over Mid. fr. Shireoaks Junctions.
.	.	.	.	.	.	.	.	Junction	Derby	L. D. & E. C.—Mid.	Warsop and Shirebrook.
.	.	.	.	.	.	.	.	Shirebrook Colliery	Derby	G. N.	Shirebrook and Pleasley.
.	.	.	.	.	.	.	.	Staveley Coal & Iron Co.'s Shirebrook Col. (Mid.)	Derby	Mid.—G. C.—L. D.&E.C.	Near Shirebrook.
.	.	.	.	.	.	.	.	Warsop Main Col. (Mid.)	Derby	Mid.—G. C.	Near Shirebrook.
G	P	.	.	H†	C†	.	.	Shirehampton	Glo'ster	Clif. Ex. Jt.(G.W.& Mid.)	Clifton and Avonmouth Docks.
G	P	.	L	H	.	5	0	Shireoaks	Notts	G. C.	Sheffield and Worksop.
.	.	.	.	.	.	.	.	Brancliffe Lime Quarry	Notts	G. C.	Shireoaks.
.	.	.	.	.	.	.	.	East Junction	Notts	G. C.—Mid.	Worksop and Mansfield.
.	.	.	.	.	.	.	.	Shireoaks Colliery	Notts	G. C.	Shireoaks.
.	.	.	.	.	.	.	.	Steetley Lime Quarry (Shireoaks)	Notts	G. C.	Shireoaks.
.	.	.	.	.	.	.	.	Steetley Lime Qry. (Steetley)	Notts	G. C.	Shireoaks.
.	.	.	.	.	.	.	.	West Junction	Notts	G. C.—Mid.	Sheffield and Mansfield.
.	.	.	.	.	.	.	.	Shireoaks Colliery	Notts	{ G. C. { Mid.	Shireoaks. Whitwell.
.	.	.	.	.	.	.	.	Shireoaks Col. Co.'s New Pit	Notts	Mid.	Whitwell.
.	.	.	.	.	.	.	.	Shirland Colliery (Shirland Gas Co.)	Derby	Mid.	Wingfield.
.	.	.	.	.	.	.	.	Shirland Gas Co.'s Siding	Derby	Mid.	Same as Shirland Col. (Wingfield).

EXPLANATION—G *Goods Station.*   P *Passenger and Parcel Station.*   P* *Passenger, but not Parcel or Miscellaneous Traffic.*
F *Furniture Vans, Carriages, Portable Engines, and Machines on Wheels.*   L *Live Stock.*
H *Horse Boxes and Prize Cattle Vans.*   H† C† *By special arrangement only.*   C *Carriages by Passenger Train.*

STATION ACCOMMODATION.						CRANE POWER.	STATIONS, &c.	COUNTY.	COMPANY.	POSITION.
						Tons Cwt.				
.	.	.	.	.	.	.	Shirleywich Salt Works	Staffs	N. S.	Weston and Ingestre.
.	.	.	.	.	.	.	Shirleywich Siding	Staffs	N. S.	Weston and Ingestre.
.	.	.	.	.	.	.	Shobnall Branch (Mid.)	Staffs	Mid.—L&NW—GN—NS	Burton-on-Trent.
.	.	.	.	.	.	.	Shobnall Junction	Staffs	L. & N. W.—Mid.	Burton-on-Trent.
.	.	.	.	.	.	.	Shobnall Wharf (Mid.)	Staffs	Mid.—L&NW—GN—NS	Burton-on-Trent.
G	P	F	L	H	C	3 0	Shoeburyness	Essex	L. T. & S.	Terminus.
.	.	.	.	.	.	.	Eastwood & Co.'s Siding ...	Essex	L. T. & S.	Shoeburyness.
.	.	.	.	.	.	.	Royal Engineers' Siding ...	Essex	L. T. & S.	Shoeburyness.
G	P	.	.	.	.	.	Sholing	Hants	L. & S.W.	Southampton and Fareham.
.	.	.	.	.	.	.	Shoreditch	Middlesex	E. L. Jt.—L. & N. W.	See London.
.	.	.	.	.	.	.	Shoreditch (N. L.)	Middlesex	N. L.—L. & N. W.	See London.
G	P	F	L	H	.	1 10	Shoreham	Kent	S. E. & C.	Swanley and Otford.
G	P	F	L	H	C	5 0	Shoreham	Sussex	L. B. & S. C.	Brighton and Worthing.
.	.	.	.	.	.	.	Beeding Siding	Sussex	L. B. & S. C.	Shoreham and Bramber.
.	.	.	.	.	.	.	Sussex Portland Cement Co.'s Siding	Sussex	L. B. & S. C.	Shoreham and Bramber.
.	.	.	.	.	.	.	Shore Road	Stirling ...	Cal.—N. B.	See Stirling.
.	.	.	.	.	.	.	Shore Road	Cheshire ..	B'head Jt.—C. L. C.	See Birkenhead.
G	P	F	L	H	C	4 0	Shorncliffe	Kent	S. E. & C.	Ashford and Folkestone.
G	P	.	.	H	C	.	Short Heath (Mid.)	Staffs	Mid.	Wolverhampton & Sutton Coldfield.
G	.	.	.	.	.	.			G. W.	Over Mid. from Wolverhampton Jn.
.	.	.	.	.	.	.	Willenhall Gas Co.'s Siding (Mid.)	Staffs	Mid.—G.W.	Adjoining Short Heath Station.
.	.	.	.	.	.	.	Shorthill Colliery	Salop	S.&W'pl.Jt.(GW & LNW)	Same as Atherton's Cruckmeole Colliery (Hanwood).
.	.	.	.	.	.	.	Short, H. O., & Son's Siding	Northumb	N. E.	Tweedmouth.
.	P	.	.	.	.	.	Shortlands	Kent	S. E. & C.	Beckenham and Bromley, South.
.	.	.	.	.	.	.	Shortlands Junction	Kent	S. E. & C.	Beckenham and Shortlands.
.	.	.	.	.	.	.	Shortridge Farm Siding ...	Northumb	N. E.	Alnmouth. Warkworth.
.	P	.	.	.	.	.	Shotley Bridge	Durham ...	N. E.	Newcastle and Blackhill.
.	.	.	.	.	.	.	Shotley Bridge Siding	Durham ...	N. E.	Blackhill. Ebchester.
G	P	F	L	H	C	.	Shottle	Derby	Mid.	Duffield and Wirksworth.
.	.	.	.	.	.	.	Shotton (W. M. & C. Q.)	Flint	W. M. & C. Q.—G. C.	See Connahs Quay and Shotton.
.	.	.	.	.	.	.	Shotton Brick Works	Flint	W.M. & C. Q.	Same as Rowley's Sid. (Connahs Quay)
.	.	.	.	.	.	.	Shotton Brick Works and Manure Siding	Durham ...	N. E.	Haswell.
.	P	.	.	.	.	.	Shotton Bridge	Durham ...	N. E.	Haswell and Thornley.
.	.	.	.	.	.	.	Shotton Colliery & Brick Wks	Durham ...	N. E.	Haswell.
G	P	F	L	H	C	1 10	Shotts	Lanark ...	Cal.	Holytown and Edinburgh.
G	.	.	.	.	.	.			N. B.	West Craigs and Morningside.
.	.	.	.	.	.	.	Baton Colliery	Lanark ...	N. B.	Branch—West Craigs and Shotts.
.	.	.	.	.	.	.	Batonrigg Colliery	Lanark ...	N. B.	Branch—West Craigs and Shotts.
.	.	.	.	.	.	.	Calderhead Foundry	Lanark ...	Cal.	Shotts.
.	.	.	.	.	.	.	Calderhead, Nos. 1 & 3 Cols.	Lanark ...	N. B.	West Craigs and Shotts.
.	.	.	.	.	.	.	Currieside Colliery (Hawk-woodburn)	Lanark ...	Cal.	Hartwood and Shotts.
.	.	.	.	.	.	.	Fortisset Colliery	Lanark ...	N. B.	West Craigs and Shotts.
G	.	.	.	.	.	.	Fortisset Mains Siding	Lanark ...	N. B.	West Craigs and Shotts.
.	.	.	.	.	.	.	Fortrigg Colliery	Lanark ...	N. B.	Branch—West Craigs and Shotts.
.	.	.	.	.	.	.	Hartwoodhill Colliery	Lanark ...	N. B.	Branch—West Craigs and Shotts.
.	.	.	.	.	.	.	Hartwoodhill Siding	Lanark ...	N. B.	West Craigs and Shotts.
.	.	.	.	.	.	.	Hassockrig Colliery	Lanark ...	N. B.	Branch—West Craigs and Shotts.
.	.	.	.	.	.	.	Hillhouserigg Colliery	Lanark ...	N. B.	Branch—West Craigs and Shotts.
.	.	.	.	.	.	.	Kepplehill Colliery	Lanark ...	N. B.	Shotts and Blackhall Junction.
.	.	.	.	.	.	.	Rimmon Colliery	Lanark ...	Cal.	Shotts.
.	.	.	.	.	.	.	Shotts Iron Works	Lanark ...	Cal.—N. B.	Near Shotts.
.	.	.	.	.	.	.	Shotts Weighs	Lanark ...	N. B.	Shotts.
.	.	.	.	.	.	.	Stane Colliery	Lanark ...	N. B.	Shotts and Blackhall Junction.
G	.	.	.	.	.	1 10	Stane Siding	Lanark ...	N. B.	Shotts and Blackhall Junction.
.	.	.	.	.	.	.	Torbothy Siding	Lanark ...	N. B.	Shotts and Blackhall Junction.
							SHREWSBURY—			
G	.	F	L	.	.	8 0	(Station)	Salop	L. & N. W.	Branch near General Station.
G	P	.	.	.	.	.	Abbey Foregate	Salop	S&W'tnJt(GW&L&NW)	General Station and Wellington.
.	.	.	.	.	.	.	Building Material Supply Stores Siding	Salop	L. & N. W.	Shrewsbury and Hadnall.
G	.	F	L	.	.	8 0	Castle Foregate	Salop	G. W.	North End of General Station.
G	.	.	.	.	.	5 0	Coleham	Salop	S & H Jt (G W & L & N W)	General Station and Craven Arms.
G	.	.	.	.	.	8 0	Coton Hill	Salop	G. W.	General Station and Leaton.
.	.	.	.	.	.	.	Crewe Line Junction	Salop	L. & N. W.—S. & H. Jt.	General Station and Whitchurch.
.	P	F	.	H	C	.	General	Salop	S & H Jt (G W & L & N W)	Craven Arms and Crewe Line Junc.

STATION ACCOMMODATION.						CRANE POWER.	STATIONS, &c.	COUNTY.	COMPANY.	POSITION.
						Tons Cwts.	SHREWSBURY—continued.			
.	.	.	.	.	.		Greenfield's Siding............	Salop	G. W.	Coton Hill.
.	.	.	.	.	.		Jones & Son's Shropshire Maltings (L. & N. W.)...	Salop	L. & N. W.—G. W..........	Shrewsbury and Hadnall.
.	.	.	.	.	.		Midland Carriage & Wagon Co.'s Siding (G. W.)......	Salop	G. W.—L. & N. W.	Near Severn Valley Junction.
G	.	.	.	.	.	10　0	New Yard, Castle Foregate	Salop	L. & N. W.	General Station and Whitchurch.
.	.	.	.	.	.		Severn Valley Junction ...	Salop	G. W.—S. & H. Jt.	Berrington and Coleham.
.	.	.	.	.	.		Treasures Siding	Salop	L. & N. W.	Shrewsbury and Hadnall.
.	.	.	.	.	.		Wellington Line Junction	Salop	S. & H. Jt.—S. & W'tn Jt.	General Station and Wellington.
.	.	.	.	.	.		Welshpool Line Junction...	Salop	S. & H. Jt.—S. & W'pl Jt.	General Station and Welshpool.
G	P	F	L	H	C	7　0	Shrivenham	Berks	G. W.	Swindon and Didcot.
.	.	.	.	.	.		Shropshire Iron Co.'s Siding	Salop	L. & N. W.	Trench.
.	.	.	.	.	.		Shropshire Maltings (L & N W)	Salop	L. & N. W.—G. W.	Same as Jones & Sons' Sid. (Shrewsbury).
.	.	.	.	.	.		Shropshire Union Co.'s Siding, connecting with Ship Canal	Cheshire...	B'head Jt. (G W & L N W)	Ellesmere Port.
.	.	.	.	.	.		Shrubbery Works	Staffs	G. W.	See Corrugated Iron Co. (Wolverhampton).
.	.	.	.	.	.		Shrub Hill	Worcester	G. W.—Mid.	See Worcester.
G	P	F	L	H	C		Shrubhill Siding (Edinburgh and District Tramway Co.)	Edinboro'	N. B.	Edinburgh, Leith Walk.
.	.	.	.	.	.		Shustoke	Warwick..	Mid.	Nuneaton and Whitacre.
.	.	.	.	.	.		Shuttle Mill Siding	Fife	N. B.	Same as Gateside Saw Mill (Gateside).
.	.	.	.	.	.		Shyflat Manure Siding........	Lanark ...	N. B.	Greengairs.
G	P	.	L	H	C		Sible Hedingham	Essex	C. V. & H.	Same as Castle Hedingham.
G	P	.	.	.	.		Sibsey	Lincoln ...	G. N.	Boston and Louth.
.	.	.	.	.	.		Sidcup	Kent	S. E. & C.	Hither Green and Dartford.
.	.	.	.	.	.		Siddall's Stone Siding	Lancs	L. & Y.	Stacksteads.
.	.	.	.	.	.		Siddick Junction	Cumb'land	C. & W. Jn.—L. & N. W.	Siddick Junction Station and Workington, Central.
.	P	.	.	.	.		Siddick Jn. Sta. (L. & N. W.)	Cumb'land	L. & N. W.—C. & W. Jn.	Maryport and Workington.
.	.	.	.	.	.		Siddick Sand Siding	Cumb'land	C. & W. Jn.	Workington.
.	.	.	.	.	.		Sideway Siding (Stafford Coal and Iron Co.) (N. S.)...	Staffs	N. S.—L. & N. W.	Trentham.
G	P	.	.	.	.		Sidlesham	Sussex ...	Selsey	Chichester and Selsey.
G	P	.	.	.	.	1　10	Sidley	Sussex ...	S. E. & C.	Crowhurst and Bexhill-on-Sea.
G	P	F	L	H	C	2　0	Sidmouth	Devon......	L. & S.W.	Branch from Sidmouth Junction.
G	P	F	L	H	C	5　0	Sidmouth Junction Station...	Devon......	L. & S.W.	Yeovil Junction and Exeter.
.	P	.	.	.	.		Sidney Parade	Dublin ...	D. W. & W.	Kingstown and Dublin, Westland Row.
.	.	.	.	.	.		Siemens, Bros. & Co.'s Siding	Staffs	L. & N. W.	Stafford.
G	P	.	L	H	.		Sigglesthorne	Yorks	N. E.	Hull and Hornsea.
.	.	.	.	.	.		Sighthill (N. B.)..................	Lanark ...	{ N. B.	} See Glasgow.
									{ N B, G N, & N E (E. Coast)	
.	.	.	.	.	.		Sighthill East Junction	Lanark ...	Cal.—N. B.	Glasgow.
.	.	.	.	.	.		Sighthill Junction	Lanark ...	N. B.	Glasgow.
.	.	.	.	.	.		Silcock, R., & Son's Siding...	Lancs	L. & Y.	Liverpool, Great Howard Street.
G	P	.	L	.	.		Sileby	Leicester..	Mid.	Leicester and Loughboro'.
.	.	.	.	.	.		Wright, W. T., & Co.—			
.	.	.	.	.	.		Albion Siding...............	Leicester..	Mid.	Sileby.
.	.	.	.	.	.		Barrow End Brick Yard	Leicester..	Mid.	Sileby.
.	.	.	.	.	.		Barrow Road Siding	Leicester..	Mid.	Sileby.
G	P	F	L	H	C	3　0	Silecroft	Cumb'land	Furness	Millom and Ravenglass.
.	.	.	.	.	.		Whicham Siding	Cumb'land	Furness	Near Silecroft Station.
.	.	.	.	.	.		Silica Co.'s Low Yard Siding	Yorks	G. C.	Oughty Bridge.
.	.	.	.	.	.		Silica Co.'s Top Yard Siding	Yorks	G. C.	Oughty Bridge.
G	P	F	L	H	C		Silkstone	Yorks	G. C.	Penistone and Barnsley.
.	.	.	.	.	.		Hall Royd (Silkstone) Col.	Yorks	G. C.	Silkstone.
.	.	.	.	.	.		Silkstone Coke Ovens	Yorks	G. C.	Silkstone.
.	.	.	.	.	.		Silkstone Fall Colliery	Yorks	G. C.	Silkstone.
.	.	.	.	.	.		West Silkstone Colliery	Yorks	G. C.	Silkstone.
.	.	.	.	.	.		Silkstone Branch	Yorks	L. & Y.	Darton.
.	.	.	.	.	.		Silkstone Coal Co.'s Siding ...	Lancs	L. & N. W.	See Tunnel End Siding (Stalybridge)
.	.	.	.	.	.		Silksworth Colliery and Depôt	Durham ...	N. E.	Ryhope.
G	P	F	L	H	C	25　0	Silloth	Cumb'land	N. B.	Branch from Carlisle.
.	.	.	.	.	.		Armstrong, Whitworth & Co.'s Battery Siding...	Cumb'land	N. B.	Branch from Silloth.
.	.	.	.	.	.		Border Counties Chemical Works (Maxwell & Co.)	Cumb'land	N. B.	Near Silloth Station.
.	.	.	.	.	.		Carr & Co.'s Siding	Cumb'land	N. B.	Silloth.

EXPLANATION—**G** *Goods Station.*　　**P** *Passenger and Parcel Station.*　　**P*** *Passenger, but not Parcel or Miscellaneous Traffic.*
F *Furniture Vans, Carriages, Portable Engines, and Machines on Wheels.*　　**L** *Live Stock.*
H *Horse Boxes and Prize Cattle Vans.*　　**C** *Carriages by Passenger Train.*

STATION ACCOMMODATION.						CRANE POWER.		STATIONS, &c.	COUNTY.	COMPANY.	POSITION.
						Tons	Cwts.	SILLOTH—continued.			
G	.	.	.	.	.	25	0	Silloth Dock	Cumb'land	N. B.	Silloth.
.	.	.	.	.	.	.	.	Solway Chemical Works ...	Cumb'land	N. B.	Near Silloth Station.
.	.	.	.	.	.	.	.	Sill's, W., Lime Works........	Notts	Mid.	Mansfield Woodhouse.
.	.	.	.	.	.	.	.	Silsden	Yorks	Mid.	See Steeton and Silsden.
.	.	.	.	.	.	.	.	Silverburn Colliery	Lanark	Cal.	Same as Cleland, Townhead.
.	.	.	.	.	.	.	.	Silverburn Siding	Fife	N. B.	Leven.
G	P	F	L	H	C	3	0	Silverdale	Lancs	Furness	Carnforth and Grange.
.	.	.	.	.	.	.	.	Northern Quarries Lime Works	Lancs	Furness	Silverdale.
.	.	.	.	.	.	.	.	Trowbarrow Lime Works ..	Lancs	Furness	Silverdale and Arnside.
G	P	F	L	H	C	10	0	Silverdale	Staffs	N. S.	Stoke and Market Drayton.
.	.	.	.	.	.	.	.	Knutton Manor Mining Co.'s Siding	Staffs	N. S.	Silverdale.
.	.	.	.	.	.	.	.	Rosemary Hill Colliery......	Staffs	N. S.	Silverdale.
.	.	.	.	.	.	.	.	Silverdale Co.'s Works......	Staffs	N. S.	Silverdale.
.	.	.	.	.	.	.	.	Silverdale Tileries Co.'s Sid.	Staffs	N. S.	Silverdale.
.	.	.	.	.	.	.	.	Silverhill Colliery	Notts	Mid.	See Stanton Iron Wks. Co. (Teversall).
.	.	.	.	.	.	.	.	Silverhill Colliery (G. N.)	Notts	G. N.—G.C.—L. D. & E.C	Teversall.
.	.	.	.	.	.	.	.	Silvermuir Junction ...~....	Lanark	Cal.	Carstairs and Lanark.
.	.	.	.	.	.	.	.	Silvermuir Junction, South	Lanark	Cal.	Carstairs and Lanark.
.	.	.	.	.	.	.	.	Silvermuir Siding	Lanark	Cal.	Cleghorn.
.	P	.	.	.	.	.	.	Silver Street (for Upper Edmonton)	Middlesex	G. E.	Seven Sisters and Enfield Town.
G	P	.	.	.	.	4	0	Silverton	Devon	G. W.	Exeter and Wellington.
.	.	.	.	.	.	.	.	Silverton Colliery	Lanark	Cal.	Hamilton, Central.
.	.	.	.	.	.	.	.	Silvertown	Essex	G. E.	See London.
.	.	.	.	.	.	.	.	Silvertown Oil Storage Co.'s Siding (G. E.)............... }	Essex	G. E.—L. & N. W.—Mid.	London, Silvertown.
.	.	.	.	.	.	.	.	Silverwood Colliery	Yorks	{ G. C.	See Dalton Main Collieries (Parkgate and Aldwarke).
.	.	.	.	.	.	.	.			{ Mid.	See Dalton Main Collieries (Parkgate and Rawmarsh).
.	.	.	.	.	.	.	.	Silvester & Co.'s Foundry .	Staffs	N. S.	Pool Dam.
.	.	.	.	.	.	.	.	Silvester's Siding	Herts	Mid.	Same as Park Str. Sid. (St. Albans).
.	.	.	.	.	.	.	.	Simmons' Siding...............	Essex	G. E.	Great Bentley.
.	.	.	.	.	.	.	.	Simon Carves Co.'s Siding ...	Yorks	E. & W. Y. Union	Robin Hood.
.	.	.	.	.	.	.	.	Simonds & Son's Siding	Lincoln	G. N.	Boston.
.	.	.	.	.	.	.	.	Simons & Co.'s Siding	Renfrew	Cal.—G. & S. W.	Renfrew.
G	P	.	.	.	.	5	0	Simonstone	Lancs	L. & Y.	Loop—Blackburn and Rose Grove.
.	.	.	.	.	.	.	.	Simonswood Siding	Lancs	L. & Y.	Kirkby.
.	.	.	.	.	.	.	.	Simon Wood Colliery	Yorks	G. C.	Same as Elsecar High Pit (Elsecar).
.	.	.	.	.	.	.	.	Simpasture Junction...........	Durham	N. E.	Darlington and Shildon.
.	.	.	.	.	.	.	.	Simpson & Co.'s Siding	Durham	N. E.	Darlington, Bank Top.
.	.	.	.	.	.	.	.	Simpson & Co.'s Siding	Notts	G. N.	See Lowfield Sidings (Newark).
.	.	.	.	.	.	.	.	Simpson Bros.' Mill	Derby	N. S.	Same as Mayfield Siding (Clifton).
.	.	.	.	.	.	.	.	Simpson's Brick Works	Northumb	N. E.	Choppington.
.	.	.	.	.	.	.	.	Simpson's Siding	Lancs	L. & Y.	Same as Aspden Colliery (Church).
.	.	.	.	.	.	.	.	Sims & Son's Siding	Derby	Mid.	Whatstandwell.
.	.	.	.	.	.	.	.	Sims', A., Siding	Derby	Mid.	Whatstandwell.
.	.	.	.	.	.	.	.	Sincil Bank Junction	Lincoln	G. N.—G. N. & G. E. Jt.	Lincoln.
.	.	.	.	.	.	.	.	Sinclair's Cooperage Siding...	Stirling	N. B.	Falkirk, Camelon.
.	.	.	.	.	.	.	.	Sinclair's Saw Mills	Perth	Cal.	Perth, North.
.	.	.	.	.	.	.	.	Sinclair's Siding	Edinboro'	N. B.	Leith, Bonnington.
.	.	.	.	.	.	.	.	Sinclairtown	Fife	N. B.	See Kirkcaldy.
G	P	.	L	H	C	.	.	Sinderby	Yorks	N. E.	Ripon and Northallerton.
.	.	.	.	.	.	.	.	Pickhill Siding	Yorks	N. E.	Sinderby.
.	.	.	.	.	.	.	.	Singer Manufacturing Co.'s Siding	Dumbartn	N. B.	Kilbowie.
G	P	.	.	.	.	1	0	Singleton	Lancs	P. & W. Jt. (L&Y&L&NW)	Fleetwood and Preston.
G	P	F	L	H	C	4	0	Singleton	Sussex	L. B. & S. C.	Midhurst and Chichester.
G	P	.	L	H	.	.	.	Sinnington	Yorks	N. E.	Kirby Moorside and Pickering.
G	P	.	.	.	.	3	0	Sion Mills	Tyrone	G. N. (I.)	Omagh and Strabane.
.	.	.	.	.	.	.	.	Sir Berkeley Sheffield's Sid.	Lincoln	G. C.	Frodingham and Scunthorpe.
G	P	.	.	H	.	1	0	Sirhowy	Mon	L. & N. W.	Nantybwch and Tredegar Jn. Sta.
.	.	.	.	.	.	.	.	Ebbw Vale Steel, Iron & Coal Co.'s Siding	Mon	L. & N. W.	Sirhowy and Tredegar.
.	.	.	.	.	.	.	.	Graham's Navigation Col.	Mon	L. & N. W.	Sirhowy and Tredegar.
.	.	.	.	.	.	.	.	Phillips & Williams' Siding	Mon	L. & N. W.	Sirhowy and Tredegar.
.	.	.	.	.	.	.	.	Tredegar Iron & Coal Co.'s Sirhowy Works	Mon	L. & N. W.	Sirhowy and Tredegar.
.	.	.	.	.	.	.	.	Sirhowy Junc. (Gellygroes)...	Mon	G. W.—L. & N. W.	Tredegar Junction.

EXPLANATION—G *Goods Station.*   P *Passenger and Parcel Station.*   P* *Passenger, but not Parcel or Miscellaneous Traffic.*
F *Furniture Vans, Carriages, Portable Engines, and Machines on Wheels.*   L *Live Stock.*
H *Horse Boxes and Prize Cattle Vans.*   C *Carriages by Passenger Train.*

STATION ACCOMMODATION.						CRANE POWER.	STATIONS, &c.	COUNTY.	COMPANY.	POSITION.
						Tons Cwts.				
.	.	.	.	.	.	.	Sirhowy Valley Colliery	Mon	L. & N. W.	Same as Burnyeat, Brown & Co.'s (Nine Mile Point).
.	.	.	.	.	.	.	Sirhowy Works	Mon	L. & N. W	See Tredegar Iron & Coal Co. (Sirhowy).
.	.	.	.	.	.	.	Sir John Jackson's Siding ...	Northumb	N. E.	Heddon-on-the-Wall.
.	.	.	.	.	.	.	Sir John Pit	Cumb'land	WC&EJt.(Fur. & LNW)	See Lindow's (Moor Row).
.	.	.	.	.	.	.	Sir Thomas Tacon's Siding...	Suffolk	G. E.	Eye.
.	P	.	.	.	.	.	Sir Watkin Wynn (private)..	Merioneth	G. W.	Bala and Llanuwchllyn.
.	.	.	.	.	.	.	Sir William Arrol's New Sid.	Lanark	Cal.	Glasgow, Bridgeton.
.	.	.	.	.	.	.	Sir William Marling's Siding	Glo'ster ..	Mid.	Ryeford.
.	.	.	.	.	.	.	Sisters Pit (Lewis Graigola Colliery Co.) (Mid.)	Glamorg'n	Mid.—G.W.—L. & N.W.	{ Glais. { Six Pit Junction.
.	.	.	.	.	.	.	Sitehill Colliery	Lanark ...	Cal.	Same as Bankend Colliery & Lime Works (Coalburn).
G	P	F	L	H	C	7 0	Sittingbourne and Milton ...	Kent	S. E. & C.	Chatham and Faversham.
.	.	.	.	.	.	.	Sittingbourne, East Junction	Kent	S. E. & C.	Newington and Sittingbourne.
.	.	.	.	.	.	.	Sittingbourne, Middle Junc.	Kent	S. E. & C.	Sittingbourne and Queenborough.
.	.	.	.	.	.	.	Sittingbourne, West Junc....	Kent	S. E. & C.	Newington and Sittingbourne.
G	P	F	L	H	C	1 0	Six Mile Bottom	Cambs.....	G. E.	Cambridge and Newmarket.
G	P	.	L	H	.	.	Sixmilebridge (G. S. & W.)...	Clare	{ G. S. & W. { M. G. W.	Limerick and Ennis. Over G.S. & W. from Athenry.
G	P	.	L	.	.	1 10	Sixmilecross	Tyrone ...	G. N. (I.)	Dungannon and Omagh.
G	.	.	.	.	.	5 0	Six Pit Junction	Glamorg'n	G. W.—Mid.	Upper Bank and Llansamlet.
.	.	.	.	.	.	.	Aber Wagon Co's Sid.(Mid.)	Glamorg'n	Mid.—G.W.—L. & N.W.	Six Pit Junction and Llansamlet.
.	.	.	.	.	.	.	Birchgrove Colliery Co.'s Siding (Mid.)	Glamorg'n	Mid.—G. W.—L. & N.W.	Llansamlet and Glais.
.	.	.	.	.	.	.	Chilian Chemical Co.'s Siding (Mid.)	Glamorg'n	Mid.—G. W.—L. & N.W.	Six Pit Junction and Llansamlet.
.	.	.	.	.	.	.	Dillwyn & Co.'s Sid. (Mid.)	Glamorg'n	Mid.—G.W.—L. & N. W.	Near Six Pit Junction.
.	.	.	.	.	.	.	Sister's Pit (Lewis Graigola Colliery Co.) (Mid.)	Glamorg'n	Mid.—G.W.—L. & N. W.	Glais and Llansamlet.
.	.	.	.	.	.	.	Velinfran Colliery Co.'s Siding (Richards, J. J., & Co.'s Brick Works) (Mid)	Glamorg'n	Mid.—G. W.—L. & N.W.	Llansamlet and Glais.
.	.	.	.	.	.	.	Sizewell Siding	Suffolk ...	G. E.	See Leiston.
G	P	F	L	H	C	.	Skares	Ayr	G. & S.W.	Annbank & Cumnock.
.	.	.	.	.	.	.	Dykes Pit...................	Ayr	G. & S.W.	Dykes Branch.
.	.	.	.	.	.	.	Hindsward Colliery	Ayr	G. & S.W.	Dykes Branch.
.	.	.	.	.	.	.	Knockterra Pit	Ayr	G. & S.W.	Skares and Cumnock.
.	.	.	.	.	.	.	Skares Quarry...............	Ayr	G. & S.W.	Dykes Branch.
.	.	.	.	.	.	.	Skares Siding	Ayr	G. & S.W.	Dykes Branch.
.	.	.	.	.	.	.	Whitehill Pit	Ayr	G. & S.W.	Dykes Branch.
.	.	.	.	.	.	.	Skaterigg Siding (N. B.)	Dumbartn	N. B.—Cal.	Glasgow, Great Western Road.
.	P	.	.	.	.	.	Skeaf	Cork	T. & C.	Ballinascarthy and Courtmacsherry.
G	P	F	L	H	C	.	Skegby (for Stanton Hill) ...	Notts	G. N.	Sutton-in-Ashfield and Shirebrook.
.	.	.	.	.	.	.	Skegby Junction	Notts	Mid.	Whiteboro'.
G	P	F	L	H	C	5 0	Skegness	Lincoln ...	G. N.	Branch—Boston and Louth.
G	P	.	.	.	.	.	Skegness Gas Co.'s Siding...	Lincoln ...	G. N.	Skegness.
.	.	.	.	.	.	.	Skelbo	Sutherl'nd	High. (Dornoch)............	The Mound and Dornoch.
.	.	.	.	.	.	.	Skelbrook Siding	Yorks ...	H. & B.	Same as Neville's (Pickburn & Brodsworth).
G	P	F	L	H	C	3 0	Skellingthorpe	Lincoln ...	L. D. & E. C.	Tuxford and Lincoln.
.	.	.	.	.	.	.	Skellyton Colliery	Lanark ...	Cal.	Larkhall.
G	P	.	.	.	.	1 10	Skelmanthorpe	Yorks ...	L. & Y.	Branch—Shepley and Denby Dale.
.	.	.	.	.	.	.	Emley Moor Siding	Yorks ...	L. & Y.	Skelmanthorpe.
G	P	.	L	H	.	1 10	Skelmersdale	Lancs ...	L. & Y.	Ormskirk and Rainford.
.	.	.	.	.	.	.	Carrington, Shaw & Co.'s Sid.	Lancs ...	L. & Y.	Skelmersdale.
.	.	.	.	.	.	.	Chapel House Col. (L. & Y.)	Lancs ...	L. & Y.—L. & N. W.	Skelmersdale.
.	.	.	.	.	.	.	L. & Y. Railway Co.'s Westhead Siding	Lancs ...	L. & Y.	Skelmersdale.
.	.	.	.	.	.	.	Mossfield Colliery (L. & Y.)	Lancs ...	L. & Y.—L. & N. W.	Skelmersdale.
.	.	.	.	.	.	.	Moss Pit Siding (Foster, Williams & Co.) (L. & Y.)	Lancs ...	L. & Y.—L. & N. W.	Skelmersdale and Rainford Junc.
.	.	.	.	.	.	.	Moss Side Siding	Lancs ...	L. & Y.	Skelmersdale.
.	.	.	.	.	.	.	Park Colliery	Lancs ...	L. & Y.	Skelmersdale.
.	.	.	.	.	.	.	White Moss Colliery (L&Y)	Lancs ...	L. & Y.—L. & N. W.	Near Skelmersdale.
.	.	.	.	.	.	.	Skelton Bridge Siding	Yorks ...	N. E.	See Saltmarshe.
.	.	.	.	.	.	.	Skelton Junction	Cheshire..	C. L. C.(G C, G N, & Mid.)	Baguley and Glazebrook.
.	.	.	.	.	.	.	Skelton Mines................	Yorks ...	N. E.	Slapewath.
.	.	.	.	.	.	.	Skelton, North Junction	Cheshire..	C. L. C.—G. C.	Baguley and Timperley.
.	.	.	.	.	.	.	Skelton Park Pit Depôt & Sid.	Yorks ...	N. E.	Slapewath.
.	.	.	.	.	.	.	Skerne Iron Works	Durham ..	N. E.	Darlington, Bank Top.

EXPLANATION—G *Goods Station.*   P *Passenger and Parcel Station.*   P* *Passenger, but not Parcel or Miscellaneous Traffic.*
F *Furniture Vans, Carriages, Portable Engines, and Machines on Wheels.*   L *Live Stock.*
H *Horse Boxes and Prize Cattle Vans.*   C *Carriages by Passenger Train.*

STATION ACCOMMODATION.						CRANE POWER.	STATIONS, &c.	COUNTY.	COMPANY.	POSITION.
						Tons Cwts	Skerne Iron Works—*continued.*			
							Pease Tubular Syndicate Construction Co.'s Siding	Durham	N. E.	Skerne Iron Works.
							Standard Wire Co.'s Siding	Durham	N. E.	Skerne Iron Works.
							Wake's, J. F., Siding	Durham	N. E.	Skerne Iron Works.
G	P	F	L	H	C		Skerries	Dublin	G. N. (I.)	Dublin and Drogheda.
							Skerrington, Nos. 19 and 20	Ayr	G. & S.W.	Hurlford.
	P						Sketty Road	Glamorg'n	Swan. & Mum.	Swansea and Mumbles Road.
							Skew Bridge	Lancs	N.U.Jt.(L.&NW.&L.&Y)	Farington and Preston.
							Skey & Co.'s Pipe Works	Warwick	Mid.	Wilnecote.
G	P	F	L	H	C	4 0 }	Skibbereen	Cork	{ C. B. & S. C.	Drimoleague and Baltimore.
G	P		L			}			{ S. & S.	Adjoining C. B. & S. C. Station.
							Skiers Spring Brick Works (Smith's)	Yorks	Mid.	Wentworth and Hoyland Common.
							Skiers Spring Siding	Yorks	G. C.	Same as Smith's Brick Wks.(Elsecar).
							Skinner's Siding	Berks	G. W.	Newbury.
	P						Skinningrove	Yorks	N. E.	Middlesbro' and Whitby.
							Skinningrove Depôts	Yorks	N. E.	Loftus.
							Skinningrove Iron Works	Yorks	N. E.	Loftus.
G	P	F	L	H	C	10 0 }	Skipton (Mid.)	Yorks	{ Mid.	Leeds and Settle.
	P			H	C	}			{ L. & Y.	Over Mid. from Colne.
							Skipton Exchange Sidings (Mid.)	Yorks	Mid.—L. & Y.	Skipton Station and Junction.
							Skipton Rock Co.'s Quarry	Yorks	Mid.	Embsay.
							Skipworth & Jones' Siding	Lancs	Trafford Park Estate	Manchester.
G	P	F	L	H	C		Skirlaugh	Yorks	N. E.	Hull and Hornsea.
							Slacks Crossing Siding	Derby	S. & M. Jt. (G. C. & Mid.)	Hayfield.
	P						Slades Green	Kent	S. E. & C.	Woolwich and Dartford.
G	P		L	H			Slaggyford	Northumb	N. E.	Haltwhistle and Alston.
							Slag Reduction Co.—			
							Siding	Derby	Mid.	Dronfield.
							Siding	Yorks	Mid.	Masboro' and Rotherham.
							Siding (G. C.)	Yorks	G. C.—G. N.	Rotherham and Masboro'.
G	P	F	L	H	C	10 0	Slaithwaite	Yorks	L. & N. W.	Huddersfield and Stalybridge.
G	P	F	L	H	C	1 10	Slamannan	Stirling	N. B.	Airdrie, Commonhead and Blackston.
G							Arnloss Siding	Stirling	N. B.	Slamannan and Avonbridge.
							Balquhatson Colliery	Stirling	N. B.	Slamannan and Avonbridge.
							Barnsmuir Colliery	Stirling	N. B.	Bch.—Longriggend & Slamannan.
							Drumclair Colliery	Stirling	N. B.	Slamannan and Avonbridge.
							East Balquhatson Colliery	Stirling	N. B.	Slamannan and Avonbridge.
							Limerigg Collieries	Stirling	N. B.	Bch.—Longriggend & Slamannan.
							Southfield Colliery	Stirling	N. B.	Longriggend and Slamannan.
							Southfield Siding	Stirling	N. B.	Longriggend and Slamannan.
							Strathavon Colliery	Stirling	N. B.	Bch.—Slamannan & Avonbridge.
G							Slapewath	Yorks	N. E.	Guisboro' and Loftus.
							Aysdalegate Mines	Yorks	N. E.	Slapewath.
							Skelton Mines	Yorks	N. E.	Slapewath.
							Skelton Park Pit Depôt and Siding	Yorks	N. E.	Slapewath.
							Slapewath Depôt & Siding	Yorks	N. E.	Slapewath.
							Slapewath Mines	Yorks	N. E.	Slapewath.
							Spa Mines	Yorks	N. E.	Slapewath.
							Spawood Mines	Yorks	N. E.	Slapewath.
G	P					1 10	Slateford	Edinboro'	Cal.	Carstairs and Edinburgh.
							Hailes Quarry	Edinboro'	Cal.	Kingsknowe and Slateford.
G							Kates Mill Siding	Edinboro'	Cal.	Colinton and Slateford.
							Kingsknowe Stone Depôt	Edinboro'	Cal.	Slateford and Curriehill.
							Slateford Stone Siding	Edinboro'	Cal.	Slateford.
							Slater, Rodger & Co.'s Bonded Store	Lanark	Cal.	Glasgow, General Terminus.
							Slater's Siding	Northumb	N. E.	Whittingham.
							Slater's Stone Quarry	Derby	Mid.	Coxbench.
							Slaughterhouse Siding	Lanark	N. B.	Coatbridge, Whifflet.
							Slaughter Siding (High Meadow Siding)	Hereford	G. W.	Symonds Yat.
G	P	F	L	H	C	5 0	Sleaford (G. N.)	Lincoln	{ G. N.	Grantham and Boston.
									{ G. E.	Over G. N. from Sleaford Junction.
							Bass & Co.'s Siding	Lincoln	G. N.	Sleaford.
							Gibson's Siding	Lincoln	G. N.	Sleaford and Rauceby.
							Kirk, Knight & Co.'s Sid.	Lincoln	G. N.	Sleaford and Rauceby.
							Sleaford, East Junction	Lincoln	G. N.—G. N. & G. E. Jt.	Sleaford and Helpringham.
							Sleaford, West Junction	Lincoln	G. N.—G. N. & G. E. Jt.	Sleaford and Ruskington.

EXPLANATION—G *Goods Station.*   P *Passenger and Parcel Station.*   P* *Passenger, but not Parcel or Miscellaneous Traffic.*
F *Furniture Vans, Carriages, Portable Engines, and Machines on Wheels.*   L *Live Stock.*
H *Horse Boxes and Prize Cattle Vans.*   C *Carriages by Passenger Train.*

G	P	F	L	H	C	Tons	Cwts	STATIONS, &c.	COUNTY.	COMPANY.	POSITION.
.	.	.	.	.	.			Sleaford & District Brick & Tile Siding	Lincoln	G. N.	Same as Burton Brick Sid (Aswarby).
G	P	F	L	H	C	3	0	Sledmere & Fimber	Yorks	N. E.	Malton and Driffield.
.	.	.	.	.	.			Slee & Co.'s Foundry	Lancs	L. & N. W.	Earlestown.
G	P	.	L	H	.			Sleights	Yorks	N. E.	Malton and Whitby.
.	.	.	.	.	.			Dorsley Bank Siding	Yorks	N. E.	Sleights and Grosmont.
.	.	.	.	.	.			Gantree Siding	Yorks	N. E.	Sleights and Grosmont.
.	.	.	.	.	.			Newbiggin Siding	Yorks	N. E.	Sleights and Grosmont.
.	.	.	.	.	.			Woodlands Sid. (Harrison's)	Yorks	N. E.	Sleights and Grosmont.
.	.	.	.	.	.			Sleight's Colliery	Notts	Mid.	Pinxton.
.	P	.	.	H	C			Sligo (M. G. W.)	Sligo	M. G. W. / G. S. & W. / S. L. & N. C.	Terminus. / Over M. G. W. from Collooney. / Over M. G. W. from Carrignagat Jn.
G	.	F	L	.	.	5	0	Sligo Quay (M. G. W.)	Sligo	M. G. W. / G. S. & W. / S. L. & N. C.	Branch from Sligo. / Over M. G. W. from Collooney. / Over M. G.W. from Carrignagat Jn.
G	P	F	L	H	C	5	0	Slinfold	Sussex	L. B. & S. C.	Guildford and Horsham.
.	.	.	.	.	.			Anderson's Siding	Sussex	L. B. & S. C.	Slinfold and Horsham.
.	.	.	.	.	.			Child & Son's Siding	Sussex	L. B. & S. C.	Slinfold.
G	P	F	L	H	C	1	0	Sling Branch	Glo'ster	S. & Wye Jt. (G.W. & Mid.)	Milkwall.
G	P	F	L	H	C	1	0	Slingsby	Yorks	N. E.	Malton and Thirsk.
.	.	.	.	.	.			Slip Siding	Cornwall	G. W.	Drinnick Mill.
.	.	.	.	.	.			Sloan & Son's Siding	Edinboro'	N. B.	Edinburgh, Leith Walk.
.	.	.	.	.	.			Sloane Square (Met. Dist.)	Middlesex	Met. Dist.—L. & N. W.	See London.
.	.	.	.	.	.			Slotburn Brick Works	Durham	N. E.	Witton-le-Wear.
G	P	F	L	H	C	8	0	Slough	Bucks	G. W.	Paddington and Reading.
.	.	.	.	.	.			Consolidated Engineering Works	Bucks	G. W.	Slough.
.	.	.	.	.	.			Gas Works	Bucks	G. W.	Slough.
.	.	.	.	.	.			Gibson's Flour Mills	Bucks	G. W.	Slough.
.	.	.	.	.	.			Nash's Brick Works Sid.	Bucks	G. W.	Slough.
.	.	.	.	.	.			Smailes Burn Mine	Durham	N. E.	Parkhead.
.	.	.	.	.	.			Smallbrook Junction	I. of W	I. of W.—I. of W. Cent.	Ryde and Newport.
.	.	.	.	.	.			Smalldale Siding	Derby	Mid.	Peak Forest.
G	P	.	L	.	.			Smallford (for Colney Heath)	Herts	G. N.	Hatfield and St. Albans.
.	.	.	.	.	.			Small Heath and Sparkbrook	Warwick	G. W.	See Birmingham.
.	.	.	.	.	.			Small Heath Mileage Depôt	Warwick	G. W.	See Birmingham.
.	.	.	.	.	.			Smallshaw's Arscott Colliery	Salop	S. & W'pl Jt. (G W & L N W)	Hanwood.
.	.	.	.	.	.			Smallthorne	Staffs	N. S.	See Ford Green and Smallthorne.
G	P	.	L	.	.			Smardale	W'morlnd	N. E.	Tebay and Kirkby Stephen.
								Smart's—			
.	.	.	.	.	.			Brickfield Siding	Herts	G. N.	Hatfield.
.	.	.	.	.	.			Twentieth Mile Siding	Herts	G. N.	Hatfield.
.	P	.	.	.	.			Smart's Brick Works	Notts	Mid.	Edwalton.
G	P	.	.	.	.			Smeafield	Northumb	N. E.	Belford and Beal.
.	.	.	.	.	.			Smeaton	Edinboro'	N. B.	Monktonhall Junc. & Hardengreen.
.	.	.	.	.	.			Carberry Colliery	Edinboro'	N. B.	Branch from Smeaton.
.	.	.	.	.	.			Thorneybank Siding	Edinboro'	N. B.	Smeaton and Hardengreen.
.	.	.	.	.	.			Smeaton Junction	Edinboro'	N. B.	Smeaton and Ormiston.
G	P	.	L	H	.			Smeeth	Kent	S. E. & C.	Ashford and Folkestone.
G	P	.	L	.	.			Smeeth Road	Norfolk	G. E.	Wisbech and Lynn.
.	.	.	.	.	.			Smellie's Saw Mill	Lanark	Cal.	Omoa.
.	.	.	.	.	.			Smellie's Siding	Renfrew	Cal.	Glasgow, Whiteinch.
.	.	.	.	.	.			Smelting Corporation, Stanlow Works	Cheshire	B'head Jt. (G W & L N W)	Ellesmere Port.
.	.	.	.	.	.			Smelt Siding (English Electric Carbon Co.)	Denbigh	G. W.	Coed Poeth.
.	.	.	.	.	.			Smethwick	Staffs	G. W.	See Handsworth & Smethwick.
								SMETHWICK—			
G	P	F	.	H	C	1	10	(Station)	Staffs	L. & N. W.	Birmingham and Wolverhampton.
.	.	.	.	.	.			Galton Junction	Staffs	G. W.—L. & N. W.	Old Hill and Birmingham.
.	P	.	.	.	.			Junction Station (G. W.)	Staffs	G. W. / L. & N. W.	Birmingham and Stourbridge Junc. / Over G. W. from Galton Junction.
.	.	.	.	.	.			Smieton & Son's Siding	Forfar	D. & A. Jt. (Cal. & N. B.)	See Panmure.
.	.	.	.	.	.			Smiles Cement Works	Yorks	N. E.	Middlesbro'.
.	.	.	.	.	.			Smith & Co.'s Malt Kiln	Yorks	N. E.	Hemingbrough.
.	.	.	.	.	.			Smith & Co.'s Siding	Leicester	Mid.	Worthington.
.	.	.	.	.	.			Smith & Lochland's Sid. (N B)	Stirling	N. B.—Cal.	Falkirk, Grahamston.
.	.	.	.	.	.			Smith & Ritchie's Siding	Edinboro'	N. B.	Edinburgh, Leith Walk.
.	.	.	.	.	.			Smith & Son's Siding	Lancs	P. & L. Jt. (L & N W. & L & Y)	Preston, Deepdale.
.	.	.	.	.	.			Smith & Son's Siding	Surrey	L. B. & S. C.	Norwood Junction.
.	.	.	.	.	.			Smith & Son's Siding	Warwick	L. & N. W.	Leamington.

EXPLANATION—G *Goods Station.*   P *Passenger and Parcel Station.*   P* *Passenger, but not Parcel or Miscellaneous Traffic.*
F *Furniture Vans, Carriages, Portable Engines, and Machines on Wheels.*   L *Live Stock.*
H *Horse Boxes and Prize Cattle Vans.*   C *Carriages by Passenger Train.*

STATION ACCOMMODATION.						CRANE POWER.	STATIONS, &c.	COUNTY.	COMPANY.	POSITION.
						Tons Cwts.	Smith & Son's Works	Lancs	G. W.	Warrington.
.	.	.	.	.	.		Smith & Wellstood Siding	Stirling	Cal.	See Bonnybridge Foundry (Bonnybridge).
.	.	.	.	.	.		Smith Bros.	Glo'ster	G. W.—Mid.	Gloucester Docks.
.	.	.	.	.	.		Smith, F. & G., Siding	Norfolk	G. E.	Ryburgh.
.	.	.	.	.	.		Smith, Marshall & Co.'s Wood Yard	L'lithgow	N. B.	Bo'ness.
							Smith, P., & Son—			
.	.	.	.	.	.		Lawkholme Works	Yorks	Mid.	Keighley.
.	.	.	.	.	.		Midland Works	Yorks	Mid.	Keighley.
.	.	.	.	.	.		Smith, Patterson & Co.'s Foundry	Durham	N. E.	Same as Pioneer Foundry (Blaydon).
.	.	.	.	.	.		Smith's Brick Works (Skiers Spring Siding)	Yorks	G. C.	Elsecar.
.	.	.	.	.	.		Smith's Brick Works	Yorks	Mid.	Same as Skiers Spring Brick Works (Wentworth and H. Common).
.	.	.	.	.	.		Smith's Brick Yard	Durham	N. E.	Billingham.
.	.	.	.	.	.		Smith's Depôt	Durham	N. E.	Waterhouses.
.	.	.	.	.	.		Smith's Flour Mill	Derby	Mid.	Langley Mill and Eastwood.
.	.	.	.	.	.		Smith's Foundry	Salop	L. & N. W.	Whitchurch.
.	.	.	.	.	.		Smith's, J., Brewery Co.'s Sid.	Yorks	N. E.	Milford Junction Station.
.	.	.	.	.	.		Smith's Saw Mill	Fife	N. B.	Ladybank.
.	.	.	.	.	.		Smith's, S., Flour Mills (Mid.)	Yorks	Mid.—G. C.	Sheffield, Wicker.
.	.	.	.	.	.		Smith's or Hartley's Brick Sid.	Lancs	L. & Y.	Aintree.
.	.	.	.	.	.		Smith's Siding	Lancs	L. & N. W.	Garston Dock.
.	.	.	.	.	.		Smith's Siding	Sussex	S. E. & C.	Robertsbridge.
.	.	.	.	.	.		Smith's Siding	Yorks	Axholme Jt (L & Y & N E)	Reedness Junction.
.	.	.	.	.	.		Smith's Siding (G.C.)	Notts	G. C.—G. N.	Worksop.
.	.	.	.	.	.		Smith's Victoria Mill	Lancs	P.&L.Jt.(L& NW.& L&Y)	Longridge.
							Smith's Timber Co.—			
.	.	.	.	.	.		Siding	N'hampt'n	Mid.	Northampton, Bridge Street.
.	.	.	.	.	.		Siding (Mid.)	Beds	Mid.—L. & N. W.	Bedford.
.	.	.	.	.	.		Siding (Mid.)	Leicester	Mid.—L. & N. W.	Leicester, East.
.	.	.	.	.	.		Smith's Wire Works (G. N.)	Yorks	G.N.—G.C.—Mid.	See Belmont Siding (Doncaster).
.	.	.	.	.	.		Smith's Wire Works & Coal Siding (L. N. W.)	Lancs	L. & N. W.—G. W.	Warrington, Bank Quay.
.	.	.	.	.	.		Smith, T. H., & Son's Siding	Herts	G. N.	Royston.
.	.	.	.	.	.		Smith, W. & A., & Bacon's Sid.	Suffolk	G. E.	Thurston.
G	P	F	L	H	C		Smitham	Surrey	S. E. & C.	Purley and Chipstead.
G	P	F	L	H	C	2 10	Smithborough	Monaghan	G. N. (I.)	Clones and Armagh.
							Smithfield	Middlesex	G. W.	See London.
G	P	.	.	.	.	2 0	Smithy Bridge	Lancs	L. & Y.	Rochdale and Littleboro'.
.	.	.	.	.	.		Smithy Wood Colliery	Yorks	G. C.—Mid.	See Newton, Chambers & Co. (Ecclesfield).
.	.	.	.	.	.		Smyllum Junction	Lanark	Cal.	Lanark.
.	.	.	.	.	.		Smyth & Co.'s Siding	Middlesex	G. E.	Lower Edmonton.
.	P*	.	.	.	.	2 10	Smyth's Siding	Down	G. N. (I.)	Scarva and Banbridge.
.	.	.	.	.	.		Snab Siding	L'lithgow	N. B.	Bo'ness.
.	.	.	.	.	.		Snailbeach District Railway Co.'s Exchange Siding	Salop	S.&W'plJt.(GW & LNW)	Pontesbury.
G	P	.	L	H	.		Snainton	Yorks	N. E.	Pickering and Seamer.
G	P	F	L	H	C	3 0	Snaith	Yorks	L. & Y.	Knottingley and Goole.
G	.	.	.	.	.	1 10	Snape	Suffolk	G. E.	Branch from Snape Junction
.	.	.	.	.	.		Newsum, Garrett & Son's Siding	Suffolk	G. E.	Snape.
G	P	.	.	H	.		Snaresbrook and Wanstead	Essex	G. E.	Stratford and Loughton.
G	P	F	.	H	C	1 10	Snarestone	Leicester	A & N Jt. (L & NW & Mid.)	Overseal and Shackerstone.
.	.	.	.	.	.		Sneaton Siding	Yorks	N. E.	Ruswarp.
.	.	.	.	.	.		Snedshill Siding	Salop	L. & N. W.	See Lilleshall Coal and Iron Co.
.	.	.	.	.	.		Snedshill Works	Salop	G. W.	See Lilleshall Coal and Iron Co.
G	P	.	L	H	C		Snelland	Lincoln	G. C.	Lincoln and Market Rasen.
G	P	F	L	H	C	1 0	Snettisham	Norfolk	G. E.	Lynn and Hunstanton.
.	.	.	.	.	.		Sneyd Colliery & Brick Wks.	Staffs	N. S.	Cobridge.
.	.	.	.	.	.		Sneyd Park Junction	Glo'ster	Clif. Ex. Jt. (G. W. & Mid.)	Bristol and Avonmouth.
.	.	.	.	.	.		Snibston Colliery (Mid.)	Leicester	Mid.—L. & N. W.	Coalville.
.	.	.	.	.	.		Sniggery Siding	Lancs	L. & Y.	Hightown.
G	P	F	L	H	C	5 0	Snodland	Kent	S. E. & C.	Strood and Maidstone, West.
.	.	.	.	.	.		Lee's Siding	Kent	S. E. & C.	Halling and Snodland.
.	.	.	.	.	.		Snow & Co.'s Siding	Somerset	S.&D.Jt.(L.&S.W. & Mid)	Glastonbury.
.	.	.	.	.	.		Snowball's Fire-Brick Works	Durham	N. E.	Derwenthaugh.
G	P	.	.	.	.		Snowdon	Carnarvon	No. Wales N. G.	Terminus.
.	.	.	.	.	.		Snowdon's Siding	Durham	N. E.	Same as Cornforth Lane Sid. (Coxhoe).

STATION ACCOMMODATION.						CRANE POWER.		STATIONS, &c.	COUNTY.	COMPANY.	POSITION.
						Tons	Cwts				
..	..	..	..	..	..			Snow Hill...............	Warwick..	G. W.	See Birmingham.
..	..	..	..	..	..			Snow Hill (S. E. & C.)	Middlesex	S. E. & C.—G. N.—Mid.	See London.
..	..	..	..	..	..			Snow Hill Junction	Middlesex	Met.—S. E. & C.	London, Aldersgate Street and Snow Hill Station.
..	..	..	..	..	..			Snow Hill Sidings	Middlesex	L. & S. W.	London, Ludgate Hill.
..	..	..	..	..	..			Snydale Branch Sidings	Yorks	Mid.	{ Normanton. { Oakenshaw.
..	..	..	..	..	..			Snydale Colliery (Victoria Colliery) (L. & Y.)	Yorks	L. & Y.—G. N.—N. E...	Featherstone.
..	..	..	..	..	..			Snydale Hall Colliery	Yorks	L. & Y.	Westhoughton.
..	..	..	..	..	..			Soames & Son's Siding	Lincoln	G. C.	Grimsby Town.
..	..	..	..	..	..			Soaphouse Siding (G. C.)	Yorks	G. C.—G. N.	See Nunnery Col. Co. (Sheffield).
G	P	F	L	H	C	1	10	Soar Lane Coal Wharf	Leicester..	Mid.	Leicester, West Bridge.
G								Soham	Cambs......	G. E.	Ely and Newmarket.
G	P	..	..	..	..			Barraway Siding	Cambs......	G. E.	Ely and Soham.
						10	0	Soho	Staffs......	L. & N. W.	Birmingham and Wolverhampton.
..	..	..	..	..	..			Avery's, or Watt & Co.'s Sid.	Staffs......	L. & N. W.	Soho and Soho Road.
..	..	..	..	..	..			Everitt, Allen & Co.'s Sid.	Staffs......	L. & N. W.	Soho and Winson Green.
..	..	..	..	..	..			Guest, Keen & Nettlefold's London Works	Staffs......	L. & N. W.	Soho and Winson Green.
..	..	..	..	..	..			Muntz Metal Co.'s Siding..	Staffs......	L. & N. W.	Soho and Winson Green.
..	..	..	..	..	..			Wiggins & Co.'s Siding......	Staffs......	L. & N. W.	Soho and Winson Green.
..	P	..	..	..	..			Soho and Winson Green	Warwick..	G. W.	Wolverhampton and Birmingham.
..	..	..	..	..	..			Soho Iron Works	Lancs	L. & N. W.	Same as Hick, Hargreaves & Co.'s Lecturers Close and Hulme Trust Siding (Bolton).
..	P	..	..	..	..			Soho Pool.......................	Warwick..	L. & N. W.	See Birmingham.
G	P	F	L	H	C	1	15	Soho Road	Staffs......	L. & N. W.	Perry Barr and Soho.
G	P	F	L	H	C	2	0	Sole Street	Kent	S. E. & C.	Meopham and Chatham.
..	..	..	..	..	..			Solihull	Warwick..	G. W.	Birmingham and Leamington.
..	..	..	..	..	..			Solway Chemical Works	Cumb'land	N. B.	Silloth.
..	..	..	..	..	..			Solway Hematite Iron Works	Cumb'land	L. & N. W.—M. & C.	See Cammell & Co. (Maryport).
G	P	F	L	H	C			Somerford	Wilts	G. W.	See Great, and Little, Somerford.
..	..	..	..	..	..			Somerleyton	Suffolk ...	G. E.	Norwich and Lowestoft.
..	..	..	..	..	..			Somerset Brick & Tile Co.'s Siding	Somerset..	S.&D.Jt. (L.&S.W.&Mid)	Evercreech Junction Station.
..	..	..	..	..	..			Somerset Road (for Harborne)	Warwick..	Mid.	See Birmingham.
..	..	..	..	..	..			Somerset Stone Quarries Sid.	Somerset..	G. W.	Frome.
G	P	F	L	H	C	1	0	Somersham	Hunts	G. N. & G. E. Jt.	St. Ives and March.
..	..	..	..	..	..			Bateman, A. J., Siding ...	Hunts	G. N. & G. E. Jt.	Somersham and Warboys.
G	..	..	..	..	..			Billup's Siding	Hunts	G. N. & G. E. Jt.	Somersham and Chatteris.
..	..	..	..	..	..			Somers Siding..................	Worcester	G. W.	Halesowen Basin.
..	..	..	..	..	..			Somers Town	Middlesex	Mid.	See London.
..	..	..	..	..	..			Somers Town Coal Depôt......	Middlesex	Mid.	See London.
G	P	..	L	H	..			Somerton	Oxon	G. W.	Oxford and Banbury.
..	..	..	..	..	..			Somervail & Co.'s Siding......	Dumbartn	N. B.	Same as Dalmuir Iron Works.
..	..	..	..	..	..			Somerville's Brewery	Edinboro'	N. B.	Duddingston & Craigmillar.
..	..	..	..	..	..			Sommerville Sid. (Creech Sid.)	Somerset..	G. W.	Taunton.
..	..	..	..	..	..			Soothill Quarry	Yorks	G. N.	Woodkirk.
..	..	..	..	..	..			Soothill Wood Colliery (G.N.)	Yorks	G. N.—G. C.	Batley.
G	P	..	L	H	..			Sorbie	Wigtown..	P.P.&W.Jt.(Cal.,G&SW, L. & N. W., & Mid.)...	Newton Stewart and Whithorn.
..	..	..	..	..	..	..	..	Soudley Siding	Glo'ster...	G. W.	Ruspidge.
..	..	..	..	..	..			Souterhouse Brick Works ...	Lanark ...	N. B.	Coatbridge, Whifflet.
..	..	..	..	..	..			Souterhouse Colliery...........	Lanark ...	N. B.	Coatbridge, Whifflet.
..	..	..	..	..	..			South Acton	Middlesex	N.&S.W.Jn.Jt.(L.& NW, Mid., & N. L.)...........	See London.
..	..	..	..	..	..			South Acton, North Junction	Middlesex	Met.Dist.—N S W Jn.Jt.	London, Mill Hill Park and Acton.
..	..	..	..	..	..			South Airdrie	Lanark ...	N. B.	See Airdrie, South.
..	..	..	..	..	..			South Airdrie Sidings	Lanark ...	N. B.	See Airdrie.
G	P	F	L	H	C	3	0	Southall	Middlesex	G. W.	London and Slough.
..	..	..	..	..	..			Brentford Gas Co.'s Works	Middlesex	G W	Southall.
..	..	..	..	..	..			Otto Monsteds Works	Middlesex	G. W.	Southall.
..	..	..	..	..	..			South Alloa	Stirling	Cal.	See Alloa, South.
G	P	F	L	H	..	5	0	Southam & Long Itchington	Warwick..	L. & N. W.	Leamington and Weedon.
..	..	..	..	..	..			Greaves, Bull & Lakin's Sid.	Warwick..	L. & N. W.	Southam and Napton.
..	..	..	..	..	..			Kaye & Co.'s Siding	Warwick..	L. & N. W.	Southam and Napton.
								SOUTHAMPTON—			
G	P	F	L	H	C	10	0	(Station, L. & S. W.)	Hants	{ L. & S. W. { M. & S. W. Jn.	Terminus. Over L. & S. W. from Andover Junc.
G	..	..	..	..	..	5	0	Bevois Park Sidings	Hants	L. & S. W.	Southampton.
..	..	..	..	..	..			Chapel Siding	Hants	L. & S. W.	Southampton.

EXPLANATION—G *Goods Station.*   P *Passenger and Parcel Station.*   P* *Passenger, but not Parcel or Miscellaneous Traffic.*
F *Furniture Vans, Carriages, Portable Engines, and Machines on Wheels.*   L *Live Stock.*
H *Horse Boxes and Prize Cattle Vans.*   C *Carriages by Passenger Train.*

STATION ACCOMMODATION.						CRANE POWER.		STATIONS, &c.	COUNTY.	COMPANY.	POSITION.
						Tons	Cwts.	SOUTHAMPTON—*continued.*			
G	P	F	L	H	C	80	0	Docks	Hants	L. & S. W.	Extension from Station.
.	.	.	.	.	.	.	.	Junction	Hants	L. & S. W.	Station and Northam Junction.
G	P	.	.	.	.	.	.	Millbrook (L. & S. W.)	Hants	{ L. & S. W. .... { M. & S. W. Jn.	Southampton and Redbridge. Over L. & S. W. from Andover Junc.
.	P	.	.	.	.	.	.	Northam	Hants	L. & S. W.	St. Denys and Southampton.
.	.	.	.	.	.	.	.	Northam Junction.............	Hants	L. & S. W.	St. Denys and Southampton.
G	.	.	.	.	.	.	.	Northam Sidings	Hants	L. & S. W.	Southampton.
G	.	.	.	.	.	12	0	Quay	Hants	L. & S. W.	Extension from Station.
.	P	.	.	.	.	.	.	Royal Pier	Hants	L. & S. W.	Extension from Station.
G	P	.	.	.	.	.	.	St. Denys	Hants	L. & S. W.	Eastleigh and Northam.
.	.	.	.	.	.	.	.	Tunnel Junction	Hants	L. & S. W.	Northam and Southampton, West.
G	P	F	L	H	C	.	.	West (L. & S. W.).............	Hants	{ L. & S. W. .... { M. & S. W. Jn.	Terminus and Millbrook. Over L. & S. W. from Andover Junc.
G	P	F	L	H	C	2	0	Southam Road & Harbury ...	Warwick..	G. W.	Banbury and Leamington.
.	.	.	.	.	.	.	.	Greaves Bull & Lakins Wks.	Warwick..	G. W.	Southam Road and Fenny Compton.
G	P	F	L	.	.	5	0	South Bank	Yorks	N. E.	Middlesbro' and Redcar.
.	.	.	.	.	.	.	.	Alliance Steel Foundry ...	Yorks	N. E.	South Bank.
.	.	.	.	.	.	.	.	Brand's Slag Works— Cargo Fleet Iron & Brick Works and Wharf	Yorks	N. E.	South Bank.
.	.	.	.	.	.	.	.	Imperial Iron Works......	Yorks	N. E.	South Bank.
.	.	.	.	.	.	.	.	Brown's Depôt..................	Yorks	N. E.	South Bank.
.	.	.	.	.	.	.	.	Cargo Fleet Salt Works and Wharf	Yorks	N. E.	South Bank.
.	.	.	.	.	.	/	.	Cargo Fleet Timber Yards and Wharves	Yorks	N. E.	South Bank.
.	.	.	.	.	.	.	.	Cargo Fleet Warrant Stores	Yorks	N. E.	South Bank.
.	.	.	.	.	.	.	.	Clay Lane Iron Works and Wharf	Yorks	N. E.	South Bank.
.	.	.	.	.	.	.	.	Cleveland Brick Works ...	Yorks	N. E.	South Bank.
.	.	.	.	.	.	.	.	Cleveland Iron & Steel Wks.	Yorks	N. E.	South Bank.
.	.	.	.	.	.	.	.	Eston Jetty	Yorks	N. E.	South Bank.
.	.	.	.	.	.	.	.	Eston Mines.....................	Yorks	N. E.	South Bank.
.	.	.	.	.	.	.	.	Evans & Son's Foundry (Cleveland Port Brick Works and Siding)	Yorks	N. E.	South Bank.
.	.	.	.	.	.	.	.	Fisher's Siding (Eston Grange Farm Siding) ...	Yorks	N. E.	South Bank.
.	.	.	.	.	.	.	.	Harris Deepwater Wharf...	Yorks	N. E.	South Bank.
.	.	.	.	.	.	.	.	Imperial Depôts	Yorks	N. E.	South Bank.
.	.	.	.	.	.	.	.	Jones & Co.'s Slag Wool Wks. (Cargo Fleet Iron Works)	Yorks	N. E.	South Bank.
.	.	.	.	.	.	.	.	Lackenby Iron Works	Yorks	N. E.	South Bank.
.	.	.	.	.	.	.	.	Lazenby Depôts	Yorks	N. E.	South Bank.
.	.	.	.	.	.	.	.	Normanby Iron Wks. & Whf.	Yorks	N. E.	South Bank.
.	.	.	.	.	.	.	.	North Eastern Brick and Tile Works	Yorks	N. E.	South Bank.
.	.	.	.	.	.	.	.	Ormesby Foundry	Yorks	N. E.	South Bank.
.	.	.	.	.	.	.	.	Ormesby Iron Wks. & Wharf	Yorks	N. E.	South Bank.
.	.	.	.	.	.	.	.	South Bank and Normanby Gas Works	Yorks	N. E.	South Bank.
.	.	.	.	.	.	.	.	South Bank Chemical Works (South Bank Iron Works)	Yorks	N. E.	South Bank.
.	.	.	.	.	.	.	.	South Bank Iron Works ...	Yorks	N. E.	South Bank.
.	.	.	.	.	.	.	.	South Bank Salt Works ...	Yorks	N. E.	South Bank.
.	.	.	.	.	.	.	.	Tees Conservancy Commissioners' Graving Dock ...	Yorks	N. E.	South Bank.
.	.	.	.	.	.	.	.	Tees Iron Works Foundry and Wharf	Yorks	N. E.	South Bank.
.	.	.	.	.	.	.	.	Tees Scoria Brick Works (Tees Iron Works)	Yorks	N. E.	South Bank.
.	.	.	.	.	.	.	.	Tees Tilery and Brick Yard	Yorks	N. E.	South Bank.
.	.	.	.	.	.	.	.	Whitehouse Siding & Depôt	Yorks	N. E.	South Bank.
.	.	.	.	.	.	.	.	Calder, Charles & Co.'s Timber Yard	Yorks	N. E.	Whitehouse Siding and Depôt.
.	.	.	.	.	.	.	.	Campbell & Co.'s Machinery Yard	Yorks	N. E.	Whitehouse Siding and Depôt.
.	.	.	.	.	.	.	.	Dock Side Timber Yard ...	Yorks	N. E.	Whitehouse Siding and Depôt.
.	.	.	.	.	.	.	.	North Ormesby Timber Yard	Yorks	N. E.	Whitehouse Siding and Depôt.
.	.	.	.	.	.	.	.	Ridley & Son's Yard	Yorks	N. E.	Whitehouse Siding and Depôt.

EXPLANATION—G *Goods Station.*   P *Passenger and Parcel Station.*   P* *Passenger, but not Parcel or Miscellaneous Traffic.*
F *Furniture Vans, Carriages, Portable Engines, and Machines on Wheels.*   L *Live Stock.*
H *Horse Boxes and Prize Cattle Vans.*   C *Carriages by Passenger Train.*

STATION ACCOMMODATION.						CRANE POWER.	STATIONS, &c.	COUNTY.	COMPANY.	POSITION.
						Tons Cwts.	SOUTH BANK—continued.			
							Whitehouse Siding and Depôt—continued:			
.	.	.	.	.	.	.	Robinson & Co.'s Timber Yard	Yorks	N. E.	Whitehouse Siding and Depôt.
.	.	.	.	.	.	.	Tees Railway and Engineering Works	Yorks	N. E.	Whitehouse Siding and Depôt.
.	.	.	.	.	.	.	Tees Side Bridge and Engineering Works ...	Yorks	N. E.	Whitehouse Siding and Depôt.
.	.	.	.	.	.	.	Watson & Co.'s Timber Yd.	Yorks	N. E.	Whitehouse Siding and Depôt.
.	.	.	.	.	.	.	South Bank Iron Works	Dumbartn	N. B.	Kirkintilloch Basin.
.	.	.	.	.	.	.	South Barr Siding	Renfrew ..	Cal.	Houston.
.	.	.	.	.	.	.	South Beach	Ayr	G. & S.W.	See Ardrossan.
.	.	.	.	.	.	.	South Benwell Colliery	Northumb	N. E.	{ Newcastle-on-Tyne. { Scotswood.
.	.	.	.	.	.	.	South Bermondsey	Surrey ...	L. B. & S. C.	See London.
.	.	.	.	.	.	.	South Bishopley Quarry	Durham ...	N. E.	Frosterley.
G	P	F	L	.	.	5 0	Southborough.................	Kent	S. E. & C.	Tonbridge and Tunbridge Wells.
.	.	.	.	.	.	.	High Brooms Brick Siding	Kent	S. E. & C.	Southborough.
.	.	.	.	.	.	.	Southborough Gas Siding..	Kent	S. E. & C.	Southborough.
.	.	.	.	.	.	.	Southbourne-on-Sea........	Hants	L. & S.W.	See Christchurch (for Southbourne-on-Sea).
.	.	.	.	.	.	.	South Brancepeth Colliery, Coke Ovens, & Brick Wks. (Page Bank Colliery, Coke Ovens, & Brick Works) ...	Durham ...	N. E.	Spennymoor.
.	.	.	.	.	.	.	South Broadrigg Brick Wks.	Lanark ...	N. B.	Westcraigs.
.	.	.	.	.	.	.	South Broadrigg Colliery ...	Lanark ...	N. B.	Westcraigs.
.	.	.	.	.	.	.	South Bromley	Middlesex	N. L.	See London.
.	.	.	.	.	.	.	South Buckley Rock Brick Co.'s Siding	Flint	W. M. & C. Q.	Buckley.
G	P	F	L	H	C	2 0	Southburn	Yorks	N. E.	Market Weighton and Driffield.
.	.	.	.	.	.	.	South Cambria Colliery........	Glamorg'n	T. V.	Cross Inn.
G	P	F	L	H	C	2 0	South Cave	Yorks	H. & B.	Howden and Hull.
.	.	.	.	.	.	.	South Church Siding...........	Durham ...	N. E.	Bishop Auckland.
.	.	.	.	.	.	.	Southcoates	Yorks	N. E.	See Hull.
.	.	.	.	.	.	.	South Cobbinshaw Junction	Edinboro'	Cal.	Branch near Cobbinshaw.
.	.	.	.	.	.	.	Southcote Junction	Berks	G. W.	Reading and Mortimer.
.	.	.	.	.	.	.	South Croydon	Surrey ...	L. B. & S. C.	See Croydon, South.
.	.	.	.	.	.	.	South Croydon Junction ...	Surrey ...	C. & O. Jt.—L. B. & S. C.	See Croydon, South Junction.
.	.	.	.	.	.	.	Southdale Siding	Derby	Mid.	Peak Forest.
.	.	.	.	.	.	.	South Derwent Col. & Ck. Wks	Durham ...	N. E.	Annfield Plain.
.	.	.	.	.	.	.	South Derwent Col. Saw Mill	Durham ...	N. E.	Annfield Plain.
.	.	.	.	.	.	.	South Derwent Colliery (Willie Pit)........................	Durham ...	N. E.	Annfield Plain.
.	.	.	.	.	.	.	South Dock	Durham ...	N. E.	See Sunderland.
.	.	.	.	.	.	.	South Dock	Glamorg'n	G. W.—L. & NW—Mid.—R. & S. B.—S. & M.	Swansea.
.	.	.	.	.	.	.	South Docks...................	Lancs	L. & Y.	See Liverpool.
.	.	.	.	.	.	.	South Docks (Millwall)........	Middlesex	G. E.	See London.
.	.	.	.	.	.	.	South Dorothea Slate Co.'s Cornwall Siding.............	Carnarvon	L. & N. W.	Nantlle.
.	.	.	.	.	.	.	South Dunraven Colliery	Glamorg'n	T. V.	Treherbert.
.	.	.	.	.	.	.	South Durham & Eldon Cols., Coke Ovens, & Brick Wks.	Durham ...	N. E.	Shildon.
.	.	.	.	.	.	.	South Durham Salt Works ...	Durham ...	N. E.	See Salt Union, Ltd. (Haverton Hill).
.	.	.	.	.	.	.	South Durham Steel and Iron Co.'s Works..................	Durham ...	N. E.	West Hartlepool.
.	P	.	.	.	.	.	South Ealing	Middlesex	Met. Dist.	Mill Hill Park and Boston Road.
G	P	F	L	H	C	10 0	South Elmsall	Yorks	H. & B.	See Moorhouse and South Elmsall.
.	.	.	.	.	.	.	South Elmsall	Yorks	W.R.&G.Jt.(G.C.&G.N.)	Doncaster and Wakefield.
.	.	.	.	.	.	.	Hinchcliffe Lime Siding	Yorks	W.R.&G.Jt.(G.C.&G.N.)	South Elmsall and Hampole.
.	.	.	.	.	.	.	South Kirkby Colliery	Yorks	W.R.&G.Jt.(G.C.&G.N.)	South Kirkby Jn. & Hemsworth Jn.
.	P	.	.	.	.	.	South Elmsall Junction ...	Yorks	S. & K. Jt.—W.R.&G. Jt.	Ackworth and South Elmsall.
.	.	.	.	.	.	.	Southend	Glamorg'n	Swan. & Mum.	Mumbles.
.	.	.	.	.	.	.	South End Co-operative Society's Siding.............	Cumb'land	Mid.	Carlisle.
G	P	F	L	H	C	5 0 }	Southend-on-Sea............	Essex	{ G. E. { L. T. & S.	Branch from Shenfield. Pitsea and Shoeburyness.
G	P	F	L	H	C	10 0 }				
.	.	.	.	.	.	.	Milton Hall Brick Co.'s Sid.	Essex	G. E.	Southend-on-Sea.
.	.	.	.	.	.	.	Sadd, J., & Son's Siding ...	Essex	G. E.	Southend-on-Sea.
.	.	.	.	.	.	.	Southend Sidings	Lanark ...	N. B.	See Coatbridge.
.	.	.	.	.	.	.	Southerham Junction	Sussex ...	L. B. & S. C.	Lewes and Glynde.

EXPLANATION— G Goods Station.　　P Passenger and Parcel Station.　　P* Passenger, but not Parcel or Miscellaneous Traffic.
F Furniture Vans, Carriages, Portable Engines, and Machines on Wheels.　　L Live Stock.
H Horse Boxes and Prize Cattle Vans.　　C Carriages by Passenger Train.

STATION ACCOMMODATION.	CRANE POWER.	STATIONS, &c.	COUNTY.	COMPANY.	POSITION.
	Tons Cwts.				
		Southerham Siding	Sussex ...	L. B. & S. C.	Lewes.
		Southern, J. W., & Son's Sid.	Lancs	Trafford Park Estate......	Manchester.
G P F L H C		Southerndown Road	Glamorg'n	Barry	Barry and Bridgend.
		Ewenny Siding	Glamorg'n	Barry	Southerndown Road and Bridgend.
		Southfield Colliery.............	Stirling ...	N. B.	Slamannan.
		Southfield Siding	Stirling ...	N. B.	Slamannan.
P		Southfields	Surrey ...	L. & S.W.	East Putney and Wimbledon.
G P F L H C	5 0	Southfleet (for Springhead)...	Kent	S. E. & C.	Farningham Road and Gravesend (West Street).
		Chamber's Siding	Kent	S. E. & C.	Southfleet.
		South Gare Battery	Yorks	N. E.	Tod Point.
		South Gare Breakwater	Yorks	N. E.	Tod Point.
		South Garesfield Colliery	Durham ...	N. E.	Lintz Green.
		South Garesfield Colliery High Pit	Durham ...	N. E.	Same as Lintz Col. (Lintz Green).
		Southgate (G. N.)	Middlesex	G. N.—N. L.—S. E. & C.	See Palmer's Green and Southgate.
		Southgate Colliery (Mid.) ...	Derby	Mid.—L. D. & E. C.	Clown.
		Southgate Gas Works	Middlesex	G. N.	New Southgate.
		South Griffin Colliery (G. W.)	Mon	G. W.—L. & N. W.	See Lancaster & Co. (Blaina).
		South Hams Brick Co.'s Wks.	Devon ...	G. W.	Steer Point.
P		South Harrow (for Roxeth and Northolt)	Middlesex	Met. Dist.	Terminus—Bch. fr. Ealing Common.
P		South Hetton	Durham ...	N. E.	Murton and Haswell.
		South Hetton Colliery	Durham ...	N. E.	Haswell.
		South Hetton Junction (Swine Lodge)	Durham ...	N. E.	Seaham.
		South Hiendley Colliery (Musgrave Siding).............	Yorks	H. & B.	Cudworth, North.
		South Hill Siding	Worcester	G. W.	Hook Norton.
		Southhook Colliery	Ayr	G. & S.W.	Crosshouse.
		Southhook Fire-Clay Works	Ayr	G. & S.W.	Crosshouse.
G P F L H C		Southill	Beds	Mid.	Bedford and Hitchin.
		South Kensington	Middlesex	Met—Met Dist—L & NW	See London.
		South Kensington Junction	Middlesex	Met.—Met. Dist.	London, South Kensington and Sloane Square.
		South Kirkby	Yorks	H. & B. / W. R.&G.Jt.(GC.&G N.)	See Hemsworth and South Kirkby. / Same as South Elmsall.
		South Kirkby (S. & K. Jt.)...	Yorks	S. & K. Jt.—G. C.	See Moorthorpe and South Kirkby.
		South Kirkby Colliery	Yorks	S. & K. Jt. (Mid. & N. E.) / W. R.&G.Jt.(G. C.&GN.)	Moorthorpe and South Kirkby. / South Elmsall.
		South Kirkby Junction.........	Yorks	S. & K Jt—W R. & G Jt.	Moorthorpe and Hemsworth.
		South Lane Siding.............	Yorks	N. E.	Cawood.
		South Leicestershire Col. & Bk. Co.'s Sid. (A & N Jt)	Leicester..	L. & N. W.—Mid. / Mid.	Hugglescote. / Coalville.
G P L		South Leigh	Oxon	G. W.	Yarnton and Witney.
		South Leith.....................	Edinboro'	Cal.—N. B.	See Leith, South.
		South Leith Junction	Edinboro'	N. B.	Edinburgh.
		South Level Sidings	Flint	L. & N. W.	Coed Talon.
		Darbyshire's	Flint	L. & N. W.	South Level Sidings.
		Peter's	Flint	L. & N. W.	South Level Sidings.
		Pontybodkin Coal and Cannel Co.	Flint	L. & N. W.	South Level Sidings.
		South Liberty Colliery	Somerset...	G. W.	Bristol, Portishead.
		South Lincolnshire Brick & Tile Co.'s Keeble's Siding..	Lincoln ...	Mid. & G. N. Jt.............	Bourne.
		South Longrigg Colliery (Hill Colliery)	Lanark ...	Cal.	Netherburn.
G P F L H C		South Lynn.....................	Norfolk ...	Mid. & G. N. Jt.	Lynn and Sutton Bridge.
		West Norfolk Manure Co.'s Siding	Norfolk ...	Mid. & G. N. Jt.	South Lynn.
		South Medomsley Colliery, Coke, and Brick Works ...	Durham ...	N. E.	Leadgate.
G P L H	2 0	South Milford.....................	Yorks	N. E.	Leeds and Selby.
		South Mill	Herts	G. E.	See Taylor&Sons(Bishops Stortford).
		South Mims (G. N.)	Middlesex	G. N.—N. L.	Same as Potters Bar.
G P F L H C	1 10	Southminster	Essex	G. E.	Branch from Woodham Ferris.
		Horner, R., Siding.............	Essex	G. E.	Southminster.
G P F L H C	2 0	South Molton	Devon ...	G. W.	Dulverton and Barnstaple.
G P F L H C	5 0	South Molton Road	Devon ...	L. & S.W.	Exeter and Barnstaple.
		South Moor Collieries and Brick Works	Durham ...	N. E.	Annfield Plain.
		Charlie Pit	Durham ...	N. E.	South Moor Cols. & Brick Works.

EXPLANATION—G *Goods Station.*   P *Passenger and Parcel Station.*   P* *Passenger, but not Parcel or Miscellaneous Traffic.*
F *Furniture Vans, Carriages, Portable Engines, and Machines on Wheels.*   L *Live Stock.*
H *Horse Boxes and Prize Cattle Vans.*   C *Carriages by Passenger Train.*

STATION ACCOMMODATION.						CRANE POWER.	STATIONS, &c.	COUNTY.	COMPANY.	POSITION.
						Tons Cwts.	South Moor Collieries and Brick Works—*continued.*			
.	.	.	.	.	.	.	Louisa Pit	Durham	N. E.	South Moor Cols. & Brick Works.
.	.	.	.	.	.	.	Morrison Pit	Durham	N. E.	South Moor Cols. & Brick Works.
.	.	.	.	.	.	.	Oxhill Siding	Durham	N. E.	South Moor Cols. & Brick Works.
.	.	.	.	.	.	.	South Normanton	Derby	Mid.	See Alfreton and South Normanton.
.	.	.	.	.	.	.	South Normanton and Black-well Gas Co.'s Siding	Derby	Mid.	Westhouses and Blackwell.
.	.	.	.	.	.	.	South Normanton Col. (G. C.)	Derby	G. C.—G. N.—L. & N. W.	Kirkby and Pinxton.
.	.	.	.	.	.	.	South Parade	Yorks	G. N.—L. & Y.	See Halifax.
.	.	.	.	.	.	.	South Pelaw Colliery	Durham	N. E.	Pelton.
.	.	.	.	.	.	.	South Pelaw Junction	Durham	N. E.	Pelton.
.	.	.	.	.	.	.	South Pontop Colliery	Durham	N. E.	Annfield Plain.
							SOUTHPORT—			
G	P	F	L	H	C	10 0	Chapel Street (L. & Y.)	Lancs	{ L. & Y.	Branch from Wigan.
.	P	.	.	H	C	.		Lancs	{ L. & N. W.	Over L. & Y. from Bootle Junction.
							Hawkshead Street Junction	Lancs	L. & Y.	Meols Cop and Central.
G	P	F	L	H	C	5 0	Lord Street	Lancs	C. L. C. (S'port Exten.).	Terminus.
.	.	.	.	.	.	.	Pearson & Knowles' Siding	Lancs	L. & Y.	Southport.
.	.	.	.	.	.	.	Roe Lane Junction	Lancs	L. & Y.	Meols Cop and Hesketh Park.
.	P	.	.	.	.	.	St. Luke's	Lancs	L. & Y.	Blowick and Chapel Street.
.	.	.	.	.	.	.	Southport Corporation Sid.	Lancs	L. & Y.	Southport.
.	.	.	.	.	.	.	Wigan Coal & Iron Co.'s Sid.	Lancs	L. & Y.	Southport.
.	.	.	.	.	.	.	Southport Corporation Siding	Lancs	L. & Y.	Southport, Charles Street.
.	.	.	.	.	.	.	Southport Gas Works	Lancs	L. & Y.	Meols Cop.
.	.	.	.	.	.	.	Southport Gas Works	Lancs	L. & Y.	Blowick.
G	.	F	L	.	.	5 0	South Queensferry	L'lithgow	N. B.	Branch from Dalmeny, Goods.
.	.	.	.	.	.	.	Distillers Co.'s Siding	L'lithgow	N. B.	South Queensferry, Goods.
.	.	.	.	.	.	.	Port Edgar Siding	L'lithgow	N. B.	Bch. from South Queensferry, Goods.
.	.	.	.	.	.	.	South Queensferry (Pass-engers)	L'lithgow	N. B.	See Dalmeny (for South Queensferry).
.	.	.	.	.	.	.	South Renfrew	Renfrew	G. & S.W.	See Renfrew.
G	P	.	L	H	.	.	Southrey	Lincoln	G. N.	Lincoln and Boston.
.	.	.	.	.	.	.	South Rhondda	Glamorg'n	G. W.	Llanharan and Bryncethin.
.	.	.	.	.	.	.	Hendrewen Colliery	Glamorg'n	G. W.	South Rhondda.
.	.	.	.	.	.	.	Raglan Colliery	Glamorg'n	G. W.	South Rhondda and Bryncethin.
.	.	.	.	.	.	.	South Rhondda Colliery	Glamorg'n	G. W.	South Rhondda and Bryncethin.
.	.	.	.	.	.	.	Southrigg Cols. Nos. 1, 2, & 3	Lanark	N. B.	Westcraigs.
.	.	.	.	.	.	.	Southsea, East	Hants	L. & S W & L B & S C Jt.	See Portsmouth, East Southsea.
G	P	F	L	H	C	10 0	South Shields	Durham	N. E.	Branch from Washington.
.	.	.	.	.	.	.	Borough Foundry	Durham	N. E.	South Shields.
.	.	.	.	.	.	.	Dean Lane Coal Depôt	Durham	N. E.	South Shields.
.	.	.	.	.	.	.	Dean Quarry Stone Co.'s Siding	Durham	N. E.	South Shields.
.	.	.	.	.	.	.	Fauld Brick Works	Durham	N. E.	South Shields.
.	.	.	.	.	.	.	Garden Lane Siding	Durham	N. E.	South Shields.
.	.	.	.	.	.	.	Harton Colliery	Durham	N. E	South Shields.
.	.	.	.	.	.	.	High Shields Depôt	Durham	N. E.	South Shields.
.	.	.	.	.	.	.	Hilda Colliery & Fuel Wks.	Durham	N. E.	South Shields.
.	.	.	.	.	.	.	Hilda Depôts	Durham	N. E.	South Shields.
.	.	.	.	.	.	.	Hilda Shipping Staithes	Durham	N. E.	South Shields.
.	.	.	.	.	.	.	Laygate Lane Siding	Durham	N. E.	South Shields.
.	.	.	.	.	.	.	Laygate Lime & Cl. Depôts	Durham	N. E.	South Shields.
.	.	.	.	.	.	.	Laygate Manure Wharf	Durham	N. E.	South Shields.
.	.	.	.	.	.	.	Marsden Limestone Quarry and Lime Works	Durham	N. E.	South Shields.
.	.	.	.	.	.	.	Marsden Manure Siding	Durham	N. E.	South Shields.
.	.	.	.	.	.	.	Marsden Paper Mills	Durham	N. E.	South Shields.
.	.	.	.	.	.	.	Maxwell Street Depôts	Durham	N. E.	South Shields.
.	.	.	.	.	.	.	Miller's Brass Foundry	Durham	N. E.	South Shields.
.	.	.	.	.	.	.	Moore's Glass Works	Durham	N. E.	South Shields.
.	.	.	.	.	.	.	North Eastern Foundry (Black's)	Durham	N. E.	South Shields.
.	.	.	.	.	.	.	South Shields Corporation Manure Wharf	Durham	N. E.	South Shields.
.	.	.	.	.	.	.	South Shields Gas Works	Durham	N. E.	South Shields.
.	.	.	.	.	.	.	South Shields Lime Depôts	Durham	N. E.	South Shields.
.	.	.	.	.	.	.	South Shields Passenger Station Depôts	Durham	N. E.	South Shields.
.	.	.	.	.	.	.	Tait's Coal Spout	Durham	N. E.	South Shields.
.	.	.	.	.	.	.	Whitburn Col. & Bk. Wks.	Durham	N. E.	South Shields.
.	P	.	.	.	.	.	South Shields (Westoe Lane)	Durham	Marsden	Near N. E. Station.

EXPLANATION—**G** *Goods Station.*   **P** *Passenger and Parcel Station.*   **P*** *Passenger, but not Parcel or Miscellaneous Traffic.*
F *Furniture Vans, Carriages, Portable Engines, and Machines on Wheels.*   **L** *Live Stock.*
H *Horse Boxes and Prize Cattle Vans.*   **C** *Carriages by Passenger Train.*

STATION ACCOMMODATION.						CRANE POWER.	STATIONS, &c.	COUNTY.	COMPANY.	POSITION.
						Tons Cwts.				
.	.	.	.	.	.		South Shields & Sunderland Water Co's Pumping Engine	Durham ...	N. E.	Seaham.
.	.	.	.	.	.		South Shore (Lytham Road)	Lancs	P & W Jt. (L & Y & L & N W)	See Blackpool.
.	.	.	.	.	.		South Shore (Waterloo Road)	Lancs	P & W Jt. (L & Y & L & N W)	See Blackpool.
.	.	.	.	.	.		South Side	Lanark ...	Cal.—G. B. & K. Jt.	See Glasgow.
.	.	.	.	.	.		South Skelton Mines	Yorks	N. E.	Boosbeck.
.	.	.	.	.	.		South Staffordshire Fire Brick Co.'s Siding	Staffs	L. & N. W.	Hednesford.
.	.	.	.	.	•	•	South Staffordshire Mond Gas Co.'s Siding	Staffs	L. & N. W.	Tipton.
.	.	.	.	.	.		South Staffordshire Tramway Co.'s Siding	Staffs	L. & N. W.	Darlaston.
.	.	.	.	.	.		South Staffordshire Water-works	Staffs	L. & N. W.	Lichfield.
.	.	.	.	.	.		South Staffordshire Water-works Crank Hall Siding	Staffs	L. & N. W.	Wednesbury.
.	.	.	.	.	.		South Stockton	Durham ...	N. E.	See Stockton-on-Tees.
.	.	.	.	.	.		South Tanfield Colliery and Coke Works	Durham ...	N. E.	Annfield Plain.
.	.	.	.	.	.		South Tottenham and Stam-ford Hill	Middlesex	Mid.—T. & H. Jt.	See London.
.	.	.	.	.	.		South Tottenham Junction ...	Middlesex	G. E.—T. & H. Jt.	London, Seven Sisters and South Tottenham Station.
.	.	.	.	.	.		South Tottenham Junction ...	Middlesex	T. & F. G. Jt.—T. & H. Jt.	Black Horse Road & South Totten-ham Station.
.	.	.	.	.	.		South Town	Suffolk ...	G. E.	See Yarmouth.
.	.	.	.	.	.		South Tyne Col. & Bk. Wks.	Northumb	N. E.	Haltwhistle.
.	.	.	.	.	.		South Tyne Paper Mills	Northumb	N. E.	Fourstones.
G	P	.	L	H	.	3 0	Southwaite	Cumb'land	L. & N. W.	Carlisle and Penrith.
.	.	.	.	.	.		South Wales and Cannock Chase Cl. & Ck. Co. (G.W.)	Worcester	G. W.—Mid.	Worcester.
.	.	.	.	.	.		South Wales and Cannock Chase Coal Co.'s Sidings ...	Salop	G. W.	Much Wenlock.
.	.	.	.	.	.		South Wales Anthracite Col-liery Co.'s Yniscedwyn Col-liery (Mid)	Brecon ...	Mid.—G. W.—L. & N. W.	Gurnos.
.	.	.	.	.	.		South Wales Portland Cement & Lime Co.'s Siding	Glamorg'n	G. W.	Bridgend.
.	.	.	.	.	.		South Wales Portland Cement Co.'s Siding	Glamorg'n	T. V.	Penarth Town.
.	.	.	.	.	.		South Wales Primrose Cl. Co.— Gwyn's Drift Colliery (Mid.)	Glamorg'n	Mid.—G. W.—L. & N. W.	Pontardawe.
.	.	.	.	.	.		Waen-y-coed Sidings (Mid.)	Glamorg'n	Mid.—G. W.—L. & N. W.	Pontardawe.
.	.	.	.	.	.		South Wales Primrose Colliery (Ynisygeinon Siding) (Mid.)	Glamorg'n	Mid.—G. W.—L. & N. W.	Ystalyfera.
.	.	.	.	.	.		South Wales Tin Plate Works (G. W.)	Carmarth'	G. W.—L. & N. W.	See Thomas, R., & Co. (Llanelly).
.	.	.	.	.	.		South Wales Wagon Co.'s Sid.	Glamorg'n	GW—L & N W—Rhy—TV	Cardiff.
.	.	.	.	.	.		Southwark and Vauxhall Waterworks	Surrey ...	L. B. & S. C.	Streatham Common.
.	.	.	.	.	.		Southwark Park	Surrey ...	S. E. & C.	See London.
G	P	F	L	H	C	5 0	Southwater	Sussex ...	L. B. & S. C.	Horsham and West Grinstead.
.	.	.	.	.	.		Southwater Brick Co.'s Sid.	Sussex ...	L. B. & S. C.	Southwater.
G	P	F	L	H	C	1 10	Southwell	Notts	Mid.	Mansfield and Newark.
.	.	.	.	.	.		Caudwell's, E., Siding	Notts	Mid.	Southwell.
.	.	.	.	.	.		South West India Dks. (L & ID)	Middlesex	G. E.—G. N.—G. W.—L. & N. W.—Mid.—N.L.	See London.
.	.	.	.	.	.		South Wexford	Wexford..	G. S. & W.	See Wexford, South.
G	.	.	.	.	.	9 0	Southwick	Durham ..	N. E.	Hylton Lane and Monkwearmouth.
.	.	.	.	.	.		Carley Lime Works	Durham ..	N. E.	Southwick.
.	.	.	.	.	.		Castletown Brick Works..	Durham ..	N. E.	Southwick.
.	.	.	.	.	.		Castletown Ship Yard	Durham ..	N. E.	Southwick.
.	.	.	.	.	.		Hylton Colliery	Durham ..	N. E.	Southwick.
.	.	.	.	.	.		North Hylton Lane Depôts	Durham ..	N. E.	Southwick.
.	.	.	.	.	.		Pratt's Depôt	Durham ..	N. E.	Southwick.
.	.	.	.	.	.		Scott's Depôt	Durham ..	N. E.	Southwick.
.	.	.	.	.	.		Thompson, R., & Son's Depôt & Shipyard	Durham ..	N. E.	Southwick.
.	.	.	.	.	.		Wearmouth Colliery	Durham ..	N. E.	Southwick.
G	P	F	L	H	C		Southwick	Kirkcud ..	G. & S. W.	Dumfries and Castle Douglas.
.	P	.	.	.	.		Southwick	Sussex ...	L. B. & S. C.	Brighton and Shoreham.
G	P	F	L	H	C		South Willingham	Lincoln ..	G. N.	Lincoln and Louth.

EXPLANATION—G *Goods Station.*   P *Passenger and Parcel Station.*   P* *Passenger, but not Parcel or Miscellaneous Traffic.*
F *Furniture Vans, Carriages, Portable Engines, and Machines on Wheels.*   L *Live Stock.*
H *Horse Boxes and Prize Cattle Vans.*   C *Carriages by Passenger Train.*

STATION ACCOMMODATION.					CRANE POWER.	STATIONS, &c.	COUNTY.	COMPANY.	POSITION.
					Tons Cwts.	South Wingfield Col. Co.'s Sid.	Derby	Mid.	Wingfield.
G	P	F	L	H	1 10	South Wishaw	Lanark	Cal.	See Wishaw, South.
						South Witham	Lincoln	Mid.	Saxby and Castle Bytham.
						Holwell Iron Co.'s Buckminster Sidings	Leicester	Mid.	Buckminster Branch.
G	P					Southwold	Suffolk	Southwold	Terminus.
						Southwood, Jones & Co.'s Sid.	Mon	L. & N. W	Penllwyn Tramway (Nine Mile Point).
						South Yardley	Worcester	G. W.	See Acocks Green & South Yardley.
						South Yorkshire Bottle Co.'s Siding	Yorks	{ G. C. / Mid.	Mexboro'. / Swinton.
						South Yorkshire Coal Co.'s Siding (Ellis, E., Col.) (G C)	Yorks	G. C.—Mid.	Doncaster.
						South Yorkshire Hoop Iron Works (Wilcock & Jones)	Yorks	Mid.	Masboro' and Rotherham.
						Sovereign Pit	Lancs	L. & N. W.	See Chowbent West Junc. Siding (Wigan Coal & Iron Co.)
G	P	F	L	H C	15 0	Sowerby Bridge	Yorks	L. & Y.	Halifax and Todmorden.
						Clay, J., & Son's Siding	Yorks	L. & Y.	Sowerby Bridge.
						Shepherd & Blackburn's Siding	Yorks	L. & Y.	Near Sowerby Bridge.
						Sowerby Bridge Flour Society's Siding	Yorks	L. & Y.	Sowerby Bridge.
						Sowerby Bridge Gas Works (Whitworth's)(CooperHouse Siding)	Yorks	L. & Y.	Luddendenfoot.
G	P		L			Spa	Kerry	G. S. & W.	Tralee and Fenit.
						SPALDING—			
G		F			1 10	(Station)	Lincoln	Mid.	Spalding Junction & North Drove.
G	P	F	L	H C	5 0	(Station, G. N.)	Lincoln	{ G. N. / G. E. / Mid. & G. N. Jt.	Peterboro' and Boston. / Over G. N. Line. / Over G. N. Line.
						Jepson's Siding	Lincoln	G. N.	Spalding.
						Junction	Lincoln	G. N.—Mid. & G. N. Jt.	Spalding and Bourne.
						Junction	Lincoln	G. N.—Mid. & G. N. Jt.	Spalding and Sutton Bridge.
						North Junction	Lincoln	G. N.—G. N. & G. E. Jt.	Spalding Station and Pinchbeck.
						South Junction	Lincoln	G. N.—G. N. & G. E. Jt.	Spalding Station and Cowbit.
G	P					Spa Mines	Yorks	N. E.	Slapewath.
						Spamount	Tyrone	C. & V. B.	Castlederg and Victoria Bridge.
						Sparkbrook	Warwick	G. W.	See Birmingham, Small Heath and Sparkbrook.
G	P	F	L	H C	1 10	Sparkford	Somerset	G. W.	Yeovil and Frome.
						Spa Road (Bermondsey)	Surrey	S. E. & C.	See London.
						Sparrow & Co.'s Lime Kilns	Devon	L. & S.W.	Plymouth, Cattewater Harbour.
						Sparrow, J., & Sons	Denbigh	G. W.—W. M. & C. Q.	Same as Ffrwd Iron Works (Moss).
						Sparrow's Siding	N'hamptn	L. & N. W.	See Gayton Sidings (Blisworth).
						Spawood Mines	Yorks	N. E.	Slapewath.
						Speakman's—			
						Bedford Colliery	Lancs	L. & N. W.	Leigh and Bedford.
						Sutton Dock	Cheshire	B'head Jt. (GW & L&NW)	Halton.
G	P	F	L	H C	2 0	Spean Bridge (N.B.)	Inverness	{ N.B. / Highland(I & F A)	Crianlarich and Fort William. / Over N.B. from Spean Bge. Junc.
						Spean Bridge Junction	Inverness	High (I.& F.A.)—N.B.	Gairlochy & Spean Bridge Station.
						Spear and Jackson's Siding (Etna Works) (Mid.)	Yorks	Mid.—G. C.	Sheffield, Wicker.
						Speculation Siding	Glo'ster	S. & Wye Jt. (G.W.& Mid)	Lydbrook, Upper.
G	P	F	L	H C	8 0	Speech House Road	Glo'ster	S. & Wye Jt. (G.W.& Mid)	Drybrook Road and Parkend.
					8 0	Bicslade Siding	Glo'ster	S. & Wye Jt. (G.W.& Mid)	Speech House Road and Parkend.
						Speech House Colliery	Glo'ster	S. & Wye Jt. (G.W.& Mid)	Speech House Road.
						Thomas & Co.'s Stone Saw Mills(Cannop StoneWks.)	Glo'ster	S. & Wye Jt. (G.W.& Mid)	Speech House Road.
						Wimberry Colliery	Glo'ster	S. & Wye Jt. (G.W.& Mid)	Speech House Road & Serridge Jn.
						Speedie Bros.' Auction Mart Siding	Stirling	N. B.	Stirling, Cowpark.
						Speedwell Iron Works	Lanark	N. B.	Coatbridge, Whifflet.
	P					Speen (for Donnington)	Berks	L'bourn Valley	Newbury and Lambourn.
G	P		L	H		Speeton	Yorks	N. E.	Bridlington and Filey.
	P					Speke	Lancs	L. & N. W.	Liverpool and Warrington.
						Spekeland Road Sidings	Lancs	L. & N. W.	See Liverpool.
						Spellow	Lancs	L. & N. W.	See Liverpool.
						Spencer & Co.'s Middleton Sid.	Derby	L. & N. W.	Steeplehouse.
						Spencer & Co.'s Siding	Wilts	G. W.	Melksham.

STATION ACCOMMODATION.						CRANE POWER.	STATIONS, &c.	COUNTY.	COMPANY.	POSITION.
						Tons Cwts.				
							Spencer & Son's Siding.........	Essex	G. E.	Stansted.
							Spencer, Chapman, & Messel's Chemical Manure Wks.(GE)	Essex	G E—G N—L N W—Mid.	London, Silvertown.
							Spencer's Brierlow Siding ...	Derby	L. & N. W.	Hindlow.
							Spencer's Lime Works	Yorks	Mid.	Same as Swinden Lime Works (Rylstone).
							Spencer's, P. W., Quarry......	Yorks	Mid.	Thornton-in-Craven.
							Spencer's Rolling Mills.........	Northumb	N. E.	Same as Newburn Rolling Mills (Newburn).
							Spencer's Siding...................	Kent	S. E. & C.	Wrotham.
							Spencer's Steel Works	Northumb	N. E.	Same as Newburn Steel Works (Newburn).
							Spen Colliery, Coke Ovens, Brick Works, and Depôts	Durham ...	N. E.	Same as Garesfield Colliery, &c. (Derwenthaugh).
							Spennithorne	Yorks	N. E.	Bedale and Leyburn.
G	P	F	L	H	C	5 0	Spennymoor	Durham ...	N. E.	Ferryhill and Bishop Auckland.
							Binchester Colliery & Coke Ovens	Durham ...	N. E.	Spennymoor.
							Carbo Syndicate Works (Tudhoe Iron Works).....	Durham ...	N. E.	Spennymoor.
							Dean & Chapter Colliery ...	Durham ...	N. E.	Spennymoor.
							Geldard's Foundry...............	Durham ...	N. E.	Spennymoor.
							Merrington Lane Foundry	Durham ...	N. E.	Spennymoor.
							Merrington Lane Siding ...	Durham ...	N. E.	Spennymoor.
							North Close Colliery (Spennymoor Cattle Dk.)	Durham ...	N. E.	Spennymoor.
							Northern Counties Electricity Supply Co.'s Wks.	Durham ...	N. E.	Spennymoor.
							South Brancepeth Colliery Coke Ovens & Bk. Wks. (Page Bank Col., Coke Ovens & Brick Works) ...	Durham ...	N. E.	Spennymoor.
							Spennymoor & Tudhoe Gas Works & Depôts.........	Durham ...	N. E.	Spennymoor.
							Spennymoor Iron Works ...	Durham ...	N. E.	Spennymoor.
							Tudhoe & Sunderland Bridge Gas Works	Durham ...	N. E.	Spennymoor.
							Tudhoe Blast Furnaces ...	Durham ...	N. E.	Spennymoor.
							Tudhoe Colliery, Coke Ovens & Brick Works	Durham ...	N. E.	Spennymoor.
							Tudhoe Grange Colliery & Coke Ovens	Durham ...	N. E.	Spennymoor.
							Tudhoe Iron & Steel Wks.	Durham ...	N. E.	Spennymoor.
							Tudhoe Slag Works	Durham ...	N. E.	Spennymoor.
							Westerton Colliery	Durham ...	N. E.	Spennymoor.
G		L					Spetchley	Worcester	Mid.	Bromsgrove and Defford.
	P						Spetisbury	Dorset......	S. & D. Jt. (L. & S. W. & Mid)	Wimborne and Blandford.
G						1 10	Spiersbridge	Renfrew...	G B & K Jt (Cal & G & S W)	Branch from Kennishead.
							Spillers & Baker's Stores	Glo'ster	G. W.—Mid.	Gloucester Docks.
							Spillers & Baker's Siding......	Glamorg'n	G W—L N W—Rhy—TV	Cardiff.
							Spillers Nephews Biscuit Wks.	Glamorg'n	T. V.	Cardiff.
							Spilman's Siding	Yorks	Axholme Jt (L & Y & N E)	Crowle.
G	P	F	L	H	C	5 0	Spilsby	Lincoln ...	G. N.	Branch—Boston and Louth.
							Robinson's Siding	Lincoln ...	G. N.	Spilsby.
							Spindleside Colliery No. 5	Lanark	Cal.	Cleland.
G	P	F	L	H	C		Spink Hill(for Mount St. Mary)	Derby......	L. D. & E. C.	Clown and Sheffield.
							Newton's Brick Yard	Derby......	L. D. & E. C.	Spink Hill.
							Park Hall Colliery.............	Derby......	L. D. & E. C.	Branch from Spink Hill.
							Spireslack Colliery...............	Ayr	Cal.	Coalburn.
G	P		L	H		4 0	Spital	Cheshire...	B'head Jt.(G W & L N W)	Birkenhead and Hooton.
							Lever Bros.' Port Sunlight Siding	Cheshire...	B'head Jt.(G W & L N W)	Spital and Bebington.
							Stourton Siding	Cheshire...	B'head Jt.(G W & L N W)	Spital and Bebington.
							Spitalfields	Middlesex	G. E.	See London.
							Spitalfields Hoist	Middlesex	G. E.	London.
							Spitalfields Hoist Junction ...	Middlesex	E. L. Jt.—G.E.	Whitechapel and Spitalfields Hoist.
							Spital Maltings	Notts	G. N. & Mid. Jt.	See Bishop & Son's (Newark). See Hole & Co.'s (Newark).
							Spittalhill Quarry & Bk. Wks.	Lanark	Cal.	See Bardykes Colliery (Newton).
							Spittle's (Cambrian) Foundry	Mon	A (N & S W) D & R—G W	Newport, Alexandra Docks.
G	P		L	H	C	2 0	Spofforth	Yorks	N. E.	Harrogate and Wetherby.
G	P		L				Spondon	Derby......	Mid.	Derby and Trent.

EXPLANATION—G *Goods Station.*   P *Passenger and Parcel Station.*   P* *Passenger, but not Parcel or Miscellaneous Traffic.*
F *Furniture Vans, Carriages, Portable Engines, and Machines on Wheels.*   L *Live Stock.*
H *Horse Boxes and Prize Cattle Vans.*   C *Carriages by Passenger Train.*

STATION ACCOMMODATION.	CRANE POWER.	STATIONS, &c.	COUNTY.	COMPANY.	POSITION.
	Tons Cwts.	Spondon—*continued.*			
. . . . . .	. .	Leach, Neal & Co.'s Siding	Derby	Mid.	Near Spondon.
. . . . . .	. .	Robinson Bros.' Siding	Derby	Mid.	Near Spondon.
. . . . . .	. .	Spon Lane	Staffs	G. W.	See West Bromwich.
G P F L H C	10 0	Spon Lane (for West Bromwich)	Staffs	L. & N. W.	Birmingham and Wolverhampton.
. . . . . .	. .	Chance Bros. & Co.'s Siding	Staffs	L. & N. W.	Spon Lane and Oldbury.
. . . . . .	. .	Metropolitan Amalgamated Railway Carriage and Wagon Co.'s Siding	Staffs	L. & N. W.	Spon Lane and Oldbury.
G	5 0	Spon Lane Basin	Staffs	L. & N. W.	Birmingham and Wolverhampton.
G P	. .	Spooner Row	Norfolk	G. E.	Wymondham and Thetford.
. P	. .	Spratton	N'hamptn	L. & N. W.	Market Harboro' and Northampton.
. . . . . .	. .	Springall's, R. F., Sid. (G.E.)	Norfolk	G. E.—G. N.—Mid.	Lynn Harbour.
. . . . . .	. .	Springbank Colliery Sidings	Lanark	N. B.	Clarkston.
. . . . . .	. .	Springbank Junction	Yorks	H. & B.	Hull.
. . . . . .	. .	Springbank Mill	Perth	Cal.	Dunblane.
. . . . . .	. .	Springbank Sidings	Lanark	N. B.	Clarkston.
. . . . . .	. .	Springburn (N. B.)	Lanark	N. B.—G. & S. W.	See Glasgow.
. . . . . .	. .	Springburn Park	Lanark	Cal.	See Glasgow.
. . . . . .	. .	Spring Colliery	Lancs	L. & N. W.	See Pearson & Knowles Coal & Iron Co. (Wigan).
G P . L H .	3 0	Springfield	Fife	N. B.	Ladybank and Cupar.
. . . . . .	. .	Brighton Brick & Tile Works and Quarry	Fife	N. B.	Springfield and Cupar.
. . . . . .	. .	Cults Lime Works	Fife	N. B.	Ladybank and Springfield.
G	. .	Cults Siding	Fife	N. B.	Ladybank and Springfield.
. . . . . .	. .	Springfield Branch (N.B.)	Stirling	N. B.—Cal.	Falkirk, Grahamston.
. . . . . .	. .	Springfield Depôt (N.B.)	Stirling	N. B.—Cal.	See Falkirk.
. . . . . .	. .	Springfield Free Warehouses (Cal.)	Renfrew	Cal.—G. & S. W.—N. B.	Glasgow, General Terminus.
. . . . . .	. .	Dk. Lane Grain Store (Cal.)	Renfrew	Cal.—G. & S. W.—N. B.	Springfield Free Warehouses.
. . . . . .	. .	McHarg's Store (Cal.)	Renfrew	Cal.—G. & S. W.—N. B.	Springfield Free Warehouses.
. . . . . .	. .	Springfield Locomotive Wks.	Durham	N. E.	Same as Stephenson, R., & Co. (Darlington).
. . . . . .	. .	Springfield Mill	Edinboro'	N. B.	Polton.
. . . . . .	. .	Springfield Quay (Cal.)	Renfrew	Cal.—G. & S. W.—N. B.	See Glasgow.
. . . . . .	. .	Springfield Shaft Works	Lanark	N. B.	Clarkston.
. . . . . .	. .	Spring Gardens Gates Siding	Durham	N. E.	West Auckland.
. . . . . .	. .	Spring Gardens Junction	Durham	N. E.	West Auckland.
. . . . . .	. .	Spring Grove	Middlesex	L. & S. W. / Met. Dist.	See Isleworth & Spring Grove. / See Osterley & Spring Grove.
. . . . . .	. .	Springhead	Kent	S. E. & C.	See Southfleet (for Springhead).
. . . . . .	. .	Springhead	Yorks	L. & N. W.	See Grotton and Springhead.
. . . . . .	. .	Springhead Loco. Siding	Yorks	H. & B.	Hull.
. . . . . .	. .	Springhead Spinning Co.'s Sid.	Yorks	L. & N. W.	Grotton and Springhead.
. . . . . .	. .	Spring Hill Colliery	Staffs	L. & N. W.	Same as Essington Farm Colliery Co.'s Siding (Bloxwich).
. . . . . .	. .	Springhill Colliery (Cauldhame Colliery)	Ayr	G. & S. W.	Dreghorn.
. . . . . .	. .	Spring Place Sidings (Kentish Town)	Middlesex	Mid.	See London.
. . . . . .	. .	Springs Branch	Lancs	L. & N. W.	Bamfurlong and Wigan.
. . . . . .	. .	Springs Branch Depôt	Lancs	L. & N. W.	See Wigan.
. P	. .	Springside	Ayr	G. & S. W.	Dreghorn and Crosshouse.
G P . L . .	7 0	Spring Vale	Lancs	L. & Y.	Bolton and Blackburn.
. . . . . .	. .	Darwen Mill Siding	Lancs	L. & Y.	Near Spring Vale.
. . . . . .	. .	Entwistle, R., & Co.'s Sid.	Lancs	L. & Y.	Spring Vale and Entwistle.
. . . . . .	. .	Spring Vale Siding	Staffs	G. W. / L. & N. W.	Bilston & Deepfields. / Deepfields and Coseley.
. . . . . .	. .	Hickman's Brick Works	Staffs	L. & N. W.	Spring Vale Siding.
. . . . . .	. .	Hickman's Iron Works	Staffs	L. & N. W.	Spring Vale Siding.
. . . . . .	. .	Hickman's Siding	Staffs	G. W.	Spring Vale Siding.
. . . . . .	. .	Meynell & Son's Siding	Staffs	L. & N. W.	Spring Vale Siding.
. . . . . .	. .	Springwell Brewery Co.'s Sid.	Yorks	L. & Y.	Heckmondwike.
. . . . . .	. .	Springwell Brick Works	Durham	N. E.	Pelaw Junction Station.
. . . . . .	. .	Springwell Colliery	Durham	N. E.	Jarrow.
. . . . . .	. .	Springwell Quarry	Durham	N. E.	Jarrow.
. . . . . .	. .	Springwood Junctions	Yorks	L&Y.—L&Y.&L&NWJt.—L. & N. W.	Huddersfield.
. . . . . .	. .	Springwood Siding	Yorks	L. & Y.	Lockwood.
. . . . . .	. .	Sproat, Marley & Co.'s Siding	Durham	N. E.	Hebburn.
G	. .	Sprotborough	Yorks	H. & B.	Wrangbrook Junction and Denaby.

EXPLANATION—G *Goods Station.*   P *Passenger and Parcel Station.*   P* *Passenger, but not Parcel or Miscellaneous Traffic.*
F *Furniture Vans, Carriages, Portable Engines, and Machines on Wheels.*   L *Live Stock.*
H *Horse Boxes and Prize Cattle Vans.*   C *Carriages by Passenger Train.*

G	P	F	L	H	C	Tons	Cwts	STATIONS, &c.	COUNTY.	COMPANY.	POSITION.
G	P	F	L	H	C	.	.	Sprouston	Roxburgh	N. E.	Berwick and Kelso.
								Sprouston Junction	Roxburgh	N. B.—N. E.	Kelso and Sprouston.
								Stableford's Brick Works (Mid.)	Leicester..	Mid.—L. & N. W.	Coalville.
								Stableford's Wagon Works (Mid.)	Leicester..	Mid.—L. & N. W.	Coalville.
G	P					.	.	Stacey, E. L., Siding	Middlesex	G. E.	Angel Road.
G	P					.	.	Stacksteads	Lancs	L. & Y.	Stubbins and Bacup.
								Brandwood Siding	Lancs	L. & Y.	Near Stacksteads.
								Siddall's Stone Siding	Lancs	L. & Y.	Stacksteads.
								Stacksteads Coal Siding	Lancs	L. & Y.	Stacksteads.
G	P	F	L	H	C	5	0	Staddlethorpe (N.E.)	Yorks	N. E.	Hull and Selby.
	P			H	C	.	.			G. C.	Over N. E. from Thorne Junction.
	P					.	.			L. & N. W.	Over N. E. from Leeds.
G	P*							Broomfleet Siding	Yorks	N. E.	Staddlethorpe.
								STAFFORD—			
G	P	F	L	H	C	10	0	(Station, L. & N. W.)	Staffs	L. & N. W.	Crewe and Lichfield.
G	P			H	C	.	.		Staffs	G. N.	Over L. & N. W. from Stafford Junc.
	P			H	C	.	.			N. S.	Over L & N W from Norton Bge. Jn.
								Bagnall's Castle Engine Wks	Staffs	L. & N. W.	Stafford and Haughton.
G	P	F	L	H	C	10	0	Common	Staffs	G. N.	Stafford Junction and Ingestre.
G								Doxey Road	Staffs	G. N.	Branch near Stafford Junction.
								Junction	Staffs	G. N.—L. & N. W.	Stafford Common & Stafford Station.
								Lilleshall Coal & Iron Co.'s Siding (G.N.)	Staffs	G. N.—L. & N. W.	Stafford Common and Stafford Junc.
								Orton & Co.'s Moss Siding	Staffs	L. & N. W.	Stafford and Milford.
								Siemens Bros. & Co.'s Sid.	Staffs	L. & N. W.	Stafford and Milford.
								Stafford Corporation—			
								Electric Light Works (G. N.)	Staffs	G. N.—L. & N. W.	Stafford Common and Stafford Junc.
								Gas Works (G. N.)	Staffs	G. N.—L. & N. W.	Stafford Common and Stafford Junc.
								Stafford Salt and Alkali Co.'s Siding	Staffs	G. N.	Stafford Common.
								Stubbs & Co.'s Siding	Staffs	G. N.	Stafford Common.
								Venables' Siding	Staffs	G. N. / L. & N. W.	Stafford Common and Stafford Junc. / Stafford and Great Bridgeford.
								Willder's Siding	Staffs	L. & N. W.	Stafford and Penkridge.
								Stafford Coal and Iron Co.'s Siding (N. S.)	Staffs	N. S.—L. & N. W.	Same as Sideway Siding (Trentham).
								Stafford Corporation—			
								Electric Light Wks. (G. N.)	Staffs	G. N.—L. & N. W.	Stafford.
								Gas Works (G. N.)	Staffs	G. N.—L. & N. W.	Stafford.
								Stafford Road Junction	Staffs	G. W.	Wolverhampton.
								Stafford Road Siding	Staffs	L. & N. W.	Same as Wolverhampton Gas Co.'s (Wolverhampton).
								Staffordshire Chemical Co's Sid.	Staffs	N. S.	Chatterley.
								Staffordshire Iron Works	Staffs	L. & N. W.	Same as Bunch & Son's Siding (Blox wich).
								Staffordshire Steel and Ingot Iron Works Siding	Staffs	G. W.	Bilston and Deepfields.
G	P					.	.	Staffordstown	Antrim	N. C. Com. (Mid.)	Cookstown Junction and Cookstown.
	P							Staincliffe and Batley Carr	Yorks	L. & N. W.	Dewsbury and Leeds.
G	P							Staincross (for Mapplewell)	Yorks	G. C.	Barnsley and Wakefield.
								Barnsley Gas Works	Yorks	G. C.	Staincross (for Mapplewell).
								East Gawber Hall Colliery	Yorks	G. C.	Staincross (for Mapplewell).
								Primrose Main Colliery	Yorks	G. C.	Staincross (for Mapplewell).
								Wallsend Main Colliery	Yorks	G. C.	Staincross (for Mapplewell).
								Wharncliffe (Carlton) New Colliery	Yorks	G. C.	Staincross (for Mapplewell).
								Wharncliffe (Woodmoor) Colliery	Yorks	G. C.	Staincross (for Mapplewell).
								Staindrop	Durham	N. E.	See Winston (for Staindrop).
								STAINES—			
G	P	F	L	H	C	6	0	(Station)	Middlesex	G. W.	Bch. from West Drayton & Yiewsley.
	P							High Street	Middlesex	L. & S. W.	Staines and Windsor.
G	P	F	L	H	C	10	0	Junction Station	Middlesex	L. & S. W.	Twickenham and Reading.
								Reservoir Siding	Middlesex	L. & S. W.	Staines.
								Staines Linoleum Co.'s Sid.	Middlesex	G. W.—L. & S. W.	Staines.
G	P		L	H	C			Stainforth and Hatfield	Yorks	G. C.	Doncaster and Thorne.
								Stainforth Junction	Yorks	G. C.	Stainforth and Thorne.
								Stainforth Junction	Yorks	G. C.—W. R. & G. Jt.	Stainforth and Bramwith.
								Stainforth Siding	Yorks	Mid.	See Craven Lime Co. (Settle).

EXPLANATION—**G** *Goods Station.*   **P** *Passenger and Parcel Station.*   **P*** *Passenger, but not Parcel or Miscellaneous Traffic.*
F *Furniture Vans, Carriages, Portable Engines, and Machines on Wheels.*   **L** *Live Stock.*
H *Horse Boxes and Prize Cattle Vans.*   **C** *Carriages by Passenger Train.*

STATION ACCOMMODATION.						CRANE POWER.		STATIONS, &c.	COUNTY.	COMPANY.	POSITION.
						Tons	Cwts.				
G	P	F	L	H	C	3	0	Stainland and Holywell Green	Yorks	L. & Y.	Branch from Greetland.
								Shaw & Son's Siding	Yorks	L. & Y.	Stainland and Holywell Green.
G	P	.	L	H	.			Stainton Dale	Yorks	N. E.	Scarborough and Whitby.
								Bent Rigg Lane Siding	Yorks	N. E.	Stainton Dale.
								Stainton Mineral Siding	Lancs	Furness	See Dalton.
G	P	.	.	.	.	5	0	Stairfoot (for Ardsley)	Yorks	G. C.	Barnsley and Doncaster.
								Barnsley Main Colliery	Yorks	G. C.	Stairfoot (for Ardsley).
								Carlton Main Col. Co.'s Grimethorpe Colliery	Yorks	G. C.	Stairfoot (for Ardsley).
								Dearne Valley Colliery	Yorks	G. C.	Stairfoot (for Ardsley).
								Houghton Main Colliery	Yorks	G. C.	Stairfoot (for Ardsley).
								Micklethwaite's, R. K., Brickyard	Yorks	G. C.	Stairfoot (for Ardsley).
								Micklethwaite's, R. K., Stone Siding	Yorks	G. C.	Stairfoot (for Ardsley).
								New Oaks Colliery	Yorks	G. C.	Stairfoot (for Ardsley).
								Ryland's Glass & Engineering Co.'s Siding	Yorks	G. C.	Stairfoot (for Ardsley).
								Stairfoot Junction	Yorks	G. C.—H. & B.	Mexboro' and Cudworth.
								Stairfoot Jn. with Nostell Line	Yorks	G. C.	Stairfoot and Staincross.
G	P	.	.	.	.	2	0	Staithes	Yorks	N. E.	Whitby and Saltburn.
								Stakepool	Lancs	G. & K. E.	Same as Pilling.
G	P	F	L	H	C	10	0	Stalbridge	Dorset	S.&D.Jt.(L.&S.W.& Mid)	Blandford and Templecombe.
G	P	.	.	.	.	10	0	Staley and Millbrook	Cheshire	L. & N. W.	Huddersfield and Stalybridge.
G	P	F	L	H	C	.	.	Stalham	Norfolk	Mid. & G. N. Jt.	North Walsham & Yarmouth Beach.
G	P	.	L	H	.			Stallingboro'	Lincoln	G. C.	Barnetby and Grimsby.
								STALYBRIDGE—			
G	P	.	L	H	.	10	0	(Station)	Lancs	L. & Y.	Bch. fr. Manchester, Miles Platting.
G	P	F	L	H	C	20	0	(Station, G.C.&L.& N. W. Jt)	Lancs	{ G. C. & L. & N. W. Jt.	Ashton and Huddersfield.
G	.	F	L	.	.	20	0			{ Mid.	Over G. C. Line.
								Junction	Lancs	G. C.—L. & Y.	Stalybridge Jt. Station and Ashton (Charlestown).
								Junction	Lancs	G. C.—L. & N. W.	Stalybridge Jt. Sta. & Huddersfield.
								Summer's Globe Iron Works	Lancs	G. C. & L. & N. W. Jt.	Stalybridge.
		.	L	.	.			Tunnel End Siding	Lancs	L. & N. W.	Stalybridge and Mossley.
								Silkstone Coal Co.	Lancs	L. & N. W.	Tunnel End Siding.
								STAMFORD—			
G	P	F	L	H	C	6	0	(Station)	N'hamptn	G. N.	Essendine and Wansford Junction.
G	P	F	L	H	C	10	0	(Station, Mid.)	N'hamptn	{ Mid.	Peterboro' and Oakham.
										{ L. & N. W.	Over Mid. from Luffenham Junc.
								Eldred's Lime Siding	Lincoln	G. N.	Stamford and Ryhall.
								Junction	N'hamptn	G. N.—Mid.	Essendine and Luffenham.
								Marquis of Exeter's Iron-stone Siding	N'hamptn	Mid.	Stamford.
								Priory Siding	Lincoln	G. N.	Ryhall and Stamford.
								Rutland Engineering Works (Blackstone & Co.) (G. N.)	Lincoln	G. N.—L. & N. W.—Mid.	Stamford and Ryhall.
G	P	F	L	H	C	1	0	Stamford Bridge	Yorks	N. E.	York and Market Weighton.
								Stamford Hill	Middlesex	{ G. E.	See London.
										{ Mid.—T. & H. Jt.	See London, South Tottenham and Stamford Hill.
								Stammerham Junction	Sussex	L. B. & S. C.	Horsham and Billingshurst.
G	P	.	L	.	.			Stanbridgeford	Beds	L. & N. W.	Dunstable and Leighton.
								Forder & Son's Sewell Lime Works	Beds	L. & N. W.	Stanbridgeford and Dunstable.
								Totternhoe Lime and Stone Co.'s Siding	Beds	L. & N. W.	Stanbridgeford and Leighton.
								Stancliffe Estates Co.'s Siding	Derby	{ L. & N. W.	Steeplehouse.
										{ Mid.	Darley Dale.
								Standard Brick Co.'s Siding	Durham	N. E.	Pelaw.
								Standard Brick Works	Durham	N. E.	Waterhouses.
								Standard Colliery	Glamorg'n	T. V.	Same as Ynishir Standard Colliery (Wattstown).
								Standard Quarry	Montgom	Cam. (W. & L.)	See Welshpool.
								Standard Sid. (Airdrie Iron Co.)	Edinboro'	N. B.	Loanhead.
								Standard Wire Co.'s Siding	Durham	N. E.	See Skerne Iron Works (Darlington).
								Standard Works	Lanark	N. B.	Airdrie, North.
								Standburn Siding	Stirling	N. B.	Bowhouse.
								Standhill Siding	Roxburgh	N. B.	Belses.
.	P	.	.	.	.			Standish	Lancs	L. & N. W.	Preston and Wigan.
								Standish Brewery	Lancs	L. & N. W.	Same as Almond's Siding (Wigan).

EXPLANATION— G Goods Station.   P Passenger and Parcel Station.   P* Passenger, but not Parcel or Miscellaneous Traffic.
F Furniture Vans, Carriages, Portable Engines, and Machines on Wheels.   L Live Stock.
H Horse Boxes and Prize Cattle Vans.   C Carriages by Passenger Train.

STATION ACCOMMODATION.						CRANE POWER.		STATIONS, &c.	COUNTY.	COMPANY.	POSITION.
						Tons	Cwts.				
G	P			L	H			Standon	Herts	G. E.	St. Margaret's and Buntingford.
G	P			L	H	1	10	Standon Bridge	Staffs	L. & N. W.	Crewe and Stafford.
								Stane Colliery	Lanark	N. B.	Shotts.
								Stane Siding	Lanark	N. B.	See Shotts.
G	P	F	L	H	C			Stanford-le-Hope	Essex	L. T. & S.	Tilbury and Southend-on-Sea.
	P							Stanford Park	N'hampton	L. & N. W.	See Yelvertoft and Stanford Park.
								Stanghow Depôts	Yorks	N. E.	Boosbeck.
								Stanghow Mines	Yorks	N. E.	Boosbeck.
	P							Stanhoe	Norfolk	G. E.	Heacham and Wells.
G	P	F	L	H	C	1	0	Stanhope	Durham	N. E.	Wearhead and Wear Valley Junc.
								Newlandside Quarry	Durham	N. E.	Stanhope.
								Parson Byers Quarry (Bell Bros.)	Durham	N. E.	Stanhope.
G								Stanhope Kilns	Durham	N. E.	Branch from Burnhill Junc. Station.
								Ashes Quarry	Durham	N. E.	Stanhope Kilns.
								Crawley Engine Siding	Durham	N. E.	Stanhope Kilns.
								Stanhope Burn Mines	Durham	N. E.	Stanhope Kilns.
								Stanhope Silkstone Colliery (L. & Y.)	Yorks	L. & Y.—G. C.	Darton.
								Stank Mines Mineral Siding	Lancs	Furness	Barrow.
								Stanley	Lancs	C. L. C. (G C, G N, & Mid.)	See Liverpool, Knotty Ash & Stanley.
								Stanley	Lancs	L. & N. W.	See Liverpool.
G	P	F	L	H	C	3	0	Stanley	Perth	Cal.	Perth and Coupar Angus.
G	P	F	L	H	C	1	10	Stanley	Yorks	Meth Jt. (G N, L&Y&N. E)	Lofthouse and Methley.
								Calder Siding	Yorks	Meth Jt. (G N, L&Y&N. E)	Stanley and Methley.
								Newmarket Colliery	Yorks	Meth Jt. (G N, L&Y&N. E)	Stanley and Methley.
								Stanley & Hyde Siding	Cambs	G. E.	Wisbech.
								Stanley & Son's Oil Soap & Manure Works	Yorks	Mid.	Swinton.
								Stanley Bros.—			
								Brick & Pipe Works (L&NW)	Warwick	L. & N. W.—Mid.	Nuneaton.
								Charity Colliery (L.N.W.)	Warwick	L. & N. W.—Mid.	Bedworth.
								Nuneaton New Col. (Mid.)	Warwick	Mid.—L. & N. W.	Stockingford.
								Stanley Colliery	Durham	N. E.	See Pease and Partners' (Crook).
								Stanley Colliery (G. N.)	Notts	G. N.—G. C.	See Mapperley Colliery Co. (West Hallam for Dale Abbey).
								Stanley Colliery (L. & Y.)	Yorks	L.& Y.—G. N.—L.& N.W.	Liversedge.
								Stanley Dock	Lancs	G. W.	See Liverpool.
								Stanley Junction	Perth	Cal.—High.	Perth and Dunkeld.
								Stanley Land & Brick Co.'s Siding	Lancs	L. & N. W.	Liverpool, Edge Hill.
								Stanley Siding	Durham	N. E.	Shield Row.
								Stanley's Siding	Yorks	G. C.	Wath.
								Stanlow Works	Cheshire	B'head Jt. (G W & L N W)	Same as Smelting Corporation (Ellesmere Port).
G	P	F	L	H	C			Stanmore	Middlesex	L. & N. W.	Branch from Harrow.
G	P		L					Stanner	Radnor	G. W.	Kington and New Radnor.
								Stannergate	Forfar	D. & A. Jt. (Cal. & N. B.)	See Dundee.
								Stanners Close Steel Works	Durham	N. E.	Wolsingham.
G	P		L			15	0	Stanningley (G. N.)	Yorks	{ G. N. / L. & Y. }	Leeds and Bradford. / Over G. N. from Bowling Junction.
								Barnes' Siding	Yorks	G. N.	Stanningley.
								Butler & Co.'s Trustee's Sid.	Yorks	G. N.	Stanningley.
								Gaunt & Co.'s Siding	Yorks	G. N.	Stanningley.
G	P	F	L	H	C			Stannington	Northumb	N. E.	Newcastle and Morpeth.
								Stanrigg Brick Works	Lanark	N. B.	Rawyards.
								Stanrigg Colliery	Lanark	N. B.	Rawyards.
								Stanrigg Oil Works	Lanark	N. B.	Rawyards.
								Stanrigg Pit, No. 5. (Airdriehill Colliery Siding)	Lanark	N. B.	Rawyards.
	P*							Stansfield Hall	Yorks	L. & Y.	Portsmouth and Todmorden.
								Stansfield Hall Siding	Lancs	L. & Y.	Todmorden.
G	P	F		H	C	1	0	Stansted	Essex	G. E.	Cambridge and Bishops Stortford.
								Hicks & Co.'s Siding	Essex	G. E.	Stansted.
								Maitland, W. F., Siding	Essex	G. E.	Stansted.
								Rochford, E., Siding	Essex	G. E.	Stansted.
								Spencer & Son's Siding	Essex	G. E.	Stansted.
G	P							Stanton	Wilts	G. W.	Swindon and Highworth.
								Stanton Colliery (J. N. Nadin & Co.) (Mid.)	Derby	Mid.—L. & N. W.	Swadlincote.
G	P							Stanton Gate	Derby	Mid.	Clay Cross and Trent.
								Ilkeston Colliery	Derby	Mid.	Branch from Stanton Gate.

EXPLANATION—G *Goods Station.*   P *Passenger and Parcel Station.*   P* *Passenger, but not Parcel or Miscellaneous Traffic.*
F *Furniture Vans, Carriages, Portable Engines, and Machines on Wheels.*   L *Live Stock.*
H *Horse Boxes and Prize Cattle Vans.*   C *Carriages by Passenger Train.*

STATION ACCOMMODATION.						CRANE POWER.		STATIONS, &c.	COUNTY.	COMPANY.	POSITION.
						Tons	Cwts.	Stanton Gate—*continued.*			
.	.	.	.	.	.	.	.	Manners Colliery	Derby	Mid.	Branch from Stanton Gate.
.	.	.	.	.	.	.	.	Mapperley Col. Co.'s Sid. ...	Derby	Mid.	Branch from Stanton Gate.
.	.	.	.	.	.	.	.	Shipley Colliery (Mundy's)	Derby	Mid.	Branch from Stanton Gate.
								Stanton Iron Co.—			
.	.	.	.	.	.	.	.	Dale Colliery	Derby	Mid.	Branch from Stanton Gate.
.	.	.	.	.	.	.	.	Hallam Fields Siding ...	Derby	Mid.	Mapperley Branch.
.	.	.	.	.	.	.	.	Old Works	Derby	Mid.	Branch from Stanton Gate.
.	.	.	.	.	.	.	.	West Hallam Colliery	Derby	Mid.	Branch from Stanton Gate.
.	.	.	.	.	.	.	.	Stanton Hill	Notts	G. N.	See Skegby (for Stanton Hill).
								Stanton House Farm Siding (Mid.)	Derby	Mid.—L. & N. W.	Swadlincote.
								Stanton Iron Co.—			
.	.	.	.	.	.	.	.	Dale Colliery	Derby	Mid.	Stanton Gate.
.	.	.	.	.	.	.	.	Draughton Crossing Siding	N'hampt'n	L. & N. W.	Lamport.
.	.	.	.	.	.	.	.	Hallam Fields Siding	Derby	Mid.	Stanton Gate.
.	.	.	.	.	.	.	.	Iron Ore Siding	Leicester..	Mid.	Holwell Junction.
.	.	.	.	.	.	.	.	Iron Ore Siding	N'hampt'n	Mid.	Wellingboro'.
.	.	.	.	.	.	.	.	Old Works	Derby	Mid.	Stanton Gate.
.	.	.	.	.	.	.	.	Siding	Lincoln ...	G. N.	Honington.
.	.	.	.	.	.	.	.	Siding	N'hampt'n	Mid.	Desboro' and Rothwell.
.	.	.	.	.	.	.	.	Siding	N'hampt'n	Mid.	Irchester.
.	.	.	.	.	.	.	.	Silverhill Colliery	Notts	G. N.—Mid.	Teversall.
.	.	.	.	.	.	.	.	Teversall Colliery (Butcherwood Colliery)...............	Notts	GN—Mid—GC—LD&EC	Teversall.
.	.	.	.	.	.	.	.	Works	Derby	G. N.	Ilkeston.
.	.	.	.	.	.	.	.	Works	Leicester..	Mid.	Old Dalby.
.	.	.	.	.	.	.	.	Staplecross	Sussex....	K. & E. S.	See Bodiam (for Staplecross and Ewhurst).
G	P	F	L	H	C	1	10	Stapleford and Sandiacre......	Notts	Mid.	Trent and Codnor Park.
.	.	.	.	.	.	.	.	Eastwoods Wagon Works	Notts	Mid.	Near Stapleford and Sandiacre.
.	.	.	.	.	.	.	.	Midland Railway Carriage & Wagon Co.'s Siding...	Derby	Mid.	Near Stapleford and Sandiacre.
.	.	.	.	.	.	.	.	Premier Gas Engineering Co.'s Siding	Derby	Mid.	Near Stapleford and Sandiacre.
.	.	.	.	.	.	.	.	Taylor Bros.' Works........	Derby	Mid.	Near Stapleford and Sandiacre.
G	P	F	L	H	C	4	0	Staple Hill	Glo'ster ...	Mid.	See Bristol.
	P							Staplehurst	Kent	S. E. & C.	Tonbridge and Ashford.
.	.	.	.	.	.	.	.	Stapleton Road	Glo'ster ...	G. W.	Bristol and Pilning.
.	.	.	.	.	.	.	.	Stapleton Road Gas Works (Bristol Gas Co.)	Glo'ster ...	{ G. W. { Mid.	Bristol, Temple Meads. Bristol, Fishponds.
.	.	.	.	.	.	.	.	Stapleton's Siding	N'hampt'n	G. N.	Peakirk.
G	P	F	L	H	C	5	0	Starbeck	Yorks	N. E.	Knaresboro' and Harrogate.
.	.	.	.	.	.	.	.	Bilton Harrogate Gas Wks.	Yorks	N. E.	Starbeck.
.	.	.	.	.	.	.	.	Bilton Junction	Yorks	N. E.	Harrogate and Ripon.
.	.	.	.	.	.	.	5	0	Crimple Siding	Yorks	N. E.	Starbeck.
.	.	.	.	.	.	.	.	Dragon Junction	Yorks	N. E.	Starbeck and Harrogate.
.	.	.	.	.	.	.	.	Starbeck Corporation Stone Siding	Yorks	N. E.	Starbeck.
.	.	.	.	.	.	.	.	Stonefall Brick Works........	Yorks	N. E.	Starbeck.
.	.	.	.	.	.	.	.	Tattersall's Malt Kilns......	Yorks	N. E.	Starbeck.
.	.	.	.	.	.	.	.	Starbeck, North Junction ...	Yorks	N. E.	Starbeck.
.	.	.	.	.	.	.	.	Starbeck, South Junction ...	Yorks	N. E.	Starbeck.
.	.	.	.	.	.	.	.	Star Brick and Tile Works...	Mon	G. W.	Llantarnam.
.	.	.	.	.	.	.	.	Star Brick Works	Lanark ...	Cal.	Glenboig.
G	P	.	.	.	.	3	0	Starcross	Devon	G. W.	Exeter and Teignmouth.
.	.	.	.	.	.	.	.	Star Fuel Works	Glamorg'n	T. V.	Cardiff Docks.
.	.	.	.	.	.	.	.	Stargate Col. & Brick Works	Durham ...	N. E.	Blaydon.
.	.	.	.	.	.	.	.	Star Iron Works............	Lanark ...	Cal.	Glasgow, Buchanan Street.
.	.	.	.	.	.	.	.	Star Pressed Brick Co.'s Sid.	N'hampt'n	Mid. & G. N. Jt.	Eye Green.
.	.	.	.	.	.	.	.	Star Siding	Lanark ...	N. B.	See Glenboig Fire-Clay Works (Coatbridge).
.	.	.	.	.	.	.	.	Statham Brick Works	Lancs ...	L. & N. W.	Warrington, Latchford.
.	.	.	.	.	.	.	.	Stathern	Leicester..	G. N. & L. & N. W. Jt.	See Harby and Stathern.
.	.	.	.	.	.	.	.	Stathern Ironstone Siding...	Leicester..	G. N. & L. & N. W. Jt....	Harby and Stathern.
.	.	.	.	.	.	.	.	Station Street (Mid.)	Staffs	Mid—L&NW—GN—NS.	See Burton-on-Trent.
.	.	.	.	.	.	.	.	Staton's Siding (L. & N. W.)	Staffs	L&NW—Mid—GN—NS.	Burton-on-Trent.
.	.	.	.	.	.	.	.	Staunton Colliery Sanitary Pipe Co.'s Siding	Leicester..	Mid.	Worthington.
G	P	.	L	.	.	3	0	Staveley	W'morlnd	L. & N. W.	Oxenholme and Windermere.
.	.	.	.	.	.	.	.	Staveley & Oakes Co.'s Siding (G.N.)......................	Leicester..	G. N.—Mid.	Waltham-on-the-Wold.

EXPLANATION—G *Goods Station.* P *Passenger and Parcel Station.* P* *Passenger, but not Parcel or Miscellaneous Traffic.*
F *Furniture Vans, Carriages, Portable Engines, and Machines on Wheels.* L *Live Stock.*
H *Horse Boxes and Prize Cattle Vans.* C *Carriages by Passenger Train.*

STATION ACCOMMODATION.						CRANE POWER.	STATIONS, &c.	COUNTY.	COMPANY.	POSITION.
						Tons Cwts.	Staveley Coal and Iron Co.—			
.	.	.	.	.	.	.	Ireland Coke Works	Derby	Mid.	Barrow Hill & Staveley Works.
.	.	.	.	.	.	.	Iron Works	Derby	Mid.	Barrow Hill & Staveley Works.
.	.	.	.	.	.	.	North Staveley Colliery ...	Derby	Mid.	{ Barrow Hill & Staveley Works. Killamarsh.
.	.	.	.	.	.	.	Shirebrook Colliery (Mid.)	Derby	Mid.—G. C.—L. D. & E.C.	Shirebrook.
.	.	.	.	.	.	.	Siding	Derby	G. C.	Staveley Works (for Barrow Hill).
.	.	.	.	.	.	.	Staveley Coal & Iron Co. or Duston Iron Ore Co.'s Sid.	N'hamptn	L. & N. W.	See Duston Siding (Northampton).
							STAVELEY TOWN—			
.	P	.	.	.	.	.	(Station)	Derby	Mid.	Barrow Hill and Clown.
G	P	F	L	H	C	1 10 }	(Station, G. C.)	Derby	{ G. C.	Sheffield and Chesterfield.
G	.	F	L	.	.	1 10 }		Derby	{ L. & N. W.	Over G. N. & G. C. Lines.
.	.	.	.	.	.	.	Duckmanton Siding	Derby	G. C.	Staveley Town.
.	.	.	.	.	.	.	Hartington Col. (G. C.)...	Derby	G. C.—G. N.—L. & N.W.	Staveley Town.
.	.	.	.	.	.	.	Ireland Colliery (G. C.)......	Derby	G. C.—G. N.—L. & N.W.	Staveley Town.
.	.	.	.	.	.	.	Markham Colliery Nos. 1 and 2 (G. C.)	Derby	G. C.—G. N.—L. & N.W.	Staveley Town.
.	.	.	.	.	.	.	St. John's Colliery (G. C.)...	Derby	G. C.—G. N.—L. & N.W.	Staveley Town.
.	.	.	.	.	.	.	Staveley Works	Derby	Mid.	See Barrow Hill and Staveley Works.
G	P	.	.	.	.	1 10 }	Staveley Works (for Bar-\ row Hill) (G. C.)........./	Derby	{ G. C.	Sheffield and Chesterfield.
G	.	.	.	.	.	1 10 }		Derby	{ L. & N. W.	Over G. N. and G. C. Lines.
.	.	.	.	.	.	.	Staveley Cl. & Ir. Co.'s Sid.	Derby	G. C.	Staveley Works (for Barrow Hill).
G	P	.	.	.	.	.	Staverton ....•....	Devon	G. W.	Totnes and Ashburton.
G	P	F	L	H	C	3 0	Staward	Northumb	N. E.	Hexham and Allendale.
G	P	F	L	H	C	.	Stechford (for Yardley).........	Worcester	L. & N. W.	Birmingham and Coventry.
.	.	.	.	.	.	.	Steel Co. of Scotland's Works	Lanark ...	Cal.	Newton.
.	.	.	.	.	.	.	Steel Co. of Scotland's Works	Lanark ...	Cal.—N. B.—G. & S. W.	Same as Blochairn Iron and Steel Works (Glasgow).
G	.	.	.	.	.	.	Steelend	Fife	N. B.	Branch—Whitemyre and Kelty.
.	.	.	.	.	.	.	Cowglen Siding	Fife	N. B.	Lilliehill Junction and Steelend.
G	.	.	.	.	.	.	Lochend Siding	Fife	N. B.	Lilliehill Junction and Steelend.
.	.	.	.	.	.	.	Sunnybraes Colliery (Saline Valley Colliery)	Fife	N. B.	Extension from Steelend.
G	P	.	L	H	.	.	Steele Road	Roxburgh	N. B.	Hawick and Carlisle.
.	.	.	.	.	.	.	Steel Peech & Tozer's Sid. (GC)	Yorks	G. C.—G. N.	Same as Ickles Siding (Rotherham).
.	.	.	.	.	.	.	Steel Peech & Tozer's Works	Yorks	Mid.	Same as Phœnix Steel Wks (Masboro').
.	.	.	.	.	.	.	Steel Railway Journal Box Co.'s Siding (Barningham's)	Lancs	L. & Y.	Pendleton.
.	.	.	.	.	.	.	Steel's Siding	Edinboro'	Cal.	Edinburgh, Lothian Road.
G	P	.	.	H	.	.	Steens Bridge.....................	Hereford ..	G. W.	Bromyard and Leominster.
G	.	F	.	.	.	5 0	Steeplehouse	Derby	L. & N. W.	Buxton and Cromford.
.	.	.	.	.	.	.	Drabble & Co.'s Black Rock Siding	Derby	L. & N. W.	Steeplehouse and Cromford.
.	.	.	.	.	.	.	Hopton Wood Stone Co.— Coal Hills Siding	Derby	L. & N. W.	Steeplehouse and Longcliffe.
.	.	.	.	.	.	.	Hopton Quarry	Derby	L. & N. W.	Steeplehouse and Longcliffe.
.	.	.	.	.	.	.	Middle Peak Siding	Derby	L. & N. W.	Steeplehouse and Longcliffe.
.	.	.	.	.	.	.	Killer's Cromford Moor Sid.	Derby	L. & N. W.	Steeplehouse and Cromford.
.	.	.	.	.	.	.	Shaw Bros.' Intake Siding	Derby	L. & N. W.	Steeplehouse and Longcliffe.
.	.	.	.	.	.	.	Spencer & Co.'s Middleton Siding	Derby	L. & N. W.	Steeplehouse and Longcliffe.
.	.	.	.	.	.	.	Stancliffe Estate Co.'s Sid.	Derby	L. & N. W.	Steeplehouse and Cromford.
G	P	.	.	.	.	.	Steer Point	Devon	G. W.	Plymstock and Yealmpton.
.	.	.	.	.	.	.	South Hams Bk. Co.'s Wks.	Devon	G. W.	Steer Point.
.	.	.	.	.	.	.	Steetley Colliery (Mid.)	Derby	Mid.—G. C.	Whitwell.
.	.	.	.	.	.	.	Steetley Lime Quarries.........	Notts	G. C.	Shireoaks.
.	.	.	.	.	.	.	Steetley Lime Works (Mid.)...	Derby	Mid.—G. C.	Whitwell.
G	P	.	L	H	.	10 0	Steeton & Silsden	Yorks	Mid.	Skipton and Keighley.
.	.	.	.	.	.	.	Stein's Brick Works	Stirling ...	{ Cal.	Same as Anchor Bk. Wks. (Denny).
.	.	.	.	.	.	.			{ Cal.	Same as Castlecary Sid. (Greenhill).
.	.	.	.	.	.	.			{ N. B.	Same as Milnquarter Brick Works (Bonnybridge).
.	.	.	.	.	.	.	Stella Coal Co.'s Emma or Towneley Cols. and Depôts	Durham ...	N. E.	Blaydon.
.	.	.	.	.	.	.	Stella Gill Junction	Durham ...	N. E.	Pelton.
.	.	.	.	.	.	.	Stenhousemuir Quarry and Brick Works	Stirling ...	Cal.	Larbert.
.	.	.	.	.	.	.	Stenhousemuir Sid. (Muirhall Siding)	Stirling ...	Cal.	See Larbert.
.	.	.	.	.	.	.	Stenhouse's Siding...............	Edinboro'	Cal.—N. B.	Leith, North.
.	.	.	.	.	.	.	Stenning & Son's Sidings... {	Surrey	L. B. & S. C.	Red Hill.
.	.	.	.	.	.	.		Sussex	L. B. & S. C.	East Grinstead.

EXPLANATION—G *Goods Station.*   P *Passenger and Parcel Station.*   P* *Passenger, but not Parcel or Miscellaneous Traffic.*

F *Furniture Vans, Carriages, Portable Engines, and Machines on Wheels.*   L *Live Stock.*

H *Horse Boxes and Prize Cattle Vans.*   C *Carriages by Passenger Train.*

STATION ACCOMMODATION.						CRANE POWER.	STATIONS, &c.	COUNTY.	COMPANY.	POSITION.
						Tons Cwts.	Stenton Iron and Steel Works	Lanark ...	Cal.	Wishaw.
							Stepends Junction	Lanark ...	N. B.	Caldercruix and Plains.
							Stepends Siding	Lanark ...	N. B.	See Caldercruix.
							Stephen & Co.'s Siding	Carmarth'	G. W.	Kidwelly.
							Stephenson & Co.'s Siding	Northumb	N. E.	Newcastle-on-Tyne.
							Stephenson, R., & Co.'s Springfield Locomotive Works ...	Durham	N. E.	Darlington, Bank Top.
							Stephenson, R., & Son's Sid.	Yorks	N. E.	Beverley.
							Stephen's Ship Yard	Lanark ...	G & P Jt (Cal & G & S W)	Same as Linthouse Ship Yard (Glasgow).
							Stephens, Smith & Co.'s Siding	Middlesex	G. E. / GN—GW—LNW—Mid	London, Millwall Docks. / London, Poplar.
							Stepney	Middlesex	G. E.	See London.
							Stepney	Yorks	N. E.	See Hull.
							Stepney Green	Middlesex	W.&B.Jt.(L.T.&S.&M D)	See London.
G	P		L	H		1 10	Steps Road	Lanark ...	Cal.	Coatbridge & Glasgow, Buchanan Str.
							Cardowan Manure Siding	Lanark ...	Cal.	Branch near Steps Road.
							Glasgow Powder Magazine	Lanark ...	Cal.	Branch near Steps Road.
G	P	F	L	H	C	5 0	Sterry, J. S., Siding (G. E.)	Norfolk	G. E.—Mid. & G. N. Jt.	Yarmouth, Vauxhall.
							Stevenage	Herts	G. N.	Hatfield and Hitchin.
							Ellis & Everard's Siding ...	Herts	G. N.	Stevenage.
							Inns Coal & Grain Siding...	Herts	G. N.	Stevenage.
							Langley Siding	Herts	G. N.	Stevenage and Knebworth.
							Wymondley Siding	Herts	G. N.	Stevenage and Hitchin.
							Steven & Struthers' Sid. (NB)	Lanark ...	N. B.—Cal.	Same as Anderston Brass Foundry (Glasgow).
							Steven's Wagon Works (G.C.)	Yorks	G. C.—G. N.	Doncaster.
							Stevenson & Co.'s Siding	Cambs	G. E.	Fordham.
							Stevenson & Mackay's Siding	Lanark ...	N. B.	Airdrie, North.
G	P	F	L	H	C	4 0	Stevenston	Ayr	Cal.	Kilwinning and Ardrossan.
G	P		L	H		3 0	Stevenston	Ayr	G. & S. W.	Kilwinning and Ardrossan.
							Ardeer Chemical Works ...	Ayr	Cal.	Branch near Stevenston.
							Ardeer Factory	Ayr	Cal.—G. & S. W.	Branch near Stevenston.
							Ardeer Foundry	Ayr	G. & S. W.	Stevenston.
							Ardeer Iron Works	Ayr	Cal. / G. & S. W.	Branch near Stevenston. / Stevenston.
							Auchenharvie Brick Works	Ayr	Cal.—G. & S. W.	Stevenston and Saltcoats.
							Auchenharvie Collieries Nos. 1, 4, and 5	Ayr	Cal.—G. & S. W.	Stevenston and Saltcoats.
							Auchenharvie Mine	Ayr	Cal.	Stevenston and Saltcoats.
							Auchenharvie Washer	Ayr	Cal.—G. & S. W.	Stevenston and Saltcoats.
							Ayrshire Foundry	Ayr	Cal. / G. & S. W.	Kilwinning and Stevenston. / Stevenston.
							Eagle Foundry	Ayr	G. & S.W.	Stevenston.
							Nobel's Explosives Works (Ardeer Explosives Works)	Ayr	Cal. / G. & S. W.	Branch near Stevenston. / Stevenston and Kilwinning.
G	P	F	L	H	C	1 0	Steventon	Berks	G. W.	Didcot and Swindon.
							Booker's Siding	Berks	G. W.	Steventon.
							Stewardson & Co.'s Siding ...	Edinboro'	N. B.	Edinburgh, Leith Walk.
							Stewart & Co.'s Siding	Edinboro'	N. B.	Leith, Bonnington.
							Stewart & Spencer's Siding ..	Kent	S. E. & C.	Strood.
							Stewart Bros.' Siding	Edinboro'	N. B.	Same as Eskbank Carpet Works (Hardengreen).
							Stewart, D. Y., & Co.'s Siding	Lanark ...	Cal.	Glasgow, Buchanan Street.
							Stewart's Foundry	Ayr	G. & S.W.	Irvine Harbour.
							Stewartfield Quarry	Lanark ...	Cal.	Same as Earnock Quarry (Meikle Earnock).
G	P	F	L	H	C	4 0	Stewarton	Ayr	G B & K Jt (Cal & G & S W)	Neilston and Kilmarnock.
							Stewarts Lane (S. E. & C.) ...	Surrey	S E & C.—GW—LNW–Mid.	See London.
							Stewarts Lane Junction	Surrey	L. B. & S. C.—S. E. & C.	London, Victoria & Wandsworth Road.
G	P	F	L	H	C	3 0	Stewartstown	Tyrone	G. N. (I.)	Dungannon and Cookstown.
G	P	F	L	H	C	5 0	Steyning	Sussex	L. B. & S. C.	Henfield and Shoreham.
G	P	F	L	H	C	2 0	Stillington	Durham ...	N. E.	Ferryhill and Stockton.
							Basic Phosphate Co.'s Wks.	Durham ...	N. E.	Stillington.
							Briquette Mills	Durham ...	N. E.	Stillington.
							Carlton Iron Works	Durham ...	N. E.	Stillington.
							Elstob Lane Siding	Durham ...	N. E.	Stillington.
							Stillington Junction Siding	Durham ...	N. E.	Stillington.
G	P						Stillorgan	Dublin	D. W. & W.	Dublin, Harcourt Street and Bray.
G	P					1 5	Stirchley	Salop	L. & N. W.	Coalport and Hadley.

EXPLANATION— G *Goods Station.*   P *Passenger and Parcel Station.*   P* *Passenger, but not Parcel or Miscellaneous Traffic.*
F *Furniture Vans, Carriages, Portable Engines, and Machines on Wheels.*   L *Live Stock.*
H *Horse Boxes and Prize Cattle Vans.*   C *Carriages by Passenger Train.*

STATION ACCOMMODATION.						CRANE POWER.	STATIONS, &c.	COUNTY.	COMPANY.	POSITION.
						Tons Cwts.	**Stirchley—**continued.			
..	..	..	..	..	..		Haybridge Iron Co.'s Old Park Siding.............	Salop	L. & N. W.	Stirchley and Malins Lee.
..	..	..	..	..	..		Lewis' Dark Lane Siding	Salop	L. & N. W.	Stirchley and Malins Lee.
..	..	..	..	..	..		Randley Brick & Tile Co.'s Siding	Salop	L. & N. W.	Stirchley and Malins Lee.
							Stirchley Iron Co.—			
..	..	..	..	..	..		Hinks Hay Siding	Salop	L. & N. W.	Stirchley and Malins Lee.
..	..	..	..	..	..		Old Park Siding	Salop	L. & N. W.	Stirchley and Malins Lee.
..	..	..	..	..	..		Wilkinson's Wrekin Chemical Works	Salop	L. & N. W.	Stirchley and Malins Lee.
							Stirchley Iron Co.—			
..	..	..	..	..	..		Hinks Hay Siding	Salop	{ G. W. { L. & N. W.	Hollinswood. Stirchley.
..	..	..	..	..	..		Old Park Siding............	Salop	{ G. W. { L. & N. W.	Hollinswood. Stirchley.
							STIRLING—			
G	P	F	L	H	C	6 0)	(Station, Cal.)................	Stirling ...	{ Cal. { N. B.	Larbert and Perth. Larbert and Alloa.
.	P	.	.	H	C	. .)				
..	..	..	..	..	..		Alloa Coal Co.'s Siding..	Stirling ...	N. B.	Cowpark.
..	..	..	..	..	..		Brisbane's, Thos., Wood Yard............	Stirling ...	N. B.	Cowpark.
G	.	.	L	.	.		Cowpark..................	Stirling ...	N. B.	Stirling (F. & C.) and Gargunnock.
..	..	..	L	.	.	1 10	Craig's Siding ...?	Stirling ...	Cal.	Stirling.
..	..	..	..	..	..		Forth Bank Siding............	Stirling ...	Cal.	Stirling.
..	..	..	..	..	..		Forth Side Sidings (War Office Sidings)........	Stirling ...	Cal.	Stirling.
..	..	..	..	..	..		Graham & Morton's Stores	Stirling ...	Cal.	Stirling.
..	..	..	..	..	..		Gray's Grain Store..........	Stirling ...	Cal.	Stirling.
..	..	..	..	..	..		Junction (Balloch Line)...	Stirling ...	Cal.—N. B.	Stirling Station and Cowpark.
..	..	..	..	..	..		Junction (Dunfermline Line)	Stirling ...	Cal.—N. B.	Bannockburn and Causewayhead.
..	..	..	..	..	..		Kerse Mill Siding	Stirling ...	Cal.	Stirling.
..	..	..	..	..	..		M'Ewan's Malt Barns Sid.	Stirling ...	N. B.	Cowpark.
..	..	..	..	..	..		Murrayshall Lime Works....	Stirling ...	N. B.	Gargunnock and Cowpark.
..	..	..	..	..	..		Polmaise Colliery	Stirling ...	Cal.	Bannockburn and Stirling.
G	.	F	L	H	C	3 0)	Shore Road	Stirling ...	{ Cal. { N. B.	Stirling. Alloa and Stirling (Cal.)
G	.	F	L	.	.	6 0)				
..	..	..	..	..	..		Speedie Bros.' Auction Mart Siding	Stirling ...	N. B.	Cowpark.
..	..	..	..	..	..		Stirling Electric Siding......	Stirling ...	Cal.	Stirling.
..	..	..	..	..	..		Stirling Gas Works	Stirling ...	Cal.	Stirling.
G	.	.	.	.	.		Wallace Street Mineral Depôt	Stirling ...	N. B.	Cowpark.
..	..	..	..	..	..		Weighs	Stirling ...	Cal.	Stirling.
..	..	..	..	..	..		Stirling Road	Lanark ...	Cal.	See Morningside.
..	..	..	..	..	..		Stirling's Boiler Works......	Lanark ...	Cal.	Shieldmuir.
..	..	..	..	..	..		Stirling's Coal Pit	Cumb'land	W C & E Jt.(Fur. & L NW)	Crossfield.
..	..	..	..	..	..		Stirling's Nos. 4, 5, 6, & 12 Pits	Cumb'land	W C & E.Jt.(Fur.& L NW)	Crossfield.
..	..	..	..	..	..		Stirling's No. 10 Pit	Cumb'land	W C & E.Jt.(Fur.& L NW)	Moor Row.
..	..	..	..	..	..		Stirrup & Pye's Siding	Staffs	N. S.	Adderley Green.
G	P	.	L	.	.		Stixwould	Lincoln ...	G. N.	Boston and Lincoln.
G	P	.	.	H	C	. .	Stoat's Nest	Surrey	L. B. & S. C.	Croydon and Earlswood.
..	..	..	..	..	..		Hall & Co.'s Siding	Surrey	L. B. & S. C.	Stoat's Nest.
..	..	..	..	..	..		Stobart & Co.'s Coal Depôt..	Durham ...	N. E.	Bishop Auckland.
..	..	..	..	..	..		Stobcross	Lanark ...	Cal.— N. B.	See Glasgow.
..	..	..	..	..	..		Stobcross Junction	Lanark ...	N. B.	Glasgow.
..	..	..	..	..	..		Stobcross Rivet Works........	Lanark ...	N. B.	Coatbridge, Whifflet.
..	..	..	..	..	..		Stobcross Weighs	Lanark ...	Cal.	Glasgow, Stobcross.
..	..	..	..	..	..		Stobhill Hospital Siding	Lanark ...	Cal.	Glasgow, Springburn Park.
G	P	F	L	H	C	1 10	Stobo	Peebles ...	Cal.	Symington and Peebles.
G	P	.	L	H	.	.	Stobs............................	Roxburgh	N. B.	Hawick and Carlisle.
G	P	.	L	H	.		Stobs Camp	Roxburgh	N. B.	Hawick and Stobs.
..	..	..	..	..	..		Stobswood Colliery	Northumb	N. E.	Widdrington.
G	P	F	L	H	C	. .	Stockbridge (L. & S. W.).....	Hants	{ L. & S. W. { M. & S. W. Jn.	Romsey and Andover. Over L. & S.W. from Andover Junc.
.	P	.	.	.	.		Stockcross and Bagnor.......	Berks	L'bourn Valley	Newbury and Lambourn.
..	..	..	..	..	..		Stocker's Siding	Edinboro'	Cal.—N. B.	Leith, North.
..	..	..	..	..	..		Stocker's Siding	Notts	G. C.	Gotham.
G	P	F	.	H	C	1 10)	Stockingford (Mid.)	Warwick..	{ Mid. { L. & N. W.	Nuneaton and Whitacre. Over Mid. from Nuneaton Junction.
G	.	F	.	.	.	.)				
..	..	..	..	..	..		Ansley Hall Coal & Iron Co.'s Colliery (Mid.)	Warwick..	Mid.—L. & N. W.	Branch from Stockingford.

EXPLANATION— G Goods Station.   P Passenger and Parcel Station.   P* Passenger, but not Parcel or Miscellaneous Traffic.
F Furniture Vans, Carriages, Portable Engines, and Machines on Wheels.   L Live Stock.
H Horse Boxes and Prize Cattle Vans.   C Carriages by Passenger Train

G	P	F	L	H	C	Tons	Cwts	STATIONS, &c.	COUNTY.	COMPANY.	POSITION.
								Stockingford (Mid.)—*continued.*			
								Chapel End Sidings (Mid).	Warwick..	Mid.—L. & N. W.	Branch from Stockingford.
								Gibson & Preston's Patent Slab Works (Mid.)	Warwick..	Mid.—L. & N. W.	Chapel End Sidings.
								Green's Wharf (Mid.)	Warwick..	Mid.—L. & N W.	Stockingford Branch.
								Haunchwood Brick & Tile Co.'s Sid. (Nowell's) (Mid)	Warwick..	Mid.—L. & N. W.	Stockingford.
								Hickman's, Sir A.—Haunchwood (or Nowell) Bk. & Col. Co.'s Sid (Mid)	Warwick..	Mid.—L. & N. W.	Stockingford.
								Tunnel Pit Siding (Mid.)	Warwick..	Mid.—L. & N. W.	Stockingford and Arley.
								Ireland & Knight's Mancetter Quarries (Mid.)	Warwick..	Mid.—L. & N. W.	Chapel End Sidings.
								Jee's Hartshill Granite and Brick Works (Mid.)	Warwick..	Mid.—L. & N. W.	Chapel End Sidings.
								Stanley Bros.' Nuneaton New Colliery (Mid.)	Warwick..	Mid.—L. & N. W.	Stockingford.
								Stockingford Colliery and Brick Works (Mid.)	Warwick..	Mid.—L. & N. W.	Branch from Stockingford.
								Trye's Siding (Mid.)	Warwick..	Mid.—L. & N. W.	Chapel End Sidings.
								STOCKPORT—			
	P		L	H	C			(Station)	Cheshire...	L. & N. W.	Crewe and Manchester.
	P			H	C					N. S.	Over L. & N. W. from Macclesfield.
G	P							Davenport	Cheshire...	L. & N. W.	Stockport Station and Buxton.
G		F	L			10	0	Edgeley	Cheshire...	L. & N. W.	Branch near Passenger Station.
								Faulder's Siding	Lancs	C. L. C. (GC, GN, & Mid.)	Stockport.
								George's Road	Lancs	C. L. C. (GC, GN, & Mid.)	Same as Wellington Road.
								Heaton Norris	Lancs	C. L. C. (GC, GN, & Mid.)	Same as Wellington Road.
G	P		L			14	0	Heaton Norris	Lancs	L. & N. W.	Stockport Station and Manchester.
								Lord Vernon's Cl. Wharves	Cheshire...	L. & N. W.	Stockport.
								Meadows' Sidings	Cheshire...	L. & N. W.	Stockport and Davenport.
									Lancs	L. & N. W.	Heaton Chapel & Heaton Norris.
								Morley & Co.'s Siding	Cheshire...	L. & N. W.	Stockport.
G						5	0	Portwood	Lancs	C. L. C. (GC, GN, & Mid.)	Northenden and Woodley Junction.
G	P					5	0	Reddish	Lancs	L. & N. W.	Stockport Station and Stalybridge.
G	P									S. & M. Jt. (G.C. & Mid.)	Ashburys and Romiley.
								Scott's Siding	Lancs	L. & N. W.	Reddish and Heaton Norris.
								Sykes' Edgeley Bleach Wks.	Cheshire...	L. & N. W.	Stockport and Cheadle.
	P	F		H	C			Tiviot Dale	Lancs	C. L. C. (GC, GN, & Mid.)	Northenden and Godley.
								Walmsley's Siding	Lancs	L. & N. W.	Reddish and Denton.
G		F	L			10	0	Wellington Road	Lancs	C. L. C. (GC, GN, & Mid.)	Branch—Cheadle and Tiviot Dale.
								Wilson & Twyford's Siding	Lancs	C.L.C. (G C, G N, & Mid.)	Branch—George's Road.
								Stockport Guardians' Woodsmoor Siding	Cheshire...	L. & N. W.	Hazel Grove.
								Stockport Sewage Works	Cheshire...	Mid.	Cheadle Heath.
								Stocksbridge	Yorks	G. C.	See Deepcar (for Stocksbridge).
								Stocksbridge Co-operative Society's Siding	Yorks	G. C.	Deepcar (for Stocksbridge).
								Stocksbriggs	Lanark	Cal.	See Auchlochan Colliery (Coalburn).
G	P	F	L	H	C	5	0	Stocksfield	Northumb	N. E.	Newcastle and Hexham.
								Mickley Colliery	Northumb	N. E.	Stocksfield and Prudhoe.
G	P	F	L	H	C	3	0	Stocksmoor	Yorks	L. & Y.	Huddersfield and Penistone.
								Stockton	Warwick..	L. & N. W.	See Napton and Stockton.
	P							Stockton Brook	Staffs	N. S.	Milton and Endon.
								STOCKTON-ON-TEES—			
	P	F		H	C			(Station)	Durham	N. E.	Northallerton and West Hartlepool.
								Ainsworth's Pottery	Durham	N. E.	North Shore.
								Atterby's Brick Siding	Durham	N. E.	Stockton, South.
								Bass & Co.'s Ale Stores	Durham	N. E.	Stockton, South.
								Blair's Engineering Works and Depôts	Durham	N. E.	North Shore.
								Blair's Sheer Legs Siding	Durham	N. E.	North Shore.
								Bon Lea Foundry	Yorks	N. E.	Stockton, South.
								Bowesfield Junction	Durham	N. E.	Stockton, South.
								Bowesfield Metal Yard	Durham	N. E.	Stockton, South.
								Bowesfield Steel Works	Durham	N. E.	Stockton, South.
								Bridge Road Depôt	Durham	N. E.	Stockton, South.
								Broadbent's Saw Mills, Timber Yards and Depôts	Durham	N. E.	North Shore.
								Brown's Foundry	Durham	N. E.	North Shore.
								Castle Wharf	Durham	N. E.	Stockton, South.
								Clarence Depôts	Durham	N. E.	North Shore.

EXPLANATION— G *Goods Station.*   P *Passenger and Parcel Station.*   P* *Passenger, but not Parcel or Miscellaneous Traffic.*
F *Furniture Vans, Carriages, Portable Engines, and Machines on Wheels.*   L *Live Stock.*
H *Horse Boxes and Prize Cattle Vans.*   C *Carriages by Passenger Train.*

STATION ACCOMMODATION.						CRANE POWER.		STATIONS, &c.	COUNTY.	COMPANY.	POSITION.
						Tons	Cwts.	STOCKTON-ON-TEES—*continued.*			
								Cleveland Steam Flour Mill	Yorks	N. E.	Stockton, South.
								Co-operative Stores and Warehouse	Durham	N. E.	North Shore.
								Corporation Store Yard	Durham	N. E.	North Shore.
								Corporation Wharves	Durham	N. E.	Stockton, South.
								Cowell, G., Siding	Durham	N. E.	Stockton, South.
								Craddock, Smith & Co.'s Siding	Durham	N. E.	Stockton, South.
								Duncan, J., Siding	Durham	N. E.	Stockton, South.
								Eaglescliffe Foundry	Durham	N. E.	Stockton, South.
								Eaglescliffe Road Brick and Tile Works	Durham	N. E.	Stockton, South.
								Forge Co.'s Siding	Durham	N. E.	North Shore.
								Gas Works	Durham	N. E.	North Shore.
								Hunton's New Brick Works	Durham	N. E.	North Shore.
								Hunton's Old Brick Works	Durham	N. E.	North Shore.
								Imperial Boiler Works	Durham	N. E.	Stockton, South.
								Iron Foundry	Durham	N. E.	Stockton, South.
								Lamb, R., Siding	Durham	N. E.	Stockton, South.
								Malleable Iron Co.'s Siding	Durham	N. E.	North Shore.
								Manure Loading Mount	Durham	N. E.	North Shore.
								Mellanby, Thos., Siding	Durham	N. E.	Stockton, South.
								Millfield Depôts	Durham	N. E.	North Shore.
								Moor Steel and Iron Works	Durham	N. E.	North Shore.
								Nattrass, F., & Son's Siding	Durham	N. E.	Stockton, South.
								North Riding Maltings	Yorks	N. E.	Stockton, South.
G			L	H		10	0	North Shore	Durham	N. E.	Branch, North of Stockton Pass.
								North Shore Junction	Durham	N. E.	North Shore.
								North Shore or Watson's Flour Mill	Durham	N. E.	North Shore.
								North Yorkshire Depôts	Yorks	N. E.	Stockton, South.
								Oxbridge Foundry	Durham	N. E.	North Shore.
								Parkfield Works	Durham	N. E.	Stockton, South.
								Pattison, Thos., Sidings	Durham	N. E.	Stockton, South.
								Perseverance Boiler Works	Durham	N. E.	North Shore.
								Phœnix Engineering Works	Durham	N. E.	North Shore.
								Portrack Lane Siding	Durham	N. E.	North Shore.
								Railway Wharf	Durham	N. E.	Stockton, South.
								Raimes & Co.'s Siding	Durham	N. E.	Stockton, South.
								Richmond Ir. & Steel Wks.	Durham	N. E.	Stockton, South.
								Roger & Co.'s Siding	Durham	N. E.	North Shore.
								Ropner Shipyard	Durham	N. E.	Stockton, South.
								Sanderson, H., Siding	Durham	N. E.	Stockton, South.
G		F	L	H		10	0	South	Durham	N. E.	Branch—Hartburn Jn. & Thornaby.
								South Stockton Ship Yard	Yorks	N. E.	Stockton, South.
								Tees Bridge Brick Works	Durham	N. E.	Stockton, South.
								Tees Bridge Depôts	Durham	N. E.	Stockton, South.
								Tees Bridge Ironworks	Durham	N. E.	Stockton, South.
								Tees Bridge Slag Crushing Works	Durham	N. E.	Stockton, South.
								Teesdale Ironworks and Wharf	Yorks	N. E.	Stockton, South.
								Tees Roller Flour Mills	Durham	N. E.	Stockton, South.
								Tees Scoria Brick Works	Durham	N. E.	Stockton, South.
								Tees Side Firewood Siding	Yorks	N. E.	Stockton, South.
								Tees Steam Saw Mills and Timber Yard	Yorks	N. E.	Stockton, South.
								Tees Union Shipping Co.'s Siding	Durham	N. E.	Stockton, South.
								Thornaby Iron Works and Wharf	Yorks	N. E.	Stockton, South.
								Thornaby Junction	Yorks	N. E.	Stockton, South.
								Thornaby Pottery	Yorks	N. E.	Stockton, South.
								Union Foundry	Yorks	N. E.	Stockton, South.
								Victoria Works	Yorks	N. E.	Stockton, South.
								Vulcan Iron Foundry	Yorks	N. E.	Stockton, South.
								Watson's Timber & Slate Yard	Durham	N. E.	Stockton, South.
								Wintersgill, B., Siding	Durham	N. E.	Stockton, South.
								Wootton, Jos., Siding	Durham	N. E.	Stockton, South.
								Wright, Robt., Siding	Durham	N. E.	Stockton, South.

EXPLANATION—G *Goods Station.*   P *Passenger and Parcel Station.*   P* *Passenger, but not Parcel or Miscellaneous Traffic.*
F *Furniture Vans, Carriages, Portable Engines, and Machines on Wheels.*   L *Live Stock.*
H *Horse Boxes and Prize Cattle Vans.*   C *Carriages by Passenger Train.*

STATION ACCOMMODATION.					CRANE POWER.	STATIONS, &c.	COUNTY.	COMPANY.	POSITION.
					Tons Cwts.	Stockwell	Surrey	C. & S. L.	See London.
						Stockwell, North	Surrey	L. B. & S. C.	See London, Clapham Road & North Stockwell
						Stockwell Street Junction	Lanark	G. & S.W.	Glasgow.
						Stockwith Siding	Notts	G. N. & G. E. Jt.	See Misterton.
G	P	.	L	.	1 15	Stogumber	Somerset	G. W.	Taunton and Watchet.
G	P	F	.	H C	. .	Stoke	Suffolk	G. E.	Haverhill and Sudbury.
G	.	.	L	.	. .	Stoke Bruern	N'hamptn	E. & W. Jn.	Towcester Junction & Salcey Forest.
G	P	.	L	.	2 0	Stoke Canon	Devon	G. W.	Exeter and Taunton.
						Stoke Canon Junction	Devon	G. W.	Silverton and Stoke Canon.
G	.	F	L	H C	1 10	Stoke D'Abernon	Surrey	L. & S.W.	See Cobham and Stoke D'Abernon.
G	.	F	L	. .	1 10	Stoke Edith (G. W.)	Hereford	G. W. / Mid.	Worcester and Hereford. / Over G. W. Line.
G	P	F	L	.	1 10	Foley's Siding	Hereford	G. W.	Stoke Edith.
						Stoke Ferry	Norfolk	G. E.	Branch from Denver Junction.
						Stoke Gifford	Glo'ster	G. W.	See Patchway and Stoke Gifford.
G	P	F	L	H C	1 10	Stoke Golding	Leicester	A.&N. Jt. (L&NW & Mid)	Nuneaton and Shackerstone.
G	P	.	.	.	}	Stoke Mandeville (Met.)	Bucks	Met. / G. C.	Rickmansworth and Aylesbury. / Over Met. Line.
						Stoke Newington	Middlesex	G. E.	See London.
G	P	F	L	H C	10 0	Stoke-on-Trent (N. S.)	Staffs	N. S. / G. W. / L. & N. W.	Colwich and Macclesfield. / Over N. S. Line. / Over N. S. Line.
G	P	F	L	H C	10 0				
G	P	F	L	H C	10 0				
						California Siding	Staffs	N. S.	Stoke-on-Trent.
						Cliff Vale Wharf	Staffs	N. S.	Stoke-on-Trent.
						Cockshute Sidings (N. S.)	Staffs	N. S.—L & N. W.	Stoke-on-Trent.
						Fenton Tileries Co.'s Works	Staffs	N. S.	Stoke-on-Trent.
						Kerr, Stuart & Co's Foundry	Staffs	N. S.	Stoke-on-Trent.
						N. S. Railway Co.'s Stores Department Siding	Staffs	N. S.	Stoke-on-Trent.
						Pratt's Siding	Staffs	N. S.	Stoke-on-Trent.
						Twyford's Works	Staffs	N. S.	Stoke-on-Trent.
						Stokes & Co.'s Sid. (L&NW)	Staffs	L. & N. W.—G. W.—Mid.	See Hatherton Siding (Walsall).
	P	.	.	.	1 10	Stokesay (S. & H. Jt.)	Salop	S & H Jt—Bishop's Castle	See Craven Arms and Stokesay.
						Stokes Bay	Hants	L. & S.W.	Branch from Fareham.
						Stokes Bay Junction	Hants	L. & S.W.	Gosport Road and Forton Junction.
						Stoke Siding	Kent	S. E. & C.	Sharnal Street.
G	P	F	L	H C	1 0	Stokesley	Yorks	N. E.	Whitby and Picton.
						Stoke Prior Junction	Worcester	G. W.—Mid.	Droitwich and Bromsgrove.
						Stoke Prior Works	Worcester	G. W.—Mid.	See Salt Union, Ltd. (Stoke Wks.).
	P	.	.	.	. .	Stoke Works (G. W.)	Worcester	G. W. / Mid.	Droitwich and Stoke Prior Junc. / Over G. W. from Stoke Prior Junc.
G	.	.	.	.	1 10	Stoke Works (Mid.)	Worcester	Mid. / G. W.	Birmingham and Spetchley. / Over Mid. from Stoke Prior Junc.
						Salt Union, Ltd., Stoke Prior Works	Worcester	G. W.—Mid.	Stoke Works.
G	P	F	L	H C	2 0	Stone (N. S.)	Staffs	N. S. / L. & N. W.	Colwich and Stoke. / Over N. S. Line.
						Stone & Co.'s Brick Works	Surrey	L. B. & S. C.	Epsom.
						Stone Bros.' Siding	Staffs	L. & N. W.	Albion.
						Stone's—			
						Sun or North Blaina Colliery (G. W.)	Mon.	G. W.—L. & N. W.	Blaina (For Outwards Traffic). / Nantyglo (For Inwards Traffic).
						Siding	Mon	L. & N. W.	Brynmawr.
						Stone's Brick Siding	Warwick	Mid.	Same as Dosthill Brick Sid. (Wilncote).
						Stone's Park Colliery	Lancs	L. & N. W.	Garswood.
						Stone's Place Sid. (GN&GEJt.)	Lincoln	G. N. & G. E. Jt.—G. C.	Lincoln.
						Stone's (Executors) Siding	Lancs	L. & N. W.	Newton-le-Willows.
						Stone's, W. H., Siding	Glamorg'n	GW—LNW—Mid—RSB	Swansea.
G	P	.	L	.	1 0	Stonea	Cambs	G. E.	Ely and March.
G	.	.	.	.	. .	Waddington Siding	Cambs	G. E.	Stonea.
						Stonebridge Mill	Lancs	P.&L.Jt.(L&NW & L&Y)	Same as Whittle & Co.'s Siding (Longridge).
						Stonebridge Park	Middlesex	Mid.	See London, Harlesden.
						Stonebriggs Siding	Ayr	G. & S.W.	Lugar.
						Stoneclough Col. Co.'s Siding	Lancs	L. & Y.	Kearsley.
						Stonecraig No. 1 Pit	Lanark	Cal.	Morningside. / Newmains.
						Stonecross Junction	Sussex	L. B. & S. C.	Polegate and Pevensey.
						Stonefall Brick Works	Yorks	N. E.	Starbeck.
						Stonefield Oil Works	Lanark	Cal.	Same as Blantyre Oil Wks (Blantyre)

EXPLANATION—G *Goods Station.*   P *Passenger and Parcel Station.*   P* *Passenger, but not Parcel or Miscellaneous Traffic.*
F *Furniture Vans, Carriages, Portable Engines, and Machines on Wheels.*   L *Live Stock.*
H *Horse Boxes and Prize Cattle Vans.*   C *Carriages by Passenger Train.*

G	P	F	L	H	C	Tons	Cwts	STATIONS, &c.	COUNTY.	COMPANY.	POSITION.
G	P	F	L	H	C	1	10	Stonehaven (Cal.)	Kinc'rdine	{ Cal.	Forfar and Aberdeen.
										N. B.	Over Cal. from Kinnaber Junction.
								Stonehead Branch (Crofthead Branch)	L'lithgow	N. B.	Crofthead.
								Stonehewer & Co's Sid. (LNW)	Staffs	L. & N. W.—Mid.	Great Bridge.
G	P	F	L	H	C	5	0	Stonehouse	Glo'ster	{ G. W.	Swindon and Gloucester.
G	P	F	L	H	C	1	10			Mid.	Gloucester and Bristol.
								Hooper & Son's Siding	Glo'ster	Mid.	Near Stonehouse.
								Jefferies Siding	Glo'ster	G. W.	Stonehouse and Stroud.
								Stonehouse Brk. & Tl. Sid.	Glo'ster	G. W.	Stonehouse.
								Stonehouse Wharf	Glo'ster	Mid.	Stonehouse and Ryeford.
G	P		L	H		2	0	Stonehouse	Lanark	Cal.	Dalserf and Strathaven.
								Avon Foundry	Lanark	Cal.	Dalserf and Stonehouse.
								Birkenshaw Col.& Bk. Wks.	Lanark	Cal.	Dalserf and Stonehouse.
								Candermain's Siding	Lanark	Cal.	Dalserf and Stonehouse.
								Canderrigg Cols. Nos. 1, 2, 3, 4, & 5	Lanark	Cal.	Dalserf and Stonehouse.
G								Cotcastle	Lanark	Cal.	Stonehouse and Strathaven.
								Overwood Quarry	Lanark	Cal.	Dalserf and Stonehouse.
								Struther's Colliery	Lanark	Cal.	Dalserf and Stonehouse.
								Swinehill Collieries Coke and Brick Works	Lanark	Cal.	Dalserf and Stonehouse.
								Watston Siding	Lanark	Cal.	Dalserf and Stonehouse.
								Stonehouse Junction	Lanark	Cal.	Dalserf and Stonehouse.
								Stonehouse Pool	Devon	L. & S.W.	See Devonport.
								Stonelaw Colliery	Lanark	Cal.	Glasgow, Rutherglen.
								Stoneybrae	Renfrew	G. & S.W.	See Paisley.
								Stoneycombe Siding	Devon	G. W.	Newton Abbot.
								Stoneyford Colliery	Derby	Mid.	Langley Mill and Eastwood.
								Stoneyford Lane Siding	Notts	Mid.	Whiteborough.
								Stoney Hill Siding	Lancs	P.&W.Jt.(L&Y&L&NW)	See Blackpool.
								Stoney Lane Siding	Notts	G. N.	Eastwood and Langley Mill.
								Stoney Stanton Sid. (L&NW)	Leicester	L. & N. W.—Mid.	See Mountsorrel Granite Co.'s Siding (Elmesthorpe).
								Stoney Street Junction	Surrey	S. E. & C.	London, Waterloo Junction Station and Cannon Street.
	P							Stoneywood	Aberdeen	G. N. of S.	Aberdeen and Dyce.
								Stoneywood	Stirling	Cal.	See Denny.
								Storefield Ironstone Siding (Davis & Co.)	N'hampt	Mid.	Glendon and Rushton.
G	P	F	L	H	C			Storeton (for Barnston)	Cheshire	N.W. & L. Jt. (G.C. and W. M. & C. Q.)	Neston & Parkgate and Birkenhead.
								Storey Lodge Colliery	Durham	N. E.	Butterknowle.
								Storforth Lane Siding	Derby	Mid.	Same as Saunder's Brick Works (Chesterfield).
								Stormstown Junc. & Siding	Glamorg'n	T. V.	Abercynon.
G								Stormy	Glamorg'n	G. W.	Bridgend and Neath.
								Jones, B. Daniel, & Co.'s Lime Works	Glamorg'n	G. W.	Bridgend and Pyle.
G	P		L							{ Cal.	Steamer from Oban.
G	P		L		C			Stornoway	Ross&Cro'	High.	Steamer from Kyle of Lochalsh.
G	P		L							N. B.	Steamer from Mallaig.
	P							Storr's Hall	Lancs	Furness	Steamer from Windermere, Lake Side.
								Storr's Mill	Yorks	Mid.	Cudworth.
								Stothert & Pitts' Siding	Somerset	Mid.	Bath.
G	P							Stoulton	Worcester	G. W.	Pershore and Norton Junction.
								STOURBRIDGE—			
								Amblecote Siding (Hall, J., & Co.)	Staffs	G. W.	Stourbridge and Brettell Lane.
G						5	0	Basin	Staffs	G. W.	Branch from Stourbridge Junction.
								Bradley & Co.'s Works	Worcester	G. W.	Stourbridge Town.
								Eveson's Coal and Coke Yard	Worcester	G. W.	Stourbridge Town.
								Gas Works	Staffs	G. W.	Stourbridge Town.
	P	F	L	H	C			Junction Station	Worcester	G. W.	Kidderminster and Dudley.
								Rufford & Co.'s Works	Worcester	G. W.	Stourbridge Junc. & Brettell Lane.
G	P	F	L			10	0	Town	Staffs	G. W.	Branch from Stourbridge Junction.
								Turney & Co.'s Works	Staffs	G. W.	Stourbridge Town.
								Waterworks	Staffs	G. W.	Stourbridge Town.
								Stourbridge Glazed Brick & Fire-Clay Co.'s Col.&Sids.	Staffs	G. W.	{ Brettell Lane. Netherton.

EXPLANATION—G Goods Station.   P Passenger and Parcel Station.   P* Passenger, but not Parcel or Miscellaneous Traffic.
F Furniture Vans, Carriages, Portable Engines, and Machines on Wheels.   L Live Stock.
H Horse Boxes and Prize Cattle Vans.   C Carriages by Passenger Train.

STATION ACCOMMODATION.						CRANE POWER.	STATIONS, &c.	COUNTY.	COMPANY.	POSITION.
G	P	F	L	H	C	Tons 4 Cwts 0	Stourport	Worcester	G. W.	Hartlebury and Bewdley.
G	G	.	.	.	.	1 10	Stourport Basin	Worcester	G. W.	Stourport.
.	P	.	.	.	.		Stourton	Yorks	E. & W. Y. U.	Rothwell and Lofthouse Junction.
.	.	.	.	.	.		Stourton Junction	Yorks	E. & W. Y. U.—Mid.	Stourton and Leeds.
.	.	.	.	.	.		Stourton Siding	Cheshire	B'head Jt. (G W & L N W)	Spital.
.	.	.	.	.	.		Stourton Sidings	Yorks	Mid.	Same as Hunslet and Stourton Sids. (Leeds).
.	.	.	.	.	.		Stour Valley Works	Staffs	G. W.	See Corrugated Iron Co. (Wolverhampton).
.	.	.	.	.	.		Stout & Son's Foundry (Fur.)	Cumb'land	Furness—L. & N. W.	Whitehaven, Preston Street.
G	P	F	L	H	C	1 10	Stow	Edinboro'	N. B.	Edinburgh and Galashiels.
G	P	.	L	H	.		Stow	Norfolk	G. E.	Ely and Lynn.
G	P	.	.	.	.		Stow Bedon	Norfolk	G. E.	Thetford and Swaffham.
.	.	.	.	.	.		Stowe	Staffs	G. N.	See Chartley & Stowe.
.	.	.	.	.	.		Stowe Siding	N'hamptn	L. & N. W.	Weedon.
.	.	.	.	.	.		Stow Heath Siding	Staffs	G. W.	Wolverhampton.
.	.	.	.	.	.		Stow Maries	Essex	G. E.	See Cold Norton (for Purleigh and Stow Maries).
G	P	F	L	H	C	5 0	Stowmarket	Suffolk	G. E.	Bury and Ipswich.
.	.	.	.	.	.		Cook, F. R., & Co.'s Siding	Suffolk	G. E.	Stowmarket.
.	.	.	.	.	.		English, J. H., Siding	Suffolk	G. E.	Stowmarket.
.	.	.	.	.	.		Free & Co.'s Siding	Suffolk	G. E.	Stowmarket.
.	.	.	.	.	.		Hewitt, W. R., & Co.'s Sid.	Suffolk	G. E.	Stowmarket.
.	.	.	.	.	.		Luck's Explosives Co.'s Sid.	Suffolk	G. E.	Stowmarket.
.	.	.	.	.	.		New Explosives Co.'s Sid.	Suffolk	G. E.	Stowmarket.
.	.	.	.	.	.		Paul, R. & W., Siding	Suffolk	G. E.	Stowmarket.
.	.	.	.	.	.		Prentice Bros.' Siding	Suffolk	G. E.	Stowmarket.
.	.	.	.	.	.		Prentice, T. P., & Co.'s Sid.	Suffolk	G. E.	Stowmarket.
.	.	.	.	.	.		Ransom, W. G., Siding	Suffolk	G. E.	Stowmarket.
G	P	F	L	H	C	4 0	Stow-on-the-Wold	Glo'ster	G. W.	Chipping Norton Jn. & Cheltenham.
G	P	F	L	H	C	1 10	Stow Park (for Marton)	Lincoln	G. N. & G. E. Jt.	Lincoln and Gainsboro'.
.	.	.	.	.	.		Stows Mine	Cornwall	L. & Looe.	Moorswater & Cheesewring Quarries.
G	P	.	L	H	C	2 0 }	Strabane	Tyrone	{ Donegal	Londonderry and Stranorlar.
G	P	F	L	.	.				{ G. N. (I.)	Omagh and Londonderry.
.	.	.	.	.	.		Strachan's Siding	Lanark	Cal.	Coatbridge, Whifflet.
.	P	.	.	.	.		Stradbally	Waterford	G. S. & W.	See Durrow and Stradbally.
.	.	.	.	.	.		Straffan	Kildare	G. S. & W.	Dublin and Kildare.
.	.	.	.	.	.		Strafford Colliery	Yorks	G. C.	Worsboro'.
.	.	.	.	.	.		Straiton Siding	Edinboro'	N. B.	Loanhead.
.	.	.	.	.	.		Strand	Glamorg'n	G. W.—L. & N. W.—Mid. R. & S. B.—S. & Mum.	See Swansea.
.	.	.	.	.	.		Strand Road (L. & Y.)	Lancs	L. & Y.—L. & N. W.	See Liverpool, Marsh Lane and Strand Road.
.	.	.	.	.	.		Strand Road Siding	Glamorg'n	G. W.—Mid.—R. & S. B.	Swansea.
.	.	.	.	.	.		Strangeways, East Junction	Lancs	G C (Wigan Jn)—L&NW	Hindley and Tyldesley.
.	.	.	.	.	.		Strangeways Hall Colliery or Amberswood West Sid. (G. C. Wigan Junction)	Lancs	G C (Wigan Jn.)—L&NW	{ See Crompton & Shawcross (Hindley and Platt Bridge).
G	P	.	.	.	.		Stranorcum	Antrim	Ballycastle	Ballymoney and Ballycastle.
G	P	F	L	H	C	3 0	Stranorlar	Donegal	Donegal	Strabane and Donegal.
							STRANRAER—			
G	P	F	L	H	C	7 0	(Station)	Wigtown	P.P.&W Jt.(Cal.,G&SW, L. & N. W. & Mid.)	Glenluce and Portpatrick.
G	P	F	L	H	C	3 10	Harbour	Wigtown	P.P.&WJt.(Cal.,G&SW, L. & N. W. & Mid.)	Branch from Stranraer Junction.
.	.	.	.	.	.		Junction	Wigtown	P.P.&WJt.(Cal.,G&SW, L. & N. W. & Mid.)	Glenluce and Portpatrick.
.	.	.	.	.	.		Stranton Saw Mill (Brown's)	Durham	N. E.	West Hartlepool.
.	.	.	.	.	.		Stranton Works	Durham	N. E.	Same as New Expanded Metal Co. (West Hartlepool).
G	P	.	L	H	.		Strata Florida	Cardigan	M. & M.	Tregaron and Aberystwyth.
.	.	.	.	.	.		Stratford	Essex	G. E.	See London.
.	.	.	.	.	.		Stratford Exchange Sids. (GE)	Essex	G. E.—N. L.	London, Stratford.
.	.	.	.	.	.		Stratford Market	Essex	G. E.	See London.
.	.	.	.	.	.		Stratford Mills Siding	Glo'ster	G. W.	Stroud.
G	P	F	L	H	C	4 0 }	Stratford-on-Avon	Warwick	{ E. & W. Jn.	Fenny Compton and Broom.
G	P	F	L	H	C	5 0 }			{ G. W.	Hatton and Honeybourne.
G	.	.	.	.	.		Clifford Siding	Warwick	E. & W. Jn.	Stratford-on-Avon.
.	.	.	.	.	.		Espley's Brick Works Sid.	Warwick	G. W.	Stratford-on-Avon.
.	.	.	.	.	.		Flower & Son's Siding	Warwick	G. W.	Stratford-on-Avon.
.	.	.	.	.	.		Gas Works	Warwick	G. W.	Stratford-on-Avon.
.	.	.	.	.	.		Stratford-on-Avon Junction	Warwick	E. & W. Jn.—G. W.	E. & W. Jn. and G. W. Stations.

EXPLANATION—G *Goods Station.*   P *Passenger and Parcel Station.*   P* *Passenger, but not Parcel or Miscellaneous Traffic.*
F *Furniture Vans, Carriages, Portable Engines, and Machines on Wheels.*   L *Live Stock.*
H *Horse Boxes and Prize Cattle Vans.*   C *Carriages by Passenger Train.*

STATION ACCOMMODATION.						CRANE POWER.		STATIONS, &c.	COUNTY.	COMPANY.	POSITION.
G	P	.	L	H	C	Tons	Cwts				
G	P	.	L	H	C	5	0	Strathaven	Lanark	Cal.	Terminus of Hamilton and Strathaven Branch.
								Strathaven Junction	Lanark	Cal.	Hamilton West and Blantyre.
								Strathaven Junction Weighs	Lanark	Cal.	Hamilton West and Blantyre.
								Strathavon Colliery	Stirling	N. B.	Slamannan.
G	P	.	L			1	10	Strathblane	Stirling	N. B.	Lennoxtown and Killearn.
								Strathbungo	Lanark	G B & K Jt (Cal & G & S W)	See Glasgow.
								Strathbungo Junction	Lanark	Cal.—G. B. & K. Jt.	Glasgow.
G	P	F	L	H	C	2	0	Strathcarron	Ross & Cro'	High.	Dingwall and Kyle of Lochalsh.
								Strathclyde Junction	Lanark	Cal.	Glasgow.
								Strathclyde Siding	Lanark	Cal.	Glasgow, Bridgeton.
								Strathearn Manure Works	Perth	Cal.	Crieff.
								Strathearn's Weldless Chain Works	Lanark	Cal.—N. B.	Same as Lanarkshire Chain Cable and Anchor Works.
G						2	0	Strathila Mills	Banff	G. N. of S.	Keith and Craigellachie.
G	P	.	L	H		1	5	Strathmiglo	Fife	N. B.	Kinross Junction and Ladybank.
G	P	.	L	H		1	0	Strathord	Perth	Cal.	Perth and Coupar Angus.
G	P	F	L	H	C	1	10	Strathpeffer	Ross & Cro'	High.	Branch from Fodderty Junction.
G	P	F	L	H	C			Strathyre	Perth	Cal.	Callander and Oban.
G	P	F	L	H	C			Stratton	Wilts	G. W.	Swindon and Highworth.
G	P	.	L	H		1	0	Stravithie	Fife	N. B.	Anstruther and St. Andrews.
	P							Strawberry Hill Junction Station	Middlesex	L. & S.W.	Twickenham and Teddington.
								Strawfrank Junction	Lanark	Cal.	Thankerton and Carstairs.
								Stream Hall Siding	Hereford	G. W.	Same as Brockhampton and Stream Hall Siding.
G	P	F	L	H	C			Streamstown Junction Station	W'meath	M. G. W.	Mullingar and Athlone.
G	P			H				Streatham (L. B. & S. C.)	Surrey	L. B. & S. C.	Tulse Hill and Mitcham Junction.
	P								Surrey	L. & S. W.	Over L.B.& S.C. from Streatham Jn.
G	P							Streatham Common	Surrey	L. B. & S. C.	Balham and Thornton Heath.
								Streatham Common Southwark & Vauxhall Water Works	Surrey	L. B. & S. C.	Streatham Common and Balham.
G	P							Streatham Hill (L. B. & S. C.)	Surrey	L. B. & S. C.	Balham and Gipsy Hill.
	P								Surrey	L. & N. W.	Over L.B.&S.C. from Clapham Junc.
								Streatham Junction	Surrey	L. B. & S. C.—L. & S. W. & L. B. & S. C. Jt.	Streatham and Tooting.
								Streatley	Oxon	G. W.	See Goring and Streatley.
								Street	Somerset	S.&D.Jt. (L.&S.W.&Mid)	See Glastonbury and Street.
	P							Street & Rathowen	Longford	M. G. W.	Mullingar and Longford.
	P							Streetly	Warwick	Mid.	Sutton Coldfield & Wolverhampton.
								Street's Siding	Surrey	L. B. & S. C.	Bramley and Wonersh.
								Street's Siding	Warwick	L. & N. W.	Kenilworth.
G	P	.	L	H				Strensall	Yorks	N. E.	York and Malton.
								Littlethorpe Brick & Tile Co.'s Siding	Yorks	N. E.	Strensall.
G	P	F	L	H	C	5	0	Stretford	Lancs	M S J & A (G C & L N W)	Manchester and Timperley.
								Stretford Bridge Junction	Salop	Bishop's Castle—S&H Jt.	Horderley and Craven Arms.
	P							Stretford Bridge Junc. Sta.	Salop	Bishop's Castle	Bishop's Castle and Stretford Bridge Junction.
G	P	.	L	H				Stretham	Cambs	G. E.	Ely and St. Ives.
G	P	F	L	H	C	5	0	Stretton	Derby	Mid.	Ambergate and Chesterfield.
	P							Stretton & Clay Mills	Staffs	N. S.	Burton and Tutbury.
								Stretton Junction	Staffs	L. & N. W.—N. S.	Burton-on-Trent.
G	P							Stretton-on-Fosse	Glo'ster	G. W.	Moreton-in-Marsh and Shipston-on-Stour.
G	P	F	L	H	C	1	5	Strichen	Aberdeen	G. N. of S.	Dyce and Fraserburgh.
								Strickland's Sidings	Sussex	L. B. & S. C.	Heathfield. / Lewes.
G	P					2	0	Strines	Derby	S. & M. Jt. (G. C. & Mid.)	Marple and New Mills.
								Stringer Bros.' Siding	Staffs	L. & N. W.	Albion.
G	P	F	L	H	C	1	10	Stromeferry	Ross & Cro'	High.	Dingwall and Kyle of Lochalsh.
G	P							Strontian	Argyll	Cal.	Steamer from Oban.
G	P	F	L	H	C	15	0	Strood	Kent	S. E. & C.	Gravesend (Central) and Chatham.
								Aveling & Porter's Siding	Kent	S. E. & C.	Strood.
								Oil Cake Mills	Kent	S. E. & C.	Strood and Cuxton.
								Stewart & Spencer's Siding	Kent	S. E. & C.	Strood and Rochester Bridge.
								Strood Junction	Kent	S. E. & C.	Strood and Cuxton.
G	P	F	L	H	C	7	0	Stroud	Glo'ster	G. W.	Swindon and Gloucester.
G	P	F	L	H	C	5	0		Glo'ster	Mid.	Branch from Dudbridge.
								Stratford Mills Siding	Glo'ster	G. W.	Stroud.
							L.	Wood & Rowe's Siding	Glo'ster	Mid.	Stroud.
								Stroud Green (G. N.)	Middlesex	G. N.—N. L.	See London.

EXPLANATION—G *Goods Station.*   P *Passenger and Parcel Station.*   P* *Passenger, but not Parcel or Miscellaneous Traffic.*
F *Furniture Vans, Carriages, Portable Engines, and Machines on Wheels.*   L *Live Stock.*
H *Horse Boxes and Prize Cattle Vans.*   C *Carriages by Passenger Train.*

STATION ACCOMMODATION.						CRANE POWER.	STATIONS, &c.	COUNTY.	COMPANY.	POSITION.
G	P	F	L	H	C	Tons Cwts.				
G	.	.	.	.	.	1 10	Struan	Perth	High..............	Blair Atholl and Kingussie.
.	.	.	.	.	.	. .	Struther's Colliery.............	Lanark ...	Cal.	Stonehouse.
.	.	.	.	.	.	. .	Stuart's Granolithic Stone Co.'s Siding.............	Middlesex	{ G. E.	London, Millwall Docks.
									GN—GW—LNW—Mid	London, Poplar.
.	.	.	.	.	.	. .	Stuart's Granolithic Works...	Edinboro'	Cal.	Edinburgh, Lothian Road.
.	.	.	.	.	.	. .	Stuart's Net Works	Edinboro'	N. B.	Musselburgh.
.	.	.	.	.	.	. .	Stuart Street Siding............	Lancs ...	L. & Y.	See Manchester Corporation.
.	P	.	.	.	.	. .	Stubber's Green Colliery	Staffs	L. & N. W	Same as Coppy Hall Col. (Pelsall).
.	.	.	.	.	.	. .	Stubbins	Lancs	L. & Y.	Bury and Bacup.
.	.	.	.	.	.	. .	Ramsbottom Gas Co.'s Sid.	Lancs	L. & Y.	Stubbins.
.	.	.	.	.	.	. .	Stubbs & Co.'s Siding	Staffs	G. N.	Stafford Common.
.	.	.	.	.	.	. .	Stubbs' Flag Yard.............	Lancs	L. & N. W.	Liverpool, Edge Hill.
.	.	.	.	.	.	. .	Stubley Siding	Lancs	L. & Y.	Portsmouth.
.	.	.	.	.	.	. .	Stubs', P., Siding	Yorks	Mid.	Same as Holmes Steel Works (Masboro').
.	.	.	.	.	.	. .	Studland Road Junction	Middlesex	L. & S.W.—Met. Dist.	London, Ravenscourt Park and Hammersmith.
G	P	.	L	H	.	1 10	Studley and Astwood Bank...	Warwick..	Mid.	Evesham and Redditch.
.	P	F	.	H	C	. .	Sturmer	Essex	G. E.	Haverhill and Sudbury.
G	P	F	L	H	C	10 0	Sturminster Newton...........	Dorset.....	S.&D. Jt. (L.&S.W.& Mid)	Blandford and Templecombe.
G	P	.	L	.	.	. .	Sturry	Kent	S. E. & C.	Canterbury, West & Ramsgate Town.
G	P	.	L	H	.	. .	Sturt Lane Junction	Surrey ..	L. & S. W.	Brookwood and Farnborough.
G	P	.	L	.	.	. .	Sturton	Notts	G. C.	Retford and Gainsboro'.
.	.	.	.	.	.	. .	Stutton.......................	Yorks	N. E.	Church Fenton and Harrogate.
.	.	.	.	.	.	. .	Subway Junction	Middlesex	G. W.	London, Paddington & Westbourne Park.
.	.	.	.	.	.	. .	Sub-Wealden Gypsum Co.'s Siding	Sussex ...	S. E. & C.	Battle.
G	P	F	L	H	C	. .	Suckley.......................	Worcester	G. W.	Bromyard and Knightwick.
.	.	.	.	.	.	. .	Sudbrook Brick Works	Mon	G. W.	Severn Tunnel Junction Station.
G	P	F	L	H	C	1 10	Sudbury	Suffolk ...	G. E.	Marks Tey and Bury St. Edmunds.
.	.	.	.	.	.	. .	Allen, R. A., & Son's Sid.	Suffolk ...	G. E.	Sudbury.
.	.	.	.	.	.	. .	Great Cornards Siding	Suffolk ...	G. E.	Sudbury.
.	.	.	.	.	.	. .	Oliver Bros.' Brewery	Suffolk ...	G. E.	Sudbury.
.	.	.	.	.	.	. .	Wheeler & Son's Siding ...	Suffolk ...	G. E.	Sudbury.
G	P	F	L	H	C	10 0	Sudbury (N. S.)	Staffs ...	{ N. S.	Derby and Uttoxeter.
.	P	.	.	.	.	. .			G. N.	Over N. S. from Egginton Junc.
G	.	F	L	.	.	10 0			L. & N. W.	Over N. S. Line.
G	P	.	L	H	C	. .	Sudbury and Wembley	Middlesex	L. & N. W.	Watford and Willesden.
.	.	.	.	.	.	. .	Eastwood & Co.'s Siding ...	Middlesex	L. & N. W	Sudbury and Harrow.
.	P	.	.	.	.	. .	Sudbury Hill (for Greenford Green)	Middlesex	Met. Dist.	Sudbury Town and South Harrow.
.	P	.	.	.	.	. .	Sudbury Town (for Horsenden)	Middlesex	Met. Dist.	Perivale-Alperton & Sudbury Hill.
.	.	.	.	.	.	. .	Sugar Tongue Siding (Fur.)..	Cumb'land	Furness—L. & N. W.	Whitehaven, Preston Street.
G	P	.	L	.	.	. .	Sulby Bridge	I. of Man..	Manx Northern	St. Johns and Ramsey.
G	P	.	L	.	.	. .	Sulby Glen	I. of Man..	Manx Northern	St. Johns and Ramsey.
.	.	.	.	.	.	. .	Sullivan's Works	Lancs	L. & N. W.—S. & M. Jt.	See United Alkali Co. (Widnes).
G	P	F	L	H	C	5 0	Sully	Glamorg'n	T. V.	Penarth and Cadoxton.
.	.	.	.	.	.	. .	Summerford Iron Works	Stirling ...	N. B.	Falkirk, Camelon.
.	.	.	.	.	.	. .	Summer Lane	Yorks	G. C.	See Barnsley.
.	.	.	.	.	.	. .	Summerlee Colliery	Lanark ...	Cal.	See Kirkwood Collieries (Langloan).
.	.	.	.	.	.	. .	Summerlee Iron Works........	Lanark ...	{ Cal.	Coatbridge.
									N. B.	Coatbridge, Sunnyside.
.	.	.	.	.	.	. .	Summers & Scott's Siding......	Glo'ster ..	G. W.—Mid.	Gloucester Docks.
G	P	.	L	.	.	1 5	Summerseat	Lancs	L. & Y.	Bury and Accrington.
.	.	.	.	.	.	. .	Brooksbottom Siding........	Lancs	L. & Y.	Near Summerseat.
.	.	.	.	.	.	. .	Northern Brick and Terra Cotta Co.'s Siding	Lancs	L. & Y.	Summerseat and Bury.
.	.	.	.	.	.	. .	Summer's Globe Iron Works	Lancs	G. C. & L. & N. W. Jt....	Stalybridge.
.	.	.	.	.	.	. .	Summer's Hawarden Bge. Sid.	Flint	G. C.	Saughall.
G	P	.	L	.	.	1 10	Summerston	Dumbartn	N. B.	Maryhill and Kilsyth.
.	.	.	.	.	.	. .	Blackhill Brick Works	Lanark ...	N. B.	Maryhill and Summerston.
.	.	.	.	.	.	. .	Blackhill Colliery	Lanark ...	N. B.	Maryhill and Summerston.
.	.	.	.	.	.	. .	Summers Town	Surrey ...	L. & S. W.	See Earlsfield and Summers Town.
.	.	.	.	.	.	. .	Summit	Lanark ...	Cal.	See Beattock.
•	.	.	.	.	.	. .	Summit Pit (G. N.)	Notts	G. N.—G.C.—L. D.& E. C.	Same as Kirkby Colliery (Sutton-in-Ashfield).
.	.	.	.	.	.	. .	Summit Siding	Fife	N. B.	See Whitemyre Junction Station.
•	.	.	••	.	.	. .	Summit Siding	Northumb	N. E.	{ Alnwick.
										Edlingham.
.	.	.	.	.	.	. .	Summit Siding	Staffs	N. S.	See Birchenwood Col. Co. (Harecastle)

EXPLANATION—G *Goods Station.*   P *Passenger and Parcel Station.*   P* *Passenger, but not Parcel or Miscellaneous Traffic.*
F *Furniture Vans, Carriages, Portable Engines, and Machines on Wheels.*   L *Live Stock.*
H *Horse Boxes and Prize Cattle Vans.*   C *Carriages by Passenger Train.*

STATION ACCOMMODATION.						CRANE POWER.	STATIONS, &c.	COUNTY.	COMPANY.	POSITION.
						Tons Cwts.	Summit Siding	W'morlnd	L. & N. W.	Same as Shap Granite and Patent Concrete Co.'s (Shap.)
						. .	Summit Siding	W'morlnd	N. E.	{ Barras. { Bowes.
						. .	Sumner & Co.'s Haigh Brewery	Lancs	L. & N. W.	Wigan.
						. .	Sunbeck Junction	Yorks	N. E.	Pilmoor and Gilling.
G	P	F	L	H	C	. .	Sunbury	Middlesex	L. & S.W.	Twickenham and Shepperton.
							East London Waterworks..	Middlesex	L. & S.W.	Sunbury.
							Kempton Park Race Station	Middlesex	L. & S.W.	Hampton and Sunbury.
							New River Waterworks ...	Middlesex	L. & S.W.	Sunbury.
							Walton's Lincrusta Siding	Middlesex	L. & S.W.	Sunbury.
							Sun or North Blaina Col. (GW)	Mon	G. W.—L. & N. W.	See Stone's.
							SUNDERLAND—			
	P						(Station)	Durham ...	N. E.	Terminus—Seaham and Sunderland Line.
							Anglo-American Oil Co.'s Sid	Durham ...	N. E.	South Dock.
							Armstrong, Addison & Co.'s Timber Yard	Durham ...	N. E.	Monkwearmouth.
							Bartram & Son's Ship Yard	Durham ...	N. E.	South Dock.
							Calder, C., & Co.'s Timber Yard	Durham ...	N. E.	South Dock.
							Cattle Dock..............	Durham ...	N. E.	Sunderland.
	P	F	L	H	C	. .	Central	Durham ...	N. E.	Monkwearmouth and Ryhope.
							Cordner's Landsale Depôt...	Durham ...	N. E.	South Dock.
							D'Arcy Street Depôts	Durham ...	N. E.	South Dock.
							Elliott & Son's Timber Yard (Thornhill Quay)...	Durham ...	N. E.	South Dock.
							Fulwell Lime Works.........	Durham ...	N. E.	Monkwearmouth.
							Haggie's, D. H. & G., Rope Works	Durham ...	N. E.	Monkwearmouth.
							Hawn's Hendon Depôts...	Durham ...	N. E.	South Dock.
							Hendon Gas Works (Sunderland Gas Co.).............	Durham ...	N. E.	South Dock.
							Hendon Paper Works	Durham ...	N. E.	South Dock.
							Jackson, T., Saw Mill	Durham ...	N. E.	South Dock.
							Lloyd's Test Works	Durham ...	N. E.	South Dock.
							Moller's Timber Yard	Durham ...	N. E.	South Dock.
G	P	F	L	H		20 0	Monkwearmouth	Durham ...	N. E.	Central Station and East Boldon.
							Monkwearmouth Fire-Brk. Works	Durham ..	N. E.	Monkwearmouth.
G						5 0	North Dock or Wearmouth Dock	Durham ...	N. E.	Branch near Monkwearmouth.
							North Eastern Marine Engineering Co.'s Siding ...	Durham ...	N. E.	South Dock.
							Old Yard	Durham ...	N. E.	Sunderland.
							Phœnix Bottle Works	Durham ...	N. E.	South Dock.
							Pier Engine Works	Durham ...	N. E.	South Dock.
							Portobello Depôts	Durham ...	N. E.	Monkwearmouth.
							Portobello Grease Works...	Durham ...	N. E.	Monkwearmouth.
							Portobello Saw Mills	Durham ...	N. E.	Monkwearmouth.
							River Wear Commissioners (Hudson & Hendon Dks.)	Durham ...	N. E.	South Dock.
							Robson's, W. & C., Timber Yard	Durham ...	N. E.	South Dock.
							Roker Park	Durham ...	N. E.	Monkwearmouth.
G			L	H		10 0	South Dock	Durham ...	N. E.	Branch—Central Station & Ryhope.
							Sunderland Corporation Manure Depôt	Durham ...	N. E.	South Dock.
							Sunderland Shipbuilding Co.'s Siding	Durham ...	N. E.	South Dock.
							Tatham Street Depôt	Durham ...	N. E.	South Dock.
							Thompson, Jos., & Co.'s Timber Yard	Durham ...	N. E.	South Dock.
							Tyzack, Sam, & Co.'s Works	Durham ...	N. E.	Monkwearmouth.
							Victoria Depôts	Durham ...	N. E.	South Dock.
							Wayman's Landsale Depôts	Durham ...	N. E.	South Dock.
							Wear Fuel and Chemical Co.'s Works...............	Durham ...	N. E.	South Dock.
							Wearmouth Foundry	Durham ...	N. E.	Monkwearmouth.
							Weiner's Timber Yard......	Durham ...	N. E.	South Dock.
							Wilson, J. & W., & Son's Timber Yard	Durham ...	N. E.	Monkwearmouth.

EXPLANATION—G *Goods Station.*   P *Passenger and Parcel Station.*   P* *Passenger, but not Parcel or Miscellaneous Traffic.*
F *Furniture Vans, Carriages, Portable Engines, and Machines on Wheels.*   L *Live Stock.*
H *Horse Boxes and Prize Cattle Vans.*   C *Carriages by Passenger Train.*

STATION ACCOMMODATION.						CRANE POWER.		STATIONS, &c.	COUNTY.	COMPANY.	POSITION.
						Tons	Cwts.				
.	.	.	.	.	.	.	.	Sunderland & South Shields Water Co.'s Pumping Station (Nimmo's Siding)...	Durham ...	N. E.	Castle Eden.
.	.	.	.	.	.	.	.	Sunderland Corporation Manure Depôt................	Durham ...	N. E.	Sunderland, South Dock.
.	.	.	.	.	.	.	.	Sunderland Forge and Engineering Co.'s Siding	Durham ...	N. E.	Pallion.
.	.	.	.	.	.	.	.	Sunderland Shipbuilding Co.'s Siding	Durham ...	N. E.	Sunderland, South Dock.
.	P	.	.	.	.	.	.	Sundridge Park	Kent	S. E. & C.	Grove Park and Bromley, North.
.	.	.	.	.	.	.	.	Sundrum, Nos. 3 and 4 (Drumdow Colliery)	Ayr	G. & S.W.	Annbank.
G	P	.	L	H	.	.	.	Sunilaws	Northumb	N. E.	Berwick and Kelso.
G	P	F	L	H	C	5	0	Sunningdale and Windlesham	Surrey	L. & S.W.	Staines and Reading.
.	.	.	.	.	.	.	.	Sunninghill	Berks	L. & S.W.	See Ascot and Sunninghill.
.	.	.	.	.	.	.	.	Sunniside Depôt	Durham ...	N. E.	Redheugh.
.	.	.	.	.	.	.	.	Sunnybraes Colliery (Saline Valley Colliery)	Fife	N. B.	Steelend.
.	.	.	.	.	.	.	.	Sunnybrow Colliery	Durham ...	N. E.	Same as Willington Colliery Coke and Brick Works (Willington).
.	.	.	.	.	.	.	.	Sunnyside................	Lanark	N. B.	See Coatbridge.
.	.	.	.	.	.	.	.	Sunnyside Blacking Mills (NB)	Stirling	N. B.—Cal.	Falkirk, Grahamston.
.	.	.	.	.	.	.	.	Sunnyside Colliery..............	Lanark ...	Cal.	Cleland.
.	.	.	.	.	.	.	.	Sunnyside Depôt and Siding	Durham ...	N. E.	Tow Law.
.	.	.	.	.	.	.	.	Sunnyside Engine Works (Lamberton's Siding).........	Lanark ...	N. B.	Coatbridge, Sunnyside.
.	.	.	.	.	.	.	.	Sunnyside Foundry (Melvin's)	Clackman'	N. B.	Alloa.
.	.	.	.	.	.	.	.	Sunnyside Iron Foundry (N.B.)	Stirling ...	N. B.—Cal.	Falkirk, Grahamston.
.	.	.	.	.	.	.	.	Sunnyside Junction	Lanark ...	N. B.	Sunnyside and Gartgill.
.	.	.	.	.	.	.	.	Sunnyside Sid. (Lambton Line)	Durham ...	N. E.	{ Fencehouses. { Penshaw.
.	.	.	.	.	.	.	.	Sun Paper Mill Co.'s Siding..	Lancs	L. & Y.	Brindle Heath.
.	.	.	.	.	.	.	.	Sun Tube Works	Lanark ...	N. B.	Greengairs.
G	P	F	L	H	C	5	0	Surbiton	Surrey	L. & S.W.	Wimbledon and Woking.
G	P	.	L	H	C	1	0	Surfleet	Lincoln	G. N.	Spalding and Boston.
.	.	.	.	.	.	.	.	Surrey Canal Junction	Surrey	S. E. & C.	London, London Bridge & New Cross.
.	.	.	.	.	.	.	.	Surrey Commercial Docks ...	Surrey	L. B. & S. C.	See London.
.	.	.	.	.	.	.	.	Sussex Brick Co.'s Siding ...	Sussex	L. B. & S. C.	Warnham.
.	.	.	.	.	.	.	.	Sussex Portland Cement Co.'s Sidings	Sussex	L. B. & S. C.	{ Glynde. { Newhaven Town. { Shoreham.
.	.	.	.	.	.	.	.	Sutcliffe's Malt Kiln (L. & Y.)	Yorks	L.&Y.—G.N.—L.&N.W.	Mirfield.
.	.	.	.	.	.	.	.	Sutherland Wharf	Staffs	N. S.	Longton.
.	.	.	.	.	.	.	.	Sutterton	Lincoln	G. N.	See Algarkirk and Sutterton.
G	P	F	L	H	C	.	.	Sutton	Cambs......	G. E.	Ely and St. Ives.
.	.	.	.	.	.	.	.	Sutton	Derby	Mid.	See Palterton & Sutton.
.	.	.	.	.	.	.	.	Sutton	Dublin	G. N. (I.)	See Baldoyle and Sutton.
.	P	.	.	.	.	.	.	Sutton	Notts	G. N.	Retford and Doncaster.
G	P	F	L	H	C	5	0	Sutton	Surrey	L. B. & S. C.	West Croydon and Epsom.
.	.	.	.	.	.	.	.	Sutton & Ash's Siding	Warwick	L. & N. W.	Birmingham, Monument Lane.
.	.	.	.	.	.	.	.	Sutton & Co.'s Siding (Mid.)	Leicester..	Mid.—L. & N. W........	Moira.
.	.	.	.	.	.	.	.	Sutton-at-Hone	Kent	S. E. & C.	See Farningham Road and Sutton-at-Hone.
G	P	F	L	H	C	.	.	Sutton Bingham	Somerset..	L. & S.W.	Yeovil Junction and Exeter.
								SUTTON BRIDGE—			
G	P	F	L	H	C	5	0	(Station)	Lincoln ...	Mid. & G. N. Jt.	South Lynn and Wisbech.
.	.	.	.	.	.	.	.	Dock Junction	Lincoln ...	Mid. & G. N. Jt.	Sutton Bridge and Long Sutton.
G	P	F	L	H	C	5	0	Sutton Coldfield	Warwick..	L. & N. W.	Birmingham and Lichfield.
.	.	.	.	.	.	.	.	Sutton Coldfield (Goods)	Warwick..	Mid.	Same as Sutton Park.
.	P	.	.	.	.	.	.	Sutton Coldfield (Pass)........	Warwick..	Mid.	Water Orton and Walsall.
.	.	.	.	.	.	.	.	Sutton Colliery	Notts	Mid.	See Blackwell Col. Co. (Whiteboro').
.	.	.	.	.	.	.	.	Sutton Dock	Cheshire..	B'headJt. (GW & LNW)	See Speakman's (Halton).
.	.	.	.	.	.	.	.	Sutton Harbour	Devon	G. W.—L. & S.W.	See Plymouth.
								Sutton Heath and Lea Green Colliery Co.—			
.	.	.	.	.	.	.	.	East Colliery	Lancs	L. & N. W.	Rainhill.
.	.	.	.	.	.	.	.	Roughdale Works	Lancs	L. & N. W.	Rainhill.
.	.	.	.	.	.	.	.	West Colliery	Lancs	L. & N. W.	Rainhill.
G	P	F	L	H	C	1	10 }	Sutton-in-Ashfield	Notts	{ G. N. { Mid.	Annesley Junction and Shirebrook. Branch from Sutton Junction.
G	P	F	L	H	C	1	10 }				
.	.	.	.	.	.	.	.	Blackmore's Siding	Notts	Mid.	Sutton-in-Ashfield.
.	.	.	.	.	.	.	.	King's Mill Sid. (Caudwell's)	Notts	Mid.	Sutton-in-Ashfield.

EXPLANATION—G Goods Station.   P Passenger and Parcel Station.   P* Passenger, but not Parcel or Miscellaneous Traffic.
F Furniture Vans, Carriages, Portable Engines, and Machines on Wheels.   L Live Stock.
H Horse Boxes and Prize Cattle Vans.   C Carriages by Passenger Train.

STATION ACCOMMODATION.						CRANE POWER.		STATIONS, &c.	COUNTY.	COMPANY.	POSITION.
						Tons	Cwts.	Sutton-in-Ashfield—*continued*.			
								Kirkby Colliery (Summit Pit) (G. N.)	Notts	G. N.—G.C.—L.D. & E.C.	Sutton-in-Ashfield and Newstead.
G								Kirkby Siding	Notts	G. N.	Sutton-in-Ashfield and Newstead.
								Meggitt & Son's Siding	Notts	Mid.	Sutton Junction and Mansfield.
G	P	F	L	H	C	2	0	Sutton Junction Station	Notts	Mid.	Nottingham and Mansfield.
								Adlington's Flour Mill	Notts	Mid.	Near Sutton Junction Station.
								Hutchinson's Siding	Derby	Mid.	Sutton Junction.
								Sutton, Little	Cheshire	B'head Jt. (G W & L N W)	See Little Sutton.
								Sutton Lodge Works	Lancs	L. & N. W.	See United Alkali Co. (St. Helens).
								Sutton Metal Co.'s Siding	Lancs	L. & N. W.	St. Helens.
	P							Sutton Oak	Lancs	L. & N. W.	St. Helens and Widnes.
								Sutton Oak Branch	Lancs	L. & N. W.	Garswood and St. Helens Junction.
G	P		L	H	C			Sutton-on-Hull	Yorks	N. E.	Hull and Hornsea.
G	P					1	10	Sutton-on-Sea	Lincoln	G. N.	Willoughby and Mablethorpe.
								Sutton-on-Trent	Notts	G. N.	See Crow Park (for Sutton-on-Trent).
G	P	F	L	H	C	1	10	Sutton Park	Warwick	Mid.	Water Orton and Walsall.
G	P	F	L	H	C	3	0	Sutton Scotney	Hants	G. W.	Newbury and Winchester.
								Sutton, Southcoates, & Drypool Gas Co.'s Siding	Yorks	N. E.	Hull, Wilmington.
G	P		L	H				Sutton Weaver	Cheshire	L. & N. W.	Crewe and Liverpool.
G	P	F	L	H	C	1	10	Swadlincote (Mid.)	Derby	Mid.	Burton and Woodville.
G		F	L							L. & N. W.	Over Mid. Line.
								Bretby Brick & Pipe Co.'s Siding (Mid)	Derby	Mid.—L. & N. W.	Near Swadlincote.
								Cartwright Col. Co.'s New Hall Field Colliery (Mid.)	Derby	Mid.—L. & N. W.	Near Swadlincote.
								Earl of Carnarvon's Sids.—Bretby Colliery Wharf (Newhall Pk Col) (Mid)	Derby	Mid.—L. & N. W.	Near Swadlincote.
								New Bretby Col. (Mid)	Derby	Mid.—L. & N. W	Near Swadlincote.
								Hall & Boardman's—Brickyard (Mid.)	Derby	Mid.—L. & N. W.	Near Swadlincote.
								Pipe Works (Mid.)	Derby	Mid.—L. & N. W.	Near Swadlincote.
								Hall's Collieries—Cadley Hill Colliery (Mid.)	Derby	Mid.—L. & N. W.	Near Swadlincote.
								Swadlincote Old Colliery (Mid.)	Derby	Mid.—L. & N. W.	Near Swadlincote.
								Stanton Colliery (J. N. Nadin & Co.) (Mid.)	Derby	Mid.—L. & N. W.	Near Swadlincote.
								Stanton House Farm Siding (Mid.)	Derby	Mid.—L. & N. W.	Near Swadlincote.
								Swadlincote Urban District Council Gas Works (Mid.)	Derby	Mid.—L. & N. W.	Near Swadlincote.
								Trent Art Tile Co.'s Siding (Mid.)	Derby	Mid.—L. & N. W.	Near Swadlincote.
								Wragg & Son's Pipe Works (Mid.)	Derby	Mid.—L. & N. W.	Near Swadlincote.
	P							Swadlincote, New	Derby	Mid.	Swadlincote Junc. and Woodville.
								Swadlincote Old Colliery (Mid)	Derby	Mid.—L. & N. W.	See Hall's Collieries (Swadlincote).
G	P	F	L	H	C	1	0	Swaffham	Norfolk	G. E.	Lynn and Dereham.
G	P	F	L					Swaffhamprior	Cambs	G. E.	Cambridge and Fordham.
								Swainson Dock	Durham	N. E.	West Hartlepool.
								Swain's Siding	Lancs	L. & Y.	Manchester, Miles Platting.
G	P	F	L	H				Swainsthorpe	Norfolk	G. E.	Norwich and Tivetshall.
								Swaithe Main Coke Ovens	Yorks	G. C.	Worsbro'.
								Swaithe Main Colliery	Yorks	G. C.	Worsbro'.
G	P	F	L			1	0	Swalwell	Durham	N. E.	Scotswood and Lanchester.
								Axwell Park Colliery (Hannington & Co.)	Durham	N. E.	Swalwell.
								Grace & Co.'s Paper Mill	Durham	N. E.	Swalwell.
								Ridley & Co.'s Steel Works	Durham	N. E.	Swalwell.
								Swalwell Bridge Depôts	Durham	N. E.	Derwenthaugh.
								Swalwell Colliery	Durham	N. E.	Derwenthaugh.
G	P	F	L	H	C	5	0	Swanage	Dorset	L. & S. W.	Branch from Wareham.
								Burt & Burt's Siding	Dorset	L. & S. W.	Swanage.
								Swanage Gas Works	Dorset	L. & S. W.	Swanage.
G	P			H				Swanbourne	Bucks	L. & N. W.	Bletchley and Verney Junction Sta.
								Swan Lane Brick & Coal Co.'s Swan Lane Colliery	Lancs	L. & N. W.	Wigan.
								Swan Lane Colliery	Lancs	L. & N. W.	Same as Swan Lane Brick and Coal Co.'s (Wigan).

STATION ACCOMMODATION.						CRANE POWER.	STATIONS, &c.	COUNTY.	COMPANY.	POSITION.
						Tons Cwts.				
G	P	F	L	H	C	1 15	Swanley Junction	Kent	S. E. & C.	St. Mary Cray and Swanley Jn. Sta.
						. .	Swanley Junction Station ...	Kent	S. E. & C.	Bromley and Rochester.
						. .	May's Siding	Kent	S. E. & C.	Swanley and Eynsford.
.	P	.	.	.	.	. .	Swannington	Leicester..	Mid.	Coalville and Ashby.
							Swannington Pumping Co.'s			
.	.	.	.	.	.	. .	Siding (Mid.)	Leicester.	Mid.—L. & N. W.	Coalville.
							Swann, Ratcliffe & Co.'s Har-			
.	.	.	.	.	.	. .	boro' Siding...................	Derby ...	L. & N. W.	Longcliffe.
.	.	.	.	.	.	. .	Swanscombe Siding	Kent	S. E. & C.	Northfleet.
							SWANSEA—			
G	P	F	L	H	C	5 0	(Station)	Glamorg'n	R. & S. B.	Terminus.
							Agglament Patent Fuel Co's			
.	.	.	.	.	.	. .	Siding	Glamorg'n	GW—LNW—Mid—RSB	East Dock.
.	P	.	.	.	.	. .	Argyle Street	Glamorg'n	Swan. & Mum.	Rutland Street and St. Helens Road.
							Atlantic Patent Fuel Co.'s			
.	.	.	.	.	.	. .	Siding	Glamorg'n	GW—LNW—Mid—RSB	Over Harbour Trust Lines.
.	.	.	.	.	.	. .	Bath & Son's Siding	Glamorg'n	GW—LNW—Mid—RSB	Over Harbour Trust Lines.
							Bristol Channel Steam Pac-			
.	.	.	.	.	.	. .	ket Co.'s Pockett's Sid.	Glamorg'n	GW—LNW—Mid—RSB	South Dock.
.	.	.	.	.	.	. .	Burrows' Sidings	Glamorg'n	G. W.	Swansea and Briton Ferry Road.
.	.	.	.	.	.	. .	Burrows' Sidings	Glamorg'n	R. & S. B.	Swansea.
							Cambrian Lubricants Co.'s			
.	.	.	.	.	.	. .	Works	Glamorg'n	GW—LNW—Mid—RSB	Over Harbour Trust Lines.
.	.	.	.	.	.	. .	Central Dry Dock	Glamorg'n	GW—LNW—Mid—RSB	North Dock.
G	.	.	.	.	.	3 0	Cobre Yard	Glamorg'n	R. & S. B.	Swansea.
							Cory Briquette Fuel Co.'s			
.	.	.	.	.	.	. .	Works	Glamorg'n	GW—LNW—Mid—RSB	East Dock.
.	.	.	.	.	.	. .	Dan-y-graig Siding	Glamorg'n	G. W.	Swansea and Briton Ferry Road.
G	P	.	.	.	.	. .	Dan-y-graig Siding	Glamorg'n	R. & S. B.	Swansea.
.	.	.	.	.	.	. .	East Dock	Glamorg'n	G. W.	Wind Str. Jn. and Briton Ferry Rd.
							East Dock Junction	Glamorg'n	G. W.—Harb.TrustLines	Swansea and Briton Ferry Road.
G	.	.	.	.	.	. .	Eastern Depôt................	Glamorg'n	G. W.	Wind Str. Jn. and Briton Ferry Rd.
.	.	.	.	.	.	. .	East or Prince of Wales Dk.	Glamorg'n	GW—LNW—Mid—RSB	Over Harbour Trust Lines.
							English Crown Spelter			
.	.	.	.	.	.	. .	Works	Glamorg'n	R. & S. B.	Swansea.
							Fish Wharf and Market			
.	.	.	.	.	.	. .	(Prince of Wales Dock)..	Glamorg'n	GW—LNW— Mid—RSB	Over Harbour Trust Lines.
							Glasbrook, Sons & Co.'s			
.	.	.	.	.	.	. .	Timber Yard	Glamorg'n	GW—LNW—Mid—RSB	South Dock.
.	.	.	.	.	.	. .	Gloucester Wagon Works	Glamorg'n	G. W.	Eastern Depôt.
							Graigola Merthyr Co.'s Pa-			
.	.	.	.	.	.	. .	tent Fuel Works..........	Glamorg'n	GW—LNW—Mid—RSB	North Dock.
.	.	.	.	.	.	. .	Gregor Bros.' Siding	Glamorg'n	GW—LNW—Mid—RSB	South Dock.
.	.	.	.	.	.	. .	Hafod Junction	Glamorg'n	G. W.	Swansea and Landore.
.	.	.	.	.	.	. .	Harrison's, J. & C., Siding	Glamorg'n	GW—LNW—Mid—RSB	East Dock.
G	P	F	L	H	C	10 0	High Street..................	Glamorg'n	G. W.	Bch.—Landore & Wind Street Junc.
							Jackson & Co.'s Oil and			
.	.	.	.	.	.	. .	Grease Works.............	Glamorg'n	GW—LNW— Mid—RSB	Over Harbour Trust Lines.
.	.	.	.	.	.	. .	Jarvis, D., Siding	Glamorg'n	GW—LNW—Mid—RSB	South Dock.
.	.	.	.	.	.	. .	Jersey Siding	Glamorg'n	GW—LNW—Mid—RSB	Over Harbour Trust Lines.
.	.	.	.	.	.	. .	Johns', D. W., Siding	Glamorg'n	GW—LNW—Mid—RSB	Over Harbour Trust Lines.
.	.	.	.	.	.	. .	Jones, M., Bros.' Siding ...	Glamorg'n	GW—LNW—Mid—RSB	South Dock.
.	.	.	.	.	.	. .	Junction	Glamorg'n	G. W.—L. & N. W.	Wind Street Junction & Victoria.
.	.	.	.	.	.	. .	Junction	Glamorg'n	G. W.—Mid.	Eastern Depôt and Upper Bank.
.	.	.	.	.	.	. .	Junction	Glamorg'n	G. W.—R. & S. B.	Over Harbour Trust Lines.
.	.	.	.	.	.	. .	Junction	Glamorg'n	G. W.—Swan. & Mum....	Over Harbour Trust Lines.
.	.	.	.	.	.	. .	Junction	Glamorg'n	L. & N. W.—R. & S. B. ...	Over Harbour Trust Lines.
.	.	.	.	.	.	. .	Junction	Glamorg'n	G.W.—L.&N.W—S.& M.	Victoria and Victoria Road.
.	.	.	.	.	.	. .	Junction	Glamorg'n	Mid.—R. & S. B.	Over Harbour Trust Lines.
.	.	.	.	.	.	. .	Junction	Glamorg'n	R. & S.B.—Swan. & Mum.	Over Harbour Trust Lines.
							Lamberts Wharfage Co.'s			
.	.	.	.	.	.	. .	Yard	Glamorg'n	GW—LNW—Mid—RSB	Over Harbour Trust Lines.
.	.	.	.	.	.	. .	Maliphant Siding	Glamorg'n	G. W.	Swansea and Landore.
.	.	.	.	.	.	. .	Mileage Siding	Glamorg'n	G. W.	East Dock Station.
.	.	.	.	.	.	. .	New Cut & Harbour Road	Glamorg'n	GW—LNW—Mid—RSB	Over Harbour Trust Lines.
.	.	.	.	.	.	. .	North Central Wgn. Wks.	Glamorg'n	G. W.	Eastern Depôt.
G	.	.	.	.	.	. .	North Dock	Glamorg'n	{ G. W.	North Dock Jn. and Wind Str. Jn.
									L & NW—Mid—R & S B	Over Harbour Trust Lines.
.	.	.	.	.	.	. .	North Dock Junction	Glamorg'n	G. W.	Swansea and Landore.
.	.	.	.	.	.	. .	Ocean Dry Dock Co.'s Sid.	Glamorg'n	GW—LNW—Mid—RSB	Over Harbour Trust Lines.
							Pacific Patent Fuel Co.'s			
.	.	.	.	.	.	. .	Siding	Glamorg'n	GW—LNW—Mid—RSB	East Dock.

EXPLANATION—G *Goods Station.*   P *Passenger and Parcel Station.*   P* *Passenger, but not Parcel or Miscellaneous Traffic.*
F *Furniture Vans, Carriages, Portable Engines, and Machines on Wheels.*   L *Live Stock.*
H *Horse Boxes and Prize Cattle Vans.*   C *Carriages by Passenger Train.*

Station Accommodation.						Crane Power.	Stations, &c.	County.	Company.	Position.
						Tons Cwts.	SWANSEA—continued.			
.	.	.	.	.	.	. .	Peels Yard	Glamorg'n	GW—LNW—Mid—RSB	Over Harbour Trust Lines.
.	.	.	.	.	.	. .	Petolite Fuel Co.'s Siding	Glamorg'n	GW—LNW—Mid—RSB	East Dock.
.	.	.	.	.	.	. .	Phœnix Dry Dock	Glamorg'n	GW—LNW—Mid—RSB	Over Harbour Trust Lines.
.	.	.	.	.	.	. .	Prince of Wales Dock	Glamorg'n	GW—LNW—Mid—RSB	See East or Prince of Wales Dock.
.	P	.	.	.	.	. .	Pritchard's Chemical Works	Glamorg'n	G. W.	East Dock and Briton Ferry Road.
.	P	.	.	.	.	. .	Rutland Street	Glamorg'n	Swan. & Mum.	Terminus.
.	P	.	.	.	.	. .	St. Helens Road	Glamorg'n	Swan. & Mum.	Rutland Street and Mumbles Road.
G	.	F	L	.	.	5 0	St. Thomas (Goods)	Glamorg'n	Mid.	Over G.W. from Swansea Junction.
.	P	.	.	H	C	. .	St. Thomas (Pass.)	Glamorg'n	Mid.	Terminus.
G	.	.	.	.	.		South Dock	Glamorg'n	G. W. / L. & N. W. / Mid.—R.&S.B.—S.&M.	Wind Str. Jn. and South Dock Jn. / Swansea. / Over Harbour Trust Lines.
.	.	.	.	.	.	. .	Stone's, W. H., Siding	Glamorg'n	GW—LNW—Mid—RSB	South Dock.
G	.	.	.	.	.		Strand	Glamorg'n	GW—LNW—Mid—RSB / Swan. & Mum.	Over Harbour Trust Lines. / Swansea.
.	.	.	.	.	.	. .	Strand Road Siding	Glamorg'n	GW—LNW—Mid—RSB	Over Harbour Trust Lines.
G	P	.	L	.	.	. .	Swansea Bay	Glamorg'n	L. & N. W.	Victoria and Llandilo.
.	.	.	.	.	.	. .	Swansea Gas Co.'s Siding	Glamorg'n	GW—LNW—Mid—RSB	South Dock.
.	.	.	.	.	.	. .	Swansea Oil and Grease Co.'s Works	Glamorg'n	GW—LNW—Mid—RSB	North Dock.
.	.	.	.	.	.	. .	Thomas' Gilwern Tin Plate Works (Mid.)	Glamorg'n	Mid.—G.W.—L. & N. W.	Swansea.
.	.	.	.	.	.	. .	Thomas, T. W., & Co.'s Sid.	Glamorg'n	GW—LNW—Mid—RSB	South Dock.
G	P	F	L	H	C	10 0	Victoria	Glamorg'n	L. & N. W.	Terminus—Swansea Section.
.	.	.	.	.	.	. .	Victoria Dry Docks Co.—Albion Dry Dock	Glamorg'n	GW—LNW—Mid—RSB	North Dock.
.	.	.	.	.	.	. .	Globe Dry Dock	Glamorg'n	GW—LNW—Mid—RSB	North Dock.
G	P	.	.	.	.	. .	Victoria Road	Glamorg'n	Swan. & Mum.	Swansea.
.	.	.	.	.	.	. .	Victoria Wharf	Glamorg'n	GW—LNW—Mid—RSB	Over Harbour Trust Lines.
.	.	.	.	.	.	. .	Vivian & Son's—Coal Siding	Glamorg'n	G. W.	High Street.
.	.	.	.	.	.	. .	Hafod Siding	Glamorg'n	G. W.	Hafod Junction.
.	.	.	.	.	.	. .	Weaver's Flour Mills	Glamorg'n	G. W.	Swansea.
.	.	.	.	.	.	. .	Wheeler & Gregory's Wagon Works	Glamorg'n	G. W.	East Dock and Briton Ferry Road.
G	.	.	.	.	.	1 10	Wind Str. (Burrows Lodge)	Glamorg'n	G. W.	Wind Str. Jn. and South Dock.
.	.	.	.	.	.	. .	Wind Street Junction	Glamorg'n	G. W.	North Dock and South Dock.
.	.	.	.	.	.	. .	Swansea Chemical Co.'s Siding (Mid.)	Glamorg'n	Mid.—G.W.—L. & N. W.	Swansea Valley Junction.
.	.	.	.	.	.	. .	Swansea Gas Co.'s Siding	Glamorg'n	GW—LNW—Mid—RSB	Swansea.
.	.	.	.	.	.	. .	Swansea Harbour Trustees' Siding (Mid.)	Glamorg'n	Mid.—G.W.—L. & N. W.	Upper Bank.
.	.	.	.	.	.	. .	Swansea Hematite Iron Works	Glamorg'n	G.W.—Mid.—L. & N. W.	Same as Baldwin's, Ltd., Landore Steel Works.
.	.	.	.	.	.	. .	Swansea Oil & Grease Co.'s Wks	Glamorg'n	GW—LNW—Mid—RSB	Swansea.
G	.	.	.	.	.	. .	Swansea Vale Spelter Co.'s Siding (Mid.)	Glamorg'n	Mid.—G. W.—L. & N. W.	Swansea Valley Junction.
							Swansea Valley Junction (G. W. & Mid. Jt.)	Glamorg'n	G. W.—Mid. / L. & N. W.	Landore and Llansamlet. / Over G. W. and Mid. Lines.
.	.	.	.	.	.	. .	Dillwyn & Co.'s Spelter Works	Glamorg'n	G. W. & Mid. Jt.	Swansea Valley Junction.
.	.	.	.	.	.	. .	Swansea Chemical Co.'s Siding (Mid.)	Glamorg'n	Mid.—G.W.—L. & N. W.	Six Pit Junction and Llansamlet.
.	.	.	.	.	.	. .	Swansea Vale Spelter Co.'s Siding (Mid.)	Glamorg'n	Mid.—G.W.—L. & N. W.	Six Pit Junction.
.	.	.	.	.	.	. .	Villiers Spelter Works (G. W. & Mid. Jt.)	Glamorg'n	G. W.—Mid.—L. & N.W.	Swansea Valley Junc. and Six Pit.
G	P	.	.	.	.	. .	Swan's Live Stock Mart Sid.	Edinboro'	N. B.	Edinburgh, Haymarket.
G	.	.	.	.	.	. .	Swan Village	Staffs	G. W.	Birmingham and Wednesbury.
G	.	.	.	.	.	8 0	Basin	Staffs	G. W.	Birmingham and Wednesbury.
.	.	.	.	.	.	. .	City of Birmingham Gas Works	Staffs	G. W.	West Bromwich and Wednesbury.
.	.	.	.	.	.	. .	Lees', J. B. & S., Timber Depôt	Staffs	G. W.	Swan Village.
G	.	.	.	.	.	5 0	Mileage Yard	Staffs	G. W.	Birmingham and Wednesbury.
G	P	F	L	H	C	2 0	Swanwick	Hants	L. & S.W.	Fareham and Southampton.
.	.	.	.	.	.	. .	Swanwick Colliery	Derby	Mid.	Butterley.
.	.	.	.	.	.	. .	Swarkestone	Derby	Mid.	See Chellaston and Swarkestone.
G	P	.	L	H	.	1 0	Swavesey (G. E.)	Cambs	G. E. / Mid.	Cambridge and St. Ives. / Over G.N. & G.E. Joint and G. E. Lines.

EXPLANATION—G Goods Station.   P Passenger and Parcel Station.   P* Passenger, but not Parcel or Miscellaneous Traffic.
F Furniture Vans, Carriages, Portable Engines, and Machines on Wheels.   L Live Stock.
H Horse Boxes and Prize Cattle Vans.   C Carriages by Passenger Train.

G	P	F	L	H	C	Tons	Cwts	STATIONS, &c.	COUNTY.	COMPANY.	POSITION.
G	**P**	F	L	H	C	.	.	Sway	Hants	L. & S.W.	Brockenhurst and Christchurch.
G	**P**	F	L	H	C	.	.	Swaythling	Hants	L. & S.W.	Eastleigh and Southampton.
G	P	.	L	.	.	2	0	Swell Tor Siding	Devon	G. W.	Princetown.
.	.	.	.	.	.	.	.	Swimbridge	Devon	G. W.	South Molton and Barnstaple.
.	.	.	.	.	.	.	.	Swindell & Collis Siding	Staffs	G. W.	Cradley Heath and Cradley.
.	.	.	.	.	.	.	.	Swinden Lime Works (Spencer's)	Yorks	Mid.	Rylstone.
G	P	F	L	H	.	.	.	Swinderby	Lincoln	Mid.	Lincoln and Newark.
G	P	F	L	H	C	8	0	Swindon	Wilts	G. W.	Didcot and Gloucester.
.	.	.	.	.	.	.	.	Gas Works	Wilts	G. W.	Swindon.
.	.	.	.	.	.	.	.	Great Western Carriage Works	Wilts	G. W.	Swindon.
.	.	.	.	.	.	.	.	Great Western Locomotive Works	Wilts	G. W.	Swindon.
.	.	.	.	.	.	.	.	Great Western Stores Depôt	Wilts	G. W.	Swindon.
.	.	.	.	.	.	.	.	Rodbourne Siding	Wilts	G. W.	Swindon.
G	P	F	L	H	C	5	0	Swindon Junction	Wilts	G. W.—M. & S. W. Jn.	Swindon (G. W.) & Swindon Town.
G	P	.	L	.	.	.	.	Swindon Town	Wilts	M. & S.W. Jn.	Cirencester and Marlboro'.
.	.	.	.	.	.	.	.	Swine	Yorks	N. E.	Hull and Hornsea.
.	.	.	.	.	.	.	.	Swinehill Collieries and Coke and Brick Works	Lanark	Cal.	Stonehouse.
G	P	F	L	H	C	1	10	Swineshead	Lincoln	G. N.	Boston and Sleaford.
G	P	F	L	H	C	3	0	Swinford	Mayo	G. S. & W.	Collooney and Claremorris.
.	.	.	.	.	.	.	.	Swinlees Branch Junction	Ayr	G. & S.W.	Kilbirnie and Dalry.
.	.	.	.	.	.	.	.	Swinnerton Sidings	Warwick	L. & N. W.	Nuneaton.
G	P	.	.	.	.	5	0	Swinton	Lancs	L. & Y.	Pendleton and Hindley.
G	P / P	F	L	H	C	5	0	Swinton	Yorks	{ G. C. / Mid.	Rotherham and Doncaster. / Masboro' and Normanton.
.	.	.	.	.	.	.	.	Manvers Main Colliery No. 2 Pit	Yorks	Mid.	Near Wath-on-Dearne.
.	.	.	.	.	.	.	.	Manvers New Colliery	Yorks	Mid.	Swinton.
.	.	.	.	.	.	.	.	Manvers Old Colliery	Yorks	Mid.	Swinton.
.	.	.	.	.	.	.	.	South Yorks Bottle Co.'s Siding	Yorks	Mid.	Swinton and Mexboro'.
.	.	.	.	.	.	.	.	Stanley & Son's Oil, Soap, and Manure Works	Yorks	Mid.	Near Wath-on-Dearne.
.	.	.	.	.	.	.	.	Wath-on-Dearne Main Col.	Yorks	Mid.	Near Wath-on-Dearne.
.	.	.	.	.	.	.	.	Swinton Junction	Yorks	G. C.—Mid.	Mexboro' and Swinton (Mid.).
.	.	.	.	.	.	.	.	Swinton Junction	Yorks	G. C.—S. & K. Jt.	Mexboro' and Bolton-on-Dearne.
.	.	.	.	.	.	.	.	Swinton, Wath Road Junc.	Yorks	Mid.—S. & K. Jt.	Swinton and Bolton-on-Dearne.
.	.	.	.	.	.	.	.	Swiss Cottage	Middlesex	Met.	See London.
.	.	.	.	.	.	.	.	Swiss Cottage (L. & N. W.)	Middlesex	L. & N. W.—N. L.	See London, Loudoun Road (for Swiss Cottage).
G	.	F	L	H	C	.	.	Swithland Siding (for Mount Sorrel)	Leicester	G. C.	Loughboro' and Leicester.
.	.	.	.	.	.	.	.	Sworder, J. & C., Siding	Herts	G. E.	Buntingford.
.	.	.	.	.	.	.	.	Sword Street Mineral Depôt	Lanark	N. B.	Glasgow, Camlachie.
.	P	.	.	.	.	.	.	Sydenham	Down	B. & C. D.	Belfast and Holywood.
.	P	.	.	.	.	.	.	Sydenham (L. B. & S. C.)	Kent	{ L. B. & S. C. / G. E.	Forest Hill and Crystal Palace. / Over L. B. & S. C. from New Cross Junction.
.	P	.	.	.	.	.	.	Sydenham & Co.'s Siding	Dorset	L. & S.W.	Hamworthy.
.	P	.	.	.	.	.	.	Sydenham Hill	Surrey	S. E. & C.	Herne Hill and Penge.
.	.	.	.	.	.	.	.	Sydenham, Lower	Kent	S. E. & C.	See Lower Sydenham.
.	.	.	.	.	.	.	.	Sydenham, Upper	Kent	S. E. & C.	See Upper Sydenham.
.	.	.	.	.	.	.	.	Sydes Siding	Lanark	Cal.	High Blantyre.
.	.	.	.	.	.	.	.	Sydney Parade	Dublin	D. W. & W.	See Dublin.
.	.	.	.	.	.	.	.	Sydney Street or College, East Junction	Lanark	G. & S.W.—N. B.	Glasgow.
.	.	.	.	.	.	.	.	Syenite Quarry	Carnarvon	Cam.	Portmadoc.
.	.	.	.	.	.	.	.	Sykehouse Mines	Cumb'land	WC&E Jt.(Fur.&LNW)	See Lindow's (Moor Row).
.	.	.	.	.	.	.	.	Sykes Junction	Lincoln	G. C.—G. N. & G. E. Jt.	Retford and Lincoln.
.	.	.	.	.	.	.	.	Sykes' Edgeley Bleach Works	Cheshire	L. & N. W.	Stockport, Edgeley.
.	.	.	.	.	.	.	.	Sylen Mountain Colliery	Carmarth'	L. & M. M.	Horeb.
.	.	.	.	.	.	.	.	Sylfaen Farm Siding	Montgom.	Cam. (W. & L.)	See Golfa.
G	P	F	L	H	C	2	0	Symington	Lanark	Cal.	Lockerbie and Carstairs.
.	.	.	.	.	.	.	.	Symington Weighs	Lanark	Cal.	Symington.
G	P	.	.	.	.	.	.	Symonds Yat	Hereford	G. W.	Ross and Monmouth.
.	.	.	.	.	.	.	.	Hadnock Siding	Hereford	G. W.	Symonds Yat.
.	.	.	.	.	.	.	.	Slaughter Siding (High Meadow Siding)	Hereford	G. W.	Symonds Yat.
.	.	.	.	.	.	.	.	Syndicate Siding	Glamorg'n	Barry	Barry.

EXPLANATION—G *Goods Station.*　　P *Passenger and Parcel Station.*　　P* *Passenger, but not Parcel or Miscellaneous Traffic.*
F *Furniture Vans, Carriages, Portable Engines, and Machines on Wheels.*　　L *Live Stock.*
H *Horse Boxes and Prize Cattle Vans.*　　C *Carriages by Passenger Train.*

STATION ACCOMMODATION.						CRANE POWER.		STATIONS, &c.	COUNTY.	COMPANY.	POSITION.
						Tons	Cwts				
G	P	F	L	H	C	1	10	Syston	Leicester..	Mid.	Leicester and Loughboro.'
.	.	.	.	.	.	.	.	Barrow Bros.' Brick Works	Leicester..	Mid.	Syston and Leicester.
.	.	.	.	.	.	.	.	Cort & Paul's Iron Works..	Leicester..	Mid.	Near Syston.
.	.	.	.	.	.	.	.	Herbert's Brick Works......	Leicester..	Mid.	Syston and Leicester.
.	.	.	.	.	.	.	.	Thurmaston Brick & Tile Co.'s Siding	Leicester..	Mid.	Syston and Leicester.

T

STATION ACCOMMODATION.						CRANE POWER.		STATIONS, &c.	COUNTY.	COMPANY.	POSITION.
.	.	.	.	.	.	.	.	Tacon, Sir Thomas, Siding ...	Suffolk	G. E.	Eye.
G	P	F	L	H	C	5	0	Tadcaster	Yorks	N. E.	Harrogate and Church Fenton.
.	.	.	.	.	.	.	.	Colley's Malt Kiln	Yorks	N. E.	Tadcaster.
.	.	.	.	.	.	.	.	Rishworth, Ingleby & Lofthouse's Mill	Yorks	N. E.	Tadcaster.
.	.	.	.	.	.	.	.	Tadcaster Tower Brewery Co.'s Siding	Yorks	N. E.	Tadcaster.
.	.	.	.	.	.	.	.	Tadcaster Brewery Co.'s Sid.	Derby	G. C.	Chesterfield.
.	.	.	.	.	.	.	.	Tadcaster Tower Brewery Co.'s Sidings	Durham	N. E.	Penshaw.
.	.	.	.	.	.	.	.		Yorks	N. E.	Tadcaster.
G	P	F	L	H	C	.	.	Tadworth and Walton-on-the-Hill	Surrey	S. E. & C.	Purley and Tattenham Corner.
.	.	.	.	.	.	.	.	Taff Bargoed Junction	Glamorg'n	G. W.—T B Jt (GW & Rhy)	Llancaiach and Bedlinog.
G	.	F	L	.	C	.	.	Taffs Well	Glamorg'n	Rhy.	Taffs Well Junction and Caerphilly.
G	P	F	L	.	.	.	.		Glamorg'n	T. V.	Cardiff and Pontypridd.
.	.	.	.	.	.	.	.	Castell Coch Siding	Glamorg'n	Rhy.	Taffs Well.
.	.	.	.	.	.	.	.	Garth Works	Glamorg'n	Rhy.	Taffs Well.
.	.	.	.	.	.	.	.	Pentyrch Siding (Melin-griffith Works)	Glamorg'n	T. V.	Taffs Well and Radyr.
.	.	.	.	.	.	.	.	Waterhouse Bros.' Taffs Well Siding	Glamorg'n	T. V.	Taffs Well and Treforest.
.	.	.	.	.	.	.	.	Taffs Well Junction	Glamorg'n	Rhy.—T. V.	Caerphilly and Radyr.
.	.	.	.	.	.	.	.	Taff Vale Little Dock	Glamorg'n	T. V.	Cardiff Docks.
.	.	.	.	.	.	.	.	Taff Vale Railway Co.'s Stores	Glamorg'n	T. V.	Cardiff Docks.
.	.	.	.	.	.	.	.	Taibach Tin Plate Works...	Glamorg'n	P. T.	Port Talbot, Central.
G	P	F	L	H	C	1	10	Tain	Ross & Cro'	High.	Invergordon and Bonar Bridge.
.	.	.	.	.	.	.	.	Glenmorangie Siding.........	Ross & Cro'	High.	Tain and Edderton.
.	.	.	.	.	.	.	.	Tait's Coal Spout............	Durham	N. E.	South Shields.
G	P	.	.	H	.	.	.	Takeley	Essex	G. E.	Bishops Stortford and Dunmow.
G	P	.	L	.	.	.	.	Talacre	Flint	L. & N. W.	Chester and Rhyl.
.	.	.	.	.	.	.	.	Talbot Road	Lancs	P.&W.Jt.(L&Y&L&NW)	See Blackpool.
.	.	.	.	.	.	.	.	Talbot Wharf Junction	Glamorg'n	P. T.—R. & S. B.	Port Talbot Dock.
G	P	.	.	.	.	.	.	Talerddig	Montgom	Cam.	Llanbrynmair and Carno.
G	P	F	L	H	C	4	0	Talgarth (Cam.)	Brecon ...	Cam.	Three Cocks and Talyllyn.
G	P	F	L	H	C	3	0			Mid.	Over Cam. from Three Cocks Junc.
.	.	.	.	.	.	.	.	Talk-o'-th'-Hill	Staffs	N. S.	Branch from Chatterley Sidings.
.	.	.	.	.	.	.	.	High Carr Siding	Staffs	N. S.	Talk-o'-th'-Hill Branch.
.	.	.	.	.	.	.	.	Oak Tree Siding	Staffs	N. S.	Talk-o'-th'-Hill.
.	.	.	.	.	.	.	.	Williamson, J. H. (Exors. of) Siding	Staffs	N. S.	Talk-o'-th'-Hill Branch.
G	P	.	.	.	.	.	.	Talley Road......................	Carmarth'	V. of T. Jt. (G W & L. N. W)	Llandilo and Llandovery.
G	P	F	L	H	C	1	10	Tallington	Lincoln ...	G. N.	Peterboro' and Grantham.
.	.	.	.	.	.	.	.	Peterboro' Corporation Water Works..............	N'hamptn	G. N.	Peterboro' and Tallington.
G	P	F	L	H	C	.	.	Tallow Road	Cork	G. S. & W.	Fermoy and Lismore.
G	P	F	L	H	C	.	.	Talsarnau	Merioneth	Cam.	Harlech and Pwllheli.
G	P	F	L	.	.	.	.	Talybont-on-Usk	Brecon ...	B. & M.	Brecon and Dowlais.
G	P	.	L	H	.	5	0	Taly-Cafn and Eglwysbach ...	Denbigh ...	L. & N. W.	Blaenau Festiniog and Llandudno Junction Station.
.	.	.	.	.	.	.	.	Talyclyn Colliery and Brick Works (G. W.)	Carmarth'	G. W.—L. & N. W.	Hendy Siding.
G	P	F	L	H	.	.	.	Talyllyn (B. & M.).............	Brecon ...	B. & M.	Brecon and Dolygaer.
.	.	.	.	.	.	.	.			Cam.	Over B. & M. from Talyllyn Junc.
.	.	.	.	.	.	.	.			Mid.	Over Cam. and B. & M. Lines.
.	.	.	.	.	.	.	.	Talyllyn Junctions..............	Brecon ...	B. & M.—Cam.	Brecon and Three Cocks.
.	.	.	.	.	.	.	.	Talysarn Siding	Carnarvon	L. & N. W.	See Robinson's Slate Qrys. (Nantlle).

EXPLANATION—G *Goods Station.*   P *Passenger and Parcel Station.*   P* *Passenger, but not Parcel or Miscellaneous Traffic.*
F *Furniture Vans, Carriages, Portable Engines, and Machines on Wheels.*   L *Live Stock.*
H *Horse Boxes and Prize Cattle Vans.*   C *Carriages by Passenger Train.*

STATION ACCOMMODATION.						CRANE POWER.		STATIONS, &c.	COUNTY.	COMPANY.	POSITION.
						Tons	Cwts.				
G	.	.	.	.	.	.	.	Talywain	Mon	G. W.	Branch near Aberyschan & Talywain.
.	.	.	.	.	.	.	.	Aberyschan Elled Colliery	Mon	G. W.	Branch from Talywain.
.	.	.	.	.	.	.	.	Castle Pond Sidings	Mon	G. W.	Talywain.
.	.	.	.	.	.	.	.	Cwmffrwd Colliery	Mon	G. W.	Branch from Talywain.
.	.	.	.	.	.	.	.	Golynos Colliery	Mon	G. W.	Branch from Talywain.
.	.	.	.	.	.	.	.	Lower Varteg Colliery	Mon	G. W.	Branch from Talywain.
.	.	.	.	.	.	.	.	Pentwyn Colliery	Mon	G. W.	Branch from Talywain.
.	.	.	.	.	.	.	.	Talywain Chemical Works Siding	Mon	G. W.	Branch from Talywain.
.	.	.	.	.	.	.	.	Talywain	Mon	G. W. & L. & N. W. Jt.	See Aberyschan and Talywain.
.	.	.	.	.	.	.	.	Tamdhu Siding	Banff	G. N. of S.	See Dalbeallie.
.	P	.	.	.	.	.	.	Tamerton Folliott	Devon	L. & S.W.	Bere Ferrers and St. Budeaux.
.	.	.	.	.	.	.	.	Tame Valley Col. & Brk. Wks.	Warwick	Mid.	Wilnecote.
G	P	F	L	H	C	10	0	Tamworth	Staffs	{ L. & N. W.	Lichfield and Nuneaton.
G	P	F	L	H	C	5	0			{ Mid.	Burton and Birmingham.
.	.	.	.	.	.	.	.	Gibbs & Canning's Brick & Pipe Works	Warwick	L. & N. W.	Tamworth and Polesworth.
.	.	.	.	.	.	.	.	Glascote Colliery Co.'s Amington Colliery	Warwick	L. & N. W.	Tamworth and Polesworth.
.	.	.	.	.	.	.	.	Tamworth Colliery Co.'s Marshall's Siding	Warwick	L. & N. W.	Tamworth and Polesworth.
G	P	F	L	H	C	2	10	Tamworth Junction	Staffs	L. & N. W.—Mid.	Lichfield and Elford.
G	P	.	L	H	.	3	0	Tandragee	Armagh	G. N. (I.)	Newry and Portadown.
.	.	.	.	.	.	.	.	Tanfield	Yorks	N. E.	Branch from Melmerby.
.	.	.	.	.	.	.	.	Tanfield Branch Junction	Durham	N. E.	Redheugh.
.	.	.	.	.	.	.	.	Tanfield Lane Manure Depôts & Sidings	Durham	N. E.	Redheugh.
.	.	.	.	.	.	.	.	Tanfield Lea Colliery & Coke Ovens	Durham	N. E.	Redheugh.
.	.	.	.	.	.	.	.	Tanfield Moor Colliery	Durham	N. E.	Redheugh.
.	.	.	.	.	.	.	.	Tanhouse Lane	Lancs	S. & M. Jt. (G. C. & Mid.)	See Widnes.
.	.	.	.	.	.	.	.	Tankersley Colliery	Yorks	G. C.	See Newton, Chambers & Co. (Westwood).
.	.	.	.	.	.	.	.	Tanlan Siding	Denbigh	L. & N. W.	Llanrwst and Trefriw.
G	P	.	L	H	.	3	0	Tannadice	Forfar	Cal.	Forfar and Brechin.
.	.	.	.	.	.	.	.	Tanner Street Junction	Essex	L. T. & S.	Barking.
.	.	.	.	.	.	.	.	Tannochside Collieries	Lanark	Cal.	Same as Tennochside Collieries (Baillieston).
G	P	.	.	.	.	.	.	Tanrallt Siding	Carnarvon	L. & N. W.	Nantlle.
G	P	.	.	.	.	.	.	Tanshelf	Yorks	L. & Y.	Pontefract and Featherstone.
G	P	.	L	.	C	2	10	Tan-y-Bwlch	Merioneth	Festiniog	Penrhyn and Dduallt.
G	P	.	L	.	C	.	.	Tan-y-Grisiau	Merioneth	Festiniog	Dduallt and Blaenau Festiniog.
G	G	.	.	.	.	.	.	Tanymanod	Merioneth	G. W.	Festiniog and Blaenau Festiniog.
.	.	.	.	.	.	.	.	Craig-ddu Quarry Siding	Merioneth	G. W.	Festiniog and Blaenau Festiniog.
G	P	F	L	H	C	5	0	Taplow	Bucks	G. W.	Reading and Slough.
.	.	.	.	.	.	.	.	Tara Street and Georges Quay	Dublin	D. W. & W. (C. of D Jn.)	See Dublin.
G	P	.	.	.	.	.	.	Tarbert	Argyll	Cal.	Steamer from Gourock or Wemyss Bay.
G	P	.	L	.	.	.	.			{ Cal.	Steamer from Oban.
G	P	.	L	.	C	.	.	Tarbert (Harris)	Inverness	{ High.	Steamer from Kyle of Lochalsh.
G	P	.	L	.	.	.	.			{ N. B.	Steamer from Mallaig.
.	.	.	.	.	.	.	.	Tarbet	Dumbartn	N. B.	See Arrochar and Tarbet.
G	P	.	L	H	.	2	0	Tarbolton	Ayr	G. & S. W.	Mauchline and Annbank.
.	.	.	.	.	.	.	.	Tarbrax Oil Works	Lanark	Cal.	Cobbinshaw.
G	P	F	L	H	C	1	10	Tarff	Kirkcud	G. & S.W.	Castle Douglas and Kirkcudbright.
.	.	.	.	.	.	.	.	Tarleton Branch	Lancs	L. & Y.	Hesketh Bank.
.	.	.	.	.	.	.	.	Tarporley	Cheshire	L. & N. W.	See Beeston Castle and Tarporley.
G	P	F	L	H	C	2	0	Tarset	Northumb	N. B.	Riccarton and Reedsmouth.
.	.	.	.	.	.	.	.	Tarvin	Cheshire	C. L. C. (GC, G N, & Mid.)	See Barrow (for Tarvin).
.	.	.	.	.	.	.	.	Tasker's Siding	Hants	L. & S.W.	Clatford.
.	.	.	.	.	.	.	.	Tate, Brown & Co.'s Siding (Heworth Quarries)	Durham	N. E.	Felling.
.	.	.	.	.	.	.	.	Tate, H., & Son's Sid. (G. E.)	Essex	GE—GN—L&NW—Mid.	London, Silvertown.
.	.	.	.	.	.	.	.	Tatham Brick Works	Denbigh	G. W.	Same as Bower's Brk. Wks. (Ruabon).
.	.	.	.	.	.	.	.	Tatham Street Depôt	Durham	N. E.	Sunderland, South Dock.
.	P	.	.	.	.	.	.	Tattenhall	Cheshire	L. & N. W.	Chester and Whitchurch.
G	P	F	L	H	C	5	0	Tattenhall Road	Cheshire	L. & N. W.	Chester and Crewe.
.	.	.	.	.	.	.	.	Jones's Aldersey's Siding	Cheshire	L. & N. W.	Tattenhall Road and Beeston Castle.
G	P	.	L	H	C	.	.	Tattenham Corner	Surrey	S. E. & C.	Branch from Purley.
.	.	.	.	.	.	.	.	Tattersall's Malt Kilns	Yorks	N. E.	Starbeck.
G	P	F	L	H	C	1	5	Tattershall	Lincoln	G. N.	Boston and Lincoln.
.	.	.	.	.	.	.	.	Tatton & Fitzgerald's Sid (GC)	Lancs	G. C.—L. & N. W.	Manchester, Ardwick.

EXPLANATION—G *Goods Station.*   P *Passenger and Parcel Station.*   P* *Passenger, but not Parcel or Miscellaneous Traffic.*
F *Furniture Vans, Carriages, Portable Engines, and Machines on Wheels.*   L *Live Stock.*
H *Horse Boxes and Prize Cattle Vans.*   C *Carriages by Passenger Train.*

STATION ACCOMMODATION.						CRANE POWER.		STATIONS, &c.	COUNTY.	COMPANY.	POSITION.
						Tons	Cwts.				
						.	.	Taucher's Siding	Banff	High.	Mulben.
G	P	F	L	H	C	14	0	Taunton	Somerset..	G. W.	Exeter and Bridgwater.
								Sommerville Siding (Creech Siding)	Somerset..	G. W.	Creech Junction and Taunton.
G	P	F	L	H	C	10	0 }	Tavistock	Devon	{ G. W.	Plymouth and Launceston.
G	P	F	L	H	C	10	0 }			{ L. & S. W.	Exeter and Plymouth.
						.	.	Crelake Siding	Devon	G. W.	Horrabridge and Tavistock.
						.	.	Tavistock Junction	Devon	G. W.	Mutley and Plympton.
						.	.	Tawe Engineering Co.'s Siding (Mid.)	Glamorg'n	Mid.—G.W.—L. & N. W.	Llansamlet.
						.	.	Tay Bridge	Forfar	N. B.	See Dundee.
						.	.	Taylor & Hubbard's Sid. (Mid)	Leicester ..	Mid.—L. & N. W.	Leicester, East.
						.	.	Taylor & Parson's Siding	Yorks	G. N.	Bradford, Great Horton.
						.	.	Taylor & Son's Foundry	Glamorg'n	G. W.	Briton Ferry.
								Taylor & Son's Sidings—			
						.	.	Anchor Maltings	Herts	G. E.	Bishops Stortford.
						.	.	South Mill	Herts	G. E.	Bishops Stortford.
						.	.	Taylor & Son's Works	Staffs	N. S.	Ford Green.
						.	.	Taylor Bros.' Works	Derby	Mid.	Stapleford and Sandiacre.
						.	.	Taylor, Dr., Siding	Essex	G. E.	Brentwood and Warley.
						.	.	Taylor, H. A. & D., Siding...	Herts	G. E.	Sawbridgeworth.
						.	.	Taylor, J., Siding	Yorks	Mid.	Guiseley.
						.	.	Taylor Pit (L. & N. W.)	Lancs	LNW—GC(WigJn)—LY	See Wigan Coal & Iron Co. (Wigan).
						.	.	Taylor, Sanderson & Co.'s Brick Works	Yorks	N. E.	Middlesbro'.
						.	.	Taylor's Siding	Brecon	L. & N. W.	Rhymney Bridge.
						.	.	Taylor's Siding (B'head Jt.)	Cheshire..	B'head Jt.—C. L. C.......	Birkenhead, Cathcart Street.
						.	.	Taylor's Hopton Bone Works	Derby	L. & N. W.	Longcliffe.
						.	.	Taylor's Siding	Herts	L. & N. W.	Bricket Wood.
						.	.	Taylor's Sid. (Watt Str. Sid.)	Lanark ...	N. B.	Rawyards.
						.	.	Taylor's, S., Siding	Derby	Mid.	Peak Forest.
						.	.	Taymouth Siding	Forfar	D. & A. Jt. (Cal. & N. B.)	See Panmure.
G	P	F	L	H	C	1	10	Taynuilt	Argyll......	Cal.	Callander and Oban.
G	P	F	L	H	C	2	0	Tayport	Fife	N. B.	Leuchars, Old and Newport, East.
						.	.	Donaldson's Wood Yard ...	Fife	N. B.	Tayport.
G	.	.	.	.	.	6	0	Harbour	Fife	N. B.	Tayport.
G	.	.	.	.	.	.	.	Morton Siding................	Fife	N. B.	Tayport and Leuchars, Old.
						.	.	Tayport Spinning Co.'s Siding (Ritchie's Siding)	Fife	N. B.	Tayport and Leuchars, Old.
						.	.	Young's Siding	Fife	N. B.	Tayport and Leuchars, Old.
						.	.	Tay Salmon Fishery Syndicate Siding	Perth	Cal.	Perth, South.
						.	.	Tay Spinning Co.'s Siding ...	Lancs	L. & Y.	Oldham (Mumps).
						.	.	Teams Siding	Durham ...	N. E.	Redheugh.
G	P	.	L	H	C	1	10	Tebay (L. & N. W. & N. E. Jt.)	W'morlnd	{ L. & N. W.	Lancaster and Penrith.
										{ N. E.	Branch from Kirkby Stephen.
						.	.	Tebay Junction	W'morlnd	L. & N. W.— N. E.	Tebay Station and Gaisgill.
G	P	F	L	H	C	5	0	Teddington & Bushey Park	Middlesex	L. & S.W.	Twickenham and Kingston.
						.	.	Hampton Court Gas Co's Sid	Middlesex	L. & S.W.	Teddington.
						.	.	Tees Bridge Brick Works ...	Durham ...	N. E.	Stockton, South.
						.	.	Tees Bridge Depôts	Durham ...	N. E.	Stockton, South.
						.	.	Tees Bridge Iron Works	Durham ...	N. E.	Stockton, South.
						.	.	Tees Bridge Slag Crushing Works	Durham ...	N. E.	Stockton, South.
						.	.	Tees Conservancy Commissioners' Graving Dock	Yorks	N. E.	South Bank.
						.	.	Teesdale Iron Works & Wharf	Yorks	N. E.	Stockton, South.
						.	.	Tees Dock Yard & Wharf......	Yorks	N. E.	Middlesbro'.
						.	.	Tees Iron Works	Yorks	N. E.	Same as Tees Scoria Brick Works.
						.	.	Tees Iron Works Foundry & Wharf	Yorks	N. E.	South Bank.
						.	.	Tees Mouth Submarine Engineering Works	Yorks	N. E.	Tod Point.
						.	.	Tees Oil and Grease Works...	Yorks	N. E.	Same as Patent Lubricating Bag Works (Middlesbro').
						.	.	Tees Powder Magazine........	Yorks	N. E.	Tod Point.
						.	.	Tees Railway & Engineering Works .... }	Yorks	N. E.	{ See Whitehouse Siding and Depôt (South Bank).
						.	.	Tees Roller Flour Mill	Durham ...	N. E.	Stockton, South.
						.	.	Tees Salt Works	Yorks	N. E.	Haverton Hill.
						.	.	Tees Saw Mills & Timber Yd.	Yorks	N. E.	Middlesbro'.
						.	.	Tees Scoria Brick Works ...	Durham ...	N. E.	Stockton, South.

STATION ACCOMMODATION.						CRANE POWER.	STATIONS, &c.	COUNTY.	COMPANY.	POSITION.
						Tons Cwts.	Tees Scoria Brick Works (Tees Iron Works)............	Yorks	N. E.	South Bank.
.	.	.	.	.	.	. .	Tees Side Bridge & Engi- neering Works	Yorks	N. E.	{ See Whitehouse Siding and Depôt (South Bank).
.	.	.	.	.	.	. .	Tees Side Firewood Siding ...	Yorks	N. E.	Stockton, South.
.	.	.	.	.	.	. .	Tees Steam Saw Mill & Timber Yard	Yorks	N. E.	Stockton, South.
.	.	.	.	.	.	. .	Tees Tilery & Brick Yards ...	Yorks	N. E.	South Bank.
.	.	.	.	.	.	. .	Tees Union Shipping Co.......	Durham ...	N. E.	Stockton, South.
.	.	.	.	.	.	. .	Teignbridge Siding	Devon ...	G. W.	Newton Abbot.
G	P	.	.	.	.	. .	Teigngrace	Devon ...	G. W. ....:	Newton Abbot and Bovey.
G	P	F	.	H	C	1 10	Teignmouth........................	Devon ...	G. W.	Exeter and Totnes.
.	.	.	.	.	.	. .	Teilo Tin Plate Co.'s Siding..	Glamorg'n	G. W. & L. & N. W. Jt.	Pontardulais.
.	.	.	.	.	.	. .	Telegraph Manufacturing Co.'s Siding	Cheshire...	C. L. C. (G C, G N, & Mid.)	Helsby.
.	.	.	.	.	.	. .	Tempest & Son's Siding	Derby...	Mid.	Same as Peckwash Mill Siding (Little Eaton).
.	.	.	.	.	.	. .	Temple (Met. Dist.)	Middlesex	Met. Dist.—L. & N. W...	See London.
.	.	.	.	.	.	. .	Temple Brick Works (N. B.)	Lanark ...	N. B.—Cal.	Glasgow, Great Western Road.
.	.	.	.	.	.	. .	Temple Gas Works	Lanark ...	Cal.	Glasgow, Dawsholm.
.	.	.	.	.	.	. .	Temple Gas Works (N. B.) ...	Lanark ...	N. B.—Cal.	Glasgow, Great Western Road.
.	.	.	.	.	.	. .	Temple Iron Works (N. B.)..	Lanark ...	N. B.—Cal.	Glasgow, Great Western Road.
.	.	.	.	.	.	. .	Temple Saw Mills (Robinson, Dunn & Co.'s Wood Yard) (N. B.)	Lanark ...	N. B.—Cal.	Glasgow, Great Western Road.
.	.	.	.	.	.	. .	Temple Siding (N. B.)	Lanark ...	N. B.—Cal.	Glasgow, Great Western Road.
							TEMPLECOMBE—			
G	.	F	L	.	.	. .	Junction	Somerset..	L. & S.W.—S. & D. Jt...	Yeovil and Shepton Mallet.
G	P	F	L	H	C	2 0	Station	Somerset..	S.&D.Jt.(L.&S.W.&Mid)	Branch—Wincanton & Henstridge.
.	P	.	.	H	C	. .	Station (L. & S. W.)........	Somerset..	{ L. & S. W. / S.&D.Jt.(L&SW&Mid.)	Salisbury and Yeovil. / Over L. & S.W. Line.
G	P	F	L	H	C	. .	Templehill Depôt	Ayr	G. & S.W.	See Troon.
.	P	.	.	.	.	. .	Temple Hirst (N. E.)	Yorks	{ N. E. / G. N.	Selby and Doncaster. / Over N. E. from Shaftholme Junc.
.	.	.	.	.	.	. .	Henwick Hall Siding	Yorks	N. E.	Temple Hirst and Selby.
.	.	.	.	.	.	. .	Temple Meads	Glo'ster ...	G. W.	See Bristol.
.	.	.	.	.	.	. .	Temple Mills Sidings (G. E.)	Middlesex	GE—L&NW—Mid—NL	London, Stratford.
G	P	F	L	H	C	. .	Templemore......................	Tipperary	G. S. & W.	Maryborough and Thurles.
G	P	.	L	.	.	. .	Templepatrick	Antrim ...	N. C. Com. (Mid.)	Antrim and Greenisland.
.	.	.	.	.	.	. .	Templeport	Cavan ...	C. & L.	See Bawnboy Road and Templeport.
G	P	.	L	H	.	. .	Temple Sowerby	W'morlnd	N. E.	Appleby and Penrith.
.	.	.	.	.	.	. .	Templetown Coke, Ballast, Washing, & Screening Wks.	Durham ...	N. E.	Blackhill.
G	P	F	L	H	C	1 10	Tempsford	Beds	G. N.	Sandy and Huntingdon.
G	P	F	L	H	C	6 0	Tenbury	Salop ...	Tenbury Jt (GW&LNW)	Branch from Woofferton.
.	.	.	.	.	.	. .	Tenbury Junction	Salop ...	G. W.—Tenbury Jt.	Bewdley and Woofferton.
G	P	F	L	H	C	1 10	Tenby	Pembroke	G. W.	Whitland and Pembroke Dock.
.	.	.	.	.	.	. .	Black Rock Siding...........	Pembroke	G. W.	Tenby and Penally.
.	.	.	.	.	.	. .	Ten Coal Exchange Co.'s Brick Works Siding	Cheshire...	G. W.	Saltney.
.	.	.	.	.	.	. .	Tendring Hundred Water Works	Essex	G. E.	Mistley.
.	.	.	.	.	.	. .	Tennant & Co.'s Siding........	Forfar...	D. & A. Jt. (Cal. & N. B.)	See Panmure.
.	.	.	.	.	.	. .	Tennant's Foundry	Lanark ...	Cal.—N. B.	Same as Whifflet Foundry (Coatbridge).
.	.	.	.	.	.	. .	Tennant's Salt Works	Durham ...	N. E.	Haverton Hill.
.	.	.	.	.	.	. .	Tennant's Siding	Lanark ...	Cal.	See United Alkali Co. (Glasgow).
.	.	.	.	.	.	. .	Tennochside Cols., Nos. 1, 2, & 3	Lanark ...	Cal.	Baillieston.
.	.	.	.	.	.	. .	Tennochside Junction	Lanark ...	Cal.	Baillieston.
G	P	F	L	H	C	. .	Tenterden Town................	Kent	K. & E. S.	Terminus.
.	.	.	.	.	.	. .	Tenters Street Depôts	Durham ...	N. E.	Bishop Auckland.
G	P	.	L	H†C†	.	. .	Tern Hill	Salop ...	G. W.	Market Drayton and Hodnet.
G	P	F	L	H	C	5 0	Terrington	Norfolk ...	Mid. & G. N. Jt.	Sutton Bridge and South Lynn.
.	.	.	.	.	.	. .	Teston Siding	Kent	S. E. & C.	Wateringbury.
G	P	F	L	H	C	6 0	Tetbury	Wilts	G. W.	Branch from Kemble Junction.
G	.	.	L	.	.	2 0	Tetbury Road	Glo'ster ...	G. W.	Swindon and Gloucester.
.	.	.	.	.	.	. .	Tetlow & Son's Siding (G. C.)	Lancs	G. C.—L. & N. W.—Mid.	Manchester, Ardwick.
G	.	.	.	.	.	. .	Teversall	Notts	{ G. N. / Mid.	Branch from Skegby. / Tibshelf and Pleasley.
G	P	.	L	H	.	. .				
							Stanton Iron Co.—			
.	.	.	.	.	.	. .	Silverhill Colliery	Notts	Mid.	Teversall.
.	.	.	.	.	.	. .	Silverhill Colliery (G. N.)	Notts	G. N.—L. D. & E. C. ...	Branch from Teversall.

EXPLANATION—G Goods Station.   P Passenger and Parcel Station.   P* Passenger, but not Parcel or Miscellaneous Traffic.
F Furniture Vans, Carriages, Portable Engines, and Machines on Wheels.   L Live Stock.
H Horse Boxes and Prize Cattle Vans.   H† C† By special arrangement only.   C Carriages by Passenger Train.

STATION ACCOMMODATION.						CRANE POWER.		STATIONS, &c.	COUNTY.	COMPANY.	POSITION.
						Tons	Cwts.				
								Teversall—*continued*.			
								Stanton Iron Co.—*continued*.			
.	.	.	.	.	.	.	.	Teversall Colliery (Butcherwood Colliery)	Notts	Mid.	Teversall.
.	.	.	.	.	.	.	.	Teversall Colliery (Butcherwood Colliery)(GN)	Notts	G. N.—G.C.—L.D.&E.C.	Teversall and Skegby.
.	.	.	.	.	.	.	.	Teversham Siding	Cambs......	G. E.	Fulbourne.
G	P	F	L	H	C	5	0	Tewkesbury............	Glo'ster ...	Mid.	Ashchurch and Malvern.
.	.	.	.	.	.	.	.	Downing's, G. & W. E., Sid.	Glo'ster ...	Mid.	Tewkesbury.
.	.	.	.	.	.	.	.	Healing & Son's Siding......	Glo'ster ...	Mid.	Tewkesbury.
.	.	.	.	.	.	.	.	Tewkesbury Quay	Glo'ster ...	Mid.	Tewkesbury.
.	.	.	.	.	.	.	.	Tewkesbury Rd. Bge. Cl. Whf.	Glo'ster ...	Mid.	Cheltenham.
G	P	F	L	H	C	1	15	Teynham	Kent	S. E. & C.	Sittingbourne and Faversham.
.	.	.	.	.	.	.	.	Thackeray's Siding	Yorks	Mid.	Leeds, Newlay and Horsforth.
.	.	.	.	.	.	.	.	Thackley	Yorks	G. N.	See Bradford.
G	P	F	L	H	C	6	0	Thame	Oxon	G. W.	Oxford and Princes Risboro'.
.	.	.	.	.	.	.	.	Penn Farm Siding............	Oxon	G. W.	Thame and Bledlow.
.	P	.	.	.	.	.	.	Thames Ditton	Surrey ...	L. & S.W.	Surbiton and Hampton Court.
G	.	.	L	H	.	4	0	Thames Haven	Essex	L. T. & S.	Branch from Thames Haven Junc.
.	.	.	.	.	.	.	.	Corringham Light Railway Siding (Kynoch & Co.)...	Essex	L. T. & S.	Branch from Thames Haven Junc.
.	.	.	.	.	.	.	.	London and Thames Haven Petroleum Oil Wharves Co.'s Siding............	Essex	L. T. & S.	Branch from Thames Haven Junc.
.	.	.	.	.	.	.	.	Thames Haven Junction	Essex	L. T. & S.	Low Street and Stanford-le-hope.
.	.	.	.	.	.	.	.	Thames Iron Works Shipbuilding and Engineering Co.'s Siding (G. E.)	Essex	G E—G N—L N W—Mid.	London, Canning Town.
.	.	.	.	.	.	.	.	Thames Paper Works	Essex	L. T. & S.	Purfleet.
.	.	.	.	.	.	.	.	Thames Wharf	Essex	Mid.	See London.
.	.	.	.	.	.	.	.	Thames Wharf, Coal	Essex	G. E.	See London.
.	.	.	.	.	.	.	.	Thames Wharf Junction	Essex	G. E.—Mid.	London, Canning Town & Victoria Docks.
G	P	.	L	H	.	2	0	Thankerton	Lanark ...	Cal.	Lockerbie and Carstairs.
.	.	.	.	.	.	.	.	Thankerton Collieries	Lanark ...	Cal.	Mossend.
.	.	.	.	.	.	.	.	Tharsis Copper Co.'s Siding	Glamorg'n	G W—L N W—Rhy—TV	Cardiff.
								Tharsis Sulphur & Copper Co.			
.	.	.	.	.	.	.	.	Siding	Lanark ...	Cal.	Glasgow, Buchanan Street.
.	.	.	.	.	.	.	.	Siding	Durham ...	N. E.	Hebburn.
G	P	.	L	.	.	2	0	Thatcham............	Berks	G. W.	Reading and Newbury.
.	P	.	.	.	.	.	.	Thatto Heath	Lancs	L. & N. W.	Liverpool and St. Helens.
.	.	.	.	.	.	.	.	Thaw & Campbell's Sid. (N.B.)	Lanark ...	N. B.—G. & S. W.	Glasgow, Haghill.
G	P	F	L	H	C	2	0	Theale	Berks	G. W.	Reading and Newbury.
.	.	.	.	.	.	.	.	Calcot Mill Siding............	Berks	G. W.	Reading and Theale.
.	.	.	.	.	.	.	.	Tyle Mill Siding	Berks	G. W.	Theale and Aldermaston.
G	P	F	L	H	C	.	.	Theddingworth	Leicester.	L. & N. W.	Market Harboro' and Rugby.
G	P	F	L	H	C	.	.	Theddlethorpe	Lincoln ...	G. N.	Louth and Mablethorpe.
.	.	.	.	.	.	.	.	The Dyke............	Sussex ...	L. B. & S. C.	See Dyke, The.
G	P	.	.	.	.	1	10	Thelwall	Cheshire...	L. & N. W.	Stockport and Warrington.
.	.	.	.	.	.	.	.	Parry's Coal Yard	Lancs	L. & N. W.	Thelwall and Latchford.
.	.	.	.	.	.	.	.	The Mound	Sutherl'nd	High.	See Mound, The.
.	P	.	.	.	.	.	.	The Oaks	Lancs	L. & Y.	Bolton and Blackburn.
G	P	.	.	.	.	.	.	Theobalds' Grove	Herts	G. E.	Edmonton and Cheshunt.
G	P	F	L	H	C	6	0	Thetford	Norfolk ...	G. E.	Norwich and Ely.
.	.	.	.	.	.	.	.	Fison & Son's Two Mile Bottom Siding	Norfolk ...	G. E.	Thetford and Brandon.
G	P	F	L	H	C	1	0	Thetford Bridge............	Norfolk ...	G. E.	Bury and Thetford.
G	P	F	.	H	C	.	.	Theydon Bois............	Essex	G. E.	Loughton and Ongar.
.	.	.	.	.	.	.	.	Thinford Junction............	Durham ...	N. E.	Shincliffe and Ferryhill.
.	.	.	.	.	.	.	.	Thingley Junction............	Wilts	G. W.	Chippenham and Melksham.
.	.	.	.	.	.	.	.	Thirdpart Siding	Ayr	G. & S.W.	Same as Gargieston Sid. (Gatehead).
G	P	F	L	H	C	5	0	Thirsk Junction Station	Yorks	N. E.	York and Northallerton.
.	.	.	.	.	.	.	.	Jackson's Siding	Yorks	N. E.	Thirsk Junction Station.
.	.	.	.	.	.	.	.	Manor House Siding........	Yorks	N. E.	Thirsk Junc. Sta. and Otterington.
G	.	.	.	.	.	5	0	Thirsk Town	Yorks	N. E.	Branch near Thirsk Junction Sta.
.	.	.	.	.	.	.	.	Thirsk, J., & Sons' Siding ...	Yorks	N. E.	Beverley.
.	.	.	.	.	.	.	.	Thirsk, J., & Sons' Siding ...	Yorks	N. E.	Same as Pocklington Flour Mills (Pocklington).
.	.	.	.	.	.	.	.	Thomas & Clements' Foundry (G. W.)............	Carmarth'	G. W.—L. & N. W.	Llanelly.
								Thomas & Co.—			
.	.	.	.	.	.	.	.	Lydney Tin Works	Glo'ster ...	S. & Wye Jt. (G.W. & Mid)	Lydney.

EXPLANATION—G *Goods Station.*   P *Passenger and Parcel Station.*   P* *Passenger, but not Parcel or Miscellaneous Traffic.*
F *Furniture Vans, Carriages, Portable Engines, and Machines on Wheels.*   L *Live Stock.*
H *Horse Boxes and Prize Cattle Vans.*   C *Carriages by Passenger Train.*

STATION ACCOMMODATION.						CRANE POWER.		STATIONS, &c.	COUNTY.	COMPANY.	POSITION.
						Tons	Cwts.	Thomas & Co.—*continued.*			
.	.	.	.	.	.	.	.	Stone Saw Mills (Cannop Stone Works)	Glo'ster ...	S. & Wye Jt.(G.W. & Mid)	Speech House Road.
.	.	.	.	.	.	.	.	Waterloo Siding..............	Glo'ster ...	S. & Wye Jt.(G.W. & Mid)	Lydbrook, Upper.
.	.	.	.	.	.	.	.	Thomas & Co.'s Avenue or Malthouse Siding	Warwick..	L. & N. W.	Leamington.
.	.	.	.	.	.	.	.	Thomas & Co.'s Iron Yard ...	Yorks	N. E.	Middlesbro'.
.	.	.	.	.	.	.	.	Thomas & Co.'s Siding	Berks	G. W.	Abingdon.
.	.	.	.	.	.	.	.	Thomas & Evans & John Dyer	Carmarth'	G. W.	Llanelly.
.	.	.	.	.	.	.	.	Thomas & Green's Siding......	Bucks	G. W.	Bourne End.
.	.	.	.	.	.	.	.	Thomas & Son's Lime Works	Glamorg'n	T. V.	Same as Llandough Lime Works (Penarth Dock).
.	.	.	.	.	.	.	.	Thomas' Brick Works	Staffs	L. & N. W.	Bloxwich.
.	.	.	.	.	.	.	.	Thomas Bros.' Timber Yard (G. W.)	Carmarth'	G. W.—L. & N. W.	Llandilo.
.	.	.	.	.	.	.	.	Thomas' Gilwern Tin Plate Works (Mid.)	Glamorg'n	Mid.—G.W.—L. & N. W.	Swansea.
.	.	.	.	.	.	.	.	Thomas' Hatherton Blast Furnaces	Staffs	L. & N. W.	Bloxwich.
.	.	.	.	.	.	.	.	Thomas, J. J., & Son (Mid.)	Glamorg'n	Mid.—G.W.—L. & N. W.	Same as Pantycelyn Colliery (Bryn-amman).
								Thomas, R., & Co.—			
.	.	.	.	.	.	.	.	Burry Tin Works (G. W.)	Carmarth'	G. W.—L. & N. W.	Llanelly.
.	.	.	.	.	.	.	.	South Wales Tin Plate Works (G. W.)	Carmarth'	G. W.—L. & N. W.	Llanelly.
.	.	.	.	.	.	.	.	Thomas' Siding	Glamorg'n	G W—L N W—Rhy—T V	Cardiff.
.	.	.	.	.	.	.	.	Thomas' Siding	Radnor ...	Cam.	Builth Road.
.	.	.	.	.	.	.	.	Thomas' Siding	Salop	Cam.	Oswestry.
.	.	.	.	.	.	.	.	Thomas, T. W., & Co.'s Sid.	Glamorg'n	G W—LNW—Mid—RSB	Swansea.
.	.	.	.	.	.	.	.	Thomasson & Co.'s Sid (G W)	Worcester	G. W.—Mid.	Worcester.
G	P	F	L	H	C	.	.	Thomastown	Kilkenny..	G. S. & W.	Waterford and Kilkenny.
.	.	.	.	.	.	.	.	Thompson & Son's Ship Yard and Depôt	Durham ...	N. E.	Southwick.
.	.	.	.	.	.	.	.	Thompson & Son's Sid. (Mid.)	Derby	Mid.—L. & N. W.	Same as Gresley Brewery Co.'s Sid.
.	.	.	.	.	.	.	.	Thompson & Southwick's Foundry	Warwick..	Mid.	Kettlebrook.
.	.	.	.	.	.	.	.	Thompson, Jos., & Co.'s Timber Yard	Durham ...	N. E.	Sunderland, South Dock.
.	.	.	.	.	.	.	.	Thompson, S., & Son's Siding (Mid.)	N'hamptn	Mid.—L. & N. W.	Peterboro'.
								Thompson's—			
.	.	.	.	.	.	.	.	Brick Works or Warrington Road Siding (C. L. C.)	Cheshire...	C. L. C.—L. & N. W.	Northwich.
.	.	.	.	.	.	.	.	Marston Siding (C. L. C.)...	Cheshire...	C. L. C.—L. & N. W. ...	Northwich.
.	.	?	.	.	.	.	.	Thompson's (Marcelus) Siding	W'morlnd	L. & N. W.	} See Kendal Bonded Stores Co.
.	.	.	.	.	.	.	.	Thompson's (Miles) Siding ...	W'morlnd	L. & N. W.	} (Kendal).
.	.	.	.	.	.	.	.	Thompson's Siding..............	Lancs	L. & Y.	Whalley.
.	.	.	.	.	.	.	.	Thomson & Balfour's Wood Yard	L'lithgow	N. B.	Bo'ness.
.	.	.	.	.	.	.	.	Thoms' Siding	Lancs	L. & N. W.	Lancaster.
G	P	.	.	.	.	3	0	Thongs Bridge	Yorks	L. & Y.	Huddersfield and Holmfirth.
.	.	.	.	.	.	.	.	Thoresby, North	Lincoln ...	G. N.	See North Thoresby.
G	P	.	.	.	.	.	.	Thorington	Essex	G. E.	Colchester and Clacton-on-Sea.
.	.	.	.	.	.	.	.	Thorley's Siding..............	Surrey ...	L. & S.W.	Wandsworth Town.
.	.	.	.	.	.	.	.	Thorlieshope Lime Works ...	Roxburgh	N. B.	Kielder.
.	P	.	.	H	C	.	.	Thornaby	Yorks	N. E.	Eaglescliffe and Middlesbro'.
.	.	.	.	.	.	.	.	Thornaby Iron Works & Wharf	Yorks	N. E.	Stockton, South.
.	.	.	.	.	.	.	.	Thornaby Junction	Yorks	N. E.	Stockton, South.
.	.	.	.	.	.	.	.	Thornaby Pottery	Yorks	N. E.	Stockton, South.
.	.	.	.	.	.	.	.	Thornbridge Siding (Cal.) ...	Stirling ...	Cal.—N. B.	Same as Laurieston Iron Works (Grangemouth).
.	.	.	.	.	.	.	.	Thornburn & Co.'s Stone Sid.	Edinboro'	Cal.	Edinburgh, Lothian Road.
G	P	F	L	H	C	1	10	Thornbury	Glo'ster ...	Mid.	Branch from Yate.
.	.	.	.	.	.	.	.	Thorncliffe	Yorks	G. C.	See Chapeltown and Thorncliffe.
.	.	.	.	.	.	.	.	Thorncliffe Colliery	Yorks	G. C.	See Newton, Chambers & Co. (Chapeltown & Thorncliffe).
.	.	.	.	.	.	.	.	Thorncliffe Collieries & Coke Ovens }	Yorks	Mid.	{ See Newton, Chambers & Co. (Chapeltown).
.	.	.	.	.	.	.	.	Thorncliffe Furnaces............	Yorks	Mid.	See Newton, Chambers & Co. (Chapeltown).
.	.	.	.	'	.	.	.	Thorncliffe Iron Works	Yorks	Mid.	See Newton, Chambers & Co. (Chapeltown).

EXPLANATION—G *Goods Station.*   P *Passenger and Parcel Station.*   P* *Passenger, but not Parcel or Miscellaneous Traffic.*
F *Furniture Vans, Carriages, Portable Engines, and Machines on Wheels.*   L *Live Stock.*
H *Horse Boxes and Prize Cattle Vans.*   C *Carriages by Passenger Train.*

						Crane Power		STATIONS, &c.	COUNTY.	COMPANY.	POSITION.
						Tons	Cwts.				
						.	.	Thorncliffe Siding	Yorks	G. C.	See Newton, Chambers & Co. (Chapeltown & Thorncliffe).
								THORNE—			
G	P	F	L	H	C	5	0	(Station)	Yorks	G. C.	Doncaster and Barnetby.
G	P	F	L	H	C	3	0 }	(Station, N. E.)	Yorks	{ N. E.	Doncaster and Goole.
	P			H	C	.	. }			{ G. C.	Over N. E. from Thorne Junction.
.	.	.	.	.	.	.	.	Junction	Yorks	G. C.—N. E.	Doncaster and Hull.
.	.	.	.	.	.	.	.	Mauds Bridge Siding	Yorks	G. C.	Thorne.
.	.	.	.	.	.	.	.	Moor End Siding	Yorks	N. E.	Thorne.
.	.	.	.	.	.	.	.	Newman & Owston's Siding	Yorks	N. E.	Goole and Thorne.
G	P	F	L	H	C	2	0	Thorner	Yorks	N. E.	Leeds and Wetherby.
.	.	.	.	.	.	.	.	Thornewell & Warham's Siding (Mid.)	Staffs	Mid—L&NW—GN—NS	Burton-on-Trent.
G	P	F	L	H	C	1	10	Thorney	Cambs......	Mid. & G. N. Jt.	Wisbech and Peterboro'.
.	.	.	.	.	.	.	.	Thorney & Wigsley Siding ...	Notts	L. D. & E. C.	Doddington & Harby.
.	.	.	.	.	.	.	.	Thorneybank Siding	Edinboro'	N. B.	Smeaton.
.	P*	.	.	.	.	.	.	Thorneyburn	Northumb	N. B.	Riccarton and Reedsmouth.
.	.	.	.	.	.	.	.	Thorneycroft's Steam Carriage & Wagon Co.'s Siding	Hants	L. & S.W.	Basingstoke.
.	.	.	.	.	.	.	.	Thorneywood	Notts	G. N.	See Nottingham.
G	P	.	.	.	.	.	.	Thornfalcon	Somerset..	G. W.	Taunton and Hatch.
G	P	F	L	H	C	3	0	Thornhill	Dumfries.	G. & S. W.	Dumfries and Sanquhar.
.	.	.	.	.	.	.	.	Gatelawbridge Brick Works and Quarry	Dumfries.	G. & S.W.	Thornhill.
.	.	.	.	.	.	.	.	Thornhill	Yorks	L. & N. W.	See Ravensthorpe and Thornhill.
G	P	F	L	H	.	5	0	Thornhill (L. & Y.)	Yorks	{ L. & Y.	Wakefield and Mirfield.
										{ G. N.	Over L. & Y. from Wakefield.
.	.	.	.	.	.	.	.	Ingham's Siding...............	Yorks	L. & Y.	Thornhill.
.	.	.	.	.	.	.	.	Kilner's Siding	Yorks	L. & Y.	Thornhill.
.	.	.	.	.	.	.	.	Thornhill Colliery (L. & Y.)	Yorks	L. & Y.—G.N.	Wakefield and Mirfield.
.	.	.	.	.	.	.	.	Thornhill Iron Co.'s Sids. } (L. & Y.) .... }	Yorks	L. & Y.—G. N.	Near Thornhill.
G	P	.	L	H	.	.	.	Thornielee	Selkirk ...	N. B.	Peebles and Galashiels.
.	.	.	.	.	.	.	.	Thornlee Colliery	Lanark ...	Cal.	Wishaw, Central.
.	P	.	.	.	.	.	.	Thornley	Durham ...	N. E.	Hartlepool and Sunderland.
G	.	.	.	.	.	2	0	Thornley Colliery Station ...	Durham ...	N. E.	Branch from Thornley.
.	.	.	.	.	.	.	.	Crows House Brick Works	Durham ...	N. E.	Thornley Colliery Station.
.	.	.	.	.	.	.	.	Ludworth Colliery	Durham ...	N. E.	Thornley Colliery Station.
.	.	.	.	.	.	.	.	Thornley Brick Works......	Durham ...	N. E.	Thornley Colliery Station.
.	.	.	.	.	.	.	.	Thornley Colliery	Durham ...	N. E.	Thornley Colliery Station.
.	.	.	.	.	.	.	.	Wheatley Hill Brick Works	Durham ...	N. E.	Thornley Colliery Station.
.	.	.	.	.	.	.	.	Wheatley Hill Colliery......	Durham ...	N. E.	Thornley Colliery Station.
.	.	.	.	.	.	.	.	Thornley's Coal Wharf........	Leicester..	Mid.	Ashby.
.	P	.	.	.	.	.	.	Thornliebank	Renfrew...	Cal.	Pollokshaws and Busby.
G	.	.	.	.	.	.	.	Thornliebank	Renfrew...	G B & K Jt (Cal & G & S W)	Kennishead and Spiersbridge.
.	.	.	.	.	.	.	.	Thornliebank Printing Co.'s Siding	Renfrew...	G B & K Jt (Cal & G & S W)	Thornliebank.
.	.	.	.	.	.	.	.	Thornly Park Junction	Renfrew...	G. & S.W.	Potterhill and Barrhead.
								THORNTON—			
G	P	.	L	.	.	1	0	(Station)	Fife	N. B.	Kirkcaldy and Markinch.
.	.	.	.	.	.	.	.	Balgonie Colliery	Fife	N. B	Branch—Thornton and Markinch.
.	.	.	.	.	.	.	.	Central Junction	Fife	N. B.	Dysart and Markinch.
.	.	.	.	.	.	.	.	East Junction.................	Fife	N. B.	Thornton and West Wemyss.
.	.	.	.	.	.	.	.	Lochty Maltings.............	Fife	N. B.	Branch—Thornton and Markinch.
.	.	.	.	.	.	.	.	North Junction	Fife	N. B.	Dysart and Markinch.
.	.	.	.	.	.	.	.	Randolph Colliery	Fife	N. B.	Dysart and Thornton.
.	.	.	.	.	.	.	.	Redford Siding	Fife	N. B.	Cardenden and Thornton.
.	.	.	.	.	.	.	.	South Junction	Fife	N. B.	Thornton and Dysart.
G	.	.	.	.	.	.	.	Thornton Bridge Siding...	Fife	N. B.	Thornton and Cardenden.
.	.	.	.	.	.	.	.	Thornton Col. (Dogton Col.)	Fife	N. B.	Cardenden and Thornton.
.	.	.	.	.	.	.	.	Thornton Gas Works........	Fife	N. B.	Thornton and Cardenden.
.	.	.	.	.	.	.	.	Thornton Wagon Works (Pickering & Co.)	Fife	N. B.	Thornton and Cardenden.
.	.	.	.	.	.	.	.	Weighs Junction.............	Fife	N. B.	Thornton and Cardenden.
.	.	.	.	.	.	.	.	West Junction	Fife	N. B.	Thornton and Cardenden.
G	P	F	L	H	C	10	0	Thornton	Yorks	G. N.	Bradford and Keighley.
.	.	.	.	.	.	.	.	Morton's Siding	Yorks	G. N.	Thornton and Queensbury.
G	P	.	.	.	.	.	.	Thornton Abbey	Lincoln ...	G. C.	Barnetby and New Holland.
.	.	.	.	.	.	.	.	Thornton & Crebbin'sSid.(GN)	Yorks	G. N.—G. C.	Bradford, Adolphus Street.
G	P	.	L	H	.	1	10	Thornton Dale	Yorks	N. E.	Pickering and Seamer.
G	P	.	.	.	.	.	.	Thorntonhall	Lanark ...	Cal.	Busby and East Kilbride.
.	.	.	.	.	.	.	.	Bogton Quarry	Lanark ...	Cal.	Thorntonhall and Hairmyres.

EXPLANATION—G Goods Station.   P Passenger and Parcel Station.   P* Passenger, but not Parcel or Miscellaneous Traffic.
F Furniture Vans, Carriages, Portable Engines, and Machines on Wheels.   L Live Stock.
H Horse Boxes and Prize Cattle Vans.   C Carriages by Passenger Train.

STATION ACCOMMODATION.						CRANE POWER.	STATIONS, &c.	COUNTY.	COMPANY.	POSITION.
G	P	.	.	L	H	Tons Cwts. 5 0	Thornton Heath	Surrey	L. B. & S. C.	Streatham Common and Croydon.
G	P	.	.	L	H	.}	Thornton-in-Craven (Mid.)	Yorks	{ Mid.	Skipton and Colne.
.	P	.	.	.	.	}			{ L. & Y.	Over Mid. from Colne Junction.
.	.	.	.	.	.		Spencer's, P. W. Quarry	Yorks	Mid.	Near Thornton.
.	.	.	.	.	.		Thornton's Siding	Surrey	S. E. & C.	Red Hill.
G	P	F	L	H	C	1 0	Thorp Arch (Boston Spa)	Yorks	N. E.	Church Fenton and Harrogate.
.	.	.	.	.	.		Thorpe	Norfolk	G. E.	See Norwich.
G	P	F	L	H	C	. .	Thorpe	N'hamptn	L. & N. W.	Peterboro' and Wellingboro'.
G	P	.	L	.	.	. .	Thorpe Cloud	Derby	L. & N. W.	Ashbourne and Buxton.
G	P	P	.	.	.		Thorpe Culvert	Lincoln	G. N.	Firsby and Skegness.
G	P	F	L	H	C	. .	Thorpe Hall Siding	Yorks	N. E.	Howden.
G	P	F	L	H	C	. .	Thorpe-le-Soken	Essex	G. E.	Colchester and Clacton-on-Sea.
.	.	.	.	.	.		Mackenzie, Donald, & Son's Siding	Essex	G. E.	Thorpe-le-Soken.
G	P	F	L	H	C	. .	Thorpe-on-the-Hill	Lincoln	Mid.	Newark and Lincoln.
.	.	.	.	.	.		Thorpe Quarry	Yorks	E. & W. Y. Union	Same as Pawson Bros. (Robin Hood).
.	.	.	.	.	.		Thorpe Road Siding	Yorks	N. E.	Same as Leeds Road Siding (Wistow).
.	.	.	.	.	.		Thorpe Siding	Yorks	E. & W. Y. Union	Robin Hood.
.	.	.	.	.	.		Armitage Bros.'	Yorks	E. & W. Y. Union	Thorpe Siding
.	.	.	.	.	.		Armitage, G., & Son's	Yorks	E. & W. Y. Union	Thorpe Siding.
.	.	.	.	.	.		Thorpe's, W. B., Siding	Rutland	Mid.	Ketton.
G	P	F	L	H	C	. .	Thorpe Thewles	Durham	N. E.	Stockton and Wellfield Junction.
G	.	.	.	.	.		Thorp Gates	Yorks	N. E.	Selby and Leeds.
G	P	F	L	.	C	5 0	Thorverton	Devon	G. W.	Exeter and Tiverton.
G	P	F	L	H	C	5 0}	Thrapston	N'hamptn	{ L. & N. W.	Peterboro' and Wellingboro'.
G	P	F	L	H	C	5 0}			{ Mid.	Huntingdon and Kettering.
.	.	.	.	.	.		Fisher's Ironstone Sidings	N'hamptn	Mid.	Near Thrapston.
.	.	.	.	.	.		Islip Iron Co.'s Siding	N'hamptn	L. & N. W.	Thrapston and Ringstead.
G	P	F	L	H	C	2 0	Three Bridges	Sussex	L. B. & S. C.	Hayward's Heath and Horley.
.	.	.	.	.	.		Caffin & Co.'s Siding	Sussex	L. B. & S. C.	Three Bridges.
G	P	F	L	H	C	4 0	Three Cocks (Cam.)	Brecon	{ Cam.	Llanidloes and Brecon.
.	.	.	.	.	.				{ Mid.	Over Cam. from Three Cocks Junc.
.	.	.	.	.	.		Pontithel Chemical Co.'s Works (Cam.)	Brecon	Cam.—Mid.	Three Cocks and Talgarth.
.	.	.	.	.	.		Three Cocks Junction	Brecon	Cam.—Mid.	Three Cocks and Hay.
G	P	.	.	.	.	3 0	Three Counties	Beds	G. N.	Hitchin and Sandy.
.	.	.	.	.	.		Arlesey Brick Co.'s Siding	Beds	G. N.	Three Counties.
.	.	.	.	.	.		Associated Portland Cement Manufacturers' Siding	Beds	G. N.	Three Counties.
.	.	.	.	.	.		Three Counties Asylum Sid.	Beds	G. N.	Three Counties.
.	.	.	.	.	.		Three Horse Shoes Siding	Cambs	G. E.	See Whittlesea.
.	.	.	.	.	.		Three Signal Bridge Junction	Yorks	G. N.—L & Y—L&NW—N. E.	Leeds.
.	.	.	.	.	.		Threlfall's Siding	Lincoln	G. N.	Horncastle.
.	.	.	.	.	.		Threlfall's Siding (G. C.)	Notts	G. C.—G. N.—Mid.	Worksop.
G	P	.	L	H	.	1 10	Threlkeld	Cumb'land	C.K.&P.(L.&N.W.&N.E. Working Companies)	Penrith and Keswick.
.	.	.	.	.	.		Threshfield	Yorks	Mid.	See Grassington and Threshfield.
.	.	.	.	.	.		Thrislington Col. & Coke Wks.	Durham	N. E.	West Cornforth.
.	.	.	.	.	.		Thrislington New Coke & Bye Product Works	Durham	N. E.	West Cornforth.
.	.	.	.	.	.		Throckley Col. & Brick Wks.	Northumb	N. E.	Newburn.
.	P*	.	.	.	.		Throsk	Stirling	Cal.	Larbert and Alloa.
.	.	.	.	.	.		Throsk Siding	Stirling	Cal.	Alloa.
G	P	F	L	H	C	. .	Throstle Nest Junction	Lancs	C. L. C. (G C, G N, & Mid.)	Manchester, Central and Didsbury.
.	.	.	.	.	.		Thrumster	Caithness	High. (W. & L.)	Wick and Lybster.
.	.	.	.	.	.		Thrushbush Quarry	Lanark	N. B.	Airdrie, North.
.	.	.	.	.	.		Thrustan's Siding (L. & N. W.)	Staffs	L. & N. W.—G. W—Mid.	Walsall.
.	.	.	.	.	.		Thrybergh Colliery	Yorks	G. C.	Kilnhurst.
.	.	.	.	.	.		Thrybergh Hall Colliery	Yorks	Mid.	See Charlesworth, J. & J. (Kilnhurst).
.	.	.	.	.	.		Thubron's Timber Yard and Creosote Works	Durham	N. E.	Redheugh.
G	P	F	L	H	C	. .	Thurgarton	Notts	Mid.	Nottingham and Newark.
.	.	.	.	.	.		Thurgoland Siding	Yorks	G. C.	Wortley.
G	P	.	L	.	.	1 5	Thurlby	Lincoln	G. N.	Bourne and Essendine.
G	P	F	L	H	C	. .	Thurles	Tipperary	G. S. & W.	Limerick Junction and Maryboro'.
.	.	.	.	.	.		Thurles Junction	Tipperary	G. S. & W.	Thurles and Goold's Cross.
.	.	.	.	.	.		Thurmaston Brick & Tile Co.'s Siding	Leicester	Mid.	Syston.
G	P	F	L	H	C	. .	Thurnby & Scraptoft	Leicester	G. N.	Leicester Branch.
.	.	.	.	.	.		Thurnscoe	Yorks	H. & B.	See Hickleton and Thurnscoe.
G	P	F	L	H	C	. .	Thursford	Norfolk	Mid. & G. N. Jt.	Melton Constable and Fakenham.

EXPLANATION— G *Goods Station.*   P *Passenger and Parcel Station.*   P* *Passenger, but not Parcel or Miscellaneous Traffic.*
F *Furniture Vans, Carriages, Portable Engines, and Machines on Wheels.*   L *Live Stock.*
H *Horse Boxes and Prize Cattle Vans.*   C *Carriages by Passenger Train.*

STATION ACCOMMODATION.						CRANE POWER.		STATIONS, &c.	COUNTY.	COMPANY.	POSITION.
						Tons	Cwts				
G	P	F	L	H	C	3	0	Thurso	Caithness..	High.	Branch from Georgemas.
G	P	F	L	H	C	.	.	Thurstaston	Cheshire...	B'head Jt. (GW & LNW)	Hooton and West Kirby.
G	P	F	L	H	C	1	10	Thurston	Suffolk ...	G. E.	Bury and Haughley.
.	.	.	.	.	.	.	.	Smith, W. & A., & Bacon's Siding	Suffolk ...	G. E.	Thurston.
G	P	.	.	.	.	.	.	Thuxton	Norfolk ...	G. E.	Wymondham and Dereham.
.	P	.	.	.	.	.	.	Thwaites	Yorks	Mid.	Bingley and Keighley.
.	.	.	.	.	.	.	.	Tibbermuir and Powbridge...	Perth	Cal.	See Almondbank.
.	.	.	.	.	.	.	.	Tibbington's Siding	Staffs	L. & N. W.	Same as Howl's Sid. (Wednesbury).
.	.	.	.	.	.	.	.	Tibble's Vi-Cocoa Siding ...	Herts	L. & N. W.	See Bushey Lodge Siding (Watford).
G	P	.	.	.	.	.	.	Tibshelf and Newton.......	Derby	Mid.	Westhouses and Teversall.
.	.	.	.	.	.	.	.	Babbington Coal Co.'s Sid.	Derby	Mid.	Newton Road.
.	.	.	.	.	.	.	.	Seeley's— Tibshelf Colliery, Nos. 1 and 2 Pits.............	Derby	Mid.	Near Tibshelf and Newton.
.	.	.	.	.	.	.	.	Tibshelf Colliery, Nos. 3 and 4 Pits.............	Derby	Mid.	Near Tibshelf and Newton.
.	.	.	.	.	.	.	.	Tibshelf Collieries (G. C.)......	Derby	G. C.—G. N.—L. & N. W.	Tibshelf Town.
.	.	.	.	.	.	.	.	Tibshelf Collieries (Nos. 1 & 2 and 3 & 4 Pits)	Derby	Mid.	See Seeley's (Tibshelf and Newton).
.	.	.	.	.	.	.	.	Tibshelf Junction	Derby	Mid.	Westhouses and Blackwell.
G	P	F	.	H	C	1	10	Tibshelf Town (G. C.)	Derby	G. C.	Chesterfield and Nottingham.
G	.	F	.	.	.	1	10			L. & N. W.	Over G. N. and G. C. Lines.
.	.	.	.	.	.	.	.	Tibshelf Collieries (G. C.)...	Derby	G. C.—G. N.—L. & N. W.	Tibshelf Town.
G	P	F	L	H	.	4	0	Ticehurst Road	Sussex	S. E. & C.	Tunbridge Wells and Hastings.
.	.	.	.	.	.	.	.	Tickle's Siding	Lancs	L. & N. W.	Same as Ramford Brick and Tile Co.'s Siding (St. Helens).
.	.	.	.	.	.	.	.	Ticknall Tramway Wharf ...	Leicester..	Mid.	Ashby.
.	.	.	.	.	.	.	.	Tidal Basin	Essex	G. E.	See London.
G	P	.	.	H	.	.	.	Tiddington	Oxon	G. W.	Oxford and Thame.
G	P	.	.	.	.	1	10	Tidenham.............	Glo'ster ...	G. W.	Chepstow and Tintern.
G	P	F	L	H	C	5	0	Tidworth	Wilts	M. & S. W. Jn.	Branch from Ludgershall.
								TILBURY—			
G	P	F	L	H	C	.	.	(Station)	Essex	L. T. & S.	Grays and Southend-on-Sea.
G	P	F	L	H	C	.	.	Dock Station	Essex	L. T. & S.	Grays and Southend-on-Sea.
.	.	.	.	.	.	.	.	Dock, North Junction	Essex	L. & I. Dks.—L. T. & S.	Tilbury Docks and Grays.
G	.	F	L	.	.	50	0			L. & I. Dks.	Branch fr. Tilbury Dock, North Jn.
G	.	F	L	.	.	50	0	Docks (L. & I. Dks.)	Essex	G. E.—Mid.	Over L. T. & S. & L. & I. Dks. Lines.
G	.	F	L	.	.	50	0			G. N.—G. W.—L. N. W.	Over N L, L T & S, & L & I Dks. Lines.
G	.	F	L	.	.	50	0			L. T. & S.	Over L. & I. Dks. Line.
.	.	.	.	.	.	.	.	East Junction.............	Essex	L. T. & S.	Tilbury and Low Street.
.	.	.	.	.	.	.	.	South Junction	Essex	L. & I. Dks.—L. T. & S.	Tilbury and Tilbury West Junction.
.	.	.	.	.	.	.	.	West Junction	Essex	L. T. & S.	Tilbury Dock Station and Tilbury.
G	P	F	L	H	C	.	.	Tile Hill	Warwick...	L. & N. W.	Birmingham and Coventry.
G	P	.	.	.	.	.	.	Tilehurst	Berks	G. W.	Reading and Didcot.
.	.	.	.	.	.	.	.	Tillanburn Siding	Lanark ...	Cal.	Omoa.
.	.	.	.	.	.	.	.	Tillery Colliery	Mon	G. W.	Abertillery.
G	P	F	L	H	.	2	0	Tillicoultry	Clackman'	N. B.	Alloa and Dollar.
.	.	.	.	.	.	.	.	Devonside Colliery.............	Clackman'	N. B.	Tillicoultry and Sauchie.
G	P	.	.	.	.	.	.	Tillietudlem	Lanark ...	Cal.	Larkhall and Lesmahagow.
.	.	.	.	.	.	.	.	Fence Colliery.............	Lanark ...	Cal.	Tillietudlem.
G	P	.	L	H	.	.	.	Tillyfourie	Aberdeen	G. N. of S.	Kintore and Alford.
G	P	.	L	H	.	.	.	Tillynaught.............	Banff	G. N. of S.	Grange and Banff.
.	P	.	.	.	.	.	.	Tillysburn	Down	B. & C. D.	Belfast and Holywood.
G	P	F	L	H	C	5	0	Tilton	Leicester..	G. N. & L. & N. W. Jt.	Market Harboro' & Melton Mowbray.
.	.	.	.	.	.	.	.	Timberland	Lincoln ...	G. N. & G. E. Jt.	See Scopwick and Timberland.
.	.	.	.	.	.	.	.	Timber Pond Siding	L'lithgow	N. B.	Bo'ness.
.	.	.	.	.	.	.	.	Timmis & Co.'s Siding	Worcester	G. W.	Lye.
.	.	.	.	.	.	.	.	Timmis' Brick Works	Staffs	N. S.	Chatterley.
G	P	.	L	H	C	.	.	Timoleague	Cork	T. & C.	Ballinascarthy and Courtmacsherry.
.	P	.	.	.	.	.	.	Timperley	Cheshire...	M.S.J.&A.(GC& L&NW)	Manchester and Altrincham.
.	.	.	.	.	.	.	.	Timperley Junction.........	Cheshire...	L. & N. W.—M. S. J. & A.	Warrington and Timperley Station.
.	.	.	.	.	.	.	.	Timperley Junction	Cheshire...	G. C.—M. S. J. & A.	Skelton, North Jn. & Timperley Sta.
.	.	.	.	.	.	.	.	Timsbury Colliery	Somerset..	G. W.	Camerton.
G	P	F	L	H	C	.	.	Tinahely	Wicklow...	D. W. & W.	Woodenbridge Junc. & Shillelagh.
.	.	.	.	.	.	.	.	Tindale Col. (St. Helens Col.)	Durham ...	N. E.	West Auckland.
G	P	.	L	H	.	.	.	Tingley (G. N.)	Yorks	G. N.	Ardsley and Morley.
.	P	.	.	.	.	.	.			L. & Y.	Over G. N. Line.
.	.	.	.	.	.	.	.	Balaclava Colliery— Tingley Colliery	Yorks	G. N.	Tingley and Morley.
.	.	.	.	.	.	.	.	West Ardsley Colliery ...	Yorks	G. N.	Tingley and Morley.
.	.	.	.	.	.	.	.	Tinker, Shenton & Co.'s Sid.	Cheshire...	S. & M. Jt. (G. C. & Mid.)	Hyde.

EXPLANATION—G *Goods Station.*   P *Passenger and Parcel Station.*   P* *Passenger, but not Parcel or Miscellaneous Traffic.*
F *Furniture Vans, Carriages, Portable Engines, and Machines on Wheels.*   L *Live Stock.*
H *Horse Boxes and Prize Cattle Vans.*   C *Carriages by Passenger Train.*

STATION ACCOMMODATION.						CRANE POWER.	STATIONS, &c.	COUNTY.	COMPANY.	POSITION.
						Tons Cwts.	Tinker's Siding	Yorks	G. C.	Hazlehead Bridge.
G	P					1 10	Tinsley	Yorks	G. C.	Sheffield and Rotherham.
							Allen, Edgar & Co.'s Siding (G. C.)	Yorks	G. C.—Mid.	Tinsley.
							Hadfield's Steel Foundry Co.— East Hecla Works(G.C.)	Yorks	G. C.—Mid.	Tinsley.
							Tinsley Works (G. C.)	Yorks	G. C.—Mid.	Tinsley.
							Imperial Steel Works	Yorks	G. C.	Tinsley.
							Sheffield Corporation Sewage Works	Yorks	G. C.	Tinsley.
							Sheffield Tube Works (Howell & Co.'s Iron Works) (G. C.)	Yorks	G. C.—Mid.	Tinsley.
							Tinsley Park Colliery	Yorks	G. C.	Tinsley.
							Tinsley, East Junction	Yorks	G. C.	Rotherham and Meadow Hall.
							Tinsley, South Junction	Yorks	G. C.	Tinsley and Meadow Hall.
							Tinsley, West Junction	Yorks	G. C.	Rotherham and Meadow Hall.
							Tinsley Colliery	Yorks	G. C.	Sheffield, Broughton Lane.
							Tinsley Iron & Wire Works	Yorks	G. C.—L. D.& E. C.—Mid.	Same as Cooke's Tinsley Iron and Wire Works.
							Tinsley Park Colliery	York	{ G. C. L. D. & E. C.—Mid.	Tinsley. Sheffield, Tinsley Road.
							Tinsley Road	Yorks	L. D. & E. C.—Mid.	See Sheffield.
							Tinsley Works	Yorks	G. C.—L.D.&E.C.—Mid.	See Hadfield's Steel Foundry Co.
G	P	F	L	H	C	5 0	Tintern	Mon	G. W.	Chepstow and Monmouth.
							Tintern Iron Works Siding	Mon	G. W.	Tintern and Tidenham.
G	P	F	L	H	C	3 0	Tintwistle	Derby	G. C.	Same as Hadfield (for Hollingworth).
							Tipperary	Tipperary	G. S. & W.	Clonmel and Limerick.
							Tippermallo Siding	Perth	Cal.	See Methven.
							TIPTON—			
G	P	F	L	H	C	10 0	(Station)	Staffs	G. W.	Dudley and Wolverhampton.
G						5 0	(Station)	Staffs	L. & N. W.	Birmingham and Wolverhampton.
G							(Station and Basin)	Staffs	G. W.	Branch from Tipton.
G							Barrows & Son's Siding	Staffs	L. & N. W.	Tipton and Princes End.
G						5 0	Basin	Staffs	L. & N. W.	Branch from Tipton Station.
G							Bloomfield Basin	Staffs	L. & N. W.	Branch near Tipton.
							Factory Basin	Staffs	G. W.	Same as Tipton Basin.
							Lloyd's Testing House	Staffs	G. W.	Tipton.
G	P					5 0}	Princes End	Staffs	{ G. W. L. & N. W.	Dudley and Wolverhampton. Tipton and Wednesbury.
	P									
							Roberts & Co.'s Siding	Staffs	L. & N. W.	Tipton and Deepfields.
							South Staffordshire Mond Gas Co.'s Siding	Staffs	L. & N. W.	Tipton and Dudley Port.
							Tipton Urban District Council Gas Siding	Staffs	L. & N. W.	Tipton and Dudley Port.
G	P		L	H			Tipton St. John's	Devon	L. & S.W.	Sidmouth Junction and Sidmouth.
							Tirbach Colliery & Brick Works (Mid.)	Glamorg'n	Mid.—G.W.—L. & N.W.	Gurnos.
							Tirdonkin Colliery Co.'s (Cefngyfelach Colliery)	Glamorg'n	G. W.	Landore.
G	P						Tiree	Argyll	Cal.	Steamer from Oban.
							Tirfounder Level	Glamorg'n	T. V.	Aberdare.
							Tirpentwys Colliery	Mon	G. W.	Pontnewynydd.
G	P	F	L*	H	C	1 10}	Tir Phil (for New Tredegar) (Rhy.)	Glamorg'n	{ Rhy. L. & N. W.	Bargoed and Rhymney. Over Rhy. from Rhymney Joint Line Junction.
G		F				1 10}				
							Powell Duffryn Co.'s New Tredegar Colliery (Rhy)	Glamorg'n	Rhy.—L. & N. W.	Branch near Tir Phil.
							Troed-y-rhiwfwch Colliery	Glamorg'n	Rhy.	Tir Phil and Pontlottyn.
G	P		L			}	Tirydail (G. W.)	Carmarth'	{ G. W. L. & N. W.	Pantyffynnon and Llandilo. Over G. W. Line.
G	P									
							Tirydail Colliery	Carmarth'	G. W.	Tirydail.
							Tirydail Tin Plate Works	Carmarth'	G. W.	Tirydail.
G	P	F	L	H	C	5 0	Tisbury	Wilts	L. & S.W.	Salisbury and Templecombe.
G	P	F	L	H	C		Tissington	Derby	L. & N. W.	Ashbourne and Buxton.
G	P	F	L	H	C	5 0	Tisted (for Selborne)	Hants	L. & S.W.	Alton and Fareham.
							Tithebarn Street (L. & Y.)	Lancs	L. & Y.—Mid.	See Liverpool, Exchange & Tithebarn Street.
G	P		L	H			Titley	Hereford	G. W.	Pembridge and Kington.
							Titterstone Siding (Field and Mackay's)	Salop	S & H Jt (G W & L N W)	Ludlow.
G	P	F	L	H	C	6 0	Tiverton	Devon	G. W.	Tiverton Junction and Cadeleigh.

EXPLANATION—G *Goods Station.* P *Passenger and Parcel Station.* P* *Passenger, but not Parcel or Miscellaneous Traffic.*
F *Furniture Vans, Carriages, Portable Engines, and Machines on Wheels.* L *Live Stock.*
L* *Live Stock in full Truck loads only.* H *Horse Boxes and Prize Cattle Vans.* C *Carriages by Passenger Train.*

STATION ACCOMMODATION.						CRANE POWER.	STATIONS, &c.	COUNTY.	COMPANY.	POSITION.
G	P	F	L	H	C	Tons 8 Cwts 0	Tiverton Junction Station ...	Devon	G. W.	Exeter and Taunton.
.	.	.	.	.	.		Cold Harbour Siding	Devon	G. W.	Branch from Tiverton Jn. Station.
.	.	.	.	.	.		Sampford Siding	Devon	G. W.	Tiverton Jn. Sta. and Burlescombe.
G	P	F	L	H	C	1 10	Tivetshall	Norfolk ...	G. E.	Norwich and Haughley.
.	.	.	.	.	.		Read, T. M., Siding	Norfolk ...	G. E.	Tivetshall.
.	.	.	.	.	.		Tiviot Dale	Lancs	C. L. C. (G C, G N, & Mid.)	See Stockport.
.	P	.	.	.	.		Tivoli	Cork	G. S. & W.	Cork and Queenstown Junction.
G	P	.	L	.	.		Tobermory	Argyll......	Cal.	Steamer from Oban.
G	P	F	L	H	C	1 5	Tochieneal	Banff	G. N. of S.	Portsoy and Elgin.
.	.	.	.	.	.		Todd Bros.' Sidings	Lancs	L. & N. W.	{ St. Helens. { Widnes.
.	.	.	.	.	.		Todd's Saw Mill.............	Lanark ...	Cal.	Lanark.
.	.	.	.	.	.		Todhill's Siding	Durham ...	N. E.	Same as Byers Green Old Station and Engine Shed (Byers Green).
.	.	.	.	.	.		Todhill's Siding (Broomhill Siding)	Ayr	G. & S. W.	Glengarnock and Kilbirnie.
.	.	.	.	.	.		Todholes Siding	Lanark ...	Cal.	See Newbigging.
G	P	F	L	H	C	7 0	Todmorden...................	Yorks	L. & Y.	Rochdale and Halifax.
.	.	.	.	.	.		Fielden's Siding.............	Lancs	L. & Y.	Todmorden.
.	.	.	.	.	.		Stansfield Hall Siding	Lancs	L. & Y.	Near Todmorden.
G	.	.	.	.	.		Tod Point.....................	Yorks	N. E.	Redcar and South Bank.
.	.	.	.	.	.		Coatham Iron Works	Yorks	N. E.	Tod Point.
							Redcar Iron Works—			
.	.	.	.	.	.		Brand's Slag Works	Yorks	N. E.	Tod Point.
							Broadbent & Co.'s Slag Wool Works	Yorks	N. E.	Tod Point.
.	.	.	.	.	.		South Gare Battery	Yorks	N. E.	Breakwater Branch.
.	.	.	.	.	.		South Gare Breakwater ...	Yorks	N. E.	Tod Point.
							Tees Mouth Submarine Engineering Works	Yorks	N. E.	Breakwater Branch.
.	.	.	.	.	.		Tees Powder Magazine......	Yorks	N. E.	Breakwater Branch.
.	.	.	.	.	.		Tod's Mill Siding	L'lithgow	N. B.	Bo'ness.
.	.	.	.	.	.		Toft's Siding	Yorks	N. E.	Marske.
.	.	.	.	.	.		Tolcarn Junction	Cornwall ..	G. W.	Newquay and St. Columb Road.
.	.	.	.	.	.		Toll Bar Depôts	Yorks	N. E.	Middlesbro'.
.	.	.	.	.	.		Toll Bar Siding	Yorks	N. E.	Middlesbro'.
.	.	.	.	.	.		Tollcross	Lanark ...	Cal.	See Glasgow.
.	.	.	.	.	.		Tollcross Estate Siding........	Lanark ...	Cal.	Glasgow.
.	.	.	.	.	.		Tollemache's (Lord) Siding	Cheshire...	L. & N. W.	Beeston Castle and Tarporley.
G	P	.	L	.	.		Toller	Dorset	G. W.	Maiden Newton and Bridport.
G	P	F	L	H	.		Tollerton	Yorks	N. E.	York and Thirsk.
.	.	.	.	.	.		Tolley, Son & Bostock Siding	Staffs	L. & N. W.	Darlaston.
G	P	F	L	H	C	1 10	Tomatin	Inverness	High.	Inverness and Aviemore.
.	.	.	.	.	.		Tomatin Distillery Siding	Inverness	High.	Tomatin.
G	P	.	.	.	.		Tomkin Road (Book to Ballyconnell)	Cavan ...	C. & L.	Belturbet and Ballyconnell.
.	.	.	.	.	.		Tonbridge Junction	Kent	S. E. & C.	Tonbridge Junc. Sta. and Penshurst.
G	P	F	L	H	C	8 0	Tonbridge Junction Station	Kent	S. E. & C.	Sevenoaks and Tunbridge Wells.
G	P	.	L	.	.	6 0	Tondu	Glamorg'n	G. W.	Bridgend and Maesteg.
.	.	.	.	.	.		Barrow Brick Works (Bryncethin Brick Works)	Glamorg'n	G. W.	Tondu and Bryncethin Junction.
.	.	.	.	.	.		Cribbw Ballast Sidings........	Glamorg'n	G. W.	Tondu and Kenfig Hill.
.	.	.	.	.	.		Cribbw Coke Ovens and Brick Works	Glamorg'n	G. W.	Tondu and Kenfig Hill.
.	.	.	.	.	.		Fountain Brick Works......	Glamorg'n	G. W.	Tondu and Kenfig Hill.
.	.	.	.	.	.		Glanant Colliery	Glamorg'n	G. W.	Tondu and Llangonoyd.
							North's—			
.	.	.	.	.	.		Navigation Colliery	Glamorg'n	G. W.	Tondu and Kenfig Hill.
.	.	.	.	.	.		Parkslip Colliery	Glamorg'n	G. W.	Tondu and Kenfig Hill.
.	.	.	.	.	.		Works and Coke Ovens...	Glamorg'n	G. W.	Tondu and Kenfig Hill.
.	.	.	.	.	.		Tondu Junction	Glamorg'n	G. W.	Tondu and Brynmenyn.
.	P	.	.	.	.		Tonevane	Kerry	T. & D.	Tralee and Castlegregory Junction.
G	P	F	L	H	C		Tonfanau	Merioneth	Cam.	Towyn and Llwyngwril.
.	.	.	.	.	.		Tong	Yorks	G. N.	See Birkenshaw and Tong.
G	P	.	L	.	.		Tonge and Breedon	Leicester ..	Mid.	Derby and Worthington.
G	P	F	L	H	C	5 0	Tongham	Surrey	L. & S.W.	Guildford and Farnham.
.	.	.	.	.	.		Aldershot Gas Co.'s Siding	Surrey	L. & S.W.	Tongham.
.	.	.	.	.	.		Ton Mawr Colliery.............	Glamorg'n	S. Wales Min.	Branch from Ton Mawr, West Junc.
.	.	.	.	.	.		Ton Mawr Junctions	Glamorg'n	P. T.—S. Wales Min. ...	Cwmavon and Cymmer.
.	.	.	.	.	.		Tonphillip Colliery.............	Glamorg'n	P. T.	Bryndu.
.	.	.	.	.	.		Tonteg Junction	Glamorg'n	Barry.	Efail-Isaf and Treforest.
.	.	.	.	.	.		Tonygregos Quarry	Glamorg'n	S. Wales Min.	Briton Ferry and Cymmer.
.	.	.	.	.	.		Ton-y-Groes Junction	Glamorg'n	P. T.	Aberavon Junction and Port Talbot.

EXPLANATION— G *Goods Station.*   P *Passenger and Parcel Station.*   P* *Passenger, but not Parcel or Miscellaneous Traffic.*
F *Furniture Vans, Carriages, Portable Engines, and Machines on Wheels.*   L *Live Stock.*
H *Horse Boxes and Prize Cattle Vans.*   C *Carriages by Passenger Train.*

STATION ACCOMMODATION.						CRANE POWER.	STATIONS, &c.	COUNTY.	COMPANY.	POSITION.
						Tons Cwts.	Tonypandy	Glamorg'n	T. V.	See Llwynypia and Tonypandy.
G	P	F	.	.	.	1 10	Tonyrefail	Glamorg'n	G. W.	Llantrisant and Penygraig.
							Cilely Colliery...............	Glamorg'n	G. W.	Tonyrefail and Penygraig.
.	P*	.	.	.	.		Tooban Junction	Donegal ...	L. & L. S.	Letterkenny and Londonderry.
G	P	.	L	H	.	2 10	Toome	Antrim ...	N.C. Com. (Mid.)	Cookstown Junc. and Magherafelt.
							Tootal, Broadhurst & Lee's Sid	Lancs	L. & Y.	Black Lane.
							Tootal Height Quarry Co.'s			
							Broomhill Siding	Lancs	P. & L. Jt. (L& NW. & L&Y)	Longridge.
							Tooth & Co.'s Siding (Mid.)...	Derby	Mid.—L. & N. W.	Woodville.
G	P	.	.	.	.		Tooting Junction Station	Surrey	L. & S W & L B & S C Jt.	Wimbledon and Streatham.
							Tooting, Upper	Surrey	L. B. & S. C.	Same as Balham.
G	P	.	L	H	C		Topcliffe	Yorks	N. E.	Thirsk and Melmerby.
							Topley Pike Stone Quarry ...	Derby	Mid.	See Newton, Chambers & Co. (Miller's Dale).
G	P	F	L	H	C	2 0	Topsham	Devon	L. & S. W.	Exeter and Exmouth.
							Digby's Siding (private) ...	Devon	L. & S. W.	Topsham.
							Ebford Siding (Odam's Manure Siding)	Devon	L. & S. W.	Topsham.
							Exeter Brick & Tile Co.'s Sid.	Devon	L. & S. W.	Topsham.
							Quay Line...................	Devon	L. & S. W.	Topsham.
							Top Yard	Sussex	L. B. & S. C.	See Brighton.
							Torbothy Siding.............	Lanark ...	N. B.	Shotts.
G	P	.	L	H	.		Torksey	Lincoln ...	G. C.	Retford and Lincoln.
							Torlundy Siding.............	Inverness	N. B.	Fort William.
.	P	.	.	.	.		Torpantau	Brecon ...	B. & M.	Dolygaer and Taiybont.
G	P	F	L	H	C	2 0	Torphins	Aberdeen	G. N. of S.	Banchory and Aboyne.
.	P	.	.	H	C		Torquay	Devon	G. W.	Newton Abbot and Kingswear.
							Torquay Gas House Siding	Devon	G. W.	Torquay and Paignton.
G	P	.	L	.	.	3 0	Torrance	Stirling ...	N. B.	Maryhill and Kilsyth.
							Hayston Sand Siding	Stirling ...	N. B.	Torrance and Gavell.
							Torrance's Siding	Edinboro'	N. B.	East Calder.
G	P	F	L	.	.	10 0	Torre	Devon	G. W.	Newton Abbot and Torquay.
G	P	F	L	H	C	10 0	Torrington	Devon	L. & S. W.	Branch from Barnstaple.
							Torry Glen Brick Works......	Lanark ...	Cal.	Glasgow, South Side.
G	P	.	L	H	.		Torver	Lancs	Furness	Foxfield and Coniston.
							Torwood Foundry (Jones and Campbell's).................	Stirling ...	Cal.	Larbert.
							Torycoed Colliery	Glamorg'n	T. V.	Cross Inn.
G	P	.	L	.	.				Cal.	Steamer from Oban.
G	P	.	L	.	.		Totaig	Inverness	High.	Steamer from Kyle of Lochalsh.
G	P	.	.	.	.				N. B.	Steamer from Mallaig.
.	P	.	.	.	.		Totland Bay	I. of W.	L. & S. W.	Steamer from Lymington Pier.
							Totley	Derby	Mid.	See Dore and Totley.
G	P	.	.	.	.		Totmonslow	Staffs	N. S. (Cheadle)	Branch from Cresswell Junction.
G	P	F	L	H	C	1 10	Totnes	Devon	G. W.	Newton Abbot and Plymouth.
							Dainton Siding	Devon	G. W.	Totnes and Newton Abbot.
G	.	.	.	.	.	5 0	Totnes Quay	Devon	G. W.	Extension from Totnes.
							Toton Sidings	Derby	Mid.	Long Eaton.
							Tottenham	Middlesex	G. E.	See London.
							Tottenham and Edmonton Gas Co.'s Siding............	Middlesex	G. E.	Angel Road.
							Tottenham Court Road.......	Middlesex	C. L.	See London.
							Tottenham, North Junction...	Middlesex	G. E.—T. & H. Jt.	London, Tottenham & Crouch Hill.
							Tottenham, West Junction ...	Middlesex	G. E.—T. & H. Jt.	London, Lea Bridge & Crouch Hill.
G	P	F	L	H	C		Totteridge & Whetstone (G.N.)	Middlesex	G. N.	Finchley and High Barnet.
.	P	.	.	.	.				N. L.	Over G. N. from Canonbury Junc.
							Totternhoe Lime and Stone Co.'s Siding.................	Beds	L. & N. W.	Stanbridgeford.
G	P	.	.	.	.	3 10	Tottington	Lancs	L. & Y.	Bury and Holcombe Brook.
							Knowles, S., & Co.'s Siding	Lancs	L. & Y.	Tottington.
							Roberts', R. K., Siding......	Lancs	L. & Y.	Tottington.
							Tottington Junction	Lancs	L. & Y.	Bury.
G	P	F	L	H	C	10 0	Totton and Eling	Hants	L. & S. W.	Southampton and Brockenhurst.
							Pamplins Siding	Hants	L. & S. W.	Totton and Eling.
							Totton Tramway	Hants	L. & S. W.	Totton and Eling.
							Touch, North Junction........	Fife	N. B.	Dunfermline.
							Touch, South Junction........	Fife	N. B.	Dunfermline.
.	P	.	.	.	.		Tovil	Kent	S. E. & C.	Maidstone West & Paddock Wood.
G	.	.	.	.	.	5 0	Tovil Siding.................	Kent	S. E. & C.	Maidstone, West.
									N. & B. Jn.	Blisworth and Banbury.
G	P	F	L	H	C	2 10	Towcester (N. & B. Jn.)	N'hampt'n	E. & W. Jn.	Over N. & B. Junction from Greens Norton Junction.

EXPLANATION—G *Goods Station.*　　P *Passenger and Parcel Station.*　　P* *Passenger, but not Parcel or Miscellaneous Traffic.*
F *Furniture Vans, Carriages, Portable Engines, and Machines on Wheels.*　　L *Live Stock.*
H *Horse Boxes and Prize Cattle Vans.*　　C *Carriages by Passenger Train.*

STATION ACCOMMODATION.						CRANE POWER.	STATIONS, &c.	COUNTY.	COMPANY.	POSITION.
						Tons Cwts.	Towcester (N. & B. Jn.)—continued.			
							Towcester Mineral and Brick Works Siding	N'hamptn	E. & W. Jn.	Towcester Junc. and Stoke Bruern.
	P						Towcester Junction	N'hamptn	E. & W. Jn.—N. & B. Jn.	Stoke Bruern and Towcester.
							Tower Bridge	Cork	C. & Muskerry	Coachford Junction and Blarney.
G	P	F	L	H	C		Tower (Duffryn Aberdare) Col.	Glamorg'n	G. W.	Hirwain.
							Tower Hill	Devon	L. & S. W.	Halwill Junction and Launceston.
							Tower Manufacturing Co.'s Works (G. W.)	Worcester	G. W.—Mid.	Worcester.
							Tower Street Siding	Edinboro'	Cal.—N.B.	Leith, South.
G	P		L	H	C	2 0	Towgood & Son's Paper Mills	N'hamptn	Mid.	Helpston.
G	P		L	H	C	1 0	Towiemore Siding	Banff	G. N. of S.	Keith and Craigellachie.
							Tow Law	Durham ...	N. E.	Bishop Auckland and Consett.
							Blackfield Depôts and Sid.	Durham ...	N. E.	Tow Law.
							Black Prince Colliery	Durham ...	N. E.	Tow Law.
							Bond's Foundry	Durham ...	N. E.	Tow Law.
							Hedley Hope Colliery	Durham ...	N. E.	Tow Law.
							High Stoop Siding and Depôts	Durham ...	N. E.	Tow Law.
							Sunnyside Depôts and Sid.	Durham ...	N. E.	Tow Law.
							Tow Law Depôts	Durham ...	N. E.	Tow Law.
							Tow Law Gas Works	Durham ...	N. E.	Tow Law.
							Tow Law Iron Works	Durham ...	N. E.	Tow Law.
							Tow Law Saw Mill	Durham ...	N. E.	Tow Law.
							West Thornley Colliery ...	Durham ...	N. E.	Tow Law.
G	P	F	L	H	C		Towneley	Lancs	L. & Y.	Burnley and Todmorden.
							Brooks & Pickup's Colliery	Lancs	L. & Y.	Towneley.
							Towneley Colliery	Lancs	L. & Y.	Towneley and Holme.
							Towneley Colliery and Depôts	Durham ...	N. E.	Same as Stella Coal Co.'s Emma Colliery and Depôts (Blaydon).
G	P		L	H	C	2 0	Town Green and Aughton ...	Lancs	L. & Y.	Liverpool and Ormskirk.
							Greenwood's Corn Mill	Lancs	L. & Y.	Town Green and Aughton.
							Pilkington's Siding	Lancs	L. & Y.	Town Green and Aughton.
							Townhead Depôt	Ayr	G. & S. W.	See Ayr.
							Townhead Mining Co.'s Sids.	Cumb'land	W C & E Jt. (Fur. & LNW)	Gillfoot.
							Townhead Siding	Lanark ...	Cal.	Blackwood.
							Townhill Junction	Fife	N. B.	Halbeath and Dunfermline.
							Townhill Junction Station ...	Fife	N. B.	Dunfermline and Cowdenbeath.
							Appin Fire-Clay Works ...	Fife	N. B.	Branch from Townhill Junction.
							Bowershall Colliery	Fife	N. B.	Townhill Junction and Steelend.
							Elgin & Wellwood Colliery	Fife	N. B.	Townhill Junction and Steelend.
							Gask Lime Siding	Fife	N. B.	Townhill Junction and Steelend.
G							Lathalmond Siding	Fife	N. B.	Townhill Junction and Steelend.
							Lilliehill Brick & Tile Works	Fife	N. B.	Branch from Townhill Junction.
							Lochside Colliery	Fife	N. B.	Townhill Junction and Kelty.
							Lochside Fire-Clay Works	Fife	N. B.	Branch from Townhill Junction.
							Muirbeath Colliery	Fife	N. B.	Whitemyre Junction and Kelty.
							Muircockhall Colliery	Fife	N. B.	Whitemyre Junction and Kelty.
							Townhill No. 7 Colliery ...	Fife	N. B.	Whitemyre Junction and Kelty.
							Townhill No. 8 Colliery ...	Fife	N. B.	Whitemyre Junction and Kelty.
							Townhill Siding	Lanark ...	Cal.	Meikle Earnock.
							Townrow's, T., Siding	Derby	Mid.	Chesterfield.
							Townsend Fold Siding	Lancs	L. & Y.	Rawtenstall.
G	P	F	L	H	C	1 0 ⎫	Towyn	Merioneth	⎧ Cam.	Barmouth and Aberdovey.
G	P					⎭			⎩ Tal-y-llyn	Terminus near Cambrian Station.
							Toxteth Dock	Lancs	L'pool O'head	See Liverpool.
							Toy Siding	Warwick..	L. & N. W.	Birmingham, Monument Lane.
							Barton's Siding	Warwick..	L. & N. W.	Toy Siding.
							Grice, Grice & Son's Siding	Warwick..	L. & N. W.	Toy Siding.
							Piggott's Siding	Warwick..	L. & N. W.	Toy Siding.
	P						Trabboch	Ayr	G. & S. W.	Annbank and Drongan.
							Trabboch Colliery	Ayr	G. & S. W.	Drongan.
							Trader's Siding (Govan) ...	Lanark ...	G & P Jt (Cal & G & S W)	Glasgow, Govan.
							Tradeston Gas Works	Renfrew...	Cal.	Glasgow, South Side.
							Tradeston Saw Mills (G. & P. Jt.) ⎫	Lanark ...	⎧ Cal.	Glasgow, Kinning Park.
							⎭		⎩ G. & S. W.	Glasgow, Eglinton Street.
							Trafalgar	Northumb	N. E.	See Newcastle.
							Trafalgar Siding	Glo'ster ...	⎧ G. W.	Bilson Junction.
									⎩ S. & Wye Jt. (G.W. & Mid)	Drybrook Road.
							Trafalgar Street	Yorks	Mid.	See Bradford.
							Trafford Park	Lancs	C. L. C. (G C, G N, & Mid)	See Manchester.
							Trafford Park (L. & Y.)	Lancs	Trafford Park Estate......	Manchester.

EXPLANATION—G Goods Station.   P Passenger and Parcel Station.   P* Passenger, but not Parcel or Miscellaneous Traffic.
F Furniture Vans, Carriages, Portable Engines, and Machines on Wheels.   L Live Stock.
H Horse Boxes and Prize Cattle Vans.   C Carriages by Passenger Train.

STATION ACCOMMODATION.						CRANE POWER.	STATIONS, &c.	COUNTY.	COMPANY.	POSITION.
						Tons Cwts.	Trafford Park Enamelling Co.'s Siding	Lancs	Trafford Park Estate	Manchester.
							Trafford Park Estate	Lancs	Manchester Ship Canal	Manchester.
							Trafford Park Estates Works Department Siding	Lancs	Trafford Park Estate	Manchester.
							Trafford Park Junction	Lancs	Manchester Ship Canal—Trafford Park Estate	See Manchester.
							Trafford Park Steel Works Co.'s Siding	Lancs	Manchester Ship Canal	Manchester.
							Trafford Power & Light Supply Siding	Lancs	Trafford Park Estate	Manchester.
							Train's Siding	Lanark	Cal.	Glasgow, Bridgeton.
G	P	F	L	H	C	5 0	Tralee	Kerry	{ G. S. & W.	Listowel and Killarney.
G	P		L	H					{ T. & D.	Adjoining G. S. & W. Station.
G	P		L	L		5 0	Tram Inn (G. W.)	Hereford	{ G. W.	Hereford and Abergavenny.
G	P		L			5 0			{ L. & N. W.	Over G. W. from Hereford.
G	P						Tramore	Waterford	W. & T.	Terminus.
							Tranent	Hadding'n	N. B.	See Prestonpans.
							Tranent Collieries	Hadding'n	N. B.	Prestonpans.
	P						Traveller's Rest	Glamorg'n	T. V.	Pontypridd and Nelson.
G	P		L	H			Trawscoed	Cardigan	M. & M.	Tregaron and Aberystwyth.
G	P	F	L	H	C	1 0	Trawsfynydd	Merioneth	G. W.	Bala and Festiniog.
G		F	L	H		4 0	Trealaw	Glamorg'n	T. V.	Pontypridd and Treherbert.
							Adare Colliery	Glamorg'n	T. V.	Trealaw and Dinas.
G			L				Blaenclydach	Glamorg'n	T. V.	Pwllyrhebog Branch.
							Blaenclydach Colliery	Glamorg'n	T. V.	Pwllyrhebog Branch.
							Blaenclydach Mileage Sid.	Glamorg'n	T. V.	Pwllyrhebog Branch.
							Clydach Vale Colliery (Phillipps Siding)	Glamorg'n	T. V.	Pwllyrhebog Branch.
							Clydach Vale Siding	Glamorg'n	T. V.	Pwllyrhebog Branch.
							Cwmclydach Colliery	Glamorg'n	T. V.	Pwllyrhebog Branch.
							Incline Top Siding (Retailer's Siding)	Glamorg'n	T. V.	Pwllyrhebog Branch.
							Llwynypia Colliery (Glamorgan Colliery)	Glamorg'n	T. V.	Trealaw and Llwynypia.
G							Llwynypia Mileage Siding	Glamorg'n	T. V.	Trealaw and Llwynypia.
							Pandy Pit (Naval Colliery)	Glamorg'n	T. V.	Trealaw and Dinas.
							Trealaw Brick Works	Glamorg'n	T. V.	Trealaw and Llwynypia.
							Treals Siding	Lancs	P.&W.Jt. (L&Y&L&NW)	See Earl of Derby's (Kirkham).
							Treaman Colliery	Glamorg'n	G. W.—T. V.	See Powell Duffryn Co.
G							Treamble	Cornwall	G. W.	Branch from Tolcarn Junction.
							East Wheal Rose Siding	Cornwall	G. W.	Tolcarn Junction & Shepherd's Sid.
							Treasures Siding	Salop	L. & N. W.	Shrewsbury.
G	P						Treborth	Carnarvon	L. & N. W.	Bangor and Carnarvon.
							Treborth Siding	Carnarvon	L. & N. W.	Same as Davies' (Menai Bridge).
							Trechmann's Cement Works	Durham	N. E.	Hartlepool.
G	P	F	L	H	C		Tredegar	Mon	L. & N. W.	Nantybwch & Tredegar Junc. Sta.
							Tredegar Iron & Coal Co.—			
							Bedwellty Pits	Glamorg'n	L. & N. W.	Bedwellty Pits and Holly Bush.
							Lower Farm Siding	Glamorg'n	L. & N. W.	Tredegar and Bedwellty Pits.
							Tredegar Yard Works	Mon	L. & N. W.	Tredegar and Sirhowy.
							Ty Trist Colliery	Mon	L. & N. W.	Tredegar and Bedwellty Pits.
							Upper Bedwellty Siding	Mon	L. & N. W.	Tredegar and Bedwellty Pits.
							Whitworth Colliery	Mon	L. & N. W.	Tredegar and Bedwellty Pits.
							Tredegar Iron & Coal Co.—			
							Bedwellty Pits	Glamorg'n	L. & N. W.	Tredegar.
							Lower Farm Siding	Glamorg'n	L. & N. W.	Tredegar.
							Pochin Pits	Mon	L. & N. W.	Holly Bush.
							Sirhowy Works	Mon	L. & N. W.	Sirhowy.
							Tredegar Yard Works	Mon	L. & N. W.	Tredegar.
							Ty Trist Colliery	Mon	L. & N. W.	Tredegar.
							Upper Bedwellty Siding	Mon	L. & N. W.	Tredegar.
							Whitworth Colliery	Mon	L. & N. W.	Tredegar.
							TREDEGAR JUNCTION—			
G	P		L	H		1 10	(Station)	Mon	{ G. W.	Crumlin, High Level & Rhymney Jn.
G	P		L						{ L. & N. W.	Nantybwch and Nine Mile Point.
							Bird-in-Hand Junction	Mon	G. W.—L. & N. W.	Rhymney Junc. & Tredegar Jn. Sta.
							Bird-in-Hand Siding	Mon	G. W.—L. & N. W.	Tredegar Jn. Sta. & Rhymney Jn. Sta.
							Brynn Tramway	Mon	L. & N. W.	Tredegar Jn. Sta. and Blackwood.
							Gwrhay Colliery	Mon	G. W.	Branch near Tredegar Junction.
							Islwyn Colliery	Mon	G. W.	Branch near Tredegar Junction.
							Manmoel Colliery	Mon	G. W.	Branch near Tredegar Junction.

EXPLANATION—G *Goods Station.*   P *Passenger and Parcel Station.*   P* *Passenger, but not Parcel or Miscellaneous Traffic.*
F *Furniture Vans, Carriages, Portable Engines, and Machines on Wheels.*   L *Live Stock.*
H *Horse Boxes and Prize Cattle Vans.*   C *Carriages by Passenger Train.*

STATION ACCOMMODATION.						CRANE POWER.	STATIONS, &c.	COUNTY.	COMPANY.	POSITION.
						Tons Cwts.	TREDEGAR JUNCTION—*continued.*			
..	..	..	..	..	..	..	Penner Junction..............	Mon	G. W.	Tredegar Junction and Crumlin.
..	..	..	..	..	..	..	Penrhiw Colliery	Mon	G. W.	Branch near Tredegar Junction.
..	..	..	..	..	..	..	Sirhowy Junc. (Gellygroes)	Mon	G. W.—L. & N. W.	Rhymney Jn. and Nine Mile Point.
..	..	..	..	..	..	..	Waterloo Colliery	Mon	G. W.	Branch near Tredegar Junction.
..	..	..	..	..	..	..	Woodfield Colliery	Mon	G. W.	Branch near Tredegar Junction.
..	..	..	..	..	..	..	Tredegar Road	Middlesex	L. & N. W.	Same as London, Bow Coal Depôt.
							Tredegar's (Lord)—			
..	..	..	..	..	..	..	Siding (B. & M.)...........	Mon	B. & M.—G. W.	Aber Bargoed.
..	..	..	..	..	..	..	Siding	Mon	L. & N. W.	Ynysddu.
..	P	..	..	..	..	..	Treeton (Mid.)	Yorks	{ Mid.	Masboro' and Woodhouse Mill.
									L. D. & E. C.	Over Midland Line.
..	..	..	..	..	..	..	Treeton Colliery.............	Yorks	Mid.	Woodhouse Mill.
..	..	..	..	..	..	..	Treeton Colliery (G. C.)	Yorks	G. C.—L. & N. W.	Woodhouse.
G	..	..	..	..	..	..	Trefeglwys	Montgom	Cam. (Van)	Caersws and Garth.
G	P	..	..	..	..	..	Trefeinon	Brecon ...	Cam.	Talyllyn and Three Cocks.
..	..	..	..	..	..	..	Treferig Branch Junction ...	Glamorg'n	T. V.	Common Bch. Jn. and Ely Valley Jn.
..	..	..	..	..	..	..	Treferig Siding	Glamorg'n	T. V.	Cross Inn.
..	..	..	..	..	..	..	Treffrys Siding	Cornwall ..	G. W.	Bridges.
G	P	..	L	H	..	5 0	Trefnant	Denbigh...	L. & N. W.	Denbigh and Rhyl.
	P								{ Barry	Efail-Isaf and Pontypridd.
G	P	..	..	..	..	1 10	Treforest	Glamorg'n	{ T. V.	Cardiff and Pontypridd.
							Waterhouse Bros.' Treforest Tin Plate Works	Glamorg'n	T. V.	Treforest and Taff's Well.
..	..	..	..	..	..	..	Treforest Junction..............	Glamorg'n	Barry—T. V.	Efail-Isaf and Treforest.
..	P	..	..	..	..	..	Trefriw	Carnarvon	L. & N. W.	See Llanrwst and Trefriw.
..	..	..	..	..	..	..	Trefynant Brick Works	Denbigh ...	G. W.	Trevor.
G	P	..	L	H	..	1 0	Tregaron	Cardigan..	M. & M.	Lampeter and Aberystwyth.
G	P	..	L	..	..	5 0	Tregarth	Carnarvon	L. & N. W.	Bangor and Bethesda.
							Tregoning & Son's Morfa Tin Plate Works (G. W.).........	Carmarth'	G. W.—L. & N. W.	Llanelly.
..	..	..	..	..	..	..	Treharne's Rock Foundry ...	Mon	L. & N. W.	Blackwood.
G	P	..	..	..	..	1 10	Treharris (G. W.)	Glamorg'n	{ G. W.	Llancaiach and Quaker's Yard.
	P								Rhy.	Over G. W. from Penallta Junction.
							Deep Navigation or Ocean Navigation Col. (G. W.)...	Glamorg'n	G. W.—Rhy.	Treharris and Llancaiach.
G	P	F	L	H	C	2 10			{ T. V.	Terminus of Rhondda Branch from Pontypridd.
	P	..	..	H	C	..	Treherbert (T. V.)..............	Glamorg'n	{ R. & S. B.	Over T. V. from Treherbert Junc.
							Blaenrhondda Colliery (North Dunraven Colliery)	Glamorg'n	T. V.	Near Treherbert.
..	..	..	..	..	..	..	Bute Merthyr Colliery	Glamorg'n	T. V.	Near Treherbert.
..	..	..	..	..	..	..	Cory Bros.& Co's Tydraw Col	Glamorg'n	T. V.	Near Treherbert.
..	..	..	..	..	..	..	Fernhill Colliery	Glamorg'n	T. V.	Near Treherbert.
..	..	..	..	..	..	..	Lady Margaret Colliery ...	Glamorg'n	T. V.	Treherbert and Treorchy.
..	..	..	..	..	..	..	Rhondda Merthyr Colliery	Glamorg'n	T. V.	Near Treherbert.
..	..	..	..	..	..	..	South Dunraven Colliery ...	Glamorg'n	T. V.	Near Treherbert.
..	..	..	..	..	..	..	Ynisfeio Colliery.............	Glamorg'n	T. V.	Treherbert and Treorchy.
..	..	..	..	..	..	..	Treherbert Junction	Glamorg'n	R. & S. B. —T. V.	Cymmer and Treherbert.
..	..	..	..	..	..	..	Trehir Quarry....................	Glamorg'n	Rhy.	Llanbradach.
..	..	..	..	..	..	..	Trelyn Colliery	Mon	G. W.	Rhymney Junction Station.
..	..	..	..	..	..	..	Trenance Siding	Cornwall ..	G. W.	St. Austell.
G	..	..	..	..	..	..	Trench	Salop	L. & N. W.	Shrewsbury and Stafford.
..	..	..	..	..	..	..	Shropshire Iron Co.'s Sid.	Salop	L. & N. W.	Trench and Hadley.
..	..	..	..	..	..	..	Trench Chemical Co.'s Sid.	Salop	L. & N. W.	Trench and Hadley.
..	..	..	..	..	..	..	Trench Iron Co.'s Siding ...	Salop	L. & N. W.	Trench and Hadley.
..	P	..	..	..	..	..	Trench Crossing	Salop	L. & N. W.	Shrewsbury and Stafford.
G	P	..	L	H	C	..	Trenholme Bar	Yorks	N. E.	Stockton and Stokesley.
G	P	..	..	..	..	5 0	Trent...........................	Derby	Mid.	Nottingham and Derby.
..	..	..	..	..	..	..	Trent Sheet & Sack Depôts	Derby	Mid.	Nottingham and Derby.
..	..	..	..	..	..	..	Trent Art Tile Co.'s Sid. (Mid.)	Derby	Mid.—L. & N. W.	Swadlincote.
..	..	..	..	..	..	..	Trent Brewery (Mid.)	Staffs	Mid.—L&NW—GN—NS	Same as Everard & Co. (Burton-on-Trent).
..	..	..	..	..	..	..	Trent Cold Storage & Ice Co.'s Siding (Mid.)	Staffs	Mid.—L N W—G N—N S	Burton-on-Trent.
..	..	..	..	..	..	..	Trent Girder Yard (Engineers' Siding)	Derby	Mid.	Long Eaton.
G	P	F	L	H	C	5 0	Trentham (N. S.)	Staffs	{ N. S.	Stoke and Stone.
									L. & N. W.	Over N. S. Line.
..	..	..	..	..	..	..	Florence Colliery	Staffs	N. S.	Trentham.
..	..	..	..	..	..	..	Sideway Siding (Stafford Coal & Iron Co.) (N. S.)..	Staffs	N. S.—L. & N. W.	Stoke and Trentham.

EXPLANATION—G *Goods Station.*   P *Passenger and Parcel Station.*   P* *Passenger, but not Parcel or Miscellaneous Traffic.*
F *Furniture Vans, Carriages, Portable Engines, and Machines on Wheels.*   L *Live Stock.*
H *Horse Boxes and Prize Cattle Vans.*   C *Carriages by Passenger Train.*

STATION ACCOMMODATION.						CRANE POWER.	STATIONS, &c.	COUNTY.	COMPANY.	POSITION.
						Tons Cwts.				
.	.	.	.	.	.	. .	Trent Iron Works	Lincoln	G. C.	Frodingham and Scunthorpe.
.	.	.	.	.	.	. .	Trent Lane Junctions	Notts	G. N.	Nottingham.
.	.	.	.	.	.	. .	Trent Valley Maltings	Staffs	L. & N. W.	Same as Evans & Co. (Lichfield).
.	.	.	.	.	.	. .	Trent Wharf Sidings	Lincoln ...	G. N. & G. E. Jt.	Gainsboro'.
G	P	F	L	H	C	3 0	Treorchy	Glamorg'n	T. V.	Treherbert and Pontypridd.
							Abergorchwy or Abergorki Colliery	Glamorg'n	T. V.	Treorchy and Treherbert.
							CoryBros.&Co.'sTynybedw Colliery	Glamorg'n	T. V.	Treorchy and Ystrad.
							Ocean Coal Co.—			
.	.	.	.	.	.	. .	Cwmpark (Park) Colliery	Glamorg'n	T. V.	Ystrad and Treorchy.
.	.	.	.	.	.	. .	Dare Pit	Glamorg'n	T. V.	Ystrad and Treorchy.
.	.	.	.	.	.	. .	Trerice Siding................	Cornwall ..	G. W.	Melangoose Mill.
.	.	.	.	.	.	. .	Tresavean Branch & Siding ..	Cornwall ..	G. W.	Redruth.
.	.	.	.	.	.	. .	Treshenkin Colliery	Glamorg'n	G. W.	Abergwynfi.
G	P	F	L	H	C	2 0	Tresmeer	Cornwall ..	L. & S.W.	Launceston and Wadebridge.
G	G					. .	Tressarrett Siding	Cornwall ..	L. & S.W.	Branch from Wadebridge.
.	.	.	.	.	.	. .	Trethosa Siding	Cornwall ..	G. W.	Drinnick Mill.
G	P					. .	Treveglwys	Montgom	Cam. (Van.)	Caersws and Cerist.
.	.	.	.	.	.	. .	Trevemper Siding	Cornwall ..	G. W.	Newquay.
.	.	.	.	.	.	. .	Trevethin Junction	Mon	G. W.	Pontypool, Crane Street and Pont-newynydd.
G	P	.	L	H	.	. .	Trevil	Mon	L. & N. W.	Abergavenny and Merthyr.
.	.	.	.	.	.	. .	Ebbw Vale Steel, Iron, and Coal Co.'s Siding	Mon	L. & N. W.	Trevil and Beaufort.
G	P	.	.	.	.	3 0	Trevor	Denbigh ...	G. W.	Ruabon and Llangollen.
.	.	.	.	.	.	. .	Garth Fire-Clay Works ...	Denbigh ...	G. W.	Trevor.
.	.	.	.	.	.	. .	Trefynant Brick Works ...	Denbigh ...	G. W.	Trevor.
.	.	.	.	.	.	. .	Trevor Hall Lime Works (Wright's)	Denbigh ...	G. W.	Trevor and Llangollen.
.	.	.	.	.	.	. .	Trevor Saw Mills	Denbigh ...	G. W.	Trevor.
.	.	.	.	.	.	. .	Trevor Hall Lime Works (Wright's)	Denbigh ...	G. W.	Trevor.
G	P	F	L	H	C	3 0	Trew and Moy	Tyrone ...	G. N. (I.)	Portadown and Dungannon.
.	P	.	.	.	.	. .	Trewythan Siding	Montgom	Cam. (Van.)	Caersws and Cerist.
.	P	.	L	.	.	. .	Triangle	Yorks	L. & Y.	Sowerby Bridge and Rishworth.
G	P	.	L	.	.	. .	Trillick	Tyrone ...	G. N. (I.)	Enniskillen and Omagh.
G	P	F	L	H	C	. .	Trim	Meath	M. G. W.	Kilmessan and Athboy.
G	P	.	L	H	C	2 0	Trimdon	Durham ...	N. E.	Ferryhill and Hartlepool.
.	.	.	.	.	.	.·.	Deaf Hill Colliery	Durham ...	N. E.	Trimdon.
.	.	.	.	.	.	. .	Grange Quarry	Durham ...	N. E.	Trimdon.
.	.	.	.	.	.	. .	Trimdon Colliery	Durham ...	N. E.	Trimdon.
.	.	.	.	.	.	. .	Trimdon Grange Colliery & Coke Works..............	Durham ...	N. E.	Trimdon.
.	.	.	.	.	.	. .	Trimdon Grange Old Station Siding	Durham ...	N. E.	Trimdon.
.	.	.	.	.	.	. .	West Moor Lime Works (Trimdon Lime Siding)...	Durham ...	N. E.	Trimdon.
.	.	.	.	.	.	. .	Wingate Limestone Quarry	Durham ...	N. E.	Trimdon.
.	.	.	.	.	.	. .	Trimdon Lime Siding	Durham ...	N. E.	Same as West Moor Lime Works (Trimdon).
G	P	F	L	H	C	. .	Trimley	Suffolk ..	G. E.	Ipswich and Felixstowe.
.	.	.	.	.	.	. .	Trimley Hall Siding	Flint	W & MJt.(G.W.& L&NW)	Same as Woolliscroft's (Llanfynydd).
.	.	.	.	.	.	. .	Trimsaran Junction	Carmarth'	B. P. & G. V.	Burry Port and Pontyeats.
.	.	.	.	.	.	. .	Trimsaran Works & Colliery	Carmarth'	B. P. & G. V.	Burry Port.
G	P	F	L	H	C	5 0	Tring	Herts	L. & N. W.	Bletchley and Watford.
.	.	.	.	.	.	. .	Mead's Siding................	Herts	L. & N. W.	Tring and Berkhamsted.
.	.	.	.	.	.	. .	Trinity and Newhaven.........	Edinboro'	N. B.	See Leith.
.	.	.	.	.	.	. .	Trinity Junction	Durham ...	N. E.	Hartlepool.
.	.	.	.	.	.	. .	Trio Mining Co.'s Pit	Cumb'land	WC& EJt.(Fur.&L&NW)	Frizington.
G	P	.	L	H	.	1 10	Troedyrhiew	Glamorg'n	T. V.	Merthyr and Pontypridd.
.	.	.	.	.	.	. .	Troedyrhiew Colliery	Glamorg'n	T. V.	Same as Tynewydd Colliery (Porth).
G	P					. .	Troedyrhiew Garth	Glamorg'n	G. W.	Bridgend and Maesteg.
.	.	.	.	.	.	. .	Elders Navigation Oakwood Colliery	Glamorg'n	G. W.	Troedyrhiew Garth and Maesteg.
.	.	.	.	.	.	. .	Garth Colliery	Glamorg'n	G. W.	Troedyrhiew Garth and Maesteg.
.	.	.	.	.	.	. .	Llwydarth Tin Works Sid.	Glamorg'n	G. W.	Troedyrhiew Garth.
.	.	.	.	.	.	. .	Tin Works	Glamorg'n	G. W.	Troedyrhiew and Maesteg.
.	.	.	.	.	.	. .	Troedyrhiwfwch Colliery Siding	Glamorg'n	Rhy.	Tir Phil.
.	.	.	.	.	.	. .	Trollope & Son's Siding	Suffolk ...	G. E.	Barnham.
.	.	.	.	.	.	. .	Trood & Co.'s Siding............	Cornwall ..	L. & S.W.	Launceston.

EXPLANATION— G *Goods Station.*   P *Passenger and Parcel Station.*   P* *Passenger, but not Parcel or Miscellaneous Traffic.*
F *Furniture Vans, Carriages, Portable Engines, and Machines on Wheels.*   L *Live Stock.*
H *Horse Boxes and Prize Cattle Vans.*   C *Carriages by Passenger Train.*

STATION ACCOMMODATION.						CRANE POWER.		STATIONS, &c.	COUNTY.	COMPANY.	POSITION.
						Tons	Cwts.				
								TROON—			
G	P	F	L	H	C	3	0	(Station)	Ayr	G. & S.W.	Ayr and Irvine.
								Ailsa Shipbuilding Co.'s Siding	Ayr	G. & S.W.	Troon Harbour.
								Gas Works	Ayr	G. & S.W.	Troon, Templehill.
G						30	0	Harbour	Ayr	G. & S.W.	Branch from Barassie Junction.
								Junction	Ayr	G. & S.W.	Troon (Passengers) and Monkton.
								Saw Mill	Ayr	G. & S.W.	Troon Harbour.
G						2	0	Templehill Depôt	Ayr	G. & S.W.	Barassie and Troon Harbour.
								Templehill Junction	Ayr	G. & S.W.	Barassie and Troon Harbour.
	P							Trooper's Lane	Antrim	N. C. Com. (Mid.)	Carrickfergus and Belfast.
								Trosnant Junction	Mon	G. W.	Pontypool, Crane Street and Panteg.
G	P	F	L	H	C	1	10	Troutbeck	Cumb'land	C. K.&P.(L.&N.W.&N.E. Working Companies)	Penrith and Keswick.
								Trowbarrow Lime Works	Lancs	Furness	Silverdale.
G	P	F	L	H	C	10	0	Trowbridge	Wilts	G. W.	Chippenham and Westbury.
G	P							Trowell	Notts	Mid.	Stanton Gate and Ilkeston Junction.
								Erewash Furnaces	Notts	Mid.	Near Trowell.
								Trowell Moor Colliery— Cossall Colliery Co.'s Sid	Notts	Mid.	Trowell Junction and Radford.
								Dunn Bros.' Siding	Notts	Mid.	Radford and Trowell Branch.
								Trowell Moor Colliery— Cossall Colliery Co.'s Siding	Notts	Mid.	Trowell.
								Dunn Bros.' Siding	Notts	Mid.	Trowell.
								Trower's Siding	Surrey	S. E. & C.	Red Hill.
								Trowse	Norfolk	G. E.	See Norwich.
								Troy	Mon	G. W.	See Monmouth.
								Trubshaw Sidings	Staffs	N. S.	Harecastle.
								Pooley & Son's Works	Staffs	N. S.	Trubshaw Sidings.
								Settle's, J., Siding	Staffs	N. S.	Trubshaw Sidings.
								Truman, Hanbury & Buxton's Siding (Mid.)	Staffs	Mid.—LNW—GN—NS	Burton-on-Trent.
G	P	F	L	H	C	12	0	Truro	Cornwall	G. W.	Plymouth and Penzance.
G						4	0	Newham	Cornwall	G. W.	Branch from Penwithers Junction.
G	P							Trusham	Devon	G. W.	Heathfield and Ashton.
								Trusty Engine Works	Glo'ster	Mid.	Same as Shillingford Engineering Works (Cheltenham).
								Truswell Brewery Co.'s Sid.	Lincoln	G. C.	Barnetby.
								Tryddyn Lodge Siding	Flint	L. & N. W.	Same as Alyn Brick Tile & Terra-Cotta Co.'s Siding (Coed Talon).
								Trye's Siding (Mid.)	Warwick	Mid.—L. & N. W.	Stockingford.
G	P							Tryfan Junction Station	Carnarvon	No. Wales N. G.	Dinas and Snowdon.
G	P	F	L	H	C	1	0	Tuam	Galway	G. S. & W.	Athenry and Claremorris.
G	P		L					Tubber (G. S. & W.)	Galway	G. S. & W. / M. G. W.	Ennis and Athenry. Over G. S. & W. from Athenry.
G	P	F	L	H	C	3	0	Tubbercurry	Sligo	G. S. & W.	Collooney and Claremorris.
								Tube Siding & Depôt	Staffs	G. W.	Wednesbury.
								Tubs Hill	Kent	S. E. & C.	See Sevenoaks.
								Tucker's Brick & Tile Siding	Leicester	G. C.	Loughborough.
								Tuckingmill Yard	Cornwall	G. W.	Carn Brea.
								Tudhoe & Sunderland Bridge Gas Works	Durham	N. E.	Spennymoor.
								Tudhoe Blast Furnaces	Durham	N. E.	Spennymoor.
								Tudhoe Colliery, Coke Ovens and Brick Works	Durham	N. E.	Spennymoor.
								Tudhoe Grange Colliery and Coke Ovens	Durham	N. E.	Spennymoor.
								Tudhoe Iron & Steel Works	Durham	N. E.	Spennymoor.
								Tudhoe Iron Works	Durham	N. E.	Same as Carbo Syndicate Works (Spennymoor).
								Tudhoe Slag Works	Durham	N. E.	Spennymoor.
								Tudor Siding	Carnarvon	L. & N. W.	Same as Jones & Ingham's Siding (Groeslon).
								Tue Brook	Lancs	L. & N. W.	See Liverpool.
								Tuffley Docks Branch	Glo'ster	Mid.	Gloucester.
								Tuffley Wharf	Glo'ster	Mid.	Gloucester.
								Tufnell Park	Middlesex	G. E.	See London.
								Tufnell Park Junction	Middlesex	G. E.—T. & H. Jt.	London, Junction Road and Upper Holloway.
								Tufts Junctions	Gloucester	S. & Wye Jt. (G W & Mid)	Whitecroft and Lydney.
								Tugby & Co.'s Pipe Wks(Mid.)	Leicester	Mid.—L. & N. W.	Moira.
G	P	F	L	H	C	0	18	Tullamore	Kings	G. S. & W.	Portarlington and Athlone.

EXPLANATION— G *Goods Station.*   P *Passenger and Parcel Station.*   P* *Passenger, but not Parcel or Miscellaneous Traffic.*   F *Furniture Vans, Carriages, Portable Engines, and Machines on Wheels.*   L *Live Stock.*   H *Horse Boxes and Prize Cattle Vans.*   C *Carriages by Passenger Train.*

STATION ACCOMMODATION.						CRANE POWER.	STATIONS, &c.	COUNTY.	COMPANY.	POSITION.
						Tons Cwts.				
G	P	.	L	H	.	1 10	Tullibardine	Perth	Cal.	Crieff Junction and Crieff.
.	.	.	.	.	.		Tullibody	Clackman'	N. B.	See Cambus (for Tullibody).
G	P	F	L	H	C	1 10	Tulloch	Inverness	N. B.	Crianlarich and Fort William.
.	.	.	.	.	.		Tulloch Siding	Perth	Cal.	Perth, North.
G	P	F	L	H	C		Tullow	Carlow ...	G. S. & W.	Terminus.
G	P	.	.	.	.		Tullygarth Colliery	Clackman'	N. B.	Clackmannan Road.
G	P	.	.	.	.		Tullymurry	Down	B. & C. D.	Downpatrick and Newcastle.
.	P	.	.	.	.	}	Tulse Hill (L. B. & S. C.) ...	Surrey	L. B. & S. C.	East Dulwich and Streatham.
.	.	.	.	.	.				L. & S. W.	Over L. B. & S.C. from Streatham Jn.
G	.	.	.	.	.		Tulse Hill Junction	Surrey ...	L. B. & S. C.—S. E. & C.	Tulse Hill and Herne Hill.
.	.	.	.	.	.		Tumble	Carmarth'	L. & M. M.	Llanelly and Cross Hands.
.	.	.	.	.	.		Canaan Colliery	Carmarth'	L. & M. M.	Tumble.
.	.	.	.	.	.		Great Mountain Colliery ...	Carmarth'	L. & M. M.	Tumble.
.	.	.	.	.	.		Little Mountain Colliery ...	Carmarth'	L. & M. M.	Tumble.
							TUNBRIDGE WELLS—			
G	P	F	L	H	C	10 0	} (Station, L. B. & S. C.) ...	Kent	L. B. & S. C.................	London and Tunbridge Wells direct Line.
.	P*	.	.	.	.				S. E. & C.	Over L. B. & S. C. from Tunbridge Wells Junction.
G	P	F	L	H	C	8 0	(Station)	Kent	S. E. & C.	Tonbridge and Hastings.
.	.	.	.	.	.		Gas Siding	Kent	S. E. & C.	Tunbridge Wells.
.	.	.	.	.	.		Junction	Kent	L. B. & S. C.—S. E. & C.	L. B. & S. C. and S. E. & C. Stations.
.	.	.	.	.	.		Tunnel End Siding	Lancs	L. & N. W.	Stalybridge.
.	.	.	.	.	.		Silkstone Coal Co.	Lancs	L. & N. W.	Tunnel End Siding.
.	.	.	.	.	.		Tunnel Junction..................	Worcester	G. W.	Worcester.
.	.	.	.	.	.		Tunnel, North Siding	Glamorg'n	Rhy.	Caerphilly.
.	.	.	.	.	.		Tunnel Pit	Glamorg'n	G. W.	Abernant.
.	.	.	.	.	.		Tunnel Pit	Glamorg'n	T. B. Jt. (G. W. & Rhy.)	See Guest, Keen, & Nettlefold (Cwm Bargoed).
.	.	.	.	.	.		Tunnel Pit (B. & M.)	Glamorg'n	B. & M.—L. & N. W. ...	See Guest, Keen & Nettlefold (Dowlais).
.	.	.	.	.	.		Tunnel Pit (Mid.)	Warwick..	Mid.—L. & N. W.	See Hickman's, Sir A. (Stockingford).
.	.	.	.	.	.		Tunnel Road Mineral Yard...	Cheshire...	{ B'head Jt(GW&L&NW)	Birkenhead, Cathcart Street.
.	.	.	.	.	.				C.L.C.(G.C,G.N,&Mid.)	Birkenhead, Shore Road.
G	P	F	L	H	C	5 0	Tunstall	Staffs	N. S.	Burslem and Kidsgrove.
.	.	.	.	.	.		Chatterley - Whitfield Collieries Siding	Staffs	N. S.	Pinnox Junction.
.	.	.	.	.	.		Pinnox Junction	Staffs	N. S.	Tunstall.
.	.	.	.	.	.		Tunstall & Co.'s Chemical Wks	Yorks	Mid.	Leeds, Newlay and Horsforth.
.	.	.	.	.	.		Tunstall Coal & Iron Co.'s Sid	Staffs	N. S.	See Chell Sidings (Black Bull).
.	.	.	.	.	.		Tunstill's Siding	Lancs	L. & Y.	Brierfield.
.	.	.	.	.	.		Tupper & Co.'s Britannia Wks	Staffs	L. & N. W.	Albion.
.	.	.	.	.	.		Turdees Branch Junction ...	Lanark ...	Cal.	Extension from Salisburgh.
.	.	.	.	.	.		Turnbull's Siding	Lanark ...	N. B.	Bishopbriggs.
.	.	.	.	.	.		Turnchapel	Devon ...	L. & S.W.	See Plymouth.
.	.	.	.	.	.		Turner & Moss' Siding.........	Lancs	L. & N. W.	Garston Docks.
.	.	.	.	.	.		Turner & Son's Lime Siding	Yorks	G. C.	Kiveton Park.
.	.	.	.	.	.		Turner & Sons' Siding	Edinboro'	N. B.	Edinburgh, Gorgie.
.	.	.	.	.	.		Turner & Son's Siding	Sussex	L. B. & S. C.	Sheffield Park.
.	.	.	.	.	.		Turner, Nott, & Co.	Glo'ster ...	G. W. — Mid.	Gloucester Docks.
.	.	.	.	.	.		Turner's, G. R., Wagon Wks.	Derby	Mid.	Langley Mill and Eastwood.
.	.	.	.	.	.		Turner's, J., Siding	Derby	Mid.	Chesterfield.
.	.	.	.	.	.		Turner's Lane Junction	Yorks	L. & Y.	Wakefield.
.	.	.	.	.	.		Turner's (New) Siding (G.C.)	Notts	G. C.—G. N.—Mid.	Worksop.
.	.	.	.	.	.		Turner's Siding	Flint	L. & N. W.	See Dundas Siding (Queensferry).
.	.	.	.	.	.		Turner's Siding	Herts	L. & N. W.	Watford.
.	.	.	.	.	.		Turner's Siding	Lancs	L. & N. W.	Patricroft.
.	.	.	.	.	.		Turner's Siding	Lancs	L. & N. W.	Preston, Charles Street.
.	.	.	.	.	.		Turner's Siding (L. & Y.)	Yorks	L. & Y.—G. N.	Dewsbury.
.	.	.	.	.	.		Turner's Stone Saw Mills ...	Glo'ster ...	S.&Wye Jt. (G.W & Mid.)	Milkwall.
.	.	.	.	.	.		Turner's Stone Yard...........	Glamorg'n	G. W.	See Canton Siding (Cardiff).
.	.	.	.	.	.		Turner's Tramway Siding ...	Staffs	L. & N. W.	Bloxwich.
.	.	.	.	.	.		Turney & Co.'s Works	Staffs	G. W.	Stourbridge.
.	P	.	.	.	.	{	Turnham Green (L. & S. W.)	Middlesex	L. & S. W.	London (Kensington) and Richmond.
									G. W.—Met	Over L&SW from Hammersmith Jn.
									Met. Dist.	Over L. & S. W. Line.
.	.	.	.	.	.		Turnham Green Junction ...	Middlesex	L. & S.W.—Met. Dist. ...	London, Turnham Green and Chiswick Park.
G	P	F	L	H	C	3 0	Turnhouse	Edinboro'	N. B.	Haymarket and Dalmeny.
G	P	F	L	H	C	1 5	Turriff	Aberdeen	G. N. of S.	Inveramsay and Macduff.
.	.	.	.	.	.		Tursdale Col. & Coke Works	Durham ...	N. E.	West Cornforth.
G	P	.	L	H	C	10 0	Turton & Edgworth	Lancs	L. & Y.	Bolton and Blackburn.

EXPLANATION—G *Goods Station.*   P *Passenger and Parcel Station.*   P* *Passenger, but not Parcel or Miscellaneous Traffic.*
F *Furniture Vans, Carriages, Portable Engines, and Machines on Wheels.*   L *Live Stock.*
H *Horse Boxes and Prize Cattle Vans.*   C *Carriages by Passenger Train.*

STATION ACCOMMODATION.						CRANE POWER.		STATIONS, &c.	COUNTY.	COMPANY.	POSITION.
						Tons	Cwts.				
G	P	F	L	H	C	.	.	Turvey	Beds	Mid.	Bedford and Northampton.
								Tushingham Bros.' Bk. Wks.	Lancs	L. & N. W.	Huyton Quarry.
G	P	F	L	H	C	10	0	Tutbury (N. S.)	Derby	N. S.	Derby and Uttoxeter.
	P									G. N.	Over N. S. from Egginton Junc.
G	P	F	L	H	C	10	0			L. & N. W.	Over N. S. Line.
.	.	.	.	.	.	.	.	Scropton Siding	Derby	N. S.	Tutbury and Sudbury.
.	.	.	.	.	.	.	.	Tuthil Limestone Quarries ...	Durham ...	N. E.	Haswell.
								TUXFORD—			
G	P	F	L	H	C	3	0	(Station)	Notts	L. D. & E. C.	Edwinstowe and Lincoln.
G	P	F	L	H	C	5	0	(Station, G. N.)	Notts	G. N.	Newark and Retford.
G	.	F	L	.	.	5	0			L. & N. W.	Over G. N. fr. Bottesford North Jn.
.	P	.	.	.	.	.	.	Dukeries Junction Station	Notts	G. N.	Crow Park and Tuxford.
.	P	.	.	.	.	.	.			L. D. & E. C.	Edwinstowe and Lincoln.
.	.	.	.	.	.	.	.	East Markham Siding	Notts	G. N.	Tuxford and Retford.
.	.	.	.	.	.	.	.	Exchange Yard	Notts	G. N.	Crow Park and Tuxford.
.	.	.	.	.	.	.	.	Junction	Notts	G. N.—L. D. & E. C. ...	Tuxford,G. N.& Tuxford, L.D.&E.C.
								Tweddle, A., & Co.'s Coal			
.	.	.	.	.	.	.	.	Dust Mill	Durham ...	N. E.	Hartlepool.
.	.	.	.	.	.	.	.	Tweedale & Smalley's Siding	Lancs	L. & Y.	Castleton.
.	.	.	.	.	.	.	.	Tweed Dock	Northumb	N. E.	Tweedmouth.
G	P	F	L	H	C	7	0	Tweedmouth	Northumb	N. E.	Berwick and Newcastle.
.	.	.	.	.	.	.	.	Allan Bros.' Siding	Northumb	N. E.	Tweedmouth.
.	.	.	.	.	.	.	.	Dixon, J., & Co.'s Siding...	Northumb	N. E.	Tweedmouth.
.	.	.	.	.	.	.	.	Scremerston Colliery	Northumb	N. E.	Tweedmouth and Scremerston.
.	.	.	.	.	.	.	.	Short, H. O., & Son's Sid.	Northumb	N. E.	Tweedmouth.
.	.	.	.	.	.	.	.	Tweed Dock	Northumb	N. E.	Tweedmouth.
.	.	.	.	.	.	.	.	West Ord Siding	Northumb	N. E.	Tweedmouth and Velvet Hall.
.	.	.	.	.	.	.	.	Twentieth Mile Siding	Herts	G. N.	See Smarts' (Hatfield).
G	P	.	L	.	.	1	5	Twenty	Lincoln ...	Mid. & G. N. Jt.	Spalding and Bourne.
.	.	.	.	.	.	.	.	Twenty Foot River Siding ...	Cambs ...	G. N. & G. E. Jt.	See Guyhirne.
.	P	.	.	.	.	.	.	Twerton-on-Avon	Somerset..	G. W.	Bristol and Bath.
G	P	F	L	H	C	10	0	Twickenham	Middlesex	L. & S.W.	Richmond and Staines.
G	P	.	L	.	.	.	.	Twizell	Northumb	N. E.	Berwick and Coldstream.
.	.	.	.	.	.	.	.	Twizell Colliery	Durham ...	N. E.	Pelton.
.	.	.	.	.	.	.	.	Two Mile Bottom Siding......	Norfolk ...	G. E.	See Fison & Son's (Thetford).
.	.	.	.	.	.	.	.	Two Pot House Siding......	Cork	G. S. & W.	Mallow.
.	.	.	.	.	.	.	.	Twrch Brick Co.'s Siding(Mid)	Glamorg'n	Mid.—G. W.—L. & N. W.	Gurnos.
G	P	F	L	H	C	4	0	Twyford	Berks	G. W.	Reading and Maidenhead.
.	.	.	.	.	.	.	.	Davis Mill Siding	Berks	G. W.	Twyford.
.	.	.	.	.	.	.	.	Twyford	Hants	L. & S.W.	See Shawford and Twyford.
.	.	.	.	.	.	.	.	Twyford Abbey	Middlesex	Met. Dist.	See Park Royal & Twyford Abbey.
.	.	.	.	.	.	.	.	Twyford's Works	Staffs	N. S.	Stoke.
G	P	.	.	.	.	.	.	Twywell	N'hamptn	Mid.	Kettering and Thrapston.
.	.	.	.	.	.	.	.	Islip Iron Co.'s Siding	N'hamptn	Mid.	Twywell and Thrapston.
.	.	.	.	.	.	.	.	Twywell Brick Co.'s Siding	N'hamptn	Mid.	Twywell and Cranford.
.	.	.	.	.	.	.	.	Tycoch Junction	Carmarth'	B. P. & G. V.—G. V. ...	Pontyeats and Kidwelly Junction.
G	P	.	L	.	.	1	10	Ty Croes	Anglesey..	L. & N. W.	Bangor and Holyhead.
G	P	.	L	.	.	.	.	Tydd	Cambs ...	Mid. & G. N. Jt.	Wisbech and Sutton Bridge.
.	.	.	.	.	.	.	.	Tydfil Engineering Co.'s Sid.	Glamorg'n	G W—L N W—Rhy—T V	Cardiff.
.	.	.	.	.	.	.	.	Tydraw Colliery	Glamorg'n	T. V.	See Cory Bros. & Co. (Treherbert).
.	.	.	.	.	.	.	.	Tygwynbach Colliery	Glamorg'n	G. W.—P. T.	Maesteg.
.	.	.	.	.	.	.	.	Tygwyn Llantwit Colliery ...	Mon	G. W.	Pontnewynydd.
.	.	.	.	.	.	.	.	Ty-Isaf Quarry	Glamorg'n	N. & Brecon.	Cilfrew.
.	.	.	.	.	.	.	.	Tyisha Saw Mills	Carmarth'	G. W.	Llangennech.
G	P	F	L	H	C	5	0	Tyldesley	Lancs	L. & N. W.	Manchester and Wigan.
								Astley & Tyldesley Coal &			
.	.	.	.	.	.	.	.	Salt Co.'s Jackson's Sid.	Lancs	L. & N. W.	Tyldesley and Leigh.
								Earl of Ellesmere's—			
.	.	.	.	.	.	.	.	Ellenbrook Colliery	Lancs	L. & N. W.	Tyldesley and Ellenbrook.
.	.	.	.	.	.	.	.	Sanderson Siding	Lancs	L. & N. W.	Walkden and Worsley.
.	.	.	.	.	.	.	.	Walkden Colliery	Lancs	L. & N. W.	Little Hulton and Walkden.
.	.	.	.	.	.	.	.	Green's Siding................	Lancs	L. & N. W.	Tyldesley and Ellenbrook.
.	.	.	.	.	.	.	.	Ramsden's Shakerley Col.	Lancs	L. & N. W.	Green's Siding.
								Tyldesley Cl. Co.'s Tyldes-			
.	.	.	.	.	.	.	.	ley Colliery	Lancs	L. & N. W.	Green's Siding.
.	.	.	.	.	.	.	.	Tyldesley Gas Works	Lancs	L. & N. W.	Tyldesley and Ellenbrook.
								Tyldesley Coal Co.—			
.	.	.	.	.	.	.	.	Peelwood Colliery	Lancs	L. & Y.	Atherton (Central).
.	.	.	.	.	.	.	.	Tyldesley Colliery	Lancs	L. & N. W.	See Green's Siding (Tyldesley).
.	.	.	.	.	.	.	.	Tyle Mill Siding	Berks	G. W.	Theale.
.	.	.	.	.	.	.	.	Tylerybont Lime Sidings......	Glamorg'n	B. & M.	See Guest, Keen and Nettlefold (Dowlais).

EXPLANATION—G *Goods Station.*   P *Passenger and Parcel Station.*   P* *Passenger, but not Parcel or Miscellaneous Traffic*
F *Furniture Vans, Carriages, Portable Engines, and Machines on Wheels.*   L *Live Stock.*
H *Horse Boxes and Prize Cattle Vans.*   C *Carriages by Passenger Train.*

Station Accommodation.						Crane Power.	STATIONS, &c.	COUNTY.	COMPANY.	POSITION.
						Tons Cwts.	Tylor's Siding	Glamorg'n	T. V.	See Davis & Sons' Ferndale Nos. 6 & 7 Collieries (Ferndale).
	P						Tylorstown	Glamorg'n	T. V.	Ferndale and Porth.
							Tylorstown Siding	Glamorg'n	T. V.	Ferndale.
G	P						Tylwch	Montgom	Cam.	Llanidloes and Builth Wells.
							Penpontbren Siding	Montgom	Cam.	Llanidloes and Tylwch.
							Tymawr Colliery	Glamorg'n	T. V.	Hafod.
							Tymawr Siding	Carmarth'	B. P. & G. V.	Burry Port.
							Tymm's Siding	Cheshire	Mac. Com. (G. C. & N. S.)	Marple, Rose Hill.
G	P		L			2 10	Tynan	Armagh	Clogher Valley	Adjoining G. N. (I.) Station.
G	P		L			5 0	Tynan and Caledon	Armagh	G. N. (I.)	Clones and Armagh.
							Tyndall Street	Glamorg'n	L. & N. W.	See Cardiff.
							Tyndall Street Junction	Glamorg'n	G. W.—Cardiff	Cardiff.
							Tyndall Street Junction	Glamorg'n	Rhy.—Cardiff	Cardiff.
G	P	F	L	H	C		Tyndrum	Perth	{ Cal. / N. B.	Callander and Oban. / Crianlarich and Fort William.
G	P	F	L	H	C					
							Tyne Bolt and Rivet Works	Durham	N. E.	Redheugh.
							Tynecastle Siding	Edinboro'	Cal.	Edinburgh, Lothian Road.
G	P					10 0	Tyne Dock	Durham	N. E.	Near South Shields.
							Fownes Forge & Engineering Co.'s Siding	Durham	N. E.	Tyne Dock.
							Hedworth Barium Co.'s Sid.	Durham	N. E.	Tyne Dock.
G	P		L	H			Tynehead	Edinboro'	N. B.	Edinburgh and Galashiels.
G	P	F	L	H	C	3 0	Tynemouth	Northumb	N. E.	{ North Shields and Cullercoats. / Branch—North Shields and Tynemouth, Passengers.
		F	L	H						
							Tynemouth, B. & T., Coal Depôts	Northumb	N. E.	Tynemouth.
							Tynemouth, B. & T., Manure Loading Wharf	Northumb	N. E.	Tynemouth.
							Tynemouth Road Coal Depôt	Northumb	N. E.	Tynemouth.
							North Shields and Tynemouth Coal Co.	Northumb	N. E.	Tynemouth Road Coal Depôt.
							Northumberland and Durham Coal Co.	Northumb	N. E.	Tynemouth Road Coal Depôt.
							Tyne River Commissioners' Siding	Northumb	N. E.	Tynemouth.
							Tynemouth Gas Co.'s Siding	Northumb	N. E.	North Shields.
							Tyne Pontoon Co.'s Siding	Northumb	N. E.	Carville.
							Tyneside Engineering Co's Sid	Glamorg'n	G W—LNW—Rhy—T V	Cardiff.
							Tynewydd Colliery (Troedyrhiew Colliery)	Glamorg'n	T. V.	Porth.
							Tynewydd Col. & Coke Ovens	Glamorg'n	G. W.	Ogmore Vale.
							Tynewydd Tin Works Siding	Mon	G. W.	Upper Pontnewydd.
							Tyning's Colliery	Somerset	G. W.—S. & D. Jt.	Radstock.
							Tynybedw Colliery	Glamorg'n	T. V.	See Cory Bros. & Co. (Treorchy).
							Tynycaeau Junction	Glamorg'n	Barry	Creigiau and St. Fagans.
							Tynycoed Junction	Glamorg'n	G. W.	Tondu and Llanharan.
							Tynycwm Quarry	Glamorg'n	{ P. T. / S. Wales Min.	Cwmavon. / Briton Ferry and Cymmer.
							Tyn-y-ffram Siding	Glamorg'n	P. T.	Port Talbot, Central.
							Tyre Mill (L. & N. W.)	Mon	L. & N. W.—G. W.	See Blaenavon Iron Wks (Blaenavon)
							Tyson & Bradley's Chemical Works	Derby	Mid.	Chesterfield.
G	P						Tytherington	Glo'ster	Mid.	Yate and Thornbury.
							Hardwicke Quarry (Tytherington Stone Co.)	Glo'ster	Mid.	Tytherington and Thornbury.
							Ty Trist Colliery	Mon	L. & N. W.	See Tredegar Ir. & Cl. Co. (Tredegar).
							Tyzack, Sam, & Co.'s Works	Durham	N. E.	Sunderland, Monkwearmouth.

U

							Ubberley Colliery	Staffs	N. S.	See Chatterley-Whitfield Collieries (Adderley Green).
G	P		L	H	C	5 0	Uckfield	Sussex	L. B. & S. C.	Lewes and Buxted.
							Uddens Siding	Dorset	L. & S. W.	{ Ringwood. / Wimborne.

STATION ACCOMMODATION.						CRANE POWER.	STATIONS, &c.	COUNTY.	COMPANY.	POSITION.
						Tons Cwts.	UDDINGSTON—			
G	P	F	L	H	C	4 10	(Station)	Lanark	Cal.	Motherwell and Rutherglen.
G	P	F	L	H	C	3 0	(Station)	Lanark	N. B.	Shettleston Junction and Bothwell.
.	.	.	.	.	.	. .	Blantyre Farm Colliery	Lanark	Cal.	Uddingston and Newton.
.	.	.	.	.	.	. .	Bothwell Park Brick Works and Quarry	Lanark	Cal.	Motherwell and Fallside.
.	.	.	.	.	.	. .	Bothwell Park Colliery	Lanark	Cal.	Motherwell and Fallside.
.	.	.	.	.	.	. .	Douglas Park Col. & Qry.	Lanark	Cal.	Motherwell and Fallside.
.	.	.	.	.	.	. .	East Parkhead Colliery	Lanark	Cal.	Motherwell and Fallside.
.	.	.	.	.	.	. .	Fallside Qry. & Brick Wks.	Lanark	Cal.	Fallside and Uddingston.
.	.	.	.	.	.	. .	Hamilton Palace Colliery	Lanark	Cal.	Motherwell and Fallside.
.	.	.	.	.	.	. .	Orbiston Colliery	Lanark	Cal.	Motherwell and Fallside.
.	.	.	.	.	.	. .	Viewpark Colliery	Lanark	{ Cal. / N. B.	Bellshill and Uddingston. / Uddingston and Uddingston West.
.	P	.	.	.	.	. .	West	Lanark	N. B.	Maryville and Uddingston.
G	P	F	L	H	C	1 5	Udny	Aberdeen	G. N. of S.	Dyce and Fraserburgh.
.	.	.	.	.	.	. .	Udston Colliery	Lanark	Cal.	High Blantyre.
G	P	F	L	.	C	1 0	Uffculme	Devon	G. W.	Branch from Tiverton Junction.
G	P	.	.	H	.	1 10	Uffington	Berks	G. W.	Didcot and Swindon.
G	P	.	.	.	.	. .	Uffington and Barnack	N'hamptn	Mid.	Peterboro' and Stamford.
.	.	.	.	.	.	. .	Ufford Bridge Siding	N'hamptn	G. N.	See Barnack.
G	P	F	L	H	C	. .	Ulbster	Caithness	High. (W. & L.)	Wick and Lybster.
G	P	F	L	H	C	. .	Ulceby	Lincoln	G. C.	Barnetby and New Holland.
.	.	.	.	.	.	. .	Ulceby Junction	Lincoln	G. C.	Ulceby and Habrough.
G	P	.	L	.	.	. .			{ Cal.	Steamer from Oban.
G	P	.	L	.	C	. .	Ullapool	Ross & Cro'	{ High.	Steamer from Kyle of Lochalsh.
G	P	.	L	.	.	. .			{ N. B.	Steamer from Mallaig.
.	.	.	.	.	.	. .	Ullbank Branch	Cumb'land	WC&EJt. (Fur. & LNW)	See Millom and Askam Iron Co.'s Ullbank Branch (Gillfoot).
.	.	.	.	.	.	. .	Ullcoats Mining Co.'s Siding	Cumb'land	WC&EJt. (Fur. & LNW)	Gillfoot.
G	P	F	L	H	C	. .			{ N. E.	York and Church Fenton.
.	P	.	.	H	C	. .			{ G. C.	Over N E fr. Knottingley, Ferry Bge Jn
.	P	.	.	H	C	. .	Ulleskelf (N. E.)	Yorks	{ G. N.	Over N. E. and S. & K. Joint Lines.
.	P	.	.	.	.	. .			{ Mid.	Over N. E. Line.
G	P	F	L	H	C	1 10	Ullesthorpe and Lutterworth	Leicester	Mid.	Rugby and Leicester.
G	P	.	L	H	.	1 5	Ullock	Cumb'land	WC&EJt. (Fur. & LNW)	Bridgefoot and Moor Row.
.	.	.	.	.	.	. .	Ullswater Lake (L. & N. W.)	Cumb'land	L. & N.W.–C.K.& P.–N.E.	See Penrith (for Ullswater Lake).
G	P	F	L	H	C	5 0	Ulverston	Lancs	Furness	Grange and Dalton.
.	.	.	.	.	.	. .	Lindal Ore Depôt Mineral Sid (Ulverston Ore Depôt)	Lancs	Furness	Ulverston and Lindal.
.	.	.	.	.	.	. .	North Lonsdale Ir. Wks. Sid.	Lancs	Furness	Ulverston and Cark-in-Cartmel.
.	.	.	.	.	.	. .	Plumpton Siding	Lancs	Furness	Ulverston and Cark-in-Cartmel.
.	.	.	.	.	.	. .	Pollitt, S., & Co's Paper Wks.	Lancs	Furness	Ulverston Canal Branch.
.	.	.	.	.	.	. .	Ulverston Gas Works	Lancs	Furness	Ulverston Canal Branch.
.	.	.	.	.	.	. .	Ulverston Ore Depôt	Lancs	Furness	Same as Lindal Ore Depôt Mineral Siding (Ulverston).
G	P	F	L	H	C	5 0	Umberleigh	Devon	L. & S.W.	Exeter and Barnstaple.
.	.	.	.	.	.	. .	Underhill Mineral Siding	Cumb'land	Furness	Green Road.
.	.	.	.	.	.	. .	Underwood Chemical Works	Stirling	N. B.	Lennoxtown.
.	.	.	.	.	.	. .	Underwood Colliery	Derby	Mid.	See Barber, Walker & Co. (Langley Mill and Eastwood).
.	.	.	.	.	.	. .	Underwood Colliery	Notts	G. N.	Eastwood and Langley Mill.
.	.	.	.	.	.	. .	Underwood Mineral Depôt	Renfrew	Cal.	See Paisley.
.	.	.	.	.	.	. .	Union Cement Co.'s Siding	Northumb	N. E.	Willington Quay.
.	.	.	.	.	.	. .	Union Dock	Durham	N. E.	See West Hartlepool.
.	.	.	.	.	.	. .	Union Foundry	Yorks	G. N.	Bradford, Dudley Hill.
.	.	.	.	.	.	. .	Union Foundry	Yorks	N. E.	Stockton, South.
.	P	.	.	.	.	. .	Union Mills	I. of Man	I. of Man	Douglas and Peel.
.	.	.	.	.	.	. .	Union Mill Siding	Lancs	L. & Y.	Rawtenstall.
.	.	.	.	.	.	. .	Union Plate Glass Co.—			
.	.	.	.	.	.	. .	Siding	Lancs	L. & N. W.	St. Helens.
.	.	.	.	.	.	. .	Siding (Pocket Nook Works)	Lancs	G. C. (St. Helens Exten.)	St. Helens.
.	.	.	.	.	.	. .	Union Tube Works	Lanark	Cal.	Calder.
.	.	.	.	.	.	. .	United Alkali Co.—			
.	.	.	.	.	.	. .	Allhusen's Works	Durham	N. E.	Gateshead.
.	.	.	.	.	.	. .	Atlas Chemical Works	Lancs	L. & N. W.–S. & M. Jt.	Widnes.
.	.	.	.	.	.	. .	Baxter Works	Lancs	L. & N. W.	St. Helens.
.	.	.	.	.	.	. .	Bold Venture Siding	Derby	Mid.	Peak Forest.
.	.	.	.	.	.	. .	Central Stores	Lancs	L. & N. W.	St. Helens.
.	.	.	.	.	.	. .	Cowpen Salt Works	Durham	N. E.	Port Clarence.
.	.	.	.	.	.	. .	Fleetwood Salt Works or Burn Naze Siding	Lancs	P. & W. Jt. (L&Y&L&NW)	Fleetwood.

EXPLANATION—G Goods Station.   P Passenger and Parcel Station.   P* Passenger, but not Parcel or Miscellaneous Traffic.
F Furniture Vans, Carriages, Portable Engines, and Machines on Wheels.   L Live Stock.
H Horse Boxes and Prize Cattle Vans.   C Carriages by Passenger Train.

STATION ACCOMMODATION.						CRANE POWER.		STATIONS, &c.	COUNTY.	COMPANY.	POSITION.
						Tons	Cwts.	United Alkali Co.—continued.			
.	.	.	.	.	.	.	.	Friar's Goose Works	Durham ...	N. E.	Gateshead.
								Gaskell Deacon & Co.—			
.	.	.	.	.	.	.	.	North Shunt Siding	Lancs	L. & N. W.	Widnes.
.	.	.	.	.	.	.	.	No. 3 Works	Lancs	L. & N. W.—S. & M. Jt..	Widnes.
.	.	.	.	.	.	.	.	Station Siding	Lancs	L. & N. W.	Widnes.
.	.	.	.	.	.	.	.	Gerard's Bridge Works.....	Lancs	L. & N. W.	St. Helens.
.	.	.	.	.	.	.	.	Globe Works	Lancs	G. C. (St. Helens Exten.)	St. Helens.
.	.	.	.	.	.	.	.	Globe Works	Lancs	L. & N. W.	St. Helens.
.	.	.	.	.	.	.	.	Golding Davies Works	Lancs	L. & N. W.—S. & M. Jt..	Widnes.
.	.	.	.	.	.	.	.	Greenbank Works	Lancs	L. & N. W.	St. Helens.
.	.	.	.	.	.	.	.	Hall & Shaw's Works	Lancs	L. & N. W.—S. & M. Jt..	Widnes.
.	.	.	.	.	.	.	.	Hardshaw Brook East Wks.	Lancs	L. & N. W.	St. Helens.
.	.	.	.	.	.	.	.	Hardshaw Brook West Wks.	Lancs	L. & N. W.	St. Helens.
.	.	.	.	.	.	.	.	Hutchinson's Works	Lancs	L. & N. W.	Widnes.
.	.	.	.	.	.	.	.	Kurtz Waste Bank Siding	Lancs	L. & N. W.	St. Helens.
.	.	.	.	.	.	.	.	Kurtz Works	Lancs	L. & N. W.	St. Helens.
.	.	.	.	.	.	.	.	Lancashire Metal Works ...	Lancs	L. & N. W.—S. & M. Jt..	Widnes.
.	.	.	.	.	.	.	.	Liver Works, Nos. 1 & 2 Sids.	Lancs	L. & N. W.—S. & M. Jt..	Widnes.
.	.	.	.	.	.	.	.	McKechnie Works............	Lancs	L. & N. W.	St. Helens.
.	.	.	.	.	.	.	.	Mathieson's Works	Lancs	L. & N. W.—S. & M. Jt..	Widnes.
.	.	.	.	.	.	.	.	Mort Liddell Works	Lancs	L. & N. W.—S. & M. Jt..	Widnes.
								Muspratt's—			
.	.	.	.	.	.	.	.	Ash House Siding	Lancs	L. & N. W.	Widnes.
.	.	.	.	.	.	.	.	North Shunt Siding	Lancs	L. & N. W.	Widnes.
.	.	.	.	.	.	.	.	Siding	Flint	L. & N. W.	Flint.
.	.	.	.	.	.	.	.	Siding	Lancs	S. & M. Jt. (G. C. & Mid.)	Widnes.
.	.	.	.	.	.	.	.	South Siding	Lancs	L. & N. W.	Widnes.
								Pilkington's—			
.	.	.	.	.	.	.	.	Mersey Chemical Works	Lancs	L. & N. W.—S. & M. Jt..	Widnes.
.	.	.	.	.	.	.	.	Mersey Manure Works...	Lancs	L. & N. W.—S. & M. Jt..	Widnes.
.	.	.	.	.	.	.	.	Siding	Durham ...	N. E.	Hebburn.
.	.	.	.	.	.	.	.	Siding (G. E.)..................	Essex	G E—G N—L NW—Mid.	London, Silvertown.
								Sullivan's—			
.	.	.	.	.	.	.	.	Carbide Works	Lancs	L. & N. W.—S. & M. Jt..	Widnes.
.	.	.	.	.	.	.	.	Chemical Works............	Lancs	L. & N. W.—S. & M. Jt..	Widnes.
.	.	.	.	.	.	.	.	Coke Works	Lancs	L. & N. W.—S. & M. Jt..	Widnes.
.	.	.	.	.	.	.	.	Sutton Lodge Works.........	Lancs	L. & N. W.	St. Helens.
.	.	.	.	.	.	.	.	Tennant's Siding	Lanark ...	Cal.	Glasgow, Buchanan Street.
								Widnes Alkali Works—			
.	.	.	.	.	.	.	.	Lugsdale Siding	Lancs	L. & N. W.	Widnes.
.	.	.	.	.	.	.	.	North Shunt Siding	Lancs	L. & N. W.	Widnes.
.	.	.	.	.	.	.	.	Siding	Lancs	S. & M. Jt. (G. C. & Mid.)	Widnes.
.	.	.	.	.	.	.	.	South Siding	Lancs	L. & N. W.	Widnes.
.	.	.	.	.	.	.	.	Works	Ayr	G. & S.W.	Irvine Harbour.
.	.	.	.	.	.	.	.	United Minera Mining Co. ...	Denbigh...	G. W.	Minera.
.	.	.	.	.	.	.	.	Unity Brook Siding	Lancs	L. & Y.	See Clifton & Kersley Co. (Dixon Fold)
.	.	.	.	.	.	.	.	Universal Colliery	Glamorg'n	Rhy.	Senghenith.
								Universal Weldless Steel			
.	.	.	.	.	.	.	.	Tubes Co.'s Siding............	Derby	L. D. & E. C.	Chesterfield.
G	P	.	.	.	.	.	.	Unston	Derby	Mid.	Sheffield and Chesterfield.
								Unsworth and Cowburn's Brookside or Bugle Horn			
.	.	.	.	.	.	.	.	Colliery	Lancs	L. & N. W.	Wigan.
G	P	F	L	H	C	3	0	Up Exe and Silverton	Devon	G. W.	Exeter and Tiverton.
G	P	F	L	H	C	3	0	Uphall	L'lithgow	N. B.	Ratho and Bathgate, Upper.
.	.	.	.	.	.	.	.	Bangour Railway Sidings...	L'lithgow	N. B.	Uphall and Livingston.
.	.	.	.	.	.	.	.	Holmes Oil Works............	L'lithgow	N. B.	Drumshoreland and Uphall.
.	.	.	.	.	.	.	.	Pumpherston No. 2 Mine...	L'lithgow	N. B.	Branch—Uphall and East Calder.
								Pumpherston No. 4 Mine			
.	.	.	.	.	.	.	.	(Pumpherston Farm Sid.)	L'lithgow	N. B.	Branch—Uphall and East Calder.
.	.	.	.	.	.	.	.	Pumpherston No. 5 Mine...	L'lithgow	N. B.	Branch—Uphall and East Calder.
.	.	.	.	.	.	.	.	Pumpherston Oil Works ...	L'lithgow	N. B.	Branch—Uphall and East Calder.
.	.	.	.	.	.	.	.	Roman Camp Branch.........	L'lithgow	N. B.	Uphall and East Calder.
.	.	.	.	.	.	.	.	Uphall Oil Works	L'lithgow	N. B.	Uphall.
								Young's Oil Co.—			
.	.	.	.	.	.	.	.	Binny Quarry	L'lithgow	N. B.	Hopetoun Branch.
.	.	.	.	.	.	.	.	Castlehill Siding............	L'lithgow	N. B.	Hopetoun Branch.
.	.	.	.	.	.	.	.	Forkneuk Pit	L'lithgow	N. B.	Hopetoun Branch.
.	.	.	.	.	.	.	.	Hopetoun Mines	L'lithgow	N. B.	Hopetoun Branch.
								Hopetoun Oil Works			
.	.	.	.	.	.	.	.	(Niddry Oil Works) ...	L'lithgow	N. B.	Hopetoun Branch.

EXPLANATION—G *Goods Station.*   P *Passenger and Parcel Station.*   P* *Passenger, but not Parcel or Miscellaneous Traffic.*
F *Furniture Vans, Carriages, Portable Engines, and Machines on Wheels.*   L *Live Stock.*
H *Horse Boxes and Prize Cattle Vans.*   C *Carriages by Passenger Train.*

STATION ACCOMMODATION.						CRANE POWER.		STATIONS, &c.	COUNTY.	COMPANY.	POSITION.
						Tons	Cwts.				
.	.	.	.	.	.	.	.	Uphall Junction	L'lithgow	N. B.	Uphall and East Calder.
.	.	.	.	.	.	.	.	Uphill	Somerset..	G. W.	See Bleadon and Uphill.
.	.	.	.	.	.	.	.	Uphill Junction	Somerset..	G. W.	Weston-super-Mare and Bleadon.
G	P	.	.	.	.	.	.	Upholland	Lancs	L. & Y.	Wigan and Rainford.
.	.	.	.	.	.	.	.	Ditton Brook Siding	Lancs	L. & Y.	Upholland.
.	.	.	.	.	.	.	.	Upholland Coal and Brick Co.'s Siding	Lancs	L. & Y.	Upholland.
G	P	F	L	H	C	3	0	Uplawmoor	Renfrew..	Cal.	Giffen and Clarkston.
.	.	.	.	.	.	.	.	Upleatham Branch Junction	Yorks	N. E.	Lazenby and Redcar.
.	.	.	.	.	.	.	.	Upleatham Mines	Yorks	N. E.	Marske.
G	P	F	L	H	C	3	0	Upminster	Essex	L. T. & S.	Barking and Pitsea.
.	.	.	.	.	.	.	.	Upminster, East Junction ...	Essex	L. T. & S.	Upminster and East Horndon.
.	.	.	.	.	.	.	.	Upminster, West Junction ...	Essex	L. T. & S.	Hornchurch and Upminster.
.	.	.	.	.	.	.	.	Upper Abercynon	Glamorg'n	T. V.	Same as Traveller's Rest.
G	P	.	.	.	.	.	.	Upper Bank (Mid.)	Glamorg'n	{ Mid.	Swansea and Morriston.
										{ G. W.	Over Midland Line.
.	.	.	.	.	.	.	.	Baldwin's Ltd., Landore Steel Works or Swansea Hematite Iron Co.'s Siding (Mid.)	Glamorg'n	Mid.—G.W.—L. & N.W.	Upper Bank and Morriston.
.	.	.	.	.	.	.	.	British Mannesman Tube Co.'s Siding (Mid.)	Glamorg'n	Mid.—G.W.—L. & N.W.	Upper Bank and Morriston.
.	.	.	.	.	.	.	.	Llanerch Colliery (Foxhole Colliery Co.) (Mid.)	Glamorg'n	Mid.—G. W.—L. & N.W.	Near Upper Bank.
.	.	.	.	.	.	.	.	Pascoe, Grenfell & Son's Copper Works (Foster's, Wm., Siding) (Mid.)......	Glamorg'n	Mid.—G.W.—L. & N.W.	Near Upper Bank.
.	.	.	.	.	.	.	.	Swansea Harbour Trustees' Siding (Mid.)	Glamorg'n	Mid.—G. W.—L. & N.W.	Upper Bank and Morriston.
.	.	.	.	.	.	.	.	Vivian & Son's White Rock Siding (Mid.)	Glamorg'n	Mid.—G. W.—L & N.W.	Near Upper Bank.
.	.	.	.	.	.	.	.	Upper Bathgate..................	L'lithgow	N. B.	See Bathgate, Upper.
.	.	.	.	.	.	.	.	Upper Batley	Yorks	G. N.	See Batley, Upper.
.	.	.	.	.	.	.	.	Upper Bedwellty Siding	Mon	L. & N.W.	See Tredegar Ir. & Cl. Co. (Tredegar).
.	.	.	.	.	.	.	.	Upper Birchwood Colliery ...	Notts	Mid.	See Birchwood, Upper Col. (Pinxton).
G	P	.	L	.	.	5	0	Upper Birstal	Yorks	L. & N.W.	Cleckheaton and Leeds.
.	P	.	.	.	.	.	.	Upper Broughton	Notts	Mid.	Nottingham and Melton Mowbray.
.	.	.	.	.	.	.	.	Upper Cymmer Colliery	Glamorg'n	T. V.	See Cymmer, Upper Colliery (Porth).
.	.	.	.	.	.	.	.	Upper Edmonton	Middlesex	G. E.	See Silver Str. (for Upper Edmonton).
.	.	.	.	.	.	.	.	Upper Forest and Worcester Steel and Tin Plate Works (Mid.)	Glamorg'n	Mid.—G. W.—L, & N.W.	Morriston.
.	.	.	.	.	.	.	.	Upper Glynrhonwy Quarry Co.'s Siding	Carnarvon	L. & N. W.	See Cambrian Sidings (Llanberis).
.	.	.	.	.	.	.	.	Upper Greenock	Renfrew...	Cal.	See Greenock, Upper.
.	.	.	.	.	.	.	.	Upper Helensburgh	Dumbartn	N. B.	See Helensburgh, Upper.
.	.	.	.	.	.	.	.	Upper Holloway..................	Middlesex	Mid.—T. & H. Jt.	See London.
.	.	.	.	.	.	.	.	Upper John Street	Kilkenny..	G. S. & W.	Same as Kilkenny.
G	P	.	L	H	.	3	0	Upperlands	Derry	N. C. Com. (Mid.)	Macfin Junction and Magherafelt.
.	.	.	.	.	.	.	.	Upper Llwydcoed Colliery (Fothergill's)	Glamorg'n	G. W.	Llwydcoed.
.	.	.	.	.	.	.	.	Upper Lydbrook	Glo'ster ...	S & Wye Jt (G W & Mid.)	See Lydbrook, Upper.
G	P	.	.	.	.	5	0	Upper Mill	Yorks	L. & N.W.	Huddersfield and Stalybridge.
.	.	.	.	.	.	.	.	Upper Mineral Siding	Edinboro'	Cal.	Leith, North.
.	.	.	.	.	.	.	.	Upper Norwood	Surrey ...	S. E. & C.	See Crystal Palace & Upper Norwood.
G	P	.	L	.	.	2	0 }	Upper Pontnewydd (G. W.)	Mon	{ G. W.	Pontypool (Crane Str.) & Newport.
G						2	0 }			{ L. & N. W.	Over G. W. from Hereford.
.	.	.	.	.	.	.	.	Avondale Tin Plate Works	Mon	G. W.	Upper Pontnewydd.
.	.	.	.	.	.	.	.	Tynewydd Tin Works Sid.	Mon	G. W.	Upper Pontnewydd.
.	.	.	.	.	.	.	.	Upper Port Glasgow	Renfrew...	G. & S.W.	See Port Glasgow.
.	P	.	.	.	.	.	.	Upper Sydenham	Kent	S. E. & C.	Nunhead and Crystal Palace.
.	.	.	.	.	.	.	.	Upperton Siding	Lanark ...	N. B.	Rawyards.
.	.	.	.	.	.	.	.	Upper Tooting	Surrey ...	L. B. & S. C.	Same as Balham.
G	P	F	L	H	C	5	0	Upper Warlingham	Surrey ...	C. & O. Jt. (L. B. & S. C. and S. E. & C.)	Croydon and Oxted.
.	.	.	.	.	.	.	.	Nichol's Lime Siding	Surrey ...	C. & O. Jt. (L. B. & S. C. and S. E. & C.)	Upper Warlingham.
.	.	.	.	.	.	.	.	Upper Wellwood No. 1........	Ayr	G. & S.W.	Muirkirk.
.	.	.	.	.	.	.	.	Upper Widnes Chemical Wks	Lancs	S. & M. Jt. (G. C. & Mid.)	Widnes.
G	P	F	L	H	C	5	0	Uppingham	Rutland ...	L. & N. W.	Branch from Seaton.
.	.	.	.	.	.	.	.	Uppingham	Rutland ...	Mid.	See Manton (for Uppingham).
G	P	.	L	H	.	1	0	Upton	Berks	G. W.	Didcot and Newbury.

EXPLANATION—G *Goods Station.*   P *Passenger and Parcel Station.*   P* *Passenger, but not Parcel or Miscellaneous Traffic*
F *Furniture Vans, Carriages, Portable Engines, and Machines on Wheels.*   L *Live Stock.*
H *Horse Boxes and Prize Cattle Vans.*   C *Carriages by Passenger Train.*

STATION ACCOMMODATION.						CRANE POWER.	STATIONS, &c.	COUNTY.	COMPANY.	POSITION.
G	P	F	L	H	C	Tons Cwts. 5 0	Upton	Cheshire...	N.W. & L. Jt. (G. C. and W. M. & C. Q.)	Neston and Birkenhead.
G	P	.	.	.	.	. .	Upton	Essex	G. E.	Same as Forest Gate.
G	P	.	.	.	.	. .	Upton and Innishannon	Cork	C. B. & S. C.	Cork and Bandon.
G	P	F	L	H	C	. .	Upton and North Elmsall ...	Yorks	H. & B.	Cudworth and Howden.
.	.	.	.	.	.	. .	Wrangbrook Siding	Yorks	H. & B.	Near Wrangbrook Junction.
G	P	F	L	H	C	. .	Upton Magna	Salop	S & W'tn Jt (GW & LNW)	Shrewsbury and Wellington.
G	P	F	L	H	C	5 0	Upton-on-Severn	Worcester	Mid.	Tewkesbury and Malvern.
.	P	.	.	.	.	. .	Upton Park	Essex	L. T. & S.	Plaistow and Barking.
G	.	.	.	.	.	. .	Upton Park Depôt	Essex	L. & N. W.	Over N. L. and L. T. & S. Lines.
.	.	.	.	.	.	. .	Upton Siding	Salop	G. W.	Shifnal.
.	.	.	.	.	.	. .	Upwell	Norfolk ...	G. E.	See Wisbech Tramway.
.	.	.	.	.	.	. .	Upwell Street Wharf	Yorks	Mid.	See Sheffield.
.	P	.	.	.	.	. .	Upwey Junction Station (GW)	Dorset......	{ G. W. .... L. & S. W.	Dorchester and Weymouth. Over G. W. from Dorchester June.
.	.	.	.	.	.	. .	Uralite Co.'s Siding	Kent	S. E. & C.	Gravesend, Central.
.	.	.	.	.	.	. .	Ure's Foundry	Stirling ...	Cal.	See Bonnybridge Foundry (Bonnybridge).
.	.	.	.	.	.	. .	Urlay Nook Siding and Depôt	Durham ...	N. E.	Eaglescliffe Junction Station.
G	P	F	L	H	C	5 0	Urmston	Lancs	C. L. C. (GC, GN, & Mid.)	Warrington & Manchester, Central.
.	.	.	.	.	.	. .	Urpeth Collieries (B. and C. Pits) and Coke Ovens	Durham ...	N. E.	Birtley.
G	P	F	L	H	C	1 5	Urquhart	Elgin&Mo'	G. N. of S.	Portsoy and Elgin.
.	P	.	.	.	.	. .	Ushaw Moor	Durham ...	N. E.	Durham, Pass. and Waterhouses.
.	.	.	.	.	.	. .	Ushaw Moor Col.& Coke Ovens	Durham ...	N. E.	Waterhouses.
.	.	.	.	.	.	. .	Usher & Co.'s Distillery	Edinboro'	N. B.	Edinburgh, St. Leonard's.
.	.	.	.	.	.	. .	Usher & Son's Brewery	Edinboro'	N. B.	Edinburgh, St. Leonard's.
G	P	F	L	H	C	5 0	Usk	Mon	G. W.	Pontypool Road and Monmouth.
.	.	.	.	.	.	. .	Davies' Siding	Mon	G. W.	Usk and Llandenny.
.	.	.	.	.	.	. .	Uskside Engineering and Rivet Works	Mon	G. W.	Newport, Dock Street.
.	.	.	.	.	.	. .	Usselby	Lincoln ...	G. C.	See Claxby and Usselby.
G	P	F	L	.	.	3 0	Usworth	Durham ...	N. E.	Washington and Pelaw.
.	.	.	.	.	.	. .	East House Depôts	Durham ...	N. E.	Usworth.
.	.	.	.	.	.	. .	Usworth Colliery	Durham ...	N. E.	Usworth.
G	P	F	L	H	C	5 0			{ N. S.	Derby and Stoke.
G	P	.	.	.	.		Uttoxeter (N. S.)	Staffs	G. N.	Over N. S. from Egginton Junction.
G	P	F	L	H	C	5 0			L. & N. W.	Over N. S. Line.
.	.	.	.	.	.	. .	Bamford & Son's Siding ...	Staffs	N. S.	Uttoxeter.
.	.	.	.	.	.	. .	Uveco Cereals Co.'s Siding ...	Cheshire...	B'head Jt—CLC—NW&L	Birkenhead.
G	P	F	L	H	C	3 0	Uxbridge	Middlesex	G. W.	Branch from West Drayton and Yiewsley.
.	.	.	.	.	.	. .	Uxbridge Road (for Shepherds Bush)	Middlesex	W Lon Jt (G W & L N W)	See London.
.	.	.	.	.	.	. .	Uxbridge Road Junction......	Middlesex	H. & C. Jt.—W. Lon. Jt.	London, Latimer Rd. & Kensington.

V

STATION ACCOMMODATION.						CRANE POWER.	STATIONS, &c.	COUNTY.	COMPANY.	POSITION.
G	P	.	.	.	.	. .	Valentia Harbour	Kerry	G. S. & W.	Terminus.
.	.	.	.	.	.	. .	Vale of Belvoir Plaster Co.'s Siding	Notts	G. N.	{ Same as Belvoir Plaster Co.'s Siding (Newark).
.	.	.	.	.	.	. .	Vale of Glamorgan Junction	Glamorg'n	Barry—G. W.	Bridgend.
.	.	.	.	.	.	. .	Vale of Mowbray Brewery (Plews & Son's)	Yorks	N. E.	Leeming Bar.
.	.	.	.	.	.	. .	Vale of Neath Brewery........	Glamorg'n	N. & Brecon	Neath.
.	.	.	.	.	.	. .	Vale Paper Works..............	Stirling ...	Cal.	Denny.
.	.	.	.	.	.	. .	Vallance Road Junction	Middlesex	Met. Dist.—W. & B. Jt.	London, Whitechapel.
G	P	F	L	H	C	1 10	Valley	Anglesey	L. & N. W.	Bangor and Holyhead.
.	.	.	.	.	.	. .	Gardner's Siding	Anglesey..	L. & N. W.	Valley and Holyhead.
.	.	.	.	.	.	. .	Valley	Yorks	Mid.	See Bradford.
.	.	.	.	.	.	. .	Valleyfield Siding	Edinboro'	N. B.	Penicuik.
.	.	.	.	.	.	. .	Van Lead Mines..................	Montgom	Cam. (Van).................	Branch from Caersws.
.	.	.	.	.	.	. .	Van Road..........................	Montgom	Cam. (Van).................	See Garth and Van Road.
.	.	.	.	.	.	. .	Varcoes Siding	Cornwall ..	G. W.	Drinnick Mill.
.	.	.	.	.	.	. .	Varley & Co.'s Waterloo Foundry	Lancs	GC(StHelen'sEx)—LNW	St. Helens.

EXPLANATION—G *Goods Station.*   P *Passenger and Parcel Station.*   P* *Passenger, but not Parcel or Miscellaneous Traffic.*
F *Furniture Vans, Carriages, Portable Engines, and Machines on Wheels.*   L *Live Stock.*
H *Horse Boxes and Prize Cattle Vans.*   C *Carriages by Passenger Train.*

STATION ACCOMMODATION.						CRANE POWER.		STATIONS, &c.	COUNTY.	COMPANY.	POSITION.
						Tons	Cwts.				
..	P	..	..	..	..	..	..	Varteg (L. & N. W.)............	Mon........	{ L. & N. W. .... { G. W.	Abersychan and Brynmawr. Over L. & N. W. from Abersychan & Talywain Junction.
..	..	..	..	..	..	..	..	Varteg Colliery	Glamorg'n	P. T.	Bryn.
..	..	..	..	..	..	..	..	Varteg Deep Black Vein Co.'s Lower Varteg Col. (G.W.)	Mon	G. W.—L. & N. W.	Abersychan and Talywain.
..	..	..	..	..	..	..	..	Varteg Hill Colliery	Mon	{ G. W. .... { L. & N. W.	Same as Vipond&Co.'sSid(Cwmavon) Same as Vipond & Co.'s Siding (Blaenavon).
..	..	..	..	..	..	..	..	Vauxhall	Norfolk ...	G. E.	See Yarmouth.
..	..	..	..	..	..	..	..	Vauxhall	Surrey	L. & S.W.	See London.
..	..	..	..	..	..	..	..	Vauxhall & Duddeston	Warwick..	L. & N. W.	See Birmingham.
..	..	..	..	..	..	..	..	Vauxhall Colliery	Denbigh ..	G. W.	Ruabon.
..	..	..	..	..	..	..	..	Vaynor	Glamorg'n	B. & M. & L. & N.W. Joint	See Pontsarn (for Vaynor).
..	..	..	..	..	..	..	..	Vaynor Limestone Quarry ...	Glamorg'n	B. & M. & L. & N.W. Joint	See Crawshay Bros. (Cefn).
..	..	..	..	..	..	..	..	Veasey, C., Siding............	Hunts	{ G. N. & G. E. Jt. ...... { Mid.	Godmanchester. Huntingdon.
..	..	..	..	..	..	..	..	Vedw Colliery.................	Mon	B. & M.	Machen.
..	..	..	..	..	..	..	..	Veitch, Moir & Erskine's Sid.	Edinboro'	N. B.	See Lindsay & Son's (Edinburgh).
..	..	..	..	..	..	..	..	Veitch's Siding	Perth	Cal.	Crieff.
..	..	..	..	..	..	..	..	Velinfran Col. (Richards, J. J., & Co's Bk. Wks.) (Mid.)	Glamorg'n	Mid.—G.W.—L. & N.W.	{ Llansamlet. { Six Pit Junction.
G	P	F	L	H	C	..	..	Velvet Hall	Northumb	N. E.	Berwick and Kelso.
..	..	..	..	..	..	..	..	West Ord Siding	Northumb	N. E.	Velvet Hall and Tweedmouth.
..	..	..	..	..	..	..	..	Venable's Siding	Staffs	{ G. N. .... { L. & N. W.	Stafford Common. Stafford.
G	P	..	L	..	..	2	0	Venn Cross	Devon	G. W.	Wiveliscombe and Dulverton.
..	..	..	..	..	..	..	..	Venning's Siding	Glamorg'n	Rhy.	See Leon's Crwys Siding (Cardiff).
G	P	F	L	H	C	10	0	Ventnor	I. of W....	I. of W.	Terminus.
G	P	F	L	H	C	..	..	Ventnor Town	I. of W....	I. of W. Cent	Terminus.
..	..	..	..	..	..	..	..	Verity's Wagon Works (G.C.)	Yorks	G. C.—Mid.	Mexboro'.
G	P	F	L	..	..	1	10	Verner's Bridge	Armagh ...	G. N. (I.)	Portadown and Dungannon.
..	..	..	..	..	..	..	..	Verney Junction	Bucks	L. & N. W.—Met.	Banbury and Aylesbury.
G G	P P	..	..	..	..	..	}	Verney Junction Station	Bucks	{ L. & N. W. .... { Met.	Bletchley and Oxford. Verney Junction and Winslow Rd.
..	..	..	..	..	..	..	..	Vernon & Son's Flour Mills...	Cheshire..	B'head Jt—CLC—NW&L	Birkenhead.
..	..	..	..	..	..	..	..	Vernon Patent Horse Shoe Co.'s Siding (N. B.)	Stirling ...	N. B.—Cal.	Falkirk, Grahamston.
..	..	..	..	..	..	..	..	Vernon Siding	Glamorg'n	R. & S. B.	Same as Ferry Tin Plate Works (Briton Ferry).
								Vernon's (Lord)—			
..	..	..	..	..	..	..	..	Coal Wharves	Cheshire...	L. & N. W.	Cheadle Hulme.
..	..	..	..	..	..	..	..	Coal Wharves	Cheshire...	L. & N. W.	Stockport, Edgeley.
..	..	..	..	..	..	..	..	Coal Wharves	Cheshire...	L. & N. W.	Macclesfield.
..	..	..	..	..	..	..	..	Poynton & Worth Colliery	Cheshire...	L. & N. W.—Mac. Com.	Poynton.
G	P	F	L	H	C	5	0	Verwood	Dorset	L. & S.W.	Salisbury and Wimborne.
..	..	..	..	..	..	..	..	Viaduct Colliery................	Mon	B. & M.	Maesycwmmer.
..	..	..	..	..	..	..	..	Viaduct Works Siding	Mon	G. W.	Blaendare Junction Station.
..	..	..	..	..	..	..	..	Vicarage Siding	Denbigh ..	G. W.	Minera.
..	..	..	..	..	..	..	..	Vicar Lane (L. & Y.)	Yorks	L. & Y.—L. & N. W. ...	See Bradford.
..	..	..	..	..	..	..	..	Vicars' Iron Works	Lancs	L. & N. W.	Earlestown.
..	..	..	..	..	..	..	..	Vickers & Son's Siding........	Lancs	L. & N. W.—S. & M. Jt.	Widnes.
..	..	..	..	..	..	..	..	Vicker's Quarry	Yorks	G. N.	Pudsey, Greenside.
..	..	..	..	..	..	..	..	Vicker's Siding	Cheshire...	L. & N. W.	Rookery Bridge.
								Vickers, Sons & Maxim's—			
..	..	..	..	..	..	..	..	Gun Range Siding...........	Cumb'land	Furness......................	Eskmeals.
..	..	..	..	..	..	..	..	Naval Construction Works	Lancs	Furness......................	See Barrow.
..	..	..	..	..	..	..	..	Siding (Mid.)	Yorks	Mid.—G. C.—L.D. & E.C.	Sheffield, Wicker.
..	..	..	..	..	..	..	..	Vi-Cocoa Siding (Tibble's) ...	Herts	L. & N. W.	See Bushey Lodge Siding (Watford).
..	P	..	..	..	..	..	..	Victoria	Cork	C. & Muskerry	Cork and Coachford Junction.
..	..	..	..	..	..	..	..	Victoria	Glamorg'n	L. & N. W.	See Swansea.
..	..	..	..	..	..	..	..	Victoria	Middlesex	L.B.&SC.—Met.Dist.— S.E.&C.—G.N.—G.W. —L. & N. W.—Mid.	} See London.
..	P	..	..	..	..	..	..	Victoria	Mon	G. W.	Aberbeeg and Ebbw Vale.
..	..	..	..	..	..	..	..	Victoria	Norfolk ...	G. E.	See Norwich.
..	..	..	..	..	..	..	..	Victoria	Notts	G. C. & G. N. Jt.	See Nottingham.
..	..	..	..	..	..	..	..	Victoria (G. C.)	Yorks	G. C.—G. N.—L. & Y.	See Sheffield.
..	..	..	..	..	..	..	..	Victoria (L. & Y.)	Lancs	L.&Y.—L.&N.W.—Mid.	See Manchester.
..	..	..	..	..	..	..	..	Victoria and Albert	Essex	G. W.	See London.
..	..	..	..	..	..	..	..	Victoria and Albert Docks ...	Essex	GE—GW—L&NW—Mid	See London.
..	..	..	..	..	..	..	..	Victoria Basin.................	Staffs	G. W.	Wolverhampton.

EXPLANATION—G *Goods Station.*   P *Passenger and Parcel Station.*   P* *Passenger, but not Parcel or Miscellaneous Traffic.*
F *Furniture Vans, Carriages, Portable Engines, and Machines on Wheels.*   L *Live Stock.*
H *Horse Boxes and Prize Cattle Vans.*   C *Carriages by Passenger Train.*

STATION ACCOMMODATION.						CRANE POWER.	STATIONS, &c.	COUNTY.	COMPANY.	POSITION.
						Tons Cwts.				
							Victoria Brick and Tile Co.'s Siding (May's Siding)	Somerset..	S. & D. Jt. (L.&S.W.&Mid)	Bath.
							Victoria Brick Co.'s Siding...	Yorks	N. E.	Castleford.
							Victoria Brick Works	Glamorg'n	Barry.	See Pwllgwaun Siding (Pontypridd).
							Victoria Brick Works	Staffs	L. & N. W.	Same as Beddow & Sons Sid. (Pelsall).
G	P					} 2 0 {	Victoria Bridge	Tyrone ...	{ C. & V. B. { G. N. (I.)	Junction with G. N. (I.).
G	P	F	L							Omagh and Strabane.
							Victoria Chemical Works	Lancs	L. & N. W.—S. & M. Jt.	Same as Bowman&Co'sSid. (Widnes).
							Victoria Coal Co.'s Siding	Yorks	L. & Y.	Wakefield.
							Victoria Colliery	Glamorg'n	G. W.	Blaengarw.
							Victoria Colliery	Glamorg'n	G. W.	Pontycymmer.
							Victoria Colliery	Lancs	L. & N. W.	Wigan.
							Victoria Colliery	Yorks	G. N.	Same as Haigh's Victoria Col. (Morley).
							Victoria Colliery	Yorks	Mid.	See Charlesworth's, J. & J. (Kilnhurst).
							Victoria Colliery (L. & Y.)	Yorks	L. & Y.—G. N.—N. E.	Same as Snydale Col. (Featherstone).
							Victoria Colliery (L. & N. W.)	Lancs	L&NW—GC. (Wigan Jn.)	See Wigan Coal & Iron Co. (Wigan).
							Victoria Col. Co.'s Victoria Col.	Lancs	G. C. (Wigan Jn.)	Hindley and Platt Bridge.
							Victoria Cotton Mills	Lancs	L. & N. W.	Same as Hayes Sid. (Leigh&Bedford).
							Victoria Depôts	Durham	N. E.	Sunderland, South Dock.
							Victoria Dock	Aberdeen	Cal.—N. B.	See Aberdeen.
							Victoria Dock	Edinboro'	Cal.—N. B.	See Leith.
							Victoria Dock	Forfar	Cal.—N. B.	See Dundee.
							Victoria Dock	Yorks	N. E.	See Hull.
							Victoria Dock (L. & I. Dks.)	Essex	L.&I.Dks—G.E—G.N.—G.W.—L.&N.W.—Mid	See London, Royal Victoria Dock.
							Victoria Dock Jetty	Edinboro'	Cal.—N. B.	See Leith.
							Victoria Docks	Essex	G. E.—G. N.—G. W.—L. & N. W.—Mid.	See London.
							Victoria Docks Junction	Essex	G. E.—Mid.	London, Canning Town and Custom House.
							Victoria Dock Sidings	Durham	N. E.	See Hartlepool.
							Victoria Dock Wharf	Edinboro'	Cal.	Leith, North.
							Victoria Dry Docks Co.—Albion Dry·Dock	Glamorg'n	GW—LNW—Mid—RSB	Swansea.
							Globe Dry Dock	Glamorg'n	GW—LNW—Mid—RSB	Swansea.
							Victoria Engine Works	Lanark	N. B.	Airdrie, North.
							Victoria Garesfield Col., Coke & Brick Wks (Highfield Sid)	Durham	N. E.	Rowlands Gill.
							Victoria Harbour	Renfrew	Cal.	See Greenock.
							Victoria Implement Works	Durham	N. E.	Darlington, Bank Top.
							Victoria Iron & Steel Works	Lanark	Cal.	Calder.
							Victoria Maltings	Fife	N. B.	Kirkcaldy.
							Victoria Mill	Lancs	P. & L. Jt. (L&NW&L&Y)	Same as Smith's Siding (Longridge).
							Victoria Mill Siding	Yorks	G. N.	Bramley.
							Victoria Park	Middlesex	G. E.—N. L.	See London.
							Victoria Park	Renfrew	N. B.	See Glasgow.
							Victoria Park or Hackney Wick Junction	Middlesex	G. E.—N. L.	London, Stratford and Hackney.
							Victoria Pits	Renfrew	G B & K Jt (Cal.&G&SW)	Nitshill.
							Victoria Road	Carmarth'	L. & M. M.	See Llanelly.
							Victoria Road	Glamorg'n	Swan. & Mum.	See Swansea.
							Victoria Saw Mills	Forfar	Cal.	Montrose.
							Victoria Siding	Cheshire	G. C.	Newton (for Hyde).
							Victoria Siding	Fife	N. B.	Kirkcaldy.
							Victoria Street Siding	Lancs	L. & N. W.—S. & M. Jt.	Same as Chapman's Siding (Widnes).
							Victoria Tube Works	Lanark	Cal.	Langloan.
							Victoria Wharf	Glamorg'n	GW—LNW—Mid—RSB	Swansea.
							Victoria Wharves	Glamorg'n	T. V.	Penarth Harbour.
							Victoria Works	Cheshire	L. & N. W.	Same as Cotton & Co.'s Siding (Holmes Chapel).
							Victoria Works	Yorks	N. E.	Stockton, South.
							Victoria Works (C. L. C)	Cheshire	C. L. C.—L. & N. W.	See Salt Union, Ltd. (Northwich).
							Victoria Works (Clarke, Chapman, & Co.)	Durham	N. E.	Gateshead.
							Victory Sid. (Allerford Sid.)	Somerset..	G. W.	Norton-Fitzwarren.
							Viewfield Colliery	Lanark	Cal.	Cobbinshaw.
							Viewpark Colliery	Lanark	Cal.—N. B.	Uddingston.
							Villier's Spelter Co.'s Siding (Mid.)	Glamorg'n	Mid.—G. W.—L. & N. W.	Six Pit.
							Villier's Spelter Works (G. W. & Mid. Jt.)	Glamorg'n	G. W.—Mid.—L. & N. W.	Swansea.

EXPLANATION—**G** *Goods Station.*   **P** *Passenger and Parcel Station.*   **P*** *Passenger, but not Parcel or Miscellaneous Traffic.*
F *Furniture Vans, Carriages, Portable Engines, and Machines on Wheels.*   **L** *Live Stock.*
H *Horse Boxes and Prize Cattle Vans.*   **C** *Carriages by Passenger Train.*

STATION ACCOMMODATION.						CRANE POWER.		STATIONS, &c	COUNTY.	COMPANY.	POSITION.
						Tons	Cwts				
.	.	.	.	.	.	.	.	Villier's Tin Plate Works ...	Glamorg'n	G. W.	Briton Ferry.
.	.	.	.	.	.	.	.	Vint & Bros.' Siding	Yorks	G. N.	Bradford, Idle.
.	.	.	.	.	.	.	.	Vinter, J. O., & Son's, Siding (G. E.)	Cambs......	G. E.—Mid.	Cambridge.
.	.	.	.	.	.	.	.	Vipond & Co.'s Varteg } Hill Colliery .... }	Mon	G. W. .... / L. & N. W.	Cwmavon. / Blaenavon.
G	P	F	L	H	C	.	.	Virginia Road	Meath......	G. N. (I.)	Kells and Oldcastle.
.	.	.	.	.	.	.	.	Virginia Siding	Cornwall ..	G. W.	Melangoose Mill.
G	P	F	L	H	C	.	.	Virginia Water	Surrey ...	L. & S.W.	Staines and Ascot.
.	.	.	.	.	.	.	.	Vittoria Wharf Shipping Sheds......................	Cheshire...	B'headJt—CLC—NW&L	Birkenhead.
								Vivian & Son's—			
.	.	.	.	.	.	.	.	Alkali Works	Glamorg'n	G. W.	Landore.
.	.	.	.	.	.	.	.	Coal Siding	Glamorg'n	G. W.	Swansea.
.	.	.	.	.	.	.	.	Hafod Siding	Glamorg'n	G. W.	Swansea.
.	.	.	.	.	.	.	.	Margam Siding	Glamorg'n	R. & S. B.	Port Talbot (Aberavon).
.	.	.	.	.	.	.	.	Morfa Siding	Glamorg'n	R. & S. B.	Port Talbot (Aberavon).
.	.	.	.	.	.	.	.	Sand Siding	Glamorg'n	R. & S. B.	Port Talbot (Aberavon).
.	.	.	.	.	.	.	.	Spelter Works	Glamorg'n	G. W.	Morriston.
.	.	.	.	.	.	.	.	White Rock Siding (Mid.)	Glamorg'n	Mid.—G. W.—L.& N.W.	Upper Bank.
.	.	.	.	.	.	.	.	Vivian Colliery	Mon	G. W.	Abertillery.
								Vivian's Boring & Exploration			
.	.	.	.	.	.	.	.	Co.'s Siding	Cumb'land	WC&EJt(Fur.&L&NW)	Frizington.
.	.	.	.	.	.	.	.	Vivian's Colliery................	Glamorg'n	G. W.	Landore.
.	.	.	.	.	.	.	.	Vivian's Loop Siding	Glamorg'n	P. T.	Same as Morfa Copper Works (Port Talbot).
.	.	.	.	.	.	.	.	Vogrie Colliery & Brick Works	Edinboro'	N. B.	Fushiebridge.
G	P	F	.	H	C	.	.	Vowchurch	Hereford ..	G. W.	Pontrilas and Dorstone.
.	.	.	.	.	.	.	.	Vron Brick Works	Denbigh ...	G. W.	Brymbo.
.	.	.	.	.	.	.	.	Vron Colliery	Denbigh ...	G. W.	Brymbo.
.	.	.	.	.	.	.	.	Vron Colliery & Brick Works	Denbigh ...	W. M. & C. Q.	Brymbo.
.	.	.	.	.	.	.	.	Vron Junction	Denbigh ...	G. W.	Brymbo.
.	.	.	.	.	.	.	.	Vron Wharf Siding	Denbigh ...	G. W.	Wrexham.
.	.	.	.	.	.	.	.	Vulcan Boiler Works	Lanark ...	Cal.	Coatbridge.
.	.	.	.	.	.	.	.	Vulcan Boiler Works	Yorks	N. E.	Middlesbro'.
.	.	.	.	.	.	.	.	Vulcan Foundry Co.'s Siding	Lancs	L. & N. W.	Earlestown.
.	.	.	.	.	.	.	.	Vulcan Iron Foundry	Yorks	N. E.	Stockton, South.
.	.	.	.	.	.	.	.	Vulcan Street Siding	Yorks	N. E.	Middlesbro'.
.	.	.	.	.	.	.	.	Vulcan Works (G. W.)	Worcester	G. W.—Mid.	Same as McKenzie & Holland's Siding (Worcester).
							.	Vynne & Everett's—			
.	.	.	.	.	.	.	.	Siding	Norfolk ...	G. E.	Narborough.
.	.	.	.	.	.	.	.	Siding (G. E.)	Norfolk ...	G. E.—G. N.—Mid.	Lynn Harbour.

W

.	P	.	L			.	.	Wadborough	Worcester	Mid.	Bromsgrove and Defford.
.	.	.	.	.	.	.	.	Waddell, Son,& Co.'s Sid (GW)	Carmarth'	G. W.—L. & N. W.	Llanelly.
G	P	F	L	H	C	.	.	Waddesdon	Bucks	O. & A. Tram...............	Quainton Rd. & Brill (Wotton Dist.)
G	P	.	.	H	C	.	. }	Waddesdon Manor (Met.)......	Bucks	{ Met. .... / { G. C.	Aylesbury and Verney Junction. / Over Met. Line.
G	P	.	L	H	.	1	10	Waddington	Lincoln ...	G. N.	Lincoln and Grantham.
.	.	.	.	.	.	.	.	Bracebridge Brick Sid.(Lincoln Brk. & Tl. Co.'s Sid.)	Lincoln ...	G. N.	Waddington and Lincoln.
.	.	.	.	.	.	.	.	Lincoln Brick Co.'s Siding	Lincoln ...	G. N.	Waddington.
.	.	.	.	.	.	.	.	Waddington Siding	Cambs......	G. E.	See Stonea.
.	.	.	.	.	.	.	.	Waddington & Son's Foundry	Lancs	Furness...............	Barrow.
.	.	.	.	.	.	.	.	Waddington's Paper Mills ...	Yorks	G. C.	Beighton.
G	P	F	L	.	.	5	0	Waddon (for Beddington and Bandon Hill)	Surrey ...	L. B. & S. C.	West Croydon and Sutton.
.	.	.	.	.	.	.	.	Brown & Co.'s Siding.........	Surrey ...	L. B. & S. C.	West Croydon and Mitcham Junc.
.	.	.	.	.	.	.	.	Wade & Co.'s Siding (Whitemoor)	Notts	Mid.	Nottingham, Radford.
G	P	F	L	H	C	2	0	Wadebridge (L. & S. W.)......	Cornwall ..	{ L. & S. W. .... / { G. W.	Okehampton and Padstow. / Over L. & S. W. from Boscarne Jn.
.	.	.	.	.	.	10	0	Wadebridge Quay	Cornwall ..	L. & S.W.	Wadebridge.

EXPLANATION—G *Goods Station.*   P *Passenger and Parcel Station.*   P* *Passenger, but not Parcel or Miscellaneous Traffic.*
F *Furniture Vans, Carriages, Portable Engines, and Machines on Wheels.*   L *Live Stock.*
H *Horse Boxes and Prize Cattle Vans.*   C *Carriages by Passenger Train.*

STATION ACCOMMODATION.						CRANE POWER.		STATIONS, &c.	COUNTY.	COMPANY.	POSITION.
						Tons	Cwts.				
								Wadebridge Junction	Cornwall ..	L. & S.W.	Wadebridge and St. Kew Highway.
								Wadham Road Siding	Essex	G. E.	See Wood Street (Walthamstow).
G	P	F	L	H	C	4	0	Wadhurst	Sussex	S. E. & C.	Tunbridge Wells and Hastings.
								Wadland's Canal Wharf (Mid.)	Derby	Mid.—L. & N. W.	Same as Robinson & Dowler's Siding.
G	P	F	L	H	C	20	0	Wadsley Bridge	Yorks	G. C.	Penistone and Sheffield.
								Moss & Gamble's Siding ...	Yorks	G. C.	Wadsley Bridge.
								Wadsworth's Siding	Glamorg'n	T. V.	Aberdare.
	P							Waenavon (L. & N. W.)	Mon	{ L. & N. W.	Abersychan and Brynmawr.
										{ G. W.	Over L. & N. W. from Abersychan & Talywain Junction.
G	P							Waenfawr..............................	Carnarvon	No. Wales N. G.	Dinas and Snowdon.
								Waen Llwyd Colliery	Mon	G. W.	Ebbw Vale.
								Waen Nantyglo Colliery	Mon	L. & N. W.	Brynmawr.
								Waen-y-Coed Sidings (Mid.)	Glamorg'n	Mid.—G. W.—L. N. W...	See (Pontardawe) South Wales Primrose Coal Co.
								Wain, A. (Exors. of), Bk. Wks.	Leicester ..	A & N Jt.(L&NW & Mid.)	Heather and Ibstock.
								Wainborfa Colliery (B. & M.)	Mon	B. & M.—G. W.	Pengam.
G	P	F	L	H	C	3	12	Wainfleet	Lincoln ...	G. N.	Firsby and Skegness.
								Wainsgrove Colliery	Derby	Mid.	Ripley.
								Wait, James, & Co.	Glo'ster ...	G. W.—Mid.	Gloucester Docks.
								WAKEFIELD—			
								Balne Lane Junction..........	Yorks	G. N.	Westgate and Wrenthorpe Junction.
								Brotherton & Co.'s Chemical and Cement Works	Yorks	G. N. & L. & Y. Jt.	Kirkgate.
								Green's Siding..................	Yorks	G. N. & L. & Y. Jt.	Kirkgate.
								Hoist Sidings..................	Yorks	G. N. & L. & Y. Jt.	Kirkgate.
								Ings Road Junction	Yorks	G. N.—L. & Y.	Kirkgate and Westgate.
								Junction	Yorks	G. N.—W. R. & G. Jt...	Westgate and Sandal.
								Kilner & Son's Glass Bottle Works	Yorks	G. N. & L. & Y. Jt.	Kirkgate.
G	P	F	L	H	C	10	0	Kirkgate (G. N. & L. & Y. Jt.)	Yorks	{ G. N.	Doncaster and Leeds.
G	P	F	L L	H	C	10	0			{ L. & Y.	Normanton and Horbury.
			L							{ L. & N. W.	Over L. & Y. from Heaton Lodge Jn.
								Park Hill Colliery (L. & Y.)	Yorks	L. & Y.—N. E.	Near Wakefield.
								Seamless Steel Boat Co.'s Siding	Yorks	G. N. & L. & Y. Jt.	Kirkgate.
								Turners Lane Junction......	Yorks	L. & Y.	Kirkgate and Park Hill Colliery.
								Victoria Coal Co.'s Siding...	Yorks	L. & Y.	Near Wakefield.
G		F	L			10	0	Westgate	Yorks	{ G. C. & Mid. Jt.	Doncaster and Leeds.
	P			H	C					{ GC,GN,Mid,&WR&GJt	Doncaster and Leeds.
								Wakefield & Co.'s Siding.....	W'morlnd	L. & N. W.	Milnthorpe.
G	P	F	L	H	C	1	10	Wakerley and Barrowden } (L. & N. W.) .... }	N'hampton	{ L. & N. W.	Market Harboro' and Peterboro'.
	P			H	C					{ G. N.	Over L. & N. W. from Longville Jn.
								Monckton's Siding............	N'hampton	L. & N. W.	Wakerley and Kingscliffe.
	.							Wake's, J. F., Siding	Durham ...	N. E.	See Skerne Iron Works (Darlington)
	P							Walberswick	Suffolk ...	Southwold	Halesworth and Southwold.
								Walbottle Col. & Brick Works	Northumb	N. E.	Newburn.
	P							Walcot	Salop	S & W'tn Jt(G W & LNW)	Shrewsbury and Wellington.
								Waldridge Colliery	Durham ...	N. E.	Pelton.
G	P	F	L	H	C			Waldron and Horeham Road	Sussex......	L. B. & S. C.	Rotherfield and Polegate.
								Waleswood Colliery	Yorks	G. C.	Woodhouse.
								Waleswood Junction............	Derby	G. C.	Kiveton Park and Killamarsh..
								Walford & Co.'s Siding	Essex	G. E.	Braintree.
								Walham Green	Middlesex	Met. Dist.	See London.
G	P		L			5	0	Walkden	Lancs	{ L. & Y.	Pendleton and Hindley.
	P									{ L. & N. W.	Bolton and Manchester.
								Earl of Ellesmere's Ellesmere Colliery	Lancs	L. & Y.	Walkden.
								Peel Hall Siding................	Lancs	L. & Y.	Walkden.
								Walkden Colliery	Lancs	L. & N. W.	See Earl of Ellesmere's (Tyldesley).
G	P	F	L			5	0	Walker	Northumb	N. E.	Loop—Newcastle and Percy Main.
								Armstrong, Whitworth & Co.'s Siding	Northumb	N. E.	Walker.
								Hunter & Co.'s Siding	Northumb	N. E.	Walker.
								Northern Wood Haskinizing Co.'s Siding	Northumb	N. E.	Walker.
								Sayer & Co.'s Foundry	Northumb	N. E.	Walker.
								Wigham, Richardson & Co.'s Neptune Siding	Northumb	N. E.	Walker.
								Walker & Co.'s Saw Mills ...	Durham ...	N. E.	West Hartlepool.
								Walker & Co.'s Siding	Ayr	G. & S.W.	Same as Hawkhill Chemical Works (Ayr).

EXPLANATION—G *Goods Station.*   P *Passenger and Parcel Station.*   P* *Passenger, but not Parcel or Miscellaneous Traffic.*
F *Furniture Vans, Carriages, Portable Engines, and Machines on Wheels.*   L *Live Stock.*
H *Horse Boxes and Prize Cattle Vans.*   C *Carriages by Passenger Train.*

STATION ACCOMMODATION.						CRANE POWER.		STATIONS, &c.	COUNTY.	COMPANY.	POSITION.
						Tons	Cwts.				
.	.	.	.	.	.	.	.	Walker & Co.'s Sugar Refinery	Renfrew ...	Cal.	Greenock, Regent Street.
.	.	.	.	.	.	.	.	Walker & Son's Siding (LNW)	Lancs	L. & N. W.—G.W.	Warrington, Bank Quay.
.	.	.	.	.	.	.	.	Walker Bros.' Siding	Lancs	L. & Y.	See Pagefield Siding.
.	.	.	.	.	.	.	.	Walker, F., Siding	Yorks	O. & I. Jt. (Mid. & N.E.)	Ilkley.
.	.	.	.	.	.	.	.	Walker, Jno., Siding	Staffs	G. W.	Brettell Lane.
.	.	.	.	.	.	.	.	Walker, P., & Son's Brewery (Mid.)	Staffs	Mid.—L&NW—GN—NS	Burton-on-Trent.
								Walker, Parker & Co.—			
.	.	.	.	.	.	.	.	Dee Bank Siding	Flint	L. & N. W.	Flint.
.	.	.	.	.	.	.	.	Siding	Cheshire..	B'head Jt (G W & L N W)	Chester.
.	.	.	.	.	.	.	.	Walker's, C. & W., Midland Iron Works	Salop	G. W.	{ Same as Midland Iron Works (Hollinswood).
.	.	.	.	.	.	.	.	Walker's, J. & T., Bone Wks.	Notts	Mid.	Nottingham, Bulwell.
.	.	.	.	.	.	.	.	Walker's Lye	Hadding'n	N. B.	Ormiston.
.	.	.	.	.	.	.	.	Walker's, P. (Trustees of) Sidings (Mid.)	Staffs	Mid.—L&NW—GN—NS	Burton-on-Trent.
.	.	.	.	.	.	.	.	Walker's Scrap Iron Yard ...	Durham ...	N. E.	Washington.
.	.	.	.	.	.	.	.	Walker's Shipbuilding Yard	Cumb'land	M. & C.	Maryport.
.	.	.	.	.	.	.	.	Walker's Siding	Ayr	G. & S. W.	Irvine Harbour.
.	.	.	.	.	.	.	.	Walker's Siding	Cheshire..	L. & N. W.	Runcorn Docks.
.	.	.	.	.	.	.	.	Walker's Siding (N. B.)	Lanark ...	N. B.—Cal.	Glasgow, Great Western Road.
.	.	.	.	.	.	.	.	Walker's Siding	Salop	L. & N. W.	Donnington.
.	.	.	.	.	.	.	.	Walker's Sid. (Sudbrook Bch.)	Mon	G. W.	Severn Tunnel Junction Station.
G	P	.	L	H	.	2	0	Walkerburn..................	Peebles ...	N. B.	Peebles and Galashiels.
G	P	.	.	.	.	4	0	Walker Gate	Northumb	N. E	Newcastle and North Shields.
.	.	.	.	.	.	.	.	Donkin & Co.'s Siding	Northumb	N. E.	Walker Gate.
.	.	.	.	.	.	.	.	Heaton Jn. or Walker Gate Carriage & Wagon Shops	Northumb	N. E.	Walker Gate.
.	.	.	.	.	.	.	.	Walker Gate Corporation Siding	Northumb	N. E.	Walker Gate.
.	.	.	.	.	.	.	.	Walker Gate Depôts.........	Northumb	N. E.	Walker Gate.
.	.	.	.	.	.	.	.	Watson & Son's Siding......	Northumb	N. E.	Walker Gate.
.	.	.	.	.	.	.	.	Walker Gate Carriage and Wagon Shops	Northumb	N. E.	{ Same as Heaton Jn. Carriage and Wagon Shops (Walker Gate).
G	P	F	L	H	C	1	10	Walkeringham	Notts	G. N. & G. E. Jt.	Doncaster and Gainsboro'.
.	.	.	.	.	.	.	.	Walkinshaw Pits	Renfrew...	Cal.	Paisley, St. James.
.	.	.	.	.	.	.	.	Walkinshaw Siding	Renfrew...	Cal.	Paisley, St. James.
.	.	.	.	.	.	.	.	Walk Mill Pit....................	Cumb'land	C. & W. Jn.	See Moresby Coal Co. (Moresby Parks)
G	P	.	.	.	.	.	.	Wall	Northumb	N. B.	Reedsmouth and Hexham.
.	.	.	.	.	.	.	.	Howford Tile Works.........	Northumb	N. B.	Wall and Hexham.
.	.	.	.	.	.	.	.	Wall & Son's Siding	Kent	S. E. & C.	Wrotham.
.	.	.	.	.	.	.	.	Wall's Siding...................	Essex	L. T. & S.	Grays.
.	.	.	.	.	.	.	.	Wall's Siding...................	Herts	Mid.	St. Albans.
.	.	.	.	.	.	.	.	Wallace & Inn's Siding	Herts	G. N.	Knebworth.
.	.	.	.	.	.	.	.	Wallace Street Mineral Depôt	Stirling ...	N. B.	See Stirling.
G	P	F	.	H	C	5	0	Wallasey	Cheshire..	Wirral	Bidston and New Brighton.
.	.	.	.	.	.	.	.	Wallasey Dock Shipping Sheds	Cheshire...	B'head Jt—CLC—NW&L	Birkenhead.
.	.	.	.	.	.	.	.	Wallasey Gas & Water Works	Cheshire...	{ B'head Jt.-CLC—NW&L Wirral.....................	Birkenhead. Liscard and Poulton.
.	.	.	.	.	.	.	.	Wallasey Lairages...............	Cheshire...	B'head Jt—CLC—NW&L	Birkenhead.
.	.	.	.	.	.	.	.	Wallasey Urban District Council Gas Works...........	Cheshire...	Wirral	Seacombe & Egremont.
G	P	.	.	.	.	.	.	Wall Grange	Staffs	N. S.	Leek and Endon.
G	P	F	L	H	C	2	0	Wallingford	Berks	G. W.	Branch from Cholsey and Moulsford.
.	.	.	.	.	.	.	.	Wallingford Gas Works ...	Berks	G. W.	Wallingford.
G	P	.	.	.	.	5	0	Wallington	Surrey ...	L. B. & S. C.	West Croydon and Sutton.
.	.	.	.	.	.	.	.	Wallis', T. & J., Mill	N'hampton	Mid.	Isham and Burton Latimer.
.	.	.	.	.	.	.	.	Wallneuk Junction	Renfrew...	G. & P. Jt.—G. & S. W.	Paisley.
.	.	.	.	.	.	.	.	Wallpaper Manufacturing Co.'s Siding..................	Middlesex	L. & N. W.	{ Same as Allan Cockshut & Co.'s Siding (London).
.	P	.	.	.	.	.	.	Wallsend	Northumb	N. E.	Newcastle and North Shields.
.	.	.	.	.	.	.	.	Church Pit	Northumb	N. E.	Wallsend.
.	.	.	.	.	.	.	.	Wallsend & Hebburn Coal Co.'s Siding...............	Northumb	N. E.	Carville.
.	.	.	.	.	.	.	.	Wallsend Colliery	Fife	N. B.	Whitemyre Junction Station.
.	.	.	.	.	.	.	.	Wallsend Main Colliery	Yorks	G. C.	Staincross (for Mapplewell).
.	.	.	.	.	.	.	.	Wallsend Siding	Glamorg'n	T. V.	Llantwit.
.	.	.	.	.	.	.	.	Wallsend Slipway & Engineering Co.'s Siding	Northumb	N. E.	Willington Quay.
.	.	.	.	.	.	.	.	Wallyford Colliery...	Edinboro'	N. B.	Inveresk.
G	P	F	L	H	C	8	0	Walmer.....................	Kent	S. E. & C.	Deal and Dover Priory.

EXPLANATION—G *Goods Station.* P *Passenger and Parcel Station.* P* *Passenger, but not Parcel or Miscellaneous Traffic.*
F *Furniture Vans, Carriages, Portable Engines, and Machines on Wheels.* L *Live Stock.*
H *Horse Boxes and Prize Cattle Vans.* C *Carriages by Passenger Train.*

STATION ACCOMMODATION.						CRANE POWER.	STATIONS, &c.	COUNTY.	COMPANY.	POSITION.
						Tons Cwts				
..	..	..	..	..	..	..	Walmsley & Smith's Corn Mill	Lancs	Furness	Barrow.
							Walmsley's—			
..	..	..	..	..	..	..	Atlas Forge Iron Works ...	Lancs	L. & N. W.	Bolton.
..	..	..	..	..	..	..	Siding	Lancs	L. & N. W.	See Lecturers Close and Hulme Trust Siding (Bolton).
G	P	F	L	H	C	..	Walmsley's Siding...............	Lancs	L. & N. W.	Stockport, Reddish.
	P			H	C	..	Walpole	Norfolk ...	Mid. & G. N. Jt.............	South Lynn and Sutton Bridge.
							WALSALL—			
	P			H	C	..	(Station)	Staffs	Mid.	Over L. & N. W. from Walsall Jn.
G	P	F	L	H	C	10 0	(Station)	Staffs	Mid.	Branch, South of Walsall (L.&N.W.)
G	P	F	L	H	C	10 0 }	(Station, L. & N. W.)	Staffs	{ L. & N. W.	Dudley and Lichfield.
G	..	F	L	..	..	10 0 }			{ G. W........................	Over Mid. & L. & N. W. Lines.
..	..	..	..	..	..	..	Brewer's Sid. (L. & N. W.)	Staffs	L. & N. W.—G. W.—Mid.	Walsall and Rushall.
..	..	..	..	..	..	..	Broadhurst & Son's Siding (L. & N.W.)...............	Staffs	L. & N. W.—G. W.—Mid.	Walsall and Rushall.
..	..	..	..	..	..	..	Hales' Siding (L. & N. W.)	Staffs	L. & N. W.—G. W.—Mid.	Walsall and Rushall.
..	..	..	..	..	..	..	Hatherton Sid. (L. & N. W.)	Staffs	L. & N. W.—G. W.—Mid.	Walsall and Rushall.
..	..	..	..	..	..	..	Stokes & Co.	Staffs	L. & N. W.—G. W.	Hatherton Siding.
..	..	..	..	..	..	..	Walsall Hardware Co. ...	Staffs	L. & N. W.—G. W.	Hatherton Siding.
..	..	..	..	..	..	..	Johnson Bros.' Sid. (LNW)	Staffs	L. & N. W.—G. W.—Mid.	Walsall and Rushall.
..	..	..	..	..	..	..	Lavender's Sid. (L. & N.W.)	Staffs	L. & N. W.—Mid.	Walsall and Rushall.
..	..	..	..	..	..	..	Neville's Siding (L. & N.W.)	Staffs	L. & N. W.—G. W.—Mid.	Walsall and Rushall.
..	..	..	..	..	..	..	Oak Tanning Co.'s Siding (L. & N.W.)	Staffs	L. & N. W.—G. W.—Mid.	Walsall and Rushall.
..	..	..	..	..	..	..	Russell & Co.'s Cyclops Iron Works	Staffs	L. & N. W.	Walsall and Wednesbury.
..	..	..	..	..	..	..	Thrustan's Sid. (L. & N.W.)	Staffs	L. & N. W.—G. W.—Mid.	Walsall and Rushall.
..	..	..	..	..	..	..	Walsall & Wolverhampton Line Jn. (Ryecroft Jn.)	Staffs	L. & N. W.—Mid.	Walsall Station & Wolverhampton.
..	..	..	..	..	..	..	Walsall Corporation Gas Works	Staffs	L. & N. W.	Walsall and Wednesbury.
..	..	..	..	..	..	..	Water Orton Line Junction	Staffs	L. & N. W.—Mid.	Walsall Station & Sutton Coldfield.
..	..	..	..	..	..	..	Walsall Corporation Siding...	Staffs	L. & N. W.	Darlaston.
..	..	..	..	..	..	..	Walsall Glue Co.'s Siding ...	Staffs	L. & N. W.	Bloxwich.
..	..	..	..	..	..	..	Walsall Hardware Co.'s Siding (L. & N. W.)	Staffs	L. & N. W.—G. W.	See Hatherton Siding (Walsall).
..	..	..	..	..	..	..	Walsall Street Basin............	Staffs	G. W.	See Wolverhampton.
G	P	F	L	..	..	..	Walsall Wood	Staffs	Mid.	Aldridge and Brownhills.
..	..	..	..	..	..	..	Jobern's Brick Works	Staffs	Mid.	Walsall Wood and Aldridge.
..	..	..	..	..	..	..	Walsall Wood Colliery......	Staffs	Mid.	Walsall Wood & Brownhills.
							Walsall Wood Colliery Co.—			
..	..	..	..	..	..	..	Ryders Hayes or Pelsall Col.	Staffs	L. & N. W.	Pelsall.
..	..	..	..	..	..	..	Walsall Wood Colliery	Staffs	L. & N. W.	Pelsall.
G	P	..	..	..	..	8 0	Walsden	Lancs	L. & Y.	Rochdale and Todmorden.
G	P	F	L	H	C	1 10	Walsingham	Norfolk ...	G. E.	Dereham and Wells.
G	P	..	L	H	..	..	Waltham	Lincoln ...	G. N.	Louth and Grimsby.
..	..	..	..	..	..	..	Waltham Abbey and Cheshunt Gas and Coke Co.'s Siding	Herts	G. E.	Waltham Cross.
G	P	F	L	H	C	4 10	Waltham Cross and Abbey ...	Herts	G. E.	Tottenham and Broxbourne.
..	..	..	..	..	..	..	Waltham Abbey & Cheshunt Gas and Coke Co.'s Siding	Herts	G. E.	Waltham Cross and Abbey.
G	..	..	L	H	..	.. }	Waltham-on-the-Wold (G.N.)	Leicester..	{ G. N.	Branch from Scalford Junction.
G	..	..	..	..	..				{ Mid.	Over G.N. from Wycombe Junction.
..	..	..	..	..	..	..	Eaton Siding (G. N.)..........	Leicester..	G. N.—Mid.	Branch from Waltham-on-the-Wold.
..	..	..	..	..	..	..	Holwell Co.'s Siding (G.N.)	Leicester..	G. N.—Mid.	Branch from Waltham-on-the-Wold.
..	..	..	..	..	..	..	Staveley & Oakes Co.'s Siding (G.N.)	Leicester..	G. N.—Mid.	Branch from Waltham-on-the-Wold.
..	..	..	..	..	..	..	Waltham Siding................	Berks	G. W.	Maidenhead.
							WALTHAMSTOW—			
..	..	..	..	..	..	..	Hoe Street	Essex	G. E.	See Hoe Street (Walthamstow).
G	..	F	L	..	..	.. }	Queen's Road	Essex	{ Mid.	} South Tottenham and Leytonstone.
..	P	..	..	..	..				{ T & F G Jt (LT & S&Mid)	
..	..	..	..	..	..	..	St. James's Street	Essex	G. E.	See St. James's Str. (Walthamstow).
..	..	..	..	..	..	..	Wood Street	Essex	G. E.	See Wood Street (Walthamstow).
..	..	..	..	..	..	..	Walthamstow Urban District Council's Sidings ...	Essex	G. E.	{ Hoe Street (Walthamstow). London, Lea Bridge.
							WALTON—			
..	..	..	..	..	..	..	New Junction, North	Cheshire...	B'head Jt.—L. & N. W.	Helsby and Warrington.
..	..	..	..	..	..	..	Old Main Line Junction ...	Cheshire...	B'head Jt.—L. & N. W.	Helsby and Warrington.
..	..	..	..	..	..	..	Old W. & S. Junction	Cheshire...	B'head Jt.—L. & N. W.	Manchester Ship Canal, Acton Grange Siding, and Warrington.
..	..	..	..	..	..	..	W. & S. Junction	Cheshire...	B'head Jt.—L. & N. W.	Helsby and Warrington.

EXPLANATION—G *Goods Station.*   P *Passenger and Parcel Station.*   P* *Passenger, but not Parcel or Miscellaneous Traffic.*
F *Furniture Vans, Carriages, Portable Engines, and Machines on Wheels.*   L *Live Stock.*
H *Horse Boxes and Prize Cattle Vans.*   C *Carriages by Passenger Train.*

STATION ACCOMMODATION.						CRANE POWER.		STATIONS, &c.	COUNTY.	COMPANY.	POSITION.
						Tons	Cwts.				
.	P	.	.	.	.	.	.	Walton	N'hamptn	Mid.	Peterboro' and Stamford.
.	.	.	.	.	.	.	.	Walton	Yorks	Mid.	See Sandal and Walton.
.	.	.	.	.	.	.	.	Walton (Mid.)	Staffs	Mid.—L. & N. W.	See Barton and Walton.
.	.	.	.	.	.	.	.	Walton (for Aintree)	Lancs	L. & N. W.	See Liverpool.
G	P	F	L	H	C	10	0	Walton and Hersham	Surrey	L. & S.W.	Surbiton and Woking.
.	.	.	.	.	.	.	.	Walton Colliery Co.'s Siding	Derby	Mid.	Chesterfield.
.	.	.	.	.	.	.	.	Walton Junction Station	Lancs	L. & Y.	See Liverpool.
.	.	.	.	.	.	.	.	Walton-on-the-Hill	Cheshire	C.L.C. (G C, G N, & Mid.)	See Liverpool.
.	.	.	.	.	.	.	.	Walton-on-the-Hill	Surrey	S. E. & C.	See Tadworth & Walton-on-the-Hill.
G	P	F	.	H	C	2	0	Walton-on-the-Naze	Essex	G. E.	Branch from Colchester.
.	.	.	.	.	.	.	.	Walton & Wood's Farnworth Brick Co.'s Siding	Lancs	L. & N. W.	Farnworth and Bold.
.	.	.	.	.	.	.	.	Walton's Lincrusta Siding	Middlesex	L. & S.W.	Sunbury.
.	.	.	.	.	.	.	.	Walworth Road (S. E. & C.)	Surrey	S E & C—G N—L & S W—Mid.	See London.
G	P	.	L	H	.	4	0	Walworth Road Coal Depôt	Surrey	Mid.	See London.
.	.	.	.	.	.	.	.	Wamphray	Dumfries	Cal.	Lockerbie and Carstairs.
G	P	F	L	H	C	.	.	Wanborough (L. & S. W.)	Surrey	L. & S. W.	Guildford and Farnham.
										S. E. & C.	Over L. & S.W. from Shalford Junc.
.	.	.	.	.	.	.	.	Coussmaker's Siding	Surrey	L. & S.W.	Wanborough.
.	.	.	.	.	.	.	.	Wanborough Brick Co.'s Siding	Surrey	L. & S.W.	Wanborough.
G	P	.	.	.	.	.	.	Wandsworth Common (L. B. & S. C.)	Surrey	L. B. & S. C.	Clapham Junction and Balham.
.	P	.	.	.	.	.	.			L. & N. W.	Over L.B.&S.C. from Clapham Junc.
G	.	F	L	.	.	.	.	Wandsworth, New	Surrey	L. B. & S. C.	Branch—Clapham Junction and Wandsworth Common.
.	.	.	.	.	.	.	.	Wandsworth Road	Surrey	L. B. & S. C.—S.E.& C.—G.N.—L.&S.W.—Mid.	See London.
.	P	.	.	.	.	.	.	Wandsworth Town	Surrey	L. & S.W.	Clapham Junction and Richmond.
.	.	.	.	.	.	.	.	Caucasian Petroleum Export Co.'s Siding	Surrey	L. & S.W.	Wandsworth Town.
.	.	.	.	.	.	.	.	Thorley's Siding	Surrey	L. & S.W.	Wandsworth Town.
G	P	.	L	H	.	3	0	Wanlockhead	Dumfries	Cal.	Branch near Elvanfoot.
G	P	F	L	H	C	1	15	Wansford (L. & N. W.)	Hunts	L. & N. W.	Market Harboro' and Peterboro'.
.	P	.	.	H	C	.	.			G. N.	Over L. & N. W. from Longville Jn.
.	.	.	.	.	.	.	.	Wansford Junction	Hunts	G. N.—L. & N. W.	Stamford and Wellingboro'.
G	P	F	L	H	C	4	18	Wansford Road	N'hamptn	G. N.	Stamford and Wansford Junction.
.	.	.	.	.	.	.	.	Wanstead	Essex	G. E.	See Snaresbrook and Wanstead.
.	P	.	.	.	.	.	.	Wanstead Park	Essex	T.&F.G.Jt.(L T&S&Mid.)	Leytonstone and East Ham.
.	P	.	.	.	.	.	.	Wanstrow	Somerset	G. W.	Witham and Shepton Mallet.
G	P	F	L	H	C	12	0	Wantage Road	Berks	G. W.	Didcot and Swindon.
.	.	.	.	.	.	.	.	Lord Wantage's Siding	Berks	G. W.	Wantage Road.
G	P	.	L	H	.	.	.	Wappenham	N'hamptn	N. & B. Jn.	Towcester and Banbury.
.	.	.	.	.	.	.	.	Wapping	Lancs	L. & N. W.	See Liverpool.
.	.	.	.	.	.	.	.	Wapping	Middlesex	E.L.Jt.(G.E.,L.B.&S.C., Met., M.D., & S.E.& C.)	See London.
.	.	.	.	.	.	.	.	Wapping and Salthouse Dock	Lancs	L. & Y.	See Liverpool.
:	.	.	.	.	.	.	.	Wapping Dock	Lancs	L'pool O'head	See Liverpool.
.	.	.	.	.	.	.	.	Wapping Siding	Durham	N. E.	Fencehouses. Penshaw.
.	.	.	.	.	.	.	.	Warboise Works	Cheshire	C.L.C. (G C, G N, & Mid.)	See Salt Union, Ltd. (Winnington).
G	P	.	L	H	.	2	0	Warboys	Hunts	G. N. & G. E. Jt.	Somersham and Ramsey.
.	.	.	.	.	.	.	.	Fuller, A., Siding	Hunts	G. N. & G. E. Jt.	Warboys.
G	.	.	.	.	.	.	.	Pidley-cum-Fenton Siding	Hunts	G. N. & G. E. Jt.	Warboys and Somersham.
.	.	.	.	.	.	.	.	Warburton	Cheshire	L. & N. W.	See Heatley and Warburton.
.	.	.	.	.	.	.	.	Warburton's Siding	Lancs	L. & Y.	Manchester, Miles Platting.
G	P	F	L	H	C	5	0	Warcop	W'morlnd	N. E.	Kirkby Stephen and Penrith.
.	P	.	.	.	.	.	.	Wardhouse	Aberdeen	G. N. of S.	Inveramsay and Keith.
G	P	.	L	.	.	10	0	Wardleworth	Lancs	L. & Y.	Rochdale and Facit.
.	.	.	.	.	.	.	.	Bright Bros.' Siding	Lancs	L. & Y.	Wardleworth and Shawclough.
.	.	.	.	.	.	.	.	Wardley	Lancs	L. & Y.	See Moorside and Wardley.
.	.	.	.	.	.	.	.	Wardley Colliery	Durham	N. E.	Jarrow.
.	.	.	.	.	.	.	.	Wardlow's Siding	Yorks	G. C.	Oughty Bridge.
.	.	.	.	.	.	.	.	Ward's Basin	Cheshire	N. S.	Congleton, Brunswick.
.	.	.	.	.	.	.	.	Ward's Saw Mill	Durham	N. E.	West Hartlepool.
.	.	.	.	.	.	.	.	Ward's Siding	Yorks	L. & N. W.	Same as Fitton&Robinson's(Morley).
.	.	.	.	.	.	.	.	Ward's, T. W.—			
.	.	.	.	.	.	.	.	Broughton Lane Sid. (G.C.)	Yorks	G. C.—Mid.	Sheffield, Broughton Lane.
.	.	.	.	.	.	.	.	Grimesthorpe Sids. (Mid.)	Yorks	Mid.—G. C.	Sheffield, Wicker.
.	.	.	.	.	.	.	.	Scrap Iron Depôt	Staffs	G. W.	Wednesbury.
.	.	.	.	.	.	.	.	Siding	Lancs	N. U. Jt. (L&N W&L&Y)	Preston, Charles Street.
G	P	F	L	H	C	5	0	Ware	Herts	G. E.	Broxbourne and Hertford.

EXPLANATION—G *Goods Station.* P *Passenger and Parcel Station.* P* *Passenger, but not Parcel or Miscellaneous Traffic.*
F *Furniture Vans, Carriages, Portable Engines, and Machines on Wheels.* L *Live Stock.*
H *Horse Boxes and Prize Cattle Vans.* C *Carriages by Passenger Train.*

STATION ACCOMMODATION.						CRANE POWER.		STATIONS, &c.	COUNTY.	COMPANY.	POSITION.
						Tons	Cwts.				
G	P	F	L	H	C	5	0	Wareham	Dorset	L. & S.W.	Poole and Dorchester.
								Sandford Pottery	Dorset	L. & S.W.	Wareham.
								Worgret Junction	Dorset	L. & S.W.	Wareham and Wool.
G	P	F				6	0	Wargrave	Berks	G. W.	Twyford and Henley-on-Thames.
								Waring & Co.'s Siding	Lancs	P & L Jt (L & N W & L & Y)	Preston, Deepdale.
								Waring Bros.' Siding	Lancs	L & Y & L U Jt (L Y & L N W)	See Withnell Mill Sids. (Brinscall).
G	P		L	H		1	0	Wark	Northumb	N. B.	Reedsmouth and Hexham.
G						4	0	Gunnerton Siding	Northumb	N. B.	Wark and Barrasford.
G	P	F	L	H	C	3	0	Warkworth	Northumb	N. E.	Berwick and Morpeth.
								Shortridge Farm Siding	Northumb	N. E.	Warkworth and Alnmouth.
								Warkworth Harbour	Northumb	N. E.	Amble.
								Warley	Essex	G. E.	See Brentwood and Warley.
	P							Warlingham	Surrey	S. E. & C.	Purley and Caterham.
								Warlingham, Upper	Surrey	C. & O. Jt. (L. B. & S. C. and S. E. & C.)	See Upper Warlingham.
								Warmanbie Quarry	Dumfries	Cal.	Annan.
G	P	F	L	H	C	12	0	Warminster	Wilts	G. W.	Westbury and Salisbury.
								Scott & Smith's Siding	Wilts	G. W.	Warminster Station Yard.
G	P		L			5	0	Warmley	Glo'ster	Mid.	Mangotsfield and Bath.
G								Warmsworth	Yorks	G. C.	Conisboro' and Doncaster.
								Lockwood & Co.'s Lime Works	Yorks	G. C.	Conisboro' and Doncaster.
G	P					1	0	Warnham	Sussex	L. B. & S. C.	Dorking and Horsham.
								Sussex Brick Co.'s Siding	Sussex	L. B. & S. C.	Warnham.
								War Office Barracks Siding	Middlesex	G. N.	Mill Hill.
								War Office Siding	Kent	S. E. & C.	Dover Priory.
								War Office Sidings	Stirling	Cal.	Same as Forth Side Sids. (Stirling).
	P*							Warren	Cheshire	Wirral	Bidston and New Brighton.
								Warren, G., Siding	Essex	G. E.	Wickford Junction Station.
								Warren's Chemical Works	Glamorg'n	G. W.	Briton Ferry.
								Warren Mines	Lincoln	G. C.	Frodingham and Scunthorpe.
								Warrenby Depôts and Siding	Yorks	N. E.	Redcar.
G	P		L			2	0	Warrenpoint	Down	{ D. N. & G.	By Steamer from Greenore.
										{ L. & N. W.	By Steamer from Holyhead, via Greenore.
G	P	F	L	H	C	1	0	Warrenpoint	Down	G. N. (I.)	Terminus.
								Warriner's Siding	Lincoln	G. C.	Lincoln.
								WARRINGTON—			
G	P		L			1	10	Arpley	Lancs	L. & N. W.	Bank Quay and Stockport.
G	P	F	L	H	C	15	0	Bank Quay (L. & N. W.)	Lancs	{ L. & N. W.	Crewe and Wigan.
										{ G. W.	Over L. & N. W. from Walton Junc.
								Blundell & Son's Siding (L. & N. W.)	Lancs	L. & N. W.—G. W.	Dallam Lane Branch.
G	P	F	L	H	C	10	0	Central	Lancs	C. L. C. (G C, G N, & Mid.)	Garston and Manchester.
								Crosfield & Son's Factory Lane Siding (L. & N. W.)	Lancs	L. & N. W.—G. W.	Bank Quay and Golborne.
								Crosfield & Son's Soap Wks.	Lancs	L. & N. W.	Bank Quay and Sankey Bridges.
								Dallam Lane Branch (L. & N. W.)	Lancs	{ L. & N. W.	Branch—North of Bank Quay.
										{ G. W.	Over L. & N. W. from Walton Junc.
								Evans, R., & Co.'s Coal Yard (L. & N. W.)	Lancs	L. & N. W.—G. W.	Dallam Lane Branch.
								Fletcher, Burrows & Co.'s Atherton Sid. (L.& N.W.)	Lancs	L. & N. W.—G. W.	Dallam Lane Branch.
								Fletcher, Russell & Co.'s Wilderspool Siding	Lancs	L. & N. W.	Arpley and Latchford.
								Greenall, Whitley & Co.'s Wilderspool Brewery	Lancs	L. & N. W.	Arpley and Latchford.
								Greening & Son's Siding	Lancs	L. & N. W.	Bank Quay and Golborne.
								Halton & Co.'s Sid. (L N W)	Lancs	L. & N. W.—G. W.	Bank Quay and Golborne.
								Lancashire Asylums Board Winwick Hall Siding	Lancs	L. & N. W.	Bank Quay and Golborne.
G	P					5	0	Latchford	Lancs	L. & N. W.	Arpley and Stockport.
								Longford Gas Wks. (L N W)	Lancs	L. & N. W.—G. W.	Bank Quay and Golborne.
								Longford Wire Co.'s Siding (L. & N. W.)	Lancs	L. & N. W.—G. W.	Dallam Lane Branch.
								Manchester Ship Canal Co.— Acton Grange Junction	Lancs	B'head Jt.—Man. Ship Canal	Bank Quay and Daresbury.
								Latchford Junction	Lancs	L. & N. W.—Man. Ship Canal	Latchford.
G						5	0	Marson Street Goods Depôt (L. & N. W.)	Lancs	L. & N. W.—G. W.	Dallam Lane Branch.

EXPLANATION— G *Goods Station.*   P *Passenger and Parcel Station.*   P* *Passenger, but not Parcel or Miscellaneous Traffic.*
F *Furniture Vans, Carriages, Portable Engines, and Machines on Wheels.*   L *Live Stock.*
H *Horse Boxes and Prize Cattle Vans.*   C *Carriages by Passenger Train.*

STATION ACCOMMODATION.						CRANE POWER.		STATIONS, &c.	COUNTY.	COMPANY.	POSITION.
						Tons	Cwts.	WARRINGTON—continued.			
.	.	.	.	.	.	.	.	Monks, Hall & Co.'s Siding	Lancs	L. & N. W.	Bank Quay and Sankey Bridges.
.	.	.	.	.	.	.	.	Peacock & Barlow's Siding (L. & N. W.)	Lancs	L. & N. W.—G. W.	Dallam Lane Branch.
								Pearson & Knowles Coal & Iron Co.—			
.	.	.	.	.	.	.	.	Bewsey & Dallam Forge Iron Works	Lancs	C. L. C. (G C, G N, & Mid.)	Warrington, Central.
.	.	.	.	.	.	.	.	Bewsey Forge Iron Wks. (L. & N. W.)	Lancs	L. & N. W.—G. W.	Dallam Lane Branch.
.	.	.	.	.	.	.	.	Coal Yard (L. & N. W.)	Lancs	L. & N. W.—G. W.	Dallam Lane Branch.
.	.	.	.	.	.	.	.	Dallam Forge Iron Wks. (L. & N. W.)	Lancs	L. & N. W.—G. W.	Dallam Lane Branch.
.	.	.	.	.	.	.	.	Pumping Siding	Lancs	L. & N. W.	Bank Quay and Moore.
.	.	.	.	.	.	.	.	Pendlebury & Co.'s Siding (L. & N. W.)	Lancs	L. & N. W.—G. W.	Dallam Lane Branch.
.	.	.	.	.	.	.	.	Pochin & Co.'s Chemical Works (L. & N. W.)	Lancs	L. & N. W.—G. W.	Bank Quay and Moore.
.	.	.	.	.	.	.	.	Richardson's Coal Siding	Lancs	L. & N. W.	Arpley and Latchford.
.	.	.	.	.	.	.	.	Richardson's Coal Siding (L. & N. W.)	Lancs	L. & N. W.—G. W.	Dallam Lane Branch.
.	.	.	.	.	.	.	.	Richmond & Co.'s Siding (L. & N. W.)	Lancs	L. & N. W.—G. W.	Dallam Lane Branch.
.	.	.	.	.	.	.	.	Robinson, Son, & Co.'s Siding (L. & N. W.)	Lancs	L. & N. W.—G. W.	Bank Quay and Moore.
.	.	.	.	.	.	.	.	Smith's Wire Works & Coal Siding (L. & N. W.)	Lancs	L. & N. W.—G. W.	Dallam Lane Branch.
.	.	.	.	.	.	.	.	Statham Brick Works	Lancs	L. & N. W.	Latchford and Arpley.
.	.	.	.	.	.	.	.	Walker & Son's Sid. (LNW)	Lancs	L. & N. W.—G. W.	Dallam Lane Branch.
.	.	.	.	.	.	.	.	Warrington Slate Co.'s Sid.	Lancs	L. & N. W.	Arpley and Bank Quay.
.	.	.	.	.	.	.	.	Warrington Slate Co.'s Siding (L. & N. W.)	Lancs	L. & N. W.—G. W.	Dallam Lane Branch.
.	.	.	.	.	.	.	.	Warrington Wire Rope Co.'s Siding (L. & N. W.)	Lancs	L. & N. W.—G. W.	Dallam Lane Branch.
.	.	.	.	.	.	.	.	Warrington Workshops Sid	Lancs	C. L. C. (G C, G N, & Mid.)	Warrington, Central.
.	.	.	.	.	.	.	.	Westwell's Sid. (L. & N. W.)	Lancs	L. & N. W.—G. W.	Bank Quay and Golborne.
.	.	.	.	.	.	.	.	White Cross Iron Works	Lancs	C. L. C. (G C, G N, & Mid.)	Warrington, Central.
.	.	.	.	.	.	.	.	White Cross Wire & Iron Co.'s Works (L. & N. W.)	Lancs	L. & N. W.	Bank Quay and Golborne.
.	.	.	.	.	.	.	.	Wigan Coal & Iron Co.'s Siding	Lancs	L. & N. W.	Arpley and Bank Quay.
.	.	.	.	.	.	.	.	Warrington & Son's Works	Staffs	N. S.	Berry Hill.
.	.	.	.	.	.	.	.	Warrington Road Sid.(C.L.C.)	Cheshire	C. L. C.—L. & N. W.	Same as Thompson's Brick Works (Northwich).
.	.	.	.	.	.	.	.	Warrington Slate Co.'s Siding	Lancs	L. & N. W.	Warrington, Arpley.
.	.	.	.	.	.	.	.	Warrington Slate Co.'s Siding (L. & N. W.)	Lancs	L. & N. W.—G. W.	Warrington, Bank Quay.
.	.	.	.	.	.	.	.	Warrington Wire Rope Co.'s Siding (L. & N. W.)	Lancs	L. & N. W —G. W.	Warrington, Bank Quay.
.	.	.	.	.	.	.	.	Warrington Workshops Sid.	Lancs	C. L. C. (G C, G N, & Mid.)	Warrington, Central.
.	.	.	.	.	.	.	.	Warrior Square (S. E. & C.)	Sussex	S. E. & C.—L. B. & S. C.	See St. Leonards.
.	.	.	.	.	.	.	.	Warriston Junction	Edinboro'	N. B.	Edinburgh.
.	.	.	.	.	.	.	.	Warrix Brick Works	Ayr	G. & S.W.	Dreghorn.
.	.	.	.	.	.	.	.	Warrix Colliery	Ayr	G. & S.W.	Dreghorn.
G	P	F	L	H	C	3	0	Warsop (L. D. & E. C.)	Notts	L. D. & E. C. / G. E. / Mid.	Langwith Junction and Tuxford. / Over L. D. & E. C. from Lincoln, Pye Wipe Junction (for Coal only). / Over L. D.& E.C. from Shirebrook Jn.
.	.	.	.	.	.	.	.	Warsop Main Colliery	Notts	L. D. & E. C.	Warsop and Langwith Junction.
.	.	.	.	.	.	.	.	Warsop Main Colliery	Notts	L. D. & E. C.	Warsop.
.	.	.	.	.	.	.	.	Warsop Main Colliery (Mid.)	Derby	Mid.—G. C.	Shirebrook.
G	P	.	L	H	C	.	.	Warthill	Yorks	N. E.	York and Market Weighton.
.	.	.	.	.	.	.	.	Warthole Lime Works	Cumb'land	M. & C.	Aspatria. / Bullgill.
G	P	.	L	H	.	.	.	Wartle	Aberdeen	G. N. of S.	Inveramsay and Macduff.
								WARWICK—			
G	P	F	L	H	C	10	0	(Station)	Warwick	G. W.	Birmingham and Leamington.
.	.	.	.	.	.	.	.	Gas Works	Warwick	G. W.	Warwick.
G	P	F	L	H	C	7	0	Milverton	Warwick	L. & N. W.	Birmingham and Leamington.
.	.	.	.	.	.	.	.	Warwick & Richardson's Sid.	Notts	G. N.—Mid.	Newark.
.	.	.	.	.	.	.	.	Warwickhill Colliery	Ayr	G. & S.W.	Cunninghamhead.
.	.	.	.	.	.	.	.	Warwick Road	Middlesex	G. W.—L. & N. W.	See London, Kensington.

EXPLANATION—G Goods Station.   P Passenger and Parcel Station.   P* Passenger, but not Parcel or Miscellaneous Traffic.
F Furniture Vans, Carriages, Portable Engines, and Machines on Wheels.   L Live Stock.
H Horse Boxes and Prize Cattle Vans.   C Carriages by Passenger Train.

G	P	F	L	H	C	Tons	Cwts	STATIONS, &c.	COUNTY.	COMPANY.	POSITION.
								Wase's Saw Mill	Durham ...	N. E.	See Longhill Sids.(West Hartlepool).
G	P	F	L	H	C	2	0	Washford	Somerset..	G. W.	Watchet and Minehead.
G	P							Washingboro'	Lincoln ...	G. N.	Lincoln and Boston.
G	P	F	L	H	C	1	0	Washington	Durham ...	N. E.	Newcastle and Leamside.
								Biddick Lane Siding	Durham ...	N. E.	Washington.
								Cook & Son's Outer Siding	Durham ...	N. E.	Washington.
								Fatfield Gears Siding	Durham ...	N. E.	Washington.
								Harraton Colliery & Depôts	Durham ...	N. E.	Washington.
								Harraton Hall Depôts	Durham ...	N. E.	Washington.
								High Barmston Depôts	Durham ...	N. E.	Washington.
								Kip Siding	Durham ...	N. E.	Washington.
								Low Barmston Depôt	Durham ...	N. E.	Washington.
								Marsh & Co.'s Brick Works	Durham ...	N. E.	Washington.
								Newall's Wire Rope Works	Durham ...	N. E.	Washington.
								North Biddick Brick and Tile Co.'s Siding	Durham ...	N. E.	Washington.
								North Biddick Colliery	Durham ...	N. E.	Washington.
								Walker's Scrap Iron Yard..	Durham ...	N. E.	Washington.
								Washington Brick Works..	Durham ...	N. E.	Washington.
								Washington Chemical Wks.	Durham ...	N. E.	Washington.
								Washington Colliery	Durham ...	N. E.	Washington.
								Washington Iron Works	Durham ...	N. E.	Washington.
								Washington Slag Works	Durham ...	N. E.	Washington.
								Wash Pit	Lancs	LY—LNW—GC(WigJn)	See Wigan Coal & Iron Co.
								Washwall's Chemical Works..	Renfrew...	Cal.	Giffnock.
G								Waskerley	Durham ...	N. E.	Consett and Tow Law.
								Baxton Bank Depôts	Durham ...	N. E.	Waskerley.
								Black Cabin Siding	Durham ...	N. E.	Waskerley.
								Meeting Slack Depôt	Durham ...	N. E.	Waskerley.
								Salter's Gate Siding and Stone Wharf	Durham ...	N. E.	Waskerley.
G	P	F	L	H	C	4	0	Watchet	Somerset..	G. W.	Taunton and Minehead.
G	P		L	H		1	0	Waterbeach	Cambs......	G. E.	Cambridge and Ely.
G	P							Waterfall	Cork	C. B. & S. C.	Cork and Bandon.
	P							Waterfall	I. of Man	Manx Northern	St. Johns and Foxdale.
G	P		L			10	0	Waterfoot (for Newchurch)..	Lancs	L. & Y.	Rawtenstall and Bacup.
								Hargreaves' Siding	Lancs	L. & Y.	Waterfoot.
								WATERFORD—			
G	P	F	L	H	C	2	10	(Station)	Waterford	G. W.	Steamer from New Milford.
G	P							(Station)	Waterford	W. & T.	Terminus.
G	P	F	L	H	C	5	0	North (G. S. & W.)	Waterford	G. S. & W. / D. W. & W.	Terminus. / Over G. S. & W. Line.
G		F	L	H		4	0	North Wharf	Waterford	G. S. & W.	Waterford.
G	P	F	L	H	C			South	Waterford	G. S. & W.	Terminus.
								Watergate Pit	Cumb'land	L. & N. W.	See Flimby Colliery Co. (Flimby).
								Waterhall Junction	Glamorg'n	P. T.	Bryndu and Pyle Junction.
								Waterhall Junction	Glamorg'n	T. V.	Radyr and Grangetown.
								Waterhall Siding	Glamorg'n	T. V.	Radyr.
								Waterhouse Bros.—			
								Taffs Well Siding	Glamorg'n	T. V.	Taffs Well.
								Treforest Tin Plate Works	Glamorg'n	T. V.	Treforest.
								Waterhouse's Siding (L. & Y.)	Yorks	L. & Y.—G. N.	Elland.
G	P		L			3	0	Waterhouses	Durham ...	N. E.	Bch.—Durham, Pass. & Brancepeth.
								Cornsay Colliery, Coke Ovens, and Brick Works	Durham ...	N. E.	Waterhouses.
								Dickens House Drift	Durham ...	N. E.	Waterhouses.
								East Hedley Hope Colliery and Coke Ovens	Durham ...	N. E.	Waterhouses.
								Esh Colliery & Coke Ovens	Durham ...	N. E.	Waterhouses.
								Flass Junction and Siding	Durham ...	N. E.	Waterhouses.
								Hamsteel's Colliery, Coke Ovens, and Brick Works	Durham ...	N. E.	Waterhouses.
								Hedley Hill Colliery and Coke Ovens	Durham ..	N. E.	Waterhouses.
								New Brancepeth Colliery, Coke Ovens & Brick Wks.	Durham ...	N. E.	Waterhouses.
								Smith's Depôt	Durham ...	N. E.	Waterhouses.
								Standard Brick Works	Durham ...	N. E.	Waterhouses.
								Ushaw Moor Colliery and Coke Ovens	Durham ...	N. E.	Waterhouses.
								Waterhouses Colliery and Coke Ovens	Durham ...	N. E.	Waterhouses.

EXPLANATION—G *Goods Station.*   P *Passenger and Parcel Station.*   P* *Passenger, but not Parcel or Miscellaneous Traffic.*
F *Furniture Vans, Carriages, Portable Engines, and Machines on Wheels.*   L *Live Stock.*
H *Horse Boxes and Prize Cattle Vans.*   C *Carriages by Passenger Train.*

STATION ACCOMMODATION.						CRANE POWER.	STATIONS, &c.	COUNTY.	COMPANY.	POSITION.
						Tons Cwts.				
G	P	F	L	H	C	4 0	Wateringbury..................	Kent	S. E. & C.	Maidstone, West & Paddock Wood.
.	.	.	.	.	.	. .	Teston Siding	Kent	S. E. & C.	East Farleigh and Wateringbury.
.	.	.	.	.	.	. .	Waterloo	Aberdeen	G. N. of S.	See Aberdeen.
.	.	.	.	.	.	. .	Waterloo	Lanark ...	Cal.	See Overtown, Waterloo.
.	.	.	.	.	.	. .	Waterloo	Lancs	L & N. W.	See Liverpool.
.	.	.	.	.	.	. .	Waterloo	Surrey	L. & S.W.—W. & C.	See London.
G	P	.	.	.	.	5 0 ⎫	Waterloo (L. & Y.)	Lancs	⎰ L. & Y.	Liverpool and Southport.
.	P	.	.	.	.	⎭			⎱ L. & N. W.	Over L. & Y. from Bootle Junction.
.	.	.	.	.	.	. .	Waterloo Colliery	Glamorg'n	G. W.	Tredegar Junction.
.	.	.	.	.	.	. .	Waterloo Colliery	Lanark ...	Cal.	Wishaw.
.	.	.	.	.	.	. .	Waterloo Foundry..............	Lancs	⎰ G.C. (St. Helens Exten.)	⎱ Same as Varley & Co.'s Siding
.	.	.	.	.	.	. .			⎱ —L. & N. W.	⎰ (St. Helens).
.	.	.	.	.	.	. .	Waterloo Junction.............	Mon	G. W.	Newport, Dock Street.
.	.	.	.	.	.	. .	Waterloo Junction	Surrey	L. & S.W.—S. E. & C. ...	London, Waterloo (L. & S. W.) and Waterloo Junction Station.
.	.	.	.	.	.	. .	Waterloo Junction Station ...	Surrey	S. E. & C.	See London.
.	.	.	.	.	.	. .	Waterloo, London Necropolis Co.'s Station	Surrey	L. & S.W.	See London.
.	.	.	.	.	.	. .	Waterloo Main Colliery	Yorks	⎰ G. N.	Leeds, Hunslet
.	.	.	.	.	.	. .			⎱ N. E.	Leeds, Marsh Lane.
.	P	.	.	.	.	. .	Waterloo Road	Lancs	P.&W.Jt. (L&Y&L&NW)	See Blackpool (South Shore).
.	P	.	.	.	.	. .	Waterloo Road	Staffs	N. S.	Hanley and Burslem.
.	.	.	.	.	.	. .	Waterloo Sid. (Thomas & Co.)	Glo'ster ...	S.& Wye Jt.(G. W.&Mid.)	Lydbrook, Upper.
.	.	.	.	.	.	. .	Waterloo Tin Plate Works ...	Glamorg'n	B. & M.	Machen.
.	.	.	.	.	.	. .	Waterlow & Son's Siding.....	Beds	G. N.	Dunstable, London Road.
G	P	.	L	H	.	. .	Water Orton	Warwick..	Mid.	Birmingham and Whitacre.
.	.	.	.	.	.	. .	Birmingham Tame & Rae District Drainage Board Sid	Warwick..	Mid.	Water Orton and Birmingham.
G	P	.	L	H	.	1 10	Waterside	Ayr	G. & S.W.	Ayr and Dalmellington.
.	.	.	.	.	.	. .	Dalmellington Iron Works (Waterside Iron Works)	Ayr	G. & S.W.	Waterside.
.	.	.	.	.	.	. .	Drumgrange Pit	Ayr	G. & S.W.	Dunaskin Junction.
.	.	.	.	.	.	. .	Dunaskin Brick Works ...	Ayr	G. & S.W.	Dunaskin Junction.
.	.	.	.	.	.	. .	Houldsworth Pit..............	Ayr	G. & S.W.	Dunaskin Junction.
.	.	.	.	.	.	. .	Jellieston Colliery	Ayr	G. & S.W.	Dunaskin Junction.
.	.	.	.	.	.	. .	Pennyvennie Nos. 1 & 2 ...	Ayr	G. & S.W.	Dunaskin Junction.
.	.	.	.	.	.	. .	Waterside	Derry	N. C. Com. (Mid.).......	See Londonderry.
.	.	.	.	.	.	. .	Waterside Iron Works.........	Ayr	G. & S.W.	Same as Dalmellington Iron Works (Waterside).
.	.	.	.	.	.	. .	Waterside Junction	Dumbartn	N. B.	Lenzie and Croy.
.	.	.	.	.	.	. .	Waterside Mills	Derby	G. C.	Dinting.
.	.	.	.	.	.	. .	Waterslack Siding..............	Lancs	Furness	Arnside.
							WATFORD—			
G	P	F	L	H	C	10 0	(Station)	Herts	L. & N. W.	Bletchley and Willesden.
.	.	.	.	.	.	. .	Benskin's Watford Brewery Co.'s Siding	Herts	L. & N. W.	High Street and Rickmansworth.
.	.	.	.	.	.	. .	Bushey Lodge Sidings	Herts	L. & N. W.	Watford and Bricket Wood.
.	.	.	.	.	.	. .	Ayre's	Herts	L. & N. W.	Bushey Lodge Sidings.
.	.	.	.	.	.	. .	Tibble's Vi-Cocoa	Herts	L. & N. W.	Bushey Lodge Sidings.
.	.	.	.	.	.	. .	Dickinson & Co.'s Croxley Green Siding	Herts	L. & N. W.	High Street and Rickmansworth.
.	P	.	.	.	.	. .	High Street.....................	Herts	L. & N. W.	Rickmansworth and Watford.
.	.	.	.	.	.	. .	Pratt's Siding	Herts	L. & N. W.	Bricket Wood and Watford.
.	.	.	.	.	.	. .	Turner's Siding	Herts	L. & N. W.	Watford and Bricket Wood.
.	.	.	.	.	.	. .	Watford Urban District Council's Siding	Herts	L. & N. W.	High Street and Rickmansworth.
.	.	.	.	.	.	. .	Wells & Co.'s Brewery	Herts	L. & N. W.	Watford and Bricket Wood.
.	.	.	.	.	.	. .	Watford Brewery Co.'s Siding	Herts	L. & N. W.	Same as Benskin's (Watford).
G	P	F	.	.	C	5 0 ⎫	Wath	Yorks	⎰ G. C.	Barnsley and Doncaster.
G	P	F	L	.	.	2 0 ⎭			⎱ H. & B.	Branch from Wrangbrook Junction.
.	.	.	.	.	.	. .	Cortonwood Colliery	Yorks	G. C.	Wath.
.	.	.	.	.	.	. .	Manvers Main Colliery......	Yorks	H. & B.	Wath and Hickleton.
.	.	.	.	.	.	. .	Stanleys Siding	Yorks	G. C.	Wath.
.	.	.	.	.	.	. .	Wath Main Colliery	Yorks	⎰ G. C.	Wath.
.	.	.	.	.	.	. .			⎱ H. & B.	Wath and Hickleton.
.	.	.	.	.	.	. .	Whitworth's Siding	Yorks	G. C.	Wath.
.	P	.	.	.	.	. .	Wath & Bolton	Yorks	Mid.	Swinton and Normanton.
.	.	.	.	.	.	. .	Wath Junction	Yorks	G. C.—Mid & N. E. Jt....	Wath and Bolton-upon-Dearne.
.	.	.	.	.	.	. .	Wath-on-Dearne Main Col.	Yorks	Mid.	Swinton.
.	.	.	.	.	.	. .	Watherston & Son's Stone Sid.	Edinboro'	Cal.	Edinburgh, Lothian Road.
.	.	.	.	.	.	. .	Watkin & Phillip's Timber Yard	Glamorg'n	G. W.	Penygraig.

EXPLANATION—G Goods Station.   P Passenger and Parcel Station.   P* Passenger, but not Parcel or Miscellaneous Traffic.
F Furniture Vans, Carriages, Portable Engines, and Machines on Wheels.   L Live Stock.
H Horse Boxes and Prize Cattle Vans.   C Carriages by Passenger Train.

STATION ACCOMMODATION.						CRANE POWER.		STATIONS, &c.	COUNTY.	COMPANY.	POSITION.
						Tons	Cwts.				
.	.	.	.	.	.	.	.	Watkins Bros.' Siding	Hereford ..	G. W.	Hereford.
.	.	.	.	.	.	.	.	Watkin's Pomona Cider Co.'s Siding	Hereford ..	G. W.	Withington.
.	.	.	.	.	.	.	.	Watkinson & Son's Mountain Colliery	Flint	W. M. & C. Q.	Buckley.
.	.	.	.	.	.	.	.	Watling Street Colliery (Owen & Dutson's Siding)	Staffs	Mid.	Brownhills.
G	P	F	L	H	C	1	0	Watlington	Oxon	G. W.	Branch from Princes Risboro'
G	P	.	.	.	.	.	.	Watnall	Notts	Mid.	Basford and Kimberley.
.	.	.	.	.	.	.	.	Watnall Colliery	Notts	Mid.	Branch from Watnall Junction.
.	.	.	.	.	.	.	.	Watnall Colliery (G. N.)	Notts	G. N.—G. C.	Kimberley.
.	.	.	.	.	.	.	.	Watney Combe & Co.'s Siding (Mid.)	Leicester ..	Mid.—L. & N. W.	Leicester, East.
.	.	.	.	.	.	.	.	Watson & Co.'s Siding	Lancs	Mid.	Carnforth.
.	.	.	.	.	.	.	.	Watson & Co.'s Timber Yard	Yorks	N. E.	See Whitehouse Siding and Depôt (South Bank).
.	.	.	.	.	.	.	.	Watson & Hartley's Siding (Fur. & Mid. Jt.)	Lancs	Fur. & Mid. Jt.—L. N. W.	Carnforth.
.	.	.	.	.	.	.	.	Watson & Son's Siding.........	Lanark ...	G B & K Jt (Cal & G & S W)	Glasgow, South Side.
.	.	.	.	.	.	.	.	Watson & Son's Siding.........	Northumb	N. E.	Walker Gate.
.	.	.	.	.	.	.	.	Watson's Brick Works........	Durham ..	N. E.	Haverton Hill.
.	.	.	...	.	.	.	.	Watson's Flour Mill	Durham ..	N. E.	Same as North Shore Flour Mill (Stockton).
.	.	.	.	.	.	.	.	Watson's Pits Nos. 1, 2, 3, & 4	Lanark ...	Cal.	Motherwell.
.	.	.	.	.	.	.	.	Watson's Siding................	Glamorg'n	T. V.	Cardiff Docks.
.	.	.	.	.	.	.	.	Watson's Timber & Slate Yard	Durham ..	N. E.	Stockton, South.
.	.	.	.	.	.	.	.	Watson's Wharf..................	Yorks	N. E.	Same as Dent's, T. R., Wharf (Middlesbro').
.	.	.	.	.	.	.	.	Watson, Todd & Co.'s Siding (L. & N. W.)	Warwick ..	L. & N. W.—Mid.	Birmingham, Monument Lane.
.	.	.	.	.	.	.	.	Watsonville Colliery............	Lanark ...	Cal.	Motherwell.
.	.	.	.	.	.	.	.	Watstonfoot Colliery	Lanark ...	N. B.	Morningside.
.	.	.	.	.	.	.	.	Watston Siding	Lanark ...	Cal.	Stonehouse.
.	.	.	.	.	.	.	.	Watt & Co.'s Siding	Staffs	L. & N. W.	Same as Avery's Siding (Soho).
.	.	.	.	.	.	.	.	Watts & Son's Sid. (G. E.)...	Cambs ...	G. E.—L. & N. W.—Mid.	Cambridge.
.	.	.	.	.	.	.	.	Watts' Siding....................	Brecon ...	Cam.	Newbridge-on-Wye.
.	.	.	.	.	.	.	.	Watt, Torrance & Co.'s Saw Mill (Cal.)	Stirling ...	Cal.—N. B.	Grangemouth.
G	P	F	L	H	C	1	10	Watten.............................	Caithness	High.	Georgemas and Wick.
.	.	.	.	.	.	.	.	Watter's Flour Mills (Mid.)...	Leicester ..	Mid.—L. & N. W.	Coalville.
.	.	.	.	.	.	.	.	Watton (B. & M.)	Brecon ...	B. & M.—Cam.—Mid.	See Brecon.
G	P	F	L	H	C	1	0	Watton	Norfolk ...	G. E.	Thetford and Swaffham.
.	.	.	.	.	.	.	.	Howlett, T. S., Siding......	Norfolk ...	G. E.	Watton.
G	.	.	.	.	.	2	10	Wattstown	Glamorg'n	T. V.	Porth and Ferndale.
.	.	.	.	.	.	.	.	National Colliery	Glamorg'n	T. V.	Tylorstown and Ynishir.
.	.	.	.	.	.	.	.	Pontygwaith Siding	Glamorg'n	T. V.	Ynishir and Tylorstown.
.	.	.	.	.	.	.	.	Ynishir Col. (House Coal)	Glamorg'n	T. V.	Porth and Ynishir.
.	.	.	.	.	.	.	.	Ynishir Standard Colliery (Steam Coal)	Glamorg'n	T. V.	Ynishir and Tylorstown.
.	.	.	.	.	.	.	.	Watt Street......................	Lanark ...	N. B.	Same as Taylor's Sid. (Rawyards).
.	.	.	.	.	.	.	.	Waulkmill Siding	Forfar	Cal.	See Arbroath.
.	.	.	.	.	.	.	.	Wauntreoda Works	Glamorg'n	T. V.	Llandaff.
.	.	.	.	.	.	.	.	Waverley	Edinboro'	N. B.	See Edinburgh.
.	.	.	.	.	.	.	.	Waverley Iron & Steel Works	Lanark ...	N. B.	Coatbridge, Sunnyside.
.	.	.	.	.	.	.	.	Waverley Mills Siding	Peebles ...	N. B.	Innerleithen.
.	.	.	.	.	.	.	.	Waverley Oil & Cake Mills ...	Edinboro'	Cal.	Edinburgh, Lothian Road.
G	P	F	L	H	C	1	10	Waverton.........................	Cheshire ..	L. & N. W.	Chester and Crewe.
.	.	.	.	.	.	.	.	Wavertree.........................	Lancs	L. & N. W.	See Liverpool.
.	.	.	.	.	.	.	.	Wavertree & Edge Hill	Lancs	C. L. C (G C, G N, & Mid.)	See Liverpool.
.	.	.	.	.	.	.	.	Wavertree Gas Works	Lancs	L. & N. W.	See Liverpool United Gas Co. (Liverpool).
.	.	.	.	.	.	.	.	Wayman's Landsale Depôts	Durham ...	N. E.	Sunderland, South Dock.
.	.	.	.	.	.	.	.	Waynes Merthyr Colliery ...	Glamorg'n	{ G. W. { T. V.	Aberdare. Same as Gadlys Works (Aberdare).
.	.	.	.	.	.	.	.	Weald Siding	Kent	S. E. & C.	Hildenborough.
.	.	.	.	.	.	.	.	Wealdstone	Middlesex	L. & N. W.	See Harrow and Wealdstone.
.	.	.	.	.	.	.	.	Wear Commissioners' Hudson and Hendon Docks...	Durham ...	N. E.	{ See River Wear Commissioners { (Sunderland).
.	.	.	.	.	.	.	.	Weardale Steel, Coal, & Coke Co.'s Siding..................	Durham ...	N. E.	Darlington, Bank Top.
.	.	.	.	.	.	.	.	Wear Fuel & Chemical Co.'s Works	Durham ...	N. E.	Sunderland, South Dock.

EXPLANATION—G *Goods Station.*   P *Passenger and Parcel Station.*   P* *Passenger, but not Parcel or Miscellaneous Traffic.*
F *Furniture Vans, Carriages, Portable Engines, and Machines on Wheels.*   L *Live Stock.*
H *Horse Boxes and Prize Cattle Vans.*   C *Carriages by Passenger Train.*

STATION ACCOMMODATION.						CRANE POWER.		STATIONS, &c.	COUNTY.	COMPANY.	POSITION.
						Tons	Cwts.				
G	P	F	L	H	C	1	10	Wearhead....................	Durham ...	N. E.	Wear Valley Extension Terminus.
.	.	.	.	.	.	.	.	Coronation Siding	Durham ...	N. E.	Wearhead.
.	.	.	.	.	.	.	.	Wearmouth Colliery	Durham ...	N. E.	Southwick.
.	.	.	.	.	.	.	.	Wearmouth Dock	Durham ...	N. E.	Same as Sunderland, North Dock.
.	.	.	.	.	.	.	.	Wearmouth Fire-Brick Wks.	Durham ...	N. E.	Sunderland, Monkwearmouth.
.	P	.	.	.	.	.	.	Wearmouth Foundry	Durham ...	N. E.	Sunderland, Monkwearmouth.
.	.	.	.	.	.	.	.	Wear Valley Junction Station	Durham ...	N. E.	Bishop Auckland and Stanhope.
.	.	.	.	.	.	.	.	Weaste (L. & N. W.)............	Lancs	L. & N. W.—G. W.	See Manchester.
.	.	.	.	.	.	.	.	Weaste Junction	Lancs	L&NW—Man.Ship Canal	Manchester.
.	.	.	.	.	.	.	.	Weaver's Flour Mills	Glamorg'n	G. W.	Swansea.
G	P	F	L	H	C	5	0	Weaverthorpe	Yorks	N. E.	Malton and Scarborough.
.	.	.	.	.	.	.	♪	Weaverthorpe Grain Warehouse	Yorks	N. E.	Weaverthorpe.
.	.	.	.	.	.	.	.	Webb & Co.'s Siding...........	Herts	G. N.	Hertingfordbury.
.	.	.	.	.	.	.	.	Webb & Son's Siding	Cheshire ...	{ G. W. / L. & N. W.	Saltney. / Saltney Wharf.
.	.	.	.	.	.	.	.	Webb & Spring's Mills........	Glo'ster ...	Mid.	Ryeford.
.	.	.	.	.	.	.	.	Webb Bros.' Siding	Glo'ster ...	Mid.	Cheltenham.
.	.	.	.	.	.	.	.	Webb, Shakespeare, & Williams' Glamorgan Tin Works	Glamorg'n	G. W. & L. & N. W. Jt...	Pontardulais.
.	.	.	.	.	.	.	.	Webb's Siding	Cork	G. S. & W.	Mallow.
.	.	.	.	.	.	.	.	Webbe's Coal Yard	Lancs	L. & N. W.	St. Helens.
.	.	.	.	.	.	.	.	Webber & Pangbourne's Sids.	Dorset......	E.& C.H.(GW&L.& SW)	Easton.
.	.	.	.	.	.	.	.	Webster & Son's Siding	Yorks	H'fax H. L. (G N & L & Y)	Halifax, Wheatley.
.	.	.	.	.	.	.	.	Webster's Brick Works } Railway Co.'s Sid.(LN W) }	Warwick.	{ L. & N. W. / Mid.	Foleshill. / Coventry.
.	.	.	.	.	.	.	.	Wedgewood's Colliery	Staffs	N. S.	Same as Jamage Colliery (Diglake).
								WEDNESBURY—			
G	P	F	L	H	C	8	0	(Station, for Darlaston) ...	Staffs	G. W.	Birmingham and Wolverhampton.
G	P	F	L	H	C	10	0)	(Station, L. & N. W.)	Staffs	{ L. & N. W.	Dudley and Walsall.
G	.	F	L	H	C	10	0)			{ Mid.	Over L. & N. W. from Walsall Jn.
.	.	.	.	.	.	.	.	Chance & Hunt's Works (G. W.)	Staffs	G. W.—L. & N. W.	Near Wednesbury.
.	.	.	.	.	.	.	.	Graham's Siding(L.& N.W.)	Staffs	L. & N. W.—G. W.	Wednesbury and Walsall.
.	.	.	.	.	.	.	.	Howl's or Tibbington's Sid.	Staffs	L. & N. W.	Princes End and Tipton.
.	.	.	.	.	.	.	.	Junction	Staffs	G. W.—L. & N. W.	G. W. and L. & N. W. Stations.
G	.	.	.	.	.	.	.	Lodge Holes Colliery........	Staffs	L. & N. W.	Darlaston and Wednesbury.
.	.	.	.	.	.	.	.	Mesty Croft Sidings.........	Staffs	L. & N. W.	Wednesbury and Walsall.
								Patent Shaft & Axletree Co.—			
.	.	.	.	.	.	.	.	Brunswick Works	Staffs	G. W.	Near Wednesbury (for Darlaston).
.	.	.	.	.	.	.	.	Brunswick Wks. (LNW)	Staffs	L. & N. W.—Mid.	Wednesbury and Darlaston.
								Lloyd's—			
.	.	.	.	.	.	.	.	Monway Works	Staffs	G. W.	Near Wednesbury (for Darlaston).
.	.	.	.	.	.	.	.	Monway Works(LNW)	Staffs	L. & N. W.—Mid.	Wednesbury and Darlaston.
.	.	.	.	.	.	.	.	Old Park Works.........	Staffs	G. W.	Near Wednesbury (for Darlaston).
.	.	.	.	.	.	.	.	Old Park Works(LNW)	Staffs	L. & N. W.—Mid.	Wednesbury and Darlaston.
.	.	.	.	.	.	◄	.	Russell's Siding	Staffs	L. & N. W.	Wednesbury and Great Bridge.
.	.	.	.	.	.	.	.	South Staffordshire Waterworks Crank Hall Siding	Staffs	L. & N. W.	Wednesbury and Walsall.
.	.	.	.	.	.	.	.	Tube Siding and Depôt...	Staffs	G. W.	Near Wednesbury.
.	.	.	.	.	.	.	.	Ward's, T. W., Scrap Iron Depôt....................	Staffs	G. W.	Wednesbury.
G	.	.	.	.	.	12	0	Wednesbury Basin	Staffs	G. W.	Birmingham and Wolverhampton.
.	.	.	.	.	.	.	.	Wednesbury Crushing Co.	Staffs	G. W.	Near Wednesbury Basin.
.	.	.	.	.	.	.	.	Williams & Son's Wed- } nesbury Oak Iron Wks. }	Staffs	{ G. W. / L. & N. W.	Wednesbury. / Ocker Hill and Princes End.
.	.	.	.	.	.	.	.	Willingsworth Iron Co.'s Siding (G. W.)	Staffs	G. W.—L. & N. W.	Near Wednesbury Basin.
.	.	.	.	.	.	.	.	Wednesbury Oak Iron Works	Staffs	G. W.—L. & N. W.	Same as Williams & Son's Siding (Wednesbury).
G	P	F	L	H	C	1	10)	Wednesfield (Mid.)	Staffs	{ Mid.	Wolverhampton & Sutton Coldfield.
G	.	F	L	.	.	1	10)			{ G. W.	Over Mid. from Wolverhampton Jn.
.	.	.	.	.	.	.	.	Patent Axle Box Co.'s Works (Mid.)	Staffs	Mid.—G. W.	Wednesfield.
G	.	.	L	.	.	.	.	Wednesfield Heath	Staffs	L. & N. W.	Birmingham and Wolverhampton.
G	P	F	L	H	C	5	0	Weedon	N'hamptn	L. & N. W.	Blisworth and Rugby.
.	.	.	.	.	.	.	.	Stowe Siding	N'hamptn	L. & N. W.	Weedon and Blisworth.
.	.	.	.	.	.	.	.	Weekday Cross Junction......	Notts	G. C.—G. N.	Nottingham.
.	.	.	.	.	.	.	.	Weekes' Siding	Kent	S. E. & C.	Cuxton.
G	P	F	L	H	C	.	.	Weeley	Essex	G. E.	Colchester and Clacton-on-Sea.
.	.	.	.	.	.	.	.	Carr, W. H., Siding	Essex	G. E.	Weeley.

STATION ACCOMMODATION.						CRANE POWER.		STATIONS, &c.	COUNTY.	COMPANY.	POSITION.
						Tons	Cwts				
G	P	.	L	H	C	3	0	Weeton.........................	Yorks	N. E.	Leeds and Harrogate.
.	.	.	.	.	.	.	.	Weiner's Timber Yard.........	Durham ...	N. E.	Sunderland, South Dock.
.	.	.	.	.	.	.	.	Welbeck	Derby	L. D. & E. C.	See Creswell and Welbeck.
G	P	.	L	H	C	3	0	Welbury.........................	Yorks .●.	N. E.	Northallerton and Stockton.
.	.	.	.	.	.	.	.	West Rounton Gate	Yorks	N. E.	Welbury.
.	.	.	.	.	.	.	.	Welby's Siding..................	Lincoln ...	G. N.	Bottesford.
.	.	.	.	.	.	.	.	Welch Whittle Colliery	Lancs	L. & N. W.	Same as Barker & Son's Sid (Coppull).
.	.	.	.	.	.	.	.	Welcome Siding (Mid.)	Staffs	Mid.—L&NW—GN—NS	See Peach & Co. (Burton-on-Trent).
G	P	F	L	H	C	5	0	Weldon and Corby.............	N'hampton	Mid.	Kettering and Manton.
.	.	.	.	.	.	.	.	Pain's Ironstone Siding	N'hampton	Mid.	Near Weldon and Corby.
.	.	.	.	.	.	.	.	Weldon and Corby Patent Brick Co.'s Siding.........	N'hampton	Mid.	Near Weldon and Corby.
G	P	F	L	H	C	1	5	Welford and Lutterworth ...	Leicester ...	L. & N. W.	Market Harboro' and Rugby.
.	.	.	.	.	.	.	.	Welford-on-Avon	Warwick..	G. W.	See Milcote.
G	P	.	.	.	.	.	.	Welford Park (for Wickham and Weston)	Berks	L'bourn Valley	Newbury and Lambourn.
.	.	.	.	.	.	.	.	Welham Junction	Leicester..	G N & L N W Jt.—L&NW	Market Harboro' & Melton Mowbray
.	.	.	.	.	.	.	.	Welham Siding	Notts	G. C.	Retford.
.	.	.	.	.	.	.	.	Wellbank Quarry	Forfar	Cal.	Gagie.
.	.	.	.	.	.	.	.	Wellbrae Quarry and Siding	Lanark	Cal.	Meikle Earnock.
.	P	.	.	.	.	.	.	Wellfield Junction Station ...	Durham ...	N. E.	Hurworth Burn and Thornley.
.	.	.	.	.	.	.	.	Wellfield Siding	Durham ...	N. E.	Castle Eden.
G	P	.	L	H	C	.	.	Well Hall	Kent	S. E. & C.	Blackheath and Dartford.
.	.	.	.	.	.	.	.	Wellhall Colliery	Lanark	N. B.	Hamilton, Burnbank.
G	P	.	.	.	.	.	.	Welling..............................	Kent	S. E. & C.	Blackheath and Dartford.
G	P	F	L	H	C	10	0	Wellingboro'	N'hamptn	L. & N. W.	Northampton and Peterboro'.
G	P	F	L	H	C	5	0			Mid.	Bedford and Kettering.
								Butlin & Co.—			
.	.	.	.	.	.	.	.	Furnaces	N'hampton	L. & N. W.	Wellingboro' and Ditchford.
.	.	.	.	.	.	.	.	Iron Works	N'hampton	Mid.	Near Wellingboro'.
.	.	.	.	.	.	.	.	Wollaston Iron Ore Siding	N'hampton	L. & N. W.	Wellingboro' and Ditchford.
.	.	.	.	.	.	.	.	Midland Brick Co.'s Siding	N'hampton	Mid.	Wellingboro'.
.	.	.	.	.	.	.	.	Neilson's Iron Ore Siding...	N'hampton	Mid.	Near Wellingboro'.
.	.	.	.	.	.	.	.	Stanton Iron Ore Co.'s Sid.	N'hampton	Mid.	Near Wellingboro'.
.	.	.	.	.	.	.	.	Wellingboro' Gas Co.'s Sid.	N'hampton	Mid.	Wellingboro'.
.	.	.	.	.	.	.	.	Wellingboro' Iron Co.'s Sid.	N'hampton	Mid.	Near Wellingboro'.
.	.	.	.	.	.	.	.	Wellingboro' Urban District Council's Siding	N'hampton	L. & N. W.	Wellingboro' and Ditchford.
.	.	.	.	.	.	.	.	Whitworth's Sid.(L.&NW.)	N'hampton	L. & N. W.—Mid.	Wellingboro' and Ditchford.
.	.	.	.	.	.	.	.	Woolston & Bull's Grain Siding (Mid.)	N'hampton	Mid.—L. & N. W.	Near Wellingboro'.
.	.	.	.	.	.	.	.	Wellingboro' Junction	N'hampton	L. & N. W.—Mid.	Wellingboro' Station and Kettering.
								WELLINGTON—			
G	.	F	L	.	.	10	0	(Station)	Salop	G. W.	Wolverhampton and Shrewsbury.
G	.	F	L	.	.	10	0	(Station)	Salop	L. & N. W.	Shrewsbury and Stafford.
.	P	F	.	H	C	.	.	(Station)	Salop	S & W'tn Jt(GW&L&NW)	Shrewsbury and Stafford Line Junc.
.	.	.	.	.	.	.	.	Groom, Sons, & Co.'s Siding	Salop	S&W'tn Jt(GW&LNW)	Wellington and Admaston.
.	.	.	.	.	.	.	.	Haybridge Iron Co.'s Siding	Salop	G. W.	Wellington and Oakengates.
.	.	.	.	.	.	.	.	Market Drayton Line Junc.	Salop	G. W.—S. & W'tn Jt. ...	Crudgington and Wellington.
.	.	.	.	.	.	.	.	Stafford Line Junction	Salop	L. & N. W.—S.& W'tn Jt.	Stafford and Shrewsbury.
.	.	.	.	.	.	.	.	Wellington Gas Co.'s Siding	Salop	S&W'tn Jt(GW&LNW)	Wellington and Admaston.
.	.	.	.	.	.	.	.	Wolverhampton Line Junc.	Salop	G. W.—S. & W'tn Jt. ...	Oakengates and Shrewsbury.
G	P	F	L	H	C	9	0	Wellington	Somerset..	G. W.	Exeter and Taunton.
.	.	.	.	.	.	.	.	Poole Siding	Somerset..	G. W	Wellington and Norton-Fitzwarren.
.	.	.	.	.	.	.	.	Wellington (Mid.)	Yorks	Mid.—E & W Y U—L & Y	See Leeds.
.	.	.	.	.	.	.	.	Wellington Bridge (G. N.) ...	Yorks	G. N.—G. C.	See Leeds.
.	.	.	.	.	.	.	.	Wellington Cast Steel Foundry	Yorks	N. E.	Middlesbro'.
G	P	F	L	H	C	.	.	Wellington College (for Crowthorne)	Berks	S. E. & C.	Guildford and Reading.
.	.	.	.	.	.	.	.	California Siding	Berks	S. E. & C.	Wellington College & Wokingham.
.	.	.	.	.	.	.	.	Wellington Road	Lancs	C. L. C. (G C, G N, & Mid.)	See Stockport.
.	.	.	.	.	.	.	.	Wellington Sidings	Middlesex	G. N.	London, Highgate.
.	.	.	.	.	.	.	.	Wellington Street	Yorks	L & Y & L & N W Jt.—NE	See Leeds.
.	.	.	.	.	.	.	.	Wellington Street (G.N.) ...	Yorks	G. N.—G. C.	See Leeds.
G	P	.	L	H	.	.	.	Wellow	Somerset..	S.&D. Jt. (L.&S. W.& Mid)	Radstock and Bath.
.	.	.	.	.	.	.	.	Fuller's Earth Union Siding	Somerset..	S.&D. Jt. (L.&S. W. & Mid)	Wellow.
G	.	.	.	.	.	.	.	Wellow Siding	I. of W. ...	I. of W. Cent...............	Yarmouth and Newport.
G	P	F	L	H	C	1	10	Wells	Norfolk ...	G. E.	Terminus.
.	.	.	.	.	.	.	.	Dewing & Kersley Siding...	Norfolk ...	G. E.	Wells.
.	.	.	.	.	.	.	.	Quay Siding....................	Norfolk ...	G. E.	Wells.
G	P	F	L	H	C	8	0	Wells..............................	Somerset..	G. W.	Witham and Yatton.
G	P	F	L	H	C	10	0			S.&D. Jt. (L.&SW & Mid)	Branch from Glastonbury.

STATION ACCOMMODATION.						CRANE POWER.		STATIONS, &c.	COUNTY.	COMPANY.	POSITION.
						Tons	Cwts.	Wells—*continued.*			
..	..	..	..	..	..	..	..	Dulcot Sidings	Somerset..	G. W.	Wells.
..	..	..	..	..	..	..	..	Gas Works	Somerset	G. W.	Wells.
..	..	..	..	..	..	..	..	Wells Junction	Somerset..	G. W.—S. & D. Jt.	Shepton Mallet and Glastonbury.
..	..	..	..	..	..	..	..	Wells & Co.'s Brewery	Herts	L. & N. W.	Watford.
..	..	..	..	..	..	..	..	Wells Coke Ovens	Yorks	G. C.	Worsbro'.
..	..	..	..	..	..	..	..	Wells', J. & G., Siding.........	Derby	Mid.	Eckington & Renishaw.
..	..	..	..	..	..	..	..	Wellsgreen Colliery	Fife	N. B.	Wemyss Castle.
..	..	..	..	..	..	..	..	Wellwood Colliery.............	Fife	N. B.	See Elgin and Wellwood Colliery (Townhill Junction Station).
..	..	..	..	..	..	..	..	Wellwood Sidings..............	Ayr	G. & S. W.	See Lower and Upper Wellwood (Muirkirk).
G	P	F	.	H	C	..	..	Welnetham	Suffolk ...	G. E.	Sudbury and Bury.
G	P	.	.	H	.	..	..	Welshampton	Salop	Cam.	Whitchurch and Ellesmere.
.	P	.	L	.	.	..	..	Welsh Main Colliery...........	Glamorg'n	S. Wales Min..............	Glyncorrwg.
G	P	.	L	.	.	..	..	Welshpool	Montgom	Cam. (W. & L.)	Near Cambrian Station.
.	P	.	.	.	.	..	..	Raven Square	Montgom	Cam. (W. & L.)	Welshpool and Golfa.
.	P	.	.	.	.	..	..	Seven Stars	Montgom	Cam. (W. & L.)	Welshpool and Raven Square.
.	P	.	.	.	.	..	..	Standard Quarry	Montgom	Cam. (W. & L.)	Welshpool and Raven Square.
G	P	F	L	H	C	5	0	Welshpool (Cam.)	Montgom	{ Cam. / S.&W'plJt(GW&LNW)	Oswestry and Newtown. / Over Cam. from Buttington Junc.
..	..	..	..	..	..	..	..	Welsh Road Siding	Flint	G. C.	Saughall.
..	..	..	..	..	..	..	..	Welsh Tin Plate Stamping Co. (G. W.)	Carmarth'	G. W.—L. & N. W.	Llanelly.
G	P	F	L	H	C	1	5	Welton	N'hamptn	L. & N. W.	Blisworth and Rugby.
..	..	..	..	..	..	..	..	Iven's Siding	N'hamptn	L. & N. W.	Welton and Weedon.
..	..	..	..	..	..	..	..	Welton	Somerset..	G. W.—S. & D. Jt.	See Midsomer-Norton and Welton.
G	P	F	L	H	C	5	0	Welwyn	Herts	G. N.	Hatfield and Hitchin.
G	P	F	L	H	C	5	0	Wem	Salop	L. & N. W.	Shrewsbury and Whitchurch.
..	..	..	..	..	..	..	..	Wembley	Middlesex	L. & N. W.	See Sudbury and Wembley.
G	P	F	L	H	C	..	..	Wembley Park	Middlesex	Met.	Baker Str. and Harrow-on-the-Hill.
G	P	F	L	H	C	3	0	Wemyss Bay	Renfrew ..	Cal.	Terminus of Bch. fr. Port Glasgow.
..	..	..	..	..	..	..	..	Wemyss Bay Junction	Renfrew ..	Cal.	Port Glasgow and Bogston.
..	..	..	..	..	..	..	..	Wemyss Brick Works	Fife	N. B.	Methil.
G	P	F	L	H	C	1	10	Wemyss Castle	Fife	N. B.	Thornton and Methil.
..	..	..	..	..	..	..	..	Michael Colliery	Fife	N. B.	Branch—West Wemyss and Wemyss Castle.
..	..	..	..	..	..	..	..	Wellsgreen Colliery	Fife	N. B.	Branch from Wemyss Castle.
..	..	..	..	..	..	..	..	Wemyss Saw Mill (Donaldson & Son's)	Fife	N. B.	Leven.
G	P	F	.	H	C	2	0	Wendling	Norfolk ...	G. E.	Swaffham and Dereham.
G	P	F	L	H	C	1	10	Wendover (Met.)	Bucks	{ Met. / G. C.	Rickmansworth and Aylesbury. / Over Met. Line.
.	P	.	.	H	C	..	..				
G	.	.	.	.	.	..	..	Wenford Bridge	Cornwall ..	L. & S. W.	Branch from Wadebridge.
G	P	.	.	.	.	..	..	Wenhaston	Suffolk ...	Southwold	Halesworth and Blythburgh.
G	P	F	L	H	C	..	..	Wennington	Lancs	Mid.	Lancaster and Skipton.
..	..	..	..	..	..	..	..	Wennington Junction	Lancs	Fur. & Mid. Jt.—Mid.	Melling and Wennington.
..	..	..	..	..	..	..	..	Wennington Siding	Essex	L. T. & S.	Rainham.
..	..	..	..	..	..	..	..	Wenn, Mrs. E., Siding........	Norfolk ...	G. E.	Downham.
G	P	.	.	.	.	..	..	Wensley	Yorks	N. E.	Leyburn and Hawes.
..	..	..	..	..	..	..	..	Wentlooge Colliery	Mon	L. & N. W.	Same as Pond's Siding (Ynysddu).
G	P	F	L	H	C	..	..	Wentworth and Hoyland Common	Yorks	Mid.	Chapeltown and Barnsley.
..	..	..	..	..	..	..	..	Lidgett's Colliery	Yorks	Mid.	Near Wentworth.
..	..	..	..	..	..	..	..	Skier's Spring Brick Works (Smith's)	Yorks	Mid.	Near Wentworth.
G	P	F	L	H	C	..	..	Wenvoe	Glamorg'n	Barry........................	Cadoxton and Creigiau.
..	..	..	..	..	..	..	..	Alps Quarry Siding	Glamorg'n	Barry........................	Wenvoe.
..	..	..	..	..	..	..	..	Wepre Hall Brick Works ...	Flint	W. M. & C. Q.	Same as Darbyshire's Brick Works (Connah's Quay).
..	..	..	..	..	..	..	..	Wepre Works (Borax Consolidated Works)	Flint	W. M. & C. Q.	Connah's Quay.
..	..	..	..	..	..	..	..	Werfa Colliery	Glamorg'n	{ G. W. / T. V.	Abernant. / Aberdare.
..	..	..	..	..	..	..	..	Wernddu Col. & Brick Works	Glamorg'n	Rhy.	Same as Caerphilly Colliery and Brick Works (Caerphilly).
..	..	..	..	..	..	..	..	Werneth	Lancs	L. & Y.	See Oldham.
..	..	..	..	..	..	..	..	Wern Siding	Carnarvon	Cam.	See Criccieth.
..	..	..	..	..	..	..	..	Wern Tin Plate Co.'s Works	Glamorg'n	G. W.	Briton Ferry.
..	..	..	..	..	..	..	..	Werrington Junction	N'hamptn	G. N.	Peterboro' and Peakirk.
..	..	..	..	..	..	..	..	Wesham Mill	Lancs	P.&W.Jt.(L&Y&L&NW)	Same as Richards, Boulder & Co.'s Siding (Kirkham).

STATION ACCOMMODATION.						CRANE POWER.	STATIONS, &c.	COUNTY.	COMPANY.	POSITION.
						Tons Cwts				
.	.	.	.	.	.	. .	West Acton	Middlesex	Met. Dist.	See Ealing Common & West Acton.
.	.	.	.	.	.	. .	West & Wright's Siding	Kent	S. E. & C.	Maidstone.
.	.	.	.	.	.	. .	West Ardsley Colliery	Yorks	G. N.	See Balaclava Colliery (Tingley).
G	P	.	.	.	.	2 0	West Auckland	Durham ...	N. E.	Barnard Castle & Bishop Auckland.
.	.	.	.	.	.	. .	Brussleton (New Winning) Pit	Durham ...	N. E.	West Auckland.
.	.	.	.	.	.	. .	Coppy Crooks Colliery (Wharf Siding)	Durham ...	N. E.	West Auckland.
.	.	.	.	.	.	. .	Davison's Wagon Repairing Works (St. Helens Col.)	Durham ...	N. E.	West Auckland.
.	.	.	.	.	.	. .	Etherley Grange & Wood-house Colliery.............	Durham ...	N. E.	West Auckland.
.	.	.	.	.	.	. .	Fieldon's Bridge Brk. Yard	Durham ...	N. E.	West Auckland.
.	.	.	.	.	.	. .	Fieldon's Bridge Junction	Durham ...	N. E.	West Auckland.
.	.	.	.	.	.	. .	Fletcher's Holme Mill Sid. (Spring Gardens)	Durham ...	N. E.	West Auckland.
.	.	.	.	.	.	. .	Fyland's Bridge Gas Works (Bishop Auckland and District Gas Co.)	Durham ...	N. E.	West Auckland.
.	.	.	.	.	.	. .	Fyland's Locomotive Shops (N. E. R.).....................	Durham ...	N. E.	West Auckland.
.	.	.	.	.	.	. .	Hummerbeck Colliery Wharf	Durham ...	N. E.	West Auckland.
.	.	.	.	.	.	. .	St. Helens Colliery (Pease & Partners)	Durham ...	N. E.	West Auckland.
.	.	.	.	.	.	. .	Spring Gardens Gates Sid.	Durham ...	N. E.	West Auckland.
.	.	.	.	.	.	. .	Spring Gardens Junction...	Durham ...	N. E.	West Auckland.
.	.	.	.	.	.	. .	Tindale Col.(St. Helens Col.)	Durham ...	N. E.	West Auckland.
.	.	.	.	.	.	. .	West Auckland Colliery ...	Durham ...	N. E.	West Auckland.
.	.	.	.	.	.	. .	West Auckland Fan Blast Siding	Durham ...	N. E.	West Auckland.
.	.	.	.	.	.	. .	Westbank Brick Works	Edinboro'	N. B.	Edinburgh, Portobello.
.	.	.	.	.	.	. .	West Bank Chemical Co.'s Sid.	Lancs	L. & N. W.—S. & M. Jt.	Widnes.
.	.	.	.	.	.	. .	West Bank Dock	Lancs	L. & N. W.—S. & M. Jt.	Widnes.
.	.	.	.	.	.	. .	West Bank Junction............	Lancs	S. & M. Jt. (G. C. & Mid.)	Widnes.
.	.	.	.	.	.	. .	West Bank Siding...............	Lancs	L. & N. W.—S. & M. Jt.	Same as Hutchinson's Trustees' Siding (Widnes).
.	.	.	.	.	.	. .	West Barns Siding	Hadding'n	N. B.	Dunbar.
.	.	.	.	.	.	. .	West Bay	Dorset......	G. W.	See Bridport.
.	.	.	.	.	.	. .	West Beach Line	Edinboro'	N. B.	Granton.
.	.	.	.	.	.	. .	West Benhar Level Crossing Siding	Lanark ...	N. B.	Westcraigs.
.	.	.	.	.	.	. .	West Boldon Junction	Durham ...	N. E.	Boldon and South Shields.
.	.	.	.	.	.	. .	Westbourne Park	Middlesex	G W—H&CJt(GW& Met.)	See London.
.	.	.	.	.	.	. .	West Bridge......................	Leicester..	Mid.	See Leicester.
.	.	.	.	.	.	. .	West Bridge Depôt	Yorks	N. E.	Middlesbro'.
.	.	.	.	.	.	. .	West Bridge Wharf	Leicester..	Mid.	Leicester, West Bridge.
.	.	.	.	.	.	. .	West Brompton	Middlesex	Met. Dist.—W. L. E. Jt.	See London.
.	.	.	.	.	.	. .	West Bromwich	Staffs	L. & N. W.	See Spon Lane (for West Bromwich).
G	P	F	L	H	C	12 0	West Bromwich & Spon Lane	Staffs	G. W.	Birmingham and Wolverhampton.
.	.	.	.	.	.	. .	Couse & Bailey's Siding ...	Staffs	G. W.	Birmingham and Wolverhampton.
.	.	.	.	.	.	. .	Spon Lane......................	Staffs	G. W.	West Bromwich.
.	.	.	.	.	.	. .	West Bromwich Corporation Siding	Staffs	L. & N. W.	Darlaston.
.	.	.	.	.	.	. .	West Bromwich Gas Co.'s Sid.	Staffs	L. & N. W.	Albion.
G	P	.	.	.	.	. .	Westbrook	Hereford..	G. W.	Dorstone and Hay.
G	.	.	.	.	.	. .	Green's Siding	Hereford..	G. W.	Westbrook and Clifford.
.	.	.	.	.	.	. .	Westburn Colliery	Lanark ...	Cal.	Newton.
.	.	.	.	.	.	. .	Westburn Sugar Refinery......	Renfrew ...	Cal.	Same as Berry Yard Sugar Refinery (Greenock).
.	.	.	.	.	.	. .	Westbury	Bucks	L. & N. W.	See Fulwell and Westbury.
G	P	F	L	H	C	2 10	Westbury	Salop	S.&W'plJt.(G W&L N W)	Shrewsbury and Welshpool.
.	.	.	.	.	.	. .	Greenwood's Sarn Terra Cotta Brick and Tile Works	Salop	S.&W'plJt.(G W&L N W)	Westbury and Yockleton.
G	P	F	L	H	C	12 0	Westbury	Wilts	G. W.	Trowbridge and Frome.
.	.	.	.	.	.	. .	Iron Works Siding............	Wilts	G. W.	Westbury.
.	.	.	.	.	.	. .	West Bush Mills Siding	Edinboro'	N. B.	Musselburgh.
.	.	.	.	.	.	. .	West Bute Dock..................	Glamorg'n	G. W—LNW—Rhy.—TV	Cardiff.
G	P	F	L	H	C	3 0	West Calder.....................	Edinboro'	Cal.	Holytown and Edinburgh.
.	.	.	.	.	.	. .	Addiewell Pits & Oil Wks.	Edinboro'	Cal.	Addiewell and West Calder.
.	.	.	.	.'	.	. .	Foulshiels Col. & Bk. Wks.	Edinboro'	Cal.	Branch near Breich.

EXPLANATION— G *Goods Station.*   P *Passenger and Parcel Station.*   P* *Passenger, but not Parcel or Miscellaneous Traffic.*
F *Furniture Vans, Carriages, Portable Engines, and Machines on Wheels.*   L *Live Stock.*
H *Horse Boxes and Prize Cattle Vans.*   C *Carriages by Passenger Train.*

STATION ACCOMMODATION.						CRANE POWER.	STATIONS, &c.	COUNTY.	COMPANY.	POSITION.
						Tons Cwts.	West Calder—continued.			
.	.	.	.	.	. .	. .	Hermand Brick Works ...	Edinboro'	Cal.	Branch near West Calder.
.	.	.	.	.	. .	. .	Hermand Oil Works (New) (Breich Oil Works)	L'lithgow	Cal.	Branch near West Calder.
.	.	.	.	.	. .	. .	Limefield Weighs	Edinboro'	Cal.	West Calder and Newpark.
.	.	.	.	.	. .	. .	Loganlea Collieries Nos.1&2	Edinboro'	Cal.	Branch near Breich.
.	.	.	.	.	. .	. .	Loganlea Collieries Nos.3&4	Edinboro'	Cal.	Branch near Breich.
.	.	.	.	.	. .	. .	Young's Paraffin Light and Mineral Oil Works	Edinboro'	Cal.	Addiewell and West Calder.
.	.	.	.	.	. .	. .	Young's Pits	Edinboro'	Cal.	Addiewell and West Calder.
.	.	.	.	.	. .	. .	West Calder Branch Junction	L'lithgow	N. B.	Livingston and Bathgate, Upper.
.	.	.	.	.	. .	. .	West Canal Wharf	Glamorg'n	G. W.	Cardiff.
.	.	.	.	.	. .	. .	West Cannock Colliery	Staffs	L. & N. W.	Hednesford.
.	.	.	.	.	. .	. .	West Carterthorne Colliery...	Durham ...	N. E.	Evenwood.
.	.	.	.	.	. .	. .	West Cheshire Water Co.'s Siding	Cheshire...	B'head Jt. (G W & L N W)	Hooton.
.	.	.	.	.	. .	. .	West Cliff	Yorks	N. E.	See Whitby.
.	P	.	.	.	. .	. .	Westcliff-on-Sea	Essex	L. T. & S.	Tilbury and Southend-on-Sea.
.	.	.	.	.	. .	. .	West Colinton Paper Mill ...	Edinboro'	Cal.	Same as Colinton Paper Mill (Colinton).
.	P	.	.	.	. .	. .	Westcombe Park	Kent	S. E. & C.	Greenwich and Woolwich.
G	P	.	L	H	. .	2 0	West Cornforth	Durham ...	N. E.	Ferryhill and Castle Eden.
.	.	.	.	.	. .	. .	Ferryhill Engine Works ...	Durham ...	N. E.	West Cornforth.
.	.	.	.	.	. .	. .	Thrislington Colliery & Coke Works..............	Durham ...	N. E.	West Cornforth.
.	.	.	.	.	. .	. .	Thrislington New Coke & Bye Product Works	Durham ...	N. E.	West Cornforth.
.	.	.	.	.	. .	. .	Tursdale Col. & Ck. Wks.	Durham ...	N. E.	West Cornforth.
G	P	.	.	.	. .	. .	Westcott	Bucks......	O. & A. Tram.	Quainton Road and Brill (Wotton District).
G	P	.	L	H	. .	1 10	Westcraigs (for Harthill)......	Lanark ...	N. B.	Caldercruix and Bathgate, Upper.
.	.	.	.	.	. .	. .	Barblues No. 10 Colliery (Blairmuckhill Colliery)	Lanark	N. B.	Westcraigs and Shotts.
.	.	.	.	.	. .	. .	Harthill Dewar Siding	Lanark	N. B.	Westcraigs and Shotts.
G	.	.	.	.	. .	1 0	Harthill Siding	Lanark	N. B.	Westcraigs and Shotts.
.	.	.	.	.	. .	. .	South Broadrigg Bk. Wks.	Lanark	N. B.	Armadale and Westcraigs.
.	.	.	.	.	. .	. .	South Broadrigg Colliery ..	Lanark	N. B.	Armadale and Westcraigs.
.	.	.	.	.	. .	. .	Southrigg Cols. Nos. 1, 2, 3	Lanark	N. B.	Armadale and Westcraigs.
.	.	.	.	.	. .	. .	West Benhar Level Crossing Siding	Lanark	N. B.	Westcraigs and Shotts.
.	.	.	.	.	. .	. .	Westrigg Colliery	Lanark	N. B.	Armadale and Westcraigs.
.	.	.	.	.	. .	. .	Woodend Nos. 4 & 5 Cols.	Lanark	N. B.	Armadale and Westcraigs.
.	.	.	.	.	. .	. .	Westcraigs Junction............	Lanark	N. B.	Armadale and Forrestfield.
.	P	.	.	.	. .	. .	West Cross Road	Glamorg'n	Swan. & Mum.	Mumbles Road and Mumbles.
.	.	.	.	.	. .	. .	West Croydon....................	Surrey	L. B. & S. C.	See Croydon, West.
.	P	.	.	.	. .	. .	West Cults	Aberdeen.	G. N. of S.	Aberdeen and Banchory.
.	.	.	.	.	. .	. .	West Cumberland Storing Co.'s Siding	Cumb'land	C. & W. Jn.—L. & N. W.	Workington.
.	.	.	.	.	. .	. .	West Derby.....................	Lancs	C. L. C.(G C,G N, & Mid.)	See Liverpool.
.	.	.	.	.	. .	. .	West Dereham	Norfolk ...	G. E.	See Abbey (for West Dereham).
G	P	F	L	H	C	2 0	West Drayton and Yiewsley	Middlesex	G. W.	Paddington and Slough.
.	.	.	.	.	. .	. .	West Durham Junction	Durham ...	N. E.	Willington.
.	.	.	.	.	. .	. .	West Durham Wallsend Col.	Durham ...	N. E.	Shildon.
G	P	F	.	H	C	2 0	West Ealing	Middlesex	G. W.	Ealing (Broadway) and Hanwell.
.	.	.	.	.	. .	. .	Ealing Town Council Siding	Middlesex	G. W.	West Ealing.
.	.	.	.	.	. .	. .	West End and Brondesbury (Mid.)	Middlesex	Mid.—S. E. & C.	See London.
.	.	.	.	.	. .	. .	West End Colliery	Yorks......	L. & N. W.	Batley.
.	.	.	.	.	. .	. .	West End Engine Works ...	Edinboro'	Cal.	Edinburgh, Lothian Road.
.	.	.	.	.	. .	. .	West End Landsale Depôts	Durham ...	N. E.	Millfield.
.	.	.	.	.	. .	. .	West End Lane (L. & N. W.)	Middlesex	L. & N. W.—N. L.	See London.
.	.	.	.	.	. .	. .	West End Mineral Depôt....	Forfar ...	Cal.	Dundee.
G	P	F	L	H	C	2 0	Westenhanger....................	Kent	S. E. & C.	Ashford and Folkestone.
.	.	.	.	.	. .	. .	Westerfield	Suffolk ...	G. E.	See Ipswich.
.	.	.	.	.	. .	. .	Wester Gartshore Colliery ...	Dumbartn	N. B.	Garngaber Junction Station.
.	.	.	.	.	. .	. .	Wester Gartshore Farm Sid.	Dumbartn	N. B.	See Garngaber Junction Station.
G	P	F	L	H	C	5 0	Westerham.......................	Kent	S. E. & C.	Branch from Dunton Green.
.	.	.	.	.	. .	. .	Westerleigh Sidings	Glo'ster ...	Mid.	Bristol, St. Philips.
.	.	.	.	.	. .	. .	Western Electric Co.'s Siding (G. E.)	Essex	GE—GN—L&NW—Mid.	London, Silvertown.
.	.	.	.	.	. .	. .	Western Petroleum Co.'s Sid.	Glo'ster ...	Clif. Ex.Jt. (G.W.&Mid.)	Bristol, Avonmouth Docks.
.	.	.	.	.	. .	. .	Western Road....................	Cork	C. & Muskerry	See Cork.

EXPLANATION—G Goods Station.   P Passenger and Parcel Station.   P* Passenger, but not Parcel or Miscellaneous Traffic.
F Furniture Vans, Carriages, Portable Engines, and Machines on Wheels.   L Live Stock.
H Horse Boxes and Prize Cattle Vans.   C Carriages by Passenger Train.

STATION ACCOMMODATION.						CRANE POWER.		STATIONS, &c.	COUNTY.	COMPANY.	POSITION.
						Tons	Cwts.				
·	·	·	·	·	·	·	·	Western Road Depôts	Durham ...	N. E.	Jarrow.
·	·	·	·	·	·	·	·	Western Tin Plate Co. (G.W.)	Carmarth'	G. W.—L. & N. W.	Llanelly.
·	·	·	·	·	·	·	·	Western Wagon Co.'s Siding	Glamorg'n	G W—LNW—Rhy—TV	Cardiff.
·	·	·	·	·	·	·	·	Westerton Colliery	Durham ...	N. E.	Spennymoor.
G	·	·	·	·	·	·	·	West Fen Drove.................	Cambs......	G. E.	Branch near Whittlesea.
·	P	·	·	·	·	·	·	West Ferry	Forfar......	D. & A. Jt. (Cal. & N. B.)	Dundee and Arbroath.
·	·	·	·	·	·	·	·	Westfield	Glo'ster ...	G. W.	Same as Notgrove.
G	P	·	L	H	·	1	10	Westfield	L'lithgow	N. B.	Bathgate (Lower) and Blackston.
·	·	·	·	·	·	·	·	Eastrigg Colliery	L'lithgow	N. B.	Bathgate (Lower) and Westfield.
·	·	·	·	·	·	·	·	Westfield Paper Mills ...	L'lithgow	N. B.	Bathgate (Lower) and Westfield.
·	·	·	·	·	·	·	·	Westfield Limestone Pit	Edinboro'	Cal.	Newpark.
·	·	·	·	·	·	·	·	Westfield Siding	Fife.........	N. B.	Kelty.
·	·	·	·	·	·	·	·	Westgarth's Engine Works and Wharf	Yorks	N. E.	Middlesbro'.
·	·	·	·	·	·	·	·	Westgate	Yorks	Mid.	See Rotherham.
·	·	·	·	·	·	·	·	Westgate	Yorks	GC,GN,Mid.,&WR&GJt.	See Wakefield.
G	P	·	·	·	·	1	10	Westgate-in-Weardale	Durham ...	N. E.	Bishop Auckland and Wearhead.
G	P	F	L	H	C	·	·	Westgate-on-Sea	Kent	S. E. & C........................	Herne Bay and Margate, West.
·	·	·	·	·	·	·	·	West Glamorgan Canister Co.'s Siding (Mid.)	Glamorg'n	Mid.—G.W.—L. & N.W.	Clydach-on-Tawe.
G	P	·	·	·	·	·	·	West Glentore Colliery........	Lanark ...	N. B.	Rawyards.
G	P	·	·	·	·	·	·	West Green	Middlesex	G. E.	Seven Sisters and Palace Gates.
G	P	F	L	H	C	5	0	West Grinstead	Sussex ...	L. B. & S. C.	Southwater and Partridge Green.
·	·	·	·	·	·	·	·	Hillman's Siding	Sussex ...	L. B. & S. C.	West Grinstead.
G	P	F	L	H	C	·	·	West Hallam (for Dale Abbey)	Derby	G. N.	Ilkeston and Derby.
·	·	·	·	·	·	·	·	Mapperley Colliery Co.'s Stanley Colliery (G. N.)	Derby	G. N.—G. C.	Ilkeston and West Hallam.
·	·	·	·	·	·	·	·	West Hallam Colliery (GN)	Derby	G. N.—G. C.	Ilkeston and West Hallam.
·	·	·	·	·	·	·	·	West Hallam Slag Siding	Derby	G. N.	Ilkeston and West Hallam.
·	·	·	·	·	·	·	·	West Hallam Colliery	Derby	Mid.	Stanton Gate.
·	·	·	·	·	·	·	·	Westham	Sussex ...	L. B. & S. C.	See Pevensey and Westham.
·	P	·	·	·	·	·	·	West Ham (L. T. & S.)........	Essex	{ L. T. & S. .... / N. L.	Bromley and Barking. / Over L. T. & S. from Bromley Junc.
·	·	·	·	·	·	·	·	West Ham Gas Co.'s Siding	Essex	G. E.	London, Stratford Market.
·	·	·	·	·	·	·	·	West Ham, South	Essex	G. E.	See London.
·	·	·	·	·	·	·	·	West Hampstead	Middlesex	Met.	See London.
·	·	·	·	·	·	·	·	West Harbour....................	Renfrew...	Cal.	Greenock, Regent Street.
G	P	F	L	H	C	3	0	West Hartlepool	Durham ...	N. E.	Stockton and Hartlepool.
·	·	·	·	·	·	·	·	Albion Saw Mill (G. Clark & Co.)	Durham ...	N. E.	West Hartlepool.
·	·	·	·	·	·	·	·	Baltic Saw Mill (Harrison & Singleton)	Durham ...	N. E.	West Hartlepool.
·	·	·	·	·	·	·	·	Belle Vue Field Siding ...	Durham ...	N. E.	West Hartlepool.
·	·	·	·	·	·	·	·	Bowers Siding	Durham ...	N. E.	West Hartlepool.
·	·	·	·	·	·	·	·	Burn Road Siding............	Durham ...	N. E.	West Hartlepool.
·	·	·	·	·	·	·	·	Burns Joinery Works and Brick Yard	Durham ...	N. E.	West Hartlepool.
·	·	·	·	·	·	·	·	Burt, Boulton & Heywood's Creosote Works	Durham ...	N. E.	West Hartlepool.
·	·	·	·	·	·	·	·	Casebourne & Co.'s Siding...	Durham ...	N. E.	West Hartlepool.
·	·	·	·	·	·	·	·	Casebourne's Cement and Brick Works, Coal Depôt & Creosote Works	Durham ...	N. E.	West Hartlepool.
G	·	·	·	·	·	80	0	Central Dock	Durham ...	N. E.	West Hartlepool.
·	·	·	·	·	·	·	·	Central Graving Docks......	Durham ...	N. E.	West Hartlepool.
·	·	·	·	·	·	·	·	Central Marine Engineering Works	Durham ...	N. E.	West Hartlepool.
·	·	·	·	·	·	·	·	Cleveland Road Siding......	Durham ...	N. E.	West Hartlepool.
·	·	·	·	·	·	·	·	Cliff House Field Siding ...	Durham ...	N. E.	West Hartlepool.
·	·	·	·	·	·	·	·	Cliff House Foundry	Durham ...	N. E.	West Hartlepool.
·	·	·	·	·	·	·	·	Cliff House "Old" Pottery	Durham ...	N. E.	West Hartlepool.
·	·	·	·	·	·	8	0	Cliff House Siding (Newburn Junction)	Durham ...	N. E.	West Hartlepool.
·	·	·	·	·	·	5	0	Coal Dock (Ballast Yard Sid.)	Durham ...	N. E.	West Hartlepool.
·	·	·	·	·	·	·	·	Co-operative Wholesale Society's Lard Refinery and Egg Warehouse	Durham ...	N. E.	West Hartlepool.
·	·	·	·	·	·	·	·	Corporation Depôts, Store, and Abbatoirs..............	Durham ...	N. E.	West Hartlepool.
·	·	·	·	·	·	·	·	Corporation Electric Light & Refuse Destructor Wks.	Durham ...	N. E.	West Hartlepool.
·	·	·	·	·	·	·	·	Corporation Flint Siding...	Durham ...	N. E.	West Hartlepool.

EXPLANATION—G Goods Station.   P Passenger and Parcel Station.   P* Passenger, but not Parcel or Miscellaneous Traffic.
F Furniture Vans, Carriages, Portable Engines, and Machines on Wheels.   L Live Stock.
H Horse Boxes and Prize Cattle Vans.   C Carriages by Passenger Train.

STATION ACCOMMODATION.						CRANE POWER.		STATIONS, &c.	COUNTY.	COMPANY.	POSITION.
						Tons	Cwts	**West Hartlepool**—*continued.*			
·	·	·	·	·	·	·	·	Coxon's Saw Mill	Durham ...	N. E.	West Hartlepool.
·	·	·	·	·	·	·	·	Erichsen, Lindhard & Co.'s Saw Mill & Timber Yard	Durham ...	N. E.	West Hartlepool.
								Gas & Water Co.—			
·	·	·	·	·	·	·	·	No. 1 Old Works	Durham ...	N. E.	West Hartlepool.
·	·	·	·	·	·	·	·	No. 2 New Works	Durham ...	N. E.	West Hartlepool.
								Gray's—			
·	·	·	·	·	·	·	·	Central Ship Yard........	Durham ...	N. E.	West Hartlepool.
·	·	·	·	·	·	·	·	Graving Dock	Durham ...	N. E.	West Hartlepool.
·	·	·	·	·	·	·	·	Old Ship Yard	Durham ...	N. E.	West Hartlepool.
·	·	·	·	·	·	·	·	Greenland Creosote Works and Saw Mill (N.E. Cos.)	Durham ...	N. E.	West Hartlepool.
·	·	·	·	·	·	·	·	Hartlepools Pulp & Paper Co.'s Works	Durham ...	N. E.	West Hartlepool.
·	·	·	·	·	·	·	·	Irvine's Shipbuilding & Dry Dock Co.'s Harbour Ship Yard	Durham ...	N. E.	West Hartlepool.
G	·	·	·	·	·	17	0	Jackson Dock	Durham ...	N. E.	West Hartlepool.
·	·	·	·	·	·	·	·	Jubilee Sidings	Durham ...	N. E.	West Hartlepool.
								Lauder, R., & Co.—			
·	·	·	·	·	·	·	·	Greenland Sleeper Saw Mill	Durham ...	N. E.	West Hartlepool.
·	·	·	·	·	·	·	·	Newburn Saw Mills	Durham ...	N. E.	West Hartlepool.
·	·	·	·	·	·	·	·	Longhill Foundry	Durham ...	N. E.	West Hartlepool.
·	·	·	·	·	·	·	·	Longhill Sidings..............	Durham ...	N. E.	West Hartlepool.
·	·	·	·	·	·	·	·	Hartlepools Cement Wks.	Durham ...	N. E.	Longhill Sidings.
·	·	·	·	·	·	·	·	Hartlepools Concrete Wks	Durham ...	N. E.	Longhill Sidings.
·	·	·	·	·	·	·	·	Wase's Saw Mill	Durham ...	N. E.	Longhill Sidings.
·	·	·	·	·	·	·	·	Lumley Steel Co.'s Siding..	Durham ...	N. E.	West Hartlepool.
·	·	·	·	·	·	·	·	Medd's Egg Packing and Pickling Works	Durham ...	N. E.	West Hartlepool.
·	·	·	·	·	·	·	·	Milton Forge & Engineering Works	Durham ...	N. E.	West Hartlepool.
·	·	·	·	·	·	·	·	Milton Saw Mills (Willson's)	Durham ...	N. E.	West Hartlepool.
·	·	·	·	·	·	·	·	New Expanded Metal Co.'s Stranton Works	Durham ...	N. E.	West Hartlepool.
·	·	·	·	·	·	·	·	N. E. R. Co.'s Dock Engineer's Works	Durham ...	N. E.	West Hartlepool.
·	·	·	·	·	·	·	·	N. E. R. Hydraulic Engine Works	Durham ...	N. E.	West Hartlepool.
·	·	·	·	·	·	·	·	N. E. R. Wagon Repairing Shops	Durham ...	N. E.	West Hartlepool.
·	·	·	·	·	·	·	·	Pearson's Saw Mill & Timber Yard	Durham ...	N. E.	West Hartlepool.
·	·	·	·	·	·	·	·	Pickering's Siding	Durham ...	N. E.	West Hartlepool.
·	·	·	·	·	·	·	·	Pounder's Boatbuilding Yard & Saw Mill	Durham ...	N. E.	West Hartlepool.
·	·	·	·	·	·	·	·	Pyman's Saw Mill & Timber Yard	Durham ...	N. E.	West Hartlepool.
·	·	·	·	·	·	·	·	Robinson, Sons & Co.'s Egg Packing & Pickling Wks.	Durham ...	N. E.	West Hartlepool.
·	·	·	·	·	·	·	·	Seaton Carew Iron Co.'s Blast Furnaces	Durham ...	N. E.	West Hartlepool.
·	·	·	·	·	·	·	·	Seaton Carew Iron Works and Coke Ovens	Durham ...	N. E.	West Hartlepool.
·	·	·	·	·	·	·	·	South Durham Steel & Iron Co.'s Works................	Durham ...	N. E.	West Hartlepool.
·	·	·	·	·	·	·	·	Stranton Saw Mill (Brown's)	Durham ...	N. E.	West Hartlepool.
·	·	·	·	·	·	·	·	Swainson Dock	Durham ...	N. E.	West Hartlepool.
·	·	·	·	·	·	5	0	Tidal Basin	Durham ...	N. E.	West Hartlepool.
·	·	·	·	·	·	80	0	Central Quay Sheers	Durham ...	N. E.	West Hartlepool.
·	·	·	·	·	·	100	0	Middleton Quay Sheers	Durham ..	N. E.	West Hartlepool.
·	·	·	·	·	·	·	·	Timber Dock	Durham ...	N. E.	West Hartlepool.
·	·	·	·	·	·	7	0	Timber Ponds Nos. 1,2,3,& 4	Durham ...	N. E.	West Hartlepool.
G	·	·	·	·	·	80	0	Union Dock	Durham ...	N. E.	West Hartlepool.
·	·	·	·	·	·	·	·	Walker & Co.'s Saw Mills..	Durham ...	N. E.	West Hartlepool.
·	·	·	·	·	·	·	·	Ward's Saw Mill............	Durham ...	N. E.	West Hartlepool.
·	·	·	·	·	·	·	·	West Hartlepool Public Coal Depôt....................	Durham ...	N. E.	West Hartlepool.
·	·	·	·	·	·	·	·	Westhead Siding	Lancs	L. & Y.	Skelmersdale.
G	P	F	L	H	C	5	0	West Hoathly....................	Sussex	L. B. & S. C.	East Grinstead & Horsted Keynes.

EXPLANATION— **G** *Goods Station.*   **P** *Passenger and Parcel Station.*   **P*** *Passenger, but not Parcel or Miscellaneous Traffic.*
F *Furniture Vans, Carriages, Portable Engines, and Machines on Wheels.*   **L** *Live Stock.*
H *Horse Boxes and Prize Cattle Vans.*   **C** *Carriages by Passenger Train.*

STATION ACCOMMODATION.						CRANE POWER.		STATIONS, &c.	COUNTY.	COMPANY.	POSITION.
						Tons	Cwts.				
								West Holmes Junction.........	Lincoln ...	G. N.—G. N. & G. E. Jt.	Lincoln.
								West Horsham	Sussex	L. B. & S. C.	See Christ's Hospital, West Horsham.
G	P	.	L	.	.	5	0	Westhoughton	Lancs	L. & Y.	Wigan and Bolton.
								Musgrave & Son's Siding...	Lancs	L. & Y.	Westhoughton.
								Snydale Hall Colliery	Notts	L. & Y.	Near Westhoughton.
								Westhoughton Colliery......	Lancs	L. & Y.	Westhoughton.
G	P	.	.	.	.			Westhouses and Blackwell ..	Derby	Mid.	Alfreton and Doe Hill.
								Blackwell Colliery Co.—			
								"A" Winning Colliery...	Derby	Mid.	Blackwell Branch.
								"B" Winning Colliery...	Derby	Mid.	Blackwell Branch.
								Hucknall Huthwaite Local Board Siding	Notts	Mid.	Blackwell Branch.
								New Hucknall Colliery......	Notts	Mid.	Blackwell Branch.
								South Normanton & Blackwell Gas Co.'s Siding ...	Derby	Mid.	Blackwell Branch.
								Tibshelf Junction	Derby	Mid.	Alfreton and Doe Hill.
								West Hunwick Col. & Bk. Wks.	Durham ...	N. E.	Hunwick.
								West Hydraulic Engineering Co.'s Siding..................	Beds	Mid.	Luton.
								West India Coal Sidings	Middlesex	Mid.	London.
								West India Docks	Middlesex	GE—GN—GW—L&ID— L & N W—Mid.—N L	See London.
G	P	.	.	.	.	3	0	West Jesmond...............	Northumb	N. E.	Jesmond and Gosforth.
								West Kensington	Middlesex	Met. Dist.—Mid.	See London.
								West Kensington Junction ...	Middlesex	Met. Dist.—Mid.	London, Hammersmith and West Kensington.
G	P	F	L	H	C	3	0	West Kilbride..................	Ayr	G. & S.W.	Ardrossan and Largs.
								West Kilburn (L. & N. W.)...	Middlesex	L. & N. W.—N. L.	See London, Queen's Park (West Kilburn).
G	P	F	.	H	C	5	0 }	West Kirby..................	Cheshire...	{ B'head Jt. (GW & LNW)	Branch from Hooton.
G	P	F	.	H	C	5	0 }			{ Wirral	Terminus.
								West Kirby Junction	Cheshire...	B'head Jt.—Wirral	Hooton and Hoylake.
								West Kirby & Hoylake Gas & Water Co.'s Siding	Cheshire...	Wirral	Hoylake.
								West Kirby & Hoylake U. D. C. Electricity Works Sid.	Cheshire...	Wirral	Hoylake.
								West Kiveton Colliery	Derby	Mid.	Killamarsh.
								West Lancashire Floor Cloth & Linoleum Co.'s Siding ...	Lancs	L. & Y.	Appley Bridge.
								Westland Row	Dublin	D. W. & W.	See Dublin.
G	P	.	.	.	.	2	0	West Leigh	Lancs	L. & N. W.	Bolton & Kenyon Junction Station.
G	P	F	L	H	C	5	0	West Leigh & Bedford.........	Lancs	G. C. (Wigan Jn.)	Lowton St. Mary's and Wigan.
								Abram Collieries	Lancs	G. C. (Wigan Jn.)	West Leigh & Bedford.
								Bickershaw Collieries	Lancs	G. C. (Wigan Jn.)	West Leigh & Bedford.
								Maypole Collieries & Brick Works	Lancs	G. C. (Wigan Jn.)	West Leigh & Bedford.
								West Leigh Coal Co.—			
								Diggle's North Siding	Lancs	L. & N. W.	Wigan.
								Diggle's South Siding	Lancs	L. & N. W.	Wigan.
								West Linton	Peebles ...	N. B.	See Broomlee (for West Linton).
								West London Junction.........	Middlesex	G. W.	London, Westbourne Park & Acton.
								West London Junction.........	Surrey ...	L. & S.W.—W. L. E. Jt.	London, Clapham Junction.
								West London, North Pole Jn.	Middlesex	G W—L & N W—W L Jt.	London, Willesden and Kensington.
								West Lothian Pottery	L'lithgow	N. B.	Bo'ness.
								West Lothian Rolling Mills & Shovel Works..................	L'lithgow	N. B.	Bathgate, Lower.
								West Marina	Sussex ...	L. B. & S. C.	See St. Leonard's.
								West Marsh Iron & Steel Wks.	Yorks	N. E.	Middlesbro'.
								West Marsh Wharf	Yorks	N. E.	Middlesbro'.
G								West Medina Cement Works	I. of W	I. of W. Cent.	Newport and Mill Hill.
G	P	F	L	H	C	5	0	West Meon	Hants	L. & S.W.	Alton and Fareham.
								West Mickley Colliery (Eltringham Colliery)	Northumb	N. E.	Prudhoe.
G	P	.	.	.	.			West Mill	Herts	G. E.	St. Margaret's and Buntingford.
								Westminster (Met. Dist.)......	Middlesex	Met. Dist.—L. & N. W.	See London.
								Westminster Colliery	Den'bigh	G. W.—W. M. & C. Q.	Moss.
								West Moor Lime Works (Trimdon Lime Siding) ...	Durham ...	N. E.	Trimdon.
G	P	F	L	H	C	.	.	West Moors Junction Station	Dorset......	L. & S.W.	Ringwood and Wimborne.
								Westmoreland Siding	Somerset...	G. W.	See Bath.
								Westmoreland Woollen Co.'s Siding.................	W'morlnd	L. & N. W.	{ See Kendal Bonded Stores Co. (Kendal).

EXPLANATION—G *Goods Station.*   P *Passenger and Parcel Station.*   P* *Passenger, but not Parcel or Miscellaneous Traffic.*
F *Furniture Vans, Carriages, Portable Engines, and Machines on Wheels.*   L *Live Stock.*
H *Horse Boxes and Prize Cattle Vans.*   C *Carriages by Passenger Train.*

STATION ACCOMMODATION.						CRANE POWER.		STATIONS, &c.	COUNTY.	COMPANY.	POSITION.
						Tons	Cwts.	West Norfolk Farmers' Manure and Chemical Co.	—		
.	.	.	.	.	.	.	.	Siding	Norfolk ...	Mid. & G. N. Jt.............	South Lynn.
.	.	.	.	.	.	.	.	Siding (G. E.).................	Norfolk ...	G. E.—G. N.—Mid.	Lynn Harbour.
.	P	.	.	.	.	.	.	West Norwood (L. B. & S. C.)	Surrey ...	{ L. B. & S. C.	Clapham Junc. and Crystal Palace.
										{ L. & N. W.	Over L.B.&S.C. from Clapham Junc.
.	.	.	.	.	.	.	.	Westoe Lane	Durham ...	Marsden	See South Shields (Westoe Lane).
								West of England Clay Co.'s			
.	.	.	.	.	.	.	.	Sidings	Cornwall ...	G. W.	Drinnick Mill.
.	.	.	.	.	.	.	.	West of England Siding ...	Cornwall ...	G. W.	Burngullow.
.	.	.	.	.	.	.	.	West of Scotland Chemical } Works }	Dumbart'n	Cal.	{ Same as Dawsholm Gas Works (Glasgow).
								West of Scotland Furniture			
.	.	.	.	.	.	.	.	Co.'s Siding	Ayr	G B & K Jt (Cal & G & S W)	Beith.
.	.	.	.	.	.	.	.	Weston	Berks	L'bourn Valley	See Welford Park (for Wickham and Weston).
.	P	.	.	.	.	.	.	Weston	Lincoln ...	Mid. & G. N. Jt.............	Sutton Bridge and Spalding.
G	P	.	.	.	.	.	.	Weston	N'hamptn	L. & N. W.	See Ashley and Weston.
.	.	.	.	.	.	.	.	Weston	Somerset...	Mid.	Mangotsfield and Bath.
.	.	.	.	.	.	.	.	Fryer's, E., Siding............	Somerset...	Mid.	Weston.
								Locksbrook Wharf Timber			
.	.	.	.	.	.	.	.	Co.'s Siding.................	Somerset...	Mid.	Weston.
.	.	.	.	.	.	.	.	Shaw's Sidings	Somerset...	Mid.	Near Weston.
.	.	.	.	.	.	.	.	Weston Brewery Siding ...	Somerset...	Mid.	Near Weston.
.	.	.	.	.	.	.	.	Weston ...:....................	Staffs	G. N.	See Ingestre (for Weston).
G	P	F	L	H	C	.	}	Weston and Ingestre (N. S.)	Staffs	{ N. S.	Colwich and Stone.
	P					.	}			{ L. & N. W.	Over N. S. Line.
.	.	.	.	.	.	.	.	Shirleywich Salt Works ...	Staffs	N. S.	Weston and Ingestre.
.	.	.	.	.	.	.	.	Shirleywich Siding	Staffs	N. S.	Weston and Ingestre.
.	.	.	.	.	.	.	.	Weston Coyney	Staffs	N. S.	Branch from Millfield Junction.
								Weston Coyney Colliery (Park Hall Colliery Co.)	Staffs	N. S.	Weston Coyney.
G	P	F	L	H	C	.	.	Weston-on-Avon...............	Glo'ster ...	G. W.	See Milcote.
.	.	.	.	.	.	.	.	Weston-on-Trent	Derby......	Mid.	Castle Donington and Chellaston.
.	.	.	.	.	.	.	.	Weston Salt Works	Staffs	G. N.	Ingestre (for Weston).
G	P	F	L	H	C	8	0	Westons Siding	Cheshire...	B'head Jt. (G W & L N W)	Same as Penks' Siding (Birkenhead).
G	P						}	Weston-super-Mare	Somerset...	{ G. W.	Loop—Yatton and Highbridge.
										{ W. C. & P.	Terminus.
.	.	.	.	.	.	.	.	Weston Wharf	N'hamptn	L. & N. W.	Northampton, Bridge Street.
.	.	.	.	.	.	.	.	Hughes & Co.'s Siding	N'hamptn	L. & N. W.	Weston Wharf.
								Northampton Brewery Co.'s			
.	.	.	.	.	..	.	.	Siding	N'hamptn	L. & N. W.	Weston Wharf.
.	.	.	.	.	.	.	.	Northampton Gas Co.'s Sid.	N'hamptn	L. & N. W.	Weston Wharf.
G	.	.	.	.	.	0	15	Weston Wharf	Salop	Cam.	Oswestry and Llynclys.
.	.	.	.	.	.	.	.	Westoning Brick Works ...	Beds	Mid.	See Forder & Son (Harlington).
.	.	.	.	.	.	.	.	West Ord Siding	Northumb	N. E.	{ Tweedmouth. Velvet Hall.
.	P	.	.	.	.	.	.	West Parade Junction	Yorks	N. E.	Hull, Pass. and Botanic Gardens.
.	.	.	.	.	.	.	.	West Park	Jersey ...	Jersey	St. Helier and St. Aubin.
.	.	.	.	.	.	.	.	West Pelton Alma Colliery ...	Durham ...	N. E.	Pelton.
.	.	.	.	.	.	.	.	West Pelton Brick Works ...	Durham ...	N. E.	Pelton.
G	P	.	L	H	C	10	0	West Pennard	Somerset...	S.&D.Jt.(L.&S.W.& Mid)	Glastonbury and Templecombe.
G	P	F	L	H	C	3	0	Westport	Mayo ...	M. G. W.	Claremorris and Achill.
G	P	.	.	.	.	.	.	Westport Quay	Mayo ...	M. G. W.	Branch from Westport.
.	.	.	.	.	.	.	.	West Rhondda Colliery	Glamorg'n	G. W.	Pontyrhyll.
.	.	.	.	.	.	.	.	West Riding Collieries.........	Yorks	N. E.	Same as Pope & Pearson's Collieries (Castleford).
.	.	.	.	.	.	.	.	West Riding Colliery	Yorks	Mid.	Normanton.
								West Riding County Asylum			
.	.	.	.	.	.	.	.	Siding	Yorks	Mid.	Menston.
.	.	.	.	.	.	.	.	Westrigg Colliery	Lanark ...	N. B.	Westcraigs.
.	.	.	.	.	.	.	.	West Road Junction............	Dublin ...	G. S. & W.—M. G. W....	Dublin.
.	.	.	.	.	.	.	.	West Rounton Gate	Yorks	N. E.	Welbury.
.	P'	.	.	.	.	.	.	West Runton	Norfolk ...	Mid. & G. N. Jt.	Melton Constable & Cromer Beach.
.	P'	.	.	.	.	.	.	West St. Leonards............	Sussex ...	S. E. & C.	Battle and St. Leonards (Warrior Square).
.	.	.	.	.	.	.	.	West Sharlston Colliery ...	Yorks	W. R. & G. Jt. (G. C. & G. N.)	See Sharlston West Col. (Hare Park).
								West Shield Row Colliery and Coke Works.................	Durham ...	N. E.	Annfield Plain.
.	.	.	.	.	.	.	.	West Siding	L'lithgow	N. B.	Same as Gaol Siding (Linlithgow).
.	.	.	.	.	.	.	.	West Silkstone Colliery	Yorks	G. C.	Silkstone.
.	.	.	.	.	.	.	.	West Silkstone Junction	Yorks	G. C.	Penistone and Silkstone.

EXPLANATION—G *Goods Station.*   P *Passenger and Parcel Station.*   P* *Passenger, but not Parcel or Miscellaneous Traffic.*
F *Furniture Vans, Carriages, Portable Engines, and Machines on Wheels.*   L *Live Stock.*
H *Horse Boxes and Prize Cattle Vans.*   C *Carriages by Passenger Train.*

Station Accommodation						Crane Power		Stations, &c.	County	Company	Position
						Tons	Cwts				
								West Sleekburn Col., "E" Pit	Northumb	N. E.	Bedlington.
								West Slit Siding	Durham	N. E.	Parkhead.
								West's Siding	Derby	G. N.	Derby.
								West Stanley Colliery	Durham	N. E.	Annfield Plain.
								West Stanley Col. & Coke Wks.	Durham	N. E.	Annfield Plain.
								West Staveley Siding	Derby	Mid.	Barrow Hill and Staveley Works.
								West Street	Renfrew	Cal.—Glas. Dist. Sub.	See Glasgow.
								West Street Junction	Lanark	Cal.	Glasgow.
								West Street Junction	Middlesex	Met.—S. E. & C.	London, Farringdon Str. & Snow Hill.
								West Tees Colliery	Durham	N. E.	Evenwood.
								West Tees Colliery, No. 1	Durham	N. E.	Evenwood.
								West Tees Colliery, No. 2	Durham	N. E.	Butterknowle.
								West Thornley Colliery	Durham	N. E.	Tow Law.
								West Thurrock Junction	Essex	L. T. & S.	Purfleet and Grays.
								West Thurrock Siding	Essex	L. T. & S.	Grays.
	P							West Timperley	Cheshire	C. L. C. (G C, G N, & Mid.)	Warrington and Northenden.
G	P					5	0	West Uddingston	Lanark	N. B.	See Uddingston, West.
G	P							West Vale	Yorks	L. & Y.	Greetland and Stainland.
								Westward Ho!	Devon	B. W. Ho! & A.	Bideford and Northam.
G	P	.	L	H	.	1	10	Westwell's Siding (L.&N.W.)	Lancs	L. & N. W —G. W.	Warrington, Bank Quay.
								West Wemyss	Fife	N. B.	Thornton and Methil.
								Duncan Colliery	Fife	N. B.	Branch from West Wemyss.
								Hugo Colliery	Fife	N. B.	Branch—West Wemyss & Wemyss Castle.
								Lady Lilian Colliery	Fife	N. B.	Branch—West Wemyss & Wemyss Castle.
G	P	F	L	H	C			West Wickham	Kent	S. E. & C.	Elmers End and Hayes.
								West Willesden	Middlesex	Mid.	See London, Harlesden (for West Willesden and Stonebridge Pk.)
G	P	.	L	H				Westwood	Yorks	G. C.	Sheffield and Barnsley.
								Newton, Chambers & Co.—			
								Newbegin Colliery	Yorks	G. C.	Westwood.
								Tankersley Colliery	Yorks	G. C.	Westwood.
								Westwood Coke Ovens	Yorks	G. C.	Westwood.
								Westwood Coke Ovens	Yorks	G. C.	See Newton, Chambers & Co. (Westwood).
										Mid.	See Newton, Chambers & Co. (Chapeltown).
								Westwood Colliery	Durham	N. E.	Ebchester.
								Westwood Colliery (Murdestoun Colliery)	Lanark	Cal.	Cleland.
								Westwood Siding	Lancs	L. & Y.	See Pearson & Knowles Coal and Iron Co. (Ince).
	P							Westwood Siding	Salop	G. W.	Presthope.
G	P							West Worthing	Sussex	L. B. & S. C.	Worthing and Goring.
								West Wycombe	Bucks	G. W. & G. C. Jt.	Princes Risboro' & High Wycombe.
								West Wylam Colliery	Northumb	N. E.	Prudhoe. Wylam.
								West Wylam Junction	Northumb	N. E.	Wylam and Prudhoe.
G	P	.	L	H	C	2	0	Wetheral	Cumb'land	N. E.	Carlisle and Hexham.
G	.	F	L	L		5	0	Corby Siding	Cumb'land	N. E.	Wetheral.
G	.	F	L	H	C	5	0	Wetherby	Yorks	N. E.	Church Fenton and Harrogate. Leeds and Harrogate.
	P										
								Wetherigg's Pottery Depôts and Brick & Tile Works	W'morlnd	N. E.	Cliburn. Clifton.
								Wetmoor Junction	Staffs	L. & N. W.—Mid.	Burton-on-Trent.
								Wetmoor Road	Staffs	G. N.	Burton-on-Trent.
								Wetmoor Sidings (Mid.)	Staffs	Mid.—G. N.	Burton-on-Trent.
G	P	.	L	H	C			Wetwang	Yorks	N. E.	Malton and Driffield.
G	P	F	L	H	C	3	0	Wexford	Wexford	D. W. & W.	Terminus.
G	P							Wexford, North Sta. & Junc.	Wexford	D. W. & W.	Terminus.
										G. S. & W.	Junction with D. W. & W.
	P			H				Wexford, South	Wexford	G. S. & W.	Wexford, North and Rosslare.
G	P	F	L	H	C			Weybourne	Norfolk	Mid. & G. N. Jt.	Melton Constable and Cromer Beach.
G	P	F	L	H	C	5	0	Weybridge	Surrey	L. & S.W.	Surbiton and Woking.
G	P	F	L	H	C	5	0	Weyhill	Hants	M. & S. W. Jn.	Savernake and Andover.
								WEYMOUTH—			
G	P	F	L	H	C	10	0	(Station)	Dorset	G. W.	Terminus.
										L. & S. W.	Over G. W. from Dorchester Junc.
G								Harbour	Dorset	W.&P. Jt. (G. W&L&SW)	Branch from Weymouth.
	P							Junction	Dorset	W.&P. Jt. (G W&L.&S W)	Upwey and Weymouth.
								Landing Stage	Dorset	G. W.	Over W. & P. Joint Tramway.

EXPLANATION—G Goods Station.   P Passenger and Parcel Station.   P* Passenger, but not Parcel or Miscellaneous Traffic.
F Furniture Vans, Carriages, Portable Engines, and Machines on Wheels.   L Live Stock.
H Horse Boxes and Prize Cattle Vans.   C Carriages by Passenger Train.

G	P	F	L	H	C	Tons	Cwts	STATIONS, &c.	COUNTY.	COMPANY.	POSITION.
								WEYMOUTH—continued.			
G	P	F	L	H	C	2	0	Quay	Dorset	G. W.	Branch from Weymouth.
G	.	.	.	.	.			Quay Tramway	Dorset	W.&P. Jt (G.W.&L&SW)	Branch from Weymouth Station.
.	P	.	.	.	.			Rodwell	Dorset	W.&P. Jt. (G.W.&L&SW)	Weymouth and Portland.
G	P	F	L	H	C	1	10	Whaley Bridge	Cheshire	L. & N. W.	Buxton and Stockport.
.	.	.	.	.	.			Bingswood Printing Co.'s Siding	Cheshire	L. & N. W.	Branch from Whaley Bridge.
.	.	.	.	.	.			Buxton Lime Firms Co.—Siding	Cheshire	L. & N. W.	Branch from Whaley Bridge.
.	.	.	.	.	.			Whaley or Gisbourne Colliery	Cheshire	L. & N. W.	Branch from Whaley Bridge.
.	.	.	.	.	.			Goyt Mill Co.'s Siding	Derby	L. & N. W.	Branch from Whaley Bridge.
G	.	.	.	.	.	2	10	Shallcross	Cheshire	L. & N. W.	Branch from Whaley Bridge.
.	.	.	.	.	.			Whaley Bridge Canal Whf.	Cheshire	L. & N. W.	Branch from Whaley Bridge.
.	.	.	.	.	.			Whaley or Gisbourne Colliery	Cheshire	L. & N. W.	See Buxton Lime Firms Co. (Whaley Bridge).
G	P	.	L	H	.	5	0	Whalley	Lancs	L. & Y.	Blackburn and Clitheroe.
.	.	.	.	.	.			Thompson's Siding	Lancs	L. & Y.	Whalley.
.	.	.	.	.	.			Whalley, G., & Co.'s Siding	Yorks	Mid.	Keighley.
.	P	.	.	.	.			Whaplode	Norfolk	Mid. & G. N. Jt.	Sutton Bridge and Spalding.
.	.	.	.	.	.			Wharncliffe Carlton (New) Col.	Yorks	G. C.	Staincross (for Mapplewell).
.	.	.	.	.	.			Wharncliffe Colliery	Yorks	G. C.	Deepcar (for Stocksbridge).
.	.	.	.	.	.			Wharncliffe Gannister } Brick Works	Yorks	N. E.	{ Same as Lowood's Wharncliffe Brick Works (Middlesbro').
.	.	.	.	.	.			Wharncliffe Silkstone Colliery	Yorks	{ G. C. { Mid.	Birdwell and Hoyland Common. Wombwell.
.	.	.	.	.	.			Wharncliffe Silkstone New Coke Works	Yorks	G. C.	Birdwell and Hoyland Common.
.	.	.	.	.	.			Wharncliffe Woodmoor Col.	Yorks	{ G. C. { H. & B.—Mid.	Staincross (for Mapplewell). Cudworth.
G	P	.	L	H	.			Wharram	Yorks	N. E.	Malton and Driffield.
.	.	.	.	.	.			Wharton	Cheshire	L. & N. W.	See Over and Wharton.
.	.	.	.	.	.			Wharton Hall Colliery	Lancs	L. & Y.	See Earl of Ellesmere's (Atherton).
.	.	.	.	.	.			Wharton's Phœnix Foundry	Cumb'land	M. & C.	Maryport.
.	.	.	.	.	.			Whateley Col. & Brick Works	Warwick	Mid.	Wilnecote.
G	P	.	L	.	.	10	0	Whatstandwell	Derby	Mid.	Ambergate and Cromford.
.	.	.	.	.	.			Jeffries Siding	Derby	Mid.	Near Whatstandwell.
.	.	.	.	.	.			Sims & Son's Siding	Derby	Mid.	Near Whatstandwell.
.	.	.	.	.	.			Sims, A., Siding	Derby	Mid.	Near Whatstandwell.
G	P	.	L	H	.	1	0	Whauphill	Wigtown	P.P.&W. Jt.(Cal., G&SW, L. & N. W., & Mid.)	Newton Stewart and Whithorn.
.	.	.	.	.	.			Wheal Anna Siding	Cornwall	G. W.	Bugle.
.	.	.	.	.	.			Wheal Busy Siding	Cornwall	G. W.	Scorrier.
.	.	.	.	.	.			Wheal Henry Siding	Cornwall	G. W.	Bugle.
.	.	.	.	.	.			Wheal Rose Siding	Cornwall	G. W.	Bugle.
.	.	.	.	.	.			Wheatcroft's Siding	Notts	Mid.	Newark.
G	P	F	L	H	C	1	0	Wheathampstead	Herts	G. N.	Hatfield and Luton.
G	P	F	L	H	C	6	0	Wheatley	Oxon	G. W.	Oxford and Thame.
.	.	.	.	.	.			Wheatley	Yorks	H'fax H. L. (G N & L & Y)	See Halifax.
.	.	.	.	.	.			Wheatley Hill Colliery & Brick Works	Durham	N. E.	Thornley Colliery Station.
.	.	.	.	.	.			Wheatsheaf (W. M. & C. Q.)	Denbigh	W. M. & C. Q.—G. C.	See Gwersyllt and Wheatsheaf.
G	.	.	.	.	.			Wheatsheaf Junction Station	Denbigh	G. W.	Wrexham and Rossett.
.	.	.	.	.	.			Clark & Reas Siding	Denbigh	G. W.	Wheatsheaf Junction.
.	.	.	.	.	.			Wheeldon's Maltings	Derby	Mid.	Derby, St. Mary's.
.	.	.	.	.	.			Wheeldon's Siding	Beds	L. & N. W.—Mid.	Bedford.
.	.	.	.	.	.			Wheeldon's Siding	Lincoln	G. N.	Grantham.
.	.	.	.	.	.			Wheeler & Co.'s Siding	Hants	L. & S. W.	Eastleigh and Bishopstoke.
.	.	.	.	.	.			Wheeler & Gregory's Wagon Works	Glamorg'n	G. W.	Swansea.
.	.	.	.	.	.			Wheeler & Gregory's Wagon Works	Somerset	G. W.—S. & D. Jt.	Radstock.
.	.	.	.	.	.			Wheeler & Son's Siding	Suffolk	G. E.	Sudbury.
.	P	.	.	H	.			Wheelock and Sandbach	Cheshire	N. S.	Branch from Harecastle.
.	.	.	.	.	.			Wheelock and Sandbach	Cheshire	N. S.	Branch from Harecastle.
.	.	.	.	.	.			Wheldale Coal Co.'s Siding	Yorks	N. E.	Castleford.
.	.	.	.	.	.			Wheldon's Siding (N. & B. Jn.)	N'hamptn	N. & B. Jn.—L. & N. W.	Blisworth.
G	P	F	L	H	C	.	.	Wherwell	Hants	L. & S. W.	Whitchurch and Fullerton.
.	.	.	.	.	.			Whessoe Brick Works	Durham	N. E.	Darlington, Bank Top.
.	.	.	.	.	.			Whessoe Foundry	Durham	N. E.	Darlington, Bank Top.
G	P	F	L	H	C			Whetstone	Leicester	G. C.	Leicester and Lutterworth.
.	.	.	.	.	.			Whetstone (G.N.)	Middlesex	G. N.—N. L.	See Totteridge and Whetstone.
.	.	.	.	.	.			Whicham Siding	Cumb'land	Furness	Silecroft.

EXPLANATION—G *Goods Station.*   P *Passenger and Parcel Station.*   P* *Passenger, but not Parcel or Miscellaneous Traffic.*
F *Furniture Vans, Carriages, Portable Engines, and Machines on Wheels.*   L *Live Stock.*
H *Horse Boxes and Prize Cattle Vans.*   C *Carriages by Passenger Train.*

Station Accommodation						Crane Power		STATIONS, &c.	COUNTY.	COMPANY.	POSITION.
						Tons	Cwts.				
..	..	..	..	..	..	..	..	Whifflet	Lanark ...	Cal.—N. B.	See Coatbridge.
..	..	..	..	..	..	..	..	Whifflet, Central Junction ...	Lanark ...	N. B.	Coatbridge.
..	..	..	..	..	..	..	..	Whifflet Foundry (Tennant's Foundry)	Lanark ...	Cal.—N. B.	Coatbridge, Whifflet.
..	..	..	..	..	..	..	..	Whifflet Forge Siding	Lanark ...	N. B.	Coatbridge, Whifflet.
..	..	..	..	..	..	..	..	Whifflet, North Junction	Lanark ...	Cal.— N. B.	Coatbridge.
G	P	F	L	H	C	5	0	Whiley Hill Siding	Durham ...	N. E.	Heighington.
..	..	..	..	..	..	..	..	Whimple	Devon	L. & S.W.	Honiton and Exeter.
..	..	..	..	..	..	..	..	Whimsey Mineral Siding	Glo'ster	G. W.	Cinderford.
..	..	..	..	..	..	..	..	Whinhill Brick Works	Clackman'	N. B.	Alloa.
..	..	..	..	..	..	..	..	Whinhill Colliery	Clackman'	N. B.	Alloa.
..	..	..	..	..	..	..	..	Whinney Hill Plastic Brick Co.'s Siding	Lancs	L. & Y.	{ Same as Hargreaves, G., & Co.'s Siding (Huncoat).
G	P	..	L	H	..	..	..	Whippingham	I. of W.	I. of W. Cent.	Newport and Ryde.
G	P	..	L	..	..	..	..	Whiskerhill Junction	Notts	G. C.	Checker House and Retford.
G	P	..	..	..	..	..	..	Whissendine	Leicester..	Mid.	Oakham and Melton Mowbray.
G	P	..	..	..	..	1	10	Whistleberry Colliery	Edinboro'	Cal.	Hamilton, Central.
..	..	..	..	..	..	..	..	Whistlefield	Dumbartn	N. B.	Craigendoran and Ardlui.
G	P	F	L	H	C	..	..	Whiston Colliery	Lancs	L. & N. W.	See Higginbottom's (Huyton Qry).
..	..	..	..	..	..	..	..	Whitacre Junction Station ...	Warwick..	Mid.	Birmingham and Tamworth.
..	..	..	..	..	..	..	..	Birmingham Corporation Water Works	Warwick..	Mid.	Near Whitacre Junction Station.
..	..	..	..	..	..	..	..	Whitaker & Son's Siding	Yorks	E. & W. Y. Union	Robin Hood.
..	..	..	..	..	..	..	..	Whitaker & Son's Siding	Yorks	N. E.	Hunmanby.
..	..	..	..	..	..	..	..	Whitaker's Brick Yard	Yorks	N. E.	Ravenscar.
..	..	..	..	..	..	..	..	Whitaker, W., & Co.'s Siding	Lancs	L. & Y.	Darwen.
G	P	..	L	H	..	1	5	Whitburn	L'lithgow	N. B.	Bathgate (Upper) and Morningside.
..	..	..	..	..	..	..	..	Whitrigg Colliery	L'lithgow	N. B.	Whitburn and Addiewell.
..	..	..	..	..	..	..	..	Whitburn Colliery	Durham ...	Marsden	Terminus.
..	..	..	..	..	..	..	..	Whitburn Col. & Brick Wks.	Durham ...	N. E.	South Shields.
								WHITBY—			
G	P	F	L	H	C	10	0	(Station)	Yorks	N. E.	Scarborough and Loftus.
..	..	..	..	..	..	..	..	Batts Foundry	Yorks	N. E.	Whitby.
..	..	..	..	..	..	..	..	Gas Works	Yorks	N. E.	Whitby and Ruswarp.
G	P	..	L	H	..	1	0	Junction	Yorks	N. E.	Whitby (West Cliff) & Scarborough.
..	..	..	..	..	..	..	..	West Cliff	Yorks	N. E.	Whitby and Saltburn.
..	..	..	..	..	..	..	..	Whitchurch	Glamorg'n	T. V.	See Llandaff (for Whitchurch).
G	P	F	L	H	C	3	0	Whitchurch	Hants	{ G. W.	Newbury and Winchester.
G	P	F	L	H	C	5	0			{ L. & S. W.	Basingstoke and Andover Junction.
G	P	F	L	H	C	5	0	Whitchurch (L. & N. W.)	Salop	{ L. & N. W.	Crewe and Shrewsbury.
										{ Cam.	Over L. & N.W. from Whitchurch Jn.
..	..	..	..	..	..	..	..	Smith's Foundry	Salop	L. & N. W.	Whitchurch.
..	..	..	..	..	..	..	..	Whitchurch Junction	Salop	Cam.—L. & N. W.	Ellesmere and Whitchurch Station.
..	P	..	..	..	..	..	..	Whiteabbey	Antrim	N. C. Com. (Mid.)	Belfast and Carrickfergus.
..	..	..	..	..	..	..	..	White & Co.'s Iron Works (C. L. C.)	Cheshire...	C. L. C.—L. & N. W.	Northwich.
..	..	..	..	..	..	..	..	White, H., & Co.'s Foundry Siding	Mon	G. W.	Risca.
..	..	..	..	..	..	..	..	White, J., & Co.'s Siding	Lancs	L. & N. W.	Widnes.
..	..	..	..	..	..	..	..	White, R., & Son's Siding	Lancs	L. & N. W.—S. & M. Jt..	Widnes.
..	..	..	..	..	..	..	..	White's Brick Siding	Kent	S. E. & C.	Erith.
..	..	..	..	..	..	..	..	Whitebank Siding (M'Intosh & Co.'s Cabinet Works) ...	Fife	N. B.	Kirkcaldy.
..	..	..	..	..	..	..	..	Whitebarn Colliery	Staffs	N. S.	Apedale.
G	P	..	L	..	..	4	0	White Bear (Adlington)	Lancs	L&Y&LU Jt(LNW&LY)	Blackburn and Boar's Head.
..	..	..	..	..	..	..	..	Duxbury Park Colliery (L. & Y. & L. U. Jt.)	Lancs	L. & N. W.	White Bear (Adlington) & Chorley.
..	..	..	..	..	..	..	..	Ellerbeck Colliery Co. (L. & Y. & L. U. Jt.)— Ellerbeck Colliery	Lancs	L. & N. W.	White Bear (Adlington) & Chorley.
..	..	..	..	..	..	..	..	Rawlinson's Siding	Lancs	L. & N. W.	White Bear (Adlington) & Chorley.
..	..	..	..	..	..	..	..	Wigan Coal & Iron Co.'s Brinks Col. (L&Y&LUJt)	Lancs	L. & N. W.	White Bear (Adlington)&Red Rock.
G	P	..	..	..	..	..	..	Whiteborough (for Hucknall Huthwaite)	Derby	Mid.	Tibshelf and Teversall.
..	..	..	..	..	..	..	..	Blackwell Colliery Co.'s Sutton Colliery	Notts	Mid.	Near Whiteborough.
..	..	..	..	..	..	..	..	Skegby Junction	Notts	Mid.	Tibshelf Junction and Teversall.
..	..	..	..	..	..	..	..	Stoneyford Lane Sidings ...	Notts	Mid.	Near Whiteborough.
..	..	..	..	..	..	..	..	Whitechapel	Middlesex	E. L. Jt.—W. & B. Jt..	See London.
..	..	..	..	..	..	..	..	Whitechapel Junction	Middlesex	E.L.Jt—Met&MetDistJt	London, Shadwell and St. Mary's (Whitechapel).

EXPLANATION—G *Goods Station.*   P *Passenger and Parcel Station.*   P* *Passenger, but not Parcel or Miscellaneous Traffic.*
F *Furniture Vans, Carriages, Portable Engines, and Machines on Wheels.*   L *Live Stock.*
H *Horse Boxes and Prize Cattle Vans.*   C *Carriages by Passenger Train.*

Station Accommodation						Crane Power		Stations, &c.	County.	Company.	Position.
						Tons	Cwts				
.	.	.	.	.	.	.	.	Whitechapel, St. Mary's	Middlesex	Met. & Met. Dist. Jt.	See London, St. Mary's (Whitechapel).
.	.	.	.	.	.	.	.	Whitechapel, Vallance Road Junction	Middlesex	Met. Dist.—W. & B. Jt.	London, St. Mary's (Whitechapel) and Stepney Green.
.	.	.	.	.	.	.	.	Whitecliffe Lime Works	Glo'ster	G. W.	Coleford.
G	P	F	L	H	C	3	0	Whitecraigs	Renfrew	Cal.	Giffen and Clarkston.
G	P	.	.	.	.	.	.	Whitecroft	Glo'ster	S. & Wye Jt. (G.W. & Mid)	Parkend and Lydney.
.	.	.	.	.	.	.	.	Norchard or Kidnall's Col.	Glo'ster	S. & Wye Jt. (G.W. & Mid)	Whitecroft and Lydney.
.	.	.	.	.	.	.	.	Park Iron Ore & Coal Co.'s Siding	Glo'ster	S. & Wye Jt. (G.W. & Mid)	Whitecroft.
.	.	.	.	.	.	.	.	Princess Royal Sidings— Flour Mill	Glo'ster	S. & Wye Jt. (G.W. & Mid)	Branch from Tufts Junction.
.	.	.	.	.	.	.	.	Park Gutter Siding	Glo'ster	S. & Wye Jt. (G.W. & Mid)	Branch from Tufts Junction.
.	.	.	.	.	.	.	.	White Cross Colliery Co.'s Peasley Cross and Sherdley Colliery	Lancs	L. & N. W.	St. Helens.
.	.	.	.	.	.	.	.	White Cross Iron Works	Lancs	C. L. C. (G C, G N, & Mid)	Warrington, Central.
.	.	.	.	.	.	.	.	Whitecross Street	Middlesex	Mid.	See London.
.	.	.	.	.	.	.	.	White Cross Wire & Iron Co.'s Works (L. & N. W.)	Lancs	L. & N. W.—G. W.	Warrington, Bank Quay.
G	P	.	L	H	.	.	.	Whitedale	Yorks	N. E.	Hull and Hornsea.
G	.	.	.	.	.	.	.	White Fen	Cambs	G. E.	Branch near Whittlesea.
G	P	.	L	.	.	10	0	Whitefield	Lancs	L. & Y.	Manchester and Radcliffe.
.	.	.	.	.	.	.	.	Whitefield Pit	Durham	N. E.	Penshaw.
G	P	.	.	.	.	5	0	Whitegate	Cheshire	C. L. C. (G C, G N, & Mid)	Cuddington and Winsford.
.	.	.	.	.	.	.	.	Whitegate Siding	Cornwall	G. W.	Drinnick Mill.
.	.	.	.	.	.	.	.	Whitegates Siding	Lanark	Cal.	Shieldmuir.
.	.	.	.	.	.	.	.	Whitehall Junction	Yorks	L. & N. W.—Mid.	Leeds.
.	.	.	.	.	.	.	.	Whitehall Quarry	Glamorg'n	T. V.	Nelson.
.	.	.	.	.	.	.	.	Whitehall Road	Yorks	L. & Y. & L. & N. W. Jt.	See Leeds.
.	.	.	.	.	.	.	.	Whitehall Siding	Devon	G. W.	Hemyock.
.	.	.	.	.	.	.	.	Whitehall Sidings	Durham	N. E.	Rowley.
G	P	.	.	.	.	.	.	White Hart Lane	Middlesex	G. E.	Seven Sisters and Enfield Town.
								WHITEHAVEN—			
.	.	.	.	.	.	.	.	Barrowmouth Cement and Plaster Works (Furness)	Cumb'land	Furness—L. & N. W.	Whitehaven.
.	P	F	.	H	C	.	.	Bransty	Cumb'land	Furness & L. & N. W. Jt.	Workington and Corkickle.
.	.	.	.	.	.	.	.	Bransty Junction	Cumb'land	Furness—L. & N. W.	Corkickle and Workington.
.	.	.	.	.	.	.	.	Bransty Quarry	Cumb'land	L. & N. W.	Whitehaven and Parton.
.	P	.	.	.	.	.	.	Corkickle (Furness)	Cumb'land	Furness / L. & N. W. / WC&E Jt. (Fur. & LNW)	Bransty Junction and St. Bees. / Over Furness from Bransty Junction. / Over Furness from Mirehouse Junc.
.	.	.	.	.	.	.	.	Croft Pit (Furness)	Cumb'land	Furness—L. & N. W.	Branch—Corkickle and St. Bees.
.	.	.	.	.	.	.	.	Dock	Cumb'land	Furness—L. & N. W.	Near Bransty.
.	.	.	.	.	.	.	.	Harbour Trustees' Lines (private)	Cumb'land	Furness—L. & N. W.	Branch from Bransty Junction.
.	.	.	.	.	.	.	.	Jackson's, J. & W., Timber Yard (Furness)	Cumb'land	Furness—L. & N. W.	Near Preston Street.
.	.	.	.	.	.	.	.	Lonsdale Hematite Smelting Co.'s Siding	Cumb'land	L. & N. W.	Whitehaven and Parton.
.	.	.	.	.	.	.	.	Mirehouse Junction	Cumb'land	Furness—W. C. & E. Jt.	Corkickle and Moor Row.
.	.	.	.	.	.	.	.	Pattinson & Son's Corn Mill (Furness)	Cumb'land	Furness—L. & N. W.	Near Preston Street.
G	.	F	L	.	.	10	0	Preston Street (Furness)	Cumb'land	Furness / L. & N. W. / WC&E Jt. (Fur. & LNW)	Branch—Corkickle and St. Bees. / Over Furness from Bransty Junction. / Over Furness from Mirehouse Junc.
.	.	.	.	.	.	.	.	Sandwith Stone Quarries (Furness)	Cumb'land	Furness—L. & N. W.	Branch from Croft Pit Branch.
.	.	.	.	.	.	.	.	Stout & Son's Foundry (Furness)	Cumb'land	Furness—L. & N. W.	Whitehaven.
.	.	.	.	.	.	.	.	Sugar Tongue Sid. (Fur.)	Cumb'land	Furness—L. & N. W.	Whitehaven.
.	.	.	.	.	.	.	.	Whitehaven Colliery Co.'s William Pit Colliery	Cumb'land	Furness—L. & N. W.	Branch from Bransty Junction.
.	.	.	.	.	.	.	.	Whitehaven Shipbuilding Co.'s Siding	Cumb'land	L. & N. W.	Whitehaven.
.	.	.	.	.	.	.	.	Whitehaven Colliery Co.'s William Pit Colliery	Cumb'land	Furness—L. & N. W.	Whitehaven, Preston Street.
.	.	.	.	.	.	.	.	Whitehaven Harbour Trustees' Lines (private)	Cumb'land	Furness—L. & N. W.	Whitehaven, Preston Street.
.	.	.	.	.	.	.	.	Whitehaven Hematite Iron Co.— Aldby Limestone Quarry	Cumb'land	WC&E Jt. (Fur. & LNW)	Cleator Moor.
.	.	.	.	.	.	.	.	Works	Cumb'land	C. & W. Jn.	Cleator Moor.

EXPLANATION—G *Goods Station.*   P *Passenger and Parcel Station.*   P* *Passenger, but not Parcel or Miscellaneous Traffic.*
F *Furniture Vans, Carriages, Portable Engines, and Machines on Wheels.*   L *Live Stock.*
H *Horse Boxes and Prize Cattle Vans.*   C *Carriages by Passenger Train.*

G	P	F	L	H	Tons	Cwts	STATIONS, &c.	COUNTY.	COMPANY.	POSITION.
							Whitehaven Hematite Iron Co.—*continued.*			
							Works, North Side	Cumb'land	WC&EJt. (Fur.&LNW)	Cleator Moor.
							Works, South Side	Cumb'land	WC&EJt. (Fur.&LNW)	Cleator Moor.
							Whitehaven Shipbuilding Co.'s Siding	Cumb'land	L. & N. W.	Whitehaven, Preston Street.
G	P			H			Whitehead	Antrim	N.C. Com. (Mid.)	Carrickfergus and Larne.
							Whitehead & Co.'s Siding	Dorset	W.&P.Jt. (GW&L.&SW)	Portland.
							Whitehead's Royal George Siding	Yorks	L. & N. W.	Greenfield.
							White Hill Bank Head Siding	Durham	N. E.	Birtley.
							Whitehill Colliery	Lanark	Cal.	Hamilton, Central.
							Whitehill Colliery Fire-Clay and Brick Works	Edinboro'	N. B.	Hawthornden.
							White Hill Manure Depôts	Durham	N. E.	Birtley.
							Whitehill Pit	Ayr	G. & S. W.	Skares.
							White Hill Point	Northumb	N. E.	Northumberland Dock.
G	P		L	H	1	5	Whitehouse	Aberdeen	G. N. of S.	Kintore and Alford.
G	P						Whitehouse	Antrim	N.C. Com. (Mid.)	Belfast and Carrickfergus.
							Whitehouse & Son's Priorfield Furnace	Staffs	L. & N. W.	Deepfields and Coseley.
							Whitehouse Junctions	Lancs	L. & Y.	Preston.
							Whitehouse Siding	Durham	N. E.	Birtley.
							Whitehouse Siding and Depôt	Yorks	N. E.	South Bank.
							Calder, Charles, & Co.'s Timber Yard	Yorks	N. E.	Whitehouse Siding and Depôt.
							Campbell & Co.'s Machinery Yard	Yorks	N. E.	Whitehouse Siding and Depôt.
							Dock Side Timber Yard	Yorks	N. E.	Whitehouse Siding and Depôt.
							North Ormesby Timber Yard	Yorks	N. E.	Whitehouse Siding and Depôt.
							Ridley & Son's Yard	Yorks	N. E.	Whitehouse Siding and Depôt.
							Robinson & Co.'s Timber Yard	Yorks	N. E.	Whitehouse Siding and Depôt.
							Tees Railway and Engineering Works	Yorks	N. E.	Whitehouse Siding and Depôt.
							Tees Side Bridge and Engineering Works	Yorks	N. E.	Whitehouse Siding and Depôt.
							Watson & Co.'s Timber Yard	Yorks	N. E.	Whitehouse Siding and Depôt.
							Whiteinch	Renfrew	Cal.	See Glasgow.
							Whiteinch (for Scotstoun)	Renfrew	Cal.	See Glasgow.
							Whiteinch, East Junction	Lanark	N. B.	Glasgow.
							Whiteinch Galvanizing Wks.	Renfrew	Cal.	Glasgow, Whiteinch.
							Whiteinch Loop Sidings	Lanark	N. B.	Glasgow, Stobcross.
							Whiteinch Shipbuilding Yard (Reid & Co.)	Renfrew	Cal.	Glasgow, Whiteinch.
								Lanark	N. B.	Glasgow, Whiteinch.
							Whiteinch, West Junction	Lanark	N. B.	Glasgow.
							Whitelaw's Siding	Dumbartn	N. B.	See Garngaber Junction Station.
							White Lea Brick Works	Durham	N. E.	East Boldon.
							White Lea Colliery	Durham	N. E.	See Pease & Partners (Crook).
							White-le-head Siding	Durham	N. E.	Redheugh.
							Whiteley & Son's Siding	Yorks	L. & Y.	Lockwood.
							Whiteley's Siding	Derby	Mid.	See Butterley Co. (Ripley).
							Whiteman's Coal Siding	Forfar	Cal.	Montrose.
							Whitemoor (G. E.)	Cambs	G. E.—G. N.	See March.
							White Moss Coal Co.'s Siding	Lancs	L. & Y.	Liverpool, Kirkdale.
							White Moss Colliery (L. & Y.)	Lancs	L. & Y.—L. & N. W.	Skelmersdale.
							Whitem's Sid. (Gould & Co.)	Cumb'land	N. B.	Kirkbride.
G			L		3	0	Whitemyre Junction	Fife	N. B.	Dunfermline (Upper) and Oakley.
							Whitemyre Junction Station	Fife	N. B.	Dunfermline (Upper) and Oakley.
G							Arthur Pit	Fife	N. B.	Branch—Whitemyre Jn. and Kelty.
							Balmule Siding	Fife	N. B.	Branch—Whitemyre Jn. and Kelty.
							Blackburn Foundry	Fife	N. B.	Whitemyre Junction Station.
G							Colton Siding	Fife	N. B.	Branch from Whitemyre Jn. Station.
G							Elgin Siding	Fife	N. B.	Branch from Whitemyre Jn. Station.
G							Lochhead Brick & Fire-Clay Works	Fife	N. B.	Branch—Whitemyre Jn. and Kelty.
							Lochhead Siding	Fife	N. B.	Branch—Whitemyre Jn. and Kelty.
							Morton's Siding	Fife	N. B.	Branch from Whitemyre Jn. Station.
							Pittencrieff Colliery (Colton Coal Depôt)	Fife	N. B.	Branch from Whitemyre Jn. Station.
							Rosebank Collieries	Fife	N. B.	Branch—Whitemyre Jn. and Kelty.

EXPLANATION—G *Goods Station.*   P *Passenger and Parcel Station.*   P* *Passenger, but not Parcel or Miscellaneous Traffic.*
F *Furniture Vans, Carriages, Portable Engines, and Machines on Wheels.*   L *Live Stock.*
H *Horse Boxes and Prize Cattle Vans.*   C *Carriages by Passenger Train.*

STATION ACCOMMODATION.						CRANE POWER.		STATIONS, &c.	COUNTY.	COMPANY.	POSITION.
						Tons	Cwts				
								Whitemyre Junction Station—*continued*.			
								Rosebank Quarry	Fife	N. B.	Branch—Whitemyre Jn. and Kelty.
G								Summit Siding	Fife	N. B.	Whitemyre Junction and Oakley.
								Wallsend Colliery	Fife	N. B.	Branch—Whitemyre Jn. and Kelty.
	P*							White Notley	Essex	G. E.	Witham and Braintree.
G	P							Whiterigg	Lanark ...	N. B.	Airdrie (Commonhead) and Long-riggend.
								Whiterigg Brick Works	Lanark ...	N. B.	Rawyards.
								Whiterigg Park Colliery	Lanark ...	N. B.	Rawyards.
								White Rock Siding (Mid.) ...	Glamorg'n	Mid.—G. W.—L. & N. W.	See Vivian & Son's (Upper Bank).
								White Rose (B. & M.)	Mon	B. & M.—G. W.	See New Tredegar and White Rose.
								White Rose Colliery (B. & M.)	Mon	B. & M.—G. W.	New Tredegar and White Rose.
								White Rose No. 2 Colliery ...	Glamorg'n	Rhy.	See Powell Duffryn Co. (Brithdir).
								Whitescut Siding	Cumb'land	N. E.	{ Brampton Junction. / { Lambley.
								Whiteshaw Tile Works	Lanark ...	Cal.	Carluke.
								Whitespot New Quarry	Ayr	Cal.	Giffen.
								Whitespot Quarry	Ayr	{ Cal. / { G. & S. W.	Giffen. / Glengarnock and Kilbirnie.
								Whitfield's Brick Siding	Glo'ster ...	Mid.	Gloucester.
								Whitfield's Collieries............	Staffs	N. S.	Black Bull.
								Whitfield's Siding	Durham ..	N. E.	Same as Brasside Manure Siding (Leamside.)
								Whitfield's Siding	Lancs	L. & N. W.	Earlestown.
								Whitgift Siding	Yorks	Axholme Jt (L & Y & N E)	Eastoft.
G	P	F	L	H	C	1	0	Whithorn	Wigtown...	{ PP & W Jt (Cal, G & S W, / { L. & N. W. & Mid.)...	} Terminus—Branch from Newton / Stewart.
G	P	F	L	H	C	1	0	Whitland	Carmarth.	G. W.	Carmarthen Junc. & New Milford.
								Cardigan Junction	Carmarth'	G. W.	Whitland and Clynderwen.
	P							Whitley Bay	Northumb	N. E.	Blyth and Tynemouth.
G	P		L	H		3	0	Whitley Bridge	Yorks	L. & Y.	Knottingley and Goole.
								Croysdale's Siding	Yorks	L. & Y.	Whitley Bridge and Hensall.
								Whitley Coal Wharf	Warwick..	L. & N. W.	Coventry.
G	P							Whitlingham	Norfolk ...	G. E.	Norwich and Yarmouth.
G	P	F	L	H	C	1	10	Whitmore.........................	Staffs	L. & N. W.	Crewe and Stafford.
G	P	F	L	H	.	1	10	Whitney-on-the-Wye	Hereford ..	Mid.	Hereford and Three Cocks.
G	P		L	H	.	1	0	Whitrigg	Cumb'land	Cal.	Brayton and Annan.
								Whitrigg Colliery	L'lithgow	N. B.	Whitburn.
								Whitrope Siding	Roxburgh	N. B.	See Riccarton.
								WHITSTABLE—			
G	P					3	10	Harbour	Kent	S. E. & C.	Branch from Canterbury, West.
G	P	F	L	H	C	1	15	Town............................	Kent	S. E. & C.	Faversham and Herne Bay.
G	P	F	L	H	C	2	0	Whitstone & Bridgerule	Devon	L. & S.W.	Holsworthy and Bude.
								Glubb's Brick & Tile Siding	Devon	L. & S.W.	Whitstone and Bridgerule.
								Whittaker Bros. & Co.'s Dye Works	Yorks	Mid.	Leeds, Newlay and Horsforth.
G	P	F	L	H	C	2	0	Whittingham	Northumb	N. E.	Alnwick and Wooperton.
								Slater's Siding	Northumb	N. E.	Whittingham.
								Whittingham Asylum Siding	Lancs	P & L Jt (L & N W & L & Y)	Grimsargh.
	P							Whittington	Derby	Mid.	Chesterfield and Killamarsh.
G	P	F		H	C			Whittington	Salop	{ Cam.	Oswestry and Ellesmere.
G	P	F	L	H	C	2	0			{ G. W.....................	Shrewsbury and Ruabon.
								Whittington Blacking Mill (Cummings, W., & Co.) ...	Derby	Mid.	Sheepbridge and Whittington Moor.
								Whittington Moor...............	Derby	Mid.	See Sheepbridge and Whittington Moor.
								Whittington Moor Potteries (Pearson & Co.)	Derby	Mid.	Sheepbridge and Whittington Moor.
								Whittington Road Public Wharf	Derby	Mid.	See Sheepbridge and Whittington Moor.
G	P	F	L	H	C	1	0	Whittlesea	Cambs......	G. E.	Peterboro' and March.
								Bundy, W. N., Siding.......	Cambs......	G. E.	Whittlesea.
								Itter, A. W., Siding..........	Cambs......	G. E.	Whittlesea and Peterboro'.
								King's Dyke Sidings.........	Cambs......	G. E.	Whittlesea and Peterboro'.
								Peed's Siding	Cambs......	G. E.	Whittlesea and Peterboro'.
								Saxon Brick Co.'s Siding...	Cambs......	G. E.	Whittlesea and Peterboro'.
G			L					Three Horse Shoes Siding	Cambs......	G. E.	Whittlesea and March.
								Whittlesea Central Brick Co.'s Siding	Cambs......	G. E.	Whittlesea and Peterboro'.
G	P	F	L	H	C	1	0	Whittlesford	Cambs......	G. E.	Cambridge and Bishops Stortford.
G						1	0	Sawston Siding	Cambs......	G. E.	Whittlesford and Shelford.

EXPLANATION—**G** *Goods Station.*   **P** *Passenger and Parcel Station.*   **P*** *Passenger, but not Parcel or Miscellaneous Traffic.*
F *Furniture Vans, Carriages, Portable Engines, and Machines on Wheels.*   **L** *Live Stock.*
H *Horse Boxes and Prize Cattle Vans.*   **C** *Carriages by Passenger Train.*

STATION ACCOMMODATION.						CRANE POWER.	STATIONS, &c.	COUNTY.	COMPANY.	POSITION.
						Tons Cwts.				
.	.	.	.	.	.	. .	Whittle, G., & Co.'s Stone-bridge Mill	Lancs	P & L Jt (L & N W & L & Y)	Longridge.
.	.	.	.	.	.	. .	Whittle's Siding (L. & Y.)	Lancs	L. & Y.—L. & N. W.	Same as Chorley Railway Wagon Co.'s Works (Chorley).
.	.	.	.	.	.	. .	Whitton	Middlesex	L. & S.W.	See Hounslow and Whitton.
.	.	.	.	.	.	. .	Whitton Junction	Middlesex	L. & S.W.	Twickenham and Feltham.
G	P	F	L	H	C	. .	Whitwell	I. of W.	I. of W. Cent.	Merstone Junc. and Ventnor Town.
G	P	F	L	H	C	1 5	Whitwell (Mid.)	Derby	{ Mid.	Mansfield and Shireoaks.
									{ G. C.	Over Mid. from Shireoaks Junctions.
.	.	.	.	.	.	. .	Duke of Portland's Sidings (Mid.)	Derby	Mid.—G. C.	Near Whitwell.
.	.	.	.	.	.	. .	Shireoaks Colliery	Notts	Mid.	Near Whitwell.
.	.	.	.	.	.	. .	Shireoaks Colliery Co.'s New Pit	Derby	Mid.	Near Whitwell.
.	.	.	.	.	.	. .	Steetley Colliery (Mid.)	Derby	Mid.—G. C.	Near Whitwell.
.	.	.	.	.	.	. .	Steetley Lime Works (Mid.)	Derby	Mid.—G. C.	Near Whitwell.
.	.	.	.	.	.	. .	Whitwell Colliery (Mid.)	Derby	Mid.—G. C.	Near Whitwell.
G	P	F	L	H	C	. .	Whitwell and Reepham	Norfolk	Mid. & G. N. Jt.	Melton Constable & Norwich, City.
.	.	.	.	.	.	. .	Whitwell Colliery	Durham	N. E.	Shincliffe.
.	.	.	.	.	.	. .	Whitwell Colliery (Mid.)	Derby	Mid.—G.C.	Whitwell.
.	.	.	.	.	.	. .	Whitwell, Hargreaves & Co.'s Siding	W'morlnd	L. & N. W.	{ See Kendal Bonded Stores Co. (Kendal).
.	.	.	.	.	.	. .	Whitwell, Hargreaves & Co.'s Siding	W'morlnd	L. & N. W.	Kendal.
.	.	.	.	.	.	. .	Whitwell, Mark & Co.'s Sid.	W'morlnd	L. & N. W.	Kendal.
G	P	.	.	.	.	1 5	Whitwick	Leicester	L. & N. W.	Loughboro' and Nuneaton.
.	.	.	.	.	.	. .	Forest Rock Granite Co.'s Siding	Leicester	L. & N. W.	Whitwick and Coalville (East).
.	.	.	.	.	.	. .	Mansfield's Siding	Leicester	L. & N. W.	Whitwick and Coalville (East).
.	.	.	.	.	.	. .	Whitwick Granite Co.'s Sid.	Leicester	L. & N. W.	Whitwick and Coalville (East).
.	.	.	.	.	.	. .	Whitwick Colliery	Leicester	L. & N. W.	Coalville, East.
.	.	.	.	.	.	. .	Whitwick Colliery and Brick Works (Mid.)	Leicester	Mid.—L. & N. W.	Coalville.
.	.	.	.	.	.	. .	Whitwood	Yorks	Mid.	See Altofts and Whitwood.
.	.	.	.	.	.	. .	Whitwood Chemical Co.—Siding	Yorks	N. E.	Castleford.
.	.	.	.	.	.	. .	Siding (L. & Y.)	Yorks	L. & Y.—Mid.	Castleford.
.	.	.	.	.	.	. .	Whitwood Collieries	Yorks	N. E.	Castleford.
.	.	.	.	.	.	. .	Whitwood Colliery (L. & Y.)	Yorks	L. & Y.—G. N.—Mid.	Castleford.
G	P	.	L	.	.	10 0	Whitworth	Lancs	L. & Y.	Rochdale and Facit.
.	.	.	.	.	.	. .	Whitworth Branch	Glamorg'n	P. T.	Branch from Tonmawr Junction.
.	.	.	.	.	.	. .	Whitworth Colliery	Glamorg'n	P. T.	Cwmavon.
.	.	.	.	.	.	. .	Whitworth Colliery	Mon	L. & N. W.	See Tredegar Iron and Coal Co. (Tredegar).
.	.	.	.	.	.	. .	Whitworth's Siding	Yorks	G. C.	Wath.
.	.	.	.	.	.	. .	Whitworth's Siding (L & N W)	N'hamptn	L. & N. W.—Mid.	Wellingboro'.
.	.	.	.	.	.	. .	Whitworth's Siding (Cooper House Siding)	Yorks	L. & Y.	{ Same as Sowerby Bridge Gas Wks. (Luddendenfoot).
.	.	.	.	.	.	. .	Whorley Hill Colliery	Durham	N. E.	Winston.
G	P	.	.	.	.	. .	Whyteleafe	Surrey	S. E. & C.	Purley and Caterham.
.	.	.	.	.	.	. .	Atkins' Siding	Surrey	S. E. & C.	Whyteleafe and Kenley.
.	.	.	.	.	.	. .	Wichnor Goods Junction	Staffs	L. & N. W.—Mid.	Lichfield and Burton.
.	.	.	.	.	.	. .	Wichnor Passenger Junction	Staffs	L. & N. W.—Mid.	Lichfield and Burton.
G	P	F	L	H	C	5 0	Wick	Caithness	High.	Terminus.
G	P	.	L	H	.	. .	Wickenby	Lincoln	G. C.	Lincoln and Market Rasen.
.	.	.	.	.	.	. .	Wicker	Yorks	Mid.	See Sheffield.
G	P	F	L	H	C	. .	Wickford Junction Station	Essex	G. E.	Shenfield and Southend.
G	.	.	.	.	.	. .	Ramsden Bellhouse Siding	Essex	G. E.	Wickford and Billericay.
.	.	.	.	.	.	. .	Warren, G., Siding	Essex	G. E.	Wickford Junction Station.
.	.	.	.	.	.	. .	Wickham	Berks	L'bourn Valley	See Welford Park (for Wickham and Weston).
.	P*	.	.	.	.	. .	Wickham	Essex	G. E.	Witham and Maldon.
G	P	F	L	H	C	5 0	Wickham	Hants	L. & S.W.	Alton and Fareham.
G	P	F	L	H	C	6 0	Wickham Market	Suffolk	G. E.	Ipswich and Beccles.
G	P	F	L	H	.	2 10	Wicklow	Wicklow	D. W. & W.	Bray and Rathdrum.
G	P	.	.	.	.	. .	Wick St. Lawrence	Somerset	W. C. & P.	Weston-super-Mare and Clevedon.
G	P	.	.	.	.	1 10	Wickwar	Glo'ster	Mid.	Gloucester and Bristol.
.	.	.	.	.	.	. .	Arnold, Perrett & Co.'s Brewery	Glo'ster	Mid.	Near Wickwar.
G	P	F	L	H	C	1 0	Widdrington	Northumb	N. E.	Morpeth and Belford.
.	.	.	.	.	.	. .	Stobswood Colliery	Northumb	N. E.	Widdrington.
.	.	.	.	.	.	. .	Widdrington Colliery	Northumb	N. E.	Widdrington.

EXPLANATION—G *Goods Station.*   P *Passenger and Parcel Station.*   P* *Passenger, but not Parcel or Miscellaneous Traffic.*
F *Furniture Vans, Carriages, Portable Engines, and Machines on Wheels.*   L *Live Stock.*
H *Horse Boxes and Prize Cattle Vans.*   C *Carriages by Passenger Train.*

Station Accommodation						Crane Power		Stations, &c.	County	Company	Position
G	P	F	L	H	C	Tons	Cwts				
G	P	F	.	H	C	.	.	Widford	Herts	G. E.	St. Margaret's and Buntingford.
G	P	F	L	H	C	1	10	Widmerpool	Notts	Mid.	Nottingham and Melton Mowbray.
								WIDNES—			
G	P	F	L	H	C	5	0	(Station)	Lancs	L. & N. W.	Liverpool and Warrington.
G	.	F	L	.	C	5	0	(Station)	Lancs	S. & M. Jt. (G. C. & Mid.)	Loop Line from C. L. C., Warrington and Garston.
.	.	.	.	.	.	.	.	Ankers & Son's Boiler Wks.	Lancs	{ L. & N. W.	Widnes.
										S. & M. Jt. (G.C. & Mid.)	Hutchinson's Estate Siding.
.	.	.	.	.	.	.	.	Arledter Size & Chemical Co.'s Siding	Lancs	{ L. & N. W.	Widnes.
										S. & M. Jt. (G.C. & Mid.)	Hutchinson's Estate Siding.
.	.	.	.	.	.	.	.	Atherton's Siding	Lancs	L. & N. W.	Widnes.
.	.	.	.	.	.	.	.	Bibby & Son's Siding	Lancs	L. & N. W.—S. & M. Jt.	Widnes.
.	.	.	.	.	.	.	.	Bibby's Siding	Lancs	S. & M. Jt. (G. C. & Mid.)	Widnes.
.	.	.	.	.	.	.	.	Bolton, T., & Son's Mersey Copper Works	Lancs	{ L. & N. W.	Widnes.
										S. & M. Jt. (G.C. & Mid.)	Hutchinson's Estate Siding.
.	.	.	.	.	.	.	.	Bone Phosphate Chemical Co.'s Siding	Lancs	L. & N. W.	Widnes.
.	.	.	.	.	.	.	.	Bowman & Co.'s Victoria Chemical Works	Lancs	{ L. & N. W.	Widnes.
										S. & M. Jt. (G.C. & Mid.)	Hutchinson's Estate Siding.
.	.	.	.	.	.	.	.	Broughton Copper Co.'s Ditton Copper Works	Lancs	{ L. & N. W.	Widnes.
										S. & M. Jt. (G.C. & Mid.)	Landowner's Branch.
.	P	.	.	H	.	.	.	Central	Lancs	S. & M. Jt. (G. C. & Mid.)	Loop Line from C. L. C., Warrington and Garston.
.	.	.	.	.	.	.	.	Chapman's Public Wharf	Lancs	S. & M. Jt. (G. C. & Mid.)	Widnes.
.	.	.	.	.	.	.	.	Chapman's Victoria Street Siding	Lancs	{ L. & N. W.	Widnes.
										S. & M. Jt. (G.C. & Mid.)	Hutchinson's Estate Siding.
.	.	.	.	.	.	.	.	Chemical Manufacturing Co.'s Siding	Lancs	{ L. & N. W.	Widnes.
										S. & M. Jt. (G.C. & Mid.)	Hutchinson's Estate Siding.
.	.	.	.	.	.	.	.	Connell & Co.'s Rosin Works	Lancs	L. & N. W.	Widnes.
.	.	.	.	.	.	.	.	Craig's Siding	Lancs	{ L. & N. W.	Widnes.
										S. & M. Jt. (G.C. & Mid.)	Hutchinson's Estate Siding.
.	.	.	.	.	.	.	.	Davies' Siding	Lancs	L. & N. W.—S. & M. Jt.	Widnes.
.	.	.	.	.	.	.	.	Dean & Marsh's Siding	Lancs	{ L. & N. W.	Widnes.
										S. & M. Jt. (G.C. & Mid.)	Hutchinson's Estate Siding.
.	.	.	.	.	.	.	.	Dennis & Co.'s Cornubia Wks	Lancs	L. & N. W.—S. & M. Jt.	Widnes.
.	.	.	.	.	.	.	.	Ditton Extract Works (Maloney & Co.)	Lancs	S. & M. Jt. (G. C. & Mid.)	Ditton Brook Iron Works.
.	.	.	.	.	.	.	.	Ditton Land Co.'s Waste Tip Siding	Lancs	S. & M. Jt. (G. C. & Mid.)	Landowner's Branch.
.	.	.	.	.	.	.	.	Ditton Oil Mills	Lancs	{ L. & N. W.	Widnes.
										S. & M. Jt. (G.C. & Mid.)	Hutchinson's Estate Siding.
G	.	F	L	.	.	6	0	Dock	Lancs	L. & N. W.	Liverpool and Warrington.
.	.	.	.	.	.	.	.	Electrical Copper Co.'s Sid.	Lancs	S. & M. Jt. (G. C. & Mid.)	Landowner's Branch.
.	.	.	.	.	.	.	.	Evans & Co.'s Siding	Lancs	L. & N. W.	Widnes.
.	.	.	.	.	.	.	.	Flewitt's Siding	Lancs	L. & N. W.	Widnes.
.	.	.	.	.	.	.	.	Foster, Dent & Co.'s Siding	Lancs	S. & M. Jt. (G. C. & Mid.)	Widnes.
.	.	.	.	.	.	.	.	Globe Chemical Works	Lancs	{ L. & N. W.	Widnes.
										S. & M. Jt. (G.C. & Mid.)	Hutchinson's Estate Siding.
.	.	.	.	.	.	.	.	Golding Davis Waste Tip Sid	Lancs	S. & M. Jt. (G. C. & Mid.)	Widnes.
									Gossage & Sons—			
.	.	.	.	.	.	.	.	East Siding	Lancs	L. & N. W.	Widnes.
.	.	.	.	.	.	.	.	West Siding	Lancs	{ L. & N. W.	Widnes.
										S. & M. Jt. (G.C. & Mid.)	Hutchinson's Estate Siding.
.	.	.	.	.	.	.	.	Greenhough's Siding	Lancs	L. & N. W.—S. & M. Jt.	Widnes.
.	.	.	.	.	.	.	.	Handley & Co.'s Siding	Lancs	L. & N. W.	Widnes.
.	.	.	.	.	.	.	.	Heyes' Siding	Lancs	L. & N. W.	Widnes.
.	.	.	.	.	.	.	.	Hues' Siding	Lancs	L. & N. W.	Widnes.
.	.	.	.	.	.	.	.	Hulme's Siding	Lancs	L. & N. W.	Widnes.
.	.	.	.	.	.	.	.	Hutchinson's Estate Siding	Lancs	S. & M. Jt. (G. C. & Mid.)	Widnes.
.	.	.	.	.	.	.	.	Hutchinson's Trustees' West Bank Siding	Lancs	{ L. & N. W.	Widnes.
										S. & M. Jt. (G.C. & Mid.)	West Bank Dock Line.
.	.	.	.	.	.	.	.	Hydraulic Stone and Cement Co.'s Siding	Lancs	L. & N. W.—S. & M. Jt.	Widnes.
.	.	.	.	.	.	.	.	Intractable Ore Co.'s Siding	Lancs	S. & M. Jt. (G. C. & Mid.)	Landowner's Branch.
.	.	.	.	.	.	.	.	Ireland's Siding	Lancs	L. & N. W.	Widnes.
.	.	.	.	.	.	.	.	Junction	Lancs	C. L. C.—S. & M. Jt.	Sankey and Widnes.
.	.	.	.	.	.	.	.	Landowner's Branch	Lancs	S. & M. Jt. (G. C. & Mid.)	Widnes.
.	.	.	.	.	.	.	.	Lewis Waste Tip Siding	Lancs	S. & M. Jt. (G. C. & Mid.)	Widnes.
.	.	.	.	.	.	.	.	Liverpool Silver and Copper Co.'s Siding	Lancs	{ L. & N. W.	Widnes.
										S. & M. Jt. (G.C. & Mid.)	Hutchinson's Estate Siding.
G	.	.	.	.	.	5	0	Lugsdale Siding	Lancs	L. & N. W.	Widnes and St. Helens.
.	.	.	.	.	.	.	.	McKechnie & Co.'s Siding	Lancs	L. & N. W.	Widnes.

EXPLANATION—G *Goods Station.*   P *Passenger and Parcel Station.*   P* *Passenger, but not Parcel or Miscellaneous Traffic.*
F *Furniture Vans, Carriages, Portable Engines, and Machines on Wheels.*   L *Live Stock.*
H *Horse Boxes and Prize Cattle Vans.*   C *Carriages by Passenger Train.*

STATION ACCOMMODATION.						CRANE POWER.		STATIONS, &c.	COUNTY.	COMPANY.	POSITION.
						Tons	Cwts.	**WIDNES**—*continued.*			
..	..	..	..	..	..	..	..	Maloney & Co.'s Siding.....	Lancs	{ L. & N. W.	Widnes.
										{ S. & M. Jt. (G. C. & Mid.)	Same as Ditton Extract Works.
..	..	..	..	..	..	..	..	Mersey & Calder Extract } Co.'s Siding .... }	Lancs	{ L. & N. W.	Widnes and Ditton.
										{ S. & M. Jt. (G. C. & Mid.)	Widnes.
..	..	..	..	..	..	..	..	Mica Boiler Covering } Co.'s Siding .... }	Lancs	{ L. & N. W.	Widnes.
										{ S. & M. Jt. (G. C. & Mid.)	Landowner's Branch.
..	..	..	..	..	..	..	..	Midwood & Son's Siding ...	Lancs	S. & M. Jt. (G. C. & Mid.)	Widnes.
..	..	..	..	..	..	..	..	**Moor Lane Junction**	Lancs	S. & M. Jt. (G. C. & Mid.)	Central Station and Hough Green.
..	..	..	..	..	..	..	..	Norman's Siding...............	Lancs	{ L. & N. W.	Widnes.
										{ S. & M. Jt. (G. C. & Mid.)	Hutchinson's Estate Siding.
..	..	..	..	..	..	..	..	Orr's Zinc White Siding...	Lancs	L. & N. W.	Widnes.
..	..	..	..	..	..	..	..	Roberts Bros.' Siding	Lancs	S. & M. Jt. (G. C. & Mid.)	Widnes.
..	..	..	..	..	..	..	..	Runcorn and Widnes Co-operative Society's Sid.	Lancs	L. & N. W.	Widnes.
..	..	..	..	..	..	..	..	Satinite Co.'s Siding........	Lancs	{ L. & N. W.	Widnes.
										{ S. & M. Jt. (G. C. & Mid.)	Hutchinson's Estate Siding.
..	..	..	..	..	..	..	..	South Junction	Lancs	S. & M. Jt. (G. C. & Mid.)	Central Station and Sankey.
..	P	..	..	..	..	..	..	Tanhouse Lane	Lancs	S. & M. Jt. (G. C. & Mid.)	Central Station and Sankey.
..	..	..	..	..	..	..	..	Todd Bros.' Siding	Lancs	L. & N. W.	Widnes.
								United Alkali Co.—			
..	..	..	..	..	..	..	..	Atlas Chemical Works...	Lancs	{ L. & N. W.	Widnes.
										{ S. & M. Jt. (G. C. & Mid.)	Hutchinson's Estate Siding.
..	..	..	..	..	..	..	..	Gaskell, Deacon & Co's Wks	Lancs	L. & N. W.—S. & M. Jt.	Widnes.
..	..	..	..	..	..	..	..	Golding Davis Works.....	Lancs	{ L. & N. W.	Widnes.
										{ S. & M. Jt. (G. C. & Mid.)	Hutchinson's Estate Siding.
..	..	..	..	..	..	..	..	Hall & Shaw's Works.....	Lancs	{ L. & N. W.	Widnes.
										{ S. & M. Jt. (G. C. & Mid.)	Hutchinson's Estate Siding.
..	..	..	..	..	..	..	..	Hutchinson's Works	Lancs	L. & N. W.	Widnes.
..	..	..	..	..	..	..	..	Lancashire Metal Works	Lancs	L. & N. W.—S. & M. Jt.	Widnes.
..	..	..	..	..	..	..	..	Liver Works, Nos. 1 } and 2 Sidings .... }	Lancs	{ L. & N. W.	Widnes.
										{ S. & M. Jt. (G. C. & Mid.)	Landowner's Branch.
..	..	..	..	..	..	..	..	Mathieson's Works	Lancs	{ L. & N. W.	Widnes.
										{ S. & M. Jt. (G. C. & Mid.)	Hutchinson's Estate Siding.
..	..	..	..	..	..	..	..	Mort Liddell Works	Lancs	{ L. & N. W.	Widnes.
										{ S. & M. Jt. (G. C. & Mid.)	Hutchinson's Estate Siding.
..	..	..	..	..	..	..	..	Muspratt's Works	Lancs	L. & N. W.—S. & M. Jt.	Widnes.
..	..	..	..	..	..	..	..	Pilkington's Works	Lancs	L. & N. W.—S. & M. Jt.	Widnes.
..	..	..	..	..	..	..	..	Sullivan's Works	Lancs	L. & N. W.—S. & M. Jt.	Widnes.
..	..	..	..	..	..	..	..	Widnes Alkali Works...	Lancs	L. & N. W.—S. & M. Jt.	Widnes.
..	..	..	..	..	..	..	..	Upper Widnes Chemical Wks	Lancs	S. & M. Jt. (G. C. & Mid.)	Widnes.
..	..	..	..	..	..	..	..	Vickers & Son's Siding...	Lancs	{ L. & N. W.	Widnes.
										{ S. & M. Jt. (G. C. & Mid.)	Hutchinson's Estate Siding.
..	..	..	..	..	..	..	..	West Bank Chemical Co.'s } Siding .... }	Lancs	{ L. & N. W.	Widnes.
										{ S. & M. Jt. (G. C. & Mid)	Hutchinson's Estate Siding.
..	..	..	..	..	..	..	..	West Bank Dock	Lancs	{ L. & N. W.	Liverpool and Warrington.
										{ S. & M. Jt. (G. C. & Mid.)	Hutchinson's Estate Siding.
..	..	..	..	..	..	..	..	West Bank Junction........	Lancs	S. & M. Jt. (G. C. & Mid.)	Moor Lane Junction and Ditton Brook Iron Works.
..	..	..	..	..	..	..	..	White, J., & Co.'s Siding	Lancs	L. & N. W.	Widnes.
..	..	..	..	..	..	..	..	White, R., & Son's Siding	Lancs	L. & N. W.—S. & M. Jt.	Widnes.
								Widnes Corporation—			
..	..	..	..	..	..	..	..	Gas Yard	Lancs	L. & N. W.	Widnes.
..	..	..	..	..	..	..	..	Highway Department Sid.	Lancs	S. & M. Jt. (G. C. & Mid.)	Widnes.
..	..	..	..	..	..	..	..	Moor Lane Depôt	Lancs	S. & M. Jt. (G. C. & Mid.)	Widnes.
								Widnes Foundry—			
..	..	..	..	..	..	..	..	Bridge Yard Siding	Lancs	L. & N. W.	Widnes.
..	..	..	..	..	..	..	..	Brookhouse Siding.........	Lancs	L. & N. W.	Widnes.
..	..	..	..	..	..	..	..	Old Side Siding	Lancs	L. & N. W.	Widnes.
..	..	..	..	..	..	..	..	Widnes Alkali Works	Lancs	L. & N. W.—S. & M. Jt...	See United Alkali Co. (Widnes).
G	P	F	L	H	C	7	10	Widney Manor	Warwick .	G. W.	Birmingham and Leamington.
								WIGAN—			
G	.	F	L	H	C	10	0	(Station)	Lancs	G. C. (Wigan Jn.)	Hindley and Wigan (Central).
G	P	F	L	H	C	10	0	(Station)	Lancs	L. & Y.	Liverpool and Bolton.
G	P	F	L	H	C	10	0	(Station)	Lancs	L. & N. W.	Preston and Warrington.
..	..	..	..	..	..	..	..	Alliance Coal & Cannel Co.'s Alliance Colliery...........	Lancs	G. C. (Wigan Jn.)	Wigan.
..	..	..	..	..	..	..	..	Almond's Standish Brewery	Lancs	L. & N. W.	Wigan and Boar's Head.
..	..	..	..	..	..	..	..	Barley Brook Siding	Lancs	L. & Y.	Wigan and Gathurst.
..	..	..	..	..	..	..	..	Bradley Manufacturing Co's Siding	Lancs	L. & N. W.	Coppull and Standish.
..	..	..	..	..	..	..	..	Canal Siding	Lancs	L. & Y.	Wigan.

EXPLANATION— **G** *Goods Station.*   **P** *Passenger and Parcel Station.*   **P*** *Passenger, but not Parcel or Miscellaneous Traffic.*
F *Furniture Vans, Carriages, Portable Engines, and Machines on Wheels.*   **L** *Live Stock.*
H *Horse Boxes and Prize Cattle Vans.*   **C** *Carriages by Passenger Train.*

STATION ACCOMMODATION.						CRANE POWER.		STATIONS, &c.	COUNTY.	COMPANY.	POSITION.
	P	F		H	C	Tons	Cwts				
								WIGAN—*continued.*			
·	P	F	·	H	C	·	·	Central	Lancs	G. C.	Terminus.
·	·	·	·	·	·	·	·	Church Iron Works	Lancs	G. C. (Wigan Jn.)	Wigan.
								Crompton & Shawcross—			
·	·	·	·	·	·	·	·	Fir Tree House Colliery...	Lancs	L. & N. W.	Wigan and Platt Bridge.
·	·	·	·	·	·	·	·	Moss Colliery	Lancs	L. & N. W.	Wigan and Platt Bridge.
								Cross, Tetley & Co.—			
·	·	·	·	·	·	·	·	Bamfurlong Colliery	Lancs	L. & N. W.	Wigan and Bamfurlong.
·	·	·	·	·	·	·	·	Mains Colliery	Lancs	L. & N. W.	Bamfurlong and Golborne.
·	·	·	·	·	·	·	·	Ellison's Church Iron Wks.	Lancs	L. & N. W.	Springs Branch.
								Garswood Coal and Iron Co.'s Long Lane Colliery	Lancs	L. & N. W.	Bamfurlong and Golborne.
								Gidlow Jackson Middle Works	Lancs	L. & N. W.	Springs Branch.
·	·	·	·	·	·	·	·	Hindley Field Colliery	Lancs	L. & N. W.	Pennington and Platt Bridge.
·	·	·	·	·	·	·	·	Ince Iron Works	Lancs	L. & N. W.	Springs Branch.
·	·	·	·	·	·	·	·	Ince Wagon & Iron Works	Lancs	G. C. (Wigan Jn.)	Wigan.
·	·	·	·	·	·	·	·	Ince Wagon Works	Lancs	L. & N. W.	Springs Branch.
·	·	·	·	·	·	·	·	Junction	Lancs	G. C.—G. C. (Wigan Jn.)	Lower Ince and Wigan.
·	·	·	·	·	·	·	·	Junction	Lancs	L. & Y.—L. & N. W.	L. & Y. & L. & N. W. Stations.
								L. & Y. Permanent Way Stores	Lancs	L. & Y.	Wigan.
								Latham Bros.—			
·	·	·	·	·	·	·	·	East Pit Colliery	Lancs	L. & N. W.	Springs Branch.
·	·	·	·	·	·	·	·	Rose Bridge Colliery	Lancs	L. & N. W.	Springs Branch.
								Lower Ince Stone Quarry and Brick Yard	Lancs	G. C. (Wigan Jn.)	Wigan.
								Melling Bros.' Ince Forge Co.'s Siding	Lancs	L. & N. W.	Springs Branch.
								Monks, Hall & Co.'s Albion Iron Works	Lancs	L. & N. W.	Springs Branch.
·	·	·	·	·	·	·	·	Moss Hall Colliery, South...	Lancs	L. & N. W.	Pennington and Platt Bridge.
								Newtown & Meadow's Sid. (Lamb & Moore's Siding)	Lancs	L. & Y.	Wigan.
·	·	·	·	·	·	·	·	Pagefield Forge Co.'s Siding	Lancs	L. & Y.	Wigan and Gathurst.
·	·	·	·	·	·	·	·	Pagefield Siding	Lancs	L. & Y.	Wigan and Gathurst.
·	·	·	·	·	·	·	·	Walker Bros.	Lancs	L. & Y.	Pagefield Siding.
·	·	·	·	·	·	·	·	Wigan Rolling Mills	Lancs	L. & Y.	Pagefield Siding.
								Pearson & Knowles Coal & Iron Co.—			
								Crow Orchard Colliery or Arley Pit	Lancs	L. & N. W.	Springs Branch.
·	·	·	·	·	·	·	·	Hindley Colliery	Lancs	L. & N. W.	Springs Branch.
·	·	·	·	·	·	·	·	Ince Moss Colliery	Lancs	L. & N. W.	Wigan and Brynn.
·	·	·	·	·	·	·	·	Moss Colliery	Lancs	L. & N. W.	Wigan and Bamfurlong.
·	·	·	·	·	·	·	·	Moss Side Iron Works...	Lancs	L. & N. W.	Wigan and Bamfurlong.
·	·	·	·	·	·	·	·	Spring Colliery	Lancs	L. & N. W.	Springs Branch.
·	·	·	·	·	·	·	·	Petford's Haigh Foundry	Lancs	L. & N. W.	Red Rock and Whelley.
·	·	·	·	·	·	·	·	Round House Branch	Lancs	L. & N. W.	Whelley and Hindley.
								Rylands & Son's Gidlow Works	Lancs	L. & N. W.	Wigan and Boars Head.
								Scowcroft & Co.'s Hindley Green Colliery	Lancs	L. & N. W.	Hindley Green and Platt Bridge.
G	·	·	·	·	·	·	·	Springs Branch Depôt	Lancs	L. & N. W.	Platt Bridge and Wigan.
								Sumner & Co.'s Haigh Brewery	Lancs	L. & N. W.	Springs Branch.
								Swan Lane Brick & Coal Co.'s Swan Lane Colliery	Lancs	L. & N. W.	Hindley Green and Howe Bridge.
								Unsworth & Cowburn's Brookside or Bugle Horn Colliery	Lancs	L. & N. W.	Hindley Green and Howe Bridge.
·	·	·	·	·	·	·	·	Victoria Colliery	Lancs	L. & N. W.	Pennington and Platt Bridge.
								West Leigh Coal Co.—			
·	·	·	·	·	·	·	·	Diggles North Siding	Lancs	L. & N. W.	Hindley Green and Platt Bridge.
·	·	·	·	·	·	·	·	Diggles South Siding	Lancs	L. & N. W.	Pennington and Platt Bridge.
								Wigan Cannel Co.'s Elms or Holme House Colliery	Lancs	L. & N. W.	Wigan and Boars Head.
								Wigan Coal & Iron Co.—			
·	·	·	·	·	·	·	·	Alexandra Pit (L & N W)	Lancs	L.&N.W.—G.C.(Wig.Jn)	Standish and Whelley.
·	·	·	·	·	·	·	·	Arley Pit (L. & N. W.)...	Lancs	L.&N.W.—G.C.(Wig.Jn)	Springs Branch.
·	·	·	·	·	·	·	·	Black Horse Siding	Lancs	L.&N.W.	Wigan and Boars Head.
·	·	·	·	·	·	·	·	Brick Works (L. & N.W.)	Lancs	L.&N.W.—G.C.(Wig.Jn)	Springs Branch.

EXPLANATION—G *Goods Station.*   P *Passenger and Parcel Station.*   P* *Passenger, but not Parcel or Miscellaneous Traffic.*
F *Furniture Vans, Carriages, Portable Engines, and Machines on Wheels.*   L *Live Stock.*
H *Horse Boxes and Prize Cattle Vans.*   C *Carriages by Passenger Train.*

STATION ACCOMMODATION.						CRANE POWER.	STATIONS, &c.	COUNTY.	COMPANY.	POSITION.
						Tons Cwts.	WIGAN—continued.			
							Wigan Coal & Iron Co.—continued.		L. & N. W.	Standish and Wigan.
•	•	•	•	•	•		Bromilow Pit	Lancs	L. & N. W.	Standish and Wigan.
•	•	•	•	•	•		Broomfield Col. (L&NW)	Lancs	L.&N.W.—G.C.(Wig.Jn)	Coppull and Standish.
•	•	•	•	•	•		Butcher Pit (L. & N. W.)	Lancs	L.&N.W.—G.C.(Wig.Jn)	Springs Branch.
•	•	•	•	•	•		California Pit (L.&N.W.)	Lancs	L.&N.W.—G.C.(Wig.Jn)	Springs Branch.
•	•	•	•	•	•		Crawford Pit (L. & N.W.)	Lancs	L.&N.W.—G.C.(Wig.Jn)	Springs Branch.
•							De Trafford Junction Iron Works	Lancs	L. & N. W.	Hindley Junction and Standish.
•							Giants Hall Col. (L&NW)	Lancs	L.&N.W.—G.C.(Wig.Jn)	Wigan and Boars Head.
•							Gidlow Lane Colliery (L. & N. W.)	Lancs	L.&N.W.—G.C.(Wig.Jn)	Wigan and Boars Head.
•							Haigh Saw Mills (L N W)	Lancs	L.&N.W.—G.C.(Wig.Jn)	Springs Branch.
•							John Pit (L. & N. W.)...	Lancs	L.&N.W.—G.C.(Wig.Jn)	Wigan and Boars Head.
•							Kirkless Hall Colliery (L. & N. W.)	Lancs	L.&N.W.—G.C.(Wig.Jn)	Springs Branch.
•							Kirkless Hall Iron and Steel Works (L.&N.W.)	Lancs	L.&N.W.—G.C.(Wig.Jn)	Hindley and Standish.
•							Kirkless Hall Iron and Steel Works Round House Sid. (L. & N.W.)	Lancs	L.&N.W.—G.C.(Wig.Jn)	Round House Branch.
•							Kirkless Hall Ore Mine and Slag Siding	Lancs	L. & N. W.	Round House Branch.
•					•		Kirkless Stores (L&NW)	Lancs	L N W—G C (Wig.Jn.)	Springs Branch.
•	•	•	•	•	•		Langtree Pit (L. & N. W.)	Lancs	L N W—G C (Wig.Jn.)	Coppull and Standish.
•	•	•	•	•	•		Lindsay Pit (L. & N. W.)	Lancs	LNW—GC(Wig Jn)—LY	Standish and Hindley.
•					•		Marsh House Coal and Lime Works (L&NW)	Lancs	L & N W—G C (Wig.Jn.)	Springs Branch.
•					•		Meadow Pit (L. & N. W.)	Lancs	L N W—G C (Wig.Jn.)	Springs Branch.
•					•		Moor Pit No. 5 (L&NW)	Lancs	L N W—G C (Wig.Jn.)	Springs Branch.
•					•		Prospect Pit (L.&N.W)	Lancs	L N W—G C (Wig.Jn.)	Wigan and Boars Head.
•					•		Taylor Pit (L. & N. W.)	Lancs	LNW—GC(Wig Jn)—LY	Springs Branch.
•					•		Victoria Col. (L. & N. W.)	Lancs	L & N W—G C (Wig.Jn.)	Boars Head and Standish.
•					•		Wash Pit (L. & N. W.)...	Lancs	L & N W—G C (Wig.Jn.)	Springs Branch.
•					•		Woodshaw Sid. (L&NW)	Lancs	L & N W—G C (Wig.Jn.)	Springs Branch.
•					•		Wigan Corporation Gas Works	Lancs	L. & Y.	Wigan.
•							Wigan Slag & Phosphate Co.'s Siding	Lancs	L. & N. W.	Springs Branch.
•							Wigan Wagon Co.'s Works	Lancs	L. & N. W.	Springs Branch.
•							Worsley Mesnes Colliery...	Lancs	L. & Y.	Wigan.
•							Worsley Mesnes Iron Works	Lancs	L. & Y.	Wigan.
•							Wright's Fir Tree House Foundry	Lancs	L. & N. W.	Wigan and Platt Bridge.
							Wigan Coal & Iron Co.—			
•							Alexandra Pit..............	Lancs	L. & Y.	Hindley.
•					•		Alexandra Pit (L. & N. W.)	Lancs	L & N W—G C (Wig.Jn.)	Wigan.
•							Arley Pit (L. & N. W.)	Lancs	L & N W—G C (Wig.Jn.)	Wigan.
•							Black Horse Siding	Lancs	L. & N. W.	Wigan.
•							Bold Hall Estate Siding ...	Lancs	L. & N. W.	St. Helens.
•							Brick Works (L. & N. W.)	Lancs	L & N W—G C (Wig.Jn.)	Wigan.
•							Brinks Col. (L&Y&LU Jt)	Lancs	{ L. & N. W. .... { L. & Y.	White Bear (Adlington). Adlington.
•							Broad Green Siding	Lancs	L. & N. W.	Liverpool, Edge Hill.
•							Bromilow Pit	Lancs	L. & N. W.	Wigan.
•					•		Broomfield Col. (L.&N.W.)	Lancs	L & N W—G C (Wig.Jn.)	Wigan.
•					•		Butcher Pit (L. & N. W.)...	Lancs	L & N W—G C (Wig.Jn.)	Wigan.
•							California Pit	Lancs	L. & Y	Hindley.
•					•		California Pit (L. & N. W.)	Lancs	L & N W—G C (Wig.Jn.)	Wigan.
•							Chowbent West Junc. Sid.	Lancs	L. & N. W.	Leigh & Bedford.
•							Eatock Pit	Lancs	L. & N. W.	Chowbent West Junction Siding.
•							Priestner Pit	Lancs	L. & N. W.	Chowbent West Junction Siding.
•							Sovereign Pit	Lancs	L. & N. W.	Chowbent West Junction Siding.
•							Crawford Pit	Lancs	L. & Y.	Hindley.
•					•		Crawford Pit (L. & N. W.)	Lancs	L & N W—G C (Wig.Jn.)	Wigan.
•							Crow Nest or Hewlett Pit (L. & Y.)	Lancs	L. & Y.—L. & N. W......	Hindley.
•					•		De Trafford Junc. Ir. Wks.	Lancs	L. & N. W.	Wigan.
•					•		Eatock Pit	Lancs	L. & Y.	Hindley.
•					•		Giants Hall Col. (L.&N.W.)	Lancs	L & N W—G C (Wig.Jn.)	Wigan.
•					•		Gidlow Lane Col. (L&NW)	Lancs	L & N W—G C (Wig.Jn.)	Wigan.
•					•		Haigh Saw Mills (L&NW)	Lancs	L & N W—G C (Wig.Jn.)	Wigan.

EXPLANATION—**G** *Goods Station.*   **P** *Passenger and Parcel Station.*   **P*** *Passenger, but not Parcel or Miscellaneous Traffic.*
F *Furniture Vans, Carriages, Portable Engines, and Machines on Wheels.*   **L** *Live Stock.*
H *Horse Boxes and Prize Cattle Vans.*   **C** *Carriages by Passenger Train.*

STATION ACCOMMODATION.						CRANE POWER.		STATIONS, &c.	COUNTY.	COMPANY.	POSITION.
						Tons	Cwts.	Wigan Coal & Iron Co.—*continued.*			
.	.	.	.	.	.	.	.	Hindley Pit	Lancs	L. & Y.	Hindley.
.	.	.	.	.	.	.	.	Iron and Steel Works	Lancs	L. & Y.	Hindley.
.	.	.	.	.	.	.	.	John Pit (L. & N. W.)	Lancs	L & N W—G C (Wig.Jn.)	Wigan.
.	.	.	.	.	.	.	.	Kirkless Hall Cl. & Ir. Sids.	Lancs	L. & Y.	Hindley.
.	.	.	.	.	.	.	.	Kirkless Hall Col. (L&NW)	Lancs	L & N W—G C (Wig.Jn.)	Wigan.
.	.	.	.	.	.	.	.	Kirkless Hall Iron and Steel Works (L. & N. W.)	Lancs	L & N W—G C (Wig.Jn.)	Wigan.
.	.	.	.	.	.	.	.	Kirkless Hall Ir.&Steel Wks. Round House Sid. (LNW)	Lancs	L & N W—G C (Wig.Jn.)	Wigan.
.	.	.	.	.	.	.	.	Kirkless Hall Ore Mine and Slag Siding	Lancs	L. & N. W.	Wigan.
.	.	.	.	.	.	.	.	Kirkless Stores (L. & N.W.)	Lancs	L & N W—G C (Wig.Jn.)	Wigan.
.	.	.	.	.	.	.	.	Ladies' Lane Col. (L. & Y.)	Lancs	L. & Y.—L. & N. W.	Hindley.
.	.	.	.	.	.	.	.	Langtree Pit (L. & N. W.)	Lancs	L & N W—G C (Wig.Jn.)	Wigan.
.	.	.	.	.	.	.	.	Lindsay Pit (L. & N. W.)...	Lancs	LNW—GC(Wig Jn)—LY	Wigan.
.	.	.	.	.	.	.	.	Manton Sidings	Notts	Mid.	Worksop.
.	.	.	.	.	.	.	.	Marsh House Coal and Lime Works (L. & N. W.)	Lancs	L & N W—G C (Wig.Jn.)	Wigan.
.	.	.	.	.	.	.	.	Meadow Pit	Lancs	L. & Y.	Hindley.
.	.	.	.	.	.	.	.	Meadow Pit (L. & N.W.)...	Lancs	L & N W—G C (Wig.Jn.)	Wigan.
.	.	.	.	.	.	.	.	Moor Pit No. 5 (L. & N.W.)	Lancs	L & N W—G C (Wig.Jn.)	Wigan.
.	.	.	.	.	.	.	.	Ordsall Lane Siding	Lancs	L. & N. W.	Manchester, Liverpool Road.
.	.	.	.	.	.	.	.	Prospect Pit (L. & N. W.)...	Lancs	L & N W—G C (Wig.Jn.)	Wigan.
.	.	.	.	.	.	.	.	Siding	Lancs	L. & Y.	Blackburn.
.	.	.	.	.	.	.	.	Siding	Lancs	L. & Y.—L. & N. W. ...	Bolton.
.	.	.	.	.	.	.	.	Siding	Lancs	L. & Y.	Darwen.
.	.	.	.	.	.	.	.	Siding	Lancs	L. & N. W.	Garston Dock.
.	.	.	.	.	.	.	.	Siding	Lancs	P.&L.Jt.(L&NW.&L&Y)	Longridge.
.	.	.	.	.	.	.	.	Siding	Lancs	P.&L.Jt.(L&NW.&L&Y)	Preston, Deepdale.
.	.	.	.	.	.	.	.	Siding	Lancs	L. & N. W.	Patricroft.
.	.	.	.	.	.	.	.	Siding	Lancs	L. & Y.	Southport, Charles Street.
.	.	.	.	.	.	.	.	Siding	Lancs	L. & N. W.	Warrington, Arpley.
.	.	.	.	.	.	.	.	Taylor Pit (L. & N. W.) ...	Isancs	LNW—GC(Wig Jn)—LY	Wigan.
.	.	.	.	.	.	.	.	Victoria Colliery (L & N W)	Lancs	L & N W—G C (Wig.Jn.)	Wigan.
.	.	.	.	.	.	.	.	Wash Pit	Lancs	L. & Y.	Hindley.
.	.	.	.	.	.	.	.	Wash Pit (L. & N. W.)......	Lancs	L & N W—G C (Wig.Jn.)	Wigan.
.	.	.	.	.	.	.	.	Woodshaw Pit..................	Lancs	L. & Y.	Hindley.
.	.	.	.	.	.	.	.	Woodshaw Siding (L&NW)	Lancs	L & N W—G C (Wig.Jn.)	Wigan.
.	.	.	.	.	.	.	.	Wigan Junc. Cols. & Bk. Wks.	Lancs	G. C. (Wigan Jn.)	Hindley and Platt Bridge.
.	.	.	.	.	.	.	.	Wigan Rolling Mills..........	Lancs	L. & Y.	See Pagefield Siding.
.	.	.	.	.	.	.	.	Wigfull & Son's Corn Mill (G C)	Yorks	G. C.—G. N.—Mid.	Sheffield, Bridgehouses.
.	.	.	.	.	.	.	.	Wiggenhall Siding..............	Norfolk ...	G. E.	See Magdalen Road.
.	.	.	.	.	.	.	.	Wiggins & Co.'s Siding	Staffs	L. & N. W.	Soho.
.	.	.	.	.	.	.	.	Wigglesworth Siding	Perth	Cal.	Coupar Angus.
.	.	.	.	.	.	.	.	Wigham, Richardson & Co.'s Neptune Siding	Northumb	N. E.	Walker.
								WIGSTON—			
.	P	.	L	H	.	.	.	(Station)	Leicester ..	Mid.	Leicester and Market Harboro'.
.	.	.	.	.	.	.	.	Dunmore & Son's Biscuit Manufactory	Leicester ..	Mid.	Near South Station.
G	P	F	L	H	.	5	0	Glen Parva	Leicester ..	L. & N. W.	Leicester and Nuneaton.
.	.	.	.	.	.	.	.	Kilby Bridge Sidings (Ellis, J., & Son)	Leicester ..	Mid.	Wigston and Great Glen.
.	.	.	.	.	.	.	.	Leicester Brick Co.'s Knighton Junc. Works	Leicester ..	Mid.	Near South Station.
.	.	.	.	.	.	.	.	Leicester Line Junction...	Leicester ..	L. & N. W.—Mid.	Nuneaton and Leicester.
.	.	.	.	.	.	.	.	Leicestershire Dairy Co.'s Siding	Leicester ..	Mid.	Near South Station.
.	.	.	.	.	.	.	.	Market Harboro' Line Junc.	Leicester ..	L. & N. W.—Mid.	Nuneaton and Great Glen.
.	.	.	.	.	.	.	.	Redshaw, Chas., Siding.....	Leicester ..	Mid.	Near South Station.
G	P	.	.	.	.	1	10	South	Leicester ..	Mid.	Rugby and Leicester.
.	.	.	.	.	.	.	.	Wigston Foundry Co.'s Siding	Leicester ..	Mid.	Near South Station.
.	.	.	.	.	.	.	.	Wright, Orson & Co.'s Sid.	Leicester ..	Mid.	Near South Station.
G	P	F	L	H	C	5	0	Wigton	Cumb'land	M. & C.	Curthwaite and Leegate.
.	.	.	.	.	.	.	.	Sheffield's Brick Works	Cumb'land	M. & C.	Wigton and Leegate.
G	P	F	L	H	C	1	0	Wigtown	Wigtown..	P.P.&W.Jt.(Cal.,G&SW, L. & N. W., & Mid.)...	Newton Stewart and Whithorn.
G	P	.	.	.	.	.	.	Wilburton	Cambs......	G. E.	Ely and St. Ives.
.	.	.	.	.	.	.	.	Wilcock & Jones' Hoop-Iron Works	Yorks	Mid.	Same as South Yorkshire Hoop-Iron Works (Masboro').

STATION ACCOMMODATION.						CRANE POWER.	STATIONS, &c.	COUNTY.	COMPANY.	POSITION.
						Tons Cwts.				
·	·	·	·	·	·	· ·	Wilderspool Brewery	Lancs	L. & N. W.	Same as Greenall, Whitley & Co.'s Siding (Warrington).
·	·	·	·	·	·	· ·	Wilderspool Siding	Lancs	L. & N. W.	Same as Fletcher, Russell & Co.'s Siding (Warrington).
·	·	·	·	·	·	· ·	Wiley's Siding	Yorks	N. E.	Brough.
·	·	·	·	·	·	· ·	Wilford Brick Co.'s Siding ...	Notts	G. C.	Ruddington.
·	·	·	·	·	·	· ·	Wilkerson & Son's Siding	Herts	G. N.	Royston.
·	·	·	·	·	·	· ·	Wilkes & Co.'s Siding	Staffs	L. & N. W.	Darlaston.
·	·	·	·	·	·	· ·	Wilkes' Siding	Staffs	L. & N. W	{ Darlaston. { Pelsall.
·	·	·	·	·	·	· ·	Wilkie & Gibb's Brick Works	Fife	N. B.	Leven.
·	·	·	·	·	·	· ·	Wilkie's Coal Siding	Stirling ...	N. B.	Falkirk, Camelon.
·	·	·	·	·	·	· ·	Wilkins and Co.'s Siding......	Derby	G. N.	Derby, Friar Gate.
·	·	·	·	·	·	· ·	Wilkinson's Malt Kiln Siding	Yorks	G. C.	Barnsley.
·	·	·	·	·	·	· ·	Wilkinson's Siding	Yorks	N. E.	Boosbeck.
·	·	·	·	·	·	· ·	Wilkinson's Wrekin Chemical Works	Salop	L. & N. W.	Stirchley.
·	·	·	·	·	·	· ·	Wilkinson's Stone Quarry ...	Lancs	P.&L.Jt. (L&NW.&L&Y)	Longridge.
G	P	·	L	H		· ·	Wilkinstown	Meath	M. G. W.	Navan and Kingscourt.
·	·	·	·	·	·	· ·	Wilks Siding	Staffs	L. & N. W.	Same as Leamore Brick Co.'s Siding (Birchills).
							Willans and Robinson's—			
·	·	·	·	·	·	· ·	Ferry Works	Flint	L. & N. W.	See Dundas Siding (Queensferry).
G	P	·	L	·	·	· ·	Siding	Warwick..	L. & N. W.	Rugby.
G	P	·	L	·	·	· ·	Willaston	Cheshire..	L. & N. W.	Crewe and Whitchurch.
·	P	·	·	·	·	· ·	Willbrook	Clare	West Clare	Ennis and Miltown Malbay.
G	P	F	L	H	C	10 0	Willder's Siding	Staffs	L. & N. W.	Stafford.
G	P	F	L	H	C	5 0 }	Willenhall	Staffs	L. & N. W.	Birmingham and Wolverhampton.
G	·	F	L	·	·	5 0 }	Willenhall (Mid.)	Staffs	{ Mid. { G. W.	Wolverhampton & Sutton Coldfield. Over Mid. from Wolverhampton Jn.
·	·	·	·	·	·	· ·	Willenhall Gas Co.'s Sid (Mid)	Staffs	Mid.—G. W.	Short Heath.
G	P	F	L	H	C	· ·	Willerby and Kirk Ella	Yorks	H. & B.	Howden and Hull.
·	·	·	·	·	·	· ·	Kirk Ella Lime Works	Yorks	H. & B.	Willerby and Little Weighton.
·	·	·	·	·	·	· ·	Willesden.....................	Middlesex	Mid.	See London, Dudding Hill (for Willesden and Neasden).
·	·	·	·	·	·	· ·	Willesden & Acton Brick Wks.	Middlesex	G. W.	Same as Acton and Willesden Brick Works (London).
·	·	·	·	·	·	· ·	Willesden Electric Light Works Siding	Middlesex	Mid.	London, Harlesden.
·	·	·	·	·	·	· ·	Willesden Green & Cricklewood	Middlesex	Met.	See London.
·	·	·	·	·	·	· ·	Willesden Junction	Middlesex	L & N W—N & S W Jn. Jt.	London, Euston and Acton.
·	·	·	·	·	·	· ·	Willesden Junction Exchange Sidings (L. & N. W.)	Middlesex	L. & N. W.—L. & S. W.	London, Willesden Junction.
·	·	·	·	·	·	· ·	Willesden Junction Station (L. & N. W.)	Middlesex	L. & N.W.—G.W.—N.L.	See London.
·	·	·	·	·	·	· ·	William Pit	Cumb'land	L. & N. W.	See Allerdale Coal Co. (Camerton).
·	·	·	·	·	·	· ·	William Pit (C. & W. Jn.) ...	Cumb'land	C. & W. Jn.—L. & N. W.	Same as St. Helens Colliery No. 3 (Workington).
·	·	·	·	·	·	· ·	William Pit (N. B.)	Stirling ...	N. B.—Cal.	Falkirk, Grahamston.
·	·	·	·	·	·	· ·	William Pit Colliery	Cumb'land	Furness—L. & N. W. ...	Same as Whitehaven Colliery Co. (Whitehaven).
·	·	·	·	·	·	· ·	Williams & Co.'s Old Union Pits and Furnaces	Staffs	L. & N. W.	Albion.
·	·	·	·	·	·	· ·	Williams & Davies' Timber Yard (G. W.)	Carmarth'	G. W.—L. & N. W.	Llanelly.
·	·	·	·	·	·	· ·	Williams & Son's Siding	Carnarvon	L. & N. W.	Llanwnda.
·	·	·	·	·	·	· ·	Williams & Son's Siding	Essex	L. T. & S.	Same as Dagenham Docks Siding (Rainham).
·	·	·	·	·	·	· ·	Williams & Son's Siding	Glamorg'n	GW—LNW—Rhy.—TV	Cardiff.
·	·	·	·	·	·	· ·	Williams & Son's Grovesend Colliery	Glamorg'n	L. & N. W.	Gorseinon.
·	·	·	·	·	·	· ·	Williams & Son's Wednesbury Oak Iron Works...............	Staffs	G. W.— L. & N. W.	Wednesbury.
·	·	·	·	·	·	· ·	Williams' Brick Siding	Surrey ...	S. E. & C.	Godstone.
·	·	·	·	·	·	· ·	Williams' Brick Works........	Flint	W. M. & C. Q.	Connah's Quay.
·	·	·	·	·	·	· ·	Williams', Chas., Sid. (Mid.)	Glamorg'n	Mid.—G.W.—L. & N.W.	Morriston.
·	·	·	·	·	·	· ·	Williams' (Executors of) Holly Bush Colliery	Mon	L. & N. W.	Holly Bush.
·	·	·	·	·	·	· ·	Williams' Foundry Siding ...	Mon	G. W.	Abertillery.
·	·	·	·	·	·	· ·	Williams, J., & Co.'s Siding..	Glo'ster ...	Mid.	Cheltenham.
·	·	·	·	·	·	· ·	Williams' Lime Siding	Glamorg'n	T. V.	Penarth Dock.

EXPLANATION—G *Goods Station.*   P *Passenger and Parcel Station.*   P* *Passenger, but not Parcel or Miscellaneous Traffic.*
F *Furniture Vans, Carriages, Portable Engines, and Machines on Wheels.*   L *Live Stock.*
H *Horse Boxes and Prize Cattle Vans.*   C *Carriages by Passenger Train.*

STATION ACCOMMODATION.						CRANE POWER.		STATIONS, &c.	COUNTY.	COMPANY.	POSITION.
						Tons	Cwts				
								Williams, R., & Son's Timber Siding	Brecon	G. W.—Mid.	Hay.
								Williams' Elwy Siding	Flint	L. & N. W.	Rhyl.
								Williams' Siding (G. N.)	Beds	G. N.—L. & N. W.	Luton.
								Williams' New Clydach Colliery	Mon	L. & N. W.	Brynmawr.
								Williamson & Son's Ship Yard	Cumb'land	L. & N. W.	Workington.
								Williamson, J. H. (Executors of), Siding	Staffs	N. S.	Talk-o'-th'-Hill.
								Williamson's Siding	Lancs	L. & N. W.	Lancaster.
								Williamthorpe Colliery	Derby	Mid.	Hasland.
								William Wright Dock (N.E.)	Yorks	N. E.—L. & N. W.	See Hull.
								Willingdon	Sussex	L. B. & S. C.	See Hampden Park (for Willingdon).
								Willingdon Junction	Sussex	L. B. & S. C.	Polegate and Eastbourne.
								Willingsworth Iron Co.'s Siding (G. W.)	Staffs	G. W.—L. & N. W.	Wednesbury.
G	P	F	L					Willington	Beds	L. & N. W.	Bedford and Cambridge.
								Willington (Mid.)	Derby	Mid.—L. & N. W.	See Repton and Willington.
								Willington Junction	Derby	Mid.—N. S.	Derby and Tutbury.
G	P		L	H		1	0	Willington	Durham	N. E.	Durham (Pass.) & Bishop Auckland.
								Bowdon Close Colliery	Durham	N. E.	Willington.
								Brancepeth Colliery	Durham	N. E.	Willington.
								West Durham Junction	Durham	N. E.	Willington.
								Willington Colliery, Coke & Brick Wks. (Sunnybrow)	Durham	N. E.	Willington.
G	P		L			10	0	Willington Quay	Northumb	N. E.	Loop—Newcastle and Percy Main.
								North Eastern Marine Engineering Co. (Northumberland Engine Works)	Northumb	N. E.	Willington Quay.
								Union Cement Co.'s Siding	Northumb	N. E.	Willington Quay.
								Wallsend Slipway & Engineering Co.'s Siding	Northumb	N. E.	Willington Quay.
G	P	F	L	H	C	1	15	Willis' Branch	Lancs	L. & N. W.	Huyton Quarry.
G	P	F	L	H	C	1	5	Williton	Somerset	G. W.	Taunton and Watchet.
								Willoughby	Lincoln	G. N.	Boston and Louth.
								Willoughby	Warwick	G. C.	See Braunston and Willoughby (for Daventry).
								Willow Bank Works	Cheshire	C. L. C. (G C, G N, & Mid.)	See Salt Union, Ltd. (Winsford and Over).
								Willow Holme Junction	Cumb'land	Cal.—Gds. Tfc. Com.	Carlisle.
								Willow Walk	Surrey	L. B. & S. C.	See London.
								Willow Walk Junction	Surrey	L. B. & S. C.—S. E. & C.	London, Willow Walk and Deptford.
								Willson's Saw Mill	Durham	N. E.	Same as Milton Saw Mill (West Hartlepool).
G	P							Wilmcote	Warwick	G. W.	Stratford-on-Avon and Hatton.
								Greaves, Bull, & Lakin's Works	Warwick	G. W.	Wilmcote.
								Wilmington	Yorks	N. E.	See Hull.
								Wilmshurst's Siding	Sussex	L. B. & S. C.	Barcombe Mills.
G	P	F	L	H	C	5	0	Wilmslow	Cheshire	L. & N. W.	Crewe and Stockport.
								Priestner's Siding	Cheshire	L. & N. W.	Wilmslow and Handforth.
G	P		L			1	10	Wilnecote	Warwick	Mid.	Tamworth and Whitacre.
								Dosthill Brick Siding (T. Stone)	Warwick	Mid.	Wilnecote and Kingsbury.
								Hathern Station Brick & Terra Cotta Co.'s Siding (Cliff Siding)	Warwick	Mid.	Wilnecote and Kingsbury.
								Hockley Hall Colliery & Brick Works	Warwick	Mid.	Wilnecote and Kingsbury.
								Peel Colliery	Staffs	Mid.	Wilnecote.
								Skey & Co.'s Pipe Works	Warwick	Mid.	Near Wilnecote.
								Tame Valley Col. & Bk. Wks.	Warwick	Mid.	Wilnecote and Kingsbury.
								Whateley Col. & Brick Wks.	Warwick	Mid.	Wilnecote and Kingsbury.
G	P		L	H		3	0	Wilpshire (for Ribchester)	Lancs	L. & Y.	Blackburn and Clitheroe.
								Cemetery Hill Siding	Lancs	L. & Y.	Wilpshire and Daisy Field.
G	P		L	H		1	10	Wilsden	Yorks	G. N.	Keighley and Bradford.
								Lodge & Flesher's Siding	Yorks	G. N.	Wilsden.
								Wilson & Twyford's Siding	Lancs	C. L. C. (G.C, G.N, & Mid.)	Stockport.
								Wilson Bros. Bobbin Co.'s Siding	Lancs	L. & N. W.	Garston Dock.
								Wilson, J. & W., & Son's Timber Yard	Durham	N. E.	Sunderland, Monkwearmouth.

EXPLANATION—G *Goods Station.*   P *Passenger and Parcel Station.*   P* *Passenger, but not Parcel or Miscellaneous Traffic.*
F *Furniture Vans, Carriages, Portable Engines, and Machines on Wheels.*   L *Live Stock.*
H *Horse Boxes and Prize Cattle Vans.*   C *Carriages by Passenger Train.*

STATION ACCOMMODATION.						CRANE POWER.	STATIONS, &c.	COUNTY.	COMPANY.	POSITION.
						Tons Cwts.	Wilson, J. H., & Co.'s Crane Works	Cheshire...	B'headJt—CLC—NW&L	Birkenhead.
							Wilson's (Executors of) Exhall Colliery (L. & N.W.)	Warwick..	L. & N. W.—Mid.	Bedworth.
							Wilson's Forge & Steel Wks.	Durham ...	N. E.	Bishop Auckland.
							Wilson's Percival Lane Siding	Cheshire...	L. & N. W.	Runcorn Docks.
							Wilson's Stone Siding	Norfolk ...	Mid. & G. N. Jt.	Massingham.
							Wilson, T. W. (Executors of) Siding	Suffolk ...	G. E.	Hadleigh.
G	P	.	L	H	.	1 10	Wilsontown	Lanark	Cal.	Branch near Auchengray.
							Climpy Colliery	Lanark	Cal.	Extension from Wilsontown.
							Wilsontown Collieries	Lanark	Cal.	Wilsontown.
							Wilsontown Junctions	Lanark	Cal.	Near Auchengray.
							Wilsontown Quarry	Lanark	Cal.	Haywood and Wilsontown.
							Wilsontown Weighs	Lanark	Cal.	Haywood and Cobbinshaw.
							Wilsthorpe Siding	Lincoln	G. N.	Essendine.
							Wilstrop Siding	Yorks	N. E.	See Marston Moor.
G	P	F	L	H	C	1 10	Wilton	Wilts	{ G. W.	Salisbury and Warminster.
G	P	F	L	H	C	2 0			{ L. & S. W.	Salisbury and Templecombe.
							Wiltshire Bacon Curing Sid.	Wilts	G. W.	Chippenham.
							Wimberry Colliery	Glo'ster	S. & Wye Jt. (G. W. & Mid.)	Speech House Road.
							WIMBLEDON—			
G	P	F	L	H	C	. .	(Station)	Surrey	L. & S. W. & L. B. & S. C. Jt.	Croydon and Tooting Lines.
G	P	F	L	H	C	10 0	(Station, L. & S. W.)	Surrey	{ L. & S. W.	Clapham Junction and Surbiton.
.	P	.	.	.	.				{ Met. Dist.	Over L. & S. W. from Putney Bridge (Fulham) Junction.
							Junction	Surrey	L. & S. W.—L. B. & S. C.	Raynes Park and Haydon's Road.
							Wimbledon Urban District Council Siding	Surrey	L. & S. W.—L. B. & S. C.	Wimbledon.
.	P						Wimbledon Park	Surrey	L. & S. W.	Wimbledon and East Putney.
G	P	F	L	H	C	2 0	Wimblington	Cambs.	G. N. & G. E. Jt.	St. Ives and March.
G	P	F	L	H	C	5 0	Wimborne (L. & S. W.)	Dorset...	{ L. & S. W.	Ringwood and Wareham.
									{ S & DJt.(L&SW & Mid.)	Over L. & S. W. from Wimborne Jn.
							Canford Siding	Dorset...	L. & S. W.—S. & D. Jt.	Wimborne.
							Uddens Siding	Dorset...	L. & S. W.	Wimborne and Ringwood.
							Wimborne Junction	Dorset...	L. & S. W.—S. & D. Jt.	Wimborne and Blandford.
G	P	F	L	H	C	10 0	Wincanton	Somerset..	S.&D.Jt.(L.&S.W.&Mid)	Templecombe and Glastonbury.
							Wincham Works (C.L.C.)	Cheshire..	C. L. C.—L. & N. W.	See Salt Union, Ltd. (Northwich).
.	P	.					Winchburgh	L'lithgow	N. B.	Ratho and Linlithgow.
							Hopetoun Quarry	L'lithgow	N. B.	Dalmeny and Philpstoun.
G	.						Myre Siding	L'lithgow	N. B.	Dalmeny and Philpstoun.
							Winchburgh Brick Works (Dougall's)	L'lithgow	N. B.	Winchburgh.
							Winchburgh Junction	L'lithgow	N. B.	Winchburgh and Philpstoun.
.	P						Winchelsea	Sussex	S. E. & C.	Hastings and Rye.
G	P	F	L	H	C	10 0	Winchester	Hants	{ G. W.	Branch from Newbury.
G	P	F	L	H	C	10 0			{ L. & S. W.	Basingstoke and Eastleigh.
							Winchester Junction	Hants	G. W.—L. & S. W.	Winchester (G.W.) and Eastleigh.
G	P	F	L	H	C	4 0	Winchfield (for Hartley Row)	Hants	L. & S. W.	Woking and Basingstoke.
G	P						Winchmore Hill (G. N.)	Middlesex	{ G. N.	Wood Green and Enfield.
.	P								{ N. L.	Over G. N. from Canonbury Junc.
.	P*								{ S. E. & C.	Over G. N. from King's Cross Junc.
							Wincobank	Yorks	G. C.	See Meadow Hall and Wincobank.
							Wincobank & Meadow Hall	Yorks	Mid.	See Sheffield.
							Windebank, J., & Son's Sid.	Somerset..	Mid.	Bath.
G	P						Winder	Cumb'land	WC&EJt.(Fur.&LNW)	Marron and Moor Row.
							Lonsdale Mining Co.'s Winder Pits	Cumb'land	WC&EJt.(Fur.&LNW)	Winder and Yeathouse.
							Postlethwaite's Eskett Mining Co.'s Siding	Cumb'land	WC&EJt.(Fur.&LNW)	Winder and Rowrah.
G	P	F	L	H	C	5 0	Windermere	W'morlnd	L. & N. W.	Branch from Oxenholme.
G	P	F	L	H	C	3 0	Windermere, Lake Side	Lancs	Furness	Branch near Ulverston.
							Winder Pits	Cumb'land	WC&EJt.(Fur.&LNW)	Same as Lonsdale Mining Co.'s Siding (Winder).
							Windhill	Yorks	G. N.	See Shipley and Windhill.
							Windlesham	Berks	L. & S. W.	See Sunningdale and Windlesham.
							Windlestone Lane Depôts	Durham	N. E.	Leasingthorne.
							Windmill Brick & Tile Co.'s Siding	Staffs	G. W.	Wolverhampton.
							Windmill Bridge Junction	Surrey	L. B. & S. C.	Croydon and Norwood.
.	P						Windmill End	Staffs	G. W.	Branch—Netherton and Old Hill.
							Windmillhill Sidings	Lanark	Cal.	Motherwell.

EXPLANATION—G *Goods Station.*   P *Passenger and Parcel Station.*   P* *Passenger, but not Parcel or Miscellaneous Traffic.*
F *Furniture Vans, Carriages, Portable Engines, and Machines on Wheels.*   L *Live Stock.*
H *Horse Boxes and Prize Cattle Vans.*   C *Carriages by Passenger Train.*

STATION ACCOMMODATION.						CRANE POWER.		STATIONS, &c.	COUNTY.	COMPANY.	POSITION.
						Tons	Cwts.				
..	..	..	..	..	..	..	..	Windmill Road Junction......	Louth	D. N. & G.—G. N. (I.) ...	Dundalk.
G	P	F	L	H	C	7	0	Windsor	Antrim ...	G. N. (I.)	See Belfast, Adelaide and Windsor.
G	P	F	L	H	C	10	0	Windsor and Eton............	Berks	{ G. W. .... { L. & S. W.	Branch from Slough. Branch from Staines.
..	..	..	..	..	..	..	..	Windsor Bridge (L. & Y.) ..	Lancs	L. & Y.—Mid.	See Manchester.
..	..	..	..	..	..	..	..	Windsor Colliery	Glamorg'n	Rhy.	Abertridwr.
..	..	..	..	..	..	..	..	Windsor Colliery	Glamorg'n	T. V.	Same as Ocean Coal Co.'s Lady Windsor Colliery (Ynysybwl).
..	..	..	..	..	..	..	..	Windsor Slipway	Glamorg'n	T. V.	Grangetown and Penarth Harbour.
..	..	..	..	..	..	..	..	Windsor Street Gas Works (L. & N. W.)	Warwick..	L. & N. W.—Mid.	See Birmingham Corporation.
..	..	..	..	..	..	..	..	Windsor Street Wharf........	Warwick..	L. & N. W.	See Birmingham.
..	..	..	..	..	..	..	..	Wind Street (Burrows Lodge)	Glamorg'n	G. W.	See Swansea.
..	..	..	..	..	..	..	..	Wind Street Junction	Glamorg'n	G. W.	Swansea.
..	..	..	..	..	..	..	..	Windyedge Colliery No. 4 ..	Lanark ...	Cal.	Same as Greenhill Collieries (Omoa).
..	..	..	..	..	..	..	..	Windyedge Pit	Ayr	G. & S.W.	Gatehead.
..	..	..	..	..	..	..	..	Windy Hill Siding	Denbigh...	W. M. & C. Q.	Moss.
G	P	..	L	H	C	3	0	Winestead Siding	Yorks	N. E.	Patrington.
G	P	..	L	H	C	..	..	Wingate	Durham ..	N. E.	Ferryhill and Hartlepool.
..	..	..	..	..	..	..	..	Carter's Brick Works	Durham ..	N. E.	Wingate.
..	..	..	..	..	..	..	..	Wingate Colliery	Durham ..	N. E.	Wingate.
..	..	..	..	..	..	..	..	Wingate Glass Brick Wks.	Durham ..	N. E.	Wingate.
..	..	..	..	..	..	..	..	Wingate Lime Stone Quarry..	Durham ..	N. E.	Trimdon.
G	P	F	L	H	C	5	0	Wingfield	Derby.....	Mid.	Clay Cross and Ambergate.
..	..	..	..	..	..	..	..	Oakerthorpe Colliery	Derby.....	Mid.	Wingfield.
..	..	..	..	..	..	..	..	Shirland Colliery (Shirland Gas Co.)	Derby.....	Mid.	Wingfield and Stretton.
..	..	..	..	..	..	..	..	South Wingfield Colliery...	Derby.....	Mid.	Stretton and Ambergate.
..	..	..	..	..	..	..	..	Wingham	Kent	S. E. & C.	See Adisham (for Wingham).
..	..	..	..	..	..	..	..	Wingmore Siding	Kent	S. E. & C.	Barham.
..	..	..	..	..	..	..	..	Winlaton Mill Rolling Mills	Durham ..	N. E.	Derwenthaugh.
G	..	..	..	..	..	..	..	Winning B. Colliery (Black-well Colliery) (G. C.).........	Derby.....	G. C.—G. N.—L. & N. W.	Kirkby and Pinxton.
..	..	..	..	..	..	..	..	Winnington	Cheshire ..	C. L. C. (GC, GN, & Mid.)	Branch near Hartford & Greenbank.
..	..	..	..	..	..	..	..	Brunner, Mond & Co.'s Chemical Works............	Cheshire ..	C. L. C. (GC, GN, & Mid.)	Winnington.
..	..	..	..	..	..	..	..	Salt Union, Limited— Hickson's Works	Cheshire ..	C. L. C. (GC, GN, & Mid.)	Winnington.
..	..	..	..	..	..	..	..	Warboise Works	Cheshire ..	C. L. C. (GC, GN, & Mid.)	Winnington.
..	..	..	..	..	..	..	..	Winnington Co-operative Society's Works	Cheshire ..	C. L. C. (GC, GN, & Mid.)	Winnington.
G	P	..	..	..	..	..	..	Winns Siding	Lincoln ...	G. C.	Frodingham and Scunthorpe.
G	P	..	..	..	..	..	..	Winscombe	Somerset..	G. W.	Yatton and Cheddar.
G	P	..	L	H	..	..	..	Winsford	Cheshire..	L. & N. W.	Crewe and Warrington.
G	P	F	L	H	..	5	0	Winsford and Over	Cheshire...	C. L. C. (GC, GN, & Mid.)	Branch from Cuddington.
..	..	..	..	..	..	..	..	Falks Junction	Cheshire...	C. L. C. (GC, GN, & Mid.)	Winsford and Over.
..	..	..	..	..	..	..	..	Garner's Siding	Cheshire...	C. L. C. (GC, GN, & Mid.)	Winsford and Over.
..	..	..	..	..	..	..	..	Hamlett's Siding	Cheshire...	C. L. C. (GC, GN, & Mid.)	Winsford and Over.
..	..	..	..	..	..	..	..	Salt Union, Ltd.— Hickson's Works	Cheshire...	C. L. C. (GC, GN, & Mid.)	Winsford and Over.
..	..	..	..	..	..	..	..	Knight's Grange Works ..	Cheshire...	C. L. C. (GC, GN, & Mid.)	Winsford and Over.
..	..	..	..	..	..	..	..	Meadow Bank Works ..	Cheshire...	C. L. C. (GC, GN, & Mid.)	Winsford and Over.
..	..	..	..	..	..	..	..	Meadow Works	Cheshire...	C. L. C. (GC, GN, & Mid.)	Winsford and Over.
..	..	..	..	..	..	..	..	Over Works...............	Cheshire...	C. L. C. (GC, GN, & Mid.)	Winsford and Over.
..	..	..	..	..	..	..	..	Soap Works...............	Cheshire...	C. L. C. (GC, GN, & Mid.)	Winsford and Over.
..	..	..	..	..	..	..	..	Willow Bank Works	Cheshire...	C. L. C. (GC, GN, & Mid.)	Winsford and Over.
G	P	F	L	H	C	5	0	Winslow	Bucks.....	L. & N. W.	Bletchley and Verney Junc. Sta.
..	P	..	..	..	..	..	..	Winslow Road	Bucks......	Met.	Aylesbury and Verney Junction.
..	..	..	..	..	..	..	..	Winson Green...................	Warwick..	{ G. W. .... { L. & N. W.	See Soho and Winson Green. See Birmingham.
G	..	..	..	..	..	..	..	Winsor Hill Siding	Somerset..	S.&D.Jt.(L.&S. W.& Mid)	Binegar and Shepton Mallet.
..	..	..	..	..	..	..	..	Winstanley Colliery	Lancs	L. & N. W.	Garswood.
G	P	F	L	H	C	5	0	Winstanley Siding.............	Lancs	L. & Y.	Pemberton.
..	..	..	..	..	..	..	..	Winston (for Staindrop)	Durham ..	N. E.	Darlington and Barnard Castle.
..	..	..	..	..	..	..	..	Newsham Siding	Durham ..	N. E.	Winston.
..	..	..	..	..	..	..	..	Whorley Hill Colliery	Durham ..	N. E.	Winston.
G	P	F	L	H	C	6	0	Winterbourne..................	Glo'ster ...	G. W.	Wootton Bassett and Patchway.
..	..	..	..	..	..	..	..	Winterset Junction	Yorks	G. C.	Ryhill and Nostell.
G	P	..	L	H	..	1	10	Wintersgill, B., Siding........	Durham ..	N. E.	Stockton, South.
..	..	..	..	..	..	..	..	Winton	Hadding'n	N. B.	Smeaton and Macmerry.
..	..	..	..	..	..	..	..	Winwick Hall Siding	Lancs	L. & N. W.	Same as Lancashire Asylums Board Siding (Warrington).

EXPLANATION—G *Goods Station.*   P *Passenger and Parcel Station.*   P* *Passenger, but not Parcel or Miscellaneous Traffic.*
F *Furniture Vans, Carriages, Portable Engines, and Machines on Wheels.*   L *Live Stock.*
H *Horse Boxes and Prize Cattle Vans.*   C *Carriages by Passenger Train.*

STATION ACCOMMODATION.						CRANE POWER.	STATIONS, &c.	COUNTY.	COMPANY.	POSITION.
G	P	F	L	H	C	Tons Cwts. 10 0	Wirksworth	Derby	Mid.	Branch from Duffield.
.	.	.	.	.	.	. .	Bowne & Shaw's Limestone Quarry	Derby	Mid.	Near Wirksworth.
.	.	.	.	.	.	. .	Butterley Co.'s Dale Quarry	Derby	Mid.	Near Wirksworth.
.	.	.	.	.	.	. .	Wirksworth Stone and Mineral Co.'s Qry. Siding	Derby	Mid.	Near Wirksworth.
							Wirksworth Stone and Mineral Co.—			
.	.	.	.	.	.	. .	Brittain's or Manystones Quarry	Derby	L. & N. W.	Longcliffe.
.	.	.	.	.	.	. .	Quarry Siding	Derby	Mid.	Wirksworth.
G	P	.	.	.	.	. .	Wirral Colliery	Cheshire...	B'head Jt. (G W & L N W)	Parkgate.
G	P	F	L	H	C	6 0 }	Wisbech	Cambs...	{ G. E. .... Mid. & G. N. Jt.........	March and Lynn. Sutton Bridge and Peterborough.
G	P	F	L	H	C	10 0 }				
G	.	.	.	.	.	. .	English Bros.' Siding	Cambs.....	G. E.	Wisbech Harbour.
G	.	.	.	.	.	5 0 }	Harbour	Cambs.....	{ G. E. .... Mid. & G. N. Jt.	Wisbech. Wisbech.
G	.	.	.	.	.	5 0 }				
.	.	.	.	.	.	. .	Ropkins & Co.'s Mill Siding	Cambs.....	G. E.	Wisbech Harbour.
.	.	.	.	.	.	. .	Stanley & Hyde Siding......	Cambs.....	G. E.	Wisbech Harbour.
.	.	.	.	.	.	. .	Wisbech Lighting Co.'s Sid.	Cambs.....	G. E.	Wisbech Harbour.
G	P	.	L	H	.	. .	Wisbech St. Mary............	Cambs.....	Mid. & G. N. Jt.	Sutton Bridge and Peterborough.
							WISBECH TRAMWAY—			
G	P*	.	.	.	.	. .	Boyce's Bridge	Cambs.....	G. E.	Wisbech Tramway.
G	P*	.	.	.	.	. .	Elm Bridge	Cambs.....	G. E.	Wisbech Tramway.
G	P*	.	.	.	.	. .	Outwell Basin	Cambs.....	G. E.	Wisbech Tramway.
G	P*	.	.	.	.	. .	Outwell Village	Cambs.....	G. E.	Wisbech Tramway.
G	P	.	L	H	.	. .	Upwell	Norfolk	G. E.	Wisbech Tramway.
G	P	F	L	H	C	3 0	Wishaw, Central	Lanark ...	Cal.	Law Junction and Holytown.
.	.	.	.	.	.	. .	Belhaven Works	Lanark ...	Cal.	Wishaw, Central and Shieldmuir.
.	.	.	.	.	.	. .	Bellevue Saw Mill	Lanark ...	Cal.	Wishaw, South.
.	.	.	.	.	.	. .	Berryhill Colliery	Lanark ...	Cal.	Wishaw, South and Shieldmuir.
.	.	.	.	.	.	. .	Brand's Siding	Lanark ...	Cal.	Wishaw.
.	.	.	.	.	.	. .	Cambusnethan Colliery......	Lanark ...	Cal.	Wishaw, South and Shieldmuir.
.	.	.	.	.	.	. .	Collyshot Mine	Lanark ...	Cal.	Wishaw.
.	.	.	.	.	.	. .	Garriongill Collieries Nos. 1, 4, & 10 Pits..............	Lanark ...	Cal.	Law Junction and Wishaw, South.
.	.	.	.	.	.	. .	Indestructible Rolled Steel Axle Box Works...........	Lanark ...	Cal.	Wishaw, South.
.	.	.	.	.	.	. .	Overtoun Forge	Lanark ...	Cal.	Law Junction and Wishaw, South.
.	.	.	.	.	.	. .	Overtoun Siding...............	Lanark ...	Cal.	Law Junction and Wishaw, South.
.	.	.	.	.	.	. .	Pather	Lanark ...	Cal.	Wishaw.
.	.	.	.	.	.	. .	Pather Iron & Steel Works	Lanark ...	Cal.	Law Junction and Wishaw, South.
.	.	.	.	.	.	. .	Stenton Iron & Steel Works	Lanark ...	Cal.	Wishaw, South and Shieldmuir.
.	.	.	.	.	.	. .	Thornlee Colliery	Lanark ...	Cal.	Wishaw, Central.
.	.	.	.	.	.	. .	Waterloo Colliery	Lanark ...	Cal.	Law Junction and Wishaw, South.
.	.	.	.	.	.	. .	Wishaw Brick & Fire-Clay Works	Lanark ...	Cal.	Wishaw, South and Shieldmuir.
.	.	.	.	.	.	. .	Wishaw Distillery (Clydesdale Distillery)	Lanark ...	Cal.	Wishaw, South and Shieldmuir.
.	.	.	.	.	.	. .	Wishaw Engine Works ...	Lanark ...	Cal.	Wishaw, South and Shieldmuir.
.	.	.	.	.	.	. .	Wishaw Foundry	Lanark ...	Cal.	Wishaw, South and Shieldmuir.
.	.	.	.	.	.	. .	Wishaw Gas Works	Lanark ...	Cal.	Wishaw, Central.
.	.	.	.	.	.	. .	Wishaw Iron Works (Glasgow Iron & Steel Works, Wishaw)	Lanark ...	Cal.	Wishaw, South and Shieldmuir.
.	.	.	.	.	.	. .	Wishaw Steel Works	Lanark ...	Cal.	Wishaw, South and Shieldmuir.
.	.	.	.	.	.	. .	Wishaw Wagon Works (Pickering & Co.)	Lanark ...	Cal.	Wishaw, South.
G	P	.	.	.	.	4 10	Wishaw, South	Lanark ...	Cal.	Law Junction and Motherwell.
G	P	F	L	H	C	1 10	Wishford	Wilts	G. W.	Salisbury and Warminster.
G	P*	.	L	.	.	. .	Wistow	Yorks	N. E.	Selby and Cawood.
.	.	.	.	.	.	. .	Brayton Siding	Yorks	N. E.	Wistow.
.	.	.	.	.	.	. .	Crosshills Siding	Yorks	N. E.	Wistow.
.	.	.	.	.	.	. .	Flaxley Siding	Yorks	N. E.	Wistow.
.	.	.	.	.	.	. .	Leeds Road Siding (Thorpe Road)	Yorks	N. E.	Wistow.
.	.	.	.	.	.	. .	Sherburn Road Siding (Selby Common Siding)	Yorks	N. E.	Wistow.
.	.	.	.	.	.	. .	Wistow Junction	Yorks	N. E.	Wistow.
G	P	F	L	H	C	3 0	Witham	Essex	G. E.	Colchester and Chelmsford.
.	.	.	.	.	.	. .	Gray's, C. H., Siding	Essex	G. E.	Witham.
G	P	.	.	H	.	. .	Witham	Somerset..	G. W.	Frome and Yeovil.

EXPLANATION—G *Goods Station.*   P *Passenger and Parcel Station.*   P* *Passenger, but not Parcel or Miscellaneous Traffic.*
F *Furniture Vans, Carriages, Portable Engines, and Machines on Wheels.*   L *Live Stock.*
H *Horse Boxes and Prize Cattle Vans.*   C *Carriages by Passenger Train.*

STATION ACCOMMODATION.						CRANE POWER.		STATIONS, &c.	COUNTY.	COMPANY.	POSITION.
						Tons	Cwts.				
.	.	.	.	.	.			Witham Hall Farm Siding ...	Durham ...	N. E.	Eaglescliffe Junction Station.
.	.	.	.	.	.			Witham Hall Quarry............	Durham ...	N. E.	Eaglescliffe Junction Station.
G	P	.	L	H	.			Withcall	Lincoln ...	G. N.	Louth and Lincoln.
G	P	F	L	H	C	3	0	Withernsea	Yorks ...	N. E.	Branch from Hull.
.	.	.	.	.	.			Hollym Gate Siding	Yorks ...	N. E.	Withernsea.
.	.	.	.	.	.			Withersfield Siding	Suffolk ...	G. E.	See Haverhill.
.	.	.	.	.	.			Withers' Siding	Hants ...	L. & S.W.	Mottisfont.
G	P	F	L	H	C	5	0	Withington	Glo'ster ...	M. & S. W. Jn.	Cirencester and Cheltenham.
G	P	F	.	H	C	2	0 }	Withington (G. W.)	Hereford ..	{ G. W.	Worcester and Hereford.
G	.	.	.	.	.	2	0 }			{ Mid.	Over G. W. Line.
.	.	.	.	.	.			Watkin's Pomona Cider Co.'s Siding	Hereford ..	G. W.	Withington.
.	P	.	.	.	.			Withington and Albert Park	Lancs	Mid.	Manchester and Stockport.
G	P	.	.	.	.	4	0	Withnell	Lancs	L&Y&LU Jt(LY&LNW)	Blackburn and Boar's Head.
.	.	.	.	.	.			Birtwistle & Co.'s Abbey Mill	Lancs	L&Y&LU Jt(LY&LNW)	Withnell and Brinscall.
.	.	.	.	.	.			Fielden's Withnell Brick & Terra Cotta Co.'s Siding	Lancs	L&Y&LU Jt(LY&LNW)	Withnell and Feniscowles.
.	.	.	.	.	.			Withnell Mill Sidings	Lancs	L&Y&LU Jt(LY&LNW)	Brinscall.
.	.	.	.	.	.			Leigh's	Lancs	L&Y&LU Jt(LY&LNW)	Withnell Mill Sidings.
.	.	.	.	.	.			Marriage & Pinnock's	Lancs	L&Y&LU Jt(LY&LNW)	Withnell Mill Sidings.
.	.	.	.	.	.			Parke'sBrk.&Fire-ClayCo.'s	Lancs	L&Y&LU Jt(LY&LNW)	Withnell Mill Sidings.
.	.	.	.	.	.			Waring Bros.	Lancs	L&Y&LU Jt(LY&LNW)	Withnell Mill Sidings.
G	P	F	L	H	C	1	10	Withyham	Sussex ...	L. B. & S. C.	East Grinstead & Tunbridge Wells.
G	.	.	.	.	.	12	0	Withymoor Basin	Staffs	G. W.	Branch—Netherton and Old Hill.
.	.	.	.	.	.			Miles, Druce & Co.'s Iron Depôt	Staffs	G. W.	Withymoor.
.	.	.	.	.	.			Pearson's, J. H., Siding ...	Staffs	G. W.	Branch—Netherton and Old Hill.
G	P	F	L	H	C	5	0	Witley and Chiddingfold......	Surrey ...	L. & S.W.	Guildford and Petersfield.
.	.	.	.	.	.			Witley Coal Co.'s Siding ,.....	Staffs	G. W.	Cradley Heath and Cradley.
G	P	F	L	H	C	4	10	Witney	Oxon	G. W.	Yarnton and Fairford.
G	P	.	L	H	.			Wittersham Road	Kent	K. & E. S.	Robertsbridge and Tenterden Town.
G	P	F	.	.	.	1	10	Witton	Warwick..	L. & N. W.	Birmingham and Wolverhampton.
.	.	.	.	.	.			Kynoch's Siding	Staffs	L. & N. W.	Witton and Perry Barr.
.	.	.	.	.	.			Witton Drift Siding	Durham ...	N. E.	Witton-le-Wear.
G	P	F	L	H	C	1	10	Witton Gilbert	Durham ...	N. E.	Durham, Pass. and Lanchester.
.	.	.	.	.	.			Aldin Grange Siding........	Durham ...	N. E.	Witton Gilbert.
.	.	.	.	.	.			Bearpark Colliery, Coke, Brick & Chemical Works	Durham ...	N. E.	Witton Gilbert.
.	.	.	.	.	.			Langley Park Colliery and Coke Works.............	Durham ...	N. E.	Witton Gilbert.
.	.	.	.	.	.			Witton Hall Works (C. L. C.)	Cheshire...	C. L. C.—L. & N. W. ...	See Salt Union, Ltd. (Northwich).
.	.	.	.	.	.			Witton Junction	Durham ...	N. E.	Bishop Auckland and Crook.
G	P	.	L	H	.	2	0	Witton-le-Wear	Durham ...	N. E.	Bishop Auckland and Wolsingham.
.	.	.	.	.	.			Harperley Depôts	Durham ...	N. E.	Witton-le-Wear.
.	.	.	.	.	.			Howden Col. & Brick Works	Durham ...	N. E.	Witton-le-Wear.
.	.	.	.	.	.			Marshall Green Colliery and Brick Works	Durham ...	N. E.	Witton-le-Wear.
.	.	.	.	.	.			Marshall Green Saw Mill...	Durham ..	N. E.	Witton-le-Wear.
.	.	.	.	.	.			North Bitchburn Colliery, Coke Ovens, and Brick and Pipe Works	Durham ...	N. E.	Witton-le-Wear.
.	.	.	.	.	.			Slotburn Brick Works	Durham ...	N. E.	Witton-le-Wear.
.	.	.	.	.	.			Witton Drift Siding	Durham ...	N. E.	Witton-le-Wear.
.	.	.	.	.	.			Witton Park Depôts	Durham ...	N. E.	Etherley.
.	.	.	.	.	.			Witton Park Iron Works.....	Durham ...	N. E.	Etherley.
.	.	.	.	.	.			Witton Park Slag Works.....	Durham ...	N. E.	Etherley.
.	.	.	.	.	.			Witton Works (C. L. C.)......	Cheshire...	C. L. C.—L. & N. W. ...	See Salt Union, Ltd. (Northwich).
G	P	F	L	H	C	2	0	Wiveliscombe	Somerset..	G. W.	Taunton and Barnstaple.
.	P	.	.	.	.			Wivelsfield	Sussex ...	L. B. & S. C.	Hayward's Heath and Burgess Hill.
.	.	.	.	.	.			Inholmes Park Siding	Sussex ...	L. B. & S. C.	Keymer Junction and Plumpton.
.	.	.	.	.	.			Keymer Bk. & Tl. Co.'s Sid.	Sussex ...	L. B. & S. C.	Plumpton and Wivelsfield.
G	P	.	.	.	.			Wixford	Warwick..	Mid.	Evesham and Alcester.
G	P	F	L	H	C	5	0	Woburn Sands	Bucks	L. & N. W.	Bedford and Bletchley.
.	.	.	.	.	.			New Fletton Brk. Co.'s Sid.	Bucks	L. & N. W.	Woburn Sands & Fenny Stratford.
.	.	.	.	.	.			Woburn Sands Gas Siding	Buck	L. & N. W.	Woburn Sands & Fenny Stratford.
G	P	F	L	H	C	10	0	Woking Junction Station ...	Surrey ...	L. & S.W.	Surbiton and Basingstoke.
G	P	F	L	H	C	8	0	Wokingham (S. E. & C.) .\....	Berks	{ S. E. & C.	Farnborough and Reading.
										{ L. & S. W.	Over S.E.& C. from Wokingham Jn.
.	.	.	.	.	.			Wokingham Junction	Berks	L. & S.W.—S. E. & C. ...	Bracknell and Wokingham.
G	P	.	L	H	.			Woldingham	Surrey ...	C. & O. Jt. (L. B. & S. C. and S. E. & C.)	Croydon and Oxted.

EXPLANATION—G *Goods Station.*   P *Passenger and Parcel Station.*   P* *Passenger, but not Parcel or Miscellaneous Traffic.*
F *Furniture Vans, Carriages, Portable Engines, and Machines on Wheels.*   L *Live Stock.*
H *Horse Boxes and Prize Cattle Vans.*   C *Carriages by Passenger Train.*

STATION ACCOMMODATION.						CRANE POWER.		STATIONS, &c.	COUNTY.	COMPANY.	POSITION.
						Tons	Cwts				
G	P	F	.	H	C	.	.	Wolf Cleugh Siding	Durham ...	N. E.	Parkhead.
						.	.	Wolferton	Norfolk ...	G. E.	Lynn and Hunstanton.
						.	.	Wolfhall Junction	Wilts	G. W.—M. & S. W. Jn.	Savernake.
						.	.	Wollaston Iron Ore Siding ...	N'hamptn	L. & N. W.	See Butlin & Co. (Wellingboro').
						.	.	Wollaton Colliery	Notts	Mid.	Nottingham, Radford.
						.	.	Wollaton Colliery Co.'s Siding	Notts	Mid.	Same as Radford Colliery (Nottingham).
						.	.	Wollaton Colliery, No. 2	Notts	Mid.	Nottingham, Radford.
						.	.	Wolseley Tool and Motor Car Co.'s Siding	Warwick..	L. & N. W.	Birmingham, Curzon Street.
G	P	F	L	H	C	2	0	Wolsingham	Durham ...	N. E.	Bishop Auckland and Stanhope.
						.	.	Stanner's Close Steel Works	Durham ...	N. E.	Wolsingham.
						.	.	Wolston.............................	Warwick..	L. & N. W.	See Brandon and Wolston.
						.	.	Wolvercot Junction	Oxon	G. W.	Oxford and Yarnton.
						.	.	Wolvercot Siding	Oxon	G. W.	See Oxford.
								WOLVERHAMPTON—			
G	P	F	L	.	.	10	0	(Station)	Staffs	Mid.	Heath Town and Wolverhampton Junction.
						.	.	Anglo-American Oil Co.'s Siding	Staffs	L. & N. W.	Wolverhampton.
						.	.	Bantock's Siding	Staffs	G. W.	Wolverhampton.
						.	.	Bayley's Siding	Staffs	L. & N. W.	Wolverhampton & Monmore Green.
						.	.	Butler's Siding	Staffs	G. W.	Low Level Station & Cannock Road.
						.	.	Cannock Road Siding........	Staffs	G. W.	Branch from Stafford Road Junc.
						.	.	Cannock Road Junction......	Staffs	G. W.	Low Level Station & Dunstall Park.
			L	.	.	10	0	Cattle Siding and Depôt...	Staffs	G. W.	Branch from Stafford Road Junc.
						.	.	Chillington Co.'s Siding...	Staffs	G. W.	Walsall Street.
								Corrugated Iron Co.—			
						.	.	Shrubbery Works	Staffs	G. W.	Walsall Street.
						.	.	Stour Valley Works	Staffs	G. W.	Walsall Street.
						.	.	Crane's Siding.................	Staffs	L. & N. W.	Wolverhampton & Monmore Green.
						.	.	Electric Construction Corporation Siding	Staffs	L. & N. W.	Wolverhampton and Bushbury.
						.	.	Gibbon's Siding	Staffs	L. & N. W.	Wolverhampton & Monmore Green.
G	.	F	L	.	.	10	0	Herbert Street	Staffs	G. W.	Branch from Stafford Road.
						.	.	Hickman's Timber Depôt...	Staffs	G. W.	Walsall Street.
.	P	.	.	.	.	.	.	High Level (L. & N. W.) ...	Staffs	{ L. & N. W.	Birmingham and Stafford.
.	P	F	.	H	C	.	.			Mid.	Over L. & N. W. Line.
						.	.	Holloway Siding	Staffs	G. W.	Near Priestfield.
						.	.	Hunt & Hunt's or Morris & Griffin's Sid. (L. & N. W.)	Staffs	L. & N. W.—G. W.	Wolverhampton.
						.	.	Junction	Staffs	G. W.—Mid.	Low Level Station and Heath Town.
						.	.	Junction	Staffs	L. & N. W.—Mid.	Wolverhampton and Heath Town.
.	P	F	L	H	C	.	.	Low Level........................	Staffs	G. W.	Birmingham and Wellington.
G	.	F	L	.	.	20	0	Mill Street	Staffs	L. & N. W.	Birmingham and Stafford.
G						5	0	Mill Street Basin	Staffs	L. & N. W.	Birmingham and Stafford.
G	P	.	.	.	.	5	0	Monmore Green	Staffs	L. & N. W.	Wolverhampton and Birmingham.
•						.	.	Osier Bed Iron Co.'s Siding (J. Lysaght & Co.)	Staffs	Mid.	Near Wolverhampton Canal Basin.
						.	.	Oxley Sidings	Staffs	G. W.	Dunstall Park and Codsall.
						.	.	Stafford Road Junction ...	Staffs	G. W.	Wolverhampton.
						.	.	Stow Heath	Staffs	G. W.	Wolverhampton and Priestfield.
G						8	0	Victoria Basin	Staffs	G. W.	Branch from Stafford Road.
G						3	0	Walsall Street Basin........	Staffs	G. W.	Branch from Priestfield.
						.	.	Windmill Brick & Tile Co.'s Siding	Staffs	G. W.	Wolverhampton.
						.	.	Wolverhampton Gas Co.'s Stafford Road Siding.....	Staffs	L. & N. W.	Wolverhampton and Bushbury.
						.	.	Wolverhampton Gas Works	Staffs	G. W.	Stafford Road.
G	P	F	L	H	C	5	0	Wolverton	Bucks	L. & N. W.	Bletchley and Blisworth.
G						.	.	Wombridge	Salop	L. & N. W.	Coalport and Hadley.
						.	.	Blockley's Hadley Lodge Siding	Salop	L. & N. W.	Hadley and Oakengates.
						.	.	Milnes & Co.'s Castle Car Works	Salop	L. & N. W.	Hadley and Trench.
						.	.	Rollison & Slater's Siding...	Salop	L. & N. W.	Wombridge and Oakengates.
G	P	.	L	.	.	4	0	Wombwell	Yorks	{ G. C.	Barnsley and Doncaster.
G	P	F	L	H	C	5	0			Mid.	Chapeltown and Barnsley.
						.	.	Barrow Colliery	Yorks	Mid.	Near Wombwell.
G	.	.	.	.	.	.	.	Birdwell and Pilley Wharf	Yorks	Mid.	Wharncliffe Branch.
						.	.	Cortonwood Colliery	Yorks	Mid.	Elsecar Branch.
						.	.	Darfield Main Colliery	Yorks	G. C.	Wombwell.

EXPLANATION—G *Goods Station.*   P *Passenger and Parcel Station.*   P* *Passenger, but not Parcel or Miscellaneous Traffic.*
F *Furniture Vans, Carriages, Portable Engines, and Machines on Wheels.*   L *Live Stock.*
H *Horse Boxes and Prize Cattle Vans.*   C *Carriages by Passenger Train.*

STATION ACCOMMODATION.						CRANE POWER.		STATIONS, &c.	COUNTY.	COMPANY.	POSITION.
						Tons	Cwts.				
								Wombwell—*continued.*			
.	.	.	.	.	.	.	.	Knoll Drift Pit	Yorks	Mid.	Near Wombwell.
.	.	.	.	.	.	.	.	Mitchell Main Colliery	Yorks	G. C.	Wombwell.
.	.	.	.	.	.	.	.	Rockingham Colliery............	Yorks	Mid.	Near Wombwell.
.	.	.	.	.	.	.	.	Wharncliffe Silkstone Col.	Yorks	Mid.	Near Wombwell.
.	.	.	.	.	.	.	.	Wombwell Main Colliery ...	Yorks	G. C.—Mid.	Wombwell.
.	.	.	.	.	.	.	.	Wombwell Pottery Siding...	Yorks	G. C.	Wombwell.
.	.	.	.	.	.	.	.	E. & J. Hoyland	Yorks	G. C.	Wombwell Pottery Siding.
.	.	.	.	.	.	.	.	Wombwell Wood Quarry ...	Yorks	G. C.—Mid.	Wombwell.
.	.	.	.	.	.	.	.	Wood Bros. & Son's Siding	Yorks	G. C.	Wombwell.
.	.	.	.	.	.	.	.	Wombwell Main Junction ...	Yorks	G. C.	Dovecliffe and Wombwell.
G	P	F	L	H	C		}	Womersley (L. & Y.)	Yorks	{ L. & Y.	Knottingley and Doncaster.
.	P	.	.	H	C	.				G. N.	Over L. & Y. Line.
.	.	.	.	.	.	.	.	Cridling Stubbs Siding.....	Yorks	L. & Y.	Womersley.
.	.	.	.	.	.	.	.	Ingle, E., & Son's Siding ...	Yorks	L. & Y.	Womersley.
.	.	.	.	.	.	.	.	Lord Hawke's Siding........	Yorks	L. & Y.	Near Womersley.
.	.	.	.	.	.	.	.	Roberts' Siding	Yorks	L. & Y.	Womersley and Knottingley.
G	P	F	L	H	C	2	0	Wonersh	Surrey	L. B. & S. C.	See Bramley and Wonersh.
.	.	.	.	.	.	.	.	Wooburn Green	Bucks	G. W.	High Wycombe and Maidenhead.
.	.	.	.	.	.	.	.	Wood & Co.'s Chain and Anchor Works	Cheshire...	G. W.	Saltney.
.	.	.	.	.	.	.	.	Wood & Co.'s Siding........	Lancs	L. & N. W.	St. Helens.
.	.	.	.	.	.	.	.	Wood & Rowe's Siding........	Glo'ster ...	Mid.	Stroud.
.	.	.	.	.	.	.	.	Wood & Son's	Worcester	G. W.	Worcester.
.	.	.	.	.	.	.	.	Wood & Son's Siding	Lancs	L. & N. W.	Garston Docks.
.	.	.	.	.	.	.	.	Wood Bros. & Son's Siding...	Yorks	G. C.	Wombwell.
.	.	.	.	.	.	.	.	Wood's Bottle Works	Edinboro'	N. B.	Edinburgh, Portobello.
.	.	.	.	.	.	.	.	Wood's Siding	Lanark ...	Cal.	Same as Shieldmuir Colliery No. 6 (Shieldmuir).
.	.	.	.	.	.	.	.	Wood's Siding	Lancs	L&Y&LU Jt(LY&LNW)	Brinscall.
G	P	F	L	H	C	1	10	Woodborough	Wilts	G. W.	Pewsey and Devizes.
G	P	F	L	H	C	1	10	Woodbridge......................	Suffolk ...	G. E.	Ipswich and Beccles.
.	.	.	.	.	.	.	.	Edwards, H., & Son's Sid.	Suffolk ...	G. E.	Woodbridge.
.	.	.	.	.	.	.	.	Hart's, J. B., Siding........	Suffolk ...	G. E.	Woodbridge.
G	P	.	L	H	C	2	0	Woodburn	Northumb	N. B.	Bellingham and Morpeth.
.	.	.	.	.	.	.	.	Newcastle and Gateshead Water Co.'s Siding	Northumb	N. B.	Near Woodburn.
G	.	.	.	.	.	.	.	Woodburn General Siding	Northumb	N. B.	Near Woodburn.
.	.	.	.	.	.	.	.	Woodburn Quarry	Northumb	N. B.	Near Woodburn.
G	P	.	.	.	.	.	.	Woodburn Junction	Yorks	G. C.	Sheffield.
G	P	.	.	.	.	1	10	Woodbury Road	Devon	L. & S. W.	Exeter and Exmouth.
G	P	.	.	.	.	.	.	Woodchester	Glo'ster ...	Mid.	Stonehouse and Nailsworth.
.	.	.	.	.	.	.	.	Baron's Product Co.'s Siding	Glo'ster ...	Mid.	Woodchester.
.	.	.	.	.	.	.	.	Dyehouse Siding............	Glo'ster ...	Mid.	Woodchester and Nailsworth.
.	.	.	.	.	.	.	.	Workman's Siding...........	Glo'ster ...	Mid.	Woodchester and Nailsworth.
.	.	.	.	.	.	.	.	Wood Colliery..................	Lancs	{ G. C. (St. Helens Exten.)	See Evans, R., & Co. (Ashton-in-Makerfield).
.	.	.	.	.	.	.	.			L. & N. W.	See Evans, R., & Co. (Earlestown).
G	P	.	.	.	.	.	.	Woodenbridge Junc. Station	Wicklow..	D. W. & W.	Wicklow and Arklow.
G	P	.	L	H	.	3	0	Woodend (for Cleator and Bigrigg)	Cumb'land	WC&EJt.(Fur.&LNW)	Moor Row and Sellafield.
.	.	.	.	.	.	.	.	Woodend Junction	Lanark ...	N. B.	Armadale and Westcraigs.
.	.	.	.	.	.	.	.	Woodend, Nos. 4 and 5 Cols.	Lanark ...	N. B.	Westcraigs.
.	.	.	.	.	.	.	.	Woodfield Colliery............	Mon	G. W.	See Tredegar Junction.
G	P	.	.	.	.	.	.	Woodford	Essex	G. E.	Stratford and Loughton.
.	.	.	.	.	.	.	.	Eagle Lane	Essex	G. E.	See George Lane Depôt, Eagle Lane.
.	.	.	.	.	.	.	.	George Lane	Essex	G. E.	See George Lane, Woodford.
								WOODFORD AND HINTON—			
G	P	.	L	H	C	.	.	(Station)	N'hampt n	G. C.	Rugby and Brackley.
.	.	.	.	.	.	.	.	Bethell's Siding	N'hampt n	G. C.	Woodford and Hinton.
.	.	.	.	.	.	.	.	North Junction	N'hampt n	G. C.	Woodford and Byfield.
.	.	.	.	.	.	.	.	South Junction	N'hampt n	G. C.	Culworth and Byfield.
.	.	.	.	.	.	.	.	West Junction	N'hampt n	E. & W. Jn.—G. C.	Morton Pinkney and Woodford.
G	P	.	.	.	.		}	Woodgrange Park (L. T. & S.)	Essex	{ L. T. & S.	Forest Gate Junction and Barking.
.	P	.	.	.	.	.				G. E.	Over L. T. & S. from Forest Gate Jn.
.	P	.	.	.	.	.				Mid.	Over L T & S fr. Woodgrange Pk. Jn.
.	.	.	.	.	.	.	.	Woodgrange Park Junction	Essex	L. T. & S.—T. & F. G. Jt.	Woodgrange Park and South Tottenham.
								WOOD GREEN—			
.	.	.	.	.	.	.	.	Alexandra Park Siding......	Middlesex	G. N.	Wood Green and New Southgate.
.	.	.	.	.	.	.	.	Noel Park	Middlesex	G. E.	See Noel Park and Wood Green.
.	.	.	.	.	.	.	.	Palace Gates	Middlesex	G. E.	See Palace Gates (Wood Green).

EXPLANATION—G *Goods Station.*　　P *Passenger and Parcel Station.*　　P* *Passenger, but not Parcel or Miscellaneous Traffic.*
F *Furniture Vans, Carriages, Portable Engines, and Machines on Wheels.*　　L *Live Stock.*
H *Horse Boxes and Prize Cattle Vans.*　　C *Carriages by Passenger Train.*

STATION ACCOMMODATION.						CRANE POWER.		STATIONS, &c.	COUNTY.	COMPANY.	POSITION.
						Tons	Cwts.	WOOD GREEN—*continued.*			
G	P	.	.	H	C	.	.	Wood Green (Alexandra Park) (G. N.)	Middlesex	G. N.	King's Cross and New Barnet.
.	P	.	.	.	.	.	.			N. L.	Over G. N. from Canonbury Junc.
.	P*	.	.	.	.	.	.			S. E. & C.	Over G. N. from Kings Cross Junc.
.	P	.	.	.	.	.	.	Wood Green (Old Bescot)	Staffs	L. & N. W.	Birmingham and Wolverhampton.
.	.	.	.	.	.	.	.	Woodhall Colliery	Lanark	Cal.	Mossend.
.	.	.	.	.	.	.	.	Woodhall Mine	Lanark	Cal.	Mossend.
G	P	.	.	.	.	.	.	Woodhall Spa	Lincoln	G. N.	Kirkstead and Horncastle.
G	P	F	L	H	C	.	.	Woodham	Surrey	L. & S.W.	See Byfleet and Woodham.
G	.	.	L	.	.	.	.	Woodham Ferris	Essex	G. E.	Wickford and Maldon.
G	P	F	L	H	C	3	0	Hogswell's Siding	Essex	G. E.	Woodham Ferris and Fambridge.
G	P	.	L	H	C	.	.	Woodhay	Hants	G. W.	Newbury and Winchester.
.	.	.	.	.	.	.	.	Woodhead	Derby	G. C.	Guide Bridge and Penistone.
.	.	.	.	.	.	.	.	Woodhead Quarry	Dumfries	Cal.	Same as Annanlea Quarry (Kirkpatrick).
.	.	.	.	.	.	.	.	Woodhill, No. 8	Ayr	G. & S.W.	Crosshouse.
.	.	.	.	.	.	.	.	Woodhorn Colliery	Northumb	N. E.	Ashington.
.	.	.	.	.	.	.	.	Woodhorn Siding	Northumb	N. E.	Newbiggin-by-the-Sea.
.	.	.	.	.	.	.	.	Woodhouse	Leicester	G. C.	See Quorn and Woodhouse.
G	P	F	L	H	C	5	0	Woodhouse (G. C.)	Yorks	G. C.	Sheffield and Worksop.
G	.	F	L	.	.	5	0			L. & N. W.	Over G. N. and G. C. Lines.
.	.	.	.	.	.	.	.	Birley Collieries (G.C.)	Yorks	G. C.—L. & N. W.	Woodhouse.
.	.	.	.	.	.	.	.	North Staveley Col. (G.C.)	Yorks	G. C.—L. & N. W.	Woodhouse.
.	.	.	.	.	.	.	.	Orgreaves Col. (G.C.)	Yorks	G. C.—L. & N. W.	Woodhouse.
.	.	.	.	.	.	.	.	Treeton Colliery (G.C.)	Yorks	G. C.—L. & N. W.	Woodhouse.
.	.	.	.	.	.	.	.	Waleswood Colliery	Yorks	G. C.	Woodhouse.
.	.	.	.	.	.	.	.	Woodthorpe Colliery	Yorks	G. C.	Woodhouse.
.	.	.	.	.	.	.	.	Woodhouse Junction	Yorks	G. C.	Woodhouse and Beighton.
.	.	.	.	.	.	.	.	Woodhouse & Rixson's Siding	Yorks	L. D. & E. C.—Mid.	Sheffield, Attercliffe.
G	P	F	L	H	C	10	0	Woodhouse Mill (Mid.)	Yorks	Mid.	Chesterfield and Treeton.
.	P	.	.	H	C	.	.			L. D. & E. C.	Over Midland Line.
.	.	.	.	.	.	.	.	Fence Colliery	Yorks	Mid.	Near Woodhouse Mill.
.	.	.	.	.	.	.	.	Orgreaves Colliery (Mid.)	Yorks	Mid.—L. D. & E. C.	Woodhouse Mill and Treeton.
.	.	.	.	.	.	.	.	Rother Vale Collieries	Yorks	Mid.	Woodhouse Mill.
.	.	.	.	.	.	.	.	Rotherwood Iron and Steel Co.'s Siding	Yorks	Mid.	Near Woodhouse Mill.
.	.	.	.	.	.	.	.	Treeton Colliery	Yorks	Mid.	Woodhouse Mill and Treeton.
.	.	.	.	.	.	.	.	Woodifield Colliery	Durham	N. E.	Crook.
.	.	.	.	.	.	.	.	Woodilee Asylum Siding	Dumbartn	N. B.	Garngaber Junction Station.
.	.	.	.	.	.	.	.	Woodilee Colliery	Dumbartn	N. B.	Kirkintilloch.
G	P	.	.	.	.	10	0	Woodkirk	Yorks	G. N.	Batley and Tingley.
.	P	.	.	.	.	.	.			L. & Y.	Over G. N. Line.
.	.	.	.	.	.	.	.	Akeroyd & Son's Siding	Yorks	G. N.	Woodkirk.
.	.	.	.	.	.	.	.	Howley Park and Great Finsdale Quarry Siding	Yorks	G. N.	Woodkirk.
.	.	.	.	.	.	.	.	Howley Park Co-operative Society's Siding	Yorks	G. N.	Woodkirk.
.	.	.	.	.	.	.	.	Pawson Bros.' Quarry	Yorks	G. N.	Woodkirk.
.	.	.	.	.	.	.	.	Soothill Quarry	Yorks	G. N.	Woodkirk.
.	.	.	.	.	.	.	.	Woodkirk Saw Mill Siding	Yorks	G. N.	Woodkirk.
G	P	.	L	H	.	.	.	Woodland	Lancs	Furness	Broughton and Coniston.
.	.	.	.	.	.	.	.	Woodland Colliery	Durham	N. E.	Butterknowle.
.	P	.	.	.	.	.	.	Woodland Junction	Durham	N. E.	Butterknowle.
.	.	.	.	.	.	.	.	Woodlands	Cork	S. & S.	Schull and Skibbereen.
.	.	.	.	.	.	.	.	Woodlands Sid. (Harrison's)	Yorks	N. E.	Grosmont. Sleights.
G	P	F	L	H	C	2	0	Woodlawn	Galway	M. G. W.	Athlone and Athenry.
.	.	.	.	.	.	.	.	Woodlea Siding (Lochview Foundry)	Stirling	N. B.	Bonnybridge (E. & G.).
G	P	F	L	H	C	10	0	Woodlesford	Yorks	Mid.	Leeds and Normanton.
.	P	.	.	.	.	.	.			L. & Y.	Over Mid. from Methley Junction.
.	.	.	.	.	.	.	.	Beeston Colliery Siding (J. & J. Charlesworth)	Yorks	Mid.	Woodlesford.
.	.	.	.	.	.	.	.	Bentley's Yorkshire Breweries Co.'s Siding	Yorks	Mid.	Near Woodlesford.
.	.	.	.	.	.	.	.	Midland Colliery	Yorks	Mid.	Rothwell Haigh.
.	.	.	.	.	.	.	.	Scott, Walter, Ltd. Siding	Yorks	Mid.	Woodlesford.
.	.	.	.	.	.	.	.	Woodlesford Brewery Co.'s Siding	Yorks	Mid.	Woodlesford.
G	P	.	.	H	.	5	0	Woodley	Cheshire	S. & M. Jt. (G. C. & Mid.)	Hyde and Marple.
.	.	.	.	.	.	.	.	Woodley Junction	Cheshire	C. L. C.—S. & M. Jt.	Stockport and Woodley.
.	.	.	.	.	.	.	.	Woodley Junction	Dumbartn	N. B.	Garngaber Junction Station.

STATION ACCOMMODATION.						CRANE POWER.		STATIONS, &c.	COUNTY.	COMPANY.	POSITION.
						Tons	Cwts.				
.	.	.	.	.	.	.	.	Woodmoor Colliery	Yorks	{ G. C.	Same as Wharncliffe Woodmoor Colliery (Staincross).
										{ H. & B.—Mid.	Same as Wharncliffe Woodmoor Colliery (Cudworth).
.	.	.	.	.	.	.	.	Woodmuir Junction	Edinboro'	Cal.	Breich and Addiewell.
.	.	.	.	.	.	.	.	Woodshaw Pit	Lancs	L. & Y.	See Wigan Coal & Iron Co. (Hindley).
.	.	.	.	.	.	.	.	Woodshaw Siding (L. & N.W.)	Lancs	L.N.W.—G.C. (Wig. Jn.)	See Wigan Coal & Iron Co. (Wigan).
.	.	.	.	.	.	.	.	Woodside	Aberdeen	G. N. of S.	See Aberdeen.
.	.	.	.	.	.	.	.	Woodside	Cheshire...	B'head Jt. (G W & L N W)	See Birkenhead.
G	.	.	.	.	.	5	0	Woodside	Lancs	L. & N. W.	Liverpool and Warrington.
G	P	F	L	H	C	3	0	Woodside	Perth	Cal.	Perth and Coupar Angus.
.	P	.	.	.	.	.	.	Woodside	Surrey ...	S. E. & C.	New Beckenham & Addiscombe Rd.
.	.	.	.	.	.	.	.	Woodside	Worcester	G. W.	See Hartshill and Woodside.
.	.	.	.	.	.	.	.	Woodside Collieries	Lanark ...	Cal.	Netherburn.
.	.	.	.	.	.	.	.	Woodside Ferry	Cheshire...	B'head Jt. (G W & L N W)	Birkenhead.
.	.	.	.	.	.	.	.	Woodside Iron & Steel Works	Lanark ...	Cal.	Langloan.
.	.	.	.	.	.	.	.	Woodside Junction	Surrey ...	S. E. & C.—W. & S. C. Jt.	Woodside and Coombe Lane.
.	.	.	.	.	.	.	.	Woodside Lairages...............	Cheshire...	B'head Jt—CLC—N W & I.	Birkenhead.
.	.	.	.	.	.	.	.	Woodside Lane Depôt (G. C.)	Yorks	G. C.—G. N.	See Sheffield Corporation Sidings.
G	P	F	L	H	C	.	.	Woodside Park (for North Finchley) (G.N.)	Middlesex	{ G. N.	Finchley and High Barnet.
.	P	.	.	.	.	.	.			{ N. L.	Over G. N. from Canonbury Junc.
.	.	.	.	.	.	.	.	Woodside Siding	Yorks	N. E.	Horsforth.
G	P	.	.	.	.	.	.	Wood Siding	Bucks	O. & A. Tram	Quainton Road & Brill (Brill Dist.)
.	.	.	.	.	.	.	.	Woodsmoor Siding	Cheshire..	L. & N. W.	Same as Stockport Guardians' (Hazel Grove).
.	.	.	.	.	.	.	.	Woodstock	Oxon	G. W.	See Blenheim and Woodstock.
.	.	.	.	.	.	.	.	Woodstock Junction	Oxon	L. & N. W.	Yarnton Jn. & Verney Jn. Station.
.	.	.	.	.	.	.	.	Woodstock Spinning Co.'s Sid.	Lancs	L. & Y.	Royton.
.	.	.	.	.	.	.	.	Woodstone Wharf	N'hamptn	L. & N. W.	See Peterboro'.
G	P	.	.	.	.	.	.	Wood Street (Walthamstow)	Essex	G. E.	Hackney Downs and Chingford.
.	.	.	.	.	.	.	.	Wadham Road Siding	Essex	G. E.	Wood Street and Highams Park.
.	.	.	.	.	.	.	.	Woodthorpe Colliery............	Yorks	G. C.	Woodhouse.
G	P	F	L	H	C	5	0	Woodvale	Lancs	C. L. C. (S'port Exten.)..	Aintree and Southport, Lord Street.
.	.	.	.	.	.	.	.	North Moss Lane Siding ...	Lancs	C. L. C. (S'port Exten.)..	Woodvale.
G	P	.	.	.	.	1	10	Woodville (Mid.)	Derby	{ Mid.	Ashby and Swadlincote.
G	.	.	.	.	.	.	.			{ L. & N. W.	Over Mid. Line.
.	.	.	.	.	.	.	.	Albion Clay Co.'s Sid. (Mid.)	Leicester	Mid.—L. & N. W.	Near Woodville.
.	.	.	.	.	.	.	.	Boothorpe Pipe Co.'s Siding (Mid.)	Derby	Mid.—L. & N. W.	Near Woodville.
.	.	.	.	.	.	.	.	Donington Pipe & Brick Sid. (Mid.)	Derby	Mid.—L. & N. W.	Near Woodville.
.	.	.	.	.	.	.	.	Ellis, Partridge & Co.'s Brick Works (Mid.)	Derby	Mid.—L. & N. W.	Near Woodville.
.	.	.	.	.	.	.	.	Ensor & Co.'s Pipe Works (Mid.)	Derby	Mid.—L. & N. W.	Near Woodville.
.	.	.	.	.	.	.	.	Granville Colliery (Mid.) ...	Derby	Mid.—L. & N. W.	Near Woodville.
.	.	.	.	.	.	.	.	Green & Co.'s Pottery Works (Mid.)	Derby	Mid.—L. & N. W.	Near Woodville.
.	.	.	.	.	.	.	.	Hilltop Pottery Co.'s Siding (Banks & Co.) (Mid.)......	Derby	Mid.—L. & N. W.	Woodville.
.	.	.	.	.	.	.	.	Jones's Siding (Mid.).........	Derby	Mid.—L. & N. W.	Woodville.
.	.	.	.	.	.	.	.	Knowles & Co.'s Brick and Sanitary Pipe Wks. (Mid.)	Derby	Mid.—L. & N. W.	Near Woodville.
.	.	.	.	.	.	.	.	Mansfield Bros.' Tile Works (Mid.)	Derby	Mid.—L. & N. W.	Near Woodville.
.	.	.	.	.	.	.	.	Mansfield's, H. R., Siding (Mid.)	Derby	Mid.—L. & N. W.	Near Woodville.
.	.	.	.	.	.	.	.	Mansfield's Sanitary Siding (Mid.)	Derby	Mid.—L. & N. W.	Near Woodville.
.	.	.	.	.	.	.	.	Mason, Cash & Co.'s Siding (Mid.)	Derby	Mid.—L. & N. W.	Near Woodville.
.	.	.	.	.	.	.	.	Outram Pottery Wks. (Mid.)	Derby	Mid.—L. & N. W.	Near Woodville.
.	.	.	.	.	.	.	.	Robinson's Siding (Mid.)...	Derby	Mid.—L. & N. W.	Woodville Branch.
.	.	.	.	.	.	.	.	Tooth & Co.'s Siding (Mid.)	Derby	Mid.—L. & N. W.	Near Woodville.
.	.	.	.	.	.	.	.	Woodville Sanitary Pipe Co.'s Siding (Mid.).........	Derby	Mid.—L. & N. W.	Near Woodville.
.	.	.	.	.	.	.	.	Woodward's Clay Sid. (Mid.)	Derby	Mid.—L. & N. W.	Near Woodville.
.	.	.	.	.	.	.	.	Wragg & Son's Bk. Wks (Mid)	Derby	Mid.—L. & N. W.	Near Woodville.
.	.	.	.	.	.	.	.	Woodward's Clay Sid. (Mid.)	Derby	Mid.—L. & N. W.	Woodville.
G	P	.	.	.	.	.	.	Woody Bay	Devon	Lyn & Barns	Barnstaple & Lynton.
G	P	F	L	H	C	5	0	Woofferton	Salop	S & H Jt (G W & L N W)	Craven Arms and Hereford.
.	.	.	.	.	.	.	.	Mainwaring's Siding.........	Salop	S & H Jt (G W & L N W)	Woofferton.

EXPLANATION— **G** *Goods Station.*   **P** *Passenger and Parcel Station.*   **P*** *Passenger, but not Parcel or Miscellaneous Traffic.*
F *Furniture Vans, Carriages, Portable Engines, and Machines on Wheels.*   **L** *Live Stock.*
H *Horse Boxes and Prize Cattle Vans.*   **C** *Carriages by Passenger Train.*

STATION ACCOMMODATION.						CRANE POWER.	STATIONS, &c.	COUNTY.	COMPANY.	POSITION.
						Tons Cwts.				
G	P	.	L	H	.	3 0	Wookey	Somerset..	G. W.	Wells and Cheddar.
G	P	F	L	H	C	. .	Wool	Dorset......	L. & S.W.	Wimborne and Dorchester.
.	.	.	.	.	.	. .	Woolard's Siding	Lancs	L. & Y.	Formby.
G	P	.	L	.	.	2 0	Woolaston	Glo'ster	G. W.	Chepstow and Gloucester.
G	P	F	L	H	C	5 0	Wooler	Northumb	N. E.	Coldstream and Alnwick.
.	.	.	.	.	.	. .	Wooley Colliery	Durham ...	N. E.	See Pease & Partners' (Crook).
G	P	.	.	.	.	5 0	Woolfold	Lancs	L. & Y.	Bury and Holcombe Brook.
.	.	.	.	.	.	. .	Woolford's Siding	Lanark	Cal.	Cobbinshaw.
.	.	.	.	.	.	. .	Woolley Colliery (L. & Y.)	Yorks	L. & Y.—G. C.—N. E.	Haigh.
.	.	.	.	.	.	. .	Woolliscroft & Son's Brick & Tile Works	Staffs	N. S.	Etruria.
.	.	.	.	.	.	. .	Woolliscroft's Ffrith Quarry or Trimley Hall Siding	Flint	W. & M. Jt.(G W & L N W)	Llanfynydd.
.	.	.	.	.	.	. .	Woolmer Green Siding	Herts	G. N.	Knebworth.
.	.	.	.	.	.	. .	Woolsthorpe Siding	Leicester..	G. N.	Bottesford.
G	P	.	L	.	.	10 0	Woolston	Hants	L. & S.W.	Southampton and Netley.
.	.	.	.	.	.	. .	Woolston & Bull's Grain Siding (Mid.)	N'hamptn	Mid.—L. & N. W.	Wellingboro'.
.	.	.	.	.	.	. .	Woolton	Lancs	C. L. C. (G C, G N, & Mid.)	See Gateacre (for Woolton).
G	P	F	L	H	C	8 0	Woolwich Arsenal	Kent	S. E. & C.	London Bridge and Dartford.
.	.	.	.	.	.	. .	Woolwich Arsenal Siding	Kent	S. E. & C.	Plumstead.
.	P	.	.	.	.	. .	Woolwich Dockyard	Kent	S. E. & C.	London Bridge and Dartford.
G	P	F	L	H	.	3 0	Woolwich, North	Essex	G. E.	Branch from Stratford.
.	.	.	.	.	.	. .	Bass & Co.'s Siding	Essex	G. E.	Woolwich, North.
.	.	.	.	.	.	. .	Henley, W. T., Telegraph Works Co.'s Siding (G E)	Essex	G E—G N—L&N W—Mid	Woolwich, North.
.	P	.	.	.	.	. .	Woolwich Town	Kent	G. E.	By Ferry from Woolwich, North.
G	P	F	L	H	C	1 0	Wooperton	Northumb	N. E.	Coldstream and Alnwick.
.	.	.	.	.	.	. .	Woore	Salop	N. S.	Pipe Gate.
.	.	.	.	.	.	. .	Wooton, Jos., Siding	Durham	N. E.	Stockton, South.
G	P	.	L	.	.	. .	Wootton	I. of W.	I. of W. Cent.	Newport and Ryde.
G	P	F	L	H	C	1 0	Wootton Bassett	Wilts	G. W.	Swindon and Chippenham.
.	.	.	.	.	.	. .	Wootton Bros.' Foundry	Leicester..	Mid.	Coalville.
.	.	.	.	.	.	. .	Wootton, North	Norfolk	G. E.	See North Wootton.
.	.	.	.	.	.	. .	Wootton Pillinge Brick Co.'s Siding	Beds	L. & N. W.	Same as Molesworth & Co.'s Siding (Millbrook for Ampthill).
							WORCESTER—			
G	.	.	L	.	.	. .	Butt's Siding	Worcester	G. W.	Branch from Foregate Street.
.	P	.	.	.	.	. .	Foregate Street	Worcester	G. W.	Shrub Hill and Henwick.
.	.	.	.	.	.	. .	Gas Works	Worcester	G. W.	Worcester.
.	.	.	.	.	.	. .	Gloucester Carriage and Wagon Works	Worcester	G. W.	Worcester.
.	.	.	.	.	.	. .	Heenan & Froude (G. W.)	Worcester	G. W.—Mid.	Worcester.
G	P	.	L	H	.	. .	Henwick (G.W.)	Worcester	G. W. / Mid.	Foregate Street & Bransford Road. / Over G. W. Line.
G	.	.	L	.	.	. .				
.	.	.	.	.	.	. .	Hill, Evans & Co.'s Siding (G. W.)	Worcester	G. W.—Mid.	Worcester.
.	.	.	.	.	.	. .	McKenzie & Holland's Siding (Vulcan Works) (G. W.)	Worcester	G. W.—Mid.	Worcester.
G	.	F	L	.	.	10 0	Midland Road	Worcester	Mid.	Over G. W. Line.
.	.	.	.	.	.	. .	Rainbow Hill Junction	Worcester	G. W.	Foregate Street and Shrub Hill.
G	.	F	L	.	.	10 0	Shrub Hill	Worcester	G. W.	Evesham and Kidderminster.
.	P	.	.	H	C	. .	Shrub Hill	Worcester	G. W. & Mid. Jt.	Evesham and Kidderminster.
.	.	.	.	.	.	. .	South Wales & Cannock Chase Cl. & Ck. Co.(G.W.)	Worcester	G. W.—Mid.	Worcester.
.	.	.	.	.	.	. .	Thomasson & Co.'s Siding (G. W.)	Worcester	G. W.—Mid.	Worcester.
.	.	.	.	.	.	. .	Tower Manufacturing Co.'s Works (G. W.)	Worcester	G. W.—Mid.	Worcester.
.	.	.	.	.	.	. .	Tunnel Junction	Worcester	G. W.	Shrub Hill and Fernhill Heath.
.	.	.	.	.	.	. .	Wood & Son's Siding	Worcester	G. W.	Butt's Branch.
G	P	F	L	H	C	4 0	Worcester Park	Surrey	L. & S.W.	Wimbledon and Leatherhead.
.	.	.	.	.	.	. .	Cunliffe's Siding	Surrey	L. & S.W.	Worcester Park.
.	.	.	.	.	.	. .	Wordie's Sid. (H. Baird & Co.)	Lanark	N. B.	Glasgow, Sighthill.
.	.	.	.	.	.	. .	Worgret Junction	Dorset	L. & S.W.	Wareham.
.	.	.	.	.	.	. .	Workhouse Siding	Denbigh	G. W.	Wrexham.
							WORKINGTON—			
G	P	F	L	H	C	3 0	(Station)	Cumb'land	L. & N. W.	Maryport and Whitehaven.
.	.	.	.	.	.	. .	Brokenshaw's Dock Siding	Cumb'land	C. & W. Jn.	Workington Dock Branch.
.	.	.	.	.	.	. .	Cammell & Co.'s Derwent Iron and Steel Works	Cumb'land	C. & W. Jn. / L. & N. W.	Branch from Harrington Junction. / Workington and Harrington.

EXPLANATION— G *Goods Station.*   P *Passenger and Parcel Station.*   P* *Passenger, but not Parcel or Miscellaneous Traffic.*
F *Furniture Vans, Carriages, Portable Engines, and Machines on Wheels.*   L *Live Stock.*
H *Horse Boxes and Prize Cattle Vans.*   C *Carriages by Passenger Train.*

STATION ACCOMMODATION.						CRANE POWER.	STATIONS, &c.	COUNTY.	COMPANY.	POSITION.
						Tons Cwts.	WORKINGTON—continued.			
G	P	F	L	H	C	3 0	Central	Cumb'land	C. & W. Jn.	Siddick Junc. and High Harrington.
.	.	.	.	.	.	.	Cloffocks Junction............	Cumb'land	C. & W. Jn.	Central Sta. & Workington Bge. Jn.
.	.	.	.	.	.	.	Jackson's Siding	Cumb'land	L. & N. W.	Merchants' Quay.
							Kirk Bros. & Co.—			
.	.	.	.	.	.	.	Marsh Sidings.........	Cumb'land	L. & N. W.	Workington and Harrington.
.	.	.	.	.	.	.	New Yard Iron Works...	Cumb'land	L. & N. W.	Workington and Harrington.
.	.	.	.	.	.	.	Lawson & Co.'s Yard........	Cumb'land	C. & W. Jn.	Workington Dock Branch.
.	.	.	.	.	.	.	Lonsdale Dock	Cumb'land	C. & W. Jn.—L. & N. W.	Workington Dock Branch.
.	.	.	.	.	.	.	Lowther Iron Works........	Cumb'land	C. & W. Jn.	Workington Dock Branch.
.	.	.	.	.	.	.	Merchants Quay............	Cumb'land	L. & N. W.	Workington.
.	.	.	.	.	.	.	Milburns Siding	Cumb'land	L. & N. W.	Workington and Harrington.
.	.	.	.	.	.	.	Moss Bay Cart Siding	Cumb'land	C. & W. Jn.	Branch from Harrington Junction.
.	.	.	.	.	.	.	Moss Bay Hematite Iron and Steel Co.'s Siding...	Cumb'land	L. & N. W.	Workington and Harrington.
.	.	.	.	.	.	.	Moss Bay Iron Works	Cumb'land	C. & W. Jn.	Branch from Harrington Junction.
.	.	.	.	.	.	.	North Western Hematite Iron and Steel Works.....	Cumb'land	C. & W. Jn.	Siddick Jn. & Workington (Central).
.	.	.	.	.	.	.	North Western Storage Co.'s Siding............	Cumb'land	C. & W. Jn.	Workington.
.	.	.	.	.	.	.	Raybould's Works...........	Cumb'land	L. & N. W.	Workington and Harrington.
.	.	.	.	.	.	.	St. Helens Colliery Co.'s Coke Ovens	Cumb'land	L. & N. W.	Workington and Siddick Junc. Sta.
.	.	.	.	.	.	.	St. Helens Colliery No. 3 William Pit (C. & W. Jn.)	Cumb'land	C. & W. Jn.—L. & N. W.	Siddick Jn. & Workington (Central).
.	.	.	.	.	.	.	Siddick Sand Siding........	Cumb'land	C. & W. Jn.	Workington and Siddick Junction.
.	.	.	.	.	.	.	West Cumberland Storing Co.'s Siding	Cumb'land	{ C. & W. Jn. .... { L. & N. W.	Workington Dock Branch. Lonsdale Dock.
.	.	.	.	.	.	.	Williamson & Son's Ship Yard	Cumb'land	L. & N. W.	Workington and Harrington.
.	.	.	.	.	.	.	Workington Bridge and Boiler Works	Cumb'land	L. & N. W.	Workington and Harrington.
.	.	.	.	.	.	.	Workington Engineering Works	Cumb'land	L. & N. W.	Workington and Harrington.
.	.	.	.	.	.	.	Workington Gas Works.....	Cumb'land	L. & N. W.	Workington and Harrington.
.	.	.	.	.	.	.	Workington Iron Co.'s Sid.	Cumb'land	L. & N. W.	Workington and Siddick Junc. Sta.
G	P	.	.	.	.	.	Workington Bridge	Cumb'land	L. & N. W.	Cockermouth and Workington.
.	.	.	.	.	.	.	Derwent Rolling Mills Barepot Siding	Cumb'land	L. & N. W.	Workington Bridge and Camerton.
.	.	.	.	.	.	.	Workington Bridge Junction	Cumb'land	C. & W. Jn.—L. & N. W.	Workington (Central) and Cockermouth Junction.
.	.	.	.	.	.	.	Workman's, J., Mill	Glo'ster	Mid.	Coaley Junction.
.	.	.	.	.	.	.	Workman's Siding.............	Glo'ster	Mid.	Woodchester.
G	P	F	L	H	C	5 0	Worksop (G. C.)	Notts	{ G. C. .... { G. N. .... { Mid.	Sheffield and Retford. Over G. C. from Retford Junction. Over G. C. from Shireoaks Junction.
.	.	.	.	.	.	.	Berry & Co.'s Siding (G.C.)	Notts	G. C.—G. N.—Mid.	Worksop.
.	.	.	.	.	.	.	Godley & Goulding's Siding (G. C.)	Notts	G. C.—G. N.—Mid.	Worksop.
.	.	.	.	.	.	.	Manton Wood Col. (G. C.)	Notts	G. C.—G. N.	Worksop.
.	.	.	.	.	.	.	Middleton's Bone Mill (G C)	Notts	G. C.—G. N.—Mid.	Worksop.
.	.	.	.	.	.	.	Oates' Siding (G. C.).........	Notts	G. C.—G. N.—Mid.	Worksop.
.	.	.	.	.	.	.	Portland Works (G. C.)	Notts	G. C.—G. N.—Mid.	Worksop.
.	.	.	.	.	.	.	Preston's Siding (G. C.)	Notts	G. C.—G. N.—Mid.	Worksop.
.	.	.	.	.	.	.	Smith's Siding (G. C.)	Notts	G. C.—G. N.	Worksop.
.	.	.	.	.	.	.	Threlfall's Siding (G. C.)...	Notts	G. C.—G. N.—Mid.	Worksop.
.	.	.	.	.	.	.	Turner's (New) Sid. (G. C.)	Notts	G. C.—G. N.—Mid.	Worksop.
.	.	.	.	.	.	.	Wigan Coal and Iron Co.'s Manton Sidings	Notts	Mid.	Worksop.
.	.	.	.	.	.	.	Worksop and Retford Brewery Co.'s Siding (G.C.)	Notts	G. C.—Mid................	Retford.
.	.	.	.	.	.	.	Worlaby Siding	Lincoln ...	G. C.	Elsham.
.	P	.	.	.	.	.	Worle	Somerset..	G. W.	Puxton and Weston-super-Mare.
G	P	.	.	.	.	.	Worle	Somerset..	W. C. & P.	Weston-super-Mare and Clevedon.
.	.	.	.	.	.	.	Worle Junction	Somerset..	G. W.	Puxton and Worle.
G	P	.	L	H	.	1 10	Worleston	Cheshire ..	L. & N. W.	Chester and Crewe.
G	P	F	L	H	C	5 0	Wormald Green	Yorks	N. E.	Leeds and Ripon.
.	.	.	.	.	.	.	Pepper's Lime Quarry	Yorks	N. E.	Wormald Green.
.	.	.	.	.	.	.	Wormald's Siding	Lancs	L. & Y.	Oldham (Mumps).
G			L			3 0 }	Wormit	Fife	N. B.	{ Dundee and St. Fort. { Dundee and Tayport.
.	P	.	.	.	.	}				
.	.	.	.	.	.	.	Wormit Junction	Fife	N. B.	Newport, West & Dundee, Esplanade.

STATION ACCOMMODATION.						CRANE POWER.		STATIONS, &c.	COUNTY.	COMPANY.	POSITION.
						Tons	Cwts.	Worms, Josse & Co.—			
..	..	..	..	..	..	..	..	Repairing Siding (G. C.) ...	Lincoln ...	G. C.—G. N.	Grimsby Town.
..	..	..	..	..	..	..	..	Siding (G. C.)	Lincoln' ..	G. C.—G. N.	Grimsby Town.
..	..	..	..	..	..	..	..	Wormwood Scrubbs	Middlesex	L. & N. W.	See London, St. Quintin Park and Wormwood Scrubbs.
G	P	F	L	H	C	..	..	Worplesdon	Surrey ...	L. & S. W.	Woking and Guildford.
..	..	..	..	..	..	..	..	Owen Stone Co.'s Siding ...	Surrey ...	L. & S. W.	Worplesdon.
G	..	..	..	..	..	5	0	Worsboro'	Yorks	G. C.	Branch—Wombwell and Penistone.
..	..	..	..	..	..	..	..	Barrow Colliery	Yorks	G. C.	Worsboro'.
..	..	..	..	..	..	..	..	Dearne & Dove's Siding ...	Yorks	G. C.	Worsboro'.
..	..	..	..	..	..	..	..	Lewden Colliery	Yorks	G. C.	Worsboro'.
..	..	..	..	..	..	..	..	New Sovereign Colliery ...	Yorks	G. C.	Worsboro'.
..	..	..	..	..	..	..	..	Strafford Colliery	Yorks	G. C.	Worsboro'.
..	..	..	..	..	..	..	..	Swaithe Main Coke Ovens	Yorks	G. C.	Worsboro'.
..	..	..	..	..	..	..	..	Swaithe Main Colliery	Yorks	G. C.	Worsboro'.
..	..	..	..	..	..	..	..	Wells Coke Ovens	Yorks	G. C.	Worsboro'.
..	..	..	..	..	..	..	..	Worsboro' Coke Ovens	Yorks	G. C.	Worsboro'.
..	..	..	..	..	..	..	..	Worsboro' Urban District Council's Siding............	Yorks	G. C.	Worsboro'.
..	..	..	..	..	..	..	..	Worsboro' Dale	Yorks	G. C.	Same as Worsboro'.
..	..	..	..	..	..	..	..	Worship Street	Middlesex	L. & N. W.	See London.
G	P	F	L	H	C	1	0	Worsley	Lancs	L. & N. W.	Bolton and Manchester.
..	..	..	..	..	..	..	..	Worsley Mesnes Colliery ...	Lancs	L. & Y.	Wigan.
..	..	..	..	..	..	..	..	Worsley Mesnes Colliery	Lancs	L. & N. W.	Garswood.
..	..	..	..	..	..	..	..	Worsley Mesnes Iron Works	Lancs	L. & Y.	Wigan.
..	..	..	..	..	..	..	..	Worsley Mesnes Iron Works	Lancs	L. & N. W.	Garswood.
G	P	F	L	H	C	..	..	Worstead	Norfolk ...	G. E.	Norwich and Cromer.
..	..	..	..	..	..	..	..	Worstead	Norfolk ...	Mid. & G. N. Jt.	See Honing (for Worstead).
G	P	F	L	H	C	10	0	Worthing	Sussex ...	L. B. & S. C.	Brighton and Ford Junction.
..	..	..	..	..	..	..	..	Cortis Siding	Sussex......	L. B. & S. C.	Worthing.
..	..	..	..	..	..	..	..	Worthing, West................	Sussex ...	L. B. & S. C	See West Worthing.
G	P	..	..	..	..	..	..	Worthington	Leicester..	Mid.	Ashby and Melbourne.
..	..	..	..	..	..	..	..	Bredon & Cloud Hill Lime Works	Leicester..	Mid.	Worthington.
..	..	..	..	..	..	..	..	Heath End Colliery	Leicester..	Mid.	Worthington and Ashby.
..	..	..	..	..	..	..	..	Lount Fire Brick & Sanitary Pipe Co.'s Siding	Derby	Mid.	Worthington.
..	..	..	..	..	..	..	..	Lount Pottery Works (Greenhaff & Co.)	Leicester..	Mid.	Worthington and Ashby.
..	..	..	..	..	..	..	..	Shield's Lime Works........	Leicester..	Mid.	Adjoining Worthington Station.
..	..	..	..	..	..	..	..	Shield's New Lime Works	Leicester..	Mid.	Worthington and Melbourne.
..	..	..	..	..	..	..	..	Smith & Co.'s Siding	Leicester..	Mid.	Worthington and Ashby.
..	..	..	..	..	..	..	..	Staunton Colliery Sanitary Pipe Co.'s Siding	Leicester..	Mid.	Worthington and Ashby.
..	..	..	..	..	..	..	..	Worthington & Co.'s Sidings (Mid.)	Staffs	Mid.—L N W—G N—N S	Burton-on-Trent.
..	..	..	..	..	..	..	..	Worthington Hall Colliery Co.'s Siding	Lancs	L. & N. W.	Coppull.
..	..	..	..	..	..	..	..	Worting Junction	Hants	L. & S. W.	Basingstoke and Micheldever.
G	P	F	L	H	C	10	0	Wortley	Yorks	G. C.	Penistone and Sheffield.
..	..	..	..	..	..	..	..	Thurgoland Siding	Yorks	G. C.	Wortley.
..	..	..	..	..	..	..	..	Wortley	Yorks	G. N.	See Leeds, Armley and Wortley.
										L. & N. W.	See Leeds, Farnley and Wortley.
										Mid.	See Leeds, Armley (for Farnley and Wortley).
..	..	..	..	..	..	..	..	Wortley Junctions............	Yorks	G. N.	Leeds.
G	P	F	L	..	..	..	..	Wotton	Bucks	O. & A. Tram	Quainton Road and Brill.
..	..	..	..	..	..	..	..	Church Siding..............	Bucks	O. & A. Tram............	Wotton and Wood Siding.
..	..	..	..	..	..	..	..	Wouldham Cement Co.'s Sid.	Essex	L. T. & S.	Grays.
G	P	F	L	H	C	1	10	Wrabness	Essex	G. E.	Manningtree and Harwich.
G	P	..	..	..	..	..	..	Wrafton	Devon	L. & S. W.	Barnstaple and Ilfracombe.
G	P	F	L	H	C	..	..	Wragby	Lincoln ...	G. N.	Lincoln and Louth.
								Wragg & Son's—			
..	..	..	..	..	..	..	..	Brick Works (Mid.)	Derby	Mid.—L. & N. W.	Woodville.
..	..	..	..	..	..	..	..	High Peak Silica Co.'s Sid.	Derby	L. & N. W.	Parsley Hay.
..	..	..	..	..	..	..	..	Pipe Works (Mid.)..........	Derby	Mid.—L. & N. W.	Swadlincote.
..	..	..	..	..	..	..	..	South Western Pottery.....	Dorset......	L. & S. W.	Parkstone.
G	P	..	..	H	..	2	0	Wrangaton	Devon	G. W.	Totnes and Plymouth.
..	..	..	..	..	..	..	..	Wrangbrook Junction	Yorks	H. & B.	Upton and Kirk Smeaton.
..	..	..	..	..	..	..	..	Wrangbrook Siding	Yorks	H. & B.	Upton and North Elmsall.
..	..	..	..	..	..	..	..	Wrawby Junction	Lincoln ...	G. C.	Barnetby and Elsham.
G	P	F	L	H	C	3	0	Wraysbury	Bucks	L. & S. W.	Staines and Windsor.

STATION ACCOMMODATION.						CRANE POWER.		STATIONS, &c.	COUNTY.	COMPANY.	POSITION.
						Tons	Cwts.				
G	P	.	.	.	.	.	.	Wrea Green	Lancs	P. & W. Jt. (L&Y&L&NW)	Lytham and Preston.
G	P	.	.	.	.	.	.	Wreay	Cumb'land	L. & N. W.	Carlisle and Penrith.
.	.	.	.	.	.	.	.	Wrecclesham Siding	Hants	L. & S. W.	Farnham.
.	.	.	.	.	.	.	.	Wreford's Siding	Kent	S. E. & C.	Dunton Green.
.	.	.	.	.	.	.	.	Wrekin Chemical Works	Salop	G. W. / L. & N. W.	Hollinswood. / Same as Wilkinson's Sid. (Stirchley).
G	P	F	L	H	C	2	0	Wrenbury	Cheshire	L. & N. W.	Crewe and Whitchurch.
.	.	.	.	.	.	.	.	Poole's Siding	Cheshire	L. & N. W.	Wrenbury and Whitchurch.
.	.	.	.	.	.	.	.	Wrenthorpe Exchange Sids.	Yorks	G. N.	Wakefield and Lofthouse.
.	.	.	.	.	.	.	.	Wrenthorpe Junctions	Yorks	G. N.	Wakefield and Leeds.
G	P	.	L	H	.	.	.	Wressle	Yorks	N. E.	Hull and Selby.
G	P	F	L	H	C	1	0	Wretham & Hockham	Norfolk	G. E.	Thetford and Swaffham.
								WREXHAM—			
G	P	F	L	H	C	8	0	(Station)	Denbigh	G. W.	Shrewsbury and Chester.
G	.	.	.	.	.	.	.	Abenbury Siding	Denbigh	Cam.	Wrexham and Marchwiel.
.	.	.	.	.	.	.	.	Bersham Colliery	Denbigh	G. W.	Wrexham and Johnstown & Hafod.
G	.	.	L	.	.	1	10	Caia	Denbigh	Cam.	Wrexham and Marchwiel.
G	P	F	L	H	C	.	.	Central Station & Junction	Denbigh	Cam. / W. M. & C. Q.	Branch from Ellesmere. / Terminus.
G	P	F	L	H	C	2	0				
G	P	F	L	H	C	.	.	Central (W. M. & C. Q.)	Denbigh	G. C.	Over W. M. & C. Q. from Hawarden Bridge Junction.
.	.	.	.	.	.	.	.	Cobden Mill Siding	Denbigh	G. W. / W. M. & C. Q.	Wrexham and Johnstown & Hafod. / Wrexham.
.	P	.	.	.	.	.	.	Exchange (W. M. & C. Q.)	Denbigh	W. M. & C. Q. / G. C.	Wrexham, Central & Connah's Quay. / Over W. M. & C. Q. from Hawarden Bridge Junction.
.	.	.	.	.	.	.	.	Junction	Denbigh	G. W.—W. M & C. Q.	Ruabon and Hope.
G	.	.	.	.	.	.	.	King's Mill Siding	Denbigh	Cam.	Wrexham and Marchwiel.
.	.	.	.	.	.	.	.	Lager Brewery Siding	Denbigh	G. W.	Wrexham and Johnstown & Hafod.
.	.	.	.	.	.	.	.	Puleston Mill	Denbigh	G. W.	Wrexham and Johnstown & Hafod.
G	.	.	.	.	.	2	0	Rhossdu	Denbigh	W. M. & C. Q.	Wrexham and Connah's Quay.
.	.	.	.	.	.	.	.	Vron Wharf Siding	Denbigh	G. W.	Wrexham and Croesnewydd.
.	.	.	.	.	.	.	.	Workhouse Siding	Denbigh	G. W.	Wrexham and Croesnewydd.
.	.	.	.	.	.	.	.	Wrexham Colliery	Denbigh	G. W. / W. M. & C. Q.	Wrexham & Wheatsheaf Junction. / Wrexham and Gwersyllt.
.	.	.	.	.	.	.	.	Wrexham Water Co.'s Works	Denbigh	G. W.	Rhos.
.	.	.	.	.	.	.	.	Wright and Eagle Range Sid.	Warwick	L. & N. W.	Birmingham, Aston.
.	.	.	.	.	.	.	.	Wright, Orson & Co.'s Siding	Leicester	Mid.	Wigston, South.
.	.	.	.	.	.	.	.	Wright, Robert, Siding	Durham	N. E.	Stockton, South.
.	.	.	.	.	.	.	.	Wright's Siding	Carnarvon	L. & N. W.	Same as Brundrit & Co.'s Siding (Penmaenmawr).
.	.	.	.	.	.	.	.	Wright's Siding	Denbigh	G. W.	Same as Trevor Hall Lime Works (Trevor).
.	.	.	.	.	.	.	.	Wright's Fir Tree House Foundry	Lancs	L. & N. W.	Wigan.
								Wright, W. T., & Co.—			
.	.	.	.	.	.	.	.	Albion Siding	Leicester	Mid.	Sileby.
.	.	.	.	.	.	.	.	Barrow End Brick Yard	Leicester	Mid.	Sileby.
.	.	.	.	.	.	.	.	Barrow Road Siding	Leicester	Mid.	Sileby.
.	.	.	.	.	.	.	.	Wrightson Colliery	Northumb	N. E.	Annitsford.
.	.	.	.	.	.	.	.	Wrigley's Siding	Lancs	L. & Y.	Heap Bridge.
G	P	F	.	H	C	.	.	Wrington	Somerset	G. W.	Congresbury and Blagdon.
.	.	.	.	.	.	.	.	Writhlington Colliery	Somerset	G. W.—S. & D. Jt.	Radstock.
G	P	F	L	H	C	5	0	Wrotham and Boro' Green	Kent	S. E. & C.	Otford and Maidstone, East.
.	.	.	.	.	.	.	.	Spencer's Siding	Kent	S. E. & C.	Wrotham and Malling.
.	.	.	.	.	.	.	.	Wall & Son's Siding	Kent	S. E. & C.	Wrotham.
G	P	.	L	H	.	10	0	Wroxall	I. of W.	I of W.	Sandown and Ventnor.
G	P	F	L	H	C	1	0	Wroxham	Norfolk	G. E.	Norwich and Cromer.
G	P	F	L	.	.	.	.	Wryde	Cambs	Mid. & G. N. Jt.	Peterboro' and Wisbech.
.	.	.	.	.	.	.	.	Wybourne's Siding	Kent	S. E. & C.	Sharnal Street.
.	.	.	.	.	.	.	.	Wycombe, High	Bucks	G. W. & G. C. Jt.	See High Wycombe.
.	.	.	.	.	.	.	.	Wycombe, West	Bucks	G. W. & G. C. Jt.	See West Wycombe.
G	P	F	L	H	C	2	0	Wye	Kent	S. E. & C.	Ashford and Canterbury, West.
.	.	.	.	.	.	.	.	Wye Colliery	Glo'ster	S. & Wye Jt. (G. W. & Mid)	Same as Speculation Siding (Lydbrook).
.	.	.	.	.	.	.	.	Wyesham Junction	Glo'ster	G. W.	Monmouth and Redbrook.
.	.	.	.	.	.	.	.	Wye Valley Junction	Glo'ster	G. W.	Chepstow and Woolaston.
G	P	.	L	H	.	2	10	Wyke & Norwood Green (L&Y)	Yorks	L. & Y. / G. N.	Halifax and Bradford. / Over L.&Y. from Bowling Junction.
G	P	.	.	H	.	.	.				
G	P	.	.	.	.	2	0	Wykeham	Yorks	N. E.	Pickering and Seamer.
.	.	.	.	.	.	.	.	Wyken Colliery	Warwick	L. & N. W.	Coventry.
G	P	.	L	H	C	2	10	Wylam	Northumb	N. E.	Newcastle and Hexham.

G	P	F	L	H	C	Tons	Cwts	STATIONS, &c.	COUNTY.	COMPANY.	POSITION.
								Wylam—*continued.*			
.	.	.	.	.	.	.	.	Clara Vale Colliery	Northumb	N. E.	Wylam.
.	.	.	.	.	.	.	.	West Wylam Colliery	Northumb	N. E.	Wylam and Prudhoe.
.	P	.	.	.	.	.	.	West Wylam Junction......	Northumb	N. E.	Wylam and Prudhoe.
.	P	.	.	.	.	.	.	Wylde Green	Warwick	L. & N. W.	Birmingham and Lichfield.
								Wylie & Lochhead's Paper			
.	.	.	.	.	.	.	.	Works	Renfrew	Cal.	Glasgow, Whiteinch.
.	.	.	.	.	.	.	.	Wyllie's Chemical Works.....	Ayr	G. & S. W.	Ayr.
G	P	F	L	H	C	1	10	Wylye	Wilts	G. W.	Salisbury and Warminster.
.	.	.	.	.	.	.	.	Wymondham	Lincoln	Mid.	See Edmondthorpe & Wymondham.
G	P	F	L	H	C	1	10	Wymondham	Norfolk	G. E.	Norwich and Thetford.
.	.	.	.	.	.	.	.	Wymondley Siding	Herts	G. N.	Stevenage.
								Wyndham Mining Co.—			
.	.	.	.	.	.	.	.	East Siding	Cumb'land	W C & E Jt. (Fur. & LNW)	Gillfoot.
.	.	.	.	.	.	.	.	Falcon Pit	Cumb'land	W C & E Jt. (Fur. & LNW)	Gillfoot.
.	.	.	.	.	.	.	.	Nos. 1, 4, and 6 Pits	Cumb'land	W C & E Jt. (Fur. & LNW)	Gillfoot.
.	.	.	.	.	.	.	.	Orgill Pit	Cumb'land	W C & E Jt. (Fur. & LNW)	Gillfoot.
.	.	.	.	.	.	.	.	Pits	Cumb'land	W C & E Jt. (Fur. & LNW)	Rowrah.
.	.	.	.	.	.	.	.	Wyndham Pits	Glamorg'n	G. W.	See North's (Ogmore Vale).
.	.	.	.	.	.	.	.	Wynn Hall Siding	Denbigh	G. W.	See Rhos.
.	P	.	.	.	.	.	.	Wynn, Sir Watkin (*private*) ...	Merioneth	G. W.	Bala Junction Sta. & Llanuwchllyn.
.	.	.	.	.	.	.	.	Wynnstay Colliery	Denbigh	G. W.	Ruabon.
G	P	F	L	H	C	.	.	Wynyard	Durham	N. E.	Stockton and Sunderland.
.	.	.	.	.	.	.	.	Wyre Dock	Lancs	L. & Y.—P. & W. Jt.	See Fleetwood.
.	.	.	.	.	.	.	.	Wyre Dock Junction........	Lancs	L. & Y.—P. & W. Jt.	Fleetwood.
G	P	.	.	.	.	.	.	Wyre Forest	Worcester	G. W.	Bewdley and Tenbury.
G	P	.	.	.	.	1	10	Wyrley and Church Bridge.	Staffs	L. & N. W.	Rugeley and Walsall.
.	.	.	.	.	.	.	.	Blewitt & Co.'s Quinton Col.	Staffs	L. & N. W.	Wyrley and Bloxwich.
.	.	.	.	.	.	.	.	Gilpin & Co.'s Siding	Staffs	L. & N. W.	Wyrley and Church Bridge.
.	.	.	.	.	.	.	.	Great Wyrley Colliery	Staffs	L. & N. W.	Wyrley and Bloxwich.
								Hawkins & Son's Cannock			
								Old Coppice Colliery or			
.	.	.	.	.	.	.	.	Cheslyn Hay Colliery ...	Staffs	L. & N. W.	Wyrley and Church Bridge.
.	.	.	.	.	.	.	.	Wyrley Grove Colliery	Staffs	L. & N. W.	See Harrison's (Brownhills).
G	P	F	.	H	C	1	10	Wyvenhoe	Essex	G. E.	Colchester and Clacton-on-Sea.
.	.	.	.	.	.	.	.	Forrestt & Son's Siding ...	Essex	G. E.	Wyvenhoe.

Y

G	P	F	L	H	C	Tons	Cwts	STATIONS, &c.	COUNTY.	COMPANY.	POSITION.
G	P	F	L	H	C	1	5	Yalding	Kent	S. E. & C.	Maidstone, West and Paddock Wood.
.	.	.	.	.	.	.	.	Yardley	Worcester	L. & N. W.	See Stechford (for Yardley).
.	.	.	.	.	.	.	.	Yardley & Co.'s Siding	Staffs	L. & N. W.	Darlaston.
G	P	F	L	H	C	2	0	Yarm	Durham	N. E.	Northallerton and Stockton.
G	P	F	L	H	C	5	0 }	Yarmouth (I. of W. Central)	I. of W	{ I. of W. Cent. / L. & S. W.	Newport and Freshwater. / Steamer from Lymington Pier.
G	P	F	L	H	C	5	0	YARMOUTH— Beach.	Norfolk	Mid. & G. N. Jt.	Terminus.
.	.	.	.	.	.	.	.	Breydon Junction	Norfolk	G. E.	Reedham & Vauxhall.
.	.	.	.	.	.	.	.	Clark, R. H., Siding	Suffolk	G. E.	South Town.
.	.	.	.	.	.	.	.	Fish Market...	Norfolk	{ G. E. / Mid. & G. N. Jt.	Extension from Vauxhall. / Yarmouth.
.	.	.	.	.	.	.	.	Jewson & Son's Siding	Suffolk	G. E.	South Town.
.	.	.	.	.	.	.	.	Junction	Norfolk	G. E.—Mid. & G. N. Jt.	Yarmouth, Vauxhall and Beach.
.	.	.	.	.	.	.	.	Lacon & Co.'s Siding (G.E.)	Norfolk	G. E.—Mid. & G. N. Jt.	Yarmouth Tramway.
								Montague Smith & Co.'s			
.	.	.	.	.	.	.	.	Siding	Norfolk	Mid. & G. N. Jt.	Yarmouth Beach.
G	P	F	L	H	C	8	0	South Town...............	Suffolk	G. E.	Terminus.
.	.	.	.	.	.	.	.	Sterry, J. S., Siding (G.E.)	Norfolk	G. E.—Mid. & G. N. Jt.	Yarmouth Tramway.
G	P	F	L	H	C	5	0	Vauxhall	Norfolk	G. E.	Terminus.
G	.	F	.	.	.	8	0	Wharf	Norfolk	Mid. & G. N. Jt.	Extension from Beach Station.
.	P	.	.	.	.	.	.	Yarnton.................	Oxon	G. W.	Oxford and Handborough.
.	.	.	.	.	.	.	.	Yarnton Junction	Oxon	G. W.—L. & N. W.	Yarnton and Verney Junc. Station.
.	.	.	.	.	.	.	.	Yarrow & Co.'s Siding	Middlesex	{ G. E. / GN—GW—LNW—Mid	London, Millwall Docks. / London, Poplar.
.	.	.	.	.	.	.	.	Yarrow Mill................	Selkirk	N. B.	Selkirk.

EXPLANATION—G *Goods Station.*   P *Passenger and Parcel Station.*   P* *Passenger, but not Parcel or Miscellaneous Traffic.*
F *Furniture Vans, Carriages, Portable Engines, and Machines on Wheels.*   L *Live Stock.*
H *Horse Boxes and Prize Cattle Vans.*   C *Carriages by Passenger Train.*

G	P	F	L	H	C	Tons	Cwts	STATIONS, &c.	COUNTY.	COMPANY.	POSITION.
G	P	F	L	H	C	1	10	Yate	Glo'ster	Mid.	Gloucester and Bristol.
								Pearson & Son's Siding	Glo'ster	Mid.	Near Yate.
								Yates, Duxbury & Son's Sid.	Lancs	L. & Y.	Same as Duxbury's Siding (Heap Bridge).
								Yates, Haywood & Co.'s Siding (G. C.)	Yorks	G. C.—G. N.	Rotherham and Masboro'.
G	P	F	L	H	C	4	0	Yates' Quarry	Cumb'land	W C & E Jt. (Fur. & L N W)	Yeathouse.
G	P	F	L	H	C	1	10	Yatton	Somerset	G. W.	Bristol and Highbridge.
G	P		L	H		1	10	Yaxham	Norfolk	G. E.	Wymondham and Dereham.
G	P	F	L	H	C	1	10	Yaxley and Farcet	Hunts	G. N.	Peterboro' and Huntingdon.
G								Yaxley Brick Co.'s Siding	Hunts	G. N.	Fletton.
G								Yeadon	Yorks	Mid.	Branch near Guiseley.
								Green Lane Mill Sid. (Mallinson, Barraclough & Co.)	Yorks	Mid.	Near Yeadon.
G	P	F	L	H	C	6	0	Yealmpton	Devon	G. W.	Branch from Plymstock.
G	P					2	0	Yeathouse	Cumb'land	W C & E Jt. (Fur. & L N W)	Bridgefoot and Moor Row.
								Yates' Quarry	Cumb'land	W C & E Jt. (Fur. & L N W)	Yeathouse and Winder.
G	P	F	L			1	0	Yeldham	Essex	C. V. & H.	Haverhill and Halstead.
								Yeld Hill Siding	Staffs	N. S.	See Goldendale Ir. Co. (Chatterley).
G	P	F	L	H	C			Yelvertoft and Stanford Park	N'hamptn	L. & N. W.	Market Harboro' and Rugby.
	P							Yelverton	Devon	G. W.	Horrabridge and Bickleigh.
								Yelverton Junction	Devon	G. W.	Horrabridge and Princetown.
G	P	F	L	H	C	5	0	Yeoford Junction Station	Devon	L. & S. W.	Exeter and Okehampton.
								Yeoman, Cherry, Curtis & Co.'s Siding (L. & N. W.)	Staffs	L. & N. W.—N. S.	Burton-on-Trent.
								YEOVIL—			
								Bradford & Son's Siding	Somerset	G. W.	Yeovil.
G								Clifton Maybank	Somerset	G. W.	Yeovil.
								Clifton Maybank Junction	Somerset	G. W.—L. & S. W.	Pen Mill and Yeovil Junc. Station.
								Gas Co.'s Siding	Somerset	L. & S. W.	Yeovil.
								Ham Hill & Doulting Stone Co.'s Siding	Somerset	G. W.	Hendford.
G		F	L			10	0	Hendford	Somerset	G. W.	Yeovil Town Station and Montacute.
								Junction	Somerset	G. W.—L. & S. W.	Durston and Yeovil Junc. Station.
G	P		L	H	C	2	0	Junction Station	Dorset	L. & S. W.	Salisbury and Exeter.
G	P	F	L	H	C	7	0	Pen Mill	Somerset	G. W.	Frome and Dorchester.
G		F	L			10	0	Town (Goods)	Somerset	L. & S. W.	Branch from Yeovil Junction.
	P			H	C			Town (Pass.)	Somerset	G. W. & L. & S. W. Jt.	Durston and Yeovil Junction.
G	P	F	L	H	C	1	10	Yetminster	Dorset	G. W.	Yeovil and Dorchester.
								Yiewsley	Middlesex	G. W.	See West Drayton and Yiewsley.
								Ynisawdre Junction	Glamorg'n	G. W.	Tondu and Brynmenyn.
								Ynisawdre Siding	Glamorg'n	G. W.	Brynmenyn.
								Ynisboeth Quarry (Richards)	Glamorg'n	T. V.	Penrhiwceiber.
								Yniscedwyn Colliery (Mid.)	Glamorg'n	Mid.—G. W.—L. & N. W.	Same as South Wales Anthracite Colliery Co. (Gurnos).
								Yniscedwyn Tin Plate Co.'s Siding (Mid.)	Glamorg'n	Mid.—G. W.—L. & N. W.	{ Glais. { Gurnos.
								Ynisci Colliery (N. & B.)	Glamorg'n	N. & Brecon—Mid.	Ystradgynlais.
								Ynisfeio Colliery	Glamorg'n	T. V.	Treherbert.
	P							Ynishir	Glamorg'n	T. V.	Ferndale and Porth.
								Ynishir Colliery (House Coal)	Glamorg'n	T. V.	Wattstown.
								Ynishir Standard Colliery (Steam Coal)	Glamorg'n	T. V.	Wattstown.
								Ynismedwy Tin Plate Works (Mid.)	Glamorg'n	Mid.—G. W.—L. & N. W.	Pontardawe.
								Ynisygeinon Junction	Glamorg'n	Mid.—N. & Brecon	Swansea and Ystradgynlais.
								Ynisygeinon Siding (Mid.)	Glamorg'n	Mid.—G. W.—L. & N. W.	Same as South Wales Primrose Colliery (Ystalyfera).
G	P							Ynys	Carnarvon	L. & N. W.	Afon Wen and Carnarvon.
								Ynysavon Colliery	Glamorg'n	P. T.	Cwmavon.
								Ynysdavid Sidings	Glamorg'n	P. T.	Cwmavon.
G	P							Ynysddu	Mon	L. & N. W.	Nine Mile Point and Tredegar Jn. Station.
								Lord Tredegar's Siding	Mon	L. & N. W.	Ynysddu and Nine Mile Point.
								Pond's Wentlooge Colliery	Mon	L. & N. W.	Ynysddu and Nine Mile Point.
								Ynysddu Chemical Works	Mon	L. & N. W.	Ynysddu and Nine Mile Point.
								Ynysfach Junction	Glamorg'n	B&M&L&NWJoint—TV	Merthyr.
								Ynysfach Siding	Glamorg'n	B. & M. & L. & N. W. Joint.	See Crawshay Bros. (Cefn.)
G	P		L	H				Ynyslas	Cardigan	Cam.	Aberystwyth and Glandyfi.
G	P							Ynysybwl	Glamorg'n	T. V.	Branch—Pontypridd & Abercynon.
								Batchelor & Snowden's Sid.	Glamorg'n	T. V.	End of Ynysybwl Branch.
								Cwm Siding	Glamorg'n	T. V.	Near Ynysybwl.

EXPLANATION— G *Goods Station.*   P *Passenger and Parcel Station.*   P* *Passenger, but not Parcel or Miscellaneous Traffic.*
F *Furniture Vans, Carriages, Portable Engines, and Machines on Wheels.*   L *Live Stock.*
H *Horse Boxes and Prize Cattle Vans.*   C *Carriages by Passenger Train.*

STATION ACCOMMODATION.						CRANE POWER.		STATIONS, &c.	COUNTY.	COMPANY.	POSITION.
						Tons	Cwts				
								Ynysybwl—*continued.*			
.	.	.	.	.	.	.	.	Darranddu Colliery	Glamorg'n	T. V.	Ynysybwl and Abercynon.
.	.	.	.	.	.	.	.	Llanwonno Colliery	Glamorg'n	T. V.	Near Ynysybwl.
.	.	.	.	.	.	.	.	Mynachdy Colliery	Glamorg'n	T. V.	Ynysybwl Branch.
								Ocean Coal Co.—			
.	.	.	.	.	.	.	.	Black Rock Junction	Glamorg'n	T. V.	Ynysybwl and Abercynon.
.	.	.	.	.	.	.	.	Lady Windsor Colliery...	Glamorg'n	T. V.	Ynysybwl and Abercynon.
.	.	.	.	.	.	.	.	Old Warehouse Siding......	Glamorg'n	T. V.	Near Ynysybwl.
.	.	.	.	.	.	.	.	Ynysybwl Branch Junction ..	Glamorg'n	T. V.	Pontypridd and Abercynon.
.	.	.	.	.	.	.	.	Ynysydwr Junction	Glamorg'n	T. V.	Cilfynydd and Travellers' Rest.
G	P	F	L	H	C	.	.	Yockleton	Salop	S.&Wpl.Jt.(GW&LNW)	Shrewsbury and Welshpool.
G	P	.	L	H	.	3	0	Yockney & Co.'s Siding	Wilts	G. W.	Corsham.
G	P	.	L	H	.	.	.	Yoker	Renfrew	Cal.	Glasgow, Central and Clydebank.
										N. B.	Glasgow, Partick and Clydebank.
								British Westinghouse Co.'s Siding	Renfrew	Cal.	Yoker and Scotstoun.
.	.	.	.	.	.	.	.	Clyde Valley Electric Works	Renfrew	Cal.	Yoker.
.	.	.	.	.	.	.	.	Yoker Distillery (Harvey's)	Renfrew	Cal.—N. B.	Yoker.
.	.	.	.	.	.	.	.	Yoker Shipbuilding Yard (Napier & Miller's)	Renfrew	Cal.—N. B.	Yoker and Clydebank.
G	P	F	L	H	C	10	0	YORK—		N. E.	Doncaster and Darlington.
.	P	.	.	H	C	.	.			G. C.	Over N. E. from Knottingley, Ferry Bridge Junction.
.	P	.	.	H	C	.	.			G. E.	Over N. E. from Doncaster.
.	P	.	.	H	C	.	.	(Station, N. E.)	Yorks	G. N.	Over N. E. from Shaftholme Junc.
.	P	.	.	H	C	.	.			L. & Y.	Over Mid. and N. E. from Normanton, Goose Hill Junction.
.	P	.	.	H	C	.	.			L. & N. W.	Over N. E. from Leeds.
.	P	.	.	H	C	.	.			Mid.	Over N. E. Line.
.	.	.	.	.	.	.	.	Anglo-American Oil Co.'s Siding	Yorks	N. E.	York.
.	.	.	.	.	.	.	.	Burton Lane Coal Siding...	Yorks	N. E.	York.
.	.	.	.	.	.	.	.	Burton Lane Junction	Yorks	N. E.	York Pass. and Bootham Junction.
.	.	.	.	.	.	.	.	Consolidated Petroleum Co.'s Siding	Yorks	N. E.	Foss Islands Branch.
.	.	.	.	.	.	.	.	Corporation Siding	Yorks	N. E.	Foss Islands Branch.
.	.	.	.	.	.	.	.	Engineering Co.'s Siding...	Yorks	N. E.	York.
G	.	F	L	.	.	5	0	Foss Islands	Yorks	N. E.	Bch.—York Pass. and Bootham Jn.
.	.	.	.	.	.	.	.	Gas Co.'s Siding................	Yorks	N. E.	Foss Islands Branch.
.	.	.	.	.	.	.	.	Holgate Dock	Yorks	N. E.	York.
.	.	.	.	.	.	.	.	Holgate Junction	Yorks	N. E.	York and Naburn.
.	.	.	.	.	.	.	.	Leetham's Siding	Yorks	N. E.	Foss Islands Branch.
.	.	.	.	.	.	.	.	North Junction	Yorks	N. E.	Holgate Junc. and Severus Junc.
.	.	.	.	.	.	.	.	Rowntree's Siding	Yorks	N. E.	Foss Islands Branch.
.	.	.	.	.	.	.	.	Severus Junction	Yorks	N. E.	North Junction and Poppleton.
.	.	.	.	.	.	.	.	Station Hotel Laundry Sid.	Yorks	N. E.	Foss Islands Branch.
.	.	.	.	.	.	.	.	Waterworks Siding	Yorks	N. E.	York.
.	.	.	.	.	.	.	.	Yorkhill	Lanark	N. B.	See Glasgow.
.	.	.	.	.	.	.	.	Yorkhill Sidings (N. B.)......	Lanark	N. B.—Cal.	Glasgow, Stobcross.
.	.	.	.	.	.	.	.	York Road (G. N.)	Middlesex	G. N.—S. E. & C.	See London, King's Cross.
.	.	.	.	.	.	.	.	Yorkshire and Derbyshire Coal and Iron Co.'s Carlton Main Colliery	Yorks	Mid.	Cudworth.
.	.	.	.	.	.	.	.	Yorkshire Engine Co.'s Siding (G. C.)	Yorks	G. C.—Mid.	Meadow Hall and Wincobank.
.	.	.	.	.	.	.	.	Yorkshire Iron and Coal Co.'s Ironworks	Yorks	G. N.	Ardsley.
.	.	.	.	.	.	.	.	Yorkshire Ir. & Cl. Co.'s Sid.	Yorks	G. N.	See Fulbeck Sidings (Caythorpe).
.	.	.	.	.	.	.	.	Yorkshire Plaster Co.'s Siding	Yorks	N. E.	Same as Hillam Gates Siding (Milford Junction Station).
.	.	.	.	.	.	.	.	Yorkshire Railway Wagon Co.'s Siding	Yorks	L. & Y.	Horbury and Ossett.
.	.	.	.	.	.	.	.	Yorkshire Tube Works........	Yorks	N. E.	Middlesbro'.
.	.	.	.	.	.	.	.	York Street Wharf	Staffs	N. S.	See Hanley.
.	.	.	.	.	.	.	.	York Town	Hants	S. E. & C.	See Blackwater and York Town.
.	.	.	.	.	.	.	.	York Town	Surrey	L. & S. W.	See Camberley and York Town.
G	P	F	L	H	C	5	0	Yorton	Salop	L. & N. W.	Shrewsbury and Whitchurch.
G	P	F	L	H	C	3	0	Youghal	Cork	G. S. & W.	Branch from Queenstown Junction.
.	.	.	.	.	.	.	.	Young & Marten Siding	Essex	G. E.	London, Stratford.
.	.	.	.	.	.	.	.	Young's Coal Depôt	Stirling	K. & B. Jt. (Cal. & N. B.)	Kilsyth, New.
.	.	.	.	.	.	.	.	Young's Engine Works	Ayr	Cal.—G. & S. W.	Ardrossan.

EXPLANATION—G *Goods Station.*   P *Passenger and Parcel Station.*   P* *Passenger, but not Parcel or Miscellaneous Traffic.*
F *Furniture Vans, Carriages, Portable Engines, and Machines on Wheels.*   L *Live Stock.*
H *Horse Boxes and Prize Cattle Vans.*   C *Carriages by Passenger Train.*

Station Accommodation						Crane Power		STATIONS, &c.	COUNTY.	COMPANY.	POSITION.
						Tons	Cwts.	**Young's Oil Co.—**			
								Binny Quarry	L'lithgow	N. B.	Uphall.
								Castlehill Siding (Hopetoun Branch)	L'lithgow	N. B.	Uphall.
								Forkneuk Pit	L'lithgow	N. B.	Uphall.
								Hopetoun Mines...............	L'lithgow	N. B.	Uphall.
								Hopetoun Oil Works (Niddry Oil Works)	L'lithgow	N. B.	Uphall.
								Young's Paraffin Light and Mineral Oil Works...........	Edinboro'	Cal.	West Calder.
								Young's Pits	Edinboro'	Cal.	West Calder.
								Young's Saw Mill	Fife	N. B.	Oakley.
								Young's Siding	Fife	N. B.	Tayport.
								Young's Siding (N. B.)	Lanark ...	N. B.—Cal.	Glasgow, Great Western Road.
								Younger & Co.'s Siding	Edinboro'	Cal.	Leith, South.
								Younger & Co.'s Siding	Edinboro'	N. B.	Same as Lochend Siding (Edinburgh)
								Younger's Ale Siding	Clackman'	N. B.	Alloa.
								Younger's Bottling Stores and Old Malt Barns	Clackman'	Cal.	Alloa.
								Younger's Maltings Siding ...	Clackman'	N. B.	Alloa.
G	P					1	0	Ystalyfera (Mid.)	Glamorg'n	{ Mid. / G. W.	Brynamman and Pontardawe. / Over Midland Line.
								South Wales Primrose Col. (Ynisygeinon Sid.) (Mid.)	Glamorg'n	Mid.—G. W.—L. & N. W.	Ystalyfera.
								Ystalyfera Iron and Tin Plate Co.'s Siding (Mid.)	Glamorg'n	Mid.—G. W.—L. & N. W.	Near Ystalyfera.
G	P	F	L	.	C	5	0	Ystrad (Rhondda Valley) ...	Glamorg'n	T. V.	Pontypridd and Treherbert.
								Cory Bros. & Co.—			
								Gelli Colliery	Glamorg'n	T. V.	Ystrad and Llwynypia.
								Pentre Colliery	Glamorg'n	T. V.	Ystrad and Treorchy.
								Davis & Sons Ferndale No. 3 Col. (Boedryngallt Col.)..	Glamorg'n	T. V.	Ystrad and Llwynypia.
								Ocean Coal Co.—			
								Eastern Pit	Glamorg'n	T. V.	Ystrad and Llwynypia.
								Maindy Colliery	Glamorg'n	T. V.	Ystrad and Llwynypia.
								Rhondda Engine Works (Llewellyn & Cubitt's) ...	Glamorg'n	T. V.	Ystrad and Treorchy.
								Ystrad Gas Works	Glamorg'n	T. V.	Ystrad and Llwynypia.
								Ystrad Mileage Siding	Glamorg'n	T. V.	Ystrad and Llwynypia.
G	P	.	L	H				Ystradgynlais (N. & B.) ...	Brecon	{ N. & Brecon / Mid.	Colbren and Ynisygeinon Junction. / Over Neath and Brecon Line.
								Penrhos Brick Works Siding (N. & B.)	Brecon ...	N. & Brecon—Mid.	Ystradgynlais and Abercrave.
								Ynisci Colliery (N. & B.) ...	Brecon ...	N. & Brecon—Mid.	Ystradgynlais.
								Ystradgynlais Col. (N. & B.)	Brecon ...	N. & Brecon—Mid.	Ystradgynlais.
G	P	F	L	H	C			Ystrad Mynach (Rhy.)........	Glamorg'n	{ Rhy. / L. & N. W.	Caerphilly and Pengam. / Over Rhy. fr. Rhymney Joint Line Jn.
G		F	L					Colliery	Glamorg'n	Rhy.	Ystrad Mynach and Penallta Junc.
								Penallta Siding	Glamorg'n	Rhy.	Penallta Junction.
								Ystrad Mynach North Junc.	Glamorg'n	G. W.—Rhy.	Rhymney Junction Station (G. W.) and Ystrad Mynach.
G	P	.	L					Ystradowen	Glamorg'n	T. V.	Llantrisant and Cowbridge.
								Ystradowen Colliery (Mid.)..	Glamorg'n	Mid.—G. W.—L. & N. W.	Gurnos.
								Ystrad, South Junction	Glamorg'n	Rhy.	Llanbradach and Ystrad Mynach.

EXPLANATION—G *Goods Station.*   P *Passenger and Parcel Station.*   P* *Passenger, but not Parcel or Miscellaneous Traffic.*
F *Furniture Vans, Carriages, Portable Engines, and Machines on Wheels.*   L *Live Stock.*
H *Horse Boxes and Prize Cattle Vans.*   C *Carriages by Passenger Train.*